ABC Thumb Index

With the help of the ABC Thumb Index at the edge of this page you can quickly find the letter you are looking for in the English-German or German-English section of this Dictionary.

You place your thumb on the letter you want at the edge of this page, then flip through the Dictionary till you come to the appropriate pages in the English-German or German-English section.

Left-handed people should use the ABC Thumb Index at the end of the book.

LANGENSCHEIDT'S SHORTER GERMAN DICTIONARY

GERMAN-ENGLISH
ENGLISH-GERMAN

New edition 1987

Edited by
THE LANGENSCHEIDT
EDITORIAL STAFF

Hodder & Stoughton

*Published in the British Commonwealth
by Hodder & Stoughton Limited*

Preface

For over 130 years Langenscheidt's bilingual dictionaries have been essential tools for the student of languages. For several decades Langenscheidt's German-English dictionaries have been used not only for academic work, but in all walks of life.

However, languages are in a constant process of change. To keep you abreast of these changes, Langenscheidt has compiled this new Dictionary. Many words which have entered the German and English languages in the last few years have been included in the vocabulary.

The Dictionary has been considerably <u>enlarged</u>, not only to accommodate the new words, but also to make space for a number of <u>user-friendly innovations.</u> The demands for more detailed notes for the user have now been met. The somewhat abstract short notes have been replaced by a more detailed and graphic explanation of the peculiarities of the Dictionary.

The Dictionary also provides clear answers to questions of declension and conjugation in more than 15,000 German noun and verb entries.

The phonetic transcription of the German and English headwords follows the principles laid down by the International Phonetic Association (IPA).

In addition to the vocabulary, this Dictionary contains <u>special quick-reference sections</u> of proper names, abbreviations, weights and measures, and an <u>alphabetical list of German and English irregular verbs.</u>

Designed for the widest possible variety of uses, this Dictionary, with its <u>more than 48,000 entries and phrases,</u> will be of great value to students, teachers and tourists, and will find a place in home and office libraries alike.

Contents

How do you use the Dictionary?

Don't be afraid of words you don't know!

This Dictionary does all that it can to make it as easy as possible for you to look up and become familiar with a word.

How and where do you find a word?

Strict alphabetical order has been maintained throughout the Dictionary. The principle parts (infinitive, preterite, and past participle) of the irregular German and English verbs as well as the irregular plural forms of English nouns have also been given in their proper alphabetical order, e.g.:

> **gebissen** *p.p. of beißen*
> **bitten** *p.p. von bite*
> **men** *pl. von man*

In the German-English section we have treated the umlauts *ä ö ü* as *a o u*, rather than as *ae oe ue*.

When trying to locate a particular German or English word, you can use the boldface **catchwords** at the top corner of each page as a guide. These catchwords show you (on the left-hand side) the *first* boldface word on the left-hand page and (on the right-hand side) the *last* boldface word on the right-hand page, e.g. **Konflikt – köstlich** on page 188 and 189.

How do you spell the word?

As in a monolingual dictionary you can check the spelling of any word in this Dictionary. In the German-English section the American spelling has been given in the following ways:

> *theat|re, Am. -er, defen|ce, Am. -se*
> *council(l)or, hono(u)r*
> *plough, Am. plow*

and in the English-German section as follows:

> *centre, Am. -ter – theatre, Am. -ter*
> *dialogue, Am. -log – programme, Am. -gram*
> *colo(u)r – hono(u)r – travel(l)er*

In a very few cases a letter in round brackets indicates that a particular word can be spelled in two different ways: *judg(e)ment = judgment* or *judgement*.

In the English-German section the dots within a headword indicate syllabification breaks.

What do the various typefaces mean?

All German and English headwords are printed **in bold face**, as are the Arabic numerals used to distinguish the various parts of speech and grammatical forms of a word:

> **klopfen 1.** *v/i. heart, pulse*: beat; ... **2.** *v/t.* knock, drive (*nail, etc.*)
>
> **feed** ... **1.** Futter *n*; ... **2.** (*fed*) *v/t.* füttern; **~back** ...

Italics are used a) for grammatical and subject label abbreviations: *adj., adv., v/i., v/t., econ., pol., zo.*, etc.; b) to indicate the gender of a German word: *m, f, n*; c) for any details added to give more precise information about a word or a particular meaning of a word, e.g.:

> **mild** ... *weather, punishment, etc.*: mild
>
> **schälen** ... pare, peel (*fruit, potatoes, etc.*)
>
> **file¹** ... *Computer*: Datei *f*
>
> **page** ... Seite *f* (*e-s Buches, e-r Zeitung etc.*)

Lightface type is used for all idiomatic phrases:

> **gut** ... *ganz* ~ not bad
>
> **Lage** ... *in der* ~ *sein zu inf.* be able to *inf.*
>
> **depend** ... *it* ~*s* F es kommt (ganz) darauf an
>
> **line** ... *hold the* ~ *teleph.* am Apparat bleiben

All translations are printed in normal type.

How do you pronounce the word?

The phonetic transcription of a word indicates how you should pronounce it. So that *everyone* could know precisely which signs represent which sounds, an international phonetic alphabet was established. As the signs used by the **I**nternational **P**honetic **A**ssociation are considered standard, we now talk of the **IPA phonetic alphabet**.

The phonetic symbols in square brackets – [ ] – are used in the Dictionary to describe how you should pronounce the German or English headword, e.g.:

> **fest** [fɛst] – **Hilfe** ['hɪlfə]
>
> **coat** [kəʊt] – **message** ['mesɪdʒ]

Guide to Pronunciation
for the German-English Section

The length of vowels is indicated by [:] following the vowel symbol, the stress by ['] preceding the stressed syllable. The glottal stop [ʔ] is the forced stop between one word or syllable and a following one beginning with a vowel, as in *unentbehrlich* [un'ʔɛnt'be:rliç]. No transcription of compounds is given if the parts appear as separate headwords.

A. Vowels

[a] as in French *carte*: *Mann* [man].

[ɑ:] as in *father*: *Wagen* ['vɑ:gən].

[e] as in *bed*: *Edikt* [e'dikt].

[e:] resembles the sound in *day*: *Weg* [ve:k].

[ə] unstressed e as in *ago*: *Bitte* ['bitə].

[ɛ] as in *fair*: *männlich* ['mɛnliç], *Geld* [gɛlt].

[ɛ:] same sound but long: *zählen* ['tsɛ:lən].

[i] as in *it*: *Wind* [vint].

[i:] as in *meet*: *hier* [hi:r].

[ɔ] as in *long*: *Ort* [ɔrt].

[ɔ:] same sound but long as in *draw*: *Komfort* [kɔm'fɔ:r].

[o] as in *molest*: *Moral* [mo'rɑ:l].

[o:] resembles the English sound in *go* [gəʊ] but without the [ʊ]: *Boot* [bo:t].

[ø:] as in French *feu*. The sound may be acquired by saying [e] through closely rounded lips: *schön* [ʃø:n].

[ø] same sound but short: *Ökonomie* [økono'mi:].

[œ] as in French *neuf*. The sound resembles the English vowel in *her*. Lips, however, must be well rounded as for [ɒ]: *öffnen* ['œfnən].

[u] as in *book*: *Mutter* ['mutər].

[u:] as in *boot*: *Uhr* [u:r].

[y] almost like the French u as in *sur*. It may be acquired by saying [ɪ] through fairly closely rounded lips: *Glück* [glyk].

[y:] same sound but long: *führen* ['fy:rən].

B. Diphthongs

[aɪ] as in *like*: *Mai* [maɪ].

[aʊ] as in *mouse*: *Maus* [maʊs].

[ɔy] as in *boy*: *Beute* ['bɔytə], *Läufer* ['lɔyfər].

C. Consonants

[b] as in *better*: *besser* ['bɛsər].

[d] as in *dance*: *du* [du:].

[f] as in *find*: *finden* ['fɪndən], *Vater* ['fɑ:tər], *Philosoph* [filo'zo:f].

[g] as in *gold*: *Gold* [gɔlt], *Geld* [gɛlt].

[ʒ] as in *measure*: *Genie* [ʒe'ni:], *Journalist* [ʒurna'lɪst].

[h] as in *house* but not aspirated: *Haus* [haʊs].

[ç] an approximation to this sound may be acquired by assuming the mouth-configuration for [ɪ] and emitting a strong current of breath: *Licht* [lɪçt], *Mönch* [mœnç], *lustig* ['lustiç].

[x] as in Scottish *loch*. Whereas [ç] is pronounced at the front of the mouth, [x] is pronounced in the throat: *Loch* [lɔx].

[j] as in *year*: *ja* [jɑ:].

[k] as in *kick*: *keck* [kɛk], *Tag* [tɑ:k], *Chronist* [kro'nɪst], *Café* [ka'fe:].

[l] as in *lump*. Pronounced like English initial "clear l": *lassen* ['lasən].

[m] as in *mouse*: *Maus* [maʊs].

[n] as in *not*: *nein* [naɪn].

[ŋ] as in *sing*, *drink*: *singen* ['zɪŋən], *trinken* ['trɪŋkən].

[p] as in *pass*: *Paß* [pas], *Trieb* [tri:p], *obgleich* [ɔp'glaɪç].

8

[r] as in *rot*. There are two pronunciations: the frontal or lingual r and the uvular r (the latter unknown in England): *rot* [ro:t].

[s] as in *miss*. Unvoiced when final, doubled, or next a voiceless consonant: *Glas* [glɑ:s], *Masse* ['masə], *Mast* [mast], *naß* [nas].

[z] as in *zero*. S voiced when initial in a word or syllable: *Sohn* [zo:n], *Rose* ['ro:zə].

[ʃ] as in *ship*: *Schiff* [ʃif], *Charme* [ʃarm], *Spiel* [ʃpi:l], *Stein* [ʃtaɪn].

[t] as in *tea*: *Tee* [te:], *Thron* [tro:n], *Stadt* [ʃtat], *Bad* [bɑ:t], *Findling* ['fintliŋ], *Wind* [vint].

[v] as in *vast*: *Vase* ['vɑ:zə], *Winter* ['vintər].

[ã, ɛ̃, õ] are nasalized vowels. Examples: *Ensemble* [ã'sã:bəl], *Terrain* [tɛ'rɛ̃:], *Bonbon* [bõ'bõ:].

List of Suffixes

The German suffixes are not transcribed unless they are parts of headwords.

-bar	[-bɑ:r]	-ist	[-ist]
-chen	[-çən]	-keit	[-kaɪt]
-d	[-t]	-lich	[-liç]
-de	[-də]	-ling	[-liŋ]
-ei	[-aɪ]	-losigkeit	[-lo:ziçkaɪt]
-en	[-ən]	-nis	[-nis]
-end	[-ənt]	-sal	[-zɑ:l]
-er	[-ər]	-sam	[-zɑ:m]
-haft	[-haft]	-schaft	[-ʃaft]
-heit	[-haɪt]	-sieren	[-zi:rən]
-ie	[-i:]	-ste	[-stə]
-ieren	[-i:rən]	-tät	[-tɛ:t]
-ig	[-iç]	-tum	[-tu:m]
-ik	[-ik]	-ung	[-uŋ]
-in	[-in]	-ungs-	[-uŋs-]
-isch	[-iʃ]		

Guide to the Phonetic Transcriptions in the English-German Section

A. Vowels and Diphthongs

[i:]	see	[si:]		[ə]	consist	[kən'sist]
[ɪ]	it	[ɪt]		[ɜ:]	bird	[bɜ:d]
[e]	get	[get]		[eɪ]	day	[deɪ]
[æ]	cat	[kæt]		[əʊ]	go	[gəʊ]
[ɑ:]	father	['fɑ:ðə]		[aɪ]	fly	[flaɪ]
[ɒ]	not	[nɒt]		[aʊ]	how	[haʊ]
[ɔ:]	saw	[sɔ:]		[ɔɪ]	boy	[bɔɪ]
[ʊ]	put	[pʊt]		[ɪə]	sheer	[ʃɪə]
[u:]	too	[tu:]		[ʊə]	tour	[tʊə]
[ʌ]	up	[ʌp]		[eə]	vary	['veərɪ]

The length of a vowel is indicated by the symbol [:], e.g. *ask* [ɑ:sk], *astir* [ə'stɜ:].

The following French nasal sounds are used occasionally: [ɑ̃] as in French *blanc*, [ɔ̃] as in French *bonbon* and [ɛ̃] as in French *vin*.

B. Consonants

[r]	bright	[braɪt]		[z]	zone	[zəʊn]
[ŋ]	ring	[rɪŋ]		[ʃ]	ship	[ʃɪp]
[ŋk]	ink	[ɪŋk]		[ʒ]	measure	['meʒə]
[j]	yes	[jes]		[tʃ]	chicken	['tʃɪkɪn]
[f]	fat	[fæt]		[dʒ]	judge	[dʒʌdʒ]
[v]	very	['verɪ]		[θ]	thin	[θɪn]
[w]	well	[wel]		[ð]	then	[ðen]
[s]	soul	[səʊl]				

To save space in the individual entries, we shall limit ourselves to a short note here on the ending -ed* and the plural -s** of the English headwords. These endings will then appear in the vocabulary without phonetics, unless they are exceptions to the rules.

* [-d] after vowels and voiced consonants; [-t] after unvoiced consonants; [-ɪd] after final d and t.

** [-z] after vowels and voiced consonants; [-s] after unvoiced consonants.

Stress

In the German and English headwords the sign ' (the stress accent) preceding a syllable indicates that this syllable is stressed.

    durchschlagen ['durçʃlɑːgən] – **durchschlagen** [durç'ʃlɑːgən]
    'nachsehen – '~senden
    record [rɪ'kɔːd] – **record** ['rekɔːd]
    gamekeeper ['geɪmkiːpə]

If in an English entry the headword is followed by a word which has the same stress, no stress accent is given for the second word – it is always stressed in exactly the same way as the word preceding it, e.g.:

    helper ['helpə] – **helpful** [~fl = 'helpfl]

What do the abbreviations and symbols tell you?

Wherever possible, we have used pictorial symbols and/or abbreviations to indicate the subject area from which a headword and/or some of its meanings are taken. A pictorial symbol or an abbreviation placed immediately after a headword applies to all translations given in the entry. Any symbol or abbreviation preceding an individual translation refers to this translation only. If the abbreviation is followed by a colon, it applies to all the following translations. Thus in the German-English section an F placed before the German or English part of an example sentence indicates that only that part of the sentence is used familiarly. On the other hand, an F: placed before the German part indicates that the example and translation belong to the same linguistic usage level.

Labels denoting figurative usage have been placed between the example phrases or sentences and their translations. This is also sometimes the case with other labels.

F	*familiar*, umgangssprachlich.	🚂	*railway, railroad*, Eisenbahn.
V	*vulgar*, vulgär.	✈	*aviation*, Flugwesen.
†	*archaic*, veraltet.	⚘	*postal affairs*, Postwesen.
↖	*rare, little used*, selten.	♪	*musical term*, Musik.
⛢	*scientific term*, wissenschaftlich.	△	*architecture*, Architektur.
♀	*botany*, Botanik, Pflanzenkunde.	∮	*electrical engineering*, Elektrotechnik.
⊕	*engineering*, Technik; *handicraft*, Handwerk.	⚖	*legal term*, Rechtswissenschaft.
⚒	*mining*, Bergbau.	𝔸	*mathematics*, Mathematik.
⚔	*military term*, militärisch.	✗	*farming*, Landwirtschaft.
⚓	*nautical term*, Schiffahrt.	⚗	*chemistry*, Chemie.
✝	*commercial term*, Handelswesen.	✚	*medicine*, Medizin.

In addition, the English-German section contains the sign △, which is intended as a warning against typical mistakes:

actual ... △ *nicht aktuell*

A further symbol is the box: □. When placed after an English adjective, this box means that the corresponding adverb is formed regularly by adding -*ly* to the adjective or by transforming -*le* to -*ly* or -*y* to -*ily*, e.g.:

beautiful □ = *beautifully*
acceptable □ = *acceptably*
happy □ = *happily*

Adverbs can also be formed by adding -*ally* to the adjective form. Such cases have been treated as follows:

authentic ... (~*ally*) = *authentically*

What does the tilde (~) mean?

One symbol which you will meet constantly in the entries is a sign indicating repetition, the tilde (~ ⚥, ~ ⚥). The boldface tilde (~) replaces either the whole headword or the part of the headword preceding the vertical bar (|). The lightface tilde (~) represents the entry immediately preceding it, which itself might have been formed with the help of a boldface tilde:

Ski ... **~fahrer** (= *Skifahrer*), **~läufer** (= *Skiläufer*)
ab|blasen ... **~bringen:** *j-n* ~ (= *abbringen*) *von* ...
foot ... **~ball** (= *football*)
happi|ly ... **~ness** (= *happiness*)

When the initial letter of an entry changes in a run-on entry from small to capital or vice versa, the simple tilde (~) is replaced by the following symbol ℒ:

dick ... **ℒkopf** (= *Dickkopf*)
Geschicht|e ... **ℒlich** (= *geschichtlich*)
representative ... *House of* **ℒs**
(= *House of Representatives*)

The same procedure has been used in the phonetics. The simple tilde is used for the whole word or for the part of the word which is repeated unchanged. Only the syllables or letters which change are added:

bewegen¹ [bə'veːgən] – **bewegen²** [~]
Beweis [bə'vaɪs] ... **ℒen** [~zən]
chap¹ [tʃæp] – **chap²** [~] – **chap³** [~]
per|suade [pə'sweɪd] ... **~suasion** [~ʒn]
destruc|tion [dɪ'strʌkʃn] ... **~tive** [~tɪv]

In addition to the symbols, you will find the following **abbreviations** for grammatical terms and special subject areas:

a.	*also,* auch.	*b.s.*	*bad sense,* in schlechtem Sinne.
abbr.	*abbreviation,* Abkürzung.		
acc.	*accusative (case),* Akkusativ.	*bsd.*	*especially,* besonders.
adj.	*adjective,* Adjektiv.		
adv.	*adverb,* Adverb.	*cj.*	*conjunction,* Konjunktion.
allg.	*commonly,* allgemein.	*co.*	*comic(al),* scherzhaft.
Am.	*American English,* amerikanisches Englisch.	*coll.*	*collectively,* als Sammelwort.
		comp.	*comparative,* Komparativ.
anat.	*anatomy,* Anatomie.	*contp.*	*contemptuously,* verächtlich.
appr.	*approximately,* etwa.		
arch.	*architecture,* Architektur.	*dat.*	*dative (case),* Dativ.
art.	*article,* Artikel.	*dem.*	*demonstrative,* hinweisend.
ast.	*astronomy,* Astronomie.		
attr.	*attributively,* attributiv.	*ea.*	*one another, each other,* einander.
biol.	*biology,* Biologie.	*eccl.*	*ecclesiastical,* kirchlich.
Brit.	*British,* britisch.	*econ.*	*economics,* Wirtschaft.
Brt.	*British English,* britisches Englisch.	*e-e, e-e, e-e a(n),* eine.	
		e.g.	*for example,* zum Beispiel.

12

e-m, e-m, e-m to a(n), einem.		*n*	*neuter,* sächlich.
e-n, e-n, e-n a(n), einen.		*nom.*	*nominative (case),* Nominativ.
eng S.	*in narrower sense,* in engerem Sinne.	*npr.*	*proper name,* Eigenname.
e-r, e-r, e-r of a(n), to a(n), einer.		*od.*	*or,* oder.
e-s, e-s, e-s of a(n), eines.		*opt.*	*optics,* Optik.
esp.	*especially,* besonders.	*orn.*	*ornithology,* Ornithologie.
et., et., et. something, etwas.		*o.s.*	*oneself,* sich.
etc., etc. and so on, und so weiter.			
		P.	*person,* Person.
f	*feminine,* weiblich.	*p.*	*person,* Person.
fig.	*figuratively,* bildlich.	*paint.*	*painting,* Malerei.
frz.	*French,* französisch.	*parl.*	*parliamentary term,* parlamentarischer Ausdruck.
gen.	*genitive (case),* Genitiv.	*pass.*	*passive voice,* Passiv.
geogr.	*geography,* Geographie.	*pers.*	*personal,* persönlich.
geol.	*geology,* Geologie.	*pharm.*	*pharmacy,* Pharmazie.
geom.	*geometry,* Geometrie.	*phls.*	*philosophy,* Philosophie.
ger.	*gerund,* Gerundium.	*phot.*	*photography,* Photographie.
Ggs.	*antonym,* Gegensatz.	*phys.*	*physics,* Physik.
gr.	*grammar,* Grammatik.	*physiol.*	*physiology,* Physiologie.
		pl.	*plural,* Plural.
h	*have,* haben.	*poet.*	*poetry,* Dichtung.
hist.	*history,* Geschichte.	*pol.*	*politics,* Politik.
hunt.	*hunting,* Jagdwesen.	*poss.*	*possessive,* besitzanzeigend.
		p.p.	*past participle,* Partizip Perfekt.
ichth.	*ichthyology,* Ichthyologie.	*p.pr.*	*present participle,* Partizip Präsens.
impers.	*impersonal,* unpersönlich.	*pred.*	*predicative,* prädikativ.
indef.	*indefinite,* unbestimmt.	*pres.*	*present,* Präsens.
inf.	*infinitive (mood),* Infinitiv.	*pret.*	*preterit(e),* Präteritum.
int.	*interjection,* Interjektion.	*print.*	*printing,* Buchdruck.
interr.	*interrogative,* fragend.	*pron.*	*pronoun,* Pronomen.
iro.	*ironically,* ironisch.	*prov.*	*provincialism,* Provinzialismus.
irr.	*irregular,* unregelmäßig.		
		prp.	*preposition,* Präposition.
j-, j-, j- someone, jemand.		*psych.*	*psychology,* Psychologie.
j-m, j-m, j-m to s.o., jemandem.			
j-n, j-n, j-n someone, jemanden.			
j-s, j-s, j-s someone's, jemandes.		*refl.*	*reflexive,* reflexiv.
		rel.	*relative,* Relativ...
konkr.	*concretely,* konkret.	*rhet.*	*rhetoric,* Rhetorik.
ling.	*linguistics,* Sprachwissenschaft.	*S., S.*	*thing,* Sache.
lit.	*literary,* nur in der Schriftsprache vorkommend.	*s.*	*see, refer to,* siehe.
		schott.	*Scottish,* schottisch.
		s-e, s-e, s-e his, one's, seine.	
m	*masculine,* männlich.	*sep.*	*separable,* abtrennbar.
m-e, m-e, m-e my, meine.		*sg.*	*singular,* Singular.
m-r	*of my, to my,* meiner.	*sl.*	*slang,* Slang.
metall.	*metallurgy,* Metallurgie.	*s-m, s-m, s-m to his, to one's,* seinem.	
meteor.	*meteorology,* Meteorologie.	*s-n, s-n, s-n his, one's,* seinen.	
min.	*mineralogy,* Mineralogie.	*s.o., s.o., s.o. someone,* jemand(en).	
mot.	*motoring,* Kraftfahrwesen.	*s-r, s-r, s-r of his, of one's, to his, to one's,* seiner.	
mount.	*mountaineering,* Bergsteigen.		
mst	*mostly, usually,* meistens.	*s-s, s-s, s-s of his, of one's,* seines.	
myth.	*mythology,* Mythologie.	*s.th., s.th., s.th. something,* etwas.	

subj.	*subjunctive (mood)*, Konjunktiv.	*vet.*	*veterinary medicine*, Tiermedizin.
sup.	*superlative*, Superlativ.	*vgl.*	*compare*, vergleiche.
surv.	*surveying*, Landvermessung.	*v/i.*	*intransitive verb*, intransitives Verb.
tel.	*telegraphy*, Telegraphie.	*v/refl.*	*reflexive verb*, reflexives Verb.
teleph.	*telephony*, Fernsprechwesen.	*v/t.*	*transitive verb*, transitives Verb.
thea.	*theatre*, Theater.		
TM	*trademark*, Warenzeichen.		
TV	*television*, Fernsehen.	*weitS.*	*in a wider sense*, in weiterem Sinne.
typ.	*typography*, Typographie.		
u., u.	*and*, und.	*z.B.*	*for example*, zum Beispiel.
univ.	*university*, Hochschulwesen. Studentensprache.	*zo.*	*zoology*, Zoologie.
		zs., zs.,	*zs. together*, zusammen.
v/aux.	*auxiliary verb*, Hilfsverb.	*Zssg(n)*	*compound word(s)*, Zusammensetzung(en).
vb.	*verb*, Verb.		

A few words on the translations

You will no doubt have already noticed that it is very rare for there to be only one translation after any headword. In most cases the headword has several translations which are related in meaning and are separated from one another by a comma. However, the headword itself can also have several very different meanings, depending on the context in which it is used.

When a word has several meanings, a semicolon is used to separate them from one another. But the various meanings of a word are often so far apart from one another that it is not enough simply to separate them by a semicolon. In such cases we use several different methods to separate the translations:

a) the headword is repeated and given a superior number:

leben[1] ... live

Leben[2] *n* ... life

Tor[1] *n* ... gate

Tor[2] *m* ... fool

chap[1] ... Riß *m*

chap[2] ... Kerl *m*

chap[3] ... Kinnbacke *f*

b) When a headword can be several different parts of speech (a noun, verb, adjective, etc.) the various translations distinguished by boldface Arabic numerals:

böse ... **1.** bad *(adjective)*

2. 2 *n* evil *(noun)*

work ... **1.** Arbeit *f (noun)*

2. *v/i.* arbeiten *(verb)*

green ... **1.** grün *(adjective)*

2. Grün *n (noun)*

In the German-English section boldface Arabic numerals are also used to distinguish transitive, intransitive and reflexive verbs (if this affects their translation) and to indicate the different meanings of nouns which can occur in more than one gender:

> **bohren** ... **1.** *v/t.* bore
> **2.** *v/i.* drill
> **Bund** ... **1.** *m* ...; **2.** *n* ...

Boldface Arabic numerals are also used to show that where there is a change of meaning a noun or verb may be differently inflected or conjugated:

> **Bau** ... *m* **1.** (-[e]s/*no pl.*) ...; **2.** (-[e]s/-ten) ...;
> **3.** (-[e]s/-e) ...
> **schwimmen** *v/i.* (*irr.*, ge-) **1.** (*sein*) ...; **2.** (*h*) ...

If grammatical indications come before the subdivision they refer to all translations following:

> **Alte** (-*n*/-*n*) **1.** *m* ...; **2.** *f* ...
> **humpeln** ... *v/i.* (ge-) **1.** (*sein*) ...; **2.** (*h*) ...

As you know, British and American English sometimes use different terms to denote the same thing. The American *sidewalk* and the British *pavement* are both "Bürgersteig" in German, whereas only in American English does *fall* have the meaning "Herbst". In this Dictionary words which are chiefly used in British English are marked *Brt.* and those which are more typically American *Am.*

Grammar in the Dictionary, too?

It is often possible for you to arrive at the correct grammatical use of a word from the "additional information" which belongs to it. If, for instance, a headword (a verb, adjective or noun) is governed by certain prepositions, these are given together with the English or German translations and placed next to the appropriate translation. If the German or English preposition is the same for all or several translations, it is given only once before or after the first translation and then also applies to the translations which follow it.

The following methods are used to relate the prepositions to their appropriate headwords:

> **abrücken** ... **1.** *v/t.* move away (*von* from) ...
> **befestigen** ... *v/t.* fasten (*an dat.* to), fix (to), attach (to) ...

dissent ... anderer Meinung sein (*from* als) ...
dissimilar ... (*to*) unähnlich (*dat.*); verschieden (von) ...

With German prepositions which can take the dative or the accusative, the case is given in brackets:

enter ... (ein)treten in (*acc.*) ...

Notes on special grammatical conventions used in the German-English section:

a) **nouns**

The inflectional forms (*genitive singular | nominative plural*) follow immediately after the indication of gender. No forms are given for compounds if the parts appear as separate headwords.

The horizontal stroke replaces the part of the word which remains unchanged in the inflexion:

Affe *m* (-*n*/-*n*) − **Affäre** *f* (-/-*n*)

The sign ⁼ indicates that an umlaut appears in the inflected form in question:

Blatt *n* (-[e]*s*/⁼*er*).

b) **verbs** (see also the list of irregular German verbs on page 744)

Verbs have been treated in the following ways:

1. bändigen *v/t.* (*ge-, h*)

The past participle of this verb is formed by means of the prefix *ge-* and the auxiliary verb *haben*: *er hat gebändigt.*

2. abfassen *v/t.* (*sep., -ge-, h*)

In conjugation the prefix *ab* must be separated from the primary verb *fassen*: *er faßt ab*; *er hat abgefaßt.*

3. verderben *v/i.* (*irr., no -ge-, sein*)

irr. following the verb refers the reader to the list of irregular German verbs in the appendix (page 744) for the principal parts of this particular verb: *es verdarb*; *es ist verdorben.*

4. abfallen *v/i.* (*irr. fallen, sep., -ge-, sein*)

A reference such as *irr. fallen* indicates that the compound verb *abfallen* is conjugated in exactly the same way as the primary verb *fallen* as given in the list of irregular verbs: *er fiel ab; er ist abgefallen.*

5. sieden *v/t. and v/i.* ([*irr.,*] ge-, h)

The square brackets indicate that *sieden* can be treated as a regular or irregular verb: *er siedete or er sott; er hat gesiedet or er hat gesotten.*

In the English-German section of the Dictionary, round brackets can be found in some entries after the square brackets for the phonetics. These round brackets indicate that the headword has a grammatical peculiarity in one of the following points:

a) **irregular plural**

   child ... (*pl. children*) **– to·ma·to** ... (*pl. -toes*)
   a·nal·y·sis ... (*pl. -ses* [-siːz])

b) **irregular verbs** (see also the list of irregular English verbs on page 746)

   go ... (*went, gone*) **– shut** ... (*shut*)
   learn ... (*learned or learnt*)
   out·grow ... (*-grew, -grown*)

c) **doubling of the final consonant**

   hit ... (*-tt-*) **– trav·el** ... (*esp. Brt. -ll-, Am. a. -l-*)

c and b)

shut ... (*-tt-; shut*) **– out·bid** ... (*-dd-; -bid*)

d) **final –c becomes –ck-**

   frol·ic ... (*-ck-*) = *frolicking*

e) **comparative and superlative forms**

   good ... (*better, best*)
   an·gry ... (*-ier, -iest*) **– sore** ... ($\sim$r, $\sim$st)

You will have seen from these notes that this Dictionary offers more than simply word-for-word equivalents as are to be found in the vocabulary sections of textbooks.

PART I

GERMAN-ENGLISH DICTIONARY

A

Aal *ichth.* [ɑ:l] *m* (-[e]s/-e) eel; **2-glatt** *adj.* (as) slippery as an eel.

Aas [ɑ:s] *n* **1.** (-es/≈-e) carrion, carcass; **2.** *fig.* (-es/Äser) beast; **'geier** *orn.* *m* vulture.

ab [ap] **1.** *prp.* (*dat.*): ~ Brüssel from Brussels onwards; ~ Fabrik, Lager *etc.* † ex works, warehouse, *etc.*; **2.** *prp.* (*dat.*, F *acc.*): ~ erstem *or* ersten März from March 1st, on and after March 1st; **3.** † *prp.* (*gen.*) less; ~ Unkosten less charges; **4.** *adv. time*: von jetzt ~ from now on, in future; ~ und zu from time to time, now and then; von da ~ from that time forward; *space: thea.* exit, *pl.* exeunt; von ... ~ from there (on).

abänder|n ['ap⁹-] *v/t.* (*sep.*, -ge-, *h*) alter, modify; *parl.* amend; **'2ung** *f* alteration, modification; *parl.* amendment (*to bill, etc.*); **'2ungsantrag** *parl.* *m* amendment.

abarbeiten ['ap⁹-] *v/t.* (*sep.*, -ge-, *h*) work off (*debt*); sich ~ drudge, toil.

Abart ['ap⁹-] *f* variety.

'Abbau *m* **1.** (-[e]s/*no pl.*) pulling down, demolition (*of structure*); dismantling (*of machine, etc.*); dismissal, discharge (*of personnel*); reduction (*of staff, prices, etc.*); cut (*of prices, etc.*); **2.** ⚒ (-[e]s/-e) working, exploitation; **'2en** *v/t.* (*sep.*, -ge-, *h*) pull *or* take down, demolish (*structure*); dismantle (*machine, etc.*); dismiss, discharge (*personnel*); reduce (*staff, prices, etc.*); cut (*prices, etc.*); ⚒ work, exploit.

'ab|beißen *v/t.* (*irr.* beißen, *sep.*, -ge-, *h*) bite off; **'~bekommen** *v/t.* (*irr.* kommen, *sep.*, *no* -ge-, *h*) get off; *s-n* Teil *or* et. ~ get one's share; et. ~ be hurt, get hurt.

abberuf|en *v/t.* (*irr.* rufen, *sep.*, *no* -ge-, *h*) recall; **'2ung** *f* recall.

'ab|bestellen *v/t.* (*sep.*, *no* -ge-, *h*) countermand, cancel one's order for (*goods, etc.*); cancel one's subscription to, discontinue (*news-paper, etc.*); **'~biegen** *v/i.* (*irr.* biegen, *sep.*, -ge-, *sein*) *p.* turn off; *road*: turn off, bend; *nach rechts* (*links*) ~ turn right (left); *von e-r Straße* ~ turn off a road.

'Abbild *n* likeness; image; **2en** ['~dən] *v/t.* (*sep.*, -ge-, *h*) figure, represent; *sie ist auf der ersten Seite abgebildet* her picture is on the front page; **~ung** ['~duŋ] *f* picture, illustration.

'abbinden *v/t.* (*irr.* binden, *sep.*, -ge-, *h*) untie, unbind, remove; ⚕ ligate, tie up.

'Abbitte *f* apology; ~ leisten *or* tun make one's apology (*bei j-m wegen* et. to s.o. for s.th.); **'2n** *v/t.* (*irr.* bitten, *sep.*, -ge-, *h*): *j-m* et. ~ apologize to s.o. for s.th.

'ab|blasen *v/t.* (*irr.* blasen, *sep.*, -ge-, *h*) blow off (*dust, etc.*); call off (*strike, etc.*), cancel; ✗ break off (*attack*); **'~blättern** *v/i.* (*sep.*, -ge-, *sein*) paint, *etc.*: scale, peel (off); ⚕ *skin*: desquamate; ♣ shed the leaves; **'~blenden** (*sep.*, -ge-, *h*) **1.** *v/t.* screen (*light*); *mot.* dim, dip (*headlights*); **2.** *v/i. mot.* dim *or* dip the headlights; *phot.* stop down; **'~blitzen** F *v/i.* (*sep.*, -ge-, *sein*) meet with a rebuff; ~ *lassen* snub; **'~brausen** (*sep.*, -ge-, *h*) **1.** *v/refl.* (*h*) have a shower(-bath), douche; **2.** F *v/i.* (*sein*) rush off; **'~brechen** (*irr.* brechen, *sep.*, -ge-) **1.** *v/t.* (*h*) break off (*a. fig.*); pull down, demolish (*building, etc.*); strike (*tent*); *fig.* stop; *das Lager* ~ break up camp, strike tents; **2.** *v/i.* (*sein*) break off, strike tents; **3.** *fig. v/i.* (*h*) stop; **'~bremsen** *v/t.* *and v/i.* (*sep.*, -ge-, *h*) slow down; brake; **'~brennen** (*irr.* brennen, *sep.*, -ge-) **1.** *v/t.* (*h*) burn down (*building, etc.*); let *or* set off (*firework*); **2.** *v/i.* (*sein*) burn away *or* down; *s. abgebrannt*; **'~bringen** *v/t.* (*irr.* bringen, *sep.*, -ge-, *h*) get off; *j-n* ~ von argue s.o. out of; dissuade s.o. from; **'~bröckeln** *v/i.* (*sep.*, -ge-, *sein*) crumble (*a.* †).

'Abbruch *m* pulling down, demolition (*of building, etc.*); rupture (*of relations*); breaking off (*of negotiations, etc.*); *fig.* damage, injury; *j-m ~ tun* damage s.o.

'ab|brühen *v/t.* (*sep., -ge-, h*) scald; *s. abgebrüht*; **'~bürsten** *v/t.* (*sep., -ge-, h*) brush off (*dirt, etc.*); brush (*coat, etc.*); **'~büßen** *v/t.* (*sep., -ge-, h*) expiate, atone for (*sin, etc.*); serve (*sentence*). [bet.]

Abc [a:be:'tse:] *n* (*-/-*) ABC, alpha-

'abdank|en *v/i.* (*sep., -ge-, h*) resign; *ruler*: abdicate; **'2ung** *f* (*-/-en*) resignation; abdication.

'ab|decken *v/t.* (*sep., -ge-, h*) uncover; untile (*roof*); unroof (*building*); clear (*table*); cover; **'~dichten** *v/t.* (*sep., -ge-, h*) make tight; seal up (*window, etc.*); ⊕ pack (*gland, etc.*); **'~dienen** *v/t.* (*sep., -ge-, h*): *s-e Zeit ~ ✕* serve one's time; **'~drängen** *v/t.* (*sep., -ge-, h*) push aside; **'~drehen** (*sep., -ge-, h*)

1. *v/t.* twist off (*wire*); turn off (*water, gas, etc.*); ⚡ switch off (*light*); **2.** ⚓, ✈ *v/i.* change one's course; **'~drosseln** *mot. v/t.* (*sep., -ge-, h*) throttle.

'Abdruck *m* (*-[e]s/~e*) impression, print, mark; cast; **'2en** *v/t.* (*sep., -ge-, h*) print; publish (*article*).

'abdrücken (*sep., -ge-, h*) **1.** *v/t.* fire (*gun, etc.*); F hug *or* squeeze affectionately; *sich ~* leave an impression *or* a mark; **2.** *v/i.* pull the trigger.

Abend ['a:bənt] *m* (*-s/-e*) evening; *am ~* in the evening, at night; *heute abend* tonight; *morgen* (*gestern*) *abend* tomorrow (last) night; *s. essen*; **'~anzug** *m* evening dress; **'~blatt** *n* evening paper; **'~brot** *n* supper, dinner; **'~dämmerung** *f* (evening) twilight, dusk; **'~essen** *n s.* Abendbrot; **'~gesellschaft** *f* evening party; **'~kasse** *thea. f* box-office; **'~kleid** *n* evening dress *or* gown; **'~land** *n* (*-[e]s/no pl.*) the Occident; **2ländisch** *adj.* ['~lɛndiʃ] western, occidental; **'~mahl** *eccl. n* (*-[e]s/-e*) the (Holy) Communion, the Lord's Supper; **'~rot** *n* evening *or* sunset glow.

abends *adv.* ['a:bənts] in the evening.

'Abend|schule *f* evening school, night-school; **'~sonne** *f* setting

sun; **'~toilette** *f* evening dress; **'~wind** *m* evening breeze; **'~zeitung** *f* evening paper.

Abenteu|er ['a:bɔytɔyər] *n* (*-s/-*) adventure; **'2erlich** *adj.* adventurous; *fig.*: strange; wild, fantastic; **~rer** ['~ɔyrər] *m* (*-s/-*) adventurer.

aber ['a:bər] **1.** *adv.* again; *Tausende und ~ Tausende* thousands upon thousands; **2.** *cj.* but; *oder ~* otherwise, (*or*) else; **3.** *int.: ~!* now then!; *~!, ~!* come, come!; *~ nein!* no!, on the contrary!; **4.** 2 *n* (*-s/-*) but.

'Aber|glaube *m* superstition; **2-gläubisch** *adj.* ['~glɔybiʃ] superstitious.

aberkenn|en ['ap?-] *v/t.* (*irr. kennen, sep., no -ge-, h*): *j-m et. ~* deprive s.o. of s.th. (*a. ⅌*); dispossess s.o. of s.th.; **'2ung** *f* (*-/-en*) deprivation (*a. ⅌*); dispossession.

aber|malig *adj.* ['~a:bərma:liç] repeated; **~mals** *adv.* ['~s] again, once more.

'ab|ernten ['ap?-] *v/t.* (*sep., -ge-, h*) reap, harvest; **~essen** ['ap?-] (*irr. essen, sep., -ge-, h*) **1.** *v/t.* clear (*plate*); **2.** *v/i.* finish eating; **'~fahren** (*irr. fahren, sep., -ge-*) **1.** *v/i.* (*sein*) leave (*nach* for), depart (for), start (for); set out *or* off (for); **2.** *v/t.* (*h*) carry *or* cart away (*load*). **'Abfahrt** *f* departure (*nach* for), start (for); setting out *or* off (for); *skiing*: downhill run; **'~sbahnsteig** *m* departure platform; **'~slauf** *m skiing*: downhill race; **'~ssignal** *n* starting-signal; **'~szeit** *f* time of departure; ⚓ *a.* time of sailing.

'Abfall *m* defection (*von* from), falling away (from); *esp. pol.* secession (from); *eccl.* apostasy (from); *often Abfälle pl.* waste, refuse, rubbish, *Am. a.* garbage; ⊕ clippings *pl.*, shavings *pl.*; *at butcher's*: offal; **'~eimer** *m* dust-bin, *Am.* ash can; **'2en** *v/i.* (*irr. fallen, sep., -ge-, sein*) *leaves, etc.*: fall (off); *ground, etc.*: slope (down); *fig.* fall away (*von* from); *esp. pol.* secede (from); *eccl.* apostatize (from); *~ gegen* come off badly by comparison with, be inferior to; **'~erzeugnis** *n* waste product; by-product.

'abfällig *adj. judgement, etc.*: adverse, unfavo(u)rable; *remark*: disparaging, depreciatory.

'**Abfallprodukt** *n* by-product; waste product.

'**ab|fangen** *v/t.* (*irr.* fangen, *sep.*, -ge-, h) catch; snatch (*ball*, etc.); intercept (*letter*, etc.); ⚓ prop; ✕ check (*attack*); ✈ flatten out; *mot.*, ✕ right; '**~färben** *v/i.* (*sep.*, -ge-, h): der Pullover färbt ab the colo(u)r of the pull-over runs (*auf acc.* on); ~ *auf* (*acc.*) influence, affect.

'**abfass|en** *v/t.* (*sep.*, -ge-, h) compose, write, pen; catch (*thief*, etc.); '**Qung** *f* composition; wording.

'**ab|faulen** *v/i.* (*sep.*, -ge-, sein) rot off; '**~fegen** *v/t.* (*sep.*, -ge-, h) sweep off; '**~feilen** *v/t.* (*sep.*, -ge-, h) file off.

abfertig|en ['apfɛrtigən] *v/t.* (*sep.*, -ge-, h) dispatch (*a.* ✈); *customs*: clear; serve, attend to (*customer*); *j-n kurz* ~ snub s.o.; '**Qung** *f* (-/-en) dispatch; *customs*: clearance; schroffe ~ snub.

'**abfeuern** *v/t.* (*sep.*, -ge-, h) fire (off), discharge.

'**abfind|en** *v/t.* (*irr.* finden, *sep.*, -ge-, h) satisfy, pay off (*creditor*); compensate; *sich mit et.* ~ resign o.s. to s.th.; put up with s.th.; '**Qung** *f* (-/-en) settlement; satisfaction; compensation; '**Qung(ssumme)** *f* indemnity; compensation.

'**ab|flachen** *v/t.* and *v/refl.* (*sep.*, -ge-, h) flatten; '**~flauen** *v/i.* (*sep.*, -ge-, sein) wind, etc.: abate; *interest*, etc.: flag; ✝ *business*: slacken; '**~fliegen** *v/i.* (*irr.* fliegen, *sep.*, -ge-, sein) leave by plane; ✈ take off, start; '**~fließen** *v/i.* (*irr.* fließen, *sep.*, -ge-, sein) drain *or* flow off *or* away.   [parture.]

'**Abflug** ✈ *m* take-off, start, de-]

'**Abfluß** *m* flowing *or* draining off *or* away; discharge (*a.* ⚕); drain (*a. fig.*); sink; outlet (*of lake*, etc.).

'**abfordern** *v/t.* (*sep.*, -ge-, h): *j-m et.* ~ demand s.th. of *or* from s.o.

Abfuhr ['apfuːr] *f* (-/-en) removal; *fig.* rebuff.

'**abführ|en** (*sep.*, -ge-, h) **1.** *v/t.* lead off *or* away; march (*prisoner*) off; pay over (*money*) (*an acc.* to); **2.** ✕ *v/i.* purge (the bowels), loosen the bowels; '**~end** ✕ *adj.* purgative, aperient, laxative; '**Qmittel** ✕ *n* purgative, aperient, laxative.

'**abfüllen** *v/t.* (*sep.*, -ge-, h) decant;

in Flaschen ~ bottle; *Bier in Fässer* ~ rack casks with beer.

'**Abgabe** *f sports*: pass; casting (*of one's vote*); sale (*of shares*, etc.); *mst* ~*n pl.* taxes *pl.*; rates *pl.*, *Am.* local taxes *pl.*; duties *pl.*; '**Qfrei** *adj.* tax-free; duty-free; '**Qnpflichtig** *adj.* taxable; dutiable; liable to tax *or* duty.

'**Abgang** *m* departure; start; *thea.* exit (*a. fig.*); retirement (*from a job*); loss, wastage; deficiency (*in weight*, etc.); ⚕ discharge; ✝ miscarriage; *nach* ~ *von der Schule* after leaving school.

'**abgängig** *adj.* missing.

'**Abgangszeugnis** *n* (school-)leaving certificate, *Am.* ⚕ diploma.

'**Abgas** *n* waste gas; *esp. mot.* exhaust gas.   [toil-worn, worn-out.]

abgearbeitet *adj.* ['apgə'arbaitət)]

'**abgeben** *v/t.* (*irr.* geben, *sep.*, -ge-, h) leave (*bei, an dat.* at); hand in (*paper*, etc.); deposit, leave (*luggage*); cast (*one's vote*); *sports*: pass (*ball*, etc.); sell, dispose of (*goods*); give off (*heat*, etc.); e-e Erklärung ~ make a statement; *s-e Meinung* ~ express one's opinion (*über acc.* on); *j-m et.* ~ *von et.* give s.o. some of s.th.; *e-n guten Gelehrten* ~ make a good scholar; *sich* ~ *mit* occupy o.s. with *s.th.*; *es gibt sich gern mit Kindern ab* she loves to be among children.

'**abge|brannt** *adj.* burnt down; F *fig.* hard up, *sl.* broke; '**~brüht** *fig. adj.* ['~bryːt] hardened, callous; '**~droschen** *adj.* trite, hackneyed; '**~feimt** *adj.* ['~faimt] cunning, crafty; '**~griffen** *adj.* worn; *book*: well-thumbed; '**~härtet** *adj.* ['~hɛrtət] hardened (*gegen* to), inured (to); '**~härmt** *adj.* ['~hɛrmt] careworn.

'**abgehen** (*irr.* gehen, *sep.*, -ge-) **1.** *v/i.* (sein) go off *or* away; leave, start, depart; *letter*, etc.: be dispatched; *post*: go; *thea.* make one's exit; *side-road*: branch off; *goods*: sell; *button*, etc.: come off; *stain*, etc.: come out; ✕ be discharged; (*von e-m Amt*) ~ give up a post; retire; *von der Schule* ~ leave school; ~ *von* digress from (*main subject*); deviate from (*rule*); alter, change (*one's opinion*); relinquish (*plan*, etc.); *diese Eigenschaft geht ihm ab* he lacks this quality; *gut* ~ end well, pass off well; *hiervon geht or gehen ... ab* ✝ less, minus; **2.** *v/t.* (*h*) measure by steps; patrol.

abge|hetzt *adj.* ['apgəhɛtst] harassed; exhausted; run down; breathless; **~kartet** F *adj.* ['~kartət]: *~e Sache* prearranged affair, put-up job; **~legen** *adj.* remote, distant; secluded; out-of-the-way; **~macht** *adj.* ['~maxt]: *~!* it's a bargain *or* deal!; **~magert** *adj.* ['~ma:gərt] emaciated; **~neigt** *adj.* ['~narkt] disinclined (*dat. for s.th.*; *zu tun to* do), averse (*to*; *from doing*), unwilling (*zu tun to* do); **~nutzt** *adj.* ['~nutst] worn-out.

Abgeordnete ['apgə?ɔrdnətə] *m, f* (*-n/-n*) deputy, delegate; *in Germany:* member of the Bundestag *or* Landtag; *Brt.* Member of Parliament, *Am.* Representative.

'abgerissen *fig. adj.* ragged; shabby; *style, speech:* abrupt, broken.

'Abgesandte *m, f* (*-n/-n*) envoy; emissary; ambassador.

'abgeschieden *fig. adj.* isolated; secluded, retired; **'2heit** *f* (*-/-en*) seclusion; retirement.

'abgeschlossen *adj. flat:* self-contained; *training, etc.:* complete.

abgeschmackt ['apgəʃmakt] *adj.* tasteless; tactless; **'2heit** *f* (*-/-en*) tastelessness; tactlessness.

'abgesehen *adj.:* *~ von* apart from, *Am. a.* aside from.

abge|spannt *fig. adj.* ['apgəʃpant] exhausted, tired, run down; **'~standen** *adj.* stale, flat; **'~storben** *adj.* numb; dead; **'~stumpft** *adj.* ['~ʃtumpft] blunt(ed); *fig.* indifferent (*gegen to*); **'~tragen** *adj.* worn-out; threadbare, shabby.

abgewöhnen *v/t.* (*sep., -ge-, h*): *j-m et. ~* break *or* cure s.o. of s.th.; *sich das Rauchen ~* give up smoking.

abgezehrt *adj.* ['apgətse:rt] emaciated, wasted.

abgießen *v/t.* (*irr. gießen, sep., -ge-, h*) pour off; 🝊 decant; ⊕ cast.

'Abglanz *m* reflection (*a. fig.*).

'abgleiten *v/i.* (*irr. gleiten, sep., -ge-, sein*) slip off; slide off (*glide*)

'Abgott *m* idol. [*off.*]

abgöttisch *adv.* ['apgœtiʃ] *j-n ~ lieben* idolize *or* worship s.o.; dote (*up*)on s.o.

'ab|grasen *v/t.* (*sep., -ge-, h*) graze; *fig.* scour; **'~grenzen** *v/t.* (*sep.,*

-ge-, h) mark off, delimit; demarcate (*a. fig.*); *fig.* define.

'Abgrund *m* abyss; precipice; chasm, gulf; *am Rande des ~s on* the brink of disaster.

'Abguß *m* cast.

'ab|hacken *v/t.* (*sep., -ge-, h*) chop *or* cut off; **'~haken** *fig. v/t.* (*sep., -ge-, h*) tick *or* check off; **'~halten** *v/t.* (*irr. halten, sep., -ge-, h*) hold (*meeting, examination, etc.*); keep out (*rain*); *j-n von der Arbeit ~* keep s.o. from his work; *j-n davon ~ et. zu tun* keep *or* restrain s.o. from doing s.th.; *et. von j-m ~* keep s.th. away from s.o.; **'~handeln** *v/t.* (*sep., -ge-, h*) discuss, treat; *j-m et. ~* bargain s.th. out of s.o.

abhanden *adv.* [ap'handən]: *~ kommen* get lost.

'Abhandlung *f* treatise (*über acc.* [*up*]on), dissertation ([*up*]on, *concerning*); essay. [*clivity.*]

'Abhang *m* slope, incline; de-]

'abhängen **1.** *v/t.* (*sep., -ge-, h*) take down (*picture, etc.*); 🝊 uncouple; **2.** *v/i.* (*irr. hängen, sep., -ge-, h*): *~ von* depend (*up*)on.

abhängig *adj.* ['aphɛŋɪç]: *~ von* dependent (*up*)on; **'2keit** *f* (*-/no pl.*) dependence (*von* [*up*]on).

ab|härmen ['aphɛrmən] *v/refl.* (*sep., -ge-, h*) pine away (*über acc. at*); **'~härten** *v/t.* (*sep., -ge-, h*) harden (*gegen to*), inure (*to*); *sich ~ harden o.s.* (*gegen to*), inure o.s. (*to*); **'~hauen** (*irr. hauen, sep., -ge-*) **1.** *v/t.* (*h*) cut *or* chop off; **2.** F *v/i.* (*sein*) be off; *hau ab! sl.* beat it!, scram!; **'~häuten** *v/t.* (*sep., -ge-, h*) skin, flay; **'~heben** (*irr. heben, sep., -ge-, h*) **1.** *v/t.* lift *or* take off; *teleph.* lift (*receiver*); (*with*)draw (*money*); *sich ~ von* stand out against; *fig. a.* contrast with; **2.** *v/i.* cut (*the cards*); *teleph.* lift the receiver; **'~heilen** *v/i.* (*sep., -ge-, sein*) heal (*up*); **'~helfen** *v/i.* (*irr. helfen, sep., -ge-, h*): *e-m Übel ~* cure *or* redress an evil; *dem ist nicht abzuhelfen* there is nothing to be done about it; **'~hetzen** *v/refl.* (*sep., -ge-, h*) tire o.s. out; rush, hurry.

Abhilfe *f* remedy, redress, relief; *~ schaffen* take remedial measures.

'abhobeln *v/t.* (*sep., -ge-, h*) plane (*away, down*).

abhold *adj.* ['aphɔlt] averse (*dat.* to *s.th.*); ill-disposed (towards *s.o.*).

'**ab**|**holen** *v/t.* (*sep.*, -ge-, h) fetch; call for, come for; *j-n von der Bahn* ~ go to meet s.o. at the station; '**~holzen** *v/t.* (*sep.*, -ge-, h) fell, cut down (*trees*); deforest; '**~hor·chen** *v/t.* (*sep.*, -ge-, h) auscultate, sound; '**~hören** *v/t.* (*sep.*, -ge-, h) listen in to, intercept (*telephone conversation*); *e-n Schüler* ~ hear a pupil's lesson.

Abitur [abi'tuːr] *n* (-s/~-e) school-leaving examination (*qualifying for university entrance*).

'**ab**|**jagen** *v/t.* (*sep.*, -ge-, h): *j-m et.* ~ recover s.th. from s.o.; '**~kanzeln** F *v/t.* (*sep.*, -ge-, h) reprimand, F tell *s.o.* off; '**~kaufen** *v/t.* (*sep.*, -ge-, h): *j-m et.* ~ buy *or* purchase s.th. from s.o.

Abkehr *fig.* (-/*no pl.*) estrangement (*von* from); withdrawal (from); '**2en** *v/t.* (*sep.*, -ge-, h) sweep off; *sich* ~ *von* turn away from; *fig.*: take no further interest in; become estranged from; withdraw from.

'**ab**|**klingen** *v/i.* (*irr. klingen*, *sep.*, -ge-, sein) fade away; *pain, etc.*: die down; *pain, illness*: ease off; '**~klopfen** (*sep.*, -ge-, h) **1.** *v/t.* knock (*dust, etc.*) off; dust (*coat, etc.*); ♪ sound, percuss; **2.** *v/i. conductor*: stop the orchestra; '**~knicken** *v/t.* (*sep.*, -ge-, h) snap *or* break off; bend off; '**~knöpfen** *v/t.* (*sep.*, -ge-, h) unbutton; F *j-m Geld* ~ get money out of s.o.; '**~kochen** (*sep.*, -ge-) **1.** *v/t.* boil; scald (*milk*); **2.** *v/i.* cook in the open air (*a.* ✕); '**~kommandieren** ✕ *v/t.* (*sep.*, *no* -ge-, h) detach, detail; second (*officer*).

Abkomme ['apkɔmə] *m* (-n/-n) descendant.

'**abkommen 1.** *v/i.* (*irr. kommen*, *sep.*, -ge-, sein) come away, get away *or* off; *von e-r Ansicht* ~ change one's opinion; *von e-m Thema* ~ digress from a topic; *vom Wege* ~ lose one's way; **2.** *♀ n* (-s/-) agreement.

abkömm·lich *adj.* ['apkœmliç] dispensable; available; *er ist nicht* ~ he cannot be spared; **2ling** ['~liŋ] *m* (-s/-e) descendant.

'**ab**|**koppeln** *v/t.* (*sep.*, -ge-, h) un-couple; '**~kratzen** (*sep.*, -ge-) **1.** *v/t.* (h) scrape off; **2.** *sl. v/i.* (sein) kick the bucket; '**~kühlen** *v/t.* (*sep.*, -ge-, h) cool; refrigerate; *sich* ~ cool down (*a. fig.*).

Abkunft ['apkunft] *f* (-/~-e) descent; origin, extraction; birth.

'**abkürz**|**en** *v/t.* (*sep.*, -ge-, h) shorten; abbreviate (*word, story, etc.*); *den Weg* ~ take a short cut; '**2ung** *f* (-/-en) abridgement; abbreviation; short cut.

'**abladen** *v/t.* (*irr. laden*, *sep.*, -ge-, h) unload; dump (*rubbish, etc.*).

'**Ablage** *f* place of deposit; filing tray; files *pl.*; cloak-room.

'**ab**|**lagern** (*sep.*, -ge-) **1.** *v/t.* (h) season (*wood, wine*); age (*wine*); *sich* ~ settle; be deposited; **2.** *v/i.* (sein) *wood, wine*: season; *wine*: age; '**~lassen** (*irr. lassen*, *sep.*, -ge-, h) **1.** *v/t.* let (*liquid*) run off; let off (*steam*); drain (*pond, etc.*); **2.** *v/i.* leave off (*von et.* [*doing*] s.th.).

'**Ablauf** *m* running off; outlet, drain; *sports*: start; *fig.* expiration, end; *nach* ~ *von* at the end of; '**2en** (*irr. laufen*, *sep.*, -ge-) **1.** *v/i.* (sein) run off; drain off; *period of time*: expire; † *bill of exchange*: fall due; *clock, etc.*: run down; *thread, film*: unwind; *spool*: run out; *gut* ~ end well; **2.** *v/t.* (h) wear out (*shoes*); scour (*region, etc.*); *sich die Beine* ~ run one's legs off; *s. Rang.*

'**Ableben** *n* (-s/ *no pl.*) death, decease (*esp.* ♌); ♌ demise.

'**ab**|**lecken** *v/t.* (*sep.*, -ge-, h) lick (off); '**~legen** (*sep.*, -ge-, h) **1.** *v/t.* take off (*garments*); leave off (*garments*); give up, break o.s. of (*habit*); file (*documents, letters, etc.*); make (*confession, vow*); take (*oath, examination*); *Zeugnis* ~ bear witness (*für* to; *von* of); *s. Rechenschaft*; **2.** *v/i.* take off one's (*hat and*) coat.

'**Ableger** ♀ *m* (-s/-) layer, shoot.

'**ablehn**|**en** (*sep.*, -ge-, h) **1.** *v/t.* decline, refuse; reject (*doctrine, candidate, etc.*); turn down (*proposal, etc.*); **2.** *v/i.* decline; *dankend* ~ decline with thanks; '**~end** *adj.* negative; '**2ung** *f* (-/-en) refusal; rejection.

'**ableit**|**en** *v/t.* (*sep.*, -ge-, h) divert (*river, etc.*); drain off *or* away (*water, etc.*); *gr.*, ♀, *fig.* derive (*aus,* *von* from); *fig.* infer (from); '2ung *f* diversion; drainage; *gr.*, Ⱥ derivation (*a. fig.*).

'ab|lenken *v/t.* (*sep.*, *-ge-*, *h*) turn aside; divert (*suspicion*, *etc.*) (*von* from); *phys.*, *etc.*: deflect (*rays*, *etc.*); *j-n von der Arbeit* ∼ distract s.o. from his work; '∼lesen *v/t.* (*irr.* *lesen*, *sep.*, *-ge-*, *h*) read (*speech*, *etc.*); read (off) (*values from instruments*); '∼leugnen *v/t.* (*sep.*, *-ge-*, *h*) deny, disavow, disown.

'ab|liefer|n *v/t.* (*sep.*, *-ge-*, *h*) deliver; hand over; surrender; '2ung *f* delivery.

'ablöschen *v/t.* (*sep.*, *-ge-*, *h*) blot (up) (*ink*); ⊕ temper (*steel*).

'ablös|en *v/t.* (*sep.*, *-ge-*, *h*) detach; take off; ⚔, *etc.*: relieve; supersede (*predecessor in office*); discharge (*debt*); redeem (*obligation*); *sich* ∼ come off; *fig.* alternate, take turns; '2ung *f* detachment; ⚔, *etc.*: relief; *fig.* supersession; discharge; redemption.

'abmach|en *v/t.* (*sep.*, *-ge-*, *h*) remove, detach; *fig.* settle, arrange (*business*, *etc.*); agree (up)on (*price*, *etc.*); '2ung *f* (*-/-en*) arrangement; settlement; agreement.

'abmager|n *v/i.* (*sep.*, *-ge-*, *sein*) lose flesh; grow lean *or* thin; '2ung *f* (*-/-en*) emaciation.

'ab|mähen *v/t.* (*sep.*, *-ge-*, *h*) mow (off); '∼malen *v/t.* (*sep.*, *-ge-*, *h*) copy.

'Abmarsch *m* start; ⚔ marching off; '2ieren *v/i.* (*sep.*, *no* *-ge-*, *sein*) start; ⚔ march off.

'abmeld|en *v/t.* (*sep.*, *-ge-*, *h*): *j-n von der Schule* ∼ give notice of the withdrawal of a pupil (from school); *sich polizeilich* ∼ give notice to the police of one's departure (from town, *etc.*); '2ung *f* notice of withdrawal; notice of departure.

'abmess|en *v/t.* (*irr.* *messen*, *sep.*, *-ge-*, *h*) measure; '2ung *f* (*-/-en*) measurement.

'ab|montieren *v/t.* (*sep.*, *no* *-ge-*, *h*) disassemble; dismantle; strip (*machinery*); remove (*tyre*, *etc.*); '∼mühen *v/refl.* (*sep.*, *-ge-*, *h*) drudge, toil; '∼nagen *v/t.* (*sep.*, *-ge-*, *h*) gnaw off (*a.* *fig.*); pick (*bone*).

Abnahme ['apnɑːmə] *f* (*-/*∼*-n*) taking off; removal; ⚕ amputation; ♱ taking delivery; ♱ purchase; ♱

sale; ⊕ acceptance (*of machine* *etc.*); administering (*of oath*); decrease, diminution; loss (*of weight*)

'abnehm|en (*irr.* *nehmen*, *sep.*, *-ge-*, *h*) **1.** *v/t.* take off; remove; *teleph.* lift (*receiver*); ⚕ amputate; gather (*fruit*); ⊕ accept (*machine*, *etc.*); *j-m et.* ∼ take s.th. from s.o.; ♱ *a.* buy *or* purchase s.th. from s.o.; *j-m zuviel* ∼ overcharge s.o.; **2.** *v/i.* decrease, diminish; decline; lose weight; *moon*: wane; *storm*: abate; *days*: grow shorter; '2er ♱ *m* (*-s/-*) buyer; customer; consumer.

'Abneigung *f* aversion (*gegen* to); disinclination (to); dislike (to, of, for); antipathy (against, to).

abnorm *adj.* [ap'nɔrm] abnormal; anomalous; exceptional; 2i'tät *f* (*-/-en*) abnormality; anomaly.

'abnötigen *v/t.* (*sep.*, *-ge-*, *h*): *j-m et.* ∼ extort s.th. from s.o

'ab|nutzen *v/t.* *and* *v/refl.* (*sep.*, *-ge-*, *h*), '∼nützen *v/t.* *and* *v/refl.* (*sep.*,*-ge-*, *h*) wear out; '2nutzung *f*, '2nützung *f* (*-/-en*) wear (and tear).

Abonn|ement [abɔn(ə)'mãː] *n* (*-s/* *-s*) subscription (*auf acc.* to); ∼ent [∼'nɛnt] *m* (*-en/-en*) subscriber; 2ieren [∼'niːrən] *v/t.* (*no* *-ge-*, *h*) subscribe to (*newspaper*); 2iert *adj.* [∼'niːrt]: ∼ *sein auf* (*acc.*) take in (*newspaper*, *etc.*).

'abordn|en ['ap⁹-] *v/t.* (*sep.*, *-ge-*, *h*) depute, delegate, *Am. a.* deputize; '2ung *f* delegation, deputation.

Abort [a'bɔrt] *m* (*-[e]s/-e*) lavatory, toilet.

'ab|passen *v/t.* (*sep.*, *-ge-*, *h*) fit, adjust; watch for, wait for (*s.o.*, *opportunity*); waylay *s.o.*; '∼pflükken *v/t.* (*sep.*, *-ge-*, *h*) pick, pluck (off), gather; '∼plagen *v/refl.* (*sep.*, *-ge-*, *h*) toil; '∼platzen *v/i.* (*sep.*, *-ge-*, *sein*) burst off; fly off; '∼prallen *v/i.* (*sep.*, *-ge-*, *sein*) rebound, bounce (off); ricochet; '∼putzen *v/t.* (*sep.*, *-ge-*, *h*) clean (off, up); wipe off; polish; '∼raten *v/i.* (*irr.* *raten*, *sep.*, *-ge-*, *h*): *j-m* ∼ *von* dissuade s.o. from, advise s.o. against; '∼räumen *v/t.* (*sep.*, *-ge-*, *h*) clear (away); '∼reagieren *v/t.* (*sep.*, *no* *-ge-*, *h*) work off (*one's anger*, *etc.*); *sich* ∼ F *a.* let off steam.

'abrechn|en (*sep.*, *-ge-*, *h*) **1.** *v/t.* deduct; settle (*account*); **2.** *v/i.*: *mit* *j-m* ∼ settle with s.o.; *fig.* settle (accounts) with s.o., F get even with s.o.; '**2ung** f settlement (of accounts); deduction, discount.

'**Abrede** f: in ~ stellen deny or question s.th.

'**abreib|en** v/t. (irr. reiben, sep., -ge-, h) rub off; rub down (body); polish; '**2ung** f rub-down; F fig. beating.

'**Abreise** f departure (nach for); '**2n** v/i. (sep., -ge-, sein) depart (nach for), leave (for), start (for), set out (for).

'**abreiß|en** (irr. reißen, sep., -ge-) **1.** v/t. (h) tear or pull off; pull down (building); s. abgerissen; **2.** v/i. (sein) break off; button, etc.: come off; '**2kalender** m tear-off calendar.

'**ab|richten** v/t. (sep., -ge-, h) train (animal), break (horse) (in); '**~riegeln** v/t. (sep., -ge-, h) bolt, bar (door); block (road).

'**Abriß** m draft; summary, abstract; (brief) outlines pl.; brief survey.

'**ab|rollen** (sep., -ge-) v/t. (h) and v/i. (sein) unroll; uncoil; unwind, unreel; roll off; '**~rücken** (sep., -ge-) **1.** v/t. (h) move off or away (von from), remove; **2.** ✕ v/i. (sein) march off, withdraw.

'**Abruf** m call; recall; auf ~ ✝ on call; '**2en** v/t. (irr. rufen, sep., -ge-, h) call off (a. ✝), call away; recall; 📞 call out.

'**ab|runden** v/t. (sep., -ge-, h) round (off); '**~rupfen** v/t. (sep., -ge-, h) pluck off.

abrupt adj. [ap'rupt] abrupt.

'**abrüst|en** ✕ v/i. (sep., -ge-, h) disarm; '**2ung** ✕ f disarmament.

'**abrutschen** v/i. (sep., -ge-, sein) slip off, glide down; ✈ skid.

'**Absage** f cancellation; refusal; '**2n** (sep., -ge-, h) **1.** v/t. cancel, call off; refuse; recall (invitation); **2.** v/i. guest: decline; j-m ~ cancel one's appointment with s.o.

'**absägen** v/t. (sep., -ge-, h) saw off; F fig. sack s.o.

'**Absatz** m stop, pause; typ. paragraph; ✝ sale; heel (of shoe); landing (of stairs); '**2fähig** ✝ adj. saleable, marketable; '**~markt** ✝ m market, outlet; '**~möglichkeit** ✝ f opening, outlet.

'**abschaben** v/t. (sep., -ge-, h) scrape off.

'**abschaff|en** v/t. (sep., -ge-, h)

abolish; abrogate (law); dismiss (servants); '**2ung** f (-/-en) abolition; abrogation; dismissal.

'**ab|schälen** v/t. (sep., -ge-, h) peel (off), pare; bark (tree); '**~schalten** v/t. (sep., -ge-, h) switch off, turn off or out; ⚡ disconnect.

'**abschätz|en** v/t. (sep., -ge-, h) estimate; value; assess; '**2ung** f valuation; estimate; assessment.

'**Abschaum** m (-[e]s/no pl.) scum; fig. a. dregs pl.

'**Abscheu** m (-[e]s/no pl.) horror (vor dat. of), abhorrence (of); loathing (of); disgust (for).

'**abscheuern** v/t. (sep., -ge-, h) scour (off); wear out; chafe, abrade.

abscheulich adj. [ap'ʃɔyliç] abominable, detestable, horrid; **2keit** f (-/-en) detestableness; atrocity.

'**ab|schicken** v/t. (sep., -ge-, h) send off, dispatch; ✉ post, esp. Am. mail; '**~schieben** v/t. (irr. schieben, sep., -ge-, h) push or shove off.

Abschied ['apʃiːt] m (-[e]s/↘-e) departure; parting, leave-taking, farewell; dismissal, ✕ discharge; ~ nehmen take leave (von of), bid farewell (to); j-m den ~ geben dismiss s.o., ✕ discharge s.o.; s-n ~ nehmen resign, retire; '**~sfeier** f farewell party; '**~sgesuch** n resignation.

'**ab|schießen** v/t. (irr. schießen, sep., -ge-, h) shoot off; shoot, discharge, fire (off) (fire-arm); launch (rocket); kill, shoot (shoot or bring) down (aircraft); s. Vogel; '**~schinden** v/refl. (irr. schinden, sep., -ge-, h) toil and moil, slave, drudge; '**~schirmen** v/t. (sep., -ge-, h) shield (gegen from); screen (from), screen off (from); '**~schlachten** v/t. (sep., -ge-, h) slaughter, butcher.

'**Abschlag** ✝ m reduction (in price); auf ~ on account; '**2en** ['apʃlaːgən] v/t. (irr. schlagen, sep., -ge-, h) knock off, beat off, strike off; cut off (head); refuse (request); repel (attack).

abschlägig adj. ['apʃlɛːgiç] negative; ~e Antwort refusal, denial.

'**Abschlagszahlung** f payment on account; instal(l)ment.

'**abschleifen** v/t. (irr. schleifen, sep., -ge-, h) grind off; fig. refine, polish.

'**Abschlepp|dienst** mot. m towing service, Am. a. wrecking service;

'²en v/t. (sep., -ge-, h) drag off; mot. tow off.

'abschließen (irr. schließen, sep., -ge-, h) **1.** v/t. lock (up); ⊕ seal (up); conclude (letter, etc.); settle (account); balance (the books); effect (insurance); contract (loan); fig. seclude, isolate; e-n Handel ~ strike a bargain; sich ~ seclude o.s.; **2.** v/i. conclude; '~d **1.** adj. concluding; final; **2.** adv. in conclusion.

'Abschluß m settlement; conclusion; ⊕ seal; '~prüfung f final examination, finals pl., Am. a. graduation; '~zeugnis n leaving certificate; diploma.

'ab|schmeicheln v/t. (sep., -ge-, h): j-m et. ~ coax s.th. out of s.o.; '~schmelzen (irr. schmelzen, sep., -ge-) v/t. (h) and v/i. (sein) melt (off); ⊕ fuse; '~schmieren v/t. (sep., -ge-, h) lubricate, grease; '~schnallen v/t. (sep., -ge-, h) unbuckle; take off (ski, etc.); '~schneiden (irr. schneiden, sep., -ge-, h) **1.** v/t. cut (off); slice off; den Weg ~ take a short cut; j-m das Wort ~ cut s.o. short; **2.** v/i.: gut ~ come out or off well.

'Abschnitt m ⚓ segment; ✝ coupon; typ. section, paragraph; counterfoil, Am. a. stub (of cheque, etc.); stage (of journey); phase (of development); period (of time).

'ab|schöpfen v/t. (sep., -ge-, h) skim (off); '~schrauben v/t. (sep., -ge-, h) unscrew, screw off.

'abschrecken v/t. (sep., -ge-, h) deter (von from); scare away; '~d adj. deterrent; repulsive, forbidding.

'abschreib|en (irr. schreiben, sep., -ge-, h) **1.** v/t. copy; write off (debt, etc.); plagiarize; in school: crib; **2.** v/i. send a refusal; '²er m copyist; plagiarist; '²ung ✝ f (-/-en) depreciation.

'abschreiten v/t. (irr. schreiten, sep., -ge-, h) pace (off); e-e Ehrenwache ~ inspect a guard of hono(u)r.

'Abschrift f copy, duplicate.

'abschürf|en v/t. (sep., -ge-, h) graze, abrade (skin); '²ung f (-/-en) abrasion.

'Abschuß m discharge (of fire-arm); launching (of rocket); hunt. shooting; shooting down, downing (of aircraft); '~rampe f launching platform.

abschüssig adj. ['apʃysiç] sloping, steep.

'ab|schütteln v/t. (sep., -ge-, h) shake off (a. fig.); fig. get rid of; '~schwächen v/t. (sep., -ge-, h) weaken, lessen, diminish; '~schweifen v/i. (sep., -ge-, sein) deviate; fig. digress; '~schwenken v/i. (sep., -ge-, sein) swerve; ⚔ wheel; '~schwören v/i. (irr. schwören, sep., -ge-, h) abjure; forswear; '~segeln v/i. (sep., -ge-, sein) set sail, sail away.

abseh|bar adj. ['apze:ba:r]: in ~er Zeit in the not-too-distant future; '~en (irr. sehen, sep., -ge-, h) **1.** v/t. (fore)see; j-m et. ~ learn s.th. by observing s.o.; es abgesehen haben auf (acc.) have an eye on, be aiming at; **2.** v/i.: ~ von refrain from; disregard.

abseits ['apzaɪts] **1.** adv. aside, apart; football, etc.: off side; **2.** prp. (gen.) aside from; off (the road).

'absend|en v/t. ([irr. senden,] sep., -ge-, h) send off, dispatch; ✉ post, esp. Am. mail; '²er ⚓ m sender.

'absengen v/t. (sep., -ge-, h) singe off.

'Absenker ♀ m (-s/-) layer, shoot.

'absetz|en (sep., -ge-, h) **1.** v/t. set or put down, deposit; deduct (sum); take off (hat); remove, dismiss (official); depose, dethrone (king); drop, put down (passenger); ✝ sell (goods); typ. set up (in type); thea.: ein Stück ~ take off a play; **2.** v/i. break off, stop, pause; '²ung f (-/-en) deposition; removal, dismissal.

'Absicht f (-/-en) intention, purpose, design; '²lich **1.** adj. intentional; **2.** adv. on purpose.

'absitzen (irr. sitzen, sep., -ge-) **1.** v/i. (sein) rider: dismount; **2.** v/t. (h) serve (sentence), F do (time).

absolut adj. [apzo'lu:t] absolute.

absolvieren [apzɔl'vi:rən] v/t. (no -ge-, h) absolve; complete (studies); get through, graduate from (school).

'absonder|n v/t. (sep., -ge-, h) separate; ✍ secrete; sich ~ withdraw; '²ung f (-/-en) separation; ✍ secretion.

ab|sorbieren [apzɔr'bi:rən] v/t. (no -ge-, h) absorb; '~speisen fig. v/t. (sep., -ge-, h) put s.o. off.

abspenstig adj. ['apʃpɛnstiç]: ~

machen entice away (*von* from).

'absperr|en v/t. (*sep.*, -ge-, h) lock; shut off; bar (*way*); block (*road*); turn off (*gas*, etc.); **'2hahn** m stopcock.

'ab|spielen v/t. (*sep.*, -ge-, h) play (*record*, etc.); play back (*tape recording*); *sich* ~ happen, take place; **'~sprechen** v/t. (*irr.* sprechen, *sep.*, -ge-, h) deny; arrange, agree; **'~springen** v/i. (*irr.* springen, *sep.*, -ge-, sein) jump down *or* off; ✈ jump, bale out, (*Am. only*) bail out; rebound. [off.\
'Absprung m jump; *sports*: take-\
'abspülen v/t. (*sep.*, -ge-, h) wash up; rinse.

'abstamm|en v/i. (*sep.*, -ge-, sein) be descended; *gr.* be derived (*both*: *von* from); **'2ung** f (-/-en) descent; *gr.* derivation.

'Abstand m distance; interval; ✝ compensation, indemnification; ~ *nehmen von* desist from.

ab|statten ['apʃtatən] v/t. (*sep.*, -ge-, h): *e-n Besuch* ~ pay a visit; *Dank* ~ return *or* render thanks; **'~stauben** v/t. (*sep.*, -ge-, h) dust.

'abstech|en (*irr.* stechen, *sep.*, -ge-, h) **1.** v/t. cut (*sods*); stick (*pig, sheep*, etc.); stab (*animal*); **2.** v/i. contrast (*von* with); **'2er** m (-s/-) excursion, trip; detour.

'ab|stecken v/t. (*sep.*, -ge-, h) unpin, undo; fit, pin (*dress*); *surv.* mark out; **'~stehen** v/i. (*irr.* stehen, *sep.*, -ge-, h) stand off; stick out, protrude; *s.* abgestanden; **'~steigen** v/i. (*irr.* steigen, *sep.*, -ge-, sein) descend; alight (*von* from) (*carriage*); get off, dismount (*from*) (*horse*); put up (*in dat.* at) (*hotel*); **'~stellen** v/t. (*sep.*, -ge-, h) put down; stop, turn off (*gas*, etc.); park (*car*); *fig.* put an end to *s.th.*; **'~stempeln** v/t. (*sep.*, -ge-, h) stamp; **'~sterben** v/i. (*irr.* sterben, *sep.*, -ge-, sein) die off; *limb*: mortify.

'Abstieg ['apʃtiːk] m (-[e]s/-e) descent; *fig.* decline.

'abstimm|en (*sep.*, -ge-, h) **1.** v/i. vote; **2.** v/t. tune in (*radio*); *fig.*: harmonize; time; ✝ balance (*books*); **'2ung** f voting; vote; tuning.

Abstinenzler [apsti'nɛntslər] m (-s/-) teetotal(l)er.

'abstoppen (*sep.*, -ge-, h) **1.** v/t.

stop; slow down; *sports*: clock; time; **2.** v/i. stop.

'abstoßen v/t. (*irr.* stoßen, *sep.*, -ge-, h) knock off; push off; clear off (*goods*); *fig.* repel; *sich die Hörner* ~ sow one's wild oats; **'~d** *fig.* *adj.* repulsive.

abstrakt *adj.* [ap'strakt] abstract.

'ab|streichen v/t. (*irr.* streichen, *sep.*, -ge-, h) take *or* wipe off; **'~streifen** v/t. (*sep.*, -ge-, h) strip off; take *or* pull off (*glove*, etc.); slip off (*dress*); wipe (*shoes*); **'~streiten** v/t. (*irr.* streiten, *sep.*, -ge-, h) contest, dispute; deny.

'Abstrich m deduction, cut; 🌡 swab.

'ab|stufen v/t. (*sep.*, -ge-, h) graduate; gradate; **'~stumpfen** (*sep.*, -ge-) **1.** v/t. (h) blunt; *fig.* dull (*mind*). **2.** *fig.* v/i. (sein) become dull.

'Absturz m fall; ✈ crash.

'ab|stürzen v/i. (*sep.*, -ge-, sein) fall down; ✈ crash; **'~suchen** v/t. (*sep.*, -ge-, h) search (*nach* for); scour *or* comb (*area*) (for).

absurd *adj.* [ap'zurt] absurd, preposterous.

Abszeß 🌡 [aps'tsɛs] m (Abszesses/ Abszesse) abscess.

Abt [apt] m (-[e]s/=e) abbot.

'abtakeln ⚓ v/t. (*sep.*, -ge-, h) unrig, dismantle, strip.

Abtei [ap'tai] f (-/-en) abbey.

Ab|'teil n compartment; **'2teilen** v/t. (*sep.*, -ge-, h) divide; ⚓ partition off; **'~teilung** f division; **'~teilung** f department; ward (*of hospital*); compartment; ✂ detachment; **~teilungsleiter** m head of a department.

'abtelegraphieren v/i. (*sep.*, *no* -ge-, h) cancel a visit, etc. by telegram.

Äbtissin [ɛp'tisin] f (-/-nen) abbess.

'ab|töten v/t. (*sep.*, -ge-, h) destroy, kill (*bacteria*, etc.); **'~tragen** v/t. (*irr.* tragen, *sep.*, -ge-, h) carry off; pull down (*building*); wear out (*garment*); pay (*debt*).

abträglich *adj.* ['aptreːkliç] injurious, detrimental.

'abtreib|en (*irr.* treiben, *sep.*, -ge-) **1.** v/t. (h) drive away *or* off; *ein Kind* ~ procure abortion; **2.** ⚓, ✈ v/i. (sein) drift off; **'2ung** f (-/-en) abortion.

'abtrennen v/t. (*sep.*, -ge-, h) detach; separate; sever (*limbs*, etc.); take (*trimmings*) off (*dress*).

'abtret|en (*irr.* treten, *sep.*, -ge-)
1. *v/t.* (h) wear down (*heels*); wear
out (*steps, etc.*); *fig.* cede, transfer;
2. *v/i.* (sein) retire, withdraw;
resign; *thea.* make one's exit; **'2er**
m (-s/-) doormat; **'2ung** *f* (-/-en)
cession, transfer.

'ab|trocknen (*sep.*, -ge-) **1.** *v/t.* (h)
dry (up); wipe (dry); *sich ~* dry
oneself, rub oneself down; **2.** *v/i.*
(sein) dry up, become dry; **'~trop-
fen** *v/i.* (*sep.*, -ge-, sein) *liquid:* drip;
dishes, vegetables: drain.

abtrünnig *adj.* ['aptrʏniç] unfaithful, disloyal; *eccl.* apostate; **2e** ['~ɡə]
m (-n/-n) deserter; *eccl.* apostate.

'ab|tun *v/t.* (*irr.* tun, *sep.*, -ge-, h)
take off; settle (*matter*); *fig.*: dispose
of; dismiss; **~urteilen** ['ap?-] *v/t.*
(*sep.*, -ge-, h) pass sentence on *s.o.*;
'~wägen *v/t.* (*irr.* wägen,) *sep.*, -ge-,
h) weigh (out); *fig.* consider care-
fully; **'~wälzen** *v/t.* (*sep.*, -ge-, h)
roll away; *fig.* shift; **'~wandeln**
v/t. (*sep.*, -ge-, h) vary, modify;
'~wandern *v/i.* (*sep.*, -ge-, sein)
wander away; migrate (*von* from).

'Abwandlung *f* modification, variation.

'abwarten (*sep.*, -ge-, h) **1.** *v/t.* wait
for, await; *s-e Zeit ~* bide one's
time; **2.** *v/i.* wait.

abwärts *adv.* ['apvɛrts] down, down-
ward(s).

'abwaschen *v/t.* (*irr.* waschen, *sep.*,
-ge-, h) wash (off, away); bathe;
sponge off; wash up (*dishes, etc.*).

'abwechseln (*sep.*, -ge-, h) **1.** *v/t.*
vary; alternate; **2.** *v/i.* vary; alternate; *mit j-m ~* take turns; **'~d** *adj.*
alternate.

'Abwechs(e)lung *f* (-/-en) change;
alternation; variation; diversion;
zur ~ for a change.

'Abweg *m: auf ~e geraten* go astray;
2ig *adj.* ['~ɡiç] erroneous, wrong.

'Abwehr *f* defen|ce, *Am.* -se; ward-
ing off (*of thrust, etc.*); **'~dienst** ⚔
m counter-espionage service; **'2en**
v/t. (*sep.*, -ge-, h) ward off; avert;
repulse, repel, ward off (*attack,
enemy*).

'abweich|en *v/i.* (*irr.* weichen, *sep.*,
-ge-, sein) deviate (*von* from),
swerve (from); differ (from); *com-
pass-needle:* deviate; **'2ung** *f* (-/-en)
deviation; difference; deflexion,
(*Am. only*) deflection.

'abweiden *v/t.* (*sep.*, -ge-, h) graze.

'abweis|en *v/t.* (*irr.* weisen, *sep.*,
-ge-, h) refuse, reject; repel (*a.* ⚔);
rebuff; **'~end** *adj.* unfriendly, cool;
'2ung *f* refusal, rejection; repulse
(*a.* ⚔); rebuff.

'ab|wenden *v/t.* ([*irr.* wenden,] *sep.*,
-ge-, h) turn away; avert (*disaster,
etc.*); parry (*thrust*); *sich ~* turn
away (*von* from); **'~werfen** *v/t.* (*irr.*
werfen, *sep.*, -ge-, h) throw off; ✈
drop (*bombs*); shed, cast (*skin, etc.*);
shed (*leaves*); yield (*profit*).

'abwert|en *v/t.* (*sep.*, -ge-, h) deval-
uate; **'2ung** *f* devaluation.

abwesen|d *adj.* ['apve:zənt] absent;
'2heit *f* (-/~ -en) absence.

'ab|wickeln (*sep.*, -ge-, h) un-
wind, unreel, wind off; transact
(*business*); **'~wiegen** *v/t.* (*irr.* wiegen,
sep., -ge-, h) weigh (out) (*goods*);
'~wischen *v/t.* (*sep.*, -ge-, h) wipe
(off); **'~würgen** *v/t.* (*sep.*, -ge-, h)
strangle, throttle, choke; *mot.* stall;
'~zahlen *v/t.* (*sep.*, -ge-, h) pay off;
pay by instal(l)ments; **'~zählen**
v/t. (*sep.*, -ge-, h) count (out, over).

'Abzahlung *f* instal(l)ment, payment on account; **'~sgeschäft** *n*
hire-purchase.

'abzapfen *v/t.* (*sep.*, -ge-, h) tap,
draw off.

'Abzehrung *f* (-/-en) wasting away,
emaciation; ✗ consumption.

'Abzeichen *n* badge; ✈ marking.

'ab|zeichnen *v/t.* (*sep.*, -ge-, h)
copy, draw; mark off; initial; tick
off; *sich ~* stand out against;
'~ziehen (*irr.* ziehen, *sep.*, -ge-)
1. *v/t.* (h) take off, remove; ⚛
subtract; strip (*bed*); bottle (*wine*);
phot. print (*film*); *typ.* pull (*proof*);
take out (*key*); *das Fell ~* skin
(*animal*); **2.** *v/i.* (sein) go away; ✗
march off; *smoke:* escape; *thunderstorm, clouds:* move on.

'Abzug *m* departure; ✗ withdrawal,
retreat; ⊕ drain; outlet; deduction
(*of sum*); *phot.* print; *typ.* proof
(-sheet).

abzüglich *prp.* (*gen.*) ['aptsy:kliç]
less, minus, deducting.

'Abzugsrohr *n* waste-pipe.

'abzweig|en ['aptsvaigən] (*sep.*, -ge-)
1. *v/t.* (h) branch; divert (*money*);
sich ~ branch off; **2.** *v/i.* (sein)
branch off; **'2ung** *f* (-/-en) branch;
road-junction.

ach *int.* [ax] oh!, ah!, alas!; ~ *so!* oh, I see!

Achse ['aksə] *f* (-/-n) axis; ⊕: axle; shaft; axle(-tree) (*of carriage*); *auf der* ~ on the move.

Achsel ['aksəl] *f* (-/-n) shoulder; *die* ~*n zucken* shrug one's shoulders; '~**höhle** *f* armpit.

acht[1] [axt] **1.** *adj.* eight; *in* ~ *Tagen* today week, this day week; *vor* ~ *Tagen* a week ago; **2.** ♀ *f* (-/-en) (figure) eight.

Acht[2] [~] *f* (-/*no pl.*) ban, outlawry; attention; *außer acht lassen* disregard; *sich in acht nehmen* be careful; be on one's guard (*vor j-m or* et. against s.o. *or* s.th.); look out (for s.o. *or* s.th.).

'**achtbar** *adj.* respectable.

'**achte** *adj.* eighth; ♀1 ['~əl] *n* (-s/-) eighth (part).

'**achten** (ge-, h) **1.** *v/t.* respect, esteem; regard; **2.** *v/i.*: ~ *auf* (*acc.*) pay attention to; *achte auf meine Worte* mark *or* mind my words; *darauf* ~, *daß* see to it that, take care that.

ächten ['ɛçtən] *v/t.* (ge-, h) outlaw, proscribe; ban.

'**Achter** *m* (-s/-) *rowing:* eight.

achtfach *adj.* ['axtfax] eightfold.

'**achtgeben** *v/i.* (*irr.* geben, *sep.*, -ge-, h) be careful; pay attention (*auf acc.* to); take care (of); *gib acht!* look *or* watch out!, be careful!

'**achtlos** *adj.* inattentive, careless, heedless.

Acht'stundentag *m* eight-hour day.

'**Achtung** *f* (-/*no pl.*) attention; respect, esteem, regard; ~*!* look out!, ✕ attention!; ~ *Stufe!* mind the step!; '♀**svoll** *adj.* respectful.

'**achtzehn** *adj.* eighteen; ~**te** *adj.* ['~tə] eighteenth.

'**achtzig** *adj.* ['axtsiç] eighty; '~**ste** *adj.* eightieth.

ächzen ['ɛçtsən] *v/i.* (ge-, h) groan, moan.

Acker ['akər] *m* (-s/ü) field; '~**bau** *m* agriculture; farming; '♀**bautreibend** *adj.* agricultural, farming; '~**geräte** *n/pl.* farm implements *pl.*; '~**land** *n* arable land; '♀**n** *v/t. and v/i.* (ge-, h) plough, till, *Am.* plow.

addi|eren [a'di:rən] *v/t.* (*no* -ge-, h) add (up); ♀**tion** [adi'tsjo:n] *f* (-/-en) addition, adding up.

Adel ['a:dəl] *m* (-s/*no pl.*) nobility, aristocracy; '♀**ig** *adj.* noble; '♀**n** *v/t.* (ge-, h) ennoble (*a. fig.*); *Brt.* knight, raise to the peerage; '~**stand** *m* nobility; aristocracy; *Brt.* peerage.

Ader ['a:dər] *f* (-/-n) ⚒, wood, *etc.*: vein; *anat.*: vein; artery; *zur* ~ *lassen* bleed.

adieu *int.* [a'djø:] good-bye, farewell, adieu, *F* cheerio.

Adjektiv *gr.* ['atjɛkti:f] *n* (-s/-e) adjective.

Adler *orn.* ['a:dlər] *m* (-s/-) eagle; '~**nase** *f* aquiline nose.

adlig ['a:dliç] *adj.* noble; ♀**e** ['~gə] *m* (-n/-n) nobleman, peer.

Admiral ⚓ [atmi'ra:l] *m* (-s/-e, ⁺e) admiral.

adopt|ieren [adɔp'ti:rən] *v/t.* (*no* -ge-, h) adopt; ♀**ivkind** [~'ti:f-] *n* adopted child.

Adressat [adrɛ'sa:t] *m* (-en/-en) addressee, consignee (*of goods*).

Adreßbuch [a'drɛs-] *n* directory.

Adress|e [a'drɛsə] *f* (-/-n) address; direction; *per* ~ care of (*abbr.* c/o); ♀**ieren** [~'si:rən] *v/t.* (*no* -ge-, h) address, direct; ✝ consign; *falsch* ~ misdirect.

adrett *adj.* [a'drɛt] smart, neat.

Adverb *gr.* [at'vɛrp] *n* (-s/-ien) adverb.

Affäre [a'fɛ:rə] *f* (-/-n) (love) affair; matter, business, incident. [key.⟩

Affe *zo.* ['afə] *m* (-n/-n) ape; mon-⟩

Affekt [a'fɛkt] *m* (-[e]s/-e) emotion; passion; ♀**iert** *adj.* [~'ti:rt] affected.

'**affig** *F adj.* foppish; affected; silly.

Afrikan|er [afri'ka:nər] *m* (-s/-) African; ♀**isch** *adj.* African.

After *anat.* ['aftər] *m* (-s/-) anus.

Agent [a'gɛnt] *m* (-en/-en) agent; broker; *pol.* (secret) agent; ~**ur** [~'tu:r] *f* (-/-en) agency.

aggressiv *adj.* [agrɛ'si:f] aggressive.

Agio ✝ ['a:ʒio] *n* (-s/*no pl.*) agio, premium.

Agitator [agi'ta:tɔr] *m* (-s/-en) agitator. [brooch.⟩

Agraffe [a'grafə] *f* (-/-n) clasp;⟩

agrarisch *adj.* [a'gra:riʃ] agrarian.

Ägypt|er [ɛ:'gyptər] *m* (-s/-) Egyptian; ♀**isch** *adj.* Egyptian.

ah *int.* [a:] ah!

aha *int.* [a'ha] aha!, I see!

Ahle ['a:lə] *f* (-/-n) awl, pricker; punch.

Ahn [ɑːn] m (-[e]s, -en/-en) ancestor; **~en** pl. a. forefathers pl.

ähneln ['ɛːnəln] v/i. (ge-, h) be like, resemble.

ahnen ['ɑːnən] v/t. (ge-, h) have a presentiment of or that; suspect; divine.

ähnlich adj. ['ɛːnlɪç] like, resembling; similar (dat. to); iro.: das sieht ihm ~ that's just like him; **'2keit** f (-/-en) likeness, resemblance; similarity.

Ahnung ['ɑːnuŋ] f (-/-en) presentiment; foreboding; notion, idea; **'2slos** adj. unsuspecting; **'2svoll** adj. full of misgivings.

Ahorn ♀ ['ɑːhɔrn] m (-s/-e) maple (-tree).

Ähre ♀ ['ɛːrə] f (-/-n) ear, head; spike; **~n lesen** glean.

Akademi|e [akadeˈmiː] f (-/-n) academy, society; **~ker** [ˈ~deːmikər] m (-s/-) university man, esp. Am. university graduate; **2sch** adj. [ˈ~deːmiʃ] academic.

Akazie ♀ [aˈkaːtsjə] f (-/-n) acacia.

akklimatisieren [aklimatiˈziːrən] v/t. and v/refl. (no -ge-, h) acclimatize, Am. acclimate.

Akkord [aˈkɔrt] m (-[e]s/-e) ♪ chord; †: contract; agreement; composition; im ~ † by the piece or job; **~arbeit** f piece-work; **~arbeiter** m piece-worker; **~lohn** m piece-wages pl.

akkredit|ieren [akrediˈtiːrən] v/t. (no -ge-, h) accredit (bei to); **2iv** [ˈ~tiːf] n (-s/-e) credentials pl.; † letter of credit.

Akku F ⊕ [ˈaku] m (-s/-s), **~mulator** ⊕ [ˌ~muˈlaːtɔr] m (-s/-en) accumulator, (storage-)battery.

Akkusativ gr. [ˈakuzatiːf] m (-s/-e) accusative (case). [acrobat.\

Akrobat [akroˈbaːt] m (-en/-en)]

Akt [akt] m (-[e]s/-e) act(ion), deed; thea. act; paint. nude.

Akte [ˈaktə] f (-/-n) document, deed; file; **~n** records pl., papers pl.; deeds pl., documents pl.; files pl.; zu den ~n to be filed; zu den ~n legen file; **'~ndeckel** m folder; **'~nmappe** f, **'~ntasche** f portfolio; briefcase; **'~nzeichen** n reference or file number.

Aktie † [ˈaktsjə] f (-/-n) share, Am. stock; ~n besitzen hold shares, Am. hold stock; **'~nbesitz** m share-

holdings pl., Am. stockholdings pl.; **'~ngesellschaft** f appr. joint-stock company, Am. (stock) corporation; **'~nkapital** n share-capital, Am. capital stock.

Aktion [akˈtsjoːn] f (-/-en) action; activity; pol., etc.: campaign, drive; ✗ operation; **~är** [ˌ~ˈnɛːr] m (-s/-e) shareholder, Am. stockholder.

aktiv adj. [akˈtiːf] active.

Aktiv|a † [akˈtiːva] n/pl. assets pl.; **~posten** [ˈ~tiːf-] m asset (a. fig.).

aktuell adj. [aktuˈel] current, present-day, up-to-date, topical.

Akust|ik [aˈkustik] f (-/no pl.) acoustics sg., pl.; **2isch** adj. acoustic.

akut adj. [aˈkuːt] acute.

Akzent [akˈtsɛnt] m (-[e]s/-e) accent; stress; **2uieren** [ˌ~uˈiːrən] v/t. (no -ge-, h) accent(uate); stress.

Akzept † [akˈtsɛpt] n (-[e]s/-e) acceptance; **~ant** † [ˌ~ˈtant] m (-en/-en) acceptor; **2ieren** [ˌ~ˈtiːrən] v/t. (no -ge-, h) accept.

Alarm [aˈlarm] m (-[e]s/-e) alarm; ~ blasen or schlagen ✗ sound or give the alarm; **~bereitschaft** f: in ~ sein stand by; **2ieren** [ˌ~ˈmiːrən] v/t. (no -ge-, h) alarm.

Alaun ♠ [aˈlaun] m (-[e]s/-e) alum.

albern adj. [ˈalbərn] silly, foolish.

Album [ˈalbum] n (-s/Alben) album.

Alge ♀ [ˈalgə] f (-/-n) alga, seaweed.

Algebra ♠ [ˈalgebra] f (-/no pl.) algebra.

Alibi ☆ [ˈaliːbi] n (-s/-s) alibi.

Alimente ☆ [aliˈmɛntə] pl. alimony.

Alkohol [ˈalkohol] m (-s/-e) alcohol; **'2frei** adj. non-alcoholic, esp. Am. soft; **~es Restaurant** temperance restaurant; **~iker** [ˈˌ~hoˈlikər] m (-s/-) alcoholic; **2isch** adj. [ˌ~ˈhoːliʃ] alcoholic; **'~schmuggler** m liquor-smuggler, Am. bootlegger; **'~verbot** n prohibition; **'~vergiftung** f alcoholic poisoning.

all¹ [al] **1.** pron. all; ~e everybody; ~es in ~em on the whole; vor ~em first of all; **2.** adj. all; every, each; any; ~e beide both of them; auf ~e Fälle in any case, at all events; ~e Tage every day; ~e zwei Minuten every two minutes.

All² [ˌ] n (-s/no pl.) the universe.

'alle F adj. all gone; ~ werden come to an end; supplies, etc.: run out.

Allee [aˈleː] f (-/-n) avenue (tree-lined) walk.

allein [a'laɪn] **1.** *adj.* alone; single; unassisted; **2.** *adv.* alone; only; **3.** *cj.* yet, only, but, however; 2**berechtigung** *f* exclusive right; 2**besitz** *m* exclusive possession; 2**herrscher** *m* absolute monarch, autocrat; dictator; **~ig** *adj.* only, exclusive, sole; 2**sein** *n* loneliness, solitariness, solitude; **~stehend** *adj. p.*: alone in the world; single; *building, etc.*: isolated, detached; 2**verkauf** *m* exclusive sale; monopoly; 2**vertreter** *m* sole representative *or* agent; 2**vertrieb** *m* sole distributors *pl.*

allemal *adv.* ['alə'maːl] always; *ein für ~* once (and) for all.

allen|falls *adv.* if need be; possibly, perhaps; at best. ~**halben** † *adv.* ['alənt'halbən] everywhere.

'**aller|'best** *adj.* best ... of all, very best; **~dings** *adv.* ['~diŋs] indeed; to be sure; ~! certainly!, *Am.* F sure!; '~**erst 1.** *adj.* first ... of all, very first; foremost; **2.** *adv.:* zu ~ first of all.

Allergie ♣ [alɛr'giː] *f* (-/-n) allergy.

'**aller|'hand** *adj.* of all kinds *or* sorts; F *das ist ja ~!* F I say!; *sl.* that's the limit!; '2**heiligen** *n* (-/*no pl.*) All Saints' Day; **~lei** *adj.* ['~laɪ] of all kinds *or* sorts; '2**lei** *n* (-s/-s) medley; '~**letzt 1.** *adj.* last of all, very last; latest (*news, fashion, etc.*); **2.** *adv.:* zu ~ last of all; '~**liebst 1.** *adj.* dearest of all, (most) lovely; **2.** *adv.:* am ~en best of all; '~**meist 1.** *adj.* most; **2.** *adv.:* am ~en mostly; chiefly; '~**nächst** *adj.* very next; '~**neu(e)st** *adj.* the very latest; '2**seelen** *n* (-/*no pl.*) All Souls' Day; '~**seits** *adv.* on all sides; universally; '~**wenigst** *adv.:* am ~en least of all.

'**alle|'samt** *adv.* one and all, all together; '~**zeit** *adv.* always, at all times, for ever.

'**all|'gegenwärtig** *adj.* omnipresent, ubiquitous; '~**ge'mein 1.** *adj.* general; common; universal; **2.** *adv.:* *im ~en* in general, generally; 2**ge'meinheit** *f* (-/*no pl.*) generality; universality; general public; 2**heilmittel** *n* panacea, cure-all (*both a. fig.*).

Allianz [ali'ants] *f* (-/-en) alliance. **alli'ier|en** *v/refl.* (*no* -ge-, *h*) ally

o.s. (*mit* to, with); 2**te** *m* (-n/-n) ally.

'**all|'jährlich 1.** *adj.* annual; **2.** *adv.* annually, every year; '2**macht** *f* (-/*no pl.*) omnipotence; ~'**mächtig** *adj.* omnipotent, almighty; ~**mählich** [~'mɛːlɪç] **1.** *adj.* gradual; **2.** *adv.* gradually, by degrees.

Allopathie ♣ [alopa'tiː] allopathy. **all|seitig** *adj.* ['alzaɪtɪç] universal; all-round; '2**strom** ≯ *m* (-[e]s/*no pl.*) alternating current/direct current (*abbr.* A.C./D.C.); '2**tag** *m* workday; week-day; *fig.* everyday life, daily routine; '~**täglich** *adj.* daily; *fig.* common, trivial; '2**tagsleben** *n* (-s/*no pl.*) everyday life; '~'**wissend** *adj.* omniscient; '2'**wissenheit** *f* (-/*no pl.*) omniscience; '~**wöchentlich** *adv.* weekly; '~**zu** *adv.* (much) too; '~**zu'viel** *adv.* too much. [alp.)

Alm [alm] *f* (-/-en) Alpine pasture,⟩ **Almosen** ['almoːzən] *n* (-s/-) alms; ~ *pl.* alms *pl.*, charity.

Alp|druck ['alp-] *m* (-[e]s/≈e), '~**drücken** *n* (-s/*no pl.*) nightmare.

Alpen ['alpən] *pl.* Alps *pl.*

Alphabet [alfa'beːt] *n* (-[e]s/-e) alphabet; **~isch** *adj.* alphabetic(al).

'**Alptraum** *m* nightmare.

als *cj.* [als] than; as, like; (in one's capacity) as; but, except; *temporal:* after, when; as; ~ *ob* as if, as though; *so viel* ~ as much as; *er ist zu dumm,* ~ *daß er es verstehen könnte* he is too stupid to understand it; ~'**bald** *adv.* immediately; ~'**dann** *adv.* then.

also ['alzo:] **1.** *adv.* thus, so; **2.** *cj.* therefore, so, consequently; *na ~!* there you are!

alt[1] *adj.* [alt] old; aged; ancient, antique; stale; second-hand.

Alt[2] ♪ [~] *m* (-s/-e) alto, contralto. **Altar** [al'taːr] *m* (-[e]s/≈e) altar. **Alteisen** ['alt⁹-] *n* scrap-iron.

'**Alte** (-n/-n) **1.** *m* old man; F: *der* ~ the governor; *hist.: die* ~n *pl.* the ancients *pl.*; **2.** *f* old woman.

'**Alter** *n* (-s/-) age; old age; seniority; *er ist in meinem* ~ he is my age; *von mittlerem* ~ middle-aged.

älter *adj.* ['ɛltər] older; senior; *der* ~e *Bruder* the elder brother.

altern ['altərn] *v/i.* (ge-, *h, sein*) grow old, age.

Alternative [altɛrna'tiːvə] *f* (-/-n)
alternative; *keine ~ haben* have no
choice.

'**Alters|grenze** *f* age-limit; retire-
ment age; '**~heim** *n* old people's
home; '**~rente** *f* old-age pension;
'2**schwach** *adj.* decrepit; senile;
'**~schwäche** *f* decrepitude; '**~ver-
sorgung** *f* old-age pension.

Altertum ['altərtuːm] *n* 1. (-s/no
pl.) antiquity; 2. (-s/-¨er) *mst Alter-
tümer pl.* antiquities *pl.*

altertümlich *adj.* ['altərtyːmliç]
ancient, antique, archaic.

'**Altertums|forscher** *m* arch(a)eol-
ogist; '**~kunde** *f* arch(a)eology.

ältest *adj.* ['ɛltəst] oldest; eldest
(*sister, etc.*); earliest (*recollections*);
'2**e** *m* (-n/-n) elder; senior; *mein ~r*
my eldest (son).

Altistin *f* [al'tistin] *f* (-/-nen) alto-
singer, contralto-singer.

'**altklug** *adj.* precocious, forward.

ältlich *adj.* ['ɛltliç] elderly, oldish.

'**Alt|material** *n* junk, scrap; sal-
vage; '**~meister** *m* doyen, dean, F
Grand Old Man (*a. sports*); *sports*:
ex-champion; '2**modisch** *adj.* old-
fashioned; '**~papier** *n* waste
paper; '**~philologe** *m* classical
philologist *or* scholar; '**~stadt** *f* old
town *or* city; '**~warenhändler** *m*
second-hand dealer; **~'weiber-
sommer** *m* Indian summer; gos-
samer.

Aluminium [alu'miːnjum] *n*
(-s/no *pl.*) aluminium, *Am.* alu-
minum.

am *prp.* [am] = *an dem.*

Amateur [ama'tøːr] *m* (-s/-e)
amateur. | (*bosse*) anvil.

Amboß ['ambɔs] *m* (*Ambosses/Am-*

ambulan|t *adj.* [ambu'lant]: *~
Behandelter* out-patient; 2**z** [~ts] *f*
(-/-en) ambulance.

Ameise *zo.* ['aːmaɪzə] *f* (-/-n) ant;
'**~nhaufen** *m* ant-hill.

Amerikan|er [ameri'kaːnər] *m*
(-s/-), **~erin** *f* (-/-nen) American;
2**isch** *adj.* American.

Amme ['amə] *f* (-/-n) (wet-)nurse.

Amnestie [amnɛs'tiː] *f* (-/-n) amnesty, general pardon.

Amor ['aːmɔr] *m* (-s/no *pl.*) Cupid.

Amortis|ation [amɔrtiza'tsjoːn] *f*
(-/-en) amortization, redemption;
2**ieren** [~'ziːrən] *v/t.* (no -ge-, h)
amortize, redeem; pay off.

Ampel ['ampəl] *f* (-/-n) hanging
lamp; traffic light.

Amphibie *zo.* [am'fiːbjə] *f* (-/-n)
amphibian.

Ampulle [am'pulə] *f* (-/-n) ampoule.

Amput|ation *&* [amputa'tsjoːn] *f*
(-/-en) amputation; 2**ieren**
[~'tiːrən] *v/t.* (no -ge-, h) amputate;
~ierte *m* (-n/-n) amputee. [bird.]

Amsel *orn.* ['amzəl] *f* (-/-n) black-]

Amt [amt] *n* (-[e]s/-¨er) office; post;
charge; office, board; official duty;
function; (telephone) exchange;
2**ieren** [~'tiːrən] *v/i.* (no -ge-, h)
hold office; officiate; 2**lich** *adj.*
official; '**~mann** *m* district administrator; *hist.* bailiff.

'**Amts|arzt** *m* medical officer of
health; '**~befugnis** *f* competence,
authority; '**~bereich** *m,* '**~bezirk**
m jurisdiction; '**~blatt** *n* gazette;
'**~eid** *m* oath of office; '**~einfüh-
rung** *f* inauguration; '**~führung** *f*
administration; '**~geheimnis** *n*
official secret; '**~gericht** *n* appr.
district court; '**~geschäfte** *n/pl.*
official duties *pl.*; '**~gewalt** *f* (official) authority; '**~handlung** *f* official act; '**~niederlegung** *f* (-/~-en)
resignation; '**~richter** *m* appr. district court judge; '**~siegel** *n* official
seal; '**~vorsteher** *m* head official.

Amulett [amu'lɛt] *n* (-[e]s/-e) amu-
let, charm.

amüs|ant *adj.* [amy'zant] amusing,
entertaining; **~ieren** [~'ziːrən] *v/t.*
(no -ge-, h) amuse, entertain; *sich ~*
amuse *or* enjoy o.s., have a good
time.

an [an] 1. *prp.* (*dat.*) at; on; upon;
in; against; to; by, near, close
to; ~ *der Themse* on the Thames;
~ *der Wand* on *or* against the wall;
es ist ~ dir it is up to you
to *inf.*; *am Leben* alive; *am 1. März*
on March 1st; *am Morgen* in the
morning; 2. *prp.* (*acc.*) to; on; on
to; at; against; about; *bis ~* as
far as, up to; 3. *adv.* on; *von heute*
~ from this day forth, from today;
von nun or jetzt ~ from now on.

analog *adj.* [ana'loːk] analogous
(*dat. or zu* to, with).

Analphabet [an(ʔ)alfa'beːt] *m* (-en/
-en) illiterate (person).

Analys|e [ana'lyːzə] *f* (-/-n) anal-
ysis; 2**ieren** [~'ziːrən] *v/t.* (no
-ge-, h) analy|se, *Am.* -ze.

Anämie ⚕ [anɛˈmiː] *f* (-/-*n*) an(a)emia.
Ananas [ˈananas] *f* (-/-, -*se*) pineapple.
Anarchie [anarˈçiː] *f* (-/-*n*) anarchy.
Anatom|ie [anatoˈmiː] *f* (-/*no pl.*) anatomy; **⁀isch** *adj.* [~ˈtoːmiʃ] anatomical.
ˈ**anbahnen** *v/t.* (*sep.*, -*ge*-, *h*) pave the way for, initiate; open up; *sich* ~ be opening up.
ˈ**Anbau** *m* **1.** ✓ (-[e]*s*/*no pl.*) cultivation; **2.** ⚠ (-[e]*s*/-*ten*) outbuilding, annex, extension, addition; ˈ**⁀en** *v/t.* (*sep.*, -*ge*-, *h*) ✓ cultivate, grow; ⚠ add (*an acc.* to); ˈ**~fläche** ✓ *f* arable land.
ˈ**anbehalten** *v/t.* (*irr. halten*, *sep.*, *no* -*ge*-, *h*) keep (*garment, etc.*) on.
anˈbei ✝ *adv.* enclosed.
ˈ**an|beißen** (*irr. beißen*, *sep.*, -*ge*-, *h*) **1.** *v/t.* bite into; **2.** *v/i.* *fish*: bite; ˈ**~bellen** *v/t.* (*sep.*, -*ge*-, *h*) bark at; **~beraumen** [ˈ~bəraʊmən] *v/t.* (*sep.*, *no* -*ge*-, *h*) appoint, fix; ˈ**~beten** *v/t.* (*sep.*, -*ge*-, *h*) adore, worship.
ˈ**Anbetracht** *m*: *in* ~ considering, in consideration of.
ˈ**anbetteln** *v/t.* (*sep.*, -*ge*-, *h*) beg from, solicit alms of.
ˈ**Anbetung** *f* (-/⚒-*en*) worship, adoration; ˈ**⁀swürdig** *adj.* adorable.
ˈ**an|bieten** *v/t.* (*irr. bieten*, *sep.*, -*ge*-, *h*) offer; ˈ**~binden** *v/t.* (*irr. binden*, *sep.*, -*ge*-, *h*) bind, tie (up); ~ *an* (*dat.*, *acc.*) tie to; *s. angebunden*; ˈ**~blasen** *v/t.* (*irr. blasen*, *sep.*, -*ge*-, *h*) blow at *or* (up)on.
ˈ**Anblick** *m* look; view; sight, aspect; ˈ**⁀en** *v/t.* (*sep.*, -*ge*-, *h*) look at; glance at; view; eye.
ˈ**an|blinzeln** *v/t.* (*sep.*, -*ge*-, *h*) wink at; ˈ**~brechen** (*irr. brechen*, *sep.*, -*ge*-) **1.** *v/t.* (*h*) break into (*provisions, etc.*); open (*bottle, etc.*); **2.** *v/i.* (*sein*) begin; *day*: break, dawn; ˈ**~brennen** (*irr. brennen*, *sep.*, -*ge*-) **1.** *v/t.* (*h*) set on fire; light (*cigar, etc.*); **2.** *v/i.* (*sein*) catch fire; burn; ˈ**~bringen** *v/t.* (*irr. bringen*, *sep.*, -*ge*-, *h*) bring; fix (*an dat.* to), attach (to); place; ✝ dispose of (*goods*); lodge (*complaint*); *s. angebracht*.
ˈ**Anbruch** *m* (-[e]*s*/*no pl.*) beginning; break (*of day*).
ˈ**anbrüllen** *v/t.* (*sep.*, -*ge*-, *h*) roar at.
Andacht [ˈandaxt] *f* (-/-*en*) devotion(s *pl.*); prayers *pl.*
andächtig *adj.* [ˈandɛçtiç] devout.
ˈ**andauern** *v/i.* (*sep.*, -*ge*-, *h*) last, continue, go on.
ˈ**Andenken** *n* (-*s*/-) memory, remembrance; keepsake, souvenir; *zum* ~ *an* (*acc.*) in memory of.
ander *adj.* [ˈandər] other; different; next; opposite; *am* ~*en Tag* (on) the next day; *e-n Tag um den* ~*en* every other day; *ein* ~*er Freund* another friend; *nichts* ~*es* nothing else.
andererseits *adv.* [ˈandərərˈzaɪts] on the other hand.
ändern [ˈɛndərn] *v/t.* (*ge*-, *h*) alter; change; *ich kann es nicht* ~ I can't help it; *sich* ~ alter; change.
ˈ**andernˈfalls** *adv.* otherwise, else.
anders *adv.* [ˈandərs] otherwise; differently (*als* from); else; *j.* ~ somebody else; *ich kann nicht* ~, *ich muß weinen* I cannot help crying; ~ *werden* change.
ˈ**anderˈseits** *adv.* *s. andererseits*.
ˈ**andersˈwo** *adv.* elsewhere.
anderthalb *adj.* [ˈandərtˈhalp] one and a half.
ˈ**Änderung** *f* (-/-*en*) change, alteration.
ander|wärts *adv.* [ˈandərˈvɛrts] elsewhere; ˈ**~ˈweitig** **1.** *adj.* other; **2.** *adv.* otherwise.
ˈ**andeut|en** *v/t.* (*sep.*, -*ge*-, *h*) indicate; hint; intimate; imply; suggest; ˈ**⁀ung** *f* intimation; hint; suggestion.
ˈ**Andrang** *m* rush; ⚕ congestion.
andre *adj.* [ˈandrə] *s. andere*.
ˈ**andrehen** *v/t.* (*sep.*, -*ge*-, *h*) turn on (*gas, etc.*); ⚡ switch on (*light*).
ˈ**androh|en** *v/t.* (*sep.*, -*ge*-, *h*): *j-m et.* ~ threaten s.o. with s.th.; ˈ**⁀ung** *f* threat.
aneignen [ˈanˀ-] *v/refl.* (*sep.*, -*ge*-, *h*) appropriate; acquire; adopt; seize; usurp.
aneinander *adv.* [anˀaɪˈnandər] together; **~geraten** *v/i.* (*irr. raten*, *sep.*, *no* -*ge*-, *sein*) clash (*mit* with).
anekeln [ˈanˀ-] *v/t.* (*sep.*, -*ge*-, *h*) disgust, sicken.
Anerbieten [ˈanˀ-] *n* (-*s*/-) offer.
anerkannt *adj.* [ˈanˀ-] acknowledged, recognized.
anerkenn|en [ˈanˀ-] *v/t.* (*irr. kennen*, *sep.*, *no* -*ge*-, *h*) acknowledge (*als* as), recognize; appreciate; own

(*child*); hono(u)r (*bill*); '2ung *f* (-/-en) acknowledgement; recognition; appreciation.

'anfahr|en (*irr. fahren, sep.,* -ge-) 1. *v/i.* (sein) start; ⚔ descend; *angefahren kommen* drive up; 2. *v/t.* (h) run into; carry, convey; *j-n* ~ let fly at s.o.; '2t *f* approach; drive.

'Anfall ⚕ *m* fit, attack; '2en (*irr. fallen, sep.,* -ge-) 1. *v/t.* (h) attack; assail; 2. *v/i.* (sein) accumulate; *money*: accrue.

anfällig *adj.* ['anfɛliç] susceptible (*für* to); prone to (*diseases, etc.*).

'Anfang *m* beginning, start, commencement; ~ *Mai* at the beginning of May, early in May; '2en *v/t. and v/i.* (*irr. fangen, sep.,* -ge-, h) begin, start, commence.

Anfäng|er ['anfɛŋ ər] *m* (-s/-) beginner; '2lich 1. *adj.* initial; 2. *adv.* in the beginning.

anfangs *adv.* ['anfaŋs] in the beginning; '2buchstabe *m* initial (letter); *großer* ~ capital letter; '2gründe [-grʏndə] *m/pl.* elements *pl.*

'anfassen (*sep.,* -ge-, h) 1. *v/t.* seize; touch; handle; 2. *v/i.* lend a hand.

anfecht|bar *adj.* ['anfɛçtbaːr] contestable; '.en *v/t.* (*irr. fechten, sep.,* -ge-, h) contest, dispute; ⚖ avoid (*contract*); '2ung *f* (-/-en) contestation; ⚖ avoidance; *fig.* temptation.

an|fertigen ['anfɛrtɪgən] *v/t.* (*sep.,* -ge-, h) make, manufacture; '~feuchten *v/t.* (*sep.,* -ge-, h) moisten, wet, damp; '~feuern *v/t.* (*sep.,* -ge-, h) fire, heat; *sports:* cheer; *fig.* encourage; '~flehen *v/t.* (*sep.,* -ge-, h) implore; '~fliegen ✈ *v/t.* (*irr. fliegen, sep.,* -ge-, h) approach, head for (*airport, etc.*); '2flug *m* ✈ approach (flight); *fig.* touch, tinge.

'anforder|n *v/t.* (*sep.,* -ge-, h) demand; request; claim; '2ung *f* demand; request; claim.

'Anfrage *f* inquiry; '2n *v/i.* (*sep.,* -ge-, h) ask (*bei j-m* s.o.); inquire (*bei j-m nach et.* of s.o. about s.th.).

an|freunden ['anfrɔyndən] *v/refl.* (*sep.,* -ge-, h): *sich* ~ *mit* make friends with; '~frieren *v/i.* (*irr. frieren, sep.,* -ge-, sein) freeze on (*an dat. or acc.* to); '~fügen *v/t.* (*sep.,* -ge-, h) join, attach (*an acc.* to); '~fühlen *v/t.* (*sep.,* -ge-, h) feel, touch; *sich* ~ feel.

Anfuhr ['anfuːr] *f* (-/-en) conveyance, carriage.

'anführ|en *v/t.* (*sep.,* -ge-, h) lead; allege; ✗ command; quote, cite (*authority, passage, etc.*); dupe, fool, trick; '2er *m* (ring)leader; '2ungszeichen *n/pl.* quotation marks *pl.*, inverted commas *pl.*

'Angabe *f* declaration; statement; instruction; F *fig.* bragging, showing off.

'angeb|en (*irr. geben, sep.,* -ge-, h) 1. *v/t.* declare; state; specify; allege; give (*name, reason*); † quote (*prices*); denounce, inform against; 2. *v/i. cards:* deal first; F *fig.* brag, show off, *Am.* blow; '2er *m* (-s/-) informer; F braggart, *Am.* blowhard; '~lich *adj.* ['~pliç] supposed; pretended, alleged.

'angeboren *adj.* innate, inborn; ⚕ congenital.

'Angebot *n* offer (*a.* †); *at auction sale:* bid; † supply.

'ange|bracht *adj.* appropriate, suitable; well-timed; '~bunden *adj.*: *kurz* ~ *sein* be short (*gegen* with).

'angehen (*irr. gehen, sep.,* -ge-) 1. *v/i.* (sein) begin; *meat, etc.*: go bad, go off; *es geht an* it will do; 2. *v/t.* (h): *j-n* ~ concern s.o.; *das geht dich nichts an* that is no business of yours.

'angehör|en *v/i.* (*sep., no* -ge-, h) belong to; '2ige ['~igə] *m, f* (-n/-n): *seine* ~*n pl.* his relations *pl.*; *die nächsten* ~*n pl.* the next of kin.

Angeklagte ⚖ ['angəklaːktə] *m, f* (-n/-n) *the* accused; prisoner (*at the bar*); defendant.

Angel ['aŋəl] *f* (-/-n) hinge; fishing-tackle, fishing-rod.

'angelegen *adj.*: *sich et.* ~ *sein lassen* make s.th. one's business; '2heit *f* business, concern, affair, matter.

'Angel|gerät *n* fishing-tackle; '2n (-ge-, h) 1. *v/i.* fish (*nach* for), angle (for) (*both a. fig.*); ~ *in* fish (*river, etc.*); 2. *v/t.* fish (*trout*); '~punkt *fig. m* pivot.

'Angel|sachse *m* Anglo-Saxon; '2sächsisch *adj.* Anglo-Saxon.

'Angelschnur *f* fishing-line.

'ange|messen *adj.* suitable, appropriate; reasonable; adequate; '~nehm *adj.* pleasant, agreeable, pleasing; *sehr* ~*!* glad *or* pleased to meet you; **~regt** *adj.* [`~re:kt`] stimulated; *discussion*: animated, lively; **`~sehen** *adj.* respected, esteemed.

'Angesicht *n* (-[e]s/-er, -e) face, countenance; *von ~ zu ~* face to face; **'2s** *prp.* (*gen.*) in view of.

angestammt *adj.* [`angəʃtamt`] hereditary, innate.

Angestellte [`angəʃtɛltə`] *m, f* (-/n/-n) employee; *die ~n pl.* the staff.

'ange|trunken *adj.* tipsy; **~wandt** *adj.* [`~vant`] applied; **~wiesen** *adj.*: *~ sein auf* (*acc.*) be dependent or thrown (up)on.

'angewöhnen *v/t.* (*sep.*, -ge-, h): *j-m et. ~* accustom s.o. to s.th.; *sich et. ~* get into the habit of s.th.; take to (*smoking*).

'Angewohnheit *f* custom, habit.

Angina *§* [an`gi:na`] *f* (-/*Anginen*) angina; tonsillitis.

'angleichen *v/t.* (*irr. gleichen*, *sep.*, -ge-, h) assimilate (*an acc.* to, with), adjust (to); *sich ~ an* (*acc.*) assimilate to *or* with, adjust *or* adapt to s.o.

Angler [`anglər`] *m* (-s/-) angler.

'angliedern *v/t.* (*sep.*, -ge-, h) join; annex; affiliate.

Anglist [an`glist`] *m* (-en/-en) professor *or* student of English, Angli(ci)st.

'angreif|en *v/t.* (*irr. greifen*, *sep.*, -ge-, h) touch; draw upon (*capital*, *provisions*); attack; affect (*health*, *material*); *⚗* corrode; exhaust; **'2er** *m* (-s/-) aggressor, assailant.

'angrenzend *adj.* adjacent; adjoining.

'Angriff *m* attack, assault; *in ~ nehmen* set about; **'~skrieg** *m* offensive war; **'2slustig** *adj.* aggressive.

Angst [anst] *f* (-/⁓e) fear, anxiety; anguish; *ich habe ~* I am afraid (*vor dat.* of); **'~hase** *m* coward.

ängstigen [`enstigən`] *v/t.* (ge-, h) frighten, alarm; *sich ~* be afraid (*vor dat.* of); be alarmed (*um* about).

ängstlich *adj.* [`enstliç`] uneasy, nervous; anxious; afraid; scrupulous; timid; **'2keit** *f* (-/*no pl.*) anxiety; scrupulousness; timidity.

'an|haben *v/t.* (*irr. haben*, *sep.*, -ge-, h) have (*garment*) on; *das kann mir nichts ~* that can't do me any harm; **'~haften** *v/i.* (*sep.*, -ge-, h) stick, adhere (*dat.* to); **'~haken** *v/t.* (*sep.*, -ge-, h) hook on; tick (off), *Am.* check (off) (*name, item*).

'anhalten (*irr. halten*, *sep.*, -ge-, h) **1.** *v/t.* stop; *j-n ~* zu et. keep s.o. to s.th.; *den Atem ~* hold one's breath; **2.** *v/i.* continue, last; stop; *um ein Mädchen ~* propose to a girl; **'~d** *adj.* continuous; persevering.

'Anhaltspunkt *m* clue.

'Anhang *m* appendix, supplement (*to book, etc.*); followers *pl.*, adherents *pl.*

'anhäng|en (*sep.*, -ge-, h) **1.** *v/t.* hang on; affix, attach, join; add; couple (on) (*coach, vehicle*); **2.** *v/i.* (*irr. hängen*) adhere to; **'2er** *m* (-s/-) adherent, follower; pendant (*of necklace, etc.*); label, tag; trailer (*behind car, etc.*).

anhänglich *adj.* [`anhenliç`] devoted, attached; **'2keit** *f* (-/*no pl.*) devotion, attachment.

Anhängsel [`anhenzəl`] *n* (-s/-) appendage.

'anhauchen *v/t.* (*sep.*, -ge-, h) breathe on; blow (*fingers*).

'anhäuf|en *v/t. and v/refl.* (*sep.*, -ge-, h) pile up, accumulate; **'2ung** *f* accumulation.

'an|heben *v/t.* (*irr. heben*, *sep.*, -ge-, h) lift, raise; **'~heften** *v/t.* (*sep.*, -ge-, h) fasten (*an acc.* to); stitch (to).

an'heim|fallen *v/i.* (*irr. fallen*, *sep.*, -ge-, sein): *j-m ~* fall to s.o.; **~stellen** *v/t.* (*sep.*, -ge-, h): *j-m et. ~* leave s.th. to s.o.

'Anhieb *m*: *auf ~* at the first go.

'Anhöhe *f* rise, elevation, hill.

'anhören *v/t.* (*sep.*, -ge-, h) listen to; *sich ~* sound.

Anilin *⚗* [ani`li:n`] *n* (-s/*no pl.*) aniline(in).

'ankämpfen *v/i.* (*sep.*, -ge-, h): *~ gegen* struggle against.

'Ankauf *m* purchase.

Anker *⚓* [`ankər`] *m* (-s/-) anchor; *vor ~ gehen* cast anchor; **'~kette** *⚓* *f* cable; **'2n** *⚓* *v/t. and v/i.* (ge-, h) anchor; **'~uhr** *f* lever watch.

'anketten *v/t.* (*sep.*, -ge-, h) chain (*an dat. or acc.* to).

'Anklage *f* accusation, charge; *ⅉ a.* indictment; **'2n** *v/t.* (*sep.*, -ge-, h) accuse (*gen. or wegen* of), charge (with); *ⅉ a.* indict (for).

'Ankläger *m* accuser; *öffentlicher ~ ⅉ* public prosecutor, *Am.* district attorney.

'anklammern *v/t.* (*sep.*, -ge-, h)

clip *s.th.* on; *sich* ~ cling (*an dat. or acc.* to).

'**Anklang** *m*: ~ *an* (*acc.*) suggestion of; ~ *finden* meet with approval.

'**an|kleben** *v/t.* (*sep.*, -ge-, *h*) stick on (*an dat. or acc.* to); glue on (to); paste on (to); gum on (to); '**~klei-den** *v/t.* (*sep.*, -ge-, *h*) dress; *sich* ~ dress (o.s.); '**~klopfen** *v/i.* (*sep.*, -ge-, *h*) knock (*an acc.* at); '**~knip-sen** ♀ *v/t.* (*sep.*, -ge-, *h*) turn or switch on; '**~knüpfen** (*sep.*, -ge-, *h*) **1.** *v/t.* tie (*an dat. or acc.* to); *fig.* begin; *Verbindungen* ~ form connexions *or* (*Am. only*) connections; **2.** *v/i.* refer (*an acc.* to); '**~kommen** *v/i.* (*irr. kommen*, *sep.*, -ge-, *sein*) arrive; ~ *auf* (*acc.*) depend (up)on; *es darauf* ~ *lassen* run the risk, risk it; *darauf kommt es an* that is the point; *es kommt nicht darauf an* it does not matter.

Ankömmling ['ankœmlɪŋ] *m* (-s/-e) new-comer, new arrival.

'**ankündig|en** *v/t.* (*sep.*, -ge-, *h*) announce; advertise; '**~ung** *f* announcement; advertisement.

Ankunft ['ankunft] *f* (-/*no pl.*) arrival.

'**an|kurbeln** *v/t.* (*sep.*, -ge-, *h*) *mot.* crank up; *die Wirtschaft* ~ F boost the economy; '**~lächeln** *v/t.* (*sep.*, -ge-, *h*), '**~lachen** *v/t.* (*sep.*, -ge-, *h*) smile at.

'**Anlage** *f* construction; installation; ⊕ plant; grounds *pl.*, park; plan, arrangement, layout; enclosure (*to letter*); ✝ investment; talent; predisposition, tendency; *öffentliche* ~ *pl.* public gardens *pl.*; '**~kapital** ✝ *n* invested capital.

'**anlangen** (*sep.*, -ge-) **1.** *v/i.* (*sein*) arrive at; **2.** *v/t.* (*h*) F touch; concern; *was mich anlangt* as far as I am concerned, (speaking) for myself.

Anlaß ['anlas] *m* (*Anlasses/Anlässe*) occasion; *ohne allen* ~ without any reason.

'**anlass|en** *v/t.* (*irr. lassen*, *sep.*, -ge-, *h*) F leave *or* keep (*garment, etc.*) on; leave (*light, etc.*) on; ⊕ start, set going; *sich gut* ~ promise well; '**~er** *mot. m* (-s/-) starter.

anläßlich *prp.* (*gen.*) ['anleslɪç] on the occasion of.

'**Anlauf** *m* start, run; '**~en** (*irr. lau-fen*, *sep.*, -ge-) **1.** *v/i.* (*sein*) run up;

start; tarnish, (grow) dim; ~ *gegen* run against; **2.** ♣ *v/t.* (*h*) call *or* touch at (*port*).

'**an|legen** (*sep.*, -ge-, *h*) **1.** *v/t.* put (*an acc.* to, against); lay out (*garden*); invest (*money*); level (*gun*); put on (*garment*); found (*town*); ✿ apply (*dressing*); lay in (*provisions*); *Feuer* ~ *an* (*acc.*) set fire to; **2.** *v/i.* ♣ land; moor; ~ *auf* (*acc.*) aim at; '**~lehnen** *v/t.* (*sep.*, -ge-, *h*) lean (*an acc.* against); leave *or* set (*door* ajar; *sich* ~ *an* (*acc.*) lean against *or* on.

Anleihe ['anlaɪə] *f* (-/-n) loan.

'**anleit|en** *v/t.* (*sep.*, -ge-, *h*) guide (*zu* to); instruct (*in dat.* in); '**~ung** *f* guidance, instruction; guide.

'**Anliegen** *n* (-s/-) desire, request.

'**an|locken** *v/t.* (*sep.*, -ge-, *h*) allure, entice; decoy; '**~machen** *v/t.* (*sep.*, -ge-, *h*) fasten (*an acc.* to), fix (to); make, light (*fire*); ⚡ switch on (*light*); dress (*salad*); '**~malen** *v/t.* (*sep.*, -ge-, *h*) paint.

'**Anmarsch** *m* approach.

anmaß|en ['anmaːsən] *v/refl.* (*sep.*, -ge-, *h*) arrogate *s.th.* to o.s.; assume (*right*); presume; '**~end** *adj.* arrogant; '**~ung** *f* (-/-en) arrogance, presumption.

'**anmeld|en** *v/t.* (*sep.*, -ge-, *h*) announce, notify; *sich* ~ *bei* make an appointment with; '**~ung** *f* announcement, notification.

'**anmerk|en** *v/t.* (*sep.*, -ge-, *h*) mark; note down; *j-m et.* ~ observe *or* perceive *s.th.* in *s.o.*; '**~ung** *f* (-/-en) remark; note; annotation; comment.

'**anmessen** *v/t.* (*irr. messen*, *sep.*, -ge-, *h*): *j-m e-n Anzug* ~ measure *s.o.* for a suit; *s. angemessen.*

'**Anmut** *f* (-/*no pl.*) grace, charm, loveliness; '**~ig** *adj.* charming, graceful, lovely.

'**an|nageln** *v/t.* (*sep.*, -ge-, *h*) nail on (*an acc.* to); '**~nähen** *v/t.* (*sep.*, -ge-, *h*) sew on (*an acc.* to).

annäher|nd *adj.* ['anneːərnt] approximate; '**~ung** *f* (-/-en) approach.

Annahme ['annaːmə] *f* (-/-n) acceptance; receiving-office; *fig.* assumption, supposition.

'**annehm|bar** *adj.* acceptable; *price:* reasonable; '**~en** (*irr. nehmen*, *sep.*, -ge-, *h*) **1.** *v/t.* accept, take; *fig.:*

suppose, take it, *Am.* guess; assume; contract (*habit*); adopt (*child*); *parl.* pass (*bill*); *sich* (*gen.*) ~ attend to *s.th.*; befriend *s.o.*; **2.** *v/i.* accept; **'2lichkeit** *f* (-/-en) amenity, agreeableness.

Annexion [anɛkˈsjoːn] *f* (-/-en) annexation.

Annonce [aˈnõːsə] *f* (-/-n) advertisement. [mous.|

anonym *adj.* [anoˈnyːm] anony-|

anordn|en [ˈanˀ-] *v/t.* (*sep.*, -ge-, *h*) order; arrange; direct; **'2ung** *f* arrangement; direction; order.

'anpacken *v/t.* (*sep.*, -ge-, *h*) seize, grasp; *fig.* tackle.

'anpass|en *v/t.* (*sep.*, -ge-, *h*) fit, adapt, suit; adjust; try *or* fit (*garment*) on; *sich* ~ adapt o.s. (*dat.* to); **'2ung** *f* (-/-en) adaptation; **'~ungs-fähig** *adj.* adaptable.

'anpflanz|en *v/t.* (*sep.*, -ge-, *h*) cultivate, plant; **'2ung** *f* cultivation; plantation.

Anprall [ˈanpral] *m* (-[e]s/%-e) impact; **'2en** *v/i.* (*sep.*, -ge-, *sein*) strike (*an acc.* against).

'anpreisen *v/t.* (*irr. preisen*, *sep.*, -ge-, *h*) commend, praise; boost, push.

'Anprobe *f* try-on, fitting.

'an|probieren *v/t.* (*sep.*, *no* -ge-, *h*) try *or* fit on; **'~raten** *v/t.* (*irr. raten*, *sep.*, -ge-, *h*) advise; **'~rechnen** *v/t.* (*sep.*, -ge-, *h*) charge; *hoch* ~ value highly.

'Anrecht *n* right, title, claim (*auf acc.* to).

'Anrede *f* address; **'2n** *v/t.* (*sep.*, -ge-, *h*) address, speak to.

'anrege|n *v/t.* (*sep.*, -ge-, *h*) stimulate; suggest; **'~end** *adj.* stimulative, stimulating; suggestive; **'2ung** *f* stimulation; suggestion.

'Anreiz *m* incentive; **'2en** *v/t.* (*sep.*, -ge-, *h*) stimulate; incite.

'an|rennen *v/i.* (*irr. rennen*, *sep.*, -ge-, *sein*): ~ *gegen* run against; *angerannt kommen* come running; **'~richten** *v/t.* (*sep.*, -ge-, *h*) prepare, dress (*food, salad*); cause, do (*damage*).

anrüchig *adj.* [ˈanryçiç] disreputable.

'anrücken *v/i.* (*sep.*, -ge-, *sein*) approach.

'Anruf *m* call (*a. teleph.*); **'2en** *v/t.* (*irr. rufen*, *sep.*, -ge-, *h*) call (*zum*

Zeugen to witness); *teleph.* ring up, F phone, *Am.* call up; hail (*ship*); invoke (*God, etc.*); appeal to (*s.o.'s help*).

'anrühren *v/t.* (*sep.*, -ge-, *h*) touch; mix.

'Ansage *f* announcement; **'2n** *v/t.* (*sep.*, -ge-, *h*) announce; **'~r** *m* (-s/-) announcer; compère, *Am.* master of ceremonies.

'ansammeln *v/t.* (*sep.*, -ge-, *h*) collect, gather; accumulate, amass; *sich* ~ collect, gather; accumulate.

ansässig *adj.* [ˈanzɛsiç] resident.

'Ansatz *m* start.

'an|schaffen *v/t.* (*sep.*, -ge-, *h*) procure, provide; purchase; *sich et.* ~ provide *or* supply o.s. with s.th.; **'~schalten** *∮ v/t.* (*sep.*, -ge-, *h*) connect; switch on (*light*).

'anschau|en *v/t.* (*sep.*, -ge-, *h*) look at, view; **'~lich** *adj.* clear, vivid; graphic.

'Anschauung *f* (-/-en) view; perception; conception; intuition; contemplation; **'~smaterial** *n* illustrative material; **'~sunterricht** [ˈanʃauuŋs-] *m* visual instruction, object-lessons *pl.*; **'~svermögen** *n* intuitive faculty.

'Anschein *m* (-[e]s/*no pl.*) appearance; **'2end** *adj.* apparent, seeming.

'an|schicken *v/refl.* (*sep.*, -ge-, *h*): *sich* ~, *et. zu tun* get ready for s.th.; prepare for s.th.; set about doing s.th.; **'~schirren** [ˈ~ʃirən] *v/t.* (*sep.*, -ge-, *h*) harness.

'Anschlag *m* ⊕ stop, catch; ♪ touch; notice; placard, poster, bill; estimate; calculation; plot; *e-n* ~ *auf j-n verüben* make an attempt on s.o.'s life; **'~brett** [ˈ~k-] *n* noticeboard, *Am.* bulletin board; **'2en** [ˈ~gən] (*irr. schlagen*, *sep.*, -ge-, *h*) **1.** *v/t.* strike (*an dat. or acc.* against), knock (against); post up (*bill*); ♪ touch; level (*gun*); estimate, rate; **2.** *v/i.* strike (*an acc.* against), knock (against); *dog:* bark; ♪ take (effect); *food:* agree (*bei* with); **'~säule** [ˈ~k-] *f* advertising pillar; **'~zettel** [ˈ~k-] *m* notice; placard, poster, bill.

'anschließen *v/t.* (*irr. schließen*, *sep.*, -ge-, *h*) fix with a lock; join, attach, annex; ⊕, ∮ connect; *sich j-m* ~ join s.o.; *sich e-r Meinung* ~ follow an opinion; **'~d** *adj.* adjacent (*an acc.* to); subsequent (to).

'Anschluß m joining; 🕿, ⚡, teleph., gas, etc.: connexion, (Am. only) connection; ~ haben an (acc.) 🕿, boat: connect with; 🕿 run in connexion with; ~ finden make friends (an acc. with), F pal up (with); teleph.: ~ bekommen get through; '~dose ⚡ f (wall) socket; '~zug 🕿 m connecting train, connexion.

'an|schmiegen v/refl. (sep., -ge-, h): sich ~ an (acc.) nestle to; '~schmieren** v/t. (sep., -ge-, h) (be)smear, grease; F fig. cheat; '~schnallen** v/t. (sep., -ge-, h) buckle on; bitte ~! 🚗 fasten seat-belts, please!; '~schnauzen** F v/t. (sep., -ge-, h) snap at, blow s.o. up, Am. a. bawl s.o. out; '~schneiden** v/t. (irr. schneiden, sep., -ge-, h) cut; broach (subject).

'Anschnitt m first cut or slice.

'an|schrauben v/t. (sep., -ge-, h) screw on (an dat. or acc. to); '~schreiben** v/t. (irr. schreiben, sep., -ge-, h) write down; sports, games: score; et. ~ lassen have s.th. charged to one's account; buy s.th. on credit; '~schreien** v/t. (irr. schreien, sep., -ge-, h) shout at.

'Anschrift f address.

an|schuldigen ['anʃuldigən] v/t. (sep., -ge-, h) accuse, incriminate; '~schwärzen** v/t. (sep., -ge-, h) blacken; fig. a. defame.

'anschwell|en (irr. schwellen, sep., -ge-) 1. v/i. (sein) swell; increase, rise; 2. v/t. (h) swell; 'Qung f swelling.

anschwemm|en ['anʃvemən] v/t. (sep., -ge-, h) wash ashore; geol. deposit (alluvium); 'Qung f (-/-en) wash; geol. alluvial deposits pl., alluvium.

'ansehen 1. v/t. (irr. sehen, sep., -ge-, h) (take a) look at; view; regard, consider (als as); et. mit ~ witness s.th.; ~ für take for; man sieht ihm sein Alter nicht an he does not look his age; 2. 2 n (-s/no pl.) authority, prestige; respect; F appearance, aspect.

ansehnlich adj. ['anze:nliç] considerable; good-looking.

'an|seilen mount. v/t. and v/refl. (sep., -ge-, h) rope; '~sengen** v/t. (sep., -ge-, h) singe; '~setzen** (sep., -ge-, h) 1. v/t. put (an acc. to); add (to); fix, appoint (date); rate; fix,

quote (prices); charge; put forth (leaves, etc.); put on (flesh); put (food) on (to boil); Rost ~ rust; 2. v/i. try; start; get ready.

'Ansicht f (-/-en) sight, view; fig. view, opinion; meiner ~ nach in my opinion; zur ~ ✝ on approval; '~s-(post)karte** f picture postcard; '~ssache** f matter of opinion.

'ansied|eln v/t. and v/refl. (sep., -ge-, h) settle; 'Qler** m settler; 'Qlung** f settlement.

'Ansinnen n (-s/-) request, demand.

'anspann|en v/t. (sep., -ge-, h) stretch; put or harness (horses, etc.) to the carriage, etc.; fig. strain, exert; 'Qung** f strain, exertion.

anspeien v/t. (irr. speien, sep., -ge-, h) spit (up)on or at.

'anspiel|en v/i. (sep., -ge-, h) cards: lead; sports: lead off; football: kick off; ~ auf (acc.) allude to, hint at; 'Qung** f (-/-en) allusion, hint.

'anspitzen v/t. (sep., -ge-, h) point, sharpen.

'Ansporn m (-[e]s/✎ -e) spur; 'Qen** v/t. (sep., -ge-, h) spur s.o. on.

'Ansprache f address, speech; e-e ~ halten deliver an address.

'ansprechen v/t. (irr. sprechen, sep., -ge-, h) speak to, address; appeal to; '~d** adj. appealing.

'an|springen (irr. springen, sep., -ge-) 1. v/i. (sein) engine: start; 2. v/t. (h) jump (up)on, leap at; '~spritzen** v/t. (sep., -ge-, h) splash (j-n mit et. s.th. on s.o.); (be-) sprinkle.

'Anspruch m claim (a. ⅈⅉ) (auf acc. to), pretension (to); ⅈⅉ title (to); ~ haben auf (acc.) be entitled to; in ~ nehmen claim s.th.; Zeit in ~ nehmen take up time; 'Qslos** adj. unpretentious; unassuming; 'Qsvoll** adj. pretentious.

'an|spülen v/t. (sep., -ge-, h) s. anschwemmen; '~stacheln** v/t. (sep., -ge-, h) goad (on).

Anstalt ['anʃtalt] f (-/-en) establishment, institution; ~en treffen zu make arrangements for.

'Anstand m 1. (-[e]s/✎e) hunt. stand; objection; 2. (-[e]s/✎ ᵘe) good manners pl.; decency, propriety.

anständig adj. ['anʃtendiç] decent; respectable; price: fair, handsome; 'Qkeit** f (-/✎ -en) decency.

'Anstands|gefühl n sense of propriety; tact; '≗los *adv.* unhesitatingly.

'an|starren *v/t.* (*sep.*, -ge-, h) stare or gaze at.

anstatt *prp.* (*gen.*) *and cj.* [an'ʃtat] instead of.

'anstaunen *v/t.* (*sep.*, -ge-, h) gaze at *s.o.* or *s.th.* in wonder.

'an|stecken *v/t.* (*sep.*, -ge-, h) pin on; put on (*ring*); ⚕ infect; set on fire; kindle (*fire*); light (*candle*, *etc.*); '≗end *adj.* infectious; contagious; *fig. a.* catching; '2ung *f* (-/-en) infection; contagion.

'an|stehen *v/i.* (*irr.* stehen, *sep.*, -ge-, h) queue up (*nach* for), *Am.* stand in line (for); '≗steigen *v/i.* (*irr.* steigen, *sep.*, -ge-, sein) ground: rise, ascend; *fig.* increase.

'an|stell|en *v/t.* (*sep.*, -ge-, h) engage, employ, hire; make (*experiments*); draw (*comparison*); turn on (*light*, *etc.*); manage; *sich ~* queue up (*nach* for), *Am.* line up (for); *sich dumm ~* set about *s.th.* stupidly; '≗ig *adj.* handy, skil(l)ful; '2ung *f* place, position, job; employment.

'Anstieg ['anʃtiːk] *m* (-[e]s/-e) ascent.

'an|stift|en *v/t.* (*sep.*, -ge-, h) instigate; '2er *m* instigator; '2ung *f* instigation.

'anstimmen *v/t.* (*sep.*, -ge-, h) strike up (*tune*).

'Anstoß *m football*: kick-off; *fig.* impulse; offen|ce, *Am.* -se; ~ *erregen* give offence (*bei* to); ~ *nehmen an* (*dat.*) take offence at; ~ *geben zu et.* start s.th., initiate s.th.; '2en (*irr.* stoßen, *sep.*, -ge-) **1.** *v/t.* (h) push, knock (*acc.* or *an* against); nudge; **2.** *v/i.* (sein) knock (*an acc.* against); border (*on, upon*); adjoin; **3.** *v/i.* (h): *mit der Zunge ~* lisp; *auf j-s Gesundheit ~* drink (to) s.o.'s health; '2end *adj.* adjoining.

'anstößig *adj.* ['anʃtøːsiç] shocking.

'an|strahlen *v/t.* (*sep.*, -ge-, h) illuminate; floodlight (*building, etc.*); *fig.* beam at *s.o.*; '≗streben *v/t.* (*sep.*, -ge-, h) aim at, aspire to, strive for.

'anstreich|en *v/t.* (*irr.* streichen, *sep.*, -ge-, h) paint; whitewash; mark; underline (*mistake*); '2er *m* (-s/-) house-painter; decorator.

anstreng|en ['anʃtreŋən] *v/t.* (*sep.*, -ge-, h) exert; try (*eyes*); fatigue; *Prozeß ~* bring an action (*gegen j-n*

against s.o.); *sich ~* exert o.s.; '≗end *adj.* strenuous; trying (*für* to); '2ung *f* (-/-en) exertion, strain, effort.

'Anstrich *m* paint, colo(u)r; coat (-ing); *fig.*: tinge; air.

'Ansturm *m* assault; onset; ~ *auf* (*acc.*) rush for; ✝ run on (*bank*).

'anstürmen *v/i.* (*sep.*, -ge-, sein) storm, rush.

'Anteil *m* share, portion; ~ *nehmen an* (*dat.*) take an interest in; sympathize with; ~nahme ['~naː-mə] *f* (-/no pl.) sympathy; interest; '≗schein ✝ *m* share-certificate.

Antenne [an'tɛnə] *f* (-/-n) aerial'.

Antialkoholiker [anti'alko'hoːlikər, ~] *m* (-s/-) teetotaller.

antik *adj.* [an'tiːk] antique.

Antilope *zo.* [anti'loːpə] *f* (-/-n) antelope.

Antipathie [antipa'tiː] *f* (-/-n) antipathy.

'antippen F *v/t.* (*sep.*, -ge-, h) tap.

Antiquar [anti'kvaːr] *m* (-s/-e) second-hand bookseller; ~iat [~ar-'jaːt] *n* (-[e]s/-e) second-hand bookshop; 2isch *adj. and adv.* [~'kvaːriʃ] second-hand.

Antiquitäten [antikvi'tɛːtən] *f/pl.* antiques *pl.*

'Anti-Rakete *f* anti-ballistic missile.

antiseptisch ⚕ *adj.* [anti'zɛptiʃ] antiseptic.

Antlitz ['antlits] *n* (-es/⚕ -e) face, countenance.

Antrag ['antraːk] *m* (-[e]s/⸚e) offer, proposal; application; request; *parl.* motion; ~ *stellen auf* (*acc.*) make an application for; *parl.* put a motion for; '≗steller *m* (-s/-) applicant; *parl.* mover; ⚖ petitioner.

'an|treffen *v/t.* (*irr.* treffen, *sep.*, -ge-, h) meet with; find; '≗treiben (*irr.* treiben, *sep.*, -ge-) **1.** *v/i.* (sein) drift ashore; **2.** *v/t.* (h) drive (on); *fig.* impel; '≗treten (*irr.* treten, *sep.*, -ge-) **1.** *v/t.* (h) enter upon (*office*); take up (*position*); set out on (*journey*); enter upon; take possession of (*inheritance*); **2.** *v/i.* (sein) take one's place; ✕ fall in.

'Antrieb *m* motive, impulse; ⊕ drive, propulsion.

'Antritt *m* (-[e]s/⚕ -e) entrance (*into office*); taking up (*of position*); setting out (*on journey*); entering into possession (*of inheritance*).

'**antun** v/t. (irr. tun, sep., -ge-, h): j-m et. ~ do s.th. to s.o.; sich et. ~ lay hands on o.s.

'**Antwort** f (-/-en) answer, reply (auf acc. to); '**2en** (ge-, h) 1. v/i. answer (j-m s.o.), reply (j-m to s.o.: both: auf acc. to); 2. v/t. answer (auf acc. to), reply (to); '**~schein** m (international) reply coupon.

'**an|vertrauen** v/t. (sep., no -ge-, h): j-m et. ~ (en)trust s.o. with s.th., entrust s.th. to s.o.; confide s.th. to s.o.; '**~wachsen** v/i. (irr. wachsen, sep., -ge-, sein) take root; fig. increase; ~ an (acc.) grow on to.

Anwalt ['anvalt] m (-[e]s/=e) lawyer; solicitor, Am. attorney; counsel; barrister, Am. counsel(l)or; fig. advocate.

'**Anwandlung** f fit; impulse.

'**Anwärter** m candidate, aspirant; expectant.

Anwartschaft ['anvartʃaft] f (-/-en) expectancy; candidacy; prospect (auf acc. of).

'**anweis|en** v/t. (irr. weisen, sep., -ge-, h) assign; instruct; direct; s. angewiesen; '**2ung** f assignment; instruction; direction; ✝: cheque, Am. check; draft; s. Postanweisung.

'**anwend|en** v/t. (irr. wenden, sep., -ge-, h) employ, use; apply (auf acc. to); s. angewandt; '**2ung** f application.

'**anwerben** v/t. (irr. werben, sep., -ge-, h) ✕ enlist, enrol(l); engage.

'**Anwesen** n estate; property.

'**anwesen|d** adj. present; '**2heit** f (-/no pl.) presence.

'**Anzahl** f (-/no pl.) number; quantity.

'**anzahl|en** v/t. (sep., -ge-, h) pay on account; pay a deposit; '**2ung** f (first) instal(l)ment; deposit.

'**anzapfen** v/t. (sep., -ge-, h) tap.

'**Anzeichen** n symptom; sign.

Anzeige ['antsaɪɡə] f (-/-en) notice, announcement; ✝ advice; advertisement; ⚕ information; '**2n** v/t. (sep., -ge-, h) announce, notify; ✝ advise; advertise; indicate; ⊕ instrument: indicate, show; thermometer: read (degrees); j-n ~ denounce s.o., inform against s.o.

'**anziehen** (irr. ziehen, sep., -ge-, h) 1. v/t. draw, pull; draw (rein); tighten (screw); put on (garment);

dress; fig. attract; 2. v/i. draw; prices: rise; '**~d** adj. attractive, interesting.

'**Anziehung** f attraction; '**~skraft** f attractive power; attraction.

'**Anzug** m (-[e]s/=e) dress; suit; 2. (-[e]s/no pl.): im ~ sein storm: be gathering; danger: be impending.

anzüglich adj. ['antsy:klɪç] personal; '**2keit** f (-/-en) personality.

'**anzünden** v/t. (sep., -ge-, h) light, kindle; strike (match); set (building) on fire.

apathisch adj. [a'pa:tiʃ] apathetic.

Apfel ['apfəl] m (-s/=) apple; '**~mus** n apple-sauce; '**~sine** [~'zi:nə] f (-/-n) orange; '**~wein** m cider.

Apostel [a'pɔstəl] m (-s/-) apostle.

Apostroph [apɔ'stro:f] m (-s/-e) apostrophe.

Apotheke [apo'te:kə] f (-/-n) chemist's shop, pharmacy, Am. drugstore; '**~r** m (-s/-) chemist, Am. druggist, pharmacist.

Apparat [apa'ra:t] m (-[e]s/-e) apparatus; device; teleph.: am ~! speaking!; teleph.: am ~ bleiben hold the line.

Appell [a'pɛl] m (-s/-e) ✕: roll-call; inspection; parade; fig. appeal (an acc. to); **2ieren** [~'li:rən] v/i. (no -ge-, h) appeal (an acc. to).

Appetit [ape'ti:t] m (-[e]s/-e) appetite; **2lich** adj. appetizing, savo(u)ry, dainty.

Applaus [a'plaus] m (-es/✦ -e) applause.

Aprikose [apri'ko:zə] f (-/-n) apricot.

April [a'pril] m (-[s]/-e) April.

Aquarell [akva'rɛl] m (-s/-e) water-colo(u)r (painting), aquarelle.

Aquarium [a'kva:rium] n (-s/ Aquarien) aquarium.

Äquator [ɛ'kva:tɔr] m (-s/✦ -en) equator.

Ära ['ɛ:ra] f (-/✦ Ären) era.

Arab|er ['arabər] m (-s/-) Arab; **2isch** adj. [a'ra:biʃ] Arabian, Arab(ic).

Arbeit ['arbaɪt] f (-/-en) work; labo(u)r, toil; employment, job; task; paper; workmanship; bei der ~ at work; sich an die ~ machen, an die ~ gehen set to work; (keine) ~ haben be in (out of) work; die ~ niederlegen stop work, down tools;

'2en (ge-, h) **1.** v/i. work; labo(u)r, toil; **2.** v/t. work; make.

'**Arbeiter** m (-s/-) worker; workman, labo(u)rer, hand; '**~in** f (-/-nen) female worker; working woman, workwoman; '**~klasse** f working class(es pl.); '**~partei** f Labo(u)r Party; '**~schaft** f (-/-en), '**~stand** m working class(es pl.), labo(u)r.

'**Arbeit|geber** m (-s/-), '**~geberin** f (-/-nen) employer; '**~nehmer** m (-s/-), '**~nehmerin** f (-/-nen) employee.

'**arbeitsam** adj. industrious.

'**Arbeits|amt** n labo(u)r exchange; '**~anzug** m overall; '**~beschaffung** f (-/-en) provision of work; '**~bescheinigung** f certificate of employment; '**~einkommen** n earned income; '**2fähig** adj. able to work; '**~gericht** n labo(u)r or industrial court; '**~kleidung** f working clothes pl.; '**~kraft** f working power; worker, hand; Arbeitskräfte pl. a. labo(u)r; '**~leistung** f efficiency; power (of engine); output (of factory); '**~lohn** m wages pl., pay; '**2los** adj. out of work, unemployed; '**~lose** m (-n/-n): die ~n pl. the unemployed pl.; '**~losenunterstützung** f unemployment benefit; ~ beziehen f be on the dole; '**~losigkeit** f (-/no pl.) unemployment; '**~markt** m labo(u)r market; '**~minister** m Minister of Labour, Am. Secretary of Labor; '**~nachweis(stelle** f) m employment registry office, Am. labor registry office; '**~niederlegung** f (-/-en) strike, Am. F a. walkout; '**~pause** f break, intermission; '**~platz** m place of work; job; '**~raum** m workroom; '**2scheu** adj. work-shy; '**~scheu** f aversion to work; '**~schutzgesetz** n protective labo(u)r law; '**~tag** m working day, workday; '**2unfähig** adj. incapable of working; disabled; '**~weise** f practice, method of working; '**~willige** m (-n/-n) non-striker; '**~zeit** f working time; working hours pl.; '**~zeug** n tools pl.; '**~zimmer** n workroom; study.

Archäo|loge [arçεo'lo:gə] m (-n/-n) arch(a)eologist; **~logie** [~o'gi:] f (-/no pl.) arch(a)eology.

Arche ['arçə] f (-/-n) ark.

Architekt [arçi'tεkt] m (-en/-en) architect; **~ur** [~'tu:r] f (-/-en) architecture.

Archiv [ar'çi:f] n (-s/-e) archives pl.; record office.

Areal [are'a:l] n (-s/-e) area.

Arena [a're:na] f (-/-Arenen) arena; bullring; (circus-)ring.

arg adj. [ark] bad; wicked; gross.

Ärger ['εrgər] m (-s/no pl.) vexation, annoyance; anger; '**2lich** adj. vexed, F mad, angry (auf, über acc. at s.th., with s.o.); annoying, vexatious; '**2n** v/t. (ge-, h) annoy, vex, irritate, fret; bother; sich ~ feel angry or vexed (über acc. at, about s.th.; with s.o.); '**~nis** n (-ses/-se) scandal, offen|ce, Am. -se.

'**Arg|list** f (-/no pl.) cunning, craft (-iness); '**2listig** adj. crafty, cunning; '**2los** adj. guileless, artless, unsuspecting; '**~wohn** ['~vo:n] m (-[e]s/no pl.) suspicion; **2wöhnen** ['~vø:nən] v/t. (ge-, h) suspect; '**2wöhnisch** adj. suspicious.

Arie ♪ ['a:rjə] f (-/-n) aria.

Aristokrat [aristo'kra:t] m (-en/-en), **~in** f (-/-nen) aristocrat; **~ie** [~kra-'ti:] f (-/-n) aristocracy.

Arkade [ar'ka:də] f (-/-n) arcade.

arm[1] adj. [arm] poor.

Arm[2] [~] m (-[e]s/-e) arm; branch (of river, etc.); F: j-n auf den ~ nehmen pull s.o.'s leg.

Armaturenbrett [arma'tu:rənbrεt] n instrument board, dash-board.

'**Arm|band** n bracelet; **~banduhr** ['armbant?-] f wrist watch; '**~bruch** m fracture of the arm.

Armee [ar'me:] f (-/-n) army.

Ärmel ['εrməl] m (-s/-) sleeve; '**~kanal** m the (English) Channel.

'**Armen|haus** n alms-house, Brt. a. workhouse; '**~pflege** f poor relief; '**~pfleger** m guardian of the poor; welfare officer; '**~unterstützung** f poor relief.

ärmlich ['εrmliç] s. armselig.

'**armselig** adj. poor; wretched; miserable; shabby; paltry.

Armut ['armu:t] f (-/no pl.) poverty.

Aroma [a'ro:ma] n (-s/Aromen, Aromata, -s) aroma, flavo(u)r; fragrance.

Arrest [a'rεst] m (-es/-e) arrest; confinement; seizure (of goods); detention (of pupil, etc.); ~ bekommen be kept in.

Art [ɑːrt] f (-/-en) kind, sort; ♀, zo. species; manner, way; nature; manners pl.; breed, race (of animals); auf die(se) ~ in this way; '2en v/i. (ge-, sein): ~ nach take after. [artery.]

Arterie anat. [ar'teːrjə] f (-/-n)]

artig adj. ['ɑːrtiç] good, well-behaved; civil, polite; '2keit f (-/-en) good behavio(u)r; politeness; civility, a. civilities pl.

Artikel [ar'tiːkəl] m (-s/-) article; commodity.

Artillerie [artilə'riː] f (-/-n) artillery.

Artist [ar'tist] m (-en/-en), ~in f (-/-nen) circus performer.

Arznei [arts'naɪ] f (-/-en) medicine, F physic; ~kunde f (-/no pl.) pharmaceutics; ~mittel n medicine, drug.

Arzt [ɑːrtst] m (-es/-e) doctor, medical man; physician.

Ärztin ['ɛːrtstin] f (-/-nen) woman or lady doctor.

ärztlich adj. ['ɛːrtstliç] medical.

As [as] n (-ses/-se) ace.

Asche ['aʃə] f (-/-n) ash(es pl.); '~n-bahn f sports: cinder-track, mot. dirt-track; '~nbecher m ash-tray; '~nbrödel ['~nbrøːdəl] n (-s/no pl.), ~nputtel ['~nputəl] n 1. (-s/no pl.) Cinderella; 2. (-s/-) drudge.

Ascher'mittwoch m Ash Wednesday.

'**aschgrau** adj. ash-grey, ashy, Am. ash-gray.

äsen hunt. ['ɛːzən] v/i. (ge-, h) graze, browse.

Asiat [az'jɑːt] m (-en/-en), ~in f (-/-nen) Asiatic, Asian; 2isch adj. Asiatic, Asian.

Asket [as'keːt] m (-en/-en) ascetic.

Asphalt [as'falt] m (-[e]s/-e) asphalt; 2ieren ['~'tiːrən] v/t. (no -ge-, h) asphalt.

aß [ɑːs] pret. of essen.

Assistent [asis'tɛnt] m (-en/-en), ~in f (-/-nen) assistant.

Ast [ast] m (-es/-e) branch, bough; knot (in timber); '~loch n knot-hole.

Astro|**naut** [astro'naʊt] m (-en/-en) astronaut; ~nom [~'noːm] m (-en/-en) astronomer.

Asyl [a'zyːl] n (-s/-e) asylum; fig. sanctuary.

Atelier [atə'lje:] n (-s/-s) studio.

Atem ['ɑːtəm] m (-s/no pl.) breath;

außer ~ out of breath; '2los adj. breathless; '~not ♂ f difficulty in breathing; '~pause f breathing-space; '~zug m breath, respiration.

Äther ['ɛːtər] m 1. (-s/no pl.) the ether; 2. ♂ (-s/-) ether; 2isch adj. [e'teːriʃ] ethereal, etheric.

Athlet [at'leːt] m (-en/-en), ~in f (-/-nen) athlete; ~ik f (-/no pl.) athletics mst sg.; 2isch adj. athletic.

atlantisch adj. [at'lantiʃ] Atlantic.

Atlas ['atlas] m 1. geogr. (-/no pl.) Atlas; 2. (-, -ses/-se, Atlanten) maps: atlas; 3. (-, -ses/-se) textiles: satin.

atmen ['ɑːtmən] v/i. and v/t. (ge-, h) breathe.

Atmosphär|**e** [atmo'sfɛːrə] f (-/-n) atmosphere; 2isch adj. atmospheric.

'**Atmung** f (-/-en) breathing, respiration.

Atom [a'toːm] n (-s/-e) atom; 2ar adj. [ato'mɑːr] atomic; ~bombe f atomic bomb, atom-bomb, A-bomb; ~energie f atomic or nuclear energy; ~forschung f atomic or nuclear research; ~kern m atomic nucleus; ~kraftwerk n nuclear power station; ~meiler m atomic pile, nuclear reactor; ~physiker m atomic physicist; ~reaktor m nuclear reactor, atomic pile; ~versuch m atomic test; ~waffe f atomic or nuclear weapon; ~wissenschaftler m atomic scientist; ~zeitalter n atomic age.

Attent|**at** [atɛn'tɑːt] n (-[e]s/-e) (attempted) assassination; fig. outrage; ~äter [~'ɛːtər] m (-s/-) assailant, assassin.

Attest [a'tɛst] n (-es/-e) certificate; 2ieren [~'tiːrən] v/t. (no -ge-, h) attest, certify.

Attraktion [atrak'tsjoːn] f (-/-en) attraction.

Attrappe [a'trapə] f (-/-n) dummy.

Attribut [atri'buːt] n (-[e]s/-e) attribute; gr. attributive.

ätz|**en** ['ɛtsən] v/t. (ge-, h) corrode; ♂ cauterize; etch (metal plate); '~end adj. corrosive, caustic (a. fig.); '2ung f (-/-en) corrosion, ♂ cauterization; etching.

au int. [aʊ] oh!; ouch!

auch cj. [aʊx] also, too, likewise; even; ~ nicht neither, nor; wo ~ (immer) wher(eso)ever; ist es ~ wahr? is it really true?

Audienz [audi'ɛnts] f (-/-en) audience, hearing.

auf [auf] **1.** prp. (dat.) (up)on; in; at; of; by; ~ dem Tisch (up)on the table; ~ dem Markt in the market; ~ der Universität at the university; ~ e-m Ball at a ball; **2.** prp. (acc.) on; in; at; to; towards (a. ~ ... zu); up; ~ deutsch in German; ~ e-e Entfernung von at a range of; ~ die Post etc. gehen go to the post-office, etc.; ~ ein Pfund gehen 20 Schilling 20 shillings go to a pound; es geht ~ neun it is getting on to nine; ~ ... hin on the strength of; **3.** adv. up(wards); ~ und ab gehen walk up and down or to and fro; **4.** cj.: ~ daß (in order) that; ~ daß nicht that not, lest; **5.** int.: ~! up!

auf|arbeiten ['auf?-] v/t. (sep., -ge-, h) work off (arrears of work); furbish up; F do up (garments); **~atmen** fig. ['auf?-] v/i. (sep., -ge-, h) breathe again.

Aufbau m (-[e]s/no pl.) building up; construction (of play, etc.); F esp. Am. setup (of organization); mot. body of car, etc.); **2en** v/t. (sep., -ge-, h) erect, build up; construct.

auf|bauschen v/t. (sep., -ge-, h) puff up; fig. exaggerate; **~beißen** v/t. (irr. beißen, sep., -ge-, h) crack; **~bekommen** v/t. (irr. kommen, sep., no -ge-, h) get open (door); be given (a task); **~bessern** v/t. (sep., -ge-, h) raise (salary); **~bewahren** v/t. (sep., no -ge-, h) keep; preserve; **~bieten** v/t. (irr. bieten, sep., -ge-, h) summon; exert; ✗ raise; **~binden** v/t. (irr. binden, sep., -ge-, h) untie; **~bleiben** v/i. (irr. bleiben, sep., -ge-, sein) sit up; door, etc.: remain open; **~blenden** (sep., -ge-, h) **1.** mot. v/i. turn up the headlights; **2.** v/t. fade in (scene); **~blicken** v/i. (sep., -ge-, h) look up; raise one's eyes; **~blitzen** v/i. (sep., -ge-, h, sein) flash (up); **~blühen** v/i. (sep., -ge-, sein) bloom; flourish.

aufbrausen fig. v/i. (sep., -ge-, sein) fly into a passion; **~d** adj. hot-tempered.

auf|brechen (irr. brechen, sep., -ge-) **1.** v/t. (h) break open; force open; **2.** v/i. (sein) burst open; set out (nach for); **~bringen** v/t. (irr. bringen, sep., -ge-, h) raise (money, troops); capture (ship); rouse or irritate s.o.

Aufbruch m departure, start.

auf|bügeln v/t. (sep., -ge-, h) iron; **~bürden** v/t. (sep., -ge-, h): j-m et. ~ impose s.th. on s.o.; **~decken** v/t. (sep., -ge-, h) uncover; spread (cloth); fig. disclose; **~drängen** v/t. (sep., -ge-, h) force, obtrude (j-m [up]on s.o.); **~drehen** v/t. (sep., -ge-, h) turn on (gas, etc.).

aufdringlich adj. obtrusive.

Aufdruck m (-[e]s/-e) imprint; surcharge.

aufdrücken v/t. (sep., -ge-, h) impress.

aufeinander adv. [auf?aɪ'nandər] one after or upon another; **2folge** f succession; **~folgend** adj. successive.

Aufenthalt m (-[e]s/-e) stay; residence; delay; 🚋 stop; **~sgenehmigung** f residence permit.

auferlegen ['auf?ɛrle:gən] v/t. (sep., no -ge-, h) impose (j-m on s.o.).

aufersteh|en ['auf?ɛrʃte:ən] v/i. (irr. stehen, sep., -ge-, sein) rise (from the dead); **2ung** f (-/-en) resurrection.

auf|essen ['auf?-] v/t. (irr. essen, sep., -ge-, h) eat up; **~fahren** v/i. (irr. fahren, sep., -ge-, sein) ascend; start up; fig. fly out; ⚓ run aground; mot. drive or run (auf acc. against, into).

Auffahrt f ascent; driving up; approach; drive, Am. driveway; **~srampe** f ramp.

auf|fallen v/i. (irr. fallen, sep., -ge-, sein) be conspicuous; j-m ~ strike s.o.; **~fallend** adj., **~fällig** adj. striking; conspicuous; flashy.

auffangen v/t. (irr. fangen, sep., -ge-, h) catch (up); parry (thrust).

auffass|en v/t. (sep., -ge-, h) conceive; comprehend; interpret; **2ung** f conception; interpretation; grasp.

auffinden v/t. (irr. finden, sep., -ge-, h) find, trace, discover, locate.

aufforder|n v/t. (sep., -ge-, h) ask, invite; call (up)on; esp. 🏛 summon; **2ung** f invitation; esp. 🏛 summons.

auffrischen (sep., -ge-) **1.** v/t. (h) freshen up, touch up; brush up (*knowledge*); revive; **2.** *v/i.* (*sein*) *wind*: freshen.

'**aufführ|en** *v/t.* (*sep.*, -*ge*-, *h*) *thea.* represent, perform, act; enumerate; enter (*in list*); einzeln ~ specify, *Am.* itemize; sich ~ behave; '**2ung** *f thea.* performance; enumeration; entry; specification; conduct.

'**Aufgabe** *f* task; problem; *school*: homework; posting, *Am.* mailing (*of letter*); booking (*of luggage*), *Am.* checking (*of baggage*); resignation (*from office*); abandonment; giving up (*business*); es sich zur ~ machen make it one's business.

'**Aufgang** *m* ascent; *ast.* rising; staircase.

'**aufgeben** (*irr. geben, sep.*, -*ge*-, *h*) **1.** *v/t.* give up, abandon; resign from (*office*); insert (*advertisement*); post, *Am.* mail (*letter*); book (*luggage*), *Am.* check (*baggage*); hand in, send (*telegram*); ✝ give (*order*); set, *Am.* assign (*homework*); set (*riddle*); **2.** *v/i.* give up *or* in.

'**Aufgebot** *n* public notice; ✕ levy; *fig.* array; banns *pl.* (*of marriage*).

'**aufgehen** *v/i.* (*irr. gehen, sep.*, -*ge*-, *sein*) open; ⚕ leave no remainder; *sewing*: come apart; *paste, star, curtain*: rise; *seed*: come up; ~ in (*dat.*) be merged in; *fig.* be devoted to (*work*); in Flammen ~ go up in flames.

aufgeklärt *adj.* ['aʊfgəkle:rt] enlightened; '**2heit** *f* (-/*no pl.*) enlightenment.

'**Aufgeld** ✝ *n* agio, premium.

aufge|legt *adj.* ['aʊfgəle:kt] disposed (*zu for*); in the mood (*zu inf.* for *ger.*, to *inf.*); gut (*schlecht*) ~ in a good (bad) humo(u)r; '**~schlossen** *fig. adj.* open-minded; **~weckt** *fig. adj.* ['~vɛkt] bright.

'**auf|gießen** *v/t.* (*irr. gießen, sep.*, -*ge*-, *h*) pour (on); make (*tea*); '**~greifen** *v/t.* (*irr. greifen, sep.*, -*ge*-, *h*) snatch up, *fig.* take up; seize.

'**Aufguß** *m* infusion.

'**auf|haben** (*irr. haben, sep.*, -*ge*-, *h*) **1.** *v/t.* have on (*hat*); have open (*door*); have to do (*task*); **2.** F *v/i.*: das Geschäft hat auf the shop is open; '**~haken** *v/t.* (*sep.*, -*ge*-, *h*) unhook; '**~halten** *v/t.* (*irr. halten, sep.*, -*ge*-, *h*) keep open; stop, detain, delay; hold up (*traffic*); sich ~ stay;

sich ~ bei dwell on; sich ~ mit spend one's time on; '**~hängen** *v/t.* (*irr. hängen, sep.*, -*ge*-, *h*) hang (up); ⊕ suspend.

'**aufheb|en** *v/t.* (*irr. heben, sep.*, -*ge*-, *h*) lift (up), raise; pick up; raise (*siege*); keep, preserve; cancel, annul, abolish; break off (*engagement*); break up (*meeting*); sich ~ neutralize; die Tafel ~ rise from the table; gut aufgehoben sein be well looked after; viel Aufhebens machen make a fuss (von about); '**2ung** *f* (-/-en) raising; abolition; annulment; breaking up.

'**auf|heitern** *v/t.* (*sep.*, -*ge*-, *h*) cheer up; sich ~ *weather*: clear up; *face*: brighten; '**~hellen** *v/t. and v/refl.* (*sep.*, -*ge*-, *h*) brighten.

'**aufhetz|en** *v/t.* (*sep.*, -*ge*-, *h*) incite, instigate *s.o.*; '**2ung** *f* (-/-en) instigation, incitement.

'**auf|holen** (*sep.*, -*ge*-, *h*) **1.** *v/t.* make up (for); ⚓ haul up; **2.** *v/i.* gain (*gegen* on); pull up (to); '**~hören** *v/i.* (*sep.*, -*ge*-, *h*) cease, stop; *Am.* quit (*all: zu tun doing*); F: da hört (sich) doch alles auf! that's the limit!, *Am.* that beats everything!; '**~kaufen** *v/t.* (*sep.*, -*ge*-, *h*) buy up.

'**aufklär|en** *v/t.* (*sep.*, -*ge*-, *h*) clear up; enlighten (*über acc.* on); ✕ reconnoit|re, *Am.* -er; sich ~ clear up; '**2ung** *f* enlightenment; ✕ reconnaissance.

'**auf|kleben** *v/t.* (*sep.*, -*ge*-, *h*) paste on, stick on, affix on; '**~klinken** *v/t.* (*sep.*, -*ge*-, *h*) unlatch; '**~knöpfen** *v/t.* (*sep.*, -*ge*-, *h*) unbutton.

'**aufkommen** **1.** *v/i.* (*irr. kommen, sep.*, -*ge*-, *sein*) rise; recover (*from illness*); come up; come into fashion *or* use; *thought*: arise; ~ für et. answer for s.th.; ~ gegen prevail against *s.o.*; **2.** ⚐ *n* (-s/*no pl.*) rise; recovery.

'**auf|krempeln** ['aʊfkrɛmpəln] *v/t.* (*sep.*, -*ge*-, *h*) turn up, roll up; tuck up; '**~lachen** *v/i.* (*sep.*, -*ge*-, *h*) burst out laughing; '**~laden** *v/t.* (*irr. laden, sep.*, -*ge*-, *h*) load; ⚡ charge.

'**Auflage** *f* edition (*of book*); circulation (*of newspaper*); ⊕ support.

'**auf|lassen** *v/t.* (*irr. lassen, sep.*, -*ge*-, *h*) F leave open (*door, etc.*); F keep on (*hat*); ⚓ cede; '**~lauern** v/i. (sep., -ge-, h): j-m ~ lie in wait for s.o.

'**Auflauf** m concourse; riot; *dish*: soufflé; '**2en** v/i. (*irr. laufen, sep., -ge-, sein*) interest: accrue; ⚓ run aground.

'**auflegen** (*sep., -ge-, h*) **1.** v/t. put on, lay on; apply (*auf acc.* to); print, publish (*book*); *teleph.* hang up; **2.** *teleph.* v/i. ring off.

'**auflehn|en** v/t. (sep., -ge-, h) lean (on); *sich* ~ lean (on); *fig.* rebel, revolt (*gegen* against); '**2ung** f (-/-en) rebellion.

'**auf|lesen** v/t. (*irr. lesen, sep., -ge-, h*) gather, pick up; '**~leuchten** v/i. (*sep., -ge-, h*) flash (up); '**~liegen** v/i. (*irr. liegen, sep., -ge-, h*) lie (*auf dat.* on).

'**auflös|bar** adj. (dis)soluble; '**~en** v/t. (*sep., -ge-, h*) undo (*knot*); break up (*meeting*); dissolve (*salt, etc.*; *marriage, business, Parliament, etc.*); solve (⚓, *riddle*); disintegrate; *fig.* aufgelöst upset; '**2ung** f (dis)solution; disintegration.

'**aufmach|en** v/t. (*sep., -ge-, h*) open; undo (*dress, parcel*); put up (*umbrella*); make up, get up; *sich* ~ *wind*: rise; set out (*nach acc.* for); make for; *die Tür* ~ answer the door; '**2ung** f (-/-en) make-up, get-up.

'**aufmarschieren** v/i. (*sep., no -ge-, sein*) form into line; ~ *lassen* ⚔ deploy.

auf'merksam adj. attentive (*gegen* to); j-n ~ *machen auf* (*acc.*) call s.o.'s attention to; **2keit** f (-/-en) attention; token.

auf'muntern v/t. (*sep., -ge-, h*) rouse; encourage; cheer up.

Aufnahme ['aufna:mə] f (-/-n) taking up (*of work*); reception; admission; *phot.*: taking; photograph, shot; shooting (*of a film*); **2fähig** adj. capable of absorbing; *mind*: receptive (*für* of); '**~gebühr** f admission fee; '**~gerät** n *phot.* camera; recorder; '**~prüfung** f entrance examination.

'**aufnehmen** v/t. (*irr. nehmen, sep., -ge-, h*) take up; pick up; take s.o. in; take down (*dictation, etc.*); take s.th. in (*mentally*); receive (*guests*); admit; raise, borrow (*money*); draw up, record; shoot (*film*); *phot.* take

(*picture*); *gut* (*übel*) ~ take well (ill); *es* ~ *mit* be a match for.

aufopfer|n ['auf?-] v/t. (*sep., -ge-, h*) sacrifice; '**2ung** f sacrifice.

'**auf|passen** v/i. (*sep., -ge-, h*) attend (*auf acc.* to); watch; *at school*: be attentive; look out; ~ *auf* (*acc.*) take care of; '**~platzen** v/i. (*sep., -ge-, sein*) burst open); '**~polieren** v/t. (*sep., no -ge-, h*) polish up; '**~prallen** v/i. (*sep., -ge-, sein*): *auf den Boden* ~ strike the ground); '**~pumpen** v/t. (*sep., -ge-, h*) blow up (*tyre, etc.*); '**~raffen** v/t. (*sep., -ge-, h*) snatch up; *sich* ~ rouse o.s. (*zu* for); muster up one's energy; '**~räumen** (*sep., -ge-, h*) **1.** v/t. put in order; tidy (up), *Am.* straighten up; clear away; **2.** v/i. tidy up; ~ *mit* do away with.

auf'recht adj. and adv. upright (a. *fig.*), erect; '**~erhalten** v/t. (*irr. halten, sep., no -ge-, h*) maintain, uphold; **2erhaltung** f (-/*no pl.*) maintenance.

aufreg|en v/t. (*sep., -ge-, h*) stir up, excite; *sich* ~ get excited *or* upset (*über acc.* about); aufgeregt excited; upset; '**2ung** f excitement, agitation.

'**auf|reiben** v/t. (*irr. reiben, sep., -ge-, h*) chafe (*skin, etc.*); *fig.*: destroy; exhaust, wear s.o. out; '**~reißen** (*irr. reißen, sep., -ge-, h*) **1.** v/t. (h) rip *or* tear up *or* open; fling open (*door*); open (*eyes*) wide; **2.** v/i. (*sein*) split open, burst.

aufreiz|en v/t. (*sep., -ge-, h*) incite, stir up; '**~end** adj. provocative; '**2ung** f instigation.

auf'richten v/t. (*sep., -ge-, h*) set up, erect; *sich* ~ stand up; straighten; sit up (*in bed*).

auf'richtig adj. sincere, candid; **2keit** f sincerity, cando(u)r.

'**aufriegeln** v/t. (*sep., -ge-, h*) unbolt.

'**Aufriß** △ m elevation.

'**aufrollen** v/t. and v/refl. (*sep., -ge-, h*) roll up; unroll.

'**Aufruf** m call, summons; '**2en** v/t. (*irr. rufen, sep., -ge-, h*) call up; call on s.o.

Aufruhr ['aufru:r] m (-[e]s/-e) uproar, tumult; riot, rebellion.

'**aufrühr|en** v/t. (*sep., -ge-, h*) stir up; revive; *fig.* rake up; '**2er** m (-s/-) rebel; '**~erisch** adj. rebellious.

'**Aufrüstung** ✕ f (re)armament.
'**auf|rütteln** v/t. (sep., -ge-, h) shake up; rouse; '~**sagen** v/t. (sep., -ge-, h) say, repeat; recite.

aufsässig adj. ['aufzεsiç] rebellious.

'**Aufsatz** m essay; composition; ⊕ top.

'**auf|saugen** v/t. (sep., -ge-, h) suck up; 🜛 absorb; '~**scheuchen** v/t. (sep., -ge-, h) scare (away); disturb; rouse; '~**scheuern** v/t. (sep., -ge-, h) scour; 🜊 chafe; '~**schichten** v/t. (sep., -ge-, h) pile up; '~**schieben** v/t. irr. schieben, sep., -ge-, h) slide open; fig.: put off; defer, postpone; adjourn.

'**Aufschlag** m striking; impact; additional or extra charge; facing (on coat), lapel (of coat); cuff (on sleeve); turn-up (on trousers); tennis: service; 2**en** ['~gən] (irr. schlagen, sep., -ge-) **1.** v/t. (h) open; turn up (sleeve, etc.); take up (abode); pitch (tent); raise (prices); cut (one's knee) open; **2.** v/i. (sein) strike, hit; ✝ rise, go up (in price); tennis: serve.

'**auf|schließen** v/t. (irr. schließen, sep., -ge-, h) unlock, open; '~**schlitzen** v/t. (sep., -ge-, h) slit or rip open.

'**Aufschluß** fig. m information.

'**auf|schnallen** v/t. (sep., -ge-, h) unbuckle; '~**schnappen** v (sep., -ge-) **1.** v/t. (h) snatch; fig. pick up; **2.** v/i. (sein) snap open; '~**schneiden** (irr. schneiden, sep., -ge-, h) **1.** v/t. cut open; cut up (meat); **2.** fig. v/i. brag, boast.

'**Aufschnitt** m (slices pl. of) cold meat, Am. cold cuts pl.

'**auf|schnüren** v/t. (sep., -ge-, h) untie; unlace; '~**schrauben** v/t. (sep., -ge-, h) screw (auf acc. on); unscrew; '~**schrecken 1.** v/t. (h) startle; **2.** v/i. (irr. schrecken, sein) start (up).

'**Aufschrei** m shriek, scream; fig. outcry.

'**auf|schreiben** v/t. (irr. schreiben, sep., -ge-, h) write down; '~**schreien** v/i. (irr. schreien, sep., -ge-, h) cry out, scream.

'**Aufschrift** f inscription; address, direction (on letter); label.

'**Aufschub** m deferment; delay; adjournment; respite.

'**auf|schürfen** v/t. (sep., -ge-, h)

graze (skin); '~**schwingen** v/refl. (irr. schwingen, sep., -ge-, h) soar, rise; sich zu et. ~ bring o.s. to do s.th.

'**Aufschwung** m fig. rise, Am. upswing; ✝ boom.

'**aufsehen 1.** v/i. (irr. sehen, sep., -ge-, h) look up; **2.** 2 n (-s/no pl.) sensation; '~ **erregen** cause a sensation; '~**erregend** adj. sensational.

'**Aufseher** m overseer; inspector.

'**aufsetzen** (sep., -ge-, h) **1.** v/t. set up; put on (hat, countenance); draw up (document); sich ~ sit up; **2.** 🜨 v/i. touch down.

'**Aufsicht** f (-/-en) inspection, supervision; store: shopwalker, Am. floor-walker; '~**sbehörde** f board of control; '~**srat** m board of directors.

'**auf|sitzen** v/i. (irr. sitzen, sep., -ge-, h) rider: mount; '~**spannen** v/t. (sep., -ge-, h) stretch; put up (umbrella); spread (sails); '~**sparen** v/t. (sep., -ge-, h) save; fig. reserve; '~**speichern** v/t. (sep., -ge-, h) store up; '~**sperren** v/t. (sep., -ge-, h) open wide; '~**spielen** (sep., -ge-, h) **1.** v/t. and v/i. strike up; **2.** v/refl. show off; sich ~ als set up for; '~**spießen** v/t. (sep., -ge-, h) pierce; with horns: gore; run through, spear; '~**springen** v/i. (irr. springen, sep., -ge-, sein) jump up; door: fly open; crack; skin: chap; '~**spüren** v/t. (sep., -ge-, h) hunt up; track down; '~**stacheln** fig. v/t. (sep., -ge-, h) goad; incite, instigate; '~**stampfen** v/i. (sep., -ge-, h) stamp (one's foot).

'**Aufstand** m insurrection; rebellion; uprising, revolt.

aufständisch adj. ['aufstεndiʃ] rebellious; '2**e** m (-n/-n) insurgent, rebel.

'**auf|stapeln** v/t. (sep., -ge-, h) pile up; ✝ store (up); '~**stechen** v/t. (irr. stechen, sep., -ge-, h) puncture; prick open; 🜊 lance; '~**stecken** v/t. (sep., -ge-, h) pin up; put up (hair); '~**stehen** v/i. (irr. stehen, sep., -ge-) **1.** (sein) stand up; rise, get up; revolt; **2.** F (h) stand open; '~**steigen** v/i. (irr. steigen, sep., -ge-, sein) rise, ascend; 🜨 take off; rider: mount.

'**aufstell|en** v/t. (sep., -ge-, h) set up, put up; ✕ draw up; post (sentries); make (assertion); set (example); erect (column); set (trap);

nominate (*candidate*); draw up (*bill*); lay down (*rule*); make out (*list*); set up, establish (*record*); '**~ung** *f* putting up; drawing up; erection; nomination; ✝ statement; list.

Aufstieg ['aufʃtiːk] *m* (-[e]s/-e) ascent, *Am. a.* ascension; *fig.* rise.

'**auf|stöbern** *fig. v/t.* (*sep.*, -ge-, h) hunt up; '**~stoßen** (*irr.* stoßen, *sep.*, -ge-) **1.** *v/t.* (h) push open; ~ auf (*acc.*) knock against; **2.** *v/i.* (h, sein) *of food:* rise, repeat; belch; '**~streichen** *v/t.* (*irr.* streichen, *sep.*, -ge-, h) spread (*butter*).

'**Aufstrich** *m* spread (*for bread*).

'**auf|stützen** *v/t.* (*sep.*, -ge-, h) prop up, support *s.th.*; sich ~ auf (*acc.*) lean on; '**~suchen** *v/t.* (*sep.*, -ge-, h) visit (*places*); go to see *s.o.*, look *s.o.* up.

'**Auftakt** *m* ♩ upbeat; *fig.* prelude, preliminaries *pl.*

'**auf|tauchen** *v/i.* (*sep.*, -ge-, sein) emerge, appear, turn up; '**~tauen** (*sep.*, -ge-) **1.** *v/t.* (h) thaw; **2.** *v/i.* (sein) thaw (*a. fig.*); '**~teilen** *v/t.* (*sep.*, -ge-, h) divide (up), share.

Auftrag ['auftraːk] *m* (-[e]s/~e) commission; instruction; mission; ⅛⅛ mandate; ✝ order; **²en** ['~gən] *v/t.* (*irr.* tragen, *sep.*, -ge-, h) serve (up) (*meal*); lay on (*paint*); wear out (*dress*); *j-m* et. ~ charge *s.o.* with *s.th.*; **~geber** ['~k-] *m* (-s/-) employer; customer; principal; **~erteilung** ['~ks'ʔɛrtaɪluŋ] *f* (-/-en) placing of an order.

'**auf|treffen** *v/i.* (*irr.* treffen, *sep.*, -ge-, sein) strike, hit; '**~treiben** *v/t.* (*irr.* treiben, *sep.*, -ge-, h) hunt up; raise (*money*); '**~trennen** *v/t.* (*sep.*, -ge-, h) rip; unstitch (*seam*).

'**auftreten 1.** *v/i.* (*irr.* treten, *sep.*, -ge-, sein) tread; *thea., witness, etc.:* appear (*als* as); behave, act; *difficulties:* arise; **2.** ♀ *n* (-s/*no pl.*) appearance; occurrence (*of events*); behavio(u)r.

'**Auftrieb** *m phys. and fig.* buoyancy; ⚓ lift; *fig.* impetus.

'**Auftritt** *m thea.* scene (*a. fig.*); appearance (*of actor*).

'**auf|trumpfen** *v/i.* (*sep.*, -ge-, h) put one's foot down; '**~tun** *v/t.* (*irr.* tun, *sep.*, -ge-, h) open; sich ~ open; *chasm:* yawn; *society:* form; '**~türmen** *v/t.* (*sep.*, -ge-, h) pile or heap

up; sich ~ tower up; pile up; *difficulties:* accumulate; '**~wachen** *v/i.* (*sep.*, -ge-, sein) awake, wake up; '**~wachsen** *v/i.* (*irr.* wachsen, *sep.*, -ge-, sein) grow up.

'**Aufwallung** *f* ebullition, surge.

Aufwand ['aufvant] *m* (-[e]s/*no pl.*) expense, expenditure (*an dat.* of); pomp; splendid *or* great display (*of words, etc.*).

'**aufwärmen** *v/t.* (*sep.*, -ge-, h) warm up.

'**Aufwarte|frau** *f* charwoman, *Am. a.* cleaning woman; '**²n** *v/i.* (*sep.*, -ge-, h) wait (up)on *s.o.*, attend on *s.o.*; wait (at table).

aufwärts *adv.* ['aufvɛrts] upward(s).

'**Aufwartung** *f* attendance; visit; *j-m s-e* ~ machen pay one's respects to *s.o.*, call on *s.o.*

'**aufwasch|en** *v/t.* (*irr.* waschen, *sep.*, -ge-, h) wash up; '**²wasser** *n* dish-water.

'**auf|wecken** *v/t.* (*sep.*, -ge-, h) awake(n), wake (up); '**~weichen** (*sep.*, -ge-) **1.** *v/t.* (h) soften; soak; **2.** *v/i.* (sein) soften, become soft; '**~weisen** *v/t.* (*irr.* weisen, *sep.*, -ge-, h) show, exhibit; produce; '**~wenden** *v/t.* ([*irr.* wenden], *sep.*, -ge-, h) spend; *Mühe* ~ take pains; '**~werfen** *v/t.* (*irr.* werfen, *sep.*, -ge-, h) raise (*a. question*).

'**aufwert|en** *v/t.* (*sep.*, -ge-, h) revalorize; revalue; '**²ung** *f* revalorization; revaluation.

'**aufwickeln** *v/t.* (*sep.*, -ge-, h) wind up, roll up.

aufwiegel|n ['aufviːgəln] *v/t.* (*sep.*, -ge-, h) stir up, incite, instigate; '**²ung** *f* (-/-en) instigation.

'**aufwiegen** *fig. v/t.* (*irr.* wiegen, *sep.*, -ge-, h) make up for.

Aufwiegler ['aufviːglər] *m* (-s/-) agitator; instigator.

'**aufwirbeln** (*sep.*, -ge-) **1.** *v/t.* (h) whirl up; raise (*dust*); *fig. viel Staub* ~ create a sensation; **2.** *v/i.* (sein) whirl up.

'**aufwisch|en** *v/t.* (*sep.*, -ge-, h) wipe up; '**²lappen** *m* floor-cloth.

'**aufwühlen** *v/t.* (*sep.*, -ge-, h) turn up; *fig.* stir.

'**aufzähl|en** *v/t.* (*sep.*, -ge-, h) count up; *fig.* enumerate, *Am. a.* call off; specify, *Am.* itemize; '**²ung** *f* (-/-en) enumeration; specification.

'**auf|zäumen** *v/t.* (*sep.*, -ge-, h)

bridle; '**~zehren** v/t. (sep., -ge-, h) consume.

'**aufzeichn|en** v/t. (sep., -ge-, h) draw; note down; record; '**2ung** f note; record.

'**auf|zeigen** v/t. (sep., -ge-, h) show; demonstrate; point out (mistakes, etc.); disclose; '**~ziehen** (irr. ziehen, sep., -ge-) 1. v/t. (h) draw or pull up; (pull) open; hoist (flag); bring up (child); mount (picture); wind (up) (clock, etc.); j-n ~ tease s.o., pull s.o.'s leg; Saiten auf e-e Violine ~ string a violin; 2. v/i. (sein) ✕ draw up; storm: approach.

'**Aufzucht** f rearing, breeding.

'**Aufzug** m ⊕ hoist; lift, Am. elevator; thea. act; attire; show.

'**aufzwingen** v/t. (irr. zwingen, sep., -ge-, h): j-m et. ~ force s.th.upon.

Augapfel ['auk?-] m eyeball. [s.o.]

Auge ['augə] n (-s/-n) eye; sight; 💐 bud; in meinen ~n in my view; im ~ behalten keep an eye on; keep in mind; aus den ~n verlieren lose sight of; ein ~ zudrücken turn a blind eye (bei to); ins ~ fallen strike the eye; große ~n machen open one's eyes wide; unter vier ~n face to face, privately; kein ~ zutun not to get a wink of sleep.

'**Augen|arzt** m oculist, eye-doctor; '**~blick** m moment, instant; '**2blicklich 1.** adj. instantaneous; momentary; present; **2.** adv. instant(aneous)ly; at present; '**~braue** f eyebrow; '**~entzündung** 🎄 f inflammation of the eye; '**~heilkunde** 🎄 f ophthalmology; '**~klinik** f ophthalmic hospital; '**~leiden** 🎄 n eye-complaint; '**~licht** n eyesight; '**~lid** n eyelid; '**~maß** n: ein gutes ~ a sure eye; nach dem ~ by eye; '**~merk** ['~merk] n (-[e]s/no pl.): sein ~ richten auf (acc.) turn one's attention to; have s.th. in view; '**~schein** m appearance; in ~ nehmen examine, view, inspect; '**2scheinlich** adj. evident; '**~wasser** n eyewash, eye-lotion; '**~wimper** f eyelash; '**~zeuge** m eyewitness.

August [au'gust] m (-[e]s, -/-e) August.

Auktion [auk'tsjo:n] f (-/-en) auction; **~ator** [~o'na:tɔr] m (-s/-en) auctioneer.

Aula ['aula] f (-/Aulen, -s) (assembly) hall, Am. auditorium.

aus [aus] **1.** prp. (dat.) out of; from; of; by; for; in; ~ Achtung out of respect; ~ London kommen come from London; ~ diesem Grunde for this reason; ~ Ihrem Brief ersehe ich I see from your letter; **2.** adv. out; over; die Schule ist ~ school is over; F: von mir ~ for all I care; auf et. ~ sein be keen on s.th.; es ist ~ mit ihm it is all over with him; das Spiel ist ~! the game is up!; er weiß weder ein noch ~ he is at his wit's end; on instruments, etc.: an — ~ on — off.

ausarbeit|en ['aus?-] v/t. (sep., -ge-, h) work out; elaborate; **2ung** f (-/-en) working-out; elaboration; composition.

aus|arten ['aus?-] v/i. (sep., -ge-, sein) degenerate; get out of hand; '**~atmen** ['aus?-] (sep., -ge-, h) **1.** v/i. breathe out; **2.** v/t. breathe out; exhale (vapour, etc.); '**~baggern** v/t. (sep., -ge-, h) dredge (river, etc.); excavate (ground).

'**Ausbau** m (-[e]s/-ten) extension; completion; development; '**2en** v/t. (sep., -ge-, h) develop; extend; finish, complete; ⊕ dismantle (engine). [sep., no -ge-, h) stipulate.)

'**ausbedingen** v/t. (irr. bedingen,)

'**ausbesser|n** v/t. (sep., -ge-, h) mend, repair, Am. F a. fix; '**2ung** f repair, mending.

'**Ausbeut|e** f (-/~-n) gain, profit; yield; ✕ output; '**2en** v/t. (sep., -ge-, h) exploit; sweat (workers); '**~ung** f (-/-en) exploitation.

'**ausbild|en** v/t. (sep., -ge-, h) form, develop; train; instruct, educate; ✕ drill; '**2ung** f development; training; instruction; education; ✕ drill.

'**ausbitten** v/t. (irr. bitten, sep., -ge-, h): sich et. ~ request s.th.; insist on s.th.

'**ausbleiben 1.** v/i. (irr. bleiben, sep., -ge-, sein) stay away, fail to appear; **2.** 2 n (-s/no pl.) non-arrival, non-appearance; absence.

'**Ausblick** m outlook (auf acc. over, on), view (of), prospect (of); fig. outlook (on).

'**aus|bohren** v/t. (sep., -ge-, h) bore, drill; '**~brechen** (irr. brechen, sep., -ge-) **1.** v/t. (h) break out; vomit; **2.** v/i. (sein) break out; fig. burst out (laughing, etc.).

'ausbreit|en v/t. (sep., -ge-, h) spread (out); stretch (out) (arms, wings); display; sich ~ spread; **'2ung** f (-/⚓-en) spreading.

'ausbrennen (irr. brennen, sep., -ge-) **1.** v/t. (h) burn out; ⚕ cauterize; **2.** v/i. (sein) burn out.

'Ausbruch m outbreak; eruption (of volcano); escape (from prison); outburst (of emotion).

'aus|brüten v/t. (sep., -ge-, h) hatch (a. fig.); **'~bürgern** v/t. (sep., -ge-, h) denationalize, expatriate.

'Ausdauer f perseverance; **'2nd** adj. persevering; ♀ perennial.

'ausdehn|en v/t. and v/refl. (sep., -ge-, h) extend (auf acc. to); expand; stretch; **'2ung** f expansion; extension; extent.

'aus|denken v/t. (irr. denken, sep., -ge-, h) think s.th. out, Am. a. think s.th. up, contrive, devise, invent; imagine; **'~dörren** v/t. (sep., -ge-, h) dry up; parch; **'~drehen** v/t. (sep., -ge-, h) turn off (radio, gas); ⚡ turn out, switch off (light).

'Ausdruck m **1.** (-[e]s/no pl.) expression; **2.** (-[e]s/⸚e) expression; term.

'ausdrück|en v/t. (sep., -ge-, h) press, squeeze (out); stub out (cigarette); fig. express; **'~lich** adj. express, explicit.

'ausdrucks|los adj. inexpressive, expressionless; blank; **'~voll** adj. expressive; **'2weise** f mode of expression; style.

'Ausdünstung f (-/-en) exhalation; perspiration; odo(u)r, smell.

auseinander adv. [ausʔa'nandər] asunder, apart; separate(d); **~bringen** v/t. (irr. bringen, sep., -ge-, h) separate, sever; **~gehen** v/i. (irr. gehen, sep., -ge-, sein) meeting, crowd: break up; opinions: differ; friends: part; crowd: disperse; roads: diverge; **~nehmen** v/t. (irr. nehmen, sep., -ge-, h) take apart or to pieces; ⊕ disassemble, dismantle; **~setzen** g v/t. (sep., -ge-, h) explain; sich mit j-m ~ ⚓ compound with s.o.; argue with s.o.; have it out with s.o.; sich mit e-m Problem ~ get down to a problem; come to grips with a problem; **2setzung** f (-/-en) explanation; discussion; settlement (with creditors, etc.); kriegerische ~ armed conflict.

auserlesen adj. ['ausʔ-] exquisite, choice; select(ed).

auserwählen ['ausʔ-] v/t. (sep., no -ge-, h) select, choose.

'ausfahr|en (irr. fahren, sep., -ge-) **1.** v/i. (sein) drive out, go for a drive; ⚓ leave (port); **2.** v/t. (h) take (baby) out (in pram); take s.o. for a drive; rut (road); ⚡ lower (undercarriage); **'2t** f drive; excursion; way out, exit (of garage, etc.); gateway; departure.

'Ausfall m falling out; ✝: loss; deficit; **'2en** v/i. (irr. fallen, sep., -ge-, sein) fall out; not to take place; turn out, prove; ~ lassen cancel; die Schule fällt aus there is no school; **'2end** adj. offensive, insulting.

'aus|fasern v/i. (sep., -ge-, sein) ravel out, fray; **'~fegen** v/t. (sep., -ge- h) sweep (out).

ausfertig|en ['ausfertigən] v/t. (sep., -ge-, h) draw up (document); make out (bill, etc.); issue (passport); **'2ung** f (-/-en) drawing up; issue; draft; copy; in doppelter ~ in duplicate. [chen find out; discover.\]

ausfindig adj. ['ausfindiç]: ~ ma-\
'Ausflucht f (-/⸚e) excuse, evasion, shift, subterfuge.

'Ausflug m trip, excursion, outing.

Ausflügler ['ausflyːklər] m (-s/-) excursionist, tripper, tourist.

'Ausfluß m flowing out; discharge (a. ⚕); outlet, outfall.

'aus|fragen v/t. (sep., -ge-, h) interrogate, Am. a. quiz; sound; **'~fransen** v/i. (sep., -ge-, sein) fray.

Ausfuhr ✝ ['ausfuːr] f (-/-en) export(ation); **~artikel** ✝ m export (article).

'ausführ|bar adj. practicable; ✝ exportable; **'~en** v/t. (sep., -ge-, h) execute, carry out, perform, Am. a. fill; ✝ export; explain; j-n ~ take s.o. out.

'Ausfuhr|genehmigung f export permit; **'~handel** m export trade.

'ausführlich 1. adj. detailed; comprehensive; circumstantial; **2.** adv. in detail, at (some) length; **2keit** f (-/no pl.) minuteness of detail; particularity; comprehensiveness; copiousness.

'Ausführung f execution, performance; workmanship; type, make;

explanation; '~sbestimmungen † f/pl. export regulations pl.

'Ausfuhr|verbot n embargo on exports; '~waren f/pl. exports pl.; '~zoll m export duty.

'ausfüllen v/t. (sep., -ge-, h) fill out or up; fill in, complete (form); Am. fill out (blank).

'Ausgabe f distribution; edition (of book); expense, expenditure; issue (of shares, etc.); issuing office.

'Ausgang m going out; exit; way out; outlet; end; result; '~skapital † n original capital; '~spunkt m starting-point; '~sstellung f starting-position.

'ausgeben v/t. (irr. geben, sep., -ge-, h) give out; spend (money); issue (shares, etc.); sich ~ für pass o.s. off for, pretend to be.

'ausge|beult adj. ['ausgəbɔylt] baggy; ~bombt adj. ['~bɔmpt] bombed out; ~dehnt adj. ['~de:nt] expansive, vast, extensive; ~dient adj. ['~di:nt] worn out; superannuated; retired, pensioned off; ~er Soldat ex-serviceman, veteran; ~fallen fig. adj. odd, queer, unusual.

'ausgehen v/i. (irr. gehen, sep., -ge-, sein) go out; take a walk; end; colour: fade; hair: fall out; money, provisions: run out; uns gehen die Vorräte aus we run out of provisions; darauf ~ aim at; gut etc. ~ turn out well, etc.; leer ~ come away empty-handed; von et. ~ start from s.th.

'ausge|lassen fig. adj. frolicsome, boisterous; '~nommen prp. 1. (acc.) except (for); 2. (nom.): Anwesende ~ present company excepted; ~prägt adj. ['~prɛːkt] marked, pronounced; ~rechnet fig. adv. ['~rɛçnət] just; ~ er he of all people; ~ heute today of all days; ~schlossen fig. adj. impossible.

'ausgestalten v/t. (sep., no -ge-, h) arrange (celebration); et. zu et. ~ develop or turn s.th. into s.th.

ausge|sucht fig. adj. exquisite, choice; ~wachsen adj. full-grown; ~zeichnet fig. adj. ['~tsaiçnət] excellent.

'ausgiebig adj. ['ausgi:biç] abundant, plentiful; meal: substantial.

'ausgießen v/t. (irr. gießen, sep., -ge-, h) pour out.

'Ausgleich ['ausglaiç] m (-[e]s/-e)

compromise; compensation; † settlement; sports: equalization (of score); tennis: deuce (score of 40 all); '2en v/t. (irr. gleichen, sep., -ge-, h) equalize; compensate (loss); balance.

'aus|gleiten v/i. (irr. gleiten, sep., -ge-, sein) slip, slide; '~graben v/t. (irr. graben, sep., -ge-, h) dig out or up (a. fig.); excavate; exhume (body).

Ausguck ⚓ ['ausguk] m (-[e]s/-e) look-out.

'Ausguß m sink; '~eimer m slop-pail.

'aus|haken v/t. (sep., -ge-, h) unhook; '~halten (irr. halten, sep., -ge-, h) 1. v/t. endure, bear, stand; ♪ sustain (note); 2. v/i. hold out; last; '~händigen ['~hɛndigən] v/t. (sep., -ge-, h) deliver up, hand over, surrender.

'Aushang m notice, placard, poster.

'aushänge|n 1. v/t. (sep., -ge-, h) hang or put out; unhinge (door); 2. v/i. (irr. hängen, sep., -ge-, h) have been hung or put out; '2~schild n signboard.

aus|harren ['ausharən] v/i. (sep., -ge-, h) persevere; hold out; '~hauchen v/t. (sep., -ge-, h) breathe out, exhale; '~heben v/t. (irr. heben, sep., -ge-, h) dig out (trench); unhinge (door); recruit, levy (soldiers); excavate (earth); rob (nest); clean out, raid (nest of criminals); '~helfen v/i. (irr. helfen, sep., -ge-, h) help out.

'Aushilf|e f (temporary) help or assistance; sie hat e-e ~ she has s.o. to help out; '2sweise adv. as a makeshift; temporarily.

'aushöhl|en v/t. (sep., -ge-, h) hollow out; '2ung f hollow.

'aus|holen (sep., -ge-, h) 1. v/i. raise one's hand (as if to strike); weit ~ go far back (in narrating s.th.); 2. v/t. sound, pump s.o.; '~horchen v/t. (sep., -ge-, h) sound, pump s.o.; '~hungern v/t. (sep., -ge-, h) starve (out); '~husten v/t. (sep., -ge-, h) cough up; '~kennen v/refl. (irr. kennen, sep., -ge-, h) know one's way (about place); be well versed, be at home (in subject); er kennt sich aus he knows what's what; '~kleiden v/t. (sep., -ge-, h) undress; ⊕ line, coat; sich ~ undress; '~klopfen v/t. (sep., -ge-, h) beat (out); dust (*garment*); knock out (*pipe*); **⸗klügeln** [ˈ⸗klyːɡəln] v/t. (sep., -ge-, h) work s.th. out; contrive; puzzle s.th. out.

'auskommen 1. v/i. (irr. kommen, sep., -ge-, sein) get out; escape; ⸗ mit manage with s.th.; get on with s.o.; ⸗ ohne do without; mit dem Geld ⸗ make both ends meet; **2.** ⸗ n (-s/no pl.) competence, competency.

'auskundschaften v/t. (sep., -ge-, h) explore; ✕ reconnoit⸗re, Am. -er, scout.

Auskunft ['auskʊnft] f (-/ːe) information; inquiry office, inquiries pl., Am. information desk; **⸗stelle** f inquiry office, inquiries pl., Am. information bureau.

'aus|lachen v/t. (sep., -ge-, h) laugh at, deride; **⸗laden** v/t. (irr. laden, sep., -ge-, h) unload; discharge (*cargo from ship*); cancel s.o.'s invitation, put off (*guest*).

'Auslage f display, show (*of goods*); in der ⸗ in the (shop) window; ⸗n pl. expenses pl.

'Ausland n (-[e]s/no pl.): das ⸗ foreign countries pl.; ins ⸗, im ⸗ abroad.

Ausländ|er ['auslɛndər] m (-s/-), **⸗erin** f (-/-nen) foreigner; alien; **⸗isch** adj. foreign; ⚤, zo. exotic.

'Auslandskorrespondent m foreign correspondent.

'aus|lassen v/t. (irr. lassen, sep., -ge-, h) let out (*water*); melt (down) (*butter*); render down (*fat*); let out (*garment*); let down (*hem*); leave out, omit (*word*); cut s.th. out; miss or cut out (*meal*); miss (*dance*); s-n Zorn an j-m ⸗ vent one's anger on s.o.; sich ⸗ über (acc.) say s.th. about; express one's opinion about; **⸗ung** f (-/-en) omission; remark, utterance; **⸗ungszeichen** gr. n apostrophe.

'aus|laufen v/i. (irr. laufen, sep., -ge-, h) run or leak out (aus et. of s.th.); leak; end (in s.th.); *machine*: run down; ⚓ (set) sail; **⸗leeren** v/t. (sep., -ge-, h) empty; ⚚ evacuate (*bowels*).

'auslegen v/t. (sep., -ge-, h) lay out; display (*goods*); explain, interpret; advance (*money*); **⸗ung** f (-/-en) explanation, interpretation.

'aus|leihen v/t. (irr. leihen, sep., -ge-, h) lend (out), esp. Am. loan;

⸗lernen v/i. (sep., -ge-, h) finish one's apprenticeship; man lernt nie aus we live and learn.

'Auslese f choice, selection; fig. pick; **⸗n** v/t. (irr. lesen, sep., -ge-, h) pick out, select; finish reading (*book*).

'ausliefer|n v/t. (sep., -ge-, h) hand or turn over, deliver (up); extradite (*criminal*); ausgeliefert sein (dat.) be at the mercy of; **⸗ung** f delivery; extradition.

'aus|liegen v/i. (irr. liegen, sep., -ge-, h) be displayed, be on show; **⸗löschen** v/t. (sep., -ge-, h) put out, switch off (*light*); extinguish (*fire*) (a. fig.); efface (*word*); wipe out, erase; **⸗losen** v/t. (sep., -ge-, h) draw (lots) for.

'auslös|en v/t. (sep., -ge-, h) ⊕ release; redeem, ransom (*prisoner*); redeem (*from pawn*); fig. cause, start; arouse (*applause*); **⸗er** m (-s/-) ⊕ release, phot. trigger.

'aus|lüften v/t. (sep., -ge-, h) air, ventilate; **⸗machen** v/t. (sep., -ge-, h) make out, sight, spot; sum: amount to; constitute, make up; put out (*fire*); ⚡ turn out, switch off (*light*); agree on, arrange; settle; es macht nichts aus it does not matter; würde es Ihnen et. ⸗, wenn ...? would you mind (ger.) ...?; **⸗malen** v/t. (sep., -ge-, h) paint; sich et. ⸗ picture s.th. to o.s., imagine s.th.

'Ausmaß n dimension (a pl.), measurement (a pl.); fig. extent.

aus|mergeln ['ausmɛrɡəln] v/t. (sep., -ge-, h) emaciate; exhaust; **⸗merzen** ['⸗mɛrtsən] v/t. (sep., -ge-, h) eliminate; eradicate; **⸗messen** v/t. (irr. messen, sep., -ge-, h) measure.

Ausnahm|e ['ausnaːmə] f (-/-n) exception; **⸗sweise** adv. by way of exception; exceptionally.

'ausnehmen v/t. (irr. nehmen, sep., -ge-, h) take out; draw (*fowl*); F fleece s.o.; fig. except, exempt; **⸗d 1.** adj. exceptional; **2.** adv. exceedingly.

'aus|nutzen v/t. (sep., -ge-, h) utilize; take advantage of; esp. ⚒, ✕ exploit; **⸗packen** (sep., -ge-, h) **1.** v/t. unpack; **2.** F fig. v/i. speak one's mind; **⸗pfeifen** thea. v/t. (irr. pfeifen, sep., -ge-, h) hiss; **⸗plaudern** v/t. (sep., -ge-, h) blab *or* let out; '**~polstern** v/t. (sep., -ge-, h) stuff, pad; wad; '**~probieren** v/t. (sep., no -ge-, h) try, test.

Auspuff mot. ['auspuf] m (-[e]s/-e) exhaust; '**~gas** mot. n exhaust gas; '**~rohr** mot. n exhaust-pipe; '**~topf** mot. m silencer, Am. muffler.

'**aus|putzen** v/t. (sep., -ge-, h) clean; '**~quartieren** v/t. (sep., no -ge-, h) dislodge; ✕ billet out; '**~radieren** v/t. (sep., no -ge-, h) erase; '**~rangieren** v/t. (sep., no -ge-, h) discard; '**~rauben** v/t. (sep., -ge-, h) rob; ransack; '**~räumen** v/t. (sep., -ge-, h) empty, clear (out); remove (*furniture*); '**~rechnen** v/t. (sep., -ge-, h) calculate, compute; reckon (out), Am. figure out *or* up (*all a. fig.*).

'**Ausrede** f excuse, evasion, subterfuge; '**2n** (sep., -ge-, h) **1.** v/i. finish speaking; **~ lassen** hear s.o. out; **2.** v/t.: j-m et. **~** dissuade s.o. from s.th.

'**ausreichen** v/i. (sep., -ge-, h) suffice; '**~d** adj. sufficient.

'**Ausreise** f departure; ♫ voyage out.

'**ausreiß|en** (irr. reißen, sep., -ge-) **1.** v/t. (h) pull *or* tear out; **2.** v/i. (sein) run away; '**2er** m runaway.

aus|renken ['ausrɛŋkən] v/t. (sep., -ge-, h) dislocate; '**~richten** v/t. (sep., -ge-, h) straighten; ✕ dress; adjust; deliver (*message*); do, effect; accomplish; obtain; arrange (*feast*); *richte ihr e-n Gruß von mir aus!* remember me to her!; '**~rotten** ['~rɔtən] v/t. (sep., -ge-, h) root out; fig. extirpate, exterminate.

'**Ausruf** m cry; exclamation; '**2en** (irr. rufen, sep., -ge-,h) **1.** v/i. cry out, exclaim; **2.** v/t. proclaim; '**~zeichen** n exclamation mark, Am. a. exclamation point; '**~ung** f (-/-en) proclamation; '**~ungszeichen** n s. Ausrufezeichen. [-ge-, h) rest.\
'**ausruhen** v/i., v/t. and v/refl. (sep.,)\
'**ausrüst|en** v/t. (sep., -ge-, h) fit out; equip; '**2ung** f outfit, equipment, fittings pl. [disseminate.\
'**aussäen** v/t. (sep., -ge-, h) sow (a. fig.).\
'**Aussage** f statement; declaration; ⚖ evidence; gr. predicate; '**2n** (sep., -ge-, h) **1.** v/t. state, declare; ⚖ depose; **2.** ⚖ v/i. give evidence.

'**Aussatz** ﹩ m (-es/no pl.) leprosy.

'**aus|saugen** v/t. (sep., -ge-, h) suck (out); fig. exhaust (*land*); '**~schalten** v/t. (sep., -ge-, h) eliminate; ⚡ cut out, switch off, turn off *or* out (*light*).

Ausschank ['ausʃaŋk] m (-[e]s/‿e) retail (*of alcoholic drinks*); public house, F pub.

'**Ausschau** f (-/no pl.): **~ halten nach** be on the look-out for, watch for.

'**ausscheid|en** (irr. scheiden, sep., -ge-) **1.** v/t. (h) separate; ﹩, ⚕, physiol. eliminate; ﹩ secrete; **2.** v/i. (sein) retire; withdraw; sports: drop out; '**2ung** f separation; elimination (a. sports); ﹩ secretion.

'**aus|schiffen** v/t. and v/refl. (sep., -ge-, h) disembark; '**~schimpfen** v/t. (sep., -ge-, h) scold, tell s.o. off, berate; '**~schirren** v/t. (sep.,-ge-, h) unharness; '**~schlachten** v/t. (sep.,-ge-, h) cut up; cannibalize (*car, etc.*); fig. exploit, make the most of; '**~schlafen** (irr. schlafen, sep., -ge-, h) **1.** v/i. sleep one's fill; **2.** v/t. sleep off (*effects of drink, etc.*).

'**Ausschlag** m ﹩ eruption, rash; deflexion (*of pointer*); *den* **~** *geben* settle it; '**2en** (irr. schlagen, sep.,-ge-) **1.** v/t. (h) knock *or* beat out; line; refuse, decline; **2.** v/i. horse: kick; pointer: deflect; **3.** v/i. (h, sein) bud; '**2gebend** adj. ['~k-] decisive.

'**ausschließ|en** (irr. schließen, sep., -ge-, h) shut *or* lock out; fig.: exclude; expel; sports: disqualify; '**~lich** adj. exclusive.

'**Ausschluß** m exclusion; expulsion; sports: disqualification.

'**ausschmücken** v/t. (sep., -ge-, h) adorn, decorate; fig. embellish.

'**Ausschnitt** m cut; décolleté, (low) neck (*of dress*); cutting, Am. clipping (*from newspaper*); fig. part, section.

'**ausschreib|en** v/t. (irr. schreiben, sep., -ge-, h) write out; copy; write out (*word*) in full; make out (*invoice*); announce; advertise; '**2ung** f (-/-en) announcement; advertisement.

'**ausschreit|en** (irr. schreiten, sep., -ge-) **1.** v/i. (sein) step out, take long strides; **2.** v/t. (h) pace (*room*), measure by steps; '**2ung** f (-/-en) excess; **~en** pl. riots pl.

'Ausschuß *m* refuse, waste, rubbish; committee, board.

'aus|schütteln *v/t.* (*sep.*, -ge-, h) shake out; **'.schütten** *v/t.* (*sep.*, -ge-, h) pour out; spill; † distribute (*dividend*); *j-m sein Herz ~ pour out one's heart to s.o.*; **'.schwärmen** *v/i.* (*sep.*, -ge-, sein) swarm out; ~ (*lassen*) ✕ extend, deploy.

'ausschweif|end *adj.* dissolute; **'.ung** *f* (-/-en) debauchery, excess.

'ausschwitzen *v/t.* (*sep.*, -ge-, h) exude.

'aussehen 1. *v/i.* (*irr. sehen, sep.*, -ge-, h) look; *wie sieht er aus?* what does he look like?; *es sieht nach Regen aus* it looks like rain; **2.** ♀ *n* (-s/ *no pl.*) look(s *pl.*), appearance.

außen *adv.* ['ausən] (on the) outside; *von ~ her* from (the) outside; *nach ~* (*hin*) outward(s); **'♀aufnahme** *f film:* outdoor shot; **'♀bordmotor** *m* outboard motor.

'aussenden *v/t.* ([*irr. senden*] *sep.*, -ge-, h) send out.

'Außen|hafen *m* outport; **'.handel** *m* foreign trade; **'.minister** *m* foreign minister; Foreign Secretary, *Am.* Secretary of State; **'.ministerium** *n* foreign ministry; Foreign Office, *Am.* State Department; **'.politik** *f* foreign policy; **'♀politisch** *adj.* of *or* referring to foreign affairs; **'.seite** *f* outside, surface; **'.seiter** *m* (-s/-) outsider; **.stände** † ['.ʃtɛndə] *pl.* outstanding debts *pl.*, *Am.* accounts *pl.* receivable; **'.welt** *f* outer *or* outside world.

außer ['ausər] **1.** *prp.* (*dat.*) out of; beside(s), *Am.* aside from; except; *~ sich sein* be beside o.s. (*vor Freude* with joy); **2.** *cj.*: *~ daß* except that; *~ wenn* unless; **'.dem** *cj.* besides, moreover.

äußere ['ɔysərə] **1.** *adj.* exterior, outer, external, outward; **2.** ♀ *n* (Äußer[e]n/*no pl.*) exterior, outside, outward appearance.

'außer|gewöhnlich *adj.* extraordinary; exceptional; **'.halb 1.** *prp.* (*gen.*) outside, out of; beyond; **2.** *adv.* on the outside.

äußerlich *adj.* ['ɔysərliç] external, outward; **'♀keit** *f* (-/-en) superficiality; formality.

äußern ['ɔysərn] *v/t.* (ge-, h) utter, express; advance; *sich ~ matter*:

manifest itself; *p.* express o.s.

'außer'ordentlich *adj.* extraordinary.

äußerst ['ɔysərst] **1.** *adj.* outermost; *fig.* utmost, extreme; **2.** *adv.* extremely, highly.

außerstande *adj.* [ausər'ʃtandə] unable, not in-a position.

'Äußerung *f* (-/-en) utterance, remark.

'aussetz|en (*sep.*, -ge-, h) **1.** *v/t.* set *or* put out; lower (*boat*); promise (*reward*); settle (*pension*); bequeath; expose (*child*); expose (*dat.* to); *et. ~ an* (*dat.*) find fault with; **2.** *v/i.* intermit; fail; *activity:* stop; suspend; *mot.* misfire; **'♀ung** *f* (-/-en) exposure (*of child, to weather, etc.*) (*a.* ♀).

'Aussicht *f* (-/-en) view (*auf acc.* of); *fig.* prospect (of), chance (of); *in ~ haben* have in prospect; **'♀slos** *adj.* hopeless, desperate; **'♀sreich** *adj.* promising, full of promise.

'aussöhn|en ['auszø:nən] *v/t.* (*sep.*, -ge-, h) reconcile *s.o.* (*mit* to *s.th.*, with *s.o.*); *sich ~* reconcile o.s. (to *s.th.*, with *s.o.*); **'♀ung** *f* (-/-en) reconciliation.

'aussondern *v/t.* (*sep.*, -ge-, h) single out; separate.

'aus|spannen (*sep.*, -ge-, h) **1.** *v/t.* stretch, extend; F *fig.* steal (*s.o.'s girl friend*); unharness (*draught animal*); **2.** *fig.* *v/i.* (take a) rest, relax; **'.speien** *v/t.* and *v/i.* (*irr. speien, sep.*, -ge-, h) spit out.

'aussperr|en *v/t.* (*sep.*, -ge-, h) shut out; lock out (*workmen*); **'♀ung** *f* (-/-en) lock-out.

'aus|spielen (*sep.*, -ge-, h) **1.** *v/t.* play (*card*); **2.** *v/i.* at cards: lead; *er hat ausgespielt* he is done for; **'.spionieren** *v/t.* (*sep.*, no -ge-, h) spy out. [cent; discussion.]

'Aussprache *f* pronunciation, ac-]

'aussprechen (*irr. sprechen, sep.*, -ge-, h) **1.** *v/t.* pronounce, express; *sich ~ für* (*gegen*) declare o.s. for (against); **2.** *v/i.* finish speaking.

'Ausspruch *m* utterance; saying; remark.

'aus|spucken *v/i.* and *v/t.* (*sep.*, -ge-, h) spit out; **'.spülen** *v/t.* (*sep.*, -ge-, h) rinse.

'Ausstand *m* strike, *Am.* F *a.* walk-out; *in den ~ treten* go on strike, *Am.* F *a.* walk out.

ausstatt|en ['aʊsʃtatən] v/t. (sep., -ge-, h) fit out, equip; furnish; supply (mit with); give a dowry to (daughter); get up (book); **'2ung** f (-/-en) outfit, equipment; furniture; supply; dowry; get-up (of book).

'aus|stechen v/t. (irr. stechen, sep., -ge-, h) cut out (a. fig.); put out (eye); **'.stehen** v/t. irr. stehen, sep., -ge-, h) 1. v/i. payments: be outstanding; 2. v/t. endure, bear; **'.steigen** v/i. (irr. steigen, sep., -ge-, sein) get out or off, alight.

'ausstell|en v/t. (sep., -ge-, h) exhibit; make out (invoice); issue (document); draw (bill); **'2er** m (-s/-) exhibitor; drawer; **'2ung** f exhibition, show; **'2ungsraum** m show-room.

'aussterben v/i. (irr. sterben, sep., -ge-, sein) die out; become extinct.

'Aussteuer f trousseau, dowry.

'ausstopfen v/t. (sep., -ge-, h) stuff; wad, pad.

'ausstoß|en v/t. (irr. stoßen, sep., -ge-, h) thrust out, eject; expel; utter (cry); heave (sigh); ✂ cashier; **'2ung** f (-/-en) expulsion.

'aus|strahlen v/t. and v/i. (sep., -ge-, h) radiate; **'.strecken** v/t. (sep., -ge-, h) stretch (out); **'.streichen** v/t. (irr. streichen, sep., -ge-, h) strike out; smooth (down); **'.streuen** v/t. (sep., -ge-, h) scatter; spread (rumours); **'.strömen** (sep., -ge-) 1. v/i. (sein) stream out; gas, light: emanate; gas, steam: escape; 2. v/t. (h) pour (out); **'.suchen** v/t. (sep., -ge-, h) choose, select.

'Austausch m exchange; **'2bar** adj. exchangeable; **'2en** v/t. (sep., -ge-, h) exchange.

'austeil|en v/t. (sep., -ge-, h) distribute; deal out (blows); **'2ung** f distribution.

Auster zo. ['aʊstər] f (-/-n) oyster.

'austragen v/t. (irr. tragen, sep., -ge-, h) deliver (letters, etc.); hold (contest).

Austral|ier [aʊ'strɑːliər] m (-s/-) Australian; **2isch** adj. Australian.

'austreib|en v/t. (irr. treiben, sep., -ge-, h) drive out; expel; **'2ung** f (-/-en) expulsion.

'aus|treten (irr. treten, sep., -ge-) 1. v/t. (h) tread or stamp out; wear out (shoes); wear down (steps);

2. v/i. (sein) emerge, come out; river: overflow its banks; retire (aus from); F ease o.s.; ~ aus leave (society, etc.); **'.trinken** (irr. trinken, sep., -ge-, h) 1. v/t. drink up; empty, drain; 2. v/i. finish drinking; **'2tritt** m leaving; retirement; **'.trocknen** (sep., -ge-) 1. v/t. (h) dry up; drain (land); parch (throat, earth); 2. v/i. (sein) dry up.

ausüb|en ['aʊsʔ-] v/t. (sep., -ge-, h) exercise; practi|se, Am. -ce (profession); exert (influence); **'2ung** f practice; exercise.

'Ausverkauf ✝ m selling off or out (of stock); sale; **'2t** ✝, thea. adj. sold out; theatre notice: 'full house.'

'Auswahl f choice; selection; ✝ assortment. [choose, select.]

'auswählen v/t. (sep., -ge-, h)

'Auswander|er m emigrant; **'2n** v/i. (sep., -ge-, sein) emigrate; **'.ung** f emigration.

auswärt|ig adj. ['aʊsvɛrtiç] out-of-town; non-resident; foreign; das Auswärtige Amt s. Außenministerium; **~s** adv. ['~s] outward(s); out of doors; out of town; abroad; ~ essen dine out.

'auswechseln 1. v/t. (sep., -ge-, h) exchange; change; replace; 2. **2** n (-s/no pl.) exchange; replacement.

'Ausweg m way out (a. fig.); outlet; fig. expedient.

'ausweichen v/i. (irr. weichen, sep., -ge-, sein) make way (for); fig. evade, avoid; **'.d** adj. evasive.

Ausweis ['aʊsvaɪs] m (-es/-e) (bank) return; identity card, Am. identification (card); **2en** ['~zən] v/t. (irr. weisen, sep., -ge-, h) turn out, expel; evict; deport; show, prove; sich ~ prove one's identity; **'.papiere** n/pl. identity papers pl.; **'.ung** ['~zuŋ] f expulsion; **'.ungsbefehl** m expulsion order.

'ausweiten v/t. and v/refl. (sep., -ge-, h) widen, stretch, expand.

'auswendig 1. adj. outward, outside; 2. adv. outwardly, outside; fig. by heart.

'aus|werfen v/t. (irr. werfen, sep., -ge-, h) throw out, cast; eject; 💰 expectorate; allow (sum of money); **'.werten** v/t. (sep., -ge-, h) evaluate; analyze, interpret; utilize, exploit; **'.wickeln** v/t. (sep., -ge-, h) unwrap; **'.wiegen** v/t. (irr. wiegen, *sep.*, -ge-, *h*) weigh out; '**~wirken** *v/refl.* (*sep.*, -ge-, *h*) take effect, operate; *sich ~ auf* (*acc.*) affect; '**2wirkung** *f* effect; '**~wischen** *v/t.* (*sep.*, -ge-, *h*) wipe out, efface; '**~wringen** *v/t.* (*irr.* wringen, *sep.*, -ge-, *h*) wring out.

'**Auswuchs** *m* excrescence, outgrowth (*a. fig.*), protuberance.

'**Auswurf** *m* expectoration; *fig.* refuse, dregs *pl.*

'**aus|zahlen** *v/t.* (*sep.*, -ge-, *h*) pay out; pay *s.o.* off; '**~zählen** *v/t.* (*sep.*, -ge-, *h*) count out.

'**Auszahlung** *f* payment.

'**Auszehrung** *f* (-/-en) consumption.

'**auszeichn|en** *v/t.* (*sep.*, -ge-, *h*) mark (out); *fig.* distinguish (*sich o.s.*); '**2ung** *f* marking; distinction; hono(u)r; decoration.

'**auszieh|en** (*irr.* ziehen, *sep.*, -ge-) **1.** *v/t.* (*h*) draw out, extract; take off (*garment*); *sich ~* undress; **2.** *v/i.* (*sein*) set out; move (out), remove, move house; '**2platte** *f* leaf (*of table*).

'**Auszug** *m* departure; ✗ marching out; removal; extract, excerpt (*from book*); summary; ✝ statement (of account). [tic, genuine.)

authentisch *adj.* [au'tɛntiʃ] authen-)

Auto ['auto] *n* (-s/-s) (motor-)car, *Am. a.* automobile; *~ fahren* drive, motor; '**~bahn** *f* motorway, autobahn; '**~biographie** *f* autobiography; '**~bus** ['~bus] *m* (-ses/-se) (motor-)bus; (motor) coach; '**~bus-**

---

haltestelle *f* bus stop; **~didakt** [~di'dakt] *m* (-en/-en) autodidact, self-taught person; '**~droschke** *f* taxi(-cab), *Am.* cab; '**~fahrer** *m* motorist; **~gramm** *n* autograph; **~'grammjäger** *m* autograph hunter; '**~händler** *m* car dealer; '**~kino** *n* drive-in cinema; **~krat** [~'kra:t] *m* (-en/-en) autocrat; **~kratie** [~a-'ti:] *f* (-/-n) autocracy; **~mat** [~'ma:t] *m* (-en/-en) automaton; slot-machine, vending machine; **~'matenrestaurant** *n* self-service restaurant, *Am.* automat; **~mation** ⊕ [~ma'tsjo:n] *f* (-/*no pl.*) automation; **2'matisch** *adj.* automatic; '**~mechaniker** *m* car mechanic; **~mobil** [~mo'bi:l] *n* (-s/-e) *s. Auto;* **2nom** *adj.* [~'no:m] autonomous; **~nomie** [~o'mi:] *f* (-/-n) autonomy.

Autor ['autɔr] *m* (-s/-en) author.

'**Autoreparaturwerkstatt** *f* car repair shop, garage. [thor(ess).)

Autorin [au'to:rin] *f* (-/-nen) au-)

autori|sieren [autori'zi:rən] *v/t.* (*no* -ge-, *h*) authorize; **~tär** *adj.* [~'tɛ:r] authoritarian; **2'tät** *f* (-/-en) authority.

'**Auto|straße** *f* motor-road; '**~vermietung** *f* (-/-en) car hire service.

avisieren [avi'zi:rən] *v/t.* (*no* -ge-, *h*) advise.

Axt [akst] *f* (-/⁼e) ax(e).

Azetylen 🜋 [atsety'le:n] *n* (-s/*no pl.*) acetylene. [**2n** *adj.* azure.)

Azur [a'tsu:r] *m* (-s/*no pl.*) azure;)

B

Bach [bax] *m* (-[e]s/⁼e) brook, *Am. a.* run.

Backbord ⬥ ['bak-] *n* (-[e]s/-e)

Backe ['bakə] *f* (-/-n) cheek.

backen ['bakən] (*irr.*, ge-, *h*) **1.** *v/t.* bake; fry; dry (*fruit*); **2.** *v/i.* bake; fry.

'**Backen|bart** *m* (side-)whiskers *pl.*, *Am. a.* sideburns *pl.*; '**~zahn** *m* molar (tooth), grinder.

Bäcker ['bekər] *m* (-s/-) baker; **~ei** [~'rai] *f* (-/-en) baker's (shop), bakery.

'**Back|fisch** *m* fried fish; *fig.* girl in her teens, teenager, *Am. a.* bobby soxer; '**~obst** *n* dried fruit; '**~ofen**

---

m oven; '**~pflaume** *f* prune; '**~pulver** *n* baking-powder; '**~stein** *m* brick; '**~ware** *f* baker's ware.

Bad [ba:t] *n* (-[e]s/⁼er) bath; *in river, etc.: a.* bathe; *s. Badeort; ein ~ nehmen* take or have a bath.

Bade|anstalt ['ba:də-] *f* (public swimming) baths *pl.*; '**~anzug** *m* bathing-costume, bathing-suit; '**~hose** *f* bathing-drawers *pl.*, (bathing) trunks *pl.*; '**~kappe** *f* bathing-cap; '**~kur** *f* spa treatment; '**~mantel** *m* bathing-gown, *Am.* bathrobe; '**~meister** *m* bath attendant; '**2n** (ge-, *h*) **1.** *v/t.* bath (*baby, etc.*); bathe (*eyes, etc.*);

2. v/i. bath, tub; have or take a bath; in river, etc.: bathe; ~ gehen go swimming; '~ofen m geyser, boiler, Am. a. water heater; '~ort m watering-place; spa; seaside resort; '~salz n bath-salt; '~strand m bathing-beach; '~tuch n bath-towel; '~wanne f bath-tub; '~zimmer n bathroom.

Bagatell|e [baga'tɛlə] f (-/-n) trifle, trifling matter, bagatelle; 2i'sieren v/t. (no -ge-, h) minimize (the importance of), Am. a. play down.

Bagger ['bagər] m (-s/-) excavator; dredge(r); '2n v/i. and v/t. (ge-, h) excavate; dredge.

Bahn [baːn] f (-/-en) course; path; 🚋 railway, Am. railroad; mot. lane; trajectory (of bullet, etc.); ast. orbit; sports: track, course, lane; skating: rink; bowling: alley; '2brechend adj. pioneer(ing), epoch-making; art: avant-gardist; '~damm m railway embankment, Am. railroad embankment; '2en v/t. (ge-, h) clear, open (up) (way); den Weg ~ prepare or pave the way (dat. for); sich e-n Weg ~ force or work or elbow one's way; '~hof m (railway-)station, Am. (railroad-)station; '~linie f railway-line, Am. railroad line; '~steig m platform; '~steigkarte f platform ticket; '~übergang m level crossing, Am. grade crossing.

Bahre ['baːrə] f (-/-n) stretcher, litter; bier.

Bai [baɪ] f (-/-en) bay; creek.

Baisse † ['bɛːs(ə)] f (-/-n) depression (on the market); fall (in prices); auf ~ spekulieren † bear, speculate for a fall, Am. sell short; '~spekulant m bear.

Bajonett ⚔ [bajo'nɛt] n (-[e]s/-e) bayonet; das ~ aufpflanzen fix the bayonet.

Bake ['baːkə] f (-/-n) ⚓ beacon; 🚋 warning-sign.

Bakterie [bak'teːrjə] f (-/-n) bacterium, microbe, germ.

bald adv. [balt] soon; shortly; before long; F almost, nearly; early; so ~ als möglich as soon as possible; ~ hier, ~ dort now here, now there; '~ig adj. ['~diç] speedy; ~e Antwort † early reply. [valerian.]

Baldrian ['baldriaːn] m (-s/-e)

Balg [balk] **1.** m (-[e]s/=e) skin, body (of doll); bellows pl.; **2.** F m, n (-[e]s/=er) brat, urchin; 2en ['balgən] v/refl. (ge-, h) scuffle (um for), wrestle (um for).

Balken ['balkən] m (-s/-) beam, rafter.

Balkon [bal'kōː; ~'koːn] m (-s/-s, -s/-e) balcony; thea. dress circle, Am. balcony; ~tür f French window.

Ball [bal] m (-[e]s/=e) ball; geogr., ast. a. globe; ball, dance; auf dem ~ at the ball. [lad.]

Ballade [ba'laːdə] f (-/-n) bal-

Ballast ['balast] m (-es/⚹-e) ballast; fig. burden, impediment; dead weight.

'ballen[1] v/t. (ge-, h) (form into a) ball; clench (fist); sich ~ (form into a) ball; cluster.

'Ballen[2] m (-s/-) bale; anat. ball; ~ Papier ten reams pl.

Ballett [ba'lɛt] n (-[e]s/-e) ballet; ~änzer [ba'lɛttɛntsər] m (-s/-) ballet-dancer.

ball|förmig adj. ['balfœrmiç] ball-shaped, globular; '2kleid n ball-dress.

Ballon [ba'lōː; ~'oːn] m (-s/-s; -s/-s, -e) balloon.

'Ball|saal m ball-room; '~spiel n ball-game, game of ball.

Balsam ['balzaːm] m (-s/-e) balsam, balm (a. fig.); 2ieren [~a'miːrən] v/t. (no -ge-, h) embalm.

Balz [balts] f (-/-en) mating season; display (by cock-bird).

Bambus ['bambus] m (-ses/-se) bamboo; '~rohr n bamboo, cane.

banal adj. [ba'naːl] commonplace, banal, trite; trivial; 2ität [~ali'tɛːt] f (-/-en) banality; commonplace; triviality.

Banane [ba'naːnə] f (-/-n) banana; ~nstecker ⚡ m banana plug.

Band [bant] **1.** m (-[e]s/=e) volume; **2.** n (-[e]s/=er) band; ribbon; tape; anat. ligament; **3.** fig. n (-[e]s/-e) bond, tie; **4.** 2 pret. of binden.

Bandag|e [ban'daːʒə] f (-/-n) bandage; 2ieren [~a'ʒiːrən] v/t. (no -ge-, h) (apply a) bandage.

Bande ['bandə] f (-/-n) billiards: cushion; fig. gang, band.

bändigen ['bɛndigən] v/t. (ge-, h) tame; break in (horse); subdue (a. fig.); fig. restrain, master.

Bandit [ban'di:t] *m* (-en/-en) bandit.

'Band|maß *n* tape measure; **'~säge** *f* band-saw; **'~scheibe** *anat. f* intervertebral disc; **'~wurm** *zo. m* tapeworm.

bang *adj.* [baŋ], **~e** *adj.* ['~ə] anxious (*um* about), uneasy (about), concerned (for); *mir ist* **~** I am afraid (*vor dat.* of); *j-m* **bange machen** frighten *or* scare s.o.; **'~en** *v/i.* (ge-, h) be anxious *or* worried (*um* about).

Bank [baŋk] *f* **1.** (-/ᵘe) bench; *school:* desk; *F durch die* **~** without exception, all through; *auf die lange* **~** schieben put off, postpone; shelve; **2.** † (-/-en) bank; *Geld auf der* **~** money in the bank; **'~anweisung** *f* cheque, *Am.* check; **'~ausweis** *m* bank return *or* statement; **'~beamte** *m* bank clerk *or* official; **'~einlage** *f* deposit.

Bankett [baŋ'kɛt] *n* (-[e]s/-e) banquet.

'Bank|geheimnis *n* banker's duty of secrecy; **'~geschäft** † *n* bank(-ing) transaction, banking operation; **'~haus** *n* bank(ing-house).

Bankier [baŋk'je:] *m* (-s/-s) banker.

'Bank|konto *n* bank(ing) account; **'~note** *f* (bank) note, *Am.* (bank) bill.

bankrott [baŋ'krɔt] **1.** *adj.* bankrupt; **2.** ♀ *m* (-[e]s/-e) bankruptcy, insolvency, failure; **~** *machen* fail, go *or* become bankrupt.

'Bankwesen *n* banking.

Bann [ban] *m* (-[e]s/-e) ban; *fig.* spell; *eccl.* excommunication; **'~en** *v/t.* (ge-, h) banish (*a. fig.*); exorcize (*devil*); avert (*danger*); *eccl.* excommunicate; spellbind.

Banner ['banər] *n* (-s/-) banner (*a. fig.*); standard; **'~träger** *m* standard-bearer.

'Bann|fluch *m* anathema; **'~meile** *f* precincts *pl.*; ⚖ area around government buildings within which processions and meetings are prohibited.

bar¹ [ba:r] **1.** *adj.:* **~**er Sache *~* destitute *or* devoid of s.th.; **~**es *Geld* ready money, cash; **~**er *Unsinn* sheer nonsense; **2.** *adv.:* **~** bezahlen pay in cash, pay money down.

Bar² [~] *f* (-/-s) bar; night-club.

Bär [bɛ:r] *m* (-en/-en) bear; *j-m e-n* **~**en *aufbinden* hoax s.o.

Baracke [ba'rakə] *f* (-/-n) barrack; **~nlager** *n* hutment.

Barbar [bar'ba:r] *m* (-en/-en) barbarian; **~ei** [~a'raɪ] *f* (-/-en) barbarism; barbarity; **2isch** [~'ba:rɪʃ] *adj.* barbarian; barbarous; *art, taste:* barbaric.

'Bar|bestand *m* cash in hand; **'~betrag** *m* amount in cash.

'Bärenzwinger *m* bear-pit.

barfuß *adj. and adv.* ['ba:r-], **~füßig** *adj. and adv.* ['~fy:sɪç] barefoot.

barg [bark] *pret. of* bergen.

'Bar|geld *n* cash, ready money; **2geldlos** *adj.* cashless; **~er** *Zahlungsverkehr* cashless money transfers *pl.*; **2häuptig** *adj. and adv.* ['~hɔʏptɪç] bare-headed, uncovered.

Bariton ♪ ['ba:rɪtɔn] *m* (-s/-e) baritone.   [launch.)

Barkasse ⚓ [bar'kasə] *f* (-/-n)

barmherzig *adj.* [barm'hɛrtsɪç] merciful, charitable; *der* **~**e *Samariter* the good Samaritan; **2**e *Schwester* Sister of Mercy *or* Charity; **2keit** *f* (-/-en) mercy, charity.

Barometer [baro'-] *n* barometer.

Baron [ba'ro:n] *m* (-s/-e) baron; **~in** *f* (-/-nen) baroness.

Barre ['barə] *f* (-/-n) bar.

Barren ['barən] *m* (-s/-) *metall.* bar, ingot, bullion; *gymnastics:* parallel bars *pl.*

Barriere [bar'jɛ:rə] *f* (-/-n) barrier.

Barrikade [bari'ka:də] *f* (-/-n) barricade; **~n** *errichten* raise barricades.

barsch *adj.* [barʃ] rude, gruff, rough.

'Bar|schaft *f* (-/-en) ready money, cash; **'~scheck** † *m* open cheque, *Am.* open check.

barst [barst] *pret. of* bersten.

Bart [ba:rt] *m* (-[e]s/-ᵉe) beard; bit (*of key*); *sich e-n* **~** *wachsen lassen* grow a beard.

bärtig *adj.* ['bɛ:rtɪç] bearded.

'bartlos *adj.* beardless.

'Barzahlung *f* cash payment; *nur gegen* **~** † terms strictly cash.

Basis ['ba:zɪs] *f* (-/Basen) base; *fig.* basis.

Baß ♪ [bas] *m* (Basses/Bässe) bass; **'~geige** *f* bass-viol.

Bassist [ba'sɪst] *m* (-en/-en) bass (singer).

Bast [bast] *m* (-es/-e) bast; velvet (*on antlers*).

Bastard ['bastart] *m* (-[e]s/-e) bas-

B

tard; half-breed; zo., & hybrid.

bast|eln ['bastəln] (ge-, h) **1.** v/t. build, F rig up; **2.** v/i. build; '**2ler** m (-s/-) amateur craftsman, do-it-yourself man.

bat [ba:t] pret. of bitten.

Bataillon [batal'joːn] n (-s/-e) battalion.

Batist [ba'tist] m (-[e]s/-e) cambric.

Batterie ✕, ⚡ [batəˈriː] f (-/-en) battery.

Bau [bau] m **1.** (-[e]s/no pl.) building, construction; build, frame; **2.** (-[e]s/-ten) building, edifice; **3.** (-[e]s/-e) burrow, den (a. fig.), earth.

'**Bau|arbeiter** m workman in the building trade; '**~art** f architecture, style; method of construction; mot. type, model.

Bauch [baux] m (-[e]s/=e) anat. abdomen, belly; paunch; ship: bottom; '**2ig** adj. big-bellied, bulgy; '**~landung** f belly landing; '**~redner** m ventriloquist; '**~schmerzen** m/pl., '**~weh** n (-s/no pl.) belly-ache, stomach-ache.

bauen ['bauən] (ge-, h) **1.** v/t. build, construct; erect, raise; build, make (nest); make (violin, etc.); **2.** v/i. build; ~ auf (acc.) trust (in); rely or count or depend on.

Bauer ['bauər] **1.** m (-n, -s/-n) farmer; peasant, countryman; chess: pawn; **2.** n, m (-s/-) (bird-)cage.

Bäuerin ['bɔʏərin] f (-/-nen) farmer's wife; peasant woman.

Bauerlaubnis ['bauʔ-] f building permit.

bäuerlich adj. ['bɔʏərliç] rural, rustic.

Bauern|fänger contp. ['bauərn-fɛŋər] m (-s/-) trickster, confidence man; '**~haus** n farm-house; '**~hof** m farm.

'**bau|fällig** adj. out of repair, dilapidated; '**2gerüst** n scaffold (-ing); '**2handwerker** m craftsman in the building trade; '**2herr** m owner; '**2holz** n timber, Am. lumber; '**2jahr** n year of construction; ~ 1969 1969 model or make; '**2kasten** m box of bricks; '**2kunst** f architecture.

'**baulich** adj. architectural; structural; in gutem ~en Zustand in good repair.

Baum [baum] m (-[e]s/=e) tree.

'**Baumeister** m architect.

baumeln ['bauməln] v/i. (ge-, h) dangle, swing; mit den Beinen ~ dangle or swing one's legs.

'**Baum|schere** f (eine a pair of) pruning-shears pl.; '**~schule** f nursery (of young trees); '**~stamm** m trunk; '**~wolle** f cotton; '**~wollen** adj. (made of) cotton.

'**Bau|plan** m architect's or building plan; '**~platz** m building plot or site, Am. location; '**~polizei** f Board of Surveyors.

Bausch [bauʃ] m (-es/-e, =e) bolster; wad; in ~ und Bogen altogether, wholesale, in the lump; '**2en** v/t. (ge-, h) swell; sich ~ bulge, swell out, billow (out).

'**Bau|stein** m brick, building stone; building block; fig. element; '**~stelle** f building site; '**~stil** m (architectural) style; '**~stoff** m building material; '**~unternehmer** m building contractor; '**~zaun** m hoarding.

Bay|er ['baɪər] m (-n/-n) Bavarian; '**2(e)risch** adj. Bavarian.

Bazill|enträger ⚕ [ba'tsilən-] m (germ-)carrier; '**~us** [~us] m (-/Bazillen) bacillus, germ.

beabsichtigen [bəˈʔapziçtigən] v/t. (no -ge-, h) intend, mean, propose (zu tun to do, doing).

be'acht|en v/t. (no -ge-, h) pay attention to; notice; observe; '**~ens-wert** adj. noteworthy, remarkable; '**~lich** adj. remarkable; considerable; **2ung** f attention; consideration; notice; observance.

Beamte [bəˈʔamtə] m (-n/-n) official, officer, Am. a. officeholder; functionary; Civil Servant. [quieting.\

be'ängstigend adj. alarming, dis-\

beanspruch|en [bəˈʔanʃpruxən] v/t. (no -ge-, h) claim, demand; require (efforts, time, space, etc.); ⊕ stress; **2ung** f (-/-en) claim; demand (gen. on); ⊕ stress, strain.

beanstand|en [bəˈʔanʃtandən] v/t. (no -ge-, h) object to; **2ung** f (-/-en) objection (gen. to).

beantragen [bəˈʔantraːgən] v/t. (no -ge-, h) apply for; ⚖, parl. move, make a motion; propose.

be'antwort|en v/t. (no -ge-, h) answer (a. fig.), reply to; **2ung** f (-/-en) answer, reply; in ~ (gen.) in answer or reply to.

be'arbeit|en v/t. (no -ge-, h) work; ✗ till; dress (leather); hew (stone); process; ♎ treat; ⚖ be in charge of (case); edit, revise (book); adapt (nach from); esp. ♪ arrange; j-n ~ work on s.o.; batter s.o.; **♀ung** f (-/-en) working; revision (of book); thea. adaptation; esp. ♪ arrangement; processing; ♎ treatment.

be'argwöhnen v/t. (no -ge-, h) suspect, be suspicious of.

beaufsichtig|en [bə'aufziçtigən] v/t. (no -ge-, h) inspect, superintend, supervise, control; look after (child); **♀ung** f (-/-en) inspection, supervision, control.

be'auftrag|en v/t. (no -ge-, h) commission (zu inf. to inf.), charge (mit with); **♀te** [⌐ktə] m (-n/-n) commissioner; representative; deputy; proxy.

be'bauen v/t. (no -ge-, h) 🏛 build on; ✗ cultivate.

beben ['be:bən] v/i. (ge-, h) shake (vor dat. with), tremble (with); shiver (with); earth: quake.

Becher ['bɛçər] m (-s/-) cup (a. fig.).

Becken ['bɛkən] n (-s/-) basin, Am. a. bowl; ♪ cymbal(s pl.); anat. pelvis.

bedacht adj. [bə'daxt]: ~ sein auf (acc.) look after, be concerned about, be careful or mindful of; darauf ~ sein zu inf. be anxious to inf.

bedächtig adj. [bə'dɛçtiç] deliberate.

bedang [bə'daŋ] pret. of bedingen.

be'danken v/refl. (no -ge-, h): sich bei j-m für et. ~ thank s.o. for s.th.

Bedarf [bə'darf] m (-[e]s/no pl.) need (an dat. of), want (of); ♱ demand (for); **~sartikel** [bə'darfs?-] m/pl. necessaries pl., requisites pl.

bedauerlich adj. [bə'dauərliç] regrettable, deplorable.

be'dauern v/t. (no -ge-, h) feel or be sorry for s.o.; pity s.o.; regret, deplore s.th.; **2.** ♀ n (-s/no pl.) regret; pity; **~swert** adj. pitiable, deplorable.

be'deck|en v/t. (no -ge-, h) cover; ✕ escort; ⚓ convoy; **~t** adj. sky: overcast; **♀ung** f cover(ing); ✕ escort; ⚓ convoy.

be'denken 1. v/t. (irr. denken, no -ge-, h) consider; think s.th. over;

j-n in s-m Testament ~ remember s.o. in one's will; **2.** ♀ n (-s/-) consideration; objection; hesitation; scruple; **~los** adj. unscrupulous.

be'denklich adj. doubtful; character: a. dubious; situation, etc.: dangerous, critical; delicate; risky.

Be'denkzeit f time for reflection; ich gebe dir e-e Stunde ~ I give you one hour to think it over.

be'deut|en v/t. (no -ge-, h) mean, signify; stand for; **~end** adj. important, prominent; sum, etc. considerable; **~sam** adj. significant.

Be'deutung f meaning, significance; importance; **2slos** adj. insignificant; meaningless; **2svoll** adj. significant; **~swandel** ling. m semantic change.

be'dien|en (no -ge-, h) **1.** v/t. serve; wait on; ⊕ operate, work (machine); ✕ serve (gun); answer (telephone); sich ~ at table: help o.s.; **2.** v/i. serve; wait (at table); cards: follow suit; **♀ung** f (-/-en) service, esp. ♱ attendance; in restaurant, etc.: service; waiter, waitress; shop assistant(s pl.).

beding|en [bə'diŋən] v/t. ([irr.,] no -ge-, h) condition; stipulate; require; cause; imply; **~t** adj. conditional (durch on); restricted; ~ sein durch be conditioned by; **♀ung** f (-/-en) condition; stipulation; **~en** pl. ♱ terms pl.; **~ungslos** adj. unconditional.

be'dräng|en v/t. (no -ge-, h) press hard, beset; **♀nis** f (-/-se) distress.

be'droh|en v/t. (no -ge-, h) threaten; menace; **~lich** adj. threatening; **♀ung** f threat, menace (gen. to).

be'drück|en v/t. (no -ge-, h) oppress; depress; deject; **♀ung** f (-/-en) oppression; depression; dejection.

bedungen [bə'duŋən] p.p. of bedingen.

be'dürf|en v/i. (irr. dürfen, no -ge-, h): e-r Sache ~ need or want or require s.th.; **♀nis** n (-ses/-se) need, want, requirement; sein ~ verrichten relieve o.s. or nature; **♀nisanstalt** [bə'dyrfnis?-] f public convenience, Am. comfort station; **~tig** adj. needy, poor, indigent.

be'ehren v/t. (no -ge-, h) hono(u)r, favo(u)r; ich beehre mich zu inf. I have the hono(u)r to inf.

be'eilen v/refl. (no -ge-, h) hasten, hurry, make haste, Am. F a. hustle.

beeindrucken [bə'aındrukən] v/t. (no -ge-, h) impress, make an impression on.

beeinfluss|en [bə'aınflussən] v/t. (no -ge-, h) influence; affect; parl. lobby; **2ung** f (-/-en) influence; parl. lobbying.

beeinträchtig|en [bə'aıntreçtigən] v/t. (no -ge-, h) impair, injure, affect (adversely); **2ung** f (-/-en) impairment (gen. of); injury (to).

be'end|en v/t. (no -ge-, h), **~igen** [~igən] v/t. (no -ge-, h) (bring to an) end, finish, terminate; **2igung** [~iguŋ] f (-/-en) ending, termination.

beengt adj. [bə'ɛŋkt] space: narrow, confined, cramped; sich ~ fühlen feel cramped (for room); feel oppressed or uneasy.

be'erben v/t. (no -ge-, h): j-n ~ be s.o.'s heir.

beerdig|en [bə'e:rdigən] v/t. (no -ge-, h) bury; **2ung** f (-/-en) burial, funeral.

Beere ['be:rə] f (-/-n) berry.

Beet ✓ [be:t] n (-[e]s/-e) bed.

befähig|en [bə'fɛ:igən] v/t. (no -ge-, h) enable (zu inf. to inf.); qualify (für, zu for); **~t** adj. [~çt] (cap)able; **2ung** f (-/-en) qualification; capacity.

befahl [bə'fa:l] pret. of befehlen.

befahr|bar adj. [bə'fa:rba:r] passable, practicable, trafficable; ♣ navigable; **~en** v/t. (irr. fahren, no -ge-, h) drive or travel on; ♣ navigate (river).

be'fallen v/t. (irr. fallen, no -ge-, h) attack; befall; disease: a. strike; fear: seize.

be'fangen adj. embarrassed; self-conscious; prejudiced (a. ⅍); ⅍ bias(s)ed; **2heit** f (-/-en) embarrassment; self-consciousness; ⅍ bias, prejudice.

be'fassen v/refl. (no -ge-, h): sich ~ mit occupy o.s. with; engage in; attend to; deal with.

Befehl [bə'fe:l] m (-[e]s/-e) command (über acc. of); order; **2en** (irr., no -ge-, h) **1.** v/t. command; order; **2.** v/i. command; **2igen** [~igən] v/t. (no -ge-, h) command. **Be'fehlshaber** m (-s/-) commander(-in-chief); **2isch** adj. imperious.

be'festig|en v/t. (no -ge-, h) fasten (an dat. to), fix (to), attach (to); ⅍ fortify; fig. strengthen; **2ung** f (-/-en) fixing, fastening; ⅍ fortification; fig. strengthening.

be'feuchten v/t. (no -ge-, h) moisten, damp; wet.

be'finden 1. v/refl. (irr. finden, no -ge-, h) be; **2.** 2 n (-s/no pl.) (state of) health.

be'flaggen v/t. (no -ge-, h) flag.

be'flecken v/t. (no -ge-, h) spot, stain (a. fig.); fig. sully.

beflissen adj. [bə'flisən] studious; **2heit** f (-/no pl.) studiousness, assiduity.

befohlen [bə'fo:lən] p.p. of befehlen.

be'folg|en v/t. (no -ge-, h) follow, take (advice); obey (rule); adhere to (principle); **2ung** f (-/_-en) observance (of); adherence (to).

be'förder|n v/t. (no -ge-, h) convey, carry; haul (goods), transport; forward; ♣ ship (a. ♠); promote (to be) (a. ⅍); **2ung** f conveyance, transport(ation), forwarding; promotion; **2ungsmittel** n (means of) transport, Am. (means of) transportation.

be'fragen v/t. (no -ge-, h) question, interview; interrogate.

be'frei|en v/t. (no -ge-, h) (set) free (von from); liberate (nation, mind, etc.) (from); rescue (captive) (from); exempt s.o. (from); deliver s.o. (aus, von from); **2er** m liberator; **2ung** f (-/-en) liberation, deliverance; exemption.

Befremden [bə'frɛmdən] n (-s/ no pl.) surprise.

befreund|en [bə'frɔyndən] v/refl. (no -ge-, h): sich mit j-m ~ make friends with s.o.; sich mit et. ~ get used to s.th., reconcile o.s. to s.th.; **~et** adj. friendly; on friendly terms; ~ sein be friends.

befriedig|en [bə'fri:digən] v/t. (no -ge-, h) satisfy; appease (hunger); meet (expectations, demand); pay off (creditor); **~end** adj. satisfactory; **2ung** f (-/-en) satisfaction.

be'fristen v/t. (no -ge-, h) set a time-limit.

be'frucht|en v/t. (no -ge-, h) fertilize; fructify; fecundate; impregnate; **2ung** f (-/-en) fertilization; fructification; fecundation; impregnation.

Befug|nis [bə'fu:knis] f (-/-se) authority, warrant; esp. ⚖ competence; 2t adj. authorized; competent.

be'fühlen v/t. (no -ge-, h) feel, touch, handle, finger.

Be'fund n (-[e]s/-e) result; finding(s pl.); ⚕ diagnosis.

be'fürcht|en v/t. (no -ge-, h) fear, apprehend; suspect; 2ung f (-/-en) fear, apprehension, suspicion.

befürworten [bə'fy:rvɔrtən] v/t. (no -ge-, h) plead for, advocate.

begabt adj. [bə'ga:pt] gifted, talented; 2ung [-buŋ] f (-/-en) gift, talent(s pl.).

begann [bə'gan] pret. of beginnen.

be'geben v/t. (irr. geben, no -ge-, h) ⚹ negotiate (bill of exchange); sich ~ happen; sich ~ nach go to, make for; sich in Gefahr ~ expose o.s. to danger.

begegn|en [bə'ge:gnən] v/i. (no -ge-, sein) meet s.o. or s.th., meet with; incident: happen to; anticipate, prevent; 2ung f (-/-en) meeting.

be'gehen v/t. (irr. gehen, no -ge-, h) walk (on); inspect; celebrate (birthday, etc.); commit (crime); make (mistake); ein Unrecht ~ do wrong.

begehr|en [bə'ge:rən] v/t. (no -ge-, h) demand, require; desire, crave (for); long for; ~lich adj. desirous, covetous.

begeister|n [bə'gaɪstərn] v/t. (no -ge-, h) inspire, fill with enthusiasm; sich ~ für feel enthusiastic about; 2ung f (-/no pl.) enthusiasm, inspiration.

Be'gier f, ~**de** [-də] f (-/-n) desire (nach for), appetite (for); concupiscence; 2ig adj. eager (nach for, auf acc. for; zu inf. to inf.), desirous (nach of; zu inf. to inf.), anxious (zu inf. to inf.).

be'gießen v/t. (irr. gießen, no -ge-, h) water; baste (roasting meat); F wet (bargain).

Beginn [bə'gin] m (-[e]s/no pl.) beginning, start, commencement; origin; 2en v/t. and v/i. (irr. no -ge-, h) begin, start, commence.

beglaubig|en [bə'glaubigən] v/t. (no -ge-, h) attest, certify; legalize, authenticate; 2ung f (-/-en) attestation, certification; legalization; 2ungsschreiben n credentials pl.

be'gleichen ⚹ v/t. (irr. gleichen, no -ge-, h) pay, settle (bill, debt).

be'gleit|en v/t. (no -ge-, h) accompany (a. ♪ auf dat. on); escort; attend (a. fig.); see (s.o. home, etc.); 2er m (-s/-) companion, attendant; escort; ♪ accompanist; 2erscheinung f attendant symptom; 2-schreiben n covering letter; 2ung f (-/-en) company; attendants pl., retinue (of sovereign, etc.); esp. ⚔ escort; ⚓, ⚔ convoy; ♪ accompaniment.

be'glückwünschen v/t. (no -ge-, h) congratulate (zu on).

begnadig|en [bə'gna:digən] v/t. (no -ge-, h) pardon; pol. amnesty; 2ung f (-/-en) pardon; pol. amnesty.

begnügen [bə'gny:gən] v/refl. (no -ge-, h): sich ~ mit content o.s. with, be satisfied with.

begonnen [bə'gɔnən] p.p. of beginnen.

be'graben v/t. (irr. graben, no -ge-, h) bury (a. fig.); inter.

Begräbnis [bə'grɛ:pnis] n (-ses/-se) burial; funeral, obsequies pl.

begradigen [bə'gra:digən] v/t. (no -ge-, h) straighten (road, frontier, etc.).

be'greif|en v/t. (irr. greifen, no -ge-, h) comprehend, understand; ~lich adj. comprehensible.

be'grenz|en v/t. (no -ge-, h) bound, border; fig. limit; 2theit f (-/-en) limitation (of knowledge); narrowness (of mind); 2ung f (-/-en) boundary; bound, limit; limitation.

Be'griff m idea, notion, conception; comprehension; im ~ sein zu inf. be about or going to inf.

be'gründ|en v/t. (no -ge-, h) establish, found; give reasons for, substantiate (claim, charge); 2ung f establishment, foundation; fig. substantiation (of claim or charge); reason.

be'grüß|en v/t. (no -ge-, h) greet, welcome; salute; 2ung f (-/-en) greeting, welcome; salutation.

begünstig|en [bə'gynstigən] v/t. (no -ge-, h) favo(u)r; encourage; patronize; 2ung (-/-en) f favo(u)ring; encouragement; patronage.

begutachten [bə'gu:t?-] v/t. (no -ge-, h) give an opinion on; examine; ~ lassen obtain expert opinion on, submit s.th. to an expert.

B

begütert adj. [bə'gy:tərt] wealthy, well-to-do.

be'haart adj. hairy.

behäbig adj. [bə'hɛ:biç] phlegmatic, comfort-loving; figure: portly.

be'haftet adj. afflicted (with disease, etc.).

behag|en [bə'ha:gən] **1.** v/i. (no -ge-, h) please or suit s.o.; **2.** ♀ n (-s/no pl.) comfort, ease; **~lich** adj. [~k-] comfortable; cosy, snug.

be'halten v/t. (irr. halten, no -ge-, h) retain; keep (für sich to o.s.); remember.

Behälter [bə'hɛltər] m (-s/-) container, receptacle; box; for liquid: reservoir; for oil, etc.: tank.

be'hand|eln v/t. (no -ge-, h) treat; deal with (a. subject); ⊕ process; 🖉 treat; dress (wound); **♀ung** f treatment; handling; ⊕ processing.

be'hängen v/t. (no -ge-, h) hang, drape (mit with); sich ~ mit cover or load o.s. with (jewellery).

beharr|en [bə'harən] v/i. (no -ge-, h) persist (auf dat. in); **~lich** adj. persistent; **♀lichkeit** f (-/no pl.) persistence.

be'hauen v/t. (no -ge-, h) hew; trim (wood).

behaupt|en [bə'hauptən] v/t. (no -ge-, h) assert; maintain; **♀ung** f (-/-en) assertion; statement.

Behausung [bə'hauzuŋ] f (-/-en) habitation; lodging.

Be'helf m (-[e]s/-e) expedient, (make)shift; s. Notbehelf; **♀en** v/refl. (irr. helfen, no -ge-, h): sich ~ mit make shift with; sich ~ ohne do without; **~sheim** n temporary home.

behend adj. [bə'hɛnt], **~e** adj. [~də] nimble, agile; smart; **♀igkeit** [~d-] f (-/no pl.) nimbleness, agility; smartness. [lodge, shelter.]

be'herbergen v/t. (no -ge-, h)

be'herrsch|en v/t. (no -ge-, h) rule (over), govern; command (situation, etc.); have command of (language); sich ~ control o.s.; **♀er** m ruler (gen. over, of); **♀ung** f (-/-en) command, control.

beherzigen [bə'hɛrtsigən] v/t. (no -ge-, h) take to heart, (bear in) mind.

be'hexen v/t. (no -ge-, h) bewitch.

be'hilflich adj.: j-m ~ sein help s.o. (bei in).

be'hindern v/t. (no -ge-, h) hinder, hamper, impede; handicap; obstruct (a. traffic, etc.).

Behörde [bə'hø:rdə] f (-/-n) authority, mst authorities pl.; board, council.

be'hüten v/t. (no -ge-, h) guard, preserve (vor dat. from).

behutsam adj. [bə'hu:tza:m] cautious, careful; **♀keit** f (-/no pl.) caution.

bei prp. (dat.) [bai] address: ~ Schmidt care of (abbr. c/o) Schmidt, ~m Buchhändler at the bookseller's, ~ uns with us; ~ der Hand nehmen take by the hand; ich habe kein Geld ~ mir I have no money about or on me; ~ der Kirche near the church; ~ guter Gesundheit in good health; wie es ~ Schiller heißt as Schiller says; die Schlacht ~ Waterloo the Battle of Waterloo; ~ e-m Glase Wein over a glass of wine; ~ alledem for all that; Stunden nehmen ~ take lessons from or with; ~ günstigem Wetter weather permitting.

'beibehalten v/t. (irr. halten, sep., no -ge-, h) keep up, retain.

'Beiblatt n supplement (zu to).

'beibringen v/t. (irr. bringen, sep., -ge-, h) bring forward; produce (witness, etc.); j-m et. ~ impart (news, etc.) to s.o.; teach s.o. s.th.; inflict (defeat, wound, etc.) on s.o.

Beichte ['baiçtə] f (-/-n) confession; **♀n** v/t. and v/i. (ge-, h) confess.

beide adj. ['baidə] both; nur wir ~ just the two of us; in ~n Fällen in either case.

beider|lei adj. ['baidərlai] of both kinds; ~ Geschlechts' of either sex; **'~seitig 1.** adj. on both sides; mutual; **2.** adv. mutually; **'~seits 1.** prp. on both sides (gen. of); **2.** adv. mutually.

'Beifahrer m (-s/-) (front-seat) passenger; assistant driver; motor racing: co-driver.

'Beifall m (-[e]s/no pl.) approbation, applause; cheers pl.

'beifällig adj. approving; favo(u)rable.

'Beifallsruf m acclaim; **~e** pl. cheers pl.

'beifügen v/t. (sep., -ge-, h) add, enclose.

'Beigeschmack m (-[e]s/no pl.

slight flavo(u)r; smack (of) (*a. fig.*).

'**Beihilfe** *f* aid; allowance; *for study*: grant; *for project*: subsidy; 🔲 aiding and abetting; j-m ~ leisten 🔲 aid and abet s.o.

'**beikommen** *v/i.* (*irr.* kommen, *sep.*, -ge-, sein) get at.

Beil [baɪl] *n* (-[e]s/-e) hatchet; chopper; cleaver; ax(e).

'**Beilage** *f* supplement (*to newspaper*); F trimmings *pl.* (*of meal*); vegetables *pl.*

beiläufig *adj.* ['baɪlɔyfɪç] casual; incidental.

'**beileg**|**en** *v/t.* (*sep.*, -ge-, h) add (*dat.* to); enclose; settle (*dispute*); '♀ung *f* (-/-en) settlement.

Beileid ['baɪlaɪt] *n* condolence; j-m sein ~ bezeigen condole with s.o. (zu on, upon).

'**beiliegen** *v/i.* (*irr.* liegen, *sep.*, -ge-, h) be enclosed (*dat.* with).

'**beimessen** *v/t.* (*irr.* messen, *sep.*, -ge-, h) attribute (*dat.* to), ascribe (to); attach (*importance* to).

'**beimisch**|**en** *v/t.* (*sep.*, -ge-, h): e-r Sache et. ~ mix s.th. with s.th.; '♀ung *f* admixture.

Bein [baɪn] *n* (-[e]s/-e) leg; bone.

'**beinah(e)** *adv.* almost, nearly.

'**Beiname** *m* appellation; nickname.

'**Beinbruch** *m* fracture of the leg.

beiordnen ['baɪ⁹-] *v/t.* (*sep.*, -ge-, h) adjoin; co-ordinate (*a. gr.*).

'**beipflichten** *v/i.* (*sep.*, -ge-, h) agree with *s.o.*; assent to *s.th.*

'**Beirat** *m* (-[e]s/⁀e) adviser, counsel(l)or; advisory board.

be'irren *v/t.* (*no* -ge-, h) confuse.

beisammen *adv.* [baɪ'zamən] together.

'**Beisein** *n* presence; im ~ (*gen.*) or von in the presence of *s.o.*, in *s.o.*'s presence.

bei'seite *adv.* aside, apart; Spaß ~! joking apart!

'**beisetz**|**en** *v/t.* (*sep.*, -ge-, h) bury, inter; '♀ung *f* (-/-en) burial, funeral.

'**Beisitzer** 🔲 *m* (-s/-) assessor; associate judge; member (*of committee*).

'**Beispiel** *n* example, instance; zum ~ for example *or* instance; '♀haft *adj.* exemplary; '♀los *adj.* unprecedented, unparalleled; unheard of.

beißen ['baɪsən] (*irr.*, ge-, h) **1.** *v/t.*; fleas, *etc.*: bite, sting; **2.** *v/i.* bite (auf *acc.* on; in *acc.* into);

fleas, *etc.*: bite, sting; *smoke*: bite, burn (in *dat.* in); *pepper*, *etc.*: bite, burn (auf *dat.* on); '♀d *adj.* biting, pungent (*both a. fig.*); *pepper*, *etc.*: hot.

'**Beistand** *m* assistance.

'**beistehen** *v/i.* (*irr.* stehen, *sep.*, -ge-, h): j-m ~ stand by *or* assist *or* help s.o.

'**beisteuern** *v/t. and v/i.* (*sep.*, -ge-, h) contribute (zu to).

Beitrag ['baɪtraːk] *m* (-[e]s/⁀e) contribution; share; subscription, *Am.* dues *pl.*; article (*in newspaper*, *etc.*).

'**bei**|**treten** *v/i.* (*irr.* treten, *sep.*, -ge-, sein) join (*political party*, *etc.*); '♀tritt *m* joining.

'**Beiwagen** *m* side-car (*of motorcycle*); trailer (*of tram*).

'**Beiwerk** *n* accessories *pl.*

'**beiwohnen** *v/i.* (*sep.*, -ge-, h) assist *or* be present at, attend.

bei'zeiten *adv.* early; in good time.

beizen ['baɪtsən] *v/t.* (ge-, h) corrode; *metall.* pickle; bate (*hides*); stain (*wood*); 🔲 cauterize; *hunt.* hawk.

bejahen [bə'jaːən] *v/t.* (*no* -ge-, h) answer in the affirmative, affirm; ~d *adj.* affirmative.

be'jahrt *adj.* aged.

Bejahung *f* (-/-en) affirmation, affirmative answer; *fig.* acceptance.

be'jammern *s.* beklagen.

be'kämpfen *v/t.* (*no* -ge-, h) fight (against), combat; *fig.* oppose.

bekannt *adj.* [bə'kant] known (*dat.* to); j-n mit j-m ~ machen introduce s.o. to s.o.; ♀e *m*, *f* (-n/-n) acquaintance, *mst* friend; ~lich *adv.* as you know; ~machen *v/t.* (*sep.*, -ge-, h) make known; ♀machung *f* (-/-en) publication; public notice; ♀schaft *f* (-/-en) acquaintance.

be'kehr|**en** *v/t.* (*no* -ge-, h) convert; ♀te *m*, *f* (-n/-n) convert; ♀ung *f* (-/-en) conversion (zu to).

be'kenn|**en** *v/t.* (*irr.* kennen, *no* -ge-, h) admit; confess; sich schuldig ~ 🔲 plead guilty; sich ~ zu declare o.s. for; profess *s.th.*; ♀tnis *n* (-ses/-se) confession; creed.

be'klagen *v/t.* (*no* -ge-, h) lament, deplore; sich ~ complain (über *acc.* of, about); ~swert *adj.* deplorable, pitiable.

Beklagte [bə'klaːktə] *m*, *f* (-n/-n) *civil case*: defendant, the accused.

be'klatschen v/t. (no -ge-, h) applaud, clap.

be'kleben v/t. (no -ge-, h) glue or stick s.th. on s.th.; mit Etiketten ~ label s.th.; mit Papier ~ paste s.th. up with paper; e-e Mauer mit Plakaten ~ paste (up) posters on a wall.

beklecker|n F [bə'klekərn] v/t. (no -ge-, h) stain (garment); sich ~ soil one's clothes. [daub; blot.]

be'klecksen v/t. (no -ge-, h) stain,

be'kleid|en v/t. (no -ge-, h) clothe, dress; hold, fill (office, etc.); ~ mit invest with; **2ung** f clothing, clothes pl.

be'klemm|en v/t. (no -ge-, h) oppress; **2ung** f (-/-en) oppression; anguish, anxiety.

be'kommen (irr. kommen, no -ge-) **1.** v/t. (h) get, receive; obtain; get, catch (illness); have (baby); catch (train, etc.); Zähne ~ teethe, cut one's teeth; **2.** v/i. (sein): j-m (gut) ~ agree with s.o.; j-m nicht or schlecht ~ disagree with s.o.

bekömmlich adj. [bə'kœmliç] wholesome (dat. to).

beköstig|en [bə'kœstigən] v/t. (no -ge-, h) board, feed; **2ung** f (-/-en) board(ing).

be'kräftig|en v/t. (no -ge-, h) confirm; **2ung** f (-/-en) confirmation.

be'kränzen v/t. (no -ge-, h) wreathe, festoon. [criticize.]

be'krittlen v/t. (no -ge-, h) carp at,

be'kümmern v/t. (no -ge-, h) afflict, grieve; trouble; s. kümmern.

be'laden v/t. (irr. laden, no -ge-, h) load; fig. burden.

Belag [bə'la:k] m (-[e]s/⸗e) covering; ⊕ coat(ing); surface (of road); foil (of mirror); ⚞ fur (on tongue); (slices of) ham, etc. (on bread); filling (of roll).

Belager|er [bə'la:gərər] m (-s/-) besieger; **2n** v/t. (no -ge-, h) besiege, beleaguer; **~ung** f siege.

Belang [bə'laŋ] m (-[e]s/-e) importance; ~e pl. interests pl.; **2en** v/t. (no -ge-, h) concern; **2los** adj. unimportant; **~losigkeit** f (-/-en) insignificance.

be'lasten v/t. (no -ge-, h) load; fig. burden; ⚖ incriminate; mortgage (estate, etc.); j-s Konto (mit e-r Summe) ~ ✝ charge or debit s.o.'s account (with a sum).

belästig|en [bə'lɛstigən] v/t. (no -ge-, h) molest; trouble; bother; **2ung** f molestation; trouble.

Be'lastung f (-/-en) load (a. ⚡, ⊕); fig. burden; ✝ debit; encumbrance; ⚖ incrimination; erbliche ~ hereditary taint; **~szeuge** ⚖ m witness for the prosecution.

be'laufen v/refl. (irr. laufen, no -ge-, h): sich ~ auf (acc.) amount to.

be'lauschen v/t. (no -ge-, h) overhear, eavesdrop on s.o.

be'leb|en fig. v/t. (no -ge-, h) enliven, animate; stimulate; **~t** adj. street: busy, crowded; stock exchange: brisk; conversation: lively, animated.

Beleg [bə'le:k] m (-[e]s/-e) proof; ⚖ (supporting) evidence; document; voucher; **2en** [⸗gən] v/t. (no -ge-, h) cover; reserve (seat, etc.); prove, verify; univ. enrol(l) or register for, Am. a. sign up for (course of lectures, term); ein Brötchen mit et. ~ put s.th. on a roll, fill a roll with s.th.; **~schaft** f (-/-en) personnel, staff; labo(u)r force; **~stelle** f reference; **2t** adj. engaged, occupied; hotel, etc.: full; voice: thick, husky; tongue: coated, furred; **~es Brot** (open) sandwich.

be'lehr|en v/t. (no -ge-, h) instruct, inform; sich ~ lassen take advice; **~end** adj. instructive; **2ung** f (-/-en) instruction; information; advice.

beleibt adj. [bə'laipt] corpulent, stout, bulky, portly.

beleidig|en [bə'laidigən] v/t. (no -ge-, h) offend (s.o.; ear, eye, etc.); insult; **~end** adj. offensive; insulting; **2ung** f (-/-en) offen|ce, Am. -se; insult.

be'lesen adj. well-read.

be'leucht|en v/t. (no -ge-, h) light (up), illuminate (a. fig.); fig. shed or throw light on; **2ung** f (-/-en) light(ing); illumination; **2ungskörper** m lighting appliance.

be'licht|en phot. v/t. (no -ge-, h) expose; **2ung** phot. f exposure.

Be'lieb|en n (-s/no pl.) will, choice; nach ~ at will; es steht in Ihrem ~ I leave it to you; **2ig 1.** adj. any; jeder **~e** anyone; **2.** adv. at pleasure; ~ viele as many as you like; **2t** adj. [⸗pt] popular (bei with); **~theit** f (-/no pl.) popularity.

be'liefer|n v/t. (no -ge-, h) supply,

furnish (*mit* with); **2ung** f (-/no pl.) supply.

bellen ['bɛlən] v/i. (ge-, h) bark.

belobigen [bə'lo:bigən] v/t. (no -ge-, h) commend, praise.

be'lohn|en v/t. (no -ge-, h) reward; recompense; **2ung** f (-/-en) reward; recompense. [j-n ~ lie to s.o.)

be'lügen v/t. (irr. lügen, no -ge-, h):)

belustig|en [bə'lustigən] v/t. (no -ge-, h) amuse, entertain; sich ~ amuse o.s.; **2ung** f (-/-en) amusement, entertainment.

bemächtigen [bə'mɛçtigən] v/refl. (no -ge-, h): sich ~ einer Sache ~ take hold of s.th., seize s.th.; sich e-r Person ~ lay hands on s.o., seize s.o.

be'malen v/t. (no -ge-, h) cover with paint; paint; daub.

bemängeln [bə'mɛŋəln] v/t. (no -ge-, h) find fault with, cavil at.

be'mannen v/t. (no -ge-, h) man.

be'merk|bar adj. perceptible; ~en v/t. (no -ge-, h) notice, perceive; remark, mention; ~enswert adj. remarkable (wegen for); **2ung** f (-/-en) remark.

bemitleiden [bə'mitlaidən] v/t. (no -ge-, h) pity, commiserate (with); ~swert adj. pitiable.

be'müh|en v/t. (no -ge-, h) trouble (j-n in or wegen et. s.o. about s.th.); sich ~ trouble o.s.; endeavo(u)r; sich um e-e Stelle ~ apply for a position; **2ung** f (-/-en) trouble; endeavo(u)r, effort.

be'nachbart adj. neighbo(u)ring; adjoining, adjacent (to).

benachrichtig|en [bə'na:xriçtigən] v/t. (no -ge-, h) inform, notify; ✝ advise; **2ung** f (-/-en) information; notification; ✝ advice.

benachteilig|en [bə'na:xtailigən] v/t. (no -ge-, h) place s.o. at a disadvantage, discriminate against s.o.; handicap; sich benachteiligt fühlen feel handicapped or at a disadvantage; **2ung** f (-/-en) disadvantage; discrimination; handicap.

be'nehmen 1. v/refl. (irr. nehmen, no -ge-, h) behave (o.s.); **2.** 2 n (-s/no pl.) behavio(u)r, conduct.

be'neiden v/t. (no -ge-, h) envy (j-n um et. s.o. s.th.); ~swert adj. enviable.

be'nennen v/t. (irr. nennen, no -ge-, h) name. [rascal; urchin.)

Bengel ['bɛŋəl] m (-s/-) (little))

benommen adj. [bə'nɔmən] bemused, dazed, stunned; ~ sein be in a daze. [require, want.)

be'nötigen v/t. (no -ge-, h) need,)

be'nutz|en v/t. (no -ge-, h) use (a. patent, etc.); make use of; avail o.s. of (opportunity); take (tram, etc.); **2ung** f use.

Benzin [bɛn'tsi:n] n (-s/-e) 🜔 benzine; mot. petrol, F juice, Am. gasoline, F gas; ~juice, Am. gasoline, F gas; ~motor m petrol engine, Am. gasoline engine; s. Tank.

beobacht|en [bə'o:baxtən] v/t. (no -ge-, h) observe; watch; police: shadow; **2er** m (-s/-) observer; **2ung** f (-/-en) observation.

beordern [bə'ɔrdərn] v/t. (no -ge-, h) order, command.

be'packen v/t. (no -ge-, h) load (mit with). [(mit with).)

be'pflanzen v/t. (no -ge-, h) plant)

bequem adj. [bə'kve:m] convenient; comfortable; p.: easy-going; lazy; ~en v/refl. (no -ge-, h): sich ~ zu condescend to; consent to; **2lichkeit** f (-/-en) convenience; comfort, ease; indolence.

be'rat|en (irr. raten, no -ge-, h) **1.** v/t. advise s.o.; consider, debate, discuss s.th.; sich ~ confer (mit j-m with s.o.; über et. on or about s.th.); **2.** v/i. confer; über et. ~ consider, debate, discuss s.th., confer on or about s.th.; **2er** m (-s/-) adviser, counsel(l)or; consultant; ~schlagen (no -ge-, h) **1.** v/i. s. beraten 2; **2.** v/refl. confer (mit j-m with s.o.; über et. on or about s.th.); **2ung** f (-/-en) advice; debate; consultation; conference; **2ungsstelle** f advisory bureau.

be'raub|en v/t. (no -ge-, h) rob, deprive (gen. of); **2ung** f (-/-en) robbery, deprivation.

be'rauschen v/t. (no -ge-, h) intoxicate (a. fig.).

be'rechn|en v/t. (no -ge-, h) calculate; ✝ charge (zu at); ~end adj. calculating, selfish; **2ung** f calculation.

berechtig|en [bə'rɛçtigən] v/t. (no -ge-, h) j-n ~ zu entitle s.o. to; authorize s.o. to; et. adj. [~çt] entitled (zu to); qualified (to); claim: legitimate; **2ung** f (-/-en) title (zu to); authorization.

be'red|en v/t. (no -ge-, h) talk s.th.

Beredsamkeit

over; persuade *s.o.*; gossip about *s.o.*; **2samkeit** [⸬tza:mkait] *f* (*-/no pl.*) eloquence; **⸱t** *adj.* [⸬t] eloquent (*a. fig.*).

Be'reich *m, n* (*-[e]s/-e*) area; reach; *fig.* scope, sphere; *science, etc.*: field, province; **2ern** *v/t.* (*no -ge-, h*) enrich; *sich ∼* enrich o.s.; **⸱erung** *f* (*-/-en*) enrichment.

be'reif|en *v/t.* (*no -ge-, h*) tire (*barrel*); tyre, (*Am. only*) tire (*wheel*); **2ung** *f* (*-/-en*) (set of) tyres *pl.*, (*Am. only*) (set of) tires *pl.*

be'reisen *v/t.* (*no -ge-, h*) tour (in), travel (over); *commercial traveller:* cover (*district*).

bereit *adj.* [bə'rait] ready, prepared; **∼en** *v/t.* (*no -ge-, h*) prepare; give (*joy, trouble, etc.*); **∼s** *adv.* already; **2schaft** *f* (*-/-en*) readiness; *police:* squad; **∼stellen** *v/t.* (*sep., -ge-, h*) place *s.th.* ready; provide; **2ung** *f* (*-/-en*) preparation; **∼willig** *adj.* ready, willing; **2willigkeit** *f* (*-/no pl.*) readiness, willingness.

be'reuen *v/t.* (*no -ge-, h*) repent (of); regret, rue.

Berg [berk] *m* (*-[e]s/-e*) mountain; hill; **∼e** *pl. von* F heaps *pl.* of, piles *pl.* of; *über den ∼ sein* be out of the wood, *Am.* be out of the woods; *über alle ∼e* off and away; *die Haare standen ihm zu ∼e* his hair stood on end; **2'ab** *adv.* downhill (*a. fig.*); **2'an** *adv. s. bergauf*; **'∼arbeiter** *m* miner; **2'auf** *adv.* uphill (*a. fig.*); **'∼bahn** 🚞 *f* mountain railway; **'∼bau** *m* (*-[e]s/pl.*) mining.

bergen ['bergən] *v/t.* (*irr., ge-, h*) save; rescue *s.o.*; ⚓ salvage, salve. 　　　　　[hilly.]

bergig *adj.* ['bergiç] mountainous,)

'Berg|kette *f* mountain chain *or* range; **'∼mann** ⚒ *m* (*-[e]s/Bergleute*) miner; **'∼predigt** *f* (*-/no pl.*) *the* Sermon on the Mount; **'∼recht** *n* mining laws *pl.*; **'∼rennen** *mot. n* mountain race; **'∼rücken** *m* ridge; **'∼rutsch** *m* landslide, landslip; **'∼spitze** *f* mountain peak; **'∼steiger** *m* (*-s/-*) mountaineer; **'∼sturz** *m s. Bergrutsch*.

'Bergung *f* (*-/-en*) ⚓ salvage; rescue; **∼sarbeiten** ['berguŋs?-] *f/pl.* salvage operations *pl.*; rescue work.

'Bergwerk *n* mine; **∼saktien** ['berkverks?-] *f/pl.* mining shares *pl.*

Bericht [bə'riçt] *m* (*-[e]s/-e*) report

(*über acc.* on); account (of); **2en** (*no -ge-, h*) **1.** *v/t.* report; *j-m et. ∼* inform s.o. of s.th.; tell s.o. about s.th.; **2.** *v/i.* report (*über acc.* on); *journalist: a.* cover (*über et. s.th.*); **∼erstatter** *m* (*-s/-*) reporter; correspondent; **∼erstattung** *f* reporting; report(s *pl.*).

berichtig|en [bə'riçtigən] *v/t.* (*no -ge-, h*) correct (*s.o.; error, mistake, etc.*); put right (*mistake*); emend (*corrupt text*); † settle (*claim, debt, etc.*); **2ung** *f* (*-/-en*) correction; emendation; settlement.

be'riechen *v/t.* (*irr. riechen, no -ge-, h*) smell *or* sniff at.

Berliner [ber'li:nər] **1.** *m* (*-s/-*) Berliner; **2.** *adj.* (*of*) Berlin.

Bernstein ['bernʃtain] *m* amber; *schwarzer ∼* jet.

bersten ['berstən] *v/i.* (*irr., ge-, sein*) burst (*fig. vor dat. with*).

berüchtigt *adj.* [bə'rüçtiçt] notorious (*wegen* for), ill-famed.

berücksichtig|en [bə'rükziçtigən] *v/t.* (*no -ge-, h*) take *s.th.* into consideration, pay regard to *s.th.*; consider *s.o.*; **2ung** *f* (*-/-en*) consideration; regard.

Beruf [bə'ru:f] *m* (*-[e]s/-e*) calling; profession; vocation; trade; occupation; **2en 1.** *v/t.* (*irr. rufen, no -ge-, h*): *j-n zu e-m Amt ∼* appoint s.o. to an office; *sich auf j-n ∼* refer to s.o.; **2.** *adj.* competent; qualified; **2lich** *adj.* professional; vocational.

Be'rufs|ausbildung *f* vocational *or* professional training; **∼beratung** *f* vocational guidance; **∼kleidung** *f* work clothes *pl.*; **∼krankheit** *f* occupational disease; **∼schule** *f* vocational school; **∼spieler** *m sports:* professional (player); **2tätig** *adj.* working; **∼tätige** [⸬gə] *pl.* working people *pl.*

Be'rufung *f* (*-/-en*) appointment (*zu* to); ⚖ appeal (*bei dat.* to); reference (*auf acc.* to); **∼sgericht** *n* court of appeal.

be'ruhen *v/i.* (*no -ge-, h*): *∼ auf* (*dat.*) rest *or* be based on; *et. auf sich ∼ lassen* let a matter rest.

beruhig|en [bə'ru:igən] *v/t.* (*no -ge-, h*) quiet, calm; soothe; *sich ∼* calm down; **2ung** *f* (*-/-en*) calming (down); soothing; comfort; **2ungsmittel** 💊 *n* sedative.

be'rühmt adj. [bǝ'ry:mt] famous (wegen for); celebrated; 2heit f (-/-en) fame, renown; famous or celebrated person, celebrity; person of note.

be'rühr|en v/t. (no -ge-, h) touch (a. fig.); touch (up)on (subject); 2ung f (-/-en) contact; touch; in ~ kommen mit come into contact with.

be'sag|en v/t. (no -ge-, h) say; mean, signify; ~t adj. [~kt] (afore-) said; above(-mentioned).

besänftigen [bǝ'zɛnftigǝn] v/t. (no -ge-, h) appease, calm, soothe.

Be'satz m (-es/ⁱⁱe) trimming; braid.

Be'satzung f ⚔ occupation troops pl.; ⚔ garrison; ⚓, ✈ crew; ~smacht ⚔ f occupying power.

be'schädig|en v/t. (no -ge-, h) damage, injure; 2ung f damage, injury (gen. to).

be'schaffen 1. v/t. (no -ge-, h) procure; provide; raise (money); **2.** adj.: gut (schlecht) ~ sein be in good (bad) condition or state; 2heit f(-/-en) state, condition; properties pl.

beschäftig|en [bǝ'ʃɛftigǝn] v/t. (no -ge-, h) employ, occupy; keep busy; sich ~ occupy or busy o.s.; 2ung f (-/-en) employment; occupation.

be'schäm|en v/t. (no -ge-, h) (put to) shame, make s.o. feel ashamed; ~end adj. shameful; humiliating; ~t adj. ashamed (über acc. of); 2ung f (-/-en) shame; humiliation.

beschatten [bǝ'ʃatǝn] v/t. (no -ge-, h) shade; fig. shadow s.o., Am. sl. tail s.o.

be'schau|en v/t. (no -ge-, h) look at, view; examine, inspect (goods, etc.); ~lich adj. contemplative, meditative.

Bescheid [bǝ'ʃaɪt] m (-[e]s/-e) answer; ⚖ decision; information (über acc. on, about); ~ geben let s.o. know; ~ bekommen be informed or notified; ~ hinterlassen leave word (bei with, at); ~ wissen be informed, know, F be in the know.

bescheiden adj. [bǝ'ʃaɪdǝn] modest, unassuming; 2heit f (-/no pl.) modesty.

bescheinig|en [bǝ'ʃaɪnigǝn] v/i. (no -ge-, h) certify, attest; den Empfang ~ acknowledge receipt; es wird hiermit bescheinigt, daß this is to certify that; 2ung f (-/-en) certification, attestation; certificate; receipt; acknowledgement.

be'schenken v/t. (no -ge-, h): j-n ~ make s.o. a present; j-n mit et. ~ present s.o. with s.th.; j-n reichlich ~ shower s.o. with gifts.

be'scher|en v/t. (no -ge-, h): j-n ~ give s.o. presents (esp. for Christmas); 2ung f (-/-en) presentation of gifts; F fig. mess.

be'schieß|en v/t. (irr. schießen, no -ge-, h) fire or shoot at or on; bombard (a. phys.), shell; 2ung f (-/-en) bombardment.

be'schimpf|en v/t. (no -ge-, h) abuse, insult; call s.o. names; 2ung f (-/-en) abuse; insult; affront.

be'schirmen v/t. (no -ge-, h) shelter, shield, guard, protect (vor dat. from); defend (against).

be'schlafen v/t. (irr. schlafen, no -ge-, h): et. ~ sleep on a matter, take counsel of one's pillow.

Be'schlag m ⊕ metal fitting(s pl.); furnishing(s pl.) (of door, etc.); shoe (of wheel, etc.); (horse)shoe; ⚖ seizure, confiscation; in ~ nehmen, mit ~ belegen seize; ⚖ seize, attach (real estate, salary, etc.); confiscate (goods, etc.); monopolize s.o.'s attention.

be'schlagen 1. v/t. (irr. schlagen, no -ge-, h) cover (mit with); ⊕ fit, mount; shoe (horse); hobnail (shoe); **2.** v/i. (irr. schlagen, no -ge-, h) window, wall, etc.: steam up; mirror, etc.: cloud or film over; **3.** adj. windows, etc.: steamed-up; fig. well versed (auf, in dat. in).

Beschlagnahme [bǝ'ʃla:kna:mǝ] f (-/-n) seizure; confiscation (of contraband goods, etc.); ⚖ sequestration, distraint (of property); ⚔ requisition (of houses, etc.); ⚔ embargo, detention (of ship); 2n v/t. (no -ge-, h) seize; attach (real estate); confiscate; ⚖ sequestrate, distrain upon (property); ⚔ requisition; ⚓ embargo.

beschleunig|en [bǝ'ʃlɔʏnigǝn] v/t. (no -ge-, h) mot. accelerate; hasten; speed up; s-e Schritte ~ quicken one's steps; 2ung f (-/-en) acceleration.

be'schließen v/t. (irr. schließen, no -ge-, h) end, close, wind up; resolve, decide.

Be'schluß m decision, resolution, Am. a. resolve; ⚖ decree; 2fähig adj.: ~ sein form or have a quorum;

~fassung f (passing of a) resolution.

be'schmieren v/t. (no -ge-, h) (be)smear (with grease, etc.).

be'schmutzen v/t. (no -ge-, h) soil (a. fig.), dirty; bespatter.

be'schneiden v/t. (irr. schneiden, no -ge-, h) clip, cut; lop (tree); trim, clip (hair, hedge, etc.); dress (vine-stock, etc.); fig. cut down, curtail, F slash.

beschönig|en [bə'ʃø:nigən] v/t. (no -ge-, h) gloss over, palliate; **2ung** f (-/-en) gloss, palliation.

beschränk|en [bə'frɛnkən] v/t. (no -ge-, h) confine, limit, restrict, Am. a. curb; **sich ~ auf** (acc.) confine o.s. to; **~t** fig. adj. of limited intelligence; **2ung** f (-/-en) limitation, restriction.

be'schreib|en v/t. (irr. schreiben, no -ge-, h) write on (piece of paper, etc.), cover with writing; describe, give a description of; **2ung** f (-/-en) description; account.

be'schrift|en v/t. (no -ge-, h) inscribe; letter; **2ung** f (-/-en) inscription; lettering.

beschuldig|en [bə'ʃuldigən] v/t. (no -ge-, h) accuse (gen. of [doing] s.th.), esp. ₰₵ charge (with); **2te** [⎣ktə] m, f (-n/-n) the accused; **2ung** f (-/-en) accusation, charge.

Be'schuß m (Beschusses/no pl.) bombardment.

be'schütz|en v/t. (no -ge-, h) protect, shelter, guard (vor dat. from); **2er** m (-s/-) protector; **2ung** f (-/-en) protection.

be'schwatzen v/t. (no -ge-, h) talk s.o. into (doing) s.th., coax s.o. into (doing s.th.).

Beschwerde [bə'ʃve:rdə] f (-/-n) trouble; complaint; complaint (über acc. about); ₰₵ objection (gegen to); **~buch** n complaints book.

beschwer|en [bə'ʃve:rən] v/t. (no -ge-, h) burden (a. fig.); weight (loose sheets, etc.); lie heavy on (stomach); weigh on (mind, etc.); **sich ~** complain (über acc. about, of; bei to); **~lich** adj. troublesome.

beschwichtigen [bə'ʃviçtigən] v/t. (no -ge-, h) appease, calm (down), soothe.

be'schwindeln v/t. (no -ge-, h) tell

a fib or lie; cheat, F diddle (um out of).

be'schwipst F adj. tipsy.

be'schwör|en v/t. (irr. schwören, no -ge-, h) take an oath on s.th.; implore or entreat s.o.; conjure (up), invoke (spirit); **2ung** f (-/-en) conjuration.

be'seelen v/t. (no -ge-, h) animate, inspire.

be'sehen v/t. (irr. sehen, no -ge-, h) look at; inspect; **sich et. ~** look at s.th.; inspect s.th.

beseitig|en [bə'zaitigən] v/t. (no -ge-, h) remove, do away with; **2ung** f (-/-en) removal.

Besen ['be:zən] m (-s/-) broom; **'~stiel** m broomstick.

besessen adj. [bə'zesən] obsessed, possessed (von by, with); **wie ~** like mad; **2e** m, f (-n/-n) demoniac.

be'setz|en v/t. (no -ge-, h) occupy (seat, table, etc.); fill (post, etc.); man (orchestra); thea. cast (play); ⚔ occupy; trim (dress, etc.); set (crown with jewels, etc.); **~t** adj. engaged, occupied; seat: taken; F bus, etc.: full up; hotel: full; teleph. engaged, Am. busy; **2ung** f (-/-en) thea. cast; ⚔ occupation.

besichtig|en [bə'ziçtigən] v/t. (no -ge-, h) view, look over; inspect (a. ⚔); visit; **2ung** f (-/-en) sightseeing; visit (gen. to); inspection (a. ⚔).

be'sied|eln v/t. (no -ge-, h) colonize, settle; populate; **2lung** f (-/-en) colonization, settlement.

be'siegeln v/t. (no -ge-, h) seal (a. fig.).

be'siegen v/t. (no -ge-, h) conquer; defeat, beat (a. sports).

be'sinn|en v/refl. (irr. sinnen, no -ge-, h) reflect, consider; **sich ~ auf** (acc.) remember, think of; **~lich** adj. reflective, contemplative.

Be'sinnung f (-/no pl.) reflection; consideration; consciousness; (wieder) zur ~ kommen recover consciousness; fig. come to one's senses; **2slos** adj. unconscious.

Be'sitz m possession; in ~ nehmen, ~ ergreifen von take possession of; **2anzeigend** gr. adj. possessive; **2en** v/t. (irr. sitzen, no -ge-, h) possess; **~er** m (-s/-) possessor, owner, proprietor; **den ~ wechseln** change hands; **~ergreifung** f taking possession (*von* of), occupation; **~tum** *n* (-s/=er), **~ung** *f* (-/-en) possession; property; estate.

be'sohlen *v/t.* (*no* -ge-, *h*) sole.

besold|en [bə'zɔldən] *v/t.* (*no* -ge-, *h*) pay a salary to (*civil servant, etc.*); pay (*soldier*); **2ung** *f* (-/-en) pay; salary.

besonder *adj.* [bə'zɔndər] particular, special; peculiar; separate; **2heit** *f* (-/-en) particularity; peculiarity; **~s** *adv.* especially, particularly; chiefly, mainly; separately.

besonnen *adj.* [bə'zɔnən] sensible, considerate, level-headed; prudent; discreet; **2heit** *f* (-/*no pl.*) considerateness; prudence; discretion; presence of mind.

be'sorg|en *v/t.* (*no* -ge-, *h*) get (*j-m et. s.o. s.th.*), procure (*s.th. for s.o.*); do, manage; **2nis** [~knis] *f* (-/-se) apprehension, fear, anxiety, concern (*über acc.* at); **~niserregend** *adj.* alarming; **~t** *adj.* [~kt] uneasy (*um* about); worried (about), concerned (about); anxious (*um* for, about); **2ung** *f* (-/-en) procurement; management; errand; **~en machen** go shopping.

be'sprech|en *v/t.* (*irr.* sprechen, *no* -ge-, *h*) discuss, talk *s.th.* over; arrange; review (*book, etc.*); **sich ~ mit** confer with (*über acc.* about); **2ung** *f* (-/-en) discussion; review; conference.

be'spritzen *v/t.* (*no* -ge-, *h*) splash, (be)spatter.

besser ['bɛsər] **1.** *adj.* better; superior; **2.** *adv.* better; '**~n** *v/t.* (ge-, *h*) (make) better, improve; reform; **sich ~** get or become better, improve, change for the better; mend one's ways; **2ung** *f* (-/-en) improvement; change for the better; reform (*of character*); **&** improvement, recovery; **gute ~!** I wish you a speedy recovery!

best [bɛst] **1.** *adj.* best; **der erste ~e** (just) anybody; **~en Dank** thank you very much; **sich von s-r ~en Seite zeigen** be on one's best behavio(u)r; **2.** *adv.* best; **am ~en** best; **aufs ~e, ~ens** in the best way possible; **zum ~en geben** recite (*poem*), tell (*story*), oblige with (*song*); **j-n zum ~en haben or halten** make fun of s.o., F pull s.o.'s leg; **ich danke ~ens!** thank you very much!

Be'stand *m* (continued) existence; continuance; stock; **✝** stock-in-trade; **✝** cash in hand; **~ haben** be lasting, last.

be'ständig *adj.* constant, steady; lasting; continual; *weather*: settled; **2keit** *f* (-/-en) constancy, steadiness; continuance.

Bestand|saufnahme **✝** [bə-'ʃtants?-] *f* stock-taking, *Am.* inventory; **~teil** *m* component, constituent; element, ingredient; part.

be'stärken *v/t.* (*no* -ge-, *h*) confirm, strengthen, encourage (*in dat.* in).

bestätig|en [bə'ʃtɛːtigən] *v/t.* confirm (*a.* **✝** *verdict*, **✝** *order*); attest; verify (*statement, etc.*); ratify (*law, treaty*); **✝** acknowledge (*receipt*); **2ung** *f* (-/-en) confirmation; attestation; verification; ratification; acknowledgement.

bestatt|en [bə'ʃtatən] *v/t.* (*no* -ge-, *h*) bury, inter; **2ung** *f* (-/-en) burial, interment; funeral; **2ungsinstitut** [bə'ʃtatuŋs?-] *n* undertakers *pl.*

'**Beste** **1.** *n* (-n/*no pl.*) the best (thing); **zu deinem ~n** in your interest; **zum ~n der Armen** for the benefit of the poor; **das ~ daraus machen** make the best of it; **2.** *m, f* (-n/-n): **er ist der ~** in his class, **in s-r Klasse** he is the best in his class.

Besteck [bə'ʃtɛk] *n* (-[e]s/-e) **&** (case *or* set of) surgical instruments *pl.*; (single set of) knife, fork and spoon; (complete set of) cutlery, *Am. a.* flatware.

be'stehen **1.** *v/t.* (*irr.* stehen, *no* -ge-, *h*) come off victorious in (*combat, etc.*); have (*adventure*); stand, undergo (well) (*test, trial*); pass (*test, examination*); **2.** *v/i.* (*irr.* stehen, *no* -ge-, *h*) be, exist; continue, last; **~ auf** (*dat.*) insist (up)on; **~ aus** consist of; **3.** **2** *n* (-s/*no pl.*) existence; continuance; passing.

be'stehlen *v/t.* (*irr.* stehlen, *no* -ge-, *h*) steal from, rob.

be'steig|en *v/t.* (*irr.* steigen, *no* -ge-, *h*) climb (up) (*mountain, tree, etc.*); mount (*horse, bicycle, etc.*); ascend (*throne*); get into or on, board (*bus, train, plane*); **2ung** *f* ascent; accession (*to throne*).

be'stell|en *v/t.* (*no* -ge-, *h*) order; **✝** *a.* place an order for; subscribe to (*newspaper, etc.*); book, reserve (*room, seat, etc.*); make an appointment with *s.o.*; send for (*taxi, etc.*); cultivate, till (*soil, etc.*); give (*message, greetings*); j-n zu sich ~ send for s.o.; **2ung** *f* order; subscription (to); booking, *esp. Am.* reservation; ⚐ cultivation; message.

'besten'falls *adv.* at (the) best.

be'steuer|n *v/t.* (*no* -ge-, *h*) tax; **2ung** *f* taxation.

besti'alisch *adj.* [best'ja:liʃ] bestial; brutal; inhuman; *weather, etc.*: F beastly; **2e** ['ə] *f* (-/-en) beast; *fig.* brute, beast, inhuman person.

be'stimmen (*no* -ge-, *h*) **1.** *v/t.* determine, decide; fix (*date, place, price, etc.*); appoint (*date, time, place, etc.*); prescribe; define (*species, word, etc.*); j-n für or zu et. ~ designate or intend s.o. for s.th.; **2.** *v/i.*: ~ über (*acc.*) dispose of.

be'stimmt 1. *adj.* voice, manner, etc.: decided, determined, firm; *time, etc.*: appointed, fixed; *point, number, etc.*: certain; *answer, etc.*: positive; *tone, answer, intention, idea*: definite (*a. gr.*); ~ nach ⚓, ✈ bound for; **2.** *adv.* certainly, surely; **2heit** *f* (-/-en) determination, firmness; certainty.

Be'stimmung *f* determination; destination (*of s.o. for the church, etc.*); designation, appointment (*of s.o. as successor, etc.*); definition; ⁂ provision (*in document*) (*amtliche*) ~en *pl.* (official) regulations *pl.*; ~sort [bə'ʃtimuŋs?-] *m* destination.

be'straf|en *v/t.* (*no* -ge-, *h*) punish (wegen, für for; mit with); **2ung** *f* (-/-en) punishment.

be'strahl|en *v/t.* (*no* -ge-, *h*) irradiate (*a.* ✻); **2ung** *f* irradiation; ✻ ray treatment, radiotherapy.

Be'streb|en *n* (-s/*no pl.*), ~ung *f* (-/-en) effort, endeavo(u)r.

be'streichen *v/t.* (*irr.* streichen, *no* -ge-, *h*) coat, cover; spread; mit Butter ~ butter.

be'streiten *v/t.* (*irr.* streiten, *no* -ge-, *h*) contest, dispute, challenge (*point, right, etc.*); deny (*facts, guilt, etc.*); defray (*expenses, etc.*); fill (*programme*).

be'streuen *v/t.* (*no* -ge-, *h*) strew, sprinkle (mit with); mit Mehl ~ flour; mit Zucker ~ sugar.

be'stürmen *v/t.* (*no* -ge-, *h*) storm, assail (*a. fig.*); pester, plague (*s.o. with questions, etc.*).

be'stürz|t *adj.* dismayed, struck with consternation (*über acc.* at); **2ung** *f* (-/-en) consternation, dismay.

Besuch [bə'zu:x] *m* (-[e]s/-e) visit (*gen., bei, in dat.* to); call (*bei* on; *in dat.* at); attendance (*gen.* at) (*lecture, church, etc.*); visitor(s *pl.*), company; **2en** *v/t.* (*no* -ge-, *h*) visit; call on, go to see; attend (*school, etc.*); frequent; ~er *m* visitor, caller; ~szeit *f* visiting hours *pl.*

be'tasten *v/t.* (*no* -ge-, *h*) touch, feel, finger; ✻ palpate.

betätigen [bə'tɛ:tigən] *v/t.* (*no* -ge-, *h*) ⊕ operate (*machine, etc.*); put on, apply (*brake*); sich ~ als act or work as; sich politisch ~ dabble in politics.

betäub|en [bə'tɔʏbən] *v/t.* (*no* -ge-, *h*) stun (*a. fig.*), daze (*by blow, noise, etc.*); deafen (*by noise, etc.*); slaughtering: stun (*animal*); ✻ an(a)esthetize; **2ung** *f* (-/-en) an(a)esthetization; ✻ an(a)esthesia; *fig.* stupefaction; **2ungsmittel** ✻ *n* narcotic, an(a)esthetic.

beteilig|en [bə'taɪligən] *v/t.* (*no* -ge-, *h*): j-n ~ give s.o. a share (*an dat.* in); sich ~ take part (*an dat.*, bei in), participate (*a.* ⁂) (*in*); **2te** [~çtə] *m*, *f* (-n/-n) person or party concerned; **2ung** *f* (-/-en) participation (*a.* ⁂, ✝), partnership; share, interest (*a.* ✝).

beten ['be:tən] *v/i.* (ge-, *h*) pray (um for), say one's prayers; *at table*: say grace.

be'teuer|n *v/t.* (*no* -ge-, *h*) protest (*one's innocence*); swear (to s.th.; that); **2ung** *f* protestation; solemn declaration.

be'titeln *v/t.* (*no* -ge-, *h*) entitle (*book, etc.*); style (*s.o. 'baron', etc.*).

Beton ⊕ [be'tõ:; be'tõ:n] *m* (-s/-s; -s/-e) concrete.

be'tonen *v/t.* (*no* -ge-, *h*) stress; *fig. a.* emphasize.

betonieren [beto'ni:rən] *v/t.* (*no* -ge-, *h*) concrete.

Be'tonung *f* (-/-en) stress; emphasis.

betör|en [bə'tø:rən] *v/t.* (*no* -ge-, *h*) dazzle, infatuate, bewitch; **2ung** *f* (-/-en) infatuation.

Betracht [bə'traxt] *m* (-[e]s/*no pl.*): in ~ ziehen take into consideration; (nicht) in ~ kommen (not to) come into question; **2en** *v/t.* (*no* -ge-, *h*) view; contemplate; *fig. a.* consider.

beträchtlich *adj.* [bə'trɛçtliç] considerable.

Be'trachtung *f* (-/-en) view; contemplation; consideration.

Betrag [bə'tra:k] *m* (-[e]s/ꞈe) amount, sum; **2en** [ˌɡən] **1.** *v/t.* (*irr. tragen, no -ge-, h*) amount to; **2.** *v/refl.* (*irr. tragen, no -ge-, h*) behave (o.s.); **3.** ꞔ *n* (-s/no pl.) behavio(u)r, conduct.

be'trauen *v/t.* (*no -ge-, h*): j-n mit et. ~ entrust or charge s.o. with s.th.

be'trauern *v/t.* (*no -ge-, h*) mourn (for, over).

Betreff [bə'trɛf] *m* (-[e]s/-e) *at head of letter:* reference; **2en** *v/t.* (*irr. treffen, no -ge-, h*) befall; refer to; concern; *was ... betrifft* as for, as to; **2end** *adj.* concerning; *das ~e Geschäft* the business referred to or in question; **2s** *prp.* (gen.) concerning; as to.

be'treiben 1. *v/t.* (*irr. treiben, no -ge-, h*) carry on (*business, etc.*); pursue (*one's studies*); operate (*railway line, etc.*); **2.** ꞔ *n* (-s/no pl.): *auf ~ von* at or by *s.o.'s* instigation.

be'treten 1. *v/t.* (*irr. treten, no -ge-, h*) step on; enter (*room, etc.*); **2.** *adj.* embarrassed, abashed.

betreu|en [bə'trɔyən] *v/t.* (*no -ge-, h*) look after; attend to; care for; **ꞔung** *f* (-/no pl.) care (*gen.* of, for).

Betrieb [bə'tri:p] *m* (-[e]s/-e) working, running, *esp. Am.* operation; business, firm, enterprise; plant, works *sg.*; workshop, *Am. a.* shop; *fig.* bustle; *in ~* working; **2sam** *adj.* active; industrious.

Be'triebs|anleitung *f* operating instructions *pl.*; **~ausflug** *m* firm's outing; **~ferien** *pl.* (firm's, works) holiday; **~führer** *m* s. Betriebsleiter; **~kapital** *n* working capital; **~kosten** *pl.* working expenses *pl.*, *Am.* operating costs *pl.* **~leiter** *m* (works) manager; superintendent; **~leitung** *f* management; **~material** *n* working materials *pl.*; 📖 rolling stock; **~rat** *m* works council; **2sicher** *adj.* safe to operate; foolproof; **~störung** *f* breakdown; **~unfall** *m* industrial accident, accident while at work.

be'trinken *v/refl.* (*irr. trinken, no -ge-, h*) get drunk.

betroffen *adj.* [bə'trɔfən] afflicted (*von* by), stricken (with); *fig.* disconcerted.

be'trüben *v/t.* (*no -ge-, h*) grieve, afflict. [deceit.\]

Be'trug *m* cheat(ing);fraud(*a. ɪ̆ꞃ*);\]

be'trüg|en *v/t.* (*irr. trügen, no -ge-, h*) deceive; cheat (*a. at games*); defraud; F skin; **2er** *m* (-s/-) cheat, deceiver, impostor, confidence man, swindler, trickster; **~erisch** *adj.* deceitful, fraudulent.

be'trunken *adj.* drunken; *pred.* drunk; **2e** *m* (-n/-n) drunk(en man).

Bett [bɛt] *n* (-[e]s/-en) bed; **~bezug** *m* plumeau case; **~decke** *f* blanket; bedspread, coverlet.

Bettel|brief ['bɛtəl-] *m* begging letter; **~ei** [~'laɪ] *f* (-/-en) begging, mendicancy; **2n** *v/i.* (ge-, h) beg (*um* for); **~ gehen** go begging; **~stab** *m*: *an den ~ bringen* reduce to beggary.

'Bett|gestell *n* bedstead; **2lägerig** *adj.* ['~lɛ:gəriç] bedridden, confined to bed, *Am. a.* bedfast; **~laken** *n* sheet.

Bettler ['bɛtlər] *m* (-s/-) beggar, *Am. sl.* panhandler.

'Bett|überzug *m* plumeau case; **~uch** ['bɛttu:x] *n* sheet; **~vorleger** *m* bedside rug; **~wäsche** *f* bedlinen; **~zeug** *n* bedding.

be'tupfen *v/t.* (*no -ge-, h*) dab.

beug|en ['bɔygən] *v/t.* (ge-, h) bend, bow; *fig.* humble, break (pride); *gr.* inflect (*word*), decline (*noun, adjective*); *sich ~* bend (*vor dat.* to), bow (to); **'2ung** *f* (-/-en) bending; *gr.* inflection, declension.

Beule ['bɔylə] *f* (-/-n) bump, swelling; boil; *on metal, etc.*: dent.

beunruhig|en [bə'unru:igən] *v/t.* (*no -ge-, h*) disturb, trouble, disquiet, alarm; *sich ~ über* (*acc.*) be uneasy about, worry about; **2ung** *f* (-/no pl.) disturbance; alarm; uneasiness.

beurkund|en [bə'u:rkundən] *v/t.* (*no -ge-, h*) attest, certify, authenticate; **2ung** *f* (-/-en) attestation, certification, authentication.

beurlaub|en [bə'u:rlaubən] *v/t.* (*no -ge-, h*) give *or* grant *s.o.* leave (of absence); give *s.o.* time off; suspend (*civil servant, etc.*); **2ung** *f* (-/-en) leave (of absence); suspension.

beurteil|en [bə'urtaɪlən] *v/t.* (*no* -ge-, *h*) judge (*nach* by); **&ung** *f* (-/-en) judg(e)ment.

Beute ['bɔytə] *f* (-/*no pl.*) booty, spoil(s *pl.*); loot; prey; *hunt.* bag; *fig.* prey, victim (*gen.* to).

Beutel ['bɔytəl] *m* (-s/-) bag; purse; pouch.

'Beutezug *m* plundering expedition.

bevölker|n [bə'fœlkərn] *v/t.* (*no* -ge-, *h*) people, populate; **&ung** *f* (-/-en) population.

bevollmächtig|en [bə'fɔlmɛçtɪgən] *v/t.* (*no* -ge-, *h*) authorize, empower; **&te** [‿çtə] *m, f* (-n/-n) authorized person *or* agent, deputy; *pol.* plenipotentiary; **&ung** *f* (-/-en) authorization.

be'vor *cj.* before.

bevormund|en *fig.* [bə'fo:rmundən] *v/t.* (*no* -ge-, *h*) patronize, keep in tutelage; **&ung** *fig.* *f* (-/-en) patronizing, tutelage.

be'vorstehen *v/i.* (*irr.* stehen, *sep.*, -ge-, *h*) be approaching, be near; *crisis, etc.*: be imminent; *j-m* ~ be in store for s.o., await s.o.; **~d** *adj.* approaching, imminent.

bevorzug|en [bə'fo:rtsu:gən] *v/t.* (*no* -ge-, *h*) prefer; favo(u)r; ⚹ privilege; **&ung** *f* (-/-en) preference.

be'wach|en *v/t.* (*no* -ge-, *h*) guard, watch; **&ung** *f* (-/-en) guard; escort.

bewaffn|en [bə'vafnən] *v/t.* (*no* -ge-, *h*) arm; **&ung** *f* (-/-en) armament; arms *pl.*

be'wahren *v/t.* (*no* -ge-, *h*) keep, preserve (*mst fig.: secret, silence, etc.*).

be'währen *v/refl.* (*no* -ge-, *h*) stand the test, prove a success; *sich* ~ *als* prove o.s. (as) (*a good teacher, etc.*); *sich* ~ *in* prove o.s. efficient in (*one's profession, etc.*); *sich nicht* ~ prove a failure.

be'wahrheiten *v/refl.* (*no* -ge-, *h*) prove (to be) true; *prophecy, etc.*: come true.

be'währt *adj.* friend, *etc.*: tried; solicitor, *etc.*: experienced; friendship, *etc.*: long-standing; remedy, *etc.*: proved, proven.

Be'währung *f* ⚹ probation; *in Zeiten der* ~ *in* times of trial; *s. bewähren*; **~sfrist** ⚹ *f* probation.

bewaldet *adj.* [bə'valdət] wooded, woody, *Am. a.* timbered.

bewältigen [bə'vɛltɪgən] *v/t.* (*no*

-ge-, *h*) overcome (*obstacle*); master (*difficulty*); accomplish (*task*).

be'wandert *adj.* (well) versed (*in dat.* in), proficient (in); *in e-m Fach gut* ~ *sein* have a thorough knowledge of a subject.

be'wässer|n *v/t.* (*no* -ge-, *h*) water (*garden, lawn, etc.*); irrigate (*land, etc.*); **&ung** *f* (-/-en) watering; irrigation.

bewegen[1] [bə've:gən] *v/t.* (*irr.*, *no* -ge-, *h*): *j-n* ~ *zu* induce or get s.o. to.

beweg|en[2] [‿] *v/t. and v/refl.* (*no* -ge-, *h*) move, stir; **&grund** [‿k-] *m* motive (*gen.*, *für* for); **~lich** *adj.* [‿k-] movable; *p., mind, etc.*: agile, versatile; active; **&lichkeit** [‿k-] *f* (-/*no pl.*) mobility; agility, versatility; **~t** *adj.* [‿kt] *sea:* rough, heavy; *fig.* moved, touched; *voice:* choked, trembling; *life:* eventful; *times, etc.*: stirring, stormy; **&ung** *f* (-/-en) movement; motion (*a. phys.*); *fig.* emotion; *in* ~ *setzen* set going *or* in motion; **~ungslos** *adj.* motionless, immobile.

be'weinen *v/t.* (*no* -ge-, *h*) weep *or* cry over; lament (for over).

Beweis [bə'vaɪs] *m* (-es/-e) proof (*für* of); (*e pl.*) evidence (*esp.* ⚹); **~en** [‿zən] *v/t.* (*irr.* weisen, *no* -ge-, *h*) prove; show (*interest, etc.*); **~führung** *f* argumentation; **~grund** *m* argument; **~material** *n* evidence; **~stück** *n* (piece of) evidence; ⚹ exhibit. [leave it at that.]

be'wenden *vb.*: *es dabei* ~ *lassen*⎫

be'werb|en *v/refl.* (*irr.* werben, *no* -ge-, *h*): *sich* ~ *um* apply for, *Am.* run for; stand for; compete for (*prize*); court (*woman*); **&er** *m* (-s/-) applicant (*um* for); candidate; competitor; suitor; **&ung** *f* application; candidature; competition; courtship; **&ungsschreiben** *n* (letter of) application.

bewerkstelligen [bə'vɛrkʃtɛlɪgən] *v/t.* (*no* -ge-, *h*) manage, effect, bring about.

be'wert|en *v/t.* (*no* -ge-, *h*) value (*auf acc.* at; *nach* by); **&ung** *f* valuation.

bewillig|en [bə'vilɪgən] *v/t.* (*no* -ge-, *h*) grant, allow; **&ung** *f* (-/-en) grant, allowance.

be'wirken *v/t.* (*no* -ge-, *h*) cause; bring about, effect.

be'wirt|en *v/t.* (*no* -ge-, h) entertain; **~schaften** *v/t.* (*no* -ge-, h) farm (*land*); **✔** cultivate (*field*); manage (*farm, etc.*); ration (*food, etc.*); control (*foreign exchange, etc.*); **2ung** *f* (-/-en) entertainment; hospitality.

bewog [bə'vo:k] *pret.* of bewegen[1]; **~en** [bə'vo:gən] *p.p.* of bewegen[1].

be'wohn|en *v/t.* (*no* -ge-, h) inhabit, live in; occupy; **2er** *m* (-s/-) inhabitant; occupant.

bewölk|en [bə'vœlkən] *v/refl.* (*no* -ge-, h) *sky:* cloud up *or* over; *brow:* cloud over, darken; **~t** *adj. sky:* clouded, cloudy, overcast; *brow:* clouded, darkened; **2ung** *f* (-/*no pl.*) clouds *pl.*

be'wunder|n *v/t.* (*no* -ge-, h) admire (*wegen for*); **~nswert** *adj.* admirable; **2ung** *f* (-/-en) admiration.

bewußt *adj.* [bə'vust] deliberate, intentional; *sich e-r Sache ~ sein* be conscious *or* aware of s.th.; *die ~e Sache* the matter in question; **~los** *adj.* unconscious; **2sein** *n* (-s/*no pl.*) consciousness.

be'zahl|en *v/t.* (*no* -ge-, h) 1. *v/t.* pay; pay for (*s.th. purchased*); pay off, settle (*debt*); 2. *v/i.* pay (*für for*); **2ung** *f* payment; settlement.

be'zähmen *v/t.* (*no* -ge-, h) tame (*animal*); restrain (*one's anger, etc.*); *sich ~* control *or* restrain o.s.

be'zauber|n *v/t.* (*no* -ge-, h) bewitch, enchant (*a. fig.*); *fig.* charm, fascinate; **2ung** *f* (-/-en) enchantment, spell; fascination.

be'zeichn|en *v/t.* (*no* -ge-, h) mark; describe (*als* as), call; **~end** *adj.* characteristic, typical (*für* of); **2ung** *f* indication (*of direction, etc.*); mark, sign, symbol; name, designation, denomination.

be'zeugen *v/t.* (*no* -ge-, h) 🏛 testify to, bear witness to (*both a. fig.*); attest.

be'zieh|en *v/t.* (*irr.* ziehen, *no* -ge-, h) cover (*upholstered furniture, etc.*); put cover on (*cushion, etc.*); move into (*flat, etc.*); enter (*university*); draw (*salary, pension, etc.*); get, be supplied with (*goods*); take in (*newspaper, etc.*); *sich ~ sky:* cloud over; *sich ~ auf* (*acc.*) refer to; **2er** *m* (-s/-) subscriber (*gen.* to).

Be'ziehung *f* relation (*zu* et. to sth.; *zu j-m* with s.o.); connexion, (*Am. only*) connection (*zu* with); *in die-*

ser ~ in this respect; **2sweise** *adv.* respectively; *or* rather.

Bezirk [bə'tsirk] *m* (-[e]s/-e) district, *Am. a.* precinct; *s. Wahlbezirk.*

Bezogene 🏛 [bə'tso:gənə] *m* (-n/-n) drawee.

Bezug [bə'tsu:k] *m* cover(ing); case; purchase (*of goods*); subscription (*to newspaper*); *in ~ auf* (*acc.*) with regard *or* reference to, as to; *~ nehmen auf* (*acc.*) refer to, make reference to.

bezüglich [bə'tsy:kliç] 1. *adj.* relative, relating (*both: auf acc.* to); 2. *prp.* (*gen.*) regarding, concerning.

Be'zugsbedingungen 🏛 *f/pl.* terms *pl.* of delivery.

be'zwecken *v/t.* (*no* -ge-, h) aim at; *~ mit* intend by.

be'zweifeln *v/t.* (*no* -ge-, h) doubt, question.

be'zwing|en *v/t.* (*irr.* zwingen, *no* -ge-, h) conquer (*fortress, mountain, etc.*); overcome, master (*feeling, difficulty, etc.*); *sich ~* keep o.s. under control, restrain o.s.; **2ung** *f* (-/-en) conquest; mastering.

Bibel ['bi:bəl] *f* (-/-n) Bible.

Biber *zo.* ['bi:bər] *m* (-s/-) beaver.

Bibliothek [biblio'te:k] *f* (-/-en) library; **~ar** [~e'ka:r] *m* (-s/-e) librarian.

biblisch *adj.* ['bi:bliʃ] biblical, scriptural; **~e Geschichte** Scripture.

bieder *adj.* ['bi:dər] honest, upright, worthy (*a. iro.*); simple-minded; '**2-keit** *f* (-/*no pl.*) honesty, uprightness; simple-mindedness.

bieg|en ['bi:gən] (*irr.*, ge-) 1. *v/t.* (h) bend; 2. *v/refl.* (h) bend; *sich vor Lachen ~* double up with laughter; 3. *v/i.* (sein): *um e-e Ecke ~* turn (round) a corner; **~sam** *adj.* ['bi:kza:m] wire, *etc.:* flexible; *body:* lithe, supple; pliant (*a. fig.*); '**2samkeit** *f* (-/*no pl.*) flexibility; suppleness; pliability; '**2ung** *f* (-/-en) bend, wind (*of road, river*); curve (*of road, arch*).

Biene *zo.* ['bi:nə] *f* (-/-n) bee; '**~n-königin** *f* queen bee; '**~nkorb** *m* (bee)hive; '**~nschwarm** *m* swarm of bees; '**~nstock** *m* (bee)hive; '**~n-zucht** *f* bee-keeping; '**~nzüchter** *m* bee-keeper.

Bier [bi:r] *n* (-[e]s/-e) beer; *helles ~* pale beer, ale; *dunkles ~* dark beer;

stout, porter; ~ vom Faß beer on draught; '~brauer m brewer; '~brauerei f brewery; '~garten m beer-garden; '~krug m beer-mug, Am. stein.

Biest [bi:st] n (-es/-er) beast, brute.

bieten ['bi:tən] (irr., ge-, h) 1. v/t. offer; ✝ at auction sale: bid; sich ~ opportunity, etc.: offer itself, arise, occur; 2. ✝ v/i. at auction sale: bid.

Bigamie [biga'mi:] f (-/-n) bigamy.

Bilanz [bi'lants] f (-/-en) balance; balance-sheet, Am. a. statement; fig. result, outcome; die ~ ziehen strike a balance; fig. take stock (of one's life, etc.).

Bild [bilt] n (-[e]s/-er) picture; image; illustration; portrait; fig. idea, notion; '~bericht m press: picture story.

bilden ['bildən] v/t. (ge-, h) form; shape; fig.: educate, train (s.o., mind, etc.); develop (mind, etc.); form, be, constitute (obstacle, etc.); sich ~ form; fig. educate o.s., improve one's mind; sich e-e Meinung ~ form an opinion.

Bilder|buch ['bildər-] n picture-book; '~galerie f picture-gallery; '~rätsel n rebus.

'Bild|fläche f: F auf der ~ erscheinen appear on the scene; F von der ~ verschwinden disappear (from the scene); '~funk m radio picture transmission; television; '~hauer m (-s/-) sculptor; ~hauerei f (-/-en) sculpture; 'Qlich adj. pictorial; word, etc.: figurative; '~nis n (-ses/-se) portrait; '~röhre f picture or television tube; '~säule f statue; '~schirm m (television) screen; 'Q'schön adj. most beautiful; '~seite f face, head (of coin); '~streifen m picture or film strip; '~telegraphie f (-/no pl.) phototelegraphy.

'Bildung f (-/-en) forming, formation (both a. gr.: of plural, etc.); constitution (of committee, etc.); education; culture; (good) breeding. [sg.; billiard-table.]

Billard ['biljart] n (-s/-e) billiards.

billig adj. ['biliç] just, equitable; fair; price: reasonable, moderate; goods: cheap, inexpensive; recht und ~ right and proper; ~en ['~gən] v/t. (ge-, h) approve of, Am. a. approbate; 'Qkeit f (-/no pl.) justness,

equity; fairness; reasonableness, moderateness; 'Qung ['~guŋ] f (-/~-en) approval, sanction.

Binde ['bində] f (-/-n) band; tie; ✿ bandage; (arm-)sling; s. Damenbinde; '~gewebe anat. n connective tissue; '~glied n connecting link; '~haut anat. f conjunctiva; '~hautentzündung ✿ f conjunctivitis; 'Qn (irr., ge-, h) 1. v/t. bind, tie (an acc. to); bind (book, etc.); make (broom, wreath, etc.); knot (tie); sich ~ bind or commit or engage o.s.; 2. v/i. bind; unite; ⊕ cement, etc.: set, harden; '~strich m hyphen; '~wort gr. n (-[e]s/=er) conjunction.

Bindfaden ['bint-] m string; packthread.

'Bindung f (-/-en) binding (a. of ski); ♪ slur, tie, ligature; fig. commitment (a. pol.); engagement; ~en pl. bonds pl., ties pl.

binnen prp. (dat., a. gen.) ['binən] within; ~ kurzem before long.

'Binnen|gewässer n inland water; '~hafen m close port; '~handel m domestic or home trade, Am. domestic commerce; '~land n inland, interior; '~verkehr m inland traffic or transport.

Binse ✿ ['binzə] f (-/-n) rush; F: in die ~n gehen go to pot; '~nwahrheit f, '~nweisheit f truism.

Biochemie [bioçe'mi:] f (-/no pl.) biochemistry.

Biograph|ie [biogra'fi:] f (-/-n) biography; Qisch adj. ['~'gra:fiʃ] biographic(al).

Biolog|ie [biolo'gi:] f (-/no pl.) biology; Qisch adj. ['~'lo:giʃ] biological.

Birke ✿ ['birkə] f (-/-n) birch(-tree).

Birne ['birnə] f (-/-n) ✿ pear; ✓ (electric) bulb; fig. sl. nob, Am. bean.

bis [bis] 1. prp. (acc.) space: to, as far as; time: till, until, by; zwei ~ drei two or three, two to three; ~ auf weiteres until further orders, for the meantime; ~ vier zählen count up to four; alle ~ auf drei all but or except three; 2. cj. till, until.

Bisamratte zo. ['bi:zam-] f muskrat.

Bischof ['biʃɔf] m (-s/=e) bishop.

bischöflich adj. ['biʃøfliç] episcopal.

bleibend B

bisher adv. [bis'he:r] hitherto, up to now, so far; **~ig** adj. until now; hitherto existing; former.

Biß [bis] **1.** m (Bisses/Bisse) bite; **2.** ♀ pret. of beißen.

bißchen ['bisçən] **1.** adj.: ein ~ a little, a (little) bit of; **2.** adv.: ein ~ a little (bit).

Bissen ['bisən] m (-s/-) mouthful, morsel; bite.

'**bissig** adj. biting (a. fig.); remark: cutting; Achtung, ~er Hund! beware of the dog!

Bistum ['bistu:m] n (-s/=er) bishopric, diocese.

bisweilen adv. [bis'vaɪlən] sometimes, at times, now and then.

Bitte ['bitə] f (-/-n) request (um for); entreaty; auf j-s ~ (hin) at s.o.'s request.

'**bitten** (irr., ge-, h) **1.** v/t.: j-n um et. ~ ask or beg s.o. for s.th.; j-n um Entschuldigung ~ beg s.o.'s pardon; dürfte ich Sie um Feuer ~? may I trouble you for a light?; bitte please; (wie) bitte? (I beg your) pardon?; bitte! offering s.th.: (please,) help yourself, (please,) do take some or one; danke (schön) — bitte (sehr)! thank you — not at all, you're welcome, don't mention it, F that's all right; **2.** v/i.: um et. ~ ask or beg for s.th.

bitter adj. ['bitər] bitter (a. fig.); frost: sharp; '**♀keit** f (-/-en) bitterness; fig. a. acrimony; '**~lich** adv. bitterly.

'**Bitt|gang** eccl. m procession; '~schrift f petition; '~steller m (-s/-) petitioner.

bläh|en ['blɛ:ən] (ge-, h) **1.** v/t. inflate, distend, swell out; belly (out), swell out (sails); sich ~ sails: belly (out), swell out; skirt: balloon out; **2.** ♀ v/i. cause flatulence; '~end adj. flatulent; '**♀ung** f (-/-en) flatulence, F wind.

Blam|age [bla'ma:ʒə] f (-/-n) disgrace, shame; **♀ieren** [~'mi:rən] v/t. (no -ge-, h) make a fool of s.o., disgrace; sich ~ make a fool of o.s.

blank adj. [blaŋk] shining, shiny, bright; polished; F fig. broke.

blanko ✝ ['blaŋko] **1.** adj. form, etc.: blank, not filled in; in blank; **2.** adv.: ~ verkaufen stock exchange: sell short; '**♀scheck** m blank cheque, Am. blank check; '**♀unterschrift** f

blank signature; '**♀vollmacht** f full power of attorney, carte blanche.

Bläschen ♀ ['blɛ:sçən] n (-s/-) vesicle, small blister.

Blase ['bla:zə] f (-/-n) bubble; blister (a. ♀); anat. bladder; bleb (in glass); ⊕ flaw; '~balg m (ein a pair of) bellows pl.; '**♀n** (irr., ge-, h) **1.** v/t. blow; blow, sound; play (wind-instrument); **2.** v/i. blow.

Blas|instrument ♪ ['bla:s-] n wind-instrument; '~kapelle f brass band.

blaß adj. [blas] pale (vor dat. with); ~ werden turn pale; keine blasse Ahnung not the faintest idea.

Blässe ['blɛsə] f (-/no pl.) paleness.

Blatt [blat] n (-[e]s/=er) leaf (of book, ♀); petal (of flower); leaf, sheet (of paper); ♪ sheet; blade (of oar, saw, airscrew, etc.); sheet (of metal); cards: hand; (news)paper.

Blattern ♀ ['blatərn] pl. smallpox.

blättern ['blɛtərn] v/i. (ge-, h): in e-m Buch ~ leaf through a book, thumb a book.

'**Blatternarb|e** f pock-mark; '**♀ig** adj. pock-marked.

'**Blätterteig** m puff paste.

'**Blatt|gold** n gold-leaf, gold-foil; '~laus zo. f plant-louse; '~pflanze f foliage plant.

blau [blau] **1.** adj. blue; F fig. drunk, tight, boozy; ~er Fleck bruise; ~es Auge black eye; mit e-m ~en Auge davonkommen get off cheaply; **2.** ♀ n (-s/no pl.) blue (colo[u]r); Fahrt ins ~e mystery tour. (blue.)

bläuen ['blɔʏən] v/t. (ge-, h) (dye)

'**blau|grau** adj. bluish grey; '**♀-jacke** ♣ f bluejacket, sailor.

'**bläulich** adj. bluish.

'**Blausäure** ♀ f (-/no pl.) hydrocyanic or prussic acid.

Blech [blɛç] n (-[e]s/-e) sheet metal; metal sheet, plate; F fig. balderdash, rubbish, Am. sl. a. baloney; '~büchse f tin, Am. can; '**♀ern** adj. (of) tin; sound: brassy; sound, voice: tinny; '~musik f brass-band music; '~waren f/pl. tinware.

Blei [blaɪ] n (-[e]s/-e) **1.** n lead; **2.** F n, m (lead) pencil.

bleiben ['blaɪbən] v/i. (irr., ge-, sein) remain, stay, be left; ruhig ~ keep calm; ~ bei keep to s.th., stick to s.th.; bitte bleiben Sie am Apparat teleph. hold the line, please; '~d *adj.* lasting, permanent; '**~lassen** *v/t.* (irr. lassen, sep., no -ge-, h) leave s.th. alone; *laß das bleiben!* don't do it!; leave it alone!; stop that (noise, etc.)!

bleich *adj.* [blaɪç] pale (vor dat. with); '**~en** (ge-) 1. *v/t.* (h) make pale; bleach; blanch; 2. *v/i.* (irr., sein) bleach; lose colo(u)r, fade; '**~süchtig** *⚕* *adj.* chlorotic, greensick.

'**bleiern** *adj.* (of lead) leaden (a. fig.). '**Blei|rohr** *n* lead pipe; '**~soldat** *m* tin soldier; '**~stift** *m* (lead) pencil; '**~stifthülse** *f* pencil cap; '**~stiftspitzer** *m* (-s/-) pencil-sharpener; '**~vergiftung** *⚕* *f* lead-poisoning.

Blend|e ['blɛndə] *f* (-/-n) *phot.* diaphragm, stop; △ blind or sham window; '**~en** (ge-) 1. *v/t.* blind; dazzle (both a. fig.); 2. *v/i. light:* dazzle the eyes; **~laterne** ['blɛnt-] *f* dark lantern.

blich [blɪç] *pret. of bleichen* ?.

Blick [blɪk] *m* (-[e]s/-e) glance, look; view (auf acc. of); auf den ersten ~ at first sight; ein böser ~ an evil or angry look; '**~en** *v/i.* (ge-, h) look, glance (auf acc., nach at); '**~fang** *m* eye-catcher.

blieb [bliːp] *pret. of bleiben.*

blies [bliːs] *pret. of blasen.*

blind *adj.* [blɪnt] blind (a. fig.: gegen, für to; vor dat. with); metal: dull, tarnished; window: opaque (with age, dirt); mirror: clouded, dull; cartridge: blank; ~er Alarm false alarm; ~er Passagier stowaway; auf e-m Auge ~ blind in one eye.

'**Blinddarm** *anat. m* blind gut; appendix; '**~entzündung** *⚕* *f* appendicitis.

Blinde ['blɪndə] (-n/-n) 1. *m* blind man; 2. *f* blind woman; '**~nanstalt** ['blɪndən?-] *f* institute for the blind; '**~nheim** *n* home for the blind; '**~nhund** *m* guide dog, *Am. a.* seeing-eye dog; '**~nschrift** *f* braille.

'**blind|fliegen** *⚹* (irr. fliegen, sep., -ge-) *v/t.* (h) and *v/i.* (sein) fly blind or on instruments; '**⚹flug** *⚹* *m* blind flying or flight; '**⚹gänger** *m* ✕ blind shell, dud; F fig. washout; '**⚹heit** *f* (-/no cj.) blindness; '**⚹lings** *adv.* ['⚹lɪŋs] blindly; at random; '**⚹schleiche** *zo. f* (-/-n) slow-worm,

---

blind-worm; '**~schreiben** *v/t. and v/i.* (irr. schreiben, sep., -ge-, h) touch-type.

blink|en ['blɪŋkən] *v/i.* (ge-, h) star, light: twinkle; metal, leather, glass, etc.: shine; signal (with lamps), flash; '**⚹er** *mot. m* (-s/-) flashing indicator; '**⚹feuer** *n* flashing light.

blinzeln ['blɪntsəln] *v/i.* (ge-, h) blink (at light, etc.); wink.

Blitz [blɪts] *m* (-es/-e) lightning; '**~ableiter** *m* (-s/-) lightning-conductor; '**⚹en** *v/i.* (ge-, h) flash; es blitzt it is lightening; '**~gespräch** *teleph. n* special priority call; '**~licht** *phot. n* flash-light; '**⚹schnell** *adv.* with lightning speed; '**~strahl** *m* flash of lightning.

Block [blɔk] *m* 1. (-[e]s/⚹e) block; slab (of cooking chocolate); block, log (of wood); ingot (of metal); parl., pol., ✝ bloc; 2. (-[e]s/⚹e, -s) block (of houses); pad, block (of paper); ~ade ✕, ⚓ [blɔkˈaːdə] *f* (-/-n) blockade; **~adebrecher** *m* (-s/-) blockade-runner; '**~haus** *n* log cabin; **⚹ieren** [~ˈkiːrən] (no -ge-, h) 1. *v/t.* block (up); lock (wheel); 2. *v/i.* brakes, etc.: jam.

blöd *adj.* [bløːt], **~e** *adj.* ['⚹də] imbecile; stupid, dull; silly; '**⚹heit** *f* (-/-en) imbecility; stupidity, dullness; silliness; '**⚹sinn** *m* imbecility; rubbish, nonsense; '**⚹sinnig** *adj.* imbecile; idiotic, stupid, foolish.

blöken ['bløːkən] *v/i.* (ge-, h) sheep, calf: bleat.

blond *adj.* [blɔnt] blond, fair (-haired).

bloß [bloːs] 1. *adj.* bare, naked; mere; ~e Worte mere words; mit dem ~en Auge wahrnehmbar visible to the naked eye; 2. *adv.* only, merely, simply, just.

Blöße ['bløːsə] *f* (-/-n) bareness, nakedness; fig. weak point or spot; sich e-e ~ geben give o.s. away; lay o.s. open to attack; keine ~ bieten be invulnerable.

'**bloß|legen** *v/t.* (sep., -ge-, h) lay bare, expose; '**~stellen** *v/t.* (sep., -ge-, h) expose, compromise, unmask; sich ~ compromise o.s.

blühen ['blyːən] *v/i.* (ge-, h) blossom, flower, bloom; fig. flourish, thrive, prosper; ✝ boom.

Blume ['bluːmə] *f* (-/-n) flower; wine: bouquet; beer: froth.

'**Blumen|beet** n flower-bed; '~**blatt** n petal; '~**händler** m florist; '~**strauß** m bouquet or bunch of flowers; '~**topf** m flowerpot; '~**zucht** f floriculture.

Bluse ['blu:zə] f (-/-n) blouse.

Blut [blu:t] n (-[e]s/no pl.) blood; ~ vergießen shed blood; böses ~ machen breed bad blood; '~**andrang** m congestion; '2**arm** adj. bloodless, an(a)emic; '~**armut** ⚕ f an(a)emia; '~**bad** n carnage, massacre; '~**bank** ⚕ f blood bank; '~**blase** f blood blister; '~**druck** m blood pressure; 2**dürstig** adj. ['~dyrstiç] bloodthirsty.

Blüte ['bly:tə] f (-/-n) blossom, bloom, flower (esp. fig. flower; prime, heyday (of life).

Blutegel ['blu:tⁿe:gəl] m (-s/-) leech.

'**bluten** v/i. (ge-, h) bleed (aus from); aus der Nase ~ bleed at the nose.

Bluterguß ⚕ ['blu:tⁿ-] m effusion of blood.

'**Blütezeit** f flowering period or time; fig. a. prime, heyday.

'**Blut|gefäß** anat. n blood-vessel; '~**gerinnsel** ⚕ ['~gərinzəl] n (-s/-) clot of blood; '~**gruppe** f blood group; '~**hund** zo. m bloodhound.

'**blutig** adj. bloody, blood-stained; es ist mein ~er Ernst I am dead serious; ~er Anfänger mere beginner, F greenhorn.

Blut|körperchen ['blu:tkœrpərçən] n (-s/-) blood corpuscle; '~**kreislauf** m (blood) circulation; '~**lache** f pool of blood; '2**leer** adj., '2**los** adj. bloodless; '~**probe** f blood test; '~**rache** f blood feud or revenge or vengeance, vendetta; '2**rot** adj. blood-red; crimson; 2**rünstig** adj. ['~rynstiç] bloodthirsty; bloody; '~**schande** f incest; '~**spender** m blood-donor; '2**stillend** adj. blood-sta(u)nching; '**sturz** ⚕ m h(a)emorrhage; '2**verwandt** adj. related to blood (mit to); '~**verwandtschaft** f blood-relationship, consanguinity; '**übertragung** f blood-transfusion; '~**ung** f (-/-en) bleeding, h(a)emorrhage; '2**unterlaufen** adj. eye: bloodshot; '~**vergießen** n bloodshed; '~**vergiftung** f blood-poisoning.

Bö [bø] f (-/-en) gust, squall.

Bock [bɔk] m (-[e]s/ᵘe) deer, hare,

rabbit: buck; he-goat, F billy-goat; sheep: ram; gymnastics: buck; e-n ~ schießen commit a blunder, sl. commit a bloomer; den ~ zum Gärtner machen set the fox to keep the geese; '2**en** v/i. (ge-, h) horse: buck; child: sulk; p. be obstinate or refractory; mot. move jerkily, Am. F a. buck; '2**ig** adj. stubborn, obstinate, pigheaded; '~**sprung** m leap-frog; gymnastics: vault over the buck; Bocksprünge machen caper, cut capers.

Boden ['bo:dən] m (-s/ᵘ) ground; ✒ soil; bottom; floor; loft; '~**kammer** f garret, attic; '2**los** adj. bottomless; fig. enormous, unheard-of; '~**personal** 🛩 n ground personnel or staff, Am. ground crew; '~**reform** f land reform; '~**satz** m grounds pl., sediment; '~**schätze** ['~ʃɛtsə] m/pl. mineral resources pl.; '2**ständig** adj. native, indigenous.

bog [bo:k] pret. of biegen.

Bogen ['bo:gən] m (-s/-, ᵘ) bow, bend, curve; 🔀 arc; △ arch; skiing: turn; skating: curve; sheet (of paper); '2**förmig** adj. arched; '~**gang** △ m arcade; '~**lampe** 🔦 f arc-lamp; '~**schütze** m archer, bowman.

Bohle ['bo:lə] f (-/-n) thick plank, board.

Bohne ['bo:nə] f (-/-n) bean; grüne ~n pl. French beans pl., Am. string beans pl.; weiße ~n pl. haricot beans pl.; F blaue ~n pl. bullets pl.; '~**stange** f beanpole (a. F fig.).

bohnern ['bo:nərn] v/t. (ge-, h) polish (floor, etc.), (bees)wax (floor).

bohr|en ['bo:rən] (ge-, h) **1.** v/t. bore, drill (hole); sink, bore (well, shaft); bore, cut, drive (tunnel, etc.); **2.** v/i. drill (a. dentistry); bore; '2**er** ⊕ m (-s/-) borer, drill.

'**böig** adj. squally, gusty; 🛩 bumpy.

Boje ['bo:jə] f (-/-n) buoy.

Bollwerk ⚔ ['bɔlvɛrk] n bastion, bulwark (a. fig.).

Bolzen ⊕ ['bɔltsən] m (-s/-) bolt.

Bombard|ement [bɔmbardə'mã:] n (-s/-s) bombardment; bombing; shelling; 2**ieren** [~'di:rən] v/t. (no -ge-, h) bomb; shell; bombard (a. fig.).

Bombe ['bɔmbə] f (-/-n) bomb; fig. bomb-shell; 2**nsicher** adj. bomb-

B

proof; F *fig.* dead sure; '∼nschaden *m* bomb damage; '∼r ✕: ✕ *m* (-s/-) bomber. [er; credit note.]

Bon ✝ [bõː] *m*(-s/-s) coupon; vouch-J
Bonbon [bõˈbõː] *m, n* (-s/-s) sweet (-meat), bon-bon, F goody, *Am.* candy. [*Am. a.* big shot.]
Bonze F ['bɔntsə] *m* (-n/-n) bigwig, J
Boot [boːt] *n* (-[e]s/-e) boat; '∼shaus *n* boat-house; '∼smann *m* (-[e]s/ *Bootsleute*) boatswain.

Bord [bɔrt] (-[e]s/-e) **1.** *n* shelf; **2.** ⚓, ✈ *m:* an ∼ on board, aboard (*ship, aircraft, etc.*); über ∼ overboard; von ∼ gehen go ashore; '∼funker ⚓, ✈ *m* wireless or radio operator; '∼stein *m* kerb, *Am.* curb.

borgen ['bɔrgən] *v/t.* (ge-, *h*) borrow (*von, bei* from, of); lend, *Am. a.* loan (*j-m et. s.th.* to s.o.).

Borke ['bɔrkə] *f* (-/-n) bark (*of tree*).

borniert *adj.* [bɔrˈniːrt] narrow-minded, of restricted intelligence.

Borsalbe ['boːr-] *f* boracic ointment.

Börse ['bœrzə] *f* (-/-n) purse; ✝ stock exchange; stock-market; money-market; '∼nbericht *m* market report; '2nfähig *adj. stock:* negotiable on the stock exchange; '∼nkurs *m* quotation; '∼nmakler *m* stock-broker; '∼nnotierung *f* (official, stock exchange) quotation; '∼npapiere *n/pl.* listed securities *pl.;* '∼nspekulant *m* stock-jobber; '∼nzeitung *f* financial newspaper.

Borst|e ['bɔrstə] *f* (-/-n) bristle (*of hog or brush, etc.*); '2ig *adj.* bristly.

Borte ['bɔrtə] *f* (-/-n) border (*of carpet, etc.*); braid, lace.

bösartig *adj.* malicious, vicious; ⚕ malignant; '2keit *f* (-/-en) viciousness; ⚕ malignity.

Böschung ['bœʃuŋ] *f* (-/-en) slope; embankment (*of railway*); bank (*of river*).

böse ['bøːzə] **1.** *adj.* bad, evil, wicked; malevolent, spiteful; angry (*über acc.* at, about; *auf j-n* with s.o.); *er meint es nicht ∼* he means no harm; **2.** 2 *n* (-n/no *pl.*) evil; 2wicht ['∼viçt] *m* (-[e]s/-er, -e) villain, rascal.

bos|haft *adj.* ['boːshaft] wicked; spiteful; malicious; '2heit *f* (-/-en) wickedness; malice; spite.

'**böswillig** *adj.* malevolent; ∼e Ab-

sicht ⚖ malice prepense; ∼es *Verlassen* ⚖ wilful desertion; '2keit *f* (-/-en) malevolence.

bot [boːt] *pret. of bieten.*

Botan|ik [boˈtaːnik] *f* (-/no *pl.*) botany; ∼iker *m* (-s/-) botanist; 2isch *adj.* botanical.

Bote ['boːtə] *m* (-n/-n) messenger; '∼ngang *m.* errand; *Botengänge machen* run errands.

'**Botschaft** *f* (-/-en) message; *pol.* embassy; *pol.* ∼er *m* (-s/-) ambassador; *in British Commonwealth countries:* High Commissioner.

Bottich ['bɔtiç] *m* (-[e]s/-e) tub; wash-tub; *brewing:* tun. vat.

Bouillon [buˈljõː] *f* (-/-s) beef tea.

Bowle ['boːlə] *f* (-/-n) vessel: bowl; cold drink consisting of fruit, hock and champagne or soda-water: appr. punch.

box|en ['bɔksən] **1.** *v/i.* (ge-, *h*) box; **2.** *v/t.* (ge-, *h*) punch *s.o.;* **3.** 2 *n* (-s/no *pl.*) boxing; pugilism; '2er *m* (-s/-) boxer; pugilist; '2handschuh *m* boxing-glove; '2kampf *m* boxing-match, bout, fight; '2sport *m* boxing.

Boykott [bɔyˈkɔt] (-[e]s/-e) boycott; 2ieren [∼ˈtiːrən] *v/t.* (*no* -ge-, *h*) boycott.

brach [braːx] **1.** *pret. of brechen;* **2.** ∼ *adv.* fallow; uncultivated (*both a. fig.*).

brachte ['braxtə] *pret. of bringen.*

Branche ✝ ['brãːʃə] *f* (-/-n) line (of business), trade; branch.

Brand [brant] *m* (-[e]s/⸚e) burning; fire, blaze; ⚕ gangrene; ✿, ✾ blight, smut, mildew; '∼blase *f* blister; '∼bombe *f* incendiary bomb; 2en ['∼dən] *v/i.* (ge-, *h*) surge (*a. fig.*), break (*an acc., gegen* against); '∼fleck *m* burn; 2ig *adj.* ['∼diç] ⚕, ✿ blighted, smutted; ⚕ gangrenous; '∼mal *n* brand; *fig.* stigma, blemish; '2marken *v/t.* (ge-, *h*) brand (*animal*); *fig.* brand or stigmatize *s.o.;* '∼mauer *f* fire (-proof) wall; '∼schaden *m* damage caused by or loss suffered by fire; '2schatzen *v/t.* (ge-, *h*) lay (*town*) under contribution; sack, pillage; '∼stätte *f,* '∼stelle *f* scene of fire; '∼stifter *m* incendiary, *Am.* F a. firebug; '∼stiftung *f* arson; '∼ung ['∼duŋ] *f* (-/-en) surf, surge, breakers *pl.;* '∼wache *f* fire-watch;

Bremsweg

'**~wunde** f burn; scald; '**~zeichen** n brand.

brannte ['brantə] *pret. of* brennen.

Branntwein ['brantvain] m brandy, spirits pl.; whisk(e)y; gin; '**~brennerei** f distillery.

braten ['brɑːtən] **1.** v/t. (irr., ge-, h) in oven: roast; grill; in frying-pan: fry; bake (apple); am Spieß ~ roast on a spit, barbecue; **2.** v/i. (irr., ge-, h) roast; grill; fry; in der Sonne ~ p. roast or grill in the sun; **3.** ♀ m (-s/-) roast (meat); joint; '♀**fett** n dripping; '♀**soße** f gravy.

'**Brat|fisch** m fried fish; '**~hering** m grilled herring; '**~huhn** n roast chicken; '**~kartoffeln** pl. fried potatoes pl.; '**~ofen** m (kitchen) oven; '**~pfanne** f frying-pan, Am. a. skillet; '**~röhre** f s. Bratofen.

Brauch [braux] m (-[e]s/ʉe) custom, usage; use, habit; practice; '♀**bar** adj. p., thing: useful; p. capable, able; thing: serviceable; '♀**en** (h) **1.** v/t. (ge-) need, want; require; take (time); use; **2.** v/aux. (no ge-): du brauchst es nur zu sagen you only have to say so; er hätte nicht zu kommen ~ he need not have come; '**~tum** n (-[e]s/ʉer) custom; tradition; folklore.

Braue ['brauə] f (-/-n) eyebrow.

brau|en ['brauən] v/t. (ge-, h) brew; '♀**er** m (-s/-) brewer; '♀**erei** [~'rai] f (-/-en) brewery; '♀**haus** n brewery.

braun adj. [braun] brown; horse: bay; ~ werden get a tan (on one's skin).

Bräune ['brɔynə] f (-/no pl.) brown colo(u)r; (sun) tan; '♀**n** (ge-, h) **1.** v/t. make or dye brown; sun: tan; **2.** v/i. tan.

'**Braunkohle** f brown coal, lignite.

'**bräunlich** adj. brownish.

Brause ['brauzə] f (-/-n) rose, sprinkling-nozzle (of watering can); s. Brausebad; s. Brauselimonade; '**~bad** n shower(-bath); '**~limonade** f fizzy lemonade; '♀**n** v/i. (ge-, h) wind, water, etc.: roar; rush; have a shower(-bath); '**~pulver** n effervescent powder.

Braut [braut] f (-/ʉe) fiancée; on wedding-day: bride; '**~führer** m best man.

Bräutigam ['brɔytigam] m (-s/-e) fiancé; on wedding-day: bridegroom, Am. a. groom.

'**Braut|jungfer** f bridesmaid; '**~kleid** n wedding-dress; '**~kranz** m bridal wreath; '**~leute** pl., '**~paar** n engaged couple; on wedding-day: bride and bridegroom; '**~schleier** m bridal veil.

brav adj. [brɑːf] honest, upright; good, well-behaved; brave.

bravo int. ['brɑːvo] bravo!, well done!

Bravour [bra'vuːr] f (-/no pl.) bravery, courage; brilliance.

Brecheisen ['brɛç'?-] n crowbar; (burglar's) jemmy, Am. a. jimmy.

'**brechen** (irr., ge-) **1.** v/t. (h) break; pluck (flower); refract (ray, etc.); fold (sheet of paper); quarry (stone); vomit; die Ehe ~ commit adultery; sich ~ break (one's leg, etc.); opt. be refracted; **2.** v/i. (h) break; vomit; mit j-m ~ break with s.o.; **3.** v/i. (sein) break, get broken; bones: break, fracture.

'**Brech|mittel** ✻ n emetic; F fig. sickener; '**~reiz** m nausea; '**~stange** f crowbar, Am. a. pry; '**~ung** opt. f (-/-en) refraction.

Brei [brai] m (-[e]s/-e) paste; pulp; mash; pap (for babies); made of oatmeal: porridge; (rice, etc.) pudding; '♀**ig** adj. pasty; pulpy; pappy.

breit adj. [brait] broad, wide; zehn Meter ~ ten metres wide; ~e Schichten der Bevölkerung large sections of or the bulk of the population; '**~beinig 1.** adj. with legs wide apart; **2.** adv.: ~ gehen straddle.

Breite ['braitə] f (-/-n) breadth, width; ast., geogr. latitude; '♀**n** v/t. (ge-, h) spread; '**~ngrad** m degree of latitude; '**~nkreis** m parallel (of latitude).

'**breit|machen** v/refl. (sep., -ge-, h) spread o.s.; take up room; '**~schlagen** v/t. (irr. schlagen, sep., -ge-, h): F j-n ~ persuade s.o.; F j-n zu et. ~ talk s.o. into (doing) s.th.; '♀**seite** ⚓ f broadside.

Bremse ['brɛmzə] f (-/-n) zo. gadfly; horse-fly; ⊕ brake; '♀**n** (ge-, h) v/i. brake, put on the brakes; slow down; **2.** v/t. brake, put on the brakes; slow down; fig. curb.

'**Brems|klotz** m brake-block; ✵ wheel chock; '**~pedal** n brake pedal; '**~vorrichtung** f brake-mechanism; '**~weg** m braking distance.

B

brenn|bar adj. ['brɛnbɑːr] combustible, burnable; **Ձdauer** f burning time; **'∼en** (irr., ge-, h) **1.** v/t. burn; distil(l) (brandy); roast (coffee); bake (brick, etc.); **2.** v/i. burn; be ablaze, be on fire; wound, eye: smart, burn; nettle: sting; vor Ungeduld ∼ burn with impatience; F darauf ∼ zu inf. be burning to inf.; es brennt! fire!

'Brenn|er m (-s/-) p. distiller; fixture: burner; **∼essel** ['brɛnnesəl] f stinging nettle; **'∼glas** n burning glass; **'∼holz** n firewood; **'∼material** n fuel; **'∼öl** n lamp-oil; fuel-oil; **'∼punkt** m focus, focal point; in den ∼ rücken bring into focus (a. fig.); im ∼ des Interesses stehen be the focus of interest; **'∼schere** f curling-tongs pl.; **'∼spiritus** m methylated spirit; **'∼stoff** m combustible; mot. fuel.

brenzlig ['brɛntsliç] **1.** adj. burnt; matter: dangerous; situation: precarious; **∼er** Geruch burnt smell, smell of burning; **2.** adv.: es riecht ∼ it smells of burning.

Bresche ['brɛʃə] f (-/-n) breach (a. fig.), gap; in die ∼ springen help s.o. out of a dilemma.

Brett [brɛt] n (-[e]s/-er) board; plank; shelf; spring-board; **'∼spiel** n game played on a board.

Brezel ['breːtsəl] f (-/-n) pretzel.

Brief [briːf] m (-[e]s/-e) letter; **'∼aufschrift** f address (on a letter); **'∼beschwerer** m (-s/-) paperweight; **'∼bogen** m sheet of notepaper; **'∼geheimnis** n secrecy of correspondence; **'∼karte** f correspondence card (with envelope); **'∼kasten** m letter-box; pillar-box; Am. mailbox; **Ձlich** adj. and adv. by letter, in writing; **'∼marke** f (postage) stamp; **'∼markensammlung** f stamp-collection; **'∼öffner** m letter-opener; **'∼ordner** m letterfile; **'∼papier** n notepaper; **'∼porto** n postage; **'∼post** f mail, post; **'∼tasche** f wallet, Am. a. billfold; **'∼taube** f carrier pigeon, homing pigeon, homer; **'∼träger** m postman, Am. mailman; **'∼umschlag** m envelope; **'∼waage** f letterbalance; **'∼wechsel** m correspondence; **'∼zensur** f postal censorship.

briet [briːt] pret. of braten.

Brikett [bri'kɛt] n (-[e]s/-s) briquet(-te).

Brillant [bril'jant] **1.** m (-en/-en) brilliant, cut diamond; **2.** Ձ adj. brilliant; **∼ring** m diamond ring.

Brille ['brilə] f (-/-n) (eine a pair of) glasses pl. or spectacles pl., goggles pl.; lavatory seat; **'∼nfutteral** n spectacle-case; **'∼nträger** m person who wears glasses.

bringen ['briŋən] v/t. (irr., ge-, h) bring; take; see (s.o. home, etc.); put (in order); make (sacrifice); yield (interest); an den Mann ∼ dispose of, get rid of; j-n dazu ∼, et. zu tun make or get s.o. to do s.th.; et. mit sich ∼ involve s.th.; j-n um et. ∼ deprive s.o. of s.th.; j-n zum Lachen ∼ make s.o. laugh.

Brise ['briːzə] f (-/-n) breeze.

Brit|e ['britə] m (-n/-n) Briton, Am. a. Britisher; die ∼n pl. the British pl.; **Ձisch** adj. British.

bröckeln ['brœkəln] v/i. (ge-, h) crumble; become brittle.

Brocken ['brɔkən] **1.** m (-s/-) piece; lump (of earth or stone, etc.); morsel (of food); F ein harter ∼ a hard nut; **2.** Ձ v/t. (ge-, h): Brot in die Suppe ∼ break bread into soup.

brodeln ['broːdəln] v/i. (ge-, h) bubble, simmer.

Brombeer|e ['brɔm-] f blackberry; **'∼strauch** m blackberry bush.

Bronch|ialkatarrh [brɔnçi'ɑːlkatar] m bronchial catarrh; **∼ien** anat. f/pl. bronchi(a) pl.; **∼itis** [∼'çiːtis] f (-/Bronchitiden) bronchitis.

Bronze ['brõːsə] f (-/-n) bronze; **'∼medaille** f bronze medal.

Brosche ['brɔʃə] f (-/-n) brooch.

broschier|en [brɔ'ʃiːrən] v/t. (no -ge-, h) sew, stitch (book); **∼t** adj. book: paper-backed, paper-bound; fabric: figured.

Broschüre [brɔ'ʃyːrə] f (-/-n) booklet; brochure; pamphlet.

Brot [broːt] n (-[e]s/-e) bread; loaf; sein ∼ verdienen earn one's living; **'∼aufstrich** m spread.

Brötchen ['brøːtçən] n (-s/-) roll.

'Brot|korb m: j-m den ∼ höher hängen put s.o. on short allowance; **Ձlos** fig. adj. unemployed; unprofitable; **'∼rinde** f crust; **'∼schneidemaschine** f bread-cutter; **'∼schnitte** f slice of bread;

'**⁀studium** n utilitarian study; '**⁀teig** m bread dough.

Bruch [brux] (-[e]s/⁀e) break(ing); breach; ⚕ fracture (of bones); ⚕ hernia; crack; fold (in paper); crease (in cloth); split (in silk); ⚕ fraction; breach (of promise); violation (of oath, etc.); violation, infringement (of law, etc.); '**⁀band** ⚕ n truss.

brüchig adj. ['bryçiç] fragile; brittle, voice: cracked.

'**Bruch|landung** ✈ f crash-landing; '**⁀rechnung** f fractional arithmetic, F fractions pl.; '**⁀strich** ∧ m fraction bar; '**⁀stück** n fragment (a. fig.); '**⁀teil** m fraction; im ⁀ e-r Sekunde in a split second; '**⁀zahl** f fraction(al) number.

Brücke ['brykə] f (-/-n) bridge; carpet: rug; sports: bridge; e-e ⁀ schlagen über (acc.) build or throw a bridge across, bridge (river); '**⁀nkopf** ⚔ m bridge-head; '**⁀npfeiler** m pier (of bridge).

Bruder ['bru:dər] m (-s/⁀) brother; eccl. (lay) brother, friar; '**⁀krieg** m fratricidal or civil war; '**⁀kuß** m fraternal kiss.

brüderlich ['bry:dərliç] **1.** adj. brotherly, fraternal; **2.** adv.: ⁀ teilen share and share alike; '2**keit** f (-/no pl.) brotherliness, fraternity.

Brühe ['bry:ə] f (-/-n) broth; stock; beef tea; F dirty water; drink: F dishwater; '2**heiß** adj. scalding hot; '**⁀würfel** m beef cube.

brüllen ['brylən] v/i. (ge-, h) roar; bellow; cattle: low; bull: bellow; vor Lachen ⁀ roar with laughter; ⁀des Gelächter roar of laughter.

brumm|en ['brumən] v/i. (ge-, h) p. speak in a deep voice, mumble; growl (a. fig.); insect: buzz; engine: buzz, boom; fig. grumble, Am. F grouch; mir brummt der Schädel my head is buzzing; '2**bär** fig. m grumbler, growler, Am. F grouch; '2**er** m (-s/-) bluebottle; dung-beetle; '**⁀ig** adj. grumbling, Am. F grouchy. [brunette.]

brünett adj. [bry'nɛt] woman:]

Brunft hunt. [brunft] f (-/⁀e) rut; '**⁀zeit** f rutting season.

Brunnen ['brunən] m (-s/-) well; spring; fountain (a. fig.); e-n ⁀ graben sink a well; '**⁀wasser** n pump-water, well-water.

Brunst [brunst] f (-/⁀e) zo. rut (of male animal), heat (of female animal); lust, sexual desire.

brünstig adj. ['brynstiç] zo. rutting, in heat; lustful.

Brust [brust] f (-/⁀e) chest, anat. thorax; breast; (woman's) breast(s pl.), bosom; aus voller ⁀ at the top of one's voice, lustily; '**⁀bild** n half-length portrait.

'**Brust|fell** anat. n pleura; '**⁀fell-entzündung** ⚕ f pleurisy; '**⁀kasten** m, '**⁀korb** m chest, anat. thorax; '**⁀schwimmen** n (-s/no pl.) breast-stroke.

Brüstung ['brystuŋ] f (-/-en) balustrade, parapet.

'**Brustwarze** anat. f nipple.

Brut [bru:t] f (-/-en) brooding, sitting; brood; hatch; fry, spawn (of fish); fig. F brood, (bad) lot.

brutal adj. [bru'ta:l] brutal; 2**ität** [⁀ali'tɛ:t] f (-/-en) brutality.

Brutapparat zo. ['bru:tʔ-] m incubator.

brüten ['bry:tən] v/i. (ge-, h) brood, sit (on egg); incubate; ⁀ über (dat.) brood over.

'**Brutkasten** ⚕ m incubator.

brutto † adv. ['bruto] gross; '2**gewicht** n gross weight; '2**register-tonne** f gross register ton; '2**verdienst** m gross earnings pl.

Bube ['bu:bə] m (-n/-n) boy, lad; knave, rogue; cards: knave, jack; '**⁀nstreich** m, '**⁀nstück** n boyish prank; knavish trick.

Buch [bu:x] n (-[e]s/⁀er) book; volume; † **⁀binder** m (book-)binder; '**⁀drucker** m printer; '**⁀druckerei** [⁀'raɪ] f printing; printing-office, Am. print shop.

Buche ♀ ['bu:xə] f (-/-n) beech.

buchen ['bu:xən] v/t. (ge-, h) book, reserve (passage, flight, etc.); book-keeping: book (item, sum), enter (transaction) in the books; et. als Erfolg ⁀ count s.th. as a success.

Bücher|abschluß † ['by:çər-] m closing of or balancing of books; '**⁀brett** n bookshelf; '**⁀ei** [⁀'raɪ] f (-/-en) library; '**⁀freund** m book-lover, bibliophil(e); '**⁀revisor** † m (-s/-en) auditor; accountant; '**⁀schrank** m bookcase; '**⁀wurm** m bookworm.

'**Buch|fink** *orn. m* chaffinch; '**~hal-ter** *m* (-s/-) book-keeper; '**~hal-tung** *f* book-keeping; '**~handel** *m* book-trade; '**~händler** *m* bookseller; '**~handlung** *f* bookshop, *Am.* bookstore.

Büchse ['byksə] *f* (-/-n) box, case; tin, *Am.* can; rifle; '**~nfleisch** *n* tinned meat, *Am.* canned meat; '**~nöffner** ['byksən⁹-] *m* tin-opener, *Am.* can opener.

Buchstab|e ['bu:xʃta:bə] *m* (-n/-n) letter, character; *typ.* type; **2ieren** [..a'bi:rən] *v/t.* (no -ge-, *h*) spell.

buchstäblich ['bu:xʃtɛ:pliç] **1.** *adj.* literal; **2.** *adv.* literally; word for word.

Bucht [buxt] *f* (-/-en) bay; bight; creek, inlet.

'**Buchung** *f* (-/-en) booking, reservation; *book-keeping*: entry.

Buckel ['bukəl] **1.** *m* (-s/-) hump, hunch; humpback, hunchback; boss, stud, knob; **2.** *f* (-/-n) boss, stud, knob.

'**buckelig** *adj. s.* bucklig.

bücken ['bykən] *v/refl.* (ge-, *h*) bend (down), stoop.

bucklig *adj.* ['bukliç] humpbacked, hunchbacked.

Bückling ['byklin] *m* (-s/-e) bloater, red herring; *fig.* bow.

Bude ['bu:də] *f* (-/-n) stall, booth; hut, cabin, *Am.* shack; F place; den; (student's, *etc.*) digs *pl.*

Budget [by'dʒe:] *n* (-s/-s) budget.

Büfett [by'fe:; by'fɛt] *n* (-[e]s/-s; -[e]s/-e) sideboard, buffet; buffet, bar, *Am. a.* counter; *kaltes* ~ buffet supper *or* lunch.

Büffel ['byfəl] *m* (-s/-) *zo.* buffalo; F *fig.* lout, blockhead.

Bug [bu:k] *m* (-[e]s/-e) ⊕ bow; ✈ nose; fold; (sharp) crease.

Bügel ['by:gəl] *m* (-s/-) bow (*of spectacles, etc.*); handle (*of handbag, etc.*); coat-hanger; stirrup; '**~brett** *n* ironing-board; '**~eisen** *n* (flat-)iron; '**~falte** *f* crease; **2n** *v/t.* (ge-, *h*) iron (*shirt, etc.*), press (*suit, skirt, etc.*).

Bühne ['by:nə] *f* (-/-n) platform (*a.* ⊕); scaffold; *thea.* stage; *fig.*: *die* ~ the stage; *die politische* ~ the political scene; **~nanweisungen** ['by:nən⁹-] *f/pl.* stage directions *pl.*; '**~nbild** *n* scene(ry); décor; stage design; '**~ndichter** *m* playwright;

dramatist; '**~nlaufbahn** *f* stage career; '**~nstück** *n* stage play.

buk [bu:k] *pret. of* backen.

Bull|auge ⊕ ['bul-] *n* porthole, bull's eye; '**~dogge** *zo.* *f* bulldog.

Bulle ['bulə] **1.** *zo. m* (-n/-n) bull; **2.** *eccl. f* (-/-n) bull.

Bummel F ['buməl] *m* (-s/-) stroll; spree, pub-crawl, *sl.* binge; **~ei** [..'laɪ] *f* (-/-en) dawdling; negligence; '**2n** *v/i.* (ge-) **1.** (*sein*) stroll, saunter; pub-crawl; **2.** (*h*) dawdle (*on way, at work*), waste time; '**~streik** *m* go-slow (strike), *Am.* slowdown; '**~zug** *m* slow train, *Am.* way train.

Bummler ['bumlər] *m* (-s/-) saunterer, stroller; loafer, *Am.* F *a.* bum; dawdler.

Bund [bunt] **1.** *m* (-[e]s/-e) *pol.* union, federation, confederacy; (waist-, neck-, wrist)band; **2.** *n* (-[e]s/-e) bundle (*of faggots*); bundle, truss (*of hay or straw*); bunch (*of radishes, etc.*).

Bündel ['byndəl] *n* (-s/-) bundle, bunch; '**2n** *v/t.* (ge-, *h*) make into a bundle, bundle up.

Bundes|bahn ['bundəs-] *f* Federal Railway (*s pl.*); '**~bank** *f* Federal Bank; '**~genosse** *m* ally; '**~gerichtshof** *m* Federal Supreme Court; '**~kanzler** *m* Federal Chancellor; '**~ministerium** *n* Federal Ministry; '**~post** *f* Federal Postal Administration; '**~präsident** *m* President of the Federal Republic; '**~rat** *m* Bundesrat, Upper House of German Parliament; '**~republik** *f* Federal Republic; '**~staat** *m* federal state; confederation; '**~tag** *m* Bundestag, Lower House of German Parliament.

bündig *adj.* ['byndiç] *style, speech:* concise, to the point, terse.

Bündnis ['byntnis] *n* (-ses/-se) alliance; agreement.

Bunker ['buŋkər] *m* (-s/-) ⚒, coal, fuel, *etc.*: bunker; bin; air-raid shelter; ✕ bunker, pill-box; ⊕ (submarine) pen.

bunt *adj.* [bunt] (multi-)colo(u)red, colo(u)rful; motley; *bird, flower, etc.*: variegated; bright, gay; *fig.* mixed, motley; full of variety; '**2druck** *m* colo(u)r-print(ing); '**2stift** *m* colo(u)r pencil, crayon.

Bürde ['byrdə] f (-/-n) burden (a. fig.: für j-n to s.o.), load.

Burg [burk] f (-/-en) castle; fortress; citadel (a. fig.).

Bürge 🏛 ['byrgə] m (-n/-n) guarantor, security, surety, bailsman; sponsor; **'2n** v/i. (ge-, h): für j-n ~ stand guarantee or surety or security for s.o., Am. a. bond s.o.; stand bail for s.o.; vouch or answer for s.o.; sponsor s.o.; für et. ~ stand security for s.th., guarantee s.th.; vouch or answer for s.th.

Bürger ['byrgər] m (-s/-) citizen; townsman; **'~krieg** m civil war.

'bürgerlich adj. civic, civil; ~e Küche plain cooking; Verlust der ~en Ehrenrechte loss of civil rights; Bürgerliches Gesetzbuch German Civil Code; **'2e** m (-n/-n) commoner.

'Bürger|meister m mayor; in Germany: a. burgomaster; in Scotland: provost; **'~recht** n civic rights pl.; citizenship; **'~schaft** f (-/-en) citizens pl.; **'~steig** m pavement, Am. sidewalk; **'~wehr** f militia.

Bürgschaft ['byrkʃaft] f (-/-en) security; bail; guarantee.

Büro [by'ro:] n (-s/-s) office; **~angestellte** m, f (-n/-n) clerk; **~arbeit** f office-work; **~klammer** f paper-clip; **~krat** [~o'kra:t] m (-en/-en) bureaucrat; **~kratie** [~okra'ti:] f (-/-n) bureaucracy; red tape; **2kratisch** adj. [~o'kra:tiʃ] bureaucratic; **~stunden** f/pl. office hours pl.; **~vorsteher** m head or senior clerk.

Bursch [burʃ] m (-en/-en), **~e** ['~ə] m (-n/-n) boy, lad, youth; F chap, Am. a. guy; ein übler ~ a bad lot, F a bad egg.

burschikos adj. [burʃi'ko:s] free and easy; esp. girl: boyish, unaffected, hearty.

Bürste ['byrstə] f (-/-n) brush; **'2n** v/t. (ge-, h) brush.   [shrub.)

Busch [buʃ] m (-es/ᵘe) bush,)

Büschel ['byʃəl] n (-s/-) bunch; tuft, handful (of hair); wisp (of straw or hair).

'Busch|holz n brushwood, underwood; **'2ig** adj. hair, eyebrows, etc.: bushy, shaggy; covered with bushes or scrub, bushy; **'~messer** n bushknife; machete; **'~neger** m maroon; **'~werk** n bushes pl., shrubbery, Am. a. brush.

Busen ['bu:zən] m (-s/-) bosom, breast (esp. of woman); fig. bosom, heart; geog. bay, gulf; **'~freund** m bosom friend.

Bussard orn. ['busart] m (-[e]s/-e) buzzard.

Buße ['bu:sə] f (-/-n) atonement (for sins), penance; repentance; satisfaction; fine; ~ tun do penance.

büßen ['by:sən] (ge-, h) 1. v/t. expiate, atone for (sin, crime); er mußte es mit s-m Leben ~ he paid for it with his life; das sollst du mir ~! you'll pay for that!; 2. v/i. atone, pay (für for).

'Büßer m (-s/-) penitent.

'buß|fertig adj. penitent, repentant, contrite; **'2fertigkeit** f (-/no pl.) repentance; contrition; **'2tag** m day of repentance; Buß- und Bettag day of prayer and repentance.

Büste ['bystə] f (-/-n) bust; **'~nhalter** m (-s/-) brassière, F bra.

Büttenpapier ['bytən-] n handmade paper.

Butter ['butər] f (-/no pl.) butter; **'~blume** ♀ f buttercup; **'~brot** n (slice or piece of) bread and butter; F: für ein ~ for a song; **'~brotpapier** n greaseproof paper; **'~dose** f butter-dish; **'~faß** n butter-churn; **'~milch** f buttermilk; **'2n** v/i. (ge-, h) churn.

C

Café [ka'fe:] n (-s/-s) café, coffee-house.

Cape [ke:p] n (-s/-s) cape.

Cell|ist ♩ [tʃe'list] m (-en/-en) violoncellist, (')cellist; **~o** ♩ ['~o] n (-s/-s, Celli) violoncello, (')cello.

Celsius ['tsɛlzius]: 5 Grad ~ (abbr. 5°C) five degrees centigrade.

Chaiselongue [ʃɛz(ə)'lõ:] f (-/-n, -s) chaise longue, lounge, couch.

Champagner [ʃam'panjər] m (-s/-) champagne.

Champignon

Champignon ♣ [ʃampinjõ] *m* (-s/-s) champignon, (common) mushroom.

Chance ['ʃãːs(ə)] *f* (-/-n) chance; *keine* ~ *haben* to stand a chance; *sich eine* ~ *entgehen lassen* miss a chance *or* an opportunity; *die* ~*n sind gleich* the chances *or* odds are even.

Chaos ['kaːɔs] *n* (-/no *pl.*) chaos.

Charakter [ka'raktər] *m* (-s/-e) character; nature; ~*bild* *n* character (sketch); ~**darsteller** *thea.* *m* character actor; ~**fehler** *m* fault in *s.o.'s* character; 2*fest* *adj.* of firm *or* strong character; 2i'**sieren** *v/t.* (no -ge-, *h*) characterize, describe (*als acc.* as); ~i'**sierung** *f* (-/-en), ~**istik** [~'ristik] *f* (-/-en) characterization; 2**istisch** *adj.* [~'ristiʃ] characteristic *or* typical (*für of*); 2**los** *adj.* characterless, without (strength of) character, spineless; ~**rolle** *thea.* *f* character role; ~**zug** *m* characteristic, feature, trait.

charm|ant *adj.* [ʃar'mant] charming, winning; 2**e** [ʃarm] *m* (-s/no *pl.*) charm, grace.

Chassis [ʃa'siː] *n* (-/-) *mot.*, *radio*: frame, chassis.

Chauffeur [ʃɔ'føːr] *m* (-s/-e) chauffeur, driver.

Chaussee [ʃo'seː] *f* (-/-n) highway, (high) road.

Chauvinismus [ʃovi'nismus] *m* (-/ no *pl.*) jingoism; chauvinism.

Chef [ʃef] *m* (-s/-s) head, chief; † principal, 7 boss; senior partner.

Chem|ie [çe'miː] *f* (-/no *pl.*) chemistry; ~**iefaser** *f* chemical fib|re, *Am.* -er; ~**ikalien** [~i'kaːljən] *f/pl.* chemicals *pl.*; ~**iker** ['çeːmikər] *m* (-s/-) (analytical) chemist; 2**isch** *adj.* ['çeːmiʃ] chemical.

Chiffr|e ['ʃifər] *f* (-/-n) number; cipher; *in advertisement:* box number; 2**ieren** [ʃi'friːrən] *v/t.* (no -ge-, *h*) cipher, code (*message, etc.*); write in code *or* cipher.

Chines|e [çi'neːzə] *m* (-n/-n) Chinese, *contp.* Chinaman; 2**isch** *adj.* Chinese.

Chinin [çi'niːn] *n* (-s/no *pl.*) quinine.

Chirurg [çi'rurk] *m* (-en/-en) surgeon; ~**ie** [~'giː] *f* (-/-en) surgery; 2**isch** *adj.* [~giʃ] surgical.

Chlor ♣ [kloːr] *n* (-s/no *pl.*) chlo-

rine; 2**en** *v/t.* (ge-, *h*) chlorinate (*water*); ~**kalk** ♣ *m* chloride of lime.

Chloroform ♣ [kloro'fɔrm] *n* (-/no *pl.*) chloroform; 2**ieren** ♣ [~'miː-rən] *v/t.* (no -ge-, *h*) chloroform.

Cholera ♣ ['koːləra] *f* (-/no *pl.*) cholera.

cholerisch *adj.* [ko'leːriʃ] choleric, irascible.

Chor [koːr] *m* **1.** △ *a.* *n* (-[e]s/-e, ⁀e) chancel, choir; (organ-)loft; **2.** (-[e]s/⁀e) *in drama:* chorus; *singers:* choir, chorus; *piece of music:* chorus; △ *a.* (-[e]s/⁀e) choral(e); hymn; ~**al** [ko'raːl] *m* (-s/⁀e) choral(e); hymn; ~'**gesang** *m* choral singing, chorus; ~'**sänger** *m* member of a choir; chorister.

Christ [krist] *m* (-en/-en) Christian; ~**baum** *m* Christmas-tree; ~**en-heit** *f* (-/no *pl.*): *die* ~ Christendom; ~**entum** *n* (-s/no *pl.*) Christianity; ~**kind** *n* (-[e]s/no *pl.*) Christ-child, Infant Jesus; 2**lich** *adj.* Christian.

Chrom ♣ [kroːm] *n* (-s/no *pl.*) metal: chromium; *pigment:* chrome.

chromatisch ♪, *opt.* *adj.* [kro'maː-tiʃ] chromatic. [icle.]

Chronik ['kroːnik] *f* (-/-en) chron-}

chronisch *adj.* ['kroːniʃ] *disease:* chronic (*a. fig.*).

Chronist [kro'nist] *m* (-en/-en) chronicler.

chronologisch *adj.* [krono'loːgiʃ] chronological. [mately.]

circa *adv.* ['tsirka] about, approxi-}

Clique ['kliːkə] *f* (-/-n) clique, set, group, coterie; ~**nwirtschaft** *f* (-/no *pl.*) cliquism.

Conférencier [kõferã'sjeː] *m* (-s/-s) compère, *Am.* master of ceremonies.

Couch [kautʃ] *f* (-/-es) couch.

Coupé [ku'peː] *n* (-s/-s) *mot.* coupé; ⅋ compartment.

Couplet [ku'pleː] *n* (-s/-s) comic *or* music-hall song.

Coupon [ku'põː] *m* (-s/-s) coupon; dividend-warrant; counterfoil.

Courtage † [kur'taːʒə] *f* (-/-n) brokerage.

Cousin [ku'zɛ̃] *m* (-s/-s), ~**e** [~iːnə] *f* (-/-n) cousin.

Creme [krɛːm, kreːm] *f* (-/-s) cream (*a. fig.: only sg.*).

Cut [kœt, kat] *m* (-s/-s), ~**away** ['kœtəveː, 'katəveː] *m* (-s/-s) cutaway (coat), morning coat.

D

da [daː] **1.** *adv. space:* there; ~ **wo** where; here and there; ~ **bin ich** here I am; ~ **haben wir's!** there we are!; **von ~ an** from there; *time:* ~ **erst** only then, not till then; **von ~ an** from that time (on), since then; **hier und ~** now and then *or* again; **2.** *cj. time:* as, when, while; **nun, ~ du es einmal gesagt hast** now (that) you have mentioned it; *causal:* as, since, because; ~ **ich krank war, konnte ich nicht kommen** as *or* since I was ill I couldn't come.

dabei *adv.* [daˈbaɪ, *when emphatic:* ˈdaːbaɪ] near (at hand), by; about, going (**zu** *inf.* to *inf.*), on the point (of *ger.*); besides; nevertheless, yet, for all that; **was ist schon ~?** what does it matter?; **lassen wir es ~** let's leave it at that; ~ **bleiben** stick to one's point, persist in it.

daˈbeiǀbleiben *v/i.* (*irr. bleiben, sep., -ge-, sein*) stay with it *or* them; **~sein** *v/i.* (*irr. sein, sep., -ge-, sein*) be present *or* there; **~stehen** *v/i.* (*irr. stehen, sep., -ge-, h*) stand by *or* near.

'dableiben *v/i.* (*irr. bleiben, sep., -ge-, sein*) stay, remain.

da capo *adv.* [daˈkaːpo] *at opera, etc.:* encore.

Dach [dax] *n* (-[e]s/⸚er) roof; *fig.* shelter; **'~antenne** *f* roof aerial; **'~decker** *m* (-s/-) roofer; tiler; slater; **'~fenster** *n* skylight; dormer window; **'~garten** *m* roof-garden; **'~gesellschaft** † *f* holding company; **'~kammer** *f* attic, garret; **'~pappe** *f* roofing felt; **'~rinne** *f* gutter, eaves *pl.*

dachte [ˈdaxtə] *pret.* of **denken**.

Dachs *zo.* [daks] *m* (-es/-e) badger; **'~bau** *m* (-[e]s/-e) badger's earth.

'Dachǀsparren *m* rafter; **'~stube** *f* attic, garret; **'~stuhl** *m* roof framework; **'~ziegel** *m* (roofing) tile.

dadurch [daˈdʊrç, *when emphatic:* ˈdaːdʊrç] **1.** *adv.* for this reason, in this manner *or* way, thus; by it *or* that; **2.** *cj.:* ~, **daß** owing to (the fact that), because; by *ger.*

dafür [daˈfyːr, *when emphatic:* ˈdaːfyːr] for it *or* that; instead (of it); in return (for it), in exchange; ~ **sein** be in favo(u)r of it; ~ **sein zu**

inf. be for *ger.*, be in favo(u)r of *ger.*; **er kann nichts ~** it is not his fault; ~ **sorgen, daß** see to it that.

Daˈfürhalten *n* (-s/*no pl.*): **nach meinem ~** in my opinion.

dagegen [daˈgeːgən, *when emphatic:* ˈdaːgeːgən] **1.** *adv.* against it *or* that; in comparison with it, compared to it; ~ **sein** be against it, be opposed to it; **ich habe nichts ~** I have no objection (to it); **2.** *cj.* on the other hand, however.

daheim *adv.* [daˈhaɪm] at home.

daher [daˈheːr, *when emphatic:* ˈdaːheːr] **1.** *adv.* from there; *prefixed to verbs of motion:* along; *fig.* from this, hence; ~ **kam es, daß** thus it happened that; **2.** *cj.* therefore; that is (the reason) why.

dahin *adv.* [daˈhin, *when emphatic:* ˈdaːhin] there, to that place; gone, past; *prefixed to verbs of motion:* along; **j-n ~ bringen, daß** induce s.o. to *inf.*; **m-e Meinung geht ~, daß** my opinion is that.

daˈhingestellt *adj.:* **es ~ sein lassen** (**,ob**) leave it undecided (whether).

dahinter *adv.* [daˈhintər, *when emphatic:* ˈdaːhintər] behind it *or* that, at the back of it; **es steckt nichts ~** there is nothing in it.

daˈhinterkommen *v/i.* (*irr. kommen, sep., -ge-, sein*) find out about it.

damalig *adj.* [ˈdaːmaːliç] then, of that time; **der ~e Besitzer** the then owner; **~s** *adv.* then, at that time.

Damast [daˈmast] *m* (-es/-e) damask.

Dame [ˈdaːmə] *f* (-/-n) lady; *dancing, etc.:* partner; *cards, chess:* queen; *s.* **Damespiel;** ~ *n* draught-board, *Am.* checkerboard.

'Damenǀbinde *f* (woman's) sanitary towel, *Am.* sanitary napkin; **'~brett** *n* tennis: women's doubles *pl.*; **'~einzel** *n* tennis: women's singles *pl.*; **'2haft** *adj.* ladylike; **'~konfektion** *f* ladies' ready-made clothes *pl.*; **'~mannschaft** *f sports:* women's team; **'~schneider** *m* ladies' tailor, dressmaker.

'Damespiel *n* (game of) draughts *pl.*, *Am.* (game of) checkers *pl.*

damit **1.** *adv.* [daˈmit, *when emphatic:* ˈdaːmit] with it *or* that, therewith, herewith; by it or that; was will er ~ sagen? what does he mean by it?; wie steht es ~? how about it?; ~ einverstanden sein agree to it; **2.** cj. (in order) that, in order to inf.; so (that); ~ nicht lest, (so as) to avoid that; for fear that (all with subjunctive). [asinine.]

dämlich F adj. ['dɛ:mlɪç] silly,

Damm [dam] m (-[e]s/⸚e) dam; dike, dyke; 🚉 embankment; embankment, Am. levee (of river); roadway; fig. barrier; '**~bruch** m bursting of a dam or dike.

dämmer|ig adj. ['dɛmərɪç] dusky; '**2licht** n twilight; '**~n** v/i. (ge-, h) dawn (a. fig.: F j-m on s.o.); grow dark or dusky; '**2ung** f (-/-en) twilight, dusk; in the morning: dawn.

Dämon ['dɛ:mɔn] m (-s/-en) demon; **2isch** adj. [dɛ'mo:nɪʃ] demoniac(al).

Dampf [dampf] m (-[e]s/⸚e) steam; vapo(u)r; '**~bad** n vapo(u)r-bath; '**~boot** n steamboat; '**2en** v/i. (ge-, h) steam.

dämpfen ['dɛmpfən] v/t. (ge-, h) deaden (pain, noise, force of blow); muffle (bell, drum, oar); damp (sound, oscillation, fig. enthusiasm); ♩ mute (stringed instrument); soften (colour, light); attenuate (wave); steam (cloth, food); stew (meat, fruit); fig. suppress, curb (emotion).

'**Dampfer** m (-s/-) steamer, steamship.

'**Dämpfer** m (-s/-) damper (a. ♩ of piano); ♩ mute (for violin, etc.).

'**Dampf|heizung** f steam-heating; '**~kessel** m (steam-)boiler; '**~maschine** f steam-engine; '**~schiff** n steamer, steamship; '**~walze** f steam-roller.

danach adv. [da'na:x, when emphatic: 'da'na:x] after it or that; afterwards; subsequently; accordingly; ich fragte ihn ~ I asked him about it; iro. er sieht ganz ~ aus he looks very much like it.

Däne ['dɛ:nə] m (-n/-n) Dane.

daneben adv. [da'ne:bən, when emphatic: 'da:ne:bən] next to it or that, beside it or that; besides, moreover; beside the mark.

da'nebengehen F v/i. (irr. gehen, sep., -ge-, sein) bullet, etc.: miss the target or mark; remark, etc.: miss one's effect, F misfire.

daniederliegen [da'ni:dər-] v/i. (irr. liegen, sep., -ge-, h) be laid up (an dat. with); trade: be depressed.

dänisch adj. ['dɛ:nɪʃ] Danish.

Dank [daŋk] **1.** m (-[e]s/no pl.) thanks pl., gratitude; reward; j-m ~ sagen thank s.o.; Gott sei ~! thank God!; **2.** ♀ prp. (dat.) owing or thanks to; '**2bar** adj. thankful, grateful (j-m to s.o.; für for); profitable; '**~barkeit** f (-/no pl.) gratitude; '**2en** v/i. (ge-, h) thank (j-m für et. s.o. for s.th.); danke (schön)! thank you (very much)!; danke thank you; nein, danke no, thank you; nichts zu ~ don't mention it; '**2enswert** adj. thing: one can be grateful for; efforts, etc.: kind; task, etc.: rewarding, worth-while; '**~gebet** n thanksgiving (prayer); '**~schreiben** n letter of thanks.

dann adv. [dan] then; ~ und wann (every) now and then.

daran adv. [da'ran, when emphatic: 'da:ran] at (or by, in, on, to) it or that; sich ~ festhalten hold on tight to it; ~ festhalten stick to it; nahe ~ sein zu inf. be on the point or verge of per.

da'rangehen v/i. (irr. gehen, sep., -ge-, sein) set to work; set about ger.

darauf adv. [da'rauf, when emphatic: 'da:rauf] space: on (top of) it or that; time: thereupon, after it or that; am Tage ~ the day after, the next or following day; zwei Jahre ~ two years later; ~ kommt es an that's what matters; **~hin** adv. [darauf'hin, when emphatic: 'da:rauf'hin] thereupon.

daraus adv. [da'raus, when emphatic: 'da:raus] out of it or that, from it or that; ~ folgt hence it follows; was ist ~ geworden? what has become of it?; ich mache mir nichts ~ I don't care or mind (about it).

darben ['darbən] v/i. (ge-, h) suffer want; starve.

darbiet|en ['da:r-] v/t. (irr. bieten, sep., -ge-, h) offer, present; perform; '**2ung** f (-/-en) thea., etc.: performance.

'**darbringen** v/t. (irr. bringen, sep., -ge-, h) offer; make (sacrifice).

darein adv. [da'raɪn, when em-

debattieren

phatic: ['dɑːraın] into it *or* that, therein.

da'rein|finden *v/refl.* (*irr.* finden, *sep.*, -ge-, h) put up with it; **~mischen** *v/refl.* (*sep.*, -ge-, h) interfere (with it); **~reden** *v/i.* (*sep.*, -ge-, h) interrupt; *fig.* interfere.

darin *adv.* [da'rin, *when emphatic*: 'dɑːrin] in it *or* that; therein; es war nichts ~ there was nothing in it *or* them.

darleg|en ['dɑːr-] *v/t.* (*sep.*, -ge-, h) lay open, expose, disclose; show; explain; demonstrate; point out; **'2ung** *f* (-/-en) exposition; explanation; statement.

Darlehen ['dɑːrleːən] *n* (-s/-) loan.

Darm [darm] *m* (-[e]s/⁼e) gut, *anat.* intestine; (sausage-)skin; *Därme pl.* intestines *pl.*, bowels *pl.*

'darstell|en *v/t.* (*sep.*, -ge-, h) represent; show, depict; delineate; describe; *actor*: interpret (*character, part*), represent (*character*); *graphic arts*: graph, plot (*curve, etc.*); '2**er** *thea.* *m* (-s/-) interpreter (*of a part*); *actor*; '2**ung** *f* representation; *thea.* performance.

'dartun *v/t.* (*irr.* tun, *sep.*, -ge-, h) prove; demonstrate; set forth.

darüber *adv.* [da'ryːbər, *when emphatic*: 'dɑːryːbər] over it *or* that; across it; in the meantime; ~ werden Jahre vergehen it will take years; wir sind ~ hinweg we got over it; ein Buch ~ schreiben write a book about it.

darum *adv.* [da'rum, *when emphatic*: 'dɑːrum] **1.** *adv.* around it *or* that; er kümmert sich nicht ~ he does not care; es handelt sich ~ zu inf. the point is to *inf.*; **2.** *cj.* therefore, for that reason; ~ ist er nicht gekommen that's (the reason) why he hasn't come.

darunter *adv.* [da'runtər, *when emphatic*: 'dɑːruntər] under it *or* that; beneath it; among them; less; zwei Jahre und ~ two years and under; was verstehst du ~? what do you understand by it?

das [das] *s. der.*

dasein ['dɑː-] **1.** *v/i.* (*irr.* sein, *sep.*, -ge-, sein) be there *or* present; exist; **2.** 2 *n* (-s/*no pl.*) existence, life; being.

daß *cj.* [das] that; ~ nicht less; es sei denn, ~ unless; ohne ~ with-out ger.; nicht ~ ich wüßte not that I know of.

'dastehen *v/i.* (*irr.* stehen, *sep.*, -ge-, h) stand (there).

Daten ['dɑːtən] *pl.* data *pl.* (*a.* ⊕), facts *pl.*; particulars *pl.*; '~verarbeitung *f* (-/-en) data processing.

datieren [da'tiːrən] *v/t.* and *v/i.* (*no* -ge-, h) date.   [(case).)

Dativ *gr.* ['dɑːtiːf] *m* (-s/-e) dative)

Dattel ['datəl] *f* (-/-n) date.

Datum ['dɑːtum] *n* (-s/Daten) date.

Dauer ['dauər] *f* (-/*no pl.*) length, duration; continuance; auf die ~ in the long run; für die ~ von for a period *or* term of; von ~ sein last well; '2**haft** *adj.* peace, *etc.*: lasting; *material, etc.*: durable; *colour, dye*: fast; '~**karte** *f* season ticket, *Am.* commutation ticket; '~**lauf** *m* jog-trot; endurance-run; '2**n** *v/i.* (ge-, h) continue, last; take (*time*); '~**welle** *f* permanent wave, F perm.

Daumen ['daumən] *m* (-s/-) thumb; j-m den ~ halten keep one's fingers crossed (for s.o.); '~**abdruck** *m* (-[e]s/⁼e) thumb-print.

Daune ['daunə] *f* (-/-n): ~(*n pl.*) down; '~**ndecke** *f* eiderdown (quilt).

davon *adv.* [da'fɔn, *when emphatic*: 'dɑːfɔn] of it *or* that; thereof; from it *or* that; off, away; was habe ich ~? what do I get from it?; das kommt ~! it serves you right!

da'von|kommen *v/i.* (*irr.* kommen, *sep.*, -ge-, sein) escape, get off; **~laufen** *v/i.* (*irr.* laufen, *sep.*, -ge-, sein) run away.

davor *adv.* [da'foːr, *when emphatic*: 'dɑːfoːr] *space*: before it *or* that, in front of it *or* that; er fürchtet sich ~ he is afraid of it.

dazu *adv.* [da'tsuː, *when emphatic*: 'dɑːtsuː] to it *or* that; for it *or* that; for that purpose; in addition to that; noch ~ at that; ~ gehört Zeit it requires time.

da'zu|gehörig *adj.* belonging to it; **~kommen** *v/i.* (*irr.* kommen, *sep.*, -ge-, sein) appear (on the scene); find time.

dazwischen *adv.* [da'tsvifən] between (them), in between; **~kommen** *v/i.* (*irr.* kommen, *sep.*, -ge-, sein) thing: intervene, happen.

Debatt|e [de'batə] *f* (-/-n) debate; **2ieren** [~'tiːrən] (*no* -ge-, h) **1.** *v/t.*

discuss; debate; **2.** *v/i.* debate (*über acc.* on).

Debüt [de'by:] *n* (-s/-s) first appearance, début.

dechiffrieren [deʃi'fri:rən] *v/t.* (*no -ge-, h*) decipher, decode.

Deck ⚓ [dek] *n* (-[e]s/-s, ⚓-e) deck; **'~adresse** *f* cover (address); **'~bett** *n* feather bed.

Decke ['dekə] *f* (-/-n) cover(ing); blanket; (travel[l]ing) rug; ceiling; **'~l** *m* (-s/-) lid, cover (*of box or pot, etc.*); lid (*of piano*); (book-)cover; **'~n** (ge-, h) **1.** *v/t.* cover; den Tisch ~ lay the table; **2.** *v/i.* paint: cover.

'Deck|mantel *m* cloak, mask, disguise; **'~name** *m* assumed name, pseudonym; **'~ung** *f* (-/-en) cover; security.

defekt [de'fekt] **1.** *adj.* defective, faulty; **2.** ⚥ *m* (-[e]s/-e) defect, fault.

defin|ieren [defi'ni:rən] *v/t.* (*no -ge-, h*) define; **⚥ition** [ˌi'tsjo:n] *f* (-/-en) definition; **~itiv** *adj.* [ˌi'ti:f] definite; definitive.

Defizit ✝ ['de:fitsit] *n* (-s/-e) deficit, deficiency.

Degen ['de:gən] *m* (-s/-) sword; *fencing*: épée.

degradieren [degra'di:rən] *v/t.* (*no -ge-, h*) degrade, *Am. a.* demote.

dehn|bar *adj.* [de:nba:r] extensible, elastic; *metal*: ductile; *notion, etc.*: vague; **'~en** *v/t.* (ge-, h) extend; stretch; **'~ung** *f* (-/-en) extension; stretch(ing).

Deich [daiç] *m* (-[e]s/-e) dike, dyke.

Deichsel ['daiksəl] *f* (-/-n) pole, shaft.

dein *poss. pron.* [dain] your; der (die, das) ~e yours; ich bin ~ I am yours; die Deinen pl. your family; **~er·seits** *adv.* ['~ər'zaits] for or on your part; **'~es'gleichen** *pron.* your like, your (own) kind, F the like(s) of you.

Dekan *eccl. and univ.* [de'ka:n] *m* (-s/-e) dean.

Deklam|ation [deklama'tsjo:n] *f* (-/-en) declamation; reciting; **⚥ieren** [ˌ'mi:rən] *v/t. and v/i.* (*no -ge-, h*) recite; declaim.

Deklin|ation *gr.* [deklina'tsjo:n] *f* (-/-en) declension; **⚥ieren** *gr.* [ˌ'ni:rən] *v/t.* (*no -ge-, h*) decline.

Dekor|ateur [dekora'tø:r] *m* (-s/-e) decorator; window-dresser; *thea.*

scene-painter; **~ation** [ˌ'tsjo:n] *f* (-/-en) decoration; (window-)dressing; *thea.* scenery; **⚥ieren** [ˌ'ri:rən] *v/t.* (*no -ge-, h*) decorate; dress (*window*).

Dekret [de'kre:t] *n* (-[e]s/-e) decree.

delikat *adj.* [deli'ka:t] delicate (*a. fig.*); delicious; *fig.* ticklish; **⚥esse** [ˌa'tesə] *f* (-/-n) delicacy; dainty.

Delphin *zo.* [dɛl'fi:n] *m* (-s/-e) dolphin.

Dement|i [de'menti] *n* (-s/-s) (formal) denial; **⚥ieren** [ˌ'ti:rən] *v/t.* (*no -ge-, h*) deny, give a (formal) denial of.

'dem|entsprechend *adv.*, **'~gemäß** *adv.* correspondingly, accordingly; **'~nach** *adv.* therefore, hence; accordingly; **'~nächst** *adv.* soon, shortly, before long.

demobili'sier|en (*no -ge-, h*) **1.** *v/t.* demobilize; disarm; **2.** *v/i.* disarm; **⚥ung** *f* (-/-en) demobilization.

Demokrat [demo'kra:t] *m* (-en/-en) democrat; **~ie** [ˌa'ti:] *f* (-/-n) democracy; **⚥isch** *adj.* [ˌ'kra:tiʃ] democratic.

demolieren [demo'li:rən] *v/t.* (*no -ge-, h*) demolish.

Demonstr|ation [demonstra'tsjo:n] *f* (-/-en) demonstration; **⚥ieren** [ˌ'stri:rən] *v/t. and v/i.* (*no -ge-, h*) demonstrate.

Demont|age [demɔn'ta:ʒə] *f* (-/-n) disassembly; dismantling; **⚥ieren** [ˌ'ti:rən] *v/t.* (*no -ge-, h*) disassemble; dismantle.

Demut ['de:mu:t] *f* (-/no pl.) humility, humbleness.

demütig *adj.* ['de:my:tiç] humble; **~en** ['~gən] *v/t.* (ge-, h) humble, humiliate.

denk|bar ['dɛŋkba:r] **1.** *adj.* conceivable; thinkable, imaginable; **2.** *adv.*: ~ einfach most simple; **'~en** (*irr.*, ge-, h) **1.** *v/i.* think; ~ an (*acc.*) think of; remember; ~ über (*acc.*) think about; j-m zu ~ geben set s.o. thinking; **2.** *v/t.* think; sich et. ~ imagine or fancy s.th.; das habe ich mir gedacht I thought as much; **'⚥mal** *n* monument; memorial; **'⚥schrift** *f* memorandum; memoir; **'⚥stein** *m* memorial stone; **'~würdig** *adj.* memorable; **'⚥zettel** *fig.* m lesson.

denn [dɛn] **1.** *cj.* for; mehr ~ je more than ever; **2.** *adv.* then; es sei ~, *daß* unless, except; *wieso* ~? how so.

dennoch *cj.* ['dennɔx] yet, still, nevertheless; though.

Denunz|iant [denun'tsjant] *m* (-en/-en) informer; **~iation** [~'tsjoːn] *f* (-/-en) denunciation; **2ieren** [~'tsiːrən] *v/t.* (no -ge-, h) inform against, denounce.

Depesche [de'pɛʃə] *f* (-/-n) dispatch; telegram, F wire; wireless.

deponieren [depo'niːrən] *v/t.* (no -ge-, h) deposit.

Depositen [depo'ziːtən] *pl.* deposits *pl.*; **~bank** *f* deposit bank.

der [deːr], **die** [diː], **das** [das] **1.** *art.* the; **2.** *dem. pron.* that, this; he, she, it; *die pl.* these, those, they, them; **3.** *rel. pron.* who, which, that.

'der'artig *adj.* such, of such a kind, of this or that kind.

derb *adj.* [dɛrp] *cloth*: coarse, rough; *shoes*, *etc.*: stout, strong; *ore*, *etc.*: massive; *p.*: sturdy; rough; *food*: coarse; *p.*, *manners*: rough, coarse; *way of speaking*: blunt, unrefined; *joke*: crude; *humour*: broad.

der'gleichen *adj.* such, of that kind; *used as a noun*: the like, such a thing; *und* ~ and the like; *nichts* ~ nothing of the kind.

der- ['deːrjeːniɡə], **'die-**, **'dasjenige** *dem. pron.* he who, she who, that which; *diejenigen pl.* those who, those which.

der- [deːr'zɛlbə], **die-**, **das'selbe** *dem. pron.* the same; he, she, it.

Desert|eur [dezɛr'tøːr] *m* (-s/-e) deserter; **2ieren** [~'tiːrən] *v/i.* (no -ge-, sein) desert.

desgleichen [des'ɡlaɪçən] **1.** *dem. pron.* such a thing; **2.** *cj.* likewise.

deshalb ['dɛshalp] **1.** *cj.* for this or that reason; therefore; **2.** *adv.*: *ich tat es nur* ~, *weil* I did it only because.   [(no -ge-, h) disinfect.]

desinfizieren [dɛsʔinfi'tsiːrən] *v/t.*

Despot [dɛs'poːt] *m* (-en/-en) despot; **2isch** *adj.* despotic.

destillieren [dɛsti'liːrən] *v/t.* (no -ge-, h) distil.

desto *adv.* ['dɛsto] (all, so much) the; ~ *besser* all the better; ~ *erstaunter* (all) the more astonished.

deswegen *cj. and adv.* ['dɛs've:ɡən] *s.* deshalb.

Detail [de'taɪ] *n* (-s/-s) detail.

Detektiv [detɛk'tiːf] *m* (-s/-e) detective.

deuten ['dɔʏtən] (ge-, h) **1.** *v/t.* interpret; read (*stars*, *dream*, *etc.*); **2.** *v/i.*: ~ *auf* (*acc.*) point at.

'deutlich *adj.* clear, distinct, plain.

deutsch *adj.* [dɔʏtʃ] German; **'2e** *m*, *f* (-n/-n) German.

'Deutung *f* (-/-en) interpretation, explanation.

Devise [de'viːzə] *f* (-/-n) motto; ~*n pl.* † foreign exchange *or* currency.

Dezember [de'tsɛmbər] *m* (-[s]/-) December.

dezent *adj.* [de'tsɛnt] *attire*, *etc.*: decent, modest; *literature*, *etc.*: decent; *behaviour*: decent, proper; *music*, *colour*: soft, restrained; *lighting*, *etc.*: subdued.

Dezernat [detsɛr'naːt] *n* (-[e]s/-e) (administrative) department.

dezimal *adj.* [detsi'maːl] decimal; **2bruch** *m* decimal fraction; **2stelle** *f* decimal place.

dezi'mieren *v/t.* (no -ge-, h) decimate; *fig. a.* reduce (drastically).

Diadem [dia'deːm] *n* (-s/-e) diadem.

Diagnose [dia'ɡnoːzə] *f* (-/-n) diagnosis.

diagonal *adj.* [diaɡo'naːl] diagonal; **2e** *f* (-/-n) diagonal.

Dialekt [dia'lɛkt] *m* (-[e]s/-e) dialect; **2isch** *adj.* dialectal.

Dialog [dia'loːk] *m* (-[e]s/-e) dialogue, *Am. a.* dialog.

Diamant [dia'mant] *m* (-en/-en) diamond.

Diät [di'ɛːt] *f* (-/no pl.) diet; *diät leben* live on a diet.

dich *pers. pron.* [diç] you; ~ (*selbst*) yourself.

dicht [diçt] **1.** *adj.* *fog*, *rain*, *etc.*: dense; *fog*, *forest*, *hair*: thick; *eyebrows*: bushy, thick; *crowd*: thick, dense; *shoe*, *etc.*: (water)tight; **2.** *adv.*: ~ *an* (*dat.*) *or* bei close to.

'dichten¹ *v/t.* (ge-, h) make tight.

'dicht|en² (ge-, h) **1.** *v/t.* compose, write; **2.** *v/i.* compose *or* write poetry; **'2er** *m* (-s/-) poet; author; **'~erisch** *adj.* poetic(al); **'2kunst** *f* poetry.

'Dichtung¹ ⊕ *f* (-/-en) seal(ing).

'Dichtung² *f* (-/-en) poetry; fiction; poem, poetic work.

dick *adj.* [dik] *wall*, *material*, *etc.*: thick; *book*: thick, bulky; *p.* fat, stout; **'2e** *f* (-/-n) thickness; bulkiness; *p.* fatness, stoutness; **'~fellig** *adj.* *p.* thick-skinned; **'~flüssig** *adj.*

thick; viscid, viscous, syrupy; **Qicht** ['ˌiçt] *n* (-[e]s/-e) thicket; **Qkopf** *m* stubborn person, F pig-headed person; **Qleibig** *adj.* ['ˌlaɪbiç] corpulent; *fig.* bulky.

die [di:] *s.* der.

Dieb [di:p] *m* (-[e]s/-e) thief, *Am.* F *a.* crook; **Qerei** [di:bəˈraɪ] *f* (-/-en) thieving, thievery.

Diebes|bande ['di:bəs-] *f* band of thieves; **Qgut** *n* stolen goods *pl.*

dieb|isch *adj.* ['di:biʃ] thievish; *fig.* malicious; **Qstahl** ['di:p-] *m* (-[e]s/ ᵁe) theft, ᵗᵗ *mst* larceny.

Diele ['di:lə] *f* (-/-n) board, plank, hall, *Am. a.* hallway.

dienen ['di:nən] *v/i.* (ge-, h) serve (*j-m s.o.*); *als* as; *zu* for; *dazu, zu inf.* to *inf.*); *womit kann ich* ᴧ? what can I do for you?

'Diener *m* (-s/-) (man-, domestic) servant; *fig.* bow (*vor dat.* to); **ᴧin** *f* (-/-nen) (woman-)servant; maid; **ᴧschaft** *f* (-/-en) servants *pl.*

'dienlich *adj.* useful, convenient; expedient, suitable.

Dienst [di:nst] *m* (-es/-e) service; duty; employment; ᴧ *haben* be on duty; *im* (*außer*) ᴧ on (off) duty.

Dienstag ['di:nsta:k] *m* (-[e]s/-e) Tuesday.

'Dienst|alter *n* seniority, length of service; **Qbar** *adj.* subject (*j-m* to s.o.); subservient (to); **ᴧbote** *m* domestic (servant), *Am.* help; **Qeifrig** *adj.* (over-)eager (in one's duty); **Qfrei** *adj.* off duty; **ᴧer Tag** day off; **ᴧherr** *m* master; employer; **ᴧleistung** *f* service; **Qlich** *adj.* official; **ᴧmädchen** *n* maid, *Am.* help; **ᴧmann** *m* (street-)porter; **ᴧstunden** *f/pl.* office hours *pl.*; **Qtauglich** *adj.* fit for service *or* duty; **Qtuend** *adj.* ['ˌtu:ənt] on duty; **Quntauglich** *adj.* unfit for service *or* duty; **ᴧweg** *m* official channels *pl.*; **ᴧwohnung** *f* official residence.

dies [di:s], **ᴧer** ['di:zər], **ᴧe** ['di:zə], **ᴧes** ['di:zəs] *adj. and dem. pron.* this; *diese pl.* these; *dieser Tage* one of these days; *used as a noun:* this one; *he,* she, it; *dies pl.* these.

Dieselmotor ['di:zəl-] *m* Diesel engine.

dies|jährig *adj.* ['di:sjɛːriç] of this year, this year's; **ᴧmal** *adv.* this time; for (this) once; **ᴧseits** ['ˌzaɪts]

1. *adv.* on this side; **2.** *prp.* (*gen.*) on this side of.

Dietrich ['di:triç] *m* (-s/-e) skeleton key; picklock.

Differenz [difəˈrɛnts] *f* (-/-en) difference; disagreement.

Diktat [dikˈtaːt] *n* (-[e]s/-e) dictation; *nach* ᴧ at *or* from dictation; **ᴧor** [ˌɔr] *m* (-s/-en) dictator; **Qorisch** *adj.* [ˌaˈtoːriʃ] dictatorial; **ᴧur** [ˌaˈtuːr] *f* (-/-en) dictatorship.

dik|tieren *v/t. and v/i.* (*no* -ge-, h) dictate.

Dilettant [dileˈtant] *m* (-en/-en) dilettante, dabbler; amateur.

Ding [diŋ] *n* (-[e]s/-e) thing; *guter* ᴧe in good spirits; *vor allen* ᴧen first of all, above all.

Diphtherie ⁊ [diftəˈriː] *f* (-/-n) diphtheria.

Diplom [diˈploːm] *n* (-[e]s/-e) diploma, certificate.

Diplomat [diploˈmaːt] *m* (-en/-en) diplomat; diplomatist; **ᴧie** [ˌaˈtiː] *f* (-/*no pl.*) diplomacy; **Qisch** *adj.* [ˌmaˈtiʃ] diplomatic (*a. fig.*).

dir *pers. pron.* [diːr] (to) you.

direkt [diˈrɛkt] **1.** *adj.* direct; **ᴧer** *Wagen* 🚃 through carriage, *Am.* through car; **2.** *adv.* direct(ly); **Qion** [ˌtsjoːn] *f* (-/-en) direction; management; board of directors; **Qor** [diˈrɛktɔr] *m* (-s/-en) director; manager; headmaster, *Am.* principal; **Qorin** [ˌtoːrin] *f* (-/-nen) headmistress, *Am.* principal; **Qrice** [ˌtriːsə)] *f* (-/-n) directress; manageress.

Dirig|ent ♪ [diriˈgɛnt] *m* (-en/-en) conductor; **Qieren** ♪ [ˌˈgiːrən] *v/t. and v/i.* (*no* -ge-, h) conduct.

Dirne ['dirnə] *f* (-/-n) prostitute.

Disharmon|ie ♪ [disharmoˈniː] *f* (-/-n) disharmony, dissonance (*both a. fig.*); **Qisch** *adj.* [ˌˈmoːniʃ] discordant, dissonant.

Diskont ⁊ [disˈkɔnt] *m* (-s/-e) discount; **Qieren** [ˌˈtiːrən] *v/t.* (*no* -ge-, h) discount.

diskret *adj.* [disˈkreːt] discreet; **Qion** [ˌeˈtsjoːn] *f* (-/*no pl.*) discretion.

Disku|ssion [diskuˈsjoːn] *f* (-/-en) discussion, debate; **Q'tieren** (*no* -ge-, h) **1.** *v/t.* discuss, debate; **2.** *v/i.:* ᴧ *über* (*acc.*) have a discussion about, debate (up)on.

dispo|nieren [dispoˈniːrən] *v/i.* (*no*

-ge-, h) make arrangements; plan ahead; dispose (*über acc.* of); **2si|tion** [ˌzi'tsjoːn] f (-/-en) disposition; arrangement; disposal.

Distanz [di'stants] f (-/-en) distance (*a. fig.*); **2ieren** [ˌ'tsiːrən] v/refl. (*no* -ge-, h): sich ~ *von* dis(as)sociate o.s. from.

Distel 💐 ['distəl] f (-/-n) thistle.

Distrikt [di'strikt] m (-[e]s/-e) district; region; area.

Disziplin [distsi'pliːn] f (-/-en) discipline.

Divid|ende ✝ [divi'dɛndə] f (-/-n) dividend; **2ieren** [ˌ'diːrən] v/t. (*no* -ge-, h) divide (*durch* by).

Diwan ['diːvaːn] m (-s/-e) divan.

doch [dɔx] **1.** *cj.* but, though; however, yet; **2.** *adv.* in answer to negative question: yes; *bist du noch nicht fertig? — ~!* aren't you ready yet? — yes, I am; *also ~!* I knew it!, I was right after all!; *komm ~ herein!* do come in!; *nicht ~!* don't!

Docht [dɔxt] m (-[e]s/-e) wick.

Dock ⚓ [dɔk] n (-[e]s/-s) dock.

Dogge *zo.* ['dɔgə] f (-/-n) Great Dane.

Dohle *orn.* ['doːlə] f (-/-n) (jack)daw.

Doktor ['dɔktər] m (-s/-en) doctor.

Dokument [doku'mɛnt] n (-[e]s/-e) document; 🔧 instrument; **~arfilm** [ˌ'taːr-] m documentary (film).

Dolch [dɔlç] m (-[e]s/-e) dagger; poniard; **~stoß** m dagger-thrust.

Dollar ['dɔlar] m (-s/-s) dollar.

dolmetsch|en ['dɔlmɛtʃən] v/i. and v/t. (ge-, h) interpret; **2er** m (-s/-) interpreter.

Dom [doːm] m (-[e]s/-e) cathedral.

Domäne [do'mɛːnə] f (-/-n) domain (*a. fig.*); province.

Domino ['doːmino] (-s/-s) **1.** m domino; **2.** n (game of) dominoes pl.

Donner ['dɔnər] m (-s/-) thunder; **2n** v/i. (ge-, h) thunder (*a. fig.*); **~schlag** m thunderclap; **~stag** m Thursday; **~wetter** n thunderstorm; F fig. telling off; F ~! my word!, by Jove!; F *zum ~!* F confound it!, *sl.* damn it.

Doppel ['dɔpəl] n (-s/-) duplicate; *tennis, etc.:* double, Am. doubles pl.; **~bett** n double bed; **~decker** m (-s/-) ✈ biplane; double-decker (bus); **~ehe** f bigamy; **~gänger** m (-s/-) double; **~punkt**

m colon; **~sinn** m double meaning, ambiguity; **2sinnig** adj. ambiguous, equivocal; **~stecker** ⚡ m two-way adapter; **2t 1.** adj. double; **2.** adv. doubly; twice; **~zentner** m quintal; **2züngig** adj. ['ˌtsyŋiç] two-faced.

Dorf [dɔrf] n (-[e]s/ᵘer) village; **~bewohner** m villager.

Dorn [dɔrn] m **1.** (-[e]s/-en) thorn (*a. fig.*), prickle, spine; *j-m ein ~ im Auge sein* be a thorn in s.o.'s flesh or side; **2.** (-[e]s/-e) tongue (*of buckle*); spike (*of running-shoe, etc.*); ⊕ punch; **2ig** adj. thorny (*a. fig.*).

dörr|en ['dœrən] v/t. (ge-, h) dry; **2fleisch** n dried meat; **2gemüse** n dried vegetables pl.; **2obst** n dried fruit.

Dorsch *ichth.* [dɔrʃ] m (-es/-e) cod(fish).

dort adv. [dɔrt] there; over there; **~her** adv. from there; **~hin** adv. there, to that place; **~ig** adj. there, in *or* of that place.

Dose ['doːzə] f (-/-n) box; tin, Am. can; **~nöffner** ['doːzən'-] m (-s/-) tin-opener, Am. can opener.

Dosis ['doːzis] f (-/Dosen) dose (*a. fig.*).

dotieren [do'tiːrən] v/t. (*no* -ge-, h) endow.

Dotter ['dɔtər] m, n (-s/-) yolk.

Dozent [do'tsɛnt] m (-en/-en) (university) lecturer, Am. assistant professor.

Drache ['draxə] m (-n/-n) dragon; **~n** m (-s/-) kite; *fig.* termagant, shrew, battle-axe.

Dragoner [dra'goːnər] m (-s/-) ✗ dragoon (*a. fig.*).

Draht [draːt] m (-[e]s/ᵘe) wire; **2en** v/t. (ge-, h) telegraph, wire; **~geflecht** n (-[e]s/-e) wire netting; **~hindernis** ✗ n wire entanglement; **2ig** adj. p. wiry; **2los** adj. wireless; **~seilbahn** f funicular (railway); **~stift** m wire tack; **~zieher** F *fig.* m (-s/-) wire-puller.

drall adj. [dral] girl, legs, etc.: plump; *woman:* buxom.

Drama ['draːma] n (-s/Dramen) drama; **~tiker** [dra'maːtikər] m (-s/-) dramatist; **2tisch** adj. [dra'maːtiʃ] dramatic.

dran F adv. [dran] s. daran; *er ist gut (übel) ~* he's well (badly) off; *ich bin ~* it's my turn.

Drang [draŋ] **1.** *m* (-[e]s/⁀⁌e) pressure, rush; *fig.* urge; **2.** ⁌ *pret.* of dringen.

drängen ['drɛŋən] (ge-, h) **1.** *v/t.* press (a. *fig.*), push; *fig.* urge; *creditor:* dun; *sich* ⁀ crowd, throng; **2.** *v/i.* press, be pressing *or* urgent.

drangsalieren [draŋza'liːrən] *v/t.* (no -ge-, h) harass, vex, plague.

drastisch *adj.* ['drastiʃ] drastic.

drauf F *adv.* [drauf] *s.* darauf; ⁀ *und dran* sein *zu inf.* be on the point of ger.; **⁌gänger** ['⁀gɛŋər] *m* (-s/-) dare-devil, *Am. sl.* a. go-getter.

draus F *adv.* [draus] *s.* daraus.

draußen *adv.* ['drausən] outside; out of doors; abroad; out at sea.

drechseln ['drɛksəln] *v/t.* (ge-, h) turn (*wood*, *etc.*); **⁌er** ['⁀slər] *m* (-s/-) turner.

Dreck F [drɛk] *m* (-[e]s/*no pl.*) dirt; mud; filth (a. *fig.*); *fig.* trash; F ⁀ *am Stecken haben* not to have a clean slate; F *das geht dich einen* ⁀ *an* that's none of your business; **⁌ig** *adj.* dirty; filthy.

Dreh|bank ['dreː-] *f* (-/⁀⁌e) (turning-) lathe; **⁌bar** *adj.* revolving, rotating; **⁌bleistift** *m* propelling pencil; **⁌buch** *n* scenario; script; **⁌bühne** *thea. f* revolving stage; **⁌en** *v/t.* (ge-, h) turn; shoot (*film*); roll (*cigarette*); *es dreht sich darum zu inf.* it is a matter of ...; **⁌kreuz** *n* turnstile; **⁌orgel** *f* barrel-organ; **⁌punkt** *m* ⊕ centre of rotation, *Am.* center of rotation, pivot (a. *fig.*); **⁌strom** ⚡ *m* three-phase current; **⁌stuhl** *m* swivel-chair; **⁌tür** *f* revolving door; **⁌ung** *f* (-/-en) turn; rotation.

drei *adj.* [drai] three; **⁌beinig** *adj.* three-legged; **⁌eck** *n* triangle; **⁌eckig** *adj.* triangular; **⁌erlei** ['⁀ər'lai] of three kinds *or* sorts; **⁌fach** *adj.* ['⁀fax] threefold, treble, triple; **⁌farbig** *adj.* three-col-o(u)r(ed); **⁌fuß** *m* tripod; **⁌jährig** *adj.* ['⁀jɛːriç] three-year-old; triennial; **⁌mal** *adv.* three times; **⁌malig** *adj.* done *or* repeated three times; three; **⁌meilenzone** ⚓, ⚖ *f* three-mile limit; **⁌rad** *n* tricycle; **⁌seitig** *adj.* three-sided; trilateral; **⁌silbig** *adj.* trisyllabic.

dreißig ['draisiç] thirty; **⁌ste** *adj.* thirtieth.

dreist *adj.* [draist] bold, audacious; cheeky, saucy; **⁌igkeit** *f* (-/-en) boldness, audacity; cheek, sauciness.

drei|stimmig ♪ *adj.* for *or* in three voices; **⁌tägig** *adj.* ['⁀tɛːgiç] three-day; **⁌teilig** *adj.* in three parts, tripartite; **⁌zehn(te)** *adj.* thirteen(th).

dresch|en ['drɛʃən] *v/t.* and *v/i.* (*irr.*, ge-, h) thresh; thrash; **⁌flegel** *m* flail; **⁌maschine** *f* threshing-machine.

dressieren [drɛ'siːrən] *v/t.* (no -ge-, h) train; break in (*horse*).

drillen ⚔, ✒ ['drilən] *v/t.* (ge-, h) drill.

Drillinge ['driliŋə] *m/pl.* triplets *pl.*

drin F *adv.* [drin] *s.* darin.

dringen ['driŋən] *v/i.* (*irr.*, ge-) **1.** (sein): ⁀ *durch* force one's way through *s.th.*, penetrate *or* pierce *s.th.*; ⁀ *aus* break forth from *s.th.*; *noise:* come from; ⁀ *in* (acc.) penetrate into; *in j-n* ⁀ urge *or* press *s.o.*; *an die Öffentlichkeit* ⁀ get abroad; **2.** (h): ⁀ *auf* (acc.) insist on, press for; **⁌d** *adj.* urgent, pressing; *suspicion:* strong.

dringlich *adj.* urgent, pressing; **⁌keit** *f* (-/no pl.) urgency.

drinnen *adv.* ['drinən] inside; in-doors.

dritt|e *adj.* ['dritə] third; **⁌el** *n* (-s/-) third; **⁌ens** *adv.* thirdly; **⁌letzt** *adj.* last but one.

Drog|e ['droːgə] *f* (-/-n) drug; **⁌erie** [drogə'riː] *f* (-/-n) chemist's (shop), *Am.* drugstore; **⁌ist** [dro-'gist] *m* (-en/-en) (retail pharmaceutical) chemist.

drohen ['droːən] *v/i.* (ge-, h) threaten, menace.

Drohne ['droːnə] *f* (-/-n) zo. drone (a. *fig.*).

dröhnen ['drøːnən] *v/i.* (ge-, h) *voice, etc.:* resound; *cannon, drum, etc.:* roar; *voice, cannon:* boom.

Drohung ['droːuŋ] *f* (-/-en) threat, menace.

drollig *adj.* ['drɔliç] amusing, quaint, comical.

Dromedar zo. [drome'daːr] *n* (-s/-e) dromedary.

drosch [drɔʃ] *pret.* of dreschen.

Droschke ['drɔʃkə] *f* (-/-n) taxi (-cab), *Am.* a. cab, hack; **⁌nkutscher** *m* cabman, driver, *Am. a.* hackman.

Drossel orn. ['drɔsəl] f (-/-n) thrush; '2n ⊕ v/t. (ge-, h) throttle.
drüben adv. ['dry:bən] over there, yonder.
drüber F adv. ['dry:bər] s. darüber.
Druck [druk] m 1. (-[e]s/ːe) pressure; squeeze (of hand, etc.); 2. typ. (-[e]s/-e) print(ing); '~bogen m printed sheet; '~buchstabe m block letter.
drucken ['drukən] v/t. (ge-, h) print; ~ lassen have s.th. printed, publish.
drücken ['drykən] (ge-, h) 1. v/t. press; squeeze (hand, etc.); force down (prices, wages, etc.); lower (record); press, push (button, etc.); F sich ~ vor (dat.) or von shirk (work, etc.); 2. v/i. shoe: pinch.
'**Drucker** m (-s/-) printer.
'**Drücker** m (-s/-) door-handle; trigger.
Drucker|**ei** [drukə'raɪ] f (-/-en) printing office, Am. printery, print shop; '~schwärze f printer's or printing-ink.
'**Druck**|**fehler** m misprint; '~fehlerverzeichnis n errata pl.; '2fertig adj. ready for press; '~kammer f pressurized cabin; '~knopf m patent fastener, snap-fastener; ⚡ push-button; '~luft f compressed air; '~pumpe f pressure pump; '~sache(n) ⚑ f printed matter, Am. a. second-class or third-class matter; '~schrift f block letters; publication; '~taste f press key.
drum F adv., cj. [drum] s. darum.
drunter F adv. ['druntər] s. darunter.
Drüse anat. ['dry:zə] f (-/-n) gland.
du pers. pron. [du:] you.
Dublette [du'blɛtə] f (-/-n) duplicate.
ducken ['dukən] v/refl. (ge-, h) duck, crouch; fig. cringe (vor dat. to, before).
Dudelsack ♪ ['du:dəl-] m bagpipes pl.
Duell [du'ɛl] n (-s/-e) duel; 2ieren [due'li:rən] v/refl. (no -ge-, h) (fight a) duel (mit with).
Duett ♪ [du'ɛt] n (-[e]s/-e) duet.
Duft [duft] m (-[e]s/ːe) scent, fragrance, perfume; '2en v/i. (ge-, h) smell, have a scent, be fragrant; '2end adj. fragrant; '2ig adj. dainty, fragrant.
duld|**en** ['duldən] (ge-, h) 1. v/t.

bear, stand, endure, suffer (pain, grief, etc.); tolerate, put up with; 2. v/i. suffer; ~sam adj. ['~t-] tolerant; '2samkeit f (-/no pl.) tolerance; 2ung ['~duŋ] f (-/⚓-en) toleration; sufferance.
dumm adj. [dum] stupid, dull, Am. F dumb; '2heit f (-/-en) stupidity, dullness; stupid or foolish action; '2kopf m fool, blockhead, Am. sl. a. dumbbell.
dumpf adj. [dumpf] smell, air, etc.: musty, fusty; atmosphere: stuffy, heavy; sound, sensation, etc.: dull; '~ig adj. cellar, etc.: damp, musty.
Düne ['dy:nə] f (-/-n) dune, sandhill.   [manure.]
Dung [duŋ] m (-[e]s/no pl.) dung,
dünge|**n** ['dyŋən] v/t. (ge-, h) dung, manure; fertilize; '2r m (-s/-) s. Dung; fertilizer.
dunkel ['duŋkəl] 1. adj. dark; dim; fig. obscure; idea, etc.: dim, faint, vague; 2. 2 n (-s/no pl.) s. Dunkelheit.
Dünkel ['dyŋkəl] m (-s/no pl.) conceit, arrogance; '2haft adj. conceited, arrogant.
'**Dunkel**|**heit** f (-/no pl.) darkness (a. fig.); fig. obscurity; '~kammer phot. f dark-room; '2n v/i. (ge-, h) grow dark, darken.
dünn adj. [dyn] paper, material, voice, etc.: thin; hair, population, etc.: thin, sparse; liquid: thin, watery; air: rare(fied).
Dunst [dunst] m (-es/ːe) vapo(u)r; haze, mist; fume.
dünsten ['dynstən] (ge-, h) 1. v/t. steam (fish, etc.); stew (fruit, etc.); 2. v/i. steam.
'**dunstig** adj. vaporous; hazy.
Duplikat [dupli'ka:t] n (-[e]s/-e) duplicate.
Dur ♪ [du:r] n (-/-) major.
durch [durç] 1. prp. (acc.) through; 2. adv.: die ganze Nacht ~ all night long; ~ und ~ through and through; thoroughly.
durcharbeiten [durç⁹-] (sep., -ge-, h) 1. v/t. study thoroughly; sich ~ durch work through (book, etc.); 2. v/i. work without a break.
durch'**aus** adv. through and through; thoroughly; by all means; absolutely; quite; ~ nicht not at all, by no means.
'**durch**|**biegen** v/t. (irr. biegen, sep.,

-ge-, h) bend; deflect (*beam*, *etc.*); sich ~ bend, *etc.*: deflect, sag; '~**blättern** v/t. (sep., -ge-, h) glance or skim through (*book*, *etc.*), *Am.* thumb through, skim; '2**blick** m: ~ auf (*acc.*) view through to, vista over, view of; '~**blicken** v/i. (sep., -ge-, h) look through; ~ lassen, daß give to understand that.

durch|'**bluten** v/t. (no -ge-, h) supply with blood; ~'**bohren** v/t. (no -ge-, h) pierce; perforate; mit Blicken ~ look daggers at s.o.

'**durch**|**braten** v/t. (irr. braten, sep., -ge-, h) roast thoroughly; ~**brechen** (irr. brechen) 1. ['~breçən] v/i. (sep., -ge-, h) break through or apart; 2. ['~] v/t. (sep., -ge-, h) break apart or in two; 3. [~'breçən] v/t. (no -ge-, h) break through, breach; run (*blockade*); crash (*sound barrier*); '~**brennen** v/i. (irr. brennen, sep., -ge-, sein) ⚡ *fuse*: blow; F *fig.* run away; *woman*: elope; '~**bringen** v/t. (irr. bringen, sep., -ge-, h) bring or get through; dissipate, squander (*money*); '2**bruch** m ✕ break-through; rupture; breach; *fig.* ultimate success.

durch'**denken** v/t. (irr. denken, no -ge-, h) think s.th. over thoroughly.

'**durch**|**drängen** v/refl. (sep., -ge-, h) force or push one's way through; ~**dringen** (irr. dringen) 1. ['~driŋən] v/i. (sep., -ge-, sein) penetrate (through); win acceptance (mit for) (*proposal*); 2. [~'driŋən] v/t. (no -ge-, h) penetrate, pierce; *water*, *smell*, *etc.*: permeate.

durcheinander [durç⁹aɪ'nandər] 1. *adv.* in confusion or disorder; pell-mell; 2. ♀ n (-s/-) muddle, mess, confusion; ~**bringen** v/t. (irr. bringen, sep., -ge-, h) confuse s.o.; *fig.* mix (*things*) up; ~**werfen** v/t. (irr. werfen, sep., -ge-, h) throw into disorder; *fig.* mix up.

durchfahr|**en** (irr. fahren) 1. ['~fɑː-rən] v/i. (sep., -ge-, sein) go or pass or drive through; 2. [~'fɑːrən] v/t. (no -ge-, h) go or pass or travel or drive through; traverse (*tract of country*, *etc.*);'2t f passage (through); gate(way); ~ **verboten**! no thorough-fare!

'**Durchfall** m 🔬 diarrh(o)ea; F *fig.* failure, *Am. a.* flunk; 2**en** (irr. fallen) 1. ['~falən] v/i. (sep., -ge-, sein)

fall through; fail, F get ploughe(d) (*in examination*); *thea.* be a failure; *sl.* be a flop; ~ lassen reject, ⊕ plough; 2. [~'falən] v/t. (no -ge-, h) fall or drop through (*space*).

'**durch**|**fechten** v/t. (irr. fechten, sep., -ge-, h) fight or see s.th. through; '~**finden** v/refl. (irr. fin-den, sep., -ge-, h) find one's way (through).

durch|**flechten** v/t. (irr. flechten, no -ge-, h) interweave, intertwine; ~'**forschen** v/t. (no -ge-, h) search through, investigate; explore (*region*, *etc.*).

'**Durchfuhr** † f (-/-en) transit.

durchführ|**bar** adj. ['durçfyːrbɑːr] practicable, feasible, workable; '~**en** v/t. (sep., -ge-, h) lead or take through or across; *fig.* carry out or through; realize; '2**ungsbestim-mung** f (implementing) regulation.

'**Durchgang** m passage; † transit; *sports*: run; '~**sverkehr** m through traffic; † transit traffic; '~**szoll** m transit duty.

'**durchgebraten** adj. well done.

'**durchgehen** (irr. gehen, sep., -ge-) 1. v/i. (sein) go or walk through; *bill*: pass, be carried; run away or off; abscond; *woman*: elope; *horse*: bolt; 2. v/t. (sein) go through (*street*, *etc.*); 3. v/t. (h, sein) go or look or read through (*work*, *book*, *etc.*); '~**d** 1. adj. continuous; ~er Zug through train; 2. adv. generally; throughout.

durch'**geistigt** adj. spiritual.

'**durch**|**greifen** v/i. (irr. greifen, sep., -ge-, h) put one's hand through; *fig.* take drastic measures or steps; '~**greifend** adj. drastic; radical, sweeping; '~**halten** (irr. halten, sep., -ge-, h) 1. v/t. keep up (*pace*, *etc.*); 2. v/i. hold out; '~**hauen** v/t. (irr. hauen, sep., -ge-, h) cut or chop through; *fig.* give s.o. a good hiding; '~**helfen** v/i. (irr. helfen, sep., -ge-, h) help through (a. *fig.*); '~**kämpfen** v/t. (sep., -ge-, h) fight out; sich ~ fight one's way through; '~**kneten** v/t. (sep., -ge-, h) knead or work thoroughly; '~**kommen** v/i. (irr. kommen, sep., -ge-, sein) come or get or pass through; *sick person*: pull through; *in examination*: pass.

durch'**kreuzen** v/t. (no -ge-, h) cross, foil, thwart (*plan*, *etc.*).

Durch|laß ['durçlas] *m* (*Durch-lasses/Durchlässe*) passage; **'2las-sen** *v/t.* (*irr. lassen, sep., -ge-, h*) let pass, allow to pass, let through; *Wasser ~* leak; **'2lässig** *adj.* pervious (to), permeable (to); leaky.

durchlaufen (*irr. laufen*) **1.** ['~lau-fən] *v/i.* (*sep., -ge-, sein*) run or pass through; **2.** ['~] *v/t.* (*sep., -ge-, h*) wear out (*shoes, etc.*); **3.** [~'laufən] *v/t.* (*no -ge-, h*) pass through (*stages, departments, etc.*); *sports:* cover (*distance*).   [live through.\
durch'leben *v/t.*(*no -ge-, h*) go or }
'durchlesen *v/t.* (*irr. lesen, sep., -ge-, h*) read through.

durchleuchten (*h*) **1.** ['~lɔyçtən] *v/i.* (*sep., -ge-*) shine through; **2.** [~'lɔyçtən] *v/t.* (*no -ge-*) ☢ X-ray; *fig.* investigate.

durchlöchern [durç'lœçərn] *v/t.* (*no -ge-, h*) perforate, make holes into *s.th.*

'durchmachen *v/t.* (*sep., -ge-, h*) go through (*difficult times, etc.*); undergo (*suffering*).   [through.\
'Durchmarsch *m* march(ing)}
'Durchmesser *m* (*-s/-*) diameter.
durch'nässen *v/t.* (*no -ge-, h*) wet through, soak, drench.

'durchnehmen *v/t.* (*irr. nehmen, sep., -ge-, h*) go through or over (*subject*); **'~pausen** *v/t.* (*sep., -ge-, h*) trace, calk (*design, etc.*).

durchqueren [durç'kve:rən] *v/t.* (*no -ge-, h*) cross, traverse.

'durch|rechnen *v/t.* (*sep., -ge-, h*) (re)calculate, check; **2reise** *f* journey or way through; **~reisen 1.** [~'rai-zən] *v/i.* (*sep., -ge-, sein*) travel or pass through; **2.** ['~raizən] *v/t.* (*no -ge-, h*) travel over or through or across; **'2reisende** *m, f* (*-n/-n*) person travel(l)ing through, *Am. a.* transient; 🚌 through passenger; **'~reißen** (*irr. reißen, sep., -ge-*) **1.** *v/i.* (*sein*) tear, break; **2.** *v/t.* (*h*) tear asunder, tear in two; **~schauen** (*h*) **1.** ['~ʃauən] *v/i. and v/t.* (*sep., -ge-*) look through; **2.** *fig.* [~'ʃauən] *v/t.* (*no -ge-*) see through.

'durchscheinen *v/i.* (*irr. scheinen, sep., -ge-, h*) shine through; **'~d** *adj.* translucent; transparent.

'durchscheuern *v/t.* (*sep., -ge-, h*) rub through; **~schießen** (*irr. schie-ßen*) **1.** ['~ʃi:sən] *v/i.* (*sep., -ge-, h*) shoot through; **2.** ['~] *v/i.* (*sep.,

-ge-, sein) *water:* shoot or race through; **3.** [~'ʃi:sən] *v/t.* (*no -ge-, h*) shoot *s.th.* through; *typ.:* space out (*lines*); interleave (*book*).

'Durchschlag *m* colander, strainer; carbon copy; **2en** (*irr. schlagen*) **1.** ['~ʃla:gən] *v/t.* (*sep., -ge-, h*) break or pass through; strain (*peas, etc.*); *sich ~* get along, make one's way; **2.** ['~] *v/i.* (*sep., -ge-, h*) *typ.* come through; take or have effect; **3.** [~'ʃla:gən] *v/t.* (*no -ge-, h*) pierce; *bullet:* penetrate; **'~end** *adj.* effective, telling; **~papier** ['~k-] *n* copying paper.

durchschneiden *v/t.* (*irr. schneiden, h*) **1.** ['~naɪdən] (*sep., -ge-*) cut through; **2.** [~'ʃnaɪdən] (*no -ge-*) cut through, cut in two.

'Durchschnitt *m* cutting through; ⊕ section, profile; ⅄ intersection; *fig.* average; *im ~* on an average; **'2lich 1.** *adj.* average; normal; **2.** *adv.* on an average; normally; **'~swert** *m* average value.

'durch|sehen (*irr. sehen, sep., -ge-, h*) **1.** *v/i.* see or look through; **2.** *v/t.* see or look through *s.th.*; look *s.th.* over, go over *s.th.*; **'~seihen** *v/t.* (*sep., -ge-, h*) filter, strain; **~setzen** *v/t.* (*h*) **1.** ['~zetsən] (*sep., -ge-*) put (*plan, etc.*) through; force through; *seinen Kopf ~* have one's way; *sich ~* opinion, *etc.*: gain acceptance; **2.** [~'zetsən] (*no -ge-*) intersperse.

'Durchsicht *f* looking through or over; examination; correction; *typ.* reading; **2ig** *adj.* glass, water, *etc.*: transparent; *fig.* clear, lucid; **'~ig-keit** *f* (*-/no pl.*) transparency; *fig.* clarity, lucidity.

'durch|sickern *v/i.* (*sep., -ge-, sein*) seep or ooze through; *news, etc.*: leak out; **~sieben** *v/t.* (*h*) **1.** ['~zi:-bən] (*sep., -ge-*) sieve, sift; bolt (*flour*); **2.** [~'zi:bən] (*no -ge-*) riddle (*with bullets*); **'~sprechen** *v/t. (irr. sprechen, sep., -ge-, h*) discuss, talk over; **'~stechen** *v/t.* (*irr. stechen, h*) **1.** ['~ʃteçən] (*sep., -ge-*) stick (*needle, etc.*) through *s.th.*; stick through *s.th.*; **2.** [~'ʃteçən] (*no -ge-*) pierce; cut through (*dike, etc.*); **'~stecken** *v/t.* (*sep., -ge-, h*) pass or stick through.

'Durchstich *m* cut(ting).

durch'stöbern *v/t.* (*no -ge-, h*) ransack (*room, pockets, etc.*); rummage through (*drawers, papers, etc.*).

'durchstreichen v/t. (*irr. streichen, sep., -ge-, h*) strike *or* cross out, cancel.

durch'streifen v/t. (*no -ge-, h*) roam *or* wander through *or* over *or* across.

durch'such|en v/t. (*no -ge-, h*) search (*a.* 🕮); **2ung** f (*-/-en*) search.

durchtrieben adj. ['durç'tri:bən] cunning, artful; **2heit** f (*-/no pl.*) cunning, artfulness.

durch'wachen v/t. (*no -ge-, h*) pass (*the night*) waking.

durch'wachsen adj. bacon: streaky.

durchwandern 1. ['∼vandərn] v/i. (*sep., -ge-, sein*) walk *or* pass through; **2.** [∼'vandərn] v/t. (*no -ge-, h*) walk *or* pass through (*place, area, etc.*).

durch'weben v/t. (*no -ge-, h*) interweave; *fig. a.* intersperse.

durchweg adv. ['durçvek] throughout, without exception.

durch'weich|en 1. ['∼vaiçən] v/i. (*sep., -ge-, sein*) soak; **2.** [∼'vaiçən] v/t. (*no -ge-, h*) soak, drench; **'∼winden** v/refl. (*irr. winden, sep., -ge-, h*) worm *or* thread one's way through; **'∼wühlen** (*h*) **1.** *fig.* ['∼vy:lən] v/refl. (*sep., -ge-*) work one's way through; **2.** [∼'vy:lən] v/t. (*no -ge-*) rummage; **'∼zählen** v/t. (*sep., -ge-, h*) count; **'∼ziehen** (*irr. ziehen*) **1.** ['∼tsi:ən] v/i. (*sep., -ge-, sein*) pass *or* go *or* come *or* march through; **2.** ['∼] v/t. (*sep., -ge-, h*) pull (*thread, etc.*) through; **3.** [∼'tsi:ən] v/t. (*no -ge-, h*) go *or* travel through; *scent, etc.*: fill, pervade (*room, etc.*).

durch'zucken v/t. (*no -ge-, h*) flash through.

'Durchzug m passage through; draught, *Am.* draft.

'durchzwängen v/refl. (*sep., -ge-, h*) squeeze o.s. through.

dürfen ['dyrfən] (*irr., h*) **1.** v/i. (*ge-*): ich darf (*nicht*) I am (not) allowed to; **2.** v/aux. (*no -ge-*): ich darf inf. I am permitted *or* allowed to inf.; I may inf.; du darfst nicht inf. you must not inf.; iro.: wenn ich bitten darf if you please.

durfte ['durftə] pret. of dürfen.

dürftig adj. ['dyrftiç] poor; scanty.

dürr adj. [dyr] wood, leaves, etc.: dry; land: barren, arid; p. gaunt, lean, skinny; **'2e** f (*-/-n*) dryness; barrenness; leanness.

Durst [durst] m (*-es/no pl.*) thirst (*nach for*); ∼ haben be thirsty.

dürsten ['dyrstən] v/i. (*ge-, h*): ∼ nach thirst for.

'durstig adj. thirsty (*nach for*).

Dusche ['duʃə] f (*-/-n*) shower (-bath); **'2n** v/refl. and v/i. (*ge-, h*) have a shower(-bath).

Düse ['dy:zə] f (*-/-n*) ⊕ nozzle; ✈ jet; **∼nantrieb** ['∼n∼] m jet propulsion; mit ∼ jet-propelled; **'∼n-flugzeug** n jet(-propelled) aircraft, F jet; **'∼njäger** ✈ m jet fighter.

düster adj. ['dy:stər] dark, gloomy (*both a. fig.*); light: dim; fig.: sad; depressing; **'2heit** f (*-/no pl.*), **'2keit** f (*-/no pl.*) gloom(iness).

Dutzend ['dutsənt] n (*-s/-e*) dozen; ein ∼ Eier a dozen eggs; ∼e von Leuten dozens of people; **'2weise** adv. by the dozen, in dozens.

Dynam|ik [dy'na:mik] f (*-/no pl.*) dynamics; **2isch** adj. dynamic(al).

Dynamit [dyna'mi:t] n (*-s/no pl.*) dynamite.

Dynamo [dy'na:mò] m (*-s/-s*), **∼ma-schine** f dynamo, generator.

D-Zug ['de:tsu:k] m express train.

E

Ebbe ['ɛbə] f (*-/-n*) ebb(-tide); low tide; **'2n** v/i. (*ge-, sein*) ebb.

eben ['e:bən] **1.** adj. even; plain, level; ⅋ plane; zu ∼er Erde on the ground floor, *Am.* on the first floor; **2.** adv. exactly; just; ∼

erst just now; **'2bild** n image, likeness; **∼bürtig** adj. ['∼byrtiç] of equal birth; j-m ∼ sein be a match for s.o., be s.o.'s equal; **'∼da** adv., **'∼da'selbst** adv. at the very (same) place, just there; quoting books:

ibidem (*abbr.* ib., ibid.); '**~'der**, '**~'die**, '**~'das** *dem. pron.* = '**~der'selbe**, '**~die'selbe**, '**~das'selbe** *dem. pron.* the very (same); '**~des'wegen** *adv.* for that very reason.

Ebene ['e:bənə] *f* (-/-n) plain; Å plane; *fig.* level.

'eben|erdig *adj. and adv.* at street level; on the ground floor, *Am.* on the first floor; '**~falls** *adv.* likewise; '**2holz** *n* ebony; '**~maß** *n* symmetry; harmony; regularity (*of features*); '**~mäßig** *adj.* symmetrical; harmonious; regular; '**~so** *adv.* just so; just as ...; likewise; '**~sosehr** *adv.*, '**~soviel** *adv.* just as much; '**~sowenig** *adv.* just as little *or* few (*pl.*), no more.

Eber *zo.* ['e:bər] *m* (-s/-) boar; '**~esche** ♀ *f* mountain-ash.

ebnen ['e:bnən] *v/t.* (ge-, h) level; *fig.* smooth.

Echo ['εço] *n* (-s/-s) echo.

echt *adj.* [εçt] genuine; true; pure; real; *colour*: fast; *document*: authentic; '**2heit** *f* (-/*no pl.*) genuineness; purity; reality; fastness; authenticity.

Eck [εk] *n* (-[e]s/-e) s. **Ecke**; '**~ball** *m sports*: corner-kick; '**~e** *f* (-/-n) corner; edge; *fig.* awkward; '**~platz** *m* corner-seat; '**~stein** *m* corner-stone; '**~zahn** *m* canine tooth.

edel ['e:dəl] *adj.* noble; *min.* precious; *organs of the body*: vital; '**~denkend** *adj.* noble-minded; '**2mann** *m* nobleman; '**2mut** *m* generosity; '**~mütig** *adj.* ['~my:tiç] noble-minded, generous; '**2stein** *m* precious stone; gem.

Edikt [e'dikt] *n* (-[e]s/-e) edict.

Efeu ♀ ['e:fɔy] *m* (-s/*no pl.*) ivy.

Effekt [e'fεkt] *m* (-[e]s/-e) effect; '**~en** *pl.* effects *pl.*; ✝: securities *pl.*; stocks *pl.*; '**~enhandel** *m* dealing in stocks; '**~hascherei** [~haʃə'raɪ] *f* (-/-en) claptrap; '**2iv** *adj.* [~'ti:v] effective; '**2uieren** [~u'i:rən] *v/t.* (*no -ge-*, h) effect; execute, *Am.* a. fill; '**2voll** *adj.* effective, striking.

egal *adj.* [e'ga:l] equal; F all the same.

Egge ['εgə] *f* (-/-n) harrow; '**2n** *v/t.* (ge-, h) harrow.

Egois|mus [ego'ismus] *m* (-/*Egois-*

men) ego(t)ism; '**~t** *m* (-en/-en) ego(t)ist; '**2tisch** *adj.* selfish, ego(t)istic(al).

ehe[1] *cj.* ['e:ə] before.

Ehe[2] [~] *f* (-/-n) marriage; matrimony; '**~anbahnung** *f* (-/-en) matrimonial agency; '**~brecher** *m* (-s/-) adulterer; '**~brecherin** *f* (-/-nen) adulteress; '**2brecherisch** *adj.* adulterous; '**~bruch** *m* adultery; '**~frau** *f* wife; '**~gatte** *m*, '**~gattin** *f* spouse; '**~leute** *pl.* married people *pl.*; '**2lich** *adj.* conjugal; *child*: legitimate; '**~losigkeit** *f* (-/*no pl.*) celibacy; single life.

ehemal|ig *adj.* ['e:əma:liç] former, ex-...; old; '**~s** *adv.* formerly.

'Ehe|mann *m* husband; '**~paar** *n* married couple.

'eher *adv.* sooner; rather; more likely; je **~**, desto besser the sooner the better.

'Ehering *m* wedding ring.

ehern *adj.* ['e:ərn] brazen, of brass.

'Ehe|scheidung *f* divorce; '**~schließung** *f* (-/-en) (contraction of) marriage; '**~stand** *m* (-[e]s/*no pl.*) married state, matrimony; '**~stifter** *m*, '**~stifterin** *f* (-/-nen) matchmaker; '**~vermittlung** *f* s. **Eheanbahnung**; '**~versprechen** *n* promise of marriage; '**~vertrag** *m* marriage contract.

Ehrabschneider ['e:r?apʃnaɪdər] *m* (-s/-) slanderer.

'ehrbar *adj.* hono(u)rable, respectable; modest; '**2keit** *f* (-/*no pl.*) respectability; modesty.

Ehre ['e:rə] *f* (-/-n) hono(u)r; zu **~**n (*gen.*) in hono(u)r of; '**2n** *v/t.* (ge-, h) hono(u)r; esteem.

'ehren|amtlich *adj.* honorary; '**2bürger** *m* honorary citizen; '**2doktor** *m* honorary doctor; '**2erklärung** *f* (full) apology; '**2gast** *m* guest of hono(u)r; '**2gericht** *n* court of hono(u)r; '**~haft** *adj.* hono(u)rable; '**2kodex** *m* code of hono(u)r; '**2legion** [~legi̯o:n] *f* (-/*no pl.*) Legion of Hono(u)r; '**2mann** *m* man of hono(u)r; '**2mitglied** *n* honorary member; '**2platz** *m* place of hono(u)r; '**2recht** *n*: bürgerliche **~e** *pl.* civil rights *pl.*; '**2rettung** *f* rehabilitation; '**~rührig** *adj.* defamatory; '**2sache** *f* affair of hono(u)r; point of hono(u)r; '**~voll** *adj.* hono(u)rable; '**~wert** *adj.* hono(u)rable;

'2wort n (-[e]s/-e) word of hono(u)r.

ehr|erbietig adj. ['e:rʔɛrbiːtiç] respectful; 2erbietung f (-/-en) reverence; '2furcht f (-/⸢-en) respect; awe; '⸜furchtgebietend adj. awe-inspiring, awesome; ⸜fürchtig adj. ['⸜fyrçtiç] respectful; 2gefühl n (-[e]s/no pl.) sense of hono(u)r; '2geiz m ambition; '⸜geizig adj. ambitious.

'ehrlich adj. honest; commerce, game: fair; opinion: candid; ~ währt am längsten honesty is the best policy; '2keit f (-/no pl.) honesty; fairness.

'ehrlos adj. dishono(u)rable, infamous; '2igkeit f (-/-en) dishonesty, infamy.

'ehr|sam adj. s. ehrbar; '2ung f (-/-en) hono(u)r (conferred on s.o.); '⸜vergessen adj. dishono(u)rable, infamous; '2verlust m ⋆⋆ m (-es/no pl.) loss of civil rights; '⸜würdig adj. venerable, reverend.

ei¹ int. [aɪ] ah!, indeed!

Ei² [⸜] n (-[e]s/-er) egg; physiol. ovum.

Eibe ♀ ['aɪbə] f (-/-n) yew(-tree).

Eiche ♀ ['aɪçə] f (-/-n) oak(-tree). ⸜l ['⸜l] f (-/-n) ♀ acorn; cards: club; ⸜lhäher orn. ['⸜hɛːər] m (-s/-) jay.

eichen¹ ['aɪçən] v/t. (ge-, h) ga(u)ge.

eichen² adj. [⸜] oaken, of oak.

Eich|hörnchen zo. ['aɪçhœrnçən] n (-s/-) squirrel; '⸜maß n standard.

Eid [aɪt] m (-es/-e) oath; '2brüchig adj.: ~ werden break one's oath.

Eidechse zo. ['aɪdɛksə] f (-/-n) lizard.

eidesstattlich ⋆⋆ adj. ['aɪdəs-] in lieu of (an) oath; ⸜e Erklärung statutory declaration.

'eidlich 1. adj. sworn; 2. adv. on oath.

'Eidotter m, n yolk.

'Eier|kuchen m omelet(te), pancake; '⸜schale f egg-shell; '⸜stock anat. m ovary; '⸜uhr f egg-timer.

Eifer ['aɪfər] m (-s/no pl.) zeal; eagerness; ardo(u)r; '⸜er m (-s/-) zealot; '⸜sucht f (-/no pl.) jealousy; '2süchtig adj. jealous (auf acc. of).

eifrig adj. ['aɪfrɪç] zealous, eager; ardent.

eigen adj. ['aɪgən] own; particular; strange, odd; in compounds: ...-owned; peculiar (dat. to); '2art f peculiarity; '⸜artig adj. peculiar;

singular; 2brötler ['⸜brøːtlər] m (-s/-) odd or eccentric person, crank; '2gewicht n dead weight; ⸜händig adj. and adv. ['⸜hɛndɪç] with one's own hands; '2heim n house of one's own; homestead; '2heit f (-/-en) peculiarity; oddity; of language: idiom; '2liebe f self-love; '2lob n self-praise; '⸜mächtig adj. arbitrary; '2name m proper name; ⸜nützig adj. ['⸜nytsɪç] self-interested, selfish; '⸜s adv. expressly, specially; on purpose.

'Eigenschaft f (-/-en) quality (of s.o.); property (of s.th.); in s-r ~ als in his capacity as; '⸜swort gr. n (-[e]s/⸜er) adjective.

'Eigensinn m (-[e]s/no pl.) obstinacy; '2ig adj. will(l)ful, obstinate.

'eigentlich 1. adj. proper; actual; true, real; 2. adv. properly (speaking).

'Eigentum n (-s/⸜er) property.

Eigentüm|er ['aɪgənty:mər] m (-s/-) owner, proprietor; '2lich adj. peculiar; odd; '⸜lichkeit f (-/-en) peculiarity.

'Eigentums|recht n ownership; copyright; '⸜wohnung f freehold flat. [dividual.]

'eigenwillig adj. self-willed; fig. in-

eign|en ['aɪgnən] v/refl. (ge-, h): sich ~ für be suited for; '2ung f (-/-en) aptitude, suitability.

'Eil|bote m ⋆ express messenger; durch ⸜n by special delivery; '⸜brief ⋆ m express letter, Am. special delivery letter.

Eile ['aɪlə] f (-/no pl.) haste, speed; hurry; '2n v/i. (ge-, sein) hasten, make haste; hurry; letter, affair: be urgent; 2nds adv. ['⸜ts] quickly, speedily.

'Eil|fracht f, '⸜gut n express goods pl., Am. fast freight; '2ig adj. hasty, speedy; urgent; es ~ haben be in a hurry.

Eimer ['aɪmər] m (-s/-) bucket, pail.

ein [aɪn] 1. adj. one; 2. indef. art. a, an.

einander adv. [aɪ'nandər] one another; each other.

ein|arbeiten ['aɪnʔ-] v/t. (sep., -ge-, h): j-n ~ in (acc.) make s.o. acquainted with; ⸜armig adj. ['aɪnʔ-] one-armed; ⸜äschern ['aɪnʔeʃərn] v/t. (sep., -ge-, h) burn to ashes; cremate (dead body); '2äscherung *f* (-/-en) cremation; **⁓atmen** ['aɪn**ʔ**-] *v/t.* (*sep., -ge-, h*) breathe, inhale; **⁓äugig** *adj.* ['aɪn**ʔ**ɔʏɡɪç] one-eyed.

'**Einbahnstraße** *f* one-way street.

'**einbalsamieren** *v/t.* (*sep., no -ge-, h*) embalm.

'**Einband** *m* (-[e]s/⁓e) binding; cover.

'**ein|bauen** *v/t.* (*sep., -ge-, h*) build in; install (*engine, etc.*); '**⁓behalten** *v/t.* (*irr. halten, sep., no -ge-, h*) detain; '**⁓berufen** *v/t.* (*irr. rufen, sep., no -ge-, h*) convene; ⚔ call up, *Am.* induct.

'**einbett|en** *v/t.* (*sep., -ge-, h*) embed; '**⁓zimmer** *n* single(-bedded) room.

'**einbild|en** *v/refl.* (*sep., -ge-, h*) fancy, imagine; '**⁓ung** *f* imagination, fancy; conceit.

'**einbinden** *v/t.* (*irr. binden, sep., -ge-, h*) bind (*books*).

'**Einblick** *m* insight (*in acc.* into).

'**einbrechen** (*irr. brechen, sep., -ge-*) **1.** *v/t.* (*h*) break open; **2.** *v/i.* (*sein*) break in; *of night, etc.*: set in; **⁓ in** (*acc.*) break into (*house*).

'**Einbrecher** *m* at night: burglar; by day: housebreaker.

'**Einbruch** *m* ⚔ invasion; housebreaking, burglary; *bei ⁓ der Nacht* at nightfall; '**⁓(s)diebstahl** *m* house-breaking, burglary.

einbürger|n ['aɪnbʏrɡərn] *v/t.* (*sep., -ge-, h*) naturalize; '**⁓ung** *f* (-/-en) naturalization.

'**Ein|buße** *f* loss; '**⁓büßen** *v/t.* (*sep., -ge-, h*) lose, forfeit.

ein|dämmen ['aɪndɛmən] *v/t.* (*sep., -ge-, h*) dam (up); embank (*river*); *fig.* check; '**⁓deutig** *adj.* unequivocal; clear, plain.

'**eindring|en** *v/i.* (*irr. dringen, sep., -ge-, sein*) enter; penetrate; intrude; **⁓ in** (*acc.*) penetrate (into); force one's way into; invade (*country*); '**⁓lich** *adj.* urgent; **⁓ling** ['⁓lɪŋ] *m* (-s/-e) intruder; invader.

'**Eindruck** *m* (-[e]s/⁓e) impression.

'**ein|drücken** *v/t.* (*sep., -ge-, h*) press in; crush (in) (*hat*); break (*pane*); '**⁓drucksvoll** *adj.* impressive; **⁓engen** ['aɪn**ʔ**-] *v/t.* (*sep., -ge-, h*) narrow; *fig.* limit.

ein|er¹ ['aɪnər], '**⁓e**, '**⁓(e)s** *indef. pron.* one.

Einer² [⁓] *m* (-s/-) ⚖ unit, digit; *rowing*: single sculler, skiff.

einerlei ['aɪnərlaɪ] **1.** *adj.* of the same kind; immaterial; *es ist mir ⁓* it is all the same to me; **2.** ⚖ *n* (-s/*no pl.*) sameness; monotony; humdrum (*of one's existence*).

einerseits *adv.* ['aɪnər'zaɪts] on the one hand.

einfach *adj.* ['aɪnfax] simple; single; plain; *meal:* frugal; *ticket:* single, *Am.* one-way; '**⁓heit** *f* (-/*no pl.*) simplicity.

einfädeln ['aɪnfɛːdəln] *v/t.* (*sep., -ge-, h*) thread; *fig.* start, set on foot; contrive.

'**Einfahrt** *f* entrance, entry.

'**Einfall** *m* ⚔ invasion; idea, inspiration; '**⁓en** *v/i.* (*irr. fallen, sep., -ge-, sein*) fall in, collapse; break in (*on a conversation*), interrupt, cut short; chime in; ♪ join in; invade; *j-m ⁓* occur to s.o.

Ein|falt ['aɪnfalt] *f* (-/*no pl.*) simplicity, silliness; **⁓fältig** *adj.* ['⁓fɛltɪç] simple; silly; '**⁓faltspinsel** *m* simpleton, *Am.* F sucker.

'**ein|farbig** *adj.* one-colo(u)red, unicolo(u)red; plain; '**⁓fassen** *v/t.* (*sep., -ge-, h*) border; set (*precious stone*); '**⁓fassung** *f* border; setting; '**⁓fetten** *v/t.* (*sep., -ge-, h*) grease; oil; '**⁓finden** *v/refl.* (*irr. finden, sep., -ge-, h*) appear; arrive; '**⁓flechten** *fig. v/t.* (*irr. flechten, sep., -ge-, h*) put in, insert; '**⁓fließen** *v/i.* (*irr. fließen, sep., -ge-, sein*) flow in; **⁓ in** (*acc.*) flow into; **⁓ lassen** mention in passing; '**⁓flößen** *v/t.* (*sep., -ge-, h*) infuse.

'**Einfluß** *m* influx; *fig.* influence; '**⁓reich** *adj.* influential.

ein|förmig *adj.* ['aɪnfœrmɪç] uniform; monotonous; '**⁓frieden** ['⁓friːdən] *v/t.* (*sep., -ge-, h*) fence, enclose; '**⁓friedung** *f* (-/-en) enclosure; '**⁓frieren** (*irr. frieren, sep., -ge-*) **1.** *v/i.* (*sein*) freeze (in); **2.** *v/t.* (*h*) freeze (*food*); '**⁓fügen** *v/t.* (*sep., -ge-, h*) put in; *fig.* insert; *sich ⁓* fit in.

Einfuhr ✝ ['aɪnfuːr] *f* (-/-en) import(ation); '**⁓bestimmungen** *f/pl.* import regulations *pl.*

'**einführen** *v/t.* (*sep., -ge-, h*) ✝ import; introduce (*s.o., custom*); insert; initiate; install (*s.o. in an office*).

'**Einfuhrwaren** ✝ *f/pl.* imports *pl.*

'**Eingabe** f petition; application.

'**Eingang** m entrance; entry; arrival (of goods); nach ~ on receipt; '~s-**buch** ⚓ n book of entries.

'**eingeben** v/t. (irr. geben, sep., -ge-, h) give, administer (medicine) (dat. to); prompt, suggest (to).

'**einge**|**bildet** adj. imaginary; conceited (auf acc. of); '~**boren** adj. native; '**2borene** m, f (-n/-n) native.

Eingebung ['aɪngəbʊŋ] f (-/-en) suggestion; inspiration.

'**einge**|**denk** adj. ['aɪngədeŋk] mindful (gen. of); '~**fallen** adj. eyes, cheeks: sunken, hollow; emaciated; ~**fleischt** fig. adj. ['~flaɪʃt] inveterate; confirmed; ~**er** Junggeselle confirmed bachelor.

'**eingehen** (irr. gehen, sep., -ge-) **1.** v/i. (sein) mail, goods: come in, arrive; ⚓, animal: die; cease (to exist); material: shrink; ~ auf (acc.) agree to; enter into; **2.** v/t. (h, sein) enter into (relationship); contract (marriage); ein Risiko ~ run a risk, esp. Am. take a chance; e-n Vergleich ~ come to terms; Verbindlichkeiten ~ incur liabilities; e-e Wette ~ make a bet; eingegangene Gelder n/pl. receipts pl.; '~**d** adj. detailed; thorough; examination: close.

Eingemachte ['aɪngəmaxtə] n (-n/no pl.) preserves pl.; pickles pl.

'**eingemeinden** v/t. (sep., no -ge-, h) incorporate (dat. into).

'**einge**|**nommen** adj. partial (für to); prejudiced (gegen against); von sich ~ conceited; '**2sandt** ⚓ n (-[e]s) letter to the editor; ~**schnappt** F fig. adj. ['~gəʃnapt] offended, touchy; '~**sessen** adj. long-established; '**2ständnis** n confession, avowal; '~**stehen** v/t. (irr. stehen, sep., no -ge-, h) confess, avow.

Eingeweide anat. ['aɪngəvaɪdə] pl. viscera pl.; intestines pl.; bowels pl.; esp. of animals: entrails pl.

'**einge**|**wöhnen** v/refl. (sep., no -ge-, h) accustom o.s. (in acc. to); acclimatize o.s., Am. acclimate o.s. (to); get used (to).

eingewurzelt adj. ['~gəvʊrtsəlt] deep-rooted, inveterate.

'**eingießen** v/t. (irr. gießen, sep., -ge-, h) pour in or out.

eingleisig adj. ['aɪnglaɪzɪç] single-track.

'**ein**|**graben** v/t. (irr. graben, sep.,

-ge-, h) dig in; bury; engrave; sich ~ ⚔ dig o.s. in, entrench o.s.; fig. engrave itself (on one's memory); '~**gravieren** v/t. (sep., no -ge-, h) engrave.

'**eingreifen 1.** v/i. (irr. greifen, sep., -ge-, h) intervene; ~ in (acc.) interfere with; encroach on (s.o.'s rights); in die Debatte ~ join in the debate; **2.** ⚔ n (-s/no pl.) intervention.

'**Eingriff** m fig. encroachment; ⚕ operation.

'**einhaken** v/t. (sep., -ge-, h) fasten; sich bei j-m ~ take s.o.'s arm.

'**Einhalt** m (-[e]s/no pl.): ~ gebieten (dat.) put a stop to; '**2en** fig. (irr. halten, sep., -ge-, h) **1.** v/t. observe, keep; **2.** v/i. stop, leave off (zu tun doing).

'**ein**|**hängen** ([irr. hängen,] sep., -ge-, h) **1.** v/t. hang in; hang up, replace (receiver); sich bei j-m ~ take s.o.'s arm, link arms with s.o.; **2.** teleph. v/i. hang up; '~**heften** v/t. (sep., -ge-, h) sew or stitch in.

'**einheimisch** adj. native (in dat. to), indigenous (to) (a. ⚘); ⚕ endemic; product: home-grown; '**2e** m, f (-n/-n) native; resident.

Einheit f (-/-en) unity; oneness; ⚛, phys., ⚔ unit; '**2lich** adj. uniform; '~**spreis** m standard price.

'**einheizen** (sep., -ge-, h) **1.** v/i. make a fire; **2.** v/t. heat (stove).

einhellig adj. ['aɪnhelɪç] unanimous.

'**einholen** (sep., -ge-, h) **1.** v/t. catch up with, overtake; make up for (lost time); make (inquiries); take (order); seek (advice); ask for (permission); buy; **2.** v/i.: ~ gehen go shopping.

'**Einhorn** zo. n unicorn.

'**einhüllen** v/t. (sep., -ge-, h) wrap (up or in); envelop.

einig adj. ['aɪnɪç] united; ~ sein agree; nicht ~ sein differ (über acc. about); ~**e** indef. pron. ['~gə] several; some; '~**en** ['~ɪgən] v/t. (ge-, h) unite; sich ~ come to terms; ~**ermaßen** adv. ['~gərˈmaːsən] in some measure; somewhat; '~**es** indef. pron. ['~gəs] some(thing); '**2keit** f (-/no pl.) unity; concord; '**2ung** ['~g-] f (-/-en) union; agreement.

'**ein**|**impfen** ['aɪnʔ-] v/t. (sep., -ge-, h) ⚕ inoculate (a. fig.); '~**jagen** v/t.

(sep., -ge-, h): *j-m Furcht* ~ scare s.o.

einjährig *adj.* ['aɪnjɛ:riç] one-year-old; *esp.* ♀ annual; *animal:* yearling.

'ein|kalkulieren *v/t. (sep., no -ge-, h)* take into account, allow for; **'~kassieren** *v/t. (sep., no -ge-, h)* cash; collect.

'Einkauf *m* purchase; *Einkäufe machen s. einkaufen* 2; **'₂en** *(sep., -ge-, h)* **1.** *v/t.* buy, purchase; **2.** *v/i.* make purchases, go shopping.

'Einkäufer *m* buyer.

'Einkaufs|netz *n* string bag; **'~preis** ✝ *m* purchase price; **'~tasche** *f* shopping-bag.

'ein|kehren *v/i. (sep., -ge-, h)* put up *or* stop *(at an inn)*; **'~kerben** *v/t. (sep., -ge-, h)* notch; **'~kerkern** *v/t. (sep., -ge-, h)* imprison; **'~klagen** *v/t. (sep., -ge-, h)* sue for; **'~klammern** *v/t. (sep., -ge-, h)* *typ.* bracket; put in brackets.

'Einklang *m* unison; harmony.

'ein|kleiden *v/t. (sep., -ge-, h)* clothe; fit out; **'~klemmen** *v/t. (sep., -ge-, h)* squeeze (in); jam; **'~klinken** *(sep., -ge-)* **1.** *v/t.* (*h*) latch; **2.** *v/i.* (*sein*) latch; engage; **'~knicken** *(sep., -ge-) v/t.* (*h*) *and v/i.* (*sein*) bend in, break; **'~kochen** *(sep., ge-)* **1.** *v/t.* (*h*) preserve; **2.** *v/i.* (*sein*) boil down *or* away.

'Einkommen *n (-s/-)* income, revenue; **'~steuer** *f* income-tax.

'einkreisen *v/t. (sep., -ge-, h)* encircle.

'Einkünfte ['aɪnkynftə] *pl.* income, revenue.

'einlad|en *v/t. (irr. laden, sep., -ge-, h)* load (in) *(goods)*; *fig.* invite; **'₂ung** *f* invitation.

'Einlage *f* enclosure *(in letter);* ✝ investment; deposit *(of money); gambling:* stake; inserted piece; ✝ arch-support; temporary filling *(of tooth);* **'₂rn** ✝ *v/t. (sep., -ge-, h)* store (up).

Einlaß ['aɪnlas] *m (Einlasses/Einlässe)* admission, admittance.

'einlassen *v/t. (irr. lassen, sep., -ge-, h)* let in, admit; ~ *in (acc.)* ⊕ imbed in; *sich* ~ *in auf (both acc.)* engage in, enter into.

'ein|laufen *v/i. (irr. laufen, sep., -ge-, sein)* come in, arrive; *ship:* enter; *material:* shrink; **'~leben**

v/refl. (sep., -ge-, h) accustom o.s. *(in acc.* to).

'einlege|n *v/t. (sep., -ge-, h)* lay *or* put in; insert; ⊕ inlay; deposit *(money);* pickle; preserve *(fruit); Berufung* ~ lodge an appeal *(bei* to); *Ehre* ~ *mit* gain hono(u)r *or* credit by; **'₂sohle** *f* insole, sock.

'einleit|en *v/t. (sep., -ge-, h)* start; introduce; **'~end** *adj.* introductory; **'₂ung** *f* introduction.

'ein|lenken *fig. v/i. (sep., -ge-, h)* come round; **'~leuchten** *v/i. (sep., -ge-, h)* be evident *or* obvious; **'~liefern** *v/t. (sep., -ge-, h)* deliver (up); *in ein Krankenhaus* ~ take to a hospital, *Am.* hospitalize; **'~lösen** *v/t. (sep., -ge-, h)* ransom *(prisoner);* redeem *(pledge);* hono(u)r *(bill);* cash *(cheque);* ✝ meet *(bill);* **'~machen** *v/t. (sep., -ge-, h)* preserve *(fruit);* tin, *Am.* can.

'einmal *adv.* once; one day; *auf* ~ all at once; *es war* ~ once (upon a time) there was; *nicht* ~ not even; **'₂eins** *n (-/-)* multiplication table; **'~ig** *adj.* single; unique.

'Einmarsch *m* marching in, entry; **'₂ieren** *v/i. (sep., no -ge-, sein)* march in, enter.

'ein|mengen *v/refl. (sep., -ge-, h),* **'~mischen** *v/refl. (sep., -ge-, h)* meddle, interfere *(in acc.* with), *esp. Am. sl.* butt in.

'Einmündung *f* junction *(of roads);* mouth *(of river).*

einmütig *adj.* ['aɪnmy:tiç] unanimous; **'₂keit** *f (-/no pl.)* unanimity.

Einnahme ['aɪnna:mə] *f (-/-)* ✖ taking, capture; *mst* ~*n pl.* takings *pl.,* receipts *pl.*

'einnehmen *v/t. (irr. nehmen, sep., -ge-, h)* take *(meal, position,* ✖*);* ✝ take *(money);* ✝ earn, make *(money);* take up, occupy *(room); fig.* captivate; **'~d** *adj.* taking, engaging, captivating.

'einnicken *v/i. (sep., -ge-, h)* doze *or* drop off.

Einöde ['aɪn⁹-] *f* desert, solitude.

ein|ordnen ['aɪn⁹-] *v/t. (sep., -ge-, h)* arrange in proper order; classify; file *(letters, etc.);* **'~packen** *v/t. (sep., -ge-, h)* pack up; wrap up; **'~pferchen** *v/t. (sep., -ge-, h)* pen in; *fig.* crowd, cram; **'~pflanzen** *v/t. (sep., -ge-, h)* plant; *fig.* implant; **'~pökeln** *v/t. (sep., -ge-, h)* pickle, salt; **`~prägen** v/t. (sep., -ge-, h) imprint; impress; **sich ~** imprint itself; commit s.th. to one's memory; **`~quartieren** v/t. (sep., no -ge-, h) quarter, billet; **`~rahmen** v/t. (sep., -ge-, h) frame; **`~räumen** fig. v/t. (sep., -ge-, h) grant, concede; **`~rechnen** v/t. (sep., -ge-, h) comprise, include; **`~reden** v/t. (sep., -ge-, h) **1.** v/t.: **j-m ~** persuade or talk s.o. into (doing) s.th.; **2.** v/i.: **auf j-n ~** talk insistently to s.o.; **`~reichen** v/t. (sep., -ge-, h) hand in, send in, present; **`~reihen** v/t. (sep., -ge-, h) insert (**unter** acc. in); class (with); place (among); **sich ~** take one's place.

einreihig adj. ['aɪnraɪç] jacket: single-breasted.

`Einreise** f entry; **`~erlaubnis f, **`~genehmigung** f entry permit.

`ein|reißen** (irr. reißen, sep., -ge-) **1.** v/t. (h) tear; pull down (building); **2.** v/i. (sein) tear; abuse, etc.: spread; **`~renken ['~rɛŋkən] v/t. (sep., -ge-, h) ♂ set; fig. set right.

`einricht|en** v/t. (sep. -ge-, h) establish; equip; arrange; set up (shop); furnish (flat); **es ~** manage; **sich ~** establish o.s., settle down; economize; **sich ~ auf** (acc.) prepare for; **`~ung f establishment; arrangement, esp. Am. setup; equipment; furniture; fittings pl. (of shop); institution.

`ein|rollen** v/t. (sep., -ge-, h) roll up or in; **sich ~** roll up; curl up; **`~rosten v/i. (sep., -ge-, sein) rust; screw, etc.: rust in; **`~rücken** (sep., -ge-) **1.** v/i. (sein) enter, march in; ╳ join the army; **2.** v/t. (h) insert (advertisement in a paper); typ. indent (line, word, etc.); **`~rühren** v/t. (sep., -ge-, h) stir (in).

eins adj. [aɪns] one.

`einsam** adj. lonely, solitary; **`2keit f (-/♀ -en) loneliness, solitude.

`einsammeln v/t. (sep., -ge-, h) gather; collect.

`Einsatz m inset; insertion (of piece of material); gambling: stake, pool; ♪ striking in, entry; employment; engagement (a. ╳); ╳ action, operation; **unter ~ s-s Lebens** at the risk of one's life.

`ein|saugen** v/t. (sep., -ge-, h) suck in; fig. imbibe; **`~schalten v/t. (sep., -ge-, h) insert; ≴ switch or turn on; **den ersten Gang ~** mot. go into first or bottom gear; **sich ~** intervene; **`~schärfen** v/t. (sep., -ge-, h) inculcate (dat. upon); **`~schätzen** v/t. (sep., -ge-, h) assess, appraise, estimate (auf acc. at); value (a. fig.); **`~schenken** v/t. (sep., -ge-, h) pour in or out; **`~schicken** v/t. (sep., -ge-, h) send in; **`~schieben** v/t. (irr. schieben, sep., -ge-, h) insert; **`~schiffen** v/t. and v/refl. (sep., -ge-, h) embark; **2schiffung** f (-/-en) embarkation; **`~schlafen** v/i. (irr. schlafen, sep., -ge-, sein) fall asleep; **~schläfern** ['~ʃlɛːfərn] v/t. (sep., -ge-, h) lull to sleep; ♨ narcotize.

`Einschlag** m striking (of lightning); impact (of missile); fig. touch; **`2en (irr. schlagen, sep., -ge-, h) **1.** v/t. drive in (nail); break (in); smash (in); wrap up; take (road); tuck in (hem, etc.); enter upon (career); **2.** v/i. shake hands; lightning, missile: strike; fig. be a success; **nicht ~** fail; (wie e-e Bombe) ~ cause a sensation; **auf j-n ~** belabour s.o.

einschlägig adj. ['aɪnʃlɛːgɪç] relevant, pertinent.

`Einschlagpapier n wrapping-paper.

`ein|schleichen** v/refl. (irr. schleichen, sep., -ge-, h) creep or sneak in; **`~schleppen v/t. (sep., -ge-, h) ♻ tow in; import (disease); **`~schleusen** fig. v/t. (sep., -ge-, h) channel or let in; **`~schließen** v/t. (irr. schließen, sep., -ge-, h) lock in or up; enclose; ╳ surround, encircle; fig. include; **`~schließlich** prp. (gen.) inclusive of; including, comprising; **`~schmeicheln** v/refl. (sep., -ge-, h) ingratiate o.s. (bei with); **`~schmeichelnd** adj. insinuating; **`~schmuggeln** v/t. (sep., -ge-, h) smuggle in; **`~schnappen** v/i. (sep., -ge-, sein) catch; fig. s. eingeschnappt; **`~schneidend** fig. adj. incisive, drastic.

`Einschnitt m cut, incision; notch.

`ein|schnüren v/t. (sep., -ge-, h) lace (up); **~schränken** ['~ʃrɛŋkən] v/t. (sep., -ge-, h) restrict, confine; reduce (expenses); **sich ~** economize; **2schränkung** f (-/-en) restriction; reduction.

`Einschreibe|brief** m registered letter; **`2n v/t. (irr. schreiben, sep.,

-ge-, h) enter; book; enrol(l); ✕ enlist, enrol(l); ⅋ register; ~ *lassen* have registered; *sich* ~ enter one's name.

'einschreiten 1. *fig. v/i.* (*irr. schreiten, sep., -ge-, sein*) step in, interpose, intervene; take action (*gegen* against); **2.** ⚥ *n* (*-s/no pl.*) intervention.

'ein|schrumpfen *v/i.* (*sep., -ge-, sein*) shrink; **'~schüchtern** *v/t.* (*sep., -ge-, h*) intimidate; bully; **'⅋schüchterung** *f* (*-/-en*) intimidation; **'~schulen** *v/t.* (*sep., -ge-, h*) put to school.

'Einschuß *m* bullet-hole; ✝ invested capital.

'ein|segnen *v/t.* (*sep., -ge-, h*) consecrate; confirm (*children*); **'⅋segnung** *f* consecration; confirmation.

'einsehen 1. *v/t.* (*irr. sehen, sep., -ge-, h*) look into; *fig.*: see, comprehend; realize; **2.** ⚥ *n* (*-s/no pl.*): *ein* ~ *haben* show consideration.

'einseifen *v/t.* (*sep., -ge-, h*) soap; lather (*beard*); F *fig.* humbug (*s.o.*).

'einseitig *adj.* ['aɪnzaɪtɪç] one-sided; ✇, *pol.*, ⚕ unilateral.

'einsend|en *v/t.* ([*irr. senden*], *sep., -ge-, h*) send in; **'⅋er** *m* (*-s/-*) sender; contributor (*to a paper*).

'einsetz|en (*sep., -ge-, h*) **1.** *v/t.* set or put in; stake (*money*); insert; institute; instal(l), appoint (*s.o.*); *fig.* use, employ; risk (*one's life*); *sich* ~ *für* stand up for; **2.** *v/i.* fever, flood, *weather*: set in; ♪ strike in; **'⅋ung** *f* (*-/-en*) insertion; appointment, installation.

'Einsicht *f* (*-/-en*) inspection; *fig.* insight, understanding; judiciousness; **'⅋ig** *adj.* judicious; sensible.

'einsickern *v/i.* (*sep., -ge-, sein*) soak in; infiltrate.

'Einsiedler *m* hermit.

'einsilbig *adj.* ['aɪnzɪlbɪç] monosyllabic; *fig.* taciturn; **'⅋keit** *f* (*-/no pl.*) taciturnity.

'einsinken *v/i.* (*irr. sinken, sep., -ge-, sein*) sink in.

'Einspänn|er ['aɪnʃpɛnər] *m* (*-s/-*) one-horse carriage; **'⅋ig** *adj.* one-horse.

'ein|sparen *v/t.* (*sep., -ge-, h*) save, economize; **'~sperren** *v/t.* (*sep., -ge-, h*) imprison; lock up, confine; **'~springen** *v/i.* (*irr. springen, sep., -ge-, sein*) ⊕ catch; *fig.* step in,

help out; *für j-n* ~ substitute for s.o.; **'~spritzen** *v/t.* (*sep., -ge-, h*) inject; **'⅋spritzung** *f* (*-/-en*) injection.

'Einspruch *m* objection, protest, veto; appeal; **'~srecht** *n* veto.

'einspurig *adj.* single-track.

einst *adv.* [aɪnst] once; one *or* some day.

'Einstand *m* entry; *tennis*: deuce.

'ein|stecken *v/t.* (*sep., -ge-, h*) put in; pocket; plug in; **'~steigen** *v/i.* (*irr. steigen, sep., -ge-, sein*) get in; ~*! ⚎* take your seats!, *Am.* all aboard!

'einstell|en *v/t.* (*sep., -ge-, h*) put in; ✕ enrol(l), enlist, *Am.* muster in; engage, employ, *Am. a.* hire; give up; stop, cease, *Am. a.* quit (*payment, etc.*); adjust (*mechanism*) (*auf acc.* to); tune in (radio) (to); *opt.* focus (on) (*a. fig.*); *die Arbeit* ~ cease working; strike, *Am. a.* walk out; *sich* ~ appear; *sich* ~ *auf* (*acc.*) be prepared for; adapt o.s. to; **'⅋ung** *f* ✕ enlistment; engagement; adjustment; focus; (mental) attitude, mentality.

'einstimm|en ♪ *v/i.* (*sep., -ge-, h*) join in; **'~ig** *adj.* unanimous; **'⅋igkeit** *f* (*-/no pl.*) unanimity.

einstöckig *adj.* ['aɪnʃtœkɪç] one-storied.

'ein|streuen *fig. v/t.* (*sep., -ge-, h*) intersperse; **'~studieren** *v/t.* (*sep., no -ge-, h*) study; *thea.* rehearse; **'~stürmen** *v/i.* (*sep., -ge-, sein*): *auf j-n* ~ rush at s.o.; **'⅋sturz** *m* falling in, collapse; **'~stürzen** *v/i.* (*sep., -ge-, sein*) fall in, collapse.

einst|weilen *adv.* ['aɪnst'vaɪlən] for the present; in the meantime; **'~weilig** *adj.* temporary.

'ein|tauschen *v/t.* (*sep., -ge-, h*) exchange (*gegen* for); **'~teilen** *v/t.* (*sep., -ge-, h*) divide (*in acc.* into); classify; **'~teilig** *adj.* one-piece; **'⅋teilung** *f* division; classification.

eintönig *adj.* ['aɪntøːnɪç] monotonous; **'⅋keit** *f* (*-/⚒ -en*) monotony.

'Eintopf(gericht *n*) *m* hot-pot; stew.

'Eintracht *f* (*-/no pl.*) harmony, concord.

einträchtig *adj.* ['aɪntrɛçtɪç] harmonious.

'eintragen *v/t.* (*irr. tragen, sep., -ge-, h*) enter; register; bring in,

yield (*profit*); **sich ~ in** (*acc.*) sign.
einträglich *adj.* ['aıntrɛːklıç] profitable.

'**Eintragung** *f* (-/-en) entry; registration.

'**ein|treffen** *v/i.* (*irr.* treffen, *sep.*, -ge-, *sein*) arrive; happen; come true; '**~treiben** *v/t.* (*irr.* treiben, *sep.*, -ge-, *h*) drive in *or* home; collect (*debts, taxes*); '**~treten** (*irr.* treten, *sep.*, -ge-) **1.** *v/i.* (*sein*) enter; occur, happen, take place; **~ für** stand up for; **~ in** (*acc.*) enter into (*rights*); enter upon (*possession*); enter (*room*); join (*the army, etc.*); **2.** *v/t.* (*h*) kick in (*door*); **sich et. ~ run** s.th. into one's foot.

'**Eintritt** *m* entry, entrance; admittance; beginning, setting-in (*of winter, etc.*); **~ frei!** admission free!; **~ verboten!** no admittance!; '**~sgeld** *n* entrance *or* admission fee; *sports:* gate money; '**~skarte** *f* admission ticket.

'**ein|trocknen** *v/i.* (*sep.*, -ge-, *sein*) dry (up); '**~trüben** *v/refl.* (*sep.*, -ge-, *h*) become cloudy *or* overcast; **~üben** ['aın?-] *v/t.* (*sep.*, -ge-, *h*) practi|se, *Am.* -ce s.th.; train *s.o.*

einver|leiben ['aınfɛrlaıbən] *v/t.* ([*sep.*,] *no* -ge-, *h*) incorporate (*dat.* in); annex (*to*); F **sich et. ~** eat *or* drink s.th.; '**2nehmen** *n* (-s/*no pl.*) agreement, understanding; **in gutem ~** on friendly terms; '**~standen** *adj.:* **~ sein** agree; '**2ständnis** *n* agreement.

'**Einwand** *m* (-[e]s/=e) objection (*gegen* to).

'**Einwander|er** *m* immigrant; '**2n** *v/i.* (*sep.*, -ge-, *sein*) immigrate; '**~ung** *f* immigration.

'**einwandfrei** *adj.* unobjectionable; perfect; faultless; *alibi:* sound.

einwärts *adv.* ['aınvɛrts] inward(s).

'**Einwegflasche** *f* one-way bottle, non-return bottle.

'**einweih|en** *v/t.* (*sep.*, -ge-, *h*) *eccl.* consecrate; inaugurate; **~ in** (*acc.*) initiate *s.o.* into; '**~ung** *f* (-/-en) consecration; inauguration; initiation.

'**einwend|en** *v/t.* ([*irr.* wenden,] *sep.*, -ge-, *h*) object; '**2ung** *f* objection.

'**einwerfen** (*irr.* werfen, *sep.*, -ge-) **1.** *v/t.* throw in (*a. fig.*); smash, break (*window-pane*); post, *Am.*

mail (*letter*); interject (*remark*); **2.** *v/i. football:* throw in.

'**einwickel|n** *v/t.* (*sep.*, -ge-, *h*) wrap (up), envelop; '**2papier** *n* wrapping-paper.

einwillig|en ['aınvılıgən] *v/i.* (*sep.*, -ge-, *h*) consent, agree (*in* to); '**2ung** *f* (-/-en) consent, agreement.

'**einwirk|en** *v/i.* (*sep.*, -ge-, *h*): **~ auf** (*acc.*) act (up)on; influence; effect; '**2ung** *f* influence; effect.

Einwohner ['aınvoːnər] *m* (-s/-), '**~in** *f* (-/-nen) inhabitant, resident.

'**Einwurf** *m* throwing in; *football:* throw-in; *fig.* objection; slit (*for letters, etc.*); slot (*for coins*).

'**Einzahl** *gr. f* (-/**~**-en) singular (number); '**2en** *v/t.* (*sep.*, -ge-, *h*) pay in; '**~ung** *f* payment; deposit (*at bank*).

einzäunen ['aıntsɔynən] *v/t.* (*sep.*, -ge-, *h*) fence in.

Einzel ['aıntsəl] *n* (-s/-) *tennis:* single, *Am.* singles *pl.*; '**~gänger** ['~gɛŋər] *m* (-s/-) outsider; F lone wolf; '**~handel** ✝ *m* retail trade; '**~händler** ✝ *m* retailer, retail dealer; '**~heit** *f* (-/-en) detail, item; **~en** *pl.* particulars *pl.*, details *pl.*; '**2n 1.** *adj.* single; particular; individual; separate; (*of shoes, etc.*: odd; **im ~en** in detail; **2.** *adv.:* **~ angeben** *or* **aufführen** specify, *esp. Am.* itemize; '**~ne** *m* (-n/-n) the individual; '**~verkauf** *m* retail sale; '**~wesen** *n* individual.

'**einziehen** (*irr.* ziehen, *sep.*, -ge-) **1.** *v/t.* (*h*) draw in; *esp.* ⊕ retract; ✗ call up *or* in, *Am.* draft, induct; ⚖ seize, confiscate; make (*inquiries*) (*über acc.* on, about); **2.** *v/i.* (*sein*) enter; move in; *liquid:* soak in; **~ in** (*acc.*) move into (*flat, etc.*).

einzig *adj.* ['aıntsıç] only; single; sole; unique; '**~artig** *adj.* unique, singular.

'**Einzug** *m* entry, entrance; moving in.

'**einzwängen** *v/t.* (*sep.*, -ge-, *h*) squeeze, jam.

Eis [aıs] *n* (-es/*no pl.*) ice; ice-cream; '**~bahn** *f* skating-rink; '**~bär** *zo. m* polar bear; '**~bein** *n* pickled pork shank; '**~berg** *m* iceberg; '**~decke** *f* sheet of ice; '**~diele** *f* ice-cream parlo(u)r.

Eisen ['aızən] *n* (-s/-) iron.

'**Eisenbahn** *f* railway, *Am.* railroad;

mit der ~ by rail, by train; '~er m (-s/-) railwayman; '~fahrt f railway journey; '~knotenpunkt m (railway) junction; '~unglück n railway accident; '~wagen m railway carriage, *Am.* railroad car; coach.

'Eisen|blech n sheet-iron; '~erz n iron-ore; '~gießerei f iron-foundry; '2haltig *adj.* ferruginous; '~hütte f ironworks *sg., pl.*; '~waren f/pl. ironmongery, *esp. Am.* hardware; '~warenhändler m ironmonger, *esp. Am.* hardware dealer.

eisern *adj.* ['aɪzərn] iron, of iron.

'Eis|gang m breaking up of the ice; ice-drift; 2gekühlt *adj.* ['~gəkyːlt] iced; '2grau *adj.* hoary; '~hockey n ice-hockey; 2ig *adj.* ['aɪziç] icy; '2kalt *adj.* icy (cold); '~kunstlauf m figure-skating; '~lauf m, '~laufen n (-s/no pl.) skating; skate; '~läufer m skater; '~meer n polar sea; '~schnellauf m speed-skating; '~scholle f ice-floe; '~schrank m s. Kühlschrank; '~vogel orn. m kingfisher; '~zapfen m icicle; '~zeit geol. f ice-age.

eitel *adj.* ['aɪtəl] vain (*auf acc.* of); conceited; mere; '2keit f (-/-en) vanity.

Eiter 🏥 ['aɪtər] m (-s/no pl.) matter, pus; '~beule f abscess; '2ig *adj.* purulent; '2n v/i. (ge-, h) fester, suppurate; '~ung f (-/-en) suppuration.

eitrig *adj.* ['aɪtriç] purulent.

'Eiweiß n (-es/-e) white of egg; 🏥 albumen; '2haltig 🏥 *adj.* albuminous.

'Eizelle f egg-cell, ovum.

Ekel ['eːkəl] 1. m (-s/no pl.) disgust (*vor dat.* at), loathing; aversion; 🏥 nausea; 2. F n (-s/-) nasty person; '2erregend *adj.* nauseating, sickening; '2haft *adj.*, '2ig *adj.* revolting; *fig.* disgusting; '2n v/refl. (ge-, h): *sich* ~ be nauseated (*vor dat.* at); *fig.* be *or* feel disgusted (at).

eklig *adj.* ['eːkliç] s. ekelhaft.

elasti|sch *adj.* [e'lastiʃ] elastic; 2zität [~tsi'tɛːt] f (-/no pl.) elasticity.

Elch zo. [ɛlç] m (-[e]s/-e) elk; moose.

Elefant zo. [ele'fant] m (-en/-en) elephant.

elegan|t *adj.* [ele'gant] elegant;

smart; 2z [~ts] f (-/no pl.) elegance.

elektrifizier|en [elektrifi'tsiːrən] v/t. (no -ge-, h) electrify; 2ung f (-/-en) electrification.

Elektri|ker [e'lɛktrikər] m (-s/-) electrician; 2sch *adj.* electric(al); 2sieren [~'ziːrən] v/t. (no -ge-, h) electrify.

Elektrizität [elektritsi'tɛːt] f (-/no pl.) electricity; ~sgesellschaft f electricity supply company; ~swerk n (electric) power station, power-house, *Am.* power plant.

Elektrode [elek'troːdə] f (-/-n) electrode.

Elektro|gerät [e'lɛktro-] n electric appliance; ~lyse [~'lyːzə] f (-/-n) electrolysis.

Elektron ⚡ [e'lɛktrɔn] n (-s/-en) electron; ~engehirn [~'troːnən-] n electronic brain; ~ik [~'troːnik] f (-/no pl.) electronics f.

Elektro'technik f electrical engineering; ~er m electrical engineer.

Element [ele'mɛnt] n (-[e]s/-e) element.

elementar *adj.* [elemen'taːr] elementary; 2schule f elementary *or* primary school, *Am.* grade school.

Elend ['eːlɛnt] 1. n (-[e]s/no pl.) misery; need, distress; 2. 2 *adj.* miserable, wretched; needy, distressed; '~sviertel n slums *pl.*

elf[1] [ɛlf] 1. *adj.* eleven; 2. 2 f (-/-en) eleven (*a. sports*).

Elf[2] [~] m (-en/-en), ~e f [ɛlfə] f (-/-n) elf, fairy.

'Elfenbein n (-[e]s/~-e) ivory; 2ern *adj.* ivory.

Elf'meter m *football*: penalty kick; ~marke f penalty spot.

'elfte *adj.* eleventh.

Elite [e'liːtə] f (-/-n) élite.

'Ellbogen *anat.* m (-s/-) elbow.

Elle ['ɛlə] f (-/-n) yard; *anat.* ulna.

Elster *orn.* ['ɛlstər] f (-/-n) magpie.

elter|lich *adj.* ['ɛltərliç] parental; 2n *pl.* parents *pl.*; '~nlos *adj.* parentless, orphaned; '2nteil m parent. [(-/-n) enamel.)

Email [e'maːj] n (-s/-s), '~le [~] f)

Emanzipation [emantsipa'tsjoːn] f (-/-en) emancipation.

Embargo [ɛm'bargo] n (-s/-s) embargo. [bolism.)

Embolie 🏥 [ɛmbo'liː] f (-/-n) em-)

Embryo *biol.* ['ɛmbryo] m (-s/-s, -nen) embryo.

Emigrant [emi'grant] *m* (-en/-en) emigrant.

empfahl [ɛm'pfɑːl] *pret. of* empfehlen.

Empfang [ɛm'pfaŋ] *m* (-[e]s/⁀e) reception (*a. radio*); receipt (*of s.th.*); *nach or bei ~* on receipt; **'2en** *v/t.* (*irr. fangen, no -ge-, h*) receive; welcome; conceive (*child*).

Empfänger [ɛm'pfɛŋər] *m* (-s/-) receiver, recipient; payee (*of money*); addressee (*of letter*); ✝ consignee (*of goods*).

em'pfänglich *adj.* susceptible (*für* to); **2keit** *f* (-/*no pl.*) susceptibility.

Em'pfangs|dame *f* receptionist; **~gerät** *n* receiver, receiving set; **~schein** *m* receipt; **~zimmer** *n* reception-room.

empfehl|en [ɛm'pfeːlən] *v/t.* (*irr., no -ge-, h*) recommend; commend; *~ Sie mich* (*dat.*) please remember me to; **~enswert** *adj.* (re)commendable; **2ung** *f* (-/-en) recommendation; compliments *pl.*

empfinden [ɛm'pfɪndən] *v/t.* (*irr. finden, no -ge-, h*) feel; perceive.

empfindlich *adj.* [ɛm'pfɪntlɪç] sensitive (*a. phot.,* ♠) (*für* gegen to); *pred. a.* susceptible (*gegen* to); delicate; tender; *p.:* touchy, sensitive; *cold:* severe; *pain, loss, etc.:* grievous; *pain:* acute; **2keit** *f* (-/-en) sensitivity; sensibility; touchiness; delicacy.

empfindsam *adj.* [ɛm'pfɪntzaːm] sensitive; sentimental; **2keit** *f* (-/-en) sensitiveness; sentimentality.

Empfindung [ɛm'pfɪnduŋ] *f* (-/-en) perception; sensation; sentiment; **2slos** *adj.* insensible; *esp. fig.* unfeeling; **~svermögen** *n* faculty of perception.

empfohlen [ɛm'pfoːlən] *p.p. of* empfehlen. [wards.]

empor *adv.* [ɛm'poːr] up, up-]

empören [ɛm'pøːrən] *v/t.* (*no -ge-, h*) incense; shock; *sich ~* revolt (*a. fig.*), rebel; grow furious (*über acc.* at); *empört* indignant, shocked (*both: über acc.* at).

em'por|kommen *v/i.* (*irr. kommen, sep., -ge-, sein*) rise (in the world); **2kömmling** [~kœmlɪŋ] *m* (-s/-e) upstart; **~ragen** *v/i.* (*sep., -ge-, h*) tower, rise; **~steigen** *v/i.* (*irr. steigen, sep., -ge-, sein*) rise, ascend.

Em'pörung *f* (-/-en) rebellion, revolt; indignation.

emsig *adj.* ['ɛmzɪç] busy, industrious, diligent; **2keit** *f* (-/*no pl.*) busyness, industry, diligence.

Ende ['ɛndə] *n* (-s/-n) end; *am ~* at *or* in the end; after all; eventually; *zu ~ gehen* end; expire; run short; **'2n** *v/i.* (*ge-, h*) end; cease, finish.

end|gültig *adj.* ['ɛntgyltɪç] final, definitive; **~lich** *adv.* finally, at last; **~los** *adj.* ['~loːs] endless; **2punkt** *m* final point; **2runde** *f* *sports:* final; **2station** ♠ *f* terminus, *Am.* terminal; **2summe** *f* (sum) total.

Endung *ling.* ['ɛnduŋ] *f* (-/-en) ending, termination.

Endzweck ['ɛnt-] *m* ultimate object.

Energie [enɛr'giː] *f* (-/-n) energy; **2los** *adj.* lacking in energy.

e'nergisch *adj.* vigorous; energetic.

eng *adj.* [ɛŋ] narrow; *clothes:* tight; close; intimate; *im ~eren Sinne* strictly speaking.

engagieren [ãga'ʒiːrən] *v/t.* (*no -ge-, h*) engage, *Am. a.* hire.

Enge ['ɛŋə] *f* (-/-n) narrowness; *fig.* straits *pl.*

Engel ['ɛŋəl] *m* (-s/-) angel.

'engherzig *adj.* ungenerous, petty.

Engländer ['ɛŋlɛndər] *m* (-s/-) Englishman; *die ~ pl.* the English *pl.*; **~in** *f* (-/-nen) Englishwoman.

englisch *adj.* ['ɛŋlɪʃ] English; British.

'Engpaß *m* defile, narrow pass, *Am. a.* notch; *fig.* bottle-neck.

en gros ✝ *adv.* [ã'groː] wholesale.

En'groshandel ✝ *m* wholesale trade.

'engstirnig *adj.* narrow-minded.

Enkel ['ɛŋkəl] *m* (-s/-) grandchild; grandson; **~in** *f* (-/-nen) granddaughter.

enorm *adj.* [e'nɔrm] enormous; *F fig.* tremendous.

Ensemble *thea.,* ♪ [ã'sãːbəl] *n* (-s/-s) ensemble; company.

entart|en [ɛnt'ʔaːrtən] *v/i.* (*no -ge-, sein*) degenerate; **2ung** *f* (-/-en) degeneration.

entbehr|en [ɛnt'beːrən] *v/t.* (*no -ge-, h*) lack; miss; want; do without; **~lich** *adj.* dispensable; superfluous; **2ung** *f* (-/-en) want, privation.

ent'bind|en (*irr. binden, no -ge-, h*)

1. v/t. dispense, release (von from); deliver (of a child); **2.** v/i. be confined; **Qung** f dispensation, release; delivery; **Qungsheim** n maternity hospital.

ent'blöß|en v/t. (no -ge-, h) bare, strip; uncover (head); **~t** adj. bare.

ent'deck|en v/t. (no -ge-, h) discover; detect; disclose; **~er** m (-s/-) discoverer; **Qung** f discovery.

Ente ['ɛntə] f (-/-n) orn. duck; false report: F canard, hoax.

ent'ehr|en v/t. (no -ge-, h) dishono(u)r; **Qung** f degradation; rape.

ent'eign|en v/t. (no -ge-, h) expropriate; dispossess; **Qung** f expropriation; dispossession.

ent'erben v/t. (no -ge-, h) disinherit.

entern ['ɛntərn] v/t. (ge-, h) board, grapple (ship).

ent'|fachen v/t. (no -ge-, h) kindle; fig. a. rouse (passions); **~'fallen** v/i. (irr. fallen, no -ge-, sein): j-m ~ escape s.o.; fig. slip s.o.'s memory; auf j-n ~ fall to s.o.'s share; s. wegfallen; **~'falten** v/t. (no -ge-, h) unfold; fig.: develop; display; sich ~ unfold; fig. develop (zu into).

ent'fern|en v/t. (no -ge-, h) remove; sich ~ withdraw; **~t** adj. distant, remote (both a. fig.); **Qung** f (-/-en) removal; distance; range; **Qungsmesser** phot. m (-s/-) range-finder.

ent'flammen (no -ge-) v/t. (h) and v/i. (sein) inflame; **~'fliehen** v/i. (irr. fliehen, no -ge-, sein) flee, escape (aus or dat. from); **~'fremden** v/t. (no -ge-, h) estrange, alienate (j-m from s.o.).

ent'führ|en v/t. (no -ge-, h) abduct, kidnap; run away with; **Qer** m abductor, kidnap(p)er; **Qung** f abduction, kidnap(p)ing.

ent'gegen 1. prp. (dat.) in opposition to, contrary to; against; **2.** adv. towards; **~gehen** v/i. (irr. gehen, sep., -ge-, sein) go to meet; **~gesetzt** adj. opposite; fig. contrary; **~halten** v/t. (irr. halten, sep., -ge-, h) hold out; fig. object; **~kommen** v/i. (irr. kommen, sep., -ge-, sein) come to meet; fig. meet s.o.'s wishes) halfway; **Qkommen** n (-s/no pl.) obligingness; **~kommend** adj. obliging; **~nehmen** v/t. (irr. nehmen, sep., -ge-, h) accept, receive; **~sehen** v/i. (dat.) (irr. sehen, sep., -ge-, h) await; look for-

ward to; **~setzen** v/t. (sep., -ge-, h) oppose; **~stehen** v/i. (irr. stehen, sep., -ge-, h) be opposed (dat. to); **~strecken** v/t. (sep., -ge-, h) hold or stretch out (dat. to); **~treten** v/i. (dat.) (irr. treten, sep., -ge-, sein) step up to s.o.; oppose; face (danger).

entgegn|en [ɛnt'ge:gnən] v/i. (no -ge-, h) reply; return; retort; **Qung** f (-/-en) reply; retort.

ent'gehen v/i. (irr. gehen, no -ge-, sein) escape.

entgeistert adj. [ɛnt'gaɪstərt] a-ghast, thunderstruck, flabbergasted.

Entgelt [ɛnt'gɛlt] n (-[e]s/no pl.) recompense; **Qen** v/t. (irr. gelten, no -ge-, h) atone or suffer or pay for.

entgleis|en [ɛnt'glaɪzən] v/i. (no -ge-, sein) run off the rails, be derailed; fig. (make a) slip; **Qung** f (-/-en) derailment; fig. slip.

ent'gleiten v/i. (irr. gleiten, no -ge-, sein) slip (dat. from).

ent'halt|en v/t. (irr. halten, no -ge-, h) contain, hold, include; sich ~ (gen.) abstain or refrain from; **~sam** adj. abstinent; **Qsamkeit** f (-/no pl.) abstinence; **Qung** f abstention.   [decapitate.\

ent'haupten v/t.(no -ge-, h) behead,\
ent'hüll|en v/t. (no -ge-, h) uncover; unveil; fig. reveal, disclose; **Qung** f (-/-en) uncovering; unveiling; fig. revelation, disclosure.

Enthusias|mus [ɛntuzi'asmus] m (-/no pl.) enthusiasm; **~t** m (-en/-en) enthusiast; film, sports: F fan; **Qtisch** adj. enthusiastic.

ent'kleiden v/t. and v/refl.(no -ge-, h) undress.

ent'kommen **1.** v/i. (irr. kommen, no -ge-, sein) escape (j-m s.o.; aus from), get away or off; **2.** Q n (-s/no pl.) escape.

entkräft|en [ɛnt'krɛftən] v/t. (no -ge-, h) weaken, debilitate; fig. refute; **Qung** f (-/-en) weakening; debility; fig. refutation.

ent'lad|en v/t. (irr. laden, no -ge-, h) unload; esp. ⚡ discharge; explode; sich ~ esp. ⚡ discharge; gun: go off; anger: vent itself; **Qung** f unloading; esp. ⚡ discharge; explosion.

ent'lang 1. prp. (dat.; acc.) along; **2.** adv. along; er geht die Straße ~ he goes along the street.

ent'larven v/t. (no -ge-, h) unmask; fig. a. expose.

ent'lass|en v/t. (irr. lassen, no -ge-, h) dismiss, discharge; F give s.o. the sack, Am. a. fire; $\mathfrak{L}$**ung** f (-/-en) dismissal, discharge; $\mathfrak{L}$**ungsgesuch** n resignation.

ent'lasten v/t. (no -ge-, h) unburden; $\frac{1}{4}$ exonerate, clear (from suspicion).

Ent'lastung f (-/-en) relief; discharge; exoneration; ~**sstraße** f by-pass (road); ~**szeuge** m witness for the defen|ce, Am. -se.

ent|'laufen v/i. (irr. laufen, no -ge-, sein) run away (dat. from); ~**ledigen** [~'le:digən] v/refl. (gen.) (no -ge-, h) rid o.s. of s.th., get rid of s.th.; acquit o.s. of (duty); execute (orders); ~'**leeren** v/t. (no -ge-, h) empty. [of-the-way.\

ent'legen adj. remote, distant, out-\

ent|'lehnen v/t. (no -ge-, h) borrow (dat. or aus from); ~'**locken** v/t. (no -ge-, h) draw, elicit (dat. from); ~'**lohnen** v/t. (no -ge-, h) pay (off); ~'**lüften** v/t. (no -ge-, h) ventilate; ~**militarisieren** [~militari'zi:rən] v/t. (no -ge-, h) demilitarize; ~**mutigen** [~'mu:tigən] v/t. (no -ge-, h) discourage; ~'**nehmen** v/t. (irr. nehmen, no -ge-, h) take (dat. from); ~ aus (with)draw from; fig. gather or learn from; ~'**rätseln** v/t. (no -ge-, h) unriddle; ~'**reißen** v/t. (irr. reißen, no -ge-, h) snatch away (dat. from); ~'**richten** v/t. (no -ge-, h) pay; ~'**rinnen** v/i. (irr. rinnen, no -ge-, sein) escape (dat. from); ~'**rollen** v/t. (no -ge-, h) unroll; ~'**rücken** v/t. (no -ge-, h) remove (dat. from), carry off or away; ~**rückt** adj. entranced; lost in thought.

ent'rüst|en v/t. (no -ge-, h) fill with indignation; sich ~ become angry or indignant (über acc. at s.th., with s.o.); ~**et** adj. indignant (über acc. at s.th., with s.o.); $\mathfrak{L}$**ung** f indignation.

ent'sag|en v/i. (no -ge-, h) renounce, resign; $\mathfrak{L}$**ung** f (-/-en) renunciation, resignation.

ent'schädig|en v/t. (no -ge-, h) indemnify, compensate; $\mathfrak{L}$**ung** f indemnification, indemnity; compensation.

ent'scheid|en (irr. scheiden, no -ge-, h) **1.** v/t. decide; sich ~ question, etc.: be decided; p.: decide (für for; gegen against; über acc. on); come to a decision; **2.** v/i. decide; ~**end** adj. decisive; crucial; $\mathfrak{L}$**ung** f decision.

entschieden adj. [ɛnt'ʃi:dən] decided; determined, resolute; $\mathfrak{L}$**heit** (-/no pl.) determination.

ent'schließen v/refl. (irr. schließen no -ge-, h) resolve, decide, determine (zu on s.th.; zu inf. to inf.); make up one's mind (zu inf. to inf.).

ent'schlossen adj. resolute, determined; $\mathfrak{L}$**heit** f (-/no pl.) resoluteness.

ent'schlüpfen v/i. (no -ge-, sein) escape, slip (dat. from).

Ent'schluß m resolution, resolve, decision, determination.

entschuldig|en [ɛnt'ʃuldigən] v/t. (no -ge-, h) excuse; sich ~ apologize (bei to; für for); sich ~ lassen beg to be excused; $\mathfrak{L}$**ung** f (-/-en) excuse; apology; ich bitte (Sie) um ~ I beg your pardon.

ent'senden v/t. (irr. senden, no -ge-, h) send off, dispatch; delegate, depute.

ent'setz|en 1. v/t. (no -ge-, h) dismiss (from a position); $\times$ relieve; frighten; sich ~ be terrified or shocked (über acc. at); **2.** $\mathfrak{L}$ n (-/no pl.) horror, fright; ~**lich** adj. horrible, dreadful, terrible, shocking.

ent'sinnen v/refl. (gen.) (irr. sinnen, no -ge-, h) remember or recall s.o., s.th.

ent'spann|en v/t. (no -ge-, h) relax; unbend; sich ~ relax; political situation: ease; $\mathfrak{L}$**ung** f relaxation; pol. détente.

ent'sprech|en v/i. (irr. sprechen, no -ge-, h) answer (description, etc.); correspond to; meet (demand); ~**end** adj. corresponding; appropriate; $\mathfrak{L}$**ung** f (-/-en) equivalent.

ent'springen v/i. (irr. springen, no -ge-, sein) escape (dat. from); river: rise, Am. head; s. entstehen.

ent'stammen v/i. (no -ge-, sein) be descended from; come from or of, originate from.

ent'steh|en v/i. (irr. stehen, no -ge-, sein) arise, originate (both: aus from); $\mathfrak{L}$**ung** f (-/-en) origin.

ent'stell|en v/t. (no -ge-, h) disfigure; deface, deform; distort; $\mathfrak{L}$**ung** f disfigurement; distortion, misrepresentation.

ent'täusch|en v/t. (no -ge-, h) disappoint; **~ung** f disappointment.

ent'thronen v/t. (no -ge-, h) dethrone.

entvölker|n [ɛnt'fœlkərn] v/t. (no -ge-, h) depopulate; **~ung** f (-/-en) depopulation.

ent'wachsen v/i. (irr. wachsen, no -ge-, sein) outgrow.

entwaffn|en [ɛnt'vafnən] v/t. (no -ge-, h) disarm; **~ung** f (-/-en) disarmament.

ent'warnen v/i. (no -ge-, h) civil defence: sound the all-clear (signal).

ent'wässer|n v/t. (no -ge-, h) drain; **~ung** f (-/-en) drainage; **⚗** dehydration.

ent'weder cj.: **~** ... oder either ... or.

ent|'weichen v/i. (irr. weichen, no -ge-, sein) escape (aus from); **~'weihen** v/t. (no -ge-, h) desecrate, profane; **~'wenden** v/t. (no -ge-, h) pilfer, purloin (j-m et. s.th. from s.o.); **~'werfen** v/t. (irr. werfen, no -ge-, h) draft, draw up (document); design; sketch, trace out, outline; plan.

ent'wert|en v/t. (no -ge-, h) depreciate, devaluate; cancel (stamp); **~ung** f depreciation, devaluation; cancellation.

ent'wickeln v/t. (no -ge-, h) develop (a. phot.); evolve; sich **~** develop.

Entwicklung [ɛnt'viklun] f (-/-en) development; evolution; **~shilfe** f development aid.

ent|'wirren v/t. (no -ge-, h) disentangle, unravel; **~'wischen** v/i. (no -ge-, sein) slip away, escape (j-m [from] s.o.; aus from); j-m **~** give s.o. the slip; **~wöhnen** [.'vø:nən] v/t. (no -ge-, h) wean.

Ent'wurf m sketch; design; plan; draft.

ent|'wurzeln v/t. (no -ge-, h) uproot; **~'ziehen** v/t. (irr. ziehen, no -ge-, h) deprive (j-m et. s.o. of s.th.); withdraw (dat. from); sich **~** avoid, elude; evade (responsibility); **~'ziffern** v/t. (no -ge-, h) decipher, make out; tel. decode.

ent'zücken **1.** v/t. (no -ge-, h) charm, delight; **2.** ⚤ n (-s/no pl.) delight, rapture(s pl.), transport(s pl.).   [ing.]

ent'zückend adj. delightful; charm-|

Ent'zug m (-[e]s/no pl.) withdrawal; cancellation (of licence); deprivation.

entzünd|bar adj. [ɛnt'tsyntbɑ:r] (in)flammable; **~en** v/t. (no -ge-, h) inflame (a. ⚚), kindle; sich **~** catch fire; ⚚ become inflamed; **~ung** f ⚚ inflammation.

ent'zwei adv. asunder, in two, to pieces; **~en** v/t. (no -ge-, h) disunite, set at variance; sich **~** quarrel, fall out (both: mit with); **~gehen** v/i. (irr. gehen, sep., -ge-, sein) break, go to pieces; **~ung** f (-/-en) disunion.

Enzian ♀ ['ɛntsjɑ:n] m (-s/-e) gentian.

Enzyklopädie [ɛntsyklopɛ'di:] f (-/-n) (en)cyclop(a)edia.

Epidemie ⚚ [epide'mi:] f (-/-n) epidemic (disease).

Epilog [epi'lo:k] m (-s/-e) epilog(ue).

episch adj. ['e:piʃ] epic.

Episode [epi'zo:də] f (-/-n) episode.

Epoche [e'pɔxə] f (-/-n) epoch.

Epos ['e:pɔs] n (-/Epen) epic (poem).

er pers. pron. [e:r] he.

erachten [ɛr'-] **1.** v/t. (no -ge-, h) consider, think, deem; **2.** ⚤ n (-s/no pl.) opinion; m-s **~s** in my opinion.

erbarmen [ɛr'barmən] **1.** v/refl. (gen.) (no -ge-, h) pity or commiserate s.o.; **2.** ⚤ n (-s/no pl.) pity, compassion, commiseration; mercy; **~swert** adj. pitiable.

erbärmlich adj. [ɛr'bɛrmliç] pitiful, pitiable; miserable; behaviour: mean.

er'barmungslos adj. pitiless, merciless, relentless.

er'bau|en v/t. (no -ge-, h) build (up), construct, raise; fig. edify; **⚤er** m (-s/-) builder; constructor; **~lich** adj. edifying; **~ung** fig. f (-/-en) edification, Am. uplift.

Erbe ['ɛrbə] **1.** m (-n/-n) heir; **2.** ⚤ n (-s/no pl.) inheritance, heritage.

er'beben v/i. (no -ge-, sein) tremble, shake, quake.

'erben v/t. (ge-, h) inherit.

er'beuten v/t. (no -ge-, h) capture.

er'bieten v/refl. (irr. bieten, no -ge-, h) offer, volunteer.

'Erbin f (-/-nen) heiress.

er'bitten v/t. (irr. bitten, no -ge-, h) beg or ask for, request, solicit.

er'bittern v/t. (no -ge-, h) embitter, exasperate; **~ung** f (-/⚛ -en) bitterness, exasperation.

Erbkrankheit ⚚ ['ɛrp-] f hereditary disease.

erblassen [ɛrˈblasən] v/i. (no -ge-, sein) grow or turn pale, lose colo(u)r.

Erblasser ⚖ [ˈɛrblasər] m (-s/-) testator; '**in** f (-/-nen) testatrix.

er'bleichen v/i. (no -ge-, sein) s. erblassen.

erblich adj. [ˈɛrplɪç] hereditary; 'keit physiol. f (-/no pl.) heredity.

er'blicken v/t. (no -ge-, h) perceive, see; catch sight of.

erblind|en [ɛrˈblɪndən] v/i. (no -ge-, sein) grow blind; ung f (-/-en) loss of sight.

er'brechen 1. v/t. (irr. brechen, no -ge-, h) break or force open; vomit; sich ⚕ vomit; 2. n (-s/no pl.) vomiting.

Erbschaft [ˈɛrpʃaft] f (-/-en) inheritance, heritage.

Erbse ⚘ [ˈɛrpsə] f (-/-n) pea; 'n-brei m pease-pudding, Am. pea purée; 'nsuppe f pea-soup.

Erb|stück [ˈɛrp-] n heirloom; pl.; 'sünde f original sin; 'teil n (portion of an) inheritance.

Erd|arbeiter [ˈeːrt-] m digger, navvy; 'ball m globe; 'beben n (-s/-) earthquake; 'beere ⚘ f strawberry; 'boden m earth; ground, soil; e [ˈeːrdə] f (-/ -n) earth; ground; soil; world; 'en ⚡ v/t. (ge-, h) earth, ground.

er'denklich adj. imaginable.

Erdgeschoß [ˈeːrt-] n ground-floor, Am. first floor.

er'dicht|en v/t. (no -ge-, h) invent, feign; 'et adj. fictitious.

erdig adj. [ˈeːrdɪç] earthy.

Erd|karte [ˈeːrt-] f map of the earth; 'kreis m earth, world; 'kugel f globe; 'kunde f geography; 'leitung ⚡ f earth-connexion, earth-wire, Am. ground wire; 'nuß f peanut; 'öl n mineral oil, petroleum.

er'dolchen v/t. (no -ge-, h) stab (with a dagger).

Erdreich [ˈeːrt-] n ground, earth.

er'dreisten v/refl. (no -ge-, h) dare, presume.

er'drosseln v/t. (no -ge-, h) strangle, throttle.

er'drücken v/t. (no -ge-, h) squeeze or crush to death; d fig. adj. overwhelming.

Erd|rutsch [ˈeːrt-] m landslip; landslide (a. pol.); 'schicht f layer of earth, stratum; 'teil m

part of the world; geogr. continent.

er'dulden v/t. (no -ge-, h) suffer, endure.

er'eifern v/refl. (no -ge-, h) get excited, fly into a passion.

er'eignen v/refl. (no -ge-, h) happen, come to pass, occur.

Ereignis [ɛrˈaiknis] n (-ses/-se) event, occurrence, reich adj. eventful.

Eremit [ere'miːt] m (-en/-en) hermit, anchorite.

ererbt adj. [ɛrˈɛrpt] inherited.

er'fahr|en 1. v/t. (irr. fahren, no -ge-, h) learn; hear; experience; 2. adj. experienced, expert, skil(l)-ful; ung f (-/-en) experience; practice; skill.

er'fassen v/t. (no -ge-, h) grasp (a. fig.), seize, catch; cover; register, record.

er'find|en v/t. (irr. finden, no -ge-, h) invent; er m inventor; 'erisch adj. inventive; ung f (-/-en) invention.

Erfolg [ɛrˈfɔlk] m (-[e]s/-e) success; result; en [gən] v/i. (no -ge-, sein) ensue, follow; happen; los adj. [k-] unsuccessful; vain; reich adj. [k-] successful.

er'forder|lich adj. necessary; required; n v/t. (no -ge-, h) demand; nis n (-ses/-se) requirement, demand, exigence, exigency.

er'forsch|en v/t. (no -ge-, h) inquire into, investigate, explore (country); er m investigator; explorer; ung f investigation; exploration.

er'freu|en v/t. (no -ge-, h) please; delight; gratify; rejoice; sich e-r Sache enjoy s.th.; 'lich adj. delightful, pleasing, pleasant, gratifying.

er'frier|en v/i. (irr. frieren, no -ge-, sein) freeze to death; ung f (-/-en) frost-bite.

er'frisch|en v/t. (no -ge-, h) refresh; ung f (-/-en) refreshment.

er'froren adj. limb: frost-bitten.

er'füll|en v/t. (no -ge-, h) fill; fig. fulfil(l); perform (mission); comply with (s.o.'s wishes); meet (requirements); ung f fulfil(l)ment; performance; compliance; ungsort ⚖, ⚖ [ɛrˈfylʊŋs-] m place of performance (of contract).

ergänz|en [ɛrˈgɛntsən] v/t. (no -ge-,

h) complete, complement; supplement; replenish (*stores*, *etc.*); **∼end** *adj.* complementary, supplementary; **Qung** *f* (-/-en) completion; supplement; replenishment; *gr.* complement; **Qungsband** *m* (-[e]s/ᵘe) supplementary volume.

er'geben 1. *v/t.* (*irr.* geben, *no* -ge-, *h*) yield, give; prove; *sich* ∼ surrender; difficulties: arise; devote o.s. to *s.th.*; *sich* ∼ *aus* result from; *sich* ∼ *in* (*acc.*) resign o.s. to; **2.** *adj.* devoted (*dat.* to); **∼st** *adv.* respectfully; **Qheit** *f* (-/*no pl.*) devotion.

Ergeb|nis [ɛr'geːpnɪs] *n* (-ses/-se) result, outcome; *sports*: score; **Qung** [∼buŋ] *f* (-/-en) resignation; ⚔ surrender.

er'gehen *v/i.* (*irr.* gehen, *no* -ge-, *sein*) be issued; ∼ *lassen* issue, publish; *über sich* ∼ *lassen* suffer, submit to; *wie ist es ihm ergangen?* how did he come off?; *sich* ∼ *in* (*dat.*) indulge in. [*rich.*]

ergiebig *adj.* [ɛr'giːbɪç] productive,)

er'gießen *v/refl.* (*irr.* gießen, *no* -ge-, *h*) flow (*in acc.* into; *über acc.* over).

er'götz|en 1. *v/t.* (*no* -ge-, *h*) delight; *sich* ∼ *an* (*dat.*) delight in; **2.** **Q** *n* (-s/*no pl.*) delight; **∼lich** *adj.* delightful.

er'greif|en *v/t.* (*irr.* greifen, *no* -ge-, *h*) seize; grasp; take (*possession*, *s.o.'s part*, *measures*, *etc.*); take to (*flight*); take up (*profession*, *pen*, *arms*); *fig.* move, affect, touch; **Qung** *f* (-/✍ -en) seizure.

Er'griffenheit *f* (-/*no pl.*) emotion.

er'gründen *v/t.* (*no* -ge-, *h*) fathom; *fig.* penetrate, get to the bottom of.

Er'guß *m* outpouring; effusion.

er'haben *adj.* elevated; *fig.* exalted, sublime; ∼ *sein über* (*acc.*) be above; **Qheit** *f* (-/✍ -en) elevation; *fig.* sublimity.

er'halt|en 1. *v/t.* (*irr.* halten, *no* -ge-, *h*) get; obtain; receive; preserve, keep; support, maintain; *sich* ∼ *von* subsist on; **2.** *adj.*: *gut* ∼ in good repair *or* condition; **Qung** *f* preservation; maintenance. [*able.*]

erhältlich *adj.* [ɛr'hɛltlɪç] obtain-)

er'hängen *v/t.* (*no* -ge-, *h*) hang; **∼härten** *v/t.* (*no* -ge-, *h*) harden; *fig.* confirm; **∼haschen** *v/t.* (*no* -ge-, *h*) snatch, catch.

er'heb|en *v/t.* (*irr.* heben, *no* -ge-, *h*) lift, raise; elevate; exalt; levy, raise, collect (*taxes*, *etc.*); *Klage* ∼ bring an action; *sich* ∼ rise; *question*, *etc.*: arise; **∼end** *fig. adj.* elevating; **∼lich** *adj.* [∼p-] considerable; **Qung** [∼buŋ] *f* (-/-en) elevation; levy (*of taxes*); revolt; rising ground.

er'heitern *v/t.* (*no* -ge-, *h*) cheer up, amuse; **∼hellen** *v/t.* (*no* -ge-, *h*) light up; *fig.* clear up; **∼'hitzen** *v/t.* (*no* -ge-, *h*) heat; *sich* ∼ get *or* grow hot; **∼'hoffen** *v/t.* (*no* -ge-, *h*) hope for.

er'höh|en *v/t.* (*no* -ge-, *h*) raise; increase; **Qung** *f* (-/-en) elevation; rise (*in prices*, *wages*); advance (*in prices*); increase.

er'hol|en *v/refl.* (*no* -ge-, *h*) recover; (take a) rest, relax; **Qung** *f* (-/-en) recovery; recreation; relaxation; **Qungsurlaub** [ɛr'hoːluŋs⁹-] *m* holiday, *Am.* vacation; recreation leave; ✚ convalescent leave, sick-leave. [*request.*]

er'hören *v/t.* (*no* -ge-, *h*) hear; grant)

erinner|n [ɛr'ɪnərn] *v/t.* (*no* -ge-, *h*): *j-n* ∼ *an* (*acc.*) remind s.o. of; *sich* ∼ (*gen.*), *sich* ∼ *an* (*acc.*) remember *s.o.* or *s.th.*, recollect *s.th.*; **Qung** *f* (-/-en) remembrance; recollection; reminder; **∼en** *pl.* reminiscences *pl.*

er'kalten *v/i.* (*no* -ge-, *sein*) cool down (*a. fig.*), get cold.

erkält|en [ɛr'kɛltən] *v/refl.* (*no* -ge-, *h*): *sich* (*sehr*) ∼ catch (a bad) cold; **Qung** *f* (-/-en) cold.

er'kennen *v/t.* (*irr.* kennen, *no* -ge-, *h*) recognize (*an dat.* by); perceive, discern; realize.

er'kenntlich *adj.* perceptible; *sich* ∼ *zeigen* show one's appreciation; **Qkeit** *f* (-/-en) gratitude; appreciation.

Er'kenntnis 1. *f* perception; realization; **2.** ⚖ *n* (-ses/-se) decision, sentence, finding.

Erker ['ɛrkər] *m* (-s/-) bay; **∼fenster** *n* bay-window.

er'klär|en *v/t.* (*no* -ge-, *h*) explain; account for; declare, state; *sich* ∼ declare (*für* for; *gegen* against); **∼lich** *adj.* explainable, explicable; **∼t** *adj.* professed, declared; **Qung** *f* explanation; declaration.

er'klingen *v/i.* (*irr.* klingen, *no* -ge-, *sein*) (re)sound, ring (out).

erkoren *adj.* [ɛr'koːrən] (s)elect, chosen.

er'krank|en *v/i.* (*no* -ge-, *sein*) fall ill, be taken ill (*an dat.* of, with); become affected; **2ung** *f* (-/-en) illness, sickness, falling ill.

er'kühnen *v/refl.* (*no* -ge-, *h*) venture, presume, make bold (*zu inf.* to *inf.*); **~kunden** *v/t.* (*no* -ge-, *h*) explore; ⚔ reconnoit|re, *Am.* -er.

erkundig|en [ɛr'kundigən] *v/refl.* (*no* -ge-, *h*) inquire (*über acc.* after; *nach* after *or* for *s.o.*; about *s.th.*); **2ung** *f* (-/-en) inquiry.

er'lahmen *fig. v/i.* (*no* -ge-, *sein*) grow weary, tire; slacken; *interest:* wane, flag; **~langen** *v/t.* (*no* -ge-, *h*) obtain, get.

Er'laß [ɛr'las] *m* (*Erlasses/Erlasse*) dispensation, exemption; remission (*of debt, penalty, etc.*); edict, decree; **2'lassen** *v/t.* (*irr. lassen, no* -ge-, *h*) remit (*debt, penalty, etc.*); dispense (*j-m et. s.o.* from s.th.); issue (*decree*); enact (*law*).

erlauben [ɛr'laubən] *v/t.* (*no* -ge-, *h*) allow, permit; *sich et. ~* indulge in s.th.; *sich ~ zu inf.* ✝ beg to *inf.*

Erlaubnis [ɛr'laupnis] *f* (-/*no pl.*) permission; authority; **~schein** *m* permit.

er'läuter|n *v/t.* (*no* -ge-, *h*) explain, illustrate; comment (up)on; **2ung** *f* explanation, illustration; comment.

Erle ⚘ ['ɛrlə] *f* (-/-n) alder.

er'leb|en *v/t.* (*no* -ge-, *h*) (live to) see; experience; go through; **2nis** [~pnis] *n* (-ses/-se) experience; adventure.

erledig|en [ɛr'le:digən] *v/t.* (*no* -ge-, *h*) dispatch; execute; settle (*matter*); **~t** *adj.* [~çt] finished, settled; *fig.:* played out; F: done for; F: *du bist für mich* ~ I am through with you; **2ung** [~gun] *f* (-/?* -en) dispatch; settlement.

er'leichter|n *v/t.* (*no* -ge-, *h*) lighten (*burden*); *fig.:* make easy, facilitate; relieve; **2ung** *f* (-/-en) ease; relief; facilitation; **~en** *pl.* facilities *pl.*

er'leiden *v/t.* (*irr. leiden, no* -ge-, *h*) suffer, endure; sustain (*damage, loss*); **~lernen** *v/t.* (*no* -ge-, *h*) learn, acquire.

er'leucht|en *v/t.* (*no* -ge-, *h*) illuminate; *fig.* enlighten; **2ung** *f* (-/-en) illumination; *fig.* enlightenment.

er'liegen *v/i.* (*irr. liegen, no* -ge-, *sein*) succumb (*dat.* to). [true.]

erlogen *adj.* [ɛr'lo:gən] false, un-]

Erlös [ɛr'lø:s] *m* (-es/-e) proceeds *pl.*

erlosch [ɛr'lɔʃ] *pret.* of erlöschen, **~en 1.** *p.p.* of erlöschen; **2.** *adj.* extinct.

er'löschen *v/i.* (*irr., no* -ge-, *sein*) go out; *fig.* become extinct; *contract:* expire.

er'lös|en *v/t.* (*no* -ge-, *h*) redeem; deliver; **2er** *m* (-s/-) redeemer, deliverer; *eccl.* Redeemer, Saviour; **2ung** *f* redemption; deliverance.

ermächtig|en [ɛr'mɛçtigən] *v/t.* (*no* -ge-, *h*) authorize; **2ung** *f* (-/-en) authorization; authority; warrant.

er'mahn|en *v/t.* (*no* -ge-, *h*) admonish; **2ung** *f* admonition.

er'mangel|n *v/i.* (*no* -ge-, *h*) be wanting (*gen.* in); **2ung** *f* (-/*no pl.*): *in ~* (*gen.*) in default of, for want of, failing.

er'mäßig|en *v/t.* (*no* -ge-, *h*) abate, reduce, cut (down); **2ung** *f* (-/-en) abatement, reduction.

er'matt|en (*no* -ge-) **1.** *v/t.* (*h*) fatigue, tire, exhaust; **2.** *v/i.* (*sein*) tire, grow weary; *fig.* slacken; **2ung** *f* (-/?* -en) fatigue, exhaustion.

er'messen 1. *v/t.* (*irr. messen, no* -ge-, *h*) judge; **2.** 2 *n* (-s/*no pl.*) judg(e)ment; discretion.

er'mitt|eln *v/t.* (*no* -ge-, *h*) ascertain, find out; ⚖ investigate; **2(e)lung** [~(ə)lun] *f* (-/-en) ascertainment; inquiry; ⚖ investigation.

er'möglichen *v/t.* (*no* -ge-, *h*) render *or* make possible.

er'mord|en *v/t.* (*no* -ge-, *h*) murder; assassinate; **2ung** *f* (-/-en) murder; assassination.

er'müd|en (*no* -ge-) **1.** *v/t.* (*h*) tire, fatigue; **2.** *v/i.* (*sein*) tire, get tired *or* fatigued; **2ung** *f* (-/?* -en) fatigue, tiredness.

er'munter|n *v/t.* (*no* -ge-, *h*) rouse, encourage, animate; **2ung** *f* (-/-en) encouragement, animation.

ermutig|en [ɛr'mu:tigən] *v/t.* (*no* -ge-, *h*) encourage; **2ung** *f* (-/-en) encouragement.

er'nähr|en *v/t.* (*no* -ge-, *h*) nourish, feed; support; **2er** *m* (-s/-) breadwinner, supporter; **2ung** *f* (-/?* -en) nourishment; support; *physiol.* nutrition.

er'nenn|en *v/t.* (*irr. nennen, no* -ge-, *h*) nominate, appoint; **2ung** *f* nomination, appointment.

er'neu|ern *v/t.* (*no* -ge-, *h*) renew,

renovate; revive; **℥erung** *f* renewal, renovation; revival; **~t** *adv.* once more.

erniedrig|en [ɛr'niːdrigən] *v/t.* (*no -ge-, h*) degrade; humiliate, humble; **℥ung** *f* (-/-en) degradation; humiliation.

Ernst [ɛrnst] **1.** *m* (-es/*no pl.*) seriousness; earnest(ness); gravity; *im ~* in earnest; **2. ℥** *adj.* = **℥haft** *adj.*, **℥lich** *adj.* serious, earnest; grave.

Ernte ['ɛrntə] *f* (-/-n) harvest; crop; **~'dankfest** *n* harvest festival; **℥n** *v/t.* (ge-, *h*) harvest, gather (in); reap (*a. fig.*).

er'nüchter|n *v/t.* (*no -ge-, h*) (make) sober; *fig.* disillusion; **℥ung** *f* (-/-en) sobering; *fig.* disillusionment.

Er'ober|er *m* (-s/-) conqueror; **℥n** *v/t.* (*no -ge-, h*) conquer; **~ung** *f* (-/-en) conquest.

er'öffn|en *v/t.* (*no -ge-, h*) open; inaugurate; disclose (*j-m et. sth.* to *s.o.*); notify; **℥ung** *f* opening; inauguration; disclosure.

erörter|n [ɛr'œrtərn] *v/t.* (*no -ge-, h*) discuss; **℥ung** *f* (-/-en) discussion.

Erpel *orn.* ['ɛrpəl] *m* (-s/-) drake.

erpicht *adj.* [ɛr'pɪçt]: *~ auf* (*acc.*) bent or intent or set or keen on.

er'press|en *v/t.* (*no -ge-, h*) extort (*von* from); blackmail; **℥er** *m* (-s/-), **℥erin** *f* (-/-nen) extort(ion)er; blackmailer; **℥ung** *f* (-/-en) extortion; blackmail.

er'proben *v/t.* (*no -ge-, h*) try, test.

erquick|en [ɛr'kvɪkən] *v/t.* (*no -ge-, h*) refresh; **℥ung** *f* (-/-en) refreshment.

er|'raten *v/t.* (*irr.* raten, *no -ge-, h*) guess, find out; **~'rechnen** *v/t.* (*no -ge-,h*) calculate, compute, work out.

erreg|bar *adj.* [ɛr're:kba:r] excitable; **~en** [~gən] *v/t.* (*no -ge-, h*) excite; cause; **℥er** [~gər] *m* (-s/-) exciter (*a. ℰ*); *ℱ* germ, virus; **℥ung** [~gʊŋ] *f* excitation; excitement.

er'reich|bar *adj.* attainable; within reach *or* call; **~en** *v/t.* (*no -ge-, h*) reach; *fig.* achieve, attain; catch (*train*); come up to (*certain standard*).

er'rett|en *v/t.* (*no -ge-, h*) rescue; **℥ung** *f* rescue.

er'richt|en *v/t.* (*no -ge-, h*) set up, erect; establish; **℥ung** *f* (-/-en) erection; establishment.

er|'ringen *v/t.* (*irr.* ringen, *no -ge-, h*) gain, obtain; achieve (*success*); **~'röten** *v/i.* (*no -ge-, sein*) blush.

Errungenschaft [ɛr'rʊŋənʃaft] *f* (-/-en) acquisition; achievement.

Er'satz *m* (-es/*no pl.*) replacement; substitute; compensation; amends *sg.*, damages *pl.*; indemnification; *s. Ersatzmann, Ersatzmittel*; *~ leisten* make amends; **~mann** *m* substitute; surrogate; **~mine** *f* refill (*for pencil*); **~mittel** *n* substitute, surrogate; **~reifen** *mot. m* spare tyre; (*Am. only*) spare tire; **~teil** ⊕ *n, m* spare (part).

er'schaff|en *v/t.* (*irr.* schaffen, *no -ge-, h*) create; **℥ung** *f* (-/*no pl.*) creation.

er'schallen *v/i.* ([*irr.* schallen,] *no -ge-, sein*) (re)sound; ring.

er'schein|en 1. *v/i.* (*irr.* scheinen, *no -ge-, sein*) appear; **2. ℥** *n* (-s/*no pl.*) appearance; **℥ung** *f* (-/-en) appearance; apparition; vision.

er|'schießen *v/t.* (*irr.* schießen, *no -ge-, h*) shoot (dead); **~'schlaffen** *v/i.* (*no -ge-, sein*) tire; relax; *fig.* languish, slacken; **~'schlagen** *v/t.* (*irr.* schlagen, *no -ge-, h*) kill, slay; **~'schließen** *v/t.* (*irr.* schließen, *no -ge-, h*) open; open up (*new market*); develop (*district*).

er'schöpf|en *v/t.* (*no -ge-, h*) exhaust; **℥ung** *f* exhaustion.

erschrak [ɛr'ʃraːk] *prēt. of* erschrecken 2.

er'schrecken 1. *v/t.* (*no -ge-, h*) frighten, scare; **2.** *v/i.* (*irr., no -ge-, sein*) be frightened (*über acc.* at); **~d** *adj.* alarming, startling.

erschrocken [ɛr'ʃrɔkən] **1.** *p.p. of* erschrecken 2; **2.** *adj.* frightened, terrified.

erschütter|n [ɛr'ʃytərn] *v/t.* (*no -ge-, h*) shake; *fig.* shock, move; **℥ung** *f* (-/-en) shock; *fig.* emotion; *ℱ* concussion; ⊕ percussion.

er'schweren *v/t.* (*no -ge-, h*) make more difficult; aggravate.

er'schwing|en *v/t.* (*irr.* schwingen, *no -ge-, h*) afford; **~lich** *adj.* within *s.o.'s* means; *prices:* reasonable.

er|'sehen *v/t.* (*irr.* sehen, *no -ge-, h*) see, learn, gather (*all: aus* from); **~'sehnen** *v/t.* (*no -ge-, h*) long for; **~'setzen** *v/t.* (*no -ge-, h*) repair; make up for, compensate (for); replace; refund.

er'sichtlich *adj.* evident, obvious.
er'sinnen *v/t.* (*irr. sinnen, no -ge-, h*) contrive, devise.
er'spar|en *v/t.* (*no -ge-, h*) save; j-m et. ~ spare s.o. s.th.; 2nis *f* (*-/-se*) saving.
er'sprießlich *adj.* useful, beneficial.
erst [e:rst] 1. *adj.*: der (die, das) ~e the first; 2. *adv.* first; at first; only; not ... till *or* until.
er'starr|en *v/i.* (*no -ge-, sein*) stiffen; solidify; congeal; set; grow numb; *fig. blood:* run cold; ~t *adj.* benumbed; 2ung *f* (*-/-en*) numbness; solidification; congealment; setting.
erstatt|en [ɛr'ʃtatən] *v/t.* (*no -ge-, h*) restore; *s.* ersetzen; Bericht ~ (make a) report; 2ung *f* (*-/-en*) restitution.
'Erstaufführung *f thea.* first night *or* performance, premiere; *film:* a. first run.
er'staun|en 1. *v/i.* (*no-ge-, sein*) be astonished (*über acc.* at); 2. *v/t.* (*no -ge-, h*) astonish; 3. 2 *n* astonishment; *in* ~ setzen astonish; ~lich *adj.* astonishing, amazing.
er'stechen *v/t.* (*irr. stechen, no -ge-, h*) stab.
er'steig|en *v/t.* (*irr. steigen, no -ge-, h*) ascend, climb; 2ung *f* ascent.
erstens *adv.* ['e:rstəns] first, firstly.
er'stick|en (*no -ge-) v/t.* (*h*) *and v/i.* (*sein*) choke, suffocate; stifle; 2ung *f* (*-/-en*) suffocation. [rate, F A 1.]
'erstklassig *adj.* first-class, first-]
er'streb|en *v/t.* (*no -ge-, h*) strive after *or* for; ~swert *adj.* desirable.
er'strecken *v/t.* (*no -ge-, h*) extend; *sich* ~ *über* (*acc.*) cover.
er'suchen 1. *v/t.* (*no -ge-, h*) request; 2. 2 *n* (*-s/-*) request.
er'|tappen *v/t.* (*no -ge-, h*) catch, surprise; *s.* frisch; ~'tönen *v/i.* (*no -ge-, sein*) (re)sound.
Ertrag [ɛr'tra:k] *m* (*-[e]s/⁀e*) produce, yield; proceeds *pl.*, returns *pl.*; ⚒ output; 2en [~gən] *v/t.* (*irr. tragen, no -ge-, h*) bear, endure; suffer; stand. [able.]
erträglich *adj.* [ɛr'trɛ:klɪç] toler-]
er'|tränken *v/t.* (*no -ge-, h*) drown; ~'trinken *v/i.* (*irr. trinken, no -ge-, sein*) be drowned, drown; ~'übrigen [ɛr'y:brɪgən] *v/t.* (*no -ge-, h*) save; spare (*time*); *sich* ~ be unnecessary; ~'wachen *v/i.* (*no -ge-, sein*) awake, wake up.

er'wachsen 1. *v/i.* (*irr. wachsen, no -ge-, sein*) arise (*aus* from); 2. *adj.* grown-up, adult; 2e *m, f* (*-n/-n*) grown-up, adult.
er'wäg|en *v/t.* (*irr. wägen, no -ge-, h*) consider, think *s.th.* over; 2ung *f* (*-/-en*) consideration.
er'wählen *v/t.* (*no -ge-, h*) choose, elect.
er'wähn|en *v/t.* (*no -ge-, h*) mention; 2ung *f* (*-/-en*) mention.
er'wärmen *v/t.* (*no -ge-, h*) warm, heat; *sich* ~ warm (up).
er'wart|en *v/t.* (*no -ge-, h*) await, wait for; *fig.* expect; 2ung *f* expectation.
er'|wecken *v/t.* (*no -ge-, h*) wake, rouse; *fig.* awake; cause (*fear*); arouse (*suspicion*); ~'wehren *v/refl.* (*gen.*) (*no -ge-, h*) keep *or* ward off; ~'weichen *v/t.* (*no -ge-, h*) soften; *fig.* move; ~'weisen *v/t.* (*irr. weisen, no -ge-, h*) prove; show (*respect*); render (*service*); do, pay (*honour*); do (*favour*).
er'weiter|n *v/t. and v/refl.* (*no -ge-, h*) expand, enlarge, extend, widen; 2ung *f* (*-/-en*) expansion, enlargement, extension.
Erwerb [ɛr'vɛrp] *m* (*-[e]s/-e*) acquisition; living; earnings *pl.*; business; 2en [~bən] *v/t.* (*irr. werben, no -ge-, h*) acquire; gain; earn.
erwerbs|los [ɛr'vɛrpslo:s] *adj.* unemployed; ~tätig *adj.* (gainfully) employed; ~unfähig *adj.* [ɛr'vɛrps⁹-] incapable of earning one's living; 2zweig *m* line of business.
Erwerbung [ɛr'vɛrbʊŋ] *f* acquisition.
erwider|n [ɛr'vi:dərn] *v/t.* (*no -ge-, h*) return; answer, reply; retort; 2ung *f* (*-/-en*) return; answer, reply.
er'wischen *v/t.* (*no -ge-, h*) catch, trap, get hold of.
er'wünscht *adj.* desired; desirable; welcome.
er'würgen *v/t.* (*no -ge-, h*) strangle, throttle. [brass.]
Erz ⚒ [e:rts] *n* (*-es/-e*) ore; *poet.*]
er'zähl|en *v/t.* (*no -ge-, h*) tell; relate; narrate; 2er *m,* 2erin *f* (*-/-nen*) narrator; writer; 2ung *f* narration; (short) story, narrative.
'Erz|bischof *eccl. m* archbishop; ~bistum *eccl. n* archbishopric; ~engel *eccl. m* archangel.

er'zeug|en v/t. (no -ge-, h) beget; produce; make, manufacture; 2er m (-s/-) father (of child); ✝ producer; 2nis n produce; production; ⊕ product; 2ung f production.

'Erz|feind m arch-enemy; '~herzog m archduke; '~herzogin f archduchess; '~herzogtum n archduchy.

er'ziehe|n v/t. (irr. ziehen, no -ge-, h) bring up, rear, raise; educate; 2er m (-s/-) educator; teacher, tutor; 2rin f (-/-nen) teacher; governess; ~risch adj. educational, pedagogic (-al).

Er'ziehung f (-/~ -en) upbringing; breeding; education; ~sanstalt [er'tsi:uŋs?-] f reformatory, approved school; ~swesen n (-s/no pl.) educational matters pl. or system.

er'ziel|en v/t. (no -ge-, h) obtain; realize (price); achieve (success); sports: score (points, goal); ~'zürnen v/t. (no -ge-, h) make angry, irritate, enrage; ~'zwingen v/t. (irr. zwingen, no -ge-, h) (en)force; compel; extort (von from).

es pers. pron. [ɛs] 1. pers.: it, he, she; wo ist das Buch? — ~ ist auf dem Tisch where is the book? — it is on the table; das Mädchen blieb stehen, als ~ seine Mutter sah the girl stopped when she saw her mother; 2. impers.: it; ~ gibt there is, there are; ~ ist kalt it is cold; ~ klopft there is a knock at the door.

Esche ♀ ['ɛʃə] f (-/-n) ash(-tree).

Esel m. ['e:zəl] m (-s/-) donkey; esp. fig. ass; ~ei [~'laɪ] f (-/-en) stupidity, stupid thing, folly; '~sbrücke f at school: crib, Am. pony; ~sohr ['e:zəls?-] n dog's ear (of book).

Eskorte [ɛs'kɔrtə] f (-/-n) ✗ escort; ⚓ convoy.

Espe ♀ ['ɛspə] f (-/-n) asp(en).

'eßbar adj. eatable, edible.

Esse ['ɛsə] f (-/-n) chimney.

essen ['ɛsən] 1. v/i. (irr. ge-, h) eat; zu Mittag ~ (have) lunch; dine, have dinner; zu Abend ~ dine, have dinner; esp. late at night: sup, have supper; auswärts ~ eat or dine out; 2. v/t. (irr. ge-, h) eat; et. zu Mittag etc. ~ have s.th. for lunch, etc.; 3. 2 n (-s/-) eating; food; meal; dish; midday meal: lunch, dinner; evening meal: dinner; last meal of the day:

supper; '2zeit f lunch-time; dinner-time; supper-time.

Essenz [ɛ'sɛnts] f (-/-en) essence.

Essig ['ɛsɪç] m (-s/-e) vinegar; '~gurke f pickled cucumber, gherkin.

'Eß|löffel m soup-spoon; '~nische f dining alcove, Am. dinette; '~tisch m dining-table; '~waren f/pl. eatables pl., victuals pl., food; '~zimmer n dining-room.

etablieren [eta'bli:rən] v/t. (no -ge-, h) establish, set up.

Etage [e'ta:ʒə] f (-/-n) floor, stor(e)y; ~nwohnung f flat, Am. a. apartment.

Etappe [e'tapə] f (-/-n) ✗ base; fig. stage, leg.

Etat [e'ta:] m (-s/-s) budget, parl. the Estimates pl.; ~sjahr n fiscal year.   [or sg.\

Ethik ['e:tik] f (-/~ -en) ethics pl.\

Etikett [eti'kɛt] n (-[e]s/-e, -s) label; ticket; tag; gummed: Am. a. sticker; ~e f (-/-n) etiquette; 2ieren [~'ti:rən] v/t. (no -ge-, h) label.

etliche indef. pron. ['ɛtliçə] some, several.

Etui [e'tvi:] n (-s/-s) case.

etwa adv. ['ɛtva] perhaps, by chance; about, Am. a. around; ~ig adj. ['~?iç] possible, eventual.

etwas ['ɛtvas] 1. indef. pron. something; anything; 2. adj. some; any; 3. adv. somewhat; 4. 2 n (-/-): das gewisse ~ certain something.

euch pers. pron. [ɔʏç] you; ~ (selbst) yourselves.

euer poss. pron. ['ɔʏər] your; der (die, das) eu(e)re yours.

Eule orn. ['ɔʏlə] f (-/-n) owl; ~n nach Athen tragen carry coals to Newcastle.

euresgleichen pron. ['ɔʏrəs'glaɪçən] people like you, F the likes of you.

Europä|er [ɔʏro'pɛ:ər] m (-s/-) European; 2isch adj. European.

Euter ['ɔʏtər] n (-s/-) udder.

evakuieren [evaku'i:rən] v/t. (no -ge-, h) evacuate.

evangeli|sch adj. [evaŋ'ge:liʃ] evangelic(al); Protestant; Lutheran; 2um [~jum] n (-s/Evangelien) gospel.

eventuell [eventu'ɛl] 1. adj. possible; 2. adv. possibly, perhaps.

ewig adj. ['e:viç] eternal; everlasting; perpetual; auf ~ for ever;

'2keit f (-/-en) eternity; F: *seit e-r ~* for ages.

exakt adj. [ε'ksakt] exact; **2heit** f (-/-en) exactitude, exactness; accuracy.

Exam|en [ε'ksaːmən] n (-s/-, *Examina*) examination, F exam; **2inieren** [~ami'niːrən] v/t. (no -ge-, h) examine.

Exekutive [εksəku'tiːvə] f (-/no pl.) executive power.

Exempel [ε'ksεmpəl] n (-s/-) example, instance.

Exemplar [εksεm'plaːr] n (-s/-e) specimen; copy (*of book*).

exerzier|en ✕ [εksεr'tsiːrən] v/i. and v/t. (no -ge-, h) drill; **2platz** ✕ m drill-ground, parade-ground.

Exil [ε'ksiːl] n (-s/-e) exile.

Existenz [εksis'tεnts] f (-/-en) existence; living, livelihood; **~minimum** n subsistence minimum.

exis'tieren v/i. (no -ge-, h) exist; subsist.

exotisch adj. [ε'ksoːtiʃ] exotic.

exped|ieren [εkspe'diːrən] v/t. (no -ge-, h) dispatch; **2ition** [~i'tsjoːn] f (-/-en) dispatch, forwarding; expedition; † dispatch or forwarding office.

Experiment [εksperi'mεnt] n (-[e]s/-e) experiment; **2ieren** [~'tiːrən] v/i. (no -ge-, h) experiment.

explo|dieren [εksplo'diːrən] v/i. (no -ge-, sein) explode, burst; **2sion** [~'zjoːn] f (-/-en) explosion; **~siv** adj. [~'ziːf] explosive.

Export [εks'pɔrt] m (-[e]s/-e) export(ation); **2ieren** [~'tiːrən] v/t. (no -ge-, h) export.

extra adj. ['εkstra] extra; special; **2blatt** n extra edition (*of newspaper*), Am. extra. [tract.]

Extrakt [εks'trakt] m (-[e]s/-e) ex-]

Extrem [εks'treːm] **1.** n (-s/-e) extreme; **2.** ⌐ adj. extreme.

Exzellenz [εkstsε'lεnts] f (-/-en) Excellency.

exzentrisch adj. [εks'tsεntriʃ] eccentric.

Exzeß [εks'tsεs] m (*Exzesses/Exzesse*) excess.

F

Fabel ['faːbəl] f (-/-n) fable (*a. fig.*); plot (*of story, book, etc.*); **2haft** adj. fabulous; marvellous; **'2n** v/i. (ge-, h) tell (tall) stories.

Fabrik [fa'briːk] f (-/-en) factory, works *sg., pl.*, mill; **~ant** [~i'kant] m (-en/-en) factory-owner, mill-owner; manufacturer; **~arbeit** f factory work; *s. Fabrikware*; **~arbeiter** m factory worker or hand; **~at** [~i'kaːt] n (-[e]s/-e) make; product; **~ationsfehler** [~a'tsjoːns-] m flaw; **~besitzer** m factory-owner; **~marke** f trade mark; **~stadt** f factory or industrial town; **~ware** f manufactured article; **~zeichen** n s. *Fabrikmarke*.

Fach [fax] n (-[e]s/⸚er) section, compartment, shelf (*of bookcase, cupboard, etc.*); pigeon-hole (*in desk*); drawer; *fig.* subject; *s. Fachgebiet*; **~arbeiter** m skilled worker; **'~arzt** m specialist (*für in*); **'~ausbildung** f professional training; **'~ausdruck** m technical term.

fächeln ['fεçəln] v/t. (ge-, h) fan *s.o.*

Fächer ['fεçər] m (-s/-) fan; **2förmig** adj. ['~fœrmiç] fan-shaped.

'Fach|gebiet n branch, field, province; **'~kenntnisse** f/pl. specialized knowledge; **'~kreis** m: *in ~n* among experts; **2kundig** adj. competent, expert; **'~literatur** f specialized literature; **'~mann** m expert; **2männisch** adj. ['~mεniʃ] expert; **'~schule** f technical school; **'~werk** △ n framework.

Fackel ['fakəl] f (-/-n) torch; **'2n** v/i. (ge-, h) hesitate, F shilly-shally; **'~zug** m torchlight procession.

fad adj. [faːt], **~e** adj. ['faːdə] food: insipid, tasteless; stale; *p.* dull, boring.

Faden ['faːdən] m (-s/⸚) thread (*a. fig.*); *fig.: an e-m ~ hängen* hang by a thread; **'~nudeln** f/pl. vermicelli *pl.*; **2scheinig** adj. ['~ʃainiç] threadbare; *excuse, etc.*: flimsy, thin.

fähig adj. ['fεːiç] capable (*zu inf. of ger.; gen.* of); able (*to inf.*); **2keit** f (-/-en) (cap)ability; talent, faculty.

Falschheit

fahl *adj.* [fɑ:l] pale, pallid; *colour*: faded; *complexion*: leaden, livid.

fahnd|en ['fɑ:ndən] *v/i.* (ge-, h): *nach j-m* ~ search for s.o.; **Qung** *f* (-/-en) search.

Fahne ['fɑ:nə] *f* (-/-n) flag; standard; banner; ♣, ✗, *fig.* colo(u)rs *pl.*; *typ.* galley-proof.

'**Fahnen|eid** *m* oath of allegiance; '**~flucht** *f* desertion; **Qflüchtig** *adj.*: ~ *werden* desert (the colo[u]rs); '**~stange** *f* flagstaff, *Am. a.* flagpole.

'**Fahr|bahn** *f*, '**~damm** *m* roadway.

Fähre ['fɛ:rə] *f* (-/-n) ferry(-boat).

fahren ['fɑ:rən] (*irr.*, ge-) **1.** *v/i.* (sein) driver, vehicle, *etc.*: drive, go, travel; *cyclist*: ride, cycle; ♣ sail; *mot.* motor; *mit der Eisenbahn* ~ go by train or rail; *spazieren* ~ go for or take a drive; *mit der Hand* ~ *über* (*acc.*) pass one's hand over; ~ *lassen* let go or slip; *gut* (*schlecht*) ~ *bei* do or fare well (badly) at or with; *er ist gut dabei gefahren* he did very well out of it; **2.** *v/t.* (h) carry, convey; drive (*car, train, etc.*); ride (*bicycle, etc.*).

'**Fahrer** *m* (-s/-) driver; '**~flucht** *f* (-/*no pl.*) hit-and-run offence, *Am.* hit-and-run offense.

'**Fahr|gast** *m* passenger; *in taxi*: fare; '**~geld** *n* fare; '**~gelegenheit** *f* transport facilities *pl.*; '**~gestell** *n* *mot.* chassis; ✈ undercarriage, landing gear; '**~karte** *f* ticket; '**~kartenschalter** *m* booking-office, *Am.* ticket office; '**Qlässig** *adj.* careless, negligent; '**~lässigkeit** *f* (-/**~**-en) carelessness, negligence; '**~lehrer** *mot.* *m* driving instructor; '**~plan** *m* timetable, *Am. a.* schedule; '**Qplanmäßig 1.** *adj.* regular, *Am.* scheduled; **2.** *adv.* on time, *Am. a.* on schedule; '**~preis** *m* fare; '**~rad** *n* bicycle, F bike; '**~schein** *m* ticket; '**~schule** *f* driving school, school of motoring; '**~stuhl** *m* lift, *Am.* elevator; '**~stuhlführer** *m* lift-boy, lift-man, *Am.* elevator operator; '**~stunde** *mot.* *f* driving lesson.

Fahrt [fɑ:rt] *f* (-/-en) ride, drive; journey, voyage, passage; trip; ~ *ins Blaue* mystery tour; *in voller* ~ (at) full speed.

Fährte ['fɛ:rtə] *f* (-/-n) track (*a. fig.*); *auf der falschen* ~ *sein* be on the wrong track.

'**Fahr|vorschrift** *f* rule of the road; '**~wasser** *n* ♣ navigable water; *fig.* track;'**~weg** *m* roadway; '**~zeug** *n* vehicle; ♣ vessel.

Fakt|or ['faktor] *m* (-s/-en) factor; **~otum** [~'to:tum] *n* (-s/-s, Faktoten) factotum; **~ur** ✝ [~'tu:r] *f* (-/-en), **~ura** ✝ [~'tu:ra] *f* (-/Fakturen) invoice.

Fakultät *univ.* [fakul'tɛ:t] *f* (-/-en) faculty.

Falke *orn.* ['falkə] *m* (-n/-n) hawk, falcon.

Fall [fal] *m* (-[e]s/⸚e) fall (*of body, stronghold, city, etc.*); *gr.*, ♣, ♬ case; *gesetzt den* ~ suppose; *auf alle Fälle* at all events; *auf jeden* ~ in any case, at any rate; *auf keinen* ~ on no account, in no case.

Falle ['falə] *f* (-/-n) trap (*a. fig.*); pitfall (*a. fig.*); *e-e* ~ *stellen* set a trap (*j-m* for s.o.).

fallen ['falən] *v/i.* (*irr.*, ge-, sein) fall, drop; ✗ be killed in action; *shot*: be heard; *flood water*: subside; *auf j-n* ~ suspicion, *etc.*: fall on s.o.; ~ *lassen* drop (*plate, etc.*). **2.** ~ *n* (-s/*no pl.*) fall(ing).

fällen ['fɛlən] *v/t.* (ge-, h) fell, cut down (*tree*); ✗ lower (*bayonet*); ♬ pass (*judgement*), give (*decision*).

'**fallenlassen** *v/t.* (*irr. lassen*, sep., no -ge-, h) drop (*plan, claim, etc.*).

fällig *adj.* ['fɛliç] due; payable; **Qkeit** *f* (-/**~**-en) maturity; '**Qkeits-termin** *m* date of maturity.

'**Fall|obst** *n* windfall; '**~reep** ♣ [~'re:p] *n* (-[e]s/-e) gangway.

falls *cj.* [fals] if; in the event of *ger.*; in case.

'**Fall|schirm** *m* parachute; '**~schirmspringer** *m* parachutist; '**~strick** *m* snare; '**~tür** *f* trap door.

falsch [falʃ] **1.** *adj.* false; wrong; *bank-note, etc.*: counterfeit; *money*: base; *bill of exchange, etc.*: forged; *p.* deceitful; **2.** *adv.*: ~ *gehen watch*: go wrong; ~ *verbunden!* *teleph.* sorry, wrong number.

fälsch|en ['fɛlʃən] *v/t.* (ge-, h) falsify; forge, fake (*document, etc.*); counterfeit (*bank-note, coin, etc.*); fake (*calculations, etc.*); tamper with (*financial account*); adulterate (*food, wine*); **Qer** *m* (-s/-) forger, faker; adulterator.

'**Falsch|geld** *n* counterfeit or bad or base money; '**~heit** *f* (-/-en) falseness, falsity; duplicity, deceitfulness; '∼meldung f false report; '∼münzer m (-s/-) coiner; '∼münzerwerkstatt f coiner's den; '2spielen v/i. (sep., -ge-, h) cheat (at cards); '∼spieler m cardsharper.

'Fälschung f (-/-en) forgery; falsification; fake; adulteration.

Falt|boot ['falt-] n folding canoe, Am. foldboat, faltboat; ∼e ['∼ə] f (-/-n) fold; pleat (in skirt, etc.); crease (in trousers); wrinkle (on face); '2en v/t. (ge-, h) fold; clasp or join (one's hands); '2ig adj. folded; pleated; wrinkled.

Falz [falts] m (-es/-e) fold; rabbet (for woodworking, etc.); bookbinding: guard; '2en v/t. (ge-, h) fold; rabbet. [informal.]

familiär adj. [famil'jɛːr] familiar;]

Familie [fa'miːljə] f (-/-n) family (a. zo., ♧).

Fa'milien|angelegenheit f family affair; ∼anschluß m: ∼ haben live as one of the family; ∼nachrichten f/pl. in newspaper: birth, marriage and death announcements pl.; ∼name m family name, surname, Am. a. last name; ∼stand m marital status.

Fanati|ker [fa'naːtikər] m (-s/-) fanatic; 2sch adj. fanatic(al).

Fanatismus [fana'tismus] m (-/no pl.) fanaticism.

fand [fant] pret. of finden.

Fanfare [fan'faːrə] f (-/-n) fanfare, flourish (of trumpets).

Fang [faŋ] m (-[e]s/∼e) capture, catch(ing); hunt. bag; '2en v/t. (irr. ge-, h) catch (animal, ball, thief, etc.); '∼zahn m fang (of dog, wolf, etc.); tusk (of boar).

Farb|band ['farp-] n (typewriter) ribbon; ∼e ['∼bə] f (-/-n) colo(u)r; paint; dye; complexion; cards: suit; 2echt adj. ['farp⁹-] colo(u)r-fast.

färben ['fɛrbən] v/t. (ge-, h) colo(u)r (glass, food, etc.); dye (material, hair, Easter eggs, etc.); tint (hair, paper, glass); stain (wood, fabrics, glass, etc.); sich ∼ take on or assume a colo(u)r; sich rot ∼ turn or go red.

'farben|blind adj. colo(u)r-blind; '2druck m (-[e]s/-e) colo(u)r print; '∼prächtig adj. splendidly colo(u)rful.

Färber ['fɛrbər] m (-s/-) dyer.

Farb|fernsehen ['farp-] n colo(u)r television; '∼film m colo(u)r film; 2ig adj. ['∼biç] colo(u)red; glass: tinted, stained; fig. colo(u)rful; 2los adj. ['∼p-] colo(u)rless; '∼photographie f colo(u)r photography; '∼stift m colo(u)red pencil; '∼stoff m colo(u)ring matter; '∼ton m tone; shade, tint.

Färbung ['fɛrbuŋ] f (-/-en) colo(u)ring (a. fig.); shade (a. fig.).

Farnkraut ♧ ['farnkraut] n fern.

Fasan orn. [fa'zaːn] m (-[e]s/-e[n]) pheasant. [val.]

Fasching ['faʃiŋ] m (-s/-e, -s) carni-]

Fasel|ei [faːzə'lai] f (-/-en) drivelling, waffling; twaddle; '2n v/i. (ge-, h) blather; F waffle.

Faser ['faːzər] f (-/-n) anat., ♧, fig. fib|re, Am. -er; cotton, wool, etc.: staple; '2ig adj. fibrous; '2n v/i. (ge-, h) wool: shed fine hairs.

Faß [fas] n (Fasses/Fässer) cask, barrel; tub; vat; '∼bier n draught beer.

Fassade △ [fa'saːdə] f (-/-n) façade, front (a. fig.); ∼nkletterer m (-s/-) cat burglar.

fassen ['fasən] (ge-, h) 1. v/t. seize, take hold of; catch, apprehend (criminal); hold; s. einfassen; fig. grasp, understand, believe; pluck up (courage); form (plan); make (decision); sich ∼ compose o.s.; sich kurz ∼ be brief; 2. v/i.: ∼ nach reach for. [ceivable.]

'faßlich adj. comprehensible, con-]

'Fassung f (-/-en) setting (of jewels); ⚡ socket; fig.: composure; draft (-ing); wording, version; die ∼ verlieren lose one's self-control; aus der ∼ bringen disconcert; '∼s-kraft f (powers of) comprehension, mental capacity; '∼svermögen n (holding) capacity; fig. s. Fassungskraft.

fast adv. [fast] almost, nearly; ∼ nichts next to nothing; ∼ nie hardly ever.

fasten ['fastən] v/i. (ge-, h) fast; abstain from food and drink; '2zeit f Lent.

'Fast|nacht f (-/no pl.) Shrovetide; carnival; '∼tag m fast-day.

fatal adj. [fa'taːl] situation, etc.: awkward; business, etc.: unfortunate; mistake, etc.: fatal.

fauchen ['fauxən] v/i. (ge-, h) cat, etc.: spit; F p. spit (with anger); locomotive, etc.: hiss.

faul adj. [faul] fruit, etc.: rotten, bad; fish, meat: putrid, bad; fig. lazy, indolent, idle; fishy; ~e Ausrede lame excuse; '~en v/i. (ge-, h) rot, go bad, putrefy.

faulenze|n ['faulentsən] v/i. (ge-, h) idle, laze, loaf; '2r m (-s/-) idler, sluggard, F lazy-bones.

'Faul|heit f (-/no pl.) idleness, laziness; '2ig adj. found.

Fäulnis ['fɔylnis] f (-/no pl.) rottenness; putrefaction; decay.

'Faul|pelz m s. Faulenzer; '~tier n zo. sloth (a. fig.).

Faust [faust] f (-/⸚e) fist; auf eigene ~ on one's own initiative; '~handschuh m mitt(en); '~schlag m blow with the fist, punch, Am. F a. slug.

Favorit [favoˈriːt] m (-en/-en) favo(u)rite.

Faxe ['faksə] f (-/-n): ~n machen (play the) fool; ~n schneiden pull or make faces.

Fazit ['faːtsit] n (-s/-e, -s) result, upshot; total; das ~ ziehen sum or total up.

Februar ['feːbruaːr] m (-[s]/-e) February.

fecht|en ['fɛçtən] v/i. (irr., ge-, h) fight; fenc. fence; '2er m (-s/-) fencer.

Feder ['feːdər] f (-/-n) feather; (ornamental) plume; pen; ⊕ spring; '~bett n feather bed; '~busch m tuft of feathers; plume; '~gewicht n boxing, etc.: featherweight; '~halter m (-s/-) penholder; '~kiel m quill; '~kraft f elasticity, resilience; '~krieg m paper war; literary controversy; '2leicht adj. (as) light as a feather; '~lesen n (-s/no pl.): nicht viel ~s machen mit make short work of; '~messer n penknife; '2n v/i. (ge-, h) be elastic; '2nd adj. springy, elastic; '~strich m stroke of the pen; '~vieh n poultry; '~zeichnung f pen-and-ink drawing.

Fee [feː] f (-/-n) fairy.

Fegefeuer ['feːgəfɔyər] n purgatory.

fegen ['feːgən] v/t. (ge-, h) sweep; clean.

Fehde ['feːdə] f (-/-n) feud; private war; in ~ liegen be at feud; F be at daggers drawn.

Fehl [feːl] m: ohne ~ without fault or blemish; '~betrag m deficit, deficiency.

fehlen ['feːlən] v/i. (ge-, h) be absent; be missing or lacking; do wrong; es fehlt ihm an (dat.) he lacks; was fehlt Ihnen? what is the matter with you?; weit gefehlt! far off the mark!

Fehler ['feːlər] m (-s/-) mistake, error, F slip; fault; ⊕ defect, flaw; '2frei adj., '2los adj. faultless, perfect; ⊕ flawless; '2haft adj. faulty; defective; incorrect.

'Fehl|geburt f miscarriage, abortion; '2gehen v/i. (irr. gehen, sep., -ge-, sein) go wrong; '~griff fig. m mistake, blunder; '~schlag fig. m failure; '2schlagen fig. v/i. (irr. schlagen, sep., -ge-, sein) fail, miscarry; '~schuß m miss; '2treten v/i. (irr. treten, sep., -ge-, sein) make a false step; '~tritt m false step; slip; fig. slip, fault; '~urteil ⁂ n error of judg(e)ment; '~zündung mot. f misfire, backfire.

Feier ['faiər] f (-/-n) ceremony; celebration; festival; festivity; '~abend m finishing or closing time; ~ machen finish, F knock off; '2lich adj. promise, oath, etc.: solemn; act: ceremonial; '~lichkeit f (-/-en) solemnity; ceremony; '2n (ge-, h) 1. v/t. hold (celebration); celebrate, observe (feast, day); 2. v/i. celebrate; rest (from work), make holiday; '~tag m holiday; festive day.

feig adj. cowardly.

feige¹ adj. ['faigə] cowardly.

Feige² [~] f (-/-n) fig; '~nbaum ♀ m fig-tree; '~nblatt n fig-leaf.

Feig|heit ['faikhait] f (-/no pl.) cowardice, cowardliness; '~ling ['~kliŋ] m (-s/-e) coward.

feil adj. [fail] for sale, to be sold; fig. venal; '~bieten v/t. (irr. bieten, sep., -ge-, h) offer for sale.

Feile ['failə] f (-/-n) file; '2n (ge-, h) 1. v/t. file (a. fig.); fig. polish; 2. v/i.: ~ an (dat.) file (at); fig. polish (up).

feilschen ['failʃən] v/i. (ge-, h) bargain (um for), haggle (for, about), Am. a. dicker (about).

fein adj. [fain] fine; material, etc.: high-grade; wine, etc.: choice; fabric, etc.: delicate, dainty; manners: polished; p. polite; distinction: subtle.

Feind [faint] *m* (-[e]s/-e) enemy (*a.* ✕.); '2**lich** *adj.* hostile, inimical; '~**schaft** *f* (-/-en) enmity; animosity; hostility; '2**selig** *adj.* hostile (*gegen* to); '~**seligkeit** *f* (-/-en) hostility; malevolence.

'fein|fühlend *adj.*, '~**fühlig** *adj.* sensitive; '2**gefühl** *n* sensitiveness; delicacy; '2**gehalt** *m* (monetary) standard; '2**heit** *f* (-/-en) fineness; delicacy, daintiness; politeness; elegance; '2**kost** *f* high-class groceries *pl.*, *Am.* delicatessen; '2**mechanik** *f* precision mechanics; '2**schmecker** *m* (-s/-) gourmet, epicure; '~**sinnig** *adj.* subtle.

feist *adj.* fat, stout.

Feld [fɛlt] *n* (-[e]s/-er) field (*a.* ✕, ✗, *sports*); ground, soil; plain; *chess*: square; △, ⊕ panel, compartment; *ins* ~ *ziehen* take the field; '~**arbeit** *f* agricultural work; '~**bett** *n* camp-bed; '~**blume** *f* wild flower; '~**dienst** ✕ *m* field service; '~**flasche** *f* water-bottle; '~**frucht** *f* fruit of the field; '~**geschrei** *n* war-cry, battle-cry; '~**herr** *m* general; '~**kessel** *m* camp-kettle; '~**lazarett** ✕ *n* fieldhospital; '~**lerche** *orn.* *f* skylark; '~**marschall** *m* Field Marshal; '2**marschmäßig** ✕ *adj.* in full marching order; '~**maus** *zo.* *f* fieldmouse; '~**messer** *m* (land) surveyor; '~**post** ✕ *f* army postal service; '~**schlacht** ✕ *f* battle; '~**stecher** *m* (-s/-) (*ein* *a pair of*) field-glasses *pl.*; '~**stuhl** *m* camp-stool; ~**webel** ['~ve:bəl] *m* (-s/-) sergeant; '~**weg** *m* (field) path; '~**zeichen** ✕ *n* standard; '~**zug** *m* ✕ campaign (*a.* *fig.*), (military) expedition; *Am.* *fig.* *a.* drive.

Felge ['fɛlgə] *f* (-/-n) felloe (*of* *cart-wheel*); rim (*of car wheel, etc.*).

Fell [fɛl] *n* (-[e]s/-e) skin, pelt, fur (*of dead animal*); coat (*of cat, etc.*); fleece (*of sheep*).

Fels [fɛls] *m* (-en/-en), ~**en** ['~zən] *m* (-s/-) rock; ~**block** ['fɛls-] *m* rock; boulder; 2**ig** *adj.* ['~ziç] rocky.

Fenchel ♀ ['fɛnçəl] *m* (-s/*no pl.*) fennel.

Fenster ['fɛnstər] *n* (-s/-) window; '~**brett** *n* window-sill; '~**flügel** *m* casement (*of casement window*); sash (*of sash window*); '~**kreuz** *n* cross-bar(s *pl.*); '~**laden** *m* shutter;

'~**rahmen** *m* window-frame; '~**riegel** *m* window-fastener; '~**scheibe** *f* (window-)pane; '~**sims** *m, n* window-sill.

Ferien ['fe:rjən] *pl.* holiday(s *pl.*), *esp. Am.* vacation; leave, *Am. a.* furlough; *parl.* recess; ⚖ vacation, recess; '~**kolonie** *f* children's holiday camp.

Ferkel ['fɛrkəl] *n* (-s/-) young pig; *contp. p.* pig.

fern [fɛrn] **1.** *adj.* far (off), distant; remote; **2.** *adv.* far (away); *von* ~ from a distance.

'Fernamt *teleph.* *n* trunk exchange, *Am.* long-distance exchange.

'fernbleiben 1. *v/i.* (*irr. bleiben, sep., -ge-; sein*) remain *or* stay away (*dat.* from); **2.** 2 *n* (-s/*no pl.*) absence (*from school, etc.*); absenteeism (*from work*).

Fern|e ['fɛrnə] *f* (-/-n) distance; remoteness; *aus der* ~ from *or* at a distance; '2**er 1.** *adj.* farther; *fig.*: further; future; **2.** *adv.* further (~*more*), in addition, also; '~*liefen* ... also ran ...; '~**flug** ✈ *m* long-distance flight; '2**gelenkt** *adj.* ['~gə-lɛŋkt] *missile*: guided; *aircraft, etc.*: remote-control(l)ed; '~**gespräch** *teleph.* *n* trunk call, *Am.* long-distance call; '2**gesteuert** *adj. s. ferngelenkt*; '~**glas** *n* binoculars *pl.*; '2**halten** *v/t. and v/refl.* (*irr. halten, sep., -ge-; h*) keep away (*von* from); '~**heizung** *f* district heating; '~**laster** F *mot.* *m* long-distance lorry, *Am.* long haul truck; '~**lenkung** *f* (-/-en) remote control; '2**liegen** *v/i.* (*irr. liegen, sep., -ge-; h*): *es liegt mir fern zu inf.* I am far from ger.; '~**rohr** *n* telescope; '~**schreiber** *m* teleprinter, *Am.* teletypewriter; '~**sehen 1.** *n* (-s/*no pl.*) television; **2.** 2 *v/i.* (*irr. sehen, sep., -ge-; h*) watch television; '~**seher** *m* television set; *p.* television viewer, televiewer; '~**sehsendung** *f* television broadcast, telecast; '~**sicht** *f* visual range.

'Fernsprech|amt *n* telephone exchange, *Am. a.* central; '~**anschluß** *m* telephone connection; '~**er** *m* telephone; '~**leitung** *f* telephone line; '~**zelle** *f* telephone box.

'fern|stehen *v/i.* (*irr. stehen, sep., -ge-; h*) have no real (point of) contact (*dat.* with); '2**steuerung** *f*

s. **Fernlenkung**; '**₂unterricht** m correspondence course or tuition; '**₂verkehr** m long-distance traffic.

Ferse ['fɛrzə] f (-/-n) heel.

fertig adj. ['fɛrtiç] ready; article, etc.: finished; clothing: ready-made; mit et. ~ werden get s.th. finished; mit et. ~ sein have finished s.th.; '**₂bringen** v/t. (irr. bringen, sep., -ge-, h) bring about; manage; '**₂keit** f (-/-en) dexterity; skill; fluency (in the spoken language); '**₂machen** v/t. (sep., -ge-, h) finish, complete; get s.th. ready; fig. finish, settle s.o.'s hash; sich ~ get ready; '**₂stellung** f completion; '**₂waren** f/pl. finished goods pl. or products pl.

fesch F adj. [fɛʃ] hat, dress, etc.: smart, stylish, chic; dashing.

Fessel ['fɛsəl] f (-/-n) chain, fetter, shackle; vet. fetlock; fig. bond, fetter, tie; '**₂ballon** m captive balloon; '**₂n** v/t. (ge-, h) chain, fetter, shackle; j-n ~ hold or arrest s.o.'s attention; fascinate s.o.

fest [fɛst] **1.** adj. firm; solid; fixed; fast; principle: firm, strong; sleep: sound; fabric: close; **2.** ₂ n (-es/-e) festival, celebration; holiday, eccl. feast; '**₂binden** v/t. (irr. binden, sep., -ge-, h) fasten, tie (an dat. to); '**₂essen** n banquet, feast; '**₂fahren** v/refl. (irr. fahren, sep., -ge-, h) get stuck; fig. reach a deadlock; '**₂halle** f (festival) hall; '**₂halten** (irr. halten, sep., -ge-, h) **1.** v/i. hold fast or tight; ~ an (dat.) adhere or keep to; **2.** v/t. hold on to; hold tight; sich ~ an (dat.) hold on to; **₂igen** ['~igən] v/t. (ge-, h) consolidate (one's position, etc.); strengthen (friendship, etc.); stabilize (currency); '**₂igkeit** ['~ç-] f (-/no pl.) firmness; solidity; '**₂land** n mainland, continent; '**₂legen** v/t. (sep., -ge-, h) fix, set; sich auf et. ~ commit o.s. to s.th.; '**₂lich** adj. meal, day, etc.: festive; reception, etc.: ceremonial; '**₂lichkeit** f (-/-en) festivity; festive character; '**₂machen** (sep., -ge-, h) **1.** v/t. fix, fasten, attach (an dat. to); ⚓ moor; **2.** ⚓ v/i. moor; put ashore; '**₂mahl** n banquet, feast; **₂nahme** ['~nɑːmə] f (-/-n) arrest; '**₂nehmen** v/t. (irr. nehmen, sep., -ge-, h) arrest, take into custody; '**₂rede** f speech

of the day; '**₂setzen** v/t. (sep., -ge-, h) fix, set; sich ~ dust, etc.: become ingrained; p. settle (down); '**₂spiel** n festival; '**₂stehen** v/i. (irr. stehen, sep., -ge-, h) stand firm; fact: be certain; '**₂stehend** adj. fixed, stationary; fact: established; '**₂stellen** v/t. (sep., -ge-, h) establish (fact, identity, etc.); ascertain, find out (fact, s.o.'s whereabouts, etc.); state; see, perceive (fact, etc.); '**₂stellung** f establishment; ascertainment; statement; '**₂tag** m festive day; festival, holiday, eccl. feast; '**₂ung** ⚔ f (-/-en) fortress; '**₂zug** m festive procession.

fett [fɛt] **1.** adj. fat; fleshy; voice: oily; land, etc.: rich; **2.** ₂ n (-[e]s/-e) fat; grease (a. ⊕); '**₂druck** typ. m bold type; '**₂fleck** m grease-spot; '**₂ig** adj. hair, skin, etc.: greasy, oily; fingers, etc.: greasy; substance: fatty.

Fetzen ['fɛtsən] m (-s/-) shred; rag, Am. a. frazzle; scrap (of paper); in ~ in rags.

feucht adj. [fɔyçt] climate, air, etc.: damp, moist; air, zone, etc.: humid; '**₂igkeit** f (-/no pl.) moisture (of substance); dampness (of place, etc.); humidity (of atmosphere, etc.).

Feuer ['fɔyər] n (-s/-) fire; light; fig. ardo(u)r; ~ fangen catch fire; fig. fall for (girl); '**₂alarm** m fire alarm; '**₂beständig** adj. fire-proof, fire-resistant; '**₂bestattung** f cremation; '**₂eifer** m ardo(u)r; '**₂fest** adj. s. feuerbeständig; '**₂gefährlich** adj. inflammable; '**₂haken** m poker; '**₂löscher** m (-s/-) fire extinguisher; '**₂melder** m (-s/-) fire-alarm; '**₂n** (ge-, h) **1.** ⚔ v/i. shoot, fire (auf acc. at, on); **2.** v/t. fig. v/t. hurl; '**₂probe** fig. f crucial test; '**₂rot** adj. fiery (red), (as) red as fire; '**₂sbrunst** f conflagration; '**₂schiff** ⚓ n lightship; '**₂schutz** m fire prevention; ⚔ covering fire; '**₂sgefahr** f danger or risk of fire; '**₂speiend** adj.: ~er Berg volcano; '**₂spritze** f fire engine; '**₂stein** m flint; '**₂versicherung** f fire insurance (company); '**₂wache** f fire station, Am. a. firehouse; '**₂wehr** f fire-brigade, Am. a. fire department; '**₂wehrmann** m fireman; '**₂werk** n (display of) fireworks pl.; '**₂werkskörper** m firework; '**₂~**

zange f (e-e a pair of) firetongs pl.; '~zeug n lighter.

feurig adj. ['fɔyriç] fiery (a. fig.); fig. ardent.

Fiasko [fi'asko] n (-s/-s) (complete) failure, fiasco; sl. flop. [primer.⟩

Fibel ['fi:bəl] f (-/-n) spelling-book,⟩

Fichte ♀ ['fiçta] f (-/-n) spruce; '~nnadel f pine-needle.

fidel adj. [fi'de:l] cheerful, merry, jolly, Am. F a. chipper.

Fieber ['fi:bər] n (-s/-) temperature, fever; ~ haben have or run a temperature; '~anfall m attack or bout of fever; '2haft adj. feverish (a. fig.); febrile; '2krank adj. ill with fever; '~mittel n febrifuge; '2n v/i. (ge-, h) have or run a temperature; ~ nach crave or long for; '~schauer m chill, shivers pl.; '~tabelle f temperature-chart; '~thermometer n clinical thermometer.

fiel [fi:l] pret. of fallen.

Figur [fi'gu:r] f (-/-en) figure; chess: chessman, piece.

figürlich adj. [fi'gy:rliç] meaning, etc.: figurative.   [pork, etc.)⟩

Filet [fi'le:] n (-s/-s)fillet (of beef,⟩

Filiale [fi'lja:lə] f (-/-n) branch.

Filigran|arbeit f [fili'gra:n(?-)] n (-s/-e) filigree.

Film [film] m (-[e]s/-e) film, thin coating (of oil, wax, etc.); phot. film; film, (moving) picture, Am. a. motion picture, F movie; e-n ~ ein!egen phot. load a camera; '~atelier n film studio; '~aufnahme f filming, shooting (of a film); film (of sporting event, etc.); '2en (ge-, h) 1. v/t. film, shoot (scene, etc.); 2. v/i. film; make a film; '~gesellschaft f film company, Am. motion-picture company; '~kamera f film camera, Am. motion-picture camera; '~regisseur m film director; '~reklame f screen advertising; '~schauspieler m film or screen actor, Am. F movie actor; '~spule f (film) reel; '~streifen m film strip; '~theater n cinema, Am. motion-picture or F movie theater; '~verleih m (-[e]s/-e) film distributors pl.; '~vorführer m projectionist; '~vorstellung f cinema performance, Am. F movie performance.

Filter ['filtər] (-s/-) 1. m (coffee-, etc.) filter; 2. ⊕ n filter; '2n v/t. (ge-, h) filter (water, air, etc.); fil-

trate (water, impurities, etc.); strain (liquid); '~zigarette f filter-tipped cigarette.

Filz [filts] m (-es/-e) felt; fig. F skinflint; '2ig adj. felt-like; of felt; fig. F niggardly, stingy; '~laus f crab louse.

Finanz|amt [fi'nants?amt] n (inland) revenue office, office of the Inspector of Taxes; ~en f/pl. finances pl.; 2iell adj. [~'tsjɛl] financial; 2ieren [~'tsi:rən] v/t. (no -ge-, h) finance (scheme, etc.); sponsor (radio programme, etc.); ~lage f financial position; ~mann m financier; ~minister m minister of finance; Chancellor of the Exchequer, Am. Secretary of the Treasury; ~ministerium n ministry of finance; Exchequer, Am. Treasury Department; ~wesen n (-s/no pl.) finances pl.; financial matters pl.

Findelkind ['findəl-] n foundling.

finden ['findən] (irr., ge-, h) 1. v/t. find; discover, come across; think, consider; wie ~ Sie ...? how do you like ...?; sich ~ thing: be found; 2. v/i.: ~ zu find one's way to.   [finder's reward.⟩

'Finder m (-s/-) finder; '~lohn m⟩

'findig adj. resourceful, ingenious.

Findling ['fintliŋ] m (-s/-e) foundling; geol. erratic block, boulder.

fing [fiŋ] pret. of fangen.

Finger ['fiŋər] m (-s/-) finger; sich die ~ verbrennen burn one's fingers; er rührte keinen ~ he lifted no finger; '~abdruck m fingerprint; '~fertigkeit f manual skill; '~hut m thimble; ♀ foxglove; '2n v/i. (ge-, h): ~ nach fumble for; '~spitze f finger-tip; '~spitzengefühl fig. n sure instinct; '~übung ♪ f finger exercise; '~zeig ['~tsaik] m (-[e]s/-e) hint, F pointer.

Fink orn. [fiŋk] m (-en/-en) finch.

finster adj. ['finstər] night, etc.: dark; shadows, wood, etc.: sombre; night, room, etc.: gloomy, murky; person, nature: sullen; thought, etc.: sinister, sombre, gloomy; '2nis f (-/no pl.) darkness, gloom.

Finte ['fintə] f (-/-n) feint; fig. a. ruse, trick.

Firma ♀ ['firma] f (-/Firmen) firm, business, company.

firmen eccl. ['firmən] v/t. (ge-, h) confirm.

'**Firmen|inhaber** *m* owner of a firm; '**~wert** *m* goodwill.

Firn [firn] *m* (-[e]s/-e) firn, névé.

First △ [first] *m* (-es/-e) ridge; '**~ziegel** *m* ridge tile.

Fisch [fiʃ] *m* (-es/-e) fish; '**~dampfer** *m* trawler; '**2en** *v/t. and v/i.* (ge-, *h*) fish; '**~er** *m* (-s/-) fisherman; '**~erboot** *n* fishing-boat; '**~erdorf** *n* fishing-village; **~erei** [~'raɪ] *f* (-/-en) fishery; fishing; '**~fang** *m* fishing; '**~geruch** *m* fishy smell; '**~gräte** *f* fish-bone; '**~grätenmuster** *n* herring-bone pattern; '**~händler** *m* fishmonger, *Am.* fish dealer; '2ig *adj.* fishy; '**~laich** *m* spawn; '**~leim** *m* fish-glue; '**~mehl** *n* fish-meal; '**~schuppe** *f* scale; '**~tran** *m* train-oil; '**~vergiftung** 𝒫 *f* fish-poisoning; '**~zucht** *f* pisciculture, fish-hatching; '**~zug** *m* catch, haul, draught (of fish).

fiskalisch *adj.* [fis'kaːliʃ] fiscal, governmental.

Fiskus ['fiskus] *m* (-/⌀ -se, Fisken) Exchequer, *esp. Am.* Treasury; government.

Fistel 𝒫 ['fistəl] *f* (-/-n) fistual; '**~stimme** ♪ *f* falsetto.

Fittich ['fitiç] *m* (-[e]s/-e) *poet.* wing; j-n unter s-e ~e nehmen take s.o. under one's wing.

fix *adj.* [fiks] salary, price, etc.: fixed; quick, clever, smart; e-e ~e Idee an obsession; ein ~er Junge a smart fellow; 2ierbad phot. [fi-'ksiːrbaːt] *n* fixing bath; **~ieren** [fi'ksiːrən] *v/t.* (no -ge-, *h*) fix (a. phot.); fix one's eyes (up)on, stare at s.o.; '2Stern ast. *m* fixed star; '2um *n* (-s/Fixa) fixed or basic salary.

flach *adj.* [flax] roof, etc.: flat; ground, etc.: flat, level, even; water, plate, fig.: shallow; △ plane.

Fläche ['fleçə] *f* (-/-n) surface, △ a. plane; sheet (of water, snow, etc.); geom. area; tract, expanse (of land, etc.); **~ninhalt** △ ['fleçən?-] *m* (surface) area; '**~nmaß** *n* square or surface measure.

'**Flach|land** *n* plain, flat country; '**~rennen** *n turf:* flat race.

Flachs ♀ [flaks] *m* (-es/*no pl.*) flax.

flackern ['flakərn] *v/i.* (ge-, *h*) light, flame, eyes, etc.: flicker, wave; voice: quaver, shake.

Flagge ✕ ['flagə] *f* (-/-n) flag,

colo(u)rs pl.; '2n *v/i.* (ge-, *h*) fly or hoist a flag; signal (with flags).

Flak ✕ [flak] *f* (-/-, -s) anti-aircraft gun; anti-aircraft artillery.

Flamme ['flamə] *f* (-/-n) flame; blaze; '**~nmeer** *n* sea of flames; '**~nwerfer** ✕ *m* (-s/-) flame-thrower.

Flanell [fla'nɛl] *m* (-s/-e) flannel; **~anzug** *m* flannel suit; **~hose** *f* flannel trousers pl., flannels pl.

Flank|e ['flaŋkə] *f* (-/-n) flank (a. △, ⊕, ✕, mount.); side; 2ieren [~'kiːrən] *v/t.* (no -ge-, *h*) flank.

Flasche ['flaʃə] *f* (-/-n) bottle; flask.

'**Flaschen|bier** *n* bottled beer; '**~hals** *m* neck of a bottle; '**~öffner** *m* (-s/-) bottle-opener; '**~zug** ⊕ *m* block and tackle.

flatter|haft *adj.* ['flatərhaft] girl, etc.: fickle, flighty; mind: fickle, volatile; '**~n** *v/i.* (ge-) **1.** (*h*, sein) bird, butterfly, etc.: flutter (about); bird, bat, etc.: flit (about); **2.** (*h*) hair, flag, garment, etc.: stream, fly; mot. wheel: shimmy, wobble; car steering: judder; **3.** (sein): auf den Boden ~ flutter to the ground.

flau *adj.* [flau] weak, feeble, faint; sentiment, reaction, etc.: lukewarm; drink: stale; colour: pale, dull; ✝ market, business, etc.: dull, slack; ~e Zeit slack period.

Flaum [flaum] *m* (-[e]s/*no pl.*) down, fluff; fuzz.

Flau|s [flaus] *m* (-es/-e), **~sch** [~ʃ] *m* (-es/-e) tuft (of wool, etc.); napped coating.

Flausen F ['flauzən] *f/pl.* whims pl., fancies pl., (funny) ideas pl.; F fibs pl.; j-m ~ in den Kopf setzen put funny ideas into s.o.'s head; j-m ~ vormachen tell s.o. fibs.

Flaute ['flautə] *f* (-/-n) ♇ dead calm; esp. ✝ dullness, slack period.

Flecht|e ['fleçtə] *f* (-/-n) braid, plait (of hair); ♀ lichen; 𝒫 herpes; '2en *v/t.* (irr., ge-, *h*) braid, plait (hair, ribbon, etc.), weave (basket, wreath, etc.); wreath (flowers); twist (rope, etc.); '**~werk** *n* wickerwork.

Fleck [flek] *m* (-[e]s/-e, -en) **1.** mark (of dirt, grease, etc.; zo.); spot (of grease, paint, etc.); smear (of oil, blood, etc.); stain (of wine, coffee, etc.); blot (of ink); place, spot; fig. blemish, spot, stain; **2.** patch (of material); bootmaking: heel-piece;

'~en m (-s/-) s. **Fleck 1**; small (market-)town, townlet; **'~enwasser** n spot or stain remover; **'~fieber** 🔬 n (epidemic) typhus; **'2ig** adj. spotted; stained.

Fledermaus zo. ['fle:dər-] f bat.

Flegel ['fle:gəl] m (-s/-) flail; fig. lout, boor; **~ei** [~'laı] f (-/-en) rudeness; loutishness; **'2haft** adj. rude-ill-mannered; loutish; **'~jahre** pl. awkward age.

flehen ['fle:ən] 1. v/i. (ge-, h) entreat, implore (zu j-m s.o.; um et. s.th.); 2. 2 n (-s/no pl.) supplication, imploration, entreaty.

Fleisch [flaɪʃ] n (-es/no pl.) flesh; meat; 🌿 pulp; **'~brühe** f meat-broth; beef tea; **'~er** m (-s/-) butcher; **~erei** [~'raɪ] f (-/-en) butcher's (shop), Am. butcher shop; **'~extrakt** m meat extract; **'2fressend** adj. carnivorous; **'~hackmaschine** f mincing machine, mincer, Am. meat grinder; **'2ig** adj. fleshy; 🌿 pulpy; **'~konserven** f/pl. tinned or potted meat, Am. canned meat; **'~kost** f meat (food); **'2lich** adj. desires, etc.: carnal, fleshly; **'2los** adj. meatless; **'~pastete** f meat pie, Am. a. potpie; **'~speise** f meat dish; **'~vergiftung** f meat or ptomaine poisoning; **'~ware** f meat (product); **'~wolf** m s. Fleischhackmaschine.

Fleiß [flaɪs] m (-es/no pl.) diligence, industry; **'2ig** adj. diligent, industrious, hard-working.

fletschen ['flɛtʃən] v/t. (ge-, h): die Zähne ~ animal: bare its teeth; p. bare one's teeth.

Flicken ['flikən] 1. m (-s/-) patch; 2. 2 v/t. (ge-, h) patch (dress, tyre, etc.); repair (shoe, roof, etc.); cobble (shoe).

'Flick|schneider m jobbing tailor; **'~schuster** m cobbler; **'~werk** n (-[e]s/no pl.) patchwork.

Flieder 🌿 ['fli:dər] m (-s/-) lilac.

Fliege ['fli:gə] f (-/-n) zo. fly; bow-tie.

'fliegen 1. v/i. (irr., ge-, sein) fly; go by air; 2. v/t. (irr., ge-, h) fly, pilot (aircraft), convey (goods, etc.) by air; 3. 2 n (-s/no pl.) flying; ✈ a. aviation.

Fliegen|fänger ['fli:gənfɛŋər] m (-s/-) fly-paper; **'~fenster** n fly-screen; **'~gewicht** n boxing, etc.:

flyweight; **'~klappe** f fly-flap, Am. fly swatter; **'~pilz** 🌿 m fly agaric.

'Flieger m (-s/-) flyer; ✈ airman, aviator; pilot; F plane, bomber; cycling: sprinter; **'~abwehr** ✈ f anti-aircraft defen|ce, Am. -se; **'~alarm** ✈ m air-raid alarm or warning; **'~bombe** ✈ f aircraft bomb; **'~offizier** ✈ m air-force officer.

flieh|en ['fli:ən] (irr., ge-) 1. v/i. (sein) flee (vor dat. from), run away; 2. v/t. (h) flee, avoid, keep away from; **'2kraft** phys. f centrifugal force.   [(floor-)tile.)

Fliese ['fli:zə] f (-/-n) (wall-)tile.{

Fließ|band ['fli:s-] n (-[e]s/¨er) conveyor-belt; assembly-line; **'2en** v/i. (irr., ge-, sein) river, traffic, etc.: flow; tap-water, etc.: run; **'2end 1.** adj. water: running; traffic: moving; speech, etc.: fluent; 2. adv.: ~ lesen (sprechen) read (speak) fluently; **'~papier** n blotting-paper.

Flimmer ['flimər] m (-s/-) glimmer, glitter; **'2n** v/i. (ge-, h) glimmer, glitter; television, film: flicker; es flimmert mir vor den Augen everything is dancing in front of my eyes.

flink adj. [fliŋk] quick, nimble, brisk.

Flinte ['flintə] f (-/-n) shotgun; die ~ ins Korn werfen throw up the sponge.

Flirt [flœrt] m (-es/-s) flirtation; **'2en** v/i. (ge-, h) flirt (mit with).

Flitter ['flitər] m (-s/-) tinsel (a. fig.), spangle; **'~kram** m cheap finery; **'~wochen** pl. honeymoon.

flitzen F ['flitsən] v/i. (ge-, sein) whisk, scamper; dash (off, etc.).

flocht [flɔxt] pret. of flechten.

Flock|e ['flɔkə] f (-/-n) flake (of snow, soap, etc.); flock (of wool); **'2ig** adj. fluffy, flaky.

flog [flo:k] pret. of fliegen.

floh¹ [flo:] pret. of fliehen.

Floh² zo. [~] m (-[e]s/¨e) flea.

Flor [flo:r] m (-s/-e) bloom, blossom; fig. bloom, prime; gauze; crêpe, crape.

Florett fenc. [flo'rɛt] n (-[e]s/-e) foil.

florieren [flo'ri:rən] v/i. (no -ge-, h) business, etc.: flourish, prosper, thrive.

Floskel ['flɔskəl] f (-/-n) flourish; empty phrase.

floß¹ [flɔs] pret. of fließen.

Floß² [flo:s] n (-es/¨e) raft, float.

Flosse ['flɔsə] f (-/-n) fin; flipper (of penguin, etc.).

flöß|en ['flø:sən] v/t. (ge-, h) raft, float (timber, etc.); **'2er** m (-s/-) rafter, raftsman.

Flöte ♪ ['flø:tə] f (-/-n) flute; **'2n** (ge-, h) **1.** v/i. (play the) flute; **2.** v/t. play on the flute.

flott adj. [flɔt] ⚓ floating, afloat; pace, etc.: quick, brisk; music, etc.: gay, lively; dress, etc.: smart, stylish; car, etc.: sporty, racy; dancer, etc.: excellent.

Flotte ['flɔtə] f (-/-n) ⚓ fleet; ♂ navy; **'~nstützpunkt** ✕ m naval base.

Flotille ⚓ [flɔ'tiljə] f (-/-n) flotilla.

Flöz geol., ⚒ [flø:ts] n (-es/-e) seam, layer, stratum.

Fluch [flu:x] m (-[e]s/=e) curse, malediction; eccl. anathema; curse, swear-word; **'2en** (ge-, h) swear, curse.

Flucht [fluxt] f (-/-en) flight (vor dat. from); escape (aus dat. from); line (of windows, etc.); suite (of rooms); flight (of stairs).

flücht|en ['flyçtən] (ge-) v/i. (sein) and v/refl. (h) flee (nach, zu to); run away; escape; **'~ig** adj. fugitive (a. fig.); thought, etc.: fleeting; fame, etc.: transient; p. careless, superficial; 🜄 volatile; **2ling** ['~lɪŋ] m (-s/-e) fugitive; pol. refugee; **'2lingslager** n refugee camp.

Flug [flu:k] m (-[e]s/=e) flight; im ~(e) rapidly; quickly; **'~abwehrrakete** f anti-aircraft missile; **'~bahn** f trajectory (of rocket, etc.); ✈ flight path; **'~blatt** n handbill, leaflet, Am. a. flier; **'~boot** ✈ n flying-boat; **'~dienst** ✈ m air service.

Flügel ['fly:gəl] m (-s/-) wing (a. △, ✈, ✕); blade, vane (of propeller, etc.); s. Fensterflügel, Türflügel, Lungenflügel; sail (of windmill, etc.); ♪ grand piano; **'~fenster** △ n casement-window; **'2lahm** adj. brokenwinged; **'~mann** ✕ m marker; **'~tür** △ f folding door.

Fluggast ['flu:k-] m (air) passenger.

flügge adj. ['flygə] fledged; ~ werden fledge; fig. begin to stand on one's own feet.

'Flug|hafen m airport; **'~linie** f ✈ air route; airline; **'~platz** m airfield, aerodrome, Am. a. airdrome;

airport; **'~sand** geol. m wind-blown sand; **'~schrift** f pamphlet; **'~sicherung** f air traffic control; **'~sport** m sporting aviation; **'~wesen** n aviation, aeronautics.

'Flugzeug n aircraft, aeroplane, F plane, Am. a. airplane; **'~bau** m aircraft construction; **'~führer** m pilot; **'~halle** f hangar; **'~rumpf** m fuselage, body; **'~träger** m aircraft carrier, Am. sl. flattop; **'~unglück** n air crash or disaster.

Flunder ichth. ['flundər] f (-/-n) flounder.

Flunker|ei F [flʊŋkə'raɪ] f (-/-en) petty lying, F fib(bing); **'2n** v/i. (ge-, h) F fib, tell fibs.

fluoreszieren [fluorɛs'tsi:rən] v/i. (no -ge-, h) fluoresce.

Flur [flu:r] **1.** f (-/-en) field, meadow; poet. lea; **2.** m (-[e]s/-e) (entrance-)hall.

Fluß [flus] m (Flusses/Flüsse) river, stream; flow(ing); fig. fluency, flux; **2'abwärts** adv. downriver, downstream; **2'aufwärts** adv. upriver, upstream; **'~bett** n river bed.

flüssig adj. ['flysiç] fluid, liquid; metal: molten, melted; ✝ money, capital, etc.: available, in hand; style: fluent, flowing; **'2keit** f (-/-en) fluid, liquid; fluidity, liquidity; availability; fluency.

'Fluß|lauf m course of a river; **'~mündung** f mouth of a river; **'~pferd** zo. n hippopotamus; **'~schiffahrt** f river navigation or traffic.

flüstern ['flystərn] v/i. and v/t. (ge-, h) whisper.

Flut [flu:t] f (-/-en) flood; high tide, (flood-)tide; fig. flood, torrent, deluge; **'2en** (ge-) **1.** v/i. (sein) water, crowd, etc.: flood, surge (über acc. over); **2.** v/t. (h) flood (dock, etc.); **'~welle** f tidal wave.

focht [fɔxt] pret. of fechten.

Fohlen zo. ['fo:lən] **1.** n (-s/-) foal; male: colt; female: filly; **2.** ♀ v/i. (ge-, h) foal.

Folge ['fɔlgə] f (-/-n) sequence, succession (of events); instalment, part (of radio series, etc.); consequence, result; series; set, suit; future; ~n pl. aftermath.

folgen v/i. (dat.) (ge-, sein) follow; succeed (j-m s.o.; auf acc. to); follow, ensue (aus from); obey (j-m s.o.); **~dermaßen** *adv.* ['~dərmɑːsən] as follows; '**~schwer** *adj.* of grave consequence, grave.

folgerichtig *adj.* logical; consistent.

folger|n ['fɔlgərn] *v/t.* (ge-, h) infer, conclude, deduce (*aus* from); '**2ung** *f* (-/-en) inference, conclusion, deduction.

'**folgewidrig** *adj.* illogical; inconsistent.

folglich *cj.* ['fɔlkliç] therefore, consequently.

folgsam *adj.* ['fɔlkzaːm] obedient; '**2keit** *f* (-/*no pl.*) obedience.

Folie ['foːljə] *f* (-/-n) foil.

Folter ['fɔltər] *f* (-/-n) torture; *auf die ~ spannen* put to the rack; *fig.* F a. keep on tenterhooks; '**2n** *v/t.* (ge-, h) torture, torment; '**~qual** *f* torture, *fig.* a. torment.

Fonds † [fõː] *m* (-/-) fund (*a. fig.*); funds *pl.*

Fontäne [fɔn'tɛːnə] *f* (-/-n) fountain.

foppen ['fɔpən] *v/t.* (ge-, h) tease, F pull s.o.'s leg; hoax, fool.

forcieren [fɔr'siːrən] *v/t.* (*no* ge-, h) force (up).

'**Förder|band** *n* (-[e]s/¨er) conveyor-belt; '**2lich** *adj.* conducive (*dat.* to), promotive (of); '**~korb** ⚒ *m* cage.

fordern ['fɔrdərn] *v/t.* (ge-, h) demand; claim (*compensation, etc.*); ask (*price, etc.*); challenge (*to duel*).

fördern ['fœrdərn] *v/t.* (ge-, h) further, advance, promote; ⚒ haul, raise (*coal, etc.*); *zutage ~* reveal, bring to light.

'**Forderung** *f* (-/-en) demand; claim; charge; challenge.

'**Förderung** *f* (-/-en) furtherance, advancement, promotion; ⚒ haulage; output. [trout.]

Forelle *ichth.* [fo'relə] *f* (-/-n)

Form [fɔrm] *f* (-/-en) form; figure, shape; model; ⊕ mo(u)ld; *sports:* form, condition; '**2al** *adj.* [~'maːl] formal; **~alität** [~ali'tɛːt] *f* (-/-en) formality; '**~at** [~'maːt] *n* (-[e]s/-e) size; *von ~* of distinction; '**~el** ['~əl] *f* (-/-n) formula; '**2ell** *adj.* [~'mɛl] formal; '**2en** *v/t.* (ge-, h) form (*object, character, etc.*); shape, fashion (*wood, metal, etc.*); mo(u)ld (*clay, character, etc.*); '**~enlehre** *gr. f* accidence; '**~fehler** *m* informality; ɪ⚖

flaw; **2ieren** [~'miːrən] *v/t.* (*no* -ge-, h) form; draw up, line up; *sich ~* line up.

förmlich ['fœrmliç] *adj.* formal; ceremonious; '**2keit** *f* (-/-en) formality; ceremoniousness.

'**formlos** *adj.* formless, shapeless; *fig.* informal.

Formular [fɔrmu'laːr] *n* (-s/-e) form, *Am. a.* blank.

formu'lieren *v/t.* (*no* -ge-, h) formulate (*question, etc.*); word, phrase (*question, contract, etc.*).

forsch *adj.* [fɔrʃ] vigorous, energetic; smart, dashing.

forsch|en ['fɔrʃən] *v/i.* (ge-, h): ~ *nach* (*dat.*) search for *or* after; ~ *in* (*dat.*) search (through); '**2er** *m* (-s/-) researcher, research worker.

'**Forschung** *f* (-/-en) research (work); '**~sreise** *f* (exploring) expedition; '**~sreisende** *m* explorer.

Forst [fɔrst] *m* (-es/-e[n]) forest; '**~aufseher** *m* (forest-)keeper, gamekeeper. [ranger.]

Förster ['fœrstər] *m* (-s/-) forester;

'**Forst|haus** *n* forester's house; '**~revier** *n* forest district; '**~wesen** *n*, '**~wirtschaft** *f* forestry.

Fort[1] ⚔ [foːr] *n* (-s/-s) fort.

fort[2] *adv.* ['fɔrt] away, gone; on; gone, lost; *in e-m ~* continuously; *und so ~* and so on *or* forth; *s. a.* weg.

'**fort|bestehen** *v/i.* (*irr.* stehen, *sep.*, *no* -ge-, h) continue, persist; '**~bewegen** *v/t.* (*sep.*, *no* -ge-, h) move (on, away); *sich ~* move, walk; '**2-dauer** *f* continuance; '**~dauern** *v/i.* (*sep.*, -ge-, h) continue, last; '**~fahren** *v/i.* (*irr.* fahren, *sep.*, -ge-) **1.** (sein) depart, leave; drive off; **2.** (h) continue, keep on (et. *zu tun* doing s.th.); '**~führen** *v/t.* (*sep.*, -ge-, h) continue, carry on; **2gang** *m* departure, leaving; continuance; '**~gehen** *v/i.* (*irr.* gehen, *sep.*, -ge-, sein) go (away), leave; '**~geschritten** *adj.* advanced; '**2kommen** *n* (-s/*no pl.*) progress; '**~laufend** *adj.* consecutive, continuous; '**~pflanzen** *v/t.* (*sep.*, -ge-, h) propagate; *sich ~ biol.* propagate, reproduce; *phys., disease, rumour:* be propagated; '**2pflanzung** *f* propagation; reproduction; '**~reißen** *v/t.* (*irr.* reißen, *sep.*, -ge-, h) avalanche, *etc.:* sweep *or* carry away; '**~schaffen** *v/t.* (*sep.*, *-ge-*, h) get *or* take away, remove; '**~schreiten** *v/i.* (*irr.* schreiten, *sep.*, *-ge-*, sein) advance, proceed, progress; '**~schreitend** *adj.* progressive; '2**schritt** *m* progress; '**~schrittlich** *adj.* progressive; '**~setzen** *v/t.* (*sep.*, *-ge-*, h) continue, pursue; '2**setzung** *f* (*-/-en*) continuation, pursuit; ~ *folgt* to be continued; '**~während 1.** *adj.* continual, continuous; perpetual; **2.** *adv.* constantly, always.

Forum ['fo:rum] *n* (*-s/*Foren, Fora *and* -s) forum.

Foto... ['fo:to-] *s. Photo...*

Foyer [foa'je:] *n* (*-s/-s*) *thea.* foyer, *Am. and parl.* lobby; *hotel:* foyer, lounge.

Fracht [fraxt] *f* (*-/-en*) goods *pl.*; ⚙ carriage, freight; ⏚, ⚓ freight (*-age*), cargo; '**~brief** *m* consignment note, *Am.*, ⚓ bill of lading; '**~dampfer** *m* cargo steamer, freighter; '**~er** *m* (*-s/-*) freighter; '2**frei** *adj.* carriage *or* freight paid; '**~führer** *m* carrier, *Am. a.* teamster; '**~geld** *n* carriage charges *pl.*, ⚓, ⚓, *Am.* freight; '**~gut** *n* goods *pl.*, freight; '**~stück** *n* package.

Frack [frak] *m* (*-[e]s/*⁀e, -s) dress coat, tail-coat, F tails; '**~anzug** *m* dress-suit.

Frag|e ['fra:gə] *f* (*-/-n*) question; *gr.*, *rhet.* interrogation; problem, point; *e-e* ~ *stellen* ask a question; *in* ~ *stellen* question; '**~ebogen** *m* questionnaire; form; '2**en** (*-ge-*, h) **1.** *v/t.* ask; question; *es fragt sich, ob* it is doubtful whether; **2.** *v/i.* ask; '**~er** *m* (*-s/-*) questioner; '**~wort** *gr. n* (*-[e]s/*⁀er) interrogative; '**~ezeichen** *n* question-mark, point of interrogation, *Am. mst* interrogation point; 2**lich** *adj.* ['fra:k-] doubtful, uncertain; in question; 2**los** *adv.* ['fra:k-] undoubtedly, unquestionably.   [fragment.]

Fragment [fra'mɛnt] *n* (*-[e]s/-e*)⟩

fragwürdig *adj.* ['fra:k-] doubtful, dubious, questionable.

Fraktion *parl.* [frak'tsjo:n] *f* (*-/-en*) (parliamentary) group.

frank|ieren [fraŋ'ki:rən] *v/t.* (*no -ge-*, h) prepay, stamp; '**~o** *adv.* ['~o] free; post(age) paid; *parcel:* carriage paid.

Franse ['franzə] *f* (*-/-n*) fringe.

Franz|ose [fran'tso:zə] *m* (*-n/-n*)

Frenchman; *die* ~*n pl.* the French *pl.*; '**~ösin** [~ø:zin] *f* (*-/-nen*) Frenchwoman; 2**ösisch** *adj.* [~ø:ziʃ] French.

fräs|en ⊕ ['frɛ:zən] *v/t.* (*ge-*, h) mill; 2**maschine** ['frɛ:s-] *f* milling-machine.

Fraß [fra:s] *m* **1.** F *m* (*-es/-e*) *sl.* grub; **2.** *pret. of* fressen.

Fratze ['fratsə] *f* (*-/-n*) grimace, F face; ~*n schneiden* make grimaces.

Frau [frau] *f* (*-/-en*) woman; lady; wife; ~ *X* Mrs *X*.

'**Frauen|arzt** *m* gyn(a)ecologist; '**~klinik** *f* hospital for women; '**~rechte** *n/pl.* women's rights *pl.*; '**~stimmrecht** *pol. n* women's suffrage; '**~zimmer** *mst contp. n* female, woman.

Fräulein ['frɔʏlaɪn] *n* (*-s/-*, F *-s*) young lady; teacher; shop-assistant; waitress; ~ *X* Miss *X*.

'**fraulich** *adj.* womanly.

frech *adj.* [frɛç] impudent, insolent, F saucy, cheeky, *Am.* F *a.* sassy, *sl.* fresh; *lie, etc.:* brazen; *thief, etc.:* bold, daring; '2**heit** *f* (*-/-en*) impudence, insolence; F sauciness, cheek; boldness.

frei *adj.* [fraɪ] free (*von* from, of); *position:* vacant; *field:* open; *parcel:* carriage-paid; *journalist, etc.:* freelance; candid, frank; licentious; ~ *Haus* ⚖ franco domicile; ~*er Tag* day off; *im Freien* in the open air.

'**Frei|bad** *n* open-air bath; ~**beuter** ['~bɔʏtər] *m* (*-s/-*) freebooter; 2**bleibend** † *adj.* *price, etc.:* subject to alteration; *offer:* conditional; '**~brief** *m* charter; *fig.* warrant; '**~denker** *m* (*-s/-*) freethinker.

Freier ['fraɪər] *m* (*-s/-*) suitor.

'**Frei|exemplar** *n* free *or* presentation copy; '**~frau** *f* baroness; '**~gabe** *f* release; 2**geben** (*irr.* geben, *sep.*, *-ge-*, h) **1.** *v/t.* release; give (*s.o. an hour, etc.*) off; **2.** *v/i.: j-m* ~ give s.o. time off; '2**gebig** *adj.* generous, liberal; '**~gebigkeit** *f* (*-/-en*) generosity, liberality; '**~gepäck** *n* free luggage; '2**haben** *v/i.* (*irr.* haben, *sep.*, *-ge-*, h) have a holiday; have a day off; '**~hafen** *m* free port; '2**halten** (*irr.* halten, *sep.*, *-ge-*, h) keep free *or* clear; *in restaurant, etc.:* treat; '**~handel** *m* free trade.

'**Freiheit** f (-/-en) liberty; freedom; *dichterische* ~ poetic licence, *Am.* poetic license.

'**Frei**|**herr** m baron; '~**karte** f free (*thea. a.* complimentary) ticket; '**♀lassen** v/t. (*irr. lassen, sep., -ge-, h*) release, set free or at liberty; *gegen Kaution* ~ 🔒 release on bail; '~**lassung** f (-/-en) release; '~**lauf** m free-wheel.

'**freilich** adv. indeed, certainly, of course; admittedly.

'**Frei**|**lichtbühne** f open-air stage or theat|re, *Am.* -er; '**♀machen** v/t. (*sep., -ge-, h*) 🖂 prepay, stamp (*letter, etc.*); *sich* ~ undress, take one's clothes off; '~**marke** f stamp; '~**maurer** m freemason; ~**maurerei** [~'raɪ] f (-/no pl.) freemasonry; '~**mut** m frankness; **♀mütig** adj. ['~myːtɪç] frank; '**♀schaffend** adj.: ~**er** *Künstler* free-lance artist; ~**schärler** ✕ ['~ʃɛːrlər] m (-s/-) volunteer, irregular; '~**schein** m licen|ce, *Am.* -se; '**♀sinnig** adj. liberal; '**♀sprechen** v/t. (*irr. sprechen, sep., -ge-, h*) *esp. eccl.* absolve (*von* from); 🔒 acquit (of); release (*apprentice*) from his articles; '~**sprechung** f (-/-en) *esp. eccl.* absolution; release from articles; = '~**spruch** 🔒 m acquittal; '~**staat** pol. m free state; '**♀stehen** v/i. (*irr. stehen, sep., -ge-, h*) house, etc.: stand empty; *es steht Ihnen frei zu* inf. you are free or at liberty to inf.; '**♀stellen** v/t. (*sep., -ge-, h*): j-n ~ exempt s.o. (*von* from) (*a.* ✕); j-m et. ~ leave s.th. open to s.o.; '~**stoß** m *football*: free kick; '~**tag** m Friday; '~**tod** m suicide; '**♀tragend** 🔺 adj. cantilever; '~**treppe** f outdoor staircase; '**♀willig 1.** adj. voluntary; **2.** adv. a. of one's own free will; ~**willige** ['~vɪlɪgə] m (-n/-n) volunteer; '~**zeit** f free or spare or leisure time; **♀zügig** adj. ['~tsyːgɪç] free to move; '**♀zügigkeit** f (-/no pl.) freedom of movement.

fremd adj. [frɛmt] strange; foreign; alien; extraneous; '~**artig** adj. strange; exotic.

Fremde ['frɛmdə] **1.** f (-/no pl.) distant or foreign parts; *in der* ~ far away from home, abroad; **2.** m, f (-n/-n) stranger; foreigner; '~**n**-**buch** n visitors' book; '~**nführer** m guide, cicerone; '~**nheim** n

boarding house; ~**nindustrie** ['frɛmdən'~] f tourist industry; '~**nlegion** ✕ f Foreign Legion; '~**nverkehr** m tourism, tourist traffic; '~**nzimmer** n spare (bed-) room; *tourism:* room.

'**Fremd**|**herrschaft** f foreign rule; '~**körper** 🟎 m foreign body; **♀ländisch** adj. ['~lɛndɪʃ] foreign, exotic; '~**sprache** f foreign language; '**♀sprachig** adj., '**♀sprachlich** adj. foreign-language; '~**wort** n (-[e]s/ּ⁀er) foreign word.

Frequenz phys. [fre'kvɛnts] f (-/-en) frequency.

fressen ['frɛsən] **1.** v/t. (*irr., ge-, h*) eat; *beast of prey:* devour; F *p.* devour, gorge; **2.** v/i. (*irr., ge-, h*) eat; F *p.* gorge; **3.** ♀ n (-s/no pl.) feed, food.

'**Freß**|**gier** f voracity, gluttony; '~**napf** m feeding dish.

Freude ['frɔydə] f (-/-n) joy, gladness; delight; pleasure; ~ *haben an* (*dat.*) find or take pleasure in.

'**Freuden**|**botschaft** f glad tidings pl.; '~**fest** n happy occasion; '~**feuer** n bonfire; '~**geschrei** n shouts pl. of joy; '~**tag** m day of rejoicing, red-letter day; '~**taumel** m transports pl. of joy.

'**freud**|**estrahlend** adj. radiant with joy; '**♀ig** adj. joyful; happy; ~**es** *Ereignis* happy event; ~**los** adj. ['frɔytloːs] joyless, cheerless.

freuen ['frɔyən] v/refl. (ge-, h): *es freut mich, daß* I am glad or pleased (that); *sich* ~ *über* (*acc.*) be pleased about or with, be glad about; *sich* ~ *auf* (*acc.*) look forward to.

Freund [frɔynt] m (-es/-e) (boy-) friend; ~**in** ['~dɪn] f (-/-nen) (girl-) friend; '**♀lich** adj. friendly, kind, nice; cheerful, bright; *climate:* mild; '~**lichkeit** f (-/-en) friendliness, kindness; '~**schaft** f (-/-en) friendship; ~ *schließen* make friends (*mit* with); '**♀schaftlich** adj. friendly.

Frevel ['freːfəl] m (-s/-) outrage (*an* dat., *gegen* on), crime (against); '**♀haft** adj. wicked, outrageous; impious; '**♀n** v/i. (*ge-, h*) commit a crime or outrage (*gegen* against).

Frevler ['freːflər] m (-s/-) evil-doer, offender; blasphemer.

Friede(n) ['friːdə(n)] m (*Friedens*/ *Frieden*) peace; *im Frieden* in peace-

time; *laß mich in Frieden!* leave me
alone!

'**Friedens|bruch** *m* violation of
(the) peace; '**~stifter** *m* peace-
maker; '**~störer** *m* (-s/-) disturber
of the peace; '**~verhandlungen** *f/pl.*
peace negotiations *pl.*; '**~vertrag**
m peace treaty.

fried|fertig *adj.* ['fri:t-] peaceable,
peace-loving; '**2hof** *m* cemetery,
graveyard; churchyard; '**~lich** *adj.*
s. friedfertig; peaceful; '**~liebend**
adj. peace-loving.

frieren ['fri:rən] *v/i.* (*irr.*, ge-)
1. (*sein*) *liquid:* freeze, become
frozen; *river, etc.:* freeze (over, up);
window-pane, etc.: freeze over;
2. (*h*) be or feel cold; *mich friert*
or *ich friere an den Füßen* my feet
are cold.

Fries △ [fri:s] *m* (-es/-e) frieze.

frisch [friʃ] **1.** *adj. food, flowers,
etc.:* fresh; *egg:* new-laid; *linen, etc.:*
clean; *auf ~er Tat ertappen* catch
red-handed; **2.** *adv.:* *~ gestrichen!*
wet paint!, *Am.* fresh paint!; **2e**
['~ə] *f* (-/no pl.) freshness.

Friseu|r [fri'zø:r] *m* (-s/-e) hair-
dresser; (*men's*) barber; '**~se** [~zə] *f*
(-/-n) (woman) hairdresser.

fri'sier|en *v/t.* (no -ge-, h): *j-n ~*
do or dress s.o.'s hair; F: *einen
Wagen ~* *mot.* tune up or soup up or
hot up a car; *sich ~* do one's hair;
2kommode *f* dressing-table; **2sa-
lon** *m* hairdressing saloon; **2tisch**
m s. Frisierkommode.

Frist [frist] *f* (-/-en) (fixed or limited)
period of time; time allowed; term;
ʒʒ prescribed time; ʒʒ, ✝ respite,
grace; '**2en** *v/t.* (ge-, h): *sein
Dasein ~* scrape along, scrape a
living.

Frisur [fri'zu:r] *f* (-/-en) hair-style,
hair-do, coiffure.

frivol *adj.* [fri'vo:l] frivolous, flippant; **2ität** [~oli'tɛ:t] *f* (-/-en)
frivolity, flippancy.

froh *adj.* [fro:] joyful, glad; cheerful; happy; gay (*a. colour*).

fröhlich *adj.* ['frø:liç] gay, merry,
cheerful, happy, *Am.* F *a.* chipper;
'**2keit** *f* (-/✓ -en) gaiety, cheerfulness; merriment.

froh|'locken *v/i.* (no -ge-, h) shout
for joy, be jubilant; exult (*über acc.*
at, in); gloat (over); '**2sinn** *m*
(-[e]s/no pl.) gaiety, cheerfulness.

fromm *adj.* [trɔm] *p.* pious, religious; *life, etc.:* godly; *prayer, etc.:*
devout; *horse, etc.:* docile; *~e Lüge*
white lie; *~er Wunsch* wishful
thinking, idle wish.

Frömmelei [frœmə'laɪ] *f* (-/-en)
affected piety, bigotry.

'**Frömmigkeit** *f* (-/-en) piety,
religiousness; godliness; devout-
ness.

Fron [fro:n] *f* (-/-en), '**~arbeit** *f*,
'**~dienst** *hist.* *m* forced or compulsory labo(u)r or service; *fig.*
drudgery.

frönen ['frø:nən] *v/i.* (*dat.*) (ge-, h)
indulge in; be a slave to.

Front [frɔnt] *f* (-/-en) △ front,
façade, face; ✕ front (line), line;
pol., ✝, *etc.:* front.

fror [fro:r] *pret. of* frieren.

Frosch *zo.* [frɔʃ] *m* (-es/⸚e) frog;
'**~perspektive** *f* worm's-eye view.

Frost [frɔst] *m* (-es/⸚e) frost; chill;
'**~beule** *f* chilblain.

frösteln ['frœstəln] *v/i.* (ge-, h)
feel chilly, shiver (with cold).

'**frostig** *adj.* frosty (*a. fig.*); *fig.* cold,
frigid, icy.

'**Frost|salbe** ❀ *f* chilblain ointment;
'**~schaden** *m* frost damage; '**~
schutzmittel** *mot.* *n* anti-freezing
mixture; '**~wetter** *n* frosty weather.

frottier|en [frɔ'ti:rən] *v/t.* (no -ge-,
h) rub; **2(hand)tuch** *n* Turkish
towel.

Frucht [fruxt] *f* (-/⸚e) ♀ fruit (*a.
fig.*); corn; crop; *fig.* reward,
result; '**2bar** *adj.* fruitful (*esp. fig.*);
fertile (*a. biol.*); '**~barkeit** *f* (-/no
pl.*) fruitfulness; fertility; '**2brin-
gend** *adj.* fruit-bearing; *fig.* fruitful; '**2en** *fig. v/i.* (ge-, h) be of use;
'**~knoten** *m* ♀ ovary; '**2los** *adj.*
fruitless; *fig. a.* ineffective.

früh [fry:] **1.** *adj.* early; *am ~en
Morgen* in the early morning; *~es
Aufstehen* early rising; *~e Anzeichen*
early symptoms; *~er former;* **2.** *adv.*
in the morning; *~ aufstehen* rise
early; *heute ~* this morning; *morgen
~* tomorrow morning; *~er* earlier;
formerly, in former times; *~estens*
at the earliest; '**2aufsteher** *m* (-s/-)
early riser, F early bird; '**2e** *f* (-/no
pl.*): *in aller ~* very early in the
morning; '**2geburt** *f* premature
birth; premature baby or animal;
'**2gottesdienst** *m* early service;

'Ջjahr n, Ջling ['‿liŋ] m (-s/-e) spring; '‿morgens adv. early in the morning; '‿reif fig. adj. precocious; 'Ջsport m early morning exercises; 'Ջstück n breakfast; '‿stücken (ge-, h) 1. v/i. (have) breakfast; 2. v/t. have s.th. for breakfast; 'Ջzug 🚂 m early train.

Fuchs [fuks] m (-es/⁺e) zo. fox (a. fig.); horse: sorrel.

Füchsin zo. ['fyksin] f (-/-nen) she-fox, vixen.

'**Fuchs|jagd** f fox-hunt(ing); '‿pelz m fox-fur; 'Ջrot adj. foxy-red, sorrel; '‿schwanz m foxtail; ⊕ pad-saw; 'Ջ'amarant(h); '‿teufels-wild F adj. mad with rage, F hopping mad.

fuchteln ['fuxtəln] v/i. (ge-, h): ~ mit (dat.) wave (one's hands) about.

Fuder ['fu:dər] n (-s/-) cart-load; tun (of wine). [♩ fugue.]

Fuge ['fu:gə] f (-/-n) ⊕ joint; seam;

füg|en ['fy:gən] v/refl. (ge-, h) submit, give in, yield (dat., in acc. to); comply (with); '‿sam adj. ['fy:k-] (com)pliant; manageable.

fühl|bar adj. ['fy:lba:r] tangible, palpable; fig. sensible, noticeable; '‿en (ge-, h) 1. v/t. feel; be aware of; sich glücklich ~ feel happy; 2. v/i.: mit j-m ~ feel for or sympathize with s.o.; 'Ջer m (-s/-) feeler (a. fig.); 'Ջung f (-/-en) touch, contact (a. ✕); ~ haben be in touch (mit with); ~ verlieren lose touch.

fuhr [fu:r] pret. of fahren.

Fuhre ['fu:rə] f (-/-n) cart-load.

führen ['fy:rən] (ge-, h) 1. v/t. lead, guide (blind person, etc.); show (zu dat. to); wield (paint-brush, etc.); ✕ command (regiment, etc.); have, bear (title, etc.); carry on (conversation, etc.); conduct (campaign, etc.); ✝ run (shop, etc.); deal in (goods); lead (life); keep (diary, etc.); ⚖ try (case); wage (war) (mit, gegen against); ~ durch show round; sich ~ conduct o.s., behave (o.s.); 2. v/i. path, etc.: lead, run, go (nach, zu to); sports, etc.: (hold the) lead, be ahead; ~ zu lead to, result in; '‿d adj. leading, prominent, Am. a. banner.

'**Führer** m (-s/-) leader (a. pol., sports); guide(-book); '‿raum ✈ m cockpit; '‿schein mot. m driving licence, Am. driver's license; '‿sitz

m mot. driver's seat, ✈ pilot's seat; '‿stand 🚂 m (driver's) cab.

'**Fuhr|geld** n, '‿lohn m cartage, carriage; '‿mann m (-[e]s/⁺er, Fuhrleute) carter, carrier, wag(g)oner; driver; '‿park m fleet (of lorries), Am. fleet (of trucks).

'**Führung** f (-/-en) leadership; conduct, management; guidance; conduct, behavio(u)r; sports, etc.: lead; '‿szeugnis n certificate of good conduct.

'**Fuhr|unternehmer** m carrier, haulage contractor, Am. a. trucker, teamster; '‿werk n (horse-drawn) vehicle; cart, wag(g)on.

Fülle ['fylə] f (-/no pl.) fullness (a. fig.); corpulence, plumpness, stoutness; fig. wealth, abundance, profusion.

füllen[1] ['fylən] v/t. (ge-, h) fill (a. tooth); stuff (cushion, poultry, etc.).

Füllen[2] zo. ['‿] n (-s/-) foal; male: colt; female: filly.

'**Füll|er** F m (-s/-), '‿feder(halter m) f fountain-pen; '‿horn n horn of plenty; '‿ung f (-/-en) filling; panel (of door, etc.).

Fund [funt] m (-[e]s/-e) finding, discovery; find.

Fundament[funda'mɛnt]n(-[e]s/-e) 🏛 foundation; fig. basis.

'**Fund|büro** n lost-property office; '‿gegenstand m object found; '‿grube fig. f rich source, mine.

fünf adj. [fynf] five; 'Ջeck n pentagon; '‿fach adj. ['‿fax] fivefold, quintuple; 'Ջkampf m sports: pentathlon; Ջlinge ['‿liŋə] m/pl. quintuplets pl.; '‿te adj. fifth; 'Ջtel n (-s/-) fifth; '‿tens adv. fifthly, in the fifth place; '‿zehn(te) adj. fifteen(th); '‿zig ['‿tsiç] fifty; '‿zigste adj. fiftieth.

fungieren [fuŋ'gi:rən] v/i. (no -ge-, h): ~ als officiate or act as.

Funk [fuŋk] m (-s/no pl.) radio, wireless; '‿anlage f radio or wireless installation or equipment; '‿bastler m do-it-yourself radio ham; '‿bild n photo-radiogram.

Funke ['fuŋkə] m (-ns/-n) spark; fig. a. glimmer.

funkeln v/i. (ge-, h) sparkle, glitter; star: twinkle, sparkle.

'**Funken**[1] esp. fig. m (-s/-) s. Funke.

'**funken**[2] v/t. (ge-, h) radio, wireless, broadcast.

'**Funk|er** *m* (-s/-) radio *or* wireless operator; '**~gerät** *n* radio (communication) set; '**~spruch** *m* radio *or* wireless message; '**~station** *f* radio *or* wireless station; '**~stille** *f* radio *or* wireless silence; '**~streifen-wagen** *m* radio patrol car.

Funktion [fuŋk'tsjoːn] *f* (-/-en) function; **~är** [~tsjoˈnɛːr] *m* (-s/-e) functionary, official; **2ieren** [~oˈniːrən] *v/i.* (*no* -ge-, *h*) function, work.

'**Funk|turm** *m* radio *or* wireless tower; '**~verkehr** *m* radio *or* wireless communication; '**~wagen** *m* radio car; '**~wesen** *n* (-s/*no pl.*) radio communication.

für *prp.* (*acc.*) [fyːr] for; in exchange *or* return for; in favo(u)r of; in s.o.'s place; *Schritt ~ Schritt* step by step; *Tag ~ Tag* day after day; *ich ~ meine Person* ... as for me, I ...; *das Für und Wider* the pros and cons *pl.*

'**Fürbitte** *f* intercession.

Furche ['furçə] *f* (-/-n) furrow (*a. in face*); rut; ⊕ groove; '**2n** *v/t.* (ge-, *h*) furrow (*a. face*); ⊕ groove.

Furcht [furçt] *f* (-/*no pl.*) fear, dread; *aus ~ vor* for fear of; '**2bar** *adj.* awful, terrible, dreadful.

fürchten ['fyrçtən] (ge-, *h*) **1.** *v/t.* fear, dread; *sich ~ vor* (*dat.*) be afraid *or* scared of; **2.** *v/i.*: *~ um* fear for.

'**fürchterlich** *adj. s.* furchtbar.

'**furcht|los** *adj.* fearless; '**2losig-keit** *f* (-/*no pl.*) fearlessness; '**~sam** *adj.* timid, timorous; '**2samkeit** *f* (-/*no pl.*) timidity.

Furie *fig.* ['fuːrjə] *f* (-/-n) fury.

Furnier ⊕ [furˈniːr] *n* (-s/-e) veneer; **2en** *v/t.* (*no* -ge-, *h*) veneer.

'**Für|sorge** *f* care; *öffentliche ~* public welfare work; '**~sorgeamt** *n* welfare department; '**~sorgeer-ziehung** *f* corrective training for juvenile delinquents; '**~sorger** *m* (-s/-) social *or* welfare worker; **2sorglich** *adj.* considerate, thoughtful, solicitous; '**~sprache** *f* intercession (*für* for, *bei* with); '**~sprecher** *m* intercessor.

Fürst [fyrst] *m* (-en/-en) prince; sovereign; '**~enhaus** *n* dynasty; '**~enstand** *m* prince's rank; '**~en-**

tum *n* (-s/*=er*) principality; '**2lich 1.** *adj.* princely (*a. fig.*), royal; *fig.* magnificent, sumptuous; **2.** *adv.*: *~ leben* live like a lord *or* king; '**~lich-keiten** *f/pl.* royalties *pl.*

Furt [furt] *f* (-/-en) ford.

Furunkel ✞ [fuˈruŋkəl] *m* (-s/-) boil, furuncle.

'**Fürwort** *gr.* *n* (-[e]s/*=er*) pronoun.

Fusel F ['fuːzəl] *m* (-s/-) low-quality spirits, F rotgut.

Fusion ✞ [fuˈzjoːn] *f* (-/-en) merger, amalgamation.

Fuß [fuːs] *m* (-es/*=e*) foot; *~ fassen* find a foothold; *fig.* become established; *auf gutem* (*schlechtem*) *~ stehen mit* be on good (bad) terms with; *zu ~* on foot; *zu ~ gehen* walk; *gut zu ~ sein* be a good walker; '**~abstreifer** *m* (-s/-) door-scraper, door-mat; '**~angel** *f* mantrap; '**~ball** *m* (association) football, F *and Am.* soccer; '**~ballspieler** *m* football player, footballer; '**~bank** *f* footstool; '**~bekleidung** *f* footwear, footgear; '**~boden** *m* floor (-ing); '**~bodenbelag** *m* floor covering; '**~bremse** *mot.* *f* foot-brake; '**2en** *v/i.* (ge-, *h*): *~ auf* (*dat.*) be based *or* founded on; '**~gänger** ['~gɛŋər] *m* (-s/-) pedestrian; '**~ge-lenk** *anat.* *n* ankle joint; '**~note** *f* footnote; '**~pfad** *m* footpath; '**~sack** *m* foot-muff; '**~sohle** *anat.* *f* sole of the foot; '**~soldat** ✕ *m* foot-soldier, infantryman; '**~spur** *f* footprint; track; **~stapfe** ['~ʃtapfə] *f* (-/-n) footprint, *fig. a.* footstep; '**~steig** *m* footpath; '**~tritt** *m* kick; '**~wanderung** *f* walking tour, hike; '**~weg** *m* footpath.

Futter ['futər] *n* **1.** (-s/*no pl.*) food, *sl.* grub, *Am.* F *a.* chow; feed, fodder; **2.** (-s/-) lining, △ casing.

Futteral [futəˈrɑːl] *n* (-s/-e) case (*for spectacles, etc.*); cover (*of umbrella*); sheath (*of knife*).

'**Futtermittel** *n* feeding stuff.

füttern ['fytərn] *v/t.* (ge-, *h*) feed; line (*dress, etc.*); △ case.

'**Futter|napf** *m* feeding bowl *or* dish; '**~neid** *fig.* *m* (professional) jealousy; '**~stoff** *m* lining (material).

'**Fütterung** *f* (-/-en) feeding; lining; △ casing.   [(tense).\

Futur *gr.* [fuˈtuːr] *n* (-s/-e) future\

G

gab [gɑ:p] *pret. of* geben.

Gabe ['gɑ:bə] *f* (-/-n) gift, present; alms; donation; *💉* dose; talent.

Gabel ['gɑ:bəl] *f* (-/-n) fork; ♀n *v/refl.* (ge-, h) fork, bifurcate; **~ung** *f* (-/-en) bifurcation.

gackern ['gakərn] *v/i.* (ge-, h) cackle.

gaffen ['gafən] *v/i.* (ge-, h) gape; stare.

Gage ['gɑ:ʒə] *f* (-/-n) salary, pay.

gähnen ['gɛ:nən] **1.** *v/i.* (ge-, h) yawn; **2.** ♀ *n* (-s/no pl.) yawning.

Gala ['gala] *f* (-/no pl.) gala; *in* ~ in full dress.

galant *adj.* [ga'lant] gallant; courteous; ♀**erie** [~ə'ri:] *f* (-/-n) gallantry; courtesy.

Galeere ♻ [ga'le:rə] *f* (-/-n) galley.

Galerie [galə'ri:] *f* (-/-n) gallery.

Galgen ['galgən] *m* (-s/-) gallows, gibbet; '**~frist** *f* respite; '**~gesicht** *n* gallows-look, hangdog look; '**~humor** *m* grim humo(u)r; '**~strick** *m*, '**~vogel** *m* gallows-bird, hangdog.

Galle *anat.* ['galə] *f* (-/-n) bile (of person); gall (of animal) (a. *fig.*); '**~nblase** *anat.* *f* gall-bladder; '**~nleiden** *✚* *n* bilious complaint; '**~nstein** *✚* *m* gall-stone, bile-stone.

Gallert ['galərt] *n* (-[e]s/-e), **~e** [ga'lɛrtə] *f* (-/-n) gelatine, jelly.

'**gallig** *fig. adj.* bilious.

Galopp [ga'lɔp] *m* (-s/-s, -e) gallop; canter; ♀**ieren** [~'pi:rən] *v/i.* (no -ge-, sein) gallop; canter.

galt [galt] *pret. of* gelten.

galvani|sch *adj.* [gal'vɑ:niʃ] galvanic; ♀**sieren** [~ani'-] *v/t.* (no -ge-, h) galvanize.

Gang[1] [gaŋ] *m* (-[e]s/ᵁe) walk; *s. Gangart*; *fig.* motion; running, working (of machine); errand; way; course (of events, of a meal, etc.); passage(-way); alley; corridor, gallery; *in vehicle, between seats:* gangway, *esp. Am.* aisle; ♻ corridor, *Am.* aisle; *fencing:* pass; *anat.* duct; *mot.* gear; erster (zweiter, dritter, vierter) ~ low or bottom (second, third, top) gear; *in* ~ bringen or setzen set going or in motion, *Am.* operate; *in* ~ kommen get going, get started; *im* ~ sein be in motion; ⊕ be working or running; *fig.* be

in progress; *in vollem* ~ in full swing.

gang[2] *adj.* [~]: ~ *und gäbe* customary, traditional.

'**Gang|art** *f* gait, walk (of person); pace (of horse); ♀**bar** *adj.* road: practicable, passable; *money:* current; *✝* goods: marketable; *s. gängig.*

Gängelband ['gɛŋəl-] *n* leading-strings *pl.*; *am* ~ führen keep in leading-strings, lead by the nose.

gängig *adj.* ['gɛŋiç] *money:* current; *✝* goods: marketable; **~er** Ausdruck current word or phrase.

Gans *orn.* [gans] *f* (-/ᵁe) goose.

Gänse|blümchen ♀ ['gɛnzəbly:m-çən] *n* (-s/-) daisy; '**~braten** *m* roast goose; '**~feder** *f* goose-quill; '**~füßchen** ['~fy:sçən] *n/pl.* quotation marks *pl.*, inverted commas *pl.*; '**~haut** *f* goose-skin; *fig. a.* goose-flesh, *Am. a.* goose pimples *pl.*; '**~klein** *n* (-s/no pl.) (goose-)giblets *pl.*; '**~marsch** *m* single or Indian file; **~rich** *orn.* ['~riç] *m* (-s/-e) gander; '**~schmalz** *n* goose-grease.

ganz [gants] **1.** *adj.* all; entire, whole; complete, total, full; den ~en Tag all day (long); **2.** *adv.* quite; entirely, *etc.* (s. **1.**); very; ~ Auge (Ohr) all eyes (ears); ~ und gar wholly, totally; ~ und gar nicht not at all; *im* ~en on the whole, generally; in all; *✝* in the lump; ♀**e** *n* (-n/no pl.) whole; totality; *aufs* ~ gehen go all out, *esp. Am. sl.* go the whole hog.

gänzlich *adj.* ['gɛntsliç] complete, total, entire.

'**Ganztagsbeschäftigung** *f* full-time job or employment.

gar [gɑ:r] **1.** *adj. food:* done; **2.** *adv.* quite, very; even; ~ *nicht* not at all.

Garage [ga'rɑ:ʒə] *f* (-/-n) garage.

Garantie [garan'ti:] *f* (-/-n) guarantee, warranty, *⚖* guaranty; ♀**ren** *v/t.* (no -ge-, h) guarantee, warrant.

Garbe ['garbə] *f* (-/-n) sheaf.

Garde ['gardə] *f* (-/-n) guard.

Garderobe [gardə'ro:bə] *f* (-/-n) wardrobe; cloakroom, *Am.* check-room; *thea.* dressing-room; '**~nfrau** *f* cloak-room attendant, *Am.* hat-check girl; **~nmarke** *f* check; **~nschrank** *m* wardrobe; **~nständer**

m coat-stand, hat-stand, hall-stand.
Garderobiere [gardəro'bje:rə] *f* (*-/-n*) *s.* **Garderobenfrau;** *thea.* wardrobe mistress.

Gardine [gar'di:nə] *f* (*-/-n*) curtain.

gär|en ['gɛ:rən] *v/i.* (*irr., ge-, h, sein*) ferment; **2mittel** *n* ferment.

Garn [garn] *n* (*-[e]s/-e*) yarn; thread; cotton; net; *j-m ins ~ gehen* fall into s.o.'s snare.

Garnele *zo.* [gar'ne:lə] *f* (*-/-n*) shrimp.

garnieren [gar'ni:rən] *v/t.* (*no -ge-, h*) trim; garnish (*esp. a dish*).

Garnison ⚔ [garni'zo:n] *f* (*-/-en*) garrison, post.

Garnitur [garni'tu:r] *f* (*-/-en*) trimming; ⊕ fittings *pl.*; set.

garstig *adj.* ['garstiç] nasty, bad; ugly.

'**Gärstoff** *m* ferment.

'**Garten** ['gartən] *m* (*-s/=*) garden; '**.anlage** *f* gardens *pl.*, park; '**.arbeit** *f* gardening; '**.bau** *m* horticulture; '**.erde** *f* (garden-)mo(u)ld; '**.fest** *n* garden-party, *Am. a.* lawn party; '**.geräte** *n/pl.* gardening-tools *pl.*; '**.stadt** *f* garden city.

Gärtner ['gɛrtnər] *m* (*-s/-*) gardener; **ei** [.'raɪ] *f* (*-/-en*) gardening, horticulture; nursery; '**.in** *f* (*-/-nen*) gardener. [tation.]

Gärung ['gɛ:ruŋ] *f* (*-/-en*) fermen-|

Gas [gɑ:s] *n* (*-es/-e*) gas; *~ geben mot.* open the throttle, *Am.* step on the gas; '**.anstalt** *f* gas-works, *Am. a.* gas plant; '**.behälter** *m* gasometer, *Am.* gas tank *or* container; '**.beleuchtung** *f* gaslight; '**.brenner** *m* gas-burner; '**.förmig** *adj.* ['.fœrmiç] gaseous; '**.hahn** *m* gas-tap; '**.herd** *m* gas-stove, *Am.* gas range; '**.leitung** *f* gas-mains *pl.*; '**.messer** *m* (*-s/-*) gas-meter; '**.ofen** *m* gas-oven; '**.pedal** *mot. n* accelerator (pedal), *Am.* gas pedal.

Gasse ['gasə] *f* (*-/-n*) lane, by-street, alley(-way); '**.nhauer** *m* (*-s/-*) street ballad, popular song; '**.njunge** *m* street arab.

Gast [gast] *m* (*-es/=e*) guest; visitor; customer (*of public house, etc.*); *thea.*: guest (artist); guest star; '**.arbeiter** *m* foreign worker; '**.bett** *n* spare bed.

Gäste|buch ['gɛstə-] *n* visitors' book; '**.zimmer** *n* guest-room; spare (bed)room; *s. Gaststube.*

'**gast|freundlich** *adj.* hospitable; '**2freundschaft** *f* hospitality; '**2geber** *m* (*-s/-*) host; '**2geberin** *f* (*-/-nen*) hostess; '**2haus** *n,* '**2hof** *m* restaurant; inn; hotel; '**2hörer** *univ. m* guest student, *Am. a.* auditor.

gastieren *thea.* [gas'ti:rən] *v/i.* (*no -ge-, h*) appear as a guest.

'**gast|lich** *adj.* hospitable; '**2mahl** *n* feast, banquet; '**2recht** *n* right of *or* to hospitality; '**2rolle** *thea. f* guest part; starring part *or* role; '**2spiel** *thea. n* guest appearance *or* performance; starring (performance); '**2stätte** *f* restaurant; '**2stube** *f* taproom; restaurant; '**2wirt** *m* innkeeper, landlord; '**2wirtin** *f* innkeeper, landlady; '**2wirtschaft** *f* inn, public house, restaurant; '**2zimmer** *n s. Gästezimmer.*

'**Gas|uhr** *f* gas-meter; '**.werk** *n s. Gasanstalt.*

Gatte ['gatə] *m* (*-n/-n*) husband; spouse, consort.

Gatter ['gatər] *n* (*-s/-*) lattice; railing, grating.

'**Gattin** *f* (*-/-nen*) wife; spouse, consort.

Gattung ['gatuŋ] *f* (*-/-en*) kind; sort; type; species; genus.

gaukeln ['gaukəln] *v/i.* (*ge-, h*) juggle; *birds, etc.*: flutter.

Gaul [gaul] *m* (*-[e]s/=e*) (old) nag.

Gaumen *anat.* ['gaumən] *m* (*-s/-*) palate.

Gauner ['gaunər] *m* (*-s/-*) scoundrel, swindler, sharper, *sl.* crook; **ei** [.'raɪ] *f* (*-/-en*) swindling, cheating, trickery.

Gaze ['gɑ:zə] *f* (*-/-n*) gauze.

Gazelle *zo.* [ga'tsɛlə] *f* (*-/-n*) gazelle.

Geächtete [gə'ɛçtətə] *m, f* (*-n/-n*) outlaw.

Gebäck [gə'bɛk] *n* (*-[e]s/-e*) baker's goods *pl.*; pastry; fancy cakes *pl.*

ge'backen *p.p. of* backen.

Gebälk [gə'bɛlk] *n* (*-[e]s/no pl.*) framework; timber-work; beams *pl.*

gebar [gə'bɑ:r] *pret. of* gebären.

Gebärde [gə'bɛ:rdə] *f* (*-/-n*) gesture; **2n** *v/refl.* (*no -ge-, h*) conduct o.s., behave; **.nspiel** *n* (*-[e]s/no pl.*) gesticulation; dumb show, pantomime; **.nsprache** *f* language of gestures.

Gebaren [gə'bɑ:rən] *n* (*-s/no pl.*) conduct, deportment, behavio(u)r.

gebären [gə'bɛ:rən] *v/t.* (*irr., no -ge-, h*) bear, bring forth (*a. fig.*); give birth to.

Ge|bäude [gə'bɔydə] *n* (*-s/-*) building, edifice, structure; **~bell** [~'bɛl] *n* (*-[e]s/no pl.*) barking.

geben ['ge:bən] *v/t.* (*irr., ge-, h*) give (*j-m et. s.o. sth.*); present (*s.o. with sth.*); put; yield *s.th.*; deal (*cards*); pledge (*one's word*); *von sich ~* emit; utter (*words*); bring up, vomit (*food*); et. (*nichts*) ~ *auf* (*acc.*) set (no) great store by; *sich geschlagen ~* give in; *sich zufrieden ~* content o.s. (*mit* with); *sich zu erkennen ~* make o.s. known; *es gibt* there is, there are; *was gibt es?* what is the matter?; *thea.: gegeben werden* be on.

Gebet [gə'be:t] *n* (*-[e]s/-e*) prayer.
ge'beten *p.p. of bitten.*
Gebiet [gə'bi:t] *n* (*-[e]s/-e*) territory; district; region; area; *fig.:* field; province; sphere.

ge'biet|en (*irr. bieten, no -ge-, h*) **1.** *v/t.* order, command; **2.** *v/i.* rule; **2er** *m* (*-s/-*) master, lord, governor; **2erin** *f* (*-/-nen*) mistress; **~erisch** *adj.* imperious; commanding.

Gebilde [gə'bildə] *n* (*-s/-*) form, shape; structure; **2t** *adj.* educated; cultured, cultivated.

Gebirg|e [gə'birgə] *n* (*-s/-*) mountains *pl.*; mountain chain *or* range; **2ig** *adj.* mountainous; **~sbewohner** *m* mountaineer; **~szug** *m* mountain range.

Ge'biß *n* (*Gebisses/Gebisse*) (set of) teeth; (set of) artificial *or* false teeth, denture; *harness:* bit.

ge|'bissen *p.p. of beißen*; **~'blasen** *p.p. of blasen*; **~'blichen** *p.p. of bleichen* 2; **~'blieben** [~'bli:bən] *p.p. of bleiben*; **~blümt** *adj.* [~'bly:mt] *pattern, design:* flowered; *material:* sprigged; **~'bogen** **1.** *p.p. of biegen*; **2.** *adj.* bent, curved; **~boren** [~'bo:rən] **1.** *p.p. of gebären*; **2.** *adj.* born; *ein ~er Deutscher* German by birth; *~e Schmidt* née Smith.

ge'borgen **1.** *p.p. of bergen*; **2.** *adj.* safe, sheltered; **2heit** *f* (*-/no pl.*) safety, security.

geborsten [gə'bɔrstən] *p.p. of bersten.*

Ge'bot *n* (*-[e]s/-e*) order; command; bid(ding), offer; *eccl.: die Zehn ~e*

pl. the Ten Commandments *pl.*; **2en** *p.p. of bieten.*

ge|bracht [gə'braxt] *p.p. of bringen*; **~brannt** [~'brant] *p.p. of brennen*; **~'braten** *p.p. of braten.*

Ge'brauch *m* **1.** (*-[e]s/no pl.*) use; *⚜* application; **2.** (*-[e]s/-e*) usage, practice; custom; **2en** *v/t.* (*no -ge-, h*) use, employ; **2t** *adj.* clothes, *etc.:* second-hand.

gebräuchlich *adj.* [gə'brɔyçliç] in use; usual, customary.

Ge'brauchs|anweisung *f* directions *pl. or* instructions *pl.* for use; **~artikel** *m* commodity, necessary, requisite; personal article; **2fertig** *adj.* ready for use; *coffee, etc.:* instant; **~muster** ✝ *n* sample; registered design.

Ge'braucht|wagen *mot. m* used car; **~waren** *f/pl.* second-hand articles *pl.*

Ge'brechen *n* (*-s/-*) defect, infirmity; affliction.

ge'brechlich *adj.* fragile; *p.:* frail, weak; infirm; **2keit** *f* (*-/-en*) fragility; infirmity.

gebrochen [gə'brɔxən] *p.p. of brechen.*

Ge'brüder [gə'bry:dər] *pl.* brothers *pl.*; **~brüll** [~'bryl] *n* (*-[e]s/no pl.*) roaring; lowing (*of cattle*).

Gebühr [gə'by:r] *f* (*-/-en*) due; duty; charge; rate; fee; **~en** *pl.*, dues *pl.*; **2en** *v/i.* (*no -ge-, h*) be due (*dat.* to); *sich ~* be proper *or* fitting; **2end** *adj.* due; becoming; proper; **2enfrei** *adj.* free of charge; **2enpflichtig** *adj.* liable to charges, chargeable.

gebunden [gə'bundən] **1.** *p.p. of binden*; **2.** *adj.* bound.

Geburt [gə'bu:rt] *f* (*-/-en*) birth; **~enkontrolle** *f*, **~enregelung** *f* birth-control; **~enziffer** *f* birth-rate.

gebürtig *adj.* [gə'byrtiç]: *~ aus a* native of.

Ge'burts|anzeige *f* announcement of birth; **~fehler** *m* congenital defect; **~helfer** *m* obstetrician; **~hilfe** *f* obstetrics, midwifery; **~jahr** *n* year of birth; **~land** *n* native country; **~ort** *m* birth-place; **~schein** *m* birth certificate; **~tag** *m* birthday; **~urkunde** *f* birth certificate.

Gebüsch [gə'byʃ] *n* (*-es/-e*) bushes *pl.*, undergrowth, thicket.

gedacht [gə'daxt] *p.p. of* denken.

Gedächtnis [gə'dɛçtnis] *n* (-ses/-se) memory; remembrance, recollection; *im* ~ *behalten* keep in mind; *zum* ~ (*gen.*) in memory of; **~feier** *f* commemoration.

Gedanke [gə'daŋkə] *m* (-ns/-n) thought; idea; *in* ~*n* (*versunken or* verloren) absorbed in thought; *sich* ~*n machen über* (*acc.*) worry about. **Ge'danken|gang** *m* train of thought; **~leser** *m*, **~leserin** *f* (-/-nen) thought-reader; **♀los** *adj.* thoughtless; **~strich** *m* dash; **♀voll** *adj.* thoughtful, pensive.

Ge|därm [gə'dɛrm] *n* (-[e]s/-e) *mst pl.* entrails *pl.*, bowels *pl.*, intestines *pl.*; **~deck** [~'dɛk] *n* (-[e]s/-e) cover; menu; *ein* ~ *auflegen* lay a place.

gedeihen [gə'daɪən] **1.** *v/i.* (*irr., no* -ge-, sein) thrive, prosper; **2.** ♀ *n* (-s/no pl.) thriving, prosperity.

ge'denken 1. *v/i.* (*gen.*) (*irr.* denken, no -ge-, h) think of; remember, recollect; commemorate; mention; ~ *zu inf.* intend to *inf.*; **2.** ♀ *n* (-s/no pl.) memory, remembrance (*an acc.* of).

Ge'denk|feier *f* commemoration; **~stein** *m* memorial stone; **~tafel** *f* commemorative *or* memorial tablet.

Ge'dicht *n* (-[e]s/-e) poem.

gediegen [gə'di:gən] *adj.* solid; pure; **♀heit** *f* (-/no pl.) solidity; purity.

gedieh [gə'di:] *pret. of* gedeihen; **~en** *p.p. of* gedeihen.

Gedräng|e [gə'drɛŋə] *n* (-s/no pl.) crowd, throng; **♀t** *adj.* crowded, packed, crammed; *style:* concise.

ge|droschen [gə'drɔʃən] *p.p. of* dreschen; **~'drückt** *fig. adj.* depressed; **~'drungen** [~'druŋən] **1.** *p.p. of* dringen; **2.** *adj.* compact, squat, thickset.

Geduld [gə'dult] *f* (-/no pl.) patience; **♀en** [~dən] *v/refl.* (*no* -ge-, h) have patience; **♀ig** *adj.* [~dıç] patient.

ge|dunsen *adj.* [gə'dunzən] bloated; **~durft** [~'durft] *p.p. of* dürfen 1; **~ehrt** *adj.* [~'e:rt] hono(u)red; *correspondence: Sehr* ~*er Herr N.!* Dear Sir, Dear Mr N.; **~eignet** *adj.* [~'aɪgnət] fit (*für, zu, als for s.th.*); suitable (to, for); qualified (for).

Gefahr [gə'fa:r] *f* (-/-en) danger, peril; risk; *auf eigene* ~ at one's

own risk; ~ *laufen zu inf.* run the risk of *ger.*

gefährden [gə'fɛːrdən] *v/t.* (*no* -ge-, h) endanger; risk.

ge'fahren *p.p. of* fahren.

gefährlich *adj.* [gə'fɛːrlıç] dangerous.

ge'fahrlos *adj.* without risk, safe.

Gefährt|e [gə'fɛːrtə] *m* (-en/-en), **~in** *f* (-/-nen) companion, fellow.

Gefälle [gə'fɛlə] *n* (-s/-) fall, slope, incline, descent, gradient, *esp. Am. a.* grade; fall (*of river, etc.*).

Ge'fallen 1. *m* (-s/-) favo(u)r; **2.** *n* (-s/no pl.): ~ *finden an* (*dat.*) take (a) pleasure in, take a fancy to *or* for; **3.** ♀ *v/i.* (*irr.* fallen, no -ge-, h) please (*j-m s.o.*); *er gefällt mir* I like him; *sich et.* ~ *lassen* put up with s.th.; **4.** ♀ *p.p. of* fallen.

gefällig *adj.* [gə'fɛlıç] pleasing, agreeable; *p.:* complaisant, obliging; kind; **♀keit** *f* (-/~-en) complaisance, kindness; favo(u)r; **~st** *adv.* (if you) please.

ge'fangen 1. *p.p. of* fangen; **2.** *adj.* captive, imprisoned; **♀e** *m* (-n/-n), *f* (-n/-n) prisoner, captive; **♀enlager** *n* prison(ers') camp; **♀ennahme** *f* (-/no pl.) capture; seizure, arrest; **~nehmen** *v/t.* (*irr.* nehmen, sep., -ge-, h) take prisoner; *fig.* captivate; **♀schaft** *f* (-/no pl.) captivity, imprisonment; **~setzen** *v/t.* (sep., -ge-, h) put in prison.

Gefängnis [gə'fɛŋnıs] *n* (-ses/-se) prison, jail, gaol, *Am. a.* penitentiary; **~direktor** *m* governor, warden; **~strafe** *f* (sentence *or* term of) imprisonment; **~wärter** *m* warder, gaoler, jailer, (prison) guard.

Gefäß [gə'fɛːs] *n* (-es/-e) vessel.

gefaßt *adj.* [gə'fast] composed; ~ *auf* (*acc.*) prepared for.

Ge|fecht [gə'fɛçt] *n* (-[e]s/-e) engagement; combat, fight; action; **~fieder** [~'fi:dər] *n* (-s/-) plumage, feathers *pl.*

ge|'fleckt *adj.* spotted; **~'flochten** [~'flɔxtən] *p.p. of* flechten; **~'flogen** [~'flo:gən] *p.p. of* fliegen; **~'flohen** [~'flo:ən] *p.p. of* fliehen; **~'flossen** [~'flɔsən] *p.p. of* fließen.

Ge|'flügel *n* (-s/no pl.) fowl; poultry; **~'flüster** [~'flystər] *n* (-s/no pl.) whisper(ing). [ten.\]

gefochten [gə'fɔxtən] *p.p. of* fech-\]

G

Ge'folg|e n (-s/no pl.) retinue, train, followers pl.; attendants pl.; **~schaft** [~kʃaft] f (-/-en) followers pl.

gefräßig adj. [gə'frɛːsɪç] greedy, voracious; **2keit** f (-/no pl.) greediness, gluttony, voracity.

ge'fressen p.p. of fressen.

ge'frier|en v/i. (irr. frieren, no -ge-, sein) congeal, freeze; **2fleisch** n frozen meat; **2punkt** m freezing-point; **2schutz(mittel)** n m antifreeze.

gefroren [gə'froːrən] p.p. of frieren; **2e** [~ə] n (-n/no pl.) ice-cream.

Gefüge [gə'fyːgə] n (-s/-) structure; texture.

ge'fügig adj. pliant; **2keit** f (-/no pl.) pliancy.

Gefühl [gə'fyːl] n (-[e]s/-e) feeling; touch; sense (für of); sensation; **2los** adj. unfeeling, insensible (gegen to); **2sbetont** adj. emotional; **2voll** adj. (full of) feeling; tender; sentimental.

ge'funden p.p. of finden; **~gangen** [~'gaŋən] p.p. of gehen.

ge'geben p.p. of geben; **~enfalls** adv. in that case; if necessary.

gegen prp. (acc.) ['geːgən] space, time: towards; against, versus; about, Am. around; by; compared with; (in exchange) for; remedy: for; freundlich sein ~ be kind to (-wards); ~ bar for cash.

'Gegen|angriff m counter-attack; **~antrag** m counter-motion; **~antwort** f rejoinder; **~befehl** m counter-order; **~beschuldigung** f countercharge; **~besuch** m return visit; **~bewegung** f counter-movement; **~beweis** m counter-evidence.

Gegend ['geːgənt] f (-/-en) region; area.

'Gegen|dienst m return service, service in return; **~druck** m counter-pressure; fig. reaction; **2ei'nander** adv. against one another or each other; **~erklärung** f counter-statement; **~forderung** f counter-claim; **~frage** f counter-question; **~geschenk** n return present; **~gewicht** n counterbalance, counterpoise; **~gift** n antidote; **~kandidat** m rival candidate; **~klage** f countercharge; **'~leistung**

f return (service), equivalent; **~lichtaufnahme** phot. ['geːgən-lıçt°-] f back-lighted shot; **~liebe** f requited love; keine ~ finden meet with no sympathy or enthusiasm; **'~maßnahme** f counter-measure; **~mittel** n remedy (gegen for); antidote (against, for); **~partei** f opposite party; **~probe** f check-test; **~satz** m contrast; opposition; im ~ zu in contrast to or with, in opposition to; **2sätzlich** adj. ['~zɛtslıç] contrary, opposite; **~seite** f opposite side; **2seitig** adj. mutual, reciprocal; **~seitigkeit** f (-/no pl.): auf ~ assurance: mutual; auf ~ beruhen be mutual; **~spieler** m games, sports: opponent; antagonist; **~spionage** f counter-espionage; **'~stand** m object; subject, topic; **'~strömung** f counter-current; **~stück** n counterpart; match; **~teil** n contrary, reverse; im ~ on the contrary; **2teilig** adj. contrary, opposite; **2**'**über** 1. adv. opposite; 2. prp. (dat.) opposite (to); to (-wards); as against; face to face with; **~'über** n (-s/-) vis-à-vis; **2'überstehen** v/i. (irr. stehen, sep., -ge-, h) (dat.) be faced with; face; **~'überstellung** esp. ⅌ f confrontation; **'~vorschlag** m counter-proposal; **~wart** ['~vart] f (-/no pl.) presence; present time; gr. present tense; **2wärtig** ['~vɛrtıç] 1. adj. present; actual; 2. adv. at present; **'~wehr** f defen|ce, Am. -se; resistance; **~wert** m equivalent; **~wind** m contrary wind, head wind; **'~wirkung** f counter-effect, reaction; **'2zeichnen** v/t. (sep., -ge-, h) countersign; '**~zug** m counter-move (a. fig.); ⚒ corresponding train.

ge'gessen [gə'gɛsən] p.p. of essen; **~glichen** [~'glıçən] p.p. of gleichen; **~gliedert** adj. articulate, jointed; **~glitten** [~'glıtən] p.p. of gleiten; **~glommen** [~'glɔmən] p.p. of glimmen.

Gegner ['geːgnər] m (-s/-) adversary, opponent; **~schaft** f (-/-en) opposition.

ge'golten [gə'gɔltən] p.p. of gelten; **~goren** [~'goːrən] p.p. of gären; **~gossen** [~'gɔsən] p.p. of gießen; **~graben** p.p. of graben; **~griffen** [~'grıfən] p.p. of greifen; **~habt** [~'haːpt] p.p. of haben.

Gehalt [gə'halt] **1.** *m* (-[e]s/-e) contents *pl.*; capacity; merit; **2.** *n* (-[e]s/-er) salary; **2en** *p.p.* of halten; **2los** [~lo:s] *adj.* empty; **~s-empfänger** [gə'halts?-] *m* salaried employee or worker; **~serhöhung** [gə'halts?-] *f* rise (in salary), *Am.* raise; **2voll** *adj.* rich; substantial; *wine*: racy.

gehangen [gə'haŋən] *p.p.* of hängen 1.

gehässig *adj.* [gə'hɛsiç] malicious, spiteful; **2keit** *f* (-/-en) malice, spitefulness.

ge'hauen *p.p.* of hauen.

Ge'häuse [gə'hɔyzə] *n* (-s/-) case, box; cabinet; shell; core (*of apple, etc.*); **~hege** [~'he:gə] *n* (-s/-) enclosure.

geheim *adj.* [gə'haım] secret; **2-dienst** *m* secret service.

Ge'heimnis *n* (-ses/-se) secret; mystery; **~krämer** *m* mystery-monger; **2voll** *adj.* mysterious.

Ge'heim|polizei *f* secret police; **~polizist** *m* detective; plain-clothes man; **~schrift** *f* cipher; *tel.* code.

ge'heißen *p.p.* of heißen.

gehen ['ge:ən] *v/i.* (*irr.*, ge-, sein) go; walk; leave; *machine*: go, work; *clock, watch*: go; *merchandise*: sell; *wind*: blow; *paste*: rise; *wie geht es Ihnen?* how are you (getting on)?; *das geht nicht* that won't do; *in sich ~* repent; *wieviel Pfennige ~ auf e-e Mark?* how many pfennigs go to a mark?; *das Fenster geht nach Norden* the window faces or looks north; *es geht nichts über* (*acc.*) there is nothing like; *wenn es nach mir ginge* if I had my way.

Geheul [gə'hɔyl] *n* (-[e]s/*no pl.*) howling.

Ge'hilf|e *m* (-n/-n), **~in** *f* (-/-nen) assistant; *fig.* helpmate.

Ge'hirn *n* (-[e]s/-e) brain(s *pl.*); **~erschütterung** *f* concussion (of the brain); **~schlag** *m* cerebral apoplexy.

gehoben [gə'ho:bən] **1.** *p.p.* of heben; **2.** *adj.* speech, style: elevated; **~e Stimmung** elated mood.

Gehöft [gə'hø:ft] *n* (-[e]s/-e) farm (-stead).

geholfen [gə'hɔlfən] *p.p.* of helfen.

Gehölz [gə'hœlts] *n* (-es/-e) wood, coppice, copse.

Gehör [gə'hø:r] *n* (-[e]s/*no pl.*)

hearing; ear; *nach dem ~* by ear; *j-m ~ schenken* lend an ear to s.o.; *sich ~ verschaffen* make o.s. heard.

ge'horchen *v/i.* (*no* -ge-, *h*) obey (*j-m* s.o.).

ge'hör|en *v/i.* (*no* -ge-, *h*) belong (*dat.* or *zu* to); *es gehört sich* it is proper or fit or right or suitable; *das gehört nicht hierher* that's not to the point; **~ig 1.** *adj.* belonging (*dat.* or *zu* to); fit, proper, right; due; F good; **2.** *adv.* duly; F thoroughly.

gehorsam [gə'ho:rza:m] **1.** *adj.* obedient; **2.** **2** *m* (-s/*no pl.*) obedience.

'Geh|steig *m*, **'~weg** *m* pavement, *Am.* sidewalk; **~werk** ⊕ *n* clockwork, works *pl.*

Geier *orn.* ['gaıər] *m* (-s/-) vulture.

Geige ♪ ['gaıgə] *f* (-/-n) violin, F fiddle; (*auf der*) *~ spielen* play (on) the violin; **~nbogen** ♪ *m* (violin-) bow; **~nkasten** ♪ *m* violin-case; **'~r** ♪ *m* (-s/-), **'~rin** ♪ *f* (-/-nen) violinist.

'Geigerzähler *phys.* *m* Geiger counter.

geil *adj.* [gaıl] lascivious, wanton; luxuriant.

Geisel ['gaızəl] *f* (-/-n) hostage.

Geiß *zo.* [gaıs] *f* (-/-en) (she-, nanny-)goat; **'~blatt** ♀ *n* (-[e]s/*no pl.*) honeysuckle, woodbine; **'~bock** *zo. m* he-goat, billy-goat.

Geißel ['gaısəl] *f* (-/-n) whip, lash; *fig.* scourge; **'2n** *v/t.* (ge-, *h*) whip, lash; *fig.* castigate.

Geist [gaıst] *m* (-es/-er) spirit; mind, intellect; wit; ghost; sprite.

'Geister|erscheinung *f* apparition; **'2haft** *adj.* ghostly.

'geistes|abwesend *adj.* absent-minded; **'2arbeiter** *m* brain-worker, white-collar worker; **'2-blitz** *m* brain-wave, flash of genius; **'2gabe** *f* talent; **'2gegenwart** *f* presence of mind; **'~gegenwärtig** *adj.* alert; quick-witted; **'~gestört** *adj.* mentally disturbed; **'~krank** *adj.* insane, mentally ill; **'2krankheit** *f* insanity, mental illness; **'~schwach** *adj.* feeble-minded, imbecile; **'~verwandt** *adj.* congenial; **'2wissenschaften** *f/pl.* the Arts *pl.*, the Humanities *pl.*; **'2zustand** *m* state of mind.

'geistig *adj.* intellectual, mental;

geistlich — spiritual; **~e Getränke** *n/pl.* spirits *pl.*

'geistlich *adj.* spiritual; clerical; sacred; **'~e** *m* (-n/-n) clergyman; minister; **'2keit** *f* (-/no *pl.*) clergy.

'geist|los *adj.* spiritless; dull; stupid; **'~reich** *adj.*, **'~voll** *adj.* ingenious, spirited.

Geiz [gaɪts] *m* (-es/no *pl.*) avarice; **'~hals** *m* miser, niggard; **'2ig** *adj.* avaricious, stingy, mean.

Gejammer [gə'jamər] *n* (-s/no *pl.*) lamentation(s *pl.*), wailing.

gekannt [gə'kant] *p.p. of* kennen.

Geklapper [gə'klapər] *n* (-s/no *pl.*) rattling.

Geklirr [gə'klɪr] *n* (-[e]s/no *pl.*), **~e** [~ə] *n* (-s/no *pl.*) clashing, clanking.

ge|klungen [~'kluŋən] *p.p. of* klingen; **~kniffen** *p.p. of* kneifen; **~'kommen** *p.p. of* kommen; **~konnt** [~'kɔnt] *p.p. of* können 1, 2.

Ge|kreisch [gə'kraɪʃ] *n* (-es/no *pl.*) screaming, screams *pl.*; shrieking; **~kritzel** [~'krɪtsəl] *n* (-s/no *pl.*) scrawl(ing), scribbling, scribble.

ge|krochen [gə'krɔxən] *p.p. of* kriechen; **~künstelt** *adj.* [~'kynstəlt] affected.

Gelächter [gə'lɛçtər] *n* (-s/-) laughter.

ge'laden *p.p. of* laden.

Ge'lage *n* (-s/-) feast; drinking-bout.

Gelände [gə'lɛndə] *n* (-s/-) ground; terrain; country; area; **2gängig** *mot. adj.* cross-country; **~lauf** *m sports:* cross-country race or run.

Geländer [gə'lɛndər] *n* (-s/-) railing, balustrade; banisters *pl.*

ge'lang *pret. of* gelingen.

ge'langen *v/i.* (no -ge-, sein): **~ an** (*acc.*) or in (*acc.*) arrive at, get or come to; **~ zu** attain (to), gain.

ge'lassen 1. *p.p. of* lassen; 2. *adj.* calm, composed.

Gelatine [ʒela'tiːnə] *f* (-/no *pl.*) gelatin(e).

ge|'laufen *p.p. of* laufen; **~läufig** *adj.* [~'lɔyfɪç] current; fluent, easy; *tongue:* voluble; familiar; **~launt** *adj.* [~'laʊnt] in a (good, *etc.*) humo(u)r or *Am.* mood.

Geläut [gə'lɔyt] *n* (-[e]s/-e), **~e** [~ə] *n* (-s/no *pl.*) ringing (of bells); chimes *pl.* (of church bells).

gelb *adj.* [gɛlp] yellow; **'~lich** *adj.*

yellowish; **'2sucht** *&* *f* (-/no *pl.*) jaundice.

Geld [gɛlt] *n* (-[e]s/-er) money; *im* **~** *schwimmen* be rolling in money; *zu* **~** *machen* turn into cash; **'~angelegenheit** *f* money-matter; **'~anlage** *f* investment; **'~ausgabe** *f* expense; **'~beutel** *m* purse; **'~entwertung** *f* devaluation of the currency; **'~erwerb** *m* money-making; **'~geber** *m* (-s/-) financial backer, investor; **'~geschäfte** *n/pl.* money transactions *pl.*; **2gierig** *adj.* greedy for money, avaricious; **'~mittel** *n/pl.* funds *pl.*, resources *pl.*; **'~schein** *m* bank-note, *Am.* bill; **'~schrank** *m* strong-box, safe; **'~sendung** *f* remittance; **'~strafe** *f* fine; **'~stück** *n* coin; **'~tasche** *f* money-bag; notecase, *Am.* billfold; **'~überhang** *m* surplus money; **'~umlauf** *m* circulation of money; **'~umsatz** *m* turnover (of money); **'~verlegenheit** *f* pecuniary embarrassment; **'~wechsel** *m* exchange of money; **'~wert** *m* (-[e]s/no *pl.*) value of money, money value.

Gelee [ʒɛ'leː] *n, m* (-s/-s) jelly.

ge'legen 1. *p.p. of* liegen; 2. *adj.* situated, *Am. a.* located; convenient, opportune; **2heit** *f* (-/-en) occasion; opportunity; chance; facility; *bei* **~** on occasion.

Ge'legenheits|arbeit *f* casual or odd job, *Am. a.* chore; **~arbeiter** *m* casual labo(u)rer, odd-job man; **~kauf** *m* bargain.

ge'legentlich 1. *adj.* occasional; 2. *prp.* (*gen.*) on the occasion of.

ge'lehr|ig *adj.* docile; **2igkeit** *f* (-/no *pl.*) docility; **2samkeit** *f* (-/no *pl.*) learning; **~t** *adj.* [~t] learned; **2te** [~ə] *m* (-n/-n) learned man, scholar.

Geleise [gə'laɪzə] *n* (-s/-) rut, track; **ⓕ** rails *pl.*, line, *esp. Am.* tracks *pl.*

Geleit [gə'laɪt] *n* (-[e]s/-e) escort; attendance; *j-m das* **~** *geben* accompany s.o.; **2en** *v/t.* (no -ge-, h) accompany, conduct; escort; **~zug** **ⓕ** *m* convoy.

Gelenk *anat.*, **⊕**, **♀** [gə'lɛŋk] *n* (-[e]s/-e) joint; **2ig** *adj.* pliable, supple.

ge'lernt *adj. worker:* skilled; trained; **~lesen** *p.p. of* lesen.

Geliebte [gə'liːptə] (-n/-n) 1. *m* lover; 2. *f* mistress, sweetheart.

geliehen [gə'liːən] *p.p. of* leihen.

ge'linde 1. *adj.* soft, smooth; gentle; 2. *adv.*: gelinde gesagt to put it mildly, to say the least.

gelingen [gə'liŋən] 1. *v/i.* (irr., no -ge-, sein) succeed; es gelingt mir zu inf. I succeed in ger.; 2. ♀ *n* (-s/no pl.) success.

ge'litten *p.p. of* leiden.

gellen ['gɛlən] (ge-, h) 1. *v/i.* shrill; yell; *of ears*: ring, tingle; 2. *v/t.* shrill; yell; '**d** *adj.* shrill, piercing.

ge'loben *v/t.* (no -ge-, h) vow, promise.

Gelöbnis [gə'løːpnis] *n* (-ses/-se) promise, pledge; vow.

ge'logen *p.p. of* lügen.

gelten ['gɛltən] (irr., ge-, h) 1. *v/t.* be worth; 2. *v/i.* be of value; be valid; go; count; *money*: be current; maxim, etc.: hold (good or true); et. ~ have credit or influence; j-m ~ concern s.o.; ~ für or als pass for, be reputed or thought or supposed to be; ~ für apply to; ~ lassen let pass, allow; **d** machen maintain, assert; s-n Einfluß bei j-m **d** machen bring one's influence to bear on s.o.; das gilt nicht that is not fair; that does not count; es galt unser Leben our life was at stake; **♀ung** *f* (-/-, -en) validity; value; currency; authority (of person); zur ~ kommen tell; take effect; show; **♀ungsbedürfnis** *n* desire to show off.   [ise; vow.\

Gelübde [gə'lypdə] *n* (-s/-) prom-\

gelungen [gə'luŋən] 1. *p.p. of* gelingen; 2. *adj.* successful; amusing, funny; F: das ist ja ~! that beats everything!

gemächlich *adj.* [gə'mɛːçliç] comfortable, easy; **♀keit** *f* (-/no pl.) ease, comfort.

Gemahl [gə'maːl] *m* (-[e]s/-e) consort; husband.

ge'mahlen *p.p. of* mahlen.

Gemälde [gə'mɛːldə] *n* (-s/-) painting, picture; **galerie** *f* picture-gallery.

gemäß *prp.* (dat.) [gə'mɛːs] according to; **igt** *adj.* moderate; temperate (a. geogr.).

gemein *adj.* [gə'maɪn] common; general; low, vulgar, mean, coarse; et. ~ haben mit have s.th. in common with.

Gemeinde [gə'maɪndə] *f* (-/-n) community; parish; municipality; eccl. congregation; **bezirk** *m* district; municipality; **rat** *m* municipal council; **steuer** *f* rate, Am. local tax; **vorstand** *m* district council.

ge'mein|gefährlich *adj.* dangerous to the public; **er Mensch public danger, Am. public enemy; ♀heit** *f* (-/-en) vulgarity; meanness; mean trick; **nützig** *adj.* of public utility; **♀platz** *m* commonplace; **sam** *adj.* common; joint; mutual; **♀schaft** *f* (-/-en) community; intercourse; **schaftlich** *adj. s.* gemeinsam; **♀-schaftsarbeit** [gə'maɪnʃafts⁹-] *f* team-work; **♀sinn** *m* (-[e]s/no pl.) public spirit; **verständlich** *adj.* popular; **♀wesen** *n* community; **♀wohl** *n* public welfare.

Ge'menge *n* (-s/-) mixture.

ge'messen 1. *p.p. of* messen; 2. *adj.* measured; formal; grave.

Gemetzel [gə'mɛtsəl] *n* (-s/-) slaughter, massacre.

gemieden [gə'miːdən] *p.p. of* meiden.

Gemisch [gə'miʃ] *n* (-es/-e) mixture; **⚗ₘ** compound, composition.

ge|mocht [gə'mɔxt] *p.p. of* mögen; **molken** [gə'mɔlkən] *p.p. of* melken.

Gemse *zo.* ['gɛmzə] *f* (-/-n) chamois.

Gemurmel [gə'murməl] *n* (-s/no pl.) murmur(ing).

Gemüse [gə'myːzə] *n* (-s/-) vegetable(s pl.); greens pl.; **anbau** *m* vegetable gardening, Am. truck farming; **garten** *m* kitchen garden; **händler** *m* greengrocer.

gemußt [gə'must] *p.p. of* müssen 1.

Gemüt [gə'myːt] *n* (-[e]s/-er) mind; feeling; soul; heart; disposition; temper; **♀lich** *adj.* good-natured; genial; comfortable, snug, cosy, cozy; **lichkeit** *f* (-/no pl.) snugness, cosiness; easy-going; genial temper.

Ge'müts|art *f* disposition, nature, temper, character; **bewegung** *f* emotion; **♀krank** *adj.* emotionally disturbed; melancholic; depressed; **krankheit** *f* mental disorder; melancholy; **ruhe** *f* composure; **verfassung** *f*, **zustand** *m* state of mind, humo(u)r.

ge'mütvoll *adj.* emotional; full of feeling.

G

genannt [gə'nant] *p.p. of* nennen.

genas [gə'nɑːs] *pret. of* genesen.

genau *adj.* [gə'nau] exact, accurate; precise; strict; as ~ *nehmen* (*mit*) be particular (about); ⚥eres full particulars *pl.*; ⚥igkeit *f* (-/-en) accuracy, exactness; precision; strictness.

genehm *adj.* [gə'neːm] agreeable, convenient; ~igen [~igən] *v/t.* (*no* -ge-, *h*) grant; approve (of); ⚥igung *f* (-/-en) grant; approval; licen|ce, *Am.* -se; permit; permission; consent.

geneigt *adj.* [gə'naikt] well disposed (*j-m* towards s.o.); inclined (*zu* to).

General ⚔ [genə'rɑːl] *m* (-s/-e, ≈e) general; ~bevollmächtigte ⚔ *m* chief representative *or* agent; ~direktor *m* general manager, managing director; ~**feldmarschall** ⚔ *m* field-marshal; ~**intendant** *thea. m* (artistic) director; ~**konsul** *m* consul-general; ~**konsulat** *n* consulate-general; ~**leutnant** ⚔ *m* lieutenant-general; ~**major** ⚔ *m* major-general; ~**probe** *thea. f* dress rehearsal; ~**stab** ⚔ *m* general staff; ~**stabskarte** ⚔ *f* ordnance (survey) map, *Am.* strategic map; ~**streik** *m* general strike; ~**versammlung** *f* general meeting; ~**vertreter** *m* general agent; ~**vollmacht** *f* full power of attorney.

Generation [genəra'tsjoːn] *f* (-/-en) generation.

generell *adj.* [genə'rɛl] general.

genes|en [gə'neːzən] **1.** *v/i.* (*irr.*, *no* -ge-, *sein*) recover (*von* from); **2.** *p.p. of* 1; ⚥ende *m, f* (-n/-n) convalescent; ⚥ung *f* (-/~ -en) recovery.

genial *adj.* [gen'jɑːl] highly gifted, ingenious; ⚥ität [~ali'tɛːt] *f* (-/*no pl.*) genius.

Genick [gə'nik] *n* (-[e]s/-e) nape of the neck), (back of the) neck.

Genie [ʒe'niː] *n* (-s/-s) genius.

ge'nieren *v/t.* (*no* -ge-, *h*) trouble, bother; *sich* ~ feel *or* be embarrassed *or* shy; be self-conscious.

genießen [gə'niːsən] *v/t.* (*irr.*, *no* -ge-, *h*) enjoy; eat; drink; et. ~ take some food *or* refreshments; *j-s* Vertrauen ~ be in s.o.'s confidence.

Genitiv *gr.* ['geːnitiːf] *m* (-s/-e) genitive (case); possessive (case).

ge|nommen [gə'nɔmən] *p.p. of* nehmen; ~'**normt** *adj.* standardized; ~**noß** [~'nɔs] *pret. of* genießen.

Genoss|e [gə'nɔsə] *m* (-n/-n) companion, mate; comrade (*a. pol.*); ⚥en *p.p. of* genießen; ~**enschaft** *f* (-/-en) company, association; co(-)operative (society); ~**in** *f* (-/-nen) (female) companion; comrade (*a. pol.*).   [cient.]

genug *adj.* [gə'nuːk] enough, suffi-]

Genüg|e [gə'nyːgə] *f* (-/*no pl.*): *zur* ~ enough, sufficiently; ⚥en *v/i.* (*no* -ge-, *h*) be enough, suffice; *das genügt* that will do; *j-m* ~ satisfy s.o.; ⚥**end** *adj.* sufficient; ⚥**sam** *adj.* [~k-] easily satisfied; frugal; ~**samkeit** [~k-] *f* (-/*no pl.*) modesty; frugality.

Genugtuung [gə'nuːktuːuŋ] *f* (-/-en) satisfaction.   [gender.]

Genus *gr.* ['geːnus] *n* (-/*Genera*)]

Genuß [gə'nus] *m* (Genusses/Genüsse) enjoyment; pleasure; use; consumption; taking (*of food*); *fig.* treat; ~**mittel** *n* semi-luxury; ~**sucht** *f* (-/*no pl.*) thirst for pleasure; ⚥**süchtig** *adj.* pleasure-seeking.

Geo|graph [geo'grɑːf] *m* (-en/-en) geographer; ~**graphie** [~a'fiː] *f* (-/*no pl.*) geography; ⚥**graphisch** *adj.* [~'grɑːfiʃ] geographic(al); ~**loge** [~'loːgə] *m* (-n/-n) geologist; ~**logie** [~lo'giː] *f* (-/*no pl.*) geology; ⚥**logisch** *adj.* [~'loːgiʃ] geologic(al); ~**metrie** [~me'triː] *f* (-/-n) geometry; ⚥**metrisch** *adj.* [~'meːtriʃ] geometric(al).

Gepäck [gə'pɛk] *n* (-[e]s/*no pl.*) luggage, ⚔ *or Am.* baggage; ~**annahme** *f* luggage (registration) counter, *Am.* baggage (registration) counter; ~**aufbewahrung** *f* (-/-en) left-luggage office, *Am.* checkroom; ~**ausgabe** *f* luggage delivery office, *Am.* baggage room; ~**netz** *n* luggage-rack, *Am.* baggage rack; ~**schein** *m* luggage-ticket, *Am.* baggage check; ~**träger** *m* porter, *Am. a.* redcap; *on bicycle*: carrier; ~**wagen** *m* luggage van, *Am.* baggage car.

ge|pfiffen [gə'pfifən] *p.p. of* pfeifen; ~**pflegt** *adj.* [~'pfleːkt] *appearance*: well-groomed; *hands, garden, etc.*: well cared-for; *garden, etc.*: well-kept.

Gepflogenheit [gə'pfloːgənhait] *f* (-/-en) habit; custom; usage.

Ge|plapper [gə'plapər] *n* (-s/*no pl.*) babbling, chattering; **~plauder** [~'plaudər] *n* (-s/*no pl.*) chatting, small talk; **~polter** [~'pɔltər] *n* (-s/*no pl.*) rumble; **~präge** [~'prɛ:gə] *n* (-s/-) impression; stamp (*a. fig.*).

ge|priesen [gə'pri:zən] *p.p.* of preisen; **~quollen** [~'kvɔlən] *p.p.* of quellen.

gerade [gə'rɑ:də] **1.** *adj.* straight (*a. fig.*); number, *etc.*: even; direct; bearing: upright, erect; **2.** *adv.* just; er schrieb ~ he was (just) writing; nun ~ now more than ever; ~ an dem Tage on that very day; **3.** ♀ *f* (-n/-n) ♋ straight line; straight (*of race-course*); linke (rechte) ~ boxing: straight left (right); **~'aus** *adv.* straight on *or* ahead; **~he'raus** *adv.* frankly; **~nwegs** *adv.* [~nvе:ks] directly; **~stehen** *v/i.* (*irr.* stehen, *sep.*, -ge-, *h*) stand erect; ~ für answer for *s.th.*; **~wegs** *adv.* [~vе:ks] straight, directly; **~'zu** *adv.* straight; almost; downright.

ge'rannt *p.p.* of rennen.

Gerassel [gə'rasəl] *n* (-s/*no pl.*) clanking; rattling.

Gerät [gə'rɛ:t] *n* (-[e]s/-e) tool, implement, utensil; ⊕ gear; *teleph.*, *radio*: set; apparatus; equipment; elektrisches ~ electric(al) appliance.

ge'raten 1. *v/i.* (*irr.* raten, *no* -ge-, *sein*) come *or* fall *or* get (*an acc.* by, upon; *auf acc.* on, upon; *in acc.* in, into); (*gut*) ~ succeed, turn out well; *in Brand* ~ catch fire; *ins Stocken* ~ come to a standstill; *in Vergessenheit* ~ fall *or* sink into oblivion; *in Zorn* ~ fly into a passion; **2.** *p.p.* of raten.

Gerate'wohl *n*: aufs ~ at random.

geräumig *adj.* [gə'rɔymiç] spacious.

Geräusch [gə'rɔyʃ] *n* (-es/-e) noise; **♀los** *adj.* noiseless; **♀voll** *adj.* noisy.

gerb|en ['gɛrbən] *v/t.* (ge-, *h*) tan; **♀er** *m* (-s/-) tanner; **♀erei** [~'raɪ] *f* (-/-en) tannery.

ge'recht *adj.* just; righteous; ♀- *werden* (*dat.*) do justice to; be fair to; meet; please *s.o.*; fulfil (*requirements*); **♀igkeit** *f* (-/*no pl.*) justice; righteousness; *j-m* ~ *widerfahren lassen* do *s.o.* justice. [rumo(u)r.]

Ge'rede *n* (-s/*no pl.*) talk; gossip;]

ge'reizt *adj.* irritable, irritated; ♀- *heit* *f* (-/*no pl.*) irritation.

ge'reuen *v/t.* (*no* -ge-, *h*): es gereut mich I repent (of) it, I am sorry for it.

Gericht [gə'riçt] *n* (-[e]s/-e) dish, course; *s.* Gerichtshof; *mst rhet. and fig.* tribunal; **♀lich** *adj.* judicial, legal.

Ge'richts|barkeit *f* (-/-en) jurisdiction; **~bezirk** *m* jurisdiction; **~diener** *m* (court) usher; **~gebäude** *n* court-house; **~hof** *m* law-court, court of justice; **~kosten** *pl.* (law-)costs *pl.*; **~saal** *m* courtroom; **~schreiber** *m* clerk (of the court); **~stand** *m* (legal) domicile; venue; **~tag** *m* court-day; **~verfahren** *n* legal proceedings *pl.*, lawsuit; **~verhandlung** *f* (court) hearing; trial; **~vollzieher** *m* (-s/-) (court-)bailiff.

gerieben [gə'ri:bən] *p.p.* of reiben.

gering *adj.* [gə'riŋ] little, small; trifling, slight; mean, low; poor; inferior; **~achten** *v/t.* (*sep.*, -ge-, *h*) think little of; disregard; **~er** *adj.* inferior, less, minor; **~fügig** *adj.* insignificant, trifling; slight; **~schätzen** *v/t.* (*sep.*, -ge-, *h*) *s.* geringachten; **~schätzig** *adj.* disdainful, contemptuous, slighting; ♀- *schätzung* *f* (-/*no pl.*) disdain; disregard; **~st** *adj.* least; *nicht im* ~en not in the least.

ge'rinnen *v/i.* (*irr.* rinnen, *no* -ge-, *sein*) curdle (*a. fig.*); congeal; coagulate, clot.

Ge'rippe *n* (-s/-) skeleton (*a. fig.*); ⊕ framework.

ge|rissen [gə'risən] **1.** *p.p.* of reißen; **2.** *fig. adj.* cunning, crafty, smart; **~ritten** [~'ritən] *p.p.* of reiten.

germanis|ch *adj.* [gɛr'mɑ:niʃ] Germanic, Teutonic; ♀**t** [~a'nist] *m* (-en/-en) Germanist, German scholar; student of German.

gern(e) *adv.* ['gɛrn(ə)] willingly, gladly; ~ *haben* or *mögen* be fond of, like; er *singt* ~ he is fond of singing, he likes to sing.

ge'rochen *p.p.* of riechen.

Geröll [gə'rœl] *n* (-[e]s/-e) boulders *pl.*

geronnen [gə'rɔnən] *p.p.* of rinnen.

Gerste ♀ ['gɛrstə] *f* (-/-n) barley; **~nkorn** *n* barleycorn; ✿ sty(e).

Gerte ['gɛrtə] *f* (-/-n) switch, twig.

Geruch [gə'rux] *m* (-[e]s/ᵘe) smell, odo(u)r; scent; *fig.* reputation; **♀los**

adj. odo(u)rless, scentless; **~ssinn** *m* (-[e]s/ *no pl.*) sense of smell.

Gerücht [gə'rʏçt] *n* (-[e]s/-e) rumo(u)r.

ge'ruchtilgend *adj.*: **~es Mittel** deodorant.

ge'rufen *p.p.* of *rufen*.

ge'ruhen *v/i.* (*no* -ge-, *h*) deign, condescend, be pleased.

Gerümpel [gə'rʏmpəl] *n* (-s/*no pl.*) lumber, junk.

Gerundium *gr.* [gə'rʊndjum] *n* (-s/*Gerundien*) gerund.

gerungen [gə'rʊŋən] *p.p.* of *ringen*.

Gerüst [gə'rʏst] *n* (-[e]s/-e) scaffold(ing); stage; trestle.

ge'salzen *p.p.* of *salzen*.

gesamt *adj.* [gə'zamt] whole, entire, total, all; **~ausgabe** *f* complete edition; **2betrag** *m* sum total; **~deutsch** *adj.* all-German.

gesandt [gə'zant] *p.p.* of *senden*; **2e** [~ə] *m* (-n/-n) envoy; **2schaft** *f* (-/-en) legation.

Ge'sang *m* (-[e]s/ːe) singing; song; **~buch** *eccl.* *n* hymn-book; **~slehrer** *m* singing-teacher; **~verein** *m* choral society, *Am.* glee club.

Gesäß *anat.* [gə'zɛːs] *n* (-es/-e) seat, buttocks *pl.*, posterior, *F* bottom, behind.

ge'schaffen *p.p.* of *schaffen 1.*

Geschäft [gə'ʃɛft] *n* (-[e]s/-e) business; transaction; affair; occupation; shop, *Am.* store; **2ig** *adj.* busy, active; **~igkeit** *f* (-/*no pl.*) activity; **2lich 1.** *adj.* business ...; commercial; **2.** *adv.* on business.

Ge'schäfts|bericht *m* business report; **~brief** *m* business letter; **~frau** *f* business woman; **~freund** *m* business friend, correspondent; **~führer** *m* manager; **~haus** *n* business firm; office building; **~inhaber** *m* owner *or* holder of a business; shopkeeper; **~jahr** *n* financial *or* business year, *Am.* fiscal year; **~lage** *f* business situation; **~leute** *pl.* businessmen *pl.*; **~mann** *m* businessman; **2mäßig** *adj.* business-like; **~ordnung** *f* standing orders *pl.*; rules *pl.* (of procedure); **~papiere** *n/pl.* commercial papers *pl.*; **~partner** *m* (business) partner; **~räume** *m/pl.* business premises *pl.*; **~reise** *f* business trip; **~reisende** *m* commercial travel(l)er, *Am.* travel(l)ing salesman; **~schluß** *m*

closing-time; *nach* ~ *a.* after business hours; **~stelle** *f* office; **~träger** *m pol.* chargé d'affaires; ♱ agent, representative; **2tüchtig** *adj.* efficient, smart; **~unternehmen** *n* business enterprise; **~verbindung** *f* business connexion *or* connection; **~viertel** *n* business cent|re, *Am.* -er; *Am.* downtown; shopping cent|re, *Am.* -er; **~zeit** *f* office hours *pl.*, business hours *pl.*; **~zimmer** *n* office, bureau; office; **~zweig** *m* branch (of business), line (of business).

geschah [gə'ʃaː] *pret.* of *geschehen.*

geschehen [gə'ʃeːən] **1.** *v/i.* (*irr.*, *no* -ge-, *sein*) happen, occur, take place; be done; *es geschieht ihm recht* it serves him right; **2.** *adj.* 1; **3.** **2** *n* (-s/-) events *pl.*, happenings *pl.*

gescheit *adj.* [gə'ʃaɪt] clever, intelligent, bright.

Geschenk [gə'ʃɛŋk] *n* (-[e]s/-e) present, gift; **~packung** *f* gift-box.

Geschicht|e [gə'ʃɪçtə] *f* **1.** (-/-n) story; tale; *fig.* affair; **2.** (-/*no pl.*) history; **2lich** *adj.* historical; **~sforscher** *m,* **~sschreiber** *m* historian.

Ge'schick *n* **1.** (-[e]s/-e) fate; destiny; **2.** (-[e]s/*no pl.*) = **~lichkeit** *f* (-/-en) skill; dexterity; aptitude; **2t** *adj.* skil(l)ful; dexterous; apt; clever.

ge'schieden [gə'ʃiːdən] *p.p.* of *scheiden*; **~schienen** [~'ʃiːnən] *p.p.* of *scheinen.*

Geschirr [gə'ʃɪr] *n* (-[e]s/-e) vessel; dishes *pl.*; china; earthenware, crockery; service; *horse:* harness.

ge'schlafen *p.p.* of *schlafen*; **~'schlagen** *p.p.* of *schlagen.*

Ge'schlecht *n* (-[e]s/-er) sex; kind; species; race; family; generation; *gr.* gender; **2lich** *adj.* sexual.

Ge'schlechts|krankheit ♱ *f* venereal disease; **~reife** *f* puberty; **~teile** *anat.* *n/pl.* genitals *pl.*; **~trieb** *m* sexual instinct *or* urge; **~verkehr** *m* (-[e]s/*no pl.*) sexual intercourse; **~wort** *gr. n* (-[e]s/ːer) article.

ge'schlichen [gə'ʃlɪçən] *p.p.* of *schleichen*; **~schliffen** [~'ʃlɪfən] **1.** *p.p.* of *schleifen*; **2.** *adj. jewel:* cut; *fig.* polished; **~schlossen**

[‿ˈʃlɔsən] **1.** *p.p.* of schließen; **2.** *adj. formation:* close; collective; **‿e** *Gesellschaft* private party; **‿schlungen** [‿ˈʃlʊŋən] *p.p.* of schlingen.

Geschmack [gəˈʃmak] *m* (-[e]s/-̈e, *co.* -̈er) taste (*a. fig.*); flavo(u)r; **‿ finden an** (*dat.*) take a fancy to; **2los** *adj.* tasteless; *pred. fig.* in bad taste; **‿(s)sache** *f* matter of taste; **2voll** *adj.* tasteful; *pred. fig.* in good taste.

ge|schmeidig *adj.* [gəˈʃmaɪdiç] supple, pliant; **‿schmissen** [‿ˈʃmɪsən] *p.p.* of schmeißen; **‿schmolzen** [‿ˈʃmɔltsən] *p.p.* of schmelzen.

Geschnatter [gəˈʃnatər] *n* (-s/*no pl.*) cackling (*of geese*); chatter(ing) (*of girls, etc.*).

ge|schnitten [gəˈʃnɪtən] *p.p.* of schneiden; **‿schoben** [‿ˈʃoːbən] *p.p.* of schieben; **‿scholten** [‿ˈʃɔltən] *p.p.* of schelten.

Geschöpf [gəˈʃœpf] *n* (-[e]s/-e) creature.

ge'schoren *p.p.* of scheren.

Geschoß [gəˈʃɔs] *n* (Geschosses/ Geschosse) projectile; missile; stor(e)y, floor.   [ßen.\

geschossen [gəˈʃɔsən] *p.p.of* schie-

Ge'schrei *n* (-[e]s/*no pl.*) cries *pl.*; shouting; *fig.* noise, fuss.

ge|schrieben [gəˈʃriːbən] *p.p.* of schreiben; **‿schrie(e)n** [‿ˈʃriː(ə)n] *p.p.* of schreien; **‿schritten** [‿ˈʃrɪtən] *p.p.* of schreiten; **‿schunden** [‿ˈʃʊndən] *p.p.* of schinden.

Geschütz [gəˈʃyts] *n* (-es/-e) gun, cannon; ordnance.

Geschwader ✕ [gəˈʃvaːdər] *n* (-s/-) ♣ squadron; ✈ wing, *Am.* group.

Geschwätz [gəˈʃvɛts] *n* (-es/*no pl.*) idle talk; gossip; **2ig** *adj.* talkative.

geschweige *cj.* [gəˈʃvaɪɡə]: **‿ (denn)** not to mention; let alone, much less.

geschwiegen [gəˈʃviːɡən] *p.p.* of schweigen.

geschwind *adj.* [gəˈʃvɪnt] fast, quick, swift; **2igkeit** [‿dɪçkaɪt] *f* (-/-en) quickness; speed, pace; *phys.* velocity; rate; *mit e-r* **‿** *von* ... at the rate of ...; **2igkeitsbegrenzung** *f* speed limit.

Geschwister [gəˈʃvɪstər] *n* (-s/-): ‿ *pl.* brother(s *pl.*) and sister(s *pl.*).

ge|schwollen [gəˈʃvɔlən] **1.** *p.p.* of schwellen; **2.** *adj. language:* bom-

bastic, pompous; **‿schwommen** [‿ˈʃvɔmən] *p.p.* of schwimmen.

geschworen [gəˈʃvoːrən] *p.p.* of schwören; **2e** [‿ə] *m, f* (-n/-n) juror; *die* **‿n** *pl.* the jury; **2engericht** *n* jury.

Geschwulst ✿ [gəˈʃvʊlst] *f* (-/-̈e) swelling; tumo(u)r.

ge|schwunden [gəˈʃvʊndən] *p.p.* of schwinden; **‿schwungen** [‿ˈʃvʊŋən] *p.p.* of schwingen.

Geschwür ✿ [gəˈʃvyːr] *n* (-[e]s/-e) abscess, ulcer.

ge'sehen *p.p.* of sehen.

Gesell [gəˈzɛl] *m* (-en/-en), **‿e** [‿ə] *m* (-n/-n) companion, fellow; ⊕ journeyman; **2en** *v/refl.* (*no -ge-*, *h*) associate, come together; *sich zu j-m* **‿** join s.o.; **2ig** *adj.* social; sociable.

Ge'sellschaft *f* (-/-en) society; company (*a.* ✝); party; *j-m* **‿** *leisten* keep s.o. company; **‿er** *m* (-s/-) companion; ✝ partner; **‿erin** *f* (-/-nen) (lady) companion; ✝ partner; **2lich** *adj.* social.

Ge'sellschafts|dame *f* (lady) companion; **‿reise** *f* party tour; **‿spiel** *n* party *or* round game; **‿tanz** *m* ball-room dance.

gesessen [gəˈzɛsən] *p.p.* of sitzen.

Gesetz [gəˈzɛts] *n* (-es/-e) law; statute; **‿buch** *n* code; statutebook; **‿entwurf** *m* bill; **‿eskraft** *f* legal force; **‿essammlung** *f* code; **2gebend** *adj.* legislative; **‿geber** *m* (-s/-) legislator; **‿gebung** *f* (-/-en) legislation; **2lich 1.** *adj.* lawful, legal; **2.** *adv.*: **‿** *geschützt* patented, registered; **2los** *adj.* lawless; **2mäßig** *adj.* legal; lawful.

ge'setzt 1. *adj.* sedate, staid; sober; mature; **2.** *cj.*: **‿** *den Fall,* (*daß*) ... suppose *or* supposing (that) ...

ge'setzwidrig *adj.* unlawful, illegal.

Ge'sicht *n* (-[e]s/-er) face; countenance; *fig.* character; *zu* **‿** *bekommen* catch sight *or* a glimpse of; *set eyes on.*

Ge'sichts|ausdruck *m* (facial) expression; **‿farbe** *f* complexion; **‿kreis** *m* horizon; **‿punkt** *m* point of view, viewpoint, aspect, *esp. Am.* angle; **‿zug** *m mst* Gesichtszüge *pl.* feature(s *pl.*), lineament(s *pl.*).

Ge'sims *n* ledge.

Gesinde [gəˈzɪndə] *n* (-s/-) (domestic) servants *pl.*; **‿l** [‿l] *n* (-s/*no pl.*) rabble, mob.

ge'sinn|t *adj. in compounds*: ...-minded; *wohl* ~ well disposed (*j-m* towards s.o.); **2ung** *f* (-/-en) mind; conviction; sentiment(s *pl.*); opinions *pl.*

gesinnungs|los *adj.* [gə'zɪnʊŋslo:s] unprincipled; **~treu** *adj.* loyal; **2wechsel** *m* change of opinion; *esp. pol.* volte-face.

ge|sittet *adj.* [gə'zɪtət] civilized; well-bred, well-mannered; **~'soffen** *p.p. of saufen*; **~sogen** [~'zo:gən] *p.p. of saugen*; **~sonnen** [~'zɔnən] **1.** *p.p. of sinnen*; **2.** *adj.* minded, disposed; **~sotten** [~'zɔtən] *p.p. of sieden*; **~'spalten** *p.p. of spalten*.

Ge'spann *n* (-[e]s/-e) team, *Am. a.* span; *oxen*: yoke; *fig.* pair, couple.

ge'spannt *adj.* tense (*a. fig.*); *rope*: tight, taut; *fig.* intent; *attention*: close; *relations*: strained; ~ *sein auf* (*acc.*) be anxious for; *auf* ~*em Fuß* on bad terms; **2heit** *f* (-/*no pl.*) tenseness, tension.

Gespenst [gə'ʃpɛnst] *n* (-es/-er) ghost, spect|re, *Am.* -er; **2isch** *adj.* ghostly.

Ge'spiel|e *m* (-n/-n), **~in** *f* (-/-nen) playmate.

gespien [gə'ʃpi:n] *p.p. of speien*.

Gespinst [gə'ʃpɪnst] *n* (-es/-e) web, tissue (*both a. fig.*); spun yarn.

gesponnen [gə'ʃpɔnən] *p.p. of spinnen*.

Gespött [gə'ʃpœt] *n* (-[e]s/*no pl.*) mockery, derision, ridicule; *zum* ~ *der Leute werden* become a laughing-stock.

Gespräch [gə'ʃprɛːç] *n* (-[e]s/-e) talk; conversation; *teleph.* call; dialogue; **2ig** *adj.* talkative.

ge|sprochen [gə'ʃrɔxən] *p.p. of sprechen*; **~'sprossen** *p.p. of sprießen*; **~sprungen** [~'ʃprʊŋən] *p.p. of springen*.

Gestalt [gə'ʃtalt] *f* (-/-en) form, figure, shape; stature; **2en** *v/t. and v/refl.* (*no -ge-, h*) form, shape; **~ung** *f* (-/-en) formation; arrangement, organization.

gestanden [gə'ʃtandən] *p.p. of stehen*.

ge'ständ|ig *adj.*: ~ *sein* confess; **2nis** [~t-] *n* (-ses/-se) confession.

Ge'stank *m* (-[e]s/*no pl.*) stench.

gestatten [gə'ʃtatən] *v/t.* (*no -ge-, h*) allow, permit.

Geste ['gɛstə] *f* (-/-n) gesture.

ge'stehen (*irr. stehen, no -ge-, h*) **1.** *v/t.* confess, avow; **2.** *v/i.* confess.

Ge|'stein *n* (-[e]s/-e) rock, stone; **~stell** [~'ʃtɛl] *n* (-[e]s/-e) stand, rack, shelf; frame; trestle, horse.

gestern *adv.* ['gɛstərn] yesterday; ~ *abend* last night.

gestiegen [gə'ʃti:gən] *p.p. of steigen*.

Ge'stirn *n* (-[e]s/-e) star; *astr.* constellation; **2t** *adj.* starry.

ge|stoben [gə'ʃto:bən] *p.p. of stieben*; **~stochen** [~'ʃtɔxən] *p.p. of stechen*; **~stohlen** [~'ʃto:lən] *p.p. of stehlen*; **~storben** [~'ʃtɔrbən] *p.p. of sterben*; **~'stoßen** *p.p. of stoßen*; **~strichen** [~'ʃtriçən] *p.p. of streichen*.

gestrig *adj.* ['gɛstriç] of yesterday, yesterday's ...

ge'stritten *p.p. of streiten*.

Gestrüpp [gə'ʃtryp] *n* (-[e]s/-e) brushwood; undergrowth.

gestunken [gə'ʃtʊŋkən] *p.p. of stinken*.

Gestüt [gə'ʃty:t] *n* (-[e]s/-e) stud farm; *horses kept for breeding, etc.*: stud.

Gesuch [gə'zu:x] *n* (-[e]s/-e) application, request; petition; **2t** *adj.* wanted; sought-after; *politeness*: studied.

gesund *adj.* [gə'zʊnt] sound, health-y; salubrious; wholesome (*a. fig.*); ~*er Menschenverstand* common sense; **~en** [~dən] *v/i.* (*no -ge-, sein*) recover.

Ge'sundheit *f* (-/*no pl.*) health (-iness); wholesomeness (*a. fig.*); *auf j-s* ~ *trinken* drink (to) s.o.'s health; **2lich** *adj.* sanitary; ~ *geht es ihm gut* he is in good health.

Ge'sundheits|amt *n* Public Health Department; **~pflege** *f* hygiene; public health service; **2schädlich** *adj.* injurious to health, unhealthy, unwholesome; **~wesen** *n* Public Health; **~zustand** *m* state of health, physical condition.

ge|sungen [gə'zʊŋən] *p.p. of singen*; **~sunken** [~'zʊŋkən] *p.p. of sinken*; **~tan** [~'ta:n] *p.p. of tun*.

Getöse [gə'tø:zə] *n* (-s/*no pl.*) din, noise.

ge'tragen 1. *p.p. of tragen*; **2.** *adj.* solemn.

Getränk [gə'trɛŋk] *n* (-[e]s/-e) drink, beverage. [venture.|

ge'trauen *v/refl.* (*no -ge-, h*) dare,|

Getreide [gə'traɪdə] n (-s/-) corn, esp. Am. grain; cereals pl.; ～(an)bau m corn-growing, esp. Am. grain growing; ～pflanze f cereal plant; ～speicher m granary, grain silo, Am. elevator.

ge'treten p.p. of treten.

ge'treu(lich) adj. faithful, loyal, true.

Getriebe [gə'tri:bə] n (-s/-) bustle; ⊕ gear(ing); ⊕ drive.

ge'trieben [gə'tri:bən] p.p. of treiben; ～troffen [～'trɔfən] p.p. of treffen; ～trogen [～'tro:gən] p.p. of trügen.

ge'trost adv. confidently.

ge'trunken p.p. of trinken.

Ge|**tue** [gə'tu:ə] n (-s/no pl.) fuss; ～tümmel [～'tyməl] n (-s/-) turmoil; ～viert [～'fi:rt] n (-[e]s/-e) square.

Gewächs [gə'vɛks] n (-es/-e) growth (a. 🜨); plant; vintage; ～haus n greenhouse, hothouse, conservatory.

ge|**wachsen 1.** p.p. of wachsen; **2.** adj.: j-m ～ sein be a match for s.o.; e-r Sache ～ sein be equal to s.th.; sich der Lage ～ zeigen rise to the occasion; ～wagt adj. [～'va:kt] risky; bold; ～wählt adj. [～'vɛ:lt] style: refined; ～'wahr adj.: ～ werden (acc. or gen.) perceive s.th.; become aware of s.th.; ～ werden, daß become aware that.

Gewähr [gə'vɛ:r] f (-/no pl.) guarantee, warrant, security; 2en v/t. (no -ge-, h) grant, allow; give, yield, afford; j-n ～ lassen let s.o. have his way; leave s.o. alone; 2leisten v/t. (no -ge-, h) guarantee.

Ge'wahrsam m (-s/-e) custody, safe keeping.

Ge'währsmann m informant, source.

Gewalt [gə'valt] f (-/-en) power; authority; control; force, violence; höhere ～ act of God; mit ～ by force; ～herrschaft f despotism, tyranny; 2ig adj. powerful, mighty; vehement; vast; ～maßnahme f violent measure; 2sam 1. adj. violent; 2. adv. a. forcibly; ～ öffnen force open; open by force; ～tat f act of violence; 2tätig adj. violent.

Gewand [gə'vant] n (-[e]s/⁓er) garment; robe; esp. eccl. vestment.

ge'wandt 1. p.p. of wenden 2; **2.** adj. agile, nimble, dexterous, adroit; clever; 2heit f (-/no pl.) agility, nimbleness; adroitness, dexterity; cleverness.

ge'wann pret. of gewinnen.

Gewäsch F [gə'vɛʃ] n (-es/no pl.) twaddle, nonsense.

ge'waschen p.p. of waschen.

Gewässer [gə'vɛsər] n (-s/-) water(s pl.).

Gewebe [gə've:bə] n (-s/-) tissue (a. anat. and fig.); fabric, web; texture.

Ge'wehr n gun; rifle; ～kolben m (rifle-)butt; ～lauf m (rifle-, gun-)barrel.

Geweih [gə'vaɪ] n (-[e]s/-e) horns pl., head, antlers pl.

Gewerbe [gə'vɛrbə] n (-s/-) trade, business; industry; ～freiheit f freedom of trade; ～schein m trade licen|ce, Am. -se; ～schule f technical school; ～steuer f trade tax; 2treibend adj. carrying on a business, engaged in trade; ～treibende m (-n/-n) tradesman.

gewerb|**lich** [gə'vɛrplɪç] commercial, industrial; ～mäßig adj. professional.

Ge'werkschaft f (-/-en) trade(s) union, Am. labor union; ～ler m (-s/-) trade(s)-unionist; 2lich adj. trade-union; ～sbund m Trade Union Congress, Am. Federation of Labor.

ge|**wesen** [gə've:zən] p.p. of sein; ～wichen [～'vɪçən] p.p. of weichen.

Gewicht [gə'vɪçt] n (-[e]s/-e) weight, Am. F a. heft; e-r Sache ～ beimessen attach importance to s.th.; ～ haben carry weight (bei dat. with); ～ legen auf et. lay stress on s.th.; ins ～ fallen be of great weight, count, matter; 2ig adj. weighty (a. fig.).

ge|**wiesen** [gə'vi:zən] p.p. of weisen; ～willt adj. [～'vɪlt] willing.

Ge|**wimmel** [gə'viməl] n (-s/no pl.) swarm; throng; ～winde ⊕ [～'vɪndə] n (-s/-) thread.

Gewinn [gə'vɪn] m (-[e]s/-e) gain; † gains pl.; profit; lottery ticket: prize; game: winnings pl.; ～anteil m dividend; ～beteiligung f profit-sharing; 2bringend adj. profitable; 2en (irr., no -ge-, h) 1. v/t. win; gain; get; 2. v/i. win; gain; fig. improve; 2end adj. manner, smile: winning, engaging; ～er m (-s/-) winner.

Ge'wirr *n* (-[e]s/-e) tangle, entanglement; *streets:* maze; *voices:* confusion.

gewiß [gə'vis] **1.** *adj.* certain; *ein gewisser Herr N.* a certain Mr. N., one Mr. N.; **2.** *adv.:* ~! certainly!, to be sure!, *Am.* sure!

Ge'wissen *n* (-s/-) conscience; ℒhaft *adj.* conscientious; ℒlos *adj.* unscrupulous; ~sbisse *m/pl.* remorse, pangs *pl.* of conscience; ~sfrage *f* question of conscience.

gewissermaßen *adv.* [gəvisər'ma:sən] to a certain extent.

Ge'wißheit *f* (-/-en) certainty; certitude.

Gewitter [gə'vitər] *n* (-s/-) (thunder)storm; ℒn *v/i.* (no -ge-, h): es *gewittert* there is a thunderstorm; ~regen *m* thunder-shower; ~wolke *f* thundercloud.

ge|woben [gə'vo:bən] *p.p. of* weben; ~'wogen **1.** *p.p. of* wägen *and* wiegen[1]; **2.** *adj.* (*dat.*) well *or* kindly disposed towards, favo(u)rably inclined towards.

gewöhnen [gə'vø:nən] *v/t.* (no -ge-, h) accustom, get used (*an acc.* to).

Gewohnheit [gə'vo:nhaɪt] *f* (-/-en) habit; custom; ℒsmäßig *adj.* habitual.

ge'wöhnlich *adj.* common; ordinary; usual, customary; habitual; common, vulgar.

ge'wohnt *adj.* customary, habitual; (es) ~ *sein zu inf.* be accustomed *or* used to *inf.*

Gewölbe [gə'vœlbə] *n* (-s/-) vault.

ge|wonnen [gə'vɔnən] *p.p. of* gewinnen; ~worben [~'vɔrbən] *p.p. of* werben; ~worden [~'vɔrdən] *p.p. of* werden; ~worfen [~'vɔrfən] *p.p. of* werfen; ~wrungen [~'vruŋən] *p.p. of* wringen.

Gewühl [gə'vy:l] *n* (-[e]s/no *pl.*) bustle; milling crowd.

gewunden [gə'vundən] **1.** *p.p. of* winden; **2.** *adj.* twisted; winding.

Gewürz [gə'vyrts] *n* (-es/-e) spice; condiment; ~nelke ♀ *f* clove.

ge'wußt *p.p. of* wissen.

Ge|'zeit *f:* *mst* ~en *pl.* tide(s *pl.*); ~'zeter *n* (-s/no *pl.*) (shrill) clamo(u)r.

ge|'ziert *adj.* affected; ~zogen [~'tso:gən] *p.p. of* ziehen.

Gezwitscher [gə'tsvitʃər] *n* (-s/no *pl.*) chirping, twitter(ing).

gezwungen [gə'tsvuŋən] **1.** *p.p. of* zwingen; **2.** *adj.* forced, constrained.

Gicht ⚕ [giçt] *f* (-/no *pl.*) gout; ℒisch ⚕ *adj.* gouty; ~knoten ⚕ *m* gouty knot.

Giebel ['gi:bəl] *m* (-s/-) gable(-end).

Gier [gi:r] *f* (-/no *pl.*) greed(iness) (*nach* for); ℒig *adj.* greedy (*nach* for, of).

'Gießbach *m* torrent.

gießen ['gi:sən] (*irr.*, ge-, h) **1.** *v/t.* pour; ⊕ cast, found; water (*flowers*); **2.** *v/i.:* es *gießt* it is pouring (with rain); ℒer *m* (-s/-) founder; ℒerei *f* (-/-en) foundry; ℒkanne *f* watering-can *or* -pot.

Gift [gift] *n* (-[e]s/-e) poison; venom (*esp. of snakes*) (*a. fig.*); malice, spite; ℒig *adj.* poisonous; venomous; malicious, spiteful; ~schlange *f* venomous *or* poisonous snake; ~zahn *m* poison-fang.

Gigant [gi'gant] *m* (-en/-en) giant.

Gimpel *orn.* ['gimpəl] *m* (-s/-) bullfinch.

ging [giŋ] *pret. of* gehen.

Gipfel ['gipfəl] *m* (-s/-) summit, top; peak; ~konferenz *pol.* f summit meeting *or* conference; ℒn *v/i.* (ge-, h) culminate.

Gips [gips] *m* (-es/-e) *min.* gypsum; ⊕ plaster (of Paris); ~abdruck *m*, ~abguß *m* plaster cast; ℒen *v/t.* (ge-, h) plaster; ~verband ⚕ *m* plaster (of Paris) dressing.

Giraffe *zo.* [gi'rafə] *f* (-/-n) giraffe.

girieren [ʒi'ri:rən] *v/t.* (no -ge-, h) endorse, indorse (*bill of exchange*).

Girlande [gir'landə] *f* (-/-n) garland.

Giro † ['ʒi:ro] *n* (-s/-s) endorsement, indorsement; ~bank *f* clearing-bank; ~konto *n* current account.

girren ['girən] *v/i.* (ge-, h) coo.

Gischt [gi∫t] *m* (-es/⚓ -e) *and* f (-/⚓ -en) foam, froth; spray; spindrift.

Gitarre ♪ [gi'tarə] *f* (-/-n) guitar.

Gitter ['gitər] *n* (-s/-) grating; lattice; trellis; railing; ~bett *n* crib; ~fenster *n* lattice-window.

Glacéhandschuh [gla'se:-] *m* kid glove.

Glanz [glants] *m* (-es/no *pl.*) brightness; lust|re, *Am.* -er; brilliancy; splendo(u)r.

glänzen ['glɛntsən] v/i. (ge-, h) glitter, shine; **'~d** adj. bright, brilliant; fig. splendid.

'Glanz|leistung f brilliant achievement or performance; **'~papier** n glazed paper; **'~punkt** m highlight; **'~zeit** f golden age, heyday.

Glas [gla:s] n (-es/ᵘer) glass; **~er** ['~zər] m (-s/-) glazier.

gläsern adj. ['glɛ:zərn] of glass; fig. glassy.

'Glas|glocke f (glass) shade or cover; globe; bell-glass; **'~hütte** f glassworks sg., pl.

glasieren [gla'zi:rən] v/t. (no -ge-, h) glaze; ice, frost (cake).

glasig adj. ['gla:ziç] glassy, vitreous.

'Glasscheibe f pane of glass.

Glasur [gla'zu:r] f (-/-en) glaze, glazing; enamel; icing, frosting (on cakes).

glatt [glat] **1.** adj. smooth (a. fig.); even; lie, etc.: flat, downright; road, etc.: slippery; **2.** adv. smoothly, evenly; **~** anliegen fit closely or tightly; **~** rasiert clean-shaven; et. **~** ableugnen deny s.th. flatly.

Glätte ['glɛtə] f (-/-n) smoothness; road, etc.: slipperiness.

'Glatteis n glazed frost, icy glaze, Am. glaze; F: j-n aufs **~** führen lead s.o. up the garden path.

'glätten v/t. (ge-, h) smooth.

Glatze ['glatsə] f (-/-n) bald head.

Glaube ['glaubə] m (-ns/ᵘ-n) faith, belief (an acc. in); **'2n** (ge-, h) **1.** v/t. believe; think, suppose, Am. a. guess; **2.** v/i. believe (j-m s.o.; an acc. in).

'Glaubens|bekenntnis n creed, profession or confession of faith; **'~lehre** f, **'~satz** m dogma, doctrine.

glaubhaft adj. ['glaup-] credible; plausible; authentic.

gläubig adj. ['glɔybiç] believing, faithful; **2e** ['~gə] m, f (-n/-n) believer; **2er** ⁺ ['~gər] m (-s/-) creditor.

glaubwürdig adj. ['glaup-] credible.

gleich [glaiç] **1.** adj. equal (an dat. in); the same; like; even, level; in **~er** Weise likewise; zur **~en** Zeit at the same time; es ist mir **~** it's all the same to me; das **~e** the same; as much; er ist nicht (mehr) der **~e**

he is not the same man; **2.** adv. alike, equally; immediately, presently, directly, at once; just; es ist **~** acht (Uhr) it is close on or nearly eight (o'clock); **'~altrig** adj. ['~altriç] (of) the same age; **'~artig** adj. homogeneous; similar; uniform; **'~bedeutend** adj. synonymous; equivalent (to); tantamount (mit to); **'~berechtigt** adj. having equal rights; **'~bleibend** adj. constant, steady; **'~en** v/i. (irr., ge-, h) equal; resemble.

'gleich|falls adv. also, likewise; **~förmig** adj. ['~fœrmiç] uniform; **~gesinnt** adj. like-minded; **2gewicht** n balance (a. fig.); equilibrium, equipoise; pol.: **~** der Kräfte balance of power; **'~gültig** adj. indifferent (gegen to); es ist mir **~** I don't care; **~,** was du tust no matter what you do; **2gültigkeit** f indifference; **2heit** f (-/-en) equality; likeness; **'2klang** m unison; consonance, harmony; **'~kommen** v/i. (irr. kommen, sep., -ge-, sein): e-r Sache **~** amount to s.th.; j-m **~** equal s.o.; **'~laufend** adj. parallel; **~lautend** adj. consonant; identical; **'~machen** v/t. (sep., -ge-, h) make equal (dat. to), equalize (to or with); **2maß** n regularity; evenness; fig. equilibrium; **'~mäßig** adj. equal; regular; constant; even; **2mut** m equanimity; **'~mütig** adj. even-tempered; calm; **~namig** adj. ['~na:miç] of the same name; **2nis** n (-ses/-se) parable; rhet. simile; **'~sam** adv. as it were, so to speak; **'~schalten** v/t. (sep., -ge-, h) ⊕ synchronize; pol. co-ordinate, unify; **'~seitig** adj. equilateral; **'~setzen** v/t. (sep., -ge-, h) equate (dat. or mit with); **'~stehen** v/i. (irr. stehen, sep., -ge-, h) be equal; **'~stellen** v/t. (sep., -ge-, h) equalize, equate (dat. with); put s.o. on an equal footing (with); **'2stellung** f equalization, equation; **'2strom** ⁴ m direct current; **'2ung** ⅍ f (-/-en) equation; **'~wertig** adj. equivalent, of the same value, of equal value; **'~zeitig** adj. simultaneous; synchronous; contemporary.

Gleis [glais] n (-es/-e) s. Geleise.

gleiten ['glaitən] v/i. (irr., ge-, sein) glide, slide.

'Gleit|flug m gliding flight, glide,

≫ volplane; '~schutzreifen *m* non-skid tyre, (*Am. only*) non-skid tire; '~schutz(vorrichtung *f*) *m* anti-skid device.

Gletscher ['glɛtʃər] *m* (-s/-) glacier; '~spalte *f* crevasse.

glich [gliç] *pret. of* gleichen.

Glied [gli:t] *n* (-[e]s/-er) *anat.* limb; member (*a. anat.*); link; ≫ rank, file; 2ern ['~dərn] *v/t.* (ge-, *h*) joint, articulate; arrange; divide (*in acc.* into); ~erung *f* (-/-en) articulation; arrangement; division; formation; ~maßen ['~tma:sən] *pl.* limbs *pl.*, extremities *pl.*

glimmen ['glimən] *v/i.* (*irr.*, ge-, *h*) fire: smo(u)lder (*a. fig.*); glimmer; glow.

glimpflich ['glimpfliç] **1.** *adj.* lenient, mild; **2.** *adv.*: ~ davonkommen get off lightly.

glitschig *adj.* ['glitʃiç] slippery.

glitt [glit] *pret. of* gleiten.

glitzern ['glitsərn] *v/i.* (ge-, *h*) glitter, glisten.

Globus ['glo:bus] *m* (-, -ses/Globen, Globusse) globe.

Glocke ['glɔkə] *f* (-/-n) bell; shade; (glass) cover.

'Glocken|schlag *m* stroke of the clock; '~spiel *n* chime(s *pl.*); '~stuhl *m* bell-cage; '~turm *m* bell tower, belfry.

Glöckner ['glœknər] *m* (-s/-) bell-ringer.

glomm [glɔm] *pret. of* glimmen.

Glorie ['glo:rjə] *f* (-/-n) glory; '~n-schein *fig. m* halo, aureola.

glorreich *adj.* ['glo:r-] glorious.

glotzen F ['glɔtsən] *v/i.* (ge-, *h*) stare.

Glück [glyk] *n* (-[e]s/*no pl.*) fortune; good luck; happiness, bliss, felicity; prosperity; *auf gut* ~ on the off chance; ~ *haben* be lucky, succeed; *das* ~ *haben zu inf.* have the good fortune to *inf.*; *j-m* ~ *wünschen* congratulate s.o. (*zu* on); *viel* ~! good luck!; *zum* ~ fortunately; 2bringend *adj.* lucky.

Glucke *orn.* ['glukə] *f* (-/-n) sitting hen. [gen.]

'glücken *v/i.* (ge-, *sein*) s. gelin-

gluckern ['glukərn] *v/i.* (ge-, *h*) water, *etc.*: gurgle.

'glücklich *adj.* fortunate; happy; lucky; '~er'weise *adv.* fortunately.

'Glücksbringer *m* (-s/-) mascot.

glück'selig *adj.* blissful, blessed, happy. [gurgle.]

glucksen ['gluksən] *v/i.* (ge-, *h*)

'Glücks|fall *m* lucky chance, stroke of (good) luck; '~göttin *f* Fortune; '~kind *n* lucky person; '~pfennig *m* lucky penny; '~pilz *m* lucky person; '~spiel *n* game of chance; *fig.* gamble; '~stern *m* lucky star; '~tag *m* happy *or* lucky day, red-letter day.

'glück|strahlend *adj.* radiant(ly happy); 2wunsch *m* congratulation, good wishes *pl.*; compliments *pl.*; ~ *zum Geburtstag* many happy returns (of the day).

Glüh|birne ≠ ['gly:-] *f* (electric-light) bulb; 2en *v/i.* (ge-, *h*) glow; 2end *adj.* glowing; *iron:* red-hot; *coal:* live; *fig.* ardent, fervid; 2(end)'heiß *adj.* burning hot; '~lampe *f* incandescent lamp; '~wein *m* mulled wine; ~würmchen *zo.* ['~vyrmçən] *n* (-s/-) glow-worm.

Glut [glu:t] *f* (-/-en) heat, glow (*a. fig.*); glowing fire, embers *pl.*; *fig.* ardo(u)r.

Gnade ['gna:də] *f* (-/-n) grace; favo(u)r; mercy; clemency; pardon; ≫ quarter.

'Gnaden|akt *m* act of grace; '~brot *n* (-[e]s/*no pl.*) bread of charity; '~frist *f* reprieve; '~gesuch *n* petition for mercy.

gnädig *adj.* ['gnɛ:diç] gracious; merciful; *address:* 2e Frau Madam.

Gnom [gno:m] *m* (-en/-en) gnome, goblin.

Gobelin [gobə'lɛ̃:] *m* (-s/-s) Gobelin tapestry.

Gold [gɔlt] *n* (-[e]s/*no pl.*) gold; '~barren *m* gold bar, gold ingot, bullion; '~borte *f* gold lace; 2en *adj.* ['~dən] gold; *fig.* golden; '~feder *f* gold nib; '~fisch *m* goldfish; 2gelb *adj.* golden-(yellow); ~gräber ['~grɛ:bər] *m* (-s/-) gold-digger; '~grube *f* gold-mine; 2haltig *adj.* gold-bearing, containing gold; 2ig *fig. adj.* ['~diç] sweet, lovely, *Am.* F *a.* cute; '~mine *f* gold-mine; '~münze *f* gold coin; '~schmied *m* goldsmith; '~schnitt *m* gilt edge; *mit* ~ gilt-edged; '~stück *n* gold coin; '~waage *f* gold-balance; '~währung *f* gold standard.

Golf[1] geogr. [gɔlf] m (-[e]s/-e) gulf.

Golf[2] [~] n (-s/no pl.) golf; '**~platz** m golf-course, (golf-)links pl.; '**~schläger** m golf-club; '**~spiel** n golf; '**~spieler** m golfer.

Gondel ['gɔndəl] f (-/-n) gondola; 🚋 mst car.

gönnen ['gœnən] v/t. (ge-, h): j-m et. ~ allow or grant or not to grudge s.o. s.th.

'**Gönner** m (-s/-) patron; Am. a. sponsor; '**2haft** adj. patronizing.

gor [go:r] pret. of gären.

Gorilla zo. [go'rila] m (-s/-s) gorilla.

goß [gɔs] pret. of gießen.

Gosse ['gɔsə] f (-/-n) gutter (a. fig.).

Gott [gɔt] m (-es, ⚔ -s/⸚er) God; god, deity; **2ergeben** adj. resigned (to the will of God).

'**Gottes|dienst** eccl. m (divine) service; '**2fürchtig** adj. godfearing; '**~haus** n church, chapel; '**~lästerer** m (-s/-) blasphemer; '**~lästerung** f blasphemy.

'**Gottheit** f (-/-en) deity, divinity.

Göttin ['gœtin] f (-/-nen) goddess.

göttlich adj. ['gœtliç] divine.

gott|'lob int. thank God or goodness!; '**~los** adj. godless; impious; F fig. deed: unholy, wicked; '**2vertrauen** n trust in God.

Götze ['gœtsə] m (-n/-n) idol; '**~nbild** n idol; '**~ndienst** m idolatry.

Gouvern|ante [guvɛr'nantə] f (-/-n) governess; **~eur** [~'nø:r] m (-s/-e) governor.

Grab [grɑ:p] n (-[e]s/⸚er) grave, tomb, sepulch|re, Am. -er.

Graben ['grɑ:bən] **1.** m (-s/⸚) ditch; ✕ trench; **2.** ⚗ v/t. (irr., ge-, h) dig; animal: burrow.

Grab|gewölbe ['grɑ:p-] n vault, tomb; '**~mal** n monument; tomb, sepulch|re, Am. -er; '**~rede** f funeral sermon; funeral oration or address; '**~schrift** f epitaph; '**~stätte** f burial-place; grave, tomb; '**~stein** m tombstone; gravestone.

Grad [grɑ:t] m (-[e]s/-e) degree; grade, rank; 15 ~ Kälte 15 degrees below zero; '**~einteilung** f graduation; '**~messer** m (-s/-) graduated scale, graduator; fig. criterion; '**~netz** n map: grid.

Graf [grɑ:f] m (-en/-en) in Britain: earl; count.

Gräfin ['grɛ:fin] f (-/-nen) countess.

Grafschaft f (-/-en) county.

Gram [grɑ:m] **1.** m (-[e]s/no pl.) grief, sorrow; **2.** ♀ adj.: j-m ~ sein bear s.o. ill will or a grudge.

grämen ['grɛ:mən] v/t. (ge-, h) grieve; sich ~ grieve (über acc. at, for, over).

Gramm [gram] n (-s/-e) gramme, Am. gram.

Grammati|k [gra'matik] f (-/-en) grammar; **2sch** adj. grammatical.

Granat min. [gra'nɑ:t] m (-[e]s/-e) garnet; **~e** ✕ f (-/-n) shell; grenade; **~splitter** ✕ m shell-splinter; **~trichter** ✕ m shell-crater; **~werfer** ✕ m (-s/-) mortar.

Granit min. [gra'ni:t] m (-s/-e) granite.

Granne ♀ ['granə] f (-/-n) awn, beard.

Graphi|k ['grɑ:fik] f (-/-en) graphic arts pl.; **2sch** adj. graphic(al).

Graphit min. [gra'fi:t] m (-s/-e) graphite.

Gras ♀ [grɑ:s] n (-es/⸚er) grass; **2bewachsen** adj. ['~bəvaksən] grass-grown, grassy; **2en** ['~zən] v/i. (ge-, h) graze; '**~halm** m blade of grass; '**~narbe** f turf, sod; '**~platz** m grass-plot, green.

grassieren [gra'si:rən] v/i. (no -ge-, h) rage, prevail.

gräßlich adj. ['grɛsliç] horrible; hideous, atrocious.

Grassteppe ['grɑ:s-] f prairie, savanna(h).

Grat [grɑ:t] m (-[e]s/-e) edge, ridge.

Gräte ['grɛ:tə] f (-/-n) (fish-)bone.

Gratifikation [gratifika'tsjo:n] f (-/-en) gratuity, bonus.

gratis adv. ['grɑ:tis] gratis, free of charge.

Gratul|ant [gratu'lant] m (-en/-en) congratulator; **~ation** [~'tsjo:n] f (-/-en) congratulation; **2ieren** [~-'li:rən] v/i. (no -ge-, h) congratulate (j-m zu et. s.o. on s.th.); j-m zum Geburtstag ~ wish s.o. many happy returns (of the day).

grau adj. [grau] grey, esp. Am. gray.

'**grauen**[1] v/i. (ge-, h) day: dawn.

'**grauen**[2] v/i. (ge-, h): mir graut vor (dat.) I shudder at, I dread; **2.** ♀ n (-s/no pl.) horror (vor dat. of); '**~erregend** adj., '**~haft** adj., '**~voll** adj. horrible, dreadful.

gräulich adj. ['grɔyliç] greyish, esp. Am. grayish.

Graupe ['graupə] f (-/-n) (peeled)

barley, pot-barley; '**.in 1.** f/pl. sleet; **2.** ♀ v/i. (ge-, h) sleet.

'**grausam** adj. cruel; '**♀keit** f (-/-en) cruelty.

'**grausen** ['grauzən] **1.** v/i. (ge-, h) s. grauen² 1; **2.** ♀ n (-s/no pl.) horror (vor dat. of).

'**grausig** adj. horrible.   [graver.)

Graveur [gra'vøːr] m (-s/-e) en-)

gravieren [gra'viːrən] v/t. (no ge-, h) engrave; '**~d** fig. adj. aggravating.

gravitätisch [gravi'tɛːtiʃ] grave; dignified; solemn; stately.

Grazie ['graːtsjə] f (-/-n) grace(fulness).

graziös adj. [gra'tsjøːs] graceful.

greifen ['graifən] v/t. and v/t. (irr., ge-, h) **1.** v/t. seize, grasp, catch hold of; ♪ touch (string); **2.** v/i.: an den Hut ~ touch one's hat; ~ nach grasp or snatch at; um sich ~ spread; j-m unter die Arme ~ give s.o. a helping hand; zu strengen Mitteln ~ resort to severe measures; zu den Waffen ~ take up arms.

Greis [grais] m (-es/-e) old man; **♀enhaft** adj. ['~zən-] senile (a. 🌣); '**~in** ['~zin] f (-/-nen) old woman.

grell adj. [grɛl] light: glaring; colour: loud; sound: shrill.

Grenze ['grɛntsə] f (-/-n) limit; territory: boundary; state: frontier, borders pl.; e-e ~ ziehen draw the line; ♀n v/i. (ge-, h): ~ an (acc.) border on (a. fig.); fig. verge on; '**♀nlos** adj. boundless.

'**Grenz|fall** m border-line case; '**~land** n borderland; '**~linie** f boundary or border line; '**~schutz** m frontier or border protection; frontier or border guard; '**~stein** m boundary stone; '**~übergang** m frontier or border crossing(-point).

Greuel ['grɔyəl] m (-s/-) horror; abomination; atrocity; '**~tat** f atrocity.

Griech|e ['griːçə] m (-n/-n) Greek; '**♀isch** adj. Greek; 🔺, features: Grecian.

griesgrämig adj. ['griːsgrɛːmiç] morose, sullen.

Grieß [griːs] m (-es/-e) gravel (a. 🌣), grit; semolina; '**~brei** m semolina pudding.

Griff [grif] **1.** m (-[e]s/-e) grip, grasp, hold; ♪ touch; handle (of knife, etc.); hilt (of sword); **2.** ♀ pret. of greifen.

Grille ['grilə] f (-/-n) zo. cricket, fig. whim, fancy; '**♀haft** adj whimsical.

Grimasse [gri'masə] f (-/-n) grimace; ~n schneiden pull faces.

Grimm [grim] m (-[e]s/no pl.) fury, rage; '**♀ig** adj. furious, fierce, grim

Grind [grint] m (-[e]s/-e) scab, scurf.

grinsen ['grinzən] **1.** v/i. (ge-, h) grin (über acc. at); sneer (at); **2.** ♀ n (-s/no pl.) grin; sneer.

Grippe 🌣 ['gripə] f (-/-n) influenza, F flu(e), grippe.

grob adj. [grɔp] coarse; gross; rude; work, skin: rough; '**♀heit** f (-/-en) coarseness; grossness; rudeness; ~en pl. rude things pl.

grölen F ['grøːlən] v/t. and v/i (ge-, h) bawl.

Groll [grɔl] m (-[e]s/no pl.) grudge, ill will; '**♀en** v/i. (ge-, h) thunder: rumble; j-m ~ bear s.o. ill will or a grudge.

Gros[1] ✝ [grɔs] n (-ses/-se) gross.

Gros[2] [groː] n (-/-) main body.

Groschen ['grɔʃən] m (-s/-) penny.

groß adj. [groːs] great; large; big figure: tall; huge; fig. great, grand; heat: intense; cold: severe; loss: heavy; die ♀en pl. the grown-ups pl.; im ~en wholesale, on a large scale; im ~en (und) ganzen on the whole; ~er Buchstabe capital (letter); das ~e Los the first prize; ich bin kein ~er Tänzer I am not much of a dancer; '**~artig** adj. great, grand, sublime; first-rate; '**♀aufnahme** f film: close-up.

Größe ['grøːsə] f (-/-n) size; largeness; height, tallness; quantity (esp. 🅐); importance: greatness; p. celebrity; thea. star.

'**Großeltern** pl. grandparents pl.

'**großenteils** adv. to a large or great extent, largely.

'**Größenwahn** m megalomania.

'**Groß|grundbesitz** m large landed property; '**~handel** ✝ m wholesale trade; '**~handelspreis** ✝ m wholesale price; '**~händler** ✝ m wholesale dealer, wholesaler; '**~handlung** ✝ f wholesale business; '**~herzog** m grand duke; '**~industrielle** m big industrialist.

Grossist [grɔ'sist] m (-en/-en) s. Großhändler.

groß|jährig adj. ['groːsjɛːriç] of age;

~ **werden** come of age; '2**jährigkeit** f (-/no pl.) majority, full (legal) age; '2**kaufmann** m wholesale merchant; '2**kraftwerk** ⚡ n superpower station; '2**macht** f great power; '2**maul** n braggart; '2**mut** f (-/no pl.) generosity; ~**mütig** adj. ['~my:tiç] magnanimous, generous; '2**mutter** f grandmother; ~**neffe** m great-nephew, grandnephew; '2**nichte** f great-niece, grand-niece; '2**onkel** m greatuncle, grand-uncle; '2**schreibung** f (-/-en) use of capital letters; capitalization; ~**sprecherisch** adj. boastful; ~**spurig** adj. arrogant; '2**stadt** f large town or city; ~**städtisch** adj. of or in a large town or city; '2**tante** f great-aunt, grandaunt.

größtenteils adv. ['grø:stəntaıls] mostly, chiefly, mainly.

'**groß|tun** v/i. (irr. tun, sep., -ge-, h) swagger, boast; sich mit et. ~ boast or brag of or about s.th.; '2**vater** m grandfather; '2**verdiener** m (-s/-) big earner; ~**wild** n big game; ~**ziehen** v/t. (irr. ziehen, sep., -ge-, h) bring up (child); rear, raise (child, animal); ~**zügig** adj. ['~tsy:giç] liberal; generous; broad-minded; planning: a. on a large scale.

grotesk adj. [gro'tesk] grotesque.

Grotte ['grɔtə] f (-/-n) grotto.

grub [gru:p] pret. of graben.

Grübchen ['gry:pçən] n (-s/-) dimple.

Grube ['gru:bə] f (-/-n) pit; ⚒ mine, pit.

Grübel|ei [gry:bə'laı] f (-/-en) brooding, musing, meditation; 2**n** ['~ln] v/i. (ge-, h) muse, meditate, ponder (all: über acc. on, over), Am. F a. mull (over).

'**Gruben|arbeiter** ⚒ m miner; '~**gas** ⚒ n fire-damp; '~**lampe** ⚒ f miner's lamp.

Gruft [gruft] f (-/⁻e) tomb, vault.

grün [gry:n] 1. adj. green; ~er Hering fresh herring; ~er Junge greenhorn; ~ und blau schlagen beat s.o. black and blue; vom ~en Tisch aus armchair (strategy, etc.); 2. 2 n (-s/no pl.) green; verdure.

Grund [grunt] m (-[e]s/⁻e) ground; soil; bottom (a. fig.); land, estate; foundation; fig.: motive; reason; argument; von ~ auf thoroughly,

fundamentally; '~**ausbildung** f basic instruction; ✕ basic (military) training; ~**bedeutung** f basic or original meaning; ~**bedingung** f basic or fundamental condition; ~**begriff** m fundamental or basic idea; ~e pl. principles pl.; rudiments pl.; ~**besitz** m land(ed property); ~**besitzer** m landowner; ~**buch** n land register.

gründ|en ['gryndən] v/t. (ge-, h) establish; † promote; sich ~ auf (acc.) be based or founded on; '2**er** m (-s/-) founder; † promoter.

'**grund'falsch** adj. fundamentally wrong; '2**farbe** f ground-colo(u)r; opt. primary colo(u)r; '2**fläche** f base; area (of room, etc.); '2**gebühr** f basic rate or fee; flat rate; '2**gedanke** m basic or fundamental idea; '2**gesetz** n fundamental law; ᵗᵗ appr. constitution; '2**kapital** † n capital (fund); '2**lage** f foundation; basis; ~**legend** adj. fundamental, basic.

gründlich adj. ['gryntliç] thorough; knowledge: profound.

'**Grund|linie** f base-line; '2**los** adj. bottomless; fig.: groundless; unfounded; ~**mauer** f foundationwall.   [Thursday.]

Grün'donnerstag eccl. m Maundy

'**Grund|regel** f fundamental rule; '~**riß** m △ ground-plan; outline; compendium; '~**satz** m principle; 2**sätzlich** ['~zetsliç] 1. adj. fundamental; 2. adv. in principle; on principle; '~**schule** f elementary or primary school; '~**stein** m △ foundation-stone; fig. corner-stone; '~**steuer** f land-tax; '2**stock** m basis, foundation; '~**stoff** m element; '~**strich** m down-stroke; '~**stück** n plot (of land); ᵗᵗ (real) estate; premises pl.; '~**stücksmakler** m real estate agent, Am. realtor; '~**ton** m ♪ keynote; ground shade.

'**Gründung** f (-/-en) foundation, establishment.

'**grund|ver'schieden** adj. entirely different; '2**wasser** geol. n (under-) ground water; '2**zahl** gr. f cardinal number; '2**zug** m main feature, characteristic.

'**grünlich** adj. greenish.

'**Grün|schnabel** fig. m greenhorn; whipper-snapper; '~**span** m (-[e]s/no pl.) verdigris.

G

grunzen ['grʊntsən] v/i. and v/t. (ge-, h) grunt.

Grupp|e ['grʊpə] f (-/-n) group; ✕ section, Am. squad; **2ieren** [~'piːrən] v/t. (no -ge-, h) group, arrange in groups; **sich ~** form groups.

Gruselgeschichte ['gruːzəl-] f tale of horror, spine-chilling story or tale, F creepy story or tale.

Gruß [gruːs] m (-es/⁓e) salutation; greeting; esp. ✕, ✈ salute; mst **Grüße** pl. regards pl.; respects pl., compliments pl.

grüßen ['gryːsən] v/t. (ge-, h) greet, esp. ✕ salute; hail; **~ Sie ihn von mir** remember me to him; **j-n ~ lassen** send one's compliments or regards to s.o.

Grütze ['grʏtsə] f (-/-n) grits pl., groats pl.

guck|en ['gʊkən] v/i. (ge-, h) look; peep, peer; **2loch** n peep- or spy-hole.

Guerilla ✕ [ge'rɪl(j)a] f (-/-s) guer(r)illa war.

gültig adj. ['gʏltɪç] valid; effective, in force; legal; coin: current; ticket: available; **2keit** f (-/no pl.) validity; currency (of money); availability (of ticket).

Gummi ['gʊmi] n, m (-s/-s) gum; (india-)rubber; **'~ball** m rubber ball; **'~band** n elastic (band); rubber band; **'~baum** ♀ m gum-tree; (india-)rubber tree.

gum'mieren v/t. (no -ge-, h) gum.

'Gummi|handschuh m rubber glove; **'~knüppel** m truncheon, Am. club; **'~schuhe** m/pl. rubber shoes pl., Am. rubbers pl.; **'~sohle** f rubber sole; **'~stiefel** m wellington (boot), Am. rubber boot; **'~zug** m elastic; elastic webbing.

Gunst [gʊnst] f (-/no pl.) favo(u)r, goodwill; **zu ~en** (gen.) in favo(u)r of.

günst|ig adj. ['gʏnstɪç] favo(u)rable; omen: propitious; **im ~sten Fall** at best; **zu ~en Bedingungen** ♣ on easy terms; **2ling** ['~lɪŋ] m (-s/-e) favo(u)rite.

Gurgel ['gʊrgəl] f (-/-n) j-m an die ~ springen leap or fly at s.o.'s throat; **2n** v/i. (ge-, h) ♣ gargle; gurgle.

Gurke ['gʊrkə] f (-/-n) cucumber; pickled: gherkin.

gurren ['gʊrən] v/i. (ge-, h) coo.

Gurt [gʊrt] m (-[e]s/-e) girdle; harness: girth; strap; belt.

Gürtel ['gʏrtəl] m (-s/-) belt; girdle; geogr. zone.

Guß [gʊs] m (Gusses/Güsse) ⊕ founding, casting; typ. fount, Am. font; rain: downpour, shower; **'~eisen** n cast iron; **2eisern** adj. cast-iron; **'~stahl** m cast steel.

gut[1] **1.** adj. good; **~e Worte** fair words; **~es Wetter** fine weather; **~er Dinge** or **~en Mutes sein** be of good cheer; **~e Miene zum bösen Spiel machen** grin and bear it; **~ so!** good!, well done!; **~ werden** get well, heal; fig. turn out well; **ganz ~** not bad; **schon ~!** never mind!, all right!; **sei so ~ und ...** (will you) be so kind as to inf.; **auf ~ deutsch** in plain German; **j-m ~ sein** love or like s.o.; **2. adv.** well; **ein ~ gehendes Geschäft** a flourishing business; **du hast ~ lachen** it's easy or very well for you to laugh; **es ~ haben** be lucky; be well off.

Gut[2] [~] n (-[e]s/⁓er) possession, property; (landed) estate; ♣ goods pl.

'Gut|achten n (-s/-) (expert) opinion; **'~achter** m (-s/-) expert; consultant; **2artig** adj. good-natured; ♣ benign; **~dünken** ['~dʏŋkən] n (-s/no pl.): **nach ~** at discretion or pleasure.

'Gute 1. n (-n/no pl.) the good; **~s tun** do good; **2. m, f** (-n/-n): **die ~n** pl. the good pl.

Güte ['gyːtə] f (-/no pl.) goodness, kindness; ♣ class, quality; **in ~** amicably; F: **meine ~!** good gracious!; **haben Sie die ~ zu** inf. be so kind as to inf.

'Güter|abfertigung f dispatch of goods; = **'~annahme** f goods office, Am. freight office; **'~bahnhof** m goods station, Am. freight depot or yard; **'~gemeinschaft** ♣♣ f community of property; **'~trennung** ♣♣ f separation of property; **'~verkehr** m goods traffic, Am. freight traffic; **'~wagen** m (goods) wag(g)on, Am. freight car; offener ~ (goods) truck; geschlossener ~ (goods) van, Am. boxcar; **'~zug** m goods train, Am. freight train.

'gut|gelaunt adj. good-humo(u)red;

'**∼gläubig** adj. acting or done in good faith; s. leichtgläubig; '**∼haben** v/t. (irr. haben, sep., -ge-, h) have credit for (sum of money); **∼haben** † n credit (balance); '**∼heißen** v/t. (irr. heißen, sep., -ge-, h) approve (of); '**∼herzig** adj. good-natured, kind-hearted.

'**gütig** adj. good, kind(ly).

'**gütlich** adv.: sich ∼ einigen settle s.th. amicably; sich ∼ tun an (dat.) regale o.s. on.

'**gut∣machen** v/t. (sep., -ge-, h) make up for, compensate, repair; **∼mütig** adj. ['∼my:tiç] good-natured; '**2mütigkeit** f (-/∼) good nature. [of an estate.]

'**Gutsbesitzer** m landowner; owner)

'**Gut∣schein** m credit note, coupon;

voucher; '**2schreiben** v/t. (irr. schreiben, sep., -ge-, h): j-m e-n Betrag ∼ put a sum to s.o.'s credit; '**∼schrift** f credit(ing).

'**Guts∣haus** n farm-house; manor house; '**∼herr** m lord of the manor; landowner; '**∼hof** m farmyard; estate, farm; '**∼verwalter** m (landlord's) manager or steward.

'**gutwillig** adj. willing, obliging.

Gymnasi∣albildung [gymna'zja:l-] f classical education; '**∼ast** [∼ast] m (-en/-en) appr. grammar-school boy; **∼um** [∼'na:zjum] n (-s/Gymnasien) appr. grammar-school.

Gymnasti∣k [gym'nastik] f (-/no pl.) gymnastics pl.; **2sch** adj. gymnastic. [(-n/-n) gyn(a)ecologist.]

Gynäkologe 🗲 [gynɛko'lo:gə] m)

H

Haar [ha:r] n (-[e]s/-e) hair; sich die ∼e kämmen comb one's hair; sich die ∼e schneiden lassen have one's hair cut; aufs ∼ to a hair; um ein ∼ by a hair's breadth; '**∼ausfall** m loss of hair; '**∼bürste** f hairbrush; '**2en** v/i. and v/refl. (ge-, h) lose or shed one's hairs; '**∼esbreite** f: um ∼ by a hair's breadth; '**2fein** adj. (as) fine as a hair; fig. subtle; '**∼gefäß** anat. n capillary (vessel); '**2ge'nau** adj. exact to a hair; '**2ig** adj. hairy, in compounds: ...-haired; '**∼klein** adv. to the last detail; '**∼klemme** f hair grip, bobby pin; '**∼nadel** f hairpin; '**∼nadelkurve** f hairpin bend; '**∼netz** n hair-net; '**∼öl** n hair-oil; '**2scharf** 1. adj. very sharp; fig. very precise; 2. adv. by a hair's breadth; '**∼schneidemaschine** f (e-e a pair of) (hair) clippers pl.; '**∼schneider** m barber, (men's) hairdresser; '**∼schnitt** m haircut; '**∼schwund** m loss of hair; '**∼spal-te'rei** f (-/-en) hair-splitting; '**2sträubend** adj. hair-raising, horrifying; '**∼tracht** f hair-style, coiffure; '**∼wäsche** f hair-wash, shampoo; '**∼wasser** n hair-lotion; '**∼wuchs** m growth of the hair; '**∼wuchsmittel** n hair-restorer.

Habe ['ha:bə] f (-/no pl.) property; belongings pl.

haben ['ha:bən] 1. v/t. (irr., ge-, h) have; F fig.: sich ∼ (make a) fuss; etwas (nichts) auf sich ∼ be of (no) consequence; unter sich ∼ be in control of, command; zu ∼ † goods: obtainable, to be had; da ∼ wir's! there we are!; 2. 2 † n (-s/-) credit (side).

Habgier ['ha:p-] f avarice, covetousness; '**2ig** adj. avaricious, covetous.

habhaft adj. ['ha:phaft]: ∼ werden (gen.) get hold of; catch, apprehend.

Habicht orn. ['ha:biçt] m (-[e]s/-e) (gos)hawk.

Hab∣seligkeiten ['ha:p-] f/pl. property, belongings pl.; '**∼sucht** f s. Habgier; '**2süchtig** adj. s. habgierig.

Hacke ['hakə] f (-/-n) 🗡 hoe, mattock; (pick)axe; heel.

Hacken ['hakən] 1. m (-s/-) heel; die ∼ zusammenschlagen ✕ click one's heels; 2. v/t. (ge-, h) hack (soil); mince (meat); chop (wood).

'**Hackfleisch** n minced meat, Am. ground meat.

Häcksel ['hɛksəl] n, m (-s/no pl.) chaff, chopped straw.

Hader ['ha:dər] m (-s/no pl.) dispute, quarrel; discord; '**2n** v/i. (ge-, h) quarrel (mit with).

Hafen ['ha:fən] m (-s/∼) harbo(u)r;

port; **anlagen** f/pl. docks pl.;
arbeiter m docker, Am. a. long-
shoreman; **damm** m jetty; pier;
stadt f seaport.

Hafer ['ha:fər] m (-s/-) oats pl.;
brei m (oatmeal) porridge;
flocken f/pl. porridge oats pl.;
grütze f groats pl., grits pl.;
schleim m gruel.

Haft ʒɪ̌ [haft] f (-/no pl.) custody,
detention, confinement; **bar** adj.
responsible, ʒɪ̌ liable (für for); **befehl** m warrant of arrest; **en** v/i.
(ge-, h) stick, adhere (an dat. to);
~ für ʒɪ̌ answer for, be liable for.

Häftling ['heftliŋ] m (-s/-e) prisoner.

Haftpflicht ʒɪ̌ f liability; **ig** adj.
liable (für for); **versicherung** f
third-party insurance.

Haftung f (-/-en) responsibility,
ʒɪ̌ liability; mit beschränkter ~
limited.

Hagel ['ha:gəl] m (-s/-) hail; fig. a.
shower, volley; **korn** n hailstone;
n v/i. (ge-, h) hail (a. fig.); **-
schauer** m shower of hail, (brief)
hailstorm.

hager adj. ['ha:gər] lean, gaunt;
scraggy, lank.

Hahn [ha:n] m 1. orn. (-[e]s/-e)
cock; rooster; 2. ⊕ (-[e]s/-e, -en)
(stop)cock, tap, Am. a. faucet;
kampf m cock-fight; **en-
schrei** m cock-crow.

Hai ichth. [haɪ] m (-[e]s/-e), **fisch**
m shark.

Hain poet. [haɪn] m (-[e]s/-e) grove;
wood.

häkel|n ['hɛ:kəln] v/t. and v/i. (ge-,
h) crochet; **2nadel** f crochet needle
or hook.

Haken ['ha:kən] 1. m (-s/-) hook
(a. boxing); peg; fig. snag, catch;
2. 2 v/i. (ge-, h) get stuck, jam.
hakig adj. hooked.

halb [halp] 1. adj. half; eine ~e
Stunde half an hour, a half-hour;
eine ~e Flasche Wein a half-bottle
of wine; ein ~es Jahr half a year;
~e Note ♪ minim, Am. a. half note;
~er Ton ♪ semitone, Am. a. half
tone; 2. adv. half; ~ voll half full;
~ soviel half as much; es schlug ~
it struck the half-hour.

halb|amtlich adj. semi-official;
2bruder m half-brother; **2dun-
kel** n semi-darkness; dusk, twilight; **er** prp. (gen.) ['halbər] on

account of; for the sake of; **2fabri-
kat** ⊕ n semi-finished product;
gar adj. underdone, Am. a. rare;
2gott m demigod; **2heit** f (-/-en)
half-measure.

halbieren ['hal'bi:rən] v/t. (no -ge-,
h) halve, divide in half; ♫ bisect.

Halb|insel f peninsula; **2jahr** n
half-year, six months pl.; **2jährig**
adj. ['.jɛ:riç] half-year, six months;
of six months; **2jährlich 1.** adj.
half-yearly; **2.** adv. a. twice a year;
kreis m semicircle; **kugel** f
hemisphere; **2laut 1.** adj. low,
subdued; **2.** adv. in an undertone;
2mast adv. (at) half-mast, Am. a.
(at) half-staff; **messer** ♫ m (-s/-)
radius; **mond** m half-moon,
crescent; **2part** adv.: ~ machen go
halves, F go fifty-fifty; **schuh** m
(low) shoe; **schwester** f half-
sister; **2tagsbeschäftigung** f part-
time job or employment; **2tot** adj.
half-dead; **2wegs** adv. ['.'ve:ks]
half-way; fig. to some extent,
tolerably; **welt** f demi-monde;
2wüchsig adj. ['.vy:ksiç] adoles-
cent, Am. a. teen-age; **zeit** f
sports: half(-time).   [dump.}

Halde ['haldə] f (-/-n) slope; ⚒ }
half [half] pret. of helfen.

Hälfte ['helftə] f (-/-n) half, ʒɪ̌
moiety; die ~ von half of.

Halfter ['halftər] m, n (-s/-) halter.

Halle ['halə] f (-/-n) hall; hotel:
lounge; tennis: covered court;
hangar.

hallen ['halən] v/i. (ge-, h) (re)sound,
ring, (re-)echo.

Hallen|bad n indoor swimming-
bath, Am. a. natatorium; **sport**
m indoor sports pl.

hallo [ha'lo:] 1. int. hallo!, hello!,
hullo!; 2. 2 fig. n (-s/-s) hullabaloo.

Halm ⚘ [halm] m (-[e]s/-e) blade;
stem, stalk; straw.

Hals [hals] m (-es/-e) neck; throat;
~ über Kopf head over heels;
auf dem ~e haben have on one's
back, be saddled with; sich den ~
verrenken crane one's neck; **ab-
schneider** fig. m extortioner, F
shark; **2band** n necklace; collar
(for dog, etc.); **entzündung** ❀ f
sore throat; **kette** f necklace;
string; chain; **kragen** m collar;
schmerzen m/pl.: ~ haben have
a sore throat; **2starrig** adj. stub-

born, obstinate; '~tuch n neckerchief; scarf; '~weite f neck size.

Halt [halt] m (-[e]s/-e) hold; foothold, handhold; support (a. fig.); fig.: stability; security, mainstay.

halt 1. int. stop!; ✗ halt!; **2.** F adv. just; das ist ~ so that's the way it is.

'**haltbar** adj. material, etc.: durable, lasting; colour: fast; fig. theory, etc.: tenable.

'**halten** (irr., ge-, h) **1.** v/t. hold (fort, position, water, etc.); maintain (position, level, etc.); keep (promise, order, animal, etc.); make, deliver (speech); give, deliver (lecture); take in (newspaper); ~ für regard as, take to be; take for; es ~ mit side with; be fond of; kurz ~ keep s.o. short; viel (wenig) ~ von think highly (little) of; sich ~ hold out; last; food: keep; sich gerade ~ hold o.s. straight; sich gut ~ in examination, etc.: do well; p. be well preserved; sich ~ an (acc.) adhere or keep to; **2.** v/i. stop, halt; ice: bear; rope, etc.: stand the strain; ~ zu stick to or by; ~ auf (acc.) set store by, value; auf sich ~ pay attention to one's appearance; have self-respect.

'**Halte|punkt** m ⚒, etc.: wayside stop, halt; shooting: point of aim; phys. critical point; '~r m (-s/-) keeper; a. owner; devices: ... holder; '~stelle f stop; ⚒ station, stop; '~signal n ⚒ stop signal.

halt|los adj. ['haltlo:s] p. unsteady, unstable; theory, etc.: baseless, without foundation; '~machen v/i. (sep., -ge-, h) stop, halt; vor nichts ~ stick or stop; at nothing; '~ung f (-/-en) deportment, carriage; pose; fig. attitude (gegenüber towards); self-control; stock exchange: tone.

hämisch adj. ['hɛ:miʃ] spiteful, malicious.

Hammel ['haməl] m (-s/-, ⸚) wether; '~fleisch n mutton; '~keule f leg of mutton; '~rippchen n (-s/-) mutton chop.

Hammer ['hamər] m (-s/⸚) hammer; (auctioneer's) gavel; unter den ~ kommen come under the hammer.

hämmern ['hɛmərn] (ge-, h) **1.** v/t. hammer; **2.** v/i. hammer (a. an dat. at door, etc.); hammer away (auf dat. at piano); heart, etc.: throb (violently), pound.

Hämorrhoiden ⚕ [hɛ:mɔroˈiːdən]

f/pl. h(a)emorrhoids pl., piles pl.

Hampelmann ['hampəlman] m jumping-jack; fig. (mere) puppet.

Hamster zo. ['hamstər] m (-s/-) hamster; '~n v/t. and v/i. (ge-, h) hoard.

Hand [hant] f (-/⸚e) hand; j-m die ~ geben shake hands with s.o.; an ~ (gen.) or von with the help or aid of; aus erster ~ first-hand, at first hand; bei der ~, zur ~ at hand; ~ und Fuß haben be sound, hold water; seine ~ im Spiele haben have a finger in the pie; '~arbeit f manual labo(u)r or work; (handi)craft; needlework; '~arbeiter m manual labo(u)rer; '~bibliothek f reference library; '~breit **1.** f (-/-) hand's breadth; **2.** ⚻ adj. a hand's breadth across; '~bremse mot. f hand-brake; '~buch n manual, handbook.

Hände|druck ['hɛndə-] m (-[e]s/⸚e) handshake; '~klatschen n (-s/no pl.) (hand-)clapping; applause.

Handel ['handəl] m **1.** (-s/no pl.) commerce; trade; business; market; traffic; transaction, deal, bargain; **2.** (-s/⸚): Händel pl. quarrels pl., contention; '~n v/i. (ge-, h) act, take action; ✝ trade (mit with s.o., in goods), deal (in goods); bargain (um for), haggle (over); ~ von treat of, deal with; es handelt sich um it concerns, it is a matter of.

'**Handels|abkommen** n trade agreement; '~bank f commercial bank; '~einig adj.: ~ werden come to terms; '~genossenschaft f traders' co-operative association; '~gericht n commercial court; '~gesellschaft f (trading) company; '~haus n business house, firm; '~kammer f Chamber of Commerce; '~marine f mercantile marine; '~minister m minister of commerce; President of the Board of Trade, Am. Secretary of Commerce; '~ministerium n ministry of commerce; Board of Trade, Am. Department of Commerce; '~reisende m commercial traveller, Am. traveling salesman, F drummer; '~schiff n merchantman; '~schiffahrt f merchant shipping; '~schule f commercial school; '~stadt f commercial town; '~üblich adj. customary in trade; '~vertrag m commercial treaty, trade agreement.

H

'**handeltreibend** adj. trading.
'**Hand|feger** m (-s/-) hand-brush; '**⚹fertigkeit** f manual skill; '**⚹fest** adj. sturdy, strong; fig. well-founded, sound; '**⚹feuerwaffen** f/pl. small arms pl.; '**⚹fläche** f flat of the hand, palm; '**⚹gearbeitet** adj. hand-made; '**⚹geld** n earnest money; ⚔ bounty; '**⚹gelenk** anat. n wrist; '**⚹gemenge** n scuffle, mélée; '**⚹gepäck** n hand luggage, Am. hand baggage; '**⚹granate** ⚔ f hand-grenade; '**⚹greiflich** adj. violent; fig. tangible, palpable; ~ werden turn violent, Am. a. get tough; '**⚹griff** m grasp; handle, grip; fig. manipulation; '**⚹habe** fig. f handle; '**⚹haben** v/t. (ge-, h) handle, manage; operate (machine, etc.); administer (law); '**⚹karren** m hand-cart; '**⚹koffer** m suitcase, Am. a. valise; '**⚹kuß** m kiss on the hand; '**⚹langer** m (-s/-) hodman, handy man; fig. dog's-body, henchman. [trader.\
'**Händler** ['hɛndlər] m (-s/-) dealer,\
'**handlich** adj. handy; manageable.
Handlung ['handluŋ] f (-/-en) act, action; deed; thea. action, plot; † shop, Am. store.

'**Handlungs|bevollmächtigte** m proxy; '**⚹gehilfe** m clerk; shop-assistant, Am. salesclerk; '**⚹reisende** m s. Handelsreisende; '**⚹weise** f conduct; way of acting.

'**Hand|rücken** m back of the hand; '**⚹schelle** f handcuff, manacle; '**⚹schlag** m handshake; '**⚹schreiben** n autograph letter; '**⚹schrift** f handwriting; manuscript; '**⚹schriftlich** 1. adj. hand-written; 2. adv. in one's own handwriting; '**⚹schuh** m glove; '**⚹streich** ⚔ m surprise attack, coup de main; im ~ nehmen take by surprise; '**⚹tasche** f handbag, Am. a. purse; '**⚹tuch** n towel; '**⚹voll** f (-/-) handful; '**⚹wagen** m hand-cart; '**⚹werk** n (handi)craft, trade; '**⚹werker** m (-s/-) (handi)craftsman, artisan; workman; '**⚹werkzeug** n (kit of) tools pl.; '**⚹wurzel** anat. f wrist; '**⚹zeichnung** f drawing.

Hanf ♀ [hanf] m (-[e]s/no pl.) hemp.
Hang [haŋ] m (-[e]s/⸗e) slope, incline, declivity; hillside; fig. inclination, propensity (zu for; zu inf. to inf.); tendency (to).

Hänge|boden ['hɛŋə-] m hanging-loft; '**⚹brücke** △ f suspension bridge; '**⚹lampe** f hanging lamp; '**⚹matte** f hammock.

hängen ['hɛŋən] 1. v/i. (irr., ge-, h) hang, be suspended; adhere, stick, cling (an dat. to); ~ an (dat.) be attached or devoted to; 2. v/t. (ge-, h) hang, suspend; '**bleiben** v/i. (irr. bleiben, sep., -ge-, sein) get caught (up) (an dat. on, in); fig. stick (in the memory).

hänseln ['hɛnzəln] v/t. (ge-, h) tease (wegen about), F rag.
Hansestadt ['hanzə-] f Hanseatic town.
Hanswurst [hans'-] m (-es/-e, F ⸗e) merry andrew; Punch; fig. contp. clown, buffoon.
Hantel ['hantəl] f (-/-n) dumb-bell.
hantieren [han'tiːrən] v/i. (no -ge-, h) be busy (mit with); work (an dat. on).
Happen ['hapən] m (-s/-) morsel, mouthful, bite; snack.
Harfe ♪ ['harfə] f (-/-n) harp.
Harke ♪ ['harkə] f (-/-n) rake; '**⚹n** v/t. and v/i. (ge-, h) rake.
harmlos adj. ['harmloːs] harmless, innocuous; inoffensive.
Harmon|ie [harmo'niː] f (-/-n) harmony (a. ♪); **⚹ieren** v/i. (no -ge-, h) harmonize (mit with); fig. a. be in tune (with); '**⚹ika** ♪ [⚹'moː-nika] f(-/-s, Harmoniken) accordion; mouth-organ; **⚹isch** [⚹'moːniʃ] harmonious.
Harn [harn] m (-[e]s/-e) urine; '**⚹blase** anat. f (urinary) bladder; **⚹en** v/i. (ge-, h) pass water, urinate.
Harnisch ['harniʃ] m (-es/-e) armo(u)r; in ~ geraten be up in arms (über acc. about).
'**Harnröhre** anat. f urethra.
Harpun|e [har'puːnə] f (-/-n) harpoon; **⚹ieren** [⚹u'niːrən] v/t. (no -ge-, h) harpoon.
hart [hart] 1. adj. hard; fig. a. harsh; heavy, severe; 2. adv. hard; ~ arbeiten work hard.
Härte ['hɛrtə] f (-/-n) hardness; fig. a. hardship; severity; **⚹n** (ge-, h) 1. v/t. harden (metal); temper (steel); case-harden (iron, steel); 2. v/i. harden, become or grow hard; steel: temper.
'**Hart|geld** n coin(s pl.), specie; '**⚹gummi** m hard rubber; † ebon-

ite, vulcanite; '2**herzig** *adj.* hard-hearted; 2**köpfig** *adj.* ['ˌkœpfiç] stubborn, headstrong; 2**näckig** *adj.* ['ˌnɛkiç] *p.* obstinate, obdurate; *effort:* dogged, tenacious; *ailment:* refractory.

Harz [haːrts] *n* (-es/-e) resin; ♪ rosin; *mot.* gum; '2**ig** *adj.* resinous.

Hasardspiel [ha'zart-] *n* game of chance; *fig.* gamble.

haschen ['haʃən] (ge-, h) 1. *v/t.* catch (hold of), snatch; *sich* ~ *children:* play tag; 2. *v/i.:* ~ *nach* snatch at; *fig.* strain after (*effect*), fish for (*compliments*).

Hase ['haːzə] *m* (-n/-n) *zo.* hare; *ein alter* ~ an old hand, an old-timer.

Haselnuß ['haːzəlnus] *f* hazel-nut.

'**Hasen**|**braten** *m* roast hare; '~**fuß** F *fig.* m coward, F funk; '~**panier** F *n: das* ~ *ergreifen* take to one's heels; '~**scharte** ♀ *f* hare-lip.

Haß [has] *m* (*Hasses/no pl.*) hatred.

'**hassen** *v/t.* (ge-, h) hate.

häßlich *adj.* ['hɛsliç] ugly; *fig. a.* nasty, unpleasant.

Hast [hast] *f* (-/*no pl.*) hurry, haste; rush; *in wilder* ~ in frantic haste; '2**en** *v/i.* (ge-, sein) hurry, hasten; rush; '2**ig** *adj.* hasty, hurried.

hätscheln ['hɛːtʃəln] *v/t.* (ge-, h) caress, fondle, pet; pamper, coddle.

hatte ['hatə] *pret.* of haben.

Haube ['haubə] *f* (-/-n) bonnet (*a.* ⊕, *mot.*); cap; *orn.* crest, tuft; *mot. Am. a.* hood.   [howitzer.]

Haubitze ['hau'bitsə] *f* (-/-n) ×]

Hauch [haux] *m* (-[e]s/⹁-e) breath; *fig.:* waft, whiff (*of perfume, etc.*); touch, tinge (*of irony, etc.*); '2**en** (ge-, h) 1. *v/i.* breathe; 2. *v/t.* breathe, whisper; *gr.* aspirate.

Haue ['hauə] *f* (-/-n) ⚒ hoe, mattock; pick; F hiding, spanking; '2**n** (*irr.*, ge-, h) 1. *v/t.* hew (*coal, stone*); cut up (*meat*); chop (*wood*); cut (*hole, steps, etc.*); beat (*child*); *sich* ~ (have a) fight; 2. *v/i.:* ~ *nach* cut at, strike out at.

Haufen ['haufən] *m* (-s/-) heap, pile (*both* F *a. fig.*); *fig.* crowd.

häufen ['hɔyfən] *v/t.* (ge-, h) heap (up), pile (up); accumulate; *sich* ~ pile up, accumulate; *fig.* become more frequent, increase.

'**häufig** *adj.* frequent; '2**keit** *f* (-/*no pl.*) frequency.

'**Häufung** *fig. f* (-/-en) increase, *fig.* accumulation.

Haupt [haupt] *n* (-[e]s/⹁er) head; *fig.* chief, head, leader; '~**altar** *m* high altar; '~**anschluß** *teleph.* m subscriber's main station; '~**bahnhof** ⊞ *m* main *or* central station; '~**beruf** *m* full-time occupation; '~**buch** ✝ *n* ledger; '~**darsteller** *thea.* m leading actor; '~**fach** *univ.* n main *or* principal subject, *Am. a.* major; '~**film** *m* feature (film); '~**geschäft** *n* main transaction; main shop; '~**geschäftsstelle** *f* head *or* central office; '~**gewinn** *m* first prize; '~**grund** *m* main reason; '~**handelsartikel** ✝ ['haupthan-dəls?-] *m* staple.   [chief(tain).]

Häuptling ['hɔyptliŋ] *m* (-s/-e)]

'**Haupt**|**linie** ⊞ *f* main *or* trunk line; '~**mann** × *m* (-[e]s/*Haupt-leute*) captain; '~**merkmal** *n* characteristic feature; '~**postamt** *n* general post office, *Am.* main post office; '~**punkt** *m* main *or* cardinal point; '~**quartier** *n* headquarters *sg. or pl.*; '~**rolle** *thea. f* lead(ing part); '~**sache** *f* main thing *or* point; '2**sächlich** *adj.* main, chief, principal; '~**satz** *gr.* m main clause; '~**stadt** *f* capital; '2**städtisch** *adj.* metropolitan; '~**straße** *f* main street; major road; '~**treffer** *m* first prize, jackpot; '~**verkehrs-straße** *f* main road; arterial road; '~**verkehrsstunden** *f/pl.*, '~**verkehrszeit** *f* rush hour(s *pl.*), peak hour(s *pl.*); '~**versammlung** *f* general meeting; '~**wort** *gr.* n (-[e]s/⹁er) substantive, noun.

Haus [haus] *n* (-es/⹁er) house; building; home, family, household; dynasty; ✝ (business) house, firm; *parl.* House; *nach* ~*e* home; *zu* ~*e* at home, F in; '~**angestellte** *f* (-n/-n) (house-)maid; '~**apotheke** *f* (household) medicine-chest; '~**arbeit** *f* housework; '~**arrest** *m* house arrest; '~**arzt** *m* family doctor; '~**aufgaben** *f/pl.* homework, F prep; '2**backen** *fig. adj.* homely; '~**bar** *f* cocktail cabinet; '~**bedarf** *m* household requirements *pl.*; '~**besitzer** *m* house-owner; '~**diener** *m* (man-)servant; *hotel:* porter, boots *sg.*

hausen ['hauzən] *v/i.* (ge-, h) live; play *or* work havoc (*in a place*).

'**Haus|flur** m (entrance-)hall, *esp. Am.* hallway; '**~frau** f housewife; '**~halt** m household; ²**halten** v/i. (*irr.* halten, *sep.*, -ge-, h) be economical (*mit* with), economize (on); **~hälterin** ['~heltərin] f (-/-nen) housekeeper; '**~halt(s)plan** *parl.* m budget; '**~haltung** f housekeeping; household, family; '**~halt-waren** f/pl. household articles *pl.*; '**~herr** m master of the family; landlord.

hausier|en [hau'zi:rən] v/i. (*no* -ge-, h) hawk, peddle (*mit* et. s.th.); ~ **gehen** be a hawker *or* pedlar; **2er** m (-s/-) hawker, pedlar.

'**Haus|kleid** n house dress; '**~knecht** m boots; '**~lehrer** m private tutor.

häuslich adj. ['hɔʏsliç] domestic; domesticated; '**2keit** f (-/*no* pl.) domesticity; family life; home.

'**Haus|mädchen** n (house-)maid; '**~mannskost** f plain fare; '**~meister** m caretaker; janitor; '**~mittel** n popular medicine; '**~ordnung** f rules *pl.* of the house; '**~rat** m household effects *pl.*; '**~recht** n domestic authority; '**~sammlung** f house-to-house collection; '**~schlüssel** m latchkey; front-door key; '**~schuh** m slipper.

Hausse ✝ ['ho:s(ə)] f (-/-n) rise, boom; '**~ier** [hos'je:] m (-s/-s) speculator for a rise, bull.

'**Haus|stand** m household; e-n ~ **gründen** set up house; '**~suchung** ⚖ f house search, domiciliary visit, *Am. a.* house check; '**~tier** n domestic animal; '**~tür** f front door; '**~verwalter** m steward; '**~wirt** m landlord; '**~wirtin** f (-/-nen) landlady.

Haut [haut] f (-/-e) skin; hide; film; *bis auf die* ~ to the skin; *aus der* ~ *fahren* jump out of one's skin; F *e-e ehrliche* ~ an honest soul; '**~abschürfung** ⚕ f skin abrasion; '**~arzt** m dermatologist; '**~ausschlag** ⚕ m rash; '2**eng** adj. *garment*: skin-tight; '**~farbe** f complexion.

Hautgout [o'gu] m (-s/*no* pl.) high taste.

häutig adj. ['hɔʏtiç] membranous, covered with skin.

'**Haut|krankheit** f skin disease; '**~pflege** f care of the skin; '**~**

schere f (e-e a pair of) cuticle scissors *pl.* [age.\]

Havarie ⚓ [hava'ri:] f (-/-n) aver-

H-Bombe ☢ ['ha:~] f H-bomb.

he int. [he:] hi!, hi there!; I say!

Hebamme ['he:p°amə] f midwife.

'**Hebe|baum** ['he:bə-] m lever (*for raising heavy objects*); '**~bühne** mot. f lifting ramp; '**~eisen** n crowbar; '**~kran** m lifting crane.

Hebel ⊕ ['he:bəl] m (-s/-) lever; '**~arm** m lever arm.

heben ['he:bən] v/t. (*irr.*, ge-, h) lift (*a.* sports), raise (*a. fig.*); heave (*heavy load*); hoist; recover (*treasure*); raise (*sunken ship*); *fig.* promote, improve, increase; *sich* ~ rise, go up.

Hecht ichth. [heçt] m (-[e]s/-e) pike.

Heck [hek] n (-[e]s/-e, -s) ⚓ stern; mot. rear; ✈ tail.

Hecke ['hekə] f (-/-n) ↗ hedge; zo. brood, hatch; '2n v/t. and v/i. (ge-, h) breed, hatch; '**~nrose** ↗ f dog-rose. [hallo!\]

heda int. ['he:da:] hi (there)!,⌐

Heer [he:r] n (-[e]s/-e) ✗ army; *fig. a.* host; '**~esdienst** m military service; '**~esmacht** f military force(s *pl.*); '**~eszug** m military expedition; '**~führer** m general; '**~lager** n (army) camp; '**~schar** f army, host; '**~straße** f military road; highway; '**~zug** m s. Heereszug.

Hefe ['he:fə] f (-/-n) yeast; barm.

Heft [heft] n (-[e]s/-e) dagger, etc.: haft; *knife*: handle; *fig.* reins *pl.*; exercise book; *periodical*, etc.: issue, number.

'**heft|en** v/t. (ge-, h) fasten, fix (*an acc.* on to); affix, attach (to); pin on (to); tack, baste (*seam*, etc.); stitch, sew (*book*); '2**faden** m basting thread.

'**heftig** adj. *storm*, *anger*, *quarrel*, etc.: violent, fierce; *rain*, etc.: heavy; *pain*, etc.: severe; *speech*, *desire*, etc.: vehement, passionate; *p.* irascible; '2**keit** f (-/~ -en) violence, fierceness; severity; vehemence; irascibility.

'**Heft|klammer** f paper-clip; '**~pflaster** n sticking plaster.

hegen ['he:gən] v/t. (ge-, h) preserve (*game*); nurse, tend (*plants*); have, entertain (*feelings*); harbo(u)r (*fears*, *suspicions*, etc.).

Hehler ɪ̃ɫ̃ ['he:lər] *m* (-s/-) receiver (of stolen goods); **~ei** [~'raɪ] *f* (-/-en) receiving (of stolen goods).

Heide ['haɪdə] **1.** *m* (-n/-n) heathen; **2.** *f* (-/-n) heath(-land); = '**~kraut** ♀ *n* heather; '**~land** *n* heath(-land).

'**Heiden|geld** F *n* pots *pl.* of money; '**~lärm** F *m* hullabaloo; '**~paß** F *m* capital fun; '**~tum** *n* (-s/*no pl.*) heathenism. [(-ish).\]

heidnisch *adj.* ['haɪdnɪʃ] heathen⌋

heikel *adj.* ['haɪkəl] *p.* fastidious, particular; *problem, etc.*: delicate, awkward.

heil [haɪl] **1.** *adj. p.* safe, unhurt; whole, sound; **2.** ♀ *n* (-[e]s/*no pl.*) welfare, benefit; *eccl.* salvation; **3.** *int.* hail!

Heiland *eccl.* ['haɪlant] *m* (-[e]s/-e) Saviour, Redeemer.

'**Heil|anstalt** *f* sanatorium, *Am. a.* sanitarium; '**~bad** *n* medicinal bath; spa; '♀**bar** *adj.* curable; '♀**en** (ge-) **1.** *v/t.* (h) cure, heal; ~ *von* cure *s.o.* of; **2.** *v/i.* (sein) heal (up); '**~gehilfe** *m* male nurse.

heilig *adj.* ['haɪlɪç] holy; sacred; solemn; *der* **Heilige Abend** Christmas Eve; ♀**e** ['~gə] *m, f* (-n/-n) saint; '**~en** ['~gən] *v/t.* (ge-) *h*) sanctify (*a. fig.*), hallow; '**~keit** *f* (-/*no pl.*) holiness, sacredness, sanctity; '**~sprechen** *v/t.* (*irr.* sprechen, *sep.*, -ge-, *h*) canonize; '♀**sprechung** *f* (-/-en) canonization; '♀**tum** *n* (-[e]s/⸚er) sanctuary; sacred relic; ♀**ung** ['~gʊŋ] *f* (-/-en) sanctification (*a. fig.*), hallowing.

'**Heil|kraft** *f* healing *or* curative power; '♀**kräftig** *adj.* healing, curative; '**~kunde** *f* medical science; '♀**los** *fig. adj.* confusion: utter, great; '**~mittel** *n* remedy, medicament; '**~praktiker** *m* non-medical practitioner; '**~quelle** *f* medicinal spring; '♀**sam** *adj.* curative; *fig.* salutary. [Army.\]

Heilsarmee ['haɪls⸚] *f* Salvation⌋

'**Heil|ung** *f* (-/-en) cure, healing, successful treatment; '**~verfahren** *n* therapy.

heim [haɪm] **1.** *adv.* home; **2.** ♀ *n* (-[e]s/-e) home; hostel; '♀**arbeit** *f* homework, outwork.

Heimat ['haɪma:t] *f* (-/⸚̃ -en) home; own country; native land; '**~land** *n* own country, native land; '♀**lich** *adj.* native; '♀**los** *adj.* homeless;

'**~ort** *m* home town *or* village; '**~vertriebene** *m* expellee.

Heimchen *zo.* ['haɪmçən] *n* (-s/-) cricket.

'**heimisch** *adj.* trade, industry, *etc.*: home, local, domestic; ♀, *zo., etc.*: native, indigenous; ~ *werden* settle down; become established; *sich* ~ *fühlen* feel at home.

Heim|kehr ['haɪmke:r] *f* (-/*no pl.*) return (home), homecoming; '♀**kehren** *v/i.* (*sep.*, -ge-, sein), '♀**kommen** *v/i.* (*irr.* kommen, *sep.*, -ge-, sein) return home.

'**heimlich** *adj.* plan, feeling, *etc.*: secret; *meeting, organization, etc.*: clandestine; *glance, movement, etc.*: stealthy, furtive.

'**Heim|reise** *f* homeward journey; '♀**suchen** *v/t.* (*sep.*, -ge-, *h*) *disaster, etc.*: afflict, strike; *disease*: haunt; *God*: visit, punish; '**~tücke** *f* underhand malice, treachery; '♀**tückisch** *adj.* malicious, treacherous, insidious; ♀**wärts** *adv.* ['~vɛrts] homeward(s); '**~weg** *m* way home; '**~weh** *n* homesickness, nostalgia; ~ *haben* be homesick.

Heirat ['haɪra:t] *f* (-/-en) marriage; '♀**en** (ge-, *h*) **1.** *v/t.* marry; **2.** *v/i.* marry, get married.

'**Heirats|antrag** *m* offer *or* proposal of marriage; '♀**fähig** *adj.* marriageable; '**~kandidat** *m* possible marriage partner; '**~schwindler** *m* marriage impostor; '**~vermittler** *m* matrimonial agent.

heiser *adj.* ['haɪzər] hoarse; husky; '♀**keit** *f* (-/*no pl.*) hoarseness; huskiness.

heiß *adj.* [haɪs] hot; *fig. a.* passionate, ardent; *mir ist* ~ I am *or* feel hot.

heißen ['haɪsən] (*irr.*, ge-, *h*) **1.** *v/t.*: *e-n Lügner* ~ call *s.o.* a liar; *willkommen* ~ welcome; **2.** *v/i.* be called; mean; *wie* ~ *Sie?* what is your name?; *was heißt das auf englisch?* what's that in English?

heiter *adj.* ['haɪtər] day, weather: bright; *sky*: bright, clear; *p., etc.*: cheerful, gay; serene; '♀**keit** *f* (-/*no pl.*) brightness; cheerfulness, gaiety; serenity.

heiz|en ['haɪtsən] (ge-, *h*) **1.** *v/t.* heat (*room, etc.*); light (*stove*); fire (*boiler*); **2.** *v/i.* stove, *etc.*: give out heat; turn on the heating; *mit*

Kohlen ~ burn coal; '2er *m* (-s/-) stoker, fireman; '2kissen *n* electric heating pad; '2körper *m* central heating: radiator; *↯* heating element; '2material *n* fuel; '2ung *f* (-/-en) heating.

Held [hɛlt] *m* (-en/-en) hero.

'**Helden|gedicht** *n* epic (poem); '2haft *adj.* heroic, valiant; '.mut *m* heroism, valo(u)r; '2mütig *adj.* ['.my:tiç] heroic; '.tat *f* heroic or valiant deed; '.tod *m* hero's death; '.tum *n* (-[e]s/*no pl.*) heroism.

helfen ['hɛlfən] *v/i.* (*dat.*) (*irr.*, *ge-*, *h*) help, assist, aid; ~ gegen be good for; *sich nicht zu ~ wissen* be helpless.

'**Helfer** *m* (-s/-) helper, assistant; '.shelfer *m* accomplice.

hell *adj.* [hɛl] sound, voice, light, etc.: clear; light, flame, etc.: bright; hair: fair; colour: light; ale: pale; '.blau *adj.* light-blue; '.blond *adj.* very fair; '.hörig *adj.* p. quick of hearing; *fig.* perceptive; △ poorly sound-proofed; '2seher *m* clairvoyant.

Helm [hɛlm] *m* ([-e]s/-e) ⚔ helmet; △ dome, cupola; ⚓ helm; '.busch *m* plume.

Hemd [hɛmt] *n* (-[e]s/-en) shirt; vest; '.bluse *f* shirt-blouse, *Am.* shirtwaist. [hemisphere.]

Hemisphäre [he:mi'sfɛ:rə] *f* (-/-n)}

hemm|en ['hɛmən] *v/t.* (*ge-*, *h*) check, stop (*movement*, etc.); stem (*stream*, *flow of liquid*); hamper (*free movement*, *activity*); be a hindrance to; *psych.*: *gehemmt sein* be inhibited; '2nis *n* (-ses/-se) hindrance, impediment; '2schuh *m* slipper; *fig.* hindrance, F drag (*für acc.* on); '2ung *f* (-/-en) stoppage, check; *psych.*: inhibition.

Hengst *zo.* [hɛŋst] *m* (-es/-e) stallion.

Henkel ['hɛŋkəl] *m* (-s/-) handle, ear.

Henker ['hɛŋkər] *m* (-s/-) hangman, executioner; F: *zum ~!* hang it (all)!

Henne *zo.* ['hɛnə] *f* (-/-n) hen.

her *adv.* [he:r] here; hither; *es ist schon ein Jahr ~, daß ... or seit ...* it is a year since ...; *wie lange ist es ~, seit ...* how long is it since ...; *hinter* (*dat.*) ~ *sein* be after; ~ *damit!* out with it!

herab *adv.* [hɛ'rap] down, downward; **.lassen** *v/t.* (*irr. lassen*, *sep.*, *-ge-*, *h*) let down, lower; *fig. sich ~* condescend; **.lassend** *adj.* condescending; **.setzen** *v/t.* (*sep.*, *-ge-*, *h*) take down; *fig.* belittle, disparage *s.o.*; *↯* reduce, lower, cut (*price*, etc.); 2setzung *fig. f* (-/-en) reduction; disparagement; **.steigen** *v/i.* (*irr. steigen*, *sep.*, *-ge-*, *sein*) climb down, descend; **.würdigen** *v/t.* (*sep.*, *-ge-*, *h*) degrade, belittle, abase.

heran *adv.* [hɛ'ran] close, near; up; *nur ~!* come on!; **.bilden** *v/t.* (*sep.*, *-ge-*, *h*) train, educate (*zu as s.th.*, to be *s.th.*); **.kommen** *v/i.* (*irr. kommen*, *sep.*, *-ge-*, *sein*) come or draw near; approach; ~ *an* (*acc.*) come up to *s.o.*; measure up to; **.wachsen** *v/i.* (*irr. wachsen*, *sep.*, *-ge-*, *sein*) grow (up) (*zu into*).

herauf *adv.* [hɛ'rauf] up(wards), up here; upstairs; **.beschwören** *v/t.* (*irr. schwören*, *sep.*, *no -ge-*, *h*) evoke, call up, conjure up (*spirit*, etc.); *fig. a.* bring about, provoke, give rise to (*war*, etc.); **.steigen** *v/i.* (*irr. steigen*, *sep.*, *-ge-*, *sein*) climb up (here), ascend; **.ziehen** (*irr. ziehen*, *sep.*, *-ge-*, *h*) **1.** *v/t.* (*h*) pull or hitch up (*trousers*, etc.); **2.** *v/i.* (*sein*) cloud, etc.: come up.

heraus *adv.* [hɛ'raus] out, out here; *zum Fenster ~* out of the window; *~ mit der Sprache!* speak out!; **.bekommen** *v/t.* (*irr. kommen*, *no -ge-*, *h*) get out; get (*money*) back; *fig.* find out; **.bringen** *v/t.* (*irr. bringen*, *sep.*, *-ge-*, *h*) bring or get out; *thea.* stage; **.finden** *v/t.* (*irr. finden*, *sep.*, *-ge-*, *h*) find out; *fig. a.* discover; 2forderer *m* (-s/-) challenger; **.fordern** *v/t.* (*sep.*, *-ge-*, *h*) challenge (*to a fight*); provoke; 2forderung *f* (-/-en) challenge; provocation; **.geben** (*irr. geben*, *sep.*, *-ge-*, *h*) **1.** *v/t.* surrender; hand over; restore; edit (*periodical*, etc.); publish (*book*, etc.); issue (*regulations*, etc.); **2.** *v/i.* give change (*auf acc.* for); 2geber *m* (-s/-) editor; publisher; **.kommen** *v/i.* (*irr. kommen*, *sep.*, *-ge-*, *sein*) come out; *fig. a.* appear, be published; **.nehmen** *v/t.* (*irr. nehmen*, *sep.*, *-ge-*, *h*) take out; *sich viel ~* take liberties; **.putzen** *v/t.* (*sep.*,

-ge-, h) dress up; sich ~ dress (o.s.) up; **~reden** v/refl. (sep., -ge-, h) talk one's way out; **~stellen** v/t. (sep., -ge-, h) put out; fig. emphasize, set forth; sich ~ emerge, turn out; **~strecken** v/t. (sep., -ge-, h) stretch out; put out; **~streichen** v/t. (irr. streichen, sep., -ge-, h) cross out, delete (word, etc.); fig. extol, praise; **~winden** fig. v/refl. (irr. winden, sep., -ge-, h) extricate o.s. (aus from).

herb adj. [herp] fruit, flavour, etc.: tart; wine, etc.: dry; features, etc.: austere; criticism, etc.: harsh; disappointment, etc.: bitter.

herbei adv. [her'baı] here; ~! come here!; **~eilen** [her'baı⁹-] v/i. (sep., -ge-, sein) come hurrying; **~führen** fig. v/t. (sep., -ge-, h) cause, bring about, give rise to; **~schaffen** v/t. (sep., -ge-, h) bring along; procure.

Herberge ['hɛrbɛrgə] f (-/-n) shelter, lodging; inn.

'Herbheit f (-/no pl.) tartness; dryness; fig.: austerity; harshness, bitterness.

Herbst [hɛrpst] m (-[e]s/-e) autumn, Am. a. fall.

Herd [heːrt] m (-[e]s/-e) hearth, fireplace; stove; fig. seat, focus.

Herde ['heːrdə] f (-/-n) herd (of cattle, pigs, etc.)(contp. a. fig.); flock (of sheep, geese, etc.).

herein adv. [hɛ'raın] in (here); ~! come in!; **~brechen** fig. v/i. (irr. brechen, sep., -ge-, sein) night: fall; ~ über (acc.) misfortune, etc.: befall; **~fallen** fig. v/i. (irr. fallen, sep., -ge-, sein) be taken in.

'her|fallen v/i. (irr. fallen, sep., -ge-, sein): ~ über (acc.) attack (a. fig.), fall upon; F fig. pull to pieces; **'2-gang** m course of events, details pl.; **~geben** v/t. (irr. geben, sep., -ge-, h) give up, part with, return; yield; sich ~ zu lend o.s. to; **'~ge-bracht** fig. adj. traditional; customary; **'~halten** v/t. (irr. halten, sep., -ge-, h) 1. v/t. hold out; 2. v/i.: ~ müssen be the one to pay or suffer (für for).

Hering ichth. ['heːrɪŋ] m (-s/-e) herring.

'her|kommen v/i. (irr. kommen, sep., -ge-, sein) come or get here; come or draw near; ~ von come from; fig. a. be due to, be caused by; **~kömmlich** adj. ['~kœmlɪç]

traditional; customary; **2kunft** ['~kunft] f (-/no pl.) origin; birth, descent; **'~leiten** v/t. (sep., -ge-, h) lead here; fig. derive (von from); **'2leitung** fig. f derivation.

Herold ['heːrɔlt] m (-[e]s/-e) herald.

Herr [hɛr] m (-n, ⚔-en/-en) lord, master; eccl. the Lord; gentleman; ~ Maier Mr Maier; mein ~ Sir; m-e ~en gentlemen; ~ der Situation master of the situation.

'Herren|bekleidung f men's clothing; **'~einzel** n tennis: men's singles pl.; **'~haus** n manor-house; **2-los** adj. ['~loːs] ownerless; **'~reiter** m sports: gentleman-jockey; **'~schneider** m men's tailor; **'~zimmer** n study; smoking-room.

herrichten ['heːr-] v/t. (sep., -ge-, h) arrange, prepare.

'herrisch adj. imperious, overbearing; voice, etc.: commanding, peremptory.

'herrlich adj. excellent, glorious, magnificent, splendid; **'2keit** f (-/-en) glory, splendo(u)r.

Herrschaft f (-/-en) rule, dominion (über acc. of); fig. mastery; master and mistress; m-e ~en ladies and gentlemen!; **'2lich** adj. belonging to a master or landlord; fig. high-class, elegant.

herrsch|en ['hɛrʃən] v/i. (ge-, h) rule (über acc. over); monarch: reign (over); govern; fig. prevail, be; **'2er** m (-s/-) ruler; sovereign, monarch; **'2sucht** f thirst for power; **'~süchtig** adj. thirsting for power; imperious.

'her|rühren v/i. (sep., -ge-, h): ~ von come from, originate with; **'~sagen** v/t. (sep., -ge-, h) recite; say (prayer); **'~stammen** v/i. (sep., -ge-, h): ~ von or aus be descended from; come from; be derived from; **'~stellen** v/t. (sep., -ge-, h) place here; ✝ make, manufacture, produce; **'2stellung** f (-/-en) manufacture, production.

herüber adv. [hɛ'ryːbər] over (here), across.

herum adv. [hɛ'rum] (a)round; about; **~führen** v/t. (sep., -ge-, h) show (a)round; ~ in (dat.) show over; **~lungern** v/i. (sep., -ge-, h) loaf or loiter or hang about; **~reichen** v/t. (sep., -ge-, h) pass or hand round; **~sprechen** v/refl. (irr.

sprechen, *sep.*, -ge-, h) get about, spread; **~treiben** *v/refl.* (*irr.* treiben, *sep.*, -ge-, h) F gad *or* knock about.

herunter *adv.* [hɛˈrʊntər] down (here); downstairs; *von oben ~* down from above; **~bringen** *v/t.* (*irr.* bringen, *sep.*, -ge-, h) bring down; *fig. a.* lower, reduce; **~kommen** *v/i.* (*irr.* kommen, *sep.*, -ge-, sein) come down(stairs); *fig.:* come down in the world; deteriorate; **~machen** *v/t.* (*sep.*, -ge-, h) take down; turn (collar, *etc.*) down; *fig.* give *s.o.* a dressing-down; *fig.:* pull to pieces; **~reißen** *v/t.* (*irr.* reißen, *sep.*, -ge-, h) pull *or* tear down; *fig.* pull to pieces; **~sein** F *fig. v/i.* (*irr.* sein, *sep.*, -ge-, sein) be low in health; **~wirtschaften** *v/t.* (*sep.*, -ge-, h) run down.

hervor *adv.* [hɛrˈfoːr] forth, out; **~bringen** *v/t.* (*irr.* bringen, *sep.*, -ge-, h) bring out, produce (*a. fig.*); yield (fruit); *fig.* utter (word); **~gehen** *v/i.* (*irr.* gehen, *sep.*, -ge-, sein) *p.* come (aus from); *fig.* come off (victorious) (from); *fact, etc.:* emerge (from); be clear *or* apparent (from); **~heben** *fig. v/t.* (*irr.* heben, *sep.*, -ge-, h) stress, emphasize; give prominence to; **~holen** *v/t.* (*sep.*, -ge-, h) produce; **~ragen** *v/i.* (*sep.*, -ge-, h) project (über *acc.* over); *fig.* tower (above); **~ragend** *adj.* projecting, prominent; *fig.* outstanding, excellent; **~rufen** *v/t.* (*irr.* rufen, *sep.*, -ge-, h) *thea.* call for; *fig.* arouse, evoke; **~stechend** *fig. adj.* outstanding; striking; conspicuous.

Herz [hɛrts] *n* (-ens/-en) *anat.* heart (*a. fig.*); *cards:* hearts *pl.*; *fig.* courage, spirit; *sich ein ~ fassen* take heart; *mit ganzem ~en* whole-heartedly; *sich et. zu ~en nehmen* take s.th. to heart; *es nicht übers ~ bringen zu inf.* not to have the heart to *inf.*; **~anfall** *m* heart attack.

Herzens|brecher *m* (-s/-) lady-killer; **~lust** *f:* *nach ~* to one's heart's content; **~wunsch** *m* heart's desire.

herz|ergreifend *fig. adj.* heart-moving; **2fehler** ⚕ *m* cardiac defect; **2gegend** *anat. f* cardiac region; **~haft** *adj.* hearty, good; **~ig** *adj.* lovely, *Am. a.* cute; **2infarkt** ⚕ *m* (-[e]s/-e) [ˈ~ɪnfarkt] *m* (-[e]s/-e) cardiac

infarction; **2klopfen** ⚕ *n* (-s/*no pl.*) palpitation; **~krank** *adj.* having heart trouble; **~lich** 1. *adj.* heart-felt; cordial, hearty; *~es Beileid* sincere sympathy; 2. *adv.:* *~ gern* with pleasure; **~los** *adj.* heartless; unfeeling.

Herzog [ˈhɛrtsoːk] *m* (-[e]s/~e, -e) duke; **~in** *f* (-/-nen) duchess; **~tum** *n* (-[e]s/~er) dukedom, duchy.

Herz|schlag *m* heartbeat; ⚕ heart failure; **~schwäche** ⚕ *f* cardiac insufficiency; **~verpflanzung** *f* heart transplant; **2zerreißend** *adj.* heart-rending.

Hetz|e [ˈhɛtsə] *f* (-/-n) hurry, rush; instigation (gegen *acc.* against); baiting (of); **2en** (ge-) 1. *v/t.* (h) course (hare); bait (bear, *etc.*); hound: hunt, chase (animal); *fig.* hurry, rush; *sich ~* hurry, rush; *e-n Hund auf j-n ~* set a dog at s.o.; 2. *v/i.* (h) *fig.:* cause discord; agitate (gegen against); 3. *fig. v/i.* (sein) hurry, rush; **~er** *fig. m* (-s/-) instigator; agitator; **2erisch** *adj.* virulent, inflammatory; **~jagd** *f* hunt(ing); *fig.:* virulent campaign; rush, hurry; **~presse** *f* yellow press.

Heu [hɔy] *n* (-[e]s/*no pl.*) hay; **~boden** *m* hayloft.

Heuchel|ei [hɔyçəˈlaɪ] *f* (-/-en) hypocrisy; **2n** (ge-, h) 1. *v/t.* simulate, feign, affect; 2. *v/i.* feign, dissemble; play the hypocrite.

Heuchler *m* (-s/-) hypocrite; **2isch** *adj.* hypocritical.

heuer [ˈhɔyər] 1. *adv.* this year; 2. ⚓ *f* (-/-en) pay, wages *pl.*; **~n** *v/t.* (ge-, h) hire; ⚓ engage, sign on (crew), charter (ship).

heulen [ˈhɔylən] *v/i.* (ge-, h) wind, *etc.:* howl; storm, wind, *etc.:* roar; siren: wail; F *p.* howl, cry.

Heu|schnupfen ⚕ *m* hay-fever; **~schrecke** *zo.* [ˈ~ʃrɛkə] *f* (-/-n) grasshopper, locust.

heut|e *adv.* [ˈhɔytə] today; *~ abend* this evening, tonight; *~ früh*, *~ morgen* this morning; *~ in acht Tagen* today *or* this day week; *~ vor acht Tagen* a week ago today; **~ig** *adj.* this day's, today's; present; **~zutage** *adv.* [ˈhɔyttsutaˈɡə] nowadays, these days.

Hexe [ˈhɛksə] *f* (-/-n) witch, sorceress; *fig.:* hell-cat; hag; **2n** *v/i.* (ge-

h) practice witchcraft; F *fig.* work miracles; '**~nkessel** *fig. m* inferno; '**~nmeister** *m* wizard, sorcerer; '**~nschuß** ✗ *m* lumbago; **~rei** [~'raɪ] *f* (-/-en) witchcraft, sorcery, magic.

Hieb [hi:p] **1.** *m* (-[e]s/-e) blow, stroke; lash, cut (*of whip, etc.*); *a.* punch (*with fist*)/ *fenc.* cut; **~e** *pl.* hiding, thrashing; **2.** ♀ *pret. of* hauen.

hielt [hi:lt] *pret. of* halten.

hier adv. [hi:r] here; in this place; **~!** present!; **~ entlang!** this way!

hier|an adv. ['hi:'ran, *when emphatic* 'hi:ran] at or by or in or on or to it or this; **~auf** adv. ['hi:'rauf, *when emphatic* 'hi:rauf] on it or this; after this or that, then; **~aus** adv. ['hi:'raus, *when emphatic* 'hi:raus] from or out of it or this; **~bei** adv. ['hi:r'baɪ, *when emphatic* 'hi:rbaɪ] here; in this case, in connection with this; **~durch** adv. ['hi:r'durç, *when emphatic* 'hi:rdurç] through here; by this, hereby; **~für** adv. ['hi:r'fy:r, *when emphatic* 'hi:rfy:r] for it or this; **~her** adv. ['hi:r'he:r, *when emphatic* 'hi:rhe:r] here, hither; *bis* **~** as far as here; **~in** adv. ['hi:'rin, *when emphatic* 'hi:rin] in it or this; in here; **~mit** adv. ['hi:r'mit, *when emphatic* 'hi:rmit] with it or this, herewith; **~nach** adv. ['hi:r'na:x, *when emphatic* 'hi:rna:x] after it or this; according to this; **~über** adv. ['hi:r'ry:bər, *when emphatic* 'hi:ry:bər] over it or this; over here; on this (subject); **~unter** adv. ['hi:r'runtər, *when emphatic* 'hi:runtər] under it or this; among these; by this or that; **~von** adv. ['hi:r'fɔn, *when emphatic* 'hi:rfɔn] of or from it or this; **~zu** adv. ['hi:r'tsu:, *when emphatic* 'hi:rtsu:] with it or this; (in addition) to this.

hiesig adj. ['hi:ziç] of or in this place or town, local.

hieß [hi:s] *pret. of* heißen.

Hilfe ['hilfə] *f* (-/-n) help; aid, assistance; succour; relief (*für* to); **~!** help!; *mit* **~** *von* with the help or aid of; '**~ruf** *m* shout or cry for help.

'**hilf|los** adj. helpless; '**~reich** adj. helpful.

'**Hilfs|aktion** *f* relief measures *pl.*;

'**~arbeiter** *m* unskilled worker or labo(u)rer; '♀**bedürftig** adj. needy, indigent; '**~lehrer** *m* assistant teacher; '**~mittel** *n* aid; device; remedy; expedient; '**~motor** *m*: *Fahrrad mit* **~** motor-assisted bicycle; '**~quelle** *f* resource; '**~schule** *f* elementary school for backward children; '**~werk** *n* relief organization.

Himbeere ♀ ['himbe:rə] *f* rasp-[berry.|

Himmel ['himəl] *m* (-s/-) sky, heavens *pl.*; *eccl.,fig.* heaven; '**~bett** *n* tester-bed; '♀**blau** adj. sky-blue; '**~fahrt** *eccl. f* ascension (of Christ); Ascension-day; '♀**schreiend** adj. crying.

'**Himmels|gegend** *f* region of the sky; cardinal point; '**~körper** *m* celestial body; '**~richtung** *f* point of the compass, cardinal point; direction; '**~strich** *m* region, climate zone.

'**himmlisch** adj. celestial, heavenly.

hin adv. [hin] there; gone; lost; **~** *und her* to and fro, *Am.* back and forth; **~** *und wieder* now and again or then; **~** *und zurück* there and back.

hinab adv. [hi'nap] down; **~steigen** *v/i.* (*irr.* steigen, *sep.*, *-ge-*, *sein*) climb down, descend.

hinarbeiten ['hin?-] *v/i.* (*sep.*, *-ge-*, *h*): **~** *auf* (*acc.*) work for or towards.

hinauf adv. [hi'nauf] up (there); upstairs; **~gehen** *v/i.* (*irr.* gehen, *sep.*, *-ge-*, *sein*) go up(stairs); *prices, wages, etc.*: go up, rise; **~steigen** *v/i.* (*irr.* steigen, *sep.*, *-ge-*, *sein*) climb up, ascend.

hinaus adv. [hi'naus] out; **~** *mit euch!* out with you!; *auf* (*viele*) *Jahre* **~** for (many) years (to come); **~gehen** *v/i.* (*irr.* gehen, *sep.*, *-ge-*, *sein*) go or walk out; **~** *über* (*acc.*) go beyond, exceed; **~** *auf* (*acc.*) *window, etc.*: look out on, overlook; *intention, etc.*: drive or aim at; **~laufen** *v/i.* (*irr.* laufen, *sep.*, *-ge-*, *sein*) run or rush out; **~** *auf* (*acc.*) come or amount to; **~schieben** *fig. v/t.* (*irr.* schieben, *sep.*, *-ge-*, *h*) put off, postpone, defer; **~werfen** *v/t.* (*irr.* werfen, *sep.*, *-ge-*, *h*) throw out (*aus* of); turn or throw or F chuck *s.o.* out.

'**Hin|blick** *m*: *im* **~** *auf* (*acc.*) in view of, with regard to; '♀**bringen** *v/t.*

(*irr.* bringen, *sep.,* -ge-, *h*) take there; while away, pass (*time*).

hinder|lich *adj.* ['hindǝrliç] hindering, impeding; *j-m* ~ *sein* be in s.o.'s way; **'~n** *v/t.* (ge-, *h*) hinder, hamper (*bei, in dat. in*); ~ *an* (*dat.*) prevent from; **'2nis** *n* (-ses/-se) hindrance; *sports:* obstacle; *turf, etc.:* fence; **'2nisrennen** *n* obstacle-race.

hin'durch *adv.* through; all through; throughout; across.

hinein *adv.* [hi'nain] in; ~ *mit dir!* in you go!; **~gehen** *v/i.* ~ *in* (*irr.* gehen, *sep.,* -ge-, *sein*) go in; ~ *in* (*acc.*) go into; *in den Topf gehen ... hinein* the pot holds *or* takes ...

'Hin|fahrt *f* journey *or* way there; **'2fallen** *v/i.* (*irr.* fallen, *sep.,* -ge-, *sein*) fall (down); **'2fällig** *adj. p.* frail; *regulation, etc.:* invalid; ~ *machen* invalidate, render invalid.

hing [hiŋ] *pret.* of *hängen* 1.

'Hin|gabe *f* devotion (*an acc.* to); **'2geben** *v/t.* (*irr.* geben, *sep.,* -ge-, *h*) give up *or* away; *sich* ~ (*dat.*) give o.s. up; devote o.s. to; **'~gebung** *f* (-/-en) devotion; **'2gehen** *v/i.* (*irr.* gehen, *sep.,* -ge-, *sein*) go *or* walk there; go (*zu* to); *path, etc.:* lead there; lead (*zu* to *a place*); **'2halten** *v/t.* (*irr.* halten, *sep.,* -ge-, *h*) hold out (*object, etc.*); put *s.o.* off.

hinken ['hiŋkǝn] *v/i.* (ge-) 1. (*h*) limp (*auf dem rechten Fuß* with one's right leg), have a limp; 2. (*sein*) limp (along).

'hin|länglich *adj.* sufficient, adequate; **'~legen** *v/t.* (*sep.,* -ge-, *h*) lay *or* put down; *sich* ~ lie down; **'~nehmen** *v/t.* (*irr.* nehmen, *sep.,* -ge-, *h*) accept, take; put up with; **'~raffen** *v/t.* (*sep.,* -ge-, *h*) *death, etc.:* snatch *s.o.* away, carry *s.o.* off; **'~reichen** *v/t.* (*sep.,* -ge-, *h*) 1. *v/t.* reach *or* stretch *or* hold out (*dat.* to); 2. *v/i.* suffice; **'~reißen** *v/t.* (*irr.* reißen, *sep.,* -ge-, *h*) carry away; enrapture, ravish; **'~reißend** *adj.* ravishing, captivating; **'~richten** *v/t.* (*sep.,* -ge-, *h*) execute, put to death; **'2richtung** *f* execution; **'~setzen** *v/t.* (*sep.,* -ge-, *h*) set *or* put down; *sich* ~ sit down; **'2sicht** *f* regard, respect; *in* ~ *auf* (*acc.*) = **'~sichtlich** *prp.* (*gen.*) with regard to, as to, concerning; **'~stellen** *v/t.*

(*sep.,* -ge-, *h*) place; put; put down; et. ~ *als* represent s.th. as; make s.th. appear (as).

hintan|setzen [hint'an-] *v/t.* (*sep.,* -ge-, *h*) set aside; **2setzung** *f* (-/-en) setting aside; **~stellen** *v/t.* (*sep.,* -ge-, *h*) set aside; **2stellung** *f* (-/-en) setting aside.

hinten *adv.* ['hintǝn] behind, at the back; in the background; in the rear.

hinter *prp.* ['hintǝr] 1. (*dat.*), behind, *Am. a.* back of; ~ *sich lassen* outdistance; 2. (*acc.*) behind; **2bein** *n* hind leg; **2bliebenen** *pl.* [~'bli:bǝnǝn] *the* bereaved *pl.*; surviving dependants *pl.*; **~bringen** *v/t.* (*irr.* bringen, *no* -ge-, *h*): *j-m* et. ~ inform s.o. of s.th. (secretly); **~ei'nander** *adv.* one after the other; in succession; **2gedanke** *m* ulterior motive; **~gehen** *v/t.* (*irr.* gehen, *no* -ge-, *h*) deceive, F double-cross; **2'gehung** *f* (-/-en) deception; **2grund** *m* background (*a. fig.*); **2halt** *m* ambush; **~haltig** *adj.* ['~hɛltiç] insidious; underhand; **2haus** *n* back *or* rear building; **~her** *adv.* behind; afterwards; **2hof** *m* backyard; **2kopf** *m* back of the head; **~lassen** *v/t.* (*irr.* lassen, *no* -ge-, *h*) leave (behind); **2'lassenschaft** *f* (-/-en) property (left), estate; **~legen** *v/t.* (*no* -ge-, *h*) deposit, lodge (*bei* with); **2'legung** *f* (-/-en) deposit(ion); **2list** *f* deceit; craftiness; insidiousness; **'~listig** *adj.* deceitful; crafty; insidious; **2mann** *m* ✕ rear-rank man; *fig.:* † subsequent endorser; *pol.:* backer; wire-puller; instigator; **2n** *F m* (-s/-) backside, behind, bottom; **2rad** *n* rear wheel; **~rücks** *adv.* ['~ryks] from behind; *fig.* behind his, *etc.* back; **2seite** *f* back; **2teil** *n* back (part); rear (part); F *s.* Hintern; **~treiben** *v/t.* (*irr.* treiben, *no* -ge-, *h*) thwart, frustrate; **2treppe** *f* backstairs *pl.*; **2tür** *f* back door; **~ziehen** *v/t.* (*irr.* ziehen, *no* -ge-, *h*) evade (*tax, duty, etc.*); **2'ziehung** *f* evasion.

hinüber *adv.* [hi'ny:bǝr] over (there); across.

Hin- und 'Rückfahrt *f* journey there and back, *Am.* round trip.

hinunter *adv.* [hi'nuntǝr] down (there); downstairs; **~schlucken**

v/t. (sep., -ge-, h) swallow (down); *fig.* swallow.

'Hinweg¹ *m* way there *or* out.

hinweg² *adv.* [hin'vɛk] away, off; **~gehen** *v/i.* (irr. gehen, sep., -ge-sein): ~ über (acc.) go *or* walk over *or* across; *fig.* pass over, ignore; **~kommen** *v/i.* (irr. kommen, sep., -ge-, sein): ~ über (acc.) get over (a. *fig.*); **~sehen** *v/i.* (irr. sehen, sep., -ge-, h): ~ über (acc.) see *or* look over; *fig.* overlook, shut one's eyes to; **~setzen** *v/refl.* (sep., -ge-, h): sich ~ über (acc.) ignore, disregard, make light of.

Hin|weis ['hinvais] *m* -es/-e) reference (auf acc. to); hint (at); indication (of); '**~weisen** (irr. weisen, sep., -ge-, h) **1.** *v/t.*: j-n ~ auf (acc.) draw *or* call s.o.'s attention to; **2.** *v/i.*: ~ auf (acc.) point at *or* to, indicate (a. *fig.*); *fig.*: point out; hint at; '2**werfen** *v/t.* (irr. werfen, sep., -ge-, h) throw down; *fig.*: dash off (sketch, etc.); say *s.th.* casually; '2**wirken** *v/i.* (sep., -ge-, h): ~ auf (acc.) work towards; use one's influence to; '2**ziehen** (irr. ziehen, sep., -ge-) **1.** *fig. v/t.* (h) attract *or* draw there; sich ~ space: extend (bis zu to); stretch (to); time: drag on; **2.** *v/i.* (sein) go *or* move there; '2**zielen** *v/i.* (sep., -ge-, h): ~ auf (acc.) aim *or* drive at.

hin'zu *adv.* there; near; in addition; **~fügen** *v/t.* (sep., -ge-, h) add (zu to) (a. *fig.*); 2**fügung** *f* (-/-en) addition; **~kommen** *v/i.* (irr. kommen, sep., -ge-, sein) come up (zu to); supervene; be added; es kommt (noch) hinzu, daß add to this that, (and) moreover; **~rechnen** *v/t.* (sep., -ge-, h) add (zu to); include (in, among); **~setzen** *v/t.* (sep., -ge-, h) s. hinzufügen; **~treten** *v/i.* (irr. treten, sep., -ge-, sein) s. hinzukommen; join; **~ziehen** *v/t.* (irr. ziehen, sep., -ge-, h) call in (doctor, etc.).

Hirn [hirn] *n* (-[e]s/-e) anat. brain; *fig.* brains *pl.*, mind; '**~gespinst** *n* figment of the mind, chimera; '2**los** *fig. adj.* brainless, senseless; '**~schale** anat. *f* brain-pan, cranium; '**~schlag** *m* apoplexy; '2**ver-brannt** *adj.* crazy, F crack-brained, cracky.

Hirsch zo. [hirʃ] *m* (-es/-e) species:

deer; stag, hart; '**~geweih** *n* (stag's) antlers *pl.*; '**~kuh** *f* hind; '**~leder** *n* buckskin, deerskin.

Hirse ♀ ['hirzə] *f* (-/-n) millet.

Hirt [hirt] *m* (-en/-en), **~e** ['~ə] *m* (-n/-n) herdsman; shepherd.

hissen ['hisən] *v/t.* (ge-, h) hoist, raise (flag); ♻ *a.* trice up (sail).

Histori|ker [hi'sto:rikər] *m* (-s/-) historian; 2**sch** *adj.* historic(al).

Hitz|e ['hitsə] *f* (-/no pl.) heat; '2**ebeständig** *adj.* heat-resistant, heat-proof; '**~ewelle** *f* heat-wave, hot spell; '2**ig** *adj. p.* hot-tempered, hot-headed; discussion: heated; '**~kopf** *m* hothead; '**~schlag** 𝓈 *m* heat-stroke.

hob [ho:p] *pret. of* heben.

Hobel ⊕ ['ho:bəl] *m* (-s/-) plane; '**~bank** *f* carpenter's bench; '2**n** *v/t.* (ge-, h) plane.

hoch [ho:x] **1.** *adj.* high; church spire, tree, etc.: tall; position, etc.: high, important; guest, etc.: distinguished; punishment, etc.: heavy, severe; age: great, old; hohe See open sea, high seas *pl.*; **2.** *adv.*: ~ lebe ...! long live ...! **3.** 2 *n* (-s/-s) cheer; toast; meteorology: high (-pressure area).

'hoch|achten *v/t.* (sep., -ge-, h) esteem highly; '2**achtung** *f* high esteem *or* respect; '**~achtungsvoll 1.** *adj.* (most) respectful; **2.** *adv.* correspondence: yours faithfully *or* sincerely, esp. Am. yours truly; '2**adel** *m* greater *or* higher nobility; '2**amt** eccl. *n* high mass; '2**antenne** *f* overhead aerial; '2**bahn** *f* elevated *or* overhead railway, Am. elevated railroad; '2**betrieb** *m* intense activity, rush; '2**burg** *fig. f* stronghold; '**~deutsch** *adj.* High *or* standard German; '2**druck** *m* high pressure (a. *fig.*); mit ~ arbeiten work at high pressure; '2**ebene** *f* plateau, tableland; '**~fahrend** *adj.* high-handed, arrogant; '**~fein** *adj.* superfine; '2**form** *f*: in ~ in top form; '2**frequenz** ≠ *f* high frequency; '2**gebirge** *n* high mountains *pl.*; '2**genuß** *m* great enjoyment; '2**glanz** *m* high polish; '2**haus** *n* multi-stor(e)y building, skyscraper; '**~herzig** *adj.* noble-minded; generous; '2**herzigkeit** *f* (-/-en) noble-mindedness; generosity; '2**konjunktur** ≠ *f* boom, business prosperity; '2**land** *n* upland(s *pl.*), highlands *pl.*; '2**mut** *m* arrogance, haughtiness; **~mütig** *adj.* ['~my:tiç] arrogant, haughty; **~näsig** F *adj.* ['~nɛːziç] stuck-up; '2**ofen** ⊕ *m* blast-furnace; '2**rot** *adj.* bright red; '2**saison** *f* peak season, height of the season; '~**schätzen** *v/t.* (*sep.*, *-ge-*, *h*) esteem highly; '2**schule** *f* university; academy; '2**seefischerei** *f* deep-sea fishing; '2**sommer** *m* midsummer; '2**spannung** *ƒ* *f* high tension *or* voltage; '2**sprung** *m* *sports:* high jump.

höchst [høːçst] **1.** *adj.* highest; *fig. a.:* supreme; extreme; **2.** *adv.* highly, most, extremely.

Hochstap|elei [hoːxʃtaːpəˈlaɪ] *f* (-/-en) swindling; '~**ler** *m* (-s/-) confidence man, swindler; **höchstens** *adv.* ['høːçstəns] at (the) most, at best.

'**Höchst|form** *f* *sports:* top form; '~**geschwindigkeit** *f* maximum speed; speed limit; '~**leistung** *f* *sports:* record (performance); ⊕ maximum output (*of machine, etc.*); '~**lohn** *m* maximum wages *pl.*; '~**maß** *n* maximum; '~**preis** *m* maximum price.

'**hoch|trabend** *fig. adj.* high-flown; pompous; '2**verrat** *m* high treason; '2**wald** *m* high forest; '2**wasser** *n* high tide *or* water; flood; '~**wertig** *adj.* high-grade, high-class; 2**wild** *n* big game; 2**wohlgeboren** *m* (-s/-) Right Hono(u)rable.

Hochzeit ['hɔxtsaɪt] *f* (-/-en) wedding; marriage; '2**lich** *adj.* bridal, nuptial; '~**sgeschenk** *n* wedding present; '~**sreise** *f* honeymoon (trip).

Hocke ['hɔkə] *f* (-/-n) *gymnastics:* squat-vault; *skiing:* crouch; '2**n** *v/i.* (*ge-*, *h*) squat, crouch; '~**r** *m* (-s/-) stool.

Höcker ['hœkər] *m* (-s/-) *surface, etc.:* bump; *camel, etc.:* hump; *p.* hump, hunch; '2**ig** *adj. animal:* humped; *p.* humpbacked, hunchbacked; *surface, etc.:* bumpy, rough, uneven.

Hode *anat.* ['hoːdə] *m* (-n/-n), *f* (-/-n), '~**n** *anat.* *m* (-s/-) testicle.

Hof [hoːf] *m* (-[e]s/ᵒe) court(yard); farm; *king, etc.:* court; *ast.* halo; *j-m den* ~ *machen* court s.o.; '~**da-**

me *f* lady-in-waiting; '2**fähig** *adj.* presentable at court.

Hoffart ['hɔfart] *f* (-/*no pl.*) arrogance, haughtiness; pride.

hoffen ['hɔfən] (*ge-*, *h*) **1.** *v/i.* hope (*auf acc.* for); trust (in); *das Beste* ~ hope for the best; **2.** *v/t.:* '~**tlich** *adv.* it is to be hoped that, I hope, let's hope.

Hoffnung ['hɔfnʊŋ] *f* (-/-en) hope (*auf acc.* for, of); *in der* ~ *zu inf.* in the hope of *ger.*, hoping to *inf.*; *s-e* ~ *setzen auf (acc.)* pin one's hopes on; '2**slos** *adj.* hopeless; '2**svoll** *adj.* hopeful; promising.

'**Hofhund** *m* watch-dog.

höfisch *adj.* ['høːfiʃ] courtly.

höflich *adj.* ['høːflɪç] polite, civil, courteous (*gegen* to); '2**keit** *f* (-/-en) politeness, civility, courtesy.

'**Hofstaat** *m* royal *or* princely household; suite, retinue.

Höhe ['høːə] *f* (-/-n) height; ⚞, ⚐, *ast.*, *geogr.* altitude; hill; peak; amount (*of bill, etc.*); size (*of sum, fine, etc.*); level (*of price, etc.*); severity (*of punishment, etc.*); ♪ pitch; *in gleicher* ~ *mit* on a level with; *auf der* ~ *sein* be up to the mark; *in die* ~ up(wards).

Hoheit ['hoːhaɪt] *f* (-/-en) *pol.* sovereignty; *title:* Highness; '~**s-gebiet** *n* (sovereign) territory; '~**s-gewässer** *n/pl.* territorial waters *pl.*; '~**szeichen** *n* national emblem.

'**Höhen|kurort** *m* high-altitude health resort; '~**luft** *f* mountain air; '~**sonne** *f* mountain sun; ⚕ ultra-violet lamp; '~**steuer** ⚞ *n* elevator; '~**zug** *m* mountain range.

'**Höhepunkt** *m* highest point; *ast.*, *fig.* culmination, zenith; *fig. a.:* climax; summit, peak.

hohl *adj.* ['hoːl] hollow (*a. fig.*); *cheeks, etc.:* sunken; *hand:* cupped; *sound:* hollow, dull.

Höhle ['høːlə] *f* (-/-n) cave, cavern; den, lair (*of bear, lion, etc.*) (*both a. fig.*); hole, burrow (*of fox, rabbit, etc.*); hollow; cavity.

'**Hohl|maß** *n* dry measure; '~**raum** *m* hollow, cavity; '~**spiegel** *m* concave mirror.

Höhlung ['høːlʊŋ] *f* (-/-en) excavation; hollow, cavity.

'**Hohlweg** *m* defile.

Hohn [hoːn] *m* (-[e]s/*no pl.*) scorn, disdain; derision.

höhnen ['høːnən] *v*/*i*. (ge-, h) sneer, jeer, mock, scoff (*über acc.* at).

'**Hohngelächter** *n* scornful *or* derisive laughter.

'**höhnisch** *adj*. scornful; sneering, derisive.

Höker ['høːkər] *m* (-s/-) hawker, huckster; '**_n** *v*/*i*. (ge-, h) huckster, hawk about.

holen ['hoːlən] *v*/*t*. (ge-, h) fetch; go for; *a.* \~ *lassen* send for; draw (*breath*); *sich e-e Krankheit* \~ catch a disease; *sich bei j-m Rat* \~ seek s.o.'s advice.

Holländer ['hɔlɛndər] *m* (-s/-) Dutchman.

Hölle ['hœlə] *f* (-/\~-n) hell.

'**Höllen**|**angst** *fig. f*: *e-e* \~ *haben* be in a mortal fright *or* F blue funk; '**_lärm** F *fig. m* infernal noise; '**_maschine** *f* infernal machine, time bomb; '**_pein** F *fig. f* torment of hell. [*a. fig.*).]

'**höllisch** *adj*. hellish, infernal (*both*)

holper|**ig** *adj*. ['hɔlpəriç] *surface, road, etc.*: bumpy, rough, uneven; *vehicle, etc.*: jolty, jerky; *verse, style, etc.*: rough, jerky; '**_n** (ge-) **1.** *v*/*i*. (sein) *vehicle*: jolt, bump; **2.** *v*/*i*. (h) *vehicle*: jolt, bump; be jolty *or* bumpy.

Holunder ♀ [hɔ'lundər] *m* (-s/-) elder.

Holz [hɔlts] *n* (-es/\"er) wood; timber, Am. lumber; Saw △ \~ *m* wooden structure; '**_bildhauer** *m* woodcarver; '**_blasinstrument** ♪ *n* woodwind instrument; '**_boden** *m* wood(en) floor; wood-loft.

hölzern *adj*. ['hœltsərn] wooden; *fig. a.* clumsy, awkward.

'**Holz**|**fäller** *m* (-s/-) woodcutter, woodman, Am. a. lumberjack, logger; '**_hacker** *m* (-s/-) woodchopper, woodcutter, Am. lumberjack; '**_händler** *m* wood *or* timber merchant, Am. lumberman; '**_haus** *n* wooden house, Am. frame house; '**Sig** *adj*. woody; '**_kohle** *f* charcoal; '**_platz** *m* wood *or* timber yard, Am. lumberyard; '**_schnitt** *m* woodcut, wood-engraving; '**_schnitzer** *m* wood-carver; '**_schuh** *m* wooden shoe, clog; '**_stoß** *m* pile *or* stack of wood; stake; '**_weg** *fig. m*: *auf dem* \~ *sein* be on the wrong track; '**_wolle** *f* wood-wool; fine wood shavings *pl.*, Am. a. excelsior.

Homöopath ♬ [homøo'paːt] *m* (-en/-en) hom(o)eopath(ist); '**_ie** [\~ˈtiː] *f* (-/no pl.) hom(o)eopathy; '**Sisch** *adj*. [\~ˈpaːtiʃ] hom(o)eopathic.

Honig ['hoːniç] *m* (-s/-e) honey; '**_kuchen** *m* honey-cake; gingerbread; '**Ssüß** *adj*. honey-sweet, honeyed (*a. fig.*); '**_wabe** *f* honeycomb.

Honor|**ar** [hono'raːr] *n* (-s/-e) fee; royalties *pl.*; salary; '**_atioren** [\~ˈtsjoːrən] *pl.* notabilities *pl.*; '**Sieren** [\~ˈriːrən] *v*/*t*. (no -ge-, h) fee, pay a fee to; ♰ *hono(u)r*, meet (*bill of exchange*).

Hopfen ['hɔpfən] *m* (-s/-) ♀ hop; *brewing*: hops *pl.*

hops|**a** *int.* ['hɔpsa] (wh)oops!; upsadaisy!; '**_en** F *v*/*i*. (ge-, sein) hop, jump.

hörbar *adj*. ['høːrbaːr] audible.

horch|**en** ['hɔrçən] *v*/*i*. (ge-, h) listen (*auf acc.* to); eavesdrop; '**Ser** *m* (-s/-) eavesdropper.

Horde ['hɔrdə] *f* (-/-n) horde, gang.

hör|**en** ['høːrən] (ge-, h) **1.** *v*/*t*. hear; listen (in) to (*radio*); attend (*lecture, etc.*); hear, learn; **2.** *v*/*i*. hear (*von dat.* from); listen; \~ *auf* (*acc.*) listen to; *schwer* \~ be hard of hearing; \~ *Sie mal!* look here! I say!; *ich say*; '**Ser** *m* (-s/-) hearer; *radio*: listener(-in); *univ.* student; *teleph.* receiver; '**Serschaft** *f* (-/-en) audience; '**Sgerät** *n* hearing aid; '**_ig** *adj.*: *j-m* \~ *sein* be enslaved to s.o.; '**Sigkeit** *f* (-/no pl.) subjection.

Horizont [hori'tsɔnt] *m* (-[e]s/-e) horizon; skyline; *s-n* \~ *erweitern* broaden one's mind; *das geht über meinen* \~ that's beyond me; **Sal** *adj.* [\~ˈtaːl] horizontal.

Hormon [hɔr'moːn] *n* (-s/-e) hormone.

Horn [hɔrn] *n* **1.** (-[e]s/\"er) horn (*of bull*); ♪, *mot., etc.*: horn; ✕ bugle; peak; **2.** (-[e]s/-e) horn, horny matter; '**_haut** *f* horny skin; *anat.* cornea (*on eye*).

Hornisse *zo.* [hɔr'nisə] *f* (-/-n) hornet.

Hornist ♪ [hɔr'nist] *m* (-en/-en) horn-player; ✕ bugler.

Horoskop [horɔ'skoːp] *n* (-s/-e) horoscope; *j-m das* \~ *stellen* cast s.o.'s horoscope.

'**Hör**|**rohr** *n* ear-trumpet; ♬ stethoscope; '**_saal** *m* lecture-hall;

'**~spiel** n radio play; '**~weite** f: in ~ within earshot.

Hose ['ho:zə] f (-/-n) (e-e a pair of) trousers pl. or Am. pants pl.; slacks pl.

'**Hosen|klappe** f flap; **~latz** ['~lats] m (-es/=e) flap; fly; '**~tasche** f trouser-pocket; '**~träger** m: (ein Paar) ~ pl. (a pair of) braces pl. or Am. suspenders pl.

Hospital [hɔspi'ta:l] n (-s/-e, =er) hospital.

Hostie eccl. ['hɔstjə] f (-/-n) host, consecrated or holy wafer.

Hotel [ho'tɛl] n (-s/-s) hotel; **~besitzer** m hotel owner or proprietor; **~gewerbe** n hotel industry; **~ier** [~'je:] m (-s/-s) hotel-keeper.

Hub ⊕ [hu:p] m (-[e]s/=e) mot. stroke (of piston); lift (of valve, etc.); '**~raum** mot. m capacity.

hübsch adj. [hypʃ] pretty, nice; good-looking, handsome; attractive.

'**Hubschrauber** ✗ m (-s/-) helicopter.

Huf [hu:f] m (-[e]s/-e) hoof; '**~eisen** n horseshoe; '**~schlag** m hoof-beat; (horse's) kick; '**~schmied** m farrier.

Hüft|e anat. ['hyftə] f (-/-n) hip; esp. zo. haunch; '**~gelenk** n hip-joint; '**~gürtel** m girdle; suspender belt, Am. garter belt.

Hügel ['hy:gəl] m (-s/-) hill(ock); **Qig** adj. hilly.

Huhn orn. [hu:n] n (-[e]s/=er) fowl, chicken; hen; junges ~ chicken.

Hühnchen ['hy:nçən] n (-s/-) chicken; ein ~ zu rupfen haben have a bone to pick (mit with).

'**Hühner|auge** ✗ ['hy:nər-] n corn; '**~ei** n hen's egg; '**~hof** m poultry-yard, Am. chicken yard; '**~hund** zo. m pointer, setter; '**~leiter** f chicken-ladder.

Huld [hult] f (-/no pl.) grace, favo(u)r; **Qigen** ['~digən] v/i. (dat.) (ge-, h) pay homage to (sovereign, lady, etc.); indulge in (vice, etc.); '**~igung** f (-/-en) homage; **Qreich** adj., **Qvoll** adj. gracious.

Hülle ['hylə] f (-/-n) cover(ing), wrapper; letter, balloon, etc.: envelope; book, etc.: jacket; umbrella, etc.: sheath; **Qn** v/t. (ge-, h) wrap, cover, envelope (a. fig.); sich in Schweigen ~ wrap o.s. in silence.

Hülse ['hylzə] f (-/-n) legume, pod

(of leguminous plant); husk, hull (of rice, etc.); skin (of pea, etc.); ✗ case; '**~nfrucht** f legume(n); leguminous plant; '**~nfrüchte** f/pl. pulse.

human adj. [hu'ma:n] humane; **Qität** [~ani'tɛ:t] f (-/no pl.) humanity.

Hummel zo. ['huməl] f (-/-n) bumble-bee.

Hummer zo. ['humər] m (-s/-) lobster.

Humor [hu'mo:r] m (-s/✗ -e) humo(u)r; **Qist** [~o'rist] m (-en/-en) humorist; **Qistisch** adj. [~o'ristiʃ] humorous.

humpeln ['humpəln] v/i. (ge-) 1. (sein) hobble (along), limp (along); 2. (h) have a limp, walk with a limp.

Hund [hunt] m (-[e]s/-e) zo. dog; ✗ tub; ast. dog, canis; auf den ~ kommen go to the dogs.

'**Hunde|hütte** f dog-kennel, Am. a. doghouse; '**~kuchen** m dog-biscuit; '**~leine** f (dog-)lead or leash; '**~peitsche** f dog-whip.

hundert ['hundərt] 1. adj. a or one hundred; 2. **2** n (-s/-e) hundred; fünf vom ~ five per cent; zu ~en by hundreds; '**Qfach** adj., '**Qfältig** adj. hundredfold; **Qjahrfeier** f centenary, Am. a. centennial; '**Qjährig** adj. ['~jɛ:riç] centenary, a hundred years old; '**Qst** adj. hundredth.

'**Hunde|sperre** f muzzling-order; '**~steuer** f dog tax.

Hündi|n zo. ['hyndin] f (-/-nen) bitch, she-dog; **Qsch** adj. doggish; fig. servile, cringing.

'**hunds|ge'mein** F adj. dirty, mean, scurvy; '**~mise'rabel** F adj. rotten, wretched, lousy; **Qtage** m/pl. dog-days pl.

Hüne ['hy:nə] m (-n/-n) giant.

Hunger ['huŋər] m (-s/no pl.) hunger (fig. nach for); ~ bekommen get hungry; ~ haben be or feel hungry; '**~kur** f starvation cure; '**~leider** F m (-s/-) starveling, poor devil; '**~lohn** m starvation wages pl.; '**Qn** v/i. (ge-, h) hunger (fig. nach after, for); go without food; ~ lassen starve z.o.; '**~snot** f famine; '**~streik** m hunger-strike; '**~tod** m death from starvation; '**~tuch** fig. n: am ~ nagen have nothing to bite.

'**hungrig** adj. hungry (fig. nach for).

Hupe mot. ['hu:pə] f (-/-n) horn,

hooter; klaxon; '⌖n v/i. (ge-, h) sound one's horn, hoot.

hüpfen ['hypfən] v/i. (ge-, sein) hip, skip; gambol, frisk (about).

Hürde ['hyrdə] f (-/-n) hurdle; fold, pen; '⌖nrennen n hurdle-race.

Hure ['huːrə] f (-/-n) whore, prostitute.   [agile, nimble.\

hurtig adj. ['hurtiç] quick, swift;\

Husar ⚔ [hu'zaːr] m (-en/-en) hussar.

husch int. [huʃ] in or like a flash; shoo!; '⌖en v/i. (ge-, sein) slip, dart; small animal: scurry, scamper, bat, etc.: flit.

hüsteln ['hyːstəln] **1.** v/i. (ge-, h) cough slightly; **2.** ⚥ n (-s/no pl.) slight cough.

husten ['huːstən] **1.** v/i. (ge-, h) cough; **2.** ⚥ m (-s/⌖-) cough.

Hut [huːt] **1.** m (-[e]s/⌖e) hat; den ~ abnehmen take off one's hat; ~ ab vor (dat.)! hats off to ...!; **2.** f (-/no pl.) care, charge; guard; auf der ~ sein be on one's guard (vor dat. against).

hüte|n ['hyːtən] v/t. (ge-, h) guard, protect, keep watch over; keep (secret); tend (sheep, etc.); das Bett ~ be confined to (one's) bed; sich ~ vor (dat.) beware of; '⌖r m (-s/-) keeper, guardian; herdsman.

'**Hut|futter** n hat-lining; '⌖krempe

f hat-brim; '⌖macher m (-s/-) hatter; '⌖nadel f hat-pin.

Hütte ['hytə] f (-/-n) hut; cottage, cabin; ⊕ metallurgical plant; mount. refuge; '⌖nwesen ⊕ n metallurgy, metallurgical engineering.

Hyäne zo. [hy'ɛ:nə] f (-/-n) hy(a)ena.

Hyazinthe ⚘ [hya'tsintə] f (-/-n) hyacinth.   [hydrant.\

Hydrant [hy'drant] m (-en/-en)\

Hydrauli|k phys. [hy'draulik] f (-/no pl.) hydraulics pl.; ⚥sch adj. hydraulic.

Hygien|e [hy'gjeːnə] f (-/no pl.) hygiene; ⚥isch adj. hygienic(al).

Hymne ['hymnə] f (-/-n) hymn.

Hypno|se [hyp'noːzə] f (-/-n) hypnosis; ⚥tisieren [⌣oti'ziːrən] v/t. and v/i. (no -ge-, h) hypnotize.

Hypochond|er [hypo'xɔndər] m (-s/-) hypochondriac; ⚥risch adj. hypochondriac.

Hypotenuse Ⱥ [hypote'nuːzə] f (-/-n) hypotenuse.

Hypothek [hypo'teːk] f (-/-en) mortgage; e-e ~ aufnehmen raise a mortgage; ⚥arisch adj. [⌣e'kaːriʃ]: ~e Belastung mortgage.

Hypothe|se [hypo'teːzə] f (-/-n) hypothesis;⚥tisch adj. hypothetical.

Hyster|ie psych. [hyste'riː] f (-/-n) hysteria; ⚥isch psych. adj. [⌣'teːriʃ] hysterical.

I

ich [iç] **1.** pers. pron. I; **2.** ⚥ n (-[s]/ -[s]) self; psych. the ego.

Ideal [ide'aːl] **1.** n (-s/-e) ideal; **2.** ⚥ adj. ideal; ⚥isieren [⌣ali'ziːrən] v/t. (no -ge-, h) idealize; ⌖ismus [⌣a'lismus] m (-/Idealismen) idealism; ⌖ist [⌣a'list] m(-en/-en)idealist.

Idee [i'deː] f (-/-n) idea, notion.

identi|fizieren [identifi'tsiːrən] v/t. (no -ge-, h) identify; sich ~ identify o.s.; ⌖sch adj. [i'dentiʃ] identical; ⚥tät [⌣'tɛːt] f (-/no pl.) identity.

Ideolog|ie [ideolo'giː] f (-/-n) ideology; ⚥isch adj. [⌣'loːgiʃ] ideological.

Idiot [idi'oːt] m (-en/-en) idiot; ⌖ie [⌣o'tiː] f (-/-n) idiocy; ⚥isch adj. [⌣'oːtiʃ] idiotic.

Idol [i'doːl] n (-s/-e) idol.

Igel zo. ['iːgəl] m (-s/-) hedgehog.

Ignor|ant [igno'rant] m (-en/-en) ignorant person, ignoramus; ⌖anz [⌣ts] f (-/no pl.) ignorance; ⚥ieren [igno'riːrən] v/t. (no -ge-, h) ignore, take no notice of.

ihm pers. pron. [iːm] p. (to) him; thing: (to) it.

ihn pers. pron. [iːn] p. him; thing: it.

'**ihnen** pers. pron. (to) them; Ihnen sg. and pl. (to) you.

ihr [iːr] **1.** pers. pron.: (2nd pl. nom.) you; (3rd sg. dat.) (to) her; **2.** poss. pron.: her; their; Ihr sg. and pl. your; der (die, das) ⌖e hers; theirs; der (die, das) Ihre sg. and pl. yours; ⌖erseits ['⌣ər'zaits] adv. on her part; on their part; Ihrerseits sg. and pl. on your part; '⌖es'gleichen pron. (of) her *or* their kind, her *or* their equal; *Ihresgleichen sg.* (of) your kind, your equal; *pl.* (of) your kind, your equals; '**~et'wegen** *adv.* for her *or* their sake, on her *or* their account; *Ihretwegen sg. or pl.* for your sake, on your account; '**~et-** '**willen** *adv.*: *um ~ s.* ihretwegen; **~ige** *poss. pron.* ['~igə]: der (die, das) ~ hers; theirs; der (die, das) *Ihrige* yours.

illegitim *adj.* [ilegi'ti:m] illegitimate.

illusorisch *adj.* [ilu'zo:riʃ] illusory, deceptive.

illustrieren [ilu'stri:rən] *v/t.* (*no* -ge-, h) illustrate.

Iltis *zo.* ['iltis] *m* (-ses/-se) fitchew, polecat.

im *prp.* [im] = in dem.   [inary.)

imaginär *adj.* [imagi'nɛ:r] imag-)

'**Imbiß** *m* light meal, snack; '**~stube** *f* snack bar.

Imker ['imkər] *m* (-s/-) bee-master, bee-keeper.

immatrikulieren [imatriku'li:rən] *v/t.* (*no* -ge-, h) matriculate, enrol(l); *sich ~ lassen* matriculate, enrol(l).

immer *adv.* ['imər] always; *~ mehr* more and more; *~ wieder* again *or* time and again; *für ~* for ever, for good; '**2grün** ♀ *n* (-s/-e) evergreen; '**~'hin** *adv.* still, yet; '**~'zu** *adv.* always, continually.

Immobilien [imo'bi:ljən] *pl.* immovables *pl.*, real estate; **~händler** *m s.* Grundstücksmakler.

immun *adj.* [i'mu:n] immune (*gegen* against, from); **2ität** [~uni'tɛ:t] *f* (-/*no pl.*) immunity.

Imperativ *gr.* ['imperati:f] *m* (-s/-e) imperative (mood).

Imperfekt *gr.* ['imperfekt] *n* (-s/-e) imperfect (tense), past tense.

Imperialis|mus [imperia'lismus] *m* (-/*no pl.*) imperialism; **~t** *m* (-en/-en) imperialist; **2tisch** *adj.* imperialistic.

impertinent *adj.* [imperti'nɛnt] impertinent, insolent.

impf|en ♣ ['impfən] *v/t.* (ge-, h) vaccinate; inoculate; '**2schein** *m* certificate of vaccination *or* inoculation; '**2stoff** ♣ *m* vaccine; serum; '**2ung** *f* (-/-en) vaccination, inoculation.

imponieren [impo'ni:rən] *v/i.* (*no* -ge-, h): *j-m ~* impress s.o.

Import ♣ [im'pɔrt] *m* (-[e]s/-e) import(ation); **~eur** ♣ [~'tø:r] *m* (-s/-e) importer; **2ieren** [~'ti:rən] *v/t.* (*no* -ge-, h) import.

imposant *adj.* [impo'zant] imposing, impressive.

imprägnieren [impre'gni:rən] *v/t.* (*no* -ge-, h) impregnate; (water-)proof (raincoat, etc.).

improvisieren [improvi'zi:rən] *v/t. and v/i.* (*no* -ge-, h) improvise.

Im'puls *m* (-es/-e) impuls; **2iv** *adj.* [~'zi:f] impulsive.   [be able.)

imstande *adj.* [im'ʃtandə]: *~ sein)*

in *prp.* (*dat.; acc.*) [in] **1.** *place:* in, at; within; into, in; *with names of important towns:* in, ☖ at, of; *with names of villages and less important towns:* at; *im Hause* in the house, indoors, in; *im ersten Stock* on the first floor; *~ der Schule* (*im Theater*) at school (the thea|tre, *Am.* -er); *~ die Schule* (*~s Theater*) to school (the theat|re, *Am.* -er); *~ England* in England; *waren Sie schon einmal in England?* have you ever been to England?; **2.** *time:* in, at, during; within; *~ drei Tagen* (with)in three days; *heute ~ vierzehn Tagen* today fortnight; *im Jahre 1960* in 1960; *im Februar* in February; *im Frühling* in (the) spring; *~ der Nacht* at night; *~ letzter Zeit* lately, of late, recently; **3.** *mode:* *~ großer Eile* in great haste; *~ Frieden leben* live at peace; *~ Reichweite* within reach; **4.** *condition, state:* *im Alter von fünfzehn Jahren* at (the age of) fifteen; *~ Behandlung* under treatment.

'**Inbegriff** *m* (quint)essence; embodiment, incarnation; paragon; '**2en** *adj.* included, inclusive (of).

'**Inbrunst** *f* (-/*no pl.*) ardo(u)r, fervo(u)r.

'**inbrünstig** *adj.* ardent, fervent.

in'dem *cj.* whilst, while; by (*ger.*); *~ er mich ansah, sagte er* looking at me he said.

Inder ['indər] *m* (-s/-) Indian.

in'des(sen) **1.** *adv.* meanwhile; **2.** *cj.* while; however.

Indianer [in'dja:nər] *m* (-s/-) (American *or* Red) Indian.

Indikativ *gr.* ['indikati:f] *m* (-s/-e) indicative (mood).

'**indirekt** *adj.* indirect.

indisch *adj.* ['indiʃ] Indian.

'indiskret *adj.* indiscreet; **♀ion** [～ε'tsjo:n] *f* (-/-en) indiscretion.

indiskutabel *adj.* ['indiskuta:bəl] out of the question.

individu|**ell** *adj.* [individu'εl] individual; **♀um** [～'vi:duum] *n* (-s/ *Individuen*) individual.

Indizienbeweis 🕮 [in'di:tsjən-] *m* circumstantial evidence.

Indoss|**ament** † [indɔsa'mεnt] *n* (-s/-e) endorsement, indorsement; **♀ieren** † [～'si:rən] *v/t.* (no -ge-, h) indorse, endorse.

Industrialisierung [industriali'zi:ruŋ] *f* (-/-en) industrialization.

Industrie [indus'tri:] *f* (-/-n) industry; **～anlage** *f* industrial plant; **～arbeiter** *m* industrial worker; **～ausstellung** *f* industrial exhibition; **～erzeugnis** *n* industrial product; **～gebiet** *n* industrial district or area; **♀ll** *adj.* [～i'εl]; **～lle** [～i'εlə] *m* (-n/-n) industrialist; **～staat** *m* industrial country.

ineinander *adv.* [in⁹ar'nandər] into one another; **～greifen** ⊕ *v/i.* (*irr.* greifen, sep., -ge-, h) gear into one another, interlock.

infam *adj.* [in'fa:m] infamous.

Infanter|**ie** ✕ [infantə'ri:] *f* (-/-n) infantry; **～ist** ✕ *m* (-en/-en) infantryman.

Infektion 🜍 [infεk'tsjo:n] *f* (-/-en) infection; **～skrankheit** 🜍 *f* infectious disease.

Infinitiv *gr.* ['infiniti:f] *m* (-s/-e) infinitive (mood).

infizieren [infi'tsi:rən] *v/t.* (no -ge-, h) infect. [flation.⎰

Inflation [infla'tsjo:n] *f* (-/-en) in-⎱

in'folge *prp.* (gen.) in consequence of, owing or due to; **～dessen** *adv.* consequently.

Inform|**ation** [infɔrma'tsjo:n] *f* (-/-en) information; **♀ieren** [～'mi:rən] *v/t.* (no -ge-, h) inform; *falsch* **～** misinform.

Ingenieur [inʒe'njø:r] *m* (-s/-e) engineer.

Ingwer ['iŋvər] *m* (-s/no pl.) ginger.

Inhaber ['inha:bər] *m* (-s/-) owner, proprietor (of business or shop); occupant (of flat); keeper (of shop); holder (of office, share, etc.); bearer (of cheque, etc.).

'Inhalt *m* (-[e]s/-e) contents pl. (of bottle, book, etc.); tenor (of speech); geom. volume; capacity (of vessel);

'Inhalts|**angabe** *f* summary; **♀los** *adj.* empty, devoid of substance; **♀reich** *adj.* full of meaning; *life*: rich, full; **～verzeichnis** *n* on parcel: list of contents; in book: table of contents.

Initiative [initsja'ti:və] *f* (-/no pl.) initiative; *die* **～** *ergreifen* take the initiative.

Inkasso † [in'kaso] *n* (-s/-s, *Inkassi*) collection.

'inkonsequen|**t** *adj.* inconsistent; **♀z** [～ts] *f* (-/-en) inconsistency.

In'krafttreten *n* (-s/no pl.) coming into force, taking effect (of new law, etc.).

'Inland *n* (-[e]s/no pl.) home (country); inland.

inländisch *adj.* ['inlεndiʃ] native; inland; home; domestic; *product*: home-made.

Inlett ['inlεt] *n* (-[e]s/-e) bedtick.

in'mitten *prp.* (gen.) in the midst of, amid(st).

'inne|**haben** *v/t.* (*irr.* haben, sep., -ge-, h) possess, hold (office, record, etc.); occupy (flat); **～halten** *v/i.* (*irr.* halten, sep., -ge-, h) stop, pause.

innen *adv.* ['inən] inside, within; indoors; *nach* **～** inwards.

'Innen|**architekt** *m* interior decorator; **～ausstattung** *f* interior decoration, fittings pl., furnishing; **～minister** *m* minister of the interior; Home Secretary, *Am.* Secretary of the Interior; **～ministerium** *n* ministry of the interior; Home Office, *Am.* Department of the Interior; **～politik** *f* domestic policy; **～seite** *f* inner side, inside; **～stadt** *f* city, *Am.* downtown.

inner *adj.* ['inər] interior; inner; 🜍, *pol.* internal; **♀e** *n* (-n/no pl.) interior; *Minister(ium) des Innern s.* Innenminister(ium); **♀eien** [～'raiən] *f/pl.* offal(s pl.); **～halb 1.** *prp.* (gen.) within; **2.** *adv.* within, inside; **～lich** *adv.* inwardly; *esp.* 🜍 internally.

innig *adj.* ['iniç] intimate, close; affectionate.

Innung ['inuŋ] *f* (-/-en) guild, corporation.

inoffiziell *adj.* ['in⁹-] unofficial.

ins *prp.* [ins] = *in das*.

Insasse ['inzasə] *m* (-n/-n) inmate; occupant, passenger (of car).

'Inschrift f inscription; legend (on coin, etc.).

Insekt zo. [in'zɛkt] n (-[e]s/-en) insect.

Insel ['inzəl] f (-/-n) island; **'~bewohner** m islander.

Inser|at [inzə'ra:t] n (-[e]s/-e) advertisement, F ad; **2ieren** [~'ri:rən] v/t. and v/i. (no -ge-, h) advertise.

insge'heim adv. secretly; **~samt** adv. altogether.

in'sofern cj. so far; **~ als** in so far as.

insolvent ✝ adj. ['inzɔlvɛnt] insolvent.

Inspekt|ion [inspɛk'tsjo:n] f (-/-en) inspection; **~or** [in'spɛktɔr] m (-s/-en) inspector; surveyor; overseer.

inspirieren [inspi'ri:rən] v/t. (no -ge-, h) inspire.

inspizieren [inspi'tsi:rən] v/t. (no -ge-, h) inspect (troops, etc.); examine (goods); survey (buildings).

Install|ateur [instala'tø:r] m (-s/-e) plumber; (gas- or electrical) fitter; **2ieren** [~'li:rən] v/t. (no -ge-, h) install.

instand adv. [in'ʃtant]: **~ halten** keep in good order; keep up; ⊕ maintain; **~ setzen** repair; **2haltung** f maintenance; upkeep.

'inständig adv.: j-n **~** bitten implore or beseech s.o.

Instanz [in'stants] f (-/-en) authority; ⚖ instance; **~enweg** ⚖ m stages of appeal; auf dem **~** through the prescribed channels.

Instinkt [in'stiŋkt] m (-[e]s/-e) instinct; **2iv** adv. [~'ti:f] instinctively.

Institut [insti'tu:t] n (-[e]s/-e) institute.

Instrument [instru'mɛnt] n (-[e]s/-e) instrument.

inszenier|en esp. thea. [instse'ni:rən] v/t. (no -ge-, h) (put on the stage; **2ung** thea. f (-/-en) staging, production.

Integr|ation [integra'tsjo:n] f (-/-en) integration; **2ieren** [~'gri:rən] v/t. (no -ge-, h) integrate.

intellektuell adj. [intelektu'ɛl] intellectual, highbrow; **2e** m (-n/-n) intellectual; highbrow.

intelligen|t adj. [inteli'gɛnt] intelligent; **2z** [~ts] f (-/-en) intelligence.

Intendant thea. [inten'dant] m (-en/-en) director. [intense.]

intensiv adj. [inten'zi:f] intensive;

interess|ant adj. [intere'sant] interesting; **2e** [~'rɛsə] n (-s/-n) interest (an dat., für in); **2engebiet** [~'resən-] n field of interest; **2engemeinschaft** [~'resən-] f community of interests; combine, pool, trust; **2ent** [~'sɛnt] m (-en/-en) interested person or party; ✝ prospective buyer, esp. Am. prospect; **~ieren** [~'si:rən] v/t. (no -ge-, h) interest (für in); sich **~** für take an interest in.

intern adj. [in'tɛrn] internal; **2at** [~'na:t] n (-[e]s/-e) boarding-school.

international adj. [internatsjo'na:l] international.

inter|'nieren v/t. (no -ge-, h) intern; **2'nierung** f (-/-en) internment; **2'nist** ✎ m (-en/-en) internal specialist, Am. internist.

inter|pretieren [interpre'ti:rən] v/t. (no -ge-, h) interpret; **2punktion** [~puŋk'tsjo:n] f (-/-en) punctuation; **2vall** [~'val] n (-s/-e) interval; **~venieren** [~ve'ni:rən] v/i. (no -ge-, h) intervene; **2'zonenhandel** m interzonal trade; **2'zonenverkehr** m interzonal traffic.

intim adj. [in'ti:m] intimate (mit with); **2ität** [~imi'tɛ:t] f (-/-en) intimacy.

'intoleran|t adj. intolerant; **2z** ['~ts] f (-/-en) intolerance.

intransitiv gr. adj. ['intranziti:f] intransitive.

Intrig|e [in'tri:gə] f (-/-n) intrigue, scheme, plot; **2ieren** [~i'gi:rən] v/i. (no -ge-, h) intrigue, scheme, plot.

Invalid|e [inva'li:də] m (-n/-n) invalid; disabled person; **~enrente** f disability pension; **~ität** [~idi'tɛ:t] f (-/no pl.) disablement, disability. [ventory, stock.)

Inventar [inven'ta:r] n (-s/-e) in-

Inventur ✝ [inven'tu:r] f (-/-en) stock-taking; **~ machen** take stock.

invest|ieren ✝ [inves'ti:rən] v/t. (no -ge-, h) invest; **2ition** ✝ [~i'tsjo:n] f (-/-en) investment.

inwie|'fern cj. to what extent; in what way or respect; **~'weit** cj. how far, to what extent.

in'zwischen adv. in the meantime, meanwhile.

Ion phys. [i'o:n] n (-s/-en) ion.

ird|en adj. ['irdən] earthen; **'~isch** adj. earthly; worldly; mortal.

Ire ['iːrə] *m* (-n/-n) Irishman; *die ~n pl.* the Irish *pl.*

irgend *adv.* ['irgənt] *in compounds*: some; any (*a. negative and in questions*); *wenn ich ~ kann* if I possibly can; '**~ein(e)** *indef. pron. and adj.* some(one); any(one); '**~einer** *indef. pron. s.* irgend jemand; '**~ein(e)s** *indef. pron.* some; any; **~ etwas** *indef. pron.* something; anything; **~ jemand** *indef. pron.* someone; anyone; '**~wann** *adv.* some time (or other); '**~wie** *adv.* somehow; anyhow; '**~wo** *adv.* somewhere; anywhere; '**~wo'her** *adv.* from somewhere; from anywhere; '**~wo'hin** *adv.* somewhere; anywhere.

'**irisch** *adj.* Irish.

Iron|ie [iro'niː] *f* (-/-n) irony; **2isch** *adj.* [i'roːnif] ironic(al).

irre ['irə] **1.** *adj.* confused; ** insane; mad; **2.** ♀ *f* (-/*no pl.*): *in die ~ gehen* go astray; **3.** ♀ *m, f* (-n/-n) lunatic; mental patient; *wie ein ~r* like a madman; '**~führen** *v/t.* (*sep., -ge-, h*) lead astray; *fig.* mislead; '**~gehen** *v/i.* (*irr. gehen, sep., -ge-, sein*) go astray, stray; lose one's way; '**~machen** *v/t.* (*sep., -ge-, h*) puzzle, bewilder; perplex; confuse; '**~n 1.** *v/i.* (*ge-, h*) err; wander; **2.** *v/refl.* (*ge-, h*) be mistaken (*in dat.* in *s.o.*, about *s.th.*); be wrong.

'**Irren|anstalt** ** *f* lunatic asylum, mental home *or* hospital; '**~arzt** ** *m* alienist, mental specialist; '**~haus** ** *n s.* Irrenanstalt.

'**irrereden** *v/i.* (*sep., -ge-, h*) rave.

'**Irr|fahrt** *f* wandering; Odyssey; '**~garten** *m* labyrinth, maze; '**~glaube** *m* erroneous belief; false doctrine, heterodoxy; heresy; '**2gläubig** *adj.* heterodox; heretical; '**2ig** *adj.* erroneous, mistaken, false, wrong.

irritieren [iri'tiːrən] *v/t.* (*no -ge-, h*) irritate, annoy; confuse.

'**Irr|lehre** *f* false doctrine, heterodoxy; heresy; '**~licht** *n* will-o'-the-wisp, jack-o'-lantern; '**~sinn** *m* insanity; madness; '**2sinnig** *adj.* insane; mad; *fig.*: fantastic; terrible; '**~sinnige** *m, f* (-n/-n) *s.* irre 3; '**~tum** *m* (-s/=er) error, mistake; *im ~ sein* be mistaken; **2tümlich** ['~tyːmliç] **1.** *adj.* erroneous; **2.** *adv.* = '2**tümlicherweise** *adv.* by mistake; mistakenly, erroneously; '**~wisch** *m s.* Irrlicht; *p.* flibbertigibbet.

Ischias ['ifias] *f, * a.: n, m* (-/*no pl.*) sciatica.

Islam ['islam, is'laːm] *m* (-s/*no pl.*) Islam.

Island|er ['iːslɛndər] *m* (-s/-) Icelander; **2isch** *adj.* Icelandic.

Isolator ** [izo'laːtɔr] *m* (-s/-en) insulator.

Isolier|band ** [izo'liːr-] *n* insulating tape; **2en** *v/t.* (*no -ge-, h*) isolate; **~masse** ** *f* insulating compound; **~schicht** ** *f* insulating layer; **~ung** *f* (-/-en) isolation (*a. **); ** quarantine; ** insulation.

Isotop ⚛, *phys.* [izo'toːp] *n* (-s/-e) isotope.

Israeli [isra'eːli] *m* (-s/-s) Israeli.

Italien|er [ital'jeːnər] *m* (-s/-) Italian; **2isch** *adj.* Italian.

I-Tüpfelchen *fig.* ['iːtypfəlçən] *n* (-s/-): *bis aufs ~* to a T.

J

ja [jaː] **1.** *adv.* yes; ♨, *parl.* aye, *Am. parl. a.* yea; *~ doch, ~ freilich* yes, indeed; to be sure; *da ist er ~!* well, there he is!; *ich sagte es Ihnen ~* I told you so; *tut es ~ nicht!* don't you dare do it!; *vergessen Sie es ~ nicht!* be sure not to forget it!; **2.** *cj.*: *~ sogar, ~ selbst* nay (even); *wenn ~* if so; *er ist ~ mein Freund* why, he is my friend; **3.** *int.*: *~, weißt du denn nicht, daß* why, don't you know that?

Jacht ♨ [jaxt] *f* (-/-en) yacht; '**~klub** *m* yacht-club.

Jacke ['jakə] *f* (-/-n) jacket.

Jackett [ʒa'ket] *n* (-s/-e, -s) jacket.

Jagd [jaːkt] *f* (-/-en) hunt(ing); *with a gun*: shoot(ing); chase; *s.* Jagdrevier; *auf (die) ~ gehen* go hunting *or* shooting, *Am. a.* be gunning; *~ machen auf (acc.)* hunt after *or* for;

'**∼aufseher** m gamekeeper, Am. game warden; '**∼bomber** ✕ m (-s/-) fighter-bomber; '**∼büchse** f sporting rifle; '**∼flinte** f sporting gun; fowling-piece; '**∼flugzeug** ✕ n fighter (aircraft); '**∼geschwader** ✕ n fighter wing, Am. fighter group; '**∼gesellschaft** f hunting or shooting party; '**∼haus** n shooting-box or -lodge, hunting-box or -lodge; '**∼hund** m hound; '**∼hütte** f shooting-box, hunting-box; '**∼pächter** m game-tenant; '**∼rennen** n steeplechase; '**∼revier** n hunting-ground, shoot; '**∼schein** m shooting licen|ce, Am. -se; '**∼schloß** n hunting seat; '**∼tasche** f game-bag.

jagen ['jɑːgən] (ge-, h) **1.** v/i. go hunting or shooting, hunt; shoot; rush, dash; **2.** v/t. hunt; chase; aus dem Hause ∼ turn s.o. out (of doors).

Jäger ['jɛːgər] m (-s/-) hunter, huntsman, sportsman; ✕ rifleman; '**∼latein** F fig. n huntsmen's yarn, tall stories pl.

Jaguar zo. ['jɑːguɑːr] m (-s/-e) jaguar.

jäh adj. [jɛː] sudden, abrupt; precipitous, steep.

Jahr [jɑːr] n (-[e]s/-e) year; ein halbes ∼ half a year, six months pl.; einmal im ∼ once a year; im ∼e 1900 in 1900; mit 18 ∼en, im Alter von 18 ∼en at (the age of) eighteen; letztes ∼ last year; das ganze ∼ durch or über all the year round; ♀aus ∼: ∼, jahrein year in, year out; year after year; '**∼buch** n yearbook, annual; '**∼ein** adv. s. jahraus.

'**jahrelang 1.** adv. for years; **2.** adj.: ∼e Erfahrung (many) years of experience.

jähren ['jɛːrən] v/refl. (ge-, h): es jährt sich heute, daß ... it is a year ago today that ..., it is a year today since ...

'**Jahres|abonnement** n annual subscription (to magazine, etc.); thea. yearly season ticket; '**∼abschluß** m annual statement of accounts; '**∼anfang** m beginning of the year; zum ∼ die besten Wünsche! best wishes for the New Year; '**∼bericht** m annual report; '**∼einkommen** n annual or yearly income; '**∼ende** n end of the year; '**∼gehalt** n annual salary; '**∼tag** m anniversary; '**∼wechsel** m turn of the year; '**∼zahl**

f date, year; '**∼zeit** f season, time of the year.

'**Jahrgang** m volume, year (of periodical, etc.); p. age-group; univ., school: year, class; wine: vintage.

Jahr'hundert n (-s/-e) century; ∼feier f centenary, Am. centennial; ∼wende f turn of the century.

jährig adj. ['jɛːrɪç] one-year-old.

jährlich ['jɛːrlɪç] **1.** adj. annual, yearly; **2.** adv. every year; yearly, once a year.

'**Jahr|markt** m fair; ∼'tausend n (-s/-e) millennium; ∼'tausendfeier f millenary; ∼'zehnt n (-[e]s/-e) decade.

'**Jähzorn** m violent (fit of) temper; irascibility; '**∼ig** adj. hot-tempered; irascible.

Jalousie [ʒaluˈziː] f (-/-n) (Venetian) blind, Am. a. window shade.

Jammer ['jamər] m (-s/no pl.) lamentation; misery; es ist ein ∼ it is a pity.

jämmerlich adj. ['jɛmərlɪç] miserable, wretched; piteous; pitiable (esp. contp.).

jammer|n ['jamərn] v/i. (ge-, h) lament (nach, um for; über acc. over); moan; wail, whine; '**∼schade** adj.: es ist ∼ it is a thousand pities, it is a great shame.

Januar ['januɑːr] m (-[s]/-e) January.

Japan|er [jaˈpɑːnər] m (-s/-) Japanese; die ∼ pl. the Japanese pl.; ♀isch adj. Japanese.

Jargon [ʒarˈgõ] m (-s/-s) jargon, cant, slang.

Jasmin ♀ [jasˈmiːn] m (-s/-e) jasmin(e), jessamin(e).

'**Jastimme** parl. f aye, Am. a. yea.

jäten ['jɛːtən] v/t. (ge-, h) weed.

Jauche ['jauxə] f (-/-n) ✔ liquid manure; sewage.

jauchzen ['jauxtsən] v/i. (ge-, h) exult, rejoice, cheer; vor Freude ∼ shout for joy.

jawohl adv. [jaˈvoːl] yes; yes, indeed; yes, certainly; that's right; ✕, etc.: yes, Sir!

'**Jawort** n consent; j-m das ∼ geben accept s.o.'s proposal (of marriage).

je [jeː] **1.** adv. ever, at any time; always; ohne ihn ∼ gesehen zu haben without ever having seen him; seit eh und ∼ since time immemorial, always; distributive with numerals:

~ **zwei** two at a time, two each, two by two, by *or* in twos; *sie bekamen* ~ **zwei Äpfel** they received two apples each; *für* ~ **zehn Wörter** for every ten words; *in Schachteln mit or zu* ~ **zehn Stück verpackt** packed in boxes of ten; **2.** *cj.*: ~ *nach Größe* according to *or* depending on size; ~ *nachdem* it depends; ~ *nachdem, was er für richtig hält* according as he thinks fit; ~ *nachdem, wie er sich fühlt* depending on how he feels; ~ *mehr, desto besser* the more the better; ~ *länger,* ~ *lieber* the longer the better; *die Birnen kosten e-e Mark* ~ *Pfund* the pears cost one mark a pound; *s. pro.*

jede|(**r, -s**) *indef. pron.* ['je:də(r, -s)] every; any; *of a group:* each; *of two persons:* either; **jeder, der wo-ever; jeden zweiten Tag** every other day; '**~n'falls** *adv.* at all events, in any case; '**~rmann** *indef. pron.* everyone, everybody; '**~r'zeit** *adv.* always, at any time; '**~s'mal** *adv.* each *or* every time; ~ *wenn* whenever.

jedoch *cj.* [je'dɔx] however, yet, nevertheless.

'**jeher** *adv.*: *von or seit* ~ at all times, always, from time immemorial.

jemals *adv.* ['je:ma:ls] ever, at any time.

jemand *indef. pron.* ['je:mant] someone, somebody; *with questions and negations:* anyone, anybody.

jene|(**r, -s**) *dem. pron.* ['je:nə(r, -s)] that (one); *jene pl.* those *pl.*

jenseitig *adj.* ['jenzaitiç] opposite.

'**jenseits 1.** *prp.* (*gen.*) on the other side of, beyond, across; **2.** *adv.* on the other side, beyond; **3.** **2** *n* (*-/no pl.*) the other *or* next world, the world to come, *the* beyond.

jetzig *adj.* ['jetziç] present, existing; *prices, etc.:* current.

jetzt *adv.* [jetst] now, at present; *bis* ~ until now; so far; *eben* ~ just now; *erst* ~ only now; *für* ~ for the present; *gleich* ~ at once, right away; *noch* ~ even now; *von* ~ *an* from now on.

jeweil|**ig** *adj.* ['je:vailiç] respective; '**~s** *adv.* ['~s] respectively, at a time; from time to time (*esp. f.*).

Joch [jɔx] *n* (*-[e]s/-e*) yoke; *in mountains:* col, pass, saddle; **Δ**

bay; '**~bein** *anat. n* cheek-bone.

Jockei ['dʒɔkei] *m* (*-s/-s*) jockey.

Jod **🜍** [jo:t] *n* (*-[e]s/no pl.*) iodine.

jodeln ['jo:dəln] *v/i.* (ge-, h) yodel.

Johanni [jo'hani] *n* (*-/no pl.*), '**~s** [.s] *n* (*-/no pl.*) Midsummer day; '**~s-beere** *f* currant; *rote* ~ red currant; '**~stag** *m eccl.* St John's day; Mid-summer day.

johlen ['jo:lən] *v/i.* (ge-, h) bawl, yell, howl.

Jolle **🛥** ['jɔlə] *f* (*-/-n*) jolly-boat, yawl, dinghy.

Jongl|**eur** [ʒõ'glø:r] *m* (*-s/-e*) juggler; **2ieren** *v/t. and v/i.* (no -ge-, h) juggle.

Journal [ʒur'na:l] *n* (*-s/-e*) journal; newspaper; magazine; diary; **🛥** log-book; '**~ist** [.a'list] *m* (*-en/-en*) journalist, *Am. a.* newspaperman.

Jubel ['ju:bəl] *m* (*-s/no pl.*) jubila-tion, exultation, rejoicing; cheer-ing; '**2n** *v/i.* (ge-, h) jubilate; exult, rejoice (*über acc.* at).

Jubil|**ar** [jubi'la:r] *m* (*-s/-e*) person celebrating his jubilee, *etc.*; '**~äum** [.ɛ:um] *n* (*-s/Jubiläen*) jubilee.

Juchten ['juxtən] *m, n* (*-s/no pl.*), '**~leder** *n* Russia (leather).

jucken ['jukən] (ge-, h) **1.** *v/i.* itch; **2.** *v/t.* irritate, (make) itch; F *sich* ~ scratch (o.s.).

Jude ['ju:də] *m* (*-n/-n*) Jew; '**2n-feindlich** *adj.* anti-Semitic; '**~n-tum** *n* (*-s/no pl.*) Judaism; '**~nver-folgung** *f* persecution of Jews, Jew-baiting, pogrom.

Jüd|**in** ['jy:din] *f* (*-/-nen*) Jewess; '**2isch** *adj.* Jewish.

Jugend ['ju:gənt] *f* (*-/no pl.*) youth; '**~amt** *n* youth welfare department; '**~buch** *n* book for the young; '**~freund** *m* friend of one's youth; school-friend; '**~fürsorge** *f* youth welfare; '**~gericht** *n* juvenile court; '**~herberge** *f* youth hostel; '**~jahre** *n/pl.* early years, youth; '**~krimi-nalität** *f* juvenile delinquency; '**2-lich** *adj.* youthful, juvenile, young; '**~liche** *m, f* (*-n/-n*) young person; juvenile; young man, youth; young girl; teen-ager; '**~liebe** *f* early *or* first love, calf-love, *Am. a.* puppy love; old sweetheart *or* flame; '**~schriften** *f/pl.* books for the young; '**~schutz** *m* protection of children and young people; '**~streich** *m* youthful prank; '**~werk** *n* early work *(of author);* ~e *pl. a.* juvenilia *pl.*; '~zeit *f* (time *or* days of) youth.

Jugoslav|e [ju:go'sla:və] *m* (-en/-en) Jugoslav, Yugoslav; ℒisch *adj.* Jugoslav, Yugoslav.

Juli ['ju:li] *m* (-[s]/-s) July.

jung *adj.* [juŋ] young; youthful; *peas:* green; *beer, wine:* new; ~es Gemüse young *or* early vegetables *pl.*; F *fig.* young people, small fry.

'**Junge 1.** *m* (-n/-n) boy, youngster; lad; fellow, chap, *Am.* guy; *cards:* knave, jack; **2.** *n* (-n/-n) young; puppy *(of dog);* kitten *(of cat);* calf *(of cow, elephant, etc.);* cub *(of beast of prey);* ~ werfen bring forth young; ein ~s a young one; ℒnhaft *adj.* boyish; '~nstreich *m* boyish prank *or* trick.

jünger ['jyŋər] *1. adj.* younger, junior; *er ist drei Jahre ~ als ich* he is my junior by three years, he is three years younger than I; **2.** ℒ *m* (-s/-) disciple.

Jungfer ['juŋfər] *f* (-/-n): *alte ~* old maid *or* spinster.

'**Jungfern|fahrt** ⚓ *f* maiden voyage *or* trip; '~flug ✈ *m* maiden flight; '~rede *f* maiden speech.

'**Jung|frau** *f* maid(en), virgin; ℒ-**fräulich** *adj.* ['~frɔʏlɪç] virginal; *fig.* virgin; '~fräulichkeit *f* (-/no *pl.*) virginity, maidenhood; '~ge-**selle** *m* bachelor; '~gesellenstand *m* bachelorhood; '~gesellin *f* (-/-nen) bachelor girl.

Jüngling ['jyŋliŋ] *m* (-s/-e) youth, young man.

jüngst [jyŋst] **1.** *adj.* youngest; *time:* (most) recent, latest; *das* ℒe *Gericht, der* ℒe *Tag* Last Judg(e)ment, Day of Judg(e)ment; **2.** *adv.* recently, lately.

'**jungverheiratet** *adj.* newly married; 'ℒen *pl. the* newlyweds *pl.*

Juni ['ju:ni] *m* (-[s]/-s) June; '~kä-**fer** *zo. m* cockchafer, June-bug.

junior ['ju:njɔr] *1. adj.* junior; **2.** ℒ *m* (-s/-en) junior *(a. sports).*

Jura ['ju:ra] *n/pl.:* ~ studieren read *or* study law.

Jurist [ju'rist] *m* (-en/-en) lawyer; law-student; ℒisch *adj.* legal.

Jury [ʒy'ri:] *f* (-/-s) jury.

justier|en ⊕ [jus'ti:rən] *v/t.* (*no* -ge-, *h*) adjust; ℒung ⊕ *f* (-/-en) adjustment.

Justiz [ju'sti:ts] *f* (-/no *pl.*) (administration of) justice; ~beamte *m* judicial officer; ~gebäude *n* courthouse; ~inspektor *m* judicial officer; ~irrtum *m* judicial error; ~-**minister** *m* minister of justice; Lord Chancellor, *Am.* Attorney General; ~ministerium *n* ministry of justice; *Am.* Department of Justice; ~mord *m* judicial murder.

Juwel [ju've:l] *m, n* (-s/-en) jewel, gem; ~en *pl.* jewel(le)ry; ~ier [~e-'li:r] *m* (-s/-e) jewel(l)er.

Jux F [juks] *m* (-es/-e) (practical) joke, fun, spree, lark; prank.

K

(Compare also C and Z)

Kabel ['ka:bəl] *n* (-s/-) cable.

Kabeljau *ichth.* ['ka:bəljau] *m* (-s/-e, -s) cod(fish).

'**kabeln** *v/t. and v/i.* (ge-, *h*) cable.

Kabine [ka'bi:nə] *f* (-/-n) cabin; *at hairdresser's, etc.:* cubicle; cage *(of lift).*

Kabinett *pol.* [kabi'nɛt] *n* (-s/-e) cabinet, government.

Kabriolett [kabrio'lɛt] *n* (-s/-e) cabriolet, convertible.

Kachel ['kaxəl] *f* (-/-n) (Dutch *or* glazed) tile; '~ofen *m* tiled stove.

Kadaver [ka'da:vər] *m* (-s/-) carcass.

Kadett [ka'dɛt] *m* (-en/-en) cadet.

Käfer *zo.* ['kɛːfər] *m* (-s/-) beetle, chafer.

Kaffee ['kafe, ka'fe:] *m* (-s/-s) coffee; (')~bohne ❦ *f* coffee-bean; (')~kanne *f* coffee-pot; (')~mühle *f* coffee-mill *or* -grinder; (')~satz *m* coffee-grounds *pl.*; (')~tasse *f* coffee-cup.

Käfig ['kɛːfiç] *m* (-s/-e) cage *(a. fig.).*

kahl *adj.* [ka:l] *p.* bald; *tree, etc.:* bare; *landscape, etc.:* barren, bleak; *rock, etc.:* naked; ℒkopf *m* baldhead, baldpate; ~köpfig *adj.* ['~kœpfiç] bald(-headed).

Kahn [kɑːn] *m* (-[e]s/⸚e) boat; river-barge; ~ *fahren* go boating; '~**fahren** *n* (-s/*no pl.*) boating.

Kai [kaɪ] *m* (-s/-e, -s) quay, wharf.

Kaiser ['kaɪzər] *m* (-s/-) emperor; '~**krone** *f* imperial crown; '2**lich** *adj.* imperial; '~**reich** *n*, '~**tum** *n* (-[e]s/⸚er) empire; '~**würde** *f* imperial status.

Kajüte ⚓ [ka'jyːtə] *f* (-/-n) cabin.

Kakao [ka'kaːo] *m* (-s/-s) cocoa; ♀ *a.* cacao.

Kakt|ee ♀ [kak'teː(ə)] *f* (-/-n), '~**us** ♀ ['⸚us] *m* (-/Kakteen, F *Kaktusse*) cactus.

Kalauer ['kɑːlaʊər] *m* (-s/-) stale joke; pun.

Kalb *zo.* [kalp] *n* (-[e]s/⸚er) calf; 2**en** ['⸚bən] *v/i.* (*ge-*, *h*) calve; '~**fell** *n* calfskin; '~**fleisch** *n* veal; '~**leder** *n* calf(-leather).

Kalbs|braten *m* roast veal; '~**keule** *f* leg of veal; '~**leder** *n* s. *Kalbleder*; '~**nierenbraten** *m* loin of veal.

Kalender [ka'lɛndər] *m* (-s/-) calendar; almanac; '~**block** *m* date-block; '~**jahr** *n* calendar year; '~**uhr** *f* calendar watch or clock.

Kali ♣ ['kaːli] *n* (-s/-s) potash.

Kaliber [ka'liːbər] *n* (-s/-) calib|re, *Am.* -er (*a. fig.*), bore (*of firearm*).

Kalk [kalk] *m* (-[e]s/-e) lime; *geol.* limestone; '~**brenner** *m* lime-burner; '2**en** *v/t.* (*ge-*, *h*) whitewash (*wall, etc.*); ✗ lime (*field*); '2**ig** *adj.* limy; '~**ofen** *m* limekiln; '~**stein** *m* limestone; '~**steinbruch** *m* limestone quarry.

Kalorie [kalo'riː] *f* (-/-n) calorie.

kalt *adj.* [kalt] climate, meal, sweat, *etc.*: cold; *p.*, manner, *etc.*: cold, chilly, frigid; *mir ist* ~ I am cold; ~*e Küche* cold dishes *pl.* or meat, *etc.*; *j-m die* ~*e Schulter zeigen* give s.o. the cold shoulder; '~**blütig** *adj.* ['⸚blyːtɪç] cold-blooded (*a. fig.*).

Kälte ['kɛltə] *f* (-/*no pl.*) cold; chill; coldness, chilliness (*both a. fig.*); *vor* ~ *zittern* shiver with cold; *fünf Grad* ~ five degrees below zero; '~**grad** *m* degree below zero; '~**welle** *f* cold spell.

'**kalt|stellen** *fig. v/t.* (*sep.*, -*ge-*, *h*) shelve, reduce to impotence; '2**welle** *f* cold wave.

kam [kɑːm] *pret. of* **kommen.**

Kamel *zo.* [ka'meːl] *n* (-[e]s/-e) camel; '~**haar** *n* *textiles*: camel hair.

Kamera *phot.* ['kamərə] *f* (-/-s) camera.

Kamerad [kamə'rɑːt] *m* (-en/-en) comrade; companion; mate, F pal, chum; '~**schaft** *f* (-/-en) comradeship, companionship; 2**schaftlich** *adj.* comradely, companionable.

Kamille ♀ [ka'milə] *f* (-/-n) camomile; '~**ntee** *m* camomile tea.

Kamin [ka'miːn] *m* (-s/-e) chimney (*a. mount.*); fireplace, fireside; '~**sims** *m, n* mantelpiece; '~**vorleger** *m* hearth-rug; '~**vorsetzer** *m* (-s/-) fender.

Kamm [kam] *m* (-[e]s/⸚e) comb; crest (*of bird or wave*); crest, ridge (*of mountain*).

kämmen ['kɛmən] *v/t.* (*ge-*, *h*) comb; *sich* (*die Haare*) ~ comb one's hair.

Kammer ['kamər] *f* (-/-n) (small) room; closet; *pol.* chamber; board; ⚖ division (*of court*); '~**diener** *m* valet; '~**frau** *f* lady's maid; '~**gericht** ⚖ *n* supreme court; '~**herr** *m* chamberlain; '~**jäger** *m* vermin exterminator; '~**musik** *f* chamber music; '~**zofe** *f* chambermaid.

'**Kamm|garn** *n* worsted (yarn); '~**rad** ⊕ *n* cogwheel.

Kampagne [kam'panjə] *f* (-/-n) campaign.

Kampf [kampf] *m* (-[e]s/⸚e) combat, fight (*a. fig.*); struggle (*a. fig.*); battle (*a. fig.*); *fig.* conflict; *sports:* contest, match; *boxing:* fight, bout; '~**bahn** *f* *sports:* stadium, arena; '2**bereit** *adj.* ready for battle.

kämpfen ['kɛmpfən] *v/i.* (*ge-*, *h*) fight (*gegen* against; *mit* with; *um* for) (*a. fig.*); struggle (*a. fig.*); *fig.* contend, wrestle (*mit* with).

Kampfer ['kampfər] *m* (-s/*no pl.*) camphor.

Kämpfer ['kɛmpfər] *m* (-s/-) fighter (*a. fig.*); ✗ combatant, warrior.

'**Kampf|flugzeug** *n* tactical aircraft; '~**geist** *m* fighting spirit; '~**platz** *m* battlefield; *fig.*, *sports:* arena; '~**preis** *m* *sports:* prize; ✝ cut-throat price; '~**richter** *m* referee, judge, umpire; '2**unfähig** *adj.* disabled.

kampieren [kam'piːrən] *v/i.* (*no* -*ge-*, *h*) camp.

Kanal [ka'nɑːl] *m* (-s/⸚e) canal; channel (*a.* ⊕, *fig.*); *geogr. the* Channel; sewer, drain; '~**isation**

[ˌ~aliza'tsjoːn] f (-/-en) *river:* canalization; *town, etc.:* sewerage; drainage; **2isieren** [ˌ~ali'ziːrən] v/t. (*no* -ge-, h) canalize; sewer.

Kanarienvogel orn. [ka'naːrjən-] m canary(-bird).

Kandare [kan'daːrə] f (-/-n) curb (-bit).

Kandid|at [kandi'daːt] m (-en/-en) candidate; applicant; **~atur** [ˌ~a'tuːr] f (-/-en) candidature, candidacy; **2ieren** [ˌ~'diːrən] v/i. (*no* -ge-, h) be a candidate (für for); ~ für apply for, stand for, *Am.* run for (*office, etc.*).

Känguruh zo. ['kɛŋguruː] n (-s/-s) kangaroo.

Kaninchen zo. [ka'niːnçən] n (-s/-) rabbit; **~bau** m rabbit-burrow.

Kanister [ka'nistər] m (-s/-) can.

Kanne ['kanə] f (-/-n) *milk, etc.:* jug; *coffee, tea:* pot; *oil, milk:* can; '**~gießer** F *fig.* m political wiseacre.

Kannibal|e [kani'baːlə] m (-n/-n) cannibal; **2isch** adj. cannibal.

kannte ['kantə] pret. of **kennen**.

Kanon ♪ ['kaːnɔn] m (-s/-s) canon.

Kanon|ade ✕ [kano'naːdə] f (-/-n) cannonade; **~e** [ˌ~'noːnə] f (-/-n) ✕ cannon, gun; F *fig.:* big shot; *esp. sports:* ace, crack.

Ka'nonen|boot ✕ n gunboat; **~donner** m boom of cannon; **~futter** *fig.* n cannon-fodder; **~kugel** f cannon-ball; **~rohr** n gun barrel.

Kanonier ✕ [kano'niːr] m (-s/-) gunner.

Kant|e ['kantə] f (-/-n) edge; brim; '**~en** m (-s/-) end of loaf; '**2en** v/t. (ge-, h) square (*stone, etc.*); set on edge; tilt; edge (*skis*); '**2ig** adj. angular, edged; square(d).

Kantine [kan'tiːnə] f (-/-n) canteen.

Kanu ['kaːnu] n (-s/-s) canoe.

Kanüle ♪ [ka'nyːlə] f (-/-n) tubule, cannula.

Kanzel ['kantsəl] f (-/-n) *eccl.* pulpit; ✈ cockpit; ✕ (gun-)turret.; '**~redner** m preacher.

Kanzlei [kants'lai] f (-/-en) office. '**Kanzler** m (-s/-) chancellor.

Kap *geogr.* [kap] n (-s/-s) headland.

Kapazität [kapatsi'tɛːt] f (-/-en) capacity; *fig.* authority.

Kapell|e [ka'pɛlə] f (-/-n) *eccl.* chapel; ♪ band; **~meister** m bandleader, conductor.

kaper|n ⚓ ['kaːpərn] v/t. (ge-, h)

capture, seize; '**2schiff** n privateer.

kapieren F [ka'piːrən] v/t. (*no* -ge-, h) grasp, get.

Kapital [kapi'taːl] **1.** n (-s/-e, -ien) capital, stock, funds *pl.*; ~ **und Zinsen** principal and interest; **2.** 2 adj. capital; **~anlage** f investment; **~flucht** f flight of capital; **~gesellschaft** f joint-stock company; **2isieren** [ˌ~ali'ziːrən] v/t. (*no* -ge-, h) capitalize; **~ismus** [ˌ~a'lismus] m (-/*no pl.*) capitalism; **~ist** [ˌ~a'list] m (-en/-en) capitalist; **~markt** [ˌ~'tɔːl-] m capital market; **~verbrechen** n capital crime.

Kapitän [kapi'tɛːn] m (-s/-e) captain; ~ **zur See** naval captain; **~leutnant** m (senior) lieutenant.

Kapitel [ka'pitəl] n (-s/-) chapter (*a. fig.*).

Kapitul|ation ✕ [kapitula'tsjoːn] f (-/-en) capitulation, surrender; **2ieren** [ˌ~'liːrən] v/i. (*no* -ge-, h) capitulate, surrender.

Kaplan *eccl.* [ka'plaːn] m (-s/*~e) chaplain.

Kappe ['kapə] f (-/-n) cap; hood (*a.* ⊕); bonnet; '**2n** v/t. (ge-, h) cut (*cable*); lop, top (*tree*).

Kapriole [kapri'oːlə] f (-/-n) *equitation:* capriole; *fig.:* caper; prank.

Kapsel ['kapsəl] f (-/-n) case, box; ♀, ♣, anat., *etc.:* capsule.

kaputt adj. [ka'put] broken; *elevator, etc.:* out of order; *fruit, etc.:* spoilt; *p.:* ruined; tired out, F fagged out; **~gehen** v/i. (irr. gehen, sep., -ge-, sein) break, go to pieces; spoil.

Kapuze [ka'puːtsə] f (-/-n) hood; *eccl.* cowl.

Karabiner [kara'biːnər] m (-s/-) carbine.

Karaffe [ka'rafə] f (-/-n) carafe (*for wine or water*); decanter (*for liqueur, etc.*).

Karambol|age [karambo'laːʒə] f (-/-n) collision, crash; *billiards:* cannon, *Am. a.* carom; **2ieren** v/i. (*no* -ge-, sein) cannon, *Am. a.* carom; F *fig.* collide.

Karat [ka'raːt] n (-[e]s/-e) carat.

Karawane [kara'vaːnə] f (-/-n) caravan.

Karbid [kar'biːt] n (-[e]s/-e) carbide.

Kardinal *eccl.* [kardi'naːl] m (-s/*~e) cardinal.   [Friday.)

Karfreitag *eccl.* [kaːr'-] m Good⌐

karg adj. [kark] soil: meagre; vegetation: scant, sparse; meal: scanty, meagre, frugal; **~en** ['~gən] v/i. (ge-, h): ~ mit be sparing of.

kärglich adj. ['kɛrkliç] scanty, meagre; poor.

kariert adj. [ka'ri:rt] check(ed), chequered, Am. checkered.

Karik|atur [karika'tu:r] f (-/-en) caricature, cartoon; **2ieren** [~ki:-rən] v/t. (no -ge-, h) caricature, cartoon.

karmesin adj. [karme'zi:n] crimson.

Karneval ['karnəval] m (-s/-e, -s) Shrovetide, carnival.

Karo ['ka:ro] n (-s/-s) square, check; cards: diamonds pl.

Karosserie mot. [karosə'ri:] f (-/-n) body.

Karotte 🌿 [ka'rɔtə] f (-/-n) carrot.

Karpfen ichth. ['karpfən] m (-s/-) carp.

Karre ['karə] f (-/-n) cart; wheelbarrow.

Karriere [kar'jɛːrə] f (-/-n) (successful) career.

Karte ['kartə] f (-/-n) card; postcard; map; chart; ticket; menu, bill of fare; list.

Kartei [kar'taɪ] f (-/-en) card-index; **~karte** f index-card, filing-card; **~schrank** m filing cabinet.

Kartell 🌿 [kar'tɛl] n (-s/-e) cartel.

'**Karten|brief** m letter-card; '**~haus** n 🚢 chart-house; fig. house of cards; '**~legerin** f (-/-nen) fortune-teller from the cards; '**~spiel** n card-playing; card-game.

Kartoffel [kar'tɔfəl] f (-/-n) potato, F spud; **~brei** m mashed potatoes pl.; **~käfer** m Colorado or potato beetle, Am. a. potato bug; **~schalen** f/pl. potato peelings pl.

Karton [kar'tõ, kar'to:n] m (-s/-s, -e) cardboard, pasteboard; cardboard box, carton. [Kartei.]

Kartothek [karto'te:k] f (-/-en) s.]

Karussell [karu'sɛl] n (-s/-s, -e) roundabout, merry-go-round, Am. a. car(r)ousel.

Karwoche eccl. ['ka:r-] f Holy or Passion Week.

Käse ['kɛːzə] m (-s/-) cheese.

Kasern|e ⚔ [ka'zɛrnə] f (-/-n) barracks pl.; **~enhof** m barrack-yard or -square; **2ieren** [~'ni:rən] v/t. (no -ge-, h) quarter in barracks, barrack.

'**käsig** adj. cheesy; complexion: pale, pasty.

Kasino [ka'zi:no] n (-s/-s) casino, club(-house); (officers') mess.

Kasperle ['kasperlə] n, m (-s/-) Punch; '**~theater** n Punch and Judy show.

Kasse ['kasə] f (-/-n) cash-box; till (in shop, etc.); cash-desk, pay-desk (in bank, etc.); pay-office (in firm); thea., etc.: box-office, booking-office; cash; bei ~ in cash.

'**Kassen|abschluß** 🌿 m balancing of the cash (accounts); '**~anweisung** f disbursement voucher; '**~bestand** m cash in hand; '**~bote** m bank messenger; '**~buch** n cash book; '**~erfolg** m thea., etc.: box-office success; '**~patient** 🌿 m panel patient; '**~schalter** m bank, etc.: teller's counter.

Kasserolle [kasə'rɔlə] f (-/-n) stewpan, casserole.

Kassette [ka'sɛtə] f (-/-n) box (for money, etc.); casket (for jewels, etc.); slip-case (for books); phot. plateholder.

kassiere|n [ka'si:rən] (no -ge-, h) 1. v/i. waiter, etc.: take the money (für for); 2. v/t. take (sum of money); collect (contributions, etc.); annul; 🌿 quash (verdict); 2r m (-s/-) cashier; bank: a. teller; collector.

Kastanie 🌿 [ka'sta:njə] f (-/-n) chestnut.

Kasten ['kastən] m (-s/⁼, 🌿 -) box; chest (for tools, etc.); case (for violin, etc.); bin (for bread, etc.).

Kasus gr. ['ka:sus] m (-/-) case.

Katalog [kata'lo:k] m (-[e]s/-e) catalogue, Am. a. catalog; **2isieren** [~ogi'zi:rən] v/t. (no -ge-, h) catalogue, Am. a. catalog.

Katarrh 🌿 [ka'tar] m (-s/-e) (common) cold, catarrh.

katastroph|al adj. [katastro'fɑ:l] catastrophic, disastrous; **2e** [~'stro:-fə] f (-/-n) catastrophe, disaster.

Katechismus eccl. [kate'çɪsmus] m (-/Katechismen) catechism.

Katego|rie [katego'ri:] f (-/-n) category; **2risch** adj. [~'go:rɪʃ] categorical.

Kater ['ka:tər] m (-s/-) zo. male cat, tom-cat; fig. s. Katzenjammer.

Katheder [ka'te:dər] n, m (-s/-) lecturing-desk. [cathedral.]

Kathedrale [kate'drɑ:lə] f (-/-n)

Katholi|k [kato'li:k] *m* (-en/-en) (Roman) Catholic; **≈sch** *adj.* [.'to:liʃ] (Roman) Catholic.

Kattun [ka'tu:n] *m* (-s/-e) calico; cotton cloth *or* fabric; chintz.

Katze zo. ['katsə] *f* (-/-n) cat; **'~njammer** F *fig. m* hangover, morning-after feeling.

Kauderwelsch ['kaudərvɛlʃ] *n* (-[s]/ *no pl.*) gibberish, F double Dutch; **'≈en** *v/i.* (ge-, h) gibber, F talk double Dutch. [chew.]

kauen ['kauən] *v/t.and v/i.* (ge-, h))

kauern ['kauərn] (ge-, h) **1.** *v/i.* crouch; squat; **2.** *v/refl.* crouch (down); squat (down); duck (down).

Kauf [kauf] *m* (-[e]s/⁀e) purchase; bargain, F good buy; acquisition; purchasing, buying; **'~brief** *m* deed of purchase; **'≈en** *v/t.* (ge-, h) buy, purchase; acquire (by purchase); *sich et.* ~ buy o.s. s.th., buy s.th. for o.s. [purchaser; customer.]

Käufer ['kɔyfər] *m* (-s/-) buyer,)

'Kauf|haus *n* department store; **'~laden** *m* shop, *Am. a.* store.

käuflich ['kɔyflɪç] **1.** *adj.* for sale; purchasable; *fig.* open to bribery, bribable; venal; **2.** *adv.*: ~ erwerben (acquire by) purchase; ~ überlassen transfer by way of sale.

'Kauf|mann *m* (-[e]s/*Kaufleute*) businessman; merchant; trader, dealer, shopkeeper; *Am. a.* storekeeper; **≈männisch** *adj.* ['.mɛnɪʃ] commercial, mercantile; **'~vertrag** *m* contract of sale.

'Kaugummi *m* chewing-gum.

kaum *adv.* [kaum] hardly, scarcely, barely; ~ *glaublich* hard to believe.

'Kautabak *m* chewing-tobacco.

Kaution [kau'tsjo:n] *f* (-/-en) security, surety; ⅇⅇ *mst* bail.

Kautschuk ['kautʃuk] *m* (-s/-e) caoutchouc, pure rubber.

Kavalier [kava'li:r] *m* (-s/-e) gentleman; beau, admirer.

Kavallerie ✕ [kavalə'ri:] *f* (-/-n) cavalry, horse.

Kaviar ['ka:viar] *m* (-s/-e) caviar(e).

keck *adj.* [kɛk] bold; impudent, saucy, cheeky; **≈heit** *f* (-/-en) boldness; impudence, sauciness, cheekiness.

Kegel ['ke:gəl] *m* (-s/-) *games*: skittle, pin; *esp.* ⒜, ⊕ cone; ~ *schieben s.* *kegeln*; **'~bahn** *f* skittle, alley, *Am.* bowling alley; **≈förmig**

adj. ['.fœrmɪç] conic(al), coniform; tapering; **'≈n** *v/i.* (ge-, h) play (at) skittles *or* ninepins, *Am.* bowl.

Kegler ['ke:glər] *m* (-s/-) skittleplayer, *Am.* bowler.

Kehl|e ['ke:lə] *f* (-/-n) throat; **'~kopf** *anat. m* larynx.

Kehre ['ke:rə] *f* (-/-n) (sharp) bend, turn; **'≈n** *v/t.* (ge-, h) sweep, brush; turn (*nach oben upwards*); *j-m den Rücken* ~ turn one's back on s.o.

Kehricht ['ke:rɪçt] *m, n* (-[e]s/*no pl.*) sweepings *pl.*, rubbish.

'Kehrseite *f* wrong side, reverse; *esp. fig.* seamy side.

'kehrtmachen *v/i.* (sep., -ge-, h) turn on one's heel; ✕ turn *or* face about. [chide.)

keifen ['kaifən] *v/i.* (ge-, h) scold,)

Keil [kail] *m* (-[e]s/-e) wedge; gore, gusset; **'~e** F *f* (-/*no pl.*) thrashing, hiding; **'~er** zo. *m* (-s/-) wild-boar; **~erei** *f* [.'rai] *f* (-/-en) row, scrap; **≈förmig** *adj.* ['.fœrmɪç] wedge-shaped, cuneiform; **'~kissen** *n* wedge-shaped bolster; **'~schrift** *f* cuneiform characters *pl.*

Keim [kaim] *m* (-[e]s/-e) ⒜, *biol.* germ; ⒝: seed-plant; shoot; sprout; *fig.* seeds *pl.*, germ, bud; **'≈en** *v/i.* (ge-, h) *seeds, etc.*: germinate; *seeds, plants, potatoes, etc.*: sprout; *fig.* b(o)urgeon; **'≈frei** *adj.* sterilized, sterile; **'≈träger** ⚹ *m* (germ-)carrier; **'~zelle** *f* germ-cell.

kein *indef. pron.* [kain] *as adj.*: ~(e) no, not any; ~ *anderer als* none other but; *as noun*: ~er, ~e, ~(e)s none, no one, nobody; ~er von *beiden* neither (of the two); ~er von *uns* none of us; **'~es'falls** *adv.*, **~eswegs** *adv.* ['.ve:ks] by no means, not at all; **'~mal** *adv.* not once, not a single time.

Keks [ke:ks] *m, n* (-, -es/-, -e) biscuit, *Am.* cookie; cracker.

Kelch [kɛlç] *m* (-[e]s/-e) cup, goblet; *eccl.* chalice, communion-cup; ⒝ calyx.

Kelle ['kɛlə] *f* (-/-n) scoop; ladle; *tool*: trowel.

Keller ['kɛlər] *m* (-s/-) cellar; basement; **~ei** [.'rai] *f* (-/-en) wine-vault; **'~geschoß** *n* basement; **'~meister** *m* cellarman.

Kellner ['kɛlnər] *m* (-s/-) waiter; **'~in** *f* (-/-nen) waitress.

Kelter ['kɛltər] f (-/-n) winepress; **'2n** v/t. (ge-, h) press.

kenn|en ['kɛnən] v/t. (irr., ge-, h) know, be acquainted with; have knowledge of s.th.; **'.enlernen** v/t. (sep., -ge-, h) get or come to know; make s.o.'s acquaintance, meet s.o.; **'2er** m (-s/-) expert, connoisseur; **'.tlich** adj. recognizable (an dat. by); ~ **machen** mark; label; **'2tnis** f (-/-se) knowledge; ~ **nehmen von** take not(ic)e of; **'2zeichen** n mark, sign; mot. registration (number), Am. license number; fig. hallmark, criterion; **'.zeichnen** v/t. (ge-, h) mark, characterize.

kentern ⚓ ['kɛntərn] v/i. (ge-, sein) capsize, keel over, turn turtle.

Kerbe ['kɛrbə] f (-/-n) notch, nick; slot; **'2n** v/t. (ge-, h) notch, nick, indent.

Kerker ['kɛrkər] m (-s/-) gaol, jail, prison; **'.meister** m gaoler, jailer.

Kerl F ['kɛrl] m (-s, ✎ -es/-e, F -s) man; fellow, F chap, bloke, esp. Am. guy.

Kern [kɛrn] m (-[e]s/-e) kernel (of nut, etc.); stone, Am. pit (of cherry, etc.); pip (of orange, apple, etc.); core (of the earth); phys. nucleus; fig. core, heart, crux; Kern-... s. a. Atom-...; **'.energie** f nuclear energy; **'.forschung** f nuclear research; **'.gehäuse** n core; **2ge'sund** adj. thoroughly healthy, F as sound as a bell; **2ig** adj. full of pips; fig.: pithy; solid; **'.punkt** m central or crucial point; **'.spaltung** f nuclear fission.

Kerze ['kɛrtsə] f (-/-n) candle; **'.n-licht** n candle-light; **'.nstärke** f candle-power.

keß F adj. [kɛs] pert, jaunty; smart.

Kessel ['kɛsəl] m (-s/-) kettle; cauldron; boiler; hollow.

Kette ['kɛtə] f (-/-n) chain; range (of mountains, etc.); necklace; **'2n** v/t. (ge-, h) chain (an acc. to).

'Ketten|hund m watch-dog; **'.rau-cher** m chain-smoker; **'.reaktion** f chain reaction.

Ketzer ['kɛtsər] m (-s/-) heretic; **.ei** [~'raɪ] f (-/-en) heresy; **2isch** adj. heretical.

keuch|en ['kɔʏçən] v/i. (ge-, h) pant, gasp; **'2husten** ✎ m (w)hooping cough. [(of mutton, pork, etc.)]

Keule ['kɔʏlə] f (-/-n) club; leg⌋

keusch adj. [kɔʏʃ] chaste, pure; **'2heit** f (-/no pl.) chastity, purity.

kichern ['kɪçərn] v/i. (ge-, h) giggle, titter.

Kiebitz ['ki:bɪts] m (-es/-e) orn. pe(e)wit; F fig. kibitzer; **'2en** F fig. v/i. (ge-, h) kibitz.

Kiefer ['ki:fər] **1.** anat. m (-s/-) jaw(-bone); **2.** ♀ f (-/-n) pine.

Kiel [ki:l] m (-[e]s/-e) ⚓ keel; quill; **'.raum** m bilge, hold; **'.wasser** n wake (a. fig.).

Kieme zo. ['ki:mə] f (-/-n) gill.

Kies [ki:s] m (-es/-e) gravel; sl. fig. dough; **'2el** ['~zəl] m (-s/-) pebble, flint; **'.weg** m gravel-walk.

Kilo ['ki:lo] n (-s/-[s]), **.gramm** [kilo'gram] n kilogram(me); **.hertz** [~'hɛrts] n (-/no pl.) kilocycle per second; **.meter** m kilomet|re, Am. -er; **.watt** n kilowatt.

Kimme ['kɪmə] f (-/-n) notch.

Kind [kɪnt] n (-[e]s/-er) child; baby.

'Kinder|arzt m p(a)ediatrician; **.ei** [~'raɪ] f (-/-en) childishness; childish trick; trifle; **'.frau** f nurse; **'.fräulein** n governess; **'.funk** m children's program(me); **'.garten** m kindergarten, nursery school; **'.lähmung** f infantile paralysis, polio(myelitis); **2leicht** adj. very easy or simple, F as easy as winking or as ABC; **'.lied** n children's song; **2los** adj. childless; **'.mäd-chen** n nurse(maid); **'.spiel** n children's game; ein ~ s. kinder-leicht; **'.stube** f nursery; fig. manners pl., upbringing; **'.wagen** m perambulator, F pram, Am. baby carriage; **'.zeit** f childhood; **'.zim-mer** n children's room.

'Kindes|alter n childhood, infancy; **'.beine** n/pl.: von ~n an from childhood, from a very early age; **'.kind** n grandchild.

'Kind|heit f (-/no pl.) childhood; **2isch** adj. childish; **'.lich** adj. childlike.

Kinn anat. [kɪn] n (-[e]s/-e) chin; **'.backe** f, **'.backen** m (-s/-) jaw (-bone); **'.haken** m boxing: hook to the chin; uppercut; **'.lade** f jaw(-bone).

Kino ['ki:no] n (-s/-s) cinema, F the pictures pl., Am. motion-picture theater, F the movies pl.; ins ~ gehen go to the cinema or F pictures, Am. F go to the movies; **'.besu-**

cher *m* cinema-goer, *Am.* F moviegoer; **~vorstellung** *f* cinema-show, *Am.* motion-picture show.

Kippe F [ˈkɪpə] *f* (-/-n) stub, fag-end, *Am. a.* butt; *auf der ~ stehen or sein* hang in the balance; **'Qn** (ge-) **1.** *v/i.* (*sein*) tip (over), topple (over), tilt (over); **2.** *v/t.* (*h*) tilt, tip over *or* up.

Kirche [ˈkɪrçə] *f* (-/-n) church.

'**Kirchen|älteste** *m* (-n/-n) churchwarden, elder; **~buch** *n* parochial register; **~diener** *m* sacristan, sexton; **~gemeinde** *f* parish; **~jahr** *n* ecclesiastical year; **~lied** *n* hymn; **~musik** *f* sacred music; **~schiff** △ *n* nave; **~steuer** *f* church-rate; **~stuhl** *m* pew; **~vorsteher** *m* churchwarden.

'**Kirch|gang** *m* church-going; **~gänger** [ˈ~ɡɛŋər] *m* (-s/-) church-goer; **~hof** *m* churchyard; **'Qlich** *adj.* ecclesiastical; **~spiel** *n* parish; **~turm** *m* steeple; **~weih** [ˈ~vaɪ] *f* (-/-en) parish fair.

Kirsche [ˈkɪrʃə] *f* (-/-n) cherry.

Kissen [ˈkɪsən] *n* (-s/-) cushion; pillow; bolster, pad.

Kiste [ˈkɪstə] *f* (-/-n) box, chest, crate.

Kitsch [kɪtʃ] *m* (-es/*no pl.*) trash, rubbish; **'Qig** *adj.* shoddy, trashy.

Kitt [kɪt] *m* (-[e]s/-e) cement; putty.

Kittel [ˈkɪtəl] *m* (-s/-) overall; smock, frock.

'**kitten** *v/t.* (ge-, *h*) cement; putt.

kitz|eln [ˈkɪtsəln] (ge-, *h*) **1.** *v/t.* tickle; **2.** *v/i.*: *meine Nase kitzelt* my nose is tickling; **'~lig** *adj.* ticklish (*a. fig.*).

Kladde [ˈkladə] *f* (-/-n) rough note-book, waste-book.

klaffen [ˈklafən] *v/i.* (ge-, *h*) gape, yawn.

kläffen [ˈklɛfən] *v/i.* (ge-, *h*) yap, yelp.

klagbar ɪ̯ɪ *adj.* [ˈklaːkbaːr] *matter, etc.*: actionable; *debt, etc.*: suable.

Klage [ˈklaːɡə] *f* (-/-n) complaint; lament; ɪ̯ɪ action, suit; **'Qn** (ge-, *h*) **1.** *v/i.* complain (*über acc. of, about; bei* to); lament; ɪ̯ɪ take legal action (*gegen* against); **2.** *v/t.*: *j-m et. ~* complain to s.o. of *or* about s.th.

Kläger ɪ̯ɪ [ˈklɛːɡər] *m* (-s/-) plaintiff; complainant.

kläglich *adj.* [ˈklɛːklɪç] pitiful, piteous, pitiable; *cries, etc.*: plaintive; *condition*: wretched, lamentable; *performance, result, etc.*: miserable, poor; *failure, etc.*: lamentable, miserable.

klamm [klam] **1.** *adj.* hands, *etc.*: numb *or* stiff with cold, clammy; **2.** ♀ *f* (-/-en) ravine, gorge, canyon.

Klammer [ˈklamər] *f* (-/-n) ⊕ clamp, cramp; (paper-)clip; *gr., typ.,* ⅄ bracket, parenthesis; **'Qn** (ge-, *h*) **1.** *v/t.* clip together; ♂ close (*wound*) with clips; *sich ~ an* (*acc.*) cling to (*a. fig.*); **2.** *v/i.* boxing: clinch.

Klang [klaŋ] **1.** *m* (-[e]s/ᵘe) sound, tone (*of voice, instrument, etc.*); tone (*of radio, etc.*); clink (*of glasses, etc.*); ringing (*of bells, etc.*); timbre; **2.** ♀ *pret. of* klingen; **~fülle** ♪ *f* sonority; **'Qlos** *adj.* toneless; **'Qvoll** *adj.* sonorous.

Klappe [ˈklapə] *f* (-/-n) flap, flap, drop leaf (*of table, etc.*); shoulder strap (*of uniform, etc.*); tailboard (*of lorry, etc.*); ⊕, ♀, *anat.* valve; ♪ key; F *fig.*: bed; trap; **'Qn** (ge-, *h*) **1.** *v/t.*: *nach oben ~* tip up; *nach unten ~* lower, put down; **2.** *v/i.* clap, flap; *fig.* come off well, work out fine, *Am. sl. a.* click.

Klapper [ˈklapər] *f* (-/-n) rattle; **'Qig** *adj.* vehicle, *etc.*: rattly, ramshackle; *furniture*: rickety; *person, horse, etc.*: decrepit; **'~kasten** F *m* wretched piano; rattletrap; **'Qn** *v/i.* (ge-, *h*) clatter, rattle (*mit et. s.th.*); *er klapperte vor Kälte mit den Zähnen* his teeth were chattering with cold; **'~schlange** *zo. f* rattlesnake, *Am. a.* rattler.

'**Klapp|kamera** *phot. f* folding camera; **~messer** *n* clasp-knife, jack-knife; **~sitz** *m* tip-up *or* flap seat; **~stuhl** *m* folding chair; **~tisch** *m* folding table, *Am. a.* gate-leg(ged) table; **~ult** [ˈklappult] *n* folding desk.

Klaps [klaps] *m* (-es/-e) smack, slap; **'Qen** *v/t.* (ge-, *h*) smack, slap.

klar *adj.* [klaːr] clear; bright; transparent, limpid; pure; *fig.*: clear, distinct, plain; evident, obvious; *sich ~ sein über* (*acc.*) be clear about; **~en Kopf bewahren** keep a clear head.

klären [ˈklɛːrən] *v/t.* (ge-, *h*) clarify; *fig.* clarify, clear up, elucidate.

'**klar|legen** v/t. (sep., -ge-, h); '**stellen** v/t. (sep., -ge-, h) clear up.
'**Klärung** f (-/-en) clarification; fig. a. elucidation.

Klasse f ['klasə] f (-/-n) class, category; school: class, form, Am. a. grade; (social) class.

'**Klassen|arbeit** f (test) paper; '**be-wußt** adj. class-conscious; '**bewußtsein** n class-consciousness; '**buch** n class-book; '**haß** m class-hatred; '**kamerad** m classmate; '**kampf** m class-war(fare); '**zimmer** n classroom, schoolroom.

klassifizier|en [klasifi'tsi:rən] v/t. (no -ge-) classify; **2ung** f (-/-en) classification.

Klass|iker ['klasikər] m (-s/-) classic; '**2isch** adj. classic(al).

klatsch [klatʃ] **1.** int. smack!, slap!; **2.** ♀ m (-es/-e) smack, slap; F fig.: gossip; scandal; '**2base** ['.ba:zə] f (-/-n) gossip; '**2e** f (-/-n) fly-flap; '**en** (ge-, h) **1.** v/t. fling, hurl; Beifall ~ clap, applaud (j-m s.o.); **2.** v/i. splash; applaud, clap; F fig. gossip; '**haft** adj. gossiping, gossipy; '**2maul** F n s. Klatschbase; '**naß** F adj. soaking wet.

Klaue ['klauə] f (-/-n) claw; paw; fig. clutch.

Klause ['klauzə] f (-/-n) hermitage; [cell.]

Klausel ♩♩ ['klauzəl] f (-/-n) clause; proviso; stipulation.

Klaviatur ♩ [klavja'tu:r] f (-/-en) keyboard, keys pl.

Klavier ♩ [kla'vi:r] n (-s/-e) piano (-forte); '**konzert** n piano concert or recital; '**lehrer** m piano teacher; '**sessel** m music-stool; '**stimmer** m (-s/-) piano-tuner; '**stunde** f piano-lesson.

kleb|en ['kle:bən] (ge-, h) **1.** v/t. glue, paste, stick; **2.** v/i. stick, adhere (an dat. to); '**end** adj. adhesive; '**2epflaster** n adhesive or sticking.plaster; '**rig** adj. adhesive, sticky; '**2stoff** m adhesive; glue.

Klecks [klɛks] m (-es/-e) blot (of ink); mark (of dirt, grease, paint, etc.); spot (of grease, paint, etc.); stain (of wine, coffee, etc.); '**2en** (ge-) **1.** v/i. (h) make a mark or spot or stain; **2.** v/i. (sein) ink, etc.: drip (down); **3.** v/t. (h): et. auf et. ~ splash or spill s.th. on s.th.

Klee ♣ [kle:] m (-s/no pl.) clover, trefoil.

Kleid [klaɪt] n (-[e]s/-er) garment; dress, frock; gown; ~er pl. clothes pl.; **2en** ['.dən] v/t. (ge-, h) dress, clothe; sich ~ dress (o.s.); j-n gut ~ suit or become s.o.

Kleider|ablage ['klaɪdər-] f cloak-room, Am. a. checkroom; '**bügel** m coat-hanger; '**bürste** f clothes-brush; '**haken** m clothes-peg; '**schrank** m wardrobe; '**ständer** m hat and coat stand; '**stoff** m dress material.

'**kleidsam** adj. becoming.

Kleidung ['klaɪduŋ] f (-/-en) clothes pl., clothing; dress; '**sstück** n piece or article of clothing; garment.

Kleie ['klaɪə] f (-/-en) bran.

klein [klaɪn] **1.** adj. little (only attr.), small; fig. a. trifling, petty; **2.** adv.: ~ schreiben write with a small (initial) letter; ~ anfangen start in a small or modest way; **3.** noun: von ~ auf from an early age; '**2auto** n baby or small car; '**2bahn** f narrow-ga(u)ge railway; '**2bildkamera** f miniature camera; '**2geld** n (small) change; '**gläubig** adj. of little faith; '**2handel** † m retail trade; '**2händler** m retailer; '**2heit** f (-/no pl.) smallness, small size; '**2holz** n firewood, matchwood, kindling.

'**Kleinigkeit** f (-/-en) trifle, triviality; '**skrämer** m pettifogger.

'**Klein|kind** n infant; '**2laut** adj. subdued; '**2lich** adj. paltry; pedantic, fussy; '**mut** m pusillanimity; '**2mütig** adj. ['.my:-tiç] pusillanimous; despondent; '**2schneiden** v/t. (irr. schneiden, sep., -ge-, h) cut into small pieces; '**staat** m small or minor state; '**stadt** f small town; '**städter** m small-town dweller, Am. a. small-towner; '**2städtisch** adj. small-town, provincial; '**vieh** n small livestock.

Kleister ['klaɪstər] m (-s/-) paste; '**2n** v/t. (ge-, h) paste.

Klemm|e ['klɛmə] f (-/-n) ⊕ clamp; ⚡ terminal; F in der ~ sitzen be in a cleft stick, F be in a jam; '**2en** v/t. (ge-, h) jam, squeeze, pinch; '**er** m (-s/-) pince-nez; '**schraube** ⊕ f set screw.

Klempner ['klɛmpnər] m (-s/-) tin-man, tin-smith, Am. a. tinner; plumber.

Klerus ['kle:rʊs] *m* (-/*no pl.*) clergy.

Klette ['klɛtə] *f* (-/-n) ♀ bur(r); *fig. a.* leech.

Kletter|er ['klɛtərər] *m* (-s/-) climber; '**2n** *v/i.* (ge-, *sein*) climb, clamber (*auf e-n Baum* [up] *a tree*); '**~pflanze** *f* climber, creeper.

Klient [kli'ɛnt] *m* (-en/-en) client.

Klima ['kli:ma] *n* (-s/-s, -te) climate; *fig. a.* atmosphere; '**~anlage** *f* air-conditioning plant; **2tisch** *adj.* [~'ma:tiʃ] climatic.

klimpern ['klɪmpərn] *v/i.* (ge-, h) jingle, chink (*mit et. s.th.*); F strum *or* tinkle away (*auf acc.* on, at *piano, guitar*).

Klinge ['klɪŋə] *f* (-/-n) blade.

Klingel ['klɪŋəl] *f* (-/-n) bell, hand-bell; '**~knopf** *m* bell-push; '**2n** *v/i.* (ge-, h) ring (the bell); *doorbell, etc.*: ring; *es klingelt* the doorbell is ringing; '**~zug** *m* bell-pull.

klingen ['klɪŋən] *v/i.* (*irr.*, ge-, h) sound; *bell, metal, etc.*: ring; *glasses, etc.*: clink; *musical instrument*: speak.

Klini|k ['kli:nɪk] *f* (-/-en) nursing home; private hospital; clinic(al hospital); '**2sch** *adj.* clinical.

Klinke ['klɪŋkə] *f* (-/-n) latch; (door-)handle.

Klippe ['klɪpə] *f* (-/-n) cliff; reef; crag; rock; *fig.* rock, hurdle.

klirren ['klɪrən] *v/i.* (ge-, h) *window-pane, chain, etc.*: rattle; *chain, swords, etc.*: clank, jangle; *keys, spurs, etc.*: jingle; *glasses, etc.*: clink, chink; *pots, etc.*: clatter; *~ mit* rattle; jingle.

Klistier ᛃ [kli'sti:r] *n* (-s/-e) enema.

Kloake [klo'a:kə] *f* (-/-n) sewer, cesspool (*a. fig.*).

Klob|en ['klo:bən] *m* (-s/-) ⊕ pulley, block; log; '**2ig** *adj.* clumsy (*a. fig.*).

klopfen ['klɔpfən] (ge-, h) **1.** *v/i. heart, pulse*: beat, throb; knock (*at door, etc.*); tap (*on shoulder*); pat (*on cheek*); *es klopft* there's a knock at the door; **2.** *v/t.* knock, drive (*nail, etc.*).

Klöppel ['klœpəl] *m* (-s/-) clapper (*of bell*); lacemaking: bobbin; beetle; '**~spitze** *f* pillow-lace, bone-lace.

Klops [klɔps] *m* (-es/-e) meat ball.

Klosett [klo'zɛt] *n* (-s/-e, -s) lavatory, (water-)closet, W.C., toilet; **~papier** *n* toilet-paper.

Kloß [klo:s] *m* (-es/⁓e) earth, clay, *etc.*: clod, lump; *cookery*: dumpling.

Kloster ['klo:stər] *n* (-s/⁓) cloister; monastery; convent, nunnery; '**~bruder** *m* friar; '**~frau** *f* nun; '**~gelübde** *n* monastic vow.

Klotz [klɔts] *m* (-es/⁓e) block, log (*a. fig.*).

Klub [klup] *m* (-s/-s) club; '**~kamerad** *m* clubmate; '**~sessel** *m* lounge-chair.

Kluft [kluft] *f* **1.** (-/⁓e) gap (*a. fig.*), crack; cleft; gulf, chasm (*both a. fig.*); **2.** F (-/-en) outfit, F togs *pl.*; uniform.

klug *adj.* [klu:k] clever; wise, intelligent, sensible; prudent; shrewd; cunning; '**2heit** *f* (-/*no pl.*) cleverness; intelligence; prudence; shrewdness; good sense.

Klump|en ['klʊmpən] *m* (-s/-) lump (*of earth, dough, etc.*); clod (*of earth, etc.*); nugget (*of gold, etc.*); heap; '**~fuß** *m* club-foot; '**2ig** *adj.* lumpy; cloddish.

knabbern ['knabərn] (ge-, h) **1.** *v/t.* nibble, gnaw; **2.** *v/i.* nibble, gnaw (*an dat.* at).

Knabe ['kna:bə] *m* (-n/-n) boy; lad; F *alter ~* F old chap.

'**Knaben|alter** *n* boyhood; '**~chor** *m* boys' choir; '**2haft** *adj.* boyish.

Knack [knak] *m* (-[e]s/-e) crack, snap, click; '**2en** (ge-, h) **1.** *v/i. wood*: crack; *fire*: crackle; click; **2.** *v/t.* crack (*nut, etc.*); F crack open (*safe*); *e-e harte Nuß zu ~ haben* have a hard nut to crack; '**2s** [~s] *m* (-es/-e) *s. Knack*; F *fig.* defect; '**2sen** *v/i.* (ge-, h) *s. knacken 1.*

Knall [knal] *m* (-[e]s/-e) crack, bang (*of shot*); bang (*of explosion*); crack (*of rifle or whip*); report (*of gun*); detonation, explosion, report; '**~bonbon** *m, n* cracker; '**~effekt** *fig. m* sensation; '**2en** *v/i.* (ge-, h) *rifle, whip*: crack; *fireworks, door, etc.*: bang; *gun*: fire; *cork, etc.*: pop; *explosive, etc.*: detonate.

knapp *adj.* [knap] *clothes*: tight, close-fitting; *rations, etc.*: scanty, scarce; *style, etc.*: concise; *lead, victory, etc.*: narrow; *majority, etc.*: bare; *mit ~er Not* entrinnen have a narrow escape; *~ werden* run short; '**2e** ♞ *m* (-n/-n) miner; '**~halten** *v/t.* (*irr. halten, sep.*, -ge-, h) keep *s.o.* short; '**2heit** *f* (-/*no pl.*) scarcity, shortage; conciseness; '~schaft ⚒ f (-/-en) miners' society.

Knarre ['knarə] f (-/-n) rattle; F rifle, gun; '2n v/i. (ge-, h) creak; voice: grate.

knattern ['knatərn] v/i. (ge-, h) crackle; machine-gun, etc.: rattle; mot. roar.

Knäuel ['knɔʏəl] m, n (-s/-) clew, ball; fig. bunch, cluster.

Knauf [knauf] m (-[e]s/⁺e) knob; pommel (of sword).

Knauser ['knauzər] m (-s/-) niggard, miser, skinflint; '~ei (~'raɪ] f (-/-en) niggardliness, miserliness; '2ig adj. niggardly, stingy; '2n v/i. (ge-, h) be stingy.

Knebel ['kne:bəl] m (-s/-) gag; '2n v/t. (ge-, h) gag; fig. muzzle (press).

Knecht [knɛçt] m (-[e]s/-e) servant; farm-labo(u)rer, farm-hand; slave; '2en v/t. (ge-, h) enslave; tyrannize; subjugate; '~schaft f (-/no pl.) servitude, slavery.

kneif|en ['knaɪfən] (irr., ge-, h) 1. v/t. pinch, nip; 2. v/i. pinch; F fig. back out, Am. F a. crawfish; '2er m (-s/-) pince-nez; '2zange f (e-e a pair of) pincers pl. or nippers pl.

Kneipe ['knaɪpə] f (-/-n) public house, tavern, F pub, Am. a. saloon; '2n v/i. (ge-, h) carouse, tipple, F booze; '~rei f (-/-en) drinking-bout, carousal.

kneten ['kne:tən] v/t. (ge-, h) knead (dough, etc.); 𝕤 a. massage (limb, etc.).

Knick [knik] m (-[e]s/-e) wall, etc.: crack; paper, etc.: fold, crease; path, etc.: bend; '2en v/t. (ge-, h) fold, crease; bend; break. [Knauser.]

Knicker F ['knikər] m (-s/-) s.↲

Knicks [kniks] m (-es/-e) curts(e)y; e-n ~ machen = '2en v/i. (ge-, h) (drop a) curts(e)y (vor dat. to).

Knie [kni:] n (-s/-) knee; '2fällig adv. on one's knees; '~kehle anat. f hollow of the knee; '2n v/i. (ge-, h) kneel, be on one's knees; '~scheibe anat. f knee-cap, knee-pan; '~strumpf m knee-length sock.

Kniff [knif] 1. m (-[e]s/-e) crease, fold; fig. trick, knack; 2. 2 pret. of kneifen; 2(e)lig adj. ['~(ə)liç] tricky; intricate.

knipsen ['knipsən] (ge-, h) 1. v/t.

clip, punch (ticket, etc.); F phot. take a snapshot of, snap; 2. F phot. v/i. take snapshots.

Knirps [knirps] m (-es/-e) little man; little chap, F nipper; '2ig adj. very small.

knirschen ['knirʃən] v/i. (ge-, h) gravel, snow, etc.: crunch, grind; teeth, etc.: grate; mit den Zähnen ~ grind or gnash one's teeth.

knistern ['knistərn] v/i. (ge-, h) woodfire, etc.: crackle; dry leaves, silk, etc.: rustle.

knitter|frei adj. ['knitər-] crease-resistant; '2n v/t. and v/i. (ge-, h) crease, wrinkle.

Knoblauch ♀ ['kno:plaux] m (-[e]s/no pl.) garlic.

Knöchel anat. ['knœçəl] m (-s/-) knuckle; ankle.

Knoch|en anat. ['knɔxən] m (-s/-) bone; '~enbruch m fracture (of a bone); '2ig adj. bony.

Knödel ['knø:dəl] m (-s/-) dumpling.

Knolle ♀ ['knɔlə] f (-/-n) tuber; bulb.

Knopf [knɔpf] m (-[e]s/⁺e) button.

knöpfen ['knœpfən] v/t. (ge-, h) button.

'**Knopfloch** n buttonhole.

Knorpel ['knɔrpəl] m (-s/-) cartilage, gristle.

Knorr|en ['knɔrən] m (-s/-) knot, knag, gnarl; '2ig adj. gnarled, knotty.

Knospe ♀ ['knɔspə] f (-/-n) bud; '2n v/i. (ge-, h) (be in) bud.

Knot|en ['kno:tən] 1. m (-s/-) knot (a. fig., ⚓); 2. 2 v/t. (ge-, h) knot; '~enpunkt m ⚙ junction; intersection; '2ig adj. knotty.

Knuff F [knuf] m (-[e]s/⁺e) poke, cuff, nudge; '2en F v/t. (ge-, h) poke, cuff, nudge.

knülle|n ['knylən] v/t. and v/i. (ge-, h) crease, crumple; '2r F m (-s/-) hit.

knüpfen ['knypfən] v/t. (ge-, h) make, tie (knot, etc.); make (net); knot (carpet, etc.); tie (shoe-lace, etc.); strike up (friendship, etc.); attach (condition, etc.) (an acc. to).

Knüppel ['knypəl] m (-s/-) cudgel.

knurren ['knurən] v/i. (ge-, h) growl, snarl; fig. grumble (über acc. at, over, about); stomach: rumble.

knusp(e)rig adj. ['knusp(ə)riç] crisp, crunchy.

Knute ['knu:tə] f (-/-n) knout.

Knüttel ['knʏtəl] m (-s/-) cudgel.

Kobold ['ko:bɔlt] m (-[e]s/-e) (hob)goblin, imp.

Koch [kɔx] m (-[e]s/⁎e) cook; '~**buch** n cookery-book, Am. cookbook; '**2en** (ge-), **1.** v/t. boil (water, egg, fish, etc.); cook (meat, vegetables, etc.) (by boiling); make (coffee, tea, etc.); **2.** v/i. water, etc.: boil (a. fig.); do the cooking; be a (good, etc.) cook; '~**er** m (-s/-) cooker.

Köcher ['kœçər] m (-s/-) quiver.

'**Koch|kiste** f haybox; '~**löffel** m wooden spoon; '~**nische** f kitchenette; '~**salz** n common salt; '~**topf** m pot, saucepan.

Köder ['kø:dər] m (-s/-) bait (a. fig.); lure (a. fig.); '**2n** v/t. (ge-, h) bait; lure; fig. a. decoy.

Kodex ['ko:dɛks] m (-es, -/-e, Kodizes) code.

Koffer ['kɔfər] m (-s/-) (suit)case; trunk; '~**radio** n portable radio (set).

Kognak ['kɔnjak] m (-s/-s, ⁎-e) French brandy, cognac.

Kohl ♀ [ko:l] m (-[e]s/-e) cabbage.

Kohle ['ko:lə] f (-/-n) coal; charcoal; ⚡ carbon; *wie auf (glühenden) ~n sitzen* be on tenterhooks.

'**Kohlen|bergwerk** n coal-mine, coal-pit, colliery; '~**eimer** m coal-scuttle; '~**händler** m coal-merchant; '~**kasten** m coal-box; '~**revier** ⚒ n coal-district; '~**säure** ♀ f carbonic acid; '~**stoff** ♀ m carbon.

'**Kohle|papier** n carbon paper; '~**zeichnung** f charcoal-drawing.

'**Kohl|kopf** ♀ m (head of) cabbage; '~**rübe** ♀ f Swedish turnip.

Koje ⚓ ['ko:jə] f (-/-n) berth, bunk.

Kokain [koka'i:n] n (-s/no pl.) cocaine, sl. coke, snow.

kokett adj. [ko'kɛt] coquettish; **2erie** [~ə'ri:] f (-/-n) coquetry, coquettishness; **~ieren** [~'ti:rən] v/i. (no ge-, h) coquet, flirt (mit with; a. fig.).

Kokosnuß ♀ ['ko:kɔs-] f coconut.

Koks [ko:ks] m (-es/-e) coke.

Kolben ['kɔlbən] m (-s/-) butt (of rifle); ⊕ piston; '~**stange** f piston-rod.

Kolchose [kɔl'ço:zə] f (-/-n) collective farm, kolkhoz.

Kolleg univ. [kɔ'le:k] n (-s/-s, -ien) course of lectures; ~**e** [~gə] m (-n/-n) colleague; **~ium** [~gjum] n (-s/Kollegien) council, board; teaching staff.

Kollekt|e eccl. [kɔ'lɛktə] f (-/-n) collection; ~**ion** ✝ [~'tsjo:n] f (-/-en) collection, range.

Koller ['kɔlər] m (-s/-) vet. staggers pl.; F fig. rage, tantrum; '**2n** v/i. **1.** (h) turkey-cock: gobble; pigeon: coo; bowels: rumble; vet. have the staggers; **2.** (sein) ball, tears, etc.: roll.

kolli|dieren [kɔli'di:rən] v/i. (no -ge-, sein) collide; fig. clash; **2sion** [~'zjo:n] f (-/-en) collision; fig. clash, conflict.

Kölnischwasser ['kœlniʃ-] n eau-de-Cologne.

Kolonialwaren [kolo'nja:l-] f/pl. groceries pl.; ~**händler** m grocer; ~**handlung** f grocer's (shop), Am. grocery.

Kolon|ie [kolo'ni:] f (-/-n) colony; **2isieren** [~i'zi:rən] v/t. (no -ge-, h) colonize.

Kolonne [ko'lɔnə] f (-/-n) column; convoy; gang (of workers, etc.).

kolorieren [kolo'ri:rən] v/t. (no -ge-, h) colo(u)r.

Kolo|ß [ko'lɔs] m (Kolosses/Kolosse) colossus; **2ssal** adj. [~'sa:l] colossal, huge (both a. fig.).

Kombin|ation [kɔmbina'tsjo:n] f (-/-en) combination; overall; flying-suit; football, etc.: combined attack; **2ieren** [~'ni:rən] (no -ge-, h) **1.** v/t. combine; **2.** v/i. reason, deduce; football, etc.: combine, move.

Kombüse ⚓ [kɔm'by:zə] f (-/-n) galley, caboose. [comet.]

Komet ast. [ko'me:t] m (-en/-en)⎰

Komfort [kɔm'fo:r] m (-s/no pl.) comfort; **2abel** adj. [~or'ta:bəl] comfortable.

Komik ['ko:mik] f (-/no pl.) humo(u)r, fun(niness); '~**er** m (-s/-) comic actor, comedian.

komisch adj. ['ko:miʃ] comic(al), funny; fig. funny, odd, queer.

Komitee [komi'te:] n (-s/-s) committee.

Kommand|ant ⚔ [kɔman'dant] m (-en/-en), ~**eur** ⚔ [~'dø:r] m (-s/-e) commander, commanding officer; **2ieren** [~'di:rən] (no -ge-, h) **1.** v/t.

order, command, be in command; **2.** *v/t.* ✗ command, be in command of; order; **~itgesellschaft** † [~ 'di:t-] *f* limited partnership; **~o** [~'mando] *n* (-s/-s) ✗ command, order; order (*pl.*), directive (*pl.*); ✗ detachment; **~obrücke** ⚓ *f* navigating bridge.

kommen ['kɔmən] *v/i.* (*irr.*, ge-, sein) come; arrive; **~ lassen** send for *s.o.*, order *s.th.*; *et.* **~ sehen** foresee; *an die Reihe* **~** it is one's turn; **~ auf** (*acc.*) think of, hit upon; remember; *zu dem Schluß* **~**, *daß* decide that; *hinter et.* **~** find s.th. out; *um et.* **~** lose s.th.; *zu et.* **~** come by s.th.; *wieder zu sich* **~** come round or to; *wie* **~** *Sie dazu!* how dare you!

Komment|ar [kɔmɛn'ta:r] *m* (-s/-e) commentary, comment; **~ator** [~ tɔr] *m* (-s/-en) commentator; **2ie-ren** [~'ti:rən] *v/t.* (no -ge-, h) comment on.

Kommissar [kɔmi'sa:r] *m* (-s/-e) commissioner; superintendent; *pol.* commissar.

Kommißbrot F [kɔ'mis-] *n* army or ration bread, *Am.* a. G.I. bread.

Kommission [kɔmi'sjo:n] *f* (-/-en) commission (*a.* †); committee; **~är** † [~o'nɛ:r] *m* (-s/-e) commission agent.

Kommode [kɔ'mo:də] *f* (-/-n) chest of drawers, *Am.* bureau.

Kommunis|mus *pol.* [kɔmu'nis-mus] *m* (-/*no pl.*) communism; **~t** *m* (-en/-en) communist; **2tisch** *adj.* communist(ic).

Komöd|iant [kɔmø'djant] *m* (-en/-en) comedian; *fig.* play-actor; **~ie** [~'mø:djə] *f* (-/-n) comedy; **~ spielen** play-act.

Kompagnon † [kɔmpan'jõ:] *m* (-s/-s) (business-)partner, associate.

Kompanie ✗ [kɔmpa'ni:] *f* (-/-n) company.

Kompaß ['kɔmpas] *m* (*Kompasses*/ *Kompasse*) compass. [petent.]

kompetent *adj.* [kɔmpe'tɛnt] com-)

komplett *adj.* [kɔm'plet] complete.

Komplex [kɔm'plɛks] *m* (-es/-e) complex (*a. psych.*); block (*of houses*).

Kompliment [kɔmpli'mɛnt] *n* (-[e]s/-e) compliment.

Komplize [kɔm'pli:tsə] *m* (-n/-n) accomplice.

komplizier|en [kɔmpli'tsi:rən] *v/t.*

(*no -ge-*, h) complicate; **~t** *adj. machine*, *etc.*: complicated; *argument*, *situation*, *etc.*: complex; **~er Bruch** 🌠 compound fracture.

Komplott [kɔm'plɔt] *n* (-[e]s/-e) plot, conspiracy.

kompo|nieren ♪ [kɔmpo'ni:rən] *v/t. and v/i.* (*no -ge-*, h) compose; **2nist** *m* (-en/-en) composer; **2si-tion** [~zi'tsjo:n] *f* (-/-en) composition.

Kompott [kɔm'pɔt] *n* (-[e]s/-e) compote, stewed fruit, *Am.* a. sauce.

komprimieren [kɔmpri'mi:rən] *v/t.* (*no -ge-*, h) compress.

Kompromi|ß [kɔmpro'mis] *m* (*Kompromisses/Kompromisse*) compromise; **2los** *adj.* uncompromising; **2ttieren** [~'ti:rən] *v/t.* (*no -ge-*, h) compromise.

Kondens|ator [kɔndɛn'za:tɔr] *m* (-s/-en) ⚡ capacitor, condenser (*a.* 🔭); **2ieren** [~'zi:rən] *v/t.* (*no -ge-*, h) condense.

Kondens|milch [kɔn'dɛns-] *f* evaporated milk; **~streifen** ✈ *m* condensation *or* vapo(u)r trail; **~was-ser** *n* water of condensation.

Konditor [kɔn'di:tɔr] *m* (-s/-en) confectioner, pastry-cook; **~ei** [~i-to'raɪ] *f* (-/-en) confectionery, confectioner's (shop); **~eiwaren** *f/pl.* confectionery.

Konfekt [kɔn'fɛkt] *n* (-[e]s/-e) sweets *pl.*, sweetmeat, *Am.* a. soft candy; chocolates *pl.*

Konfektion [kɔnfɛk'tsjo:n] *f* (-/-en) (manufacture of) ready-made clothing; **~sanzug** [kɔnfɛk'tsjo:ns⁹-] *m* ready-made suit; **~sgeschäft** *n* ready-made clothes shop.

Konfer|enz [kɔnfe'rɛnts] *f* (-/-en) conference; **2ieren** [~'ri:rən] *v/i.* (*no -ge-*, h) confer (*über acc.* on).

Konfession [kɔnfɛ'sjo:n] *f* (-/-en) confession, creed; denomination; **2ell** *adj.* [~o'nɛl] confessional, denominational; **~sschule** [~'sjo:ns-] *f* denominational school.

Konfirm|and *eccl.* [kɔnfir'mant] *m* (-en/-en) candidate for confirmation, confirmee; **~ation** [~'tsjo:n] *f* (-/-en) confirmation; **2ieren** [~ 'mi:rən] *v/t.* (*no -ge-*, h) confirm.

konfiszieren 🏛 [kɔnfis'tsi:rən] *v/t.* (*no -ge-*, h) confiscate, seize.

Konfitüre [kɔnfi'ty:rə] *f* (-/-n) preserve(s *pl.*), (whole-fruit) jam.

Konflikt [kɔn'flikt] *m* (-[e]s/-e) conflict. [*mit* agree *or* concur with.]

konform *adv.* [kɔn'fɔrm]: ~ *gehen*]

konfrontieren [kɔnfrɔn'tiːrən] *v/t.* (*no* -ge-, *h*) confront (*mit* with).

konfus *adj.* [kɔn'fuːs] *p.*, *a.* ideas: muddled; *p.* muddle-headed.

Kongreß [kɔn'grɛs] *m* (Kongresses/ Kongresse) congress; *Am. parl. Congress;* ~**halle** *f* congress hall.

König ['køːnɪç] *m* (-s/-e) king; 2**lich** *adj.* ['~k-] royal; regal; 2**reich** ['~k-] *n* kingdom; ~**swürde** ['~ks-] *f* royal dignity, kingship; '~**tum** *n* (-s/=er) monarchy; kingship.

Konjug|ation *gr.* [kɔnjuga'tsjoːn] *f* (-/-en); 2**ieren** [~'giːrən] *v/t.* (*no* -ge-, *h*) conjugate.

Konjunkt|iv *gr.* ['kɔnjuŋktiːf] *m* (-s/-e) subjunctive (mood); ~**ur** †' [~'tuːr] *f* (-/-en) trade *or* business cycle; economic *or* business situation.

konkret *adj.* [kɔn'kreːt] concrete.

Konkurrent [kɔnku'rɛnt] *m* (-en/ -en) competitor, rival.

Konkurrenz [kɔnku'rɛnts] *f* (-/-en) competition; competitors *pl.*, rivals *pl.*; *sports*: event; 2**fähig** *adj.* able to compete; competitive; ~**geschäft** *n* rival business *or* firm; ~**kampf** *m* competition.

konkur'rieren *v/i.* (*no* -ge-, *h*) compete (*mit* with; *um* for).

Konkurs †, 🏛 [kɔn'kurs] *m* (-es/-e) bankruptcy, insolvency; failure; ~ *anmelden* file a petition in bankruptcy; *in* ~ *gehen or geraten* become insolvent, go bankrupt; ~**er- klärung** 🏛 *f* declaration of insolvency; ~**masse** 🏛 *f* bankrupt's estate; ~**verfahren** 🏛 *n* bankruptcy proceedings *pl.*; ~**verwalter** 🏛 *m* trustee in bankruptcy; liquidator.

können ['kœnən] **1.** *v/i.* (irr., ge-, *h*): *ich kann nicht* I can't, I am not able to; **2.** *v/t.* (irr., ge-, *h*) know, understand; *e-e Sprache* ~ know a language, have command of a language; **3.** *v/aux.* (irr., *no* -ge-, *h*) be able to *inf.*, be capable of *ger.*; be allowed *or* permitted to *inf.*; *es kann sein* it may be; *du kannst hingehen* you may go there; *er kann schwimmen* he can swim, he knows how to swim; **4.** 2 *n* (-s/*no pl.*) ability; skill; proficiency.

Konnossement †' [kɔnɔsə'mɛnt] *n* (-[e]s/-e) bill of lading.

konnte ['kɔntə] *pret.* of *können.*

konsequen|t *adj.* [kɔnze'kvɛnt] consistent; 2**z** [~ts] *f* (-/-en) consistency; consequence; *die* ~*en ziehen* do the only thing one can.

konservativ *adj.* [kɔnzɛrva'tiːf] conservative.

Konserven [kɔn'zɛrvən] *f/pl.* tinned *or Am.* canned foods *pl.*; ~**büchse** *f*, ~**dose** *f* tin, *Am.* can; ~**fabrik** *f* tinning factory, *Am.* cannery.

konservieren [kɔnzɛr'viːrən] *v/t.* (*no* -ge-, *h*) preserve.

Konsonant *gr.* [kɔnzo'nant] *m* (-en/ -en) consonant.

Konsortium †' [kɔn'zɔrtsjum] *n* (-s/Konsortien) syndicate.

konstruieren [kɔnstru'iːrən] *v/t.* (*no* -ge-, *h*) *gr.* construe; ⊕: construct; design.

Konstruk|teur ⊕ [kɔnstruk'tøːr] *m* (-s/-e) designer; ~**tion** ⊕ [~'tsjoːn] *f* (-/-en) construction; ~**tionsfeh- ler** ⊕ *m* constructional defect.

Konsul *pol.* ['kɔnzul] *m* (-s/-n) consul; ~**at** *pol.* [~'laːt] *n* (-[e]s/-e) consulate; 2**ieren** *v/t.* (*no* -ge-, *h*) consult, seek *s.o.*'s advice.

Konsum [kɔn'zuːm] *m* **1.** (-s/*no pl.*) consumption; **2.** (-s/-s) co-operative shop, *Am.* co-operative store, F co-op; **3.** (-s/*no pl.*) consumers' co-operative society, F co-op; ~**ent** [~u'mɛnt] *m* (-en/-en) consumer; 2**ieren** [~u'miːrən] *v/t.* (*no* -ge-, *h*) consume; ~**verein** *m* s. Konsum 3.

Kontakt [kɔn'takt] *m* (-[e]s/-e) contact (*a.* 𝕗); *in* ~ *stehen mit* be in contact *or* touch with.

Kontinent ['kɔntinɛnt] *m* (-[e]s/-e) continent.

Kontingent [kɔntɪŋ'gɛnt] *n* (-[e]s/ -e) ✕ contingent, quota (*a.* †').

Konto †' ['kɔnto] *n* (-s/Konten, Kontos, Konti) account; '~**auszug** †' *m* statement of account; ~**korrent- konto** †' [~kɔ'rɛnt-] *n* current account.

Kontor [kɔn'toːr] *n* (-s/-e) office; ~**ist** [~o'rɪst] *m* (-en/-en) clerk.

Kontrast [kɔn'trast] *m* (-es/-e) contrast.

Kontroll|e [kɔn'trɔlə] *f* (-/-n) control; supervision; check; 2**ieren** [~'liːrən] *v/t.* (*no* -ge-, *h*) control; supervise; check.

Kontroverse [kɔntro'vɛrzə] f (-/-n) controversy.

konventionell adj. [kɔnvɛntsjo'nɛl] conventional.

Konversation [kɔnvɛrza'tsjoːn] f (-/-en) conversation; **~slexikon** n encyclop(a)edia.

Konzentr|ation [kɔntsɛntra'tsjoːn] f (-/-en) concentration; **2ieren** [~'triːrən] v/t. (no -ge-, h) concentrate, focus (attention, etc.) (auf acc. on); sich ~ concentrate (auf acc. on).

Konzern ✝ [kɔn'tsɛrn] m (-s/-e) combine, group.

Konzert ♩ [kɔn'tsɛrt] n (-[e]s/-e) concert; recital; concerto; **~saal** ♩ m concert-hall.

Konzession [kɔntsɛ'sjoːn] f (-/-en) concession; licen|ce, Am. -se; **2ieren** [~o'niːrən] v/t. (no -ge-, h) license.

Kopf [kɔpf] m (-[e]s/ᵘe) head; top; brains pl.; pipe: bowl; ein fähiger ~ a clever fellow; ~ hoch! chin up!; j-m über den ~ wachsen outgrow s.o.; fig. get beyond s.o.; **~arbeit** f brain-work; **~bahnhof** 🚂 m terminus, Am. terminal; **~bedeckung** f headgear, headwear.

köpfen ['kœpfən] v/t. (no -ge-, h) behead, decapitate; football: head (ball).

Kopf|ende n head; **~hörer** m headphone, headset; **~kissen** n pillow; **2los** adj. headless; fig. confused; **~nicken** n (-s/no pl.) nod; **~rechnen** n (-s/no pl.) mental arithmetic; **~salat** m cabbage-lettuce; **~schmerzen** m/pl. headache; **~sprung** m header; **~tuch** n scarf; **2über** adv. head first, headlong; **~weh** n (-[e]s/-e) s. Kopfschmerzen; **~zerbrechen** n (-s/no pl.): j-m ~ machen puzzle s.o.

Kopie [ko'piː] f(-/-n) copy; duplicate; phot., film: print; **~rstift** m indelible pencil.

Koppel ['kɔpəl] 1. f (-/-n) hounds: couple; horses: string; paddock; 2. ✕ n (-s/-) belt; **2n** v/t. (ge-, h) couple (a. ⊕, 🚗).

Koralle [ko'ralə] f (-/-n) coral; **~nfischer** m coral-fisher.

Korb [kɔrp] m (-[e]s/ᵘe) basket; fig. refusal; Hahn im ~ cock of the walk; **~möbel** n/pl. wicker furniture. [twine; cord.]

Kordel ['kɔrdəl] f (-/-n) string,

Korinthe [ko'rintə] f (-/-n) currant.

Kork [kɔrk] m (-[e]s/-e), **~en** m (-s/-) cork; **~(en)zieher** m (-s/-) corkscrew.

Korn [kɔrn] 1. n (-[e]s/ᵘer) seed; grain; 2. n (-[e]s/-, corn, cereals pl.; 3. n (-[e]s/🔍-e) front sight; 4. F m (-[e]s/-) (German) corn whisky.

körnig adj. ['kœrnɪç] granular; in compounds: ...-grained.

Körper ['kœrpər] m (-s/-) body (a. phys., ♩); ♩ solid; **~bau** m build, physique; **2behindert** adj. ['~bəhindərt] (physically) disabled, handicapped; **~beschaffenheit** f constitution, physique; **~fülle** f corpulence; **~geruch** m body-odo(u)r; **~größe** f stature; **~kraft** f physical strength; **2lich** adj. physical; corporal; bodily; **~pflege** f care of the body, hygiene; **~schaft** f (-/-en) body; ⚖ body (corporate), corporation; **~verletzung** ⚖ f bodily harm, physical injury.

korrekt adj. [kɔ'rɛkt] correct; **2or** m (-s/-en) (proof-)reader; **2ur** [~'tuːr] f (-/-en) correction; **2urbogen** m proof-sheet.

Korrespond|ent [kɔrɛspɔn'dɛnt] m (-en/-en) correspondent; **~enz** [~ts] f (-/-en) correspondence; **2ieren** [~'diːrən] v/i. (no -ge-, h) correspond (mit with).

korrigieren [kɔri'giːrən] v/t. (no -ge-, h) correct.

Korsett [kɔr'zɛt] n (-[e]s/-e, -s) corset, stays pl.

Kosename ['koːzə-] m pet name.

Kosmetik [kɔs'meːtik] f (-/no pl.) beauty culture; **~erin** f (-/-nen) beautician, cosmetician.

Kost [kɔst] f (-/no pl.) food, fare; board; diet; **2bar** adj. present, etc.: costly, expensive; health, time, etc.: valuable; mineral, etc.: precious.

kosten¹ v/t. (ge-, h) taste, try, sample.

Kosten² 1. pl. cost(s pl.); expense(s pl.), charges pl.; auf ~ (gen.) at the expense of; 2. 2 v/t. (ge-, h) cost; take, require (time, etc.); **~anschlag** m estimate, tender; **2frei** 1. adj. free; 2. adv. free of charge; **2los** s. kostenfrei.

Kost|gänger ['kɔstgɛŋər] m (-s/-) boarder; **~geld** n board-wages pl.

köstlich adj. ['kœstlɪç] delicious.

'**Kost**|**probe** f taste, sample (a. fig.);
2**spielig** adj. ['ʃpiːliç] expensive,
costly.

Kostüm [kɔs'tyːm] n (-s/-e) costume, dress; suit; ~**fest** n fancy-dress ball.

Kot [koːt] m (-[e]s/no pl.) mud, mire; excrement.

Kotelett [kot(ə)'let] n (-[e]s/-s, ✕ -e) pork, veal, lamb: cutlet; pork, veal, mutton: chop; ~**en** pl. sidewhiskers pl., Am. a. sideburns pl.

'**Kot**|**flügel** m mudguard, Am. a. fender; 2**ig** adj. muddy, miry.

Krabbe zo. ['krabə] f (-/-n) shrimp, crab.

krabbeln ['krabəln] v/i. (ge-, sein) crawl.

Krach [krax] m (-[e]s/-e, -s) crack, crash (a. ✝); quarrel, sl. bust-up; F row; ~ **machen** sl. kick up a row; 2**en** v/i. (ge-) 1. (h) thunder: crash; cannon: roar, thunder; 2. (sein) crash (a. ✝), smash.

krächzen ['krɛçtsən] v/t. and v/i. (ge-, h) croak.

Kraft [kraft] 1. f (-/̈-e) strength; force (a. ✕); power (a. ⚡, ⊕); energy; vigo(u)r; efficacy; in ~ sein (setzen, treten) be in (put into, come into) operation or force; außer ~ setzen repeal, abolish (law); 2. ✝ prp. (gen.) by virtue of; '~**an**-**lage** ⚡ f power plant; '~**brühe** f beef tea; '~**fahrer** m driver, motorist; '~**fahrzeug** n motor vehicle.

kräftig adj. ['krɛftiç] strong (a. fig.), powerful; fig. nutritious, rich; ~**en** ['~gən] (ge-, h) 1. v/t. strengthen; 2. v/i. give strength.

'**kraft**|**los** adj. powerless, feeble; weak; 2**probe** f trial of strength; 2**rad** n motor cycle; 2**stoff** mot. m fuel; '~**voll** adj. powerful (a. fig.); 2**wagen** m motor vehicle; 2**werk** ⚡ n power station.

Kragen ['kraːgən] m (-s/-) collar; '~**knopf** m collar-stud, Am. collar button.

Krähe orn. ['krɛː] f (-/-n) crow; 2**n** v/i. (ge-, h) crow.

Kralle ['kralə] f (-/-n) claw (a. fig.); talon, clutch.

Kram [kraːm] m (-[e]s/no pl.) stuff, odds and ends pl.; fig. affairs pl., business.

Krämer ['krɛːmər] m (-s/-) shopkeeper.

Krampf ✳ [krampf] m (-[e]s/̈-e) cramp; spasm, convulsion; '~**ader** ✳ f varicose vein; '2**haft** adj. spasmodic, convulsive; laugh: forced.

Kran ⊕ [kraːn] m (-[e]s/̈-e, -e) crane.

krank adj. [kraŋk] sick; organ, etc.: diseased; ~ sein p. be ill, esp. Am. be sick; animal: be sick or ill; ~ werden p. fall ill or esp. Am. sick; animal: fall sick; '2**e** m, f (-n/-n) sick person, patient, invalid.

kränkeln ['krɛŋkəln] v/i. (ge-, h) be sickly, be in poor health.

'**kranken** fig. v/i. (ge-, h) suffer (an dat. from).

kränken ['krɛŋkən] v/t. (ge-, h) offend, injure; wound or hurt s.o.'s feelings; sich ~ feel hurt (über acc. at, about).

'**Kranken**|**bett** n sick-bed; '~**geld** n sick-benefit; '~**haus** n hospital; '~**kasse** f health insurance (fund); '~**kost** f invalid diet; '~**lager** n s. Krankenbett; '~**pflege** f nursing; '~**pfleger** m male nurse; '~**schein** m medical certificate; '~**schwester** f (sick-)nurse; '~**versicherung** f health or sickness insurance; '~**wagen** m ambulance; '~**zimmer** n sick-room.

'**krank**|**haft** adj. morbid, pathological; '2**heit** f (-/-en) illness, sickness; disease.

'**Krankheits**|**erreger** ✳ m pathogenic agent; '~**erscheinung** f symptom (a. fig.).

'**kränklich** adj. sickly, ailing.

'**Kränkung** f (-/-en) insult, offen|ce, Am. -se.

Kranz [krants] m (-es/̈-e) wreath; garland.

Kränzchen fig. ['krɛntsçən] n (-s/-) tea-party, F hen-party.

kraß adj. [kras] crass, gross.

kratzen ['kratsən] (ge-, h) 1. v/i. scratch; 2. v/t. scratch; sich ~ scratch (o.s.).

kraulen ['kraulən] (ge-) 1. v/t. (h) scratch gently; 2. v/i. (sein) sports: crawl.

kraus adj. [kraus] curly, curled; crisp, frizzy; die Stirn ~ ziehen knit one's brow; '2**e** f (-/-n) ruff(le), frill.

kräuseln ['krɔyzəln] v/t. (ge-, h) curl, crimp (hair, etc.); pucker *(lips)*; *sich ~ hair*: curl; *waves, etc.*: ruffle; *smoke*: curl *or* wreath up.

Kraut ⚘ [kraut] *n* **1.** (-[e]s/⁻er) plant; herb; **2.** (-[e]s/*no pl.*) tops *pl.*; cabbage; weed.

Krawall [kra'val] *m* -[e]s/-e) riot; shindy, F row, *sl.* rumpus.

Krawatte [kra'vatə] *f* (-/-n) (neck-) tie.

Kreatur [krea'tu:r] *f* (-/-en) creature.

Krebs [kre:ps] *m* (-es/-e) *zo.* crayfish, *Am. a.* crawfish; *ast.* Cancer, Crab; ⚕ cancer; ~e *pl.* ✝ returns *pl.*

Kredit ✝ [kre'di:t] *m* (-[e]s/-e) credit; *auf ~* on credit; **2fähig** ✝ *adj.* credit-worthy.

Kreide ['kraidə] *f* (-/-n) chalk; *paint.* crayon.

Kreis [krais] *m* (-es/-e) circle *(a. fig.)*; *ast.* orbit; ⚡ circuit; district, *Am.* county; *fig.*: sphere, field; range.

kreischen ['kraiʃən] (ge-, h) **1.** *v/i.* screech, scream; squeal, shriek; *circular saw, etc.*: grate (on the ear); **2.** *v/t.* shriek, screech *(insult, etc.).*

Kreisel ['kraizəl] *m* -s/-) (whipping-)top; **2kompaß** *m* gyro-compass.

kreisen ['kraizən] *v/i.* (ge-, h) (move in a) circle; revolve, rotate; 🦅, *bird*: circle; *bird*: wheel; *blood, money*: circulate.

kreis|förmig *adj.* ['kraisfœrmiç] circular; **2lauf** *m physiol., money, etc.*: circulation; *business, trade*: cycle; **2laufstörungen** ⚕ *f/pl.* circulatory trouble; **~rund** *adj.* circular; **2säge** ⊕ *f* circular saw, *Am. a.* buzz saw; **2verkehr** *m* roundabout (traffic).

Krempe ['krempə] *f* (-/-n) brim *(of hat).*

Krempel F ['krempəl] *m* (-s/*no pl.*) rubbish, stuff, lumber.

krepieren [kre'pi:rən] *v/i.* (*no* -ge-, sein) *shell*: burst, explode; *sl.* kick the bucket, peg *or* snuff out; *animal*: die, perish.

Krepp [krep] *m* (-s/-s, -e) crêpe; crape; **~apier** ['krɛppapi:r] *n* crêpe paper; **~sohle** *f* crêpe(-rubber) sole.

Kreuz [krɔyts] **1.** *n* (-es/-e) cross *(a. fig.)*; crucifix; *anat.* small of the back; ♯ sacral region; *cards*: club(s *pl.*); ♪ sharp; *zu ~(e) kriechen* eat

humble pie; **2.** ⚢ *adv.*: *~ und quer* in all directions; criss-cross.

'kreuzen (ge-, h) **1.** *v/t.* cross, fold *(arms, etc.)*; ⚢, *zo.* cross(-breed), hybridize; *sich ~ roads*: cross, intersect; *plans, etc.*: clash; **2.** ⚓ *v/i.* cruise.

'Kreuzer ⚓ *m* (-s/-) cruiser.

'Kreuz|fahrer *hist. m* crusader; **~fahrt** *f hist.* crusade; ⚓ cruise; **~feuer** ✗ *n* cross-fire *(a. fig.)*; **2igen** ['~igən] *v/t.* (ge-, h) crucify; **~igung** *f* (-/-en) crucifixion; **~otter** *zo. f* common viper; **~ritter** *hist. m* knight of the Cross; **~schmerzen** *m/pl.* back ache; **~spinne** *zo. f* garden- *or* cross-spider; **~ung** *f* (-/-en) ⚡, *roads, etc.*: crossing, intersection; *roads*: crossroads; ⚢, *zo.* cross-breeding, hybridization; **~verhör** ⚖ *n* cross-examination; *ins ~ nehmen* cross-examine; **2weise** *adv.* crosswise, crossways; **~worträtsel** *n* cross-word (puzzle); **~zug** *hist. m* crusade.

kriech|en ['kri:çən] *v/i.* (*irr.*, ge-, sein) creep, crawl; *fig.* cringe (*vor dat.* to, before); **2er** *contp. m* (-s/-) toady; **2erei** *contp.* [~'rai] *f* (-/-en) toadyism.

Krieg [kri:k] *m* (-[e]s/-e) war; *im ~* at war; *s. führen.*

kriegen F ['kri:gən] *v/t.* (ge-, h) catch, seize; get.

Krieg|er ['kri:gər] *m* (-s/-) warrior; **~erdenkmal** *n* war memorial; **2erisch** *adj.* warlike; militant; **2führend** *adj.* belligerent; **~führung** *f* warfare.

Kriegs|beil *fig. n*: *das ~ begraben* bury the hatchet; **2beschädigt** *adj.* war-disabled; **~beschädigte** *m* (-n/-n) disabled ex-serviceman; **~dienst** ✗ *m* war service; **~dienstverweigerer** ✗ *m* (-s/-) conscientious objector; **~erklärung** *f* declaration of war; **~flotte** *f* naval force; **~gefangene** *m* prisoner of war; **~gefangenschaft** ✗ *f* captivity; **~gericht** ⚖ *n* court martial; **~gewinnler** ['~gɔvinlər] *m* (-s/-) war profiteer; **~hafen** *m* naval port; **~kamerad** *m* wartime comrade; **~list** *f* stratagem; **~macht** *f* military forces *pl.*; **~minister** *hist. m* minister of war; Secretary of State for War,

Am. Secretary of War; '**~ministerium** *hist. n* ministry of war; War Office, *Am.* War Department; '**~rat** *m* council of war; '**~schauplatz** ✕ *m* theat|re *or Am.* -er of war; '**~schiff** *n* warship; '**~schule** *f* military academy; '**~teilnehmer** *m* combatant; ex-serviceman, *Am.* veteran; '**~treiber** *m* (-s/-) warmonger; '**~verbrecher** *m* war criminal; '**~zug** *m* (military) expedition, campaign.

Kriminal|beamte [krimi'nɑ:l-] *m* criminal investigator, *Am.* plainclothes man; **~film** *m* crime film; thriller; **~polizei** *f* criminal investigation department; **~roman** *m* detective *or* crime novel, thriller, *sl.* whodun(n)it.

kriminell *adj.* [krimi'nɛl] criminal; ♀e *m* (-n/-n) criminal.

Krippe ['krɪpə] *f* (-/-n) crib, manger; crèche.

Krise ['kri:zə] *f* (-/-n) crisis.

Kristall [krɪs'tal] **1.** *m* (-s/-e) crystal; **2.** *n* (-s/*no pl.*) crystal(-glass); ♀**isieren** [,i'zi:rən] *v/i.* and *v/refl.* (no -ge-, h) crystallize.

Kriti|k [kri'ti:k] *f* (-/-en) criticism; ♪, *thea.*, *etc.*: review, criticism; F *unter aller ~* beneath contempt; *~ üben an* (*dat.*) *s.* kritisieren; **~ker** ['kri:tikər] *m* (-s/-) critic; *books*: reviewer; ♀**sch** *adj.* ['kri:tiʃ] critical (*gegenüber of*); ♀**sieren** [kriti'zi:rən] *v/t.* (no -ge-, h) criticize; review (*book*).

kritt|eln ['krɪtəln] *v/t.* (ge-, h) find fault (*an dat.* with), cavil (*at*); ♀**ler** ['...lər] *m* (-s/-) fault-finder, caviller.

Kritzel|ei [krɪtsə'laɪ] *f* (-/-en) scrawl(ing), scribble, scribbling; ♀**n** *v/t.* and *v/i.* (ge-, h) scrawl, scribble.

kroch [krɔx] *pret. of* kriechen.

Krokodil [kroko'di:l] *n* (-s/-e) crocodile.

Krone ['kro:nə] *f* (-/-n) crown; coronet (*of duke, earl, etc.*).

krönen ['krø:nən] *v/t.* (ge-, h) crown (*zum König* king) (*a. fig.*).

'**Kron|leuchter** *m* chandelier; lust|re, *Am.* -er; electrolier; '**~prinz** *m* crown prince; '**~prinzessin** *f* crown princess.

'**Krönung** *f* (-/-en) coronation, crowning; *fig.* climax, culmination.

'**Kronzeuge** ⚖ *m* chief witness; King's evidence, *Am.* State's evidence.

Kropf 🦅 [krɔpf] goit|re, *Am.* -er.

Kröte *zo.* ['krø:tə] *f* (-/-n) toad.

Krücke ['krʏkə] *f* (-/-n) crutch.

Krug [kru:k] *m* (-[e]s/ᵁe) jug, pitcher; jar; mug; tankard.

Krume ['kru:mə] *f* (-/-n) crumb; 🌱 topsoil.

Krümel ['kry:məl] *m* (-s/-) small crumb; ♀**n** *v/t.* and *v/i.* (ge-, h) crumble.

krumm *adj.* [krum] *p.* bent, stooping; *limb, nose, etc.*: crooked; *spine*: curved; *deal, business, etc.*: crooked; '**~beinig** *adj.* bandy- or bow-legged.

krümmen ['krʏmən] *v/t.* (ge-, h) bend (*arm, back, etc.*); crook (*finger, etc.*); curve (*metal sheet, etc.*); *sich ~ person, snake, etc.*: writhe; *worm, etc.*: wriggle; *sich vor Schmerzen ~* writhe with pain; *sich vor Lachen ~* be convulsed with laughter.

'**Krümmung** *f* (-/-en) road, curve: bend; arch, road, etc.: curve; river, path, etc.: turn, wind, meander; earth's surface, spine, etc.: curvature.

Krüppel ['krʏpəl] *m* (-s/-) cripple.

Kruste ['krustə] *f* (-/-n) crust.

Kübel ['ky:bəl] *m* (-s/-) tub; pail, bucket.

Kubik|meter [ku'bi:k-] *n, m* cubic met|re, *Am.* -er; **~wurzel** ⯑ *f* cube root.

Küche ['kʏçə] *f* (-/-n) kitchen; cuisine, cookery; *s. kalt.*

Kuchen ['ku:xən] *m* (-s/-) cake, flan; pastry.

'**Küchen|gerät** *n*, '**~geschirr** *n* kitchen utensils *pl.*; '**~herd** *m* (kitchen-)range; cooker, stove; '**~schrank** *m* kitchen cupboard *or* cabinet; '**~zettel** *m* bill of fare, menu.

Kuckuck *orn.* ['kukuk] *m* (-s/-e) cuckoo.

Kufe ['ku:fə] *f* (-/-n) ⛷ skid; *sleigh, etc.*: runner.

Küfer ['ky:fər] *m* (-s/-) cooper; cellarman.

Kugel ['ku:gəl] *f* (-/-n) ball; ✕ bullet; ⯑, *geogr.* sphere; *sports*: shot, weight; ♀**förmig** *adj.* ['...fœrmiç] spherical, ball-shaped, globular; '**~gelenk** ⊕, *anat. n* ball-and-socket joint; '**~lager** ⊕ *n* ball-bearing; '2n (ge-) **1.** v/i. (sein) ball, etc.: roll; **2.** v/t. (h) roll (ball, etc.); sich ~ children, etc.: roll about; F double up (vor with laughter); '~schreiber m ball(-point)-pen; '~stoßen v/i. (-s/no pl.) sports: putting the shot or weight.

Kuh zo. [ku:] f (-/=e) cow.

kühl adj. [ky:l] cool (a. fig.); '2anlage f cold-storage plant; '2e f (-/no pl.) cool(ness); '~en v/t. (ge-, h) cool (wine, wound, etc.); chill (wine, etc.); '2er mot. m (-s/-) radiator; '2raum m cold-storage chamber; '2schrank m refrigerator, F fridge.

kühn adj. [ky:n] bold (a. fig.), daring, audacious. [a. city barn.]

'**Kuhstall** m cow-house, byre, Am.]

Küken orn. ['ky:kən] n (-s/-) chick.

kulant ✝ adj. [ku'lant] firm, etc.: accommodating, obliging; price, terms, etc.: fair, easy.

Kulisse [ku'lisə] f (-/-n) thea. wing, side-scene; fig. front; ~n pl. a. scenery; hinter den ~n behind the scenes.

Kult [kult] m (-[e]s/-e) cult, worship.

kultivieren [kulti'vi:rən] v/t. (no -ge-, h) cultivate (a. fig.).

Kultur [kul'tu:r] f (-/-en) ✎ cultivation; fig.: culture; civilization; 2ell adj. [~u'rel] cultural; 2film [~'tu:r-] m educational film; ~geschichte f history of civilization (a. fig.); ~volk n civilized people.

Kultus ['kultus] m (-/Kulte) s. Kult; '~minister m minister of education and cultural affairs; '~ministerium n ministry of education and cultural affairs.

Kummer ['kumər] m (-s/no pl.) grief, sorrow; trouble, worry.

kümmer|lich adj. ['kymərliç] life, etc.: miserable, wretched; conditions, etc.: pitiful, pitiable; result, etc.: poor; resources: scanty; '~n v/t. (ge-, h): es kümmert mich I bother, I worry; sich ~ um look after, take care of; see to; meddle with.

'**kummervoll** adj. sorrowful.

Kump|an F [kum'pɑ:n] m (-s/-e) companion; F mate, chum, Am. F a. buddy; ~el ['~pəl] m (-s/-, F -s) ⛏ pitman, collier; F work-mate; F s. Kumpan.

Kunde ['kundə] **1.** m (-n/-n) cus-

tomer, client; **2.** f (-/-n) knowledge.

Kundgebung ['kunt-] f (-/-en) manifestation; pol. rally.

kündig|en ['kyndigən] (ge-, h) **1.** v/i.: j-m ~ give s.o. notice; **2.** v/t. ✝ call in (capital); ⚖ cancel (contract); pol. denounce (treaty); '2ung f (-/-en) notice; ✝ calling in; ⚖ cancellation; pol. denunciation.

'**Kundschaft** f (-/-en) customers pl., clients pl.; custom, clientele; '~er ⚔ m (-s/-) scout; spy.

künftig ['kynftiç] **1.** adj. event, years, etc.: future; event, programme, etc.: coming; life, world, etc.: next; **2.** adv. in future, from now on.

Kunst [kunst] f (-/=e) art; skill; '~akademie f academy of arts; '~ausstellung f art exhibition; '~druck m art print(ing); '~dünger m artificial manure, fertilizer; '2fertig adj. skilful, skilled; '2fertigkeit f artistic skill; '~gegenstand m objet d'art; '2gerecht adj. skilful; professional; expert; '~geschichte f history of art; '~gewerbe n arts and crafts pl.; applied arts pl.; '~glied n artificial limb; '~griff m trick, dodge; artifice, knack; '~händler m art-dealer; '~kenner m connoisseur of or in art; '~leder n imitation or artificial leather.

Künstler ['kynstlər] m (-s/-) artist; ♪, thea. performer; '2isch adj. artistic.

künstlich adj. ['kynstliç] eye, flower, light, etc.: artificial; teeth, hair, etc.: false; fibres, dyes, etc.: synthetic.

'**Kunst|liebhaber** m art-lover; '~maler m artist, painter; '~reiter m equestrian; circus-rider; ~schätze ['~fetsə] m/pl. art treasures pl.; '~seide f artificial silk, rayon; '~stück n feat, trick, F stunt; '~tischler m cabinet-maker; '~verlag m art publishers pl.; '2voll adj. artistic, elaborate; '~werk n work of art.

kunterbunt F fig. adj. ['kuntər-] higgledy-piggledy.

Kupfer ['kupfər] n (-s/no pl.) copper; '~geld n copper coins pl., F coppers pl.; '2n adj. (of) copper; '2rot adj. copper-colo(u)red; '~stich m copper-plate engraving.

Kupon [ku'põ:] m (-s/-s) s. Coupon.

Kuppe ['kupə] f (-/-n) rounded hilltop; nail: head.

Kuppel ◬ ['kupəl] f (-/-n) dome, cupola, vault; **~ei** ⚷ [~'lai] f (-/-en) procuring; **2n** (ge-, h) **1.** v/t. s. koppeln; **2.** mot. v/i. declutch.

Kuppl|er ['kuplər] m (-s/-) pimp, procurer; **~ung** f (-/-en) ⊕ coupling (a. ⚙); mot. clutch.

Kur [ku:r] f (-/-en) course of treatment, cure.

Kür [ky:r] f (-/-en) sports: s. Kürlauf; voluntary exercise.

Kuratorium [kura'to:rium] n (-s/ Kuratorien) board of trustees.

Kurbel ⊕ ['kurbəl] f (-/-n) crank, winch, handle; **2n** (ge-, h) **1.** v/t. shoot (film); in die Höhe ~ winch up (load, etc.); wind up (car window, etc.); **2.** v/i. crank. [pumpkin.\]

Kürbis ♧ ['kyrbis] m (-ses/-se)\
'Kur|gast m visitor to or patient at a health resort or spa; **~haus** n spa hotel.

Kurier [ku'ri:r] m (-s/-e) courier, express (messenger).

kurieren [ku'ri:rən] v/t. (no -ge-, h) cure.

kurios adj. [kur'jo:s] curious, odd, strange, queer. [skating.\]

'Kürlauf m sports: free (roller)\
'Kur|ort m health resort; spa; **~pfuscher** m quack (doctor); **~pfusche'rei** f (-/-en) quackery.

Kurs [kurs] m (-es/-e) ✝ currency; ✝ rate, price; ⚓ and fig. course; course, class; **~bericht** ✝ m market-report; **~buch** 🕮 n railway guide, Am. railroad guide.

Kürschner ['kyrʃnər] m (-s/-) furrier.

kursieren [kur'zi:rən] v/i. (no -ge-, h) money, etc.: circulate, be in circulation; rumour, etc.: circulate, be afloat, go about.

Kursivschrift typ. [kur'zi:f-] f italics pl. [class.\]

Kursus ['kurzus] m (-/Kurse) course,\
'Kurs|verlust ✝ m loss on the stock exchange; **~wert** ✝ m market value; **~zettel** ✝ m stock exchange list.

Kurve ['kurvə] f (-/-n) curve; road, etc.: a. bend, turn.

kurz [kurts] **1.** adj. space: short; time, etc.: short, brief; **~ und bündig** brief, concise; **~e Hose** shorts pl.; mit **~en Worten** with a few words; den **kürzeren ziehen** get the worst of it; **2.** adv. in short; **~ angebunden**

sein be curt or sharp; **~ und gut** in short, in a word; **~ vor London** short of London; **sich ~ fassen** be brief or concise; in **~em** before long, shortly; vor **~em** a short time ago; zu **~ kommen** come off badly, get a raw deal; um es ~ zu sagen to cut a long story short; **2arbeit** ✝ f short-time work; **2arbeiter** ✝ m short-time worker; **~atmig** adj. ['~ʔa:tmiç] short-winded.

Kürze ['kyrtsə] f (-/no pl.) shortness; brevity; in **~** shortly, before long; **2n** v/t. (ge-, h) shorten (dress, etc.) (um by); abridge, condense (book, etc.); cut, reduce (expenses, etc.).

'kurz|er'hand adv. without hesitation; on the spot; **2film** m short (film); **2form** f shortened form; **~fristig** adj. short-term; ✝ bill, etc.: short-dated; **2geschichte** f (short) short story; **~lebig** adj. ['~le:biç] short-lived; **2nachrichten** f/pl. news summary.

kürzlich adv. ['kyrtsliç] lately, recently, not long ago.

'Kurz|schluß ⚡ m short circuit, F short; **~schrift** f shorthand, stenography; **2sichtig** adj. short-sighted, near-sighted; **2um** adv. in short, in a word.

Kürzung f (-/-en) shortening (of dress, etc.); abridg(e)ment, condensation (of book, etc.); cut, reduction (of expenses, etc.).

'Kurz|waren f/pl. haberdashery, Am. dry goods pl., notions pl.; **~weil** f (-/no pl.) amusement, entertainment; **2weilig** adj. amusing, entertaining; **~welle** ⚡ f short wave; radio: short-wave band.

Kusine [ku'zi:nə] f (-/-n) s. Cousine.

Kuß [kus] m (Kusses/Küsse) kiss; **2echt** adj. kiss-proof. [kiss.\]

küssen ['kysən] v/t. and v/i.(ge-, h)\
'kußfest adj. s. kußecht.

Küste ['kystə] f (-/-n) coast; shore.

'Küsten|bewohner m inhabitant of a coastal region; **~fischerei** f inshore fishery or fishing; **~gebiet** n coastal area or region; **~schiffahrt** f coastal shipping.

Küster eccl. ['kystər] m (-s/-) verger, sexton, sacristan.

Kutsch|bock ['kutʃ-] m coach-box; **~e** f (-/-n) carriage, coach; **~enschlag** m carriage-door, coach-door; **~er** m (-s/-) coachman; **2ie-**

ren [ˌʌˈtʃiːrən] (no -ge-) **1.** v/t. (h) drive s.o. in a coach; **2.** v/i. (h) (drive a) coach; **3.** v/i. (sein) (drive or ride in a) coach.

Kutte [ˈkʊtə] f (-/-n) cowl.

Kutter ⚓ [ˈkʊtər] m (-s/-) cutter.

Kuvert [kuˈvɛrt; kuˈvɛːr] n (-[e]s/-e; -s/-s) envelope; at table: cover.

Kux ⚒ [kuks] m (-es/-e) mining share.

L

Lab zo. [laːp] n (-[e]s/-e) rennet.

labil adj. [laˈbiːl] unstable (a. ⊕, ⚕); phys., ⚗ labile.

Labor [laˈboːr] n (-s/-s, -e) s. Laboratorium; **~ant** [laboˈrant] m (-en/-en) laboratory assistant; **~atorium** [laboraˈtoːrjum] n (-s/ Laboratorien) laboratory; **2ieren** [ˌʌoˈriːrən] v/i. (no -ge-, h): ~ an (dat.) labo(u)r under, suffer from.

Labyrinth [labyˈrɪnt] n (-[e]s/-e) labyrinth, maze.

Lache [ˈlaxə] f (-/-n) pool, puddle.

lächeln [ˈlɛçəln] **1.** v/i. (ge-, h) smile (über acc. at); höhnisch ~ sneer (über acc. at); **2.** ⚺ n (-s/no pl.) smile; höhnisches ~ sneer.

lachen [ˈlaxən] **1.** v/i. (ge-, h) laugh (über acc. at); **2.** ⚺ n (-s/no pl.) laugh(ter).

lächerlich adj. [ˈlɛçərlɪç] ridiculous, laughable, ludicrous, absurd; derisory, scoffing; ~ machen ridicule; sich ~ machen make a fool of o.s. (guest).

Lachs ichth. [laks] m (-es/-e) salmon.

Lack [lak] m (-[e]s/-e) (gum-)lac; varnish; lacquer, enamel; **2ieren** [laˈkiːrən] v/t. (no -ge-, h) lacquer, varnish, enamel; **~leder** n patent leather; **~schuhe** m/pl. patent leather shoes pl., F patents pl.

Lade|fähigkeit [ˈlaːdə-] f loading capacity; **~fläche** f loading area; **~hemmung** ⚔ f jam, stoppage; **~linie** ⚓ f load-line.

laden[1] [ˈlaːdən] v/t. (irr., ge-, h) load; load (gun), charge (a. ⚡); freight, ship; ⚖ cite, summon; invite, ask (guest).

Laden[2] [ˌʌ] m (-s/-ʺ) shop, Am. store; shutter; **~besitzer** m s. Ladeninhaber; **~dieb** m shop-lifter; **~diebstahl** m shop-lifting; **~hüter** m drug on the market; **~inhaber** m shopkeeper, Am. store-

keeper; **~kasse** f till; **~preis** m selling-price, retail price; **~schild** n shopsign; **~schluß** m closing time; nach ~ after hours; **~tisch** m counter.

'Lade|platz m loading-place; **~rampe** f loading platform or ramp; **'~raum** m loading space; ⚓ hold; **'~schein** ⚓ m bill of lading.

'Ladung f (-/-en) loading; load, freight; ⚓ cargo; ⚡ charge (a. of gun); ⚖ summons.

lag [laːk] pret. of liegen.

Lage [ˈlaːgə] f (-/-n) situation, position; site, location (of building); state, condition; attitude; geol. layer, stratum; round (of beer, etc.); in der ~ sein zu inf. be able to inf., be in a position to inf.; versetzen Sie sich in meine ~ put yourself in my place.

Lager [ˈlaːgər] n (-s/-) couch, bed; den, lair (of wild animals); geol. deposit; ⊕ bearing; warehouse, storehouse, depot; store, stock (✝ pl. a. Läger); ⚔, etc.: encampment; auf ~ ✝ on hand, in stock; **~buch** n stock-book; **~feuer** n camp-fire; **~geld** n storage; **~haus** n warehouse; **'2n** (ge-, h) **1.** v/i. lie down, rest; ⚔ (en)camp; ✝ be stored; **2.** v/t. lay down; ⚔ (en)camp; ✝ store, warehouse; sich ~ lie down, rest; **~platz** m ✝ depot; resting-place; ⚔, etc.: camp-site; **~raum** m store-room; **~ung** f (-/-en) storage (of goods).

Lagune [laˈguːnə] f (-/-n) lagoon.

lahm adj. [laːm] lame; **~en** v/i. (ge-, h) be lame.

lähmen [ˈlɛːmən] v/t. (ge-, h) (make) lame; paraly|se, Am. -ze (a. fig.).

'lahmlegen v/t. (sep., -ge-, h) paraly|se, Am. -ze; obstruct.

'Lähmung ⚕ f (-/-en) paralysis.

Laib [laɪp] m (-[e]s/-e) loaf.

Laich [laɪç] *m* (-[e]s/-e) spawn;
'**2en** *v/i.* (ge-, h) spawn.

Laie ['laɪə] *m* (-n/-n) layman;
amateur; '**2nbühne** *f* amateur
theat|re, *Am.* -er.

Lakai [la'kaɪ] *m* (-en/-en) lackey
(*a. fig.*), footman.

Lake ['la:kə] *f* (-/-n) brine, pickle.

Laken ['la:kən] *n* (-s/-) sheet.

lallen ['lalən] *v/i. and v/t.* (ge-, h)
stammer; babble.

Lamelle [la'mɛlə] *f* (-/-n) lamella,
lamina; ♀ gill (*of mushrooms*).

lamentieren [lamɛn'ti:rən] *v/i.* (no
-ge-, h) lament (*um* for; *über acc.*
over).

Lamm *zo.* [lam] *n* (-[e]s/-er) lamb;
'**.fell** *n* lambskin; '2**fromm** *adj.*
(as) gentle *or* (as) meek as a lamb.

Lampe ['lampə] *f* (-/-n) lamp.

'**Lampen|fieber** *n* stage fright;
'**.licht** *n* lamplight; '**.schirm** *m*
lamp-shade.

Lampion [lã'pjõ:] *m*, *n* (-s/-s) Chinese lantern.

Land [lant] *n* (-[e]s/-er, *poet.* -e)
land; country; territory; ground,
soil; *an ~ gehen* go ashore; *auf dem
~e* in the country; *aufs ~ gehen* go
into the country; *außer ~es gehen*
go abroad; *zu ~e* by land; '**.arbei-
ter** *m* farm-hand; '**.besitz** *m*
landed property; ⚖ real estate;
'**.besitzer** *m* landowner, landed
proprietor; '**.bevölkerung** *f* rural
population.

Lande|bahn ✈ ['landə-] *f* runway;
'**.deck** ⚓ *n* flight-deck.   [land.|

land|einwärts *adv.* upcountry, in-
landen ['landən] (ge-) **1.** *v/i.* (sein)
land; **2.** *v/t.* (h) ⚓ disembark
(*troups*); ✈ land, set down (*troups*).

'**Landenge** *f* neck of land, isthmus.

Landeplatz ✈ ['landə-] *m* landing-
field.

Ländereien [lɛndə'raɪən] *pl.* landed
property, lands *pl.*, estates *pl.*

Länderspiel ['lɛndər-] *n* sports:
international match.

Landes|grenze ['landəs-] *f* frontier,
boundary; '**.innere** *n* interior, inland, upcountry; '**.kirche** *f* national church; *Brt.* Established Church;
'**.regierung** *f* government; *in
Germany:* Land government; '**.
sprache** *f* native language, vernacular; '2**üblich** *adj.* customary;
'**.verrat** *m* treason; '**.verräter** *m*

traitor to his country; '**.verteidi-
gung** *f* national defen|ce, *Am.* -se.

'**Land|flucht** *f* rural exodus; '**.frie-
densbruch** ⚖ *m* breach of the
public peace; '**.gericht** *n* appr.
district court; '**.gewinnung** *f*
(-/-en) reclamation of land; '**.gut** *n*
country-seat, estate; '**.haus** *n*
country-house, cottage; '**.karte** *f*
map; '**.kreis** *m* rural district;
'2**läufig** *adj.* ['~lɔʏfiç] customary,
current, common.

ländlich *adj.* ['lɛntliç] rural, rustic.

'**Land|maschinen** *f/pl.* agricultural
or farm equipment; '**.partie** *f*
picnic, outing, excursion into the
country; '**.plage** iro. *f* nuisance;
'**.rat** *m* (-[e]s/-e) appr. district
president; '**.ratte** ⚓ *f* landlubber;
'**.recht** *n* common law; '**.regen** *m*
persistent rain.

'**Landschaft** *f* (-/-en) province,
district, region; countryside, scenery; *esp. paint.* landscape; '2**lich**
adj. provincial; scenic (*beauty, etc.*).

'**Landsmann** *m* (-[e]s/*Landsleute*)
(fellow-)countryman, compatriot;
was sind Sie für ein ~? what's your
native country?

'**Land|straße** *f* highway, high road;
'**.streicher** *m* (-s/-) vagabond,
tramp, *Am. sl.* hobo; '**.streit-
kräfte** *f/pl.* land forces *pl.*, the
Army; ground forces *pl.*; '**.strich**
m tract of land, region; '**.tag** *m*
Landtag, Land parliament.

Landung ['landuŋ] *f* (-/-en) ⚓, ✈
landing; disembarkation; arrival;
'**.sbrücke** ⚓ *f* floating: landing-
stage; pier; '**.ssteg** ⚓ *m* gangway,
gang-plank.

'**Land|vermesser** *m* (-s/-) surveyor;
'**.vermessung** *f* land-surveying;
'2**wärts** *adv.* [~'vɛrts] landward(s);
'**.weg** *m*: *auf dem ~e* by land;
'**.wirt** *m* farmer, agriculturist;
'**.wirtschaft** *f* agriculture, farming; '2**wirtschaftlich** *adj.* agricultural; *~e Maschinen f/pl. s.
Landmaschinen*; '**.zunge** *f* spit.

lang [laŋ] **1.** *adj.* long; *p.* tall; *er
machte ein ~es Gesicht* his face fell;
2. *adv.* long; *e-e Woche ~* for a
week; *über kurz oder ~* sooner or
later; *~(e) anhaltend* continuous;
~(e) entbehrt long-missed; *~(e) er-
sehnt* long-wished-for; *das ist
schon ~(e) her* that was a long time

ago; ~ **und breit** at (full or great) length; **noch** ~(e) nicht not for a long time yet; far from ger.; **wie** ~e lernen Sie schon Englisch? how long have you been learning English?; **'atmig** adj. ['~a:tmiç] long-winded; **'~e** adv. s. lang 2.

'Länge ['lɛŋə] f (-/-n) length; tallness; geogr., ast. longitude; **der** ~ **nach** (at) full length, lengthwise.

'langen ['laŋən] v/i. (ge-, h) suffice, be enough; ~ **nach** reach for.

'Längen|grad m degree of longitude; **'~maß** n linear measure.

'länger 1. adj. longer; ~**e Zeit** (for) some time; **2.** adv. longer; **ich kann es nicht** ~ **ertragen** I cannot bear it any longer; **je** ~, **je lieber** the longer the better.

'Langeweile f (-, Langenweile/no pl.) boredom, tediousness, ennui.

'lang|fristig adj. long-term; **'~jährig** adj. of long standing; ~**e Erfahrung** (many) years of experience; **'2lauf** m skiing: cross-country run or race.

'länglich adj. longish, oblong.

'Langmut f (-/no pl.) patience, forbearance.

längs [lɛŋs] **1.** prp. (gen., dat.) along(side of); ~ **der Küste fahren** ⚓ (sail along the) coast; **2.** adv. lengthwise; **'2achse** f longitudinal axis.

'lang|sam adj. slow; **2schläfer** ['~ʃlɛːfər] m (-s/-) late riser, lieabed; **'2spielplatte** f long-playing record.

längst [lɛŋst] adv. long ago or since; **ich weiß es** ~ I have known it for a long time; **'~ens** adv. at the longest; at the latest; at the most.

'lang|stielig adj. long-handled; ♀ long-stemmed, long-stalked; **'2-streckenlauf** m long-distance run or race; **'2weile** f (-, Langenweile/no pl.) s. Langeweile; **'~weilen** v/t. (ge-, h) bore; sich ~ be bored; **'~weilig** adj. tedious, boring, dull; ~e Person bore; **'2welle** f ♀ long wave; radio: long wave band; **~wierig** adj. ['~viːriç] protracted, lengthy; ♀ lingering.

'Lanze ['lantsə] f (-/-n) spear, lance.

Lappalie [la'paːljə] f (-/-n) trifle.

Lapp|en ['lapən] m (-s/-) patch; rag; duster; (dish- or floor-)cloth; anat., ♀ lobe; **'2ig** adj. flabby.

läppisch adj. ['lɛpiʃ] foolish, silly.

Lärche ♀ ['lɛrçə] f (-/-n) larch.

Lärm [lɛrm] m (-[e]s/no pl.) noise; din; ~ **schlagen** give the alarm; **2en** v/i. (ge-, h) make a noise; **2end** adj. noisy.

Larve ['larfə] f (-/-n) mask; face (often iro.); zo. larva, grub.

las [laːs] pret. of lesen.

lasch F adj. [laʃ] limp, lax.

Lasche ['laʃə] f (-/-n) strap; tongue (of shoe).

lassen ['lasən] (irr., h) **1.** v/t. (ge-) let; leave; **laß das!** don't!; **laß das Weinen!** stop crying!; **ich kann es nicht** ~ I cannot help (doing) it; **sein Leben** ~ **für** sacrifice one's life for; **2.** v/i. (ge-): **von et.** ~ desist from s.th., renounce s.th.; do without s.th.; **3.** v/aux. (no -ge-) allow, permit, let; make, cause; **drucken** ~ **have** s.th. printed; **gehen** ~ let s.o. go; **ich habe ihn dieses Buch lesen** ~ I have made him read this book; **von sich hören** ~ send word; **er läßt sich nichts sagen** he won't take advice; **es läßt sich nicht leugnen** there is no denying (the fact).

lässig adj. ['lɛsiç] indolent, idle; sluggish; careless.

Last [last] f (-/-en) load; burden; weight; cargo, freight; fig. weight, charge, trouble; **zu** ~**en von** ♰ to the debit of; **j-m zur** ~ **fallen** be a burden to s.o.; **j-m et. zur** ~ **legen** lay s.th. at s.o.'s door or to s.o.'s charge; **'2auto** n s. Lastkraftwagen.

'lasten v/i. (ge-, h): ~ **auf** (dat.) weigh or press (up)on; **'Laufzug** m goods lift, Am. freight elevator.

Laster ['lastər] n (-s/-) vice.

Lästerer ['lɛstərər] m (-s/-) slanderer, backbiter.

'lasterhaft adj. vicious; corrupt.

Läster|maul ['lɛstər-] n s. Lästerer; **'2n** v/i. (ge-, h) slander, calumniate, defame; abuse; **'~ung** f (-/-en) slander, calumny.

lästig adj. ['lɛstiç] troublesome, annoying; uncomfortable, inconvenient.

'Last|kahn m barge, lighter; **'~kraftwagen** m lorry, Am. truck; **'~schrift** ♰ f debit; **'~tier** n pack animal; **'~wagen** m s. Lastkraftwagen.

Latein [la'tain] n (-s/no pl.) Latin; **2isch** adj. Latin.

Laterne [la'tɛrnə] f (-/-n) lantern; street-lamp; **~npfahl** m lamp-post.

latschen F ['la:tʃən] v/i. (ge-, sein) shuffle (along).

Latte ['latə] f (-/-n) pale; lath; sports: bar; **~nkiste** f crate; lath; **verschlag** m latticed partition; **~nzaun** m paling, Am. picket fence.

Lätzchen ['lɛtsçən] n (-s/-) bib, feeder.

lau adj. [lau] tepid, lukewarm (a. fig.).

Laub [laup] n (-[e]s/no pl.) foliage, leaves pl.; **~baum** m deciduous tree.

Laube ['laubə] f (-/-n) arbo(u)r, bower; **~ngang** m arcade.

'Laub|frosch zo. m tree-frog; **~säge** f fret-saw.

Lauch ♀ [laux] m (-[e]s/-e) leek.

Lauer ['lauər] f (-/no pl.): auf der ~ liegen or sein lie in wait or ambush, be on the look-out; **2n** v/i. (ge-, h) lurk (auf acc. for); ~ auf (acc.) watch for; **2nd** adj. louring, lowering.

Lauf [lauf] m (-[e]s/⁼e) run(ning); sports: a. run, heat; race; current (of water); course; barrel (of gun); (♪ run; im ~e der Zeit in (the) course of time; **~bahn** f career; **~bursche** m errand-boy, office-boy; **~disziplin** f sports: running event.

'laufen (irr., ge-) 1. v/i. run; walk; flow; time: pass, go by, elapse; leak; die Dinge ~ lassen let things slide; j-n ~ lassen let s.o. go; 2. v/t. (sein, h) run; walk; **~d** adj. running; current; regular; ~en Monats ♱ instant; auf dem ~en sein be up to date, be fully informed.

Läufer ['lɔyfər] m (-s/-) runner (a. carpet); chess: bishop; football: half-back.

'Lauf|masche f ladder, Am. a. run; **~paß** F m (-es/-, sl. walking papers pl.; **~planke** ♣ f gang-board, gang-plank; **~schritt** m: im ~ running; **~steg** m footbridge; ♣ gangway.

Lauge ['laugə] f (-/-n) lye.

Laun|e ['launə] f (-/-n) humo(u)r; mood; temper; caprice, fancy, whim; guter ~ in (high) spirits; **2enhaft** adj. capricious; **2isch** adj. moody; wayward.

Laus zo. [laus] f (-/⁼e) louse; **~bub**

['~bu:p] m (-en/-en) young scamp, F young devil, rascal.

lausch|en ['lauʃən] v/i. (ge-, h) listen; eavesdrop; **'~ig** adj. snug, cosy; peaceful.

laut [laut] 1. adj. loud (a. fig.); noisy; 2. adv. aloud; loud(ly); (sprechen Sie) ~er! speak up!, Am. louder!; 3. prp. (gen., dat.) according to; ♱ as per; 4. ♀ m (-[e]s/-e) sound; **2e** ♪ f (-/-n) lute; **~en** v/i. (ge-, h) sound; words, etc.: run; read; ~ auf (acc.) passport, etc.: be issued to.

läuten ['lɔytən] (ge-, h) 1. v/i. ring; toll; es läutet the bell is ringing; 2. v/t. ring; toll.

'lauter adj. pure; clear; genuine; sincere; mere, nothing but, only.

läuter|n ['lɔytərn] v/t. (ge-, h) purify; ⊕ cleanse; refine; **'2ung** f (-/-en) purification; refining.

'laut|los adj. noiseless; mute; silent; silence: hushed; **2schrift** f phonetic transcription; **2sprecher** m loud-speaker; **2stärke** f sound intensity; radio: sound-volume; **2-stärkeregler** ['~re:glər] m (-s/-) volume control.

'lauwarm adj. tepid, lukewarm.

Lava geol. ['la:va] f (-/Laven) lava.

Lavendel ♀ [la'vɛndəl] m (-s/-) lavender.

lavieren [la'vi:rən] v/i. (no -ge-, h, sein) ♣ tack (a. fig.).

Lawine [la'vi:nə] f (-/-n) avalanche.

lax adj. [laks] lax, loose; morals: a. easy.

Lazarett [latsa'rɛt] n (-[e]s/-e) (military) hospital.

leben¹ ['le:bən] (ge-, h) 1. v/i. live; be alive; ~ Sie wohl! good-bye!, farewell!; j-n hochleben lassen cheer s.o.; at table: drink s.o.'s health; von et. ~ live on s.th.; hier lebt es sich gut it is pleasant living here; 2. v/t. live (one's life).

Leben² [~] n (-s/-) life; stir, animation, bustle; am ~ bleiben remain alive, survive; am ~ erhalten keep alive; ein neues ~ beginnen turn over a new leaf; ins ~ rufen call into being; sein ~ aufs Spiel setzen risk one's life; sein ~ lang all one's life; ums ~ kommen lose one's life; perish.

lebendig adj. [le'bɛndiç] living; pred.: alive; quick; lively.

'Lebens|alter n age; **'~anschau-**

ung f outlook on life; '**~art** f manners pl., behavio(u)r; '**~auffassung** f philosophy of life; '**~bedingungen** f/pl. living conditions pl.; '**~beschreibung** f life, biography; '**~dauer** f span of life; ⊕ durability; '**2echt** adj. true to life; '**~erfahrung** f experience of life; '**2-fähig** adj. ✿ and fig. viable; '**~gefahr** f danger of life; **~!** danger (of death)!; unter ~ at the risk of one's life; '**2gefährlich** adj. dangerous (to life), perilous; '**~gefährte** m life's companion; '**~größe** f life-size; in ~ at full length; '**~kraft** f vital power, vigo(u)r, vitality; '**2länglich** adj. for life, lifelong; '**~lauf** m course of life; personal record, curriculum vitae; '**2lustig** adj. gay, merry; '**~mittel** pl. food (-stuffs pl.), provisions pl., groceries pl.; '**2müde** adj. weary or tired of life; '**~notwendig** adj. vital, essential; '**~retter** m life-saver, rescuer; '**~standard** m standard of living; '**~unterhalt** m livelihood; s-n ~ verdienen earn one's living; '**~versicherung** f life-insurance; '**~wandel** m life, (moral) conduct; '**~weise** f mode of living, habits pl.; gesunde ~ regimen; '**~weisheit** f worldly wisdom; '**2wichtig** adj. vital, essential; **~e** Organe pl. vitals pl.; '**~zeichen** n sign of life; '**2zeit** f lifetime; auf ~ for life.

Leber anat. ['le:bər] f (-/-n) liver; '**~fleck** m mole; '**2krank** adj., '**2-leidend** adj. suffering from a liver-complaint; '**~tran** m cod-liver oil; '**~wurst** f liver-sausage, Am. liverwurst.

'**Lebewesen** n living being, creature.

Lebe'wohl n (-[e]s/-e, -s) farewell.

leb|haft adj. ['le:phaft] lively; vivid; spirited; interest: keen; traffic: busy; '**2kuchen** m gingerbread; '**~los** adj. lifeless; '**2zeiten** pl.: zu s-n ~ in his lifetime.

lechzen ['lɛçtsən] v/i. (ge-, h): ~ nach languish or yearn or pant for.

Leck [lɛk] **1.** n (-[e]s/-e) leak; **2.** 2 adj. leaky; ~ werden ⚓ spring a leak.

lecken ['lɛkən] (ge-, h) **1.** v/t. lick; **2.** v/i. lick; leak.

lecker adj. ['lɛkər] dainty; delicious; '**2bissen** m dainty, delicacy.

Leder ['le:dər] n (-s/-) leather; in

~ gebunden leather-bound; '**2n** adj. leathern, of leather.

ledig adj. ['le:dɪç] single, unmarried; child: illegitimate; **~lich** adv. ['~k-] solely, merely.

Lee ⚓ [le:] f (-/no pl.) lee (side).

leer [le:r] **1.** adj. empty; vacant; void; vain; blank; **2.** adv.: ~ laufen ⊕ idle; '**2e** f (-/no pl.) emptiness, void (a. fig.); phys. vacuum; '**~en** v/t. (ge-, h) empty; clear (out); pour out; '**2gut** ✝ n empties pl.; '**2lauf** m ⊕ idling; mot. neutral gear; fig. waste of energy; '**~stehend** adj. flat: empty, unoccupied, vacant.

legal adj. [le'ga:l] legal, lawful.

Legat [le'ga:t] **1.** m (-en/-en) legate; **2.** ᵍᵗᶻ n (-[e]s/-e) legacy.

legen ['le:gən] (ge-, h) **1.** v/t. lay; place, put; sich ~ wind, etc.: calm down, abate; cease; Wert ~ auf (acc.) attach importance to; **2.** v/i. hen: lay.

Legende [le'gɛndə] f (-/-n) legend.

legieren [le'gi:rən] v/t. (no -ge-, h) ⊕ alloy; cookery: thicken (mit with).

Legislative [le:gisla'ti:və] f (-/-n) legislative body or power.

legitim adj. [legi'ti:m] legitimate; **~ieren** [~i'mi:rən] v/t. (no -ge-, h) legitimate; authorize; sich ~ prove one's identity.

Lehm [le:m] m (-[e]s/-e) loam; mud; '**2ig** adj. loamy.

Lehn|e ['le:nə] f (-/-n) support; arm, back (of chair); '**2en** (ge-, h) **1.** v/i. lean (an dat. against); **2.** v/t. lean, rest (an acc., gegen against); sich ~ an (acc.) lean against; sich ~ auf (acc.) rest or support o.s. (up-) on; sich aus dem Fenster ~ lean out of the window; '**~sessel** m, '**~stuhl** m armchair, easy chair.

Lehrbuch ['le:r-] n textbook.

Lehre ['le:rə] f (-/-n) rule, precept; doctrine; system; science; theory; lesson, warning; moral (of fable); instruction, tuition; ⊕ ga(u)ge; ⊕ pattern; in der ~ sein be apprenticed (bei to); in die ~ geben apprentice, article (both: bei, zu to); '**2n** v/t. (ge-, h) teach, instruct; show.

'**Lehrer** m (-s/-) teacher; master, instructor; '**~in** f (-/-nen) (lady) teacher; (school)mistress; '**~kollegium** n staff (of teachers).

'**Lehr|fach** n subject; '**~film** m instructional film); '**~gang** m course (of instruction); '**~geld** n premium; '**~herr** m master, sl. boss; '**~jahre** n/pl. (years pl. of) apprenticeship; '**~junge** m s. Lehrling; '**~körper** m teaching staff; univ. professorate, faculty; '**~kraft** f teacher; professor; '**~ling** m (-s/-e) apprentice; '**~mädchen** n girl apprentice; '**~meister** m master; '**~methode** f method of teaching; '**~plan** m curriculum, syllabus; '**2reich** adj. instructive; '**~satz** m Å theorem; doctrine; eccl. dogma; '**~stoff** m subject-matter, subject(s pl.); '**~stuhl** m professorship; '**~vertrag** m articles pl. of apprenticeship, indenture(s pl.); '**~zeit** f apprenticeship.

Leib [laɪp] m (-[e]s/-er) body; belly, anat. abdomen; womb; bei lebendigem ~e alive; mit ~ und Seele body and soul; sich j-n vom ~e halten keep s.o. at arm's length; '**~arzt** m physician in ordinary, personal physician; '**~chen** n (-s/-) bodice.

Leibeigen|e ['laɪpˀaɪɡənə] m (-n/-n) bond(s)man, serf; '**~schaft** f (-/no pl.) bondage, serfdom.

Leibes|erziehung ['laɪbəs-] f physical training; '**~frucht** f f(o)etus; '**~kraft** f: aus Leibeskräften pl. with all one's might; '**~übung** f bodily or physical exercise.

'**Leib|garde** f body-guard; '**~gericht** n favo(u)rite dish; '**2haftig** adj. [~'haftɪç]: der ~e Teufel the devil incarnate; '**2lich** adj. bodily, corpor(e)al; '**~rente** f life-annuity; '**~schmerzen** m/pl. stomach-ache, belly-ache, f colic; '**~wache** f body-guard; '**~wäsche** f underwear.

Leiche ['laɪçə] f (-/-n) (dead) body, corpse.

Leichen|beschauer ts ['laɪçənbəʃaʊər] m (-s/-) appr. coroner; '**~bestatter** m (-s/-) undertaker, Am. a. mortician; '**~bittermiene** F f woebegone look or countenance; '**2blaß** adj. deadly pale; '**~halle** f mortuary; '**~schau** ts f appr. (coroner's) inquest; '**~schauhaus** n morgue; '**~tuch** n (-[e]s/-er) shroud; '**~verbrennung** f cremation; '**~wagen** m hearse. [Leiche.]

Leichnam ['laɪçnaːm] m (-[e]s/-e) s.]

leicht [laɪçt] **1.** adj. light; easy; slight; tobacco: mild; **2.** adv.: es ~

nehmen take it easy; '**2athlet** m athlete; '**2athletik** f athletics pl., Am. track and field events pl.; '**~fertig** adj. light(-minded); careless; frivolous, flippant; '**2fertigkeit** f levity; carelessness, frivolity, flippancy; '**2gewicht** n boxing: light-weight; '**~gläubig** adj. credulous; '**~hin** adv. lightly, casually; **2igkeit** ['~ɪç-] f (-/-en) lightness; ease, facility; '**~lebig** adj. easy-going; '**2metall** n light metal; '**2sinn** m (-[e]s/no pl.) frivolity, levity, carelessness; '**~sinnig** adj. light-minded, frivolous; careless; '**~verdaulich** adj. easy to digest; '**~verständlich** adj. easy to understand.

leid [laɪt]° **1.** adv.: es tut mir ~ I am sorry (um for), I regret; **2.** ⚥ n (-[e]s/no pl.) injury, harm; wrong; grief, sorrow; **~en** ['~dən] (irr., ge-, h) **1.** v/i. suffer (an dat. from); **2.** v/t.: (nicht) ~ können (dis)like; **2en** ['~dən] n (-s/-) suffering; ⚕ complaint; **~end** adj. ['~dənt] ailing.

'**Leidenschaft** f (-/-en) passion; '**2lich** adj. passionate; ardent; vehement; '**2slos** adj. dispassionate.

'**Leidens|gefährte** m, '**~gefährtin** f fellow-sufferer.

leid|er adv. ['laɪdər] unfortunately; int. alas!; ~ muß ich inf. I'm (so) sorry to inf.; ich muß ~ gehen I am afraid I have to go; '**~ig** adj. disagreeable; '**~lich** adj. ['laɪt-] tolerable; fairly well; '**2tragende** ['laɪt-] m, f (-n/-n) mourner; er ist der ~ dabei he is the one who suffers for it; **2wesen** ['laɪt-] n (-s/no pl.): zu meinem ~ to my regret.

Leier ♪ ['laɪər] f (-/-n) lyre; '**~kasten** m barrel-organ; '**~kastenmann** m organ-grinder.

Leih|bibliothek ['laɪ-] f, '**~bücherei** f lending or circulating library, Am. a. rental library; '**2en** v/t. (irr., ge-, h) lend; borrow (von from); '**~gebühr** f lending fee(s pl.); '**~haus** n pawnshop, Am. a. loan office; '**2weise** adv. as a loan.

Leim [laɪm] m (-[e]s/-e) glue; F aus dem ~ gehen get out of joint; F auf den ~ gehen fall for it, fall into the trap; '**2en** v/t. (ge-, h) glue; size.

Lein ♀ [laɪn] m (-[e]s/-e) flax.

Leine ['laɪnə] f (-/-n) line, cord; (dog-)lead, leash.

leinen ['laɪnən] **1.** *adj.* (of) linen; **2.** ⚥ *n* (-s/-) linen; *in ~* gebunden cloth-bound; '**2schuh** *m* canvas shoe.

'**Lein|öl** *n* linseed-oil; '**~samen** *m* linseed; '**~wand** *f* (-/no pl.) linen (cloth); *paint.* canvas; *film:* screen.

leise *adj.* ['laɪzə] low, soft; gentle; slight, faint; *~r stellen* turn down (*radio*).

Leiste ['laɪstə] *f* (-/-n) border, ledge; △ fillet; *anat.* groin.

leisten ['laɪstən] **1.** *v/t.* (ge-, h) do; perform; fulfil(l); take (*oath*); render (*service*); *ich kann mir das ~* I can afford it; **2.** ⚥ *m* (-s/-) last; boot-tree, *Am. a.* shoetree; '**2bruch** 🞍 *m* inguinal hernia.

'**Leistung** *f* (-/-en) performance; achievement; work(manship); result(s *pl.*); ⊕ capacity; output (*of factory*); benefit (*of insurance company*); '**2sfähig** *adj.* productive, efficient; ⊕ *a.* powerful; '**~sfähigkeit** *f* efficiency; ⊕ productivity; ⊕ capacity, producing-power.

Leit|artikel ['laɪt-] *m* leading article, leader, editorial; '**~bild** *n* image; example.

leiten ['laɪtən] *v/t.* (ge-, h) lead, guide; conduct (*a. phys.*, ♪); *fig.* direct, run, manage, operate; preside over (*meeting*); '**~d** *adj.* leading; *phys.* conductive; *~e Stellung* key position.

'**Leiter 1.** *m* (-s/-) leader; conductor (*a. phys.*, ♪); guide; manager; **2.** *f* (-/-n) ladder; '**~in** *f* (-/-nen) leader; conductress, guide; manageress; '**~wagen** 🞍 *m* rack-wag(g)on.

'**Leit|faden** *m* manual, textbook, guide; '**~motiv** ♪ *n* leit-motiv; '**~spruch** *m* motto; '**~tier** *n* leader; '**~ung** *f* (-/-en) lead(ing), conducting, guidance; management, direction, administration, *Am. a.* operation; *phys.* conduction; ⚡ *eel* circuit; *tel.* line; mains *pl.* (*for gas, water, etc.*); pipeline; *die ~ ist besetzt teleph.* the line is engaged *or Am.* busy.

'**Leitungs|draht** *m* conducting wire, conductor; '**~rohr** *n* conduit(-pipe); main (*for gas, water, etc.*); '**~wasser** *n* (-s/ᵘ) tap water.

'**Leitwerk** 🞍 *n* tail unit *or* group, empennage.

Lekt|ion [lɛk'tsjoːn] *f* (-/-en) lesson; **~or** ['lɛktɔr] *m* (-s/-en) lecturer; reader; **~üre** [ˌ/ˈtyːrə] *f* **1.** (-/no pl.) reading; **2.** (-/-n) books *pl.*

Lende *anat.* ['lɛndə] *f* (-/-n) loin(s *pl.*).

lenk|bar *adj.* ['lɛŋkbaːr] guidable, manageable, tractable; docile; ⊕ steerable, dirigible; '**~en** *v/t.* (ge-, h) direct, guide; turn; rule; govern; drive (*car*); ♆ steer; *Aufmerksamkeit ~ auf* (*acc.*) draw attention to; '**2rad** *mot. n* steering wheel; '**2säule** *mot. f* steering column; '**2stange** *f* handle-bar (*of bicycle*); '**2ung** *mot. f* (-/-en) steering-gear.

Lenz [lɛnts] *m* (-es/-e) spring.

Leopard *zo.* [leo'part] *m* (-en/-en) leopard.

Lepra 🞍 ['leːpra] *f* (-/no pl.) leprosy.

Lerche *orn.* ['lɛrçə] *f* (-/-n) lark.

lern|begierig *adj.* ['lɛrn-] eager to learn, studious; '**~en** *v/t. and v/i.* (ge-, h) learn; study.

Lese ['leːzə] *f* (-/-n) gathering; *s. Weinlese;* '**2buch** *n* reader; '**~lampe** *f* reading-lamp.

lesen ['leːzən] (*irr.*, ge-, h) **1.** *v/t.* read; ⚘ gather; *Messe ~ eccl.* say mass; **2.** *v/i.* read; *univ.* (give a) lecture (*über acc.* on); '**~swert** *adj.* worth reading.

'**Leser** *m* (-s/-), '**~in** *f* (-/-nen) reader; ⚘ gatherer; vintager; '**2lich** *adj.* legible; '**~zuschrift** *f* letter to the editor.

'**Lesezeichen** *n* book-mark.

'**Lesung** *parl. f* (-/-en) reading.

letzt *adj.* [lɛtst] last; final; ultimate; *~e Nachrichten pl.* latest news *pl.*; *~e Hand anlegen* put the finishing touches (*an acc.* to); *das ~ e* the last thing; *der ~ere* the latter; *der (die, das) Letzte* the last (one); *zu guter Letzt* last but not least; finally; '**~ens** *adv.*, '**~hin** *adv.* lately, of late; '**~lich** *adv. s. letztens;* finally; ultimately.

Leucht|e ['lɔyçtə] *f* (-/-n) (*fig.* shining) light, lamp (*a. fig.*), luminary (*a. fig., esp. p.*); '**2en** *v/i.* (ge-, h) (give) light, shine (forth); beam, gleam; '**~en** *n* (-s/no pl.) shining, light, luminosity; '**2end** *adj.* shining, bright; luminous; brilliant (*a. fig.*); '**~er** *m* (-s/-) candlestick; *s. Kronleuchter;* '**~feuer** *n* ♆, ✈, *etc.*; beacon(-light), flare (light); '**~käfer** *zo. m* glow-worm; '**~kugel** ✕ *f*

Very light; flare; '**∼turm** *m* lighthouse; '**∼ziffer** *f* luminous figure.

leugnen ['lɔʏgnən] *v/t.* (ge-, h) deny; disavow; contest.

Leukämie ⚕ [lɔʏkɛ'miː] *f* (-/-n) leuk(a)emia.

Leumund ['lɔʏmʊnt] *m* (-[e]s/*no pl.*) reputation, repute; character; '**∼szeugnis** t⁵⁵ *n* character reference.

Leute ['lɔʏtə] *pl.* people *pl.*; persons *pl.*; ✕, *pol.* men *pl.*; *workers*: hands *pl.*; ✝ folks *pl.*; domestics *pl.*, servants *pl.*

Leutnant ✕ ['lɔʏtnant] *m* (-s/-s, ✕ -e) second lieutenant.

leutselig *adj.* affable.

Lexikon ['lɛksikɔn] *n* (-s/*Lexika, Lexiken*) dictionary; encyclop(a)edia.

Libelle *zo.* [li'bɛlə] *f* (-/-n) dragonfly.

liberal *adj.* [libe'raːl] liberal.

Licht [liçt] **1.** *n* (-[e]s/-er) light; brightness; lamp; candle; *hunt.* eye; **∼ machen** ⚡ switch *or* turn on the light(s *pl.*); *das* ∼ *der Welt erblicken* see the light, be born; **2.** ♀ *adj.* light, bright; clear; *∼er Augenblick* ⚕ lucid interval; '**∼anlage** *f* lighting plant; '**∼bild** *n* photo (-graph); '**∼bildervortrag** *m* slide lecture; '**∼blick** *fig. m* bright spot; '**∼bogen** ⚡ *m* arc; '♀**durchlässig** *adj.* translucent; '♀**echt** *adj.* fast (to light), unfading; '♀**empfindlich** *adj.* sensitive to light, *phot.* sensitive; ∼ *machen* sensitize.

lichten *v/t.* (ge-, h) clear (*forest*); *den Anker* ∼ ⚓ weigh anchor; *sich* ∼ *hair*, *crowd*: thin.

lichterloh *adv.* ['liçtɐ'loː] blazing, in full blaze.

'**Licht|geschwindigkeit** *f* speed of light; '**∼hof** *m* glass-roofed court; patio; halo (*a. phot.*); '**∼leitung** *f* lighting mains *pl.*; '**∼maschine** *mot. f* dynamo, generator; '**∼pause** *f* blueprint; '**∼quelle** *f* light source, source of light; '**∼reklame** *f* neon sign; '**∼schacht** *m* well; '**∼schalter** *m* (light) switch; '**∼schein** *m* gleam of light; '♀**scheu** *adj.* shunning the light; '**∼signal** *n* light *or* luminous signal; '**∼spieltheater** *n s. Filmtheater, Kino*; '**∼strahl** *m* ray *or* beam of light (*a. fig.*); '♀**undurchlässig** *adj.* opaque; [ing, glade.|

'**Lichtung** *f* (-/-en) clearing, open-|

'**Lichtzelle** *f s. Photozelle.*

Lid [liːt] *n* (-[e]s/-er) eyelid.

lieb *adj.* [liːp] dear; nice, kind; *child*: good; *in letters*: *∼er Herr N.* dear Mr N.; *∼er Himmel!* good Heavens!, dear me!; *es ist mir* ∼, *daß I am glad that;* '♀**chen** *n* (-s/-) sweetheart.

Liebe ['liːbə] *f* (-/*no pl.*) love (*zu* of, for); *aus* ∼ for love; *aus* ∼ *zu* for the love of; '♀**n** (ge-, h) **1.** *v/t.* love; be in love with; be fond of, like; **2.** *v/i.* (be in) love; '**∼nde** *m, f* (-n/-n): *die* ∼*n pl.* the lovers *pl.*

'**liebens|wert** *adj.* lovable; charming; '**∼würdig** *adj.* lovable, amiable; *das ist sehr* ∼ *von Ihnen* that is very kind of you; '♀**würdigkeit** *f* (-/-en) amiability, kindness.

'**lieber 1.** *adj.* dearer; **2.** *adv.* rather, sooner; ∼ *haben* prefer, like better.

'**Liebes|brief** *m* love-letter; '**∼dienst** *m* favo(u)r, kindness; good turn; '**∼erklärung** *f: e-e* ∼ *machen* declare one's love; '**∼heirat** *f* love-match; '**∼kummer** *m* lover's grief; '**∼paar** *n* (courting) couple, lovers *pl.*; '**∼verhältnis** *n* love-affair.

'**liebevoll** *adj.* loving, affectionate.

lieb|gewinnen ['liːp-] *v/t.* (*irr. gewinnen, sep., no -ge-, h*) get *or* grow fond of; '**∼haben** *v/t.* (*irr. haben, sep., -ge-, h*) love, be fond of; '♀**haber** *m* (-s/-) lover; beau; *fig.* amateur; ♀**haberei** *fig.* [∼'raɪ] *f* (-/-en) hobby; '♀**haberpreis** *m* fancy price; '♀**haberwert** *m* sentimental value; '**∼kosen** *v/t.* (*no -ge-, h*) caress, fondle; '**∼kosung** *f* (-/-en) caress; '**∼lich** *adj.* lovely, charming, delightful.

Liebling ['liːplɪŋ] *m* (-s/-e) darling; favo(u)rite; *esp.* pet; *esp. form of address*: darling, *esp. Am.* honey; '**∼sbeschäftigung** *f* favo(u)rite occupation, hobby.

lieb|los *adj.* ['liːp-] unkind; careless; '♀**schaft** *f* (-/-en) (love-)affair; '♀**ste** *m, f* (-n/-n) sweetheart; darling.

Lied [liːt] *n* (-[e]s/-er) song; tune.

liederlich *adj.* ['liːdɐlɪç] slovenly, disorderly; careless; loose, dissolute.

lief [liːf] *pret. of laufen.*

Lieferant [liːfə'rant] *m* (-en/-en) supplier, purveyor; caterer.

Liefer|auto ['liːfɐr-] *n s. Liefer-|*

wagen; '**2bar** *adj.* to be delivered; available; '**˞bedingungen** *f/pl.* terms *pl.* of delivery; '**˞frist** *f* term of delivery; '**2n** *v/t.* (ge-, h) deliver; *j-m et.* ˞ furnish *or* supply s.o. with s.th.; '**˞schein** *m* delivery note; '**˞ung** *f* (-/-en) delivery; supply; consignment; instal(l)ment (*of book*); '**˞ungsbedingungen** *f/pl.* s. Lieferbedingungen; '**˞wagen** *m* deliveryvan, *Am.* delivery wagon.

Liege ['liːgə] *f* (-/-n) couch; bedchair.

liegen ['liːgən] *v/i.* (*irr.*, ge-, h) lie; *house, etc.*: be (situated); *room*: face; *an wem liegt es?* whose fault is it? *es liegt an* or *bei ihm zu inf.* it is for him to *inf.*; *es liegt daran, daß* the reason for it is that; *es liegt mir daran zu inf.* I am anxious to *inf.*; *es liegt mir nichts daran* it does not matter *or* it is of no consequence to me; '**˞bleiben** *v/i.* (*irr. bleiben*, *sep.*, -ge-, *sein*) stay in bed; break down (*on the road, a. mot., etc.*); *work, etc.*: stand over; fall behind; ✝ *goods:* remain on hand; '**˞lassen** *v/t.* (*irr. lassen*, *sep.*, -ge-, h) leave; leave behind; leave alone; leave off (*work*); *j-n links* ˞ ignore s.o., give s.o. the cold shoulder; '**2schaften** *f/pl.* real estate.

'**Liege|stuhl** *m* deck-chair; '**˞wagen** 🚃 *m* couchette coach.

lieh [liː] *pret. of leihen.*

ließ [liːs] *pret. of lassen.*

Lift [lift] *m* (-[e]s/-e, -s) lift, *Am.* elevator.

Liga ['liːga] *f* (-/Ligen) league.

Likör [li'køːr] *m* (-s/-e) liqueur, cordial.

lila *adj.* ['liːla] lilac.

Lilie 🌿 ['liːljə] *f* (-/-n) lily.

Limonade [limo'naːdə] *f* (-/-n) soft drink, fruit-juice; lemonade.

Limousine *mot.* [limu'ziːnə] *f* (-/-n) limousine, saloon car, *Am.* sedan.

lind *adj.* [lint] soft, gentle; mild.

Linde 🌿 ['lində] *f* (-/-n) lime(-tree), linden(-tree).

linder|n ['lindərn] *v/t.* (ge-, h) soften; mitigate; alleviate, soothe; allay, ease (*pain*); '**2ung** *f* (-/˞-en) softening; mitigation; alleviation; easing.

Lineal [line'aːl] *n* (-s/-e) ruler.

Linie ['liːnjə] *f* (-/-n) line; '**˞papier** *n* ruled paper; '**˞nrichter** *m*

sports: linesman; '**2ntreu** *pol. adj.*: ˞ *sein* follow the party line.

lin(i)ieren [li'niːrən; lini'iːrən] *v/t.* (*no* -ge-, h) rule, line.

link *adj.* [liŋk] left; **˞e** *Seite* left (-hand) side, left; *of cloth:* wrong side; '**2e** *f* (-/-n/-n) the left (hand); *pol.* the Left (Wing); *boxing:* the left; '**˞isch** *adj.* awkward, clumsy.

links *adv.* on *or* to the left; **2händer** ['˞hendər] *m* (-s/-) left-hander, *Am. a.* southpaw.

Linse ['linzə] *f* (-/-n) 🌿 lentil; *opt.* lens.

Lippe ['lipə] *f* (-/-n) lip; '**˞nstift** *m* lipstick.

liquidieren [likvi'diːrən] *v/t.* (*no* -ge-, h) liquidate (*a. pol.*); wind up (*business company*); charge (*fee*).

lispeln ['lispəln] *v/i. and v/t.* (ge-, h) lisp; whisper.

List [list] *f* (-/-en) cunning, craft; artifice, ruse, trick; stratagem.

Liste ['listə] *f* (-/-n) list, roll.

listig *adj.* cunning, crafty, sly.

Liter ['liːtər] *n, m* (-s/-) lit|re, *Am.* -er.

literarisch *adj.* [lite'raːriʃ] literary.

Literatur [litera'tuːr] *f* (-/-en) literature; **˞beilage** *f* literary supplement (*in newspaper*); **˞geschichte** *f* history of literature; **˞verzeichnis** *n* bibliography.

litt [lit] *pret. of leiden.*

Litze ['litsə] *f* (-/-n) lace, cord, braid; ⚡ strand(ed wire).

Livree [li'vreː] *f* (-/-n) livery.

Lizenz [li'tsɛnts] *f* (-/-en) licen|ce, *Am.* -se; **˞inhaber** *m* licensee.

Lob [loːp] *n* (-[e]s/*no pl.*) praise; commendation; '**2en** ['loːbən] *v/t.* (ge-, h) praise; '**2enswert** *adj.* ['loːbəns-] praise-worthy, laudable; **˞gesang** ['loːp-] *m* hymn, song of praise; **˞hudelei** ['loːp:huˑdəˈlaɪ] *f* (-/-en) adulation, base flattery.

löblich *adj.* ['løːpliç] s. lobenswert.

Lobrede ['loːp-] *f* eulogy, panegyric.

Loch [lɔx] *n* (-[e]s/˞-er) hole; '**2en** *v/t.* (ge-, h) perforate, pierce; punch (*ticket, etc.*); '**˞er** *m* (-s/-) punch, perforator; '**˞karte** *f* punch(ed) card.

Locke ['lɔkə] *f* (-/-n) curl, ringlet. '**locken¹** *v/t. and v/refl.* (ge-, h) curl.

'**locken²** *v/t.* (ge-, h) *hunt.:* bait; decoy (*a. fig.*); *fig.* allure, entice.

'Locken|kopf m curly head; **~wickler** ['~viklər] m (-s/-) curler, roller.

locker adj. ['lɔkər] loose; slack; **'~n** v/t. (ge-, h) loosen; slacken; relax (grip); break up (soil); sich ~ loosen, (be)come loose; give way; fig. relax.

'lockig adj. curly.

'Lock|mittel n s. Köder; **'~vogel** m decoy (a. fig.); Am. a. stool pigeon (a. fig.).

lodern ['lo:dərn] v/i. (ge-, h) flare, blaze.

Löffel ['lœfəl] m (-s/-) spoon; ladle; **'2n** v/t. (ge-, h) spoon up; ladle out; **'~voll** m (-/-) spoonful.

log [lo:k] pret. of lügen.

Loge ['lo:ʒə] f (-/-n) thea. box; free-masonry: lodge; **'~nschließer** thea. m (-s/-) box-keeper.

logieren [lo'ʒi:rən] v/i. (no -ge-, h) lodge, stay, Am. a. room (all: bei with; in dat. at).

logisch ['lo:giʃ] logical; **'~erweise** adv. logically.

Lohn [lo:n] m (-[e]s/⁀e) wages pl., pay(ment); hire; fig. reward; **'~büro** n pay-office; **'~empfänger** m wage-earner; **'2en** v/t. (ge-, h) compensate, reward; sich ~ pay; es lohnt sich zu inf. it is worth while ger., it pays to inf.; **'2end** adj. paying; advantageous; fig. rewarding; **'~erhöhung** f increase in wages, rise, Am. raise; **'~forderung** f demand for higher wages; **'~steuer** f tax on wages or salary; **'~stopp** m (-s/no pl.) wage freeze; **'~tarif** m wage rate; **'~tüte** f pay envelope.

lokal [lo'ka:l] 1. adj. local; 2. 2 n (-[e]s/-e) locality, place; restaurant; public house, F pub, F local, Am. saloon.

Lokomotiv|e [lokomo'ti:və] f (-/-n) (railway) engine, locomotive; **'~führer** [~ti:f-] m engine-driver, Am. engineer.

Lorbeer ['lɔrbeːr] m (-s/-en) laurel, bay.

Lore ['lo:rə] f (-/-n) lorry, truck.

Los¹ ['lo:s] n (-es/-e) lot; lottery ticket; fig. fate, destiny, lot; das Große ~ ziehen win the first prize, Am. sl. hit the jackpot; durchs ~ entscheiden decide by lot.

los² [~] 1. pred. adj. loose; free; was ist ~? what is the matter?, F what's up?, Am. F what's cooking?; ~ sein

be rid of; 2. int.: ~! go (on or ahead)!

losarbeiten ['lo:sʔ-] v/i. (sep., -ge-, h) start work(ing).

lösbar adj. ['lø:sba:r] soluble, 🜂 a. solvable.

'los|binden v/t. (irr. binden, sep., -ge-, h) untie, loosen; **'~brechen** (irr. brechen, sep., -ge-) 1. v/t. (h) break off; 2. v/i. (sein) break or burst out.

Lösch|blatt ['lœʃ-] n blotting-paper; **'2en** v/t. (ge-, h) extinguish, put out (fire, light); blot out (writing); erase (tape recording); cancel (debt); quench (thirst); slake (lime); ⚓ unload; **'~er** m (-s/-) blotter; **'~papier** n blotting-paper.

lose adj. ['lo:zə] loose.

'Lösegeld n ransom.

losen ['lo:zən] v/i. (ge-, h) cast or draw lots (um for).

lösen ['lø:zən] v/t. (ge-, h) loosen, untie; buy, book (ticket); solve (task, doubt, etc.); break off (engagement); annul (agreement, etc.); 🜂 dissolve; ein Schuß löste sich the gun went off.

'los|fahren v/i. (irr. fahren, sep., -ge-, sein) depart, drive off; **'~gehen** v/i. (irr. gehen, sep., -ge-, sein) go or be off; come off, get loose; gun: go off; begin, start; F auf j-n ~ fly at s.o.; **'~haken** v/t. (sep., -ge-, h) unhook; **'~kaufen** v/t. (sep., -ge-, h) ransom, redeem; **'~ketten** v/t. (sep., -ge-, h) unchain; **'~kommen** v/i. (irr. kommen, sep., -ge-, sein) get loose or free; **'~lachen** v/i. (sep., -ge-, h) laugh out; **'~lassen** v/t. (irr. lassen, sep., -ge-, h) let go; release.

löslich 🜂 adj. ['lø:sliç] soluble.

'los|lösen v/t. (sep., -ge-, h) loosen, detach; sever; **'~machen** v/t. (sep., -ge-, h) unfasten, loosen; sich ~ disengange (o.s.) (von from); **'~reißen** v/t. (irr. reißen, sep., -ge-, h) tear off; sich ~ break away, esp. fig. tear o.s. away (both: von from); **'~sagen** v/refl. (sep., -ge-, h): sich ~ von renounce; **'~schlagen** (irr. schlagen, sep., -ge-) 1. v/t. knock off; 2. v/i. open the attack; auf j-n ~ attack s.o.; **'~schnallen** v/t. (sep., -ge-, h) unbuckle; **'~schrauben** v/t. (sep., -ge-, h) unscrew, screw off; **'~sprechen** v/t. (irr. sprechen, *sep.*, -ge-, *h*) absolve (*von* of, from); acquit (of); free (from, of); '**~stür-zen** *v/i.* (*sep.*, -ge-, *sein*) ~ *auf* (*acc.*) rush at.

Losung ['loːzuŋ] *f* 1. (-/-en) ✕ pass-word, watchword; *fig.* slogan; 2. *hunt.* (-/*no pl.*) droppings *pl.*, dung.

Lösung ['løːzuŋ] *f* (-/-en) solution; '**~smittel** *n* solvent.

'**los|werden** *v/t.* (*irr.* werden, *sep.*, -ge-, *sein*) get rid of, dispose of; '**~ziehen** *v/i.* (*irr.* ziehen, *sep.*, -ge-, *sein*) set out, take off, march away.

Lot [loːt] *n* (-[e]s/-e) plumb(-line), plummet.

löten ['løːtən] *v/t.* (ge-, *h*) solder.

Lotse ['loːtsə] *m* (-n/-n) pilot; '**2n** *v/t.* (ge-, *h*) ⚓ pilot (*a. fig.*).

Lotterie [lɔtəˈriː] *f* (-/-n) lottery; '**~gewinn** *m* prize; '**~los** *n* lottery ticket.

Lotto ['lɔto] *n* (-s/-s) numbers pool, lotto.

Löwe *zo.* ['løːvə] *m* (-n/-n) lion.

'**Löwen|anteil** F *m* lion's share; '**~maul** ♣ *n* (-[e]s/*no pl.*) snapdragon; '**~zahn** ♣ *m* (-[e]s/*no pl.*) dandelion.

'**Löwin** *zo.* *f* (-/-nen) lioness.

loyal *adj.* [loaˈjaːl] loyal.

Luchs *zo.* [luks] *m* (-es/-e) lynx.

Lücke ['lykə] *f* (-/-n) gap; blank, void (*a. fig.*); '**~nbüßer** *m* stopgap; '**2nhaft** *adj.* full of gaps; *fig.* defec-tive, incomplete; '**2nlos** *adj.* with-out a gap; *fig.*: unbroken; com-plete; **~er Beweis** close argument.

lud [luːt] *pret.* *of* laden.

Luft [luft] *f* (-/⸚e) air; breeze; breath; **frische ~ schöpfen** take the air; **an die ~ gehen** go for an airing; **aus der ~ gegriffen** (totally) un-founded, fantastic; **es liegt et. in der ~** there is s.th. in the wind; **in die ~ fliegen** be blown up, explode; **in die ~ gehen** explode, *sl.* blow one's top; **in die ~ sprengen** blow up; F **j-n an die ~ setzen** turn s.o. out, *Am. sl.* give s.o. the air; **sich** *or* **s-n Gefühlen ~ machen** give vent to one's feelings.

'**Luft|alarm** *m* air-raid alarm; '**~an-griff** *m* air raid; '**~aufnahme** *f* aerial photograph; '**~ballon** *m* (air-)balloon; '**~bild** *n* aerial photo-graph, airview; '**~blase** *f* air-bubble; '**~brücke** *f* air-bridge; *for supplies, etc.*: air-lift.

Lüftchen ['lyftçən] *n* (-s/-) gentle breeze.

'**luft|dicht** *adj.* air-tight; '**2druck** *phys. m* (-[e]s/*no pl.*) atmospheric *or* air pressure; '**2druckbremse** ⊕ *f* air-brake; '**~durchlässig** *adj.* per-meable to air.

lüften ['lyftən] *v/t.* air; 2. *v/i.* air; raise (*hat*); lift (*veil*); disclose (*secret*).

'**Luft|fahrt** *f* aviation, aeronautics; '**~feuchtigkeit** *f* atmospheric humidity; '**2gekühlt** ⊕ *adj.* air-cooled; '**~hoheit** *f* air sovereignty; '**2ig** *adj.* airy; breezy; flimsy; '**~kissen** *n* air-cushion; '**~klappe** *f* air-valve; '**~korridor** *m* air corri-dor; '**~krankheit** *f* airsickness; '**~krieg** *m* aerial warfare; '**~kurort** *m* climatic health resort; '**~lande-truppen** *f/pl.* airborne troops *pl.*; '**2leer** *adj.* void of air, evacuated; **~er Raum** vacuum; '**~linie** *f* air line, bee-line; '**~loch** *n* ✈ air-pocket; vent(-hole); '**~post** *f* air mail; '**~pumpe** *f* air-pump; '**~raum** *m* airspace; '**~röhre** *anat. f* windpipe, trachea; '**~schacht** *m* air-shaft; '**~schaukel** *f* swing-boat; '**~schiff** *n* airship; '**~schloß** *n* castle in the air *or* in Spain; '**~schutz** *m* air-raid protection; '**~schutzkeller** *m* air-raid shelter; '**~sprünge** ['~ʃpryŋə] *m/pl.*: ~ ma-chen cut capers *pl.*; gambol; '**~stützpunkt** ✕ *m* air base. [tion.]

'**Lüftung** *f* (-/-en) airing; ventila-⸗

'**Luft|veränderung** *f* change of air; '**~verkehr** *m* air-traffic; '**~ver-kehrsgesellschaft** *f* air transport company, airway, *Am.* airline; '**~verteidigung** ✕ *f* air defen|ce, *Am.* -se; '**~waffe** ✕ *f* air force; '**~weg** *m* airway; **auf dem ~** by air; '**~zug** *m* draught, *Am.* draft.

Lüge ['lyːgə] *f* (-/-n) lie, falsehood; **j-n ~n strafen** give the lie to s.o.

lügen ['lyːgən] *v/i.* (*irr.*, ge-, *h*) (tell a) lie; '**~haft** *adj.* lying, mendacious; un-true, false.

Lügner ['lyːgnər] *m* (-s/-), '**~in** *f* (-/-nen) liar; '**2isch** *adj.* s. lügen-haft.

Luke ['luːkə] *f* (-/-n) dormer- *or* garret-window; hatch.

Lümmel ['lyməl] *m* (-s/-) lout, boor; saucy fellow; '**2n** *v/refl.* (ge-, *h*) loll, lounge, sprawl.

L

Lump

Lump [lump] *m* (-en/-en) ragamuffin, beggar; cad, *Am. sl.* rat, heel; scoundrel.

'Lumpen 1. *m* (-s/-) rag; **2.** ♀ *vb.*: *sich nicht ~ lassen* come down handsomely; '**~pack** *n* rabble, riffraff; '**~sammler** *m* rag-picker.

'lumpig *adj.* ragged; *fig.*: shabby, paltry; mean.

Lunge ['luŋə] *f* (-/-n) *anat.* lungs *pl.*; *of animals:* a. lights *pl.*

'Lungen|entzündung ♣ *f* pneumonia; '**~flügel** *anat. m* lung; '**⚥krank** ♣ *adj.* suffering from consumption, consumptive; '**~kranke** *m, f* consumptive (patient); '**~krankheit** ♣ *f* lung-disease; '**~schwindsucht** ♣ *f* (pulmonary) consumption.

lungern ['luŋərn] *v/i.* (ge-, h) *s. herumlungern.*

Lupe ['lu:pə] *f* (-/-n) magnifying-glass; *unter die ~ nehmen* scrutinize, take a good look at.

Lust [lust] *f* (-/⁓e) pleasure, delight; desire; lust; ~ *haben zu inf.* have a mind to *inf.*, feel like *ger.*; *haben Sie ~ auszugehen?* would you like to go out?

lüstern *adj.* ['lʏstərn] desirous (*nach*

of), greedy (of, for); lewd, lascivious, lecherous.

'lustig *adj.* merry, gay; jolly, cheerful; amusing, funny; *sich ~ machen über (acc.)* make fun of; '**⚥keit** *f* (-/no *pl.*) gaiety, mirth; jollity, cheerfulness; fun.

Lüstling ['lʏstlɪŋ] *m* (-s/-e) voluptuary, libertine.

'lust|los *adj.* dull, spiritless; ♣ flat; '**⚥mord** *m* rape and murder; '**⚥spiel** *n* comedy.

lutschen ['lutʃən] *v/i. and v/t.* (ge-, h) suck. [ward.]

Luv ⚓ [lu:f] *f* (-/no *pl.*) luff, windward.]

luxuriös *adj.* [luksu'rjø:s] luxurious.

Luxus ['luksus] *m* (-/no *pl.*) luxury (*a. fig.*); '**~artikel** *m* luxury; '**~ausgabe** *f* de luxe edition (*of books*); '**~ware** *f* luxury (article); fancy goods *pl.*

Lymph|drüse *anat.* ['lymf-] *f* lymphatic gland; '**⚥e** *f* (-/-n) lymph; ♣ vaccine; '**~gefäß** *anat. n* lymphatic vessel.

lynchen ['lynçən] *v/t.* (ge-, h) lynch.

Lyrik ['ly:rɪk] *f* (-/no *pl.*) lyric verses *pl.*, lyrics *pl.*; '**~er** *m* (-s/-) lyric poet.

'lyrisch *adj.* lyric; lyrical (*a. fig.*).

M

Maat ⚓ [ma:t] *m* (-[e]s/-e[n]) (ship's) mate.

Mache F ['maxə] *f* (-/no *pl.*) make-believe, window-dressing, *sl.* eyewash; *et. in der ~ haben* have s.th. in hand.

machen ['maxən] (ge-, h) **1.** *v/t.* make; do; produce, manufacture; give (*appetite, etc.*); sit for, undergo (*examination*); come *or* amount to; make (*happy, etc.*); *was macht das (aus)?* what does that matter?; *das macht nichts!* never mind!, that's (quite) all right!; *da(gegen) kann man nichts ~* that cannot be helped; *ich mache mir nichts daraus* I don't care about it; *mach, daß du fortkommst!* off with you!; *j-n ~ lassen, was er will* let s.o. do as he pleases; *sich ~ an (acc.)* go *or* set about; *sich et. ~ lassen* have s.th. made; **2.** F *v/i.*: *na, mach schon!*

hurry up!; '**⚥schaften** *f/pl.* machinations *pl.*

Macht [maxt] *f* (-/⁓e) power; might; authority; control (*über acc.* of); *an der ~ pol.* in power; '**~befugnis** *f* authority, power; '**~haber** *pol. m* (-s/-) ruler.

mächtig *adj.* ['mɛçtɪç] powerful (*a. fig.*); mighty; immense, huge; ~ *sein (gen.)* be master of *s.th.*; have command of (*language*).

'Macht|kampf *m* struggle for power; '**⚥los** *adj.* powerless; '**~politik** *f* power politics *sg.*, *pl.*; policy of the strong hand; '**~spruch** *m* authoritative decision; '**~vollkommenheit** *f* authority; '**~wort** *n* (-[e]s/-e) word of command; *ein ~ sprechen* put one's foot down.

'Machwerk *n* concoction, F put-up job; *elendes ~* bungling work.

Mädchen ['mɛːtçən] n (-s/-) girl; maid(-servant); ~ für alles maid of all work; fig. a. jack of all trades; '2chaft adj. girlish; '~name m girl's name; maiden name; '~schule f girls' school.

Made zo. ['maːdə] f (-/-n) maggot, mite; fruit: worm.

Mädel ['mɛːdəl] n (-s/-, F -s) girl, lass(ie).

madig adj. ['maːdiç] maggoty, full of mites; fruit: wormeaten.

Magazin [maga'tsiːn] n (-s/-e) store, warehouse; ×, in rifle, periodical: magazine.

Magd [maːkt] f (-/-e) maid(-servant).

Magen ['maːgən] m (-s/-, a. -) stomach, F tummy; animals: maw; '~beschwerden f/pl. stomach or gastric trouble, indigestion; '~bitter m (-s/-) bitters pl.; '~geschwür ﾟ n gastric ulcer; '~krampf m stomach cramp; '~krebs ﾟ m stomach cancer; '~leiden n gastric complaint; '~säure f gastric acid.

mager adj. ['maːgər] meag|re, Am. -er (a. fig.); p., animal, meat: lean, Am. a. scrawny; '2milch f skim milk.

Magie [ma'giː] f (-/no pl.) magic; ~r ['maːgjər] m (-s/-) magician.

magisch adj. ['maːgiʃ] magic(al).

Magistrat [magis'traːt] m (-[e]s/-e) municipal or town council.

Magnet [ma'gneːt] m (-[e]s, -en/-e[n]) magnet (a. fig.); lodestone; 2isch adj. magnetic; 2isieren [~eti'ziːrən] v/t. (no -ge-, h) magnetize; '~nadel [~'gneːt-] f magnetic needle.

Mahagoni [maha'goːni] n (-s/no pl.) mahogany (wood).

mähen ['mɛːən] v/t. (ge-, h) cut, mow, reap.

Mahl [maːl] n (-[e]s/-er, -e) meal, repast.

'**mahlen** (irr., ge-, h) **1.** v/t. grind, mill; **2.** v/i. tyres: spin.

'**Mahlzeit** f s. Mahl; F feed.

Mähne ['mɛːnə] f (-/-n) mane.

mahn|en ['maːnən] v/t. (ge-, h) remind, admonish (both: an acc. of); j-n wegen e-r Schuld ~ press s.o. for payment, dun s.o.; '2mal n (-[e]s/-e) memorial; '2ung f (-/-en) admonition; † reminder, dunning; '2zettel m reminder.

Mai [maɪ] m (-[e]s, -/-e) May; '~baum m maypole; ~glöckchen ﾟ ['~glœkçən] n (-s/-) lily of the valley; '~käfer zo. m cockchafer, may-beetle, may-bug.

Mais ﾟ [maɪs] m (-es/-e) maize, Indian corn, Am. corn.

Majestät [majɛ'stɛːt] f (-/-en) majesty; 2isch adj. majestic; ~s-beleidigung f lese-majesty.

Major × [ma'joːr] m (-s/-e) major.

Makel ['maːkəl] m (-s/-) stain, spot; fig. a. blemish, fault; '2los adj. stainless, spotless; fig. a. unblemished, faultless, immaculate.

mäkeln F ['mɛːkəln] v/i. (ge-, h) find fault (an dat. with), carp (at), F pick (at).

Makler † ['maːklər] m (-s/-) broker; '~gebühr † f brokerage.

Makulatur ⊕ [makula'tuːr] f (-/-en) waste paper.

Mal[1] [maːl] n (-[e]s/-e) mark, sign; sports: start(ing-point), goal; spot, stain; mole.

Mal[2] [~] **1.** n (-[e]s/-e) time; für dieses ~ this time; zum ersten ~e for the first time; mit e-m ~e all at once, all of a sudden; **2.** ﾟ adv. times, multiplied by; drei ~ fünf ist fünfzehn three times five is or are fifteen; F s. einmal.

'**malen** v/t. (ge-, h) paint, portray.

'**Maler** m (-s/-) painter; artist; ~ei [~'raɪ] f (-/-en) painting; '2isch adj. pictorial, painting; fig. picturesque.

'**Malkasten** m paint-box.

'**malnehmen** ﾟ v/t. (irr. nehmen, sep., -ge-, h) multiply (mit by).

Malz [malts] n (-es/no pl.) malt; '~bier n malt beer.

Mama [ma'maː, F 'mama] f (-/-s) mamma, mammy, F ma, Am. F a. mummy, mom.

man indef. pron. [man] one, you, we; they, people; ~ sagte mir I was told.   [manager.]

Manager ['mɛnidʒər] m (-s/-)

manch [manç], '~er, '~e, '~es adj. and indef. pron. many a; ~e pl. some, several; ~erlei adj. ['~ər'laɪ] diverse, different; all sorts of, ... of several sorts; auf ~e Art in various ways; used as a noun: many or various things; '~mal adv. sometimes, at times.

Mandant ﾟﾟ [man'dant] m (-en/-en) client.

Mandarine ♀ [manda'ri:nə] f (-/-n) tangerine.

Mandat [man'da:t] n (-[e]s/-e) authorization; ⚖ brief; *pol.* mandate; *parl.* seat.

Mandel ['mandəl] f (-/-n) ♀ almond; *anat.* tonsil; '~baum ♀ m almond-tree; '~entzündung ⚕ f tonsillitis. [ring, manège.)

Manege [ma'nɛ:ʒə] f (-/-n) (circus-)

Mangel[1] ['maŋəl] m 1. (-s/*no pl.*) want, lack, deficiency; shortage; penury; *aus* ~ *an (dat.)* for want of; *~ leiden an (dat.)* be in want of; 2. (-s/¨) defect, shortcoming.

Mangel[2] [~] f (-/-n) mangle; calender.

'**mangelhaft** *adj.* defective; deficient; unsatisfactory; '2igkeit f (-/*no pl.*) defectiveness; deficiency.

'**mangeln**[1] *v/i.* (ge-, h) *es mangelt an Brot* there is a lack *or* shortage of bread, bread is lacking *or* wanting; *es mangelt ihm an (dat.)* he is in need of *or* short of *or* wanting in, he wants *or* lacks.

'**mangeln**[2] *v/t.* (ge-, h) mangle (*clothes, etc.*); ⊕ calender (*cloth, paper*).

'**mangels** *prp.* (*gen.*) for lack *or* want of; *esp.* ⚖ in default of.

'**Mangelware** † f scarce commodity; goods *pl.* in short supply.

Manie [ma'ni:] f (-/-n) mania.

Manier [ma'ni:r] f (-/-en) manner; 2lich *adj.* well-behaved; polite, mannerly. [manifesto.)

Manifest [mani'fɛst] n (-es/-e))

Mann [man] m (-[e]s/¨er) man; husband.

'**mannbar** *adj.* marriageable; '2keit f (-/*no pl.*) puberty, manhood.

Männchen ['mɛnçən] n (-s/-) little man; *zo.* male; *birds:* cock.

'**Mannes**|**alter** n virile age, manhood; '~kraft f virility.

mannig|**fach** ['maniç-], '~**faltig** *adj.* manifold, various, diverse; 2**faltigkeit** f (-/*no pl.*) manifoldness, variety, diversity.

männlich *adj.* ['mɛnliç] male; *gr.* masculine; *fig.* manly; 2**keit** f (-/*no pl.*) manhood, virility.

'**Mannschaft** f (-/-en) (body of) men; ⚓ crew; *sports:* team, side; '~**führer** m *sports:* captain; '~**geist** m (-es/*no pl.*) *sports:* team spirit.

Manöv|**er** [ma'nø:vər] n (-s/-) manœuvre, *Am.* maneuver; 2**rieren** [~'vri:rən] *v/i.* (*no* -ge-, h) manœuvre, *Am.* maneuver.

Mansarde [man'zardə] f (-/-n) attic, garret; ~**nfenster** n dormer-window.

mansche|**n** F ['manʃən] (ge-, h) 1. *v/t.* mix, work; 2. *v/i.* dabble (*in dat.* in); 2'**rei** F f (-/-en) mixing, F mess; dabbling.

Manschette [man'ʃɛtə] f (-/-n) cuff; ~**knopf** m cuff-link.

Mantel ['mantəl] m (-s/¨) coat; overcoat, greatcoat; cloak, mantle (*both a. fig.*); ⊕ case, jacket; (outer) cover (*of tyre*).

Manuskript [manu'skript] n (-[e]s/-e) manuscript; *typ.* copy.

Mappe ['mapə] f (-/-n) portfolio, brief-case; folder; *s. a.* Schreibmappe, Schulmappe.

Märchen ['mɛ:rçən] n (-s/-) fairy-tale; *fig.* (cock-and-bull) story, fib; '~**buch** n book of fairy-tales; '2**haft** *adj.* fabulous (*a. fig.*). [ten.)

Marder *zo.* ['mardər] m (-s/-) mar-)

Marine [ma'ri:nə] f (-/-n) marine; ✕ navy, naval forces *pl.*; ~**minister** m minister of naval affairs; First Lord of the Admiralty, *Am.* Secretary of the Navy; ~**ministerium** n ministry of naval affairs; *the* Admiralty, *Am.* Department of the Navy.

marinieren [mari'ni:rən] *v/t.* (*no* -ge-, h) pickle, marinade.

Marionette [mario'nɛtə] f (-/-n) puppet, marionette; ~**ntheater** n puppet-show.

Mark [mark] 1. f (-/-) *coin:* mark; 2. n (-[e]s/*no pl.*) *anat.* marrow; ♀ pith; *fig.* core.

markant *adj.* [mar'kant] characteristic; striking; (well-)marked.

Marke ['markə] f (-/-n) mark, sign, token; ♥, *etc.:* stamp; † brand, trade-mark; coupon; '~**nartikel** † m branded *or* proprietary article.

mar'kier|**en** (*no* -ge-, h) 1. *v/t.* mark (*a. sports*); brand (*cattle, goods, etc.*); 2. F *fig. v/i.* put it on; 2**ung** f (-/-en) mark(ing).

'**markig** *adj.* marrowy; *fig.* pithy.

Markise [mar'ki:zə] f (-/-n) blind, (window-)awning.

'**Markstein** m boundary-stone, landmark (*a. fig.*).

Markt [markt] *m* (-[e]s/⸚e) 🕆 market; *s. Marktplatz*; fair; *auf den ~ bringen* 🕆 put on the market; '**~flecken** *m* small market-town; '**~platz** *m* market-place; '**~schreier** *m* (-s/-) quack; puffer.

Marmelade [marmə'la:də] *f* (-/-n) jam; marmalade *(made of oranges)*.

Marmor ['marmɔr] *m* (-s/-e) marble; **Sieren** [⸍ο'ri:rən] *v/t.* (no -ge-, h) marble, vein, grain; **Sn** *adj.* ['⸍ɔrn] (of) marble. [whim, caprice.]

Marotte [ma'rɔtə] *f* (-/-n) fancy,⎦

Marsch [marʃ] **1.** *m* (-es/⸚e) march *(a. ♪)*; **2.** *f* (-/-en) marsh, fen.

Marschall ['marʃal] *m* (-s/⸚e) marshal.

'**Marsch|befehl** ⚔ *m* marching orders *pl.*; **Sieren** [⸍'fi:rən] *v/i.* (no -ge-, sein) march; '**~land** *n* marshy land.

Marter ['martər] *f* (-/-n) torment, torture; '**Sn** *v/t.* (ge-, h) torment, torture; '**~pfahl** *m* stake.

Märtyrer ['mertyrər] *m* (-s/-) martyr; '**~tod** *m* martyr's death; '**~tum** *n* (-s/no pl.) martyrdom.

Marxi|mus *pol.* [mar'ksismus] *m* (-/no pl.) Marxism; **~t** *pol. m* (-en/-en) Marxian, Marxist; **Stisch** *pol. adj.* Marxian, Marxist.

März [merts] *m* (-[e]s/-e) March.

Marzipan [martsi'pa:n] *n*, ⚒ *m* (-s/-e) marzipan, marchpane.

Masche ['maʃə] *f* (-/-n) mesh; knitting: stitch; F *fig.* trick, line; '**Snfest** *adj.* ladder-proof, Am. runproof.

Maschine [ma'ʃi:nə] *f* (-/-n) machine; engine.

maschinell *adj.* [maʃi'nel] mechanical; *~e Bearbeitung* machining.

Ma'schinen|bau ⊕ *m* (-[e]s/no pl.) mechanical engineering; '**~gewehr** ⚔ *n* machine-gun; **Smäßig** *adj.* mechanical; automatic; **~pistole** ⚔ *f* sub-machine-gun; **~schaden** *m* engine trouble; **~schlosser** *m* (engine) fitter; **~schreiberin** *f* (-/-nen) typist; **~schrift** *f* typescript.

Maschin|erie [maʃinə'ri:] *f* (-/-n) machinery; **~ist** [⸍'nist] *m* (-en/-en) machinist.

Masern ⚕ ['ma:zərn] *pl.* measles *pl.*

Mask|e ['maskə] *f* (-/-n) mask *(a. fig.)*; '**~enball** *m* fancy-dress *or* masked ball; **~erade** [⸍'ra:də] *f* (-/-n) masquerade; **Sieren** [⸍'ki:-

rən] *v/t.* (no -ge-, h) mask; *sich ~* put on a mask; dress o.s. up *(als as)*.

Maß [ma:s] **1.** *n* (-es/-e) measure; proportion; *fig.* moderation; **~e** *pl. und Gewichte pl.* weights and measures *pl.*; **~e** *pl.* room, etc.: measurements *pl.*; **2.** *f* (-/-[e]) *appr.* quart *(of beer)*; **3.** **2** *pret. of* messen.

Massage [ma'sa:ʒə] *f* (-/-n) massage.

'**Maßanzug** *m* tailor-made *or* bespoke suit, Am. a. custom(-made) suit.

Masse ['masə] *f* (-/-n) mass; bulk; substance; multitude; crowd; ⸏⸏ assets *pl.*, estate; *die breite ~* the rank and file; F e-e ~ a lot of, F lots *pl.* or heaps pl. of.

'**Maßeinheit** *f* measuring unit.

'**Massen|flucht** *f* stampede; '**~grab** *n* common grave; '**~güter** 🕆 ['⸍gy:tər] *n/pl.* bulk goods *pl.*; '**Shaft** *adj.* abundant; '**~produktion** ⊕ *f* mass production; '**~versammlung** *f* mass meeting, Am. a. rally; '**Sweise** *adv.* in masses, in large numbers.

Masseu|r [ma'sø:r] *m* (-s/-e) masseur; **~se** [⸍zə] *f* (-/-n) masseuse.

'**maß|gebend** *adj.* standard; authoritative, decisive; *board:* competent; *circles:* influential, leading; '**~halten** *v/i.* (*irr.* halten, sep., -ge-, h) keep within limits, be moderate.

mas'sieren *v/t.* (no -ge-, h) massage, knead.

'**massig** *adj.* massy, bulky; solid.

mäßig *adj.* ['me:siç] moderate; *food, etc.*: frugal; 🕆 *price:* moderate, reasonable; *result, etc.*: poor; **~en** ['⸍gən] *v/t.* (ge-, h) moderate; *sich ~* moderate *or* restrain o.s.; '**Sung** *f* (-/-en) moderation; restraint.

massiv [ma'si:f] **1.** *adj.* massive, solid; **2.** **2** *geol. n* (-s/-e) massif.

'**Maß|krug** *m* beer-mug, Am. a. stein; '**Slos** *adj.* immoderate; boundless; exorbitant, excessive; extravagant; '**~nahme** ['⸍na:mə] *f* (-/-n) measure, step, action; '**Sregeln** *v/t.* (ge-, h) reprimand; inflict disciplinary punishment on; '**~schneider** *m* bespoke *or* Am. custom tailor; '**~stab** *m* measure, rule(r); *maps, etc.*: scale; *fig.* yardstick, standard; '**Svoll** *adj.* moderate.

M

Mast[1] ⚓ [mast] *m* (-es/-e[n]) mast.

Mast[2] 🌱 [~] *f* (-/-en) fattening; mast, food; **~darm** *anat. m* rectum.

mästen ['mɛstən] *v/t.* (ge-, h) fatten, feed; stuff (*geese, etc.*).

'**Mastkorb** ⚓ *m* mast-head, crows-nest.

Material [mater'jɑ:l] *n* (-s/-ien) material; substance; stock, stores *pl.*; *fig.*: material, information; evidence; **~ismus** *phls.* [~a'lɪsmus] *m* (-/*no pl.*) materialism; **~ist** [~a'lɪst] *m* (-en/-en) materialist; **2istisch** *adj.* [~a'lɪstɪʃ] materialistic.

Materie [ma'te:rjə] *f* (-/-n) matter (*a. fig.*), stuff; *fig.* subject; **2ll** *adj.* [~er'jɛl] material.

Mathemati|k [matema'ti:k] *f* (-/*no pl.*) mathematics *sg.*; **~ker** [~'ma:-tikər] *m* (-s/-) mathematician; **2sch** *adj.* [~'ma:tiʃ] mathematical.

Matinee *thea.* [mati'ne:] *f* (-/-n) morning performance.

Matratze [ma'tratsə] *f* (-/-n) mattress.

Matrone [ma'tro:nə] *f* (-/-n) matron; **2nhaft** *adj.* matronly.

Matrose ⚓ [ma'tro:zə] *m* (-n/-n) sailor, seaman.

Matsch [matʃ] *m* (-es/*no pl.*), **~e** F ['~ə] *f* (-/*no pl.*) pulp, squash; mud, slush; **2ig** *adj.* pulpy, squashy; muddy, slushy.

matt *adj.* [mat] faint, feeble; *voice, etc.*: faint; *eye, colour, etc.*: dim; *colour, light,* ✝ *stock exchange, style, etc.*: dull; *metal*: tarnished; *gold, etc.*: dead, dull; *chess*: mated; ⚡ *bulb*: non-glare; ~ *geschliffen glass*: ground, frosted, matted; ~ *setzen at chess*: (check)mate *s.o.*

Matte ['matə] *f* (-/-n) mat.

'**Mattigkeit** *f* (-/*no pl.*) exhaustion, feebleness; faintness.

'**Mattscheibe** *f phot.* focus(s)ing screen; *television*: screen.

Mauer ['mauər] *f* (-/-n) wall; **~blümchen** *fig.* ['~bly:mçən] *n* (-s/-) wall-flower; **2n** (ge-, h) **1.** *v/i.* make a wall, lay bricks; **2.** *v/t.* build (in stone or brick); **~stein** *m* brick; **~werk** *n* masonry, brickwork.

Maul [maul] *n* (-[e]s/ⁿer) mouth; *sl.*: halt's ~ ! shut up!; **2en** F *v/i.* (ge-, h) sulk, pout; **~esel** *zo. m* mule, hinny; **~held** F *m* braggart;

~korb *m* muzzle; **~schelle** F *f* box on the ear; **~tier** *zo. n* mule; **~wurf** *zo. m* mole; **~wurfshügel** *m* molehill.

Maurer ['maurər] *m* (-s/-) brick-layer, mason; **~meister** *m* master mason; **~polier** *m* bricklayers' foreman.

Maus *zo.* [maus] *f* (-/ⁿe) mouse; **~efalle** ['~zə-] *f* mousetrap; **2en** ['~zən] (ge-, h) **1.** *v/i.* catch mice; **2.** F *v/t.* pinch, pilfer, F swipe.

Mauser ['mauzər] *f* (-/*no pl.*) mo(u)lt(ing); *in der* ~ *sein* be mo(u)lting; **2n** *v/refl.* (ge-, h) mo(u)lt.

Maximum ['maksimum] *n* (-s/*Maxima*) maximum.

Mayonnaise [majo'nɛ:zə] *f* (-/-n) mayonnaise.

Mechani|k [me'ça:nik] *f* **1.** (-/*no pl.*) mechanics *mst sg.*; **2.** ⊕ (-/-en) mechanism; **~ker** *m* (-s/-) mechanic; **2sch** *adj.* mechanical; **2sieren** [~ani'zi:rən] *v/t.* (*no -ge-*, h) mechanize; **~smus** ⊕ [~a'nɪsmus] *m* (-/*Mechanismen*) mechanism; *clock, watch, etc.*: works *pl.*

meckern ['mɛkərn] *v/i.* (ge-, h) bleat; *fig.* grumble (*über acc.* over, at, about), carp (*at*); nag (*at*); *sl.* grouse, *Am. sl.* gripe.

Medaill|e [me'daljə] *f* (-/-n) medal; **~on** [~'jõ:] *n* (-s/-s) medallion; locket.

Medikament [medika'mɛnt] *n* (-[e]s/-e) medicament, medicine.

Medizin [medi'tsi:n] *f* **1.** (-/*no pl.*) (science of) medicine; **2.** (-/-en) medicine, F physic; **~er** *m* (-s/-) medical man; medical student; **2isch** *adj.* medical; medicinal.

Meer [me:r] *n* (-[e]s/-e) sea (*a. fig.*), ocean; **~busen** *m* gulf, bay; **~enge** *f* strait(s *pl.*); **~esspiegel** *m* sea level; **~rettich** 🌱 *m* horse-radish; **~schweinchen** *zo. n* guinea-pig.

Mehl [me:l] *n* (-[e]s/-e) flour; meal; **~brei** *m* pap; **2ig** *adj.* floury, mealy, farinaceous; **~speise** *f* sweet dish, pudding; **~suppe** *f* gruel.

mehr [me:r] **1.** *adj.* more; *er hat* ~ *Geld als ich* he has (got) more money than I; **2.** *adv.* more; *nicht* ~ no more, no longer, not any longer; *ich habe nichts* ~ I have nothing left; **2arbeit** *f* additional

work; overtime; '**&ausgaben** f/pl.
additional expenditure; '**&betrag**
m surplus; '**&deutig** adj. ambiguous; '**&einnahme(n** pl.) f additional receipts pl.; '**~en** v/t. (ge-, h)
augment, increase; sich ~ multiply,
grow; '**~ere** adj. and indef. pron.
several, some; '**~fach 1.** adj. manifold, repeated; **2.** adv. repeatedly,
several times; '**&gebot** n higher bid;
'**&heit** f (-/-en) majority, plurality;
'**&kosten** pl. additional expense;
'**~malig** adj. repeated, reiterated;
~mals adv. ['~ma:ls] several times,
repeatedly; '**~sprachig** _♪_ adj.: polyglot; '**~stimmig** _♪_ adj.: **~er** Gesang part-song; '**&verbrauch** m
excess consumption; '**&wertsteuer**
✝ f (-/no pl.) value-added tax; '**&zahl** f majority; gr. plural (form);
die ~ (gen.) most of.

meiden ['maɪdən] v/t. (irr., ge-, h)
avoid, shun, keep away from.

Meile ['maɪlə] f (-/-n) mile; '**~nstein** f milestone.

mein poss. pron. [maɪn] my; der
(die, das) **~e** my; die **&en** pl. my
family, F my people or folks pl.;
ich habe das **~e** getan I have done
all I can; **~e** Damen und Herren!
Ladies and Gentlemen!

Meineid _♫♫_ ['maɪnⁱ-] m. perjury;
'**&ig** adj. perjured.

meinen ['maɪnən] v/t. (ge-, h)
think, believe, be of (the) opinion,
Am. a. reckon, guess; say; mean;
wie ~ Sie das? what do you mean
by that?; ~ Sie das ernst? do you
(really) mean it?; es gut ~ mean
well.

meinetwegen adv. ['maɪnət'-] for
my sake; on my behalf; because of
me, on my account; for all I care;
I don't mind or care.

'**Meinung** f (-/-en) opinion (über
acc., von about, of); die öffentliche
~ (the) public opinion; meiner ~
nach in my opinion, to my mind;
j-m (gehörig) die ~ sagen give s.o.
a piece of one's mind; '**~saustausch**
['maɪnʊŋs⁹-] m exchange of views
(über acc. on); '**~sverschiedenheit**
f difference of opinion (über acc.
on); disagreement.

Meise orn. ['maɪzə] f (-/-n) titmouse.

Meißel ['maɪsəl] m (-s/-) chisel; '**&n**
v/t. and v/i. (ge-, h) chisel; carve.

meist [maɪst] **1.** adj. most; die **~en**
Leute most people; die **~e** Zeit most
of one's time; **2.** adv.: s. meistens;
am **~en** most (of all); **&bietende**
['~bi:təndə] m (-n/-n) highest bidder; **~ens** adv. ['~əns], '**~en'teils**
adv. mostly, in most cases; usually.

Meister ['maɪstər] m (-s/-) master,
sl. boss; sports: champion; '**&haft
1.** adj. masterly; **2.** adv. in a masterly manner or way; '**&n** v/t. (ge-,
h) master; '**~schaft** f 1. (-/no pl.)
mastery; **2.** sports: championship, title; '**~stück** n, '**~werk** n
masterpiece.

'**Meistgebot** n highest bid, best
offer.

Melancholie [melaŋko'li:] f (-/-n)
melancholy; **&isch** adj. [~'ko:liʃ]
melancholy; ~ sein F have the blues.

Meldeamt ['meldə-] n registration
office; '**~liste** f sports: list of entries; '**&n** v/t. (ge-, h) announce;
j-m et. ~ inform s.o. of s.th.; officially: notify s.th. to s.o.; j-n ~
enter s.o.'s name (für, zu for); sich
~ report o.s. (bei to); school, etc.:
put up one's hand; answer the telephone; enter (one's name) (für, zu
for examination, etc.); sich ~ zu
apply for; sich auf ein Inserat ~
answer an advertisement.

'**Meldung** f (-/-en) information, advice; announcement; report; registration; application; sports: entry.

melken ['melkən] v/t. (irr.) ge-, h)
milk; '**&r** m (-s/-) milker.

Melodie [melo'di:] f (-/-n) melody; tune, air; **&isch** adj. [~'lo:diʃ]
melodious, tuneful.

Melone [me'lo:nə] f (-/-n) _♀_ melon;
F bowler(-hat), Am. derby.

Membran [mɛm'brɑ:n] f (-/-en),
~e f (-/-n) membrane; teleph. a.
diaphragm.

Memme F ['memə] f (-/-n) coward;
poltroon.

Memoiren [memo'a:rən] pl. memoirs pl.

Menagerie [menaʒə'ri:] f (-/-n)
menagerie.

Menge ['meŋə] f (-/-n) quantity;
amount; multitude; crowd; in
großer ~ in abundance; persons,
animals: in crowds; e-e ~ Geld
plenty of money, F lots pl. of
money; e-e ~ Bücher a great many
books; '**&n** v/t. (ge-, h) mix, blend;
sich ~ mix (unter acc. with), mingle

(with); *sich* ~ *in* (acc.) meddle *or* interfere with.

Mensch [menʃ] *m* (-en/-en) human being; man; person, individual; *die* ~*en pl.* people *pl.*, the world, mankind; *kein* ~ nobody.

'**Menschen**|**affe** *zo.* *m* anthropoid ape; '~**alter** *n* generation, age; '~**feind** *m* misanthropist; '2**feindlich** *adj.* misanthropic; '~**fresser** *m* (-s/-) cannibal, man-eater; '~**freund** *m* philanthropist; '2**freundlich** *adj.* philanthropic; '~**gedenken** *n* (-s/*no pl.*): *seit* ~ from time immemorial, within the memory of man; '~**geschlecht** *n* human race, mankind; '~**haß** *m* misanthropy; '~**kenner** *m* judge of men *or* human nature; '~**kenntnis** *f* knowledge of human nature; '~**leben** *n* human life; '2**leer** *adj.* deserted; '~**liebe** *f* philanthropy; '~**menge** *f* crowd (of people), throng; '2**möglich** *adj.* humanly possible; '~**raub** *m* kidnap(p)ing; '~**rechte** *n/pl.* human rights *pl.*; '2**scheu** *adj.* unsociable, shy; '~**seele** *f: keine* ~ not a living soul; '~**verstand** *m* human understanding; *gesunder* ~ common sense, F horse sense; '~**würde** *f* dignity of man. ~**race**, mankind.|

'**Menschheit** *f* (-/*no pl.*) human|
'**menschlich** *adj.* human; *fig.* humane; '2**keit** *f* (-/*no pl.*) human nature; humanity, humaneness.

Mentalität [mentali'tɛ:t] *f* (-/-en) mentality.

merk|**bar** *adj.* ['mɛrkba:r] *s.* merklich; '2**blatt** *n* leaflet, instructional pamphlet; '2**buch** *n* notebook; '~**en** (ge-, h) **1.** *v/i.*: ~ *auf* (acc.) pay attention to, listen to; **2.** *v/t.* notice, perceive, find out, discover; *sich et.* ~ remember s.th.; bear s.th. in mind; '~**lich** *adj.* noticeable, perceptible; '2**mal** *n* (-[e]s/-e) mark, sign; characteristic, feature.

'**merkwürdig** *adj.* noteworthy, remarkable; strange, odd, curious; ~**erweise** *adv.* ['~gər'~] strange to say, strangely enough; '2**keit** *f* (-/-en) remarkableness; curiosity, peculiarity.

meßbar *adj.* ['mɛsba:r] measurable.

Messe ['mɛsə] *f* (-/-n) ✝ fair; *eccl.* mass; ✕, ⚓ mess.

messen ['mɛsən] *v/t.* (irr., ge-, h) measure; ⚓ sound; *sich mit j-m* ~ compete with s.o.; *sich nicht mit j-m* ~ *können* be no match for s.o.; *gemessen an* (dat.) measured against, compared with.

Messer ['mɛsər] *n* (-s/-) knife; ✂ scalpel; *bis aufs* ~ to the knife; *auf des* ~*s Schneide* on a razor-edge *or* razor's edge; '~**griff** *m* knifehandle; '~**held** *m* stabber; '~**klinge** *f* knife-blade; '~**schmied** *m* cutler; '~**schneide** *f* knife-edge; '~**stecher** *m* (-s/-) stabber; 2**stecherei** [~ʃte-çə'raɪ] *f* (-/-en) knifing, knifebattle; '~**stich** *m* stab with a knife.

Messing ['mɛsiŋ] *n* (-s/*no pl.*) brass; '~**blech** *n* sheet-brass.

'**Meß**|**instrument** *n* measuring instrument; '~**latte** *f* surveyor's rod; '~**tisch** *m* surveyor's *or* plane table.

Metall [me'tal] *n* (-s/-e) metal; ~**arbeiter** *m* metal worker; 2**en** *adj.* (of) metal, metallic; ~**geld** *n* coin(s *pl.*), specie; ~**glanz** *m* metallic lust|re, *Am.* -er; 2**haltig** *adj.* metalliferous; ~**industrie** *f* metallurgical industry; ~**waren** *f/pl.* hardware.

Meteor *ast.* [mete'o:r] *m* (-s/-e) meteor; ~**ologe** [~oro'lo:gə] *m* (-n/-n) meteorologist; ~**ologie** [~orolo'gi:] *f* (-/*no pl.*) meteorology.

Meter ['me:tər] *n, m* (-s/-) met|re, *Am.* -er; '~**maß** *n* tape-measure.

Method|**e** [me'to:də] *f* (-/-n) method; ⊕ *a.* technique; 2**isch** *adj.* methodical. [metropolis.]

Metropole [metro'po:lə] *f* (-/-n)|

Metzel|**ei** [mɛtsə'laɪ] *f* (-/-en) slaughter, massacre; '2**n** *v/t.* (ge-, h) butcher, slaughter, massacre.

Metzger ['mɛtsgər] *m* (-s/-) butcher; ~**ei** [~'raɪ] *f* (-/-en) butcher's (shop).

Meuchel|**mord** ['mɔʏçəl-] *m* assassination; '~**mörder** *m* assassin.

Meute ['mɔʏtə] *f* (-/-n) pack of hounds; *fig.* gang; '~**rei** [~'raɪ] *f* (-/-en) mutiny; '~**rer** *m* (-s/-) mutineer; '2**risch** *adj.* mutinous; '2**rn** *v/i.* (ge-, h) mutiny (*gegen* against).

mich *pers. pron.* [miç] me; ~ (*selbst*) myself.

mied [mi:t] *pret. of* meiden.

Mieder ['mi:dər] *n* (-s/-) bodice; corset; '~**waren** *f/pl.* corsetry.

Miene ['mi:nə] *f* (-/-n) countenance, air; feature; *gute* ~ *zum bösen Spiel machen* grin and bear it; ~ **machen zu** inf. offer or threaten to inf.

mies F adj. [mi:s] miserable, poor; out of sorts; seedy.

Miet|e ['mi:tə] f (-/-n) rent; hire; **zur ~ wohnen** live in lodgings, be a tenant; **'2en** v/t. (ge-, h) rent (land, building, etc.); hire (horse, etc.); (take on) lease (land, etc.); ⚓, ✈ charter; **'~er** m (-s/-) tenant; lodger, Am. a. roomer; ⚵ lessee; **'2frei** adj. rent-free; **'~shaus** n block of flats, Am. apartment house; **'~vertrag** m tenancy agreement; lease; **'~wohnung** f lodgings pl., flat, Am. apartment.

Migräne ⚕ [mi'grɛ:nə] f (-/-n) migraine, megrim; sick headache.

Mikrophon [mikro'fo:n] n (-s/-e) microphone, F mike.

Mikroskop [mikro'sko:p] n (-s/-e) microscope; **2isch** adj. microscopic(al).

Milbe zo. ['milbə] f (-/-n) mite.

Milch [milç] f (-/no pl.) milk; milt, soft roe (of fish); **'~bar** f milk-bar; **'~bart** fig. m stripling; **'~brötchen** n (French) roll; **'~gesicht** n baby face; **'~glas** n frosted glass; **2ig** adj. milky; **'~kanne** f milk-can; **'~kuh** f milk cow (a. fig.); **'~mäd-chen** F n milkmaid, dairymaid; **'~mann** F m milkman, dairyman; **'~pulver** n milk-powder; **'~reis** m rice-milk; **'~straße** ast. f Milky Way, Galaxy; **'~wirtschaft** f dairy-farm(ing); **'~zahn** m milktooth.

mild [milt] 1. adj. weather, punishment, etc.: mild; air, weather, light, etc.: soft; wine, etc.: mellow, smooth; reprimand, etc.: gentle; 2. adv.: et. ~ **beurteilen** take a lenient view of s. th.

milde ['mildə] 1. adj. s. mild 1; 2. adv.: ~ **gesagt** to put it mildly; 3. 2 f (-/no pl.) mildness; softness; smoothness; gentleness.

milder|n ['mildərn] v/t. (ge-, h) soften, mitigate; soothe, alleviate (pain, etc.); **~de Umstände** ⚵ extenuating circumstances; **'2ung** f (-/-en) softening, mitigation, alleviation.

'mild|herzig adj. charitable; **'2her-zigkeit** f (-/no pl.) charitableness; **'~tätig** adj. charitable; **'2tätigkeit** f charity.

Milieu [mil'jø:] n (-s/-s) surroundings pl., environment; class, circles pl.; local colo(u)r.

Militär [mili'tɛ:r] 1. n (-s/no pl.) military, armed forces pl.; army; 2. m (-s/-s) military man, soldier; **~attaché** [‿ataʃe:] m (-s/-s) military attaché; **~dienst** m military service; **2isch** adj. military; **~musik** f military music; **~regierung** f military government; **~zeit** f (-/no pl.) term of military service.

Miliz ⚔ [mi'li:ts] f (-/-en) militia; **~soldat** ⚔ m militiaman.

Milliarde [mil'jardə] f (-/-n) thousand millions, milliard, Am. billion.

Millimeter [mili'-] n, m millimet|re, Am. -er.

Million [mil'jo:n] f (-/-en) million; **~är** [‿o'nɛ:r] m (-s/-e) millionaire.

Milz anat. [milts] f (-/-en) spleen, milt.

minder ['mindər] 1. adv. less; **nicht ~** no less, likewise; 2. adj. less(er); smaller; minor; inferior; **'~begabt** adj. less gifted; **~bemittelt** adj. ['‿bəmitəlt] of moderate means; **'2betrag** m deficit, shortage; **'2einnahme** f shortfall in receipts; **'2gewicht** n short weight; **'2heit** f (-/-en) minority; **~jährig** adj. ['‿jɛ:riç] under age, minor; **'2jährigkeit** f (-/no pl.) minority; **'~n** v/t. and v/refl. (ge-, h) diminish, lessen, decrease; **'2ung** f (-/-en) decrease, diminution; **'~wertig** adj. inferior, of inferior quality; **'2wertigkeit** f (-/no pl.) inferiority; ⚕ inferior quality; **'2wertigkeits-komplex** m inferiority complex.

mindest adj. ['mindəst] least; slightest; minimum; **nicht die ~e Aussicht** not the slightest chance; **nicht im ~en** not in the least; **zum ~en** at least; **'2alter** n minimum age; **'2anforderungen** f/pl. minumum requirements pl.; **'2betrag** m lowest amount; **'2einkommen** n minimum income; **'~ens** adv. at least; **'2gebot** n lowest bid; **'2lohn** m minimum wage; **'2maß** n minimum; **auf ein ~ herabsetzen** minimize; **'2preis** m minimum price.

Mine ['mi:nə] f (-/-n) ⚒, ⚔, ⚓ mine; pencil: lead; ball-point-pen: refill.

M

Mineral [minə'ra:l] n (-s/-e, -ien) mineral; 2isch adj. mineral; ~ogie [~alo'gi:] f (-/no pl.) mineralogy; ~wasser n (-s/⸗) mineral water.

Miniatur [minia'tu:r] f (-/-en) miniature; ~gemälde n miniature.

Minirock ['mini-] m miniskirt.

Minister [mi'nistər] m (-s/-) minister; Secretary (of State), Am. Secretary; ~ium [~'te:rjum] n (-s/Ministerien) ministry; Office, Am. Department; ~präsident m prime minister, premier; in Germany, etc.: minister president; ~rat m (-[e]s/⸗e) cabinet council.

minus adv. ['mi:nus] minus, less, deducting.

Minute [mi'nu:tə] f (-/-n) minute; ~nzeiger m minute-hand.

mir pers. pron. [mi:r] (to) me.

Misch|ehe ['miʃ?-] f mixed marriage; intermarriage; 2en v/t. (ge-, h) mix, mingle; blend (coffee, tobacco, etc.); alloy (metal); shuffle (cards); sich ~ in (acc.) interfere in; join in (conversation); sich ~ unter (acc.) mix or mingle with (the crowd); ~ling [~liŋ] m (-s/-e) half-breed, half-caste; ♀, zo. hybrid; ~masch F [~maʃ] m (-es/-e) hotchpotch, jumble; ~ung f (-/-en) mixture; blend; alloy.

miß|achten [mis'-] v/t. (no ge-, h) disregard, ignore, neglect; slight, despise; 2achtung f disregard, neglect; ~behagen 1. v/i. (no -ge-, h) displease; 2. 2 n discomfort, uneasiness; 2bildung f malformation, deformity; ~billigen v/t. (no -ge-, h) disapprove (of); 2billigung f disapproval; 2brauch m abuse; misuse; ~brauchen v/t. (no -ge-, h) abuse; misuse; ~bräuchlich adj. [~brɔyçliç] abusive; improper; ~deuten v/t. (no -ge-, h) misinterpret; 2deutung f misinterpretation.

missen ['misən] v/t. (ge-, h) miss; do without, dispense with.

'Miß|erfolg m failure; fiasco; ~ernte f bad harvest, crop failure.

Misse|tat ['misə-] f misdeed; crime; ~täter m evil-doer, offender; criminal.

miß|fallen v/i. (irr. fallen, no -ge-, h): j-m ~ displease s.o.; 2fallen n (-s/no pl.) displeasure, dislike; ~fällig 1. adj. displeasing; shock-ing; disparaging; 2. adv.: sich ~ äußern über (acc.) speak ill of; '2geburt f monster, freak (of nature), deformity; '2geschick n bad luck, misfortune; mishap; ~gestimmt fig. adj. [~gə'ʃtimt] s. mißmutig; ~glücken v/i. (no -ge-, sein) fail; ~gönnen v/t. (no -ge-, h): j-m et. ~ envy or grudge s.o. s.th.; ~griff m mistake, blunder; '2gunst f envy, jealousy; '~günstig adj. envious, jealous; ~handeln v/t. (no -ge-, h) ill-treat; maul, sl. manhandle; 2handlung f ill-treatment; mauling, sl. manhandling; ⚖ assault and battery; '2heirat f misalliance; ~hellig adj. dissonant, dissentient; 2helligkeit f (-/-n) dissonance, dissension, discord.

Mission [mis'jo:n] f (-/-en) mission (a. pol. and fig.); ~ar [~o'na:r] m (-s/-e) missionary.

'Miß|klang m dissonance, discord (both a. fig.); '~kredit fig. m (-[e]s/no pl.) discredit; in ~ bringen bring discredit upon s.o.

miß|lang pret. of mißlingen; '~lich adj. awkward; unpleasant; ~liebig adj. ['~li:biç] unpopular; ~lingen [~'liŋən] v/i. (irr., no -ge-, sein) fail; 2lingen n (-s/no pl.) failure; 2mut m ill humo(u)r; discontent; '~mutig adj. ill-humo(u)red; discontented; ~raten 1. v/i. (irr. raten, no -ge-, sein) fail; turn out badly; 2. adj. wayward; ill-bred; 2stand m nuisance; grievance; 2stimmung f ill humo(u)r; '2ton m (-[e]s/⸗e) dissonance, discord (both a. fig.); ~trauen v/i. (no -ge-, h): j-m distrust or mistrust s.o.; '2trauen n (-s/no pl.) distrust, mistrust; '~trauisch adj. distrustful; suspicious; '2vergnügen n (-s/no pl.) displeasure; '~vergnügt adj. displeased; discontented; '2verhältnis n disproportion; incongruity; '2verständnis n misunderstanding; dissension; '~verstehen v/t. (irr. stehen, no -ge-, h) misunderstand, mistake (intention, etc.); '2wirtschaft f maladministration, mismanagement.

Mist [mist] m (-es/-e) dung, manure; dirt; F fig. trash, rubbish; ~beet n hotbed.

Mistel ♀ ['mistəl] f (-/-n) mistletoe.

'Mist|gabel f dung-fork; **~haufen** m dung-hill.

mit [mit] **1.** prp. (dat.) with; ~ 20 Jahren at (the age of) twenty; ~ e-m Schlage at a blow; ~ Gewalt by force; ~ der Bahn by train; **2.** adv. also, too; ~ dabeisein be there too, be (one) of the party.

Mit|arbeiter ['mit⁹-] m co-worker; writing, art, etc.: collaborator; colleague; newspaper, etc.: contributor (an dat. to); **2benutzen** v/t. (sep., no -ge-, h) use jointly or in common; **~besitzer** m joint owner; **~bestimmungsrecht** n right of co-determination; **~bewerber** m competitor; **~bewohner** m coinhabitant, fellow-lodger; **2bringen** v/t. (irr. bringen, sep., -ge-, h) bring along (with one); **~bringsel** ['~briŋzəl] n (-s/-) little present; **~bürger** m fellow-citizen; **2einander** adv. [mit⁹ai'nandər] together, jointly; with each other, with one another; **~empfinden** ['mit⁹-] n (-s/no pl.) sympathy; **~erbe** ['mit⁹-] m co-heir; **~esser** ♂ ['mit⁹-] m (-s/-) blackhead; **2fahren** v/i. (irr. fahren, sep., -ge-, sein): mit j-m ~ drive or go with s.o.; j-n ~ lassen give s.o. a lift; **2fühlen** v/i. (sep., -ge-, h) sympathize (mit with); **2geben** v/t. (irr. geben, sep., -ge-, h) give along (dat. with); **~gefühl** n sympathy; **2gehen** v/i. (irr. gehen, sep., -ge-, sein): mit j-m ~ go with s.o.; **~gift** f (-/-en) dowry, marriage portion.

'Mitglied n member; **~erversammlung** f general meeting; **~erzahl** f membership; **~sbeitrag** m subscription; **~schaft** f (-/no pl.) membership.

mit|'hin adv. consequently, therefore; **2inhaber** ['mit⁹-] m copartner; **2kämpfer** m fellowcombatant; **2kommen** v/i. (irr. kommen, sep., -ge-, sein) come along (mit with); fig. be able to follow; **2läufer** pol. m nominal member; contp. trimmer.

'Mitleid n (-[e]s/no pl.) compassion, pity; sympathy; aus ~ out of pity; ~ haben mit have or take pity on; **~enschaft** f (-/no pl.): in ~ ziehen affect; implicate, involve; damage; **2ig** adj. compassionate, pitiful; **2(s)los** adj. ['~t-] pitiless, merciless;

2(s)voll adj. ['~t-] pitiful, compassionate.

'mit|machen (sep., -ge-, h) **1.** v/i. make one of the party; **2.** v/t. take part in, participate in; follow; go with (fashion); go through (hardships); **2mensch** m fellow creature; **~nehmen** v/t. (irr. nehmen, sep., -ge-, h) take along (with one); fig. exhaust, wear out; j-n (im Auto) ~ give s.o. a lift; **~nichten** adv. [~'niçtən] by no means, not at all; **~rechnen** v/t. (sep., -ge-, h) include (in the account); nicht ~ leave out of account; nicht mitgerechnet not counting; **~reden** (sep., -ge-, h) **1.** v/i. join in the conversation; **2.** v/t.: ein Wort or Wörtchen mitzureden haben have a say (bei in); **~reißen** v/t. (irr. reißen, sep., -ge-, h) tear or drag along; fig. sweep along.

'Mitschuld f complicity (an dat. in); **2ig** adj. accessary (an dat. to crime); **~ige** m accessary, accomplice.

'Mitschüler m schoolfellow.

'mitspiel|en (sep., -ge-, h) **1.** v/i. play (bei with); sports: be on the team; thea. appear, star (in a play); join in a game; matter: be involved; j-m arg or übel ~ play s.o. a nasty trick; **2.** fig. v/t. join in (game); **2er** m partner.

'Mittag m midday, noon; heute 2 at noon today; zu ~ essen lunch, dine; **~essen** n lunch(eon), dinner; **'2s** adv. at noon.

'Mittags|pause f lunch hour; **~ruhe** f midday rest; **~schlaf** m, **~schläfchen** n after-dinner nap, siesta; **~stunde** f noon; **~tisch** fig. m lunch, dinner; **~zeit** f noontide; lunch-time, dinner-time.

Mitte ['mitə] f (-/-n) middle; cent|re, Am. -er; die goldene ~ the golden or happy mean; aus unserer ~ from among us; ~ Juli in the middle of July; ~ Dreißig in the middle of one's thirties.

'mitteil|en v/t. (sep., -ge-, h): j-m et. ~ communicate s.th. to s.o.; impart s.th. to s.o.; inform s.o. of s.th.; make s.th. known to s.o.; **~sam** adj. communicative; **~ung** f (-/-en) communication; information; communiqué.

Mittel ['mitəl] n (-s/-) means sg.,

M

way; remedy (gegen for); average; Ⱥ mean; phys. medium; ~ pl. a. means pl., funds pl., money; ~ pl. und Wege ways and means pl.; '**alter** n Middle Ages pl.; ²**alterlich** adj. medi(a)eval; ²**bar** adj. mediate, indirect; '**ding** n: ein ~ zwischen … und … something between … and …; '**finger** m middle finger; '**gebirge** n highlands pl.; ²**groß** adj. of medium height; medium-sized; '**läufer** m sports: centre half back, Am. center half back; '**los** adj. without means, destitute; ²**mäßig** adj. middling; mediocre; '**mäßigkeit** f (-/no pl.) mediocrity; '**punkt** m cent|re, Am. -er; fig. a. focus; ²s prp. (gen.) by (means of); through; '**schule** f intermediate school, Am. high school; '**smann** m (-[e]s/⸗er, Mittelsleute) mediator, go-between; '**stand** m middle classes pl.; '**stürmer** m sports: centre forward, Am. center forward; '**weg** fig. m middle course; '**wort** gr. n (-[e]s/⸗er) participle.

mitten adv. [⸗mitən]: ~ in or on or auf or unter (acc.) dat.) in the midst or middle of; ~ entzwei right in two; ~ im Winter in the depth of winter; ~ in der Nacht in the middle or dead of night; ~ ins Herz right into the heart; **~'drin** F adv. right in the middle; **~'durch** F adv. right through or across.

Mitter|nacht [⸗mitər⸗] f midnight; um ~ at midnight; ²**nächtig** adj. [⸗⸗nɛçtiç], ²**nächtlich** adj. midnight.

Mittler [⸗mitlər] 1. m (-s/-) mediator, intercessor; 2. ♀ adj. middle, central; average, medium; '²**weile** adv. meanwhile, (in the) meantime.

Mittwoch [⸗mitvɔx] m (-[e]s/-e) Wednesday; '²s adv. on Wednesday(s), every Wednesday.

mit|'unter adv. now and then, sometimes; '**verantwortlich** adj. jointly responsible; '²**welt** f (-/no pl.): die ~ our, etc. contemporaries pl.

'**mitwirk|en** v/i. (sep., -ge-, h) co-operate (bei in), contribute (to), take part (in); '²**ende** m (-n/-n) thea. performer, actor, player (a. ♪); die ~n pl. the cast; '²**ung** f (-/no pl.) co(-)operation, contribution.

'**Mitwisser** m (-s/-) confidant; t⅟z accessary. [rechnen.] '**mitzählen** v/t. (sep., -ge-, h) s. mit-|

Mix|becher m (cocktail-)shaker; ²**en** v/t. (ge-, h) mix; '**tur** [⸗'u:r] f (-/-en) mixture.

Möbel [⸗møːbəl] n (-s/-) piece of furniture; ~ pl. furniture; '**händler** m furniture-dealer; '**spediteur** m furniture-remover; '**stück** n piece of furniture; '**tischler** m cabinet-maker; '**wagen** m pantechnicon, Am. furniture truck.

mobil adj. [mo'biːl] ✕ mobile; F active, nimble; ~ machen ✕ mobilize; ²**iar** [⸗il'jaːr] n (-s/-e) furniture; movables pl.; **isieren** [⸗ili'ziːrən] v/t. (no -ge-, h) ✕ mobilize; ✝ realize (property, etc.); ²**machung** ✕ [mo'biːlmaxuŋ] f (-/-en) mobilization.

möblieren [mø'bliːrən] v/t. (no -ge-, h) furnish; möbliertes Zimmer furnished room, F bed-sitter.

mochte [⸗mɔxtə] pret. of mögen.

Mode [⸗moːdə] f (-/-n) fashion, vogue; use, custom; die neueste ~ the latest fashion; in ~ in fashion or vogue; aus der ~ kommen grow or go out of fashion; die ~ bestimmen set the fashion; '**artikel** m/pl. fancy goods pl., novelties pl.; '**farbe** f fashionable colo(u)r.

Modell [mo'dɛl] n (-s/-e) ⊕, fashion, paint.: model; pattern, design; ⊕ mo(u)ld; j-m ~ stehen paint. pose for s.o.; **eisenbahn** f model railway; ²**ieren** [⸗'liːrən] v/t. (no -ge-, h) model, mo(u)ld, fashion.

'**Moden|schau** f dress parade, fashion-show; '**zeitung** f fashion magazine.

Moder [⸗moːdər] m (-s/no pl.) must, putrefaction; '**geruch** m musty smell; '²**ig** adj. musty, putrid.

modern[1] [⸗moːdərn] v/i. (ge-, h) putrefy, rot, decay.

modern[2] adj. [mo'dɛrn] modern; progressive; up-to-date; fashionable; **isieren** [⸗i'ziːrən] v/t. (no -ge-, h) modernize, bring up to date.

'**Mode|salon** m fashion house; '**schmuck** m costume jewel(le)ry; '**waren** f/pl. fancy goods pl.; '**zeichner** m fashion-designer.

modifizieren [modifi'tsiːrən] v/t. (no -ge-, h) modify.

M

modisch adj. ['moːdiʃ] fashionable, stylish.

Modistin [mo'distin] f (-/-nen) milliner.

Mogel|ei F [moː'gəˈlaɪ] f (-/-en) cheat; **'2n** F v/i. (ge-, h) cheat.

mögen ['møːgən] (irr., h) **1.** v/i. (ge-) be willing; ich mag nicht I don't like to; **2.** v/t. (ge-) want, wish; like, be fond of; nicht ~ dislike; not to be keen on (food, etc.); lieber ~ like better, prefer; **3.** v/aux. (no -ge-) may, might; ich möchte wissen I should like to know; ich möchte lieber gehen I would rather go; das mag (wohl) sein that's (well) possible; wo er auch sein mag wherever he may be; mag er sagen, was er will let him say what he likes.

möglich ['møːklɪç] **1.** adj. possible; practicable, feasible; market, criminal, etc.: potential; alle ~en all sorts of things; alles ~e all sorts of things; sein ~stes tun do one's utmost or level best; nicht ~! you don't say (so)!; so bald etc. wie ~ = **2.** adv.: ~st bald etc. as soon, etc., as possible; **'~er'weise** adv. possibly, if possible; perhaps; **'2keit** f (-/-en) possibility; chance; nach ~ if possible.

Mohammedan|er [mohame'daː-nər] m (-s/-) Muslim, Moslem, Mohammedan; **2isch** adj. Muslim, Moslem, Mohammedan.

Mohn [moːn] m (-[e]s/-e) poppy.

Möhre ♀ ['møːrə] f (-/-n) carrot.

Mohrrübe ♀ ['moːr-] f carrot.

Molch zo. [mɔlç] m (-[e]s/-e) salamander; newt.

Mole ♁ ['moːlə] f (-/-n) mole, jetty.

molk [mɔlk] pret. of melken.

Molkerei [mɔlkəˈraɪ] f (-/-en) dairy; **~produkte** n/pl. dairy products pl.

Moll ♪ [mɔl] n (-/-) minor (key).

mollig F adj. ['mɔlɪç] snug, cosy, plump, rounded.

Moment [mo'mɛnt] **1.** m (-[e]s/-e) moment, instant; im ~ at the moment; **2.** n motive; fact(or); ⊕ momentum; ⊕ impulse (a. fig.); **2an** [~'taːn] **1.** adj. momentary; **2.** adv. at the moment, for the time being; **~aufnahme** phot. f snapshot, instantaneous photograph.

Monarch [mo'narç] m (-en/-en) monarch; **~ie** [~çi:] f (-/-n) monarchy.

Monat ['moːnat] m (-[e]s/-e) month; **2elang 1.** adj. lasting for months;

2. adv. for months; **'2lich 1.** adj. monthly; **2.** adv. monthly, a month.

Mönch [mœnç] m (-[e]s/-e) monk, friar.

'Mönchs|kloster n monastery; **'~kutte** f (monk's) frock; **'~leben** n monastic life; **'~orden** m monastic order; **'~zelle** f monk's cell.

Mond [moːnt] m (-[e]s/-e) moon; hinter dem ~ leben be behind the times; **'~fähre** f lunar module; **'~finsternis** f lunar eclipse; **'2'hell** adj. moonlit; **'~schein** m (-[e]s/no pl.) moonlight; **'~sichel** f crescent; **'2süchtig** adj. moonstruck.

Mono|log [mono'loːk] m (-s/-e) monologue, Am. a. monolog; soliloquy; **~'pol** ✝ n (-s/-e) monopoly; **2polisieren** [~poli'ziːrən] v/t. (no -ge-, h) monopolize; **~'ton** adj. monotonous; **~tonie** [~toˈniː] f (-/-n) monotony.

Monstrum ['mɔnstrum] n (-s/Monstren, Monstra) monster.

Montag ['moːn-] m Monday; **'2s** adv. on Monday(s), every Monday.

Montage ⊕ [mɔn'taːʒə] f (-/-n) mounting, fitting; setting up; assemblage, assembly.

Montan|industrie [mɔn'taːn-] f coal and steel industries pl.; **~union** f European Coal and Steel Community.

Mont|eur [mɔn'tøːr] m (-s/-e) ⊕ fitter, assembler; esp. mot., ✈ mechanic; **~euranzug** m overall; **2ieren** [~'tiːrən] v/t. (no -ge-, h) mount, fit; set up; assemble; **~ur** ✕ [~'tuːr] f (-/-en) regimentals pl.

Moor [moːr] n (-[e]s/-e) bog; swamp; **'~bad** n mud-bath; **'2ig** adj. boggy, marshy.

Moos ♀ [moːs] n (-es/-e) moss; **'2ig** adj. mossy.

Moped mot. ['moːpet] n (-s/-s) moped.

Mops zo. [mɔps] m (-es/⸚e) pug; **'2en** v/t. (ge-, h) F pilfer, pinch; sl.: sich ~ be bored stiff.

Moral [moˈraːl] f (-/⸚, -en) morality; morals pl.; moral; ✕, etc.: morale; **2isch** adj. moral; **2isieren** [~ali'ziːrən] v/i. (no -ge-, h) moralize.

Morast [moˈrast] m (-es/-e, ⸚e) slough, morass; s. Moor; mire, mud; **2ig** adj. marshy; muddy, miry.

Mord [mɔrt] m (-[e]s/-e) murder

M

(an dat. of); e-n ~ begehen commit murder; '~anschlag m murderous assault; ♀en ['~dən] v/i. (ge-, h) commit murder(s).

Mörder ['mœrdər] m (-s/-) murderer; ♀isch adj. murderous; climate, etc.: deadly; † competition: cut-throat.

'**Mord|gier** f lust of murder, bloodthirstiness; ♀gierig adj. bloodthirsty; '~kommission f homicide squad; '~prozeß ﬃ m murder trial.

'**Mords|angst** F f blue funk, sl. mortal fear; '~glück F n stupendous luck; '~kerl F m devil of a fellow; '~spektakel F m hullabaloo.

Morgen ['morgən] 1. m (-s/-) morning; measure: acre; am ~ s. morgens; 2. ♀ adv. tomorrow; ~ früh (abend) tomorrow morning (evening or night); ~ in acht Tagen tomorrow week; '~ausgabe f morning edition; '~blatt n morning paper; '~dämmerung f dawn, daybreak; '~gebet n morning prayer; '~gymnastik f morning exercises pl.; '~land n (-[e]s/no pl.) Orient, East; '~rock m peignoir, dressing-gown, wrapper (for woman); '~röte f dawn; '♀s adv. in the morning; '~zeitung f morning paper.

'**morgig** adj. of tomorrow.

Morphium pharm. ['mɔrfium] n (-s/no pl.) morphia, morphine.

morsch adj. [mɔrʃ] rotten, decayed; brittle.

Mörser ['mœrzər] m (-s/-) mortar (a. ✕).

Mörtel ['mœrtəl] m (-s/-) mortar.

Mosaik [moza'i:k] n (-s/-en) mosaic; '~fußboden m mosaic or tessellated pavement.

Moschee [mɔ'ʃe:] f (-/-n) mosque.

Moschus ['mɔʃus] m (-/no pl.) musk.

Moskito zo. [mɔs'ki:to] m (-s/-s) mosquito; '~netz n mosquito-net.

Moslem ['mɔslɛm] m (-s/-s) Muslim, Moslem.

Most [mɔst] m (-es/-e) must, grapejuice; of apples: cider; of pears: perry. \} mustard.\}

Mostrich ['mɔstriç] m (-[e]s/no pl.)

Motiv [mo'ti:f] n (-s/-e) motive, reason; paint., ♪ motif; ♀ieren [~i'vi:rən] v/t. (no -ge-, h) motivate.

Motor [mo'to:r] m (-s/-en) engine, esp. ⚙ motor; '~boot n motor boat; '~defekt m engine or ⚙ motor

trouble; '~haube f bonnet, Am. hood; ♀isieren [motori'zi:rən] v/t. (no -ge-, h) motorize; ~isierung [motori'zi:ruŋ] f (-/no pl.) motorization; '~rad n motor (bi)cycle; '~radfahrer m motor cyclist; '~roller m (motor) scooter; '~sport m motoring.

Motte zo. ['mɔtə] f (-/-n) moth.

'**Motten|kugel** f moth-ball; ♀sicher adj. mothproof; ♀zerfressen adj. moth-eaten.

Motto ['mɔto] n (-s/-s) motto.

Möwe orn. ['mø:və] f (-/-n) sea-gull, (sea-)mew.

Mücke zo. ['mykə] f (-/-n) midge, gnat, mosquito; aus e-r ~ e-n Elefanten machen make a mountain out of a molehill; '~nstich m gnatbite. \} (hypocrite.\}

Mucker ['mukər] m (-s/-) bigot,\}

müd|e ['my:də] tired, weary; e-r Sache ~ sein be weary or tired of s.th.; '♀igkeit f (-/no pl.) tiredness, weariness.

Muff [muf] m 1. (-[e]s/-e) muff; 2. (-[e]s/no pl.) mo(u)ldy or musty smell; '~e ⊕ f (-/-n) sleeve, socket; ♀eln F v/i. (ge-, h) munch; mumble; ♀ig adj. smell, etc.: musty, fusty; air: close; fig. sulky, sullen.

Mühe ['my:ə] f (-/-n) trouble, pains pl.; (nicht) der ~ wert (not) worth while; j-m ~ machen give s.o. trouble; sich ~ geben take pains (mit over, with s.th.); ♀los adj. effortless, easy; ♀n v/refl. (ge-, h) take pains, work hard; ♀voll adj. troublesome, hard; laborious.

Mühle ['my:lə] f (-/-n) mill.

'**Müh|sal** f (-/-e) toil, trouble; hardship; ♀sam, ♀selig 1. adj. toilsome, troublesome; difficult; 2. adv. laboriously; with difficulty.

Mulatte [mu'latə] m (-n/-n) mulatto.

Mulde ['muldə] f (-/-n) trough; depression, hollow.

Mull [mul] m (-[e]s/-e) mull.

Müll [myl] m (-[e]s/no pl.) dust, rubbish, refuse, Am. a. garbage; '~abfuhr f removal of refuse; '~eimer m dust-bin, Am. garbage can.

Müller ['mylər] m (-s/-) miller.

'**Müll|fahrer** m dust-man, Am. garbage collector; '~haufen m dustheap; '~kasten m s. Mülleimer; '~kutscher m s. Müllfahrer; '~wa-

gen *m* dust-cart, *Am.* garbage cart.

Multipli|kation ♈ [multiplika-'tsjo:n] *f* (-/-en) multiplication; **⦵zieren** ♈ [~'tsi:rən] *v/t.* (*no* -ge-, *h*) multiply (*mit* by).

Mumie ['mu:mjə] *f* (-/-n) mummy.

Mumps 𝒮 [mumps] *m*, F *f* (-/*no pl.*) mumps.

Mund [munt] *m* (-[e]s/=er) mouth; *den ~ halten* hold one's tongue; *den ~ voll nehmen* talk big; *sich den ~ verbrennen* put one's foot in it; *nicht auf den ~ gefallen sein* have a ready *or* glib tongue; *j-m über den ~ fahren* cut s.o. short; '~**art** *f* dialect; '**⦵artlich** *adj.* dialectal.

Mündel ['myndəl] *m*, *n* (-s/-), *girl:* *a.* *f* (-/-n) ward, pupil; '**⦵sicher** *adj.:* *~e Papiere n/pl.* ♰ gilt-edged securities *pl.*

münden ['myndən] *v/i.* (ge-, h): *~ in* (*acc.*) river, *etc.:* fall *or* flow into; *street, etc.:* run into.

'mund|faul *adj.* too lazy to speak; '~**gerecht** *adj.* palatable (*a. fig.*); '**⦵harmonika** ♪ *f* mouth-organ; '**⦵höhle** *anat.* *f* oral cavity.

mündig 🕮 *adj.* ['myndiç] of age; *~ werden* come of age; '**⦵keit** *f* (-/*no pl.*) majority.

mündlich ['myntliç] **1.** *adj.* oral, verbal; **2.** *adv.* *a.* by word of mouth.

'Mund|pflege *f* oral hygiene; '~**raub** 🕮 *m* theft of comestibles; '~**stück** *n* mouthpiece (*of musical instrument, etc.*); tip (*of cigarette*) *bar*; '**⦵tot** *adj.:* *~ machen* silence *or* gag s.o.

'Mündung *f* (-/-en) mouth; *a.* estuary (*of river*); muzzle (*of fire-arms*).

'Mund|vorrat *m* provisions *pl.*, victuals (*pl.*); '~**wasser** *n* (-s/=) mouth-wash, gargle; '~**werk** F *fig. n:* *ein gutes ~ haben* have the gift of the gab.

Munition [muni'tsjo:n] *f* (-/-en) ammunition.

munkeln F ['muŋkəln] (ge-, *h*) **1.** *v/i.* whisper; **2.** *v/t.* whisper, rumo(u)r; *man munkelt* there is a rumo(u)r afloat; (lively; merry.)

munter *adj.* ['muntər] awake; *fig.:*

Münz|e ['myntsə] *f* (-/-n) coin; (small) change; medal; mint; *für bare ~ nehmen* take at face value; *j-m et. mit gleicher ~ heimzahlen* pay s.o. back in his own coin; '~**einheit** *f* (monetary) unit, standard of

currency; '**⦵en** *v/t.* (ge-, h) coin, mint; *gemünzt sein auf* (*acc.*) be meant for, be aimed at; '~**fernsprecher** *teleph.* *m* coin-box telephone; '~**fuß** *m* standard (of coinage); '~**wesen** *n* monetary system.

mürbe *adj.* ['myrbə] tender; *pastry, etc.:* crisp, short; *meat:* well-cooked; *material:* brittle; F *fig.* worn-out, demoralized; F *j-n ~ machen* break s.o.'s resistance; F *~ werden* give in.

Murmel ['murməl] *f* (-/-n) marble; '**⦵n** *v/t. and v/i.* (ge-, h) mumble, murmur; '~**tier** *zo. n* marmot.

murren ['murən] *v/i.* (ge-, h) grumble, F grouch (*both:* über *acc.*, over, about).

mürrisch *adj.* ['myriʃ] surly, sullen.

Mus [mu:s] *n* (-es/-e) pap; stewed fruit.

Muschel ['muʃəl] *f* (-/-n) *zo.:* mussel; shell, conch; *teleph.* ear-piece.

Museum [mu'ze:um] *n* (-s/Museen) museum.

Musik [mu'zi:k] *f* (-/*no pl.*) music; ~**alienhandlung** *f* [~i'ka:ljən-] *f* music-shop; **⦵alisch** [~i'ka:-liʃ] *adj.* musical; ~**ant** [~i'kant] *m* (-en/-en) musician; ~**automat** *m* juke-box; ~**er** ['mu:zikər] *m* (-s/-) musician; bandsman; ~**instrument** *n* musical instrument; ~**lehrer** *m* music-master; ~**stunde** *f* music-lesson; ~**truhe** *f* radio-gram(ophone), *Am.* radio-phonograph.

musizieren [muzi'tsi:rən] *v/i.* (*no* -ge-) make *or* have music.

Muskat ♀ [mus'ka:t] *m* (-[e]s/-e) nutmeg; ~**nuß** ♀ *f* nutmeg.

Muskel ['muskəl] *m* (-s/-n) muscle; '~**kater** F *m* stiffness and soreness, *Am.* *a.* charley horse; '~**kraft** *f* muscular strength; '~**zerrung** 𝒮 *f* pulled muscle.

Muskul|atur [muskula'tu:r] *f* (-/-en) muscular system, muscles *pl.*; **⦵ös** [~'lø:s] *adj.* muscular, brawny.

Muß [mus] *n* (-/*no pl.*) necessity; *es ist ein ~* it is a must.

Muße ['mu:sə] *f* (-/*no pl.*) leisure; spare time; *mit ~* at one's leisure.

Musselin [musə'li:n] *m* (-s/-e) muslin.

müssen ['mysən] (*irr.*, h) **1.** *v/i.* (ge-): *ich muß* I must; **2.** *v/aux.* (*no* -ge-): *ich muß* I must, I have to;

I am obliged *or* compelled *or* forced to; I am bound to; *ich habe gehen ~* I had to go; *ich müßte (eigentlich) wissen* I ought to know.

müßig *adj.* ['myːsiç] idle; superfluous; useless; **2gang** *m* idleness, laziness; **2gänger** ['~gɛŋər] *m* (-s/-) idler, loafer; lazy-bones.

mußte ['mustə] *pret. of* müssen.

Muster ['mustər] *n* (-s/-) model, example, paragon; design, pattern; specimen; sample; **2betrieb** *m* model factory *or* ✔ farm; **2gatte** *m* model husband; **2gültig, 2haft** **1.** *adj.* model, exemplary, perfect; **2.** *adv.*: *sich ~ benehmen* be on one's best behavio(u)r; **2kollektion** ✝ *f* range of samples; **2n** *v/t.* (ge-, h) examine; eye; ✗ inspect, review; figure, pattern (*fabric, etc.*); **2schutz** *m* protection of patterns and designs; **2ung** *f* (-/-en) examination; ✗ review; pattern (*of fabric, etc.*); **2werk** *n* standard work.

Mut [muːt] *m* (-[e]s/*no pl.*) courage; spirit; pluck; *~ fassen* pluck up courage, summon one's courage; *den ~ sinken lassen* lose courage *or* heart; *guten ~(e)s sein* be of good cheer; **2ig** *adj.* courageous, plucky; **2los** *adj.* discouraged; despondent; **2losigkeit** *f* (-/*no pl.*) discouragement; despondency; **2maßen** ['~maːsən] *v/t.* (ge-, h) suppose, guess, surmise; **2maßlich** *adj.* presumable; supposed; *heir*: presumptive; **2maßung** *f* (-/-en) supposition, surmise; *bloße ~en pl.* guesswork.

Mutter ['mutər] *f* **1.** (-/-) mother; **2.** ⊕ (-/-n) nut; **2brust** *f* mother's breast; **2leib** *m* womb.

mütterlich *adj.* ['mytərliç] motherly; maternal; **2erseits** *adv.* ['~ərzaits] on *or* from one's mother's side; *uncle, etc.*: maternal.

2Mutterliebe *f* motherly love; **2los** *adj.* motherless; **2mal** *n* birth-mark, mole; **2milch** *f* mother's milk; **2schaft** *f* (-/*no pl.*) maternity, motherhood; **2seelenallein** *adj.* all *or* utterly alone; **2söhnchen** ['~zøːnçən] *n* (-s/-) milksop, *sl.* sissy; **2sprache** *f* mother tongue; **2witz** *m* (-es/*no pl.*) mother wit.

Mutwill|e *m* wantonness; mischievousness; **2ig** *adj.* wanton; mischievous; wilful.

Mütze ['mytsə] *f* (-/-n) cap.

Myrrhe ['myrə] *f* (-/-n) myrrh.

Myrte ⚘ ['myrtə] *f* (-/-n) myrtle.

mysteri|ös *adj.* [myster'jøːs] mysterious; **2um** [~'teːrjum] *n* (-s/*Mysterien*) mystery.

Mystifi|kation [mystifika'tsjoːn] *f* (-/-en) mystification; **2zieren** [~'tsiːrən] *v/t.* (*no* -ge-, h) mystify.

Mysti|k ['mystik] *f* (-/*no pl.*) mysticism; **2sch** *adj.* mystic(al).

Myth|e ['myːtə] *f* (-/-n) myth; **2isch** *adj.* mythic; *esp. fig.* mythical; **2ologie** [mytolo'giː] *f* (-/-en) mythology; **2ologisch** *adj.* [myto-'loːgiʃ] mythological; **2os** ['~ɔs] *m* (-/*Mythen*), **2us** ['~us] *m* (-/*Mythen*) myth.

N

na *int.* [na] now!, then!, well!, *Am. a.* hey!

Nabe ['naːbə] *f* (-/-n) hub.

Nabel *anat.* ['naːbəl] *m* (-s/-) navel.

nach [naːx] **1.** *prp.* (*dat.*) direction, *striving*: after; to(wards), for (*a. ~ ... hin or zu*); *succession*: after; *time*: after, past; *manner, measure, example*: according to; *~ Gewicht* by weight; *~ deutschem Geld* in German money; *e-r ~ dem andern* one by one; *fünf Minuten ~ eins* five minutes past one; **2.** *adv.* after;

~ und ~ little by little, gradually; *~ wie vor* now as before, still.

nachahm|en ['naːx⁹aːmən] *v/t.* (*sep.*, -ge-, h) imitate, copy; counterfeit; **2ens|wert** *adj.* worthy of imitation, exemplary; **2er** *m* (-s/-) imitator; **2ung** *f* (-/-en) imitation; copy; counterfeit, fake.

Nachbar ['naxbaːr] *m* (-n, -s/-n), **2in** *f* (-/-nen) neighbo(u)r; **2schaft** *f* (-/-en) neighbo(u)rhood, vicinity. [ment.)

Nachbehandlung ✂ *f* after-treat-

'nachbestell|en v/t. (sep., no -ge-, h) repeat one's order for s.th.; **'2ung** f repeat (order).

'nachbeten v/t. (sep., -ge-, h) echo.

'Nachbildung f copy, imitation; replica; dummy.

'nachblicken v/i. (sep., -ge-, h) look after.

nachdem cj. [na'de:m] after, when; je ~ according as.

'nachdenk|en v/i. (irr. denken, sep., -ge-, h) think (über acc. over, about); reflect, meditate (über acc. on); **'2en** n (-s/no pl.) reflection, meditation; musing; **'~lich** adj. meditative, reflecting; pensive.

'Nachdichtung f free version.

'Nachdruck m 1. (-[e]s/no pl.) stress, emphasis; 2. typ. (-[e]s/-e) reprint; unlawfully: piracy, pirated edition; **'2en** v/t. (sep., -ge-, h) reprint; unlawfully: pirate.

nachdrücklich ['na:xdryklıç] 1. adj. emphatic, energetic; forcible; positive; 2. adv.: ~ betonen emphasize.

nacheifern ['na:x⁹-] v/i. (sep., -ge-, h) emulate s.o.

nacheinander adv. [na:x⁹aɪ'nan-dər] one after another, successively; by or in turns.

nachempfinden ['na:x⁹-] v/t. (irr. empfinden, sep., no -ge-, h) s. nachfühlen.

nacherzähl|en ['na:x⁹-] v/t. (sep., no -ge-, h) repeat; retell; dem Englischen nacherzählt adapted from the English; **2ung** ['na:x⁹-] f repetition; story retold, reproduction.

'Nachfolge f succession; **2n** v/i. (sep., -ge-, h) follow s.o.; j-m im Amt ~ succeed s.o. in his office; **'~r** m (-s/-) follower; successor.

'nachforsch|en v/i. (sep., -ge-, h) investigate; search for; **'2ung** f investigation, inquiry, search.

'Nachfrage f inquiry; † demand; **'2n** v/i. (sep., -ge-, h) inquire (nach after).

'nach|fühlen v/t. (sep., -ge-, h): es j-m ~ feel or sympathize with s.o.; **'~füllen** v/t. (sep., -ge-, h) fill up, refill; **'~geben** v/i. (irr. geben, sep., -ge-, h) give way (dat. to); fig. give in, yield (to); **2gebühr** ['—] f surcharge; **~gehen** v/i. (irr. gehen, sep., -ge-, sein) follow (s.o., business, trade, etc.); pursue (pleasure); attend to (business); investigate

s.th.; watch: be slow; **'2geschmack** m (-[e]s/no pl.) after-taste.

nachgiebig adj. ['na:xgi:bıç] elastic, flexible; fig. a. yielding, compliant; **'2keit** f (-/-en) flexibility; compliance.

'nachgrübeln v/i. (sep., -ge-, h) ponder, brood (both: über acc. over), muse (on).

nachhaltig adj. ['na:xhaltıç] lasting, enduring.

nach'her adv. afterwards; then; bis ~! see you later!, so long!

'Nachhilfe f help, assistance; **'~lehrer** m coach, private tutor; **'~unterricht** m private lesson(s pl.), coaching.

'nach|holen v/t. (sep., -ge-, h) make up for, make good; **'2hut** ✗ f (-/-en) rear(-guard); die ~ bilden bring up the rear (a. fig.); **'~jagen** v/i. (sep., -ge-, sein) chase or pursue s.o.; **'~klingen** v/i. (irr. klingen, sep., -ge-, h) resound, echo.

'Nachkomme m (-n/-n) descendant; ~n pl. esp. ⚖ issue; **'2n** v/i. (irr. kommen, sep., -ge-, sein) follow; come later; obey (order); meet (liabilities); **~nschaft** f (-/-en) descendants pl., esp. ⚖ issue.

'Nachkriegs... post-war.

Nachlaß ['na:xlas] m (Nachlasses/ Nachlasse, Nachlässe) † reduction, discount; assets pl., estate, inheritance (of deceased).

'nachlassen (irr. lassen, sep., -ge-, h) 1. v/t. reduce (price); 2. v/i. deteriorate; slacken, relax; diminish; pain, rain, etc.: abate; storm: calm down; strength: wane; interest: flag.

'nachlässig adj. careless, negligent.

'nach|laufen v/i. (irr. laufen, sep., -ge-, sein) run (dat. after); **'~lesen** v/t. (irr. lesen, sep., -ge-, h) in book: look up; ✗ glean; **'~liefern** † v/t. (sep., -ge-, h) deliver subsequently; repeat delivery of; **'~lösen** v/t. (sep., -ge-, h): e-e Fahrkarte ~ take a supplementary ticket; buy a ticket en route; **'~machen** v/t. (sep., -ge-, h) imitate (j-m et. s.o. in s.th.); copy; counterfeit, forge; **'~messen** v/t. (irr. messen, sep., -ge-, h) measure again.

'Nachmittag m afternoon; **'2s** adv. in the afternoon; **'~svorstellung** thea. f matinée.

Nach|nahme ['na:xna:mə] f (-/-n)

cash on delivery, *Am.* collect on delivery; *per ~ schicken* send C.O.D.; '**~name** *m* surname, last name; '**~porto** ⚖ *n* surcharge.

'**nach|prüfen** *v/t.* (*sep.*, -ge-, *h*) verify; check; '**~rechnen** *v/t.* (*sep.*, -ge-, *h*) reckon over again; check (*bill*).

'**Nachrede** *f*: *üble ~* 🖞 defamation (of character); *oral*: slander, *written*: libel; '**2n** *v/t.* (*sep.*, -ge-, *h*): *j-m Übles ~* slander s.o.

Nachricht ['na:xriçt] *f* (-/-en) news; message; report; information, notice; *~ geben s. benachrichtigen*; '**~enagentur** *f* news agency; '**~endienst** *m* news service; ✗ intelligence service; '**~ensprecher** *m* newscaster; '**~enwesen** *n* (-s/*no pl.*) communications *pl.*

'**nachrücken** *v/i.* (*sep.*, -ge-, *sein*) move along.

'**Nach|ruf** *m* obituary (notice); '**~ruhm** *m* posthumous fame.

'**nachsagen** *v/t.* (*sep.*, -ge-, *h*) repeat; *man sagt ihm nach, daß he is* said to *inf.*

'**Nachsaison** *f* dead *or* off season.

'**nachschicken** *v/t.* (*sep.*, -ge-, *h*) *s. nachsenden.*

'**nachschlage|n** *v/t.* (*irr. schlagen, sep.*, -ge-, *h*) consult (*book*); look up (*word*); '**2werk** *n* reference-book.

'**Nach|schlüssel** *m* skeleton key; '**~schrift** *f* in *letter*: postscript; '**~schub** *esp.* ✗ *m* supplies *pl.*; '**~schubweg** ✗ *m* supply line.

'**nach|sehen** (*irr. sehen, sep.*, -ge-, *h*) **1.** *v/i.* look after; *~, ob* (go and) see whether; **2.** *v/t.* look after; examine, inspect; check; overhaul (*machine*); *s. nachschlagen*; *j-m et. ~* indulge s.o. in s.th.; '**~senden** *v/t.* ([*irr. senden,*] *sep.*, -ge-, *h*) send after; send on, forward (*letter*) (*j-m to* s.o.).

'**Nachsicht** *f* indulgence; '**2ig** *adj.*, '**2svoll** *adj.* indulgent, forbearing.

'**Nachsilbe** *gr. f* suffix.

'**nach|sinnen** *v/i.* (*irr. sinnen, sep.*, -ge-, *h*) muse, meditate (*über acc.* [*up*]*on*); '**~sitzen** *v/i.* (*irr. sitzen, sep.*, -ge-, *h*) *pupil*: be kept in.

'**Nach|sommer** *m* St. Martin's summer, *esp. Am.* Indian summer; '**~speise** *f* dessert; '**~spiel** *fig. n* sequel.

'**nach|spionieren** *v/i.* (*sep.*, *no* -ge-, *h*) spy (*dat.* *on*); '**~sprechen** *v/i. and v/t.* (*irr. sprechen, sep.*, -ge-, *h*) repeat; '**~spülen** *v/t.* (*sep.*, -ge-, *h*) rinse; '**~spüren** *v/i.* (*sep.*, -ge-, *h*) (*dat.*) track, trace.

nächst [nɛ:çst] **1.** *adj.* succession, *time*: next; *distance, relation*: nearest; **2.** *prp.* (*dat.*) next to, next after; '**2beste** *m, f, n* (-*n*/-*n*): *der* (*die*) *~* anyone; *das ~* anything; *er fragte den ~n he asked the next person he met.

'**nachstehen** *v/i.* (*irr. stehen, sep.*, -ge-, *h*): *j-m in nichts ~* be in no way inferior to s.o.

'**nachstell|en** (*sep.*, -ge-, *h*) **1.** *v/t.* place behind; put back (*watch*); ⊕ adjust (*screw, etc.*); **2.** *v/i.*: *j-m ~* be after s.o.; '**2ung** *fig. f* persecution.

'**Nächstenliebe** *f* charity.

'**nächstens** *adv.* shortly, (very) soon, before long.

'**nach|streben** *v/i.* (*sep.*, -ge-, *h*) *s. nacheifern*; '**~suchen** *v/i.* (*sep.*, -ge-, *h*): *~ um* apply for, seek.

Nacht [naxt] *f* (-/⸚e) night; *bei ~, des ~s s. nachts*; '**~arbeit** *f* night-work; '**~asyl** *n* night-shelter; '**~ausgabe** *f* night edition (*of newspaper*); '**~dienst** *m* night-duty.

'**Nachteil** *m* disadvantage, drawback; *im ~ sein* be at a disadvantage; '**2ig** *adj.* disadvantageous.

'**Nacht|essen** *n* supper; '**~falter** *zo. m* (-s/-) moth; '**~gebet** *n* evening prayer; '**~geschirr** *n* chamber-pot; '**~hemd** *n* night-gown, *Am. a.* night robe; *for men*: night-shirt.

Nachtigall *orn.* ['naxtigal] *f* (-/-en) nightingale.

'**Nachtisch** *m* (-es/*no pl.*) sweet, dessert.

'**Nachtlager** *n* (a) lodging for the night; bed.

nächtlich *adj.* ['nɛçtliç] nightly, nocturnal.

'**Nacht|lokal** *n* night-club; '**~mahl** *n* supper; '**~portier** *m* night-porter; '**~quartier** *n* night-quarters *pl.*

Nachtrag ['na:xtra:k] *m* (-[e]s/⸚e) supplement; '**2en** *v/t.* (*irr. tragen, sep.*, -ge-, *h*) carry (*j-m et. s.th. after* s.o.); add; † post up (*ledger*); *j-m et. ~* bear s.o. a grudge; '**2end** *adj.* unforgiving, resentful.

namenlos

nachträglich *adj.* ['nɑːxtrɛːklɪç] additional; subsequent.

nachts *adv.* [naxts] at *or* by night.

'Nacht|schicht *f* night-shift; **'2~schlafend** *adj.:* zu ~er Zeit in the middle of the night; **'~schwärmer** *fig. m* night-reveller; **'~tisch** *m* bedside table; **'~topf** *m* chamber-pot; **'~vorstellung** *thea. f* night performance; **'~wache** *f* night-watch; **'~wächter** *m* (night-)watchman; **~wandler** ['~vandlər] *m* (-s/-) sleep-walker; **'~zeug** *n* night-things *pl.*

'nachwachsen *v/i.* (irr. wachsen, sep., -ge-, sein) grow again.

'Nachwahl *parl. f* by-election.

Nachweis ['nɑːxvaɪs] *m* (-es/-e) proof, evidence; **'2bar** *adj.* demonstrable; traceable; **2en** ['~zən] *v/t.* (irr. weisen, sep., -ge-, h) point out, show; trace; prove; **'~lich** *adj. s.* nachweisbar.

'Nach|welt *f* posterity; **'~wirkung** *f* after-effect; consequences *pl.*; aftermath; **'~wort** *n* (-[e]s/-e) epilog(ue); **'~wuchs** *m* (-[e]s/no pl.) rising generation.

'nach|zahlen *v/t.* (sep., -ge-, h) pay in addition; **'~zählen** *v/t.* (sep., -ge-, h) count over (again), check; **'2zahlung** *f* additional payment.

Nachzügler ['nɑːxtsyːglər] *m* (-s/-) straggler, late-comer.

Nacken ['nakən] *m* (-s/-) nape (of the neck), neck.

nackt *adj.* [nakt] naked, nude; bare (*a. fig.*); young birds: unfledged; *truth:* plain.

Nadel ['nɑːdəl] *f* (-/-n) needle; pin; brooch; **'~arbeit** *f* needlework; **'~baum** ♀ *m* conifer(ous tree); **'~stich** *m* prick; stitch; *fig.* pinprick.

Nagel ['nɑːgəl] *m* (-s/~) anat., ⊕ nail; *of wood:* peg; spike; stud; die Arbeit brennt mir auf den Nägeln it's a rush job; **'~haut** *f* cuticle; **'~lack** *m* nail varnish; **'2n** *v/t.* (ge-, h) nail (an *or* auf acc. to); **'~necessaire** ['~nesɛːr] *n* (-s/-s) manicure-case; **'2neu** F *adj.* bran(d)-new; **'~pflege** *f* manicure.

nage|n ['nɑːgən] (ge-, h) **1.** *v/i.* gnaw; ~ an (dat.) gnaw at; pick (bone); **2.** *v/t.* gnaw; **'2tier** *zo. n* rodent, gnawer.

nah *adj.* [nɑː] near, close (bei to); nearby; *danger:* imminent.

'Näharbeit ['nɛː-] *f* needlework, sewing.

'Nahaufnahme *f film:* close-up.

nahe *adj.* ['nɑːə] *s.* nah.

Nähe ['nɛːə] *f* (-/no pl.) nearness, proximity; vicinity; in der ~ close by.

'nahe|gehen *v/i.* (irr. gehen, sep., -ge-, sein) (dat.) affect, grieve; **'~kommen** *v/i.* (irr. kommen, sep., -ge-, sein) (dat.) approach; get at (truth); **'~legen** *v/t.* (sep., -ge-, h) suggest; **'~liegen** *v/i.* (irr. liegen, sep., -ge-, h) suggest itself, be obvious.

nahen ['nɑːən] **1.** *v/i.* (ge-, sein) approach; **2.** *v/refl.* (ge-, h) approach (j-m s.o.).

nähen ['nɛːən] *v/t. and v/i.* (ge-, h) sew, stitch.

näher *adj.* ['nɛːər] nearer, closer; *road:* shorter; das Nähere (further) particulars *pl. or* details *pl.*

'Näherin *f* (-/-nen) seamstress.

'nähern *v/t.* (ge-, h) approach (dat. to); sich ~ approach (j-m s.o.).

'nahezu *adv.* nearly, almost.

'Nahkampf ✗ *m* close combat.

nahm [nɑːm] *pret. of* nehmen.

'Näh|maschine *f* sewing-machine; **'~nadel** *f* sewing-needle.

nähren ['nɛːrən] *v/t.* (ge-, h) nourish (*a. fig.*), feed; nurse (child); sich ~ von live *or* feed on.

nahrhaft *adj.* ['nɑːrhaft] nutritious, nourishing.

'Nahrung *f* (-/no pl.) food, nourishment, nutriment.

'Nahrungs|aufnahme *f* intake of food; **'~mittel** *n/pl.* food(-stuff), victuals *pl.*

'Nährwert *m* nutritive value.

Naht [nɑːt] *f* (-/~e) seam; ✁ suture.

'Nahverkehr *m* local traffic.

'Nähzeug *n* sewing-kit.

naiv *adj.* [na'iːf] naïve, naive, simple; **2ität** [naivi'tɛːt] *f* (-/no pl.) naïveté, naivety, simplicity.

Name ['nɑːmə] *m* (-ns/-n) name; im ~n (gen.) on behalf of; dem ~n nach nominal(ly), in name only; dem ~n nach kennen know by name; die Dinge beim rechten ~n nennen call a spade a spade; darf ich um Ihren ~n bitten? may I ask your name?

'namen|los *adj.* nameless, anonymous; *fig.* unutterable; '⁓s **1.** *adv.* named, by the name of, called; **2.** *prp.* (*gen.*) in the name of.

'**Namens|tag** *m* name-day; '⁓**vetter** *m* namesake; '⁓**zug** *m* signature.

namentlich ['nɑːməntlɪç] **1.** *adj.* nominal; **2.** *adv.* by name; especially, in particular.

'**namhaft** *adj.* notable; considerable; ⁓ **machen** name.

nämlich ['nɛːmlɪç] **1.** *adj. the* same; **2.** *adv.* namely, that is (to say).

nannte ['nantə] *pret.* of **nennen**.

Napf [napf] *m* (-[e]s/⸚e) bowl, basin.

Narb|e ['narbə] *f* (-/-n) scar; '⁓**ig** *adj.* scarred; *leather*: grained.

Narko|se ⚕ [nar'koːzə] *f* (-/-n) narcosis; ⁓**tisieren** [⸚oti'ziːrən] *v/t.* (*no* -ge-, *h*) narcotize.

Narr [nar] *m* (-en/-en) fool; jester; **zum** ⸚**en halten** = ⁇**en** *v/t.* (ge-, *h*) make a fool of, fool.

'**Narren|haus** *F n* madhouse; '⁓**kappe** *f* fool's-cap; '⁓**sicher** *adj.* foolproof.

'**Narrheit** *f* (-/-en) folly.

Närrin ['nɛrɪn] *f* (-/-nen) fool, foolish woman.

'**närrisch** *adj.* foolish, silly; odd.

Narzisse ⚘ [nar'tsɪsə] *f* (-/-n) narcissus; **gelbe** ⁓ daffodil.

nasal *adj.* [na'zɑːl] nasal; ⁓**e Sprechweise** twang.

nasch|en ['naʃən] (ge-, *h*) **1.** *v/i.* nibble (*an dat.* at); **gern** ⁓ **haben** a sweet tooth; **2.** *v/t.* nibble; eat *s.th.* on the sly; ⁇**ereien** [⸚'raɪən] *f/pl.* dainties *pl.*, sweets *pl.*; '⁓**haft** *adj.* fond of dainties *or* sweets.

Nase ['nɑːzə] *f* (-/-n) nose; **die** ⁓ **rümpfen** turn up one's nose (*über acc.* at).

näseln ['nɛːzəln] *v/i.* (ge-, *h*) speak through the nose, nasalize; snuffle.

'**Nasen|bluten** *n* (-s/*no pl.*) nosebleeding; '⁓**loch** *n* nostril; '⁓**spitze** *f* tip of the nose.

naseweis *adj.* ['nɑːzəvaɪs] pert, saucy.

nasführen ['nɑːs-] *v/t.* (ge-, *h*) fool, dupe.

Nashorn *zo.* ['nɑːs-] *n* rhinoceros.

naß *adj.* [nas] wet; damp, moist.

Nässe ['nɛsə] *f* (-/*no pl.*) wet(ness); moisture; ⚗ humidity; '⁓**n** (ge-, *h*) **1.** *v/t.* wet; moisten; **2.** ⚕ *v/i.* discharge.

'**naßkalt** *adj.* damp and cold, raw.

Nation [na'tsjoːn] *f* (-/-en) nation.

national *adj.* [natsjo'nɑːl] national; ⁇**hymne** *f* national anthem; ⁇**ismus** [⸚a'lɪsmus] *m* (-/*Nationalismen*) nationalism; ⁇**ität** [⸚ali'tɛːt] *f* (-/-en) nationality; ⁇**mannschaft** *f* national team.

Natter ['natər] *f* (-/-n) *zo.* adder, viper; *fig.* serpent.

Natur [na'tuːr] *f* **1.** (-/*no pl.*) nature; **2.** (-/-en) constitution; temper(ament), disposition, nature; **von** ⁓ by nature.

Naturalien [natu'rɑːljən] *pl.* natural produce *sg.*; **in** ⁓ in kind.

naturalisieren [naturali'ziːrən] *v/t.* (*no* -ge-, *h*) naturalize.

Naturalismus [natura'lɪsmus] *m* (-/*no pl.*) naturalism.

Naturanlage [na'tuːr⁇] *f* (natural) disposition.

Naturell [natu'rel] *n* (-s/-e) natural disposition, nature, temper.

Na'tur|ereignis *n*, **⁓erscheinung** *f* phenomenon; **⁓forscher** *m* naturalist, scientist; ⁇**gemäß** *adj.* natural; **⁓geschichte** *f* natural history; **⁓gesetz** *n* law of nature, natural law; ⁇**getreu** *adj.* true to nature; life-like; **⁓kunde** *f* (natural) science.

natürlich [na'tyːrlɪç] **1.** *adj.* natural; genuine; innate; unaffected; **2.** *adv.* naturally, of course.

Na'tur|produkte *n/pl.* natural products *pl.* or produce *sg.*; **⁓schutz** *m* wild-life conservation; **⁓schutzgebiet** *n*, **⁓schutzpark** *m* national park, wild-life (p)reserve; **⁓trieb** *m* instinct; **⁓wissenschaft** *f* (natural) science; **⁓wissenschaftler** *m* (natural) scientist.

Nebel ['neːbəl] *m* (-s/-) fog; mist; haze; smoke; ⁇**haft** *fig. adj.* nebulous, hazy, dim; '⁓**horn** *n* fog-horn.

neben *prp.* (*dat.*; *acc.*) ['neːbən] beside, by (the side of); near to; against, compared with; apart *or* *Am. a.* aside from, besides.

neben|'an *adv.* next door; close by; ⁇**anschluß** *teleph.* ['neːbən⁇] *m* extension (line); ⁇**arbeit** ['neːbən⁇] *f* extra work; ⁇**ausgaben** ['neːbən⁇] *f/pl.* incidental expenses *pl.*, extras *pl.*; ⁇**ausgang** ['neːbən⁇] *m* side-exit, side-door; '⁇**bedeutung** *f* secondary meaning, connotation;

~'bei adv. by the way; besides; '2beruf m side-line; '~beruflich adv. as a side-line; in one's spare time; '2beschäftigung f s. Nebenberuf; '2buhler ['~buːlər] m (-s/-) rival; ~ei'nander adv. side by side; ~ bestehen co-exist; '2eingang ['neːbən²-] m side-entrance; 2einkünfte ['neːbən²-] pl., 2einnahmen ['neːbən²-] f/pl. casual emoluments pl., extra income; 2erscheinung ['neːbən²-] f accompaniment; '2fach n subsidiary subject, Am. minor (subject); '2fluß m tributary (river); '2gebäude n annex(e); outhouse; '2geräusch n radio: atmospherics pl., interference, jamming; '2gleis 🚂 n siding, side-track; '2handlung thea. f underplot; '2haus n adjoining house; ~'her adv.], ~'hin adv. by his or her side; s. nebenbei; '2kläger 🜨 m co-plaintiff; '2kosten pl. extras pl.; '2mann m person next to one; '2produkt n by-product; '2rolle f minor part (a. thea.); '2sache f minor matter, side issue; '~sächlich adj. subordinate, incidental, unimportant; '2satz gr. m subordinate clause; '2stehend adj. in the margin; '2stelle f teleph. agency; teleph. extension; '2straße f by-street, by-road; '2strecke 🚂 f branch line; '2tisch m next table; '2tür f side-door; '2verdienst m incidental or extra earnings pl.; '2zimmer n adjoining room.

'neblig adj. foggy, misty, hazy.

nebst prp. (dat.) [neːpst] together with, besides; including.

neck|en ['nɛkən] v/t. (ge-, h) tease, banter, sl. kid; 2erei [~'raɪ] f (-/-en) teasing, banter; '~isch adj. playful; droll.

Neffe ['nɛfə] m (-n/-n) nephew.

negativ [nega'tiːf] 1. adj. negative; 2. 2 n (-s/-e) negative.

Neger ['neːgər] m (-s/-) negro; '~in f (-/-nen) negress.

nehmen ['neːmən] v/t. (irr., ge-, h) take; receive; charge (money); zu sich ~ take, have (meal); j-m et. ~ take s.th. from s.o.; ein Ende ~ come to an end; es sich nicht ~ lassen zu inf. insist upon ger.; streng genommen strictly speaking.

Neid [naɪt] m (-[e]s/no pl.) envy; 2en ['naɪdən] v/t. (ge-, h): j-m et.

~ envy s.o. s.th.; ~er ['~dər] m (-s/-) envious person; ~hammel F ['naɪt-] m dog in the manger; 2isch adj. ['~diʃ] envious (auf acc. of); ~los adj. ['naɪt-] ungrudging.

Neige ['naɪgə] f (-/-n) decline; barrel: dregs pl.; glass: heeltap; zur ~ gehen (be on the) decline; esp. 🌙 run short; 2n (ge-, h) 1. v/t. and v/refl. bend, incline; 2. v/i.: er neigt zu Übertreibungen he is given to exaggeration.

'Neigung f (-/-en) inclination (a. fig.); slope, incline.

nein adv. [naɪn] no. [tar.]

Nektar ['nɛktaːr] m (-s/no pl.) nec-]

Nelke 🌷 ['nɛlkə] f (-/-n) carnation, pink; spice: clove.

nennen ['nɛnən] v/t. (irr., ge-, h) name; call; term; mention; nominate (candidate); sports: enter (für for); sich ... ~ be called ...; '~swert adj. worth mentioning.

'Nenn|er ♈ m (-s/-) denominator; '~ung f (-/-en) naming; mentioning; nomination (of candidates); sports: entry; '~wert m nominal or face value; zum ~ 🌙 at par.

Neon 🜍 ['neːɔn] n (-s/no pl.) neon; '~röhre f neon tube.

Nerv [nɛrf] m (-s/-en) nerve; j-m auf die ~en fallen or gehen get on s.o.'s nerves.

'Nerven|arzt m neurologist; '2aufreibend adj. trying; '~heilanstalt f mental hospital; '~kitzel m (-s/no pl.) thrill, sensation; '2krank adj. neurotic; '2leidend adj. neuropathic, neurotic; '~schwäche f nervous debility; '2stärkend adj. tonic; '~system n nervous system; '~zusammenbruch m nervous breakdown.

nerv|ig adj. ['nɛrviç] sinewy; ~ös adj. [~'vøːs] nervous; 2osität [~ozi'tɛːt] f (-/no pl.) nervousness.

Nerz zo. ['nɛrts] m (-es/-e) mink.

Nessel 🌿 ['nɛsəl] f (-/-n) nettle.

Nest [nɛst] n (-es/-er) nest; F fig. bed; F fig. hick or one-horse town.

nett adj. [nɛt] nice; neat, pretty, Am. a. cute; pleasant; kind.

netto 🌙 adv. ['nɛto] net, clear.

Netz [nɛts] n (-es/-e) net; fig. network; '~anschluß 🔌 m mains connection, power supply; '~haut anat. f retina; '~spannung 🔌 f mains voltage.

neu adj. [nɔʏ] new; fresh; recent; modern; ~ere Sprachen modern languages; ~este Nachrichten latest news; von ~em anew, afresh; ein ~es Leben beginnen turn over a new leaf; was gibt es Neues? what is the news?, Am. what is new?

'Neu|anschaffung f (-/-en) recent acquisition; '**2artig** adj. novel; '~auflage typ. f, '~ausgabe typ. f new edition; reprint; '~bau m (-[e]s/-ten) new building; '2bearbeitet adj. revised; '~e m (-n/-n) new man; new-comer; novice; '2entdeckt adj. recently discovered.

neuer|dings adv. ['nɔʏər'dɪŋs] of late, recently; '2er m (-s/-) innovator.

Neuerscheinung ['nɔʏ⁹-] f new book or publication.

'Neuerung f (-/-en) innovation.

'neu|geboren adj. new-born; '~gestalten v/t. (sep., -ge-, h) reorganize; '2gestaltung f reorganization; '2gier f, 2gierde ['~də] f (-/no pl.) curiosity, inquisitiveness; '~gierig adj. curious (auf acc. about, of), inquisitive (nach acc. about), inquisitive, sl. nos(e)y; ich bin ~, ob I wonder whether or if; '2heit f (-/-en) newness, freshness; novelty.

'Neuigkeit f (-/-en) (e-e a piece of) news.

'Neu|jahr n New Year('s Day); '~land n (-[e]s/no pl.): ~ erschließen break fresh ground (a. fig.); '2lich adv. the other day, recently; '~ling m (-s/-e) novice; contp. greenhorn; '2modisch adj. fashionable; '~mond m (-[e]s/no pl.) new moon.

neun adj. [nɔʏn] nine; '~te adj. ninth; '2tel n (-s/-) ninth part; '~tens adv. ninthly; '~zehn adj. nineteen; '~zehnte adj. nineteenth; '~zig adj. ['~tsɪç] ninety; '~zigste adj. ninetieth.

'Neu|philologe m student or teacher of modern languages; '~regelung f reorganization, rearrangement.

neutr|al adj. [nɔʏ'traːl] neutral; **2alität** [~ali'tɛːt] f (-/no pl.) neutrality; **2um** gr. ['nɔʏtrum] n (-s/Neutra, Neutren) neuter.

'neu|vermählt adj. newly married; die 2en pl. the newly-weds pl.; '2wahl parl. f new election; '~wertig adj. as good as new; '2zeit f (-/no pl.) modern times pl.

nicht adv. [nɪçt] not; auch ~ nor; ~ anziehend unattractive; ~ besser no better; ~ bevollmächtigt non-commissioned; ~ einlösbar ✝ inconvertible; ~ erscheinen fail to attend.

'Nicht|achtung f disregard; '2amtlich adj. unofficial; '~angriffspakt pol. m non-aggression pact; '~annahme f non-acceptance; '~befolgung f non-observance.

Nichte ['nɪçtə] f (-/-n) niece.

'nichtig adj. null, void; invalid; vain, futile; für ~ erklären declare null and void, annul; '2keit f (-/-en) nullity; vanity, futility.

'Nichtraucher m non-smoker.

nichts [nɪçts] 1. indef. pron. nothing, naught, not anything; 2. 2 n (-/no pl.) nothing(ness); fig.: nonentity; void; '~ahnend adj. unsuspecting; '2destoweniger adv. nevertheless; '~nutzig adj. ['~nutsɪç] good-for-nothing, worthless; '~sagend adj. insignificant; '2tuer ['~tuːər] m (-s/-) idler; '~würdig adj. vile, base, infamous.

'Nicht|vorhandensein n absence; lack; '~wissen f ignorance.

nick|en ['nɪkən] v/i. (ge-, h) nod; bow; '2erchen F n (-s/-): ein ~ machen take a nap, have one's forty winks.

nie adv. [niː] never, at no time.

nieder ['niːdər] 1. adj. low; base, mean, vulgar; value, rank: inferior; 2. adv. down.

'Nieder|gang m decline; '2gedrückt adj. dejected, downcast; '2gehen v/i. (irr. gehen, sep., -ge-, sein) go down; ✈ descend; storm: break; '2geschlagen adj. dejected, downcast; '2hauen v/t. (irr. hauen, sep., -ge-, h) cut down; '2kommen v/i. (irr. kommen, sep., -ge-, sein) be confined; be delivered (mit of); '~kunft ['~kunft] f (-/⁻e) confinement, delivery; '~lage f defeat; ✝ warehouse; branch; '2lassen v/t. (irr. lassen, sep., -ge-, h) let down; sich ~ settle (down); bird: alight; sit down; establish o.s.; settle (in dat. at); '~lassung f (-/-en) establishment; settlement; branch, agency; '2legen v/t. (sep., -ge-, h) lay or put down; resign (position); retire from (business); abdicate; die Arbeit ~ (go on) strike, down tools,

Am. F *a.* walk out; *sich* ~ lie down, go to bed; '2**machen** *v/t.* (*sep.*, -ge-, h) cut down; massacre; '~**schlag** *m* 🔫 precipitate; sediment; precipitation (*of rain, etc.*); *radioactive:* fall-out; *boxing:* knockdown, knock-out; '2**schlagen** *v/t.* (*irr. schlagen, sep.*, -ge-, h) knock down; *boxing: a.* floor; cast down (*eyes*); suppress; put down, crush (*rebellion*); 🔫 quash; *sich* ~ 🔫 precipitate; '2**schmettern** *fig. v/t.* (*sep.*, -ge-, h) crush; '2**setzen** *v/t.* (*sep.*, -ge-, h) set or put down; *sich* ~ sit down; *birds:* perch, alight; '2**strecken** *v/t.* (*sep.*, -ge-, h) lay low, strike to the ground; floor; '2**trächtig** *adj.* base, mean; F beastly; '~**ung** *f* (-/-en) lowlands *pl.*

niedlich *adj.* ['ni:tliç] neat, nice, pretty, *Am. a.* cute.   [nail.]
Niednagel ['ni:t-] *m* agnail, hang-
niedrig *adj.* ['ni:driç] low (*a. fig.*); moderate; *fig.* mean, base.
niemals *adv.* ['ni:ma:ls] never, at no time.
niemand *indef. pron.* ['ni:mant] nobody, no one, none; '2**sland** *n* (-[e]s/no pl.) no man's land.
Niere ['ni:rə] *f* (-/-n) kidney; '~**nbraten** *m* loin of veal.
niesel|n F ['ni:zəln] *v/i.* (ge-, h) drizzle; '2**regen** F *m* drizzle.
niesen ['ni:zən] *v/i.* (ge-, h) sneeze.
Niet ⊕ ['ni:t] *m* (-[e]s/-e) rivet; '~**e** *f* (-/-n) *lottery:* blank; F *fig.* washout; '2**en** ⊕ *v/t.* (ge-, h) rivet.
Nilpferd *zo.* ['ni:l-] *n* hippopotamus.
Nimbus ['nimbus] *m* (-/-se) halo (*a. fig.*), nimbus.
nimmer *adv.* ['nimər] never; '~**mehr** *adv.* nevermore; '2**satt** *m* (-, -[e]s/-e) glutton; '2**wiedersehen** F *n: auf* ~ never to meet again; *er verschwand auf* ~ he left for good.   [dat. at.)
nippen ['nipən] *v/i.* (ge-, h) sip (*an*)
Nipp|es ['nipəs] *pl.*, '~**sachen** *pl.* (k)nick-(k)nacks *pl.*
nirgend|s *adv.* ['nirgənts], '~**(s)wo** *adv.* nowhere.
Nische ['ni:ʃə] *f* (-/-n) niche, recess.
nisten ['nistən] *v/i.* (ge-, h) nest.
Niveau [ni'vo:] *n* (-s/-s) level; *fig. a.* standard.
nivellieren [nivε'li:rən] *v/t.* (*no* -ge-, h) level, grade.

Nixe ['niksə] *f* (-/-n) water-nymph, mermaid.
noch [nɔx] **1.** *adv.* still; yet; ~ *ein* another, one more; ~ *einmal* once more or again; ~ *etwas* something more; ~ *etwas?* anything else?; ~ *heute* this very day; ~ *immer* still; ~ *nicht* not yet; ~ *nie* never before; ~ *so ever so;* ~ *im 19. Jahrhundert* as late as the 19th century; *es wird* ~ *2 Jahre dauern* it will take two more or another two years; **2.** *cj.: s. weder;* '~**malig** *adj.* ['~ma:liç] repeated; '~**mals** *adv.* ['~ma:ls] once more or again.
Nomad|e [no'ma:də] *m* (-n/-n) nomad; '2**isch** *adj.* nomadic.
Nominativ *gr.* ['no:minati:f] *m* (-s/-e) nominative (case).
nominieren [nomi'ni:rən] *v/t.* (*no* -ge-, h) nominate.
Nonne ['nɔnə] *f* (-/-n) nun; '~**nkloster** *n* nunnery, convent.
Nord *geogr.* [nɔrt], '~**en** *m* (-s/no pl.) north; '2**isch** *adj.* ['~diʃ] northern.
nördlich *adj.* ['nœrtliç] northern, northerly.
'**Nord|licht** *n* northern lights *pl.*; '~**ost(en** *m*) north-east; '~**pol** *m* North Pole; '2**wärts** *adv.* ['~vɛrts] northward(s), north; '~**west(en** *m*) north-west.
nörg|eln ['nœrgəln] *v/i.* (ge-, h) nag, carp (*an dat.* at); grumble; '2**ler** ['~lər] *m* (-s/-) faultfinder, grumbler.
Norm [nɔrm] *f* (-/-en) standard; rule; norm.
normal *adj.* [nɔr'ma:l] normal; regular; *measure, weight, time:* standard; ~**isieren** [~ali'zi:rən] *v/refl.* (*no* -ge-, h) return to normal.
'**norm|en** *v/t.* (ge-, h), ~**ieren** [~'mi:rən] *v/t.* (*no* -ge-, h) standardize.
Not [no:t] *f* (-/¨e) need, want; necessity; difficulty, trouble; misery; danger, emergency, distress (*a.* ⚓); ~ *leiden* suffer privations; *in* ~ *geraten* become destitute, get into trouble; *in* ~ *sein* to be in trouble; *zur* ~ at a pinch; *es tut not, daß* it is necessary that.   [notary.]
Notar [no'ta:r] *m* (-s/-e) (public)
'**Not|ausgang** *m* emergency exit; '~**behelf** *m* makeshift, expedient, stopgap; '~**bremse** *f* emergency

brake; **'brücke** f temporary bridge; **~durft** ['~durft] f (-/no pl.): s-e ~ verrichten relieve o.s.; **'2dürftig** adj. scanty, poor; temporary.

Note ['no:tə] f (-/-n) note (a. ♪); pol. note, memorandum; school: mark.

'Noten|bank ✝ f bank of issue; **'~schlüssel** ♪ m clef; **'~system** ♪ n staff.

'Not|fall m case of need, emergency; **'2falls** adv. if necessary; **'2gedrungen** adv. of necessity, needs.

notier|en [no'ti:rən] v/t. (no -ge-, h) make a note of, note (down); ✝ quote; **2ung** ✝ f (-/-en) quotation.

nötig adj. ['nø:tiç] necessary; ~ haben need; **~en** ['~gən] v/t. (ge-, h) force, oblige, compel; press, urge (guest); **'~en'falls** adv. if necessary; **'2ung** f (-/-en) compulsion; pressing; ♔ intimidation.

Notiz [no'ti:ts] f (-/-en) notice, note; memorandum; ~ nehmen von take notice of; pay attention to; keine ~ nehmen von ignore; sich ~en machen take notes; **~block** m pad, Am. a. scratch pad; **~buch** n notebook.

'Not|lage f distress; emergency; **'2landen** ✈ v/i. (-ge-, sein) make a forced or emergency landing; **'~landung** ✈ f forced or emergency landing; **'2leidend** adj. needy, destitute; distressed; **'~lösung** f expedient; **'~lüge** f white lie.

notorisch adj. [no'to:riʃ] notorious.

'Not|ruf teleph. m emergency call; **'~signal** n emergency or distress signal; **'~sitz** mot. m dick(e)y(-seat), Am. a. rumble seat; **'~stand** m emergency; **'~standsarbeiten** f/pl. relief works pl.; **'~standsgebiet** n distressed area; **'~standsgesetze** n/pl. emergency laws pl.; **'~verband** m first-aid dressing; **'~verordnung** f emergency decree; **'~wehr** f self-defen|ce, Am. -se; **'2wendig** adj. necessary; **'~wendigkeit** f (-/-en) necessity, **'~zucht** f (-/no pl.) rape.

Novelle [no'vɛlə] f (-/-n) short story, novella; parl. amendment.

November [no'vɛmbər] m (-[s]/-) November. [time.)

Nu [nu:] m (-/no pl.): im ~ in no

Nuance [ny'ã:sə] f (-/-n) shade.

nüchtern adj. ['nyçtərn] empty, fasting; sober (a. fig.); matter-of-fact; writings: jejune; prosaic; cool; plain; **'2heit** f (-/no pl.) sobriety; fig. soberness.

Nudel ['nu:dəl] f (-/-n) noodle.

null [nul] **1.** adj. null; nil; tennis: love; ~ und nichtig null and void; **2.** 2 f (-/-en) nought, cipher (a. fig.); zero; **2punkt** m zero.

numerieren [numə'ri:rən] v/t. (no -ge-, h) number; numerierter Platz reserved seat.

Nummer ['numər] f (-/-n) number (a. newspaper, thea.); size (of shoes, etc.); thea. turn; sports: event; **'~nschild** mot. n number-plate.

nun [nu:n] **1.** adv. now, at present; then; ~? well?; ~ also well then; **2.** int. now then!; **'~mehr** adv. now.

nur adv. [nu:r] only; (nothing) but; merely; ~ noch only.

Nuß [nus] f (-/Nüsse) nut; **'~kern** m kernel; **'~knacker** m (-s/-) nutcracker; **'~schale** f nutshell.

Nüstern ['ny:stərn] f/pl. nostrils pl.

nutz adj. [nuts] s. nütze; **'2anwendung** f practical application; **'~bar** adj. useful; **'~bringend** adj. profitable.

nütze adj. ['nytsə] useful; zu nichts ~ sein be of no use, be good for nothing.

Nutzen ['nutsən] **1.** m (-s/-) use; profit, gain; advantage; utility; **2.** 2 v/i. and v/t. (ge-, h) s. nützen.

nützen ['nytsən] (ge-, h) **1.** v/i.: zu et. ~ be of use or useful for s.th.; j-m ~ serve s.o.; es nützt nichts zu inf. it is no use ger.; **2.** v/t. use, make use of; put to account; avail o.s. of, seize (opportunity).

'Nutz|holz n timber; **'~leistung** f capacity.

nützlich adj. ['nytsliç] useful, of use; advantageous.

'nutz|los adj. useless; **2nießer** ['~ni:sər] m (-s/-) usufructuary; **'2nießung** f (-/-en) usufruct.

'Nutzung f (-/-en) using; utilization.

Nylon ['nailɔn] n (-s/no pl.) nylon; **~strümpfe** ['~ʃtrympfə] m/pl. nylons pl., nylon stockings pl.

Nymphe ['nymfə] f (-/-n) nymph.

O

o int. [o:] oh!, ah!; ~ **weh!** alas!, oh dear (me)!

Oase [o'a:zə] f (-/-n) oasis.

ob cj. [ɔp] whether, if; *als* ~ as if, as though.

Obacht ['o:baxt] f (-/no pl.): ~ **geben auf** (acc.) pay attention to, take care of, heed.

Obdach ['ɔpdax] n (-[e]s/no pl.) shelter, lodging; **2los** adj. unsheltered, homeless; '~**lose** m, f (-n/-n) homeless person; '~**losenasyl** n casual ward.

Obduktion ⚕ [ɔpduk'tsjo:n] f (-/-en) post-mortem (examination), autopsy; **2zieren** ⚕ [~'tsi:rən] v/t. (no -ge-, h) perform an autopsy on.

oben adv. ['o:bən] above; *mountain:* at the top; *house:* upstairs; on the surface; *von* ~ from above; *von* ~ *bis unten* from top to bottom; *von* ~ *herab behandeln* treat haughtily; '~**an** adv. at the top; '~**auf** adv. on the top; on the surface; ~**drein** adv. ['~'draɪn] into the bargain, at that; ~**erwähnt** adj. ['o:bən'ʔɛrvɛːnt], ~**genannt** adj. above-mentioned, aforesaid; '~**hin** adv. superficially, perfunctorily.

ober ['o:bər] **1.** adj. upper, higher; *fig. a.* superior; **2.** **2** m (-s/-) (head) waiter; *German cards:* queen.

Ober|arm ['o:bər?-] m upper arm; ~**arzt** ['o:bər?-] m head physician; ~**aufseher** ['o:bər?-] m superintendent; ~**aufsicht** ['o:bər?-] f superintendence; '~**befehl** ⚔ m supreme command; '~**befehlshaber** ⚔ m commander-in-chief; '~**bekleidung** f outer garments pl., outer wear; '~**bürgermeister** m chief burgomaster; Lord Mayor; '~**deck** ⚓ n upper deck; '~**fläche** f surface; '2**flächlich** adj. ['~flɛçlɪç] superficial; *fig. a.* shallow; '2**halb** prp. (gen.) above; '~**hand** fig. f: *die* ~ *gewinnen über* (acc.) get the upper hand of; '~**haupt** n head, chief; '~**haus** Brt. parl. n House of Lords; '~**hemd** n shirt; '~**herrschaft** f supremacy.

'Oberin f (-/-nen) eccl. Mother Superior; *at hospital:* matron.

ober|irdisch adj. ['o:bər?-] over-ground, above ground; ⚡ overhead; '2**kellner** m head waiter; '2**kiefer** anat. m upper jaw; '2**körper** m upper part of the body; '2**land** n upland; '2**lauf** m upper course (of river); '2**leder** n upper; '2**leitung** f chief management; ⚡ overhead wires pl.; '2**leutnant** ⚔ m (Am. first) lieutenant; '2**licht** n skylight; '2**lippe** f upper lip; '2**schenkel** m thigh; '2**schule** f secondary school, Am. a. high school.

'oberst 1. adj. uppermost, topmost, top; highest (a. fig.); fig. chief, principal; rank, etc.: supreme; **2.** **2** ⚔ m (-en, -s/-en, -e) colonel.

'Ober|staatsanwalt ⚖ m chief public prosecutor; '~**stimme** ♪ f treble, soprano.

'Oberst|leutnant ⚔ m lieutenant-colonel.

'Ober|tasse f cup; '~**wasser** fig. n: ~ **bekommen** get the upper hand.

obgleich cj. [ɔp'glaɪç] (al)though.

'Obhut f (-/no pl.) care, guard; protection; custody; *in (seine)* ~ *nehmen* take care or charge of.

obig adj. ['o:bɪç] above(-mentioned), aforesaid.

Objekt [ɔp'jɛkt] n (-[e]s/-e) object (a. gr.); project; ✝ a. transaction.

objektiv [ɔpjɛk'ti:f] **1.** adj. objective; impartial, detached; actual, practical; **2.** **2** n (-s/-e) object-glass, objective; phot. lens; **2ität** [~ivi-'tɛ:t] f (-/no pl.) objectivity; impartiality.

obligat adj. [obli'ga:t] obligatory; indispensable; inevitable; **2ion** ✝ [~a'tsjo:n] f (-/-en) bond, debenture; ~**orisch** adj. [~a'to:rɪʃ] obligatory (für on), compulsory, mandatory.

'Obmann m chairman; ✝ foreman (of jury); umpire; ✝ shop-steward, spokesman.

Oboe ♪ [o'bo:ə] f (-/-n) oboe, hautboy.

Obrigkeit ['o:brɪçkaɪt] f (-/-en) the authorities pl.; government; '2**lich** adj. magisterial, official; '~**sstaat** m authoritarian state.

ob'schon cj. (al)though.

Observatorium ast. [ɔpzɛrva'to:rjum] n (-s/Observatorien) observatory.

Obst [o:pst] n (-es/no pl.) fruit; '~bau m fruit-culture, fruit-growing; '~baum m fruit-tree; '~ernte f fruit-gathering; fruit-crop; '~garten m orchard; '~händler m fruiterer, Am. fruitseller; '~züchter m fruiter, fruit-grower.

obszön adj. [ɔps'tsøːn] obscene, filthy.

ob'wohl cj. (al)though.

Ochse zo. ['ɔksə] m (-n/-n) ox; bullock; '~nfleisch n beef.

öde ['øːdə] 1. adj. deserted, desolate; waste; fig. dull, tedious; 2. ♀ f (-/-n) desert, solitude; fig. dullness, tedium.

oder cj. ['oːdər] or.

Ofen ['oːfən] m (-s/ü) stove; oven; kiln; furnace; '~heizung f heating by stove; '~rohr n stove-pipe.

offen adj. ['ɔfən] open (a. fig.); position: vacant; hostility: overt; fig. frank, outspoken.

'**offen|bar** 1. adj. obvious, evident; apparent; 2. adv. a. it seems that; ~en [ɔfən'-] v/t. (no -ge-, h) reveal, disclose; manifest; sich j-m ~ open one's heart to s.o.; ♀ung [ɔfən'-] f (-/-en) manifestation; revelation; ♀ungseid 🏛 [ɔfən'baːruŋs-] m oath of manifestation.

'**Offenheit** fig. f (-/no pl.) openness, frankness.

'**offen|herzig** adj. open-hearted, sincere; frank; '~kundig adj. public; notorious; '~sichtlich adj. manifest, evident, obvious.

offensiv adj. [ɔfɛn'ziːf] offensive; ♀e [~və] f (-/-n) offensive.

'**offenstehen** v/i. (irr. stehen, sep., -ge-, h) stand open; † bill: be outstanding; be open (j-m to s.o.); es steht ihm offen zu inf. he is free or at liberty to inf.

öffentlich ['œfəntliç] 1. adj. public; ~es Ärgernis public nuisance; ~er Dienst Civil Service; 2. adv. publicly, in public; ~ auftreten make a public appearance; ♀keit f (-/no pl.) publicity; the public; in aller ~ in public.

offerieren [ɔfə'riːrən] v/t. (no -ge-, h) offer. [tender.]

Offerte [ɔ'fɛrtə] f (-/-n) offer;

offiziell adj. [ɔfi'tsjɛl] official.

Offizier ✕ [ɔfi'tsiːr] m (-s/-e) (com-

missioned) officer; ~skorps ✕ [~skoːr] n (-/-) body of officers, the officers pl.; ~smesse f ✕ officers' mess; ♣ a. wardroom.

offiziös adj. [ɔfi'tsjøːs] officious, semi-official.

öffn|en ['œfnən] v/t. (ge-, h) open; a. uncork (bottle); 🜊 dissect (body); sich ~ open; '~er m (-s/-) opener; '♀ung f (-/-en) opening, aperture; '♀ungszeiten f/pl. hours pl. of opening, business hours pl.

oft adv. [ɔft] often, frequently.

öfters adv. ['œftərs] s. oft.

'**oftmal|ig** adj. frequent, repeated; '~s adv. s. oft.

oh int. [oː] o(h)!

ohne ['oːnə] 1. prp. (acc.) without; 2. cj.: ~ daß, ~ zu inf. without ger.; ~'dies adv. anyhow, anyway; ~'gleichen adv. unequal(l)ed, matchless; ~'hin adv. s. ohnedies.

'**Ohn|macht** f (-/-en) powerlessness; impotence; 🜊 faint, unconsciousness; in ~ fallen faint, swoon; ~machtsanfall 🜊 ['oːnmaxts?-] m fainting fit, swoon; 2mächtig adj. powerless; impotent; 🜊 unconscious; ~ werden faint, swoon.

Ohr [oːr] n (-[e]s/-en) ear; fig. a. hearing; ein ~ haben für have an ear for; ganz ~ sein be all ears; F j-n übers ~ hauen cheat s.o., sl. do s.o. (in the eye); bis über die ~en up to the ears or eyes.

Öhr [øːr] n (-[e]s/-e) eye (of needle).

'**Ohren|arzt** m aurist, ear specialist; '♀betäubend adj. deafening; '~leiden n ear-complaint; '~schmalz n ear-wax; '~schmaus m treat for the ears; '~schmerzen m/pl. earache; '~zeuge m ear-witness.

Ohr|feige f box on the ear(s), slap in the face (a. fig.); '♀feigen v/t. (ge-, h); j-n ~ box s.o.'s ear(s), slap s.o.'s face; '~läppchen [~lɛpçən] n (-s/-) lobe of ear; '~ring m earring.

Ökonom|ie [økono'miː] f (-/-n) economy; ♀isch adj. [~'noːmiʃ] economical.

Oktav [ɔk'taːf] n (-s/-e) octavo; ~e ♪ [~və] f (-/-n) octave.

Oktober [ɔk'toːbər] m (-[s]/-) October.

Okul|ar opt. [oku'laːr] n (-s/-e) eyepiece, ocular; ♀ieren ✿ v/t. (no -ge-, h) inoculate, graft.

Öl [ø:l] *n* (-[e]s/-e) oil; ~ *ins Feuer gießen* add fuel to the flames; ~ *auf die Wogen gießen* pour oil on the (troubled) waters; '~**baum** ♀ *m* olive-tree; '~**berg** *eccl. m* (-[e]s/*no pl.*) Mount of Olives; '2en *v/t.* (ge-, h) oil; ⊕ *a.* lubricate; '~**farbe** *f* oil-colo(u)r, oil-paint; '~**gemälde** *n* oil-painting; '~**heizung** *f* oil heating; '2**ig** *adj.* oily (*a. fig.*).

Oliv|**e** [o'li:və] *f* (-/-n) olive; ~**enbaum** ♀ *m* olive-tree; 2**grün** *adj.* olive(-green).

Öl|**male'rei** *f* oil-painting; '~**quelle** *f* oil-spring, gusher; oil-well; '~**ung** *f* (-/-en) oiling; ⊕ *a.* lubrication; *Letzte* ~ *eccl.* extreme unction.

Olympi|**ade** [olymp'ja:də] *f* (-/-n) Olympiad; *a.* Olympic Games *pl.*; 2**sch** *adj.* [o'lympiʃ] Olympic; *Olympische Spiele pl.* Olympic Games *pl.*

'**Ölzweig** *m* olive-branch.

Omelett [ɔm(ə)'lɛt] *n* (-[e]s/-e, -s), ~**e** [~'lɛt] *f* (-/-n) omelet(te).

Om|**en** ['o:mən] *n* (-s/-, *Omina*) omen, augury; 2**inös** *adj.* [omi'nø:s] ominous.

Omnibus ['ɔmnibus] *m* (-ses/-se) (omni)bus; (motor-)coach; '~**haltestelle** *f* bus-stop.

Onkel ['ɔŋkəl] *m* (-s/-, F -s) uncle.

Oper ['o:pər] *f* (-/-n) ♪ opera; opera-house.

Operat|**eur** [opəra'tø:r] *m* (-s/-e) operator; ♂ surgeon; ⚔, ✗ [~'tsjo:n] *f* (-/-en) operation; ~**ions-saal** ♂ *m* operating room, *Am.* surgery; 2**iv** *adj.* [~'ti:f] operative. **Operette** ♪ [opə'rɛtə] *f* (-/-n) operetta.

operieren [opə'ri:rən] (*no* -ge-, h) **1.** *v/t.*: *j-n* ~ ♂ operate (up)on s.o. (*wegen* for); **2.** ⚔, ✗ *v/i.* operate; *sich* ~ *lassen* ♂ undergo an operation.

'**Opern**|**glas** *n*, ~**gucker** F ['~gukər] *m* (-s/-) opera-glass(es *pl.*); '~**haus** *n* opera-house; '~**sänger** *m* opera-singer, operatic singer; '~**text** *m* libretto, book (of an opera).

Opfer ['ɔpfər] *n* (-s/-) sacrifice; offering; victim (*a. fig.*); *ein* ~ *bringen* make a sacrifice; *j-m zum* ~ *fallen* be victimized by s.o.; '~**gabe** *f* offering; '2**n** (ge-, h) **1.** *v/t.* sacrifice; immolate; *sich für et.* ~ sacrifice o.s. for s.th.; **2.** *v/i.* (make a)

sacrifice (*dat.* to); '~**stätte** *f* place of sacrifice; '~**tod** *m* sacrifice of one's life; '~**ung** *f* (-/-en) sacrificing, sacrifice; immolation.

Opium ['o:pjum] *n* (-s/*no pl.*) opium.

opponieren [ɔpo'ni:rən] *v/i.* (*no* -ge-, h) be opposed (*gegen* to), resist.

Opposition [ɔpozi'tsjo:n] *f* (-/-en) opposition (*a. parl.*); ~**führer** *parl. m* opposition leader; ~**spartei** *parl. f* opposition party.

Optik ['ɔptik] *f* (-/⚓-en) optics; *phot.* lens system; *fig.* aspect; ~**er** *m* (-s/-) optician.

Optim|**ismus** [ɔpti'mismus] *m* (-/*no pl.*) optimism; ~**ist** *m* (-en/-en) optimist; 2**istisch** *adj.* optimistic.

'**optisch** *adj.* optic(al); ~**e** *Täuschung* optical illusion.

Orakel [o'ra:kəl] *n* (-s/-) oracle; 2**haft** *adj.* oracular; 2**n** *v/i.* (*no* -ge-, h) speak oracularly; '~**spruch** *m* oracle.

Orange [o'rã:ʒə] *f* (-/-n) orange; 2**farben** *adj.* orange-colo(u)red); ~**nbaum** ♀ *m* orange-tree.

Oratorium ♪ [ora'to:rjum] *n* (-s/*Oratorien*) oratorio.

Orchester ♪ [ɔr'kɛstər] *n* (-s/-) orchestra.   [orchid.]

Orchidee ♀ [ɔrçi'de:ə] *f* (-/-n)]

Orden ['ɔrdən] *m* (-s/-) order (*a. eccl.*); order, medal, decoration.

'**Ordens**|**band** *n* ribbon (of an order); '~**bruder** *eccl. m* brother, friar; '~**gelübde** *eccl. n* monastic vow; '~**schwester** *eccl. f* sister, nun; '~**verleihung** *f* conferring (of) an order.

ordentlich *adj.* ['ɔrdəntliç] tidy; orderly; proper; regular; respectable; good, sound; ~**er** *Professor univ.* professor in ordinary.

ordinär *adj.* [ɔrdi'nɛ:r] common, vulgar, low.

ordn|**en** ['ɔrdnən] *v/t.* (ge-, h) put in order; arrange, fix (up); settle (*a.* ✝ *liabilities*); '2**er** *m* (-s/-) at festival, *etc.*: steward; *for papers, etc.*: file.

'**Ordnung** *f* (-/-en) order; arrangement; system; rules *pl.*, regulations *pl.*; class; *in* ~ *bringen* put in order.

'**ordnungs|gemäß**, '**~mäßig 1.** *adj.* orderly, regular; **2.** *adv.* duly; '**2ruf** *parl. m* call to order; '**2strafe** *f* disciplinary penalty; fine; '**~widrig** *adj.* contrary to order, irregular; '**2zahl** *f* ordinal number.

Ordonnanz ✕ [ɔrdɔˈnants] *f* (-/-en) orderly.

Organ [ɔrˈɡaːn] *n* (-s/-e) organ.

Organisat|ion [ɔrɡaniza'tsjoːn] *f* (-/-en) organization; **~ionstalent** *n* organizing ability; **~or** [~ˈzaːtɔr] *m* (-s/-en) organizer; **2orisch** *adj.* [~ˈaːtoːriʃ] organizational, organizing.

or'ganisch *adj.* organic.

organi'sieren *v/t.* (*no* -ge-, *h*) organize; *sl.* scrounge; (*nicht*) *organisiert(er Arbeiter)* (non-)unionist.

Organismus [ɔrɡaˈnɪsmʊs] *m* (-/Organismen) organism; **⚥** *a.* system.

Organist ♪ [ɔrɡaˈnɪst] *m* (-en/-en) organist.

Orgel ♪ [ˈɔrɡəl] *f* (-/-n) organ, Am. a. pipe organ; '**2bauer** *m* organbuilder; '**~pfeife** *f* organ-pipe; '**~spieler** ♪ *m* organist.

Orgie [ˈɔrɡjə] *f* (-/-n) orgy.

Oriental|e [orien'taːlə] *m* (-n/-n) oriental; **2isch** *adj.* oriental.

orientier|en [orien'tiːrən] *v/t.* (*no* -ge-, *h*) inform, instruct; *sich ~ orient(ate) o.s.* (*über acc.* of); *gut orientiert sein über* (*acc.*) be well informed about, be familiar with; **2ung** *f* (-/-en) orientation; *fig. a.* information; *die ~ verlieren* lose one's bearings.

Origin|al [orig'naːl] **1.** *n* (-s/-e) original; **2.** **2** *adj.* original; **~alität** [~aliˈtɛːt] *f* (-/-en) originality; **2ell** *adj.* [~ˈnɛl] original; *design, etc.:* ingenious.

Orkan [ɔrˈkaːn] *m* (-[e]s/-e) hurricane; typhoon; **2artig** *adj.* storm; violent; *applause:* thunderous, frenzied.

Ornat [ɔrˈnaːt] *m* (-[e]s/-e) robe(s *pl.*), vestment.

Ort [ɔrt] *m* (-[e]s/-e) place; site; spot, point; locality; place, village, town; *~ der Handlung thea.* scene (of action); *an ~ und Stelle* on the spot; *höher(e)n ~(e)s* at higher quarters; '**2en** *v/t.* (ge-, *h*) locate.

ortho|dox *adj.* [ɔrto'dɔks] orthodox; **2graphie** [~ɡraˈfiː] *f* (-/-n) orthography; **~graphisch** *adj.* [~'ɡraːfiʃ] orthographic(al); **2päde ⚥** [~ˈpɛːdə] *m* (-n/-n) orthop(a)edist; **2pädie ⚥** [~pɛˈdiː] *f* (-/*no pl.*) orthop(a)edics, orthop(a)edy; **~pädisch** *adj.* [~ˈpɛːdiʃ] orthop(a)edic.

örtlich *adj.* [ˈœrtliç] local; **⚥** *a.* topical; **2keit** *f* (-/-en) locality.

'**Orts|angabe** *f* statement of place; '**2ansässig** *adj.* resident, local; '**~ansässige** [ˈ~ɡə] *m* (-n/-n) resident; '**~beschreibung** *f* topography; '**~besichtigung** *f* local inspection.

'**Ortschaft** *f* (-/-en) place, village.

'**Orts|gespräch** *teleph. n* local call; '**~kenntnis** *f* knowledge of a place; '**2kundig** *adj.* familiar with the locality; '**~name** *m* place-name; '**~verkehr** *m* local traffic; '**~zeit** *f* local time.

Öse [ˈøːzə] *f* (-/-n) eye, loop; eyelet (*of shoe*).

Ost *geogr.* [ɔst] east; '**~en** *m* (-s/*no pl.*) east; *the* East; *der Ferne (Nahe) ~ the* Far (Near) East.

ostentativ *adj.* [ɔstentaˈtiːf] ostentatious.

Oster|ei [ˈoːstər ?-] *n* Easter egg; '**~fest** *n* Easter; '**~hase** *m* Easter bunny *or* rabbit; '**~lamm** *n* paschal lamb; '**~n** *n* (-/-) Easter.

Österreich|er [ˈøːstəraɪçər] *m* (-s/-) Austrian; **2isch** *adj.* Austrian.

östlich [ˈœstliç] **1.** *adj.* eastern; *wind, etc.:* easterly; **2.** *adv.:* ~ *von* east of.

ost|wärts *adv.* [ˈɔstvɛrts] eastward(s); '**2wind** *m* east(erly) wind.

Otter *zo.* [ˈɔtər] **1.** *m* (-s/-) otter; **2.** *f* (-/-n) adder, viper.

Ouvertüre ♪ [uverˈtyːrə] *f* (-/-n) overture.

oval [oˈvaːl] **1.** *adj.* oval; **2.** **2** *n* (-s/-e) oval.

Ovation [ovaˈtsjoːn] *f* (-/-en) ovation; *j-m ~en bereiten* give s.o. ovations.

Oxyd 🜍 [ɔˈksyːt] *n* (-[e]s/-e) oxide; **2ieren** [~yˈdiːrən] (*no* -ge-) **1.** *v/t.* (*h*) oxidize; **2.** *v/i.* (*sein*) oxidize.

Ozean [ˈoːtseaːn] *m* (-s/-e) ocean.

P

Paar [pɑ:r] **1.** *n* (-[e]s/-e) pair; couple; **2.** 2 *adj.*: ein ~ a few, some; j-m ein ~ Zeilen schreiben drop s.o. a few lines; '2**en** *v/t.* (ge-, h) pair, couple, mate (*animals*); sich ~ (form a) pair; *animals*: mate; *fig.* join, unite; '~**lauf** *m sports*: pair-skating; '~**läufer** *m sports*: pair-skater; '2**mal** *adv.*: ein ~ several or a few times; '~**ung** *f* (-/-en) coupling; mating, copulation; *fig.* union; '2**weise** *adv.* in pairs or couples, by twos.

Pacht [paxt] *f* (-/-en) lease, tenure, tenancy; *money payment*: rent; '2**en** *v/t.* (ge-, h) (take on) lease; rent.

Pächter ['pɛçtər] *m* (-s/-), '~**in** *f* (-/-nen) lessee, lease-holder; tenant.

'**Pacht|ertrag** *m* rental; '~**geld** *n* rent; '~**vertrag** *m* lease; '2**weise** *adv.* on lease.

Pack [pak] **1.** *m* (-[e]s/-e, ~e) s. *Packen²*; **2.** *n* (-[e]s/no pl.) rabble.

Päckchen ['pɛkçən] *n* (-s/-) small parcel, *Am. a.* package; ein ~ *Zigaretten* a pack(et) of cigarettes.

packen¹ ['pakən] (ge-, h) **1.** *v/t.* pack (up); seize, grip, grasp, clutch; collar; *fig.* grip, thrill; F *pack dich!* F clear out!, *sl.* beat it!; **2.** *v/i.* pack (up); **3.** 2 *n* (-s/no pl.) packing.

Packen² [~] *m* (-s/-) pack(et), parcel, bale.

'**Packer** *m* (-s/-) packer; ~**ei** [~'raɪ] *f* **1.** (-/-en) packing-room; **2.** (-/no pl.) packing.

'**Pack|esel** *fig. m* drudge; '~**material** *n* packing materials *pl.*; '~**papier** *n* packing-paper, brown paper; '~**pferd** *n* pack-horse; '~**ung** *f* (-/-en) pack(age), packet; 2 pack; e-e ~ *Zigaretten* a pack(et) of cigarettes; '~**wagen** *m s. Gepäck-wagen.*

Pädagog|e [pedaˈgoːgə] *m* (-n/-n) pedagog(ue), education(al)ist; ~**ik** *f* (-/no pl.) pedagogics, pedagogy; 2**isch** *adj.* pedagogic(al).

Paddel ['padəl] *n* (-s/-) paddle; '~**boot** *n* canoe; '2**n** *v/i.* (ge-, h, sein) paddle, canoe.

Page ['pɑːʒə] *m* (-n/-n) page.

pah *int.* [pɑ:] pah!, pooh!, pshaw!

Paket [paˈkeːt] *n* (-[e]s/-e) parcel, packet, package; ~**annahme** & *f* parcel counter; ~**karte** & *f* dispatch-note; ~**post** *f* parcel post; ~**zustellung** & *f* parcel delivery.

Pakt [pakt] *m* (-[e]s/-e) pact; agreement; treaty.

Palast [paˈlast] *m* (-es/ue) palace.

Palm|e & *f* ['palmə] *f* (-/-n) palm (-tree); '~**öl** *n* palm-oil; '2**sonntag** *eccl. m* Palm Sunday.

panieren [paˈniːrən] *v/t.* (no -ge-, h) crumb.

Pani|k ['paːnɪk] *f* (-/-en) panic, stampede; 2**sch** *adj.* panic; von ~em Schrecken erfaßt panic-stricken.

Panne ['panə] *f* (-/-en) breakdown, *mot. a.* engine trouble; *tyres*: puncture; *fig.* blunder.

panschen ['panʃən] (ge-, h) **1.** *v/i.* splash (about); **2.** *v/t.* adulterate (*wine, etc.*).

Panther *zo.* ['pantər] *m* (-s/-) panther.

Pantine [panˈtiːnə] *f* (-/-n) clog.

Pantoffel [panˈtɔfəl] *m* (-s/-n, F -) slipper; *unter dem ~ stehen* be henpecked; ~**held** F *m* henpecked husband.

pantschen ['pantʃən] *v/i.* and *v/t.* (ge-, h) s. *panschen.*

Panzer ['pantsər] *m* (-s/-) armo(u)r; ✗ tank; *zo.* shell; '~**abwehr** ✗ *f* anti-tank defen|ce, *Am.* -se; '~**glas** *n* bullet-proof glass; '~**hemd** *n* coat of mail; '~**kreuzer** ✗ *m* armo(u)red cruiser; '2**n** *v/t.* (ge-, h) armo(u)r; '~**platte** *f* armo(u)r-plate; '~**schiff** ✗ *n* ironclad; '~**schrank** *m* safe; '~**ung** *f* (-/-en) armo(u)r-plating; '~**wagen** *m* armo(u)red car; ✗ tank.

Papa [paˈpɑː, F 'papa] *m* (-s/-s) papa, F pa, dad(dy), *Am. a.* pop.

Papagei *orn.* ['papaˈgaɪ] *m* (-[e]s, -en/-e[n]) parrot.

Papier [paˈpiːr] *n* (-s/-e) paper; ~**e** *pl.* papers *pl.*, documents *pl.*; papers *pl.*, identity card; ein Bogen ~ a sheet of paper; 2**en** *adj.* (of) paper; *fig.* dull; ~**fabrik** *f* paper-mill; ~**geld** *n* (-[e]s/no pl.) paper-money; bank-notes *pl.*, *Am.* bills *pl.*; ~**korb** *m* waste-paper-basket; ~**schnitzel** F *n* *or m/pl.* scraps *pl.* of paper; **~tüte** *f* paper-bag; **~waren** *f/pl.* stationery.

'Papp|band *m* (-[e]s/⁐e) paperback; **'~deckel** *m* pasteboard, cardboard.

Pappe ['papə] *f* (-/-n) pasteboard, cardboard.

Pappel ♀ ['papəl] *f* (-/-n) poplar.

päppeln F ['pɛpəln] *v/t.* (ge-, h) feed (with pap).

papp|en F ['papən] (ge-, h) **1.** *v/t.* paste; **2.** *v/i.* stick; **'~ig** *adj.* sticky; **'²karton** *m*, **'²schachtel** *f* cardboard box, carton.

Papst [pɑːpst] *m* (-es/⁐e) pope.

päpstlich *adj.* ['pɛːpstliç] papal.

'Papsttum *n* (-s/*no pl.*) papacy.

Parade [pa'rɑːdə] *f* (-/-n) parade; ✗ review; *fencing:* parry.

Paradies [para'diːs] *n* (-es/-e) paradise; **²isch** *fig. adj.* [~'diːziʃ] heavenly, delightful.   [ical.\]

paradox *adj.* [para'dɔks] paradox-\]

Paragraph [para'grɑːf] *m* (-en, -s/-en) article, section; paragraph; section-mark.

parallel *adj.* [para'leːl] parallel; **²e** *f* (-/-n) parallel.

Paralys|e ℀ [para'lyːzə] *f* (-/-n) paralysis; **²ieren** ℀ [~y'ziːrən] *v/t.* (*no* -ge-, h) paralyse.

Parasit [para'ziːt] *m* (-en/-en) parasite.

Parenthese [paren'teːzə] *f* (-/-n) parenthesis.

Parforcejagd [par'fɔrs-] *f* hunt (-ing) on horseback (with hounds), *after hares:* coursing.

Parfüm [par'fyːm] *n* (-s/-e, -s) perfume, scent; **~erie** [~ymə'riː] *f* (-/-n) perfumery; **²ieren** [~y'miːrən] *v/t.* (*no* -ge-, h) perfume, scent.

pari ✝ *adv.* ['pɑːri] par; *al ~* at par.

parieren [pa'riːrən] (*no* -ge-, h) **1.** *v/t. fencing:* parry (*a. fig.*); pull up (*horse*); **2.** *v/i.* obey (*j-m* s.o.).

Park [park] *m* (-s/-s, -e) park; **~anlage** *f* park; **'~aufseher** *m* parkkeeper; **²en** (ge-, h) **1.** *v/i.* park; *~ verboten!* no parking!; **2.** *v/t.* park.

Parkett [par'ket] *n* (-[e]s/-e) parquet; *thea.* (orchestra) stalls *pl.*, *esp. Am.* orchestra or parquet.

'Park|gebühr *f* parking-fee; **'~licht** *n* parking light; **'~platz** *m* (car-)park, parking lot; **'~uhr** *mot. f* parking meter.

Parlament [parla'ment] *n* (-[e]s/-e) parliament; **²arisch** *adj.* [~'tɑːriʃ] parliamentary.

Parodie [paro'diː] *f* (-/-n) parody; **²ren** *v/t.* (*no* -ge-, h) parody.

Parole [pa'roːlə] *f* (-/-n) ✗ password, watchword; *fig.* slogan.

Partei [par'taɪ] *f* (-/-en) party (*a. pol.*); *j-s ~ ergreifen* take s.o.'s part, side with s.o.; **~apparat** *pol. m* party machinery; **~gänger** [~gɛŋər] *m* (-s/-) partisan; **²isch** *adj.*, **²lich** *adj.* partial (*für* to); prejudiced (*gegen* against); **²los** *pol. adj.* independent; **~mitglied** *pol. n* party member; **~programm** *pol. n* platform; **~tag** *pol. m* convention; **~zugehörigkeit** *pol. f* party membership.

Parterre [par'ter] *n* (-s/-s) ground floor, *Am.* first floor; *thea.:* pit, *Am.* parterre, *Am.* parquet circle.

Partie [par'tiː] *f* (-/-n) ✝ parcel, lot; outing, excursion; *cards, etc.:* game; ♪ part; *marriage:* match.

Partitur ♪ [parti'tuːr] *f* (-/-en) score.

Partizip *gr.* [parti'tsiːp] *n* (-s/-ien) participle.

Partner ['partnər] *m* (-s/-), **'~in** *f* (-/-nen) partner; *film: a.* co-star; **'~schaft** *f* (-/-en) partnership.

Parzelle [par'tsɛlə] *f* (-/-n) plot, lot, allotment.

Paß [pas] *m* (Passes/Pässe) pass; passage; *football, etc.:* pass; passport.

Passage [pa'sɑːʒə] *f* (-/-n) passage; arcade.

Passagier [pasa'ʒiːr] *m* (-s/-e) passenger, *in taxis: a.* fare; **~flugzeug** *n* air liner.

Passah ['pasa] *n* (-s/*no pl.*), **'~fest** *n* Passover.

Passant [pa'sant] *m* (-en/-en), **~in** *f* (-/-nen) passer-by.

'Paßbild *n* passport photo(graph).

passen ['pasən] (ge-, h) **1.** *v/i.* fit (*j-m* s.o.; *auf acc. or für or zu et.* s.th.); suit (*j-m* s.o.), be convenient; *cards, football:* pass; *~ zu* go with, match (with); **2.** *v/refl.* be fit or proper; **'~d** *adj.* fit, suitable, convenient (*für* for).

passier|bar *adj.* [pa'siːrbɑːr] passable, practicable; **~en** (*no* -ge-) **1.** *v/i.* (sein) happen; **2.** *v/t.* (h) pass (over or through); **²schein** *m* pass, permit.

Passion [pa'sjo:n] f (-/-en) passion; hobby; *eccl.* Passion.

passiv ['pasi:f] 1. *adj.* passive; 2. ♀ *gr. n* (-s/⁹⌐) passive (voice); **2a** ♀ [pa'si:va] *pl.* liabilities *pl.*

Paste ['pastə] f (-/-n) paste.

Pastell [pa'stɛl] n (-[e]s/-e) pastel.

Pastete [pa'ste:tə] f (-/-n) pie; **~nbäcker** m pastry-cook.

Pate ['pa:tə] 1. m (-n/-n) godfather; godchild; 2. f (-/-n) godmother; '**~kind** n godchild; '**~nschaft** f (-/-en) sponsorship.

Patent [pa'tɛnt] n (-[e]s/-e) patent; ✕ commission; *ein ~ anmelden* apply for a patent; **~amt** n Patent Office; **~anwalt** m patent agent; **2ieren** [~'ti:rən] v/t. (no -ge-, h) patent; *et. ~ lassen* take out a patent for s.th.; **~inhaber** m patentee; **~urkunde** f letters patent.

Patient [pa'tsjɛnt] m (-en/-en), **~in** f (-/-nen) patient.

Patin ['pa:tin] f (-/-nen) godmother.

Patriot [patri'o:t] m (-en/-en), **~in** f (-/-nen) patriot.

Patron [pa'tro:n] m (-s/-e) patron, protector; *contp.* fellow, bloke, customer; **~at** [~o'na:t] n (-[e]s/-e) patronage; **~e** [pa'tro:nə] f (-/-n) cartridge, *Am. a.* shell.

Patrouill|e ✕ [pa'truljə] f (-/-n) patrol; **2ieren** ✕ [~'ji:rən] v/i. (no -ge-, h) patrol.

Patsch|e F ['patʃə] f (-/no pl.): *in der ~ sitzen* be in a fix *or* scrape; '**2en** F (ge-) 1. v/i. (h, sein) splash; 2. v/t. (h) slap; '**2naß** *adj.* dripping wet, drenched.

patzig F *adj.* ['patsiç] snappish.

Pauke ♪ ['paukə] f (-/-n) kettle-drum; '**2n** F v/i. *and* v/t. (ge-, h) *school:* cram.

Pauschal|e [pau'ʃa:lə] f (-/-n), **~summe** f lump sum.

Pause ['pauzə] f (-/-n) pause, stop, interval; *school:* break, *Am.* recess; *thea.* interval, *Am.* intermission; ♪ rest; *drawing:* tracing; '**2n** v/t. (ge-, h) trace; '**2nlos** *adj.* uninterrupted, incessant; '**~nzeichen** n *wireless:* interval signal.

pau'sieren v/i. (no -ge-, h) pause.

Pavian zo. ['pa:viaːn] m (-s/-e) baboon.

Pavillon ['paviljõ] m (-s/-s) pavilion.

Pazifist [patsi'fist] m (-en/-en) pacif(ic)ist.

Pech [pɛç] n 1. (-[e]s /-e) pitch; 2. F *fig.* (-[e]s/no pl.) bad luck; '**~strähne** F f run of bad luck; '**~vogel** F m unlucky fellow.

pedantisch *adj.* [pe'dantiʃ] pedantic; punctilious, meticulous.

Pegel ['pe:gəl] m (-s/-) water-ga(u)ge.

peilen ['paɪlən] v/t. (ge-, h) sound (*depth*); take the bearings of (*coast*).

Pein [paɪn] f (-/no pl.) torment, torture, anguish; **2igen** [~igən] v/t. (ge-, h) torment; **~iger** ['~igər] m (-s/-) tormentor.

'**peinlich** *adj.* painful, embarrassing; particular, scrupulous, meticulous.

Peitsche ['paɪtʃə] f (-/-n) whip; '**2n** v/t. (ge-, h) whip; '**~nhieb** m lash.

Pelikan *orn.* ['pe:lika:n] m (-s/-e) pelican.

Pell|e ['pɛlə] f (-/-n) skin, peel; '**2en** v/t. (ge-, h) skin, peel; '**~kartoffeln** f/pl. potatoes *pl.* (boiled) in their jackets *or* skins.

Pelz [pɛlts] m (-es/-e) fur; *garment:* *mst* furs *pl.*; '**2gefüttert** *adj.* fur-lined; '**~händler** m furrier; '**~handschuh** m furred glove; '**2ig** *adj.* furry; 🌿 *tongue:* furred; '**~mantel** m fur coat; '**~stiefel** m fur-lined boot; '**~tiere** n/pl. fur-covered animals *pl.*

Pendel ['pɛndəl] n (-s/-) pendulum; '**2n** v/i. (ge-, h) oscillate, swing; shuttle, *Am.* commute; '**~tür** f swing-door; '**~verkehr** 🚃 m shuttle service.

Pension [pã'sjõː, pen'zjo:n] f (-/-en) (old-age) pension, retired pay; board; boarding-house; **~är** [~o'nɛ:r] m (-s/-e) (old-age) pensioner; boarder; **~at** [~o'na:t] n (-[e]s/-e) boarding-school; **2ieren** [~o'ni:rən] v/t. (no -ge-, h) pension (off); *sich ~ lassen* retire; **~sgast** m boarder.

Pensum ['pɛnzum] n (-s/Pensen, Pensa) task, lesson.

perfekt 1. *adj.* [pɛr'fɛkt] perfect; *agreement:* settled; 2. ♀ *gr.* ['~] n (-[e]s/-e) perfect (tense).

Pergament [pɛrga'mɛnt] n (-[e]s/-e) parchment.

Period|e [pe'rjo:də] f (-/-n) period; 🩸 periods *pl.*; **2isch** *adj.* periodic (-al).

Peripherie [perife'ri:] f (-/-n) circumference; outskirts *pl.* (*of town*).

Perle ['pɛrlə] f (-/-n) pearl; *of glass*: bead; 'Ձn v/i. (ge-, h) sparkle; '~nkette f pearl necklace; '~nschnur f string of pearls or beads.

'Perl|muschel zo. f pearl-oyster; ~mutt ['~mʊt] n (-s/no pl.), ~'mutter f (-/no pl.) mother-of-pearl.

Person [pɛr'zo:n] f (-/-en) person; *thea.* character.

Personal [pɛrzo'na:l] n (-s/no pl.) staff, personnel; ~abteilung f personnel office; ~angaben f/pl. personal data pl.; ~ausweis m identity card; ~chef m personnel officer or manager or director; ~ien [~jən] pl. particulars pl., personal data pl.; ~pronomen gr. n personal pronoun.

Per'sonen|verzeichnis n list of persons; *thea.* dramatis personae pl.; ~wagen ⊕ m (passenger-)carriage or Am. car, coach; *mot.* (motor-)car; ~zug ⊕ m passenger train.

personifizieren [pɛrzonifi'tsi:rən] v/t. (no -ge-, h) personify.

persönlich adj. [pɛr'zø:nlɪç] personal; *opinion, letter*: a. private; Ձkeit f (-/-en) personality; personage.

Perücke [pe'rʏkə] f (-/-n) wig.

Pest [pɛst] f (-/no pl.) plague.

Petersilie [petər'zi:ljə] f (-/-n) parsley.

Petroleum [pe'tro:leʊm] n (-s/no pl.) petroleum; *for lighting, etc.*: paraffin, *esp.* Am. kerosene.

Pfad [pfa:t] m (-[e]s/-e) path, track; '~finder m boy scout; '~finderin f (-/-nen) girl guide, Am. girl scout.

Pfahl [pfa:l] m (-[e]s/ⁿe) stake, pale, pile.

Pfand [pfant] n (-[e]s/ⁿer) pledge; † deposit, security; *real estate*: mortgage; *game*: forfeit; '~brief † m debenture (bond).

pfänden [['pfɛndən] v/t. (ge-, h) seize s.th.; distrain upon s.o. or s.th.

'**Pfand|haus** n s. Leihhaus; '~leiher m (-s/-) pawnbroker; '~schein m pawn-ticket. [distraint.]

'**Pfändung** f [(-/-en) seizure;]

Pfann|e ['pfanə] f (-/-n) pan; '~kuchen m pancake.

Pfarr|bezirk ['pfar-] m parish; '~er m (-s/-) parson; *Church of England*: rector, vicar; *dissenters*: minister; '~gemeinde f parish; '~haus n

parsonage; *Church of England*: rectory, vicarage; ~kirche f parish church; '~stelle f (church) living.

Pfau orn. [pfaʊ] m (-[e]s/-en) peacock.

Pfeffer ['pfɛfər] m (-s/-) pepper; '~gurke f gherkin; Ձig adj. peppery; '~kuchen m gingerbread; '~minze ♀ ['~mɪntsə] f (-/no pl.) peppermint; '~minzplätzchen n peppermint; Ձn v/t. (ge-, h) pepper; '~streuer m (-s/-) pepperbox, pepper-castor, pepper-caster.

Pfeife ['pfaɪfə] f (-/-n) whistle; ✕ fife; pipe (of organ, etc.); (tobacco-) pipe; 'Ձn (irr., ge-, h) 1. v/i. whistle (dat. to, for); radio: howl; pipe; 2. v/t. whistle; pipe; '~nkopf m pipe-bowl.

Pfeil [pfaɪl] m (-[e]s/-e) arrow.

Pfeiler ['pfaɪlər] m (-s/-) pillar (a. fig.); pier (of bridge, etc.).

'**pfeil|'schnell** adj. (as) swift as an arrow; '~spitze f arrow-head.

Pfennig ['pfɛnɪç] m (-[e]s/-e) coin: pfennig; fig. penny, farthing.

Pferch [pfɛrç] m (-[e]s/-e) fold, pen; 'Ձen v/t. (ge-, h) fold, pen; fig. cram.

Pferd zo. [pfe:rt] n (-[e]s/-e) horse; zu ~ on horseback.

Pferde|geschirr ['pfe:rdə-] n harness; '~koppel f (-/-n) paddock, Am. a. corral; '~rennen n horse-race; '~schwanz m horse's tail; *hair-style*: pony-tail; '~stall m stable; '~stärke ⊕ f horsepower.

pfiff [pfɪf] pret. of pfeifen.

Pfiff [pfɪf] m (-[e]s/-e) whistle; fig. trick; 'Ձig adj. cunning, artful.

Pfingst|en eccl. ['pfɪŋstən] n (-/-), '~fest eccl. n Whitsun(tide); '~montag eccl. m Whit Monday; '~rose ♀ f peony; '~sonntag eccl. m Whit Sunday.

Pfirsich ['pfɪrzɪç] m (-[e]s/-e) peach.

Pflanz|e ['pflantsə] f (-/-n) plant; 'Ձen v/t. (ge-, h) plant, set; pot; '~enfaser f vegetable fib|re, Am. -er; '~enfett n vegetable fat; 'Ձenfressend adj. herbivorous; '~er m (-s/-) planter; '~ung f (-/-en) plantation.

Pflaster ['pflastər] n (-s/-) ✚ plaster; *road*: pavement; '~er m (-s/-) paver, pavio(u)r; 'Ձn v/t. (ge-, h) ✚ plaster; pave (road); '~stein m paving-stone; cobble.

P

Pflaume ['pflaumə] f (-/-n) plum; *dried*: prune.

Pflege ['pfle:gə] f (-/-n) care; ⚕ nursing; cultivation (*of art, garden, etc.*); ⊕ maintenance; *in ~ geben* put out (*child*) to nurse; *in ~ nehmen* take charge of; '**~bedürftig** adj. needing care; **~befohlene** ['~bəfo:lənə] m, f (-n/-n) charge; '**~eltern** pl. foster-parents pl.; '**~heim** ⚕ n nursing home; '**~kind** n foster-child; '**~n** (ge-, h) 1. v/t. take care of; attend (to); ⚕ nurse; maintain; cultivate (*art, garden*); 2. v/i.: ~ *zu inf.* be accustomed *or* used *or* wont to *inf.*, be in the habit of *ger.*; *sie pflegte zu sagen* she used to say; '**~r** m (-s/-) fosterer; ⚕ male nurse; trustee; ⚖ guardian, curator; '**~rin** f (-/-nen) nurse.

Pflicht [pflɪçt] f (-/-en) duty (*gegen* to); obligation; '**Øbewußt** adj. conscious of one's duty; '**Øeifrig** adj. zealous; '**~erfüllung** f performance of one's duty; '**~fach** n *school, univ.*: compulsory subject; '**~gefühl** n sense of duty; '**Øgemäß** adj. dutiful; '**Øgetreu** adj. dutiful, loyal; '**Øschuldig** adj. in duty bound; '**Øvergessen** adj. undutiful, disloyal; '**~verteidiger** ⚖ m assigned counsel.

Pflock [pflɔk] m (-[e]s/⁺e) plug, peg.

pflücken ['pflʏkən] v/t. (ge-, h) pick, gather, pluck. [*Am.* plow.\]

Pflug [pflu:k] m (-[e]s/⁺e) plough,\]

pflügen ['pfly:gən] v/t. *and* v/i. (ge-, h) plough, *Am.* plow.

Pforte ['pfɔrtə] f (-/-n) gate, door.

Pförtner ['pfœrtnər] m (-s/-) gatekeeper, door-keeper, porter, janitor.

Pfosten ['pfɔstən] m (-s/-) post.

Pfote ['pfo:tə] f (-/-n) paw.

Pfropf [pfrɔpf] m (-[e]s/-e) s. Pfropfen.

'**Pfropfen 1.** m (-s/-) stopper; plug; ⚕ clot (of blood); 2. 2 v/t. (ge-, h) stopper; cork; *fig.* cram; ⚘ graft.

Pfründe *eccl.* ['pfrʏndə] f (-/-n) prebend; benefice, (church) living.

Pfuhl [pfu:l] m (-[e]s/-e) pool, puddle; *fig.* sink, slough.

pfui *int.* [pfui] fie!, for shame!

Pfund [pfʊnt] n (-[e]s/-e) pound; **Øig** F adj. ['~dɪç] great, *Am.* swell; '**Øweise** adv. by the pound.

pfusch|en F ['pfuʃən] (ge-, h) 1. v/i. bungle; 2. v/t. bungle, botch; **Øerei** F [~'rai] f (-/-en) bungle, botch.

Pfütze ['pfʏtsə] f (-/-n) puddle, pool.

Phänomen [feno'me:n] n (-s/-e) phenomenon; **Øal** adj. [~e'na:l] phenomenal.

Phantasie [fanta'zi:] f (-/-n) imagination, fancy; vision; ♪ fantasia; **Øren** (*no -ge-, h*) 1. v/i. dream; ramble; ⚕ be delirious *or* raving; ♪ improvise; 2. v/t. dream; ♪ improvise.

Phantast [fan'tast] m (-en/-en) visionary, dreamer; **Øisch** adj. fantastic; *fig.* great, terrific.

Phase ['fa:zə] f (-/-n) phase (*a.* ⚡), stage.

Philanthrop [filan'tro:p] m (-en/-en) philanthropist.

Philolog [filo'lo:gə] m (-n/-n), **~in** f (-/-nen) philologist; **~ie** [~o'gi:] f (-/-n) philology.

Philosoph [filo'zo:f] m (-en/-en) philosopher; **~ie** [~o'fi:] f (-/-n) philosophy; **Øieren** [~o'fi:rən] v/i. (*no -ge-, h*) philosophize (*über acc.* on); **Øisch** adj. [~'zo:fiʃ] philosophical.

Phlegma ['flɛgma] n (-s/*no pl.*) phlegm; **Øtisch** adj. [~'ma:tiʃ] phlegmatic.

phonetisch adj. [fo'ne:tiʃ] phonetic.

Phosphor ⚗ ['fɔsfɔr] m (-s/*no pl.*) phosphorus.

Photo F ['fo:to] 1. n (-s/-s) photo; 2. m (-s/-s) = '**~apparat** m camera.

Photograph [foto'gra:f] m (-en/-en) photographer; **~ie** [~a'fi:] f 1. (-/-n) photograph, F: photo, picture; 2. (-/*no pl.*) *as an art*: photography; **Øieren** [~a'fi:rən] (*no -ge-, h*) 1. v/t. photograph; take a picture of; *sich ~ lassen* have one's photo(graph) taken; 2. v/i. photograph; **Øisch** adj. [~'gra:fiʃ] photographic.

Photo|ko'pie f photostat; **~ko'piergerät** n photostat; '**~zelle** f photoelectric cell.

Phrase ['fra:zə] f (-/-n) phrase.

Physik [fy'zi:k] f (-/*no pl.*) physics *sg.*; **Øalisch** adj. [~i'ka:liʃ] physical; **~er** ['fy:zikər] m (-s/-) physicist.

physisch adj. ['fy:ziʃ] physical.

Pian|ist [pia'nist] m (-en/-en) pianist; **~o** [pi'a:no] n (-s/-s) piano.

Picke ⊕ ['pikə] f (-/-n) pick(axe).

Pickel ['pikəl] m (-s/-) ⚕ pimple; ⊕

pick(axe); ice-pick; '≗ig *adj.* pimpled, pimply.

picken ['pikən] *v/i. and v/t.* (ge-, h) pick, peck.

picklig *adj.* ['pikliç] *s.* pickelig.

Picknick ['piknik] *n* (-s/-e, -s) picnic.

piekfein F *adj.* ['piːk'-] smart, tiptop, slap-up.

piep(s)en ['piːp(s)ən] *v/i.* (ge-, h) cheep, chirp, peep; squeak.

Pietät [pie'tɛːt] *f* (-/*no pl.*) reverence; piety; ≗los *adj.* irreverent; ≗voll *adj.* reverent.

Pik [piːk] 1. *m* (-s/-e, -s) peak; 2. F *m* (-s/-e): e-n ~ auf j-n haben bear s.o. a grudge; 3. *n* (-s/-s) *cards*: spade(s *pl.*).

pikant *adj.* [pi'kant] piquant, spicy (*both a. fig.*); *das Pikante* the piquancy.

Pike ['piːkə] *f* (-/-n) pike; *von der ~ auf dienen* rise from the ranks.

Pilger ['pilgər] *m* (-s/-) pilgrim; '≗fahrt *f* pilgrimage; '≗n *v/i.* (ge-, sein) go on *or* make a pilgrimage; wander.

Pille ['pilə] *f* (-/-n) pill.

Pilot [pi'loːt] *m* (-en/-en) pilot.

Pilz ♀ [pilts] *m* (-es/-e) fungus, *edible*: mushroom, *inedible*: toadstool.

pimp(e)lig F *adj.* ['pimp(ə)liç] sickly; effeminate.

Pinguin *orn.* ['piŋguiːn] *m* (-s/-e) penguin.

Pinsel ['pinzəl] *m* (-s/-) brush; F *fig.* simpleton; '≗n *v/i. and v/t.* (ge-, h) paint; daub; '≗strich *m* stroke of the brush.

Pinzette [pin'tsɛtə] *f* (-/-n) (e-e a pair of) tweezers *pl.*

Pionier [pio'niːr] *m* (-s/-e) pioneer, *Am. a.* trail blazer; ✗ engineer.

Pirat [pi'raːt] *m* (-en/-en) pirate.

Pirsch *hunt.* [pirʃ] *f* (-/*no pl.*) deerstalking, *Am. a.* still hunt.

Piste ['pistə] *f* (-/-n) *skiing, etc.*: course; ✗ runway.

Pistole [pis'toːlə] *f* (-/-n) pistol, *Am.* F *a.* gun, rod, ✗ntasche *f* holster.

placieren [pla'siːrən] *v/t.* (no -ge-, h) place; *sich ~ sports*: be placed (*second, etc.*).

Plackerei F [plakə'raɪ] *f* (-/-en) drudgery.

plädieren [plɛ'diːrən] *v/i.* (no -ge-, h) plead (*für* for).

Plädoyer ⚖ [plɛdoa'je:] *n* (-s/-s) pleading.

Plage ['plaːgə] *f* (-/-n) trouble, nuisance, F plague; torment; '≗n *v/t.* (ge-, h) torment; trouble, bother; F plague; *sich ~* toil, drudge.

Plagiat [plag'jaːt] *n* (-[e]s/-e) plagiarism; *ein ~ begehen* plagiarize.

Plakat [pla'kaːt] *n* (-[e]s/-e) poster, placard, bill; ✗säule *f* advertisement pillar.

Plakette [pla'kɛtə] *f* (-/-n) plaque.

Plan [plaːn] *m* (-[e]s/⁺e) plan; design, intention; scheme.

Plane ['plaːnə] *f* (-/-n) awning, tilt.

'planen *v/t.* (ge-, h) plan; scheme.

Planet [pla'neːt] *m* (-en/-en) planet.

planieren ⊕ [pla'niːrən] *v/t.* (no -ge-, h) level.

Planke ['plaŋkə] *f* (-/-n) plank, board.

plänkeln ['plɛŋkəln] *v/i.* (ge-, h) skirmish (*a. fig.*).

'plan|los 1. *adj.* planless, aimless, desultory; 2. *adv.* at random; '≗mäßig 1. *adj.* systematic, planned; 2. *adv.* as planned.

planschen ['planʃən] *v/i.* (ge-, h) splash, paddle.

Plantage [plan'taːʒə] *f* (-/-n) plantation.

Plapper|maul F ['plapər-] *n* chatterbox; '≗n F *v/i.* (ge-, h) chatter, prattle, babble.

plärren F ['plɛrən] *v/i. and v/t.* (ge-, h) blubber; bawl.

Plasti|k [plastik] 1. *f* (-/*no pl.*) plastic art; 2. *f* (-/-en) sculpture; ✗ plastic; 3. ⊕ *n* (-s/-s) plastic; '≗sch *adj.* plastic; three-dimensional.

Platin [pla'tiːn] *n* (-s/*no pl.*) platinum.

plätschern ['plɛtʃərn] *v/i.* (ge-, h) dabble, splash; *water*: ripple, murmur.

platt *adj.* [plat] flat, level, even; *fig.* trivial, commonplace, trite; F *fig.* flabbergasted.

Plättbrett ['plɛt-] *n* ironing-board.

Platte ['platə] *f* (-/-n) plate; dish; sheet (*of metal, etc.*); flag, slab (*of stone*); *mountain*: ledge; top (*of table*); tray, salver; disc, record; F *fig.* bald pate; *kalte ~* cold meat.

plätten ['plɛtən] *v/t.* (ge-, h) iron.

'Platten|spieler *m* record-player; **'_teller** *m* turn-table.

'Platt|form *f* platform; **'_fuß** *m* flat-foot; F *mot.* flat; **'_heit** *fig.* *f* (-/-en) triviality; commonplace, platitude, *Am. sl.* a. bromide.

Platz [plats] *m* (-es/_e) place; spot, *Am. a.* point; room, space; site; seat; square; *round:* circus; *sports:* ground; *tennis:* court; ~ *behalten* remain seated; ~ *machen* make way or room (*dat.* for); ~ *nehmen* take a seat, sit down, *Am. a.* have a seat; *ist hier noch ~?* is this seat taken or engaged *or* occupied?; *den dritten ~ belegen sports:* be placed third, come in third; **'_anweiserin** *f* (-/-nen) usherette.

Plätzchen ['plɛtsçən] *n* (-s/-) snug place; spot; biscuit, *Am.* cookie.

'platzen *v/i.* (ge-, *sein*) burst; explode; crack, split.

'Platz|patrone *f* blank cartridge; **'_regen** *m* downpour.

Plauder|ei [plaudə'raɪ] *f* (-/-en) chat; talk; small talk; **'_n** *v/i.* (ge-, *h*) (have a) chat (*mit* with), talk (to); chatter.

plauz *int.* [plauts] bang!

Pleite F ['plaɪtə] **1.** *f* (-/-en) smash; *fig.* failure; *Am. sl.* bust. **2.** F *adj.* (dead) broke, *Am. sl.* bust.

Plissee [pli'se:] *n* (-s/-s) pleating; **_rock** *m* pleated skirt.

Plomb|e ['plɔmbə] *f* (-/-n) (lead) seal; stopping, filling (*of tooth*); **2ieren** [_'bi:rən] *v/t.* (no -ge-, *h*) seal; stop, fill (*tooth*).

plötzlich *adj.* ['plœtslɪç] sudden.

plump *adj.* [plump] clumsy; **_s** *int.* plump, plop; **'_sen** *v/i.* (ge-, *sein*) plump, plop, flop.

Plunder F ['plundər] *m* (-s/*no pl.*) lumber, rubbish, junk.

plündern ['plyndərn] (ge-, *h*) **1.** *v/t.* plunder, pillage, loot, sack; **2.** *v/i.* plunder, loot. [(number).]

Plural *gr.* ['plu:ra:l] *m* (-s/-e) plural**)**

plus *adv.* [plus] plus.

Plusquamperfekt *gr.* ['pluskvamperfɛkt] *n* (-s/-e) pluperfect (tense), past perfect.

Pöbel ['pø:bəl] *m* (-s/*no pl.*) mob, rabble; **2haft** *adj.* low, vulgar.

pochen ['pɔxən] *v/i.* (ge-, *h*) knock, rap, tap; *heart:* beat, throb, thump; *auf sein Recht* ~ stand on one's rights.

Pocke 🜚 ['pɔkə] *f* (-/-n) pock; **_n** 🜚 *pl.* smallpox; **'2nnarbig** *adj.* pock-marked.

Podest [po'dɛst] *n, m* (-es/-e) pedestal (*a. fig.*).

Podium ['po:dium] *n* (-s/*Podien*) podium, platform, stage.

Poesie [poe'zi:] *f* (-/-n) poetry.

Poet [po'e:t] *m* (-en/-en) poet; **2isch** *adj.* poetic(al).

Pointe [po'ɛ̃:tə] *f* (-/-n) point.

Pokal [po'ka:l] *m* (-s/-e) goblet; *sports:* cup; **_endspiel** *n sports:* cup final; **_spiel** *n football:* cup-tie.

Pökel|fleisch ['pø:kəl-] *n* salted meat; '2n *v/t.* (ge-, *h*) pickle, salt.

Pol [po:l] *m* (-s/-e) pole; ⚡ *a.* terminal; **2ar** *adj.* [po'la:r] polar (*a.* ⚡).

Pole ['po:lə] *m* (-n/-n) Pole.

Polemi|k [po'le:mik] *f* (-/-en) polemic(s *pl.*); **2sch** *adj.* polemic (-al); **2sieren** [_emi'zi:rən] *v/i.* (no -ge-, *h*) polemize.

Police [po'li:s(ə)] *f* (-/-n) policy.

Polier ⊕ [po'li:r] *m* (-s/-e) foreman; **2en** *v/t.* (no -ge-, *h*) polish, burnish; furbish.

Politi|k [poli'ti:k] *f* (-/⚡ -en) policy; politics *sg.*, *pl.*; **_ker** [po'li:tikər] *m* (-s/-) politician; statesman; **2sch** *adj.* [po'li:tiʃ] political; **2sieren** [_iti'zi:rən] *v/i.* (no -ge-, *h*) talk politics.

Politur [poli'tu:r] *f* (-/-en) polish; lust|re, *Am.* -er, finish.

Polizei [poli'tsaɪ] *f* (-/⚡ -en) police; **_beamte** *m* police officer; **_knüppel** *m* truncheon, *Am.* club; **_kommissar** *m* inspector; **2lich** *adj.* (of or by the) police; **_präsident** *m* president of police; *Brt.* Chief Constable, *Am.* Chief of Police; **_präsidium** *n* police headquarters *pl.*; **_revier** *n* police-station; police precinct; **_schutz** *m:* *unter* ~ under police guard; **_streife** *f* police patrol; police squad; **_stunde** *f* (-/*no pl.*) closing-time; **_verordnung** *f* police regulation(s *pl.*); **_wache** *f* police-station.

Polizist [poli'tsɪst] *m* (-en/-en) policeman, constable, *sl.* bobby, cop; **_in** *f* (-/-nen) policewoman.

polnisch *adj.* ['pɔlnɪʃ] Polish.

Polster ['pɔlstər] *n* (-s/-) pad; cushion; bolster; *s. Polsterung;* **'_möbel** *n/pl.* upholstered furniture; upholstery; **'2n** *v/t.* (ge-, *h*) upholster, stuff; pad, wad; '~sessel *m*, '~stuhl *m* upholstered chair; '~ung *f* (-/-en) padding, stuffing; upholstery.

poltern ['pɔltərn] *v/i.* (ge-, h) make a row; rumble; *p.* bluster.

Polytechnikum [poly'tɛçnikum] *n* (-s/Polytechnika, Polytechniken) polytechnic (school).

Pommes frites [pɔm'frit] *pl.* chips *pl.*, *Am.* French fried potatoes *pl.*

Pomp [pɔmp] *m* (-[e]s/no *pl.*) pomp, splendo(u)r; 2**haft** *adj.*, 2**ös** *adj.* [~'pøːs] pompous, splendid.

Pony ['pɔni] 1. *zo.* *n* (-s/-s) pony; 2. *m* (-s/-s) hairstyle: bang, fringe.

popul|är *adj.* [popu'lɛːr] popular; 2**arität** [~ari'tɛːt] *f* (-/no *pl.*) popularity.

Por|e ['poːrə] *f* (-/-n) pore; 2**ös** *adj.* [po'røːs] porous; permeable.

Portemonnaie [pɔrtmɔ'nɛː] *n* (-s/-s) purse.

Portier [pɔr'tjeː] *m* (-s/-s) *s.* Pförtner.

Portion [pɔr'tsjoːn] *f* (-/-en) portion, share; ✕ ration; helping, serving; zwei ~en Kaffee coffee for two.

Porto ['pɔrto] *n* (-s/-s, Porti) postage; 2**frei** *adj.* post-free; prepaid, *esp. Am.* postpaid; 2**pflichtig** *adj.* subject to postage.

Porträt [pɔr'trɛː; ~t] *n* (-s/-s; -[e]s/-e) portrait, likeness; 2**ieren** [~ɛ'tiːrən] *v/t.* (no -ge-, h) portray.

Portugies|e [pɔrtu'giːzə] *m* (-n/-n) Portuguese; die ~n *pl.* the Portuguese *pl.*; 2**isch** *adj.* Portuguese.

Porzellan [pɔrtsɛ'laːn] *n* (-s/-e) porcelain, china.

Posaune [po'zaunə] *f* (-/-n) ♪ trombone; *fig.* trumpet.

Pose ['poːzə] *f* (-/-n) pose, attitude; *fig. a.* air.

Position [pozi'tsjoːn] *f* (-/-en) position; social standing; ⚓ station.

positiv *adj.* ['poːzitiːf] positive.

Positur [pozi'tuːr] *f* (-/-en) posture; sich in ~ setzen strike an attitude.

Posse *thea.* ['pɔsə] *f* (-/-n) farce.

'**Possen** *m* (-s/-) trick, prank; 2**haft** *adj.* farcical, comical; '~reißer *m* (-s/-) buffoon, clown.

possessiv *gr. adj.* ['pɔsɛsiːf] possessive.

pos'sierlich *adj.* droll, funny.

Post [pɔst] *f* (-/-en) post, *Am.* mail; mail, letters *pl.*; post office; mit der ersten ~ by the first delivery; '~amt *n* post office; '~anschrift *f* mailing address; '~anweisung *f* postal order; '~beamte *m* post-office clerk; '~bote *m* postman, *Am.* mailman; '~dampfer *m* packet-boat.

Posten ['pɔstən] *m* (-s/-) post, place, station; job; ✕ sentry, sentinel; item; entry; *goods:* lot, parcel.

'**Postfach** *n* post-office box.

pos'tieren *v/t.* (no -ge-, h) post, station, place; sich ~ station o.s.

'**Post|karte** *f* postcard, *with printed postage stamp: Am. a.* postal card; '~kutsche *f* stage-coach; 2**lagernd** *adj.* to be (kept until) called for, poste restante, *Am.* (in care of) general delivery; '~leitzahl *f* post-code; '~minister *m* minister of post; *Brt. and Am.* Postmaster General; '~paket *n* postal parcel; '~schalter *m* (post-office) window; '~scheck *m* postal cheque, *Am.* postal check; '~schließfach *n* post-office box; '~sparbuch *n* post-office savings-book; '~stempel *m* postmark; 2**wendend** *adv.* by return of post; '~wertzeichen *n* (postage) stamp; '~zug 🚂 *m* mail-train.

Pracht [praxt] *f* (-/⚡-en, ⚡e) splendo(u)r, magnificence; luxury.

prächtig *adj.* ['prɛçtiç] splendid, magnificent; gorgeous; grand.

'**prachtvoll** *adj. s.* prächtig.

Prädikat [predi'kaːt] *n* (-[e]s/-e) *gr.* predicate; *school, etc.*: mark.

prägen ['prɛːgən] *v/t.* (ge-, h) stamp; coin (*word, coin*).

prahlen ['praːlən] *v/i.* (ge-, h) brag, boast (mit of); ~ mit show off *s.th.*

'**Prahler** *m* (-s/-) boaster, braggart; ~**ei** [~'raɪ] *f* (-/-en) boasting, bragging; 2**isch** *adj.* boastful; ostentatious.

Prakti|kant [prakti'kant] *m* (-en/-en) probationer; '~ker *m* (-s/-) practical man; expert; ~**kum** ['~kum] *n* (-s/Praktika, Praktiken) practical course; 2**sch** *adj.* practical, useful, handy; ~er Arzt general practitioner; 2**zieren** ⚕, ⚖ [~'tsiːrən] *v/i.* (no -ge-, h) practi|se, *Am.* -ce medicine or the law. [prelate.)

Prälat *eccl.* ['prɛ'laːt] *m* (-en/-en))

Praline [pra'liːnə] *f* (-/-n): ~n *pl.* chocolates *pl.*

prall *adj.* [pral] tight; plump; *sun:* blazing; **'₂en** *v/i.* (ge-, sein) bounce *or* bound (*auf acc., gegen* against).

Prämi|e ['prɛːmjə] *f* (-/-n) † premium; prize; bonus; **₂(i)eren** [prɛ'miːrən, premi'iːrən] *v/t.* (*no* -ge-, *h*) award a prize to.

prang|en ['praŋən] *v/i.* (ge-, *h*) shine, make a show; **'₂er** *m* (-s/-) pillory.

Pranke ['praŋkə] *f* (-/-n) paw.

pränumerando *adv.* [prɛːnumə-'rando] beforehand, in advance.

Präpa|rat [prɛpa'raːt] *n* (-[e]s/-e) preparation; *microscopy:* slide; **₂'rieren** *v/t.* (*no* -ge-, *h*) prepare.

Präposition *gr.* [prepozi'tsjoːn] *f* (-/-en) preposition.

Prärie [prɛ'riː] *f* (-/-n) prairie.

Präsens *gr.* ['prɛːzɛns] *n* (-/Präsentia, Präsenzien) present (tense).

Präsi|dent [prɛzi'dɛnt] *m* (-en/-en) president; chairman; **₂'dieren** *v/i.* (*no* -ge-, *h*) preside (*über acc.* over); be in the chair; **~dium** [~'ziːdjum] *n* (-s/Präsidien) presidency, chair.

prasseln ['prasəln] *v/i.* (ge-, *h*) *fire:* crackle; *rain:* patter.

prassen ['prasən] *v/i.* (ge-, *h*) feast, carouse.

Präteritum *gr.* [prɛ'teːritum] *n* (-s/Präterita) preterite (tense); past tense.

Praxis ['praksis] *f* **1.** (-/no *pl.*) practice; **2.** (-/Praxen) practice (*of doctor or lawyer*).

Präzedenzfall [prɛtse'dɛnts-] *m* precedent; 🏛 *a.* case-law.

präzis *adj.* [prɛ'tsiːs], **~e** *adj.* [~zə] precise.

predig|en ['preːdigən] *v/i. and v/t.* (ge-, *h*) preach; **'₂er** *m* (-s/-) preacher; clergyman; **₂t** ['~diçt] *f* (-/-en) sermon (*a. fig.*); *fig.* lecture.

Preis [prais] *m* (-es/-e) price; cost; *competition:* prize; reward; praise; *um jeden* ~ at any price *or* cost; **'~ausschreiben** *n* (-s/-) competition; [praise.]

preisen ['praizən] *v/t.* (*irr.*,ge-, *h*)

Preis|erhöhung *f* rise *or* increase in price(s); **'~gabe** *f* abandonment; revelation (*of secret*); **'₂geben** *v/t.* (*irr. geben, sep.,* -ge-, *h*) abandon; reveal, give away (*secret*); disclose, expose; **'₂gekrönt** *adj.* prize-winning, prize (*novel, etc.*); **'~gericht** *n* jury; **'~lage** *f* range of

prices; **'~liste** *f* price-list; **'~nachlaß** *m* price cut; discount; **'~richter** *m* judge, umpire; **'~schießen** *n* (-s/-) shooting competition; **'~stopp** *m* (-s/no *pl.*) price freeze; **'~träger** *m* (-s/-) prize-winner; **₂wert** *adj.:* ~ *sein* be a bargain.

prell|en ['prɛlən] *v/t.* (ge-, *h*) *fig.* cheat, defraud (*um of*); *sich et.* ~ contuse *or* bruise s.th.; **'₂ung** 🩹 *f* (-/-en) contusion.

Premier|e *thea.* [prəm'jɛːrə] *f* (-/-n) première, first night; **~minister** [~'je:-] *m* prime minister.

Presse ['prɛsə] *f* **1.** (-/-n) ⊕, *typ.* press; squeezer; **2.** (-/no *pl.*) *newspapers generally: the* press; **'~amt** *n* public relations office; **'~freiheit** *f* freedom of the press; **'~meldung** *f* news item; **₂n** *v/t.* (ge-, *h*) press; squeeze; **'~photograph** *m* press-photographer; **'~vertreter** *m* reporter; public relations officer.

Preßluft ['pres-] *f* (-/no *pl.*) compressed air.

Prestige [pres'tiːʒə] *n* (-s/no *pl.*) prestige; ~ *verlieren a.* lose face.

Preuß|e ['prɔysə] *m* (-n/-n) Prussian; **₂isch** *adj.* Prussian.

prickeln ['prikəln] *v/i.* (ge-, *h*) prick(le), tickle; itch; *fingers:* tingle.

Priem [priːm] *m* (-[e]s/-e) quid.

pries [priːs] *pret. of* preisen.

Priester ['priːstər] *m* (-s/-) priest; **'~in** *f* (-/-nen) priestess; **₂lich** *adj.* priestly, sacerdotal; **'~rock** *m* cassock.

prim|a F *adj.* ['priːma] first-rate, F A 1; † *a.* prime; F swell; **~är** *adj.* [pri'mɛːr] primary.

Primel 💐 ['priːməl] *f* (-/-n) primrose.

Prinz [prints] *m* (-en/-en) prince; **~essin** [~'tsɛsin] *f* (-/-nen) princess; **'~gemahl** *m* prince consort.

Prinzip [prin'tsiːp] *n* (-s/-ien) principle; *aus* ~ on principle; *im* ~ in principle, basically.

Priorität [priori'tɛːt] *f* **1.** (-/-en) priority; **2.** (-/no *pl.*) *time:* priority.

Prise ['priːzə] *f* (-/-n) ⚓ prize; *e-e* ~ a pinch of (*salt, snuff*).

Prisma ['prisma] *n* (-s/Prismen) prism. [bed.]

Pritsche ['pritʃə] *f* (-/-n) bat; plank-]

privat *adj.* [pri'vaːt] private; **₂adresse** *f* home address; **₂mann** *m* (-[e]s/Privatmänner, Privatleute) private person *or* gentleman; **&patient** ⚕ *m* paying patient; **&person** *f* private person; **&schule** *f* private school.

Privileg [privi'le:k] *n* (-[e]s/-ien, -e) privilege.

pro *prp.* [pro:] per; ~ *Jahr* per annum; ~ *Kopf* per head; ~ *Stück* a piece.

Probe ['pro:bə] *f* (-/-n) experiment; trial, test; *metall.* assay; sample; specimen; proof; probation; check; *thea.* rehearsal; audition; *auf* ~ on probation, on trial; *auf die* ~ *stellen* (put to the) test; '**~abzug** *typ.*, *phot.* *m* proof; '**~exemplar** *n* specimen copy; '**~fahrt** *f* ⚓ trial trip; *mot.* trial run; '**~flug** *m* test *or* trial flight; '**&n** *v/t.* (ge-, h) exercise; *thea.* rehearse; '**~nummer** *f* specimen copy *or* number; '**~seite** *typ. f* specimen page; '**~sendung** *f* goods on approval; '**&weise** *adv.* on trial; *p. a.* on probation; '**~zeit** *f* time of probation.

probieren [pro'bi:rən] *v/t.* (*no* -ge-, *h*) try, test; taste (*food*.)

Problem [pro'ble:m] *n* (-s/-e) problem; **&atisch** *adj.* [~e'mɑ:tiʃ] problematic(al).

Produkt [pro'dukt] *n* (-[e]s/-e) product (*a.* ⚗); ⚘ produce; result; **~ion** [~'tsjo:n] *f* (-/-en) production; output; **&iv** *adj.* [~'ti:f] productive.

Produz|ent [produ'tsɛnt] *m* (-en/-en) producer; **&ieren** [~'tsi:rən] *v/t.* (*no* -ge-, *h*) produce; *sich* ~ perform; *contp.* show off.

professionell *adj.* [profɛsio'nɛl] professional, by trade.

Profess|or [pro'fɛsɔr] *m* (-s/-en) professor; **~ur** [~'su:r] *f* (-/-en) professorship, chair.

Profi ['pro:fi] *m* (-s/-s) *sports*: professional, F pro.

Profil [pro'fi:l] *n* (-s/-e) profile; [*on tyre*: tread.]

Profit [pro'fi:t] *m* (-[e]s/-e) profit; **&ieren** [~i'ti:rən] *v/i.* (*no* -ge-, *h*) profit (*von* by).

Prognose [pro'gno:zə] *f* (-/-n) ⚕ prognosis; *meteor.* forecast.

Programm [pro'gram] *n* (-s/-e) program(me); *politisches* ~ political program(me), *Am.* platform.

Projektion [projɛk'tsjo:n] *f* (-/-en) projection; **~sapparat** [projɛk'tsjo:nsˀ-] *m* projector.

proklamieren [prokla'mi:rən] *v/t.* (*no* -ge-, *h*) proclaim.

Prokur|a ✝ [pro'ku:ra] *f* (-/*Prokuren*) procuration; **~ist** [~ku'rist] *m* (-en/-en) confidential clerk.

Proletari|er [prole'tɑ:rjər] *m* (-s/-) proletarian; **&sch** *adj.* proletarian.

Prolog [pro'lo:k] *m* (-[e]s/-e) prolog(ue).

prominen|t *adj.* [promi'nɛnt] prominent; **&z** [~ts] *f* (-/*no pl.*) notables *pl.*, celebrities *pl.*; high society.

Promo|tion *univ.* [promo'tsjo:n] *f* (-/-en) graduation; **&vieren** [~'vi:rən] *v/i.* (*no* -ge-, *h*) graduate (*an dat.* from), take one's degree.

Pronomen *gr.* [pro'no:mɛn] *n* (-s/-, *Pronomina*) pronoun.

Propeller [pro'pɛlər] *m* (-s/-) ⚓, ✈ (screw-)propeller, screw; ✈ airscrew.

Prophe|t [pro'fe:t] *m* (-en/-en) prophet; **&tisch** *adj.* prophetic; **&zeien** [~e'tsaɪən] *v/t.* (*no* -ge-, *h*) prophesy; predict, foretell; **~'zeiung** *f* (-/-en) prophecy; prediction.

Proportion [propɔr'tsjo:n] *f* (-/-en) proportion.

Prosa ['pro:za] *f* (-/*no pl.*) prose.

prosit *int.* ['pro:zit] your health!, here's to you!, cheers!

Prospekt [pro'spɛkt] *m* (-[e]s/-e) prospectus; brochure, leaflet, folder.

prost *int.* [pro:st] *s. prosit.*

Prostituierte [prostitu'i:rtə] *f* (-n/-n) prostitute.

Protest [pro'tɛst] *m* (-es/-e) protest; ~ *einlegen or erheben gegen* (enter a) protest against.

Protestant *eccl.* [protɛs'tant] *m* (-en/-en) Protestant; **&isch** *adj.* Protestant.

protes'tieren *v/i.* (*no* -ge-, *h*): *gegen et.* ~ protest against s.th., object to s.th.

Prothese ⚕ [pro'te:zə] *f* (-/-n) pro(s)thesis; *dentistry*: *a.* denture; artificial limb.

Protokoll [proto'kɔl] *n* (-s/-e) record, minutes *pl.* (*of meeting*); *diplomacy*: protocol; *das* ~ *aufnehmen* take down the minutes; *das* ~ *führen* keep the minutes; *zu* ~ *geben* ⚖ depose, state in evidence; *zu* ~ *nehmen* take down, record; **&ieren** [~'li:rən] (*no* -ge-, *h*) **1.** *v/t.* record, take down (on record); **2.** *v/i.* keep the minutes.

Protz *contp.* [prɔts] *m* (-en, -es/

-e[n] braggart, F show-off; '2en
v/i. (ge-, h) show off (mit dat. with);
'2ig adj. ostentatious, showy.
Proviant [pro'vjant] m (-s/✐-e)
provisions pl., victuals pl.
Provinz [pro'vints] f (-/-en) province; fig. the provinces pl.; 2ial adj.
[~'tsja:l], 2iell adj. [~'tsjɛl] provincial.
Provis|ion ✝ [provi'zjo:n] f (-/-en)
commission; 2orisch adj. [~'zo:riʃ]
provisional, temporary.
provozieren [provo'tsi:rən] v/t. (no
-ge-, h) provoke.
Prozent [pro'tsɛnt] n (-[e]s/-e) per
cent; ~satz m percentage; 2ual adj.
[~u'a:l] percental; ~er Anteil percentage.
Prozeß [pro'tsɛs] m (Prozesses/Pro-
zesse) process; ♊: action, lawsuit;
trial; (legal) proceedings pl.; e-n ~
gewinnen win one's case; e-n ~
gegen j-n anstrengen bring an action
against s.o., sue s.o.; j-m den ~
machen try s.o., put s.o. on trial;
kurzen ~ machen mit make short
work of.
prozessieren [protsɛ'si:rən] v/i. (no
-ge-, h): mit j-m ~ go to law a-
gainst s.o., have the law of s.o
Prozession [protsɛ'sjo:n] f (-/-en)
procession.
prüde adj. ['pry:də] prudish.
prüf|en ['pry:fən] v/t. (ge-, h) ex-
amine; try, test; quiz; check,
verify; '~end adj. look: searching,
scrutinizing; '2er m (-s/-) examiner;
'2ling m (-s/-e) examinee; '2stein
fig. m touchstone; '2ung f (-/-en)
examination; school, etc.: a. F exam;
test; quiz; verification, checking,
check-up; e-e ~ machen go in for
or sit for or take an examination.
'**Prüfungs|arbeit** f, '~aufgabe f
examination-paper; '~ausschuß m,
'~kommission f board of exam-
iners.
Prügel ['pry:gəl] 1. m (-s/-) cudgel,
club, stick; 2. F fig. pl. beating,
thrashing; ~ei f [~'laɪ] f (-/-en)
fight, row; '~knabe m scapegoat;
'2n F v/t. (ge-, h) cudgel, flog; beat
(up), thrash; sich ~ (have a) fight.
Prunk [pruŋk] m (-[e]s/no pl.)
splendo(u)r; pomp, show; '2en
v/i. (ge-, h) make a show (mit of),
show off (mit et. s.th.); '2voll adj.
splendid, gorgeous.

Psalm eccl. [psalm] m (-s/-en)
psalm.
Pseudonym [psɔ^do'ny:m] n (-s/-e)
pseudonym.
pst int. [pst] hush!
Psychi|ater [psyçi'a:tər] m (-s/-)
psychiatrist, alienist; 2sch adj.
['psy:çiʃ] psychic(al).
Psycho|analyse [psyço^ana'ly:zə] f
(-/no pl.) psychoanalysis; ~analy-
tiker [~tikər] m (-s/-) psycho-
analyst; ~loge [~'lo:gə] m (-n/-n)
psychologist; ~se [~'ço:zə] f (-/-n)
psychosis; panic.
Pubertät [puber'tɛ:t] f (-/no pl.)
puberty.
Publikum ['pu:blikum] n (-s/no
pl.) the public; audience; spectators
pl., crowd; readers pl.
publiz|ieren [publi'tsi:rən] v/t. (no
-ge-, h) publish; 2ist m (-en/-en)
publicist; journalist.
Pudding ['pudiŋ] m (-s/-e, -s)
cream.
Pudel zo. ['pu:dəl] m (-s/-) poodle;
'2naß F adj. dripping wet,
drenched.
Puder ['pu:dər] m (-s/-) powder;
'~dose f powder-box; compact; 2n
v/t. (ge-, h) powder; sich ~ powder
o.s. or one's face; '~quaste f
powder-puff; '~zucker m pow-
dered sugar.
Puff F [puf] m (-[e]s/✐e, -e) poke,
nudge; '2en (ge-, h) 1. F v/t. nudge;
2. v/i. pop; '2er ✐ m (-s/-) buffer.
Pullover [pu'lo:vər] m (-s/-) pullover, sweater.
Puls ✐ [puls] m (-es/-e) pulse;
'~ader anat. f artery; 2ieren [~'zi:-
rən] v/i. (no -ge-, h) pulsate, throb;
'~schlag ✐ m pulsation.
Pult [pult] n (-[e]s/-e) desk.
Pulver ['pulfər] n (-s/-) powder;
gunpowder; F fig. cash, sl. brass,
dough; '2erig adj. powdery; 2eri-
sieren [~vəri'zi:rən] v/t. (no -ge-, h)
pulverize; 2rig adj. ['~friç] powdery.
Pump F [pump] m (-[e]s/-e): auf ~
on tick; '~e f (-/-n) pump; '2en
(ge-, h) 1. v/i. pump; 2. v/t. pump;
F fig.: give s.th. on tick; borrow (et.
von j-m s.th. from s.o.).
Punkt [puŋkt] m (-[e]s/-e) point (a.
fig.); dot; typ., gr. full stop, period;
spot, place; fig. item; article, clause
(of agreement); der springende ~ the

point; *toter* ~ deadlock, dead end; *wunder* ~ tender subject, sore point; ~ *zehn Uhr* on the stroke of ten, at 10 (o'clock) sharp; *in vielen* ~*en* on many points, in many respects; *nach* ~*en siegen sports*: win on points; Ձieren [~'ti:rən] *v/t. (no -ge-, h)* dot, point; ⚹ puncture, tap; *drawing, painting*: stipple.

pünktlich *adj.* ['pyŋktliç] punctual; ~ *sein* be on time; Ձkeit *f (-/no pl.)* punctuality.

Punsch [punʃ] *m (-es/-e)* punch.

Pupille *anat.* [pu'pilə] *f (-/-n)* pupil.

Puppe ['pupə] *f (-/-n)* doll (*a. fig.*); puppet (*a. fig.*); *tailoring*: dummy; *zo.* chrysalis, pupa; '~nspiel *n* puppet-show; '~nstube *f* doll's room; '~nwagen *m* doll's pram, *Am.* doll carriage *or* buggy.

pur *adj.* [pu:r] pure, sheer.

Püree [py're:] *n (-s/-s)* purée, mash.

Purpur ['purpur] *m (-s/no pl.)* purple; Ձfarben *adj.*, Ձn *adj.*, Ձrot *adj.* purple.

Purzel|baum ['purtsəl-] *m* somersault; *e-n* ~ *schlagen* turn a somersault; Ձn *v/i. (ge-, sein)* tumble.

Puste F ['pu:stə] *f (-/no pl.)* breath; *ihm ging die* ~ *aus* he got out of breath.

Pustel ⚹ ['pustəl] *f (-/-n)* pustule, pimple.

pusten ['pu:stən] *v/i. (ge-, h)* puff, pant; blow.

Pute *orn.* ['pu:tə] *f (-/-n)* turkey (-hen); '~r *orn. m (-s/-)* turkey (-cock); Ձr'rot *adj.* (as) red as a turkey-cock.

Putsch [putʃ] *m (-es/-e)* putsch, insurrection; riot; Ձen *v/i. (ge-, h)* revolt, riot.

Putz [puts] *m (-es/-e) on garments*: finery; ornaments *pl.*; trimming; △ roughcast, plaster; Ձen *v/t. (ge-, h)* clean, cleanse; polish, wipe; adorn; snuff (*candle*); polish, *Am.* shine (*shoes*); *sich* ~ smarten *or* dress o.s. up; *sich die Nase* ~ blow *or* wipe one's nose; *sich die Zähne* ~ brush one's teeth; '~frau *f* charwoman, *Am. a.* scrubwoman; Ձig *adj.* droll, funny; '~lappen *m* cleaning rag; '~zeug *n* cleaning utensils *pl.*

Pyjama [pi'dʒa:ma] *m (-s/-s)* (*ein a suit of*) pyjamas *pl. or Am. a.* pajamas *pl.*

Pyramide [pyra'mi:də] *f (-/-n)* pyramid (*a. ⚹*); ✕ stack (*of rifles*); Ձnförmig *adj.* [~nfœrmiç] pyramidal.

Q

Quacksalber ['kvakzalbər] *m (-s/-)* quack (doctor); ~ei F [~'raɪ] *f (-/-en)* quackery; Ձn *v/i. (ge-, h)* (play the) quack.

Quadrat [kva'dra:t] *n (-[e]s/-e)* square; *2 Fuß im* ~ 2 feet square; *ins* ~ *erheben* square; Ձisch *adj.* square; Å *equation*: quadratic; ~meile *f* square mile; ~meter *n, m* square met|re, *Am.* -er; ~wurzel Å *f* square root; ~zahl Å *f* square number.

quaken ['kva:kən] *v/i. (ge-, h) duck*: quack; *frog*: croak. {squeak.}

quäken ['kvɛ:kən] *v/i. (ge-, h)*

Quäker ['kvɛ:kər] *m (-s/-)* Quaker, member of the Society of Friends.

Qual [kva:l] *f (-/-en)* pain; torment; agony.

quälen ['kvɛ:lən] *v/t. (ge-, h)* torment (*a. fig.*); torture; ago-

nize; *fig.* bother, pester; *sich* ~ toil, drudge.

Qualifikation [kvalifika'tsjo:n] *f (-/-en)* qualification.

qualifizieren [kvalifi'tsi:rən] *v/t. and v/refl. (no -ge-, h)* qualify (*zu* for).

Qualit|ät [kvali'tɛ:t] *f (-/-en)* quality; Ձativ [~a'ti:f] **1.** *adj.* qualitative; **2.** *adv.* as to quality.

Quali'täts|arbeit *f* work of high quality; ~stahl *m* high-grade steel; ~ware *f* high-grade *or* quality goods *pl.*

Qualm [kvalm] *m (-[e]s/no pl.)* dense smoke; fumes *pl.*; vapo(u)r, steam; Ձen *(ge-, h)* **1.** *v/i.* smoke, give out vapo(u)r *or* fumes; F p. smoke heavily; **2.** F *v/t.* puff (away) at (*cigar, pipe, etc.*); Ձig *adj.* smoky.

'**qualvoll** adj. very painful; pain: excruciating; fig. agonizing, harrowing.

Quantit|ät [kvanti'tɛ:t] f (-/-en) quantity; **ℒativ** [..a'ti:f] **1.** adj. quantitative; **2.** adv. as to quantity.

Quantum ['kvantum] n (-s/Quanten) quantity, amount; quantum (a. phys.).

Quarantäne [karan'tɛ:nə] f (-/-n) quarantine; in ~ legen (put in) quarantine.   [curd(s pl.).]

Quark [kvark] m (-[e]s/no pl.)]

Quartal [kvar'ta:l] n (-s/-e) quarter (of a year); univ. term.

Quartett [kvar'tɛt] n (-[e]s/-e) ♪ quartet(te); cards: four.

Quartier [kvar'ti:r] n (-s/-e) accommodation; ✕ quarters pl., billet.   [(powder-)puff.]

Quaste ['kvastə] f (-/-n) tassel;]

Quatsch F [kvatʃ] m (-es/no pl.) nonsense, fudge, sl. bosh, rot, Am. sl. a. baloney; **2en** F v/i. (ge-, h) twaddle, blether, sl. talk rot; (have a) chat; '**_kopf** F m twaddler.

Quecksilber ['kvɛk-] n mercury, quicksilver.

Quelle ['kvɛlə] f (-/-n) spring, source (a. fig.); oil: well; fig. fountain, origin; **2n** v/i. (irr., ge-, sein) gush, well; **_nangabe** ['kvɛlən?-] f mention of sources used); '**_nforschung** f original research.

Quengel|ei F [kvɛŋə'laɪ] f (-/-en) grumbling, whining; nagging; '**2n** F v/i. (ge-, h) grumble, whine; nag.

quer adv. [kve:r] crossways, crosswise; F fig. wrong; F ~ gehen go wrong; ~ über (acc.) across.

'**Quer|e** f (-/no pl.): der ~ nach crossways, crosswise; F j-m in die ~

kommen cross s.o.'s path; fig. thwart s.o.'s plans; '**_frage** f cross-question; '**_kopf** fig. m wrong-headed fellow; '**2schießen** F v/i. (irr. schießen, sep., -ge-, h) try to foil s.o.'s plans; '**_schiff** 🏛 n transept; '**_schläger** ✕ m ricochet; '**_schnitt** m cross-section (a. fig.); '**_straße** f cross-road; zweite ~ rechts second turning to the right; '**_treiber** m (-s/-) schemer; **_trei-be'rei** f (-/-en) intriguing, machination.

Querulant [kveru'lant] m (-en/-en) querulous person, grumbler, Am. sl. a. griper.

quetsch|en ['kvɛtʃən] v/t. (ge-, h) squeeze; ⚕ bruise, contuse; sich den Finger ~ jam one's finger; '**2ung** ⚕ f (-/-en), '**2wunde** ⚕ f bruise, contusion.

quick adj. [kvik] lively, brisk.

quieken ['kvi:kən] v/i. (ge-, h) squeak, squeal.

quietsch|en ['kvi:tʃən] v/i. (ge-, h) squeak, squeal; door-hinge, etc.: creak, squeak; brakes, etc.: screech; '**_ver'gnügt** F adj. (as) jolly as a sandboy.

Quirl [kvirl] m (-[e]s/-e) twirling-stick; '**2en** v/t. (ge-, h) twirl.

quitt adj. [kvit]: ~ sein mit j-m be quits or even with s.o.; jetzt sind wir ~ that leaves us even; **_ieren** [~'ti:rən] v/t. (no -ge-, h) receipt (bill, etc.); quit, abandon (post, etc.); '**2ung** f (-/-en) receipt; fig. answer; gegen ~ against receipt.

quoll [kvɔl] pret. of quellen.

Quot|e ['kvo:tə] f (-/-en) quota; share, portion; **_ient** Ⓐ [kvo'tsjɛnt] m (-en/-en) quotient.

R

Rabatt † [ra'bat] m (-[e]s/-e) discount, rebate.

Rabe orn. ['ra:bə] m (-n/-n) raven; '**2n_schwarz** F adj. raven, jet-black.

rabiat adj. [ra'bja:t] rabid, violent.

Rache ['raxə] f (-/no pl.) revenge, vengeance; retaliation.

Rachen anat. ['raxən] m (-s/-) throat, pharynx; jaws pl.

rächen ['rɛçən] v/t. (ge-, h) avenge,

revenge; sich ~ an (dat.) revenge o.s. or be revenged on.

'**Rachen|höhle** anat. f pharynx; '**_katarrh** ⚕ m cold in the throat.

'**rach|gierig** adj., '**_süchtig** adj. revengeful, vindictive.

Rad [ra:t] n (-[e]s/⸗er) wheel; (bi)cycle, F bike; (ein) ~ schlagen peacock: spread its tail; sports: turn cart-wheels; unter die Räder *kommen* go to the dogs; '~achse *f* axle(-tree).

Radar ['ra:da:r, ra'da:r] *m, n* (-s/-s) radar.

Radau F [ra'dau] *m* (-s/*no pl.*) row, racket, hubbub.

radebrechen ['ra:də-] *v/t.* (ge-, h) speak (*language*) badly, murder (*language*).

radeln ['ra:dəln] *v/i.* (ge-, sein) cycle, pedal, F bike.

Rädelsführer ['re:dəls-] *m* ringleader.

Räderwerk ⊕ ['re:dər-] *n* gearing.

'**rad|fahren** *v/i.* (irr. fahren, sep., -ge-, sein) cycle, (ride a bicycle) pedal, F bike; '♀**fahrer** *m* cyclist, Am. a. cycler *or* wheelman.

radier|en [ra'di:rən] *v/t.* (no -ge-, h) rub out, erase; *art:* etch; ♀**gummi** *m* (india-)rubber, *esp. Am.* eraser; ♀**messer** *n* eraser; ♀**ung** *f* (-/-en) etching.

Radieschen ♀ [ra'di:sçən] *n* (-s/-) (red) radish.

radikal *adj.* [radi'ka:l] radical.

Radio ['ra:djo] *n* (-s/-s) radio, wireless; *im ~* on the radio, on the air; ♀**aktiv** *phys. adj.* [radjoak'ti:f] radio(-)active; ~**er** *Niederschlag* fall-out; '~**apparat** *m* radio *or* wireless (set).

Radium ⚛ ['ra:djum] *n* (-s/*no pl.*) radium.

Radius ⚛ ['ra:djus] *m* (-/Radien) radius.

'**Rad|kappe** *f* hub cap; '~**kranz** *m* rim; '~**rennbahn** *f* cycling track; '~**rennen** *n* cycle race; '~**sport** *m* cycling; '~**spur** *f* rut, track.

raffen ['rafən] *v/t.* (ge-, h) snatch up; gather (*dress*).

raffiniert *adj.* [rafi'ni:rt] refined; *fig.* clever, cunning.

ragen ['ra:gən] *v/i.* (ge-, h) tower, loom.

Ragout [ra'gu:] *n* (-s/-s) ragout, stew, hash.

Rahe ⚓ ['ra:ə] *f* (-/-n) yard.

Rahm [ra:m] *m* (-[e]s/*no pl.*) cream.

Rahmen ['ra:mən] 1. *m* (-s/-) frame; *fig.:* frame, background, setting; scope; *aus dem ~ fallen* be out of place; 2. ♀ *v/t.* (ge-, h) frame.

Rakete [ra'ke:tə] *f* (-/-n) rocket; *e-e ~ abfeuern or starten* launch a rocket; *dreistufige ~* three-stage rocket; ~**nantrieb** [ra'ke:tən⁹-] *m*

rocket propulsion; *mit ~* rocket-propelled; ~**nflugzeug** *n* rocket (-propelled) plane; ~**ntriebwerk** *n* propulsion unit.

Ramm|bär ⊕ ['ram-] *m*, '~**bock** *m*, '~**e** *f* (-/-n) ram(mer); '♀**en** *v/t.* (ge-, h) ram.

Rampe ['rampə] *f* (-/-n) ramp, ascent; '~**nlicht** *n* footlights *pl.*; *fig.* limelight.

Ramsch [ramʃ] *m* (-es/♀ -e) junk, trash; *im ~ kaufen* buy in the lump; '~**verkauf** *m* jumble-sale; '~**ware** *f* job lot.

Rand [rant] *m* (-[e]s/⁼er) edge, brink (*a. fig.*); *fig.* verge; border; brim (*of hat, cup, etc.*); rim (*of plate, etc.*); margin (*of book, etc.*); lip (*of wound*); *Ränder pl. under the eyes:* rings *pl.*, circles *pl.*; *vor Freude außer ~ und Band geraten* be beside o.s. with joy; *er kommt damit nicht zu ~e* he can't manage it; '~**bemerkung** *f* marginal note; *fig.* comment.

rang¹ [raŋ] *pret. of ringen.*

Rang² [~] *m* (-[e]s/⁼e) rank, order; ✕ rank; position; *thea.* tier; *erster ~ thea.* dress-circle, *Am.* first balcony; *zweiter ~ thea.* upper circle, *Am.* second balcony; *ersten ~es* first-class, first-rate; *j-m den ~ ablaufen* get the start *or* better of s.o.

Range ['raŋə] *m* (-n/-n), *f* (-/-n) rascal; romp.

rangieren [rã'ʒi:rən] (no -ge-, h) 1. 🚂 *v/t.* shunt, *Am. a.* switch; 2. *fig. v/i.* rank.

'**Rang|liste** *f sports, etc.:* ranking list; ✕ army-list, navy *or* air-force list; '~**ordnung** *f* order of precedence.

Ranke ♀ ['raŋkə] *f* (-/-n) tendril; runner.

Ränke ['rɛŋkə] *m/pl.* intrigues *pl.*

'**ranken** *v/refl.* (ge-, h) creep, climb.

rann [ran] *pret. of rinnen.*

rannte ['rantə] *pret. of rennen.*

Ranzen ['rantsən] *m* (-s/-) knapsack; satchel.

ranzig *adj.* ['rantsiç] rancid, rank.

Rappe *zo.* ['rapə] *m* (-n/-n) black horse.

rar *adj.* [ra:r] rare, scarce.

Rarität [rari'tɛ:t] *f* (-/-en) rarity; curiosity, curio.

rasch *adj.* [raʃ] quick, swift, brisk; hasty; prompt.

rascheln ['raʃəln] v/i. (ge-, h) rustle.

rasen[1] ['rɑːzən] v/i. (ge-) **1.** (h) rage, storm, rave; **2.** (sein) race, speed; **~d** adj. raving, frenzied; speed: tearing; pains: agonizing; headache: splitting; j-n ~ machen drive s.o. mad.

Rasen[2] [~] m (-s/-) grass; lawn; turf; **~platz** m lawn, grass-plot.

Raserei F [rɑːzəˈraɪ] f (-/-en) rage, fury; frenzy, madness; F mot. scorching; j-n zur ~ bringen drive s.o. mad.

Rasier|apparat [raˈziːr-] m (safety) razor; **2en** v/t. (no -ge-, h) shave; sich ~ (lassen get a) shave; **~klinge** f razor-blade; **~messer** n razor; **~pinsel** m shaving-brush; **~seife** f shaving-soap; **~wasser** n aftershave lotion; **~zeug** n shaving kit.

Rasse ['rasə] f (-/-n) race; zo. breed.

rasseln ['rasəln] v/i. (ge-, h) rattle.

'**Rassen|frage** f (-/no pl.) racial issue; **~kampf** m race conflict; '**~problem** n racial issue; '**~schranke** f colo(u)r bar; '**~trennung** f (-/no pl.) racial segregation; '**~unruhen** f/pl. race riots pl.

'**rasserein** adj. thoroughbred, purebred.

'**rassig** adj. thoroughbred; fig. racy.

Rast [rast] f (-/-en) rest, repose; break, pause; **2en** v/i. (ge-, h) rest, repose; **2los** adj. restless; **~platz** m resting-place; mot. picnic area.

Rat [rɑːt] m **1.** (-[e]s/no pl.) advice, counsel; suggestion; fig. way out; zu ~e ziehen consult; j-n um ~ fragen ask s.o.'s advice; **2.** (-[e]s/=e) council, board; council(l)or, alderman.

Rate ['rɑːtə] f (-/-n) instal(l)ment (a. ✝); auf ~n ✝ on hire-purchase.

'**raten** (irr., ge-, h) **1.** v/i. advise, counsel (j-m zu inf. s.o. to inf.); **2.** v/t. guess, divine.

'**raten|weise** adv. by instal(l)ments; '**2zahlung** ✝ f payment by instal(l)ments.

'**Rat|geber** m (-s/-) adviser, counsel(l)or; '**~haus** n town hall, Am. a. city hall.

ratifizieren [ratifiˈtsiːrən] v/t. (no -ge-, h) ratify.

Ration [raˈtsjoːn] f (-/-en) ration, allowance; **2ell** adj. [~oˈnɛl] rational; efficient; economical; **2ieren** [~oˈniːrən] v/t. (no -ge-, h) ration.

rat|los adj. puzzled, perplexed, at a loss; '**~sam** adj. advisable; expedient; '**2schlag** m (piece of) advice, counsel.

Rätsel ['rɛːtsəl] n (-s/-) riddle, puzzle; enigma, mystery; '**2haft** adj. puzzling; enigmatic(al), mysterious.

Ratte zo. ['ratə] f (-/-n) rat.

rattern ['ratərn] v/i. (ge-, h, sein) rattle, clatter.

Raub [raup] m (-[e]s/no pl.) robbery; kidnap(p)ing; piracy (of intellectual property); booty, spoils pl.; '**~bau** m (-[e]s/no pl.): ~ treiben ✗ exhaust the land; ⚒ rob a mine; ~ treiben mit undermine (one's health); **2en** ['~bən] v/t. (ge-, h) rob, take by force, steal; kidnap; j-m et. ~ rob or deprive s.o. of s.th.

Räuber ['rɔʏbər] m (-s/-) robber; '**~bande** f gang of robbers; '**2isch** adj. rapacious, predatory.

'**Raub|fisch** ichth. m fish of prey; '**~gier** f rapacity; '**2gierig** adj. rapacious; '**~mord** m murder with robbery; '**~mörder** m murderer and robber; '**~tier** zo. n beast of prey; '**~überfall** m hold-up, armed robbery; '**~vogel** orn. m bird of prey; '**~zug** m raid.

Rauch [raux] m (-[e]s/no pl.) smoke; fume; '**2en** (ge-, h) **1.** v/i. smoke; fume; p. (have a) smoke; **2.** v/t. smoke (cigarette); '**~er** m (-s/-) smoker; s. Raucherabteil. [eel.]

Räucheraal ['rɔʏçərʔ-] m smoked]

Raucherabteil 🚃 ['rauxərʔ-] n smoking-car(riage), smoking-compartment, smoker.

'**Räucher|hering** m red or smoked herring, kipper; '**2n** (ge-, h) **1.** v/t. smoke, cure (meat, fish); **2.** v/i. burn incense.

'**Rauch|fahne** f trail of smoke; '**~fang** m chimney, flue; '**~fleisch** n smoked meat; '**2ig** adj. smoky; '**~tabak** m tobacco; '**~waren** f/pl. tobacco products pl.; furs pl.; '**~zimmer** n smoking-room.

Räud|e ['rɔʏdə] f (-/-n) mange, scab; '**2ig** adj. mangy, scabby.

Rauf|bold contp. ['raufbɔlt] m (-[e]s/-e) brawler, rowdy, Am. sl. tough; '**2en** (ge-, h) **1.** v/t. pluck, pull; sich die Haare ~ tear one's hair; **2.** v/i. fight, scuffle; **~erei** [~əˈraɪ] f (-/-en) fight, scuffle.

Q
R

rauh adj. [rau] rough; rugged; *weather*: inclement, raw; *voice*: hoarse; *fig.*: harsh; coarse, rude; F: in ~en Mengen galore; **Sreif** m (-[e]s/no pl.) hoar-frost, *poet.* rime.

Raum [raum] m (-[e]s/̈e) room, space; expanse; area; room; premises pl.; **~anzug** m space suit.

räumen ['rɔyman] v/t. (ge-, h) remove, clear (away); leave, give up, *esp.* ✠ evacuate; vacate (*flat*).

'Raum|fahrt f astronautics; **~flug** m space flight; **~inhalt** m volume, capacity; **~kapsel** f capsule.

räumlich adj. ['rɔymliç] relating to space, of space, spatial.

'Raum|meter n, m cubic met|re, *Am.* -er; **~schiff** n space craft *or* ship; **~sonde** ♀ f space probe; **~station** f space station.

'Räumung f (-/-en) clearing, removal; *esp.* ✠ clearance; vacating (*of flat*), *by force*: eviction; ✠ evacuation (*of town*); **~sverkauf** ✠ m clearance sale.

raunen ['raunan] (ge-, h) 1. v/i. whisper, murmur; 2. v/t. whisper, murmur; *man raunt* rumo(u)r has it.

Raupe zo. ['raupə] f (-/-n) caterpillar; **~nschlepper** ⊕ m caterpillar tractor.

raus int. [raus] get out!, *sl.*beat it!, [scram!]

Rausch [rauʃ] m (-es/̈e) intoxication, drunkenness; *fig.* frenzy, transport(s pl.); e-n ~ haben be drunk; **Sen** v/i. (ge-) 1. (h) *leaves, rain, silk*: rustle; *water, wind*: rush; *surf*: roar; *applause*: thunder; 2. (sein) *movement*: sweep; **'~gift** n narcotic (drug), F dope.

räuspern ['rɔyspərn] v/refl. (ge-, h) clear one's throat.

Razzia ['ratsja] f (-/Razzien) raid, round-up.

reagieren [rea'giːrən] v/i. (no -ge-, h) react (auf acc. [up]on; to); *fig. and* ⊕ a. respond (to).

Reaktion [reak'tsjoːn] f (-/-en) reaction (a. pol.); *fig. a.* response (auf acc. to); **~är** [~o'nɛːr] 1. m (-s/-e) reactionary; 2. ♀ adj. reactionary.

Reaktor phys. [re'aktɔr] m (-s/-en) (nuclear) reactor, atomic pile.

real adj. [re'aːl] real; concrete; **~isieren** [reali'ziːrən] v/t. (no -ge-,

h) realize; **Sismus** [rea'lismʊs] m (-/no pl.) realism; **~istisch** adj. [rea'listiʃ] realistic; **Sität** [reali'tɛːt] f (-/-en) reality; **Sschule** f non-classical secondary school.

Rebe ♀ ['reːbə] f (-/-n) vine.

Rebell [re'bɛl] m (-en/-en) rebel; **Sieren** [~'liːrən] v/i. (no -ge-, h) rebel, revolt, rise; **Sisch** adj. rebellious.

Reb|huhn orn. ['rep-] n partridge; **~laus** zo. ['reːp-] f vine-fretter, phylloxera; **~stock** ♀ ['reːp-] m vine.

Rechen ['reçən] m (-s/-) rake; grid.

Rechen|aufgabe ['reçən-] f sum, (arithmetical) problem; **~fehler** m, arithmetical error, miscalculation; **~maschine** f calculating-machine; **~schaft** f (-/no pl.): ~ ablegen give *or* render an account (über acc. of), account *or* answer (for); zur ~ ziehen call to account (wegen for); **~schieber** ✄ m slide-rule.

rechne|n ['reçnən] (ge-, h) 1. v/t. reckon, calculate; estimate, value; charge; ~ zu rank with *or* among(st); 2. v/i. count; ~ auf (acc.) *or* mit count *or* reckon *or* rely (up)on; **~risch** adj. arithmetical.

'Rechnung f (-/-en) calculation, sum, reckoning; account, bill; invoice (*of goods*); *in restaurant*: bill, *Am.* check; score; auf ~ on account; ~ legen render an account (über acc. of); e-r Sache ~ tragen make allowance for s.th.; es geht auf meine ~ *in restaurants*: it is my treat, *Am.* F this is on me; **'~sprüfer** m auditor.

recht¹ [reçt] 1. adj. right; real; legitimate; right, correct; zur ~en Zeit in due time, at the right moment; ein ~er Narr a regular fool; mir ist es ~ I don't mind; ~ haben be right; j-m ~ geben agree with s.o.; 2. adv. right(ly); well; very; rather; really; correctly; ganz ~! quite (so)!; es geschieht ihm ~ it serves him right; ~ gern gladly, with pleasure; ~ gut quite good *or* well; ich weiß nicht ~ I wonder.

Recht² [~] n (-[e]s/-e) right (auf acc. to), title (to), claim (on), interest (in); privilege; power, authority; ♀♀ law; justice; ~ sprechen administer justice; mit ~ justly.

ˈ**Rechte** *f* (-*n*/-*n*) right hand; *boxing*: right; *pol. the* Right.
Rechteck [ˈrɛçtˀ-] *n* (-[e]s/-e) rectangle; ˈ**&ig** *adj.* rectangular.
recht|fertigen [ˈrɛçtfɛrtigən] *v/t.* (ge-, *h*) justify; defend, vindicate; ˈ**&fertigung** *f* (-/-en) justification; vindication, defen|ce, *Am.* -se; ˈ**~gläubig** *adj.* orthodox; **~haberisch** *adj.* [ˈ~hɑːbəriʃ] dogmatic; ˈ**~lich** *adj.* legal, lawful, legitimate; honest, righteous; ˈ**~los** *adj.* without rights; outlawed; ˈ**&losigkeit** *f* (-/*no pl.*) outlawry; ˈ**~mäßig** *adj.* legal, lawful, legitimate; ˈ**&mäßigkeit** *f* (-/*no pl.*) legality, legitimacy.
rechts *adv.* [rɛçts] on *or* to the right (hand).
ˈ**Rechts|anspruch** *m* legal right *or* claim (*auf acc.* on, to), title (to); ˈ**~anwalt** *m* lawyer, solicitor; barrister, *Am.* attorney (at law); **~**ˈ**außen** *m* (-/-) *football*: outside right; ˈ**~beistand** *m* legal adviser, counsel.
ˈ**recht|schaffen** **1.** *adj.* honest, righteous; **2.** *adv.* thoroughly, downright, F awfully; ˈ**&schreibung** *f* (-/-en) orthography, spelling.
ˈ**Rechts|fall** *m* case, cause; ˈ**~frage** *f* question of law; issue of law; ˈ**~gelehrte** *m* jurist, lawyer; ˈ**&gültig** *adj. s. rechtskräftig*; ˈ**~kraft** *f* (-/*no pl.*) legal force *or* validity; ˈ**&kräftig** *adj.* valid, legal; *judgement*: final; ˈ**~kurve** *f* right-hand bend; ˈ**~lage** *f* legal position *or* status; ˈ**~mittel** *n* legal remedy; ˈ**~nachfolger** *m* assign, assignee; ˈ**~person** *f* legal personality; ˈ**~pflege** *f* administration of justice, judicature.
ˈ**Rechtsprechung** *f* (-/-en) jurisdiction.
ˈ**Rechts|schutz** *m* legal protection; ˈ**~spruch** *m* legal decision; judg(e)ment; sentence; verdict (*of jury*); ˈ**~steuerung** *mot. f* (-/-en) right-hand drive; ˈ**~streit** *m* action, lawsuit; ˈ**~verfahren** *n* (legal) proceedings *pl.*; ˈ**~verkehr** *mot. m* right-hand traffic; ˈ**~verletzung** *f* infringement; ˈ**~vertreter** *m s. Rechtsbeistand*; ˈ**~weg** *m*: *den ~ beschreiten* take legal action, go to law; *unter Ausschluß des ~es* eliminating legal proceedings; ˈ**&widrig** *adj.* illegal, unlawful; ˈ**~wissenschaft** *f* jurisprudence.
ˈ**recht|wink(e)lig** *adj.* right-angled; ˈ**~zeitig** **1.** *adj.* punctual; opportune; **2.** *adv.* in (due) time, punctually, *Am.* on time.
Reck [rɛk] *n* (-[e]s/-e) *sports*: horizontal bar.
recken [ˈrɛkən] *v/t.* (ge-, *h*) stretch; *sich ~* stretch o.s.
Redakt|eur [redakˈtøːr] *m* (-s/-e) editor; **~ion** [~ˈtsjoːn] *f* (-/-en) editorship; editing, wording; editorial staff, editors *pl.*; editor's *or* editorial office; **&ionell** *adj.* [~tsjoˈnɛl] editorial.
Rede [ˈreːdə] *f* (-/-n) speech; oration; language; talk, conversation; discourse; *direkte ~ gr.* direct speech; *indirekte ~ gr.* reported *or* indirect speech; *e-e ~ halten* make *or* deliver a speech; *zur ~ stellen* call to account (*wegen* for); *davon ist nicht die ~* that is not the point; *davon kann keine ~ sein* that's out of the question; *es ist nicht der ~ wert* it is not worth speaking of; ˈ**&gewandt** *adj.* eloquent; ˈ**~kunst** *f* rhetoric; ˈ**&n** (ge-, *h*) **1.** *v/t.* speak; talk; **2.** *v/i.* speak (*mit* to); talk (to), chat (with); discuss (*über et.* s.th.); *sie läßt nicht mit sich ~* she won't listen to reason.
Redensart [ˈreːdənsˀ-] *f* phrase, expression; idiom; proverb, saying.
redigieren [rediˈgiːrən] *v/t.* (*no* -ge-, *h*) edit; revise.
redlich [ˈreːtliç] **1.** *adj.* honest, upright; sincere; **2.** *adv.*: *sich ~ bemühen* take great pains.
Redner [ˈreːdnər] *m* (-s/-) speaker; orator; ˈ**~bühne** *f* platform; ˈ**&isch** *adj.* oratorical, rhetorical; ˈ**~pult** *n* speaker's desk.
redselig *adj.* [ˈreːtzeːliç] talkative.
reduzieren [reduˈtsiːrən] *v/t.* (*no* -ge-, *h*) reduce (*auf acc.* to).
Reede ⚓ [ˈreːdə] *f* (-/-n) roads *pl.*, roadstead; ˈ**~r** *m* (-s/-) shipowner; **~**ˈ**rei** *f* (-/-en) shipping company *or* firm.
reell [reˈɛl] **1.** *adj.* respectable, honest; *business firm*: solid; *goods*: good; *offer*: real; **2.** *adv.*: *~ bedient werden* get good value for one's money.
Refer|at [refeˈrɑːt] *n* (-[e]s/-e) report; lecture; paper; *ein ~ halten*

esp. univ. read a paper; **~endar** [~ɛn'daːr] *m* (-s/-e) ɪ̣ɪ̣ junior lawyer; *at school:* junior teacher; **~ent** [~'rɛnt] *m* (-en/-en) reporter, speaker; **~enz** [~'rɛnts] *f* (-/-en) reference; **2ieren** [~'riːrən] *v/i* (no -ge-, h) report (*über acc.* [up]on); (give a) lecture (on); *esp. univ.* read a paper (on).

reflektieren [reflɛk'tiːrən] (no -ge-, h) **1.** *phys. v/t.* reflect; **2.** *v/i.* reflect (*über acc.* [up]on); **~** *auf* (*acc.*) ☂ think of, be interested in.

Reflex [re'flɛks] *m* (-es/-e) *phys.* reflection *or* reflexion; ﹩ reflex (action); **2iv** *gr. adj.* [~'ksiːf] reflexive.

Reform [re'fɔrm] *f* (-/-en) reform; **~er** *m* (-s/-) reformer; **2ieren** [~'miːrən] *v/t.* (no -ge-, h) reform.

Refrain [rə'frɛ̃ː] *m* (-s/-s) refrain, chorus, burden.

Regal [re'gaːl] *n* (-s/-e) shelf.

rege *adj.* ['reːɡə] active, brisk, lively; busy.

Regel ['reːɡəl] *f* (-/-n) rule; regulation; standard; *physiol.* menstruation, menses *pl.*; *in der* **~** as a rule; **'2los** *adj.* irregular; disorderly; **'2mäßig** *adj.* regular; **2n** *v/t.* (ge-, h) regulate, control; arrange, settle; put in order; **'2recht** *adj.* regular; **~ung** *f* (-/-en) regulation, control; arrangement, settlement; **'2widrig** *adj.* contrary to the rules, irregular; abnormal; *sports:* foul.

regen[1] ['reːɡən] *v/t. and v/refl.* (ge-, h) move, stir.

Regen[2] [~] *m* (-s/-) rain; *vom* **~** *in die Traufe kommen* jump out of the frying-pan into the fire, get from bad to worse; **'2arm** *adj.* dry; **'~bogen** *m* rainbow; **'~bogenhaut** *anat.* *f* iris; **'2dicht** *adj.* rain-proof; **'~guß** *m* downpour; **'~mantel** *m* waterproof, raincoat, mac(k)intosh, *F* mac; **'2reich** *adj.* rainy; **'~schauer** *m* shower (of rain); **'~schirm** *m* umbrella; **'~tag** *m* rainy day; **'~tropfen** *m* raindrop; **'~wasser** *n* rain-water; **'~wetter** *n* rainy weather; **'~wolke** *f* rain-cloud; **'~wurm** *zo.* *m* earthworm, *Am. a.* angleworm; **'~zeit** *f* rainy season.

Regie [re'ʒiː] *f* (-/-n) management; *thea., film:* direction; *unter der* **~** *von* directed by.

regier|**en** [re'ɡiːrən] (no -ge-, h)

1. *v/i.* reign; **2.** *v/t.* govern (*a. gr.*), rule; **2ung** *f* (-/-en) government, *Am.* administration; reign.

Re'gierungs|**antritt** *m* accession (to the throne); **~beamte** *m* government official; *Brt.* Civil Servant; **~bezirk** *m* administrative district; **~gebäude** *n* government offices *pl.*

Regiment [regi'mɛnt] *n* **1.** (-[e]s/-e) government, rule; **2.** ✕ (-[e]s/-er) regiment.

Regisseur [reʒi'søːr] *m* (-s/-e) *thea.* stage manager, director; *film:* director.

Regist|**er** [re'ɡɪstər] *n* (-s/-) register (*a. ♪*), record; index; **~ratur** [~ra'tuːr] *f* (-/-en) registry; registration.

registrier|**en** [regis'triːrən] *v/t.* (no -ge-, h) register, record; **2kasse** *f* cash register.

reglos *adj.* ['reːkloːs] motionless.

regne|**n** ['reːɡnən] *v/i.* (ge-, h) rain; *es regnet in Strömen* it is pouring with rain; **'~risch** *adj.* rainy.

Regreß ɪ̣ɪ̣, ☂ [re'grɛs] *m* (Regresses/Regresse) recourse; **2pflichtig** ɪ̣ɪ̣, ☂ *adj.* liable to recourse.

regulär *adj.* [regu'lɛːr] regular.

regulier|**bar** *adj.* [regu'liːrbaːr] adjustable, controllable; **~en** *v/t.* (no -ge-, h) regulate, adjust; control.

Regung ['reːɡuŋ] *f* (-/-en) movement, motion; emotion; impulse; **'2slos** *adj.* motionless.

Reh *zo.* [re:] *n* (-[e]s/-e) deer, roe; *female:* doe.

rehabilitieren [rehabili'tiːrən] *v/t.* (no -ge-, h) rehabilitate.

'Reh|**bock** *zo.* *m* roebuck; **'2braun** *adj.*, **'2farben** *adj.* fawn-colo(u)red; **'~geiß** *zo.* *f* doe; **'~kalb** *zo.* *n*, **'~kitz** *zo.* ['~kɪts] *n* (-es/-e) fawn.

Reib|**e** ['raɪbə] *f* (-/-n), **~eisen** ['raɪpʔ-] *n* grater.

reib|**en** ['raɪbən] (*irr.*, ge-, h) **1.** *v/i.* rub (*an dat.* [up]on); **2.** *v/t.* rub, grate; pulverize; *wund* **~** chafe, gall; **2erei** *F fig.* [~'raɪ] *f* (-/-en) (constant) friction; **2ung** *f* (-/-en) friction; **'~ungslos** *adj.* frictionless; *fig.* smooth.

reich[1] *adj.* [raɪç] rich (*an dat.* in); wealthy; ample, abundant, copious.

Reich[2] [~] *n* (-es/-e) empire; kingdom (*of animals, vegetables, minerals*); *poet., rhet., fig.* realm.

reichen ['raɪçən] (ge-, h) **1.** *v/t.* offer; serve (*food*); *j-m et.* **~** hand *or* pass s.th. to s.o.; *sich die Hände* ~ join hands; **2.** *v/i.* reach; extend; suffice; *das reicht!* that will do!

reich|haltig *adj.* ['raɪçhaltɪç] rich; abundant, copious; '**~lich 1.** *adj.* ample, abundant, copious, plentiful; ~ *Zeit* plenty of time; **2.** *F adv.* rather, fairly, F pretty, plenty; '**2tum** *m* (-s/-er) riches *pl.*; wealth (*an dat.* of).

'**Reichweite** *f* reach; ⚔ range; *in* ~ within reach, near at hand.

reif[1] *adj.* [raɪf] ripe, mature.

Reif[2] [~] *m* (-[e]s/*no pl.*) white or hoar-frost, *poet.* rime.

'**Reife** *f* (-/*no pl.*) ripeness, maturity.

'**reifen**[1] *v/i.* (ge-) **1.** (*sein*) ripen, mature; **2.** (*h*): *es hat gereift* there is a white or hoar-frost.

'**Reifen**[2] *m* (-s/-) hoop; ring; tyre, (*Am. only*) tire; *as ornament:* circlet; ~ *wechseln mot.* change tyres; '**~panne** *mot. f* puncture, *Am. a.* blowout.

'**Reife|prüfung** *f s. Abitur;* '**~zeugnis** *n s. Abschlußzeugnis.*

'**reiflich** *adj.* mature, careful.

Reihe ['raɪə] *f* (-/-n) row; line; rank; series; number; *thea.* row, tier; *der* ~ *nach* by turns; *ich bin an der* ~ *it* is my turn.

'**Reihen|folge** *f* succession, sequence; *alphabetische* ~ alphabetical order; '**~haus** *n* terrace-house, *Am.* row house; '**2weise** *adv.* in rows.

Reiher *orn.* ['raɪər] *m* (-s/-) heron.

Reim [raɪm] *m* (-[e]s/-e) rhyme; '**2en** (ge-) **1.** *v/i.* rhyme; **2.** *v/t.* *and v/refl.* rhyme (*auf acc.* with).

rein *adj.* [raɪn] pure; clean; clear; ~*e Wahrheit* plain truth; '**2ertrag** *m* net proceeds *pl.*; '**2fall** *F m* letdown; '**2gewicht** *n* net weight; '**2gewinn** *m* net profit; '**2heit** *f* (-/*no pl.*) purity; cleanness.

'**reinig|en** *v/t.* (ge-, *h*) clean(se); *fig.* purify; '**2ung** *f* (-/-en) clean(s)-ing; *fig.* purification; cleaners *pl.*; *chemische* ~ dry cleaning; '**2ungsmittel** *n* detergent, cleanser.

'**rein|lich** *adj.* clean; cleanly; neat, tidy; '**2machefrau** *f* charwoman; '**~rassig** *adj.* pedigree, thoroughbred, *esp. Am.* purebred; '**2schrift** *f* fair copy.

Reis[1] ♠ [raɪs] *m* (-es/-e) rice.

Reis[2] ♀ [~] *n* (-es/-er) twig, sprig.

Reise ['raɪzə] *f* (-/-n) journey; ⚓,

⚓ voyage; travel; tour; trip; passage; '**~büro** *n* travel agency *or* bureau; '**~decke** *f* travel(l)ing-rug; '**2fertig** *adj.* ready to start; '**~führer** *m* guide(-book); '**~gepäck** *n* luggage, *Am.* baggage; '**~gesellschaft** *f* tourist party; '**~kosten** *pl.* travel(l)ing-expenses *pl.*; '**~leiter** *m* courier; '**2n** *v/i.* (ge-, *sein*) travel, journey; ~ *nach* go to; *ins Ausland* ~ go abroad; '**~nde** *m, f* (-n/-n) (♣ commercial) travel(l)er; *in trains:* passenger; *for pleasure:* tourist; **~necessaire** ['~nesɛːr] *n* (-s/-s) dressing-case; '**~paß** *m* passport; '**~scheck** *m* traveller's cheque, *Am.* traveler's check; '**~schreibmaschine** *f* portable typewriter; '**~tasche** *f* travel(l)ing-bag, *Am.* grip(sack).

Reisig ['raɪzɪç] *n* (-s/*no pl.*) brushwood.

Reißbrett ['raɪs-] *n* drawing-board.

reißen ['raɪsən] **1.** *v/t.* (irr., ge-, *h*) tear; pull; *an sich* ~ seize; *sich* ~ scratch o.s. (*an dat.* with); *sich* ~ *um* scramble for; **2.** *v/i.* (irr., ge-, *sein*) break; burst; split; tear; *mir riß die Geduld* I lost (all) patience; **3.** ♀ ♂ *no n* (-s/*no pl.*) rheumatism; '**~d** *adj.* rapid; *animal:* rapacious; *pain:* acute; *~en Absatz finden* sell like hot cakes.

'**Reiß|er** *F m* (-s/-) draw, box-office success; thriller; '**~feder** *f* drawing-pen; '**~leine** ♀ *f* rip-cord; '**~nagel** *m s. Reißzwecke*; '**~schiene** *f* (T-)square; '**~verschluß** *m* zipfastener, zipper, *Am. a.* slide fastener; '**~zeug** *n* drawing instruments *pl.*; '**~zwecke** *f* drawing-pin, *Am.* thumbtack.

Reit|anzug ['raɪt-] *m* riding-dress; '**~bahn** *f* riding-school, manège; riding-track; '**2en** (*irr.*, ge-) **1.** *v/i.* (*sein*) ride, go on horseback; **2.** *v/t.* (*h*) ride; '**~er** *m* (-s/-) rider, horseman; ✕, *police:* trooper; *filing:* tab; '**~e'rei** *f* (-/-en) cavalry; '**~erin** *f* (-/-nen) horsewoman; '**~gerte** *f* riding-whip; '**~hose** *f* (riding-) breeches *pl.*; '**~knecht** *m* groom; '**~kunst** *f* horsemanship; '**~lehrer** *m* riding master; '**~peitsche** *f* riding-whip; '**~pferd** *zo. n* riding-horse, saddle-horse; '**~schule** *f* riding-school; '**~stiefel** *m/pl.* riding-boots *pl.*; '**~weg** *m* bridle-path.

Q
R

Reiz [raɪts] *m* (-es/-e) irritation; charm, attraction; allurement; '2**bar** *adj.* sensitive; irritable, excitable, *Am.* sore; '2**en** (ge-, h) 1. *v/t.* irritate (*a.* ♣); excite; provoke; nettle; stimulate, rouse; entice, (al)lure, tempt, charm, attract; 2. *v/i.* cards: bid; '2**end** *adj.* charming, attractive; *Am.* cute; lovely; '2**los** *adj.* unattractive; '**.mittel** *n* stimulus; ♣ stimulant; '**.ung** *f* (-/-en) irritation; provocation; '2**voll** *adj.* charming, attractive.

rekeln F ['reːkəln] *v/refl.* (ge-, h) loll, lounge, sprawl.

Reklamation [reklamaˈtsjoːn] *f* (-/-en) claim; complaint, protest.

Reklame [reˈklaːmə] *f* (-/-n) advertising; advertisement, F ad; publicity; ~ *machen* advertise; ~ *machen für et.* advertise s.th.

rekla'mieren (*no -ge-*, h) 1. *v/t.* (re)claim; 2. *v/i.* complain (*wegen* about).

Rekonvaleszen|t [rekɔnvalesˈtsɛnt] *m* (-en/-en), **.tin** *f* (-/-nen) convalescent; **.z** [.ts] *f* (-/*no pl.*) convalescence.

Rekord [reˈkɔrt] *m* (-[e]s/-e) *sports*, *etc.*: record.

Rekrut ✗ [reˈkruːt] *m* (-en/-en) recruit; 2**ieren** ✗ [.uˈtiːrən] *v/t.* (*no -ge-*, h) recruit.

Rektor ['rɛktɔr] *m* (-s/-en) headmaster, rector, *Am.* principal; *univ.* chancellor, rector, *Am.* president.

relativ *adj.* [relaˈtiːf] relative.

Relief [relˈjɛf] *n* (-s/-s, -e) relief.

Religi|on [reliˈgjoːn] *f* (-/-en) religion; 2**ös** *adj.* [.øːs] religious; pious, devout; **.osität** [.oziˈtɛːt] *f* (-/*no pl.*) religiousness; piety.

Reling ⚓ ['reːlɪŋ] *f* (-/-s, -e) rail.

Reliquie [reˈliːkvi̯ə] *f* (-/-n) relic.

Ren *zo.* [rɛn; reːn] *n* (-s/-s; -s/-e) reindeer.

Renn|bahn ['rɛn-] *f* racecourse, *Am.* race track, *horse-racing: a. the* turf; *mot.* speedway; '**.boot** *n* racing boat, racer.

rennen ['rɛnən] 1. *v/i.* (*irr.*, ge-, sein) run; race; 2. *v/t.* (*irr.*, ge-, h): *j-n zu Boden* ~ run s.o. down; 3. 2 *n* (-s/-) run(ning); race; heat.

'**Renn|fahrer** *m mot.* racing driver, racer; racing cyclist; '**.läufer** *m* ski racer; '**.mannschaft** *f* racecrew; '**.pferd** *zo. n* racehorse, racer;

'**.rad** *n* racing bicycle, racer; '**.sport** *m* racing; *horse-racing: a. the* turf; '**.stall** *m* racing stable; '**.strecke** *f* racecourse, *Am.* race track; *mot.* speedway; distance (to be run); '**.wagen** *m* racing car, racer.

renommiert *adj.* [renɔˈmiːrt] famous, noted (*wegen* for).

renovieren [renoˈviːrən] *v/t.* (*no -ge-*, h) renovate, repair; redecorate (*interior of house*).

rent|abel *adj.* [rɛnˈtaːbəl] profitable, paying; 2**e** *f* (-/-n) income, revenue; annuity; (old-age) pension; rent; 2**enempfänger** ['rɛntən-²] *m s. Rentner*; rentier.

Rentier *zo.* ['rɛn-] *n s. Ren.*

rentieren [rɛnˈtiːrən] *v/refl.* (*no -ge-*, h) pay.

Rentner ['rɛntnər] *m* (-s/-) (old-age) pensioner.

Reparatur [reparaˈtuːr] *f* (-/-en) repair; **.werkstatt** *f* repair-shop; *mot. a.* garage, service station.

repa'rieren *v/t.* (*no -ge-*, h) repair, *Am.* F fix.

Report|age [repɔrˈtaːʒə] *f* (-/-n) reporting, commentary, coverage; **.er** [reˈpɔrtər] *m* (-s/-) reporter.

Repräsent|ant [reprɛzɛnˈtant] *m* (-en/-en) representative; **.antenhaus** *Am. parl. n* House of Representatives; 2**ieren** (*no -ge-*, h) 1. *v/t.* represent; 2. *v/i.* cut a fine figure.

Repressalie [reprɛˈsaːli̯ə] *f* (-/-n) reprisal.

reproduzieren [reprodʊˈtsiːrən] *v/t.* (*no -ge-*, h) reproduce.

Reptil *zo.* [rɛpˈtiːl] *n* (-s/-ien, ♣ -e) reptile.

Republik [repuˈbliːk] *f* (-/-en) republic; **.aner** *pol.* [.iˈkaːnər] *m* (-s/-) republican; 2**anisch** *adj.* [.iˈkaːnɪʃ] republican.

Reserve [reˈzɛrvə] *f* (-/-n) reserve; **.rad** *mot. n* spare wheel.

reser'vier|en *v/t.* (*no -ge-*, h) reserve; ~ *lassen* book (*seat, etc.*); **.t** *adj.* reserved (*a. fig.*).

Resid|enz [reziˈdɛnts] *f* (-/-en) residence; 2**ieren** *v/i.* (*no -ge-*, h) reside.

resignieren [reziˈgniːrən] *v/i.* (*no -ge-*, h) resign.

Respekt [reˈspɛkt] *m* (-[e]s/*no pl.*) respect; 2**ieren** [.ˈtiːrən] *v/t.* (*no*

-ge-, h) respect; 2**los** adj. irreverent, disrespectful; 2**voll** adj. respectful.

Ressort [rɛ'soːr] n (-s/-s) department; province.

Rest [rɛst] m (-es/-e, ✝ -er) rest, remainder; residue (a. 🜍.); esp. ✝ remnant (of cloth); leftover (of food); das gab ihm den ∼ that finished him (off).

Restaurant [rɛsto'rãː] n (-s/-s) restaurant.

'**Rest|bestand** m remnant; '∼**betrag** m remainder, balance; '2**lich** adj. remaining; '2**los** adv. completely; entirely; '∼**zahlung** f payment of balance; final payment.

Resultat [rezul'taːt] n (-[e]s/-e) result, outcome; sports: score.

retten ['rɛtən] v/t. (ge-, h) save; deliver, rescue.

Rettich 🜍 ['rɛtiç] m (-s/-e) radish.

'**Rettung** f (-/-en) rescue; deliverance; escape.

'**Rettungs|boot** n lifeboat; '∼**gürtel** m lifebelt; '2**los** adj. irretrievable, past help or hope, beyond recovery; '∼**mannschaft** f rescue party; '∼**ring** m life-buoy.

Reu|e ['rɔʏə] f (no pl.) repentance (über acc. of), remorse (at); 2**en** v/t. (ge-, h): et. reut mich I repent (of) s.th.; 2**evoll** adj. repentant; 2(**müt)ig** adj. ['∼(my:t)iç] repentant.

Revanche [re'vãː∫(ə)] f (-/-n) revenge; ∼**spiel** n return match.

revan'chieren v/refl. (no -ge-, h) take or have one's revenge (an dat. on); return (für et. s.th.).

Revers 1. [re've:r] n, m (-/-) lapel (of coat); 2. [re'vɛrs] m (-es/-e) declaration; 🜨🜨 bond.

revidieren [revi'diːrən] v/t. (no -ge-, h) revise; check; ✝ audit.

Revier [re'viːr] n (-s/-e) district, quarter; s. Jagdrevier.

Revision [revi'zjoːn] f (-/-en) revision (a. typ.); ✝ audit; 🜨🜨 appeal; ∼ einlegen 🜨🜨 lodge an appeal.

Revolt|e [re'vɔltə] f (-/-n) revolt, uprising; 2**ieren** [∼'tiːrən] v/i. (no -ge-, h) revolt, rise (in revolt).

Revolution [revolu'tsjoːn] f (-/-en) revolution; ∼**är** [∼o'nɛːr] 1. m (-s/-e) revolutionary; 2. 2 adj. revolutionary.

Revolver [re'vɔlvər] m (-s/-) revolver, Am. F a. gun.

Revue [rə'vyː] f (-/-n) review; thea. revue, (musical) show; ∼ passieren lassen pass in review.

Rezens|ent [retsɛn'zɛnt] m (-en/-en) critic, reviewer; 2**ieren** v/t. (no -ge-, h) review, criticize; ∼**ion** [∼'zjoːn] f (-/-en) review, critique.

Rezept [re'tsɛpt] n (-[e]s/-e) 🝊 prescription; cooking: recipe (a. fig.).

Rhabarber 🜍 [ra'barbər] m (-s/no pl.) rhubarb.

rhetorisch adj. [re'toːri∫] rhetorical.

rheumati|sch 🝊 adj. [rɔʏ'maːti∫] rheumatic; 2**smus** 🝊 [∼a'tismus] m (-/Rheumatismen) rheumatism.

rhythm|isch adj. ['rytmi∫] rhythmic(al); 2**us** ['∼us] m (-/Rhythmen) rhythm.

richten ['riçtən] v/t. (ge-, h) set right, arrange, adjust; level, point (gun) (auf acc. at); direct (gegen at); 🜨🜨 judge; execute; zugrunde ∼ ruin, destroy; in die Höhe ∼ raise, lift up; sich ∼ nach conform to, act according to; take one's bearings from; gr. agree with; depend on; price: be determined by; ich richte mich nach Ihnen I leave it to you.

'**Richter** m (-s/-) judge; 2**lich** adj. judicial; '∼**spruch** m judg(e)ment, sentence.

'**richtig** 1. adj. right, correct, accurate; proper; true; just; ein ∼er Londoner a regular cockney; 2. adv.: ∼ gehen clock: go right; 2**keit** f (-/no pl.) correctness; accuracy; justness; '∼**stellen** v/t. (sep., -ge-, h) put or set right, rectify.

'**Richt|linien** f/pl. (general) directions pl., rules pl.; '∼**preis** ✝ m standard price; '∼**schnur** f ⊕ plumb-line; fig. rule (of conduct), guiding principle.

'**Richtung** f (-/-en) direction; course; way; fig. line; ∼**sanzeiger** mot. ['riçtuŋs∼] m (-s/-) flashing indicator, trafficator; '2**weisend** adj. directive, leading, guiding.

'**Richtwaage** ⊕ f level.

rieb [riːp] pret. of reiben.

riechen ['riːçən] (irr., ge-, h) 1. v/i. smell (nach of; an dat. at); sniff (an dat. at); 2. v/t. smell; sniff.

rief [riːf] pret. of rufen.

riefeln ⊕ ['riːfəln] v/t. (ge-, h) flute, ' [groove.

Riegel ['riːgəl] m (-s/-) bar, bolt; bar, cake (of soap); bar (of chocolate).

Riemen ['riːmən] *m* (-s/-) strap, thong; belt; ⏚ oar.

Ries [riːs] *n* (-es/-e) ream.

Riese ['riːzə] *m* (-n/-n) giant.

rieseln ['riːzəln] *v/i.* (ge-) **1.** (*sein*) *small stream:* purl, ripple; trickle; **2.** (*h*): es rieselt it drizzles.

ries|engroß *adj.* ['riːzən-], '**~enhaft** *adj.*, '**~ig** *adj.* gigantic, huge; '**⏚in** *f* (-/-nen) giantess.

riet [riːt] *pret. of* raten.

Riff [rif] *n* (-[e]s/-e) reef.

Rille ['rilə] *f* (-/-n) groove; ⊕ a. flute. [tance.]

Rimesse ✝ [ri'mɛsə] *f* (-/-n) remit-

Rind *zo.* [rint] *n* (-[e]s/-er) ox; cow; neat; *~er pl.* (horned) cattle *pl.*; zwanzig *~er* twenty head of cattle.

Rinde ['rində] *f* (-/-n) ♀ bark; rind (*of fruit, bacon, cheese*); crust (*of bread*).

'**Rinder|braten** *m* roast beef; '**~herde** *f* herd of cattle; '**~hirt** *m* cowherd, *Am.* cowboy.

'**Rind|fleisch** *n* beef; '**~(s)leder** *n* neat's-leather, cow-hide; '**~vieh** *n* (horned) cattle *pl.*, neat *pl.*

Ring [riŋ] *m* (-[e]s/-e) ring; circle; link (*of chain*); ✝ ring, pool, trust, *Am.* F combine; '**~bahn** *f* circular railway.

ringel|n ['riŋəln] *v/refl.* (ge-, h) curl, coil; '**⏚natter** *zo.* *f* ringsnake.

ring|en ['riŋən] (*irr.*, ge-, h) **1.** *v/i.* wrestle; struggle (um for); nach Atem *~* gasp (for breath); **2.** *v/t.* wring (*hands, washing*); '**⏚er** *m* (-s/-) wrestler.

ring|förmig *adj.* ['riŋfœrmiç] annular, ring-like; '**⏚kampf** *m sports:* wrestling(-match); '**⏚richter** *m boxing:* referee.

rings *adv.* [riŋs] around; '**~herum** *adv.*, '**~um** *adv.*, '**~um'her** *adv.* round about, all (a)round.

Rinn|e ['rinə] *f* (-/-n) groove, channel; gutter (*of roof or street*); gully; '**⏚en** *v/i.* (*irr.*, ge-, sein) run, flow; drip; leak; '**~sal** *n* (-[e]s/-e) [' .zaːl] watercourse, streamlet; '**~stein** *m* gutter; sink (*of kitchen unit*).

Rippe ['ripə] *f* (-/-n) rib; ⏃ groin; bar (*of chocolate*); '**~n** *v/t.* (ge-, h) rib; '**~nfell** *anat.* *n* pleura; '**~nfellentzündung** ✻ *f* pleurisy; '**~nstoß** *m* dig in the ribs; nudge.

Risiko ['riːziko] *n* (-s/-s, Risiken)

risk; ein *~* eingehen take a risk.

risk|ant *adj.* [ris'kant] risky; '**~ieren** *v/t.* (*no* -ge-, h) risk.

Riß [ris] **1.** *m* (Risses/Risse) rent, tear; split (*a. fig.*); crack; *in skin:* chap; scratch; ⊕ draft, plan; *fig.* rupture; **2.** ⏁ *pret. of* reißen.

rissig *adj.* ['risiç] full of rents; *skin, etc.:* chappy; *~* werden crack.

Rist [rist] *m* (-es/-e) instep; back of the hand; wrist.

Ritt [rit] **1.** *m* (-[e]s/-e) ride; **2.** ⏁ *pret. of* reiten.

'**Ritter** *m* (-s/-) knight; zum *~* schlagen knight; '**~gut** *n* manor; '**⏚lich** *adj.* knightly, chivalrous; '**~lichkeit** *f* (-/-en) gallantry, chivalry.

rittlings *adv.* ['ritliŋs] astride (auf e-m Pferd a horse).

Ritz [rits] *m* (-es/-e) crack, chink; scratch; '**~e** *f* (-/-n) crack, chink; fissure; '**⏚en** *v/t.* (ge-, h) scratch; cut.

Rival|e [ri'vaːlə] *m* (-n/-n), '**~in** *f* (-/-nen) rival; **⏁isieren** [..ali'ziːrən] *v/i.* (*no* -ge-, h) rival (mit j-m s.o.); **~ität** [..ali'tɛːt] *f* (-/-en) rivalry.

Rizinusöl ['riːtsinus?-] *n* (-[e]s/*no pl.*) castor oil.

Robbe *zo.* ['rɔbə] *f* (-/-n) seal.

Robe ['roːbə] *f* (-/-n) gown; robe.

Roboter ['rɔbɔtər] *m* (-s/-) robot.

robust *adj.* [ro'bust] robust, sturdy, vigorous.

roch [rɔx] *pret. of* riechen.

röcheln ['rœçəln] (ge-, h) **1.** *v/i.* rattle; **2.** *v/t.* gasp out (*words*).

Rock [rɔk] *m* (-[e]s/⸚e) skirt; coat, jacket; '**~schoß** *m* coat-tail.

Rodel|bahn ['roːdəl-] *f* toboggan-run; '**⏚n** *v/i.* (ge-, h, sein) toboggan, *Am.* a. coast; '**~schlitten** *m* sled(ge), toboggan.

roden ['roːdən] *v/t.* (ge-, h) clear (*land*); root up, stub (*roots*).

Rogen *ichth.* ['roːgən] *m* (-s/-) roe, spawn.

Roggen ♀ ['rɔgən] *m* (-s/-) rye.

roh *adj.* [roː] raw; *fig.:* rough, rude; cruel, brutal; *oil, metal:* crude; '**⏚bau** *m* (-[e]s/-ten) rough brickwork; '**⏚eisen** *n* pig-iron.

Roheit ['roːhait] *f* (-/-en) rawness; roughness (*a. fig.*); *fig.:* rudeness; brutality.

'**Roh|ling** *m* (-s/-e) brute, ruffian; '**~material** *n* raw material; '**~produkt** *n* raw product.

Rohr [roːr] n (-[e]s/-e) tube, pipe; duct; ♀: reed; cane.

Röhre ['røːrə] f (-/-n) tube, pipe; duct; radio: valve, Am. (electron) tube.

Rohr|leger m (-s/-) pipe fitter, plumber; '∼leitung f plumbing; pipeline; '∼post f pneumatic dispatch or tube; '∼stock m cane; '∼zucker m cane-sugar.

Rohstoff m raw material.

Rolladen ['rɔlaːdən] m (-s/ᵘ, -) rolling shutter.

Rollbahn ✈ f taxiway, taxi-strip.

Rolle ['rɔlə] f (-/-n) roll; roller; coil (of rope, etc.); pulley; beneath furniture: cast|or, -er; mangle; thea. part, role; fig. figure; ∼ Garn reel of cotton, Am. spool of thread; das spielt keine ∼ that doesn't matter, it makes no difference; Geld spielt keine ∼ money (is) no object; aus der ∼ fallen forget o.s.

'rollen (ge-) 1. v/i. (sein) roll; ✈ taxi; 2. v/t. (h) roll; wheel; mangle (laundry).

Rollenbesetzung thea. f cast.

Roller m (-s/-) children's toy: scooter; mot. (motor) scooter.

Roll|feld ✈ n manœuvring area, Am. maneuvering area; '∼film phot. m roll film; '∼kragen m turtle neck; '∼schrank m roll-fronted cabinet; '∼schuh m roller-skate; '∼schuhbahn f roller-skating rink; '∼stuhl m wheel chair; '∼treppe f escalator; '∼wagen m lorry, truck.

Roman [ro'maːn] m (-s/-e) novel, (work of) fiction; novel of adventure and fig.: romance; ∼ist [∼a'nist] m (-en/-en) Romance scholar or student; ∼schriftsteller m novelist.

Romanti|k [ro'mantik] f (-/no pl.) romanticism; 2sch adj. romantic.

Röm|er ['røːmər] m (-s/-) Roman; '2isch adj. Roman.

röntgen ['rœntɡən] v/t. (ge-, h) X-ray; '2aufnahme f, '2bild n X-ray; '2strahlen m/pl. X-rays pl.

rosa adj. ['roːza] pink.

Rose ['roːzə] f (-/-n) ♀ rose; 𝄢 erysipelas.

Rosen|kohl ♀ m Brussels sprouts pl.; '∼kranz eccl. m rosary; '2rot adj. rose-colo(u)red, rosy; '∼stock ♀ m (-[e]s/ᵘe) rose-bush.

'rosig adj. rosy (a. fig.), rose-colo(u)red, roseate.

Rosine [ro'ziːnə] f (-/-n) raisin.

Roß zo. [rɔs] n (Rosses/Rosse, F Rösser) horse, poet. steed; '∼haar n horsehair.

Rost [rɔst] m 1. (-es/no pl.) rust; 2. (-es/-e) grate; gridiron; grill; '∼braten m roast joint.

'rosten v/i. (ge-, h, sein) rust.

rösten ['røːstən] v/t. (ge-, h) roast, grill; toast (bread); fry (potatoes).

'Rostfleck m rust-stain; in cloth: iron-mo(u)ld; '2frei adj. rustless, rustproof, esp. steel: stainless; '2ig adj. rusty, corroded.

rot [roːt] 1. adj. red; 2. 2 n (-s/-, F -s) red.

Rotationsmaschine typ. [rota-'tsjoːns-] f rotary printing machine.

'rot|backig adj. ruddy; '∼blond adj. sandy.

Röte ['røːtə] f (-/no pl.) redness, red (colo[u]r); blush; '2n v/t. (ge-, h) redden; paint or dye red; sich ∼ redden; flush, blush.

'rot|gelb adj. reddish yellow; '∼glühend adj. red-hot; '2haut f red-skin.

rotieren [ro'tiːrən] v/i. (no -ge-, h) rotate, revolve.

Rot|käppchen ['roːtkɛpçən] n (-s/-) Little Red Riding Hood; '∼kehlchen orn. n (-s/-) robin (redbreast).

rötlich adj. ['røːtliç] reddish.

'Rot|stift m red crayon or pencil; '∼tanne ♀ f spruce (fir).

Rotte ['rɔtə] f (-/-n) band, gang.

'Rot|wein m red wine; claret; '∼wild zo. n red deer.

Rouleau [ru'loː] n (-s/-s) s. Rollladen; blind, Am. (window) shade.

Route ['ruːtə] f (-/-n) route.

Routine [ru'tiːnə] f (-/no pl.) routine, practice.

Rübe ♀ ['ryːbə] f (-/-n) beet; weiße ∼ (Swedish) turnip, Am. a. rutabaga; rote ∼ red beet, beet(root); gelbe ∼ carrot.

Rubin [ru'biːn] m (-s/-e) ruby.

ruch|bar adj. ['ruːxbaːr]: ∼ werden become known, get about or abroad; '∼los adj. wicked, profligate.

Ruck [ruk] m (-[e]s/-e) jerk, Am. F yank; jolt (of vehicle).

Rück|antwort ['ryk?-] f reply; Postkarte mit ∼ reply postcard; mit bezahlter ∼ telegram: reply paid;

Q
R

'⊕bezüglich *gr. adj.* reflexive; '⊾blick *m* retrospect(ive view) (*auf acc.* at); reminiscences *pl.*

rücken¹ ['rykən] (ge-) **1.** *v/t.* (h) move, shift; **2.** *v/i.* (sein) move; *näher* ~ near, approach.

Rücken² [~] *m* (-s/-) back; ridge (*of mountain*); '⊾deckung *fig. f* backing, support; '⊾lehne *f* back (*of chair, etc.*); '⊾mark *anat. n* spinal cord; '⊾schmerzen *m/pl.* pain in the back, back ache; '⊾schwimmen *n* (-s/*no pl.*) backstroke swimming; '⊾wind *m* following *or* tail wind; '⊾wirbel *anat. m* dorsal vertebra.

Rück|erstattung ['ryk⁹-] *f* restitution; refund (*of money*), reimbursement (*of expenses*); '⊾fahrkarte *f* return (ticket), *Am. a.* round-trip ticket; '⊾fahrt *f* return journey *or* voyage; *auf der* ~ on the way back; '⊾fall *m* relapse; '⊕fällig *adj.*: ~ *werden* relapse; '⊾flug *m* return flight; '⊾frage *f* further inquiry; '⊾gabe *f* return, restitution; '⊾gang *fig. m* retrogression; † recession, decline; '⊕gängig *adj.*: ~ *machen* cancel; '⊾grat *anat. n* (-[e]s/-e) spine, backbone (*both a. fig.*); '⊾halt *m* support; '⊕haltlos *adj.* unreserved, frank; '⊾hand *f* (-/*no pl.*) *tennis*: backhand (stroke); '⊾kauf *m* repurchase; ⊾kehr ['⊾ke:r] *f* (-/*no pl.*) return; '⊾kopp(e)lung ⊕ *f* (-/-en) feedback; '⊾lage *f* reserve(s *pl.*); savings *pl.*, ⊕läufig *fig. adj.* ['⊾lɔyfiç] retrograde; '⊾licht *mot. n* tail-light, tail-lamp, rear-light; '⊕lings *adv.* backwards; from behind; '⊾marsch *m* march back *or* home; retreat; '⊾porto ⊕ *n* return postage; '⊾reise *f* return journey, journey back *or* home.

'**Rucksack** *m* knapsack, rucksack.

Rück|schlag *m* backstroke; *fig.* setback; '⊾schluß *m* conclusion, inference; '⊾schritt *fig. m* retrogression, set-back; *pol.* reaction; '⊾seite *f* back, reverse; *a.* tail (*of coin*); '⊾sendung *f* return; '⊾sicht *f* respect, regard, consideration (*auf j-n* for s.o.); '⊕sichtslos *adj.* inconsiderate (*gegen* of), regardless (of); ruthless; reckless; ⊾es *Fahren mot.* reckless driving; '⊕sichtsvoll

adj. regardful (*gegen* of); considerate, thoughtful; '⊾sitz *mot. m* back-seat; '⊾spiegel *mot. m* rearview mirror; '⊾spiel *n sports*: return match; '⊾sprache *f* consultation; ~ *nehmen mit* consult (*lawyer*), consult with (*fellow workers*); *nach* ~ *mit* on consultation with; '⊾stand *m* arrears *pl.*; backlog; ⊕ residue; *im* ~ *sein mit* be in arrears *or* behind with; '⊕ständig *fig. adj.* old-fashioned, backward; ⊾e *Miete* arrears of rent; '⊾stoß *m* recoil; kick (*of gun*); '⊾strahler *m* (-s/-) rear reflector, cat's eye; '⊾tritt *m* withdrawal, retreat; resignation; '⊾trittbremse *f* back-pedal brake, *Am.* coaster brake; '⊾versicherung *f* reinsurance; ⊕wärts *adv.* ['⊾verts] back, backward(s); '⊾wärtsgang *mot. m* reverse (gear); '⊾weg *m* way back, return.

'**ruckweise** *adv.* by jerks.

rück|wirkend *adj.* reacting; ⊭, *etc.*: retroactive, retrospective; '⊕wirkung *f* reaction; '⊕zahlung *f* repayment; '⊕zug *m* retreat.

Rüde ['ry:də] **1.** *zo. m* (-n/-n) male dog *or* fox *or* wolf; large hound; **2.** ⊕ *adj.* rude, coarse, brutal.

Rudel ['ru:dəl] *n* (-s/-) troop; pack (*of wolves*); herd (*of deer*).

Ruder ['ru:dər] *n* (-s/-) oar; rudder (*a.* ✈); helm; '⊾boot *n* row(ing)-boat; '⊾er *m* (-s/-) rower, oarsman; '⊾fahrt *f* row; '⊕n (ge-) **1.** *v/i.* (h, sein) row; **2.** *v/t.* (h) row; '⊾regatta ['⊾regata] *f* (-/Ruderregatten) boat race, regatta; '⊾sport *m* rowing.

Ruf [ru:f] *m* (-[e]s/-e) call; cry, shout; summons; *univ.* call; reputation, repute; fame; standing, credit; '⊕en (*irr.*, ge-, h) **1.** *v/i.* call; cry, shout; **2.** *v/t.* call; ~ *lassen* send for.

'**Ruf|name** *m* Christian *or* first name; '⊾nummer *f* telephone number; '⊾weite *f* (-/*no pl.*): *in* ~ within call *or* earshot.

Rüge ['ry:gə] *f* (-/-n) rebuke, censure, reprimand; '⊕n *v/t.* (ge-, h) rebuke, censure, blame.

Ruhe ['ru:ə] *f* (-/*no pl.*) rest, repose; sleep; quiet, calm; tranquillity; silence; peace; composure; *sich zur* ~ *setzen* retire; ~! quiet!, silence!; *immer mit der* ~! take it easy!; *lassen Sie mich in* ~! let me alone!; '⊕bedürftig *adj.*: ~ *sein* want *or* need rest; **˷gehalt** *n* pension; **ℓlos** *adj.* restless; **ℓn** *v/i.* (ge-, *h*) rest, repose; sleep; *laß die Vergangenheit ˷!* let bygones be bygones!; **˷pause** *f* pause; null; **˷platz** *m* resting-place; **˷stand** *m* (-[e]s/*no pl.*) retirement; *im ˷* retired; *in den ˷ treten* retire; *in den ˷ versetzen* superannuate, pension off, retire; **˷stätte** *f*: *letzte ˷* last resting-place; **˷störer** *m* (-s/-) disturber of the peace, peacebreaker; **˷störung** *f* disturbance (of the peace), disorderly behavio(u)r, riot.

'ruhig *adj.* quiet, still; *mind, water:* tranquil, calm; silent; ⊕ smooth.

Ruhm [ru:m] *m* (-[e]s/*no pl.*) glory, fame, renown.

rühm|en ['ry:mən] *v/t.* (ge-, *h*) praise, glorify; *sich e-r Sache ˷* boast of s.th.; **˷lich** *adj.* glorious, laudable.

'ruhm|los *adj.* inglorious; **˷reich** *adj.* glorious.

Ruhr 𝔰 [ru:r] *f* (-/*no pl.*) dysentery.

Rühr|ei ['ry:r²-] *n* scrambled egg; **ℓen** (ge-, *h*) **1.** *v/t.* stir, move; *fig.* touch, move, affect; *sich ˷* stir, move, bustle; **2.** *v/i.*: *an et. ˷* touch s.th.; *wir wollen nicht daran ˷* let sleeping dogs lie; **ℓend** *adj.* touching, moving; **ℓig** *adj.* active, busy; enterprising; nimble; **ℓselig** *adj.* sentimental; **˷ung** *f* (-/*no pl.*) emotion, feeling.

Ruin [ru'i:n] *m* (-s/*no pl.*) ruin; decay; **˷e** *f* (-/-n) ruin (*a pl.*); *fig.* ruin, wreck; **ℓieren** [rui'ni:rən] *v/t.* (*no* -ge-, *h*) ruin; destroy, wreck; spoil; *sich ˷* ruin o.s.

rülpsen ['rylpsən] *v/i.* (ge-, *h*) belch.

Rumän|e [ru'mɛ:nə] *m* (-n/-n) Ro(u)manian; **ℓisch** *adj.* Ro(u)manian.

Rummel F ['ruməl] *m* (-s/*no pl.*) hurly-burly, row; bustle; revel; *in publicity:* F ballyhoo; **˷platz** *m* fun fair, amusement park.

rumoren [ru'mo:rən] *v/i.* (*no* -ge-, *h*) make a noise or row; *bowels:* rumble.

Rumpel|kammer F ['rumpəl-] *f* lumber-room; **ℓn** *v/i.* (ge-, *h*, *sein*) rumble.

Rumpf [rumpf] *m* (-[e]s/⁀e) *anat.* trunk, body; torso (*of statue*); ⊕ hull, frame, body; ✈ fuselage, body.

rümpfen ['rympfən] *v/t.* (ge-, *h*): *die Nase ˷* turn up one's nose, sniff (*über acc.* at).

rund [runt] **1.** *adj.* round (*a. fig.*); circular; **2.** *adv.* about; **˷blick** *m* panorama, view all (a)round; **ℓe** ['rundə] *f* (-/-n) round; *sports:* lap; *boxing:* round; round, patrol; beat (*of policeman*); *in der or die ˷* (a)round; **˷en** ['˷dən] *v/refl.* (ge-, *h*) (grow) round; **ℓfahrt** *f* drive round (*town, etc.*); *s. Rundreise;* **ℓflug** *m* circuit (*über* of); **ℓfrage** *f* inquiry, poll.

'Rundfunk *m* broadcast(ing); broadcasting service; broadcasting company; radio, wireless; *im ˷* over the wireless, on the radio *or* air; **˷anstalt** *f* broadcasting company; **˷ansager** *m* (radio) announcer; **˷gerät** *n* radio *or* wireless set; **˷gesellschaft** *f* broadcasting company; **˷hörer** *m* listener(-in), *˷ pl. a.* (radio) audience; **˷programm** *n* broadcast *or* radio program(me); **˷sender** *m* broadcast transmitter; broadcasting *or* radio station; **˷sendung** *f* broadcast; **˷sprecher** *m* broadcaster, broadcast speaker, (radio) announcer; **˷station** *f* broadcasting *or* radio station; **˷übertragung** *f* radio transmission, broadcast(ing); broadcast (*of programme*).

'Rund|gang *m* tour, round, circuit; **˷gesang** *m* glee, catch; **ℓhe'raus** *adv.* in plain words, frankly, plainly; **ℓhe'rum** *adv.* round about, all (a)round; **ℓlich** *adj.* round(ish); rotund, plump; **˷reise** *f* circular tour *or* trip, sight-seeing trip, *Am. a.* round trip; **˷schau** *f* panorama; *newspaper:* review; **˷schreiben** *n* circular (letter); **ℓ'weg** *adv.* flatly, plainly.

Runz|el ['runtsəl] *f* (-/-n) wrinkle; **ℓelig** *adj.* wrinkled; **ℓeln** *v/t.* (ge-, *h*) wrinkle; *die Stirn ˷* knit one's brows, frown; **ℓig** *adj.* wrinkled.

Rüpel ['ry:pəl] *m* (-s/-) boor, lout; **ℓhaft** *adj.* coarse, boorish, rude.

rupfen ['rupfən] *v/t.* (ge-, *h*) pull up *or* out, pick; pluck (*fowl*) (*a. fig.*). [*fig.* rude.\]

ruppig *adj.* ['rupiç] ragged, shabby;\]

Rüsche ['ry:ʃə] *f* (-/-n) ruffle, frill.

Ruß [ru:s] *m* (-es/*no pl.*) soot.

Q
R

Russe ['rusə] *m* (-n/-n) Russian.
Rüssel ['rysəl] *m* (-s/-) trunk (*of elefant*); snout (*of pig*). [*adj.* sooty.]
ruß|en *v/i.* (ge-, h) smoke; **~ig|**
russisch *adj.* Russian.
rüsten ['rystən] (ge-, h) **1.** *v/t. and v/refl.* prepare, get ready (*zu* for); **2.** *esp.* ✗ *v/i.* arm.
rüstig *adj.* ['rystiç] vigorous, strong; **2keit** *f* (-/*no pl.*) vigo(u)r.
Rüstung *f* (-/-en) preparations *pl.*; ✗ arming, armament; armo(u)r; **~sindustrie** ['rystuŋs⁹-] *f* armament industry.

'Rüstzeug *n* (set of) tools *pl.*, implements *pl.*; *fig.* equipment.
Rute ['ru:tə] *f* (-/-n) rod; switch; *fox's tail*: brush.
Rutsch [rutʃ] *m* (-es/-e) (land)slide; F short trip; **~bahn** *f*, **~e** *f* (-/-n) slide, chute; **2en** *v/i.* (ge-, sein) glide, slide; slip; *vehicle*: skid; **2ig** *adj.* slippery.
rütteln ['rytəln] (ge-, h) **1.** *v/t.* shake, jog; jolt; **2.** *v/i.* shake, jog; *car*: jolt; *an der Tür ~* rattle at the door; *daran ist nicht zu ~* that's a fact.

S

Saal [za:l] *m* (-[e]s/*Säle*) hall.
Saat ['za:t] *f* (-/-en) sowing; standing *or* growing crops *pl.*; seed (*a. fig.*); **~feld** ✗ *n* cornfield; **~gut** ✗ *n* (-[e]s/*no pl.*) seeds *pl.*; **~kartoffel** ✗ *f* seed-potato.
Sabbat ['zabat] *m* (-s/-e) Sabbath.
sabbern F ['zabərn] *v/i.* (ge-, h) slaver, slobber, *Am. a.* drool; twaddle, *Am. sl. a.* drool.
Säbel ['zɛ:bəl] *m* (-s/-) sab|re, *Am.* -er; *mit dem ~ rasseln pol.* rattle the sabre; **~beine** *n/pl.* bandy legs *pl.*; **2beinig** *adj.* bandy-legged; **~hieb** *m* sabre-cut; **2n** F *fig. v/t.* (ge-, h) hack.
Sabot|age [zabo'ta:ʒə] *f* (-/-n) sabotage; **~eur** [~'ø:r] *m* (-s/-e) saboteur; **2ieren** *v/t.* (*no* -ge-, h) sabotage.
Sach|bearbeiter ['zax-] *m* (-s/-) official in charge; *social work*: case worker; **~beschädigung** *f* damage to property; **2dienlich** *adj.* relevant, pertinent; useful, helpful.
'Sache *f* (-/-n) thing; affair, matter, concern; ⚖ case; point; issue; *~n pl.* things *pl.*; *beschlossene ~* foregone conclusion; *e-e ~ für sich a* matter apart; *(nicht) zur ~ gehörig* (ir)relevant, *pred. a.* to (off) the point; *bei der ~ bleiben* stick to the point; *gemeinsame ~ machen mit* make common cause with.
'sach|gemäß *adj.* appropriate, proper; **2kenntnis** *f* expert knowledge; **~kundig** *adj. s.* sachverständig; **2lage** *f* state of affairs,

situation; **~lich 1.** *adj.* relevant, pertinent, *pred. a.* to the point; matter-of-fact, business-like; unbias(s)ed; objective; **2.** *adv.*: *~ einwandfrei od. richtig* factually correct.
sächlich *gr. adj.* ['zɛçliç] neuter.
'Sachlichkeit *f* (-/*no pl.*) objectivity; impartiality; matter-of-factness.
'Sach|register *n* (subject) index; **~schaden** *m* damage to property.
Sachse ['zaksə] *m* (-n/-n) Saxon.
sächsisch *adj.* ['zɛksiʃ] Saxon.
sacht *adj.* [zaxt] soft, gentle; slow.
Sach|verhalt ['zaxfɛrhalt] *m* (-[e]s/
-e) facts *pl.* (of the case); **2verständig** *adj.* expert; **~verständige** *m* (-n/-n) expert, authority; ⚖ expert witness; **~wert** *m* real value.
Sack [zak] *m* (-[e]s/╪e) sack; bag; *mit ~ und Pack* with bag and baggage; **~gasse** *f* blind all╪y, cul-de-sac, impasse (*a. fig.*), *Am. a.* dead end (*a. fig.*); *fig.* deadlock; **~leinwand** *f* sackcloth.
Sadis|mus [za'dismus] *m* (-/*no pl.*) sadism; **~t** *m* (-en/-en) sadist; **2tisch** *adj.* sadistic.
säen ['zɛ:ən] *v/t. and v/i.* (ge-, h) sow (*a. fig.*).
Saffian ['zafja:n] *m* (-s/*no pl.*) morocco.
Saft [zaft] *m* (-[e]s/╪e) juice (*of vegetables or fruits*); sap (*of plants*) (*a. fig.*); **2ig** *adj. fruits, etc.*: juicy; *meadow, etc.*: lush; *plants*: sappy (*a. fig.*); *joke, etc.*: spicy, coarse; **2los** *adj.* juiceless; sapless (*a. fig.*).

Sage ['zaːgə] f (-/-n) legend, myth; *die* ~ *geht* the story goes.

Säge ['zɛːgə] f (-/-n) saw; **~blatt** n saw-blade; **~bock** m saw-horse, *Am. a.* sawbuck; **~fisch** *ichth. m* sawfish; **~mehl** n sawdust.

sagen ['zaːgən] (ge-, h) **1.** v/t. say; *j-m et.* ~ tell s.o. s.th., say s.th. to s.o.; *j-m* ~ *lassen, daß* send s.o. word that; *er läßt sich nichts* ~ he will not listen to reason; *das hat nichts zu* ~ that doesn't matter; *j-m gute Nacht* ~ bid s.o. good night; **2.** v/i. say; *es ist nicht zu* ~ it is incredible or fantastic; *wenn ich so* ~ *darf* if I may express myself in these terms; *sage und schreibe* believe it or not; no less than, as much as.

'sägen v/t. and v/i. (ge-, h) saw.

'sagenhaft adj. legendary, mythical; F *fig.* fabulous, incredible.

Säge|späne ['zɛːgəʃpɛːnə] m/pl. sawdust; **~werk** n sawmill.

sah [zaː] pret. of sehen.

Sahne ['zaːnə] f (-/no pl.) cream.

Saison [zɛ'zõː] f (-/-s) season; **Qbe- dingt** adj. seasonal.

Saite ['zaitə] f (-/-n) string, chord (a. fig.); **~ninstrument** ['zaitən°-] n stringed instrument.

Sakko ['zako] m, n (-s/-s) lounge coat; **~anzug** m lounge suit.

Sakristei [zakris'tai] f (-/-en) sac- risty, vestry.

Salat [za'laːt] m (-[e]s/-e) salad; ♀ lettuce.

Salbe ['zalbə] f (-/-n) ointment; **Qen** v/t. (ge-, h) rub with ointment; anoint; **~ung** f (-/-en) anointing, unction (a. fig.); **Qungsvoll** fig. adj. unctuous.

saldieren ♣ [zal'diːrən] v/t. (no -ge-, h) balance, settle.

Saldo ♣ ['zaldo] m (-s/Salden, Sal- dos, Saldi) balance; *den* ~ *ziehen* strike the balance; **~vortrag** ♣ m balance carried down.

Saline [za'liːnə] f (-/-n) salt-pit, salt-works.

Salmiak ♠ [zal'mjak] m, n (-s/no pl.) sal-ammoniac, ammonium chloride; **~geist** m (-es/no pl.) liquid ammonia.

Salon [za'lõː] m (-s/-s) drawing- room, *Am. a.* parlor; ♣ saloon; **Qfähig** adj. presentable; **~löwe** fig. m lady's man, carpet-knight;

~wagen 🚃 m salooncar, saloon carriage, *Am.* parlor car.

Salpeter ♠ [zal'peːtər] m (-s/no pl.) saltpetre; **~re** *Am.* -er; nit|re, *Am.* -er.

Salto ['zalto] m (-s/-s, Salti) somer- sault; ~ *mortale* break-neck leap; *e-n* ~ *schlagen* turn a somersault.

Salut [za'luːt] m (-[e]s/-e) salute; ~ *schießen* fire a salute; **Qieren** [~'tiːrən] v/i. (no -ge-, h) (stand at the) salute.

Salve ['zalvə] f (-/-n) volley; ♣ broadside; salute.

Salz [zalts] n (-es/-e) salt; **~berg- werk** n salt-mine; **Qen** v/t. (irr.) ge-, h) salt; **~faß** n, **~fäßchen** ['~fɛsçən] n (-s/-) salt-cellar; **~gurke** f pickled cucumber; **Qhal- tig** adj. saline, saliferous; **~hering** m pickled herring; **Qig** adj. salt(y); *s. salzhaltig*; **~säure** ♠ f hydro- chloric or muriatic acid; **~wasser** n (-s/¿) salt water, brine; **~werk** n salt-works, saltern.

Same ['zaːmə] m (-ns/-n), **~n** m (-s/-) ♀ seed (a. fig.); biol. sperm, semen; **~nkorn** ♀ n grain of seed.

Sammel|büchse ['zaməl-] f col- lecting-box; **~lager** n collecting point; *refugees, etc.*: assembly camp; **Qn** (ge-, h) **1.** v/t. gather; collect (stamps, etc.); sich ~ gather; fig.: concentrate; compose o.s.; **2.** v/i. collect money (für for) **~platz** m meeting-place, place of appointment; ✕, ♣ rendezvous.

Samml|er ['zamlər] m (-s/-) col- lector; **~ung** f **1.** (-/-en) collection; **2.** fig. (-/no pl.) composure; con- centration.

Samstag ['zams-] m Saturday.

samt[1] [zamt] **1.** adv.: ~ *und sonders* one and all; **2.** prp. (dat.) together or along with.

Samt[2] [~] m (-[e]s/-e) velvet.

sämtlich ['zɛmtlɪç] **1.** adj. all (to- gether); complete; **2.** adv. all (to- gether or of them).

Sanatorium [zana'toːrjum] n (-s/ Sanatorien) sanatorium, *Am. a.* sanitarium.

Sand [zant] m (-[e]s/-e) sand; *j-m* ~ *in die Augen streuen* throw dust into s.o.'s eyes; *im* ~ *verlaufen* end in smoke, come to nothing.

Sandale [zan'daːlə] f (-/-n) sandal.

Sand|bahn f sports: dirt-track; **~bank** f sandbank; **~boden** m

S

sandy soil; '**~grube** f sand-pit; **2ig** adj. ['~diç] sandy; '**~korn** n grain of sand; '**~mann** fig. m (-[e]s/no pl.) sandman, dustman; '**~papier** n sandpaper; '**~sack** m sand-bag; '**~stein** m sandstone.

sandte ['zantə] pret. of senden.

'**Sand|torte** f Madeira cake; '**~uhr** f sand-glass; '**~wüste** f sandy desert.

sanft adj. [zanft] soft; gentle, mild; smooth; slope, death, etc.: easy; **~er** Zwang non-violent coercion; mit **~er** Stimme softly, gently; **~mütig** adj. ['~my:tiç] gentle, mild; meek.

sang [zaŋ] pret. of singen.

Sänger ['zɛŋər] m (-s/-) singer.

Sanguini|ker [zaŋgu'i:nikər] m (-s/-) sanguine person; **2sch** adj. sanguine.

sanier|en [za'ni:rən] v/t. (no -ge-, h) improve the sanitary conditions of; esp. ✝: reorganize; readjust; **2ung** f (-/-en) sanitation; esp. ✝: reorganization; readjustment.

sanitär adj. [zani'tɛ:r] sanitary.

Sanität|er [zani'tɛ:tər] m (-s/-) ambulance man; ⚔ medical orderly.

sank [zaŋk] pret. of sinken.

Sankt [zaŋkt] Saint, St.

sann [zan] pret. of sinnen.

Sard|elle ichth. [zar'dɛlə] f (-/-n) anchovy; **~ine** ichth. [~'i:nə] f (-/-n) sardine.

Sarg [zark] m (-[e]s/ue) coffin, Am. a. casket; '**~deckel** m coffin-lid.

Sarkas|mus [zar'kasmus] m (-/⚹ Sarkasmen) sarcasm; **2tisch** adj. [~tiʃ] sarcastic.

saß [za:s] pret. of sitzen.

Satan ['za:tan] m (-s/-e) Satan; fig. devil; **2isch** fig. adj. [za'tɑ:niʃ] satanic.

Satellit ast., pol. [zatɛ'li:t] m (-en/-en) satellite; **~enstaat** pol. m satellite state.

Satin [sa'tɛ̃:] m (-s/-s) satin; sateen.

Satir|e [za'ti:rə] f (-/-n) satire; **~iker** [~ikər] m (-s/-) satirist; **2isch** adj. satiric(al).

satt adj. [zat] satisfied, satiated, full; colour: deep, rich; sich **~ essen** eat one's fill; ich bin **~** I have had enough; F et. **~** haben be tired or sick of s.th., sl. be fed up with s.th.

Sattel ['zatəl] m (-s/u) saddle; '**~gurt** m girth; **2n** v/t. (ge-, h) saddle.

'**Sattheit** f (-/no pl.) satiety, fullness; richness, intensity (of colours).

sättig|en ['zɛtigən] (ge-, h) 1. v/t. satisfy, satiate; 🜍, phys. saturate; 2. v/i. food: be substantial; **2ung** f (-/-en) satiation; 🜍, fig. saturation.

Sattler ['zatlər] m (-s/-) saddler; **~ei** [~'rai] f (-/-en) saddlery.

'**sattsam** adv. sufficiently.

Satz [zats] m (-es/ue) gr. sentence, clause; phls. maxim; ♪ proposition, theorem; ♪ movement; tennis, etc.: set; typ. setting, composition; sediment, dregs pl., grounds pl.; rate (of prices, etc.); set (of stamps, tools, etc.); leap, bound.

'**Satzung** f (-/-en) statute, by-law; **2sgemäß** adj. statutory.

'**Satzzeichen** gr. n punctuation mark.

Sau [zau] f 1. (-/ue) zo. sow; fig. contp. filthy swine; 2. hunt. (-/-en) wild sow.

sauber adj. ['zaubər] clean; neat (a. fig.), tidy; attitude: decent; iro. fine, nice; **2keit** f (-/no pl.) clean-(li)ness; tidiness, neatness; decency (of attitude).

'**säuber|n** ['zɔybərn] v/t. (ge-, h) clean(se); tidy, clean up (room, etc.); clear (von of); purge (of, from) (a. fig., pol.); **2ungsaktion** pol. f purge.

sauer ['zauər] 1. adj. sour (a. fig.), acid (a. 🜍); cucumber: pickled; task, etc.: hard, painful; fig. morose, surly; 2. adv.: **~** reagieren auf et. take s.th. in bad part.

säuer|lich adj. ['zɔyərliç] sourish, acidulous; '**~n** v/t. (ge-, h) (make) sour, acidify (a. 🜍); leaven (dough).

'**Sauer|stoff** 🜍 m (-[e]s/no pl.) oxygen; '**~teig** m leaven.

saufen ['zaufən] v/t. and v/i. (irr., ge-, h) animals: drink; F p. sl. soak, lush.

Säufer F ['zɔyfər] m (-s/-) sot, sl. soak.

saugen ['zaugən] ([irr.,] ge-, h) 1. v/i. suck (an et. s.th.); 2. v/t. suck.

säuge|n ['zɔygən] v/t. (ge-, h) suckle, nurse; **2tier** n mammal.

Säugling ['zɔyklɪŋ] m (-s/-e) baby, suckling; '**~sheim** n baby-farm, baby-nursery.

'**Saug|papier** n absorbent paper; '**~pumpe** f suction-pump; '**~wirkung** f suction-effect.

Säule ['zɔʏlə] f (-/-n) ⚛, anat. column (a. of smoke, mercury, etc.); pillar, support (both a. fig.); '~ngang m colonnade; '~nhalle f pillared hall; portico.

Saum [zaum] m (-[e]s/ue) seam, hem; border, edge.

säum|en ['zɔʏmən] v/t. (ge-, h) hem; border, edge; die Straßen ~ line the streets; '~ig adj. payer: dilatory.

'**Saum|pfad** m mule-track; '~tier n sumpter-mule.

Säure ['zɔʏrə] f (-/-n) sourness; acidity (a. 🜊 of stomach); 🜊 acid.

Saure'gurkenzeit f silly or slack season.

säuseln ['zɔʏzəln] (ge-, h) 1. v/i. leaves, wind: rustle, whisper; 2. v/t. p. say airily, purr.

sausen ['zauzən] v/i. (ge-) 1. (sein) F rush, dash; bullet, etc.: whiz(z), whistle; 2. (h) wind: whistle, sough.

'**Saustall** m pigsty; F fig. a. horrid mess.

Saxophon ♪ [zakso'foːn] n (-s/-e) saxophone.

Schab|e ['ʃaːbə] f (-/-n) zo. cockroach; ⊕ s. Schabeisen; '~efleisch n scraped meat; '~eisen ⊕ n scraper, shaving-tool; '~emesser ⊕ n scraping-knife; '2en v/t. (ge-, h) scrape (a. ⊕); grate, rasp; scratch; '~er ⊕ m (-s/-) scraper.

Schabernack ['ʃaːbərnak] m (-[e]s/-e) practical joke, hoax, prank.

schäbig adj. ['ʃɛːbiç] shabby (a. fig.), F seedy, Am. F a. dowdy, tacky; fig. mean.

Schablone [ʃa'bloːnə] f (-/-n) model, pattern; stencil; fig.: routine; cliché; 2nhaft adj., 2nmäßig adj. according to pattern; fig.: mechanical; attr. a. routine.

Schach [ʃax] n (-s/-s) chess; ~! check!; ~ und matt! checkmate!; in or im ~ halten keep s.o. in check; '~brett n chessboard.

schachern ['ʃaxərn] v/i. (ge-, h) haggle (um about, over), chaffer (about, over), Am. a. dicker; ~ mit barter (away).

'**Schach|feld** n square; '~figur f chess-man, piece; fig. pawn; '2-'matt adj. (check)mated; fig. tired out, worn out; '~spiel n game of chess. [a. pit.]

Schacht [ʃaxt] m (-[e]s/ue) shaft; ⚒)

Schachtel ['ʃaxtəl] f (-/-n) box; F alte ~ old frump.

'**Schachzug** m move (at chess); geschickter ~ clever move (a. fig.).

schade pred. adj. ['ʃaːdə]: es ist ~ it is a pity; wie ~! what a pity!; zu ~ für too good for.

Schädel ['ʃɛːdəl] m (-s/-) skull; cranium; '~bruch 🜊 m fracture of the skull.

schaden ['ʃaːdən] 1. v/i. (ge-, h) damage, injure, harm, hurt (j-m s.o.); be detrimental (to s.o.); das schadet nichts it does not matter, never mind; 2. 2 m (-s/-) damage (an dat. to); injury, harm; infirmity; hurt; loss; '2ersatz m indemnification, compensation; damages pl.; ~ verlangen claim damages; ~ leisten pay damages; auf ~ (ver)klagen 🜊🜊 sue for damages; '2freude f malicious enjoyment of others' misfortunes, schadenfreude; '~froh adj. rejoicing over others' misfortunes.

schadhaft adj. ['ʃaːthaft] damaged; defective, faulty; building, etc.: dilapidated; pipe, etc.: leaking; tooth, etc.: decayed.

schädig|en ['ʃɛːdigən] v/t. (ge-, h) damage, impair; wrong, harm; '2ung f (-/-en) damage (gen. to), impairment (of); prejudice (to).

schädli|ch adj. ['ʃɛːtliç] harmful, injurious; noxious; detrimental, prejudicial; '2ng m (-s/-e) zo. pest; ♣ destructive weed; noxious person; ~e pl. 🜊 a. vermin.

schadlos adj. ['ʃaːtloːs]: sich ~ halten recoup or idemnify o.s. (für for).

Schaf [ʃaːf] n (-[e]s/-e) zo. sheep; fig. simpleton; '~bock zo. m ram.

Schäfer ['ʃɛːfər] m (-s/-) shepherd; '~hund m sheep-dog; Alsatian (wolf-hound).

Schaffell ['ʃaːfɛl] n sheepskin.

schaffen ['ʃafən] 1. v/t. (irr., ge-, h) create, produce; 2. v/t. (ge-, h) convey, carry, move; take, bring; cope with, manage; 3. v/i. (ge-, h) be busy, work.

Schaffner ['ʃafnər] m (-s/-) 🚃 guard, Am. conductor; tram, bus: conductor.

'**Schafhirt** m shepherd.   [fold.)

Schafott [ʃa'fɔt] n (-[e]s/-e) scaf-)

'**Schaf|pelz** m sheepskin coat; '~stall m fold.

Schaft [ʃaft] *m* (-[e]s/-̈e) shaft (*of lance, column, etc.*); stick (*of flag*); stock (*of rifle*); shank (*of tool, key, etc.*); leg (*of boot*); **stiefel** *m* high boot; ~ *pl. a.* Wellingtons *pl.*

'**Schaf|wolle** *f* sheep's wool; '**zucht** *f* sheep-breeding, sheep-farming.

schäkern ['ʃɛːkərn] *v/i.* (ge-, h) jest, joke; flirt.

schal¹ *adj.* [ʃaːl] insipid; stale; *fig. a.* flat.

Schal² [~] *m* (-s/-e, -s) scarf, muffler; comforter.

Schale ['ʃaːlə] *f* (-/-n) bowl; ⊕ scale (*of scales*); shell (*of eggs, nuts, etc.*); peel, skin (*of fruit*); shell, crust (*of tortoise*); paring, peeling; F: *sich in ~ werfen* doll o.s. up.

schälen ['ʃɛːlən] *v/t.* (ge-, h) remove the peel or skin from; pare, peel (*fruit, potatoes, etc.*); *sich ~ skin:* peel or come off.

Schalk [ʃalk] *m* (-[e]s/-e, -̈e) rogue, wag; '**2haft** *adj.* roguish, waggish.

Schall [ʃal] *m* (-[e]s/-̈e, -̈e) sound; '**dämpfer** *m* sound absorber; *mot.* silencer, *Am.* muffler; silencer (*on fire-arms*); '**2dicht** *adj.* sound-proof; '**2en** *v/i.* (irr., ge-, h) sound; ring, peal; '**2end** *adj.:* ~es Gelächter roars *pl.* or a peal of laughter; '**mauer** *f* sound barrier; '**platte** *f* record, disc, disk; '**welle** *f* sound-wave.

schalt [ʃalt] *pret. of* schelten.

'**Schaltbrett** ⚡ *n* switchboard.

schalten ['ʃaltən] (ge-, h) **1.** *v/i.* ⚡ switch; *mot.* change or shift gears; direct, rule; **2.** *v/t.* ⊕ actuate; operate, control.

'**Schalter** *m* (-s/-) ⚡, *theatre, etc.:* booking-office; ☞, *bank, etc.:* counter; ⚡ switch; ⊕, *mot.* controller.

'**Schalt|hebel** *m mot.* gear lever; ⊕, ⚡ control lever; ⚡ switch lever; '**jahr** *n* leap-year; '**tafel** ⚡ *f* switchboard, control panel; '**tag** *m* intercalary day.

Scham [ʃaːm] *f* (-/no *pl.*) shame; bashfulness, modesty; *anat.* privy parts *pl.*, genitals *pl.*

schämen ['ʃɛːmən] *v/refl.* (ge-, h) be or feel ashamed (*gen. or wegen of*).

'**Scham|gefühl** *n* sense of shame; '**2haft** *adj.* bashful, modest; '**haftigkeit** *f* (-/no *pl.*) bashfulness,

modesty; '**2los** *adj.* shameless; impudent; '**losigkeit** *f* (-/-en) shamelessness; impudence; '**2rot** *adj.* blushing; ~ *werden* blush; '**röte** *f* blush; '**teile** *anat. m/pl.* privy parts *pl.*, genitals *pl.*

Schande ['ʃandə] *f* (-/-̈n) shame, disgrace.

schänden ['ʃɛndən] *v/t.* (ge-, h) dishono(u)r, disgrace; desecrate, profane; rape, violate; disfigure.

Schandfleck *fig.* ['ʃant-] *m* blot, stain; eyesore.

schändlich *adj.* ['ʃɛntliç] shameful, disgraceful, infamous; '**2keit** *f* (-/-en) infamy.

'**Schandtat** *f* infamous act(ion).

'**Schändung** *f* (-/-en) dishono(u)ring; profanation; desecration; rape, violation; disfigurement.

Schanze ['ʃantsə] *f* (-/-n) ✕ entrenchment; ⚓ quarter-deck; *sports:* ski-jump; '**2n** *v/i.* (ge-, h) throw up entrenchments, entrench.

Schar [ʃaːr] *f* (-/-en) troop, band; geese, etc.: flock; 🜨 ploughshare, *Am.* plowshare; '**2en** *v/t.* (ge-, h) assemble, collect; *sich ~ a.* flock (*um round*).

scharf [ʃarf] **1.** *adj.* sharp; edge: keen; *voice, sound:* piercing, shrill; *smell, taste:* pungent; *pepper, etc.:* hot; *sight, hearing, intelligence, etc.:* keen; *answer, etc.:* cutting; ✕ *ammunition:* live; ~ *sein auf* (*acc.*) be very keen on; **2.** *adv.:* ~ *ansehen* look sharply at; ~ *reiten* ride hard; '**2blick** *fig. m* (-[e]s/no *pl.*) clear-sightedness.

Schärfe ['ʃɛrfə] *f* (-/-n) sharpness; keenness; pungency; '**2n** *v/t.* (ge-, h) put an edge on, sharpen; strengthen (*memory*); sharpen (*sight, hearing, etc.*).

'**Scharf|macher** *fig. m* (-s/-) firebrand, agitator; '**richter** *m* executioner; '**schütze** ✕ *m* sharpshooter, sniper; '**2sichtig** *adj.* sharp-sighted; *fig.* clear-sighted; '**sinn** *m* (-[e]s/no *pl.*) sagacity; acumen; '**2sinnig** *adj.* sharp-witted, shrewd; sagacious.

Scharlach ['ʃarlax] *m* **1.** (-s/-e) scarlet; **2.** 🖋 (-s/no *pl.*) scarlet fever; '**2rot** *adj.* scarlet.

Scharlatan ['ʃarlatan] *m* (-s/-e) charlatan, quack (doctor); mountebank.

Scharmützel [ʃarˈmytsəl] *n* (-s/-) skirmish.

Scharnier ⊕ [ʃarˈniːr] *n* (-s/-e) hinge, joint.

Schärpe [ˈʃɛrpə] *f* (-/-n) sash.

scharren [ˈʃarən] (ge-, h) **1.** *v/i.* scrape (*mit den Füßen* one's feet); *hen, etc.*: scratch; *horse*: paw; **2.** *v/t. horse*: paw (*ground*).

Schart|e [ˈʃartə] *f* (-/-n) notch, nick; *mountains*: gap, *Am.* notch; *e-e ~ auswetzen* repair a fault; wipe out a disgrace; **'2ig** *adj.* jagged, notchy.

Schatten [ˈʃatən] *m* (-s/-) shadow (*a. fig.*); shade (*a. paint.*); **~bild** *n* silhouette; **'2haft** *adj.* shadowy; **'~kabinett** *pol. n* shadow cabinet; **'~riß** *m* silhouette; **'~seite** *f* shady side; *fig.* seamy side.

schattier|en [ʃaˈtiːrən] *v/t.* (*no* -ge-, h) shade, tint; **2ung** *f* (-/-en) shading; shade (*a. fig.*), tint.

'schattig *adj.* shady.

Schatz [ʃats] *m* (-es/¨e) treasure; *fig.* sweetheart, darling; **'~amt** † *n* Exchequer, *Am.* Treasury (Department); **'~anweisung** † *f* Treasury Bond, *Am. a.* Treasury Note.

schätzen [ˈʃɛtsən] *v/t.* (ge-, h) estimate; value (*auf acc. at*); price (at); rate; appreciate; esteem; *sich glücklich ~ zu inf.* be delighted to *inf.*; **'~swert** *adj.* estimable.

'Schatz|kammer *f* treasury; **'~meister** *m* treasurer.

'Schätzung *f* **1.** (-/-en) estimate, valuation; rating; **2.** (-/*no pl.*) appreciation, estimation; esteem.

'Schatzwechsel † *m* Treasury Bill.

Schau [ʃau] *f* (-/-en) inspection, show, exhibition; *zur ~ stellen* exhibit, display.

Schauder [ˈʃaudər] *m* (-s/-) shudder(ing), shiver, tremor; *fig.* horror, terror; **'2haft** *adj.* horrible, dreadful; *F fig. a.* awful; **'2n** *v/i.* (ge-, h) shudder, shiver (*both: vor dat. at*).

schauen [ˈʃauən] *v/i.* (ge-, h) look (*auf acc. at*).

Schauer [ˈʃauər] *m* (-s/-) *rain, etc.*: shower (*a. fig.*); shudder(ing), shiver; attack, fit; thrill; **'2lich** *adj.* dreadful, horrible; **'2n** *v/i.* (ge-, h) *s. schaudern*; **'~roman** *m* penny dreadful, thriller.

Schaufel [ˈʃaufəl] *f* (-/-n) shovel,

dust-pan; **'2n** *v/t. and v/i.* (ge-, h) shovel.

'Schaufenster *n* shop window, *Am. a.* show-window; **'~bummel** *m: e-n ~ machen* go window-shopping; **'~dekoration** *f* window-dressing; **'~einbruch** *m* smash-and-grab raid.

Schaukel [ˈʃaukəl] *f* (-/-n) swing; **'2n** (ge-, h) **1.** *v/i.* swing; *ship, etc.*: rock; **2.** *v/t.* rock (*baby, etc.*); **'~pferd** *n* rocking-horse; **'~stuhl** *m* rocking-chair, *Am. a.* rocker.

Schaum [ʃaum] *m* (-[e]s/¨e) foam; *beer, etc.*: froth, head; *soap*: lather; **'~bad** *n* bubble bath.

schäumen [ˈʃɔymən] *v/i.* (ge-, h) foam, froth; lather; *wine, etc.*: sparkle.

'Schaum|gummi *n, m* foam rubber; **'2ig** *adj.* foamy, frothy; **'~wein** *m* sparkling wine.

'Schau|platz *m* scene (of action), theat|re, *Am.* -er; **'~prozeß** ɪ‡ɜ *m* show trial.

schaurig *adj.* [ˈʃauriç] horrible, horrid.

'Schau|spiel *n* spectacle; *thea.* play; **'~spieler** *m* actor, player; **'~spielhaus** *n* playhouse, theat|re, *Am.* -er; **'~spielkunst** *f* (-/*no pl.*) dramatic art, *the* drama; **'~steller** *m* (-s/-) showman.

Scheck † [ʃɛk] *m* (-s/-s) cheque, *Am.* check; **'~buch** *n*, **'~heft** *n* chequebook, *Am.* checkbook.

'scheckig *adj.* spotted; *horse*: piebald.

scheel [ʃeːl] **1.** *adj.* squint-eyed, cross-eyed; *fig.* jealous, envious; **2.** *adv.*: *j-n ~ ansehen* look askance at s.o.

Scheffel [ˈʃɛfəl] *m* (-s/-) bushel; **'2n** *v/t.* (ge-, h) amass (*money, etc.*).

Scheibe [ˈʃaibə] *f* (-/-n) disk, disc (*a. of sun, moon*); *esp. ast.* orb; slice (*of bread, etc.*); pane (*of window*); *shooting*: target; **'~nhonig** *m* honey in combs; **'~nwischer** *mot. m* (-s/-) wind-screen wiper, *Am.* windshield wiper.

Scheide [ˈʃaidə] *f* (-/-n) sword, *etc.*: sheath, scabbard; border, boundary; **'~münze** *f* small coin; **'2n** (*irr.*, ge-) **1.** *v/t.* (h) separate; **ʔ‿** analyse; ɪ‡ɜ divorce; *sich ~ lassen von* ɪ‡ɜ divorce (*one's husband or wife*); **2.** *v/i.* (sein) depart; part (*von* with); *aus dem Dienst* ~ retire from service; *aus dem Leben* ~ depart from this life; '**~wand** f partition; '**~weg** fig. m cross-roads sg.

'**Scheidung** f (-/-en) separation; 🙤 divorce; '**~sgrund** 🙤 m ground for divorce; '**~sklage** 🙤 f divorce-suit; *die* ~ *einreichen* file a petition for divorce.

Schein [ʃaɪn] m 1. (-[e]s/no pl.) shine; *sun, lamp, etc.*: light; *fire*: blaze; *fig.* appearance; 2. (-[e]s/-e) certificate; receipt; bill; (bank-) note; '**2bar** adj. seeming, apparent; '**2en** v/i. (irr., ge-, h) shine; *fig.* seem, appear, look; '**~grund** m pretext, preten|ce, *Am.* -se; '**2hei-lig** adj. sanctimonious, hypocritical; '**~tod** ✝ m suspended animation; '**2tot** adj. in a state of suspended animation; '**~werfer** m (-s/-) reflector, projector; ✗, ⚓, ✈ searchlight; *mot.* headlight; *thea.* spotlight.

Scheit [ʃaɪt] n (-[e]s/-e) log, billet.

Scheitel ['ʃaɪtəl] m (-s/-) crown or top of the head; *hair*: parting; summit, peak; *esp.* ⚕ vertex; '**2n** v/t. (ge-, h) part (*hair*).

Scheiterhaufen ['ʃaɪtər-] m (funeral) pile; stake.

'**scheitern** v/i. (ge-, sein) ⚓ run aground, be wrecked; *fig.* fail, miscarry. [box on the ear.)

Schelle ['ʃɛlə] f (-/-n) (little) bell;)

'**Schellfisch** *ichth.* m haddock.

Schelm [ʃɛlm] m (-[e]s/-e) rogue; '**~enstreich** m roguish trick; '**2isch** adj. roguish, arch.

Schelte ['ʃɛltə] f (-/-n) scolding; '**2n** (*irr.*, ge-, h) 1. v/t. scold, rebuke; 2. v/i. scold.

Schema ['ʃeːma] n (-s/-s, -ta, Schemen) scheme; model, pattern; arrangement; '**2tisch** adj. [ʃeˈmaːtiʃ] schematic.

Schemel ['ʃeːməl] m (-s/-) stool.

Schemen ['ʃeːmən] m (-s/-) phantom, shadow; '**2haft** adj. shadowy.

Schenke ['ʃɛŋkə] f (-/-n) public house, F pub; tavern, inn.

Schenkel ['ʃɛŋkəl] m (-s/-) anat. thigh; *anat.* shank; *triangle, etc.*: leg; ⚕ angle: side.

schenken ['ʃɛŋkən] v/t. (ge-, h) give; remit (*penalty, etc.*); *j-m et.* ~ give s.o. s.th., present s.o. with s.th., make s.o. a present of s.th.

'**Schenkung** 🙤 f (-/-en) donation; '**~surkunde** ['ʃɛŋkuŋs⁹-] f deed of gift.

Scherbe ['ʃɛrbə] f (-/-n), '**~n** m (-s/-) (broken) piece, fragment.

Schere ['ʃeːrə] f (-/-n) (e-e a pair of) scissors *pl.*; *zo. crab, etc.*: claw; '**2n** v/t. 1. (*irr.*, ge-, h) shear (*a. sheep*), clip, shave (*beard*); cut (*hair*); clip, prune (*hedge*); 2. (ge-, h): *sich um et.* ~ trouble about s.th.; '**~nschleifer** m (-s/-) knife-grinder; '**~rei** [~'raɪ] f (-/-en) trouble, bother.

Scherz [ʃɛrts] m (-es/-e) jest, joke; ~ *beiseite* joking apart; *im* ~, *zum* ~ in jest or joke; ~ *treiben mit* make fun of; '**2en** v/i. (ge-, h) jest, joke; '**2haft** adj. joking, sportive.

scheu [ʃɔy] 1. adj. shy, bashful, timid; *horse*: skittish; ~ *machen* frighten; 2. 2 f (-/no pl.) shyness; timidity; aversion (*vor dat.* to).

scheuchen ['ʃɔyçən] v/t. (ge-, h) scare, frighten (away).

'**scheuen** (ge-, h) 1. v/i. shy (*vor dat.* at), take fright (at); 2. v/t. shun, avoid; fear; *sich* ~ *vor* (*dat.*) shy at, be afraid of.

Scheuer|lappen ['ʃɔyər-] m scouring-cloth, floor-cloth; '**~leiste** f skirting-board; '**2n** (ge-, h) 1. v/t. scour, scrub; chafe; 2. v/i. chafe.

'**Scheuklappe** f blinker, *Am. a.* blinder.

Scheune ['ʃɔynə] f (-/-n) barn.

Scheusal ['ʃɔyzaːl] n (-[e]s/-e) monster.

scheußlich adj. ['ʃɔyslɪç] hideous, atrocious (F *a. fig.*), abominable (F *a. fig.*); '**2keit** f 1. (-/no pl.) hideousness; 2. (-/-en) abomination; atrocity.

Schi [ʃiː] m (-s/-er) etc. s. Ski, etc.

Schicht [ʃɪçt] f (-/-en) layer; *geol.* stratum (*a. fig.*); at work: shift; (social) class, rank, order of life; '**2en** v/t. (ge-, h) arrange or put in layers, pile up; classify; '**2weise** adv. in layers; *work*: in shifts.

Schick [ʃɪk] 1. m (-[e]s/no pl.) chic, elegance, style; 2. 2 adj. chic, stylish, fashionable.

schicken ['ʃɪkən] v/t. (ge-, h) send (*nach, zu* to); remit (*money*); *nach j-m* ~ send for s.o.; *sich* ~ *für* become, suit, befit s.o.; *sich* ~ *in* put up with, resign o.s. to s.th.

'**schicklich** adj. becoming, proper,

Schinderei

seemly; '2**keit** f (-/no pl.) propriety, seemliness.

'**Schicksal** n [-[e]s/-e) fate, destiny.

Schiebe|dach mot. ['ʃiːbə-] n sliding roof; '**~fenster** n sash-window; '2n (irr., ge-, h) **1.** v/t. push, shove; shift (blame) (auf acc. on to); F fig. sell on the black market; **2.** F fig. v/i. profiteer; '**~r** m (-s/-) bolt (of door); ⊕ slide; fig. profiteer, black marketeer, sl. spiv; '**~tür** f sliding door.

'**Schiebung** fig. f (-/-en) black marketeering, profiteering; put-up job.

schied [ʃiːt] pret. of scheiden.

Schieds|gericht ['ʃiːts-] n court of arbitration, arbitration committee; '**~richter** m arbitrator; tennis, etc.: umpire; football, etc.: referee; '2**richterlich** adj. arbitral; '**~spruch** m award, arbitration.

schief [ʃiːf] **1.** adj. sloping, slanting; oblique; face, mouth: wry; fig. false, wrong; ~e Ebene ⚔ inclined plane; **2.** adv.: j-n ~ ansehen look askance at s.o.

Schiefer ['ʃiːfər] m (-s/-) slate; splinter; '**~stift** m slate-pencil; '**~tafel** f slate.

'**schiefgehen** v/i. (irr. gehen, sep., -ge-, sein) go wrong or awry.

schielen ['ʃiːlən] v/i. (ge-, h) squint, be cross-eyed; ~ auf (acc.) squint at; leer at.

schien [ʃiːn] pret. of scheinen.

Schienbein ['ʃiːn-] n shin(-bone), tibia.

Schiene ['ʃiːnə] f (-/-n) 🚃, etc.: rail; ⚕ splint; '2n v/t. (ge-, h) splint.

schießen ['ʃiːsən] (irr., ge-) **1.** v/t. (h) shoot; tot ~ shoot dead; ein Tor ~ score (a goal); Salut ~ fire a salute; **2.** v/i. (h): auf j-n ~ shoot or fire at; gut ~ be a good shot; **3.** v/i. (sein) shoot, dart, rush.

'**Schieß|pulver** n gunpowder; '**~scharte** ⚔ f loop-hole, embrasure; '**~scheibe** f target; '**~stand** m shooting-gallery or -range.

Schiff [ʃif] n (-[e]s/-e) ⚓ ship, vessel; 🏛 church: nave.

Schiffahrt ['ʃiffaːrt] f (-/-en) navigation.

'**schiff|bar** adj. navigable; '2**bau** m shipbuilding; '2**bauer** m (-s/-) ship-builder; '2**bruch** m shipwreck (a. fig.); ~ erleiden be shipwrecked; fig. make or suffer shipwreck; '**~brüchig** adj. shipwrecked; '**~en** v/i. (ge-, sein) navigate, sail; '2**er** m (-s/-) sailor; boatman; navigator; skipper.

'**Schiffs|junge** m cabin-boy; '**~kapitän** m (sea-)captain; '**~ladung** f shipload; cargo; '**~makler** m shipbroker; '**~mannschaft** f crew; '**~raum** m hold; tonnage; '**~werft** f shipyard, esp. ⚔ dockyard, Am. a. navy yard.

Schikan|e [ʃiˈkaːnə] f (-/-n) vexation, nasty trick; 2**ieren** [~kaˈniːrən] v/t. (no -ge-, h) vex, ride.

Schild [ʃilt] **1.** ⚔ m (-[e]s/-e) shield, buckler; **2.** n (-[e]s/-er) shop, etc.: sign(board), facia; name-plate; traffic: signpost; label; cap: peak; '**~drüse** anat. f thyroid gland.

'**Schilder|haus** ⚔ n sentry-box; '**~maler** m sign-painter; '2**n** v/t. (ge-, h) describe, delineate; '**~ung** f (-/-en) description, delineation.

'**Schild|kröte** zo. f tortoise; turtle; '**~wache** ⚔ f sentinel, sentry.

Schilf ⚘ [ʃilf] n (-[e]s/-e) reed; '2**ig** adj. reedy; '**~rohr** n reed.

schillern ['ʃilərn] v/i. (ge-, h) show changing colo(u)rs; be iridescent.

Schimmel ['ʃiməl] m **1.** zo. (-s/-) white horse; **2.** ⚘ (-s/no pl.) mo(u)ld, mildew; '2**ig** adj. mo(u)ldy, musty; '2**n** v/i. (ge-, h) become mo(u)ldy, Am. a. mo(u)ld.

Schimmer ['ʃimər] m (-s/no pl.) glimmer, gleam (a. fig.); 2**n** v/i. (ge-, h) glimmer, gleam.

Schimpanse zo. [ʃimˈpanzə] m (-n/-n) chimpanzee.

Schimpf [ʃimpf] m (-[e]s/-e) insult, disgrace; mit ~ und Schande ignominiously; '2**en** (ge-, h) **1.** v/i. rail (über acc., auf acc. at, against); **2.** v/t. scold; j-n e-n Lügner ~ call s.o. a liar; '2**lich** adj. disgraceful (für to), ignominious (to); '**~name** m abusive name; '**~wort** n term of abuse; ~e pl. a. invectives pl.

Schindel ['ʃindəl] f (-/-n) shingle.

schinden ['ʃindən] v/t. (irr., ge-, h) flay, skin (rabbit, etc.); sweat (worker); sich ~ drudge, slave, sweat.

'**Schinder** m (-s/-) knacker; fig. sweater, slave-driver; **~ei** fig. [~ˈraɪ] *f* (-/-en) sweating; drudgery, grind.

Schinken ['ʃiŋkən] *m* (-s/-) ham.

Schippe ['ʃipə] *f* (-/-n) shovel; '2n *v/t.* (ge-, h) shovel.

Schirm [ʃirm] *m* (-[e]s/-e) umbrella; parasol, sunshade; *lamp:* shade; *cap:* peak, visor; '~futteral *n* umbrella-case; '~herr *m* protector; patron; '~herrschaft *f* protectorate; patronage; *unter der ~ von event:* under the auspices of; '~mütze *f* peaked cap; '~ständer *m* umbrella-stand.

Schlacht ⚔ [ʃlaxt] *f* (-/-en) battle (*bei* of); '~bank *f* shambles; '2en *v/t.* (ge-, h) slaughter, butcher.

Schlächter ['ʃlɛçtər] *m* (-s/-) butcher.

Schlacht|feld ⚔ *n* battle-field; '~haus *n*, '~hof *m* slaughter-house, abattoir; '~kreuzer ⚓ *m* battle-cruiser; '~plan *m* ⚔ plan of action (*a. fig.*); '~schiff ⚓ *n* battleship; '~vieh *n* slaughter cattle.

Schlack|e ['ʃlakə] *f* (-/-n) wood, *coal:* cinder; *metall.* dross (*a. fig.*); slag; *geol.* scoria; '2ig *adj.* drossy, slaggy; *F weather:* slushy.

Schlaf [ʃlaːf] *m* (-[e]s/*no pl.*) sleep; *im ~*(e) in one's sleep; *e-n leichten (festen) ~ haben* be a light (sound) sleeper; *in tiefem ~e liegen* be fast asleep; '~abteil ⚏ *n* sleeping-compartment; '~anzug *m* (*ein a pair of*) pyjamas *pl. or Am.* pajamas *pl.*

Schläfchen ['ʃlɛːfçən] *n* (-s/-) doze, nap, F forty winks *pl.*; *ein ~ machen* take a nap, F have one's forty winks.

'**Schlafdecke** *f* blanket.

Schläfe ['ʃlɛːfə] *f* (-/-n) temple.

'**schlafen** ['ʃlaːfən] *v/i.* (*irr.*, ge-, h) sleep; *~ gehen, sich ~ legen* go to bed.

schlaff *adj.* [ʃlaf] slack, loose; *muscles, etc.:* flabby, flaccid; *plant, etc.:* limp; *discipline, morals, etc.:* lax; '2heit *f* (-/*no pl.*) slackness; flabbiness; limpness; *fig.* laxity.

'**Schlaf|gelegenheit** *f* sleeping accommodation; '~kammer *f* bedroom; '~krankheit ⚕ *f* sleeping-sickness; '~lied *n* lullaby; '~los *adj.* sleepless; '~losigkeit *f* (-/*no pl.*) sleeplessness, ⚕ insomnia; '~mittel *n* soporific; '~mütze *f* nightcap; *fig.* sleepyhead.

schläfrig *adj.* ['ʃlɛːfriç] sleepy, drowsy; '2keit *f* (-/*no pl.*) sleepiness, drowsiness.

'**Schlaf|rock** *m* dressing-gown, *Am. a.* robe; '~saal *m* dormitory; '~sack *m* sleeping-bag; '~stelle *f* sleeping-place; night's lodging; '~tablette ⚕ *f* sleeping-tablet; '2trunken *adj.* very drowsy; '~wagen ⚏ *m* sleeping-car(riage), *Am. a.* sleeper; '~wandler ['~vandlər] *m* (-s/-) sleep-walker, somnambulist; '~zimmer *n* bedroom.

Schlag [ʃlaːk] *m* (-[e]s/~e) blow (*a. fig.*); stroke (*of clock, piston*) (*a. tennis, etc.*); slap (*with palm of hand*); punch (*with fist*); kick (*of horse's hoof*); ⚡ shock; beat (*of heart or pulse*); clap (*of thunder*); warbling (*of bird*); door (*of carriage*); ⚕ apoplexy; *fig.* race, kind, sort; breed (*esp. of animals*); *Schläge bekommen* get a beating; *~ sechs Uhr* on the stroke of six; '~ader *anat.* f artery; '~anfall ⚕ *m* (stroke of) apoplexy, stroke; '2artig 1. *adj.* sudden, abrupt; 2. *adv.* all of a sudden; '~baum *m* turnpike.

schlagen ['ʃlaːgən] (*irr.*, ge-, h) 1. *v/t.* strike, beat, hit; punch; slap; beat, defeat; fell (*trees*); fight (*battle*); *Alarm ~* sound the alarm; *zu Boden ~* knock down; *in den Wind ~* cast or fling to the winds; *sich ~* (have a) fight; *sich et. aus dem Kopf or Sinn ~* put s.th. out of one's mind, dismiss s.th. from one's mind; 2. *v/i.* strike, beat; *heart, pulse:* beat, throb; *clock:* strike; *bird:* warble; *das schlägt nicht in mein Fach* that is not in my line; *um sich ~* lay about one; '~d *fig. adj.* striking.

Schlager ['ʃlaːgər] *m* (-s/-) ♪ song hit; *thea.* hit, draw, box-office success; *book:* best seller.

Schläger ['ʃlɛːgər] *m* (-s/-) rowdy, hooligan; *cricket, etc.:* batsman; *horse:* kicker; *cricket, etc.:* bat; *golf:* club; *tennis, etc.:* racket; *hockey, etc.:* stick; '~ei [~'raɪ] *f* (-/-en) tussle, fight.

'**schlag|fertig** *fig. adj.* quick at repartee; '~e *Antwort* repartee; '2fertigkeit *fig. f* (-/*no pl.*) quickness at repartee; '2instrument ♪ *n* percussion instrument; '2kraft *f* (-/*no pl.*) striking power (*a. ⚔*); '2loch *n* pot-hole; '2mann *m rowing:* stroke; '2ring *m* knuckle-duster, *Am. a.* brass knuckles *pl.*;

'2̶sahne *f* whipped cream; '2̶-schatten *m* cast shadow; '2̶seite ⚓ *f* list; ~ haben ⚓ list; F *fig.* be half-seas-over; '2̶uhr *f* striking clock; '2̶werk *n* clock: striking mechanism; '2̶wort *n* catchword; slogan; '2̶zeile *f* headline; banner headline, *Am.* banner; '2̶zeug ♪ *n in orchestra:* percussion instruments *pl.; in band:* drums *pl.,* percussion; '2̶zeuger ♪ *m* (-s/-) *in orchestra:* percussionist; *in band:* drummer.

schlaksig *adj.* ['ʃlaːksiç] gawky.

Schlamm [ʃlam] *m* (-[e]s/~-e, ~e) mud, mire; '~bad *n* mud-bath; '2̶ig *adj.* muddy, miry.

Schlämmkreide ['ʃlɛm-] *f* (-/*no pl.*) whit(en)ing.

Schlamp|e ['ʃlampə] *f* (-/-n) slut, slattern; '2̶ig *adj.* slovenly, slip-shod.

schlang [ʃlaŋ] *pret. of* schlingen.

Schlange ['ʃlaŋə] *f* (-/-n) *zo.* snake, *rhet.* serpent (*a. fig.*); *fig.*: snake in the grass; queue, *Am. a.* line; ~ stehen queue up (*um* for), *Am.* line up (for).

schlängeln ['ʃlɛŋəln] *v/refl.* (ge-, h): *sich ~ durch person:* worm one's way *or* o.s. through; *path, river, etc.*: wind (one's way) through, meander through.

'**Schlangenlinie** *f* serpentine line.

schlank *adj.* [ʃlaŋk] slender, slim; '2̶heit *f* (-/*no pl.*) slenderness, slimness; '2̶heitskur *f*: e-e ~ *machen* slim.

schlapp F *adj.* [ʃlap] tired, exhausted, worn out; '2̶e F *f* (-/-n) reverse, set-back; defeat; '~machen F *v/i.* (*sep.,* -ge-, h) break down, faint.

schlau *adj.* [ʃlau] sly, cunning, crafty, clever, F cute.

Schlauch [ʃlaux] *m* (-[e]s/~-e) tube; hose; *car, etc.*: inner tube; '~boot *n* rubber dinghy, pneumatic boat.

Schlaufe ['ʃlaufə] *f* (-/-n) loop.

schlecht [ʃlɛçt] **1.** *adj.* bad; wicked; poor; *temper:* ill; *quality:* inferior; ~e *Laune haben* be in a bad temper; ~e *Aussichten* poor prospects; ~e *Zeiten* hard times; *mir ist* ~ I feel sick; **2.** *adv.* badly, ill; '~erdings *adv.* ['~ər'dɪŋs] absolutely, down-right, utterly; '~gelaunt *adj.* ['~gə-launt] ill-humo(u)red, in a bad temper; '~hin *adv.* plainly, simply; '2̶igkeit *f* (-/-en) badness; wicked-

ness; ~en *pl.* base acts *pl.*, mean tricks *pl.*; '~machen *v/t.* (*sep.,* -ge-, h) run down, backbite; '~weg *adv.* ['~vɛk] plainly, simply.

schleich|en ['ʃlaiçən] *v/i.* (*irr.,* ge-, sein) creep (*a. fig.*): sneak, steal; '2̶er *m* (-s/-) creeper; *fig.* sneak; '2̶handel *m* illicit trade; smuggling; contraband; '2̶händler *m* smuggler, contrabandist; black marketeer; '2̶weg *m* secret path.

Schleier ['ʃlaiər] *m* (-s/-) veil (*a. fig.*); mist: *a.* haze; *den ~ nehmen* take the veil; '2̶haft *fig. adj.* mysterious, inexplicable.

Schleife ['ʃlaifə] *f* (-/-n) loop (*a. ✕*); slip-knot; bow; *wreath:* streamer; loop, horse-shoe bend.

'**schleif|en 1.** *v/t.* (*irr.,* ge-, h) whet (*knife, etc.*): cut (*glass, precious stones*); polish (*a. fig.*); **2.** *v/t.* (ge-, h) ♪ slur; drag, trail; ✕ raze (*fortress, etc.*); **3.** *v/i.* (ge-, h) drag, trail; '2̶stein *m* grindstone, whet-stone.

Schleim [ʃlaim] *m* (-[e]s/-e) slime; ✹ mucus, phlegm; '~haut *anat. f* mucous membrane; '2̶ig *adj.* slimy (*a. fig.*): mucous.

schlemm|en ['ʃlɛmən] *v/i.* (ge-, h) feast, gormandize; '2̶er *m* (-s/-) glutton, gormandizer; '2̶erei [~'rai] *f* (-/-en) feasting; gluttony.

schlen|dern ['ʃlɛndərn] *v/i.* (ge-, sein) stroll, saunter; '2̶drian ['~driːan] *m* (-[e]s/*no pl.*) jogtrot; beaten track.

schlenkern ['ʃlɛŋkərn] (ge-, h) **1.** *v/t.* dangle, swing; **2.** *v/i.:* mit *den Armen ~* swing one's arms.

Schlepp|dampfer ['ʃlɛp-] *m* steam tug, tug(boat); '~e *f* (-/-n) train (*of woman's dress*); '2̶en (ge-, h) **1.** *v/t.* carry with difficulty, haul, *Am.* F *a.* tote; ⚓, ✕, *mot.* tow, haul; ⚓ tug; ✝ tout (*customers*); *sich ~* drag o.s.; **2.** *v/i.* *dress:* drag, trail; '2̶end *adj. speech:* drawling; *gait:* shuffling; *style:* heavy; *conversation, etc.*: tedious; '~er *m* (-s/-) steam tug, tug(boat); '~tau *n* tow(ing)-rope; *ins* ~ *nehmen* take in or on tow (*a. fig.*).

Schleuder ['ʃlɔidər] *f* (-/-n) sling, catapult (*a. ✕*), *Am. a.* slingshot; spin drier; '2̶n (ge-, h) **1.** *v/t.* fling, hurl (*a. fig.*); sling, catapult (*a. ✕*); spin-dry (*washing*); **2.** *mot. v/i.*

S

skid; '**~preis** † m ruinous or give-away price; zu **~en** dirt-cheap.

schleunig adj. ['ʃlɔʏniç] prompt, speedy, quick.

Schleuse ['ʃlɔʏzə] f (-/-n) lock, sluice; '**2n** v/t. (ge-, h) lock (boat) (up or down), fig. manœuvre, Am. maneuver.

schlich [ʃliç] pret. of schleichen.

schlicht adj. [ʃliçt] plain, simple; modest, unpretentious; hair: smooth, sleek; '**~en** fig. v/t. (ge-, h) settle, adjust; settle by arbitration; '**2er** fig. m (-s/-) mediator; arbitrator.

schlief [ʃliːf] pret. of schlafen.

schließ|en ['ʃliːsən] (irr., ge-, h) 1. v/t. shut, close; shut down (factory, etc.); shut up (shop); contract (marriage); conclude (treaty, speech, etc.); parl. close (debate); in die Arme **~** clasp in one's arms; in sich **~** comprise, include; Freundschaft **~** make friends (mit with); 2. v/i. shut, close; school: break up; aus et. **~** auf (acc.) infer or conclude s.th. from s.th.; '**2fach** & n post-office box; '**~lich** adv. finally, eventually; at last; after all.

Schliff [ʃlif] 1. m (-[e]s/-e) polish (a. fig.); precious stones, glass: cut; 2. 2 pret. of schleifen.

schlimm [ʃlim] 1. adj. bad; evil, wicked, nasty; serious; F **~** bad, sore; **~er** worse; am **~sten**, das 2ste the worst; es wird immer **~er** things are going from bad to worse; 2. adv.: **~** daran sein be badly off; '**~sten**|**falls** adv. at (the) worst.

Schling|e ['ʃliŋə] f (-/-n) loop, sling (a. &); noose; coil (of wire or rope); hunt. snare (a. fig.); den Kopf in die **~** stecken put one's head in the noose; '**~el** m (-s/-) rascal, naughty boy; '**2en** v/t. (irr., ge-, h) wind, twist; plait; den Arme **~** um (acc.) fling one's arms round; sich um et. **~** wind round; '**~pflanze** & f creeper, climber.

Schlips [ʃlips] m (-es/-e) (neck)tie.

Schlitten ['ʃlitən] m (-s/-) sled(ge); sleigh; sports: toboggan.

'**Schlittschuh** m skate; **~** laufen skate; '**~läufer** m skater.

Schlitz [ʃlits] m (-es/-e) slit, slash; slot; '**2en** v/t. (ge-, h) slit, slash.

Schloß [ʃlɔs] 1. n (Schlosses/Schlösser) lock (of door, gun, etc.); castle, palace; ins **~** fallen door: snap to; hinter **~** und Riegel behind prison bars; 2. 2 pret. of schließen.

Schlosser ['ʃlɔsər] m (-s/-) locksmith; mechanic, fitter.

Schlot [ʃloːt] m (-[e]s/-e, **~**e) chimney; flue; ♪, ⚙ funnel; '**~feger** m (-s/-) chimney-sweep(er).

schlotter|ig adj. ['ʃlɔtəriç] shaky, tottery; loose; '**~n** v/i. (ge-, h) garment: hang loosely; p. shake, tremble (both: vor dat. with).

Schlucht [ʃluxt] f (-/-en) gorge, mountain cleft; ravine, Am. a. gulch.

schluchzen ['ʃluxtsən] v/i. (ge-, h) sob.

Schluck [ʃluk] m (-[e]s/-e, **~**e) draught, swallow; mouthful, sip; '**~auf** m (-s/no pl.) hiccup (pl.); '**schlucken** 1. v/t. and v/i. (ge-, h) swallow (a. fig.); 2. 2 m (-s/no pl.) hiccup (pl.).

schlug [ʃluːk] pret. of schlagen.

Schlummer ['ʃlumər] m (-s/no pl.) slumber; '**2n** v/i. (ge-, h) slumber.

Schlund [ʃlunt] m (-[e]s/**~**e) anat. pharynx; fig. abyss, chasm, gulf.

schlüpf|en ['ʃlʏpfən] v/i. (ge-, sein) slip, slide; in die Kleider **~** slip on one's clothes; aus den Kleidern **~** slip out of or slip off one's clothes; '**2er** m (-s/-) (ein a pair of) knickers pl. or drawers pl. or F panties pl.; briefs pl.

Schlupfloch ['ʃlupf-] n loop-hole.

'**schlüpfrig** adj. slippery; fig. lascivious.

'**Schlupfwinkel** m hiding-place.

schlurfen ['ʃlurfən] v/i. (ge-, sein) shuffle, drag one's feet.

schlürfen ['ʃlʏrfən] v/t. and v/i. (ge-, h) drink or eat noisily; sip.

Schluß [ʃlus] m (Schlusses/Schlüsse) close, end; conclusion; parl. closing (of debate).

Schlüssel ['ʃlʏsəl] m (-s/-) key (zu of; fig. to); ♪ clef; fig.: code; quota; '**~bart** m key-bit; '**~bein** anat. n collar-bone, clavicle; '**~bund** m, n (-[e]s/-e) bunch of keys; '**~industrie** f key industry; '**~loch** n keyhole; '**~ring** m key-ring.

'**Schluß**|**folgerung** f conclusion, inference; '**~formel** f in letter: complimentary close.

schlüssig adj. ['ʃlʏsiç] evidence:

conclusive; *sich* ~ *werden* make up one's mind (*über acc.* about).

'Schluß|licht *n* 🚲, *mot.*, *etc.*: taillight; *sports:* last runner; bottom club; **'~runde** *f sports:* final; **'~schein** ✝ *m* contract-note.

Schmach [ʃmɑːx] *f* (-/*no pl.*) disgrace; insult; humiliation.

schmachten [ˈʃmaxtən] *v/i.* (ge-, h) languish (*nach* for), pine (for).

schmächtig *adj.* [ˈʃmɛçtiç] slender, slim; *ein* ~*er Junge* a (mere) slip of a boy; **2ment** *n* ... (-/*no pl.*) melt (*a. fig.*); liquefy; *fig.* melt away, dwindle; **2**) (*h*) melt; smelt, fuse (*ore, etc.*); liquefy; **~erei** [~ˈrai] *f* (-/-en), **~hütte** *f* foundry; **~ofen** *m* smelting furnace; **'~tiegel** *m* melting-pot, crucible.

schmackhaft *adj.* [ˈʃmakhaft] palatable, savo(u)ry.

schmäh|en [ˈʃmɛːən] *v/t.* (ge-, h) abuse, revile; decry, disparage; slander, defame; **~lich** *adj.* ignominious, disgraceful; **2schrift** *f* libel, lampoon; **2ung** *f* (-/-en) abuse; slander, defamation.

schmal *adj.* [ʃmɑːl] narrow; *figure:* slender, slim; *face:* thin; *fig.* poor, scanty.

schmäler|n [ˈʃmɛːlərn] *v/t.* (ge-, h) curtail; impair; belittle; **2ung** *f* (-/-en) curtailment; impairment; detraction.

'Schmal|film *phot. m* substandard film; **'~spur** 🚲 *f* narrow ga(u)ge; **'~spurbahn** 🚲 *f* narrow-ga(u)ge railway; **2spurig** 🚲 *adj.* narrow-ga(u)ge.

Schmalz [ʃmalts] *n* (-es/-e) grease; lard; **2ig** *adj.* greasy; lardy; F *fig.* soppy, sentimental.

schmarotz|en [ʃmaˈrɔtsən] *v/i.* (*no* -ge-, h) sponge (*bei* on); **2er** *m* (-s/-) 🌿, *zo.* parasite; *fig. a.* sponge.

Schmarre F [ˈʃmarə] *f* (-/-n) slash, cut; scar.

Schmatz [ʃmats] *m* (-es/⁺e) smack, loud kiss; **2en** *v/i.* (ge-, h) smack (*mit den Lippen* one's lips); eat noisily.

Schmaus [ʃmaʊs] *m* (-es/⁺e) feast, banquet; fig. treat; **2en** [~zən] *v/i.* (ge-, h) feast, banquet.

schmecken [ˈʃmɛkən] (ge-, h) 1. *v/t.* taste, sample; 2. *v/i.:* ~ *nach* taste *or* smack of (*both a. fig.*); *dieser Wein schmeckt mir* I like *or* enjoy this wine.

Schmeichel|ei [ʃmaiçəˈlai] *f* (-/-en) flattery; cajolery; **2haft** *adj.* flattering; **2n** *v/i.* (ge-, h): *j-m* ~ flatter s.o.; cajole s.o.

Schmeichler [ˈʃmaiçlər] *m* (-s/-) flatterer; **2isch** *adj.* flattering; cajoling.

schmeiß|en F [ˈʃmaisən] (*irr.*, ge-, h) 1. *v/t.* throw, fling, hurl; slam, bang (*door*); 2. *v/i.:* *mit Geld um sich* ~ squander one's money; **'2fliege** *zo. f* blowfly, bluebottle.

Schmelz [ʃmelts] *m* 1. (-es/-e) enamel; 2. *fig.* (-es/*no pl.*) bloom; ♪ sweetness, mellowness; **2en** (*irr.*, ge-) 1. *v/i.* (sein) melt (*a. fig.*); liquefy; *fig.* melt away, dwindle; **2**) (*h*) melt; smelt, fuse (*ore, etc.*); liquefy; **~erei** [~ˈrai] *f* (-/-en), **~hütte** *f* foundry; **~ofen** *m* smelting furnace; **'~tiegel** *m* melting-pot, crucible.

Schmerbauch [ˈʃmeːr-] *m* paunch, pot-belly, F corporation; *Am. sl. a.* bay window.

Schmerz [ʃmerts] *m* (-es/-en) pain (*a. fig.*); ache; *fig.* grief, sorrow; **2en** (ge-, h) 1. *v/i.* pain (*a. fig.*), hurt; ache; 2. *v/t.* pain (*a. fig.*), hurt; *fig.* grieve, afflict; **2haft** *adj.* painful; **2lich** *adj.* painful, grievous; **2lindernd** *adj.* soothing; **2los** *adj.* painless.

Schmetter|ling *zo.* [ˈʃmɛtərliŋ] *m* (-s/-e) butterfly; **2n** (ge-, h) 1. *v/t.* dash (*zu Boden* to the ground); rend (*in Stücke* to pieces); 2. *v/i.* crash; *trumpet, etc.:* bray, blare; *bird:* warble.

Schmied [ʃmiːt] *m* (-[e]s/-e) (black-) smith; **~e** [ˈ~də] *f* (-/-n) forge, smithy; **~eeisen** [ˈ~dəˀ-] *n* wrought iron; **'~ehammer** *m* sledge(-hammer); **2en** [ˈ~dən] *v/t.* (ge-, h) forge; make, devise, hatch (*plans*).

schmiegen [ˈʃmiːgən] *v/refl.* (ge-, h) nestle (*an acc.* to).

schmiegsam *adj.* [ˈʃmiːkzɑːm] pliant, flexible; supple (*a. fig.*); **2keit** *f* (-/*no pl.*) pliancy, flexibility; suppleness (*a. fig.*).

Schmier|e [ˈʃmiːrə] *f* (-/-n) grease; *thea. contp.* troop of strolling players, *sl.* penny gaff; **2en** *v/t.* (ge-, h) smear; ⊕ grease, oil, lubricate; butter (*bread*); spread (*butter, etc.*); scrawl, scribble; *painter:* daub; **~enkomödiant** [ˈ~kɔmødjant] *m* (-en/-en) strolling actor, barnstormer, *sl.* ham (actor); **~erei** [~ˈrai] *f* (-/-en) scrawl; *paint.* daub; **2ig** *adj.* greasy; dirty; *fig.:* filthy;

S

Schmiermittel

F smarmy; '~mittel ⊕ *n* lubricant.

Schminke ['ʃmɪŋkə] *f* (-/-n) make-up (*a. thea.*), paint; rouge; *thea.* grease-paint; 'ℒn *v/t. and v/refl.* (ge-, h) paint, make up; rouge (o.s.); put on lipstick.

Schmirgel ['ʃmɪrgəl] *m* (-s/*no pl.*) emery; 'ℒn *v/t.* (ge-, h) (rub with) emery; '~papier *n* emery-paper.

Schmiß [ʃmɪs] **1.** *m* (*Schmisses*/ *Schmisse*) gash, cut; (duelling-) scar; **2.** F *m* (*Schmisses*/*no pl.*) verve, go, *Am. sl. a.* pep; **3.** ℒ *pret. of* schmeißen.

schmoll|en ['ʃmɔlən] *v/i.* (ge-, h) sulk, pout; '~winkel *m* sulking-corner.

schmolz [ʃmɔlts] *pret. of* schmelzen.

Schmor|braten ['ʃmoːr-] *m* stewed meat; 'ℒen *v/t. and v/i.* (ge-, h) stew (*a. fig.*).

Schmuck [ʃmuk] **1.** *m* (-[e]s/~-e) ornament; jewel(le)ry, jewels *pl.*; **2.** ℒ *adj.* neat, smart, spruce, trim.

schmücken ['ʃmʏkən] *v/t.* (ge-, h) adorn, trim; decorate.

'schmuck|los *adj.* unadorned; plain; 'ℒsachen *f/pl.* jewel(le)ry, jewels *pl.*

Schmuggel ['ʃmugəl] *m* (-s/*no pl.*), ~ei [~'laɪ] *f* (-/-en) smuggling; 'ℒn *v/t. and v/i.* (ge-, h) smuggle; '~ware *f* contraband, smuggled goods *pl.* [smuggler.]

Schmuggler ['ʃmuglər] *m* (-s/-)]

schmunzeln ['ʃmʊntsəln] *v/i.* (ge-, h) smile amusedly.

Schmutz [ʃmuts] *m* (-es/*no pl.*) dirt; filth; *fig. a.* smut; 'ℒen *v/i.* (ge-, h) soil, get dirty; '~fink *fig. m* mudlark; '~fleck *m* smudge, stain; *fig.* blemish; 'ℒig *adj.* dirty; filthy; *fig. a.* mean, shabby.

Schnabel ['ʃnaːbəl] *m* (-s/~) bill, *esp. bird of prey:* beak.

Schnalle ['ʃnalə] *f* (-/-n) buckle; 'ℒn *v/t.* (ge-, h) buckle; strap.

schnalzen ['ʃnaltsən] *v/i.* (ge-, h): mit den Fingern ~ snap one's fingers; mit der Zunge ~ click one's tongue.

schnappen ['ʃnapən] (ge-, h) **1.** *v/i.* lid, spring, *etc.*: snap; *lock:* catch; nach *et.* ~ snap *or* snatch at; nach Luft ~ gasp for breath; **2.** F *v/t.* catch, *sl.* nab (*criminal*).

'Schnapp|messer *n* flick-knife; '~schloß *n* spring-lock; '~schuß *phot. m* snapshot.

Schnaps [ʃnaps] *m* (-es/~e) strong liquor, *Am.* hard liquor; brandy; ein (*Glas*) ~ a dram.

schnarch|en ['ʃnarçən] *v/i.* (ge-, h) snore; 'ℒer *m* (-s/-) snorer.

schnarren ['ʃnarən] *v/i.* (ge-, h) rattle; jar.

schnattern ['ʃnatərn] *v/i.* (ge-, h) cackle; *fig. a.* chatter, gabble.

schnauben ['ʃnaubən] (ge-, h) **1.** *v/i.* snort; vor Wut ~ foam with rage; **2.** *v/t.*: sich die Nase ~ blow one's nose. [pant, puff, blow; wheeze.]

schnaufen ['ʃnaufən] *v/i.* (ge-, h)]

Schnauz|bart ['ʃnauts-] *m* m(o)ustache; '~e *f* (-/-n) snout, muzzle; ⊕ nozzle; *teapot, etc.:* spout; *sl. fig.* potato-trap; 'ℒen F *v/i.* (ge-, h) jaw.

Schnecke zo. ['ʃnɛkə] *f* (-/-n) snail; slug; '~nhaus *n* snail's shell; '~n-tempo *n*: im ~ at a snail's pace.

Schnee [ʃneː] *m* (-s/*no pl.*) snow; '~ball *m* snowball; '~ballschlacht *f* pelting-match with snowballs; ℒbedeckt *adj.* snow-covered, *mountain-top:* snow-capped; 'ℒblind *adj.* snow-blind; '~blindheit *f* snow-blindness; '~brille *f* (e-e a pair of) snow-goggles *pl.*; '~fall *m* snow-fall; '~flocke *f* snow-flake; '~gestöber *n* (-s/-) snow-storm; ~glöckchen ♀ ['~glœkçən] *n* (-s/-) snowdrop; '~grenze *f* snow-line; '~mann *m* snow man; '~pflug *m* snow-plough, *Am.* snowplow; '~schuh *m* snow-shoe; '~sturm *m* snow-storm, blizzard; '~wehe *f* (-/-n) snow-drift; 'ℒweiß *adj.* snow-white.

Schneid F [ʃnaɪt] *m* (-[e]s/*no pl.*) pluck, dash, *sl.* guts *pl.*

Schneide ['ʃnaɪdə] *f* (-/-n) edge; '~mühle *f* sawmill; 'ℒn (*irr.*, ge-, h) **1.** *v/t.* cut; carve (*meat*); pare, clip (*finger-nails, etc.*); **2.** *v/i.* cut.

'Schneider *m* (-s/-) tailor; ~ei [~'raɪ] *f* **1.** (-/*no pl.*) tailoring; dressmaking; **2.** (-/-en) tailor's shop; dressmaker's shop; '~in *f* (-/-nen) dressmaker; '~meister *m* master tailor; 'ℒn (ge-, h) **1.** *v/i.* tailor; do tailoring; do dressmaking; **2.** *v/t.* make, tailor.

'Schneidezahn *m* incisor.

'schneidig *fig. adj.* plucky, dashing, keen; smart, *Am. sl. a.* nifty.

schneien ['ʃnaɪən] *v/i.* (ge-, h) snow.

schnell [ʃnɛl] **1.** adj. quick, fast; rapid; swift; speedy; reply, etc.: prompt; sudden; **2.** adv.: ~ fahren drive fast; ~ handeln act promptly or without delay; (mach) ~! be quick!, hurry up!

Schnelläufer [ˈʃnɛlɔyfər] m sprinter; speed skater.

'schnell|en (ge-) v/t. (h) and v/i. (sein) jerk; '**2feuer** ✕ n rapid fire; '**2hefter** m (-s/-) folder.

'Schnelligkeit f (-/no pl.) quickness, fastness; rapidity; swiftness; promptness; speed, velocity.

'Schnell|imbiß m snack (bar); '~imbißstube f snack bar; '~kraft f (-/no pl.) elasticity; '~verfahren n ⁴⁵ summary proceeding; ⊕ high-speed process; '~zug 🚂 m fast train, express (train).

schneuzen [ˈʃnɔytsən] v/refl. (ge-, h) blow one's nose.

schniegeln [ˈʃniːgəln] v/refl. (ge-, h) dress or smarten or spruce (o.s.) up.

Schnipp|chen [ˈʃnɪpçən] n: F j-m ein ~ schlagen outwit or overreach s.o.; '**2isch** adj. pert, snappish, Am. F a. snippy.

Schnitt [ʃnɪt] **1.** m (-[e]s/-e) cut; dress, etc.: cut, make, style; pattern; book: edge; Ⓐ (inter)section; fig.: average; F profit; **2.** ♀ pret. of schneiden; '**~blumen** f/pl. cut flowers pl.; '**~e** f (-/-n) slice; '**~er** m (-s/-) reaper, mower; '**~fläche** Ⓐ f section(al plane); '**2ig** adj. streamline(d); '**~muster** n pattern; '**~punkt** m (point of) intersection; '**~wunde** f cut, gash.

Schnitzel [ˈʃnɪtsəl] **1.** n (-s/-) schnitzel; **2.** F n, m (-s/-) chip; paper: scrap; ~ pl. ⊕ parings pl., shavings pl.; paper: a. clippings pl.; '**2n** v/t. (ge-, h) chip, shred, whittle.

schnitzen [ˈʃnɪtsən] v/t. (ge-, h) carve, cut (in wood).

'Schnitzer m (-s/-) carver; F fig. blunder, Am. sl. a. boner; '**~ei** [~ˈraɪ] f **1.** (-/-en) carving, carved work; **2.** (-/no pl.) carving.

schnöde adj. [ˈʃnøːdə] contemptuous; disgraceful; base, vile; ~r Mammon filthy lucre.

Schnörkel [ˈʃnœrkəl] m (-s/-) flourish (a. fig.), scroll (a. Ⓐ).

schnorr|en F [ˈʃnɔrən] v/t. and v/i. (ge-, h) cadge; '**2er** m (-s/-) cadger.

schnüff|eln [ˈʃnyfəln] v/i. (ge-, h) sniff, nose (both: an dat. at); fig. nose about, Am. F a. snoop around; '**2ler** fig. m (-s/-) spy, Am. F a. snoop; F sleuth(-hound).

Schnuller [ˈʃnʊlər] m (-s/-) dummy, comforter.

Schnulze F [ˈʃnʊltsə] f (-/-n) sentimental song or film or play, F tear-jerker.

Schnupf|en [ˈʃnʊpfən] **1.** m (-s/-) cold, catarrh; **2.** ♀ v/i. (ge-, h) take snuff; '**~er** m (-s/-) snuff-taker; '**~tabak** m snuff.

schnuppe F adj. [ˈʃnʊpə]: das ist mir ~ I don't care (F a damn); '**~rn** v/i. (ge-, h) sniff, nose (both: an dat. at).

Schnur [ʃnuːr] f (-/¨e, ✂ -en) cord; string, twine; line; 🔌 flex.

Schnür|band [ˈʃnyːr-] n lace; '**~chen** [ˈ~çən] n: wie am ~ like clock-work; '**2en** v/t. (ge-, h) lace (up) (bind with) cord, tie up.

'schnurgerade adj. dead straight.

Schnurr|bart [ˈʃnʊr-] m mo(u)stache; '**2en** v/i. (ge-, h) **1.** v/i. wheel, etc.: whir(r); cat: purr (a. fig.); F fig. cadge; **2.** F fig. v/t. cadge.

Schnür|senkel [ˈʃnyːrzɛŋkəl] m (-s/-) shoe-lace, shoe-string; '**~stiefel** m lace-boot.

schnurstracks adv. [ˈʃnuːrˈʃtraks] direct, straight; on the spot, at once, sl. straight away.

schob [ʃoːp] pret. of schieben.

Schober [ˈʃoːbər] m (-s/-) rick, stack.

Schock [ʃɔk] **1.** n (-[e]s/-e) three-score; **2.** ♀ m (-[e]s/-s, ✂ -e) shock; **2ieren** [ˈkiːrən] v/t. (no -ge-, h) shock, scandalize.

Schokolade [ʃokoˈlaːdə] f (-/-n) chocolate.

scholl [ʃɔl] pret. of schallen.

Scholle [ˈʃɔlə] f (-/-n) clod (of earth), poet. glebe; floe (of ice); ichth. plaice.

schon adv. [ʃoːn] already; ~ lange for a long time; ~ gut! all right!; ~ der Gedanke the very idea; ~ der Name the bare name; hast du ~ einmal ...? have you ever ...?; mußt du ~ gehen? need you go yet?; ~ um 8 Uhr as early as 8 o'clock.

schön [ʃøːn] **1.** adj. beautiful; man: handsome (a. fig.); weather: fair, fine (a. iro.); das ~e Geschlecht the

fair sex; die ∼en Künste the fine
arts; ∼e Literatur belles-lettres pl.;
2. adv.: ∼ warm nice and warm;
du hast mich ∼ erschreckt you gave
me quite a start.

schonen ['ʃoːnən] v/t. (ge-, h) spare
(j-n s.o.; j-s Leben s.o.'s life); take
care of; husband (strength, etc.);
sich ∼ take care of o.s., look after
o.s.

'**Schönheit** f **1.** (-/no pl.) beauty;
of woman: a. pulchritude; **2.** (-/-en)
beauty; beautiful woman, belle;
'**∼spflege** f beauty treatment.

'**schöntun** v/i. (irr. tun, sep., -ge-, h)
flatter (j-m s.o.); flirt (dat. with).

'**Schonung** f **1.** (-/no pl.) mercy;
sparing, forbearance; careful treatment; **2.** (-/-en) tree-nursery;
'**∼slos** adj. unsparing, merciless,
relentless. [a. crest.]

Schopf [ʃɔpf] m (-[e]s/∺e) tuft; orn.]

schöpfen ['ʃœpfən] v/t. (ge-, h)
scoop, ladle; draw (water at well);
draw, take (breath); take (courage);
neue Hoffnung ∼ gather fresh hope;
Verdacht ∼ become suspicious.

'**Schöpf|er** m (-s/-) creator; '**2e-
risch** adj. creative; '**∼ung** f (-/-en)
creation.

schor [ʃoːr] pret. of scheren.

Schorf [ʃɔrf] m (-[e]s/-e) scurf;
scab, crust; '**2ig** adj. scurfy; scabby.

Schornstein ['ʃɔrn-] m chimney;
⚓, ⊕ funnel; '**∼feger** m (-s/-)
chimney-sweep(er).

Schoß **1.** [ʃoːs] m (-es/∺e) lap; womb;
coat: tail; **2.** ⅔ [ʃɔs] pret. of schießen.

Schote ['ʃoːtə] f (-/-n) pod, husk.

Schott|e ['ʃɔtə] m (-n/-n) Scot,
Scotchman, Scotsman; die ∼n pl.
the Scotch pl.; '**2er** m (-s/-) gravel;
(road-)metal; '**2isch** adj. Scotch,
Scottish.

schräg [ʃrɛːk] **1.** adj. oblique, slanting; sloping; **2.** adv.: ∼ gegenüber
diagonally across (von from).

schrak [ʃraːk] pret. of schrecken **2.**

Schramme ['ʃramə] f (-/-en) scratch;
skin: a. abrasion; '**2n** v/t. (ge-, h)
scratch; graze, abrade (skin).

Schrank [ʃraŋk] m (-[e]s/∺e) cupboard, esp. Am. closet; wardrobe.

'**Schranke** f (-/-n) barrier (a. fig.);
⛫ a. (railway-)gate; ⅔⅔ bar; ∼n pl.
fig. bounds pl., limits pl.; '**2nlos**
fig. adj. boundless; unbridled; '**∼n-
wärter** ⛫ m gate-keeper.

'**Schrankkoffer** m wardrobe trunk.

Schraube ['ʃraubə] f (-/-n) ⊕ screw;
⚓ screw(-propeller); '**2n** v/t. (ge-,
h) screw.

'**Schrauben|dampfer** ⚓ m screw
(steamer); '**∼mutter** ⊕ f nut;
'**∼schlüssel** ⊕ m spanner, wrench;
'**∼zieher** ⊕ m screwdriver.

Schraubstock ⊕ ['ʃraup-] m vice,
Am. vise.

Schrebergarten ['ʃreːbər-] m allotment garden.

Schreck [ʃrek] m (-[e]s/-e) fright,
terror; consternation; '**∼bild** n
bugbear; '**∼en** m (-s/-) fright, terror,
consternation; '**2en** (ge-) **1.** v/t. (h)
frighten, scare; **2.** v/i. (irr., sein):
only in compounds; '**∼ensbotschaft**
f alarming or terrible news; '**∼ens-
herrschaft** f reign of terror; '**2haft**
adj. fearful, timid; '**2lich** adj. terrible, dreadful (both a. F fig.);
'**∼schuß** m scare shot; fig. warning
shot.

Schrei [ʃrai] m (-[e]s/-e) cry; shout;
scream.

schreiben ['ʃraibən] **1.** v/t. and v/i.
(irr., ge-, h) write (j-m to s.o.; über
acc. on); mit der Maschine ∼
type(write); **2.** v/t. (irr., ge-, h)
spell; **3.** 2 n (-s/-) letter.

'**Schreiber** m (-s/-) writer; secretary, clerk.

schreib|faul adj. ['ʃraip-] lazy in
writing; '**2feder** f pen; '**2fehler** m
mistake in writing or spelling, slip
of the pen; '**2heft** n exercise-book;
'**2mappe** f writing-case; '**2ma-
schine** f typewriter; (mit der) ∼
schreiben type(write); '**2material**
n writing-materials pl., stationery;
'**2papier** n writing-paper; '**2-
schrift** typ. f script; '**2tisch** m
(writing-)desk; '**2ung** f ['∼buŋ] f
(-/-en) spelling; '**2unterlage** f
desk pad; '**2waren** f/pl. writing-
materials pl., stationery; '**2waren-
händler** m stationer; '**2zeug** n
writing-materials pl.

'**schreien** (irr., ge-, h) **1.** v/t. shout;
scream; **2.** v/i. cry (out) (vor dat.
with pain, etc.; nach for bread,
etc.); shout (vor with); squeak
(with); '**∼d** adj. colour: loud; injustice: flagrant.

schreiten ['ʃraitən] v/i. (irr., ge-,
sein) step, stride (über acc. across);
fig. proceed (zu to).

schrie [ʃriː] *pret. of* schreien.

schrieb [ʃriːp] *pret. of* schreiben.

Schrift [ʃrift] *f* (-/-en) (hand-)writing, hand; *typ.* type; character, letter; writing; publication; *die Heilige ~* the (Holy) Scriptures *pl.*; '**~art** *f* type; '**2deutsch** *adj.* literary German; '**~führer** *m* secretary; '**~leiter** *m* editor; '**2lich 1.** *adj.* written, in writing; **2.** *adv.* in writing; '**~satz** *m* 🕮 pleadings *pl.*; *typ.* composition, type-setting; '**~setzer** *m* compositor, type-setter; '**~sprache** *f* literary language; '**~steller** *m* (-s/-) author, writer; '**~stück** *n* piece of writing, paper, document; '**~tum** *n* (-s/*no pl.*) literature; '**~wechsel** *m* exchange of letters, correspondence; '**~zeichen** *n* character, letter.

schrill *adj.* [ʃril] shrill, piercing.

Schritt [ʃrit] **1.** *m* (-[e]s/-e) step (*a. fig.*); pace (*a. fig.*); *~e unternehmen* take steps; **2.** ♀ *pret. of* schreiten; '**~macher** *m* (-s/-) *sports:* pace-maker; '**~weise 1.** *adj.* gradual; **2.** *adv.* step by step.

schroff *adj.* [ʃrɔf] rugged, jagged; steep, precipitous; *fig.* harsh, gruff; *~er Widerspruch* glaring contradiction.

schröpfen [ˈʃrœpfən] *v/t.* (ge-, h) 🩸 cup; *fig.* milk, fleece.

Schrot [ʃroːt] *m, n* (-[e]s/-e) crushed grain; small shot; '**~brot** *n* wholemeal bread; '**~flinte** *f* shotgun.

Schrott [ʃrɔt] *m* (-[e]s/-e) scrap (-iron *or* -metal).

schrubben [ˈʃrubən] *v/t.* (ge-, h) scrub.

Schrulle [ˈʃrulə] *f* (-/-n) whim, fad.

schrumpf|en [ˈʃrumpfən] *v/i.* (ge-, sein) shrink (*a.* ⊕, 🩸, *fig.*); '**2ung** *f* (-/-en) shrinking; shrinkage.

Schub [ʃuːp] *m* (-[e]s/~e) push, shove; *phys.,* ⊕ thrust; *bread, people, etc.:* batch; '**~fach** *n* drawer; '**~karren** *m* wheelbarrow; '**~kasten** *m* drawer; '**~kraft** *phys.,* ⊕ *f* thrust; '**~lade** *f* (-/-n) drawer.

Schubs F [ʃups] *m* (-es/-e) push; '**2en** F *v/t.* (ge-, h) push.

schüchtern *adj.* [ˈʃʏçtərn] shy, bashful, timid; *girl:* coy; '**2heit** *f* (-/*no pl.*) shyness, bashfulness, timidity; coyness (*of girl*).

schuf [ʃuːf] *pret. of* schaffen 1.

Schuft [ʃuft] *m* (-[e]s/-e) scoundrel, rascal; cad; '**2en** F *v/i.* (ge-, h) drudge, slave, plod; '**2ig** *adj.* scoundrelly, rascally; caddish.

Schuh [ʃuː] *m* (-[e]s/-e) shoe; *j-m et. in die ~e schieben* put the blame for s.th. on s.o.; *wissen, wo der ~ drückt* know where the shoe pinches; '**~anzieher** *m* (-s/-) shoehorn; '**~band** *n* shoe-lace *or* -string; '**~creme** *f* shoe-cream, shoepolish; '**~geschäft** *n* shoe-shop; '**~löffel** *m* shoehorn; '**~macher** *m* (-s/-) shoemaker; '**~putzer** *m* (-s/-) shoeblack, *Am. a.* shoeshine; '**~sohle** *f* sole; '**~spanner** *m* (-s/-) shoetree; '**~werk** *n,* '**~zeug** F *n* foot-wear, boots and shoes *pl.*

Schul|amt *n* school-board; '**~arbeit** *f* homework; '**~bank** *f* (school-)desk; '**~beispiel** *n* test-case, typical example; '**~besuch** *m* (-[e]s/*no pl.*) attendance at school; '**~bildung** *f* education; *höhere ~* secondary education; '**~buch** *n* school-book.

Schuld [ʃult] *f* **1.** (-/*no pl.*) guilt; fault, blame; *es ist se ~* it is his fault, he is to blame for it; **2.** (-/-en) debt; *~en machen* contract *or* incur debts; '**2bewußt** *adj.* conscious of one's guilt; '**2en** [ˈʃuldən] *v/t.* (ge-, h): *j-m et. ~* owe s.o. s.th.; *j-m Dank ~* be indebted to s.o. (*für* for); '**2haft** *adj.* [ˈ..thaft] culpable.

'**Schuldiener** *m* school attendant *or* porter.

schuldig *adj.* [ˈʃuldiç] guilty (*e-r Sache* of s.th.); respect, *etc.:* due; *j-m et. ~ sein* owe s.o. s.th.; *Dank ~ sein* be indebted *to s.o.* (*für* for); *für ~ befinden* 🕮 find guilty; '**2e** [ˈ..gə] *m, f* (-n/-n) guilty person; culprit; '**2keit** *f* (-/*no pl.*) duty, obligation.

'**Schuldirektor** *m* headmaster, *Am. a.* principal.

'**schuld|los** *adj.* guiltless, innocent; '**2losigkeit** *f* (-/*no pl.*) guiltlessness, innocence; '**2ner** [ˈ..dnər] *m* (-s/-) debtor; '**2schein** *m* evidence of debt, certificate of indebtedness, IOU (= I owe you); '**2verschreibung** *f* bond, debt certificate.

Schule [ˈʃuːlə] *f* (-/-n) school; *höhere ~* secondary school, *Am. a.* high school; *auf or in der ~* at school; *in die ~ gehen* go to school; '**2n** *v/t.* (ge-, h) train, school; *pol.* indoctrinate.

S

Schüler ['ʃyːlər] *m* (-s/-) schoolboy, pupil; *phls.*, *etc.*: disciple; '~austausch *m* exchange of pupils; '~in *f* (-/-nen) schoolgirl.

'Schul|ferien *pl.* holidays *pl.*, vacation; '~fernsehen *n* educational TV; '~funk *m* educational broadcast; '~gebäude *n* school(house); '~geld *n* school fee(s *pl.*), tuition; '~hof *m* playground, *Am. a.* schoolyard; '~kamerad *m* schoolfellow; '~lehrer *m* schoolmaster, teacher; '~mappe *f* satchel; '2meistern *v/t.* (ge-, h) censure pedantically; '~ordnung *f* school regulations *pl.*; '2pflichtig *adj.* schoolable; '~rat *m* supervisor of schools, school inspector; '~schiff *n* training-ship; '~schluß *m* end of school; end of term; '~schwänzer *m* (-s/-) truant; '~stunde *f* lesson.

Schulter ['ʃʊltər] *f* (-/-n) shoulder; '~blatt *anat. n* shoulder-blade; '2n *v/t.* (ge-, h) shoulder.

'Schul|unterricht *m* school, lessons *pl.*; school instruction; '~versäumnis *f* (-/no *pl.*) absence from school; '~wesen *n* educational system; '~zeugnis *n* report.

schummeln F ['ʃʊməln] *v/i.* (ge-, h) cheat, *Am.* F a. chisel.

Schund [ʃʊnt] **1.** *m* (-[e]s/no *pl.*) trash, rubbish (*both a. fig.*); **2.** 2 *pret. of* schinden; '~literatur *f* trashy literature; '~roman *m* trashy novel, *Am. a.* dime novel.

Schuppe ['ʃʊpə] *f* (-/-n) scale; ~n *pl. on head:* dandruff; '~en **1.** *m* (-s/-) shed; *mot.* garage; ✈ hangar; **2.** 2 *v/t.* (ge-, h) scale (*fish*); *sich* ~ *skin:* scale off; '2ig *adj.* scaly.

Schür|eisen ['ʃyːr?-] *n* poker; '2en *v/t.* (ge-, h) poke; stoke; *fig.* fan, foment.

schürfen ['ʃʏrfən] (ge-, h) **1.** ⚒ *v/i.* prospect (*nach* for); **2.** *v/t.* ⚒ prospect for; *sich den Arm* ~ graze one's arm.

Schurk|e ['ʃʊrkə] *m* (-n/-n) scoundrel, knave; ~erei [~'raɪ] *f* (-/-en) rascality, knavish trick; '2isch *adj.* scoundrelly, knavish.

Schürze ['ʃʏrtsə] *f* (-/-n) apron; *children:* pinafore; '2n *v/t.* (ge-, h) tuck up (*skirt*); tie (*knot*); purse (*lips*); '~njäger *m* skirt-chaser, *Am. sl.* wolf.

Schuß [ʃʊs] *m* (Schusses/Schüsse) shot (*a. sports*); *ammunition:* round; *sound:* report; charge; *wine, etc.:* dash (*a. fig.*); *in* ~ *sein* be in full swing, be in full working order.

Schüssel ['ʃʏsəl] *f* (-/-n) basin (*for water, etc.*); bowl, dish, tureen (*for soup, vegetables, etc.*).

'Schuß|waffe *f* fire-arm; '~weite *f* range; '~wunde *f* gunshot wound.

Schuster ['ʃuːstər] *m* (-s/-) shoemaker; '2n *fig. v/i.* (ge-, h) s. pfuschen.

Schutt [ʃʊt] *m* (-[e]s/no *pl.*) rubbish, refuse; rubble, debris.

Schüttel|frost 🧪 *m* ['ʃʏtəl-] *m* shivering-fit; '2n *v/t.* (ge-, h) shake; den *Kopf* ~ shake one's head; *j-m die Hand* ~ shake hands with s.o.

schütten ['ʃʏtən] (ge-, h) **1.** *v/t.* pour; spill (*auf acc.* on); **2.** *v/i.:* *es schüttet* it is pouring with rain.

Schutz [ʃʊts] *m* (-es/no *pl.*) protection (*gegen*, *vor dat.* against), defen|ce, *Am.* -se (against, from); shelter (from); safeguard; cover; '~brille *f* (*e-e a pair of*) goggles *pl.*

Schütze ['ʃʏtsə] *m* (-n/-n) marksman, shot; ✗ rifleman; '2n *v/t.* (ge-, h) protect (*gegen*, *vor dat.* against, from), defend (against, from), guard (against, from); shelter (from); safeguard (*rights, etc.*).

Schutzengel ['ʃʊts?-] *m* guardian angel.

'Schützen|graben ✗ *m* trench; '~könig *m* champion shot.

'Schutz|haft ⚖ *f* protective custody; '~heilige *m* patron saint; '~herr *m* patron, protector; '~impfung 🧪 *f* protective inoculation; *smallpox:* vaccination.

Schützling ['ʃʏtslɪŋ] *m* (-s/-e) protégé, *female:* protégée.

'schutz|los *adj.* unprotected; defen|celess, *Am.* -seless; '2mann *m* (-[e]s/-er, Schutzleute) policeman, (police) constable, *sl.* bobby, *sl.* cop; '2marke *f* trade mark, brand; '2-mittel *n* preservative; 🧪 prophylactic; '2patron *m* patron saint; '2umschlag *m* (dust-)jacket, wrapper; '~zoll *m* protective duty.

Schwabe ['ʃvaːbə] *m* (-n/-n) Swabian.

schwäbisch *adj.* ['ʃvɛːbiʃ] Swabian.

schwach *adj.* [ʃvax] *resistance, team, knees* (*a. fig.*), *eyes, heart, voice, character, tea, gr. verb,* ✝ *demand,* *etc.*: weak; *person, etc.*: infirm; *person, recollection, etc.*: feeble; *sound, light, hope, idea, etc.*: faint; *consolation, attendance, etc.*: poor; *light, recollection, etc.*: dim; *resemblance*: remote; *das* ~*e Geschlecht* the weaker sex; ~*e Seite* weak point or side.

Schwäche ['ʃvɛçə] *f* (-/-n) weakness (*a. fig.*); infirmity; *fig.* foible; *e-e* ~ *haben für* have a weakness for; '**2n** *v/t.* (ge-, h) weaken (*a. fig.*); impair (*health*).

'**Schwach|heit** *f* (-/-en) weakness; *fig. a.* frailty; '~**kopf** *m* simpleton, soft(y), *Am.* F *a.* sap(head); **2köpfig** *adj.* ['~kœpfɪç] weak-headed, soft, *Am. sl. a.* sappy.

schwäch|lich *adj.* ['ʃvɛçlɪç] weakly, feeble; delicate, frail; '**2ling** *m* (-s/-e) weakling (*a. fig.*).

'**schwach|sinnig** *adj.* weak- or feeble-minded; '**2strom ⚡** *m* (-[e]s/*no pl.*) weak current.

Schwadron ✕ [ʃva'droːn] *f* (-/-en) squadron; **2ieren** [~o'niːrən] *v/t.* (*no* -ge-, h) swagger, vapo(u)r.

Schwager ['ʃvaːɡər] *m* (-s/⁼) brother-in-law.

Schwägerin ['ʃvɛːɡərɪn] *f* (-/-nen) sister-in-law.   [swallow.\

Schwalbe *orn.* ['ʃvalbə] *f* (-/-n)\

Schwall [ʃval] *m* (-[e]s/-e) swell, flood; *words*: torrent.

Schwamm [ʃvam] **1.** *m* (-[e]s/⁼e) sponge; ♣ fungus; ♣ dry-rot; **2.** ♀ *pret. of* schwimmen; **2ig** *adj.* spongy; *face, etc.*: bloated.

Schwan *orn.* [ʃvaːn] *m* (-[e]s/⁼e) swan.

schwand [ʃvant] *pret. of* schwinden.

schwang [ʃvaŋ] *pret. of* schwingen.

schwanger *adj.* ['ʃvaŋər] pregnant, with child, in the family way.

schwängern ['ʃvɛŋərn] *v/t.* (ge-, h) get with child, impregnate (*a. fig.*).

'**Schwangerschaft** *f* (-/-en) pregnancy.

schwanken ['ʃvaŋkən] *v/i.* (ge-) **1.** (h) *earth, etc.*: shake, rock; *prices*: fluctuate; *branches, etc.*: sway; *fig.* waver, oscillate, vacillate; **2.** (sein) stagger, totter.

Schwanz [ʃvants] *m* (-es/⁼e) tail (*a.* ✕, *ast.*); *fig.* train.

schwänz|eln ['ʃvɛntsəln] *v/i.* (ge-, h) wag one's tail; *fig.* fawn (*um* [up]on); '~**en** *v/t.* (ge-, h) cut (*lecture, etc.*);

die Schule ~ play truant, *Am. a.* play hooky.

Schwarm [ʃvarm] *m* (-[e]s/⁼e) bees, *etc.*: swarm; *birds*: a. flight, flock; *fish*: school, schoal; *birds, girls, etc.*: bevy; F *fig.* fancy, craze; *p.*: idol, hero; flame.

schwärmen ['ʃvɛrmən] *v/i.* (ge-, h) bees, *etc.*: swarm; *fig.*: revel; rave (*von about, of*), gush (*over*); ~ *für* be wild about, adore *s.o.*

'**Schwärmer** *m* (-s/-) enthusiast; *esp. eccl.* fanatic; visionary; *fireworks*: cracker, squib; *zo.* hawkmoth; ~**ei** [~'raɪ] *f* (-/-en) enthusiasm (*für* for); idolization; ecstasy; *esp. eccl.* fanaticism; '**2isch** *adj.* enthusiastic; gushing, raving; adoring; *esp. eccl.* fanatic(al).

Schwarte ['ʃvartə] *f* (-/-n) *bacon*: rind; F *fig.* old book.

schwarz *adj.* [ʃvarts] black (*a. fig.*); dark; dirty; ~*es Brett* notice-board, *Am.* bulletin board; ~*es Brot* brown bread; *der Mann* bog(e)y; ~*er Markt* black market; ~ *auf weiß* in black and white; *auf die* ~*e Liste setzen* blacklist; '**2arbeit** *f* illicit work; '**2brot** *n* brown bread; '**2e** *m, f* (-n/-n) black.

Schwärze ['ʃvɛrtsə] *f* (-/*no pl.*) blackness (*a. fig.*); darkness; '**2n** *v/t.* (ge-, h) blacken.

'**schwarz|fahren** F *v/i.* (*irr.* fahren, *sep.,* -ge-, sein) travel without a ticket; *mot.* drive without a licence; '**2fahrer** *m* fare-dodger; *mot.* person driving without a licence; '**2fahrt** *f* ride without a ticket; *mot.* drive without a licence; '**2handel** *m* illicit trade, black marketeering; '**2händler** *m* black marketeer; '**2hörer** *m* listener without a licence.

'**schwärzlich** *adj.* blackish.

'**Schwarz|markt** *m* black market; '~**seher** *m* pessimist; *TV*: viewer without a licence; '~**sender** *m* pirate broadcasting station; '~'**weißfilm** *m* black-and-white film.

schwatzen ['ʃvatsən] *v/i.* (ge-, h) chat; chatter, tattle.

schwätz|en ['ʃvɛtsən] *v/i.* (ge-, h) *s. schwatzen*; '**2er** *m* (-s/-) chatterbox; tattler, prattler; gossip.

'**schwatzhaft** *adj.* talkative, garrulous.

Schwebe *fig.* ['ʃveːbə] *f* (-/*no pl.*): *in der* ~ *sein* be in suspense; *law,*

S

rule, etc.: be in abeyance; **~bahn** *f* aerial railway *or* ropeway; **'2n** *v/i.* (ge-, h) be suspended; *bird:* hover (*a. fig.*); glide; *fig.* be pending (*a. ʦ*); *in Gefahr* ~ be in danger.

Schwed|e ['ʃveːdə] *m* (-n/-n) Swede; **'2isch** *adj.* Swedish.

Schwefel ⚗ ['ʃveːfəl] *m* (-s/*no pl.*) sulphur, *Am. a.* sulfur; **'~säure** *f* (-/*no pl.*) sulphuric acid, *Am. a.* sulfuric acid.

Schweif [ʃvaɪf] *m* (-[e]s/-e) tail (*a. ast.*); *fig.* train; **'2en** (ge-) **1.** *v/i.* (sein) rove, ramble; **2.** ⊕ *v/t.* (h) curve; scallop.

schweigen ['ʃvaɪgən] **1.** *v/i.* (*irr.*, ge-, h) be silent; **2.** **2** *n* (-s/*no pl.*) silence; **'~d** *adj.* silent.

schweigsam *adj.* ['ʃvaɪkzaːm] taciturn; **'2keit** *f* (-/*no pl.*) taciturnity.

Schwein [ʃvaɪn] *n* **1.** (-[e]s/-e) *zo.* pig, hog, swine (*all a. contp. fig.*); **2.** F (-[e]s/*no pl.*): ~ *haben* be lucky.

'Schweine|braten *m* roast pork; **'~fleisch** *n* pork; **'~hund** F *contp.* *m* swine; **~rei** [~'raɪ] *f* (-/-en) mess; dirty trick; smut(ty story); **'~stall** *m* pigsty (*a. fig.*).

'schweinisch *fig. adj.* swinish; smutty.

'Schweinsleder *n* pigskin.

Schweiß [ʃvaɪs] *m* (-es/-e) sweat, perspiration; **'2en** ⊕ *v/t.* (ge-, h) weld; **'~er** ⊕ *m* (-s/-) welder; **'~fuß** *m* perspiring foot; **'2ig** *adj.* sweaty, damp with sweat.

Schweizer ['ʃvaɪtsər] *m* (-s/-) Swiss; *on farm:* dairyman.

schwelen ['ʃveːlən] *v/i.* (ge-, h) smo(u)lder (*a. fig.*).

schwelg|en ['ʃvelgən] *v/i.* (ge-, h) lead a luxurious life; revel; *fig.* revel (*in dat. in*); **'2er** *m* (-s/-) revel(l)er; epicure; **2erei** [~'raɪ] *f* (-/-en) revel(ry), feasting; **'~erisch** *adj.* luxurious; revel(l)ing.

Schwell|e ['ʃvelə] *f* (-/-n) sill, threshold (*a. fig.*); 🚆 sleeper, *Am.* tie; **'2en 1.** *v/i.* (*irr.*, ge-, sein) swell (out); **2.** *v/t.* (ge-, h) swell; **'~ung** *f* (-/-en) swelling.

Schwemme ['ʃvemə] *f* (-/-n) watering-place; horse-pond; *at tavern, etc.:* taproom; 🐟 glut (*of fruit, etc.*).

Schwengel ['ʃveŋəl] *m* (-s/-) clapper (*of bell*); handle (*of pump*).

schwenk|en ['ʃveŋkən] (ge-) **1.** *v/t.* (h) swing; wave (*hat, etc.*); brandish (*stick, etc.*); rinse (*washing*); **2.** *v/i.* (sein) turn, wheel; **'2ung** *f* (-/-en) turn; *fig.* change of mind.

schwer [ʃveːr] **1.** *adj.* heavy; *problem, etc.*: hard, difficult; *illness, mistake, etc.*: serious; *punishment, etc.*: severe; *fault, etc.*: grave; *wine, cigar, etc.*: strong; *~e Zeiten* hard times; *2 Pfund ~ sein* weigh two pounds; **2.** *adv.*: *~ arbeiten* work hard; *~ hören* be hard of hearing; **'2e** *f* (-/*no pl.*) heaviness; *phys.* gravity (*a. fig.*); severity; **'2fällig** *adj.* heavy, slow; clumsy; **'2gewicht** *n sports:* heavy-weight; *fig.* main emphasis; **'2gewichtler** *m* (-s/-) *sports:* heavy-weight; **'2hörig** *adj.* hard of hearing; **'2industrie** *f* heavy industry; **'2kraft** *phys. f* (-/*no pl.*) gravity; **'~lich** *adv.* hardly, scarcely; **'2mut** *f* (-/*no pl.*) melancholy; **'~mütig** *adj.* [~'myːtɪç] melancholy; **'2punkt** *m* centre of gravity, *Am.* center of gravity; *fig.*: crucial point; emphasis.

Schwert [ʃveːrt] *n* (-[e]s/-er) sword.

'Schwer|verbrecher *m* felon; **'2verdaulich** *adj.* indigestible, heavy; **'2verständlich** *adj.* difficult *or* hard to understand; **'2verwundet** *adj.* seriously wounded; **'2wiegend** *fig. adj.* weighty, momentous [*nurse.*]

Schwester ['ʃvestər] *f* (-/-n) sister;)

schwieg [ʃviːk] *pret. of* schweigen.

Schwieger|eltern ['ʃviːgər-] *pl.* parents-in-law *pl.*; **'~mutter** *f* mother-in-law; **'~sohn** *m* son-in-law; **'~tochter** *f* daughter-in-law; **'~vater** *m* father-in-law.

Schwiel|e ['ʃviːlə] *f* (-/-n) callosity; **'2ig** *adj.* callous.

schwierig *adj.* ['ʃviːrɪç] difficult, hard; **'2keit** *f* (-/-en) difficulty, trouble.

Schwimm|bad ['ʃvɪm-] *n* swimming-bath, *Am.* swimming pool; **'2en** *v/i.* (*irr.*, ge-) **1.** (sein) swim; *thing:* float; *ich bin über den Fluß geschwommen* I swam across the river; *in Geld ~* be rolling in money; **2.** (h) swim; *ich habe lange unter Wasser geschwommen* I swam under water for a long time; **'~gür-**

tel m swimming-belt; lifebelt; '~**haut** f web; '~**lehrer** m swimming-instructor; '~**weste** f life-jacket.

Schwindel ['ʃvɪndəl] m (-s/no pl.) 🐝 vertigo, giddiness, dizziness; F fig.: swindle, humbug, sl. eyewash; cheat, fraud; '~**anfall** 🐝 m fit of dizziness; 'Se**rregend** adj. dizzy (a. fig.); '~**firma** ✝ f long firm, Am. wildcat firm; 'Sn v/i. (ge-, h) cheat, humbug, swindle.

schwinden ['ʃvɪndən] v/i. (irr., ge-, sein) dwindle, grow less; strength, colour, etc.: fade.

'**Schwindl|er** m (-s/-) swindler, cheat, humbug; liar; 'Si**g** 🐝 adj. giddy, dizzy.

Schwind|sucht 🐝 ['ʃvɪnt-] f (-/no pl.) consumption; 'Ssüchtig 🐝 adj. consumptive.

Schwing|e ['ʃvɪŋə] f (-/-n) wing, poet. pinion; swingle; 'Sen (irr., ge-, h) 1. v/t. swing; brandish (weapon); swingle (flax); 2. v/i. swing; ⊕ oscillate; sound, etc.: vibrate; '~**ung** f (-/-en) oscillation; vibration.

Schwips F [ʃvɪps] m (-es/-e): e-n ~ haben be tipsy, have had a drop too much.

schwirren ['ʃvɪrən] v/i. (ge-) 1. (sein) whir(r); arrow, etc.: whiz(z); insects: buzz; rumours, etc.: buzz, circulate; 2. (h): mir schwirrt der Kopf my head is buzzing.

'**Schwitz|bad** n sweating-bath, hot-air bath, vapo(u)r bath; 'Sen (ge-, h) 1. v/i. sweat, perspire; 2. F fig. v/t.: Blut und Wasser ~ be in great anxiety.

schwoll [ʃvɔl] pret. of schwellen.

schwor [ʃvoːr] pret. of schwören.

schwören ['ʃvøːrən] (irr., ge-, h) 1. v/t. swear; e-n Meineid ~ commit perjury; j-m Rache ~ vow vengeance against s.o.; 2. v/i. swear (bei by); ~ auf (acc.) have great belief in, F swear by.

schwül adj. [ʃvyːl] sultry, oppressively hot; 'Se f (-/no pl.) sultriness.   [bast.]

Schwulst [ʃvʊlst] m (-es/⁀e) bom-/

schwülstig adj. ['ʃvʏlstɪç] bombastic, turgid.

Schwund [ʃvʊnt] m (-[e]s/no pl.) dwindling; wireless, etc.: fading; 🐝 atrophy.

Schwung [ʃvʊŋ] m (-[e]s/⁀e) swing;

fig. verve, go; flight (of imagination); buoyancy; 'Shaft ✝ adj. flourishing, brisk; '~**rad** ⊕ n flywheel; watch, clock: balance-wheel; 'Svoll adj. full of energy or verve; attack, translation, etc.: spirited; style, etc.: racy.

Schwur [ʃvuːr] m (-[e]s/⁀e) oath; '~**gericht** 🖳 n England, Wales: appr. court of assize.

sechs [zɛks] 1. adj. six; 2. 2 f (-/-en) six; 'Se**ck** n (-[e]s/-e) hexagon; '~**eckig** adj. hexagonal; '~**fach** adj. sixfold, sextuple; '~**mal** adv. six times; 'Smonatig adj. lasting or of six months, six-months ...; '~**monatlich** 1. adj. six-monthly; 2. adv. every six months; '~**stündig** adj. ['~ʃtʏndɪç] lasting or of six hours, six-hour ...; 'Stagerennen n cycling: six-day race; '~**tägig** adj. ['~tɛːgɪç] lasting or of six days.

sechs|te adj. [zɛkstə] sixth; 'Stel n (-s/-) sixth (part); '~**tens** adv. sixthly, in the sixth place.

sech|zehn(te) adj. ['zɛç-] sixteen(th); ~**zig** adj. ['~tsɪç] sixty; '~**zigste** adj. sixtieth.

See [zeː] 1. m (-s/-n) lake; 2. f (-/no pl.) sea; an die ~ gehen go to the seaside; in ~ gehen or stechen put to sea; auf ~ at sea; auf hoher ~ on the high seas; zur ~ gehen go to sea; 3. f (-/-n) sea, billow; '~**bad** n seaside resort; '~**fahrer** m sailor, navigator; '~**fahrt** f navigation; voyage; 'Sfest adj. seaworthy; ~ sein be a good sailor; '~**gang** m (motion of the) sea; '~**hafen** m seaport; '~**handel** ✝ m maritime trade; '~**herrschaft** f naval supremacy; '~**hund** zo. m seal; 'Skrank adj. seasick; '~**krankheit** f (-/no pl.) seasickness; '~**krieg** m naval war(fare).

Seele ['zeːlə] f (-/-n) soul (a. fig.); mit or von ganzer ~ with all one's heart.

'**Seelen|größe** f (-/no pl.) greatness of soul or mind; '~**heil** n salvation, spiritual welfare; 'Slos adj. soulless; '~**qual** f anguish of mind, (mental) agony; '~**ruhe** f peace of mind; coolness.

'**seelisch** adj. psychic(al), mental.

'**Seelsorge** f (-/no pl.) cure of souls; ministerial work; '~**r** m (-s/-) pastor, minister.

S

'**See|macht** f naval power; '**~mann** m (-[e]s/*Seeleute*) seaman, sailor; '**~meile** f nautical mile; '**~not** f (-/no pl.) distress (at sea); '**~räuber** m pirate; **~räuberei** [~'raɪ] f (-/-en) piracy; '**~recht** n maritime law; '**~reise** f voyage; '**~schiff** n seagoing ship; '**~schlacht** f naval battle; '**~schlange** f sea serpent; '**~sieg** m naval victory; '**~stadt** f seaside town; '**~streitkräfte** f/pl. naval forces pl.; ²**tüchtig** adj. seaworthy; '**~warte** f naval observatory; '**~weg** m sea-route; *auf dem ~ by sea*; '**~wesen** n (-s/no pl.) maritime or naval affairs pl.

Segel ['ze:gəl] n (-s/-) sail; *unter ~ gehen* set sail; '**~boot** n sailing-boat, *Am.* sailboat; *sports:* yacht; '**~fliegen** n (-s/no pl.) gliding, soaring; '**~flug** m gliding flight, glide; '**~flugzeug** n glider; ²**n** (ge-) **1.** v/i. (h, sein) sail; *sports:* yacht; **2.** v/t. (h) sail; '**~schiff** n sailing-ship, sailing-vessel; '**~sport** m yachting; '**~tuch** n (-[e]s/-e) sailcloth, canvas.

Segen ['ze:gən] m (-s/-) blessing (a. fig.), *esp. eccl.* benediction; ²**sreich** adj. blessed.

Segler ['ze:glər] m (-s/-) sailingvessel, sailing-ship; *fast, good, etc.* sailer; yachtsman.

segn|en ['ze:gnən] v/t. (ge-, h) bless; '²**ung** f (-/-en) s. Segen.

sehen ['ze:ən] (*irr.*, ge-, h) **1.** v/i. see; *gut ~ have* good eyes; *~ auf* (*acc.*) look at; be particular about; *~ nach* look for; look after; **2.** v/t. see; notice, watch, observe; '**~swert** adj. worth seeing; '²**swürdigkeit** f (-/-en) object of interest, curiosity; *~en pl.* sights pl. (of a place).

Seher ['ze:ər] m (-s/-) seer, prophet; '**~blick** m (-[e]s/no pl.) prophetic vision; '**~gabe** f (-/no pl.) gift of prophecy.

'**Seh|fehler** m visual defect; '**~kraft** f vision, eyesight.

Sehne ['ze:nə] f (-/-n) *anat.* sinew, tendon; string (*of bow*); Å chord.

'**sehnen** v/refl. (ge-, h) long (*nach* for), yearn (for, after); *sich danach ~ zu inf.* be longing to *inf.* [nerve.]

'**Sehnerv** *anat.* m visual or optic [

'**sehnig** adj. sinewy (a. fig.), stringy.

'**sehn|lich** adj. longing; ardent; passionate; '²**sucht** f longing, yearning; '**~süchtig** adj., '**~suchtsvoll** adj. longing, yearning; *eyes, etc.:* a. wistful.

sehr adv. [ze:r] *before adj. and adv.:* very, most; *with vb.:* (very) much, greatly.

'**Seh|rohr** 🜨 n periscope; '**~weite** f range of sight, visual range; *in ~* within eyeshot or sight.

seicht adj. [zaɪçt] shallow; *fig. a.* superficial.

Seide ['zaɪdə] f (-/-n) silk. |silk.)

'**seiden** adj. silk, silken (a. fig.);] '²**flor** m silk gauze; '²**glanz** m silky lust|re, *Am.* -er; '²**händler** m mercer; '²**papier** n tissue(-paper); '²**raupe** zo. f silkworm; '²**spinnerei** f silk-spinning mill; '²**stoff** m silk cloth or fabric.

'**seidig** adj. silky.

Seife ['zaɪfə] f (-/-n) soap.

'**Seifen|blase** f soap-bubble; '**~kistenrennen** n soap-box derby; '**~lauge** f (soap-)suds pl.; '**~pulver** n soap-powder; '**~schale** f soapdish; '**~schaum** m lather.

'**seifig** adj. soapy.

seih|en ['zaɪən] v/t. (ge-, h) strain, filter; '²**er** m (-s/-) strainer, colander.

Seil [zaɪl] n (-[e]s/-e) rope; '**~bahn** f funicular or cable railway; '**~er** m (-s/-) rope-maker; '**~tänzer** m ropedancer.

sein[1] [zaɪn] **1.** v/i. (*irr.*, ge-, sein) be; exist; **2.** ² n (-s/no pl.) being; existence.

sein[2] *poss. pron.* [~] his, her, its (*in accordance with gender of possessor*); *der (die, das) ~e* his, hers, its; *~ Glück machen* make one's fortune; *die Seinen pl.* his family or people.

'**seiner**|'**seits** adv. for his part; '**~zeit** adv. then, at that time; in those days.

'**seines|gleichen** pron. his equal(s pl.); *j-n wie ~ behandeln* treat s.o. as one's equal; *er hat nicht ~* he has no equal; there is no one like him.

seit [zaɪt] **1.** prp. (*dat.*): *~ 1945* since 1945; *~ drei Wochen* for three weeks; **2.** cj. since; *es ist ein Jahr her, ~* ... it is a year now since ...; '**~dem** [~'de:m] **1.** adv. since or from that time, ever since; **2.** cj. since.

Seite ['zaɪtə] *f* (-/-n) side (*a. fig.*); flank (*a.* ✕, △); page (*of book*).

'**Seiten|ansicht** *f* profile, side-view; '**～blick** *m* side-glance; '**～flügel** △ *m* wing; '**～hieb** *fig. m* innuendo, sarcastic remark; '**～s** *prp.* (*gen.*) on the part of; by; '**～schiff** △ *n* church: aisle; '**～sprung** *fig. m* extra-marital adventure; '**～straße** *f* bystreet; '**～stück** *fig. n* counterpart (*zu of*); '**～weg** *m* by-way.

seit|her *adv.* since (then, that time).

'**seit|lich** *adj.* lateral; '**～wärts** *adv.* ['～vɛrts] sideways; aside.

Sekret|är [zekre'tɛ:r] *m* (-s/-e) secretary; bureau; **～ariat** [～ari'a:t] *n* (-[e]s/-e) secretary's office; secretariat(e); **～ärin** *f* (-/-nen) secretary.

Sekt [zɛkt] *m* (-[e]s/-e) champagne.

Sekt|e ['zɛktə] *f* (-/-n) sect; **～ierer** [～'ti:rər] *m* (-s/-) sectarian.

Sektor ['zɛktɔr] *m* (-s/-en) ⚔, ✕, *pol.* sector; *fig.* field, branch.

Sekunde [ze'kundə] *f* (-/-n) second; **～nbruchteil** *m* split second; **～n-zeiger** *m* second-hand.

selb *adj.* [zɛlp] same; **～er** F *pron.* ['～bər] *s. selbst 1.*

selbst [zɛlpst] **1.** *pron.* self; personally; *ich ～* I myself; *von ～ p.* of one's own accord; *thing:* by itself, automatically; **2.** *adv.* even; **3.** ⚥ *n* (-/*no pl.*) (one's own) self; ego.

selbständig *adj.* ['zɛlpʃtɛndiç] independent; *sich ～ machen* set up for o.s.; '**Ｑkeit** *f* (-/*no pl.*) independence.

'**Selbst|anlasser** *mot.* ⚙ *m* self-starter; '**～anschluß** *teleph. m* automatic connection; '**～bedienungsladen** *m* self-service shop; '**～beherr-schung** *f* self-command, self-control; '**～bestimmung** *f* self-determination; '**～betrug** *m* self-deception; '**Ｑbewußt** *adj.* self-confident, self-reliant; '**～bewußtsein** *n* self-confidence, self-reliance; '**～binder** *m* (-s/-) tie; '**～erhaltung** *f* self-preservation; '**～erkenntnis** *f* self-knowledge; '**～erniedrigung** *f* self-abasement; '**Ｑgefällig** *adj.* (self-)complacent; '**～gefälligkeit** *f* (-/*no pl.*) (self-)complacency; '**～ge-fühl** *n* (-[e]s/*no pl.*) self-reliance; '**Ｑgemacht** *adj.* ['～gəmaxt] home-made; '**Ｑgerecht** *adj.* self-right-

eous; '**～gespräch** *n* soliloquy, monolog(ue); '**Ｑherrlich 1.** *adj.* high-handed, autocratic(al); **2.** *adv.* with a high hand; '**～hilfe** *f* self-help; '**～kostenpreis** ✝ *m* cost price; '**～laut** *gr. m* vowel; '**Ｑlos** *adj.* unselfish, disinterested; '**～mord** *m* suicide; '**～mörder** *m* suicide; '**Ｑmörderisch** *adj.* suicidal; '**Ｑsicher** *adj.* self-confident, self-assured; '**～sucht** *f* (-/*no pl.*) selfishness, ego(t)ism; '**Ｑsüchtig** *adj.* selfish, ego(t)istic(al); '**Ｑtätig** ⊕ *adj.* self-acting, automatic; '**～täu-schung** *f* self-deception; '**～über-windung** *f* (-/*no pl.*) self-conquest; '**～unterricht** *m* self-instruction; '**～verleugnung** *f* self-denial; '**～versorger** *m* (-s/-) self-supporter; '**Ｑverständlich 1.** *adj.* self-evident, obvious; **2.** *adv.* of course, naturally; *～! a.* by all means!; '**～ver-ständlichkeit** *f* **1.** (-/-en) matter of course; **2.** (-/*no pl.*) matter-of-factness; '**～verteidigung** *f* self-defen|ce, *Am.* -se; '**～vertrauen** *n* self-confidence, self-reliance; '**～verwaltung** *f* self-government, autonomy; '**Ｑzufrieden** *adj.* self-satisfied; '**～zufriedenheit** *f* self-satisfaction; '**～zweck** *m* (-[e]s/*no pl.*) end in itself.

selig *adj.* ['ze:liç] *eccl.* blessed; late, deceased; *fig.* blissful, overjoyed; '**Ｑkeit** *f* (-/-en) bliss, very great joy.

Sellerie ♧ ['zɛləri:] *m* (-s/-[s]), *f* (-/-) celery.

selten ['zɛltən] **1.** *adj.* rare; scarce; **2.** *adv.* rarely, seldom; '**Ｑheit** *f* (-/-en) rarity, scarcity; rarity, curio(sity); '**Ｑheitswert** *m* (-[e]s/*no pl.*) scarcity value.

Selterswasser ['zɛltərs-] *n* (-s/-) seltzer (water), soda-water.

seltsam *adj.* ['zɛltza:m] strange, odd.

Semester *univ.* [ze'mestər] *n* (-s/-) term.

Semikolon *gr.* [zemi'ko:lɔn] *n* (-s/-s, *Semikola*) semicolon.

Seminar [zemi'na:r] *n* (-s/-e) *univ.* seminar; seminary (*for priests*).

Senat [ze'na:t] *m* (-[e]s/-e) senate; *parl.* Senate.

send|en ['zɛndən] *v/t.* **1.** [*irr.,*] *ge-, h*) send; forward; **2.** (*ge-, h*) transmit; broadcast, *Am. a.* radio(broad-

S

cast); telecast; '2er m (-s/-) transmitter; broadcasting station.

'Sende|raum m (broadcasting) studio; '~zeichen n interval signal.

'Sendung f (-/-en) ✝ consignment, shipment; broadcast; telecast; fig. mission. [🐾 .)

Senf [zɛnf] m (-[e]s/-e) mustard (a.)

sengen ['zɛŋən] v/t. (ge-, h) singe, scorch; '~d adj. heat: parching.

senil adj. [ze'niːl] senile; 2ität [~ili'tɛːt] f (-/no pl.) senility.

senior adj. ['zeːnioʀ] senior.

Senk|blei ['zɛŋk-] n ⚓ plumb, plummet; ♇ a. sounding-lead; '2e geogr. f (-/-en) depression, hollow; '2en v/t. (ge-, h) lower; sink (a. voice); let down; bow (head); cut (prices, etc.); sich ~ land, buildings, etc.: sink, subside; ceiling, etc.: sag; '~fuß ♂ m flat-foot; '~fußeinlage f arch support; '~grube f cesspool; '2recht adj. vertical, esp. ♈ perpendicular; '~ung f (-/-en) geogr. depression, hollow; lowering, reduction (of prices); ♂ sedimentation.

Sensation [zɛnza'tsjoːn] f (-/-en) sensation; 2ell adj. [~o'nɛl] sensational; ~slust f (-/no pl.) sensationalism; ~spresse f yellow press.

Sense ['zɛnzə] f (-/-n) scythe.

sensi|bel adj. [zɛn'ziːbəl] sensitive; 2bilität [~ibili'tɛːt] f (-/no pl.) sensitiveness.

sentimental adj. [zɛntimɛn'taːl] sentimental; 2ität [~ali'tɛːt] f (-/-en) sentimentality.

September [zɛp'tɛmbər] m (-[s]/-) September.

Serenade ♪ [zere'naːdə] f (-/-n) serenade.

Serie ['zeːrjə] f (-/-n) series; set; billiards: break; 2nmäßig 1. adj. standard; 2. adv.: ~ herstellen produce in mass; '~nproduktion f mass production.

seriös adj. [ze'rjøːs] serious; trustworthy, reliable.

Serum ['zeːrum] n (-s/Seren, Sera) serum.

Service¹ [zɛr'viːs] n (-s/-) service, set.

Service² ['zøːrvis] m, n (-/-s) service.

servieren [zɛr'viːrən] v/t. (no -ge-, h) serve; 2wagen m trolley(-table).

Serviette [zɛr'vjɛtə] f (-/-n) (table-) napkin.

Sessel ['zɛsəl] m (-s/-) armchair, easy chair; '~lift m chair-lift.

seßhaft adj. ['zɛshaft] settled, established; resident.

Setzei ['zɛts?-] n fried egg.

'setzen (ge-) 1. v/t. (h) set, place, put; typ. compose; ♪ plant; erect, raise (monument); stake (money) (auf acc. on); sich ~ sit down, take a seat; bird: perch; foundations of house, sediment, etc.: settle; 2. v/i. (h): ~ auf (acc.) back (horse, etc.); 3. v/i. (sein): ~ über (acc.) leap (wall, etc.); clear (hurdle, etc.); take (ditch, etc.).

'Setzer typ. m (-s/-) compositor, type-setter; ~ei typ. [~'raɪ] f (-/-en) composing-room.

Seuche ['zɔʏçə] f (-/-n) epidemic (disease).

seufz|en ['zɔʏftsən] v/i. (ge-, h) sigh; '2er m (-s/-) sigh.

sexuell adj. [zɛksu'ɛl] sexual.

sezieren [ze'tsiːrən] v/t. (no -ge-, h) dissect (a. fig.).

sich refl. pron. [ziç] oneself; sg. himself, herself, itself; pl. themselves; sg. yourself, pl. yourselves; each other, one another; sie blickte ~ um she looked about her.

Sichel ['ziçəl] f (-/-n) sickle; s. Mondsichel.

sicher ['ziçər] 1. adj. secure (vor dat. from), safe (from); proof (against); hand: steady; certain, sure; positive; aus ~er Quelle from a reliable source; ~ sein to be sure of s.th.; 2. adv. s. sicherlich; um ~ zu gehen to be on the safe side, to make sure.

'Sicherheit f (-/-en) security; safety; surety, certainty; positiveness; assurance (of manner); in ~ bringen place in safety; '~snadel f safety-pin; '~sschloß n safety-lock.

'sicher|lich adv. surely, certainly; undoubtedly; er wird ~ kommen he is sure to come; '~n v/t. (ge-, h) secure (a. ✕, ⊕); guarantee (a. ✝); protect, safeguard; sich et. ~ secure (prize, seat, etc.); '~stellen v/t. (sep., -ge-, h) secure; 2ung f (-/-en) securing; safeguard(ing); ✝ security, guaranty; ⊕ safety device; ⚡ fuse.

Sicht [ziçt] f (-/no pl.) visibility;

view; *in* ~ *kommen* come in(to) view or sight; *auf lange* ~ in the long run; *auf* or *bei* ~ **†** at sight; '**⌾bar** *adj.* visible; '**⌾en** *v/t.* (ge-, h) **⚓** sight; *fig.* sift; '**⌾lich** *adv.* visibly; '**~vermerk** *m* visé, visa (*on passport*).

sickern ['zikərn] *v/i.* (ge-, sein) trickle, ooze, seep.

sie *pers. pron.* [zi:] *nom.: sg.* she, *pl.* they; *acc.: sg.* her, *pl.* them; *Sie nom. and acc.: sg. and pl.* you.

Sieb [zi:p] *n* (-[e]s/-e) sieve; riddle (*for soil, gravel, etc.*).

sieben[1] ['zi:bən] *v/t.* (ge-, h) sieve, sift; riddle.

sieben[2] [~] **1.** *adj.* seven; **2.** ⚲ *f* (-/-) (number) seven; *böse* ~ shrew, vixen; '**~fach** *adj.* sevenfold; '**~mal** *adv.* seven times; '**⌾sachen** F *f/pl.* belongings *pl.*, F traps *pl.*; '**~te** *adj.* seventh; '**⌾tel** *n* (-s/-) seventh (part); '**~tens** *adv.* seventhly, in the seventh place.

sieb|zehn(te) *adj.* ['zi:p-] seventeen(th); **~zig** *adj.* ['~tsiç] seventy; '**⌾zigste** *adj.* seventieth.

siech *adj.* [zi:ç] sickly; '**⌾tum** *n* (-s/-*no pl.*) sickliness, lingering illness.

Siedehitze ['zi:də-] *f* boiling-heat.

siedeln ['zi:dəln] *v/i.* (ge-, h) settle; *Am. a.* homestead.

siede|n ['zi:dən] *v/t. and v/i.* ([irr.,] ge-, h) boil, simmer; '**⌾punkt** *m* boiling-point (*a. fig.*).

Siedler ['zi:dlər] *m* (-s/-) settler; *Am. a.* homesteader; '**~stelle** *f* settler's holding; *Am. a.* homestead. [ing estate.)

'**Siedlung** *f* (-/-en) settlement; hous-)

Sieg [zi:k] *m* (-[e]s/-e) victory (*über acc.* over); *sports:* a. win; *den* ~ *davontragen* win the day, be victorious.

Siegel ['zi:gəl] *n* (-s/-) seal (*a. fig.*); signet; '**~lack** *m* sealing-wax; '**⌾n** *v/t.* (ge-, h) seal; '**~ring** *m* signetring.

sieg|en ['zi:gən] *v/i.* (ge-, h) be victorious (*über acc.* over), conquer *s.o.*; *sports:* win; '**⌾er** *m* (-s/-) conqueror, *rhet.* victor; *sports:* winner.

Siegeszeichen ['zi:gəs-] *n* trophy.

'**siegreich** *adj.* victorious, triumphant.

Signal [zi'gnɑ:l] *n* (-s/-e) signal; **⌾isieren** [~ali'zi:rən] *v/t.* (*no* -ge-, h) signal.

Silbe ['zilbə] *f* (-/-n) syllable; '**~ntrennung** *f* syllabi(fi)cation.

Silber ['zilbər] *n* (-s/*no pl.*) silver; *s. Tafelsilber*; '**⌾n** *adj.* (of) silver; '**~zeug** F *n* silver plate, *Am. a.* silverware.

Silhouette [zilu'ɛtə] *f* (-/-n) silhouette; skyline.

Silvester [zil'vɛstər] *n* (-s/-), **~abend** *m* new-year's eve.

simpel ['zimpəl] **1.** *adj.* plain, simple; stupid, silly; **2.** ⚲ *m* (-s/-) simpleton.

Sims [zims] *m, n* (-es/-e) ledge; sill (*of window*); mantelshelf (*of fireplace*); shelf; **△** cornice.

Simul|ant [zimu'lant] *m* (-en/-en) *esp.* ✗, **⚓** malingerer; **⌾ieren** (*no* -ge-, h) **1.** *v/t.* sham, feign, simulate (*illness, etc.*); **2.** *v/i.* sham, feign; *esp.* ✗, **⚓** malinger.

Sinfonie ♩ [zinfo'ni:] *f* (-/-n) symphony.

sing|en ['ziŋən] *v/t. and v/i.* (*irr.*, ge-, h) sing; *vom Blatt* ~ sing at sight; *nach Noten* ~ sing from music; '**⌾sang** F *m* (-[e]s/*no pl.*) singsong; '**⌾spiel** *n* musical comedy; '**⌾stimme** ♩ *f* vocal part.

Singular *gr.* ['ziŋgulɑ:r] *m* (-s/-e) singular (number).

'**Singvogel** *m* song-bird, songster.

sinken ['ziŋkən] *v/i.* (*irr.*, ge-, sein) sink; *ship:* a. founder, go down; **†** *prices:* fall, drop, go down; *den Mut* ~ *lassen* lose courage.

Sinn [zin] *m* (-[e]s/-e) sense; taste (*für* for); tendency; sense, meaning; *von* ~*en sein* be out of one's senses; *im* ~ *haben* have in mind; *in gewissem* ~*e* in a sense; '**~bild** *n* symbol, emblem; '**⌾bildlich** *adj.* symbolic(al), emblematic; '**⌾en** *v/i.* (*irr.*, ge-, h): *auf Rache* ~ meditate revenge.

'**Sinnen|lust** *f* sensuality; '**~mensch** *m* sensualist; '**~rausch** *m* intoxication of the senses.

sinnentstellend *adj.* ['zin⁹-] garbling, distorting. [world.)

'**Sinnenwelt** *f* (-/*no pl.*) material)

'**Sinnes|änderung** *f* change of mind; '**~art** *f* disposition, mentality; '**~organ** *n* sense-organ; '**~täuschung** *f* illusion, hallucination.

'**sinn|lich** *adj.* sensual; material; '**⌾lichkeit** *f* (-/*no pl.*) sensuality; '**~los** *adj.* senseless; futile, useless;

'2losigkeit f (-/-en) senselessness; futility, uselessness; '~reich adj. ingenious; '~verwandt adj. synonymous.

Sipp|e ['zipə] f (-/-n) tribe; (blood-) relations pl.; family; '~schaft contp. f (-/-en) relations pl.; fig. clan, clique; die ganze ~ the whole lot.

Sirene [zi're:nə] f (-/-n) siren.

Sirup ['zi:rup] m (-s/-e) syrup, Am. sirup; treacle, molasses sg.

Sitte ['zitə] f (-/-n) custom; habit; usage; ~n pl. morals pl.; manners pl.

'Sitten|bild n, '~gemälde n genre (-painting); fig. picture of manners and morals; '~gesetz n moral law; '~lehre f ethics pl.; '2los adj. immoral; '~losigkeit f (-/-en) immorality; '~polizei f appr. vice squad; '~prediger m moralizer; '~richter fig. m censor, moralizer; '2streng adj. puritanic(al).

'sittlich adj. moral; '2keit f (-/no pl.) morality; '2keitsverbrechen n sexual crime.

'sittsam adj. modest; '2keit f (-/no pl.) modesty.

Situation [zitua'tsjo:n] f (-/-en) situation.

Sitz [zits] m (-es/-e) seat (a. fig.); fit (of dress, etc.).

'sitzen v/i. (irr., ge-, h) sit, be seated; dress, etc.: fit; blow, etc.: tell; F fig. do time; ~ bleiben remain seated, keep one's seat; '~bleiben v/i. (irr. bleiben, sep., -ge-, sein) girl at dance: F be a wallflower; girl: be left on the shelf; at school: not to get one's remove; ~ auf (dat.) be left with (goods) on one's hands; '~d adj.: ~e Tätigkeit sedentary work; '~lassen v/t. (irr. lassen, sep., [no] -ge-, h) leave s.o. in the lurch, let s.o. down; girl: jilt (lover); leave (girl) high and dry; auf sich ~ pocket (insult, etc.).

'Sitz|gelegenheit f seating accommodation, seats pl.); ~ bieten für seat; '~platz m seat; '~streik m sit-down or stay-in strike.

'Sitzung f (-/-en) sitting (a. parl., paint.); meeting, conference; '~speriode f session.

Skala ['ska:la] f (-/Skalen, Skalas) scale (a. ♪); dial (of radio set); fig. gamut; gleitende ~ sliding scale.

Skandal [skan'da:l] m (-s/-e) scandal; row, riot; 2ös adj. [~a'lø:s] scandalous.

Skelett [ske'lɛt] n (-[e]s/-e) skeleton.

Skep|sis ['skɛpsis] f (-/no pl.) scepticism, Am. a. skepticism; ~tiker ['~tikər] m (-s/-) sceptic, Am. a. skeptic; '2tisch adj. sceptical, Am. a. skeptical.

Ski [ʃi:] m (-s/-er, ✎ -) ski; ~ laufen or fahren ski; '~fahrer m, '~läufer m skier; '~lift m ski-lift; '~sport m (-[e]s/no pl.) skiing.

Skizz|e ['skitsə] f (-/-n) sketch (a. fig.); 2ieren [~'tsi:rən] v/t. (no -ge-, h) sketch, outline (both a. fig.).

Sklav|e ['skla:və] m (-n/-n) slave (a. fig.); '~enhandel m slave-trade; '~enhändler m slave-trader; ~e'rei f (-/-en) slavery; '2isch adj. slavish.

Skonto † ['skɔnto] m, n (-s/-s, ✎ Skonti) discount.

Skrupel ['skru:pəl] m (-s/-) scruple; '2los adj. unscrupulous.

Skulptur [skulp'tu:r] f (-/-en) sculpture.

Slalom ['sla:lɔm] m (-s/-s) skiing, etc.: slalom.

Slaw|e ['sla:və] m (-n/-n) Slav; '2isch adj. Slav(onic).

Smaragd [sma'rakt] m (-[e]s/-e) emerald; 2grün adj. emerald.

Smoking ['smo:kiŋ] m (-s/-s) dinner-jacket, Am. a. tuxedo, F tux.

so [zo:] 1. adv. so, thus; like this or that; as; ~ ein such a; ~ ... wie as ...; as; nicht ~ ... wie not so ... as; ~ oder ~ by hook or by crook; 2. cj. so, therefore, consequently; ~ daß so that; ~bald cj. [zo'-]: ~ (als) as soon as.

Socke ['zɔkə] f (-/-n) sock; '~l m (-s/-) △ pedestal, socle; socket (of lamp); '~n m (-s/-) sock; '~nhalter m/pl. suspenders pl., Am. garters pl.

Sodawasser ['zo:da-] n (-s/⁼) soda(-water).

Sodbrennen ✎ ['zo:t-] n (-s/no pl.) heartburn.

soeben adv. [zo'-] just (now).

Sofa ['zo:fa] n (-s/-s) sofa.

sofern cj. [zo'-] if, provided that; ~ nicht unless.

soff [zɔf] pret. of saufen.

sofort adv. [zo'-] at once, immediately, directly, right or straight away; '~ig adj. immediate, prompt.

Sog [zo:k] 1. m (-[e]s/-e) suction; ♫

wake (a. fig.), undertow; **2.** ♀ pret. of saugen.

so|gar adv. [zo'-] even; **~genannt** adj. ['zo:-] so-called; **~gleich** adv. [zo'-] s. sofort.

Sohle ['zo:lə] f (-/-n) sole; bottom (of valley, etc.); ✗ floor.

Sohn [zo:n] m (-[e]s/⸚e) son.

solange cj. [zo'-]: ~ (als) so or as long as.   [such.]

solch pron. [zɔlç] such; als ~e(r) as

Sold ✗ [zɔlt] m (-[e]s/⸗e) pay.

Soldat [zɔl'da:t] m (-en/-en) soldier; der unbekannte ~ the Unknown Warrior or Soldier.   [cenary.]

Söldner ['zœldnər] m (-s/-) mer-

Sole ['zo:lə] f (-/-n) brine, salt water.

solid adj. [zo'li:t] solid (a. fig.); basis, etc.: sound; † firm, etc.: sound, solvent; prices: reasonable, fair; p. steady, staid, respectable.

solidarisch [zoli'da:riʃ]: sich ~ erklären mit declare one's solidarity with.

solide adj. [zo'li:də] s. solid.

Solist [zo'list] m (-en/-en) soloist.

Soll † [zɔl] n (-[s]/-[s]) debit; (output) target.

'sollen (h) **1.** v/i. (ge-): ich sollte (eigentlich) I ought to; **2.** v/aux. (irr., no -ge-): er soll he shall; he is to; he is said to; ich sollte I should; er sollte (eigentlich) zu Hause sein he ought to be at home; er sollte seinen Vater niemals wiedersehen he was never to see his father again.

Solo ['zo:lo] n (-s/-s, Soli) solo.

somit cj. [zo'-] thus; consequently.

Sommer ['zɔmər] m (-s/-) summer; **'~frische** f (-/-n) summer-holidays pl.; summer-resort; **Ϩlich** adj. summer-like, summer(l)y; **'~spros-se** f freckle; **Ϩsprossig** adj. freckled; **'~wohnung** f summer residence, Am. cottage, summer house; **'~zeit** f **1.** (-/-en) season: summer-time; **2.** (-/no pl.) summer time, Am. daylight-saving time.

Sonate ♪ [zo'na:tə] f (-/-n) sonata.

Sonde ['zɔndə] f (-/-n) probe.

Sonder|angebot ['zɔndər-] n special offer; **'~ausgabe** f special (edition); **Ϩbar** adj. strange, odd; **'~beilage** f inset, supplement (of newspaper); **'~berichterstatter** m special correspondent; **Ϩlich 1.** adj. special, peculiar; **2.** adv.: nicht ~

not particularly; **'~ling** m (-s/-e) crank, odd person; **'Ϩn 1.** cj. but; nicht nur, ~ auch not only, but (also); **2.** v/t. (ge-, h): die Spreu vom Weizen ~ sift the chaff from the wheat; **'~recht** n privilege; **'~zug** 🚂 m special (train).

sondieren [zɔn'di:rən] (no -ge-, h) **1.** v/t. ♛ probe (a. fig.); **2.** fig. v/i. make tentative inquiries.

Sonn|abend ['zɔn⁹-] m (-s/-e) Saturday; **'~e** f (-/-n) sun; **'Ϩen** v/t. (ge-, h) (expose to the) sun; sich ~ sun o.s. (a. fig. in dat. in), bask in the sun.

'Sonnen|aufgang m sunrise; **'~bad** n sun-bath; **'~brand** m sunburn; **'~bräune** f sunburn, tan, Am. (sun)tan; **'~brille** f (ee a pair of) sunglasses pl.; **'~finsternis** f solar eclipse; **'~fleck** m sun-spot; **'Ϩklar** fig. adj. (as) clear as daylight; **'~licht** n (-[e]s/no pl.) sunlight; **'~schein** m (-[e]s/no pl.) sunshine; **'~schirm** m sunshade, parasol; **'~segel** n awning; **'~seite** f sunny side (a. fig.); **'~stich** ♛ m sunstroke; **'~strahl** m sunbeam; **'~uhr** f sun-dial; **'~untergang** m sunset, sundown; **'Ϩverbrannt** adj. sunburnt, tanned; **'~wende** f solstice.

'sonnig adj. sunny (a. fig.).

'Sonntag m Sunday.

'Sonntags|anzug m Sunday suit or best; **'~fahrer** mot. contp. m Sunday driver; **'~kind** n person born on a Sunday; fig. person born under a lucky star; **'~rückfahrkarte** 🚂 f week-end ticket; **'~ruhe** f Sunday rest; **'~staat** F co. m (-[e]s/no pl.) Sunday go-to-meeting clothes pl.

sonor adj. [zo'no:r] sonorous.

sonst [zɔnst] **1.** adv. otherwise, with pron. else; usually, normally; wer ~? who else?; wie ~ as usual; ~ nichts nothing else; **2.** cj. otherwise, or else; **'~ig** adj. other; **'~wie** adv. in some other way; **'~wo** adv. elsewhere, somewhere else.

Sopran ♪ [zo'pra:n] m (-s/-e) soprano; sopranist; **~istin** ♪ [~a'nistin] f (-/-nen) soprano, sopranist.

Sorge ['zɔrgə] f (-/-n) care; sorrow; uneasiness, anxiety; ~ tragen für take care of; sich ~n machen um be anxious or worried about; mach dir keine ~n don't worry.

'sorgen (ge-, h) 1. v/i.: ~ für care for, provide for; take care of, attend to; dafür ~, daß take care that; 2. v/refl.: sich ~ um be anxious or worried about; **'~frei** adj., **'~los** adj. carefree, free from care; **'~voll** adj. full of cares; face: worried, troubled.

Sorg|falt ['zɔrkfalt] f (-/no pl.) care(fulness); **2fältig** adj. ['~fɛltiç] careful; **2lich** adj. careful, anxious; **2los** adj. carefree; thoughtless; negligent; careless; **2sam** adj. careful.

Sort|e ['zɔrtə] f (-/-n) sort, kind, species, Am. a. stripe; **2ieren** [~'ti:rən] v/t. (no -ge-, h) (as)sort; arrange; **~iment** [~i'mɛnt] n (-[e]s/-e) assortment.

Soße ['zo:sə] f (-/-n) sauce; gravy.

sott [zɔt] pret. of sieden.

Souffl|eurkasten thea. [su'flø:r-] m prompt-box, prompter's box; **~euse** thea. [~'zø:] f (-/-n) prompter; **2ieren** thea. (no -ge-, h) 1. v/i. prompt (j-m s.o.); 2. v/t. prompt.

Souverän [suvə're:n] 1. m (-s/-e) sovereign; 2. 2 adj. sovereign; fig. superior; **~ität** [~ɛni'tɛ:t] f (-/no pl.) sovereignty.

so|viel [zo'-] 1. cj. so or as far as; ~ ich weiß so far as I know; 2. adv.: doppelt ~ twice as much; **~'weit** 1. cj.: ~ es mich betrifft in so far as it concerns me, so far as I am concerned; 2. adv.: ~ ganz gut not bad (for a start); **~wieso** adv. [zovi'zo:] in any case, anyhow, anyway.

Sowjet [zɔ'vjɛt] m (-s/-s) Soviet; **2isch** adj. Soviet.

sowohl cj. [zo'-]: ~ ... als (auch) ... both ... and ..., ... as well as ...

sozial adj. [zo'tsja:l] social; **2demokrat** m social democrat; **~isieren** [~ali'zi:rən] v/t. (no -ge-, h) socialize; **2isierung** [~ali'zi:ruŋ] f (-/-en) socialization; **2ist** m [~a'list] m (-en/-en) socialist; **~istisch** adj. [~a'listiç] socialist.

Sozius ['zo:tsjus] m (-/-se) † partner; mot. pillion-rider; **'~sitz** mot. m pillion.

sozusagen adv. [zotsu'za:gən] so to speak, as it were.

Spachtel ['ʃpaxtəl] m (-s/-), f (-/-n) spatula.

spähe|n ['ʃpɛ:ən] v/i. (ge-, h) look

out (nach for); peer; **'2r** m (-s/-) look-out; ✕ scout.

Spalier [ʃpa'li:r] n (-s/-e) trellis, espalier; fig. lane; ~ bilden form a lane.

Spalt [ʃpalt] m (-[e]s/-e) crack, split, rift, crevice, fissure; **'~e** f (-/-n) s. Spalt; typ. column; **'2en** v/t. ([irr.] ge-, h) split (a. fig. hairs), cleave (block of wood, etc.); sich ~ split (up); **'~ung** f (-/-en) splitting, cleavage; fig. split; eccl. schism.

Span [ʃpa:n] m (-[e]s/⁼e) chip, shaving, splinter.

Spange ['ʃpaŋə] f (-/-n) clasp; buckle; clip; slide (in hair); strap (of shoes); bracelet.

Span|ier ['ʃpa:njər] m (-s/-) Spaniard; **2isch** adj. Spanish.

Spann [ʃpan] 1. m (-[e]s/-e) instep; 2. 2 pret. of spinnen; **'~e** f (-/-n) span; ✍, orn. spread (of wings); † margin; **'2en** (ge-, h) 1. v/t. stretch (rope, muscles, etc.); cock (rifle); bend (bow, etc.); tighten (spring, etc.); vor den Wagen ~ harness to the carriage; s. gespannt; 2. v/i. be (too) tight; **2end** adj. exciting, thrilling, gripping; **'~kraft** f (-/no pl.) elasticity; fig. energy; **'~ung** f (-/-en) tension (a. fig.); ⚡ voltage; ⊕ strain, stress; ⚠ span; fig. close attention.

Spar|büchse ['ʃpa:r-] f money-box; **2en** (ge-, h) 1. v/t. save (money, strength, etc.); put by; 2. v/i. save; economize, cut down expenses; ~ mit be chary of (praise, etc.); **'~er** m (-s/-) saver.

Spargel ✍ ['ʃpargəl] m (-s/-) asparagus.

'Spar|kasse f savings-bank; **'~konto** n savings-account.

spärlich adj. ['ʃpɛ:rliç] crop, dress, etc.: scanty; population, etc.: sparse; hair: thin.

Sparren ['ʃparən] m (-s/-) rafter, spar.

'sparsam 1. adj. saving, economical (mit of); 2. adv.: ~ leben lead a frugal life, economize; ~ umgehen mit use sparingly, be frugal of; **'2keit** f (-/no pl.) economy, frugality.

Spaß [ʃpa:s] m (-es/⁼e) joke, jest; fun, lark; amusement; aus or im or zum ~ in fun; ~ beiseite joking apart; er hat nur ~ gemacht he

S

was only joking; '⸚en v/i. (ge-, h) joke, jest, make fun; *damit ist nicht zu ~* that is no joking matter; '⸚haft adj., '⸚ig adj. facetious, waggish; funny; '⸚macher m (-s/-), '⸚vogel m wag, joker.

spät [ʃpɛːt] 1. adj. late; advanced; *zu ~* too late; *am ⸚en Nachmittag* late in the afternoon; *wie ~ ist es?* what time is it?; 2. adv. late; *er kommt 5 Minuten zu ~* he is five minutes late (*zu* for); *~ in der Nacht* late at night.

Spaten [ʃpaːtən] m (-s/-) spade.

'späte|r 1. adj. later; 2. adv. later on; afterward(s); *früher oder ~* sooner or later; '⸚stens adv. ['⸚stəns] at the latest.

Spatz orn. [ʃpats] m (-en, -es/-en) sparrow.

spazieren [ʃpaˈtsiːrən] v/i. (no -ge-, sein) walk, stroll; ⸚fahren (irr. fahren, sep., -ge-) 1. v/i. (sein) go for a drive; take (*baby*) out (in pram); ⸚gehen v/i. (irr. gehen, sep., -ge-, sein) go for a walk.

Spa'zier|fahrt f drive, ride; ⸚gang m walk, stroll; *e-n ~ machen* go for a walk; ⸚gänger m [-ɡɛŋər] m (-s/-) walker, stroller; ⸚weg m walk.

Speck [ʃpɛk] m (-[e]s/-e) bacon.

Spedi|teur [ʃpediˈtøːr] m (-s/-e) forwarding agent; (furniture) remover; ⸚tion f [-ˈtsjoːn] f (-/-en) forwarding agent or agency.

Speer [ʃpeːr] m (-[e]s/-e) spear; *sports:* javelin; '⸚werfen n (-s/no pl.) javelin-throw(ing); '⸚werfer m (-s/-) javelin-thrower.

Speiche ['ʃpaɪçə] f (-/-n) spoke.

Speichel ['ʃpaɪçəl] m (-s/no pl.) spit(tle), saliva; '⸚lecker fig. m (-s/-) lickspittle, toady.

Speicher ['ʃpaɪçər] m (-s/-) granary, warehouse; garret, attic.

speien ['ʃpaɪən] (irr., ge-, h) 1. v/t. spit out (*blood, etc.*); volcano, etc.: belch (*fire, etc.*); 2. v/i. spit; vomit, be sick.

Speise ['ʃpaɪzə] f (-/-n) food, nourishment; meal; dish; '⸚eis n ice-cream; '⸚kammer f larder, pantry; '⸚karte f bill of fare, menu; '⸚n (ge-, h) 1. v/i. s. essen 1; *at restaurants:* take one's meals; 2. v/t. feed; ⊕, ⚡ a. supply (*mit* with); '⸚nfolge f menu; '⸚röhre anat. f

gullet, (o)esophagus; '⸚saal m dining-hall; '⸚schrank m (meat-) safe; '⸚wagen ⚙ m dining-car, diner; '⸚zimmer n dining-room.

Spektakel F [ʃpɛkˈtaːkəl] m (-s/-) noise, din.

Spekul|ant [ʃpekuˈlant] m (-en/-en) speculator; ⸚ation f [-aˈtsjoːn] f (-/-en) speculation; ⚡ a. venture; 2ieren [-ˈliːrən] v/i. (no -ge-, h) speculate (*auf acc.* on).

Spelunke [ʃpeˈluŋkə] f (-/-n) den; drinking-den, *Am.* F a. dive.

Spende ['ʃpɛndə] f (-/-n) gift; alms pl.; contribution; '2n v/t. (ge-, h) give; donate (*money to charity, blood, etc.*); *eccl.* administer (*sacraments*); bestow (*praise*) (*dat.* on); '⸚r m (-s/-) giver; donor.

spen'dieren v/t. (no -ge-, h): *j-m et. ~* treat s.o. to s.th., stand s.o. s.th.

Sperling orn. ['ʃpɛrliŋ] m (-s/-e) sparrow.

Sperr|e ['ʃpɛrə] f (-/-n) barrier; 🚉 barrier, *Am.* gate; toll-bar; ⊕ lock(ing device), detent; barricade; ✝, ⚓ embargo; ✕ blockade; *sports:* suspension; '2en (ge-, h) 1. v/t. close; ✝, ⚓ embargo; cut off (*gas supply, electricity, etc.*); stop (*cheque, etc.*); *sports:* suspend; 2. v/i. jam, be stuck; '⸚holz n plywood; '⸚konto ⚡ n blocked account; '⸚kreis ⚡ m wave-trap; '⸚sitz *thea.* m stalls pl., *Am.* orchestra; '⸚ung f (-/-en) closing; stoppage (*of cheque, etc.*); ✝, ⚓ embargo; ✕ blockade; '⸚zone f prohibited area.

Spesen ['ʃpeːzən] pl. expenses pl., charges pl.

Spezial|ausbildung [ʃpeˈtsjaːlʔ-] f special training; ⸚fach n special(i)ty; ⸚geschäft ✝ n one-line shop, *Am.* specialty store; 2isieren [-aliˈziːrən] v/refl. (no -ge-, h) specialize (*auf acc.* in); ⸚ist [-aˈlist] m (-en/-en) specialist; 2ität f [-aliˈtɛːt] f (-/-en) special(i)ty.

speziell adj. [ʃpeˈtsjɛl] specific, special, particular.

spezifisch adj. [ʃpeˈtsiːfiʃ]: *~es Gewicht* specific gravity.

Sphäre ['ʃfɛːrə] f (-/-n) sphere (a. fig.).

Spick|aal ['ʃpik-] m smoked eel; '2en (ge-, h) 1. v/t. lard; fig. (inter-)

lard (*mit* with); F: *j-n* ~ grease s.o.'s palm; **2.** F *fig. v/i.* crib.

spie [ʃpiː] *pret. of* speien.

Spiegel ['ʃpiːgəl] *m* (-s/-) mirror (*a. fig.*), looking-glass; '~**bild** *n* reflected image; 'ℒ**blank** *adj.* mirror-like; ~**ei** ['ʃpiːgəlˀ-] *n* fried egg; 'ℒ**glatt** *adj.* water: glassy, unrippled; *road, etc.*: very slippery; '~**n** (ge-, h) **1.** *v/i.* shine; **2.** *v/refl.* be reflected; '~**schrift** *f* mirror-writing.

Spieg(e)lung ['ʃpiːg(ə)luŋ] *f* (-/-en) reflection, reflexion; mirage.

Spiel [ʃpiːl] *n* (-[e]s/-e) play (*a. fig.*); game (*a. fig.*); match; ♪ playing; *ein* ~ *Karten* a pack of playing-cards, *Am.* ~ a deck; *auf dem* ~ *stehen* be at stake; *aufs* ~ *setzen* jeopardize, stake; '~**art** ℒ, *zo. f* variety; '~**ball** *m tennis:* game ball; *billiards:* red ball; *fig.* plaything, sport; '~**bank** *f* (-/-en) gaming-house; 'ℒ**en** (ge-, h) **1.** *v/i.* play; gamble; ~ *mit* play with; *fig.* a. toy with; **2.** *v/t.* play (*tennis, violin, etc.*); *thea.* act, play (*part*); *mit j-m Schach* ~ play s.o. at chess; *den Höflichen* ~ do the polite; 'ℒ**end** *fig. adv.* easily; '~**er** *m* (-s/-) player; gambler; '~**erei** *f* (-/-en) pastime; child's amusement; '~**ergebnis** *n sports:* result, score; '~**feld** *n sports:* (playing-)field; pitch; '~**film** *m* feature film *or* picture; '~**gefährte** *m* playfellow, playmate; '~**karte** *f* playing-card; '~**leiter** *m thea.* stage manager; *cinematography:* director; *sports:* referee; '~**marke** *f* counter, *sl.* chip; '~**plan** *m thea., etc.:* program(me); repertory; '~**platz** *m* playground; '~**raum** *fig. m* play, scope; '~**regel** *f* rule (of the game); '~**sachen** *f/pl.* playthings *pl.*, toys *pl.*; '~**schuld** *f* gambling-debt; '~**schule** *f* infant-school, kindergarten; '~**tisch** *m* card-table; gambling-table; '~**uhr** *f* musical box, *Am.* music box; '~**verderber** *m* (-s/-) spoil-sport, killjoy; wet blanket; '~**waren** *f/pl.* playthings *pl.*, toys *pl.*; '~**zeit** *f thea.* season; *sports:* time of play; '~**zeug** *n* toy(s *pl.*), plaything(s *pl.*).

Spieß [ʃpiːs] *m* (-es/-e) spear, pike; spit; *den* ~ *umdrehen* turn the tables; '~**bürger** *m* bourgeois, Philistine, *Am.* a. Babbitt; 'ℒ**bürgerlich** *adj.* bourgeois, Philistine;

'~**er** *m* (-s/-) s. Spießbürger; '~**geselle** *m* accomplice; '~**ruten** *f/pl.:* ~ *laufen* run the gauntlet (*a. fig.*).

spinal *adj.* [ʃpiˈnaːl]: ~**e** *Kinderlähmung* ℒ infantile paralysis, poliomyelitis, F polio.

Spinat ℒ [ʃpiˈnaːt] *m* (-[e]s/-e) spinach.

Spind [ʃpint] *n, m* (-[e]s/-e) wardrobe, cupboard; ⚔, *sports, etc.:* locker.

Spindel ['ʃpindəl] *f* (-/-n) spindle; 'ℒ**dürr** *adj.* (as) thin as a lath.

Spinn|**e** *zo.* ['ʃpinə] *f* (-/-n) spider; 'ℒ**en** (*irr.*, ge-, h) **1.** *v/t.* spin (*a. fig.*); hatch (*plot, etc.*); **2.** *v/i.* cat: purr; F *fig.* be crazy, *sl.* be nuts; '~**engewebe** *n* cobweb; '~**er** *m* (-s/-) spinner; F *fig.* silly; '~**erei** *f* (-/-en) spinning; spinning-mill; '~**maschine** *f* spinning-machine; '~**webe** *f* (-/-n) cobweb.

Spion [ʃpiˈoːn] *m* (-s/-e) spy, intelligencer; *fig.* judas; '~**age** [~oˈnaːʒə] *f* (-/no *pl.*) espionage; ℒ**ieren** [~oˈniːrən] *v/i.* (no -ge-, h) (play the) spy.

Spiral|**e** [ʃpiˈraːlə] *f* (-/-n) spiral (*a.* ⚙), helix; ℒ**förmig** *adj.* [~fœrmiç] spiral, helical.   [its *pl.*]

Spirituosen [ʃpirituˈoːzən] *pl.* spir-|

Spiritus ['ʃpiːritus] *m* (-/-se) spirit, alcohol; '~**kocher** *m* (-s/-) spirit stove.

Spital [ʃpiˈtaːl] *n* (-s/⸚er) hospital; alms-house; home for the aged.

spitz [ʃpits] **1.** *adj.* pointed (*a. fig.*); ⦞ *angle:* acute; *fig.* poignant; ~**e** *Zunge* sharp tongue; **2.** *adv.:* ~ *zulaufen* taper (off); 'ℒ**bube** *m* thief, rogue, rascal (*both a. co.*); ℒ**büberei** [~byːbəˈraɪ] *f* (-/-en) roguery, rascality (*both a. co.*); ~**bübisch** *adj.* ['~byːbiʃ] *eyes, smile, etc.:* roguish.

'**Spitze** *f* (-/-n) point (*of pencil, weapon, jaw, etc.*); tip (*of nose, finger, etc.*); nib (*of tool, etc.*); spire; head (*of enterprise, etc.*); lace; *an der* ~ *liegen sports:* be in the lead; *j-m die* ~ *bieten* make head against s.o.; *auf die* ~ *treiben* carry to an extreme; '~**el** *m* (-s/-) (common) informer; 'ℒ**en** *v/t.* (ge-, h) point, sharpen; *den Mund* ~ purse (up) one's lips; *die Ohren* ~ prick up one's ears (*a. fig.*).

'**Spitzen**|**leistung** *f* top performance; ⊕ maximum capacity; '~lohn m top wages pl.

'spitz|findig adj. subtle, captious; '2findigkeit f (-/-en) subtlety, captiousness; '2hacke f pickax(e), pick; '~ig adj. pointed; fig. a. poignant; '2marke typ. f head(ing); '2name m nickname.

Splitter ['ʃplitər] m (-s/-) splinter, shiver; chip; '2frei adj. glass: shatterproof; '2ig adj. splintery; '2n v/i. (ge-, h, sein) splinter, shiver; '2nackt F adj. stark naked, Am. a. mother-naked; '~partei pol. f splinter party.

spontan adj. [ʃpɔn'taːn] spontaneous.

sporadisch adj. [ʃpo'raːdiʃ] sporadic.

Sporn [ʃpɔrn] m (-[e]s/Sporen) spur; die Sporen geben put or set spurs to (horse); sich die Sporen verdienen win one's spurs; '2en v/t. (ge-, h) spur.

Sport [ʃpɔrt] m (-[e]s/⊗-e) sport; fig. hobby; ~ treiben go in for sports; '~ausrüstung f sports equipment; '~geschäft n sporting-goods shop; '~kleidung f sport clothes pl., sportswear; '~lehrer m games-master; '2lich adj. sporting, sportsmanlike; figure: athletic; '~nachrichten f/pl. sports news sg., pl.; '~platz m sports field; stadium.

Spott [ʃpɔt] m (-[e]s/no pl.) mockery; derision; scorn; (s-n) ~ treiben mit make sport of; '2billig F adj. dirt-cheap.

Spötte|lei [ʃpœtə'laɪ] f (-/-en) raillery, banter, jeer; '2ln v/i. (ge-, h) sneer (über acc. at), jeer (at).

'spotten v/i. (ge-, h) mock (über acc. at); jeer (at); jeder Beschreibung ~ beggar description.

Spötter ['ʃpœtər] m (-s/-) mocker, scoffer; ~ei [~'raɪ] f (-/-en) mockery.

'spöttisch adj. mocking; sneering; ironical.

'Spott|name m nickname; '~preis m ridiculous price; für e-n ~ for a mere song; '~schrift f lampoon, satire.

sprach [ʃpraːx] pret. of sprechen.

'Sprache f (-/-n) speech; language (a. fig.); diction; zur ~ bringen bring up, broach; zur ~ kommen come up (for discussion).

'Sprach|eigentümlichkeit f idiom;

'~fehler ⚥ m impediment (in one's speech); '~führer m language guide; '~gebrauch m usage; '~gefühl n (-[e]s/no pl.) linguistic instinct; 2kundig adj. ['~kundiç] versed in languages; '~lehre f grammar; '~lehrer m teacher of languages; '2lich adj. linguistic; grammatical; '2los adj. speechless; '~rohr n speaking-trumpet, megaphone; fig.: mouthpiece; organ; '~schatz m vocabulary; '~störung ⚥ f impediment (in one's speech); '~wissenschaft f philology, science of language; linguistics pl.; '~wissenschaftler m philologist; linguist; '2wissenschaftlich adj. philological; linguistic.

sprang [ʃpraŋ] pret. of springen.

Sprech|chor ['ʃpreç-] m speaking chorus; '2en (irr., ge-, h) 1. v/t. speak (language, truth, etc.); ⚖ pronounce (judgement); say (prayer); j-n zu ~ wünschen wish to see s.o.; j-n schuldig ~ ⚖ pronounce s.o. guilty; F Bände ~ speak volumes (für for); 2. v/i. speak; talk (both: mit to, with; über acc., von of, about); er ist nicht zu ~ you cannot see him; '~er m (-s/-) speaker; radio: announcer; spokesman; '~fehler m slip of the tongue; '~stunde f consulting-hours pl.; '~übung f exercise in speaking; '~zimmer n consulting-room, surgery.

spreizen ['ʃpraɪtsən] v/t. (ge-, h) spread (out); a. straddle (legs); sich ~ pretend to be unwilling.

Spreng|bombe ✕ ['ʃpreŋ-] f high-explosive bomb, demolition bomb; '~el eccl. m (-s/-) diocese, see; parish; '2en (ge-) 1. v/t. (h) sprinkle, water (road, lawn, etc.); blow up, blast (bridge, rocks, etc.); burst open (door, etc.); spring (mine, etc.); gambling: break (bank); break up (meeting, etc.); 2. v/i. (sein) gallop; '~stoff m explosive; '~ung f (-/-en) blowing-up, blasting; explosion; '~wagen m water(ing)-cart.

Sprenkel ['ʃpreŋkəl] m (-s/-) speckle, spot; '2n v/t. (ge-, h) speckle, spot.

Spreu [ʃprɔʏ] f (-/no pl.) chaff; s. sondern 2.

Sprich|wort ['ʃpriç-] n (-[e]s/⸚er) proverb, adage; '2wörtlich adj. proverbial (a. fig.).

S

sprießen ['ʃpriːsən] v/i. (irr., ge-, sein) sprout; germinate.

Spring|brunnen ['ʃpriŋ-] m fountain; '**2en** v/i. (irr., ge-, sein) jump, leap; *ball, etc.*: bounce; *swimming*: dive; burst, crack, break; *in die Augen* ~ strike the eye; ~ *über (acc.)* jump (over), leap, clear; '**~er** m (-s/-) jumper; *swimming*: diver; *chess*: knight; '**~flut** f spring tide.

Sprit [ʃprɪt] m (-[e]s/-e) spirit, alcohol; F *mot.* fuel, petrol, *sl.* juice, *Am.* gasoline, F gas.

Spritz|e ['ʃprɪtsə] f (-/-n) syringe (a. ⚕), squirt; ⊕ fire-engine; *j-m e-e* ~ *geben* ⚕ give s.o. an injection; '**2en** (ge-) 1. v/t. (h) sprinkle, water (*road, lawn, etc.*); splash (*water, etc.*) (*über acc.* on, over); 2. v/i. (h) splash; *pen*: splutter; 3. v/i. (sein) F *fig.* dash, flit; ~ *aus blood, etc.*: spurt *or* spout from (*wound, etc.*); '**~er** m (-s/-) splash; '**~tour** f: *e-e* ~ *machen* go for a spin.

spröde adj. ['ʃprøːdə] *glass, etc.*: brittle; *skin*: chapped, chappy; *esp. girl*: prudish, prim, coy.

Sproß [ʃprɔs] 1. m (Sprosses/Sprosse) ♀ shoot, sprout, scion (a. *fig.*); *fig.* offspring; 2. ♀ *pret. of* sprießen.

Sprosse ['ʃprɔsə] f (-/-n) rung, round, step.   [Sproß 1.; *co.* son.]

Sprößling ['ʃprœslɪŋ] m (-s/-e) ♀ s.]

Spruch [ʃprʊx] m (-[e]s/¨e) saying; dictum; ⚖ sentence; ⚖ verdict; '**~band** n banner; '**2reif** adj. ripe for decision.

Sprudel ['ʃpruːdəl] m (-s/-) mineral water; '**2n** v/i. (ge-) 1. (h) bubble, effervesce; 2. (sein): ~ *aus or von* gush from.

sprüh|en ['ʃpryːən] (ge-) 1. v/t. (h) spray, sprinkle (*liquid*); throw off (*sparks*); *Feuer* ~ *eyes*: flash fire; 2. v/i. (h): ~ *vor* sparkle with (*wit, etc.*); *es sprüht* it is drizzling; 3. v/i. (sein) *sparks*: fly; '**2regen** m drizzle.

Sprung [ʃprʊŋ] m (-[e]s/¨e) jump, leap, bound; *swimming*: dive; crack, fissure; '**~brett** n *sports*: springboard; *fig.* stepping-stone; '**~feder** f spiral spring.

Spuck|e F ['ʃpukə] f (-/*no pl.*) spit(tle); '**2en** (ge-, h) 1. v/t. spit (out) (*blood, etc.*); 2. v/i. spit; *engine*: splutter; '**~napf** m spittoon, *Am. a.* cuspidor.

Spuk [ʃpuːk] m (-[e]s/-e) apparition, ghost, *co.* spook; F *fig.* noise; '**2en** v/i. (ge-, h): ~ *in (dat.)* haunt (*a place*); *hier spukt es* this place is haunted.

Spule ['ʃpuːlə] f (-/-n) spool, reel; bobbin; ⚡ coil; '**2n** v/t. (ge-, h) spool, reel.

spülen ['ʃpyːlən] (ge-, h) 1. v/t. rinse (*clothes, mouth, cup, etc.*); wash up (*dishes, etc.*); *an Land* ~ wash ashore; 2. v/i. flush the toilet.

Spund [ʃpunt] m (-[e]s/¨e) bung; plug; '**~loch** n bunghole.

Spur [ʃpuːr] f (-/-en) trace (a. *fig.*); track (a. *fig.*); print (a. *fig.*); rut (of *wheels*); *j-m auf der* ~ *sein* be on s.o.'s track.

spür|en ['ʃpyːrən] v/t. (ge-, h) feel; sense; perceive; *fig. a.* flair (*für* for).

Spurweite 🚂 f ga(u)ge.

sputen ['ʃpuːtən] v/refl. (ge-, h) make haste, hurry up.

Staat [ʃtaːt] m 1. F (-[e]s/*no pl.*) pomp, state; finery; ~ *machen mit* make a parade of; 2. (-[e]s/-en) state; government; '**~enbund** m (-[e]s/¨e) confederacy, confederation; '**2enlos** adj. stateless; '**2lich** adj. state; national; political; public.

'Staats|angehörige m, f (-n/-n) national, citizen, *esp. Brt.* subject; '**~angehörigkeit** f (-/*no pl.*) nationality, citizenship; '**~anwalt** ⚖ m public prosecutor, *Am.* prosecuting attorney; '**~beamte** m Civil Servant, *Am. a.* public servant; '**~begräbnis** n state *or* national funeral; '**~besuch** m official *or* state visit; '**~bürger** m citizen; '**~bürgerkunde** f (-/*no pl.*) civics sg.; '**~bürgerschaft** f (-/-en) citizenship; '**~dienst** m Civil Service; '**2eigen** adj. state-owned; '**~feind** m public enemy; '**2feindlich** adj. subversive; '**~gewalt** f (-/*no pl.*) supreme power; '**~haushalt** m budget; '**~hoheit** f (-/*no pl.*) sovereignty; '**~kasse** f treasury, *Brt.* exchequer; '**~klugheit** f (-/*no pl.*) political wisdom; '**~kunst** f (-/*no pl.*) statesmanship; '**~mann** m statesman; '**2männisch** adj. '**~männisch]** statesmanlike; '**~oberhaupt** n head of (the) state; '**~papiere** n/pl. Government securities pl.; '**~rat** m Privy Council; '**~recht** n public law; '**~schatz** m *s.* Staatskasse;

'**⁓schulden** f/pl. national debt; '**⁓sekretär** m under-secretary of state; '**⁓streich** m coup d'état; '**⁓trauer** f national mourning; '**⁓vertrag** m treaty; '**⁓wesen** n polity; '**⁓wirtschaft** f public sector of the economy; '**⁓wissenschaft** f political science; '**⁓wohl** n public weal.

Stab [ʃtaːp] m (-[e]s/⁓e) staff (a. fig.); bar (of metal, wood); crosier, staff (of bishop); wand (of magician); relay-race, ♪ conducting: baton; pole-vaulting: pole.

stabil adj. [ʃtaˈbiːl] stable (a. ✝); health: robust.

stabilisier|en [ʃtabiliˈziːrən] v/t. (no -ge-, h) stabilize (a. ✝); ⁓ung f (-/-en) stabilization (a. ✝).

stach [ʃtax] pret. of stechen.

Stachel ['ʃtaxəl] m (-s/-n) prickle (of plant, hedgehog, etc.); sting (of bee, etc.); tongue (of buckle); spike (of sports shoe); fig.: sting; goad; '**⁓beere** ♀ f gooseberry; '**⁓draht** m barbed wire; '**⁓ig** adj. prickly, 'stachlig adj. s. stachelig. } [thorny. ∫

Stadi|on ['ʃtaːdjɔn] n (-s/Stadien) stadium; '**⁓um** ['⁓um] n (-s/Stadien) stage, phase.

Stadt [ʃtat] f (-/⁓e) town; city.

Städt|chen ['ʃtɛːtçən] n (-s/-) small town; '**⁓ebau** m (-[e]s/no pl.) town-planning; '**⁓er** m (-s/-) townsman; ⁓ pl. townspeople pl.

'**Stadt|gebiet** n urban area; '**⁓gespräch** n teleph. local call; fig. town talk, talk of the town; '**⁓haus** n town house.

städtisch adj. ['ʃtɛːtiʃ] municipal.

'**Stadt|plan** m city map; plan (of a town); '**⁓planung** f town-planning; '**⁓rand** m outskirts pl. (of a town); '**⁓rat** m (-[e]s/⁓e) town council; town council(l)or; '**⁓teil** m, '**⁓viertel** n quarter.

Staffel ['ʃtafəl] f (-/-n) relay; relay-race; '**⁓ei** paint. ['⁓laɪ] f (-/-en) easel; '**⁓lauf** m relay-race; '**⁓n** v/t. (ge-, h) graduate (taxes, etc.); stagger (hours of work, etc.).

Stahl¹ [ʃtaːl] m (-[e]s/⁓e, -e) steel.

stahl² [⁓] pret. of stehlen.

stählen ['ʃtɛːlən] v/t. (ge-, h) ⊕ harden (a. fig.), temper.

'**Stahl|feder** f steel pen; steel spring; '**⁓kammer** f strong-room; '**⁓stich** m steel engraving.

stak [ʃtaːk] pret. of stecken 2.

Stall [ʃtal] m (-[e]s/⁓e) stable (a. fig.); cow-house, cowshed; pigsty, Am. a. pigpen; shed; '**⁓knecht** m stableman; '**⁓ung** f (-/-en) stabling, ⁓en pl. stables pl.

Stamm [ʃtam] m (-[e]s/⁓e) ♀ stem (a. gr.), trunk; fig.: race; stock; family; tribe; '**⁓aktie** ✝ f ordinary share, Am. common stock; '**⁓baum** m family or genealogical tree, pedigree (a. zo.); '**⁓buch** n album; book that contains the births, deaths, and marriages in a family; zo. stud-book; '⁓eln (ge-, h) 1. v/t. stammer (out); 2. v/i. stammer; '**⁓eltern** pl. ancestors pl., first parents pl.; '⁓en v/i. (ge-, sein): ⁓ von or aus come from (town, etc.), Am. a. hail from; date from (certain time); gr. be derived from; aus gutem Haus ⁓ be of good family; '**⁓gast** m regular customer or guest, F regular.

stämmig adj. ['ʃtɛmiç] stocky; thickset, squat(ty).

'**Stamm|kapital** ✝ n share capital, Am. capital stock; '**⁓kneipe** F f one's favo(u)rite pub, local; '**⁓kunde** m regular customer, patron; '**⁓tisch** m table reserved for regular guests; '**⁓utter** [ʃtammˈʊtər] f (-/⁓⁓) ancestress; '**⁓vater** m ancestor; '⁓verwandt adj. cognate, kindred; pred. of the same race.

stampfen ['ʃtampfən] (ge-) 1. v/t. (h) mash (potatoes, etc.); aus dem Boden ⁓ conjure up; 2. v/i. (h) stamp (one's foot); horse: paw; 3. v/i. (sein): ⁓ durch plod through; ♣ pitch through.

Stand [ʃtant] 1. m (-[e]s/⁓e) stand (-ing), standing or upright position; footing, foothold; s. Standplatz; stall; fig.: level; state; station, rank, status; class; profession; reading (of thermometer, etc.); ast. position; sports: score; auf den neuesten ⁓ bringen bring up to date; e-n schweren ⁓ haben have a hard time (of it); 2. ♀ pret. of stehen.

Standarte [ʃtanˈdartə] f (-/-n) standard, banner.

'**Standbild** n statue.

'**Ständchen** n (-s/-) serenade; j-m ein ⁓ bringen serenade s.o.

Ständer ['ʃtɛndər] m (-s/-) stand; post, pillar, standard.

S

'**Standes|amt** *n* registry (office),
register office; '**2amtlich** *adj.*: **~e
Trauung** civil marriage; '**~beamte**
m registrar; '**~dünkel** *m* pride of
place; '**2gemäß** *adj.*, '**2mäßig** *adj.*
in accordance with one's rank;
'**~person** *f* person of rank or position; '**~unterschied** *m* social difference.

'**standhaft** *adj.* steadfast; firm;
constant; **~ bleiben** stand pat; resist
temptation; '**2igkeit** *f* (-/*no pl.*)
steadfastness; firmness.

'**standhalten** *v/i.* (*irr.* halten, sep.,
-ge-, *h*) hold one's ground; *j-m* or
e-r Sache **~** resist *s.o.* or *s.th.*

ständig *adj.* ['ʃtɛndiç] permanent;
constant; *income, etc.*: fixed.

'**Stand|ort** *m* position (*of ship, etc.*);
⚔ garrison, post; '**~platz** *m* stand;
'**~punkt** *fig. m* point of view, stand-
point, angle, *Am. a.* slant; '**~quar-
tier** ⚔ *n* fixed quarters *pl.*; '**~recht**
⚔ *n* martial law; '**~uhr** *f* grand-
father's clock.

Stange ['ʃtaŋə] *f* (-/-*n*) pole; rod,
bar (*of iron, etc.*); staff (*of flag*);
Anzug or *Kleid von der* **~** *sl.* reach-
me-down, *Am.* F hand-me-down.

stank [ʃtaŋk] *pret. of* stinken.

Stänker|(er) *contp.* ['ʃtɛŋkər(ər)] *m*
(-*s*/-) mischief-maker, quarrel(l)er;
'**2n** F *v/i.* (ge-, *h*) make mischief.

Stanniol [ʃta'njɔːl] *n* (-*s*/-*e*) tin foil.

Stanze ['ʃtantsə] *f* (-/-*n*) stanza; ⊕
punch, stamp, die; '**2n** ⊕ *v/t.* (ge-,
h) punch, stamp.

Stapel ['ʃtaːpəl] *m* (-*s*/-) pile, stack;
⚓ stocks *pl.*; *vom* or *von* **~** *lassen* ⚓
launch; *vom* or *von* **~** *laufen* ⚓ be
launched; '**~lauf** ⚓ *m* launch; '**2n**
v/t. (ge-, *h*) pile (up), stack; '**~platz**
m dump; emporium.

stapfen ['ʃtapfən] *v/i.* (ge-, *sein*)
plod (*durch* through).

Star 1. [ʃtaːr] *m* (-[*e*]*s*/-*e*) *orn.*
starling; 𝔰 cataract; *j-m den* **~** *stechen* open *s.o.'s* eyes; 2. [staːr] *m*
(-*s*/-*s*) *thea., etc.*: star.

starb [ʃtarp] *pret. of* sterben.

stark [ʃtark] 1. *adj.* strong (*a. fig.*),
stout, corpulent; *fig.*: intense; large;
~e Erkältung bad cold; **~er Raucher**
heavy smoker; **~e Seite** strong point,
forte; 2. *adv.* very much; **~ erkältet
sein** have a bad cold; **~ übertrieben**
grossly exaggerated.

Stärke ['ʃtɛrkə] *f* (-/-*n*) strength (*a.*

fig.); stoutness, corpulence; *fig.*:
intensity; largeness; strong point,
forte; 🜂 starch; '**2n** *v/t.* (ge-, *h*)
strengthen (*a. fig.*); starch (*linen,
etc.*); *sich* **~** take some refresh-
ment(s).

'**Starkstrom** 𝔰 *m* heavy current.

'**Stärkung** *f* (-/-*en*) strengthening;
fig. a. refreshment; '**~smittel** *n*
restorative; 𝔰 *a.* tonic.

starr [ʃtar] 1. *adj.* rigid (*a. fig.*),
stiff; *gaze*: fixed; **~** *vor* (*dat.*) numb
with (*cold, etc.*); transfixed with
(*horror, etc.*); dumbfounded with
(*amazement, etc.*); 2. *adv.*: *j-n* **~** *ansehen* stare at *s.o.*; '**~en** *v/i.* (ge-, *h*)
stare (*auf acc.* at); *vor Schmutz* **~** be
covered with dirt; '**2heit** *f* (-/*no pl.*)
rigidity (*a. fig.*), stiffness; '**2kopf** *m*
stubborn or obstinate fellow; '**~köp-
fig** *adj.* ['~kœpfiç] stubborn, obstinate; '**2krampf** 𝔰 *m* (-[*e*]*s*/*no pl.*)
tetanus; '**2sinn** *m* (-[*e*]*s*/*no pl.*)
stubbornness, obstinacy; '**~sinnig**
adj. stubborn, obstinate.

Start [ʃtart] *m* (-[*e*]*s*/-*s*, 𝔰 *-e* start
(*a. fig.*); 𝔰 take-off; '**~bahn** 𝔰 *f*
runway; '**2bereit** *adj.* ready to
start; 𝔰 ready to take off; '**2en**
(ge-) 1. *v/i.* (sein) start; 𝔰 take off;
2. *v/t.* (*h*) start; *fig. a.* launch; '**~er**
m (-*s*/-) *sports*: starter; '**~platz** *m*
starting-place.

Station [ʃta'tsjɔːn] *f* (-/-*en*) station;
ward (*of hospital*); (*gegen*) *freie* **~**
board and lodging (found); **~** *machen* break one's journey; '**~svor-
steher** 🚃 *m* station-master, *Am. a.*
station agent.

Statist [ʃta'tist] *m* (-*en*/-*en*) *thea.*
supernumerary (actor), F super;
film: extra; '**~ik** *f* (-/-*en*) statistics
pl., *sg.*; '**~iker** *m* (-*s*/-) statistician;
'**2isch** *adj.* statistic(al).

Stativ [ʃta'tiːf] *n* (-*s*/-*e*) tripod.

Statt [ʃtat] 1. *f* (-/*no pl.*): *an Eides*
~ in lieu of an oath; *an Kindes* **~** *annehmen* adopt; 2. 2 *prp.* (*gen.*) instead of; **~** *zu inf.* instead of *ger.*;
~ *meiner* in my place.

Stätte ['ʃtɛtə] *f* (-/-*n*) place, spot;
scene (*of events*).

'**statt|finden** *v/i.* (*irr.* finden, sep.,
-ge-, *h*) take place, happen; '**~haft**
adj. admissible, allowable; legal.

'**Statthalter** *m* (-*s*/-) governor.

'**stattlich** *adj.* stately; impressive;
sum of money, etc.: considerable.

Steigerungsstufe

Statue ['ʃta:tuə] *f* (-/-n) statue.

statuieren [ʃtatu'i:rən] *v/t.* (*no* -ge-, *h*): *ein Exempel* ~ make an example (*an dat.* of).

Statur [ʃta'tu:r] *f* (-/-en) stature, size.

Statut [ʃta'tu:t] *n* (-[e]s/-en) statute; ~*en pl.* regulations *pl.*; † articles *pl.* of association.

Staub [ʃtaup] *m* (-[e]s/⊕ -e, ⸚e) dust; powder.

Staubecken ['ʃtauˀ-] *n* reservoir.

stauben ['ʃtaubən] *v/i.* (ge-, *h*) give off dust, make *or* raise a dust.

stäuben ['ʃtɔybən] (ge-, *h*) **1.** *v/t.* dust; **2.** *v/i.* spray.

'Staub|faden *φ m* filament; **'2ig** *adj.* ['-biç] dusty; ~**sauger** ['-p-] *m* (-s/-) vacuum cleaner; ~**tuch** ['-p-] *n* (-[e]s/⸚er) duster.

stauchen ['ʃtauxən] *v/t.* (ge-, *h*) upset, jolt.

'Staudamm *m* dam.

Staude φ ['ʃtaudə] *f* (-/-n) perennial (plant); head (of lettuce).

stau|en ['ʃtauən] *v/t.* (ge-, *h*) dam (up) (*river*, *etc.*); ⚓ stow; *sich* ~ *waters*, *etc.*: be dammed (up); *vehicles*: be jammed; '**2er** *φ m* (-s/-) stevedore.

staunen ['ʃtaunən] **1.** *v/i.* (ge-, *h*) be astonished (*über acc.* at); **2.** ♀ *n* (-s/*no pl.*) astonishment; '~**swert** *adj.* astonishing. [temper.]

Staupe *vet.* ['ʃtaupə] *f* (-/-n) dis-]

'Stau|see *m* reservoir; '~**ung** *f* (-/-en) damming (up) (*of water*); stoppage; ✿ congestion (*a.* of traffic); jam; ⚓ stowage.

stechen ['ʃtɛçən] (*irr.*, ge-, *h*) **1.** *v/t.* prick; *insect*, *etc.*: sting; *flea*, *mosquito*, *etc.*: bite; *card*: take, trump (*other card*); ⊕ engrave (*in or auf acc.* on); cut (*lawn*, *etc.*); *sich in den Finger* ~ prick one's finger; **2.** *v/i.* prick; stab (*nach* at); *insect*, *etc.*: sting; *flea*, *mosquito*, *etc.*: bite; *sun*: burn; *j-m in die Augen* ~ strike s.o.'s eye; '~**d** *adj.* pain, look, *etc.*: piercing; *pain*: stabbing.

Steck|brief 🜨 ['ʃtɛk-] *m* warrant of apprehension; '**2brieflich** 🜨 *adv.*: *er wird* ~ *gesucht* a warrant is out against him; '~**dose** φ *f* (wall) socket; '**2en 1.** *v/t.* (ge-, *h*) put; *esp.* ⊕ insert (*in acc.* into); F stick; pin (*an acc.* to, on); ⚘ set, plant; **2.** *v/i.* ([*irr.*,] ge-, *h*) be; stick, be

stuck; *tief in Schulden* ~ be deeply in debt; '~**en** *m* (-s/-) stick; '**2en-bleiben** *v/i.* (*irr.* bleiben, *sep.*, -ge-, *sein*) get stuck; *speaker*, *etc.*: break down; '~**enpferd** *n* hobby-horse, *fig.* hobby; '~**er** *φ m* (-s/-) plug; '~**kontakt** *φ m* (-s/-) Steckdose; '~**nadel** *f* pin.

Steg [ʃte:k] *m* (-[e]s/-e) foot-bridge; ⚓ landing-stage; '~**reif** *m* (-[e]s/-e): *aus dem* ~ extempore, offhand (*both a. attr.*); *aus dem* ~ *sprechen* extemporize, F ad-lib.

stehen ['ʃte:ən] *v/i.* (*irr.*, ge-, *h*) stand; be; be written; *dress*: suit, become (*j-m* s.o.); ~ *vor* be faced with; *gut* ~ *mit* be on good terms with; *es kam ihm or ihn teuer zu* ~ it cost him dearly; *wie steht's mit* ...? what about ...?; *wie steht das Spiel?* what's the score?; ~ *bleiben* remain standing; '~**bleiben** *v/i.* (*irr.* bleiben, *sep.*, -ge-, *sein*) stand (still), stop; leave off reading, *etc.*; '~**lassen** *v/t.* (*irr.* lassen, *sep.*, [*no*] -ge-, *h*) turn one's back (up)on; leave (*meal*) untouched; leave (behind); forget; leave alone.

'Steher *m* (-s/-) *sports*: stayer.

'Steh|kragen *m* stand-up collar; '~**lampe** *f* standard lamp; '~**leiter** *f* (e-e a pair of) steps *pl.*, step-ladder.

stehlen ['ʃte:lən] (*irr.*, ge-, *h*) **1.** *v/t.* steal; *j-m Geld* ~ steal s.o.'s money; **2.** *v/i.* steal.

'Stehplatz *m* standing-room; '~**inhaber** *m Am.* F standee; *in bus*, *etc.*: straphanger.

steif *adj.* [ʃtaif] stiff (*a. fig.*); numb (*vor Kälte* with cold); '~**halten** *v/t.* (*irr.* halten, *sep.*, -ge-, *h*): F *die Ohren* ~ keep a stiff upper lip.

Steig [ʃtaik] *m* (-[e]s/-e) steep path; '~**bügel** *m* stirrup.

steigen ['ʃtaigən] **1.** *v/i.* (*irr.*, ge-, *sein*) flood, barometer, spirits, prices, *etc.*: rise; *mists*, *etc.*: ascend; *blood, tension, etc.*: mount; prices, *etc.*: increase; *auf e-n Baum* ~ climb a tree; **2.** ♀ *n* (-s/*no pl.*) rise; *fig. a.* increase.

steigern ['ʃtaigərn] *v/t.* (ge-, *h*) raise; increase; enhance; *gr.* compare.

'Steigerung *f* (-/-en) raising; increase; enhancement; *gr.* comparison; '~**sstufe** *gr. f* degree of comparison.

Steigung ['ʃtaɪɡʊŋ] f (-/-en) rise, gradient, ascent, grade.

steil adj. [ʃtaɪl] steep; precipitous.

Stein [ʃtaɪn] m (-[e]s/-e) stone (a. ♀, ♂), Am. F a. rock; s. Edel2; '2'**alt** F adj. (as) old as the hills; '**bruch** m quarry; '**druck** m 1. (-[e]s/no pl.) lithography; 2. (-[e]s/-e) lithograph; '**drucker** m lithographer; '2**ern** adj. stone-..., of stone; fig. stony; '**gut** n (-[e]s/-e) crockery, stoneware, earthenware; '2**ig** adj. stony; 2**igen** ['ʃtaɪɡən] v/t. (ge-, h) stone; **igung** ['ʃtaɪɡʊŋ] f (-/-en) stoning; '**kohle** f mineral coal; pit-coal; '**metz** ['mets] m (-en/-en) stonemason; '**obst** n stone-fruit; '2'**reich** adj. immensely rich; '**salz** n (-es/no pl.) rock-salt; '**setzer** m (-s/-) pavio(u)r; '**wurf** m throwing of a stone; fig. stone's throw; '**zeit** f (-/no pl.) stone age.

Steiß [ʃtaɪs] m (-es/-e) buttocks pl., rump; '**bein** anat. n coccyx.

Stelldichein co. ['ʃtɛldɪç'ʔaɪn] n (-[s]/-[s]) meeting, appointment, rendezvous, Am. F a. date.

Stelle ['ʃtɛlə] f (-/-n) place; spot; point; employment, situation, post, place, F job; agency, authority; passage (of book, etc.); freie ~ vacancy; an deiner ~ in your place, if I were you; auf der ~ on the spot; zur ~ sein be present.

'**stellen** v/t. (ge-, h) put, place, set, stand; regulate (watch, etc.); set (watch, trap, task, etc.); stop (thief, etc.); hunt down (criminal); furnish, supply, provide; Bedingungen ~ make conditions; e-e Falle ~ a. lay a snare; sich ~ give o.s. up (to the police); stand, place o.s. (somewhere); sich krank ~ feign or pretend to be ill.

'**Stellen|angebot** n position offered, vacancy; '**gesuch** n application for a post; '2**weise** adv. here and there, sporadically.

'**Stellung** f (-/-en) position, posture; position, situation, (place of) employment; position, rank, status; arrangement (a. gr.); ✗ position; ~ nehmen give one's opinion (zu on), comment (upon); **nahme** ['~naː-mə] f (-/-en) attitude (zu to[wards]); opinion (on); comment (on); '2**slos** adj. unemployed.

'**stellvertret|end** adj. vicarious,

representative; acting, deputy; ~**er** Vorsitzender vice-chairman, deputy chairman; '2**er** m representative; deputy; proxy; '2**ung** f representation; substitution; proxy.

Stelz|bein contp. ['ʃtɛlts-] n wooden leg; '**e** f (-/-n) stilt; '2**en** mst iro. v/i. (ge-, sein) stalk.

stemmen ['ʃtɛmən] v/t. (ge-, h) lift (weight); sich ~ press (gegen against); fig. resist or oppose s.th.

Stempel ['ʃtɛmpəl] m (-s/-) stamp; ⊕ piston; ♀ pistil; '**geld** F n the dole; '**kissen** n ink-pad; '2**n** (ge-, h) 1. v/t. stamp; hallmark (gold, silver); 2. v/i. F: ~ gehen be on the dole.

Stengel ♀ ['ʃtɛŋəl] m (-s/-) stalk, stem.

Steno F ['ʃteno] f (-/no pl.) s. Stenographie; **gramm** n (-s/-e) stenograph; **graph** [~'ɡraːf] m (-en/-en) stenographer; **graphie** [~a'fiː] f (-/-n) stenography, shorthand; 2**graphieren** [~a'fiːrən] (no -ge-, h) 1. v/t. take down in shorthand; 2. v/i. know shorthand; 2**graphisch** [~'ɡraːfɪʃ] 1. adj. shorthand, stenographic; 2. adv. in shorthand; ~**typistin** [~ty'pɪstɪn] f (-/-nen) shorthand-typist.

Stepp|decke ['ʃtɛp-] f quilt, Am. a. comforter; 2**en** (ge-, h) 1. v/t. quilt; stitch; 2. v/i. tap-dance.

Sterbe|bett ['ʃtɛrbə-] n deathbed; '**fall** m (case of) death; '**kasse** f burial-fund.

'**sterben** 1. v/i. (irr., ge-, sein) die (a. fig.) (an dat. of); esp. ⚖ decease; 2. 2 n (-s/no pl.): im ~ liegen be dying.

sterblich ['ʃtɛrplɪç] 1. adj. mortal; 2. adv.: ~ verliebt sein be desperately in love (in acc. with); '2**keit** f (-/no pl.) mortality; '2**keitsziffer** f death-rate, mortality.

stereotyp adj. [stereo'tyːp] typ. stereotyped (a. fig.); **ieren** typ. [~y'piːrən] v/t. (no -ge-, h) stereotype.

steril adj. [ʃteˈriːl] sterile; **isieren** [~ili'ziːrən] v/t. (no -ge-, h) sterilize.

Stern [ʃtɛrn] m (-[e]s/-e) star (a. fig.); '**bild** ast. n constellation; '**deuter** m (-s/-) astrologer; '**deutung** f astrology; '**enbanner** n Star-Spangled Banner, Stars and Stripes pl., Old Glory; '**fahrt**

stilliegen

mot. f motor rally; '~gucker F *m* (-s/-) star-gazer; 'Qhell *adj.* starry, starlit; '~himmel *m* (-s/*no pl.*) starry sky; '~kunde *f* (-/*no pl.*) astronomy; '~schnuppe *f* (-/-n) shooting star; '~warte *f* observatory.

stet *adj.* [ʃteːt], '~ig *adj.* continual, constant; steady; 'Qigkeit *f* (-/*no pl.*) constancy, continuity; steadiness; ~ *adv.* always; constantly.

Steuer ['ʃtɔʏər] 1. *n* (-s/-) ♫ helm, rudder; steering-wheel; 2. *f* (-/-n) tax; duty; rate, local tax; '~amt *n s. Finanzamt* ~beamte *m* revenue officer; '~berater *m* (-s/-) tax adviser; '~bord ♫ *n* (-[e]s/-e) starboard; '~erhebung *f* levy of taxes; '~erklärung *f* tax-return; '~ermäßigung *f* tax allowance; 'Qfrei *adj.* tax-free; *goods:* duty-free; '~freiheit *f* (-/*no pl.*) exemption from taxes; '~hinterziehung *f* tax-evasion; '~jahr *n* fiscal year; '~klasse *f* tax-bracket; '~knüppel ✈ *m* control lever *or* stick; '~mann *m* (-[e]s/¨er, Steuerleute) ♫ helmsman, steersman, *Am. a.* wheelsman; coxwain (*a. rowing*); 'Qn (ge-) 1. *v/t.* (h) ♫, ✈ steer, navigate, pilot; ⊕ control; *fig.* direct, control; 2. *v/i.* (h) check *s.th.*; 3. *v/i.* (sein): ~ *in* (*acc.*) ♫ enter (*harbour, etc.*); ~ *nach* ♫ be bound for; 'Qpflichtig *adj.* taxable; *goods:* dutiable; '~rad ⊕ *n* steering-wheel; '~ruder ♫ *n* helm, rudder; '~satz *m* rate of assessment; '~ung *f* (-/-en) ♫, ⊕ steering; ⊕, ✈ control (*a. fig.*); ✈ controls *pl.*; '~veranlagung *f* tax assessment; '~zahler *m* (-s/-) taxpayer; ratepayer.

Steven ['ʃteːvən] *m* (-s/-) stem; stern-post.

Stich [ʃtiç] *m* (-[e]s/-e) prick (*of needle, etc.*); sting (*of insect, etc.*); stab (*of knife, etc.*); *sewing:* stitch; *cards:* trick; ⊕ engraving; ✿ stab; ~ *halten* hold water; *im* ~ *lassen* abandon, desert, forsake.

Stichel|ei *fig.* [ʃtiçə'laɪ] *f* (-/-en) gibe, jeer; 'Qn *fig. v/i.* (ge-, h) gibe (*gegen* at), jeer (at).

'Stich|flamme *f* flash; 'Qhaltig *adj.* valid, sound; ~ *sein* hold water; '~probe *f* random test *or* sample, *Am. a.* spot check; '~tag *m* fixed day; '~wahl *f* second ballot; '~-

wort *n* 1. *typ.* (-[e]s/¨er) head-word; 2. *thea.* (-[e]s/-e) cue; '~wunde *f* stab.

sticken ['ʃtikən] *v/t. and v/i.* (ge-, h) embroider.

'Stick|garn *n* embroidery floss; '~husten ✿ *m* (w)hooping cough; 'Qig *adj.* stuffy; close; '~stoff ♔ *m* (-[e]s/*no pl.*) nitrogen.

stieben ['ʃtiːbən] *v/i.* (*irr.,*) ge-, h, sein) sparks, *etc.:* fly about.

Stief... ['ʃtiːf-] step...

Stiefel ['ʃtiːfəl] *m* (-s/-) boot; '~knecht *m* bootjack; '~schaft *m* leg of a boot.

'Stief|mutter *f* (-/¨) stepmother; ~mütterchen ♀ *f* '~mytərçən] *n* (-s/-) pansy; '~vater *m* stepfather.

stieg [ʃtiːk] *pret. of* steigen.

Stiel [ʃtiːl] *m* (-[e]s/-e) handle; helve (*of weapon, tool*); haft (*of axe*); stick (*of broom*); ♀ stalk.

Stier [ʃtiːr] 1. *zo. m* (-[e]s/-e) bull; 2. ♀ *adj.* staring; 'Qen *v/i.* (ge-, h) stare (*auf acc.* at); '~kampf *m* bull-fight.

stieß [ʃtiːs] *pret. of* stoßen.

Stift [ʃtift] 1. *m* (-[e]s/-e) pin; peg; tack; pencil, crayon; F *fig.:* youngster; apprentice; 2. *n* (-[e]s/-e, -er) charitable institution; 'Qen *v/t.* (ge-, h) endow, give, *Am. a.* donate; found; *fig.* cause; make (*mischief, peace*); '~er *m* (-s/-) donor; founder; *fig.* author; '~ung *f* (-/-en) (charitable) endowment, donation; foundation.

Stil [ʃtiːl] *m* (-[e]s/-e) style (*a. fig.*); 'Qgerecht *adj.* stylish; Qisieren [ʃtili'ziːrən] *v/t.* (*no* -ge-, h) stylize; Qistisch [ʃti'listiʃ] *adj.* stylistic.

still *adj.* [ʃtil] still, quiet; silent; ♥ dull, slack; secret; ~! silence!; *im* ~*en* secretly; ~*er Gesellschafter* ✶ sleeping *or* silent partner; *der* Qe *Ozean* the Pacific (Ocean); 'Qe *f* (-/*no pl.*) stillness, quiet(ness); silence; *in aller* ~ quietly, silently; privately; 'Qeben *paint.* ['ʃtiːlbən] *n* (-s/-) still life; '~egen ['ʃtiːlgən] *v/t.* (*sep.*, -ge-, h) shut down (*factory, etc.*); stop (*traffic*); '~en *v/t.* (ge-, h) soothe (*pain*); appease (*appetite*); quench (*thirst*); sta(u)nch (*blood*); nurse (*baby*); '~halten *v/i.* (*irr.* halten, *sep.*, -ge-, h) keep still; '~iegen ['ʃtiːligən] *v/i.* (*irr.* liegen, *sep.*, -ge-, h) factory, *etc.*: be shut down; *traffic*: be suspended; *machines, etc.*: be idle.

stillos *adj.* ['ʃti:llo:s] without style.

'stillschweigen 1. *v/i.* (*irr. schweigen, sep., ge-, h*) be silent; ~ *zu et.* ignore s.th.; **2.** ♀ *n* (-s/*no pl.*) silence; secrecy; ~ *bewahren* observe secrecy; *et. mit* ~ *übergehen* pass s.th. over in silence; **'~d** *adj.* silent; *agreement, etc.*: tacit.

'Still|stand *m* (-[e]s/*no pl.*) standstill; *fig.*: stagnation (*a.* ♠); deadlock; **'♀stehen** *v/i.* (*irr. stehen, sep., -ge-, h*) stop; be at a standstill; *stillgestanden!* ✗ attention!

'Stil|möbel *n/pl.* period furniture; **'♀voll** *adj.* stylish.

Stimm|band *anat.* ['ʃtim-] *n* (-[e]s/*⁻er*) vocal c(h)ord; **'♀berechtigt** *adj.* entitled to vote; **'~e** *f* (-/-n) voice (*a.* ♪, *fig.*); vote; comment; ♪ part; **'♀en** (*ge-, h*) **1.** *v/t.* tune (*piano, etc.*); *j-n fröhlich* ~ put s.o. in a merry mood; **2.** *v/i.* be true or right; *sum, etc.*: be correct; ~ *für* vote for; **'~enmehrheit** *f* majority or plurality of votes; **'~enthaltung** *f* abstention; **'~enzählung** *f* counting of votes; **'~gabel** ♪ *f* tuning-fork; **'~recht** *n* right to vote; *pol.* franchise; **'~ung** *f* (-/-en) ♪ tune; *fig.* mood, humo(u)r; **'♀ungsvoll** *adj.* impressive; **'~zettel** *m* ballot, voting-paper.

stinken ['ʃtiŋkən] *v/i.* (*irr., ge-, h*) stink (*nach of*); *fig.* be fishy.

Stipendium *univ.* [ʃti'pɛndiʊm] *n* (-s/*Stipendien*) scholarship; exhibition.

stipp|en ['ʃtipən] *v/t.* (*ge-, h*) dip, steep; **'♀visite** F *f* flying visit.

Stirn [ʃtirn] *f* (-/-en) forehead, brow; *fig.* face, cheek; *j-m die* ~ *bieten* make head against s.o.; *s. runzeln;* **'~runzeln** *n* (-s/*no pl.*) frown(ing).

stob [ʃto:p] *pret. of* stieben.

stöbern F ['ʃtø:bərn] *v/i.* (*ge-, h*) rummage (*about*) (*in dat. in*).

stochern ['ʃtɔxərn] *v/i.* (*ge-, h*): ~ *in* (*dat.*) poke (*fire*); pick (*teeth*).

Stock [ʃtɔk] *m* **1.** (-[e]s/*⁻e*) stick; cane; ♪ baton; beehive; ♀ stock; **2.** (-[e]s/-) stor(e)y, floor; *im ersten* ~ on the first floor, *Am.* on the second floor; **'♀be'trunken** F *adj.* dead drunk; **'♀blind** F *adj.* stone-blind; **'♀dunkel** F *adj.* pitch-dark.

Stöckelschuh ['ʃtœkəl-] *m* high-heeled shoe.

'stocken *v/i.* (*ge-, h*) stop; *liquid*: stagnate (*a. fig.*); *speaker*: break down; *voice*: falter; *traffic*: be blocked; *ihm stockte das Blut* his blood curdled.

'Stock|engländer F *m* thorough or true-born Englishman; **'♀finster** F *adj.* pitch-dark; **'~fleck** *m* spot of mildew; **'♀(fleck)ig** *adj.* foxy, mildewy; **'♀nüchtern** F *adj.* (as) sober as a judge; **'~schnupfen** ✎ *m* chronic rhinitis; **'♀taub** F *adj.* stone-deaf; **'~ung** *f* (-/-en) stop (-page); stagnation (*of liquid*) (*a. fig.*); block (*of traffic*); **'~werk** *n* stor(e)y, floor.

Stoff [ʃtɔf] *m* (-[e]s/-e) matter, substance; material, fabric, textile; material, stuff; *fig.*: subject(-matter); food; **'♀lich** *adj.* material.

stöhnen ['ʃtø:nən] *v/i.* (*ge-, h*) groan, moan.

Stolle ['ʃtɔlə] *f* (-/-n) loaf-shaped Christmas cake; **'~n** *m* (-s/-) *s.* Stolle; ✗ tunnel, gallery (*a.* ✗).

stolpern ['ʃtɔlpərn] *v/i.* (*ge-, sein*) stumble (*über acc. over*), trip (*over*) (*both a. fig.*).

stolz [ʃtɔlts] **1.** *adj.* proud (*auf acc. of*) (*a. fig.*); haughty; **2.** ♀ *m* (-es/*no pl.*) pride (*auf acc. in*); haughtiness; **~ieren** [~'tsi:rən] *v/i.* (*no -ge-, sein*) strut, flaunt.

stopfen ['ʃtɔpfən] (*ge-, h*) **1.** *v/t.* stuff; fill (*pipe*); cram (*poultry, etc.*); darn (*sock, etc.*); *j-m den Mund* ~ stop s.o.'s mouth; **2.** ✎ *v/i.* cause constipation.

'Stopf|garn *n* darning-yarn; **'~nadel** *f* darning-needle.

Stoppel ['ʃtɔpəl] *f* (-/-n) stubble; **'~bart** F *m* stubbly beard; **'♀ig** *adj.* stubbly.

stopp|en ['ʃtɔpən] (*ge-, h*) **1.** *v/t.* stop; time, F clock; **2.** *v/i.* stop; **'♀licht** *mot. n* stop-light; **'♀uhr** *f* stop-watch.

Stöpsel ['ʃtœpsəl] *m* (-s/-) stopper, cork; plug (*a.* ♀); F *fig.* whippersnapper; **'♀n** *v/t.* (*ge-, h*) stopper, cork; plug (*up*).

Storch *orn.* [ʃtɔrç] *m* (-[e]s/*⁻e*) stork.

stören ['ʃtø:rən] (*ge-, h*) **1.** *v/t.* disturb; trouble; *radio*: jam (*reception*); *lassen Sie sich nicht* ~*!* don't let me disturb you!; *darf ich Sie* kurz ~? may I trouble you for a minute?; **2.** *v/i.* be intruding; be in the way; **2fried** ['~friːt] *m* (-[e]s/-e) troublemaker; intruder.

störr|ig *adj.* ['ʃtœ:rɪç], **'~isch** *adj.* stubborn, obstinate; *a.* horse: restive.

'Störung *f* (-/-en) disturbance; trouble (*a.* ⊕); breakdown; *radio*: jamming, interference.

Stoß [ʃtoːs] *m* (-es/-̈e) push, shove; thrust (*a.* fencing); kick; butt; shock; knock, strike; blow; swimming, billiards: stroke; jolt (*of car, etc.*); pile, stock, heap; '~dämpfer *mot. m* shock-absorber; **2en** (*irr.*, ge-) **1.** *v/t.* (*h*) push, shove; thrust (*weapon, etc.*); kick; butt; knock, strike; pound (*pepper, etc.*); sich ~ an (*dat.*) strike or knock against; *fig.* take offence at; **2.** *v/i.* (*h*) thrust (*nach an.*); kick (at); butt (at); goat, etc.: butt; car: jolt; ~ an (*acc.*) adjoin, border on; **3.** *v/i.* (*sein*): F ~ auf (*acc.*) come across; meet with (*opposition, etc.*); ~ gegen or an (*acc.*) knock or strike against.

'Stoß|seufzer *m* ejaculation; '~stange *mot. f* bumper; '2weise *adv.* by jerks; by fits and starts; '~zahn *m* tusk.

stottern ['ʃtɔtərn] (ge-, *h*) **1.** *v/t.* stutter (out); stammer; **2.** *v/i.* stutter; stammer; F *mot.* conk (out).

Straf|anstalt ['ʃtraːf˘-] *f* penal institution; prison; *Am.* penitentiary; '~arbeit *f* imposition, F impo(t); **2bar** *adj.* punishable, penal; '~e *f* (-/-n) punishment; ⚖, ✝, sports, *fig.* penalty; fine; bei ~ von on or under pain of; zur ~ as a punishment; '2en *v/t.* (ge-, *h*) punish.

straff *adj.* [ʃtraf] tight; rope: *a.* taut; *fig.* strict, rigid.

'straf|fällig *adj.* liable to prosecution; '2gesetz *n* penal law; '2gesetzbuch *n* penal code.

sträf|lich ['ʃtreːflɪç] culpable; reprehensible; inexcusable; **2ling** ['~lɪŋ] *m* (-s/-e) convict, *Am.* sl. a. lag.

'straf|los *adj.* unpunished; '2losigkeit *f* (-/no pl.) impunity; '2porto *n* surcharge; '2predigt *f* severe lecture; j-m e-e ~ halten lecture s.o. severely; '2prozeß *m* criminal action; '2raum *m* football: penalty

area; '2stoß *m* football: penalty kick; '2verfahren *n* criminal proceedings *pl.*

Strahl [ʃtraːl] *m* (-[e]s/-en) ray (*a. fig.*); beam; flash (*of lightning, etc.*); jet (*of water, etc.*); '2en *v/i.* (ge-, *h*) radiate, shine (vor *dat.* with); *fig.* beam (vor *dat.* with), shine (with); '~ung *f* (-/-en) radiation, rays *pl.*

Strähne ['ʃtreːnə] *f* (-/-n) lock, strand (*of hair*); skein, hank (*of yarn*); *fig.* stretch.

stramm *adj.* [ʃtram] tight; rope: *a.* taut; stalwart; *soldier*: smart.

strampeln ['ʃtrampəln] *v/i.* (ge-, *h*) kick.

Strand [ʃtrant] *m* (-[e]s/-e) beach; '~anzug *m* beach-suit; **2en** ['~dən] *v/i.* (ge-, *h*) ⚓ strand, run ashore; *fig.* fail, founder; '~gut *n* stranded goods *pl.*; *fig.* wreckage; '~korb *m* roofed wicker chair for use on the beach; **~promenade** ['~promənaːdə] *f* (-/-n) promenade, *Am.* boardwalk.

Strang [ʃtraŋ] *m* (-[e]s/-̈e) cord (*a. anat.*); rope; halter (*for hanging s.o.*); trace (*of harness*); 🚂 track; über die Stränge schlagen kick over the traces.

Strapaze [ʃtraˈpaːtsə] *f* (-/-n) fatigue; toil; **2ieren** [~aˈtsiːrən] *v/t.* (no -ge-, *h*) fatigue, strain (*a. fig.*); wear out (*fabric, etc.*); **2ierfähig** *adj.* [~aˈtsiːr-] long-lasting; **2iös** *adj.* [~aˈtsjøːs] fatiguing.

Straße ['ʃtraːsə] *f* (-/-n) road, highway; street (*of town, etc.*); strait; auf der ~ on the road; in the street.

'Straßen|anzug *m* lounge-suit, *Am.* business suit; '~bahn *f* tram(way), tram-line, *Am.* street railway; streetcar line; s. Straßenbahnwagen; '~bahnhaltestelle *f* tram stop, *Am.* streetcar stop; '~bahnwagen *m* tram(-car), *Am.* streetcar; '~beleuchtung *f* street lighting; '~damm *m* roadway; '~händler *m* hawker; '~junge *m* street arab, *Am.* street Arab; '~kehrer *m* (-s/-) scavenger, street orderly; '~kreuzung *f* crossing, cross roads; '~reinigung *f* street-cleaning, scavenging; '~rennen *n* road-race.

strategisch *adj.* [ʃtraˈteːgɪʃ] strategic(al).

sträuben ['ʃtrɔybən] *v/t.* (ge-, *h*) ruffle up (*its feathers, etc.*); sich ~

hair: stand on end; *sich* ~ *gegen* kick against *or* at.

Strauch [ʃtraux] *m* (-[e]s/⁼er) shrub; bush.

straucheln [ˈʃtrauxəln] *v/i.* (ge-, sein) stumble (*über acc.* over, at), trip (over) (*both a. fig.*).

Strauß [ʃtraus] *m* **1.** *orn.* (-es/-e) ostrich; **2.** (-es/⁼e) bunch (*of flowers*), bouquet; *strife*, combat.

Strebe [ˈʃtreːbə] *f* (-/-n) strut, support, brace.

'**streben 1.** *v/i.* (ge-, h): ~ *nach* strive for *or* after, aspire to *or* after; **2.** 2 *n* (-s/*no pl.*) striving (*nach* for, after), aspiration (for, after); effort, endeavo(u)r.

'**Streber** *m* (-s/-) pusher, careerist; *at school*: *sl.* swot.

strebsam *adj.* [ˈʃtreːpzaːm] assiduous; ambitious; '2keit *f* (-/*no pl.*) assiduity; ambition.

Strecke [ˈʃtrɛkə] *f* (-/-n) stretch; route; tract, extent; distance (*a. sports*); course; 🚉, *etc.*: section, line; *hunt.* bag; *zur* ~ *bringen hunt.* bag, hunt down (*a. fig.*); '2n *v/t.* (ge-, h) stretch, extend; dilute (*fluid*); *sich* ~ stretch (o.s.); *die Waffen* ~ lay down one's arms; *fig. a.* give in.

Streich [ʃtraiç] *m* (-[e]s/-e) stroke; blow; *fig.* trick, prank; *j-m e-n* ~ *spielen* play a trick on s.o.; '2eln [ˈ~əln] *v/t.* (ge-, h) stroke, caress; pat; '2en (*irr.*, ge-) **1.** *v/t.* (h) rub; spread (*butter, etc.*); paint; strike out, delete, cancel (*a. fig.*); strike, lower (*flag, sail*); **2.** *v/i.* (sein) prowl (*um round*); **3.** *v/i.* (h): *mit der Hand über et.* ~ pass one's hand over s.th.; '~holz *n* match; '~instrument ♪ *n* stringed instrument; '~orchester *n* string band; '~riemen *m* strop.

Streif [ʃtraif] *m* (-[e]s/-e) *s.* Streifen; '~band *n* (-[e]s/⁼er) wrapper; ~e *f* (-/-n) patrol; patrolman; raid.

'**streifen** (ge-) **1.** *v/t.* (h) stripe, streak; graze, touch lightly in passing, brush; touch (up)on (*subject*); **2.** *v/i.* (sein): ~ *durch* rove, wander through; **3.** *v/i.* (h): ~ *an* (*acc.*) graze, brush; *fig.* border *or* verge on; **4.** 2 *m* (-s/-) strip; stripe; streak.

'**streif**|**ig** *adj.* striped; '2licht *n* sidelight; '2schuß ✕ *m* grazing shot; '2zug *m* ramble; ✕ raid.

Streik [ʃtraik] *m* (-[e]s/-s) strike, *Am.* F *a.* walkout; *in den* ~ *treten* go on strike, *Am.* F *a.* walk out; '~brecher *m* (-s/-) strike-breaker, blackleg, scab; '2en *v/i.* (ge-, h) (be on) strike; go on strike, *Am.* F *a.* walk out; '~ende [ˈ~əndə] *m, f* (-n/-n) striker; '~posten *m* picket.

Streit [ʃtrait] *m* (-[e]s/-e) quarrel; dispute; conflict; 🏛 litigation; '2bar *adj.* pugnacious; '2en *v/i. and v/refl.* (*irr.*, ge-, h) quarrel (*mit* with; *wegen* for; *über acc.* about); '~frage *f* controversy, (point of) issue; '2ig *adj.* debatable, controversial; *j-m et.* ~ *machen* dispute s.o.'s right to s.th.; '~igkeiten *f/pl.* quarrels *pl.*; disputes *pl.*; '~kräfte ✕ [ˈ~krɛftə] *f/pl.* (military *or* armed) forces *pl.*; '2lustig *adj.* pugnacious, aggressive; '2süchtig *adj.* quarrelsome; pugnacious.

streng [ʃtrɛŋ] **1.** *adj.* severe; stern; strict; austere; *discipline, etc.*: rigorous; *weather, climate*: inclement; *examination*: stiff; **2.** *adv.*: ~ *vertraulich* in strict confidence; '2e *f* (-/*no pl.*) *s.* streng 1: severity; sternness; strictness; austerity; rigo(u)r; inclemency; stiffness; '~genommen *adv.* strictly speaking; '~gläubig *adj.* orthodox.

Streu [ʃtrɔy] *f* (-/-en) litter; '2en *v/t.* (ge-, h) strew, scatter; '~zucker *m* castor sugar.

Strich [ʃtriç] **1.** *m* (-[e]s/-e) stroke; line; dash; tract (*of land*); *j-m e-n* ~ *durch die Rechnung machen* queer s.o.'s pitch; **2.** 2 *pret. of streichen*; '~regen *m* local shower; '2weise *adv.* here and there.

Strick [ʃtrik] *m* (-[e]s/-e) cord; rope; halter, rope (*for hanging s.o.*); F *fig.* (young) rascal; '2en *v/t. and v/i.* (ge-, h) knit; '~garn *n* knitting-yarn; '~jacke *f* cardigan, jersey; '~leiter *f* rope-ladder; '~nadel *f* knitting-needle; '~waren *f/pl.* knitwear; '~zeug *n* knitting(-things *pl.*).

Striemen [ˈʃtriːmən] *m* (-s/-) weal, wale.

Strippe F [ˈʃtripə] *f* (-/-n) band; string; shoe-lace; *an der* ~ *hängen* be on the phone.

stritt [ʃtrit] *pret. of streiten*; '~ig *adj.* debatable, controversial; *~er Punkt* (point of) issue.

Stroh [ʃtroː] *n* (-[e]s/*no pl.*) straw;

thatch; '**~dach** n thatch(ed roof); '**~halm** m straw; nach e-m ~ greifen catch at a straw; '**~hut** m straw hat; '**~mann** m man of straw; scarecrow; fig. dummy; '**~sack** m straw mattress; '**~witwe** F f grass widow.

Strolch [ʃtrɔlç] m (-[e]s/-e) scamp, F vagabond; '**Ωen** v/i. (ge-, sein): ~ durch rove.

Strom [ʃtroːm] m (-[e]s/ᵘe) stream (a. fig.); (large) river; ⚡ current (a. fig.); es regnet in Strömen it is pouring with rain; Ω'**ab**(wärts) adv. down-stream; Ω'**auf**(wärts) adv. up-stream.

strömen [ˈʃtrøːmən] v/i. (ge-, sein) stream; flow, run; rain: pour; people: stream, pour (aus out of; in acc. into).

'**Strom|kreis** ⚡ m circuit; '**~linienform** f (-/no pl.) streamline shape; 'Ω**linienförmig** adj. streamline(d); '**~schnelle** f (-/-n) rapid, Am. a. riffle; '**~sperre** f f stoppage of current.   [trend, tendency.]

'**Strömung** f (-/-en) current; fig.a.

'**Stromzähler** ⚡ m electric meter.

Strophe [ˈʃtroːfə] f (-/-n) stanza, verse.

strotzen [ˈʃtrɔtsən] v/i. (ge-, h): ~ von abound in; teem with (blunders, etc.); burst with (health, etc.).

Strudel [ˈʃtruːdəl] m (-s/-) eddy, whirlpool; fig. whirl; 'Ω**n** v/i. (ge-, h) swirl, whirl.   [ture.]

Struktur [ʃtrʊkˈtuːr] f (-/-en) struc-

Strumpf [ʃtrʊmpf] m (-[e]s/ᵘe) stocking; '**~band** n (-[e]s/ᵘer) garter; '**~halter** m (-s/-) suspender, Am. garter; '**~waren** f/pl. hosiery.

struppig adj. [ˈʃtrʊpɪç] hair: rough, shaggy; dog, etc.: shaggy.

Stube [ˈʃtuːbə] f (-/-n) room.

'**Stuben|hocker** fig. m (-s/-) stay-at-home; '**~mädchen** n chambermaid; 'Ω**rein** adj. house-trained.

Stück [ʃtyk] n (-[e]s/-e) piece (a. ♪); fragment; head (of cattle); lump (of sugar); thea. play; aus freien ~en of one's own accord; in ~e gehen or schlagen break to pieces; '**~arbeit** f piece-work; 'Ω**weise** adv. piece by piece; (by) piecemeal; ✝ by the piece; '**~werk** fig. n patchwork.

Student [ʃtuˈdɛnt] m (-en/-en), **~in** f (-/-nen) student, undergraduate.

Studie [ˈʃtuːdjə] f (-/-n) study (über

acc., zu of, in) (a. art, literature); paint, etc.: sketch; '**~nrat** m (-[e]s/ᵘe) appr. secondary-school teacher; '**~nreise** f study trip.

studier|en [ʃtuˈdiːrən] (no -ge-, h) 1. v/t. study, read (law, etc.); 2. v/i. study; be a student; Ω**zimmer** n study.

Studium [ˈʃtuːdjʊm] n (-s/Studien) study (a. fig.); studies pl.

Stufe [ˈʃtuːfə] f (-/-n) step; fig.: degree; grade; stage.

'**Stufen|folge** fig. f gradation; '**~leiter** f step-ladder; fig. scale; 'Ω**weise** 1. adj. gradual; 2. adv. gradually, by degrees.

Stuhl [ʃtuːl] m (-[e]s/ᵘe) chair, seat; in a church: pew; weaving: loom; ⚕. Stuhlgang; '**~bein** n leg of a chair; '**~gang** ⚕ m (-[e]s/no pl.) stool; motion; '**~lehne** f back of a chair.

stülpen [ˈʃtylpən] v/t. (ge-, h) put (über acc. over); clap (hat) (auf acc. on).

stumm adj. [ʃtʊm] dumb, mute; fig. a. silent; gr. silent, mute.

Stummel [ˈʃtʊməl] m (-s/-) stump;}

'**Stummfilm** m silent film.   [stub.]

Stümper F [ˈʃtympər] m (-s/-) bungler; '**~ei** f [~ˈraɪ] f (-/-en) bungling; bungle; 'Ω**haft** adj. bungling; botch; 'Ω**n** F v/i. (ge-, h) bungle, botch.

stumpf [ʃtʊmpf] 1. adj. blunt; ℞ angle: obtuse; senses: dull, obtuse; apathetic; 2. Ω m (-[e]s/ᵘe) stump, stub; mit ~ und Stiel root and branch; 'Ω**sinn** m (-[e]s/no pl.) stupidity, dul(l)ness; '**~sinnig** adj. stupid, dull.

Stunde [ˈʃtʊndə] f (-/-n) hour; lesson, Am. a. period; 'Ω**n** v/t. (ge-, h) grant respite for.

'**Stunden|kilometer** m kilometre per hour, Am. kilometer per hour; 'Ω**lang** 1. adj.: nach ~em Warten after hours of waiting; 2. adv. for hours (and hours); '**~lohn** m hourly wage; '**~plan** m timetable, Am. schedule; 'Ω**weise** 1. adj.: ~ Beschäftigung part-time employment; 2. adv. by the hour; '**~zeiger** m hour-hand.

stündlich [ˈʃtʏntlɪç] 1. adj. hourly; 2. adv. hourly, every hour; at any hour.

'**Stundung** f (-/-en) respite.

stur F *adj.* [ʃtuːr] *gaze:* fixed, staring; *p.* pigheaded, mulish.

Sturm [ʃturm] *m* (-[e]s/ᵉe) storm (*a. fig.*); ♆ gale.

stürm|en ['ʃtyrmən] (ge-) **1.** *v/i.* (h) ✕ storm (*a. fig.*); **2.** *v/i.* (h) *wind:* storm, rage; es stürmt it is stormy weather; **3.** *v/i.* (sein) rush; '2**er** *m* (-s/-) football, *etc.:* forward; '**⹁isch** *adj.* stormy; *fig.:* impetuous, tumultuous.

'**Sturm|schritt** ✕ *m* double-quick step; '**⹁trupp** ✕ *m* storming-party; '**⹁wind** *m* storm-wind.

Sturz [ʃturts] *m* (-es/ᵉe) fall, tumble, overthrow (*of government, etc.*); *fig.* ruin; ✝ slump; '**⹁bach** *m* torrent.

stürzen ['ʃtyrtsən] (ge-) **1.** *v/i.* (sein) (have a) fall, tumble; *fig.* rush, plunge (*in acc.* into); **2.** *v/t.* (h) throw; overthrow (*government, etc.*); *fig.* plunge (*in acc.* into), precipitate (into); j-n ins Unglück ᵕ ruin s.o.; sich in Schulden ᵕ plunge into debt.

'**Sturz|flug** ✈ *m* (nose)dive; '**⹁helm** *m* crash-helmet.

Stute *zo.* ['ʃtuːtə] *f* (-/-n) mare.

Stütze ['ʃtytsə] *f* (-/-n) support, prop, stay (*all a. fig.*).

stutzen ['ʃtutsən] (ge-) **1.** *v/t.* cut (hedge); crop (ears, tail, hair); clip (hedge, wing); trim (hair, beard, hedge); dock (tail); lop (tree); **2.** *v/i.* start (bei at); stop dead or short.

'**stützen** *v/t.* (ge-, h) support, prop, stay (*all a. fig.*); ᵕ auf (*acc.*) base or found on; sich ᵕ auf (*acc.*) lean on; *fig.* rely (up)on; argument, *etc.:* be based on.

'**Stutz|er** *m* (-s/-) dandy, fop, *Am. a.* dude; '2**ig** *adj.* suspicious; ᵕ machen make suspicious.

'**Stütz|pfeiler** 🏛 *m* abutment; '**⹁punkt** *m* phys. fulcrum; ✕ base.

Subjekt [zup'jɛkt] *n* (-[e]s/-e) *gr.* subject; *contp.* individual; 2**iv** *adj.* [⹁'tiːf] subjective; **⹁ivität** [⹁ivi'tɛːt] *f* (-/no pl.) subjectivity.

Substantiv *gr.* ['zupstantiːf] *n* (-s/-e) noun, substantive; (*a. fig.*); 2**isch** *gr. adj.* ['⹁viʃ] substantival.

Substanz [zup'stants] *f* (-/-en) substance (*a. fig.*).

subtra|hieren ♈ [zuptra'hiːrən] *v/t.* (*no* -ge-, h) subtract; 2**ktion** ♈

[⹁k'tsjoːn] *f* (-/-en) subtraction.

Such|dienst ['zuːx-] *m* tracing service; '**⹁e** *f* (-/no pl.) search (nach for); auf der ᵕ nach in search of; '2**en** (ge-, h) **1.** *v/t.* seek (advice, *etc.*); search for; look for; Sie haben hier nichts zu ᵕ you have no business to be here; **2.** *v/i.:* ᵕ nach seek for or after; search for; look for; '**⹁er** *phot. m* (-s/-) view-finder.

Sucht [zuxt] *f* (-/ᵉe) mania (nach for), rage (for), addiction (to).

süchtig *adj.* ['zyçtiç] having a mania (nach for); ᵕ sein be a drug addict; 2**e** ['⹁gə] *m, f* (-n/-n) drug addict or fiend.

Süd *geogr.* [zyːt], ᵕ**en** ['⹁dən] *m* (-s/no pl.) south; **⹁früchte** ['zyːt-fryçtə] *f/pl.* fruits from the south; '2**lich 1.** *adj.* south(ern); southerly; **2.** *adv.:* ᵕ von (to the) south of; **⹁'ost** *geogr.*, **⹁'osten** *m* (-s/no pl.) south-east; 2**östlich** *adj.* south-east(ern); **⹁pol** *geogr. m* (-s/no pl.) South Pole; 2**wärts** *adv.* ['⹁verts] southward(s); **⹁'west** *geogr.*, **⹁'westen** *m* (-s/no pl.) south-west; 2**westlich** *adj.* south-west(ern); '**⹁wind** *m* south-wind.

süffig F *adj.* ['zyfiç] palatable, tasty.

suggerieren [zuge'riːrən] *v/t.* (*no* -ge-, h) suggest.

suggestiv *adj.* [zuges'tiːf] suggestive.

Sühne ['zyːnə] *f* (-/-n) expiation, atonement; 2**n** *v/t.* (ge-, h) expiate, atone for.

Sülze ['zyltsə] *f* (-/-n) jellied meat.

summ|arisch *adj.* [zu'maːriʃ] summary (*a. 🏛*); '2**e** *f* (-/-n) sum (*a. fig.*); (sum) total; amount.

'**summen** (ge-, h) **1.** *v/i.* bees, *etc.:* buzz, hum; **2.** *v/t.* hum (song, *etc.*).

sum'mieren *v/t.* (*no* -ge-, h) sum or add up; sich ᵕ run up.

Sumpf [zumpf] *m* (-[e]s/ᵉe) swamp, bog, marsh; 2**ig** *adj.* swampy, boggy, marshy.

Sünd|e ['zyndə] *f* (-/-n) sin (*a. fig.*); '**⹁enbock** F *m* scapegoat; '**⹁er** *m* (-s/-) sinner; 2**haft** ['⹁haft] **1.** *adj.* sinful; **2.** *adv.:* F ᵕ teuer awfully expensive; 2**ig** ['⹁diç] *adj.* sinful; 2**igen** ['⹁digən] *v/i.* (ge-, h) (commit a) sin.

Superlativ ['zuːperlatiːf] *m* (-s/-e) *gr.* superlative degree; in ᵕen sprechen speak in superlatives.

Suppe ['zupə] f (-/-n) soup; broth.
'**Suppen|löffel** m soup-spoon; '~schöpfer m soup ladle; '~schüssel f tureen; '~teller m soup-plate.

surren ['zurən] v/i. (ge-, h) whir(r); insects: buzz.

Surrogat [zuro'ga:t] n (-[e]s/-e) substitute.

suspendieren [zuspen'di:rən] v/t. (no -ge-, h) suspend.

süß adj. [zy:s] sweet (a. fig.); '2e f (-/no pl.) sweetness; '~en v/t. (ge-, h) sweeten; '2igkeiten pl. sweets pl., sweetmeats pl., Am. a. candy; '~lich adj. sweetish; mawkish (a. fig.); '2stoff m saccharin(e); '2wasser n (-s/-) fresh water.

Symbol [zym'bo:l] n (-s/-e) symbol; ~ik f (-/no pl.) symbolism; 2isch adj. symbolic(al).

Symmetr|ie [zyme'tri:] f (-/-n) symmetry; 2isch adj. [~'me:triʃ] symmetric(al).

Sympath|ie [zympa'ti:] f (-/-n) liking; 2isch adj. [~'pa:tiʃ] likable; er ist mir ~ I like him;

2isieren [~i'zi:rən] v/i. (no -ge-, h) sympathize (mit with).

Symphonie ♪ [zymfo'ni:] f (-/-n) symphony; ~orchester n symphony orchestra.

Symptom [zymp'to:m] n (-s/-e) symptom; 2atisch adj. [~o'ma:tiʃ] symptomatic (für of). [synagogue.]

Synagoge [zyna'go:gə] f (-/-n)|

synchronisieren [zynkroni'zi:rən] v/t. (no -ge-, h) synchronize; dub.

Syndik|at [zyndi'ka:t] n (-[e]s/-e) syndicate; ~us ['zyndikus] m (-/-se, Syndizi) syndic. [syncope.]

Synkope ♪ [zyn'ko:pə] f (-/-n)|

synonym [zyno'ny:m] **1.** adj. synonymous; **2.** 2 n (-s/-e) synonym.

Syntax gr. ['zyntaks] f (-/-en) syntax.

synthetisch adj. [zyn'te:tiʃ] synthetic.

System [zys'te:m] n (-s/-e) system; scheme; 2atisch adj. [~ema:tiʃ] systematic(al), methodic(al).

Szene ['stse:nə] f (-/-n) scene (a. fig.); in ~ setzen stage; ~rie [stsenə'ri:] f (-/-n) scenery.

T

Tabak ['ta:bak, 'tabak, ta'bak] m (-s/-e) tobacco; (')~händler m tobacconist; (')~sbeutel m tobacco-pouch; (')~sdose f snuff-box; (')~waren pl. tobacco products pl., F smokes pl.

tabellarisch [tabε'la:riʃ] **1.** adj. tabular; **2.** adv. in tabular form.

Tabelle [ta'bεlə] f (-/-n) table; schedule.

Tablett [ta'blεt] n (-[e]s/-e, -s) tray; of metal: salver; ~e pharm. f (-/-n) tablet; lozenge.

Tachometer [taxo'-] n, m (-s/-) ⊕ tachometer; mot. a. speedometer.

Tadel ['ta:dəl] m (-s/-) blame; censure; reprimand, rebuke, reproof; reproach; at school: bad mark; '2los adj. faultless, blameless; excellent, splendid; '2n v/t. (ge-, h) blame (wegen for); censure; reprimand, rebuke, reprove; scold; find fault with.

Tafel ['ta:fəl] f (-/-n) table; plate (a. book illustration); slab; on houses, etc.: tablet, plaque; slate; black-

board; signboard, notice-board, Am. billboard; cake, bar (of chocolate, etc.); dinner-table; dinner; 2förmig adj. ['~fœrmiç] tabular; '~geschirr n dinner-service, dinner-set; '~land n table-land, plateau; '2n v/i. (ge-, h) dine; feast, banquet; '~service n s. Tafelgeschirr; '~silber n silver plate, Am. silverware.

Täf(e)lung ['tε:f(ə)luŋ] f (-/-en) wainscot, panelling.

Taft [taft] m (-[e]s/-e) taffeta.

Tag [ta:k] m (-[e]s/-e) day; officially: a. date; am or bei ~e by day; e-s ~es one day; den ganzen ~ all day long; ~ für ~ day by day; über ~e ⚒ aboveground; unter ~e ⚒ underground; heute vor acht ~en a week ago; heute in acht (vierzehn) ~en today or this day week (fortnight), a week (fortnight) today; denkwürdiger or freudiger ~ red-letter day; freier ~ day off; guten ~! how do you do?; good morning!; good afternoon!; F hallo!, hullo!, Am.

hello!; *am hellichten* ~*e* in broad daylight; *es wird* ~ it dawns; *an den* ~ *bringen* (*kommen*) bring (come) to light; *bis auf den heutigen* ~ to this day; $\mathfrak{L}$**'aus** *adv.*: ~, *tagein* day in, day out.

Tage|blatt *n* daily (paper); '~**buch** *n* journal, diary.

tagein *adv.* [ta:k'aın] *s.* tagaus.

tage|lang *adv.* ['ta:gə-] day after day, for days together; $\mathfrak{L}$**lohn** *m* day's or daily wages *pl.*; $\mathfrak{L}$**löhner** ['~lø:nər] *m* (-s/-) day-labo(u)rer; '~**n** *v/i.* (ge-, h) dawn; hold a meeting, meet, sit; $\underset{\mathtt{t}}{\mathtt{t}}$ be in session; '$\mathfrak{L}$**reise** *f* day's journey.

Tages|anbruch *m* ['ta:gəs?-] *m* daybreak, dawn; *bei* ~ at daybreak *or* dawn; '~**befehl** ✕ *m* order of the day; '~**bericht** *m* daily report, bulletin; '~**einnahme** † *f* receipts *pl. or* takings *pl.* of the day; '~**gespräch** *n* topic of the day; '~**kasse** *f thea.* box-office, booking-office; *s.* Tageseinnahme; '~**kurs** † *m* current rate; *stock exchange*: quotation of the day; '~**licht** *n* daylight; '~**ordnung** *f* order of the day, agenda; *das ist an der* ~ that is the order of the day, that is quite common; '~**presse** *f* daily press; '~**zeit** *f* time of day; daytime; *zu jeder* ~ at any hour, at any time of the day; '~**zeitung** *f* daily (paper).

tage|weise *adv.* ['ta:gə-] by the day; '$\mathfrak{L}$**werk** *n* day's work; man-day.

täglich *adj.* ['tɛ:klıç] daily.

tags *adv.* [ta:ks]: ~ *darauf* the following day, the day after; ~ *zuvor* (on) the previous day, the day before.

'**Tagschicht** *f* day shift.

tagsüber *adv.* ['ta:ks?-] during the day, in the day-time.

Tagung ['ta:guŋ] *f* (-/-en) meeting.

Taille ['taljə] *f* (-/-n) waist; bodice (*of dress*).

Takel ⚓ ['ta:kəl] *n* (-s/-) tackle; '~**age** ⚓ [taka'la:ʒə] *f* (-/-n) rigging, tackle; '$\mathfrak{L}$**n** ⚓ *v/t.* (ge-, h) rig (*ship*); '~**werk** ⚓ *n s.* Takelage.

Takt [takt] *m* **1.** (-[e]s/-e) ♪ time, measure; bar; *mot.* stroke; *den* ~ *halten* ♪ keep time; *den* ~ *schlagen* ♪ beat time; **2.** (-[e]s/*no pl.*) tact; '$\mathfrak{L}$**fest** *adj.* steady in time or measure; *fig.* firm; '~**ik** ✕ *f* (-/-en) tactics *pl. and sg.* (*a. fig.*); '~**iker** *m* (-s/-)

tactician; '$\mathfrak{L}$**isch** *adj.* tactical; '$\mathfrak{L}$**los** *adj.* tactless; '~**stock** *m* baton; '~**strich** ♪ *m* bar; '$\mathfrak{L}$**voll** *adj.* tactful.

Tal [ta:l] *n* (-[e]s/~er) valley, *poet. a.* dale; *enges* ~ glen.

Talar [ta'la:r] *m* (-s/-e) $\underset{\mathtt{t}}{\mathtt{t}}$, *eccl.*, *univ.* gown; $\underset{\mathtt{t}}{\mathtt{t}}$ robe.

Talent [ta'lɛnt] *n* (-[e]s/-e) talent, gift, aptitude, ability; $\mathfrak{L}$**iert** *adj.* [~'ti:rt] talented, gifted.

'**Talfahrt** *f* downhill journey; ⚓ passage downstream.

Talg [talk] *m* (-[e]s/-e) suet; *melted*: tallow; '~**drüse** *anat.* *f* sebaceous gland; $\mathfrak{L}$**ig** *adj.* ['~gıç] suety; tallowish, tallowy; '~**licht** *n* tallow candle.

Talisman ['ta:lısman] *m* (-s/-e) talisman, (good-luck) charm.

'**Talsperre** *f* barrage, dam.

Tampon ['tã'põ:, 'tampɔn] *m* (-s/-s) tampon, plug.

Tang ♣ [taŋ] *m* (-[e]s/-e) seaweed.

Tank [taŋk] *m* (-[e]s/-s, -e) tank; '$\mathfrak{L}$**en** *v/i.* (ge-, h) get (some) petrol, *Am.* get (some) gasoline; '~**er** ⚓ *m* (-s/-) tanker; '~**stelle** *f* petrol station, *Am.* gas *or* filling station; '~**wagen** *m mot.* tank truck, *Am. a.* gasoline truck, tank trailer; 🚒 tank-car; '~**wart** ['~vart] *m* (-[e]s/-e) pump attendant.

Tanne ♣ ['tanə] *f* (-/-n) fir(-tree).

'**Tannen|baum** *m* fir-tree; '~**nadel** *f* fir-needle; '~**zapfen** *m* fir-cone.

Tante ['tantə] *f* (-/-n) aunt.

Tantieme [tã'tje:mə] *f* (-/-n) royalty, percentage, share in profits.

Tanz [tants] *m* (-es/~e) dance.

tänzeln ['tɛntsəln] *v/i.* (ge-, h, sein) dance, trip, frisk; (h) dance.

'**tanzen** (ge-) *v/i.* (h, sein) *and v/t.*

Tänzer ['tɛntsər] *m* (-s/-), '~**in** *f* (-/-nen) dancer; *thea.* ballet-dancer; partner.

'**Tanz|lehrer** *m* dancing-master; '~**musik** *f* dance-music; '~**saal** *m* dancing-room, ball-room, dance-hall; '~**schule** *f* dancing-school; '~**stunde** *f* dancing-lesson.

Tapete [ta'pe:tə] *f* (-/-n) wallpaper, paper-hangings *pl.*

tapezier|en [tape'tsi:rən] *v/t.* (*no* -ge-, h) paper; $\mathfrak{L}$**er** *m* (-s/-) paperhanger; upholsterer.

tapfer *adj.* ['tapfər] brave; valiant, heroic; courageous; '$\mathfrak{L}$**keit** *f* (-/*no* *pl.*) bravery, valo(u)r; heroism; courage.

tappen ['tapən] *v/i.* (ge-, *sein*) grope (about), fumble.   [awkward.]

täppisch *adj.* ['tɛpiʃ] clumsy,)

tapsen F ['tapsən] *v/i.* (ge-, *sein*) walk clumsily.

Tara † ['tɑːra] *f* (-/*Taren*) tare.

Tarif [ta'riːf] *m* (-s/-e) tariff, (table of) rates *pl.*, price-list; **2lich** *adv.* according to tariff; **~lohn** *m* standard wage(s *pl.*); collective *or* wage agreement.

tarn|en ['tarnən] *v/t.* (ge-, h) camouflage; *esp. fig.* disguise; **2ung** *f* (-/-en) camouflage.

Tasche ['taʃə] *f* (-/-n) pocket (*of garment*); (hand)bag; pouch; *s.* Aktentasche, Schultasche.

'**Taschen|buch** *n* pocket-book; '**~dieb** *m* pickpocket, *Am. sl.* dip; '**~geld** *n* pocket-money; '*monthly*' allowance; '**~lampe** *f* (electric) torch, *esp. Am.* flashlight; '**~messer** *n* pocket-knife; '**~spielerei** *f* juggle(ry); '**~tuch** *n* (pocket) handkerchief; '**~uhr** *f* (pocket-)watch; '**~wörterbuch** *n* pocket dictionary.

Tasse ['tasə] *f* (-/-n) cup.

Tastatur [tasta'tuːr] *f* (-/-en) keyboard, keys *pl.*

Tast|e ['tastə] *f* (-/-n) key; '**2en** (ge-, h) **1.** *v/i.* touch; grope (*nach* for, after), fumble (for); **2.** *v/t.* touch, feel; *sich* ~ feel *or* grope one's way; '**~sinn** *m* (-[e]s/*no pl.*) sense of touch.

Tat [tɑːt] **1.** *f* (-/-en) action, act, deed; offen|ce, *Am.* -se, crime; *in der* ~ indeed, in fact, as a matter of fact, really; *auf frischer* ~ *ertappen* catch *s.o.* red-handed; *zur* ~ *schreiten* proceed to action; *in die* ~ *umsetzen* implement, carry into effect; **2.** 2 *pret. of* tun; '**~bestand** *m* facts *pl.* of the case; '**2enlos** *adj.* inactive, idle.

Täter ['tɛːtər] *m* (-s/-) perpetrator; offender, culprit.

tätig *adj.* ['tɛːtiç] active; busy; ~ *sein bei* work at; be employed with; '**~en** † [~gən] *v/t.* (ge-, h) effect, transact; conclude; '**2keit** *f* (-/-en) activity; occupation, business, job; profession.

'**Tat|kraft** *f* (-/*no pl.*) energy; enterprise; '**2kräftig** *adj.* energetic, active.

tätlich *adj.* ['tɛːtliç] violent; ~ *werden gegen* assault; '**2keiten** *f/pl.* (acts *pl.* of) violence; $\frac{r}{r}$ assault (and battery).

Tatort $\frac{r}{r}$ ['tɑːt²-] *m* (-[e]s/-e) place *or* scene of a crime.

tätowieren [teto'viːrən] *v/t.* (*no -ge-*, h) tattoo.

'**Tat|sache** *f* (matter of) fact; '**~sachenbericht** *m* factual *or* documentary report, matter-of-fact account; '**2sächlich** *adj.* actual, real.   [pat.\

tätscheln ['tɛtʃəln] *v/t.* (ge-, h) pet,)

Tatze ['tatsə] *f* (-/-n) paw, claw.

Tau¹ [tau] *n* (-[e]s/-e) rope, cable.

Tau² [~] *m* (-[e]s/*no pl.*) dew.

taub *adj.* [taup] deaf (*fig.*: *gegen* to); *fingers, etc.*: benumbed, numb; *nut*: deaf, empty; *rock*: dead; ~ *es Ei* addle egg; *auf e-m Ohr* ~ *sein* be deaf of *or* in one ear.

Taube *orn.* ['taubə] *f* (-/-n) pigeon; '**~nschlag** *m* pigeon-house.

'**Taub|heit** *f* (-/*no pl.*) deafness; numbness; '**2stumm** *adj.* deaf and dumb; '**~stumme** *m, f* (-/n-/-en) deaf mute.

tauch|en ['tauxən] (ge-) **1.** *v/t.* (h) dip, plunge; **2.** *v/i.* (h, *sein*) dive, plunge; *submarine*: submerge; '**2er** *m* (-s/-) diver; '**2sieder** *m* (-s/-) immersion heater.

tauen ['tauən] *v/i.* (ge-) **1.** (h, *sein*): *der Schnee* qr *es taut* the snow *or* it is thawing; *der Schnee ist von den Dächern getaut* the snow has melted off the roofs; **2.** (h): *es taut* dew is falling.

Taufe ['taufə] *f* (-/-n) baptism, christening; '**2n** *v/t.* (ge-, h) baptize, christen.

Täufling ['tɔyfliŋ] *m* (-s/-e) child *or* person to be baptized.

'**Tauf|name** *m* Christian name, *Am. a.* given name; '**~pate 1.** *m* godfather; **2.** *f* godmother; '**~patin** *f* godmother; '**~schein** *m* certificate of baptism.

taug|en ['taugən] *v/i.* (ge-, h) be good, be fit, be of use (*all:* *zu* for); (*zu*) *nichts* ~ be good for nothing, be no good, be of no use; '**2enichts** *m* (-, -es/-e) good-for-nothing, *Am. sl.* dead beat; '**~lich** *adj.* ['tauk-] good, fit, useful (*all:* *für*, *zu* for, *to inf.*); able; ✕, ⚓ able-bodied.

Taumel ['tauməl] *m* (-s/*no pl.*)

T

giddiness; rapture, ecstasy; **'~ig**
adj. reeling; giddy; **'~n** *v/i.* (ge-,
sein) reel, stagger; be giddy.

Tausch [tauʃ] *m* (-es/-e) exchange;
barter; **'~en** *v/t.* (ge-, h) exchange;
barter (*gegen* for).

täuschen ['tɔyʃən] *v/t.* (ge-, h)
deceive, delude, mislead (on purpose); cheat; *sich ~ deceive o.s.*; be
mistaken; *sich ~ lassen* let o.s. be
deceived; **'~d** *adj.* deceptive, delusive; *resemblance:* striking.

'Tauschhandel *m* barter.

'Täuschung *f* (-/-en) deception,
delusion.

tausend *adj.* ['tauzənt] a thousand;
'~fach *adj.* thousandfold; **'2fuß** *zo.*
m, **2füß(l)er** *zo.* ['~fy:s(l)ər] *m*
(-s/-) millepede, milliped(e), *Am. a.*
wireworm; **'~st** *adj.* thousandth;
'2stel *n* (-s/-) thousandth (part).

'Tau|tropfen *m* dew-drop; **'~wetter**
n thaw.

Taxameter [taksa'-] *m* taximeter.

Taxe ['taksə] *f* (-/-n) rate; fee;
estimate; *s. Taxi.*

Taxi ['taksi] *n* (-[s]/-[s]) taxi(-cab),
cab, *Am. a.* hack.

ta'xieren *v/t.* (no -ge-, h) rate,
estimate; *officially:* value, appraise.

'Taxistand *m* cabstand.

Technik ['tɛçnik] *f* **1.** (-/no *pl.*)
technology; engineering; **2.** (-/-en)
skill, workmanship; technique,
practice; ♪ execution; **'~er** *m* (-s/-)
(technical) engineer; technician;
~um ['~um] *n* (-s/*Technika, Tech-
niken*) technical school.

'technisch *adj.* technical; **~e** *Hochschule* school of technology.

Tee [te:] *m* (-s/-s) tea; **'~büchse** *f*
tea-caddy; **'~gebäck** *n* scones *pl.*,
biscuits *pl.*, *Am. a.* cookies *pl.*;
'~kanne *f* teapot; **'~kessel** *m* tea-
kettle; **'~löffel** *m* tea-spoon.

Teer [te:r] *m* (-[e]s/-e) tar; **'2en** *v/t.*
(ge-, h) tar.

'Tee|rose ♀ *f* tea-rose; **'~sieb** *n*
tea-strainer; **'~tasse** *f* teacup;
'~wärmer *m* (-s/-) tea-cosy.

Teich [taiç] *m* (-[e]s/-e) pool,
pond.

Teig [taik] *m* (-[e]s/-e) dough, paste;
2ig *adj.* ['~giç] doughy, pasty;
'~waren *f/pl.* farinaceous food;
noodles *pl.*

Teil [tail] *m, n* (-[e]s/-e) part; portion, share; component; ♣ party;

zum ~ partly, in part; *ich für mein
~ ...* for my part I ...; **2bar** *adj.*
divisible; **'~chen** *n* (-s/-) particle;
2en *v/t.* (ge-, h) divide; *fig.* share;
'2haben *v/i.* (*irr. haben, sep.,* -ge-,
h) participate, (have a) share (*both:
an dat.* in); **'~haber** † *m* (-s/-)
partner; **~nahme** ['~na:mə] *f* (-/no
pl.) participation (*an dat.* in); *fig.:*
interest (in); sympathy (with);
2nahmslos *adj.* ['~na:mslo:s] indifferent, unconcerned; passive;
apathetic; **'~nahmslosigkeit** *f*
(-/no *pl.*) indifference; passiveness,
apathy; **'2nehmen** *v/i.* (*irr. nehmen,
sep.,* -ge-, h): *~ an (dat.)* take part *or*
participate in; join in; be present
at, attend at; *fig.* sympathize with;
'~nehmer *m* (-s/-) participant;
member; *univ., etc.:* student; con-
testant; *sports:* competitor; *teleph.*
subscriber; **2s** *adv.* [~s] partly;
'~strecke *f* section; stage, leg; ⚏
fare stage; **'~ung** *f* (-/-en) division;
2weise *adv.* partly, partially, in
part; **'~zahlung** *f* (payment by)
instal(l)ments.

Teint [tɛ̃:] *m* (-s/-s) complexion.

Tele|fon [tele'fo:n] *n* (-s/-e) *etc. s.
Telephon, etc.;* **~graf** [~'gra:f] *m*
(-en/-en) *etc. s. Telegraph, etc.;*
~gramm [~'gram] *n* (-s/-e) telegram, wire; *overseas:* cable(gram).

Telegraph [tele'gra:f] *m* (-en/-en)
telegraph; **~enamt** [~ən?-] *n* telegraph office; **2ieren** [~a'fi:rən] *v/t.
and v/i.* (no -ge-, h) telegraph, wire;
overseas: cable; **2isch** [~'gra:fiʃ]
1. *adj.* telegraphic; **2.** *adv.* by telegram, by wire; by cable; **~ist**
[~a'fist] *m* (-en/-en), **~istin** *f* (-/-nen)
telegraph operator, telegrapher,
telegraphist.

Teleobjektiv *phot.* ['te:le-] *n* tele-
photo lens.

Telephon [tele'fo:n] *n* (-s/-e) telephone, F phone; *am ~* on the
(tele)phone; *ans ~ gehen* answer the
(tele)phone; *~ haben* be on the
(tele)phone; **~anschluß** *m* telephone connexion *or* connection; *~-
buch *n* telephone directory; **~ge-
spräch** *n* (tele)phone call; conversation *or* chat over the (tele-)
phone; **~hörer** *m* (telephone) receiver, handset; **2ieren** [~o'ni:rən]
v/i. (no -ge-, h) telephone, F phone;
mit j-m ~ ring s.o. up, *Am.* call

s.o. up; **≗isch** adv. [~'fo:niʃ] by (tele)phone, over the (tele)phone; **~ist** [~ʊ'nɪst] m (-en/-en), **~istin** f (-/-nen) (telephone) operator, telephonist; **~vermittlung** f s. Telephonzentrale; **~zelle** f telephone kiosk or box, call-box, Am. telephone booth; **~zentrale** f (telephone) exchange.

Teleskop opt. [tele'sko:p] n (-s/-e) telescope.

Teller ['tɛlər] m (-s/-) plate.

Tempel ['tɛmpəl] m (-s/-) temple.

Temperament [tɛmpəra'mɛnt] n (-[e]s/-e) temper(ament); fig. spirit(s pl.); **≗los** adj. spiritless; **≗voll** adj. (high-)spirited.

Temperatur [tɛmpəra'tu:r] f (-/-en) temperature; j-s ~ messen take s.o.'s temperature.

Tempo ['tɛmpo] n (-s/-s, Tempi) time; pace; speed; rate.

Tendenz [tɛn'dɛnts] f (-/-en) tendency; trend; **≗iös** adj. [~'tsjø:s] tendentious.

Tennis ['tɛnɪs] n (-/no pl.) (lawn) tennis; **'~ball** m tennis-ball; **'~platz** m tennis-court; **'~schläger** m (tennis-)racket; **'~spieler** m tennis player; **'~turnier** n tennis tournament.

Tenor ♪ [te'no:r] m (-s/⁻e) tenor.

Teppich ['tɛpɪç] m (-s/-e) carpet; **'~kehrmaschine** f carpet-sweeper.

Termin [tɛr'mi:n] m (-s/-e) appointed time or day; ᵗʰ, ✝ date, term; sports: fixture; äußerster ~ final date, dead(-)line; **~geschäfte** ✝ n/pl. futures pl.; **~kalender** m appointment book or pad; ᵗʰ causelist, Am. calendar; **~liste** ᵗʰ f causelist, Am. calendar.

Terpentin [tɛrpɛn'ti:n] n (-s/-e) turpentine.

Terrain [tɛ'rɛ̃:] n (-s/-s) ground; plot; building site.

Terrasse [tɛ'rasə] f (-/-n) terrace; **≗nförmig** adj. [~nfœrmɪç] terraced, in terraces.

Terrine [tɛ'ri:nə] f (-/-n) tureen.

Territorium [tɛri'to:rjum] n (-s/ Territorien) territory.

Terror ['tɛrɔr] m (-s/no pl.) terror; **≗isieren** [~ori'zi:rən] v/t. (no -ge-, h) terrorize.

Terz ♪ [tɛrts] f (-/-en) third; **~ett** ♪ [~'tsɛt] n (-[e]s/-e) trio.

Testament [tɛsta'mɛnt] n (-[e]s/-e

(last) will, (often: last will and) testament; eccl. Testament; **≗arisch** [~'ta:rɪʃ] 1. adj. testamentary; 2. adv. by will; **~svollstrecker** m (-s/-) executor; officially: administrator.

testen ['tɛstən] v/t. (ge-, h) test.

teuer adj. ['tɔyər] dear (a. fig.), expensive; wie ~ ist es? how much is it?

Teufel ['tɔyfəl] m (-s/-) devil; der ~ the Devil, Satan; zum ~! F dickens!, hang it!; wer zum ~? F who the devil or deuce?; der ~ ist los the fat's in the fire; scher dich zum ~! F go to hell!, go to blazes!; **~ei** [~'laɪ] f (-/-en) devilment, mischief, devilry, Am. deviltry; **'~skerl** F m devil of a fellow.

'teuflisch adj. devilish, diabolic(al).

Text [tɛkst] m (-es/-e) text; words pl. (of song); book, libretto (of opera); **'~buch** n book; libretto.

Textil|ien [tɛks'ti:ljən] pl., **~waren** pl. textile fabrics pl., textiles pl.

'textlich adv. concerning the text.

Theater [te'a:tər] n 1. (-s/-) theat|re, Am. -er; stage; 2. F (-s/no pl.) playacting; **~besucher** m playgoer; **~karte** f theatre ticket; **~kasse** f box-office; **~stück** n play; **~vorstellung** f theatrical performance; **~zettel** m playbill.

theatralisch adj. [tea'tra:lɪʃ] theatrical, stagy.

Theke ['te:kə] f (-/-n) at inn: bar, Am. a. counter; at shop: counter.

Thema ['te:ma] n (-s/Themen, Themata) theme, subject; topic (of discussion).

Theolog|e [teo'lo:gə] m (-n/-n) theologian, divine; **~ie** [~o'gi:] f (-/-n) theology.

Theoret|iker [teo're:tikər] m (-s/-) theorist; **≗isch** adj. theoretic(al).

Theorie [teo'ri:] f (-/-n) theory.

Therapie ⚕ [tera'pi:] f (-/-n) therapy. [spa.]

Thermalbad [tɛr'ma:l-] n thermal

Thermometer [tɛrmo'-] n (-s/-) thermometer; **~stand** m (thermometer) reading.

Thermosflasche ['tɛrmɔs-] f vacuum bottle or flask, thermos (flask).

These ['te:zə] f (-/-n) thesis.

Thrombose ⚕ [trɔm'bo:zə] f (-/-n) thrombosis.

Thron [tro:n] m (-[e]s/-e) throne; **'~besteigung** f accession to the

T

throne; '**～erbe** m heir to the throne, heir apparent; '**～folge** f succession to the throne; '**～folger** m (-s/-) successor to the throne; '**～rede** parl. f Queen's or King's Speech.

Thunfisch ichth. ['tu:n-] m tunny, tuna.

Tick F [tik] m (-[e]s/-s, -e) crotchet, fancy, kink; e-n ～ haben have a bee in one's bonnet.

ticken ['tikən] v/i. (ge-, h) tick.

tief [ti:f] 1. adj. deep (a. fig.); fig.: profound; low; im ～sten Winter in the dead or depth of winter; 2. adv.: bis ～ in die Nacht far into the night; das läßt ～ blicken that speaks volumes; zu ～ singen sing flat; 3. ♀ meteor. n (-[e]s/-s) depression, low(-pressure area); '♀**bau** m civil or underground engineering; '♀**druckgebiet** meteor. n s. Tief; '♀**e** f (-/-n) depth (a. fig.); fig. profundity; '♀**ebene** f low plain, lowland; '♀**enschärfe** phot. f depth of focus; '♀**flug** m low-level flight; '♀**gang** ♣ m draught, Am. draft; **～gebeugt** fig. adj. ['~gəbɔykt] deeply afflicted, bowed down; **～gekühlt** adj. deep-frozen; '**～greifend** adj. fundamental, radical; '♀**land** n lowland(s pl.); '**～liegend** adj. eyes: sunken; fig. deep-seated; '♀**schlag** m boxing: low hit; '**～schürfend** fig. adj. profound; thorough; '♀**see** f deep sea; '**～sinnig** adj. thoughtful, pensive; F melancholy; '♀**stand** m (-[e]s/no pl.) low level.

Tiegel ['ti:gəl] m (-s/-) saucepan, stew-pan; ⊕ crucible.

Tier [ti:r] n (-[e]s/-e) animal; beast; brute; großes ～ fig. sl. bigwig, big bug, Am. big shot; '**～arzt** m veterinary (surgeon), F vet, Am. a. veterinarian; '**～garten** m zoological gardens pl., zoo; '**～heilkunde** f veterinary medicine; '♀**isch** adj. animal; fig. bestial, brutish, savage; '**～kreis** ast. m zodiac; **～quälerei** [~kvɛ:lə'raɪ] f (-/-en) cruelty to animals; '**～reich** n (-[e]s/no pl.) animal kingdom; '**～schutzverein** m Society for the Prevention of Cruelty to Animals.

Tiger zo. ['ti:gər] m (-s/-) tiger; '**～in** zo. f (-/-nen) tigress.

tilg|en ['tilgən] v/t. (ge-, h) extinguish; efface; wipe or blot out, erase; fig. obliterate; annul, cancel;

discharge, pay (debt); redeem (mortgage, etc.); '♀**ung** f (-/-en) extinction; extermination; cancel(l)ing; discharge, payment; redemption.

Tinktur [tiŋk'tu:r] f (-/-en) tincture.

Tinte ['tintə] f (-/-n) ink; in der ～ sitzen F be in a scrape.

'**Tinten|faß** n ink-pot, desk: inkwell; '**～fisch** ichth. m cuttle-fish; '**～fleck** m, '**～klecks** m (ink-)blot; '**～stift** m indelible pencil.

Tip [tip] m (-s/-s) hint, tip; '♀**pen** (ge-, h) 1. v/i. F type; fig. guess; j-m auf die Schulter ～ tap s.o. on his shoulder; 2. v/t. tip; foretell, predict; F type.

Tiroler [ti'ro:lər] 1. m (-s/-) Tyrolese; 2. adj. Tyrolese.

Tisch [tiʃ] m (-es/-e) table; bei ～ at table; den ～ decken lay the table or cloth, set the table; reinen ～ machen make a clean sweep (damit of it); zu ～ bitten invite or ask to dinner or supper; bitte zu ～! dinner is ready!; '**～decke** f tablecloth; '♀**fertig** adj. food: ready-prepared; '**～gast** m guest; '**～gebet** n: das ～ sprechen say grace; '**～gesellschaft** f dinner-party; '**～gespräch** n table-talk; '**～lampe** f table-lamp; desk lamp.

Tischler ['tiʃlər] m (-s/-) joiner; carpenter; cabinet-maker; **～ei** [~'raɪ] f (-/-en) joinery; joiner's workshop.

'**Tisch|platte** f top (of a table), table top; leaf (of extending table); '**～rede** f toast, after-dinner speech; '**～tennis** n table tennis, ping-pong; '**～tuch** n table-cloth; '**～zeit** f dinner-time.

Titan [ti'ta:n] m (-en/-en) Titan; ♀**isch** adj. titanic.

Titel ['ti:təl] m (-s/-) title; e-n ～ (inne)haben sports: hold a title; '**～bild** n frontispiece; cover picture (of magazine, etc.); '**～blatt** n title-page; cover (of magazine); '**～halter** m (-s/-) sports: title-holder; '**～kampf** m boxing: title fight; '**～rolle** thea. f title-role.

titulieren [titu'li:rən] v/t. (no -ge-, h) style, call, address as.

Toast [to:st] m (-es/-e, -s) toast (a. fig.).

tob|en ['to:bən] v/i. (ge-, h) rage, rave, storm, bluster; children: romp; ♀**sucht** ✠ ['to:p-] f (-/no pl.)

raving madness, frenzy; **~süchtig**
adj. ['to:p-] raving mad, frantic.

Tochter ['tɔxtər] *f* (-/⸚) daughter;
'**~gesellschaft** † *f* subsidiary
company.

Tod [to:t] *m* (-[e]s/⸚ -e) death; *z̄z*
decease.

Todes|angst ['to:dəs⁹-] *f* mortal
agony; *fig.* mortal fear; *Todesängste
ausstehen* be scared to death, be
frightened out of one's wits; '**~an-
zeige** *f* obituary (notice); '**~fall** *m*
(case of) death; *Todesfälle pl.* deaths
pl., ⚔ casualties *pl.*; '**~kampf** *m*
death throes *pl.*, mortal agony;
'**~strafe** *f* capital punishment,
death penalty; *bei ~ verboten* forbidden on *or* under pain *or* penalty
of death; '**~ursache** *f* cause of
death; '**~urteil** *n* death *or* capital
sentence, death-warrant.

'**Tod|feind** *m* deadly *or* mortal
enemy; '**²krank** *adj.* dangerously
ill.

tödlich *adj.* ['tø:tlɪç] deadly; fatal;
wound: a. mortal.

'**tod|müde** *adj.* dead tired; '**~-
schick** F *adj.* dashing, gorgeous;
'**~sicher** F *adj.* cock-sure; '**²sünde**
f deadly *or* mortal sin.

Toilette [toa'lɛtə] *f* (-/-n) *dress(ing)*:
toilet; lavatory, gentlemen's *or*
ladies' room, *esp. Am.* toilet.

Toi'letten|artikel *m/pl.* toilet ar-
ticles *pl.*, *Am. a.* toiletry; **~papier**
n toilet-paper; **~tisch** *m* toilet
(-table), dressing-table, *Am. a.*
dresser.

toleran|t *adj.* [tole'rant] tolerant
(*gegen* of); **²z** [**~ts**] *f* **1.** (-/*no pl.*)
tolerance, toleration (*esp. eccl.*);
2. ⊕ (-/-en) tolerance, allowance.

toll [tɔl] **1.** *adj.* (raving) mad, frantic,
mad, crazy, wild (*all a. fig.*);
fantastic; *noise, etc.*: frightful, F
awful; *das ist ja ~* F that's (just)
great; **2.** *adv.*: *es ~ treiben* carry on
like mad; *es zu ~ treiben* go too far;
'**~en** *v/i.* (ge-, h, sein) *children*:
romp; '**²haus** *n* bedlam; '**²heit**
f (-/-en) madness; mad trick;
'**~kühn** *adj.* foolhardy, rash; '**²wut**
vet. f rabies.

Tolpatsch F ['tɔlpatʃ] *m* (-es/-e)
awkward *or* clumsy fellow; '**²ig** F
adj. awkward, clumsy.

Tölpel F ['tœlpəl] *m* (-s/-) awkward
or clumsy fellow; boob(y).

Tomate ⚘ [to'ma:tə] *f* (-/-n) tomato.

Ton¹ [to:n] *m* (-[e]s/-e) clay.

Ton² [**~**] *m* (-[e]s/⸚e) sound; ♪ tone
(*a. of language*); ♪ *single*: note; accent, stress; *fig.* tone; *paint.* tone,
tint, shade; *guter ~* good form; *den
~ angeben* set the fashion; *zum
guten ~ gehören* be the fashion;
große Töne reden or F *spucken* F
talk big, boast; '**~abnehmer** *m*
pick-up; '**²angebend** *adj.* setting
the fashion, leading; '**~arm** *m*
pick-up arm (*of record-player*); '**~-
art** ♪ *f* key; '**~band** *n* recording
tape; '**~bandgerät** *n* tape recorder.

tönen ['tø:nən] (ge-, h) **1.** *v/i.* sound,
ring; **2.** *v/t.* tint, tone, shade.

tönern *adj.* ['tø:nərn] (of) clay,
earthen.

'**Ton|fall** *m in speaking*: intonation,
accent; '**~film** *m* sound film; '**~lage**
f pitch; '**~leiter** ♪ *f* scale, gamut;
'**²los** *adj.* soundless; *fig.* toneless;
'**~meister** *m* sound engineer.

Tonne ['tɔnə] *f* (-/-n) *large*: tun;
smaller: barrel, cask; ⚓ *measure of
weight*: ton.

'**Tonsilbe** *gr. f* accented syllable.

Tonsur [tɔn'zu:r] *f* (-/-en) tonsure.

'**Tönung** *paint. f* (-/-en) tint, tinge,
shade.

'**Tonwaren** *f/pl. s.* Töpferware.

Topf [tɔpf] *m* (-[e]s/⸚e) pot.

Töpfer ['tœpfər] *m* (-s/-) potter;
stove-fitter; **~ei** [**~**'raɪ] *f* (-/-en)
pottery; '**~ware** *f* pottery, earthenware, crockery.

topp¹ *int.* [tɔp] done!, agreed!

Topp² ⚓ [**~**] *m* (-s/-e, -s) top, mast-
head.

Tor¹ [to:r] *n* (-[e]s/-e) gate; gate-
way (*a. fig.*); *football*: goal; *skiing*:
gate.

Tor² [**~**] *m* (-en/-en) fool.

Torf [tɔrf] *m* (-[e]s/*no pl.*) peat.

Torheit ['to:rhaɪt] *f* (-/-en) folly.

'**Torhüter** *m* gate-keeper; *sports*:
goalkeeper.

töricht *adj.* ['tø:rɪçt] foolish, silly.

Törin ['tø:rɪn] *f* (-/-nen) fool(ish
woman).

torkeln ['tɔrkəln] *v/i.* (ge-, h, sein)
reel, stagger, totter.

'**Tor|latte** *f sports*: cross-bar; '**~lauf**
m skiing: slalom; '**~linie** *f sports*:
goal-line.

Tornister [tɔr'nɪstər] *m* (-s/-) knapsack; satchel.

T

torpedieren [tɔrpe'diːrən] v/t. (no -ge-, h) torpedo (a. fig.).

Torpedo [tɔr'peːdo] m (-s/-s) torpedo; ~**boot** n torpedo-boat.

'**Tor**|**pfosten** m gate-post; sports: goal-post; '~**schuß** m shot at the goal; '~**schütze** m sports: scorer.

Torte ['tɔrtə] f (-/-n) fancy cake, Am. layer cake; tart, Am. pie.

Tortur [tɔr'tuːr] f (-/-en) torture; fig. ordeal.

Tor|**wart** ['toːrvart] m (-[e]s/-e) sports: goalkeeper; '~**weg** m gate-way.

tosen ['toːzən] v/i. (ge-, h, sein) roar, rage; '~**d** adj. applause: thunderous.

tot adj. [toːt] dead (a. fig.); deceased; ~**er Punkt** ⊕ dead cent|re, Am. -er; fig.: deadlock; fatigue; ~**es Rennen** sports: dead heat.

total adj. [to'taːl] total, complete.

'**tot**|**arbeiten** v/refl. (sep., -ge-, h) work o.s. to death; '**2e** (-n/-n) **1.** m dead man; (dead) body, corpse; die ~**n** pl. the dead pl., the deceased pl. or departed pl.; ✗ casualties pl.; **2.** f dead woman.

töten ['tøːtən] v/t. (ge-, h) kill; destroy; murder; deaden (nerve, etc.).

'**Toten**|**bett** n deathbed; '**2blaß** adj. deadly or deathly pale; '~**blässe** f deadly paleness or pallor; '**2bleich** adj. s. totenblaß; '~**gräber** ['~grɛːbər] m (-s/-) grave-digger (a. zo.); '~**hemd** n shroud; '~**kopf** m death's-head (a. zo.); emblem of death: a. skull and cross-bones; '~**liste** f death-roll (a. ✗), esp. ✗ casualty list; '~**maske** f death-mask; '~**messe** eccl. f mass for the dead, requiem; '~**schädel** m death's-head, skull; '~**schein** m death certificate; '**2still** adj. (as) still as the grave; '~**stille** f dead(ly) silence, deathly stillness.

'**tot**|**geboren** adj. still-born; '**2ge-burt** f still birth; '~**lachen** v/refl. (sep., -ge-, h) die of laughing.

Toto ['toːto] m, F a. n (-s/-s) football pools pl.

'**tot**|**schießen** v/t. (irr. schießen, sep., -ge-, h) shoot dead, kill; '**2schlag** ⅍ m manslaughter, homicide; '~**schlagen** v/t. (irr. schlagen, sep., -ge-, h) kill (a. time), slay; '~**schweigen** v/t. (irr. schwei-gen, sep., -ge-, h) hush up; '~**ste-**

chen v/t. (irr. stechen, sep., -ge-, h) stab to death; '~**stellen** v/refl. (sep., -ge-, h) feign death.

'**Tötung** f (-/-en) killing, slaying; ⅍ homicide; fahrlässige ~ ⅍ man-slaughter.

Tour [tuːr] f (-/-en) tour; excursion, trip; ⊕ turn, revolution; auf ~**en kommen** mot. pick up speed; '~**en-wagen** mot. m touring car.

Tourist [tu'rist] m (-en/-en), ~**in** f (-/-nen) tourist.

Tournee [tur'neː] f (-/-s, -n) tour.

Trab [traːp] m (-[e]s/no pl.) trot.

Trabant [tra'bant] m (-en/-en) satellite.

traben [tra'bən] v/i. (ge-, h, sein) trot; **2rennen** ['traː-] n trotting race.

Tracht [traxt] f (-/-en) dress, cos-tume; uniform; fashion; load; e-e (gehörige) ~ Prügel a (sound) thrash-ing; '**2en** v/i. (ge-, h): ~ nach et. strive for; j-m nach dem Leben ~ seek s.o.'s life.

trächtig adj. ['trɛçtiç] (big) with young, pregnant. [tradition.\]

Tradition [tradi'tsjoːn] f (-/-en)

traf [traːf] pret. of treffen.

Trag|**bahre** ['traːk-] f stretcher, litter; '**2bar** adj. portable; dress: wearable; fig.: bearable; reason-able; ~**e** ['~gə] f (-/-n) hand-barrow; s. Tragbahre.

träge adj. ['trɛːgə] lazy, indolent; phys. inert (a. fig.).

tragen ['traːgən] (irr., ge-, h) **1.** v/t. carry; bear (costs, name, respon-sibility, etc.); bear, endure; support; bear, yield (fruit, ✝ interest, etc.); wear (dress, etc.); bei sich ~ have about one; sich gut ~ material: wear well; zur Schau ~ show off; **2.** v/i. tree: bear, yield; gun, voice: carry; ice: bear.

Träger ['trɛːgər] m (-s/-) carrier; porter (of luggage); holder, bearer (of name, licence, etc.); wearer (of dress); (shoulder-)strap (of slip, etc.); ⊕ support; △ girder.

Trag|**fähigkeit** ['traːk-] f carrying or load capacity; ⅏ tonnage; '~**flä-che** ⅍ f, '~**flügel** ⅍ m wing, plane.

Trägheit ['trɛːkhaɪt] f (-/no pl.) laziness, indolence; phys. inertia (a. fig.).

tragisch adj. ['traːgiʃ] tragic (a. fig.); fig. tragical.

Tragödie [tra'gø:djə] f (-/-n) tragedy.

Trag|riemen ['trɑ:k-] m (carrying) strap; sling (of gun); '**~tier** n pack animal; '**~tüte** f carrier-bag; '**~weite** f range; fig. import(ance), consequences pl.; von großer ~ of great moment.

Train|er ['trɛ:nər] m (-s/-) trainer; coach; **ℒieren** [~'ni:rən] (no -ge-, h) 1. v/t. train; coach; 2. v/i. train; **~ing** ['~iŋ] n (-s/-s) training; '**~ings-anzug** m sports: track suit.

traktieren [trak'ti:rən] v/t. (no -ge-, h) treat (badly).

Traktor ⊕ ['traktɔr] m (-s/-en) tractor.

trällern ['trɛlərn] v/t. and v/i. (ge-, h) troll.

trampel|n ['trampəln] v/i. (ge-, h) trample, stamp; '**ℒpfad** m beaten track.

Tran [trɑ:n] m (-[e]s/-e) train-oil, whale-oil.

Träne ['trɛ:nə] f (-/-n) tear; in ~n ausbrechen burst into tears; '**ℒn** v/i. (ge-, h) water; '**~ngas** n tear-gas.

Trank [traŋk] 1. m (-[e]s/ᵘe) drink, beverage; ᵍ potion; 2. ℒ pret. of trinken.

Tränke ['trɛŋkə] f (-/-n) watering-place; '**ℒn** v/t. (ge-, h) water (animals); soak, impregnate (material).

Trans|formator ⚡ [transfɔr'mɑ:tɔr] m (-s/-en) transformer; **~fusion** ⚕ [~u'zjo:n] f (-/-en) transfusion.

Transistorradio [tran'zistɔr-] n transistor radio or set.

transitiv gr. adj. ['tranziti:f] transitive.

transparent [transpa'rɛnt] 1. adj. transparent; 2. ℒ n (-[e]s/-e) transparency; in political processions, etc.: banner.

transpirieren [transpi'ri:rən] v/i. (no -ge-, h) perspire.

Transplantation ⚕ [transplanta'tsjo:n] f transplant (operation).

Transport [trans'pɔrt] m (-[e]s/-e) transport(ation), conveyance, carriage; **ℒabel** adj. [~'tɑ:bəl] (trans-)portable; **~er** m (-s/-) ⚓, (troop-)transport; ℒ transport (aircraft or plane); **ℒfähig** adj. transportable, sick person: a. trans-

ferable; **ℒieren** [~'ti:rən] v/t. (no -ge-, h) transport, convey, carry; **~unternehmen** n carrier.

Trapez [tra'pe:ts] n (-es/-e) Å trapezium, Am. trapezoid; gymnastics: trapeze.

trappeln ['trapəln] v/i. (ge-, h) horse: clatter; children, etc.: patter.

Trass|ant ⚕ [tra'sant] m (-en/-en) drawer; **~at** ⚕ [~'sɑ:t] m (-en/-en) drawee; '**~e** ⚕ f (-/-n) line; **ℒieren** [~'si:rən] v/t. (no -ge-, h) ⚕ lay or trace out; ~ auf (acc.) ⚕ draw on.

trat [trɑ:t] pret. of treten.

Tratte ⚕ ['tratə] f (-/-n) draft.

Traube ['traubə] f (-/-n) bunch of grapes; grape; cluster; '**~nsaft** m grape-juice; '**~nzucker** m grape-sugar, glucose.

trauen ['trauən] (ge-, h) 1. v/t. marry; sich ~ lassen get married; 2. v/i. trust (j-m s.o.), confide (dat. in); ich traute meinen Ohren nicht I could not believe my ears.

Trauer ['trauər] f (-/no pl.) sorrow, affliction; for dead person: mourning; '**~botschaft** f sad news; '**~fall** m death; '**~feier** f funeral ceremonies pl., obsequies pl.; '**~flor** m mourning-crape; '**~geleit** n funeral procession; '**~gottesdienst** m funeral service; '**~kleid** n mourning (-dress); '**~marsch** m funeral march; '**ℒn** v/i. (ge-, h) mourn (um for); be in mourning; '**~spiel** n tragedy; '**~weide** ♀ f weeping willow; '**~zug** m funeral procession.

Traufe ['traufə] f (-/-n) eaves pl.; gutter; s. Regen².

träufeln ['trɔyfəln] v/t. (ge-, h) drop, drip, trickle.   [cosy, snug.]

traulich adj. ['traulɪç] intimate;]

Traum [traum] m (-[e]s/ᵘe) dream (a. fig.); reverie; das fällt mir nicht im ~ ein! I would not dream of (doing) it!; '**~bild** n vision; '**~deuter** m (-s/-) dream-reader.

träum|en ['trɔymən] v/i. and v/t. (ge-, h) dream; 'ℒer m (-s/-) dreamer (a. fig.); **ℒerei** [~'rai] f (-/-en) dreaming; fig. a. reverie (a. ♪), day-dream, musing; **~erisch** adj. dreamy; musing.

traurig adj. ['trauriç] sad (über acc. at), Am. F blue; wretched.

'**Trau|ring** m wedding-ring; '**~schein** m marriage certificate or lines pl.; '**~ung** f (-/-en) marriage, wedding; '**~zeuge** *m* witness to a marriage.

Trecker ⊕ ['trɛkər] *m* (-s/-) tractor.

Treff [trɛf] *n* (-s/-s) *cards*: club(s *pl.*).

treffen¹ ['trɛfən] (*irr., ge-*) **1.** *v/t.* (*h*) hit (*a. fig.*), strike; concern; *disadvantageously*: affect; meet; *nicht ~ miss; e-e Entscheidung ~* come to a decision; *Maßnahmen ~* take measures *or* steps; *Vorkehrungen ~* take precautions *or* measures; *sich ~* happen; meet; gather, assemble; *a.* have an appointment (*mit with*), F have a date (*with*); *das trifft sich gut!* that's lucky!, how fortunate!; *sich getroffen fühlen* feel hurt; *wen trifft die Schuld?* who is to blame?; *das Los traf ihn* the lot fell on him; *du bist gut getroffen paint., phot.* this is a good likeness of you; *vom Blitz getroffen* struck by lightning; **2.** *v/i.* (*h*) hit; **3.** *v/i.* (*sein*): *~ auf* (*acc.*) meet with; encounter (*a.* ✕).

Treffen² [~] *n* (-s/-) meeting; rally; gathering; ✕ encounter; '**2d** *adj.* remark: appropriate, to the point.

'**Treff|er** *m* (-s/-) hit (*a. fig.*); prize; '**~punkt** *m* meeting-place.

Treibeis ['traɪp-] *n* drift-ice.

treiben¹ ['traɪbən] (*irr., ge-*) **1.** *v/t.* (*h*) drive; ⊕ put in motion, propel; drift (*smoke, snow*); put forth (*leaves*); force (*plants*); *fig.* impel, urge, press (*j-n zu inf. s.o. to inf.*); carry on (*business, trade*); *Musik* (*Sport*) *~* go in for music (sports); *Sprachen ~* study languages; *es zu weit ~* go too far; *wenn er es weiterhin so treibt* if he carries *or* goes on like that; *was treibst du da?* what are you doing there?; **2.** *v/i.* (*sein*) drive; float, drift; **3.** *v/i.* (*h*) 🍺 shoot; *dough*: ferment, work.

Treiben² [~] *n* (-s/*no pl.*) driving; doings *pl.*, goings-on *pl.*; *geschäftiges ~* bustle; '**2d** *adj.*: *~e Kraft* driving force.

Treib|haus ['traɪp-] *n* hothouse; '**~holz** *n* drift-wood; '**~jagd** *f* battue; '**~riemen** *m* driving-belt; '**~stoff** *m* fuel; propell|ant, -ent (*of rocket*).

trenn|en ['trɛnən] *v/t.* (*ge-, h*) separate, sever; rip (*seam*); *teleph.*, 🗲 cut off, disconnect; isolate; segregate; *sich ~* separate (*von from*), part (*from or with s.o.*); with

s.th.); '**2schärfe** *f* *radio*: selectivity; '**2ung** *f* (-/-en) separation; disconne|xion, -ction; segregation (*of races, etc.*); '**2(ungs)wand** *f* partition (wall). [(-bit).\

Trense ['trɛnzə] *f* (-/-n) snaffle\

Treppe ['trɛpə] *f* (-/-n) staircase, stairway, (e-e a flight *or* pair of) stairs *pl.*; *zwei ~n hoch* on the second floor, *Am.* on the third floor.

'**Treppen|absatz** *m* landing; '**~geländer** *n* banisters *pl.*; '**~haus** *n* staircase; '**~stufe** *f* stair, step.

Tresor [tre'zo:r] *m* (-s/-e) safe; *bank*: strong-room, vault.

treten ['tre:tən] (*irr., ge-*) **1.** *v/i.* (*h*) tread, step (*j-n or j-m auf die Zehen* on s.o.'s toes); **2.** *v/i.* (*sein*) tread, step (*j-m auf die Zehen* on s.o.'s toes); walk; *ins Haus ~* enter the house; *j-m unter die Augen ~* appear before s.o., face s.o.; *j-m zu nahe ~* offend s.o.; *zu j-m ~* step *or* walk up to s.o.; *über die Ufer ~* overflow its banks; **3.** *v/t.* (*h*) tread; kick; *mit Füßen ~* trample upon.

treu *adj.* [trɔy] faithful, loyal; '**2bruch** *m* breach of faith, perfidy; '**2e** *f* (-/*no pl.*), faith(fulness), loyalty; **2händer** ['~hɛndər] *m* (-s/-) trustee; '**~herzig** *adj.* guileless; ingenuous, simpleminded; '**~los** *adj.* faithless (*gegen* to), disloyal (*to*); perfidious.

Tribüne [tri'by:nə] *f* (-/-n) platform; *sports, etc.*: (grand) stand.

Tribut [tri'bu:t] *m* (-[e]s/-e) tribute.

Trichter ['trɪçtər] *m* (-s/-) funnel; *made by bomb, shell, etc.*: crater; horn (*of wind instruments, etc.*).

Trick [trɪk] *m* (-s/-e, -s) trick; '**~film** *m* animation, animated cartoon.

Trieb [tri:p] **1.** *m* (-[e]s/-e) 🍺 sprout, (new) shoot; driving force; impulse; instinct; (sexual) urge; desire; **2.** ♀ *pret. of* treiben; '**~feder** *f* main-spring; *fig.* driving force, motive; '**~kraft** *f* motive power; *fig.* driving force, motive; '**~wagen** 🚋 *m* rail-car, rail-motor; '**~werk** ⊕ *n* gear (drive), (driving) mechanism, transmission; engine.

triefen ['tri:fən] *v/i.* ([*irr.,*] *ge-, h*) drip (*von* with); *eye*: run.

triftig *adj.* ['trɪftiç] valid.

Trigonometrie Ⓐ [trigonome'tri:] *f* (-/*no pl.*) trigonometry.

Trikot [tri'ko:] (-s/-s) **1.** *m* stockinet; **2.** *n* tights *pl.*; vest; **⸗agen** [⸗o'ta:-ʒən] *f/pl.* hosiery.

Triller ♪ ['trilər] *m* (-s/-) trill, shake, quaver; **⸗2n** ♪ *v/i. and v/t.* (ge-, h) trill, shake, quaver; *bird:* a. warble.

trink|bar *adj.* ['triŋkba:r] drinkable; **'⸗2becher** *m* drinking-cup; **'⸗en** (*irr.*, ge-, h) **1.** *v/t.* drink, take, have (*tea, etc.*); **2.** *v/i.* drink; *⸗ auf* (*acc.*) drink to, toast; **'2er** *m* (-s/-) drinker; drunkard; **'2gelage** *n* drinking-bout; **'2geld** *n* tip, gratuity; *j-m e-e Mark ⸗ geben* tip s.o. one mark; **'2glas** *n* drinking-glass; **'2halle** *f at spa:* pump-room; **'2kur** *f:* *e-e ⸗ machen* drink the waters; **'2spruch** *m* toast; **'2wasser** *n* (-s/*no pl.*) drinking-water.

Trio ['tri:o] *n* (-s/-s) trio (*a.* ♪).

trippeln ['tripəln] *v/i.* (ge-, sein) trip.

Tritt [trit] *m* (-[e]s/-e) tread, step; footprint; *noise:* footfall, (foot)step; kick; ⊕ treadle; *s.* Trittbrett, Trittleiter; *im* (*falschen*) *⸗* in (out of) step; *⸗ halten* keep step; **'⸗brett** *n* step, footboard; *mot.* running-board; **'⸗leiter** *f* stepladder, (e-e a pair *or* set of) steps *pl.*

Triumph [tri'umf] *m* (-[e]s/-e) triumph; **2al** *adj.* [⸗'fa:l] triumphant; **⸗bogen** *m* triumphal arch; **2ieren** [⸗'fi:rən] *v/i.* (*no* ge-, h) triumph (*über acc.* over).

trocken *adj.* ['trɔkən] dry (*a. fig.*); *soil, land:* arid; **'2dock** ⚓ *n* dry dock; **'2haube** *f* (hood of) hairdrier; **'2heit** *f* (-/*no pl.*) dryness; drought, aridity; **'⸗legen** *v/t.* (*sep.*, -ge-, h) dry up; drain (*land*); change the napkins of, *Am.* change the diapers of (*baby*); **'2obst** *n* dried fruit.

trocknen ['trɔknən] (ge-) **1.** *v/i.* (sein) dry; **2.** *v/t.* (h) dry.

Troddel ['trɔdəl] *f* (-/-n) tassel.

Trödel Ⓕ ['trø:dəl] *m* (-s/*no pl.*) second-hand articles *pl.*; lumber, *Am.* junk; rubbish; **'2n** Ⓕ *fig. v/i.* (ge-, h) dawdle, loiter.

Trödler ['trø:dlər] *m* (-s/-) second-hand dealer, *Am.* junk dealer, junkman; *fig.* dawdler, loiterer.

troff [trɔf] *pret.* of triefen.

Trog¹ [tro:k] *m* (-[e]s/⸚e) trough.

trog² [⸗] *pret.* of trügen.

Trommel ['trɔməl] *f* (-/-n) drum; ⊕ *a.* cylinder, barrel; **'⸗fell** *n* drumskin; *anat.* ear-drum; **'2n** *v/i. and v/t.* (ge-, h) drum.

Trommler ['trɔmlər] *m* (-s/-) drummer.

Trompete [trɔm'pe:tə] *f* (-/-n) trumpet; **2n** *v/i. and v/t.* (*no* ⸗ge-, h) trumpet; **⸗r** *m* (-s/-) trumpeter.

Tropen ['tro:pən]: *die ⸗ pl.* the tropics *pl.*

Tropf Ⓕ [trɔpf] *m* (-[e]s/⸚e) simpleton; *armer ⸗* poor wretch.

tröpfeln ['trœpfəln] (ge-) **1.** *v/i.* (h) drop, drip, trickle; *tap:* a. leak; *es tröpfelt rain:* a few drops are falling; **2.** *v/i.* (sein): *⸗ aus or von* trickle *or* drip from; **3.** *v/t.* (h) drop, drip.

tropfen¹ ['trɔpfən] (ge-) **1.** *v/i.* (h) drop, drip, trickle; *tap:* a. leak; *candle:* gutter; **2.** *v/i.* (sein): *⸗ aus or von* trickle *or* drip from; **3.** *v/t.* (h) drop, drip.

Tropfen² [⸗] *m* (-s/-) drop; *ein ⸗ auf den heißen Stein* a drop in the ocean *or* bucket; **2förmig** *adj.* ['⸗fœrmiç] drop-shaped; **2weise** *adv.* drop by drop, by drops.

Trophäe [tro'fɛ:ə] *f* (-/-n) trophy.

tropisch *adj.* ['tro:piʃ] tropical.

Trosse ['trɔsə] *f* (-/-n) cable; ⚓ *a.* hawser.

Trost [tro:st] *m* (-es/*no pl.*) comfort, consolation; *das ist ein schlechter ⸗* that is cold comfort; *du bist wohl nicht (recht) bei ⸗!* Ⓕ you must be out of your mind!

tröst|en ['trø:stən] *v/t.* (ge-, h) console, comfort; *sich ⸗* console o.s. (*mit with*); *⸗ Sie sich!* be of good comfort!, cheer up!; **'⸗lich** *adj.* comforting.

'trost|los *adj.* disconsolate, inconsolable; *land, etc.:* desolate; *fig.* wretched; **'2losigkeit** *f* (-/*no pl.*) desolation; *fig.* wretchedness; **'2preis** *m* consolation prize, booby prize; **'⸗reich** *adj.* consolatory, comforting.

Trott [trɔt] *m* (-[e]s/-e) trot; Ⓕ *fig.* jogtrot, routine; **'⸗el** Ⓕ *m* (-s/-) idiot, fool, ninny; **'2en** *v/i.* (ge-, sein) trot.

trotz [trɔts] **1.** *prp.* (*gen.*) in spite of, despite; *⸗ alledem* for all that; **2.** ⚥ *m* (-es/*no pl.*) defiance; obstinacy; **⸗dem** *cj.* ['⸗de:m] nevertheless; (al)though; **'⸗en** *v/i.* (ge-,

trotzig

h) (*dat.*) defy, dare; brave (*danger*); be obstinate; sulk; '**∼ig** *adj.* defiant; obstinate; sulky.

trüb *adj.* [try:p], **∼e** *adj.* ['∼bə] *liquid*: muddy, turbid, thick; *mind, thinking*: confused, muddy, turbid; *eyes, etc.*: dim, dull; *weather*: dull, cloudy, dreary (*all a. fig.*); *experiences*: sad.

Trubel ['tru:bəl] *m* (-s/*no pl.*) bustle.

trüben ['try:bən] *v/t.* (ge-, h) make thick *or* turbid *or* muddy; dim; darken; spoil (*pleasures, etc.*); blur (*view*); dull (*mind*); *sich ∼ liquid*: become thick *or* turbid *or* muddy; dim, darken; *relations*: become strained.

Trüb∣sal ['try:pza:l] *f* (-/✧-e): *∼ blasen* mope, F be in the dumps, have the blues; '**2selig** *adj.* sad, gloomy, melancholy; wretched, miserable; dreary; '**∼sinn** *m* (-[e]s/*no pl.*) melancholy, sadness, gloom; '**2sinnig** *adj.* melancholy, gloomy, sad; **∼ung** *f* (-/-en) *liquid*: muddiness, turbidity (*both a. fig.*); dimming, darkening.

Trüffel ✧ ['tryfəl] *f* (-/-n), F *m* (-s/-) truffle.

Trug[1] [tru:k] *m* (-[e]s/*no pl.*) deceit, fraud; delusion (*of senses*).

trug[2] [∼] *pret.* of tragen.

'**Trugbild** *n* phantom; illusion.

trüg∣en ['try:gən] (*irr.*, ge-, h) 1. *v/t.* deceive; 2. *v/i.* be deceptive; '**∼e-risch** *adj.* deceptive, delusive; treacherous.

'**Trugschluß** *m* fallacy, false conclusion.

Truhe ['tru:ə] *f* (-/-n) chest, trunk; *radio, etc.*: cabinet, console.

Trümmer ['trymər] *pl.* ruins *pl.*; rubble, debris; ⚓, ✈ wreckage; '**∼haufen** *m* heap of ruins or rubble.

Trumpf [trumpf] *m* (-[e]s/✧e) *cards*: trump (*card*) (*a. fig.*); *s-n ∼ ausspielen* play one's trump card.

Trunk [truŋk] *m* (-[e]s/✧e) drink; draught; drinking; '**2en** *adj.* drunken; *pred.* drunk (*a. fig. von, vor* with); intoxicated; '**∼enbold** *contp.* [' ∼bɔlt] *m* (-[e]s/-e) drunkard, sot; '**∼enheit** *f* (-/*no pl.*) drunkenness, intoxication; *∼ am Steuer* 🚗 drunken driving, drunkenness at the wheel; '**∼sucht** *f* alcoholism, dipsomania; '**2süchtig** *adj.* addicted to drink, given to drinking.

Trupp [trup] *m* (-s/-s) troop, band, gang; ✗ detachment.

'**Truppe** *f* (-/-n) ✗ troop, body; ✗ unit; *thea.* company, troupe; *∼n pl.* ✗ troops *pl.*, forces *pl.*; *die ∼n pl.* ✗ the (fighting) services *pl.*, the armed forces *pl.*

'**Truppen∣gattung** *f* arm, branch, division; '**∼schau** *f* military review; '**∼transporter** ⚓, ✈ *m* (troop-) transport; '**∼übungsplatz** *m* training area.

Truthahn *orn.* ['tru:t-] *m* turkey (-cock).

Tschech∣e ['tʃɛçə] *m* (-n/-n), '**∼in** *f* (-/-nen) Czech; '**2isch** *adj.* Czech.

Tube ['tu:bə] *f* (-/-n) tube.

tuberkul∣ös 🩺 *adj.* [tuberku'lø:s] tuberculous, tubercular; **2ose** *f* [∼o:zə] *f* (-/-n) tuberculosis.

Tuch [tu:x] *n* 1. (-[e]s/-e) cloth; fabric; 2. (-[e]s/✧er) *head covering*: kerchief; shawl, scarf; *round neck*: neckerchief; duster; rag; '**∼füh-lung** *f* (-/*no pl.*) close touch.

tüchtig ['tyçtiç] 1. *adj.* able, fit; clever; proficient; efficient; excellent; good; thorough; 2. *adv.* vigorously; thoroughly; F awfully; '**2keit** *f* (-/*no pl.*) ability, fitness; cleverness; proficiency; efficiency; excellency.

'**Tuchwaren** *f/pl.* drapery, cloths *pl.*

Tück∣e ['tykə] *f* (-/-n) malice, spite; '**2isch** *adj.* malicious, spiteful; treacherous.

tüfteln F ['tyftəln] *v/i.* (ge-, h) puzzle (*an dat.* over).

Tugend ['tu:gənt] *f* (-/-en) virtue; **∼bold** ['∼bɔlt] *m* (-[e]s/-e) paragon of virtue; '**2haft** *adj.* virtuous.

Tülle [tyl] *m* (-s/-e) tulle.

Tulpe ✧ ['tulpə] *f* (-/-n) tulip.

tummel∣n ['tuməln] *v/refl.* (ge-, h) *children*: romp; hurry; bestir o.s.; '**2platz** *m* playground; *fig.* arena.

Tümmler ['tymlər] *m* (-s/-) *orn.* tumbler; *zo.* porpoise.

Tumor 🩺 ['tu:mɔr] *m* (-s/-en) tumo(u)r.

Tümpel ['tympəl] *m* (-s/-) pool.

Tumult [tu'mult] *m* (-[e]s/-e) tumult; riot, turmoil, uproar; row.

tun [tu:n] 1. *v/t.* (*irr.*, ge-, h) do; make; put (*to school, into the bag, etc.*); *dazu ∼* add to it; contribute; *ich kann nichts dazu ∼* I cannot help it; *es ist mir darum zu ∼* I am anxious about (it); *zu* ~ *haben* have to do; be busy; *es tut nichts* it doesn't matter; **2.** *v/i.* (*irr.*, ge-, *h*) do; make; *so* ~ *als ob* make as if; pretend to *inf.*; *das tut gut!* that is a comfort!; *that's good!*; **3.** ♀ *n* (-*s*/*no pl.*) doings *pl.*; proceedings *pl.*; action; ~ *und Treiben* ways and doings *pl.*

Tünche ['tynçə] *f* (-/-*n*) whitewash (*a. fig.*); '**2n** *v/t.* (ge-, *h*) whitewash.

Tunichtgut ['tu:niçtgu:t] *m* (-, -[*e*]*s*/-*e*) ne'er-do-well, good-for-nothing.

Tunke ['tuŋkə] *f* (-/-*n*) sauce; '**2n** *v/t.* (ge-, *h*) dip, steep.

tunlichst *adv.* ['tu:nliçst] if possible.

Tunnel ['tunəl] *m* (-*s*/-, -*s*) tunnel; subway.

Tüpfel ['typfəl] *m*, *n* (-*s*/-) dot, spot; '**2n** *v/t.* (ge-, *h*) dot, spot.

tupfen ['tupfən] **1.** *v/t.* (ge-, *h*) dab; dot, spot; **2.** ♀ *m* (-*s*/-) dot, spot.

Tür [ty:r] *f* (-/-*en*) door; *mit der* ~ *ins Haus fallen* blurt (things) out; *j-n vor die* ~ *setzen* turn s.o. out; *vor der* ~ *stehen* be near or close at hand; *zwischen* ~ *und Angel in passing*; '~**angel** *f* (door-)hinge.

Turbine ⊕ [tur'bi:nə] *f* (-/-*n*) turbine; ~**flugzeug** *n* turbo-jet.

Turbo-Prop-Flugzeug ['turbo-'prɔp-] *n* turbo-prop.

'**Tür|flügel** *m* leaf (of a door); ~**füllung** *f* (door-)panel; '~**griff** *m* door-handle.

Türk|e ['tyrkə] *m* (-*n*/-*n*) Turk; '~**in** *f* (-/-*nen*) Turk(ish woman); '**2is** *min.* [~'ki:s] *m* (-*es*/-*e*) turquoise; '**2isch** *adj.* Turkish.

'**Türklinke** *f* door-handle; latch.

Turm [turm] *m* (-[*e*]*s*/-*e*) tower; *a.* steeple (*of church*); *chess*: castle, rook.

Türm|chen ['tyrmçən] *n* (-*s*/-) tur-

ret; '**2en** (ge-) **1.** *v/t.* (*h*) pile up; *sich* ~ tower; **2.** F *v/i.* (*sein*) bolt, F skedaddle, *Am. sl. a.* skiddoo.

'**turm|hoch** *adv.*: *j-m* ~ *überlegen sein* stand head and shoulders above s.o.; '~**spitze** *f* spire; '**2-springen** *n* (-*s*/*no pl.*) *swimming*: high diving; '**2uhr** *f* tower-clock, church-clock.

turnen ['turnən] **1.** *v/i.* (ge-, *h*) do gymnastics; **2.** ♀ *n* (-*s*/*no pl.*) gymnastics *pl.*

'**Turn|er** *m* (-*s*/-), '~**erin** *f* (-/-*nen*) gymnast; '~**gerät** *n* gymnastic apparatus; '~**halle** *f* gym(nasium); '~**hemd** *n* (gym-)shirt; '~**hose** *f* shorts *pl.*

Turnier [tur'ni:r] *n* (-*s*/-*e*) tournament.

'**Turn|lehrer** *m* gym master; '~**lehrerin** *f* gym mistress; '~**schuh** *m* gym-shoe; '~**stunde** *f* gym lesson; '~**unterricht** *m* instruction in gymnastics; '~**verein** *m* gymnastic or athletic club.

'**Tür|pfosten** *m* door-post; '~**rahmen** *m* door-case, door-frame; '~**schild** *n* door-plate.

Tusche ['tuʃə] *f* (-/-*n*) India(n) or Chinese ink; '**2ln** *v/i.* (ge-, *h*) whisper; '**2n** *v/t.* (ge-, *h*) draw in India(n) ink.

Tüte ['ty:tə] *f* (-/-*n*) paper-bag.

tuten ['tu:tən] *v/i.* (ge-, *h*) toot(le); *mot.* honk, blow one's horn.

Typ [ty:p] *m* (-*s*/-*en*) type; ⊕ *a.* model; '~**e** *f* (-/-*n*) *typ.* type; F *fig.* (queer) character.

Typhus 🕮 ['ty:fus] *m* (-/*no pl.*) typhoid (fever).

'**typisch** *adj.* typical (*für* of).

Tyrann [ty'ran] *m* (-*en*/-*en*) tyrant; ~**ei** [~'naɪ] *f* (-/*no pl.*) tyranny; **2isch** *adj.* [ty'raniʃ] tyrannical; **2isieren** [~i'zi:rən] *v/t.* (*no* -ge-, *h*) tyrannize (over) s.o., oppress, bully.

U

U-Bahn ['u:-] *f s. Untergrundbahn*.

übel ['y:bəl] **1.** *adj.* evil, bad; *nicht* ~ not bad, pretty good; *mir wird* ~ I am or feel sick; **2.** *adv.* ill; ~ *gelaunt sein* be in a bad mood; *es gefällt mir nicht* ~ I rather like it;

3. ♀ *n* (-*s*/-) evil; *s. Übelstand*; *das kleinere* ~ *wählen* choose the lesser evil; '~**gelaunt** *adj.* ill-humo(u)red; '**2keit** *f* (-/-*en*) sickness, nausea; '~**nehmen** *v/t.* (*irr. nehmen, sep.,* -ge-, *h*) take s.th. ill or amiss; '**2-**

U V

stand *m* grievance; **Ꞛtäter** *m* evil-doer, wrongdoer.

'übelwollen 1. *v/i.* (*sep.*, -ge-, *h*): *j-m* ~ wish s.o. ill; be ill-disposed towards s.o.; **2.** Ꞛ *n* (*-s/no pl.*) ill will, malevolence; **'~d** *adj.* malevolent.

üben ['y:bən] (ge-, *h*) **1.** *v/t.* exercise; practiꞅe, *Am. a.* -ce; *Geduld* ~ exercise patience; *Klavier* ~ practiꞅe the piano; **2.** *v/i.* exercise; practiꞅe, *Am. a.* -ce.

über ['y:bər] **1.** *prp.* (*dat.*; *acc.*) over, above; across (*river, etc.*); via, by way of (*Munich, etc.*); *sprechen* ~ (*acc.*) talk about *or* of; ~ *Politik sprechen* talk politics; *nachdenken* ~ (*acc.*) think about *or* of; *ein Buch schreiben* ~ (*acc.*) write a book on; ~ *Nacht bleiben bei* stay overnight at; ~ *s-e Verhältnisse leben* live beyond one's income; ~ *kurz oder lang* sooner *or* later; **2.** *adv.*: *die ganze Zeit* ~ all along; *j-m in et.* ~ *sein* excel s.o. in s.th.

über'all *adv.* everywhere, anywhere, *Am. a.* all over.

über'|anstrengen *v/t.* (*no -ge-, h*) overstrain; *sich* ~ overstrain o.s.; **~'arbeiten** *v/t.* (*no -ge-, h*) retouch (*painting, etc.*); revise (*book, etc.*); *sich* ~ overwork o.s.

überaus *adv.* ['y:bər⁹-] exceedingly, extremely.

'überbelichten *phot. v/t.* (*no -ge-, h*) over-expose.

über'bieten *v/t.* (*irr. bieten, no -ge-, h*) at *auction*: outbid; *fig.*: beat; surpass.

Überbleibsel ['y:bərblaipsəl] *n* (*-s/-*) remnant, *Am.* F *a.* holdover; ~ *pl. a.* remains *pl.*

'Überblick *fig. m* survey, general view (*both*: über *acc. of*).

über'|blicken *v/t.* (*no -ge-, h*) overlook; *fig.* survey, have a general view of; **~'bringen** *v/t.* (*irr. bringen, no -ge-, h*) deliver; Ꞛ**'bringer** *m* (*-s/-*) bearer; **~'brücken** *v/t.* (*no -ge-, h*) bridge; *fig.* bridge over *s.th.*; **~'dachen** *v/t.* (*no -ge-, h*) roof over; **~'dauern** *v/t.* (*no -ge-, h*) outlast, outlive; **~'denken** *v/t.* (*irr. denken, no -ge-, h*) think *s.th.* over.

über'dies *adv.* besides, moreover.

über'drehen *v/t.* (*no -ge-, h*) overwind (*watch, etc.*); strip (*screw*).

'Überdruck *m* **1.** (*-[e]s/-e*) overprint; *typ. a.* surcharge; **2.** ⊕ (*-[e]s/-e*) overpressure.

Über'|druß ['y:bərdrus] *m* (*Überdrusses/no pl.*) satiety; *bis zum* ~ to satiety; Ꞛ**'drüssig** *adj.* (*gen.*) ['y:-sıç] disgusted with, weary *or* sick of.

Über'eif|er ['y:bər⁹-] *m* over-zeal; Ꞛ**'rig** *adj.* ['y:bər⁹-] over-zealous.

über'eil|en *v/t.* (*no -ge-, h*) precipitate, rush; *sich* ~ hurry too much; **~t** *adj.* precipitate, rash.

übereinander *adv.* [y:bər⁹aɪ'nandər] one upon the other; **~schlagen** *v/t.* (*irr. schlagen, sep., -ge-, h*) cross (*one's legs*).

über'ein|kommen *v/i.* (*irr. kommen, sep., -ge-, sein*) agree; Ꞛ**kommen** *n* (*-s/-*), Ꞛ**kunft** [~kunft] *f* (*-/-e*) agreement; **~stimmen** *v/i.* (*sep., -ge-, h*) *p.* agree (*mit with*); *thing*: correspond (*with, to*); Ꞛ**stimmung** *f* agreement; correspondence; *in* ~ *mit* in agreement *or* accordance with.

über'|fahren 1. ['~faːrən] *v/i.* (*irr. fahren, sep., -ge-, sein*) cross; **2.** [~'faːrən] *v/t.* (*irr. fahren, no -ge-, h*) run over; disregard (*traffic sign, etc.*); Ꞛ**fahrt** *f* passage; crossing.

'Überfall *m* ✕ surprise; ✕ invasion (*auf acc. of*); ✕ raid; hold-up; assault ([up]on).

über'fallen *v/t.* (*irr. fallen, no -ge-, h*) ✕ surprise; ✕ invade; ✕ raid; hold up; assault.

'über'fällig *adj.* overdue; Ꞛ**fallkommando** *n* flying squad, *Am.* riot squad.

über'fliegen *v/t.* (*irr. fliegen, no -ge-, h*) fly over *or* across; *fig.* glance over, skim (*through*); *den Atlantik* ~ fly (across) the Atlantic.

'überfließen *v/i.* (*irr. fließen, sep., -ge-, sein*) overflow.

über'flügeln *v/t.* (*no -ge-, h*) ✕ outflank; *fig.* outstrip, surpass.

'Über|fluß *m* (*Überflusses/no pl.*) abundance (*an dat. of*); superfluity (*of*); ~ *haben an* (*dat.*) abound in (*of*); Ꞛ**flüssig** *adj.* superfluous; redundant.

über'fluten *v/t.* (*no -ge-, h*) overflow, flood (*a city*).

'Überfracht *f* excess freight.

über'führen *v/t.* **1.** [~'fyːrən] (*sep., -ge-, h*) convey (*dead body*).

2. [ˌˈfyːrən] (no -ge-, h) s. 1; ⚖ convict (gen. of); ²ˈführung f (-/-en) conveyance (of dead body); bridge, Am. overpass; ⚖ conviction (gen. of).   [dat. u.]

'**Überfülle** f superabundance (an)

über|'**füllen** v/t. (no -ge-, h) overfill; cram; overcrowd; sich den Magen ∼ glut o.s.; ∼'**füttern** v/t. (no -ge-, h) overfeed.

'**Übergabe** f delivery; handing over; surrender (a. ✗).

'**Übergang** m bridge; 🚃 crossing; fig. transition (a. ♪); esp. ⚖ devolution; '∼**sstadium** n transition stage.

über|'**geben** v/t. (irr. geben, no -ge-, h) deliver up; hand over; surrender (a. ✗); sich ∼ vomit, be sick; ∼**gehen 1.** ['∼ɡeːən] v/i. (irr. gehen, sep., -ge-, sein) pass over; work, duties: devolve (auf acc. [up]on); ∼ in (acc.) pass into; ∼ zu et. proceed to s.th.; **2.** [∼'ɡeːən] v/t. (irr. gehen, no -ge-, h) pass over, ignore.

'**Übergewicht** n (-[e]s/no pl.) overweight; fig. a. preponderance (über acc. over).

über|'**gießen** v/t. (irr. gießen, no -ge-, h): mit Wasser ∼ pour water over s.th.; mit Fett ∼ baste (roasting meat).

über|'**greifen** v/i. (irr. greifen, sep., -ge-, h): ∼ auf (acc.) encroach (up-)on (s.o.'s rights); fire, epidemic, etc.: spread to; ²**griff** m encroachment (auf acc. [up]on), inroad (on); '∼**haben** F v/t. (irr. haben, sep., -ge-, h) have (coat, etc.) on; fig. have enough of, sl. be fed up with.

über|'**handnehmen** v/i. (irr. nehmen, sep., -ge-, h) be rampant, grow or wax rife.

'**überhängen 1.** v/i. (irr. hängen, sep., -ge-, h) overhang; **2.** v/t. (sep., -ge-, h) put (coat, etc.) round one's shoulders; sling (rifle) over one's shoulder.

über'**häufen** v/t. (no -ge-, h): ∼ mit swamp with (letters, work, etc.); overwhelm with (inquiries, etc.).

über'**haupt** adv.: wer will denn ∼, daß er kommt? who wants him to come anyhow?; wenn ∼ if at all; ∼ nicht not at all; ∼ kein no ... whatever.

überheblich adj. [yːbərˈheːplɪç] presumptuous, arrogant; ²**keit** f

(-/⚲-en) presumption, arrogance.

über|'**hitzen** v/t. (no -ge-, h) overheat (a. ✝); ⊕ superheat; ∼'**holen** v/t. (no -ge-, h) overtake (a. mot.); esp. sports: outstrip (a. fig.); overhaul, esp. Am. a. service; ∼'**holt** adj. outmoded; pred. a. out of date; ∼'**hören** v/t. (no -ge-, h) fail to hear, miss; ignore.

'**überirdisch** adj. supernatural; unearthly.

'**überkippen** v/i. (sep., -ge-, sein) p. overbalance, lose one's balance.

über'**kleben** v/t. (no -ge-, h) paste over.

'**Überkleidung** f outer garments pl.

'**überklug** adj. would-be wise, sapient.

'**überkochen** v/i. (sep., -ge-, sein) boil over; F leicht ∼ be very irritable.

über|'**kommen** v/t. (irr. kommen, no -ge-, h): Furcht überkam ihn he was seized with fear; ∼'**laden** v/t. (irr. laden, no -ge-, h) overload; overcharge (battery, picture, etc.).

'**Überland**|**flug** m cross-country flight; '∼**zentrale** ⚡ f long-distance power-station.

über|'**lassen** v/t. (irr. lassen, no -ge-, h): j-m et. ∼ let s.o. have s.th.; fig. leave s.th. to s.o.; j-n sich selbst ∼ leave s.o. to himself; j-n s-m Schicksal ∼ leave or abandon s.o. to his fate; ∼'**lasten** v/t. (no -ge-, h) overload; fig. overburden.

über|'**laufen 1.** ['∼laʊfən] v/i. (irr. laufen, sep., -ge-, sein) run over; boil over; ✗ desert (zu to); **2.** [∼'laʊfən] v/t. (irr. laufen, no -ge-, h): es überlief mich kalt a shudder passed over me; überlaufen werden von doctor, etc.: be besieged by (patients, etc.); **3.** adj. [∼'laʊfən] place, profession, etc.: overcrowded; ²**läufer** m ✗ deserter; pol. renegade, turncoat.

'**überlaut** adj. too loud.

über'**leben** v/t. (no -ge-, h) **1.** v/t. survive, outlive; **2.** v/i. survive; ²**de** m, f (-n/-n) survivor.

'**überlebensgroß** adj. bigger than life-size(d).

überlebt adj. [yːbərˈleːpt] outmoded, disused, out of date.

'**überlegen**¹ v/t. (sep., -ge-, h) give (child) a spanking.

über'**leg**|**en**² **1.** v/t. and v/refl. (no

-ge-, h) consider, reflect upon, think about; *ich will es mir* ~ I will think it over; *es sich anders* ~ change one's mind; **2.** *v/i.* (*no* -ge-, h): *er überlegt noch* he hasn't made up his mind yet; **3.** *adj.* superior (*dat.* to; *an dat.* in); **2enheit** *f* (*-/no pl.*) superiority; preponderance; ~**t** *adj.* [~kt] deliberate; prudent; **2ung** [~guŋ] *f* (*-/-en*) consideration, reflection; *nach reiflicher* ~ after mature deliberation.

über'lesen *v/t.* (*irr.* lesen, *no* -ge-, h) read *s.th.* through quickly, run over *s.th.*; overlook.

über'liefer|n *v/t.* (*no* -ge-, h) hand down *or* on (*dat.* to); **2ung** *f* tradition.

über'listen *v/t.* (*no* -ge-, h) outwit, F outsmart.

'**Über|macht** *f* (*-/no pl.*) superiority; *esp.* ✕ superior forces *pl.*; *in der* ~ *sein* be superior in numbers; **2mächtig** *adj.* superior.

über'malen *v/t.* (*no* -ge-, h) paint out; ~'**mannen** *v/t.* (*no* -ge-, h) overpower, overcome, overwhelm (*all. a. fig.*).

'**Über|maß** *n* (*-es/no pl.*) excess (*an dat.* of); **2mäßig 1.** *adj.* excessive; immoderate; **2.** *adv.* excessively, Am. *a.* overly; ~ *trinken* drink to excess.

'**Übermensch** *m* superman; **2lich** *adj.* superhuman.

über'mitt|eln *v/t.* (*no* -ge-, h) transmit; convey; **2lung** *f* (*-/-en*) transmission; conveyance.

'**übermorgen** *adv.* the day after tomorrow.

über'müd|et *adj.* overtired; **2ung** *f* (*-/~-en*) overfatigue.

'**Über|mut** *m* wantonness; frolicsomeness; **2mütig** *adj.* [~my:tiç] wanton; frolicsome.

'**übernächst** *adj. the* next but one; ~*e Woche* the week after next.

über'nacht|en *v/i.* (*no* -ge-, h) stay overnight (*bei at a friend's* [*house*], *with friends*), spend the night (at, with); **2ung** *f* (*-/-en*) spending the night; ~ *und Frühstück* bed and breakfast.

Übernahme [~'ya:bərna:mə] *f* (*-/-n*) field of application *s.* übernehmen 1: taking over; undertaking; assumption; adoption.

'**übernatürlich** *adj.* supernatural.

übernehmen *v/t.* **1.** [~'ne:mən] (*irr.* nehmen, *no* -ge-, h) take over (*business, etc.*); undertake (*responsibility, etc.*); take (*lead, risk, etc.*); assume (*direction of business, office, etc.*); adopt (*idea, custom, etc.*); *sich* ~ overreach o.s.; **2.** ✕ ['~ne:mən] (*irr.* nehmen, *sep.*, -ge-, h) slope, shoulder (*arms*).

'**über|ordnen** *v/t.* (*sep.*, -ge-, h): *j-n j-m* ~ set s.o. over s.o.; '~**parteilich** *adj.* non-partisan; '**2produktion** *f* over-production.

über'prüf|en *v/t.* (*no* -ge-, h) reconsider; verify; check; review; screen *s.o.*; **2ung** *f* reconsideration; checking; review.

über|'queren *v/t.* (*no* -ge-, h) cross; ~'**ragen** *v/t.* (*no* -ge-, h) tower above (*a. fig.*), overtop; *fig.* surpass.

überrasch|en [y:bər'raʃən] *v/t.* (*no* -ge-, h) surprise; catch (*bei at, in*); **2ung** *f* (*-/-en*) surprise.

über'red|en *v/t.* (*no* -ge-, h) persuade (*zu inf.* to *inf.*, into *ger.*); talk (*into ger.*); **2ung** *f* (*-/~-en*) persuasion.

über'reich|en *v/t.* (*no* -ge-, h) present; **2ung** *f* (*-/~-en*) presentation.

über|'reizen *v/t.* (*no* -ge-, h) overexcite; ~'**reizt** *adj.* overstrung; ~'**rennen** *v/t.* (*irr.* rennen, *no* -ge-, h) overrun.

'**Überrest** *m* remainder; ~*e pl.* remains *pl.*; *sterbliche* ~*e pl.* mortal remains *pl.*

über'rump|eln *v/t.* (*no* -ge-, h) (take by) surprise; **2(e)lung** *f* (*-/~-en*) surprise.

über'rund|en *v/t.* (*no* -ge-, h) *sports:* lap; *fig.* surpass; **2ung** *f* (*-/-en*) lapping.

übersät *adj.* [y:bər'zɛ:t] studded, dotted.

über'sättig|en *v/t.* (*no* -ge-, h) surfeit (*a. fig.*); 🌰 supersaturate; **2ung** *f* (*-/-en*) surfeit (*a. fig.*); 🌰 supersaturation.

'**Überschallgeschwindigkeit** *f* supersonic speed.

über|'schatten *v/t.* (*no* -ge-, h) overshadow (*a. fig.*); ~'**schätzen** *v/t.* (*no* -ge-, h) overrate, overestimate.

'**Überschlag** *m gymnastics:* somersault; ✈ loop; ⚡ flashover; *fig.*

estimate, approximate calculation;
2en (*irr. schlagen*) **1.** ['~∫la:gən] *v/t.*
(*sep.*, *-ge-*, *h*) cross (*one's legs*);
2. ['~∫la:gən] *v/i.* (*sep.*, *-ge-*, *sein*)
voice: become high-pitched; **3.**
[~'∫la:gən] *v/t.* (*no -ge-*, *h*) skip
(*page*, *etc.*): make a rough estimate
of (*cost*, *etc.*); *sich ~ fall head over
heels*; *car, etc.*: (be) turn(ed) over;
⊼ loop the loop; *voice*: become
high-pitched; *~ vor* (*dat.*) outdo
(*one's friendliness*, *etc.*); **4.** *adj.*
[~'∫la:gən] lukewarm, tepid.

'**überschnappen** *v/i.* (*sep.*, *-ge-*,
sein) *voice*: become high-pitched;
F *p.* go mad, turn crazy.

über|**schneiden** *v/refl.* (*irr. schnei-
den*, *no -ge-*, *h*) overlap; intersect;
~'**schreiben** *v/t.* (*irr. schreiben*, *no
-ge-*, *h*) superscribe, entitle; make
s.th. over (*dat.* to); ~'**schreiten**
v/t. (*irr. schreiten*, *no -ge-*, *h*) cross;
transgress (*limit*, *bound*); infringe
(*rule*, *etc.*); exceed (*speed limit, one's
instructions, etc.*); *sie hat die 40 bereits überschritten* she is on the
wrong side of 40.

'**Über**|**schrift** *f* heading, title;
headline; '~**schuh** *m* overshoe.

'**Über**|**schuß** *m* surplus, excess;
profit; 2**schüssig** *adj.* ['~∫ysiç]
surplus, excess.

über'schütten *v/t.* (*no -ge-*, *h*): ~
mit pour (*water*, *etc.*) on; *fig.*: overwhelm with (*inquiries*, *etc.*); shower
(*gifts*, *etc.*) upon.

überschwemm|**en** [y:bər'∫vemən]
v/t. (*no -ge-*, *h*) inundate, flood
(*both a. fig.*); 2**ung** *f* (*-/-en*) inunda-
tion, flood(ing).

überschwenglich *adj.* ['y:bər-
∫vɛŋliç] effusive, gushy.

'**Übersee**: *nach ~ gehen* go overseas; '~**dampfer** ⚓ *m* transoceanic
steamer; '~**handel** *m* (*-s/no pl.*)
oversea(s) trade.

über'sehen *v/t.* (*irr. sehen*, *no -ge-*,
h) survey; overlook (*printer's error*,
etc.); *fig.* ignore, disregard.

über'send|**en** *v/t.* (*irr. senden*, *no
-ge-*, *h*) send, transmit; consign;
2**ung** *f* sending, transmission; ✝
consignment.

'**übersetzen**[1] (*sep.*, *-ge-*) **1.** *v/i.* (*sein*)
cross; **2.** *v/t.* (*h*) ferry.

über'setz|**en**[2] *v/t.* (*no -ge-*, *h*)
translate (*in acc.* into), render (into);
⊕ gear; 2**er** *m* (*-s/-*) translator;

2**ung** *f* (*-/-en*) translation (*aus
from*; *in acc.* into); rendering; ⊕
gear(ing), transmission.

'**Übersicht** *f* (*-/-en*) survey (*über
acc.* of); summary; 2**lich** *adj.*
clear(ly arranged).

über|**siedeln** ['y:bərzi:dəln] *v/i.*
(*sep.*, *-ge-*, *sein*) and [~'zi:dəln] *v/i.*
(*no -ge-*, *sein*) remove (*nach* to);
2**siedelung** [~'zi:dəluŋ] *f* (*-/-en*),
2**siedlung** [~zi:dluŋ, ~'zi:dluŋ] *f*
(*-/-en*) removal (*nach* to).

'**übersinnlich** *adj.* transcendental;
forces: psychic.

über'spann|**en** *v/t.* (*no -ge-*, *h*)
cover (*mit* with); *den Bogen ~* go
too far; ~**t** *adj.* extravagant; *p.*
eccentric; *claims*, *etc.*: exaggerated;
2**theit** *f* (*-/*⚹*-en*) extravagance;
eccentricity.

über'spitzt *adj.* oversubtle; exaggerated.

überspringen 1. ['~∫priŋən] *v/i.*
(*irr. springen*, *sep.*, *-ge-*, *sein*) ⚡
spark: jump; *in a speech, etc.*: ~ *von
… zu …* jump or skip from (*one
subject*) to (*another*); **2.** [~'∫priŋən]
v/t. (*irr. springen*, *no -ge-*, *h*) jump,
clear; skip (*page*, *etc.*); jump (*class*).

überstehen (*irr. stehen*) **1.** ['~∫te:ən]
v/i. (*sep.*, *-ge-*, *h*) jut (out or forth),
project; **2.** [~'∫te:ən] *v/t.* (*no -ge-*, *h*)
survive (*misfortune*, *etc.*); weather
(*crisis*); get over (*illness*).

über|'**steigen** *v/t.* (*irr. steigen*, *no
-ge-*, *h*) climb over; *fig.* exceed;
~'**stimmen** *v/t.* (*no -ge-*, *h*) out-
vote, vote down.

'**überstreifen** *v/t.* (*sep.*, *-ge-*, *h*)
slip *s.th.* over.

überströmen 1. ['~∫trø:mən] *v/i.*
(*sep.*, *-ge-*, *sein*) overflow (*vor dat.*
with); **2.** [~'∫trø:mən] *v/t.* (*no -ge-*,
h) flood, inundate.

'**Überstunden** *f/pl.* overtime; ~
machen work overtime.

über'stürz|**en** *v/t.* (*no -ge-*, *h*)
rush, hurry (up or on); *sich ~* act
rashly; *events*: follow in rapid
succession; 2**t** *adj.* precipitate, rash;
2**ung** *f* (*-/*⚹*-en*) precipitancy.

über|'**teuern** *v/t.* (*no -ge-*, *h*) over-
charge; ~'**tölpeln** *v/t.* (*no -ge-*, *h*)
dupe, take in; ~'**tönen** *v/t.* (*no
-ge-*, *h*) drown.

Übertrag ✝ ['y:bərtra:k] *m* (*-[e]s/
⁼e*) carrying forward; sum carried
forward.

über'trag|bar adj. transferable; ⚓
negotiable; ✍ communicable; **~en**
[~gən] **1.** v/t. (irr. tragen, no -ge-, h)
⚓ carry forward; make over (property) (auf acc. to); ✍ transfuse
(blood); delegate (rights, etc.) (dat.
to); render (book, etc.) (in acc. into);
transcribe (s.th. written in shorthand); ♪, ⊕, phys., radio: transmit; radio: a. broadcast; im Fernsehen ~ televise; ihm wurde eine
wichtige Mission ~ he was charged
with an important mission; **2.** adj.
figurative; 2ung [~guŋ] f (-/-en)
field of application s. übertragen 1:
carrying forward; making over;
transfusion; delegation; rendering,
free translation; transcription;
transmission; broadcast; ~ im Fernsehen telecast.

über'treffen v/t. (irr. treffen, no
-ge-, h) excel s.o. (an dat. in; in dat.
in, at); surpass (in), exceed (in).

über'treib|en v/t. (irr. treiben, no
-ge-, h) **1.** v/t. overdo; exaggerate,
overstate; v/i. exaggerate, draw
the long bow; 2ung f (-/-en) exaggeration, overstatement.

'übertreten[1] v/i. (irr. treten, sep.,
-ge-, sein) sports: cross the take-off
line; fig. go over (zu to); zum
Katholizismus ~ turn Roman
Catholic.

über'tret|en[2] v/t. (irr. treten, no
-ge-, h) transgress, violate, infringe
(law, etc.); sich den Fuß ~ sprain one's
ankle; 2ung f (-/-en) transgression,
violation, infringement.

'Übertritt m going over (zu to)
eccl. conversion (to).

übervölker|n [y:bər'fœlkərn] v/t.
(no -ge-, h) over-populate; 2ung f
(-/-en) over-population.

über'vorteilen v/t. (no -ge-, h)
overreach, F do.

über'wach|en v/t. (no -ge-, h)
supervise, superintend; control;
police: keep under surveillance,
shadow; 2ung f (-/-en) supervision, superintendence; control;
surveillance.

überwältigen [y:bər'vɛltigən] v/t.
(no -ge-, h) overcome, overpower,
overwhelm (all a. fig.); **~d** fig. adj.
overwhelming.

über'weis|en v/t. (irr. weisen, no
-ge-, h) remit (money) (dat. or an
acc. to); (zur Entscheidung etc.) ~

refer (to); 2ung f (-/-en) remittance;
reference (an acc. to); parl. devolution.

überwerfen (irr. werfen) **1.** ['~vɛr-
fən] v/t. (sep., -ge-, h) slip (coat) on;
2. [.'vɛrfən] v/refl. (no -ge-, h) fall
out (mit with).

über'wiegen (irr. wiegen, no -ge-, h)
1. v/t. outweigh; **2.** v/i. preponder-
ate; predominate; **~wiegend** adj.
preponderant; predominant; **~-
'winden** v/t. (irr. winden, no -ge-, h)
overcome (a. fig.), subdue; sich ~ zu
inf. bring o.s. to inf.; **~'wintern**
v/i. (no -ge-, h) (pass the) winter.

'Über|wurf m wrap; **~zahl** f
(-/-en) numerical superiority; in
der ~ superior in numbers; 2zählig
adj. ['~tse:liç] supernumerary; surplus.

über'zeug|en v/t. (no -ge-, h) con-
vince (von of); satisfy (of); 2ung f
(-/-en) conviction.

überziehe|n v/t. (irr. ziehen)
1. ['~tsi:ən] (sep., -ge-, h) put on;
2. [.'tsi:ən] (no -ge-, h) cover; put
clean sheets on (bed); ⚓ overdraw
(account); sich ~ sky: become over-
cast; 2r m (-s/-) overcoat, topcoat.

'Überzug m cover; case, tick; ⊕
coat(ing).

üblich adj. ['y:pliç] usual, custom-
U-Boot ♣, ⚔ ['u:'] n submarine, in
Germany: a. U-boat.

übrig adj. ['y:briç] left, remaining;
die ~e Welt the rest of the world;
die ~en pl. the others pl., the rest;
im ~en for the rest; by the way; ~
haben have s.th. left; keine Zeit ~
haben have no time to spare; etwas
~ haben für care for, have a soft
spot for; ein ~es tun go out of one's
way; **~bleiben** v/i. (irr. bleiben,
sep., -ge-, sein) be left; remain; es
blieb ihm nichts anderes übrig he
had no (other) alternative (als but);
~ens adv. ['~gəns] by the way;
~lassen ['~ç-] v/t. (irr. lassen, sep.,
-ge-, h) leave; viel zu wünschen ~
leave much to be desired.

'Übung f (-/-en) exercise; practice;
drill; **'~shang** m skiing: nursery
slope.

Ufer ['u:fər] n (-s/-) shore (of sea,
lake); bank (of river, etc.).

Uhr [u:r] f (-/-en) clock; watch; um
vier ~ at four o'clock; **'~armband**
n (-[e]s/~er) watch-strap; **'~feder** f

watch-spring; '**~macher** m (-s/-)
watch-maker; '**~werk** n clockwork;
watch-work; '**~zeiger** m hand (of
clock or watch); '**~zeigersinn** m
(-[e]s/no pl.): im ~ clockwise; entgegen dem ~ counter-clockwise.

Uhu orn. ['u:hu:] m (-s/-s) eagle-owl.

Ulk [ulk] m (-[e]s/-e) fun, lark; '**2en**
v/i. (ge-, h) (sky)lark, joke; '**2ig** adj.
funny.

Ulme ♀ ['ulmə] f (-/-n) elm.

Ultimatum [ulti'ma:tum] n (-s/Ul-
timaten, -s) ultimatum; j-m ein ~
stellen deliver an ultimatum to s.o.

Ultimo ✝ ['ultimo] m (-s/-s) last
day of the month.

Ultrakurzwelle phys. [ultra'-] f
ultra-short wave, very-high-fre-
quency wave.

um [um] **1.** prp. (acc.) round, about;
~ vier Uhr at four o'clock; ~ sein Leben laufen run for one's life; et. ~
einen Meter verfehlen miss s.th. by
a metre; et. ~ zwei Mark verkaufen
sell s.th. at two marks; **2.** prp. (gen.):
~ seinetwillen for his sake; **3.** cj.: ~
so besser all the better, so much the
better; ~ so mehr (weniger) all the
more (less); ~ zu (in order to); **4.**
adv.: er drehte sich ~ he turned
round.

um|ändern ['um⁹-] v/t. (sep., -ge-,
h) change, alter; **~arbeiten** ['um⁹-]
v/t. (sep., -ge-, h) make over (coat,
etc.); revise (book, etc.); ~ zu make
into.

um'armen v/t. (no -ge-, h) hug,
embrace; sich ~ embrace; **2ung** f
(-/-en) embrace, hug.

'**Umbau** m (-[e]s/-e, -ten) rebuilding;
reconstruction; '**2en** v/t. (sep.,
-ge-, h) rebuild; reconstruct.

'**umbiegen** v/t. (irr. biegen, sep.,
-ge-, h) bend; turn up or down.

'**umbild|en** v/t. (sep., -ge-, h)
remodel, reconstruct; reorganize,
reform; reshuffle (cabinet); **2ung** f
(-/-en) remodel(l)ing, reconstruction; reorganization, pol. reshuffle.

'**um|binden** v/t. (irr. binden, sep.,
-ge-, h) put on (apron, etc.); '**~blät-
tern** (sep., -ge-, h) **1.** v/t. turn over;
2. v/i. turn over the page; '**~brechen**
v/t. (irr. brechen) **1.** ✏ ['~brɛçən]
(sep., -ge-, h) dig, break up (ground);
2. typ. [~'brɛçən] (no -ge-, h) make
up; '**~bringen** v/t. (irr. bringen,
sep., -ge-, h) kill; sich ~ kill o.s.;

'**2bruch** m typ. make-up; fig.:
upheaval; radical change; '**~bu-
chen** v/t.⁺ (sep., -ge-, h) ✝ transfer
or switch to another account; book
for another date; **~disponieren**
v/i. (sep., no -ge-, h) change one's
plans.

'**umdreh|en** v/t. (sep., -ge-, h) turn;
s. Spieß; sich ~ turn round; '**2ung**
[um'-] f (-/-en) turn; phys., ⊕ rotation, revolution.

um|fahren (irr. fahren) **1.** ['~fa:rən]
v/t. (sep., -ge-, h) run down;
2. [~'fa:rən] (no -ge-, h) drive round; ⊕
sail round; ♣ double (cape); '**~
fallen** v/i. (irr. fallen, sep., -ge-,
sein) fall; collapse; tot ~ drop dead.

'**Umfang** m (-[e]s/no pl.) circumference, circuit; perimeter; girth
(of body, tree, etc.); fig.: extent;
volume; in großem ~ on a large
scale; '**2reich** adj. extensive,
voluminous; spacious.

um'fassen v/t. (no -ge-, h) clasp,
embrace (a. fig.); ⚔ envelop; fig.
comprise, cover, comprehend; **~d**
adj. comprehensive, extensive,
sweeping, drastic.

'**umform|en** v/t. (sep., -ge-, h)
remodel, recast, transform (a. ⚡);
⚡ convert; '**2er** ⚡ m (-s/-) trans-
former; converter.

'**Umfrage** f poll; öffentliche ~
public opinion poll.

'**Umgang** m **1.** (-[e]s/⁼e) 🏛 gallery,
ambulatory; eccl. procession (round
the fields, etc.); **2.** (-[e]s/no pl.) intercourse (mit with); company; ~ ha-
ben mit associate with.

umgänglich adj. ['umgɛnlɪç] sociable, companionable, affable.

'**Umgangs|formen** f/pl. manners
pl.; '**~sprache** f colloquial usage;
in der deutschen ~ in colloquial
German.

um'garnen v/t. (no -ge-, h) ensnare.

um'geb|en 1. v/t. (irr. geben, no
-ge-, h) surround; mit e-r Mauer ~
wall in; **2.** adj. surrounded (von
with, by) (a. fig.); **2ung** f (-/-en)
environs pl. (of town, etc.); surroundings pl., environment (of
place, person, etc.).

umgeh|en 1. v/i. (irr. gehen) ['~ge:ən]
v/i. (sep., -ge-, sein) make a detour;
rumour, etc.: go about, be afloat;

ghost: walk; ~ *mit* use *s.th.*; deal with *s.o.*; keep company with; *ein Gespenst soll im Schlosse* ~ the castle is said to be haunted; **2.** [~'ɡe:ən] *v/t.* (*no* -ge-, *h*) go round; ✕ flank; bypass (*town, etc.*); *fig.* avoid, evade; circumvent, elude (*law, etc.*); **~end** *adj.* immediate; **2ungsstraße** [um'ɡe:uŋs-] *f* bypass.

umgekehrt ['umɡəke:rt] **1.** *adj.* reverse; inverse, inverted; *in* ~*er Reihenfolge* in reverse order; *im* ~*en Verhältnis zu* in inverse proportion to; **2.** *adv.* vice versa.

'umgraben *v/t.* (*irr. graben, sep.*, -ge-, *h*) dig (up).

um'grenzen *v/t.* (*no* -ge-, *h*) encircle; enclose; *fig.* circumscribe, limit.

'umgruppier|en *v/t.*(*sep.,no-ge-,h*) regroup; **2ung** *f* (-/-en) regrouping.

'um|haben F *v/t.* (*irr. haben, sep.*, -ge-, *h*) have (*coat, etc.*) on; **'2hang** *m* wrap; cape; **'~hängen** *v/t.* (*sep.*, -ge-, *h*) rehang (*pictures*); sling (*rifle*) over one's shoulder; *sich den Mantel* ~ put one's coat round one's shoulders; **'~hauen** *v/t.* (*irr. hauen, sep.*, -ge-, *h*) fell, cut down; F: *die Nachricht hat mich umgehauen* I was bowled over by the news.

um'her|blicken *v/i.* (*sep.*, -ge-, *h*) look about (one); **~streifen** *v/i.* (*sep.*, -ge-, *sein*) rove.

um'hinkönnen *v/i.* (*irr. können, sep.*, -ge-, *h*): *ich kann nicht umhin, zu sagen* I cannot help saying.

um'hüll|en *v/t.* (*no* -ge-, *h*) wrap up (*mit in*), envelop (in); **2ung** *f* (-/-en) wrapping, wrapper, envelopment.

Umkehr ['umke:r] *f* (-/*no pl.*) return; **2en** (*sep.*, -ge-) **1.** *v/i.* (*sein*) return, turn back; **2.** *v/t.* (*h*) turn out (*one's pocket, etc.*); invert (*a. ♪*); reverse (*a. ⚡, ⅄*); **'~ung** *f* (-/-en) reversal; inversion.

'umkippen (*sep.*, -ge-) **1.** *v/t.* (*h*) upset, tilt; **2.** *v/i.* (*sein*) upset, tilt (over); F faint.

um'klammer|n *v/t.* (*no* -ge-, *h*) clasp; *boxing*: clinch; **2ung** *f* (-/-en) clasp; *boxing*: clinch.

'umkleide|n *v/refl.* (*sep.*, -ge-, *h*) change (one's clothes); **2eraum** *m* dressing-room.

'umkommen *v/i.* (*irr. kommen, sep.*, -ge-, *sein*) be killed (*bei in*), die (in), perish (in); *vor Langeweile* ~ die of boredom.

'Umkreis *m* (-es/*no pl.*) ⚡ circumscribed circle; *im* ~ *von* within a radius of.

um'kreisen *v/t.* (*no* -ge-, *h*) circle round.

um|krempeln *v/t.* (*sep.*, -ge-, *h*) tuck up (*shirt-sleeves, etc.*); change (*plan, etc.*); (*völlig*) ~ turn *s.th.* inside out; **'~laden** *v/t.* (*irr. laden, sep.*, -ge-, *h*) reload; ✝, ⚓ transship.

'Umlauf *m* circulation; *phys.*, ⊕ rotation; circular (letter); *in* ~ setzen *or* bringen circulate, put into circulation; *im* ~ *sein* circulate, be in circulation; *rumours:* a. be afloat; *außer* ~ setzen withdraw from circulation; **'~bahn** *f* orbit; **2en** (*irr. laufen*) **1.** ['~laufən] *v/t.* (*sep.*, -ge-, *h*) knock over; **2.** ['~laufən] *v/i.* (*sep.*, -ge-, *sein*) circulate; make a detour; **3.** [~'laufən] *v/t.* (*no* -ge-, *h*) run round.

'Umlege|kragen *m* turn-down collar; **2n** *v/t.* (*sep.*, -ge-, *h*) lay down; ⊕ throw (*lever*); storm, *etc.*: beat down (*wheat, etc.*); re-lay (*cable, etc.*); put (*coat, etc.*) round one's shoulders; apportion (*costs, etc.*); *fig. sl.* do *s.o.* in.

'umleiten *v/t.* (*sep.*, -ge-, *h*) divert; **'2ung** *f* diversion, detour.

'umliegend *adj.* surrounding; circumjacent.

um'nacht|et *adj.*: geistig ~ mentally deranged; **2ung** *f* (-/⚡-en): *geistige* ~ mental derangement.

'um|packen *v/t.* (*sep.*, -ge-, *h*) repack; **'~pflanzen** *v/t.* **1.** ['~pflantsən] (*sep.*, -ge-, *h*) transplant; **2.** [~'pflantsən] (*no* -ge-, *h*): ~ *mit* plant *s.th.* round with; **'~pflügen** *v/t.* (*sep.*, -ge-, *h*) plough, *Am.* plow.

um'rahmen *v/t.* (*no* -ge-, *h*) frame; *musikalisch* ~ put into a musical setting.

umrand|en [um'randən] *v/t.* (*no* -ge-, *h*) edge, border; **2ung** *f* (-/-en) edge, border.

um'ranken *v/t.* (*no* -ge-, *h*) twine (*mit* with).

'umrechn|en *v/t.* (*sep.*, -ge-, *h*) convert (*in acc.* into); **2ung** *f* (-/*no* *pl.*) conversion; '2**ungskurs** *m* rate of exchange.

um|reißen *v/t.* (*irr. reißen*) **1.** ['~raısən] (*sep.*, *-ge-*, *h*) pull down; knock *s.o.* over; **2.** [~'raısən] (*no -ge-*, *h*) outline.   [round (*a. fig.*).\

um'ringen *v/t.* (*no -ge-*, *h*) sur-\ '**Um|riß** *m* outline (*a. fig.*), contour; '2**rühren** *v/t.* (*sep.*, *-ge-*, *h*) stir; '2**satteln** (*sep.*, *-ge-*, *h*) **1.** *v/t.* resaddle; **2.** F *fig. v/i.* change one's studies *or* occupation; ~ **von** ... **auf** (*acc.*) change from ... to ...; '~**satz** ⚕ *m* turnover; sales *pl.*; return(s *pl.*); stock exchange: business done.

umschalt|en (*sep.*, *-ge-*, *h*) **1.** *v/t.* ⊕ change over; ⚡ commutate; ⚡, ⊕ switch; **2.** ⚡, ⊕ *v/i.* switch over; '2**er** *m* ⊕ change-over switch; ⚡ commutator; '2**ung** *f* (*-/-en*) ⊕ change-over; ⚡ commutation.

'**Umschau** *f* (*-/no pl.*): ~ **halten** nach look out for, be on the look-out for; '2**en** *v/refl.* (*sep.*, *-ge-*, *h*) look round (*nach* for); look about (for) (*a. fig.*), look about one.

umschicht|en *v/t.* (*sep.*, *-ge-*, *h*) pile afresh; *fig.* regroup (*a.* ✝); '~**ig** *adv.* by *or* in turns; '2**ung** *fig.* *f* (*-/-en*) regrouping; *soziale ~en pl.* social upheavals *pl.*

um'schiff|en *v/t.* (*no -ge-*, *h*) circumnavigate; double (*cape*); 2**ung** *f* (*-/✎ -en*) circumnavigation; doubling.

'**Umschlag** *m* envelope; cover; wrapper; jacket; turn-up, *Am. a.* cuff (*of trousers*); ✂ compress; ✂ poultice; trans-shipment (*of goods*); *fig.* change, turn; '2**en** (*irr. schlagen*, *sep.*, *-ge-*) **1.** *v/t.* (*h*) knock *s.o.* down; cut down, fell (*tree*); turn (*leaf*); turn up (*sleeves*, *etc.*); turn down (*collar*); trans-ship (*goods*); **2.** *v/i.* (*sein*) turn over, upset; ⚓ capsize, upset; *wine*, *etc.*: turn sour; *fig.* turn (*in acc.* into); '~**hafen** *m* port of trans-shipment.

um|schließen *v/t.* (*irr. schließen*, *no -ge-*, *h*) embrace, surround (*a.* ✗), enclose; ✗ invest; ~'**schlingen** *v/t.* (*irr. schlingen*, *no -ge-*, *h*) embrace.

'**um|schmeißen** F *v/t.* (*irr. schmeißen*, *sep.*, *-ge-*, *h*) *s.* umstoßen; '~**schnallen** *v/t.* (*sep.*, *-ge-*, *h*) buckle on.

umschreib|en *v/t.* (*irr. schreiben*) **1.** ['~ʃraıbən] (*sep.*, *-ge-*, *h*) rewrite; transfer (*property*, *etc.*) (*auf acc.* to); **2.** [~'ʃraıbən] (*no -ge-*, *h*) ♈ circumscribe; paraphrase; 2**ung** *f* (*-/-en*) **1.** ['~ʃraıbuŋ] rewriting; transfer (*auf acc.* to); **2.** [~'ʃraıbuŋ] ♈ circumscription; paraphrase.

'**Umschrift** *f* circumscription; *phonetics:* transcription.

'**umschütten** *v/t.* (*sep.*, *-ge-*, *h*) pour into another vessel; spill.

'**Um|schweife** *pl.*: ~ **machen** beat about the bush; *ohne* ~ pointblank; '2**schwenken** *fig. v/i.* (*sep.*, *-ge-*, *sein*) veer *or* turn round; '~**schwung** *fig. m* revolution; revulsion (*of public feeling*, *etc.*); change (*in the weather*, *etc.*); reversal (*of opinion*, *etc.*).

um'seg|eln *v/t.* (*no -ge-*, *h*) sail round; double (*cape*); circumnavigate (*globe*, *world*); 2(**e**)**lung** *f* (*-/-en*) sailing round (*world*, *etc.*); doubling; circumnavigation.

'**um|sehen** *v/refl.* (*irr. sehen*, *sep.*, *-ge-*, *h*) look round (*nach* for); look about (for) (*a. fig.*), look about one; '~**sein** F *v/i.* (*irr. sein*, *sep.*, *-ge-*, *sein*) *time:* be up; *holidays*, *etc.:* be over; '~**setzen** *v/t.* (*sep.*, *-ge-*, *h*) transpose (*a.* ♪); ✓ transplant; ✝ turn over; spend (*money*) (*in acc.* on *books*, *etc.*); *in die Tat* ~ realize, convert into fact.

'**Umsicht** *f* (*-/no pl.*) circumspection; 2**ig** *adj.* circumspect.

'**umsied|eln** (*sep.*, *-ge-*, *h*) **1.** *v/t.* (*h*) resettle; **2.** *v/i.* (*sein*) (re)move (*nach*, *in acc.* to); 2**lung** *f* (*-/✎ -en*) resettlement; evacuation; removal.

um'sonst *adv.* gratis, free of charge; in vain; to no purpose; *nicht* ~ not without good reason.

umspann|en *v/t.* **1.** ['~ʃpanən] (*sep.*, *-ge-*, *h*) change (*horses*); ⚡ transform; **2.** [~'ʃpanən] (*no -ge-*, *h*) span; *fig. a.* embrace; '2**er** ⚡ *m* (*-s/-*) transformer.

'**umspringen** *v/i.* (*irr. springen*, *sep.*, *-ge-*, *sein*) shift, veer (round); ~ *mit* treat badly, *etc.*

'**Umstand** *m* circumstance; fact, detail; *unter diesen Umständen* in *or* under the circumstances; *unter keinen Umständen* in *or* under no circumstances, on no account; *unter Umständen* possibly; *ohne*

Umstände without ceremony; *in anderen Umständen sein* be in the family way.

umständlich *adj.* ['umʃtɛntliç] *story, etc.*: long-winded; *method, etc.*: roundabout; *p.* fussy; *das ist (mir) viel zu* ~ that is far too much trouble (for me); **2keit** *f* (-/~-en) long-windedness; fussiness.

'**Umstands|kleid** *n* maternity robe; '~**wort** *gr. n* (-[e]s/⁓er) adverb.

'**umstehend** 1. *adj.*: *auf der* ~*en Seite* overleaf; 2. *adv.* overleaf; **2en** ['~dən] *pl. the* bystanders *pl.*

'**Umsteige|karte** *f* transfer; **2n** *v/i.* (*irr.* steigen, *sep.*, -ge-, sein) change (*nach* for); **⛴** *a.* change trains (for).

Umsteigkarte ['umʃtaık-] *f s. Umsteigekarte.*

umstell|en *v/t.* 1. ['~ʃtɛlən] (*sep.*, -ge-, h) transpose (*a. gr.*); shift (*furniture*) about *or* round; convert (*currency, production*) (*auf acc.* to); *sich* ~ change one's attitude; accommodate o.s. to new conditions; adapt o.s. (*auf acc.* to); 2. [~'ʃtɛlən] (*no* -ge-, h) surround; **2ung** [~'ʃtɛluŋ] *f* transposition; *fig.*: conversion; adaptation; change.

'**um|stimmen** *v/t.* (*sep.*, -ge-, h) ♪ tune to another pitch; *j-n* ~ change s.o.'s mind, bring s.o. round; '~**stoßen** *v/t.* (*irr.* stoßen, *sep.*, -ge-, h) knock over; upset; *fig.* annul; **⚖** overrule, reverse; upset (*plan*).

um|'stricken *fig. v/t.* (*no* -ge-, h) ensnare; ~**stritten** *adj.* [~'ʃtrɪtən] disputed, contested; controversial.

'**Um|sturz** *m* subversion, overturn; '**2stürzen** (*sep.*, -ge-) 1. *v/t.* (h) upset, overturn (*a. fig.*); *fig.* subvert; 2. *v/i.* (sein) upset, overturn; fall down; '**2stürzlerisch** *adj.* ['~lərɪʃ] subversive.

'**Umtausch** *m* (-es/⁓-e) exchange; **⊤** conversion (*of currency, etc.*); '**2en** *v/t.* (*sep.*, -ge-, h) exchange (*gegen* for); **⊤** convert.

'**umtun** F *v/t.* (*irr.* tun, *sep.*, -ge-, h) put (*coat, etc.*) round one's shoulders; *sich* ~ *nach* look about for.

'**umwälz|en** *v/t.* (*sep.*, -ge-, h) roll round; *fig.* revolutionize; '~**end** *adj.* revolutionary; '**2ung** *fig. f* (-/-en) revolution, upheaval.

'**umwandeln** *v/t.* (*sep.*, -ge-, h) transform (*in acc.* into); **⚡**, **⊤** con-

vert (*into*); **⚖** commute (*into*); '**2lung** *f* transformation; **⚡**, **⊤** conversion; **⚖** commutation.

'**um|wechseln** *v/t.* (*sep.*, -ge-, h) change; '**2weg** *m* roundabout way *or* route; detour; *auf ~en* in a roundabout way; '~**wehen** *v/t.* (*sep.*, -ge-, h) blow down *or* over; '**2welt** *f* (-/⁓) environment; '~**wenden** 1. *v/t.* (*sep.*, -ge-, h) turn over; 2. *v/refl.* (*irr.* wenden,] *sep.*, -ge-, h) look round (*nach* for).

um|'werben *v/t.* (*irr.* werben, *no* -ge-, h) court, woo.

'**umwerfen** *v/t.* (*irr.* werfen, *sep.*, -ge-, h) upset (*a. fig.*), overturn; *sich e-n Mantel* ~ throw a coat round one's shoulders.

um|'wickeln *v/t.* (*no* -ge-, h): *et. mit Draht* ~ wind wire round s.th.; ~**wölken** [~'vœlkən] *v/refl.* (*no* -ge-, h) cloud over (*a. fig.*); ~**zäunen** [~'tsɔʏnən] *v/t.* (*no* -ge-, h) fence (in).

umziehen (*irr.* ziehen) 1. ['~tsiːən] *v/i.* (*sep.*, -ge-, sein) (re)move (*nach* to); move house; 2. [~'tsiːən] *v/refl.* (*sep.*, -ge-, h) change (one's clothes); 3. [~'tsiːən] *v/refl.* (*no* -ge-, h) cloud over.

umzingeln [um'tsɪŋəln] *v/t.* (*no* -ge-, h) surround, encircle.

'**Umzug** *m* procession; move (*nach* to), removal (*to*); change of residence.

unab|änderlich *adj.* [unˀapˈˀɛndərliç] unalterable; ~**hängig** ['~hɛŋiç] 1. *adj.* independent (*von* of); 2. *adv.*: ~ *von* irrespective of; '**2hängigkeit** *f* (-/*no pl.*) independence (*von* of); ~**kömmlich** adj. ['~kœmliç]: *er ist im Moment* ~ cannot spare him at the moment, we cannot do without him at the moment; ~'**lässig** *adj.* incessant, unremitting; ~**sehbar** *adj.* ['~'zeːbaːr] incalculable; *in ~er Ferne* in a distant future; ~'**sichtlich** *adj.* unintentional; inadvertent; ~'**wendbar** *adj.* [~'vɛntbaːr] inevitable, inescapable.

unachtsam *adj.* ['unˀ-] careless, heedless; **2keit** *f* (-/⁓-en) carelessness, heedlessness.

unähnlich *adj.* ['unˀ-] unlike, dissimilar (*dat.* to).

unan|fechtbar *adj.* [unˀanˈ-] unimpeachable, unchallengeable, incontestable; '**~gebracht** adj. inappropriate; pred. a. out of place; '**~gefochten 1.** adj. undisputed; unchallenged; **2.** adv. without any hindrance; '**~gemessen** adj. unsuitable; improper; inadequate; '**~genehm** adj. disagreeable, unpleasant; awkward; troublesome; **~'nehmbar** adj. unacceptable (für to); '**2nehmlichkeit** f (-/-en) unpleasantness; awkwardness; troublesomeness; **~en** pl. trouble, inconvenience; '**~sehnlich** adj. unsightly; plain; '**~ständig** adj. indecent; obscene; '**2ständigkeit** f (-/-en) indecency; obscenity; '**~tastbar** adj. unimpeachable; inviolable.

unappetitlich adj. ['un⁹-] food, etc.: unappetizing; sight, etc.: distasteful, ugly.

Unart ['un⁹-] **1.** f bad habit; **2.** m (-[e]s/-e) naughty child; '**2ig** adj. naughty; '**~igkeit** f (-/-en) naughty behavio(u)r, naughtiness.

unauf|dringlich adj. ['un⁹auf-] unobtrusive; unostentatious; '**~fällig** adj. inconspicuous; unobtrusive; **~'findbar** adj. [~'fintba:r] undiscoverable; untraceable; **~gefordert** ['~gəfɔrdərt] **1.** adj. unasked; **2.** adv. without being asked, of one's own accord; **~'hörlich** adj. incessant, continuous, uninterrupted; '**~merksam** adj. inattentive; '**2merksamkeit** f (-/-en) inattention, inattentiveness; '**~richtig** adj. insincere; '**2richtigkeit** f (-/-en) insincerity; **~schiebbar** adj. [~'ʃi:pba:r] urgent; **~** sein brook no delay.

unaus|bleiblich adj. [un⁹aus'blaipliç] inevitable; das **~** war bound to happen; '**~führbar** adj. impracticable; **~'geglichen** adj. ['~gəgliçən] unbalanced (a. ✝); **~'löschlich** adj. indelible; fig. a. inextinguishable; **~'sprechlich** adj. unutterable; unspeakable; inexpressible; **~'stehlich** adj. unbearable, insupportable.

unbarmherzig adj. merciless, unmerciful; '**2keit** f (-/no pl.) mercilessness, unmercifulness.

unbe|absichtigt adj. ['unbə⁹apziçtiçt] unintentional, undesigned; '**~achtet** adj. unnoticed; **~anstandet** adj. ['unbə⁹-] unopposed, not

objected to; '**~baut** adj. 🖍 untilled; land: undeveloped; '**~dacht** adj. inconsiderate; imprudent; '**~denklich 1.** adj. unobjectionable; **2.** adv. without hesitation; '**~deutend** adj. insignificant; slight; '**~dingt 1.** adj. unconditional; obedience, etc.: implicit; **2.** adv. by all means; under any circumstances; **~'fahrbar** adj. impracticable, impassable; '**~fangen** adj. unprejudiced, unbias(s)ed; ingenuous; unembarrassed; '**~friedigend** adj. unsatisfactory; '**~friedigt** adj. ['~çt] dissatisfied; disappointed; '**~fugt** adj. unauthorized; incompetent; '**2fugte** m (-n/-n) unauthorized person; **~n** ist der Zutritt verboten! no trespassing; '**~gabt** adj. untalented; **~'greiflich** adj. inconceivable, incomprehensible; '**~grenzt** adj. unlimited; boundless; '**~gründet** adj. unfounded; '**2hagen** n uneasiness; discomfort; '**~haglich** adj. uneasy; uncomfortable; **~'helligt** adj. [~'hɛliçt] unmolested; '**~herrscht** adj. lacking self-control; '**2herrschtheit** f (-/no pl.) lack of self-control; **~'hindert** adj. unhindered, free; **~'holfen** adj. ['~bəhɔlfən] clumsy, awkward; '**2holfenheit** f (-/no pl.) clumsiness, awkwardness; **~'irrt** adj. unswerving; '**~kannt** adj. unknown; **~e** Größe ⚛ unknown quantity (a. fig.); **~'kümmert** adj. unconcerned (um, wegen about), careless (of, about); '**~lebt** adj. inanimate; street, etc.: unfrequented; '**~lehrbar** adj.: **~** sein take no advice; '**~liebt** adj. unpopular; sich **~** machen get o.s. disliked; '**~mannt** adj. unmanned; '**~merkt** adj. unnoticed; **~'mittelt** adj. impecunious, without means; **~'nommen** adj. [~'nɔmən]: es bleibt ihm **~** zu inf. he is at liberty to inf.; '**~nutzt** adj. unused; **~'quem** adj. uncomfortable, inconvenient; '**2quemlichkeit** f lack of comfort; inconvenience; '**~rechtigt** adj. unauthorized; unjustified; **~schadet** prp. (gen.) [~'ʃa:dət] without prejudice to; **~'schädigt** adj. ['~çt] uninjured, undamaged; '**~scheiden** adj. immodest; **~'scholten** adj. ['~ʃɔltən] blameless, irreproachable; '**~schränkt** adj. unrestricted; absolute; **~schreiblich** *adj.* [~'ʃraıpliç] indescribable; ~'**sehen** *adv.* unseen; without inspection; '~**setzt** *adj.* unoccupied; vacant; ~**siegbar** *adj.* [~'ziːkbaːr] invincible; '~**sonnen** *adj.* thoughtless, imprudent; rash; '2**sonnenheit** *f* (-/-en) thoughtlessness, rashness; '~**ständig** *adj.* inconstant; unsteady; *weather:* changeable, unsettled (*a.* ✝); *p.* erratic; '2**ständigkeit** *f* (-/no pl.) inconstancy; changeability; ~**stätigt** *adj.* ['~çt] unconfirmed; *letter, etc.:* unacknowledged; ~**stechlich** *adj.* incorruptible, unbribable; 2'**stechlichkeit** *f* (-/no pl.) incorruptibility; '~**stimmt** *adj.* indeterminate (*a.* ⅍); indefinite (*a. gr.*); uncertain; *feeling, etc.:* vague; '2**stimmtheit** *f* (-/no pl.) indeterminateness, indetermination; indefiniteness; uncertainty; vagueness; ~**streitbar** *adj.* incontestable; indisputable; '~**stritten** *adj.* uncontested, undisputed; '~**teiligt** *adj.* unconcerned (*an dat.* in); indifferent; ~**trächtlich** *adj.* inconsiderable, insignificant. [flexible.]

unbeugsam *adj.* [un'bɔykzaːm] in-'**unbewacht** *adj.* unwatched, unguarded (*a. fig.*); '~**waffnet** *adj.* unarmed; *eye:* naked; '~**weglich** *adj.* immovable; motionless; '~**wiesen** *adj.* unproven; '~**wohnt** *adj.* uninhabited; unoccupied, vacant; '~**wußt** *adj.* unconscious; ~**zähmbar** *adj.* indomitable.

'**Un|bilden** *pl.:* ~ *der Witterung* inclemency of the weather; '~**bildung** *f* lack of education.

'**un|billig** *adj.* unfair; '~**blutig** 1. *adj.* bloodless; 2. *adv.* without bloodshed.

unbotmäßig *adj.* ['unboːt-] insubordinate; '2**keit** *f* (-/-en) insubordination.

'**un|brauchbar** *adj.* useless; '~**christlich** *adj.* unchristian.

und *cj.* [unt] and; F: *na* ~? so what? '**Undank** *m* ingratitude; '2**bar** *adj.* ungrateful (*gegen* to); *task, etc.:* thankless; '~**barkeit** *f* ingratitude, ungratefulness; *fig.* thanklessness.

un|denkbar *adj.* unthinkable; inconceivable; ~'**denklich** *adj.:* seit ~*en Zeiten* from time immemorial; '~**deutlich** *adj.* indistinct; *speech:* a. inarticulate; *fig.* vague, indis-

tinct; '~**deutsch** *adj.* un-German; '~**dicht** *adj.* leaky; '2**ding** *n:* es wäre ein ~, zu behaupten, daß ... it would be absurd to claim that ...

'**unduldsam** *adj.* intolerant; '2**keit** *f* intolerance.

undurch|'dringlich *adj.* impenetrable; *countenance:* impassive; ~'**führbar** *adj.* impracticable; '~**lässig** *adj.* impervious, impermeable; '~**sichtig** *adj.* opaque; *fig.* mysterious.

uneben *adj.* ['un?-] *ground:* uneven, broken; *way, etc.:* bumpy; '2**heit** *f* 1. (-/no pl.) unevenness; 2. (-/-en) bump.

un|echt *adj.* ['un?-] *jewellery, etc.:* imitation; *hair, teeth, etc.:* false; *money, jewellery, etc.:* counterfeit; *picture, etc.:* fake; ⅍ *fraction:* improper; '~**ehelich** *adj.* illegitimate. **Unehr|e** ['un?-] *f* dishono(u)r; *j-m* ~ *machen* discredit s.o.; '2**enhaft** *adj.* dishono(u)rable; '2**lich** *adj.* dishonest; '~**lichkeit** *f* dishonesty. **uneigennützig** *adj.* ['un?-] disinterested, unselfish.

uneinig *adj.* ['un?-]: ~ *sein* be at variance (*mit* with); disagree (*über acc.* on); '2**keit** *f* variance, disagreement.

un|ein'nehmbar *adj.* impregnable; '~**empfänglich** *adj.* insusceptible (*für* of, to).

unempfindlich *adj.* ['un?-] insensitive (*gegen* to); '2**keit** *f* insensitiveness (*gegen* to).

un'endlich 1. *adj.* endless, infinite (*both a. fig.*); 2. *adv.* infinitely (*a. fig.*); ~ *lang* endless; ~ *viel* no end of (*money, etc.*); '2**keit** *f* (-/no pl.) endlessness, infinitude, infinity (*all a. fig.*).

unent|behrlich *adj.* [un?ɛnt'beːrliç] indispensable; ~'**geltlich** 1. *adj* gratuitous, gratis; 2. *adv.* gratis, free of charge; ~'**rinnbar** *adj.* ineluctable; ~'**schieden** 1. *adj.* undecided; ~ *enden game:* end in a draw or tie; 2. 2 *n* (-s/-) draw, tie; '~**schlossen** *adj.* irresolute; '2**schlossenheit** *f* irresolution, irresolution; ~**schuldbar** *adj.* [~'ʃultbaːr] inexcusable; ~**wegt** *adv.* [~'veːkt] untiringly; continuously; '~**wirrbar** *adj.* inextricable.

uner|bittlich *adj.* [un?ɛr'bitliç] inexorable; *fact:* stubborn; '~**fahren**

adj. inexperienced; **~findlich** *adj.* [~'fintliç] incomprehensible; **~forschlich** *adj.* inscrutable; **~freulich** *adj.* unpleasant; **~füllbar** *adj.* unrealizable; **~giebig** *adj.* unproductive (*an dat.* of); **~heblich** *adj.* irrelevant (*für* to); inconsiderable; **~hört** *adj.* **1.** ['~hø:rt] unheard; **2.** [~'hø:rt] unheard-of; outrageous; **~kannt** *adj.* unrecognized; **~klärlich** *adj.* inexplicable; **~läßlich** *adj.* [~'lesliç] indispensable (*für* to, for); **~laubt** *adj.* ['~laupt] unauthorized; illegal, illicit; *~e Handlung* ₺ tort; **~ledigt** *adj.* ['~le:diçt] unsettled (*a.* ✝); **~meßlich** *adj.* ['~mesliç] immeasurable, immense; **~müdlich** *adj.* [~'my:tliç] *p.* indefatigable, untiring; *efforts, etc.*: untiring, unremitting; **~quicklich** *adj.* unpleasant, unedifying; **~'reichbar** *adj.* inattainable; inaccessible; *pred. a.* above or beyond or out of reach; **~'reicht** *adj.* unrival(l)ed, unequal(l)ed; **~sättlich** *adj.* [~'zetliç] insatiable, insatiate; **~schöpflich** *adj.* inexhaustible.

unerschrocken *adj.* ['~n⁹-] intrepid, fearless; **2heit** *f* (*-/no pl.*) intrepidity, fearlessness.

uner|schütterlich *adj.* [~n⁹er'ʃytərliç] unshakable; **~'schwinglich** *adj.* *price*: prohibitive; *pred. a.* above or beyond or out of reach (*für* of); **~'setzlich** *adj.* irreplaceable; *loss, etc.*: irreparable; **~'träglich** *adj.* intolerable, unbearable; **~wartet** *adj.* unexpected; **~wünscht** *adj.* undesirable, undesired.

unfähig *adj.* incapable (*zu inf.* of *ger.*); unable (to *inf.*); inefficient; **2keit** *f* incapability (*zu inf.* of *ger.*); inability (to *inf.*); inefficiency.

Unfall *m* accident; *e-n ~ haben* meet with *or* have an accident; **~station** *f* emergency ward; **~versicherung** *f* accident insurance.

un'faßlich *adj.* incomprehensible, inconceivable; *das ist mir ~* that is beyond me.

un'fehlbar 1. *adj.* infallible (*a. eccl.*); *decision, etc.*: unimpeachable; *instinct, etc.*: unfailing; **2.** *adv.* without fail; inevitably; **2keit** *f* (*-/no pl.*) infallibility.

'un|fein *adj.* indelicate; *pred. a.* lacking in refinement; **'~fern** *prp.* (*gen. or von*) not far from; **'~fertig** *adj.* unfinished; *fig. a.* half-baked; **~flätig** *adj.* ['~fle:tiç] dirty, filthy.

unfolgsam *adj.* disobedient; **'2keit** *f* disobedience.

un|förmig *adj.* ['unfœrmiç] misshapen; shapeless; **'~frankiert** *adj.* unstamped; **'~frei** *adj.* not free; & unstamped; **'~freiwillig** *adj.* involuntary; *humour*: unconscious; **'~freundlich** *adj.* unfriendly (*zu* with), unkind (to); *climate, weather*: inclement; *room, day*: cheerless; **'2friede(n)** *m* discord.

'unfruchtbar *adj.* unfruitful; sterile; **'2keit** *f* (*-/no pl.*) unfruitfulness; sterility.

Unfug ['unfu:k] *m* (*-[e]s/no pl.*) mischief.

Ungar ['uŋgar] *m* (*-n/-n*) Hungarian; **'2isch** *adj.* Hungarian.

'ungastlich *adj.* inhospitable.

unge|achtet *prp.* (*gen.*) ['uŋgə⁹axtət] regardless of; despite; **~ahnt** *adj.* ['uŋgə⁹-] undreamt-of; unexpected; **~bärdig** *adj.* ['~bɛ:rdiç] unruly; **~beten** *adj.* uninvited, unasked; *~er Gast* intruder, *sl.* gatecrasher; **~bildet** *adj.* uneducated; **~bräuchlich** *adj.* unusual; **~braucht** *adj.* unused; **~bührlich** *adj.* improper, undue, unseemly; **~bunden** *adj. book*: unbound; *fig.*: free; single; **~deckt** *adj. table*: unlaid; *sports*, ✕, ✝: uncovered; *paper currency*: fiduciary.

Ungeduld *f* impatience; **'2ig** *adj.* impatient.

'ungeeignet *adj.* unfit (*für* for *s.th.*, to do *s.th.*); *p. a.* unqualified; *moment*: inopportune.

ungefähr ['uŋgəfɛ:r] **1.** *adj.* approximate, rough; **2.** *adv.* approximately, roughly, about, *Am.* F *a.* around; *von ~* by chance; **~det** *adj.* unendangered, safe; **'~lich** *adj.* harmless; *pred. a.* not dangerous.

'unge|fällig *adj.* disobliging; **~halten** *adj.* displeased (*über acc.* at); **~hemmt 1.** *adj.* unchecked; **2.** *adv.* without restraint; **~heuchelt** *adj.* unfeigned.

ungeheuer ['uŋgəhɔyər] **1.** *adj.* vast, huge, enormous; **2.** 2 *n* (*-s/-*) monster; **~lich** *adj.* [~'hɔyərliç] monstrous.

U V

'ungehobelt adj. not planed; fig. uncouth, rough.

'ungehörig adj. undue, improper; **2keit** f (-/♀-en) impropriety.

'ungehorsam 1. adj. disobedient; **2.** ♀ m disobedience.

'unge|künstelt adj. unaffected; **'~kürzt** adj. unabridged.

'ungelegen adj. inconvenient, inopportune; **'2heiten** f/pl. inconvenience; trouble; j-m ~ machen put s.o. to inconvenience.

'unge|lehrig adj. indocile; **'~lenk** adj. awkward, clumsy; **'~lernt** adj. unskilled; **'~mütlich** adj. uncomfortable; room: a. cheerless; p. nasty; **'~nannt** adj. unnamed; p. anonymous.

'ungenau adj. inaccurate, inexact; **'2igkeit** f inaccuracy, inexactness.

'ungeniert adj. free and easy, unceremonious; undisturbed.

'unge|nießbar adj. ['ungəni:sba:r] uneatable; undrinkable; F p. unbearable, pred. a. in a bad humo(u)r; **'~nügend** adj. insufficient; **'~pflegt** adj. unkempt; **'~rade** adj. odd; **'~raten** adj. spoilt, undutiful.

'ungerecht adj. unjust (gegen to); **'2igkeit** f (-/-en) injustice.

'un|gern adv. unwillingly, grudgingly; reluctantly; **'~geschehen** adj.: ~ machen undo s.th.

'Ungeschick n (-[e]s/no pl.), **'~lichkeit** f awkwardness, clumsiness, maladroitness; **'2t** adj. awkward, clumsy, maladroit.

'unge|schlacht adj. ['ungəʃlaxt] hulking; uncouth; **'~schliffen** adj. unpolished, rough (both a. fig.); **'~schminkt** adj. not made up; fig. unvarnished.

'ungesetzlich adj. illegal, unlawful, illicit; **'2keit** f (-/-en) illegality, unlawfulness.

'unge|sittet adj. uncivilized; unmannerly; **'~stört** adj. undisturbed, uninterrupted; **'~straft 1.** adj. unpunished; **2.** adv. with impunity; ~ davonkommen get off or escape scot-free.

ungestüm ['ungəʃty:m] **1.** adj. impetuous; violent; **2.** ♀ n (-[e]s/no pl.) impetuosity; violence.

'unge|sund adj. climate: unhealthy; appearance: a. unwholesome; food: unwholesome; **'~teilt** adj. undivided (a. fig.); **~trübt** adj.

['~try:pt] untroubled; unmixed; **2tüm** ['~ty:m] n (-[e]s/-e) monster; **~übt** adj. ['~°y:pt] untrained; inexperienced; **'~waschen** adj. unwashed.

'ungewiß adj. uncertain; j-n im ungewissen lassen keep s.o. in suspense; **'2heit** f (-/♀-en) uncertainty; suspense.

'unge|wöhnlich adj. unusual, uncommon; **'~wohnt** adj. unaccustomed; unusual; **'~zählt** adj. numberless, countless; **'2ziefer** ['~tsi:fər] n (-s/-) vermin; **'~ziemend** adj. improper, unseemly; **'~zogen** adj. ill-bred, rude, uncivil; child: naughty; **'~zügelt** adj. unbridled.

'ungezwungen adj. unaffected, easy; **'2heit** f (-/♀-en) unaffectedness, ease, easiness.

'Unglaube(n) m unbelief, disbelief.

'ungläubig adj. incredulous, unbelieving (a. eccl.); infidel; **'2e** m, f unbeliever; infidel.

'unglaub|lich adj. [un'glaupliç] incredible; **'~würdig** adj. p. untrustworthy; thing: incredible; ~e Geschichte cock-and-bull story.

'ungleich 1. adj. unequal, different; uneven; unlike; **2.** adv. (by) far, much; **'~artig** adj. heterogeneous; **'2heit** f difference, inequality; unevenness; unlikeness; **'~mäßig** adj. uneven; irregular.

'Unglück n (-[e]s/♀-e) misfortune; bad or ill luck; accident; calamity; disaster; misery; **'2lich** adj. unfortunate, unlucky; unhappy; **2-licher'weise** adv. unfortunately, unluckily; **'2selig** adj. unfortunate; disastrous.

'Unglücks|fall m misadventure; accident; **'~rabe** F m unlucky fellow.

'Un|gnade f (-/no pl.) disgrace, disfavo(u)r; in ~ fallen bei fall into disgrace with, incur s.o.'s disfavo(u)r; **'2gnädig** adj. ungracious, unkind.

'ungültig adj. invalid; ticket: not available; money: not current; ♂ʰ (null and) void; **'2keit** f invalidity; ♂ʰ a. voidness.

'Un|gunst f disfavo(u)r; inclemency (of weather); zu meinen ~en to my disadvantage; **'2günstig** adj. unfavo(u)rable; disadvantageous.

'un|gut adj.: ~es Gefühl misgiving;

nichts für ~*!* no offen|ce, *Am.* -se!; '~**haltbar** *adj. shot:* unstoppable; *theory, etc.:* untenable; '~**handlich** *adj.* unwieldy, bulky.

'**Unheil** *n* mischief; disaster, calamity; '2**bar** *adj.* incurable; '2**voll** *adj.* sinister, ominous.

'**unheimlich 1.** *adj.* uncanny (*a. fig.*), weird; sinister; F *fig.* tremendous, terrific; **2.** F *fig. adv.:* ~ *viel* heaps of, an awful lot of.

'**unhöflich** *adj.* impolite, uncivil; '2**keit** *f* impoliteness, incivility.

Unhold ['unhɔlt] *m* (-[e]s/-e) fiend.

'**un|hörbar** *adj.* inaudible; '~**hygienisch** *adj.* unsanitary, insanitary.

Uni ['uni] *f* (-/-s) F varsity.

Uniform [uni'fɔrm] *f* (-/-en) uniform.

Unikum ['u:nikum] *n* (-s/*Unika*, -s) unique (thing); queer fellow.

uninteress|ant *adj.* ['un⁹-] uninteresting, boring; '~**iert** *adj.* uninterested (*an dat.* in).

Universität [univerzi'tɛ:t] *f* (-/-en) university.

Universum [uni'vɛrzum] *n* (-s/*no pl.*) universe.

Unke ['uŋkə] *f* (-/-n) *zo.* fire-bellied toad; F *fig.* croaker; '2**n** F *v/i.* (ge-, h) croak.

'**unkenntlich** *adj.* unrecognizable; '2**lichkeit** *f* (-/*no pl.*): *bis zur* ~ past all recognition; '2**nis** *f* (-/*no pl.*) ignorance.

'**unklar** *adj.* not clear; *meaning, etc.:* obscure; *answer, etc.:* vague; *im* ~*en sein* be in the dark (*über acc.* about); '2**heit** *f* want of clearness; vagueness; obscurity.

'**unklug** *adj.* imprudent, unwise.

'**Unkosten** *pl.* cost(s *pl.*), expenses *pl.*; *sich in* (*große*) ~ *stürzen* go to great expense.

'**Unkraut** *n* weed.

'**un|kündbar** *adj.* ['unkyntba:r] *loan, etc.:* irredeemable; *employment:* permanent; ~**kundig** *adj.* ['~kundiç] ignorant (*gen.* of); '~**längst** *adv.* lately, recently, the other day; '~**lauter** *adj. competition:* unfair; '~**leidlich** *adj.* intolerable, insufferable; '~**leserlich** *adj.* illegible; ~**leugbar** *adj.* ['~lɔykba:r] undeniable; '~**logisch** *adj.* illogical; '~**lösbar** *adj.* unsolvable, insoluble.

'**Unlust** *f* (-/*no pl.*) reluctance (*zu*

inf. to *inf.*); '2**ig** *adj.* reluctant.

'**un|manierlich** *adj.* unmannerly; '~**männlich** *adj.* unmanly; ~**maßgeblich** *adj.* ['~gə:pliç]: *nach m-r* ~*en Meinung* in my humble opinion; '~**mäßig** *adj.* immoderate; intemperate; '2**menge** *f* enormous *or* vast quantity *or* number.

'**Unmensch** *m* monster, brute; '2~**lich** *adj.* inhuman, brutal; '~**lichkeit** *f* inhumanity, brutality.

'**un|mißverständlich** *adj.* unmistakable; '~**mittelbar** *adj.* immediate, direct; '~**möbliert** *adj.* unfurnished; '~**modern** *adj.* unfashionable, outmoded.

'**unmöglich** *adj.* impossible; '2**keit** *f* impossibility.

'**Unmoral** *f* immorality; '2**isch** *adj.* immoral.

'**unmündig** *adj.* under age.

'**un|musikalisch** *adj.* unmusical; '2**mut** *m* (-[e]s/*no pl.*) displeasure (*über acc.* at, over); '~**nachahmlich** *adj.* inimitable; '~**nachgiebig** *adj.* unyielding; '~**nachsichtig** *adj.* strict, severe; inexorable; ~**nahbar** *adj.* inaccessible, unapproachable; '~**natürlich** *adj.* unnatural; affected; '~**nötig** *adj.* unnecessary, needless; '~**nütz** *adj.* useless; ~**ordentlich** *adj.* ['un⁹-] untidy; *room, etc.:* *a.* disorderly; 2**ordnung** ['un⁹-] *f* disorder, mess.

'**unpartei|isch** *adj.* impartial, unbias(s)ed; '2**ische** *m* (-n/-n) referee; umpire; '2**lichkeit** *f* impartiality.

'**un|passend** *adj.* unsuitable; improper; inappropriate; '~**passierbar** *adj.* impassable.

unpäßlich *adj.* ['unpɛsliç] indisposed, unwell; '2**keit** *f* (-/-en) indisposition.

'**un|persönlich** *adj.* impersonal (*a. gr.*); '~**politisch** *adj.* unpolitical; '~**praktisch** *adj.* unpractical, *Am. a.* impractical; '2**rat** *m* (-[e]s/*no pl.*) filth; rubbish; ~**wittern** smell a rat.

'**unrecht 1.** *adj.* wrong; ~ *haben* be wrong; *j-m* ~ *tun* wrong s.o.; **2.** 2 *n* (-[e]s/*no pl.*): *mit or zu* ~ wrongly; *ihm ist* ~ *geschehen* he has been wronged; '~**mäßig** *adj.* unlawful; '2**mäßigkeit** *f* unlawfulness.

'**unreell** *adj.* dishonest; unfair.

'**unregelmäßig** *adj.* irregular (*a. gr.*); '2**keit** *f* (-/-en) irregularity.

U
V

'**unreif** adj. unripe, immature (both a. fig.); '**2e** f unripeness, immaturity (both a. fig.).

'**un|rein** adj. impure (a. eccl.); unclean (a. fig.); '**~reinlich** adj. uncleanly; **~rettbar** adv.: ~ verloren irretrievably lost; '**~richtig** adj. incorrect, wrong.

Unruh ['unru:] f (-/-en) balance (-wheel); **2e** f (-/-n) restlessness, unrest (a. pol.); uneasiness; disquiet(ude); flurry; alarm; ~n pl. disturbances pl., riots pl.; '**2ig** adj. restless; uneasy; sea: rough, choppy.

'**unrühmlich** adj. inglorious.

uns pers. pron. [uns] us; dat.: a. to us; ~ (selbst) ourselves, after prp.: us; ein Freund von ~ a friend of ours.

'**un|sachgemäß** adj. inexpert; '**~sachlich** adj. not objective; personal; **~säglich** adj. [~'ze:kliç] unspeakable; untold; '**~sanft** adj. ungentle; '**~sauber** adj. dirty; fig. a. unfair (a. sports); '**~schädlich** adj. innocuous, harmless; '**~scharf** adj. blurred; pred. a. out of focus; **~schätzbar** adj. inestimable, invaluable; '**~scheinbar** adj. plain, Am. a. homely.

'**unschicklich** adj. improper, indecent; '**2keit** f (-/-en) impropriety, indecency.

unschlüssig adj. ['unʃlysiç] irresolute; '**2keit** f (-/no pl.) irresoluteness, irresolution.

'**un|schmackhaft** adj. insipid; unpalatable, unsavo(u)ry; '**~schön** adj. unlovely, unsightly; fig. unpleasant.

'**Unschuld** f (-/no pl.) innocence; '**2ig** adj. innocent (an dat. of).

'**unselbständig** adj. dependent (on others); '**2keit** f (lack of in)dependence.

unser ['unzər] 1. poss. pron. our; der (die, das) ~e ours; die ~en pl. our relations pl.; 2. pers. pron. of us; wir waren ~ drei there were three of us.

'**unsicher** adj. unsteady; unsafe, insecure; uncertain; '**2heit** f unsteadiness; insecurity, unsafeness; uncertainty.

'**unsichtbar** adj. invisible.

'**Unsinn** m (-[e]s/no pl.) nonsense; '**2ig** adj. nonsensical.

'**Unsitt|e** f bad habit; abuse; '**2lich**

adj. immoral; indecent (a. 🚻); '**~lichkeit** f (-/-en) immorality.

'**un|solid(e)** adj. p. easy-going; life: dissipated; † unreliable; '**~sozial** adj. unsocial, antisocial; '**~sportlich** adj. unsportsmanlike; unfair (gegenüber to).

'**unstatthaft** adj. inadmissible.

'**unsterblich** adj. immortal.

Un'sterblichkeit f immortality.

'**un|stet** adj. unsteady; character, life: unsettled; **2stimmigkeit** ['~ʃtimiçkait] f (-/-en) discrepancy; dissension; '**~sträflich** adj. blameless; '**~streitig** adj. incontestable; '**~sympathisch** adj. disagreeable; er ist mir ~ I don't like him; '**~tätig** adj. inactive; idle.

'**untauglich** adj. unfit (a. 🏹); unsuitable; '**2keit** f (-/no pl.) unfitness (a. 🏹).

un'teilbar adj. indivisible.

unten adv. ['untən] below; downstairs; von oben bis ~ from top to bottom.

unter ['untər] 1. prp. (dat.; acc.) below, under; among; ~ anderem among other things; ~ zehn Mark (for) less than ten marks; ~ Null below zero; ~ aller Kritik beneath contempt; ~ diesem Gesichtspunkt from this point of view; 2. adj. lower; inferior; die ~en Räume the downstair(s) rooms.

Unter|abteilung ['untər⁹-] f subdivision; **~arm** ['untər⁹-] m forearm; '**~bau** m (-[e]s/-ten) 🏛 substructure (a. 🚂), foundation.

unter|'bieten v/t. (irr. bieten, no -ge-, h) underbid; † undercut, undersell (competitor); lower (record); **~'binden** v/t. (irr. binden, no -ge-, h) 🩺 ligature; fig. stop; **~'bleiben** v/i. (irr. bleiben, no -ge-, sein) remain undone; not to take place.

unter'brech|en v/t. (irr. brechen, no -ge-, h) interrupt (a. 🔌); break, Am. a. stop over; 🔌 break (circuit); **2ung** f (-/-en) interruption; break, Am. a. stopover. [mit.]

unter'breiten v/t. (no -ge-, h) sub-]

'**unterbring|en** v/t. (irr. bringen, sep-, -ge-, h) place (a. †); accommodate, lodge; '**2ung** f (-/-en) accommodation; † placement.

unterdessen adv. ['untər'desən] (in the) meantime, meanwhile.

unter'drück|en v/t. (no -ge-, h) oppress (subjects, etc.); repress (revolt, sneeze, etc.); suppress (rising, truth, yawn, etc.); put down (rebellion, etc.); **Sung** f (-/-en) oppression; repression; suppression; putting down.

unterernähr|t adj. ['untɐrʔ-] underfed, undernourished; **'Sung** f (-/no pl.) underfeeding, malnutrition.

Unter'führung f subway, Am. underpass.

'Untergang m (-[e]s/ꞏꞏe) ast. setting; ⚓ sinking; fig. ruin.

Unter'gebene m (-n/-n) inferior, subordinate; contp. underling.

'untergehen v/i. (irr. gehen, sep., -ge-, sein) ast. set; ⚓ sink, founder; fig. be ruined.

untergeordnet adj. ['untɐrgəʔordnət] subordinate; importance: secondary. [underweight.\
'Untergewicht n (-[e]s/no pl.)\
unter'graben fig. v/t. (irr. graben, no -ge-, h) undermine.

'Untergrund m (-[e]s/no pl.) subsoil; '**hahn** f underground (railway), in London: tube; Am. subway; '**bewegung** f underground movement.

'unterhalb prp. (gen.) below, underneath.

'Unterhalt m (-[e]s/no pl.) support, subsistence, livelihood; maintenance.

unter'halt|en v/t. (irr. halten, no -ge-, h) maintain; support; entertain, amuse; sich ~ converse (mit with; über acc. on, about), talk (with; on, about); sich gut ~ enjoy o.s.; **Sung** f maintenance, upkeep; conversation, talk; entertainment.

'Unterhändler m negotiator; ⚔ Parlementaire.

'Unter|haus parl. n (-es/no pl.) House of Commons; '**hemd** n vest, undershirt; '**holz** n (-es/no pl.) underwood, brushwood; '**hose** f (e-e a pair of) drawers pl., pants pl.; **Sirdisch** adj. subterranean, underground (both a. fig.).

unter'joch|en v/t. (no -ge-, h) subjugate, subdue; **Sung** f (-/-en) subjugation.

'Unter|kiefer m lower jaw; '**kleid** n slip; '**kleidung** f underclothes pl., underclothing, underwear.

'unterkommen 1. v/i. (irr. kommen, sep., -ge-, sein) find accommodation; find employment; **2.** **S** n (-s/ꞏ) accommodation; employment, situation.

'unter|kriegen F v/t. (sep., -ge-, h) bring to heel; sich nicht ~ lassen not to knuckle down or under; **Skunft** ['kunft] f (-/ꞏe) accommodation, lodging; ⚔ quarters pl.; **Slage** f base; pad; fig.: voucher; ~n pl. documents pl.; data pl.

unter'lass|en v/t. (irr. lassen, no -ge-, h) omit (zu tun doing, to do); neglect (to do, doing); fail (to do); **Sung** f (-/-en) omission; neglect; failure; **Sungssünde** f sin of omission.

'unterlegen¹ v/t. (sep., -ge-, h) lay or put under; give (another meaning).

unter'legen² adj. inferior (dat. to); **Se** m (-n/-n) loser; underdog; **Sheit** f (-/no pl.) inferiority.

'Unterleib m abdomen, belly.

unter'liegen v/i. (irr. liegen, no -ge-, sein) be overcome (dat. by); be defeated (by), sports: a. lose (to); fig.: be subject to; be liable to; es unterliegt keinem Zweifel, daß ... there is no doubt that ...

'Unter|lippe f lower lip; '**mieter** m subtenant, lodger, Am. a. roomer.

unter'nehmen 1. v/t. (irr. nehmen, no -ge-, h) undertake; take (steps); **2.** **S** n (-s/-) enterprise; ✝ a. business; ⚔ operation.

unter'nehm|end adj. enterprising; **Ser** ✝ m (-s/-) entrepreneur; contractor; employer; **Sung** f (-/-en) enterprise, undertaking; ⚔ operation; **ungslustig** adj. enterprising.

'Unter|offizier ⚔ m non-commissioned officer; **Sordnen** v/t. (sep., -ge-, h) subordinate (dat. to); sich ~ submit (to).

Unter'redung f (-/-en) conversation, conference.

Unterricht ['untərɪçt] m (-[e]s/ꞏe) instruction, lessons pl.

unter'richten v/t. (no -ge-, h): ~ in (dat.) instruct in, teach (English, etc.); von inform s.o. of.

'Unterrichts|ministerium n ministry of education; '**stunde** f lesson, (teaching) period; '**wesen** n (-s/no pl.) education; teaching.

'Unterrock m slip.

U V

unter'sagen v/t. (no -ge-, h) forbid (j-m et. s.o. to do s.th.).

'Untersatz m stand; saucer.

unter'schätzen v/t. (no -ge-, h) undervalue; underestimate, underrate.

unter'scheid|en v/t. and v/i. (irr. scheiden, no -ge-, h) distinguish (zwischen between; von from); sich ~ differ (von from); **2ung** f distinction.

'Unterschenkel m shank.

'unterschieb|en v/t. (irr. schieben, sep., -ge-, h) push under; fig.: attribute (dat. to); substitute (statt for); **'2ung** f substitution.

Unterschied ['untərʃiːt] m (-[e]s/-e) difference; distinction; zum ~ von in distinction from or to; **'2lich** adj. different; differential; variable, varying; **'2slos** adj. indiscriminate; undiscriminating.

unter'schlag|en v/t. (irr. schlagen, no -ge-, h) embezzle; suppress (truth, etc.); **2ung** f (-/-en) embezzlement; suppression.

'Unterschlupf m (-[e]s/ʺe, -e) shelter, refuge.

unter'schreiben v/t. and v/i. (irr. schreiben, no -ge-, h) sign.

'Unterschrift f signature.

'Untersee|boot ⚓, ✗ n s. U-Boot; **~kabel** n submarine cable.

unter'setzt adj. thick-set, squat.

unterst adj. ['untərst] lowest, undermost.

'Unterstand ✗ m shelter, dug-out.

unter'stehen (irr. stehen, no -ge-, h) **1.** v/i. (dat.) be subordinate to; be subject to (law, etc.); **2.** v/refl. dare; unterstéh dich! don't you dare!; **~stellen** v/t. **1.** ['~ʃtelən] (sep., -ge-, h) put or place under; garage (car); sich ~ take shelter (vor dat. from); **2.** [~'ʃtelən] (no -ge-, h) (pre)suppose, assume; impute (dat. to); j-m ~ put (troops, etc.) under s.o.'s command; **2'stellung** f (-/-en) assumption, supposition; imputation; **~streichen** v/t. (irr. streichen, no -ge-, h) underline, underscore (both a. fig.).

unter'stütz|en v/t. (no -ge-, h) support; back up; **2ung** f (-/-en) support (a. ✗); assistance, aid; relief.

unter'such|en v/t. (no -ge-, h) examine (a. ✗); inquire into, investigate (a. ⚖️); explore; ⚖️ try;

analy|se, Am. -ze (a. 🜛); **2ung** f (-/-en) examination (a. ✗); inquiry (gen. into), investigation (a. ⚖️); exploration; analysis (a. 🜛).

Unter'suchungs|gefangene m prisoner on remand; **~gefängnis** n remand prison; **~haft** f detention on remand; **~richter** m investigating judge.

Untertan ['untərtaːn] m (-s, -en/ -en) subject. (missive.)

untertänig adj. ['untərtɛːniç] sub-)

'Unter|tasse f saucer; **'2tauchen** (sep., -ge-) **1.** v/i. (sein) dive, dip; duck; fig. disappear; **2.** v/t. (h) duck.

'Unterteil n, m lower part.

unter'teil|en v/t. (no -ge-, h) subdivide; **2ung** f subdivision.

'Unter|titel m subheading; subtitle; a. caption (of film); **'~ton** m undertone; **2vermieten** v/t. (no -ge-, h) sublet.

unter'wander|n pol. v/t. (no -ge-, h) infiltrate; **2ung** pol. f infiltration.

'Unterwäsche f s. Unterkleidung.

unterwegs adv. [untər'veːks] on the or one's way.

unter'weis|en v/t. (irr. weisen, no -ge-, h) instruct (in dat. in); **2ung** f instruction.

'Unterwelt f underworld (a. fig.).

unter'werf|en v/t. (irr. werfen, no -ge-, h) subdue (dat. to), subjugate (to); subject (to); submit (to); sich ~ submit (to); **2ung** f (-/-en) subjugation, subjection; submission (unter acc. to).

unterworfen adj. [untər'vorfən] subject (dat. to).

unterwürfig adj. [untər'vyrfiç] submissive; subservient; **2keit** f (-/no pl.) submissiveness; subservience.

unter'zeichn|en v/t. (no -ge-, h) sign; **2er** m signer, the undersigned; subscriber (gen. to); signatory (gen. to treaty); **2erstaat** m signatory state; **2ete** m, f (-n/-n) the undersigned; **2ung** f signature, signing.

unterziehen v/t. (irr. ziehen) **1.** ['~tsiːən] (sep., -ge-, h) put on underneath; **2.** [~'tsiːən] (no -ge-, h) subject (dat. to); sich e-r Operation ~ undergo an operation; sich e-r Prüfung ~ go in or sit for an examination; sich der Mühe ~ zu inf. take the trouble to inf.

'Untiefe f shallow, shoal.

'Untier n monster (a. fig.).

un|tilgbar adj. [un'tilkbɑːr] indelible; † government annuities: irredeemable; ~'tragbar adj. unbearable, intolerable; costs: prohibitive; ~'trennbar adj. inseparable.

'untreu adj. untrue (dat. to), disloyal (to); husband, wife: unfaithful (to); '2e f disloyalty; unfaithfulness, infidelity.

un|'tröstlich adj. inconsolable, disconsolate; ~trüglich adj. [~'tryːkliç] infallible, unerring.

'Untugend f vice, bad habit.

unüber|legt adj. ['unʔyːbər-] inconsiderate, thoughtless; '~sichtlich adj. badly arranged; difficult to survey; involved; mot. corner: blind; ~'trefflich adj. unsurpassable; ~windlich adj. [~'vintliç] invincible; fortress: impregnable; obstacle, etc.: insurmountable; difficulties, etc.: insuperable.

unum|gänglich adj. [un'ʔum'ɡɛnliç] absolutely necessary; ~schränkt adj. [~'ʃrɛŋkt] absolute; ~stößlich adj. [~'ʃtøːsliç] irrefutable; incontestable; irrevocable; ~wunden adj. ['~vʊndən] frank, plain.

ununterbrochen adj. ['unʔʊntər-brɔxən] uninterrupted; incessant.

unver|'änderlich adj. unchangeable; invariable; ~'antwortlich adj. irresponsible; inexcusable; ~'besserlich adj. incorrigible; '~bindlich adj. not binding or obligatory; answer, etc.: non-committal; ~'blümt adj. [~'blyːmt] plain, blunt; ~'bürgt adj. [~'byrkt] unwarranted; news: unconfirmed; '~dächtig adj. unsuspected; '~daulich adj. indigestible (a. fig.); '~dient adj. undeserved; '~dorben adj. unspoiled, unspoilt; fig.: uncorrupted; pure, innocent; '~drossen adj. indefatigable, unflagging; '~dünnt adj. undiluted, Am. a. straight; ~'einbar adj. incompatible; '~fälscht adj. unadulterated; fig. genuine; '~fänglich adj. ['~feŋliç] not captious; ~froren adj. ['~froːrən] unabashed, impudent; '2frorenheit f (-/-en) impudence, F cheek; '~gänglich adj. imperishable; '~geßlich adj. unforgettable; ~'gleichlich adj. incomparable; '~hältnismäßig adj. disproportionate; '~heiratet adj. unmarried, single; '~hofft adj. unhoped-for, unexpected; '~hohlen adj. unconcealed; '~käuflich adj. unsal(e)able; not for sale; ~'kennbar adj. unmistakable; ~'letzbar adj. invulnerable; fig. a. inviolable; ~'meidlich adj. [~'maitliç] inevitable; '~mindert adj. undiminished; '~mittelt adj. abrupt.

'Unvermögen n (-s/no pl.) inability; impotence; '2d adj. impecunious, without means.

'unvermutet adj. unexpected.

'Unver|nunft f unreasonableness, absurdity; '2nünftig adj. unreasonable, absurd; '2richteterdinge adv. without having achieved one's object.

'unverschämt adj. impudent, impertinent; '2heit f (-/-en) impudence, impertinence.

'unver|schuldet adj. not in debt; through no fault of mine, etc.; '~sehens adv. unawares, suddenly, all of a sudden; ~'sehrt adj. ['~zeːrt] uninjured; ~'söhnlich adj. implacable, irreconcilable; '~sorgt adj. unprovided for; '2stand m injudiciousness; folly, stupidity; '~ständig adj. injudicious; foolish; ~'ständlich adj. unintelligible; incomprehensible; das ist mir ~ that is beyond me; '~sucht adj.: nichts ~ lassen leave nothing undone; ~'träglich adj. unsociable; quarrelsome; '~wandt adj. steadfast; ~'wundbar adj. [~'vʊntbaːr] invulnerable; ~'wüstlich adj. [~'vyːstliç] indestructible; fig. irrepressible; ~'zagt adj. ['~tsaːkt] intrepid, undaunted; ~'zeihlich adj. unpardonable; ~'zinslich adj. bearing no interest; non-interest-bearing; ~'züglich adj. [~'tsyːkliç] immediate, instant.

'unvollendet adj. unfinished.

'unvollkommen adj. imperfect; '2heit f imperfection.

'unvollständig adj. incomplete; '2keit f (-/no pl.) incompleteness.

'unvorbereitet adj. unprepared; extempore.

'unvoreingenommen adj. unbias(s)ed, unprejudiced; '2heit f freedom from prejudice.

'unvor|hergesehen adj. unforeseen; '~schriftsmäßig adj. irregular.

unvorsichtig adj. incautious; imprudent; '2**keit** f incautiousness; imprudence.

unvor|'**stellbar** adj. unimaginable; '**~tellbar** adj. unprofitable (dress, etc.: unbecoming. [truth.]

unwahr adj. untrue; '2**heit** f un-]

'**unwahrscheinlich** adj. improbable, unlikely; '2**keit** f (-/-en) improbability, unlikelihood.

'**un**|**wegsam** adj. pathless, impassable; '**~weit** prp. (gen. or von) not far from; '**~wesen** n (-s/no pl.) nuisance; sein ~ treiben be up to one's tricks; '**~wesentlich** adj. unessential, immaterial (für to); '2**wetter** n thunderstorm; '**~wichtig** adj. unimportant, insignificant.

unwider|'**legbar** adj. [unvi:dər'le:kba:r] irrefutable; '**~ruflich** adj. irrevocable (a. ✝).

unwider'**stehlich** adj. irresistible; 2**keit** f (-/no pl.) irresistibility.

unwieder'**bringlich** adj. irretrievable.

'**Unwill**|**e** m (-ns/no pl.), '**~en** m (-s/no pl.) indignation (über acc. at), displeasure (at, over); '2**ig** adj. indignant (über acc. at), displeased (at, with); unwilling; '2**kürlich** adj. involuntary.

'**unwirklich** adj. unreal.

'**unwirksam** adj. ineffective, inefficient; laws, rules, etc.: inoperative; '**~** inactive; '2**keit** f (-/no pl.) ineffectiveness, inefficiency; '**~** inactivity.

unwirsch adj. ['unvirʃ] testy.

'**unwirt**|**lich** adj. inhospitable, desolate; '**~schaftlich** adj. uneconomic(al).

'**unwissen**|**d** adj. ignorant; '2**heit** f (-/no pl.) ignorance; '**~tlich** adj. unwitting, unknowing.

'**unwohl** adj. unwell, indisposed; '2**sein** n (-s/no pl.) indisposition.

'**unwürdig** adj. unworthy (gen. of).

un|**zählig** adj. ['un'tsɛ:liç] innumerable; '2**zart** adj. indelicate.

Unze ['untsə] f (-/-n) ounce.

'**Unzeit** f: zur ~ inopportunely; '2**gemäß** adj. old-fashioned; inopportune; '2**ig** adj. untimely; unseasonable; fruit: unripe.

unzer|'**brechlich** adj. unbreakable; **~'reißbar** adj. untearable; **~'stör-bar** adj. indestructible; **~'trenn-lich** adj. inseparable.

'**un**|**ziemlich** adj. unseemly; '2**zucht** f (-/no pl.) lewdness; ½½ sexual offen|ce, Am. -se; '**~züchtig** adj. lewd; obscene.

'**unzufrieden** adj. discontented (mit with), dissatisfied (with, at); '2**heit** f discontent, dissatisfaction.

'**unzugänglich** adj. inaccessible.

'**unzulänglich** adj. ['untsulɛnliç] insufficient; '2**keit** f (-/-en) insufficiency; shortcoming.

'**unzulässig** adj. inadmissible; esp. ½½ influence: undue.

'**unzurechnungsfähig** adj. irresponsible; '2**keit** f irresponsibility.

'**unzu**|**reichend** adj. insufficient; '**~sammenhängend** adj. incoherent; '**~träglich** adj. unwholesome; '**~treffend** adj. incorrect; inapplicable (auf acc. to).

'**unzuverlässig** adj. unreliable, untrustworthy; friend: a. uncertain; '2**keit** f unreliability, untrustworthiness.

'**unzweckmäßig** adj. inexpedient; '2**keit** f inexpediency.

'**un**|**zweideutig** adj. unequivocal; unambiguous; '**~zweifelhaft 1.** adj. undoubted, undubitable; **2.** adv. doubtless.

üppig adj. ['ʏpiç] ♀ luxuriant, exuberant, opulent; food: luxurious, opulent; figure: voluptuous; '2**keit** f (-/♀ -en) luxuriance, luxuriancy, exuberance; voluptuousness.

ur|**alt** adj. ['u:r'alt] very old; (as) old as the hills; '2**aufführung** ['u:r'-] f world première.

Uran [u'ra:n] n (-s/no pl.) uranium.

urbar adj. ['u:rba:r] arable, cultivable; ~ machen reclaim; '2**machung** f (-/-en) reclamation.

'**Ur**|**bevölkerung** f aborigines pl.; '**~bild** n original, prototype; '2**eigen** adj. one's very own; '**~enkel** m great-grandson; '**~großeltern** pl. great-grandparents pl.; '**~groß-mutter** f great-grandmother; '**~großvater** m great-grandfather.

'**Urheber** m (-s/-) author; '2**recht** n copyright (an dat. in); '**~schaft** f (-/no pl.) authorship.

Urin [u'ri:n] m (-s/-e) urine; 2**ieren** [~i'ni:rən] v/i. (no -ge-, h) urinate.

'**Urkund**|**e** f [document; deed]; '**~en-fälschung** f forgery of documents; 2**lich** adj. ['~tliç] documentary.

Urlaub ['uːrlaʊp] *m* (-[e]s/-e) leave (of absence) (*a.* ✗); holiday(s *pl.*), *esp. Am.* vacation; **⁓er** ['⁓bər] *m* (-s/-) holiday-maker, *esp. Am.* vacationist, vacationer.

Urne ['urnə] *f* (-/-n) urn; ballot-box.

'ur|plötzlich 1. *adj.* very sudden, abrupt; **2.** *adv.* all of a sudden; **⁓sache** *f* cause; reason; *keine* **⁓***!* don't mention it, *Am. a.* you are welcome; **'⁓sächlich** *adj.* causal; **⁰schrift** *f* original (text); **⁰-sprung** *m* origin, source; **⁓sprünglich** *adj.* ['⁓ʃpryŋlɪç] original; **⁰stoff** *m* primary matter.

Urteil ['urtaɪl] *n* (-s/-e) judg(e)-ment; ⚖ *a.* sentence; *meinem* **⁓** *nach* in my judg(e)ment; *sich ein* **⁓** *bilden* form a judg(e)ment (*über acc.* of, on); **⁰en** *v/i.* (ge-, h) judge (*über acc.* of; *nach* by, from); **'⁓s-kraft** *f* (-/⚹ **⁓e**) discernment.

'Ur|text *m* original (text); **'⁓wald** *m* primeval *or* virgin forest; **⁰-wüchsig** *adj.* ['⁓vyːksɪç] original; *fig.*: natural; rough; **'⁓zeit** *f* primitive times *pl.*   [sils *pl.*)

Utensilien [uten'ziːljən] *pl.* uten-)

Utop|ie [uto'piː] *f* (-/-n) Utopia; **⁰isch** *adj.* [u'toːpiʃ] Utopian, utopian.

V

Vagabund [vaga'bʊnt] *m* (-en/-en) vagabond, vagrant, tramp, *Am.* hobo, F bum.

Vakuum ['vaːkuˀʊm] *n* (-s/*Vakua, Vakuen*) vacuum.

Valuta [va'luːta] *f* (-/*Valuten*) value; currency.

Vanille [va'nɪljə] *f* (-/*no pl.*) vanilla.

variabel *adj.* [vari'aːbəl] variable.

Varia|nte [vari'antə] *f* (-/-n) variant; **⁓tion** [⁓'tsjoːn] *f* (-/-en) variation.

Varieté [varie'teː] *n* (-s/-s), **⁓theater** *n* variety theatre, music-hall, *Am.* vaudeville theater.

variieren [vari'iːrən] *v/i. and v/t.* (*no -ge-*, h) vary.

Vase ['vaːzə] *f* (-/-n) vase.

Vater ['faːtər] *m* (-s/⁓) father; **'⁓land** *n* native country *or* land, mother country; **'⁓landsliebe** *f* patriotism.   [paternal.)

väterlich *adj.* ['fɛːtərlɪç] fatherly,)

'Vater|schaft *f* (-/*no pl.*) paternity, fatherhood; **'⁓unser** *eccl. n* (-s/-) Lord's Prayer.

Vati ['faːti] *m* (-s/-s) dad(dy).

Veget|arier [vege'taːrjər] *m* (-s/-) vegetarian; **⁰arisch** *adj.* vegetarian; **⁓ation** [⁓a'tsjoːn] *f* (-/-en) vegetation; **⁰ieren** [⁓'tiːrən] *v/i.* (*no -ge-*, h) vegetate.

Veilchen ⚘ ['faɪlçən] *n* (-s/-) violet.

Vene *anat.* ['veːnə] *f* (-/-n) vein.

Ventil [vɛn'tiːl] *n* (-s/-e) valve (*a.* ♪); ♪ stop (*of organ*); *fig.* vent,

outlet; **⁓ation** [⁓ila'tsjoːn] *f* (-/-en) ventilation; **⁓ator** [⁓i'laːtər] *m* (-s/-en) ventilator, fan.

verab|folgen [fɛr'ap-] (*no -ge-*, h) deliver; give; ⚕ administer (*medicine*); **⁓reden** *v/t.* (*no -ge-*, h) agree upon, arrange; appoint, fix (*time, place*); *sich* **⁓** make an appointment, *Am.* F (have a) date; **⁰redung** *f* (-/-en) agreement; arrangement; appointment, *Am.* F date; **⁓reichen** *v/t.* (*no -ge-*, h) *s.* verabfolgen; **⁓scheuen** *v/t.* (*no -ge-*, h) abhor, detest, loathe; **⁓schieden** [⁓'ʃiːdən] *v/t.* (*no -ge-*, h) dismiss; retire (*officer*); ✗ discharge (*troops*); *parl.* pass (*bill*); *sich* **⁓** take leave (*von* of), say goodbye (*to*); **⁰schiedung** *f* (-/-en) dismissal; discharge; passing.

ver|achten *v/t.* (*no -ge-*, h) despise; **⁓ächtlich** *adj.* [⁓'ɛçtlɪç] contemptuous; contemptible; **⁰achtung** *f* contempt; **⁓allgemeinern** [⁓ˀalgə'maɪnərn] *v/t.* (*no -ge-*, h) generalize; **⁓altet** *adj.* antiquated, obsolete, out of date.

Veranda [ve'randa] *f* (-/*Veranden*) veranda(h), *Am. a.* porch.

veränder|lich *adj.* changeable; variable (*a.* ♔, *gr.*); **⁓n** *v/t. and v/refl.* (*no -ge-*, h) alter, change; vary; **⁰ung** *f* change, alteration (*in dat.* in; *an dat.* to); variation.   [timidated, scared.)

verängstigt *adj.* [fɛr'ɛŋstɪçt] in-)

ver'anlag|en v/t. (no -ge-, h) of taxation: assess; **∼t** adj. [∼kt] talented; **Qung** [∼guŋ] f (-/-en) assessment; fig. talent(s pl.); ♂ predisposition.

ver'anlass|en v/t. (no -ge-, h) cause, occasion; arrange; **Qung** f (-/-en) occasion, cause; auf m-e ∼ at my request or suggestion.

ver'anschaulichen v/t. (no -ge-, h) illustrate; **∼'anschlagen** v/t. (no -ge-, h) rate, value, estimate (all: auf acc. at).

ver'anstalt|en v/t. (no -ge-, h) arrange, organize; give (concert, ball, etc.); **Qung** f (-/-en) arrangement; event; sports: event, meeting, Am. meet.

ver'antwort|en v/t. (no -ge-, h) take the responsibility for; account for; **∼lich** adj. responsible; j-n ∼ machen für hold s.o. responsible for.

Ver'antwortung f (-/-en) responsibility; die ∼ tragen be responsible; zur ∼ ziehen call to account; **Qslos** adj. irresponsible.

ver|'arbeiten v/t. (no -ge-, h) work up; ⊕ process, manufacture (both: zu into); digest (food) (a. fig.); **∼'ärgern** v/t. (no -ge-, h) vex, annoy.

ver'arm|en v/i. (no -ge-, sein) become poor; **∼t** adj. impoverished.

ver|'ausgaben v/t. (no -ge-, h) spend (money); sich ∼ run short of money; fig. spend o.s.; **∼'äußern** v/t. (no -ge-, h) sell; alienate.

Verb gr. [verp] n (-s/-en) verb.

Ver'band m (-[e]s/∸e) ♂ dressing, bandage; association, union; ✗ formation, unit; **∼(s)kasten** m first-aid box; **∼(s)zeug** n dressing (material).

ver'bann|en v/t. (no -ge-, h) banish (a. fig.), exile; **Qung** f (-/-en) banishment, exile.

ver|barrikadieren [ferbarika'di:-rən] v/t. (no -ge-, h) barricade; block (street, etc.); **∼'bergen** v/t. (irr. bergen, no -ge-, h) conceal, hide.

ver'besser|n v/t. (no -ge-, h) improve; correct; **Qung** f improvement; correction.

ver'beug|en v/refl. (no -ge-, h) bow (vor dat. to); **Qung** f bow.

ver|'biegen v/t. (irr. biegen, no

-ge-, h) bend, twist, distort; **∼'bieten** v/t. (irr. bieten, no -ge-, h) forbid, prohibit; **∼'billigen** v/t. (no -ge-, h) reduce in price, cheapen.

ver'bind|en v/t. (irr. binden, no -ge-, h) ♂ dress; tie (together); bind (up); link (mit to); join, unite, combine; connect (a. teleph.); teleph. put s.o. through (mit to); j-m die Augen ∼ blindfold s.o.; sich ∼ join, unite, combine (a. ♋); ich bin Ihnen sehr verbunden I am greatly obliged to you; falsch verbunden! teleph. wrong number!; **∼lich** adj. [∼tlɪç] obligatory; obliging; **Qlichkeit** f (-/-en) obligation, liability; obligingness, civility.

Ver'bindung f union; alliance; combination; association (of ideas); connexion, (Am. only) connection (a. teleph., ⛟, ⚓, ⊕); relation; communication (a. teleph.); 🎵 compound; geschäftliche ∼ business relations pl.; teleph.: ∼ bekommen (haben) get (be) through; die ∼ verlieren mit lose touch with; in ∼ bleiben (treten) keep (get) in touch (mit with); sich in ∼ setzen mit communicate with, esp. Am. contact s.o.; **∼sstraße** f communication road, feeder road; **∼stür** f communication door.

ver'bissen [fer'bɪsən] adj. dogged; crabbed; **∼'bitten** v/refl. (irr. bitten, no -ge-, h): das verbitte ich mir! I won't suffer or stand that!

ver'bitter|n v/t. (no -ge-, h) embitter; **Qung** f (-/♋, -en) bitterness (of heart).

verblassen [fer'blasən] v/i. (no -ge-, sein) fade (a. fig.).

Verbleib [fer'blaɪp] m (-[e]s/no pl.) whereabouts sg., pl.; **Qen** [∼bən] v/i. (irr. bleiben, no -ge-, sein) be left, remain.

ver'blend|en v/t. (no -ge-, h) ⚠ face (wall, etc.); fig. blind, delude; **Qung** f (-/♋, -en) ⚠ facing; fig. blindness, delusion. [faded.)

verblichen [fer'blɪçən] colour:)

verblüff|en [fer'blyfən] v/t. (no -ge-, h) amaze; perplex, puzzle; dumbfound; **Qung** f (-/♋, -en) amazement, perplexity.

ver'blühen v/i. (no -ge-, sein) fade, wither; **∼'bluten** v/i. (no -ge-, sein) bleed to death.

ver'borgen adj. hidden; secret;
♀heit f (-/no pl.) concealment;
secrecy.

Verbot [fɛr'boːt] n (-[e]s/-e) prohibition; **♀en** adj. forbidden, prohibited; Rauchen ~ no smoking.

Ver'brauch m (-[e]s/♀ ⁺e) consumption (an dat. of); **♀en** v/t. (no -ge-, h) consume, use up; wear out; **~er** m (-s/-) consumer; **♀t** adj. air: stale; p. worn out.

ver'brechen 1. v/t. (irr. brechen, no -ge-, h) commit; was hat er verbrochen? what is his offen|ce, Am. -se?, what has he done?; 2. ♀ n (-s/-) crime, offen|ce, Am. -se.

Ver'brecher m (-s/-) criminal; **♀isch** adj. criminal; **~tum** n (-s/no pl.) criminality.

ver'breit|en v/t. (no -ge-, h) spread, diffuse; shed (light, warmth, happiness); sich ~ spread; sich ~ über (acc.) enlarge (up)on (theme); **~ern** v/t. and v/refl. (no -ge-, h) widen, broaden; **♀ung** f (-/♀ -en) spread (-ing), diffusion.

ver'brenn|en (irr. brennen, no -ge-)
1. v/i. (sein) burn; 2. v/t. (h) burn (up); cremate (corpse); **♀ung** f (-/-en) burning, combustion; cremation (of corpse); wound: burn.

ver'bringen v/t. (irr. bringen, no -ge-, h) spend, pass.

verbrüder|n [fɛr'bryːdərn] v/refl. (no -ge-, h) fraternize; **♀ung** f (-/-en) fraternization.

ver'brühen v/t. (no -ge-, h) scald; sich ~ scald o.s.; **~'buchen** v/t. (no -ge-, h) book.

Verbum gr. ['vɛrbum] n (-s/Verba) verb.

verbünden [fɛr'byndən] v/refl. (no -ge-, h) ally o.s. (mit to, with).

Verbundenheit [fɛr'bundənhaɪt] f (-/no pl.) bonds pl., ties pl.; solidarity; affection.

Ver'bündete m, f (-n/-n) ally, confederate; die ~n pl. the allies pl.

ver|'bürgen v/t. (no -ge-, h) guarantee, warrant; sich ~ für answer or vouch for; **~'büßen** v/t. (no -ge-, h): e-e Strafe ~ serve a sentence, serve (one's) time.

Verdacht [fɛr'daxt] m (-[e]s/no pl.) suspicion; in ~ haben suspect.

verdächtig adj. [fɛr'dɛçtɪç] suspected (gen. of); pred. suspect; suspicious; **~en** [~gən] v/t. (no

-ge-, h) suspect s.o. (gen. of); cast suspicion on; **♀ung** [~guŋ] f (-/-en) suspicion; insinuation.

verdamm|en [fɛr'damən] v/t. (no -ge-, h) condemn, damn (a. eccl.); **♀nis** f (-/no pl.) damnation; **~t**
1. adj. damned; F: ~! damn (it)!, confound it!; **-2.** F adv.: ~ kalt beastly cold; **♀ung** f (-/♀ -en) condemnation, damnation.

ver'dampfen (no -ge-) v/t. (h) and v/i. (sein) evaporate; **~'danken** v/t. (no -ge-, h): j-m et. ~ owe s.th. to s.o. [ben.]

verdarb [fɛr'darp] pret. of verder-)

verdau|en [fɛr'daʊən] v/t. (no -ge-, h) digest; **~'lich** adj. digestible; leicht ~ easy to digest, light; **♀ung** f (-/no pl.) digestion; **♀ungsstörung** f indigestion.

Ver'deck n (-[e]s/-e) ⚓ deck; hood (of carriage, car, etc.); top (of vehicle); **♀en** v/t. (no -ge-, h) cover; conceal, hide.

ver'denken v/t. (irr. denken, no -ge-, h): ich kann es ihm nicht ~, daß I cannot blame him for ger.

Verderb [fɛr'dɛrp] m (-[e]s/no pl.) ruin; **♀en** [~bən] 1. v/i. (irr., no -ge-, sein) spoil (a. fig.); rot; meat, etc.: go bad; fig. perish; 2. v/t. (irr., no -ge-, h) spoil; fig. a.: corrupt; ruin; er will es mit niemandem ~ he tries to please everybody; sich den Magen ~ upset one's stomach; **~en** [~bən] n (-s/no pl.) ruin; **♀lich** adj. [~plɪç] pernicious; food: perishable; **~nis** [~pnɪs] f (-/♀ -se) corruption; depravity; **♀t** adj. [~pt] corrupt, depraved.

ver|'deutlichen v/t. (no -ge-, h) make plain or clear; **~'dichten** v/t. (no -ge-, h) condense; sich ~ condense; suspicion: grow stronger; **~'dicken** v/t. and v/refl. (no -ge-, h) thicken; **~'dienen** v/t. (no -ge-, h) merit, deserve; earn (money).

Ver'dienst (-es/-e) 1. m gain, profit; earnings pl.; 2. n merit; es ist sein ~, daß it is owing to him that; **♀voll** adj. meritorious, deserving; **~spanne** † f profit margin.

ver|'dient adj. p. of merit; (well-)deserved; sich ~ gemacht haben um deserve well of; **~'dolmetschen** v/t. (no -ge-, h) interpret (a. fig.); **~'doppeln** v/t. and v/refl. (no -ge-, h) double.

verdorben [fɛr'dɔrbən] 1. *p.p.* of
verderben; 2. *adj. meat*: tainted;
stomach: disordered, upset; *fig.*
corrupt, depraved.

ver|dorren [fɛr'dɔrən] *v/i.* (no
-ge-, sein) wither (up); **~'drängen**
v/t. (no -ge-, h) push away, thrust
aside; *fig.* displace; *psych.* repress;
~'drehen *v/t.* (no -ge-, h) distort,
twist (*both a. fig.*); roll (*eyes*); *fig.*
pervert; j-m den Kopf ~ turn s.o.'s
head; **~'dreht** F *fig. adj.* crazy;
~'dreifachen *v/t. and v/refl.* (no
-ge-, h) triple.

verdrieß|en [fɛr'driːsən] *v/t.* (*irr.*,
no -ge-, h) vex, annoy; **~lich** *adj.*
vexed, annoyed; sulky; *thing*: annoying.

ver|droß [fɛr'drɔs] *pret.* of ver-
drießen; **~drossen** [~'drɔsən] 1. *p.p.*
of verdrießen; 2. *adj.* sulky; list-
less.

ver'drucken *typ. v/t.* (no -ge-, h)
misprint.

Verdruß [fɛr'drus] *m* (Verdrusses/%
Verdrusse) vexation, annoyance.

ver'dummen (no -ge-) 1. *v/t.* (h)
make stupid; 2. *v/i.* (sein) become
stupid.

ver'dunk|eln *v/t.* (no -ge-, h)
darken, obscure (*both a. fig.*);
black out (*window*); sich ~ darken;
2(e)lung *f* (-/%-en) darkening;
obscuration; black-out; ⅛ collu-
sion.

ver|'dünnen *v/t.* (no -ge-, h) thin;
dilute (*liquid*); **~'dunsten** *v/i.* (no
-ge-, sein) volatilize, evaporate;
~'dursten *v/i.* (no -ge-, sein) die
of thirst; **~dutzt** *adj.* [~'duts]
nonplussed.

ver'ed|eln *v/t.* (no -ge-, h) ennoble;
refine; improve; ⚘ graft; process
(*raw materials*); **2(e)lung** *f* (-/%
-en) refinement; improvement;
processing.

ver'ehr|en *v/t.* (no -ge-, h) revere,
venerate; worship; admire, adore;
2er *m* (-s/-) worship(p)er; admirer,
adorer; **2ung** *f* (-/%-en) reverence,
veneration; worship; adoration.

vereidigen [fɛr'aɪdigən] *v/t.* (no
-ge-, h) swear (*witness*); *at entrance
into office*: swear s.o. in.

Verein [fɛr'aɪn] *m* (-[e]s/-e) union;
society, association; club.

ver'einbar *adj.* compatible (*mit*
with), consistent (*with*); **~en** *v/t.*

(no -ge-, h) agree upon, arrange;
2ung *f* (-/-en) agreement, arrangement.

ver'einen *v/t.* (no -ge-, h) s. vereinigen.

ver'einfach|en *v/t.* (no -ge-, h)
simplify; **2ung** *f* (-/-en) simplifi-
cation.

ver'einheitlichen *v/t.* (no -ge-, h)
unify, standardize.

ver'einig|en *v/t.* (no -ge-, h) unite,
join; associate; sich ~ unite; join;
associate o.s.; **2ung** *f.* 1. (-/%-en)
union; 2. (-/-en) union; society,
association.

ver'ein|samen *v/i.* (no -ge-, sein)
grow lonely or solitary; **~zelt** *adj.*
isolated; sporadic.

ver|'eiteln *v/t.* (no -ge-, h) frus-
trate; **~'ekeln** *v/t.* (no -ge-, h):
er hat mir das Essen verekelt he
spoilt my appetite; **~'enden** *v/i.*
(no -ge-, sein) *animals*: die, perish;
~enge(r)n [~'ɛŋə(r)n] *v/t. and
v/refl.* (no -ge-, h) narrow.

ver'erb|en *v/t.* (no -ge-, h) leave,
bequeath; *biol.* transmit; sich ~ be
hereditary; sich ~ auf (*acc.*) descend (up)on; **2ung** *f* (-/%-en)
biol. transmission; *physiol.* heredity; **2ungslehre** *f* genetics.

verewig|en [fɛr'e:vigən] *v/t.* (no
-ge-, h) perpetuate; **~t** *adj.* [~çt]
deceased, late.

ver'fahren 1. *v/i.* (*irr. fahren*, no
-ge-, sein) proceed; ~ mit deal with;
2. *v/t.* (*irr. fahren*, no -ge-, h) mis-
manage, muddle, bungle; sich ~
miss one's way; 3. **2** *n* (-s/-) procedure; proceeding(s); ⊕ proc-
ess.

Ver'fall *m* (-[e]s/no pl.) decay, decline; dilapidation (*of house, etc.*);
⅛ forfeiture; expiration; maturity
(*of bill of exchange*); **2en** 1. *v/i.*
(*irr. fallen*, no -ge-, sein) decay;
house: dilapidate; *document, etc.*:
expire; *pawn*: become forfeited;
right: lapse; *bill of exchange*: fall
due; *sick person*: waste away; ~ auf
(*acc.*) hit upon (*idea, etc.*); ~ in
(*acc.*) fall into; j-m ~ become s.o.'s
slave; 2. *adj.* ruinous; addicted
(*dat.* to drugs, *etc.*); **~serscheinung**
[fɛr'fals⁹-] *f* symptom of decline;
~tag *m* day of payment.

ver|'fälschen *v/t.* (no -ge-, h) fal-
sify; adulterate (*wine, etc.*); **~fäng-**

lich *adj.* [ˈfɛnliç] *question*: captious, insidious; risky; embarrassing; **~färben** *v/refl.* (*no* -ge-, *h*) change colo(u)r.

ver'fass|en *v/t.* (*no* -ge-, *h*) compose, write; **2er** *m* (-s/-) author.

Ver'fassung *f* state, condition; *pol.* constitution; disposition (*of mind*); **2smäßig** *adj.* constitutional; **2swidrig** *adj.* unconstitutional.

ver|'faulen *v/i.* (*no* -ge-, *sein*) rot, decay; **~'fechten** *v/t.* (*irr. fechten, no* -ge-, *h*) defend, advocate.

ver'fehl|en *v/t.* (*no* -ge-, *h*) miss; **2ung** *f* (-/-en) offen|ce, *Am.* -se.

ver|feinden [fɛrˈfaɪndən] *v/t.* (*no* -ge-, *h*) make enemies of; **~mit** make an enemy of; **~feinern** [ˈfaɪnɐn] *v/t. and v/refl.* (*no* -ge-, *h*) refine; **~fertigen** [ˈfɛrtɪgən] *v/t.* (*no* -ge-, *h*) make, manufacture; compose.

ver'film|en *v/t.* (*no* -ge-, *h*) film, screen; **2ung** *f* (-/-en) film-version.

ver|'finstern *v/t.* (*no* -ge-, *h*) darken, obscure; *sich* ~ darken; **~'flachen** (*no* -ge-) *v/i.* (*sein*) *and v/refl.* (*h*) (become) shallow (*a. fig.*); **~'flechten** *v/t.* (*irr. flechten, no* -ge-, *h*) interlace; *fig.* involve; **~'fliegen** (*irr. fliegen, no* -ge-) 1. *v/i.* (*sein*) evaporate; *time*: fly; *fig.* vanish; 2. *v/refl.* (*h*) *bird*: stray; ✈ lose one's bearings, get lost; **~'fließen** *v/i.* (*irr. fließen, no* -ge-, *sein*) *colours*: blend; *time*: elapse; **~flossen** *adj.* [ˈflɔsən] *time*: past; F *ein* ~*er Freund* a late friend, an ex-friend.

ver|'fluchen *v/t.* (*no* -ge-, *h*) curse, *Am.* F cuss; **~t** *adj.* damned; ~*l damn* (*it*)!, confound it!

ver|flüchtigen [fɛrˈflyçtɪgən] *v/t.* (*no* -ge-, *h*) volatilize; *sich* ~ evaporate (*a. fig.*); F *fig.* vanish; **~flüssigen** [ˈflysɪgən] *v/t. and v/refl.* (*no* -ge-, *h*) liquefy.

ver'folg|en *v/t.* (*no* -ge-, *h*) pursue, persecute; follow (*tracks*); trace; *thoughts, dream*: haunt; *gerichtlich* ~ prosecute; **2er** *m* (-s/-) pursuer; persecutor; **2ung** *f* (-/-en) pursuit; persecution; pursuance; *gerichtliche* ~ prosecution; **2ungswahn** 🜂 *m* persecution mania.

ver|frachten [fɛrˈfraxtən] *v/t.* (*no* -ge-, *h*) freight, *Am. a.* ship (*goods*);

⚓ ship; F *j-n* ~ *in* (*acc.*) bundle s.o. in(to) (*train, etc.*); **~'froren** *adj.* chilled through; **~'früht** *adj.* premature.

verfüg|bar *adj.* [fɛrˈfyːkbaːr] available; **~en** [ˈgən] (*no* -ge-, *h*) 1. *v/t.* decree, order; 2. *v/i.*: ~ *über* (*acc.*) have at one's disposal; dispose of; **2ung** [ˈgʊŋ] *f* (-/-en) decree, order; disposal; *j-m zur* ~ *stehen* (*stellen*) be (place) at s.o.'s disposal.

ver'führ|en *v/t.* (*no* -ge-, *h*) seduce; **2er** *m* (-s/-) seducer; **~erisch** *adj.* seductive; enticing, tempting; **2ung** *f* seduction.

vergangen *adj.* [fɛrˈgaŋən] gone, past; *im* ~*en Jahr* last year; **2heit** *f* (-/-en) past; *gr.* past tense.

vergänglich *adj.* [fɛrˈgɛŋliç] transient, transitory.

vergas|en [fɛrˈgaːzən] *v/t.* (*no* -ge-, *h*) gasify; gas *s.o.*; **2er** *mot.* *m* (-s/-) carburet(t)or.

vergaß [fɛrˈgaːs] *pret. of* vergessen.

ver'geb|en *v/t.* (*irr. geben, no* -ge-, *h*) give away (*j-n to s.o.*); confer (on), bestow (on); place (*order*); forgive; *sich et.* ~ compromise one's dignity; **~ens** *adv.* [~s] in vain; **~lich** [~pliç] 1. *adj.* vain; 2. *adv.* in vain; **2ung** [~bʊŋ] *f* (-/~-en) bestowal, conferment (*both*: *an acc.* on); forgiveness, pardon.

vergegenwärtigen [fɛrgeːgən'vɛrtɪgən] *v/t.* (*no* -ge-, *h*) represent; *sich et.* ~ visualize s.th.

ver'gehen *v/i.* (*irr. gehen, no* -ge-, *sein*) pass (away); fade (away); ~ *vor* (*dat.*) die of; 2. *v/refl.* (*irr. gehen, no* -ge-, *h*): *sich an j-m* ~ assault s.o., violate s.o.; *sich gegen das Gesetz* ~ offend against or violate the law; 3. **2** *n* (-s/-) offen|ce, *Am.* -se.

ver'gelt|en *v/t.* (*irr. gelten, no* -ge-, *h*) repay, requite; reward; retaliate; **2ung** *f* (-/-en) requital; retaliation, retribution.

vergessen [fɛrˈgɛsən] 1. *v/t.* (*irr., no* -ge-, *h*) forget; leave; 2. *p.p. of* 1; **2heit** *f* (-/no pl.): *in* ~ *geraten* sink *or* fall into oblivion.

vergeßlich *adj.* [fɛrˈgɛsliç] forgetful.

vergeud|en [fɛrˈgɔʏdən] *v/t.* (*no* -ge-, *h*) dissipate, squander, waste *(time, money)*; ⚥ung *f* (-/⚥-en) waste.

vergewaltig|en [fɛrgə'valtigən] *v/t.* (*no* -ge-, *h*) violate; rape; ⚥ung *f* (-/-en) violation; rape.

ver|gewissern [fɛrgə'wisərn] *v/refl.* (*no* -ge-, *h*) make sure (e-r Sache of s.th.); **~'gießen** *v/t.* (*irr.* gießen, *no* -ge-, *h*) shed (*tears, blood*); spill (*liquid*).

ver'gift|en *v/t.* (*no* -ge-, *h*) poison (*a. fig.*); *sich* ~ take poison; ⚥ung *f* (-/-en) poisoning.

Vergißmeinnicht ⚘ [fɛr'gismaɪnɪçt] *n* (-[e]s/-[e]) forget-me-not.

ver'gittern [fɛr'gitərn] *v/t.* (*no* -ge-, *h*) grate.

Vergleich [fɛr'glaɪç] *m* (-[e]s/-e) comparison; ⚖: agreement; compromise, composition; ⚥**bar** *adj.* comparable (*mit* to); ⚥**en** *v/t.* (*irr.* gleichen, *no* -ge-, *h*) compare (*mit* with, to); *sich* ~ *mit* ⚖ come to terms with; *verglichen mit* as against, compared to; ⚥**sweise** *adv.* comparatively.

vergnügen [fɛr'gny:gən] 1. *v/t.* (*no* -ge-, *h*) amuse; *sich* ~ enjoy o.s.; 2. ⚥ *n* (-s/-) pleasure, enjoyment; entertainment; ~ *finden an* (*dat.*) take pleasure in; *viel* ~*!* have a good time! [gay.\
vergnügt *adj.* [fɛr'gny:kt] merry,\
Ver'gnügung *f* (-/-en) pleasure, amusement, entertainment; **~s-reise** *f* pleasure-trip, tour; ⚥s-**süchtig** *adj.* pleasure-seeking.

ver|golden [fɛr'goldən] *v/t.* (*no* -ge-, *h*) gild; **~'göttern** *fig.* [~'gœtərn] *v/t.* (*no* -ge-, *h*) idolize, adore; **~'graben** *v/t.* (*irr.* graben, *no* -ge-, *h*) bury (*a. fig.*); *sich* ~ bury o.s.; **~'greifen** *v/refl.* (*irr.* greifen, *no* -ge-, *h*) sprain (*one's hand, etc.*); *sich* ~ *an* (*dat.*) lay (violent) hands on, attack, assault; embezzle (*money*); encroach upon (*s.o.'s property*); **~griffen** *adj.* [~'grɪfən] *goods*: sold out; *book*: out of print.

vergrößer|n [fɛr'grø:sərn] *v/t.* (*no* -ge-, *h*) enlarge (*a. phot.*); opt. magnify; *sich* ~ enlarge; ⚥ung *f* 1. (-/-en) phot. enlargement; opt. magnification; 2. (-/⚥-en) enlargement; increase; extension; ⚥ungs-**glas** *n* magnifying glass.

Vergünstigung [fɛr'gynstɪguŋ] *f* (-/-en) privilege.

---

ver'güt|en [fɛr'gy:tən] *v/t.* (*no* -ge-, *h*) compensate (*j-m et.* s.o. for s.th.); reimburse (*money spent*); ⚥ung *f* (-/-en) compensation; reimbursement.

ver'haft|en *v/t.* (*no* -ge-, *h*) arrest; ⚥ung *f* (-/-en) arrest.

ver'halten 1. *v/t.* (*irr.* halten, *no* -ge-, *h*) keep back; catch *or* hold (*one's breath*); suppress, check; *sich* ~ *thing*: be; *p.* behave; *sich ruhig* ~ keep quiet; 2. ⚥ *n* (-s/*no pl.*) behavio(u)r, conduct.

Verhältnis [fɛr'hɛltnis] *n* (-ses/-se) proportion, rate; relation(s *pl.*) (*zu* with); F liaison, love-affair; F mistress; **~se** *pl.* conditions *pl.*, circumstances *pl.*; means *pl.*; ⚥**mäßig** *adv.* in proportion; comparatively; **~wort** *gr.* *n* (-[e]s/⸗er) preposition.

Ver'haltungsmaßregeln *f/pl.* instructions *pl.*

ver'hand|eln (*no* -ge-, *h*) 1. *v/i.* negotiate, treat (*über* acc., *wegen* for); ⚖ try (*über et.* s.th.); 2. *v/t.* discuss; ⚥**lung** *f* negotiation; discussion; ⚖ trial, proceedings *pl.*

ver'häng|en *v/t.* (*no* -ge-, *h*) cover (over), hang; inflict (*punishment*) (*über* acc. upon); ⚥**nis** *n* (-ses/-se) fate; **~nisvoll** *adj.* fatal; disastrous.

ver'härmt *adj.* [fɛr'hɛrmt] careworn; **~harren** [~'harən] *v/i.* (*no* -ge-, *h, sein*) persist (*auf dat., bei,* in *dat.* in), stick (to); **~'härten** *v/t.* *and v/refl.* (*no* -ge-, *h*) harden; **~haßt** *adj.* [~'hast] hated; hateful, odious; **~'hätscheln** *v/t.* (*no* -ge-, *h*) coddle, pamper, spoil; **~'hauen** *v/t.* (*irr.* hauen, *no* -ge-, *h*) thrash.

verheer|en [fɛr'he:rən] *v/t.* (*no* -ge-, *h*) devastate, ravage, lay waste; **~end** *fig.* *adj.* disastrous; ⚥ung *f* (-/-en) devastation.

ver|hehlen [fɛr'he:lən] *v/t.* (*no* -ge-, *h*) *s.* verheimlichen; **~'heilen** *v/i.* (*no* -ge-, *sein*) heal (up).

ver'heimlich|en *v/t.* (*no* -ge-, *h*) hide, conceal; ⚥ung *f* (-/⚥-en) concealment.

ver'heirat|en *v/t.* (*no* -ge-, *h*) marry (*mit* to); *sich* ~ marry; ⚥ung *f* (-/⚥-en) marriage.

ver'heiß|en *v/t.* (*irr.* heißen, *no* -ge-, *h*) promise; ⚥ung *f* (-/-en) promise; **~ungsvoll** *adj.* promising.

ver'helfen *v/i.* (*irr.* helfen, *no* -ge-,

h): *j-m zu et.* ~ help s.o. to s.th.

ver'herrlich|en *v/t.* (*no -ge-, h*) glorify; **~ung** *f* (*-/~-en*) glorification.

ver'hetzen *v/t.* (*no -ge-, h*) instigate; **~hexen** *v/t.* (*no -ge-, h*) bewitch.

ver'hinder|n *v/t.* (*no -ge-, h*) prevent; **~ung** *f* (*-/~-en*) prevention.

ver'höhn|en *v/t.* (*no -ge-, h*) deride, mock (at), taunt; **~ung** *f* (*-/-en*) derision, mockery; error.

Verhör ⚖ [fɛr'høːr] *n* (*-[e]s/-e*) interrogation, questioning (*of prisoners, etc.*); examination; **~en** *v/t.* (*no -ge-, h*) examine, hear; interrogate; *sich* ~ hear it wrong.

ver'hüllen *v/t.* (*no -ge-, h*) cover, veil; **~hungern** *v/i.* (*no -ge-, sein*) starve; **~hüten** *v/t.* (*no -ge-, h*) prevent.

ver'irr|en *v/refl.* (*no -ge-, h*) go astray, lose one's way; **~t** *adj.:* **~es Schaf** stray sheep; **~ung** *fig. f* (*-/-en*) aberration; error.

ver'jagen *v/t.* (*no -ge-, h*) drive away.

verjähr|en ⚖ [fɛr'jɛːrən] *v/i.* (*no -ge-, sein*) become prescriptive; **~ung** *f* (*-/-en*) limitation, (negative) prescription.

verjüngen [fɛr'jyŋən] *v/t.* (*no -ge-, h*) make young again, rejuvenate; reduce (*scale*); *sich* ~ grow young again, rejuvenate; taper off.

Ver'kauf *m* sale; **~en** *v/t.* (*no -ge-, h*) sell; *zu* ~ for sale; *sich gut* ~ sell well.

Ver'käuf|er *m* seller; vendor; shop-assistant, salesman, *Am. a.* (sales-) clerk; **~erin** *f* (*-/-nen*) seller; vendor; shop-assistant, saleswoman, shop girl, *Am. a.* (sales)clerk; **2lich** *adj.* sal(e)able; for sale.

Ver'kaufs|automat *m* slot-machine, vending machine; **~schlager** *m* best seller.

Verkehr [fɛr'keːr] *m* (*-[e]s/~-e*) traffic; transport(ation); communication; correspondence; ⚓, ✈, ⚞, *etc.:* service; commerce, trade; intercourse (*a. sexually*); *aus dem* ~ *ziehen* withdraw from service; withdraw (*money*) from circulation; **2en** (*no -ge-, h*) **1.** *v/t.* convert (*in acc.* into), turn (*into*); **2.** *v/i. ship, bus, etc.:* run, ply (*zwischen dat.* between); *bei j-m* ~ go to *or* visit

s.o.'s house; ~ *in* (*dat.*) frequent (*public house, etc.*); ~ *mit* associate *or* mix with; have (sexual) intercourse with.

Ver'kehrs|ader *f* arterial road; **~ampel** *f* traffic lights *pl.*, traffic signal; **~büro** *n* tourist bureau; **~flugzeug** *n* air liner; **~insel** *f* refuge, island; **~minister** *m* minister of transport; **~mittel** *n* (means of) conveyance *or* transport, *Am.* transportation; **~polizist** *m* traffic policeman *or* constable, *sl.* traffic cop; **2reich** *adj.* congested with traffic, busy; **~schild** *n* traffic sign; **~schutzmann** *m s.* Verkehrspolizist; **~stauung** *f*, **~stockung** *f* traffic block, traffic jam; **~störung** *f* interruption of traffic; ⚞, *etc.:* breakdown; **~straße** *f* thoroughfare; **~teilnehmer** *m* road user; **~unfall** *m* traffic accident; **~verein** *m* tourist agency; **~verhältnisse** *pl.* traffic conditions *pl.*; **~vorschrift** *f* traffic regulation; **~wesen** *n* (*-s/no pl.*) traffic; **~zeichen** *n* traffic sign.

ver'kehrt *adj.* inverted, upside down; *fig.* wrong; **~'kennen** *v/t.* (*irr. kennen, no -ge-, h*) mistake; misunderstand, misjudge.

Ver'kettung *f* (*-/-en*) concatenation (*a. fig.*).

ver'klagen ⚖ *v/t.* (*no -ge-, h*) sue (*auf acc., wegen* for); bring an action against *s.o.*; **~'kleben** *v/t.* (*no -ge-, h*) paste *s.th.* up.

ver'kleid|en *v/t.* (*no -ge-, h*) disguise; ⊕: line; face; wainscot; encase; *sich* ~ disguise o.s.; **2ung** *f* (*-/-en*) disguise; ⊕: lining; facing; panel(l)ing, wainscot(t)ing.

verkleiner|n [fɛr'klaɪnərn] *v/t.* (*no -ge-, h*) make smaller, reduce, diminish; *fig.* belittle, derogate; **2ung** *f* (*-/-en*) reduction, diminution; *fig.* derogation.

ver'kling|en *v/i.* (*irr. klingen, no -ge-, sein*) die away; **~knöchern** [~'knœçərn] (*no -ge-*) **1.** *v/t.* (*h*) ossify; **2.** *v/i.* (*sein*) ossify; *fig. a.* fossilize; **~'knoten** *v/t.* (*no -ge-, h*) knot; **~'knüpfen** *v/t.* (*no -ge-, h*) knot *or* tie (together); *fig.* connect, combine; **~'kohlen** (*no -ge-*) **1.** *v/t.* (*h*) carbonize, char; F: *j-n* ~ pull s.o.'s leg; **2.** *v/i.* (*sein*) char; **~'kommen 1.** *v/i.* (*irr. kommen, no -ge-,* *sein*) decay; *p.*: go downhill *or* to the dogs; become demoralized; **2.** *adj.* decayed; depraved, corrupt; **~'korken** *v/t.* (*no* -ge-, *h*) cork (up).

ver'körper|n *v/t.* (*no* -ge-, *h*) personify, embody; represent; *esp. thea.* impersonate; **2ung** *f* (-/-en) personification, embodiment; impersonation.

ver|'krachen F *v/refl.* (*no* -ge-, *h*) fall out (*mit* with); **~'krampft** *adj.* cramped; **~'kriechen** *v/refl.* (*irr.* kriechen, *no* -ge-, *h*) hide; **~'krümmt** *adj.* crooked; **~'krüppelt** *adj.* [~'krypəlt] crippled; stunted; **~krustet** *adj.* [~'krustət] (en)crusted; caked; **~'kühlen** *v/refl.* (*no* -ge-, *h*) catch (a) cold.

ver'kümmer|n *v/i.* (*no* -ge-, *sein*) ♀, **~** become stunted; ♀ atrophy; *fig.* waste away; **~t** *adj.* stunted; atrophied; rudimentary (*a. biol.*).

verkünd|en [fɛr'kyndən] *v/t.* (*no* -ge-, *h*), **~igen** *v/t.* (*no* -ge-, *h*) announce; publish, proclaim; pronounce (*judgement*); **2igung** *f*, **2ung** *f* (-/-en) announcement; proclamation; pronouncement.

ver'kuppeln *v/t.* (*no* -ge-, *h*) ⊕ couple; *fig.* pander; **~'kürzen** *v/t.* (*no* -ge-, *h*) shorten; abridge; beguile (*time, etc.*); **~'lachen** *v/t.* (*no* -ge-, *h*) laugh at; **~'laden** *v/t.* (*irr.* laden, *no* -ge-, *h*) load, ship; 🚂 entrain (*esp. troops*).

Verlag [fɛr'lɑːk] *m* (-[e]s/-e) publishing house, *the* publishers *pl.*; *im* **~** *von* published by.

ver'lagern *v/t.* (*no* -ge-, *h*) displace, shift; *sich* **~** shift.

Ver'lags|buchhändler *m* publisher; **~buchhandlung** *f* publishing house; **~recht** *n* copyright.

ver'langen **1.** *v/t.* (*no* -ge-, *h*) demand; require; desire; **2.** *v/i.* (*no* -ge-, *h*): **~** *nach* ask for; long for; **3.** **2** *n* (-s/❨~) desire; longing (*nach* for); demand, request; *auf* **~** on demand; *auf* **~** *von* at the request of, at *s.o.'s* request.

ver'länger|n [fɛr'lɛŋɔrn] *v/t.* (*no* -ge-, *h*) lengthen; prolong; extend; **2ung** *f* (-/-en) lengthening; prolongation, extension.

ver'langsamen *v/t.* (*no* -ge-, *h*) slacken, slow down.

ver'lassen *v/t.* (*irr.* lassen, *no* -ge-, *h*) leave; forsake, abandon, desert;

sich **~** *auf* (*acc.*) rely on; **2heit** *f* (-/*no pl.*) abandonment; loneliness.

verläßlich *adj.* [fɛr'lɛslɪç] reliable.

Ver'lauf *m* lapse, course (*of time*); progress, development (*of matter*); course (*of disease, etc.*); *im* **~** (*gen.*) *or* *von* in the course of; *e-n schlimmen* **~** *nehmen* take a bad turn; **2en** (*irr.* laufen, *no* -ge-) **1.** *v/i.* (*sein*) *time*: pass, elapse; *matter*: take its course; turn out, develop; *road, etc.*: run, extend; **2.** *v/refl.* (*h*) lose one's way, go astray; *crowd*: disperse; *water*: subside.

ver'lauten *v/i.* (*no* -ge-, *sein*): **~** *lassen* give to understand, hint; *wie verlautet* as reported.

ver'leb|en *v/t.* (*no* -ge-, *h*) spend, pass; **~t** *adj.* [~pt] worn out.

ver'leg|en **1.** *v/t.* (*no* -ge-, *h*) mislay; transfer, shift, remove; ⊕ lay (*cable, etc.*); bar (*road*); put off, postpone; publish (*book*); *sich* **~** *auf* (*acc.*) apply o.s. to; **2.** *adj.* embarrassed; *at a loss* (*um* for *answer, etc.*); **2enheit** *f* (-/❨~-en) embarrassment; difficulty; predicament; **2er** *m* (-s/-) publisher; **2ung** *f* (-/-en) transfer, removal; ⊕ laying; *time*: postponement.

ver'leiden *v/t.* (*no* -ge-, *h*) *s.* verekeln.

ver'leih|en *v/t.* (*irr.* leihen, *no* -ge-, *h*) lend, *Am. a.* loan; hire *or* let out; bestow (*right, etc.*) (*j-m on s.o.*); award (*price*); **2ung** *f* (-/-en) lending, loan; bestowal.

ver'leiten *v/t.* (*no* -ge-, *h*) mislead; induce; seduce; 🔨 suborn; **~'lernen** *v/t.* (*no* -ge-, *h*) unlearn, forget; **~'lesen** *v/t.* (*irr.* lesen, *no* -ge-, *h*) read out; call (*names*) over; pick (*vegetables, etc.*); *sich* **~** read wrong.

verletz|en [fɛr'lɛtsən] *v/t.* (*no* -ge-, *h*) hurt, injure; *fig. a.*: offend; violate; **~end** *adj.* offensive; **2te** [~tə] *m, f* (-n/-n) injured person; *die* **~n** *pl.* the injured *pl.*; **2ung** *f* (-/-en) hurt, injury, wound; *fig.* violation.

ver'leugn|en *v/t.* (*no* -ge-, *h*) deny; disown; renounce (*belief, principle, etc.*); *sich* **~** *lassen* have o.s. denied (*vor j-m to s.o.*); **2ung** *f* (-/-en) denial; renunciation.

verleumd|en [fɛr'lɔymdən] *v/t.* (*no* -ge-, *h*) slander, defame; **~erisch** *adj.* slanderous; **2ung** *f* (-/-en) slander, defamation, *in writing*: libel.

ver'lieb|en *v/refl.* (no -ge-, h): sich ~ in (acc.) fall in love with; **~t** *adj.* [~pt] in love (in *acc.* with); amorous; **2theit** *f* (-/~ -en) amorousness.

verlieren [fɛr'liːrən] (*irr.*, no -ge-, h) **1.** *v/t.* lose; shed (*leaves, etc.*); sich ~ lose o.s.; disappear; **2.** *v/i.* lose.

ver'lob|en *v/t.* (no -ge-, h) engage (mit to); sich ~ become engaged; **2te** [~ptə] (-n/-n) **1.** *m* fiancé; die ~n *pl.* the engaged couple *sg.*; **2.** *f* fiancée; **2ung** [~buŋ] *f* (-/-en) engagement.

ver'lock|en *v/t.* (no -ge-, h) allure, entice; tempt; **~end** *adj.* tempting; **2ung** *f* (-/-en) allurement, enticement.

verlogen *adj.* [fɛr'loːgən] mendacious; **2heit** *f* (-/~ -en) mendacity.

verlor [fɛr'loːr] *pret.* of verlieren; **~en 1.** *p.p.* of verlieren; **2.** *adj.* lost; *fig.* forlorn; **~e Eier** poached eggs; **~engehen** *v/i.* (*irr. gehen, sep.*, -ge-, sein) be lost.

ver'los|en *v/t.* (no -ge-, h) raffle; **2ung** *f* (-/-en) lottery, raffle.

ver'löten *v/t.* (no -ge-, h) solder.

Verlust [fɛr'lust] *m* (-es/-e) loss; **~e** *pl.* ✕ casualties *pl.*

ver'machen *v/t.* (no -ge-, h) bequeath, leave *s.th.* (dat. to).

Vermächtnis [fɛr'mɛçtnis] *n* (-ses/-se) will; legacy, bequest.

vermähl|en [fɛr'mɛːlən] *v/t.* (no -ge-, h) marry (mit to); sich ~ (mit) marry (*s.o.*); **2ung** *f* (-/-en) wedding, marriage.

ver'mehr|en *v/t.* (no -ge-, h) increase (*um* by), augment; multiply; add to; durch Zucht ~ propagate; breed; sich ~ increase, augment; multiply (*a. biol.*); propagate (itself), *zo.* breed; **2ung** *f* (-/~ -en) increase; addition (gen. to); propagation.

ver'meid|en *v/t.* (*irr. meiden*, no -ge-, h) avoid; **2ung** *f* (-/~ -en) avoidance.

ver|meintlich *adj.* [fɛr'maintliç] supposed; **~'mengen** *v/t.* (no -ge-, h) mix, mingle, blend.

Vermerk [fɛr'mɛrk] *m* (-[e]s/-e) note, entry; **2en** *v/t.* (no -ge-, h) note down, record.

ver'mess|en 1. *v/t.* (*irr. messen*, no -ge-, h) measure; survey (*land*); **2.** *adj.* presumptuous; **2enheit** *f* (-/~ -en) presumption; **2ung** *f* (-/-en) measurement; survey (*of land*).

ver'miete|n *v/t.* (no -ge-, h) let, *esp. Am.* rent; hire (out); ⚖ lease; zu ~ on *or* for hire; Haus zu ~ house to (be) let; **2r** *m* landlord; ⚖ lessor; letter, hirer.

ver'mindern *v/t.* (no -ge-, h) diminish, lessen; reduce, cut.

ver'misch|en *v/t.* (no -ge-, h) mix, mingle, blend; **~t** *adj.* mixed; *news, etc.*: miscellaneous; **2ung** *f* (-/~ -en) mixture.

ver'mi|ssen *v/t.* (no -ge-, h) miss; **~ßt** *adj.* [~'mist] missing; **2ßte** *m, f* (-n/-n) missing person; die ~n *pl.* the missing *pl.*

vermitt|eln [fɛr'mitəln] (no -ge-, h) **1.** *v/t.* mediate (settlement, peace); procure, get; give (impression, etc.); impart (knowledge) (j-m to s.o.); **2.** *v/i.* mediate (zwischen dat. between); intercede (bei with, für for), intervene; **2ler** *m* mediator; go-between; † agent; **2lung** *f* (-/-en) mediation; intercession, intervention; *teleph.* (telephone) exchange.

ver'modern *v/i.* (no -ge-, sein) mo(u)lder, decay, rot.

ver'mögen 1. *v/t.* (*irr. mögen*, no -ge-, h): ~ zu *inf.* be able to *inf.*; et. ~ bei j-m have influence with s.o.; **2.** **2** *n* (-s/-) ability, power; property; fortune; means *pl.*; ⚖ assets *pl.*; **~d** *adj.* wealthy; *pred.* well off; **2sverhältnisse** *pl.* pecuniary circumstances *pl.*

vermut|en [fɛr'muːtən] *v/t.* (no -ge-, h) suppose, presume, *Am. a.* guess; conjecture, surmise; **~lich 1.** *adj.* presumable; **2.** *adv.* presumably; I suppose; **2ung** *f* (-/-en) supposition, presumption; conjecture, surmise.

vernachlässig|en [fɛr'naːxlɛsigən] *v/t.* (no -ge-, h) neglect; **2ung** *f* (-/~ -en) neglect(ing).

ver'narben *v/i.* (no -ge-, sein) cicatrize, scar over.   [with.]

ver'narrt *adj.*: ~ in (acc.) infatuated]

ver'nehm|en *v/t.* (*irr. nehmen*, no -ge-, h) hear, learn; examine, interrogate; **~lich** *adj.* audible, distinct;

Qung 🏛 f (-/-en) interrogation, questioning; examination.

ver'neig|en v/refl. (no -ge-, h) bow (vor dat. to); **Qung** f bow.

vernein|en [fɛr'naɪnən] (no -ge-, h) **1.** v/t. answer in the negative; deny; **2.** v/i. answer in the negative; **~end** adj. negative; **Qung** f (-/-en) negation; denial; gr. negative.

vernicht|en [fɛr'nɪçtən] v/t. (no -ge-, h) annihilate; destroy; dash (hopes); **~end** adj. destructive (a. fig.); look: withering; criticism: scathing; defeat, reply: crushing; **Qung** f (-/~-en) annihilation; destruction.

ver'nickeln [fɛr'nɪkəln] v/t. (no -ge-, h) nickel(-plate); **~'nieten** v/t. (no -ge-, h) rivet.

Vernunft [fɛr'nʊnft] f (-/no pl.) reason; ~ annehmen listen to or hear reason; j-n zur ~ bringen bring s.o. to reason or to his senses.

vernünftig adj. [fɛr'nʏnftɪç] rational; reasonable; sensible.

ver'öden (no -ge-) **1.** v/t. (h) make desolate; **2.** v/i. (sein) become desolate.

ver'öffentlich|en v/t. (no -ge-, h) publish; **Qung** f (-/-en) publication.

ver'ordn|en v/t. (no -ge-, h) decree; order (a. 🏛); 🌿 prescribe (j-m to or for s.o.); **Qung** f decree, order; 🌿 prescription.

ver'pachten v/t. (no -ge-, h) rent, 🏛 lease (building, land).

Ver'pächter m landlord, 🏛 lessor.

ver'pack|en v/t. (no -ge-, h) pack (up); wrap up; **Qung** f packing (material); wrapping.

ver|'passen v/t. (no -ge-, h) miss (train, opportunity, etc.); **~patzen** F [~'patsən] v/t. (no -ge-, h) s. verpfuschen; **~'pesten** v/t. (no -ge-, h) fumes: contaminate (the air); **~'pfänden** v/t. (no -ge-, h) pawn, pledge (a. fig.); mortgage.

ver'pflanz|en v/t. (no -ge-, h) transplant (a. 🌿); **Qung** f transplantation; 🌿 a. transplant.

ver'pfleg|en v/t. (no -ge-, h) board; supply with food, cater; **Qung** f (-/~-en) board; food-supply; provisions pl.

ver'pflicht|en v/t. (no -ge-, h) oblige; engage; **Qung** f (-/-en) obligation, duty; ✝, 🏛 liability; engagement, commitment.

ver'pfusch|en F v/t. (no -ge-, h) bungle, botch; make a mess of; **~t** adj. life: ruined, wrecked.

ver|'pönt adj. [fɛr'pø:nt] taboo; **~'prügeln** F v/t. (no -ge-, h) thrash, flog, F wallop; **~'puffen** fig. v/i. (no -ge-, sein) fizzle out.

Ver'putz △ m (-es/~-e) plaster; **Qen** △ v/t. (no -ge-, h) plaster.

ver'quicken v/t. (no -ge-, h) mix up; **~'quollen** adj. wood: warped; face: bloated; eyes: swollen; **~rammeln** [~'raməln] v/t. (no -ge-, h) bar(ricade).

Verrat [fɛr'ra:t] m (-[e]s/no pl.) betrayal (an dat. of); treachery (to); 🏛 treason (to); **Qen** v/t. (irr. raten, no -ge-, h) betray, give s.o. away; give away (secret); sich ~ betray o.s., give o.s. away.

Verräter [fɛr'rɛ:tər] m (-s/-) traitor (an dat. to); **Qisch** adj. treacherous; fig. telltale.

ver'rechn|en v/t. (no -ge-, h) reckon up; charge; settle; set off (mit against); account for; ~ mit offset against; sich ~ miscalculate, make a mistake (a. fig.); fig. be mistaken; sich um e-e Mark ~ be one mark out; **Qung** f settlement; clearing; booking or charging (to account); **Qungsscheck** m collection-only cheque or Am. check.

ver'regnet adj. rainy, rain-spoilt.

ver'reis|en v/i. (no -ge-, sein) go on a journey; **~t** adj. out of town; (geschäftlich) ~ away (on business).

ver'renk|en v/t. (no -ge-, h) 🌿: wrench; dislocate, luxate; sich et. ~ 🌿 dislocate or luxate s.th.; sich den Hals ~ crane one's neck; **Qung** 🌿 f (-/-en) dislocation, luxation.

ver|'richten v/t. (no -ge-, h) do, perform; execute; sein Gebet ~ say one's prayer(s); **~'riegeln** v/t. (no -ge-, h) bolt, bar.

verringer|n [fɛr'rɪŋərn] v/t. (no -ge-, h) diminish, lessen; reduce, cut; sich ~ diminish, lessen; **Qung** f (-/-en) diminution; reduction, cut.

ver|'rosten v/i. (no -ge-, sein) rust; **~rotten** [~'rɔtən] v/i. (no -ge-, sein) rot.

ver'rück|en v/t. (no -ge-, h) displace, (re)move, shift; **~t** adj. mad, crazy (both a. fig.: nach about); wie ~ like mad; j-n ~ machen drive s.o. mad; **2te** (*-n/-n*) **1.** *m* lunatic, madman; **2.** *f* lunatic, madwoman; **2theit** *f* (*-/-en*) madness; foolish action; craze.

Ver'ruf *m* (*-[e]s/no pl.*): in ~ bringen bring discredit (up)on; *in* ~ kommen get into discredit; **2en** *adj.* ill-reputed, ill-famed.

ver'rutsch|en *v/i.* (*no -ge-, sein*) slip; ~ **t** *adj.* not straight.

Vers [fɛrs] *m* (*-es/-e*) verse.

ver'sagen 1. *v/t.* (*no -ge-, h*) refuse, deny (*j-m et.* s.o. s.th.); *sich et.* ~ deny o.s. s.th.; **2.** *v/i.* (*no -ge-, h*) fail, break down; *gun:* misfire; **3.** 2 *n* (*-s/no pl.*) failure. [ure.\
Ver'sager *m* (*-s/-*) misfire; *p.* fail-|
ver'salzen *v/t.* (*irr. salzen,*] *no -ge-, h*) oversalt; *F fig.* spoil.

ver'samm|eln *v/t.* (*no -ge-, h*) assemble; *sich* ~ assemble, meet; **2lung** *f* assembly, meeting.

Versand [fɛr'zant] *m* (*-[e]s/no pl.*) dispatch, *Am. a.* shipment; mailing; ~ *ins Ausland a.* export(ation); **~abteilung** *f* forwarding department; **~geschäft** *n,* **~haus** *n* mail-order business *or* firm *or* house.

ver'säum|en *v/t.* (*no -ge-, h*) neglect (*one's duty, etc.*); miss (*opportunity, etc.*); lose (*time*); ~ *zu inf.* fail *or* omit to *inf.*; **2nis** *n* (*-ses/-se*) neglect, omission, failure.

ver'|schachern *F v/t.* (*no -ge-, h*) barter (away); **~'schaffen** *v/t.* (*no -ge-, h*) procure, get; *sich* ~ obtain, get; raise (*money*); *sich Respekt* ~ make o.s. respected; **~'schämt** *adj.* bashful; **~'schanzen** *v/refl.* (*no -ge-, h*) entrench o.s.; *sich* ~ *hinter* (*dat.*) (take) shelter behind; **~'schärfen** *v/t.* (*no -ge-, h*) heighten, intensify; aggravate; *sich* ~ get worse; **~'scheiden** *v/i.* (*irr. scheiden, no -ge-, sein*) pass away; **~'schenken** *v/t.* (*no -ge-, h*) give *s.th.* away; make a present of; **~'scherzen** *v/t.* (*no -ge-, h*) forfeit; **~'scheuchen** *v/t.* (*no -ge-, h*) frighten *or* scare away; *fig.* banish; **~'schicken** *v/t.* (*no -ge-, h*) send (away), dispatch, forward.

ver'schieb|en *v/t.* (*irr. schieben, no -ge-, h*) displace, shift, (re)move; 🚂 shunt; put off, postpone; *F fig.* † sell underhand; ~ **t** *adj.* ~ schief; **2ung** *f* shift(ing); postponement.

verschieden *adj.* [fɛr'ʃiːdən] differ-

ent (*von* from); dissimilar, unlike; *aus* ~ **en** *Gründen* for various *or* several reasons; *Verschiedenes* various things *pl.*, *esp.* † sundries *pl.*; **~artig** *adj.* of a different kind, various; **2heit** *f* (*-/-en*) difference; diversity, variety; **~tlich** *adv.* repeatedly; at times.

ver'schiff|en *v/t.* (*no -ge-, h*) ship; **2ung** *f* (*-/💢-en*) shipment.

ver'|schimmeln *v/i.* (*no -ge-, sein*) get mo(u)ldy, *Am.* mo(u)ld; **~'schlafen 1.** *v/t.* (*irr. schlafen, no -ge-, h*) miss by sleeping; sleep (*afternoon, etc.*) away; sleep off (*headache, etc.*); **2.** *v/i.* (*irr. schlafen, no -ge-, h*) oversleep (o.s.); **3.** *adj.* sleepy, drowsy.

Ver'schlag *m* shed; box; crate; **2en** [~gən] **1.** *v/t.* (*irr. schlagen, no -ge-, h*) board up; nail up; *es verschlug ihm die Sprache* it dum(b)founded him; **2.** *adj.* cunning; *eyes: a.* shifty; **~enheit** *f* (*-/no pl.*) cunning.

verschlechter|n [fɛr'ʃlɛçtərn] *v/t.* (*no -ge-, h*) deteriorate, make worse; *sich* ~ deteriorate, get worse; **2ung** *f* (*-/💢-en*) deterioration; change for the worse.

ver'schleiern *v/t.* (*no -ge-, h*) veil (*a. fig.*).

Verschleiß [fɛr'ʃlais] *m* (*-es/💢-e*) wear (and tear); **2en** *v/t.* (*[irr.,]*] *no -ge-, h*) wear out.

ver'|schleppen *v/t.* (*no -ge-, h*) carry off; *pol.* displace (*person*); abduct; kidnap; delay; protract; neglect (*disease*); **~'schleudern** *v/t.* (*no -ge-, h*) dissipate, waste; † sell at a loss, sell dirt-cheap; **~'schließen** *v/t.* (*irr. schließen, no -ge-, h*) shut, close; lock (*door*); lock up (*house*).

verschlimmern [fɛr'ʃlimərn] *v/t.* (*no -ge-, h*) make worse, aggravate; *sich* ~ get worse.

ver'schlingen *v/t.* (*irr. schlingen, no -ge-, h*) devour; wolf (down) (*one's food*); intertwine, entwine, interlace; *sich* ~ intertwine, entwine, interlace.

verschli|ß [fɛr'ʃlis] *pret. of* verschleißen; **~ssen** [~sən] *p.p. of* verschleißen.

verschlossen *adj.* [fɛr'ʃlɔsən] closed, shut; *fig.* reserved; **2heit** *f* (*-/no pl.*) reserve.

ver'schlucken v/t. (no -ge-, h) swallow (up); sich ~ swallow the wrong way.

Ver'schluß m lock; clasp; lid; plug; stopper (of bottle); seal; fastener, fastening; phot. shutter; unter ~ under lock and key.

ver|'schmachten v/i. (no -ge-, sein) languish, pine away; vor Durst ~ die or be dying of thirst, be parched with thirst; ~'schmähen v/t. (no -ge-, h) disdain, scorn.

ver'schmelz|en (irr. schmelzen, no -ge-) v/t. (h) and v/i. (sein) melt, fuse (a. fig.); blend; fig.: amalgamate; merge (mit in, into); 2ung f (-/~-en) fusion; † merger; fig. amalgamation.

ver|'schmerzen v/t. (no -ge-, h) get over (the loss of); ~'schmieren v/t. (no -ge-, h) smear (over); blur; ~schmitzt adj. [~'ʃmɪtst] cunning; roguish; arch; ~'schmutzen (no -ge-) 1. v/t. (h) soil, dirty; pollute (water); 2. v/i. (sein) get dirty; ~'schnaufen F v/i. and v/refl. (no -ge-, h) stop for breath; ~'schneiden v/t. (irr. schneiden, no -ge-, h) cut badly; blend (wine, etc.); geld, castrate; ~'schneit adj. covered with snow; mountains: a. snow-capped; roofs: a. snow-covered.

Ver'schnitt m (-[e]s/no pl.) blend.

ver'schnupf|en F fig. v/t. (no -ge-, h) nettle, pique; ~t ~ adj.: ~ sein have a cold.

ver|'schnüren v/t. (no -ge-, h) tie up, cord; ~schollen adj. [~'ʃɔlən] not heard of again; missing; ♣ presumed dead; ~'schonen v/t. (no -ge-, h) spare; j-n mit et. ~ spare s.o. s.th.

verschöne|(r)n [fɛr'ʃø:nə(r)n] v/t. (no -ge-, h) embellish, beautify; 2rung f (-/-en) embellishment.

ver|'schossen adj. [fɛr'ʃɔsən] colour: faded; F ~ sein in (acc.) be madly in love with; ~schränken [~'ʃrɛŋkən] v/t. (no -ge-, h) cross, fold (one's arms).

ver'schreib|en v/t. (irr. schreiben, no -ge-, h) use up (in writing); ♣ prescribe (j-m for s.o.); ♣ assign (j-m to s.o.); sich ~ make a slip of the pen; sich e-r Sache ~ devote o.s. to s.th.; 2ung f (-/-en) assignment; prescription.

ver|schroben adj. [fɛr'ʃro:bən] ec-centric, queer, odd; ~'schrotten v/t. (no -ge-, h) scrap; ~schüchtert adj. [~'ʃʏçtərt] intimidated.

ver'schulden 1. v/t. (no -ge-, h) be guilty of; be the cause of; 2. 2 n (-s/no pl.) fault.

ver|'schuldet adj. indebted, in debt; ~'schütten v/t. (no -ge-, h) spill (liquid); block (up) (road); bury s.o. alive; ~schwägert adj. [~'ʃvɛːgərt] related by marriage; ~'schweigen v/t. (irr. schweigen, no -ge-, h) conceal (j-m et. s.th. from s.o.).

verschwend|en [fɛr'ʃvɛndən] v/t. (no -ge-, h) waste, squander (an acc. on); lavish (on); 2er m (-s/-) spendthrift, prodigal; ~erisch adj. prodigal, lavish (both: mit of); wasteful; 2ung f (-/~-en) waste; extravagance.

verschwiegen adj. [fɛr'ʃviːgən] discreet; place: secret, secluded; 2heit f (-/no pl.) discretion; secrecy.

ver|'schwimmen v/i. (irr. schwimmen, no -ge-, sein) become indistinct or blurred; ~'schwinden v/i. (irr. schwinden, no -ge-, sein) disappear, vanish; F verschwinde! go away!, sl. beat it!; 2'schwinden n (-s/no pl.) disappearance; ~schwommen adj. [~'ʃvɔmən] vague (a. fig.); blurred; fig. woolly.

ver'schwör|en v/refl. (irr. schwören, no -ge-, h) conspire; 2er m (-s/-) conspirator; 2ung f (-/-en) conspiracy, plot.

ver'seh|en 1. v/t. (irr. sehen, no -ge-, h) fill (an office); look after (house, etc.); mit et. ~ furnish or supply with; sich ~ make a mistake; ehe man sich's versieht all of a sudden; 2. 2 n (-s/-) oversight, mistake, slip; aus ~ = ~tlich adv. by mistake; inadvertently. [disabled person.)

Versehrte [fɛr'zeːrtə] m (-n/-n)]

ver'send|en v/t. ([irr. senden,] no -ge-, h) send, dispatch, forward, Am. ship; by water: ship; ins Ausland ~ a. export; 2ung f (-/~-en) dispatch, shipment, forwarding.

ver|'sengen v/t. (no -ge-, h) singe, scorch; ~'senken v/t. (no -ge-, h) sink; sich ~ in (acc.) immerse o.s. in; ~sessen adj. [~'zɛsən]: ~ auf (acc.) bent on, mad after.

ver'setz|en v/t. (no -ge-, h) displace, remove; transfer (*officer*); *at school*: remove, move up, *Am.* promote; transplant (*tree, etc.*); pawn, pledge; F *fig.* stand (*lover, etc.*) up; ~ in (*acc.*) put *or* place into (*situation, condition*); j-m e-n Schlag ~ give *or* deal s.o. a blow; *in Angst* ~ frighten *or* terrify *s.o.*; *in den Ruhestand* ~ pension *s.o.* off, retire *s.o.*; *versetzt werden* be transferred; *at school*: go up; ~ *Sie sich in m-e Lage* put *or* place yourself in my position; *Wein mit Wasser* ~ mix wine with water, add water to wine; et. ~ reply s.th.; ℒ**ung** f (-/-en) removal; transfer; *at school*: remove, *Am.* promotion.

ver'**seuch|en** v/t. (*no* -ge-, h) infect; contaminate; ℒ**ung** f (-/ℛ -en) infection; contamination.

ver'**sicher|n** v/t. (*no* -ge-, h) assure (a. one's life); protest, affirm; insure (one's property or life); *sich* ~ insure *or* assure o.s.; *sich* ~ (, daß) make sure (that); ℒ**te** m, f (-n/-n) insurant, *the* insured *or* assured, policy-holder; ℒ**ung** f assurance, affirmation; insurance; (life-)assurance; insurance company.

Ver'**sicherungs|gesellschaft** f insurance company, ~**police** f, ~**schein** m policy of assurance, insurance policy.

ver'**sickern** v/i. (*no* -ge-, sein) trickle away; ~'**siegeln** v/t. (*no* -ge-, h) seal (up); ~'**siegen** v/i. (*no* -ge-, sein) dry up, run dry; ~'**silbern** v/t. (*no* -ge-, h) silver; F *fig.* realize, convert into cash; ~'**sinken** v/i. (*irr.* sinken, *no* -ge-, sein) sink; *s.* versunken; ~'**sinnbildlichen** v/t. (*no* -ge-, h) symbolize.

Version [ver'zjo:n] f (-/-en) version.
'**Versmaß** n met|re, *Am.* -er.

ver**söhn|en** [fer'zø:nən] v/t. (*no* -ge-, h) reconcile (mit to, with); *sich* (*wieder*) ~ become reconciled; ~**lich** adj. conciliatory; ℒ**ung** f (-/ℛ -en) reconciliation.

ver'**sorg|en** v/t. (*no* -ge-, h) provide (mit with), supply (with); take care of, look after; ~**t** adj. [~kt] provided for; ℒ**ung** f [~gun] f (-/-en) providing (mit with), supplying (with); supply, provision.

ver**spät|en** v/refl. (*no* -ge-, h) be late; ~**et** adj. belated, late, *Am.*

tardy; ℒ**ung** f (-/-en) lateness, *Am.* tardiness; ~ *haben* be late; *mit* 2 *Stunden* ~ two hours behind schedule.

ver'**speisen** v/t. (*no* -ge-, h) eat (up); ~'**sperren** v/t. (*no* -ge-, h) lock (up); bar, block (up), obstruct (a. view); ~'**spielen** v/t. (*no* -ge-, h) *at cards, etc.*: lose (money); ~'**spielt** adj. playful; ~'**spotten** v/t. (*no* -ge-, h) scoff at, mock (at), deride, ridicule; ~'**sprechen** v/t. (*irr.* sprechen, *no* -ge-, h) promise; *sich* ~ make a mistake in speaking; *sich viel* ~ *von* expect much of; ℒ'**sprechen** n (-s/ℛ -) promise; ~'**sprühen** v/t. (*no* -ge-, h) spray; ~'**spüren** v/t. (*no* -ge-, h) feel; perceive, be conscious of.

ver'**staatlich|en** v/t. (*no* -ge-, h) nationalize; ℒ**ung** f (-/ℛ -en) nationalization.

Verstand [fer'ʃtant] m (-[e]s/*no pl.*) understanding; intelligence, intellect, brains *pl.*; mind, wits *pl.*; reason; (common) sense.

Verstandes|kraft [fer'ʃtandəs-] f intellectual power *or* faculty; ℒ**mäßig** adj. rational; intellectual; ~**mensch** m matter-of-fact person.

ver**ständ|ig** adj. [fer'ʃtendiç] intelligent; reasonable, sensible; judicious; ~**igen** [~gən] v/t. (*no* -ge-, h) inform (von of), notify (of); *sich mit j-m* ~ make o.s. understood to s.o.; come to an understanding with s.o.; ℒ**igung** f [~gun] f (-/ℛ -en) information; understanding, agreement; *teleph.* communication; ~**lich** adj. [~tliç] intelligible; understandable; j-m et. ~ *machen* make s.th. clear to s.o.; *sich* ~ *machen* make o.s. understood.

Verständnis [fer'ʃtentnis] n (-ses/ℛ -se) comprehension, understanding; insight; appreciation (für of); ~ *haben für* appreciate; ℒ**los** adj. uncomprehending; *look, etc.*: blank; unappreciative; ℒ**voll** adj. understanding; appreciative; sympathetic; *look*: knowing.

ver'**stärk|en** v/t. (*no* -ge-, h) strengthen, reinforce (a. ⊕, ⚔); amplify (*radio signals, etc.*); intensify; ℒ**er** m (-s/-) *in radio, etc.*: amplifier; ℒ**ung** f (-/ℛ -en) strengthening, reinforcement (a. ⚔); amplification; intensification.

ver'staub|en v/i. (no -ge-, sein) get dusty; **~t** adj. [~pt] dusty.

ver'stauch|en ✚ v/t. (no -ge-, h) sprain; *sich den Fuß* ~ sprain one's foot; **2ung** ✚ f (-/-en) sprain.

ver'stauen v/t. (no -ge-, h) stow away.

Versteck [fɛr'ʃtɛk] n (-[e]s/-e) hiding-place; *for gangsters, etc.:* Am. F a. hide-out; *~ spielen* play at hide-and-seek; **2en** v/t. (no -ge-, h) hide, conceal; *sich* ~ hide.

ver'stehen v/t. (irr. stehen, no -ge-, h) understand, see, F get; comprehend; realize; know (*language*); es ~ zu inf. know how to inf.; *Spaß* ~ take a joke; *zu* ~ geben intimate; ~ *Sie?* do you see?; *ich* ~! I see!; *verstanden?* (do you) understand?, F (do you) get me?; *falsch* ~ misunderstand; ~ *Sie mich recht!* don't misunderstand me!; *was* ~ *Sie unter* (dat.)? what do you mean *or* understand by ...?; *er versteht et. davon* he knows a thing or two about it; *sich* ~ understand one another; *sich* ~ *auf* (acc.) know well, be an expert at *or* in; *sich mit j-m gut* ~ get on well with s.o.; *es versteht sich von selbst* it goes without saying.

ver'steifen v/t. (no -ge-, h) ⊕ strut, brace; stiffen; *sich* ~ stiffen; *sich* ~ *auf* (acc.) make a point of, insist on.

ver'steiger|n v/t. (no -ge-, h) (sell by *or* Am. at) auction; **2ung** f (sale by *or* Am. at) auction, auction-sale.

ver'steinern (no -ge-) v/t. (h) and v/i. (sein) turn into stone, petrify (*both a. fig.*).

ver'stell|bar adj. adjustable; **~en** v/t. (no -ge-, h) shift; adjust; disarrange; bar, block (*up*), obstruct; disguise (*voice, etc.*); *sich* ~ play or act a part; dissemble, feign; **2ung** f (-/-~-en) disguise; dissimulation.

ver|'steuern v/t. (no -ge-, h) pay duty or tax on; **~stiegen** fig. adj. [~'ʃtiːɡən] eccentric.

ver'stimm|en v/t. (no -ge-, h) put out of tune; fig. put out of humo(u)r; **~t** adj. out of tune; fig. out of humo(u)r, F cross; **2ung** f ill humo(u)r; disagreement; ill feeling.

ver'stockt adj. stubborn, obdurate; **2heit** f (-/no pl.) obduracy.

verstohlen adj. [fɛr'ʃtoːlən] furtive.

ver'stopf|en v/t. (no -ge-, h) stop (up); clog, block (up), obstruct; jam, block (*passage, street*); ✚ constipate; **2ung** ✚ f (-/~-en) constipation.

verstorben adj. [fɛr'ʃtɔrbən] late, deceased; **2e** m, f (-n/-n) the deceased, Am. ⚕ a. decedent; *die* ~n pl. the deceased pl., the departed pl.

ver'stört adj. scared; distracted, bewildered; **2heit** f (-/no pl.) distraction, bewilderment.

Ver'stoß m offen|ce, Am. -se; contravention (*gegen* of *law*); infringement (on *trade name, etc.*); blunder; **2en** (irr. stoßen, no -ge-, h) **1.** v/t. expel (*aus* from); repudiate, disown (*wife, child, etc.*); **2.** v/i.: ~ *gegen* offend against; contravene (*law*); infringe (*rule, etc.*).

ver|'streichen (irr. streichen, no -ge-) **1.** v/i. (sein) *time:* pass, elapse; expire; **2.** v/t. (h) spread (*butter, etc.*); **~'streuen** v/t. (no -ge-, h) scatter.

ver'stümmel|n [fɛr'ʃtyməln] v/t. (no -ge-, h) mutilate; garble (*text, etc.*); **2ung** f (-/-en) mutilation.

ver'stummen v/i. (no -ge-, sein) grow silent or dumb.

Verstümmlung [fɛr'ʃtymluŋ] f (-/-en) mutilation.

Versuch [fɛr'zuːx] m (-[e]s/-e) attempt, trial; *phys., etc.:* experiment; *e-n* ~ *machen mit* give s.o. or s.th. a trial; try one's hand at s.th.; have a go at s.th.; **2en** v/t. (no -ge-, h) try, attempt; taste; *j-n* ~ tempt s.o.; *es* ~ *mit* give s.o. or s.th. a trial.

Ver'suchs|anstalt f research institute; **~kaninchen** fig. n guinea-pig; **2weise** adv. by way of trial or (an) experiment; on trial; **~zweck** m: *zu* ~en pl. for experimental purposes pl.

Ver'suchung f (-/-en) temptation; *j-n in* ~ *bringen* tempt s.o.; *in* ~ *sein* be tempted.

ver|'sündigen v/refl. (no -ge-, h) sin (*an* dat. against); **~sunken** fig. adj. [~'zuŋkən]: ~ *in* (acc.) absorbed or lost in; **~'süßen** v/t. (no -ge-, h) sweeten.

ver'tag|en v/t. (no -ge-, h) adjourn; parl. prorogue; *sich* ~ adjourn, Am.

a. recess; **2ung** *f* adjournment; *parl.* prorogation.

ver'tauschen *v/t. (no -ge-, h)* exchange *(mit for).*

verteidig|en [fɛr'taɪdɪgən] *v/t. (no -ge-, h)* defend; *sich ~* defend o.s.; **2er** *m (-s/-)* defender; ᵗ½, *fig.* advocate; ᵗ½ counsel for the defen|ce, *Am.* -se, *Am.* attorney for the defendant *or* defense; *football:* fullback; **2ung** *f (-/~-en)* defen|ce, *Am.* -se.

Ver'teidigungs|bündnis *n* defensive alliance; **~minister** *m* minister of defence; *Brt.* Minister of Defence, *Am.* Secretary of Defense; **~ministerium** *n* ministry of defence; *Brt.* Ministry of Defence, *Am.* Department of Defense.

ver'teil|en *v/t. (no -ge-, h)* distribute; spread *(colour, etc.);* **2er** *m (-s/-)* distributor; **2ung** *f (-/~-en)* distribution.

ver'teuern *v/t. (no -ge-, h)* raise *or* increase the price of.

ver'tief|en *v/t. (no -ge-, h)* deepen *(a. fig.); sich ~* deepen; *sich ~ in (acc.)* plunge in(to); become absorbed in; **2ung** *f (-/~-en)* hollow, cavity; recess.

vertikal *adj.* [vɛrti'kɑːl] vertical.

ver'tilg|en *v/t. (no -ge-, h)* exterminate; F consume, eat (up) *(food);* **2ung** *f (-/~-en)* extermination.

ver'tonen ♪ *v/t. (no -ge-, h)* set to music.

Vertrag [fɛr'traːk] *m (-[e]s/~e)* agreement, contract; *pol.* treaty; **2en** [~gən] *v/t. (irr. tragen, no -ge-, h)* endure, bear, stand; *diese Speise kann ich nicht ~* this food does not agree with me; *sich ~ things:* be compatible *or* consistent; *colours:* harmonize; *p.:* agree; get on with one another; *sich wieder ~* be reconciled, make it up; **2lich** [~klɪç] **1.** *adj.* contractual, stipulated; **2.** *adv.* as stipulated; *~ verpflichtet sein* be bound by contract; *sich ~ verpflichten* contract *(zu for s.th.; zu inf.* to *inf.).*

verträglich *adj.* [fɛr'trɛːklɪç] sociable.

Ver'trags|bruch *m* breach of contract; **2brüchig** *adj.: ~ werden* commit a breach of contract; **~entwurf** *m* draft agreement; **~partner** *m* party to a contract.

ver'trauen 1. *v/i. (no -ge-, h)* trust *(j-m s.o.); ~ auf (acc.)* trust *or* confide in; **2.** **2** *n (-s/no pl.)* confidence, trust; *im ~* confidentially, between you and me; **~erweckend** *adj.* inspiring confidence; promising.

Ver'trauens|bruch *m* breach *or* betrayal of trust; **~frage** *parl. f: die ~ stellen* put the question of confidence; **~mann** *m (-[e]s/~er,* Vertrauensleute) spokesman; shopsteward; confidential agent; **~sache** *f: das ist ~* that is a matter of confidence; **~stellung** *f* position of trust; **2voll** *adj.* trustful, trusting; **~votum** *parl. n* vote of confidence; **2würdig** *adj.* trustworthy, reliable.

ver'traulich *adj.* confidential, in confidence; intimate, familiar; **2keit** *f (-/-en)* confidence; intimacy, familiarity.

ver'traut *adj.* intimate, familiar; **2e** *(-n/-n)* **1.** *m* confidant, intimate friend; **2.** *f* confidante, intimate friend; **2heit** *f (-/~-en)* familiarity.

ver'treib|en *v/t. (irr. treiben, no -ge-, h)* drive away; expel *(aus* from); turn out; ♱ sell; distribute *(goods); sich die Zeit ~* pass one's time, kill time; **2ung** *f (-/~-en)* expulsion.

ver'tret|en *v/t. (irr. treten, no -ge-, h)* represent *(s.o., firm, etc.);* substitute for *s.o.;* attend to, look after *(s.o.'s interests);* hold *(view); parl.* sit for *(borough);* answer for *s.th.; j-s Sache ~* ᵗ½ plead s.o.'s case *or* cause; *sich den Fuß ~* sprain one's foot; F *sich die Beine ~* stretch one's legs; **2er** *m (-s/-)* representative; ♱ *a.* agent; proxy, agent; substitute, deputy; exponent; (sales) representative; door-to-door salesman; commercial travel(l)er, *esp. Am.* travel(l)ing salesman; **2ung** *f (-/-en)* representation *(a. pol.);* ♱ agency; *in office:* substitution; *in ~* by proxy; *gen.:* acting for.

Vertrieb ♱ [fɛr'triːp] *m (-[e]s/-e)* sale; distribution; **~ene** [~bənə] *m, f (-n/-n)* expellee.

ver'trocknen *v/i. (no -ge-, sein)* dry up; **~'trödeln** F *v/t. (no -ge-, h)* dawdle away, waste *(time);* **~'trösten** *v/t. (no -ge-, h)* put off; **~'tuschen** F *v/t. (no -ge-, h)* hush up; **~'übeln** *v/t. (no -ge-, h)* take *s.th.*

U
V

amiss; ~'**üben** v/t. (no -ge-, h) commit, perpetrate.

ver'**unglück|en** v/i. (no -ge-, sein) meet with or have an accident; fig. fail, go wrong; tödlich ~ be killed in an accident; 2te m, f (-n/-n) casualty.

verun|**reinigen** [fer'unraɪnɪgən] v/t. (no -ge-, h) soil, dirty; defile; contaminate (air); pollute (water); ~**stalten** [~ʃtaltən] v/t. (no -ge-, h) disfigure.

ver'**untreu|en** v/t. (no -ge-, h) embezzle; 2**ung** f (-/-en) embezzlement.

ver'**ursachen** v/t. (no -ge-, h) cause.

ver'**urteil|en** v/t. (no -ge-, h) condemn (zu to) (a. fig.), sentence (to); convict (wegen of); 2te m, f (-n/-n) convict; 2**ung** f (-/-en) condemnation (a. fig.), conviction.

ver'**vielfältigen** [fer'fiːlfɛltɪgən] v/t. (no -ge-, h) manifold; ~**vollkommnen** [~'fɔlkɔmnən] v/t. (no -ge-, h) perfect; sich ~ perfect o.s.

vervollständig|en [fer'fɔlʃtɛndɪgən] v/t. (no -ge-, h) complete; 2**ung** f (-/~-en) completion.

ver'|**wachsen 1.** v/i. (irr. wachsen, no -ge-, sein): miteinander ~ grow together; **2.** adj. deformed; humpbacked, hunchbacked; ~'**wackeln** phot. v/t. (no -ge-, h) blur.

ver'**wahr|en** v/t. (no -ge-, h) keep; sich ~ gegen protest against; ~**lost** adj. [~loːst] child, garden, etc.: uncared-for, neglected; degenerate; 2**ung** f keeping; charge; custody; fig. protest; j-m et. in ~ geben give s.th. into s.o.'s charge; in ~ nehmen take charge of. [fig. deserted.]

verwaist adj. [fer'vaɪst] orphan(ed);

ver'**walt|en** v/t. (no -ge-, h) administer, manage; 2**er** m (-s/-) administrator, manager; steward (of estate); 2**ung** f (-/-en) administration; management.

ver'**wand|eln** v/t. (no -ge-, h) change, turn, transform; sich ~ change (all: in acc. into); 2**lung** f (-/-en) change; transformation.

verwandt adj. [fer'vant] related (mit to); languages, tribes, etc.: kindred; languages, sciences: cognate (with); pred. akin (to) (a. fig.); 2e m, f (-n/-n) relative, relation; 2**schaft** f (-/-en) relationship; re-

lations pl.; geistige ~ congeniality.

ver'**warn|en** v/t. (no -ge-, h) caution; 2**ung** f caution.

ver'**wässern** v/t. (no -ge-, h) water (down), dilute; fig. water down, dilute.

ver'**wechs|eln** v/t. (no -ge-, h) mistake (mit for); confound, mix up, confuse (all: mit with); 2(e)-**lung** f (-/-en) mistake; confusion.

verwegen adj. [fer've:gən] daring, bold, audacious; 2**heit** f (-/~-en) boldness, audacity, daring.

ver'|**wehren** v/t. (no -ge-, h): j-m et. ~ (de)bar s.o. from (doing) s.th.; den Zutritt ~ deny or refuse admittance (zu to); ~'**weichlicht** adj. effeminate, soft.

ver'**weiger|n** v/t. (no -ge-, h) deny, refuse; disobey (order); 2**ung** f denial, refusal.

ver'**weilen** v/i. (no -ge-, h) stay, linger; bei et. ~ dwell (up)on s.th.

Verweis [fer'vaɪs] m (-es/-e) reprimand; rebuke, reproof; reference (auf acc. to); 2**en** [~zən] v/t. (irr. weisen, no -ge-, h): j-n des Landes ~ expel s.o. from Germany, etc.; j-m et. ~ reprimand s.o. for s.th.; j-n ~ auf (acc.) or an (acc.) refer s.o. to.

ver'**welken** v/i. (no -ge-, sein) fade, wither (up).

ver'**wend|en** v/t. ([irr. wenden,] no -ge-, h) employ, use; apply (für for); spend (time, etc.) (auf acc. on); sich bei j-m ~ für intercede with s.o. for; 2**ung** f (-/~-en) use, employment; application; keine ~ haben für have no use for.

ver'**werf|en** v/t. (irr. werfen, no -ge-, h) reject; ⅓ quash (verdict); ~**lich** adj. abominable.

ver'**werten** v/t. (no -ge-, h) turn to account, utilize.

ver'**wes|en** [fer've:zən] v/i. (no -ge-, sein) rot, decay; 2**ung** f (-/~-en) decay.

ver'**wick|eln** v/t. (no -ge-, h) entangle (in acc. in); sich ~ entangle o.s. (in) (a. fig.); ~**elt** fig. adj. complicated; 2(**e**)**lung** f (-/-en) entanglement; fig. a. complication.

ver'**wilder|n** v/i. (no -ge-, sein) run wild; ~**t** adj. garden, etc.: uncultivated, weed-grown; fig. wild, unruly. [-ge-, h) get over s.th.]

ver'**winden** v/t. (irr. winden, no

ver'wirklich|en v/t. (no -ge-, h) realize; sich ~ be realized, esp. Am. materialize; come true; **2ung** f (-/⸚-en) realization.

ver'wirr|en v/t. (no -ge-, h) entangle; j-n ~ confuse s.o.; embarrass s.o.; **~t** fig. adj. confused; embarrassed; **2ung** fig. f (-/-en) confusion.

ver'wischen v/t. (no -ge-, h) wipe or blot out; efface (a. fig.); blur, obscure; cover up (one's tracks).

ver'witter|n geol. v/i. (no -ge-, sein) weather; **~t** adj. geol. weathered; weather-beaten (a. fig.).

ver'witwet adj. widowed.

verwöhn|en [fɛr'vøːnən] v/t. (no -ge-, h) spoil; **~t** adj. fastidious, particular.

verworren adj. [fɛr'vɔrən] ideas, etc.: confused; situation, plot: intricate.

verwund|bar adj. [fɛr'vuntbaːr] vulnerable (a. fig.); **~en** [~dən] v/t. (no -ge-, h) wound.

ver'wunder|lich adj. astonishing; **2ung** f (-/⸚-en) astonishment.

Ver'wund|ete m (-n/-n) wounded (soldier), casualty; **~ung** f (-/-en) wound, injury.

ver'wünsch|en v/t. (no -ge-, h) curse; **2ung** f (-/-en) curse.

ver'wüst|en v/t. (no -ge-, h) lay waste, devastate, ravage (a. fig.); **2ung** f (-/-en) devastation, ravage.

verzag|en [fɛr'tsaːgən] v/i. (no -ge-, h) despond (an dat. of); **~t** adj. [~kt] despondent; **2theit** [~kt-] f (-/no pl.) despondency, -cy.

ver|'zählen v/refl. (no -ge-, h) miscount; **~'zärteln** [~'tsɛːrtəln] v/t. (no -ge-, h) coddle, pamper; **~'zaubern** v/t. (no -ge-, h) bewitch, enchant, charm; **~'zehren** v/t. (no -ge-, h) consume (a. fig.).

ver'zeichn|en v/t. (no -ge-, h) note down; record; list; fig. distort; ~ können, zu ~ haben score (success, etc.); **~et** paint. adj. out of drawing; **2is** n (-ses/-se) list, catalog(ue); register; inventory; index (of book); table, schedule.

verzeih|en [fɛr'tsaɪən] v/t. (irr., no -ge-, h) **1.** v/i. pardon, forgive; ~ Sie! I beg your pardon!; excuse me!; sorry!; **2.** v/t. pardon, forgive (j-m et. s.o. s.th.); **~lich** adj. pardonable; **2ung** f (-/no pl.) pardon; ~! I beg your pardon!, sorry!

ver'zerr|en v/t. (no -ge-, h) distort; sich ~ become distorted; **2ung** f distortion.

ver'zetteln v/t. (no -ge-, h) enter on cards; sich ~ fritter away one's energies.

Verzicht [fɛr'tsiçt] m (-[e]s/-e) renunciation (auf acc. of); **2en** v/i. (no -ge-, h) renounce (auf et. s.th.); do without (s.th.).

verzieh [fɛr'tsiː] pret. of verzeihen.

ver'ziehen¹ (irr. ziehen, no -ge-) **1.** v/i. (sein) (re)move (nach to); **2.** v/t. (h) spoil (child); distort; das Gesicht ~ make a wry face, screw up one's face, grimace; ohne e-e Miene zu ~ without betraying the least emotion; sich ~ wood: warp; crowd, clouds: disperse; storm, clouds: blow over; F disappear.

ver'ziehen² p.p. of verzeihen.

ver'zier|en v/t. (no -ge-, h) adorn, decorate; **2ung** f (-/-en) decoration; ornament.

verzins|en [fɛr'tsinzən] v/t. (no -ge-, h) pay interest on; sich ~ yield interest; **2ung** f (-/⸚-en) interest.

ver'zöger|n v/t. (no -ge-, h) delay, retard; sich ~ be delayed; **2ung** f (-/-en) delay, retardation.

ver'zollen v/t. (no -ge-, h) pay duty on; haben Sie et. zu ~? have you anything to declare?

verzück|t adj. [fɛr'tsykt] ecstatic, enraptured; **2ung** f (-/⸚-en) ecstasy, rapture; in ~ geraten go into ecstasies (wegen over).

Ver'zug m (-[e]s/no pl.) delay; † default; in ~ geraten come in default; im ~ sein (be in) default.

ver'zweif|eln v/i. (no -ge-, h, sein) despair (an dat. of); es ist zum Verzweifeln it is enough to drive one mad; **~elt** adj. hopeless; desperate; **2lung** [~luŋ] f (-/no pl.) despair; j-n zur ~ bringen drive s.o. to despair.

verzweig|en [fɛr'tsvaɪgən] v/refl. (no -ge-, h) ramify; trees: branch (out); road: branch; business firm, etc.: branch out; **2ung** f (-/-en) ramification; branching.

verzwickt adj. [fɛr'tsvikt] intricate, complicated.

Veteran [vete'raːn] m (-en/-en) ⚔ veteran (a. fig.), ex-serviceman.

Veterinär [veteri'nɛːr] m (-s/-e) veterinary (surgeon), F vet.

Veto ['veːto] n (-s/-s) veto; ein ~

einlegen gegen put a veto on, veto *s.th.*

Vetter ['fɛtər] *m* (-s/-n) cousin; '**~nwirtschaft** *f* (-/*no pl.*) nepotism.

vibrieren [vi'bri:rən] *v/i.* (*no* -ge-, *h*) vibrate.

Vieh [fi:] *n* (-[e]s/*no pl.*) livestock; cattle; animal, brute, beast; F *fig.* brute, beast; '**~bestand** *m* livestock; '**~händler** *m* cattle-dealer; '**~hof** *m* stockyard; '**²isch** *adj.* bestial, beastly, brutal; '**~wagen** 🚋 *m* stock-car; '**~weide** *f* pasture; '**~zucht** *f* stock-farming, cattle-breeding; '**~züchter** *m* stock-breeder, stock-farmer, cattle-breeder, *Am. a.* rancher.

viel [fi:l] 1. *adj.* much; *~e pl.* many; a lot (of), lots of; plenty of (*cake, money, room, time, etc.*); *das ~e Geld* all that money; *seine ~en Geschäfte pl.* his numerous affairs *pl.*; *sehr ~e pl.* a great many *pl.*; *ziemlich ~* a good deal of; *ziemlich ~e pl.* a good many *pl.*; *~ zuviel* far too much; *sehr ~* a great *or* good deal; 2. *adv.* much; *~ besser much or* a good deal *or* a lot better; *et. ~ lieber tun* prefer to do *s.th.*

viel|beschäftigt *adj.* ['fi:lbəʃɛftiçt] very busy; '**~deutig** *adj.* ambiguous; **~erlei** *adj.* ['~ər'laɪ] of many kinds, many kinds of; multifarious; **~fach** ['~fax] 1. *adj.* multiple; 2. *adv.* in many cases, frequently; **~fältig** *adj.* ['~fɛltiç] multiple, manifold, multifarious; '**~leicht** *adv.* perhaps, maybe; **~mals** *adv.* ['~ma:ls]: *ich danke Ihnen ~* many thanks, thank you very much; *sie läßt (dich) ~ grüßen* she sends you her kind regards; *ich bitte ~ um Entschuldigung* I am very sorry, I do beg your pardon; '**~mehr** *cj.* rather; '**~sagend** *adj.* significant, suggestive; **~seitig** *adj.* ['~zaɪtiç] many-sided, versatile; '**~versprechend** *adj.* (very) promising.

vier [fi:r] four; *zu ~t* four of us *or* them; *auf allen ~en* on all fours; *unter ~ Augen* confidentially, privately; *um halb ~* at half past three; '**~beinig** *adj.* four-legged; '**²eck** *n* square, quadrangle; '**~eckig** *adj.* square, quadrangular; **~erlei** *adj.* ['~ər'laɪ] of four different kinds, four kinds of; **~fach** *adj.* ['~fax] fourfold; *~e Ausfertigung* four

copies; **²füßer** *zo.* ['~fy:sər] *m* (-s/-) quadruped; **~füßig** *adj.* ['~fy:siç] four-footed; *zo.* quadruped; **²füßler** *zo.* ['~fy:slər] *m* (-s/-) quadruped; **~händig** ♩ *adv.* ['~hɛndiç]: *~ spielen* play a duet; **~jährig** *adj.* ['~jɛ:riç] four-year-old, of four; **²linge** ['~liŋə] *m/pl.* quadruplets *pl.*, F quads *pl.*; '**~mal** *adv.* four times; **~schrötig** *adj.* ['~ʃrø:tiç] square-built, thickset; **~seitig** *adj.* ['~zaɪtiç] four-sided; 🔺 quadrilateral; **²sitzer** *esp. mot. m* (-s/-) four-seater; **~stöckig** *adj.* ['~ʃtœkiç] four-storeyed, four-storied; '**²takt-motor** *mot. m* four-stroke engine; '**~te** *adj.* fourth; '**~teilen** *v/t.* (ge-, *h*) quarter.

Viertel ['firtəl] *n* (-s/-) fourth (part); quarter; *~ fünf, (ein) ~ nach vier* a quarter past four; *drei ~ vier* a quarter to four; **~'jahr** *n* three months *pl.*, quarter (of a year); **²'jährlich**, **²'jährlich** 1. *adj.* quarterly; 2. *adv.* every three months, quarterly; '**~note** ♩ *f* crotchet, *Am. a.* quarter note; '**~pfund** *n*, **~'pfund** *n* quarter of a pound; **~'stunde** *f* quarter of an hour, *Am.* quarter hour.

vier|tens *adv.* ['fi:rtəns] fourthly; **²'vierteltakt** ♩ *m* common time.

vierzehn *adj.* ['firtse:n] fourteen; *~ Tage pl.* a fortnight, *Am.* two weeks *pl.*; '**~te** *adj.* fourteenth.

vierzig *adj.* ['firtsiç] forty; '**~ste** *adj.* fortieth.

Vikar *eccl.* [vi'ka:r] *m* (-s/-e) curate.

Villa ['vila] *f* (-/*Villen*) villa.

violett *adj.* [vio'lɛt] violet.

Violine ♩ [vio'li:nə] *f* (-/-n) violin.

Viper *zo.* ['vi:pər] *f* (-/-n) viper.

virtuos *adj.* [virtu'o:s] masterly; **²e** [~zə] *m* (-n/-n), **²in** [~zin] *f* (-/-nen) virtuoso; **²ität** [~ozi'tɛ:t] *f* (-/*no pl.*) virtuosity.

Virus 🔬 ['vi:rus] *n, m* (-/*Viren*) virus.

Vision [vi'zjo:n] *f* (-/-en) vision.

Visitation [vizita'tsjo:n] *f* (-/-en) search; inspection.

Visite 🔬 [vi'zi:tə] *f* (-/-n) visit; **~nkarte** *f* visiting-card, *Am.* calling card.

Visum ['vi:zum] *n* (-s/*Visa, Visen*) visa, visé.

Vitalität [vitali'tɛ:t] *f* (-/*no pl.*) vitality.

Vitamin [vita'mi:n] *n* (-s/-e) vita-

[vicar.]
[min.]

Vize|kanzler [ˈfiːtsə-] *m* vice-chancellor; **˷könig** *m* viceroy; **˷konsul** *m* vice-consul; **˷präsident** *m* vice-president.

Vogel [ˈfoːgəl] *m* (-s/ᵘ) bird; F e-n ˷ **haben** have a bee in one's bonnet, *sl.* have bats in the belfry; *den* ˷ **abschießen** carry off the prize, *Am. sl.* take the cake; **˷bauer** *n, m* (-s/-) bird-cage; **˷flinte** *f* fowling-piece; **Ꝼfrei** *adj.* outlawed; **˷futter** *n* food for birds, bird-seed; **˷kunde** *f* (-/no *pl.*) ornithology; **˷liebhaber** *m* bird-fancier; **˷nest** *n* bird's nest, bird-nest; **˷perspektive** *f* (-/no *pl.*), **˷schau** *f* (-/no *pl.*) bird's-eye view; **˷scheuche** *f* (-/-n) scarecrow (*a. fig.*); **˷'Strauß-Politik** *f* ostrich policy; *˷* **betreiben** hide one's head in the sand (like an ostrich); **˷warte** *f* ornithological station; **˷zug** *m* passage *or* migration of birds.

Vokab|el [voˈkaːbəl] *f* (-/-n) word; **˷ular** [˷abuˈlaːr] *n* (-s/-e) vocabulary.

Vokal *ling.* [voˈkaːl] *m* (-s/-e) vowel.

Volk [fɔlk] *n* **1.** (-[e]s/ᵘer) people; nation; swarm (*of bees*) covey (*of partridges*); **2.** (-[e]s/no *pl.*) populace, *the* common people; *contp. the* common *or* vulgar herd; *der Mann aus dem* ˷*e* the man in the street *or Am.* on the street.

Völker|bund [ˈfœlkər-] *m* (-[e]s/no *pl.*) League of Nations; **˷kunde** *f* (-/no *pl.*) ethnology; **˷recht** *n* (-[e]s/no *pl.*) international law, law of nations; **˷wanderung** *f* age of national migrations.

'Volks|abstimmung *pol. f* plebiscite; **˷ausgabe** *f* popular edition (*of book*); **˷bücherei** *f* free *or* public library; **˷charakter** *m* national character; **˷dichter** *m* popular *or* national poet; **˷entscheid** *pol.* [ˈ˷ɛnt[ʃaɪt] *m* (-[e]s/-e) referendum; plebiscite; **˷fest** *n* fun fair, amusement park *or* grounds *pl.*; public merry-making; national festival; **˷gunst** *f* popularity; **˷herrschaft** *f* democracy; **˷hochschule** *f* adult education (courses *pl.*); **˷lied** *n* folk-song; **˷menge** *f* crowd (*of people*), multitude; **˷partei** *f* people's party; **˷republik** *f* people's republic; **˷schule** *f* elementary *or* primary school, *Am.*

a. grade school; **˷schullehrer** *m* elementary *or* primary teacher, *Am.* grade teacher; **˷sprache** *f* vernacular; **˷stamm** *m* tribe, race; **˷stück** *thea. n* folk-play; **˷tanz** *m* folk-dance; **˷tracht** *f* national costume; **Ꝼtümlich** *adj.* [ˈ˷tyːmlɪç] national; popular; **˷versammlung** *f* public meeting; **˷vertreter** *parl. m* deputy, representative; member of parliament; *Brt.* Member of Parliament, *Am.* Representative; **˷vertretung** *parl. f* representation of the people; parliament; **˷wirt** *m* (political) economist; **˷wirtschaft** *f* economics, political economy; **˷wirtschaftler** [ˈ˷viːrt] *m* (-s/-) s. Volkswirt; **˷zählung** *f* census.

voll [fɔl] **1.** *adj.* full; filled; whole, complete, entire; *figure, face:* full, round; *figure:* buxom; ˷*er Knospen* full of buds; *aus* ˷*em Halse* at the top of one's voice; *aus* ˷*em Herzen* from the bottom of one's heart; *in* ˷*er Blüte* in full blossom; *in* ˷*er Fahrt* at full speed; *mit* ˷*en Händen* lavishly, liberally; *mit* ˷*em Recht* with perfect right; *um das Unglück* ˷*zumachen* to make things worse; **2.** *adv.* fully, in full; ˷ *und ganz* fully, entirely; *j-n nicht für* ˷ *ansehen* or *nehmen* have a poor opinion of s.o., think little of s.o.

'voll|auf *adv.*, **˷'auf** *adv.* abundantly, amply, F plenty; **˷automatisch** *adj.* fully automatic; **Ꝼbad** *n* bath; **Ꝼbart** *m* beard; **Ꝼbeschäftigung** *f* full employment; **Ꝼbesitz** *m* full possession; **Ꝼblut(pferd)** *zo. n* thoroughbred (horse); **˷bringen** *v/t.* (*irr. bringen, no -ge-, h*) accomplish, achieve; perform; **Ꝼdampf** *m* full steam; F: *mit* ˷ *at* or *in* full blast; **˷enden** *v/t.* (*no -ge-, h*) finish, complete; **˷endet** *adj.* perfect; **˷ends** *adv.* [ˈ˷ɛnts] entirely, wholly, altogether; **Ꝼendung** *f* (-/˷ -en) finishing, completion; *fig.* perfection.

Völlerei [fœlˈraɪ] *f* (-/˷ -en) gluttony.

voll|'führen *v/t.* (*no -ge-, h*) execute, carry out; **˷füllen** *v/t.* (*sep.*, *-ge-, h*) fill (up); **Ꝼgas** *mot. n:* ˷ *geben* open the throttle; *mit* ˷ *with* the throttle full open; at full speed; **˷gepfropft** *adj.* [ˈ˷gəpfrɔpft] crammed, packed; **~gießen** v/t. (irr. gießen, sep., -ge-, h) fill (up); **²gummi** n, m solid rubber.

völlig adj. ['fœliç] entire, complete; silence, calm, etc.: dead.

voll|jährig adj. ['fɔljɛːriç]: ~ sein be of age; ~ werden come of age; **²jährigkeit** f (-/no pl.) majority; **~kommen** adj. perfect; **²kommenheit** f (-/~-en) perfection; **²kornbrot** n whole-meal bread; **~machen** v/t. (sep., -ge-, h) fill (up); F soil, dirty; um das Unglück vollzumachen to make things worse; **²macht** f (-/-en) full power, authority; ⚖ power of attorney; ~ haben be authorized; **²matrose** ⚓ m able-bodied seaman; **²milch** f whole milk; **²mond** m full moon; **~packen** v/t. (sep., -ge-, h) stuff, cram; '**²pension** f (-/-en) full board; **~schenken** v/t. (sep., -ge-, h) fill (up); '**~schlank** adj. stout, corpulent; '**~ständig** adj. complete; **~stopfen** v/t. (sep., -ge-, h) stuff, cram; sich ~ stuff o.s.; sich die Taschen ~ stuff one's pockets; **~'strecken** v/t. (no -ge-, h) execute; **²streckung** f (-/-en) execution; **~tönend** adj. sonorous, rich; **²treffer** m direct hit; **²versammlung** f plenary meeting or assembly; General Assembly (of the United Nations); '**~wertig** adj. equivalent, equal in value; full; '**~zählig** adj. complete; **~'ziehen** v/t. (irr. ziehen, no -ge-, h) execute; consummate (marriage); sich ~ take place; **²ziehung** f (-/~-en), **²zug** m (-[e]s/no pl.) execution.

Volontär [volɔn'tɛːr] m (-s/-e) unpaid assistant.

Volt ⚡ [vɔlt] n (-, -[e]s/-) volt.

Volumen [vo'luːmən] n (-s/-, Volumina) volume.

vom prp. [fɔm] = von dem

von prp. (dat.) [fɔn] space, time: from; instead of gen.: of; passive: by; ~ Hamburg from Hamburg; ~ nun an from now on; ~ morgen an from tomorrow (on), beginning tomorrow; ein Freund ~ mir a friend of mine; die Einrichtung ~ Schulen the erection of schools; ~ dem or vom Apfel essen eat (some) of the apple; der Herzog ~ Edinburgh the Duke of Edinburgh; ein Gedicht ~ Schiller a poem by

Schiller; ~ selbst by itself; ~ selbst, ~ sich aus by oneself; ~ drei Meter Länge three metres long; ein Betrag ~ 300 Mark a sum of 300 marks; e-e Stadt ~ 10 000 Einwohnern a town of 10,000 inhabitants; reden ~ talk of or about s.th.; speak on (scientific subject); ~ mir aus as far as I am concerned; I don't mind, for all I care; das ist nett ~ ihm that is nice of him; ich habe ~ ihm gehört I have heard of him; **²statten** adv. [~'ʃtatən]: gut ~ gehen go well.

vor prp. (dat.; acc.) [foːr] space: in front of, before; time: before; ~ langer Zeit a long time ago; ~ einigen Tagen a few days ago; (heute) ~ acht Tagen a week ago (today); am Tage ~ (on) the day before, on the eve of; 5 Minuten ~ 12 five minutes to twelve, Am. five minutes of twelve; fig. at the eleventh hour; ~ der Tür stehen be imminent, be close at hand; ~ e-m Hintergrund against a background; ~ Zeugen in the presence of witnesses; ~ allen Dingen above all; (dicht) ~ dem Untergang stehen be on the brink or verge of ruin; ~ Hunger sterben die of hunger; ~ Kälte zittern tremble with cold; schützen (verstecken) ~ protect (hide) from or against; ~ sich gehen take place, pass off; ~ sich hin lächeln smile to o.s.; sich fürchten ~ be afraid of, fear.

Vor|abend ['foːrʔ-] m eve; **~ahnung** f presentiment, foreboding.

voran adv. [fo'ran] at the head (dat. of), in front (of), before; Kopf ~ head first; **~gehen** v/i. (irr. gehen, sep., -ge-, sein) lead the way; precede; **~kommen** v/i. (irr. kommen, sep., -ge-, sein) make progress; fig. get on (in life).

Voran|schlag ['foːrʔan-] m (rough) estimate; '**~zeige** f advance notice; film: trailer.

vorarbeite|n ['foːrʔ-] v/t. and v/i. (sep., -ge-, h) work in advance; **²r** m foreman.

voraus adv. [fo'raus] in front (dat. of), ahead (of); im ~ in advance, beforehand; **~bestellen** v/t. (sep., no -ge-, h) s. vorbestellen; **~bezahlen** v/t. (sep., no -ge-, h) pay in advance, prepay; **~gehen** v/i. (irr. gehen, sep., -ge-, sein) go on before; s. vorangehen; **²sage** f prediction;

prophecy; forecast (*of weather*); **˜sagen** v/t. (*sep.*, *-ge-*, *h*) foretell, predict; prophesy; forecast (*weather, etc.*); **˜schicken** v/t. (*sep.*, *-ge-*, *h*) send on in advance; *fig.* mention beforehand, premise; **˜sehen** v/t. (*irr.* sehen, *sep.*, *-ge-*, *h*) foresee; **˜setzen** v/t. (*sep.*, *-ge-*, *h*) (pre)suppose, presume, assume; *vorausgesetzt, daß* provided that; **2setzung** f (*-/-en*) (pre)supposition, assumption; prerequisite; **2sicht** f foresight; *aller ˜ nach* in all probability; **˜sichtlich** adj. presumable, probable, likely; **2zahlung** f advance payment *or* instal(l)ment.

'**Vor|bedacht 1.** m (*-[e]s/no pl.*): *mit ˜* deliberately, on purpose; **2.** 2 adj. premeditated; **˜bedeutung** f foreboding, omen, portent; **˜bedingung** f prerequisite.

Vorbehalt ['fo:rbəhalt] m (*-[e]s/-e*) reservation, reserve; **2en 1.** v/t. (*irr.* halten, *sep.*, *no -ge-*, *h*): *sich ˜ reserve* (*right, etc.*); **2.** adj.: *Änderungen ˜ subject to change* (*without notice*); **2los** adj. unreserved, unconditional.

vorbei adv. ['fɔr'baɪ] *space:* along, by, past (*all: an dat. s.o., s.th.*); *time:* over, gone; *3 Uhr ˜* past three (o'clock); **˜fahren** v/i. (*irr.* fahren, *sep.*, *-ge-*, *sein*) drive past; **˜gehen** v/i. (*irr.* gehen, *sep.*, *-ge-*, *sein*) pass, go by; *pain:* pass (off); *storm:* blow over; *˜ an* (*dat.*) pass; *im Vorbeigehen* in passing; **˜kommen** v/i. (*irr.* kommen, *sep.*, *-ge-*, *sein*) pass by; F drop in; F *˜ an* (*dat.*) get past (*obstacle, etc.*); **˜lassen** v/t. (*irr.* lassen, *sep.*, *-ge-*, *h*) let pass.

'**Vorbemerkung** f preliminary remark *or* note.

'**vorbereit|en** v/t. (*sep.*, *no -ge-*, *h*) prepare (*für, auf acc.* for); **2ung** f preparation (*für, auf acc.* for).

'**Vorbesprechung** f preliminary discussion *or* talk.

'**vor|bestellen** v/t. (*sep.*, *no -ge-*, *h*) order in advance; book (*room, etc.*); **˜bestraft** adj. previously convicted.

'**vorbeug|en** (*sep.*, *-ge-*, *h*) **1.** v/i. prevent (*e-r Sache* s.th.); **2.** v/t. *and* v/refl. bend forward; **˜end** adj. preventive; *ℱ a.* prophylactic; **2ung** f prevention.

'**Vorbild** n model; pattern; example; prototype; **2lich** adj. exemplary; **˜ung** ['˜duŋ] f preparatory training.

'**vor|bringen** v/t. (*irr.* bringen, *sep.*, *-ge-*, *h*) bring forward, produce; advance (*opinion*); ᵗᵗ prefer (*charge*); utter, say, state; **˜datieren** v/t. (*sep.*, *no -ge-*, *h*) post-date.

vorder adj. ['fɔrdər] front, fore.

'**Vorder|achse** f front axle; **˜ansicht** f front view; **˜bein** n foreleg; **˜fuß** m forefoot; **˜grund** m foreground (*a. fig.*); **˜haus** n front building; **˜mann** m man in front (*of s.o.*); **˜rad** n front wheel; **˜radantrieb** mot. ['fɔrdərra:tˀ-] m front-wheel drive; **˜seite** f front (side); obverse (*of coin*); **˜sitz** m front seat; **2st** adj. foremost; **˜teil** n, m front (part); **˜tür** f front door; **˜zahn** m front tooth; **˜zimmer** n front room.

'**vordrängen** v/refl. (*sep.*, *-ge-*, *h*) press *or* push forward.

'**vordring|en** v/i. (*irr.* dringen, *sep.*, *-ge-*, *sein*) advance; **˜lich** adj. urgent.

'**Vordruck** m (*-[e]s/-e*) form, *Am. a.* blank.

voreilig adj. ['fo:rˀ-] hasty, rash, precipitate; *˜e Schlüsse ziehen* jump to conclusions.

voreingenommen adj. ['fo:rˀ-] prejudiced, bias(s)ed; **2heit** f (*-/no pl.*) prejudice, bias.

vor|enthalten ['fo:rˀ-] v/t. (*irr.* halten, *sep.*, *no -ge-*, *h*) keep back, withhold (*j-m et.* s.th. from s.o.); **2entscheidung** ['fo:rˀ-] f preliminary decision; **˜erst** adv. ['fo:rˀ-] for the present, for the time being.

Vorfahr ['fo:rfɑ:r] m (*-en/-en*) ancestor.

'**vorfahr|en** v/i. (*irr.* fahren, *sep.*, *-ge-*, *sein*) drive up; pass; *den Wagen ˜ lassen* order the car; **2t(srecht** n) f right of way, priority.

'**Vorfall** m incident, occurrence, event; **2en** v/i. (*irr.* fallen, *sep.*, *-ge-*, *sein*) happen, occur.

'**vorfinden** v/t. (*irr.* finden, *sep.*, *-ge-*, *h*) find.

'**Vorfreude** f anticipated joy.

'**vorführ|en** v/t. (*sep.*, *-ge-*, *h*) bring forward, produce; bring (*dat.* before); show, display, exhibit; demonstrate (*use of s.th.*); show, present (*film*); **2er** m projectionist (*in cinema theatre*); '**Qung** f presentation, showing; ⊕ demonstration; ⚬⚬ production (*of prisoner*); *thea., film*: performance.

'**Vor|gabe** f *sports*: handicap; *athletics*: stagger; *golf, etc.*: odds *pl.*; '**⚬gang** m incident, occurrence, event; *facts pl.*; file, record(s *pl.*); *biol.*, ⊕ process; **⚬gänger** ['⚬ɡɛŋər] m (-s/-), '**⚬gängerin** f (-/-nen) predecessor; '**⚬garten** m front garden.

'**vorgeben** v/t. (*irr. geben, sep., -ge-, h*) *sports*: give (*j-m s.o.*); *fig.* pretend, allege.

'**Vor|gebirge** n promontory, cape, headland; foot-hills *pl.*; '**⚬gefühl** n presentiment, foreboding.

'**vorgehen 1.** v/i. (*irr. gehen, sep., -ge-, sein*) ✗ advance; F lead the way; go on before; *watch, clock*: be fast, gain (*fünf Minuten five minutes*); take precedence (*dat.* of, over), be more important (*than*); take action, act; proceed (*a.* ⚬⚬; *gegen* against); go on, happen, take place; **2.** ♀ n (-s/no *pl.*) action, proceeding.

'**Vor|geschmack** m (-[e]s/no *pl.*) foretaste; '**⚬gesetzte** ['⚬ɡəzɛtstə] m (-n/-n) superior; *esp. Am.* F boss; '**Qgestern** adv. the day before yesterday; '**Qgreifen** v/i. (*irr. greifen, sep., -ge-, h*) anticipate (*j-m or e-r Sache s.o. or s.th.*).

'**vorhaben 1.** v/t. (*irr. haben, sep., -ge-, h*) intend, mean; be going to do *s.th.*; *nichts* ⚬ be at a loose end; *haben Sie heute abend et. vor?* have you anything on tonight?; *was hat er jetzt wieder vor?* what is he up to now?; *was hast du mit ihm vor?* what are you going to do with him?; **2.** ♀ n (-s/-) intention, purpose, ⚬⚬ intent; plan; project.

'**Vorhalle** f vestibule, (entrance-) hall; lobby; porch.

'**vorhalt|en** (*irr. halten, sep., -ge-, h*) **1.** v/t.: *j-m et.* ⚬ hold s.th. before s.o.; *fig.* reproach s.o. with s.th.; **2.** v/i. last; '**Qung** f remonstrance; *j-m* ⚬**en machen** remonstrate with s.o. (*wegen* on).

vorhanden adj. [for'handən] at hand, present; available (*a.* ♱); ♱ on hand, in stock; ⚬ *sein* exist; ♀**sein** n presence, existence.

'**Vor|hang** m curtain; '**⚬hänge-schloß** n padlock.

'**vorher** adv. before, previously; in advance, beforehand.

vor'her|bestellen v/t. (*sep., no -ge-, h*) s. vorbestellen; **⚬bestimmen** v/t. (*sep., no -ge-, h*) determine beforehand, predetermine; **⚬gehen** v/i. (*irr. gehen, sep., -ge-, sein*) precede; **⚬ig** adj. preceding, previous.

'**Vorherr|schaft** f predominance; '**Qschen** v/i. (*sep., -ge-, h*) predominate, prevail; '**Qschend** adj. predominant, prevailing.

Vor'her|sage f s. Voraussage; **Qsagen** v/t. (*sep., -ge-, h*) s. voraussagen; **Qsehen** v/t. (*irr. sehen, sep., -ge-, h*) foresee; **Qwissen** v/t. (*irr. wissen, sep., -ge-, h*) know beforehand, foreknow.

'**vorhin** adv., ⚬'**hin** adv. a short while ago, just now.

'**Vor|hof** m outer court, forecourt; *anat.* auricle (*of heart*); '**⚬hut** ✗ f vanguard.

'**vor|ig** adj. last; **⚬jährig** adj. ['⚬jɛːrɪç] of last year, last year's.

'**Vor|kämpfer** m champion, pioneer; '**⚬kehrung** f (-/-nen) precaution; **⚬en treffen** take precautions; '**⚬kenntnisse** f/pl. preliminary or basic knowledge (*in dat.* of); mit guten ⚬n in (*dat.*) well grounded in.

'**vorkommen 1.** v/i. (*irr. kommen, sep., -ge-, sein*) be found; occur, happen; *es kommt mir vor* it seems to me; **2.** ♀ n (-s/-) occurrence.

'**Vor|kommnis** n (-ses/-se) occurrence; event; '**⚬kriegszeit** f prewar times *pl.*

'**vorlad|en** ⚬⚬ v/t. (*irr. laden, sep., -ge-, h*) summon; '**Qung** ⚬⚬ f summons.

'**Vorlage** f copy; pattern; *parl.* bill; presentation; production (*of document*); *football*: pass.

'**vorlassen** v/t. (*irr. lassen, sep., -ge-, h*) let *s.o.* pass, allow *s.o.* to pass; admit.

'**Vorläuf|er** m, '**⚬erin** f (-/-nen) forerunner; '**Qig 1.** adj. provisional, temporary; **2.** adv. provisionally, temporarily; for the present, for the time being.

'**vorlaut** adj. forward, pert.

'**Vorleben** n past (*life*), antecedents *pl.*

'**vorlege|n** v/t. (*sep., -ge-, h*) put (*lock*) on; produce (*document*); submit (*plans, etc. for discussion, etc.*); propose (*plan, etc.*); present (*bill, etc.*); j-m et. ~ lay *or* place *or* put s.th. before s.o.; show s.o. s.th.; *at table*: help s.o. to s.th.; j-m e-e *Frage* ~ put a question to s.o.; *sich* ~ lean forward; '2r m (-s/-) rug.

'**vorles|en** v/t. (*irr.* lesen, *sep.*, -ge-, h) read aloud; j-m et. ~ read (out) s.th. to s.o.; '2ung f lecture (*über acc.* on; *vor dat.* to); e-e ~ halten (give a) lecture.

'**vorletzt** adj. last but one; ~e Nacht the night before last.

'**Vorlieb|e** f (-/no pl.) predilection, preference; 2nehmen [~'li:p-] v/i. (*irr.* nehmen, *sep.*, -ge-, h) be satisfied (*mit* with); ~ mit dem, was da ist at meals: take pot luck.

'**vorliegen** v/i. (*irr.* liegen, *sep.*, -ge-, h) lie before s.o.; be there, exist; da muß ein Irrtum ~ there must be a mistake; was liegt gegen ihn vor? what is the charge against him?; '~d adj. present, in question.

'**vor|lügen** v/t. (*irr.* lügen, *sep.*, -ge-, h): j-m et. ~ tell s.o. lies; '~machen v/t. (*sep.*, -ge-, h): j-m et. ~ show s.o. how to do s.th.; *fig.* impose upon s.o.; sich (selbst) et. ~ fool o.s.

'**Vormacht** f (-/◌̸ ̈e), '~stellung f predominance; supremacy; hegemony.

'**Vormarsch** ⚔ m advance.

'**vormerken** v/t. (*sep.*, -ge-, h) note down, make a note of; reserve; sich ~ lassen für put one's name down for.

'**Vormittag** m morning, forenoon; '2s adv. in the morning.

'**Vormund** m (-[e]s/-e, ̈er) guardian; '~schaft f (-/-en) guardianship.

vorn adv. [fɔrn] in front; nach ~ forward; von ~ from the front; ich sah sie von ~ I saw her face; von ~ anfangen begin at the beginning; noch einmal von ~ anfangen begin anew, make a new start.

'**Vorname** m Christian name, first name, *Am. a.* given name.

vornehm ['foːrneːm] **1.** adj. of (superior) rank, distinguished; aristocratic; noble; fashionable; ~e Gesinnung high character; **2.** adv.: ~ tun give o.s. airs; '~en v/t. (*irr.* nehmen, *sep.*, -ge-, h) take s.th. in

hand; deal with; make (*changes, etc.*); take up (*book*); F *sich* j-n ~ take s.o. to task (*wegen* for, about); sich ~ resolve (up)on s.th.; resolve (zu inf. to inf.), make up one's mind (to inf.); sich vorgenommen haben a. be determined (zu inf. to inf.); '2heit f (~/-no pl.) refinement; elegance; high-mindedness.

'**vorn|herein** adv., '~he'rein adv.: von ~ from the first *or* start *or* beginning.

Vorort ['foːrʔ-] m (-[e]s/-e) suburb; '~(s)verkehr m suburban traffic; '~(s)zug m local (train).

'**Vor|posten** m outpost (a. ⚔); '~rang m (-[e]s/no pl.) precedence (vor dat. of, over), priority (over); '~rat m store, stock (an dat. of); Vorräte pl. a. provisions pl., supplies pl.; 2rätig adj. ['~rɛːtɪç] available; ✝ a. on hand, in stock; '2rechnen v/t. (*sep.*, -ge-, h) reckon up (j-m to s.o.); '~recht n privilege; '~rede f preface, introduction; '~redner m previous speaker; '~richtung ⊕ f contrivance, device; '2rücken (*sep.*, -ge-) **1.** v/t. (h) move (chair, etc.) forward; **2.** v/i. (sein) advance; '~runde f sports: preliminary round; '2sagen v/i. (*sep.*, -ge-, h): j-m ~ prompt s.o.; '~saison f off *or* dead season; '~satz m intention, purpose, design; 2sätzlich adj. ['~zetslɪç] intentional, deliberate; ~er Mord ᵗᵗ wil(l)ful murder; '~schein m: zum ~ bringen bring forward, produce; zum ~ kommen appear, turn up; '2schieben v/t. (*irr.* schieben, *sep.*, -ge-, h) push s.th. forward; slip (bolt); s. vorschützen; '2schießen v/t. (*irr.* schießen, *sep.*, -ge-, h) advance (money).

'**Vorschlag** m proposition, proposal; suggestion; offer; 2en ['~gən] v/t. (*irr.* schlagen, *sep.*, -ge-, h) propose; suggest; offer.

'**Vor|schlußrunde** f sports: semifinal; '2schnell adj. hasty, rash; '2schreiben v/t. (*irr.* schreiben, *sep.*, -ge-, h): j-m et. ~ write s.th. out for s.o.; *fig.* prescribe.

'**Vorschrift** f direction, instruction; prescription (*esp.* ⚕); order (a. ⚕); regulation(s pl.); 2mäßig adj. according to regulations; ~e Kleidung regulation dress; '2swidrig *adj. and adv.* contrary to regulations.

'**Vor|schub** m: ~ leisten (dat.) countenance (fraud, etc.); further, encourage; ⚖ aid and abet; '**~schule** f preparatory school; '**~schuß** m advance; for barrister: retaining fee, retainer; '**2schützen** v/t. (sep., -ge-, h) pretend, plead (sickness, etc. as excuse); '**2schweben** v/i. (sep., -ge-, h): mir schwebt et. vor I have s.th. in mind.

'**vorseh|en** v/t. (irr. sehen, sep., -ge-, h) plan; design; für ~ provide; sich ~ take care, be careful; sich ~ vor (dat.) guard against; '**2ung** f (-/~-en) providence.

'**vorsetzen** v/t. (sep., -ge-, h) put forward; place or put or set before, offer;

'**Vorsicht** f caution; care; ~! caution!, danger!; look out!, be careful!; ~, Glas! Glass, with care!; ~, Stufe! mind the step!; '**2ig** adj. cautious; careful; ~! F steady!

'**vorsichts|halber** adv. as a precaution; '**2maßnahme** f, '**2maßregel** f precaution(ary measure); ~n treffen take precautions.

'**Vorsilbe** gr. f prefix.

'**vorsingen** v/t. (irr. singen, sep., -ge-, h): j-m et. ~ sing s.th. to s.o.

'**Vorsitz** m (-es/no pl.) chair, presidency; den ~ führen or haben be in the chair, preside (bei over; at); den ~ übernehmen take the chair; **~ende** ['~əndə] (-n/-n) **1.** m chairman, president; **2.** f chairwoman.

'**Vorsorg|e** f (-/no pl.) provision, providence; precaution; ~ treffen make provision; '**2en** v/i. (sep., -ge-, h) provide; **2lich** ['~kliç] **1.** adj. precautionary; **2.** adv. as a precaution.

'**Vorspeise** f appetizer, hors d'œuvre.

'**vorspieg|eln** v/t. (sep., -ge-, h) pretend; j-m et. ~ delude s.o. (with false hopes, etc.); '**2(e)lung** f preten|ce, Am. -se.

'**Vorspiel** n prelude; '**2en** v/t. (sep., -ge-, h): j-m et. ~ play s.th. to s.o.

'**vor|sprechen** (irr. sprechen, sep., -ge-, h) **1.** v/t. pronounce (j-m et. s.th. to or for s.o.); **2.** v/i. call (bei on s.o.; at an office); thea. audition; '**~springen** v/i. (irr. springen, sep., -ge-, sein) jump forward; project; '**2sprung** m △ projection;

sports: lead; fig. start, advantage (vor dat. of); '**2stadt** f suburb; '**~städtisch** adj. suburban; '**2stand** m board of directors, managing directors pl.

'**vorsteh|en** v/i. (irr. stehen, sep., -ge-, h) project, protrude; fig.: direct; manage (both: e-r Sache s.th.); '**2er** m director, manager; head, chief.

'**vorstell|en** v/t. (sep., -ge-, h) put forward; put (clock) on; introduce (j-n j-m s.o. to s.o.); mean, stand for; represent; sich ~ bei have an interview with; sich et. ~ imagine or fancy s.th.; '**2ung** f introduction, presentation; interview (of applicant for post); thea. performance; fig.: remonstrance; idea, conception; imagination; '**2ungsvermögen** n imagination.

'**Vor|stoß** ⚔ m thrust, advance; '**~strafe** f previous conviction; '**2strecken** v/t. (sep., -ge-, h) thrust out, stretch forward; advance (money); '**~stufe** f first step or stage; '**2täuschen** v/t. (sep., -ge-, h) feign, pretend.

'**Vorteil** ['fortail] m advantage (a. sports); profit; tennis: (ad)vantage; '**2haft** adj. advantageous (für to), profitable (to).

'**Vortrag** ['fo:rtra:k] m (-[e]s/~e) performance; execution (esp. ♪); recitation (of poem); ♪ recital; lecture; report; ✝ balance carried forward; e-n ~ halten (give a) lecture (über acc. on); '**2en** ['~gən] v/t. (irr. tragen, sep., -ge-, h) ✝ carry forward; report on; recite (poem); perform, esp. ♪ execute; lecture on; state, express (opinion); **~ende** ['~gəndə] m (-n/-n) performer; lecturer; speaker.

'**vor|trefflich** adj. [fo:r'trefliç] excellent; '**~treten** v/i. (irr. treten, sep., -ge-, sein) step forward; fig. project, protrude, stick out; '**2tritt** m (-[e]s/no pl.) precedence.

'**vorüber** adv. ['fo'ry:bər] space: by, past; time: gone by, over; **~gehen** v/i. (irr. gehen, sep., -ge-, sein) pass, go by; **~gehend** adj. passing; temporary; **2gehende** [~də] m (-n/-n) passer-by; **~ziehen** v/i. (irr. ziehen, sep., -ge-, sein) march past, pass by; storm: blow over.

'**Vor|übung** ['fo:r⁹-] f preliminary

practice; **_untersuchung** 🕮 ['fo:r?-] f preliminary inquiry.
Vorurteil ['fo:r?-] n prejudice; '**_s-los** adj. unprejudiced, unbias(s)ed.
'**Vor|verkauf** thea. m booking in advance; im ~ bookable (bei at); '**_verlegen** v/t. (sep., no -ge-, h) advance; '**_wand** m (-[e]s/-e) pretext, preten|ce, Am. -se.
vorwärts adv. ['fo:rverts] forward, onward, on; ~! go ahead!; '**_kommen** v/i. (irr. kommen, sep., -ge-, sein) (make) progress; fig. make one's way, get on (in life).
vorweg adv. [for'vek] beforehand; '**_nehmen** v/t. (irr. nehmen, sep., -ge-, h) anticipate.
'**vor|weisen** v/t. (irr. weisen, sep., -ge-, h) produce, show; '**_werfen** v/t. (irr. werfen, sep., -ge-, h) throw or cast before; j-m et. ~ reproach s.o. with s.th.; '**_wiegend 1.** adj. predominant, preponderant; **2.** adv. predominantly, chiefly, mainly, mostly; '**_witzig** adj. forward, pert; inquisitive.
'**Vorwort** n (-[e]s/-e) preface (by author); foreword.
'**Vorwurf** m reproach; subject (of drama, etc.); j-m e-n ~ or Vorwürfe

machen reproach s.o. (wegen with); '**_svoll** adj. reproachful.
'**vor|zählen** v/t. (sep., -ge-, h) enumerate, count out (both: j-m to s.o.); '**_zeichen** n omen; '**_zeichnen** v/t. (sep., -ge-, h): j-m et. ~ draw or sketch s.th. for s.o.; show s.o. how to draw s.th.; fig. mark out, destine; '**_zeigen** v/t. (sep., -ge-, h) produce, show.
'**Vorzeit** f antiquity; in literature often: times of old, days of yore; '**_ig** adj. premature.
'**vor|ziehen** v/t. (irr. ziehen, sep., -ge-, h) draw forth; draw (curtains); fig. prefer; '**_zimmer** n antechamber, anteroom; waiting-room; '**_zug** fig. m preference; advantage; merit; priority; '**_züglich** adj. [~'tsy:kliç] excellent, superior, exquisite.
'**Vorzugs|aktie** f preference share or stock, Am. preferred stock; '**_preis** m special price; '**_weise** adv. preferably; chiefly.
Votum ['vo:tum] n (-s/Voten, Vota) vote.
vulgär adj. [vul'gɛ:r] vulgar.
Vulkan [vul'ka:n] m (-s/-e) volcano; **_isch** adj. volcanic.

W

Waag|e ['va:gə] f (-/-n) balance, (e-e a pair of) scales pl.; die ~ halten (dat.) counterbalance; '**_erecht** adj., **_recht** adj. ['va:k-] horizontal, level; '**_schale** ['va:k-] f scale.
Wabe ['va:bə] f (-/-n) honeycomb.
wach adj. [vax] awake; hell~ wide awake; ~ werden awake, wake up; '**_e** f (-/-n) watch; guard; guardhouse, guardroom; police-station; sentry, sentinel; ~ haben be on guard; ~ halten keep watch; '**_en** v/i. (ge-, h) (keep) watch (über acc. over); sit up (bei with); '**_hund** m watch-dog.
Wacholder 💲 [va'xɔldər] m (-s/-) juniper.
'**wach|rufen** v/t. (irr. rufen, sep., -ge-, h) rouse, evoke; '**_rütteln** v/t. (sep., -ge-, h) rouse (up); fig. rouse, shake up.
Wachs [vaks] n (-es/-e) wax.

'**wachsam** adj. watchful, vigilant; '**_keit** f (-/no pl.) watchfulness, vigilance.
wachsen[1] ['vaksən] v/i. (irr., ge-, sein) grow; fig. increase.
wachsen[2] [~] v/t. (ge-, h) wax.
wächsern adj. ['vɛksərn] wax; fig. waxen, waxy.
'**Wachs|kerze** f, '**_licht** n wax candle; '**_tuch** n waxcloth, oilcloth.
Wachstum ['vakstu:m] n (-s/no pl.) growth; fig. increase.
Wächte mount. ['vɛçtə] f (-/-n) cornice.
Wachtel orn. ['vaxtəl] f (-/-n) quail.
Wächter ['vɛçtər] m (-s/-) watcher, guard(ian); watchman.
'**Wacht|meister** m sergeant; '**_turm** m watch-tower.
wackel|ig adj. ['vakəliç] shaky (a. fig.), tottery; furniture, etc.: rickety;

tooth, etc.: loose; '2**kontakt** ∉ *m* loose connexion *or* (*Am. only*) connection; '~**n** *v/i.* (ge-, h) shake; *table, etc.*: wobble; *tooth, etc.*: be loose; *tail, etc.*: wag; ~ *mit* wag *s.th.*

wacker *adj.* ['vakər] honest, upright; brave, gallant.

wacklig *adj.* ['vakliç] *s.* wackelig.

Wade ['va:də] *f* (-/-n) calf; '~**nbein** *anat. n* fibula.

Waffe ['vafə] *f* (-/-n) weapon (*a. fig.*); ~**n** *pl. a.* arms *pl.*

Waffel ['vafəl] *f* (-/-n) waffle; wafer.

'**Waffen|fabrik** *f* armaments factory, *Am. a.* armory; '~**gattung** *f* arm; '~**gewalt** *f* (-/*no pl.*): *mit* ~ by force of arms; '2**los** *adj.* weaponless, unarmed; '~**schein** *m* firearm certificate, *Am.* gun license; '~**stillstand** *m* armistice (*a. fig.*), truce.

Wage|hals ['va:gəhals] *m* daredevil; '2**halsig** *adj.* daring, foolhardy; *attr. a.* daredevil; '~**mut** *m* daring

wagen[1] ['va:gən] *v/t.* (ge-, h) venture; risk, dare; *sich* ~ venture (*an acc.* [up]on).

Wagen[2] [~] *m* (-s/-, ≈) carriage (*a.* 🚂); *Am.* 🚂 car; 🚂 coach; wag(g)on; cart; car; lorry, truck; van.

wägen ['ve:gən] *v/t.* (*irr.*,) ge-, h) weigh (*a. fig.*).

'**Wagen|heber** *m* (-s/-) (lifting) jack; '~**park** *m* (-[e]s/*no pl.*) fleet of vehicles; '~**schmiere** *f* grease; '~**spur** *f* rut.

Waggon [va'gõ:] *m* (-s/-s) (railway) carriage, *Am.* (railroad) car.

wag|halsig *adj.* ['va:khalsiç] *s.* wagehalsig; '2**nis** *n* (-ses/-se) venture, risk.

Wahl [va:l] *f* (-/-en) choice; alternative; selection; *pol.* election; *e-e* ~ *treffen* make a choice; *s-e* ~ *treffen* take one's choice; *ich hatte keine (andere)* ~ I had no choice.

wählbar *adj.* ['ve:lba:r] eligible; '2**keit** *f* (-/*no pl.*) eligibility.

wahl|berechtigt *adj.* ['va:lbəreçtiçt] entitled to vote; '2**beteiligung** *f* percentage of voting, F turn-out; '2**bezirk** *m* constituency.

'**wählen** (ge-, h) 1. *v/t.* choose; *pol.* elect; *teleph.* dial; 2. *v/i.* choose, take one's choice; *teleph.* dial (the number).

'**Wahlergebnis** *n* election return.

'**Wähler** *m* (-s/-) elector, voter; '2**isch** *adj.* particular (*in dat.* in, about, as to), nice (about), fastidious, F choosy; '~**schaft** *f* (-/-en) constituency, electorate.

'**Wahl|fach** *n* optional subject, *Am. a.* elective; '2**fähig** *adj.* having a vote; eligible; '~**gang** *m* ballot; '~**kampf** *m* election campaign; '~**kreis** *m* constituency; '~**lokal** *n* polling station; '2**los** *adj.* indiscriminate; '~**recht** *n* (-[e]s/*no pl.*) franchise; '~**rede** *f* electoral speech.

'**Wählscheibe** *teleph. f* dial.

'**Wahl|spruch** *m* device, motto; '~**stimme** *f* vote; '~**urne** *f* ballot-box; '~**versammlung** *f* electoral rally; '~**zelle** *f* polling-booth; '~**zettel** *m* ballot, voting-paper.

Wahn [va:n] *m* (-[e]s/*no pl.*) delusion, illusion; mania; '~**sinn** *m* (-[e]s/*no pl.*) insanity, madness (*both a. fig.*); '2**sinnig** *adj.* insane, mad (*vor dat.* with) (*both a. fig.*); ~**sinnige** ['~gə] *m* (-n/-n) madman, lunatic; '~**vorstellung** *f* delusion, hallucination; '~**witz** *m* (-es/*no pl.*) madness, insanity; '2**witzig** *adj.* mad, insane.

wahr *adj.* [va:r] true; real; genuine; '~**en** *v/t.* (ge-, h) safeguard (*interests, etc.*); maintain (*one's dignity*); *den Schein* ~ keep up *or* save appearances.

währen ['ve:rən] *v/i.* (ge-, h) last, continue.

'**während** 1. *prp.* (*gen.*) during; pending; 2. *cj.* while, whilst; while, whereas.

'**wahrhaft** *adv.* really, truly, indeed; ~**ig** [~'haftiç] 1. *adj.* truthful, veracious; 2. *adv.* really, truly, indeed.

'**Wahrheit** *f* (-/-en) truth; *in* ~ in truth; *j-m die* ~ *sagen* give s.o. a piece of one's mind; '2**sgetreu** *adj.* true, faithful; '~**sliebe** *f* (-/*no pl.*) truthfulness, veracity; '2**sliebend** *adj.* truthful, veracious.

'**wahr|lich** *adv.* truly, really; '~**nehmbar** *adj.* perceivable, perceptible; '~**nehmen** *v/t.* (*irr.* nehmen, *sep.*, -ge-, h) perceive, notice; avail o.s. of (*opportunity*); safeguard (*interests*); '2**nehmung** *f* (-/-en) perception, observation; '~**sagen** *v/i.* (*sep.*, -ge-, h) tell *or* read fortunes;

sich ~ *lassen* have one's fortune told; '⊋**sagerin** f (-/-nen) fortune-teller; '⊾**scheinlich 1.** adj. probable; likely; **2.** adv.: *ich werde* ~ *gehen* I am likely to go; ⊋**scheinlichkeit** f (-/⊾-en) probability, likelihood; *aller* ~ *nach* in all probability or likelihood.

'**Wahrung** f (-/no pl.) maintenance; safeguarding.

Währung ['vɛːruŋ] f (-/-en) currency; standard; '⊾**sreform** f currency or monetary reform.

'**Wahrzeichen** n landmark.

Waise ['vaizə] f (-/-n) orphan; '⊾**n-haus** n orphanage.

Wal zo. [vaːl] m (-[e]s/-e) whale.

Wald [valt] m (-[e]s/⁻er) wood, forest; '⊾**brand** m forest fire; ⊋**ig** adj. ['⊾diç] wooded, woody; ⊋**reich** adj. ['⊾t-] rich in forests; ⊾**ung** ['⊾duŋ] f (-/-en) forest.

Walfänger ['vaːlfɛŋər] m (-s/-) whaler.

walken ['valkən] v/t. (ge-, h) full (*cloth*); mill (*cloth, leather*).

Wall [val] m (-[e]s/⁻e) rampart (a. fig.); dam; mound. [ing.]

Wallach ['valax] m (-[e]s/-e) geld-]

wallen ['valən] v/i. (ge-, h, sein) hair, articles of dress, etc.: flow; simmer; boil (a. fig.).

wall|fahren ['valfaːrən] v/i. (ge-, sein) (go on a) pilgrimage; ⊋**fahrer** m pilgrim; ⊋**fahrt** f pilgrimage; '⊾**fahrten** v/i. (ge-, sein) (go on a) pilgrimage.

'**Wallung** f (-/-en) ebullition; ⁂ congestion; (*Blut*) *in* ~ *bringen* make s.o.'s blood boil, enrage.

Walnuß ['val-] f walnut; '⊾**baum** ⁑ m walnut(-tree).

Walroß zo. ['val-] n walrus.

walten ['valtən] v/i. (ge-, h): *s-s Amtes* ~ attend to one's duties; *Gnade* ~ *lassen* show mercy.

Walze ['valtsə] f (-/-n) roller, cylinder; ⊕ a. roll; ⊕, ♪ barrel; ⊋**n** v/t. (ge-, h) roll (a. ⊕).

wälzen ['vɛltsən] v/t. (ge-, h) roll; roll (*problem*) round in one's mind; shift (*blame*) (*auf* acc. [up]on); *sich* ~ roll; wallow (*in mud, etc.*); welter (*in blood, etc.*).

Walzer ♪ ['valtsər] m (-s/-) waltz.

Wand [vant] **1.** f (-/⁻e) wall; partition; **2.** ⊋ pret. of *winden*.

Wandel ['vandəl] m (-s/no pl.)

change; '⊋**bar** adj. changeable; variable; '⊾**gang** m, '⊾**halle** f lobby; '⊋**n** (ge-) **1.** v/i. (sein) walk; **2.** v/refl. (h) change.

Wander|er ['vandərər] m (-s/-) wanderer; hiker; '⊾**leben** n (-s/no pl.) vagrant life; ⊋**n** v/i. (ge-, sein) wander; hike; '⊾**niere** ⁜ f floating kidney; '⊾**prediger** m itinerant preacher; '⊾**preis** m challenge trophy; '⊾**schaft** f (-/no pl.) wanderings pl.; *auf* (*der*) ~ *on the tramp*; '⊾**ung** f (-/-en) walking-tour; hike.

'**Wand|gemälde** n mural (painting); '⊾**kalender** m wall-calendar; '⊾**karte** f wall-map.

Wandlung ['vandluŋ] f (-/-en) change, transformation; eccl. transubstantiation; ⁜⁜ redhibition.

'**Wand|schirm** m folding-screen; '⊾**schrank** m wall-cupboard; '⊾**spiegel** m wall-mirror; '⊾**tafel** f blackboard; '⊾**teppich** m tapestry; '⊾**uhr** f wall-clock.

wandte ['vantə] pret. of *wenden* 2.

Wange ['vaŋə] f (-/-n) cheek.

Wankel|mut ['vaŋkəlmuːt] m fickleness, inconstancy; ⊋**mütig** adj. ['⊾myːtiç] fickle, inconstant.

wanken ['vaŋkən] v/i. (ge-, h, sein) totter, stagger (a. fig.); house, etc.: rock; fig. waver.

wann adv. [van] when; *s. dann*; *seit* ~? how long?, since when?

Wanne ['vanə] f (-/-n) tub; bath (-tub), F tub; '⊾**nbad** n bath, F tub.

Wanze zo. ['vantsə] f (-/-n) bug, Am. a. bedbug.

Wappen ['vapən] n (-s/-) (coat of) arms pl.; '⊾**kunde** f (-/no pl.) heraldry; '⊾**schild** m, n escutcheon; '⊾**tier** n heraldic animal.

wappnen fig. ['vapnən] v/refl. (ge-, h): *sich* ~ *gegen* be prepared for; *sich mit Geduld* ~ have patience.

war [vaːr] pret. of *sein*[1].

warb [varp] pret. of *werben*.

Ware ['vaːrə] f (-/-n) commodity, article of trade; ~*n* pl. a. goods pl., merchandise, wares pl.

'**Waren|aufzug** m hoist; '⊾**bestand** m stock (on hand); '⊾**haus** n department store; '⊾**lager** n stock; warehouse, Am. a. stock room; '⊾**probe** f sample; '⊾**zeichen** n trade mark.

warf [varf] pret. of *werfen*.

warm adj. [varm] warm (a. fig.); meal: hot; schön ~ nice and warm.

Wärme ['vɛrmə] f (-/⚕-n) warmth; pinys. heat; '**~grad** m degree of heat; '**2n** v/t. (ge-, h) warm; sich die Füße ~ warm one's feet.

'**Wärmflasche** f hot-water bottle.

'**warmherzig** adj. warm-hearted.

Warm'wasser|heizung f hot-water heating; **~versorgung** f hot-water supply.

warn|en ['varnən] v/t. (ge-, h) warn (vor dat. of, against), caution (against); **2signal** n danger-signal (a. fig.); **2streik** m token strike; **2ung** f (-/-en) warning, caution; **2ungstafel** ['varnuŋs-] f notice-board.

Warte fig. ['vartə] f (-/-n) point of view.

warten ['vartən] v/i. (ge-, h) wait (auf acc. for); be in store (for s.o.); j-n ~ lassen keep s.o. waiting.

Wärter ['vɛrtər] m (-s/-) attendant; keeper; (male) nurse.

'**Warte|saal** m, '**~zimmer** n waiting-room.

Wartung ⊕ ['vartuŋ] f (-/⚕-en) maintenance.

warum adv. [va'rum] why.

Warze ['vartsə] f (-/-n) wart; nipple.

was [vas] **1.** interr. pron. what; ~ kostet das Buch? how much is this book?; F ~ rennst du denn so (schnell)? why are you running like this?; ~ für (ein) ...! what a(n) ...!; ~ für ein ...? what ...?; **2.** rel. pron. what; ~ (auch immer), alles ~ what(so)ever; ..., ~ ihn völlig kalt ließ ... which left him quite cold; **3.** F indef. pron. something; ich will dir mal ~ sagen I'll tell you what.

wasch|bar adj. ['vaʃbɑːr] washable; **2becken** n wash-basin, Am. wash-bowl.

Wäsche ['vɛʃə] f (-/-n) wash(ing); laundry; linen (a. fig.); underwear; in der ~ sein be at the wash; sie hat heute große ~ she has a large wash today.

waschecht adj. ['vaʃʔ-] washable; colour: a. fast; fig. dyed-in-the-wool.

'**Wäsche|klammer** f clothes-peg, clothes-pin; '**~leine** f clothes-line.

'**waschen** v/t. (irr., ge-, h) wash;

sich ~ (have a) wash; sich das Haar or den Kopf ~ wash or shampoo one's hair or head; sich gut ~ (lassen) wash well.

Wäscher|ei [vɛʃə'raɪ] f (-/-en) laundry; '**~in** f (-/-nen) washer-woman, laundress.

'**Wäscheschrank** m linen closet.

'**Wasch|frau** f s. Wäscherin; '**~haus** n wash-house; '**~kessel** m copper; '**~korb** m clothes-basket; '**~küche** f wash-house; '**~lappen** m face-cloth, Am. washrag, wash-cloth; '**~maschine** f washing machine, washer; '**~pulver** n washing powder; '**~raum** m lavatory, Am. a. washroom; '**~schüssel** f wash-basin; '**~tag** m wash(ing)-day; '**~ung** f (-/-en) wash; ablution; '**~weib** contp. n gossip; '**~wanne** f wash-tub.

Wasser ['vasər] n (-s/-, ⚌) water; ~ lassen make water; zu ~ und zu Land(e) by sea and land; '**~ball** m **1.** beach-ball; water-polo ball; **2.** (-[e]s/no pl.) water-polo; '**~ball-spiel** n **1.** (-[e]s/no pl.) water-polo; **2.** water-polo match; '**~behälter** m reservoir, water-tank; '**~blase** ⚕ f water-blister; '**~dampf** m steam; **2dicht** adj. waterproof; water-tight; '**~eimer** m water-pail, bucket; '**~fall** m waterfall, cascade; cataract; '**~farbe** f water-colo(u)r; '**~flugzeug** n waterplane, seaplane; '**~glas** n **1.** tumbler; **2.** ⚗ (-es/no pl.) water-glass; '**~graben** m ditch; '**~hahn** m tap, Am. a. faucet; '**~hose** f waterspout.

wässerig adj. ['vɛsəriç] watery; washy (a. fig.); j-m den Mund ~ machen make s.o.'s mouth water.

'**Wasser|kanne** f water-jug, ewer; '**~kessel** m kettle; '**~klosett** n water-closet, W.C.; '**~kraft** f water-power; '**~kraftwerk** n hy-droelectric power station or plant, water-power station; '**~krug** m water-jug, ewer; '**~kur** f water-cure, hydropathy; '**~lauf** m water-course; '**~leitung** f water-supply; '**~leitungsrohr** n water-pipe; '**~mangel** m shortage of water; **2n** v/i. (ge-, h) alight on water; splash down.   [(salted herring, etc.).]

wässern ['vɛsərn] v/t. (ge-, h) soak

'**Wasser|pflanze** f aquatic plant; '**~rinne** f gutter; '**~rohr** n water-pipe; '**~schaden** *m* damage caused by water; '**~scheide** *f* watershed, *Am. a.* divide; '**2scheu** *adj.* afraid of water; '**~schlauch** *m* water-hose; '**~spiegel** *m* water-level; '**~sport** *m* aquatic sports *pl.*; '**~spülung** *f* (-/-en) flushing (system); '**~stand** *m* water-level; '**~standsanzeiger** ['vasərʃtants⁹-] *m* water-gauge; '**~stiefel** *m* waders *pl.*; '**~stoff** *m* (-[e]s/*no pl.*) hydrogen; '**~stoffbombe** *f* hydrogen bomb, H-bomb; '**~strahl** *m* jet of water; '**~straße** *f* waterway; '**~tier** *n* aquatic animal; '**~verdrängung** *f* (-/-en) displacement; '**~versorgung** *f* water-supply; '**~waage** *f* spirit-level, water-level; '**~weg** *m* waterway; *auf dem ~* by water; '**~welle** *f* water-wave; '**~werk** *n* waterworks *sg., pl.*; '**~zeichen** *n* watermark.

wäßrig *adj.* ['vesriç] *s.* wässerig.

waten ['vɑːtən] *v/i.* (ge-, sein) wade.

watscheln ['vɑːtʃəln] *v/i.* (ge-, sein, h) waddle.

Watt¹ *n* [vat] *n* (-s/-) watt.

Watt|e ['vatə] *f* (-/-n) cotton-wool; surgical cotton; wadding; '**~ebausch** *m* wad; **2ieren** [~'tiːrən] *v/t.* wad, pad.

weben ['veːbən] *v/t. and v/i.* ([*irr.,*] ge-, h) weave.

'**Weber** *m* (-s/-) weaver; **~ei** [~'raɪ] *f* **1.** (-/*no pl.*) weaving; **2.** (-/-en) weaving-mill.

Webstuhl ['veːpʃtuːl] *m* loom.

Wechsel ['veksəl] *m* (-s/-) change; allowance; † bill (of exchange); *hunt.* runway; *eigener ~* † promissory note; '**~beziehung** *f* correlation; '**~fälle** ['~fɛlə] *pl.* vicissitudes *pl.*; '**~fieber** ♯ *n* (-s/*no pl.*) intermittent fever; malaria; '**~frist** † *f* usance; '**~geld** *n* change; '**~kurs** *m* rate of exchange; '**~makler** † *m* bill-broker; **2n** (ge-) **h) 1.** *v/t.* change; vary; exchange (*words, etc.*); *den Besitzer ~* change hands; *die Kleider ~* change (one's clothes); **2.** *v/i.* change; vary; alternate; '**~nehmer** † *m* (-s/-) payee; '**~seitig** *adj.* ['~zaitiç] mutual, reciprocal; '**~strom** ⚡ *m* alternating current; '**~stube** *f* exchange office; '**2weise** *adv.* alternately, by *or* in turns; '**~wirkung** *f* interaction.

wecke|n ['vɛkən] *v/t.* (ge-, h) wake

(up), waken; arouse (*a. fig.*); '**2r** *m* (-s/-) alarm-clock.

wedeln ['veːdəln] *v/i.* (ge-, h): ~ *mit* wag (*tail*).

weder *cj.* ['veːdər]: ~ ... *noch* neither ... nor.

Weg¹ [veːk] *m* (-[e]s/-e) way (*a. fig.*); road (*a. fig.*); path; route; walk; *auf halbem ~* half-way; *am ~e* by the roadside; *aus dem ~e* steer clear of; *aus dem ~e räumen* remove (*a. fig.*); *in die ~e leiten* set on foot, initiate.

weg² *adv.* [vɛk] away, off; gone; *geh ~!* be off (with you)!; ~ *mit ihm!* off with him!; *Hände ~!* hands off!; F *ich muß ~* I must be off; F *ganz ~ sein* be quite beside o.s.; '**~bleiben** F *v/i.* (*irr.* bleiben, *sep.,* -ge-, sein) stay away; be omitted; '**~bringen** *v/t.* (*irr.* bringen, *sep.,* -ge-, h) take away; *a.* remove (*things*).

wegen *prp.* (*gen.*) ['veːgən] because of, on account of, owing to.

weg|fahren ['vɛk-] (*irr.* fahren, *sep.,* -ge-) **1.** *v/t.* (h) remove; cart away; **2.** *v/i.* (sein) leave; '**~fallen** *v/i.* (*irr.* fallen, *sep.,* -ge-, sein) be omitted; be abolished; '**2gang** *m* (-[e]s/*no pl.*) going away, departure; '**~gehen** *v/i.* (*irr.* gehen, *sep.,* -ge-, sein) go away *or* off; *merchandise:* sell; '**~haben** F *v/t.* (*irr.* haben, *sep.,* -ge-, h): *e-n ~* be tight; *have a screw loose; er hat noch nicht weg, wie man es machen muß* he hasn't got the knack of it yet; '**~jagen** *v/t.* (*sep.,* -ge-, h) drive away; '**~kommen** F *v/i.* (*irr.* kommen, *sep.,* -ge-, sein) get away; be missing; *gut* (*schlecht*) ~ come off well (badly); *mach, daß du wegkommst!* be off (with you)!; '**~lassen** *v/t.* (*irr.* lassen, *sep.,* -ge-, h) let *s.o.* go; leave out, omit; '**~laufen** *v/i.* (*irr.* laufen, *sep.,* -ge-, sein) run away; '**~legen** *v/t.* (*sep.,* -ge-, h) put away; '**~machen** F *v/t.* (*sep.,* -ge-, h) remove, *a.* take out (*stains*); '**~müssen** F *v/i.* (*irr.* müssen 1, *sep.,* -ge-, h): *ich muß weg* I must be off; **2nahme** ['~nɑːmə] *f* (-/-n) taking (away); '**~nehmen** *v/t.* (*irr.* nehmen, *sep.,* -ge-, h) take up, occupy (*time, space*); *j-m et.* ~ take s.th. away from s.o.; '**~raffen** *fig.* *v/t.* (*sep.,* -ge-, h) carry off.

W

Wegrand ['ve:k-] *m* wayside.

weg|räumen ['vɛk-] *v/t.* (*sep.*, -ge-, *h*) clear away, remove; '**∼schaffen** *v/t.* (*sep.*, -ge-, *h*) remove; '**∼schikken** *v/t.* (*sep.*, -ge-, *h*) send away or off; '**∼sehen** *v/i.* (*irr. sehen, sep.*, -ge-, *h*) look away; ∼ **über** (*acc.*) overlook, shut one's eyes to; '**∼setzen** *v/t.* (*sep.*, -ge-, *h*) put away; *sich* ∼ *über* (*acc.*) disregard, ignore; '**∼streichen** *v/t.* (*irr. streichen, sep.*, -ge-, *h*) strike off or out; '**∼tun** *v/t.* (*irr. tun, sep.*, -ge-, *h*) put away or aside.

Wegweiser ['ve:kvaɪzər] *m* (-s/-) signpost, finger-post; *fig.* guide.

weg|wenden ['vɛk-] *v/t.* (*irr. wenden,*] *sep.*, -ge-, *h*) turn away, avert (one's eyes); *sich* ∼ turn away; '**∼werfen** *v/t.* (*irr. werfen, sep.*, -ge-, *h*) throw away; '**∼werfend** *adj.* disparaging; '**∼wischen** *v/t.* (*sep.*, -ge-, *h*) wipe off; '**∼ziehen** (*irr. ziehen, sep.*, -ge-, *h*) **1.** *v/t.* (*h*) pull or draw away; **2.** *v/i.* (*sein*) (re)move.

weh [ve:] **1.** *adj.* sore; **2.** *adv.*: ∼ *tun* ache, hurt; *j-m* ∼ *tun* pain or hurt s.o.; *fig. a.* grieve s.o.; *sich* ∼ *tun* hurt o.s.; *mir tut der Finger* ∼ my finger hurts.

Wehen¹ ⚕ ['ve:ən] *f/pl.* labo(u)r, travail.

wehen² [∼] (ge-, *h*) **1.** *v/t.* blow; **2.** *v/i.* blow; *es weht ein starker Wind* it is blowing hard.

weh|klagen *v/i.* (ge-, *h*) lament (*um* for, over); '**∼leidig** *adj.* snivel(l)ing; *voice:* plaintive; '**∼mut** *f* (-/*no pl.*) wistfulness; '**∼mütig** *adj.* ['∼my:tiç] wistful.

Wehr¹ [ve:r] **1.** *f* (-/-en): *sich zur* ∼ *setzen* offer resistance (*gegen* to), show fight; **2.** *n* (-[e]s/-e) weir; '**∼dienst** ✕ *m* military service; '**2en** *v/refl.* (ge-, *h*) defend o.s., offer resistance (*gegen* to); '**2fähig** ✕ *adj.* able-bodied; '**2los** *adj.* defenceless, *Am.* defenseless; '**∼pflicht** ✕ *f* (-/*no pl.*) compulsory military service, conscription; '**2pflichtig** ✕ *adj.* liable to military service.

Weib [vaɪp] *n* (-[e]s/-er) woman; wife; '**∼chen** *zo. n* (-s/-) female.

Weiber|feind ['vaɪbər-] *m* woman-hater; '**∼held** *contp. m* ladies' man; '**∼volk** F *n* (-[e]s/*no pl.*) womenfolk.

weib|isch *adj.* ['vaɪbiʃ] womanish, effeminate; '**∼lich** *adj.* ['∼p-] female; *gr.* feminine; womanly, feminine.

weich *adj.* [vaɪç] soft (*a. fig.*); *meat, etc.*: tender; *egg:* soft-boiled; ∼ *werden* soften; *fig.* relent.

Weiche¹ 🚊 ['vaɪçə] *f* (-/-n) switch; ∼*n pl.* points pl.

Weiche² *anat.* [∼] *f* (-/-n) flank, side.

weichen¹ ['vaɪçən] *v/i.* (*irr.*, ge-, *sein*) give way, yield (*dat.* to); *nicht von der Stelle* ∼ not to budge an inch; *j-m nicht von der Seite* ∼ stick to s.o.

weichen² [∼] *v/i.* (ge-, *h*, *sein*) soak.

'Weichensteller 🚊 *m* (-s/-) points-man, switch-man.

'weich|herzig *adj.* soft-hearted, tender-hearted; '**∼lich** *adj.* somewhat soft; *fig.* effeminate; **2ling** ['∼lɪŋ] *m* (-s/-e) weakling, milksop, molly(-coddle), *sl.* sissy; **2tier** *n* mollusc.

Weide¹ ♀ ['vaɪdə] *f* (-/-n) willow.

Weide² ♫ [∼] *f* (-/-n) pasture; *auf der* ∼ out at grass; '**∼land** *n* pasture(-land); '**2n** (ge-, *h*) **1.** *v/t.* feed, pasture, graze; *sich* ∼ *an* (*dat.*) gloat over; feast on; **2.** *v/i.* pasture, graze.

'Weiden|korb *m* wicker basket, osier basket; '**∼rute** *f* osier switch.

weidmännisch *hunt. adj.* ['vaɪtmɛnɪʃ] sportsmanlike.

weiger|n ['vaɪgərn] *v/refl.* (ge-, *h*) refuse, decline; '**2ung** *f* (-/-en) refusal.

Weihe *eccl.* ['vaɪə] *f* (-/-n) consecration; ordination; '**2n** *eccl. v/t.* (ge-, *h*) consecrate; *j-n zum Priester* ∼ ordain s.o. priest.

Weiher ['vaɪər] *m* (-s/-) pond.

'weihevoll *adj.* solemn.

Weihnachten ['vaɪnaxtən] *n* (-s/*no pl.*) Christmas, Xmas.

'Weihnachts|abend *m* Christmas eve; '**∼baum** *m* Christmas-tree; '**∼ferien** *pl.* Christmas holidays *pl.*; '**∼fest** *n* Christmas; '**∼geschenk** *n* Christmas present; '**∼gratifikation** *f* Christmas bonus; '**∼karte** *f* Christmas card; '**∼lied** *n* carol, Christmas hymn; '**∼mann** *m* Father Christmas, Santa Claus; '**∼markt** *m* Christmas fair; '**∼zeit** *f* (-/*no pl.*) Christmas(-tide) (*in Germany beginning on the first Advent Sunday*).

W

'**Weih|rauch** *eccl. m* incense; '~**wasser** *eccl. n* (-s/*no pl.*) holy water.

weil *cj.* [vaɪl] because, since, as.

Weil|chen ['vaɪlçən] *n* (-s/-): *ein ~ a* little while, a spell; '~**e** *f* (-/*no pl.*): *e-e ~* a while.

Wein [vaɪn] *m* (-[e]s/-e) wine; ⚥ vine; *wilder* ~ ✿ Virginia creeper; '~**bau** *m* (-[e]s/*no pl.*) vine-growing, viticulture; '~**beere** *f* grape; '~**berg** *m* vineyard; '~**blatt** *n* vine-leaf.

wein|en ['vaɪnən] *v/i.* (ge-, h) weep (*um, vor dat.* for), cry (*vor dat.* for joy, *etc.*, *with* hunger, *etc.*); '~**erlich** *adj.* tearful, lachrymose; whining.

'**Wein|ernte** *f* vintage; '~**essig** *m* vinegar; '~**faß** *n* wine-cask; '~**flasche** *f* wine-bottle; '~**geist** *m* (-[e]s/*no pl.*) spirit(*s pl.*) of wine; '~**glas** *n* wineglass; '~**handlung** *f* wine-merchant's shop; '~**karte** *f* wine-list; '~**keller** *m* wine-vault; '~**kelter** *f* winepress; '~**kenner** *m* connoisseur of *or* in wines.

'**Weinkrampf** 🜊 *m* paroxysm of weeping.

'**Wein|kühler** *m* wine-cooler; '~**lese** *f* vintage; '~**presse** *f* winepress; '~**ranke** *f* vine-tendril; '~**rebe** *f* vine; '²**rot** *adj.* claret-colo(u)red; '~**stock** *m* vine; '~**traube** *f* grape, bunch of grapes.

weise[1] ['vaɪzə] **1.** *adj.* wise; sage; **2.** ⚥ *m* (-n/-n) wise man, sage.

Weise[2] [~] *f* (-/-n) ♪ melody, tune; *fig.* manner, way; *auf diese ~* in this way.

weisen ['vaɪzən] (*irr.*, ge-, h) **1.** *v/t.*: *j-m die Tür ~* show s.o. the door; *von der Schule ~* expel from school; *von sich ~* reject (*idea, etc.*); deny (*charge, etc.*); **2.** *v/i.*: *~ auf* (*acc.*) point at *or* to.

Weis|heit ['vaɪshaɪt] *f* (-/✿-en) wisdom; *am Ende s-r ~ sein* be at one's wit's end; '~**heitszahn** *m* wisdom-tooth; '²**machen** *v/t.* (sep., -ge-, h): *j-m et. ~* make s.o. believe s.th.

weiß *adj.* [vaɪs] white; '²**blech** *n* tin(-plate); '²**brot** *n* white bread; '²**e** *m* (-n/-n) white (man); '~**en** *v/t.* (ge-, h) whitewash; '~**glühend** *adj.* white-hot, incandescent; '²**kohl** *m* white cabbage; '~**lich** *adj.* whitish; '²**waren** *pl.* linen goods *pl.*; '²**wein** *m* white wine.

Weisung ['vaɪzʊŋ] *f* (-/-en) direction, directive.

weit [vaɪt] **1.** *adj.* distant (*von* from); *world, garment:* wide; *area, etc.:* vast; *garment:* loose; *journey, way:* long; *conscience:* elastic; **2.** *adv.:* ~ *entfernt* far away; ~ *entfernt von a.* a long distance from; *fig.* far from; ~ *und breit* far and wide; ~ *über sechzig* (*Jahre alt*) well over sixty; *bei ~em* (by) far; *von ~em* from a distance.

weit|ab *adv.* ['vaɪt-] far away (*von* from); '~**aus** *adv.* (by) far, much; '²**blick** *m* (-[e]s/*no pl.*) far-sightedness; '~**blickend** *adj.* far-sighted, far-seeing; '~**en** *v/t. and v/refl.* (ge-, h) widen.

'**weiter 1.** *adj.* particulars, *etc.:* further; *charges, etc.:* additional, extra; ~*e fünf Wochen* another five weeks; *bis auf ~es* until further notice; *ohne ~es* without any hesitation; off-hand; **2.** *adv.* furthermore, moreover; ~*!* go on!; *nichts ~* nothing more; *und so ~* and so on; *bis hierher und nicht ~* so far and no farther; '²**e** *n* (-n/*no pl.*) *the* rest; *further details pl.*

'**weiter|befördern** *v/t.* (sep., no -ge-, h) forward; '~**bestehen** *v/i.* (*irr. stehen*, sep., no -ge-, h) continue to exist, survive; '~**bilden** *v/t.* (sep., -ge-, h) give *s.o.* further education; ~ *sich ~* improve one's knowledge; continue one's education; '~**geben** *v/t.* (*irr. geben*, sep., -ge-, h) pass (*dat., an acc.* to); '~**gehen** *v/i.* (*irr. gehen*, sep., -ge-, sein) pass *or* move on, walk along; *fig.* continue, go on; '~**hin** *adv.* in (the) future; furthermore; *et. ~ tun* continue doing *or* to do s.th.; '~**kommen** *v/i.* (*irr. kommen*, sep., -ge-, sein) get on; '~**können** *v/i.* (*irr. können*, sep., -ge-, h) be able to go on; '~**leben** *v/i.* (sep., -ge-, h) live on, survive (*a. fig.*); '~**machen** *v/t. and v/i.* (sep., -ge-, h) carry on.

'**weit|gehend** *adj.* powers: large; support: generous; '~**gereist** *adj.* travel(l)ed; '~**greifend** *adj.* far-reaching; '~**herzig** *adj.* broad-minded; '~**hin** *adv.* far off; '~**läufig** ['~lɔʏfɪç] **1.** *adj.* house, *etc.:* spacious; *story, etc.:* detailed; *relative:* distant; **2.** *adv.:* ~ *erzählen* (tell in) detail; *er ist ~ verwandt mit mir* hé is a distant relative of mine; '**～reichend** *adj.* far-reaching; '**～schweifig** *adj.* diffuse, prolix; '**～sichtig** *adj.* ✻ far-sighted; *fig. a.* far-seeing; '**～sichtigkeit** *f* (-/-en) far-sightedness; '**～sprung** *m* (-[e]s/no *pl.*) long jump, *Am.* broad jump; '**～tragend** *adj.* ✕ long-range; *fig.* far-reaching; '**～verbreitet** *adj.* widespread.

Weizen ♀ ['vaitsən] *m* (-s/-) wheat; '**～brot** *n* wheaten bread; '**～mehl** *n* wheaten flour.

welch [vɛlç] **1.** *interr. pron.* what; which; **～er?** which one?; **～er von beiden?** which of the two? **2.** *rel. pron.* who, that; which, that; **3.** *f indef. pron.:* es gibt **～e,** die sagen, daß ... there are some who say that ...; es sollen viele Ausländer hier sein, hast du schon **～e** gesehen? many foreigners are said to be here, have you seen any yet?

welk *adj.* [vɛlk] faded, withered; *skin:* flabby, flaccid; '**～en** *v/i.* (ge-, sein) fade, wither. [iron.\

Wellblech ['vɛlblɛç] *n* corrugated\

Welle ['vɛlə] *f* (-/-n) wave (*a. fig.*); ⊕ shaft.

'**wellen** *v/t. and v/refl.* (ge-, h) wave; '**2bereich** ⚡ *m* wave-range; '**～förmig** *adj.* ['**～fœrmiç**] undulating, undulatory; '**2länge** ⚡ *f* wavelength; '**2linie** *f* wavy line; '**2reiten** *n* (-s/no *pl.*) surf-riding.

'**wellig** *adj.* wavy.

'**Wellpappe** *f* corrugated cardboard *or* paper.

Welt [vɛlt] *f* (-/-en) world; die ganze **～** the whole world, all the world; auf der **～** in the world, auf der ganzen **～** all over the world; zur **～** bringen give birth to, bring into the world.

'**Welt|all** *n* universe, cosmos; '**～anschauung** *f* Weltanschauung; '**～ausstellung** *f* world fair; '**2bekannt** *adj.* known all over the world; '**2berühmt** *adj.* world-famous; '**～bürger** *m* cosmopolite; '**2erschütternd** *adj.* world-shaking; '**2fremd** *adj.* wordly innocent; '**～friede(n)** *m* universal peace; '**～geschichte** *f* (-/no *pl.*) universal history; '**2gewandt** *adj.* knowing the ways of the world; '**～handel** *m* (-s/no *pl.*) world trade; '**～karte** *f* map of the world; '**2klug** *adj.*

wordly-wise; '**～krieg** *m* world war; der zweite **～** World War II; '**～lage** *f* international situation; '**～lauf** *m* course of the world; '**2lich 1.** *adj.* wordly; secular, temporal; **2.** *adv.:* **～** gesinnt wordly-minded; '**～literatur** *f* world literature; '**～macht** *f* world-power; '**2männisch** *adj.* ['**～mɛniʃ**] man-of-the-world; '**～markt** *m* (-[e]s/no *pl.*) world market; '**～meer** *n* ocean; '**～meister** *m* world champion; '**～meisterschaft** *f* world championship; '**～raum** *m* (-[e]s/no *pl.*) (outer) space; '**～reich** *n* universal empire; das Britische **～** the British Empire; '**～reise** *f* journey round the world; '**～rekord** *m* world record; '**～ruf** *m* (-[e]s/no *pl.*) world-wide reputation; '**～schmerz** *m* Weltschmerz; '**～sprache** *f* world *or* universal language; '**～stadt** *f* metropolis; '**2weit** *adj.* world-wide; '**～wunder** *n* wonder of the world.

Wende ['vɛndə] *f* (-/-n) turn (*a. swimming*); *fig. a.* turning-point; '**～kreis** *m geogr.* tropic; *mot.* turning-circle.

Wendeltreppe ['vɛndəl-] *f* winding staircase, (e-e a flight of) winding stairs *pl.*, spiral staircase.

'**Wende|marke** *f sports:* turning-point; '**2n 1.** *v/t.* (ge-, h) turn (coat, etc.); turn (hay) about; **2.** *v/refl.* ([irr.] ge-, h): sich **～** an (acc.) turn to; address o.s. to; apply to (wegen for); **3.** *v/i.* (ge-, h) ⊕, *mot.* turn; bitte **～!** please turn over!; '**～punkt** *m* turning-point.

'**wend|ig** *adj.* nimble, agile (both *a. fig.*); *mot.,* ⚓ easily steerable; *mot.* flexible; '**2ung** *f* (-/-en) turn (*a. fig.*); ✕ facing; *fig.:* change; expression; idiom.

wenig ['ve:niç] **1.** *adj.* little; **～e** *pl.* few *pl.*; **～er** less; **～er** *pl.* fewer; ein klein **～** Geduld a little bit of patience; das **～e** the little; **2.** *adv.* little; **～er** less; **2er** *a.* minus; am **～sten** least (of all); '**2keit** *f* (-/-en): meine **～** my humble self; '**～stens** *adv.* ['**～stəns**] at least.

wenn *cj.* [vɛn] when; if; **～** ... nicht if ... not, unless; **～** auch (al)though, even though; **～** auch noch so however; und **～** nun ...? what if ...?; wie wäre es, **～** wir jetzt heimgingen? what about going home now?

wer [ve:r] **1.** *interr. pron.* who; which; ~ *von euch?* which of you?; **2.** *rel. pron.* who; ~ *auch (immer)* who(so)ever; **3.** F *indef. pron.* somebody; anybody; *ist schon* ~ *gekommen?* has anybody come yet?

Werbe|abteilung ['vɛrbə-] *f* advertising *or* publicity department; **'~film** *m* advertising film.

'werb|en (*irr.*, ge-, h) **1.** *v/t.* canvass (*votes, subscribers, etc.*); ⚔ recruit, enlist; **2.** *v/i.*: ~ *für* advertise, *Am. a.* advertize; make propaganda for; canvass for; **2ung** *f* (-/-en) advertising, publicity, *Am. a.* advertizing; propaganda; canvassing; ⚔ enlistment, recruiting.

Werdegang ['ve:rdə-] *m* career; ⊕ process of manufacture.

'werden 1. *v/i.* (*irr.*, ge-, sein) become, get; grow; turn (*pale, sour, etc.*); *was ist aus ihm geworden?* what has become of him?; *was will er (einmal)* ~? what is he going to be?; **2.** 2 *n* (-s/*no pl.*): *noch im* ~ *sein* in embryo.

werfen ['vɛrfən] (*irr.*, ge-, h) **1.** *v/t.* throw (*nach at*); zo. throw (*young*); cast (*shadow, glance, etc.*); *Falten* ~ fall in folds; set badly; **2.** *v/i.* throw; zo. litter; ~ *mit* throw (*auf acc., nach at*). [dockyard.]

Werft ⚓ [vɛrft] *f* (-/-en) shipyard,)

Werk [vɛrk] *n* (-[e]s/-e) work; act; ⊕ works *pl.*; works *sg.*, *pl.*, factory; *das* ~ *e-s Augenblicks* the work of a moment; *zu* ~*e gehen* proceed; **'~bank** ⊕ *f* work-bench; **'~meister** *m* foreman; **~statt** *f* ['~ʃtat] *f* (-/-en) workshop; **'~tag** *m* workday; **2tätig** *adj.* working; **'~zeug** *n* tool; implement; instrument.

Wermut ['ve:rmu:t] *m* (-[e]s/*no pl.*) ♥ wormwood; verm(o)uth.

wert [ve:rt] **1.** *adj.* worth; worthy (*gen. of*); ~, *getan zu werden* worth doing; **2.** 2 *m* (-[e]s/-e) value (*a.* ⚔, ♠, *phys., fig.*); worth (*a. fig.*); *Briefmarken im* ~ *von 2 Schilling 2 shillings' worth of stamps; großen* ~ *legen auf* (*acc.*) set a high value (up)on.

'Wert|brief *m* money-letter; **2en** *v/t.* (ge-, h) value; appraise; **'~gegenstand** *m* article of value; **2los** *adj.* worthless, valueless; **'~papiere** *n/pl.* securities *pl.*; **'~sachen** *pl.* valuables *pl.*; **'~ung** *f* (-/-en)

valuation; appraisal; *sports:* score; **2voll** *adj.* valuable, precious.

Wesen ['ve:zən] *n* **1.** (-s/*no pl.*) entity, essence; nature, character; *viel* ~*s machen um* make a fuss of; **2.** (-s/-) being; creature; **2los** *adj.* unreal; **2lich** *adj.* essential, substantial.

weshalb [vɛs'halp] **1.** *interr. pron.* why; **2.** *cj.* that's why.

Wespe zo. ['vɛspə] *f* (-/-n) wasp.

West *geogr.* [vɛst] west; **'~en** *m* (-s/*no pl.*) west; *the* West.

Weste ['vɛstə] *f* (-/-n) waistcoat, ♣ *and Am.* vest; *e-e reine* ~ *haben* have a clean slate.

'west|lich *adj.* west; westerly; western; **2wind** *m* west(erly) wind.

Wett|bewerb ['vɛtbəvɛrp] *m* (-[e]s/-e) competition (*a.* ♠); **'~büro** *n* betting office; **'~e** *f* (-/-n) wager, bet; *e-e* ~ *eingehen* lay *or* make a bet; **'~eifer** *m* emulation, rivalry; **2eifern** *v/i.* (ge-, h) vie (*mit* with; *in dat.* in; *um* for); **2en** (ge-, h) **1.** *v/t.* wager, bet; **2.** *v/i.*: *mit j-m um et.* ~ wager *or* bet s.o. s.th.; ~ *auf* (*acc.*) wager *or* bet on, back.

Wetter¹ ['vɛtər] *n* (-s/-) weather.

Wetter² [~] *m* (-s/-) better.

'Wetter|bericht *m* weather-forecast; **2fest** *adj.* weather-proof; **'~karte** *f* weather-chart; **'~lage** *f* weather-conditions *pl.*; **'~leuchten** *n* (-s/*no pl.*) sheet-lightning; **'~vorhersage** *f* (-/-n) weather-forecast; **'~warte** *f* weather-station.

'Wett|kampf *m* contest, competition; **'~kämpfer** *m* contestant; **'~lauf** *m* race; **'~läufer** *m* racer, runner; **2machen** *v/t.* (*sep.*, -ge-, h) make up for; **'~rennen** *n* race; **'~rüsten** *n* (-s/*no pl.*) armament race; **'~spiel** *n* match, game; **'~streit** *n* contest. [sharpen.]

wetzen ['vɛtsən] *v/t.* (ge-, h) whet,)

wich [viç] *pret. of* weichen¹.

Wichse ['viksə] *f* **1.** (-/-n) blacking; polish; **2.** F *pl.* (-/*no pl.*) thrashing; **2n** *v/t.* (ge-, h) black; polish.

wichtig *adj.* ['viçtiç] important; *sich* ~ *machen* show off; **2keit** *f* (-/~-en) importance; **2tuer** ['~tu:-ər] *m* (-s/-) pompous fellow; **'~tuerisch** *adj.* pompous.

Wickel ['vikəl] *m* (-s/-) roll(er); ♠: compress; packing; **2n** *v/t.* (ge-, h) wind; swaddle (*baby*); wrap.

Widder zo. ['vidər] m (-s/-) ram.
wider prp. (acc.) ['vi:dər] against,
contrary to; '**~borstig** adj. cross-
grained; '**~fahren** v/i. (irr. fahren,
no -ge-, sein) happen (dat. to);
'2**haken** m barb; '2**hall** ['~hal] m
(-[e]s/-e) echo, reverberation; fig.
response; '**~hallen** v/i. (sep., -ge-,
h) (re-)echo (von with), resound
(with); **~legen** v/t. (no -ge-, h)
refute, disprove; '**~lich** adj. repugnant, repulsive; disgusting; '**~na-
türlich** adj. unnatural; '2**rechtlich** adj. illegal, unlawful; '2**rede** f
contradiction; '2**ruf** m ɪ̃ɫ̃ revoca-
tion; retraction; '**~rufen** v/t. (irr.
rufen, no -ge-, h) revoke; retract (a.
ɪ̃ɫ̃); '**~ruflich** adj. revocable; 2**sa-
cher** ['~zaxər] m (-s/-) adversary;
'2**schein** m reflection; '**~setzen**
v/refl. (no -ge-, h): sich e-r Sache ~
oppose or resist s.th.; '**~setzlich**
adj. refractory; insubordinate; '**~
sinnig** adj. absurd; **~spenstig** adj.
['~ʃpɛnstiç] refractory; '2**spenstig-
keit** f (-/⁊-en) refractoriness;
'**~spiegeln** v/t. (sep., -ge-, h)
reflect (a. fig.); sich ~ in (dat.) be
reflected in; **~sprechen** v/i. (irr.
sprechen, no -ge-, h): j-m ~ con-
tradict s.o.; '2**spruch** m contradiction; opposition; im ~ zu in contradiction to; **~sprüchlich** adj.
['~ʃpry:çliç] contradictory; '**~
spruchslos 1.** adj. uncontradicted;
2. adv. without contradiction;
'2**stand** m resistance (a. ⚡); opposition; ~ leisten offer resistance
(dat. to); auf heftigen ~ stoßen meet
with stiff opposition; '**~stands-
fähig** adj. resistant (a. ⊕); '**~ste-
hen** v/i. (irr. stehen, no -ge-, h)
resist (e-r Sache s.th.); **~streben**
v/i. (no -ge-, h): es widerstrebt mir,
dies zu tun I hate doing or to do
that, I am reluctant to do that;
'**~strebend** adv. reluctantly; '2**~
streit** m (-[e]s/⁊-e) antagonism;
fig. conflict; '**~wärtig** adj. ['~vɛrtiç]
unpleasant, disagreeable; disgusting; '2**wille** m aversion (gegen to,
for, from); dislike (to, of, for);
disgust (at, for); reluctance, un-
willingness; '**~willig** adj. reluctant,
unwilling.

widm|en ['vitmən] v/t. (ge-, h)
dedicate; '2**ung** f (-/-en) dedica-
tion.

widrig adj. ['vi:driç] adverse; **~en-
falls** adv. ['~gən-] failing which,
in default of which.
wie [vi:] **1.** adv. how; ~ alt ist er?
what is his age?; ~ spät ist es? what
is the time?; **2.** cj.: ein Mann ~ er
a man such as he, a man like him;
~ er dies hörte hearing this; ich
hörte, ~ er es sagte I heard him
saying so.
wieder adv. ['vi:dər] again, anew;
immer ~ again and again; 2**aufbau**
m (-[e]s/no pl.) reconstruction;
rebuilding; **~aufbauen** v/t. (sep.,
-ge-, h) reconstruct; 2**aufleben**
v/i. (sep., -ge-, sein) revive; 2**aufleben** n (-s/no pl.) revival; 2**aufnahme** f resumption; **~aufneh-
men** v/t. (irr. nehmen, sep., -ge-, h)
resume; 2**beginn** m recommence-
ment; re-opening; **~bekommen**
v/t. (irr. kommen, sep., no -ge-, h)
get back; **~beleben** v/t. (sep., no
-ge-, h) resurrect; 2**belebung** f
(-/-en) revival; fig. a. resurrection;
2**belebungsversuch** m attempt at
resuscitation; **~bringen** v/t. (irr.
bringen, sep., -ge-, h) bring back;
restore, give back; **~einsetzen** v/t.
(sep., -ge-, h) restore; **~einstellen**
v/t. (sep., -ge-, h) re-engage; 2**ergreifung** f reseizure; **~erkennen**
v/t. (irr. kennen, sep., no -ge-, h)
recognize (an dat. by); **~erstatten**
v/t. (sep., no -ge-, h) restore;
reimburse, refund (money); **~ge-
ben** v/t. (irr. geben, sep., -ge-, h)
give back, return; render, reproduce; '**~gutmachen** v/t. (sep.,
-ge-, h) make up for; 2**gutma-
chung** f (-/-en) reparation; **~her-
stellen** v/t. (sep., -ge-, h) restore;
~holen v/t. (h) **1.** [**~**ho:lən] (no
-ge-) repeat; **2.** ['~ho:lən] (sep.,
-ge-) fetch back; 2**holung** f (-/-en)
repetition; **~käuen** ['~kɔyən] (sep.,
-ge-, h) **1.** v/i. ruminate, chew the
cud; **2.** F fig. v/t. repeat over and
over; 2**kehr** ['~ke:r] f (-/no pl.)
return; recurrence; '**~kehren** v/i.
(sep., -ge-, sein) return; recur;
'**~kommen** v/i. (irr. kommen, sep.,
-ge-, sein) come back, return;
'**~sehen** v/t. and v/refl. (irr. sehen,
sep., -ge-, h) see or meet again;
2**sehen** n (-s/no pl.) meeting again;
auf ~! good-bye!; '**~tun** v/t. (irr.
tun, sep., -ge-, h) do again, repeat;

W

'∼um adv. again, anew; **'∼vereinigen** v/t. (sep., no -ge-, h) reunite; **'²vereinigung** f reunion; pol. reunification; **'²verheiratung** f remarriage; **'²verkäufer** m reseller; retailer; **'²wahl** f re-election; **'∼wählen** v/t. (sep., -ge-, h) reelect; **²'zulassung** f readmission.

Wiege ['vi:gə] f (-/-n) cradle.

wiegen¹ ['vi:gən] v/t. and v/i. (irr., ge-, h) weigh.

wiegen² [∼] v/t. (ge-, h) rock; in Sicherheit ∼ rock in security, lull into (a false sense of) security.

'Wiegenlied n lullaby.

wiehern ['vi:ərn] v/i. (ge-, h) neigh.

Wiener ['vi:nər] m (-s/-) Viennese; **'²isch** adj. Viennese.

wies [vi:s] pret. of **weisen**.

Wiese ['vi:zə] f (-/-n) meadow.

wie'so interr. pron. why; why so.

wie'viel adv. how much; ∼ pl. how many pl.; **∼te** adv. [∼tə]: den ∼ten haben wir heute? what's the date today?

wild [vilt] **1.** adj. wild; savage; ∼es Fleisch 🜊 proud flesh; ∼e Ehe concubinage; ∼er Streik ✝ wildcat strike; **2.** ♀ n (-[e]s/no pl.) game.

'Wild|bach m torrent; **'∼bret** ['∼bret] n (-s/no pl.) game; venison.

Wilde ['vildə] m (-n/-n) savage.

Wilder|er ['vildərər] m (-s/-) poacher; **'²n** v/i. (ge-, h) poach.

'Wild|fleisch n s. Wildbret; **'²-'fremd** F adj. quite strange; **'∼hüter** m gamekeeper; **'∼leder** n buckskin; **'²ledern** adj. buckskin; doeskin; **'∼nis** f (-/-se) wilderness, wild (a. fig.); **'∼schwein** n wildboar.

Wille ['vilə] m (-ns/🜊 -n) will; s-n ∼n durchsetzen have one's way; gegen s-n ∼n against one's will; j-m s-n ∼n lassen let s.o. have his (own) way; **'²nlos** adj. lacking will-power.

'Willens|freiheit f (-/no pl.) freedom of (the) will; **'∼kraft** f (-/no pl.) will-power; **'∼schwäche** f (-/no pl.) weak will; **'²stark** adj. strong-willed; **'∼stärke** f (-/no pl.) strong will, will-power.

'will|ig adj. willing, ready; **∼'kommen** adj. welcome; **²kür** ['∼ky:r] f (-/no pl.) arbitrariness; **'∼kürlich** adj. arbitrary.

wimmeln ['viməln] v/i. (ge-, h) swarm (von with), teem (with).

wimmern ['vimərn] v/i. (ge-, h) whimper, whine.

Wimpel ['vimpəl] m (-s/-) pennant, pennon, streamer.

Wimper ['vimpər] f (-/-n) eyelash.

Wind [vint] m (-[e]s/-e) wind; **'∼beutel** m cream-puff; F fig. windbag.

Winde ['vində] f (-/-n) windlass; reel.

Windel ['vindəl] f (-/-n) diaper, (baby's) napkin; ∼n pl. a. swaddlingclothes pl.

'winden v/t. (irr., ge-, h) wind; twist, twirl; make, bind (wreath); sich ∼ vor (dat.) writhe with.

'Wind|hose f whirlwind, tornado; **'∼hund** m greyhound; **²ig** adj. ['∼diç] windy; F fig. excuse: thin, lame; **'∼mühle** f windmill; **'∼pocken** 🜊 pl. chicken-pox; **'∼richtung** f direction of the wind; **'∼rose** ⚓ f compass card; **'∼schutzscheibe** f wind-screen, Am. windshield; **'∼stärke** f wind velocity; **²still** adj. calm; **'∼stille** f calm; **'∼stoß** m blast of wind, gust.

'Windung f (-/-en) winding, turn; bend (of way, etc.); coil (of snake, etc.).

Wink [viŋk] m (-[e]s/-e) sign; wave; wink; fig.: hint; tip.

Winkel ['viŋkəl] m (-s/-) 🜊 angle; corner, nook; ²ig adj. angular; street: crooked; **'∼zug** m subterfuge, trick, shift.

'winken v/i. (ge-, h) make a sign; beckon; mit dem Taschentuch ∼ wave one's handkerchief.

winklig adj. ['viŋkliç] s. winkelig.

winseln ['vinzəln] v/i. (ge-, h) whimper, whine.

Winter ['vintər] m (-s/-) winter; im ∼ in winter; **²lich** adj. wintry; **'∼schlaf** m hibernation; **'∼sport** m winter sports pl.

Winzer ['vintsər] m (-s/-) vinedresser; vine-grower; vintager.

winzig adj. ['vintsiç] tiny, diminutive.

Wipfel ['vipfəl] m (-s/-) top.

Wippe ['vipə] f (-/-n) seesaw; **'²n** v/i. (ge-, h) seesaw.

wir pers. pron. [vi:r] we; ∼ drei the three of us.

Wirbel ['virbəl] m (-s/-) whirl, swirl; eddy; flurry (of blows, etc.); anat. vertebra; **'²ig** adj. giddy,

W

vertiginous; wild; '2n v/i. (ge-, h) whirl; drums: roll; '~säule anat. f spinal or vertebral column; '~sturm m cyclone, tornado, Am. a. twister; '~tier n vertebrate; '~wind m whirlwind (a. fig.).

wirk|en ['virkən] (ge-, h) **1.** v/t. knit, weave; work (wonders); **2.** v/i.: ~ als or function as; ~ auf (acc.) produce an impression on; beruhigend ~ have a soothing effect; '~lich adj. real, actual; true, genuine; '2lichkeit f (-/-en) reality; in ~ in reality; '~sam adj. effective, efficacious; '2samkeit f (-/⸢-en) effectiveness, efficacy; '2ung f (-/-en) effect.

'**Wirkungs|kreis** m sphere or field of activity; '2los adj. ineffective, inefficacious; '~losigkeit f (-/no pl.) ineffectiveness, inefficacy; '2voll adj. s. wirksam.

wirr adj. [vir] confused; speech: incoherent; hair: dishevel(l)ed; '2en pl. disorders pl.; troubles pl.; 2warr ['~var] m (-s/no pl.) confusion, muddle.

Wirsingkohl ['virziŋ-] m (-[e]s/no pl.) savoy.

Wirt [virt] m (-[e]s/-e) host; landlord; innkeeper.

'**Wirtschaft** f (-/-en) housekeeping; economy; trade and industry; economics pl.; s. Wirtshaus; F mess; '2en v/i. (ge-, h) keep house; economize; F bustle (about); '~erin f (-/-nen) housekeeper; '2lich adj. economic; economical.

'**Wirtschafts|geld** n housekeeping money; '~jahr n financial year; '~krise f economic crisis; '~politik f economic policy; '~prüfer m (-s/-) chartered accountant, Am. certified public accountant.

'**Wirtshaus** n public house, F pub.

Wisch [viʃ] m (-[e]s/-e) wisp (of straw, etc.); contp. scrap of paper; '2en v/t. (ge-, h) wipe.

wispern ['vispərn] v/t. and v/i. (ge-, h) whisper.

Wiß|begierde ['vis-] f (-/no pl.) thirst for knowledge; '2begierig adj. eager for knowledge.

wissen ['visən] **1.** v/t. (irr., ge-, h) know; man kann nie ~ you never know, you never can tell; **2.** 2 n (-s/no pl.) knowledge; meines ~s to my knowledge, as far as I know.

'**Wissenschaft** f (-/-en) science; knowledge; '~ler m (-s/-) scholar; scientist; researcher; '2lich adj. scientific.

'**Wissens|drang** m (-[e]s/no pl.) urge or thirst for knowledge; '2~wert adj. worth knowing.

'**wissentlich** adj. knowing, conscious.

wittern ['vitərn] v/t. (ge-, h) scent, smell; fig. a. suspect.

'**Witterung** f (-/⸢-en) weather; hunt. scent; ~sverhältnisse ['~sfer-heltnisə] pl. meteorological conditions pl. [m (-s/-) widower.]

Witwe ['vitvə] f (-/-n) widow; '~r]

Witz [vits] m **1.** (-es/no pl.) wit; **2.** (-es/-e) joke; ~e reißen crack jokes; '~blatt n comic paper; '2ig adj. witty; funny.

wo [vo:] **1.** adv. where?; **2.** cj.: F ach ~! nonsense!

wob [vo:p] pret. of weben.

wo'bei adv. at what?; at which; in doing so.

Woche ['vɔxə] f (-/-n) week; heute in e-r ~ today week.

'**Wochen|bett** n childbed; '~blatt n weekly (paper); '~ende n weekend; '2lang **1.** adj.: nach ~em Warten after (many) weeks of waiting; **2.** adv. for weeks; '~lohn m weekly pay or wages pl.; '~markt m weekly market; '~schau f news-reel; '~tag m week-day.

wöchentlich ['vœçəntliç] **1.** adj. weekly; **2.** adv. weekly, every week; einmal ~ once a week.

Wöchnerin ['vœçnərin] f (-/-nen) woman in childbed.

wo'|durch adv. by what?, how?; by which, whereby; ~'für adv. for what?, what ... for?; (in return) for which. [gen[1].]

wog [vo:k] pret. of wägen and wie-]

Woge ['vo:gə] f (-/-n) wave (a. fig.), billow; die ~n glätten pour oil on troubled waters; '2n v/i. (ge-, h) surge (a. fig.), billow; wheat: a. wave; heave.

wo'|her adv. from where?, where ... from?; ~ wissen Sie das? how do you (come to) know that?; ~'hin adv. where (... to)?

wohl [vo:l] **1.** adv. well; sich nicht ~ fühlen be unwell; ~ oder übel willy-nilly; leben Sie ~! farewell!; er wird ~ reich sein he is rich, I suppose;

2. ♀ n (-[e]s/no pl.): ~ und Wehe weal and woe; auf Ihr ~! your health!, here is to you!

'**Wohl|befinden** n well-being; good health; '~**behagen** n comfort, ease; '**2behalten** adv. safe; '**2bekannt** adj. well-known; '~**ergehen** n (-s/no pl.) welfare, prosperity; **2er-zogen** adj. ['~ ⁹ɛrtso:gən] well-bred, well-behaved; '~**fahrt** f (-/no pl.) welfare; public assistance; '~**ge-fallen** n (-s/no pl.) pleasure; sein ~ haben an (dat.) take delight in; '**2gemeint** adj. well-meant, well-intentioned; **2gemut** adj. ['~gə-mu:t] cheerful; '**2genährt** adj. well-fed; '~**geruch** m scent, perfume; '**2gesinnt** adj. well-disposed (j-m towards s.o.); '**2habend** adj. well-to-do; '~**ig** adj. comfortable; cosy, snug; '~**klang** m (-[e]s/no pl.) melodious sound, harmony; **2-klingend** adj. melodious, harmonious; '~**laut** m s. Wohlklang; '~**leben** n (-s/no pl.) luxury; '**2riechend** adj. fragrant; '**2schmeckend** adj. savo(u)ry; '~**sein** n well-being; good health; '~**stand** m (-[e]s/no pl.) prosperity, wealth; '~**tat** f kindness, charity; fig. comfort, treat; '~**täter** m benefactor; '**2tätig** adj. charitable, beneficent; '~**tä-tigkeit** f charity; '**2tuend** adj. ['~tu:-ənt] pleasant, comfortable; '**2tun** v/i. (irr. tun, sep., -ge-, h) do good; '**2verdient** adj. well-deserved; p. of great merit; '~**wollen** n (-s/no pl.) goodwill; benevolence; favo(u)r; '**2wollen** v/i. (sep., -ge-, h) be well-disposed (j-m towards s.o).

wohn|en ['vo:nən] v/i. (ge-, h) live (in dat. in, at; bei j-m with s.o.); reside (in, at; with); '**2haus** n dwelling-house; block of flats, Am. apartment house; '~**haft** adj. resident, living; '~**lich** adj. comfortable; cosy, snug; '**2ort** m dwelling-place, residence; esp. ⚖ domicile; '**2sitz** m residence; mit ~ in resident in or at; ohne festen ~ without fixed abode; '**2ung** f (-/-en) dwelling, habitation; flat, Am. apartment.

'**Wohnungs|amt** n housing office; '~**not** f housing shortage; '~**pro-blem** n housing problem.

'**Wohn|wagen** m caravan, trailer; '~**zimmer** n sitting-room, esp. Am. living room.

wölb|en ['vœlbən] v/t. (ge-, h) vault; arch; sich ~ arch; '**2ung** f (-/-en) vault, arch; curvature.

Wolf zo. [vɔlf] m (-[e]s/⸚e) wolf.
Wolke ['vɔlkə] f (-/-n) cloud.
'**Wolken|bruch** m cloud-burst; '~**kratzer** m (-s/-) skyscraper; '**2los** adj. cloudless.
'**wolkig** adj. cloudy, clouded.
'**Woll|decke** ['vɔl-] f blanket; '~**e** f (-/-n) wool.
wollen[1] ['vɔlən] (h) **1.** v/t. (ge-) wish, desire; want; lieber ~ prefer; nicht ~ refuse; er weiß, was er will he knows his mind; **2.** v/i. (ge-): ich will schon, aber ... I want to, but ...; **3.** v/aux. (no -ge-) be willing; intend, be going to; be about to; lieber ~ prefer; nicht ~ refuse; er hat nicht gehen ~ he refused to go.
woll|en[2] adj. [~] wool(l)en; '~**ig** adj. wool(l)y; '**2stoff** m wool(l)en.
Wol|lust ['vɔlust] f (-/⸚e) voluptuousness; **2lüstig** adj. ['~lystiç] voluptuous.
'**Wollwaren** pl. wool(l)en goods pl.
wo|'mit adv. with what, what ... with?; with which; ~'**möglich** adv. perhaps, maybe.
Wonn|e ['vɔnə] f (-/-n) delight, bliss; '**2ig** adj. delightful, blissful.
wo|ran adv. [vo:'ran]: ~ denkst du? what are you thinking of?; ich weiß nicht, ~ ich mit ihm bin I don't know what to make of him; ~ liegt es, daß ...? how is it that ...?; ~'**rauf** adv. on what?, what ... on?; whereupon, after which; ~ wartest du? what are you waiting for?; ~'**raus** adv. from what?; what ... of?; from which; ~**rin** adv. [~'rin] in what?; in which.
Wort [vɔrt] n **1.** (-[e]s/⸚er) word; er kann seine Wörter noch nicht he hasn't learnt his words yet; **2.** (-[e]s/-e) word; term, expression; ums ~ bitten ask permission to speak; das ~ ergreifen begin to speak; parl. rise to speak, address the House, esp. Am. take the floor; das ~ führen be the spokesman; ~ halten keep one's word; '**2brüchig** adj.: er ist ~ geworden he has broken his word.
'**Wörter|buch** ['vœrtər-] n dictionary; '~**verzeichnis** n vocabulary, list of words.
'**Wort|führer** m spokesman; '**2ge-treu** adj. literal; '**2karg** adj. taci-

turn; **~klauberei** [⌣klaubə'raɪ] f (-/-en) word-splitting; **'~laut** m (-[e]s/no pl.) wording; text. [eral.\
wörtlich adj. ['vœrtlɪç] verbal, literally]\
'Wort|schatz m (-es/no pl.) vocabulary; **'~schwall** m (-[e]s/no pl.) verbiage; **'~spiel** n pun (über acc., mit [up]on), play upon words; **'~stellung** gr. f word order, order of words; **'~stamm** ling. m stem; **'~streit** m, **'~wechsel** m dispute.\
wo|rüber adv. [vo:'ry:bər] over or upon what?, what ... over or about or on?; over or upon which, about which; **~rum** adv. [⌣'rum] about what?, what ... about?; about or for which; ~ handelt es sich? what is it about?; **~runter** adv. [⌣'runtər] under or among what?, what ... under?; under or among which; **~'von** adv. of or from what?, what ... from or of?; about what?, what ... about?; of or from which; **~'vor** adv. of what?, what ... of?; of which; **~'zu** adv. for what?, what ... for?; for which.\
Wrack [vrak] n (-[e]s/-e, -s) ⚓ wreck (a. fig.).\
wrang [vraŋ] pret. of wringen.\
wring|en ['vrɪŋən] v/t. (irr., ge-, h) wring; **'2maschine** f wringing-machine.\
Wucher ['vu:xər] m (-s/no pl.) usury; ~ treiben practise usury; **'~er** m (-s/-) usurer; **'~gewinn** m excess profit; **'2isch** adj. usurious; **'2n** v/i. (ge-, h) grow exuberantly; **'~ung** f (-/-en) ⚕ exuberant growth; ⚕ growth; **'~zinsen** m/pl. usurious interest.\
Wuchs [vu:ks] **1.** m (-es/⸚e) growth; figure, shape; stature; **2.** ⚲ pret. of wachsen.\
Wucht [vuxt] f (-/⚲-en) weight; force; **'2ig** adj. heavy.\
Wühl|arbeit fig. ['vy:l-] f insidious agitation, subversive activity; **'2en** v/i. (ge-, h) dig; pig: root; fig. agitate; ~ in (dat.) rummage (about) in; **'~er** m (-s/-) agitator.\
Wulst [vulst] m (-es/⸚e), f (-/⸚e) pad; bulge; △ roll(-mo[u]lding); ⊕ bead; **'2ig** adj. lips: thick.\
wund adj. [vunt] sore; ~e Stelle sore; ~er Punkt tender spot; 2e ['⸚də] f (-/-n) wound; alte ~n wieder aufreißen reopen old sores.\
Wunder ['vundər] n (-s/-) miracle;

fig. a. wonder, marvel; ~ wirken pills, etc.: work marvels; kein ~, wenn man bedenkt ... no wonder, considering ...; **'2bar** adj. miraculous; fig. a. wonderful, marvel-(l)ous; **'~kind** n infant prodigy; **'2lich** adj. queer, odd; **'2n** v/t. (ge-, h) surprise, astonish; sich ~ be surprised or astonished (über acc. at); **'2schön** adj. very beautiful; **'~tat** f wonder, miracle; **'~täter** m wonder-worker; **'2tätig** adj. wonder-working; **'2voll** adj. wonderful; **'~werk** n marvel, wonder.\
Wund|fieber ⚕ n wound-fever; **'~starrkrampf** ⚕ m tetanus.\
Wunsch [vunʃ] m (-es/⸚e) wish, desire; request; auf ~ by or on request; if desired; nach ~ as desired; mit den besten Wünschen zum Fest with the compliments of the season.\
Wünschelrute ['vynʃəl-] f divining-rod, dowsing-rod; **~ngänger** ['⸚gɛŋər] m (-s/-) diviner, dowser.\
wünschen ['vynʃən] v/t. (ge-, h) wish, desire; wie Sie ~ as you wish; was ~ Sie? what can I do for you?; **'~swert** adj. desirable.\
'wunsch|gemäß adv. as requested or desired, according to one's wishes; **'2zettel** m list of wishes.\
wurde ['vurdə] pret. of werden.\
Würde ['vyrdə] f (-/-n) dignity; unter seiner ~ beneath one's dignity; **'2los** adj. undignified; **'~nträger** m dignitary; **'2voll** adj. dignified; grave.\
'würdig adj. worthy (gen. of); dignified; grave; **~en** ['⸚gən] v/t. (ge-, h) appreciate, value; mention hono(u)rably; laud, praise; j-n keines Blickes ~ ignore s.o. completely; **2ung** ['⸚guŋ] f (-/-en) appreciation, valuation.\
Wurf [vurf] m (-[e]s/⸚e) throw, cast; zo. litter.\
Würfel ['vyrfəl] m (-s/-) die; cube (a. Å); **'~becher** m dice-box; **'2n** v/i. (ge-, h) (play) dice; **'~spiel** n game of dice; **'~zucker** m lump sugar. [tile.]\
'Wurfgeschoß n missile, projec-]\
würgen ['vyrgən] (ge-, h) **1.** v/t. choke, strangle; **2.** v/i. choke; retch.\
Wurm zo. [vurm] m (-[e]s/⸚er) worm; **'2en** F v/t. (ge-, h) vex; rankle (j-n in s.o.'s mind); **'2-stichig** adj. worm-eaten.

Wurst [vurst] *f* (-/ⁱᵉ) sausage; F *das ist mir ganz* ~ I don't care a rap.

Würstchen ['vyrstçən] *n* (-s/-) sausage; *heißes* ~ hot sausage, *Am.* hot dog.

Würze ['vyrtsə] *f* (-/-n) seasoning, flavo(u)r; spice, condiment; *fig.* salt.

Wurzel ['vurtsəl] *f* (-/-n) root (*a. gr.*, Ⱥ); ~ *schlagen* strike *or* take root (*a. fig.*); 'Ꝛ̃n *v/i.* (ge-, h) (strike *or* take) root; ~ *in* (*dat.*) take one's root in, be rooted in.

'**würz|en** *v/t.* (ge-, h) spice, season, flavo(u)r; '~**ig** *adj.* spicy, well-seasoned, aromatic.

wusch [vu:ʃ] *pret. of* waschen.

wußte ['vustə] *pret. of* wissen.

Wust F [vu:st] *m* (-es/*no pl.*) tangled mass; rubbish; mess.

wüst *adj.* [vy:st] desert, waste; confused; wild, dissolute; rude; 'Ꝛ̃e *f* (-/-n) desert, waste; 'Ꝛ̃ling ['~lɪŋ] *m* (-s/-e) debauchee, libertine, rake.

Wut [vu:t] *f* (-/*no pl.*) rage, fury; *in* ~ in a rage; '~**anfall** *m* fit of rage.

wüten ['vy:tən] *v/i.* (ge-, h) rage (*a. fig.*); '~**d** *adj.* furious, enraged (*über acc.* at; *auf acc.* with), *esp. Am.* F a. mad (*über acc.*, *auf acc.* at).

Wüterich ['vy:tərɪç] *m* (-[e]s/-e) berserker; bloodthirsty man. [rage.]

'**wutschnaubend** *adj.* foaming with⟩

X, Y

X-Beine ['iks-] *n/pl.* knock-knees *pl.*; '**X-beinig** *adj.* knock-kneed.

x-beliebig *adj.* [iksbə'li:bɪç] any (... you please); *jede*(*r, -s*) ~e ... any ...

x-mal *adv.* ['iks-] many times, *sl.* umpteen times.

X-Strahlen ['iks-] *m/pl.* X-rays *pl.*

x-te *adj.* ['ikstə]: *zum* ~*n Male* for the umpteenth time.

Xylophon ♪ [ksylo'fo:n] *n* (-s/-e) xylophone.

Yacht ⚓ [jaxt] *f* (-/-en) yacht.

Z

Zacke ['tsakə] *f* (-/-n) *s.* Zacken.

'**Zacken** 1. *m* (-s/-) (sharp) point; prong; tooth (*of comb, saw, rake*); jag (*of rock*); 2. Ꝛ̃ *v/t.* (ge-, h) indent, notch; jag.

'**zackig** *adj.* indented, notched; *rock:* jagged; pointed; ⚔ F *fig.* smart.

zaghaft *adj.* ['tsa:khaft] timid; 'Ꝛ̃ig-keit *f* (-/*no pl.*) timidity.

zäh *adj.* [tsɛ:] tough, tenacious (*both a. fig.*); *liquid:* viscid, viscous; *fig.* dogged; '~**flüssig** *adj.* viscid, viscous, sticky; 'Ꝛ̃igkeit *f* (-/*no pl.*) toughness, tenacity (*both a. fig.*); viscosity; *fig.* doggedness.

Zahl [tsa:l] *f* (-/-en) number; figure, cipher; 'Ꝛ̃bar *adj.* payable.

'**zählbar** *adj.* countable.

zahlen ['tsa:lən] (ge-, h) 1. *v/i.* pay; *at restaurant:* ~ (, *bitte*)! the bill, please!, *Am.* the check, please!; 2. *v/t.* pay.

zählen ['tsɛ:lən] (ge-, h) 1. *v/t.* count, number; ~ *zu* count *or* number among; 2. *v/i.* count; ~ *auf* (*acc.*) count (up)on, rely (up)on.

'**Zahlen|lotto** *n s.* Lotto; 'Ꝛ̃mäßig 1. *adj.* numerical; 2. *adv.:* *j-m* ~ *überlegen sein* outnumber s.o.

'**Zähler** *m* (-s/-) counter; Ⱥ numerator; *for gas, etc.:* meter.

'**Zahl|karte** *f* money-order form (*for paying direct into the postal cheque account*); 'Ꝛ̃los *adj.* numberless, innumerable, countless; '~**meister** ⚔ *m* paymaster; 'Ꝛ̃reich 1. *adj.* numerous; 2. *adv.* in great number; '~**tag** *m* pay-day; '~**ung** *f* (-/-en) payment.

'**Zählung** *f* (-/-en) counting.

'**Zahlungs|anweisung** *f* order to pay; '~**aufforderung** *f* request for payment; '~**bedingungen** *f/pl.* terms *pl.* of payment; '~**befehl** *m* order to pay; '~**einstellung** *f* suspension of payment; '2**fähig** adj. solvent; '~**fähigkeit** f solvency; '~**frist** f term for payment; '~**mittel** n currency; gesetzliches ~ legal tender; '~**schwierigkeiten** f/pl. financial or pecuniary difficulties pl.; '~**termin** m date of payment; '2**unfähig** adj. insolvent; '~**unfähigkeit** f insolvency;

Zahlwort gr. n (-[e]s/=er) numeral.

zahm adj. [tsa:m] tame (a. fig.), domestic(ated).

zähm|en ['tsɛ:mən] v/t. (ge-, h) tame (a. fig.), domesticate; '2**ung** f (-/⚓-en) taming (a. fig.), domestication.

Zahn [tsa:n] m (-[e]s/=e) tooth; ⊕ tooth, cog; Zähne bekommen cut one's teeth; '~**arzt** m dentist, dental surgeon; '~**bürste** f toothbrush; '~**creme** f tooth-paste; '2**en** v/i. (ge-, h) teethe, cut one's teeth; '~**ersatz** m denture; '~**fäule** ['~fɔylə] f (-/no pl.) dental caries; '~**fleisch** n gums pl.; '~**füllung** f filling, stopping; '~**geschwür** ⚕ n gumboil; '~**heilkunde** f dentistry; '2**los** adj. toothless; '~**lücke** f gap between the teeth; '~**pasta** ['~pasta] f (-/Zahnpasten), '~**paste** f tooth-paste; '~**rad** ⊕ n cog-wheel; '~**radbahn** f rack-railway; '~**schmerzen** m/pl. toothache; '~**stocher** m (-s/-) toothpick.

Zange ['tsaŋə] f (-/-n) (e-e a pair of) tongs pl. or pliers pl. or pincers pl.; ⚙, zo. forceps sg., pl.

Zank [tsaŋk] m (-[e]s/no pl.) quarrel, F row; '~**apfel** m bone of contention; '2**en** (ge-, h) 1. v/i. scold (mit j-m s.o.); 2. v/refl. quarrel, wrangle.

zänkisch adj. ['tsɛŋkiʃ] quarrelsome.

Zäpfchen ['tsɛpfçən] n (-s/-) small peg; anat. uvula.

Zapfen ['tsapfən] 1. m (-s/-). plug; peg, pin; bung (of barrel); pivot; ♀ cone; 2. ♀ v/t. (ge-, h) tap; '~**streich** ✕ m tattoo, retreat, Am. a. taps pl.

'**Zapf|hahn** m tap, Am. faucet; '~**säule** mot. f petrol pump.

zappel|ig adj. ['tsapəliç] fidgety; '~**n** v/i. (ge-, h) struggle; fidget.

zart adj. [tsa:rt] tender; soft; gentle; delicate; '~**fühlend** adj. delicate; 2**gefühl** n (-[e]s/no pl.) delicacy (of feeling).

zärtlich adj. ['tsɛ:rtliç] tender; fond, loving; '2**keit** f 1. (-/no pl.) tenderness; fondness; 2. (-/-en) caress.

Zauber ['tsaubər] m (-s/-) spell, charm, magic (all a. fig.); fig.: enchantment; glamo(u)r; '~**ei** [~'rai] f (-/-en) magic, sorcery; witchcraft; conjuring; '~**er** m (-s/-) sorcerer, magician; conjurer; '~**flöte** f magic flute; '~**formel** f spell; '2**haft** adj. magic(al); fig. enchanting; '~**in** f (-/-nen) sorceress, witch; fig. enchantress; '~**kraft** f magic power; '~**kunststück** n conjuring trick; '2**n** (ge-, h) 1. v/i. practise magic or witchcraft; do conjuring tricks; 2. v/t. conjure; '~**spruch** m spell; '~**stab** m (magic) wand; '~**wort** n (-[e]s/-e) magic word, spell.

zaudern ['tsaudərn] v/i. (ge-, h) hesitate; linger, delay.

Zaum [tsaum] m (-[e]s/=e) bridle; im ~ halten keep in check.

zäumen ['tsɔymən] v/t. (ge-, h) bridle.

'**Zaumzeug** n bridle.

Zaun [tsaun] m (-[e]s/=e) fence; '~**gast** m deadhead; '~**könig** orn. m wren; '~**pfahl** m pale.

Zebra zo. ['tse:bra] n (-s/-s) zebra; '~**streifen** m zebra crossing.

Zech|e ['tsɛçə] f (-/-n) score, reckoning, bill; ⚒ mine; coal-pit, colliery; F die ~ bezahlen foot the bill, F stand treat; '2**en** v/i. (ge-, h) carouse, tipple; '~**gelage** n carousal, carouse; '~**preller** m (-s/-) bilk(er).

Zeh [tse:] m (-[e]s/-en), '~**e** f (-/-n) toe; '~**enspitze** f point or tip of the toe; auf ~n on tiptoe.

zehn adj. [tse:n] ten; '2**er** m (-s/-) ten; coin: F ten-pfennig piece; '~**fach** adj. ['~fax] tenfold; '~**jährig** adj. ['~jɛːriç] ten-year-old, of ten (years); '~**kampf** m sports: decathlon; '~**mal** adv. ten times; ~**te** ['~tə] 1. adj. tenth; 2. 2 † m (-n/-n) tithe; 2**tel** ['~təl] n (-s/-) tenth (part); ~**tens** adv. ['~təns] tenthly.

zehren ['tse:rən] v/i. (ge-, h) make thin; ~ von live on s.th.; fig. live off (the capital); ~ an prey (up)on (one's mind); undermine (one's health).

Zeichen ['tsaiçən] n (-s/-) sign; token; mark; indication, symptom;

signal; zum ~ (gen.) in sign of, as a sign of; '**~block** m drawing-block; '**~brett** n drawing-board; '**~lehrer** m drawing-master; '**~papier** n drawing-paper; '**~setzung** gr. f (/no pl.) punctuation; '**~sprache** f sign-language; '**~stift** m pencil, crayon; '**~trickfilm** m animation, animated cartoon; '**~unterricht** m drawing-lessons pl.

zeichn|en ['tsaɪçnən] (ge-, h) **1.** v/t. draw (plan, etc.); design (pattern); mark; sign; subscribe (sum of money) (zu to); subscribe for (shares); **2.** v/i. draw; sie zeichnet gut she draws well; **2er** m (-s/-) draftsman, draughtsman; designer; subscriber (gen. for shares); **2ung** f (-/-en) drawing; design; illustration; zo. marking (of skin, etc.); subscription.

Zeige|finger ['tsaɪgə-] m forefinger, index (finger); '**2n** (ge-, h) **1.** v/t. show; point out; indicate; demonstrate; sich ~ appear; **2.** v/i.: ~ auf (acc.) point at; ~ nach point to; '**~r** m (-s/-) hand (of clock, etc.); pointer (of dial, etc.); '**~stock** m pointer.

Zeile ['tsaɪlə] f (-/-n) line; row; j-m ein paar ~n schreiben drop s.o. a line or a few lines.   [siskin.|

Zeisig orn. ['tsaɪzɪç] m (-[e]s/-e)

Zeit [tsaɪt] f (-/-en) time; epoch, era, age; period, space (of time); term; freie ~ spare time; mit der ~ in the course of time; von ~ zu ~ from time to time; vor langer ~ long ago, a long time ago; zur ~ (gen.) in the time of; at (the) present; zu meiner ~ in my time; zu s-r ~ in due course (of time); das hat ~ there is plenty of time for that; es ist höchste ~ it is high time; j-m ~ lassen give s.o. time; laß dir ~! take your time!; sich die ~ vertreiben pass the time, kill time.

'**Zeit|abschnitt** m epoch, period; '**~alter** n age; '**~angabe** f exact date and hour; date; '**~aufnahme** phot. f time-exposure; '**~dauer** f length of time, period (of time); '**~enfolge** gr. f sequence of tenses; '**~geist** m (-es/no pl.) spirit of the time(s), zeitgeist; '**2gemäß** adj. modern, up-to-date; '**~genosse** m contemporary; '**2genössisch** adj. ['~gənœsɪʃ] contemporary; '**~geschichte** f contemporary history;

'**~gewinn** m gain of time; '**2ig 1.** adj. early; **2.** adv. on time; '**~karte** f season-ticket, Am. commutation ticket; '**~lang** f: e-e ~ for some time, for a while; '**2lebens** adv. for life, all one's life; '**2lich 1.** adj. temporal; **2.** adv. as to time; '**2los** adj. timeless; '**~lupe** phot. f slow motion; '**~lupenaufnahme** phot.f slow-motion picture; '**2nah** adj. current, up-to-date; '**~ordnung** f chronological order; '**~punkt** m moment; time; date; '**~rafferaufnahme** phot. f time-lapse photography; '**2raubend** adj. time-consuming; pred. a. taking up much time; '**~raum** m space (of time); period; '**~rechnung** f chronology; era; '**~schrift** f journal, periodical, magazine; review; '**~tafel** f chronological table.

'**Zeitung** f (-/-en) (news)paper, journal.

'**Zeitungs|abonnement** n subscription to a paper; '**~artikel** m newspaper article; '**~ausschnitt** m (press or newspaper) cutting, (Am. only) (newspaper) clipping; '**~kiosk** ['~kiɔsk] m (-[e]s/-e) news-stand; '**~notiz** f press item; '**~papier** n newsprint; '**~verkäufer** m newsvendor; news-boy, news-man; '**~wesen** n journalism, the press.

'**Zeit|verlust** m loss of time; '**~verschwendung** f waste of time; '**~vertreib** ['~fɛrtraɪp] m (-[e]s/-e) pastime; zum ~ to pass the time; '**2weilig** adj. ['~vaɪlɪç] temporary; '**2weise** adv. for a time, at times, occasionally; '**~wort** gr. n (-[e]s/ⸯer) verb; '**~zeichen** n time-signal.

Zell|e ['tsɛlə] f (-/-n) cell; '**~stoff** m, **~ulose** ⊕ [~u'lo:zə] f (-/-n) cellulose.

Zelt [tsɛlt] n (-[e]s/-e) tent; '**2en** v/i. (ge-, h) camp; '**~leinwand** f canvas; '**~platz** m camping-ground.

Zement [tse'mɛnt] m (-[e]s/-e) cement; **2ieren** [~'ti:rən] v/t. (no -ge-, h) cement.   [(a. fig.).|

Zenit [tse'ni:t]m (-[e]s/no pl.) zenith

zens|ieren [tsɛn'zi:rən] v/t. (no -ge-, h) censor (book, etc.); at school: mark, Am. a. grade; **2or** ['~ɔr] m (-s/-en) censor; **2ur** [~'zu:r] f **1.** (-/no pl.) censorship; **2.** (-/-en) at school: mark, Am. a. grade;

Z

(school) report, *Am.* report card.

Zentimeter [tsɛnti'-] *n, m* centimet|re, *Am.* -er.

Zentner ['tsɛntnər] *m* (-*s*/-) (*Brt. appr.*) hundredweight.

zentral *adj.* [tsɛn'trɑːl] central; **2e** *f* (-/-*n*) central office; *teleph.* (telephone) exchange, *Am. a.* central; **2heizung** *f* central heating.

Zentrum ['tsɛntrum] *n* (-*s*/*Zentren*) cent|re, *Am.* -er.

Zepter ['tsɛptər] *n* (-*s*/-) scept|re, [*Am.* -er.]

zer|beißen [tsɛr'-] *v/t.* (*irr. beißen, no* -*ge*-, *h*) bite to pieces; **~'bersten** *v/i.* (*irr. bersten, no* -*ge*-, *sein*) burst asunder.

zer'brech|en (*irr. brechen, no* -*ge*-) **1.** *v/t.* (*h*) break (to pieces); *sich den Kopf* ~ rack one's brains; **2.** *v/i.* (*sein*) break; **~lich** *adj.* breakable, fragile.

zer|'bröckeln *v/t.* (*h*) *and v/i.* (*sein*) (*no* -*ge*-) crumble; **~'drücken** *v/t.* (*no* -*ge*-, *h*) crush; crease (*dress*).

Zeremon|ie [tseremo'niː, ~'moːnjə] *f* (-/-*n*) ceremony; **2iell** *adj.* [~o'njɛl] ceremonial; **~iell** [~o'njɛl] *n* (-*s*/-*e*) ceremonial.

zer'fahren *adj. road*: rutted; *p.*: flighty, giddy; scatter-brained; absent-minded.

Zer'fall *m* (-[*e*]*s*/*no pl.*) ruin, decay; disintegration; **2en** *v/i.* (*irr. fallen, no* -*ge*-, *sein*) fall to pieces, decay; disintegrate; *in mehrere Teile* ~ fall into several parts.

zer|'fetzen *v/t.* (*no* -*ge*-, *h*) tear in *or* to pieces; **~'fleischen** *v/t.* (*no* -*ge*-, *h*) mangle; lacerate; **~'fließen** *v/i.* (*irr. fließen, no* -*ge*-, *sein*) melt (away); *ink, etc.*: run; **~'fressen** *v/t.* (*irr. fressen, no* -*ge*-, *h*) eat away; ⚗ corrode; **~'gehen** *v/i.* (*irr. gehen, no* -*ge*-, *sein*) melt, dissolve; **~'gliedern** *v/t.* (*no* -*ge*-, *h*) dismember; *anat.* dissect; *fig.* analy|se, *Am.* -ze; **~'hacken** *v/t.* (*no* -*ge*-, *h*) cut (in)to pieces; mince; chop (up) (*wood, meat*); **~'kauen** *v/t.* (*no* -*ge*-, *h*) chew; **~'kleinern** *v/t.* (*no* -*ge*-, *h*) mince (*meat*); chop up (*wood*); grind.

zer'knirsch|t *adj.* contrite; **2ung** *f* (-/⚒ -*en*) contrition.

zer|'knittern *v/t.* (*no* -*ge*-, *h*) (c)rumple, wrinkle, crease; **~'knüllen** *v/t.* (*no* -*ge*-, *h*) crumple up (*sheet of paper*); **~'kratzen** *v/t.* (*no* -*ge*-, *h*) scratch; **~'krümeln** *v/t.* (*no* -*ge*-, *h*) crumble; **~'lassen** *v/t.* (*irr. lassen, no* -*ge*-, *h*) melt; **~'legen** *v/t.* (*no* -*ge*-, *h*) take apart *or* to pieces; carve (*joint*); ⚗, *gr.*, *fig.* analy|se, *Am.* -ze; **~'lumpt** *adj.* ragged, tattered; **~'mahlen** *v/t.* (*irr. mahlen, no* -*ge*-, *h*) grind; **~malmen** [~'malmən] *v/t.* (*no* -*ge*-, *h*) crush; crunch; **~'mürben** *v/t.* (*no* -*ge*-, *h*) wear down *or* out; **~'platzen** *v/i.* (*no* -*ge*-, *sein*) burst; explode; **~'quetschen** *v/t.* (*no* -*ge*-, *h*) crush, squash; mash (*esp. potatoes*).

Zerrbild ['tsɛr-] *n* caricature.

zer|'reiben *v/t.* (*irr. reiben, no* -*ge*-, *h*) rub to powder, grind down, pulverize; **~'reißen** (*irr. reißen, no* -*ge*-) **1.** *v/t.* (*h*) tear, rip up; *in Stücke* ~ tear to pieces; **2.** *v/i.* (*sein*) tear; *rope, string*: break.

zerren ['tsɛrən] (*ge*-, *h*) **1.** *v/t.* tug, pull; drag; ⚕ strain; **2.** *v/i.*: ~ *an* (*dat.*) pull at.

zer'rinnen *v/i.* (*irr. rinnen, no* -*ge*-, *sein*) melt away; *fig.* vanish.

'Zerrung ⚕ *f* (-/-*en*) strain.

zer|rütten [tsɛr'rytən] *v/t.* (*no* -*ge*-, *h*) derange, unsettle; disorganize; ruin, shatter (*one's health or nerves*); wreck (*marriage*); **~'sägen** *v/t.* (*no* -*ge*-, *h*) saw up; **~schellen** [~'ʃɛlən] *v/i.* (*no* -*ge*-, *sein*) be dashed *or* smashed; ⚓ be wrecked; ✈ crash; **~'schlagen 1.** *v/t.* (*irr. schlagen, no* -*ge*-, *h*) break *or* smash (to pieces); *sich* ~ come to nothing; **2.** *adj.* battered; *fig.* knocked up; **~'schmettern** *v/t.* (*no* -*ge*-, *h*) smash, dash, shatter; **~'schneiden** *v/t.* (*irr. schneiden, no* -*ge*-, *h*) cut in two; cut up, cut to pieces.

zer'setz|en *v/t. and v/refl.* (*no* -*ge*-, *h*) decompose; **2ung** *f* (-/⚒ -*en*) decomposition.

zer|'spalten *v/t.* ([*irr. spalten,*] *no* -*ge*-, *h*) cleave, split; **~'splittern** (*no* -*ge*-) **1.** *v/t.* (*h*) split (up), splinter; fritter away (*one's energy, etc.*); **2.** *v/i.* (*sein*) split (up), splinter; **~'sprengen** *v/t.* (*no* -*ge*-, *h*) burst (asunder); disperse (*crowd*); **~'springen** *v/i.* (*irr. springen, no* -*ge*-, *sein*) burst; *glass*: crack; *mein Kopf zerspringt mir* I've got a splitting headache; **~'stampfen** *v/t.* (*no* -*ge*-, *h*) crush; pound.

zer'stäub|en v/t. (no -ge-, h) spray; **2er** m (-s/-) sprayer, atomizer.

zer'stör|en v/t. (no -ge-, h) destroy; **2er** m (-s/-) destroyer (a. ♣); **2ung** f destruction.

zer'streu|en v/t. (no -ge-, h) disperse, scatter; dissipate (doubt, etc.); fig. divert; sich ~ disperse, scatter; fig. amuse o.s.; **~t** fig. adj. absent(-minded); **2theit** f (-/~-en) absent-mindedness; **2ung** f **1.** (-/-en) dispersion; diversion, amusement; **2.** phys. (-/no pl.) dispersion (of light).

zerstückeln [tsɛr'ʃtykəln] v/t. (no -ge-, h) cut up, cut (in)to pieces; dismember (body, etc.).

zer'teilen v/t. and v/refl. (no -ge-, h) divide (in acc. into); **~'trennen** v/t. (no -ge-, h) rip (up) (dress); **~'treten** v/t. (irr. treten, no -ge-, h) tread down; crush; tread or stamp out (fire); **~'trümmern** v/t. (no -ge-, h) smash.

Zerwürfnis [tsɛr'vyrfnis] n (-ses/ -se) dissension, discord.

Zettel ['tsetəl] m (-s/-) slip (of paper), scrap of paper; note; ticket; label, sticker; tag; s. Anschlagzettel; s. Theaterzettel; **~-kartei** f, **~kasten** m card index.

Zeug [tsɔʏk] n (-[e]s/-e) stuff (a. fig. contp.), material; cloth; tools pl.; things pl.

Zeuge ['tsɔʏgə] m (-n/-n) witness; **2n** (ge-, h) **1.** v/i. witness; ⚖ give evidence; für (gegen, von) et. ~ testify for (against, of) s.th.; ~ von be evidence of, bespeak (courage, etc.); **2.** v/t. beget.

Zeugin ['tsɔʏgin] f (-/-nen) (female) witness.

Zeugnis ['tsɔʏknis] n (-ses/-se) ⚖ testimony, evidence; certificate; (school) report, Am. report card.

Zeugung ['tsɔʏguŋ] f (-/-en) procreation; **2sfähig** adj. capable of begetting; **~skraft** f generative power; **2sunfähig** adj. ['tsɔʏguŋs?-] impotent.

Zick|lein zo. ['tsiklaɪn] n (-s/-) kid; **~zack** ['~tsak] m (-[e]s/-e) zigzag; im ~ fahren etc. zigzag.

Ziege zo. ['tsi:gə] f (-/-n) (she-)goat, nanny(-goat).

Ziegel ['tsi:gəl] m (-s/-) brick; tile (of roof); **~dach** n tiled roof; **~ei** ['~laɪ] f (-/-en) brickworks sg., pl., brickyard; **~stein** m brick.

'Ziegen|bock zo. m he-goat; **'~fell** n goatskin; **'~hirt** m goatherd; **'~-leder** n kid(-leather); **'~peter** ♫ m (-s/-) mumps.

Ziehbrunnen ['tsi:-] m draw-well.

ziehen ['tsi:ən] (irr., ge-) **1.** v/t. (h) pull, draw; draw (line, weapon, lots, conclusion, etc.); drag; ♀ cultivate; zo. breed; take off (hat); dig (ditch); draw, extract (tooth); ⊞ extract (root of number); Blasen ~ ⚕ raise blisters; e-n Vergleich ~ draw or make a comparison; j-n ins Vertrauen ~ take s.o. into one's confidence; in Erwägung ~ take into consideration; in die Länge ~ draw out; fig. protract; Nutzen ~ aus derive profit or benefit from; an sich ~ draw to one; Aufmerksamkeit etc. auf sich ~ attract attention, etc.; et. nach sich ~ entail or involve s.th.; **2.** v/i. (h) pull (an dat. at); chimney, cigar, etc.: draw; puff (an e-r Zigarre at a cigar); tea: infuse, draw; play: draw (large audiences); F ✝ goods: draw (customers), take; es zieht there is a draught, Am. there is a draft; **3.** v/i. (sein) move, go; march; (re)move (nach to); birds: migrate; **4.** v/refl. (h) extend, stretch, run; wood: warp; sich in die Länge ~ drag on.

'Zieh|harmonika ♩ f accordion; **'~ung** f (-/-en) drawing (of lots).

Ziel [tsi:l] n (-[e]s/-e) aim (a. fig.); mark; sports: winning-post, goal (a. fig.); target; ⚔ objective; destination (of voyage); fig. end, purpose, target, object(ive); term; sein ~ erreichen gain one's end(s pl.); über das ~ hinausschießen overshoot the mark; zum ~e führen succeed, be successful; sich zum ~ setzen zu inf. aim at ger., Am. aim to inf.; **'~band** n sports: tape; **2-bewußt** adj. purposeful; **2en** v/i. (ge-, h) (take) aim (auf acc. at); **'~fernrohr** n telescopic sight; **2-los** adj. aimless, purposeless; **'~-scheibe** f target, butt; ~ des Spottes butt or target (of derision); **2-strebig** adj. purposive.

ziemlich ['tsi:mliç] **1.** adj. fair, tolerable; considerable; **2.** adv.

pretty, fairly, tolerably, rather; about.

Zier [tsi:r] *f* (-/no pl.), **~de** ['~də] *f* (-/-n) ornament; *fig. a.* hono(u)r (für to); **2en** *v/t.* (ge-, h) ornament, adorn; decorate; *sich ~* be affected; *esp. of woman:* be prudish; refuse; **2lich** *adj.* delicate; neat; graceful, elegant; **~lichkeit** *f* (-/~-en) delicacy; neatness; gracefulness, elegance; **~pflanze** *f* ornamental plant.

Ziffer ['tsifər] *f* (-/-n) figure, digit; **~blatt** *n* dial(-plate), face.

Zigarette [tsiga'retə] *f* (-/-n) cigaret(te); **~nautomat** [~n⁹-] *m* cigarette slot-machine; **~netui** [~n⁹-] *n* cigarette-case; **~nspitze** *f* cigarette-holder; **~nstummel** *m* stub, *Am. a.* butt.

Zigarre [tsi'garə] *f* (-/-n) cigar.

Zigeuner [tsi'gɔynər] *m* (-s/-), **~in** *f* (-/-nen) gipsy, gypsy.

Zimmer ['tsimər] *n* (-s/-) room; apartment; **~antenne** *f radio, etc.:* indoor aerial, *Am. a.* indoor antenna; **~einrichtung** *f* furniture; **~flucht** *f* suite (of rooms); **~mädchen** *n* chamber-maid; **~mann** *m* (-[e]s/Zimmerleute) carpenter; **2n** (ge-, h) **1.** *v/t.* carpenter; *fig.* frame; **2.** *v/i.* carpenter; **~pflanze** *f* indoor plant; **~vermieterin** *f* (-/-nen) landlady. [prudish; affected.]

zimperlich *adj.* ['tsimpərliç] prim;]

Zimt [tsimt] *m* (-[e]s/-e) cinnamon.

Zink [tsiŋk] *n* (-[e]s/no pl.) zinc; **~blech** *n* sheet zinc.

Zinke ['tsiŋkə] *f* (-/-n) prong; tooth (of comb or fork); **~n** *m* (-s/-) *s. Zinke.*

Zinn [tsin] *n* (-[e]s/no pl.) tin.

Zinne ['tsinə] *f* (-/-n) pinnacle; battlement.

Zinnober [tsi'no:bər] *m* (-s/-) cinnabar; **2rot** *adj.* vermilion.

Zins [tsins] *m* (-es/-en) rent; tribute; *mst ~en pl.* interest; **~en tragen** yield *or* bear interest; **2bringend** *adj.* bearing interest; **~eszins** ['~zɛs-] *m* compound interest; **2frei** *adj.* rent-free; free of interest; **~fuß** *m*, **~satz** *m* rate of interest.

Zipf|el ['tsipfəl] *m* (-s/-) tip, point, end; corner (of handkerchief, etc.); lappet (of garment); **2elig** *adj.* having points *or* ends; **~elmütze** *f* jelly-bag cap; nightcap.

Zirkel ['tsirkəl] *m* (-s/-) circle (a. fig.); ⚬ (ein a pair of) compasses *pl. or* dividers *pl.*

zirkulieren [tsirku'li:rən] *v/i.* (no -ge-, h) circulate.

Zirkus ['tsirkus] *m* (-/-se) circus.

zirpen ['tsirpən] *v/i.* (ge-, h) chirp, cheep.

zisch|eln ['tsiʃəln] *v/t. and v/i.* (ge-, h) whisper; **~en** *v/i.* (ge-, h) hiss; whiz(z).

ziselieren [tsize'li:rən] *v/t.* (no -ge-, h) chase.

Zit|at [tsi'tɑ:t] *n* (-[e]s/-e) quotation; **2ieren** [~'ti:rən] *v/t.* (no -ge-, h) summon; quote.

Zitrone [tsi'tro:nə] *f* (-/-n) lemon; **~nlimonade** *f* lemonade; lemon squash; **~npresse** *f* lemon-squeezer; **~nsaft** *m* lemon juice.

zittern ['tsitərn] *v/i.* (ge-, h) tremble, shake (vor *dat.* with).

zivil [tsi'vi:l] **1.** *adj.* civil; civilian; *price:* reasonable; **2.** 2 *n* (-s/no pl.) civilians *pl.*; *s. Zivilkleidung*; **2bevölkerung** *f* civilian population, civilians *pl.*; **2isation** [~liza'tsjo:n] *f* (-/~-en) civilization; **~isieren** [~ili'zi:rən] *v/t.* (no -ge-, h) civilize; **2ist** [~i'list] *m* (-en/-en) civilian; **2kleidung** *f* civilian *or* plain clothes *pl.*

Zofe ['tso:fə] *f* (-/-n) lady's maid.

zog [tso:k] *pret. of ziehen.*

zögern ['tsø:gərn] **1.** *v/i.* (ge-, h) hesitate; linger; delay; **2.** 2 *n* (-s/no pl.) hesitation; delay.

Zögling ['tsø:kliŋ] *m* (-s/-e) pupil.

Zoll [tsɔl] *m* **1.** (-[e]s/-) inch; **2.** (-[e]s/~e) customs *pl.*, duty; *the* Customs *pl.*; **~abfertigung** *f* customs clearance; **~amt** *n* custom-house; **~beamte** *m* customs officer; **~behörde** *f the* Customs *pl.*; **~erklärung** *f* customs declaration; **2frei** *adj.* duty-free; **~kontrolle** *f* customs examination; **2pflichtig** *adj.* liable to duty; **~stock** *m* foot-rule; **~tarif** *m* tariff.

Zone ['tso:nə] *f* (-/-n) zone.

Zoo [tso:] *m* (-[s]/-s) zoo.

Zoolog|e [tso⁹o'lo:gə] *m* (-n/-n) zoologist; **~ie** [~o'gi:] *f* (-/no pl.) zoology; **2isch** *adj.* [~'lo:giʃ] zoological.

Zopf [tsɔpf] *m* (-[e]s/~e) plait, tress; pigtail; *alter ~* antiquated ways *pl. or* custom.

Z

Zorn [tsɔrn] *m* (-[e]s/*no pl.*) anger; '**2ig** *adj.* angry (*auf* j-n with s.o.; *auf* et. at s.th.).

Zote ['tso:tə] *f* (-/-n) filthy *or* smutty joke, obscenity.

Zott|el ['tsɔtəl] *f* (-/-n) tuft (of hair); tassel; '**2ig** *adj.* shaggy.

zu [tsu:] **1.** *prp.* (*dat.*) direction: to, towards, up to; at, in; on; in addition to, along with; *purpose:* for; ~ *Beginn* at the beginning *or* outset; ~ *Weihnachten* at Christmas; *zum ersten Mal* for the first time; ~ e-m ... *Preise* at a ... price; ~ *meinem Erstaunen* to my surprise; ~ *Tausenden* by thousands; ~ *Wasser* by water; ~ *zweien* by twos; *zum Beispiel* for example; **2.** *adv.* too; *direction:* towards, to; F closed, shut; *with inf.:* to; *ich habe* ~ *arbeiten* I have to work.

'**zubauen** *v/t.* (*sep.*, -ge-, h) build up *or* in; block.

Zubehör ['tsu:bəhø:r] *n*, *m* (-[e]s/-e) appurtenances *pl.*, fittings *pl.*, Am. F fixings *pl.*; *esp.* ⊕ accessories *pl.*

'**zubereit|en** *v/t.* (*sep.*, *no* -ge-, h) prepare; '**2ung** *f* preparation.

'**zu|billigen** *v/t.* (*sep.*, -ge-, h) grant; '**binden** *v/t.* (*irr. binden*, *sep.*, -ge-, h) tie up; '**blinzeln** *v/i.* (*sep.*, -ge-, h) wink at s.o.; '**bringen** *v/t.* (*irr. bringen*, *sep.*, -ge-, h) pass, spend (*time*).

Zucht [tsuxt] *f* **1.** (-/*no pl.*) discipline; breeding, rearing; *rearing of bees, etc.*: culture; ♀ cultivation; **2.** (-/-en) breed; race; '**bulle** *zo.* *m* bull (for breeding).

zücht|en ['tsʏçtən] *v/t.* (ge-, h) breed (*animals*); grow, cultivate (*plants*); '**2er** *m* (-s/-) breeder (*of animals*); grower (*of plants*).

'**Zucht|haus** *n* penitentiary; *punishment:* penal servitude; **häusler** ['hɔʏslər] *m* (-s/-) convict; '**hengst** *zo.* *m* stud-horse, stallion.

züchtig *adj.* ['tsʏçtɪç] chaste, modest; '**en** [''gən] *v/t.* (ge-, h) flog.

'**zucht|los** *adj.* undisciplined; '**2losigkeit** *f* (-/*no pl.*) want of discipline; '**2stute** *zo.* *f* brood-mare.

zucken ['tsukən] *v/i.* (ge-, h) jerk; move convulsively, twitch (*all:* mit et. s.th.); *with pain:* wince; *lightning:* flash.

zücken ['tsʏkən] *v/t.* (ge-, h) draw (*sword*); F pull out (*purse, pencil*).

Zucker ['tsukər] *m* (-s/*no pl.*) sugar; '**dose** *f* sugar-basin, Am. sugar bowl; '**erbse** ♀ *f* green pea; '**guß** *m* icing, frosting; '**hut** *m* sugarloaf; '**2ig** *adj.* sugary; '**krank** *adj.* diabetic; '**2n** *v/t.* (ge-, h) sugar; '**rohr** ♀ *n* sugar-cane; '**rübe** ♀ *f* sugar-beet; '**2'süß** *adj.* (as) sweet as sugar; '**wasser** *n* sugared water; '**zange** *f* (e-e a pair of) sugar-tongs *pl.*

zuckrig *adj.* ['tsukrɪç] sugary.

'**Zuckung** ♀ *f* (-/-en) convulsion.

'**zudecken** *v/t.* (*sep.*, -ge-, h) cover (up).

zudem *adv.* [tsu'de:m] besides, moreover.

'**zu|drehen** *v/t.* (*sep.*, -ge-, h) turn off (*tap*); j-m *den Rücken* ~ turn one's back on s.o.; '**dringlich** *adj.* importunate, obtrusive; '**drücken** *v/t.* (*sep.*, -ge-, h) close, shut; '**erkennen** *v/t.* (*irr. kennen*, *sep.*, *no* -ge-, h) award (a. ⚖); adjudge (*dat.* to) (a. ⚖).

zuerst *adv.* [tsu'-] first (of all); at first; *er kam* ~ *an* he was the first to arrive.

'**zufahr|en** *v/i.* (*irr. fahren*, *sep.*, -ge-, sein) drive on; ~ *auf* (*acc.*) drive to (-wards); *fig.* rush at s.o.; '**2t** *f* approach; drive, Am. driveway; '**2tsstraße** *f* approach (road).

Zufall *m* chance, accident; *durch* ~ by chance, by accident; '**2en** *v/i.* (*irr. fallen*, *sep.*, -ge-, sein) *eyes:* be closing (*with sleep*); *door:* shut (of) itself; j-m ~ fall to s.o.('s share).

'**zufällig 1.** *adj.* accidental; *attr.* chance; casual; **2.** *adv.* accidentally, by chance.

'**zufassen** *v/i.* (*sep.*, -ge-, h) seize (hold of) s.th.; (mit) ~ lend *or* give a hand.

'**Zuflucht** *f* (-/✎ ⸗e) refuge, shelter, resort; s-e ~ *nehmen zu* have recourse to s.th., take refuge in s.th.

'**Zufluß** *m* afflux; influx (a. ⸸); affluent, tributary (*of river*); ⸸ supply.

'**zuflüstern** *v/t.* (*sep.*, -ge-, h): j-m et. ~ whisper s.th. to s.o.

zufolge *prp.* (*gen.*; *dat.*) [tsu'fɔlgə] according to.

zufrieden *adj.* [tsu'-] content(ed), satisfied; '**2heit** *f* (-/*no pl.*) contentment, satisfaction; '**lassen** *v/t.* (*irr. lassen*, *sep.*, -ge-, h) let s.o. alone;

~stellen v/t. (sep., -ge-, h) satisfy; **~stellend** adj. satisfactory.

'zu|frieren v/i. (irr. frieren, sep., -ge-, sein) freeze up or over; **'~fügen** v/t. (sep., -ge-, h) add; do, cause; inflict (wound, etc.) (j-m [up]on s.th.); **²fuhr** ['~fuːr] f (-/-en) supply; supplies pl.; influx; **'~führen** v/t. (sep., -ge-, h) carry, lead, bring; ⊕ feed; supply (a. ⊕).

Zug [tsuːk] m (-[e]s/=e) draw(ing), pull(ing); ⊕ traction; ✗ expedition, campaign; procession; migration (of birds); drift (of clouds); range (of mountains); 🚂 train; feature; trait (of character); bent, tendency, trend; draught, Am. draft (of air); at chess: move; drinking: draught, Am. draft; at cigarette, etc.: puff.

'Zu|gabe f addition; extra; thea. encore; **'~gang** m entrance; access; approach; **²gänglich** adj. ['~gɛnliç] accessible (für to); **²geben** v/t. (irr. geben, sep., -ge-, h) add; fig.: allow; confess; admit.

zugegen adj. [tsu'-] present (bei at.).

'zugehen v/i. (irr. gehen, sep., -ge-, sein) door, etc.: close, shut; p. move on, walk faster; happen; auf j-n ~ go up to s.o., move or walk towards s.o.

'Zugehörigkeit f (-/no pl.) membership (zu to) (society, etc.); belonging (to).

Zügel ['tsyːgəl] m (-s/-) rein; bridle (a. fig.); **²los** adj. unbridled; fig.: unrestrained; licentious; **²n** v/t. (ge-, h) rein (in); fig. bridle, check.

'Zuge|ständnis n concession; **²-stehen** v/t. (irr. stehen, sep., -ge-, h) concede.

'zugetan adj. attached (dat. to).

'Zugführer 🚂 m guard, Am. conductor. [-ge-, h) add.]

'zugießen v/t. (irr. gießen, sep.,)

zug|ig adj. ['tsuːgiç] draughty, Am. drafty; **²kraft** ['~k-] f ⊕ traction; fig. attraction, draw, appeal; **~kräftig** adj. ['~k-]: ~ sein be a draw.

zugleich adv. [tsu'-] at the same time; together.

'Zug|luft f (-/no pl.) draught, Am. draft; **'~maschine** f traction-engine, tractor; **~pflaster** 🇫 n blister.

table: help o.s.; lend a hand; **'~griff** m grip, clutch.

zugrunde adv. [tsu'grundə]: ~ gehen perish; ~ richten ruin.

'Zugtier n draught animal, Am. draft animal.

zu|gunsten prp. (gen.) [tsu'gunstən] in favo(u)r of; **~'gute** adv.: j-m et. ~ halten give s.o. credit for s.th.; ~ kommen be for the benefit (dat.).

'Zugvogel m bird of passage. [of.)]

'zuhalten v/t. (irr. halten, sep., -ge-, h) hold (door) to; sich die Ohren ~ stop one's ears. [home.)]

Zuhause [tsu'hauzə] n (-/no pl.))

'zu|heilen v/i. (sep., -ge-, sein) heal up, skin over; **'~hören** v/i. (sep., -ge-, h) listen (dat. to).

'Zuhörer m hearer, listener; ~ pl. audience; **'~schaft** f (-/🇫-en) audience.

'zu|jubeln v/i. (sep., -ge-, h) cheer; **'~kleben** v/t. (sep., -ge-, h) paste or glue up; gum (letter) down; **'~knallen** v/t. (sep., -ge-, h) bang, slam (door, etc.); **'~knöpfen** v/t. (sep., -ge-, h) button (up); **'~kommen** v/i. (irr. kommen, sep., -ge-, sein): auf j-n ~ come up to s.o.; j-m ~ be due to s.o.; j-m et. ~ lassen let s.o. have s.th.; send s.o. s.th.; **'~korken** v/t. (sep., -ge-, h) cork (up).

Zu|kunft ['tsuːkunft] f (-/no pl.) future; gr. future (tense); **²künftig** 1. adj. future; ~er Vater father-to-be; 2. adv. in future.

'zu|lächeln v/i. (sep., -ge-, h) smile at or (up)on; **'²lage** f extra pay, increase; rise, Am. raise (in salary or wages); **'~langen** v/i. (sep., -ge-, h) at table: help o.s.; **'~lassen** v/t. (irr. lassen, sep., -ge-, h) leave (door) shut; keep closed; fig.: admit s.o.; license; allow, suffer; admit of (only one interpretation, etc.); **'~lässig** adj. admissible, allowable; **'²lassung** f (-/-en) admission; permission; licen|ce, Am. -se.

'zulegen v/t. (sep., -ge-, h) add; F sich et. ~ get o.s. s.th.

zuleide adv. [tsu'laɪdə]: j-m et. ~ tun do s.o. harm, harm or hurt s.o.

'zuleiten v/t. (sep., -ge-, h) let in (water, etc.); conduct to; pass on to s.o.

zu|letzt adv. [tsu'-] finally, at last; er kam ~ an he was the last to arrive; **~'liebe** adv.: j-m ~ for s.o.'s sake.

zum prp. [tsum] = zu dem.

'**zumachen** v/t. (sep., -ge-, h) close, shut; button (up) (coat); fasten.

zumal cj. [tsu'-] especially, particularly. [up.]

'**zumauern** v/t. (sep., -ge-, h) wall)

zumut|en ['tsu:mu:tən] v/t. (sep., -ge-, h): j-m et. ~ expect s.th. of s.o.; sich zuviel ~ overtask o.s., overtax one's strength, etc.; '**Qung** f (-/-en) exacting demand, exaction; fig. impudence.

zunächst [tsu'-] **1.** prp. (dat.) next to; **2.** adv. first of all; for the present.

'**zu|nageln** v/t. (sep., -ge-, h) nail up; '**~nähen** v/t. (sep., -ge-, h) sew up; **Qnahme** ['tsu:na:mə] f (-/-n) increase, growth; '**Qname** m surname.

zünden ['tsyndən] v/i. (ge-, h) kindle; esp. mot. ignite; fig. arouse enthusiasm.

Zünd|holz ['tsynt-] n match; '**~kerze** mot. f spark(ing)-plug, Am. spark plug; '**~schlüssel** mot. m ignition key; '**~schnur** f fuse; '**~stoff** fig. m fuel; '**~ung** mot. ['~duŋ] f (-/-en) ignition.

'**zunehmen** v/i. (irr. nehmen, sep., -ge-, h) increase (an dat. in); grow; put on weight; moon: wax; days: grow longer.

'**zuneig|en** (sep., -ge-, h) **1.** v/i. incline to(wards); **2.** v/refl. incline to(wards); sich dem Ende ~ draw to a close; **Qung** f (-/~ -en) affection.

Zunft [tsunft] f (-/-̈e) guild, corporation.

Zunge ['tsuŋə] f (-/-n) tongue.

züngeln ['tsyŋəln] v/i. (ge-, h) play with its tongue; flame: lick.

'**zungen|fertig** adj. voluble; '**Qfertigkeit** f (-/no pl.) volubility; '**Qspitze** f tip of the tongue.

zunichte adv. [tsu'niçtə]: ~ machen or werden bring or come to nothing.

zunicken v/i. (sep., -ge-, h) nod to.

zu|nutze adv. [tsu'nutsə]: sich et. ~ machen turn s.th. to account, utilize s.th.; '**~oberst** adv. at the top, uppermost.

zupfen ['tsupfən] (ge-, h) **1.** v/t. pull, tug, twitch; **2.** v/i. pull, tug, twitch (all: an dat. at).

zur prp. [tsu:r] = zu der.

'**zurechnungsfähig** adj. of sound mind; **tt** responsible; '**Qkeit tt** f (-/no pl.) responsibility.

zurecht|finden [tsu'-] v/refl. (irr. finden, sep., -ge-, h) find one's way; **~kommen** v/i. (irr. kommen, sep., -ge-, sein) arrive in time; ~ (mit) get on (well) (with); manage s.th.; **~legen** v/t. (sep., -ge-, h) arrange; sich e-e Sache ~ think s.th. out; **~machen** F v/t. (sep., -ge-, h) get ready, prepare, Am. F fix; adapt (für to, for purpose); sich ~ of woman: make (o.s.) up; **~weisen** v/t. (irr. weisen, sep., -ge-, h) reprimand; **Qweisung** f reprimand.

'**zu|reden** v/i. (sep., -ge-, h): j-m ~ try to persuade s.o.; encourage s.o.; '**~reiten** v/t. (irr. reiten, sep., -ge-, h) break in; '**~riegeln** v/t. (sep., -ge-, h) bolt (up).

zürnen ['tsyrnən] v/i. (ge-, h) be angry (j-m with s.o.).

zurück adv. [tsu'ryk] back; backward(s); behind; **~behalten** v/t. (irr. halten, sep., no -ge-, h) keep back, retain; **~bekommen** v/t. (irr. kommen, sep., no -ge-, h) get back; **~bleiben** v/i. (irr. bleiben, sep., -ge-, sein) remain or stay behind; fall behind, lag; **~blicken** v/i. (sep., -ge-, h) look back; **~bringen** v/t. (irr. bringen, sep., -ge-, h) bring back; **~datieren** v/t. (sep., no -ge-, h) date back, antedate; **~drängen** v/t. (sep., -ge-, h) push back; fig. repress; **~erobern** v/t. (sep., no -ge-, h) reconquer; **~erstatten** v/t. (sep., no -ge-, h) restore, return; refund (expenses); **~fahren** (irr. fahren, sep., -ge-) **1.** v/i. (sein) drive back; fig. start; **2.** v/t. (h) drive back; **~fordern** v/t. (sep., -ge-, h) reclaim; **~führen** v/t. (sep., -ge-, h) lead back; ~ auf (acc.) reduce to (rule, etc.); refer to (cause, etc.); **~geben** v/t. (irr. geben, sep., -ge-, h) give back, return, restore; **~gehen** v/i. (irr. gehen, sep., -ge-, sein) go back; return; **~gezogen** adj. retired; **~greifen** fig. v/i. (irr. greifen, sep., -ge-, h): ~ auf (acc.) fall back (up)on; **~halten** (irr. halten, sep., -ge-) **1.** v/t. hold back; **2.** v/i.: ~ mit keep back; **~haltend** adj. reserved; **Qhaltung** f (-/~ -en) reserve; **~kehren** v/i. (sep., -ge-, sein) return; **~kommen**

Z

v/i. (irr. kommen, sep., -ge-, sein) come back; return (fig. auf acc. to); **~lassen** *v/t.* (irr. lassen, sep., -ge-, h) leave (behind); **~legen** *v/t.* (sep., -ge-, h) lay aside; cover (distance, way); **~nehmen** *v/t.* (irr. nehmen, sep., -ge-, h) take back; withdraw, retract (words, etc.); **~prallen** *v/i.* (sep., -ge-, sein) rebound; start; **~rufen** *v/t.* (irr. rufen, sep., -ge-, h) call back; sich ins Gedächtnis ~ recall; **~schicken** *v/t.* (sep., -ge-, h) send back; **~schlagen** (irr. schlagen, sep., -ge-, h) **1.** *v/t.* drive (ball) back; repel (enemy); turn down (blanket); **2.** *v/i.* strike back; **~schrecken** *v/i.* (sep., -ge-, sein) **1.** (irr. schrecken) shrink back (vor dat. from spectacle, etc.); **2.** shrink (vor dat. from work, etc.); **~setzen** *v/t.* (sep., -ge-, h) put back; fig. slight, neglect; **~stellen** *v/t.* (sep., -ge-, h) put back (a. clock); fig. defer, postpone; **~strahlen** *v/t.* (sep., -ge-, h) reflect; **~streifen** *v/t.* (sep., -ge-, h) turn or tuck up (sleeve); **~treten** *v/i.* (irr. treten, sep., -ge-, sein) step or stand back; fig.: recede; resign; withdraw; **~weichen** *v/i.* (irr. weichen, sep., -ge-, sein) fall back; recede (a. fig.); **~weisen** *v/t.* (irr. weisen, sep., -ge-, h) decline, reject; repel (attack); **~zahlen** *v/t.* (sep., -ge-, h) pay back (a. fig.); **~ziehen** (irr. ziehen, sep., -ge-, h) **1.** *v/t.* (h) draw back; fig. withdraw; sich ~ retire, withdraw; ✗ retreat; **2.** *v/i.* (sein) move or march back.

'**Zuruf** *m* call; '**~en** *v/t.* (irr. rufen, sep., -ge-, h) call (out), shout (j-m et. s.th. to s.o.).

'**Zusage** *f* promise; assent; '**~en** (sep., -ge-, h) **1.** *v/t.* promise; **2.** *v/i.* promise to come; j-m ~ food, etc.: agree with s.o.; accept s.o.'s invitation; suit s.o.

zusammen *adv.* [tsu'zamən] together; at the same time; alles ~ (all) in all; ~ betragen amount to, total (up to); **2arbeit** *f* (-/no pl.) co-operation; team-work; **~arbeiten** *v/i.* (sep., -ge-, h) work together; co-operate; **~beißen** *v/t.* (irr. beißen, sep., -ge-, h): die Zähne ~ set one's teeth; **~brechen** *v/i.* (irr. brechen, sep., -ge-, sein) break down; collapse; **2bruch** *m* breakdown; collapse; **~drücken** *v/t.*

(sep., -ge-, h) compress, press together; **~fahren** fig. *v/i.* (irr. fahren, sep., -ge-, sein) start (bei at; vor dat. with); **~fallen** *v/i.* (irr. fallen, sep., -ge-, sein) fall in, collapse; coincide; **~falten** *v/t.* (sep., -ge-, h) fold up; **~fassen** *v/t.* (sep., -ge-, h) summarize, sum up; **2fassung** *f* (-/-en) summary; **~fügen** *v/t.* (sep., -ge-, h) join (together); **~halten** (irr. halten, sep., -ge-, h) **1.** *v/t.* hold together; **2.** *v/i.* hold together; friends: F stick together; **2hang** *m* coherence, coherency, connection; context; **~hängen** (sep., -ge-, h) **1.** *v/i.* (irr. hängen) cohere; fig. be connected; **2.** *v/t.* hang together; **~klappen** *v/t.* (sep., -ge-, h) fold up; close (clasp-knife); **~kommen** *v/i.* (irr. kommen, sep., -ge-, sein) meet; **2kunft** [~kunft] *f* (-/⁀e) meeting; **~laufen** *v/i.* (irr. laufen, sep., -ge-, sein) run or crowd together; ⚕ converge; milk: curdle; **~legen** *v/t.* (sep., -ge-, h) lay together; fold up; club (money) (together); **~nehmen** fig. *v/t.* (irr. nehmen, sep., -ge-, h) collect (one's wits); sich ~ be on one's good behavio(u)r; pull o.s. together; **~packen** *v/t.* (sep., -ge-, h) pack up; **~passen** *v/i.* (sep., -ge-, h) match, harmonize; **~rechnen** *v/t.* (sep., -ge-, h) add up; **~reißen** F *v/refl.* (irr. reißen, sep., -ge-, h) pull o.s. together; **~rollen** *v/t. and v/refl.* (sep., -ge-, h) coil (up); **~rotten** *v/refl.* (sep., -ge-, h) band together; **~rücken** (sep., -ge-, h) **1.** *v/t.* (h) move together; **2.** *v/i.* (sein) close up; **~schlagen** (irr. schlagen, sep., -ge-) **1.** *v/t.* clap (hands) (together); F smash to pieces; beat s.o. up; **2.** *v/i.* (sein) ~ über (dat.) close over; **~schließen** *v/refl.* (irr. schließen, sep., -ge-, h) join; unite; **2schluß** *m* union; **~schrumpfen** *v/i.* (sep., -ge-, sein) shrivel (up), shrink; **~setzen** *v/t.* (sep., -ge-, h) put together; compose; compound (a. ♫, word); ⊕ assemble; sich ~ aus consist of; **2setzung** *f* (-/-en) composition; compound (⊕ assembly); **~stellen** *v/t.* (sep., -ge-, h) put together; compile; combine; **2stoß** *m* collision (a. fig.); ✗ encounter; fig. clash; **~stoßen** *v/i.* (irr. stoßen, sep., -ge-, sein) collide (a. fig.); adjoin; fig. clash;

~ *mit* knock (*heads, etc.*) together; **~stürzen** *v/i.* (*sep.*, *-ge-*, *sein*) collapse; *house, etc.*: fall in; **~tragen** *v/t.* (*irr. tragen, sep., -ge-, h*) collect; compile (*notes*); **~treffen** *v/i.* (*irr. treffen, sep., -ge-, sein*) meet; coincide; **2treffen** *n* (*-s/no pl.*) meeting; encounter (*of enemies*); coincidence; **~treten** *v/i.* (*irr. treten, sep., -ge-, sein*) meet; *parl. a.* convene; **~wirken** *v/i.* (*sep., -ge-, h*) co-operate; **2wirken** *n* (*-s/no pl.*) co-operation; **~zählen** *v/t.* (*sep., -ge-, h*) add up, count up; **~ziehen** *v/t.* (*irr. ziehen, sep., -ge-, h*) draw together; contract; concentrate (*troops*); *sich* ~ contract.

'Zusatz *m* addition; admixture, *metall.* alloy; supplement.

zusätzlich *adj.* ['tsu:zɛtsliç] additional.

'zuschau|en *v/i.* (*sep., -ge-, h*) look on (*e-r Sache* at s.th.); *j-m* ~ watch s.o. (*bei et.* doing s.th.); **'2er** *m* (*-s/-*) spectator, looker-on, onlooker; **'2erraum** *thea. m* auditorium.

'zuschicken *v/t.* (*sep., -ge-, h*) send (*dat.* to); mail; consign (*goods*).

'Zuschlag *m* addition; extra charge; excess fare; 🚂 surcharge; *at auction*: knocking down; **2en** ['~gən] (*irr. schlagen, sep., -ge-*) **1.** *v/i.* (*h*) strike; **2.** *v/i.* (*sein*) *door*: slam (to); **3.** *v/t.* (*h*) bang, slam (*door*) (to); *at auction*: knock down (*dat.* to).

'zu|schließen *v/t.* (*irr. schließen, sep., -ge-, h*) lock (up); **'~schnallen** *v/t.* (*sep., -ge-, h*) buckle (up); **'~schnappen** (*sep., -ge-*) **1.** *v/i.* (*h*) *dog*: snap; **2.** *v/i.* (*sein*) *door*: snap to; **'~schneiden** *v/t.* (*irr. schneiden, sep., -ge-, h*) cut up; cut (*suit*) (to size); **'2schnitt** *m* (*-[e]s/*⚒*-e*) cut; style; **'~schnüren** *v/t.* (*sep., -ge-, h*) lace up; cord up; **'~schrauben** *v/t.* (*sep., -ge-, h*) screw up *or* tight; **'~schreiben** *v/t.* (*irr. schreiben, sep., -ge-, h*): *j-m et.* ~ ascribe *or* attribute s.th. to s.o.; **'2schrift** *f* letter.

zuschulden *adv.* [tsu'-]: *sich et.* ~ *kommen lassen* make o.s. guilty of s.th.

'Zu|schuß *m* allowance; subsidy, grant (*of government*); **'2schütten** *v/t.* (*sep., -ge-, h*) fill up (*ditch*); F add; **'2sehen** *v/i.* (*irr. sehen, sep., -ge-, h*) *s. zuschauen*; ~, *daß* see (to it) that; **2sehends** *adv.* ['~ts] visibly; **'2senden** *v/t.* ([*irr. senden,*] *sep., -ge-, h*) *s. zuschicken*; **'2setzen** (*sep., -ge-, h*) **1.** *v/t.* add; lose (*money*); **2.** *v/i.* lose money; *j-m* ~ press s.o. hard.

'zusicher|n *v/t.* (*sep., -ge-, h*): *j-m et.* ~ assure s.o. of s.th.; promise s.o. s.th.; **'2ung** *f* promise, assurance.

'zu|spielen *v/t.* (*sep., -ge-, h*) *sports*: pass (*ball*) (*dat.* to) **'~spitzen** *v/t.* (*sep., -ge-, h*) point; *sich* ~ taper (off); *fig.* come to a crisis; **'2spruch** *m* (*-[e]s/no pl.*) encouragement; consolation; ✝ custom; **'2stand** *m* condition, state; *in gutem* ~ *house*: in good repair.

zustande *adv.* [tsu'ʃtandə]: ~ *bringen* bring about; ~ *kommen* come about; *nicht* ~ *kommen* not to come off.

'zuständig *adj.* competent; **'2keit** *f* [(*-/-en*) competence.]

zustatten *adv.* [tsu'ʃtatən]: *j-m* ~ *kommen* be useful to s.o.

'zustehen *v/i.* (*irr. stehen, sep., -ge-, h*) be due (*dat.* to).

'zustell|en *v/t.* (*sep., -ge-, h*) deliver (*a.* 🚂); ⚖ serve (*j-m* on s.o.); **'2ung** *f* delivery; ⚖ service.

'zustimm|en *v/i.* (*sep., -ge-, h*) agree (*dat.*: to *s.th.*; with *s.o.*); consent (to *s.th.*); **'2ung** *f* consent.

'zustoßen *fig. v/i.* (*irr. stoßen, sep., -ge-, sein*): *j-m* ~ happen to s.o.

zutage *adv.* [tsu'tɑ:gə]: ~ *treten* come to light.

Zutaten ['tsu:tɑ:tən] *f/pl.* ingredients *pl.* (*of food*); trimmings *pl.* (*of dress*).

zuteil *adv.* [tsu'taɪl]: *j-m* ~ *werden* [fall to s.o.'s share.]

'zuteil|en *v/t.* (*sep., -ge-, h*) allot, apportion; **'2ung** *f* allotment, apportionment; ration.

'zutragen *v/refl.* (*irr. tragen, sep., -ge-, h*) happen.

'zutrauen **1.** *v/t.* (*sep., -ge-, h*): *j-m et.* ~ credit s.o. with s.th.; *sich zuviel* ~ overrate o.s.; **2.** **2** *n* (*-s/no pl.*) confidence (*zu* in).

'zutraulich *adj.* confiding, trustful, trusting; *animal*: friendly, tame.

'zutreffen *v/i.* (*irr. treffen, sep., -ge-, h*) be right, be true; ~ *auf* (*acc.*) be true of; **'~d** *adj.* right, correct; applicable.

'zutrinken *v/i.* (*irr. trinken, sep., -ge-, h*): *j-m* ~ drink to s.o.

'Zutritt m (-[e]s/no pl.) access; admission; ~ verboten! no admittance! [bottom.]

zuunterst adv. [tsu'-] right at the]

zuverlässig adj. ['tsu:ferlɛsɪç] reliable; certain; **'2keit** f (-/no pl.) reliability; certainty.

Zuversicht ['tsu:ferzɪçt] f (-/no pl.) confidence; **'2lich** adj. confident.

zuviel adv. [tsu'-] too much; e-r ~ one too many.

zuvor adv. [tsu'-] before, previously; first; **~kommen** v/i. (irr. kommen, sep., -ge-, sein): j-m ~ anticipate s.o.; e-r Sache ~ anticipate or prevent s.th.; **~kommend** adj. obliging; courteous.

Zuwachs ['tsu:vaks] m (-es/no pl.) increase; **'2en** v/i. (irr. wachsen, sep., -ge-, sein) become overgrown; wound: close.

zu|wege adv. [tsu've:gə]: ~ bringen bring about; **~'weilen** adv. sometimes.

'zu|weisen v/t. (irr. weisen, sep., -ge-, h) assign; **~wenden** v/t. ([irr. wenden] sep., -ge-, h) (dat.) turn to(wards); fig.: give; bestow on; sich ~ (dat.) turn to(wards).

zuwenig adv. [tsu'-] too little.

'zuwerfen v/t. (irr. werfen, sep., -ge-, h) fill up (pit); slam (door) (to); j-m ~ throw (ball, etc.) to s.o.; cast (look) at s.o.

zuwider prp. (dat.) [tsu'-] contrary to, against; repugnant, distasteful; **~handeln** v/i. (sep., -ge-, h) (dat.) act contrary or in opposition to; esp. ﬥﬦ contravene; **2handlung** ﬥﬦ f contravention.

'zu|winken v/i. (sep., -ge-, h) (dat.) wave to; beckon to; **'~zahlen** v/t. (sep., -ge-, h) pay extra; **'~zählen** v/t. (sep., -ge-, h) add; **'~ziehen** (irr. ziehen, sep., -ge-) **1.** v/t. (h) draw together; draw (curtains); consult (doctor, etc.); sich ~ incur (s.o.'s displeasure, etc.); ﬧ catch (disease); **2.** v/i. (sein) move in; **~züglich** prp. (gen.) ['tsy:k-] plus.

Zwang [tsvaŋ] **1.** m (-[e]s/⸢e) compulsion, coercion; constraint; ﬥﬦ duress(e); force; check or restrain o.s.; **2.** 2 pret. of zwingen.

zwängen ['tsvɛŋən] v/t. (ge-, h) press, force.

'zwanglos fig. adj. free and easy,

informal; **2igkeit** f (-/-en) ease, informality.

'Zwangs|arbeit f hard labo(u)r; **~jacke** f strait waistcoat or jacket; **~lage** f embarrassing situation; **2läufig** fig. adj. ['-lɔʏf-] necessary; **~maßnahme** f coercive measure; **~vollstreckung** ﬥﬦ f distraint, execution; **~vorstellung** f obsession, hallucination; **2weise** adv. by force; **~wirtschaft** f (-/⸢ -en) controlled economy.

zwanzig adj. ['tsvantsɪç] twenty; **~ste** adj. ['-stə] twentieth.

zwar cj. [tsva:r] indeed, it is true; und ~ and that, that is.

Zweck [tsvɛk] m (-[e]s/-e) aim, end, object, purpose; design; keinen ~ haben be of no use; s-n ~ erfüllen answer its purpose; zu dem ~ (gen.) for the purpose of; **2dienlich** adj. serviceable, useful, expedient.

Zwecke ['tsvɛkə] f (-/-n) tack; drawing-pin, Am. thumbtack.

'zweck|los adj. aimless, purposeless; useless; **~mäßig** adj. expedient, suitable; **2mäßigkeit** f (-/no pl.) expediency.

zwei adj. [tsvaɪ] two; **'~beinig** adj. two-legged; **2bettzimmer** n double (bedroom); **~deutig** adj. ['-dɔʏtɪç] ambiguous; suggestive; **~erlei** adj. ['-ˈɔr'laɪ] of two kinds, two kinds of; **~fach** adj. ['-fax] double, twofold.

Zweifel ['tsvaɪfəl] m (-s/-) doubt; **2haft** adj. doubtful, dubious; **2los** adj. doubtless; **2n** v/i. (ge-, h) doubt (an e-r Sache s.th.; an j-m s.o.).

Zweig [tsvaɪk] m (-[e]s/-e) branch (a. fig.); kleiner ~ twig; **~geschäft** n, **~niederlassung** f, **~stelle** f branch.

zwei|jährig adj. ['tsvaɪjɛ:rɪç] two-year-old, of two (years); **2kampf** m duel, single combat; **'~mal** adv. twice; **'~malig** adj. (twice) repeated; **~motorig** adj. ['-mo:torɪç] two- or twin-engined; **'~reihig** adj. having two rows; suit: double-breasted; **'~schneidig** adj. double-or two-edged (both a. fig.); **'~seitig** adj. two-sided; contract, etc.: bilateral; fabric: reversible; **2sitzer** esp. mot. m (-s/-) two-seater; **'~sprachig** adj. bilingual; **'~stimmig** adj. for two voices; **~stöckig**

adj. ['~ʃtœkiç] two-stor|eyed, -ied;
'**~stufig** ⊕ *adj.* two-stage; **~stün-
dig** *adj.* ['~ʃtyndiç] of *or* lasting
two hours, two-hour.
zweit *adj.* [tsvaɪt] second; *ein* ~er
another; *aus* ~er *Hand* second-
hand; *zu* ~ by twos; *wir sind zu* ~
there are two of us.   [engine.)
'**Zweitaktmotor** *mot. m* two-stroke)
'**zweit'best** *adj.* second-best.
'**zweiteilig** *adj. garment:* two-piece.
zweitens *adv.* ['tsvaɪtəns] secondly.
'**zweitklassig** *adj.* second-class,
second-rate.
Zwerchfell *anat.* ['tsverç-] *n* diaphragm.
Zwerg [tsverk] *m* (-[e]s/-e) dwarf;
☨enhaft *adj.* ['~ɡən-] dwarfish.
Zwetsch(g)e ['tsvɛtʃ(g)ə] *f* (-/-n)
plum.
Zwick|el ['tsvikəl] *m* (-s/-) *sewing:*
gusset; **☨en** *v/t. and v/i.* (ge-, h)
pinch, nip; '**~er** *m* (-s/-) (*ein a pair
of*) eye-glasses *pl.,* pince-nez;
'**~mühle** *fig. f* dilemma, quandary,
fix.
Zwieback ['tsvi:bak] *m* (-[e]s/☨e, -e)
rusk, zwieback.
Zwiebel ['tsvi:bəl] *f* (-/-n) onion;
bulb (*of flowers, etc.*).
Zwie|gespräch ['tsvi:-] *n* dialog(ue);
'**~licht** *n* (-[e]s/*no pl.*) twilight;
'**~spalt** *m* (-[e]s/-e, ☨e) disunion;
conflict; **☨spältig** *adj.* ['~ʃpeltiç]
disunited; *emotions:* conflicting;
'**~tracht** *f* (-/no *pl.*) discord.
Zwilling|e ['tsviliŋə] *m/pl.* twins
pl.; '**~sbruder** *m* twin brother;
'**~sschwester** *f* twin sister.
Zwinge ['tsviŋə] *f* (-/-n) ferrule (*of
stick, etc.*); ⊕ clamp; **☨n** *v/t.* (irr.,
ge-, h) compel, constrain; force;
☨nd *adj.* forcible; *arguments:*
cogent, compelling; *imperative:*
'**~r** *m* (-s/-) outer court; kennel(s
pl.); bear-pit.
zwinkern ['tsviŋkərn] *v/i.* (ge-, h)
wink, blink.
Zwirn [tsvirn] *m* (-[e]s/-e) thread,
cotton; '**~sfaden** *m* thread.

zwischen *prp.* (*dat.; acc.*) ['tsviʃən]
between (*two*); among (*several*);
'**☨bilanz** ☨ *f* interim balance;
'**☨deck** ⚓ *n* steerage; **~'durch** F
adv. in between; for a change;
'**☨ergebnis** *n* provisional result;
'**☨fall** *m* incident; '**☨händler** ☨ *m*
middleman; '**☨landung** ✈ *f* intermediate landing, stop, *Am. a.* stop-
over; (*Flug*) *ohne* ~ non-stop (flight);
'**☨pause** *f* interval, intermission;
'**☨prüfung** *f* intermediate examination; '**☨raum** *m* space, interval;
'**☨ruf** *m* (loud) interruption; '**☨spiel**
n interlude; '**~staatlich** *adj.* international; *Am. between States:* inter-
state; '**☨station** *f* intermediate station; '**☨stecker** ⚡ *m* adapter;
'**☨stück** *n* intermediate piece, connexion, (*Am. only*) connection;
'**☨stufe** *f* intermediate stage; '**☨-
wand** *f* partition (wall); '**☨zeit** *f*
interval; *in der* ~ in the meantime.
Zwist [tsvist] *m* (-es/-e), '**~igkeit** *f*
(-/-en) discord; disunion; quarrel.
zwitschern ['tsvitʃərn] *v/i.* (ge-, h)
twitter, chirp.
Zwitter ['tsvitər] *m* (-s/-) hermaph-
rodite.
zwölf *adj.* [tsvœlf] twelve; *um* ~
(*Uhr*) at twelve (o'clock); (*um*) ~
Uhr mittags (at) noon; (*um*) ~ *Uhr
nachts* (at) midnight; '**☨finger-
darm** *anat. m* duodenum; **~te** *adj.*
['~tə] twelfth.
Zyankali [tsyan'ka:li] *n* (-s/no *pl.*)
potassium cyanide.
Zyklus ['tsy:klus, 'tsy:k-] *m* (-/Zy-
klen) cycle; course, set (*of lectures,
etc.*).
Zylind|er [tsi'lindər, tsy'-] *m* (-s/-)
A, ⊕ cylinder; chimney (*of lamp*);
top hat; **☨risch** *adj.* [~driʃ]
cylindrical.
Zyni|ker ['tsy:nikər] *m* (-s/-) cynic;
'**☨isch** *adj.* cynical; **~smus** [tsy-
'nismus] *m* (-/Zynismen) cynicism.
Zypresse ♣ [tsy'presə] *f* (-/-n)
cypress.
Zyste ⚕ ['tsystə] *f* (-/-n) cyst.

Z

PART II

ENGLISH-GERMAN
DICTIONARY

A

a [ə, betont: eɪ], *vor Vokal*: **an** [ən, betont: æn] *unbestimmter Artikel*: ein(e); per, pro, je; *not a(n)* kein(e); *all of a size* alle gleich groß; £ *10 a year* zehn Pfund im Jahr; *twice a week* zweimal die *od.* in der Woche.

A 1 F ['eɪ'wʌn] Ia, prima.

a·back [ə'bæk]: *taken* ~ *fig.* überrascht, verblüfft; bestürzt.

a·ban·don [ə'bændən] auf-, preisgeben; verlassen; überlassen; **~ed:** *be found* ~ verlassen aufgefunden werden (*Fahrzeug etc.*).

a·base [ə'beɪs] erniedrigen, demütigen; **~ment** [~mənt] Erniedrigung *f*, Demütigung *f*.

a·bashed [ə'bæʃt] verlegen.

a·bate [ə'beɪt] *v/t.* verringern; *Mißstand* abstellen; *v/i.* abnehmen, nachlassen; **~ment** [~mənt] Verminderung *f*; Abschaffung *f*.

ab·at·toir ['æbətwɑː] Schlachthof *m*.

ab·bess ['æbɪs] Äbtissin *f*.

ab·bey ['æbɪ] Kloster *n*; Abtei *f*.

ab·bot ['æbət] Abt *m*.

ab·bre·vi·ate [ə'briːvɪeɪt] (ab)kürzen; **~a·tion** [æbriːvɪ'eɪʃn] Abkürzung *f*, Kurzform *f*.

ABC ['eɪbiː'siː] Abc *n*, Alphabet *n*.

ABC weap·ons *pl.* ABC-Waffen *pl.*

ab·di·cate ['æbdɪkeɪt] *Amt, Recht etc.* aufgeben, verzichten auf (*acc.*); ~ (*from*) *the throne* abdanken; **~ca·tion** [æbdɪ'keɪʃn] Verzicht *m*; Abdankung *f*.

ab·do·men *anat.* ['æbdəmən] Unterleib *m*; **ab·dom·i·nal** *anat.* [æb'dɒmɪnl] Unterleibs...

ab·duct 🏛 [æb'dʌkt] *j-n* entführen.

a·bet [ə'bet] (-*tt*-): *aid and* ~ 🏛 Beihilfe leisten (*dat.*); begünstigen; **~tor** [~ə] Anstifter *m*; (Helfers)Helfer *m*.

a·bey·ance [ə'beɪəns] Unentschiedenheit *f*; *in* ~ 🏛 in der Schwebe.

ab·hor [əb'hɔː] (-*rr*-) verabscheuen; **~rence** [əb'hɒrəns] Abscheu *m* (*of vor dat.*); **~rent** □ [~t] zuwider (*to dat.*); abstoßend.

a·bide [ə'baɪd] *v/i.*: ~ *by the law, etc.*

sich an das Gesetz *etc.* halten; *v/t.*: *I can't* ~ *him* ich kann ihn nicht ausstehen.

a·bil·i·ty [ə'bɪlətɪ] Fähigkeit *f*.

ab·ject □ ['æbdʒekt] verächtlich, erbärmlich; *in* ~ *poverty* in äußerster Armut.

ab·jure [əb'dʒʊə] abschwören; entsagen (*dat.*).

a·blaze [ə'bleɪz] in Flammen; *fig.* glänzend, funkelnd (*with vor dat.*).

a·ble □ ['eɪbl] fähig; geschickt; *be* ~ *to do* imstande sein zu tun; tun können; **~-bod·ied** kräftig; ~ *seaman* Vollmatrose *m*.

ab·nor·mal □ [æb'nɔːml] abnorm, ungewöhnlich; anomal.

a·board [ə'bɔːd] an Bord; *all...!* 🚢 alle Mann *od.* Reisenden an Bord!; ~ alles einsteigen!; ~ *a bus* in e-m Bus; *go* ~ *a train* in e-n Zug einsteigen.

a·bode [ə'bəʊd] *a. place of* ~ Aufenthaltsort *m*, Wohnsitz *m*; *of* (*od. with*) *no fixed* ~ ohne festen Wohnsitz.

a·bol·ish [ə'bɒlɪʃ] abschaffen, aufheben.

ab·o·li·tion [æbə'lɪʃn] Abschaffung *f*, Aufhebung *f*; **~ist** *hist.* [~ʃənɪst] Gegner *m* der Sklaverei.

A-bomb ['eɪbɒm] = *atom(ic)* bomb.

a·bom·i·na·ble □ [ə'bɒmɪnəbl] abscheulich, scheußlich; **~nate** [~eɪt] verabscheuen; **~na·tion** [əbɒmɪ'neɪʃn] Abscheu *m*.

ab·o·rig·i·nal [æbə'rɪdʒənl] **1.** □ eingeboren, Ur...; **2.** Ureinwohner *m*; **~ne** [~niː] Ureinwohner *m* (*bsd. Australiens*).

a·bort [ə'bɔːt] 🏥 e-e Fehlgeburt herbeiführen bei *od.* haben; *Raumflug etc.* abbrechen; *fig.* fehlschlagen, scheitern; **a·bor·tion** 🏥 [~ʃn] Fehlgeburt *f*; Schwangerschaftsunterbrechung *f*, -abbruch *m*, Abtreibung *f*; *have an* ~ abtreiben (*lassen*); **a·bor·tive** □ *fig.* [~ɪv] mißlungen, erfolglos.

a·bound [ə'baʊnd] reichlich vorhanden sein; Überfluß haben, reich sein (*in an dat.*); voll sein (*with von*).

a·bout [ə'baʊt] **1.** *prp.* um (...herum);

bei (*dat.*); (irgendwo) herum in (*dat.*); um, gegen, etwa; im Begriff, dabei; über (*acc.*); *I had no money ∼ me* ich hatte kein Geld bei mir; *what are you ∼?* was macht ihr da?; **2.** *adv.* herum, umher; in der Nähe; etwa, ungefähr.

a·bove [əˈbʌv] **1.** *prp.* über, oberhalb; *fig.* über, erhaben über; *∼ all* vor allem; **2.** *adv.* oben; darüber; **3.** *adj.* obig, obenerwähnt.

a·breast [əˈbrest] nebeneinander; *keep od. be ∼ of fig.* Schritt halten mit.

a·bridge [əˈbrɪdʒ] (ab-, ver)kürzen; **a·bridg(e)·ment** [∼mənt] (Ab-, Ver)Kürzung *f*; Kurzfassung *f*; Abriß *m*.

a·broad [əˈbrɔːd] im *od.* ins Ausland; überall(hin); *the news soon spread ∼* die Nachricht verbreitete sich rasch.

a·brupt [əˈbrʌpt] abrupt; jäh; zusammenhanglos; schroff.

ab·scess ✚ [ˈæbsɪs] Abszeß *m*.

ab·scond [əbˈskɒnd] sich davonmachen.

ab·sence [ˈæbsəns] Abwesenheit *f*; Mangel *m*.

ab·sent 1. □ [ˈæbsənt] abwesend; fehlend; nicht vorhanden; *be ∼* fehlen (*from school* in der Schule; *from work* am Arbeitsplatz); **2.** [æbˈsent]: *∼ o.s.* von (*dat.*) fernbleiben; **∼-mind·ed** □ [ˈæbsəntˈmaindid] zerstreut, geistesabwesend.

ab·so·lute □ [ˈæbsəluːt] absolut; unumschränkt; vollkommen; ✚ rein, unvermischt; unbedingt.

ab·so·lu·tion *eccl.* [æbsəˈluːʃn] Absolution *f*.

ab·solve [əbˈzɒlv] frei-, lossprechen; △ *nicht absolvieren*.

ab·sorb [əbˈsɔːb] absorbieren, auf-, einsaugen; *fig.* ganz in Anspruch nehmen; **∼ing** *fig.* [∼ɪŋ] fesselnd, packend.

ab·sorp·tion [əbˈsɔːpʃn] Absorption *f*; *fig.* Vertieftsein *n*.

ab·stain [əbˈsteɪn] sich enthalten (*from gen.*).

ab·ste·mi·ous □ [æbˈstiːmɪəs] enthaltsam; mäßig.

ab·sten·tion [əbˈstenʃn] Enthaltung *f*; *pol.* Stimmenthaltung *f*.

ab·sti|nence [ˈæbstɪnəns] Abstinenz *f*, Enthaltsamkeit *f*; **∼nent** □ [∼t] abstinent, enthaltsam.

ab·stract 1. □ [ˈæbstrækt] abstrakt; **2.** [∼] *das* Abstrakte; Auszug *m*; **3.** [æbˈstrækt] abstrahieren; entwenden; *e-n wichtigen Punkt aus e-m Buch etc.* herausziehen; **∼ed** □ *fig.* zerstreut; **ab·strac·tion** [∼kʃn] Abstraktion *f*; abstrakter Begriff.

ab·struse □ [æbˈstruːs] dunkel, schwer verständlich.

ab·surd □ [əbˈsɜːd] absurd; lächerlich.

a·bun|dance [əˈbʌndəns] Überfluß *m*; Fülle *f*; Überschwang *m*; **∼dant** □ [∼t] reich(lich).

a·buse 1. [əˈbjuːs] Mißbrauch *m*; Beschimpfung *f*; **2.** [∼z] mißbrauchen; beschimpfen; **a·bu·sive** □ [∼sɪv] ausfallend, Schimpf...

a·but [əˈbʌt] (-*tt*-) (an)grenzen (*on* an).

a·byss [əˈbɪs] Abgrund *m* (*a. fig.*).

ac·a·dem·ic [ækəˈdemɪk] **1.** Hochschullehrer *m*; △ *nicht Akademiker*. **2.** (*∼ally*) akademisch; **a·cad·e·mi·cian** [əkædəˈmɪʃn] Akademiemitglied *n*; △ *nicht Akademiker*.

a·cad·e·my [əˈkædəmɪ] Akademie *f*; *∼ of music* Musikhochschule.

ac·cede [ækˈsiːd]: *∼ to* zustimmen (*dat.*); *Amt* antreten; *Thron* besteigen.

ac·cel·e|rate [əkˈseləreɪt] *v/t.* beschleunigen; *v/i.* schneller werden, *mot. a.* beschleunigen, Gas geben; **∼ra·tion** [əkseləˈreɪʃn] Beschleunigung *f*; **∼ra·tor** [əkˈseləreɪtə] Gaspedal *n*.

ac·cent 1. [ˈæksənt] Akzent *m* (*a. gr.*); **2.** [ækˈsent] = **ac·cen·tu·ate** [ækˈsentjʊeɪt] akzentuieren, betonen.

ac·cept [əkˈsept] annehmen; akzeptieren; hinnehmen; **ac·cep·ta·ble** □ [∼əbl] annehmbar; **∼ance** [∼əns] Annahme *f*; Aufnahme *f*.

ac·cess [ˈækses] Zugang *m* (*to* zu); *fig.* Zutritt *m* (*to* bei, zu); *easy of ∼* zugänglich (*Person*); *∼ road* Zufahrtsstraße *f*; (Autobahn)Zubringerstraße *f*.

**ac·ces·sa·ry* ½ [əkˈsesərɪ] s. accessory.

ac·ces|si·ble □ [əkˈsesəbl] (leicht) zugänglich; **∼sion** [∼ʃn] Zuwachs *m*, Zunahme *f*; Antritt *m* (*e-s Amtes*); *∼ to power* Machtübernahme *f*; *∼ to the throne* Thronbesteigung *f*.

ac·ces·so·ry [əkˈsesərɪ] **1.** zusätzlich; **2.** ½ Kompli|ze *m*, -zin *f*, Mitschuldige(r m) f; *mst accessories pl.* Zubehör n, *Mode a.* Accessoires *pl.*; ⊕ Zubehör(teile *pl.*) n.

ac·ci·dent ['æksɪdənt] Zufall m; Un(glücks)fall m; *by* ~ zufällig; **~·den·tal** □ [æksɪ'dentl] zufällig; versehentlich.

ac·claim [ə'kleɪm] freudig begrüßen.

ac·cla·ma·tion [æklə'meɪʃn] lauter Beifall; Lob n.

ac·cli·ma·tize [ə'klaɪmətaɪz] (sich) akklimatisieren *od.* eingewöhnen.

ac·com·mo·date [ə'kɒmədeɪt] (sich) anpassen (*to dat. od.* an *acc.*); unterbringen, beherbergen; Platz haben für; *j-m* aushelfen (*with* mit *Geld*); **~·da·tion** [əkɒmə'deɪʃn] Anpassung f; Unterbringung f, (Platz m für) Unterkunft f, Quartier n.

ac·com·pa·ni·ment ♪ [ə'kʌmpənɪmənt] Begleitung f; **~·ny** [ə'kʌmpənɪ] begleiten (*a. ♪*); *accompanied with* verbunden mit.

ac·com·plice [ə'kʌmplɪs] Komplize m, -zin f.

ac·com·plish [ə'kʌmplɪʃ] vollenden; ausführen; *Zweck* erreichen; **~ed** vollendet, perfekt; **~·ment** [~mənt] Vollendung f, Ausführung f; Fähigkeit f, Talent n.

ac·cord [ə'kɔːd] **1.** Übereinstimmung f; △ *nicht* Akkord; *of one's own* ~ aus eigenem Antrieb; *with one* ~ einstimmig; **2.** *v/i.* übereinstimmen; *v/t.* gewähren; **~·ance** [~əns] Übereinstimmung f; *in* ~ *with* laut (*gen.*), gemäß (*dat.*); **~·ant** [~t] übereinstimmend; **~·ing** [~ɪŋ]: ~ *to* gemäß (*dat.*), nach; **~·ing·ly** [~ɪŋlɪ] (dem-) entsprechend.

ac·cost [ə'kɒst] *j-n bsd. auf der Straße* ansprechen.

ac·count [ə'kaʊnt] **1.** *econ.* Rechnung f, Berechnung f; *econ.* Konto n; Rechenschaft f; Bericht m; *by all* ~ nach allem, was man so hört; *of no* ~ ohne Bedeutung; *on no* ~ auf keinen Fall; *on* ~ *of* wegen; take *into* ~, take ~ *of* in Betracht *od.* Erwägung ziehen, berücksichtigen; *turn s.th. to* (*good*) ~ et. (gut) ausnutzen; *keep* ~*s* die Bücher führen; *call to* ~ zur Rechenschaft ziehen; *give* (an) ~ *of* Rechenschaft ablegen über (*acc.*); *give an* ~ *of* Bericht erstatten über (*acc.*); **2.** *v/i.:* ~ *for* Rechenschaft über *et.* ablegen, (sich) erklären; **~·coun·ta·ble** □ [~əbl] verant-

wortlich; erklärlich; **ac·coun·tant** [~ənt] Buchhalter m; **~·ing** [~ɪŋ] Buchführung f.

ac·cu·mu·late [ə'kjuːmjʊleɪt] (sich) (an)häufen *od.* ansammeln; **~·la·tion** [əkjuːmjʊ'leɪʃn] Ansammlung f.

ac·cu·ra·cy ['ækjʊrəsɪ] Genauigkeit f; **~·rate** □ [~rət] genau; richtig.

ac·cu·sa·tion [ækjuː'zeɪʃn] Anklage f; An-, Beschuldigung f.

ac·cu·sa·tive *gr.* [ə'kjuːzətɪv] *a.* ~ *case* Akkusativ m.

ac·cuse [ə'kjuːz] anklagen; beschuldigen; *the* ~*d* der *od.* die Angeklagte, die Angeklagten; **ac·cus·er** [~ə] Ankläger(in); **ac·cus·ing** □ [~ɪŋ] anklagend, vorwurfsvoll.

ac·cus·tom [ə'kʌstəm] gewöhnen (*to* an *acc.*); **~ed** gewohnt, üblich; gewöhnt (*to* an *acc.*, zu *inf.*).

ace [eɪs] As n (*a. fig.*); *have an* ~ *up one's sleeve, Am. have an* ~ *in the hole fig.* (noch) e-n Trumpf in der Hand haben; *within an* ~ um ein Haar.

ache [eɪk] **1.** schmerzen, weh tun; **2.** anhaltender Schmerz.

a·chieve [ə'tʃiːv] zustande bringen; *Ziel* erreichen; **~·ment** [~mənt] Zustandebringen n, Ausführung f; Leistung f.

ac·id ['æsɪd] **1.** sauer; *fig.* beißend, bissig; ~ *rain* saurer Regen; **2.** 🜆 Säure f; **a·cid·i·ty** [ə'sɪdətɪ] Säure f.

ac·knowl·edge [ək'nɒlɪdʒ] anerkennen; zugeben; *Empfang* bestätigen; **ac·knowl·edg(e)·ment** [~mənt] Anerkennung f; (Empfangs)Bestätigung f; Eingeständnis n.

a·corn ♀ ['eɪkɔːn] Eichel f.

a·cous·tics [ə'kuːstɪks] *pl.* Akustik f (*e-s Raumes*).

ac·quaint [ə'kweɪnt] bekannt machen; ~ *s.o. with s.th.* j-m et. mitteilen; *be* ~*ed with* kennen; **~·ance** [~əns] Bekanntschaft f; Bekannte(r m) f.

ac·qui·esce [ækwɪ'es] (*in*) hinnehmen (*acc.*); einwilligen (in *acc.*).

ac·quire [ə'kwaɪə] erwerben; sich aneignen (*Kenntnisse*).

ac·qui·si·tion [ækwɪ'zɪʃn] Erwerb m; Erwerbung f; Errungenschaft f.

ac·quit [ə'kwɪt] (*-tt-*) 🜩 j-n freisprechen (*of a charge* von e-r Anklage); ~ *o.s. of e-e Pflicht* erfüllen; ~ *o.s. well* s-e Sache gut machen; **~·tal** 🜩 [~tl] Freispruch m.

a·cre ['eɪkə] Acre m (*4047 qm*).

ac·rid ['ækrɪd] scharf, beißend.

a·cross [ə'krɒs] **1.** *adv.* (quer) hin- *od.* herüber; querdurch; drüben, auf der anderen Seite; über Kreuz; **2.** *prp.* (quer) über (*acc.*); (quer) durch; auf der anderen Seite von (*od. gen.*), jenseits (*gen.*); über (*dat.*); *come* ~, *run* ~ stoßen auf (*acc.*).

act [ækt] **1.** *v/i.* handeln; sich benehmen; wirken; funktionieren; (Theater) spielen (*a. fig.*), auftreten; *v/t. thea.* spielen (*a. fig.*), *Stück* aufführen; ~ *out* szenisch darstellen, vorspielen; **2.** Handlung *f*, Tat *f*, Maßnahme *f*, Akt *m*; *thea.* Akt *m*; Gesetz *n*, Beschluß *m*; Urkunde *f*, Vertrag *m*; ~**ing** ['æktɪŋ] **1.** Handeln *n*; *thea.* Spiel(en) *n*; **2.** tätig; amtierend.

ac·tion ['ækʃn] Handlung *f* (*a. thea.*), Tat *f*; Action *f* (*spannende Handlung*); Aktion *f*; Tätigkeit *f*, Funktion *f*; (Ein)Wirkung *f*; ⚖ Klage *f*, Prozeß *m*; ✗ Gefecht *n*, Kampfhandlung *f*; ⊕ Mechanismus *m*; *take* ~ Schritte unternehmen, handeln.

ac·tive ['æktɪv] aktiv; tätig, rührig; lebhaft, rege; wirksam; *econ.* lebhaft; ~ *voice gr.* Aktiv *n*, Tatform *f*; **ac·tiv·ist** [~vɪst] Aktivist(in); **ac·tiv·i·ty** [æk'tɪvətɪ] Tätigkeit *f*; Aktivität *f*; Betriebsamkeit *f*; *bsd. econ.* Lebhaftigkeit *f*.

ac·tor ['æktə] Schauspieler *m*; **ac·tress** [~trɪs] Schauspielerin *f*.

ac·tu·al [ ] ['æktʃʊəl] wirklich, tatsächlich, eigentlich; △ *nicht aktuell*.

a·cute [ ] [ə'kju:t] (~*r*, ~*st*) spitz; scharf(sinnig); brennend (*Frage*); ⚕ akut.

ad F [æd] = *advertisement*.

ad·a·mant [ ] *fig.* ['ædəmənt] unerbittlich.

a·dapt [ə'dæpt] anpassen (*to dat. od.* an *acc.*); *Text* bearbeiten (*from* nach); ⊕ umstellen (*to auf acc.*); umbauen (*to für*); **ad·ap·ta·tion** [ædæp'teɪʃn] Anpassung *f*; Bearbeitung *f*; **a·dapt·er**, **a·dapt·or** [ə'dæptə] Adapter *m*.

add [æd] *v/t.* hinzufügen; ~ *up* zusammenzählen, addieren; *v/i.*: ~ *to* vermehren, beitragen zu, hinzukommen zu; ~ *up fig.* F e-n Sinn ergeben.

ad·dict ['ædɪkt] Süchtige(r *m*) *f*; *alcohol* (*drug*) ~ Alkohol- (Drogen*od.* Rauschgift)Süchtige(r *m*) *f*; *Fuß-*

ball- etc. Fanatiker(in), *Film- etc.* Narr *m*; ~**ed** [ə'dɪktɪd] süchtig, abhängig (*to* von); *be* ~ *to alcohol* (*drugs, television, etc.*) alkohol- (drogen-, fernseh- *etc.*)süchtig sein; **ad·dic·tion** [~ʃn] Sucht *f*, Zustand *a.* Süchtigkeit *f*.

ad·di·tion [ə'dɪʃn] Hinzufügen *n*; Zusatz *m*; Zuwachs *m*; Anbau *m*; ∆ Addition *f*; *in* ~ außerdem; *in* ~ *to* außer (*dat.*); ~**al** [~l] zusätzlich.

ad·dress [ə'dres] **1.** *Worte* richten (*to* an *acc.*), *j-n* anreden *od.* ansprechen; **2.** Adresse *f*, Anschrift *f*; Rede *f*; Ansprache *f*; ~**ee** [ædre'si:] Empfänger(in).

ad·ept ['ædept] **1.** erfahren, geschickt (*at, in* in *dat.*); **2.** Meister *m*, Experte *m* (*at, in* in *dat.*).

ad·e·qua·cy ['ædɪkwəsɪ] Angemessenheit *f*; ~**quate** [ ] [~kwət] angemessen.

ad·here [əd'hɪə] (*to*) kleben, haften (an *dat.*); *fig.* festhalten (an *dat.*); **ad·her·ence** [~rəns] Anhaften *n*; *fig.* Festhalten *n*; **ad·her·ent** [~rənt] Anhänger(in).

ad·he·sive [əd'hi:sɪv] **1.** [ ] klebend; ~ *plaster* Heftpflaster *n*; ~ *tape* Klebestreifen *m*; *Am.* Heftpflaster *n*; **2.** Klebstoff *m*.

ad·ja·cent [ ] [ə'dʒeɪsnt] angrenzend, anstoßend (*to* an *acc.*); benachbart.

ad·jec·tive *gr.* ['ædʒɪktɪv] Adjektiv *n*, Eigenschaftswort *n*.

ad·join [ə'dʒɔɪn] (an)grenzen an (*acc.*).

ad·journ [ə'dʒɜ:n] verschieben, (*v/i.* sich) vertagen; ~**ment** [~mənt] Vertagung *f*, -schiebung *f*.

ad·just [ə'dʒʌst] anpassen; in Ordnung bringen; *Streit* beilegen; *Mechanismus u. fig.* einstellen (*to auf acc.*); ~**ment** [~mənt] Anpassung *f*; Ordnung *f*; ⊕ Einstellung *f*; Beilegung *f*.

ad·min·is·ter [əd'mɪnɪstə] verwalten; spenden; *Arznei* geben, verabreichen; ~ *justice* Recht sprechen; ~**tra·tion** [ədmɪnɪ'streɪʃn] Verwaltung *f*; *pol. bsd. Am.* Regierung *f*; *bsd. Am.* Amtsperiode *f* (*e-s Präsidenten*); ~**tra·tive** [ ] [əd'mɪnɪstrətɪv] Verwaltungs...; ~**tra·tor** [~reɪtə] Verwaltungsbeamte(r) *m*.

ad·mi·ra·ble [ ] ['ædmərəbl] bewundernswert; großartig.

ad·mi·ral ['ædmrəl] Admiral *m*.

ad·mi·ra·tion [ædmə'reɪʃn] Bewunderung f.

ad·mire [əd'maɪə] bewundern; verehren; **ad·mir·er** [~rə] Verehrer m.

ad·mis·si·ble □ [əd'mɪsəbl] zulässig; **~sion** [~ʃn] Zulassung f; Eintritt(sgeld n) m; Eingeständnis n; **~ free** Eintritt frei.

ad·mit [əd'mɪt] (-tt-) v/t. (her)einlassen (to, into in acc.), eintreten lassen; zulassen (to zu); zugeben; **~tance** [~əns] Einlaß m, Ein-, Zutritt m; no **~** Zutritt verboten.

ad·mix·ture [æd'mɪkstʃə] Beimischung f, Zusatz m.

ad·mon·ish [əd'mɒnɪʃ] ermahnen; warnen (of, against vor dat.); **ad·mo·ni·tion** [ædmə'nɪʃn] Ermahnung f; Warnung f.

a·do [ə'du:] (pl. -dos) Getue n, Lärm m; without much od. more od. further **~** ohne weitere Umstände.

ad·o·les·cence [ædə'lesns] Adoleszenz f, Reifezeit f; **~cent** [~t] 1. jugendlich, heranwachsend; 2. Jugendliche(r m) f.

a·dopt [ə'dɒpt] adoptieren; sich zu eigen machen, übernehmen; **~ed child** Adoptivkind n; **a·dop·tion** [~pʃn] Adoption f; **a·dop·tive** □ [~tɪv] Adoptiv...; angenommen; **~ child** Adoptivkind n; **~ parents** pl. Adoptiveltern pl.

a·dor·a·ble □ [ə'dɔ:rəbl] anbetungswürdig; F entzückend; **ad·o·ra·tion** [ædə'reɪʃn] Anbetung f, Verehrung f; **a·dore** [ə'dɔ:] anbeten, verehren.

a·dorn [ə'dɔ:n] schmücken, zieren; **~ment** [~mənt] Schmuck m.

a·droit □ [ə'drɔɪt] geschickt.

ad·ult [ædʌlt] 1. erwachsen; 2. Erwachsene(r m) f; **~ education** Erwachsenenbildung f.

a·dul·ter·ate [ə'dʌltəreɪt] verfälschen; **~er** [~rə] Ehebrecher m; **~ess** [~rɪs] Ehebrecherin f; **~ous** □ [~rəs] ehebrecherisch; **~y** [~rɪ] Ehebruch m.

ad·vance [əd'vɑ:ns] 1. v/i. vorrücken, -dringen; vorrücken (Zeit); steigen; Fortschritte machen; v/t. vorrücken; Ansicht etc. vorbringen; Geld vorauszahlen; vorschießen; (be)fördern; Preis erhöhen; beschleunigen; 2. Vorrücken n, Vorstoß m (a. fig.); Fortschritt m; Vorschuß m; Erhöhung f; in **~** im voraus; **~d** fortgeschritten; **~ for one's years** weit od.

reif für sein Alter; **~ment** [~mənt] Förderung f; Fortschritt m.

ad·van·tage [əd'vɑ:ntɪdʒ] Vorteil m; Überlegenheit f; Gewinn m; take **~** of ausnutzen; **~·ta·geous** □ [ædvən'teɪdʒəs] vorteilhaft.

ad·ven·ture [əd'ventʃə] Abenteuer n, Wagnis n; Spekulation f; **~tur·er** [~rə] Abenteurer m; Spekulant m; **~tur·ess** [~rɪs] Abenteu(r)erin f; **~tur·ous** □ [~rəs] abenteuerlich; verwegen, kühn.

ad·verb gr. ['ædvɜ:b] Adverb n, Umstandswort n.

ad·ver·sa·ry ['ædvəsərɪ] Gegner(in), Feind(in); **ad·verse** □ ['ædvɜ:s] widrig; feindlich; ungünstig, nachteilig (to für); **ad·ver·si·ty** [əd'vɜ:sətɪ] Unglück n.

ad·ver·tise ['ædvətaɪz] ankündigen, bekanntmachen; inserieren; Reklame machen (für); **~tise·ment** [əd'vɜ:tɪsmənt] Anzeige f, Ankündigung f, Inserat n; Reklame f; **~tis·ing** ['ædvətaɪzɪŋ] 1. Reklame f, Werbung f; 2. Anzeigen..., Reklame..., Werbe...; **~ agency** Anzeigenannahme f; Werbeagentur f.

ad·vice [əd'vaɪs] Rat(schlag) m; Nachricht f, Meldung f; take medical **~** e-n Arzt zu Rate ziehen; take my **~** hör auf mich.

ad·vi·sa·ble □ [əd'vaɪzəbl] ratsam; **ad·vise** [əd'vaɪz] v/t. j-n beraten; j-m raten; bsd. econ. benachrichtigen; avisieren; v/i. sich beraten; **ad·vis·er**, Am. a. **ad·vi·sor** [~ə] Berater m; **ad·vi·so·ry** [~ərɪ] beratend.

ad·vo·cate 1. ['ædvəkət] Anwalt m; Verfechter m; Befürworter m; 2. [~keɪt] verteidigen, befürworten.

aer·i·al ['eərɪəl] 1. □ luftig; Luft...; **~ view** Luftaufnahme f; 2. Antenne f.

aer·o- ['eərəʊ] Aero..., Luft...

aer·o·bics [eə'rəʊbɪks] sg. Sport: Aerobic n; **~·drome** bsd. Brt. ['eərədrəʊm] Flugplatz m; **~·dy·nam·ic** [eərəʊdaɪ'næmɪk] (**~ally**) aerodynamisch; **~·dy·nam·ics** sg. Aerodynamik f; **~·nau·tics** [eərə'nɔ:tɪks] sg. Luftfahrt f; **~·plane** Brt. ['eərəpleɪn] Flugzeug n.

aes·thet·ic [i:s'θetɪk] ästhetisch; **~s** sg. Ästhetik f.

a·far [ə'fɑ:] fern, weit (weg).

af·fa·ble □ ['æfəbl] leutselig.

af·fair [ə'feə] Geschäft n, Angelegenheit f, Sache f; F Ding n,

Sache *f;* Liebesaffäre *f,* Verhältnis *n.*

af·fect [ə'fekt] (ein- *od.* sich aus-)wirken auf (*acc.*); rühren; *Gesundheit* angreifen; lieben, vorziehen; nachahmen; vortäuschen; **af·fec·ta·tion** [æfek'teɪʃn] Vorliebe *f;* Affektiertheit *f;* Verstellung *f;* ∼**ed** □ gerührt; befallen (*von Krankheit*); angegriffen (*Augen etc.*); geziert, affektiert; **af·fec·tion** [∼kʃn] Zuneigung *f;* **af·fec·tion·ate** □ [∼ʃnət] liebevoll.

af·fil·i·ate [ə'fɪlɪeɪt] *als Mitglied* aufnehmen; angliedern; ∼**d company** *econ.* Tochtergesellschaft *f.*

af·fin·i·ty [ə'fɪnətɪ] (geistige) Verwandtschaft *f;* ⚗ Affinität *f;* Neigung *f* (*for,* to zu).

af·firm [ə'fɜːm] versichern, beteuern; bestätigen; **af·fir·ma·tion** [æfə'meɪʃn] Versicherung *f;* Beteuerung *f;* Bestätigung *f;* **af·fir·ma·tive** [ə'fɜːmətɪv] **1.** □ bejahend; **2.** *answer in the* ∼ bejahen.

af·fix [ə'fɪks] (*to*) anheften, -kleben (an *acc.*), befestigen (an *dat.*); bei-, hinzufügen (*dat.*).

af·flict [ə'flɪkt] betrüben, heimsuchen, plagen; **af·flic·tion** [∼kʃn] Betrübnis *f;* Gebrechen *n;* Elend *n,* Not *f.*

af·flu·ence ['æfluəns] Überfluß *m;* Wohlstand *m;* ∼**ent** [∼t] **1.** □ reich (-lich); ∼ *society* Wohlstandsgesellschaft *f;* **2.** Nebenfluß *m.*

af·ford [ə'fɔːd] sich leisten; gewähren, bieten; *I can* ∼ *it* ich kann es mir leisten.

af·front [ə'frʌnt] **1.** beleidigen; **2.** Beleidigung *f.*

a·field [ə'fiːld] im Feld; (weit) weg.

a·float [ə'fləʊt] ⚓ *u. fig.* flott; schwimmend; auf See; *set* ∼ ⚓ flottmachen; in Umlauf bringen.

a·fraid [ə'freɪd]: *be* ∼ *of* sich fürchten *od.* Angst haben vor (*dat.*); *I'm* ∼ *she won't come* ich fürchte, sie wird nicht kommen; *I'm* ∼ *I must go now* leider muß ich jetzt gehen.

a·fresh [ə'freʃ] von neuem.

Af·ri·can ['æfrɪkən] **1.** afrikanisch; **2.** Afrikaner(in); *Am. a.* Neger(in).

af·ter ['ɑːftə] **1.** *adv.* hinterher, nachher, danach; **2.** *prp.* nach; hinter (*dat.*) (... her); ∼ *all* schließlich (doch); **3.** *cj.* nachdem; **4.** *adj.* später; Nach...; ∼**·ef·fect** ⚕ Nachwirkung *f*

(*a. fig.*); *fig.* Folge *f;* ∼**·glow** Abendrot *n;* ∼**·math** [∼mæθ] Nachwirkungen *pl.,* Folgen *pl.;* ∼**·noon** [ɑːftə'nuːn] Nachmittag *m; this* ∼ heute nachmittag; *good* ∼*!* guten Tag*!;* ∼**·taste** ['ɑːfteteɪst] Nachgeschmack *m;* ∼**·thought** nachträglicher Einfall; ∼**·wards,** *Am. a.* ∼**·ward** [∼wəd(z)] nachher, später.

a·gain [ə'gen] wieder(um); ferner; ∼ *and* ∼ *, time and* ∼ immer wieder; *as much* ∼ noch einmal soviel.

a·gainst [ə'genst] gegen; *räumlich:* gegen; an, vor (*dat. od. acc.*); *fig.* im Hinblick auf (*acc.*); *as* ∼ verglichen mit; *he was* ∼ *it* er war dagegen.

age [eɪdʒ] **1.** (Lebens)Alter *n;* Zeit (-alter *n*) *f;* Menschenalter *n;* (*old*) ∼ (hohe) Alter; (*come*) *of* ∼ mündig *od.* volljährig (werden); *be over* ∼ die Altersgrenze überschritten haben; *under* ∼ minderjährig; unmündig; *wait for* ∼*s* F e-e Ewigkeit warten; **2.** alt werden *od.* machen; ∼**d** ['eɪdʒɪd] alt, betagt; [eɪdʒd]: ∼ *twenty* 20 Jahre alt; ∼**less** ['eɪdʒlɪs] zeitlos; ewig jung.

a·gen·cy ['eɪdʒənsɪ] Tätigkeit *f;* Vermittlung *f;* Agentur *f,* Büro *n.*

a·gen·da [ə'dʒendə] Tagesordnung *f.*

a·gent ['eɪdʒənt] Handelnde(r *m*) *f;* (Stell)Vertreter(in); Agent *m* (*a. pol.*); Wirkstoff *m,* Mittel *n,* Agens *n.*

ag·glom·er·ate [ə'glɒməreɪt] (sich) zusammenballen; (sich) (an)häufen.

ag·gra·vate ['ægrəveɪt] erschweren, verschlimmern; F ärgern.

ag·gre·gate 1. ['ægrɪgeɪt] (sich) anhäufen; vereinigen (*to* mit); sich belaufen auf (*acc.*); **2.** □ [∼gət] (an)gehäuft; gesamt; **3.** [∼] Anhäufung *f;* Gesamtmenge *f,* Summe *f;* Aggregat *n.*

ag·gres·sion [ə'greʃn] Angriff *m;* ∼**sive** □ [∼sɪv] aggressiv, Angriffs...; *fig.* energisch; ∼**·sor** [∼sə] Angreifer *m.*

ag·grieved [ə'griːvd] verletzt, gekränkt.

a·ghast [ə'gɑːst] entgeistert, entsetzt.

ag·ile □ ['ædʒaɪl] flink, behend; **a·gil·i·ty** [ə'dʒɪlətɪ] Behendigkeit *f.*

ag·i·tate ['ædʒɪteɪt] *v/t.* hin u. her bewegen, schütteln; *fig.* aufregen; erörtern; *v/i.* agitieren; ∼**·ta·tion** [ædʒɪ'teɪʃn] heftige Bewegung, Erschütterung *f;* Aufregung *f;* Agitation *f*; **~·ta·tor** [ˈædʒɪteɪtə] Agitator *m*, Aufwiegler *m*.

a·glow [əˈgləʊ] glühend; *be ~* strahlen (*with* vor).

a·go [əˈgəʊ]: *a year ~* vor e-m Jahr.

ag·o·nize [ˈægənaɪz] (sich) quälen.

ag·o·ny [ˈægənɪ] heftiger Schmerz, *a. seelische* Qual; Pein *f*; Agonie *f*, Todeskampf *m*.

a·grar·i·an [əˈgreərɪən] Agrar...

a·gree [əˈgriː] *v/i*. übereinstimmen; sich vertragen; einig werden, sich einigen (*on, upon* über *acc*.); übereinkommen; ~ *to* zustimmen (*dat*.), einverstanden sein mit; **~·a·ble** □ [əˈgrɪəbl] (*to*) angenehm (für); übereinstimmend (mit); **~·ment** [əˈgriːmənt] Übereinstimmung *f*; Vereinbarung *f*; Abkommen *n*; Vertrag *m*.

ag·ri·cul·tur·al [ægrɪˈkʌltʃərəl] landwirtschaftlich; **~e** [ˈægrɪkʌltʃə] Landwirtschaft *f*; **~·ist** [ægrɪˈkʌltʃərɪst] Landwirt *m*.

a·ground ⚓ [əˈgraʊnd] gestrandet; *run* ~ stranden, auf Grund laufen.

a·head [əˈhed] vorwärts, voraus; vorn; *go* ~! nur zu!, mach nur!; *straight* ~ geradeaus.

aid [eɪd] **1.** helfen (*dat*.; *in* bei *et*.); fördern; **2.** Hilfe *f*, Unterstützung *f*.

ail [eɪl] *v/i* kränkeln (*dat*.); ~ schmerzen, weh tun (*dat*.); *what ~s him?* was fehlt ihm?; **~·ing** [ˈeɪlɪŋ] leidend; **~·ment** [~mənt] Leiden *n*.

aim [eɪm] **1.** *v/i*. zielen (*at* auf *acc*., nach); ~ *at fig*. beabsichtigen; *be ~ing to do s.th.* vorhaben, et. zu tun; *v/t*. ~ *at Waffe etc.* richten auf *od*. gegen (*acc*.); **2.** Ziel *n* (*a. fig*.); Absicht *f*; *take ~ at* zielen auf (*acc*.) *od*. nach; **~·less** □ [ˈeɪmlɪs] ziellos.

air¹ [eə] **1.** Luft *f*; Luftzug *m*; Miene *f*, Aussehen *n*; *by ~* auf dem Luftwege; *in the open* ~ im Freien; *on the* ~ im Rundfunk *od*. Fernsehen; *be on the* ~ senden (*Sender*); *go off the* ~ die Sendung beenden (*Person*); sein Programm beenden (*Sender*); *give o.s.* ~s, *put on* ~s vornehm tun; **2.** (aus)lüften; *fig*. an die Öffentlichkeit bringen; erörtern.

air² [~] Arie *f*, Weise *f*, Melodie *f*.

air|base ✈ [ˈeəbeɪs] Luftstützpunkt *m*; **~·bed** Luftmatratze(*n*) *f*; **~·borne** in der Luft (*Flugzeug*); ✈ Luftlande...; **~·brake** ⊕ Druckluftbremse *f*; **~· con·di·tioned** mit Klimaanlage;

~·craft (*pl*. *-craft*) Flugzeug *n*; **~·craft car·ri·er** Flugzeugträger *m*; **~·field** Flugplatz *m*; **~ force** ✕ Luftwaffe *f*; **~ host·ess** ✈ Stewardess *f*; **~·jack·et** Schwimmweste *f*; **~·lift** ✈ Luftbrücke *f*; **~·line** ✈ Fluggesellschaft *f*; **~·lin·er** ✈ Verkehrsflugzeug *n*; **~·mail** Luftpost *f*; *by* ~ mit Luftpost; **~·man** (*pl*. *-men*) Flieger *m* (*Luftwaffe*); **~·plane** *Am*. Flugzeug *n*; **~ pock·et** ✈ Luftloch *n*; **~ pol·lu·tion** Luftverschmutzung *f*; **~·port** Flughafen *m*; **~ raid** Luftangriff *m*; **~·raid pre·cau·tions** *pl*. Luftschutz *m*; **~·raid shel·ter** Luftschutzraum *m*; **~·route** ✈ Flugroute *f*; **~·sick** luftkrank; **~·space** Luftraum *m*; **~·strip** (behelfsmäßige) Start- u. Landebahn; **~·ter·mi·nal** Flughafenabfertigungsgebäude *n*; **~·tight** luftdicht; **~ traf·fic** Flugverkehr *m*; **~·traf·fic con·trol** ✈ Flugsicherung *f*; **~·traf·fic con·trol·ler** ✈ Fluglotse *m*; **~·way** ✈ Fluggesellschaft *f*; **~·wor·thy** flugtüchtig.

air·y □ [ˈeərɪ] (*-ier, -iest*) luftig; *contp*. überspannt.

aisle *arch*. [aɪl] Seitenschiff *n*; Gang *m*.

a·jar [əˈdʒɑː] halb offen, angelehnt.

a·kin [əˈkɪn] verwandt (*to* mit).

a·lac·ri·ty [əˈlækrətɪ] Munterkeit *f*; Bereitwilligkeit *f*, Eifer *m*.

a·larm [əˈlɑːm] **1.** Alarm(zeichen *n*) *m*; Wecker *m*; Angst *f*; **2.** alarmieren; beunruhigen; **~ clock** Wecker *m*.

al·bum [ˈælbəm] Album *n*.

al·bu·mi·nous [ælˈbjuːmɪnəs] eiweißhaltig.

al·co·hol [ˈælkəhɒl] Alkohol *m*; **~·ic** [ælkəˈhɒlɪk] **1.** alkoholisch; **2.** Alkoholiker(in); **~·is·m** [ˈælkəhɒlɪzəm] Alkoholismus *m*.

al·cove [ˈælkəʊv] Nische *f*; Laube *f*.

al·der·man [ˈɔːldəmən] (*pl*. *-men*) Ratsherr *m*, Stadtrat *m*.

ale [eɪl] Ale *n* (*helles, obergäriges Bier*).

a·lert [əˈlɜːt] **1.** □ wachsam; munter; **2.** Alarm(bereitschaft *f*) *m*; *on the* ~ auf der Hut; in Alarmbereitschaft; **3.** warnen (*to* vor *dat*.), alarmieren.

al·i·bi [ˈælɪbaɪ] Alibi *n*; F Entschuldigung *f*, Ausrede *f*.

a·li·en [ˈeɪljən] **1.** fremd; ausländisch; **2.** Fremde(r *m*) *f*, Ausländer(in);

~ate [~eɪt] veräußern; entfremden (*from dat.*).

a·light [əˈlaɪt] **1.** in Flammen; erhellt; **2.** ab-, aussteigen; ✈ niedergehen, landen; sich niederlassen (*on, upon* auf *dat. od. acc.*).

a·lign [əˈlaɪn] (sich) ausrichten (*with* nach); ~ *o.s. with* sich anschließen an (*acc.*).

a·like [əˈlaɪk] **1.** *adj.* gleich; **2.** *adv.* gleich, ebenso.

al·i·men·ta·ry [ælɪˈmentərɪ] nahrhaft; ~ *canal* Verdauungskanal *m*.

al·i·mo·ny ⚖ [ˈælɪmənɪ] Unterhalt *m*.

alive [əˈlaɪv] lebendig; (noch) am Leben; empfänglich (*to* für); lebhaft; belebt (*with* von).

all [ɔːl] **1.** *adj.* all; ganz; jede(r, -s); **2.** *pron.* alles; alle *pl.*; **3.** *adv.* ganz, völlig; *Wendungen:* ~ *at once* auf einmal; ~ *the better* desto besser; ~ *but* beinahe, fast; ~ *in Am.* F fertig, ganz erledigt; ~ *right* (alles) in Ordnung; *for* ~ *that* dessenungeachtet, trotzdem; *for* ~ *(that) I care* meinetwegen; *for* ~ *I know* soviel ich weiß; *at* ~ überhaupt; *not at* ~ überhaupt nicht; *the score was two* ~ das Spiel stand zwei zu zwei.

all-A·mer·i·can [ˌɔːləˈmerɪkən] rein amerikanisch; die ganzen USA vertretend.

al·lay [əˈleɪ] beruhigen; lindern.

al·le·ga·tion [ælɪˈɡeɪʃn] *unerwiesene* Behauptung.

al·lege [əˈledʒ] behaupten; **~d** □ angeblich.

al·le·giance [əˈliːdʒəns] (Untertanen)Treue *f*.

al·ler|gic [əˈlɜːdʒɪk] allergisch; **~gy** [ˈælədʒɪ] Allergie *f*.

al·le·vi·ate [əˈliːvɪeɪt] lindern, vermindern.

al·ley [ˈælɪ] (enge *od.* schmale) Gasse; Garten-, Parkweg *m*; *Bowling, Kegeln:* Bahn *f*; △ *nicht Allee.*

al·li·ance [əˈlaɪəns] Bündnis *n*.

al·lo|cate [ˈæləkeɪt] zuteilen, anweisen; **~ca·tion** [æləˈkeɪʃn] Zuteilung *f*.

al·lot [əˈlɒt] (*-tt-*) zuteilen, an-, zuweisen; **~ment** [~mənt] Zuteilung *f*; Parzelle *f*.

al·low [əˈlaʊ] erlauben, bewilligen, gewähren; zugeben; ab-, anrechnen, vergüten; ~ *for* berücksichtigen (*acc.*); **~·a·ble** □ [əˈlaʊəbl] erlaubt,

zulässig; **~ance** Erlaubnis *f*; Bewilligung *f*; Taschengeld *n*, Zuschuß *m*; Vergütung *f*; *fig.* Nachsicht *f*; *make* **~**(*s*) *for s.th.* et. in Betracht ziehen.

al·loy 1. [ˈælɔɪ] Legierung *f*; **2.** [əˈlɔɪ] legieren.

all-round [ˈɔːlraʊnd] vielseitig; **~er** [ɔːlˈraʊndə] Alleskönner *m*; *Sport:* Allroundsportler *m*, -spieler *m*.

al·lude [əˈluːd] anspielen (*to* auf *acc.*).

al·lure [əˈljʊə] (an-, ver)locken; **~ment** [~mənt] Verlockung *f*.

al·lu·sion [əˈluːʒn] Anspielung *f*.

al·ly 1. [əˈlaɪ] (sich) vereinigen, verbünden (*to, with* mit); **2.** [ˈælaɪ] Verbündete(r *m*) *f*, Bundesgenoss|e *m*, -in *f*; *the Allies pl.* die Alliierten *pl.*

al·ma·nac [ˈɔːlmənæk] Almanach *m*.

al·might·y [ɔːlˈmaɪtɪ] allmächtig; *the* ♀ *der Allmächtige.*

al·mond ♀ [ˈɑːmənd] Mandel *f*.

al·mo·ner *Brt.* [ˈɑːmənə] Sozialarbeiter(in) im Krankenhaus.

al·most [ˈɔːlməʊst] fast, beinah(e).

alms [ɑːmz] *pl.* Almosen *n*.

a·loft [əˈlɒft] (hoch) (dr)oben.

a·lone [əˈləʊn] allein; *let od. leave* ~ in Ruhe *od.* bleiben lassen; *let* ~ ... abgesehen von ...

a·long [əˈlɒŋ] **1.** *adv.* weiter, vorwärts; da; dahin; *all* ~ die ganze Zeit; ~ *with* (zusammen) mit; *come* ~ mitkommen, -gehen; *get* ~ vorwärts-, weiterkommen; *auskommen*, sich vertragen (*with s.o.* mit j-m); *take* ~ mitnehmen; **2.** *prp.* entlang, längs; **~side** [~ˈsaɪd] Seite an Seite; neben.

a·loof [əˈluːf] abseits; reserviert, zurückhaltend.

a·loud [əˈlaʊd] laut.

al·pha·bet [ˈælfəbɪt] Alphabet *n*.

al·pine [ˈælpaɪn] alpin, (Hoch)Gebirgs...

al·read·y [ɔːlˈredɪ] bereits, schon.

al·right [ɔːlˈraɪt] = *all right.*

al·so [ˈɔːlsəʊ] auch, ferner; △ *nicht also.*

al·tar [ˈɔːltə] Altar *m*.

al·ter [ˈɔːltə] (sich) (ver)ändern; ab-, umändern; **~a·tion** [ɔːltəˈreɪʃn] Änderung *f* (*to an dat.*), Veränderung *f*.

al·ter|nate 1. [ˈɔːltəneɪt] abwechseln (lassen); *alternating current* ⚡ Wechselstrom *m*; **2.** □ [ɔːlˈtɜːnət] abwechselnd; **3.** *Am.* [~] Stellvertreter *m*; **~na·tion** [ɔːltəˈneɪʃn] Abwechslung *f*; Wechsel *m*; **~na·tive**

[ɔːlˈtɜːnətɪv] **1.** ☐ alternativ, wahlweise; ~ *society* alternative Gesellschaft; **2.** Alternative *f*, Wahl *f*, Möglichkeit *f*.

al·though [ɔːlˈðou] obwohl, obgleich.

al·ti·tude [ˈæltɪtjuːd] Höhe *f*; *at an* ~ *of* in e-r Höhe von.

al·to·geth·er [ɔːltəˈgeðə] im ganzen, insgesamt; ganz (u. gar), völlig.

a·lu·min·i·um [æljuˈmɪnjəm], *Am.* **a·lu·mi·num** [əˈluːmɪnəm] Aluminium *n*.

al·ways [ˈɔːlweɪz] immer, stets.

am [æm; *im Satz* əm] *1. sg. pres. von* be.

a·mal·gam·ate [əˈmælgəmeɪt] amalgamieren; verschmelzen.

a·mass [əˈmæs] an-, aufhäufen.

am·a·teur [ˈæmətə] Amateur *m*; Dilettant(in).

a·maze [əˈmeɪz] in Erstaunen setzen, verblüffen; **~·ment** [~mənt] Staunen *n*, Verblüffung *f*; **a·maz·ing** ☐ [~ɪŋ] erstaunlich, verblüffend.

am·bas·sa·dor *pol.* [æmˈbæsədə] Botschafter *m* (*to* in e-m *Land*); Gesandte(r) *m*; **~·dress** *pol.* [~drɪs] Botschafterin *f* (*to* in e-m *Land*).

am·ber *min.* [ˈæmbə] Bernstein *m*.

am·bi·gu·i·ty [æmbɪˈgjuːɪtɪ] Zwei-, Mehrdeutigkeit *f*; **am·big·u·ous** ☐ [æmˈbɪgjʊəs] zwei-, vieldeutig; doppelsinnig.

am·bi·tion [æmˈbɪʃn] Ehrgeiz *m*; Streben *n*; **~·tious** ☐ [~ʃəs] ehrgeizig; begierig (*of* nach).

am·ble [ˈæmbl] **1.** Paßgang *m*; **2.** im Paßgang gehen *od.* reiten; schlendern.

am·bu·lance [ˈæmbjʊləns] ✗ Feldlazarett *n*; Krankenwagen *m*.

am·bush [ˈæmbuʃ] **1.** Hinterhalt *m*; *be od. lie in* ~ *for s.o.* j-m auflauern; **2.** auflauern (*dat.*); überfallen.

a·me·li·o·rate [əˈmiːljəreɪt] *v/t.* verbessern; *v/i.* besser werden.

a·men *int.* [ɑːˈmen] amen.

a·mend [əˈmend] verbessern, berichtigen; *Gesetz* abändern, ergänzen; **~·ment** [~mənt] Besserung *f*; Verbesserung *f*; *parl.* Abänderungs-, Ergänzungsantrag *m* (*zu* e-m *Gesetz*); *Am.* Zusatzartikel *m* zur Verfassung; **~s** *pl.* (Schaden)Ersatz *m*; *make*~ Schadenersatz leisten; *make* ~ *to s.o. for s.th.* j-n für et. entschädigen.

a·men·i·ty [əˈmiːnətɪ] *oft* amenities

pl. Annehmlichkeiten *pl.*

A·mer·i·can [əˈmerɪkən] **1.** amerikanisch; ~ *plan* Vollpension *f*; **2.** Amerikaner(in); **~·is·m** [~ɪzəm] Amerikanismus *m*; **~·ize** [~aɪz] (sich) amerikanisieren.

a·mi·a·ble ☐ [ˈeɪmjəbl] liebenswürdig, freundlich.

am·i·ca·ble ☐ [ˈæmɪkəbl] freundschaftlich; gütlich.

a·mid(st) [əˈmɪd(st)] inmitten (*gen.*), (mitten) in *od.* unter.

a·miss [əˈmɪs] verkehrt, falsch, übel; *take* ~ übelnehmen.

am·mo·ni·a [əˈməunjə] Ammoniak *n*.

am·mu·ni·tion [æmjʊˈnɪʃn] Munition *f*.

am·nes·ty [ˈæmnɪstɪ] **1.** Amnestie *f* (*Straferlaß*); **2.** begnadigen.

a·mok [əˈmɒk]: *run* ~ Amok laufen.

a·mong(st) [əˈmʌŋ(st)] (mitten) unter, zwischen.

am·o·rous ☐ [ˈæmərəs] verliebt (*of* in *acc.*).

a·mount [əˈmaʊnt] **1.** (*to*) sich belaufen (auf *acc.*); hinauslaufen (auf *acc.*); **2.** Betrag *m*, (Gesamt)Summe *f*; Menge *f*.

am·ple ☐ [ˈæmpl] (~*r*, ~*st*) weit, groß, geräumig; reich(lich), beträchtlich.

am·pli·fi·ca·tion [æmplɪfɪˈkeɪʃn] Erweiterung *f*; *rhet.* weitere Ausführung; *phys.* Verstärkung *f*; **~·fi·er** *ᶎ* [ˈæmplɪfaɪə] Verstärker *m*; **~·fy** [~faɪ] erweitern; *ᶎ* verstärken; weiter ausführen; **~·tude** [~tjuːd] Umfang *m*, Weite *f*, Fülle *f*.

am·pu·tate [ˈæmpjʊteɪt] amputieren.

a·muck [əˈmʌk] = amok.

a·muse [əˈmjuːz] (*o.s. sich*) amüsieren, unterhalten, belustigen; **~·ment** [~mənt] Unterhaltung *f*, Vergnügen *n*, Zeitvertreib *m*; **a·mus·ing** ☐ [~ɪŋ] amüsant, unterhaltend.

an [æn, ən] *unbestimmter Artikel vor vokalisch anlautenden Wörtern*: ein(e).

a·nae·mi·a *ᶎ* [əˈniːmjə] Blutarmut *f*, Anämie *f*.

an·aes·thet·ic [ænɪsˈθetɪk] **1.** (~*ally*) betäubend, Narkose...; **2.** Betäubungsmittel *n*.

a·nal *anat.* [ˈeɪnl] anal, Anal...

a·nal·o·gous ☐ [əˈnæləgəs] analog, entsprechend; **~·gy** [~dʒɪ] Analogie *f*, Entsprechung *f*.

an·a·lyse *bsd. Brt.*, *Am.* **-lyze** ['ænə-laɪz] analysieren; zerlegen; **a·nal·y·sis** [ə'næləsɪs] (*pl.* **-ses** [-siːz]) Analyse *f*.

an·arch·y ['ænəkɪ] Anarchie *f*, Gesetzlosigkeit *f*; Chaos *n*.

a·nat·o·mize [ə'nætəmaɪz] *≈* zerlegen; zergliedern; **~·my** [~ɪ] Anatomie *f*; Zergliederung *f*, Analyse *f*.

an·ces·tor ['ænsestə] Vorfahr *m*, Ahn *m*; **~·tral** [æn'sestrəl] angestammt; **~·tress** [~ɪ] Ahnen *pl*.

an·chor ['æŋkə] **1.** Anker *m*; *at* ~ vor Anker; **2.** verankern; **~·age** [~rɪdʒ] Ankerplatz *m*.

an·cho·vy *zo.* ['æntʃəvɪ] An(s)chovis *f*, Sardelle *f*.

an·cient ['eɪnʃənt] **1.** alt, antik; uralt; **2.** *the* ~*s* *pl. hist.* die Alten, die antiken Klassiker.

and [ænd, ənd] und.

a·ne·mi·a *Am.* = anaemia.

an·es·thet·ic *Am.* = anaesthetic.

a·new [ə'njuː] von neuem.

an·gel ['eɪndʒəl] Engel *m*; △ *nicht* Angel.

an·ger ['æŋgə] **1.** Zorn *m*, Ärger *m* (*at* über *acc.*); **2.** erzürnen, (ver)ärgern.

an·gi·na *≈* [æn'dʒaɪnə] Angina *f*, Halsentzündung *f*.

an·gle ['æŋgl] **1.** Winkel *m*; *fig.* Standpunkt *m*; **2.** angeln (*for* nach); **~·r** [~ə] Angler(in).

An·gli·can ['æŋglɪkən] **1.** *eccl.* anglikanisch; *Am.* britisch, englisch; **2.** *eccl.* Anglikaner(in).

An·glo-Sax·on ['æŋgləʊ'sæksən] **1.** angelsächsisch; **2.** Angelsachse *m*; *ling.* Altenglisch *n*.

an·gry ['æŋgrɪ] (-*ier*, -*iest*) zornig, verärgert, böse (*at*, *with* über *acc.*, mit *dat.*).

an·guish ['æŋgwɪʃ] (Seelen)Qual *f*, Schmerz *m*; **~·ed** [~ʃt] qualvoll.

an·gu·lar □ ['æŋgjʊlə] winkelig, Winkel...; knochig.

an·i·mal ['ænɪml] **1.** Tier *n*; **2.** tierisch.

an·i·mate ['ænɪmeɪt] beleben, beseelen; aufmuntern, anregen; △ *nicht animieren*; ~*d* lebendig, lebhaft, angeregt; ~ *cartoon* Zeichentrickfilm *m*; **~·ma·ted** [~] **~·ma·tion** [ænɪ'meɪʃn] Leben *n*, Lebhaftigkeit *f*, Feuer *n*; Animation *f*, Herstellung *f* von (Zeichen)Trickfilmen; (Zeichen)Trickfilm *m*.

an·i·mos·i·ty [ænɪ'mɒsətɪ] Animosität *f*, Feindseligkeit *f*.

an·kle *anat.* ['æŋkl] (Fuß)Knöchel *m*.

an·nals ['ænlz] *pl.* Jahrbücher *pl.*

an·nex 1. [ə'neks] anhängen; annektieren; **2.** ['æneks] Anhang *m*; Anbau *m*; **~·a·tion** [ænek'seɪʃn] Annexion *f*, Einverleibung *f*.

an·ni·hi·late [ə'naɪəleɪt] vernichten.

an·ni·ver·sa·ry [ænɪ'vɜːsərɪ] Jahrestag *m*; Jahresfeier *f*.

an·no·tate ['ænəʊteɪt] mit Anmerkungen versehen; kommentieren; **~·ta·tion** [ænəʊ'teɪʃn] Kommentieren *n*; Anmerkung *f*.

an·nounce [ə'naʊns] ankündigen; bekanntgeben; *Rundfunk*, *TV*: ansagen; durchsagen; △ *nicht annoncieren*; **~·ment** [~mənt] Ankündigung *f*; Bekanntgabe *f*; *Rundfunk*, *TV*: Ansage *f*; Durchsage *f*; **an·nounc·er** [~ə] *Rundfunk*, *TV*: Ansager(in), Sprecher(in).

an·noy [ə'nɔɪ] ärgern; belästigen; **~·ance** [~əns] Störung *f*, Belästigung *f*; Ärgernis *n*; **~·ing** [~ɪŋ] ärgerlich, lästig.

an·nu·al ['ænjʊəl] **1.** □ jährlich, Jahres...; **2.** ♀ einjährige Pflanze; Jahrbuch *n*.

an·nu·i·ty [ə'njuːɪtɪ] (Jahres)Rente *f*.

an·nul [ə'nʌl] (-*ll*-) für ungültig erklären, annullieren; **~·ment** [~mənt] Annullierung *f*, Aufhebung *f*.

an·o·dyne *≈* ['ænəʊdaɪn] **1.** schmerzstillend; **2.** schmerzstillendes Mittel.

a·noint [ə'nɔɪnt] salben.

a·nom·a·lous □ [ə'nɒmələs] anomal, abnorm, regelwidrig.

a·non·y·mous □ [ə'nɒnɪməs] anonym, ungenannt.

an·o·rak ['ænəræk] Anorak *m*.

an·oth·er [ə'nʌðə] ein anderer; ein zweiter; noch eine(r, -s).

an·swer ['ɑːnsə] **1.** *v/t. et.* beantworten; *j-m* antworten; entsprechen (*dat.*); *Zweck* erfüllen; ⊕ *dem Steuer* gehorchen; *e-r Vorladung* Folge leisten; *e-r Beschreibung* entsprechen; ~ *the bell od. door* (die Haustür) aufmachen; ~ *the telephone* ans Telefon gehen; *v/i.* antworten (*to* auf *acc.*); entsprechen (*to dat.*); ~ *back* freche Antworten geben; widersprechen; ~ *for* einstehen für; **2.** Antwort *f* (*to* auf *acc.*); **~·a·ble** [~rəbl] verantwortlich.

ant *zo.* [ænt] Ameise *f*.

an·tag·o|nis·m [æn'tægənɪzəm] Widerstreit m; Widerstand m; Feindschaft f; **~nist** [~ɪst] Gegner(in); **~nize** [~naɪz] ankämpfen gegen; sich j-n zum Feind machen.

an·te·ced·ent [æntɪ'si:dənt] **1.** □ vorhergehend, früher (to als); **2.** ~s pl. Vorgeschichte f; Vorleben f.

an·te·lope zo. ['æntɪləʊp] Antilope f.

an·ten·na¹ zo. [æn'tenə] (pl. -nae [-ni:]) Fühler m.

an·ten·na² Am. [~] Antenne f.

an·te·ri·or [æn'tɪərɪə] vorhergehend, früher (to als); vorder.

an·te-room ['æntɪrʊm] Vorzimmer n; Wartezimmer n.

an·them ['ænθəm] Hymne f.

an·ti- ['æntɪ] Gegen..., gegen ... eingestellt od. wirkend, Anti..., anti...; **~air·craft** ✕ Flieger-, Flugabwehr...; **~bi·ot·ic** [~baɪ'ɒtɪk] Antibiotikum n.

an·tic·i·pate [æn'tɪsɪpeɪt] vorwegnehmen; zuvorkommen (dat.); voraussehen, (-)ahnen; erwarten; **an·tic·i·pa·tion** [æntɪsɪ'peɪʃn] Vorwegnahme f; Zuvorkommen n; Voraussicht f; Erwartung f; in ~ im voraus.

an·ti·clock·wise Brt. [æntɪ'klɒkwaɪz] entgegen dem Uhrzeigersinn.

an·tics ['æntɪks] pl. Gekasper n; Mätzchen pl.; △ nicht antik, Antike.

an·ti|dote ['æntɪdəʊt] Gegengift n, -mittel n; **~freeze** Frostschutzmittel n; **~mis·sile** ✕ [æntɪ'mɪsaɪl] Raketenabwehr...

an·tip·a·thy [æn'tɪpəθɪ] Abneigung f.

an·ti·quat·ed ['æntɪkweɪtɪd] veraltet, altmodisch.

an·tique [æn'tiːk] **1.** antik, alt; **2.** Antiquität f; △ nicht Antike; ~ dealer Antiquitätenhändler(in); ~ shop, bsd. Am. ~ store Antiquitätenladen m; **an·tiq·ui·ty** [æn'tɪkwətɪ] Altertum n, Vorzeit f.

an·ti·sep·tic [æntɪ'septɪk] **1.** antiseptisch; **2.** antiseptisches Mittel.

ant·lers ['æntləz] pl. Geweih n.

a·nus anat. ['eɪnəs] After m.

an·vil ['ænvɪl] Amboß m.

anx·i·e·ty [æŋ'zaɪətɪ] Angst f; Sorge f (for um); ✚ Beklemmung f.

anx·ious □ ['æŋkʃəs] besorgt, beunruhigt (about wegen); △ nicht ängstlich; eifrig, gespannt (for auf acc.); bestrebt (to do zu tun).

an·y ['enɪ] **1.** adj. u. pron. (irgend-)

eine(r, -s), (irgend)welche(r, -s); (irgend) etwas, jede(r, -s) (beliebige); einige pl., welche pl.; ~ not keiner; **2.** adv. irgend(wie), ein wenig, etwas, (noch) etwas; **~·bod·y** (irgend) jemand; jeder; **~·how** irgendwie; trotzdem, jedenfalls; wie dem auch sei; **~·one** = anybody; **~·thing** (irgend) etwas; alles; ~ but alles andere als; ~ else? sonst noch etwas?; not ~ nichts; **~·way** = anyhow; **~·where** irgendwo(hin); überall.

a·part [ə'pɑːt] einzeln, getrennt, für sich; beiseite; △ nicht apart; ~ from abgesehen von.

a·part·heid [ə'pɑːtheɪt] Apartheid f, Politik f der Rassentrennung.

a·part·ment [ə'pɑːtmənt] Zimmer n; Am. Wohnung f; ~s pl. Brt. (möblierte) (Miet)Wohnung f; ~ house Am. Mietshaus n.

ap·a|thet·ic [æpə'θetɪk] (~ally) apathisch, teilnahmslos, gleichgültig; **~thy** ['æpəθɪ] Apathie f, Teilnahmslosigkeit f, Gleichgültigkeit f.

ape [eɪp] **1.** zo. (Menschen)Affe m; **2.** nachäffen.

a·pe·ri·ent [ə'pɪərɪənt] Abführmittel n.

ap·er·ture ['æpətjʊə] Öffnung f.

a·pi|a·ry ['eɪpjərɪ] Bienenhaus n; **~cul·ture** [~kʌltʃə] Bienenzucht f.

a·piece [ə'piːs] für jedes od. pro Stück, je.

a·pol·o|get·ic [əpɒlə'dʒetɪk] (~ally) verteidigend; rechtfertigend; entschuldigend; **~gize** [ə'pɒlədʒaɪz] sich entschuldigen (for für; to bei); **~gy** [~ɪ] Entschuldigung f; Rechtfertigung f; make od. offer s.o. an ~ (for s.th.) sich bei j-m (für et.) entschuldigen.

a·pos·tle [ə'pɒsl] Apostel m.

a·pos·tro·phe ling. [ə'pɒstrəfɪ] Apostroph m.

ap·pal(l) [ə'pɔːl] (-ll-) erschrecken, entsetzen; **~ling** □ [~ɪŋ] erschreckend, entsetzlich.

ap·pa·ra·tus [æpə'reɪtəs] Apparat m, Vorrichtung f, Gerät n.

ap·par·el [ə'pærəl] Kleidung f.

ap·par·ent □ [ə'pærənt] sichtbar; anscheinend; offenbar.

ap·pa·ri·tion [æpə'rɪʃn] Erscheinung f, Gespenst n.

ap·peal [ə'piːl] **1.** ⚖ Berufung od.

Revision einlegen, Einspruch erheben, Beschwerde einlegen; appellieren, sich wenden (*to* an~acc.); ~ *to* gefallen (*dat.*), zusagen (*dat.*), wirken auf (*acc.*); *j-n* dringend bitten (*for* um); **2.** ⚖ Revision *f*, Berufung *f*; Beschwerde *f*; Einspruch *m*; Appell *m* (*to* an *acc.*); Aufruf *m*; ⚔ Appell; Wirkung *f*, Reiz *m*; Bitte *f* (*to* an *acc.*; *for* um); ~ *for mercy* ⚖ Gnadengesuch *n*; ~**ing** □ [~ɪŋ] flehend; ansprechend.

ap·pear [əˈpɪə] (er)scheinen; sich zeigen; *öffentlich* auftreten; sich ergeben *od.* herausstellen; **~·ance** [~rəns] Erscheinen *n*; Auftreten *n*; Äußere(s) *n*, Erscheinung *f*, Aussehen *n*; Anschein *m*, äußerer Schein; *to all* ~(*s*) allem Anschein nach.

ap·pease [əˈpiːz] beruhigen; besänftigen; stillen; mildern; beilegen.

ap·pend [əˈpend] an-, hinzu-, beifügen; **~·age** [~ɪdʒ] Anhang *m*, Anhängsel *n*, Zubehör *n*.

ap·pen|di·ci·tis ⚕ [əpendɪˈsaɪtɪs] Blinddarmentzündung *f*; **~·dix** [əˈpendɪks] (*pl. -dixes, -dices* [-dɪsiːz]) Anhang *m*; *a. vermiform~* ⚕ Wurmfortsatz *m*, Blinddarm *m*.

ap·per·tain [æpəˈteɪn] gehören (*to* zu).

ap·pe|tite [ˈæpɪtaɪt] (*for*) Appetit *m* (auf *acc.*); *fig.* Verlangen *n* (nach); **~·tiz·er** [~zə] Appetithappen *m*, pikante Vorspeise; **~·tiz·ing** □ [~ɪŋ] appetitanregend.

ap·plaud [əˈplɔːd] applaudieren, Beifall spenden; loben; **ap·plause** [~z] Applaus *m*, Beifall *m*.

ap·ple ♀ [ˈæpl] Apfel *m*; **~·cart**: *upset s.o.'s* ~ F j-s Pläne über den Haufen werfen; **~ pie** (*warmer*) gedeckter Apfelkuchen; *in* ~*pie order* F in schönster Ordnung; **~ sauce** Apfelmus *n*; *Am. sl.* Schmus *m*, Quatsch *m*.

ap·pli·ance [əˈplaɪəns] Vorrichtung *f*; Gerät *n*; Mittel *n*.

ap·plic·a·ble □ [ˈæplɪkəbl] anwendbar (*to* auf *acc.*).

ap·pli|cant [ˈæplɪkənt] Antragsteller(in), Bewerber(in) (*for* um); **~·ca·tion** [æplɪˈkeɪʃn] (*to*) Anwendung *f* (auf *acc.*); Bedeutung *f* (für); Gesuch *n* (*for* um); Bewerbung *f* (*for* um).

ap·ply [əˈplaɪ] *v/t.* (*to*) (auf)legen,

auftragen (auf *acc.*); anwenden (auf *acc.*); verwenden (für); ~ *o.s. to* sich widmen (*dat.*); *v/i.* (*to*) passen, zutreffen, sich anwenden lassen (auf *acc.*); gelten (für); sich wenden (an *acc.*); sich bewerben (*for* um), beantragen (*for acc.*).

ap·point [əˈpɔɪnt] bestimmen, festsetzen; verabreden; ernennen (*s.o. governor* j-n zum ...); berufen (*to* auf *e-n Posten*); ~**ment** [~mənt] Bestimmung *f*; Verabredung *f*; Termin *m* (*geschäftlich, beim Arzt etc.*); Ernennung *f*, Berufung *f*; Stelle *f*; ~ *book* Terminkalender *m*.

ap·por·tion [əˈpɔːʃn] ver-, zuteilen; ~**ment** [~mənt] Ver-, Zuteilung *f*.

ap·prais|al [əˈpreɪzl] (Ab)Schätzung *f*; **~e** [əˈpreɪz] (ab)schätzen, taxieren.

ap·pre|cia·ble □ [əˈpriːʃəbl] nennenswert, spürbar; **~·ci·ate** [~ʃɪeɪt] *v/t.* schätzen, würdigen; dankbar sein für; *v/i.* im Wert steigen; **~·ci·a·tion** [əpriːʃɪˈeɪʃn] Schätzung *f*, Würdigung *f*; Anerkennung *f*; Verständnis *n* (*of* für); Einsicht *f*; Dankbarkeit *f*; *econ.* Wertsteigerung *f*.

ap·pre·hend [æprɪˈhend] ergreifen, fassen; begreifen; befürchten; ~**hen·sion** [~ʃn] Ergreifung *f*, Festnahme *f*; Besorgnis *f*; ~**hen·sive** □ [~sɪv] ängstlich, besorgt (*for* um; *that* daß).

ap·pren·tice [əˈprentɪs] **1.** Auszubildende(r *m*) *f*, Lehrling *m*; **2.** in die Lehre geben; ~**ship** [~ʃɪp] Lehrzeit *f*, Lehre *f*, Ausbildung *f*.

ap·proach [əˈprəʊtʃ] **1.** *v/i.* näherkommen, sich nähern; *v/t.* sich nähern (*dat.*); herangehen *od.* -treten an (*acc.*); **2.** (Heran)Nahen *n*; Ein-, Zu-, Auffahrt *f*; Annäherung *f*; Methode *f*.

ap·pro·ba·tion [æprəˈbeɪʃn] Billigung *f*, Beifall *m*.

ap·pro·pri·ate 1. [əˈprəʊprɪeɪt] sich aneignen; verwenden; *parl.* bewilligen; **2.** □ [~ɪt] (*for, to*) angemessen (*dat.*), passend (für, zu).

ap·prov|al [əˈpruːvl] Billigung *f*; Anerkennung *f*; Beifall *m*; **~e** [~v] billigen, anerkennen; ~**ed** bewährt.

ap·prox·i·mate 1. [əˈprɒksɪmeɪt] sich nähern; **2.** □ [~mət] annähernd, ungefähr.

a·pri·cot ♀ [ˈeɪprɪkɒt] Aprikose *f*.

A·pril [ˈeɪprəl] April *m*.

a·pron [ˈeɪprən] Schürze *f*; ~**string**

Schürzenband *n*; *be tied to one's wife's* (*mother's*) ~*s fig.* unterm Pantoffel stehen (der Mutter am Schürzenzipfel hängen).

apt □ ['æpt] geeignet, passend; treffend; begabt; ~ *to* geneigt zu; **ap·ti·tude** ['æptɪtjuːd] (*for*) Begabung *f* (für), Befähigung *f* (für), Talent *n* (zu); ~ *test* Eignungsprüfung *f*.

a·quat·ic [ə'kwætɪk] Wassertier *n*, -pflanze *f*; ~*s sg.* Wassersport *m*.

aq·ue·duct ['ækwɪdʌkt] Aquädukt *m*.

aq·ui·line ['ækwɪlaɪn] Adler...; gebogen; ~ *nose* Adlernase *f*.

Ar·ab ['ærəb] Araber(in); **Ar·a·bic** [~ɪk] **1.** arabisch; **2.** *ling.* Arabisch *n*.

ar·a·ble ['ærəbl] anbaufähig; Acker...

ar·bi·tra·ry □ ['ɑːbɪtrəri] willkürlich, eigenmächtig; ~**trate** [~reɪt] entscheiden, schlichten; ~**tra·tion** [ɑːbɪ'treɪʃn] Schlichtung *f*; ~**tra·tor** *ᵗⱼʃ* [ə'bɪtreɪtə] Schiedsrichter *m*; Schlichter *m*.

ar·bo(u)r ['ɑːbə] Laube *f*.

arc [ɑːk] (*ᵗⱼ* Licht)Bogen *m*; **ar·cade** [ɑː'keɪd] Arkade *f*; Bogen-, Laubengang *m*; Durchgang *m*, Passage *f*.

arch[1] [ɑːtʃ] **1.** Bogen *m*; Gewölbe *n*; *anat.* Rist *m*, Spann *m* (*Fuß*); **2.** (sich) wölben; krümmen; ~ *over* überwölben.

arch[2] [~] erste(r, -s), oberste(r, -s), Haupt..., Erz...

arch[3] □ [~] schelmisch.

ar·cha·ic [ɑː'keɪɪk] (~*ally*) veraltet.

arch·an·gel ['ɑːkeɪndʒəl] Erzengel *m*; ~**bish·op** ['ɑːtʃ'bɪʃəp] Erzbischof *m*.

ar·cher ['ɑːtʃə] Bogenschütze *m*; ~**y** [~rɪ] Bogenschießen *n*.

ar·chi·tect ['ɑːkɪtekt] Architekt *m*; Urheber(in), Schöpfer(in); ~**tec·ture** [~ktʃə] Architektur *f*, Baukunst *f*.

ar·chives ['ɑːkaɪvz] *pl.* Archiv *n*.

arch·way ['ɑːtʃweɪ] (Bogen)Gang *m*.

arc·tic ['ɑːktɪk] **1.** arktisch, nördlich, Nord...; *Polar...*; **2.** *Am.* wasserdichter Überschuh.

ar·dent □ ['ɑːdənt] heiß, glühend; *fig.* leidenschaftlich, heftig; eifrig.

ar·do(u)r *fig.* ['ɑːdə] Leidenschaft (-lichkeit) *f*, Heftigkeit *f*, Feuer *n*; Eifer *m*.

ar·du·ous □ ['ɑːdjuəs] mühsam; zäh.

are [ɑː, *unbetont:* ə] *pres. pl. u.* 2. *sg. von be.*

ar·e·a ['eərɪə] Areal *n*; (Boden)Fläche

f, Flächenraum *m*; Gegend *f*, Gebiet *n*, Zone *f*; Bereich *m*; ~ *code Am. teleph.* Vorwählnummer *f*, Vorwahl *f*.

Ar·gen·tine ['ɑːdʒəntaɪn] **1.** argentinisch; **2.** Argentinier(in).

a·re·na [ə'riːnə] Arena *f*.

ar·gue ['ɑːgjuː] *v/t.* (das Für u. Wider) erörtern, diskutieren; *v/i.* streiten; argumentieren, Gründe (für u. wider) anführen, Einwendungen machen.

ar·gu·ment ['ɑːgjumənt] Argument *n*, Beweis(grund) *m*; Streit *m*, Wortwechsel *m*, Auseinandersetzung *f*.

ar·id □ ['ærɪd] dürr, trocken (*a. fig.*).

a·rise [ə'raɪz] (*arose, arisen*) entstehen; auftauchen, -treten, -kommen; **a·ris·en** [ə'rɪzn] *p.p von arise.*

ar·is·toc·ra·cy [ærɪ'stɒkrəsɪ] Aristokratie *f*, Adel *m*; ~**to·crat** ['ærɪstəkræt] Aristokrat(in); ~**to·crat·ic** (~*ally*) [ærɪstə'krætɪk] aristokratisch.

a·rith·me·tic [ə'rɪθmətɪk] Rechnen *n*.

ark [ɑːk] Arche *f*.

arm[1] [ɑːm] Arm *m*; Armlehne *f*; *keep s.o. at* ~'*s length* sich j-n vom Leibe halten; *infant in* ~*s* Säugling *m*.

arm[2] [~] **1.** *mst* ~*s pl.* Waffen *pl.*; Waffengattung *f*; ~*s control* Rüstungskontrolle *f*; ~*s race* Wettrüsten *n*, Rüstungswettlauf *m*; *up in* ~*s* kampfbereit; *fig.* in Harnisch; **2.** (sich) bewaffnen; (sich) wappnen *od.* rüsten.

ar·ma·da [ɑː'mɑːdə] Kriegsflotte *f*.

ar·ma·ment ['ɑːməmənt] (Kriegsaus)Rüstung *f*; Aufrüstung *f*.

ar·ma·ture *ᵗⱼ* ['ɑːmətjuə] Anker *m*.

arm·chair ['ɑːm'tʃeə] Lehnstuhl *m*, Sessel *m*.

ar·mi·stice ['ɑːmɪstɪs] Waffenstillstand *m* (*a. fig.*).

ar·mo(u)r ['ɑːmə] **1.** *ᵡ* Rüstung *f*, Panzer *m* (*a. fig., zo.*); **2.** panzern; ~*ed car* gepanzertes Fahrzeug (*für Geldtransporte etc.*); ~**y** [~rɪ] Waffenkammer *f*; Waffenfabrik *f*.

arm·pit ['ɑːmpɪt] Achselhöhle *f*.

ar·my ['ɑːmɪ] Heer *n*, Armee *f*; *fig.* Menge *f*; ~ *chaplain* Militärgeistliche(r) *m*.

a·ro·ma [ə'rəumə] Aroma *n*, Duft *m*; **ar·o·mat·ic** [ærə'mætɪk] (~*ally*) aromatisch, würzig.

a·rose [əˈrəʊz] *pret. von* arise.

a·round [əˈraʊnd] **1.** *adv.* (rings)herum, (rund)herum, ringsumher, überall; um, herum; in der Nähe; da; **2.** *prp.* um, um... herum, rund um; in (*dat.*) ... herum; ungefähr, etwa.

a·rouse [əˈraʊz] (auf)wecken; *fig.* aufrütteln, erregen.

ar·range [əˈreɪndʒ] (an)ordnen; in die Wege leiten, arrangieren; vereinbaren, ausmachen; ♪ arrangieren, bearbeiten (*a. thea.*); **~·ment** [~mənt] Anordnung *f*, Zusammenstellung *f*, Verteilung *f*, Disposition *f*; Vereinbarung *f*, Absprache *f*; ♪ Arrangement *n*, Bearbeitung *f* (*a. thea.*); *make* ~s Vorkehrungen *od.* Vorbereitungen treffen.

ar·ray [əˈreɪ] ✗ Schlachtordnung *f*; Schar *f*, Aufgebot *n*.

ar·rear [əˈrɪə] *mst* ~s *pl.* Rückstand *m*, Rückstände *pl.*; Schulden *pl.*

ar·rest [əˈrest] **1.** ⚖ Verhaftung *f*, Festnahme *f*; ⚠ *nicht Arrest* (*Schule etc.*); **2.** ⚖ verhaften, festnehmen; an-, aufhalten; *fig.* fesseln.

ar·riv·al [əˈraɪvl] Ankunft *f*; Erscheinen *n*; Ankömmling *m*; ~s *pl.* ankommende Züge *pl. od.* Schiffe *pl. od.* Flugzeuge *pl.*; **ar·rive** [~v] (an)kommen, eintreffen, erscheinen; ~ *at fig.* erreichen (*acc.*).

ar·ro·gance [ˈærəgəns] Arroganz *f*, Anmaßung *f*, Überheblichkeit *f*; **~·gant** [~t] arrogant, anmaßend, überheblich.

ar·row [ˈærəʊ] Pfeil *m*; ~·**head** Pfeilspitze *f*.

ar·se·nal [ˈɑːsənl] Arsenal *n*, Zeughaus *n*.

ar·se·nic ⚗ [ˈɑːsnɪk] Arsen *n*.

ar·son ⚖ [ˈɑːsn] Brandstiftung *f*.

art [ɑːt] Kunst *f*; *fig.* List *f*; Kniff *m*; ⚠ *nicht Art*; ~s *pl.* Geisteswissenschaften *pl.*; *Faculty of* ~s, *Am.* ~s *Department* philosophische Fakultät *f*.

ar·te·ri·al [ɑːˈtɪərɪəl] *anat.* Schlagader...; ~ *road* Hauptstraße *f*; **ar·te·ry** [ˈɑːtərɪ] *anat.* Arterie *f*, Schlag-, Pulsader *f*; *fig.* Verkehrsader *f*.

art·ful □ [ˈɑːtfl] schlau, verschmitzt.

ar·ti·cle [ˈɑːtɪkl] Artikel *m* (*a. gr.*).

ar·tic·u·late **1.** [ɑːˈtɪkjʊleɪt] deutlich (aus)sprechen; zusammenfügen; **2.** □ [~lət] deutlich; ⚕, *zo.* gegliedert; **~·la·tion** [ɑːtɪkjʊˈleɪʃn] (deutliche

Aussprache; *anat.* Gelenk(verbindung *f*) *n*.

ar·ti·fice [ˈɑːtɪfɪs] Kunstgriff *m*, List *f*; ~·**fi·cial** □ [ɑːtɪˈfɪʃl] künstlich, Kunst...; ~ *person* juristische Person.

ar·til·le·ry [ɑːˈtɪlərɪ] Artillerie *f*.

ar·ti·san [ɑːtɪˈzæn] Handwerker *m*.

art·ist [ˈɑːtɪst] Künstler(in); *variety* ~ Artist(in); **ar·tis·tic** [ɑːˈtɪstɪk] (~*ally*) künstlerisch, Kunst...

art·less □ [ˈɑːtlɪs] ungekünstelt, schlicht; arglos.

as [æz, əz] **1.** *adv.* so, ebenso; wie; (*in der Eigenschaft*) als; **2.** *cj.* (gerade) wie, so wie; ebenso wie; als, während; obwohl, obgleich; da, weil; *besondere Wendungen:* ~ ... ~ (eben)so ... wie; ~ *for*, ~ *to* was ... (an)betrifft; ~ *from* von e-m *Zeitpunkt an*, ab; ~ *it were* sozusagen; ~ *Hamlet* als Hamlet.

as·cend [əˈsend] *v/i.* (auf-, empor-, hinauf)steigen; *v/t.* be-, ersteigen; *Fluß etc.* hinauffahren.

as·cen·dan·cy, **~·den·cy** [əˈsendənsɪ] [~ənsɪ] Überlegenheit *f*, Einfluß *m*; ~·**sion** [~ʃn] Aufsteigen *n* (*bsd. ast.*); Aufstieg *m* (*e-s Ballons etc.*); ♀ (*Day*) Himmelfahrt(stag *m*) *f*; ~·**t** [~t] Aufstieg *m*; Steigung *f*.

as·cer·tain [æsəˈteɪn] ermitteln.

as·cet·ic [əˈsetɪk] (~*ally*) asketisch.

as·cribe [əˈskraɪb] zuschreiben (*to dat.*).

a·sep·tic ⚕ [æˈseptɪk] **1.** aseptisch, keimfrei; **2.** aseptisches Mittel.

ash¹ [æʃ] ♀ Esche *f*; Eschenholz *n*.

ash² [~] *a.* ~es *pl.* Asche *f*; *Ash Wednesday* Aschermittwoch *m*.

a·shamed [əˈʃeɪmd] beschämt; *be* ~ *of* sich schämen für (*od. gen.*).

ash can *Am.* [ˈæʃkæn] = *dustbin.*

ash·en [ˈæʃn] Aschen...; aschfahl.

a·shore [əˈʃɔː] *am od.* ans Ufer *od.* Land; *run* ~ stranden.

ash|tray [ˈæʃtreɪ] Asch(en)becher *m*; ~·**y** [~ɪ] (-*ier*, -*iest*) = *ashen*.

A·sian [ˈeɪʃn, ˈeɪʒn], **A·si·at·ic** [eɪʃɪˈætɪk] **1.** asiatisch; **2.** Asiat(in).

a·side [əˈsaɪd] **1.** beiseite (*a. thea.*), seitwärts; ~ *from Am.* abgesehen von; **2.** *thea.* Aparte *n*.

ask [ɑːsk] *v/t.* fragen (*s.th. nach et.*); verlangen (*of, from s.o.* von j-m); bitten (*s.o.* [*for*] *s.th.* j. um et.; *that* darum, daß); erbitten; ~ (*s.o.*) *a question* (j-m) e-e Frage stellen;

v/i.: ~ *for* bitten um; fragen nach; *he* ~*ed for it od. for trouble* er wollte es ja so haben; *to be had for the* ~*ing* umsonst zu haben.

a·skance [ə'skæns]: *look* ~ *at s.o.* j-n von der Seite ansehen; j-n schief *od.* mißtrauisch ansehen.

a·skew [ə'skju:] schief.

a·sleep [ə'sli:p] schlafend; *be (fast, sound)* ~ (fest) schlafen; *fall* ~ einschlafen.

as·par·a·gus ♀ [ə'spærəgəs] Spargel *m*.

as·pect ['æspekt] Lage *f*; Aspekt *m*, Seite *f*, Gesichtspunkt *m*.

as·phalt ['æsfælt] **1.** Asphalt *m*; **2.** asphaltieren.

as·pic ['æspɪk] Aspik *m*, Gelee *n*.

as·pi·rant [ə'spaɪərənt] Bewerber(in); ~**ra·tion** [æspə'reɪʃn] Ambition *f*, Bestrebung *f*.

as·pire [ə'spaɪə] streben, trachten (*to, after* nach).

ass *zo.* [æs] Esel *m*; △ *nicht* As.

as·sail [ə'seɪl] angreifen; *be* ~*ed with doubts* von Zweifeln befallen werden; **as·sai·lant** [~ənt] Angreifer(in).

as·sas·sin [ə'sæsɪn] Mörder(in) (aus politischen Gründen), Attentäter(in); ~**ate** *bsd. pol.* [~eɪt] ermorden; *be* ~*d* e-m Attentat *od.* Mordanschlag zum Opfer fallen; ~**a·tion** [əsæsɪ'neɪʃn] (*of*) *bsd.* politischer Mord (*an dat.*), Ermordung *f* (*gen.*), (geglücktes) Attentat (auf *acc.*).

as·sault [ə'sɔːlt] **1.** Angriff *m*; **2.** angreifen, überfallen; ⚖ tätlich angreifen *od.* beleidigen.

as·say [ə'seɪ] **1.** (Erz-, Metall)Probe *f*; **2.** *v/t.* prüfen, untersuchen.

as·sem·blage [ə'semblɪdʒ] (An-)Sammlung *f*; ⊕ Montage *f*; ~**ble** [~bl] (sich) versammeln; ⊕ montieren; ~**bly** [~ɪ] Versammlung *f*, Gesellschaft *f*; ⊕ Montage *f*; ~ *line* ⊕ Fließband *n*.

as·sent [ə'sent] **1.** Zustimmung *f*; **2.** (*to*) zustimmen (*dat.*); billigen.

as·sert [ə'sɜːt] behaupten; geltend machen; ~ *o.s.* sich behaupten *od.* durchsetzen; **as·ser·tion** [ə'sɜːʃn] Behauptung *f*; Erklärung *f*; Geltendmachung *f*.

as·sess [ə'ses] *Kosten etc.* festsetzen; (zur Steuer) veranlagen (*at* mit); *fig.* abschätzen, beurteilen; ~**ment** [~mənt] Festsetzung *f*; (Steuer-)

Veranlagung *f*; *fig.* Einschätzung *f*.

as·set ['æset] *econ.* Aktivposten *m*; *fig.* Plus *n*, Gewinn *m*; ~*s pl.* Vermögen *n*; *econ.* Aktiva *pl.*; ⚖ Konkursmasse *f*.

as·sid·u·ous □ [ə'sɪdjʊəs] emsig, fleißig; aufmerksam.

as·sign [ə'saɪn] an-, zuweisen; bestimmen; zuschreiben; **as·sig·na·tion** [æsɪg'neɪʃn] (*bsd.* heimliches) Treffen (*e-s Liebespaares*); = ~**ment** [ə'saɪnmənt] An-, Zuweisung *f*; Aufgabe *f*; Auftrag *m*; ⚖ Übertragung *f*.

as·sim·i·late [ə'sɪmɪleɪt] (sich) angleichen *od.* anpassen (*to, with dat.*); ~**la·tion** [əsɪmɪ'leɪʃn] Assimilation *f*, Angleichung *f*, Anpassung *f*.

as·sist [ə'sɪst] j-m beistehen, helfen; unterstützen; ~**ance** [~əns] Beistand *m*, Hilfe *f*; **as·sis·tant** [~t] **1.** stellvertretend, Hilfs...; **2.** Assistent(in), Mitarbeiter(in); *shop* ~ *Brt.* Verkäufer(in).

as·siz·es *Brt. hist.* [ə'saɪzɪz] *pl.* Sitzung(en *pl.*) *f* des periodischen Geschworenengerichts.

as·so·ci·ate 1. [ə'səʊʃɪeɪt] vereinigen, -binden; assoziieren; ~ *with* verkehren mit; **2.** [~ʃɪət] verbunden; ~ *member* außerordentliches Mitglied; **3.** [~] Kolleg(e *m*, -in *f*; Teilhaber(in); ~**a·tion** [əsəʊsɪ'eɪʃn] Vereinigung *f*, Verbindung *f*; Verein *m*; Assoziation *f*.

as·sort [ə'sɔːt] sortieren, aussuchen, zusammenstellen; ~**ment** [~mənt] Sortieren *n*; *econ.* Sortiment *n*, Auswahl *f*.

as·sume [ə'sjuːm] annehmen; vorgeben; übernehmen; **as·sump·tion** [ə'sʌmpʃn] Annahme *f*; Übernahme *f*; ♀ (*Day*) *eccl.* Mariä Himmelfahrt *f*.

as·sur·ance [ə'ʃʊərəns] Zu-, Versicherung *f*; Zuversicht *f*; Sicherheit *f*, Gewißheit *f*; Selbstsicherheit *f*; (*life*) ~ *bsd. Brt.* (Lebens)Versicherung *f*; ~**e** [ə'ʃʊə] versichern; *bsd. Brt.* j-s Leben versichern; ~**ed 1.** (*adv.* ~**ed·ly** [~rɪdlɪ]) sicher; **2.** Versicherte(r *m*) *f*.

asth·ma ✻ ['æsmə] Asthma *n*.

a·stir [ə'stɜː] auf(gestanden); auf den Beinen; voller *od.* in Aufregung.

as·ton·ish [ə'stɒnɪʃ] in Erstaunen setzen; *be* ~*ed* erstaunt sein (*at* über *acc.*); ~**ing** □ [~ɪŋ] erstaunlich;

~ment [~mənt] (Er)Staunen *n*, Verwunderung *f*.

as·tound [əˈstaʊnd] verblüffen.

a·stray [əˈstreɪ]: *go* ~ vom Weg abkommen; *fig.* auf Abwege geraten; irregehen; *lead* ~ *fig.* verleiten, verleiten; vom rechten Weg abbringen.

a·stride [əˈstraɪd] rittlings (*of* auf *dat.*).

as·trin·gent s^r [əˈstrɪndʒənt] **1.** □ adstringierend; **2.** Adstringens *n*.

as·trol·o·gy [əˈstrɒlədʒɪ] Astrologie *f*.

as·tro·naut [ˈæstrənɔːt] Astronaut *m*, (Welt)Raumfahrer *m*.

as·tron·o·my [əˈstrɒnəmɪ] Astronomie *f*.

as·tute □ [əˈstjuːt] scharfsinnig; schlau; **~ness** [~nɪs] Scharfsinn *m*.

a·sun·der [əˈsʌndə] auseinander; entzwei.

a·sy·lum [əˈsaɪləm] Asyl *n*.

at [æt, *unbetont:* ət] *prp.* an; auf; aus; bei; für; in; mit; nach; über; um; von; vor; zu; ~ *school* in der Schule; ~ *the age of* im Alter von.

ate [et] *pret. von* eat 1.

a·the·is·m [ˈeɪθɪɪzm] Atheismus *m*.

ath·lete [ˈæθliːt] (*bsd.* Leicht)Athlet *m*; **~let·ic** [æθˈletɪk] (~ally) athletisch; **~let·ics** *sg. od. pl.* (*bsd.* Leicht)Athletik *f*.

At·lan·tic [ətˈlæntɪk] **1.** atlantisch; **2.** *a.* ~ *Ocean* Atlantik *m*.

at·mo·sphere [ˈætməsfɪə] Atmosphäre *f* (*a. fig.*); **~spher·ic** [ætməsˈferɪk] (~ally) atmosphärisch.

at·om [ˈætəm] Atom *n* (*a. fig.*); ~ **bomb** Atombombe *f*.

a·tom·ic [əˈtɒmɪk] (~ally) atomar, Atom...; ~ **age** Atomzeitalter *n*; ~ **bomb** Atombombe *f*; ~ **en·er·gy** Atomenergie *f*; ~ **pile** Atomreaktor *m*; ~ **pow·er** Atomkraft *f*; **~pow·ered** atomgetrieben; ~ **waste** Atommüll.

at·om·ize [ˈætəmaɪz] in Atome auflösen; atomisieren; zerstäuben; **~iz·er** [~ə] Zerstäuber *m*.

a·tone [əˈtəʊn]: ~ *for* et. wiedergutmachen; **~ment** [~mənt] Buße *f*, Sühne *f*.

a·tro·cious □ [əˈtrəʊʃəs] scheußlich, gräßlich; grausam; **~c·i·ty** [əˈtrɒsɪtɪ] Scheußlichkeit *f*, Gräßlichkeit *f*; Greueltat *f*, Greuel *m*.

at·tach [əˈtætʃ] *v/t.* (*to*) anheften, ankleben (an *acc.*), befestigen, anbringen (an *dat.*); *Wert, Wichtigkeit etc.* beimessen (*dat.*); ~ *o.s. to* sich anschließen (*dat.*, an *acc.*); **~ed** zugetan; **~ment** [~mənt] Befestigung *f*; ~ *for*, ~ *to* Bindung *f* an (*acc.*); Anhänglichkeit *f* an (*acc.*), Neigung *f* zu.

at·tack [əˈtæk] **1.** angreifen (*a. fig.*); befallen (*Krankheit*); *Arbeit* in Angriff nehmen; **2.** Angriff *m*; s^r Anfall *m*; Inangriffnahme *f*.

at·tain [əˈteɪn] *Ziel* erreichen, erlangen; **~ment** [~mənt] Erreichung *f*; Erlangen *n*; **~s** *pl.* Kenntnisse *pl.*, Fertigkeiten *pl.*

at·tempt [əˈtempt] **1.** versuchen; **2.** Versuch *m*; Attentat *n*.

at·tend [əˈtend] *v/t.* begleiten; bedienen; pflegen; s^r behandeln; *j-m* aufwarten; beiwohnen (*dat.*), anwesend sein bei, teilnehmen an, *Schule etc.* besuchen; *e-e Vorlesung etc.* hören; *v/i.* achten, hören (*to* auf *acc.*); ~ *to* erledigen; **~ance** [~əns] Begleitung *f*; Dienst *m*; (Auf)Wartung *f*, Pflege *f*; s^r Behandlung *f*; Anwesenheit *f* (*at* bei); Besuch *m* (*der Schule etc.*); Besucher(zahl *f*) *pl.*; **~ant** [~t] Aufseher(in); ⊕ Bedienungsmann *m*.

at·ten·tion [əˈtenʃn] Aufmerksamkeit *f* (*a. fig.*); **~tive** □ [~tɪv] aufmerksam.

at·tic [ˈætɪk] Dachboden *m*; Dachstube *f*.

at·tire [əˈtaɪə] **1.** kleiden; **2.** Kleidung *f*.

at·ti·tude [ˈætɪtjuːd] (Ein)Stellung *f*; Haltung *f*.

at·tor·ney [əˈtɜːnɪ] Bevollmächtigte(r) *m*; *Am.* Rechtsanwalt *m*; *power of* ~ Vollmacht *f*; 2 *General Brt.* erster Kronanwalt; *Am.* Justizminister *m*.

at·tract [əˈtrækt] anziehen, *Aufmerksamkeit* erregen; *fig.* reizen; **at·trac·tion** [~kʃn] Anziehung(skraft) *f*, Reiz *m*; Attraktion *f*, *thea. etc.* Zugnummer *f*, -stück *n*; **at·trac·tive** □ [~tɪv] anziehend; attraktiv; reizvoll; **at·trac·tive·ness** [~nɪs] Reiz *m*.

at·trib·ute¹ [əˈtrɪbjuːt] beimessen, zuschreiben; zurückführen (*to* auf *acc.*).

at·tri·bute² [ˈætrɪbjuːt] Attribut *n* (*a. gr.*), Eigenschaft *f*, Merkmal *n*.

at·tune [əˈtjuːn]: ~ *to fig.* einstellen auf (*acc.*).

avow

au·burn ['ɔ:bən] kastanienbraun.

auc|tion ['ɔ:kʃn] 1. Auktion *f*; *sell by* (*Am. at*) ~ versteigern; *put up for* (*Am. at*) ~ zur Versteigerung anbieten; 2. *mst* ~ *off* versteigern; **~·tio·neer** [ɔ:kʃəˈnɪə] Auktionator *m*.

au·da·cious □ [ɔ:ˈdeɪʃəs] kühn; dreist; **~·ci·ty** [ɔ:ˈdæsətɪ] Kühnheit *f*; Dreistigkeit *f*.

au·di·ble □ ['ɔ:dəbl] hörbar.

au·di·ence ['ɔ:djəns] Publikum *n*, Zuhörer(schaft *f*) *pl.*, Zuschauer *pl.*, Besucher *pl.*, Leser(kreis *m*) *pl.*; Audienz *f*; *give* ~ *to* Gehör schenken (*dat.*).

au·di·o|cas·sette ['ɔ:drəʊkæˈset] Text-, Tonkassette *f*; **~·vis·u·al** [ɔ:drəʊˈvɪzjʊəl]: ~ *aids pl.* audiovisuelle Unterrichtsmittel *pl.*

au·dit *econ.* ['ɔ:dɪt] 1. Bücherrevision *f*; 2. *Rechnungen* prüfen; **au·di·tor** [~ə] (Zu)Hörer(in); *econ.* Bücherrevisor *m*, Buchprüfer *m*; **au·di·to·ri·um** [ɔ:dɪˈtɔ:rɪəm] Zuschauerraum *m*; *Am.* Vortrags-, Konzertsaal *m*.

au·ger ⊕ ['ɔ:gə] *großer* Bohrer.

aught [ɔ:t] (irgend) etwas; *for* ~ *I care* meinetwegen; *for* ~ *I know* soviel ich weiß.

aug·ment [ɔ:gˈment] vergrößern.

au·gur ['ɔ:gə]: ~ *ill* (*well*) ein schlechtes (gutes) Zeichen *od.* Omen sein (*for* für).

Au·gust¹ ['ɔ:gəst] August *m*.

au·gust² □ [ɔ:ˈgʌst] erhaben.

aunt [ɑ:nt] Tante *f*; **~·ie**, **~·y** ['ɑ:ntɪ] Tantchen *n*.

aus|pices ['ɔ:spɪsɪz] *pl.* Schirmherrschaft *f*; **~·pi·cious** □ [ɔ:ˈspɪʃəs] günstig.

aus|tere □ [ɒˈstɪə] streng; herb; hart; einfach; **~·ter·i·ty** [ɒˈsterətɪ] Strenge *f*; Härte *f*; Einfachheit *f*.

Aus·tra·li·an [ɒˈstreɪljən] 1. australisch; 2. Australier(in).

Aus·tri·an ['ɒstrɪən] 1. österreichisch; 2. Österreicher(in).

au·then·tic [ɔ:ˈθentɪk] (~*ally*) authentisch; zuverlässig; echt.

au·thor ['ɔ:θə] Urheber(in); Autor(in), Verfasser(in); **~·i·ta·tive** □ [ɔ:ˈθɒrɪtətɪv] maßgebend; gebieterisch; zuverlässig; **~·i·ty** [~rətɪ] Autorität *f*; (Amts)Gewalt *f*; Nachdruck *m*, Gewicht *n*; Vollmacht *f*; Einfluß *m* (*over* auf *acc.*); Ansehen *n*; Quelle *f*; Fachmann *m*; *mst authorities pl.* Behörde *f*; **~·ize**

['ɔ:θəraɪz] *j-n* autorisieren, ermächtigen, bevollmächtigen, berechtigen; *et.* gutheißen; **~·ship** [~ʃɪp] Urheberschaft *f*.

au·to·graph ['ɔ:təgrɑ:f] Autogramm *n*.

au·to·mat *TM* ['ɔ:təmæt] Automatenrestaurant *n* (*in den USA*).

au·to|mate ['ɔ:təmeɪt] automatisieren; **~·mat·ic** [ɔ:təˈmætɪk] (~*ally*) 1. automatisch; 2. Selbstladepistole *f*, -gewehr *n*; *mot.* Auto *n* mit Automatik; **~·ma·tion** [~ˈmeɪʃn] Automation *f*; **~·ma·ton** *fig.* [ɔ:ˈtɒmətən] (*pl.* -*ta* [-tə], -*tons*) Roboter *m*.

au·to·mo·bile *bsd. Am.* ['ɔ:təməbi:l] Auto *n*, Automobil *n*.

au·ton·o·my [ɔ:ˈtɒnəmɪ] Autonomie *f*.

au·tumn ['ɔ:təm] Herbst *m*; **au·tum·nal** □ [ɔ:ˈtʌmnəl] herbstlich, Herbst...

aux·il·i·a·ry [ɔ:gˈzɪljərɪ] helfend, Hilfs...

a·vail [əˈveɪl] 1. ~ *o.s. of* sich *e-r Sache* bedienen, et. nutzen; 2. Nutzen *m*; *of no*, *to no* ~ nutzlos; **a·vai·la·ble** □ [~əbl] verfügbar, vorhanden; erreichbar; *econ.* lieferbar, vorrätig, erhältlich.

av·a·lanche ['ævəlɑ:nʃ] Lawine *f*.

av·a|rice ['ævərɪs] Habsucht *f*; **~·ri·cious** □ [ævəˈrɪʃəs] habgierig, -süchtig.

a·venge [əˈvendʒ] rächen; **a·veng·er** [~ə] Rächer(in).

av·e·nue ['ævənju:] Allee *f*; Boulevard *m*, Prachtstraße *f*.

a·ver [əˈvɜ:] (-*rr*-) behaupten.

av·e·rage ['ævərɪdʒ] 1. Durchschnitt *m*; ⚓ Havarie *f*; 2. □ durchschnittlich, Durchschnitts...; 3. durchschnittlich betragen (ausmachen, haben, leisten, erreichen *etc.*); *a.* ~ *out* den Durchschnitt ermitteln.

a·verse [əˈvɜ:s] abgeneigt (*to dat.*); **a·ver·sion** [~ʃn] Widerwille *m*, Abneigung *f*.

a·vert [əˈvɜ:t] abwenden (*a. fig.*).

a·vi·a·ry ['eɪvɪərɪ] Vogelhaus *n*, Voliere *f*.

a·vi·a·tion ✈ [eɪvɪˈeɪʃn] Luftfahrt *f*; **~·tor** ['eɪvɪeɪtə] Flieger *m*.

av·id □ ['ævɪd] gierig (*for* nach); begeistert, passioniert.

a·void [əˈvɔɪd] (ver)meiden; ausweichen; **~·ance** [~əns] Vermeidung *f*.

a·vow [əˈvaʊ] bekennen, (ein)gestehen; anerkennen; **~·al** [~əl] Bekenntnis *n*, (Ein)Geständnis *n*; **~ed·ly** [~ɪdlɪ] eingestandenermaßen.

a·wait [ə'weɪt] erwarten.

a·wake [ə'weɪk] **1.** wach, munter; *be ~ to* sich e-r *Sache* (voll) bewußt sein; **2.** *a.* **a·wak·en** [~ən] (*awoke od. awaked, awaked od. awoken od. awoken*) *v/t.* (auf)wecken; *~ s.o. to s.th.* j-m et. zum Bewußtsein bringen; *v/i.* auf-, erwachen; **a·wak·en·ing** [~ənɪŋ] Erwachen *n*.

a·ward [ə'wɔːd] **1.** Belohnung *f*; Preis *m*, Auszeichnung *f*; **2.** zuerkennen, *Preis etc.* verleihen.

a·ware [ə'weə] *be ~ of s.th.* von et. wissen, sich e-r *Sache* bewußt sein; *become ~ of s.th.* et. gewahr werden *od.* merken.

a·way [ə'weɪ] (hin)weg, fort; entfernt; immer weiter, d(a)rauflos; *Sport:* auswärts; *~ (game)* Auswärtsspiel *n*; *~ (win)* Auswärtssieg *m*.

awe [ɔː] **1.** Ehrfurcht *f*, Scheu *f*, Furcht *f*; **2.** (Ehr)Furcht einflößen (*dat.*).

aw·ful □ ['ɔːfl] furchtbar, schrecklich.

a·while [ə'waɪl] e-e Weile.

awk·ward □ ['ɔːkwəd] ungeschickt, unbeholfen, linkisch; unangenehm; dumm, ungünstig (*Zeitpunkt etc.*).

awl [ɔːl] Ahle *f*, Pfriem *m*.

aw·ning ['ɔːnɪŋ] Plane *f*; Markise *f*.

a·woke [ə'wəuk] *pret. von awake* 2; *a.*

a·wok·en [~ən] *p.p. von awake* 2.

a·wry [ə'raɪ] schief; *fig.* verkehrt.

ax(e) [æks] Axt *f*, Beil *n*.

ax·is ['æksɪs] (*pl. -es* [-siːz]) Achse *f*.

ax·le ⊕ ['æksl] *a.* **~·tree** (Rad)Achse *f*, Welle *f*.

ay(e) [aɪ] Ja *n*; *parl.* Jastimme *f*; *the ~s have it* der Antrag ist angenommen.

az·ure ['æʒə] azur-, himmelblau.

B

bab·ble ['bæbl] **1.** stammeln; plappern, schwatzen; plätschern (*Bach*); **2.** Geplapper *n*, Geschwätz *n*.

babe [beɪb] kleines Kind, Baby *n*; *Am.* F Puppe *f* (*Mädchen*).

ba·boon *zo.* [bə'buːn] Pavian *m*.

ba·by ['beɪbɪ] **1.** Säugling *m*, kleines Kind, Baby *n*; *Am.* F Puppe *f* (*Mädchen*); **2.** Baby..., Kinder...; klein; *~ car·riage Am.* Kinderwagen *m*; **~·hood** [~hʊd] frühe Kindheit, Säuglingsalter *n*; **~·mind·er** *Brt.* [~maɪndə] Tagesmutter *f*; **~·sit** *(-tt-, -sat)* babysitten; **~·sit·ter** [~ə] Babysitter(in).

bach·e·lor ['bætʃələ] Junggeselle *m*; *univ.* Bakkalaureus *m* (*Grad*).

back [bæk] **1.** Rücken *m*; Rückseite *f*; Rücklehne *f*; Hinterende *n*; *Fußball:* Verteidiger *m*; **2.** *adj.* Hinter..., Rück..., hintere(r, -s), rückwärtig; entlegen; rückläufig; rückständig; alt, zurückliegend (*Zeitung etc.*); **3.** *adv.* zurück; rückwärts; **4.** *v/t.* mit e-m Rücken versehen; (*a. ~ up*) unterstützen; hinten grenzen an

(*acc.*); zurückbewegen, zurückstoßen mit (*Auto*); wetten *od.* setzen auf (*acc.*); *econ. Scheck* indossieren; *v/i.* sich rückwärts bewegen, zurückgehen *od.* -treten *od.* -fahren, *mot. a.* zurückstoßen; **~ al·ley** *Am.* finstere Seitengasse; **~·bite** ['bækbaɪt] (*-bit, -bitten*) verleumden; **~·bone** Rückgrat *n*; **~·break·ing** [~ɪŋ] erschöpfend, mörderisch (*Arbeit*); **~·comb** *Haar* toupieren; **~·er** [~ə] Unterstützer(in); Wetter(in); **~·fire** *mot.* Früh-, Fehlzündung *f*; **~·ground** Hintergrund *m*; **~·hand** *Sport:* Rückhand *f*; **~·ing** [~ɪŋ] Unterstützung *f*; ⊕ versteifende Ausfütterung, Verstärkung *f*; ♩ Begleitung *f* (*e-s Popsängers*); **~ num·ber** alte Nummer (*e-r Zeitung*); **~ seat** Rücksitz *m*; **~·side** Gesäß *n*, Hintern *m*, Po *m*; **~ stairs** Hintertreppe *f*; **~ street** Seitenstraße *f*; **~·stroke** *Sport:* Rückenschwimmen *n*; **~ talk** *Am.* F freche Antwort(en *pl.*); **~·track** *fig.* e-n Rückzieher machen; **~·ward** [~wəd] **1.** *adj.* Rück-

(wärts)...; langsam; zurückgeblieben; rückständig; zurückhaltend; **2.** *adv.* (*a.* **~wards** [~wədz]) rückwärts, zurück; **~yard** *Brt.* Hinterhof *m*; *Am.* Garten *m* hinter dem Haus.

ba·con ['beɪkən] Speck *m*.

bac·te·ri·a *biol.* [bæk'tɪərɪə] *pl.* Bakterien *pl.*

bad ☐ [bæd] (*worse, worst*) schlecht, böse, schlimm; *go* ~ schlecht werden, verderben; *he is in a* ~ *way* es geht ihm schlecht, er ist übel dran; *he is* ~*ly off* es geht ihm sehr schlecht; ~*ly wounded* schwerverwundet; *want* ~*ly* F dringend brauchen.

bade [beɪd] *pret. von* bid 1.

badge [bædʒ] Abzeichen *n*; Dienstmarke *f*.

bad·ger ['bædʒə] **1.** *zo.* Dachs *m*; **2.** plagen, *j-m* zusetzen.

bad·lands ['bædlændz] *pl.* Ödland *n*.

baf·fle ['bæfl] *j-n* verwirren; *Plan etc.* vereiteln, durchkreuzen.

bag [bæg] **1.** Beutel *m*, Sack *m*; Tüte *f*; Tasche *f*; ~ *and baggage* (mit) Sack und Pack; **2.** (-*gg-*) in e-n Beutel *etc.* tun; in e-n Beutel verpacken *od.* abfüllen; *hunt.* zur Strecke bringen; (sich) bauschen.

bag·gage *bsd. Am.* ['bægɪdʒ] (Reise-) Gepäck *n*; **~car** ⊕ Gepäckwagen *m*; **~ check** *Am.* Gepäckschein *m*; **~room** *Am.* Gepäckaufbewahrung *f*.

bag·gy F ['bægɪ] (-*ier, -iest*) sackartig; schlaff (heruntterhängend); ausgebeult (*Hose*).

bag·pipes ['bægpaɪps] *pl.* Dudelsack *m*.

bail [beɪl] **1.** Bürge *m*; Bürgschaft *f*; Kaution *f*; *admit to* ~ ⚖ gegen Kaution freilassen; *go od. stand* ~ *for s.o.* ⚖ für *j-n* Kaution stellen; **2.** ~ *out* ⚖ *j-n* gegen Kaution freibekommen; *Am.* ✈ (mit dem Fallschirm) abspringen.

bai·liff ['beɪlɪf] ⚖ *bsd.* Gerichtsvollzieher *m*; (Guts)Verwalter *m*.

bait [beɪt] **1.** Köder *m* (*a. fig.*); **2.** mit e-m Köder versehen; *fig.* ködern; *fig.* quälen, piesacken.

bake [beɪk] backen, im (Back)Ofen braten; *Ziegel* brennen; dörren; ~*d beans pl.* Bohnen *pl.* in Tomatensoße; ~*d potatoes pl.* ungeschälte, im Ofen gebackene *Kartoffeln*; Folienkartoffeln *pl.*; **bak·er** ['beɪkə] Bäcker

m; **bak·er·y** [~ərɪ] Bäckerei *f*; **baking-pow·der** [~ɪŋpaʊdə] Backpulver *n*.

bal·ance ['bæləns] **1.** Waage *f*; Gleichgewicht *n* (*a. fig.*); Harmonie *f*; *econ.* Bilanz *f*; *econ.* Saldo *m*, Kontostand *m*, Guthaben *n*; F Rest *m*; *a.* ~ *wheel* Unruh *f* (*der Uhr*); *keep one's* ~ das Gleichgewicht halten; *lose one's* ~ das Gleichgewicht verlieren; *fig.* die Fassung verlieren; ~ *of payments* econ. Zahlungsbilanz *f*; ~ *of power* pol. Kräftegleichgewicht *n*; ~ *of trade* (Außen)Handelsbilanz *f*; **2.** *v/t.* (ab-, er)wägen; im Gleichgewicht halten, balancieren; ausgleichen; *v/i.* balancieren, sich ausgleichen.

bal·co·ny ['bælkənɪ] Balkon *m* (*a. thea.*).

bald ☐ [bɔːld] kahl; *fig.* dürftig; *fig.* unverblümt; ⚠ *nicht bald.*

bale¹ *econ.* [beɪl] Ballen *m*.

bale² *Brt.* ✈ [~]: ~ *out* (mit dem Fallschirm) abspringen.

bale·ful ☐ ['beɪlfl] verderblich; unheilvoll; haßerfüllt (*Blick*).

balk [bɔːk] **1.** ✇ (Furchen)Rain *m*; Balken *m*; Hindernis *n*; **2.** *v/t.* (ver)hindern, vereiteln; *v/i.* stutzen; scheuen.

ball¹ [bɔːl] **1.** Ball *m*; Kugel *f*; *anat.* (Hand-, Fuß)Ballen *m*; Knäuel *m, n*; Kloß *m*; ~*s pl.* V Eier *pl.* (*Hoden*); *keep the* ~ *rolling* das Gespräch *od.* die Sache in Gang halten; *play* ~ F mitmachen; **2.** (sich) (zusammen-) ballen.

ball² [~] Ball *m*, Tanzveranstaltung *f*.

bal·lad ['bæləd] Ballade *f*; Lied *n*.

bal·last ['bæləst] **1.** Ballast *m*; Schotter *m*; **2.** mit Ballast beladen; beschottern.

ball-bear·ing ⊕ ['bɔːl'beərɪŋ] Kugellager *n*.

bal·let ['bæleɪ] Ballett *n*.

bal·lis·tics ✕, *phys.* [bə'lɪstɪks] *sg.* Ballistik *f*.

bal·loon [bə'luːn] **1.** Ballon *m*; **2.** im Ballon aufsteigen; sich blähen.

bal·lot ['bælət] **1.** Wahl-, Stimmzettel *m*; geheime Wahl; **2.** (geheim) abstimmen; ~ *for* losen um; **~box** Wahlurne *f*.

ball-point (pen) ['bɔːlpɔɪnt('pen)] Kugelschreiber *m*.

ball·room ['bɔːlrʊm] Ball-, Tanzsaal *m*.

B

balm [bɑ:m] Balsam *m* (*a. fig.*).

balm·y □ ['bɑ:mɪ] (*-ier, -iest*) lind, mild (*Wetter*); *bsd. Am. sl.* bekloppt, verrückt.

ba·lo·ney *Am. sl.* [bə'ləʊnɪ] Quatsch *m*.

bal·us·trade [bælə'streɪd] Balustrade *f*, Brüstung *f*; Geländer *n*.

bam·boo ♀ [bæm'bu:] (*pl. -boos*) Bambus(rohr *n*) *m*.

bam·boo·zle F [bæm'bu:zl] betrügen, übers Ohr hauen.

ban [bæn] **1.** (*amtliches*) Verbot, Sperre *f*; *eccl.* Bann *m*; **2.** (*-nn-*) verbieten.

ba·nal [bə'nɑ:l] banal, abgedroschen.

ba·na·na ♀ [bə'nɑ:nə] Banane *f*.

band [bænd] **1.** Band *n*; Streifen *m*; Schar *f*, Gruppe *f*; (*bsd. Räuber*)Bande *f*; ♪ Kapelle *f*, (*Tanz-, Unterhaltungs*)Orchester *n*, (*Jazz-, Rock-*)Band *f*; **2.** △ *nicht Buch-Band, Tonband*; ~ *together* sich zusammentun *od.* zusammenrotten.

ban·dage ['bændɪdʒ] **1.** Binde *f*; Verband *m*; **2.** bandagieren; verbinden.

ban·dit ['bændɪt] Bandit *m*.

band·|-mas·ter ['bændmɑ:stə] Kapellmeister *m*; ~**stand** Musikpavillon *m*, -podium *n*; ~**wag·on** *Am.* Wagen *m* mit Musikkapelle; *jump on the* ~ sich der erfolgversprechenden Sache anschließen.

ban·dy¹ ['bændɪ] ~ *words* (*with s.o.*) sich (mit j-m) streiten; ~ *about Gerüchte etc.* in Umlauf setzen *od.* weitererzählen.

ban·dy² [~] (*-ier, -iest*) krumm; ~**legged** säbel-, O-beinig.

bane [beɪn] Ruin *m*, Fluch *m*; ~**ful** □ ['beɪnfl] verderblich.

bang [bæŋ] **1.** heftiger Schlag; Knall *m*; *mst* ~*s pl.* Ponyfrisur *f*; **2.** dröhnend (zu)schlagen.

ban·ish ['bænɪʃ] verbannen; ~**ment** [~mənt] Verbannung *f*.

ban·is·ter ['bænɪstə] *a.* ~*s pl.* Treppengeländer.

bank [bæŋk] **1.** Damm *m*; Ufer *n*; (Fels-, Sand-, Wolken-, ♣ Blut*etc.*)Bank *f*; *econ.* Bank(haus *n*) *f*; ~ *of issue* Notenbank *f*; △ *nicht Sitz-Bank*; **2.** *v/t.* eindämmen; *econ.* Geld auf e-r Bank einzahlen; ♣ *Blut etc.* konservieren u. aufbewahren; *v/i.* *econ.* Bankgeschäfte machen; *econ.* ein Bankkonto haben; ~ *on* sich verlassen auf (*acc.*); ~**bill** ['bæŋkbɪl]

Bankwechsel *m*; *Am.* = *banknote*; ~**book** Kontobuch *n*, *a.* Sparbuch *n*; ~**er** [~ə] Bankier *m*; ~ **hol·i·day** *Brt.* Bankfeiertag *m* (*gesetzlicher Feiertag*); ~**ing** [~ɪŋ] Bankgeschäft *n*, Bankwesen *n*; *attr.* Bank...; ~**note** Banknote *f*, Geldschein *m*; ~ **rate** Diskontsatz *m*.

bank·rupt ♣♣ ['bæŋkrʌpt] **1.** Zahlungsunfähige(r *m*) *f*; **2.** bankrott, zahlungsunfähig; *go* ~ in Konkurs gehen, Bankrott machen; **3.** bankrott machen; ~**cy** ♣♣ [~sɪ] Bankrott *m*, Konkurs *m*.

ban·ner ['bænə] Banner *n*; Fahne *f*.

banns [bænz] *pl.* Aufgebot *n*.

ban·quet ['bæŋkwɪt] Bankett *n*, Festessen *n*.

ban·ter ['bæntə] necken.

bap·tis·m ['bæptɪzəm] Taufe *f*; ~**tize** [bæp'taɪz] taufen.

bar [bɑ:] **1.** Stange *f*, Stab *m*; Barren *m*; Riegel *m*; Schranke *f*; Sandbank *f*; (*Ordens*)Spange *f*; ♪ Takt(strich) *m*; dicker Strich; ♣♣ (Gerichts-)Schranke *f*; ♣♣ Anwaltschaft *f*; Bar *f* (*im Hotel etc.*); *fig.* Hindernis *n*; **2.** (*-rr-*) zu-, verriegeln; versperren; einsperren; (ver)hindern; ausschließen.

barb [bɑ:b] Widerhaken *m*.

bar·bar·i·an [bɑ:'beərɪən] **1.** barbarisch; **2.** Barbar(in).

bar·be·cue ['bɑ:bɪkju:] **1.** Bratrost *m*, Grill *m*; Grillfleisch *n* (*bsd. Ochse*); Grillparty *f*; **2.** *bsd. Ochse* auf dem Rost braten, grillen.

barbed wire [bɑ:bd 'waɪə] Stacheldraht *m*.

bar·ber ['bɑ:bə] (Herren)Friseur *m*.

bare [beə] **1.** (~*r*, ~*st*) nackt, bloß; kahl; bar, leer; **2.** entblößen; ~**faced** □ ['beəfeɪst] frech; ~**foot**, ~**footed** barfuß; ~**head·ed** barhäuptig; ~**ly** [~lɪ] kaum.

bar·gain ['bɑ:gɪn] **1.** Vertrag *m*, Abmachung *f*; Geschäft *n*, Handel *m*, Kauf *m*; vorteilhafter Kauf; *a* (*dead*) ~ spottbillig; *it's a* ~*!* abgemacht!; *into the* ~ obendrein; **2.** (ver)handeln; übereinkommen; ~ **sale** Ausverkauf *m*.

barge [bɑ:dʒ] **1.** Flußboot *n*, Lastkahn *m*; Hausboot *n*; **2.** ~ *in*(*to*) hereinplatzen (in *acc.*).

bark¹ [bɑ:k] **1.** ♀ Borke *f*, Rinde *f*; **2.** abrinden; *Knie* abschürfen.

bark² [~] **1.** bellen; ~ *up the wrong*

tree F auf dem Holzweg sein; an der falschen Adresse sein; **2.** Bellen *n*.

bar·ley ♀ ['bɑːlɪ] Gerste *f*; Graupe *f*.

barn [bɑːn] Scheune *f*; (Vieh)Stall *m*; **~storm** *Am. pol.* ['bɑːnstɔːm] herumreisen u. (Wahl)Reden halten.

ba·rom·e·ter [bə'rɒmɪtə] Barometer *n*.

bar·on ['bærən] Baron *m*; Freiherr *m*; **~ess** [~ɪs] Baronin *f*; Freifrau *f*.

bar·racks ['bærəks] *sg.* ✕ Kaserne *f*; *contp.* Mietskaserne *f*; △ *nicht Baracke*.

bar·rage ['bærɑːʒ] Staudamm *m*; ✕ Sperrfeuer *n*; *fig.* Hagel *m* (*Wort-, Rede-*)Schwall *m*.

bar·rel ['bærəl] **1.** Faß *n*, Tonne *f*; (*Gewehr*)Lauf *m*; ⊕ Trommel *f*, Walze *f*; **2.** in Fässer füllen; **~·or·gan** ♪ Drehorgel *f*.

bar·ren □ ['bærən] unfruchtbar; dürr, trocken; tot (*Kapital*).

bar·ri·cade [bærɪ'keɪd] **1.** Barrikade *f*; **2.** verbarrikadieren; sperren.

bar·ri·er ['bærɪə] Schranke *f* (*a. fig.*), Barriere *f*, Sperre *f*; Hindernis *n*.

bar·ris·ter *Brt.* ['bærɪstə] (plädierender) Rechtsanwalt, Barrister *m*.

bar·row ['bærəʊ] Karre *f*.

bar·ter ['bɑːtə] **1.** Tausch(handel) *m*; **2.** tauschen (*for* gegen).

base¹ □ [beɪs] (~*r*, ~*st*) gemein.

base² [~] **1.** Basis *f*; Grundlage *f*; Fundament *n*; Fuß *m*; ♫ Base *f*; ✕ Standort *m*; ✕ Stützpunkt *m*; **2.** gründen, stützen (*on, upon* auf *acc.*).

base|ball ['beɪsbɔːl] Baseball(spiel *n*) *m*; **~·board** *Am.* Scheuerleiste *f*; **~·less** ['beɪslɪs] grundlos; **~·ment** [~mənt] Fundament *n*; Kellergeschoß *n*.

base·ness ['beɪsnɪs] Gemeinheit *f*.

bash·ful □ ['bæʃfl] schüchtern.

ba·sic¹ ['beɪsɪk] **1.** grundlegend, Grund...; ♫ basisch; **2.** ~*s pl.* Grundlagen *pl.*

BA·SIC² [~] BASIC *n* (*e-e Computersprache*).

ba·si·cal·ly ['beɪsɪkəlɪ] im Grunde.

ba·sin ['beɪsn] Becken *n*, Schale *f*; Schüssel *f*; Tal-, Wasser-, Hafenbecken *n*.

ba·sis ['beɪsɪs] (*pl. -ses* [-siːz]) Basis *f*; Grundlage *f*.

bask [bɑːsk] sich sonnen (*a. fig.*).

bas·ket ['bɑːskɪt] Korb *m*; **~·ball** Basketball(spiel *n*) *m*.

bass¹ ♪ [beɪs] Baß *m*.

bass² *zo.* [bæs] (Fluß-, See)Barsch *m*.

bas·tard ['bɑːstəd] **1.** □ unehelich; unecht; Bastard...; **2.** Bastard *m*.

baste¹ [beɪst] *Braten* mit Fett begießen.

baste² [~] (an)heften.

bat¹ [bæt] *zo.* Fledermaus *f*; *as blind as a* ~ stockblind.

bat² [~] *Sport:* **1.** Schlagholz *n*, Schläger *m*; **2.** (*-tt-*) *den Ball* schlagen; am Schlagen *od.* dran sein.

batch [bætʃ] Schub *m* (*Brote*); Stoß *m*, Stapel *m* (*Briefe etc.*).

bate [beɪt]: *with* ~*d breath* mit angehaltenem Atem.

bath [bɑːθ] **1.** (*pl. baths* [~ðz]) (Wannen)Bad *n*; *have a* ~ *Brt.*, *take a* ~ *Am.* baden, ein Bad nehmen; ~*s pl.* Bad *n*; Badeanstalt *f*; Badeort *m*; **2.** *Brt. v/t. Kind etc.* baden; *v/i.* baden, ein Bad nehmen.

bathe [beɪð] *v/t. Wunde etc.*, *bsd. Am. Kind etc.* baden; *v/i. etc.* baden; schwimmen; *bsd. Am.* baden, ein Bad nehmen.

bath·ing ['beɪðɪŋ] Baden *n*; *attr.* Bade...; **~·suit** Badeanzug *m*.

bath|robe ['bɑːθrəʊb] Bademantel *m*; *Am.* Morgen-, Schlafrock *m*; **~·room** Badezimmer *n*; ~*towel* Badetuch *n*; **~·tub** Badewanne *f*.

bat·on ['bætən] Stab *m*; ♪ Taktstock *m*; Schlagstock *m*, Gummiknüppel *m*.

bat·tal·i·on ✕ [bə'tæljən] Bataillon *n*.

bat·ten ['bætn] Latte *f*.

bat·ter ['bætə] **1.** *Sport:* Schläger *m*; Rührteig *m*; **2.** heftig schlagen; *Ehefrau, Kind etc.* mißhandeln; verbeulen; ~ *down od. in* Tür einschlagen; **~·y** [~rɪ] Batterie *f*; *assault and* ~ ⚖ tätlicher Angriff; **~·y-op·e·rat·ed** batteriebetrieben.

bat·tle ['bætl] **1.** Schlacht *f* (*of* bei); **2.** streiten, kämpfen; **~·ax(e)** Streitaxt *f*; F alter Drachen (*bösartige Frau*); **~·field**, **~·ground** Schlachtfeld *n*; **~·ments** [~mənts] *pl.* Zinnen *pl.*; **~·plane** ✕ Kampfflugzeug *n*; **~·ship** ✕ Schlachtschiff *n*.

baulk [bɔːk] = *balk*.

Ba·var·i·an [bə'veərɪən] **1.** bay(e)risch; **2.** Bayer(in).

bawd·y ['bɔːdɪ] (*-ier, -iest*) obszön.

bawl [bɔːl] brüllen, schreien, grölen; ~ *out Befehl* brüllen.

bay¹ [beɪ] **1.** rotbraun; **2.** Braune(r) *m* (*Pferd*).

B

bay² [~] Bai f, Bucht f; Erker m.
bay³ ⚘ [~] a. ~ **tree** Lorbeer(baum) m.
bay⁴ [~] 1. bellen, Laut geben (Hund);
2. hold od. keep at ~ j-n in Schach
halten; et. von sich fernhalten.
bay·o·net ⚔ ['beɪənɪt] Bajonett n.
bay·ou Am. ['baːruː] sumpfiger Flußarm.
bay win·dow ['beɪˈwɪndəu] Erker-
fenster n; Am. sl. Vorbau m (Bauch).
ba·za(a)r [bəˈzaː] Basar m.
be [biː, bɪ] (was od. were, been) sein;
zur Bildung des Passivs: werden;
stattfinden; werden (beruflich); he
wants to ~ ... er möchte ... werden;
how much are the shoes? was kosten die Schuhe? ~ reading beim
Lesen sein, gerade lesen; there is,
there are es gibt.
beach [biːtʃ] 1. Strand m; 2. ⚓ auf
den Strand setzen od. ziehen; ~ **ball**
Wasserball m; ~ **bug·gy** mot. Strand-
buggy m; ~ **comb·er** ['biːtʃ-
kəumə] Nichtstuer m.
bea·con ['biːkən] Leuchtfeuer n;
Funkfeuer n.
bead [biːd] (Glas- etc.)Perle f; Tropfen m; ~s pl. a. Rosenkranz m; ~**y**
['biːdɪ] (-ier, -iest) klein, rund u.
glänzend (Augen).
beak [biːk] Schnabel m; ⊕ Tülle f.
bea·ker ['biːkə] Becher m.
beam [biːm] 1. Balken m; Waage-
balken m; Strahl m; ⚡ (Funk)Leit-,
Richtstrahl m; 2. ausstrahlen, strahlen (a. fig. with vor dat.).
bean [biːn] ⚘ Bohne f; Birne f
(Kopf); be full of ~s F voller Le-
ben(skraft) stecken.
bear¹ zo. [beə] Bär m.
bear² [~] (bore, borne od. pass. geboren [werden]: born) v/t. tragen; gebären; ein Gefühl hegen; ertragen;
aushalten; mst negativ: ausstehen,
leiden; ~ down überwinden, bewältigen; ~out bestätigen; v/i. tragen;
zo. trächtig sein; ~·a·ble □
['beərəbl] erträglich.
beard [bɪəd] Bart m; ⚘ Grannen pl.;
~ed ['bɪədɪd] bärtig.
bear·er ['beərə] Träger(in); econ.
Überbringer(in), (Wertpapier)Inha-
ber(in).
bear·ing ['beərɪŋ] (Er)Tragen n; Betragen n; fig. Beziehung f; Lage f,
Richtung f, Orientierung f; take
one's ~s sich orientieren; lose one's
~s die Orientierung verlieren.

beast [biːst] Vieh n, Tier n; Bestie f;
~·ly ['biːstlɪ] (-ier, -iest) scheußlich.
beat [biːt] 1. (beat, beaten od. beat)
v/t. schlagen; (ver)prügeln; besiegen; übertreffen; ~ it! F hau ab!; that
~s all! das ist doch der Gipfel od. die
Höhe!; that ~s me das ist mir zu
hoch; down econ. Preis drücken,
herunterhandeln; ~ out Melodie etc.
trommeln; Feuer ausschlagen; ~ up
j-n zusammenschlagen; v/i. schlagen; ~ about the bush wie die Katze
um den heißen Brei herumschleichen; 2. Schlag m; ♪ Takt(schlag) m;
Jazz: Beat m; Pulsschlag m; Runde
f, Revier n (e-s Polizisten); 3. (dead)
F wie erschlagen, fix u. fertig; ~en
['biːtn] p.p. von beat; vielbegangen
(Weg); off the ~ track abgelegen; fig.
ungewohnt.
beau·ti·cian [bjuːˈtɪʃn] Kosmetikerin
f; ~·ful □ ['bjuːtəfl] schön; ~·fy
[~ɪfaɪ] schön(er) machen.
beau·ty ['bjuːtɪ] Schönheit f; Sleeping ⚘ Dornrös-chen n; ~ parlo(u)r, ~
shop Schönheitssalon m.
bea·ver ['biːvə] zo. Biber m; Biber-
pelz m.
be·came [bɪˈkeɪm] pret. von become.
be·cause [bɪˈkɒz] weil; ~ of wegen.
beck·on ['bekən] (zu)winken.
be·come [bɪˈkʌm] (-came, -come)
v/i. werden (of aus); v/t. sich schik-
ken für; j-m stehen, j-n kleiden; △
nicht bekommen; **be·com·ing** □
[~ɪŋ] passend; schicklich; kleidsam.
bed [bed] 1. Bett n; Lager n (e-s
Tieres); ✿ Beet n; Unterlage f; ~ and
breakfast Zimmer n mit Frühstück;
2. (-dd-): ~ down sein Nachtlager
aufschlagen; ~**clothes** ['bedkləuðz]
pl. Bettwäsche f; ~**ding** [~ɪŋ] Bett-
zeug n; Streu f.
bed·lam ['bedləm] Tollhaus n.
bed·rid·den ['bedrɪdn] bettlägerig;
~**room** Schlafzimmer n; ~**side**: at
the ~ am (a. Kranken)Bett; ~ lamp
Nachttischlampe f; ~**sit** F, ~**sit·ter**
[~ə], ~**sit·ting room** [~ɪŋ] Brt.
möbliertes Zimmer; Einzimmerap-
partement n; ~**spread** Tagesdecke
f; ~**stead** Bettgestell n; ~**time**
Schlafenszeit f.
bee [biː] zo. Biene f; have a ~ in one's
bonnet F e-n Tick haben.
beech ⚘ [biːtʃ] Buche f; ~**nut** Buch-
ecker f.
beef [biːf] 1. Rindfleisch n; 2. F

meckern (*about* über *acc.*); ~ **tea**
Fleischbrühe *f*; ~**y** ['bi:fɪ] (*-ier*,
-iest) fleischig; kräftig, bullig.

bee·hive ['bi:haɪv] Bienenkorb *m*,
-stock *m*; ~**keep·er** Bienenzüchter
m, Imker *m*; ~**line** kürzester Weg;
make a ~ for schnurstracks losgehen
auf (*acc.*).

been [bi:n, bɪn] *p.p. von* be.

beer [bɪə] Bier *n*.

beet ♀ [bi:t] (Runkel)Rübe *f*, Bete *f*;
Am. = beetroot.

bee·tle¹ *zo.* ['bi:tl] Käfer *m*.

bee·tle² [~] 1. überhängend; buschig
(*Brauen*); 2. *v/i.* überhängen.

beet·root ♀ ['bi:tru:t] Rote Bete *od.*
Rübe.

be·fall [bɪ'fɔ:l] (*-fell*, *-fallen*) *v/t.* j-m
zustoßen; △ *nicht* befallen; *v/i.* sich
ereignen.

be·fit [bɪ'fɪt] (*-tt-*) sich schicken für.

be·fore [bɪ'fɔ:] 1. *adv.* räumlich: vorn,
voran; *zeitlich:* vorher, früher, schon
(*früher*); 2. *cj.* bevor, ehe, bis; 3. *prp.*
vor; ~**hand** zuvor, (im) voraus.

be·friend [bɪ'frend] sich *j-s* annehmen; △ *nicht* befreunden.

beg [beg] (*-gg-*) *v/t. et.* erbetteln;
erbitten (*of* von), bitten um; *j-n*
bitten; *v/i.* betteln; bitten, flehen;
betteln gehen; sich erlauben.

be·gan [bɪ'gæn] *pret. von* begin.

be·get [bɪ'get] (*-tt-*; *-got*, *-gotten*)
(er)zeugen.

beg·gar ['begə] 1. Bettler(in); F Kerl
m; 2. arm machen; *fig.* übertreffen; it
~s all description es spottet jeder
Beschreibung.

be·gin [bɪ'gɪn] (*-nn-*; *began*, *begun*)
beginnen, anfangen; ~**ner** [~ə] An-
fänger(in); ~**ning** Beginn *m*, Anfang
m.

be·gone *int.* [bɪ'gɒn] fort!

be·got [bɪ'gɒt] *pret. von* beget; ~**ten**
[~tn] *p.p. von* beget.

be·grudge [bɪ'grʌdʒ] mißgönnen.

be·guile [bɪ'gaɪl] täuschen; betrügen
(*of*, *out of* um); sich *die Zeit* vertreiben.

be·gun [bɪ'gʌn] *p.p. von* begin.

be·half [bɪ'ha:f]: on (*Am. a.* in) ~ of
im Namen von (*od. gen.*).

be·have [bɪ'heɪv] sich (gut) benehmen.

be·hav·io(u)r [bɪ'heɪvjə] Benehmen
n, Betragen *n*, Verhalten *n*; ~**al**
psych. [~rəl] Verhaltens...

be·head [bɪ'hed] enthaupten.

be·hind [bɪ'haɪnd] 1. *adv.* hinten,
dahinter; zurück; 2. *prp.* hinter; 3. F
Hinterteil *n*, Hintern *m*; ~**hand** im
Rückstand.

be·hold [bɪ'həʊld] (*-held*) 1. erblik-
ken, sehen; △ *nicht* behalten; 2. *int.*
siehe (da)!; ~**er** [~ə] Betrachter(in).

be·ing ['bi:ɪŋ] (Da)Sein *n*; Wesen *n*;
in ~ wirklich (vorhanden).

be·lat·ed [bɪ'leɪtɪd] verspätet.

belch [beltʃ] 1. aufstoßen, rülpsen;
ausspeien; 2. Rülpser *m*.

be·lea·guer [bɪ'li:gə] belagern.

bel·fry ['belfrɪ] Glockenturm *m*,
-stuhl *m*.

Bel·gian ['beldʒən] 1. belgisch; 2.
Belgier(in).

be·lie [bɪ'laɪ] Lügen strafen.

be·lief [bɪ'li:f] Glaube *m* (*in* an *acc.*).

be·liev·a·ble □ [bɪ'li:vəbl] glaubhaft.

be·lieve [bɪ'li:v] glauben (*in* an *acc.*);
be·liev·er *eccl.* [~ə] Gläubige(r *m*) *f*.

be·lit·tle *fig.* [bɪ'lɪtl] herabsetzen.

bell [bel] Glocke *f*; Klingel *f*; ~**boy**
Am. ['belbɔɪ] (Hotel)Page *m*.

belle [bel] Schöne *f*, Schönheit *f*.

bell·hop *Am.* ['belhɒp] (Hotel)Page
m.

~**bel·lied** ['belɪd] ...bäuchig.

bel·lig·er·ent [bɪ'lɪdʒərənt] 1. krieg-
führend; streit-, kampflustig; aggressiv; 2. kriegführendes Land.

bel·low ['beləʊ] 1. brüllen; 2. Gebrüll
n; ~**s** Blasebalg *m*.

bel·ly ['belɪ] 1. Bauch *m*; 2. sich
bauchen; (an)schwellen; bauschen;
~**ache** F Bauchweh *n*.

be·long [bɪ'lɒŋ] gehören (*to* gehören *dat. od.* zu; ~**ings** [~ɪŋz] *pl.*
Habseligkeiten *pl.*

be·loved [bɪ'lʌvd] 1. (innig) geliebt;
2. Geliebte(r *m*) *f*.

be·low [bɪ'ləʊ] 1. *adv.* unten; 2. *prp.*
unter.

belt [belt] 1. Gürtel *m*; ⚔ Koppel *n*;
Zone *f*, Gebiet *n*; ⊕ Treibriemen *m*;
2. *a.* ~ up den Gürtel (*gen.*) zumachen; ~**ed** ['beltɪd] mit e-m Gürtel.

be·moan [bɪ'məʊn] betrauern, beklagen.

bench [bentʃ] (Sitz)Bank *f*; Richter-
bank *f*; Richter *m od. pl.*; Werkbank
f.

bend [bend] 1. Biegung *f*, Kurve *f*;
drive s.o. round the ~ F j-n noch
wahnsinnig machen; 2. (*bent*) (sich)
biegen; *Gedanken etc.* richten (*to*, *on*
auf *acc.*); (sich) beugen; sich neigen.

be·neath [bɪ'niːθ] = *below*.

ben·e·dic·tion [benɪ'dɪkʃn] Segen *m*.

ben·e·fac·tor ['benɪfæktə] Wohltäter *m*.

be·nef·i·cent □ [bɪ'nefɪsnt] wohltätig.

ben·e·fi·cial □ [benɪ'fɪʃl] wohltuend, zuträglich, nützlich.

ben·e·fit ['benɪfɪt] 1. Nutzen *m*, Vorteil *m*; Wohltätigkeitsveranstaltung *f*; (*Sozial-, Versicherungs- etc.*)Leistung *f*; Rente *f*; Unterstützung *f*; 2. nützen; begünstigen; ~ *by od. from* Vorteil haben von *od.* durch, Nutzen ziehen aus.

be·nev·o|lence [bɪ'nevələns] Wohlwollen *n*; ~**lent** □ [~t] wohlwollend; gütig, mildtätig.

be·nign □ [bɪ'naɪn] freundlich, gütig; ⚕ gutartig.

bent [bent] 1. *pret. u. p.p. von* bend 2; ~ *on doing* entschlossen zu tun; 2. *fig.* Hang *m*, Neigung *f*; Veranlagung *f*.

ben·zene 🜊 ['benziːn] Benzol *n*.

ben·zine 🜊 ['benziːn] Leichtbenzin *n*; △ *nicht* Benzin.

be·queath ⚖ [bɪ'kwiːð] vermachen.

be·quest ⚖ [bɪ'kwest] Vermächtnis *n*.

be·reave [bɪ'riːv] (*bereaved od. bereft*) berauben.

be·reft [bɪ'reft] *pret. u. p.p. von* bereave.

be·ret ['bereɪ] Baskenmütze *f*.

ber·ry ♦ ['berɪ] Beere *f*.

berth [bɜːθ] 1. ♣ Liege-, Ankerplatz *m*; ♣ Koje *f*; 🛏 (Schlafwagen)Bett *n*; 2. *v/t.* ♣ vor Anker legen; *v/i.* ♣ anlegen.

be·seech [bɪ'siːtʃ] (*besought od. beseeched*) (inständig) bitten (um); anflehen.

be·set [bɪ'set] (*-tt-; beset*) heimsuchen, bedrängen; ~ *with difficulties* mit vielen Schwierigkeiten verbunden; △ *nicht besetzen*.

be·side *prp.* [bɪ'saɪd] neben; ~ *o.s.* außer sich (*with vor*); ~ *the point*, ~ *the question* nicht zur Sache gehörig; ~**s** [~z] 1. *adv.* außerdem; 2. *prp.* abgesehen von, außer.

be·siege [bɪ'siːdʒ] belagern; △ *nicht besiegen*.

be·smear [bɪ'smɪə] beschmieren.

be·sought [bɪ'sɔːt] *pret. u. p.p. von* beseech.

be·spat·ter [bɪ'spætə] bespritzen.

best [best] 1. *adj.* (*sup. von* good 1) beste(r, -s) höchste(r, -s), größte(r, -s), meiste; ~ *man* Trauzeuge *m* (*des Bräutigams*); 2. *adv.* (*sup. von* well[2] 1) am besten; 3. *der, die, das* Beste; *All the* ~! Alles Gute!, Viel Glück!; *to the* ~ *of* ... nach bestem ...; *make the* ~ *of* das Beste machen aus; *at* ~ bestenfalls; *be at one's* ~ in Hochod. Höchstform sein.

bes·ti·al □ ['bestjəl] tierisch, viehisch.

be·stow [bɪ'stəʊ] geben, schenken, verleihen (*on, upon dat.*).

best·sell·er [best'selə] Bestseller *m*, Verkaufsschlager *m* (*bsd. Buch*).

bet [bet] 1. Wette *f*; 2. (-*tt-; bet od. betted*) wetten; *you* ~ F und ob!

be·tray [bɪ'treɪ] verraten (*a. fig.*); verleiten; ~**al** [~əl] Verrat *m*; ~**er** [~ə] Verräter(in).

bet·ter ['betə] 1. *adj.* (*comp. von* good 1) besser; *he is* ~ es geht ihm besser; 2. *das* Bessere; ~**s** *pl.* Höherstehende *pl.*, Vorgesetzte *pl.*; *get the* ~ *of* die Oberhand gewinnen über (*acc.*); *et.* überwinden; 3. *adv.* (*comp. von* well[2] 1) besser; mehr; *so much the* ~ desto besser; *you had* ~ (*Am.* F *you* ~) *go* es wäre besser, wenn du gingest; 4. *v/t.* verbessern; *v/i.* sich bessern.

be·tween [bɪ'twiːn] 1. *adv.* dazwischen; *few and far* ~ F (ganz) vereinzelt; 2. *prp.* zwischen; unter; ~ *you and me* unter uns *od.* im Vertrauen (gesagt).

bev·el ['bevl] (*bsd. Brt.* -*ll-*, *Am.* -*l-*) abkanten, abschrägen.

bev·er·age ['bevərɪdʒ] Getränk *n*.

bev·y ['bevɪ] Schwarm *m*, Schar *f*.

be·wail [bɪ'weɪl] be-, wehklagen.

be·ware [bɪ'weə] (*of*) sich in acht nehmen (*vor dat.*), sich hüten (*vor dat.*); △ *nicht bewahren*; ~ *of the dog!* Warnung vor dem Hunde!

be·wil·der [bɪ'wɪldə] verwirren, irremachen; ~**ment** [~mənt] Verwirrung *f*.

be·witch [bɪ'wɪtʃ] bezaubern, behexen.

be·yond [bɪ'jɒnd] 1. *adv.* darüber hinaus; 2. *prp.* jenseits; über ... (*acc.*) hinaus.

bi- [baɪ] zwei(fach, -mal).

bi·as ['baɪəs] 1. *adj. u. adv.* schief, schräg; 2. Neigung *f*; Vorurteil *n*; 3. (-*s-*, -*ss-*) *mst ungünstig* beeinflussen; ~(*s*)*ed bsd.* ⚖ befangen.

bi·ath|lete [baɪˈæθliːt] *Sport*: Biathlet *m*; **~lon** [~ən] *Sport*: Biathlon *n*.

bib [bɪb] (Sabber)Lätzchen *n*.

Bi·ble [ˈbaɪbl] Bibel *f*.

bib·li·cal □ [ˈbɪblɪkl] biblisch, Bibel...

bib·li·og·ra·phy [bɪblɪˈɒgrəfɪ] Bibliographie *f*.

bi·car·bon·ate [🜍] [baɪˈkɑːbənɪt] *a*. ~ *of soda* doppeltkohlensaures Natron.

bi·cen·te·na·ry [baɪsenˈtiːnərɪ] *Am*. **~ten·ni·al** [~ˈtenɪəl] Zweihundertjahrfeier *f*, zweihundertjähriges Jubiläum.

bi·ceps *anat*. [ˈbaɪseps] Bizeps *m*.

bick·er [ˈbɪkə] (sich) zanken; flackern; plätschern; prasseln.

bi·cy·cle [ˈbaɪsɪkl] **1.** Fahrrad *n*; **2.** radfahren, radeln.

bid [bɪd] **1.** (*-dd-*; *bid od. bade, bid od. bidden*) gebieten, befehlen; (ent)bieten; *Karten*: reizen; ~ *farewell* Lebewohl sagen; **2.** *econ*. Gebot *n*, Angebot *n*; *Karten*: Reizen *n*; **~den** [ˈbɪdn] *p.p. von bid 1*.

bide [baɪd] (*bode od. bided, bided*): ~ *one's time* den rechten Augenblick abwarten.

bi·en·ni·al □ [baɪˈenɪəl] zweijährlich; zweijährig (*Pflanzen*); **~ly** [~lɪ] alle zwei Jahre.

bier [bɪə] (Toten)Bahre *f*; △ *nicht Bier*.

big [bɪg] (*-gg-*) groß; erwachsen; (hoch)schwanger; F wichtig(tuerisch); ~ *business* Großunternehmertum *n*; ~ *shot* F hohes Tier (*Person*); *talk* ~ den Mund vollnehmen.

big·a·my [ˈbɪgəmɪ] Bigamie *f*.

big·ot [ˈbɪgət] selbstgerechte *od*. intolerante Person *f*; **~ed** selbstgerecht, intolerant.

big·wig F [ˈbɪgwɪg] hohes Tier (*Person*).

bike F [baɪk] (Fahr)Rad *n*.

bi·lat·er·al □ [baɪˈlætərəl] bilateral.

bile [baɪl] Galle *f* (*a. fig*.).

bi·lin·gual [baɪˈlɪŋgwəl] zweisprachig.

bil·i·ous □ [ˈbɪljəs] gallig; *fig*. gereizt.

bill¹ [bɪl] Schnabel *m*; Spitze *f*.

bill² [~] *econ*. Rechnung *f*; *pol*. Gesetzentwurf *m*; 🜪 Klageschrift *f*; *a*. ~ *of exchange econ*. Wechsel *m*; Plakat *n*; *Am*. Banknote *f*, Geldschein *m*; ~ *of fare* Speisekarte *f*; ~ *of*

lading Seefrachtbrief *m*, Konnossement *n*; ~ *of sale* 🜪 Verkaufsurkunde *f*; **2.** (durch Anschlag) ankündigen.

bill·board *Am*. [ˈbɪlbɔːd] Reklametafel *f*.

bill·fold *Am*. [ˈbɪlfəʊld] Brieftasche *f*.

bil·li·ards [ˈbɪljədz] *sg*. Billiard(spiel) *n*.

bil·li·on [ˈbɪljən] Milliarde *f*.

bil·low [ˈbɪləʊ] Woge *f*; (*Rauch- etc.*) Schwade *f*; **~y** [~ɪ] wogend; in Schwaden ziehend; gebläht, gebauscht.

bil·ly *Am*. [ˈbɪlɪ] (Gummi)Knüppel *m*; **~goat** *zo*. Ziegenbock *m*.

bin [bɪn] (großer) Behälter.

bind [baɪnd] (*bound*) *v/t*. (an-, ein-, um-, auf-, fest-, ver)binden; *a*. vertraglich binden, verpflichten; (*Buch*) einfassen; *v/i*. binden; **~er** [ˈbaɪndə] (*bsd. Buch*)Binder(in); Einband *m*, (*Akten- etc.*)Deckel *m*, Hefter *m*; **~ing** [~ɪŋ] **1.** bindend, verbindlich; **2.** (*Buch*)Einband *m*; Einfassung *f*, Borte *f*.

bin·oc·u·lars [bɪˈnɒkjʊləz] *pl*. Feldstecher *m*, Fern-, Opernglas *n*.

bi·o·chem·is·try [baɪəʊˈkemɪstrɪ] Biochemie *f*.

bi·og·ra·pher [baɪˈɒgrəfə] Biograph *m*; **~phy** [~ɪ] Biographie *f*.

bi·o·log·i·cal □ [baɪəʊˈlɒdʒɪkl] biologisch; **bi·ol·o·gy** [baɪˈɒlədʒɪ] Biologie *f*.

bi·ped *zo*. [ˈbaɪped] Zweifüßer *m*.

birch [bɜːtʃ] **1.** ♀ Birke *f*; (Birken-)Rute *f*; **2.** (mit der Rute) züchtigen.

bird [bɜːd] Vogel *m*; ~ *of prey* Raubvogel *m*; ~ *sanctuary* Vogelschutzgebiet *n*; **~'s-eye** [ˈbɜːdzaɪ]: ~ *view* Vogelperspektive *f*.

bi·ro *TM* [ˈbaɪrəʊ] (*pl. -ros*) Kugelschreiber *m*.

birth [bɜːθ] Geburt *f*; Ursprung *m*, Entstehung *f*; Herkunft *f*; *give* ~ *to* gebären, zur Welt bringen; **~con·trol** Geburtenregelung *f*; **~day** [ˈbɜːθdeɪ] Geburtstag *m*; **~mark** Muttermal *n*; **~place** Geburtsort *m*; ~ *rate* Geburtenziffer *f*.

bis·cuit *Brt*. [ˈbɪskɪt] Keks *m*, *n*, Plätzchen *n*; △ *nicht Biskuit*.

bish·op [ˈbɪʃəp] Bischof *m*; *Schach*: Läufer *m*; **~ric** [~rɪk] Bistum *n*.

bi·son *zo*. [ˈbaɪsn] Bison *m*, Amer. Büffel; Europäischer Wisent *m*.

bit [bɪt] **1.** Bißchen *n*, Stück(chen) *n*;

Gebiß n (am Zaum); (Schlüssel)Bart m; Computer: Bit n; a (little) ~ ein (kleines) bißchen; **2.** pret. von bite 2.
bitch [bɪtʃ] zo. Hündin f; contp. Miststück n, -weib n.
bite [baɪt] **1.** Beißen n; Biß m; Bissen m, Happen m; ⊕ Fassen n; **2.** (bit, bitten) (an)beißen; stechen (Insekt); brennen (Pfeffer); schneiden (Kälte); beißen (Rauch); ⊕ fassen; fig. verletzen.
bit·ten [ˈbɪtn] p.p. von bite 2.
bit·ter [ˈbɪtə] **1.** □ bitter; fig. verbittert; **2.** ~s pl. Magenbitter m.
biz F[bɪz] = business.
blab F [blæb] (-bb-) (aus)schwatzen.
black [blæk] **1.** □ schwarz; dunkel; finster; ~ eye blaues Auge; have s.th. in ~ and white etw. schwarz auf weiß haben od. besitzen; be ~ and blue blaue Flecken haben; beat s.o. ~ and blue j-n grün u. blau schlagen; **2.** schwärzen; wichsen; ~ out verdunkeln; **3.** Schwarz n; Schwärze f; Schwarze(r m) f, Neger(in); ~**ber·ry** ♣ [ˈblækberɪ] Brombeere f; ~**bird** zo. Amsel f; ~**board** (Schul-, Wand)Tafel f; △ nicht Schwarzes Brett; ~**en** [~ən] v/t. schwärzen; fig. anschwärzen; v/i. schwarz werden; ~**guard** [ˈblægɑːd] **1.** Lump m, Schuft m; **2.** □ gemein, schuftig; ~**head** ✽ Mitesser m; ~**ice** Glatteis n; ~**ing** [~ɪŋ] schwarze Schuhwichse; ~**ish** □ [~ɪʃ] schwärzlich; ~**jack** bsd. Am. Totschläger m (Waffe); ~**leg** Brt. Streikbrecher m; ~**let·ter** print. Fraktur f; ~**mail 1.** Erpressung f; **2.** j-n erpressen; ~**mail·er** [~ə] Erpresser(in); ~ **mar·ket** schwarzer Markt; ~**ness** [~nɪs] Schwärze f; ~**out** Verdunkelung f; thea., ✽, Raumfahrt: Blackout n; ✽ Ohnmacht f; ~ **pud·ding** Blutwurst f; ~ **sheep** fig. schwarzes Schaf; ~**smith** Grobschmied m.
blad·der anat. [ˈblædə] Blase f.
blade [bleɪd] ♣ Blatt n, Halm m; (Säge-, Schulter- etc.)Blatt n; (Propeller)Flügel m; Klinge f.
blame [bleɪm] **1.** Tadel m; Schuld f; **2.** tadeln; be to ~ for schuld sein an (dat.); △ nicht blamieren; ~**less** □ [~lɪs] untadelig.
blanch [blɑːntʃ] bleichen; erbleichen (lassen).
blanc·mange [bləˈmɒnʒ] Pudding m.
bland □ [blænd] mild, sanft.

blank [blæŋk] **1.** □ leer; unausgefüllt, unbeschrieben; econ. Blanko...; verdutzt; △ nicht blank (glänzend); ~ cartridge ✗ Platzpatrone f; ~ cheque (Am. check) econ. Blankoscheck m; **2.** Leere f; leerer Raum, Lücke f; unbeschriebenes Blatt, Formular n; Lotterie: Niete f.
blan·ket [ˈblæŋkɪt] **1.** (Woll)Decke f; wet ~ Spielverderber m; **2.** zudecken.
blare [bleə] brüllen, plärren (Radio etc.), schmettern (Trompete).
blas·pheme [blæsˈfiːm] lästern; ~**phe·my** [ˈblæsfəmɪ] Gotteslästerung f.
blast [blɑːst] **1.** Windstoß m; Ton m (e-s Blasinstruments); ⊕ Gebläse(luft f) n; Druckwelle f; ♣ Mehltau m; **2.** v/t. vernichten; sprengen; ~ off (into space) Rakete, Astronauten in den Weltraum schießen; v/i.: ~ off abheben, starten (Rakete); ~! verdammt!; ~**fur·nace** ⊕ [ˈblɑːstfɜːnɪs] Hochofen m; ~**off** Start m (Rakete).
bla·tant □ [ˈbleɪtənt] lärmend; kraß; unverhohlen.
blaze [bleɪz] **1.** Flamme(n pl.) f, Feuer n; heller Schein; fig. Ausbruch m; go to ~s! zum Teufel mit dir!; **2.** brennen, flammen, lodern, leuchten; △ nicht blasen.
blaz·er [ˈbleɪzə] Blazer m.
bla·zon [ˈbleɪzn] Wappen n.
bleach [bliːtʃ] bleichen.
bleak □ [bliːk] öde, kahl; rauh; fig. trüb, freudlos, finster.
blear·y □ [ˈblɪərɪ] (-ier, -iest) trübe, verschwommen; ~**eyed** mit trüben Augen; verschlafen.
bleat [bliːt] **1.** Blöken n; **2.** blöken.
bled [bled] pret. u. p.p. von bleed.
bleed [bliːd] (bled) v/i. bluten; v/t. ✽ zur Ader lassen; fig. F schröpfen; ~**ing** [ˈbliːdɪŋ] **1.** ✽ Bluten n, Blutung f; ✽ Aderlaß m; **2.** sl. verflixt.
bleep [bliːp] **1.** Piepton m; **2.** j-n anpiepsen (über Funkrufempfänger).
blem·ish [ˈblemɪʃ] **1.** (a. Schönheits)Fehler m; Makel m; **2.** entstellen.
blend [blend] **1.** (sich) (ver)mischen; Wein etc. verschneiden; △ nicht blenden; **2.** Mischung f; econ. Verschnitt m; ~**er** [ˈblendə] Mixer m, Mixgerät n.
bless [bles] (blessed od. blest) segnen; preisen; be ~ed with gesegnet sein mit; (God) ~ you! alles Gute!;

Gesundheit!; ~ *me!*, ~ *my heart!*, ~ *my soul!* F du meine Güte!; ~**ed** *adj.* □ ['blesɪd] glückselig, gesegnet; ~**ing** [~ɪŋ] Segen *m*.

blest [blest] *pret. u. p.p. von* bless.

blew [blu:] *pret. von* blow[2] 1.

blight [blaɪt] 1. Mehltau *m*; *fig.* Gifthauch *m*; 2. vernichten.

blind □ [blaɪnd] 1. blind (*fig. to* gegen[über]); verborgen, geheim; schwererkennbar; ~ *alley* Sackgasse *f*; ~*ly fig.* blindlings; 2. Rouleau *n*, Rollo *n*; *the* ~ *pl.* die Blinden *pl.*; 3. blenden; *fig.* blind machen (*to* für, gegen); ~**ers** *Am.* ['blaɪndəz] *pl.* Scheuklappen *pl.*; ~**fold** 1. blindlings; 2. *j-m* die Augen verbinden; 3. Augenbinde *f*; ~**worm** *zo.* Blindschleiche *f*.

blink [blɪŋk] 1. Blinzeln *n*; Schimmer *m*; 2. *v/i.* blinzeln, zwinkern; blinken; schimmern; *v/t. fig.* ignorieren; ~**ers** ['blɪŋkəz] *pl.* Scheuklappen *pl.*

bliss [blɪs] Seligkeit *f*, Wonne *f*.

blis·ter ['blɪstə] 1. Blase *f* (*auf der Haut, im Lack*); ♂ Zugpflaster *n*; 2. Blasen hervorrufen auf (*dat.*); Blasen ziehen.

blitz [blɪts] 1. heftiger (Luft)Angriff; 2. schwer bombardieren; △ *nicht* Blitz; blitzen.

bliz·zard ['blɪzəd] Schneesturm *m*.

bloat·ed ['bləʊtɪd] (an)geschwollen; (auf)gedunsen; *fig.* aufgeblasen; ~**er** [~ə] Bückling *m*.

block [blɒk] 1. Block *m*, Klotz *m*; Baustein *m*; Verstopfung *f*, (Verkehrs)Stockung *f*; *a.* ~ *of flats* Brt. Wohn-, Mietshaus *n*; *Am.* (Häuser-)Block *m*; 2. formen; verhindern; *a.* ~ *up* (ab-, ver)sperren, blockieren.

block·ade [blɒ'keɪd] 1. Blockade *f*; 2. blockieren.

block·head ['blɒkhed] Dummkopf *m*; ~ *let·ters pl.* Blockschrift *f*.

bloke Brt. F ['bləʊk] Kerl *m*.

blond [blɒnd] 1. Blonde(r) *m*; 2. blond; hell (*Haut*); ~**e** [~] 1. blond; 2. Blondine *f*.

blood [blʌd] Blut *n*; *fig.* Blut *n*; Abstammung *f*; *attr.* Blut...; *in cold* ~ kaltblütig; ~**-cur·dling** ['blʌdkɜ:-dlɪŋ] grauenhaft; ~**shed** Blutvergießen *n*; ~**shot** blutunterlaufen; ~**thirst·y** □ blutdürstig; ~**ves·sel** *anat.* Blutgefäß *n*; ~**y** □ [~ɪ] (*-ier, -iest*) blutig; Brt. F verdammt, verflucht.

bloom [blu:m] 1. *poet.* Blume *f*, Blüte *f*; *fig.* Blüte(zeit) *f*; △ *nicht allg.* Blume; 2. blühen; *fig.* (er)strahlen.

blos·som ['blɒsəm] 1. Blüte *f*; 2. blühen.

blot [blɒt] 1. Klecks *m*; *fig.* Makel *m*; 2. (*-tt-*) *v/t.* beklecksen, beflecken; (ab)löschen; ausstreichen; *v/i.* klecksen.

blotch [blɒtʃ] Klecks *m*; Hautfleck *m*; ~**y** ['blɒtʃɪ] (*-ier, -iest*) fleckig (*Haut*).

blot·ter ['blɒtə] (Tinten)Löscher *m*; *Am.* Eintragungsbuch *n*; ~**ting-pa·per** [~ʌŋpeɪpə] Löschpapier *n*.

blouse [blaʊz] Bluse *f*.

blow[1] [bləʊ] Schlag *m*, Stoß *m*.

blow[2] 1. (*blew, blown*) *v/i.* blasen, wehen; schnaufen; platzen (*Reifen*); ⚡ durchbrennen (*Sicherung*); ~ *up in* die Luft fliegen; *v/t.* blasen, wehen; ~ *one's nose* sich die Nase putzen; ~ *one's top* F an die Decke gehen (*vor Wut*); ~ *out* ausblasen; ~ *up* sprengen; *Foto* vergrößern; 2. Blasen *n*, Wehen *n*; ~**dry** ['bləʊdraɪ] fönen; ~**fly** *zo.* Schmeißfliege *f*; ~**n** [bləʊn] *p.p. von* blow[2] 1; ~**pipe** ['bləʊpaɪp] ⊕ Lötrohr *n*; Blasrohr *n*; ~**up** Explosion *f*; *phot.* Vergrößerung *f*.

bludg·eon ['blʌdʒən] Knüppel *m*.

blue [blu:] 1. blau; F melancholisch, traurig, schwermütig; 2. Blau *n*; *out of the* ~ *fig.* aus heiterem Himmel; ~**ber·ry** ♀ ['blu:bərɪ] Blau-, Heidelbeere *f*; ~**bot·tle** *zo.* Schmeißfliege *f*; ~**col·lar work·er** (Fabrik)Arbeiter(in).

blues [blu:z] *pl. od. sing.* ♪ Blues *m*; F Melancholie *f*; *have the* ~ F den Moralischen haben.

bluff [blʌf] 1. □ schroff, steil; derb; 2. Steilufer *n*; Bluff *m*; 3. bluffen.

blu·ish ['blu:ɪʃ] bläulich.

blun·der ['blʌndə] 1. Fehler *m*, Schnitzer *m*; 2. e-n (groben) Fehler machen; stolpern; verpfuschen; △ *nicht plündern*.

blunt [blʌnt] 1. □ stumpf (*a. fig.*); grob, rauh; 2. abstumpfen; ~**ly** ['blʌntlɪ] frei heraus.

blur [blɜ:] 1. Fleck *m*; undeutlicher Eindruck *m*, verschwommene Vorstellung; 2. (*-rr-*) *v/t.* beflecken; verwischen, -schmieren; *phot.*, *TV* verwackeln, -zerren; *Sinn* trüben.

blurt [blɜ:t]: ~ *out* herausplatzen mit.

B

blush [blʌʃ] 1. Schamröte f; Erröten n; 2. erröten, rot werden.

blus·ter ['blʌstə] 1. Brausen n, Toben n (a. fig.); fig. Poltern n; 2. brausen; fig. poltern, toben.

boar zo. [bɔː] Eber m; Keiler m.

board [bɔːd] 1. Brett n; (Anschlag-) Brett n; Konferenztisch m; Ausschuß m, Kommission f; Behörde f; Verpflegung f; Pappe f, Karton m; Sport: (Surf)Board n; △ nicht Bücher-Bord; on ~ a train in e-m Zug; ~ of directors econ. Verwaltungsrat m; ♀ of Trade Brt. Handelsministerium n, Am. Handelskammer f; 2. v/t. dielen, verschalen; beköstigen; an Bord gehen; ⊕ entern; einsteigen in (ein Fahr- od. Flugzeug); v/i. in Kost sein, wohnen; ~·er [-də] Kostgänger(in); Pensionsgast m; Internatsschüler(in); ~·ing-house [~ɪŋhaʊs] Pension f, Fremdenheim n; ~·ing-school [~ɪŋskuːl] Internat n; ~·walk bsd. Am. Strandpromenade f.

boast [bəʊst] 1. Prahlerei f; 2. (of, about) sich rühmen (gen.), prahlen (mit); ~·ful [ˈbəʊstfl] prahlerisch.

boat [bəʊt] Boot n; Schiff n; ~·ing [ˈbəʊtɪŋ] Bootsfahrt f.

bob [bɒb] 1. Quaste f; Ruck m; Knicks m; kurzer Haarschnitt; Brt. F hist. Schilling m; 2. (-bb-) v/t. Haar kurz schneiden; ~bed hair Bubikopf m; v/i. springen, tanzen; knicksen.

bob·bin [ˈbɒbɪn] Spule f (a. ⚡).

bob·by Brt. F [ˈbɒbɪ] Bobby m (Polizist).

bob·sleigh [ˈbɒbsleɪ] Sport: Bob m.

bode [bəʊd] pret. von bide.

bod·ice [ˈbɒdɪs] Mieder n; Oberteil n (e-s Kleides).

bod·i·ly [ˈbɒdɪlɪ] körperlich.

bod·y [ˈbɒdɪ] Körper m, Leib m; Leiche f; Körperschaft f; Hauptteil m; mot. Karosserie f; ✗ Truppenkörper m; ~guard Leibwache f; Leibwächter m; ~work Karosserie f.

Boer [ˈbəʊə] Bure m; attr. Buren...

bog [bɒg] 1. Sumpf m, Moor n; 2. (-gg-): get ~ged down fig. sich festfahren.

bo·gus [ˈbəʊgəs] falsch; Schwindel...

boil¹ ✗ [bɔɪl] Geschwür n, Furunkel m, n.

boil² [~] 1. kochen, sieden; 2. Kochen n, Sieden n; ~·er [ˈbɔɪlə] (Dampf-)

Kessel m; Boiler m; ~·er suit Overall m; ~·ing [~ɪŋ] kochend, siedend; ~·ing-point Siedepunkt m (a. fig.).

bois·ter·ous □ [ˈbɔɪstərəs] ungestüm; heftig, laut; lärmend.

bold □ [bəʊld] kühn; keck, dreist, unverschämt; steil; as ~ as brass F frech wie Oskar; ~·ness [ˈbəʊldnɪs] Kühnheit f; Keckheit f; Dreistigkeit f.

bol·ster [ˈbəʊlstə] 1. Keilkissen n; Nackenrolle f; △ nicht Polster; 2. ~ up fig. (unter)stützen; j-m Mut machen.

bolt [bəʊlt] 1. Bolzen m; Riegel m; Blitz(strahl) m; plötzlicher Satz, Fluchtversuch m; 2. adv. ~ upright kerzengerade; 3. v/t. verriegeln; F hinunterschlingen; v/i. davonlaufen, ausreißen; scheuen; durchgehen (Pferd).

bomb [bɒm] 1. Bombe f; the ~ die Atombombe; 2. bombardieren.

bom·bard [bɒmˈbɑːd] bombardieren (a. fig.).

bomb|-proof [ˈbɒmpruːf] bombensicher; ~·shell Bombe f (a. fig.).

bond [bɒnd] econ. Schuldverschreibung f, Obligation f; ⊕ Haftfestigkeit f; ~s pl. Bande (der Freundschaft etc.); in ~ econ. unter Zollverschluß; ~·age lit. [ˈbɒndɪdʒ] Hörigkeit f; Knechtschaft f.

bone [bəʊn] 1. Knochen m; Gräte f; △ nicht Bein; ~s pl. a. Gebeine pl.; ~ of contention Zankapfel m; have a ~ to pick with s.o. mit j-m ein Hühnchen zu rupfen haben; make no ~s about nicht lange fackeln mit; keine Skrupel haben hinsichtlich (gen.); 2. die Knochen auslösen (aus); entgräten.

bon·fire [ˈbɒnfaɪə] Feuer n im Freien; Freudenfeuer n.

bon·net [ˈbɒnɪt] Haube f; Brt. Motorhaube f.

bon·ny bsd. schott. [ˈbɒnɪ] (-ier, -iest) hübsch; rosig (Baby); gesund.

bo·nus econ. [ˈbəʊnəs] Bonus m, Prämie f; Gratifikation f.

bon·y [ˈbəʊnɪ] (-ier, -iest) knöchern; knochig.

boob sl. [buːb] Blödmann m; Brt. (grober) Fehler; ~s pl. F Titten pl. (Busen).

boo·by [ˈbuːbɪ] Trottel m.

book [bʊk] 1. Buch n; Heft n; Liste f; Block m; 2. buchen; eintragen;

B

Fahrkarte etc. lösen; *Platz etc.* (vor-) bestellen, reservieren lassen; *Gepäck* aufgeben; ~ *in bsd. Brt.* sich (*im Hotel*) eintragen; ~ *in at* absteigen in (*dat.*); ~*ed up* ausgebucht, -verkauft, belegt (*Hotel*); ~**case** ['bʊkeɪs] Bücherschrank *m*; ~**ing** [~ɪŋ] Buchen *n*, (Vor)Bestellung *f*; ~**ing-clerk** Schalterbeamte|r(e) *m*, -in *f*; ~**ing-office** Fahrkartenausgabe *f*, -schalter *m*; *thea.* Kasse *f*; ~**keep·er** Buchhalter(in); ~**keep·ing** Buchhaltung *f*, -führung *f*; ~**let** [~lɪt] Büchlein *n*, Broschüre *f*; ~**mark(·er)** [~ə] Lesezeichen *n*; ~**sell·er** Buchhändler(in); ~**shop**, *Am.* ~**store** Buchhandlung *f*.

boom[1] [buːm] **1.** *econ.* Boom *m*, Aufschwung *m*, Hochkonjunktur *f*, Hausse *f*; **2.** in die Höhe treiben *od.* gehen.

boom[2] [~] dröhnen, donnern.

boon [buːn] Segen *m*, Wohltat *f*.

boor *fig.* [bʊə] Bauer *m*, Lümmel *m*; ~**ish** [~'bʊərɪʃ] bäuerisch, ungehobelt.

boost [buːst] hochschieben; *Preise* in die Höhe treiben; *Wirtschaft* ankurbeln; verstärken (*a.* ⚡); *fig.* fördern, Auftrieb geben.

boot[1] [buːt]: *to* ~ obendrein.

boot[2] [~] [buːt] *Stiefel m; Brt. mot.* Kofferraum *m*; △ *nicht Boot*; ~**ee** ['buːtiː] (*Damen*)Halbstiefel *m*.

booth [buːð] (*Markt- etc.*)Bude *f*; (*Messe*)Stand *m*; (*Wahl-, etc.*) Kabine *f*; (*Fernsprech*)Zelle *f*.

boot·lace ['buːtleɪs] Schnürsenkel *m*; ~**leg·ger** [~legə] Alkoholschmuggler *m*.

boo·ty ['buːtɪ] Beute *f*, Raub *m*.

booze F [buːz] **1.** saufen; **2.** Alkohol *m* (*Getränk*); Sauferei *f*.

bop·per ['bɒpə] = *teeny-bopper*.

bor·der ['bɔːdə] **1.** Rand *m*, Saum *m*, Einfassung *f*; Rabatte *f*; Grenze *f*; **2.** einfassen; (um)säumen; grenzen (*on, upon an acc.*).

bore[1] [bɔː] **1.** Bohrloch *n*; Kaliber *n*; *fig.* langweiliger Mensch; langweilige Sache; *Brt.* F lästige Sache; **2.** bohren; langweilen; *j-m* lästig sein.

bore[2] [~] *pret. von bear*[1].

bor·ing [bɔːrɪŋ] langweilig.

born [bɔːn] *p.p. von bear*[2] gebären.

borne [bɔːn] *p.p. von bear*[2] tragen.

bo·rough ['bʌrə] Stadtteil *m*; Stadtgemeinde *f*; Stadtbezirk *m*.

bor·row ['bɒrəʊ] (sich) *et.* borgen *od.* (aus)leihen; △ *nicht j-m et. borgen*.

bos·om ['bʊzəm] Busen *m*; *fig.* Schoß *m*.

boss F [bɒs] **1.** Boss *m*, Chef *m*; *bsd. Am. pol.* (Partei-, Gewerkschafts-) Bonze *m*; **2.** *a.* ~ *about*, ~ *around* herumkommandieren; ~**y** F ['bɒsɪ] (*-ier, -iest*) herrisch.

bo·tan·i·cal □ [bə'tænɪkl] botanisch; **bot·a·ny** ['bɒtənɪ] Botanik *f*.

botch [bɒtʃ] **1.** Pfusch(arbeit *f*) *m*; **2.** verpfuschen.

both [bəʊθ] beide(s); ~ ... *and* sowohl ... als (auch).

both·er ['bɒðə] **1.** Belästigung *f*, Störung *f*, Plage *f*, Mühe *f*; **2.** belästigen, stören, plagen; *don't* ~*!* bemühen Sie sich nicht!

bot·tle ['bɒtl] **1.** Flasche *f*; **2.** in Flaschen abfüllen; ~**neck** Flaschenhals *m*, Engpaß *m* (*e-r Straße*) (*a. fig.*).

bot·tom ['bɒtəm] unterster Teil, Boden *m*, Fuß *m*, Unterseite *f*; Grund *m*; F Hintern *m*, Popo *m*; *be at the* ~ *of hinter e-r Sache* stecken; *get to the* ~ *of s.th.* e-r Sache auf den Grund gehen.

bough [baʊ] Ast *m*, Zweig *m*.

bought [bɔːt] *pret. u. p.p. von buy*.

boul·der ['bəʊldə] Geröllblock *m*, Findling *m*.

bounce [baʊns] **1.** Aufprall(en *n*) *m*, Aufspringen *n* (*e-s Balles etc.*); Schwung *m* (*Lebensfreude, -kraft*); **2.** aufspringen *od.* springen (lassen) (*Ball*); F platzen (*ungedeckter Scheck*); *she* ~*d the baby on her knee* sie ließ das Kind auf den Knien reiten; **bounc·ing** ['baʊnsɪŋ] stramm (*Baby*).

bound[1] [baʊnd] **1.** *pret. u. p.p. von bind*; **2.** *adj.* verpflichtet; bestimmt; unterwegs (*for nach*).

bound[2] [~] *mst* ~*s pl.* Grenze *f*, *fig. a.* Schranke *f*.

bound[3] [~] **1.** Sprung *m*; **2.** (hoch)springen; auf-, abprallen.

bound·a·ry ['baʊndərɪ] Grenze *f*.

bound·less □ ['baʊndlɪs] grenzenlos.

boun|te·ous □ ['baʊntɪəs], ~**ti·ful** □ [~fl] freigebig, reichlich.

boun·ty ['baʊntɪ] Mildtätigkeit *f*, Freigebigkeit *f*; Spende *f*; Prämie *f*.

bou·quet [bʊ'keɪ] Bukett *n*, Strauß *m*; Blume *f* (*des Weins*).

bout [baʊt] Boxen, Ringen, Fechten:
Kampf m; (Verhandlungs)Runde f;
♣ Anfall m; (Trink)Gelage n.

bou·tique [buːˈtiːk] Boutique f.

bow¹ [baʊ] 1. Verbeugung f; 2. v/i.
sich verbeugen od. -neigen (to vor
dat.); fig. sich beugen od. unterwerfen (to dat.); v/t. biegen; beugen,
neigen.

bow² ♣ [ᴧ] Bug m.

bow³ [bəʊ] 1. Bogen m; Schleife f; 2.
geigen; ~·legged O-beinig.

bow·els [ˈbaʊəlz] pl. anat. Eingeweide pl.; das Innere.

bowl¹ [bəʊl] Schale f, Schüssel f,
Napf m; (Pfeifen)Kopf m; geogr.
Becken n; Am. Stadion n; △ nicht
Bowle (Getränk).

bowl² [ᴧ] 1. (Bowling-, Kegel- etc.)
Kugel f; 2. v/t. rollen; Bowlingkugel,
Kricketball werfen; v/i. bowlen,
Bowling spielen; kegeln; Kricket:
werfen; ~·ing [ˈbəʊlɪŋ] Bowling n;
Kegeln n.

box¹ [bɒks] ♣ Buchsbaum m; Kasten
m, Kiste f; Büchse f; Schachtel f; ⊕
Gehäuse n; thea. Loge f; Box f; 2. in
Kästen etc. tun.

box² [ᴧ] 1. Sport: boxen; ~ s.o.'s ears
j-n ohrfeigen; 2. ~ on the ear Ohr-
feige f; ~·er [ˈbɒksə] Boxer m; ~·ing
[ᴧɪŋ] Boxen n, Boxsport m; ♀·ing
Day Brt. der zweite Weihnachtsfeiertag.

box-of·fice [ˈbɒksɒfɪs] Theaterkasse
f.

boy [bɔɪ] Junge m, Knabe m, Bursche
m; ~·friend Freund m; ~ scout Pfadfinder m.

boy·cott [ˈbɔɪkɒt] boykottieren.

boy·hood [ˈbɔɪhʊd] Knabenalter n,
Kindheit f, Jugend(zeit) f; ~·ish □
[ˈbɔɪɪʃ] jungenhaft.

bra [brɑː] BH m (Büstenhalter).

brace [breɪs] 1. ⊕ Strebe f, Stützbal-
ken m; Klammer f; Paar n (a. Wild,
Geflügel); (a. a pair of) ~s pl. Brt.
Hosenträger pl.; 2. verstreben, -stei-
fen, stützen; spannen; fig. stärken.

brace·let [ˈbreɪslɪt] Armband n.

brack·et [ˈbrækɪt] 1. ⊕ Träger m,
Halter m, Stütze f; (Wand)Arm (e-r
Leuchte); Winkelstütze f; arch. Kon-
sole f; print. (mst eckige) Klammer;
(bsd. Alters-, Steuer)Klasse f; lower
income ~ niedrige Einkommens-
gruppe; 2. einklammern; fig. gleich-
stellen.

brack·ish [ˈbrækɪʃ] brackig, salzig.

brag [bræg] 1. Prahlerei f; 2. (-gg-)
prahlen (about, of mit).

brag·gart [ˈbrægət] 1. Prahler m; 2.
prahlerisch.

braid [breɪd] 1. (Haar)Flechte f, Zopf
m; Borte f, Tresse f; 2. flechten; mit
Borte besetzen.

brain [breɪn] anat. Gehirn n; oft ~s
pl. fig. Gehirn n, Verstand m, Intelligenz f, Kopf m; ~s trust Brt., Am. ~
trust [ˈbreɪn(z)trʌst] Gehirntrust m
(bsd. politische od. wirtschaftliche Be-
ratergruppe); ~·wash j-n e-r Gehirnwäsche unterziehen; ~·wash·ing
Gehirnwäsche f; ~·wave F Geistes-
blitz m.

brake [breɪk] 1. ⊕ Bremse f; 2. bremsen.

bram·ble ♀ [ˈbræmbl] Brombeer-
strauch m.

bran [bræn] Kleie f.

branch [brɑːntʃ] 1. Ast m, Zweig m;
Fach n; Linie f (des Stammbaumes);
Zweigstelle f; 2. sich verzweigen;
abzweigen.

brand [brænd] 1. econ. (Handels-,
Schutz)Marke f, Warenzeichen n;
Sorte f, Klasse f (e-r Ware); Brand-
mal n; △ nicht Brand; ~ name Mar-
kenbezeichnung f, -name m; 2. ein-
brennen; brandmarken.

bran·dish [ˈbrændɪʃ] schwingen.

bran(d)-new [ˈbræn(d)ˈnjuː] nagel-
neu.

bran·dy [ˈbrændɪ] Kognak m, Weinbrand m.

brass [brɑːs] Messing n; F Unverschämtheit f; ~ band Blaskapelle f; ~
knuckles pl. Am. Schlagring m.

bras·sière [ˈbræsɪə] Büstenhalter m.

brat contp. [bræt] Balg m, n, Gör n
(Kind).

brave [breɪv] 1. □ (~r, ~st) tapfer,
mutig, unerschrocken; △ nicht
brav; 2. trotzen; mutig begegnen
(dat.); **brav·er·y** [ˈbreɪvərɪ] Tapferkeit f.

brawl [brɔːl] 1. Krawall m; Rauferei
f; 2. Krawall machen; raufen.

brawn·y [ˈbrɔːnɪ] (-ier, -iest) muskulös.

bray [breɪ] 1. Eselsschrei m; 2.
schreien; schmettern; dröhnen.

bra·zen □ [ˈbreɪzn] unverschämt,
unverfroren, frech.

Bra·zil·ian [brəˈzɪljən] 1. brasilia-
nisch; 2. Brasilianer(in).

breach [briːtʃ] **1.** Bruch *m*; *fig.* Verletzung *f*; ✕ Bresche *f*; **2.** e-e Bresche schlagen in (*acc.*).

bread [bred] Brot *n*; *brown* ~ Schwarzbrot *m*; *know which side one's* ~ *is buttered* F s-n Vorteil (er)kennen.

breadth [bredθ] Breite *f*, Weite *f*; *fig.* Größe *f*; (*Tuch*)Bahn *f*.

break [breik] **1.** Bruch *m*; Lücke *f*; Pause *f* (*Brt. a. Schule*), Unterbrechung *f*; *econ.* (*Preis- etc.*)Sturz *m*; (*Tages*)Anbruch *m*; *fig.* Zäsur *f*, Einschnitt *m*; *bad* ~ F Pech *n*; *lucky* ~ F Dusel *m*, Schwein *n* (*Glück*); *without a* ~ ununterbrochen; **2.** (*broke*, *broken*) *v/t.* ab-, auf-, durchbrechen; *v/t.* (zer)brechen; unterbrechen; übertreten; *Tier* abrichten, *Pferd* zureiten; *Bank* sprengen; *Vorrat* anbrechen; *Nachricht* (schonend) mitteilen; ruinieren; *v/i.* brechen; eindringen *od.* -brechen in (*acc.*); hervorbrechen; aus-, los-, anauf-, hervorbrechen; umschlagen (*Wetter*); *mit Adverbien:* ~ *away* abbrechen; sich losmachen *od.* losreißen; ~ *down* ein-, niederreißen, *Haus* abbrechen; zusammenbrechen (*a. fig.*); versagen; ~ *in* einbrechen, -dringen; ~ *off* abbrechen; *fig. a.* Schluß machen mit; ~ *out* ausbrechen; ~ *through* durchbrechen; *fig.* den Durchbruch schaffen; ~ *up* abbrechen, beendigen, schließen; (sich) auflösen; zerbrechen, auseinandergehen (*Ehe etc.*); ~**a·ble** ['breikəbl] zerbrechlich; ~**age** [~idʒ] Bruch *m*; ~**a·way** Trennung *f*, Bruch *m*; *Brt.* Splitter...; ~**down** Zusammenbruch *m* (*a. fig.*); ⊕ Maschinenschaden *m*; *mot.* Panne *f*.

break·fast ['brekfəst] **1.** Frühstück *n*; **2.** frühstücken.

break|through *fig.* ['breikθruː] Durchbruch *m*; ~**up** Auflösung *f*; Zerfall *m*; Zerrüttung *f*; Zusammenbruch *m*.

breast [brest] Brust *f*; Busen *m*; *fig.* Herz *n*; *make a clean* ~ *of s.th.* et. offen gestehen; ~**stroke** ['brest-strəuk] *Sport:* Brustschwimmen *n*.

breath [breθ] Atem(zug) *m*; Hauch *m*; *waste one's* ~ s-e Worte verschwenden.

breath·a|lyse, *Am.* **-lyze** ['breθəlaiz] *Verkehrsteilnehmer* (ins Röhrchen) blasen *od.* pusten lassen; ~**lys·er,**

Am. **-lyz·er** [~ə] Alkoholtestgerät *n*, F Röhrchen *n*.

breathe [briːð] *v/i.* atmen; leben; *v/t.* (aus-, ein)atmen; hauchen, flüstern.

breath|less □ ['breθlis] atemlos; ~**tak·ing** atemberaubend.

bred [bred] *pret. u. p.p. von* **breed** 2.

breech·es ['britʃiz] *pl.* Knie-, Reithosen *pl.*

breed [briːd] **1.** Zucht *f*, Rasse *f*; (*Menschen*)Schlag *m*; **2.** (*bred*) *v/t.* erzeugen; auf-, erziehen; züchten; *v/i.* sich fortpflanzen; ~**er** ['briːdə] Züchter(in); Zuchttier *n*; ~**ing** [~iŋ] (*Tier*)Zucht *f*; Erziehung *f*; (*gutes*) Benehmen *n*.

breeze [briːz] Brise *f*; ~**y** **breez·y** ['briːzi] (*-ier, -iest*) windig, luftig; heiter, unbeschwert.

breth·ren ['breðrən] *pl.* Brüder *pl.*

brev·i·ty ['brevəti] Kürze *f*.

brew [bruː] **1.** *v/t. u. v/i.* brauen; zubereiten; *fig.* aushecken; **2.** Gebräu *n*; ~**er** ['bruːə] (*Bier*)Brauer *m*; ~**er·y** ['bruəri] Brauerei *f*.

bri·ar ['braiə] = **brier.**

bribe [braib] **1.** Bestechung(sgeld *n*, -geschenk *n*) *f*; **2.** bestechen; **brib·er·y** ['braibəri] Bestechung *f*.

brick [brik] **1.** Ziegel(stein) *m*; *drop a* ~ *Brt.* F ins Fettnäpfchen treten; **2.** ~ *up od. in* zumauern; ~**lay·er** ['brikleiə] Maurer *m*; ~**works** *sg.* Ziegelei *f*.

brid·al □ ['braidl] Braut...

bride [braid] Braut *f*; ~**groom** ['braidgrum] Bräutigam *m*; ~**s·maid** [~zmeid] Brautjungfer *f*.

bridge [bridʒ] **1.** Brücke *f*; **2.** e-e Brücke schlagen über (*acc.*); *fig.* überbrücken.

bri·dle ['braidl] **1.** Zaum *m*; Zügel *m*; **2.** *v/t.* (auf)zäumen; zügeln; *v/i. a.* ~ *up* den Kopf zurückwerfen; ~**path** Reitweg *m.*

brief [briːf] **1.** □ kurz, bündig; **2.** ⚖ schriftliche Instruktion; △ *nicht Brief*; **3.** kurz zusammenfassen; instruieren; ~**case** ['briːfkeis] Aktenmappe *f*.

briefs [briːfs] *pl.* (*a pair of* ~ ein) Slip (*kurze Unterhose*).

bri·er ♦ ['braiə] Dorn-, Hagebuttenstrauch *m*; Wilde Rose.

bri·gade ✕ ['brigeid] Brigade *f*.

bright [brait] □ hell, glänzend; klar; heiter; lebhaft; gescheit; △ *nicht breit*; ~**en** ['braitn] *v/t.* auf-, erhel-

len; polieren; aufheitern; *v/i.* sich
aufhellen; **~ness** [~nɪs] Helligkeit *f*;
Glanz *m*; Klarheit *f*; Heiterkeit *f*;
Aufgewecktheit *f*, Intelligenz *f*.
bril|liance, ~lian·cy ['brɪljəns, ~sɪ]
Glanz *m*; durchdringender Verstand; **~liant** [~t] **1.** □ glänzend;
hervorragend, brillant; **2.** Brillant *m*.
brim [brɪm] **1.** Rand *m*; Krempe *f*; **2.**
(-*mm*-) bis zum Rande füllen *od.* voll
sein; **~ful(l)** ['brɪm'fʊl] randvoll.
brine [braɪn] Salzwasser *n*; Sole *f*.
bring [brɪŋ] (*brought*) (mit-, her-)
bringen; △ *nicht fort-, wegbringen*;
j-n veranlassen; *Klage* erheben;
Grund etc. vorbringen; ~ *about* zustande bringen; bewirken; ~ *back*
zurückbringen; ~ *forth* hervorbringen; ~ *home to j-n* überzeugen; ~ *in*
(her)einbringen; ᵗᵗ *Spruch* fällen; ~
off et. fertigbringen, schaffen; ~ *on*
verursachen; ~ *out* herausbringen; ~
round wieder zu sich bringen; *Kranken* durchbringen; ~ *up* auf-, großziehen; erziehen; zur Sprache bringen; *bsd. Brt. et.* (er)brechen.
brink [brɪŋk] Rand *m* (*a. fig.*).
brisk □ [brɪsk] lebhaft, munter;
frisch; flink; belebend.
bris|tle ['brɪsl] **1.** Borste *f*; **2.** (sich)
sträuben; hochfahren, zornig werden; ~ *with fig.* starren von; **~tly** [~lɪ]
(-*ier*, -*iest*) stopp(e)lig, Stoppel...
Brit·ish ['brɪtɪʃ] britisch; *the* ~ *pl.* die
Briten *pl.*
brit·tle ['brɪtl] zerbrechlich, spröde.
broach [brəʊtʃ] *Thema* anschneiden.
broad □ [brɔːd] breit; weit; hell
(*Tag*); deutlich (*Wink etc.*); derb
(*Witz*); allgemein; weitherzig; liberal; **~cast** ['brɔːdkɑːst] **1.** (-*cast od.*
-*casted*) *fig.* Nachricht verbreiten;
im Rundfunk *od.* Fernsehen bringen,
ausstrahlen, übertragen; senden; im Rundfunk *od.* Fernsehen
sprechen *od.* auftreten; **2.** Rundfunk-, Fernsehsendung *f*; **~·cast·er**
[~ə] Rundfunk-, Fernsehsprecher(in); **~en** [~dn] verbreitern, erweitern; ~ *jump Am. Sport:* Weitsprung *m*; **~·mind·ed** liberal.
bro·cade [brəʊˈkeɪd] Brokat *m*.
bro·chure ['brəʊʃə] Broschüre *f*,
Prospekt *m*.
brogue [brəʊg] derber Straßenschuh.
broil *bsd. Am.* [brɔɪl] = *grill* 1.
broke [brəʊk] **1.** *pret. von break* **2**;

2. F pleite, abgebrannt; **bro·ken**
['brəʊkən] **1.** *p.p. von break* **2**; **2.** ~
health zerrüttete Gesundheit; **~hearted** verzweifelt, untröstlich.
bro·ker *econ.* ['brəʊkə] Makler *m*.
bron·co *Am.* ['brɒŋkəʊ] (*pl.* -*cos*)
(halb)wildes Pferd.
bronze [brɒnz] **1.** Bronze *f*; **2.** bronzen, Bronze...; **3.** bronzieren.
brooch [brəʊtʃ] Brosche *f*, Spange *f*.
brood [bruːd] **1.** Brut *f*; *attr.* Brut...;
2. brüten (*a. fig.*); **~·er** ['bruːdə]
Brutkasten *m*.
brook [brʊk] Bach *m*.
broom [bruːm] Besen *m*; **~·stick**
['bruːmstɪk] Besenstiel *m*.
broth [brɒθ] Fleischbrühe *f*.
broth·el ['brɒθl] Bordell *n*.
broth·er ['brʌðə] Bruder *m*, ~(*s*) *and*
sister(*s*) Geschwister *pl.*; **~·hood**
[~hʊd] Bruderschaft *f*; Brüderlichkeit *f*; **~-in-law** [~rɪnlɔː] (*pl.* -*s-in-law*) Schwager *m*; **~·ly** [~lɪ] brüderlich.
brought [brɔːt] *pret. u. p.p. von bring.*
brow [braʊ] (Augen)Braue *f*; Stirn *f*;
Rand *m* (*e-s Steilhanges*); **~·beat**
['braʊbiːt] (-*beat*, -*beaten*) einschüchtern; tyrannisieren.
brown [braʊn] **1.** braun; **2.** Braun *n*;
3. bräunen; braun werden.
browse [braʊz] **1.** Grasen *n*; *fig.*
Schmökern *n*; **2.** grasen, weiden; *fig.*
schmökern.
bruise [bruːz] **1.** ᵗ Quetschung *f*,
Prellung *f*, Bluterguß *m*; **2.** (zer-)
quetschen; *j-n* grün u. blau schlagen.
brunch F [brʌntʃ] Brunch *m* (*spätes*
reichliches Frühstück, das das Mittag-
essen ersetzt).
brunt [brʌnt]: *bear the* ~ *of* die
Hauptlast von *et.* tragen.
brush [brʌʃ] **1.** Bürste *f*; Pinsel *m*;
(*Fuchs*)Rute *f*; Scharmützel *n*; Unterholz *n*; **2.** bürsten; fegen; streifen;
~ *against s.o.* in *j-n* streifen; ~ *away*, ~
off wegbürsten, abwischen; ~ *aside*,
~ *away fig. et.* abtun; ~ *up Kenntnis-*
se auffrischen, -frischen; **~·up**
['brʌʃʌp]: *give one's English a* ~ s-e
Englischkenntnisse auffrischen;
~·wood Gestrüpp *n*, Unterholz *n*.
brusque □ [brʊsk] brüsk, barsch.
Brus·sels sprouts ♀ ['brʌsl'spraʊts]
pl. Rosenkohl *m*.
bru·tal □ ['bruːtl] viehisch; brutal;
roh; **~·i·ty** [bruːˈtælətɪ] Brutalität *f*,

Roheit *f*; **brute** [bru:t] **1.** tierisch; unvernünftig; brutal, roh; **2.** Vieh *n*; F Untier *n*, Scheusal *n*.

bub·ble ['bʌbl] **1.** Blase *f*; *fig.* Schwindel *m*; **2.** sprudeln.

buc·ca·neer [bʌkə'nɪə] Seeräuber *m*.

buck [bʌk] **1.** *zo.* Bock *m*; *Am. sl.* Dollar *m*; **2.** *v/i.* bocken; ~ *up!* Kopf hoch!; *v/t.* ~ *off Reiter* (durch Bocken) abwerfen.

buck·et ['bʌkɪt] Eimer *m*, Kübel *m*.

buck·le ['bʌkl] **1.** Schnalle *f*, Spange *f*; △ *nicht* Buckel *f*; **2.** *v/t. a.* ~ *up* zu-, festschnallen; ~ *on* anschnallen; *v/i.* ⊕ sich (ver)biegen; ~ *down to a task* F sich hinter e-e Aufgabe klemmen.

buck\shot *hunt.* ['bʌkʃɒt] Rehposten *m*; **~skin** Wildleder *n*.

bud [bʌd] **1.** ♀ Knospe *f*; *fig.* Keim *m*; **2.** (*-dd-*) *v/i.* knospen, keimen; *a* ~*ding lawyer* ein angehender Jurist.

bud·dy *Am.* F ['bʌdɪ] Kamerad *m*.

budge [bʌdʒ] (sich) bewegen.

bud·ger·i·gar *zo.* ['bʌdʒərɪgɑ:] Wellensittich *m*.

bud·get ['bʌdʒɪt] Vorrat *m*; Staatshaushalt *m*; Etat *m*, Finanzen *pl*.

bud·gie *zo.* F ['bʌdʒɪ] = *budgerigar*.

buff¹ [bʌf] **1.** Ochsenleder *n*; Lederfarbe *f*; **2.** lederfarben.

buff² F [~] Film- *etc.* Fan *m*.

buf·fa·lo *zo.* ['bʌfələʊ] (*pl. -loes, -los*) Büffel *m*.

buff·er ['bʌfə] ⊕ Puffer *m*; Prellbock *m* (*a. fig.*).

buf·fet¹ ['bʌfɪt] **1.** (Faust)Schlag *m*; **2.** schlagen; ~ *about* durchrütteln, -schütteln.

buf·fet² [~] Büfett *n*, Anrichte *f*.

buf·fet³ ['bʊfeɪ] Büfett *n*, Theke *f*; Tisch *mit Speisen u. Getränken*.

buf·foon [bə'fu:n] Possenreißer *m*.

bug [bʌg] **1.** *zo.* Wanze *f*; *Am. zo.* Insekt *n*; F Bazillus *m*; F Abhörvorrichtung *f*, Wanze *f*; *Computer:* Fehler *m* im Programm (*in Soft- od. Hardware*); **2.** (*-gg-*) F *Gespräch* abhören; F Wanzen anbringen in (*dat.*); *Am.* F ärgern, wütend machen.

bug·gy ['bʌgɪ] *mot.* Buggy *m* (*Freizeitauto*); *Am.* Kinderwagen *m*.

bu·gle ['bju:gl] Wald-, Signalhorn *n*.

build [bɪld] **1.** (*built*) (er)bauen, errichten; △ *nicht* bilden; **2.** Körperbau *m*, Figur *f*; ~**er** ['bɪldə] Erbauer *m*, Baumeister *m*; Bauunternehmer

m; ~**ing** [~ɪŋ] (Er)Bauen *n*; Bau *m*, Gebäude *n*; *attr.* Bau...

built [bɪlt] *pret. u. p.p. von build 1.*

bulb [bʌlb] ♀ Zwiebel *f*, Knolle *f*; ≠ (Glüh)Birne *f*.

bulge [bʌldʒ] **1.** (Aus)Bauchung *f*; Anschwellung *f*; **2.** sich (aus)bauchen; hervorquellen.

bulk [bʌlk] Umfang *m*; Masse *f*; Hauptteil *m*, ⊕ Ladung *f*; *in* ~ *econ.* lose; in großer Menge; ~**y** ['bʌlkɪ] (*-ier, -iest*) umfangreich; unhandlich, sperrig.

bull¹ *zo.* [bʊl] Bulle *m*, Stier *m*.

bull² [~] päpstliche Bulle.

bull·dog *zo.* ['bʊldɒg] Bulldogge *f*.

bull\doze F ['bʊldəʊz] terrorisieren; **~·doz·er** ⊕ [~ə] Bulldozer *m*, Planierraupe *f*.

bul·let ['bʊlɪt] Kugel *f*; ~-*proof* kugelsicher.

bul·le·tin ['bʊlɪtɪn] Bulletin *n*, Tagesbericht *m*; ~ *board Am.* Schwarzes Brett.

bul·lion ['bʊljən] Gold-, Silberbarren *m*; Gold-, Silberlitze *f*.

bul·ly ['bʊlɪ] **1.** Maulheld *m*; Tyrann *m*; **2.** einschüchtern, tyrannisieren.

bul·wark ['bʊlwək] Bollwerk *n* (*a. fig.*).

bum *Am.* F [bʌm] **1.** Nichtstuer *m*, Herumtreiber *m*; Gammler *m*; **2.** *v/t.* (*-mm-*) schnorren; ~ *around* herumgammeln.

bum·ble-bee *zo.* ['bʌmblbi:] Hummel *f*.

bump [bʌmp] **1.** heftiger Schlag *od.* Stoß; Beule *f*; **2.** stoßen; zusammenstoßen (mit), rammen; ~ *into fig. j-n* zufällig treffen; ~ *off F j-n* umlegen, umbringen.

bum·per¹ ['bʌmpə] **1.** volles Glas (*Wein*); **2.** riesig; ~ *crop* Rekordernte *f*.

bum·per² *mot.* [~] Stoßstange *f*; ~-*to*-~ Stoßstange an Stoßstange.

bump·y ['bʌmpɪ] (*-ier, -iest*) holp(e)rig.

bun [bʌn] süßes Brötchen; (Haar-)Knoten *m*.

bunch [bʌntʃ] **1.** Bund *n*, Büschel *n*; Haufen *m*; ~ *of grapes* Weintraube *f*; **2.** *a.* ~ *up* bündeln.

bun·dle ['bʌndl] **1.** Bündel *n* (*a. fig.*), Bund *f*; **2.** *v/t. a.* ~ *up* bündeln.

bung [bʌŋ] Spund *m*.

bun·ga·low ['bʌŋgələʊ] Bungalow *m*.

bun·gle ['bʌŋgl] **1.** Stümperei *f*,

bunion 418

Pfusch(arbeit f) m; 2. (ver)pfuschen.

bun·ion 🐝 [ˈbʌnjən] entzündeter Fußballen.

bunk [bʌŋk] Schlafkoje f.

bun·ny [ˈbʌnɪ] Häschen n.

buoy ⚓ [bɔɪ] 1. Boje f; 2. ~ed up fig. von neuem Mut erfüllt; ~**ant** [ˈbɔɪənt] schwimmfähig; tragend (Wasser etc.); fig. heiter.

bur·den [ˈbɜːdn] 1. Last f; Bürde f; ⚓ Tragfähigkeit f; 2. belasten; ~**some** [~səm] lästig, drückend.

bu·reau [ˈbjʊərəʊ] (pl. -reaux, -reaus) Büro n, Geschäftszimmer n; Brt. Schreibtisch m, -pult n; Am. (bsd. Spiegel)Kommode f; ~**c·ra·cy** [bjʊəˈrɒkrəsɪ] Bürokratie f.

bur|glar [ˈbɜːglə] Einbrecher m; ~**glar·ize** Am. [~raɪz] = burgle; ~**glar·y** [~rɪ] Einbruch(sdiebstahl) m; ~**gle** [~gl] einbrechen (in acc.).

bur·i·al [ˈberɪəl] Begräbnis n.

bur·ly [ˈbɜːlɪ] (-ier, -iest) stämmig, kräftig.

burn [bɜːn] 1. 🐝 Brandwunde f; verbrannte Stelle; 2. (burnt od. burned) (ver-, an)brennen; ~ down ab-, niederbrennen; ~ out ausbrennen; ~ up auflodern; verbrennen; verglühen (Rakete etc.); ~**ing** [ˈbɜːnɪŋ] brennend (a. fig.).

bur·nish [ˈbɜːnɪʃ] polieren.

burnt [bɜːnt] pret. u. p.p. von burn 2.

burp F [bɜːp] rülpsen, aufstoßen; ein Bäuerchen machen (lassen) (Baby).

bur·row [ˈbʌrəʊ] 1. Höhle f, Bau m; 2. (sich ein-, ver)graben.

burst [bɜːst] 1. Bersten n; Riß m; fig. Ausbruch m; 2. (burst) v/i. bersten, platzen; zerspringen; explodieren; ~ from sich losreißen von; ~ in on od. upon hereinplatzen bei j-m; ~ into tears in Tränen ausbrechen; ~ out herausplatzen; v/t. (auf)sprengen.

bur·y [ˈberɪ] be-, vergraben; beerdigen.

bus [bʌs] (pl. -es, -ses) (Omni)Bus m.

bush [bʊʃ] Busch m; Gebüsch n.

bush·el [ˈbʊʃl] Scheffel m (= Brt. 36,37 l, Am. 35,24 l).

bush·y [ˈbʊʃɪ] (-ier, -iest) buschig.

busi·ness [ˈbɪznɪs] Geschäft n; Beschäftigung f; Beruf m; Angelegenheit f; Aufgabe f; econ. Handel m; ~ of the day Tagesordnung f; on ~ geschäftlich; you have no ~ doing

(od. to do) that Sie haben kein Recht, das zu tun; this is none of your ~ das geht Sie nichts an; s. mind 2; ~**hours** pl. Geschäftszeit f; ~**like** geschäftsmäßig, sachlich; ~**man** (pl. -men) Geschäftsmann m; ~**trip** Geschäftsreise f; ~**wom·an** (pl. -women) Geschäftsfrau f.

bust¹ [bʌst] Büste f.

bust² Am. F [~] Pleite f.

bus·tle [ˈbʌsl] 1. Geschäftigkeit f; geschäftiges Treiben; 2. ~ about geschäftig hin u. her eilen.

bus·y □ [ˈbɪzɪ] 1. (-ier, -iest) beschäftigt; geschäftig; fleißig (at bei, an dat.); lebhaft; Am. teleph. besetzt; 2. (mst ~ o.s.) sich beschäftigen (with mit); ~**bod·y** aufdringlicher Mensch, Gschaftlhuber m.

but [bʌt, bət] 1. cj. aber, jedoch, sondern; außer, als; ohne daß; dennoch; a. ~ that daß nicht; he could not ~ laugh er mußte einfach lachen, 2. prp. außer; all ~ him alle außer ihm; the last ~ one der vorletzte; the next ~ one der übernächste; nothing ~ nichts als; ~ for wenn nicht gewesen wäre, ohne; 3. nach Negation: der (die od. das) nicht; there is no one ~ knows es gibt niemand, der es nicht weiß; 4. adv. nur; erst; gerade; all ~ fast, beinahe.

butch·er [ˈbʊtʃə] 1. Fleischer m, Metzger m; 2. (fig. ab-, hin)schlachten; ~**y** [~rɪ] Schlachthaus n; fig. Gemetzel n.

but·ler [ˈbʌtlə] Butler m.

butt¹ [bʌt] 1. Stoß m; (dickes) Ende (e-s Baumes etc.); Stummel m, Kippe f; (Gewehr)Kolben m; Schießstand m; fig. Zielscheibe f; 2. (mit dem Kopf) stoßen; ~ in F sich einmischen (on in acc.).

butt² [~] Wein-, Bierfaß n; Regentonne f.

but·ter [ˈbʌtə] 1. Butter f; F Schmeichelei f; 2. mit Butter bestreichen; ~**cup** 🌼 Butterblume f; ~**fly** zo. Schmetterling m; ~**y** [~rɪ] butter(-artig), Butter...

but·tocks [ˈbʌtəks] pl. Gesäß n, F od. zo. Hinterteil n.

but·ton [ˈbʌtn] 1. Knopf m; 🌼 Knospe f; 2. mst ~ up zuknöpfen; ~**hole** Knopfloch n.

but·tress [ˈbʌtrɪs] 1. Strebepfeiler m; fig. Stütze f; 2. (unter)stützen.

bux·om [ˈbʌksəm] drall, stramm.

C

buy [baɪ] **1.** F Kauf *m*; **2.** (*bought*) *v/t.* (an-, ein)kaufen (*of*, *from* von; *at* bei); ~ *out j-n* abfinden, auszahlen; *Firma* aufkaufen; ~ **up** aufkaufen; **~·er** ['baɪə] (Ein)Käufer(in).

buzz [bʌz] **1.** Summen *n*, Surren *n*; Stimmengewirr *n*; **2.** *v/i.* summen, surren; ~ *about* herumschwirren; ~ *off! Brt.* F schwirr ab!, hau ab!

buz·zard *zo.* ['bʌzəd] Bussard *m*.

buzz·er ⚡ ['bʌzə] Summer *m*.

by [baɪ] **1.** *prp. räumlich:* bei; an, neben; *Richtung:* durch; über; an (*dat.*) entlang *od.* vorbei; *zeitlich:* an, bei; spätestens bis, bis zu; *Urheber, Ursache:* von, durch (*bsd. beim Passiv*); *Mittel, Werkzeug:* durch, mit; *Art u. Weise:* bei; *Schwur:* bei; *Maß:* um, bei; *Richtschnur:* gemäß, bei; ~ *the dozen* dutzendweise; ~ *o.s.* allein; ~ *land* zu Lande; ~ *rail* per

Bahn; *day* ~ *day* Tag für Tag; ~ *twos* zu zweien; **2.** *adv.* dabei; vorbei; beiseite; ~ *and* ~ bald; nach u. nach; ~ *the* ~ nebenbei bemerkt; ~ *and large* im großen u. ganzen.

by- [baɪ] Neben...; Seiten...

bye *int.* F [baɪ], *a.* **bye-bye** [~'baɪ] Wiedersehen!, Tschüs!

by·e·lec·tion ['baɪlekʃn] Nachwahl *f*; **~gone 1.** vergangen; **2.** *let* ~*s be* ~*s* laß(t) das Vergangene ruhen; **~pass 1.** Umgehungsstraße *f*; ⚕ Bypass *m*; **2.** umgehen; vermeiden; **~path** Seitenstraße *f*; **~prod·uct** Nebenprodukt *n*; **~road** Seitenstraße *f*; **~stand·er** Zuschauer(in); **~street** Neben-, Seitenstraße *f*.

byte [baɪt] *Computer:* Byte *n*.

by·way ['baɪweɪ] Seitenstraße *f*; **~word** Sprichwort *n*; Inbegriff *m*; *be a* ~ *for* gleichbedeutend sein mit.

C

cab [kæb] Droschke *f*, Taxi *n*; Führerstand *m* (*Lokomotive*); Führerhaus *n* (*Lastwagen*), Führerhaus *n* (*a. Kran*).

cab·bage ♦ ['kæbɪdʒ] Kohl *m*.

cab·in ['kæbɪn] Hütte *f*; ⚓ Kabine *f* (*a. Seilbahn*), Kajüte *f*; ✈ Kanzel *f*; **~boy** ⚓ junger Kabinensteward; **~ cruis·er** ⚓ Kabinenkreuzer *m*.

cab·i·net ['kæbɪnɪt] *pol.* Kabinett *n*; Schrank *m*, Vitrine *f*; (Radio)Gehäuse *n*; **~mak·er** Kunsttischler *m*; **~ meet·ing** Kabinettssitzung *f*; **~mak·er** Kunsttischler *m*.

ca·ble ['keɪbl] **1.** Kabel *n*; ⚓ Ankertau *n*; **2.** telegrafieren; *j-m Geld* telegrafisch anweisen; **~car** *Seilbahn:* Kabine *f*, Wagen *m*; **~gram** [~græm] (Übersee)Telegramm *n*; ~ **tel·e·vi·sion** Kabelfernsehen *n*.

cab·rank ['kæbræŋk], **~stand** Taxi-, Droschkenstand *m*.

ca·ca·o ♦ [kə'kɑːəʊ] (*pl. -os*) Kakaobaum *m*, -bohne *f*.

cack·le ['kækl] **1.** Gegacker *n*, Geschnatter *n*; **2.** gackern, schnattern.

cad [kæd] Schuft *m*, Schurke *m*.

ca·dav·er ⚕ [kə'deɪvə] Leichnam *m*; △ *nicht Kadaver.*

ca·dence ['keɪdəns] ♪ Kadenz *f*; Tonfall *m*; Rhythmus *m*.

ca·det ⚔ [kə'det] Kadett *m*.

caf·é, caf·e ['kæfeɪ] Café *n*.

caf·e·te·ri·a [kæfɪ'tɪərɪə] Selbstbedienungsrestaurant *n*.

cage [keɪdʒ] **1.** Käfig *m*; ⚒ Förderkorb *m*; **2.** einsperren.

cag·ey □ F ['keɪdʒɪ] (*-gier, -giest*) verschlossen; vorsichtig; *Am.* schlau, gerissen.

ca·jole [kə'dʒəʊl] *j-m* schmeicheln; *j-n* beschwatzen.

cake [keɪk] **1.** Kuchen *m*, Torte *f*; Tafel *f* (*Schokolade*), Riegel *m* (*Seife*); **2.** ~*d with mud* schmutzverkrustet.

ca·lam·i·tous □ [kə'læmɪtəs] katastrophal; **~ty** [~tɪ] großes Unglück, Katastrophe *f*.

cal·cu·late ['kælkjʊleɪt] *v/t.* kalkulieren; be-, aus-, errechnen; *Am.* F vermuten; *v/i.* rechnen (*on, upon* mit, auf *acc.*); **~la·tion** [kælkjʊ-'leɪʃn] Berechnung *f* (*a. fig.*), Ausrechnung *f*; *econ.* Kalkulation *f*; Überlegung *f*; **~la·tor** ['kælkjʊleɪtə] Rechner *m* (*Gerät*).

cal·dron [ˈkɔːldrən] = *cauldron*.
cal·en·dar [ˈkælɪndə] 1. Kalender *m*; Liste *f*; 2. registrieren.
calf¹ [kɑːf] (*pl.* calves [~vz]) Wade *f*.
calf² [~] (*pl.* calves) Kalb *n*; **~skin** Kalb(s)fell *n*.
cal·i·bre, *Am.* **-ber** [ˈkælɪbə] Kaliber *n*.
cal·i·co [ˈkælɪkəʊ] (*pl.* -coes, -cos) Kaliko *m*.
call [kɔːl] 1. Ruf *m*; *teleph.* Anruf *m*, Gespräch *n*; Ruf *m*, Berufung *f* (*to in ein Amt*; *auf e-n Lehrstuhl*); Aufruf *m*, Aufforderung *f*; Signal *n*; (kurzer) Besuch; Kündigung *f* (*von Geldern*); *on* ~ auf Abruf; *make a* ~ telefonieren; 2. *v/t.* (herbei)rufen; (ein)berufen; *teleph.* j-n anrufen; berufen, ernennen (*to* zu); nennen; *Aufmerksamkeit* lenken (*to* auf *acc.*); *be* ~*ed* heißen; ~ *s.o. names* j-n beschimpfen, beleidigen; ~ *up* *teleph.* anrufen; *v/i.* rufen; *teleph.* anrufen; e-n (kurzen) Besuch machen (*on s.o.*, *at s.o.'s* [*house*] bei j-m); ~ *at a port* e-n Hafen anlaufen; ~ *for* rufen nach; *et.* anfordern; *et.* abholen; *to be* ~*ed for* postlagernd; ~ *on s.o.* j-n besuchen; ~ *on*, ~ *upon* sich an *j-n* wenden (*for* wegen); appellieren an (*acc.*) (*to do* zu tun); **~box** [ˈkɔːlbɒks] *Am.* Fernsprechzelle *f*; **~er** [ˈkɔːlə] *teleph.* Anrufer(in); Besucher(in); **~girl** Callgirl *n*; **~ing** [~ɪŋ] Rufen *n*; Berufung *f*; Beruf *m*.
cal·lous □ [ˈkæləs] schwielig; *fig.* dickfellig, herzlos.
cal·low [ˈkæləʊ] nackt (*ungefiedert*); *fig.* unerfahren.
calm [kɑːm] 1. □ still, ruhig; 2. (*Wind*)Stille *f*, Ruhe *f*; 3. *oft* ~ *down* besänftigen, (sich) beruhigen.
cal·o·rie *phys.* [ˈkælərɪ] Kalorie *f*; **~con·scious** kalorienbewußt.
ca·lum·ni·ate [kəˈlʌmnɪeɪt] verleumden; **cal·um·ny** [ˈkæləmnɪ] Verleumdung *f*.
calve [kɑːv] kalben.
calves [kɑːvz] *pl. von calf¹,²*.
cam·bric [ˈkeɪmbrɪk] Kambrik *m* (*feines Gewebe*).
came [keɪm] *pret. von come.*
cam·el *zo.*, ♣ [ˈkæml] Kamel *n*.
cam·er·a [ˈkæmərə] Kamera *f*, Fotoapparat *m*; *in* ~ ⚖ unter Ausschluß der Öffentlichkeit.
cam·o·mile ♀ [ˈkæməmaɪl] Kamille *f*.

cam·ou·flage ✕ [ˈkæmʊflɑːʒ] 1. Tarnung *f*; 2. tarnen.
camp [kæmp] 1. Lager *n*; ✕ Feldlager *n*; ~ *bed* Feldbett *n*; 2. lagern; ~ *out* zelten, campen.
cam·paign [kæmˈpeɪn] 1. ✕ Feldzug *m*; *fig.* Kampagne *f*, Feldzug *m*, Aktion *f*; *pol.* Wahlkampf *m*; 2. ✕ an e-m Feldzug teilnehmen; *fig.* kämpfen, zu Felde ziehen; *pol.* sich am Wahlkampf beteiligen, Wahlkampf machen; *Am.* kandidieren (*for* für).
camp|ground [ˈkæmpɡraʊnd], **~site** Lagerplatz *m*; Zelt-, Campingplatz *m*.
cam·pus [ˈkæmpəs] Campus *m*, Universitätsgelände *n*.
can¹ *v/aux.* [kæn, kən] (*pret. could*; *verneint: cannot, can't*) ich; du etc. kann(st) etc.; dürfen, können.
can² [~] 1. Kanne *f*; (Blech-, Konserven)Dose *f*, (~)Büchse *f*; 2. (-*nn*-) (in Büchsen) einmachen, eindosen.
Ca·na·di·an [kəˈneɪdjən] 1. kanadisch; 2. Kanadier(in).
ca·nal [kəˈnæl] Kanal *m* (*a. anat.*).
ca·nard [kæˈnɑːd] (Zeitungs)Ente *f*.
ca·nar·y *zo.* [kəˈneərɪ] Kanarienvogel *m*.
can·cel [ˈkænsl] (*bsd. Brt.* -*ll*-, *Am.* -*l*-) (durch-, aus)streichen; entwerten; rückgängig machen; absagen; *be* ~(*l*)*ed* ausfallen.
can·cer *ast.*, ♍ [ˈkænsə] Krebs *m*; **~ous** [~rəs] krebsartig; krebsbefallen.
can·did □ [ˈkændɪd] aufrichtig, offen.
can·di·date [ˈkændɪdət] Kandidat(in) (*for* für), Bewerber(in) (*for* um).
can·died [ˈkændɪd] kandiert.
can·dle [ˈkændl] Kerze *f*; Licht *n*; *burn the* ~ *at both ends* mit s-r Gesundheit Raubbau treiben; **~stick** Kerzenleuchter *m*.
can·do(u)r [ˈkændə] Aufrichtigkeit *f*, Offenheit *f*.
can·dy [ˈkændɪ] 1. Kandis(zucker) *m*; *Am.* Süßigkeiten *pl.*; 2. *v/t.* kandieren.
cane [keɪn] 1. ♀ Rohr *n*; (Rohr)Stock *m*; 2. (mit dem Stock) züchtigen.
ca·nine [ˈkeɪnaɪn] Hunde...
canned *Am.* [kænd] Dosen..., Büchsen...
can·ne·ry *Am.* [ˈkænərɪ] Konservenfabrik *f*.

can·ni·bal [ˈkænɪbl] Kannibale *m*.

can·non [ˈkænən] Kanone *f*.

can·not [ˈkænɒt] *s.* can¹.

can·ny □ [ˈkænɪ] (*-ier, -iest*) gerissen, schlau.

ca·noe [kəˈnuː] **1.** Kanu *n*, Paddelboot *n*; **2.** Kanu fahren, paddeln.

can·on [ˈkænən] Kanon *m*; Regel *f*, Richtschnur *f*; **~ize** [~aɪz] heiligsprechen.

can·o·py [ˈkænəpɪ] Baldachin *m*; *arch.* Vordach *n*.

cant [kænt] Fachsprache *f*; Gewäsch *n*; frömmlerisches Gerede.

can't [kɑːnt] = *cannot*.

can·tan·ker·ous F □ [kænˈtæŋkərəs] zänkisch, mürrisch.

can·teen [kænˈtiːn] ⚔ Feldflasche *f*; Kantine *f*; ⚔ Kochgeschirr *n*; Besteck(kasten *m*) *n*.

can·ter [ˈkæntə] **1.** Kanter *m* (*kurzer, leichter Galopp*); **2.** kantern.

can·vas [ˈkænvəs] Segeltuch *n*; Zelt-, Packleinwand *f*; Segel *pl.*; *paint.* Leinwand *f*; Gemälde *n*.

can·vass [~] **1.** *pol.* Wahlfeldzug *m*; *econ.* Werbefeldzug *m*; **2.** *v/t.* eingehend untersuchen *od.* erörtern *od.* prüfen; *pol.* werben um (*Stimmen*); *v/i. pol.* e-n Wahlfeldzug veranstalten.

can·yon [ˈkænjən] Cañon *m*.

cap [kæp] **1.** Kappe *f*; Mütze *f*; Haube *f*; *arch.* Aufsatz *m*; Zündkapsel *f*; ⚕ Pessar *n*; **2.** (*-pp-*) (mit e-r Kappe *etc.*) bedecken; *fig.* krönen; übertreffen.

ca·pa·bil·i·ty [keɪpəˈbɪlətɪ] Fähigkeit *f*; **~ble** □ [ˈkeɪpəbl] fähig (*of zu*).

ca·pa·cious □ [kəˈpeɪʃəs] geräumig.

ca·pac·i·ty [kəˈpæsətɪ] (Raum)Inhalt *m*; Fassungsvermögen *n*; Kapazität *f*; Aufnahmefähigkeit *f*; *geistige* (*od.* ⊕ Leistungs)Fähigkeit *f* (*for ger. zu inf.*); *in my* ~ *as* in meiner Eigenschaft als.

cape¹ [keɪp] Kap *n*, Vorgebirge *n*.

cape² [~] Cape *n*, Umhang *m*.

ca·per [ˈkeɪpə] **1.** Kapriole *f*, Luftsprung *m*; *cut* ~*s* = **2.** Freuden- *od.* Luftsprünge machen.

ca·pil·la·ry *anat.* [kəˈpɪlərɪ] Haar-, Kapillargefäß *n*.

cap·i·tal [ˈkæpɪtl] **1.** □ Kapital...; Tod(es)...; Haupt...; großartig, prima; ~ *crime* Kapitalverbrechen *n*; ~ *punishment* Todesstrafe *f*; **2.** Hauptstadt *f*; Kapital *n*; *mst* ~ *letter*

Großbuchstabe *m*; **~·ism** [~ɪzəm] Kapitalismus *m*; **~·ist** [~ɪst] Kapitalist *m*; **~·ize** [~əlaɪz] kapitalisieren; groß schreiben.

ca·pit·u·late [kəˈpɪtjʊleɪt] kapitulieren (*to* vor *dat.*).

ca·price [kəˈpriːs] Laune *f*; **ca·pricious** □ [~ʃəs] kapriziös, launisch.

Cap·ri·corn *ast.* [ˈkæprɪkɔːn] Steinbock *m*.

cap·size [kæpˈsaɪz] *v/i.* kentern; *v/t.* zum Kentern bringen.

cap·sule [ˈkæpsjuːl] Kapsel *f*; (Raum)Kapsel *f*.

cap·tain [ˈkæptɪn] (An)Führer *m*; Kapitän *m*; ⚔ Hauptmann *m*.

cap·tion [ˈkæpʃn] Überschrift *f*, Titel *m*; Bildunterschrift *f*; *Film:* Untertitel *m*.

cap·ti·vate *fig.* [ˈkæptɪveɪt] gefangennehmen, fesseln; **~tive** [ˈkæptɪv] **1.** gefangen; gefesselt; *hold* ~ gefangenhalten; *take* ~ gefangennehmen; **2.** Gefangene(r *m*) *f*; **~tiv·i·ty** [kæpˈtɪvɪtɪ] Gefangenschaft *f*.

cap·ture [ˈkæptʃə] **1.** Eroberung *f*; Gefangennahme *f*; **2.** fangen; erobern; erbeuten; ♣ kapern.

car [kɑː] Auto *n*, Wagen *m*; (Eisenbahn-, Straßenbahn)Wagen *m*; Gondel *f* (*e-s Ballons etc.*); Kabine *f* (*e-s Aufzugs*); *by* ~ mit dem Auto, im Auto.

car·a·mel [ˈkærəmel] Karamel *m*; Karamelle *f*.

car·a·van [ˈkærəvæn] Karawane *f*; *Brt.* Wohnwagen *m*, -anhänger *m*; ~ *site* Campingplatz *m* für Wohnwagen.

car·a·way ♀ [ˈkærəweɪ] Kümmel *m*.

car·bine ⚔ [ˈkɑːbaɪn] Karabiner *m*.

car·bo·hy·drate 🜄 [ˈkɑːbəʊˈhaɪdreɪt] Kohle(n)hydrat *n*.

car·bon [ˈkɑːbən] 🜄 Kohlenstoff *m*; *a.* ~ *copy* Durchschlag *m*; *a.* ~ *paper* Kohlepapier *n*.

car·bu·ret·tor, *a.* **-ret·ter** *bsd. Brt.*, *Am.* **-ret·or**, *a.* **-ret·er** ⊕ [kɑːbjʊˈretə] Vergaser *m*.

car·case, **car·cass** [ˈkɑːkəs] Kadaver *m*, Aas *n*; *Fleischerei:* Rumpf *m*.

card [kɑːd] Karte *f*; *have a* ~ *up one's sleeve fig.* (noch) e-n Trumpf in der Hand haben; **~board** [ˈkɑːdbɔːd] Pappe *f*; ~ *box* Pappkarton *m*.

car·di·ac 🜄 [ˈkɑːdiæk] Herz...

car·di·gan [ˈkɑːdɪgən] Strickjacke *f*.

car·di·nal [ˈkɑːdɪnl] **1.** □ Grund...,

Haupt..., Kardinal...; scharlachrot; ~ *number* Grundzahl *f*; 2. *eccl.* Kardinal *m.*

card-in·dex ['kɑːdɪndeks] Kartei *f.*

card-sharp·er ['kɑːdʃɑːpə] Falschspieler *m.*

care [keə] 1. Sorge *f*; Sorgfalt *f*; Vorsicht *f*; Obhut *f*, Pflege *f*; *medical* ~ ärztliche Behandlung; ~ *of* (*abbr. c/o*) ... per Adresse, bei ...; *take* ~ *of* aufpassen auf (*acc.*); *with* ~! Vorsicht!; 2. Lust haben (*to inf.* zu); ~ *for* sorgen für, sich kümmern um; sich etwas machen aus; *I don't* ~! F meinetwegen!; *I couldn't* ~ *less* F es ist mir völlig egal; *well* ~*d-for* gepflegt.

ca·reer [kə'rɪə] 1. Karriere *f*, Laufbahn *f*; 2. Berufs...; Karriere...; rasen.

care·free ['keəfriː] sorgenfrei, sorglos.

care·ful □ ['keəfl] vorsichtig; sorgsam bedacht (*of* auf *acc.*); sorgfältig; *be* ~! gib acht!; ~**ness** [~nɪs] Vorsicht *f*; Sorgfalt *f.*

care·less □ ['keəlɪs] sorglos; nachlässig; unachtsam; leichtsinnig; ~**ness** [~nɪs] Sorglosigkeit *f*; Nachlässigkeit *f*; Fahrlässigkeit *f.*

ca·ress [kə'res] 1. Liebkosung *f*; 2. liebkosen, streicheln.

care·tak·er ['keəteɪkə] Hausmeister *m*; (*Haus- etc.*)Verwalter *m.*

care·worn ['keəwɔːn] abgehärmt.

car·go ['kɑːɡəʊ] (*pl. -goes, Am. a. -gos*) Ladung *f.*

car·i·ca·ture ['kærɪkətjʊə] 1. Karikatur *f*; 2. karikieren; ~**tur·ist** [~rɪst] Karikaturist *m.*

car·mine ['kɑːmaɪn] Karmin(rot) *n.*

car·nal □ ['kɑːnl] fleischlich; sinnlich.

car·na·tion [kɑːˈneɪʃn] ⚘ (Garten-) Nelke *f*; Blaßrot *n.*

car·ni·val ['kɑːnɪvl] Karneval *m.*

car·niv·o·rous □ *zo.* [kɑːˈnɪvərəs] fleischfressend.

car·ol ['kærəl] Weihnachtslied *n.*

carp *zo.* [kɑːp] Karpfen *m.*

car-park *Brt.* ['kɑːpɑːk] Parkplatz *m*; Parkhaus *n.*

car·pen·ter ['kɑːpɪntə] Zimmermann *m*; ~**try** [~rɪ] Zimmerhandwerk *n*; Zimmermannsarbeit *f.*

car·pet ['kɑːpɪt] 1. Teppich *m*; *bring on the* ~ aufs Tapet bringen; 2. mit e-m Teppich belegen.

car|pool ['kɑːpuːl] Fahrgemeinschaft *f*; ~**port** überdachter Abstellplatz (*für Autos*).

car·riage ['kærɪdʒ] Beförderung *f*, Transport *m*; Fracht(gebühr) *f*; Kutsche *f*; *Brt.* 🚋(Personen)Wagen *m*; ⊕ Fahrgestell *n* (*a.* ✈); (Körper-) Haltung *f*; ~**way** Fahrbahn *f.*

car·ri·er ['kærɪə] Spediteur *m*; Träger *m*; Gepäckträger *m*; ~**bag** Trag(e)tasche *f*, -tüte *f*; ~ **pi·geon** Brieftaube *f.*

car·ri·on ['kærɪən] Aas *n*; *attr.* Aas...

car·rot ⚘ ['kærət] Karotte *f*, Möhre, Mohrrübe *f.*

car·ry ['kærɪ] *v/t. wohin* bringen, führen, tragen (*a. v/i.*), fahren, befördern; (*bei sich*) haben *od.* tragen; *Ansicht* durchsetzen; *Gewinn, Preis* davontragen; *Ernte, Zinsen* tragen; (*weiter*)führen; *Mauer* ziehen; *Antrag* durchbringen; *be carried* angenommen werden (*Antrag*); ~ *the day* den Sieg davontragen; ~ *s.th. too far et.* übertreiben, et. zu weit treiben; *get carried away fig.* die Kontrolle über sich verlieren; ~ *forward, ~ over econ.* übertragen; ~ *on* fortsetzen, weiterführen; *Geschäft etc.* betreiben; ~ *out, ~ through* durchführen, ausführen; ~**cot** *Brt.* ['kærɪkɒt] (Baby)Trag(e)tasche *f.*

cart [kɑːt] 1. Karren *m*; Wagen *m*; *put the* ~ *before the horse fig.* das Pferd beim Schwanz aufzäumen; 2. karren, fahren.

car·ti·lage *anat.* ['kɑːtɪlɪdʒ] Knorpel *m.*

car·ton ['kɑːtən] Karton *m*; *a* ~ *of cigarettes* e-e Stange Zigaretten.

car·toon [kɑːˈtuːn] Cartoon *m*, *n*; Karikatur *f*; Zeichentrickfilm *m*; ~**ist** [~ɪst] Karikaturist *m.*

car·tridge ['kɑːtrɪdʒ] Patrone *f*; *phot.* (Film)Patrone *f* (*e-r Kleinbildkamera*), (Film)Kassette *f* (*e-r Film- od. Kassettenkamera*); ~**pen** Patronenfüllhalter *m.*

cart-wheel ['kɑːtwiːl] Wagenrad *n*; *turn* ~s radschlagen.

carve [kɑːv] *Fleisch* vorschneiden, zerlegen; schnitzen; meißeln; **carv·er** ['kɑːvə] (Holz)Schnitzer *m*; Bildhauer *m*; Tranchierer *m*; Tranchiermesser *n*; **carv·ing** [~ɪŋ] Schnitzerei *f.*

car wash ['kɑːwɒʃ] Autowäsche *f*; Waschanlage *f*, -straße *f.*

cas·cade [kæˈskeɪd] Wasserfall *m*.

case[1] [keɪs] **1.** Behälter *m*; Kiste *f*, Kasten *m*; Etui *n*; Gehäuse *n*; Schachtel *f*; (*Glas*)Schrank *m*; (*Kissen*)Bezug *m*; ⊕ Verkleidung *f*; **2.** in ein Gehäuse *od.* Etui stecken; ⊕ verkleiden.

case[2] [~] Fall *m* (*a.* 🏛); *gr.* Kasus *m*, Fall *m*; ⚕ (Krankheits)Fall *m*, Patient(in); F komischer Kauz; Sache *f*, Angelegenheit *f*.

case·ment [ˈkeɪsmənt] Fensterflügel *m*; *a.* ~ window Flügelfenster *n*.

cash [kæʃ] **1.** Bargeld *n*; Barzahlung *f*; ~ down gegen bar; ~ on delivery Lieferung *f* gegen bar, (per) Nachnahme *f*; **2.** Scheck etc. einlösen; ~·**book** [ˈkæʃbʊk] Kassenbuch *n*; ~·**desk** [~] Kasse *f* (*im Warenhaus etc.*); ~·**di·spens·er** Geldautomat *m*, Bankomat *m*; ~·**ier** [kæˈʃɪə] Kassierer(in); ~'s desk *od.* office Kasse *f*; ~·**less** [~lɪs] bargeldlos; ~·**o·mat** [kæʃəʊˈmæt] = ~ dispenser; ~ **re·gis·ter** Registrierkasse *f*.

cas·ing [ˈkeɪsɪŋ] (Schutz)Hülle *f*; Verschalung *f*, -kleidung *f*, Gehäuse *n*.

cask [kɑːsk] Faß *n*.

cas·ket [ˈkɑːskɪt] Kästchen *n*; *Am.* Sarg *m*.

cas·se·role [ˈkæsərəʊl] Kasserolle *f*.

cas·sette [kəˈset] (Film-, Band-etc.)Kassette *f*; ⚠ nicht Geld- etc. Kassette; ~·**deck** Kassettendeck *n*; ~·**ra·di·o** Radiorecorder *m*; ~·**re·cord·er** Kassettenrecorder *m*.

cas·sock *eccl.* [ˈkæsək] Soutane *f*.

cast [kɑːst] **1.** Wurf *m*; ⊕ Guß(form *f*) *m*; Abguß *m*, Abdruck *m*; Schattierung *f*, Anflug *m*; Form *f*, Art *f*; Auswerfen *n* (*der Angel etc.*); *thea.* Besetzung *f*; **2.** (*cast*) *v/t.* (ab-, aus-, hin-, um-, weg)werfen; *zo.* Haut etc. abwerfen; *Zähne etc.* verlieren; verwerfen; gestalten; ⊕ gießen; *a.* ~ up ausrechnen, zusammenzählen; *thea. Stück* besetzen; *Rollen* verteilen (to an *acc.*); be ~ in a lawsuit 🏛 e-n Prozeß verlieren; ~ lots losen (for um); ~ in one's lot with s.o. j-s Los teilen; ~ aside *Gewohnheit etc.* ablegen; *Freund etc.* fallenlassen; ~ away wegwerfen; be ~ away ⚓ verschlagen werden; be ~ down niedergeschlagen sein; ~ off *Kleidung* ausrangieren; *Freund etc.* fallenlassen; *Stricken etc.: Maschen* abnehmen;

v/i. ⊕ sich gießen lassen; sich (ver-)werfen (*Holz*); ~ about for, ~ around for suchen (nach), *fig. a.* sich umsehen nach.

cas·ta·net [kæstəˈnet] Kastagnette *f*.

cast·a·way [ˈkɑːstəweɪ] **1.** ausgestoßen; ausrangiert, abgelegt (*Kleidung etc.*); ⚓ schiffbrüchig; **2.** Ausgestoßene(r *m*) *f*; ⚓ Schiffbrüchige(r *m*) *f*.

caste [kɑːst] Kaste *f* (*a. fig.*).

cast·er [ˈkɑːstə] = castor[2].

cast·i·gate [ˈkæstɪgeɪt] züchtigen; *fig.* geißeln.

cast iron [ˈkɑːstˈaɪən] Gußeisen *n*; **cast-i·ron** gußeisern.

cas·tle [ˈkɑːsl] Burg *f*, Schloß *n*; *Schach:* Turm *m*.

cast·or[1] [ˈkɑːstə] ~ oil Rizinusöl *n*.

cast·or[2] [~] Laufrolle *f* (*unter Möbeln*); (Salz-, Zucker- etc.)Streuer *m*.

cas·trate [kæˈstreɪt] kastrieren.

cas·u·al □ [ˈkæʒjʊəl] zufällig; gelegentlich; flüchtig; lässig; ~ wear Freizeitkleidung *f*; ~·**ty** [~tɪ] Unfall *m*; Verunglückte(r *m*) *f*, Opfer *n*; ⚔ Verwundete(r *m*), Gefallene(r *m*); casualties *pl.* Opfer *pl.*, ⚔ *mst* Verluste *pl.*; ~ ward, ~ department Unfallstation *f*.

cat *zo.* [kæt] Katze *f*.

cat·a·logue, *Am.* **-log** [ˈkætəlɒg] **1.** Katalog *m*, *Am. univ.* Vorlesungsverzeichnis *n*; **2.** katalogisieren.

cat·a·pult [ˈkætəpʌlt] *Brt.* Schleuder *f*; Katapult *n, m*.

cat·a·ract [ˈkætərækt] Wasserfall *m*; Stromschnelle *f*; ⚕ grauer Star.

ca·tarrh ⚕ [kəˈtɑː] Katarrh *m*; Schnupfen *m*.

ca·tas·tro·phe [kəˈtæstrəfɪ] Katastrophe *f*.

catch [kætʃ] **1.** Fangen *n*; Fang *m*, Beute *f*; Stocken *n* (*des Atems*); Halt *m*, Griff *m*; ⊕ Haken *m*; (Tür)Klinke *f*; Verschluß *m*; *fig.* Haken *m*; **2.** (*caught*) *v/t.* (auf-, ein)fangen; packen, fassen, ergreifen; überraschen, ertappen; *Blick etc.* auffangen; *Zug etc.* (noch) kriegen, erwischen; erfassen, verstehen; einfangen (*Atmosphäre*); sich *e-e Krankheit* holen; ~ (a) cold sich erkälten; ~ the eye ins Auge fallen; ~ s.o.'s eye j-s Aufmerksamkeit auf sich lenken; ~ s.o. up j-n einholen; be caught up in verwickelt sein in (*acc.*); **3.** *v/i.* sich verfangen, hängenbleiben; fassen, greifen; ineinandergreifen (*Räder*);

klemmen; einschnappen (*Schloß etc.*); ~ **on** F einschlagen, Anklang finden; F kapieren; ~ **up with** einholen; ~**er** [ˈkætʃə] Fänger *m*; ~**ing** [~ɪŋ] packend; *fig.* ansteckend; ~**word** Schlagwort *n*; Stichwort *n*; ~**y** □ [~ɪ] (*-ier, -iest*) eingängig (*Melodie*).

cat·e·chis·m [ˈkætɪkɪzəm] Katechismus *m*.

ca·te·gor·i·cal □ [kætɪˈgɒrɪkl] kategorisch; ~**go·ry** [ˈkætɪgərɪ] Kategorie *f*.

ca·ter [ˈkeɪtə]: ~ **for** Speisen u. Getränke liefern für; *fig.* sorgen für.

cat·er·pil·lar [ˈkætəpɪlə] *zo.* Raupe *f*; *TM* Raupenfahrzeug *n*; ~ **tractor** *TM* Raupenschlepper *m*.

cat·gut [ˈkætgʌt] Darmsaite *f*.

ca·the·dral [kəˈθiːdrəl] Dom *m*, Kathedrale *f*.

Cath·o·lic [ˈkæθəlɪk] **1.** katholisch; **2.** Katholik(in).

cat·kin ♀ [ˈkætkɪn] Kätzchen *n*.

cat·tle [ˈkætl] Vieh *n*.

cat·ty F [ˈkætɪ] (*-ier, iest*) boshaft, gehässig.

caught [kɔːt] *pret. u. p.p. von catch 2.*

caul·dron [ˈkɔːldrən] großer Kessel.

cau·li·flow·er ♀ [ˈkɒlɪflaʊə] Blumenkohl *m*.

caus·al □ [ˈkɔːzl] ursächlich.

cause [kɔːz] **1.** Ursache *f*; Grund *m*; ⁂⁂ Klagegrund *m*; ⁂⁂ Fall *m*, Sache *f*; Angelegenheit *f*, Sache *f*; **2.** verursachen; veranlassen; ~**less** □ [ˈkɔːzlɪs] grundlos.

cause·way [ˈkɔːzweɪ] Damm *m*.

caus·tic [ˈkɔːstɪk] (*~ally*) ätzend; *fig.* beißend, scharf.

cau·tion [ˈkɔːʃn] **1.** Vorsicht *f*; Warnung *f*; Verwarnung *f*; △ *nicht Kaution*; **2.** warnen; verwarnen; ⁂⁂ belehren.

cau·tious □ [ˈkɔːʃəs] behutsam, vorsichtig; ~**ness** [~nɪs] Behutsamkeit *f*, Vorsicht *f*.

cav·al·ry *bsd. hist.* ✕ [ˈkævlrɪ] Kavallerie *f*.

cave [keɪv] **1.** Höhle *f*; **2.** *v/i.* ~ **in** einstürzen; klein beigeben.

cav·ern [ˈkævən] (große) Höhle; ~**ous** *fig.* [~əs] hohl.

cav·i·ty [ˈkævətɪ] Höhle *f*; Loch *n*.

caw [kɔː] **1.** krächzen; **2.** Krächzen *n*.

cease [siːs] *v/i.* aufhören, zu Ende gehen; *v/t.* aufhören (*to do, doing* zu tun); ~**fire** ✕ [ˈsiːsfaɪə] Feuereinstellung *f*; Waffenruhe *f*; ~**less** □ [~lɪs] unaufhörlich.

cede [siːd] abtreten, überlassen.

cei·ling [ˈsiːlɪŋ] (Zimmer-)Decke *f*; *fig.* Höchstgrenze *f*; ~ **price** Höchstpreis *m*.

cel·e·brate [ˈselɪbreɪt] feiern; ~**brated** gefeiert, berühmt (*for* für, wegen); ~**bra·tion** [selɪˈbreɪʃn] Feier *f*.

ce·leb·ri·ty [sɪˈlebrətɪ] Berühmtheit *f*.

ce·ler·i·ty [sɪˈlerətɪ] Geschwindigkeit *f*.

cel·er·y ♀ [ˈselərɪ] Sellerie *m*, *f*.

ce·les·ti·al □ [sɪˈlestjəl] himmlisch.

cel·i·ba·cy [ˈselɪbəsɪ] Ehelosigkeit *f*.

cell [sel] Zelle *f*; ⚡ *a.* Element *n*.

cel·lar [ˈselar] Keller *m*.

cel·list ♪ [ˈtʃelɪst] Cellist(in); ~**lo** ♪ [~əʊ] (*pl. -los*) (Violon)Cello *n*.

cel·lo·phane *TM* [ˈseləʊfeɪn] Zellophan *n*.

cel·lu·lar [ˈseljʊlə] Zell(en)...

Cel·tic [ˈkeltɪk] keltisch.

ce·ment [sɪˈment] **1.** Zement *m*; Kitt *m*; **2.** zementieren; (ver)kitten.

cem·e·tery [ˈsemɪtrɪ] Friedhof *m*.

cen·sor [ˈsensə] **1.** Zensor *m*; **2.** zensieren; ~**ship** [~ʃɪp] Zensur *f*.

cen·sure [ˈsenʃə] **1.** Tadel *m*, Verweis *m*; △ *nicht Zensur*; **2.** tadeln.

cen·sus [ˈsensəs] Volkszählung *f*.

cent [sent] Hundert *n*; *Am.* Cent *m* (= $^1\!/_{100}$ *Dollar*); *per* ~ Prozent *n*.

cen·te·na·ry [senˈtiːnərɪ] Hundertjahrfeier *f*, hundertjähriges Jubiläum.

cen·ten·ni·al [senˈtenjəl] **1.** hundertjährig; **2.** *Am.* = centenary.

cen·ter *Am.* [ˈsentə] = centre.

cen·ti·grade [ˈsentɪgreɪd]: *10 degrees* ~ 10 Grad Celsius; ~**me·tre**, *Am.* ~**me·ter** Zentimeter *m*, *n*; ~**pede** *zo.* [~piːd] Tausendfüß(l)er *m*.

cen·tral [ˈsentrəl] zentral; Haupt..., Zentral...; Mittel...; ~ **heating** Zentralheizung *f*; ~**ize** [~aɪz] zentralisieren.

cen·tre, *Am.* **-ter** [ˈsentə] **1.** Zentrum *n*, Mittelpunkt *m*; ~ *of gravity phys.* Schwerpunkt *m*; **2.** (sich) konzentrieren; zentrieren.

cen·tu·ry [ˈsentʃʊrɪ] Jahrhundert *n*.

ce·ram·ics [sɪˈræmɪks] *pl.* Keramik *f*, keramische Erzeugnisse *n/pl.*

ce·re·al [ˈsɪərɪəl] **1.** Getreide...; **2.** Getreide(pflanze *f*) *n*; Getreideflokken(gericht n) pl., Frühstückskost f (aus Getreide).

cer·e·bral anat. [ˈserɪbrəl] Gehirn...

cer·e·mo|ni·al [serɪˈməʊnjəl] **1.** □ zeremoniell; **2.** Zeremoniell n; **~ni·ous** □ [~jəs] zeremoniell; förmlich; **~ny** [ˈserɪmənɪ] Zeremonie f; Feier(lichkeit) f; Förmlichkeit(en pl.) f.

cer·tain □ [ˈsɜːtn] sicher, gewiß; zuverlässig; bestimmt; gewisse(r, -s); **~ly** [~lɪ] sicher, gewiß; in Antworten: sicherlich, bestimmt, natürlich; **~ty** [~tɪ] Sicherheit f, Bestimmtheit f, Gewißheit f.

cer·tif·i·cate 1. [səˈtɪfɪkət] Zeugnis n; Bescheinigung f; ~ of birth Geburtsurkunde f; General ♀ of Education advanced level (A level) Brt. Schule: etwa Abitur(zeugnis) n; General ♀ of Education ordinary level (O level) Schule: etwa mittlere Reife; medical ~ ärztliches Attest; **2.** [~keɪt] bescheinigen; **~ti·fy** [ˈsɜːtɪfaɪ] et. bescheinigen; beglaubigen.

cer·ti·tude [ˈsɜːtɪtjuːd] Sicherheit f, Bestimmtheit f, Gewißheit f.

ces·sa·tion [seˈseɪʃn] Aufhören n.

chafe [tʃeɪf] v/t. (auf)scheuern, wund reiben; ärgern; v/i. sich aufscheuern od. wund scheuern; scheuern; sich ärgern.

chaff [tʃɑːf] **1.** Spreu f; Häcksel n; F Neckerei f; **2.** F necken.

chaf·finch zo. [ˈtʃæfɪntʃ] Buchfink m.

cha·grin [ˈʃægrɪn] **1.** Ärger m; **2.** ärgern.

chain [tʃeɪn] **1.** Kette f; fig. Fessel f; ~ reaction Kettenreaktion f; ~-smoke Kette rauchen; ~-smoker Kettenraucher m; ~ store Kettenladen m; **2.** (an)ketten; fesseln.

chair [tʃeə] Stuhl m; Lehrstuhl m; Vorsitz m; be in the ~ den Vorsitz führen; ~ lift [ˈtʃeəlɪft] Sessellift m; **~·man** (pl. -men) Vorsitzende(r) m, Präsident m; **~·man·ship** [~ʃɪp] Vorsitz m; **~·wom·an** (pl. -women) Vorsitzende f.

chal·ice [ˈtʃælɪs] Kelch m.

chalk [tʃɔːk] **1.** Kreide f; **2.** mit Kreide schreiben od. zeichnen; ~ up Sieg verbuchen.

chal·lenge [ˈtʃælɪndʒ] **1.** Herausforderung f; ⚔ Anruf m; bsd. ⚖ Ablehnung f; **2.** herausfordern; anrufen; ablehnen; anzweifeln.

cham·ber [ˈtʃeɪmbə] parl., zo., ⚘, ⊕, Kammer f; **~s** pl. Geschäfts-

räume pl.; **~maid** Zimmermädchen n.

cham·ois [ˈʃæmwɑː] Gemse f; a. ~ leather [mst. ˈʃæmleðə] Wildleder n.

champ F [tʃæmp] = champion (Sport).

cham·pagne [ʃæmˈpeɪn] Champagner m.

cham·pi·on [ˈtʃæmpjən] **1.** Verfechter m, Fürsprecher m; Sport: Sieger m; Meister m; **2.** verfechten, eintreten für, verteidigen; **3.** Meister...; **~·ship** Sport: Meisterschaft f.

chance [tʃɑːns] **1.** Zufall m; Schicksal n; Risiko n; Chance f, (günstige) Gelegenheit; Aussicht f (of auf acc.); Möglichkeit f; by ~ zufällig; take a ~ es darauf ankommen lassen; take no ~s nichts riskieren (wollen); **2.** zufällig; **3.** v/i. geschehen; I ~d to meet her zufällig traf ich sie; v/t. riskieren.

chan·cel·lor [ˈtʃɑːnsələ] Kanzler m.

chan·de·lier [ʃændəˈlɪə] Kronleuchter m.

change [tʃeɪndʒ] **1.** Veränderung f, Wechsel m; Abwechslung f; Wechselgeld n; Kleingeld n; for a ~ zur Abwechslung; ~ for the better (worse) Besserung f (Verschlechterung f); **2.** v/t. (ver)ändern, umändern; (aus)wechseln; (aus-, ver)tauschen (for gegen); mot. ⊕ schalten; ~ over umschalten; umstellen; ~ trains umsteigen; v/i. sich (ver)ändern, wechseln; sich umziehen; **~·ble** □ [ˈtʃeɪndʒəbl] veränderlich; **~·less** □ [~lɪs] unveränderlich; **~·o·ver** Umstellung f.

chan·nel [ˈtʃænl] **1.** Kanal m; Flußbett n; Rinne f; (Fernseh- etc.)Kanal m, (-)Programm n; fig. Kanal m, Weg m; **2.** (bsd. Brt. -ll-; Am. -l-) furchen; aushöhlen; fig. lenken.

chant [tʃɑːnt] **1.** (Kirchen)Gesang m; Singsang m; **2.** singen; in Sprechchören rufen; Sprechchöre anstimmen.

cha·os [ˈkeɪɒs] Chaos n.

chap¹ [tʃæp] **1.** Riß m, Sprung m; **2.** (-pp-) rissig machen od. werden.

chap² [tʃæp] Bursche m, Kerl m, Junge m.

chap³ [~] Kinnbacke(n m) f; Maul n.

chap·el [ˈtʃæpl] Kapelle f; Gottesdienst m.

chap·lain [ˈtʃæplɪn] Kaplan m.

chap·ter [ˈtʃæptə] Kapitel n.

char [tʃɑː] (*-rr-*) verkohlen.

char·ac·ter [ˈkærəktə] Charakter *m*; Eigenschaft *f*; Schrift(zeichen *n*) *f*; Persönlichkeit *f*; *Roman etc.*: Figur *f*, Gestalt *f*; *thea.* Rolle *f*; (*bsd.* guter) Ruf; Zeugnis *n*; **~·is·tic** [kærəktəˈrɪstɪk] **1.** (*~ally*) charakteristisch (*of* für); **2.** Kennzeichen *n*; **~·ize** [ˈkærəktəraɪz] charakterisieren.

char·coal [ˈtʃɑːkəʊl] Holzkohle *f*.

charge [tʃɑːdʒ] **1.** Ladung *f*; (Spreng)Ladung *f*; *bsd. fig.* Last *f*; Verantwortung *f*; Aufsicht *f*, Leitung *f*; Obhut *f*; Schützling *m*; ✕ Angriff *m*; Beschuldigung *f*, ✞ *a.* (Punkt *m* der) Anklage *f*; Preis *m*, Kosten *pl.*; Gebühr *f*; *free of ~* kostenlos; *be in ~ of* verantwortlich sein für; *have ~ of* in Obhut *od.* Verwahrung haben, betreuen; *take ~* die Leitung *etc.* übernehmen, die Sache in die Hand nehmen; **2.** *v/t.* laden; beladen, belasten; beauftragen; belehren; ✞ beschuldigen, anklagen (*with gen.*); in Rechnung stellen; berechnen, (als Preis) fordern; ✕ angreifen; *v/i.* stürmen; *~ at s.o.* auf j-n losgehen.

char·i·ot *poet. od. hist.* [ˈtʃærɪət] Streit-, Triumphwagen *m*.

char·i·ta·ble □ [ˈtʃærɪtəbl] mild (-tätig), wohltätig.

char·i·ty [ˈtʃærətɪ] Nächstenliebe *f*; Wohltätigkeit *f*; Güte *f*; Nachsicht *f*; milde Gabe.

char·la·tan [ˈʃɑːlətən] Scharlatan *m*; Quacksalber *m*, Kurpfuscher *m*.

charm [tʃɑːm] **1.** Zauber *m*; Charme *m*, Reiz *m*; Talisman *m*, Amulett *n*; **2.** bezaubern, entzücken; **~·ing** □ [ˈtʃɑːmɪŋ] charmant, bezaubernd.

chart [tʃɑːt] **1.** ⚓ Seekarte *f*; Tabelle *f*; **~s** *pl.* Charts *pl.*, Hitliste(n *pl.*) *f*; **2.** auf e-r Karte einzeichnen.

char·ter [ˈtʃɑːtə] **1.** Urkunde *f*, Freibrief *m*; Chartern *n*; **2.** konzessionieren; ⚓, ✈ chartern, mieten; **~ flight** Charterflug *m*.

char·wom·an [ˈtʃɑːwʊmən] (*pl. -women*) Putzfrau *f*, Raumpflegerin *f*.

chase [tʃeɪs] **1.** Jagd *f*; Verfolgung *f*; gejagtes Wild; **2.** jagen, hetzen; Jagd machen auf (*acc.*); rasen, rennen.

chas·m [ˈkæzəm] Kluft *f*, Abgrund *m* (*a. fig.*); Riß *m*, Spalte *f*.

chaste □ [tʃeɪst] rein, keusch, unschuldig; schlicht (*Stil*).

chas·tise [tʃæˈstaɪz] züchtigen.

chas·ti·ty [ˈtʃæstətɪ] Keuschheit *f*.

chat [tʃæt] **1.** Geplauder *n*, Schwätzchen *n*, Plauderei *f*; **2.** plaudern.

chat·tels [ˈtʃætlz] *pl. mst* goods and ~ bewegliches Eigentum.

chat·ter [ˈtʃætə] **1.** plappern; schnattern; klappern; **2.** Geplapper *n*; Klappern *n*; **~·box** F Plappermaul *n*; **~·er** [⌐rə] Schwätzer(in).

chat·ty [ˈtʃætɪ] (*-ier, -iest*) gesprächig.

chauf·feur [ˈʃəʊfə] Chauffeur *m*.

chau·vi F [ˈʃəʊvɪ] Chauvi *m*; **~·vin·ist** [⌐nɪst] Chauvinist *m*.

cheap □ [tʃiːp] billig; *fig.* schäbig, gemein; **~·en** [ˈtʃiːpən] (sich) verbilligen; *fig.* herabsetzen.

cheat [tʃiːt] **1.** Betrug *m*, Schwindel *m*; Betrüger(in); **2.** betrügen.

check [tʃek] **1.** Schach(stellung *f*) *n*; Hemmnis *n*, Hindernis *n* (*on* für); Einhalt *m*; Kontrolle *f* (*on gen.*); Kontrollabschnitt *m*, -schein *m*; *Am.* Gepäckschein *m*; *Am.* Garderobenmarke *f*; *Am. econ.* = *cheque*; *Am.* Rechnung *f* (*im Restaurant od. Kaufhaus*); karierter Stoff; **2.** *v/i.* an-, innehalten; *Am.* e-n Scheck ausstellen; ~ *in* sich (*in e-m Hotel*) anmelden; einstempeln; ✈ einchecken; ~ *out* (*aus e-m Hotel*) abreisen; ausstempeln; ~ *up* (*on*) F (*e-e Sache*) nachprüfen; (*e-e Sache, j-n*) überprüfen; *v/t.* hemmen, hindern, aufhalten; zurückhalten; kontrollieren, über-, nachprüfen; *Am. auf e-r Liste* abhaken; *Am. Kleider* in der Garderobe abgeben; *Am.* Gepäck aufgeben; ~ *card Am. econ.* [ˈtʃekaːd] Scheckkarte *f*; **~ed** [⌐t] kariert; **~ers** *Am.* [⌐əz] *sg.* Damespiel *n*; **~·in** Anmeldung *f* (*in e-m Hotel*); Einstempeln *n*; ✈ Einchecken *n*; **~·ing ac·count** *Am. econ.* Girokonto *n*; **~·list** Check-, Kontroll-, Vergleichsliste *f*; **~·mate 1.** (Schach)Matt *n*; **2.** (schach)matt setzen; **~·out** Abreise *f* (*aus e-m Hotel*); Ausstempeln *n*; *a.* ~ *counter* Kasse *f* (*bsd. im Supermarkt*); **~·point** Kontrollpunkt *m*; **~·room** *Am.* Garderobe *f*; Gepäckaufbewahrung *f*; **~·up** Überprüfung *f*, Kontrolle *f*; ✚ Check-up *m*, (umfangreiche) Vorsorgeuntersuchung *f*.

cheek [tʃiːk] Backe *f*, Wange *f*; F

Unverschämtheit f; **~·y** □ F [ˈtʃiːkɪ] (-ier, -iest) frech.

cheer [tʃɪə] **1.** Stimmung f, Fröhlichkeit f; Hoch(ruf m) n, Beifall(sruf m; **~s**! prost!; *three* **~s**! dreimal hoch!; **2.** v/t. mit Beifall begrüßen; a. **~** *on* anspornen; a. **~** *up* aufheitern; v/i. hoch rufen, jubeln; a. **~** *up* Mut fassen; **~** *up*! Kopf hoch!; **~·ful** □ [ˈtʃɪəfl] vergnügt; **~·i·o** *int.* F [ˌ~rɪˈəʊ] mach's gut!, tschüs!; **~·less** □ [ˌ~lɪs] freudlos; **~·y** □ [ˌ~rɪ] (-ier, -iest) vergnügt.

cheese [tʃiːz] Käse m.

chee·tah *zo.* [ˈtʃiːtə] Gepard m.

chef [ʃef] Küchenchef m; Koch m; △ *nicht* Chef.

chem·i·cal [ˈkemɪkl] **1.** □ chemisch; **2.** Chemikalie f.

che·mise [ʃəˈmiːz] (Damen)Hemd n.

chem|ist [ˈkemɪst] Chemiker(in); Apotheker(in); Drogist(in); **~·'s** *shop* Apotheke f; Drogerie f; **~·is·try** [ˌ~rɪ] Chemie f.

cheque *Brt. econ.* [tʃek] (*Am.* check) Scheck m; *crossed* **~** Verrechnungsscheck m; **~ ac·count** *Brt. econ.* Girokonto n; **~ card** *Brt. econ.* Scheckkarte f.

chequ·er *Brt.* [ˈtʃekə] Karomuster n.

cher·ish [ˈtʃerɪʃ] Andenken an j-n *etc.* hochhalten; hegen, pflegen.

cher·ry ♀ [ˈtʃerɪ] Kirsche f.

chess [tʃes] Schach(spiel) n; *a game of* **~** e-e Partie Schach; **~·board** [ˈtʃesbɔːd] Schachbrett n; **~·man** (*pl. -men*), **~·piece** Schachfigur f.

chest [tʃest] Kiste f, Kasten m, Truhe f; *anat.* Brustkasten m; *get s.th. off one's* **~** F sich et. von der Seele reden; **~** *of drawers* Kommode f.

chest·nut [ˈtʃesnʌt] **1.** ♀ Kastanie f; **2.** kastanienbraun.

chew [tʃuː] kauen; nachsinnen, grübeln (*on, over* über *acc.*); **~·ing-gum** [ˈtʃuːɪŋʌm] Kaugummi m.

chick [tʃɪk] Küken n, junger Vogel; F Biene f, Puppe f (*Mädchen*).

chick·en [ˈtʃɪkɪn] Huhn n; Küken n; (*Brat*)Hähnchen n, (-)Hühnchen n; **~·heart·ed** furchtsam, feige; **~·pox** ♂ [ˌ~pɒks] Windpocken *pl.*

chic·o·ry ♀ [ˈtʃɪkərɪ] Chicorée f, m.

chief [tʃiːf] **1.** □ oberste(r, -s), Ober..., Haupt...; wichtigste(r, -s); **~** *clerk* Bürovorsteher m; **2.** Oberhaupt n, Chef m; Häuptling m; *...-in-chief* Ober...; **~·ly** [ˈtʃiːflɪ]

hauptsächlich; **~·tain** [ˌ~tən] Häuptling m.

chil·blain [ˈtʃɪlbleɪn] Frostbeule f.

child [tʃaɪld] (*pl. children*) Kind n; *from a* **~** von Kindheit an; *with* **~** schwanger; **~ a·buse** ⚖ Kindesmißhandlung f; **~·birth** [ˈtʃaɪldbɜːθ] Geburt f, Niederkunft f; **~·hood** [ˌ~hʊd] Kindheit f; **~·ish** □ [ˌ~ɪʃ] kindlich; kindisch; **~·like** kindlich; **~·mind·er** *Brt.* [ˌ~maɪndə] Tagesmutter f; **chil·dren** [ˈtʃɪldrən] *pl. v.* child.

chill [tʃɪl] **1.** eisig, frostig; **2.** Frost m, Kälte f; ♂ Fieberschauer m; Erkältung f; **3.** abkühlen; j-n frösteln lassen; **~ed** gekühlt; **~·y** [ˈtʃɪlɪ] (-ier, -iest) kalt, frostig.

chime [tʃaɪm] **1.** Glockenspiel n; Geläut n; *fig.* Einklang m; **2.** läuten; **~** *in* sich (ins Gespräch) einmischen.

chim·ney [ˈtʃɪmnɪ] Schornstein m; Rauchfang m; (Lampen)Zylinder m; **~·sweep** Schornsteinfeger m.

chimp *zo.* [tʃɪmp], **chim·pan·zee** *zo.* [ˌ~ənˈziː] Schimpanse m.

chin [tʃɪn] **1.** Kinn n; (*keep your*) **~** *up*! Kopf hoch!, halt die Ohren steif! **chi·na** [ˈtʃaɪnə] Porzellan n.

Chi·nese [tʃaɪˈniːz] **1.** chinesisch; **2.** Chinese m, -in f; *ling.* Chinesisch n; *the* **~** *pl.* die Chinesen *pl.*

chink [tʃɪŋk] Ritz m, Spalt m.

chip [tʃɪp] **1.** Splitter m, Span m, Schnitzel n, m ; dünne Scheibe; Spielmarke f; *Computer*: Chip m; *have a* **~** *on one's shoulder* F sich ständig angegriffen fühlen; *e-n* Komplex haben (*about* wegen); **~s** *pl. Brt.* Pommes frites *pl.*; *Am.* (Kartoffel)Chips *pl.*; **2.** (-pp-) v/t. schnitzeln; an-, abschlagen; v/i. abbröckeln; **~·munk** *zo.* [ˈtʃɪpmʌŋk] nordamerikanisches gestreiftes Eichhörnchen.

chirp [tʃɜːp] **1.** zirpen, zwitschern, piepsen; **2.** Gezirp n, Zwitschern n, Piepsen n.

chis·el [ˈtʃɪzl] **1.** Meißel m; **2.** (*bsd. Brt. -ll-, Am. -l-*) meißeln.

chit-chat [ˈtʃɪttʃæt] Plauderei f.

chiv·al|rous □ [ˈʃɪvlrəs] ritterlich; **~·ry** [ˌ~ɪ] *hist.* Rittertum n; Ritterlichkeit f.

chive(s *pl.*) ♀ [tʃaɪv(z)] Schnittlauch m.

chlo·ri·nate [ˈklɔːrɪneɪt] *Wasser etc.* chloren; **~·rine** ⚗ [ˌ~riːn] Chlor n; **chlor·o·form** [ˈklɒrəfɔːm]

chocolate

1. $\curlywedge_m$, $\cancel{s}$ Chloroform n; 2. chloroformieren.

choc·o·late ['tʃɒkələt] Schokolade f; Praline f; ~s pl. Pralinen pl., Konfekt n.

choice [tʃɔɪs] 1. Wahl f; Auswahl f; 2. ☐ auserlesen, ausgesucht, vorzüglich.

choir ['kwaɪə] Chor m.

choke [tʃəʊk] 1. v/t. (er)würgen, (a. v/i.) ersticken; ~ back Ärger etc. unterdrücken, Tränen zurückhalten; ~ down hinunterwürgen; a. ~ up verstopfen; 2. mot. Choke m, Luftklappe f.

choose [tʃuːz] (chose, chosen) (aus-)wählen, aussuchen; ~ to do vorziehen zu tun.

chop [tʃɒp] 1. Hieb m, Schlag m; Kotelett n; 2. (-pp-) v/t. hauen, hacken, zerhacken; ~ down fällen; v/i. hacken; ~·per ['tʃɒpə] Hackmesser n, -beil n; F Hubschrauber m; Am. sl. Maschinengewehr n; ~·py [~ɪ] (-ier, -iest) unruhig (See); ~·stick Eßstäbchen n.

cho·ral ['kɔːrəl] Chor...; ~(e) ♪ [kɒˈrɑːl] Choral m.

chord ♪ [kɔːd] Saite f; Akkord m.

chore Am. [tʃɔː] schwierige od. unangenehme Aufgabe; mst ~s pl. Hausarbeit f.

cho·rus ['kɔːrəs] Chor m; Kehrreim m, Refrain m; Tanzgruppe f (e-r Revue).

chose [tʃəʊz] pret. von choose; **chosen** ['tʃəʊzn] p.p. von choose.

Christ [kraɪst] Christus m; △ nicht der Christ.

chris·ten ['krɪsn] taufen; ~·ing [~ɪŋ] Taufe f; attr. Tauf...

Chris·tian ['krɪstjən] 1. christlich; ~ name Vorname m; 2. Christ(in); ~·ti·an·i·ty [krɪstɪˈænətɪ] Christentum n.

Christ·mas ['krɪsməs] Weihnachten n u. pl.; at ~ zu Weihnachten; ~ Day der erste Weihnachtsfeiertag; ~ Eve Heiliger Abend.

chrome [krəʊm] Chrom n; **chromi·um** $\curlywedge_m$ ['krəʊmjəm] Chrom n; ~·plated verchromt.

chron·ic ['krɒnɪk] (~ally) chronisch (mst ♣); dauernd; ~·i·cle [~l] 1. Chronik f; 2. aufzeichnen.

chron·o·log·i·cal ☐ [krɒnəˈlɒdʒɪkl] chronologisch; **chro·nol·o·gy** [krəˈnɒlədʒɪ] Zeitrechnung f; Zeitfolge f.

chub·by F ['tʃʌbɪ] (-ier, -iest) rundlich; pausbäckig.

chuck F [tʃʌk] werfen, schmeißen; ~ out j-n rausschmeißen; et. wegschmeißen; ~ up Job etc. hinschmeißen.

chuck·le ['tʃʌkl] 1. ~ (to o.s.) (still-vergnügt) in sich hineinlachen; 2. leises Lachen.

chum F [tʃʌm] Kamerad m, Kumpel m; ~·my ['tʃʌmɪ] (-ier, -iest) dick befreundet.

chump [tʃʌmp] Holzklotz m; F Trottel m.

chunk [tʃʌŋk] Klotz m, Klumpen m.

church [tʃɜːtʃ] Kirche f; attr. Kirch(en)...; ~ service Gottesdienst m; ~·war·den ['tʃɜːtʃ'wɔːdn] Kirchenvorsteher m; ~·yard Kirchhof m.

churl·ish ☐ ['tʃɜːlɪʃ] grob, flegelhaft.

churn [tʃɜːn] 1. Butterfaß n; 2. buttern; aufwühlen.

chute [ʃuːt] Stromschnelle f; Rutsche f, Rutschbahn f; F Fallschirm m.

ci·der ['saɪdə] (Am. hard ~) Apfelwein m; (sweet) ~ Am. Apfelmost m, -saft m.

ci·gar [sɪˈgɑː] Zigarre f.

cig·a·rette, Am. a. **-ret** [sɪgəˈret] Zigarette f.

cinch F [sɪntʃ] todsichere Sache.

cin·der ['sɪndə] Schlacke f; ~s pl. Asche f; **Cin·de·rel·la** [sɪndəˈrelə] Aschenbrödel n, -puttel n; ~·path, ~·track Sport: Aschenbahn f.

cin·e·cam·e·ra ['sɪnɪkæmərə] (Schmal)Filmkamera f; ~·film Schmalfilm m.

cin·e·ma Brt. ['sɪnəmə] Kino n; Film m.

cin·na·mon ['sɪnəmən] Zimt m.

ci·pher ['saɪfə] Ziffer f; Null f (a. fig.); Geheimschrift f, Chiffre f.

cir·cle ['sɜːkl] 1. Kreis m; Bekannten-etc. Kreis m; fig. Kreislauf m; thea. Rang m; Ring m; 2. (um)kreisen.

cir·cuit ['sɜːkɪt] Kreislauf m; ⚡ Stromkreis m; Rundreise f; Sport: Zirkus m; short ~ ⚡ Kurzschluß m; ~·cu·i·tous ☐ [səˈkjuːɪtəs] weitschweifig; ~ route Umweg m.

cir·cu·lar ['sɜːkjʊlə] 1. ☐ kreisförmig; Kreis...; ~ letter Rundschreiben n; 2. Rundschreiben n, Umlauf m.

cir·cu·late ['sɜːkjʊleɪt] v/i. umlaufen, zirkulieren; v/t. in Umlauf setzen;

classify

~**lat·ing** [~ɪŋ]: ~ *library* Leihbücherei *f*; ~**la·tion** [sɜːkjʊˈleɪʃn] Zirkulation *f*, Kreislauf *m*; (Blut)Kreislauf *m*; *fig.* Umlauf *m*; Verbreitung *f*, Auflage(nhöhe) *f* (*e-r Zeitung, e-s Buches etc.*).

cir·cum-... [ˈsɜːkəm] (her)um; ~**fer·ence** [səˈkʌmfərəns] (Kreis)Umfang *m*, Peripherie *f*; ~**nav·i·gate** [sɜːkəmˈnævɪgeɪt] umschiffen; ~**scribe** [ˈsɜːkəmskraɪb] Ⓐ umschreiben; *fig.* begrenzen; ~**spect** □ [~spekt] um-, vorsichtig; ~**stance** [~stəns] Umstand *m*, Einzelheit *f*; ~*s pl. a.* Verhältnisse *pl.*; *in od. under no* ~s unter keinen Umständen, auf keinen Fall; *in od. under the* ~s unter diesen Umständen; ~**stan·tial** [sɜːkəmˈstænʃl] umständlich; ~ *evidence* Ⓐ Indizien(beweis *m*) *pl.*; ~**vent** [~ˈvent] überlisten; vereiteln.

cir·cus [ˈsɜːkəs] Zirkus *m*; (runder) Platz.

cis·tern [ˈsɪstən] Wasserbehälter *m*; Spülkasten *m* (*in der Toilette*).

ci·ta·tion [saɪˈteɪʃn] Ⓐ Vorladung *f*; Anführung *f*, Zitat *n*; **cite** [saɪt] Ⓐ vorladen; anführen; zitieren.

cit·i·zen [ˈsɪtɪzn] (Staats)Bürger(in); Städter(in); ~**ship** [~ʃɪp] Bürgerrecht *n*; Staatsbürgerschaft *f*.

cit·y [ˈsɪtɪ] **1.** (Groß)Stadt *f*; *the* ⊘ die (Londoner) City; **2.** städtisch, Stadt...; ~ *centre Brt.* Innenstadt *f*, City *f*; ~ *council(l)or* Stadtrat(smitglied *n*) *m*; ~ *editor Am.* Lokalredakteur *m*; *Brt.* Wirtschaftsredakteur *m*; ~ *hall* Rathaus *n*; *bsd. Am.* Stadtverwaltung *f*.

civ·ic [ˈsɪvɪk] (staats)bürgerlich; städtisch; ~*s sg.* Staatsbürgerkunde *f*.

civ·il [ˈsɪvl] staatlich, Staats...; (staats)bürgerlich, Bürger...; Zivil...; Ⓐ zivilrechtlich; höflich; ~ *rights pl.* (Staats)Bürgerrechte *pl.*; ~ *rights activist* Bürgerrechtler(in); ~ *rights movement* Bürgerrechtsbewegung *f*; ~ *servant* Staatsbeamte(r) *m*; ~ *service* Staatsdienst *m*, öffentlicher Dienst *m*; Beamtenschaft *f*; ~ *war* Bürgerkrieg *m*.

ci·vil·i·an [sɪˈvɪljən] Zivilist *m*; ~**ty** [~lətɪ] Höflichkeit *f*.

civ·i·li·za·tion [sɪvɪlaɪˈzeɪʃn] Zivilisation *f*, Kultur *f*; ~**ze** [ˈsɪvɪlaɪz] zivilisieren.

clad [klæd] **1.** *pret. u. p.p. von clothe*; **2.** *adj.* gekleidet.

claim [kleɪm] **1.** Anspruch *m*; Anrecht *n* (*to auf acc.*); Forderung *f*; *Am.* Stück *n* Staatsland; *Am.* Claim *m*; **2.** beanspruchen; fordern; behaupten; **clai·mant** [ˈkleɪmənt] Ansprucherhebende(r *m*) *f*.

clair·voy·ant [kleəˈvɔɪənt] Hellseher(in).

clam·ber [ˈklæmbə] klettern.

clam·my □ [ˈklæmɪ] (*-ier, -iest*) feuchtkalt, klamm.

clam·o(u)r [ˈklæmə] **1.** Geschrei *n*, Lärm *m*; **2.** schreien (*for nach*).

clamp ⊕ [klæmp] **1.** Klammer *f*; **2.** mit Klammer(n) befestigen.

clan [klæn] Clan *m*, Sippe *f* (*a. fig.*).

clan·des·tine □ [klænˈdestɪn] heimlich, Geheim...

clang [klæŋ] **1.** Klang *m*, Geklirr *n*; **2.** schallen (lassen).

clank [klæŋk] **1.** Gerassel *n*, Geklirr *n*; **2.** rasseln *od.* klirren (mit).

clap [klæp] **1.** Klatschen *n*; Schlag *m*, Klaps *m*; **2.** (*-pp-*) schlagen *od.* klatschen (mit).

clar·et [ˈklærət] roter Bordeaux; Rotwein *m*; Weinrot *n*; *sl.* Blut *n*.

clar·i·fy [ˈklærɪfaɪ] *v/t.* (auf)klären, erhellen, klarstellen; *v/i.* sich (auf)klären.

clar·i·net ♪ [klærɪˈnet] Klarinette *f*.

clar·i·ty [ˈklærətɪ] Klarheit *f*.

clash [klæʃ] **1.** Geklirr *n*; Zusammenstoß *m*; Widerstreit *m*, Konflikt *m*; **2.** klirren (mit); zusammenstoßen; nicht zusammenpassen *od.* harmonieren.

clasp [klɑːsp] **1.** Haken *m*, Klammer *f*; Schnalle *f*, Spange *f*; *fig.* Umklammerung *f*, Umarmung *f*; **2.** ein-, zuhaken; *fig.* umklammern, umfassen; ~**knife** [ˈklɑːspnaɪf] Taschenmesser *n*.

class [klɑːs] **1.** Klasse *f*; (Bevölkerungs)Schicht *f*; (Schul)Klasse *f*; (Unterrichts)Stunde *f*; Kurs *m*; *Am. univ.* Studenten *pl. e-s Jahrgangs*; ~*mate* Mitschüler(in); ~*room* Klassenzimmer *n*; **2.** (in Klassen) einteilen, einordnen.

clas·sic [ˈklæsɪk] **1.** Klassiker *m*; **2.** *adj.* (~*ally*) erstklassig; klassisch; ~**si·cal** □ [~kl] klassisch.

clas·si·fi·ca·tion [klæsɪfɪˈkeɪʃn] Klassifizierung *f*, Einteilung *f*; ~**fy** [ˈklæsɪfaɪ] klassifizieren, einstufen.

clatter

430

clat·ter ['klætə] 1. Geklapper *n*; 2. klappern (mit).

clause [klɔːz] ᵗᵗ Klausel *f*, Bestimmung *f*; *gr.* Satz(teil *n*) *m*.

claw [klɔː] 1. Klaue *f*, Kralle *f*, Pfote *f*; (*Krebs*)Schere *f*; 2. (zer)kratzen; umkrallen, packen.

clay [kleɪ] Ton *m*; Erde *f*.

clean [kliːn] 1. *adj.* □ rein; sauber, glatt, eben; *sl.* clean (*nicht mehr drogenabhängig*); 2. *adv.* völlig, ganz u. gar; 3. reinigen, säubern, putzen; ~ out reinigen; ~ up gründlich reinigen; aufräumen; **~·er** ['kliːnə] Reiniger *m*; Rein(e)machefrau *f*; *mst* ~s *pl.*, ~'s (chemische) Reinigung (*Geschäft*); **~·ing** [~ɪŋ] Reinigung *f*, Putzen *n*; *do the* ~ saubermachen, putzen; *spring-cleaning* Frühjahrsputz *m*; **~·li·ness** ['klenlɪnɪs] Reinlichkeit *f*; **~·ly** 1. *adv.* ['kliːnlɪ] rein; sauber; 2. *adj.* ['klenlɪ] (*-ier, -iest*) reinlich.

cleanse [klenz] reinigen, säubern; **cleans·er** ['klenzə] Reinigungsmittel *n*.

clear [klɪə] 1. □ klar; hell; rein; frei (*of* von); ganz; voll; *econ.* rein, netto; 2. *v/t.* reinigen (*of, from* von); *Wald* lichten, roden; wegräumen (*a.* ~ *away*); *Tisch* abräumen; räumen, leeren; *Hindernis* nehmen; *econ.* verzollen; ᵗᵗ freisprechen; ~ *out* säubern; ausräumen u. wegtun; ~ *up* aufräumen; aufklären; *v/i.* aufklaren (*Wetter*); ~ *out* F abhauen; ~ *up* aufräumen; sich aufhellen, aufklaren (*Wetter*); **~·ance** ['klɪərəns] Räumung *f*; Rodung *f*; ⊕ lichter Abstand; *econ.* Zollabfertigung *f*; Freigabe *f*; ⚓ Auslaufgenehmigung *f*; **~·ing** [~rɪŋ] Aufklärung *f*; Lichtung *f*, Rodung *f*.

cleave [kliːv] (*cleaved od. cleft od. clove, cleaved od. cleft od. cloven*) spalten.

cleav·er ['kliːvə] Hackmesser *n*.

clef ♪ [klef] Schlüssel *m*.

cleft [kleft] 1. Spalt *m*, Spalte *f*; 2. *pret. u. p.p. von* cleave.

clem·en·cy ['klemənsɪ] Milde *f*, Gnade *f*; **~t** □ [~t] mild.

clench [klentʃ] *Lippen etc.* (fest) zusammenpressen; *Zähne* zusammenbeißen; *Faust* ballen.

cler·gy ['klɜːdʒɪ] Geistlichkeit *f*; **~·man** (*pl. -men*) Geistliche(r) *m*.

cler·i·cal □ ['klerɪkl] geistlich; Schreib(...)

clerk [klɑːk] Schriftführer(in), Sekretär(in); kaufmännische(r) Angestellte(r), (Büro- *etc.*) Angestellte(r *m*) *f*, (Bank-, Post)Beamt|e(r) *m*, -in *f*; *Am.* Verkäufer(in).

clev·er □ ['klevə] klug, gescheit; geschickt.

click [klɪk] 1. Klicken *n*, Knacken *n*; ⊕ Sperrhaken *m*, -klinke *f*; 2. klicken, knacken; zu-, einschnappen; *mit der Zunge* schnalzen.

cli·ent ['klaɪənt] ᵗᵗ Klient(in), Mandant(in); Kund|e *m*, -in *f*.

cliff [klɪf] Klippe *f*, Felsen *m*.

cli·mate ['klaɪmɪt] Klima *n*.

cli·max ['klaɪmæks] 1. *rhet.* Steigerung *f*; Gipfel *m*, Höhepunkt *m*, *physiol. a.* Orgasmus *m*; 2. (sich) steigern.

climb [klaɪm] klettern; (er-, be)steigen; **~·er** ['klaɪmə] Kletterer *m*, Bergsteiger(in); *fig.* Aufsteiger *m*; ⚘ Kletterpflanze *f*; **~·ing** [~ɪŋ] Klettern *n*; *attr.* Kletter...

clinch [klɪntʃ] 1. ⊕ Vernietung *f*; *Boxen:* Clinch *m*; F Umarmung *f*; 2. *v/t.* ⊕ vernieten; festmachen; (vollends) entscheiden; *v/i. Boxen:* clinchen.

cling [klɪŋ] (*clung*) (*to*) festhalten (an *dat.*), sich klammern (an *acc.*); sich (an)schmiegen (an *acc.*).

clin·ic ['klɪnɪk] Klinik *f*; **~·i·cal** □ [~l] klinisch.

clink [klɪŋk] 1. Klirren *n*, Klingen *n*; 2. klingen *od.* klirren (lassen); klimpern mit.

clip¹ [klɪp] 1. Schneiden *n*; Schur *f*; F (Faust)Schlag *m*; 2. (*-pp-*) (be)schneiden; ab-, ausschneiden; *Schafe etc.* scheren.

clip² [~] 1. Klipp *m*, Klammer *f*, Spange *f*; 2. (*-pp-*) *a.* ~ *on* befestigen, anklammern.

clip|per ['klɪpə]: (*a pair of*) ~s *pl.* (e-e) Haarschneide-, Schermaschine *f*, (*Nagel- etc.*) Schere *f*; ⚓ Klipper *m*; ✈ Clipper *m*; **~·pings** [~ɪŋz] *pl.* Abfälle *pl.*, Schnitzel *pl.*; *bsd. Am.* (*Zeitungs- etc.*) Ausschnitte *pl.*

clit·o·ris *anat.* ['klɪtərɪs] Klitoris *f*.

cloak [kləʊk] 1. Mantel *m*; 2. *fig.* verhüllen; **~·room** ['kləʊkrʊm] Garderobe *f*; *Brt.* Toilette *f*.

clock [klɒk] 1. (Wand-, Stand-, Turm)Uhr *f*; 2. die Zeit (*e-s Läufers*) stoppen; ~ *in*, ~ *on* einstempeln; ~ *out*, ~ *off* ausstempeln; **~·wise**

['klɒkwaɪz] im Uhrzeigersinn; **~work** Uhrwerk *n*; *like* ~ wie am Schnürchen.

clod [klɒd] (Erd)Klumpen *m*.

clog [klɒg] **1.** Klotz *m*; Holzschuh *m*, Pantine *f*; **2.** (*-gg-*) (be)hindern, hemmen; (sich) verstopfen; klumpig werden.

clois·ter ['klɔɪstə] Kreuzgang *m*; Kloster *n*.

close 1. *adj.* □ [kləus] knapp, kurz, geschlossen, *nur pred.*: zu; verborgen; verschwiegen; knapp; nah; eng; knapp, bündig; dicht; genau (*Übersetzung*); schwül; geizig, knaus(e)rig; *keep a* ~ *watch on* scharf im Auge behalten (*acc.*); ~ *fight* Handgemenge *n*; ~ *season hunt.* Schonzeit *f*; **2.** *adv.* eng, nahe, dicht; ~ *by*, ~ *to* ganz in der Nähe, nahe *od.* dicht bei; **3.** [kləuz] Schluß *m*; (Ab)Schluß *m*; *come to a* ~ sich dem Ende nähern; [kləus] Einfriedung *f*; Hof *m*; **4.** [kləuz] *v/t.* (ab-, ver-, zu)schließen; *Straße* (ab)sperren; *v/i.* (sich) schließen; handgemein werden; *mit Adverbien:* ~ *down* schließen; stillegen; stillgelegt werden; *Rundfunk, TV:* das Programm beenden, Sendeschluß haben; ~ *in* bedrohlich nahekommen; hereinbrechen (*Nacht*); kürzer werden (*Tage*); ~ *up* (ab-, ver-, zu-) schließen; blockieren; aufschließen, -rücken; **~d** geschlossen, *pred.* zu.

clos|et ['klɒzɪt] **1.** (Wand)Schrank *m*; ⚠ *nicht Klosett*; **2.** *be ~ed with* mit *j-m* geheime Besprechungen führen.

close-up ['kləusʌp] *phot., Film:* Großaufnahme *f*.

clos·ing-time ['kləuzɪŋtaɪm] Laden-, Geschäftsschluß *m*; Polizeistunde *f* (*e-s Pubs*).

clot [klɒt] **1.** Klumpen *m*, Klümpchen *n*; *Brt.* F Trottel *m*; **2.** (*-tt-*) gerinnen; Klumpen bilden.

cloth [klɒθ] (*pl. cloths* [~θs, ~ðz]) Stoff *m*, Tuch *n*; Tischtuch *n*; *the* ~ der geistliche Stand; *lay the* ~ den Tisch decken; **~bound** in Leinen gebunden.

clothe [kləuð] (*clothed od. clad*) (an-, be)kleiden; einkleiden.

clothes [kləuðz] *pl.* Kleider *pl.*, Kleidung *f*; Wäsche *f*; **~·bas·ket** ['kləuðzbɑːskɪt] Wäschekorb *m*; **~horse** Wäscheständer *m*; **~line** Wäscheleine *f*; **~peg** *Brt.*, *Am.*

~**pin** Wäscheklammer *f*.

cloth·ing ['kləuðɪŋ] (Be)Kleidung *f*.

cloud [klaud] **1.** Wolke *f* (*a. fig.*); Trübung *f*, Schatten *m*; **2.** (sich) be-, umwölken (*a. fig.*); (sich) trüben; **~burst** ['klaudbɜːst] Wolkenbruch *m*; **~·less** □ [~lɪs] wolkenlos; **~y** □ [~ɪ] (*-ier, -iest*) wolkig, bewölkt; Wolken...; trüb; unklar.

clout F [klaut] Schlag *m*; *bsd. Am.* Macht *f*, Einfluß *m*.

clove[1] [kləuv] (Gewürz)Nelke *f*; ~ *of garlic* Knoblauchzehe *f*.

clove[2] [~] *pret. von cleave*[1]; **clo·ven** ['kləuvn] **1.** *p.p. von cleave*[1]; **2.** ~ *hoof zo.* Huf *m* der Paarzeher.

clo·ver ♣ ['kləuvə] Klee *m*.

clown [klaun] Clown *m*, Hanswurst *m*; Bauer *m*, ungehobelter Kerl; **~·ish** □ ['klaunɪʃ] clownisch.

club [klʌb] **1.** Keule *f*; (Gummi-) Knüppel *m*; (Golf)Schläger *m*; Klub *m*; **~s** *pl.* Karten: Kreuz *n*; **2.** (*-bb-*) *v/t.* einknüppeln auf (*acc.*), (nieder-) knüppeln; *v/i.*: ~ *together* sich zusammentun, **~foot** (*pl. -feet*) ['klʌbfut] Klumpfuß *m*.

cluck [klʌk] **1.** gackern; glucken; **2.** Gackern *n*; Glucken *n*.

clue [kluː] Anhaltspunkt *m*, Fingerzeig *m*, Spur *f*.

clump [klʌmp] **1.** Klumpen *m*; (*Baum- etc.*)Gruppe *f*; **2.** trampeln.

clum·sy □ ['klʌmzɪ] (*-ier, -iest*) unbeholfen, ungeschickt, plump.

clung [klʌŋ] *pret. u. p.p. von cling.*

clus·ter ['klʌstə] **1.** Traube *f*; Büschel *n*; Haufen *m*; **2.** büschelartig wachsen; sich drängen.

clutch [klʌtʃ] **1.** Griff *m*; ⊕ Kupplung *f*; Klaue *f*; **2.** (er)greifen.

clut·ter ['klʌtə] **1.** Wirrwarr *m*; Unordnung *f*; **2.** *a.* ~ *up* zu voll machen *od.* stellen; überladen.

coach [kəutʃ] **1.** Kutsche *f*; *Brt.* 🚌 (Personen)Wagen *m*; Omnibus, *bsd.* Reisebus *m*; Einpauker *m*; *Sport:* Trainer *m*; **2.** einpauken; *Sport:* trainieren; **~·man** ['kəutʃmən] (*pl. -men*) Kutscher *m*.

co·ag·u·late [kəu'ægjuleɪt] gerinnen (lassen).

coal [kəul] (Stein)Kohle *f*; *carry ~s to Newcastle* Eulen nach Athen tragen.

co·a·lesce [kəuə'les] verschmelzen, zusammenwachsen; sich vereinigen *od.* verbinden.

co·a·li·tion [kəʊə'lɪʃn] **1.** *pol.* Koalition *f*; Bündnis *n*, Zusammenschluß *m*; **2.** *pol.* Koalitions...

coal|-mine ['kəʊlmaɪn], **~-pit** Kohlengrube *f*.

coarse ☐ [kɔːs] (~*r*, ~*st*) grob; ungeschliffen.

coast [kəʊst] **1.** Küste *f*; *Am.* Rodelbahn *f*; **2.** die Küste entlangfahren; im Leerlauf (*Auto*) *od.* im Freilauf (*Fahrrad*) fahren; *Am.* rodeln; **~-er** ['kəʊstə] *Am.* Rodelschlitten; ♣ Küstenfahrer *m*; **~-guard** Küstenwache *f*; **~-guard** Angehörige(r) *m* der Küstenwache; **~-line** Küstenlinie *f*, -strich *m*.

coat [kəʊt] **1.** Jackett *n*, Jacke *f*, Rock *m*; Mantel *m*; Pelz *m*, Fell *n*, Haut *f*, Gefieder *n*; Überzug *m*, Anstrich *m*, Schicht *f*; ~ *of arms* Wappen (-schild *m*, *n*) *n*; **2.** überziehen, beschichten; (an)streichen; **~-hang·er** ['kəʊthæŋə] Kleiderbügel *m*; **~-ing** ['kəʊtɪŋ] Überzug *m*, Anstrich *m*, Schicht *f*; Mantelstoff *m*.

coax [kəʊks] überreden, beschwatzen.

cob [kɒb] kleines starkes Pferd; Schwan *m*; Maiskolben *m*.

cob|bled ['kɒbld]: ~ *street* Straße *f* mit Kopfsteinpflaster; **~-bler** [~ə] (Flick)Schuster *m*; Stümper *m*.

cob-web ['kɒbweb] Spinn(en)gewebe *n*.

co·caine [kəʊ'keɪn] Kokain *n*.

cock [kɒk] **1.** *zo. etc.* Hahn *m*; (An-)Führer *m*; Heuhaufen *m*; **2.** *a.* ~ *up* aufrichten; *Gewehrhahn* spannen.

cock·a·too *zo.* [kɒkə'tuː] Kakadu *m*.

cock-chaf·er ['kɒktʃeɪfə] Maikäfer *m*.

cock|-eyed F ['kɒkaɪd] schielend; (krumm u.) schief.

cock|ney ['kɒknɪ] *mst* ♀ Cockney *m*, waschechter Londoner.

cock|pit ['kɒkpɪt] ✈, ♣ Cockpit (*a. e-s Rennwagens*); Hahnenkampfplatz *m*.

cock|roach *zo.* ['kɒkrəʊtʃ] Schabe *f*.

cock|sure F ['kɒk'ʃʊə] absolut sicher; anmaßend; **~-tail** Cocktail *m*; **~-y** ☐ F ['kɒkɪ] (-*ier*, -*iest*) großspurig, anmaßend.

co·co ♀ ['kəʊkəʊ] (*pl.* -cos) Kokospalme *f*.

co·coa ['kəʊkəʊ] Kakao *m*.

co·co·nut ['kəʊkənʌt] Kokosnuß *f*.

co·coon [kə'kuːn] (*Seiden*)Kokon *m*.

cod *zo.* [kɒd] Kabeljau *m*, Dorsch *m*.

cod·dle ['kɒdl] verhätscheln.

code [kəʊd] **1.** Gesetzbuch *n*; Kodex *m*; (*Telegramm-*)Schlüssel *m*; Code *m*, Chiffre *f*; **2.** verschlüsseln, codieren, chiffrieren.

cod|fish *zo.* ['kɒdfɪʃ] = *cod*; **~-liv·er oil** Lebertran *m*.

co-ed F ['kəʊ'ed] Schülerin *f od.* Studentin *f* e-r gemischten Schule; **~-u-ca·tion** [kəʊedju:'keɪʃn] Koedukation *f*, Gemeinschaftserziehung *f*.

co·erce [kəʊ'ɜːs] (er)zwingen.

co·ex·ist ['kəʊɪg'zɪst] gleichzeitig *od.* nebeneinander bestehen *od.* leben; **~-ence** [~əns] Koexistenz *f*.

cof·fee ['kɒfɪ] Kaffee *m*; **~-bean** Kaffeebohne *f*; **~-pot** Kaffeekanne *f*; **~-set** Kaffeeservice *n*; **~-ta·ble** Couchtisch *m*.

cof·fer ['kɒfə] (Geld- *etc.*)Kasten *m*.

cof·fin ['kɒfɪn] Sarg *m*.

cog ⊕ [kɒg] (Rad)Zahn *m*.

co·gent ☐ ['kəʊdʒənt] zwingend.

cog·i·tate ['kɒdʒɪteɪt] (nach)denken.

cog·wheel ⊕ ['kɒgwiːl] Zahnrad *n*.

co·her|ence [kəʊ'hɪərəns] Zusammenhang *m*; **~-ent** ☐ [~t] zusammenhängend.

co·he|sion [kəʊ'hiːʒn] Zusammenhalt *m*; **~-sive** [~sɪv] (fest) zusammenhaltend.

coif·fure [kwɑː'fjʊə] Frisur *f*.

coil [kɔɪl] **1.** *a.* ~ *up* aufwickeln; (sich) zusammenrollen; **2.** Rolle *f*; Spirale *f*; Wicklung *f*; Spule *f*; Windung *f*; ⊕ (Rohr)Schlange *f*.

coin [kɔɪn] **1.** Münze *f*; **2.** prägen (*a. fig.*); münzen.

co·in|cide [kəʊɪn'saɪd] zusammentreffen; übereinstimmen; **~-ci-dence** [kəʊ'ɪnsɪdəns] Zusammentreffen *n*; Zufall *m*; *fig.* Übereinstimmung *f*.

coke¹ [kəʊk] Koks *m* (*a. sl.* = *Kokain*).

Coke² TM F [~] Coke *n*, Cola *n*, *f*, Coca *n*, *f* (*Coca-Cola*).

cold [kəʊld] **1.** ☐ kalt; **2.** Kälte *f*, Frost *m*; Erkältung *f*; **~-blood·ed** [~'blʌdɪd] kaltblütig; **~-heart·ed** kalt-, hartherzig; **~-ness** ['kəʊldnɪs] Kälte *f*; **~ war** *pol.* kalter Krieg.

cole·slaw ['kəʊlslɔː] Krautsalat *m*.

col·ic ✿ ['kɒlɪk] Kolik *f*.

col·lab·o|rate [kə'læbəreɪt] zusammenarbeiten; **~-ra·tion** [kəlæbə-'reɪʃn] Zusammenarbeit *f*; *in* ~ *with* gemeinsam mit.

col|lapse [kə'læps] **1.** zusammen-, einfallen; zusammenbrechen; **2.** Zusammenbruch *m*; **~lap·si·ble** [~əbl] zusammenklappbar.

col·lar ['kɒlə] **1.** Kragen *m*; Halsband *n*; Kummet *n*; **2.** beim Kragen packen; *j-n* festnehmen, F schnappen; **~bone** *anat.* Schlüsselbein *n*.

col·league ['kɒliːg] Kolleg|e *m*, -in *f*, Mitarbeiter(in).

col|lect 1. *eccl.* ['kɒlekt] Kollekte *f*; **2.** *v/t.* [kə'lekt] (ein)sammeln; *Gedanken etc.* sammeln; einkassieren; abholen; *v/i.* sich (ver)sammeln; **~lect·ed** □ *fig.* gesammelt; **~lec·tion** [~kʃn] Sammlung *f*; *econ.* Eintreibung *f*; *eccl.* Kollekte *f*; **~lec·tive** □ [~tɪv] gesammelt; Sammel...; **~ bargaining** *econ.* Tarifverhandlungen *pl.*; **~lec·tive·ly** [~lɪ] insgesamt; zusammen; **~lec·tor** [~ə] Sammler(in); Steuereinnehmer *m*; Fahrkartenabnehmer *m*; ⚡ Stromabnehmer *m*.

col|lege ['kɒlɪdʒ] College *n* (*Teil e-r Universität*); Hochschule *f*; höhere Lehranstalt.

col·lide [kə'laɪd] zusammenstoßen.

col|li·er ['kɒliə] Bergmann *m*; ⚓ Kohlenschiff *n*; **~lie·ry** [~jəri] Kohlengrube *f*.

col·li·sion [kə'lɪʒn] Zusammenstoß *m*, -prall *m*, Kollision *f*.

col·lo·qui·al □ [kə'ləʊkwɪəl] umgangssprachlich, familiär.

col·lo·quy ['kɒləkwɪ] Gespräch *n*.

co·lon ['kəʊlən] Doppelpunkt *m*.

colo·nel ✕ ['kɜːnl] Oberst *m*.

co·lo·ni·al □ [kə'ləʊnjəl] Kolonial...; **~is·m** *pol.* [~lɪzəm] Kolonialismus *m*.

col·o|nize ['kɒlənaɪz] kolonisieren, besiedeln; sich ansiedeln; **~ny** [~nɪ] Kolonie *f*; Siedlung *f*.

co·los·sal □ [kə'lɒsl] kolossal, riesig.

col·o(u)r ['kʌlə] **1.** Farbe *f*; *fig.* Anschein *m*; Vorwand *m*; **~s** *pl.* Fahne *f*, Flagge *f*; *what ~ is ...?* welche Farbe hat ...?; **2.** *v/t.* färben; an-, bemalen, anstreichen; *fig.* beschönigen; *v/i.* sich (ver)färben; erröten; **~ bar** Rassenschranke *f*; **~blind** farbenblind; **~ed 1.** bunt; farbig; ~ *man* Farbige(r) *m*; **2.** *oft contp.* Farbige(r *m*) *f*; **~fast** farbecht; **~ film** *phot.* Farbfilm *m*; **~ful** [~fl] farbenreich, -freudig; lebhaft; **~ing** [~rɪŋ] Färbemittel *n*; Gesichtsfarbe *f*;

fig. Beschönigung *f*; **~less** □ [~lɪs] farblos; **~ line** Rassenschranke *f*; **~ set** Farbfernseher *m*; **~ tel·e·vi·sion** Farbfernsehen *n*.

colt [kəʊlt] Hengstfüllen *n*, -fohlen *n*.

col·umn ['kɒləm] Säule *f*; *print.* Spalte *f*; ✕ Kolonne *f*; **~ist** [~nɪst] Kolumnist(in).

comb [kəʊm] **1.** Kamm *m*; (Flachs-) Hechel *f*; **2.** *v/t.* kämmen; striegeln; *Flachs* hecheln.

com|bat ['kɒmbæt] **1.** Kampf *m*; *single* ~ Zweikampf *m*; **2.** (*-tt-*, *Am. a. -t-*) kämpfen gegen, bekämpfen; **~ba·tant** [~ənt] Kämpfer *m*.

com·bi·na·tion [kɒmbɪ'neɪʃn] Verbindung *f*; *mst* ~*s pl.* Hemdhose *f* mit langem Bein; **~bine** [kəm'baɪn] (sich) verbinden *od.* vereinigen.

com·bus·ti·ble [kəm'bʌstəbl] **1.** brennbar; **2.** Brennstoff *m*, -material *n*; **~tion** [~tʃən] Verbrennung *f*.

come [kʌm] (*came*, *come*) kommen; *to* ~ künftig, kommend; ~ *about* geschehen, passieren; ~ *across* auf *j-n od. et.* stoßen; F ankommen (*Rede etc.*); ~ *along* mitkommen; ~ *apart* auseinanderfallen; ~ *at* auf *j-n od. et.* losgehen; ~ *back* zurückkommen; ~ *by* zu *et.* kommen; ~ *down* herunterkommen (*a. fig.*); einstürzen; sinken (*Preis*); überliefert werden; ~ *down with* F erkranken an (*dat.*); ~ *for* abholen kommen, kommen wegen; ~ *loose* sich ablösen, abgehen; ~ *off* ab-, losgehen, sich lösen; stattfinden; ~ *on!* los!, vorwärts!, komm!; ~ *over* vorbeikommen (*Besucher*); ~ *round* vorbeikommen (*Besucher*); wiederkehren; F wieder zu sich kommen; anders überlegen; ~ *through* durchkommen; *Krankheit etc.* überstehen, -leben; ~ *to* sich belaufen auf; wieder zu sich kommen; *what's the world coming to?* wohin ist die Welt geraten?; ~ *to see* besuchen; ~ *up to* entsprechen (*dat.*), heranreichen an (*acc.*); **~back** ['kʌmbæk] Comeback *n*.

co·me·di·an [kə'miːdjən] Komödienschauspieler(in); Komiker(in); Lustspieldichter *m*.

com·e·dy ['kɒmədɪ] Komödie *f*, Lustspiel *n*.

come·ly ['kʌmlɪ] (*-ier*, *-iest*) attraktiv, gutaussehend.

com·fort ['kʌmfət] **1.** Behaglichkeit *f*; Trost *m*; Wohltat *f*, Erquickung *f*;

_a._ ~s _pl._ Komfort _m;_ **2.** trösten;
com·for·ta·ble □ [~əbl] komforta-
bel, behaglich, bequem; tröstlich;
~·er [~ə] Tröster _m;_ Wollschal _m;_
bsd. _Brt._ Schnuller _m; Am._ Steppdecke _f;_ **~·less** □ [~lɪs] unbequem;
trostlos; ~ **sta·tion** _Am._ Bedürfnisanstalt _f._
com·ic ['kɒmɪk] (_~ally_) komisch;
Komödien..., Lustspiel...
com·i·cal □ ['kɒmɪkl] komisch,
spaßig.
com·ics ['kɒmɪks] _pl._ Comics _pl.,_
Comic-Hefte _pl._
com·ing ['kʌmɪŋ] **1.** kommend;
künftig; **2.** Kommen _n._
com·ma ['kɒmə] Komma _n._
com·mand [kə'mɑːnd] **1.** Herrschaft
_f,_ Beherrschung _f_ (_a._ _fig._); Befehl _m;_
✕ Kommando _n; be (have) at ~ zur
Verfügung stehen (haben); **2.** befehlen; ✕ kommandieren; verfügen
über (_acc._); beherrschen; **~·er** [~ə] ✕
Kommandeur _m,_ Befehlshaber _m;_ ♣
Fregattenkapitän _m;_ **~·er-in-chief**
✕ [~ərɪn't∫iːf] (_pl._ _commanders-in-
chief_) Oberbefehlshaber _m;_ **~·ing** □
[kə'mɑːndɪŋ] kommandierend, be-
fehlshabend; gebieterisch; **~·ment**
[~mənt] Gebot _n;_ **~ mod·ule** _Raum-
fahrt:_ Kommandokapsel _f._
com·man·do ✕ [kə'mɑːndəʊ] (_pl._
-dos, -does) Kommando _n._
com·mem·o·rate [kə'meməreɪt] gedenken (_gen._), _j-s_ Gedächtnis feiern;
~·ra·tion [kəmemə'reɪ∫n]: _in ~ of_
zum Gedenken _od._ Gedächtnis an
(_acc._); **~·ra·tive** □ [kə'memərətɪv]
Gedenk..., Erinnerungs...
com·mence [kə'mens] anfangen, beginnen; **~·ment** [~mənt] Anfang _m,_
Beginn _m._
com·mend [kə'mend] empfehlen;
anvertrauen.
com·ment ['kɒment] **1.** Kommentar
_m;_ Erläuterung _f;_ Bemerkung _f;_
Stellungnahme _f; no ~! kein Kommentar!;_ **2.** (_on, upon_) erläutern
(_acc._); sich (kritisch) äußern (über
acc.); **~·men·ta·ry** ['kɒməntərɪ]
Kommentar _m;_ **~·men·tate** [~eɪt]: ~
on Rundfunk, TV: kommentieren
(_acc._); **~·men·ta·tor** [~ə] Kommen-
tator _m, Rundfunk, TV: a._ Reporter
_m._
com·merce ['kɒmɜːs] Handel _m;_
Verkehr _m._
com·mer·cial □ [kə'mɜː∫l] **1.** kauf-

männisch, Handels..., Geschäfts...;
handelsüblich; ~ _travel(l)er_ Hand-
lungsreisende(r) _m;_ **2.** _Rundfunk,
TV:_ Werbespot _m,_ -sendung _f;_ **~·ize**
[~∫əlaɪz] kommerzialisieren, ver-
markten.
com·mis·e·rate [kə'mɪzəreɪt]: ~ _with_
Mitleid empfinden mit; **~·ra·tion**
[kəmɪzə'reɪ∫n] Mitleid _n_ (_for_ mit).
com·mis·sa·ry ['kɒmɪsərɪ] Kommissar _m._
com·mis·sion [kə'mɪ∫n] **1.** Auftrag
_m;_ Übertragung _f_ (_von Macht etc._);
Begehung _f_ (_e-s Verbrechens_); Provision _f;_ Kommission _f;_ ✕ (_Offiziers-_)
Patent _n;_ **2.** beauftragen, bevollmächtigen; _et._ in Auftrag geben; _j-n_
zum Offizier ernennen; _Schiff_ in
Dienst stellen; **~·er** [~ə] Bevoll-
mächtigte(r _m_) _f;_ (_Regierungs-_)Kom-
missar _m._
com·mit [kə'mɪt] (_-tt-_) anvertrauen,
übergeben; ṭʒ _j-n_ einweisen; ṭʒ _j-n_
übergeben; _Verbrechen_ begehen;
bloßstellen; ~ (_o.s._ sich) verpflichten; **~·ment** [~mənt] Verpflichtung
_f;_ ~ **tal** ṭʒ [~l] Einweisung _f;_ **~·tee**
[~ɪ] Ausschuß _m,_ Komitee _n._
com·mod·i·ty [kə'mɒdətɪ] Ware _f,_
Gebrauchsartikel _m._
com·mon ['kɒmən] **1.** □ allgemein,
gewöhnlich; gemein(sam), gemein-
schaftlich; öffentlich; gewöhnlich,
minderwertig; F ordinär; ♀ _Council_
Gemeinderat _m;_ **2.** Gemeindeland _n;_
_in ~_ gemeinsam; _in ~ with_ genau wie;
~·er [~ə] Bürgerliche(r _m_) _f;_ ~ _law_
(_ungeschriebenes englisches_) Ge-
wohnheitsrecht; ♀ **Mar·ket** _econ.
pol._ Gemeinsamer Markt; **~·place 1.**
Gemeinplatz _m;_ **2.** alltäglich; abgedroschen; **~s** _pl. das gemeine Volk;
House of ♀ parl._ Unterhaus _n;_ ~
sense gesunder Menschenverstand;
~·wealth [~welθ] Gemeinwesen _n,_
Staat _m;_ Republik _f; the ♀ (of
Nations)_ das Commonwealth.
com·mo·tion [kə'məʊ∫n] Aufruhr
_m,_ Erregung _f._
com·mu·nal □ ['kɒmjʊnl] Gemeinde...; Gemeinschafts...
com·mune 1. [kə'mjuːn] sich vertraulich besprechen; **2.** ['kɒmjuːn]
Kommune _f;_ Gemeinde _f._
com·mu·ni·cate [kə'mjuːnɪkeɪt] _v/t._
mitteilen; _v/i._ sich besprechen; sich
in Verbindung setzen (_with_ s.o. mit
j-m); (_durch e-e Tür_) verbunden

sein; **~·ca·tion** [kəmju:nɪ'keɪʃn] Mitteilung f; Verständigung f; Verbindung f; **~s** pl. Verbindung f, Verkehrswege pl.; **~s satellite** Nachrichtensatellit m; **~·ca·tive** [kə'mju:nɪkətɪv] mitteilsam, gesprächig.

com·mu·nion [kə'mju:njən] Gemeinschaft f; ♀ eccl. Kommunion f, Abendmahl n.

com·mu·nis|m ['kɒmjʊnɪzəm] Kommunismus m; **~·t** [~ɪst] 1. Kommunist(in); 2. kommunistisch.

com·mu·ni·ty [kə'mju:nətɪ] Gemeinschaft f; Gemeinde f; Staat m.

com|mute [kə'mju:t] ♀♀ Strafe mildernd umwandeln; ⨯ etc. pendeln; **~·mut·er** [~ə] Pendler(in); **~ train** Pendler-, Vorort-, Nahverkehrszug m.

com·pact 1. ['kɒmpækt] Vertrag m; Puderdose f; Am. mot. Kompaktauto n; 2. [kəm'pækt] adj. dicht, fest; knapp, bündig; **~ disc** Compact Disc f (Schallplatte); 3. v/t. fest verbinden.

com·pan|ion [kəm'pænjən] Begleiter(in); Gefährt|e m, -in f; Gesellschafter(in); Handbuch n, Leitfaden m; **~·ion·a·ble** [~əbl] gesellig; **~·ion·ship** [~ʃɪp] Gesellschaft f.

com·pa·ny ['kʌmpənɪ] Gesellschaft f; Begleitung f; ⨯ Kompanie f; econ. (Handels)Gesellschaft f; ♣ Mannschaft f; thea. Truppe f; have ~ Gäste haben; keep ~ with verkehren mit.

com·pa·ra·ble □ ['kɒmpərəbl] vergleichbar; **~·par·a·tive** [kəm'pærətɪv] 1. □ vergleichend; verhältnismäßig; 2. a. ~ degree gr. Komparativ m; **~·pare** [~'peə] 1. beyond ~, without ~, past ~ unvergleichlich; 2. v/t. vergleichen; (as) ~d with im Vergleich zu; v/i. sich vergleichen (lassen); **~·pa·ri·son** [~'pærɪsn] Vergleich m.

com·part·ment [kəm'pɑ:tmənt] Abteilung f, Fach n; ⨯ Abteil n.

com|pass ['kʌmpəs] Bereich m; ♪ Umfang m; Kompaß m; pair of ~es pl. Zirkel m.

com·pas·sion [kəm'pæʃn] Mitleid n; **~·ate** [~ət] mitleidig.

com·pat·i·ble □ [kəm'pætəbl] vereinbar; ✦ verträglich; passend.

com·pat·ri·ot [kəm'pætrɪət] Landsmann m, -männin f.

com·pel [kəm'pel] (-ll-) (er)zwingen; **~·ling** □ [~ɪŋ] zwingend.

com·pen|sate ['kɒmpenseɪt] j-n entschädigen; et. ersetzen; ausgleichen; **~·sa·tion** [kɒmpen'seɪʃn] Ersatz m; Ausgleich m; (Schaden)Ersatz m, Entschädigung f; Am. Bezahlung f, Gehalt n.

com|père, ~·pere Brt. ['kɒmpeə] 1. Conférencier m; 2. konferieren, ansagen.

com·pete [kəm'pi:t] sich (mit)bewerben (for um); konkurrieren.

com·pe|tence ['kɒmpɪtəns] Können n, Fähigkeit f; ♀♀ Zuständigkeit f; **~·tent** □ [~t] hinreichend; (leistungs)fähig, tüchtig; sachkundig.

com·pe·ti·tion [kɒmpɪ'tɪʃn] Wettbewerb m; Konkurrenz f.

com·pet·i·tive □ [kəm'petətɪv] konkurrierend; **~·tor** [~ə] Mitbewerber(in); Konkurrent(in); Sport: (Wettbewerbs)Teilnehmer(in).

com·pile [kəm'paɪl] zusammentragen, zusammenstellen, sammeln.

com·pla|cence, ~·cen·cy [kəm'pleɪsns, ~sɪ] Selbstzufriedenheit f, -gefälligkeit f; **~·cent** □ [~nt] selbstzufrieden, -gefällig.

com·plain [kəm'pleɪn] sich beklagen od. beschweren; klagen (of über acc.); **~·t** [~t] Klage f, Beschwerde f, ✦ a. Leiden n.

com·plai·sant □ [kəm'pleɪzənt] gefällig, entgegenkommend.

com·ple|ment 1. ['kɒmplɪmənt] Ergänzung f; a. full ~ volle Anzahl; 2. [~mənt] ergänzen; **~·men·ta·ry** [kɒmplɪ'mentərɪ] (sich gegenseitig) ergänzend.

com|plete [kəm'pli:t] 1. □ vollständig, ganz, vollkommen; vollzählig; 2. vervollständigen; vervollkommnen; abschließen; **~·ple·tion** [~i:ʃn] Vervollständigung f; Abschluß m; Erfüllung f.

com·plex ['kɒmpleks] 1. □ zusammengesetzt; komplex, vielschichtig; kompliziert; 2. Komplex m; Komplex m (a. psych.); **~·ion** [kəm'plekʃn] Aussehen n, Charakter m; Gesichtsfarbe f, Teint m; **~·i·ty** [~sətɪ] Vielschichtigkeit f.

com·pli|ance [kəm'plaɪəns] Einwilligung f; Einverständnis n; in ~ with gemäß; **~·ant** □ [~t] willfährig, unterwürfig.

com·pli|cate ['kɒmplɪkeɪt] komplizieren; **~·cat·ed** kompliziert; **~·ca·tion** [kɒmplɪˈkeɪʃn] Komplikation f (a. ♂); Kompliziertheit f.

com·plic·i·ty [kəmˈplɪsɪtɪ] Mitschuld f (in an dat.).

com·pli·ment 1. [ˈkɒmplɪmənt] Kompliment n; Empfehlung f; Gruß m; **2.** [~ment] v/t. (on) beglückwünschen (zu); j-m ein Kompliment machen (wegen); **~·men·ta·ry** [kɒmplɪˈmentərɪ] höflich.

com·ply [kəmˈplaɪ] sich fügen; nachkommen, entsprechen (with dat.).

com·po·nent [kəmˈpəʊnənt] Bestandteil m; ⊕, ⚡ Bauelement n.

com|pose [kəmˈpəʊz] zusammensetzen od. -stellen; ♪ komponieren; verfassen; ordnen; print. (ab)setzen; ~ o.s. sich beruhigen; **~posed** □ ruhig, gesetzt; **~·er** [~ə] Komponist(in); Verfasser(in). **~·pos·ite** [ˈkɒmpəzɪt] zusammengesetzt, gemischt; **~·po·si·tion** [kɒmpəˈzɪʃn] Zusammensetzung f; Abfassung f; Komposition f; Schriftstück n, Dichtung f; Aufsatz m; **~·po·sure** [kəmˈpəʊʒə] Fassung f, (Gemüts-)Ruhe f.

com·pound¹ [ˈkɒmpaʊnd] Lager n; Gefängnishof m; (Tier)Gehege n.

com·pound² 1. [~] zusammengesetzt; ~ interest Zinseszinsen pl.; **2.** Zusammensetzung f; Verbindung f; gr. zusammengesetztes Wort; **3.** [kəmˈpaʊnd] v/t. zusammensetzen; steigern, bsd. verschlimmern.

com·pre·hend [kɒmprɪˈhend] umfassen; begreifen, verstehen.

com·pre·hen|si·ble □ [kɒmprɪˈhensəbl] verständlich; **~·sion** [~ʃn] Begreifen n, Verständnis n; Fassungskraft f, Begriffsvermögen n, Verstand m, Einsicht f; past. unfaßbar, unfaßlich; **~·sive** [~sɪv] **1.** □ umfassend; **2.** a. ~ school Brt. Gesamtschule f.

com|press [kəmˈpres] zusammendrücken; **~ed air** Druckluft f; **~·pres·sion** [~ʃn] phys. Verdichtung f; ⊕ Druck m.

com·prise [kəmˈpraɪz] einschließen, umfassen, enthalten.

com·pro·mise [ˈkɒmprəmaɪz] **1.** Kompromiß m; **2.** v/t. (o.s. sich) bloßstellen; v/i. e-n Kompromiß schließen.

com·pul|sion [kəmˈpʌlʃn] Zwang m; **~·sive** □ [~sɪv] zwingend, Zwangs...;

psych. zwanghaft; **~·so·ry** □ [~sərɪ] obligatorisch; Zwangs...; Pflicht...

com·punc·tion [kəmˈpʌŋkʃn] Gewissensbisse pl.; Reue f; Bedenken pl.

com·pute [kəmˈpjuːt] (be-, er)rechnen; schätzen.

com·put·er [kəmˈpjuːtə] Computer m, Rechner m; **~·con·trolled** computergesteuert; **~·ize** [~raɪz] mit Computern ausstatten, auf Computer umstellen; Information in e-m Computer speichern.

com·rade [ˈkɒmreɪd] Kamerad m; (Partei)Genosse m.

con¹ abbr. [kɒn] = contra.

con² F [~] (-nn-) reinlegen, betrügen.

con·ceal [kənˈsiːl] verbergen; verheimlichen.

con·cede [kənˈsiːd] zugestehen, einräumen; gewähren; nachgeben.

con·ceit [kənˈsiːt] Einbildung f, Dünkel m; gesuchte Metapher; **~ed** □ eingebildet (of auf acc.).

con·cei|va·ble □ [kənˈsiːvəbl] denkbar, begreiflich; **~ve** [kənˈsiːv] v/i. schwanger werden; v/t. Kind empfangen; sich denken, planen, ausdenken.

con·cen·trate [ˈkɒnsəntreɪt] **1.** (sich) zusammenziehen, vereinigen; (sich) konzentrieren; **2.** Konzentrat n.

con·cept [ˈkɒnsept] Begriff m; Gedanke m; △ nicht Konzept.

con·cep·tion [kənˈsepʃn] Begreifen n; Vorstellung f, Begriff m, Idee f; biol. Empfängnis f.

con|cern [kənˈsɜːn] **1.** Angelegenheit f; Interesse n; Sorge f; Beziehung f (with zu); Geschäft n, (industrielles) Unternehmen; △ nicht Konzern; **2.** betreffen, angehen, interessieren; beunruhigen; interessieren, beschäftigen; **~ed** □ interessiert, beteiligt (in an dat.); besorgt; **~ing** prp. [~ɪŋ] betreffend, über, wegen, hinsichtlich.

con·cert 1. [ˈkɒnsət] Konzert n; **2.** [~sɜːt] Einverständnis n; **~ed** □ [kənˈsɜːtɪd] gemeinsam; ♪ mehrstimmig.

con·ces·sion [kənˈseʃn] Zugeständnis n; Konzession f.

con·cil·i|ate [kənˈsɪlɪeɪt] aus-, versöhnen; **~·a·to·ry** [~ɪətərɪ] versöhnlich, vermittelnd.

con·cise □ [kənˈsaɪs] kurz, bündig, knapp; **~·ness** [~nɪs] Kürze f.

con·clude [kən'klu:d] schließen, beschließen, beenden; abschließen; folgern, schließen (*from* aus); sich entscheiden; *to be* ~*d* Schluß folgt.

con·clu·sion [kən'klu:ʒn] Schluß *m*, Ende *n*; Abschluß *m*; Schluß *m*; (Schluß)Folgerung *f*; Beschluß *m*; *s.* *jump*; ~**sive** □ [~sɪv] überzeugend; endgültig.

con·coct [kən'kɒkt] zusammenbrauen; *fig.* aushecken, sich ausdenken; ~**coc·tion** [~kʃn] Gebräu *n*; *fig.* Erfindung *f*.

con·cord ['kɒnkɔ:d] Eintracht *f*; Übereinstimmung *f* (*a. gr.*); ♪ Harmonie *f*.

con·course ['kɒnkɔ:s] Zusammen-, Auflauf *m*; Menge *f*; freier Platz.

con·crete ['kɒnkri:t] **1.** □ fest; konkret; Beton...; **2.** Beton *m*; **3.** betonieren.

con·cur [kən'kɜ:] (-*rr*-) übereinstimmen; ~**rence** [~'kʌrəns] Zusammentreffen *n*; Übereinstimmung *f*; △ *nicht* Konkurrenz.

con·cus·sion [kən'kʌʃn]: ~ *of the brain* ⚕ Gehirnerschütterung *f*.

con|demn [kən'dem] verdammen; ⚕ *u. fig.* verurteilen (*to death* zum Tode); für unbrauchbar *od.* unbewohnbar *etc.* erklären; ~**dem·na·tion** [kɒndem'neɪʃn] ⚕ *u. fig.* Verurteilung *f*; Verdammung *f*, Mißbilligung *f*.

con|den·sa·tion [kɒnden'seɪʃn] Verdichtung *f*; ~**dense** [kən'dens] (sich) verdichten; ⊕ kondensieren; zusammenfassen, kürzen; ~**dens·er** ⊕ [~ə] Kondensator *m*.

con·de|scend [kɒndɪ'send] sich herablassen, geruhen; ~**scen·sion** [~ʃn] Herablassung *f*.

con·di·ment ['kɒndɪmənt] Würze *f*.

con·di·tion [kən'dɪʃn] **1.** Zustand *m*; (körperlicher *od.* Gesundheits)Zustand *m*; *Sport*: Kondition *f*, Form *f*; Bedingung *f*; ~*s pl.* Verhältnisse *pl.*, Umstände *pl.*; *on* ~ *that* unter der Bedingung, daß; *out of* ~ in schlechter Verfassung, in schlechtem Zustand; **2.** bedingen; in ein bestimmten Zustand bringen; ~**al** [~l] **1.** □ bedingt (*on, upon* durch); Bedingungs...; **2.** *a.* ~ *clause gr.* Bedingungs-, Konditionalsatz *m*; *a.* ~ *mood gr.* Konditional *m*.

con|dole [kən'dəʊl] kondolieren (*with dat.*); ~**do·lence** [~əns] Beileid *n*.

con·done [kən'dəʊn] verzeihen, vergeben.

con·du·cive [kən'dju:sɪv] dienlich, förderlich (*to dat.*).

con|duct 1. ['kɒndʌkt] Führung *f*; Verhalten *n*, Betragen *n*; **2.** [kən'dʌkt] führen; ♪ dirigieren; ~*ed tour (of)* Führung *f* (durch); Gesellschaftsreise *f* (durch); ~**duc·tion** [~kʃn] Leitung *f*; ~**duc·tor** [~tə] Führer *m*; Leiter *m*; Schaffner *m*; *Am.* 🚃 Zugbegleiter *m*; ♪ (Orchester)Dirigent *m*, (Chor)Leiter *m*; ⚡ Blitzableiter *m*.

cone [kəʊn] Kegel *m*; Eistüte *f*; ♣ Zapfen *m*.

con·fec·tion [kən'fekʃn] Konfekt *n*; △ *nicht* Konfektion; ~**er** [~ə] Konditor *m*; ~**ery** [~ərɪ] Süßigkeiten *pl.*, Süß-, Konditoreiwaren *pl.*; Konfekt *n*; Konditorei *f*; Süßwarengeschäft *n*.

con·fed·e|ra·cy [kən'fedərəsɪ] Bündnis *n*; *the* 2 *Am. hist.* die Konföderation; ~**rate 1.** [~rət] verbündet; **2.** [~] Bundesgenosse *m*; **3.** [~reɪt] (sich) verbünden; ~**ra·tion** [kənfedə'reɪʃn] Bund *m*, Bündnis *n*; Staatenbund *m*.

con·fer [kən'fɜ:] (-*rr*-) *v/t.* übertragen, verleihen; *v/i.* sich besprechen.

con·fe·rence ['kɒnfərəns] Konferenz *f*.

con·fess [kən'fes] bekennen, gestehen; beichten; ~**fes·sion** [~ʃən] Geständnis *n*; Bekenntnis *n*; Beichte *f*; ~**fes·sion·al** [~nl] Beichtstuhl *m*; ~**fes·sor** [~esə] Bekenner *m*; Beichtvater *m*.

con·fide [kən'faɪd] *v/t.* anvertrauen; *v/i.*: ~ *in s.o.* j-m vertrauen.

con·fi·dence ['kɒnfɪdəns] Vertrauen *n*; Zuversicht *f*; ~ **man** (*pl.* -men) Betrüger *m*; ~ **trick** aufgelegter Schwindel.

con·fi|dent □ ['kɒnfɪdənt] zuversichtlich; ~**den·tial** □ [kɒnfɪ'denʃl] vertraulich.

con·fid·ing □ [kən'faɪdɪŋ] vertrauensvoll.

con·fine [kən'faɪn] begrenzen; beschränken; einsperren; *be* ~*d of* entbunden werden von; *be* ~*d to bed* das Bett hüten müssen; ~**ment** [~mənt] Haft *f*; Beschränkung *f*; Entbindung *f*.

con·firm [kən'fɜ:m] (be)kräftigen; bestätigen; *eccl.* konfirmieren; *eccl.*

firmen; **~·fir·ma·tion** [kɒnfə-
'meɪʃn] Bestätigung *f*; *eccl.* Kon-
firmation *f*; *eccl.* Firmung *f*.

con·fis|cate ['kɒnfɪskeɪt] beschlag-
nahmen; **~·ca·tion** [kɒnfɪ'skeɪʃn]
Beschlagnahme *f*.

con·fla·gra·tion [kɒnflə'greɪʃn] (*bsd.*
Groß)Brand.

con·flict 1. ['kɒnflɪkt] Konflikt *m*; **2.**
[kən'flɪkt] in Konflikt stehen; **~·ing**
[~ɪŋ] widersprüchlich.

con·form [kən'fɔːm] (sich) anpassen
(*to dat.*, an *acc.*).

con·found [kən'faʊnd] *j-n* verwirren,
-blüffen; **~** *it!* F verdammt!; **~·ed** □
F verdammt.

con|front [kən'frʌnt] gegenübertre-
ten, -stehen (*dat.*); sich stellen
(*dat.*); konfrontieren; **~·fron·ta·
tion** [kɒnfrʌn'teɪʃn] Konfrontation
f.

con|fuse [kən'fjuːz] verwechseln;
verwirren; **~·fused** □ verwirrt; verlegen; verworren; **~·fu·sion** [~uːʒn]
Verwirrung *f*; Verlegenheit *f*; Ver-
wechslung *f*.

con·geal [kən'dʒiːl] erstarren (lassen), gerinnen (lassen).

con|gest·ed [kən'dʒestɪd] überfüllt;
verstopft; **~·ges·tion** [~tʃən] Blutan-
drang *m*; *a. traffic* ~ Verkehrs-
stockung *f*, -stauung *f*.

con·glom·e·ra·tion [kənglɒmə'reɪʃn]
Anhäufung *f*; Konglomerat *n*.

con·grat·u|late [kən'grætjuleɪt] be-
glückwünschen, *j-m* gratulieren;
~·la·tion [~grætjʊ'leɪʃn] Glückwunsch *m*; **~s!** ich gratuliere!, herz-
lichen Glückwunsch!

con·gre|gate ['kɒŋɡrɪgeɪt] (sich)
(ver)sammeln; **~·ga·tion** [kɒŋɡrɪ-
'ɡeɪʃn] Versammlung *f*; *eccl.* Gemeinde *f*.

con·gress ['kɒŋɡres] Kongreß *m*; ℓ
Am. parl. der Kongreß; ℓ·**man** (*pl.*
-*men*) *Am. parl.* Kongreßabgeord-
nete(r) *m*; ℓ·**wom·an** (*pl.* -*women*)
Am. pl. Kongreßabgeordnete *f*.

con|ic *bsd.* ⊕ ['kɒnɪk], **~·i·cal** □ [~kl]
konisch, kegelförmig.

co·ni·fer ⚘ ['kɒnɪfə] Nadelbaum *m*.

con·jec·ture [kən'dʒektʃə] **1.** Mut-
maßung *f*; **2.** mutmaßen.

con·ju·gal □ ['kɒndʒʊɡl] ehelich.

con·ju|gate *gr.* ['kɒndʒʊɡeɪt] kon-
jugieren, beugen; **~·ga·tion** *gr.*
[kɒndʒʊ'ɡeɪʃn] Konjugation *f*, Beugung *f*.

con·junc·tion [kən'dʒʌŋkʃn] Verbindung *f*; *gr.* Konjunktion *f*.

con·junc·ti·vi·tis ⚕ [kəndʒʌŋktɪ'vaɪ-
tɪs] Bindehautentzündung *f*.

con|jure ['kʌndʒə] Teufel *etc.* be-
schwören; zaubern; **~·jur·er** [~rə]
Zauber|er *m*, -in *f*, Zauberkünst-
ler(in); **~·jur·ing trick** [~rɪŋ trɪk]
Zauberkunststück *n*; **~·jur·or** [~rə]
= conjurer.

con|nect [kə'nekt] verbinden; ⚡ an-
schließen, (zu)schalten; 🚗, 🚂 *etc.*
Anschluß haben (*with* an *acc.*);
~·nect·ed □ verbunden; (logisch)
zusammenhängend (*Rede etc.*); *be*
well ~ gute Beziehungen haben;
~·nec·tion, *Brt. a.* **~·nex·ion** [~kʃn]
Verbindung *f*; ⚡ Schaltung *f*; Anschluß *m*; Zusammenhang *m*; Verwandtschaft *f*.

con·quer ['kɒŋkə] erobern; (be)sie-
gen; **~·or** [~rə] Eroberer *m*.

con·quest ['kɒŋkwest] Eroberung *f*
(*a. fig.*); erobertes Gebiet; Besiegung *f*; Bezwingung *f*.

con·science ['kɒnʃəns] Gewissen *n*.

con·sci·en·tious □ [kɒnʃɪ'enʃəs] gewissenhaft; Gewissens...; **~** *objector*
Wehrdienstverweigerer *m* (*aus Über-
zeugung*); **~·ness** [~nɪs] Gewissen-
haftigkeit *f*.

con·scious □ ['kɒnʃəs] bei Bewußtsein; bewußt; *be* ~ *of* sich bewußt
sein (*gen.*); **~·ness** [~nɪs] Bewußtsein
n.

con|script ✗ **1.** [kən'skrɪpt] einzie-
hen, -berufen; **2.** ['kɒnskrɪpt] Wehr-
pflichtige(r) *m*; **~·scrip·tion** ✗
[kən'skrɪpʃn] Einberufung *f*, Einzie-
hung *f*.

con·se|crate ['kɒnsɪkreɪt] weihen,
einsegnen; widmen; **~·cra·tion**
[kɒnsɪ'kreɪʃn] Weihe *f*; Einsegnung
f.

con·sec·u·tive □ [kən'sekjʊtɪv] aufeinanderfolgend; fortlaufend.

con·sent [kən'sent] **1.** Zustimmung *f*;
2. einwilligen, zustimmen.

con·se|quence ['kɒnsɪkwəns] Folge *f*,
Konsequenz *f*; Einfluß *m*; Bedeutung *f*; **~·quent·ly** [~tlɪ] folglich,
daher.

con·ser·va|tion [kɒnsə'veɪʃn] Erhal-
tung *f*; Naturschutz *m*; Umwelt-
schutz *m*; **~·tion·ist** [~ʃnɪst] Natur-
schützer(in); Umweltschützer(in);
~·tive □ [kən'sɜːvətɪv] **1.** erhaltend;
konservativ; vorsichtig; **2.** ℓ *pol.*

Konservative(r *m*) *f*; **~·to·ry** [kɒn-ˈsɜːvətrɪ] Treib-, Gewächshaus *n*; ♪ Konservatorium *n*; **con·serve** [kən-ˈsɜːv] erhalten.

con·sid·er [kənˈsɪdə] *v/t.* betrachten; sich überlegen, erwägen; in Betracht ziehen, berücksichtigen; meinen; *v/i.* nachdenken, überlegen; **~·e·ra·ble** □ [~rəbl] ansehnlich, beträchtlich; **~·e·ra·bly** [~lɪ] ziemlich, (sehr) viel; **~·er·ate** □ [~rət] rücksichtsvoll; **~·e·ra·tion** [kənsɪdəˈreɪʃn] Betrachtung *f*, Erwägung *f*, Überlegung *f*; Rücksicht *f*; Gesichtspunkt *m*; *take into* ~ in Erwägung *od.* in Betracht ziehen, berücksichtigen; **~·er·ing** [~ˈsɪdərɪŋ] **1.** *prp.* in Anbetracht (*gen.*); **2.** *adv.* F den Umständen entsprechend.

con·sign [kənˈsaɪn] übergeben; anvertrauen; *econ.* Waren zusenden; **~·ment** *econ.* [~mənt] Über-, Zusendung *f*; (Waren)Sendung *f*.

con·sist [kənˈsɪst]: ~ *in* bestehen in (*dat.*); ~ *of* bestehen *od.* sich zusammensetzen aus.

con·sis·tence, **~·ten·cy** [kənˈsɪstəns, ~sɪ] Konsistenz *f*, Beschaffenheit *f*; Übereinstimmung *f*; Konsequenz *f*; **~·tent** □ [~ənt] übereinstimmend, vereinbar (*with* mit); konsequent; *Sport etc.*: beständig (*Leistung*).

con·so·la·tion [kɒnsəˈleɪʃn] Trost *m*; **~·sole** [kənˈsəʊl] trösten.

con·sol·i·date [kənˈsɒlɪdeɪt] festigen; *fig.* zusammenschließen, -legen.

con·so·nant [ˈkɒnsənənt] **1.** □ übereinstimmend; Mitlaut *m*. **2.** *gr.* Konsonant *m*, Mitlaut *m*.

con·spic·u·ous □ [kənˈspɪkjʊəs] sichtbar; auffallend; hervorragend; *make o.s.* ~ sich auffällig benehmen.

con·spi·ra·cy [kənˈspɪrəsɪ] Verschwörung *f*; **~·spi·ra·tor** [~tə] Verschwörer *m*; **~·spire** [~ˈspaɪə] sich verschwören.

con·sta·ble *Brt.* [ˈkʌnstəbl] Polizist *m* (auf Streife), Wachtmeister *m*; **~·stab·u·la·ry** [kənˈstæbjʊlərɪ] Polizei(truppe) *f*.

con·stan·cy [ˈkɒnstənsɪ] Standhaftigkeit *f*; Beständigkeit *f*; **~·stant** □ [~t] beständig, unveränderlich; treu.

con·ster·na·tion [kɒnstəˈneɪʃn] Bestürzung *f*.

con·sti·pat·ed ☞ [ˈkɒnstɪpeɪtɪd] ver-

stopft; **~·pa·tion** ☞ [kɒnstɪˈpeɪʃn] Verstopfung *f*.

con·stit·u·en·cy [kənˈstɪtjʊənsɪ] Wählerschaft *f*; Wahlkreis *m*; **~·ent** [~t] **1.** e-n (Bestand)Teil bildend; *pol.* konstituierend; **2.** (wesentlicher) Bestandteil; *pol.* Wähler(in).

con·sti·tute [ˈkɒnstɪtjuːt] ein-, errichten; ernennen; bilden, ausmachen.

con·sti·tu·tion [kɒnstɪˈtjuːʃn] *pol.* Verfassung *f*; Konstitution *f*, körperliche Verfassung; Zusammensetzung *f*; **~·al** □ [~nl] **1.** □ konstitutionell; *pol.* verfassungsmäßig; **2.** (Verdauungs)Spaziergang *m*.

con·strain [kənˈstreɪn] zwingen; **~ed** gezwungen, unnatürlich; **~t** [~t] Zwang *m*.

con·strict [kənˈstrɪkt] zusammenziehen; **~·stric·tion** [~kʃn] Zusammenziehung *f*.

con·struct [kənˈstrʌkt] bauen, errichten, konstruieren; *fig.* bilden; **~·struc·tion** [~kʃn] Konstruktion *f*; Bau *m*; *fig.* Auslegung *f*; ~ *site* Baustelle *f*; **~·struc·tive** □ [~tɪv] aufbauend, schöpferisch, konstruktiv; positiv; **~·struc·tor** [~ə] Erbauer *m*, Konstrukteur *m*.

con·strue [kənˈstruː] *gr.* konstruieren; auslegen; auffassen.

con·sul [ˈkɒnsəl] Konsul *m*; **~-general** Generalkonsul *m*; **~·su·late** [~sjʊlət] Konsulat *n* (*a. Gebäude*).

con·sult [kənˈsʌlt] *v/t.* konsultieren, um Rat fragen; in *e-m Buch* nachschlagen; *v/i.* sich beraten.

con·sul·tant [kənˈsʌltənt] (fachmännische[r]) Berater(in); *Brt.* Facharzt *m* (*an e-m Krankenhaus*); **~·ta·tion** [kɒnsəlˈteɪʃn] Konsultation *f*, Beratung *f*, Rücksprache *f*; ~ *hour* Sprechstunde *f*; **~·ta·tive** [kənˈsʌltətɪv] beratend.

con·sume [kənˈsjuːm] *v/t.* essen, trinken; verbrauchen; zerstören, vernichten (*durch Feuer*); *fig.* verzehren (*durch Haß etc.*); **~·sum·er** [~ə] *econ.* Verbraucher(in).

con·sum·mate 1. □ [kənˈsʌmɪt] vollendet; **2.** [ˈkɒnsəmeɪt] vollenden.

con·sump·tion [kənˈsʌmpʃn] Verbrauch *m*; *veraltet* ☞ Schwindsucht *f*; **~·tive** □ [~tɪv] verzehrend; *veraltet* ☞ schwindsüchtig.

con·tact [ˈkɒntækt] **1.** Berührung *f*; Kontakt *m*; *make* ~s Verbindungen anknüpfen *od.* herstellen; ~ *lenses pl.* Haft-, Kontaktschalen *pl.*; **2.** sich in Verbindung setzen, Kontakt aufnehmen mit.

con·ta·gious □ *⚕* [kən'teɪdʒəs] ansteckend (*a. fig.*).

con·tain [kən'teɪn] enthalten, (um-)fassen; ~ *o.s.* an sich halten, sich beherrschen; **~er** [~ə] Behälter *m*; *econ.* Container *m*; **~er·ize** *econ.* [~əraɪz] auf Containerbetrieb umstellen; in Containern transportieren.

con·tam·i·nate [kən'tæmɪneɪt] verunreinigen; infizieren, vergiften; (*a.* radioaktiv) verseuchen; **~na·tion** [kɔntæmɪ'neɪʃn] Verunreinigung *f*; Vergiftung *f*; (*a.* radioaktive) Verseuchung.

con·tem·plate ['kɔntempleɪt] betrachten; beabsichtigen, vorhaben; **~pla·tion** [kɔntem'pleɪʃn] Betrachtung *f*; Nachdenken *n*; **~pla·tive** □ ['kɔntempleɪtɪv] nachdenklich; [kən'templətɪv] beschaulich.

con·tem·po·ra·ne·ous □ [kɔntempə'reɪnjəs] gleichzeitig; **~ry** [kən'tempərərɪ] **1.** zeitgenössisch; **2.** Zeitgenosse *m*, -in *f*.

con·tempt [kən'tempt] Verachtung *f*; **~temp·ti·ble** □ [~əbl] verachtenswert; **~temp·tu·ous** □ [~juəs] geringschätzig, verächtlich.

con·tend [kən'tend] *v/i.* kämpfen, ringen (*for* um); *v/t.* behaupten; **~er** [~ə] *bsd. Sport:* Wettkämpfer(in).

con·tent [kən'tent] **1.** zufrieden; **2.** befriedigen; ~ *o.s.* sich begnügen; **3.** Zufriedenheit *f*; *to one's heart's* ~ nach Herzenslust; ['kɔntent] Gehalt *m*; ~s *pl.* (*stofflicher*) Inhalt; **~ed** □ [kən'tentɪd] zufrieden.

con·ten·tion [kən'tenʃn] Streit *m*; Argument *n*, Behauptung *f*.

con·tent·ment [kən'tentmənt] Zufriedenheit *f*.

con·test 1. ['kɔntest] Streit *m*; Wettkampf *m*; **2.** [kən'test] sich bewerben um, kandidieren für; (be)streiten, anfechten; um *et.* streiten; **~tes·tant** [~ənt] Wettkämpfer(in), (Wettkampf)Teilnehmer(in).

con·text ['kɔntekst] Zusammenhang *m*.

con·ti·nent ['kɔntɪnənt] **1.** □ enthaltsam, mäßig; **2.** Kontinent *m*, Erdteil *m*; *the* ♀ *Brt.* das (europäische) Festland; **~nen·tal** [kɔntɪ'nentl] **1.** □

kontinental, Kontinental...; **2.** Kontinentaleuropäer(in).

con·tin·gen·cy [kən'tɪndʒənsɪ] Zufälligkeit *f*; Möglichkeit *f*, Eventualität *f*; **~t** [~t] **1.** □: *be* ~ *on od. upon* abhängen von; **2.** Kontingent *n*.

con·tin·u·al □ [kən'tɪnjʊəl] fortwährend, unaufhörlich; **~u·a·tion** [kəntɪnjʊ'eɪʃn] Fortsetzung *f*; Fortdauer *f*; ~ *school* Fortbildungsschule *f*; ~ *training* berufliche Fortbildung; **~ue** [kən'tɪnju:] *v/t.* fortsetzen, -fahren mit; beibehalten; *to be* ~d Fortsetzung folgt; *v/i.* fortdauern, andauern, anhalten; fortfahren, weitermachen; **con·ti·nu·i·ty** [kɔntɪ'nju:ətɪ] Kontinuität *f*; **~u·ous** □ [kən'tɪnjʊəs] ununterbrochen; ~ *form gr.* Verlaufsform *f*.

con·tort [kən'tɔ:t] entstellen; verzerren; **~tor·tion** [~ɔ:ʃn] Verdrehung *f*; Verzerrung *f*.

con·tour ['kɔntʊə] Umriß *m*.

con·tra ['kɔntrə] wider, gegen.

con·tra·band *econ.* ['kɔntrəbænd] unter Ein- *od.* Ausfuhrverbot stehende Ware.

con·tra·cep·tion *⚕* [kɔntrə'sepʃn] Empfängnisverhütung *f*; **~tive** *⚕* [~tɪv] empfängnisverhütend(es Mittel).

con·tract 1. [kən'trækt] *v/t.* zusammenziehen; sich *e-e Krankheit* zuziehen; *Schulden* machen; *e-e Ehe etc.* schließen; *v/i.* sich zusammenziehen, schrumpfen; *⚙* e-n Vertrag schließen; sich vertraglich verpflichten; **2.** ['kɔntrækt] Kontrakt *m*, Vertrag *m*; **~trac·tion** [kən'trækʃn] Zusammenziehung *f*; *gr.* Kurzform *f*; **~trac·tor** [~tə]: *a. building* ~ Bauunternehmer *m*.

con·tra·dict [kɔntrə'dɪkt] widersprechen (*dat.*); **~dic·tion** [~kʃn] Widerspruch *m*; **~dic·to·ry** □ [~tərɪ] (sich) widersprechend.

con·tra·ry ['kɔntrərɪ] **1.** □ entgegengesetzt; widrig; ~ *to* im Gegensatz zu; ~ *to expectations* wider Erwarten; **2.** Gegenteil *n*; *on the* ~ im Gegenteil.

con·trast 1. ['kɔntrɑ:st] Gegensatz *m*; Kontrast *m*; **2.** [kən'trɑ:st] *v/t.* gegenüberstellen, vergleichen; *v/i.* sich unterscheiden, abstechen (*with* von).

con·trib·ute [kən'trɪbju:t] beitragen, -steuern; spenden (*to* für); **~tri-**

bu·tion [kɒntrɪˈbjuːʃn] Beitrag *m*; Spende *f*; **~·trib·u·tor** [kənˈtrɪbjʊtə] Beitragende(r *m f*); Mitarbeiter(in) (*an e-r Zeitung*); **~·trib·u·to·ry** [~ərɪ] beitragend.

con|trite □ [ˈkɒntraɪt] zerknirscht; **~·tri·tion** [kənˈtrɪʃn] Zerknirschung *f*.

con·trive [kənˈtraɪv] ersinnen, (sich) ausdenken, planen; zustande bringen; es fertigbringen (*to inf.* zu *inf.*); **~d** gekünstelt (*Freundlichkeit etc.*).

con·trol [kənˈtrəʊl] **1.** Kontrolle *f*, Herrschaft *f*, Macht *f*, Gewalt *f*, Beherrschung *f*; Aufsicht *f*; ⊕ Steuerung *f*; *mst* **~s** *pl.* ⊕ Steuervorrichtung *f*; △ *nicht* Kontrolle (*Überprüfung*); *lose* ~ die Herrschaft *od.* Gewalt *od.* Kontrolle verlieren; **2.** (*-ll-*) beherrschen, die Kontrolle haben über (*acc.*); *e-r Sache* Herr werden, (erfolgreich) bekämpfen; kontrollieren, überwachen; *econ.* (staatlich) lenken; *Preise* binden; ≴, ⊕ steuern, regeln, regulieren; △ *nicht* kontrollieren (*überprüfen*); **~ desk** ≴ Schalt-, Steuerpult *n*; **~ pan·el** ≴ Schalttafel *f*; Bedienungsfeld *n*; **~ tow·er** ✈ Kontrollturm *m*, Tower *m*.

con·tro·ver|sial □ [kɒntrəˈvɜːʃl] umstritten; **~·sy** [ˈkɒntrəvɜːsɪ] Kontroverse *f*, Streit *m*.

con·tuse ≴ [kənˈtjuːz] quetschen.

con·va·lesce [kɒnvəˈles] gesund werden, genesen; **~·les·cence** [~ns] Rekonvaleszenz *f*, Genesung *f*; **~·les·cent** [~t] **1.** □ genesend; **2.** Rekonvaleszent(in), Genesende(r *m*) *f*.

con·vene [kənˈviːn] (sich) versammeln; zusammentreten (*Parlament etc.*); einberufen.

con·ve·ni|ence [kənˈviːnjəns] Bequemlichkeit *f*; Angemessenheit *f*; Vorteil *m*; *Brt.* Toilette *f*; *all* (*modern*) **~s** *pl.* aller Komfort; *at your earliest* ~ möglichst bald; **~·ent** [~t] bequem; günstig.

con·vent [ˈkɒnvənt] (Nonnen)Kloster *n*.

con·ven·tion [kənˈvenʃn] Versammlung *f*; Konvention *f*, Übereinkommen *n*, Abkommen *n*; Sitte *f*; **~·al** □ [~nl] herkömmlich, konventionell.

con·verge [kənˈvɜːdʒ] konvergieren; zusammenlaufen, -strömen.

con·ver·sant [kənˈvɜːsənt] vertraut.

con·ver·sa·tion [kɒnvəˈseɪʃn] Gespräch *n*, Unterhaltung *f*; **~·al** □ [~nl] Unterhaltungs...; umgangssprachlich.

con·verse 1. □ [ˈkɒnvɜːs] umgekehrt; **2.** [kənˈvɜːs] sich unterhalten.

con·ver·sion [kənˈvɜːʃn] Um-, Verwandlung *f*; *econ.* ⊕ Umstellung *f*; ⊕ Umbau *m*; ≴ Umformung *f*; *eccl.* Konversion *f*; *pol.* Übertritt *m*; *econ.* Konvertierung *f*; Umstellung *f* (*e-r Währung etc.*).

con|vert 1. [ˈkɒnvɜːt] Bekehrte(r *m f*); *eccl. a.* Konvertit(in); **2.** [kənˈvɜːt] (sich) um- *od.* verwandeln; *econ.* ⊕ umstellen (*to auf acc.*); ⊕ umbauen (*into* zu); ≴ verwandeln; *eccl.* bekehren; *econ.* konvertieren, umwandeln; *Währung etc.* umstellen; **~·vert·er** ≴ [~ə] Umformer *m*; **~·vert·i·ble 1.** □ [~əbl] um-, verwandelbar; *econ.* konvertierbar; **2.** *mot.* Kabrio(lett) *n*.

con·vey [kənˈveɪ] befördern, transportieren, bringen; überbringen, -mitteln; übertragen; mitteilen; **~·ance** [~əns] Beförderung *f*, Transport *m*; Übermittlung *f*; Verkehrsmittel *n*; ⚖ Übertragung *f*; **~·er**, **~·or** ⊕ [~ɪə] = **~ er belt** Förderband *n*.

con|vict 1. [ˈkɒnvɪkt] Strafgefangene(r) *m*, Sträfling *m*; **2.** ⚖ [kənˈvɪkt] *j-n* überführen; **~·vic·tion** [~kʃn] ⚖ Verurteilung *f*; Überzeugung *f*.

con·vince [kənˈvɪns] überzeugen.

con·viv·i·al □ [kənˈvɪvɪəl] gesellig.

con·voy [ˈkɒnvɔɪ] **1.** ♣ Geleitzug *m*, Konvoi *m*; (Wagen)Kolonne *f*; (Geleit)Schutz *m*; **2.** Geleitschutz geben (*dat.*), eskortieren.

con·vul|sion ≴ [kənˈvʌlʃn] Zuckung *f*, Krampf *m*; **~·sive** □ [~sɪv] krampfhaft, -artig, konvulsiv.

coo [kuː] gurren.

cook [kʊk] **1.** Koch *m*; Köchin *f*; **2.** kochen; *Bericht etc.* frisieren; **~ up** F sich ausdenken, erfinden; **~·book** *Am.* [ˈkʊkbʊk] Kochbuch *n*; **~·er** *Brt.* [~ə] Ofen *m*, Herd *m*; **~·e·ry** [~ərɪ] Kochen *n*; Kochkunst *f*; ~ *book Brt.* Kochbuch *n*; **~·ie** *Am.* [~ɪ] (süßer) Keks, Plätzchen *n*; **~·ing** □ Küche *f* (*Kochweise*); **~·y** *Am.* [~ɪ] = *cookie*.

cool [kuːl] **1.** □ kühl; *fig.* kaltblütig, gelassen; unverfroren; *bsd. Am.* F klasse, prima, cool; **2.** Kühle *f*; F

(Selbst)Beherrschung f; 3. (sich) abkühlen; ~ **down**, ~ **off** sich beruhigen.

coon zo. F [ku:n] Waschbär m.

coop [ku:p] 1. Hühnerstall m; 2. ~ **up**, ~ **in** einsperren, -pferchen.

co-op F ['kəʊɒp] Co-op m (Genossenschaft u. Laden).

co(-)op·e·rate [kəʊ'ɒpəreɪt] mitwirken; zusammenarbeiten; ~**ra·tion** [kəʊpə'reɪʃn] Mitwirkung f; Zusammenarbeit f; ~**ra·tive** [kəʊ'ɒpərətɪv] 1. ☐ zusammenarbeitend; mitarbeitend; 2. a. ~ **society** Genossenschaft f; Co-op m, Konsumverein m; a. ~ **store** Co-op m, Konsumladen m; ~**ra·tor** [~reɪtə] Mitarbeiter(in).

co(-)or·di·nate 1. ☐ [kəʊ'ɔ:dɪnət] koordiniert, gleichgeordnet; 2. [~neɪt] koordinieren, aufeinander abstimmen; ~**na·tion** [kəʊɔ:dɪ'neɪʃn] Koordination f; harmonisches Zusammenspiel.

cop F [kɒp] Bulle m (Polizist).

cope [kəʊp]: ~ **with** gewachsen sein, fertig werden mit.

cop·i·er ['kɒpɪə] Kopiergerät n, Kopierer m; = **copyist**.

co·pi·ous ☐ ['kəʊpjəs] reich(lich); weitschweifig.

cop·per¹ ['kɒpə] 1. min. Kupfer n; Kupfermünze f; 2. kupfern, Kupfer...

cop·per² F [~] Bulle m (Polizist).

cop·pice, copse ['kɒpɪs, kɒps] Unterholz n, Dickicht n.

cop·y ['kɒpɪ] 1. Kopie f; Abschrift f; Nachbildung f; Durchschlag m; Muster n; Exemplar n (e-s Buches); (Zeitungs)Nummer f; druckfertiges Manuskript; fair od. clean ~ Reinschrift f; 2. kopieren; abschreiben; Computer: Daten übertragen; nachbilden; nachahmen; ~**book** Schreibheft n; ~**ing** [~ɪŋ] Kopier...; ~**ist** [~ɪst] Abschreiber m, Kopist m; ~**right** Urheberrecht n, Copyright n.

cor·al zo. ['kɒrəl] Koralle f.

cord [kɔ:d] 1. Schnur f, Strick m; anat. Band n, Schnur f, Strang m; 2. (zu)schnüren, binden.

cor·di·al ['kɔ:djəl] 1. ☐ herzlich; 🏵 stärkend; 2. belebendes Mittel, Stärkungsmittel n; Fruchtsaftkonzentrat n; Likör m; ~**i·ty** [kɔ:dɪ'ælətɪ] Herzlichkeit f.

cor·don ['kɔ:dn] 1. Kordon m, Po-

stenkette f; 2. ~ **off** abriegeln, absperren.

cor·du·roy ['kɔ:dərɔɪ] Kord(samt) m; (a pair of) ~**s** pl. (e-e) Kordhose.

core [kɔ:] 1. Kerngehäuse n; fig. Herz n, Mark n, Kern m; 2. entkernen.

cork [kɔ:k] 1. Kork m; 2. a. ~ **up** zu-, verkorken; ~**screw** ['kɔ:kskru:] Korkenzieher m.

corn [kɔ:n] 1. (Samen-, Getreide-) Korn n; Getreide n; a. Indian ~ Am. Mais m; 🏵 Hühnerauge n; 2. (ein-) pökeln.

cor·ner ['kɔ:nə] 1. Ecke f; Winkel m; Kurve f; Fußball etc.: Eckball m, Ecke f; fig. schwierige Lage, Klemme f, Enge f; 2. Ecke...; ~**kick** Fußball: Eckstoß m; 3. in die Ecke (fig. Enge) treiben; econ. aufkaufen; ~**ed** ...eckig.

cor·net ['kɔ:nɪt] ♪ Kornett n; Brt. Eistüte f.

corn·flakes ['kɔ:nfleɪks] pl. Cornflakes pl.

cor·nice arch. ['kɔ:nɪs] Gesims n, Sims m.

cor·o·na·ry anat. ['kɒrənərɪ] koronar; ~ **artery** Koronar-, Kranzarterie f.

cor·o·na·tion [kɒrə'neɪʃn] 1. Krönung f.

cor·o·ner 🏛 ['kɒrənə] Coroner m (richterlicher Beamter zur Untersuchung der Todesursache in Fällen gewaltsamen od. unnatürlichen Todes); ~'s **inquest** gerichtliches Verfahren zur Untersuchung der Todesursache.

cor·o·net ['kɒrənɪt] Adelskrone f.

cor·po·ral ['kɔ:pərəl] 1. ☐ körperlich; 2.✕ Unteroffizier m; ~**ra·tion** [kɔ:pə'reɪʃn] Körperschaft f; Stadtverwaltung f; Vereinigung f, Gesellschaft f; Am. Aktiengesellschaft f.

corpse [kɔ:ps] Leichnam m, Leiche f.

cor·pu|lence, ~len·cy ['kɔ:pjʊləns, ~sɪ] Beleibtheit f; ~**lent** [~t] beleibt.

cor·ral Am. [kɔ:'ra:l, Am. kə'ræl] Korral m, Hürde f, Pferch m; 2. (-ll-) Vieh in e-n Pferch treiben.

cor|rect [kə'rekt] 1. adj. ☐ korrekt, richtig; 2. v/t. korrigieren; zurechtweisen; strafen; ~**rec·tion** [~kʃn] Berichtigung f; Korrektur f; Verweis m; Strafe f; house of ~ (Jugend-) Strafanstalt f, (-)Gefängnis n.

cor·re|spond [kɒrɪ'spɒnd] entsprechen (with, to dat.); korrespondieren; ~**spon·dence** [~əns] Übereinstimmung *f*; Korrespondenz *f*, Briefwechsel *m*; ~ *course* Fernkurs *m*; **~spon·dent** [~t] **1.** □ entsprechend; **2.** Briefpartner(in); Korrespondent(in); **~spon·ding** □ [~ɪŋ] entsprechend.

cor·ri·dor [ˈkɒrɪdɔː] Korridor *m*, Gang *m*; ~ *train* D-Zug *m*.

cor·rob·o·rate [kəˈrɒbəreɪt] bekräftigen, bestätigen.

cor|rode [kəˈrəʊd] zerfressen; korrodieren; **~·ro·sion** [~ʒn] Zerfressen *n*; ⊕ Korrosion *f*; Rost *m*; **~ro·sive** [~sɪv] **1.** □ zerfressend, ätzend; **2.** Korrosions-, Ätzmittel *n*.

cor·ru·gate [ˈkɒrʊgeɪt] runzeln; ⊕ wellen, riefen; ~*d iron* Wellblech *n*.

cor|rupt [kəˈrʌpt] **1.** □ verdorben; korrupt, bestechlich, käuflich; **2.** *v/t.* verderben; bestechen; *v/i.* verderben; **~rupt·i·ble** □ [~əbl] verderblich; korrupt, bestechlich, käuflich; **~rup·tion** [~pʃn] Verdorbenheit, Verworfenheit *f*; Fäulnis *f*; Korruption *f*, Bestechlichkeit *f*; Verfälschung *f*.

cor·set [ˈkɔːsɪt] Korsett *n*.

cos|met·ic [kɒzˈmetɪk] **1.** (*~ally*) kosmetisch, Schönheits...; **2.** kosmetisches Mittel, Schönheitsmittel *n*; **~·me·ti·cian** [kɒzməˈtɪʃn] Kosmetiker(in).

cos·mo·naut [ˈkɒzmənɔːt] Kosmonaut *m*, (sowjetischer) (Welt)Raumfahrer.

cos·mo·pol·i·tan [kɒzməˈpɒlɪtən] **1.** kosmopolitisch; **2.** Weltbürger(in).

cost [kɒst] **1.** Preis *m*; Kosten *pl.*; Schaden *m*; △ *nicht Kost* (*Essen*); ~ *of living* Lebenshaltungskosten *pl.*; **2.** (*cost*) kosten; **~·ly** [ˈkɒstlɪ] (*-ier, -iest*) kostspielig; teuer erkauft.

cos·tume [ˈkɒstjuːm] Kostüm *n*, Kleidung *f*, Tracht *f*.

co·sy [ˈkəʊzɪ] **1.** □ (*-ier, -iest*) behaglich, gemütlich; **2.** = *egg-cosy, tea-cosy.*

cot [kɒt] Feldbett *n*; *Brt.* Kinderbett *n*.

cot|tage [ˈkɒtɪdʒ] Cottage *n*, (kleines) Landhaus; *Am.* Ferienhaus *n*, -häuschen *n*; ~ *cheese* Hüttenkäse *m*; **~·tag·er** [~ə] Cottagebewohner(in); *Am.* Urlauber(in) in e-m Ferienhaus.

cot·ton [ˈkɒtn] **1.** Baumwolle *f*; Baumwollstoff *m*; (Baumwoll)Garn *n*, (-)Zwirn *m*; **2.** baumwollen,

Baumwoll...; **3.** ~ *on to et.* kapieren, verstehen; **~·wood** ♥ *e-e* amer. Pappel; ~ *wool Brt.* (Verband)Watte *f*.

couch [kaʊtʃ] **1.** Couch *f*, Sofa *n*; Liege *f*; **2.** (*ab*)fassen, formulieren.

cou·chette 🚄 [kuːˈʃet] Liegewagenplatz *m*; *a.* ~ *coach* Liegewagen *m*.

cou·gar *zo.* [ˈkuːgə] Puma *m*.

cough [kɒf] **1.** Husten *m*; **2.** husten.

could [kʊd] *pret. von* can[1].

coun·cil [ˈkaʊnsl] Rat(sversammlung *f*) *m*; ~ *house Brt.* gemeindeeigenes Wohnhaus (*mit niedrigen Mieten*); **~·ci(l)·lor** [~sələ] Ratsmitglied *n*, Stadtrat *m*, Stadträtin *f*.

coun·sel [ˈkaʊnsl] **1.** Beratung *f*; Rat(schlag) *m*; *Brt.* ⚖ (Rechts)Anwalt *m*; ~ *for the defence* (*Am. defense*) Verteidiger *m*; ~ *for the prosecution* Anklagevertreter *m*; **2.** (*bsd. Brt. -ll-, Am. -l-*) *j-n* beraten; *j-m* raten; **~·se(l)·lor** [~sələ] Berater *m*; *a.* ~*-at-law Am.* ⚖ (Rechts)Anwalt *m*.

count[1] [kaʊnt] Graf *m* (*nicht britisch*).

count[2] [~] **1.** Rechnung *f*, Zählung *f*; ⚖ Anklagepunkt *m*; **2.** *v/t.* zählen; aus-, berechnen; *fig.* halten für; ~ *down Geld* hinzuzählen; (*a. v/i.*) den Countdown durchführen (*für e-e Rakete etc.*), letzte (Start)Vorbereitungen treffen (*für*); *v/i.* zählen; rechnen; (*on, upon*) zählen, sich verlassen (auf *acc.*); gelten (*for little* wenig); **~·down** [ˈkaʊntdaʊn] Countdown *m*, *n* (*beim Raketenstart etc.*), letzte (Start)Vorbereitungen *pl.*

coun·te·nance [ˈkaʊntɪnəns] Gesichtsausdruck *m*; Fassung *f*.

count·er[1] [ˈkaʊntə] Zähler *m*; Zählgerät *n*; *Brt.* Spielmarke *f*.

coun·ter[2] [~] Ladentisch *m*, Theke *f*; (Bank-, Post)Schalter *m*.

coun·ter[3] [~] **1.** (ent)gegen, Gegen...; **2.** entgegentreten (*dat.*), entgegnen (*dat.*), bekämpfen; abwehren.

coun·ter·act [kaʊntəˈrækt] entgegenwirken (*dat.*); neutralisieren; bekämpfen.

coun·ter·bal·ance 1. [ˈkaʊntəbæləns] Gegengewicht *n*; **2.** [kaʊntəˈbæləns] aufwiegen, ausgleichen.

coun·ter·clock·wise *Am.* [kaʊntəˈklɒkwaɪz] = *anticlockwise.*

coun·ter·es·pi·o·nage [ˈkaʊntərˈespɪənɑːʒ] Spionageabwehr *f*.

coun·ter·feit [ˈkaʊntəfɪt] **1.** □ nachgemacht, falsch, unecht; **2.** Fälschung *f*; Falschgeld *n*; **3.** *Geld, Unterschrift etc.* fälschen.

coun·ter·foil [ˈkaʊntəfɔɪl] Kontrollabschnitt *m*.

coun·ter·mand [kaʊntəˈmɑːnd] widerrufen; *Ware* abbestellen.

coun·ter·pane [ˈkaʊntəpeɪn] = *bedspread*.

coun·ter·part [ˈkaʊntəpɑːt] Gegenstück *n*; genaue Entsprechung.

coun·ter·sign [ˈkaʊntəsaɪn] gegenzeichnen, mit unterschreiben.

coun·tess [ˈkaʊntɪs] Gräfin *f*.

count·less [ˈkaʊntlɪs] zahllos.

coun·try [ˈkʌntrɪ] **1.** Land *n*; Gegend *f*; Heimatland *n*; **2.** Land..., ländlich; **~man** (*pl. -men*) Landbewohner *m*; Bauer *m*; *a. fellow ~* Landsmann *m*; **~ road** Landstraße *f*; **~side** (ländliche) Gegend; Landschaft *f*; **~wom·an** (*pl. -women*) Landbewohnerin *f*; Bäuerin *f*; *a. fellow ~* Landsmännin *f*.

coun·ty [ˈkaʊntɪ] *Brt.* Grafschaft *f*; *Am.* (Land)Kreis *m* (*einzelstaatlicher Verwaltungsbezirk*); **~ seat** *Am.* Kreis(haupt)stadt *f*; **~ town** *Brt.* Grafschaftshauptstadt *f*.

coup [kuː] Coup *m*; Putsch *m*.

cou·ple [ˈkʌpl] **1.** Paar *n*; *a ~ of* F ein paar; **2.** (zusammen)koppeln; ⊕ kuppeln; *zo.* (sich) paaren.

coup·ling ⊕ [ˈkʌplɪŋ] Kupplung *f*.

cou·pon [ˈkuːpɒn] Gutschein *m*, Kupon *m*, Bestellzettel *m*.

cour·age [ˈkʌrɪdʒ] Mut *m*; **cou·ra·geous** [kəˈreɪdʒəs] mutig, beherzt.

cou·ri·er [ˈkʊrɪə] Kurier *m*, Eilbote *m*; Reiseleiter *m*.

course [kɔːs] **1.** Lauf *m*, Gang *m*; Weg *m*; ♣, ≫, *fig.* Kurs *m*; *Sport:* (Renn-)Bahn *f*, (-)Strecke *f*, (*Golf*)Platz *m*; Gang *m* (*Speisen*); Reihe *f*; Folge *f*; Kurs *m*; ♣ Kur *f*; *of ~* natürlich, selbstverständlich; **2.** hetzen, jagen; strömen (*Tränen etc.*).

court [kɔːt] **1.** Hof *m* (*a. e-s Fürsten*); kleiner Platz; *Sport:* Platz *m*, (Spiel)Feld *n*; ♣♣ Gericht(shof *m*) *n*; Gerichtssaal *m*; **2.** *j-m* den Hof machen; werben um.

cour·te·ous [ˈkɜːtjəs] höflich; **~sy** [~ɪsɪ] Höflichkeit *f*; Gefälligkeit *f*.

court-house [ˈkɔːthaʊs] Gerichtsgebäude *n*; **~ier** [~jə] Höfling *m*; **~ly** [~lɪ] höfisch; höflich; **~ mar·tial** (*pl.*

~s martial, ~ martials) Kriegsgericht *n*; **~-mar·tial** [~ˈmɑːʃl] (*bsd. Brt. -ll-, Am. -l-*) vor ein Kriegsgericht stellen; **~room** Gerichtssaal *m*; **~ship** [ˈkɔːtʃɪp] Werben *n*; **~yard** Hof *m*.

cous·in [ˈkʌzn] Cousin *m*, Vetter *m*; Cousine *f*, Kusine *f*.

cove [kəʊv] kleine Bucht.

cov·er [ˈkʌvə] **1.** Decke *f*; Deckel *m*; (Buch)Deckel *m*, Einband *m*; Umschlag *m*; Hülle *f*; Schutzhaube *f*, -platte *f*; Abdeckhaube *f*; Briefumschlag *m*; Deckung *f*; Schutz *m*; Dickicht *n*; Decke *f*, Mantel *m* (*Bereifung*); *fig.* Deckmantel *m*; *take ~* in Deckung gehen; *under plain ~* in neutralem Umschlag; *under separate ~* mit getrennter Post; **2.** (be-, zu)decken; einschlagen, -wickeln; verbergen, -decken; schützen; *Weg* zurücklegen; *econ.* decken; *mit e-r Schußwaffe* zielen auf (*acc.*); ✗ *Gelände* bestreichen; umfassen; *fig.* erfassen; *Presse, Rundfunk, TV:* berichten über (*acc.*); **~ up** ab-, zudecken; *fig.* verbergen, -heimlichen; **~ up for s.o.** j-n decken; **~age** [~rɪdʒ] Berichterstattung *f* (*of über acc.*); **~ girl** Covergirl *n*, Titelblattmädchen *n*; **~ing** [~rɪŋ] Decke *f*; Überzug *m*; (*Fußboden*)Belag *m*; **~ sto·ry** Titelgeschichte *f*.

cov·ert □ [ˈkʌvət] heimlich, versteckt.

cov·et [ˈkʌvɪt] begehren; **~ous** □ [~əs] (be)gierig; habsüchtig.

cow¹ *zo.* [kaʊ] Kuh *f*.

cow² [~] einschüchtern, ducken.

cow·ard [ˈkaʊəd] **1.** □ feig(e); **2.** Feigling *m*; **~ice** [~ɪs] Feigheit *f*; **~ly** [~lɪ] feig(e).

cow·boy [ˈkaʊbɔɪ] Cowboy *m*.

cow·er [ˈkaʊə] kauern; sich ducken.

cow·herd [ˈkaʊhɜːd] Kuhhirt *m*; **~hide** Rind(s)leder *n*; **~house** Kuhstall *m*.

cowl [kaʊl] Mönchskutte *f* (*mit Kapuze*); Kapuze *f*; Schornsteinkappe *f*.

cow·shed [ˈkaʊʃed] Kuhstall *m*; **~slip** ♀ Schlüsselblume *f*; *Am.* Sumpfdotterblume *f*.

cox [kɒks] = *coxswain*.

cox·comb [ˈkɒkskəʊm] Geck *m*.

cox·swain [ˈkɒkswein, ♣ *mst* ˈkɒksn] Bootsführer *m*; *Rudern:* Steuermann *m*.

coy □ [kɔɪ] schüchtern; spröde.

credible

coy·ote zo. [ˈkɔɪəʊt] Kojote m, Prärie-wolf m.

co·zy Am. □ [ˈkəʊzɪ] (-ier, -iest) = cosy.

crab [kræb] Krabbe f, Taschenkrebs m; F Nörgler(in).

crack [kræk] **1.** Krach m, Knall m; Spalte f, Spalt m, Schlitz m; F derber Schlag; F Versuch m; Witz m; **2.** erstklassig; **3.** v/t. knallen mit; knacken lassen; zerbrechen, (zer-) sprengen; schlagen, hauen; (auf-) knacken; ~ a joke e-n Witz reißen; v/i. krachen, knallen, knacken; (zer-) springen, (-)platzen; überschlagen (Stimme); a. ~ up fig. zusammenbre-chen; get ~ing F loslegen; **~·er** [ˈkrækə] Cracker m, Kräcker m (un-gesüßtes, keksartiges Kleingebäck); Schwärmer m, Frosch m (Feuer-werkskörper); **~·le** [~kl] knattern, knistern, krachen.

cra·dle [ˈkreɪdl] **1.** Wiege f; fig. Kind-heit f; **2.** wiegen; betten.

craft[1] [krɑːft] □ Boot(e pl.) n, Schiff(e pl.) n; ✈ Flugzeug(e pl.) n; (Welt)Raumfahrzeug(e pl.) n.

craft[2] [~] Handwerk n, Gewerbe n; Schlauheit f, List f; △ nicht Kraft; **~s·man** [ˈkrɑːftsmən] (pl. -men) (Kunst)Handwerker m; **~·y** □ [~ɪ] (-ier, -iest) gerissen, listig, schlau.

crag [kræg] Klippe f, Felsenspitze f.

cram [kræm] (-mm-) (voll)stopfen; nudeln, mästen; mit j-m pauken; für e-e Prüfung pauken.

cramp [kræmp] **1.** Krampf m; ⊕ Klammer f; fig. Fessel f; **2.** einen-gen, hemmen.

cran·ber·ry ♥ [ˈkrænbərɪ] Preisel-beere f.

crane [kreɪn] **1.** zo. Kranich m; ⊕ Kran m; **2.** den Hals recken; ~ one's neck sich den Hals verrenken (for nach).

crank [kræŋk] **1.** ⊕ Kurbel f; ⊕ Schwengel m; F Spinner m, komi-scher Kauz; **2.** (an)kurbeln; **~·shaft** ⊕ [ˈkræŋkʃɑːft] Kurbelwelle f; **~·y** □ [~ɪ] (-ier, -iest) wacklig; verschro-ben; Am. schlechtgelaunt.

cran·ny [ˈkrænɪ] Riß m, Ritze f.

crape [kreɪp] Krepp m, Flor m.

craps Am. [kræps] sg. ein Würfelspiel.

crash [kræʃ] **1.** Krach(en n) m; Unfall m, Zusammenstoß m; ✈ Absturz m; bsd. econ. Zusammenbruch m, (Börsen)Krach m; **2.** v/t. zertrüm-

mern; e-n Unfall haben mit; ✈ abstürzen mit; v/i. (krachend) zer-bersten, -brechen; krachend ein-stürzen, zusammenkrachen; bsd. econ. zusammenbrechen; krachen (against, into gegen); mot. zusam-menstoßen, verunglücken; ✈ ab-stürzen; **3.** Schnell..., Sofort...; ~ **bar·ri·er** [ˈkræˌbærɪə] Leitplanke f; ~ **course** Schnell-, Intensivkurs m; ~ **di·et** radikale Schlankheitskur; ~ **hel·met** Sturzhelm m; **~·land** ✈ e-e Bruchlandung machen (mit); ~ **land·ing** ✈ Bruchlandung f.

crate [kreɪt] (Latten)Kiste f.

cra·ter [ˈkreɪtə] Krater m; Trichter m.

crave [kreɪv] v/t. dringend bitten od. flehen um; v/i. sich sehnen (for nach); **crav·ing** [ˈkreɪvɪŋ] heftiges Verlangen.

craw·fish zo. [ˈkrɔːfɪʃ] Flußkrebs m.

crawl [krɔːl] **1.** Kriechen n; **2.** krie-chen; schleichen; wimmeln; krib-beln; Schwimmen: kraulen; it makes one's flesh ~ man bekommt e-e Gänsehaut davon.

cray·fish zo. [ˈkreɪfɪʃ] Flußkrebs m.

cray·on [ˈkreɪən] Zeichenstift m, Pastellstift m.

craze [kreɪz] Verrücktheit f, F Fim-mel m; be the ~ Mode sein; **cra·zy** □ [ˈkreɪzɪ] (-ier, -iest) verrückt (about nach).

creak [kriːk] knarren, quietschen.

cream [kriːm] **1.** Rahm m, Sahne f; Creme f; Auslese f, das Beste; **2.** a. ~ off den Rahm abschöpfen von, ab-sahnen (a. fig.); **~·er·y** [ˈkriːmərɪ] Molkerei f; Milchgeschäft n; **~·y** □ [~ɪ] (-ier, -iest) sahnig; weich.

crease [kriːs] **1.** (Bügel)Falte f; **2.** (zer)knittern.

cre·ate [kriːˈeɪt] (er)schaffen; her-vorrufen; verursachen; kreieren; **~·a·tion** [~ˈeɪʃn] (Er)Schaffung f; Erzeugung f; Schöpfung f; **~·a·tive** □ [~ˈeɪtɪv] schöpferisch; **~·a·tor** [~ə] Schöpfer m; (Er)Schaffer m; **crea·ture** [ˈkriːtʃə] Geschöpf n; Kreatur f.

crèche [kreɪʃ] (Kinder)Krippe f.

cre·dence [ˈkriːdns] Glaube m; **~·den·tials** [krɪˈdenʃlz] pl. Beglaubi-gungsschreiben n; Referenzen pl.; Zeugnisse pl.; (Ausweis)Papiere pl.

cred·i·ble □ [ˈkredəbl] glaubwürdig; glaubhaft.

cred|it [ˈkredɪt] **1.** Glaube(n) *m*; Ruf *m*, Ansehen *n*; Verdienst *n*; *econ.* Guthaben *n*; *econ.* Kredit *m*; ~ *card econ.* Kreditkarte *f*; **2.** *j-m* glauben; *j-m* trauen; *econ.* gutschreiben; ~ *s.o. with s.th.* j-m et. zutrauen; j-m et. zuschreiben; **~·i·ta·ble** □ [~əbl] achtbar, ehrenvoll (*to* für); **~·i·tor** [~ə] Gläubiger *m*; **~·u·lous** □ [~jʊləs] leichtgläubig.

creed [kriːd] Glaubensbekenntnis *n*.

creek [kriːk] *Brt.* kleine Bucht; *Am.* Bach *m*.

creel [kriːl] Fischkorb *m*.

creep [kriːp] (*crept*) kriechen; schleichen (*a. fig.*); ~ *in* (sich) hinein- od. hereinschleichen; sich einschleichen (*Fehler etc.*); *it makes my flesh* ~ *ich bekomme e-e Gänsehaut davon;* **~·er** ♀ [ˈkriːpə] Kriech-, Kletterpflanze *f*; **~s** *pl.* F: *the sight gave me the* ~ bei dem Anblick bekam ich e-e Gänsehaut.

crept [krept] *pret. u. p.p. von creep.*

cres·cent [ˈkresnt] **1.** zunehmend; halbmondförmig; **2.** Halbmond *m*.

cress ♀ [kres] Kresse *f*.

crest [krest] (Hahnen-, Berg- *etc.*) Kamm *m*; Mähne *f*; Federbusch *m*; *family* ~ *Heraldik:* Familienwappen *n*; **~·fal·len** [ˈkrestfɔːlən] niedergeschlagen.

cre·vasse [krɪˈvæs] (Gletscher)Spalte *f*; *Am.* Deichbruch *m*.

crev·ice [ˈkrevɪs] Riß *m*, Spalte *f*.

crew[1] [kruː] ♣, ✈ Besatzung *f*, ♣ *a.* Mannschaft *f*; (*Arbeits*)Gruppe *f*; Belegschaft *f*.

crew[2] [~] *pret. von crow 2.*

crib [krɪb] **1.** Krippe *f*; *Am.* Kinderbett *n*; F *Schule:* Klatsche *f*, Spickzettel *m*; **2.** (*-bb-*) F abschreiben, spicken.

crick [krɪk] *a* ~ *in one's back* (*neck*) ein steifer Rücken (Hals).

crick·et [ˈkrɪkɪt] *zo.* Grille *f*; *Sport:* Kricket *n*; *not* ~ F nicht fair.

crime [kraɪm] ✠ Verbrechen *n*; *coll.* Verbrechen *pl.*; ~ *novel* Kriminalroman *m.*

crim·i·nal [ˈkrɪmɪnl] **1.** □ verbrecherisch; Kriminal..., Straf...; **2.** Verbrecher(in), Kriminelle(r *m*) *f.*

crimp [krɪmp] kräuseln.

crim·son [ˈkrɪmzn] karmesinrot; puterrot.

cringe [krɪndʒ] sich ducken.

crin·kle [ˈkrɪŋkl] **1.** Falte *f*, im Ge-

sicht: Fältchen *n*; **2.** (sich) kräuseln; knittern.

crip·ple [ˈkrɪpl] **1.** Krüppel *m*; **2.** zum Krüppel machen; *fig.* lähmen.

cri·sis [ˈkraɪsɪs] (*pl. -ses* [-siːz]) Krisis *f*, Krise *f*; Wende-, Höhepunkt *m.*

crisp [krɪsp] **1.** □ kraus; knusp(e)rig, mürbe (*Gebäck*); frisch; klar; steif; **2.** (sich) kräuseln; knusp(e)rig machen od. werden; **3.** ~**s** *pl.*, *a. potato* ~**s** *pl. Brt.* (Kartoffel)Chips *pl.*; **~·bread** [ˈkrɪspbred] Knäckebrot *n.*

criss·cross [ˈkrɪskrɒs] **1.** Netz *n* sich schneidender Linien; **2.** (durch-) kreuzen.

cri·te·ri·on [kraɪˈtɪərɪən] (*pl. -ria* [-rɪə], *-rions*) Kriterium *n.*

crit|ic [ˈkrɪtɪk] Kritiker(in); △ *nicht Kritik*; **~·i·cal** □ [~kl] kritisch; bedenklich; **~·i·cis·m** [~ɪsɪzəm] Kritik *f* (*of an dat.*); **~·i·cize** [~saɪz] kritisieren; kritisch beurteilen; tadeln.

cri·tique [krɪˈtiːk] kritischer Essay, Kritik *f.*

croak [krəʊk] krächzen; quaken.

cro·chet [ˈkrəʊʃeɪ] **1.** Häkelei *f*; Häkelarbeit *f*; **2.** häkeln.

crock·er·y [ˈkrɒkərɪ] Geschirr *n.*

croc·o·dile *zo.* [ˈkrɒkədaɪl] Krokodil *n.*

crone F [krəʊn] altes Weib.

cro·ny F [ˈkrəʊnɪ] alter Freund.

crook [krʊk] **1.** Krümmung *f*; Haken *m*; Hirtenstab *m*; F Gauner *m*; **2.** (sich) krümmen *od.* (ver)biegen; **~ed** [ˈkrʊkɪd] krumm; bucklig; F unehrlich; [krʊkt] Krück...

croon [kruːn] schmalzig singen; summen; **~·er** [ˈkruːnə] Schnulzensänger(in).

crop [krɒp] **1.** *zo.* Kropf *m*; Peitschenstiel *m*; Reitpeitsche *f*; (Feld-) Frucht *f*, *bsd.* Getreide *n*; Ernte *f*; kurzer Haarschnitt *m*; **2.** (*-pp-*) abfressen, abweiden; *Haar* kurz schneiden; ~ *up fig.* plötzlich auftauchen.

cross [krɒs] **1.** Kreuz *n* (*a. fig. Leiden*); Kreuzung *f*; **2.** □ sich kreuzend, quer (liegend, laufend *etc.*); ärgerlich, böse; entgegengesetzt; Kreuz..., Quer...; **3.** *v/t.* kreuzen; überqueren; *fig.* durchkreuzen; j-m in die Quere kommen; ~ *off*, ~ *out* aus-, durchstreichen; ~ *o.s.* sich bekreuzigen; *keep one's fingers ~ed* den Daumen halten; *v/i.* sich kreuzen; **~·bar** [ˈkrɒsbɑː] *Fußball:* Torlatte *f*; **~·breed** (Rassen)Kreuzung *f*; **~coun·try** Querfeldein..., Gelände...; ~ *skiing* Skilanglauf *m*; **~ex·am·i·na·tion** Kreuzverhör *n*; **~ex·am·ine** ins Kreuzverhör nehmen; **~eyed** schielen; *be* ~ schielen; **~ing** [~ɪŋ] Kreuzung *f*; Übergang *m*; ⚓ Überfahrt *f*; **~road** Querstraße *f*; **~roads** *pl. od. sg.* Straßenkreuzung *f*; *fig.* Scheideweg *m*; **~sec·tion** Querschnitt *m*; **~walk** *Am.* Fußgängerübergang *m*; **~wise** kreuzweise; **~word** (*puz·zle*) Kreuzworträtsel *n*.

crotch [krɒtʃ] Schritt *m* (*des Körpers, der Hose*).

crotch·et ['krɒtʃɪt] Haken *m*; *bsd. Br.* ♩ Viertelnote *f*.

crouch [krautʃ] **1.** sich ducken; **2.** Hockstellung *f*.

crow [krəʊ] **1.** *zo.* Krähe *f*; Krähen *n*; **2.** (*crowed od.* crew, *crowed*) krähen; (*crowed*) F prahlen (*about* mit).

crow·bar ['krəʊbɑ:] Brecheisen *n*.

crowd [kraʊd] **1.** Masse *f*, Menge *f*, Gedränge *n*; F Bande *f*; **2.** sich drängen; *Straßen etc.* bevölkern; vollstopfen; **~ed** ['kraʊdɪd] überfüllt, voll.

crown [kraʊn] **1.** Krone *f*; Kranz *m*; Gipfel *m*; Scheitel *m*; **2.** krönen; *Zahn* überkronen; *to* ~ *all* zu allem Überfluß.

cru·cial □ ['kru:ʃl] entscheidend, kritisch.

cru·ci·fix ['kru:sɪfɪks] Kruzifix *n*; **~fix·ion** [kru:sɪ'fɪkʃn] Kreuzigung *f*; **~fy** ['kru:sɪfaɪ] kreuzigen.

crude □ [kru:d] roh; unfertig; unreif; unfein; grob; Roh...; grell.

cru·el □ [krʊəl] (*-ll-*) grausam; roh, gefühllos; **~ty** ['krʊəltɪ] Grausamkeit *f*; ~ *to animals* Tierquälerei *f*; ~ *to children* Kindesmißhandlung *f*.

cru·et ['kru:ɪt] Essig-, Ölfläschchen *n*.

cruise ⚓ [kru:z] **1.** Kreuzfahrt *f*, Seereise *f*; ~ *missile* ⚔ ✈ Marschflugkörper *m*; **2.** kreuzen, e-e Kreuzfahrt machen; *mit* Reisegeschwindigkeit fliegen *od.* fahren; **cruis·er** ['kru:zə] ⚔ ✈ Kreuzer *m*; Jacht *f*; Kreuzfahrtschiff *n*; *Am.* (*Funk-*)Streifenwagen *m*.

crumb [krʌm] **1.** Krume *f*; Brocken *m*; **2.** panieren; zerkrümeln; **crumble** ['krʌmbl] (zer)bröckeln; *fig.* zugrunde gehen.

crum·ple ['krʌmpl] *v/t.* zerknittern;

v/i. knittern; zusammengedrückt werden.

crunch [krʌntʃ] (zer)kauen; zermalmen; knirschen.

cru·sade [kru:'seɪd] Kreuzzug *m* (*a. fig.*); **~sad·er** *hist.* [~ə] Kreuzfahrer *m*.

crush [krʌʃ] **1.** Druck *m*; Gedränge *n*; (*Frucht*)Saft *m*; F Schwärmerei *f*; *have a* ~ *on* s.o. in j-n verliebt od. verknallt sein; **2.** *v/t.* (zer-, aus)quetschen; zermalmen; *fig.* vernichten; *v/i.* sich drängen; **~bar·ri·er** ['krʌʃbærɪə] Barriere *f*, Absperrung *f*.

crust [krʌst] **1.** Kruste *f*; Rinde *f*; **2.** verkrusten; verharschen.

crus·ta·cean *zo.* [krʌ'steɪʃn] Krebs-, Krusten-, Schalentier *n*.

crust·y □ ['krʌstɪ] (*-ier, -iest*) krustig; *fig.* mürrisch, barsch.

crutch [krʌtʃ] Krücke *f*.

cry [kraɪ] **1.** Schrei *m*; Geschrei *n*; Ruf *m*; Weinen *n*; Gebell *n*; **2.** schreien; (aus)rufen; weinen; ~ *for* verlangen nach.

crypt [krɪpt] Gruft *f*; **cryp·tic** ['krɪptɪk] (*~ally*) verborgen, geheim; rätselhaft.

crys·tal ['krɪstl] Kristall *m*; *Am.* Uhrglas *n*; **~line** [~təlaɪn] kristallen; **~lize** [~aɪz] kristallisieren.

cub [kʌb] **1.** Junge(s) *n*; Flegel *m*; Anfänger *m*; **2.** (*Junge*) werfen.

cube [kju:b] Würfel *m* (*a.* ♣); *phot.* Blitzwürfel *m*; ♣ Kubikzahl *f*; ~ *root* ♣ Kubikwurzel *f*; **cu·bic** ['kju:bɪk] (*~ally*), **cu·bi·cal** □ [~kl] würfelförmig, kubisch; Kubik...

cu·bi·cle ['kju:bɪkl] Kabine *f*.

cuck·oo *zo.* ['kʊku:] (*pl. -oos*) Kuckuck *m*.

cu·cum·ber ['kju:kʌmbə] Gurke *f*; *as cool as a* ~ *fig.* eiskalt, gelassen.

cud [kʌd] wiedergekäutes Futter; *chew the* ~ wiederkäuen; *fig.* überlegen.

cud·dle ['kʌdl] *v/t.* an sich drücken; schmusen (mit).

cud·gel ['kʌdʒəl] **1.** Knüppel *m*; **2.** (*bsd. Brt. -ll-, Am. -l-*) prügeln.

cue [kju:] *Billard:* Queue *n*; *thea. etc.*, *a. fig.* Stichwort *n*; Wink *m*.

cuff [kʌf] **1.** Manschette *f*; Handschelle *f*; (*Ärmel-, Am. a.* Hosen-)Aufschlag *m*; Schlag *m* (*mit der offenen Hand*); Klaps *m*; **2.** (*mit der flachen Hand*) schlagen.

cui·sine [kwiˈziːn] Küche f (*Koch-kunst*).

cul·mi·nate [ˈkʌlmɪneɪt] gipfeln (*in* in *dat.*).

cu·lottes [kjuˈlɒts] *pl.* (*a pair of* ein) Hosenrock *m*.

cul·pa·ble □ [ˈkʌlpəbl] strafbar.

cul·prit [ˈkʌlprɪt] Angeklagte(r *m*) f; Schuldige(r *m*) f, Täter(in).

cul·ti·vate [ˈkʌltɪveɪt] ✍ kultivieren, bestellen, an-, bebauen; *Freund-schaft etc.* pflegen; **~·vat·ed** ✍ bebaut; *fig.* gebildet, kultiviert; **~·va·tion** [kʌltɪˈveɪʃn] ✍ Kultivierung f, (An-, Acker)Bau *m*; *fig.* Pflege f.

cul·tu·ral □ [ˈkʌltʃərəl] kulturell; Kultur...

cul·ture [ˈkʌltʃə] Kultur f; Zucht f; **~d** kultiviert (*a. fig.*); Zucht...

cum·ber·some [ˈkʌmbəsəm] lästig, hinderlich; klobig.

cu·mu·la·tive □ [ˈkjuːmjʊlətɪv] sich (an-, auf)häufend, anwachsend; Zusatz...

cun·ning [ˈkʌnɪŋ] **1.** □ schlau, listig, gerissen; geschickt; *Am.* niedlich; **2.** List f, Schlauheit f, Gerissenheit f; Geschicklichkeit f.

cup [kʌp] **1.** Tasse f; Becher *m*; Schale f; Kelch *m*; *Sport:* Cup *m*, Pokal *m*; **~ final** Pokalendspiel *n*; **~ winner** Pokalsieger *m*; **2.** (*-pp-*) *die Hand* hohl machen; *she ~ped her chin in her hand* sie stützte das Kinn in die Hand; **~·board** [ˈkʌbəd] (Geschirr-, Speise-, *Brt. a.* Wäsche-, Kleider)Schrank *m*; **~ bed** Schrankbett *n*.

cu·pid·i·ty [kjuːˈpɪdətɪ] Habgier f.

cu·po·la [ˈkjuːpələ] Kuppel *m*.

cur [kɜː] Köter *m*; Schurke *m*.

cur·a·ble [ˈkjʊərəbl] heilbar.

cu·rate [ˈkjʊərət] Hilfsgeistliche(r *m*.

curb [kɜːb] **1.** Kandare f (*a. fig.*); *bsd. Am.* = *kerb*(*stone*); **2.** an die Kandare legen (*a. fig.*); *fig.* zügeln.

curd [kɜːd] **1.** Quark *m*; **2.** *mst* **cur·dle** [ˈkɜːdl] gerinnen (lassen); *the sight made my blood ~* bei dem Anblick erstarrte mir das Blut in den Adern.

cure [kjʊə] **1.** Kur f; Heilmittel *n*; Heilung f; Seelsorge f; Pfarre f; **2.** heilen; pökeln; räuchern; trocknen.

cur·few ✗ [ˈkɜːfjuː] Ausgangsverbot *n*, -sperre f.

cu·ri·o [ˈkjʊərɪəʊ] (*pl. -os*) Rarität f; **~·os·i·ty** [kjʊərɪˈɒsətɪ] Neugier f; Rarität f; **~·ous** □ [ˈkjʊərɪəs] neu-

gierig; wißbegierig; seltsam, merk-würdig.

curl [kɜːl] **1.** Locke f; **2.** (sich) kräuseln *od.* locken; **~·er** [ˈkɜːlə] Lockenwickler *m*; **~·y** [~ɪ] (*-ier, -iest*) gekräuselt; gelockt, lockig.

cur·rant [ˈkʌrənt] ♣ Johannisbeere f; Korinthe f.

cur·ren·cy [ˈkʌrənsɪ] Umlauf *m*; *econ.* Laufzeit f; *econ.* Währung f; *foreign ~* Devisen *pl.*; **~·rent** [~t] **1.** □ umlaufend; *econ.* gültig (*Geld*); allgemein (bekannt); geläufig; laufend (*Jahr etc.*); gegenwärtig, aktuell; **2.** Strom *m* (*a. ⚡*); Strömung f (*a. fig.*); (*Luft*)Zug *m*; **~·rent account** *econ.* Girokonto *n*.

cur·ric·u·lum [kəˈrɪkjʊləm] (*pl. -la* [-lə], *-lums*) Lehr-, Stundenplan *m*; **~ vi·tae** [~ˈvaɪtiː] Lebenslauf *m*.

cur·ry¹ [ˈkʌrɪ] Curry *m, n*.

cur·ry² [~] *Pferd* striegeln.

curse [kɜːs] **1.** Fluch *m*; △*nicht Kurs*; **2.** (ver)fluchen; strafen; **curs·ed** □ [ˈkɜːsɪd] verflucht.

cur·sor [ˈkɜːsə] ⚙ Läufer *m*, Schieber *m* (*am Rechenschieber*); *Computer:* Positionsanzeiger *m* (*auf dem Bildschirm*).

cur·so·ry □ [ˈkɜːsrɪ] flüchtig, oberflächlich.

curt □ [kɜːt] kurz, knapp; barsch.

cur·tail [kɜːˈteɪl] beschneiden; *fig.* beschränken; kürzen (*of* um).

cur·tain [ˈkɜːtn] **1.** Vorhang *m*, Gardine f; *draw the ~s* den Vorhang *od.* die Vorhänge zuziehen *od.* aufziehen; **2. ~ off** mit Vorhängen abteilen.

curt·s(e)y [ˈkɜːtsɪ] **1.** Knicks *m*; **2.** knicksen (*to vor dat.*).

cur·va·ture [ˈkɜːvətʃə] Krümmung f.

curve [kɜːv] **1.** Kurve f; Krümmung f; **2.** (sich) krümmen *od.* biegen.

cush·ion [ˈkʊʃn] **1.** Kissen *n*, Polster *n*; *Billardtisch:* Bande f; **2.** polstern.

cuss F [kʌs] **1.** Fluch *m*; **2.** (ver)fluchen.

cus·tard [ˈkʌstəd] Eiercreme f.

cus·to·dy [ˈkʌstədɪ] Haft f; Gewahrsam *m*; Obhut f.

cus·tom [ˈkʌstəm] Gewohnheit f, Brauch *m*, Sitte f; *econ.* Kundschaft f; **~·a·ry** □ [~ərɪ] gewöhnlich, üblich; **~·built** nach Kundenangaben gefertigt; **~·er** [~ə] Kunde *m*, -in f; F Bursche *m*; **~·house** Zollamt *n*; **~·made** maßgefertigt, Maß...

cus·toms [ˈkʌstəmz] *pl.* Zoll *m*; **~**

clear·ance Zollabfertigung *f*; ~ **of-fi·cer**, ~ **of·fi·cial** Zollbeamte(r) *m*.

cut [kʌt] 1. Schnitt *m*; Hieb *m*; Stich *m*; (Schnitt)Wunde *f*; Einschnitt *m*; Graben *m*; Kürzung *f*; Ausschnitt *m*; Wegabkürzung *f* (*mst short-~*); (*Holz*)Schnitt *m*; (*Kupfer*)Stich *m*; Schliff *m*; Schnitte *f*, Scheibe *f*; *Karten*: Abheben *n*; cold ~s *pl*. Küche: Aufschnitt *m*; give s.o. the ~ direct F j-n ostentativ schneiden; 2. (*-tt-*; *cut*) schneiden; schnitzen; gravieren; ab-, an-, auf-, aus-, be-, durch-, zer-, zuschneiden; kürzen; *Edelstein etc.* schleifen; *Karten* abheben; j-n beim *Begegnen* schneiden; ~ teeth zahnen; ~ short j-n unterbrechen; ~ across quer durch... gehen (*um abzukürzen*); ~ back *Pflanze* beschneiden, stutzen; kürzen; einschränken; herabsetzen; ~ down *Bäume* fällen; verringern, einschränken, reduzieren; ~ in F sich einschalten; ~ in on s.o. mot. j-n schneiden; ~ off abschneiden; *teleph.* *Teilnehmer* trennen; j-n enterben; ~ out ausschneiden; *Am. Vieh* aussondern (*aus der Herde*); *fig.* j-n ausstechen; be ~ out for das Zeug zu et. haben; ~ up zerschneiden; be ~ up F tief betrübt sein; **~·back** [ˈkʌtbæk] Kürzung *f*; Herabsetzung *f*, Verringerung *f*.

cute □ F [kjuːt] (*~r*, *~st*) schlau; *Am.* niedlich, süß.

cu·ti·cle [ˈkjuːtɪkl] Nagelhaut *f*.

cut·le·ry [ˈkʌtlərɪ] (Tisch-, Eß)Besteck *n*.

cut·let [ˈkʌtlɪt] Schnitzel *n*; Hacksteak *n*.

cut|-price *econ.* [ˈkʌtpraɪs], **~·rate** ermäßigt, herabgesetzt; Billig...; **~·ter** [~ə] (Blech-, Holz)Schneider *m*; Schnitzer *m*; Zuschneider(in); (Glas- *etc.*)Schleifer *m*; *Film*: Cutter(in); ⊕ Schneidewerkzeug *n*, -maschine *f*; ⚓ Kutter *m*; *Am.* leichter Schlitten; **~·throat** Mörder *m*; Killer *m*; **~·ting** [~ɪŋ] 1. □ schneidend; scharf; ⊕ Schneid..., Fräs...; 2. Schneiden *n*; 🔪 *etc.* Einschnitt *m*; 🌱 Steckling *m*; *bsd. Brt.* (*Zeitungs-*)Ausschnitt *m*; ~s *pl.* Schnipsel *pl.*; ⊕ Späne *pl.*

cy·cle¹ [ˈsaɪkl] Zyklus *m*; Kreis(lauf) *m*; Periode *f*.

cy·cle² [~] 1. Fahrrad *n*; 2. radfahren; **cy·clist** [~lɪst] Radfahrer(in); Motorradfahrer(in).

cy·clone [ˈsaɪkləʊn] Wirbelsturm *m*.

cyl·in·der [ˈsɪlɪndə] Zylinder *m*, Walze *f*; ⊕ Trommel *f*.

cym·bal ♪ [ˈsɪmbl] Becken *n*.

cyn|ic [ˈsɪnɪk] Zyniker *m*; **~·i·cal** □ [~kl] zynisch.

cy·press 🌱 [ˈsaɪprɪs] Zypresse *f*.

cyst 🔬 [sɪst] Zyste *f*.

czar *hist.* [zɑː] = tsar.

Czech [tʃek] 1. tschechisch; 2. Tscheche *m*, -in *f*; *ling.* Tschechisch *n*.

Czech·o·slo·vak [ˈtʃekəʊˈsləʊvæk] 1. Tschechoslowake *m*, -in *f*; 2. tschechoslowakisch.

D

dab [dæb] 1. Klaps *m*; Tupfen *m*, Klecks *m*; 2. (*-bb-*) leicht schlagen *od.* klopfen; be-, abtupfen.

dab·ble [ˈdæbl] bespritzen; betupfen; plätschern; sich oberflächlich *od.* (*contr.*) in dilettantischer Weise befassen (*at*, *in* mit).

dachs·hund *zo.* [ˈdækshʊnd] Dackel *m*.

dad F [dæd], **~·dy** F [ˈdædɪ] Papa *m*, Vati *m*.

dad·dy-long·legs *zo.* [ˈdædɪˈlɒŋlegz] Schnake *f*; *Am.* Weberknecht *m*.

daf·fo·dil 🌱 [ˈdæfədɪl] gelbe Narzisse.

daft F [dɑːft] blöde, doof.

dag·ger [ˈdægə] Dolch *m*; be at ~s drawn *fig.* auf Kriegsfuß stehen.

dai·ly [ˈdeɪlɪ] 1. täglich; 2. Tageszeitung *f*; Putzfrau *f*.

dain·ty [ˈdeɪntɪ] 1. □ (*-ier*, *-iest*) lecker; zart; zierlich, niedlich, reizend; wählerisch; 2. Leckerbissen m.

dair·y ['deərı] Molkerei f; Milchwirtschaft f; Milchgeschäft n; ~ **cattle** Milchvieh n; ~**man** (pl. -men) Melker m; Milchmann m.

dai·sy ♀ ['deɪzɪ] Gänseblümchen n.

dale dial. od. poet. [deɪl] Tal n.

dal·ly ['dælɪ] (ver)trödeln; schäkern.

dam[1] zo. [dæm] Mutter(tier n) f.

dam[2] [~] 1. Deich m, (Stau)Damm m; 2. (-mm-) a. ~ up stauen, (ab-, ein-) dämmen (a. fig.).

dam·age ['dæmɪdʒ] 1. Schaden m, (Be)Schädigung f; ~s pl. ⚖ Schadensersatz m; 2. (be)schädigen.

dam·ask ['dæməsk] Damast m.

dame Am. F [deɪm] Weib n; △ nicht Dame.

damn [dæm] 1. verdammen; verurteilen; ~ (it)! F verflucht!, verdammt!; 2. adj. u. adv. F = damned; 3. I don't care a ~ F das ist mir völlig gleich(gültig) od. egal; **dam·na·tion** [dæm'neɪʃn] Verdammung f; Verurteilung f; ~**ed** F [dæmd] verdammt; ~**ing** ['dæmɪŋ] vernichtend, belastend.

damp [dæmp] 1. □ feucht, klamm; 2. Feuchtigkeit f; 3. a. ~**en** ['dæmpən] an-, befeuchten; dämpfen; ~**ness** [~nɪs] Feuchtigkeit f.

dance [dɑːns] 1. Tanz m; Tanz(veranstaltung f) m; 2. tanzen (lassen); **danc·er** ['dɑːnsə] Tänzer(in); **danc·ing** [~ɪŋ] Tanzen n; attr. Tanz...

dan·de·li·on ♀ ['dændɪlaɪən] Löwenzahn m.

dan·dle ['dændl] wiegen, schaukeln.

dan·druff ['dændrʌf] (Kopf)Schuppen pl.

Dane [deɪn] Dän|e m, -in f.

dan·ger ['deɪndʒə] 1. Gefahr f; be in ~ of doing s.th. Gefahr laufen et. zu tun; be out of ~ ⚕ über den Berg sein; 2. Gefahren...; ~ area, ~ zone Gefahrenzone f, -bereich m; ~**ous** □ [~rəs] gefährlich.

dan·gle ['dæŋgl] baumeln (lassen).

Da·nish ['deɪnɪʃ] 1. dänisch; 2. ling. Dänisch n.

dank [dæŋk] feucht, naß(kalt).

dap·per ['dæpə] adrett; flink.

dap·pled ['dæpld] scheckig.

dare [deə] v/i. es wagen; I ~ say, I ~say ich glaube wohl; allerdings; v/t. et. wagen; j-n herausfordern; trotzen (dat.); ~**dev·il** ['deədevl]

Draufgänger m, Teufelskerl m; **dar·ing** □ [~rɪŋ] 1. kühn; waghalsig; 2. Mut m, Kühnheit f.

dark [dɑːk] 1. □ dunkel; brünett; geheim(nisvoll); trüb(selig); 2. Dunkel(heit f) n; before (at, after) ~ vor (bei, nach) Einbruch der Dunkelheit; keep s.o. in the ~ about s.th. j-n über et. im ungewissen lassen; 2 **Ag·es** pl. das frühe Mittelalter; ~**en** ['dɑːkən] (sich) verdunkeln od. verfinstern; ~**ness** [~nɪs] Dunkelheit f, Finsternis f.

dar·ling ['dɑːlɪŋ] 1. Liebling m; 2. Lieblings...; geliebt.

darn [dɑːn] stopfen, ausbessern.

dart [dɑːt] 1. Wurfspieß m; Wurfpfeil m; Sprung m, Satz m; ~s sg. Darts n (Wurfpfeilspiel); ~**board** Dartsscheibe f; 2. v/t. werfen, schleudern; v/i. schießen, stürzen.

dash [dæʃ] 1. Schlag m; Klatschen n; Schwung m; Ansturm m; fig. Anflug m; Prise f; Schuß m (Rum etc.); (Feder)Strich m; Gedankenstrich m; Sport: Sprint m; 2. v/t. schlagen, werfen, schleudern, schmettern; Hoffnung zunichte machen; v/i. stürzen, stürmen, jagen, rasen; schlagen; ~**board** mot. ['dæʃbɔːd] Armaturenbrett n; ~**ing** □ [~ɪŋ] schneidig, forsch; flott, F fesch.

da·ta ['deɪtə] pl., a. sg. Daten pl., Einzelheiten pl., Angaben pl., Unterlagen pl.; Computer: Daten pl.; ~ **bank** Datenbank f; ~ **in·put** Dateneingabe f; ~ **out·put** Datenausgabe f; ~ **pro·cess·ing** Datenverarbeitung f; ~ **pro·tec·tion** Datenschutz m; ~ **typ·ist** Datentypist(in).

date[1] ♀ [deɪt] Dattel f.

date[2] [~] 1. Datum n; Zeit(punkt m) f; Termin m; Verabredung f; Am. F (Verabredungs)Partner(in); out of ~ veraltet, unmodern; up to ~ zeitgemäß, modern, auf dem laufenden; 2. datieren; Am. F sich verabreden mit, ausgehen mit, (regelmäßig) gehen mit; **dat·ed** ['deɪtɪd] veraltet, überholt.

da·tive gr. ['deɪtɪv] a. ~ case Dativ m, dritter Fall.

daub [dɔːb] (be)schmieren; (be)klecksen.

daugh·ter ['dɔːtə] Tochter f; ~**in-law** [~rɪnlɔː] (pl. daughters-in-law) Schwiegertochter f.

daunt [dɔːnt] entmutigen; ~**less** ['dɔːntlɪs] furchtlos, unerschrocken.

daw *zo.* [dɔː] Dohle *f.*

daw·dle F ['dɔːdl] (ver)trödeln.

dawn [dɔːn] **1.** (Morgen)Dämmerung *f*, Tagesanbruch *m*; **2.** dämmern, tagen; *it ~ed on od. upon him fig.* es wurde ihm langsam klar.

day [deɪ] Tag *m*; *oft ~s pl.* (Lebens)Zeit *f*; *~ off* (dienst)freier Tag; *carry od. win the ~* den Sieg davontragen; *any ~* jederzeit; *these ~s* heutzutage; *the other ~* neulich; *this ~ week* heute in e-r Woche; heute vor e-r Woche; *let's call it a ~!* machen wir Schluß für heute!, Feierabend!; **~·break** Tagesanbruch *m*; **~·light** Tageslicht *n*; *in broad ~* am hellichten Tag; **~·time**: *in the ~* am Tag, bei Tage.

daze [deɪz] **1.** blenden; betäuben; **2.** *in a ~* benommen, betäubt.

dead [ded] **1.** tot; unempfindlich (*to* für); matt (*Farbe etc.*); blind (*Fenster etc.*); erloschen (*Feuer*); schal (*Getränk*); tief (*Schlaf*); *econ.* still, ruhig, flau; *econ.* tot (*Kapital etc.*); völlig, absolut, total; *~ bargain* Spottpreis *m*; *~ letter* unzustellbarer Brief; *~ loss* Totalverlust *m*; *a ~ shot* ein Meisterschütze; **2.** *adv.* gänzlich, völlig, total; plötzlich, abrupt; genau, (haar)scharf; *~ tired* todmüde; *~ against* ganz u. gar gegen; **3.** *the ~* der, die, das Tote; die Toten *pl.*; *in the ~ of winter* im tiefsten Winter; *in the ~ of night* mitten in der Nacht; **~·cen·tre**, *Am.* **~·cen·ter** genaue Mitte; **~·en** ['dedn] abstumpfen; dämpfen; (ab)schwächen; **~ end** Sackgasse *f* (*a. fig.*); **~ heat** *Sport*: totes Rennen; **~·line** *Am.* Sperrlinie *f*, Todesstreifen *m* (*im Gefängnis*); letzter (Ablieferungs)Termin; Stichtag *m*; **~·lock** *fig.* toter Punkt; **~·locked** *fig.* festgefahren (*Verhandlungen*); **~·ly** [~lɪ] (-*ier*, -*iest*) tödlich.

deaf [def] **1.** □ taub; *~ and dumb* taubstumm; **2.** *the ~ pl.* die Tauben *pl.*; **~·en** ['defn] taub machen; betäuben.

deal [diːl] **1.** Teil *m*; Menge *f*; *Karten*: Geben *n*; F Geschäft *n*; Abmachung *f*; *a good ~* ziemlich viel; *a great ~* sehr viel; **2.** (*dealt*) *v/t.* (aus-, ver-, zu)teilen; *Karten* geben; *e-n Schlag* versetzen; *v/i.* handeln (*in mit* e-r *Ware*); *sl.* dealen (*mit Rauschgift handeln*); *Karten*: geben; *~ with sich befassen mit, behandeln; econ.* Han-

del treiben mit, in Geschäftsverbindung stehen mit; **~·er** ['diːlə] *econ.* Händler(in); *Karten*: Geber(in); *sl.* Dealer *m* (*Rauschgifthändler*); **~·ing** [~ɪŋ] Verhalten *n*, Handlungsweise *f*; *econ.* Geschäftsgebaren *n*; *~s pl.* Umgang *m*, (Geschäfts)Beziehungen *pl.*; **~t** [delt] *pret. u. p.p. von* deal 2.

dean [diːn] Dekan *m.*

dear [dɪə] **1.** □ teuer; lieb; **2.** Liebste(r *m*) *f*, Schatz *m*; *my ~* m-e Liebe, mein Lieber; **3.** *int.* (*oh*) *~!, ~ ~!, ~ me!* F du liebe Zeit!, ach herrje!; **~·ly** ['dɪəlɪ] innig, von ganzem Herzen; teuer (*im Preis*).

death [deθ] Tod *m*; Todesfall *m*; **~·bed** ['deθbed] Sterbebett *n*; **~·less** [~lɪs] unsterblich; **~·ly** [~lɪ] (-*ier*, -*iest*) tödlich; **~·war·rant** ᵗᵗₛ Hinrichtungsbefehl *m*; *fig.* Todesurteil *n.*

de·bar [dɪ'bɑː] (-*rr*-): *~ from doing s.th.* j-n hindern et. zu tun.

de·base [dɪ'beɪs] erniedrigen.

de·ba·ta·ble □ [dɪ'beɪtəbl] strittig; umstritten; **de·bate** [dɪ'beɪt] **1.** Debatte *f*; **2.** debattieren; erörtern; sich et. überlegen.

de·bil·i·tate [dɪ'bɪlɪteɪt] schwächen.

deb·it *econ.* ['debɪt] **1.** Debet *n*, Soll *n*; (Konto)Belastung *f*; *~ and credit* Soll *n* u. Haben *n*; **2.** j-n, *ein Konto* belasten.

de·bris ['debriː] Trümmer *pl.*

debt [det] Schuld *f*; *be in ~* verschuldet sein; *be out of ~* schuldenfrei sein; **~·or** ['detə] Schuldner(in).

de·bug ⊕ [diː'bʌg] (-*gg*-) Fehler beseitigen (*a. Computer*).

de·bunk ['diː'bʌŋk] den Nimbus nehmen (*dat.*).

dé·but, *bsd. Am.* **de·but** ['deɪbuː] Debüt *n.*

dec·ade ['dekeɪd] Jahrzehnt *n.*

dec·a|dence ['dekədəns] Dekadenz *f*, Verfall *m*; **~·dent** □ [~t] dekadent.

de·caf·fein·at·ed ['diː'kæfɪneɪtɪd] koffeinfrei.

de·camp [dɪ'kæmp] *bsd.* ✕ das Lager abbrechen; F verschwinden.

de·cant [dɪ'kænt] abgießen; umfüllen; **~·er** [~ə] Karaffe *f.*

de·cath|lete [dɪ'kæθliːt] *Sport*: Zehnkämpfer *m*; **~·lon** [~lɒn] *Sport*: Zehnkampf *m.*

de·cay [dɪ'keɪ] **1.** Verfall *m*; Zerfall *m*; Fäule *f*; **2.** verfallen; (ver)faulen.

de·cease bsd. ⚖️ [dɪˈsiːs] 1. Tod m, Ableben n; 2. sterben; **~d** bsd. ⚖️ 1. the ~ der od. die Verstorbene; der Verstorbenen pl.; 2. ver-, gestorben.

de·ceit [dɪˈsiːt] Täuschung f; Betrug m; **~·ful** [~fl] falsch; betrügerisch.

de·ceive [dɪˈsiːv] betrügen; täuschen; **de·ceiv·er** [~ə] Betrüger(in).

De·cem·ber [dɪˈsembə] Dezember m.

de·cen|cy [ˈdiːsnsɪ] Anstand m; **~t** [~t] anständig; F annehmbar, (ganz) anständig; F nett; ⚠ nicht dezent.

de·cep|tion [dɪˈsepʃn] Täuschung f; **~tive** [~tɪv]: be ~ täuschen, trügen (Sache).

de·cide [dɪˈsaɪd] (sich) entscheiden; bestimmen; sich entschließen; **de·cid·ed** □ entschieden; bestimmt; entschlossen.

dec·i·mal [ˈdesɪml] a. ~ fraction Dezimalbruch m; attr. Dezimal...

de·ci·pher [dɪˈsaɪfə] entziffern.

de·ci|sion [dɪˈsɪʒn] Entscheidung f; Entschluß m; Entschlossenheit f; make a ~ e-e Entscheidung treffen; reach od. come to a ~ zu e-m Entschluß kommen; **~sive** □ [dɪˈsaɪsɪv] entscheidend; ausschlaggebend; entschieden.

deck [dek] 1. ⚓ Deck n (a. e-s Busses); Am. Pack m Spielkarten; Laufwerk n (e-s Plattenspielers); tape~ Tapedeck n; 2. ~ out schmücken; **~-chair** [ˈdektʃeə] Liegestuhl m.

de·claim [dɪˈkleɪm] deklamieren, vortragen.

dec·la·ra·ble [dɪˈkleərəbl] zollpflichtig.

dec·la·ra·tion [dekləˈreɪʃn] Erklärung f; Zollerklärung f.

de·clare [dɪˈkleə] (sich) erklären, bekanntgeben; behaupten; deklarieren, verzollen.

de·clen·sion gr. [dɪˈklenʃn] Deklination f.

dec·li·na·tion [deklɪˈneɪʃn] Neigung f; Abweichung f; **de·cline** [dɪˈklaɪn] 1. Abnahme f; Niedergang m, Verfall m; 2. v/t. neigen; (höflich) ablehnen; gr. deklinieren; v/i. sich neigen; abnehmen; verfallen.

de·cliv·i·ty [dɪˈklɪvətɪ] Abhang m.

de·clutch mot. [ˈdiːˈklʌtʃ] auskuppeln.

de·code [ˈdiːˈkəud] entschlüsseln.

de·com·pose [diːkəmˈpəuz] zerlegen; (sich) zersetzen; verwesen.

dec·o·rate [ˈdekəreɪt] verzieren, schmücken; tapezieren; (an)streichen; dekorieren; **~ra·tion** [dekəˈreɪʃn] Verzierung f, Schmuck m, Dekoration f; Orden m; **~ra·tive** □ [ˈdekərətɪv] dekorativ; Zier...; **~ra·tor** [~reɪtə] Dekorateur m; Maler m u. Tapezierer m.

dec·o·rous □ [ˈdekərəs] anständig; **de·co·rum** [dɪˈkɔːrəm] Anstand m.

de·coy 1. [ˈdiːkɔɪ] Lockvogel m (a. fig.); Köder m (a. fig.); 2. [dɪˈkɔɪ] ködern; locken (into in acc.); verleiten (into zu).

de·crease 1. [ˈdiːkriːs] Abnahme f; 2. [diːˈkriːs] (sich) vermindern.

de·cree [dɪˈkriː] 1. Dekret n, Verordnung f, Erlaß m; ⚖️ Entscheid m; 2. ⚖️ entscheiden; verordnen, verfügen.

ded·i·cate [ˈdedɪkeɪt] widmen; **~cat·ed** engagiert; **~ca·tion** [dedɪˈkeɪʃn] Widmung f; Hingabe f.

de·duce [dɪˈdjuːs] ableiten; folgern.

de·duct [dɪˈdʌkt] abziehen; einbehalten; **de·duc·tion** [~kʃn] Abzug m; econ. a. Rabatt m; Schlußfolgerung f, Schluß m.

deed [diːd] 1. Tat f; Heldentat f; ⚖️ (Vertrags-, bsd. Übertragungs)Urkunde f; 2. Am. ⚖️ urkundlich übertragen (to dat., auf acc.).

deem [diːm] v/t. halten für; v/i. denken, urteilen (of über acc.).

deep [diːp] 1. □ tief; gründlich; schlau; vertieft; dunkel (a. fig.); verborgen; 2. Tiefe f; poet. Meer n; **~en** [ˈdiːpən] (sich) vertiefen; (sich) verstärken; **~-freeze** 1. (-froze, -frozen) tiefkühlen u. einfrieren; 2. Tiefkühl-, Gefriergerät n; 3. Tiefkühl..., Gefrier...; ~ cabinet Tiefkühltruhe f, Gefriertruhe f; **~-fro·zen** tiefgefroren; ~ food Tiefkühlkost f; **~-fry** fritieren; **~ness** [~nɪs] Tiefe f.

deer zo. [dɪə] Rotwild n; Hirsch m.

de·face [dɪˈfeɪs] entstellen; unkenntlich machen; ausstreichen.

def·a·ma·tion [defəˈmeɪʃn] Verleumdung f; **de·fame** [dɪˈfeɪm] verleumden.

de·fault [dɪˈfɔːlt] 1. Nichterscheinen n vor Gericht; Sport: Nichtantreten n; econ. Verzug m; 2. ~ on etc. Verbindlichkeiten nicht nachkommen; im Verzug sein; nicht (vor Gericht) erscheinen; Sport: nicht antreten.

de·feat [dɪˈfiːt] 1. Niederlage f; Besiegung *f*; Vereitelung *f*; **2.** besiegen; vereiteln, zunichte machen.

de·fect [dɪˈfekt] Defekt *m*, Fehler *m*; Mangel *m*; **de·fec·tive** □ [~ɪv] mangelhaft; schadhaft, defekt.

de·fence, *Am.* **de·fense** [dɪˈfens] Verteidigung *f*; Schutz *m*; *witness for the* ~ Entlastungszeuge *m*; **~·less** [~lɪs] schutzlos, wehrlos.

de·fend [dɪˈfend] *(from, against)* verteidigen (gegen), schützen (vor *dat.*, gegen); **de·fen·dant** [~ənt] Angeklagte(r *m*) *f*; Beklagte(r *m*) *f*; **de·fend·er** [~ə] Verteidiger(in).

de·fen·sive [dɪˈfensɪv] **1.** Defensive *f*, Verteidigung *f*, Abwehr *f*; **2.** □ defensiv; Verteidigungs..., Abwehr...

de·fer [dɪˈfɜː] *(-rr-)* auf-, verschieben; *Am.* ✕ (vom Wehrdienst) zurückstellen; sich fügen, nachgeben. **def·er·ence** [ˈdefərəns] Ehrerbietung *f*; Nachgiebigkeit *f*; **~·en·tial** □ [defəˈrenʃl] ehrerbietig.

de·fi·ance [dɪˈfaɪəns] Herausforderung *f*; Trotz *m*; **~·ant** □ [~t] herausfordernd; trotzig.

de·fi·cien·cy [dɪˈfɪʃnsɪ] Unzulänglichkeit *f*; Mangel *m*; = *deficit*; **~·t** □ [~t] mangelhaft, unzureichend.

def·i·cit *econ.* [ˈdefɪsɪt] Fehlbetrag *m*.

de·file 1. [ˈdiːfaɪl] Engpaß *m*; **2.** [dɪˈfaɪl] beschmutzen.

de·fine [dɪˈfaɪn] definieren; erklären, genau bestimmen; **def·i·nite** □ [ˈdefɪnɪt] bestimmt; deutlich, genau; **def·i·ni·tion** [defɪˈnɪʃn] Definition *f*, (Begriffs)Bestimmung *f*, Erklärung *f*; **de·fin·i·tive** □ [dɪˈfɪnɪtɪv] endgültig; maßgeblich.

de·flect [dɪˈflekt] ablenken; abweichen.

de·form [dɪˈfɔːm] entstellen, verunstalten; **~ed** deformiert, verunstaltet; verwachsen; **de·for·mi·ty** [~ətɪ] Entstelltheit *f*; Mißbildung *f*.

de·fraud [dɪˈfrɔːd] betrügen (*of* um).

de·frost [diːˈfrɒst] *v/t.* Windschutzscheibe entfrosten; *Kühlschrank etc.* abtauen, *Tiefkühlkost* auftauen; *v/i.* ab-, auftauen.

deft □ [deft] gewandt, flink.

de·fy [dɪˈfaɪ] herausfordern; trotzen (*dat.*).

de·gen·er·ate 1. [dɪˈdʒenəreɪt] entarten; **2.** □ [~rət] entartet.

deg·ra·da·tion [degrəˈdeɪʃn] Erniedrigung *f*; **de·grade** [dɪˈgreɪd] *v/t.* erniedrigen, demütigen.

de·gree [dɪˈgriː] Grad *m*; Stufe *f*, Schritt *m*; Rang *m*; Stand *m*; *by* ~*s* allmählich; *take one's* ~ e-n akademischen Grad erwerben, promovieren.

de·hy·drat·ed [ˈdiːˈhaɪdreɪtɪd] Trokken...

de·i·fy [ˈdiːɪfaɪ] vergöttern; vergöttlichen.

deign [deɪn] sich herablassen.

de·i·ty [ˈdiːɪtɪ] Gottheit *f*.

de·ject·ed □ [dɪˈdʒektɪd] niedergeschlagen, mutlos, deprimiert; **~·tion** [~kʃn] Niedergeschlagenheit *f*.

de·lay [dɪˈleɪ] **1.** Aufschub *m*; Verzögerung *f*; **2.** *v/t.* ver-, aufschieben; verzögern; aufhalten; *v/i.* ~ *in doing s.th.* es verschieben, et. zu tun.

del·e·gate 1. [ˈdelɪgeɪt] abordnen; übertragen; **2.** [~gət] *(Am. parl.* Kongreß)Abgeordnete(r *m*) *f*; **~·ga·tion** [delɪˈgeɪʃn] Abordnung *f*; *Am. parl.* Kongreßabgeordnete *pl.*

de·lete [dɪˈliːt] tilgen, (aus)streichen, (aus)radieren.

de·lib·e·rate 1. [dɪˈlɪbəreɪt] *v/t.* überlegen, erwägen; *v/i.* nachdenken, beraten; **2.** □ [~rət] bedachtsam; wohlüberlegt; vorsätzlich; **~·ra·tion** [dɪlɪbəˈreɪʃn] Überlegung *f*; Beratung *f*; Bedächtigkeit *f*.

del·i·ca·cy [ˈdelɪkəsɪ] Delikatesse *f*, Leckerbissen *m*; Zartheit *f*; Schwächlichkeit *f*; Feingefühl *n*; **~·cate** □ [~kət] schmackhaft, lecker; zart; fein; schwach; heikel; empfindlich; *a.* feinfühlig; wählerisch; **~·ca·tes·sen** [delɪkəˈtesn] Delikatessen *pl.*, Feinkost *f*; Delikatessen-, Feinkostgeschäft *n*.

de·li·cious □ [dɪˈlɪʃəs] köstlich.

de·light [dɪˈlaɪt] **1.** Lust *f*, Freude *f*, Wonne *f*; **2.** entzücken; (sich) erfreuen; ~ *in* (große) Freude haben an (*dat.*); **~·ful** □ [~fl] entzückend.

de·lin·e·ate [dɪˈlɪnɪeɪt] entwerfen; schildern.

de·lin·quen·cy [dɪˈlɪŋkwənsɪ] Kriminalität *f*; Straftat *f*; ~ Straffälligkeit *f*; **2.** Straffällige(r *m*) *f*; *s. juvenile 1.*

de·lir·i·ous □ [dɪˈlɪrɪəs] 🌶 phantasierend; wahnsinnig; **~·um** [~əm] Delirium *n*.

de·liv·er [dɪˈlɪvə] befreien; über-, aus-, abliefern; *bsd. econ.* liefern; *Botschaft* ausrichten; äußern; *Rede etc.* halten; *Schlag* austeilen; werfen;

✻ entbinden; *be* ~*ed of a child* entbunden werden, entbinden; **~ance** [~rəns] Befreiung *f*; (Meinungs)Äußerung *f*; **~er** [~rə] Befreier(in); Überbringer(in); **~y** [~rɪ] (Ab-, Aus)Lieferung *f*; **&** Zustellung *f*; Übergabe *f*; Halten *n* (*e-r Rede etc.*); **⚓** Entbindung *f*; **~y van** *Brt.* Lieferwagen *m*.

dell [del] kleines Tal.

de·lude [dɪ'lu:d] täuschen; verleiten.

del·uge ['delju:dʒ] **1.** Überschwemmung *f*; **2.** überschwemmen.

de·lu·sion [dɪ'lu:ʒn] Täuschung *f*, Verblendung *f*, Wahn *m*; **~sive** □ [~sɪv] trügerisch, täuschend.

de·mand [dɪ'mɑ:nd] **1.** Verlangen *n*; Forderung *f*; Anforderung (*on an acc.*), Inanspruchnahme *f* (*on gen.*); *econ.* Nachfrage *f*, Bedarf *m*; **⚖** Rechtsanspruch *m*; **2.** verlangen, fordern; erfordern; **~ing** [~ɪŋ] fordernd; anspruchsvoll; schwierig.

de·mean [dɪ'mi:n]: ~ *o.s.* sich benehmen; sich erniedrigen; **de·mea·no(u)r** [~ə] Benehmen *n*.

de·ment·ed □ [dɪ'mentɪd] wahnsinnig.

dem·i- ['demɪ] Halb...

dem·i·john ['demɪdʒɒn] große Korbflasche, Glasballon *m*.

de·mil·i·ta·rize ['di:'mɪlɪtəraɪz] entmilitarisieren.

de·mo·bi·lize [di:'məʊbɪlaɪz] demobilisieren.

de·moc·ra·cy [dɪ'mɒkrəsɪ] Demokratie *f*.

dem·o·crat ['deməkræt] Demokrat(in); **~ic** [demə'krætɪk] (~*ally*) demokratisch.

de·mol·ish [dɪ'mɒlɪʃ] demolieren; ab-, ein-, niederreißen; zerstören; **dem·o·li·tion** [demə'lɪʃn] Demolierung *f*; Niederreißen *n*, Abbruch *m*.

de·mon ['di:mən] Dämon *m*; Teufel *m*.

dem·on·strate ['demənstreɪt] anschaulich darstellen; beweisen; demonstrieren; **~stra·tion** [demən-'streɪʃn] Demonstration *f*, Kundgebung *f*; Demonstration *f*, Vorführung *f*; anschauliche Darstellung; Beweis *m*; (Gefühls)Äußerung *f*.

de·mon·stra·tive □ [dɪ'mɒnstrə-tɪv] überzeugend; demonstrativ; *be* ~ s-e Gefühle (offen) zeigen; **~stra·tor** ['demənstreɪtə] Demonstrant(in); Vorführer(in).

de·mote [di:'məʊt] degradieren.

de·mur [dɪ'mɜ:] (-*rr*-) Einwendungen machen.

de·mure □ [dɪ'mjʊə] ernst; prüde.

den [den] Höhle *f*, Bau *m*; Bude *f*; Arbeitszimmer *n*.

de·ni·al [dɪ'naɪəl] Leugnen *n*; Verneinung *f*; abschlägige Antwort.

den·ims ['denɪmz] *pl.* Overall *m* od. Jeans *pl.* aus Köper

de·nom·i·na·tion [dɪnɒmɪ'neɪʃn] *eccl.* Sekte *f*; *eccl.* Konfession *f*; *econ.* Nennwert *m* (*von Banknoten etc.*).

de·note [dɪ'nəʊt] bezeichnen; bedeuten.

de·nounce [dɪ'naʊns] anzeigen; brandmarken; *Vertrag* kündigen.

dense □ [dens] (~*r*, ~*st*) dicht, dick (*Nebel*); beschränkt; **den·si·ty** ['densətɪ] Dichte *f*.

dent [dent] **1.** Beule *f*, Delle *f*; Kerbe *f*; **2.** ver-, einbeulen.

den·tal ['dentl] Zahn...; ~ *plaque* Zahnbelag *m*; ~ *plate* Zahnprothese *f*; ~ *surgeon* Zahnarzt *m*; **~tist** [~tɪst] Zahnarzt *m*, -ärztin *f*; **~tures** [~ʃəz] *pl.* (künstliches) Gebiß.

de·nun·ci·a·tion [dɪnʌnsɪ'eɪʃn] Anzeige *f*, Denunziation *f*; **~tor** [dɪ-'nʌnsɪeɪtə] Denunziant(in).

de·ny [dɪ'naɪ] ab-, bestreiten, (ab-) leugnen; verweigern, abschlagen; *j-n* abweisen.

de·part [dɪ'pɑ:t] abreisen; abfahren, abfliegen; abweichen.

de·part·ment [dɪ'pɑ:tmənt] Abteilung *f*; Bezirk *m*; *econ.* Branche *f*; *pol.* Ministerium *n*; ♀ *of Defense Am.* Verteidigungsministerium *n*; ♀ *of the Environment Brt.* Umweltschutzministerium *n*; ♀ *of the Interior Am.* Innenministerium *n*; ♀ *of State Am.*, *State* ♀ *Am.* Außenministerium *n*; ~ *store* Warenhaus *n*.

de·par·ture [dɪ'pɑ:tʃə] Abreise *f*, **⚓** *etc.* Abfahrt *f*, **✈** Abflug *m*; Abweichung *f*; ~ *gate* **✈** Flugsteig *m*; ~ *lounge* **✈** Abflughalle *f*.

de·pend [dɪ'pend]: ~ *on*, ~ *upon* abhängen von; angewiesen sein auf (*acc.*); sich verlassen auf (*acc.*); ankommen auf (*acc.*); *it* ~*s* Er kommt (ganz) darauf an.

de·pen·da·ble [dɪ'pendəbl] zuverlässig; **~dant** [~ənt] Abhängige(r *m*) *f*, *bsd.* (Familien)Angehörige(r *m*) *f*; **~dence** [~əns] Abhängigkeit *f*; Vertrauen *n*; **~den·cy** [~ənsɪ] *pol.*

Schutzgebiet *n*; ~**dent** [~ənt] **1.** □ (*on*) abhängig (von); angewiesen (auf *acc.*); **2.** *Am.* = *dependant*.

de·pict [dɪ'pɪkt] darstellen; schildern.

de·plor|a·ble □ [dɪ'plɔ:rəbl] bedauerlich, beklagenswert; ~**e** [dɪ'plɔ:] beklagen, bedauern.

de·pop·u·late [di:'pɒpjʊleɪt] (sich) entvölkern.

de·port [dɪ'pɔ:t] *Ausländer* abschieben; ~ *o.s.* sich *gut etc.* benehmen; ~**ment** [~mənt] Benehmen *n*.

de·pose [dɪ'pəʊz] absetzen; *ža* unter Eid aussagen.

de·pos|it [dɪ'pɒzɪt] **1.** Ablagerung *f*; Lager *n*; (*Bank*)Einlage *f*; Hinterlegung *f*; Anzahlung *f*; make a ~ e-e Anzahlung leisten; ~ *account Brt.* Termineinlagekonto *n*; **2.** (nieder-, ab-, hin)legen; *Geld* einzahlen; *Betrag* anzahlen; hinterlegen; (sich) ablagern; **dep·o·si·tion** [depə'zɪʃn] Absetzung *f*; (zu Protokoll gegebene) eidliche Aussage; ~**i·tor** [dɪ'pɒzɪtə] Hinterleger(in); Einzahler(in); Kontoinhaber(in).

dep·ot ['depəʊ] Depot *n*; Lagerhaus *n*; *Am.* ['di:pəʊ] Bahnhof *m*.

de·prave [dɪ'preɪv] moralisch verderben.

de·pre·ci·ate [dɪ'pri:ʃɪeɪt] *Wert* mindern.

de·press [dɪ'pres] (nieder)drücken; *Preise etc.* senken, drücken; deprimieren, bedrücken; ~**ed** deprimiert, niedergeschlagen; **de·pres·sion** [~eʃn] Vertiefung *f*, Senke *f*; Depression *f*, Niedergeschlagenheit *f*; *econ.* Depression *f*, Flaute *f*, Wirtschaftskrise *f*; *𝄐* Schwäche *f*.

de·prive [dɪ'praɪv]: ~ *s.o. of s.th.* j-m et. entziehen *od.* nehmen; ~**d** benachteiligt, unterprivilegiert.

depth [depθ] Tiefe *f*; *attr.* Tiefen...

dep·u|ta·tion [depjʊ'teɪʃn] Abordnung *f*; ~**tize** ['depjʊtaɪz]: ~ *for s.o.* j-n vertreten; ~**ty** [~ɪ] *parl.* Abgeordnete(r *m*) *f*; Stellvertreter(in), Beauftragte(r *m*) *f*; Bevollmächtigte(r *m*) *f*; *a.* ~ *sheriff Am.* Hilfssheriff *m*.

de·rail *⚏* [dɪ'reɪl] *v/i.* entgleisen; *v/t.* zum Entgleisen bringen.

de·range [dɪ'reɪndʒ] in Unordnung bringen; stören; verrückt *od.* wahnsinnig machen; ~**d** geistesgestört.

der·e·lict ['derəlɪkt] verlassen; nachlässig.

de·ride [dɪ'raɪd] verlachen, -spotten; **de·ri·sion** [dɪ'rɪʒn] Hohn *m*, Spott *m*; **de·ri·sive** □ [dɪ'raɪsɪv] spöttisch, höhnisch.

de·rive [dɪ'raɪv] herleiten, (her)kommen (*from* aus); *et.* gewinnen (*from* aus); *Nutzen etc.* ziehen (*from* aus).

de·rog·a·to·ry □ [dɪ'rɒgətərɪ] abfällig, geringschätzig.

der·rick ['derɪk] ⊕ Derrickkran *m*; *⚓* Ladebaum *m*; Bohrturm *m*.

de·scend [dɪ'send] ⊕ (her-, hin)absteigen, herunter-, hinuntersteigen, herabkommen; *⚏* niedergehen; (ab)stammen; *on*, ~ *upon* herfallen über (*acc.*); einfallen in (*acc.*); **de·scen·dant** [~ənt] Nachkomme *m*.

de·scent [dɪ'sent] Herab-, Hinuntersteigen *n*, Abstieg *m*; *⚏* Niedergehen *n*; Abhang *m*, Gefälle *n*; Abstammung *f*; *fig.* Niedergang *m*, Abstieg *m*.

de·scribe [dɪ'skraɪb] beschreiben.

de·scrip|tion [dɪ'skrɪpʃn] Beschreibung *f*, Schilderung *f*; Art *f*; ~**tive** □ [~tɪv] beschreibend; anschaulich.

des·e·crate ['desɪkreɪt] entweihen.

de·seg·re·gate [di:'segrɪgeɪt] die Rassentrennung aufheben in (*dat.*).

des·ert¹ ['dezət] **1.** Wüste *f*; **2.** Wüsten...

de·sert² [dɪ'zɜ:t] *v/t.* verlassen; *v/i.* desertieren; ~**er** *⚔* [~ə] Deserteur *m*, Fahnenflüchtige(r) *m*; **de·ser·tion** [~ʃn] (*ža 𝄐.* böswilliges) Verlassen; *⚔* Fahnenflucht *f*.

de·serve [dɪ'zɜ:v] verdienen; **de·serv·ed·ly** [~ɪdlɪ] mit Recht; **de·serv·ing** [~ɪŋ] würdig (*of gen.*); verdienstvoll, verdient.

de·sign [dɪ'zaɪn] **1.** Plan *m*; Entwurf *m*, Zeichnung *f*; Muster *n*; Vorhaben *n*, Absicht *f*; have ~s on *od.* against et. im Schilde führen gegen; **2.** entwerfen, ⊕ konstruieren; gestalten, planen; bestimmen.

des·ig|nate ['dezɪgneɪt] bezeichnen; ernennen, bestimmen; ~**na·tion** [dezɪg'neɪʃn] Bezeichnung *f*; Bestimmung *f*, Ernennung *f*.

de·sign·er [dɪ'zaɪnə] (Muster)Zeichner(in); Designer(in); ⊕ Konstrukteur *m*; (Mode)Schöpfer(in).

de·sir|a·ble □ [dɪ'zaɪərəbl] wünschenswert; angenehm; ~**e** [dɪ'zaɪə]

1. Wunsch m, Verlangen n; Begierde f; **2.** verlangen, wünschen; begehren; **~ous** □ [~rəs] begierig.

de·sist [dɪˈzɪst] ablassen (*from* von).

desk [desk] n; Pult n; Schreibtisch m.

des·o·late □ [ˈdesələt] einsam; verlassen; öde.

de·spair [dɪˈspeə] **1.** Verzweiflung f; **2.** verzweifeln (*of an dat.*); **~ing** □ [~rɪŋ] verzweifelt.

de·spatch [dɪˈspætʃ] = dispatch.

des·per|ate □ [ˈdespərət] verzweifelt; hoffnungslos; f schrecklich; **~a·tion** [despəˈreɪʃn] Verzweiflung f.

des·pic·a·ble □ [ˈdespɪkəbl] verachtenswert, verabscheuungswürdig.

de·spise [dɪˈspaɪz] verachten.

de·spite [dɪˈspaɪt] **1.** Verachtung f; *in ~ of* zum Trotz, trotz; **2.** *prp. a. ~ of* trotz.

de·spon·dent □ [dɪˈspɒndənt] mutlos, verzagt.

des·pot [ˈdespɒt] Despot m, Tyrann m; **~is·m** [~pətɪzəm] Despotismus m.

des·sert [dɪˈzɜːt] Nachtisch m, Dessert n; *attr.* Dessert...

des|ti·na·tion [destɪˈneɪʃn] Bestimmung(sort m) f; **~tined** [ˈdestɪnd] bestimmt; **~ti·ny** [~ɪ] Schicksal n.

des·ti·tute □ [ˈdestɪtjuːt] mittellos, notleidend; *~ of bar* (*gen.*), ohne.

de·stroy [dɪˈstrɔɪ] zerstören, vernichten; töten, *Tier a.* einschläfern; **~er** [~ə] Zerstörer(in); ♣ ✕ Zerstörer m.

de·struc·tion [dɪˈstrʌkʃn] Zerstörung f, Vernichtung f; Tötung f, *e-s Tiers a.* Einschläferung f; **~tive** □ [~tɪv] zerstörend, vernichtend; zerstörerisch.

de·sul·to·ry □ [ˈdesəltərɪ] unstet; planlos; oberflächlich.

de·tach [dɪˈtætʃ] losmachen, (ab)lösen; absondern; ✕ abkommandieren; **~ed** einzeln (stehend); unvoreingenommen; distanziert; **~ment** [~mənt] Loslösung f; (Ab)Trennung f; ✕ (Sonder)Kommando n.

de·tail [ˈdiːteɪl] **1.** Detail n, Einzelheit f; eingehende Darstellung; ✕ (Sonder)Kommando n; *in ~* ausführlich; **2.** genau schildern; ✕ abkommandieren; **~ed** detailliert, ausführlich.

de·tain [dɪˈteɪn] aufhalten; *j-n in* (Untersuchungs)Haft (be)halten.

de·tect [dɪˈtekt] entdecken; (auf)finden; **de·tec·tion** [~kʃn] Entdeckung

f; **de·tec·tive** [~tɪv] Kriminalbeamte(r) m, Detektiv m; *~ novel, ~ story* Kriminalroman m.

de·ten·tion [dɪˈtenʃn] Vorenthaltung f; Aufhaltung f; Haft f.

de·ter [dɪˈtɜː] (*-rr-*) abschrecken (*from* von).

de·ter·gent [dɪˈtɜːdʒənt] Reinigungsmittel n; Waschmittel n; Geschirrspülmittel n.

de·te·ri·o·rate [dɪˈtɪərɪəreɪt] (sich) verschlechtern; verderben; entarten.

de·ter|mi·na·tion [dɪtɜːmɪˈneɪʃn] Entschlossenheit f; Entscheidung f, Entschluß m; **~mine** [dɪˈtɜːmɪn] bestimmen; (sich) entscheiden; sich entschließen; **~mined** entschlossen.

de·ter|rence [dɪˈterəns] Abschreckung f; **~rent** [~t] **1.** abschreckend; **2.** Abschreckungsmittel n.

de·test [dɪˈtest] verabscheuen; **~a·ble** □ [~əbl] abscheulich.

de·throne [dɪˈθrəʊn] entthronen.

de·to·nate [ˈdetəneɪt] explodieren (lassen).

de·tour [ˈdiːtʊə] Umweg m; Umleitung f.

de·tract [dɪˈtrækt]: *~ from s.th.* et. beeinträchtigen; et. schmälern.

de·tri·ment [ˈdetrɪmənt] Schaden m.

deuce [djuːs] Zwei f (*im Spiel*); *Tennis:* Einstand m; f Teufel m; *how the ~* wie zum Teufel.

de·val·u·a·tion [ˈdiːvæljuˈeɪʃn] Abwertung f; **~e** [ˈdiːˈvæljuː] abwerten.

dev·a·state [ˈdevəsteɪt] verwüsten; **~stat·ing** □ [~ɪŋ] verheerend, -nichtend; f umwerfend; **~sta·tion** [devəˈsteɪʃn] Verwüstung f.

de·vel·op [dɪˈveləp] (sich) entwickeln; (sich) entfalten; *Gelände* erschließen; *Altstadt etc.* sanieren; ausbauen; (sich) zeigen; **~ing** [~ɪŋ] *phot.* Entwickler m; (Stadt)Planer m; **~ing** [~ɪŋ] Entwicklungs...; *~ country econ.* Entwicklungsland n; **~ment** [~mənt] Entwicklung f; Entfaltung f; Erschließung f; Ausbau m; *~ aid econ.* Entwicklungshilfe f.

de·vi·ate [ˈdiːvɪeɪt] abweichen; **~a·tion** [diːvɪˈeɪʃn] Abweichung f.

de·vice [dɪˈvaɪs] Vor-, Einrichtung f, Gerät n; Erfindung f; Plan m; Kunstgriff m, Kniff m; Devise f, Motto n; *leave s.o. to his own ~s* j-n sich selbst überlassen.

dev·il ['devl] Teufel m (a. fig.); **~ish** □ [~lʃ] teuflisch.

de·vi·ous □ ['diːvjəs] abwegig; gewunden; unaufrichtig; *take a ~ route* e-n Umweg machen.

de·vise □ [dɪ'vaɪz] ausdenken, ersinnen; ⚖ vermachen.

de·void [dɪ'vɔɪd]: *~ of* bar (*gen.*), ohne.

de·vote [dɪ'vəʊt] widmen, *et.* hingeben, opfern (*to dat.*); △ *nicht* devot; **de·vot·ed** □ ergeben; eifrig, begeistert; zärtlich; **dev·o·tee** [devəʊ'tiː] begeisterter Anhänger; **de·vo·tion** [dɪ'vəʊʃn] Ergebenheit f; Hingabe f; Frömmigkeit f, Andacht f.

de·vour [dɪ'vaʊə] verschlingen.

de·vout □ [dɪ'vaʊt] andächtig; fromm; sehnlichst.

dew [djuː] Tau m; **~y** ['djuːɪ] (*-ier, -iest*) (tau)feucht.

dex·ter·i·ty [dek'sterətɪ] Gewandtheit f; **~ter·ous, ~trous** □ ['dekstrəs] gewandt.

di·ag·nose ['daɪəɡnəʊz] diagnostizieren; **~no·sis** [daɪəɡ'nəʊsɪs] (*pl. -ses* [-siːz]) Diagnose f.

di·a·gram ['daɪəɡræm] graphische Darstellung, Schema n, Plan m.

di·al ['daɪəl] **1.** Zifferblatt n; *teleph.* Wählscheibe f; ⊕ Skala f; **2.** (*bsd. Brt. -ll-, Am. -l-*) *teleph.* wählen; *~ direct* durchwählen (*to nach*); *direct ~(l)ing* Durchwahl f.

di·a·lect ['daɪəlekt] Dialekt m; Mundart f.

di·a·logue, *Am.* **-log** ['daɪəlɒɡ] Dialog m, Gespräch n.

di·am·e·ter [daɪ'æmɪtə] Durchmesser m; *in ~* im Durchmesser.

di·a·mond ['daɪəmənd] Diamant m; Rhombus m; *Baseball:* Spielfeld n; *Karten:* Karo n.

di·a·per *Am.* ['daɪəpə] Windel f.

di·a·phragm ['daɪəfræm] *anat.* Zwerchfell n; *opt.* Blende f; *teleph.* Membran(e) f.

di·ar·rh(o)e·a ⸸ [daɪə'rɪə] Durchfall m.

di·a·ry ['daɪərɪ] Tagebuch n.

dice [daɪs] **1.** *pl. von* die[2]; **2.** würfeln; **~box** ['daɪsbɒks], **~cup** Würfelbecher m.

dick *Am. sl.* [dɪk] Schnüffler m (*Detektiv*).

dick·(e)y(-bird) ['dɪkɪ(bɜːd)] Piepvögelchen n.

dic|tate [dɪk'teɪt] diktieren; *fig.* vor- schreiben; **~ta·tion** [~ʃn] Diktat n.

dic·ta·tor [dɪk'teɪtə] Diktator m; **~ship** [~ʃɪp] Diktatur f.

dic·tion ['dɪkʃn] Ausdruck(sweise f) m, Stil m.

dic·tion·a·ry ['dɪkʃnrɪ] Wörterbuch n.

did [dɪd] *pret. von* do.

die[1] [daɪ] sterben; umkommen; untergehen; absterben; *~ away* sich legen (*Wind*); verklingen (*Ton*); verlöschen (*Licht*); *~ down* nachlassen; herunterbrennen; schwächer werden; *~ off* wegsterben; *~ out* aussterben (*a. fig.*).

die[2] [~] (*pl.* dice [daɪs]) Würfel m; (*pl.* dies [daɪz]) Prägestock m, -stempel m.

die-hard ['daɪhɑːd] Reaktionär m.

di·et ['daɪət] **1.** Diät f; Nahrung f, Kost f; *be on a ~* diät leben; **2.** diät leben.

dif·fer ['dɪfə] sich unterscheiden; anderer Meinung sein (*with, from* als); abweichen.

dif·fe|rence ['dɪfrəns] Unterschied m; Differenz f; Meinungsverschiedenheit f; **~rent** □ [~t] verschieden; andere(r, -s); anders (*from* als); **~ren·ti·ate** [dɪfə'renʃɪeɪt] (sich) unterscheiden.

dif·fi|cult ['dɪfɪkəlt] schwierig; **~cul·ty** [~ɪ] Schwierigkeit f.

dif·fi|dence ['dɪfɪdəns] Schüchternheit f; **~dent** □ [~t] schüchtern.

dif·fuse 1. *fig.* [dɪ'fjuːz] verbreiten; **2.** □ [as] weitverbreitet, zerstreut (*bsd. Licht*); weitschweifig; **~fu·sion** [~ʒn] Verbreitung f.

dig [dɪɡ] **1.** (*-gg-; dug*) graben (in *dat.*); *oft ~ up* umgraben; *oft ~ up, ~ out* ausgraben (*a. fig.*); **2.** F Ausgrabung(sstätte) f; F Puff m, Stoß m; **~s** *pl. Brt.* F Bude f, (Studenten)Zimmer n.

di·gest [dɪ'dʒest] *v/t.* verdauen (*a. fig.*); ordnen; *v/i.* verdaulich sein; **2.** [daɪdʒest] Abriß m; Auslese f, Auswahl f; **~i·ble** □ [dɪ'dʒestəbl] verdaulich; **di·ges·tion** [~tʃən] Verdauung f; **di·ges·tive** □ [~tɪv] verdauungsfördernd.

dig·ger ['dɪɡə] (*bsd.* Gold)Gräber m.

di·git ['dɪdʒɪt] Ziffer f; *three-~ number* dreistellige Zahl; **di·gi·tal** □ [~tl] digital, Digital...; *~ clock, ~ watch* Digitaluhr f.

dig·ni·fied ['dıgnıfaıd] würdevoll, würdig.

dig·ni·ta·ry ['dıgnıtərı] Würdenträger(in).

dig·ni·ty ['dıgnıtı] Würde f.

di·gress [daı'gres] abschweifen.

dike¹ [daık] 1. Deich m, Damm m; Graben m; 2. eindeichen, -dämmen.

dike² sl. [∼] Lesbe f (Lesbierin).

di·lap·i·dat·ed [dı'læpıdeıtıd] verfallen, baufällig, klapp(e)rig.

di·late [daı'leıt] (sich) ausdehnen; Augen weit öffnen; **dil·a·to·ry** □ ['dılətərı] verzögernd, hinhaltend; aufschiebend; langsam.

dil·i·gence ['dılıdʒəns] Fleiß m; **∼gent** □ [∼nt] fleißig, emsig.

di·lute [daı'lju:t] 1. verdünnen; verwässern; 2. verdünnt.

dim [dım] 1. □ (-mm-) trüb(e); dunkel; matt; 2. (-mm-) (sich) verdunkeln; abblenden; (sich) trüben; matt werden.

dime Am. [daım] Zehncentstück n.

di·men·sion [dı'menʃn] Dimension f, Abmessung f; **∼s** pl. a. Ausmaß n; **∼al** [∼ʃnl] dimensional; **three-∼** dreidimensional.

di·min·ish [dı'mınıʃ] (sich) vermindern; abnehmen.

di·min·u·tive □ [dı'mınjʊtıv] klein, winzig.

dim·ple ['dımpl] Grübchen n.

din [dın] Getöse n, Lärm m.

dine [daın] essen, speisen; bewirten; **∼ in** od. **out** zu Hause od. auswärts essen; **din·er** ['daınə] Speisende(r m) f; Gast m (im Restaurant); bsd. Am. 🚃 Speisewagen m; Am. Speiselokal n.

din·gy □ ['dındʒı] (-ier, -iest) schmutzig.

din·ing· car 🚃 ['daınıŋkɑ:] Speisewagen m; **∼ room** Eß-, Speisezimmer n.

din·ner ['dınə] (Mittag-, Abend)Essen n; Festessen n; **∼jack·et** Smoking m; **∼par·ty** Tischgesellschaft f; **∼ser·vice, ∼set** Speiseservice n, Tafelgeschirr n.

dint [dınt] 1. Beule f; by ∼ of kraft, vermöge (gen.); 2. ver-, einbeulen.

dip [dıp] 1. (-pp-) v/t. (ein)tauchen; senken; schöpfen; ∼ the headlights bsd. Brt. mot. abblenden; v/i. (unter)tauchen; sinken; sich neigen, sich senken; 2. (Ein-, Unter)Tauchen n; kurzes Bad; Senkung f,

Neigung f, Gefälle n; Dip m (Soße).

diph·ther·i·a 🔬 [dıf'θıərıə] Diphtherie f.

di·plo·ma [dı'pləʊmə] Diplom n.

di·plo·ma·cy [dı'pləʊməsı] Diplomatie f.

dip·lo·mat ['dıpləmæt] Diplomat m; **∼ic** [dıplə'mætık] (∼ally) diplomatisch.

di·plo·ma·tist fig. [dı'pləʊmətıst] Diplomat(in).

dip·per ['dıpə] Schöpfkelle f.

dire ['daıə] (∼r, ∼st) gräßlich, schrecklich.

di·rect [dı'rekt] 1. adj. □ direkt; gerade; unmittelbar; offen, aufrichtig; ∼ current ⚡ Gleichstrom m; ∼ train durchgehender Zug; 2. adv. direkt, unmittelbar; 3. richten; lenken, steuern; leiten; anordnen; j-n anweisen; j-m den Weg zeigen; Brief adressieren; Regie führen bei.

di·rec·tion [dı'rekʃn] Richtung f; Leitung f, Führung f; Adresse f (e-s Briefes etc.); Film etc.: Regie f; mst ∼s pl. Anweisung f, Anleitung f; ∼s for use Gebrauchsanweisung f; △ nicht Direktion; **∼find·er** [∼faındə] (Funk)Peiler m, Peilempfänger m; **∼in·di·ca·tor** mot. Fahrtrichtungsanzeiger m, Blinker m; 🚉 Kursweiser m.

di·rec·tive [dı'rektıv] richtungweisend, leitend.

di·rect·ly [dı'rektlı] 1. adv. sofort; 2. cj. sobald, sowie.

di·rec·tor [dı'rektə] Direktor m; Film etc.: Regisseur m; board of ∼s Aufsichtsrat m.

di·rec·to·ry [dı'rektərı] Adreßbuch n; telephone ∼ Telefonbuch n.

dirge [dɜ:dʒ] Klagelied n.

dir·i·gi·ble ['dırıdʒəbl] 1. lenkbar; 2. lenkbares Luftschiff.

dirt [dɜ:t] Schmutz m; (lockere) Erde; **∼cheap** F ['dɜ:t'tʃi:p] spottbillig; **∼y** [∼ı] 1. □ (-ier, -iest) schmutzig (a. fig.); 2. beschmutzen; schmutzig werden.

dis·a·bil·i·ty [dısə'bılətı] Unfähigkeit f.

dis·a·ble [dıs'eıbl] (⚔ kampf)unfähig machen; ⚔ dienstuntauglich machen; **∼d** 1. arbeits-, erwerbsunfähig, invalid(e); ⚔ dienstuntauglich; ⚔ kriegsversehrt; körperlich od. geistig behindert; 2. the ∼ pl. die Behinderten pl.

dis·ad·van·tage [dɪsəd'vɑ:ntɪdʒ] Nachteil *m*; Schaden *m*; **~ta·geous** □ [dɪsædvɑ:n'teɪdʒəs] nachteilig, ungünstig.

dis·a·gree [dɪsə'gri:] nicht übereinstimmen; uneinig sein; nicht bekommen (*with* s.o. j-m); **~a·ble** □ [~'ɪəbl] unangenehm; **~ment** [~ɪ:mənt] Verschiedenheit *f*, Unstimmigkeit *f*; Meinungsverschiedenheit *f*.

dis·ap·pear [dɪsə'pɪə] verschwinden; **~ance** [~rəns] Verschwinden *n*.

dis·ap·point [dɪsə'pɔɪnt] *j-n* enttäuschen; *Hoffnungen etc.* zunichte machen; **~ment** [~mənt] Enttäuschung *f*.

dis·ap·prov|al [dɪsə'pru:vl] Mißbilligung *f*; **~e** [ˈdɪsə'pru:v] mißbilligen; dagegen sein.

dis|arm [dɪs'ɑ:m] *v/t.* entwaffnen (*a. fig.*); *v/i.* ✕ *pol.* abrüsten; **~ar·ma·ment** [~əmənt] Entwaffnung *f*; ✕ *pol.* Abrüstung *f*.

dis·ar·range [ˈdɪsə'reɪndʒ] in Unordnung bringen.

dis·ar·ray [ˈdɪsə'reɪ] Unordnung *f*.

di·sas|ter [dɪ'zɑ:stə] Unglück(sfall *m*) *n*, Katastrophe *f*; **~trous** □ [~trəs] katastrophal, verheerend.

dis·band [dɪs'bænd] (sich) auflösen.

dis·be|lief [ˈdɪsbɪ'li:f] Unglaube *m*, Zweifel *m* (*in an dat.*); **~lieve** [~'li:v] *et.* bezweifeln, nicht glauben.

disc [dɪsk] Scheibe *f* (*a. anat., zo.,* ⊕); (Schall)Platte *f*; Parkscheibe *f*; ⚠ *nicht Diskus*! *slipped* ~ 🦴 Bandscheibenvorfall *m*.

dis·card [dɪ'skɑ:d] *Karten, Kleid etc.* ablegen; *Freund etc.* fallenlassen.

di·scern [dɪ'sɜ:n] wahrnehmen, erkennen; **~ing** □ [~ɪŋ] kritisch, scharfsichtig; **~ment** [~mənt] Einsicht *f*; Scharfblick *m*; Wahrnehmen *n*.

dis·charge [dɪs'tʃɑ:dʒ] **1.** *v/t.* entladen; *j-n* befreien, entbinden; *j-n* entlassen; *Gewehr etc.* abfeuern; von sich geben, ausströmen, -senden; 🦴 absondern; *Pflicht etc.* erfüllen; *Zorn etc.* auslassen (*on dat.*); *Schuld* bezahlen; *Wechsel* einlösen; *v/i.* ⚡ sich entladen; sich ergießen, münden (*Fluß*); 🦴 eitern; **2.** Entladung *f* (*e-s Schiffes etc.*); Abfeuern *n* (*e-s Gewehrs etc.*); Ausströmen *n*; 🦴 Absonderung *f*; 🦴 Ausfluß *m*; Ausstoßen *n*; ⚡ Entladung *f*; Entlassung

f; Entlastung *f*; Erfüllung *f* (*e-r Pflicht*).

di·sci·ple [dɪ'saɪpl] Schüler *m*; Jünger *m*.

dis·ci·pline ['dɪsɪplɪn] **1.** Disziplin *f*; Bestrafung *f*; **2.** disziplinieren; bestrafen; *well* ~*d* diszipliniert; *badly* ~*d* disziplinlos, undiszipliniert.

disc jock·ey ['dɪskdʒɒkɪ] Disk-, Discjockey *m*.

dis·claim [dɪs'kleɪm] ab-, bestreiten; *Verantwortung* ablehnen; 🏛 verzichten auf (*acc.*).

dis|close [dɪs'kləʊz] bekanntgeben, -machen; enthüllen, aufdecken; **~clo·sure** [~əʊʒə] Enthüllung *f*.

dis·co F ['dɪskəʊ] **1.** (*pl. -cos*) Disko *f* (*Diskothek*); **2.** Disko...; ~ *sound* Diskosound *m*.

dis·col·o(u)r [dɪs'kʌlə] (sich) verfärben.

dis·com·fort [dɪs'kʌmfət] **1.** Unbehagen *n*; Beschwerden *pl.*; **2.** *j-m* Unbehagen verursachen.

dis·con·cert [dɪskən'sɜ:t] aus der Fassung bringen.

dis·con·nect [ˈdɪskə'nekt] trennen (*a. 🦶*); ⊕ auskuppeln; ⚡ *Gerät* abschalten; *Gas, Strom, Telefon* abstellen; *teleph. Gespräch* unterbrechen; **~ed** □ zusammenhang(s)los.

dis·con·so·late □ [dɪs'kɒnsələt] untröstlich, tieftraurig.

dis·con·tent [ˈdɪskən'tent] Unzufriedenheit *f*; **~ed** □ unzufrieden.

dis·con·tin·ue [ˈdɪskən'tɪnju:] aufgeben, aufhören mit; unterbrechen.

dis·cord ['dɪskɔ:d], **~ance** [dɪs'kɔ:dəns] Uneinigkeit *f*; 🎵 Mißklang *m*; **~ant** □ [~t] nicht übereinstimmend; 🎵 unharmonisch, mißtönend.

dis·co·theque ['dɪskətek] Diskothek *f*.

dis·count ['dɪskaʊnt] **1.** *econ.* Diskont *m*; Abzug *m*, Rabatt *m*; **2.** *econ.* diskontieren; abziehen, abrechnen; *Nachricht* mit Vorsicht aufnehmen.

dis·cour·age [dɪs'kʌrɪdʒ] entmutigen; abschrecken; **~ment** [~mənt] Entmutigung *f*; Hindernis *n*, Schwierigkeit *f*.

dis·course 1. ['dɪskɔ:s] Rede *f*; Abhandlung *f*; Predigt *f*; **2.** [dɪ'skɔ:s] e-n Vortrag halten (*on, upon* über *acc.*).

dis·cour·te|ous □ [dɪs'kɜ:tjəs] unhöflich; **~sy** [~təsɪ] Unhöflichkeit *f*.

dis·cov|er [dɪ'skʌvə] entdecken; ausfindig machen; feststellen; **~e·ry** [~ərɪ] Entdeckung f.

dis·cred·it [dɪsˈkredɪt] **1.** Zweifel m; Mißkredit m, schlechter Ruf; **2.** nicht glauben; in Mißkredit bringen.

di·screet □ [dɪˈskriːt] besonnen, vorsichtig; diskret, verschwiegen.

di·screp·an·cy [dɪˈskrepənsɪ] Widerspruch m, Unstimmigkeit f.

di·scre·tion [dɪˈskreʃn] Besonnenheit f, Klugheit f; Takt m; Verschwiegenheit f; Belieben n.

di·scrim·i·nate [dɪˈskrɪmɪneɪt] unterscheiden; **~** *against* benachteiligen; **~·nat·ing** □ [~ɪŋ] unterscheidend; kritisch, urteilsfähig; **~·na·tion** [dɪskrɪmɪˈneɪʃn] Unterscheidung f; unterschiedliche (*bsd.* nachteilige) Behandlung; Urteilskraft f.

dis·cus [ˈdɪskəs] *Sport:* Diskus m; **~** throw Diskuswerfen n; **~** thrower Diskuswerfer(in).

di·scuss [dɪˈskʌs] diskutieren, erörtern, besprechen; **di·scus·sion** [~ʌʃn] Diskussion f, Besprechung f.

dis·dain [dɪsˈdeɪn] **1.** Verachtung f; **2.** geringschätzen, verachten; verschmähen.

dis·ease [dɪˈziːz] Krankheit f; **~d** krank.

dis·em·bark [ˈdɪsɪmˈbɑːk] v/t. ausschiffen; v/i. von Bord gehen.

dis·en·chant·ed [dɪsɪnˈtʃɑːntɪd]: be **~** *with* sich keinen Illusionen mehr hingeben über (*acc.*).

dis·en·gage [ˈdɪsɪnˈgeɪdʒ] (sich) freimachen *od.* lösen; ⊕ loskuppeln.

dis·en·tan·gle [ˈdɪsɪnˈtæŋgl] entwirren; herauslösen (*from* aus).

dis·fa·vo(u)r [ˈdɪsˈfeɪvə] Mißfallen n; Ungnade f.

dis·fig·ure [dɪsˈfɪɡə] entstellen.

dis·grace [dɪsˈgreɪs] **1.** Ungnade f; Schande f; **2.** Schande bringen über (*acc.*), j-m Schande bereiten; be **~d** in Ungnade fallen; **~·ful** □ [~fl] schändlich; skandalös.

dis·guise [dɪsˈgaɪz] **1.** verkleiden (*as* als); verstellen; verschleiern, -bergen; **2.** Verkleidung f; Verstellung f; Verschleierung f; *thea. u. fig.* Maske f; *in* **~** maskiert, verkleidet; *fig.* verkappt; *in* **~** *of* verkleidet als.

dis·gust [dɪsˈgʌst] **1.** Ekel m, Abscheu m; **2.** (an)ekeln; empören, entrüsten; **~·ing** □ [~ɪŋ] ekelhaft.

dish [dɪʃ] **1.** flache Schüssel; (Ser-

vier)Platte f; Gericht n, Speise f; *the* **~es** *pl.* das Geschirr; **2.** *mst* **~** *up* anrichten; auftischen, -tragen; **~** *out* F austeilen; **~·cloth** [ˈdɪʃklɒθ] Geschirrspültuch n.

dis·heart·en [dɪsˈhɑːtn] entmutigen.

di·shev·el(l)ed [dɪˈʃevld] zerzaust.

dis·hon·est □ [dɪsˈɒnɪst] unehrlich, unredlich; **~·y** [~ɪ] Unredlichkeit f.

dis·hon·o(u)r [dɪsˈɒnə] **1.** Unehre f, Schande f; **2.** entehren; schänden; *econ. Wechsel* nicht honorieren *od.* einlösen; **~·o(u)·ra·ble** □ [~rəbl] schändlich, unehrenhaft.

dish|**rag** [ˈdɪʃræg] = dishcloth; **~·wash·er** Spüler(in); Geschirrspülmaschine f, -spüler m; **~·wa·ter** Spülwasser n.

dis·il·lu·sion [dɪsɪˈluːʒn] **1.** Ernüchterung f, Desillusion f; **2.** ernüchtern, desillusionieren; be **~ed** *with* sich keinen Illusionen mehr hingeben über (*acc.*).

dis·in·clined [ˈdɪsɪnˈklaɪnd] abgeneigt.

dis·in·fect [ˈdɪsɪnˈfekt] desinfizieren; **~·fec·tant** [~ənt] Desinfektionsmittel n.

dis·in·her·it [dɪsɪnˈherɪt] enterben.

dis·in·te·grate [dɪsˈɪntɪgreɪt] (sich) auflösen; ver-, zerfallen.

dis·in·terest·ed □ [dɪsˈɪntrəstɪd] uneigennützig, selbstlos; objektiv, unvoreingenommen; △ *mst nicht* desinteressiert.

disk [dɪsk] *bsd. Am.* = *Brt. disc;* *Computer:* Diskette f; **~** *drive* Diskettenlaufwerk n, F Floppy f.

disk·ette [ˈdɪskət, dɪˈsket] *Computer:* Diskette f.

dis·like [dɪsˈlaɪk] **1.** Abneigung f, Widerwille m (*of, for* gegen); *take a* **~** *to* s.o. gegen j-n e-e Abneigung fassen; **2.** nicht mögen.

dis·lo·cate [ˈdɪsləkeɪt] ♂ verrenken; verlagern.

dis·lodge [dɪsˈlɒdʒ] vertreiben, verjagen; entfernen; *Stein etc.* lösen.

dis·loy·al □ [ˈdɪsˈlɔɪəl] treulos.

dis·mal □ [ˈdɪzməl] trüb(e), trostlos, elend.

dis·man·tle [dɪsˈmæntl] abbrechen, niederreißen; ♣ abtakeln; ⊕ abwracken; ⊕ demontieren.

dis·may [dɪsˈmeɪ] **1.** Schrecken m, Bestürzung f; *in* **~**, *with* **~** bestürzt; *to one's* **~** zu s-m Entsetzen; **2.** v/t. erschrecken, bestürzen.

dis·miss [dɪs'mɪs] v/t. entlassen; wegschicken; ablehnen; *Thema etc.* fallenlassen; ⚡ abweisen; **~·al** [~l] Entlassung f; Aufgabe f; ⚡ Abweisung f.

dis·mount ['dɪs'maunt] v/t. aus dem Sattel heben; *Reiter* abwerfen; demontieren; ⊕ auseinandernehmen; v/i. absteigen, absitzen (*from* von *Fahrrad, Pferd etc.*).

dis·o·be·di·ence [dɪsə'biːdjəns] Ungehorsam m; **~·ent** □ [~t] ungehorsam.

dis·o·bey ['dɪsə'beɪ] nicht gehorchen, ungehorsam sein (gegen).

dis·or·der [dɪs'ɔ:də] 1. Unordnung f; Aufruhr m; ⚡ Störung f; 2. in Unordnung bringen; ⚡ angreifen; **~·ly** [~lɪ] unordentlich; ordnungswidrig; unruhig; aufrührerisch.

dis·or·gan·ize [dɪs'ɔːgənaɪz] durcheinanderbringen; desorganisieren.

dis·own [dɪs'əun] nicht anerkennen; *Kind* verstoßen; ablehnen.

di·spar·age [dɪ'spærɪdʒ] verächtlich machen, herabsetzen; geringschätzen.

di·spar·i·ty [dɪ'spærətɪ] Ungleichheit f; **~ of** od. *in age* Altersunterschied m.

dis·pas·sion·ate □ [dɪ'spæʃnət] leidenschaftslos; objektiv.

di·spatch [dɪ'spætʃ] 1. schnelle Erledigung; (Ab)Sendung f; Abfertigung f; Eile f; (Eil)Botschaft f; Bericht m (*e-s Korrespondenten*); 2. schnell erledigen; absenden, abschicken, *Telegramm* aufgeben, abfertigen.

di·spel [dɪ'spel] (*-ll-*) *Menge etc.* zerstreuen (*a. fig.*), *Nebel* zerteilen.

dis·pen·sa·ble [dɪ'spensəbl] entbehrlich; **~·ry** [~rɪ] Werks-, Krankenhaus-, Schul-, ⚔ Lazarettapotheke f.

dis·pen·sa·tion [dɪspen'seɪʃn] Austeilung f; Befreiung f (*with* von); Dispens m; *göttliche* Fügung.

di·spense [dɪ'spens] austeilen; *Recht* sprechen; *Arzneien* zubereiten u. abgeben; **~ with** auskommen ohne; überflüssig machen; **dis·pens·er** [~ə] Spender m, *für Klebestreifen a.* Abroller m, (*Briefmarken- etc.*)Automat m.

di·sperse [dɪ'spɜ:s] verstreuen; (sich) zerstreuen.

di·spir·it·ed [dɪ'spɪrɪtɪd] entmutigt.

dis·place [dɪs'pleɪs] verschieben; ablösen, entlassen; verschleppen; ersetzen; verdrängen.

di·splay [dɪ'spleɪ] 1. Entfaltung f; (Her)Zeigen n; (protzige) Zurschaustellung; Sichtanzeige f; *econ.* Display n, Auslage f; *be on* ~ ausgestellt sein; 2. entfalten; zur Schau stellen; zeigen.

dis·please [dɪs'pliːz] *j-m* mißfallen; **~·pleased** ungehalten; **~·pleas·ure** [~'pleʒə] Mißfallen n.

dis·po·sa·ble [dɪ'spəuzəbl] Einweg...; Wegwerf...; **~·pos·al** [~zl] Beseitigung f (*von Müll etc.*), Entsorgung f; Verfügung(srecht n) f; *be* (*put*) *at s.o.'s* ~ *j-m* zur Verfügung stehen (stellen); **~·pose** [~'əuz] v/t. (an)ordnen, einrichten; geneigt machen, veranlassen; v/i. ~ *of* verfügen über (*acc.*); erledigen; loswerden; beseitigen; **~·posed** geneigt; ...gesinnt; **~·po·si·tion** [dɪspə'zɪʃn] Disposition f; Anordnung f; Neigung f; Veranlagung f, Art f.

dis·pos·sess ['dɪspə'zes] enteignen, vertreiben; berauben (*of gen.*).

dis·pro·por·tion·ate □ ['dɪsprə'pɔ:-[nət] unverhältnismäßig.

dis·prove ['dɪs'pruːv] widerlegen.

di·spute [dɪ'spjuːt] 1. Disput m, Kontroverse f; Streit m; Auseinandersetzung f; 2. streiten (über *acc.*); bezweifeln.

dis·qual·i·fy [dɪs'kwɒlɪfaɪ] unfähig od. untauglich machen; für untauglich erklären; *Sport:* disqualifizieren.

dis·qui·et [dɪs'kwaɪət] beunruhigen.

dis·re·gard ['dɪsrɪ'gɑːd] 1. Nichtbeachtung f; Mißachtung f; 2. nicht beachten.

dis·rep·u·ta·ble □ [dɪs'repjutəbl] übel; verrufen; **~·re·pute** ['dɪsrɪ-'pjuːt] schlechter Ruf.

dis·re·spect ['dɪsrɪ'spekt] Respektlosigkeit f; Unhöflichkeit f; **~·ful** □ [~fl] respektlos; unhöflich.

dis·rupt [dɪs'rʌpt] unterbrechen.

dis·sat·is·fac·tion ['dɪssætɪs'fækʃn] Unzufriedenheit f; **~·fy** ['dɪs'sætɪs-faɪ] nicht befriedigen; *j-m* mißfallen.

dis·sect [dɪ'sekt] zerlegen, -gliedern.

dis·sem·ble [dɪ'sembl] v/t. verbergen; v/i. sich verstellen, heucheln.

dis·sen·sion [dɪ'senʃn] Meinungsverschiedenheit(en *pl.*) f, Differenz(en *pl.*) f; Uneinigkeit f; **~·t** [~t]

1. abweichende Meinung; 2. anderer Meinung sein (*from* als); ~**t·er** [~ə] Andersdenkende(r *m*) *f*.

dis·si·dent ['dɪsɪdənt] 1. andersdenkend; 2. Andersdenkende(r *m*) *f*; *pol*. Dissident(in), Regime-, Systemkritiker(in).

dis·sim·i·lar □ ['dɪˈsɪmɪlə] unähnlich (*dat.*); verschieden (von).

dis·sim·u·la·tion [dɪsɪmjʊˈleɪʃn] Verstellung *f*.

dis·si·pate ['dɪsɪpeɪt] (sich) zerstreuen; verschwenden; ~**pat·ed** ausschweifend, zügellos.

dis·so·ci·ate [dɪˈsəʊʃɪeɪt] trennen; ~ *o.s.* sich distanzieren, abrücken.

dis·so·lute □ ['dɪsəluːt] ausschweifend, zügellos; ~**lu·tion** [dɪsəˈluːʃn] Auflösung *f*; Zerstörung *f*; ⚖ Aufhebung *f*, Annullierung *f*.

dis·solve [dɪˈzɒlv] *v/t*. (auf)lösen; schmelzen; *v/i*. sich auflösen.

dis·so·nant □ ['dɪsənənt] ♪ dissonant, mißtönend; *fig*. unstimmig.

dis·suade [dɪˈsweɪd] *j-m* abraten (*from* von).

dis·tance ['dɪstəns] 1. Abstand *m*; Entfernung *f*; Ferne *f*; Strecke *f*; *fig*. Distanz *f*, Zurückhaltung *f*; *at a* ~ von weitem; *in einiger Entfernung*; *keep s.o. at a* ~ j-m gegenüber reserviert sein; ~ *race* Sport: Langstreckenlauf *m*; ~ *runner* Sport: Langstreckenläufer(in) *f*. 2. hinter sich lassen; ~**tant** □ [~t] entfernt; fern; zurückhaltend; Fern...; ~ *control* Fernsteuerung *f*.

dis·taste [dɪsˈteɪst] Widerwille *m*, Abneigung *f*; ~**ful** □ [~fl]: *be* ~ *to s.o.* j-m zuwider sein.

dis·tem·per [dɪˈstempə] Krankheit *f* (*bsd. von Tieren*); (Hunde)Staupe *f*.

dis·tend [dɪˈstend] (sich) (aus)dehnen; (auf)blähen; sich weiten.

dis·til(l) [dɪˈstɪl] (*-ll-*) herabtropfen (lassen); 🜍 destillieren; **dis·til·le·ry** [~ləri] (Branntwein)Brennerei *f*.

dis·tinct □ [dɪˈstɪŋkt] verschieden; getrennt; deutlich, klar, bestimmt; ~**tinc·tion** [~kʃn] Unterscheidung *f*; Unterschied *m*; Auszeichnung *f*; Rang *m*; ~**tinc·tive** □ [~tɪv] unterscheidend; kennzeichnend, bezeichnend.

dis·tin·guish [dɪˈstɪŋgwɪʃ] unterscheiden; auszeichnen; ~ *o.s.* sich auszeichnen; ~**ed** berühmt; ausgezeichnet; vornehm.

dis·tort [dɪˈstɔːt] verdrehen; verzerren.

dis·tract [dɪˈstrækt] ablenken; zerstreuen; beunruhigen; verwirren; verrückt machen; ~**ed** □ beunruhigt, besorgt; (*by, with*) außer sich (*vor dat.*); wahnsinnig (*vor Schmerzen etc.*); **dis·trac·tion** [~kʃn] Ablenkung *f*; Zerstreutheit *f*; Verwirrung *f*; Zerstreuung *f*; Raserei *f*.

dis·traught [dɪˈstrɔːt] = *distracted*.

dis·tress [dɪˈstres] 1. Qual *f*; Kummer *m*, Sorge *f*; Elend *n*, Not *f*; 2. in Not bringen; quälen; beunruhigen; betrüben; *j-n* erschöpfen; ~**ed** beunruhigt, besorgt; betrübt; notleidend; ~ *area* Brt. Notstandsgebiet *n*.

dis·trib·ute [dɪˈstrɪbjuːt] ver-, austeilen; einteilen; verbreiten; ~**tri·bu·tion** [dɪstrɪˈbjuːʃn] Ver-, Austeilung *f*; Verleih *m* (*von Filmen*); Verbreitung *f*; Einteilung *f*.

dis·trict ['dɪstrɪkt] Bezirk *m*; Gegend *f*.

dis·trust [dɪsˈtrʌst] 1. Mißtrauen *n*; 2. mißtrauen (*dat.*); ~**ful** □ [~fl] mißtrauisch.

dis·turb [dɪˈstɜːb] stören; beunruhigen; ~**ance** [~əns] Störung *f*; Unruhe *f*; ~ *of the peace* ⚖ Störung *f* der öffentlichen Sicherheit u. Ordnung; *cause a* ~ für Unruhe sorgen; ruhestörenden Lärm machen; ~**ed** geistig gestört; verhaltensgestört.

dis·used [dɪsˈjuːzd] nicht mehr benutzt (*Maschine etc.*), stillgelegt (*Bergwerk etc.*).

ditch [dɪtʃ] Graben *m*.

di·van [dɪˈvæn, *Am.* ˈdaɪvæn] Diwan *m*; ~ *bed* Bettcouch *f*.

dive [daɪv] 1. (*dived od. Am. a. dove, dived*) (unter)tauchen; *vom Sprungbrett* springen; e-n Hecht- *od.* Kopfsprung machen; hechten (*for* nach); e-n Sturzflug machen; 2. Schwimmen: Springen *n*; Kopf-, Hechtsprung *m*; Sturzflug *m*; F Spelunke *f*; **div·er** ['daɪvə] Taucher(in) *f*; *Sport:* Wasserspringer(in).

di·verge [daɪˈvɜːdʒ] auseinanderlaufen; abweichen; **di·ver·gence** [~əns] Abweichung *f*; **di·ver·gent** □ [~t] abweichend.

di·vers ['daɪvɜːz] mehrere.

di·verse □ [daɪˈvɜːs] verschieden; mannigfaltig; **di·ver·si·fy** [~sɪfaɪ] verschieden(artig) *od.* abwechslungsreich gestalten; **di·ver·sion**

[~ɜːʃn] Ablenkung f; Zeitvertreib m; **di·ver·si·ty** [~ɜːsətɪ] Verschiedenheit f; Mannigfaltigkeit f.

di·vert [daɪˈvɜːt] ablenken; j-n zerstreuen, unterhalten; *Verkehr* umleiten.

di·vide [dɪˈvaɪd] 1. v/t. teilen; ver-, aus-, aufteilen; trennen; einteilen; & dividieren (*by* durch); v/i. sich teilen; zerfallen; & sich dividieren lassen; sich trennen *od.* auflösen; 2. *geogr.* Wasserscheide f; **di·vid·ed** geteilt; ~ *highway Am.* Schnellstraße f; ~ *skirt* Hosenrock m.

div·i·dend *econ.* [ˈdɪvɪdend] Dividende f.

di·vid·ers [dɪˈvaɪdəz] *pl.* (*a pair of* ~) ein) Stechzirkel m.

di·vine [dɪˈvaɪn] 1. □ (~r, ~st) göttlich; ~ *service* Gottesdienst m; 2. Geistliche(r) m; 3. weissagen; ahnen.

div·ing [ˈdaɪvɪŋ] Tauchen n; *Sport*: Wasserspringen n; *attr.* Tauch..., Taucher..., & Sturzflug...; ~**board** Sprungbrett n; ~**suit** Taucheranzug m.

di·vin·i·ty [dɪˈvɪnətɪ] Gottheit f; Göttlichkeit f; Theologie f.

di·vis·i·ble □ [dɪˈvɪzəbl] teilbar; **di·vi·sion** [~ɪʒn] Teilung f; Trennung f; Abteilung f; ✕, & Division f.

di·vorce [dɪˈvɔːs] 1. (Ehe)Scheidung f; *get a* ~ geschieden werden (*from* von); 2. *Ehe* scheiden; sich scheiden lassen von; *they have been* ~d sie haben sich scheiden lassen; **di·vor·cee** [dɪvɔːˈsiː] Geschiedene(r m) f.

diz·zy □ [ˈdɪzɪ] (*-ier, -iest*) schwind(e)lig.

do [duː] (*did, done*) v/t. tun, machen; (zu)bereiten; *Zimmer* aufräumen; *Geschirr* abwaschen; *Rolle* spielen; *Wegstrecke* zurücklegen, schaffen; ~ *you know him? – no, I don't* kennst du ihn? – nein; *what can I* ~ *for you?* was kann ich für Sie tun?, womit kann ich (Ihnen) dienen?; ~ *London* F London besichtigen; *have one's hair done* sich die Haare machen *od.* frisieren lassen; *have done reading* fertig sein mit Lesen; v/i. tun, handeln; sich befinden; genügen; *that will* ~ das genügt; *how* ~ *you* ~? guten Tag! (*bei der Vorstellung*); ~ *be quick* beeile dich doch; ~ *you like London? – I* ~ *l* ~ gefällt Ihnen London? – ja; ~ *well* s-e Sache gut machen; gute

Geschäfte machen; *mit Adverbien u. Präpositionen*: ~ *away with* beseitigen, weg-, abschaffen; *I'm done in* F ich bin geschafft; ~ *up Kleid etc.* zumachen; *Haus etc.* instand setzen; *Päckchen* zurechtmachen; ~ *o.s. up* sich zurechtmachen; *I'm done up* F ich bin geschafft; *I could* ~ *with ...* ich könnte ... brauchen *od.* vertragen; ~ *without* auskommen *od.* sich behelfen ohne.

do·cile □ [ˈdəʊsaɪl] gelehrig; fügsam.

dock[1] [dɒk] stutzen, kupieren; *fig.* kürzen.

dock[2] [~] 1. & Dock n; Kai m, Pier m; ✚ Anklagebank f; 2. v/t. *Schiff* (ein-)docken; *Raumschiff* koppeln; v/i. & anlegen; andocken, ankoppeln (*Raumschiff*); ~**ing** [ˈdɒkɪŋ] Docking n, Ankopp(e)lung f (*von Raumschiffen*); ~**yard** & (*bsd. Brt.* Marine)Werft f.

doc·tor [ˈdɒktə] 1. Doktor m; Arzt m; 2. F verarzten; F (ver)fälschen.

doc·trine [ˈdɒktrɪn] Doktrin f, Lehre f.

doc·u·ment 1. [ˈdɒkjʊmənt] Urkunde f; 2. [~ment] (urkundlich) belegen.

doc·u·men·ta·ry [dɒkjʊˈmentrɪ] 1. urkundlich; *Film etc.*: Dokumentar...; 2. Dokumentarfilm m.

dodge [dɒdʒ] 1. Sprung m zur Seite; Kniff m, Trick m; 2. (rasch) zur Seite springen, ausweichen; F sich drücken (vor *dat.*).

doe *zo.* [dəʊ] Hirschkuh f; Rehgeiß f; Ricke f; Häsin f.

dog [dɒg] 1. *zo.* Hund m; 2. (-*gg*-) j-n beharrlich verfolgen; ~**eared** [ˈdɒgɪəd] mit Eselsohren (*Buch*); ~**ged** □ verbissen, hartnäckig.

dog·ma [ˈdɒgmə] Dogma n; Glaubenssatz m; ~**t·ic** [dɒgˈmætɪk] (~*ally*) dogmatisch.

dog-tired F [ˈdɒgˈtaɪəd] hundemüde.

do·ings [ˈduːɪŋz] *pl.* Handlungen *pl.*, Taten *pl.*, Tätigkeit f; Begebenheiten *pl.*; Treiben n, Betragen n.

do-it-your·self [duːɪtjɔːˈself] 1. Heimwerken n; 2. Heimwerker...

dole [dəʊl] 1. milde Gabe; *Brt.* F Stempelgeld n; *be od. go on the* ~ *Brt.* F stempeln gehen; 2. ~ *out* sparsam ver- *od.* austeilen.

dole·ful □ [ˈdəʊlfl] trübselig.

doll [dɒl] Puppe f.

dol·lar ['dɒlə] Dollar *m*.

dol·phin *zo.* ['dɒlfɪn] Delphin *m*.

do·main [dəʊ'meɪn] Domäne *f*; *fig.* Gebiet *n*, Bereich *m*.

dome [dəʊm] Kuppel *f*; △ *nicht Dom*; **~d** gewölbt.

Domes·day Book ['du:mzdeɪbʊk] *Reichsgrundbuch Englands* (1086).

do·mes·tic [də'mestɪk] **1.** (~*ally*) häuslich; inländisch, einheimisch; zahm; ~ *animal* Haustier *n*; ~ *flight* ✈ Inlandsflug *m*; ~ *trade* Binnenhandel *m*; **2.** Hausangestellte(r *m*) *f*; **~·ti·cate** [~eɪt] zähmen.

dom·i·cile ['dɒmɪsaɪl] Wohnsitz *m*.

dom·i·nant □ ['dɒmɪnənt] (vor)herrschend; **~nate** [~eɪt] (be)herrschen; **~na·tion** [~'neɪʃn] Herrschaft *f*; **~neer·ing** □ [~'ɪərɪŋ] herrisch, tyrannisch; überheblich.

do·min·ion [də'mɪnjən] Herrschaft *f*; (Herrschafts)Gebiet *n*; ♀ Dominion *n* (*im Brit. Commonwealth*).

don [dɒn] anziehen; *Hut* aufsetzen.

do·nate [dəʊ'neɪt] schenken, stiften; **do·na·tion** [~eɪʃn] Schenkung *f*.

done [dʌn] **1.** *p.p. von* do; **2.** *adj.* getan; erledigt; fertig; gar *gekocht*.

don·key ['dɒŋkɪ] *zo.* Esel *m*; *attr.* Hilfs...

do·nor ['dəʊnə] (✚ *bsd.* Blut-, Organ)Spender(in).

doom [du:m] **1.** Schicksal *n*, Verhängnis *n*; **2.** verurteilen, -dammen; **~s·day** ['du:mzdeɪ]: *till* ~ F bis zum Jüngsten Tag.

door [dɔ:] Tür *f*; Tor *n*; *next* ~ nebenan; **~·han·dle** ['dɔ:hændl] Türklinke *f*; **~·keep·er** Pförtner *m*; **~·man** (*pl. -men*) (livrierter) Portier; **~·step** Türstufe *f*; **~·way** Türöffnung *f*, Tür/Eingang *m*.

dope [dəʊp] **1.** Schmiere *f*; *bsd.* ✈ Lack *m*; F Stoff *m*, Rauschgift *n*; F Betäubungsmittel *n*; *Sport:* Dopingmittel *n*; *Am.* F Rauschgiftsüchtige(r *m*) *f*; *sl.* Trottel *m*; *sl.* (vertrauliche) Informationen *pl.*, Geheimtip *m*; **2.** ✈ lackieren; F *j-m* Stoff geben; *Sport:* dopen; ~ **ad·dict**, ~ **fiend** F Rauschgift-, Drogensüchtige(r *m*) *f*; ~ **test** Dopingkontrolle *f*.

dorm F [dɔ:m] = *dormitory*.

dor·mant *mst fig.* ['dɔ:mənt] schlafend, ruhend; untätig.

dor·mer (win·dow) ['dɔ:mə('wɪndəʊ)] stehendes Dachfenster.

dor·mi·to·ry ['dɔ:mɪtrɪ] Schlafsaal

m; *bsd. Am.* Studentenwohnheim *n*.

dose [dəʊs] **1.** Dosis *f*; △ *nicht Dose*; **2.** *j-m* e-e Medizin geben.

dot [dɒt] **1.** Punkt *m*; Fleck *m*; *on the* ~ F auf die Sekunde pünktlich; **2.** (-*tt*-) punktieren; tüpfeln; *fig.* sprenkeln; **~ted line** punktierte Linie.

dote [dəʊt]: ~ *on*, ~ *upon* vernarrt sein *in* (*acc.*), abgöttisch lieben (*acc.*); **dot·ing** □ ['dəʊtɪŋ] vernarrt.

dou·ble □ ['dʌbl] **1.** doppelt; zu zweien; gekrümmt; zweideutig; Doppelte(s) *n*; Doppelgänger(in); *Film, TV:* Double *n*; *mst* ~*s sg., pl. Tennis:* Doppel *n*; *men's od. women's* ~*s sg., pl.* Herren- *od.* Damendoppel *n*; **3.** (sich) verdoppeln; *Film, TV: j-n* doubeln; *a.* ~ *up* falten; *Decke* zusammenlegen; ~ *back* kehrtmachen; ~ *up* zusammenkrümmen; sich krümmen (*with* vor *dat.*); **~breast·ed** zweireihig (*Jakkett*); **~check** genau nachprüfen; ~ **chin** Doppelkinn *n*; **~cross** ein doppeltes *od.* falsches Spiel treiben mit; **~deal·ing 1.** betrügerisch; **2.** Betrug *m*; **~deck·er** [~ə] Doppeldecker *m*; **~edged** zweischneidig; zweideutig; **~en·try** *econ.* doppelte Buchführung; **~ fea·ture** *Film:* Doppelprogramm *n*; ~ **head·er** *Am.* [~ə] Doppelveranstaltung *f*; **~park** *mot.* in zweiter Reihe parken; **~quick** F im Eiltempo, fix.

doubt [daʊt] **1.** *v/i.* zweifeln; *v/t.* bezweifeln; mißtrauen (*dat.*); **2.** Zweifel *m*; *be in* ~ *about* Zweifel haben an (*dat.*); *no* ~ ohne Zweifel; **~ful** □ ['daʊtfl] zweifelhaft; **~less** [~lɪs] ohne Zweifel.

douche [du:ʃ] **1.** Spülung *f* (*a.* ✚); Spülapparat *m*; △ *nicht Dusche*; **2.** spülen (*a.* ✚); △ *nicht duschen*.

dough [dəʊ] Teig *m*; **~nut** ['dəʊnʌt] Krapfen *m*, Berliner (Pfannkuchen) *m*, Schmalzkringel *m*.

dove[1] *zo.* ['dʌv] Taube *f*.

dove[2] *Am.* ['dəʊv] *pret. von* dive 1.

dow·el ⊕ ['daʊəl] Dübel *m*.

down[1] [daʊn] Daunen *pl.*; Flaum *m*; Düne *f*; **~s** *pl.* Hügelland *n*.

down[2] [~] **1.** *adv.* nach unten, her-, hinunter, her-, hinab, abwärts; unten; **2.** *prp.* her-, hinab, her-, hinunter; ~ *the river* flußabwärts; **3.** *adj.* nach unten gerichtet; deprimiert, niedergeschlagen; ~ *platform* Abfahrtsbahnsteig *m* (*in London*); ~

train Zug *m* (von London fort); **4.** *v/t.* niederschlagen; *Flugzeug* abschießen; F *Getränk* runterkippen; ~ *tools* die Arbeit niederlegen, in den Streik treten; **~·cast** ['dɑunkɑːst] niedergeschlagen; **~·fall** Platzregen *m*; *fig.* Sturz *m*; **~·hill 1.** *adv.* bergab; **2.** *adj.* abschüssig; *Skisport:* Abfahrts...; **3.** Abhang *m*; *Skisport:* Abfahrt *f*; **~·pay·ment** *econ.* Anzahlung *f*; **~·pour** Regenguß *m*, Platzregen *m*; **~·right 1.** *adv.* völlig, ganz u. gar, ausgesprochen; **2.** *adj.* glatt (*Lüge etc.*); ausgesprochen; **~·stairs** die Treppe her- *od.* hinunter; (nach) unten; **~·stream** stromabwärts; **~·to–earth** realistisch; **~·town** *Am.* **1.** *adv.* im *od.* ins Geschäftsviertel; **2.** *adj.* im Geschäftsviertel (gelegen *od.* tätig); **3.** Geschäftsviertel *n*, Innenstadt *f*, City *f*; **~·ward(s)** [~wəd(z)] abwärts, nach unten.

down·y ['dɑuni] (*-ier, -iest*) flaumig.

dow·ry ['dɑuəri] Mitgift *f*.

doze [dəuz] **1.** dösen, ein Nickerchen machen; **2.** Nickerchen *n*.

doz·en ['dʌzn] Dutzend *n*.

drab [dræb] trist; düster; eintönig.

draft [drɑːft] **1.** Entwurf *m*; *econ.* Tratte *f*; Abhebung *f* (*von Geld*); ✗ (Sonder)Kommando *n*; *Am.* ✗ Einberufung *f*; *bsd. Brit.* = draught; **2.** entwerfen; aufsetzen; ✗ abkommandieren; *Am.* ✗ einziehen, -berufen; **~·ee** *Am.* ✗ [drɑːf'tiː] Wehrdienstpflichtige(r) *m*; **~·s·man** *bsd. Am.* ['drɑːftsmən] (*pl. -men*) *s.* draughtsman; **~·y** *Am.* [~ɪ] (*-ier, -iest*) = draughty.

drag [dræg] **1.** Schleppen *n*, Zerren *n*; ✦ Schleppnetz *n*; Egge *f*; Schlepp-, Zugseil *n*; *fig.* Hemmschuh *m* F *et.* Langweiliges *n*; **2.** (*-gg-*) (sich) schleppen, zerren, ziehen, schleifen; *a.* ~ *behind* zurückbleiben, nachhinken; ~ *on* weiterschleppen; *fig.* sich dahinschleppen; *fig.* sich in die Länge ziehen; **~·lift** ['dræglɪft] Schlepplift *m*.

drag·on ['drægən] Drache *m*; **~·fly** *zo.* Libelle *f*.

drain [dreɪn] **1.** Abfluß(kanal *m*, -rohr *n*) *m*; Entwässerungsgraben *m*; *fig.* Belastung *f*; **2.** *v/t.* abfließen lassen; entwässern; austrinken, leeren; *fig.* aufbrauchen, -zehren; *v/i.* ~ *off*, ~ *away* abfließen, ablaufen;

~·age ['dreɪnɪdʒ] Abfließen *n*, Ablaufen *n*; Entwässerung(sanlage *f*, -ssystem *n*) *f*; Abwasser *n*; **~·pipe** Abflußrohr *n*.

drake *zo.* [dreɪk] Enterich *m*, Erpel *m*; △ *nicht* Drache.

dram F [dræm] Schluck *m*.

dra|ma ['drɑːmə] Drama *n*; in Falten legen; **2.** *mst* ~*s pl. Am.* Gardinen *pl.*; **~·mat·ic** [drə'mætɪk] (~*ally*) dramatisch; **~·ma·tist** ['dræmətɪst] Dramatiker *m*; **~·ma·tize** [~taɪz] dramatisieren.

drank [dræŋk] *pret. von* drink 2.

drape [dreɪp] **1.** drapieren; in Falten legen; **2.** *mst* ~*s pl. Am.* Gardinen *pl.*; **drap·er·y** ['dreɪpərɪ] Textilhandel *m*; Stoffe *pl.*; Faltenwurf *m*.

dras·tic ['dræstɪk] (~*ally*) drastisch.

draught [drɑːft] (Luft)Zug *m*; Zug *m*, Schluck *m*; Fischzug *m*; ✦ Tiefgang *m*; ~ *beer* Faßbier *n*; **~·horse** ['drɑːfthɔːs] Zugpferd *n*; **~·man** [~smən] (*pl. -men*) *Brt.* Damestein *m*; ⊕ (Konstruktions-, Muster)Zeichner *m*; **~·y** [~ɪ] (*-ier, -iest*) zugig.

draw [drɔː] **1.** (*drew, drawn*) ziehen; an-, auf-, ein-, zuziehen; ✗ *Blut* abnehmen; *econ.* Geld abheben; *Tränen* hervorlocken; *Kunden etc.* anziehen, anlocken; *j-s Aufmerksamkeit* lenken (*to auf acc.*); *Bier* abzapfen; ausfischen; *Tier* ausnehmen, -weiden; *Luft* schöpfen, ziehen (lassen) (*Tee*); (in Worten) schildern; *Schriftstück* ab-, verfassen; *fig.* entlocken; zeichnen, malen; *fig.* ziehen, Zug haben (*Kamin*); sich zusammenziehen; sich nähern (*to dat.*); *Sport:* unentschieden spielen; ~ *near* sich nähern; ~ *on*, ~ *upon* in Anspruch nehmen; ~ *out* in die Länge ziehen; ~ *up Schriftstück* aufsetzen; halten; vorfahren; **2.** Zug *m* (*Ziehen*); *Lotterie:* Ziehung *f*; *Sport:* Unentschieden *n*; Attraktion *f*, (Kassen)Schlager *m*; **~·back** ['drɔːbæk] Nachteil *m*, Hindernis *n*; **~·er** ['drɔːə] Zeichner *m*; *econ.* Aussteller *m*, Trassant *m* (*e-s Wechsels*); [drɔː] Schubfach *n*, -lade *f*; (*a pair of*) ~*s pl.* (eine) Unterhose; (ein) (Damen-) Schlüpfer *m*; *mst chest of* ~*s* Kommode *f*.

draw·ing ['drɔːɪŋ] Ziehen *n*; Zeichnen *n*; Zeichnung *f*; ~ **ac·count** *econ.* Girokonto *n*; **~·board** Reißbrett *n*; **~·pin** *Brt.* Reißzwecke *f*, -nagel *m*, Heftzwecke *f*; **~room** = *living room*; Salon *m*.

drawl [drɔ:l] 1. gedehnt sprechen; 2. gedehntes Sprechen.

drawn [drɔ:n] 1. *p.p. von draw 1*; 2. *adj. Sport*: unentschieden; abgespannt.

dread [dred] 1. (große) Angst, Furcht *f*; 2. (sich) fürchten; **~ful** □ ['dredfl] schrecklich, furchtbar.

dream [dri:m] 1. Traum *m*; 2. (*dreamed od. dreamt*) träumen; **~er** ['dri:mə] Träumer(in); **~t** [dremt] *pret. u. p.p. von dream 2*; **~y** □ ['dri:mɪ] (*-ier, -iest*) träumerisch, verträumt.

drear·y □ ['drɪərɪ] (*-ier, -iest*) trübselig; trüb(e); langweilig.

dredge [dredʒ] 1. Schleppnetz *n*; Bagger(maschine *f*) *m*; 2. (aus)baggern.

dregs [dregz] *pl*. Bodensatz *m*; *fig.* Abschaum *m*.

drench [drentʃ] durchnässen.

dress [dres] 1. Anzug *m*; Kleidung *f*; Kleid *n*; 2. (sich) ankleiden *od.* anziehen; schmücken, dekorieren; zurechtmachen; *Speisen* zubereiten; *Salat* anmachen; *Abendkleidung* anziehen; ✗ verbinden; frisieren; ~ *down j-m e-e Standpauke halten*; ~ *up* (sich) fein machen; sich kostümieren *od.* verkleiden (*bsd. Kinder*); ~ **cir·cle** *thea*. ['dres'sɜ:kl] erster Rang; ~ **de·sign·er** Modezeichner(in); **~er** [~ə] Anrichte *f*; Toilettentisch *m*.

dress·ing ['dresɪŋ] An-, Zurichten *n*; Ankleiden *n*; ✗ Verband *m*; Appretur *f*; Dressing *n* (*Salatsoße*); Füllung *f*; **~down** Standpauke *f*; **~gown** Morgenrock *m*, -mantel *m*; *Sport*: Bademantel *m*; **~ta·ble** Toilettentisch *m*.

dress·mak·er ['dresmeɪkə] (Damen-)Schneider(in).

drew [dru:] *pret. von draw 1*.

drib·ble ['drɪbl] tröpfeln (lassen); sabbern, geifern; *Fußball*: dribbeln.

dried [draɪd] getrocknet, Dörr...

dri·er ['draɪə] = *dryer*.

drift [drɪft] 1. (Dahin)Treiben *n*; (Schnee)Verwehung *f*; (Schnee-, Sand)Wehe *f*; *fig.* Tendenz *f*; 2. (dahin)treiben; wehen; aufhäufen.

drill [drɪl] 1. Drillbohrer *m*; Furche *f*; ✔ Drill-, Sämaschine *f*; ✗ Drill *m* (*a. fig.*); ✗ Exerzieren *n*; 2.

bohren; ✗, *fig.* drillen, einexerzieren.

drink [drɪŋk] 1. Getränk *n*; 2. (*drank, drunk*) trinken; ~ *to s.o.* j-m zuprosten *od.* zutrinken; **~er** ['drɪŋkə] Trinker(in).

drip [drɪp] 1. Tröpfeln *n*; ✗ Tropf *m*; 2. (*-pp-*) tropfen *od.* tröpfeln (lassen); triefen; **~dry shirt** [drɪp'draɪ ʃɜːt] bügelfreies Hemd; **~ping** ['drɪpɪŋ] Bratenfett *n*.

drive [draɪv] 1. (Spazier)Fahrt *f*; Auffahrt *f*; Fahrweg *m*; ⊕ Antrieb *m*; *mot.* (*Links- etc.*)Steuerung *f*; *psych.* Trieb *m*; *fig.* Kampagne *f*; *fig.* Schwung *m*, Elan *m*, Dynamik *f*; 2. (*drove, driven*) *v/t.* (an-, ein)treiben; *Auto etc.* fahren, lenken, steuern; (im Auto *etc.*) fahren; ~ *(an)treiben; zwingen; a. ~ off* vertreiben; *v/i.* treiben; (Auto) fahren; ~ *off wegfahren; what are you driving at?* F worauf wollen Sie hinaus?

drive-in ['draɪvɪn] 1. Auto...; ~ *cinema, Am.* ~ *motion-picture theater* Autokino *n*; 2. Autokino *n*; Drive-in-Restaurant *n*; Autoschalter *m*, Drive-in-Schalter *m* (*e-r Bank*).

driv·el ['drɪvl] 1. (*bsd. Brt. -ll-, Am. -l-*) faseln; 2. Geschwätz *n*, Gefasel *n*.

driv·en ['drɪvn] *p.p. von drive 2*.

driv·er ['draɪvə] *mot.* Fahrer(in); (*Lokomotiv*)Führer *m*; **~'s li·cense** *Am.* Führerschein *m*.

driv·ing ['draɪvɪŋ] (an)treibend; ⊕ Antriebs..., Treib..., Trieb...; *mot.* Fahr...; ~ **li·cense** Führerschein *m*.

driz·zle ['drɪzl] 1. Sprühregen *m*; 2. sprühen, nieseln.

drone [drəun] 1. *zo.* Drohne *f* (*a. fig.*); 2. summen; dröhnen.

droop [dru:p] (schlaff) herabhängen; den Kopf hängenlassen; schwinden.

drop [drɒp] 1. Tropfen *m*; Fallen *n*, Fall *m*; *fig.* Fall *m*, Sturz *m*; Bonbon *m*, *n*; *fruit* **~s** *pl.* Drops *m*, *n od. pl.*; 2. (*-pp-*) *v/t.* tropfen (lassen); fallen lassen; *Bemerkung, Thema etc.* fallenlassen; *Brief* einwerfen; *Fahrgast* absetzen; senken; ~ *s.o. a few lines* *pl.* j-m ein paar Zeilen schreiben; *v/i.* tropfen; (herab-, herunter)fallen; umsinken, fallen; ~ *in* (kurz) hereinschauen; ~ *off abfallen*; zurückgehen, nachlassen; F einnicken;

~ *out* herausfallen; aussteigen (*of aus*); *a.* ~ *out of school* (*university*) die Schule (das Studium) abbrechen; **~out** ['drɒpaʊt] Drop-out *m*, Aussteiger *m* (*aus der Gesellschaft*); (Schul-, Studien)Abbrecher *m*.

drought [draʊt] Trockenheit *f*, Dürre *f*.

drove [drəʊv] **1.** Herde *f* (*Vieh*); Schar *f* (*Menschen*); **2.** *pret. von* drive 2.

drown [draʊn] *v/t.* ertränken; überschwemmen; *fig.* übertönen; *v/i.* ertrinken.

drowse [draʊz] dösen; ~ *off* eindösen; **drow·sy** ['draʊzɪ] (*-ier, -iest*) schläfrig; einschläfernd.

drudge [drʌdʒ] sich (ab)placken, schuften; **drudg·er·y** ['drʌdʒərɪ] (stumpfsinnige) Plackerei *od.* Schinderei.

drug [drʌg] **1.** Arzneimittel *n*, Medikament *n*; Droge *f*, Rauschgift *n*; *be on* (*off*) ~*s* rauschgift- *od.* drogensüchtig (clean) sein; **2.** (*-gg-*) *j-m* Medikamente geben; *j-n unter* Drogen setzen; in ein Betäubungsmittel beimischen (*dat.*); betäuben (*a. fig.*); ~ **a·buse** Drogenmißbrauch *m*; Medikamentenmißbrauch *m*; ~ **ad·dict** Drogen-, Rauschgiftsüchtige(r *m*) *f*; **~·gist** *Am.* ['drʌgɪst] Apotheker(in); Inhaber(in) e-s Drugstores; **~·store** *Am.* Apotheke *f*; Drugstore *m*.

drum [drʌm] **1.** ♪ Trommel *f*; *anat.* Trommelfell *n*; ~*s pl.* ♪ Schlagzeug *n*; **2.** (*-mm-*) trommeln; **~·mer ♪** ['drʌmə] Trommler *m*; Schlagzeuger *m*.

drunk [drʌŋk] **1.** *p.p. von* drink 2; **2.** *adj.* betrunken; *get* ~ sich betrinken; **3.** Betrunkene(r *m*) *f*; = **~·ard** ['drʌŋkəd] Trinker(in), Säufer(in); **~·en** *adj.* ['drʌŋkən] betrunken; ~ *driving* Trunkenheit *f* am Steuer.

dry [draɪ] **1.** □ (*-ier, -iest*) trocken; trocken, herb (*Wein*); F durstig; F trocken (*ohne Alkohol*); ~ *goods pl.* Textilien *pl.*; **2.** trocknen; dörren; ~ *up* austrocknen; versiegen; **~·clean** ['draɪˈkliːn] chemisch reinigen; ~ **clean·er's** chemische Reinigung; **~·er** □ *a. drier* Trockenapparat *m*, Trockner *m*.

du·al □ ['djuːəl] doppelt, Doppel...; ~ *carriageway Brt.* Schnellstraße *f* (*mit Mittelstreifen*).

dub [dʌb] (*-bb-*) Film synchronisieren.

du·bi·ous □ ['djuːbjəs] zweifelhaft.

duch·ess ['dʌtʃɪs] Herzogin *f*.

duck [dʌk] **1.** *zo.* Ente *f*; Ducken *n*; F Schatz *m* (*Anrede, oft unübersetzt*); **2.** (unter)tauchen; (sich) ducken; **~·ling** *zo.* ['dʌklɪŋ] Entchen *n*.

due [djuː] **1.** zustehend; gebührend; gehörig, angemessen; fällig; *zeitlich* fällig, erwartet; *in* ~ *time* zur rechten Zeit; ~ *to* wegen (*gen.*); *be* ~ *to j-m* gebühren, zustehen; kommen von, zurückzuführen sein auf; **2.** *adv.* direkt, genau; **3.** Recht *n*, Anspruch *m*; ~*s pl.* Gebühr(en *pl.*) *f*; Beitrag *m*.

du·el ['djuːəl] **1.** Duell *n*; **2.** (*bsd. Brt. -ll-, Am. -l-*) sich duellieren.

dug [dʌg] *pret. u. p.p. von* dig 1.

duke [djuːk] Herzog *m*.

dull [dʌl] **1.** □ dumm; träge, schwerfällig; stumpf; matt (*Auge etc.*); schwach (*Gehör*); langweilig; abgestumpft, teilnahmslos; dumpf; trüb(e); *econ.* flau; **2.** stumpf machen *od.* werden; (sich) trüben; mildern, dämpfen; *Schmerz* betäuben; *fig.* abstumpfen.

du·ly *adv.* ['djuːlɪ] ordnungsgemäß; gebührend; rechtzeitig.

dumb □ ['dʌm] stumm; sprachlos; *bsd. Am.* F doof, dumm, blöd; **dum(b)·found·ed** ['dʌmˈfaʊndɪd] verblüfft, sprachlos.

dum·my ['dʌmɪ] Attrappe *f*; Kleider-, Schaufensterpuppe *f*; Dummy *m*, Puppe *f* (*für Unfalltests*); *Brt.* Schnuller *m*; *attr.* Schein...

dump [dʌmp] **1.** *v/t.* (hin)plumpsen *od.* (hin)fallen lassen; auskippen; *Schutt etc.* abladen; *econ. Waren zu* Dumpingpreisen verkaufen; **2.** Plumps *m*; (Schutt-, Müll)Abladeplatz *m*; ✗ Depot *n*, Lager(platz *m*) *n*; **~·ing** *econ.* ['dʌmpɪŋ] Dumping *n*, Ausfuhr *f* zu Schleuderpreisen.

dune [djuːn] Düne *f*.

dung [dʌŋ] **1.** Dung *m*; **2.** düngen.

dun·ga·rees [dʌŋgəˈriːz] *pl.* (*a pair of* ~ e-e) Arbeitshose.

dun·geon ['dʌndʒən] (Burg)Verlies *n*.

dunk F [dʌŋk] (ein)tunken.

dupe [djuːp] anführen, täuschen.

du·plex ['djuːpleks] doppelt, Doppel...; ~ (*apartment*) *Am.* Maison(n)ette(wohnung) *f*; ~ (*house*) *Am.* Doppel-, Zweifamilienhaus *n*.

du·pli·cate 1. ['djuːplɪkət] doppelt; ~ *key* Zweit-, Nachschlüssel *m*; **2.** [~]

Duplikat *n*; Zweit-, Nachschlüssel *m*; 3. [⁓keıt] doppelt ausfertigen; kopieren, vervielfältigen.

du·plic·i·ty [dju:'plısətı] Doppelzüngigkeit *f*.

dur·a·ble □ ['djʊərəbl] haltbar; dauerhaft; **du·ra·tion** [djʊə'reıʃn] Dauer *f*.

du·ress [djʊə'res] Zwang *m*.

dur·ing *prp.* ['djʊərıŋ] während.

dusk [dʌsk] (Abend)Dämmerung *f*; ⁓·y □ ['dʌskı] (*-ier, -iest*) dämmerig, düster (*a. fig.*); schwärzlich.

dust [dʌst] 1. Staub *m*; 2. *v/t.* abstauben; (be)streuen; *v/i.* Staub wischen, abstauben; ⁓·bin *Brt.* ['dʌstbın] Abfall-, Mülleimer *m*; Abfall-, Mülltonne *f*; ⁓·cart *Brt.* Müllwagen *m*; ⁓·er [⁓ə] Staublappen *m*, -wedel *m*; *Schule:* Tafelschwamm *m*, -tuch *n*; ⁓·cov·er, ⁓·jack·et Schutzumschlag *m* (*e-s Buches*); ⁓·man (*pl. -men*) *Brt.* Müllmann *m*; ⁓·y □ [⁓ı] (*-ier, -iest*) staubig.

Dutch [dʌtʃ] 1. *adj.* holländisch; 2. *adv.:* go ⁓ getrennte Kasse machen; 3. *ling.* Holländisch *n*; the ⁓ die Holländer *pl.*

du·ty ['dju:tı] Pflicht *f*; Ehrerbietung *f*; *econ.* Abgabe *f*; Zoll *m*; Dienst *m*; be on ⁓ Dienst haben; be off ⁓ dienstfrei haben; ⁓-free zollfrei.

dwarf [dwɔ:f] 1. (*pl. dwarfs* [⁓fs], *dwarves* [⁓vz]) Zwerg(in) *f*; 2. verkleinern, klein erscheinen lassen.

dwell [dwel] (*dwelt od. dwelled*) wohnen; verweilen (*on, upon* bei); ⁓·ing ['dwelıŋ] Wohnung *f*.

dwelt [dwelt] *pret. u. p.p. von* dwell.

dwin·dle ['dwındl] (dahin)schwinden, abnehmen.

dye [daı] 1. Farbe *f*; of the deepest ⁓ *fig.* von der übelsten Sorte; 2. färben.

dy·ing ['daıŋ] 1. sterbend; Sterbe...; 2. Sterben *n*.

dyke [daık] = dike[1], [2].

dy·nam·ic [daı'næmık] dynamisch, kraftgeladen; ⁓s *mst sg.* Dynamik *f*.

dy·na·mite ['daınəmaıt] 1. Dynamit *n*; 2. (mit Dynamit) sprengen.

dys·en·te·ry ⚕ ['dısntrı] Ruhr *f*.

dys·pep·si·a ⚕ [dıs'pepsıə] Verdauungsstörung *f*.

E

each [i:tʃ] jede(r, -s); ⁓ other einander, sich; je, pro Person, pro Stück.

ea·ger □ ['i:gə] begierig; eifrig; ⁓·ness ['i:gənıs] Begierde *f*; Eifer *m*.

ea·gle ['i:gl] *zo.* Adler *m*; *Am. hist.* Zehndollarstück *n*; ⁓·eyed scharfsichtig.

ear [ıə] Ähre *f*; *anat.* Ohr *n*; Öhr *n*; Henkel *m*; keep an ⁓ to the ground die Ohren offenhalten; ⁓·drum *anat.* ['ıədrʌm] Trommelfell *n*; ⁓·ed mit (...) Ohren, -ohrig.

earl [ɜ:l] *englischer* Graf.

ear·lobe ['ıələʊb] Ohrläppchen *n*.

ear·ly ['ɜ:lı] früh; Früh...; Anfangs..., erste(r, -s); bald(ig); as ⁓ as May schon im Mai; as ⁓ as possible so bald wie möglich; ⁓ bird Frühaufsteher(in); ⁓ warning system ⚔ Frühwarnsystem *n*.

ear·mark ['ıəma:k] 1. Kennzeichen *n*; Merkmal *n*; 2. kennzeichnen; zurücklegen (*for* für).

earn [ɜ:n] verdienen; einbringen.

ear·nest ['ɜ:nıst] 1. □ ernst(lich, -haft); ernstgemeint; 2. Ernst *m*; in ⁓ im Ernst; ernsthaft.

earn·ings ['ɜ:nıŋz] *pl.* Einkommen *n*.

ear|phones ['ıəfəʊnz] *pl.* Ohrhörer *pl.*; Kopfhörer *pl.*; ⁓·piece *teleph.* Hörmuschel *f*; ⁓·ring Ohrring *m*; ⁓·shot: within (out of) ⁓ in (außer) Hörweite.

earth [ɜ:θ] 1. Erde *f*; Land *n*; 2. *v/t.* ⚡ erden; ⁓·en ['ɜ:θn] irden; ⁓·en·ware [⁓nweə] 1. Töpferware *f*; Steingut *n*; 2. irden; ⁓·ly ['ɜ:θlı] irdisch; F denkbar; ⁓·quake Erdbeben *n*; ⁓·worm *zo.* Regenwurm *m*.

ease [i:z] 1. Bequemlichkeit *f*, Behagen *n*; Ruhe *f*; Ungezwungenheit *f*;

Leichtigkeit f; at ~ bequem, behaglich; ill at ~ unruhig; befangen; **2.** v/t. erleichtern; lindern; beruhigen; bequem(er) machen; v/i. mst ~ off, ~ up nachlassen, sich entspannen (Lage); (bei der Arbeit) kürzertreten.

ea·sel ['iːzl] Staffelei f.

east [iːst] **1.** Ost(en m); the ♀ der Osten, die Oststaaten pl. (der USA); pol. der Osten; der Orient; **2.** Ost..., östlich; **3.** ostwärts, nach Osten.

East·er ['iːstə] Ostern n; attr. Oster...

east·er·ly ['iːstəlɪ] östlich, Ost...; nach Osten; **east·ern** [~n] östlich, Ost...; **east·ward(s)** [~wəd(z)] östlich, nach Osten.

eas·y ['iːzɪ] ☐ (-ier, -iest) leicht, einfach; bequem; frei von Schmerzen; gemächlich, gemütlich; ruhig; ungezwungen; in ~ circumstances wohlhabend; on ~ street Am. in guten Verhältnissen; go ~, take it ~ sich Zeit lassen, langsam tun; sich nicht aufregen; take it ~! immer mit der Ruhe!; ~ **chair** Sessel m; **~·go·ing** gelassen.

eat [iːt] **1.** (ate, eaten) (zer-)fressen; ~ out auswärts essen; **2.** ~s pl. F Fressalien pl.; **ea·ta·ble** ['iːtəbl] **1.** eß-, genießbar; **2.** ~s pl. Eßwaren pl.; **~·en** ['iːtn] p.p. von eat 1; **~·er** [~ə] Esser(in).

eaves [iːvz] pl. Dachrinne f, Traufe f; **~·drop** ['iːvzdrɒp] (-pp-) (heimlich) lauschen od. horchen.

ebb [eb] **1.** Ebbe f; fig. Tiefstand m; fig. Abnahme f; **2.** verebben; fig. abnehmen, sinken; ~ **tide** ['eb'taɪd] Ebbe f.

eb·o·ny ['ebənɪ] Ebenholz n.

ec·cen·tric [ɪk'sentrɪk] **1.** (~ally) exzentrisch; überspannt; **2.** Exzentriker m, Sonderling m.

ec·cle·si·as·tic [ɪkliːzɪ'æstɪk] (~ally), **~·ti·cal** [~kl] geistlich, kirchlich.

ech·o ['ekəʊ] **1.** (pl. -oes) Echo n; **2.** widerhallen; fig. echoen, nachsprechen.

e·clipse [ɪ'klɪps] **1.** ast. Finsternis f; **2.** verfinstern; be ~d by fig. verblassen neben (dat.).

e·co·cide [iːkəsaɪd] Umweltzerstörung f.

e·co·lo·gi·cal ☐ [iːkə'lɒdʒɪkl] ökologisch; **~·lo·gist** [iːˈkɒlədʒɪst] Ökologe m; **~·lo·gy** [~ɪ] Ökologie f.

ec·o·nom·ic [iːkə'nɒmɪk] (~ally) wirtschaftlich, Wirtschafts...; ~ aid

Wirtschaftshilfe f; ~ growth Wirtschaftswachstum n; **~·i·cal** ☐ [~kl] wirtschaftlich, sparsam; **~·ics** sg. Volkswirtschaft(slehre) f.

e·con·o·mist [ɪ'kɒnəmɪst] Volkswirt m; **~·mize** [~aɪz] sparsam wirtschaften (mit); **~·my** [~ɪ] **1.** Wirtschaft f; Wirtschaftlichkeit f, Sparsamkeit f; Einsparung f; **2.** Spar...; ~ class ✈ Economyklasse f.

e·co·sys·tem ['iːkəʊsɪstəm] Ökosystem n.

ec·sta·sy ['ekstəsɪ] Ekstase f, Verzückung f; **~·tic** [ɪk'stætɪk] (~ally) verzückt.

ed·dy ['edɪ] **1.** Wirbel m; **2.** wirbeln.

edge [edʒ] **1.** Schneide f; Rand m; Kante f; Schärfe f; △ nicht (Straßen-, Haus)Ecke; be on ~ nervös od. gereizt sein, **2.** schärfen; (um)säumen; (sich) drängen; **~·ways, ~·wise** ['edʒweɪz, ~waɪz] seitlich, von der Seite.

edg·ing ['edʒɪŋ] Einfassung f; Rand m.

edg·y ['edʒɪ] (-ier, -iest) scharf(kantig); F nervös; F gereizt.

ed·i·ble ['edɪbl] eßbar.

e·dict ['iːdɪkt] Edikt n.

ed·i·fice ['edɪfɪs] Gebäude n.

ed·i·fy·ing ☐ ['edɪfaɪɪŋ] erbaulich.

ed·it ['edɪt] Text redigieren, redigieren; Zeitung als Herausgeber leiten; **e·di·tion** [ɪ'dɪʃn] (Buch)Ausgabe f; Auflage f; **ed·i·tor** ['edɪtə] Herausgeber(in); Redakteur(in); **ed·i·to·ri·al** [edɪ'tɔːrɪəl] **1.** Leitartikel m; **2.** ☐ Redaktions...

ed·u·cate ['edjʊkeɪt] erziehen; unterrichten; **~·cat·ed** gebildet; **~·ca·tion** [edjʊ'keɪʃn] Erziehung f; (Aus)Bildung f; Bildungs-, Schulwesen n; Ministry of ♀ Unterrichtsministerium n; **~·ca·tion·al** ☐ [~nl] erzieherisch, Erziehungs...; Bildungs...; **~·ca·tor** ['edjʊkeɪtə] Erzieher(in).

eel zo. [iːl] Aal m.

ef·fect [ɪ'fekt] **1.** Wirkung f; Erfolg m, Ergebnis n; Auswirkung(en pl.) f; Effekt m, Eindruck m; ⊕ Leistung f; ~s pl. econ. Effekten pl.; persönliche Habe; be of ~ Wirkung haben; take ~ in Kraft treten; in ~ tatsächlich, praktisch; to the ~ des Inhalts; **2.** bewirken; ausführen; **ef·fec·tive** ☐ [~ɪv] wirksam; eindrucksvoll; tatsächlich, wirklich; ⊕ nutzbar; ~ date Tag m des Inkrafttretens.

ef·fem·i·nate □ [ɪˈfemɪnət] verweichlicht; weibisch.

ef·fer|vesce [efəˈves] brausen, sprudeln; **~·ves·cent** [~nt] sprudelnd, schäumend.

ef·fi·cien|cy [ɪˈfɪʃənsɪ] Leistung(s-fähigkeit) f; ~ engineer, ~ expert econ. Rationalisierungsfachmann m; **~t** □ [~t] wirksam; leistungsfähig, tüchtig.

ef·flu·ent [ˈefluənt] Abwasser n, Abwässer pl.

ef·fort [ˈefət] Anstrengung f, Bemühung f (at um); Mühe f; without ~ = **~·less** □ [~lɪs] mühelos, ohne Anstrengung.

ef·fron·te·ry [ɪˈfrʌntərɪ] Frechheit f.

ef·fu·sive □ [ɪˈfjuːsɪv] überschwenglich.

egg[1] [eg]: ~ on anstacheln.

egg[2] [~] Ei n; put all one's ~s in one basket alles auf eine Karte setzen; as sure as ~s is ~s F todsicher; **~·co·sy** [~kəʊzɪ] Eierwärmer m; **~·cup** Eierbecher m; **~·head** F Eierkopf m (Intellektueller).

e·go·is|m [ˈeɡəʊɪzəm] Egoismus m, Selbstsucht f; **~t** [~ɪst] Egoist(in), selbstsüchtiger Mensch.

e·go·tis|m [ˈeɡəʊtɪzəm] Egotismus m, Selbstgefälligkeit f; **~t** [~ɪst] Egotist(in), selbstgefälliger od. geltungsbedürftiger Mensch.

E·gyp·tian [ɪˈdʒɪpʃn] 1. ägyptisch; 2. Ägypter(in).

ei·der·down [ˈaɪdədaʊn] Eiderdaunen pl.; Daunendecke f.

eight [eɪt] 1. acht; 2. Acht f; **eigh·teen** [ˈeɪˈtiːn] 1. achtzehn; 2. Achtzehn f; **eigh·teenth** [~θ] achtzehnte(r); **~fold** [ˈeɪtfəʊld] achtfach; **~h** [eɪtθ] 1. achte(r, -s); 2. Achtel n; **~h·ly** [ˈeɪtθlɪ] achtens; **eigh·ti·eth** [ˈeɪtɪɪθ] achtzigste(r, -s); **eigh·ty** [ˈeɪtɪ] 1. achtzig; 2. Achtzig f.

ei·ther [ˈaɪðə; Am. ˈiːðə] jede(r, -s) (von zweien); eine(r, -s) (von zweien); beides; ~ ... or entweder ... oder; not ~ auch nicht.

e·jac·u·late [ɪˈdʒækjʊleɪt] v/t. Worte etc. aus-, hervorstoßen; physiol. Samen ausstoßen; v/i. physiol. ejakulieren, e-n Samenerguß haben.

e·ject [ɪˈdʒekt] vertreiben; hinauswerfen; entlassen, -fernen (from aus e-m Amt).

eke [iːk]: ~ out Vorräte etc. strecken; Einkommen aufbessern; ~ out a living sich (mühsam) durchschlagen.

e·lab·o·rate 1. □ [ɪˈlæbərət] sorgfältig (aus)gearbeitet; kompliziert; 2. [~reɪt] sorgfältig ausarbeiten.

e·lapse [ɪˈlæps] verfließen, -streichen.

e·las|tic [ɪˈlæstɪk] 1. (~ally) elastisch, dehnbar; ~ band Brt. = 2. Gummiring m, -band n; **~·ti·ci·ty** [elæˈstɪsətɪ] Elastizität f.

e·lat·ed [ɪˈleɪtɪd] begeistert, stolz.

el·bow [ˈelbəʊ] 1. Ellbogen m; Biegung f; ⊕ Knie n; at one's ~ bei der Hand; out at ~s fig. heruntergekommen; 2. mit dem Ellbogen (weg)stoßen; ~ one's way through sich (mit den Ellbogen) e-n Weg bahnen durch.

el·der[1] ♀ [ˈeldə] Holunder m.

el·der[2] [~] 1. ältere(r, -s); 2. der, die Ältere; (Kirchen)Älteste(r) m; **~·ly** [~lɪ] ältlich, ältere(r, -s).

el·dest [ˈeldɪst] älteste(r, -s).

e·lect [ɪˈlekt] 1. gewählt; 2. (aus-, er)wählen.

e·lec|tion [ɪˈlekʃn] 1. Wahl f; 2. pol. Wahl...; **~·tor** [~tə] Wähler(in); Am. pol. Wahlmann m; hist. Kurfürst m; **~·to·ral** [~ərəl] Wahl..., Wähler...; ~ college Am. pol. Wahlmänner pl.; **~·to·rate** pol. [~ərət] Wähler(schaft f) pl.

e·lec|tric [ɪˈlektrɪk] (~ally) elektrisch, Elektro...; fig. elektrisierend; **~·tri·cal** □ [~kl] elektrisch; Elektro...; ~ engineer Elektroingenieur m, -techniker m; **~·tric chair** elektrischer Stuhl; **~·tri·cian** [ɪlekˈtrɪʃn] Elektriker m; **~·tri·ci·ty** [~ɪsətɪ] Elektrizität f.

e·lec·tri·fy [ɪˈlektrɪfaɪ] elektrifizieren; elektrisieren (a. fig.).

e·lec·tro- [ɪˈlektrəʊ] Elektro...

e·lec·tro·cute [ɪˈlektrəkjuːt] auf dem elektrischen Stuhl hinrichten; durch elektrischen Strom töten.

e·lec·tron [ɪˈlektrɒn] Elektron n.

e·lec·tron·ic [ɪlekˈtrɒnɪk] 1. (~ally) elektronisch, Elektronen...; ~ data processing elektronische Datenverarbeitung; 2. ~s sg. Elektronik f; pl. Elektronik f (e-s Geräts).

el·e|gance [ˈelɪɡəns] Eleganz f; **~·gant** □ [~t] elegant; geschmackvoll; erstklassig.

el·e|ment [ˈelɪmənt] Element n; Urstoff *m*; (Grund)Bestandteil *m*; ~*s pl.* Anfangsgründe *pl.*, Grundlage(n *pl.*) *f*; Elemente *pl.*, Naturkräfte *pl.*; ~·men·tal □ [eli'mentl] elementar; wesentlich.

el·e·men·ta·ry □ [eli'mentəri] elementar; Anfangs..; ~ school *Am.* Grundschule *f.*

el·e·phant *zo.* ['elifənt] Elefant *m.*

el·e·vate ['eliveit] erhöhen; *fig.* erheben; ~·vat·ed erhöht; *fig.* gehoben, erhaben; ~ (railroad) *Am.* Hochbahn *f*; ~·va·tion [eli'veiʃn] Erhebung *f*; Erhöhung *f*; Höhe *f*; Erhabenheit *f*; ~·va·tor ⊕ ['eliveitə] *Am.* Lift *m*, Fahrstuhl *m*, Aufzug *m*; ✍ Höhenruder *n.*

e·lev·en [i'levn] 1. elf; 2. Elf *f*; ~th [~θ] 1. elfte(r, -s); 2. Elftel *n.*

elf [elf] (*pl. elves*) Elf(e *f*) *m*; Kobold *m.*

e·lic·it [i'lisit] *et.* entlocken (*from dat.*); ans (Tages)Licht bringen.

el·i·gi·ble □ ['elidʒəbl] geeignet, annehmbar, akzeptabel; berechtigt.

e·lim·i·nate [i'limineit] entfernen, beseitigen; ausscheiden; ~·na·tion [ilimi'neiʃn] Entfernung *f*, Beseitigung *f*; Ausscheidung *f.*

é·lite [ei'li:t] Elite *f*; Auslese *f.*

elk *zo.* [elk] Elch *m.*

el·lipse ⅄ [i'lips] Ellipse *f.*

elm ⅄ [elm] Ulme *f*, Rüster *f.*

el·o·cu·tion [elə'kju:ʃn] Vortrag(s-kunst *f*, -sweise *f*) *m*; Sprechtechnik *f.*

e·lon·gate ['i:lɒŋgeit] verlängern.

e·lope [i'ləup] (mit s-m *od.* s-r Geliebten) ausreißen, *od.* durchbrennen.

el·o·quence ['eləkwəns] Beredsamkeit *f*; ~·quent □ [~t] beredt.

else [els] sonst, weiter; anderer(r, -s); ~·where ['els'weə] anderswo(hin).

e·lu·ci·date [i'lu:sideit] erklären.

e·lude [i'lu:d] geschickt entgehen, ausweichen, sich entziehen (*alle dat.*); *fig.* nicht einfallen (*dat.*).

e·lu·sive □ [i'lu:siv] schwerfaßbar.

elves [elvz] *pl. von* elf.

e·ma·ci·ated [i'meiʃieitid] abgezehrt, ausgemergelt.

em·a|nate ['eməneit] ausströmen; ausgehen (*from* von); ~·na·tion [emə'neiʃn] Ausströmen *n*; *fig.* Ausstrahlung *f.*

e·man·ci|pate [i'mænsipeit] emanzipieren; befreien; ~·pa·tion [imænsi'peiʃn] Emanzipation *f*; Befreiung *f.*

em·balm [im'ba:m] (ein)balsamieren.

em·bank·ment [im'bæŋkmənt] Eindämmung *f*; (Erd)Damm *m*; (Bahn-, Straßen)Damm *m*; Uferstraße *f.*

em·bar·go [em'ba:gəu] (*pl. -goes*) Embargo *n*, (Hafen-, Handels)Sperre *f.*

em·bark [im'ba:k] ✈, ✍ an Bord nehmen *od.* gehen, ✍ ⌂ *a.* (sich) einschiffen; *Waren* verladen; ~ on, ~ upon *et.* anfangen *od.* beginnen.

em·bar·rass [im'bærəs] in Verlegenheit bringen, verlegen machen, in e-e peinliche Lage versetzen; ~·ing □ [~iŋ] unangenehm, peinlich; ~·ment [~mənt] Verlegenheit *f.*

em·bas·sy ['embəsi] Botschaft *f.*

em·bed [im'bed] (*-dd-*) (ein)betten, (ein)lagern.

em·bel·lish [im'beliʃ] verschönern; *fig.* ausschmücken, beschönigen.

em·bers ['embəz] *pl.* Glut *f.*

em·bez·zle [im'bezl] unterschlagen; ~·ment [~mənt] Unterschlagung *f.*

em·bit·ter [im'bitə] verbittern.

em·blem ['embləm] Sinnbild *n*; Wahrzeichen *n.*

em·bod·y [im'bɒdi] verkörpern; enthalten.

em·bo·lis·m ⅄ ['embəlizəm] Embolie *f.*

em·brace [im'breis] 1. (sich) umarmen; einschließen; 2. Umarmung *f.*

em·broi·der [im'brɔidə] (be)sticken; *fig.* ausschmücken; ~·y [~əri] Stickerei *f*; *fig.* Ausschmückung *f.*

em·broil [im'brɔil] (in Streit) verwickeln; verwirren.

e·men·da·tion [i:men'deiʃn] Verbesserung *f*, Berichtigung *f.*

em·e·rald ['emərəld] 1. Smaragd *m*; 2. smaragdgrün.

e·merge [i'mɜːdʒ] auftauchen; hervorkommen; *fig.* sich erheben; sich zeigen.

e·mer|gen·cy [i'mɜːdʒənsi] Not (-lage) *f*, ~-fall *m*, -stand *m*; *attr.* Not...; ~ brake Notbremse *f*; ~ call *Am.* Notruf *m*; ~ exit Notausgang *m*; ~ landing ✍ Notlandung *f*; ~ number Notruf(nummer *f*) *m*; ~ ward ⚕ Notaufnahme *f*; ~·gent [~t] auftauchend; *fig.* (jung u.) aufstrebend (*Nationen*).

em·i|grant ['emigrənt] Auswanderer *m*, *bsd. pol.* Emigrant(in); ~·grate [~reit] auswandern, *bsd. pol.* emigrieren; **~·gra·tion** [emɪˈɡreɪʃn] Auswanderung *f*, *bsd. pol.* Emigration *f*.

em·i·nence [ˈemɪnəns] (An)Höhe *f*; hohe Stellung; Ruhm *m*, Bedeutung *f*; ⅋ Eminenz *f* (*Titel*); **~·nent** □ [~t] *fig.* ausgezeichnet, hervorragend; **~·nent·ly** [~lɪ] ganz besonders, äußerst.

e·mit [ɪˈmɪt] (*-tt-*) aussenden, -stoßen, -strahlen, -strömen; von sich geben.

e·mo·tion [ɪˈməʊʃn] (Gemüts)Bewegung *f*, Gefühl(sregung *f*) *n*; Rührung *f*; **~·al** □ [~l] emotional; gefühlsmäßig; gefühlsbetont; **~·al·ly** [~lɪ] emotional, gefühlsmäßig; **~ disturbed** seelisch gestört; **~ ill** gemütskrank; **~·less** [~lɪs] gefühllos; unbewegt.

em·per·or [ˈempərə] Kaiser *m*.

em·pha|sis [ˈemfəsɪs] (*pl. -ses* [-siːz]) Gewicht *n*; Nachdruck *m*; **~·size** [~saɪz] nachdrücklich betonen; **~·tic** [ɪmˈfætɪk] (*~ally*) nachdrücklich; deutlich; bestimmt.

em·pire [ˈempaɪə] (Kaiser)Reich *n*; Herrschaft *f*; *the British* ⅋ das britische Weltreich.

em·pir·i·cal □ [emˈpɪrɪkl] erfahrungsgemäß.

em·ploy [ɪmˈplɔɪ] **1.** beschäftigen, anstellen; an-, verwenden, gebrauchen; **2.** Beschäftigung *f*; *in the ~ of* angestellt bei; **~·ee** [emplɔɪˈiː] Angestellte(r *m*) *f*, Arbeitnehmer(in); **~·er** [ɪmˈplɔɪə] Arbeitgeber(in); **~·ment** [~mənt] Beschäftigung *f*, Arbeit *f*; **~ agency, ~ bureau** Stellenvermittlung(sbüro *n*) *f*; **~ market** Arbeits-, Stellenmarkt *m*; **~ service agency** *Brt.* Arbeitsamt *n*.

em·pow·er [ɪmˈpaʊə] ermächtigen; befähigen.

em·press [ˈempris] Kaiserin *f*.

emp|ti·ness [ˈemptɪnɪs] Leere *f* (*a. fig.*); **~·ty** □ [ˈemptɪ] **1.** (*-ier, -iest*) leer (*a. fig.*); **~ of** ohne; **2.** (aus-, ent)leeren; sich leeren.

em·u·late [ˈemjʊleɪt] wetteifern mit; nacheifern (*dat.*); es gleichtun (*dat.*).

e·mul·sion [ɪˈmʌlʃn] Emulsion *f*.

en·a·ble [ɪˈneɪbl] befähigen *j-m* ermöglichen; ermächtigen.

en·act [ɪˈnækt] verfügen, -ordnen; *Gesetz* erlassen; *thea.* aufführen.

e·nam·el [ɪˈnæml] **1.** Email(le *f*) *n*; *anat.* (Zahn)Schmelz *m*; Glasur *f*;

Lack *m*; Nagellack *m*; **2.** (*bsd. Brt. -ll-, Am. -l-*) emaillieren; glasieren; lackieren.

en·am·o(u)red [ɪˈnæməd]: **~ of** verliebt in.

en·camp·ment *bsd.* ✗ [ɪnˈkæmpmənt] (Feld)Lager *n*.

en·cased [ɪnˈkeɪst]: **~ in** gehüllt in (*acc.*).

en·chant [ɪnˈtʃɑːnt] bezaubern; **~·ing** □ [~ɪŋ] bezaubernd; **~·ment** [~mənt] Bezauberung *f*; Zauber *m*.

en·cir·cle [ɪnˈsɜːkl] einkreisen, umzingeln; umfassen, umschlingen.

en·close [ɪnˈkləʊz] einzäunen; einschließen; beifügen; **en·clo·sure** [~əʊʒə] Einzäunung *f*; eingezäuntes Grundstück; Anlage *f* (*zu e-m Brief*).

en·com·pass [ɪnˈkʌmpəs] umgeben.

en·coun·ter [ɪnˈkaʊntə] **1.** Begegnung *f*; Gefecht *n*; **2.** begegnen (*dat.*); auf *Schwierigkeiten etc.* stoßen; mit *j-m feindlich* zusammenstoßen.

en·cour·age [ɪnˈkʌrɪdʒ] ermutigen; fördern; **~·ment** [~mənt] Ermutigung *f*; Anfeuerung *f*; Unterstützung *f*.

en·croach [ɪnˈkrəʊtʃ] (*on, upon*) eingreifen (*in j-s Recht etc.*), eindringen (*in acc.*); über Gebühr in Anspruch nehmen (*acc.*); **~·ment** [~mənt] Ein-, Übergriff *m*.

en·cum|ber [ɪnˈkʌmbə] belasten; (be)hindern; **~·brance** [~brəns] Last *f*, Belastung *f*, Hindernis *n*, Behinderung *f*; *without ~* ohne (Familien-) Anhang.

en·cy·clo·p(a)e·di·a [ensaɪkləˈpiːdjə] Enzyklopädie *f*.

end [end] **1.** Ende *n*; Ziel *n*, Zweck *m*; *no ~ of* unendlich viel(e), unzählige; *in the ~* am Ende; *on ~* aufrecht; *stand on ~* zu Berge stehen (*Haare*); *to no ~* vergebens; *go off the deep ~ fig.* in die Luft gehen; *make both ~s meet* gerade auskommen; **2.** enden; beend(ig)en.

en·dan·ger [ɪnˈdeɪndʒə] gefährden.

en·dear [ɪnˈdɪə] beliebt machen (*to s.o.* bei *j-m*); **~·ing** □ [~rɪŋ] gewinnend; liebenswert; **~·ment** [~mənt] Liebkosung *f*; *term of ~* Kosewort *n*.

en·deav·o(u)r [ɪnˈdevə] **1.** Bestreben *n*, Bemühung *f*; **2.** sich bemühen.

end|ing [ˈendɪŋ] Ende *n*; Schluß *m*; *gr.* Endung *f*; **~·less** □ [~lɪs] endlos, unendlich; ⊕ ohne Ende.

en·dive ♀ ['endɪv] Endivie f.

en·dorse [ɪn'dɔːs] econ. Scheck etc. indossieren; et. vermerken (on auf der Rückseite e-r Urkunde); gutheißen; **~ment** [~mənt] Aufschrift f, Vermerk m; econ. Indossament n.

en·dow [ɪn'daʊ] fig. ausstatten; ~ s.o. with s.th. j-m et. stiften; **~ment** [~mənt] Stiftung f; mst ~s pl. Begabung f, Talent n.

en·dur|ance [ɪn'djʊərəns] Ausdauer f; Ertragen n; beyond ~, past ~ unerträglich; **~e** [ɪn'djʊə] ertragen.

en·e·my ['enəmɪ] **1.** Feind m; the ♀ der Teufel; **2.** feindlich.

en·er|get·ic [enə'dʒetɪk] (~ally) energisch; **~gy** ['enədʒɪ] Energie f; ~ crisis Energiekrise f.

en·fold [ɪn'fəʊld] einhüllen; umfassen.

en·force [ɪn'fɔːs] (mit Nachdruck, a. gerichtlich) geltend machen; erzwingen; aufzwingen (upon dat.); durchführen; **~ment** [~mənt] Erzwingung f; Geltendmachung f; Durchführung f.

en·fran·chise [ɪn'fræntʃaɪz] j-m das Wahlrecht verleihen; j-m die Bürgerrechte verleihen.

en·gage [ɪn'geɪdʒ] v/t. anstellen; verpflichten; Künstler etc. engagieren; in Anspruch nehmen; × angreifen; be ~d verlobt sein (to mit); beschäftigt sein (in mit); besetzt sein; ~ the clutch mot. ⚙ in Gang einlegen; v/i. sich verpflichten (to do zu tun); garantieren (for für); sich beschäftigen (in mit); × angreifen; ⊕ greifen (Zahnräder); **~ment** [~mənt] Verpflichtung f; Verlobung f; Verabredung f; Beschäftigung f; × Gefecht n; ⊕ Ineinandergreifen n.

en·gag·ing [ɪn'geɪdʒɪŋ] einnehmend; gewinnend (Lächeln etc.).

en·gine [ɪn'dʒɪn] Maschine f; Motor m; 🚂 Lokomotive f; **~-driv·er** Brt. 🚂 Lokomotivführer m.

en·gi·neer [endʒɪ'nɪə] **1.** Ingenieur m; Techniker m; Mechaniker m; Am. 🚂 Lokomotivführer m; × Pionier m; **2.** als Ingenieur tätig sein; bauen; **~ing** [~rɪŋ] **1.** Maschinen- u. Gerätebau m; Ingenieurwesen n; **2.** technisch; Ingenieur...

En·glish ['ɪŋglɪʃ] **1.** englisch; **2.** ling. Englisch n; the ~ pl. die Engländer pl.; in plain ~ fig. unverblümt; **~man** (pl. -men) Engländer m;

~wom·an (pl. -women) Engländerin f.

en·grave [ɪn'greɪv] (ein)gravieren, (-)meißeln, (-)schnitzen; fig. einprägen; **en·grav·er** [~ə] Graveur m; **en·grav·ing** [~ɪŋ] (Kupfer-, Stahl-) Stich m; Holzschnitt m.

en·grossed [ɪn'grəʊst] (in) (voll) in Anspruch genommen (von), vertieft, -sunken (in acc.).

en·gulf [ɪn'gʌlf] verschlingen (a. fig.).

en·hance [ɪn'hɑːns] erhöhen.

e·nig·ma [ɪ'nɪgmə] Rätsel n; **en·ig·mat·ic** [enɪg'mætɪk] (~ally) rätselhaft.

en·joy [ɪn'dʒɔɪ] sich erfreuen an (dat.); genießen; did you ~ it? hat es Ihnen gefallen?; ~ o.s. sich amüsieren, sich gut unterhalten; ~ yourself! viel Spaß!; I ~ my dinner es schmeckt mir; **~·a·ble** □ [~əbl] angenehm, erfreulich; **~ment** [~mənt] Genuß m, Freude f.

en·large [ɪn'lɑːdʒ] (sich) vergrößern od. erweitern, ausdehnen; phot. vergrößern, sich vergrößern lassen; sich verbreiten od. auslassen (on, upon über acc.); **~ment** [~mənt] Erweiterung f; Vergrößerung f (a. phot.).

en·light·en [ɪn'laɪtn] fig. erleuchten; j-n aufklären; **~ment** [~mənt] Aufklärung f.

en·list [ɪn'lɪst] v/t. × anwerben; j-n gewinnen; ~ed men pl. Am. × Unteroffiziere pl. und Mannschaften pl.; v/i. sich freiwillig melden.

en·liv·en [ɪn'laɪvn] beleben.

en·mi·ty ['enmətɪ] Feindschaft f.

en·no·ble [ɪ'nəʊbl] adeln; veredeln.

e·nor|mi·ty [ɪ'nɔːmətɪ] Ungeheuerlichkeit f; **~mous** □ [~əs] ungeheuer.

e·nough [ɪ'nʌf] genug.

en·quire, en·qui·ry [ɪn'kwaɪə, ~rɪ] = inquire, inquiry.

en·rage [ɪn'reɪdʒ] wütend machen; **~d** wütend (at über acc.).

en·rap·ture [ɪn'ræptʃə] entzücken, hinreißen; **~d** entzückt, hingerissen.

en·rich [ɪn'rɪtʃ] be-, anreichern.

en·rol(l) [ɪn'rəʊl] (-ll-) v/t. j-n in e-e Liste eintragen; univ. j-n immatrikulieren; × anwerben; aufnehmen; v/i. sich einschreiben (lassen), univ. sich immatrikulieren; **~ment** [~mənt] Eintragung f, -schreibung f, univ. Immatrikulation f; bsd. × An-

E

werbung f; Einstellung f; Aufnahme f; Schüler-, Studenten-, Teilnehmerzahl f.

en·sign ['ensaɪn] Fahne f; Flagge f; Abzeichen n; Am. ♣ ['ensn] Leutnant m zur See.

en·sue [ɪn'sjuː] (darauf, nach)folgen.

en·sure [ɪn'ʃʊə] sichern.

en·tail [ɪn'teɪl] ɪtɪ als Erbgut vererben; fig. mit sich bringen.

en·tan·gle [ɪn'tæŋgl] verwickeln; **~ment** [~mənt] Verwicklung f; ✕ Drahtverhau m.

en·ter ['entə] v/t. (hinein)gehen, (-)kommen in (acc.), (ein)treten in (acc.), betreten; einsteigen od. einfahren etc. in (acc.); eindringen in (acc.); econ. eintragen, (ver)buchen; Protest erheben; Namen eintragen, -schreiben, j-n aufnehmen; Sport: melden, nennen; ~ s.o. at school j-n zur Schule anmelden; v/i. eintreten, herein-, hineinkommen, -gehen; in ein Land einweisen; Sport: sich melden (for für); ~ into fig. eingehen auf (acc.); ~ on od. upon an inheritance e-e Erbschaft antreten.

en·ter·prise ['entəpraɪz] Unternehmen n (a. econ.); econ. Unternehmertum n; Unternehmungsgeist m; **~pris·ing** □ [~ɪŋ] unternehmungslustig; wagemutig; kühn.

en·ter·tain [entə'teɪn] unterhalten; bewirten; in Erwägung ziehen; Zweifel etc. hegen; **~er** [~ə] Entertainer(in), Unterhaltungskünstler(in); **~ment** [~mənt] Unterhaltung f; Entertainment n; Bewirtung f.

en·thral(l) fig. [ɪn'θrɔːl] (-ll-) fesseln, bezaubern.

en·throne [ɪn'θrəʊn] inthronisieren.

en·thu·si·as·m [ɪn'θjuːzɪæzəm] Begeisterung f; **~t** [~st] Enthusiast(in); **~tic** [ɪnθjuːzɪ'æstɪk] (~ally) begeistert.

en·tice [ɪn'taɪs] (ver)locken; **~ment** [~mənt] Verlockung f, Reiz m.

en·tire □ [ɪn'taɪə] ganz, vollständig; ungeteilt; **~ly** [~lɪ] völlig; ausschließlich.

en·ti·tle [ɪn'taɪtl] betiteln; berechtigen (to zu).

en·ti·ty ['entɪtɪ] Wesen n; Dasein n.

en·trails ['entreɪlz] pl. Eingeweide pl.; fig. das Innere.

en·trance ['entrəns] Eintritt m; Einfahrt f; Eingang m; Einlaß m.

en·treat [ɪn'triːt] inständig bitten,

anflehen; **en·trea·ty** [~ɪ] dringende od. inständige Bitte.

en·trench ✕ [ɪn'trentʃ] verschanzen (a. fig.).

en·trust [ɪn'trʌst] anvertrauen (s.th. to s.o. j-m et.); betrauen.

en·try ['entrɪ] Einreise f; Einlaß m, Zutritt m; Eingang m; Einfahrt f; Beitritt m (into zu); Eintragung f; Sport: Meldung f, Nennung f; **~ permit** Einreisegenehmigung f; **~ visa** Einreisevisum n; book-keeping by double (single) ~ econ. doppelte (einfache) Buchführung; no ~! Zutritt verboten!, mot. keine Einfahrt!

en·twine [ɪn'twaɪn] ineinanderschlingen.

e·nu·me·rate [ɪ'njuːməreɪt] aufzählen.

en·vel·op [ɪn'veləp] (ein)hüllen, einwickeln.

en·ve·lope ['envələʊp] Briefumschlag m.

en·vi·a·ble □ ['envɪəbl] beneidenswert; **~ous** □ [~əs] neidisch.

en·vi·ron·ment [ɪn'vaɪərənmənt] Umgebung f, sociol. a. Milieu n; Umwelt f (a. sociol.); **~men·tal** □ [ɪnvaɪərən'mentl] sociol. Milieu...; Umwelt...; **~ law** Umweltschutzgesetz n; **~ pollution** Umweltverschmutzung f; **~men·tal·ist** [~əlɪst] Umweltschützer(in); **~s** ['envɪrənz] pl. Umgebung f (e-r Stadt).

en·vis·age [ɪn'vɪzɪdʒ] sich et. vorstellen.

en·voy ['envɔɪ] Gesandte(r) m.

en·vy ['envɪ] 1. Neid m; 2. beneiden.

ep·ic ['epɪk] 1. episch; 2. Epos n.

ep·i·dem·ic [epɪ'demɪk] 1. (~ally) seuchenartig; **~ disease** = 2. Epidemie f, Seuche f.

ep·i·der·mis [epɪ'dɜːmɪs] Oberhaut f.

ep·i·lep·sy ✿ ['epɪlepsɪ] Epilepsie f.

ep·i·logue, Am. a. **-log** ['epɪlɒg] Nachwort n.

e·pis·co·pal □ eccl. [ɪ'pɪskəpl] bischöflich.

ep·i·sode ['epɪsəʊd] Episode f.

ep·i·taph ['epɪtɑːf] Grabinschrift f; Gedenktafel f.

e·pit·o·me [ɪ'pɪtəmɪ] Verkörperung f, Inbegriff m.

e·poch ['iːpɒk] Epoche f, Zeitalter n.

eq·ua·ble □ ['ekwəbl] ausgeglichen (a. Klima).

e·qual ['iːkwəl] 1. □ gleich; gleichmäßig; ~ to fig. gewachsen (dat.); ~ opportunities pl. Chancengleichheit f; ~ rights pl. for women Gleichberechtigung f der Frau; **2.** Gleiche(r m) f; **3.** (bsd. Brt. -ll-, Am. -l-) gleichen (dat.); **~·i·ty** [iːˈkwɒlətɪ] Gleichheit f; **~·i·za·tion** [iːkwəlaɪˈzeɪʃn] Gleichstellung f; Ausgleich m; **~ize** [ˈiːkwəlaɪz] gleichmachen, -stellen, angleichen; Sport: ausgleichen.

equa·nim·i·ty [iːkwəˈnɪmətɪ] Gleichmut m.

e·qua·tion [ɪˈkweɪʒn] Ausgleich m; ⅍ Gleichung f.

e·qua·tor [ɪˈkweɪtə] Äquator m.

e·qui·lib·ri·um [iːkwɪˈlɪbrɪəm] Gleichgewicht n.

e·quip [ɪˈkwɪp] (-pp-) ausrüsten; **~·ment** [~mənt] Ausrüstung f; Einrichtung f.

eq·ui·ty [ˈekwɪtɪ] Gerechtigkeit f, Billigkeit f.

e·quiv·a·lent [ɪˈkwɪvələnt] **1.** □ gleichwertig; gleichbedeutend (to mit); **2.** Äquivalent n, Gegenwert m.

e·quiv·o·cal □ [ɪˈkwɪvəkl] zweideutig; zweifelhaft.

e·ra [ˈɪərə] Zeitrechnung f; Zeitalter n.

e·rad·i·cate [ɪˈrædɪkeɪt] ausrotten.

e·rase [ɪˈreɪz] ausradieren, -streichen, löschen (a. Tonband); fig. auslöschen; **e·ras·er** [~ə] Radiergummi m.

ere [eə] **1.** cj. ehe, bevor; **2.** prp. vor (dat.).

e·rect [ɪˈrekt] **1.** □ aufrecht; **2.** aufrichten; Denkmal etc. errichten; aufstellen; **e·rec·tion** [~kʃn] Errichtung f; physiol. Erektion f.

er·mine zo. [ˈɜːmɪn] Hermelin n.

e·ro·sion [ɪˈrəʊʒn] Zerfressen n; geol. Erosion f, Auswaschung f.

e·rot·ic [ɪˈrɒtɪk] (~ally) erotisch; **~·i·cis·m** [~ɪsɪzəm] Erotik f.

err [ɜː] (sich) irren.

er·rand [ˈerənd] Botengang m, Auftrag m, Besorgung f; go on od. make an ~ e-e Besorgung machen; **~·boy** Laufbursche m.

er·rat·ic [ɪˈrætɪk] (~ally) sprunghaft, unstet, unberechenbar.

er·ro·ne·ous □ [ɪˈrəʊnjəs] irrig.

er·ror [ˈerə] Irrtum m, Fehler m; ~s excepted Irrtümer vorbehalten.

e·rupt [ɪˈrʌpt] ausbrechen (Vulkan etc.); durchbrechen (Zähne); **e·rup-**

tion [~pʃn] (Vulkan)Ausbruch m; ⅍ Ausbruch m e-s Ausschlags; ⅍ Ausschlag m.

es·ca·late [ˈeskəleɪt] eskalieren (Krieg etc.); steigen, in die Höhe gehen (Preise); **~·la·tion** [ɪˈskəˈleɪʃn] Eskalation f.

es·ca·la·tor [ˈeskəleɪtə] Rolltreppe f.

es·ca·lope [ˈeskələʊp] (bsd. Wiener) Schnitzel n.

es·cape [ɪˈskeɪp] **1.** entgehen; entkommen, -rinnen; entweichen; j-m entfallen; **2.** Entrinnen n, Entweichen n; Flucht f; have a narrow ~ mit knapper Not davonkommen; ~ chute ✈ Notrutsche f.

es·cort 1. [ˈeskɔːt] ✕ Eskorte f; Geleit(schutz m) n; **2.** [ɪˈskɔːt] ✕ eskortieren; ✕, ♣ Geleit(schutz) geben; geleiten.

es·cutch·eon [ɪˈskʌtʃən] Wappenschild m, n.

es·pe·cial [ɪˈspeʃl] besondere(r, -s); vorzüglich; **~·ly** [~lɪ] besonders.

es·pi·o·nage [espɪəˈnɑːʒ] Spionage f.

es·pla·nade [espləˈneɪd] (bsd. Strand)Promenade f.

es·pres·so [eˈspresəʊ] (pl. -sos) Espresso m (Kaffee).

Es·quire [ɪˈskwaɪə] (abbr. Esq.) auf Briefen: John Smith Esq. Herrn John Smith.

es·say 1. [eˈseɪ] versuchen; probieren; **2.** [ˈeseɪ] Versuch m; Aufsatz m, kurze Abhandlung, Essay m, n.

es·sence [ˈesns] Wesen n (e-r Sache); Essenz f; Extrakt m.

es·sen·tial [ɪˈsenʃl] **1.** □ (to für) wesentlich; wichtig; **2.** mst ~s pl. das Wesentliche, in der Hauptsache.

es·tab·lish [ɪˈstæblɪʃ] festsetzen; errichten, gründen; einrichten; j-n einsetzen; ~ o.s. sich niederlassen; Q̂ed Church Staatskirche f; **~·ment** [~mənt] Er-, Einrichtung f; Gründung f; the Q̂ das Establishment, die etablierte Macht, die herrschende

es·tate [ɪˈsteɪt] (großes) Grundstück, Landsitz m, Gut n; ⅌ Besitz m, (Erb)Masse f, Nachlaß m; housing ~ (Wohn)Siedlung f; industrial ~ Industriegebiet n; real ~ Liegenschaften pl.; (Am. real) **~ a·gent** Grundstücks-, Immobilienmakler m; **~ car** Brt. mot. Kombiwagen m.

es·teem [ɪˈstiːm] **1.** Achtung f, An-

sehen *n* (*with* bei); **2.** achten, (hoch-)
schätzen; ansehen *od.* betrachten
als.

es·thet·ic(s) *Am.* [es'θetɪk(s)] =
aesthetic(s).

es·ti·ma·ble ['estɪməbl] schätzens-
wert.

es·ti·mate 1. ['estɪmeɪt] (ab-, ein-)
schätzen; veranschlagen; **2.** [~mɪt]
Schätzung *f*; (Kosten)Voranschlag
m; **~ma·tion** [estɪ'meɪʃn] Schätzung *f*; Meinung *f*; Achtung *f*.

es·trange [ɪ'streɪndʒ] entfremden.

es·tu·a·ry ['estjʊərɪ] *den Gezeiten
ausgesetzte* weite Flußmündung.

etch [etʃ] ätzen; radieren; **~ing**
['etʃɪŋ] Radierung *f*; Kupferstich *m.*

e·ter·nal □ [ɪ'tɜːnl] immerwährend,
ewig; **~ni·ty** [~ətɪ] Ewigkeit *f.*

e·ther ['i:θə] Äther *m*; **e·the·re·al** □
[i:'θɪərɪəl] ätherisch (*a. fig.*).

eth·i·cal □ ['eθɪkl] sittlich, ethisch;
~ics [~] *sg.* Sittenlehre *f*, Ethik *f.*

Eu·ro- ['jʊərəʊ] europäisch, Euro...

Eu·ro·pe·an [jʊərə'pɪən] **1.** europäisch; **~** (*Economic*) *Community*
Europäische (Wirtschafts)Gemein-
schaft; **2.** Europäer(in).

e·vac·u·ate [ɪ'vækjʊeɪt] entleeren;
evakuieren; *Haus etc.* räumen.

e·vade [ɪ'veɪd] (geschickt) ausweichen (*dat.*); umgehen.

e·val·u·ate [ɪ'væljʊeɪt] schätzen; abschätzen, bewerten, beurteilen.

e·va·nes·cent [i:və'nesnt] vergänglich.

e·van·gel·i·cal □ [i:væn'dʒelɪkl]
evangelisch.

e·vap·o·rate [ɪ'væpəreɪt] verdunsten,
-dampfen (lassen); **~d** *milk* Kon-
densmilch *f*; **~ra·tion** [ɪvæpə'reɪʃn]
Verdunstung *f*, -dampfung *f.*

e·va·sion [ɪ'veɪʒn] Entkommen *n*;
Umgehung *f*, Vermeidung *f*; Ausflucht *f*; **~sive** □ [~sɪv] auswei-
chend; *be* **~** ausweichen.

eve [i:v] Vorabend *m*; Vortag *m*; *on
the* **~** *of* unmittelbar vor (*dat.*); am
Vorabend (*gen.*).

e·ven ['i:vn] **1.** *adj.* □ eben, gleich;
gleichmäßig; ausgeglichen; glatt;
gerade (*Zahl*); unparteiisch; *get* **~**
with s.o. fig. mit j-m abrechnen; **2.**
adv. selbst, sogar, auch; *not* **~** nicht
einmal; **~** *though*, **~** *if* wenn auch; **3.**
ebnen, glätten; **~** *out* sich einpen-
deln.

eve·ning ['i:vnɪŋ] Abend *m*; **~** *class-*

es *pl.* Abendkurs *m*; **~** *dress* Gesellschaftsanzug *m*; Frack *m*, Smoking
m; Abendkleid *n.*

e·ven·song ['i:vnsɒŋ] Abendgottes-
dienst *m.*

e·vent [ɪ'vent] Ereignis *n*, Vorfall *m*;
sportliche Veranstaltung; *Sport*:
Disziplin *f*; *Sport*: Wettbewerb *m*;
at all **~s** auf alle Fälle; *in the* **~** *of* im
Falle (*gen.*); **~ful** [~fl] ereignisreich.

e·ven·tu·al □ [ɪ'ventʃʊəl] schließlich; △ *nicht* eventuell; **~ly** schließlich, endlich.

ev·er ['evə] je, jemals; immer; **~** *so*
noch so (sehr); *as soon as* **~** *I can*
sobald ich nur irgend kann; **~** *after*,
~ *since* von der Zeit an, seitdem; **~** *and
again* dann u. wann, hin u. wieder;
for **~** für immer, auf ewig; *Yours* ... **~** ...
Viele Grüße, Dein(e) *od.* Ihr(e), ...
(*Briefschluß*); **~glade** *Am.* sumpfi-
ges Flußgebiet; **~green 1.** immer-
grün; unverwüstlich, *bsd.* immer
wieder gern gehört; **~** *song* Evergreen *m*; **2.** immergrüne Pflanze;
~last·ing □ ewig; dauerhaft;
~more [~'mɔ:] immerfort.

ev·ery ['evrɪ] jede(r, -s); alle(r, -s); **~**
now and then dann u. wann; **~** *one of
them* jeder von ihnen; **~** *other day*
jeden zweiten Tag, alle zwei Tage;
~bod·y jeder(mann); **~day** All-
tags...; **~one** jeder(mann); **~thing**
alles; **~where** überall; überallhin.

e·vict [ɪ'vɪkt] *rt* zur Räumung zwingen; *j-n* gewaltsam vertreiben.

ev·i·dence ['evɪdəns] **1.** Beweis(material *n*) *m*, Beweise *pl.*; (Zeugen-)
Aussage *f*; *give* **~** (als Zeuge) aussagen; *in* **~** als Beweis; deutlich sichtbar; **2.** be-, nachweisen, zeugen von;
~dent □ [~t] augenscheinlich,
offenbar, klar.

e·vil ['i:vl] **1.** □ (*bsd. Brt. -ll-, Am. -l-*)
übel, schlimm, böse; *the* ♀ *One der
Böse* (*Teufel*); **2.** Übel *n*; *das Böse*; **~-
mind·ed** [~'maɪndɪd] bösartig.

e·vince [ɪ'vɪns] zeigen, bekunden.

e·voke [ɪ'vəʊk] (herauf)beschwören;
Erinnerungen wachrufen.

e·vo·lu·tion [i:və'lu:ʃn] Evolution *f*,
Entwicklung *f.*

e·volve [ɪ'vɒlv] (sich) entwickeln.

ewe *zo.* [ju:] Mutterschaf *n.*

ex [eks] *prp. econ.* ab *Fabrik etc.*;
Börse: ohne.

ex- [~] ehemalig, früher.

ex·act [ɪg'zækt] **1.** □ genau; **2.** *Zah-*

lung eintreiben; *Gehorsam* fordern; **~ing** [~ɪŋ] streng, genau; **~·i·tude** [~ɪtjuːd] = *exactness*; **~ly** [~lɪ] exakt, genau; *als Antwort:* ganz recht, genau; **~ness** [~nɪs] Genauigkeit *f.*

ex·ag·ge·rate [ɪgˈzædʒəreɪt] übertreiben; **~ra·tion** [ɪgzædʒəˈreɪʃn] Übertreibung *f.*

ex·alt [ɪgˈzɔːlt] erhöhen, erheben; preisen; **ex·al·ta·tion** [egzɔːlˈteɪʃn] Begeisterung *f.*

ex·am F [ɪgˈzæm] Examen *n.*

ex·am·i·na·tion [ɪgzæmɪˈneɪʃn] Examen *n*, Prüfung *f*; Untersuchung *f*; Vernehmung *f*; **~ine** [ɪgˈzæmɪn] untersuchen; ⚖️ vernehmen, -hören; *Schule etc.:* prüfen (*in in dat.*; *on über acc.*).

ex·am·ple [ɪgˈzɑːmpl] Beispiel *n*; Vorbild *n*, Muster *n*; *for ~* zum Beispiel.

ex·as·pe·rate [ɪgˈzæspəreɪt] wütend machen; **~rat·ing** □ [~ɪŋ] ärgerlich.

ex·ca·vate [ˈekskəveɪt] ausgraben, -heben, -schachten.

ex·ceed [ɪkˈsiːd] überschreiten; übertreffen; **~ing** □ [~ɪŋ] übermäßig; **~ing·ly** [~lɪ] außerordentlich, überaus.

ex·cel [ɪkˈsel] (*-ll-*) *v/t.* übertreffen; *v/i.* sich auszeichnen; **~lence** [ˈeksələns] ausgezeichnete Qualität; hervorragende Leistung; **Ex·cel·len·cy** [~ənsɪ] Exzellenz *f*; **~lent** □ [~ənt] ausgezeichnet, hervorragend.

ex·cept [ɪkˈsept] 1. ausnehmen, -schließen; 2. *prp.* ausgenommen, außer; *~ for* abgesehen von; **~ing** *prp.* [~ɪŋ] ausgenommen.

ex·cep·tion [ɪkˈsepʃn] Ausnahme *f*; Einwendung *f*, Einwand *m* (*to* gegen); *by way of ~* ausnahmsweise; *make an ~* e-e Ausnahme machen; *take ~ to* Anstoß nehmen an (*dat.*); **~al** □ [~nl] außergewöhnlich; **~al·ly** [~ʃnəlɪ] un-, außergewöhnlich.

ex·cerpt [ˈeksɜːpt] Auszug *m.*

ex·cess [ɪkˈses] Übermaß *n*; Überschuß *m*; Ausschweifung *f*; *attr.* Mehr...; *~ fare* (Fahrpreis)Zuschlag *m*; *~ baggage bsd. Am.*, *~ luggage bsd. Brt.* ✈ Übergepäck *n*; *~ postage* Nachgebühr *f*; **ex·ces·sive** □ [~ɪv] übermäßig, übertrieben.

ex·change [ɪksˈtʃeɪndʒ] 1. (aus-, ein-, um)tauschen (*for* gegen); wechseln; 2. (Aus-, Um)Tausch *m*; (*bsd.* Geld-)

Wechsel *m*; *a. bill of ~* Wechsel *m*; Börse *f*; Wechselstube *f*; Fernsprechamt *n*; *foreign ~*(*s pl.*) Devisen *pl.*; *rate of ~*, *~ rate* Wechselkurs *m*; *~ office* Wechselstube *f*; *~ student* Austauschstudent(in), -schüler(in).

ex·cheq·uer [ɪksˈtʃekə] Staatskasse *f*; *Chancellor of the ♀ Brt.* Schatzkanzler *m*, Finanzminister *m.*

ex·cise[1] [ˈeksaɪz] Verbrauchssteuer *f.*

ex·cise[2] ⚕ [~] herausschneiden.

ex·ci·ta·ble [ɪkˈsaɪtəbl] reizbar, (leicht) erregbar.

ex·cite [ɪkˈsaɪt] er-, anregen; reizen; **ex·cit·ed** □ erregt, aufgeregt; **ex·cite·ment** [~mənt] Auf-, Erregung *f*; Reizung *f*; **ex·cit·ing** □ [~ɪŋ] erregend, aufregend, spannend.

ex·claim [ɪkˈskleɪm] (aus)rufen.

ex·cla·ma·tion [ekskləˈmeɪʃn] Ausruf *m*, (Auf)Schrei *m*; *~ mark*, *Am. a. ~ point* Ausrufe-, Ausrufungszeichen *n.*

ex·clude [ɪkˈskluːd] ausschließen.

ex·clu·sion [ɪkˈskluːʒn] Ausschließung *f*, Ausschluß *m*; **~sive** □ [~sɪv] ausschließlich; exklusiv; Exklusiv...; *~ of* abgesehen von, ohne.

ex·com·mu·ni·cate [ekskəˈmjuːnɪkeɪt] exkommunizieren; **~ca·tion** [ˈekskəmjuːnɪˈkeɪʃn] Exkommunikation *f.*

ex·cre·ment [ˈekskrɪmənt] Kot *m.*

ex·crete [ekˈskriːt] ausscheiden.

ex·cru·ci·at·ing □ [ɪkˈskruːʃɪeɪtɪŋ] entsetzlich, scheußlich.

ex·cur·sion [ɪkˈskɜːʃn] Ausflug *m.*

ex·cu·sa·ble □ [ɪkˈskjuːzəbl] entschuldbar; **ex·cuse** 1. [ɪkˈskjuːz] entschuldigen; *~ me* entschuldige(n Sie); 2. [~s] Entschuldigung *f.*

ex·e·cute [ˈeksɪkjuːt] ausführen; vollziehen; ♪ vortragen; hinrichten; *Testament* vollstrecken; **~cu·tion** [eksɪˈkjuːʃn] Ausführung *f*; Vollziehung *f*; (Zwangs)Vollstreckung *f*; Hinrichtung *f*; ♪ Vortrag *m*; *put od. carry a plan into ~* e-n Plan ausführen *od.* verwirklichen; **~cu·tion·er** [~ʃnə] Henker *m*, Scharfrichter *m*; **~c·u·tive** [ɪgˈzekjʊtɪv] 1. □ vollziehend, ausübend, *pol.* Exekutiv...; *econ.* leitend; *~ board* Vorstand *m*; *~ committee* Exekutivausschuß *m*; 2. *pol.* Exekutive *f*, vollziehende Gewalt; *econ.* leitender Angestellter; **~cu·tor** [~ə] Erbschaftsverwalter *m*, Testamentsvollstrecker *m.*

ex·em·pla·ry □ [ɪgˈzemplərɪ] vor-
bildlich.

ex·em·pli·fy [ɪgˈzemplɪfaɪ] veran-
schaulichen.

ex·empt [ɪgˈzempt] **1.** befreit, frei; **2.**
ausnehmen, befreien.

ex·er·cise [ˈeksəsaɪz] **1.** Übung f;
Ausübung f; ~ *Schule:* Übung(sar-
beit) f, Schulaufgabe f; ⚔ Manöver
n; (körperliche) Bewegung; *do one's*
~s Gymnastik machen; *take* ~ sich
Bewegung machen; *Am.* ~s *pl.*
Feierlichkeiten *pl.*; ~ *book* Schul-,
Schreibheft n; **2.** üben; ausüben;
(sich) bewegen; sich Bewegung machen; ⚔ exerzieren.

ex·ert [ɪgˈzɜːt] *Einfluß etc.* ausüben; ~
o.s. sich anstrengen *od.* bemühen;
ex·er·tion [~ɜːʃn] Ausübung f; Anstrengung f, Strapaze f.

ex·hale [eksˈheɪl] ausatmen; *Gas, Geruch etc.* verströmen; *Rauch* ausstoßen.

ex·haust [ɪgˈzɔːst] **1.** erschöpfen; entleeren; auspumpen; **2.** ⊕ Abgas n,
Auspuffgase *pl.*; Auspuff m; ~ *fumes*
pl. Abgase *pl.*; ~ *pipe* Auspuffrohr n;
~**ed** erschöpft (*a. fig.*); vergriffen
(*Auflage*); **ex·haus·tion** [~tʃən] Erschöpfung f; **ex·haus·tive** □ [~tɪv]
erschöpfend.

ex·hib·it [ɪgˈzɪbɪt] **1.** ausstellen; ⚖
vorzeigen, *Beweise* beibringen; *fig.*
zeigen; **2.** Ausstellungsstück n; Be-
weisstück n; **ex·hi·bi·tion** [eksɪ-
ˈbɪʃn] Ausstellung f; Zurschaustellung f; *Brt.* Stipendium n.

ex·hil·a·rate [ɪgˈzɪləreɪt] auf-, erhei-
tern.

ex·hort [ɪgˈzɔːt] ermahnen.

ex·ile [ˈeksaɪl] **1.** Verbannung f; Exil
n; Verbannte(r m) f; im Exil Leben-
de(r m) f; **2.** in die Verbannung *od.*
ins Exil schicken.

ex·ist [ɪgˈzɪst] existieren; vorhanden
sein; leben; bestehen; ~**ence** [~əns]
Existenz f; Vorhandensein n, Vorkommen n; Leben n, Dasein n; △
nicht Existenz (Lebensunterhalt);
~**ent** [~t] vorhanden.

ex·it [ˈeksɪt] **1.** Abgang m; Ausgang
m; (Autobahn)Ausfahrt f; Ausreise
f; **2.** *thea.* (geht) ab.

ex·o·dus [ˈeksədəs] Auszug m; Ab-
wanderung f; *general* ~ allgemeiner
Aufbruch.

ex·on·e·rate [ɪgˈzɒnəreɪt] entlasten,
entbinden, befreien.

ex·or·bi·tant □ [ɪgˈzɔːbɪtənt] übertrieben, maßlos; unverschämt (*Preis
etc.*).

ex·or·cize [ˈeksɔːsaɪz] *böse Geister* be-
schwören, austreiben (*from aus*); befreien (*of von*).

ex·ot·ic [ɪgˈzɒtɪk] (~*ally*) exotisch;
fremdländisch; fremd(artig).

ex·pand [ɪkˈspænd] (sich) ausbreiten; (sich) ausdehnen *od.* erweitern;
~ *on* sich auslassen über (*acc.*);
ex·panse [~ns] Ausdehnung f, Weite f; **ex·pan·sion** [~ʃn] Ausbreitung
f; *phys.* Ausdehnung n; *fig.* Erweiterung f, Ausweitung f; **ex·pan·sive**
□ [~sɪv] ausdehnungsfähig; ausgedehnt, weit; *fig.* mitteilsam.

ex·pat·ri·ate [eksˈpætrɪeɪt] *j-n* aus-
bürgern, *j-m* die Staatsangehörigkeit aberkennen.

ex·pect [ɪkˈspekt] erwarten; F annehmen; *be* ~*ing* in anderen Umständen
sein; **ex·pec·tant** □ [~ənt] erwar-
tend (*of acc.*); ~ *mother* werdende
Mutter; **ex·pec·ta·tion** [ekspek-
ˈteɪʃn] Erwartung f; Hoffnung f,
Aussicht f.

ex·pe·dient [ɪkˈspiːdjənt] **1.** □
zweckmäßig; ratsam; **2.** (Hilfs-)
Mittel n, (Not)Behelf m.

ex·pe·di·tion [ekspɪˈdɪʃn] Eile f; ⚔
Feldzug m; (Forschungs)Reise f,
Expedition f; ~**tious** □ [~ʃəs]
schnell.

ex·pel [ɪkˈspel] (-*ll*-) ausstoßen; vertreiben, -jagen; hinauswerfen; ausschließen.

ex·pend [ɪkˈspend] *Geld* ausgeben;
aufwenden; verbrauchen; **ex·pen-
di·ture** [~dɪtʃə] Ausgabe f; Aufwand
m; **ex·pense** [ɪkˈspens] Ausgabe f;
Kosten *pl.*; ~*s pl.* Unkosten *pl.*,
Spesen *pl.*, Auslagen *pl.*; *at the* ~ *of*
auf Kosten (*gen.*); *at any* ~ um jeden
Preis; **ex·pen·sive** □ [~sɪv] kostspielig, teuer.

ex·pe·ri·ence [ɪkˈspɪərɪəns] **1.** Erfahrung f; (Lebens)Praxis f; Erlebnis n;
2. erfahren, erleben; ~**d** erfahren.

ex·per·i·ment 1. [ɪkˈsperɪmənt] Versuch m; **2.** [~ment] experimentieren;
~**men·tal** □ [eksperɪˈmentl] Versuchs...

ex·pert [ˈekspɜːt] **1.** □ [*pred.* eksˈpɜːt]
erfahren, geschickt; fachmännisch;
2. Fachmann m; Sachverständige(r
m) f.

ex·pi·ra·tion [ekspɪˈreɪʃn] Ausatmung f; Ablauf m, Ende n; **ex·pire** [ık'sparə] ausatmen; sein Leben od. s-n Geist aushauchen; ablaufen, verfallen, erlöschen.

ex·plain [ık'spleın] erklären, erläutern; *Gründe* auseinandersetzen.

ex·pla·na·tion [eksplə'neıʃn] Erklärung f; Erläuterung f; **ex·plan·a·to·ry** □ [ık'splænətərı] erklärend.

ex·pli·ca·ble □ ['eksplıkəbl] erklärlich.

ex·pli·cit □ [ık'splısıt] deutlich.

ex·plode [ık'spləʊd] explodieren (lassen); *fig.* ausbrechen (*with in acc.*), platzen (*with* vor); *fig.* sprunghaft ansteigen.

ex·ploit **1.** ['eksplɔıt] Heldentat f; **2.** [ık'splɔıt] ausbeuten; *fig.* ausnutzen; **ex·ploi·ta·tion** [eksplɔı'teıʃn] Ausbeutung f, Auswertung f, Verwertung f, Abbau f; *fig.* Ausnutzung f.

ex·plo·ra·tion [eksplɔ:'reıʃn] Erforschung f; **ex·plore** [ık'splɔ:] erforschen; **ex·plor·er** [~rə] Forscher(in); Forschungsreisende(r m) f.

ex·plo·sion [ık'spləʊʒn] Explosion f; *fig.* Ausbruch m; *fig.* sprunghafter Anstieg; **~sive** [~əʊsıv] **1.** □ explosiv; *fig.* aufbrausend; *fig.* sprunghaft ansteigend; **2.** Sprengstoff m.

ex·po·nent [ek'spəʊnənt] Exponent m; Vertreter m.

ex·port **1.** [ık'spɔ:t] exportieren, ausführen; **2.** ['ekspɔ:t] Export(artikel) m, Ausfuhr(artikel m) f; **ex·por·ta·tion** [ekspɔ:'teıʃn] Ausfuhr f.

ex·pose [ık'spəʊz] aussetzen; *phot.* belichten; ausstellen; *fig.* entlarven, bloßstellen, *et.* aufdecken; **ex·po·si·tion** [ekspə'zıʃn] Ausstellung f.

ex·po·sure [ık'spəʊʒə] Aussetzen n; Ausgesetztsein n; *fig.* Bloßstellung f; Aufdeckung f; Enthüllung f, Entlarvung f; *phot.* Belichtung f; *phot.* Aufnahme f; **~ meter** Belichtungsmesser m.

ex·pound [ık'spaʊnd] erklären, auslegen.

ex·press [ık'spres] **1.** □ ausdrücklich, deutlich; Expreß..., Eil...; **~ compa·ny** *Am.* (Schnell)Transportunternehmen n; **~ train** Schnellzug m; **2.** Eilbote m; Schnellzug m; *by* **~** = **3.** *adv.* durch Eilboten; als Eilgut; **4.** äußern, ausdrücken; auspressen; **ex·pres·sion** [~eʃn] Ausdruck m; **ex·pres·sion·less** □ [~lıs] ausdruckslos; **ex·pres·sive** □ [~sıv]

ausdrückend (*of acc.*); ausdrucksvoll; **~ly** [~lı] ausdrücklich, eigens; **~way** *bsd. Am.* Schnellstraße f.

ex·pro·pri·ate [eks'prəʊprıeıt] enteignen.

ex·pul·sion [ık'spʌlʃn] Vertreibung f; Ausweisung f.

ex·pur·gate ['ekspɜ:geıt] reinigen.

ex·qui·site □ ['ekskwızıt] auserlesen, vorzüglich; fein; heftig.

ex·tant [ek'stænt] (noch) vorhanden.

ex·tend [ık'stend] *v/t.* ausdehnen; ausstrecken; erweitern; verlängern; *Hilfe etc.* gewähren; ⚔ ausschwärmen lassen; *v/i.* sich erstrecken.

ex·ten|sion [ık'stenʃn] Ausdehnung f; Erweiterung f; Verlängerung f; Aus-, Anbau m; *teleph.* Nebenanschluß m, Apparat m; **~ cord** ⚡ Verlängerungsschnur f; **~sive** [~sıv] ausgedehnt, umfassend.

ex·tent [ık'stent] Ausdehnung f, Weite f, Größe f, Umfang m; Grad m; *to the* **~** *of* bis zum Betrag von; *to some od. a certain* **~** bis zu e-m gewissen Grade, einigermaßen.

ex·ten·u·ate [ek'stenjueıt] abschwächen, mildern; beschönigen; *extenuating circumstances pl.* ⚖ mildernde Umstände *pl.*

ex·te·ri·or [ek'stıərıə] **1.** äußerlich, äußere(r, -s), Außen...; **2.** *das* Äußere; *Film:* Außenaufnahme f.

ex·ter·mi·nate [ek'stɜ:mıneıt] ausrotten (*a. fig.*), vernichten, *Ungeziefer, Unkraut a.* vertilgen.

ex·ter·nal □ [ek'stɜ:nl] äußere(r, -s), äußerlich, Außen...

ex·tinct [ık'stıŋkt] erloschen; ausgestorben; **ex·tinc·tion** [~kʃn] Erlöschen n; Aussterben n, Untergang m; (Aus)Löschen n; Vernichtung f, Zerstörung f.

ex·tin·guish [ık'stıŋgwıʃ] (aus)löschen; vernichten; **~er** [~ə] (Feuer-)Löschgerät n.

ex·tort [ık'stɔ:t] erpressen (*from* von); **ex·tor·tion** [~ʃn] Erpressung f.

ex·tra ['ekstrə] **1.** *adj.* Extra..., außer..., Außer...; Neben..., Sonder...; **~ pay** Zulage f; **~ time** *Sport:* (Spiel-) Verlängerung f; **2.** *adv.* besonders; **3.** *et.* Zusätzliches, Extra n; Zuschlag m; Extrablatt n; *thea., Film:* Statist(in).

ex·tract **1.** ['ekstrækt] Auszug m; **2.** [ık'strækt] (heraus)ziehen; herauslocken; ab-, herleiten; **ex·trac·tion** [⸤kʃn] (Heraus)Ziehen n; Herkunft f.

ex·tra|dite [ˈekstrədaɪt] ausliefern; j-s Auslieferung erwirken; **~·di·tion** [ekstrəˈdɪʃn] Auslieferung f.

extra·or·di·na·ry □ [ɪkˈstrɔːdnrɪ] außerordentlich; ungewöhnlich; außerordentlich, Sonder...

ex·tra·ter·res·tri·al □ [ˈekstrətɪˈrestrɪəl] außerirdisch.

ex·trav·a|gence [ɪkˈstrævəgəns] Übertriebenheit f; Verschwendung f; Extravaganz f; **~·gant** □ [⸤t] übertrieben; überspannt; verschwenderisch; extravagant.

ex·treme [ɪkˈstriːm] **1.** □ äußerste(r, -s), größte(r, -s), höchste(r, -s); außergewöhnlich; **2.** das Äußerste; Extrem n; höchster Grad; **~·ly** [⸤lɪ] äußerst, höchst.

ex·trem·is·m bsd. pol. [ɪkˈstriːmɪzm] Extremismus m; **~·ist** [⸤ɪst] Extremist(in).

ex·trem·i·ty [ɪkˈstremətɪ] das Äußerste; höchste Not; äußerste Maßnahme; extremities pl. Gliedmaßen pl., Extremitäten pl.

ex·tri·cate [ˈekstrɪkeɪt] herauswinden, -ziehen, befreien.

ex·tro·vert [ˈekstrəʊvɜːt] Extrovertierte(r m) f.

ex·u·be|rance [ɪgˈzjuːbərəns] Fülle f; Überschwang m; **~·rant** □ [⸤t] reichlich, üppig; überschwenglich; ausgelassen.

ex·ult [ɪgˈzʌlt] frohlocken, jubeln.

eye [aɪ] **1.** Auge n; Blick m; Öse f; see ~ to ~ with s.o. mit j-m völlig übereinstimmen; be up to the ~s in work bis über die Ohren in Arbeit stecken; with an ~ to s.th. im Hinblick auf et.; **2.** ansehen; mustern; **~·ball** [ˈaɪbɔːl] Augapfel m; **~·brow** Augenbraue f; **~·catch·ing** [⸤ɪŋ] ins Auge fallend, auffallend; **~·d** ...äugig; **~·glass** Augenglas n; (a pair of) ~es pl. (e-e) Brille; **~·lash** Augenwimper f; **~·lid** Augenlid n; **~·lin·er** Eyeliner m; **~·o·pen·er:** that was an ~ to me das hat mir die Augen geöffnet; **~·shad·ow** Lidschatten m; **~·sight** Augen(licht n) pl., Sehkraft f; **~·strain** Ermüdung f od. Überanstrengung f der Augen; **~·wit·ness** Augenzeug|e m, -in f.

F

fa·ble [ˈfeɪbl] Fabel f; Sage f; Lüge f.

fab|ric [ˈfæbrɪk] Gewebe n, Stoff m; Bau m; Gebäude n; Struktur f; △ nicht Fabrik; **~·ri·cate** [⸤eɪt] fabrizieren (mst fig. = erdichten, fälschen).

fab·u·lous □ [ˈfæbjʊləs] sagenhaft, der Sage angehörend; sagen-, fabelhaft.

fa·çade arch. [fəˈsɑːd] Fassade f.

face [feɪs] **1.** Gesicht n; Gesicht(sausdruck m) n, Miene f; (Ober)Fläche f; Vorderseite f; Zifferblatt n; ~ to ~ with Auge in Auge mit; save od. lose one's ~ das Gesicht wahren od. verlieren; on the ~ of it auf den ersten Blick; pull a long ~ ein langes Gesicht machen; have the ~ to do s.th. die Stirn haben, et. zu tun; **2.** v/t. ansehen; gegenüberstehen (dat.); (hinaus)gehen auf (acc.); die Stirn bieten (dat.); einfassen; arch. beklei-

den; v/i. ~ about sich umdrehen; **~·cloth** [ˈfeɪsklɒθ] Waschlappen m; **~·d** in Zssgn: mit (e-m) ... Gesicht; **~·flan·nel** Brt. = face-cloth; **~·lift·ing** [⸤ɪŋ] Facelifting n, Gesichtsstraffung f; fig. Renovierung f, Verschönerung f.

fa·ce·tious □ [fəˈsiːʃəs] witzig.

fa·cial [ˈfeɪʃl] **1.** □ Gesichts...; **2.** Kosmetik: Gesichtsbehandlung f.

fa·cile [ˈfæsaɪl] leicht; oberflächlich; **fa·cil·i·tate** [fəˈsɪlɪteɪt] erleichtern; **fa·cil·i·ty** [⸤ətɪ] Leichtigkeit f; Oberflächlichkeit f; mst facilities pl. Erleichterung(en pl.) f; Einrichtung(en pl.) f, Anlage(n pl.) f.

fac·ing [ˈfeɪsɪŋ] Verkleidung f; **~s** pl. Schneiderei: Besatz m.

fact [fækt] Tatsache f, Wirklichkeit f, Wahrheit f; Tat f; in ~ in der Tat, tatsächlich.

fac·tion *bsd. pol.* [ˈfækʃn] Splitter-
gruppe *f*; Zwietracht *f*.

fac·ti·tious □ [fækˈtɪʃəs] künstlich.

fac·tor [ˈfæktə] *fig.* Umstand *m*, Moment *n*, Faktor *m*; Agent *m*; *Schott.*
Verwalter *m*.

fac·to·ry [ˈfæktrɪ] Fabrik *f*.

fac·ul·ty [ˈfækəltɪ] Fähigkeit *f*; Kraft
f; *fig.* Gabe *f*; *univ.* Fakultät *f*.

fad [fæd] Mode(erscheinung, -tor-
heit) *f*; (vorübergehende) Laune.

fade [feɪd] (ver)welken (lassen), verblassen; schwinden; immer schwächer werden (*Person*); △ *nicht* fade;
Film, Rundfunk, TV: ~ in auf- od.
eingeblendet werden; auf- od. ein-
blenden; ~ out aus- od. abgeblendet
werden; aus- od. abblenden.

fag¹ [fæg] F Plackerei *f*, Schinderei *f*;
Brt. Schule: Schüler, *der für e-n älte-
ren Dienste verrichtet*.

fag² *sl.* [~] *Brt.* Glimmstengel *m* (*Zigarette*); *Am.* Schwule(r) *m* (*Homosexueller*).

fail [feɪl] **1.** *v/i.* versagen; mißlingen,
fehlschlagen; versiegen; nachlas-
sen; Bankrott machen; durchfallen
(*Kandidat*); *v/t.* im Stich lassen, verlassen; *j-n in e-r Prüfung* durchfallen
lassen; *he ~ed to come* er kam nicht;
he cannot ~ to er muß (einfach); **2.**
without ~ mit Sicherheit, ganz bestimmt; **~ing** [ˈfeɪlɪŋ] **1.** Fehler *m*,
Schwäche *f*; **2.** in Ermang(e)lung
(*gen.*); **~ure** [~jə] Fehlen *n*; Ausbleiben *n*; Versagen *n*; Fehlschlag *m*,
Mißerfolg *m*; Verfall *m*; Versäumnis
n; Bankrott *m*; Versager *m*.

faint [feɪnt] **1.** □ schwach, matt; **2.**
ohnmächtig werden, in Ohnmacht
fallen (*with* vor); **3.** Ohnmacht *f*; **~-
heart·ed** □ [ˈfeɪntˈhɑːtɪd] verzagt.

fair¹ [feə] **1.** *adj.* □ gerecht, ehrlich,
anständig, fair; ordentlich; schön
(*Wetter*), günstig (*Wind*); reichlich;
hell (*Haut, Haar, Teint*), blond
(*Haar*); freundlich, sauber, in Reinschrift; schön, hübsch, nett; **2.** *adv.*
gerecht, ehrlich, anständig, fair; in
Reinschrift; direkt.

fair² [~] (Jahr)Markt *m*; Volksfest *n*;
Ausstellung *f*, Messe *f*.

fair·ly [ˈfeəlɪ] ziemlich; völlig; **~ness**
[~nɪs] Schönheit *f*; Blondheit *f*;
Anständigkeit *f*, *bsd. Sport:* Fair-
neß *f*; Ehrlichkeit *f*; Gerechtigkeit
f.

fai·ry [ˈfeərɪ] Fee *f*; Zauberin *f*; Elf(e

f) *m*; **~·land** Feen-, Märchenland *n*;
~·tale Märchen *n* (*a. fig.*):

faith [feɪθ] Glaube *m*; Vertrauen *n*;
Treue *f*; **~·ful** □ [ˈfeɪθfl] treu; ehrlich; *Yours ~ly* Mit freundlichen
Grüßen (*Briefschluß*); **~·less** □ [~lɪs]
treulos; ungläubig.

fake [feɪk] **1.** Schwindel *m*; Fälschung *f*; Schwindler *m*; **2.** fälschen;
imitieren, nachmachen; vortäu-
schen, simulieren; **3.** gefälscht.

fal·con *zo.* [ˈfɔːlkən] Falke *m*.

fall [fɔːl] **1.** Fall(en *n*) *m*; Sturz *m*;
Verfall *m*; Einsturz *m*; *Am.* Herbst
m; Sinken *n* (*der Preise etc.*); Gefälle
n; *mst* ~s *pl.* Wasserfall *m*; △ *nicht*
gr., ♣, ⚕ Fall; ⚕, ♣ Fall; **2.** (fell, fallen) fallen,
stürzen; ab-, einfallen; sinken; sich
legen (*Wind*); in e-n Zustand verfallen; ~ ill od. sick krank werden; ~ in
love with sich verlieben in (*acc.*); ~
short of den Erwartungen etc. nicht
entsprechen; ~ back zurückweichen; ~ back on *fig.* zurückgreifen
auf (*acc.*); ~ for hereinfallen auf (*j-n,
et.*); F sich in *j-n* verknallen; ~ off
zurückgehen (*Geschäfte, Zuschauer-
zahlen etc.*), nachlassen; ~ on herfallen über (*acc.*); ~ out sich streiten
(*with mit*); ~ through durchfallen (*a.
fig.*); ~ to reinhauen, tüchtig zugreifen (*beim Essen*).

fal·la·cious □ [fəˈleɪʃəs] trügerisch.

fal·la·cy [ˈfæləsɪ] Trugschluß *m*.

fall·en [ˈfɔːlən] *p.p. von* fall 2.

fall guy *Am.* F [ˈfɔːlgaɪ] *der* Lackierte,
der Dumme.

fal·li·ble □ [ˈfæləbl] fehlbar.

fall·ing star *ast.* [ˈfɔːlɪŋstɑː] Sternschnuppe *f*.

fall·out [ˈfɔːlaut] Fallout *m*, radio-
aktiver Niederschlag.

fal·low [ˈfæləʊ] *zo.* falb; ✔ brach(liegend).

false □ [fɔːls] falsch; **~·hood** [ˈfɔːls-
hʊd], **~·ness** [~nɪs] Falschheit *f*; Un-
wahrheit *f*.

fal·si·fi·ca·tion [fɔːlsɪfɪˈkeɪʃn] (Ver-)
Fälschung *f*; **~·fy** [ˈfɔːlsɪfaɪ] (ver)fäl-
schen; **~·ty** [~tɪ] Falschheit *f*, Un-
wahrheit *f*.

fal·ter [ˈfɔːltə] schwanken; stocken
(*Stimme*); stammeln; *fig.* zaudern.

fame [feɪm] Ruf *m*, Ruhm *m*; **~d**
berühmt (*for* wegen).

fa·mil·i·ar [fəˈmɪljə] **1.** □ vertraut;
gewohnt; familiär; **2.** Vertraute(r *m*)
f; **~·i·ty** [fəmɪlɪˈærətɪ] Vertrautheit

f; (plumpe) Vertraulichkeit; **~ize** [fə'mɪljəraɪz] vertraut machen.

fam·i·ly ['fæməlɪ] **1.** Familie *f*; **2.** Familien..., Haus...; *be in the ~ way* F in anderen Umständen sein; *~ allowance* Kindergeld *n*; *~ planning* Familienplanung *f*; *~ tree* Stammbaum *m*.

fam·ine ['fæmɪn] Hungersnot *f*; Knappheit *f* (*of* an *dat.*); **~ished** [~ʃt] verhungert; *be ~* F am Verhungern sein.

fa·mous □ ['feɪməs] berühmt; △ *nicht famos.*

fan¹ [fæn] **1.** Fächer *m*; Ventilator *m*; *~ belt* ⊕ Keilriemen *m*; **2.** (*-nn-*) (zu)fächeln; an-, *fig.* entfachen.

fan² [~] (*Sport- etc.*)Fan *m*; *~ club* Fanklub *m*; *~ mail* Verehrerpost *f*.

fa·na·tic [fə'nætɪk] **1.** (*~ally*), *a.* **~·i·cal** □ [~kl] fanatisch; **2.** Fanatiker(in).

fan·ci·er ['fænsɪə] (*Tier-, Pflanzen-*)Liebhaber(in), (-)Züchter(in).

fan·ci·ful □ ['fænsɪfl] phantastisch.

fan·cy ['fænsɪ] **1.** Phantasie *f*; Einbildung(skraft) *f*; Schrulle *f*; Vorliebe *f*; Liebhaberei *f*; **2.** Phantasie...; Mode...; *~ ball* Kostümfest *n*, Maskenball *m*; *~ dress* (Masken)Kostüm *n*; *~ goods pl.* Modeartikel *pl.*, -waren *pl.*; **3.** sich einbilden; Gefallen finden an (*dat.*); *just ~!* denken Sie nur!; **~-free** frei u. ungebunden; **~·work** feine Handarbeit, Stickerei *f*.

fang [fæŋ] Reiß-, Fangzahn *m*; Hauer *m*; Giftzahn *m*.

fan·tas·tic [fæn'tæstɪk] (*~ally*) phantastisch; **~·ta·sy** ['fæntəsɪ] Phantasie *f*.

far [fɑː] (*farther, further; farthest, furthest*) **1.** *adj.* fern, entfernt, weit; **2.** *adv.* fern; weit; (sehr) viel; *as ~ as* bis; *in so ~ as* insofern als; **~·a·way** ['fɑːrəweɪ] weit entfernt.

fare [feə] **1.** Fahrgeld *n*; Fahrgast *m*; Verpflegung *f*, Kost *f*; **2.** *ge*·leben; *he ~d well* es (er)ging ihm gut; **~·well** ['feə'wel] **1.** *int.* lebe(n Sie) wohl!; **2.** Abschied *m*, Lebewohl *n*.

far-fetched *fig.* ['fɑː'fetʃt] weithergeholt, gesucht.

farm [fɑːm] **1.** Bauernhof *m*, Gut *n*, Gehöft *n*, Farm *f*; Züchterei *f*; *chicken ~* Hühnerfarm *f*; **2.** (ver-)pachten; *Land, Vieh* bewirtschaften; *Geflügel etc.* züchten; **~·er** ['fɑːmə] Bauer *m*, Landwirt *m*, Farmer

m; (*Geflügel- etc.*)Züchter *m*; Pächter *m*; **~·hand** Landarbeiter(in); **~·house** Bauernhaus *n*; **~·ing** [~ŋ] **1.** Acker..., landwirtschaftlich; **2.** Landwirtschaft *f*; **~·stead** Bauernhof *m*, Gehöft *n*; **~·yard** Wirtschaftshof *n* (*e-s Bauernhofs*).

far|-off ['fɑː'rɒf] entfernt, fern; **~·sight·ed** *bsd. Am.* weitsichtig; *fig.* weitblickend.

far·ther ['fɑːðə] *comp. von far*; **~·thest** ['fɑːðɪst] *sup. von far.*

fas·ci·nate ['fæsɪneɪt] faszinieren; **~·nat·ing** □ [~ŋ] faszinierend; **~·na·tion** [fæsɪ'neɪʃn] Zauber *m*, Reiz *m*, Faszination *f*.

fas·cis·m *pol.* ['fæʃɪzəm] Faschismus *m*; **~·t** *pol.* [~ɪst] **1.** Faschist *m*; **2.** faschistisch.

fash·ion ['fæʃn] Mode *f*; Art *f*; feine Lebensart; Form *f*; Schnitt *m*; *in (out of) ~* (un)modern; *~ parade, ~ show* Mode(n)schau *f*; **2.** gestalten; *Kleid* machen; **~·a·ble** □ [~nəbl] modern, elegant.

fast¹ [fɑːst] **1.** Fasten *n*; **2.** fasten.

fast² [~] schnell; fest; treu; echt, beständig (*Farbe*); flott; △ *nicht fast*; *be ~* vorgehen (*Uhr*); **~·back** *mot.* ['fɑːstbæk] (Wagen *m* mit) Fließheck *n*; **~ breed·er, ~·breed·er re·ac·tor** *phys.* schneller Brüter; **~ food** Schnellgericht(*e pl.*) *n*; **~·food res·tau·rant** Schnellimbiß *m*, -gaststätte *f*; **~ lane** *mot.* Überholspur *f*.

fas·ten ['fɑːsn] *v/t.* befestigen; anheften; fest zumachen; zubinden; *Augen etc.* heften (*on, upon* auf *acc.*); *v/i.* schließen (*Tür*); △ *nicht fasten*; *~ on, ~ upon* sich klammern an (*acc.*); *fig.* sich stürzen auf (*acc.*); **~·er** [~ə] Verschluß *m*, Halter *m*; **~·ing** [~ŋ] Verschluß *m*, Halterung *f*.

fas·tid·i·ous □ [fə'stɪdɪəs] anspruchsvoll, heikel, wählerisch, verwöhnt.

fat [fæt] **1.** □ (*-tt-*) fett; dick; fettig; **2.** Fett *n*; **3.** (*-tt-*) fett machen *od.* werden; mästen.

fa·tal □ ['feɪtl] verhängnisvoll, fatal (*to* für); Schicksals...; tödlich; **~·i·ty** [fə'tælətɪ] Verhängnis *n*; Unglücks-, Todesfall *m*; Todesopfer *n*.

fate [feɪt] Schicksal *n*; Verhängnis *n*.

fa·ther ['fɑːðə] Vater *m*; ♀ **Christmas** *bsd. Brt.* der Weihnachtsmann, der Nikolaus; **~·hood** [~hʊd] Vaterschaft *f*; **~-in-law** [~rɪnlɔː] (*pl.*

fathers-in-law) Schwiegervater *m*; **~·less** [~lɪs] vaterlos; **~·ly** [~lɪ] väterlich.

fath·om ['fæðəm] **1.** ⚓ Faden *m* (*Tiefenmaß*); **2.** ⚓ loten; *fig.* ergründen; **~·less** [~lɪs] unergründlich.

fa·tigue [fə'tiːg] **1.** Ermüdung *f*; Strapaze *f*; **2.** ermüden.

fat|ten ['fætn] fett machen *od.* werden; mästen; *Boden* düngen; **~·ty** [~tɪ] (*-ier, -iest*) fett(ig).

fat·u·ous □ ['fætjʊəs] albern.

fau·cet *Am.* □ ['fɔːsɪt] (Wasser)Hahn *m*.

fault [fɔːlt] Fehler *m*; Defekt *m*; Schuld *f*; *find* ~ *with* et. auszusetzen haben an (*dat.*); *be at* ~ Schuld haben; **~·less** □ [~lɪs] fehlerfrei, -los; **~·y** □ [~ɪ] (*-ier, -iest*) fehlerhaft, ⊕ *a.* defekt.

fa·vo(u)r ['feɪvə] **1.** Gunst *f*; Gefallen *m*; Begünstigung *f*; *in* ~ *of* zugunsten von *od. gen.*; *do s.o. a* ~ j-m e-n Gefallen tun; **2.** begünstigen; bevorzugen, vorziehen; wohlwollend gegenüberstehen; *Sport:* favorisieren, beehren; **fa·vo(u)·ra·ble** □ [~rəbl] günstig; **fa·vo(u)·rite** [~rɪt] **1.** Liebling *m*; *Sport:* Favorit *m*; **2.** Lieblings...

fawn¹ [fɔːn] **1.** *zo.* (Reh)Kitz *n*; Rehbraun *n*; **2.** rehbraun.

fawn² [~] (mit dem Schwanz) wedeln (*Hund*); *fig.* katzbuckeln (*on, upon* vor *dat.*).

fear [fɪə] **1.** Furcht *f* (*of* vor *dat.*); Befürchtung *f*; Angst *f*; **2.** (be)fürchten; sich fürchten vor (*dat.*); **~·ful** □ ['fɪəfl] furchtsam; furchtbar; **~·less** □ [~lɪs] furchtlos.

fea·si·ble □ ['fiːzəbl] durchführbar.

feast [fiːst] **1.** *eccl.* Fest *n*, Feiertag *m*; Festessen *n*; *fig.* Fest *n*, (Hoch)Genuß *m*; **2.** *v/t.* festlich bewirten; *v/i.* sich gütlich tun (*on* an *dat.*).

feat [fiːt] (Helden)Tat *f*; Kunststück *n*.

fea·ther ['feðə] **1.** Feder *f*; *a.* **~s** Gefieder *n*; *birds of a* ~ Leute vom gleichen Schlag; *in high* ~ (bei) bester Laune; in Hochform; **2.** mit Federn schmücken; **~ bed** Matratze *f* mit Feder- *od.* Daunenfüllung; △ *nicht Federbett*; **~·bed** (*-dd-*) verwöhnen; **~·brained**, **~·head·ed** unbesonnen; albern; **~ed** be-, gefiedert; **~·weight** *Sport:* Federgewicht(ler *m*) *n*; Leichtgewicht *n* (*Person*); *fig.* unbedeutende Person;

et. Belangloses; **~·y** [~rɪ] be-, gefiedert; feder(art)ig.

fea·ture ['fiːtʃə] **1.** (Gesichts-, Grund-, Haupt-, Charakter)Zug *m*; (charakteristisches) Merkmal; *Rundfunk, TV:* Feature *n*; *a.* ~ *article*, ~ *story* Zeitung: Feature *n*; *a.* ~ *film* Haupt-, Spielfilm *m*; **~s** *pl.* Gesicht *n*; **2.** kennzeichnen; sich auszeichnen durch; groß herausbringen *od.* -stellen; *Film:* in der Hauptrolle zeigen.

Feb·ru·a·ry ['februərɪ] Februar *m*.

fed [fed] *pret. u. p.p. von* feed 2.

fed·e·ral □ ['fedərəl] Bundes...; *USA:* Zentral..., Unions..., National...; ♀ *Bureau of Investigation* (*abbr. FBI*) amer. Bundeskriminalpolizei; ~ *government* Bundesregierung *f*; **~·rate** [~eɪt] (sich) zu e-m (Staaten)Bund zusammenschließen; **~·ra·tion** [fedə'reɪʃn] Föderation *f* (*a. econ., pol.*); (politischer) Zusammenschluß *m*; *econ.* (Dach)Verband *m*; *pol.* Staatenbund *m*.

fee [fiː] Gebühr *f*; Honorar *n*; (Mitglieds)Beitrag *m*; Eintrittsgeld *n*.

fee·ble □ ['fiːbl] (*~r, ~st*) schwach.

feed [fiːd] **1.** Futter *n*; Nahrung *f*; Fütterung *f*; ⊕ Zuführung *f*, Speisung *f*; **2.** (*fed*) *v/t.* füttern; ernähren; ⊕ (ein)speisen; weiden lassen; *be fed up with* et. *od.* j-n satt haben; *well fed* wohlgenährt; *v/i.* (fr)essen; sich ernähren; weiden; **~·back** ['fiːdbæk] ⚡, *Kybernetik:* Feedback *n*, Rückkoppelung *f*; *Rundfunk, TV:* Feedback *n* (*mögliche Einflußnahme des Publikums auf den Verlauf e-r Sendung*); Zurückleitung *f* (*von Informationen*) (*to an acc.*); **~·er** [~ə] Fütterer *m*; *Am.* Viehmäster *m*; Esser(in); **~·er road** Zubringer (-straße *f*) *m*; **~·ing-bot·tle** [~ɪŋbɒtl] (Säuglings-, Saug)Flasche *f*.

feel [fiːl] **1.** (*felt*) (sich) fühlen; befühlen; empfinden; sich anfühlen; *I* ~ *like doing* ich möchte am liebsten tun; **2.** Gefühl *n*; Empfindung *f*; **~·er** *zo.* ['fiːlə] Fühler *m*; **~·ing** [~ɪŋ] Gefühl *n*.

feet [fiːt] *pl. von* foot 1.

feign [feɪn] *Interesse etc.* vortäuschen, *Krankheit a.* simulieren.

feint [feɪnt] Finte *f*; ✗ Täuschungsmanöver *n*.

fell [fel] **1.** *pret. von* fall 2; **2.** niederschlagen; fällen.

fel·low ['feləʊ] **1.** Gefährt|e *m*, -in *f*; Kamerad(in); Gleiche(r, -s); Gegenstück *n*; *univ.* Fellow *m*, Mitglied *n* e-s College; Kerl *m*, Bursche *m*, Mensch *m*; *old* ~ F alter Junge; *the* ~ *of a glove* der andere Handschuh; **2.** Mit...; ~ *being* Mitmensch *m*; ~ *countryman* Landsmann *m*; ~ *travel(l)er* Mitreisende(r) *m*, Reisegefährte *m*; **~·ship** [~ʃɪp] Gemeinschaft *f*; Kameradschaft *f*.

fel·o·ny 𝔷𝔷 ['feləni] (schweres) Verbrechen, Kapitalverbrechen *n*.

felt¹ [felt] *pret. u. p.p. von feel* 1.

felt² [~] Filz *m*; ~ *tip*, ~*tip(ped) pen* Filzschreiber *m*, -stift *m*.

fe·male ['fi:meɪl] **1.** weiblich; **2.** Weib *n*; *zo.* Weibchen *n*.

fem·i·nine □ ['femɪnɪn] weiblich, Frauen...; weiblich; **~·nis·m** [~ɪzəm] Feminismus *m*; **~·nist** [~ɪst] **1.** Feminist(in); **2.** feministisch.

fen [fen] Fenn *n*, Moor *n*; Marsch *f*.

fence [fens] **1.** Zaun *m*; F Hehler *m*; **2.** *v/t.* ~ *in* ein-, umzäunen; einsperren; ~ *off* abzäunen; *v/i.* Sport: fechten; *sl.* Hehlerei treiben; **fenc·er** ['fensə] Sport: Fechter *m*, Fechterin *f*; **fenc·ing** [~ɪŋ] Einfriedung *f*; Sport: Fechten *n*; *attr.* Fecht...

fend [fend]: ~ *off* abwehren; ~ *for o.s.* für sich selbst sorgen; **~·er** ['fendə] Schutzvorrichtung *f*; Schutzblech *n*; *Am. mot.* Kotflügel *m*; Kamingitter *n*, -vorsetzer *m*.

fen·nel ♀ ['fenl] Fenchel *m*.

fer·ment 1. ['fɜ:ment] Ferment *n*; Gärung *f*; **2.** [fə'ment] gären (lassen); **~·men·ta·tion** [fɜ:men'teɪʃn] Gärung *f*.

fern ♀ [fɜ:n] Farn(kraut *n*) *n*.

fe·ro·cious □ [fə'rəʊʃəs] wild; grausam; **~·ci·ty** [fə'rɒsətɪ] Wildheit *f*.

fer·ret ['ferɪt] **1.** *zo.* Frettchen *n*; *fig.* Spürhund *m*; **2.** herumstöbern; ~ *out* aufspüren, -stöbern.

fer·ry ['ferɪ] **1.** Fähre *f*; **2.** übersetzen; **~·boat** Fährboot *n*, Fähre *f*; **~·man** (*pl. -men*) Fährmann *m*.

fer·tile □ ['fɜ:taɪl] fruchtbar; reich (*of, in* an *dat.*); **~·til·i·ty** [fə'tɪlətɪ] Fruchtbarkeit *f* (*a. fig.*); **~·ti·lize** ['fɜ:tɪlaɪz] fruchtbar machen; befruchten; düngen; **~·ti·liz·er** [~ə] (*bsd. Kunst*)Dünger *m*, Düngemittel *n*.

fer·vent □ ['fɜ:vənt] heiß; inbrünstig, glühend; leidenschaftlich.

fer·vo(u)r ['fɜ:və] Glut *f*; Inbrunst *f*.

fes·ter ['festə] eitern; verfaulen.

fes·ti·val ['festəvl] Fest *n*; Feier *f*; Festspiele *pl.*; **~·tive** □ [~tɪv] festlich; **~·tiv·i·ty** [fe'stɪvətɪ] Festlichkeit *f*.

fes·toon [fe'stu:n] Girlande *f*.

fetch [fetʃ] holen; Preis erzielen; Seufzer ausstoßen; **~·ing** □ F ['fetʃɪŋ] reizend.

fet·id □ ['fetɪd] stinkend.

fet·ter ['fetə] **1.** Fessel *f*; **2.** fesseln.

feud [fju:d] Fehde *f*; Lehen *n*; **~·al** □ ['fju:dl] feudal, Lehns...; **feu·dal·is·m** [~əlɪzəm] Feudalismus *m*, Feudalsystem *n*.

fe·ver ['fi:və] Fieber *n*; **~·ish** □ [~rɪʃ] fieb(e)rig; *fig.* fieberhaft.

few [fju:] wenige; *a.* ~ ein paar, einige; *no* ~ *than* nicht weniger als; *quite a* ~, *a good* ~ e-e ganze Menge.

fi·an·cé [fɪ'ã:nseɪ] Verlobte(r) *m*; **~·e** [~] Verlobte *f*.

fib F [fɪb] **1.** Flunkerei *f*, Schwindelei *f*; **2.** (*-bb-*) schwindeln, flunkern.

fi·bre, *Am.* **-ber** ['faɪbə] Faser *f*; Charakter *m*; **fi·brous** □ ['faɪbrəs] faserig.

fick·le ['fɪkl] wankelmütig; unbeständig; **~·ness** [~nɪs] Wankelmut *m*.

fic·tion ['fɪkʃn] Erfindung *f*; Prosaliteratur *f*, Belletristik *f*; Romane *pl.*; **~·al** □ [~l] erdichtet; Roman...

fic·ti·tious □ [fɪk'tɪʃəs] erfunden.

fid·dle □ ['fɪdl] **1.** Fiedel *f*, Geige *f*; *play first* (*second*) ~ *bsd. fig.* die erste (zweite) Geige spielen; (*as*) *fit as a* ~ kerngesund; **2.** ♪ fiedeln; *a.* ~ *about od. around* (*with*) herumfingern (an *dat.*), spielen (mit); **~·r** [~ə] Geiger(in); **~·sticks** *int.* dummes Zeug!

fi·del·i·ty [fɪ'delətɪ] Treue *f*; Genauigkeit *f*.

fidg·et F ['fɪdʒɪt] **1.** nervöse Unruhe; **2.** nervös machen *od.* sein; **~·y** [~ɪ] zapp(e)lig, nervös.

field [fi:ld] Feld *n*; (Spiel)Platz *m*; Arbeitsfeld *n*; Gebiet *n*; Bereich *m*; *hold the* ~ das Feld behaupten; ~ *events pl. Sport:* Sprung- u. Wurfdisziplinen *pl.*; **~·glass·es** *pl.* (*a pair of* ~ ein) Feldstecher *m od.* Fernglas *n*; **~·mar·shal** ✗ Feldmarschall *m*; **~·of·fi·cer** ✗ Stabsoffizier *m*; ~ *sports pl.* Sport *m* im Freien (*bsd. Jagen, Schießen, Fischen*); **~·work** praktische (wissenschaftliche) Arbeit, *Archäologie etc.*: *a.* Arbeit *f* im Gelände; *Markt-, Meinungsforschung:* Feldarbeit *f.*

fiend [fiːnd] Satan *m,* Teufel *m; in Zssgn:* Süchtige(r *m*) *f;* Fanatiker(in); △ *nicht* Feind; **~ish** □ [ˈfiːndɪʃ] teuflisch, boshaft.

fierce [fɪəs] (*~r, ~st*) wild; scharf; heftig; **~ness** [ˈfɪəsnɪs] Wildheit *f,* Schärfe *f;* Heftigkeit *f.*

fi·er·y □ [ˈfaɪərɪ] (*-ier, -iest*) feurig; hitzig.

fif|teen [ˈfɪfˈtiːn] 1. fünfzehn; 2. Fünfzehn *f;* **~teenth** [~ˈtiːnθ] fünfzehnte(r, -s); **~th** [fɪfθ] 1. fünfte(r, -s); 2. Fünftel *n;* **~th·ly** [ˈfɪfθlɪ] fünftens; **~ti·eth** [ˈfɪftɪɪθ] fünfzigste(r, -s); **~ty** [~ɪ] 1. fünfzig; 2. Fünfzig *f;* **~ty-fif·ty** F halbe-halbe.

fig ♀ [fɪg] Feige(nbaum *m*) *f.*

fight [faɪt] 1. Kampf *m;* ⚔ Gefecht *n;* Schlägerei *f; Boxen:* Kampf *m,* Fight *m;* Kampflust *f;* 2. (*fought*) *v/t.* bekämpfen; kämpfen gegen *v/i.* mit, *Sport: a.* boxen gegen; *v/i.* kämpfen, sich schlagen; *Sport:* boxen; **~er** [ˈfaɪtə] Kämpfer *m; Sport:* Boxer *m,* Fighter *m; a.* **~ plane** ✈ Jagdflugzeug *n;* **~ing** [~ɪŋ] Kampf *m.*

fig·u·ra·tive □ [ˈfɪgjʊrətɪv] bildlich.

fig·ure [ˈfɪgə] 1. Figur *f;* Gestalt *f;* Zahl *f,* Ziffer *f;* Preis *m; be good at ~s* ein guter Rechner sein; 2. *v/t.* abbilden, darstellen; *Am.* F meinen, glauben; sich *et.* vorstellen; **~ out** rauskriegen; *Problem* lösen; verstehen; **~ up** zusammenzählen; *v/i.* erscheinen, vorkommen; **~ on** *bsd. Am.* rechnen mit; **~ skat·er** *Sport:* Eiskunstläufer(in); **~ skat·ing** *Sport:* Eiskunstlauf *m.*

fil·a·ment [ˈfɪləmənt] Faden *m,* Faser *f;* ♀ Staubfaden *m;* ⚡ Glüh-, Heizfaden *m.*

fil·bert ♀ [ˈfɪlbət] Haselnuß *f.*

filch F [fɪltʃ] klauen, stibitzen.

file[1] [faɪl] 1. Ordner *m,* Karteikasten *m;* Akte *f;* Akten *pl.,* Ablage *f; Computer:* Datei *f;* Reihe *f;* ⚔ Rotte *f; on ~* bei den Akten; 2. *v/t. Briefe etc.* einordnen, ablegen, zu den Akten nehmen; *Antrag* einreichen, *Berufung* einlegen; *v/i.* hintereinander marschieren.

file[2] [~] 1. Feile *f;* 2. feilen.

fi·li·al □ [ˈfɪljəl] kindlich, Kindes...

fil·ing [ˈfaɪlɪŋ] Ablegen *n* (*von Briefen etc.*); **~ cabinet** Aktenschrank *m.*

fill [fɪl] 1. (sich) füllen; an-, aus-,

erfüllen; *Auftrag* ausführen; **~ in** einsetzen; *Am. a.* **~ out** *Formular* ausfüllen; **~ up** vollfüllen; sich füllen; **~ her up!** F volltanken, bitte!; 2. Füllung *f; eat one's ~* sich satt essen.

fil·let, *Am. a.* **fil·et** [ˈfɪlɪt] Filet *n.*

fill·ing [ˈfɪlɪŋ] Füllung *f;* ⚕ (Zahn-) Plombe *f,* (-)Füllung *f;* **~ station** Tankstelle *f.*

fil·ly [ˈfɪlɪ] Stutenfohlen *n; fig.* wilde Hummel (*Mädchen*).

film [fɪlm] 1. Häutchen *n;* Membran(e) *f;* Film *m* (*a. phot. u. bsd. Brt. Kinofilm*); Trübung *f* (*des Auges*); Nebelschleier *m; take od. shoot a ~* e-n Film drehen; 2. (ver)filmen; sich verfilmen lassen.

fil·ter [ˈfɪltə] 1. Filter *m;* 2. filtern; **~ tip** Filter *m;* Filterzigarette *f;* **~tipped:** **~ cigarette** Filterzigarette *f.*

filth [fɪlθ] Schmutz *m;* **~·y** □ [ˈfɪlθɪ] (*-ier, -iest*) schmutzig; *fig.* unflätig.

fin [fɪn] *zo.* Flosse *f* (*a. sl. = Hand*).

fi·nal [ˈfaɪnl] 1. □ letzte(r, -s); End..., Schluß...; endgültig; **~ storage** Endlagerung *f* (*von Atommüll etc.*); 2. *Sport:* Finale *n,* Endkampf, -lauf *m,* -runde *f,* -spiel *n; mst* **~s** *pl.* Schlußexamen, -prüfung *f;* **~ist** [~nəlɪst] *Sport:* Finalist(in), Endkampfteilnehmer(in); **~·ly** [~lɪ] endlich, schließlich; endgültig.

fi·nance [faɪˈnæns] 1. Finanzwesen *n;* **~s** *pl.* Finanzen *pl.;* 2. *v/t.* finanzieren; *v/i.* Geldgeschäfte machen; **fi·nan·cial** □ [~nʃl] finanziell; **fi·nan·cier** [~ˈnsɪə] Finanzier *m.*

finch *zo.* [fɪntʃ] Fink *m.*

find [faɪnd] 1. (*found*) finden; (an-) treffen; auf-, herausfinden; ⚖ *j-n* für (*nicht*) *schuldig* erklären; beschaffen; versorgen; 2. Fund *m,* Entdeckung *f;* **~·ings** [ˈfaɪndɪŋz] *pl.* Befund *m;* ⚖ Feststellung *f,* Spruch *m.*

fine[1] □ [faɪn] 1. *adj.* (*~r, ~st*) schön; fein; verfeinert; rein; spitz, dünn; scharf; geziert; vornehm; *I'm ~* mir geht es gut; 2. *adv.* gut, bestens.

fine[2] [~] 1. Geldstrafe *f,* Bußgeld *n;* 2. zu e-r Geldstrafe verurteilen.

fi·ne·ry [ˈfaɪnərɪ] Glanz *m;* Putz *m,* Staat *m.*

fin·ger [ˈfɪŋgə] 1. Finger *m; s. cross* 2; 2. betasten, (herum)fingern an (*dat.*); **~nail** Fingernagel *m;* **~print** Fingerabdruck *m;* **~tip** Fingerspitze *f.*

fin·i·cky [ˈfɪnɪkɪ] wählerisch.

fin·ish ['fɪnɪʃ] **1.** v/t. beenden, vollenden; fertigstellen; abschließen; vervollkommnen; erledigen; v/i. enden, aufhören; ~ **with** mit j-m, et. Schluß machen; *have* ~ed *with* j-m, et. nicht mehr brauchen; **2.** Vollendung f, letzter Schliff; *Sport:* Endspurt m, Finish n; Ziel n; ~**ing line** [~ɪŋlaɪn] *Sport:* Ziellinie f.

Finn [fɪn] Finn|e m, -in f; ~**ish** ['fɪnɪʃ] **1.** finnisch; **2.** *ling.* Finnisch n.

fir ♀ [fɜ:] *a.* ~**tree** Tanne f; ~**cone** ['fɜ:kəʊn] Tannenzapfen m.

fire ['faɪə] **1.** Feuer n; *be on* ~ in Flammen stehen, brennen; *catch* ~ Feuer fangen, in Brand geraten; *set on* ~, *set* ~ *to* anzünden; **2.** v/t. anentzünden; *fig.* anfeuern; abfeuern; *Ziegel etc.* brennen; F rausschmeißen (*entlassen*); heizen; v/i. Feuer fangen (*a. fig.*); feuern; ~**a·larm** [~rəlɑ:m] Feuermelder m; ~**arms** pl. Feuer-, Schußwaffen pl.; ~**bri·gade** Feuerwehr f; ~**bug** F Feuerteufel m; ~**crack·er** Frosch m (*Feuerwerkskörper*); ~ **de·part·ment** Am. Feuerwehr f; ~**en·gine** [~rendʒɪn] (Feuer)Spritze f; ~**es·cape** [~rɪskeɪp] Feuerleiter f, -treppe f; ~**ex·tin·guish·er** [~rɪkstɪŋwɪʃə] Feuerlöscher m; ~**guard** Kamingitter n; ~**man** Feuerwehrmann m; Heizer m; ~**place** (offener) Kamin; ~**plug** Hydrant m; ~**proof** feuerfest; ~**rais·ing** Brt. [~ɪŋ] Brandstiftung f; ~**side** Herd m; Kamin m; ~**sta·tion** Feuerwache f; ~**wood** Brennholz n; ~**works** pl. Feuerwerk n.

fir·ing squad ⚔ ['faɪərɪŋskwɒd] Exekutionskommando n.

firm[1] [fɜ:m] fest; derb; standhaft; ⚠ *nicht firm.*

firm[2] [~] Firma f, Betrieb m, Unternehmen n.

first [fɜ:st] **1.** *adj.* □ erste(r, -s); beste(r, -s); **2.** *adv.* erstens; zuerst; ~ *of all* an erster Stelle; zu allererst; **3.** Erste(r, -s); *at* ~ zuerst, anfangs; *from the* ~ von Anfang an; ~ **aid** Erste Hilfe; ~**aid** ['fɜ:steɪd] Erste-Hilfe-...; ~ *kit* Verband(s)kasten m, -zeug n; ~**born** erstgeborene(r, -s), älteste(r, -s); ~ **class** 1. Klasse (*e-s Verkehrsmittels*); ~**class** erstklassig; ~**ly** [~lɪ] erstens; ~**hand** aus erster Hand; ~ **name** Vorname m; Beiname m; ~**rate** erstklassig.

firth [fɜ:θ] Förde f, Meeresarm m.

fish [fɪʃ] **1.** Fisch(e pl.) m; *a queer* ~ F ein komischer Kauz; **2.** fischen, angeln; ~ *around* kramen (*for* nach); ~**bone** ['fɪʃbəʊn] Gräte f.

fish·er·man ['fɪʃəmən] (pl. -men) Fischer m; ~**ry** [~rɪ] Fischerei f.

fish·ing ['fɪʃɪŋ] Fischen n, Angeln n; ~**line** Angelschnur f; ~**rod** Angelrute f; ~**tack·le** Angelgerät n.

fish|mon·ger bsd. Brt. ['fɪʃmʌŋɡə] Fischhändler m; ~**y** □ [~ɪ] (-*ier*, -*iest*) Fisch...; F verdächtig, faul.

fis·sile ⊕ ['fɪsaɪl] spaltbar; ~**sion** ['fɪʃn] Spaltung f; ~**sure** ['fɪʃə] Spalt m, Riß m.

fist [fɪst] Faust f.

fit[1] [fɪt] **1.** □ (-*tt*-) geeignet, passend; tauglich; *Sport:* fit, in (guter) Form; **2.** (-*tt*-; *fitted*, Am. a. *fit*) v/t. passen für od. dat.; anpassen; passend machen; befähigen; geeignet machen (*for*, *to* für; zu); ~ *in* j-m e-n Termin geben, j-n, et. einschieben; *a.* ~ *on* anprobieren; *a.* ~ *out* ausrüsten, -statten, einrichten, versehen (*with* mit); *a.* ~ *up* ausrüsten, -statten, einrichten; montieren; v/i. passen; sitzen (*Kleid*); **3.** Sitz m (*Kleid*).

fit[2] [~] Anfall m; ✠ Ausbruch m; Anwandlung f; *by* ~s *and starts* ruckweise; *give s.o. a* ~ F j-n auf die Palme bringen; j-m e-n Schock versetzen.

fit|ful □ ['fɪtfl] ruckartig; *fig.* unstet; ~**ness** [~nɪs] Tauglichkeit f; bsd. *Sport:* Fitneß f, (gute) Form; ~**ted** zugeschnitten, nach Maß (gearbeitet); Einbau...; ~ *carpet* Spannteppich m, Teppichboden m; ~ *kitchen* Einbauküche f; ~**ter** [~ə] Monteur m; Installateur m; ~**ting** [~ɪŋ] **1.** passend; **2.** Montage f; Anprobe f; ~*s* pl. Einrichtung f; Armaturen pl.

five [faɪv] **1.** fünf; **2.** Fünf f.

fix [fɪks] **1.** v/t. befestigen, anheften; fixieren; *Blick etc.* heften, richten (*on* auf acc.); fesseln; aufstellen; bestimmen, festsetzen; reparieren, instand setzen; bsd. Am. et. zurechtmachen; *ein Essen* zubereiten; ⚠ *nicht fix*; ~ *up* in Ordnung bringen, regeln; j-n unterbringen; v/i. fest werden; ~ *on* sich entschließen für od. zu; **2.** F Klemme f; sl. Schuß m (*Heroin etc.*); ~**ed** □ fest; bestimmt; starr; ~**ing** ['fɪksɪŋ] Befestigen n;

Instandsetzen *n*; Fixieren *n*; Aufstellen *n*, Montieren *n*; Besatz *m*, Versteifung *f*; *Am.* ⁓s *pl.* Zubehör *n*, Ausrüstung *f*; ⁓**ture** [⁓stʃə] fest angebrachtes Zubehörteil, feste Anlage; Inventarstück *n*; *lighting* ⁓ Beleuchtungskörper *m*.

fizz [fɪz] **1.** zischen, sprudeln; **2.** Zischen *n*; F Schampus *m* (*Sekt*).

flab·ber·gast F [ˈflæbəga:st] verblüffen; *be* ⁓*ed* platt sein.

flab·by □ [ˈflæbɪ] (*-ier, -iest*) schlaff.

flac·cid □ [ˈflæksɪd] schlaff, schlapp.

flag [flæg] **1.** Flagge *f*; Fahne *f*; Fliese *f*; ⚜ Schwertlilie *f*; **2.** (*-gg-*) beflaggen; durch Flaggen signalisieren; mit Fliesen belegen; ermatten, mutlos werden; ⁓**pole** [ˈflægpəʊl] = *flagstaff*.

fla·grant □ [ˈfleɪgrənt] abscheulich; berüchtigt; offenkundig.

flag|staff [ˈflægsta:f] Fahnenstange *f*, -mast *m*; ⁓**stone** Fliese *f*.

flair [fleə] Talent *n*; Gespür *n*, (feine) Nase.

flake [fleɪk] **1.** Flocke *f*; Schicht *f*; **2.** (sich) flocken; abblättern; **flak·y** [ˈfleɪkɪ] (*-ier, -iest*) flockig; blätt(e)-rig; ⁓ *pastry* Blätterteig *m*.

flame [fleɪm] **1.** Flamme *f* (*a. fig.*); *be in* ⁓s in Flammen stehen; **2.** flammen, lodern.

flam·ma·ble *Am. u.* ⊕ [ˈflæməbl] = *inflammable*.

flan [flæn] Obst-, Käsekuchen *m*.

flank [flæŋk] **1.** Flanke *f*; **2.** flankieren.

flan·nel [ˈflænl] Flanell *m*; Waschlappen *m*; ⁓*s pl.* Flanellhose *f*.

flap [flæp] **1.** (Ohr)Läppchen *n*; Rockschoß *m*; (*Hut*)Krempe *f*; Klappe *f*; Klaps *m*; (Flügel)Schlag *m*; **2.** *v/t.* (*-pp-*) klatschen(d schlagen); *v/i.* lose herabhängen; flattern.

flare [fleə] **1.** flackern; sich nach außen erweitern, sich bauschen; ⁓ *up* aufflammen; *fig.* aufbrausen; **2.** flackerndes Licht; Lichtsignal *n*.

flash [flæʃ] **1.** Aufblitzen *n*, -leuchten *n*, Blitz *m*; *Rundfunk etc.*: Kurzmeldung *f*; *phot.* F Blitz *m* (*Blitzlicht*); *bsd. Am.* F Taschenlampe *f*; *like a* ⁓ wie der Blitz; *in a* ⁓ im Nu; ⁓ *of lightning* Blitzstrahl *m*; **2.** (auf)blitzen; auflodern (lassen); *Blick etc.* werfen; flitzen; funken; telegrafieren; *it* ⁓*ed on me* mir kam plötzlich der Gedanke; ⁓**back** [ˈflæʃbæk]

Film, Roman: Rückblende *f*; ⁓**light** *phot.* Blitzlicht *n*; ⚓ Leuchtfeuer; *bsd. Am.* Taschenlampe *f*; ⁓**y** □ [⁓ɪ] (*-ier, -iest*) auffallend, -fällig.

flask [fla:sk] Taschenflasche *f*; Thermosflasche *f*.

flat [flæt] **1.** □ (*-tt-*) flach, platt; schal; *econ.* flau; klar; glatt; *mot.* platt (*Reifen*); ♪ erniedrigt (*Note*); ⁓ *price* Einheitspreis *m*; **2.** *adv.* glatt; völlig; *fall* ⁓ danebengehen; *sing* ⁓ zu tief singen; **3.** Fläche *f*, Ebene *f*; Flachland *n*; Untiefe *f*; (Miet)Wohnung *f*; ♪ B *n*; F Simpel *m*; *bsd. Am.* *mot.* Reifenpanne *f*, Plattfuß *m*; ⁓**foot** [ˈflætfʊt] (*pl. -feet*) *sl.* Bulle *m* (*Polizist*); ⁓**foot·ed** plattfüßig; ⁓**i·ron** Plätteisen *n*; ⁓**ten** [⁓tn] (sich) ab-, verflachen.

flat·ter [ˈflætə] schmeicheln (*dat.*); △ *nicht flattern*; ⁓**er** [⁓rə] Schmeichler(in); ⁓**y** [⁓rɪ] Schmeichelei *f*.

fla·vo(u)r [ˈfleɪvə] **1.** Geschmack *m*; Aroma *n*; Blume *f* (*Wein*); *fig.* Beigeschmack *m*; Würze *f*; **2.** würzen; ⁓**ing** [⁓ərɪŋ] Würze *f*, Aroma *n*; ⁓**less** [⁓lɪs] geschmacklos, fad.

flaw [flɔː] **1.** Sprung *m*, Riß *m*; Fehler *m*; ⚓ Bö *f*; **2.** zerbrechen; beschädigen; ⁓**less** □ [ˈflɔːlɪs] fehlerlos.

flax ♀ [flæks] Flachs *m*, Lein *m*.

flea *zo.* [fliː] Floh *m*.

fleck [flek] Fleck(en) *m*; Tupfen *m*.

fled [fled] *pret. u. p.p. von flee.*

fledged [fledʒd] flügge; **fledg(e)-ling** [ˈfledʒlɪŋ] Jungvogel *m*; *fig.* Grünschnabel *m*.

flee [fliː] (*fled*) fliehen; meiden.

fleece [fliːs] **1.** Vlies *n*; **2.** scheren; **fleec·y** [ˈfliːsɪ] (*-ier, -iest*) wollig; flockig.

fleet [fliːt] **1.** □ schnell; **2.** ⚓ Flotte *f*; ♀ *Street das Londoner Presseviertel*; *die (Londoner) Presse.*

flesh [fleʃ] *lebendiges* Fleisch; ⁓**y** [ˈfleʃɪ] (*-ier, -iest*) fleischig; dick.

flew [fluː] *pret. von fly 2.*

flex[1] *bsd. anat.* [fleks] biegen.

flex[2] *bsd. Brit.* ⚡ [⁓] (Anschluß-*f*, Verlängerungs)Kabel *n*, (-)Schnur *f*.

flex·i·ble □ [ˈfleksəbl] flexibel, biegsam; *fig.* anpassungsfähig.

flick [flɪk] schnippen; schnellen.

flick·er [ˈflɪkə] **1.** flackern; flattern; flimmern; **2.** Flackern *n*, Flimmern *n*; Flattern *n*; *Am.* Buntspecht *m*.

fli·er [ˈflaɪə] = *flyer.*

flight [flaɪt] Flucht *f*; Flug *m* (*a. fig.*);

Schwarm *m* (*Vögel etc.*; *a.* ✈, ✕); *a.*
~ *of stairs* Treppe *f*; *put to* ~ in die
Flucht schlagen; *take* (*to*) ~ die
Flucht ergreifen; **~·less** *zo.* [.ʌlɪs]
flugunfähig; **~·y** □ ['flaɪtɪ] (*-ier,
-iest*) launisch.

flim·sy ['flɪmzɪ] (*-ier, -iest*) dünn;
zart; *fig.* fadenscheinig.

flinch [flɪntʃ] zurückweichen;
zucken.

fling [flɪŋ] **1.** Wurf *m*; Schlag *m*; *have
one's od. a* ~ sich austoben; **2.** (*flung*)
v/i. eilen; ausschlagen (*Pferd*); *fig.*
toben; *v/t.* werfen, schleudern; ~
o.s. sich stürzen; ~ *open* aufreißen.

flint [flɪnt] Feuerstein *m*.

flip [flɪp] **1.** Klaps *m*; Ruck *m*; **2.**
(*-pp-*) schnippen, schnipsen.

flip·pant □ ['flɪpənt] respektlos,
schnodd(e)rig.

flip·per ['flɪpə] *zo.* Flosse *f*; *Sport:*
(Schwimm)Flosse *f*.

flirt [flɜːt] **1.** flirten; = *flip 2*; *be a* ~
gern flirten; **flir·ta·tion** [flɜː'teɪʃn]
Flirt *m*.

flit [flɪt] (*-tt-*) flitzen, huschen.

float [fləʊt] **1.** Schwimmer *m*; Floß *n*;
Plattformwagen *m*; **2.** *v/t.* überfluten; flößen; tragen (*Wasser*); ♣ flott
machen; *fig.* in Gang bringen; *econ.*
Gesellschaft gründen; *econ.* Wertpapiere *etc.* in Umlauf bringen; verbreiten; *v/i.* schwimmen, treiben;
schweben; umlaufen, in Umlauf
sein; **~·ing** ['fləʊtɪŋ] **1.** schwimmend, treibend, Schwimm...; *econ.*
umlaufend (*Geld etc.*); frei beweglich
(*Wechselkurs*); frei konvertierbar
(*Währung*); ~ *voter* *pol.* Wechsel-
wähler *m*; **2.** *econ.* Floating *n*.

flock [flɒk] **1.** Herde *f* (*bsd. Schafe od.
Ziegen*) (*a. fig.*); Schar *f*; △ *nicht*
Flocke; **2.** sich scharen; zs.-strömen.

floe [fləʊ] (treibende) Eisscholle.

flog [flɒg] (*-gg-*) peitschen; prügeln;
~·ging ['flɒgɪŋ] Tracht *f* Prügel.

flood [flʌd] **1.** *a.* **~·tide** Flut *f* (*Überschwemmung*); **2.** überfluten, überschwemmen; **~·gate** ['flʌdgeɪt]
Schleusentor *n*; **~·light** ⚡ Flutlicht
n.

floor [flɔː] **1.** (Fuß)Boden *m*; Stock
(*-werk n*) *m*; Tanzfläche *f*; ✓ Tenne
f; *first* ~ *Brt.* erster Stock, *Am.*
Erdgeschoß *n*; *second* ~ *Brt.* zweiter Stock, *Am.* erster Stock; ~
leader Am. parl. Fraktionsvorsit-
zende(r) *Am.*; ~ *show* Nachtklubvor-

stellung *f*; *take the* ~ das Wort ergreifen; **2.** dielen; zu Boden schlagen; verblüffen; **~·board** ['flɔːbɔːd]
(Fußboden)Diele *f*; **~·cloth** Putz-
lappen *m*; **~·ing** [.rɪŋ] Dielung *f*;
Fußboden *m*; ~ **lamp** Stehlampe *f*;
~·walk·er *Am.* = shopwalker.

flop [flɒp] **1.** (*-pp-*) schlagen; flattern; (hin)plumpsen; sich fallen lassen; ╇ durchfallen, danebengehen,
ein Reinfall sein; **2.** Plumps *m*; ╇
Flop *m*, Mißerfolg *m*, Reinfall *m*,
Pleite *f*; Versager *m*.

flor·id □ ['flɒrɪd] rot, gerötet.

flor·ist ['flɒrɪst] Blumenhändler *m*.

flounce[1] [flaʊns] Volant *m*.

flounce[2] [.] ~ *off* davonstürzen.

floun·der[1] *zo.* ['flaʊndə] Flunder *f*.

floun·der[2] [.] zappeln; strampeln;
fig. sich verhaspeln.

flour ['flaʊə] (feines) Mehl.

flour·ish ['flʌrɪʃ] **1.** Schnörkel *m*;
schwungvolle Bewegung; ♪ Tusch
m; **2.** *v/i.* blühen, gedeihen; *v/t.*
schwenken.

flout [flaʊt] (ver)spotten.

flow [fləʊ] **1.** Fließen *n*, Strömen *n*
(*beide a. fig.*), Rinnen *n*; Fluß *m*,
Strom *m* (*beide a. fig.*); ♣ Flut *f*; **2.**
fließen, strömen, rinnen; wallen
(*Haar*).

flow·er ['flaʊə] **1.** Blume *f*; Blüte *f* (*a.
fig.*); Zierde *f*; **2.** blühen; **~·bed**
Blumenbeet *n*; **~·pot** Blumentopf *m*;
~·y [.rɪ] (*-ier, -iest*) Blumen...; *fig.*
blumig (*Stil*).

flown [fləʊn] *p.p. von fly 2*.

fluc·tu|ate ['flʌktjʊeɪt] schwanken;
~·a·tion [flʌktjʊ'eɪʃn] Schwankung
f.

flu ╇ [fluː] Grippe *f*.

flue [fluː] Rauchfang *m*, Esse *f*.

flu·en|cy *fig.* ['fluːənsɪ] Fluß *m*; **~·t** □
[.t] fließend; flüssig; gewandt (*Red-
ner*).

fluff [flʌf] **1.** Flaum *m*; Flocke *f*; *fig.*
Schnitzer *m*; **2.** *Kissen* aufschütteln;
Federn aufplustern (*Vogel*); **~·y**
['flʌfɪ] (*-ier, -iest*) flaumig; flockig.

flu·id ['fluːɪd] **1.** flüssig; **2.** Flüssigkeit *f*.

flung [flʌŋ] *pret. u. p.p. von fling
2*.

flunk *Am. fig.* ╇ [flʌŋk] durchfallen
(lassen).

flu·o·res·cent [flʊə'resnt] fluoreszie-
rend.

flur·ry ['flʌrɪ] Nervosität *f*; Bö *f*;

Am. a. (Regen)Schauer *m;* Schnee-gestöber *n.*

flush [flʌʃ] **1.** ⊕ in gleicher Ebene; reichlich; (über)voll; **2.** Erröten *n;* Erregung *f;* Spülung *f;* (Wasser-)Spülung *f (in der Toilette);* **3.** *v/t. a.* ~ *out* (aus)spülen; ~ *down* hinunter-spülen; ~ *the toilet* spülen; *v/i.* errö-ten, rot werden; spülen *(Toilette od. Toilettenbenutzer).*

flus·ter ['flʌstə] **1.** Aufregung *f;* **2.** nervös machen, durcheinanderbrin-gen.

flute [fluːt] **1.** ♪ Flöte *f;* Falte *f;* **2.** (auf der) Flöte spielen; riefeln; fälteln.

flut·ter ['flʌtə] **1.** Geflatter *n;* Er-regung *f;* F Spekulation *f;* **2.** *v/t.* aufregen; *v/i.* flattern.

flux *fig.* [flʌks] Fluß *m.*

fly [flaɪ] **1.** *zo.* Fliege *f;* Flug *m;* Hosenschlitz *m;* Zeltklappe *f;* **2.** *(flew, flown)* fliegen (lassen); stür-men, stürzen; flattern, wehen; ver-fliegen *(Zeit); Drachen* steigen las-sen; ⚡ überfliegen; ~ *at s.o.* auf j-n losgehen; ~ *into a passion od. rage* in Wut geraten; ~ **er** ['flaɪə] Flieger *m; Am.* Flugblatt *n,* Reklamezettel *m;* ~ **ing** [~ɪŋ] fliegend; Flug...; ~ *saucer* fliegende Untertasse; ~ *squad* Überfallkommando *n (der Polizei);* ~ **o·ver** *Brt.* (Straßen-, Eisenbahn)Überführung *f;* ~ **weight** Boxen: Fliegengewicht(ler *m) n;* ~ **wheel** Schwungrad *n.*

foal *zo.* [fəʊl] Fohlen *n.*

foam [fəʊm] **1.** Schaum *m;* ~ *rubber* Schaumgummi *m;* **2.** schäumen; ~ **y** ['fəʊmɪ] *(-ier, -iest)* schaumig.

fo·cus ['fəʊkəs] **1.** *(pl. -cuses, -ci* [-saɪ]) (sich) im Brennpunkt vereini-gen; *opt.* einstellen *(a. fig.);* konzen-trieren.

fod·der ['fɒdə] (Trocken)Futter *n.*

foe *poet.* [fəʊ] Feind *m,* Gegner *m.*

fog [fɒg] **1.** (dichter) Nebel; *fig.* Um-nebelung *f; phot.* Schleier *m;* **2.** *(-gg-) mst fig.* umnebeln; *phot.* ver-schleiern; ~ **gy** □ ['fɒgɪ] *(-ier, -iest)* neb(e)lig; nebelhaft.

foi·ble *fig.* ['fɔɪbl] (kleine) Schwäche *f.*

foil¹ [fɔɪl] Folie *f; fig.* Hintergrund *m.*

foil² [~] vereiteln.

foil³ [~] *Fechten:* Florett *n.*

fold¹ [fəʊld] **1.** Schafhürde *f; fig.* Herde *f;* **2.** einpferchen.

fold² [~] **1.** Falte *f;* Falz *m;* **2.** ...fach, ...fältig; **3.** *v/t.* falten; falzen; *Arme*

kreuzen; ~ *(up)* einwickeln; *v/i.* sich falten; *Am.* F eingehen; ~ **er** ['fəʊldə] Mappe *f,* Schnellhefter *m;* Faltpro-spekt *m.*

fold·ing ['fəʊldɪŋ] zusammenlegbar; Klapp...; ~ **bed** Klappbett *n;* ~ **bi·cy·cle** Klapprad *n;* ~ **boat** Falt-boot *n;* ~ **chair** Klappstuhl *m;* ~ **door(s** *pl.)* Falttür *f.*

fo·li·age ['fəʊlɪɪdʒ] Laub(werk) *n.*

folk [fəʊk] *pl.* Leute *pl.;* ~s *pl.* F m-e *etc.* Leute *pl. (Angehörige);* △ *nicht Volk;* ~ **lore** ['fəʊkləː] Volkskunde *f;* Volkssagen *pl.;* ~ **song** Volkslied *n;* Folksong *m.*

fol·low ['fɒləʊ] folgen *(dat.);* folgen auf *(acc.);* be-, verfolgen; *s-m Beruf etc.* nachgehen; ~ *through* Plan *etc.* bis zum Ende durchführen; ~ *up e-r Sache* nachgehen; *e-e Sache* weiter-verfolgen; ~ **er** [~ə] Nachfolger(in); Verfolger(in); Anhänger(in); ~ **ing** [~ɪŋ] **1.** Anhängerschaft *f,* Anhänger *pl.;* Gefolge *n; the* ~ das Folgende; die Folgenden *pl.;* **2.** folgende(r, -s); **3.** im Anschluß an *(acc.).*

fol·ly ['fɒlɪ] Torheit *f;* Narrheit *f.*

fond □ [fɒnd] zärtlich; vernarrt *(of in acc.);* be ~ *of* gern haben, lieben; **fon·dle** ['fɒndl] liebkosen; strei-cheln; (ver)hätscheln; ~ **ness** [~nɪs] Zärtlichkeit *f,* Zuneigung *f;* Vorliebe *f.*

font [fɒnt] Taufstein *m; Am.* Quelle *f.*

food [fuːd] Speise *f,* Nahrung *f;* Essen *n;* Futter *n;* Lebensmittel *pl.*

fool [fuːl] **1.** Narr *m,* Närrin *f,* Dummkopf *m; make a* ~ *of s.o.* j-n zum Narren halten; *make a* ~ *of o.s.* sich lächerlich machen; **2.** *Am.* F närrisch, dumm; **3.** *v/t.* narren; be-trügen *(out of* um *et.);* ~ *away* F vertrödeln; *v/i.* herumalbern; *(her-um)spielen;* ~ *(a)round bsd. Am.* Zeit vertrödeln.

fool·e·ry ['fuːlərɪ] Torheit *f;* ~ **har·dy** □ [~haːdɪ] tollkühn; ~ **ish** □ [~ɪʃ] dumm, töricht; unklug; ~ **ish·ness** [~ɪʃnɪs] Dummheit *f;* ~ **proof** kin-derleicht; todsicher.

foot [fʊt] **1.** *(pl. feet)* Fuß *m (a. Maß* = 0,3048 *m);* Fußende *n;* ✕ Infante-rie *f; on* ~ zu Fuß; *im Gange, in* Gang; **2.** *mst* ~ *up* addieren; ~ *it* zu Fuß gehen; ~ **ball** ['fʊtbɔːl] *Brt.* Fußball(spiel *n) m; Am.* Football (-spiel *n) m; Brt.* Fußball *m; Am.* Football-Ball *m;* ~ **board** Trittbrett n; **~bridge** Fußgängerbrücke f; **~fall** Tritt m, Schritt m (Geräusch); **~gear** Schuhwerk n; **~hold** fester Stand; fig. Halt m.

foot·ing ['fʊtɪŋ] Halt m, Stand m; Grundlage f, Basis f; Stellung f; fester Fuß; Verhältnis n; ⚖ Zustand m; Endsumme f; be on a friendly ~ with s.o. ein gutes Verhältnis zu j-m haben; lose one's ~ ausgleiten.

foot|lights thea. ['fʊtlaɪts] pl. Rampenlicht(er pl.) n; Bühne f; **~loose** frei, unbeschwert; ~ and fancy-free frei u. ungebunden; **~path** (Fuß-)Pfad m; **~print** Fußabdruck m; ~s pl. a. Fußspur(en pl.) f; **~sore** wund an den Füßen; **~step** Tritt m, Schritt m; Fußstapfe f; **~wear** = footgear.

fop [fɒp] Geck m, Fatzke m.

for [fɔː, fə] 1. prp. mst für; Zweck, Ziel, Richtung: zu; nach; warten, hoffen etc. auf (acc.); sich sehnen etc. nach; Grund, Anlaß: aus, vor (dat.), wegen; Zeitdauer: ~ three days drei Tage (lang); seit drei Tagen; Entfernung: I walked ~ a mile ich ging eine Meile (weit); Austausch: (an)statt; in der Eigenschaft als; I ~ one ich zum Beispiel; ~ sure sicher!, gewiß!; 2. cj. denn.

for·age ['fɒrɪdʒ] a. ~ about (herum-)stöbern, (-)wühlen (in in dat.; for nach).

for·ay ['fɒreɪ] räuberischer Einfall.

for·bear¹ [fɔː'beə] (-bore, -borne) v/t. unterlassen; v/i. sich enthalten (from gen.); Geduld haben.

for·bear² ['fɔːbeə] Vorfahr m.

for·bid [fə'bɪd] (-dd-; -bade od. -bad [-bæd], -bidden od. -bid) verbieten; hindern; **~ding** □ [~ɪŋ] abstoßend.

force [fɔːs] 1. Stärke f, Kraft f, Gewalt f; Nachdruck m; Zwang m; Heer m; Streitmacht f; in ~ in großer Zahl od. Menge; the (police) ~ die Polizei; armed ~s pl. (Gesamt)Streitkräfte pl.; come (put) in(to) ~ in Kraft treten (setzen); 2. zwingen, nötigen; erzwingen; aufzwingen; Gewalt antun (dat.); beschleunigen; aufbrechen; künstlich reif machen; ~ open aufbrechen; **~d:** ~ landing Notlandung f; ~ march Gewaltmarsch m; **~ful** □ ['fɔːsfl] energisch, kraftvoll (Person); eindrucksvoll, überzeugend.

for·ceps ⚕ ['fɔːseps] Zange f.

for·ci·ble □ ['fɔːsəbl] gewaltsam; Zwangs...; eindringlich; wirksam.

ford [fɔːd] 1. Furt f; 2. durchwaten.

fore [fɔː] 1. adv. vorn; 2. Vorderteil m, n; come to the ~ sich hervortun; 3. adj. vorder; Vorder...; **~arm** ['fɔːrɑːm] Unterarm m; **~bear** ['fɔːbeə] = forbear²; **~bod·ing** [fɔː'bəʊdɪŋ] (böses) Vorzeichen; Ahnung f; **~cast** ['fɔːkɑːst] 1. Vorhersage f; 2. (-cast od. -casted) vorhersehen; voraussagen; **~fa·ther** Vorfahr m; **~fin·ger** Zeigefinger m; **~foot** (pl. -feet) zo. Vorderfuß m; **~gone** ['fɔːgɒn] von vornherein feststehend; ~ conclusion ausgemachte Sache, Selbstverständlichkeit f; **~ground** ['fɔːgraʊnd] Vordergrund m; **~hand** 1. Sport: Vorhand(schlag m) f; 2. Sport: Vorhand...; **~head** ['fɒrɪd] Stirn f.

for·eign ['fɒrən] fremd, ausländisch, -wärtig, Auslands..., Außen...; ~ affairs Außenpolitik f; ~ language Fremdsprache f; ~ minister pol. Außenminister m; ♀ Office Brt. pol. Außenministerium n; ~ policy Außenpolitik f; ♀ Secretary Brt. pol. Außenminister m; ~ trade econ. Außenhandel m; ~ worker Gastarbeiter m; **~er** [~ə] Ausländer(in), Fremde(r m) f.

fore|knowl·edge ['fɔː'nɒlɪdʒ] Vorherwissen n; **~leg** zo. ['fɔːleg] Vorderbein n; **~man** (pl. -men) ⚖ Obmann m; Vorarbeiter m, (Werk-)Meister m, Polier m, ⚒ Steiger m; **~most** vorderste(r, -s), erste(r, -s); **~name** Vorname m; **~run·ner** Vorläufer(in); **~see** [fɔː'siː] (-saw, -seen) vorhersehen; **~shad·ow** ahnen lassen, andeuten; **~sight** ['fɔːsaɪt] fig. Weitblick m, (weise) Voraussicht.

for·est ['fɒrɪst] 1. Wald m (a. fig.), Forst m; ~ ranger Am. Förster m; 2. aufforsten.

fore·stall [fɔː'stɔːl] et. vereiteln; j-m zuvorkommen.

for·est|er ['fɒrɪstə] Förster m; Waldarbeiter m; **~ry** [~rɪ] Forstwirtschaft f; Waldgebiet n.

fore|taste ['fɔːteɪst] Vorgeschmack m; **~tell** [fɔː'tel] (-told) vorhersagen; **~thought** ['fɔːθɔːt] Vorsorge f, -bedacht m.

for·ev·er, for ev·er [fə'revə] für immer.

fore|wom·an (*pl. -women*) Aufseherin *f*; Vorarbeiterin *f*; **~word** Vorwort *n*.

for·feit ['fɔ:fɪt] **1.** Verwirkung *f*; Strafe *f*; Pfand *n*; **2.** verwirken; einbüßen.

forge[1] [fɔ:dʒ] *mst* ~ *ahead* sich vor(wärts)arbeiten.

forge[2] [~] **1.** Schmiede *f*; **2.** schmieden (*fig. sich ausdenken*); fälschen; **forg·er** ['fɔ:dʒə] Fälscher; **for·ge·ry** [~ərɪ] Fälschen *n*; Fälschung *f*.

for·get [fə'get] (*-got, -gotten*) vergessen; **~ful** [~fl] vergeßlich; **~me-not** ♀ Vergißmeinnicht *n*.

for·give [fə'gɪv] (*-gave, -given*) vergeben, -zeihen; **~ness** [~nɪs] Verzeihung *f*; **for·giv·ing** □ [~ɪŋ] versöhnlich; nachsichtig.

for·go [fɔ:'gəʊ] (*-went, -gone*) verzichten auf (*acc.*).

fork [fɔ:k] **1.** (Eß-, Heu-, Mist-*etc.*)Gabel *f*; **2.** (sich) gabeln; **~ed** gegabelt, gespalten; **~lift** ['fɔ:klɪft], *a.* ~ **truck** Gabelstapler *m*.

for·lorn [fə'lɔ:n] verloren, -lassen.

form [fɔ:m] **1.** Form *f*; Gestalt *f*; Formalität *f*; Formular *n*; (Schul-)Bank *f*; (Schul-)Klasse *f*; Kondition *f*; geistige Verfassung *f*; **2.** (sich) formen, (sich) bilden, gestalten; ✕ (sich) aufstellen.

form·al □ ['fɔ:ml] förmlich; formell; äußerlich; **for·mal·i·ty** [fɔ:'mælətɪ] Förmlichkeit *f*; Formalität *f*.

for·ma·tion [fɔ:'meɪʃn] Bildung *f*; **~tive** ['fɔ:mətɪv] bildend; gestaltend; ~ *years pl.* Entwicklungsjahre *pl.*

for·mer ['fɔ:mə] vorig, früher; ehemalig, vergangen; erstere(r, -s); jene(r, -s); **~ly** [~lɪ] ehemals, früher.

for·mi·da·ble □ ['fɔ:mɪdəbl] furchtbar, schrecklich; ungeheuer.

for·mu·la ['fɔ:mjʊlə] (*pl. -las, -lae* [-li:]) Formel *f*; Rezept *n* (*zur Zubereitung*); △ *nicht Formular*; **~late** [~leɪt] formulieren.

for·sake [fə'seɪk] (*-sook, -saken*) aufgeben; verlassen; **~sak·en** [~ən] *p.p. von forsake;* **~sook** [fə'sʊk] *pret. von forsake;* **~swear** [fɔ:'sweə] (*-swore, -sworn*) abschwören, entsagen.

fort ✕ [fɔ:t] Fort *n*, Festung *f*.

forth [fɔ:θ] vor(wärts); voran; heraus, hinaus, hervor; weiter, fort; **~com·ing** ['fɔ:θ'kʌmɪŋ] erscheinend; bereit; bevorstehend; F entgegenkommend; ~ **with** [~'wɪθ] sogleich.

for·ti·eth ['fɔ:tɪɪθ] vierzigste(r, -s).

for·ti·fi·ca·tion [fɔ:tɪfɪ'keɪʃn] Befestigung *f*; **~fy** ['fɔ:tɪfaɪ] ✕ befestigen; *fig.* (ver)stärken; **~tude** [~tju:d] Seelenstärke *f*; Tapferkeit *f*.

for·night ['fɔ:tnaɪt] vierzehn Tage.

for·tu·i·tous □ [fɔ:'tju:ɪtəs] zufällig.

for·tu·nate ['fɔ:tʃnət] glücklich; *be* ~ Glück haben; **~ly** [~lɪ] glücklicherweise.

for·tune ['fɔ:tʃn] Glück *n*; Schicksal *n*; Zufall *m*; Vermögen *n*; **~tell·er** Wahrsager(in).

for·ty ['fɔ:tɪ] **1.** vierzig; **~niner** *Am. kalifornischer Goldsucher von 1849;* ~ *winks pl.* F Nickerchen *n*; **2.** Vierzig *f*.

for·ward ['fɔ:wəd] **1.** *adj.* vorder; bereit(willig); fortschrittlich; vorwitzig, keck; **2.** *adv. a.* ~**s** vor(wärts); **3.** *Fußball:* Stürmer *m*; **4.** befördern, (ver)senden, schicken; *Brief etc.* nachsenden; **~ing a·gent** [~ɪŋeɪdʒənt] Spediteur *m*.

fos·ter-child ['fɔstətʃaɪld] (*pl. -children*) Pflegekind *n*; **~par·ents** *pl.* Pflegeeltern *pl.*

fought [fɔ:t] *pret. u. p.p. von fight* 2.

foul [faʊl] **1.** □ stinkend, widerlich, schlecht, übel(riechend); schlecht, stürmisch (*Wetter*); widrig (*Wind*); *Sport:* regelwidrig, unfair; *fig.* widerlich, ekelhaft; *fig.* abscheulich, gemein; △ *nicht faul;* **2.** *Sport:* Foul *n*, Regelverstoß *m*; **3.** *a.* ~ *up* be-, verschmutzen, verunreinigen; *Sport:* foulen.

found [faʊnd] **1.** *pret. u. p.p. von find* 1; **2.** (be)gründen; stiften; ⊕ gießen.

foun·da·tion [faʊn'deɪʃn] *arch.* Grundmauer *f*, Fundament *n*; *fig.* Gründung *f*, Errichtung *f*; (gemeinnützige) Stiftung; *fig.* Grund(lage *f*) *m*, Basis *f*.

found·er[1] ['faʊndə] Gründer(in), Stifter(in).

foun·der[2] [~] ♣ sinken; *fig.* scheitern.

found·ling ['faʊndlɪŋ] Findling *m*.

foun·dry ⊕ ['faʊndrɪ] Gießerei *f*.

foun·tain ['faʊntɪn] Quelle *f*; Springbrunnen *m*; ~ **pen** Füllfederhalter *m*.

four 492

four [fɔ:] 1. vier; 2. Vier f; *Rudern:* Vierer m; **on all ~s** auf allen vieren; **~-square** [fɔ:'skweə] viereckig; *fig.* unerschütterlich; **~-stroke** ['fɔ:-strəuk] *mot.* Viertakt...; **~-teenth** ['fɔ:'ti:nθ] 1. vierzehn; 2. Vierzehn f; **~-teenth** [~'ti:nθ] vierzehnte(r, -s); **~th** [fɔ:θ] 1. vierte(r, -s); 2. Viertel n; **~th·ly** ['fɔ:θlɪ] viertens.

fowl [faul] Geflügel n; Huhn n; Vogel m; **~ing piece** ['faulɪŋpi:s] Vogelflinte f.

fox [fɔks] 1. Fuchs m; 2. überlisten; **~glove** ♀ ['fɔksglʌv] Fingerhut m; **~y** [~ɪ] (-ier, -iest) fuchsartig; schlau, gerissen.

frac·tion ['frækʃn] Bruch(teil) m; △ *nicht* parl. Fraktion.

frac·ture ['fræktʃə] 1. (*bsd.* Knochen)Bruch m; 2. brechen.

fra·gile ['frædʒaɪl] zerbrechlich.

frag·ment ['frægmənt] Bruchstück n.

fra·grance ['freɪgrəns] Wohlgeruch m, Duft m; **~grant** □ [~t] wohlriechend.

frail □ [freɪl] ge-, zerbrechlich; zart, schwach; **~ty** ['freɪltɪ] Zartheit f; Zerbrechlichkeit f; Schwäche f.

frame [freɪm] 1. Rahmen m; Gefüge n; Gerüst n; (Brillen)Gestell n; Körper m; (An)Ordnung f; *phot.* (Einzel)Bild n; **~ of mind** Gemütsverfassung f, Stimmung f; 2. bilden, formen, bauen; entwerfen; (ein)rahmen; sich entwickeln; **~-up** *bsd.* Am. F ['freɪmʌp] abgekartetes Spiel; **~work** ⊕ Gerippe n; Rahmen m; *fig.* Struktur f, System n.

fran·chise ⚖ ['fræntʃaɪz] Wahlrecht n; Bürgerrecht n; *bsd.* Am. Konzession f.

frank [fræŋk] 1. □ frei(mütig), offen; 2. *Brief* maschinell frankieren.

frank·fur·ter ['fræŋkfɜ:tə] Frankfurter Würstchen n.

frank·ness ['fræŋknɪs] Offenheit f.

fran·tic ['fræntɪk] (**~ally**) wahnsinnig.

fra·ter·nal □ [frə'tɜ:nl] brüderlich; **~ni·ty** [~nətɪ] Brüderlichkeit f; Bruderschaft f; Am. univ. Verbindung f.

fraud [frɔ:d] Betrug m; F Schwindel m; **~u·lent** □ ['frɔ:djʊlənt] betrügerisch.

fray [freɪ] (sich) abnutzen; (sich) durchscheuern, (sich) ausfransen.

freak [fri:k] 1. Mißbildung f, Mißge-

burt f, Monstrosität f; außergewöhnlicher Umstand; Grille f, Laune f; *mst in Zssgn:* Süchtige(r m) f; Freak m, Narr m, Fanatiker m; **~ of nature** Laune f der Natur; **film ~** Kinonarr m, -fan m; 2. **~ out** *sl.* ausflippen.

freck·le ['frekl] Sommersprosse f; **~d** sommersprossig.

free [fri:] 1. □ (~r, ~st) frei; freigebig (**of** mit); freiwillig; **he is ~ to inf.** es steht ihm frei, zu *inf.*; **~ and easy** zwanglos; sorglos; **make ~** sich Freiheiten erlauben; **set ~** freilassen; 2. (*freed*) befreien; freilassen, *et.* freimachen; **~dom** ['fri:dəm] Freiheit f; freie Benutzung; Offenheit f; Zwanglosigkeit f; (plumpe) Vertraulichkeit f; **~ of a city** (Ehren)Bürgerrecht n; **~-hold·er** Grundeigentümer m; **~lance** frei(beruflich tätig), freischaffend; **2·ma·son** Freimaurer m; **~way** *Am.* Schnellstraße f; **~-wheel** ⊕ ['fri:'wi:l] 1. Freilauf m; 2. im Freilauf fahren.

freeze [fri:z] 1. (*froze, frozen*) *v/i.* (ge)frieren; erstarren; *v/t.* gefrieren lassen; *Fleisch etc.* einfrieren, tiefkühlen; *econ. Preise etc.* einfrieren; 2. Frost m, Kälte f; *econ. pol.* Einfrieren n; **wage~,~ on wages** Lohnstopp m; **~-dry** ['fri:z'draɪ] gefriertrocknen; **freez·er** ['fri:zə] *a.* **deep ~** Gefriertruhe f, Tiefkühl-, Gefriergerät n; Gefrierfach n; **freez·ing** □ [~ɪŋ] eisig; ⊕ Gefrier...; **~ compartment** Gefrier-, Tiefkühlfach n; **~ point** Gefrierpunkt m.

freight [freɪt] 1. Fracht(geld) n; *attr.* Am. Güter...; 2. be-, verfrachten; **~ car** *Am.* ⚐ ['freɪtka:] Güterwagen m; **~er** [~ə] Frachter m, Frachtschiff n; Fracht-, Transportflugzeug n; **~ train** *Am.* Güterzug m.

French [frentʃ] 1. französisch; **take ~ leave** heimlich weggehen; **~ doors** pl. *Am.* = **French window**(s); **~ fries** pl. bsd. Am. Pommes frites pl.; **~ window**(s pl.) Terrassen-, Balkontür f; 2. *ling.* Französisch n; **the ~** pl. die Franzosen pl.; **~man** ['frentʃmən] (pl. -men) Franzose m.

fren·zied ['frenzɪd] wahnsinnig, **~zy** [~ɪ] wilde Aufregung; Ekstase f; Raserei f.

fre·quen·cy ['fri:kwənsɪ] Häufigkeit f; ⚡ Frequenz f; **~t** 1. □ [~t] häufig; 2. [frɪ'kwent] (oft) besuchen.

fruity

fresh □ [freʃ] frisch; neu; unerfahren; *Am.* F frech; **~en** ['freʃn] frisch machen *od.* werden; **~** *up* neuer *od.* schöner machen; **~** (*o.s.*) *up* sich frisch machen; **~man** (*pl. -men*) *univ.* Student *m* im ersten Jahr; **~ness** [~nɪs] Frische *f*; Neuheit *f*; Unerfahrenheit *f*; **~ wa·ter** Süßwasser *n*; **~·wa·ter** Süßwasser...

fret [fret] 1. Aufregung *f*; Ärger *m*; ♪ Bund *m*, Griffleiste *f*; 2. (*-tt-*) zerfressen; (sich) ärgern; (sich) grämen; **~** *away*, **~** *out* aufreiben.

fret·ful □ ['fretfl] ärgerlich.

fret-saw ['fretsɔː] Laubsäge *f*.

fret-work ['fretwɜːk] (geschnitztes) Gitterwerk; Laubsägearbeit *f*.

fri·ar ['fraɪə] Mönch *m*.

fric·tion ['frɪkʃn] Reibung *f* (*a. fig.*).

Fri·day ['fraɪdɪ] Freitag *m*.

fridge F [frɪdʒ] Kühlschrank *m*.

friend [frend] Freund(in); Bekannte(r *m*) *f*; *make* **~** *with* sich anfreunden mit, Freundschaft schließen mit; **~·ly** ['frendlɪ] freund(schaft)-lich; **~ship** [~ʃɪp] Freundschaft *f*.

frig·ate ⚓ ['frɪgɪt] Fregatte *f*.

fright [fraɪt] Schrecken *m*; *fig.* Vogelscheuche *f*; **~en** ['fraɪtn] erschrecken; *be* **~** *ed of s.th.* vor et. Angst haben; **~·en·ing** □ [~ɪŋ] furchterregend; **~·ful** □ [~fl] schrecklich.

frig·id □ ['frɪdʒɪd] kalt, frostig; *psych.* frigid(e).

frill [frɪl] Krause *f*, Rüsche *f*.

fringe [frɪndʒ] 1. Franse *f*; Rand *m*; Ponyfrisur *f*; **~** *benefits pl. econ.* Gehalts-, Lohnnebenleistungen *pl.*; **~** *event* Randveranstaltung *f*; **~** *group* Soziologie: Randgruppe *f*; 2. mit Fransen besetzen.

Fri·si·an ['frɪzɪən] friesisch.

frisk [frɪsk] 1. Luftsprung *m*; 2. herumtollen; F filzen; *j-n*, *et.* durchsuchen; **~·y** □ ['frɪskɪ] (*-ier, -iest*) lebhaft, munter.

frit·ter ['frɪtə] 1. Pfannkuchen *m*, Krapfen *m*. 2. **~** *away* vertun, -trödeln, -geuden.

fri·vol·i·ty [frɪ'vɒlɪtɪ] Frivolität *f*, Leichtfertigkeit *f*; **friv·o·lous** □ ['frɪvələs] frivol, leichtfertig.

friz·zle ['frɪzl] *Küche:* brutzeln.

friz·z·y □ ['frɪzɪ] (*-ier, -iest*) gekräuselt, kraus (*Haar*).

fro [frəʊ]: *to and* **~** hin und her.

frock [frɒk] Kutte *f*; (*Frauen*)Kleid *n*; Kittel *m*; Gehrock *m*.

frog *zo.* [frɒg] Frosch *m*; **~·man** ['frɒgmən] (*pl. -men*) Froschmann *m*.

frol·ic ['frɒlɪk] 1. Herumtoben *n*, -tollen *n*; Ausgelassenheit *f*; Streich *m*, Jux *m*; 2. (*-ck-*) herumtoben, -tollen; **~some** □ [~səm] lustig, fröhlich.

from [frɒm, frəm] von; aus, von ... her; von ... (an); aus, vor, wegen; nach, gemäß; *defend* **~** schützen vor (*dat.*); **~** *amidst* mitten aus.

front [frʌnt] 1. Stirn *f*; Vorderseite *f*; ✕ Front *f*; Hemdbrust *f*; Strandpromenade *f*; Kühnheit *f*, Frechheit *f*; *at the* **~** vorn; *in* **~** *of* räumlich vor; 2. Vorder...; **~** *door* Haustür *f*; **~** *entrance* Vordereingang *m*; 3. *a.* **~** *on*, **~** *towards* die Front haben nach; gegenüberstehen, gegenübertreten (*dat.*); **~·age** ['frʌntɪdʒ] (Vorder-)Front *f* (*e-s Hauses*); **~·al** □ [~tl] Stirn...; Front..., Vorder...

fron·tier ['frʌntɪə] (Landes)Grenze *f*; *Am. hist.* Grenzland *n*, Grenze *f* (*zum Wilden Westen*); *attr.* Grenz...

front| page ['frʌntpeɪdʒ] *Zeitung:* Titelseite *f*; **~-wheel drive** *mot.* Vorderradantrieb *m*.

frost [frɒst] 1. Frost *m*; *a. hoar* **~**, *white* **~** Reif *m*; 2. (*mit Zucker*) bestreuen, glasieren, mattieren; **~ed** *glass* Milchglas *n*; **~·bite** ['frɒstbaɪt] Erfrierung *f*; **~·bit·ten** erfroren; **~·y** □ [~ɪ] (*-ier, -iest*) eisig, frostig (*a. fig.*).

froth [frɒθ] 1. Schaum *m*; 2. schäumen; zu Schaum schlagen; **~·y** □ ['frɒθɪ] (*-ier, -iest*) schäumend, schaumig; *fig.* seicht.

frown [fraʊn] 1. Stirnrunzeln *n*; finsterer Blick; 2. *v/i.* die Stirn runzeln; finster blicken; **~** *on od. upon s.th.* et. mißbilligen.

froze [frəʊz] *pret. von* freeze 1; **fro·zen** ['frəʊzn] 1. *p.p. von* freeze 1; 2. *adj.* (ein)gefroren; (ein-, zu)gefroren; Gefrier...; **~** *food* Tiefkühlkost *f*.

fru·gal □ ['fruːgl] einfach; sparsam.

fruit [fruːt] 1. Frucht *f*; Früchte *pl.*; Obst *n*; 2. Frucht tragen; **~·er·er** ['fruːtərə] Obsthändler *m*; **~·ful** □ [~fl] fruchtbar; **~·less** □ [~lɪs] unfruchtbar; **~·y** □ [~ɪ] (*-ier, -iest*) frucht-, obstartig; fruchtig (*Wein*); klangvoll, sonor (*Stimme*).

frus|trate [frʌˈstreɪt] vereiteln; enttäuschen; frustrieren; **~·tra·tion** [~eɪʃn] Vereitelung *f*; Enttäuschung *f*; Frustration *f*.

fry [fraɪ] 1. Gebratene(s) *n*; Fischbrut *f*; 2. braten, backen; **~·ing-pan** [ˈfraɪɪŋpæn] Bratpfanne *f*.

fuch·sia ⚘ [ˈfjuːʃə] Fuchsie *f*.

fuck V [fʌk] 1. ficken, vögeln; ~ *it!* Scheiße!; *get ~ed!* der Teufel soll dich holen!; 2. *int.* Scheiße!; **~·ing** V [ˈfʌkɪŋ] Scheiß..., verflucht, -dammt (*oft nur verstärkend*); ~ *hell!* verdammte Scheiße!

fudge [fʌdʒ] 1. F zurechtpfuschen; 2. Unsinn *m*; *Art* Fondant *m*.

fu·el [fjʊəl] 1. Brennmaterial *n*; Betriebs-, *mot.* Kraftstoff *m*; 2. (*bsd. Brt. -ll-, Am. -l-*) *mot.*, ✈ (auf)tanken.

fu·gi·tive [ˈfjuːdʒɪtɪv] 1. flüchtig (*a. fig.*); 2. Flüchtling *m*.

ful·fil, *Am. a.* **-fill** [fʊlˈfɪl] (*-ll-*) erfüllen; vollziehen; **~·ment** [~mənt] Erfüllung *f*.

full [fʊl] 1. □ voll; Voll...; vollständig, völlig; reichlich; ausführlich; *of* ~ *age* volljährig; 2. *adv.* völlig, ganz; genau; 3. *das* Ganze; Höhepunkt *m*; *in* ~ völlig; ausführlich; *to the* ~ vollständig; **~·blood·ed** [ˈfʊlblʌdɪd] vollblütig; kräftig; reinrassig; ~ **dress** Gesellschaftsanzug *m*; ~ **dress** formell, Gala...; **~·fledged** *Am.* = *fully-fledged*; **~·grown** ausgewachsen; **~·length** in voller Größe; bodenlang; abendfüllend (*Film etc.*); ~ **moon** Vollmond *m*; ~ **stop** *ling.* Punkt *m*; ~ **time** *Sport*: Spielende *n*; **~·time** ganztägig, Ganztags...; ~ *job* Ganztagsbeschäftigung *f*.

ful·ly [ˈfʊlɪ] voll, völlig, ganz; **~·fledged** flügge; fig. richtig; **~·grown** *Brt.* = *full-grown*.

fum·ble [ˈfʌmbl] tasten; fummeln.

fume [fjuːm] 1. rauchen; aufgebracht sein; 2. *~s pl.* Dämpfe *pl.*, Dünste *pl.*

fu·mi·gate [ˈfjuːmɪgeɪt] ausräuchern, desinfizieren.

fun [fʌn] Scherz *m*, Spaß *m*; *make ~ of* sich lustig machen über (*acc.*).

func·tion [ˈfʌŋkʃn] 1. Funktion *f*; Beruf *m*; Tätigkeit *f*; Aufgabe *f*; Feierlichkeit *f*; 2. funktionieren; **~·a·ry** [~ərɪ] Funktionär *m*.

fund [fʌnd] 1. Fonds *m*; *~s pl.* Staats-papiere *pl.*; Geld(mittel *pl.*) *n*; *a ~ of fig.* ein Vorrat an (*dat.*); 2. *Schuld* fundieren; *Geld* anlegen; das Kapital aufbringen für.

fun·da·men·tal [fʌndəˈmentl] 1. grundlegend; Grund...; 2. *~s pl.* Grundlage *f*, -züge *pl.*, -begriffe *pl.*

fu·ne·ral [ˈfjuːnərəl] Beerdigung *f*; *attr.* Trauer..., Begräbnis...; **~·re·al** □ [fjuːˈnɪərɪəl] traurig, düster.

fun-fair [ˈfʌnfeə] Rummelplatz *m*.

fu·nic·u·lar [fjuːˈnɪkjʊlə] *a.* ~ *railway* (Draht)Seilbahn *f*.

fun·nel [ˈfʌnl] Trichter *m*; Rauchfang *m*; ⚓, 🚂 Schornstein *m*.

fun·nies *Am.* [ˈfʌnɪz] *pl.* Comics *pl.*

fun·ny □ [ˈfʌnɪ] (*-ier, -iest*) lustig, spaßig, komisch.

fur [fɜː] 1. Pelz *m*; Belag *m* (*auf der Zunge*); Kesselstein *m*; **~s** *pl.* Pelzwaren *pl.*; 2. mit Pelz besetzen *od.* füttern.

fur·bish [ˈfɜːbɪʃ] putzen, polieren.

fu·ri·ous □ [ˈfjʊərɪəs] wütend; wild.

furl [fɜːl] *Fahne, Segel* auf-, einrollen; *Schirm* zusammenrollen.

fur·lough ✕ [ˈfɜːləʊ] Urlaub *m*.

fur·nace [ˈfɜːnɪs] Schmelz-, Hochofen *m*; (Heiz)Kessel *m*.

fur·nish [ˈfɜːnɪʃ] versehen (*with* mit); *et.* liefern; möblieren; ausstatten.

fur·ni·ture [ˈfɜːnɪtʃə] Möbel *pl.*, Einrichtung *f*; Ausstattung *f*; *sectional* ~ Anbaumöbel *pl.*

fur·ri·er [ˈfʌrɪə] Kürschner *m*.

fur·row [ˈfʌrəʊ] 1. Furche *f*; 2. furchen.

fur·ry [ˈfɜːrɪ] aus Pelz, pelzartig; belegt (*Zunge*).

fur·ther [ˈfɜːðə] 1. *comp. von far*; 2. fördern; **~·ance** [~rəns] Förderung *f*; **~·more** [~ˈmɔː] ferner, überdies; **~·most** [~məʊst] weiteste(r, -s) entfernteste(r, -s).

fur·thest [ˈfɜːðɪst] *sup. von far*.

fur·tive □ [ˈfɜːtɪv] verstohlen.

fu·ry [ˈfjʊərɪ] Raserei *f*, Wut *f*; Furie *f*.

fuse [fjuːz] 1. schmelzen; *⚡* durchbrennen; 2. *⚡* Sicherung *f*; Zünder *m*; Zündschnur *f*.

fu·se·lage ✈ [ˈfjuːzɪlɑːʒ] (Flugzeug-)Rumpf *m*.

fu·sion [ˈfjuːʒn] Verschmelzung *f*, Fusion *f*; *nuclear* ~ Kernfusion *f*.

fuss F [fʌs] 1. Lärm *m*; Wesen *n*, Getue *n*; 2. viel Aufhebens machen (*about* um, von); (sich) aufregen; **~·y**

□ ['fʌsɪ] (*-ier*, *-iest*) aufgeregt, hektisch; kleinlich, pedantisch; heikel, wählerisch.

fus·ty ['fʌstɪ] (*-ier*, *-iest*) muffig; *fig.* verstaubt.

fu·tile □ ['fju:taɪl] nutz-, zwecklos.

fu·ture ['fju:tʃə] **1.** (zu)künftig; **2.** Zukunft *f*; *gr.* Futur *n*, Zukunft *f*; *in* ~ in Zukunft, künftig.

fuzz[1] [fʌz] **1.** feiner Flaum; Fusseln *pl.*; **2.** fusseln, (zer)fasern.

fuzz[2] *sl.* [~] Bulle *m* (*Polizist*).

G

gab F [gæb] Geschwätz *n*; *have the gift of the* ~ ein gutes Mundwerk haben.

gab·ar·dine ['gæbədi:n] Gabardine *m* (*Wollstoff*).

gab·ble ['gæbl] **1.** Geschnatter *n*, Geschwätz *n*; **2.** schnattern, schwatzen.

gab·er·dine ['gæbədi:n] *hist.* Kaftan *m* (*der Juden*); = *gabardine*.

ga·ble *arch.* ['geɪbl] Giebel *m*.

gad F [gæd] (*-dd-*): ~ *about*, ~ *around* (viel) unterwegs sein (*in dat.*).

gad·fly *zo.* ['gædflaɪ] Bremse *f*.

gad·get ⊕ ['gædʒɪt] Apparat *m*, Gerät *n*, Vorrichtung *f*; *oft contp.* technische Spielerei.

gag [gæg] **1.** Knebel *m* (*a. fig.*); F Gag *m*; **2.** (*-gg-*) knebeln; *fig.* mundtot machen.

gage *Am.* [geɪdʒ] = *gauge*; △ *nicht Gage*.

gai·e·ty ['geɪətɪ] Fröhlichkeit *f*.

gai·ly ['geɪlɪ] *adv. von gay 1.*

gain [geɪn] **1.** Gewinn *m*; Vorteil *m*; **2.** gewinnen; erreichen; bekommen; zunehmen an (*dat.*); vorgehen (um) (*Uhr*); ~ *in* zunehmen an (*dat.*).

gait [geɪt] Gang(art *f*) *m*; Schritt *m*.

gai·ter ['geɪtə] Gamasche *f*.

gal F [gæl] Mädel *n*.

gal·ax·y *ast.* ['gæləksɪ] Milchstraße *f*, Galaxis *f*.

gale [geɪl] Sturm *m*.

gall [gɔ:l] **1.** *veraltet* Galle *f*; wundgeriebene Stelle; F Frechheit *f*; **2.** wund reiben; ärgern.

gal·lant ['gælənt] stattlich; tapfer; galant, höflich; ~ *lan·try* [~rɪ] Tapferkeit *f*; Galanterie *f*.

gal·le·ry ['gælərɪ] Galerie *f*; Empore *f*.

gal·ley ['gælɪ] ♣ Galeere *f*; ♣ Kombüse *f*; *a.* ~ *proof print.* Fahne(nabzug *m*) *f*.

gal·lon ['gælən] Gallone *f* (*4,54 Liter, Am. 3,78 Liter*).

gal·lop ['gæləp] **1.** Galopp *m*; **2.** galoppieren (lassen).

gal·lows ['gæləʊz] *sg.* Galgen *m*.

ga·lore [gə'lɔ:] in rauhen Mengen.

gam·ble ['gæmbl] **1.** (um Geld) spielen; **2.** F Glücksspiel *n*; ~ **r** [~ə] Spieler(in).

gam·bol ['gæmbl] **1.** Luftsprung *m*; **2.** (*bsd. Brt. -ll-, Am. -l-*) (herum-) tanzen, (-)hüpfen.

game [geɪm] **1.** (Karten-, Ball-*etc.*)Spiel *n*; (einzelnes) Spiel (*a. fig.*); *hunt.* Wild *n*; Wildbret *n*; ~*s pl.* Spiele *pl.*; *Schule:* Sport *m*; **2.** mutig; bereit (*for* zu; *to do* zu tun); ~ **·keep·er** ['geɪmki:pə] Wildhüter *m*.

gam·mon *bsd. Brt.* ['gæmən] schwachgepökelter *od.* -geräucherter Schinken.

gan·der *zo.* ['gændə] Gänserich *m*.

gang [gæŋ] **1.** (Arbeiter)Trupp *m*; Gang *f*, Bande *f*; Clique *f*; Horde *f*; △ *nicht der Gang*; **2.** ~ *up* sich zusammentun, *contp.* sich zusammenrotten.

gang·ster ['gæŋstə] Gangster *m*.

gang·way ['gæŋweɪ] (Durch)Gang *m*; ♣ Fallreep *n*; ♣ Laufplanke *f*.

gaol [dʒeɪl], ~ **bird** ['dʒeɪlbɜ:d], ~ **er** [~ə] *s. jail etc.*

gap [gæp] Lücke *f*; Kluft *f*; Spalte *f*.

gape [geɪp] gähnen; klaffen; gaffen.

gar·age ['gæra:ʒ] **1.** Garage *f*; (Reparatur)Werkstatt *f* (*u.* Tankstelle *f*); **2.** *Auto* in e-r Garage ab- *od.* unterstellen; *Auto* in die Garage fahren.

gar·bage *bsd. Am.* ['gɑ:bɪdʒ] Abfall *m*, Müll *m*; ~ *can* Abfall-, Mülleimer *m*; Abfall-, Mülltonne *f*; ~ **truck** Müllwagen *m*.

gar·den ['gɑːdn] **1.** Garten *m*; **2.** im Garten arbeiten; Gartenbau treiben; ~**er** [~ə] Gärtner(in); ~**ing** [~ɪŋ] Gartenarbeit *f*.

gar·gle ['gɑːgl] **1.** gurgeln; **2.** Gurgeln *n*; Gurgelwasser *n*.

gar·ish □ ['geərɪʃ] grell, auffallend.

gar·land ['gɑːlənd] Girlande *f*.

gar·lic ♀ ['gɑːlɪk] Knoblauch *m*.

gar·ment ['gɑːmənt] Gewand *n*.

gar·nish ['gɑːnɪʃ] garnieren; zieren.

gar·ret ['gærət] Dachstube *f*.

gar·ri·son ✕ ['gærɪsn] Garnison *f*.

gar·ru·lous □ ['gærələs] schwatzhaft.

gar·ter ['gɑːtə] Strumpfband *n*; *Am.* Socken-, Strumpfhalter *m*.

gas [gæs] **1.** Gas *n*; *Am.* F Benzin *n*; **2.** (-ss-) *v/t.* vergasen; *v/i.* F faseln; *a.* ~ **up** *Am.* F *mot.* (auf)tanken; ~·**e·ous** ['gæsjəs] gasförmig.

gash [gæʃ] **1.** klaffende Wunde; Hieb *m*; Riß *m*; **2.** tief (ein)schneiden in (*acc.*).

gas·ket ⊕ ['gæskɪt] Dichtung *f*.

gas·light ['gæslaɪt] Gasbeleuchtung *f*; ~ **me·ter** Gasuhr *f*; ~·**o·lene**, ~·**o·line** *Am.* [~əliːn] Benzin *n*.

gasp [gɑːsp] **1.** Keuchen *n*, schweres Atmen; **2.** keuchen; ~ **for breath** nach Luft schnappen, nach Atem ringen.

gas·sta·tion *Am.* ['gæssteɪʃn] Tankstelle *f*; ~ **stove** Gasofen *m*, -herd *m*; ~·**works** *sg.* Gaswerk *n*.

gate [geɪt] Tor *n*; Pforte *f*; Schranke *f*, Sperre *f*; ✈ Flugsteig *m*; ~·**crash** ['geɪtkræʃ] uneingeladen kommen *od.* (hin)gehen (zu); sich ohne zu bezahlen hinein- *od.* hereinschmuggeln; sich ohne zu bezahlen schmuggeln in (*acc.*); ~·**post** Tor-, Türpfosten *m*; ~·**way** Tor(weg *m*) *n*, Einfahrt *f*.

gath·er ['gæðə] **1.** *v/t.* (ein-, ver-) sammeln; ernten; pflücken; schließen (*from* aus); zusammenziehen, kräuseln; ~ *speed* schneller werden; *v/i.* sich (ver)sammeln; sich vergrößern; reifen (*Abszeß*); eitern (*Wunde*); **2.** Falte *f*; ~·**ing** [~rɪŋ] Versammlung *f*; Zusammenkunft *f*.

gau·dy □ ['gɔːdɪ] (-*ier*, -*iest*) auffällig, bunt, grell (*Farbe*); protzig.

gauge [geɪdʒ] **1.** (Normal)Maß *n*; ⊕ Lehre *f*; ⬛ Spurweite *f*; Meßgerät *n*;

fig. Maßstab *m*; **2.** eichen; (aus)messen; *fig.* abschätzen.

gaunt □ [gɔːnt] hager; ausgemergelt.

gaunt·let ['gɔːntlɪt] Schutzhandschuh *m*; *fig.* Fehdehandschuh *m*; *run the* ~ Spießruten laufen.

gauze [gɔːz] Gaze *f*.

gave [geɪv] *pret. von* give.

gav·el ['gævl] Hammer *m* (*e-s Vorsitzenden od. Auktionators*).

gaw·ky ['gɔːkɪ] (-*ier*, -*iest*) unbeholfen, linkisch.

gay [geɪ] **1.** □ lustig, fröhlich; bunt, (farben)prächtig; F schwul (*homosexuell*); **2.** F Schwule(r) *m* (*Homosexueller*).

gaze [geɪz] **1.** (starrer) Blick; ⚠ *nicht* Gaze; **2.** starren; ~ *at* starren auf (*acc.*), anstarren.

ga·zette [gə'zet] Amtsblatt *n*.

ga·zelle *zo.* [gə'zel] Gazelle *f*.

gear [gɪə] **1** ⊕ Getriebe *n*; *mot.* Gang *m*; *mst in Zssgn*: Vorrichtung *f*, Gerät *n*; *in* ~ mit eingelegtem Gang; *out of* ~ im Leerlauf; *change* ~(s), *Am.* *shift* ~(s) *mot.* schalten; *landing* ~ ✈ Fahrgestell *n*; *steering* ~ ⚓ Ruderanlage *f*; *mot.* Lenkung *f*; **2.** einschalten; ⊕ greifen; ~·**le·ver** ['gɪəliːvə], *Am.* ~·**shift** *mot.* Schalthebel *m*.

geese [giːs] *pl. von* goose.

geld·ing *zo.* ['geldɪŋ] Wallach *m*.

gem [dʒem] Edelstein *m*; Gemme *f*; *fig.* Glanzstück *n*.

gen·der ['dʒendə] *gr.* Genus *n*, Geschlecht *n*; *coll.* F Geschlecht *n*.

gen·e·ral ['dʒenərəl] **1.** □ allgemein; allgemeingültig; ungefähr; Haupt..., General...; 9 *Certificate of Education s. certificate* 1; ~ *education* Allgemeinbildung *f*; ~ *knowledge* Allgemeinbildung *f*; ~ *election Brt. pol.* allgemeine Wahlen *pl.*; ~ *practitioner* praktischer Arzt; **2.** ✕ General *m*; Feldherr *m*; *in* ~ im allgemeinen; ~·**i·ty** [dʒenə'rælətɪ] Allgemeinheit *f*; *die große Masse*; ~ *gemeinern; *gen·er·al·ly* [~lɪ] im allgemeinen, überhaupt; gewöhnlich.

gen·e·rate ['dʒenəreɪt] erzeugen; ~·**ra·tion** [dʒenə'reɪʃn] (Er)Zeugung *f*; Generation *f*; Menschenalter *n*; ~·**ra·tor** ['dʒenəreɪtə] Erzeuger *m*; ⊕ Generator *m*; *bsd. Am. mot.* Lichtmaschine *f*.

gen·e·ros·i·ty [dʒenə'rɒsətɪ] Großmut *f*; Großzügigkeit *f*; ~·**rous** □ ['dʒenərəs] großmütig, großzügig.

ge·ni·al □ ['dʒi:njəl] freundlich; angenehm; wohltuend; △ *nicht genial.*

gen·i·tive *gr.* ['dʒenɪtɪv] *a.* ~ *case* Genitiv *m,* zweiter Fall.

ge·ni·us ['dʒi:njəs] Geist *m;* Genie *n.*

gent F [dʒent] Herr *m;* ~*s sg.* Brt. F Herrenklo *n.*

gen·teel □ [dʒen'ti:l] vornehm; elegant.

gen·tile ['dʒentaɪl] **1.** heidnisch, nichtjüdisch; **2.** Heid|e *m,* -in *f.*

gen·tle □ ['dʒentl] (~*f,* ~*st*) sanft; mild; zahm; leise, sacht; vornehm; ~**man** (*pl.* -men) Herr *m;* Gentleman *m;* ~**man·ly** [~mənlɪ] gentlemanlike, vornehm; ~**ness** [~nɪs] Sanftheit *f;* Milde *f,* Güte *f,* Sanftmut *f.*

gen·try ['dʒentrɪ] niederer Adel; Oberschicht *f.*

gen·u·ine □ ['dʒenjʊɪn] echt; aufrichtig.

ge·og·ra·phy [dʒɪ'ɒɡrəfɪ] Geographie *f.*

ge·ol·o·gy [dʒɪ'ɒlədʒɪ] Geologie *f.*

ge·om·e·try [dʒɪ'ɒmɪtrɪ] Geometrie *f.*

germ *biol.,* ♀ [dʒɜ:m] Keim *m.*

Ger·man ['dʒɜ:mən] **1.** deutsch; **2.** Deutsche(r *m*) *f;* *ling.* Deutsch *n.*

ger·mi·nate ['dʒɜ:mɪneɪt] keimen (lassen).

ger·und *gr.* ['dʒerənd] Gerundium *n.*

ges·tic·u·late [dʒe'stɪkjʊleɪt] gestikulieren; ~**la·tion** [dʒestɪkjʊ'leɪʃn] Gebärdenspiel *n.*

ges·ture ['dʒestʃə] Geste *f,* Gebärde *f.*

get [get] (-*tt*-) *got, got* od. *Am. gotten* v/t. erhalten, bekommen, F kriegen; besorgen; holen; bringen; erwerben; verdienen; ergreifen, fassen, fangen; (veran)lassen; *mit adv. mst* bringen, machen; *have got* haben; *have got to* müssen; ~ *one's hair cut* sich die Haare schneiden lassen; ~ *by heart* auswendig lernen; v/i. gelangen, geraten, kommen; gehen; werden; ~ *ready* sich fertig machen; ~ *about* auf den Beinen sein; herumkommen; sich verbreiten (*Gerücht*); ~ *ahead* vorankommen; ~ *ahead of* übertreffen (*acc.*); ~ *along* vorwärtskommen; auskommen (*with* mit); ~ *at* herankommen an (*acc.*); sagen wollen; ~ *away* loskommen; entkommen; ~ *in* einsteigen (in); ~ *off*

aussteigen (aus); ~ *on* einsteigen (in); ~ *out* heraus-, hinausgehen; aussteigen (of aus); ~ *over s.th.* über et. hinwegkommen; ~ *to* kommen nach; ~ *together* zusammenkommen; ~ *up* aufstehen; ~**a·way** ['getəweɪ] Flucht *f;* ~ *car* Fluchtauto *n;* ~**up** Aufmachung *f.*

ghast·ly ['ɡɑ:stlɪ] (-*ier,* -*iest*) gräßlich; schrecklich; (toten)bleich; gespenstisch.

gher·kin ['ɡɜ:kɪn] Gewürzgurke *f.*

ghost [ɡəʊst] Geist *m,* Gespenst *n;* *fig.* Spur *f;* ~**ly** ['ɡəʊstlɪ] (-*ier,* -*iest*) geisterhaft.

gi·ant ['dʒaɪənt] **1.** riesig; **2.** Riese *m.*

gib·ber ['dʒɪbə] kauderwelschen; ~**ish** [~rɪʃ] Kauderwelsch *n.*

gib·bet ['dʒɪbɪt] Galgen *m.*

gibe [dʒaɪb] **1.** spotten (*at* über *acc.*); **2.** höhnische Bemerkung.

gib·lets ['dʒɪblɪts] *pl.* Hühner-, Gänseklein *n.*

gid·di·ness ['ɡɪdɪnɪs] ♨ Schwindel *m;* Unbeständigkeit *f;* Leichtsinn *m;* ~**dy** □ ['ɡɪdɪ] (-*ier,* -*iest*) schwind(e)lig; leichtfertig; unbeständig; albern.

gift [ɡɪft] Geschenk *n;* Talent *n;* △ *nicht Gift;* ~**ed** ['ɡɪftɪd] begabt.

gi·gan·tic [dʒaɪ'ɡæntɪk] (~*ally*) gigantisch, riesenhaft, riesig, gewaltig.

gig·gle ['ɡɪɡl] **1.** kichern; **2.** Gekicher *n.*

gild [ɡɪld] (*gilded* od. *gilt*) vergolden; verschönen; ~*ed youth* Jeunesse *f* dorée.

gill [ɡɪl] *zo.* Kieme *f;* ♀ Lamelle *f.*

gilt [ɡɪlt] **1.** *pret. u. p.p. von gild;* **2.** Vergoldung *f.*

gim·mick F ['ɡɪmɪk] Trick *m.*

gin [dʒɪn] Gin *m* (*Wacholderschnaps*).

gin·ger ['dʒɪndʒə] **1.** Ingwer *m;* rötliches od. gelbliches Braun *f;* **2.** rötlich od. gelblichbraun; ~**bread** Pfefferkuchen *m;* ~**ly** [~lɪ] zimperlich; behutsam, vorsichtig.

gip·sy ['dʒɪpsɪ] Zigeuner(in).

gi·raffe *zo.* [dʒɪ'rɑ:f] Giraffe *f.*

gir·der ⊕ ['ɡɜ:də] Tragbalken *m.*

gir·dle ['ɡɜ:dl] Hüfthalter *m,* -gürtel *m,* Korselett *n,* Miederhose *f.*

girl [ɡɜ:l] Mädchen *n;* ~**friend** ['~frend] Freundin *f;* ~ **guide** [~ɡaɪd] Pfadfinderin *f* (*in Großbritannien*); ~**hood** [~hʊd] Mädchenzeit *f,* Mädchenjahre *pl.,* Jugend(zeit) *f;* ~**ish** □ [~lɪʃ] mädchenhaft; Mädchen...; ~ **scout** Pfadfinderin f (in den USA).

gi·ro ['dʒaɪrəʊ] 1. Postscheckdienst m (in Großbritannien); 2. Postscheck...

girth [gɜ:θ] (Sattel)Gurt m; (a. Körper)Umfang m.

gist [dʒɪst] das Wesentliche.

give [gɪv] (gave, given) geben; ab-, übergeben; her-, hingeben; überlassen; zum besten geben; schenken; gewähren; von sich geben; ergeben; ~ birth to zur Welt bringen; ~ away her-, weggeben, verschenken; j-n, et. verraten; ~ back zurückgeben; ~ in Gesuch einreichen, Prüfungsarbeit abgeben; nachgeben; aufgeben; ~ off Geruch verbreiten; ausstoßen, -strömen; ~ out aus-, verteilen; zu Ende gehen (Kräfte, Vorräte); ~ up (es) aufgeben; aufhören mit; j-n ausliefern; ~ o.s. up sich (freiwillig) stellen (to the police der Polizei); ~ and take ['gɪvən'teɪk] (Meinungs)Austausch m; Kompromiß m, n; **giv·en** ['gɪvn] 1. p.p. von give; 2. be ~ to verfallen sein; neigen zu; **giv·en name** Am. Vorname m.

gla|cial □ ['gleɪsjəl] eisig; Eis...; Gletscher...; ~**ci·er** ['glæsjə] Gletscher m.

glad □ [glæd] (-dd-) froh, erfreut; freudig; ~**den** ['glædn] erfreuen.

glade [gleɪd] Lichtung f; Am. sumpfige Niederung.

glad|ly ['glædlɪ] gern(e); ~**ness** [~nɪs] Freude f.

glam|or·ous, -our·ous □ ['glæmərəs] bezaubernd; ~**o(u)r** ['glæmə] 1. Zauber m, Glanz m, Reiz m; 2. bezaubern.

glance [glɑ:ns] 1. (schneller od. flüchtiger) Blick (at auf acc.); △ nicht Glanz; at a ~ mit e-m Blick; 2. (auf)leuchten, (-)blitzen; mst ~ off abprallen; ~ at flüchtig ansehen; anspielen auf (acc.).

gland anat. [glænd] Drüse f.

glare [gleə] 1. grelles Licht; wilder, starrer Blick; 2. grell leuchten; wild blicken; (~ at an)starren.

glass [glɑ:s] 1. Glas n; Spiegel m; Opern-, Fernglas n; Barometer n; (a pair of) ~es pl. (e-e) Brille; 2. gläsern; Glas...; 3. verglasen; ~ **case** ['glɑ:skeɪs] Vitrine f; Schaukasten m; ~**ful** [~fʊl] ein Glas(voll); ~**house** Treibhaus n; ✕ F Bau m;

~**ware** Glas(waren pl.) n; ~**y** [~ɪ] (-ier, -iest) gläsern; glasig.

glaze [gleɪz] 1. Glasur f; 2. v/t. verglasen; glasieren; polieren; v/i. trüb(e) od. glasig werden (Auge); **gla·zi·er** ['gleɪzjə] Glaser m.

gleam [gli:m] 1. Schimmer m, Schein m; 2. schimmern.

glean [gli:n] v/t. sammeln; v/i. Ähren lesen.

glee [gli:] Fröhlichkeit f; ~**ful** □ ['gli:fl] ausgelassen, fröhlich.

glen [glen] Bergschlucht f.

glib □ [glɪb] (-bb-) gewandt; schlagfertig.

glide [glaɪd] 1. Gleiten n; ✈ Gleitflug m; 2. (dahin)gleiten (lassen); e-n Gleitflug machen; **glid·er** ✈ ['glaɪdə] Segelflugzeug n; Segelflieger(in); **glid·ing** ✈ [~ɪŋ] das Segelfliegen.

glim·mer ['glɪmə] 1. Schimmer m; min. Glimmer m; 2. schimmern.

glimpse [glɪmps] 1. flüchtiger Blick (at auf acc.); Schimmer m; flüchtiger Eindruck; 2. flüchtig (er)blicken.

glint [glɪnt] 1. blitzen, glitzern; 2. Lichtschein m.

glis·ten ['glɪsn] glitzern, glänzen.

glit·ter ['glɪtə] 1. glitzern, funkeln, glänzen; 2. Glitzern n, Funkeln n, Glanz m.

gloat [gləʊt]: ~ over sich hämisch od. diebisch freuen über (acc.); ~**ing** □ ['gləʊtɪŋ] hämisch, schadenfroh.

globe [gləʊb] (Erd)Kugel f; Globus m.

gloom [glu:m] Düsterkeit f; Dunkelheit f; gedrückte Stimmung, Schwermut f; ~**y** □ ['glu:mɪ] (-ier, -iest) dunkel; düster; schwermütig, traurig.

glo|ri·fy ['glɔ:rɪfaɪ] verherrlichen; ~**ri·ous** □ [~ɪəs] herrlich; glorreich; ~**ry** [~ɪ] 1. Ruhm m; Herrlichkeit f, Pracht f; Glorienschein m; 2. ~ in sich freuen über (acc.).

gloss [glɒs] 1. Glosse f, Bemerkung f; Glanz m; 2. Glossen machen (zu); Glanz geben (dat.); ~ over beschönigen.

glos·sa·ry ['glɒsərɪ] Glossar n, Wörterverzeichnis n (mit Erklärungen).

gloss·y □ ['glɒsɪ] (-ier, -iest) glänzend.

glove [glʌv] Handschuh m; ~ **compartment** mot. Handschuhfach n.

glow [gləʊ] **1.** Glühen *n*; Glut *f*; **2.** glühen.

glow·er ['glaʊə] finster blicken.

glow-worm zo. ['gləʊwɜːm] Glühwürmchen *n*.

glu·cose ['gluːkəʊs] Traubenzucker *m*.

glue [gluː] **1.** Leim *m*; **2.** kleben.

glum □ [glʌm] (-mm-) bedrückt, niedergeschlagen.

glut [glʌt] (-tt-) übersättigen, -schwemmen; *~ o.s. with* od. *on* sich vollstopfen mit.

glu·ti·nous □ ['gluːtɪnəs] klebrig.

glut·ton ['glʌtn] Unersättliche(r *m*) *f*; Vielfraß *m*; **~ous** □ [~əs] gefräßig; **~y** [~ɪ] Gefräßigkeit *f*.

gnarled [nɑːld] knorrig; knotig (*Hände*).

gnash [næʃ] knirschen (mit).

gnat zo. [næt] (Stech)Mücke *f*.

gnaw [nɔː] (zer)nagen; (zer)fressen.

gnome [nəʊm] Gnom *m*; Gartenzwerg *m*.

go [gəʊ] **1.** (*went, gone*) gehen, fahren, fliegen; weggehen, aufbrechen, abfahren; abreisen; verkehren (*Fahrzeuge*); vergehen (*Zeit*); werden; führen (*to* nach); sich erstrecken, reichen (*to* bis zu); ausgehen, ablaufen, ausfallen; gehen, arbeiten, funktionieren, kaputtgehen; *let ~* loslassen; *~ shares* teilen; *I must be ~ing* ich muß weg od. fort; *~ to bed* ins Bett gehen; *~ to school* zur Schule gehen; *~ to see* besuchen; *~ ahead* vorangehen; vorausgehen; *-fahren*; *~ ahead with s.th.* et. durchführen, et. machen; *~ at* losgehen auf (*acc.*); *~ between* vermitteln (zwischen); *~ by* sich richten nach; *~ for holen*; *~ for a walk* e-n Spaziergang machen, spazierengehen; *~ in for an examination* e-e Prüfung machen; *~ off* fortgehen; *~ on* weitergehen, *-fahren*; *fig. ~* fortfahren (*doing zu tun*); *fig.* vor sich gehen, vorgehen; *~ out* hinausgehen; ausgehen (*with* mit) (*a. Licht etc.*); *~ through* durchgehen; durchmachen; *~ up* steigen; hinaufgehen, *-steigen*; *~ without* sich behelfen ohne, auskommen ohne; **2.** F Mode *f*; Schwung *m*, Schneid *m*; *on the ~* auf den Beinen; *in* Gange; *it is no ~* es geht nicht; *in one ~* auf Anhieb; *have a ~ at* es versuchen mit.

goad [gəʊd] **1.** Stachelstock *m*; *fig.* Ansporn *m*; **2.** *fig.* anstacheln.

go-a·head F ['gəʊəhed] zielstrebig; unternehmungslustig.

goal [gəʊl] Mal *n*; Ziel *n*; *Fußball*: Tor *n*; **~-keep·er** ['gəʊlkiːpə] Torwart *m*.

goat zo. [gəʊt] Ziege *f*, Geiß *f*.

gob·ble ['gɒbl] **1.** kollern (*Truthahn*); schlingen; *mst ~ up* verschlingen; **2.** Kollern *n*; **~r** [~ə] Truthahn *m*; gieriger Esser.

go-be·tween ['gəʊbɪtwiːn] Vermittler(in), Mittelsmann *m*.

gob·let ['gɒblɪt] Kelchglas *n*; Pokal *m*, Becher *m*.

gob·lin ['gɒblɪn] Kobold *m*.

god [gɒd] *eccl.* ♀ Gott *m*; *fig.* Abgott *m*; **~-child** ['gɒdtʃaɪld] (*pl. -children*) Patenkind *n*; **~-dess** ['gɒdɪs] Göttin *f*; **~-fa·ther** Pate *m* (*a. fig.*), Taufpate *m*; **~-for·sak·en** *contp.* gottverlassen; **~-head** Gottheit *f*; **~-less** [~lɪs] gottlos; **~-like** göttlich; **~-ly** [~lɪ] (*-ier, -iest*) gottesfürchtig; fromm; **~-moth·er** (Tauf)Patin *f*; **~-par·ent** (Tauf)Pate *m*, (-)Patin *f*; **~-send** Geschenk *n* des Himmels.

go-get·ter F ['gəʊˈgetə] Draufgänger *m*.

gog·gle ['gɒgl] **1.** glotzen; **2.** *~s pl.* Schutzbrille *f*; **~-box** *Brt.* F Glotze *f* (*Fernseher*).

go·ing ['gəʊɪŋ] **1.** gehend; im Gange (befindlich); *be ~ to inf.* im Begriff sein zu *inf.*; gleich *tun* wollen od. werden; **2.** Gehen *n*; Vorwärtskommen *n*; Straßenzustand *m*; Geschwindigkeit *f*, Leistung *f*; **~-s-on** F [~zˈɒn] Treiben *n*, Vorgänge *pl.*

gold [gəʊld] **1.** Gold *n*; **2.** golden; **dig·ger** *Am.* ['gəʊlddɪgə] Goldgräber *m*; **~-en** *mst fig.* [~ən] golden, goldgelb; **~-finch** zo. Stieglitz *m*; **~-fish** zo. Goldfisch *m*; **~-smith** Goldschmied *m*.

golf [gɒlf] **1.** Golf(spiel) *n*; **2.** Golf spielen; **~ club** ['gɒlfklʌb] Golfschläger *m*; Golfklub *m*; **~ course**, **~ links** *pl.* od. *sg.* Golfplatz *m*.

gon·do·la ['gɒndələ] Gondel *f*.

gone [gɒn] **1.** *p.p. von* go 1; **2.** *adj.* fort; F futsch; vergangen; tot; F hoffnungslos.

good [gʊd] **1.** (*better, best*) gut; artig; gütig; gründlich; *~ at* geschickt od. gut in (*dat.*); **2.** Nutzen *m*, Wert *m*,

Vorteil m; *das* Gute, Wohl n; **~s** pl. *econ.* Waren pl., Güter pl.; *that's* no ~ das nützt nichts; *for* ~ für immer; **~·by(e) 1.** [gʊdˈbaɪ]: wish s.o. ~, say ~ *to* s.o. j-m auf Wiedersehen sagen; **2.** *int.* [gʊdˈbaɪ] (auf) Wiedersehen!; ♀ **Fri·day** Karfreitag m; **~·hu·mo(u)red** ☐ gutgelaunt; gutmütig; **~·look·ing** [~ɪŋ] gutaussehend; **~·ly** [ˈgʊdlɪ] anmutig, hübsch; *fig.* ansehnlich; **~·na·tured** ☐ gutmütig; **~ness** [~nɪs] Güte f; *das* Beste; thank ~! Gott sei Dank! (*my*) ~! ~, gracious! du meine Güte!, du lieber Himmel!; *for* ~' sake um Himmels willen!; ~ knows weiß der Himmel; **~·will** Wohlwollen n; *econ.* Kundschaft f; *econ.* Firmenwert m.

good·y [ˈgʊdɪ] Bonbon m, n.

goose zo. [guːs] (pl. **geese**) Gans f (a. fig.).

goose·ber·ry ♀ [ˈgʊzbərɪ] Stachelbeere f.

goose·flesh [ˈguːsfleʃ], **~ pim·ples** pl. Gänsehaut f.

go·pher zo. [ˈgəʊfə] Taschenratte f; *Am.* Ziesel m.

gore [gɔː] durchbohren, aufspießen (*mit den Hörnern etc.*).

gorge [gɔːdʒ] **1.** Kehle f, Schlund m; enge (Fels)Schlucht f; **2.** (ver)schlingen; (sich) vollstopfen.

gor·geous ☐ [ˈgɔːdʒəs] prächtig.

go·ril·la zo. [gəˈrɪlə] Gorilla m.

gor·y [ˈgɔːrɪ] (-ier, -iest) blutig; *fig.* blutrünstig.

gosh *int.* F [gɒʃ]: by ~ Mensch!

gos·ling [ˈgɒzlɪŋ] junge Gans.

go-slow *Brt. econ.* [gəʊˈsləʊ] Bummelstreik m.

Gos·pel *eccl.* [ˈgɒspəl] Evangelium n.

gos·sa·mer [ˈgɒsəmə] Altweibersommer m.

gos·sip [ˈgɒsɪp] **1.** Klatsch m, Tratsch m; Klatschbase f; **2.** klatschen, tratschen.

got [gɒt] pret. u. p.p. von **get**.

Goth·ic [ˈgɒθɪk] gotisch; Schauer...; ~ *novel* Schauerroman m.

got·ten *Am.* [ˈgɒtn] p.p. von **get**.

gouge [gaʊdʒ] **1.** ⊕ Hohlmeißel m; **2.** ~ *out* ausmeißeln; ~ *out* s.o.'s *eye* j-m ein Auge ausstechen.

gourd ♀ [gʊəd] Kürbis m.

gout ✽ [gaʊt] Gicht f.

gov·ern [ˈgʌvn] v/t. regieren, beherrschen; lenken; leiten; v/i. herrschen; **~ess** [~ɪs] Erzieherin f; **~ment** [~mənt] Regierung(sform) f; Herrschaft f (*of über* acc.); Ministerium n; attr. Staats...; ~·**men·tal** [gʌvənˈmentl] Regierungs...; **gov·er·nor** [ˈgʌvənə] Gouverneur m; Direktor m, Präsident m; F Alte(r) m (*Vater, Chef*).

gown [gaʊn] **1.** (Frauen)Kleid n; Robe f, Talar m; **2.** kleiden.

grab [græb] **1.** (-bb-) (hastig od. gierig) ergreifen, packen, fassen; **2.** (hastiger od. gieriger) Griff; ⊕ Greifer m.

grace [greɪs] **1.** Gnade f; Gunst f; (Gnaden)Frist f; Grazie f, Anmut f; Anstand m; Zier(de) f; Reiz m; Tischgebet n; *Your* ♀ Eure Hoheit (*Herzog*); Eure Exzellenz (*Erzbischof*); **2.** zieren, schmücken; begünstigen, auszeichnen; **~·ful** ☐ [ˈgreɪsfl] anmutig; **~·less** ☐ [~lɪs] ungraziös, linkisch; ungehobelt.

gra·cious ☐ [ˈgreɪʃəs] gnädig.

gra·da·tion [grəˈdeɪʃn] Abstufung f.

grade [greɪd] **1.** Grad m, Rang m; Stufe f; Qualität f; bsd. *Am.* = gradient; *Am.* *Schule*: Klasse f; Note f; make the ~ es schaffen, Erfolg haben; ~ *crossing* bsd. *Am.* schienengleicher Bahnübergang; **2.** abstufen; einstufen; ⊕ planieren.

gra·di·ent [ˈgreɪdɪənt] etc. Steigung f.

grad·u·al ☐ [ˈgrædʒʊəl] stufenweise, allmählich; **~·al·ly** [~lɪ] nach u. nach; allmählich; **~·ate 1.** [~ʊeɪt] graduieren; (sich) abstufen; die Abschlußprüfung machen; promovieren; **2.** [~ʊət] univ. Hochschulabsolvent(in), Akademiker(in); Graduierte(r m) f; *Am.* Schulabgänger(in); **~·a·tion** [grædjʊˈeɪʃn] Gradeinteilung f; univ., *Am. a. Schule:* (Ab-)Schlußfeier f; univ. Erteilung f od. Erlangung f e-s akademischen Grades.

graft [grɑːft] **1.** ✿ Pfropfreis n; *Am.* Schiebung f; *Am.* Schmiergelder pl.; **2.** ✿ pfropfen; ✽ verpflanzen.

grain [greɪn] (Samen)Korn n; Getreide n; Gefüge n; *fig.* Natur f; Gran n (*Gewicht*).

gram [græm] Gramm n.

gram·mar [ˈgræmə] Grammatik f; ~ *school* *Brt.* etwa (humanistisches) Gymnasium; *Am.* etwa Grundschule f.

gram·mat·i·cal □ [grəˈmætɪkl] grammatisch.

gramme [græm] = gram.

gra·na·ry [ˈgrænərɪ] Kornspeicher m.

grand □ [grænd] 1. fig. großartig; erhaben; groß; Groß..., Haupt...; ⌀ Old Party Am. Republikanische Partei; 2. (pl. grand) F Riese m (1000 Dollar od. Pfund); **~child** [ˈgræntʃaɪld] (pl. -children) Enkel(in).

gran·deur [ˈgrændʒə] Größe f, Hoheit f; Erhabenheit f.

grand·fa·ther [ˈgrændfɑːðə] Großvater m.

gran·di·ose □ [ˈgrændɪəʊs] großartig.

grand|moth·er [ˈgrænmʌðə] Großmutter f; **~·par·ents** [~npeərənts] pl. Großeltern pl; **~ pi·an·o** ♪ (pl. -os) (Konzert)Flügel m; **~stand** Sport: Haupttribüne f.

grange [greɪndʒ] (kleiner) Gutshof.

gran·ny F [ˈgrænɪ] Oma f.

grant [grɑːnt] 1. Gewährung f; Unterstützung f; Stipendium n; 2. gewähren; bewilligen; verleihen; z͡t͡z übertragen; zugestehen; ~ed, but zugeben, aber; take for ~ed als selbstverständlich annehmen.

gran·u·lat·ed [ˈgrænjʊleɪtɪd] körnig, granuliert; ~ sugar Kristallzucker m; **~ule** [~juːl] Körnchen n.

grape [greɪp] Weinbeere f, -traube f; **~·fruit** ♀ [ˈgreɪpfruːt] Grapefruit f, Pampelmuse f; **~·vine** ♀ Weinstock m.

graph [græf] graphische Darstellung; **~·ic** [ˈgræfɪk] (~ally) graphisch; anschaulich; ~ arts pl. Graphik f, graphische Kunst.

grap·ple [ˈgræpl] ringen, kämpfen; ~ with s.th. fig. sich mit et. herumschlagen.

grasp [grɑːsp] 1. Griff m; Bereich m; Beherrschung f; Fassungskraft f; 2. (er)greifen, packen; begreifen.

grass [grɑːs] Gras n; Rasen m; Weide(land n) f; sl. Grass n (Marihuana); **~·hop·per** zo. [ˈgrɑːshɒpə] Heuschrecke f; **~ wid·ow** Strohwitwe f; Am. geschiedene Frau; Am. (von ihrem Mann) getrennt lebende Frau; **~ wid·ow·er** Strohwitwer m; Am. geschiedener Mann; Am. (von s-r Frau) getrennt lebender Mann; **gras·sy** [~ɪ] (-ier, -iest) grasbedeckt, Gras...

grate [greɪt] 1. (Kamin)Gitter n; (Feuer)Rost m; 2. reiben, raspeln; knirschen (mit); ~ on s.o.'s nerves an j-s Nerven zerren.

grate·ful □ [ˈgreɪtfl] dankbar.

grat·er [ˈgreɪtə] Reibe f.

grat·i·fi·ca·tion [grætɪfɪˈkeɪʃn] Befriedigung f; Freude f; △ nicht Gratifikation; **~·fy** [ˈgrætɪfaɪ] erfreuen; befriedigen.

grat·ing¹ □ [ˈgreɪtɪŋ] kratzend, knirschend, quietschend; schrill; unangenehm.

grat·ing² [~] Gitter(werk) n.

grat·i·tude [ˈgrætɪtjuːd] Dankbarkeit f.

gra·tu·i·tous □ [grəˈtjuːɪtəs] unentgeltlich; freiwillig; **~·ty** [~ˈtjuːətɪ] Abfindung f; Gratifikation f; Trinkgeld n.

grave¹ □ [greɪv] (~r, ~st) ernst; (ge)wichtig; gemessen.

grave² [~] Grab n; **~·dig·ger** [ˈgreɪvdɪgə] Totengräber m (a. zo.).

grav·el [ˈgrævl] 1. Kies m; Schotter m; ✗ Harngrieß m; 2. (bsd. Brt. -ll-, Am. -l-) mit Kies bestreuen.

grave|stone [ˈgreɪvstəʊn] Grabstein m; **~·yard** Friedhof m.

grav·i·ta·tion [grævɪˈteɪʃn] phys. Schwerkraft f; fig. Hang m, Neigung f.

grav·i·ty [ˈgrævətɪ] Schwere f, Ernst m; phys. Schwerkraft f.

gra·vy [ˈgreɪvɪ] Bratensaft m; Bratensoße f.

gray bsd. Am. [greɪ] grau.

graze¹ [greɪz] Vieh weiden (lassen); (ab)weiden; (ab)grasen.

graze² [~] 1. streifen; schrammen; Haut (ab-, auf)schürfen, (auf-) schrammen; 2. Abschürfung f, Schramme f.

grease 1. [griːs] Fett n; Schmiere f; 2. [griːz] (be)schmieren.

greas·y □ [ˈgriːzɪ] (-ier, -iest) fett(ig), ölig; schmierig.

great □ [greɪt] groß, Groß...; F großartig; **~·grand·child** [greɪtˈgrænt-ʃaɪld] (pl. -children) Urenkel(in); **~-grand·fa·ther** Urgroßvater m; **~-grand·moth·er** Urgroßmutter f; **~-grand·par·ents** pl. Urgroßeltern pl.; **~·ly** [ˈgreɪtlɪ] sehr; **~·ness** [~nɪs] Größe f; Stärke f.

greed [griːd] Gier f; **~·y** □ [ˈgriːdɪ] (-ier, -iest) gierig (for auf acc., nach); habgierig; gefräßig.

G

Greek [griːk] **1.** griechisch; **2.** Griech|e *m*, -in *f*; *ling.* Griechisch *n*.

green [griːn] **1.** □ grün (*a. fig.*); frisch (*Fisch etc.*); neu; Grün...; **2.** Grün *n*; Grünfläche *f*, Rasen *m*; *∼s pl.* grünes Gemüse, Blattgemüse *n*; **∼back** *Am.* F ['griːnbæk] Dollarschein *m*; **∼ belt** Grüngürtel *m* (*um e-e Stadt*); **∼·gro·cer** *bsd. Brt.* Obst- u. Gemüsehändler(in); **∼·gro·cer·y** *bsd. Brt.* Obst- u. Gemüsehandlung *f*; **∼horn** Greenhorn *n*, Grünschnabel *m*; **∼house** Gewächs-, Treibhaus *n*; **∼ish** [∼ɪʃ] grünlich.

greet [griːt] grüßen; **∼·ing** ['griːtɪŋ] Begrüßung *f*, Gruß *m*; *∼s pl.* Grüße *pl.*

gre·nade ✕ [grɪˈneɪd] Granate *f*.

grew [gruː] *pret. von* grow.

grey [greɪ] **1.** □ grau; **2.** Grau *n*; **3.** grau machen *od.* werden; **∼hound** *zo.* ['greɪhaʊnd] Windhund *m*.

grid [grɪd] Gitter *n*; ⚡ *etc.* Versorgungsnetz *n*; **2.** ⚡ Gitter...; *Am.* F Football...; **∼·i·ron** ['grɪdaɪən] (Brat)Rost *m*.

grief [griːf] Gram *m*, Kummer *m*; *come to* ∼ zu Schaden kommen.

griev|ance ['griːvns] Beschwerde *f*; Mißstand *m*; **∼e** [griːv] *v/t.* betrüben, bekümmern, *j-m* Kummer bereiten; *v/i.* bekümmert sein; ∼ *for* trauern um; **∼ous** □ ['griːvəs] kränkend, schmerzlich; schlimm.

grill [grɪl] **1.** grillen; **2.** Grill *m*; Bratrost *m*; Gegrillte(s) *n*; *a.* **∼-room** Grillroom *m*.

grim □ [grɪm] (*-mm-*) grimmig; schrecklich; erbittert; F schlimm.

gri·mace [grɪˈmeɪs] **1.** Fratze *f*, Grimasse *f*; **2.** Grimassen schneiden.

grime [graɪm] Schmutz *m*; Ruß *m*; **grim·y** □ ['graɪmɪ] (*-ier, -iest*) schmutzig; rußig.

grin [grɪn] **1.** Grinsen *n*; **2.** (*-nn-*) grinsen.

grind [graɪnd] **1.** (*ground*) (zer)reiben; mahlen; schleifen; *Leierkasten etc.* drehen; *fig.* schinden; mit *den Zähnen* knirschen; **2.** Schinderei *f*, Schufterei *f*; △ *nicht Grind*; **∼·er** ['graɪndə] (*Messer- etc.*)Schleifer *m*; ⊕ Schleifmaschine *f*; ⊕ Mühle *f*; **∼·stone** Schleifstein *m*.

grip [grɪp] **1.** (*-pp-*) packen, fassen (*a. fig.*); **2.** Griff *m* (*a. fig.*); *fig.* Gewalt *f*, Herrschaft *f*; *Am.* Reisetasche *f*.

gripes [graɪps] *pl.* Bauchschmerzen *pl.*, Kolik *f*.

grip·sack *Am.* ['grɪpsæk] Reisetasche *f*.

gris·ly ['grɪzlɪ] (*-ier, -iest*) gräßlich, schrecklich.

gris·tle ['grɪsl] Knorpel *m* (*im Fleisch*).

grit [grɪt] **1.** Kies *m*; Sand(stein) *m*; *fig.* Mut *m*; **2.** (*-tt-*): ∼ *one's teeth* die Zähne zusammenbeißen.

griz·zly (bear) ['grɪzlɪ(beə)] Grizzly (-bär) *m*, Graubär *m*.

groan [grəʊn] **1.** stöhnen, ächzen; **2.** Stöhnen *n*, Ächzen *n*.

gro·cer ['grəʊsə] Lebensmittelhändler *m*; **∼·ies** [∼rɪz] *pl.* Lebensmittel *pl.*; **∼·y** [∼ɪ] Lebensmittelgeschäft *n*.

grog·gy F ['grɒgɪ] (*-ier, -iest*) schwach *od.* wackelig (auf den Beinen).

groin *anat.* [grɔɪn] Leiste(ngegend) *f*.

groom [grʊm] **1.** Pferdepfleger *m*, Stallbursche *m*; = *bridegroom*; **2.** pflegen; *j-n* aufbauen, lancieren.

groove [gruːv] Rinne *f*, Furche *f*; Rille *f*, Nut *f*; **groov·y** *sl.* ['gruːvɪ] (*-ier, -iest*) klasse, toll.

grope [grəʊp] tasten; *sl. Mädchen* befummeln.

gross [grəʊs] **1.** □ dick, fett; grob, derb; *econ.* Brutto...; **2.** Gros *n* (*12 Dutzend*); *in the* ∼ im ganzen.

gro·tesque □ [grəʊˈtesk] grotesk.

ground[1] [graʊnd] **1.** *pret. u. p.p. von* grind 1; **2.** ∼ *glass* Mattglas *n*.

ground[2] [graʊnd] **1.** Grund *m*, Boden *m*; Gebiet *n*; (*Spiel- etc.*)Platz *m*; (*Beweg- etc.*)Grund *m*; ⚡ Erde *f*; *∼s pl.* Grundstück *n*, Park(s *pl.*) *m*, Gärten *pl.*; (*Kaffee*)Satz *m*; *on the* ∼(*s*) *of* auf Grund (*gen.*); *stand od. hold od. keep one's* ∼ sich behaupten; **2.** niederlegen; (be)gründen; *j-m* die Anfangsgründe beibringen; ⚡ erden; **∼ crew** ✈ Bodenpersonal *n*; **∼ floor** *bsd. Brt.* [graʊndˈfloː] Erdgeschoß *n*; **∼ forc·es** *pl.* ✕ Bodentruppen *pl.*, Landstreitkräfte *pl.*; **∼·hog** *zo.* Amer. Waldmurmeltier *n*; **∼·ing** [∼ɪŋ] ⚡ Erdung *f*; Grundlagen *pl.*, -kenntnisse *pl.*; **∼·less** □ [∼lɪs] grundlos, unbegründet; **∼·nut** *Brt.* ♀ Erdnuß *f*; **∼ staff** *Brt.* ✈ Bodenpersonal *n*; **∼·work** Grundlage *f*.

sta·tion Raumfahrt: Bodenstation *f*; **∼·work** Grundlage *f*.

group [gruːp] **1.** Gruppe *f*; **2.** (sich) gruppieren.

group·ie F ['gru:pɪ] Groupie n (aufdringlicher weiblicher Fan).

group·ing ['gru:pɪŋ] Gruppierung f.

grove [grəʊv] Wäldchen n, Gehölz n.

grov·el ['grɒvl] (bsd. Brt. -ll-, Am. -l-) (am Boden) kriechen.

grow [grəʊ] (grew, grown) v/i. wachsen; werden; ~ into hineinwachsen in; werden zu, sich entwickeln zu; ~ on j-m lieb werden od. ans Herz wachsen; ~ out of herauswachsen aus; entstehen aus; ~ up aufwachsen, heranwachsen; sich entwickeln; v/t. ♀ anpflanzen, anbauen, züchten; ~·er ['grəʊə] Züchter m, Erzeuger m, in Zssgn ...bauer m.

growl [graʊl] knurren, brummen.

grown [grəʊn] 1. p.p. von grow; 2. adj. erwachsen; bewachsen; ~·up ['grəʊnʌp] 1. erwachsen; 2. Erwachsene(r m) f; **growth** [grəʊθ] Wachstum n; (An)Wachsen n; Entwicklung f; Erzeugnis n; ✗ Gewächs n, Wucherung f.

grub [grʌb] 1. zo. Raupe f, Larve f, Made f; F Futter n (Essen); 2. (-bb-) graben; sich abmühen; ~·by ['grʌbɪ] (-ier, -iest) schmutzig.

grudge [grʌdʒ] 1. Groll m; 2. mißgönnen; ungern geben od. tun etc.

gru·el [grʊəl] Haferschleim m.

gruff □ ['grʌf] grob, schroff, barsch.

grum·ble ['grʌmbl] 1. murren; 2. Murren n; ~·r fig. [~ə] Brummbär m.

grunt [grʌnt] 1. grunzen; brummen; stöhnen; 2. Grunzen n; Stöhnen n.

guar·an·tee [gærən'tiː] 1. Garantie f; Bürgschaft f; Sicherheit f; Zusicherung f; 2. sich verbürgen für; garantieren; ~·tor [~'tɔː] Bürge m; Bürgin f; ~·ty ['gærəntɪ] Garantie f; Bürgschaft f; Sicherheit f.

guard [gɑːd] 1. Wacht f; ✗ Wache f; Wächter m, Wärter m; ⬛ Schaffner m; Schutz(vorrichtung f) m; ⬛s Garde f; be on ~ Wache haben; be on (off) one's ~ (nicht) auf der Hut sein; 2. v/t. bewachen, (be)schützen (from vor dat.); v/i. sich hüten (against vor dat.); ~·ed ['gɑːdɪd] vorsichtig, zurückhaltend; ~·i·an [~jən] Hüter m, Wächter m; ⚖︎⚖︎ Vormund m; attr. Schutz...; ~·i·an·ship ⚖︎⚖︎ [~ʃɪp] Vormundschaft f.

gue(r)·ril·la ✗ [gə'rɪlə] Guerilla m; ~ warfare Guerillakrieg m.

guess [ges] 1. Vermutung f; 2. vermuten; schätzen; raten; Am. glau-

ben, denken; ~·ing game Ratespiel n; ~·work ['geswɜːk] (reine) Vermutung(en pl.).

guest [gest] 1. Gast m; 2. Gast...; ~·house ['gesthaʊs] (Hotel)Pension f, Fremdenheim n; ~·room Gast-, Gäste-, Fremdenzimmer n.

guf·faw [gʌ'fɔː] 1. schallendes Gelächter; 2. schallend lachen.

guid·ance ['gaɪdns] Führung f; (An-) Leitung f.

guide [gaɪd] 1. (Reise-, Fremden-) Führer(in); ⊕ Führung f; a. ~·book (Reise- etc.)Führer m (Buch); a ~ to London ein London-Führer; s. girl guide; 2. leiten; führen; lenken; **guid·ed mis·sile** ✗ Lenkflugkörper m; **guid·ed tour** Führung f; ~·line ['gaɪdlaɪn] Richtlinie f, -schnur f (on gen.).

guild hist. [gɪld] Gilde f, Zunft f; **♀·hall** ['gɪld'hɔːl] Rathaus n (von London).

guile [gaɪl] Arglist f; ~·ful □ ['gaɪlfl] arglistig; ~·less □ [~lɪs] arglos.

guilt [gɪlt] Schuld f; Strafbarkeit f; ~·less □ ['gɪltlɪs] schuldlos, unkundig; ~·y □ [~ɪ] (-ier, -iest) schuldig (of gen.).

guin·ea ['gɪnɪ] Guinee f (21 Schilling alter Währung); ~·pig zo. Meerschweinchen n.

guise [gaɪz] Erscheinung f, Gestalt f; fig. Maske f.

gui·tar ♪ [gɪ'tɑː] Gitarre f.

gulch bsd. Am. [gʌlʃ] tiefe Schlucht.

gulf [gʌlf] Meerbusen m, Golf m; Abgrund m; Strudel m.

gull zo. [gʌl] Möwe f.

gul·let anat. ['gʌlɪt] Schlund m, Speiseröhre f, Gurgel f.

gulp [gʌlp] 1. (großer) Schluck; 2. oft ~ down Getränk hinunterstürzen; Speise hinunterschlingen.

gum [gʌm] 1. Gummi m, n; Klebstoff m; ~s, Am. ~·drop Gummibonbon m, n; ~s pl. anat. Zahnfleisch n; Am. Gummischuhe pl.; 2. (-mm-) gummieren; kleben.

gun [gʌn] 1. Gewehr n; Flinte f; Geschütz n, Kanone f; Am. Revolver m; big F fig. hohes Tier; 2. (-nn-): mst ~ down niederschießen; ~·bat·tle Feuergefecht n, Schießerei f; ~·boat ['gʌnbəʊt] Kanonenboot n; ~·fight Am. = gun battle; ~·fire Schüsse pl.; ✗ Geschützfeuer n; ~·li·cence Waffenschein m; ~·man (*pl. -men*) Bewaffnete(r) *m*; Revolverheld *m*; **~ner** ⚔ [~ə] Kanonier *m*; **~point:** *at* ~ mit vorgehaltener Waffe, mit Waffengewalt; **~powder** Schießpulver *n*; **~run·ner** Waffenschmuggler *m*; **~run·ning** Waffenschmuggel *m*; **~shot** Schuß *m*; *within* (*out of*) ~ in (außer) Schußweite; **~smith** Büchsenmacher *m*.

gur·gle ['gɜːgl] 1. glucksen, gluckern, gurgeln; 2. Glucksen *n*, Gurgeln *n*.

gush [gʌʃ] 1. Schwall *m*, Strom *m* (*a. fig.*); 2. sich ergießen, schießen (*from* aus); *fig.* schwärmen.

gust [gʌst] Windstoß *m*, Bö *f*.

gut [gʌt] *anat.* Darm *m*; ♪ Darmsaite

f; **~s** *pl.* Eingeweide *pl.*; *das* Innere; *fig.* Schneid *m*, Mumm *m*.

gut·ter ['gʌtə] Dachrinne *f*; Gosse *f* (*a. fig.*), Rinnstein *m*.

guy F [gaɪ] Kerl *m*, Typ *m*.

guz·zle ['gʌzl] saufen; fressen.

gym F [dʒɪm] = *gymnasium*; *gymnastics*; **~na·si·um** [dʒɪm'neɪzɪəm] Turn-, Sporthalle *f*; △ *nicht Gymnasium*; **~nas·tics** [~'næstɪks] *sg.* Turnen *n*, Gymnastik *f*.

gy·n(a)e·col·o·gist [gaɪnə'kɒlədʒɪst] Gynäkologe *m*, -in *f*, Frauenarzt *m*, -ärztin *f*; **~gy** [~dʒɪ] Gynäkologie *f*, Frauenheilkunde *f*.

gyp·sy *bsd. Am.* ['dʒɪpsɪ] = *gipsy*.

gy·rate [dʒaɪə'reɪt] kreisen, sich (im Kreis) drehen, (herum)wirbeln.

H

hab·er·dash·er ['hæbədæʃə] *Brt.* Kurzwarenhändler *m*; *Am.* Herrenausstatter *m*; **~y** [~rɪ] *Brt.* Kurzwaren(geschäft *n*) *pl.*; *Am.* Herrenbekleidungsartikel *pl.*; *Am.* Herrenmodengeschäft *n*.

hab·it ['hæbɪt] (An)Gewohnheit *f*; *bsd.* Ordenskleidung *f*; ~ *of mind* Geistesverfassung *f*; *drink has become a* ~ *with him* er kommt vom Alkohol nicht mehr los; **~i·ta·ble** □ [~əbl] bewohnbar.

ha·bit·u·al □ [hə'bɪtjʊəl] gewohnt, gewöhnlich; Gewohnheits...

hack¹ [hæk] (zer)hacken.

hack² [~] Reitpferd *n*; Mietpferd *n*; Klepper *m*; *a.* ~ *writer* Schreiberling *m*; **~neyed** ['hæknɪd] abgedroschen.

had [hæd] *pret. u. p.p. von have.*

had·dock *zo.* ['hædək] Schellfisch *m*.

h(a)e·mor·rhage 🏥 ['hemərɪdʒ] Blutung *f*.

hag *fig.* [hæg] häßliches altes Weib, Hexe *f*.

hag·gard □ ['hægəd] verhärmt.

hag·gle ['hægl] feilschen, schachern.

hail [heɪl] 1. Hagel *m*; (Zu)Ruf *m*; 2. (nieder)hageln (lassen); rufen; (be-)grüßen; ~ *from* stammen aus; **~stone** ['heɪlstəʊn] Hagelkorn *n*; **~storm** Hagelschauer *m*.

hair [heə] *einzelnes* Haar; *coll.* Haar *n*, Haare *pl.*; **~breadth** ['heəbredθ]: *by a* ~ um Haaresbreite; **~brush** Haarbürste *f*; **~cut** Haarschnitt *m*; **~do** (*pl. -dos*) F Frisur *f*; **~dress·er** Friseur *m*, Friseuse *f*; **~dri·er**, **~dry·er** [~draɪə] Trockenhaube *f*; Haartrockner *m*; *TM* Fön *m*; **~grip** *Brt.* Haarklammer *f*, -klemme *f*; **~less** [~lɪs] ohne Haare, kahl; **~pin** Haarnadel *f*; ~ *bend* Haarnadelkurve *f*; **~rais·ing** [~reɪzɪŋ] haarsträubend; **~'s breadth** = *hairbreadth*; **~slide** *Brt.* Haarspange *f*; **~splitting** Haarspalterei *f*; **~spray** Haarspray *m, n*; **~style** Frisur *f*; **~styl·ist** Hair-Stylist *m*, Haarstilist *m*, Damenfriseur *m*; **~y** [~rɪ] (*-ier, -iest*) behaart; haarig.

hale [heɪl]: ~ *and hearty* gesund u. munter.

half [hɑːf] 1. (*pl. halves* [~vz]) Hälfte *f*; *by halves* nur halb; *go halves* halbe-halbe machen, teilen; 2. halb; ~ *an hour* e-e halbe Stunde; ~ *a pound* ein halbes Pfund; ~ *past ten* halb elf (Uhr); ~ *way up* auf halber Höhe; **~back** ['hɑːfbæk] *Fußball:* Läufer *m*; **~breed** [~briːd] Halbblut *n*; **~broth·er** Halbbruder *m*; **~caste** Halbblut *n*; **~heart·ed** □

[~'haːtɪd] lustlos, lau; **~-length:** ~ portrait Brustbild n; **~-mast:** fly at ~ auf halbmast wehen; **~-pen·ny** ['heɪpnɪ] (pl. -pennies, -pence) halber Penny; ~ **sis·ter** Halbschwester f; **~-term** Brt. univ. kurze Ferien in der Mitte e-s Trimesters; **~-time** ['haːf'taɪm] Sport: Halbzeit f; ~ **way** halb; auf halbem Weg, in der Mitte; **~-wit·ted** schwachsinnig.

hal·i·but zo. ['hælɪbət] Heilbutt m.

hall [hɔːl] Halle f, Saal m; Flur m, Diele f; Herrenhaus n; univ. Speisesaal m; ~ of residence Studentenwohnheim n.

hal·lo Brt. [hə'ləʊ] = hello.

hal·low ['hæləʊ] heiligen, weihen; **♀·e'en** [hæləʊ'iːn] Abend m vor Allerheiligen.

hal·lu·ci·na·tion [həluːsɪ'neɪʃn] Halluzination f.

hall·way bsd. Am. ['hɔːlweɪ] Halle f, Diele f; Korridor m.

ha·lo ['heɪləʊ] (pl. -loes, -los) ast. Hof m; Heiligenschein m.

halt [hɔːlt] **1.** Halt(estelle f) m; Stillstand m; **2.** (an)halten.

hal·ter ['hɔːltə] Halfter m, n; Strick m.

halve [hɑːv] halbieren; **~s** [hɑːvz] pl. von half 1.

ham [hæm] Schinken m; ~ and eggs Schinken mit (Spiegel)Ei.

ham·burg·er ['hæmbɜːgə] Am. Rinderhack n; a. ♀ steak Hamburger m, Frikadelle f (aus Rinderhack).

ham·let ['hæmlɪt] Weiler m.

ham·mer ['hæmə] **1.** Hammer m; **2.** hämmern.

ham·mock ['hæmək] Hängematte f.

ham·per[1] ['hæmpə] (Trag)Korb m (mit Deckel); Geschenk-, Freßkorb m.

ham·per[2] [~] (be)hindern; stören.

ham·ster zo. ['hæmstə] Hamster m.

hand [hænd] **1.** Hand f (a. fig.); Handschrift f; Handbreite f; (Uhr)Zeiger m; Mann m, Arbeiter m; Karten: Blatt n; at ~ bei der Hand; nahe bevorstehend; at first ~ aus erster Hand; a good (poor) ~ at (un)geschickt in (dat.); ~ and glove ein Herz und eine Seele; change ~s den Besitzer wechseln; lend a ~ (mit) anfassen; off ~ aus dem Handgelenk od. Stegreif; on ~ econ. vorrätig, auf

Lager; bsd. Am. zur Stelle, bereit; on one's ~s auf dem Hals; on the one ~ einerseits; on the other ~ andererseits; **2.** ein-, aushändigen, (über)geben, (-)reichen; ~ around herumreichen; ~ down herunterreichen; vererben; ~ in et. hinein-, hereinreichen; Prüfungsarbeit etc. abgeben; Bericht, Gesuch einreichen; ~ on weiterreichen, -geben; ~ out aus-, verteilen; ~ over übergeben; aushändigen; ~ up hinauf-, heraufreichen; **~-bag** ['hændbæg] Handtasche f; **~-bill** Handzettel m, Flugblatt n; **~-brake** ⊕ Handbremse f; **~-cuffs** pl. Handschellen pl.; **~-ful** [~fʊl] Handvoll f; F Plage f.

hand·i·cap ['hændɪkæp] **1.** Handikap n; Sport: Vorgabe f; Vorgaberennen n, -spiel n, -kampf m; fig. Behinderung f, Benachteiligung f, Nachteil m; s. mental, physical; **2.** (-pp-) (be)hindern, benachteiligen, belasten; Sport: mit Handikaps belegen; **~ped 1.** gehandikapt, behindert, benachteiligt; s. mental, physical; **2.** the ~ pl. ♿ die Behinderten pl.

hand·ker·chief ['hæŋkətʃɪf] (pl. -chiefs) Taschentuch n.

han·dle ['hændl] **1.** Griff m; Stiel m; Henkel m; (Pumpen- etc.)Schwengel m; fig. Handhabe f; fly off the ~ F wütend werden; **2.** anfassen; handhaben; behandeln; △ nicht handeln; **~-bar(s)** pl. Lenkstange f.

hand|lug·gage ['hændlʌgɪdʒ] Handgepäck n; **~-made** handgearbeitet; **~-rail** Geländer m; **~-shake** Händedruck m; **~-some** □ ['hænsəm] (~r, ~st) ansehnlich; hübsch; anständig; **~-work** Handarbeit f; **~-writ·ing** Handschrift f; **~-writ·ten** handgeschrieben; **~-y** □ [~ɪ] (-ier, -iest) geschickt; handlich; nützlich; zur Hand; come in ~ sich als nützlich erweisen; sehr gelegen kommen.

hang[1] [hæŋ] **1.** (hung) v/t. hängen; auf-, einhängen; verhängen; hängenlassen; Tapete ankleben; v/i. hängen; schweben; sich neigen; ~ about, ~ around herumlungern; ~ back zögern; ~ on sich klammern (to an acc.) (a. fig.); ~ up teleph. einhängen, auflegen; she hung up on me sie legte einfach auf; **2.** Fall m, Sitz m (e-s Kleides etc.); get the ~ of s.th. et. kapieren, den Dreh rauskriegen (bei et.).

hang² [~] (*hanged*) (auf)hängen; ~ *o.s.* sich erhängen.

han·gar ['hæŋə] Hangar *m*, Flugzeughalle *f*.

hang·dog ['hæŋdɒg] Armesünder...

hang·er ['hæŋə] Kleiderbügel *m*; ~**on** *fig.* [~ər'ɒn] (*pl.* hangers-on) Klette *f*.

hang|-glid·er ['hæŋglaɪdə] (Flug-) Drachen *m*; Drachenflieger(in); ~**glid·ing** [~ɪŋ] Drachenfliegen *n*.

hang·ing ['hæŋɪŋ] 1. hängend; Hänge...; 2. (Er)Hängen *n*; ~**s** Tapete *f*, Wandbehang *m*, Vorhang *m*.

hang·man ['hæŋmən] (*pl.* -men) Henker *m*.

hang·nail ⚕ ['hæŋneɪl] Niednagel *m*.

hang·o·ver F ['hæŋəʊvə] Katzenjammer *m*, Kater *m*.

han·ker ['hæŋkə] sich sehnen (*after*, *for* nach).

hap·haz·ard ['hæp'hæzəd] 1. Zufall *m*; *at* ~ aufs Geratewohl; 2. □ willkürlich, plan-, wahllos.

hap·pen ['hæpən] sich ereignen, geschehen; *he* ~*ed to be at home* er war zufällig zu Hause; ~ *on*, ~ *upon* zufällig treffen auf (*acc.*); ~ *in Am.* F hereinschneien; ~**ing** ['hæpnɪŋ] Ereignis *n*, Vorkommnis *n*; Happening *n*.

hap·pi|·ly ['hæpɪlɪ] glücklich(erweise); ~**ness** [~nɪs] Glück(seligkeit *f*) *n*.

hap·py □ ['hæpɪ] (-*ier*, -*iest*) glücklich; beglückt; erfreut; erfreulich; geschickt; treffend; F beschwipst; ~**go-luck·y** unbekümmert.

ha·rangue [hə'ræŋ] 1. Strafpredigt *f*; 2. *v/t. j-m* e-e Strafpredigt halten.

har·ass ['hærəs] belästigen, quälen.

har·bo(u)r ['hɑ:bə] 1. Hafen *m*; Zufluchtsort *m*; 2. beherbergen; *fig.* hegen (*Gedanken, Rache etc.*).

hard [hɑ:d] 1. *adj.* □ hart; schwer; mühselig; streng; ausdauernd; fleißig; heftig; hart (*Droge*), Getränk *a.* stark; ~ *of hearing* schwerhörig; 2. *adv.* stark; tüchtig; mit Mühe; ~ *by* nahe bei; ~ *up* in Not; ~**boiled** ['hɑ:dbɔɪld] hart(gekocht); *fig.* hart, unsentimental, nüchtern; ~ *cash* Bargeld *n*; klingende Münze; ~ *core* harter Kern (*e-r Bande etc.*); ~**core** zum harten Kern gehörend; hart (*Pornographie*); ~**cov·er** *print.* 1. gebunden; 2. Hard cover *n*, gebundene Ausgabe; ~**en** [~n] härten; hart ma-

chen *od.* werden; (sich) abhärten; *fig.* (sich) verhärten (*to* gegen); *econ.* sich festigen (*Preise*); ~**hat** Schutzhelm *m* (*für Bauarbeiter etc.*); ~**head·ed** nüchtern, praktisch; *bsd. Am.* starr-, dickköpfig; ~ *la·bo(u)r* ⚖ Zwangsarbeit *f*; ~ *line bsd. pol.* harter Kurs; ~**line** *bsd. pol.* hart, kompromißlos; ~**heart·ed** □ hart (-herzig); ~**ly** [~lɪ] kaum; streng; mit Mühe; ~**ness** [~nɪs] Härte *f*; Schwierigkeit *f*; Not *f*; ~**ship** [~ʃɪp] Bedrängnis *f*, Not *f*; Härte *f*; ~**shoul·der** *mot.* Standspur *f*; ~**ware** Eisenwaren *pl.*; Haushaltswaren *pl.*; *Computer:* Hardware *f* (*technischphysikalische Teile*); *Sprachlabor:* Hardware *f*, technische Ausrüstung; **har·dy** □ [~ɪ] (-*ier*, -*iest*) kühn; widerstandsfähig, hart; abgehärtet; winterfest (*Pflanze*).

hare *zo.* [heə] Hase *m*; ~**bell** ⚘ ['heəbel] Glockenblume *f*; ~**brained** verrückt (*Person, Plan*); ~**lip** *anat.* [~'lɪp] Hasenscharte *f*.

hark [hɑ:k]: ~ *back* F zurückgreifen, -kommen, *a.* zeitlich: zurückgehen (*to* auf *acc.*).

harm [hɑ:m] 1. Schaden *m*; Unrecht *n*, Böse(s) *n*; 2. beschädigen, verletzen; schaden, Leid zufügen (*dat.*); ~**ful** □ ['hɑ:mfl] schädlich; ~**less** [~lɪs] harmlos; unschädlich.

har·mo|ni·ous □ [hɑ:'məʊnjəs] harmonisch; ~**nize** ['hɑ:mənaɪz] *v/t.* in Einklang bringen; *v/i.* harmonieren; ~**ny** [~ɪ] Harmonie *f*.

har·ness ['hɑ:nɪs] 1. Harnisch *m*; (*Pferde- etc.*)Geschirr *n*; *die in* ~ *fig.* in den Sielen sterben; 2. anschirren; *Naturkräfte etc.* nutzbar machen.

harp [hɑ:p] 1. ♪ Harfe *f*; 2. ♪ Harfe spielen; ~ *on fig.* herumreiten auf (*dat.*).

har·poon [hɑ:'pu:n] 1. Harpune *f*; 2. harpunieren.

har·row ✗ ['hærəʊ] 1. Egge *f*; 2. eggen.

har·row·ing □ ['hærəʊɪŋ] quälend, qualvoll, erschütternd.

harsh □ [hɑ:ʃ] rauh; herb; grell; streng; schroff; barsch.

hart *zo.* [hɑ:t] Hirsch *m*.

har·vest ['hɑ:vɪst] 1. Ernte(zeit) *f*; (Ernte)Ertrag *m*; 2. ernten; einbringen; ~**er** [~ə] *bsd.* Mähdrescher *m*.

has [hæz] 3. *sg. pres. von* have.

hash¹ [hæʃ] 1. Haschee *n*; *fig.* Durcheinander n; make a ~ of verpfuschen; 2. Fleisch zerhacken, -kleinern.

hash² F [~] Hasch n (Haschisch).

hash·ish ['hæʃiːʃ] Haschisch n.

hasp [hɑːsp] Schließband n, (Verschluß)Spange f.

haste [heɪst] Eile f; Hast f; make ~ sich beeilen; **has·ten** ['heɪsn] j-n antreiben; (sich beeilen); et. beschleunigen; **hast·y** □ ['heɪstɪ] (-ier, -iest) (vor)eilig; hastig; hitzig, heftig.

hat [hæt] Hut m.

hatch¹ [hæt] a. ~ out ausbrüten; ausschlüpfen.

hatch² [~] ♣, ⚓ Luke f; Durchreiche f (für Speisen); ~**back** mot. ['hætʃbæk] (Wagen m mit) Hecktür f.

hatch·et ['hætʃɪt] (Kriegs)Beil n.

hatch·way ♣ ['hætʃweɪ] Luke f.

hate [heɪt] 1. Haß m; 2. hassen; ~**ful** □ ['heɪtfl] verhaßt; abscheulich; **ha·tred** [~rɪd] Haß m.

haugh·ti·ness ['hɔːtɪnɪs] Stolz m; Hochmut m; ~**ty** □ [~ɪ] stolz; hochmütig.

haul [hɔːl] 1. Ziehen n; (Fisch)Zug m; Transport(weg) m; 2. ziehen; schleppen; transportieren; ⚔ fördern; ♣ abdrehen.

haunch [hɔːntʃ] Hüfte f; zo. Keule f; Am. a. ~es pl. Gesäß n; zo. Hinterbacken pl.

haunt [hɔːnt] 1. Aufenthaltsort m; Schlupfwinkel m; 2. oft besuchen; heimsuchen; verfolgen; spuken in (dat.); ~**ing** □ ['hɔːntɪŋ] quälend; unvergeßlich, eindringlich.

have [hæv] (had) v/t. haben; bekommen; Mahlzeit einnehmen; ~ to do tun müssen; I had my hair cut ich ließ mir die Haare schneiden; he will ~ it that ... er behauptet, daß ...; I had better go es wäre besser, wenn ich ginge; I had rather go ich möchte lieber gehen; ~ about one bei od. an sich haben; ~ on anhaben; ~ it out with sich auseinandersetzen mit; v/aux. haben; bei v/i. oft sein; ~ come gekommen sein.

ha·ven ['heɪvn] Hafen m (mst fig.).

hav·oc ['hævək] Verwüstung f; play ~ with verwüsten, zerstören; verheerend wirken auf (acc.), übel mitspielen (dat.).

haw [hɔː] Mehlbeere f.

Ha·wai·i·an [həˈwaɪən] 1. hawaiisch; 2. Hawaiianer(in); ling. Hawaiisch n.

hawk¹ zo. [hɔːk] Habicht m, Falke m.

hawk² [~] hausieren (gehen) mit; auf der Straße verkaufen.

haw·thorn ♀ ['hɔːθɔːn] Weißdorn m.

hay [heɪ] 1. Heu n; 2. Heu machen; ~**cock** ['heɪkɒk] Heuhaufen m; ~**fe·ver** Heuschnupfen m; ~**loft** Heuboden m; ~**rick**, ~**stack** Heumiete f.

haz·ard ['hæzəd] 1. Zufall m; Gefahr f, Wagnis n; Hasard(spiel) n; 2. wagen; ~**ous** □ [~əs] gewagt.

haze [heɪz] Dunst m, feiner Nebel.

ha·zel ['heɪzl] 1. ♀ Haselnuß f, Hasel(nuß)strauch m; 2. (hasel)nußbraun; ~**nut** ♀ Haselnuß f.

haz·y □ ['heɪzɪ] (-ier, -iest) dunstig, diesig; fig. unklar.

H-bomb ⚔ ['eɪtʃbɒm] H-Bombe f, Wasserstoffbombe f.

he [hiː] 1. er; 2. Er m; zo. Männchen n; 3. adj. in Zssgn, bsd. zo.: männlich, ...männchen n; ~**goat** Ziegenbock m.

head [hed] 1. Kopf m (a. fig.); Haupt n (a. fig.); nach Zahlwort (pl. ~): Kopf m, Person f, Stück n (Vieh etc.); Leiter(in); Chef m; Kopfende n (e-s Bettes etc.); Kopfseite f (e-r Münze); Gipfel m; Quelle f; Vorderteil n; ♣ Bug m; Hauptpunkt m, Abschnitt m; Überschrift f; come to a ~ eitern (Geschwür); fig. sich zuspitzen, zur Entscheidung kommen; get it into one's ~ that ... es sich in den Kopf setzen, daß; lose one's ~ den Kopf od. die Nerven verlieren; ~ over heels über Hals über Kopf; 2. Ober..., Haupt..., Chef..., oberste(r, -s), erste(r, -s); 3. v/t. (an)führen; an der Spitze von et. stehen; vorausgehen (dat.); mit e-r Überschrift versehen; ~ off ablenken; v/i. gehen, fahren; sich bewegen (for auf acc. ... zu), lossteuern, -gehen (for auf acc.); ♣ zusteuern (for auf acc.); entspringen (Fluß); ~**ache** ['hedeɪk] Kopfweh n; ~**band** Stirnband n; ~**dress** Kopfschmuck m; ~**gear** Kopfbedeckung f; Zaumzeug n; ~**ing** [~ɪŋ] Brief-, Titelkopf m, Rubrik f; Überschrift f, Titel m; Kopfballspiel n; ~**land** [~lənd] Vorgebirge n, Kap n; ~**light** mot. Scheinwerfer(licht n) m; ~**line** Überschrift f; Schlagzeile f; ~s pl. Rundfunk, TV: das Wichtigste in Schlagzeilen; **~·long 1.** *adj.* ungestüm; **2.** *adv.* kopfüber; **~·mas·ter** *Schule*: Direktor *m*, Rektor *m*; **~·mis·tress** *Schule*: Direktorin *f*, Rektorin *f*; **~·on** frontal; ~ *collision* Frontalzusammenstoß *m*; **~·phones** *pl.* Kopfhörer *pl.*; **~·quar·ters** *pl.* ✗ Hauptquartier *n*; Zentrale *f*; **~·rest**, **~·re·straint** Kopfstütze *f*; **~·set** *bsd. Am.* Kopfhörer *pl.*; **~·start** *Sport*: Vorgabe *f*, -sprung (a. *fig.*); **~·strong** halsstarrig; **~·wa·ters** *pl.* Quellgebiet *n*; **~·way** *fig.* Fortschritt(e *pl.*) *m*; *make* ~ (gut) vorankommen; **~·word** Stichwort *n* (*in e-m Wörterbuch*); **~·y** □ [~ɪ] (-*ier*, -*iest*) ungestüm; voreilig; zu Kopfe steigend.

heal [hi:l] heilen; ~ *over*, ~ *up* (zu)heilen.

health [helθ] Gesundheit *f*; ~ *club* Fitneßclub *m*; ~ *food* Reformkost *f*; ~ *food shop* (*bsd. Am. store*) Reformhaus *n*; ~ *insurance* Krankenversicherung *f*; ~ *resort* Kurort *m*; ~ *service* Gesundheitsdienst *m*; **~·ful** □ ['helθfl] gesund; heilsam; **~·y** □ [~ɪ] (-*ier*, -*iest*) gesund.

heap [hi:p] **1.** Haufe(n) *m*; **2.** *a.* ~ *up* aufhäufen, *fig. a.* anhäufen.

hear [hɪə] (*heard*) hören; erfahren; anhören, *j-m* zuhören; erhören; *Zeugen* vernehmen; *Lektion* abhören; **~·d** [hɜːd] *pret. u. p.p. von* hear; **~·er** ['hɪərə] (Zu)Hörer(in); **~·ing** [~rɪŋ] Gehör *n*; ⚖ Verhandlung *f*; ⚖ Vernehmung *f*; *bsd. pol.* Hearing *n*, Anhörung *f*; *within* (*out of*) ~ in (außer) Hörweite; **~·say** Gerede *n*; *by* ~ vom Hörensagen.

hearse [hɜːs] Leichenwagen *m*.

heart [hɑːt] *anat.* Herz *n* (a. *fig.*); Innere(s) *n*; Kern *m*; *fig.* Liebling *m*, Schatz *m*; *by* ~ auswendig; *out of* ~ mutlos; *cross my* ~ Hand aufs Herz, auf Ehre u. Gewissen; *lay to* ~ sich zu Herzen nehmen; *lose* ~ den Mut verlieren; *take* ~ sich ein Herz fassen; **~·ache** ['hɑːteɪk] Kummer *m*; ~ **at·tack** ⚕ Herzanfall *m*; ⚕ Herzinfarkt *m*; **~·beat** Herzschlag *m*; **~·break** Leid *n*, großer Kummer; **~·break·ing** □ [~ɪ] herzzerreißend; **~·brok·en** gebrochen, verzweifelt; **~·burn** ⚕ Sodbrennen *n*; **~·en** [~n] ermutigen; **~·fail·ure** ⚕ Herzinsuffizienz *f*; ⚕ Herzversagen *n*; **~·felt** innig, tiefempfunden.

hearth [hɑːθ] Herd *m* (a. *fig.*).

heart|less □ ['hɑːtlɪs] herzlos; **~·rend·ing** □ ['hɑːtrendɪŋ] herzzerreißend; ~ **trans·plant** ⚕ Herzverpflanzung *f*, -transplantation *f*; **~·y** □ [~ɪ] (-*ier*, -*iest*) herzlich; aufrichtig; gesund; herzhaft.

heat [hi:t] **1.** Hitze *f*; Wärme *f*; Eifer *m*; *Sport*: Vorlauf *m*; *zo.* Läufigkeit *f*; **2.** heizen; (sich) erhitzen (a. *fig.*); **~·ed** □ ['hi:tɪd] erhitzt; *fig.* erregt; **~·er** ⊕ [~ə] Heizgerät *n*, Ofen *m*.

heath [hi:θ] Heide *f*; ⚘ Heidekraut *n*.

hea·then ['hi:ðn] **1.** Heide|*m*, -in *f*; **2.** heidnisch.

heath·er ⚘ ['heðə] Heidekraut *n*.

heat|ing ['hi:tɪŋ] Heizung *f*; *attr.* Heiz...; ~ **·proof**, **~·re·sis·tant**, **~·re·sist·ing** hitzebeständig; ~ **shield** *Raumfahrt*: Hitzeschild *m*; **~·stroke** ⚕ Hitzschlag *m*; ~ **wave** Hitzewelle *f*.

heave [hi:v] **1.** Heben *n*; **2.** (*heaved*, *bsd.* ⚓ *hove*) *v/t.* heben; *Seufzer* ausstoßen; *Anker* lichten; *v/i.* sich heben u. senken, wogen.

heav·en ['hevn] Himmel *m*; **~·ly** [~lɪ] himmlisch.

heav·i·ness ['hevɪnɪs] Schwere *f*, Druck *m*; Schwerfälligkeit *f*; Schwermut *f*.

heav·y □ ['hevɪ] (-*ier*, -*iest*) schwer; schwermütig; schwerfällig; trüb; drückend; heftig (*Regen etc.*); unwegsam (*Straße*); Schwer...; ~ **cur·rent** ⚡ Starkstrom *m*; **~·du·ty** ⊕ Hochleistungs...; strapazierfähig; **~·hand·ed** □ ungeschickt; **~·heart·ed** niedergeschlagen; **~·weight** *Boxen*: Schwergewicht(ler *m*) *n*.

He·brew ['hi:bru:] **1.** hebräisch; **2.** Hebräer(in), Jude *m*, Jüdin *f*; *ling.* Hebräisch *n*.

heck·le ['hekl] *j-m* zusetzen; *e-n Redner* durch Zwischenrufe *od.* -fragen aus der Fassung bringen *od.* in die Enge treiben.

hec·tic ['hektɪk] (~*ally*) hektisch.

hedge [hedʒ] **1.** Hecke *f*; **2.** *v/t.* mit e-r Hecke einfassen *od.* umgeben; *v/i.* ausweichen, sich nicht festlegen (wollen); **~·hog** *zo.* ['hedʒhɒg] Igel *m*; *Am.* Stachelschwein *n*; **~·row** Hecke *f*.

heed [hi:d] **1.** Beachtung *f*, Aufmerksamkeit *f*; *take* ~ *of*, *give od.* pay~ *to* achtgeben auf (*acc.*), beachten; **2.** beachten, achten auf (*acc.*); **~·less** □

['hi:dlɪs] unachtsam; unbekümmert (*of* um).

heel [hi:l] **1.** Ferse *f*; Absatz *m*; *Am. sl.* Lump *m*; *head over* ~*s* Hals über Kopf; *down at* ~ mit schiefen Absätzen; *fig.* abgerissen; schlampig; **2.** Absätze machen auf.

hef·ty ['heftɪ] (*-ier, -iest*) kräftig, stämmig; mächtig (*Schlag etc.*), gewaltig.

heif·er *zo.* ['hefə] Färse *f*, junge Kuh.

height [haɪt] Höhe *f*; Höhepunkt *m*; ~**en** ['haɪtn] erhöhen; vergrößern.

hei·nous ['heɪnəs] abscheulich.

heir [eə] Erbe *m*; ~ *apparent* rechtmäßiger Erbe; ~**ess** ['eərɪs] Erbin *f*; ~**loom** ['eəlu:m] Erbstück *n*.

held [held] *pret. u. p.p. von* hold 2.

hel·i·cop·ter ✈ ['helɪkɒptə] Hubschrauber *m*, Helikopter *m*; ~**port** ✈ Hubschrauberlandeplatz *m*.

hell [hel] **1.** Hölle *f*; *attr.* Höllen...; *what the* ~...? F was zum Teufel ...?; *raise* ~ F e-n Mordskrach schlagen; **2.** *int.* F verdammt!, verflucht!; ~**bent** ['helbent] ganz versessen, wie wild (*for, on auf acc.*); ~**ish** □ [~ɪʃ] höllisch.

hel·lo *int.* [hə'ləʊ] hallo!

helm ⏚ [helm] Ruder *n*, Steuer *n*; △ *nicht* Helm.

hel·met ['helmɪt] Helm *m*.

helms·man ⏚ ['helmzmən] (*pl. -men*) Steuermann *m*.

help [help] **1.** Hilfe *f*; (Hilfs)Mittel *n*; (Dienst)Mädchen *n*; **2.** helfen; ~ *o.s.* sich bedienen, zulangen; *I cannot* ~ *it* ich kann es nicht ändern; *I could not* ~ *laughing* ich mußte einfach lachen; ~**er** ['helpə] Helfer(in); ~**ful** □ [~fl] hilfreich; nützlich; ~**ing** [~ɪŋ] Portion *f* (*Essen*); ~**less** □ [~lɪs] hilflos; ~**less·ness** [~nɪs] Hilflosigkeit *f*.

hel·ter-skel·ter ['heltə'skeltə] **1.** *adv.* holterdiepolter, Hals über Kopf; **2.** *adj.* hastig, überstürzt; **3.** *Brt.* Rutschbahn *f*.

helve [helv] Stiel *m*, Griff *m*.

Hel·ve·tian [hel'vi:ʃjən] Helvetier(in); *attr.* Schweizer...

hem [hem] **1.** Saum *m*; **2.** (*-mm-*) säumen; ~ *in* einschließen.

hem·i·sphere *geogr.* ['hemɪsfɪə] Halbkugel *f*, Hemisphäre *f*.

hem·line ['hemlaɪn] (Kleider)Saum *m*.

hem·lock ♣ ['hemlɒk] Schierling *m*.

hemp ♣ [hemp] Hanf *m*.

hem·stitch ['hemstɪtʃ] Hohlsaum *m*.

hen [hen] *zo.* Henne *f*, Huhn *n*; Weibchen *n* (*von Vögeln*).

hence [hens] hieraus; daher; *a week* ~ in *od.* nach e-r Woche; ~**forth** ['hens'fɔ:θ], ~**for·ward** [~'fɔ:wəd] von nun an.

hen·|house ['henhaʊs] Hühnerstall *m*; ~**pecked** unter dem Pantoffel (stehend).

her [hɜ:, hə] sie; ihr; ihr(e); sich.

her·ald ['herəld] **1.** *hist.* Herold *m*; **2.** ankündigen; ~ *in* einführen; ~**ry** [~rɪ] Wappenkunde *f*, Heraldik *f*.

herb ♣ [hɜ:b] Kraut *n*; **her·ba·ceous** ♣ [hɜ:'beɪʃəs] krautartig; ~ *border* (Stauden)Rabatte *f*; **herb·age** ['hɜ:bɪdʒ] Gras *n*; Weide *f*; **her·biv·o·rous** □ *zo.* [hɜ:'bɪvərəs] pflanzenfressend.

herd [hɜ:d] **1.** Herde *f* (*a. fig.*), *wildlebender Tiere a.* Rudel *n*; **2.** *v/t.* Vieh hüten; *v/i. a.* ~ *together* in e-r Herde leben; sich zusammendrängen; ~**s·man** ['hɜ:dzmən] (*pl. -men*) Hirt *m*.

here [hɪə] hier; hierher; ~ *you are* hier(, bitte); ~'*s to you!* auf dein Wohl!

here·|a·bout(s) ['hɪərəbaʊt(s)] hier herum, in dieser Gegend; ~**af·ter** [hɪər'ɑ:ftə] **1.** künftig; **2.** *das* Jenseits; ~**by** ['hɪə'baɪ] hierdurch.

he·red·i·ta·ry [hɪ'redɪtərɪ] erblich; Erb...; ~**ty** [~] Erblichkeit *f*; ererbte Anlagen *pl.*, Erbmasse *f*.

here·|in ['hɪər'ɪn] hierin; ~**of** [~'ɒv] hiervon.

her·e·|sy ['herəsɪ] Häresie *f*, Ketzerei *f*; ~**tic** [~tɪk] Häretiker(in), Ketzer(in).

here·|up·on ['hɪərə'pɒn] hierauf; ~**with** hiermit.

her·i·tage ['herɪtɪdʒ] Erbschaft *f*.

her·mit ['hɜ:mɪt] Einsiedler *m*.

he·ro ['hɪərəʊ] (*pl. -roes*) Held *m*; ~**ic** [hɪ'rəʊɪk] (~*ally*) heroisch; heldenhaft; Helden...

her·o·in ['herəʊɪn] Heroin *n*.

her·o·ine ['herəʊɪn] Heldin *f*; ~**is·m** [~ɪzəm] Heldenmut *m*, -tum *n*.

her·on *zo.* ['herən] Reiher *m*.

her·ring *zo.* ['herɪŋ] Hering *m*.

hers [hɜ:z] der, die, das ihr(ig)e; ihr.

her·self [hɜ:'self] sie selbst; ihr selbst; sich; *by* ~ von selbst, allein, ohne Hilfe.

H

hes·i|tant □ ['hezitənt] zögernd, zaudernd, unschlüssig; **~tate** [~eɪt] zögern, zaudern, unschlüssig sein, Bedenken haben; **~ta·tion** [hezi-'teɪʃn] Zögern n, Zaudern n, Unschlüssigkeit f; without ~ ohne zu zögern, bedenkenlos.

hew [hju:] (hewed, hewed od. hewn) hauen, hacken; ~ down fällen, umhauen; **~n** [hju:n] p.p. von hew.

hey int. [heɪ] ei!, hei!; he!, heda!

hey·day ['heɪdeɪ] Höhepunkt m, Blüte f.

hi int. [haɪ] hallo!; he!, heda!

hi·ber·nate zo. ['haɪbəneɪt] Winterschlaf halten.

hic|cup, ~·cough ['hɪkʌp] **1.** Schluckauf m; **2.** den Schluckauf haben.

hid [hɪd] pret. von hide²; **~·den** ['hɪdn] p.p. von hide².

hide¹ [haɪd] Haut f, Fell n.

hide² [~] (hid, hidden) (sich) verbergen, ~stecken; **~-and-seek** ['haɪnd-'si:k] Versteckspiel n; **~·a·way** F [~əweɪ] Versteck n; **~·bound** engstirnig.

hid·e·ous □ ['hɪdɪəs] scheußlich.

hide-out ['haɪdaʊt] Versteck n.

hid·ing¹ ['haɪdɪŋ] Tracht f Prügel.

hid·ing² [~] Verstecken n, ~bergen n, **~·place** Versteck n.

hi-fi ['haɪ'faɪ] **1.** (pl. hi-fis) Hi-Fi n; Hi-Fi-Anlage f; **2.** Hi-Fi-...

high [haɪ] **1.** adj. □ hoch; vornehm; gut, edel (Character); stolz; hochtrabend; angegangen (Fleisch); extrem; stark; üppig, flott (Leben); F blau (betrunken); F high (im Drogenrausch; in euphorischer Stimmung); Haupt..., Hoch..., Ober...; with a ~ hand arrogant, anmaßend; in ~ spirits guter Laune; ~ society High-Society f, gehobene Gesellschaftsschicht; ≈ Tech = ≈ Technology Hochtechnologie f; ~ time höchste Zeit; ~ words heftige Worte; **2.** meteor. Hoch n; **3.** adv. hoch; stark, heftig; **~·ball** Am. F ['haɪbɔːl] Highball m (Whisky-Cocktail); **~·brow** F **1.** Intellektuelle(r m) f; **2.** betont intellektuell; **~·class** erstklassig; **fi·del·i·ty** High-Fidelity f; **~·fi·del·i·ty** High-Fidelity-...; **~·grade** hochwertig; **~·hand·ed** □ anmaßend; ~ jump Sport: Hochsprung m; ~ **jump·er** Sport: Hochspringer(in); **~·land** ['haɪlənd] mst ~s pl. Hochland n; **~·lights** pl. fig. Höhe-

punkte pl.; **~·ly** [~lɪ] hoch; sehr; speak ~ of s.o. j-n loben; **~·mind·ed** hochgesinnt; hoch (Ideale); **~·ness** [~nɪs] Höhe f; fig. Hoheit f; **~·pitched** schrill (Ton); steil (Dach); **~·pow·ered** ⊕ Hochleistungs..., Groß..., stark; dynamisch; **~·pres·sure** meteor., ⊕ Hochdruck...; **~·rise 1.** Hoch...; Hochhaus...; **2.** Hochhaus n; **~·road** Hauptstraße f; ~ **school** bsd. Am. High-School f; **~·street** Hauptstraße f, **~·strung** reizbar, nervös; ~ **tea** Brt. (frühes) Abendessen; ~ **wa·ter** Hochwasser n; **~·way** bsd. Am. od. ₴₺ Highway m, Haupt(verkehrs)straße f; ≈ Code Brt. Straßenverkehrsordnung f; **~·way·man** (pl. -men) Straßenräuber m.

hi·jack ['haɪdʒæk] **1.** Flugzeug entführen; j-n, Geldtransport etc. überfallen; **2.** (Flugzeug)Entführung f; Überfall m; **~·er** [~ə] (Flugzeug)Entführer m, Luftpirat m; Räuber m.

hike F [haɪk] **1.** wandern; **2.** Wanderung f; Am. Erhöhung f (Preis etc.); **hik·er** ['haɪkə] Wanderer m; **hik·ing** [~ɪŋ] Wandern n.

hi·lar·i·ous □ [hɪ'leərɪəs] ausgelassen; **~·ty** [hɪ'lærətɪ] Ausgelassenheit f.

hill [hɪl] Hügel m, Berg m; **~·bil·ly** Am. F ['hɪlbɪlɪ] Hinterwäldler m; ~ music Hillbilly-Musik f; **~·ock** ['hɪlək] kleiner Hügel; **~·side** ['hɪl'saɪd] Hang m; **~·top** Gipfel m; **~·y** ['hɪlɪ] (-ier, -iest) hügelig.

hilt [hɪlt] Griff m (bsd. am Degen).

him [hɪm] ihn; ihm; sich; **~·self** [hɪm'self] sich; sich (selbst); (er, ihm, ihn) selbst; by ~ von selbst, allein, ohne Hilfe.

hind¹ zo. [haɪnd] Hirschkuh f.

hind² [~] Hinter...

hind·er¹ ['haɪndə] hintere(r, ~s); Hinter...

hin·der² ['hɪndə] hindern (from an, dat.); hemmen.

hind·most ['haɪndməʊst] hinterste(r, ~s), letzte(r, ~s).

hin·drance ['hɪndrəns] Hindernis n.

hinge [hɪndʒ] **1.** Türangel f; Scharnier n; fig. Angelpunkt m; **2.** ~ on, ~ upon fig. abhängen von.

hint [hɪnt] **1.** Wink m; Anspielung f; take a ~ e-n Wink verstehen; **2.** andeuten; anspielen (at auf acc.).

hin·ter·land ['hɪntəlænd] Hinterland *n*.

hip[1] *anat*. [hɪp] Hüfte *f*.

hip[2] ♀ [~] Hagebutte *f*.

hip·pie, hip·py ['hɪpɪ] Hippie *m*.

hip·po *zo*. F ['hɪpəʊ] (*pl*. -pos) = **~·pot·a·mus** *zo*. [hɪpə'pɒtəməs] (*pl*. -muses, -mi [-maɪ]) Fluß-, Nilpferd *n*.

hire ['haɪə] 1. Miete *f*; Entgelt *n*, Lohn *m*; *for* ~ zu vermieten; frei (*Taxi*); ~ *car* Leih-, Mietwagen *m*; ~ *charge* Leihgebühr *f*; ~ *purchase* Brt. *econ*. Kauf *m* auf Raten- *od*. Teilzahlung; 2. mieten; *j-n* anstellen; ~ *out* vermieten.

his [hɪz] sein(e); seine(r, -s).

hiss [hɪs] 1. zischen; zischeln; *a*. ~ *at* auszischen; 2. Zischen *n*.

his|to·ri·an [hɪ'stɔːrɪən] Historiker *m*; **~·tor·ic** [hɪ'stɒrɪk] (*~ally*) historisch, geschichtlich; **~·tor·i·cal** [~kl] historisch, geschichtlich; Geschichts...; **~·to·ry** ['hɪstərɪ] Geschichte *f*; ~ *of civilization* Kulturgeschichte *f*; *contemporary* ~ Zeitgeschichte *f*.

hit [hɪt] 1. Schlag *m*, Stoß *m*; *fig*. (Seiten)Hieb *m*; (Glücks)Treffer *m*; Hit *m* (*Buch, Schlager etc.*); 2. (*-tt-; hit*) schlagen, stoßen; treffen; auf *et*. stoßen; ~ *it off with* F sich gut vertragen mit; ~ *on*, ~ *upon* (zufällig) stoßen auf (*acc.*), finden; **~·and-run** [hɪtənd'rʌn] 1. *a*. ~ *accident* Unfall *m* mit Fahrerflucht; 2. ~ *driver* unfallflüchtiger Fahrer.

hitch [hɪtʃ] 1. Ruck *m*; ♣ Knoten *m*; Schwierigkeit *f*, Problem *n*, Haken *m*; 2. (ruckartig) ziehen, rücken; befestigen, festmachen, -haken, anbinden, ankoppeln; **~·hike** ['hɪtʃhaɪk] per Anhalter fahren, trampen; **~·hik·er** Anhalter(in), Tramper(in).

hith·er ['hɪðə]: ~ *and thither* hierhin u. dorthin; **~·to** bisher.

hive [haɪv] Bienenstock *m*; Bienenschwarm *m*.

hoard [hɔːd] 1. Vorrat *m*, Schatz *m*; 2. *a*. ~ *up* horten, hamstern.

hoard·ing ['hɔːdɪŋ] Bauzaun *m*; Brt. Reklametafel *f*.

hoar·frost ['hɔː'frɒst] (Rauh)Reif *m*.

hoarse [hɔːs] (*~r, ~st*) heiser, rauh.

hoar·y ['hɔːrɪ] (*-ier, -iest*) (alters)grau.

hoax [həʊks] 1. Falschmeldung *f*; (übler) Scherz *m*; 2. *j-n* hereinlegen.

hob·ble ['hɒbl] 1. Hinken *n*, Humpeln *n*; 2. *v/i*. humpeln, hinken (*a. fig.*); *v/t*. an den Füßen fesseln.

hob·by ['hɒbɪ] *fig*. Steckenpferd *n*, Hobby *n*; **~·horse** Steckenpferd *n*; Schaukelpferd *n*.

hob·gob·lin ['hɒbgɒblɪn] Kobold *m*.

ho·bo *Am*. ['həʊbəʊ] (*pl*. -boes, -bos) Wanderarbeiter *m*; Landstreicher *m*.

hock[1] [hɒk] Rheinwein *m*.

hock[2] *zo*. [~] Sprunggelenk *n*.

hock·ey ['hɒkɪ] Brt., Am. *field* ~ *Sport*: Hockey *n*; *Am*. Eishockey *n*.

hoe ♂ [həʊ] 1. Hacke *f*; 2. hacken.

hog [hɒg] (Mast)Schwein *n*; *Am*. Schwein *n*; **~·gish** □ ['hɒgɪʃ] schweinisch; gefräßig.

hoist [hɔɪst] 1. (Lasten)Aufzug *m*, Winde *f*; 2. hochziehen; hissen.

hold [həʊld] 1. Halten *n*; Halt *m*; Griff *m*; Gewalt *f*, Macht *f*, Einfluß *m*; ♣ Lade-, Frachtraum *m*; *catch* (*od. get, lay, take, seize*) ~ *of* erfassen, ergreifen; sich aneignen; *keep* ~ *of* festhalten; 2. (*held*) halten; (fest)halten; (zurück-, einbe)halten; abhalten (*from* von); an-, aufhalten; *Wahlen, Versammlung etc.* abhalten; *Sport*: *Meisterschaft etc.* austragen; beibehalten; innehaben; besitzen; *Amt* bekleiden; *Platz* einnehmen; *Rekord* halten; fassen, enthalten; behaupten, *Ansicht* vertreten; fesseln, in Spannung halten; stand-, aushalten; (sich) festhalten; sich verhalten; anhalten, andauern (*Wetter*); ~ *one's ground*, ~ *one's own* sich behaupten; ~ *the line* *teleph*. am Apparat bleiben; *a*. ~ *good* (weiterhin) gelten; ~ *still* stillhalten; ~ *against j-m et.* vorhalten *od*. vorwerfen; *j-m et.* übelnehmen; ~ *back* (sich) zurückhalten; *fig*. zurückhalten mit; ~ *forth* sich auslassen *od*. verbreiten (*on* über *acc*); ~ *off* (sich) fernhalten; *et*. aufschieben; ausbleiben; ~ *on* (sich) festhalten (*to* an *dat*.); aus-, durchhalten; andauern; *teleph*. am Apparat bleiben; ~ *on to et*. behalten; ~ *over* vertagen, -schieben; ~ *together* zusammenhalten; hinstellen (*as als Beispiel etc*.); aufhalten, verzögern; *j-n, Bank etc*. überfallen; **~·all** ['həʊldɔːl] Reisetasche *f*; **~·er** [~ə] Pächter *m*; Halter *m* (*Gerät*); Inhaber(in) (*bsd. econ*.);

~·ing [~ɪŋ] Halten n; Halt m; Pacht-gut n; Besitz m; **~ company** econ. Holding-, Dachgesellschaft f; **~·up** Verzögerung f; Stockung f; (a. Verkehrs-) (bewaffneter) (Raub-) Überfall m.

hole [həʊl] **1.** Loch n; Höhle f; F fig. Klemme f; **pick ~s in** bekritteln; **2.** aushöhlen; durchlöchern.

hol·i·day ['hɒlədɪ] Feiertag m; freier Tag; bsd. Brt. mst **~s** pl. Ferien pl., Urlaub m; **~-mak·er** Urlauber(in).

hol·i·ness ['həʊlɪnɪs] Heiligkeit f; His **♀** Seine Heiligkeit (der Papst).

hol·ler Am. F ['hɒlə] schreien.

hol·low ['hɒləʊ] **1.** □ hohl; leer; falsch; **2.** Höhle f, (Aus)Höhlung f; (Land)Senke f; **3.** **~ out** aushöhlen.

hol·ly ♀ ['hɒlɪ] Stechpalme f.

hol·o·caust ['hɒləkɔːst] Massenver-nichtung f, -sterben n, (bsd. Brand-) Katastrophe f; **the ♀** hist. der Holo-caust.

hol·ster ['həʊlstə] (Pistolen)Halfter m, n.

ho·ly ['həʊlɪ] (-ier, -iest) heilig; **♀** Thursday Gründonnerstag m; **~** water Weihwasser n; **♀** Week Kar-woche f.

home [həʊm] **1.** Heim n; Haus n, Wohnung f; Heimat f; Sport: Heim-spiel n; Heimsieg m; **at ~** zu Hause; **make oneself at ~** es sich bequem machen; **at ~ and abroad** im In-u. Ausland; **2.** adj. (ein)heimisch, in-ländisch; wirkungsvoll (Schlag etc.); **3.** adv. heim, nach Hause; zu Hause, daheim; ins Ziel od. Schwarze; **strike ~** sitzen, treffen; **~ com-put·er** Heimcomputer m; **♀ Coun-ties** pl. die an London angrenzenden Grafschaften; **~ e·co·nom·ics** sg. Hauswirtschaft(slehre) f; **~·felt** ['həʊmfelt] tief empfunden; **~·less** [~lɪs] heimatlos; **~·like** anheimelnd, gemütlich; **~·ly** [~lɪ] (-ier, -iest) freundlich (with zu); vertraut; ein-fach; Am. unscheinbar, reizlos; **~·made** selbstgemacht, Hausma-cher...; **♀ Of·fice** Brt. pol. Innen-ministerium n; **♀ Sec·re·ta·ry** Brt. pol. Innenminister m; **~·sick:** be **~** Heimweh haben; **~·sick·ness** Heimweh n; **~·stead** Gehöft n; ⚖ in USA: Heimstätte f; **~ team** Sport: Gastgeber pl.; **~·ward** [~wəd] **1.** adj. Heim..., Rück...; **2.** adv. Am. heimwärts, nach Hause; **~·wards**

[~wədz] adv. = homeward **2**; **~·work** Hausaufgabe(n pl.) f, Schul-arbeiten pl.

hom·i·cide ⚖ ['hɒmɪsaɪd] Tötung f; Totschlag m; Mord m; Totschlä-ger(in); Mörder(in); **~ squad** Mord-kommission f.

ho·mo F ['həʊməʊ] (pl. -mos) Homo m (Homosexueller).

ho·mo·ge·ne·ous □ [hɒmə'dʒiːnjəs] homogen, gleichartig.

ho·mo·sex·u·al [hɒməʊ'seksjʊəl] **1.** □ homosexuell; **2.** Homosexuelle(r m) f.

hone ⊕ [həʊn] feinschleifen.

hon·est □ ['ɒnɪst] ehrlich, recht-schaffen; aufrichtig; echt; **~·es·ty** [~ɪ] Ehrlichkeit f, Rechtschaffenheit f; Aufrichtigkeit f.

hon·ey ['hʌnɪ] Honig m; fig. Liebling m; **~·comb** [~kəʊm] (Honig)Wabe f; **~ed** [~ɪd] honigsüß; **~·moon 1.** Flit-terwochen pl.; **2.** s-e Hochzeitsreise machen.

honk mot. [hɒŋk] hupen.

hon·ky-tonk Am. sl. ['hɒŋkɪtɒŋk] Spelunke f.

hon·or·a·ry ['ɒnərərɪ] Ehren...; eh-renamtlich.

hon·o(u)r ['ɒnə] **1.** Ehre f; fig. Zierde f; **~s** pl. besondere Auszeichnung(en pl.), Ehren pl.; **Your ♀** Euer Ehren; **2.** (be)ehren; econ. honorieren; **~·a·ble** □ [~rəbl] ehrenvoll; redlich, ehrbar; ehrenwert.

hood [hʊd] Kapuze f; mot. Verdeck n; Am. (Motor)Haube f; ⊕ Kappe f.

hood·lum Am. F ['huːdləm] Rowdy m; Ganove m.

hood·wink ['hʊdwɪŋk] j-n reinlegen.

hoof [huːf] (pl. hoofs [~fs], hooves [~vz]) Huf m.

hook [hʊk] **1.** Haken m; Angelhaken m; Sichel f; **by ~ or by crook** so oder so; **2.** (sich) (zu-, fest)haken; angeln (a. fig.); **~ed** krumm, Haken...; F süchtig (on nach) (a. fig.); **~ on heroin** (television) heroin- (fern-seh)süchtig; **~·y** ['hʊkɪ]: **play ~** Am. F (bsd. die Schule) schwänzen.

hoo·li·gan ['huːlɪgən] Rowdy m; **~·is·m** [~ɪzəm] Rowdytum n.

hoop [huːp] **1.** (Faß- etc.)Reif(en) m; ⊕ Ring m; **2.** Fässer binden.

hoot [huːt] **1.** Schrei m (der Eule); höhnischer, johlender Schrei; mot. Hupen n; **2.** v/i. heulen; johlen; mot. hupen; v/t. auspfeifen, auszischen.

Hoo·ver *TM* ['hu:və] 1. Staubsauger *m*; 2. *mst* ♀ (staub)saugen, *Teppich etc. a.* absaugen.

hooves [hu:vz] *pl. von* hoof.

hop¹ [hop] Sprung *m*; F Tanz *m*; 2. (*-pp-*) hüpfen; springen (über *acc.*); *be ~ping mad* F e-e Stinkwut (im Bauch) haben.

hop² ♀ [~] Hopfen *m*.

hope [həʊp] 1. Hoffnung *f*; 2. hoffen (*for* auf *acc.*); *~ in* vertrauen auf (*acc.*); **~·ful** □ ['həʊpfl] hoffnungsvoll; **~·less** □ [~lıs] hoffnungslos; verzweifelt.

horde [hɔːd] Horde *f*.

ho·ri·zon [hə'raızn] Horizont *m*.

hor·i·zon·tal [hɒrı'zɒntl] horizontal, waag(e)recht.

horn [hɔːn] Horn *n*; Schalltrichter *m*; *mot.* Hupe *f*; ~*s pl.* Geweih *n*; ~ *of plenty* Füllhorn *m*.

hor·net *zo.* ['hɔːnɪt] Hornisse *f*.

horn·y ['hɔːnɪ] (*-ier, -iest*) hornig, schwielig; ∨ geil (*Mann*).

hor·o·scope ['hɒrəskəʊp] Horoskop *n*.

hor·ri·ble □ ['hɒrəbl] schrecklich, furchtbar, scheußlich; F gemein; **~·rid** □ ['hɒrɪd] gräßlich, abscheulich; schrecklich; **~·ri·fy** [~faɪ] erschrecken; entsetzen; **~·ror** [~ə] Entsetzen *n*, Schauder *m*; Schrecken *m*; Greuel *m*.

horse [hɔːs] *zo.* Pferd *n*; Bock *m*, Gestell *n*; *wild ~s will not drag me there* keine zehn Pferde bringen mich dort hin; ~**·back** ['hɔːsbæk]: *on ~* zu Pferde, beritten; ~**·chest·nut** ♀ Roßkastanie *f*; ~**·hair** Roßhaar *n*; ~**·man** (*pl. -men*) (geübter) Reiter; ~**·man·ship** [~mənʃɪp] Reitkunst *f*; ~ **op·e·ra** F Western *m* (*Film*); ~**·pow·er** *phys.* Pferdestärke *f*; ~ **rac·ing** Pferderennen *n od. pl.*; ~**·rad·ish** Meerrettich *m*; ~**·shoe** Hufeisen *n*; ~**·wom·an** (*pl. -women*) (geübte) Reiterin.

hor·ti·cul·ture ['hɔːtɪkʌltʃə] Gartenbau *m*.

hose¹ [həʊz] Schlauch *m*.

hose² [~] *pl.* Strümpfe *pl.*, Strumpfwaren *pl.*; △ *nicht* Hose.

ho·sier·y ['həʊʒərɪ] Strumpfwaren *pl.*

hos·pi·ta·ble □ ['hɒspɪtəbl] gastfrei.

hos·pi·tal ['hɒspɪtl] Krankenhaus *n*, Klinik *f*; ✗ Lazarett *n*; *in* (*Am. in the*) ~ im Krankenhaus; ~**·i·ty** [hɒspɪ'tælətɪ] Gastfreundschaft *f*, Gastlichkeit *f*; **~·ize** ['hɒspɪtəlaɪz] ins Krankenhaus einliefern *od.* -weisen.

host¹ [həʊst] Gastgeber *m*; (Gast-)Wirt *m*; *Rundfunk, TV:* Talkmaster *m*; Showmaster *m*; Moderator *m*; *your ~ was ...* durch die Sendung führte Sie ...

host² [~] Menge *f*, Masse *f*.

host³ *eccl.* [~] *oft* ♀ Hostie *f*.

hos·tage ['hɒstɪdʒ] Geisel *m, f*; *take s.o. ~* j-n als Geisel nehmen.

hos·tel ['hɒstl] *bsd. Brt.* (*Studenten-, Arbeiter- etc.*) (Wohn)Heim *n*; *mst youth ~* Jugendherberge *f*.

host·ess ['həʊstɪs] Gastgeberin *f*; (Gast)Wirtin *f*; Hostess *f*; ✈ Stewardeß *f*.

hos·tile ['hɒstaɪl] feindlich (gesinnt); *~ to foreigners* ausländerfeindlich; **~·til·i·ty** [hɒ'stɪlətɪ] Feindseligkeit *f* (*to* gegen).

hot [hɒt] (*-tt-*) heiß; scharf; beißend; hitzig, heftig; eifrig; warm (*Speise, Fährte*); F heiß, gestohlen; radioaktiv; ~**·bed** ['hɒtbed] Mistbeet *n*; *fig.* Brutstätte *f*.

hotch·potch ['hɒtʃpɒtʃ] Mischmasch *m*; Gemüsesuppe *f*.

hot dog [hɒt'dɒg] Hot dog *n, m*.

ho·tel [həʊ'tel] Hotel *n*.

hot·head ['hɒthed] Hitzkopf *m*; ~**·house** Treibhaus *n*; ~ **line** *pol.* heißer Draht; ~**·pot** Eintopf *m*; ~ **spot** *bsd. pol.* Unruhe-, Krisenherd *m*; ~**·spur** Hitzkopf *m*; ~**·wa·ter** Heißwasser...; ~ *bottle* Wärmflasche *f*.

hound [haʊnd] 1. Jagdhund *m*; *fig.* Hund *m*; 2. jagen, hetzen.

hour ['aʊə] Stunde *f*; Zeit *f*, Uhr *f*; **~·ly** [~lɪ] stündlich.

house 1. [haʊs] Haus *n*; *the* ♀ das Unterhaus; die Börse; 2. [haʊz] *v/t.* unterbringen; *v/i.* hausen; ~**·a·gent** ['haʊsedʒənt] Häusermakler *m*; ~**·bound** *fig.* ans Haus gefesselt; ~**·hold** Haushalt *m*; *attr.* Haushalts...; Haus...; ~**·hold·er** Hausherr *m*; ~**·hus·band** *bsd. Am.* Hausmann *m*; ~**·keep·er** Haushälterin *f*; ~**·keep·ing** Haushaltung *f*, Haushaltsführung *f*; ~**·maid** Hausmädchen *n*; ~**·man** (*pl. -men*) *Brt.* ✗ Medizinalassistent *m*; △ *nicht* Hausmann; ~**·warm·ing (par·ty)** [~wɔːmɪŋ(pɑːtɪ)] Einzugsparty *f*;

H

~·wife ['haʊswaɪf] (*pl.* *-wives*) Hausfrau *f*; ['hazɪf] Nähetui *n*; **~·work** Hausarbeit *f*; △ *nicht Hausaufgabe*(*n*).

hous·ing ['haʊzɪŋ] Unterbringung *f*; Wohnung *f*; **~ estate** *Brt.* Wohnsiedlung *f*.

hove [həʊv] *pret. u. p.p. von* heave 2.

hov·el ['hɒvl] Schuppen *m*; Hütte *f*.

hov·er ['hɒvə] schweben; lungern; *fig.* schwanken; **~·craft** (*pl. -craft*[s]) Hovercraft *n*, Luftkissenfahrzeug *n*.

how [haʊ] wie; **~** *do you do? bei der Vorstellung:* guten Tag!; **~** *about* ...? wie steht's mit ...?

how·dy *Am. int.* F ['haʊdɪ] Tag!

how·ev·er [haʊ'evə] **1.** *adv.* wie auch (immer), wenn auch noch so ...; **2.** *cj.* (je)doch.

howl [haʊl] **1.** heulen; brüllen; **2.** Heulen *n*, Geheul *n*; **~·er** F ['haʊlə] grober Schnitzer.

hub [hʌb] (Rad)Nabe *f*; *fig.* Mittel-, Angelpunkt *m*.

hub·bub ['hʌbʌb] Tumult *m*.

hub·by F ['hʌbɪ] (Ehe)Mann *m*.

huck·le·ber·ry ♀ ['hʌklberɪ] amerikanische Heidelbeere.

huck·ster ['hʌkstə] Hausierer(in).

hud·dle ['hʌdl] **1.** *a.* **~** *together* (sich) zusammendrängen, zusammenpressen; **~** (*o.s.*) *up* sich zusammenkauern; **2.** (wirrer) Haufen, Wirrwarr *m*, Durcheinander *n*.

hue¹ [hjuː] Farbe *f*; (Farb)Ton *m*.

hue² [~]: **~** *and cry fig.* großes Geschrei.

huff [hʌf] Verärgerung *f*; Verstimmung *f*; *be in a* **~** verärgert *od.* -stimmt sein.

hug [hʌg] **1.** Umarmung *f*; **2.** (*-gg-*) an sich drücken, umarmen; *fig.* festhalten an (*dat.*); sich dicht am *Weg etc.* halten.

huge [hjuːdʒ] ungeheuer, riesig; **~·ness** ['hjuːdʒnɪs] ungeheure Größe.

hulk·ing ['hʌlkɪŋ] sperrig, klotzig; ungeschlacht, schwerfällig.

hull [hʌl] **1.** ♀ Schale *f*, Hülse *f*; ⚓ Rumpf *m*; **2.** enthülsen; schälen.

hul·la·ba·loo ['hʌləbə'luː] (*pl. -loos*) Lärm *m*.

hul·lo *int.* [hə'ləʊ] hallo!

hum [hʌm] (*-mm-*) summen; brummen.

hu·man ['hjuːmən] **1.** □ menschlich, Menschen...; △ *nicht human*; **~·ly**

possible menschenmöglich; **~** *being* Mensch *m*; **~** *rights pl.* Menschenrechte *pl.*; **2.** Mensch *m*; **~·e** □ [hjuː'meɪn] human, menschenfreundlich; **~·i·tar·i·an** [hjuːmænɪ'teərɪən] **1.** Menschenfreund *m*; **2.** menschenfreundlich; **~·i·ty** [hjuː'mænətɪ] die Menschheit; die Menschen *pl.*; Humanität *f*, Menschlichkeit *f*; *humanities pl.* Geisteswissenschaften *pl.*; Altphilologie *f*.

hum·ble ['hʌmbl] **1.** □ (**~r**, **~st**) demütig; bescheiden; **2.** erniedrigen; demütigen.

hum·ble-bee *zo.* ['hʌmblbiː] Hummel *f*.

hum·ble·ness ['hʌmblnɪs] Demut *f*.

hum·drum ['hʌmdrʌm] eintönig.

hu·mid ['hjuːmɪd] feucht, naß; **~·i·ty** [hjuː'mɪdətɪ] Feuchtigkeit *f*.

hu·mil·i·ate [hjuː'mɪlɪeɪt] erniedrigen, demütigen; **~·a·tion** [hjuːmɪlɪ'eɪʃn] Erniedrigung *f*, Demütigung *f*; **~·ty** [hjuː'mɪlətɪ] Demut *f*.

hum·ming·bird *zo.* ['hʌmɪŋbɜːd] Kolibri *m*.

hu·mor·ous □ ['hjuːmərəs] humoristisch, humorvoll; spaßig.

hu·mo(u)r ['hjuːmə] **1.** Laune *f*, Stimmung *f*; Humor *m*; *das* Spaßige; *out of* **~** schlecht gelaunt; **2.** *j-m* s-n Willen lassen; eingehen auf (*acc.*).

hump [hʌmp] **1.** Höcker *m* (*e-s Kamels*), Buckel *m*; **2.** krümmen; *Brt.* F auf den Rücken nehmen, tragen; **~** *o.s. Am. sl.* sich ranhalten; **~·back(ed)** ['hʌmpbæk(t)] = hunchback(ed).

hunch [hʌntʃ] **1.** = hump 1; dickes Stück; Ahnung *f*, Gefühl *n*; **2.** *a.* **~** *up* krümmen; **~·back** ['hʌntʃbæk] Buckel *m*; Bucklige(r *m*) *f*; **~·backed** buck(e)lig.

hun·dred ['hʌndrəd] **1.** hundert; **2.** Hundert *n* (*Einheit*); Hundert *f* (*Zahl*); **~·th** [~θ] **1.** hundertste(r, -s); **2.** Hundertstel *n*; **~·weight** *in GB:* *appr.* Zentner *m* (= 50,8 *kg*).

hung [hʌŋ] **1.** *pret. u. p.p. von* hang¹; **2.** *adj.* abgehangen (*Fleisch*).

Hun·gar·i·an [hʌŋ'geərɪən] **1.** ungarisch; **2.** Ungar(in); *ling.* Ungarisch *n*.

hun·ger ['hʌŋgə] **1.** Hunger *m* (*a. fig.*: *for* nach); **2.** hungern (*for, after* nach); **~** *strike* Hungerstreik *m*.

hun·gry □ ['hʌŋgrɪ] (*-ier*, *-iest*) hungrig.

hunk [hʌŋk] dickes Stück.

hunt [hʌnt] **1.** Jagd *f* (*a. fig.*: *for* nach); Jagd(revier *n*) *f*; Jagd(gesellschaft) *f*; **2.** jagen; *Revier* bejagen; hetzen; ~ *out*, ~ *up* aufspüren; ~ *after*, ~ *for* Jagd machen auf (*acc.*); **~er** ['hʌntə] Jäger *m*; Jagdpferd *n*; **~ing** [~ɪŋ] Jagen *n*; *attr.* Jagd...; **~ing-ground** Jagdrevier *n*.

hur·dle ['hɜːdl] *Sport:* Hürde *f* (*a. fig.*); **~r** [~ə] *Sport:* Hürdenläufer(in); **~race** *Sport:* Hürdenrennen *n*.

hurl [hɜːl] **1.** Schleudern *n*; **2.** schleudern; *Worte* ausstoßen.

hur·ri·cane ['hʌrɪkən] Hurrikan *m*, Wirbelsturm *m*; Orkan *m*.

hur·ried □ ['hʌrɪd] eilig; übereilt.

hur·ry ['hʌrɪ] **1.** (große) Eile, Hast *f*; *be in a* (*no*) ~ es (nicht) eilig haben; *not ... in a* ~ F nicht so bald, nicht so leicht; **2.** *v/t.* (an)treiben; drängen; *et.* beschleunigen; eilig schicken *od.* bringen; *v/i.* eilen, hasten; ~ *up* sich beeilen.

hurt [hɜːt] **1.** Schmerz *m*; Verletzung *f*, Wunde *f*; Schaden *m*; **2.** (*hurt*) verletzen, -wunden (*a. fig.*); schmerzen, weh tun; schaden (*dat.*); **~ful** □ ['hɜːtfl] verletzend.

hus·band ['hʌzbənd] **1.** (Ehe)Mann *m*; **2.** haushalten mit; verwalten; **~ry** [~rɪ] ♪ Landwirtschaft *f*; *fig.* Haushalten *n*, sparsamer Umgang (*of* mit).

hush [hʌʃ] **1.** *int.* still!; **2.** Stille *f*; **3.** zum Schweigen bringen; besänftigen, beruhigen; ⚠ *nicht huschen*; ~ *up* vertuschen; **~money** ['hʌʃmʌnɪ] Schweigegeld *n*.

husk [hʌsk] **1.** ♀ Hülse *f*, Schote *f*, Schale *f* (*a. fig.*); **2.** enthülsen; **husk·y** ['hʌskɪ] **1.** □ (*-ier*, *-iest*) hülsig; trocken; heiser; F stramm, stämmig; **2.** F stämmiger Kerl.

hus·sy ['hʌsɪ] Fratz *m*, Göre *f*; Flittchen *n*.

hus·tle ['hʌsl] **1.** *v/t.* (an)rempeln; stoßen; drängen; *v/i.* (sich) drängen;

hasten, hetzen; sich beeilen; **2.** ~ *and bustle* Gedränge *n*; Gehetze *n*; Getriebe *n*.

hut [hʌt] Hütte *f*; ✕ Baracke *f*.

hutch [hʌtʃ] (*bsd. Kaninchen*)Stall *m*.

hy·a·cinth ♀ ['haɪəsɪnθ] Hyazinthe *f*.

hy·ae·na zo. [haɪˈiːnə] Hyäne *f*.

hy·brid biol. ['haɪbrɪd] Bastard *m*, Mischling *m*, Kreuzung *f*; *attr.* Bastard...; Zwitter...; **~ize** [~aɪz] kreuzen.

hy·drant ['haɪdrənt] Hydrant *m*.

hy·draul·ic [haɪˈdrɔːlɪk] (*~ally*) hydraulisch; **~s** *sg.* Hydraulik *f*.

hy·dro- ['haɪdrəʊ] Wasser...; **~car·bon** Kohlenwasserstoff *m*; **~chlor·ic ac·id** [ˌrəˈklɒrɪkˈæsɪd] Salzsäure *f*; **~foil** ♣ [~fɔɪl] Tragflächen-, Tragflügelboot *n*; **~gen** [~ədʒən] Wasserstoff *m*; **~gen bomb** Wasserstoffbombe *f*; **~plane** ✈ Wasserflugzeug *n*; ♣ Gleitboot *n*.

hy·e·na zo. [haɪˈiːnə] Hyäne *f*.

hy·giene ['haɪdʒiːn] Hygiene *f*; **hy·gien·ic** [haɪˈdʒiːnɪk] (*~ally*) hygienisch.

hymn [hɪm] **1.** Hymne *f*; Lobgesang *m*; Kirchenlied *n*; **2.** preisen.

hy·per- ['haɪpə] hyper..., Hyper..., über..., höher, größer; **~mar·ket** Großmarkt *m*, Verbrauchermarkt *m*; **~sen·si·tive** [haɪpəˈsensətɪv] überempfindlich (*to* gegen).

hy·phen ['haɪfn] Bindestrich *m*; **~ate** [~eɪt] mit Bindestrich schreiben.

hyp·no·tize ['hɪpnətaɪz] hypnotisieren.

hy·po·chon·dri·ac ['haɪpəʊˈkɒndrɪæk] Hypochonder *m*.

hy·poc·ri·sy [hɪˈpɒkrəsɪ] Heuchelei *f*; **hyp·o·crite** ['hɪpəkrɪt] Heuchler(in); Scheinheilige(r *m*) *f*; **hyp·o·crit·i·cal** □ [hɪpəˈkrɪtɪkl] heuchlerisch, scheinheilig.

hy·poth·e·sis [haɪˈpɒθɪsɪs] (*pl. -ses* [-siːz]) Hypothese *f*.

hys·te·ri·a ✻ [hɪˈstɪərɪə] Hysterie *f*; **~ter·i·cal** □ [~ˈsterɪkl] hysterisch; **~ter·ics** [~ɪks] *pl.* hysterischer Anfall; *go into* ~ hysterisch werden; F e-n Lachkrampf bekommen.

I

I [aɪ] ich; *it is* ~ ich bin es.
ice [aɪs] **1.** Eis *n*; **2.** gefrieren lassen; *a.*
~ *up* vereisen; *Kuchen* mit Zuckerguß überziehen; in Eis kühlen; **~age**
['aɪseɪdʒ] Eiszeit *f*; **~berg** [~bɜːg]
Eisberg *m* (*a. fig.*); **~bound** eingefroren; **~box** Eisfach *n*; *Am.* Kühlschrank *m*; **~cream** (Speise)Eis *n*; ~
cube Eiswürfel *m*; ~ **floe** Eisscholle
f; **~lolly** *Brt.* Eis *n* am Stiel; ~ **rink**
(Kunst)Eisbahn *f*; ~ **show** Eisrevue
f.
i·ci·cle ['aɪsɪkl] Eiszapfen *m*.
ic·ing ['aɪsɪŋ] Zuckerguß *m*; Vereisung *f*.
i·cy □ ['aɪsɪ] (*-ier, -iest*) eisig (*a. fig.*),
vereist.
i·dea [aɪ'dɪə] Idee *f*; Begriff *m*; Vorstellung *f*; Gedanke *m*; Meinung *f*;
Ahnung *f*; Plan *m*; **~l** [~l] **1.** □ ideell;
(nur) eingebildet; ideal; **2.** Ideal *n*;
~l·is·m [~ɪzəm] Idealismus *m*; **~l·ize**
[~aɪz] idealisieren.
i·den·ti·cal □ [aɪ'dentɪkl] identisch,
gleich(bedeutend); **~fi·ca·tion** [aɪdentɪfɪ'keɪʃn] Identifizierung *f*;
Ausweis *m*; **~fy** [aɪ'dentɪfaɪ] identifizieren; ausweisen; erkennen; **~ty**
[~tɪ] Identität *f*; Persönlichkeit *f*,
Eigenart *f*; **~card** (Personal)Ausweis
m, Kennkarte *f*; ~ *disk, Am.* ~ *tag* ⚔
Erkennungsmarke *f*.
i·de·o·log·i·cal □ [aɪdɪə'lɒdʒɪkl]
ideologisch; **~ol·o·gy** [aɪdɪ'ɒlədʒɪ]
Ideologie *f*.
id·i·om ['ɪdɪəm] Idiom *n*; Redewendung *f*; **~o·mat·ic** [ɪdɪə'mætɪk]
(*~ally*) idiomatisch.
id·i·ot ['ɪdɪət] Idiot(in), Schwachsinnige(r *m*) *f*; **~ic** [ɪdɪ'ɒtɪk] (*~ally*)
blödsinnig.
i·dle ['aɪdl] **1.** □ (*~r, ~st*) müßig,
untätig; träge, faul; *econ.* unproduktiv, tot; ungenutzt; beiläufig; ~
hours pl. Mußestunden *pl.*; **2.** *v/t.*
mst ~ *away* vertrödeln; *v/i.* faulenzen; ⊕ leer laufen; **~ness** [~nɪs]
Untätigkeit *f*, Müßiggang *m*; Faulheit *f*; Muße *f*; Zwecklosigkeit *f*.
i·dol ['aɪdl] Idol *n* (*a. fig.*), Götzenbild
n; **~a·trous** [aɪ'dɒlətrəs] abgöttisch; **~a·try** Götzenanbetung *f*; *fig.*
abgöttische Verehrung *f*, Vergötterung *f*; **~ize** ['aɪdəlaɪz] abgöttisch
verehren, vergöttern.

i·dyl·lic [aɪ'dɪlɪk] (*~ally*) idyllisch.
if [ɪf] **1.** wenn, falls; ob; **2.** Wenn *n*.
ig·nite [ɪg'naɪt] anzünden, (sich) entzünden; *mot.* zünden; **ig·ni·tion**
[ɪg'nɪʃən] An-, Entzünden *n*; *mot.*
Zündung *f*.
ig·no·ble □ [ɪg'nəʊbl] gemein, unehrenhaft.
ig·no·min·i·ous □ [ɪgnə'mɪnɪəs]
schändlich, schimpflich.
ig·no·rance ['ɪgnərəns] Unwissenheit *f*; **ig·no·rant** [~t] unwissend;
ungebildet; F ungehobelt; **ig·nore**
[ɪg'nɔː] ignorieren, nicht beachten;
🏛 verwerfen.
ill [ɪl] **1.** (*worse, worst*) krank;
schlimm, schlecht; übel; böse; *fall* ~,
be taken ~ krank werden; **2.** ~*s pl.*
Übel *n*, Mißstand *m*; **~ad·vised** □
['ɪlæd'vaɪzd] schlecht beraten; unbesonnen, unklug; **~bred** schlechterzogen; ungezogen; ~ **breed·ing**
schlechtes Benehmen.
il·le·gal □ [ɪ'liːgl] unerlaubt; 🏛 illegal, ungesetzlich; ~ *parking* Falschparken *n*.
il·le·gi·ble □ [ɪ'ledʒəbl] unleserlich.
il·le·git·i·mate □ [ɪlɪ'dʒɪtɪmət] illegitim; unrechtmäßig; unehelich.
ill·fat·ed ['ɪl'feɪtɪd] unglücklich,
Unglücks...; **~fa·vo(u)red** häßlich;
~hu·mo(u)red schlechtgelaunt.
il·lib·e·ral □ [ɪ'lɪbərəl] engstirnig;
intolerant; knaus(e)rig.
il·li·cit □ [ɪ'lɪsɪt] unerlaubt.
il·lit·e·rate [ɪ'lɪtərət] **1.** □ unwissend,
ungebildet; **2.** Analphabet(in).
ill·judged ['ɪl'dʒʌdʒd] unbesonnen,
unklug; **~man·nered** ungezogen,
mit schlechten Umgangsformen;
~na·tured □ boshaft, bösartig.
ill·ness ['ɪlnɪs] Krankheit *f*.
il·lo·gi·cal □ [ɪ'lɒdʒɪkl] unlogisch.
ill·tem·pered ['ɪl'tempəd] schlechtgelaunt, übellaunig; **~timed** ungelegen, unpassend, zur unrechten
Zeit.
il·lu·mi·nate [ɪ'ljuːmɪneɪt] be-, erleuchten (*a. fig.*); *fig.* erläutern, erklären; **~nat·ing** [~ɪŋ] Leucht...;
fig. aufschlußreich; **~na·tion** [ɪljuːmɪ'neɪʃn] Er-, Beleuchtung *f*; *fig.*
Erläuterung *f*, Erklärung *f*; **~s** *pl.*
Illumination *f*, Festbeleuchtung *f*.
ill·use ['ɪl'juːz] mißhandeln.

il·lu·sion [ɪ'luːʒn] Illusion *f*, Täuschung *f*; **~·sive** [~sɪv], **~·so·ry** □ [~ərɪ] illusorisch, trügerisch.

il·lus·trate ['ɪləstreɪt] illustrieren, bebildern; erläutern; **~·tra·tion** [ɪlə-'streɪʃn] Erläuterung *f*; Illustration *f*; Bild *n*, Abbildung *f*; **~·tra·tive** □ ['ɪləstrətɪv] erläuternd.

ill will ['ɪl'wɪl] Feindschaft *f*.

im·age ['ɪmɪdʒ] Bild *n*; Statue *f*; Götzenbild *n*; Ebenbild *n*; Image *n*; **im·ag·e·ry** [~ərɪ] Bilder *pl.*; Bildersprache *f*, Metaphorik *f*.

i·ma·gi·na·ble □ [ɪ'mædʒɪnəbl] denkbar; **~·ry** [~ərɪ] eingebildet, imaginär; **~·tion** [ɪmædʒɪ'neɪʃn] Einbildung(skraft) *f*; **~·tive** □ [ɪ'mædʒɪnətɪv] ideen-, einfallsreich; **i·ma·gine** [ɪ'mædʒɪn] sich *et*. einbilden *od.* vorstellen *od.* denken.

im·bal·ance [ɪm'bæləns] Unausgewogenheit *f*; *pol. etc.* Ungleichgewicht *n*.

im·be·cile □ ['ɪmbɪsiːl] 1. schwachsinnig; 2. Schwachsinnige(r *m*) *f*; *contp.* Idiot *m*, Trottel *m*.

im·bibe [ɪm'baɪb] trinken; *fig.* sich zu eigen machen.

im·bue *fig.* [ɪm'bjuː] durchdringen, erfüllen (*with* mit).

im·i·tate ['ɪmɪteɪt] nachahmen, imitieren; **~·ta·tion** [ɪmɪ'teɪʃn] 1. Nachahmung *f*; Imitation *f*; 2. nachgemacht, unecht, künstlich, Kunst...

im·mac·u·late □ [ɪ'mækjʊlət] unbefleckt, rein; fehlerlos.

im·ma·te·ri·al □ [ɪmə'tɪərɪəl] unkörperlich; unwesentlich (*to* für).

im·ma·ture □ [ɪmə'tjʊə] unreif.

im·mea·su·ra·ble □ [ɪ'meʒərəbl] unermeßlich.

im·me·di·ate □ [ɪ'miːdjət] unmittelbar; unverzüglich, sofortig; **~·ly** [~lɪ] 1. *adv.* sofort; 2. *cj.* sobald; sofort, als.

im·mense □ [ɪ'mens] riesig; *fig. a.* enorm, immens; prima, großartig.

im·merse [ɪ'mɜːs] (ein-, unter)tauchen; *fig.* versenken *od.* vertiefen (*in* in *acc.*); **im·mer·sion** [~ʃn] Ein-, Untertauchen *n*; **~ heater** Tauchsieder *m*.

im·mi·grant ['ɪmɪgrənt] Einwander|er *m*, -in *f*, Immigrant(in); **~·grate** [~greɪt] *v/i.* einwandern; *v/t.* ansiedeln (*into* in *dat.*); **~·gra·tion**

[ɪmɪ'greɪʃn] Einwanderung *f*, Immigration *f*.

im·mi·nent □ ['ɪmɪnənt] nahe bevorstehend; **~** *danger* drohende Gefahr.

im·mo·bile [ɪ'məʊbaɪl] unbeweglich.

im·mod·e·rate □ [ɪ'mɒdərət] maßlos.

im·mod·est □ [ɪ'mɒdɪst] unbescheiden; unanständig.

im·mor·al □ [ɪ'mɒrəl] unmoralisch.

im·mor·tal [ɪ'mɔːtl] 1. □ unsterblich; 2. Unsterbliche(r *m*) *f*; **~·i·ty** [ɪmɔː'tælətɪ] Unsterblichkeit *f*.

im·mo·va·ble [ɪ'muːvəbl] 1. □ unbeweglich; unerschütterlich; unnachgiebig; 2. **~s** *pl.* Immobilien *pl.*

im·mune [ɪ'mjuːn] (*against, from, to*) immun (gegen); geschützt (gegen), frei (von); **im·mu·ni·ty** [~tɪ] Immunität *f*; Unempfindlichkeit *f*.

im·mu·ta·ble □ [ɪ'mjuːtəbl] unveränderlich.

imp [ɪmp] Teufelchen *n*; Racker *m*.

im·pact ['ɪmpækt] (Zusammen)Stoß *m*; Anprall *m*; Einwirkung *f*.

im·pair [ɪm'peə] beeinträchtigen.

im·part [ɪm'pɑːt] (*to dat.*) geben; mitteilen; vermitteln.

im·par·tial □ [ɪm'pɑːʃl] unparteiisch; **~·ti·al·i·ty** [ɪmpɑːʃɪ'ælətɪ] Unparteilichkeit *f*, Objektivität *f*.

im·pass·a·ble □ [ɪm'pɑːsəbl] unpassierbar.

im·passe [æm'pɑːs] Sackgasse *f* (*a. fig.*); *fig.* toter Punkt.

im·pas·sioned [ɪm'pæʃnd] leidenschaftlich.

im·pas·sive □ [ɪm'pæsɪv] teilnahmslos; unbewegt (*Gesicht*).

im·pa·tience [ɪm'peɪʃns] Ungeduld *f*; **~·tient** □ [~t] ungeduldig.

im·peach [ɪm'piːtʃ] anklagen (*for, of, with gen.*); anfechten, anzweifeln.

im·pec·ca·ble □ [ɪm'pekəbl] sünd(en)los; untadelig, einwandfrei.

im·pede [ɪm'piːd] (be)hindern.

im·ped·i·ment [ɪm'pedɪmənt] Hindernis *n*.

im·pel [ɪm'pel] (-*ll*-) (an)treiben.

im·pend·ing [ɪm'pendɪŋ] nahe bevorstehend; **~** *danger* drohende Gefahr.

im·pen·e·tra·ble □ [ɪm'penɪtrəbl] undurchdringlich; *fig.* unergründlich; *fig.* unzugänglich (*to dat.*).

im·per·a·tive [ɪmˈperətɪv] **1.** □ notwendig, dringend, unbedingt erforderlich; befehlend; gebieterisch; *gr.* imperativisch; **2.** Befehl *m*; *a.* ~ *mood gr.* Imperativ *m*, Befehlsform *f*.

im·per·cep·ti·ble □ [ɪmpəˈseptəbl] unmerklich.

im·per·fect [ɪmˈpɜːfɪkt] **1.** □ unvollkommen; unvollendet; **2.** *a.* ~ *tense gr.* Imperfekt *n*.

im·pe·ri·al·is·m *pol.* [ɪmˈpɪərɪəlɪzəm] Imperialismus *m*; ~**t** *pol.* [~ɪst] Imperialist *m*.

im·per·il [ɪmˈperəl] (*bsd. Brt.* -ll-, *Am.* -l-) gefährden.

im·pe·ri·ous □ [ɪmˈpɪərɪəs] herrisch, gebieterisch; dringend.

im·per·me·a·ble □ [ɪmˈpɜːmjəbl] undurchlässig.

im·per·son·al □ [ɪmˈpɜːsnl] unpersönlich.

im·per·so·nate [ɪmˈpɜːsəneɪt] *thea. etc.* verkörpern, darstellen.

im·per·ti|nence [ɪmˈpɜːtɪnəns] Unverschämtheit *f*, Ungehörigkeit *f*, Frechheit *f*; ~**nent** □ [~t] unverschämt, ungehörig, frech.

im·per·turb·a·ble □ [ɪmpəˈtɜːbəbl] unerschütterlich, gelassen.

im·per·vi·ous □ [ɪmˈpɜːvjəs] unzugänglich (*to* für); undurchlässig.

im·pe·tu·ous □ [ɪmˈpetjʊəs] ungestüm, heftig, impulsiv.

im·pe·tus [ˈɪmpɪtəs] Antrieb *m*, Schwung *m*.

im·pi·e·ty [ɪmˈpaɪətɪ] Gottlosigkeit *f*; Respektlosigkeit *f*.

im·pinge [ɪmˈpɪndʒ]: ~ *on*, ~ *upon* sich auswirken auf (*acc.*), beeinflussen (*acc.*).

im·pi·ous □ [ˈɪmpɪəs] gottlos; pietätlos; respektlos.

im·plac·a·ble □ [ɪmˈplækəbl] unversöhnlich, unnachgiebig.

im·plant [ɪmˈplɑːnt] ♣ einpflanzen; *fig.* einprägen.

im·ple|ment 1. [ˈɪmplɪmənt] Werkzeug *n*; Gerät *n*; **2.** [~ment] ausführen.

im·pli|cate [ˈɪmplɪkeɪt] verwickeln; zur Folge haben; ~**ca·tion** [ɪmplɪˈkeɪʃn] Verwick(e)lung *f*; Implikation *f*, Einbeziehung *f*; Folgerung *f*.

im·pli·cit □ [ɪmˈplɪsɪt] unausgesprochen; bedingungslos, blind (*Glaube etc.*).

im·plore [ɪmˈplɔː] inständig bitten, anflehen; (er)flehen.

im·ply [ɪmˈplaɪ] implizieren, (mit) einbegreifen; bedeuten; andeuten.

im·po·lite □ [ɪmpəˈlaɪt] unhöflich.

im·pol·i·tic □ [ɪmˈpɒlɪtɪk] unklug.

im·port 1. [ˈɪmpɔːt] *econ.* Import *m*, Einfuhr *f*; *econ.* Import-, Einfuhrartikel *m*; Bedeutung *f*; Wichtigkeit *f*; ~**s** *pl. econ.* (Gesamt)Import *m*, (-)Einfuhr *f*; Importgüter *pl.*; **2.** [ɪmˈpɔːt] *econ.* importieren, einführen; bedeuten.

im·por·tance [ɪmˈpɔːtəns] Bedeutung *f*, Wichtigkeit *f*; ~**tant** □ [~t] bedeutend, wichtig; wichtigtuerisch.

im·por·ta·tion [ɪmpɔːˈteɪʃn] *s.* import 1 *econ.*

im·por·tu|nate □ [ɪmˈpɔːtjʊnət] lästig; zudringlich; ~**tune** [ɪmˈpɔːtjuːn] dringend bitten; belästigen.

im·pose [ɪmˈpəʊz] *v/t.* auferlegen, -bürden, -drängen, -zwingen (*on, upon dat.*); *v/i.* ~ *on*, ~ *upon j-m* imponieren, *j-n* beeindrucken; *j-n* ausnutzen; sich *j-m* aufdrängen; *j-m* zur Last fallen; ~**pos·ing** □ [~ɪŋ] imponierend, eindrucksvoll, imposant.

im·pos·si·bil·i·ty [ɪmpɒsəˈbɪlətɪ] Unmöglichkeit *f*; ~**ble** [ɪmˈpɒsəbl] unmöglich.

im·pos·tor [ɪmˈpɒstə] Betrüger *m*.

im·po|tence [ˈɪmpətəns] Unfähigkeit *f*; Hilflosigkeit *f*; Schwäche *f*; ♣ Impotenz *f*; ~**tent** □ [~t] unfähig; hilflos; schwach; ♣ impotent.

im·pov·er·ish [ɪmˈpɒvərɪʃ] arm machen; *Boden* auslaugen.

im·prac·ti·ca·ble □ [ɪmˈpræktɪkəbl] unbrauchbar; unpassierbar (*Straße*).

im·prac·ti·cal □ [ɪmˈpræktɪkl] unpraktisch; theoretisch; unbrauchbar.

im·preg|na·ble □ [ɪmˈpregnəbl] uneinnehmbar; ~**nate** [ˈɪmpregneɪt] *biol.* schwängern; ♠ sättigen; ⊕ imprägnieren.

im·press [ɪmˈpres] (auf-, ein-) drücken; (deutlich) klarmachen; einschärfen; *j-n* beeindrucken; *j-n* mit *et.* erfüllen; ~**pres·sion** [~ʃn] Eindruck *m*; *print.* Abdruck *m*, Abzug *m*; Auflage *f*; *be under the* ~ *that* den Eindruck haben, daß; **im·pres·sive** □ [~sɪv] eindrucksvoll.

im·print 1. [ɪmˈprɪnt] aufdrücken, -prägen; *fig.* einprägen (*on, in dat.*); **2.** [ˈɪmprɪnt] Eindruck *m*; Stempel *m* (*a. fig.*); *print.* Impressum *n*.

im·pris·on ⚖ [ɪmˈprɪzn] inhaftieren; **~ment** ⚖ [~mənt] Freiheitsstrafe *f*, Gefängnis(strafe *f*) *n*, Haft *f*.

im·prob·a·ble □ [ɪmˈprɒbəbl] unwahrscheinlich.

im·prop·er □ [ɪmˈprɒpə] ungeeignet, unpassend; unanständig, unschicklich (*Benehmen etc.*); ungenau.

im·pro·pri·e·ty [ɪmprəˈpraɪətɪ] Unschicklichkeit *f*.

im·prove [ɪmˈpruːv] *v/t.* verbessern; veredeln, -feinern; *v/i.* sich (ver)bessern; **~ on, ~ upon** übertreffen; **~ment** [~mənt] (Ver)Besserung *f*; Fortschritt *m* (*on, upon* gegenüber *dat.*).

im·pro·vise [ˈɪmprəvaɪz] improvisieren.

im·pru·dent □ [ɪmˈpruːdənt] unklug.

im·pu·dence [ˈɪmpjʊdəns] Unverschämtheit *f*, Frechheit *f*; **~dent** □ [~t] unverschämt, frech.

im·pulse [ˈɪmpʌls] Impuls *m*, (An-)Stoß *m*; *fig.* (An)Trieb *m*; **im·pul·sive** □ [ɪmˈpʌlsɪv] (an)treibend; *fig.* impulsiv.

im·pu·ni·ty [ɪmˈpjuːnɪtɪ] Straflosigkeit *f*; *with* ~ ungestraft.

im·pure □ [ɪmˈpjʊə] unrein (*a. eccl.*), schmutzig; verfälscht; *fig.* schlecht, unmoralisch.

im·pute [ɪmˈpjuːt] zuschreiben (*to dat.*); ~ *s.th. to s.o.* j-m e-r Sache bezichtigen; j-m et. unterstellen.

in [ɪn] **1.** *prp.* in (*dat.*), innerhalb (*gen.*); an (*dat.*) (~ *the morning,* ~ *number,* ~ *itself, professor* ~ *the university*); auf (*dat.*) (~ *the street,* ~ *English*); auf (*acc.*) (~ *this manner,* ~ *English*); aus (*coat* ~ *velvet*); bei (~ *Shakespeare,* ~ *crossing the road*); mit (*engaged* ~ *reading,* ~ *a word*); nach (~ *my opinion*); über (*acc.*) (*rejoice* ~ *s.th.*); unter (*dat.*) (~ *the circumstances,* ~ *the reign of, one* ~ *ten*); vor (*dat.*) (*cry out* ~ *alarm*); zu (*grouped* ~ *tens,* ~ *excuse,* ~ *honour of*); ~ *1989 1989;* ~ *that* ... insofern als, weil; **2.** *adv.* innen, drinnen; herein; hinein; in, in Mode; *be* ~ *et.* zu erwarten haben; *e-e Prüfung etc.* vor sich haben; *be* ~ *with* gut mit

j-m stehen; **3.** *adj.* hereinkommend; Innen...

in·a·bil·i·ty [ɪnəˈbɪlətɪ] Unfähigkeit *f*.

in·ac·ces·si·ble □ [ɪnækˈsesəbl] unzugänglich, unerreichbar (*to* für *od. dat.*).

in·ac·cu·rate □ [ɪnˈækjʊrət] ungenau; unrichtig.

in·ac·tive □ [ɪnˈæktɪv] untätig; *econ.* lustlos, flau; 🜛 unwirksam; **~tiv·i·ty** [ɪnækˈtɪvɪtɪ] Untätigkeit *f*; *econ.* Lustlosigkeit *f*, Flauheit *f*; 🜛 Unwirksamkeit *f*.

in·ad·e·quate □ [ɪnˈædɪkwət] unangemessen; unzulänglich, ungenügend.

in·ad·mis·si·ble □ [ɪnədˈmɪsəbl] unzulässig, unerlaubt.

in·ad·ver·tent □ [ɪnədˈvɜːtənt] unachtsam; unbeabsichtigt, versehentlich.

in·a·li·en·a·ble □ [ɪnˈeɪljənəbl] unveräußerlich.

i·nane □ *fig.* [ɪˈneɪn] leer; albern.

in·an·i·mate □ [ɪnˈænɪmət] leblos; unbelebt (*Natur*); geistlos, langweilig.

in·ap·pro·pri·ate □ [ɪnəˈprəʊprɪət] unpassend, ungeeignet.

in·apt □ [ɪnˈæpt] ungeeignet, unpassend.

in·ar·tic·u·late □ [ɪnɑːˈtɪkjʊlət] unartikuliert, undeutlich (ausgesprochen), unverständlich; unfähig (, deutlich) zu sprechen.

in·as·much [ɪnəzˈmʌtʃ]: ~ *as* insofern als.

in·at·ten·tive □ [ɪnəˈtentɪv] unaufmerksam.

in·au·di·ble □ [ɪnˈɔːdəbl] unhörbar.

in·au·gu·ral [ɪˈnɔːgjʊrəl] Antrittsrede *f*; *attr.* Antritts...; **~rate** [~reɪt] (feierlich) einführen; einweihen; einleiten; **~ra·tion** [ɪnɔːgjʊˈreɪʃn] Amtseinführung *f*; Einweihung *f*; Beginn *m*; ♀ *Day Am.* Tag *m* der Amtseinführung des neugewählten Präsidenten der USA (*20. Januar*).

in·born [ɪnˈbɔːn] angeboren.

in·built [ˈɪnbɪlt] eingebaut, Einbau...

in·cal·cu·la·ble □ [ɪnˈkælkjʊləbl] unberechenbar.

in·can·des·cent □ [ɪnkænˈdesnt] (weiß)glühend.

in·ca·pa·ble □ [ɪnˈkeɪpəbl] unfähig, nicht imstande (*of doing* zu tun); hilflos.

in·ca·pa·ci|tate [ɪnkə'pæsɪteɪt] unfähig machen; **~ty** [~sətɪ] Unfähigkeit f.

in·car·nate [ɪn'kɑːnət] eccl. fleischgeworden; fig. verkörpert.

in·cau·tious □ [ɪn'kɔːʃəs] unvorsichtig.

in·cen·di·a·ry [ɪn'sendjərɪ] 1. Brand...; fig. aufwiegelnd, -hetzend; 2. Brandstifter m; Aufwiegler m.

in·cense¹ ['ɪnsens] Weihrauch m.

in·cense² [ɪn'sens] in Wut bringen.

in·cen·tive [ɪn'sentɪv] Ansporn m, Antrieb m.

in·ces·sant □ [ɪn'sesnt] unaufhörlich.

in·cest ['ɪnsest] Inzest m, Blutschande f.

inch [ɪntʃ] 1. Inch m (= 2,54 cm), Zoll m (a. fig.); by ~es allmählich; every ~ durch u. durch; 2. (sich) zentimeterweise od. sehr langsam bewegen.

in·ci|dence ['ɪnsɪdəns] Vorkommen n; **~dent** [~t] Vorfall m, Ereignis n, Vorkommnis n; **~den·tal** □ [ɪnsɪ'dentl] zufällig; gelegentlich; Neben...; beiläufig; ~ly nebenbei.

in·cin·e|rate [ɪn'sɪnəreɪt] verbrennen; **~ra·tor** [~ə] Verbrennungsofen m; Verbrennungsanlage f.

in·cise [ɪn'saɪz] ein-, aufschneiden; einritzen, -schnitzen; **in·ci·sion** [ɪn'sɪʒn] (Ein)Schnitt m; **in·ci·sive** □ [ɪn'saɪsɪv] (ein)schneidend; scharf; **in·ci·sor** [~aɪzə] anat. Schneidezahn m.

in·cite [ɪn'saɪt] anspornen, anregen; anstiften; **~ment** [~mənt] Anregung f; Ansporn m; Anstiftung f.

in·clem·ent □ [ɪn'klemənt] rauh (Klima).

in·cli·na·tion [ɪnklɪ'neɪʃn] Neigung f (a. fig.); **in·cline** [ɪn'klaɪn] 1. v/i. sich neigen, (schräg) abfallen; ~ to fig. zu et. neigen; v/t. neigen; geneigt machen; 2. Gefälle n; (Ab)Hang m.

in·close [ɪn'kləʊz], **in·clos·ure** [~əʊ-ʒə] s. enclose, enclosure.

in·clude [ɪn'kluːd] einschließen; enthalten; **in·clud·ed** eingeschlossen; mit inbegriffen; tax ~ inklusive Steuer; **in·clud·ing** einschließlich; **in·clu·sion** [~ʒn] Einschluß m, Einbeziehung f; **in·clu·sive** □ [~sɪv] einschließlich, inklusive (of gen.); be ~ of einschließen (acc.); ~ terms pl. Pauschalpreis m.

in·co·her|ence [ɪnkəʊ'hɪərəns] Zu-

sammenhang(s)losigkeit f; **~ent** □ [~t] (logisch) unzusammenhängend, unklar, unverständlich.

in·come econ. ['ɪnkʌm] Einkommen n, Einkünfte pl.; ~ tax econ. Einkommensteuer f.

in·com·ing ['ɪnkʌmɪŋ] hereinkommend; ankommend; nachfolgend, neu; ~ orders pl. econ. Auftragseingänge pl.

in·com·mu·ni·ca·tive □ [ɪnkə'mjuː-nɪkətɪv] nicht mitteilsam, verschlossen.

in·com·pa·ra·ble □ [ɪn'kɒmpərəbl] unvergleichlich.

in·com·pat·i·ble □ [ɪnkəm'pætəbl] unvereinbar; unverträglich.

in·com·pe|tence [ɪn'kɒmpɪtəns] Unfähigkeit f; Inkompetenz f; **~tent** □ [~t] unfähig; nicht fach- od. sachkundig; unzuständig, inkompetent.

in·com·plete □ [ɪnkəm'pliːt] unvollständig; unvollkommen.

in·com·pre·hen·si·ble □ [ɪnkɒm-prɪ'hensəbl] unbegreiflich, unfaßbar; **~sion** [~ʃn] Unverständnis n.

in·con·cei·va·ble □ [ɪnkən'siːvəbl] unbegreiflich, unfaßbar; undenkbar.

in·con·clu·sive □ [ɪnkən'kluːsɪv] nicht überzeugend; ergebnis-, erfolglos.

in·con·gru·ous □ [ɪn'kɒŋgrʊəs] nicht übereinstimmend; nicht passend.

in·con·se|quent □ [ɪn'kɒnsɪkwənt] inkonsequent, folgewidrig; **~quen·tial** □ [ɪnkɒnsɪ'kwenʃl] unbedeutend.

in·con·sid·e·ra·ble □ [ɪnkən'sɪdə-rəbl] unbedeutend; **~er·ate** □ [~rət] unüberlegt; rücksichtslos.

in·con·sis|ten·cy [ɪnkən'sɪstənsɪ] Unvereinbarkeit f; Inkonsequenz f; **~tent** □ [~t] unvereinbar; widersprüchlich; unbeständig; inkonsequent.

in·con·so·la·ble □ [ɪnkən'səʊləbl] untröstlich.

in·con·spic·u·ous □ [ɪnkən'spɪk-jʊəs] unauffällig.

in·con·stant □ [ɪn'kɒnstənt] unbeständig, veränderlich.

in·con·ti·nent □ [ɪn'kɒntɪnənt] zügellos; ✗ inkontinent.

in·con·ve·ni·ence [ɪnkən'viːnjəns] 1. Unbequemlichkeit f; Unannehmlichkeit f; 2. belästigen, stören;

~·ent □ [~t] unbequem; ungelegen, lästig.

in·cor·po·rate [ɪn'kɔːpəreɪt] (sich) verbinden od. -vereinigen od. zusammenschließen; *Idee etc.* einverleiben; aufnehmen, eingliedern, inkorporieren; *econ.*, 🏛 als Gesellschaft eintragen (lassen); **~·rat·ed** *econ.*, 🏛 als (*Am.* Aktien)Gesellschaft eingetragen; **~·ra·tion** [ɪnkɔː-pə'reɪʃn] Vereinigung *f*, -bindung *f*, Zusammenschluß *m*; Eingliederung *f*; *econ.*, 🏛 Eintragung *f* als (*Am.* Aktien)Gesellschaft.

in·cor·rect [ɪnkə'rekt] unrichtig, falsch; inkorrekt.

in·cor·ri·gi·ble □ [ɪn'kɒrɪdʒəbl] un-verbesserlich.

in·cor·rup·ti·ble □ [ɪnkə'rʌptəbl] unbestechlich; unvergänglich.

in·crease 1. [ɪn'kriːs] zunehmen, (an)wachsen, (an)steigen, (sich) vergrößern od. -mehren od. erhöhen od. steigern od. verstärken; **2.** ['ɪnkriːs] Zunahme *f*, Vergrößerung *f*; (An-)Wachsen *n*, Steigen *n*, Steigerung *f*; Zuwachs *m*; **in·creas·ing·ly** [ɪn-'kriːsɪŋlɪ] zunehmend, immer mehr; *~ difficult* immer schwieriger.

in·cred·i·ble □ [ɪn'kredəbl] unglaublich, unglaubhaft.

in·cre·du·li·ty [ɪnkrɪ'djuːlətɪ] Un-gläubigkeit *f*; **in·cred·u·lous** □ [ɪn-'kredjʊləs] ungläubig, skeptisch.

in·crim·i·nate [ɪn'krɪmɪneɪt] be-schuldigen; *j-n* belasten.

in·cu·bate ['ɪnkjʊbeɪt] ausbrüten; **~·ba·tor** [~ə] Brutapparat *m*; Brut-kasten *m*.

in·cum·bent □ [ɪn'kʌmbənt] obliegend; *it is ~ on her* es ist ihre Pflicht.

in·cur [ɪn'kɜː] (-*rr*-) sich *et.* zuziehen, auf sich laden, geraten in (*acc.*); *Schulden* machen; *Verpflichtung* ein-gehen; *Verlust* erleiden.

in·cu·ra·ble □ [ɪn'kjʊərəbl] unheil-bar.

in·cu·ri·ous □ [ɪn'kjʊərɪəs] nicht neugierig, gleichgültig, uninteres-siert.

in·cur·sion [ɪn'kɜːʃn] (feindlicher) Einfall; plötzlicher Angriff; Ein-dringen *n*.

in·debt·ed [ɪn'detɪd] *econ.* verschul-det; *fig.* (zu Dank) verpflichtet.

in·de·cent [ɪn'diːsnt] unanständig, anstößig; 🏛 unsittlich, unzüchtig; *~ assault* 🏛 Sittlichkeitsverbrechen *n*.

in·de·ci·sion [ɪndɪ'sɪʒn] Unent-schlossenheit *f*; **~·sive** □ [~'saɪsɪv] unbestimmt, ungewiß; unentschlos-sen, unschlüssig.

in·deed [ɪn'diːd] **1.** *adv.* in der Tat, tatsächlich, wirklich; allerdings; *thank you very much ~!* vielen herz-lichen Dank!; **2.** *int.* ach wirklich!

in·de·fat·i·ga·ble □ [ɪndɪ'fætɪgəbl] unermüdlich.

in·de·fen·si·ble □ [ɪndɪ'fensəbl] un-haltbar.

in·de·fi·na·ble □ [ɪndɪ'faɪnəbl] un-definierbar, unbestimmbar.

in·def·i·nite □ [ɪn'defɪnət] unbe-stimmt; unbegrenzt; unklar.

in·del·i·ble □ [ɪn'delɪbl] unauslösch-lich, untilgbar; *fig.* unvergeßlich; *~ pencil* Kopier-, Tintenstift *m*.

in·del·i·cate □ [ɪn'delɪkət] unfein, derb; taktlos.

in·dem·ni·fy [ɪn'demnɪfaɪ] *j-n* ent-schädigen (*for* für); versichern; 🏛 *j-m* Straflosigkeit zusichern; **~·ty** [~ətɪ] Schadenersatz *m*, Entschädi-gung *f*, Abfindung *f*; Versicherung *f*; 🏛 Straflosigkeit *f*.

in·dent [ɪn'dent] einkerben, aus-zacken; *print.* Zeile einrücken; 🏛 *Vertrag* mit Doppel ausfertigen; *~ on s.o. for s.th. bsd. Brt. econ.* et. bei j-m bestellen.

in·den·tures *econ.*, 🏛 [ɪn'dentʃəz] *pl.* Ausbildungs-, Lehrvertrag *m*.

in·de·pen·dence [ɪndɪ'pendəns] Un-abhängigkeit *f*; Selbständigkeit *f*; Auskommen *n*; ♀ *Day Am.* Unab-hängigkeitstag *m* (*4. Juli*); **~·dent** □ [~t] unabhängig; selbständig.

in·de·scri·ba·ble □ [ɪndɪ'skraɪbəbl] unbeschreiblich.

in·de·struc·ti·ble □ [ɪndɪ'strʌktəbl] unzerstörbar; unverwüstlich.

in·de·ter·mi·nate □ [ɪndɪ'tɜːmɪnət] unbestimmt; unklar, vage.

in·dex ['ɪndeks] **1.** (*pl.* -*dexes*, -*dices* [-dɪsiːz]) (Inhalts-, Namens-, Sach-, Stichwort)Verzeichnis *n*, Register *n*, Index *m*; Index-, Meßziffer *f*; ⊕ Zeiger *m*; Anzeichen *n*; *cost of living ~* Lebenshaltungskosten-Index *m*; **2.** mit e-m Inhaltsverzeichnis verse-hen; in ein Verzeichnis aufnehmen; **~ card** Karteikarte *f*; **~ fin·ger** Zei-gefinger *m*.

In·di·an ['ɪndjən] **1.** indisch; india-nisch, Indianer...; **2.** Inder(in); *a. American ~*, *Red ~* Indianer(in);

~ corn 🌿 Mais *m*; **~ file:** *in ~* im Gänsemarsch; **~ pud·ding** Maismehlpudding *m*; **~ sum·mer** Altweiber-, Nachsommer *m*.

In·dia rub·ber, in·dia-rub·ber ['ɪndjə'rʌbə] Radiergummi *m*; *attr.* Gummi...

in·di·cate ['ɪndɪkeɪt] (an)zeigen; hinweisen *od.* -deuten auf (*acc.*); andeuten; *mot.* blinken; **~·ca·tion** [ˌɪndɪ'keɪʃn] (An)Zeichen *n*, Hinweis *m*, Andeutung *f*; **in·dic·a·tive** [ɪn'dɪkətɪv] *a.* ~ *mood gr.* Indikativ *m*; **~·ca·tor** ['ɪndɪkeɪtə] (An)Zeiger *m*; *mot.* Richtungsanzeiger *m*, Blinker *m*.

in·di·ces ['ɪndɪsiːz] *pl. von* index.

in·dict ⚖ [ɪn'daɪt] anklagen (*for wegen*); **~·ment** ⚖ [ˌ~mənt] Anklage *f*.

in·dif·fer·ence [ɪn'dɪfrəns] Gleichgültigkeit *f*, Interesselosigkeit *f*; **~·ent** □ [ˌ~t] gleichgültig (*to gegen*), interesselos (*to gegenüber*); durchschnittlich, mittelmäßig.

in·di·gent ['ɪndɪdʒənt] arm.

in·di·ges|ti·ble □ [ɪndɪ'dʒestəbl] unverdaulich; **~·tion** [ˌ~tʃən] Verdauungsstörung *f*, Magenverstimmung *f*.

in·dig|nant □ [ɪn'dɪgnənt] entrüstet, empört, ungehalten (*at, over, about* über *acc.*); **~·na·tion** [ɪndɪg'neɪʃn] Entrüstung *f*, Empörung *f* (*at, over, about* über *acc.*); **~·ni·ty** [ɪn'dɪgnətɪ] Demütigung *f*, unwürdige Behandlung.

in·di·rect □ [ɪndɪ'rekt] indirekt (*a. gr.*); *by ~ means* auf Umwegen.

in·dis|creet □ [ɪndɪ'skriːt] unbesonnen; taktlos; indiskret; **~·cre·tion** [ˌ~reʃn] Unbesonnenheit *f*; Taktlosigkeit *f*; Indiskretion *f*.

in·dis·crim·i·nate □ [ɪndɪ'skrɪmɪnət] unterschieds-, wahllos; willkürlich.

in·dis·pen·sa·ble □ [ɪndɪ'spensəbl] unentbehrlich, unerläßlich.

in·dis|posed [ɪndɪ'spəʊzd] indisponiert; unpäßlich; abgeneigt; **~·po·si·tion** [ɪndɪspə'zɪʃn] Abneigung *f* (*to gegen*); Unpäßlichkeit *f*.

in·dis·pu·ta·ble □ [ɪndɪ'spjuːtəbl] unbestreitbar, unstreitig.

in·dis·tinct □ [ɪndɪ'stɪŋkt] undeutlich; unklar, verschwommen.

in·dis·tin·guish·a·ble □ [ɪndɪ'stɪŋgwɪʃəbl] nicht zu unterscheiden(d).

in·di·vid·u·al [ɪndɪ'vɪdjʊəl] **1.** □ persönlich; individuell; besondere(r, -s); einzeln, Einzel...; **2.** Individuum *n*, Einzelne(r *m*) *f*; **~·is·m** [ˌ~ɪzəm] Individualismus *m*; **~·ist** [ˌ~ɪst] Individualist(in); **~·i·ty** [ɪndɪvɪdjʊ'ælɪtɪ] Individualität *f*, (persönliche) Note; **~·ly** [ɪndɪ'vɪdjʊəlɪ] einzeln, jede(r, -s) für sich.

in·di·vis·i·ble □ [ɪndɪ'vɪzəbl] unteilbar.

in·do·lent □ ['ɪndələnt] träge, faul, arbeitsscheu; 🕮 schmerzlos.

in·dom·i·ta·ble □ [ɪn'dɒmɪtəbl] unbezähmbar, nicht unterzukriegen(d).

in·door ['ɪndɔː] zu *od.* im Hause (befindlich), Haus..., Zimmer..., Innen..., *Sport:* Hallen...; **~s** ['ɪn'dɔːz] zu *od.* im Hause; im *od.* ins Haus.

in·dorse [ɪn'dɔːs] = *endorse etc.*

in·duce [ɪn'djuːs] veranlassen; hervorrufen, bewirken; **~·ment** [ˌ~mənt] Anlaß *m*; Anreiz *m*, Ansporn *m*.

in·duct [ɪn'dʌkt] einführen, -setzen; **in·duc·tion** [ˌ~kʃn] Einführung *f*, Einsetzung *f* (*in Amt, Pfründe*); ⚡ Induktion *f*.

in·dulge [ɪn'dʌldʒ] nachsichtig sein gegen, gewähren lassen, *j-m* nachgeben; ~ *in s.th.* sich et. gönnen *od.* leisten; **in·dul·gence** [ˌ~əns] Nachsicht *f*, Nachgiebigkeit *f*; Schwäche *f*, Leidenschaft *f*; **in·dul·gent** □ [ˌ~nt] nachsichtig, -giebig.

in·dus·tri·al □ [ɪn'dʌstrɪəl] industriell, Industrie..., Gewerbe..., Betriebs...; ~ *area* Industriegebiet *n*; **~·ist** *econ.* [ˌ~əlɪst] Industrielle(r *m*) *f*; **~·ize** *econ.* [ˌ~əlaɪz] industrialisieren. △ *nicht* Industrie...

in·dus·tri·ous □ [ɪn'dʌstrɪəs] fleißig; △ *nicht* Industrie...

in·dus·try ['ɪndʌstrɪ] *econ.* Industrie (-zweig *m*) *f*; Gewerbe(zweig *m*) *n*; Fleiß *m*.

in·ed·i·ble □ [ɪn'edɪbl] ungenießbar, nicht eßbar.

in·ef·fa·ble □ [ɪn'efəbl] unaussprechlich, unbeschreiblich.

in·ef·fec|tive □ [ɪnɪ'fektɪv], **~·tu·al** □ [ˌ~tʃʊəl] unwirksam, wirkungslos; untauglich.

in·ef·fi·cient □ [ɪnɪ'fɪʃnt] unfähig, untauglich; leistungsschwach, unproduktiv.

in·el·e·gant □ [ɪn'elɪgənt] unelegant; schwerfällig.

in·el·i·gi·ble □ [ɪn'elɪdʒəbl] nicht

wählbar; ungeeignet; nicht berechtigt; *bsd.* ✗ untauglich.

in·ept □ [ɪˈnept] unpassend; ungeschickt; albern, töricht.

in·e·qual·i·ty [ɪnɪˈkwɒlətɪ] Ungleichheit *f*.

in·ert □ [ɪˈnɜːt] *phys.* träge (*a. fig.*); ⚗ inaktiv; **in·er·tia** [ɪˈnɜːʃjə] Trägheit *f* (*a. fig.*).

in·es·ca·pa·ble □ [ɪnɪˈskeɪpəbl] unvermeidlich.

in·es·sen·tial □ [ɪnɪˈsenʃl] unwesentlich, unwichtig (*to* für).

in·es·ti·ma·ble □ [ɪnˈestɪməbl] unschätzbar.

in·ev·i·ta·ble □ [ɪnˈevɪtəbl] unvermeidlich; zwangsläufig.

in·ex·act □ [ɪnɪɡˈzækt] ungenau.

in·ex·cu·sa·ble □ [ɪnɪˈskjuːzəbl] unverzeihlich, unentschuldbar.

in·ex·haus·ti·ble □ [ɪnɪɡˈzɔːstəbl] unerschöpflich; unermüdlich.

in·ex·o·ra·ble □ [ɪnˈeksərəbl] unerbittlich.

in·ex·pe·di·ent □ [ɪnɪkˈspiːdjənt] unzweckmäßig; nicht ratsam.

in·ex·pen·sive □ [ɪnɪkˈspensɪv] nicht teuer, billig, preiswert.

in·ex·pe·ri·ence [ɪnɪkˈspɪərɪəns] Unerfahrenheit *f*; **~d** unerfahren.

in·ex·pert □ [ɪnˈekspɜːt] unerfahren; ungeschickt.

in·ex·plic·a·ble □ [ɪnɪkˈsplɪkəbl] unerklärlich.

in·ex·pres·si·ble □ [ɪnɪkˈspresəbl] unaussprechlich, unbeschreiblich; **~ve** [~sɪv] ausdruckslos.

in·ex·tri·ca·ble □ [ɪnˈekstrɪkəbl] unentwirrbar.

in·fal·li·ble □ [ɪnˈfæləbl] unfehlbar.

in·fa|mous □ [ˈɪnfəməs] berüchtigt; schändlich, niederträchtig; **~my** [~ɪ] Ehrlosigkeit *f*; Schande *f*; Niedertracht *f*.

in·fan|cy [ˈɪnfənsɪ] frühe Kindheit; ⚤ Minderjährigkeit *f*; *in its* ~ *fig.* in den Anfängen *od.* Kinderschuhen steckend; **~t** [~t] Säugling *m*; Kleinkind *n*; ⚤ Minderjährige(r *m*) *f*.

in·fan·tile [ˈɪnfəntaɪl] kindlich; Kindes..., Kinder...; infantil, kindisch.

in·fan·try ✗ [ˈɪnfəntrɪ] Infanterie *f*.

in·fat·u·at·ed [ɪnˈfætjʊeɪtɪd] vernarrt (*with* in *acc.*).

in·fect [ɪnˈfekt] ✱ *j-n, et.* infizieren, *j-n* anstecken (*a. fig.*); verseuchen, -unreinigen; **in·fec·tion** [~kʃn] ✱ Infektion *f*, Ansteckung *f* (*a. fig.*);

in·fec·tious □ [~kʃəs] ✱ infektiös, ansteckend (*a. fig.*).

in·fer [ɪnˈfɜː] (*-rr-*) folgern, schließen (*from* aus); **~ence** [ˈɪnfərəns] (Schluß)Folgerung *f*.

in·fe·ri·or [ɪnˈfɪərɪə] **1.** (*to*) untergeordnet (*dat.*), (*im Rang*) tieferstehend, niedriger, geringer (als); minderwertig; *be* ~ *to s.o.* j-m untergeordnet sein; j-m unterlegen sein; **2.** Untergebene(r *m*) *f*; **~·i·ty** [ɪnfɪərɪˈɒrətɪ] Unterlegenheit *f*; geringerer Wert *od.* Stand, Minderwertigkeit *f*; ~ *complex psych.* Minderwertigkeitskomplex *m*.

in·fer|nal □ [ɪnˈfɜːnl] höllisch, Höllen...; **~no** [~əʊ] (*pl. -nos*) Inferno *n*, Hölle *f*.

in·fer·tile [ɪnˈfɜːtaɪl] unfruchtbar.

in·fest [ɪnˈfest] heimsuchen; verseuchen, befallen; *fig.* überschwemmen (*with* mit).

in·fi·del·i·ty [ɪnfɪˈdelətɪ] (*bsd.* eheliche) Untreue.

in·fil·trate [ˈɪnfɪltreɪt] *v/t.* eindringen in (*acc.*); einsickern in (*acc.*), durchdringen; *pol.* unterwandern; *pol.* einschleusen; *v/i.* eindringen (*into* in *acc.*); *pol.* unterwandern (*into acc.*), sich einschleusen (*into* in *acc.*).

in·fi·nite □ [ˈɪnfɪnət] unendlich.

in·fin·i·tive [ɪnˈfɪnɪtɪv] *a.* ~ *mood gr.* Infinitiv *m*, Nennform *f*.

in·fin·i·ty [ɪnˈfɪnətɪ] Unendlichkeit *f*.

in·firm □ [ɪnˈfɜːm] schwach; gebrechlich; **in·fir·ma·ry** [~ˈmərɪ] Krankenhaus *n*; Krankenstube *f*, -zimmer *n* (*in Internaten etc.*); **in·fir·mi·ty** [~ətɪ] Schwäche *f* (*a. fig.*); Gebrechlichkeit *f*.

in·flame [ɪnˈfleɪm] entflammen (*mst fig.*); ✱ (sich) entzünden; erregen; erzürnen.

in·flam·ma·ble [ɪnˈflæməbl] leicht entzündlich; feuergefährlich; **~tion** ✱ [ɪnfləˈmeɪʃn] Entzündung *f*; **~to·ry** [ɪnˈflæmətərɪ] ✱ entzündlich; *fig.* aufrührerisch, Hetz...

in·flate [ɪnˈfleɪt] aufpumpen, -blasen, -blähen (*a. fig.*); *econ.* Preise etc. in die Höhe treiben; **in·fla·tion** [~ʃn] Aufblähung *f*; *econ.* Inflation *f*.

in·flect *gr.* [ɪnˈflekt] flektieren, beugen; **in·flec·tion** [~kʃn] *gr.* = *inflexion*.

in·flex|i·ble □ [ɪnˈfleksəbl] unbiegsam, starr (*a. fig.*); *fig.* unbeugsam;

~ion *bsd. Brt.* [~kʃn] *gr.* Flexion *f*, Beugung *f*; ♪ Modulation *f*.

in·flict [ɪnˈflɪkt] (*on, upon*) *Leid etc.* zufügen (*dat.*); *Wunde etc.* beibringen (*dat.*); *Schlag* versetzen (*dat.*); *Strafe* verhängen (über *acc.*); aufbürden, -drängen (*dat.*); **in·flic·tion** [~kʃn] Zufügung *f*; Verhängung *f* (*e-r Strafe*); Plage *f*.

in·flu·ence [ˈɪnfluəns] **1.** Einfluß *m*; **2.** beeinflussen; **~en·tial** □ [ɪnfluˈenʃl] einflußreich.

in·flu·en·za [ɪnfluˈenzə] Grippe *f*.

in·flux [ˈɪnflʌks] Einströmen *n*; *econ.* (*Waren*)Zufuhr *f*; *fig.* (Zu)Strom *m*.

in·form [ɪnˈfɔːm] benachrichtigen, unterrichten (*of* von), informieren (*of* über *acc.*); **~** *against.* *on* od. *upon s.o.* j-n anzeigen; j-n denunzieren.

in·for·mal [ɪnˈfɔːml] formlos, zwanglos; **~·i·ty** [ɪnfɔːˈmælətɪ] Formlosigkeit *f*; Ungezwungenheit *f*.

in·for·ma·tion [ɪnfəˈmeɪʃn] Auskunft *f*; Nachricht *f*; Information *f*; **~** *storage Computer:* Datenspeicherung *f*; **~·tive** [ɪnˈfɔːmətɪv] informativ; lehrreich; mitteilsam.

in·form·er [ɪnˈfɔːmə] Denunziant(in); Spitzel *m*.

in·fre·quent □ [ɪnˈfriːkwənt] selten.

in·fringe [ɪnˈfrɪndʒ]: **~** *on,* **~** *upon Rechte, Vertrag etc.* verletzen.

in·fu·ri·ate [ɪnˈfjʊərɪeɪt] wütend machen.

in·fuse [ɪnˈfjuːz] *Tee* aufgießen; *fig.* einflößen; *fig.* erfüllen (*with* mit); **in·fu·sion** [~ʒn] Aufguß *m*, Tee *m*; Einflößen *n*; 🏥 Infusion *f*.

in·ge·ni·ous □ [ɪnˈdʒiːnjəs] genial; geist-, sinnreich; erfinderisch; raffiniert; **~·nu·i·ty** [ɪndʒɪˈnjuːɪtɪ] Genialität *f*; Einfallsreichtum *m*.

in·gen·u·ous □ [ɪnˈdʒenjuəs] offen, aufrichtig; unbefangen; naiv.

in·got [ˈɪŋgət] (*Gold- etc.*)Barren *m*.

in·gra·ti·ate [ɪnˈgreɪʃɪeɪt]: **~** *o.s. with s.o.* sich bei j-m beliebt machen.

in·grat·i·tude [ɪnˈgrætɪtjuːd] Undankbarkeit *f*.

in·gre·di·ent [ɪnˈgriːdjənt] Bestandteil *m*; *Küche:* Zutat *f*.

in·grow·ing [ˈɪngrəʊɪŋ] nach innen wachsend; eingewachsen.

in·hab·it [ɪnˈhæbɪt] bewohnen, leben in (*dat.*); **~·it·a·ble** [~əbl] bewohn-

bar; **~·i·tant** [~ənt] Bewohner(in); Einwohner(in).

in·hale [ɪnˈheɪl] einatmen, 🏥 *a.* inhalieren.

in·her·ent □ [ɪnˈhɪərənt] anhaftend; innewohnend, angeboren, eigen (*in dat.*).

in·her·it [ɪnˈherɪt] erben; **~·i·tance** [~əns] Erbe *n*, Erbschaft *f*; *biol.* Vererbung *f*.

in·hib·it [ɪnˈhɪbɪt] hemmen (*a. psych.*), hindern; **~ed** *psych.* gehemmt; **in·hi·bi·tion** *psych.* [ɪnhɪˈbɪʃn] Hemmung *f*.

in·hos·pi·ta·ble □ [ɪnˈhɒspɪtəbl] ungastlich; unwirtlich (*Gegend etc.*).

in·hu·man □ [ɪnˈhjuːmən] unmenschlich; **~·e** □ [ɪnhjuːˈmeɪn] inhuman; menschenunwürdig.

in·im·i·cal □ [ɪˈnɪmɪkl] feindselig (*to* gegen); nachteilig (*to* für).

in·im·i·ta·ble □ [ɪˈnɪmɪtəbl] unnachahmlich.

i·ni·tial [ɪˈnɪʃl] **1.** □ anfänglich, Anfangs...; **2.** Initiale *f*, (großer) Anfangsbuchstabe *f*; **~·tial·ly** [~ʃəlɪ] am od. zu Anfang; **~·ti·ate 1.** [~ʃɪət] Eingeweihte(r *m*) *f*; **2.** [~ʃɪeɪt] beginnen, einweihen; einführen, in die Wege leiten; einführen, einweihen; aufnehmen; **~·ti·a·tion** [ɪnɪʃɪˈeɪʃn] Einführung *f*; Aufnahme *f*; **~** *fee bsd. Am.* Aufnahmegebühr *f* (*Vereinigung*); **~·ti·a·tive** [ɪˈnɪʃɪətɪv] Initiative *f*; erster Schritt; Entschlußkraft *f*, Unternehmungsgeist *m*; *take the* **~** die Initiative ergreifen; *on one's own* **~** aus eigenem Antrieb.

in·ject [ɪnˈdʒekt] injizieren, einspritzen; **in·jec·tion** 🏥 [~kʃn] Injektion *f*, Spritze *f*.

in·ju·di·cious □ [ɪndʒuːˈdɪʃəs] unklug, unüberlegt.

in·junc·tion [ɪnˈdʒʌŋkʃn] ⚖ gerichtliche Verfügung; ausdrücklicher Befehl.

in·jure [ˈɪndʒə] verletzen, -wunden; (be)schädigen; schaden (*dat.*); kränken; **in·ju·ri·ous** □ [ɪnˈdʒʊərɪəs] schädlich; beleidigend; *be* **~** *to* schaden (*dat.*); **~** *to health* gesundheitsschädlich; **in·ju·ry** [ˈɪndʒərɪ] Verletzung *f*; Unrecht *n*; Schaden *m*; Kränkung *f*.

in·jus·tice [ɪnˈdʒʌstɪs] Ungerechtigkeit *f*; Unrecht *n*; *do s.o. an* **~** j-m unrecht tun.

ink [ɪŋk] Tinte *f*; *mst printer's* **~**

Druckerschwärze f; attr. Tinten...

ink·ling ['ɪŋklɪŋ] Andeutung f; dunkle od. leise Ahnung.

ink|pad ['ɪŋkpæd] Stempelkissen n; **~·y** [~ɪ] (-ier, -iest) voll Tinte, Tinten...; tinten-, pechschwarz.

in·laid ['ɪnleɪd] eingelegt, Einlege...; **~ work** Einlegearbeit f.

in·land 1. adj. ['ɪnlənd] inländisch, einheimisch; Binnen...; **2.** [~] das Landesinnere; Binnenland n. **3.** adv. ['ɪnlænd] landeinwärts; **~ rev·e·nue** Brt. Steuereinnahmen pl.; ⚖ **Rev·e·nue** Brt. Finanzamt n.

in·lay ['ɪnleɪ] Einlegearbeit f; (Zahn-)Füllung f, Plombe f.

in·let ['ɪnlet] Meeresarm m; Flußarm m; ⊕ Einlaß m.

in·mate ['ɪnmeɪt] Insass|e m, -in f; Mitbewohner(in).

in·most ['ɪnməʊst] = innermost.

inn [ɪn] Gasthaus n, Wirtshaus n.

in·nate [ɪ'neɪt] angeboren.

in·ner ['ɪnə] innere(r, -s); Innen...; verborgen; **~·most** innerste(r, -s) (a. fig.).

in·nings ['ɪnɪŋz] (pl. innings) Kriket, Baseball: Spielzeit f (e-s Spielers od. e-r Mannschaft).

inn·keep·er ['ɪnkiːpə] Gastwirt(in).

in·no|cence ['ɪnəsns] Unschuld f; Harmlosigkeit f; Naivität f; **~·cent** [~t] **1.** □ unschuldig; harmlos; arglos, naiv; **2.** Unschuldige(r m) f; Einfältige(r m) f.

in·noc·u·ous □ [ɪ'nɒkjʊəs] harmlos.

in·no·va·tion [ɪnəʊ'veɪʃn] Neuerung f.

in·nu·en·do [ɪnjuː'endəʊ] (pl. -does, -dos) (versteckte) Andeutung.

in·nu·mer·a·ble □ [ɪ'njuːmərəbl] unzählig, zahllos.

i·noc·u|late [ɪ'nɒkjʊleɪt] (ein)impfen; **~·la·tion** 🗲 [ɪnɒkjʊ'leɪʃn] Impfung f.

in·of·fen·sive □ [ɪnə'fensɪv] harmlos.

in·op·er·a·ble [ɪn'ɒpərəbl] 🗲 inoperabel, nicht operierbar; undurchführbar (Plan etc.).

in·op·por·tune □ [ɪn'ɒpətjuːn] opportun, unangebracht, ungelegen.

in·or·di·nate □ [ɪ'nɔːdɪnət] unmäßig.

in·pa·tient 🗲 ['ɪnpeɪʃnt] stationärer Patient, stationäre Patientin.

in·put ['ɪnpʊt] Input m: econ. (von außen bezogene) Produktionsmittel pl.; Arbeitsaufwand m; Energiezufuhr f; 🗲 Eingang m (an Geräten); Computer: (Daten- od. Programm-) Eingabe f.

in·quest 🏛 ['ɪnkwest] gerichtliche Untersuchung; coroner's ~ s. coroner.

in·quir|e [ɪn'kwaɪə] fragen od. sich erkundigen (nach); **~ into** untersuchen; **in·quir·ing** □ [~rɪŋ] forschend; wißbegierig; **in·quir·y** [~rɪ] Erkundigung f, Nachfrage f; Untersuchung f; Ermittlung f; make inquiries Erkundigungen einziehen.

in·qui·si·tion [ɪnkwɪ'zɪʃn] 🏛 Untersuchung f; Verhör n; eccl. hist. Inquisition f; **in·quis·i·tive** □ [ɪn'kwɪzətɪv] neugierig; wißbegierig.

in·road fig. ['ɪnrəʊd] (into, on) Eingriff m (in acc.); übermäßige Inanspruchnahme (gen.).

in·sane □ [ɪn'seɪn] geisteskrank, wahnsinnig.

in·san·i·ta·ry [ɪn'sænɪtərɪ] unhygienisch.

in·san·i·ty [ɪn'sænətɪ] Geisteskrankheit f, Wahnsinn m.

in·sa·tia·ble □ [ɪn'seɪʃjəbl] unersättlich.

in·scribe [ɪn'skraɪb] (ein-, auf-)schreiben, einmeißeln, -ritzen; Buch mit e-r Widmung versehen.

in·scrip·tion [ɪn'skrɪpʃn] In-, Aufschrift f; Widmung f.

in·scru·ta·ble □ [ɪn'skruːtəbl] unerforschlich, unergründlich.

in·sect zo. ['ɪnsekt] Insekt n, Kerbtier n; **in·sec·ti·cide** [ɪn'sektɪsaɪd] Insektenvertilgungsmittel n, Insektizid n.

in·se·cure □ [ɪnsɪ'kjʊə] unsicher; nicht sicher od. fest.

in·sen·si·ble □ [ɪn'sensəbl] unempfindlich (to gegen); bewußtlos; unmerklich; gefühllos, gleichgültig; **~·tive** [~sətɪv] unempfindlich, gefühllos (to gegen); unempfänglich.

in·sep·a·ra·ble □ [ɪn'sepərəbl] untrennbar; unzertrennlich.

in·sert 1. [ɪn'sɜːt] einfügen, -setzen, -führen, (hinein)stecken; Münze einwerfen; inserieren; **2.** ['ɪnsɜːt] Beilage f; **in·ser·tion** [ɪn'sɜːʃn] Einfügen n, -setzen n, -führen n, Hineinstecken n; Einfügung f; Einwurf m (e-r Münze); Anzeige f, Inserat n.

in·shore ['ɪn'ʃɔ:] an od. nahe der Küste; Küsten...

in·side [ɪn'saɪd] **1.** Innenseite f; das Innere; turn ~ out umkrempeln; auf den Kopf stellen; **2.** adj. inner(e, -s), Innen...; Insider...; **3.** adv. im Innern, (dr)innen; ~ of a week F innerhalb e-r Woche; **4.** prp. innen in; in ... (hinein); **in·sid·er** [~ə] Eingeweihte(r m) f, Insider m.

in·sid·i·ous □ [ɪn'sɪdɪəs] heimtückisch.

in·sight ['ɪnsaɪt] Einsicht f, Einblick m; Verständnis n.

in·sig·ni·a [ɪn'sɪgnɪə] pl. Insignien pl.; Abzeichen pl.

in·sig·nif·i·cant [ɪnsɪg'nɪfɪkənt] bedeutungslos; unbedeutend.

in·sin·cere □ [ɪnsɪn'sɪə] unaufrichtig.

in·sin·u|ate [ɪn'sɪnjʊeɪt] andeuten, anspielen auf (acc.); **~·a·tion** [ɪn-sɪnjʊ'eɪʃn] Anspielung f, Andeutung f.

in·sip·id [ɪn'sɪpɪd] geschmacklos, fad.

in·sist [ɪn'sɪst] bestehen, beharren (on, upon auf dat.); **in·sis·tence** [~əns] Bestehen n, Beharren n; Beharrlichkeit f; **in·sis·tent** □ [~t] beharrlich, hartnäckig.

in·so·lent □ ['ɪnsələnt] unverschämt.

in·sol·u·ble □ [ɪn'sɒljʊbl] unlöslich; unlösbar (Problem etc.).

in·sol·vent [ɪn'sɒlvənt] zahlungsunfähig, insolvent.

in·som·ni·a [ɪn'sɒmnɪə] Schlaflosigkeit f.

in·spect [ɪn'spekt] untersuchen, prüfen, nachsehen; besichtigen, inspizieren; **in·spec·tion** [~kʃn] Prüfung f, Untersuchung f, Kontrolle f; Inspektion f; **in·spec·tor** [~ktə] Aufsichtsbeamte(r) m, Inspektor m; (Polizei)Inspektor m, (-)Kommissar m.

in·spi·ra·tion [ɪnspə'reɪʃn] Inspiration f, Eingebung f; **in·spire** [ɪn-'spaɪə] inspirieren; hervorrufen; Hoffnung etc. wecken; Respekt etc. einflößen.

in·stall [ɪn'stɔ:l] ⊕ installieren, einrichten, aufstellen, einbauen, Leitung legen; in ein Amt etc. einsetzen; **in·stal·la·tion** [ɪnstə'leɪʃn] ⊕ Installation f, Einrichtung f, -bau m; ⊕ fertige Anlage; Einsetzung f, -führung f (in ein Amt).

in·stal·ment, Am. a. **-stall-** [ɪn'stɔ:l-mənt] econ. Rate f; (Teil)Lieferung f (e-s Buches etc.); Fortsetzung f (e-s Romans etc.); Rundfunk, TV: (Sende)Folge f.

in·stance ['ɪnstəns] Beispiel n; (besonderer) Fall; ⚖ Instanz f; for ~ zum Beispiel; at s.o.'s ~ auf j-s Veranlassung (hin).

in·stant ['ɪnstənt] **1.** sofortig; unmittelbar; econ. Fertig...; ~ coffee löslicher od. Pulverkaffee, Instantkaffee m; **2.** Augenblick m; **in·stan-ta·ne·ous** □ [ɪnstən'teɪnjəs] sofortig, augenblicklich; Moment...; **~·ly** ['ɪnstəntlɪ] sofort, unverzüglich.

in·stead [ɪn'sted] statt dessen, dafür; ~ of an Stelle von, (an)statt.

in·step anat. ['ɪnstep] Spann m, Rist m.

in·sti|gate ['ɪnstɪgeɪt] anstiften; aufhetzen; veranlassen; **~·ga·tor** [~ə] Anstifter(in); (Auf)Hetzer(in).

in·stil, Am. a. **-still** fig. [ɪn'stɪl] (-ll-) beibringen, einflößen (into dat.).

in·stinct ['ɪnstɪŋkt] Instinkt m; **in·stinc·tive** □ [ɪn'stɪŋktɪv] instinktiv.

in·sti·tute ['ɪnstɪtjuːt] **1.** Institut n; (gelehrte etc.) Gesellschaft; **2.** einrichten, gründen; einführen; einleiten; **~·tu·tion** [ɪnstɪ'tjuːʃn] Institut n, Anstalt f; Einführung f; Institution f, Einrichtung f.

in·struct [ɪn'strʌkt] unterrichten, belehren; j-n anweisen; **in·struc·tion** [~kʃn] Unterricht m; Anweisung f, Instruktion f; Computer: Befehl m; ~s for use Gebrauchsanweisung f; operating ~s Bedienungsanleitung f; **in·struc·tive** □ [~ktɪv] instruktiv, lehrreich; **in·struc·tor** [~ə] Lehrer m; Ausbilder m; Am. univ. Dozent m.

in·stru·ment ['ɪnstrʊmənt] Instrument n; Werkzeug n (a. fig.); ~ panel ⊕ Armaturenbrett n; **~·men·tal** □ [ɪnstrʊ'mentl] behilflich, dienlich; ♪ Instrumental...

in·sub·or·di|nate [ɪnsə'bɔ:dənət] aufsässig; **~·na·tion** ['ɪnsəbɔ:dɪ-'neɪʃn] Auflehnung f.

in·suf·fe·ra·ble □ [ɪn'sʌfərəbl] unerträglich, unausstehlich.

in·suf·fi·cient □ [ɪnsə'fɪʃnt] unzulänglich, ungenügend.

in·su·lar □ ['ɪnsjʊlə] Insel...; fig. engstirnig.

interloper

in·su|late ['ɪnsjʊleɪt] isolieren; **~la·tion** [ɪnsjʊ'leɪʃn] Isolierung f; Isoliermaterial n.

in·sult 1. ['ɪnsʌlt] Beleidigung f; **2.** [ɪn'sʌlt] beleidigen.

in·sur|ance [ɪn'ʃʊərəns] Versicherung f; Versicherungssumme f; ~ **company** Versicherungsgesellschaft f; ~ **policy** Versicherungspolice f; **~e** [ɪn'ʃʊə] versichern (against gegen).

in·sur·gent [ɪn'sɜːdʒənt] **1.** aufständisch; **2.** Aufständische(r m) f.

in·sur·moun·ta·ble □ fig. [ɪnsə'maʊntəbl] unüberwindlich.

in·sur·rec·tion [ɪnsə'rekʃn] Aufstand m.

in·tact [ɪn'tækt] unberührt; unversehrt, intakt.

in·tan·gi·ble □ [ɪn'tændʒəbl] nicht greifbar; unbestimmt.

in·te|gral □ ['ɪntɪɡrəl] ganz, vollständig; wesentlich; **~·grate** [~eɪt] v/t. integrieren, zu e-m Ganzen zusammenfassen; einbeziehen, -gliedern; Am. die Rassenschranken aufheben zwischen; v/i. sich integrieren; **~·grat·ed** einheitlich; ⊕ eingebaut; ohne Rassentrennung; **~·gra·tion** [ɪntɪ'ɡreɪʃn] Integration f.

in·teg·ri·ty [ɪn'teɡrətɪ] Integrität f, Rechtschaffenheit f; Vollständigkeit f.

in·tel|lect ['ɪntəlekt] Intellekt m, Verstand m; **~·lec·tual** [ɪntə'lektjʊəl] **1.** □ intellektuell, Verstandes..., geistig; **2.** Intellektuelle(r m) f.

in·tel·li·gence [ɪn'telɪdʒəns] Intelligenz f, Verstand m; Nachrichten pl., Informationen pl.; a. ~ **department** Geheimdienst m; **~·gent** □ [~t] intelligent, klug.

in·tel·li·gi·ble □ [ɪn'telɪdʒəbl] verständlich (to für).

in·tem·per·ate □ [ɪn'tempərət] unmäßig, maßlos; trunksüchtig.

in·tend [ɪn'tend] beabsichtigen, vorhaben, planen; **~ed for** bestimmt für od. zu.

in·tense □ [ɪn'tens] stark, heftig; angespannt; ernsthaft.

in·ten|si·fy [ɪn'tensɪfaɪ] intensivieren; (sich) verstärken; **~·si·ty** [~sətɪ] Intensität f; **~·sive** [~sɪv] intensiv; stark, heftig; ~ **care unit** ⚕ Intensivstation f.

in·tent [ɪn'tent] **1.** □ gespannt, aufmerksam; ~ **on** fest entschlossen zu (dat.); konzentriert auf (acc.); **2.**

Absicht f, Vorhaben n; to all ~s and purposes in jeder Hinsicht; **in·ten·tion** [~ʃn] Absicht f; ⚹⚹ Vorsatz m; **in·ten·tion·al** □ [~nl] absichtlich, vorsätzlich.

in·ter [ɪn'tɜː] (-rr-) bestatten.

in·ter- ['ɪntə] zwischen, Zwischen...; gegenseitig, einander.

in·ter·act [ɪntər'ækt] aufeinander (ein)wirken, sich gegenseitig beeinflussen.

in·ter·cede [ɪntə'siːd] vermitteln, sich einsetzen (with bei; for für).

in·ter|cept [ɪntə'sept] abfangen; aufhalten; **~·cep·tion** [~pʃn] Abfangen n; Aufhalten n.

in·ter·ces·sion [ɪntə'seʃn] Fürbitte f, -sprache f.

in·ter·change 1. [ɪntə'tʃeɪndʒ] austauschen; **2.** ['ɪntə'tʃeɪndʒ] Austausch m; kreuzungsfreier Verkehrsknotenpunkt.

in·ter·course ['ɪntəkɔːs] Verkehr m; a. sexual ~ (Geschlechts)Verkehr m.

in·ter|dict 1. [ɪntə'dɪkt] untersagen, verbieten (s.th. to s.o. j-m et.; s.o. from doing j-m zu tun); **2.** ['ɪntədɪkt], **~·dic·tion** [ɪntə'dɪkʃn] Verbot n.

in·terest ['ɪntrɪst] **1.** Interesse n (in an dat., für), (An)Teilnahme f; Nutzen m; econ. Anteil m, Beteiligung f; econ. Zins(en pl.) m; Interessenten pl., Interessengruppe(n pl.) f; take an ~ in sich interessieren (in für); **2.** interessieren (in für et.); **~·ing** □ [~ɪŋ] interessant.

in·ter·face ['ɪntəfeɪs] Computer: Schnittstelle f.

in·ter|fere [ɪntə'fɪə] sich einmischen (with in acc.); stören; **~·fer·ence** [~rəns] Einmischung f; Störung f.

in·ter·i·or [ɪn'tɪərɪə] **1.** □ innere(r, -s), Innen...; Binnen...; Inlands...; ~ **decorator** Innenarchitekt(in); **2.** das Innere; Interieur n; pol. innere Angelegenheiten pl.; Department of the ♀ Am. Innenministerium n.

in·ter|ject [ɪntə'dʒekt] Bemerkung einwerfen; **~·jec·tion** [~kʃn] Einwurf m; Ausruf m; ling. Interjektion f.

in·ter·lace [ɪntə'leɪs] (sich) (ineinander) verflechten.

in·ter·lock [ɪntə'lɒk] ineinandergreifen; (miteinander) verzahnen.

in·ter·lop·er ['ɪntələʊpə] Eindringling m.

in·ter·lude ['ɪntəluːd] Zwischenspiel n; Pause f; ~s of bright weather zeitweilig schön.

in·ter·me·di·a·ry [ɪntə'miːdjəri] Vermittler(in); ~ate □ [~ət] in der Mitte liegend, Mittel..., Zwischen...; ~range missile Mittelstreckenrakete f.

in·ter·ment [ɪn'tɜːmənt] Beerdigung f, Bestattung f.

in·ter·mi·na·ble □ [ɪn'tɜːmɪnəbl] endlos.

in·ter·mis·sion [ɪntə'mɪʃn] Aussetzen n, Unterbrechung f; bsd. Am. thea., Film etc.: Pause f.

in·ter·mit·tent □ [ɪntə'mɪtənt] (zeitweilig) aussetzend, periodisch (auftretend); ~ fever ⚕ Wechselfieber n.

in·tern¹ [ɪn'tɜːn] internieren.

in·tern² Am. ⚕ ['ɪntɜːn] Medizinalassistent(in).

in·ter·nal □ [ɪn'tɜːnl] innere(r, -s); einheimisch, Inlands...; ~combustion engine Verbrennungsmotor m.

in·ter·na·tion·al [ɪntə'næʃənl] 1. □ international; ~ law ⚖ Völkerrecht n; 2. Sport: Internationale m, f, Nationalspieler(in); internationaler Wettkampf; Länderspiel n.

in·ter·po·late [ɪn'tɜːpəleɪt] einfügen.

in·ter·pose [ɪntə'pəʊz] v/t. Veto einlegen; Wort einwerfen; v/i. eingreifen.

in·ter·pret [ɪn'tɜːprɪt] auslegen, erklären, deuten, interpretieren; dolmetschen; ~pre·ta·tion [ɪntɜːprɪ'teɪʃn] Auslegung f, Deutung f, Interpretation f; ~pret·er [ɪn'tɜːprɪtə] Dolmetscher(in); Interpret(in).

in·ter·ro·gate [ɪn'terəgeɪt] (be-, aus-) fragen; verhören; ~ga·tion [~'geɪʃn] Befragung f; Verhör m; Frage f; note od. mark od. point of ~ ling. Fragezeichen n; ~ga·tive [ɪntə-'rɒgətɪv] fragend, Frage...; gr. Interrogativ..., Frage...

in·ter·rupt [ɪntə'rʌpt] unterbrechen; ~rup·tion [~pʃn] Unterbrechung f.

in·ter·sect [ɪntə'sekt] durchschneiden; sich schneiden od. kreuzen; ~sec·tion [~kʃn] Schnittpunkt m; (Straßen- etc.-)Kreuzung f.

in·ter·sperse [ɪntə'spɜːs] einstreuen, hier u. da einfügen.

in·ter·state Am. [ɪntə'steɪt] zwischen den einzelnen Bundesstaaten.

in·ter·twine [ɪntə'twaɪn] (sich ineinander) verschlingen.

in·ter·val ['ɪntəvl] Intervall n (a. ♪), Abstand m; Pause f; at ~s of in Abständen von.

in·ter·vene [ɪntə'viːn] einschreiten, intervenieren; dazwischenliegen; (unerwartet) dazwischenkommen; ~ven·tion [~'venʃn] Eingreifen n, -griff m, Intervention f.

in·ter·view ['ɪntəvjuː] 1. Presse, TV: Interview n; Unterredung f; (Vorstellungs)Gespräch n; 2. j-n interviewen, befragen; ein Vorstellungsgespräch führen mit; ~er [~ə] Interviewer(in); Leiter(in) e-s Vorstellungsgesprächs.

in·ter·weave [ɪntə'wiːv] (-wove, -woven) (miteinander) verweben, -flechten, -schlingen.

in·tes·tate ⚖ [ɪn'testeɪt]: die ~ ohne Testament sterben.

in·tes·tine anat. [ɪn'testɪn] Darm m; ~s pl. Eingeweide pl.

in·ti·ma·cy ['ɪntɪməsɪ] Intimität f (a. sexuell), Vertrautheit f; Vertraulichkeit f.

in·ti·mate¹ ['ɪntɪmət] 1. □ intim (a. sexuell), vertraut; vertraulich; 2. Vertraute(r m) m/f.

in·ti·mate² ['ɪntɪmeɪt] andeuten; ~ma·tion [ɪntɪ'meɪʃn] Andeutung f.

in·tim·i·date [ɪn'tɪmɪdeɪt] einschüchtern; ~da·tion [ɪntɪmɪ'deɪʃn] Einschüchterung f.

in·to ['ɪntʊ, 'ɪntə] in (acc.) ... hinein; gegen (acc.); ⟋ in (acc.); 4 ~ 20 goes five times 4 geht fünfmal in 20.

in·tol·er·a·ble □ [ɪn'tɒlərəbl] unerträglich.

in·tol·er·ance [ɪn'tɒlərəns] Intoleranz f, Unduldsamkeit (of gegen); ~rant [~t] intolerant, unduldsam (of gegen).

in·to·na·tion [ɪntəʊ'neɪʃn] gr. Intonation f, Tonfall m; ♪ Intonation f.

in·tox·i·cant [ɪn'tɒksɪkənt] 1. berauschend; 2. bsd. berauschendes Getränk; ~cate [~eɪt] berauschen (a. fig.), betrunken machen; ~ca·tion [ɪntɒksɪ'keɪʃn] Rausch m (a. fig.).

in·trac·ta·ble □ [ɪn'træktəbl] unlenksam, eigensinnig; schwer zu handhaben(d).

in·tran·si·tive □ gr. [ɪn'trænsɪtɪv] intransitiv.

in·tra·ve·nous ℱ [ɪntrə'viːnəs] intravenös.

in·trep·id □ [ɪn'trepɪd] unerschrocken.

in·tri·cate □ ['ɪntrɪkət] verwickelt, kompliziert.

in·trigue [ɪn'triːg] 1. Intrige f; Machenschaft f; 2. faszinieren, interessieren; intriguieren.

in·trin·sic [ɪn'trɪnsɪk] (~ally) wirklich, wahr, inner(lich).

in·tro·duce [ɪntrə'djuːs] vorstellen (to dat.), j-n bekannt machen (to mit); einführen; einleiten; ~**duc·tion** [~'dʌkʃn] Vorstellung f; Einführung f; Einleitung f; letter of ~ Empfehlungsschreiben n; ~**duc·to·ry** [~təri] einleitend, Einführungs..., Einleitungs...

in·tro·spec·tion [ɪntrəʊ'spekʃn] Selbstbeobachtung f; ~**tive** [~tɪv] selbstbeobachtend.

in·tro·vert psych. ['ɪntrəʊvɜːt] introvertierter Mensch; ~**ed** psych. introvertiert, in sich gekehrt.

in·trude [ɪn'truːd] sich einmischen; sich ein- od. aufdrängen; stören; am I intruding? störe ich?; **in·trud·er** [~də] Eindringling m; **in·tru·sion** [~ʒn] Aufdrängen n; Einmischung f; Auf-, Zudringlichkeit f; Störung f; Verletzung f; **in·tru·sive** □ [~sɪv] aufdringlich.

in·tu·i·tion [ɪntjuː'ɪʃn] Intuition f; Ahnung f; ~**tive** □ [ɪn'tjuːɪtɪv] intuitiv.

in·un·date ['ɪnʌndeɪt] überschwemmen, -fluten (a. fig.).

in·vade [ɪn'veɪd] eindringen in, einfallen in, ⚔ a. einmarschieren in (acc.); fig. überlaufen, -schwemmen; ~**r** [~ə] Eindringling m.

in·va·lid[1] ['ɪnvəlɪd] 1. dienstunfähig; kränklich, invalide; Kranken...; 2. Invalide m, f.

in·val·id[2] □ [ɪn'vælɪd] (rechts)ungültig; ~**i·date** [~eɪt] Argument entkräften; ⚖ ungültig machen.

in·val·u·a·ble □ [ɪn'væljʊəbl] unschätzbar.

in·var·i·a·ble □ [ɪn'veərɪəbl] unveränderlich; ~**bly** [~lɪ] ausnahmslos.

in·va·sion [ɪn'veɪʒn] Invasion f, Einfall m; fig. Eingriff m, Verletzung f.

in·vec·tive [ɪn'vektɪv] Schmähung f, Beschimpfung f.

in·vent [ɪn'vent] erfinden; **in·ven-**

tion [~ʃn] Erfindung(sgabe) f; **in·ven·tive** □ [~tɪv] erfinderisch; **in·ven·tor** [~ə] Erfinder(in); **in·ven·to·ry** ['ɪnvəntri] Inventar n; Bestandsverzeichnis n; Am. Inventur f.

in·verse ['ɪn'vɜːs] 1. □ umgekehrt; 2. Umkehrung f, Gegenteil n; **in·ver·sion** [ɪn'vɜːʃn] Umkehrung f; gr. Inversion f.

in·vert [ɪn'vɜːt] umkehren; gr. Satz etc. umstellen; ~**ed** commas pl. Anführungszeichen pl.

in·ver·te·brate zo. [ɪn'vɜːtɪbrət] 1. wirbellos; 2. wirbelloses Tier.

in·vest [ɪn'vest] investieren, anlegen.

in·ves·ti·gate [ɪn'vestɪgeɪt] untersuchen; überprüfen; Untersuchungen od. Ermittlungen anstellen (into über acc.), nachforschen; ~**ga·tion** [ɪnvestɪ'geɪʃn] Untersuchung f; Ermittlung f, Nachforschung f; ~**ga·tor** [ɪn'vestɪgeɪtə] Untersuchungs-, Ermittlungsbeamte(r) m; private ~ Privatdetektiv m.

in·vest·ment econ. [ɪn'vestmənt] Investition f, (Kapital)Anlage f.

in·vet·e·rate □ [ɪn'vetərət] unverbesserlich; unversöhnlich; hartnäckig.

in·vid·i·ous □ [ɪn'vɪdɪəs] verhaßt; gehässig, boshaft, gemein; ungerecht.

in·vig·o·rate [ɪn'vɪgəreɪt] kräftigen, stärken, beleben.

in·vin·ci·ble □ [ɪn'vɪnsəbl] unbesiegbar; unüberwindlich.

in·vi·o·la·ble □ [ɪn'vaɪələbl] unverletzlich, unantastbar; ~**te** [~lət] unverletzt; unversehrt.

in·vis·i·ble □ [ɪn'vɪzəbl] unsichtbar.

in·vi·ta·tion [ɪnvɪ'teɪʃn] Einladung f; Aufforderung f; **in·vite** [ɪn'vaɪt] einladen; auffordern; Gefahr etc. herausfordern; ~ s.o. in j-n hereinbitten; **in·vit·ing** □ [~ɪŋ] einladend, verlockend.

in·voice econ. ['ɪnvɔɪs] 1. (Waren-) Rechnung f; Lieferschein m; 2. in Rechnung stellen, berechnen.

in·voke [ɪn'vəʊk] anrufen; zu Hilfe rufen (acc.); appellieren an (acc.); Geist heraufbeschwören.

in·vol·un·ta·ry □ [ɪn'vɒləntəri] unfreiwillig; unabsichtlich; unwillkürlich.

in·volve [ɪn'vɒlv] verwickeln, hineinziehen (in in acc.); umfassen; zur Folge haben, mit sich bringen; be-

treffen; **~d** kompliziert; betroffen
(*Person*); **~ment** [~mənt] Verwick-
lung f; Beteiligung f; Engagement n;
(Geld)Verlegenheit f.

in·vul·ne·ra·ble □ [ɪn'vʌlnərəbl]
unverwundbar; *fig.* unanfechtbar.

in·ward ['ɪnwəd] **1.** *adj.* innere(r, -s),
innerlich; **2.** *adv. mst* ~s einwärts,
nach innen.

i·o·dine [♫ ['aɪədiːn] Jod n.

i·on *phys.* ['aɪən] Ion n.

IOU ['aɪəʊ'juː] (= *I owe you*)
Schuldschein m.

I·ra·ni·an [ɪ'reɪnjən] **1.** iranisch, persisch; **2.** Iraner(in), Perser(in); *ling.*
Iranisch n, Persisch n.

I·ra·qi [ɪ'rɑːkɪ] **1.** irakisch; **2.** Ira-
ker(in); *ling.* Irakisch n.

i·ras·ci·ble □ [ɪ'ræsəbl] jähzornig.

i·rate □ [aɪ'reɪt] zornig, wütend.

ir·i·des·cent [ɪrɪ'desnt] schillernd.

i·ris ['aɪərɪs] *anat.* Regenbogenhaut f,
Iris f; ♀ Schwertlilie f, Iris f.

I·rish ['aɪərɪʃ] **1.** irisch; **2.** *ling.* Irisch
n; *the* ~ *pl.* die Iren *pl.*; **~man** (*pl.
-men*) Ire m; **~wom·an** (*pl. -wom-
en*) Irin f.

irk·some □ ['ɜːksəm] lästig, ärgerlich.

i·ron ['aɪən] **1.** Eisen n; *a. flat-*~
Bügeleisen n; ~s *pl.* Hand- u. Fuß-
schellen *pl.*; *strike while the* ~ *is hot
fig.* das Eisen schmieden, solange es
heiß ist; **2.** eisern (*a. fig.*), Eisen...,
aus Eisen; **3.** bügeln, plätten; ~ *out
fig. et.* ausbügeln, *Schwierigkeiten*
beseitigen; ♀ **Cur·tain** *pol.* Eiserner
Vorhang.

i·ron·ic [aɪ'rɒnɪk] (~*ally*), **i·ron·i·cal**
□ [~kl] ironisch, spöttisch.

i·ron|ing ['aɪənɪŋ] Bügel-, Plättwä-
sche f; **~board** Bügel-, Plättbrett n;
~ **lung** ♫ eiserne Lunge; **~mon·ger**
Brt. [~mʌŋgə] Eisenwarenhändler
m; **~mon·ger·y** *Brt.* [~ərɪ] Eisenwaren *pl.*; **~works** *sg.* Eisenhütte f.

i·ron·y ['aɪərənɪ] Ironie f.

ir·ra·tion·al □ [ɪ'ræʃənl] irrational;
unvernünftig; vernunftlos (*Tier*).

ir·rec·on·ci·la·ble □ [ɪ'rekənsaɪləbl]
unversöhnlich; unvereinbar.

ir·re·cov·er·a·ble □ [ɪrɪ'kʌvərəbl]
unersetzlich; unwiederbringlich.

ir·re·fu·ta·ble □ [ɪ'refjʊtəbl] unwi-
derlegbar, nicht zu widerlegen(d).

ir·reg·u·lar □ [ɪ'regjʊlə] unregelmäßig; uneben; ungleichmäßig; regelwidrig; ungesetzlich; ungehörig.

ir·rel·e·vant □ [ɪ'reləvənt] irrele-

vant, nicht zur Sache gehörig; uner-
heblich, belanglos (*to* für).

ir·rep·a·ra·ble □ [ɪ'repərəbl] irrepa-
rabel, nicht wiedergutzumachen(d).

ir·re·place·a·ble □ [ɪrɪ'pleɪsəbl] unersetzlich.

ir·re·pres·si·ble □ [ɪrɪ'presəbl] nicht
zu unterdrücken(d); unerschütterlich; un(be)zähmbar.

ir·re·proa·cha·ble □ [ɪrɪ'prəʊtʃəbl]
einwandfrei, tadellos, untadelig.

ir·re·sis·ti·ble □ [ɪrɪ'zɪstəbl] unwi-
derstehlich.

ir·res·o·lute □ [ɪ'rezəluːt] unentschlossen.

ir·re·spec·tive □ [ɪrɪ'spektɪv] ~ *of*
ungeachtet (*gen.*), ohne Rücksicht
auf (*acc.*); unabhängig von.

ir·re·spon·si·ble □ [ɪrɪ'spɒnsəbl]
unverantwortlich; verantwortungs-
los.

ir·re·trie·va·ble □ [ɪrɪ'triːvəbl] unwiederbringlich, unersetzlich; nicht
wiedergutzumachen(d).

ir·rev·e·rent □ [ɪ'revərənt] respektlos.

ir·rev·o·ca·ble □ [ɪ'revəkəbl] unwiderruflich, unabänderlich, endgültig.

ir·ri·gate ['ɪrɪgeɪt] (künstlich) bewässern.

ir·ri·ta|ble □ ['ɪrɪtəbl] reizbar; **~nt**
[~ənt] Reizmittel n; **~te** [~teɪt] reizen; ärgern; **~ting** □ [~tɪŋ] aufreizend; ärgerlich (*Sache*); **~tion** [ɪrɪ-
'teɪʃn] Reizung f; Gereiztheit f, Ärger m.

is [ɪz] **3.** *sg. pres. von* be.

Is·lam ['ɪzlɑːm] der Islam.

is·land ['aɪlənd] Insel f; *a. traffic* ~
Verkehrsinsel f; **~er** [~ə] Inselbe-
wohner(in).

isle *poet.* [aɪl] Insel f.

is·let ['aɪlɪt] Inselchen n.

i·so|late ['aɪsəleɪt] absondern; isolie-
ren; **~lat·ed** einzeln, isoliert; ~
einzeln; △ *nicht* ≠ *isoliert*; **~la·tion**
[aɪsə'leɪʃn] Isolierung f; Absonderung f; ~ **ward** ♫ Isolierstation f.

Is·rae·li [ɪz'reɪlɪ] **1.** israelisch; **2.** Israeli m, Bewohner(in) des Staates
Israel.

is·sue ['ɪʃuː] **1.** Herauskommen n;
Herausfließen n; Abfluß m; ♫
Nachkommen(schaft f) *pl.*; *econ.*
Ausgabe f (*von Banknoten etc.*); Er-
teilung f (*von Befehlen etc.*); *print.*
Ausgabe f, Exemplar n (*e-s Buches*);

print. Ausgabe *f*, Nummer *f* (*e-r Zeitung*); *bsd.* ⚖ Streitfrage *f*; *fig.* Ausgang, Ergebnis *n*; *at* ~ zur Debatte stehend; *point at* ~ strittiger Punkt; **2.** *v/i.* herauskommen; ausfließen, -strömen; herkommen, -rühren (*from* von); *v/t. econ.*, *Material etc.* ausgeben; *Befehl* erteilen; *Buch, Zeitung* herausgeben, veröffentlichen.

isth·mus ['ɪsməs] Landenge *f*.

it [ɪt] es; er, ihn, sie; *nach prp.*: *by* ~ dadurch; *for* ~ dafür.

I·tal·i·an [ɪ'tæljən] **1.** italienisch; **2.** Italiener(in); *ling.* Italienisch *n*.

i·tal·ics *print.* [ɪ'tælɪks] Kursivschrift *f*.

itch [ɪtʃ] **1.** ✿ Krätze *f*; Jucken *n*; Verlangen *n*; **2.** jucken; *I* ~ *all over* es juckt mich überall; *be* ~*ing to inf.* darauf brennen, zu *inf.*

i·tem ['aɪtəm] Punkt *m*; Gegenstand *m*; Posten *m*, Artikel *m*; *a. news* ~ (Zeitungs)Notiz *f*, (kurzer) Artikel; Rundfunk, *TV*: (kurze) Meldung; ~**ize** [~aɪz] einzeln angeben *od.* aufführen.

i·tin·e·rant □ [ɪ'tɪnərənt] reisend; umherziehend, Reise..., Wander...; ~**ra·ry** [aɪ'tɪnərərɪ] Reiseroute *f*, Reisebeschreibung *f*.

its [ɪts] sein(e), ihr(e), dessen, deren.

it·self [ɪt'self] sich; (sich) selbst; *by* ~ (für sich) allein; von selbst; *in* ~ an sich.

i·vo·ry ['aɪvərɪ] Elfenbein *n*.

i·vy ✿ ['aɪvɪ] Efeu *m*.

J

jab [dʒæb] **1.** (-*bb*-) stechen; (zu)stoßen; **2.** Stich *m*, Stoß *m*; F ✿ Spritze *f*.

jab·ber ['dʒæbə] (daher)plappern.

jack [dʒæk] **1.** ⊕ Hebevorrichtung *f*; ⊕ Wagenheber *m*; ⚡ Klinke *f*; ⚡ Steckdose *f*, Buchse *f*; ⚓ Gösch *f*, kleine Bugflagge; *Kartenspiel*: Bube *m*; **2.** ~ *up Auto* aufbocken.

jack·al *zo.* ['dʒækɔːl] Schakal *m*.

jack|ass ['dʒækæs] Esel *m* (*a. fig.*); ~**boots** ✗ Reitstiefel *pl.*; hohe Wasserstiefel *pl.*; ~**daw** *zo.* Dohle *f*.

jack·et ['dʒækɪt] Jacke *f*, Jackett *n*; ⊕ Mantel *m*; Schutzumschlag *m* (*e-s Buches*); *Am.* (Schall)Plattenhülle *f*.

jack|-knife ['dʒæknaɪf] **1.** (*pl. -knives*) Klappmesser *n*; **2.** zusammenklappen, -knicken; ~ **of all trades** Alleskönner *m*, Hansdampf in allen Gassen; ~**pot** Haupttreffer *m*, -gewinn *m*; *hit the* ~ F den Haupttreffer machen; *fig.* das große Los ziehen.

jade [dʒeɪd] Jade *m*, *f*; Jadegrün *n*.

jag [dʒæg] Zacken *m*; ~**ged** ['dʒægɪd] gezackt; zackig.

jag·u·ar *zo.* ['dʒægjʊə] Jaguar *m*.

jail [dʒeɪl] **1.** Gefängnis *n*; **2.** einsperren; ~**bird** F ['dʒeɪlbɜːd] Knastbruder *m*; ~**er** [~ə] Gefängnisaufseher *m*; ~**house** *Am.* Gefängnis *n*.

jam¹ [dʒæm] Konfitüre *f*, Marmelade *f*.

jam² [~] **1.** Gedränge *n*, Gewühl *n*; ⊕ Klemmen *n*, Blockierung *f*; Stauung *f*, Stockung *f*; *traffic* ~ Verkehrsstau *m*; *be in a* ~ F in der Klemme sein; **2.** (-*mm*-) ⊕ (sich) (ver)klemmen, blockieren; (hinein)zwängen, (-)stopfen; einklemmen; pressen, quetschen; ~ *the brakes on*, ~ *on the brakes* auf die Bremse steigen.

jamb [dʒæm] (Tür-, Fenster)Pfosten *m*.

jam·bo·ree [dʒæmbə'riː] Jamboree *n*, Pfadfindertreffen *n*.

jan·gle ['dʒæŋgl] klimpern *od.* klirren (mit); bimmeln (lassen).

jan·i·tor ['dʒænɪtə] Hausmeister *m*.

Jan·u·a·ry ['dʒænjʊərɪ] Januar *m*.

Jap·a·nese [dʒæpə'niːz] **1.** japanisch; **2.** Japaner(in); *ling.* Japanisch *n*; *the* ~ *pl.* die Japaner *pl.*

jar¹ [dʒaː] **1.** Krug *m*, Topf *m*; (Marmelade- *etc.*)Glas *n*.

jar² [~] **1.** (-*rr*-) knarren, kreischen; quietschen; sich nicht vertragen; erschüttern (*a. fig.*); **2.** Knarren *n*,

Kreischen *n*, Quietschen *n*; Erschütterung *f* (*a. fig.*); Schock *m*.

jar·gon ['dʒɑːgən] Jargon *m*, Fachsprache *f*.

jaun·dice ᵃ ['dʒɔːndɪs] Gelbsucht *f*; **~d** ᵃ gelbsüchtig; *fig.* neidisch, eifersüchtig, voreingenommen.

jaunt [dʒɔːnt] **1.** Ausflug *m*, Spritztour *f*; **2.** e-n Ausflug machen; **jaun·ty** □ ['dʒɔːntɪ] (*-ier, -iest*) munter, unbeschwert; flott.

jav·e·lin ['dʒævlɪn] *Sport:* Speer *m*; ~ (*throw[ing]*), *throwing the* ~ Speerwerfen *n*; ~ *thrower* Speerwerfer(in).

jaw [dʒɔː] *anat.* Kinnbacken *m*, Kiefer *m*; **~s** *pl.* Rachen *m*; Maul *n*; Schlund *m*; ⊕ Backen *pl.*; **~bone** *anat.* ['dʒɔːbəʊn] Kieferknochen *m*.

jay *zo.* [dʒeɪ] Eichelhäher *m*; **~walk** ['dʒeɪwɔːk] unachtsam über die Straße gehen; **~walk·er** unachtsamer Fußgänger.

jazz ♪ [dʒæz] Jazz *m*.

jeal·ous □ ['dʒeləs] eifersüchtig (*of* auf *acc.*); neidisch; **~y** [~sɪ] Eifersucht *f*; Neid *m*; △ *nicht Jalousie*.

jeans [dʒiːnz] *pl.* Jeans *pl.*

jeep *TM* [dʒiːp] Jeep *m*.

jeer [dʒɪə] **1.** Spott *m*; höhnische Bemerkung; **2.** spotten (*at* über *acc.*); verspotten, -höhnen.

jel·lied ['dʒelɪd] eingedickt (*Fruchtsaft*); in Gelee.

jel·ly ['dʒelɪ] **1.** Gallert(e *f*) *n*; Gelee *n*; **2.** gelieren; **~ba·by** *Brt.* Gummibärchen *n*; **~bean** Gummi-, Geleebonbon *m*; **~fish** *zo.* Qualle *f*.

jeop·ar·dize ['dʒepədaɪz] gefährden; **~dy** [~dɪ] Gefahr *f*.

jerk [dʒɜːk] **1.** (plötzlicher) Ruck, Sprung *m*, Satz *m*; ᵃ Zuckung *f*, Zucken *n*; **2.** (plötzlich) ziehen, zerren, reißen (*an dat.*); schleudern, schnellen; **~y** □ ['dʒɜːkɪ] (*-ier, -iest*) ruckartig; holprig; abgehackt (*Sprache*).

jer·sey ['dʒɜːzɪ] Pullover *m*.

jest [dʒest] **1.** Spaß *m*; **2.** scherzen; **~er** ['dʒestə] (Hof)Narr *m*.

jet [dʒet] **1.** (Wasser-, Gas- *etc.*)Strahl *m*; ⊕ Düse *f*; = ~ *engine*, ~ *plane*; **2.** (*-tt-*) hervorschießen, (her)ausströmen; ✈ jetten; **~en·gine** ⊕ Düsen-, Strahltriebwerk *n*; **~lag** körperliche Anpassungsschwierigkeiten *pl.* durch die Zeitverschiebung bei weiten Flugreisen; **~plane** Düsenflug-

zeug *n*, Jet *m*; **~pro·pelled** ['dʒetprəpeld] mit Düsenantrieb, Düsen...; ~ *pro·pul·sion* ⊕ Düsen-, Strahlantrieb *m*; ~ *set* Jet-set *m*; **set·ter** Angehörige(r *m*) *f* des Jet-set.

jet·ty ⚓ ['dʒetɪ] Mole *f*; Pier *m*.

Jew [dʒuː] Jude *m*, Jüdin *f*; *attr.* Juden...

jew·el ['dʒuːəl] Juwel *m*, *n*, Edelstein *m*; Schmuckstück *n*; **~ler**, *Am.* **~er** [~ə] Juwelier *m*; **~lery**, *Am.* **~ry** [~lrɪ] Juwelen *pl.*; Schmuck *m*.

Jew·ess ['dʒuːɪs] Jüdin *f*; **~ish** [~ɪʃ] jüdisch.

jib ⚓ [dʒɪb] Klüver *m*.

jif·fy F ['dʒɪfɪ]: *in a* ~ im Nu, sofort.

jig·saw ['dʒɪgsɔː] Laubsäge *f*; = ~ *puz·zle* Puzzle(spiel) *n*.

jilt [dʒɪlt] *Mädchen* sitzenlassen; *Liebhaber* den Laufpaß geben.

jin·gle ['dʒɪŋgl] **1.** Geklingel *n*, Klimpern *n*; Spruch *m*, Vers *m*; *advertising* ~ Werbespruch *m*; **2.** klingeln; klimpern (mit); klinge(l)n lassen.

jit·ters F ['dʒɪtəz] *pl.*: *the* ~ Bammel *m*, das große Zittern.

job [dʒɒb] (ein Stück) Arbeit *f*; *econ.* Akkordarbeit *f*; Beruf *m*, Beschäftigung *f*, Stellung *f*, Stelle *f*, Arbeit *f*, Job *m*; Aufgabe *f*, Sache *f*; *by the* ~ im Akkord; *out of* ~ arbeitslos; **~ber** *Brt.* ['dʒɒbə] Börsenspekulant *m*; **~hop·ping** *Am.* [~hɒpɪŋ] häufiger Arbeitsplatzwechsel; **~hunt·er** Arbeit(s)suchende(r *m*) *f*; **~hunt·ing**: *be* ~ auf Arbeitssuche sein; **~less** [~lɪs] arbeitslos; **~work** Akkordarbeit *f*.

jock·ey ['dʒɒkɪ] Jockei *m*.

joc·u·lar □ ['dʒɒkjʊlə] lustig; spaßig.

jog [dʒɒg] **1.** (leichter) Stoß, Schubs; *Sport:* Dauerlauf *m*; Trott *m*; **2.** (*-gg-*) *v/t.* (an)stoßen, (*fig.* auf)rütteln; *v/i. mst* ~ *along*, ~ *on* dahintrotten, -zuckeln; *Sport:* Dauerlauf machen, joggen; **~ging** ['dʒɒgɪŋ] *Sport:* Dauerlauf *m*, Jogging *n*, Joggen *n*.

join [dʒɔɪn] **1.** *v/t.* verbinden, zusammenfügen (*to* mit); vereinigen; sich anschließen (*dat. od.* an *acc.*), sich gesellen zu; eintreten in (*acc.*), beitreten (*dat.*); ~ *hands* sich die Hände reichen; *fig.* sich zusammentun; *v/i.* sich verbinden *od.* vereinigen; ~ *in* teilnehmen an (*dat.*), mitmachen bei, sich beteiligen an (*dat.*); ~ *up* Soldat werden; **2.** Verbindungsstelle *f*, Naht *f*.

join·er ['dʒɔɪnə] Tischler *m*, Schreiner *m*; **~·y** *bsd. Brt.* [~ərɪ] Tischlerhandwerk *n*; Tischlerarbeit *f*.

joint [dʒɔɪnt] **1.** Verbindung(sstelle) *f*; Naht(stelle) *f*; *anat.*, ⊕ Gelenk *m*; ♘ Knoten *m*; *Brt.* Braten *m*; *sl.* Spelunke *f*; *sl.* Joint *m* (*Marihuanazigarette*); *out of* ~ ausgerenkt; *fig.* aus den Fugen; **2.** □ gemeinsam; Mit...; ~ *heir* Miterbe *m*; ~ *stock econ.* Aktienkapital *n*; **3.** verbinden, zusammenfügen; *Braten* zerlegen; **~·ed** ['dʒɔɪntɪd] gegliedert; Glieder...; **~·stock** *econ.* Aktien...; ~ *company Brt.* Aktiengesellschaft *f*.

joke [dʒəʊk] **1.** Witz *m*; Scherz *m*, Spaß *m*; *practical* ~ Streich *m*; **2.** scherzen, Witze machen; **jok·er** ['dʒəʊkə] Spaßvogel *m*; *Kartenspiel*: Joker *m*.

jol·ly ['dʒɒlɪ] **1.** *adj.* (*-ier, -iest*) lustig, fidel, vergnügt; **2.** *adv. Brt.* □ mächtig, sehr; ~ *good* prima.

jolt [dʒəʊlt] **1.** stoßen, rütteln, holpern; *fig.* aufrütteln; **2.** Ruck *m*, Stoß *m*; *fig.* Schock *m*.

jos·tle ['dʒɒsl] **1.** (an)rempeln; drängeln; **2.** Stoß *m*, Rempelei *f*; Zusammenstoß *m*.

jot [dʒɒt] **1.** *not a* ~ keine Spur, kein bißchen; **2.** (*-tt-*): ~ *down* schnell hinschreiben *od.* notieren.

jour·nal ['dʒɜːnl] Journal *n*; (*Fach-*) Zeitschrift *f*; (*Tages*)Zeitung *f*; Tagebuch *n*; **~·is·m** ['dʒɜːnəlɪzəm] Journalismus *m*; **~·ist** [~ɪst] Journalist(in).

jour·ney ['dʒɜːnɪ] **1.** Reise *f*; Fahrt *f*; **2.** reisen; **~·man** (*pl. -men*) Geselle *m*.

jo·vi·al □ ['dʒəʊvjəl] heiter, jovial.

joy [dʒɔɪ] Freude *f*; *for* ~ vor Freude; **~·ful** □ ['dʒɔɪfʊl] freudig; erfreut; **~·less** □ [~lɪs] freudlos, traurig; **~·stick** ✈ Steuerknüppel *m* (F *a. für Computerspiele*).

ju·bi·lant □ ['dʒuːbɪlənt] jubelnd, überglücklich.

ju·bi·lee ['dʒuːbɪliː] Jubiläum *n*.

judge [dʒʌdʒ] **1.** ♿ Richter *m*; Schieds-, Preisrichter *m*; Kenner(in), Sachverständige(r *m*) *f*; **2.** *v/i.* urteilen; *v/t.* ♿ *Fall* verhandeln, die Verhandlung führen über (*acc.*); ♿ ein Urteil fällen über (*acc.*); richten; beurteilen; halten für.

judg(e)·ment ['dʒʌdʒmənt] ♿ Urteil *n*; Urteilsvermögen *n*; Meinung *f*, Ansicht *f*, Urteil *n*; *göttliches* (*Straf-*) Gericht; *pass* ~ on ♿ ein Urteil fällen über (*acc.*); ♄ *Day, Day of* ♄ *eccl.* Tag *m* des Jüngsten Gerichts.

ju·di·cial □ [dʒuː'dɪʃl] ♿ gerichtlich, Gerichts...; kritisch; unparteiisch.

ju·di·cia·ry ♿ [dʒuː'dɪʃɪərɪ] Richter (-stand *m*) *pl.*

ju·di·cious □ [dʒuː'dɪʃəs] klug, weise.

jug [dʒʌg] Krug *m*, Kanne *f*.

jug·gle ['dʒʌgl] jonglieren (mit); manipulieren, *Bücher etc.* frisieren; **~·r** [~ə] Jongleur *m*; Schwindler(in).

juice [dʒuːs] Saft *m*; *sl. mot.* Sprit *m*; **juic·y** □ ['dʒuːsɪ] (*-ier, -iest*) saftig; F pikant, gepfeffert.

juke·box ['dʒuːkbɒks] Musikbox *f*, Musikautomat *m*.

Ju·ly [dʒuː'laɪ] Juli *m*.

jum·ble ['dʒʌmbl] **1.** Durcheinander *n*; **2.** *a.* ~ *together*, ~ *up* durcheinanderbringen, -werfen; ~ *sale Brt.* Wohltätigkeitsbasar *m*.

jum·bo ['dʒʌmbəʊ] *a.* ~*-sized* riesig.

jump [dʒʌmp] **1.** Sprung *m*, the ~s *pl.* große Nervosität; *high* (*long*) ~ *Sport:* Hoch-(Weit)sprung *m*; *get the* ~ *on* F zuvorkommen; **2.** *v/i.* springen; zusammenzucken, -fahren, hochfahren; ~ *at the chance* mit beiden Händen zugreifen; ~ *to conclusions* übereilte Schlüsse ziehen; *v/t.* (hinweg)springen über (*acc.*); überspringen; springen lassen; ~ *the queue Brt.* sich vordränge(l)n; ~ *the lights* bei Rot über die Kreuzung fahren, F bei Rot drüberfahren; **~·er** ['dʒʌmpə] Springer(in); *Brt.* Pullover *m*; *Am.* Trägerkleid *n*; **~·ing jack** Hampelmann *m*; **~·y** [~ɪ] (*-ier, -iest*) nervös.

junc|tion ['dʒʌŋkʃn] Verbindung *f*; (Straßen)Kreuzung *f*; ♅ Knotenpunkt *m*; **~·ture** [~ktʃə]: *at this* ~ an dieser Stelle, in diesem Augenblick.

June [dʒuːn] Juni *m*.

jun·gle ['dʒʌŋgl] Dschungel *m*.

ju·ni·or ['dʒuːnjə] **1.** jüngere(r, -s); untergeordnet, rangniedriger; *Sport:* Junioren-, Jugend...; **2.** Jüngere(r *m*) *f*; F Junior *m*; *Am. univ.* Student (-in) im vorletzten Studienjahr.

junk¹ ⚓ [dʒʌŋk] Dschunke *f*.

junk² F [~] Plunder *m*, alter Kram; *sl.* Stoff *m* (*bsd. Heroin*); ~ *food* kalo-

J

rienreiches aber minderwertiges Nahrungsmittel; **~·ie,** **~·y** *sl.* ['dʒʌŋkɪ] Fixer(in), Junkie *m;* **~ yard** Schrottplatz *m.*

jur·is·dic·tion ['dʒʊərɪs'dɪkʃn] Gerichtsbarkeit *f;* Zuständigkeit(sbereich *m*) *f.*

ju·ris·pru·dence [dʒʊərɪs'pruːdəns] Rechtswissenschaft *f.*

ju·ror ⚖ ['dʒʊərə] Geschworene(r *m*) *f.*

ju·ry ['dʒʊərɪ] ⚖ *die* Geschworenen *pl.;* Jury *f,* Preisrichter *pl.;* **~·man** *(pl. -men)* ⚖ Geschworene(r) *m;* **~·wom·an** *(pl. -women)* ⚖ Geschworene *f.*

just □ [dʒʌst] **1.** *adj.* gerecht; berechtigt; angemessen; **2.** *adv.* gerade, (so)eben; gerade, genau, eben; gerade (noch), ganz knapp; nur, bloß; F

einfach, wirklich; **~** *now* gerade (jetzt); (so)eben.

jus·tice ['dʒʌstɪs] Gerechtigkeit *f;* Rechtmäßigkeit *f;* Berechtigung *f,* Recht *n;* Gerichtsbarkeit *f,* Justiz *f;* ⚖ Richter *m;* ♀ *of the Peace* Friedensrichter *m;* *court of* **~** Gericht(shof *m*) *n.*

jus·ti·fi·ca·tion [dʒʌstɪfɪ'keɪʃn] Rechtfertigung *f;* **~·fy** ['dʒʌstɪfaɪ] rechtfertigen.

just·ly ['dʒʌstlɪ] mit *od.* zu Recht.

jut [dʒʌt] *(-tt-):* **~** *out* vorspringen, hervorragen, -stehen.

ju·ve·nile ['dʒuːvɪnaɪl] **1.** jung, jugendlich; Jugend...; für Jugendliche; **~** *court* Jugendgericht *n;* **~** *delinquency* Jugendkriminalität *f;* **~** *delinquent* jugendlicher Straftäter; **2.** Jugendliche(r *m*) *f.*

J

K

kan·ga·roo *zo.* [kæŋgə'ruː] *(pl. -roos)* Känguruh *n.*

keel ⚓ [kiːl] **1.** Kiel *m;* **2.** **~** *over* kieloben legen; umschlagen, kentern.

keen □ [kiːn] scharf *(a. fig.);* schneidend *(Kälte);* heftig; stark, groß *(Appetit etc.);* **~** *on* F scharf *od.* erpicht auf *(acc.); be* **~** *on hunting* ein leidenschaftlicher Jäger sein; **~·ness** ['kiːnnɪs] Schärfe *f;* Heftigkeit *f;* Scharfsinn *m.*

keep [kiːp] **1.** (Lebens)Unterhalt *m; for* **~** s F für immer; **2.** *(kept)* *v/t.* (auf-, [bei]be-, er-, fest-, zurück-)halten; unterhalten, sorgen für; *Gesetze etc.* einhalten, befolgen; *Ware, Tagebuch* führen; *Geheimnis* für sich behalten; *Versprechen* halten, einlösen; (auf)bewahren; abhalten, hindern *(from* von); *Vieh* halten; *Bett* hüten; (be)schützen; **~** *s.o. company* j-m Gesellschaft leisten; **~** *company with* verkehren mit; **~** *one's head* die Ruhe bewahren; **~** *early hours* früh zu Bett gehen; **~** *one's temper* sich beherrschen; **~** *time* richtig gehen *(Uhr);* Takt, Schritt halten; **~** *s.o. waiting* j-n

warten lassen; **~** *away* fernhalten; **~** *s.th. from s.o.* j-m et. vorenthalten *od.* verschweigen *od.* verheimlichen; **~** *in Schüler* nachsitzen lassen; **~** *on Kleid* anbehalten, *Hut* aufbehalten; **~** *up* aufrechterhalten; *Mut* bewahren; instand halten; fortfahren mit, weitermachen; nicht schlafen lassen; **~** *it up* so weitermachen; *v/i.* bleiben; sich halten; fortfahren, weitermachen; **~** *doing* immer wieder tun; **~** *going* weitergehen; **~** *away* sich fernhalten; **~** *from doing s.th.* et. nicht tun; **~** *off* weg-, fernbleiben; **~** *on* fortfahren *(doing* zu tun); **~** *on talking* weiterreden; **~** *to* sich halten an *(acc.);* **~** *up* stehen bleiben; andauern, anhalten; **~** *up with Schritt* halten mit; **~** *up with the Joneses* nicht hinter den Nachbarn zurückstehen (wollen).

keep·er ['kiːpə] Wärter(in), Wächter(in), Aufseher(in); Verwalter(in); Inhaber(in); **~·ing** [~ɪŋ] Verwahrung *f;* Obhut *f; be in (out of)* **~** *with* ... (nicht) übereinstimmen mit ...; **~·sake** [~seɪk] Andenken *n (Geschenk).*

keg [keg] Fäßchen *n,* kleines Faß.

ken·nel ['kenl] Hundehütte *f*; ~*s pl.* Hundezwinger *m*; Hundepension *f*.

kept [kept] *pret. u. p.p. von* keep 2.

kerb [kɜːb], ~**stone** ['kɜːbstəʊn] Bordstein *m*.

ker·chief ['kɜːtʃɪf] (Hals-, Kopf-) Tuch *n*.

ker·nel ['kɜːnl] Kern *m* (*a. fig.*).

ket·tle ['ketl] (Koch)Kessel *m*; ~**drum** *♪* (Kessel)Pauke *f*.

key [kiː] **1.** Schlüssel *m*; (*Schreibmaschinen-, Klavier- etc.*)Taste *f*; (*Druck*)Taste *f*; *♪* Tonart *f*; *fig.* Ton *m*; *fig.* Schlüssel *m*, Lösung *f*; *attr.* Schlüssel...; **2.** anpassen (*to an acc.*); ~*ed up* nervös, aufgeregt, überdreht; ~**board** ['kiːbɔːd] Klaviatur *f*, Tastatur *f*; ~**hole** Schlüsselloch *n*; ~**man** (*pl. -men*) Schlüsselfigur *f*; ~**mon·ey** *Brt.* Abstand(ssumme *f*) *m* (*für e-e Wohnung*); ~**note** *♪* Grundton *m*; *fig.* Grundgedanke *m*, Tenor *m*; ~ **ring** Schlüsselring *m*; ~**stone** *arch.* Schlußstein *m*; *fig.* Grundpfeiler *m*; ~**word** Schlüssel-, Stichwort *n*.

kick [kɪk] **1.** (Fuß)Tritt *m*; Stoß *m*; F Kraft *f*, Feuer *n*; F Nervenkitzel *m*; *get a ~ out of s.th.* e-n Riesenspaß an et. haben; *for ~s* (nur) zum Spaß; **2.** *v/t.* (mit dem Fuß) stoßen od. treten; *Fußball:* schießen, treten, kicken; ~ *off sich* verschaffen; ~ *up hochschleudern*; ~ *up a fuss od. row* F Krach schlagen; *v/i.* (mit dem Fuß) treten od. stoßen; (hinten) ausschlagen; strampeln; ~ *off Fußball:* anstoßen, den Anstoß ausführen; ~**er** ['kɪkə] Fußballspieler *m*; ~**off** Fußball: Anstoß *m*.

kid [kɪd] **1.** Zicklein *n*, Kitz *n*; Ziegenleder *n*; F Kind *n*; ~ *brother* F kleiner Bruder; **2.** (*-dd-*) *v/t.* j-n aufziehen; ~ *s.o.* j-m et. vormachen; *v/i.* Spaß machen; *he is only ~ding* er macht das nur Spaß; *no ~ding!* im Ernst!; ~ **glove** Glacéhandschuh *m* (*a. fig.*).

kid·nap ['kɪdnæp] (*-pp-, Am. a. -p-*) entführen, kidnappen; ~**per**, *Am. a.* ~**er** [~ə] Entführer(in), Kidnapper(in); ~**ping**, *Am. a.* ~**ing** [~ɪŋ] Entführung *f*, Kidnapping *n*.

kid·ney ['kɪdnɪ] *anat.* Niere *f* (*a. als Speise*); ~ *bean* ♀ Weiße Bohne; ~ *machine* künstliche Niere.

kill [kɪl] **1.** töten (*a. fig.*); umbringen; vernichten; beseitigen; *Tiere* schlach-

ten; *hunt.* erlegen, schießen; *be ~ed in an accident* tödlich verunglücken; ~ *time* die Zeit totschlagen; **2.** Tötung *f*; *hunt.* Jagdbeute *f*; ~**er** ['kɪlə] Mörder(in), F Killer *m*; ~**ing** ☐ [~ɪŋ] mörderisch, tödlich.

kiln [kɪln] Brenn-, Darrofen *m*.

ki·lo F ['kiːləʊ] (*pl. -los*) Kilo *n*.

kil·o|gram(me) ['kɪləgræm] Kilogramm *n*; ~**me·tre**, *Am.* ~**me·ter** Kilometer *m*.

kilt [kɪlt] Kilt *m*, Schottenrock *m*.

kin [kɪn] Verwandtschaft *f*, Verwandte *pl.*

kind [kaɪnd] **1.** ☐ gütig, freundlich, liebenswürdig, nett; **2.** Art *f*, Sorte *f*; Art *f*, Gattung *f*, Geschlecht *n*; △ *nicht Kind*; *pay in ~* in Naturalien zahlen; *fig.* mit gleicher Münze heimzahlen.

kin·der·gar·ten ['kɪndəgɑːtn] Kindergarten *m*.

kind-heart·ed ['kaɪnd'hɑːtɪd] gütig.

kin·dle ['kɪndl] anzünden; (sich) entzünden (*a. fig.*).

kin·dling ['kɪndlɪŋ] Material *n* zum Anzünden, Anmachholz *n*.

kind|ly ['kaɪndlɪ] *adj.* (*-ier, -iest*) *u. adv.* freundlich, liebenswürdig, nett; gütig; ~**ness** [~nɪs] Güte *f*; Freundlichkeit *f*, Liebenswürdigkeit *f*; Gefälligkeit *f*.

kin·dred ['kɪndrɪd] **1.** verwandt; *fig.* gleichartig; ~ *spirits pl.* Gleichgesinnte *pl.*; **2.** Verwandtschaft *f*.

king [kɪŋ] König *m* (*a. fig. u. Schach, Kartenspiel*); ~**dom** ['kɪŋdəm] Königreich *n*; *eccl.* Reich *n* Gottes; *animal* (*mineral, vegetable*) ~ Tier-(Mineral-, Pflanzen)reich *n*; ~**ly** ['kɪŋlɪ] (*-ier, -iest*) königlich; ~**size(d)** extrem groß.

kink [kɪŋk] Schleife *f*, Knoten *m*; *fig.* Schrulle *f*, Tick *m*, Spleen *m*; ~**y** ['kɪŋkɪ] (*-ier, -iest*) schrullig, spleenig.

ki·osk ['kiːɒsk] Kiosk *m*; *Brt.* Telefonzelle *f*.

kip·per ['kɪpə] Räucherhering *m*.

kiss [kɪs] **1.** Kuß *m*; **2.** (sich) küssen.

kit [kɪt] Ausrüstung *f* (*a. ✗ u. Sport*); Werkzeug(e *pl.*) *n*; Werkzeugtasche *f*, -kasten *m*; Bastelsatz *m*; *s. first-aid*; ~**bag** ['kɪtbæg] Seesack *m*.

kitch·en ['kɪtʃɪn] Küche *f*; *attr.* Küchen...; ~**ette** [kɪtʃɪ'net] Kleinküche *f*, Kochnische *f*; ~ **gar·den** ['kɪtʃɪn-'gɑːdn] Küchen-, Gemüsegarten *m*.

kite [kaɪt] (Papier-, Stoff)Drachen *m*; *zo.* Milan *m*.

kit·ten ['kɪtn] Kätzchen *n*.

knack [næk] Kniff *m*, Trick *m*, Dreh *m*; Geschick *n*, Talent *n*.

knave [neɪv] Schurke *m*, Spitzbube *m*; *Kartenspiel:* Bube *m*, Unter *m*.

knead [niːd] kneten; massieren.

knee [niː] Knie *n*; ⊕ Kniestück *n*; **~cap** *anat.* ['niːkæp] Kniescheibe *f*; **~joint** *anat.* Kniegelenk *n* (*a.* ⊕); **~l** [niːl] (*knelt, Am. a. kneeled*) knien (*to* vor *dat.*); **~length** knielang (*Rock etc.*).

knell [nel] Totenglocke *f*.

knelt [nelt] *pret. u. p.p. von* kneel.

knew [njuː] *pret. von* know.

knick·er|bock·ers ['nɪkəbɒkəz] *pl.* Knickerbocker *pl.*, Kniehosen *pl.*; **~s** *Brt.* F [~z] *pl.* (Damen)Schlüpfer *m*.

knick-knack ['nɪknæk] Nippsache *f*.

knife [naɪf] 1. (*pl. knives* [~vz]) Messer *n*; 2. schneiden; mit e-m Messer verletzen; erstechen.

knight [naɪt] 1. Ritter *m*; *Schach:* Springer *m*; 2. zum Ritter schlagen; **~hood** ['naɪthʊd] Ritterwürde *f*, -stand *m*; Ritterschaft *f*.

knit [nɪt] (*-tt-; knit od. knitted*) *v/t.* stricken; *a.* ~ *together* zusammenfügen, verbinden; ~ *one's brows* die Stirn runzeln; *v/i.* stricken; zusammenwachsen (*Knochen*); **~ting** ['nɪtɪŋ] Stricken *n*; Strickzeug *n*; *attr.* Strick...; **~wear** Strickwaren *pl.*

knives [naɪvz] *pl. von* knife 1.

knob [nɒb] Knopf *m*, Knauf *m*; Buckel *m*; Brocken *m*.

knock [nɒk] 1. Stoß *m*; Klopfen (*a. mot.*), Pochen *n*; *there is a* ~ es klopft; 2. *v/i.* schlagen, pochen, klopfen; stoßen (*against, into* gegen); ~ *about,* ~ *around* F sich herumtreiben; F herumliegen; ~ *at the door* an die Tür klopfen; ~ *off* F Feierabend *od.* Schluß machen, aufhören; *v/t.* stoßen, schlagen; F schlechtmachen, verreißen; ~ *about,* ~ *around* herumstoßen, übel zurich-

ten; ~ *down* niederschlagen, umwerfen; um-, überfahren; *Auktion:* et. zuschlagen (*to s.o.* j-m); *Preis* herabsetzen; ⊕ auseinandernehmen, zerlegen; *Haus* abreißen; *Baum* fällen; *be* ~ed *down* überfahren werden; ~ *off* herunterstoßen; abschlagen; F aufhören mit; F hinhauen (*schnell erledigen*); *vom Preis* abziehen, nachlassen; *Brt.* F ausrauben; ~ *out* (her)ausschlagen, (her)ausklopfen; k.o. schlagen; *fig.* F umwerfen, schocken; *be* ~ed *out of* ausscheiden aus (*e-m Wettbewerb*); ~ *over* umwerfen, umstoßen; um-, überfahren; *be* ~ed *over* überfahren werden; ~ *up* hochschlagen; *Brt.* F rasch auf die Beine stellen, improvisieren; **~er** ['nɒkə] Türklopfer *m*; **~kneed** [~'niːd] X-beinig; **~out** [~kaʊt] *Boxen:* Knockout *m*, K.o. *m.*

knoll [nəʊl] kleiner runder Hügel; △ *nicht* Knolle.

knot [nɒt] 1. Knoten *m*; Astknorren *m*; ⚓ Knoten *m*, Seemeile *f*; Gruppe *f*, Knäuel *m*, *n* (*Menschen*); 2. (*-tt-*) (ver)knoten, (-)knüpfen; **~ty** ['nɒtɪ] (*-ier, -iest*) knotig; knorrig; *fig.* verzwickt.

know [nəʊ] (*knew, known*) wissen; kennen; erfahren; (wieder)erkennen, unterscheiden; (es) können *od.* verstehen; ~ *French* Französisch können; *come to* ~ erfahren; *get to* ~ kennenlernen; ~ *one's business,* ~ *the ropes,* ~ *a thing or two,* ~ *what's what* F sich auskennen, Erfahrung haben; *you* ~ wissen Sie; **~how** ['nəʊhaʊ] Know-how *n*, praktische (Sach-, Spezial)Kenntnis(se *pl.*) *f*; **~ing** □ [~ɪŋ] klug; schlau; verständnisvoll; wissend; **~ing·ly** [~lɪ] wissend; absichtlich, bewußt; **~ledge** ['nɒlɪdʒ] Kenntnis(se *pl.*) *f*, Wissen *n*; *to my* ~ meines Wissens; **~n** [nəʊn] *p.p. von* know; bekannt; *make* ~ bekanntmachen.

knuck·le ['nʌkl] 1. (Finger)Knöchel *m*; 2. ~ *down to work* sich an die Arbeit machen.

Krem·lin ['kremlɪn]: *the* ~ der Kreml.

L

lab F [læb] Labor *n*.

la·bel ['leɪbl] 1. Etikett *n*, Aufkleber *m*; Schild(chen) *n*; Aufschrift *f*, Beschriftung *f*; (Schall)Plattenfirma *f*; 2. (*bsd. Brt. -ll-, Am. -l-*) etikettieren, beschriften; *fig.* abstempeln als.

la·bor·a·to·ry [lə'bɒrətərɪ] Laboratorium *n*; ~ *assistant* Laborant(in).

la·bo·ri·ous □ [lə'bɔːrɪəs] mühsam; schwerfällig (*Stil*).

la·bo(u)r ['leɪbə] 1. (schwere) Arbeit *f*; Mühe *f*; ⚕ Wehen *pl.*; Arbeiter *pl.*, Arbeitskräfte *pl.*; *Labour pol.* die Labour Party; *hard* ~ ⚖ Zwangsarbeit *f*; 2. Arbeiter..., Arbeits...; 3. *v/i.* arbeiten; sich abmühen, sich quälen; ~ *under* leiden unter (*dat.*), zu kämpfen haben mit; *v/t.* ausführlich behandeln; ~**ed** schwerfällig (*Stil*); mühsam (*Atem etc.*); ~**er** [~rə] *bsd.* ungelernter Arbeiter; **Labour Ex·change** *Brt.* F *od. hist.* Arbeitsamt *n*; **La·bour Par·ty** *pol.* Labour Party *f*; **la·bor u·ni·on** *Am. pol.* Gewerkschaft *f*.

lace [leɪs] 1. Spitze *f*; Borte *f*; Schnürsenkel *m*; 2. ~ *up* (zu-, zusammen-) schnüren; Schuhe zubinden; ~*d with brandy* mit e-m Schuß Weinbrand.

la·ce·rate ['læsəreɪt] zerfleischen, -schneiden, -kratzen, aufreißen; *j-s Gefühle* verletzen.

lack [læk] 1. (*of*) Fehlen *n* (von), Mangel *m* (an *dat.*); △ *nicht* Lack; 2. *v/t.* nicht haben; *he* ~*s money* es fehlt ihm an Geld; *v/i.* *be* ~*ing* fehlen; *he is* ~*ing in courage* ihm fehlt der Mut; ~**lus·tre**, *Am.* ~**lus·ter** ['læklʌstə] glanzlos, matt.

la·con·ic [lə'kɒnɪk] (~*ally*) lakonisch, wortkarg, kurz und prägnant.

lac·quer ['lækə] 1. Lack *m*; Haarspray *m*, *n*; Nagellack *m*; 2. lackieren.

lad [læd] Bursche *m*, Junge *m*.

lad·der ['lædə] Leiter *f*; *Brt.* Laufmasche *f*; ~**proof** (lauf)maschenfest (*Strumpf*).

la·den ['leɪdn] (schwer) beladen.

la·ding ['leɪdɪŋ] Ladung *f*, Fracht *f*.

la·dle ['leɪdl] 1. Schöpf-, Suppen-) Kelle *f*, Schöpflöffel *m*; 2. ~ *out* Suppe austeilen.

la·dy ['leɪdɪ] Dame *f*; Lady *f* (*a.*

Titel); ~ *doctor* Ärztin *f*; *Ladies*('), *Am. Ladies' room* Damentoilette *f*; ~**bird** *zo.* Marienkäfer *m*; ~**like** damenhaft; ~**ship** [~ʃɪp]: *her od. your* ~ Ihre Ladyschaft.

lag [læg] 1. (-*gg*-) ~ *behind* zurückbleiben; sich verzögern; 2. ~ Verzögerung *f*; Zeitabstand *m*, -differenz *f*.

la·ger ['lɑːgə] Lagerbier *n*; △ *nicht* Lager.

la·goon [lə'guːn] Lagune *f*.

laid [leɪd] *pret. u. p.p. von* lay³.

lain [leɪn] *p.p. von* lie² 2.

lair [leə] Lager *n*, Höhle *f*, Bau *m* (*e-s wilden Tieres*).

la·i·ty ['leɪətɪ] Laien *pl.*

lake [leɪk] See *m*.

lamb [læm] 1. Lamm *n*; 2. lammen.

lame [leɪm] 1. □ lahm (*a. fig. = unbefriedigend*); 2. lähmen.

la·ment [lə'ment] 1. Wehklage *f*; Klagelied *n*; 2. (be)klagen; (be)trauern; **lam·en·ta·ble** □ ['læməntəbl] beklagenswert; kläglich; **lam·en·ta·tion** [læmen'teɪʃn] Wehklage *f*.

lamp [læmp] Lampe *f*; Laterne *f*.

lam·poon [læm'puːn] 1. Schmähschrift *f*; 2. verspotten, -unglimpfen.

lamp|post ['læmppəʊst] Laternenpfahl *m*; ~**shade** Lampenschirm *m*.

lance [lɑːns] Lanze *f*.

land [lænd] 1. Land *n*; Boden *m*, Land-; Grundbesitz *m*; Land *n*, Staat *m*, Nation *f*; *by* ~ auf dem Landweg; ~*s pl.* Ländereien *pl.*; 2. landen; *Fracht* löschen; F *j-n od. et.* erwischen, kriegen; F *in Schwierigkeiten etc.* bringen; ~**a·gent** ['lændeɪdʒənt] Gutsverwalter *m*; ~**ed** Land..., Grund...; ~**hold·er** Grundbesitzer(in).

land·ing ['lændɪŋ] Landung *f*; Anlegen *n* (*Schiff*); Anlegestelle *f*; Treppenabsatz *m*; Flur *m*, Gang *m* (*am Ende e-r Treppe*); ~**field** ✈ Landebahn *f*; ~**gear** ✈ Fahrgestell *n*; ~**stage** Landungsbrücke *f*, -steg *m*.

land|la·dy ['lænleɪdɪ] Vermieterin *f*; Wirtin *f*; ~**lord** [~lɔːd] Vermieter *m*; Wirt *m*; Hauseigentümer *m*; Grundbesitzer *m*; ~**lub·ber** ⚓ *contp.* [~dlʌbə] Landratte *f*; ~**mark** Grenzstein *m*; Orientierungspunkt *m*; Wahrzeichen *n*; *fig.* Markstein *m*; ~**own·er** Grundbesitzer(in);

~·scape ['lænskeip] Landschaft *f (a. paint.)*; **~·slide** Erdrutsch *m (a. pol.)*; a ~ *victory pol.* ein überwältigender Wahlsieg; **~·slip** (kleiner) Erdrutsch.

lane [lein] Feldweg *m*; Gasse *f*, Sträßchen *n*; ♣ (Fahrt)Route *f*; ✈ Flugschneise *f*; *mot.* Fahrbahn *f*, Spur *f*; *Sport:* (einzelne) Bahn.

lan·guage ['læŋgwidʒ] Sprache *f*; ~ *laboratory* Sprachlabor *n*.

lan·guid □ ['læŋgwid] matt; träg(e).

lank □ [læŋk] dünn, dürr; strähnig *(Haar)*; **~·y** □ ['læŋki] *(-ier, -iest)* schlaksig.

lan·tern ['læntən] Laterne *f*.

lap¹ [læp] Schoß *m*.

lap² [~] 1. *Sport:* Runde *f*; 2. *(-pp-) Sport: Gegner* überrunden; *Sport:* e-e Runde zurücklegen; wickeln; einhüllen.

lap³ [~] *(-pp-) v/t.:* ~ *up* auflecken, -schlecken; *v/i.* plätschern *(against* gegen).

la·pel [lə'pel] Revers *n*, *m*.

lapse [læps] 1. Verlauf *m (der Zeit)*; (kleiner) Fehler *od.* Irrtum; ⚖ Verfall *m*; 2. verfallen; ⚖ verfallen, erlöschen; abfallen *(vom Glauben)*.

lar·ce·ny ⚖ ['lɑːsəni] Diebstahl *m*.

larch ♀ [lɑːtʃ] Lärche *f*.

lard [lɑːd] 1. Schweinefett *n*, -schmalz *n*; 2. *Fleisch* spicken; **~·der** ['lɑːdə] Speisekammer *f*; Speiseschrank *m*.

large □ [lɑːdʒ] *(~r, ~st)* groß; umfassend, weitgehend, ausgedehnt; *at* ~ in Freiheit, auf freiem Fuß; ganz allgemein; in der Gesamtheit; (sehr) ausführlich; **~·ly** ['lɑːdʒli] zum großen Teil, im wesentlichen; **~·minded** tolerant; **~·ness** [~nis] Größe *f*.

lar·i·at *bsd. Am.* ['læriət] Lasso *n*, *m*.

lark¹ *zo.* [lɑːk] Lerche *f*.

lark² *F* [~] Jux *m*, Spaß *m*.

lark·spur ♀ ['lɑːkspɜː] Rittersporn *m*.

lar·va *zo.* ['lɑːvə] *(pl. -vae* [-viː]*)* Larve *f*.

lar·ynx *anat.* ['læriŋks] Kehlkopf *m*.

las·civ·i·ous □ [lə'siviəs] lüstern.

la·ser *phys.* ['leizə] Laser *m*; ~ **beam** Laserstrahl *m*.

lash [læʃ] 1. Peitschenschnur *f*; Peitschenhieb *m*; Wimper *f*; 2. peitschen, schlagen; (fest)binden; ~ *out* (wild) um sich schlagen; *fig.* heftig angreifen.

lass, **~·ie** [læs, 'læsi] Mädchen *n*.

las·si·tude ['læsitjuːd] Mattigkeit *f*.

las·so [læ'suː] *(pl. -sos, -soes)* Lasso *n*, *m*.

last¹ [lɑːst] 1. *adj.* letzte(r, -s); vorige(r, -s); äußerste(r, -s); neueste(r, -s); ~ *but one* vorletzte(r, -s); ~ *night* gestern abend; 2. *der, die, das* Letzte; ⚠ *nicht Last; at* ~ endlich; *to the* ~ bis zum Schluß; 3. *adv.* zuletzt; ~ *but not least* nicht zuletzt.

last² [~] (an-, fort)dauern; (sich) halten *(Farbe etc.)*; (aus)reichen.

last³ [~] (Schuhmacher)Leisten *m*.

last·ing □ ['lɑːstiŋ] dauerhaft; beständig.

last·ly ['lɑːstli] schließlich, zum Schluß.

latch [lætʃ] 1. Klinke *f*; Schnappschloß *n*; 2. ein-, zuklinken; ~·**key** ['lætʃkiː] Hausschlüssel *m*.

late □ [leit] *(~r, ~st)* spät; jüngste(r, -s), letzte(r, -s); frühere(r, -s), ehemalig; verstorben; *be* ~ zu spät kommen, sich verspäten; *at (the)* ~*st* spätestens; *as* ~ *as* noch, erst; *of* ~ kürzlich; ~*r on* später; ~·**ly** ['leitli] kürzlich.

la·tent □ ['leitənt] verborgen, latent.

lat·er·al □ ['lætərəl] seitlich, Seiten...

lath [lɑːθ] Latte *f*.

lathe ⊕ [leið] Drehbank *f*.

la·ther ['lɑːðə] 1. (Seifen)Schaum *m*; 2. *v/t.* einseifen; *v/i.* schäumen.

Lat·in ['lætin] 1. *ling.* lateinisch; romanisch; südländisch; 2. *ling.* Latein *n*; Roman|e *m*, -in *f*, Südländer(in).

lat·i·tude ['lætitjuːd] *geogr.* Breite *f*; *fig.* Spielraum *m*.

lat·ter ['lætə] letztere(r, -s) *(von zweien)*; letzte(r, -s), spätere(r, -s); ~·**ly** [~li] in letzter Zeit.

lat·tice ['lætis] Gitter *n*.

lau·da·ble □ ['lɔːdəbl] lobenswert.

laugh [lɑːf] 1. Lachen *n*, Gelächter *n*; 2. lachen; ~ *at j-n* auslachen; *have the last* ~ *(am Ende)* doch noch gewinnen; ~·**a·ble** □ ['lɑːfəbl] lächerlich; ~·**ter** [~tə] Lachen *n*, Gelächter *n*.

launch [lɔːntʃ] 1. *Schiff* vom Stapel laufen lassen; *Boot* aussetzen; schleudern; *Rakete* starten; abschießen; *fig.* in Gang setzen; 2. ♣ Barkasse *f*; ~·**ing** ['lɔːntʃiŋ] ♣ Stapellauf *m*; Abschuß *m (e-r Rakete)*; ~**·**

Start(en n) m; ~ **pad** Abschußrampe f; ~ **site** Abschußbasis f.

laun|de·rette [lɔːndəˈret], bsd. Am. ~**·dro·mat** [ˈlɔːndrəmæt] Waschsalon m, Münzwäscherei f; ~**dry** [~rɪ] Wäscherei f; schmutzige od. gewaschene Wäsche.

laur·el ♀ [ˈlɒrəl] Lorbeer m (a. fig.).

lav·a·to·ry [ˈlævətərɪ] Toilette f, Klosett n; public ~ Bedürfnisanstalt f.

lav·en·der ♀ [ˈlævəndə] Lavendel m.

lav·ish [ˈlævɪʃ] **1.** □ freigebig, verschwenderisch; **2.** ~ s.th. on s.o. j-n mit et. überhäufen od. überschütten.

law [lɔː] Gesetz n; Recht n; (Spiel-) Regel f; Rechtswissenschaft f; Jura pl.; F die Polizei; ~ and order Recht od. Ruhe u. Ordnung; ~**·a·bid·ing** [ˈlɔːəbaɪdɪŋ] gesetzestreu; ~**court** Gericht(shof m) n; ~**·ful** □ [~fl] gesetzlich; rechtmäßig, legitim; rechtsgültig; ~**·less** □ [~lɪs] gesetzlos; gesetzwidrig; zügellos.

lawn [lɔːn] Rasen m.

law|suit [ˈlɔːsjuːt] Prozeß m; ~**yer** [~jə] (Rechts)Anwalt m, (-)Anwältin f.

lax □ [læks] locker, lax; schlaff; lasch; ~**·a·tive** ♣ [ˈlæksətɪv] **1.** abführend; **2.** Abführmittel n.

lay[1] [leɪ] pret. von lie[2] 2.

lay[2] [~] eccl. weltlich; Laien...

lay[3] [~] (laid) v/t. legen; umlegen; Plan schmieden; Tisch decken; Eier legen; beruhigen, besänftigen; auferlegen; Klage vorbringen, Anklage erheben; Wette abschließen; Summe wetten; ~ in einlagern, sich eindecken mit; ~ low niederstrecken, -werfen; ~ off econ. Arbeiter vorübergehend entlassen, Arbeit einstellen; ~ open offen legen; ~ out ausbreiten; Garten etc. anlegen; entwerfen, planen; print. Buch gestalten; ~ up Vorräte hinlegen, sammeln; be laid up das Bett hüten müssen; v/i. (Eier) legen.

lay-by Brt. mot. [ˈleɪbaɪ] Parkbucht f, -streifen m; Park-, Rastplatz m.

lay·er [ˈleɪə] Lage f, Schicht f.

lay·man [ˈleɪmən] (pl. -men) Laie m.

lay|off [ˈleɪɒf] vorübergehende Arbeitseinstellung, Feierschicht(en pl.) f; ~**out** Layout n; Plan m; print. Layout n, Gestaltung f.

la·zy □ [ˈleɪzɪ] (-ier, -iest) faul; träg(e), langsam; müde od. faul machend.

---

lead[1] [led] ♠ Blei n; ♣ Lot n.

lead[2] [liːd] **1.** Führung f; Leitung f; Spitzenposition f; Beispiel n; thea. Hauptrolle f; thea. Hauptdarsteller(in); Sport u. fig. Führung f, Vorsprung m; Kartenspiel: Vorhand f; Leitung f; (Hunde)Leine f; Hinweis m, Tip m, Anhaltspunkt m; **2.** (led) v/t. führen; leiten; (an)führen; verleiten, bewegen (to zu); Karte ausspielen; ~ on F j-n anführen, auf den Arm nehmen; v/i. führen; vorangehen; Sport: in Führung liegen; ~ off den Anfang machen; ~ up to führen zu, hinführen auf.

lead·en [ˈledn] bleiern (a. fig.), Blei...

lead·er [ˈliːdə] (An)Führer(in), Leiter(in); Erste(r m) f; Brt. Leitartikel m; ~**·ship** [~ʃɪp] Führung f, Leitung f.

lead-free [ˈledfriː] bleifrei.

lead·ing [ˈliːdɪŋ] leitend; führend; Haupt...

leaf [liːf] **1.** (pl. leaves [~vz]) Blatt n; (Tür- etc.)Flügel m; (Tisch)Klappe f; **2.** ~ through durchblättern; ~**·let** [ˈliːflɪt] Prospekt m; Broschüre f, Informationsblatt n; Merkblatt n; ~**y** [~ɪ] (-ier, -iest) belaubt.

league [liːg] Liga f (a. hist. u. Sport); Bund m.

leak [liːk] **1.** Leck n, undichte Stelle (a. fig.); **2.** lecken, leck sein; tropfen; ~ out auslaufen, -strömen, entweichen; fig. durchsickern; ~**·age** [ˈliːkɪdʒ] Lecken n, Auslaufen n, -strömen n; fig. Durchsickern n; ~**y** [~ɪ] (-ier, -iest) leck, undicht.

lean[1] [liːn] (bsd. Brt. leant od. bsd. Am. leaned) (sich) lehnen; (sich) stützen; (sich) neigen; ~ on, ~ upon sich verlassen auf (acc.).

lean[2] [~] **1.** mager; **2.** das Magere (von gekochtem Fleisch).

leant bsd. Brt. [lent] pret u. p.p. von lean[1].

leap [liːp] **1.** Sprung m, Satz m; **2.** (leapt od. leaped) (über)springen; ~ at fig. sich stürzen auf; ~**t** [lept] pret. u. p.p. von leap 2; ~**year** [ˈliːpjɜː] Schaltjahr n.

learn [lɜːn] (learned od. learnt) (er)lernen; erfahren, hören; ~**ed** [ˈlɜːnɪd] gelehrt; ~**er** [~ə] Anfänger(in); Lernende(r m) f; ~ driver mot. Fahrschüler(in); ~**·ing** [~ɪŋ] (Er)Lernen n; Gelehrsamkeit f; ~**t** [lɜːnt] pret. u. p.p. von learn.

lease [li:s] **1.** Pacht f, Miete f; Pacht-, Mietvertrag m; **2.** (ver)pachten, (ver)mieten.

leash [li:ʃ] (Hunde)Leine f.

least [li:st] **1.** adj. (sup. von little 1) kleinste(r, -s), geringste(r, -s), wenigste(r, -s); **2.** adv. (sup. von little 2) am wenigsten; ~ of all am allerwenigsten; **3.** das Geringste, das Mindeste, das Wenigste; at ~ wenigstens; to say the ~ gelinde gesagt.

leath·er [ˈleðə] **1.** Leder n; **2.** ledern; Leder...

leave [li:v] **1.** Erlaubnis f; a. ~ of absence Urlaub m; Abschied m; take (one's) ~ sich verabschieden; **2.** (left) v/t. (hinter-, über-, übrig-, ver-, zurück)lassen; stehen-, liegenlassen, vergessen; vermachen, -erben; v/i. (fort-, weg)gehen, abreisen, abfahren, abfliegen.

leav·en [ˈlevn] Sauerteig m; Hefe f.

leaves [li:vz] pl. von leaf 1; Laub n.

leav·ings [ˈli:vɪŋz] pl. Überreste pl.

lech·er·ous □ [ˈletʃərəs] lüstern.

lec·ture [ˈlektʃə] **1.** univ. Vorlesung f; Vortrag m; Strafpredigt f; △ nicht Lektüre; **2.** v/i. univ. e-e Vorlesung halten; e-n Vortrag halten; v/t. tadeln, abkanzeln; **~tur·er** [~rə] univ. Dozent(in); Redner(in).

led [led] pret. u. p.p. von lead² 2.

ledge [ledʒ] Leiste f; Sims m, n; Riff n; (Fels)Vorsprung m.

ledg·er econ. [ˈledʒə] Hauptbuch n.

leech [li:tʃ] zo. Blutegel m; fig. Blutsauger m, Schmarotzer m.

leek ♣ [li:k] Lauch m, Porree m.

leer [lɪə] **1.** anzüglicher (Seiten)Blick; **2.** anzüglich od. lüstern blicken; schielen (at nach).

lee·ward ⌘ [ˈli:wəd] leewärts; **~·way** ⌘ Abtrift f; fig. Rückstand m; fig. Spielraum m.

left¹ [left] pret. u. p.p. von leave 2.

left² [~] **1.** adj. linke(r, -s); **2.** adv. (nach) links; **3.** Linke f (a. pol., Boxen), linke Seite; on od. to the ~ links; **~·hand** [ˈlefthænd] linke(r, -s); ~ drive mot. Linkssteuerung f; **~·hand·ed** □ [ˈlefthændɪd] linkshändig; für Linkshänder.

left·-lug·gage of·fice Brt. 🚉 [ˈleft-ˈlʌgɪdʒɒfɪs] Gepäckaufbewahrung f; **~·o·vers** pl. (Speise)Reste pl.; **~·wing** pol. linke(r, -s), linksgerichtet.

leg [leg] Bein n; Keule f; (Stiefel-) Schaft m; ⚕ Schenkel m; pull s.o.'s ~

j-n auf den Arm nehmen (hänseln); stretch one's ~s sich die Beine vertreten.

leg·a·cy [ˈlegəsɪ] Vermächtnis n.

le·gal □ [ˈli:gl] legal, gesetz-, rechtmäßig; gesetz-, rechtlich; juristisch, Rechts...; **~·ize** [~aɪz] legalisieren, rechtskräftig machen.

le·ga·tion [lɪˈgeɪʃn] Gesandtschaft f.

le·gend [ˈledʒənd] Legende f, Sage f; Bildunterschrift f; **le·gen·da·ry** [~ərɪ] legendär, sagenhaft.

leg·gings [ˈlegɪŋz] pl. Gamaschen pl.; -schutz m.

le·gi·ble □ [ˈledʒəbl] leserlich.

le·gion fig. [ˈli:dʒən] Legion f, Heer n.

le·gis·la|tion [ledʒɪsˈleɪʃn] Gesetzgebung f; **~·tive** pol. [ˈledʒɪslətɪv] **1.** □ gesetzgebend, legislativ; **2.** Legislative f, gesetzgebende Gewalt; **~·tor** [~eɪtə] Gesetzgeber m.

le·git·i·mate □ [lɪˈdʒɪtɪmət] legitim; gesetz-, rechtmäßig, berechtigt; ehelich.

lei·sure [ˈleʒə] Muße f, Freizeit f; at ~ frei, unbeschäftigt; ohne Hast; **~·ly** [~lɪ] gemächlich.

lem·on [ˈlemən] Zitrone f; **~·ade** [lemɪˈneɪd] Zitronenlimonade f; ~ **squash** Zitronenwasser n.

lend [lend] (lent) j-m et. (ver-, aus)leihen, borgen; △ nicht sich et. leihen.

length [leŋθ] Länge f; Strecke f; (Zeit)Dauer f; at ~ endlich, schließlich; ausführlich; go to any od. great od. considerable ~s sehr weit gehen; **~·en** [ˈleŋθən] verlängern; länger werden; **~·ways** [~weɪz], **~·wise** [~waɪz] der Länge nach; **~·y** □ [~ɪ] (-ier, -iest) sehr lang.

le·ni·ent □ [ˈli:njənt] mild(e), nachsichtig.

lens opt. [lenz] Linse f.

lent¹ [lent] pret. u. p.p. von lend.

Lent² [~] Fastenzeit f.

len·til ♣ [ˈlentɪl] Linse f.

leop·ard zo. [ˈlepəd] Leopard m.

le·o·tard [ˈli:əʊtɑ:d] (Tänzer)Trikot n; Gymnastikanzug m.

lep·ro·sy ⚕ [ˈleprəsɪ] Lepra f.

les·bi·an [ˈlezbɪən] **1.** lesbisch; **2.** Lesbierin f, F Lesbe f.

less [les] **1.** adj. u. adv. (comp. von little 1, 2) kleiner, geringer, weniger; **2.** prp. weniger, minus, abzüglich.

less·en [ˈlesn] (sich) vermindern od. -ringern; abnehmen; herabsetzen.

less·er ['lesə] kleiner, geringer.

les·son ['lesn] Lektion f; (Haus)Aufgabe f; (Unterrichts)Stunde f; fig. Lektion f, Lehre f; ~s pl. Unterricht m.

lest [lest] damit nicht; daß.

let [let] (let) lassen; vermieten, -pachten; ~ alone in Ruhe lassen; geschweige denn; ~ down herab-, herunterlassen; Kleider verlängern; j-n im Stich lassen; ~ go loslassen; ~ o.s. go sich gehenlassen; ~ in (her)einlassen; ~ o.s. in for s.th. sich aufhalsen od. einbrocken; ~ s.o. in on s.th. j-n in et. einweihen; ~ off abschießen; j-n laufenlassen; aussteigen lassen; ~ out hinauslassen; Schrei ausstoßen; ausplaudern; vermieten; ~ up aufhören.

le·thal ['li:θl] tödlich; Todes...

leth·ar·gy ['leθədʒɪ] Lethargie f.

let·ter ['letə] 1. Buchstabe m; print. Type f; Brief m, Schreiben n; ~s pl. Literatur f; attr. Brief...; 2. beschriften; **~box** Briefkasten m; **~card** Kartenbrief m; **~ car·ri·er** Am. Briefträger m; **~ed** (literarisch) gebildet; **~ing** [~rɪŋ] Beschriftung f.

let·tuce ꝗ ['letɪs] (bsd. Kopf)Salat m.

leu·k(a)e·mia ꝗ [lju:'ki:mɪə] Leukämie f.

lev·el ['levl] 1. waag(e)recht; eben; gleich; ausgeglichen; my ~ best f mein möglichstes; ~ crossing Brt. schienengleicher Bahnübergang; 2. Ebene f, ebene Fläche; (gleiche) Höhe, (Wasser- etc.)Spiegel m, (-)Stand m; Wasserwaage f; fig. Niveau n, Stand m, Stufe f; sea ~ Meeresspiegel m; on the ~ f ehrlich, aufrichtig; 3. (bsd. Brt. -ll-, Am. -l-) ebnen, planieren; niederschlagen, fällen; ~ at Waffe richten auf (acc.); Anklage erheben gegen (acc.); **~head·ed** vernünftig, nüchtern.

le·ver ['li:və] Hebel m; **~age** [~rɪdʒ] Hebelkraft f, -wirkung f.

lev·y ['levɪ] 1. Steuereinziehung f; Steuer f; ꝗ Aushebung f; 2. Steuern einziehen, erheben; ꝗ ausheben.

lewd ☐ [lju:d] unanständig, obszön; schmutzig.

li·a·bil·i·ty [laɪə'bɪlətɪ] ꝗ Haftung f, Haftpflicht f; liabilities pl. Verbindlichkeiten pl.; econ. Passiva pl.

li·a·ble ['laɪəbl] ꝗ haftbar, -pflichtig; be ~ for haften für; be ~ to neigen zu; anfällig sein für.

li·ar ['laɪə] Lügner(in).

lib F [lɪb] abbr. für liberation.

li·bel ꝗ ['laɪbl] 1. Verleumdung f od. Beleidigung f (durch Veröffentlichung); 2. (bsd. Brt. -ll-, Am. -l-) (schriftlich) verleumden od. beleidigen.

lib·e·ral ['lɪbərəl] 1. ☐ liberal (a. pol.), aufgeschlossen; großzügig; reichlich; 2. Liberale(r m) f (a. pol.); **~i·ty** [lɪbə'rælɪtɪ] Großzügigkeit f; Aufgeschlossenheit f.

lib·e·rate ['lɪbəreɪt] befreien; **~ra·tion** [lɪbə'reɪʃn] Befreiung f; **~ra·tor** ['lɪbəreɪtə] Befreier m.

lib·er·ty ['lɪbətɪ] Freiheit f; take liberties sich Freiheiten herausnehmen; be at ~ frei sein.

li·brar·i·an [laɪ'breərɪən] Bibliothekar(in); **li·bra·ry** ['laɪbrərɪ] Bibliothek f; Bücherei f.

lice [laɪs] pl. von louse.

li·cence, Am. **-cense** ['laɪsəns] Lizenz f, Konzession f; Freiheit f; Zügellosigkeit f; license plate Am. mot. Nummernschild n; driving ~ Führerschein m.

li·cense, **-cence** [~] e-e Lizenz od. Konzession erteilen; (amtlich) genehmigen od. zulassen.

li·cen·tious ☐ [laɪ'senʃəs] ausschweifend, zügellos.

li·chen ꝗ, ꝗ ['laɪkən] Flechte f.

lick [lɪk] 1. Lecken n; Salzlecke f; 2. v/t. (ab-, auf-, be)lecken; F verdreschen, -prügeln; F schlagen, besiegen; v/i. lecken; züngeln (Flammen).

lic·o·rice ['lɪkərɪs] = liquorice.

lid [lɪd] Deckel m; (Augen)Lid n.

lie[1] [laɪ] 1. Lüge f; give s.o. the ~ j-n Lügen strafen; 2. lügen.

lie[2] [laɪ] 1. Lage f; 2. (lay, lain) liegen; ~ behind fig. dahinterstecken; ~ down sich hinlegen; let sleeping dogs ~ fig. daran rühren wir lieber nicht; **~down** F [laɪ'daʊn] Nickerchen n; **~in** ['laɪɪn]: have a ~ Brt. F sich gründlich ausschlafen.

lieu [lju:]: in ~ statt dessen; in ~ of an Stelle von (od. gen.), anstatt (gen.).

lieu·ten·ant [lef'tenənt; ꝗ lə'tenənt; Am. lu:'tenənt] Leutnant m.

life [laɪf] (pl. lives [~vz]) Leben n; Menschenleben n; Lebensbeschreibung f, Biographie f; for ~ fürs (ganze) Leben; bsd. ꝗ lebenslänglich; ~ imprisonment, ~ sentence lebenslängliche Freiheitsstrafe; **as·sur·ance** Lebensversicherung f; **~belt** ['laɪfbelt] Rettungsgürtel m; **~boat** Rettungsboot n; **~guard** ✕ Leibgarde f; Bademeister m; Rettungsschwimmer m; **~ in·sur·ance** Lebensversicherung f; **~jack·et** Schwimmweste f; **~less** □ [~lɪs] leblos; matt, schwung-, lustlos; **~like** lebensecht; **~long** lebenslang; **~ pre·serv·er** Am. [~prɪzɜːvə] Schwimmweste f; Rettungsgürtel m; **~time** Lebenszeit f.

lift [lɪft] **1.** (Hoch-, Auf)Heben n; phys., ✈ Auftrieb m; bsd. Brt. Lift m, Aufzug m, Fahrstuhl m; give s.o. a ~ j-n aufmuntern; j-m Auftrieb geben; j-n (im Auto) mitnehmen; **2.** v/t. (hoch-, auf)heben; erheben; Verbot aufheben; Gesichtshaut straffen; F klauen, stehlen; v/i. sich heben (Nebel); ~ off abheben (Rakete etc.); **~-off** ['lɪftɒf] Start m, Abheben n (Rakete etc.).

lig·a·ture ['lɪgətʃʊə] Binde f; ✍ Verband m.

light¹ [laɪt] **1.** Licht n (a. fig.); Lampe f; Leuchten n, Glanz m; Aspekt m, Gesichtspunkt m; Can you give me a ~, please? Haben Sie Feuer?; put a ~ to anzünden; **2.** licht, hell; blond; **3.** (lit od. lighted) v/t. ~ (up) be-, erleuchten; anzünden; v/i. sich entzünden, brennen; ~ up aufleuchten.

light² adj. □ u. adv. [~] leicht (a. fig.); make ~ of et. leichtnehmen.

light·en¹ ['laɪtn] v/t. erhellen; aufhellen; aufheitern; v/i. hell(er) werden, sich aufhellen.

light·en² [~] leichter machen od. werden; erleichtern.

light·er ['laɪtə] Anzünder m; Feuerzeug n; ♣ Leichter m.

light|-head·ed ['laɪthedɪd] benommen, benebelt; leichtfertig, töricht; **~-heart·ed** □ fröhlich, unbeschwert; **~house** Leuchtturm m.

light·ing ['laɪtɪŋ] Beleuchtung f; Anzünden n.

light|-mind·ed ['laɪt'maɪndɪd] leichtfertig; **~ness** ['laɪtnɪs] Leichtheit f; Leichtigkeit f.

light·ning ['laɪtnɪŋ] Blitz m; attr. blitzschnell, Blitz...; **~ con·duc·tor,** Am. **~ rod** ✍ Blitzableiter m.

light·weight ['laɪtweɪt] Boxen: Leichtgewicht(ler m) n.

like [laɪk] **1.** gleich; ähnlich; (so) wie;

F als ob; ~ that so; feel ~ Lust haben auf od. zu; what is he ~? wie ist er?; that is just ~ him! das sieht ihm ähnlich!; **2.** der, die, das gleiche, et. Gleiches; his ~ seinesgleichen; the ~ dergleichen; the ~s of you Leute wie du; my ~s and dislikes was ich mag und was ich nicht mag; **3.** v/t. gern haben, (gern) mögen; gern tun etc.; how do you ~ it? wie gefällt es dir?; wie findest du es?; I ~ that! iro. das hab' ich gern!; I should ~ to come ich würde gern kommen; v/i. wollen; as you ~ wie du willst; if you ~ wenn Sie wollen; **~·li·hood** ['laɪklɪhʊd] Wahrscheinlichkeit f; **~·ly** [~lɪ] **1.** adj. (-ier, -iest) wahrscheinlich; geeignet; **2.** adv. wahrscheinlich; not ~! F bestimmt nicht!

lik·en ['laɪkən] vergleichen (to mit).

like|ness ['laɪknɪs] Ähnlichkeit f; (Ab)Bild n; Gestalt f; **~·wise** [~waɪz] gleich-, ebenfalls; auch.

lik·ing ['laɪkɪŋ] (for) Vorliebe f (für), Gefallen n (an dat.).

li·lac ['laɪlək] **1.** lila; **2.** ♀ Flieder m.

lil·y ♀ ['lɪlɪ] Lilie f; ~ of the valley Maiglöckchen n; **~·white** schneeweiß.

limb [lɪm] (Körper)Glied n; Ast m.

lim·ber ['lɪmbə]: ~ up Sport: Lockerungsübungen machen.

lime¹ [laɪm] Kalk m; Vogelleim m; △ nicht Leim.

lime² ♀ [~] Linde f; Limone f.

lime·light fig. ['laɪmlaɪt] Rampenlicht n.

lim·it ['lɪmɪt] **1.** fig. Grenze f; within ~s inGrenzen; off ~s Am. Zutritt verboten (to für); that is the ~! das ist der Gipfel!, das ist (doch) die Höhe!; go to the ~ bis zum Äußersten gehen; **2.** beschränken (to auf acc.).

lim·i·ta·tion [lɪmɪ'teɪʃn] Ein-, Beschränkung f; fig. Grenze f.

lim·it·ed ['lɪmɪtɪd] beschränkt, begrenzt; ~ (liability) company Brt. Gesellschaft f mit beschränkter Haftung; **~·less** [~lɪs] grenzenlos.

limp [lɪmp] **1.** hinken, humpeln; **2.** Hinken n, Humpeln n; **3.** schlaff, schwach, müde; weich.

lim·pid □ ['lɪmpɪd] klar, durchsichtig.

line [laɪn] **1.** Linie f; Zeile f; Vers m; Strich m; Falte f, Runzel f, Furche f; Reihe f; (Menschen)Schlange f;

(*Ahnen-* etc.)Reihe *f*, Linie *f*; (*Bahn-*, *Verkehrs-* etc.)Linie *f*, Strecke *f*; (*Eisenbahn-*, *Verkehrs-* etc.)Gesellschaft *f*; *tel.*, *teleph.* Leitung *f*; Branche *f*, Fach *n*, Gebiet *n*; *Sport*: (*Ziel-* etc.)Linie *f*; Leine *f*; (*Angel*)Schnur *f*; Äquator *m*; Richtung *f*; *econ.* Posten *m* (*Ware*). dat. Grenze *f*; ~*s pl. thea.* Rolle *f*, Text *m*; *be in* ~ *for* gute Aussichten haben auf (*acc.*); *be in* ~ *with* übereinstimmen mit; *draw the* ~ haltmachen, e-e Grenze ziehen (*at bei*); *hold the* ~ *teleph.* am Apparat bleiben; *stand in* ~ *Am.* Schlange stehen; 2. lin(i)ieren; *Gesicht* furchen, zeichnen; *Weg* etc. säumen; *Kleid* füttern; ⊕ auskleiden; ~ *up* (sich) in e-r Reihe aufstellen.

lin·e·a·ments ['lɪnɪəmənts] *pl.* Gesichtszüge *pl.*

lin·e·ar ['lɪnɪə] linear, geradlinig; *Längen...*

lin·en ['lɪnɪn] 1. Leinen *n*; (*Bett-*, *Tisch-* etc.)Wäsche *f*; 2. leinen, Leinen...; ~**clos·et**, ~**cup·board** Wäscheschrank *m*.

lin·er ['laɪnə] Linien-, Passagierschiff *n*; Verkehrsflugzeug *n*; = *eyeliner.*

lin·ger ['lɪŋɡə] zögern; verweilen, sich aufhalten; dahinsiechen; *a.* ~ *on* sich hinziehen.

lin·ge·rie ['lɛ̃ːnʒəriː] Damenunterwäsche *f*.

lin·i·ment *pharm.* ['lɪnɪmənt] Liniment *n*, Einreibemittel *n*.

lin·ing ['laɪnɪŋ] Futter(stoff *m*) *n*; (*Brems*)Belag *m*; ⊕ Aus-, Verkleidung *f*.

link [lɪŋk] 1. (Ketten)Glied *n*; Manschettenknopf *m*; *fig.* (Binde)Glied *n*, Verbindung *f*; 2. (sich) verbinden; ~ *up* miteinander verbinden; *Raumschiff* (an)koppeln.

links [lɪŋks] *pl.* Dünen *pl.*; *a.* golf ~ Golfplatz *m*.

link-up ['lɪŋkʌp] Zusammenschluß *m*, Verbindung *f*; Kopplung(smanöver *n*) *f* (*Raumschiff*).

lin·seed ['lɪnsiːd] ♣ Leinsamen *m*; ~ *oil* Leinöl *n*.

li·on *zo.* ['laɪən] Löwe *m*; ~**ess** *zo.* [~nɪs] Löwin *f*.

lip [lɪp] Lippe *f*; (*Tassen-* etc.)Rand *m*; *sl.* Unverschämtheit *f*; ~**stick** ['lɪpstɪk] Lippenstift *m*.

liq·ue·fy ['lɪkwɪfaɪ] (sich) verflüssigen.

liq·uid ['lɪkwɪd] 1. flüssig; feucht (schimmernd) (*Augen*); 2. Flüssigkeit *f*.

liq·ui·date ['lɪkwɪdeɪt] liquidieren (*a. econ.*); *Schuld(en)* tilgen.

liq·uid|ize ['lɪkwɪdaɪz] zerkleinern, pürieren (*im Mixer*); ~**iz·er** [~ə] Mixgerät *n*, Mixer *m*.

liq·uor ['lɪkə] *Brt.* alkoholisches Getränk; *Am.* Schnaps *m*; △ *nicht* Likör.

liq·uo·rice ['lɪkərɪs] Lakritze *f*.

lisp [lɪsp] 1. Lispeln *n*; 2. lispeln.

list [lɪst] 1. Liste *f*, Verzeichnis *n*; 2. (*in e-e Liste*) eintragen; verzeichnen, auflisten.

lis·ten ['lɪsn] (*to*) lauschen, horchen (*auf acc.*); anhören (*acc.*); zuhören (*dat.*); hören (*auf acc.*); ~ *in* (*im Radio*) hören (*to acc.*); *am Telefon* mithören; ~**er** [~ə] Zuhörer(in); (*Rundfunk*)Hörer(in).

list·less ['lɪstlɪs] teilnahms-, lustlos.

lit [lɪt] *pret. u. p.p. von* light[1] 3.

lit·e·ral □ ['lɪtərəl] (wort)wörtlich; buchstäblich; prosaisch.

lit·e·ra|ry □ ['lɪtərərɪ] literarisch, Literatur...; ~**ture** [~rət͜ʃə] Literatur *f*.

lithe □ [laɪð] geschmeidig, gelenkig.

lit·i·ga·tion ${}^{t}_{t}$ [lɪtɪˈɡeɪʃn] Prozeß *m*.

li·tre, *Am.* **-ter** ['liːtə] Liter *n*, *m*.

lit·ter ['lɪtə] 1. Sänfte *f*; Tragbahre *f*, Trage *f*; Streu *f*; *zo.* Wurf *m*; Abfall *m*, *bsd.* herumliegendes Papier; Durcheinander *n*, Unordnung *f*; 2. *v/t. zo. Junge* werfen; verstreuen; ~*ed with* übersät sein mit; *v/i. zo. Junge* werfen; ~ **bas·ket**, ~ **bin** Abfallkorb *m*.

lit·tle ['lɪtl] 1. *adj.* (*less*, *least*) klein; gering(fügig), unbedeutend; wenig; ~ *one* Kleiner *m*, Kleine *f*, Kleines *n* (*Kind*); 2. *adv.* (*less*, *least*) wenig, kaum; überhaupt nicht; 3. Kleinigkeit *f*; *a* ~ ein bißchen, etwas; ~ *by* ~ nach und nach; *not a* ~ nicht wenig.

live[1] [lɪv] *v/i.* leben; wohnen; ~ *to see* erleben; ~ *off* von *s-m* Kapital etc. leben; *auf j-s* Kosten leben; ~ *on* leben von; ~ *through* durchmachen, -stehen; ~ *up to s-m* Ruf gerecht werden, *s-n* Grundsätzen gemäß leben; *Versprechen* halten, *Erwartungen* erfüllen; ~ *with* mit *j-m* zusammenleben; mit et. leben; *v/t. Leben* führen; ~ *s.th. down* et. durch guten Lebenswandel vergessen lassen.

live[2] [laɪv] 1. *adj.* lebend, lebendig;

wirklich, richtig; aktuell; glühend; scharf (*Munition*); ⚡ stromführend, geladen; *Rundfunk, TV*: direkt, Direkt...; live, Live-..., Original...; **2.** *adv. Rundfunk, TV*: direkt, live, original.

live·li·hood ['laɪvlɪhʊd] (Lebens)Unterhalt *m*; **~·li·ness** [~nɪs] Lebhaftigkeit *f*; **~·ly** [~lɪ] (*-ier, -iest*) lebhaft, lebendig; aufregend; schnell; bewegt.

liv·er *anat.* ['lɪvə] Leber *f*.

liv·e·ry ['lɪvərɪ] Livree *f*; (Amts-) Tracht *f*.

lives [laɪvz] *pl. von* life.

live·stock ['laɪvstɒk] Vieh(bestand *m*) *n*.

liv·id □ ['lɪvɪd] bläulich; F fuchsteufelswild.

liv·ing ['lɪvɪŋ] **1.** □ lebend(ig); *the ~ image of* das genaue Ebenbild *gen.*; **2.** *das* Leben; Lebensweise *f*; Lebensunterhalt *m*; *eccl.* Pfründe *f*; *the ~ pl.* die Lebenden *pl.*; *standard of ~* Lebensstandard *m*; **~ room** Wohnzimmer *n*.

liz·ard ['lɪzəd] Eidechse *f*.

load [ləʊd] **1.** Last *f* (*a. fig.*); Ladung *f*; Belastung *f*; **2.** (auf-, be)laden; *Schußwaffe* laden; *j-n* überhäufen (*with* mit); *~ a camera* e-n Film einlegen; **~·ing** ['ləʊdɪŋ] Laden *n*; Ladung *f*, Fracht *f*; *attr.* Lade...

loaf¹ [ləʊf] (*pl. loaves* [~vz]) Laib *m* (Brot); Brot *n*.

loaf² [~] herumlungern; **~·er** ['ləʊfə] Faulenzer(in).

loam [ləʊm] Lehm *m*; **~·y** ['ləʊmɪ] (*-ier, -iest*) lehmig.

loan [ləʊn] **1.** (Ver)Leihen *n*; Anleihe *f*; Darlehen *n*; Leihgabe *f*; *on ~* leihweise; **2.** *bsd. Am.* an *j-n* ausleihen.

loath □ [ləʊθ] abgeneigt; *be ~ to do s.th.* et. ungern tun; **~·e** [ləʊð] sich ekeln vor (*dat.*); verabscheuen; **~·ing** ['ləʊðɪŋ] Ekel *m*; Abscheu *m*; **~·some** □ [~ðsəm] abscheulich, ekelhaft; verhaßt.

loaves [ləʊvz] *pl. von* loaf¹.

lob·by ['lɒbɪ] **1.** Vorhalle *f*; *thea., Film*: Foyer *n*; *parl.* Wandelhalle *f*; *pol.* Lobby *f*, Interessengruppe *f*; **2.** *pol.* Abgeordnete beeinflussen.

lobe *anat.*, ♥ [ləʊb] Lappen *m*; *a. ear~* Ohrläppchen *n*.

lob·ster *zo.* ['lɒbstə] Hummer *m*.

lo·cal □ ['ləʊkl] **1.** örtlich, Orts-...,

lokal, Lokal...; *~ government* Gemeindeverwaltung *f*; **2.** Einheimische(r *m*) *f*; *a. ~ train* Nahverkehrszug *m*; *the ~ Brt.* F bsd. die Stammkneipe; **~·i·ty** [ləʊ'kælətɪ] Örtlichkeit *f*; Lage *f*; **~·ize** ['ləʊkəlaɪz] lokalisieren.

lo·cate [ləʊ'keɪt] *v/t.* ausfindig machen; orten; *be ~d* liegen, sich befinden; **lo·ca·tion** [~ɪʃn] Lage *f*; Standort *m*; Platz (*for* für); *Film*: Gelände *n* für Außenaufnahmen; *on ~* auf Außenaufnahme.

loch *schott.* [lɒk] See *m*.

lock¹ [lɒk] **1.** (*Tür-, Gewehr- etc.*) Schloß *n*; Schleuse(nkammer) *f*; ⊕ Sperrvorrichtung *f*; **2.** (ab-, ver-, zu)schließen, zu- versperren; umschließen, umfassen; sich schließen lassen; ⊕ blockieren; *~ away* wegschließen; *~ in* einschließen, -sperren; *~ out* aussperren; *~ up* abschließen; wegschließen; einsperren.

lock² [~] (Haar)Locke *f*.

lock·er ['lɒkə] Schrank *m*, Spind *m*; Schließfach *n*; *~ room* Umkleideraum *m*; **~·et** [~ɪt] Medaillon *n*; **~-out** *econ.* Aussperrung *f*; **~·smith** Schlosser *m*; **~-up** (Haft)Zelle *f*; F Gefängnis *n*.

lo·co *Am. sl.* ['ləʊkəʊ] bekloppt.

lo·co·mo·tion [ləʊkə'məʊʃn] Fortbewegung(sfähigkeit) *f*; **~·tive** ['ləʊkəməʊtɪv] **1.** (Fort)Bewegungs-...; **2.** *a. ~ engine* Lokomotive *f*.

lo·cust *zo.* ['ləʊkəst] Heuschrecke *f*.

lodge [lɒdʒ] **1.** Häuschen *n*, Jagd-, Skihütte *f etc.*; Pförtnerhaus *n*, -loge *f*; (Freimaurer)Loge *f*; **2.** *v/i.* (*bsd.* vorübergehend *od.* in Untermiete) wohnen; stecken(bleiben) (*Kugel etc.*), (fest)sitzen; *v/t.* aufnehmen, beherbergen, unterbringen; *Kugel* jagen (*in* in *dat.*); *Schlag* versetzen; *Beschwerde einlegen; *Klage* einreichen; **lodg·er** ['lɒdʒə] Untermieter(in); **lodg·ing** [~ɪŋ] Unterkunft *f*; *~s pl. bsd.* möbliertes Zimmer.

loft [lɒft] (Dach)Boden *m*; Heuboden *m*; Empore *f*; **~·y** □ ['lɒftɪ] (*-ier, -iest*) hoch; erhaben; stolz.

log [lɒg] (Holz)Klotz *m*, (*gefällter*) Baumstamm *m*; ♩ Log *n*; = **~-book** ['lɒgbʊk], ♩ Logbuch *n*; *mot.* Fahrtenbuch *n*; *Brt. mot.* Kraftfahrzeugbrief *m*; *~ cab·in* Blockhaus *n*, -hütte *f*; **~·ger·head** [~əhed]: *be at ~s* sich in den Haaren liegen.

lo·gic ['lɒdʒɪk] Logik f; **∼·al** □ [∼kl] logisch.

loins [lɔɪnz] pl. anat. Lende f; Kochkunst: Lende(nstück n) f.

loi·ter ['lɔɪtə] trödeln, schlendern, bummeln; herumlungern.

loll [lɒl] (sich) rekeln od. lümmeln; ∼ **out** heraushängen (Zunge).

lol|li·pop ['lɒlɪpɒp] Lutscher m; Eis n am Stiel; ∼ **man**, ∼ **woman** Brt. Schülerlotse m; **∼·ly** F ['lɒlɪ] Lutscher m; ice(d) ∼ Eis n am Stiel.

lone|li·ness ['ləʊnlɪnɪs] Einsamkeit f; **∼·ly** [∼lɪ] (-ier, -iest), **∼·some** □ [∼səm] einsam.

long¹ [lɒŋ] **1.** (e-e) lange Zeit; before ∼ bald; for ∼ lange; take ∼ lange brauchen od. dauern; **2.** adj. lang; langfristig; in the ∼ run schließlich; be ∼ lange brauchen od. dauern; **3.** adv. lange; as od. so ∼ as solange, vorausgesetzt, daß; ∼ ago vor langer Zeit; no ∼er nicht mehr, nicht länger; so ∼! F bis dann!, tschüs!

long² [∼] sich sehnen (for nach).

long-dis·tance ['lɒŋ'dɪstəns] Fern...; Langstrecken...; ∼ call teleph. Ferngespräch n; ∼ runner Sport: Langstreckenläufer m.

lon·gev·i·ty [lɒn'dʒevətɪ] Langlebigkeit f.

long·hand ['lɒŋhænd] Schreibschrift f.

long·ing ['lɒŋɪŋ] **1.** □ sehnsüchtig; **2.** Sehnsucht f, Verlangen n.

lon·gi·tude geogr. ['lɒndʒɪtjuːd] Länge f.

long jump ['lɒŋdʒʌmp] Sport: Weitsprung m; **∼·shore·man** [∼ʃɔːmən] (pl. -men) Hafenarbeiter m; **∼·sight·ed** □ [lɒŋ'saɪtɪd] weitsichtig; **∼·stand·ing** sein langer Zeit bestehend; alt; **∼·term** langfristig; auf lange Sicht; **∼ wave** ∮ Langwelle f; **∼·wind·ed** □ langatmig.

loo Brt. F [luː] Klo n.

look [lʊk] **1.** Blick m; Miene f, (Gesichts)Ausdruck m; (good) ∼s pl. gutes Aussehen; have a ∼ at s.th. sich et. ansehen; I don't like the ∼ of it es gefällt mir nicht; **2.** sehen, blicken, schauen (at, on auf acc., nach); nachsehen; krank etc. aussehen; aufpassen, achten; nach e-r Richtung liegen, gehen (Fenster etc.); ∼ here! schau mal (her); hör mal (zu)!; ∼ like aussehen wie; it ∼s as if es sieht (so) aus, als ob; ∼ after aufpassen auf (acc.), sich kümmern um, sorgen für; ∼ ahead nach vorne sehen; fig. vorausschauen; ∼ around sich umsehen; ∼ at ansehen; ∼ back sich umsehen; fig. zurückblicken; ∼ down herab-, heruntersehen (a. fig. on s.o. auf j-n); ∼ for suchen; ∼ forward to freuen auf (acc.); ∼ in F hereinschauen (on bei) (als Besucher); F TV fernsehen; ∼ into untersuchen, prüfen; ∼ on zusehen, -schauen (dat.); ∼ on to liegen zu, (hinaus)gehen auf (acc.) (Fenster, etc.); ∼ on, ∼ upon betrachten, ansehen (as als); ∼ out hinaus-, heraussehen; aufpassen, sich vorsehen; Ausschau halten (for nach); ∼ over et. durchsehen; j-n mustern; ∼ round sich umsehen; ∼ through et. durchsehen; ∼ up aufblicken, -sehen; et. nachschlagen; j-n aufsuchen.

look·ing-glass ['lʊkɪŋglɑːs] Spiegel m.

look-out ['lʊkaʊt] Ausguck m; Ausschau f; fig. F Aussicht(en pl.) f; that is my ∼ F das ist meine Sache.

loom [luːm] **1.** Webstuhl m; **2.** a. ∼ up undeutlich sichtbar werden od. auftauchen.

loop [luːp] **1.** Schlinge f, Schleife f; Schlaufe f; Öse f; ✈ Looping m, n; Computer: Programmschleife f; **2.** v/t. in Schleifen legen; schlingen; v/i. e-e Schleife machen; sich schlingen; **∼·hole** ['luːphəʊl] ✗ Schießscharte f; fig. Hintertürchen n; a ∼ in the law e-e Gesetzeslücke.

loose [luːs] **1.** □ (∼r, ∼st) los(e); locker; weit; frei; ungenau; liederlich; let ∼ loslassen; freilassen; **2.** be on the ∼ frei herumlaufen; **loos·en** ['luːsn] (sich) lösen, (sich) lockern; ∼ up Sport: Lockerungsübungen machen.

loot [luːt] **1.** plündern; **2.** Beute f.

lop [lɒp] (-pp-) Baum beschneiden, stutzen; ∼ off abhauen, abhacken; **∼·sid·ed** □ ['lɒp'saɪdɪd] schief; einseitig.

lo·qua·cious □ [ləʊ'kweɪʃəs] redselig, geschwätzig.

lord [lɔːd] Herr m, Gebieter m; Lord m; the ♀ der Herr (Gott); my ∼ [mɪ'lɔːd] Mylord, Euer Gnaden, Euer Ehren (Anrede); ♀ Mayor Brt. Oberbürgermeister m; the ♀'s Prayer das Vaterunser; the ♀'s Supper das Abendmahl; **∼·ly** ['lɔːdlɪ]

L

(-ier, -iest) vornehm, edel; gebieterisch; hochmütig, arrogant; ~**ship** [~ʃɪp]: *his od. your* ~ seine *od.* Euer Lordschaft.

lore [lɔː] Kunde *f*; Überlieferungen *pl.*

lor·ry *Brt.* ['lɔrɪ] Last(kraft)wagen *m*, Lastauto *n*, Laster *m*; 🚬 Lore *f*.

lose [luːz] (*lost*) *v/t.* verlieren; verpassen, -säumen; *et.* nicht mitbekommen; nachgehen (*Uhr*); *j-n s-e Stellung kosten*; ~ *o.s.* sich verirren; sich verlieren; *v/i.* Verluste erleiden; verlieren; nachgehen (*Uhr*); **los·er** ['luːzə] Verlierer(in).

loss [lɒs] Verlust *m*; Schaden *m*; *at a* ~ *econ.* mit Verlust; *be at a* ~ nicht mehr weiterwissen.

lost [lɒst] **1.** *pret. u. p.p. von lose*; **2.** *adj.* verloren; verlorengegangen; verirrt; verschwunden, verloren, -geudet (*Zeit*); versäumt (*Gelegenheit*); *be* ~ *in thought* in Gedanken versunken *od.* -tieft sein; ~ *property office* Fundbüro *n*.

lot [lɒt] Los *n*; *econ.* Partie *f*, Posten (*Ware*); *bsd. Am.* Bauplatz *m*; *bsd. Am.* Parkplatz *m*; *bsd. Am.* Filmgelände *n*; F Gruppe *f*, Gesellschaft *f*; Los *n*, Schicksal *n*; △ *nicht* Lot; *the* ~ F alles, das Ganze; *a* ~ *of* F, ~*s of* F viel, e-e Menge; ~*s and* ~*s of* F jede Menge; *a bad* ~ F ein übler Kerl; *cast od. draw* ~*s* losen.

loth [ləʊθ] = *loath*.

lo·tion ['ləʊʃn] Lotion *f*.

lot·te·ry ['lɒtərɪ] Lotterie *f*.

loud [laʊd] laut (*a. adv.*); *fig.* schreiend, grell (*Farben etc.*); ~**speak·er** ['laʊd'spiːkə] Lautsprecher *m*.

lounge [laʊndʒ] **1.** faulenzen; herumlungern; schlendern; **2.** Bummel *m*; Wohnzimmer *n*; Aufenthaltsraum *m*, Lounge *f* (*e-s Hotels*); Warteraum *m*, Lounge *f* (*e-s Flughafens*); ~ *suit* Straßenanzug *m*.

louse *zo.* [laʊs] (*pl. lice* [laɪs]) Laus *f*; **lou·sy** ['laʊzɪ] (-*ier, -iest*) verlaust; F miserabel, saumäßig.

lout [laʊt] Flegel *m*, Lümmel *m*.

lov·a·ble □ ['lʌvəbl] liebenswert; reizend.

love [lʌv] **1.** Liebe *f* (*of, for, to, towards* zu); Liebling *m*, Schatz *m*; *Brt.* m-e Liebe, mein Lieber, mein Liebes (*Anrede*); *Tennis*: null; *be in* ~ *with s.o.* in j-n verliebt sein; *fall in* ~ *with s.o.* sich in j-n verlieben; *make* ~ sich lieben, miteinander schlafen; *give my* ~ *to her* grüße sie herzlich von mir; *send one's* ~ *to j-n* grüßen lassen; ~ *from* herzliche Grüße von (*Briefschluß*); **2.** lieben; gern mögen; ~ **af·fair** Liebesaffäre *f*; ~**ly** ['lʌvlɪ] (-*ier, -iest*) lieblich, wunderschön, entzückend, reizend; **lov·er** [~ə] Liebhaber *m*, Geliebte(r) *m*; Geliebte *f*; Liebhaber(in), (*Tier- etc.*)Freund(in).

lov·ing □ ['lʌvɪŋ] liebevoll, liebend.

low¹ [ləʊ] **1.** *adj.* nieder, niedrig (*a. fig.*); tief; gering(schätzig); knapp (*Vorrat*); gedämpft, schwach (*Licht*); schwach, matt; niedergeschlagen; *sozial* untere(r, -s), niedrig; gewöhnlich, niedrig (*denkend od. gesinnt*); gemein; tief (*Ton*); leise (*Ton, Stimme*); **2.** *adv.* niedrig; tief (*a. fig.*); leise; **3.** *meteor.* Tief(druckgebiet) *n*; Tiefstand *m*, -punkt *m*.

low² [~] brüllen, muhen (*Rind*).

low·brow F ['ləʊbraʊ] **1.** geistig Anspruchslose(r *m*) *f*; **2.** geistig anspruchslos.

low·er ['ləʊə] **1.** niedriger, tiefer; geringer; leiser; untere(r, -s), Unter...; **2.** *v/t.* herunterlassen; niedriger machen; *Augen, Stimme, Preis etc.* senken; (ab)schwächen; *Standard* herabsetzen; erniedrigen; ~ *o.s.* sich herablassen; sich demütigen; *v/i.* fallen, sinken.

low|land ['ləʊlənd] *mst* ~*s pl.* Tiefland *n*; ~**li·ness** [~lɪnɪs] Niedrigkeit *f*; Bescheidenheit *f*; ~**ly** [~lɪ] (-*ier, -iest*) niedrig; bescheiden; ~**necked** (tief) ausgeschnitten (*Kleid*); ~**pitched** ♪ tief; ~**pres·sure** *meteor.* Tiefdruck...; ⊕ Niederdruck...; ~**rise** *bsd. Am.* niedrig (gebaut); ~**spir·it·ed** niedergeschlagen.

loy·al □ ['lɔɪəl] loyal, treu; ~**ty** [~tɪ] Loyalität *f*, Treue *f*.

loz·enge ['lɒzɪndʒ] Raute *f*; Pastille *f*.

lu·bri|cant ['luːbrɪkənt] Schmiermittel *n*; ~**cate** [~keɪt] schmieren, ölen; ~**ca·tion** [luːbrɪ'keɪʃn] Schmieren *n*, Ölen *n*.

lu·cid □ ['luːsɪd] klar; deutlich.

luck [lʌk] Schicksal *n*; Glück *n*; *bad* ~, *hard* ~ Unglück *n*, Pech *n*; *good* ~ Glück *n*; *good* ~! viel Glück!; *be in* (*out of*) ~ (kein) Glück haben; ~**i·ly** ['lʌkɪlɪ] glücklicherweise, zum Glück; ~**y** □ [~ɪ] (-*ier, -iest*) glücklich; Glücks...; *be* ~ Glück haben.

lu·cra·tive □ [ˈluːkrətɪv] einträglich, lukrativ.

lu·di·crous □ [ˈluːdɪkrəs] lächerlich.

lug [lʌg] (*-gg-*) zerren, schleppen.

lug·gage *bsd. Brt.* [ˈlʌgɪdʒ] (Reise-)Gepäck *n*; ~ **car·ri·er** Gepäckträger *m (am Fahrrad)*; ~ **rack** Gepäcknetz *n*, -ablage *f*; ~ **van** *bsd. Brt.* Gepäckwagen *m*.

luke·warm [ˈluːkwɔːm] lau(warm); *fig.* lau, mäßig.

lull [lʌl] **1.** beruhigen; sich legen *od.* beruhigen; *mst* ~ *to sleep* einlullen; **2.** Pause *f*; Flaute *f (a. econ.)*, Windstille *f*.

lul·la·by [ˈlʌləbaɪ] Wiegenlied *n*.

lum·ba·go ✿ [lʌmˈbeɪgəʊ] Hexenschuß *m*.

lum·ber [ˈlʌmbə] **1.** *bsd. Am.* Bau-, Nutzholz *n*; *bsd. Brt.* Gerümpel *n*; **2.** *v/t.* ~ *s.o. with s.th. Brt.* F j-m et. aufhalsen; *v/i.* rumpeln, poltern *(Wagen)*; schwerfällig gehen, trampeln; ~**jack**, ~**man** (*pl. -men*) *bsd. Am.* Holzfäller *m*; -arbeiter *m*; ~ **mill** Sägewerk *n*; ~ **room** Rumpelkammer *f*; ~**yard** Holzplatz *m*, -lager *n*.

lu·mi·na·ry [ˈluːmɪnərɪ] Himmelskörper *m*; *fig.* Leuchte *f*, Koryphäe *f*; ~**nous** □ [~əs] leuchtend, Leucht...

lump [lʌmp] **1.** Klumpen *m*; Beule *f*; Stück *n (Zucker etc.)*; △ *nicht* Lump; *in the* ~ in Bausch und Bogen; ~ *sugar* Würfelzucker *m*; ~ *sum* Pauschalsumme *f*; **2.** *v/t.* zusammentun, -stellen, -legen, -werfen, -fassen; *v/i.* Klumpen bilden; ~**y** □ [~ɪ] (*-ier, -iest*) klumpig.

lu·na·cy [ˈluːnəsɪ] Wahnsinn *m*.

lu·nar [ˈluːnə] Mond...; ~ *module* Raumfahrt: Mond(lande)fähre *f*.

lu·na·tic [ˈluːnətɪk] **1.** irr-, wahnsinnig; **2.** Irre(r *m*) *f*, Wahnsinnige(r *m*) *f*, Geisteskranke(r *m*) *f*.

lunch [lʌntʃ], *formell* **lun·cheon** [ˈlʌntʃən] **1.** Lunch *m*, Mittagessen

n; **2.** zu Mittag essen; ~ **hour**, ~ **time** Mittagszeit *f*, -pause *f*.

lung *anat.* [lʌŋ] Lunge(nflügel *m*) *f*; *the* ~*s pl.* die Lunge.

lunge [lʌndʒ] **1.** *Fechten:* Ausfall *m*; **2.** *v/i. Fechten:* e-n Ausfall machen *(at* gegen); losstürzen *(at* auf *acc.)*.

lurch [lɜːtʃ] **1.** taumeln, torkeln; **2.** *leave in the* ~ im Stich lassen.

lure [ljʊə] **1.** Köder *m*; *fig.* Lockung *f*; **2.** ködern; (an)locken.

lu·rid □ [ˈljʊərɪd] grell, schreiend *(Farben etc.)*; schockierend, widerlich.

lurk [lɜːk] lauern; ~ *about*, ~ *around* herumschleichen.

lus·cious □ [ˈlʌʃəs] köstlich, lecker; üppig; knackig *(Mädchen)*.

lush [lʌʃ] saftig, üppig.

lust [lʌst] **1.** sinnliche Begierde, Lust *f*; Gier *f*; △ *nicht* Lust *(Freude etc.)*; **2.** ~ *after*, ~ *for* begehren; gierig sein nach.

lus·tre, *Am.* **-ter** [ˈlʌstə] Glanz *m*, Schimmer *m*; ~**trous** □ [~rəs] glänzend, schimmernd.

lust·y □ [ˈlʌstɪ] (*-ier, -iest*) kräftig, stark u. gesund, vital; kraftvoll.

lute ♩ [luːt] Laute *f*.

Lu·ther·an [ˈluːθərən] lutherisch.

lux·ate ✿ [ˈlʌkseɪt] verrenken.

lux·u·ri·ant □ [lʌgˈzjʊərɪənt] üppig; ~**ri·ate** [~ɪeɪt] schwelgen *(in* in *dat.)*; ~**ri·ous** □ [~rɪəs] luxuriös, üppig; Luxus...; ~**ry** [ˈlʌkʃərɪ] Luxus *m*; Komfort *m*; Luxusartikel *m*; *attr.* Luxus...

lye [laɪ] Lauge *f*.

ly·ing [ˈlaɪɪŋ] **1.** *p.pr. von lie*[1] 2 *u. lie*[2] 2; **2.** *adj.* lügnerisch, verlogen; ~**in** [~ˈɪn] Wochenbett *n*.

lymph [lɪmf] Lymphe *f*.

lynch [lɪntʃ] lynchen; ~ *law* [ˈlɪntʃlɔː] Lynchjustiz *f*.

lynx *zo.* [lɪŋks] Luchs *m*.

lyr·ic [ˈlɪrɪk] **1.** lyrisch; **2.** lyrisches Gedicht *n*; ~*s pl.* Lyrik *f*; (Lied)Text *m*; ~**i·cal** □ [~kl] lyrisch, gefühlvoll; schwärmerisch.

L

M

ma F [mɑ:] Mama f, Mutti f.
ma·am [mæm] Majestät (*Anrede für die Königin*); (*königliche*) Hoheit (*Anrede für Prinzessinnen*); F [məm] gnä' Frau (*Anrede*).
mac *Brt.* F [mæk] = *mackintosh*.
ma·cad·am [məˈkædəm] Schotterdecke f (*Straßenbau*).
mac·a·ro·ni [mækəˈrəʊnɪ] Makkaroni *pl.*
mac·a·roon [mækəˈruːn] Makrone f.
mach·i·na·tion [mækɪˈneɪʃn] (tückischer) Anschlag; ~s *pl.* Ränke *pl.*
ma·chine [məˈʃiːn] **1.** Maschine f; Mechanismus m; **2.** maschinell herstellen *od.* drucken; mit der (Näh-)Maschine nähen; **~made** maschinell hergestellt.
ma·chin·e·ry [məˈʃiːnərɪ] Maschinen *pl.*; Maschinerie f; **~ist** [~ɪst] Maschinenbauer m; Maschinist m; Maschinennäherin f.
mack *Brt.* F [mæk] = *mackintosh*.
mack·e·rel *zo.* [ˈmækrəl] Makrele f.
mack·in·tosh *bsd. Brt.* [ˈmækɪntɒʃ] Regenmantel m.
mac·ro· [ˈmækrəʊ] Makro..., (sehr) groß.
mad □ [mæd] wahnsinnig, verrückt; toll(wütig); F wütend; *fig.* wild; *go* ~, *Am. get* ~ verrückt *od.* wahnsinnig werden; *drive s.o.* ~ j-n verrückt *od.* wahnsinnig machen; *like* ~ wie toll, wie verrückt (*arbeiten etc.*).
mad·am [ˈmædəm] gnädige Frau, gnädiges Fräulein (*Anrede*).
mad|cap [ˈmædkæp] **1.** verrückt; **2.** verrückter Kerl; **~den** [~n] verrückt *od.* rasend machen; **~den·ing** □ [~ɪŋ] verrückt *od.* rasend machend.
made [meɪd] *pret. u. p.p. von make* 1; ~ *of gold* aus Gold.
mad|house [ˈmædhaʊs] Irrenhaus n; **~ly** [~lɪ] toll, verrückt; wie besessen; F irre, wahnsinnig; **~man** (*pl. -men*) Wahnsinnige(r) m, Verrückte(r) m; **~ness** [~nɪs] Wahnsinn m; (*Toll*)Wut f; **~wom·an** (*pl. -women*) Wahnsinnige f, Verrückte f.
mag·a·zine [mægəˈziːn] Magazin n; (*Munitions*)Lager n; Zeitschrift f.
mag·got *zo.* [ˈmægət] Made f, Larve f.
Ma·gi [ˈmeɪdʒaɪ] *pl.*: *the (three)* ~ die

(drei) Weisen aus dem Morgenland, die Heiligen Drei Könige.
ma·gic [ˈmædʒɪk] **1.** (~*ally*) *a.* **~al** □ [~l] magisch, Zauber...; **2.** Zauberei f; Zauber m; *fig.* Wunder n; **ma·gi·cian** [məˈdʒɪʃn] Zauberer m; Zauberkünstler m.
ma·gis|tra·cy [ˈmædʒɪstrəsɪ] Richteramt n; *die* Richter *pl.*; **~trate** [~eɪt] (Polizei-, Friedens)Richter m; △ *nicht Magistrat.*
mag·na·nim·i·ty [mægnəˈnɪmətɪ] Großmut m; **~nan·i·mous** □ [mægˈnænɪməs] großmütig, hochherzig.
mag·net [ˈmægnɪt] Magnet m; **~ic** [mægˈnetɪk] (~*ally*) magnetisch, Magnet...
mag·nif·i·cence [mægˈnɪfɪsns] Pracht f, Herrlichkeit f; **~cent** □ [~t] prächtig, herrlich.
mag·ni|fy [ˈmægnɪfaɪ] vergrößern; ~*ing glass* Vergrößerungsglas n, Lupe f; **~tude** [~tjuːd] Größe f; Wichtigkeit f.
mag·pie *zo.* [ˈmægpaɪ] Elster f.
ma·hog·a·ny [məˈhɒgənɪ] Mahagoni(holz) n.
maid [meɪd] *veraltet od. lit.* (junges) Mädchen, (junge) unverheiratete Frau; (*Dienst*)Mädchen n, Hausangestellte f; *old* ~ alte Jungfer; ~ *of all work* Mädchen n für alles; ~ *of honour* Ehren-, Hofdame f; *bsd. Am.* (erste) Brautjungfer.
maid·en [ˈmeɪdn] **1.** = *maid*; **2.** jungfräulich; unverheiratet; *fig.* Jungfern..., Erstlings...; ~ *name* Mädchenname m (*e-r Frau*); **~head** *veraltet* Jungfräulichkeit f; **~hood** *lit.* [~hʊd] Jungmädchenzeit f; **~ly** [~lɪ] jungfräulich; mädchenhaft.
mail¹ [meɪl] (Ketten)Panzer m.
mail² [~] **1.** Post(dienst m) f; Post (-sendung) f; *by* ~ mit der Post; **2.** *bsd. Am.* mit der Post schicken, aufgeben; **~·a·ble** *Am.* [ˈmeɪləbl] postversandfähig; **~bag** Postsack m; *Am.* Posttasche f (*e-s Briefträgers*); **~box** *Am.* Briefkasten m; ~ *car·ri·er Am.*, **~man** (*pl. -men*) *Am.* Briefträger m, Postbote m; ~ **or·der** Bestellung f (*von Waren*) durch die Post; **~·or·der firm**, *bsd. Am.* **~·or·der house** Versandgeschäft n, -haus n.

maim [meɪm] verstümmeln, zum Krüppel machen.

main [meɪn] **1.** Haupt..., größte(r, -s), wichtigste(r, -s); hauptsächlich; *by ~ force* mit äußerster Kraft; ~ *road* Haupt(verkehrs)straße f; **2.** mst ~*s pl.* Haupt(gas-, -wasser-, -strom-)leitung f; (Strom)Netz n; *in the ~* in der Hauptsache, im wesentlichen; **~·land** [~lənd] Festland n; **~·ly** [~lɪ] hauptsächlich; **~·spring** Hauptfeder f (*e-r Uhr*); *fig.* Triebfeder f; **~·stay** ♣ Großstag n; *fig.* Hauptstütze f; ♀ **Street** *Am.* provinziell-materialistisch; ♀ **Street·er** *Am.* provinzieller Spießer.

main·tain [meɪnˈteɪn] (aufrecht)erhalten, beibehalten; instand halten; ⊕ *a.* warten; unterstützen; unterhalten; behaupten.

main·te·nance [ˈmeɪntənəns] Erhaltung f; Unterhalt m; Instandhaltung f, ⊕ *a.* Wartung f.

maize *bsd. Brt.* ♀ [meɪz] Mais m.

ma·jes·tic [məˈdʒestɪk] (~ally) majestätisch; **~·ty** [ˈmædʒəstɪ] Majestät f; Würde f, Hoheit f.

ma·jor [ˈmeɪdʒə] **1.** größere(r, -s) *fig. a.* bedeutend, wichtig; ♪ voll-jährig; *C* ~ ♪ C-Dur n; ~ *key* ♪ Dur(tonart f) n; ~ *league Am. Baseball:* oberste Spielklasse; ~ *road* Haupt(verkehrs)straße f; **2.** Major m; ♪ Volljährige(r m) f; *Am. univ.* Hauptfach n; ♪ Dur n; **~·gen·er·al** ♪ Generalmajor m; **~·i·ty** [məˈdʒɔrətɪ] Mehrzahl f; ♪ Volljährigkeit f; ♪ Majorsrang m.

make [meɪk] **1.** (*made*) *v/t.* machen; anfertigen, herstellen, erzeugen; (zu)bereiten; bilden; (er)schaffen; (aus)machen; (er)geben; machen zu; ernennen zu; *j-n* lassen, veranlassen zu, bringen zu, zwingen zu; verdienen; sich erweisen als, abgeben; schätzen auf (*acc.*); F *et.* erreichen, *et.* schaffen; *Fehler* machen; *Frieden etc.* schließen; *e-e Rede* halten; F *Strecke* zurücklegen; *Uhrzeit* feststellen; ~ *s.th. do*, ~ *do* with *s.th.* mit et. auskommen, sich mit et. behelfen; *do you* ~ *one of us?* machen Sie mit?; *what do you* ~ *of it?* was halten Sie davon?; ~ *friends* with sich anfreunden mit; ~ *good* wiedergutmachen; *Versprechen etc.* halten, erfüllen; ~ *haste* sich beeilen; ~ *way* Platz machen; vorwärtskommen;

v/i. sich anschicken (*to do* zu tun); sich begeben; führen, gehen (*Weg etc.*); *mit Adverbien u. Präpositionen:* ~ *away with* sich davonmachen mit (*Geld etc.*); bескleiten; ~ *for* zugehen auf (*acc.*); sich aufmachen nach; ~ *into* verarbeiten zu; ~ *off* sich davonmachen, sich aus dem Staub machen; ~ *out* ausfindig machen; erkennen; verstehen; entziffern; *Rechnung etc.* ausstellen; ~ *over Eigentum* übertragen; ~ *up* ergänzen, vollständigen; zusammenstellen; bilden, ausmachen; sich et. ausdenken; *Streit* beilegen; (sich) zurechtmachen *od.* schminken; ~ *up one's mind* sich entschließen; *be made up of* bestehen aus, sich zusammensetzen aus; ~ *up (for)* nach-, aufholen; für et. entschädigen; **2.** Mach-, Bauart f; (Körper)Bau m; Form f; Fabrikat n, Erzeugnis n; **~·be·lieve** [ˈmeɪkbɪliːv] Schein m, Vorwand m, Verstellung f; **~·r** [~ə] Hersteller m; ♀ Schöpfer m (*Gott*); **~·shift 1.** Notbehelf m; **2.** behelfsmäßig, Behelfs...; **~·up** *typ.* Umbruch m; Aufmachung f; Schminke f, Make-up n.

mak·ing [ˈmeɪkɪŋ] Machen n; Erzeugung f, Herstellung f; *this will be the* ~ *of him* damit ist er ein gemachter Mann; *he has the* ~*s of* er hat das Zeug *od.* die Anlagen zu.

mal- [mæl] *s. bad(ly).*

mal·ad·just·ed [mæləˈdʒʌstɪd] schlecht angepaßt *od.* angeglichen; **~·ment** [~mənt] schlechte Anpassung.

mal·ad·min·i·stra·tion [ˈmælədmɪnɪsˈtreɪʃn] schlechte Verwaltung; *pol.* Mißwirtschaft f.

mal·a·dy [ˈmælədɪ] Krankheit f.

mal·con·tent [ˈmælkəntent] **1.** unzufrieden; **2.** Unzufriedene(r m) f.

male [meɪl] **1.** männlich; Männer...; **2.** Mann m; *zo.* Männchen n.

mal·e·dic·tion [mælɪˈdɪkʃn] Fluch m, Verwünschung f.

mal·e·fac·tor [ˈmælɪfæktə] Übeltäter m.

ma·lev·o·lence [məˈlevələns] Bosheit f; **~·lent** □ [~t] feindselig.

mal·for·ma·tion [mælfɔːˈmeɪʃn] Mißbildung f.

mal·ice [ˈmælɪs] Bosheit f; Groll m.

ma·li·cious □ [məˈlɪʃəs] boshaft; böswillig; **~·ness** [~nɪs] Bosheit f.

ma·lign [məˈlaɪn] **1.** □ schädlich; **2.**

M

verleumden; **ma·lig·nant** □ [mə-ˈlɪgnənt] bösartig (a. 🐾); boshaft; **ma·lig·ni·ty** [⁓ətɪ] Bösartigkeit f (a. 🐾); Bosheit f.

mall Am. [mɔːl, mæl] Einkaufszentrum n.

mal·le·a·ble [ˈmælɪəbl] hämmerbar; fig. formbar, geschmeidig.

mal·let [ˈmælɪt] Holzhammer m; (Krocket-, Polo)Schläger m.

mal·nu·tri·tion [ˈmælnjuːˈtrɪʃn] Unterernährung f; Fehlernährung f.

mal·o·dor·ous □ [mælˈəʊdərəs] übelriechend.

mal·prac·tice 🏛 [ˈmælˈpræktɪs] 🖳 falsche Behandlung; Amtsvergehen n; Untreue (im Amt etc.).

malt [mɔːlt] Malz n.

mal·treat [mælˈtriːt] schlecht behandeln; mißhandeln.

ma·ma, mam·ma [məˈmɑː] Mama f, Mutti f.

mam·mal zo. [ˈmæml] Säugetier n.

mam·moth [ˈmæməθ] 1. Mammut n; 2. riesig.

mam·my F [ˈmæmɪ] Mami f; Am. contp. farbiges Kindermädchen.

man [mæn] 1. [in nachgestellten Zssgn: -mən] (pl. men [men; in nachgestellten Zssgn: -mən]) Mann m; Mensch(en pl.) m; Menschheit f; Diener m; Angestellte(r) m; Arbeiter m; 🛡 Mann m, (einfacher) Soldat; F (Ehe)Mann m; F Freund m; F Geliebte(r) m; (Schach)Figur f; Damestein m; the ⁓ in (Am. a. on) the street der Mann auf der Straße, der Durchschnittsbürger; 2. männlich; 3. (-nn-)🛡, ⚓ bemannen; ⁓ o.s. sich ermannen.

man·age [ˈmænɪdʒ] v/t. handhaben; verwalten; Betrieb etc. leiten od. führen; Gut etc. bewirtschaften; Künstler, Sportler managen; mit j-m fertig werden; et. fertigbringen; F Arbeit, Essen etc. bewältigen, schaffen; ⁓ to inf. es fertigbringen, zu inf.; v/i. die Aufsicht haben, das Geschäft führen; auskommen; F es schaffen; F es einrichten, es ermöglichen; ⁓·a·ble □ [⁓əbl] handlich; lenksam; ⁓·ment [⁓mənt] Verwaltung f; econ. Management n, Unternehmensführung f; econ. (Geschäfts)Leitung f, Direktion f; Bewirtschaftung f; Geschicklichkeit f, (kluge) Taktik; ⁓ studies Betriebswirtschaft f; labo(u)r and ⁓ Arbeitnehmer u. Arbeitgeber.

man·ag·er [ˈmænɪdʒə] Verwalter m; econ. Manager m; econ. Geschäftsführer m, Leiter m, Direktor m; thea. Intendant m; thea. Regisseur m; Manager m (e-s Schauspielers etc.); (Guts)Verwalter m; Sport: Cheftrainer m; be a good ⁓ gut od. sparsam wirtschaften können; ⁓·ess [ˈmænɪdʒəˈres] Verwalterin f; econ. Managerin f; econ. Geschäftsführerin f, Leiterin f, Direktorin f; Managerin f (e-s Schauspielers etc.).

man·a·ge·ri·al econ. [mænəˈdʒɪərɪəl] geschäftsführend, leitend; ⁓ position leitende Stellung; ⁓ staff leitende Angestellte pl.

man·ag·ing econ. [ˈmænɪdʒɪŋ] geschäftsführend; Betriebs...

man·date [ˈmændeɪt] Mandat n; Befehl m; Auftrag m; Vollmacht f; **⁓·da·to·ry** [⁓ətərɪ] vorschreibend, befehlend; obligatorisch.

mane [meɪn] Mähne f.

ma·neu·ver [məˈnuːvə] = manoeuvre.

man·ful □ [ˈmænfl] mannhaft, beherzt.

mange vet. [meɪndʒ] Räude f.

manger [ˈmeɪndʒə] Krippe f.

man·gle [ˈmæŋgl] 1. (Wäsche)Mangel f; 2. mangeln; übel zurichten, zerfleischen; fig. verstümmeln.

mang·y □ [ˈmeɪndʒɪ] (-ier, -iest) vet. räudig; fig. schäbig.

man·hood [ˈmænhʊd] Mannesalter n; Männlichkeit f; die Männer pl.

ma·ni·a [ˈmeɪnjə] Wahn(sinn) m; fig. (for) Sucht f (nach), Leidenschaft (für), Manie f (für); **⁓·c** [ˈmeɪnɪæk] Wahnsinnige(r m) f; fig. Fanatiker m.

man·i·cure [ˈmænɪkjʊə] 1. Maniküre f; 2. maniküren.

man·i·fest [ˈmænɪfest] 1. □ offenbar, -kundig, deutlich (erkennbar); 2. v/t. offenbaren, kundtun, deutlich zeigen; 3. ⚓ Ladungsverzeichnis n; **⁓·fes·ta·tion** [mænɪfeˈsteɪʃn] Offenbarung f; Kundgebung f; △ nicht Manifest; **⁓·fes·to** [mænɪˈfestəʊ] (pl. -tos, -toes) Manifest n; pol. Grundsatzerklärung f, Programm n (e-r Partei).

man·i·fold [ˈmænɪfəʊld] 1. □ mannigfaltig; 2. vervielfältigen.

ma·nip·u·late [məˈnɪpjʊleɪt] manipulieren; (geschickt) handhaben; **⁓·la·tion** [mənɪpjʊˈleɪʃn] Manipula-

mark

tion f; Handhabung f, Behandlung f, Verfahren n; Kniff m.

man|jack [mænˈdʒæk]: *every* ~ jeder einzelne; **~kind** [mænˈkaɪnd] die Menschheit, die Menschen *pl.*; [ˈmænkaɪnd] die Männer *pl.*; **~ly** [ˈmænlɪ] (*-ier, -iest*) männlich; mannhaft.

man·ner [ˈmænə] Art f, Weise f, Art f u. Weise f; Stil(art f) m; Art f (*sich zu geben*); ~s *pl.* Benehmen n, Manieren *pl.*; Sitten *pl.*; *in a* ~ gewissermaßen; **~ed** ...geartet; gekünstelt; **~ly** [~lɪ] manierlich, gesittet, anständig.

ma·noeu·vre, *Am.* **ma·neu·ver** [məˈnuːvə] **1.** Manöver n (*a. fig.*); **2.** manövrieren (*a. fig.*).

man-of-war *veraltet* [ˈmænəvˈwɔː] (*pl.* men-of-war) Kriegsschiff n.

man·or *Brt.* [ˈmænə] *hist.* Rittergut n; (Land)Gut n; *sl.* Polizeibezirk m; *lord of the* ~ Gutsherr m; = **~-house** Herrenhaus n, -sitz m.

man·pow·er [ˈmænpaʊə] menschliche Arbeitskraft; Menschenpotential n; Arbeitskräfte *pl.*

man·ser·vant [ˈmænsɜːvənt] (*pl.* menservants) Diener m.

man·sion [ˈmænʃn] (herrschaftliches) Wohnhaus.

man·slaugh·ter *rt* [ˈmænslɔːtə] Totschlag m, fahrlässige Tötung.

man·tel|piece [ˈmæntlpiːs], **~shelf** (*pl. -shelves*) Kaminsims m.

man·tle [ˈmæntl] **1.** ⊕ Glühstrumpf m; *fig.* Hülle f; *a* ~ *of snow* e-e Schneedecke; △ *nicht* Mantel. **2.** (sich) überziehen; einhüllen.

man·u·al [ˈmænjʊəl] **1.** □ Hand...; *mit der Hand (gemacht);* **2.** Handbuch n.

man·u·fac|ture [mænjʊˈfæktʃə] **1.** Herstellung f, Fabrikation f; Fabrikat n; **2.** (an-, ver)fertigen, erzeugen, herstellen, fabrizieren; verarbeiten; **~tur·er** [~rə] Hersteller m, Erzeuger m; Fabrikant m; **~tur·ing** [~ɪŋ] Herstellungs...; Fabrik...; Gewerbe...; Industrie...

ma·nure [məˈnjʊə] **1.** Dünger m, Mist m, Dung m; **2.** düngen.

man·u·script [ˈmænjʊskrɪpt] Manuskript n; Handschrift f.

man·y [ˈmenɪ] **1.** (*more, most*) viel(e); ~ (*a*) manche(r, -s), manch eine(r, -s); ~ *times* oft; *as* ~ ebensoviel(e); *be one too* ~ *for s.o.* j-m überlegen sein; **2.** viele; Menge f; *a*

good ~ ziemlich viel(e); *a great* ~ sehr viele.

map [mæp] **1.** (Land- *etc.*)Karte f; (Stadt- *etc.*)Plan m; △ *nicht* Mappe; **2.** (*-pp-*) e-e Karte machen von; *auf* e-r Karte eintragen; ~ *out fig.* planen; einteilen.

ma·ple ♀ [ˈmeɪpl] Ahorn m.

mar [mɑː] (*-rr-*) schädigen; verderben.

ma·raud [məˈrɔːd] plündern.

mar·ble [ˈmɑːbl] **1.** Marmor m; Murmel f; **2.** marmorn.

March¹ [mɑːtʃ] März m.

march² [~] **1.** Marsch m; *fig.* Fortgang m; *the* ~ *of events* der Lauf der Dinge; **2.** marschieren (lassen); *fig.* fort-, vorwärtsschreiten.

mar·chio·ness f [ˈmɑːʃənɪs] Marquise f.

mare [meə] *zo.* Stute f; △ *nicht* Mähre; ~'s *nest fig.* Schwindel m; (Zeitungs)Ente f.

mar·ga·rine [mɑːdʒəˈriːn], *Brt.* F **marge** [mɑːdʒ] Margarine f.

mar·gin [ˈmɑːdʒɪn] Rand m (*a. fig.*); Grenze f (*a. fig.*); Spielraum m; Verdienst-, Gewinn-, Handelsspanne f; *by a narrow* ~ *fig.* mit knapper Not; **~al** □ [~l] am Rande (befindlich); Rand...; ~ *note* Randbemerkung f.

ma·ri·na [məˈriːnə] Boots-, Jachthafen m.

ma·rine [məˈriːn] Marine f; △ *nicht* (*Kriegs*)Marine; ⚓, ✗ Marineinfanterist m; *paint.* Seestück n; *attr.* See...; Meeres...; Marine...; Schiffs...; **mar·i·ner** [ˈmærɪnə] Seemann m.

mar·i·tal □ [ˈmærɪtl] ehelich, Ehe...; ~ *status* ✗ Familienstand m.

mar·i·time [ˈmærɪtaɪm] an der See liegend od. lebend; See...; Küsten...; Schiffahrts...

mark¹ [mɑːk] (deutsche) Mark; △ *nicht das* Mark.

mark² [~] **1.** Marke f, Markierung f, Bezeichnung f; Zeichen n (*a. fig.*); Merkmal n; (Körper)Mal n; Ziel n (*a. fig.*); (*Fuß-, Brems- etc.*)Spur f (*a. fig.*); (Fabrik-, Waren)Zeichen n, (Schutz-, Handels)Marke f; *econ.* Preisangabe f; (Schul)Note f, Zensur f; Punkt m; *Sport:* Startlinie f; *fig.* Norm f; *fig.* Bedeutung f, Rang m; *a man of* ~ e-e bedeutende Persönlichkeit; *be up to the* ~ *gesund-*

heitlich auf der Höhe sein; *be wide of the ~* fig. sich gewaltig irren; den Kern der Sache nicht treffen; *hit the ~* fig. (ins Schwarze) treffen; *miss the ~* danebenschießen; fig. sein Ziel verfehlen; **2.** v/t. (be)zeichnen; markieren; kennzeichnen; be(ob)achten, achtgeben auf (*acc.*); sich *et.* merken; Zeichen hinterlassen auf (*dat.*); *Schule:* benoten, zensieren; notieren, vermerken; *econ. Waren* auszeichnen; *econ.* den Preis festsetzen; *Sport: s-n Gegenspieler* decken; *~ my words* denke an m-e Worte; *to ~ the occasion* zur Feier des Tages; *~ time* auf der Stelle treten (*a. fig.*); *~ down* notieren, vermerken; *econ.* im Preis herabsetzen; *~ off* abgrenzen; *bsd. auf e-r Liste* abhaken; *~ out durch Striche etc.* markieren, bezeichnen; *~ up econ.* im Preis heraufsetzen; v/i. markieren; achtgeben, aufpassen; *Sport:* decken; **~ed** □ auffallend; merklich; ausgeprägt.

mar·ket ['mɑːkɪt] **1.** Markt(platz) *m*; *Am.* (Lebensmittel)Geschäft *n*, Laden *m*; *econ.* Absatz *m*; *econ.* (for) Nachfrage *f* (nach), Bedarf *m* (an); *in the ~* auf dem Markt; *be on the ~* (zum Verkauf) angeboten werden; *play the ~* (an der Börse) spekulieren; **2.** v/t. auf den Markt bringen; verkaufen; v/i. *bsd. Am.* go ~ing einkaufen gehen; **~·a·ble** □ [~əbl] marktfähig; -gängig; **~·gar·den** *Brt.* Handelsgärtnerei *f*; **~·ing** [~ɪŋ] *econ.* Marketing *n*, Absatzpolitik *f*; Marktbesuch *m*.

marks·man ['mɑːksmən] (*pl. -men*) guter Schütze.

mar·ma·lade ['mɑːməleɪd] *bsd.* Orangenmarmelade *f*.

mar·mot *zo.* ['mɑːmət] Murmeltier *n*.

ma·roon [məˈruːn] **1.** kastanienbraun; **2.** *auf e-r einsamen Insel* aussetzen; **3.** Leuchtrakete *f*.

mar·quee [mɑːˈkiː] Festzelt *n*.

mar·quis ['mɑːkwɪs] Marquis *m*.

mar·riage ['mærɪdʒ] Heirat *f*, Hochzeit *f*; Ehe(stand *m*) *f*; *civil ~* standesamtliche Trauung; **mar·ria·gea·ble** [~dʒəbl] heiratsfähig; **~ ar·ti·cles** *pl.* Ehevertrag *m*; **~ cer·tif·i·cate**, **~ lines** *pl. bsd. Brt.* F Trauschein *m*; **~ por·tion** Mitgift *f*.

mar·ried ['mærɪd] verheiratet; ehe-

lich, Ehe...; *~ couple* Ehepaar *n*; *~ life* Ehe(leben *n*) *f*.

mar·row ['mærəʊ] *anat.* (Knochen-)Mark *n*; fig. Kern *m*, das Wesentlichste; (*vegetable*) *~ Brt.* ⚓ Kürbis *m*.

mar·ry ['mærɪ] v/t. (ver)heiraten; *eccl.* trauen; *get married* to sich verheiraten mit; v/i. (sich ver)heiraten.

marsh [mɑːʃ] Sumpf *m*; Morast *m*.

mar·shal ['mɑːʃl] **1.** ✕ Marschall *m*; *hist.* Hofmarschall *m*; Zeremonienmeister *m*; *Am.* Branddirektor *m*; *Am.* Polizeidirektor *m*; *Am.* Bezirkspolizeichef *m*; *US ~ Am.* (Bundes-)Vollzugsbeamte(r) *m*; **2.** (*bsd. Brt. -ll-, Am. -l-*) ordnen, aufstellen; führen; 🚂 (Zug) zusammenstellen.

marsh·y ['mɑːʃɪ] (*-ier, -iest*) sumpfig, morastig.

mart [mɑːt] Markt *m*; Auktionsraum *m*.

mar·ten *zo.* ['mɑːtɪn] Marder *m*.

mar·tial □ ['mɑːʃl] kriegerisch; militärisch; Kriegs...; *~ law* ✕ Kriegsrecht *n*; (*state of*) *~ law* ✕ Ausnahmezustand *m*.

mar·tyr ['mɑːtə] **1.** Märtyrer(in) (*to gen.*); **2.** (zu Tode) martern.

mar·vel ['mɑːvl] **1.** Wunder *n*, *et.* Wunderbares; **2.** (*bsd. Brt. -ll-, Am. -l-*) sich wundern; **~·(l)ous** □ ['mɑːvələs] wunderbar; erstaunlich.

mar·zi·pan [mɑːzɪˈpæn] Marzipan *n*.

mas·ca·ra [mæˈskɑːrə] Wimperntusche *f*.

mas·cot ['mæskət] Maskottchen *n*.

mas·cu·line ['mæskjʊlɪn] männlich; Männer...

mash [mæʃ] **1.** Gemisch *n*; Maische *f*; Mengfutter *n*; **2.** zerdrücken; (ein)maischen; *~ed potatoes pl.* Kartoffelbrei *m*.

mask [mɑːsk] **1.** Maske *f*; **2.** maskieren; fig. verbergen; tarnen; *~ed* maskiert; *~ ball* Maskenball *m*.

ma·son ['meɪsn] Steinmetz *m*; *Am.* Maurer *m*; *mst* ♀ Freimaurer *m*; **~·ry** [~rɪ] Mauerwerk *n*.

masque *thea. hist.* [mɑːsk] Maskenspiel *n*; △ *nicht* Maske.

mas·que·rade [mæskəˈreɪd] **1.** Maskenball *m*; fig. Maske, *f*, Verkleidung *f*; **2.** fig. sich maskieren.

mass [mæs] **1.** *eccl. a.* ♀ Messe *f*; Masse *f*; Menge *f*; *the ~es pl.* die (breite) Masse; ~ media pl. Massenmedien pl.; ~ meeting Massenversammlung f; 2. (sich) (an)sammeln.

mas·sa·cre ['mæsəkə] 1. Blutbad n; 2. niedermetzeln.

mas·sage ['mæsɑ:ʒ] 1. Massage f; 2. massieren.

mas·sif ['mæsi:f] (Gebirgs)Massiv n.

mas·sive ['mæsɪv] massiv; groß u. schwer; fig. gewaltig.

mast ⚓ [mɑ:st] Mast m.

mas·ter ['mɑ:stə] 1. Meister m; Herr m (a. fig.); Gebieter m; bsd. Brt. Lehrer m; Kapitän m (e-s Handelsschiffs); (junger) Herr (Anrede); univ. Rektor m (e-s College); 2 of Arts (abbr. MA) Magister m Artium; ~ of ceremonies bsd. Am. Conférencier m; 2. Meister...; Haupt..., hauptsächlich; fig. führend; 3. Herr sein od. herrschen über (acc.); Sprache etc. meistern, beherrschen; ~·build·er Baumeister m; ~·ful □ [~fl] herrisch; meisterhaft; ~·key Hauptschlüssel m; ~·ly [~lɪ] meisterhaft, virtuos; ~·piece Meisterstück n; ~·ship [~ʃɪp] Meisterschaft f; Herrschaft f; bsd. Brt. Lehramt n; ~·y [~rɪ] Herrschaft f; Überlegenheit f; Oberhand f; Meisterschaft f; Beherrschung f.

mas·ti·cate ['mæstɪkeɪt] (zer)kauen.

mas·tur·bate ['mæstəbeɪt] masturbieren.

mat [mæt] 1. Matte f; Deckchen n; Unterlage f, -setzer m; 2. (-tt-) (sich) verflechten od. -filzen; fig. bedecken; 3. mattiert, matt.

match¹ [mætʃ] Zünd-, Streichholz n.

match² [~] 1. der, die, das gleiche; Partie f, Wettspiel n, -kampf m, Treffen n, Match n, m; Heirat f; be a ~ for j-m gewachsen sein; find od. meet one's ~ s-n Meister finden; 2. v/t. passend machen, anpassen; passen zu; et. Passendes finden od. geben zu; es aufnehmen mit; passend verheiraten; be well ~ed gut zusammenpassen; v/i. zusammenpassen; gloves to ~ dazu passende Handschuhe.

match·box ['mætʃbɒks] Zünd-, Streichholzschachtel f; ~ car TM Matchbox-Auto n.

match·less □ ['mætʃlɪs] unvergleichlich, einzigartig; ~·mak·er Ehestifter(in).

mate¹ [meɪt] s. checkmate.

mate² [~] 1. Gefährt|e m, -in f; (Arbeits)Kamerad(in); Gatt|e m, -in f; Männchen n, Weibchen n (von Tieren); Gehilf|e m, -in f ⚓ Maat m; 2. (sich) verheiraten; (sich) paaren.

ma·te·ri·al □ [mə'tɪərɪəl] 1. materiell; körperlich; materialistisch; wesentlich; 2. Material n; Stoff m; Werkstoff m; writing ~s pl. Schreibmaterial(ien) pl.

ma·ter|nal □ [mə'tɜ:nl] mütterlich, Mutter...; mütterlicherseits; ~·ni·ty [~ətɪ] 1. Mutterschaft f; 2. Schwangerschafts..., Umstands...; ~ hospital Entbindungsklinik f; ~ ward Entbindungsstation f.

math Am. F [mæθ] Mathe f (Mathematik).

math·e·ma·ti·cian [mæθəmə'tɪʃn] Mathematiker m; ~·mat·ics [~'mætɪks] mst sg. Mathematik f.

maths Brt. F [mæθs] Mathe f (Mathematik).

mat·i·née thea., ♪ ['mætɪneɪ] Nachmittagsvorstellung f, Frühvorstellung f; △ nicht Matinee.

ma·tric·u·late [mə'trɪkjʊleɪt] (sich) immatrikulieren (lassen).

mat·ri·mo·ni·al □ [mætrɪ'məʊnjəl] ehelich, Ehe...; ~·ny ['mætrɪmənɪ] Ehe(stand m) f.

ma·trix ⊕ ['meɪtrɪks] (pl. -trices [-trɪsi:z], -trixes) Matrize f.

ma·tron ['meɪtrən] Matrone f; Hausmutter f; Brt. Oberschwester f.

mat·ter ['mætə] 1. Materie f, Material n, Substanz f, Stoff m; ⚕ Eiter m; Gegenstand m; Sache f; Angelegenheit f; Anlaß m, Veranlassung f (for zu); printed ~ ⚑ Drucksache f; what's the ~ (with you)? was ist los (mit Ihnen)?; no ~ es hat nichts zu sagen; no ~ who gleichgültig, wer; ~ of course e-e Selbstverständlichkeit; for that ~, for the ~ of that was das betrifft; a ~ of fact e-e Tatsache; 2. von Bedeutung sein; it doesn't ~ es macht nichts; ~·of-fact sachlich, nüchtern.

mat·tress ['mætrɪs] Matratze f.

ma·ture [mə'tjʊə] 1. □ (~r, ~st) reif (a. fig.); econ. fällig; fig. reiflich erwogen; 2. v/t. zur Reife bringen; v/i. reifen; econ. fällig werden; **ma·tu·ri·ty** [~rətɪ] Reife f; econ. Fälligkeit f.

maud·lin □ ['mɔ:dlɪn] rührselig.

maul [mɔ:l] übel zurichten, roh umgehen mit; fig. verreißen.

M

Maun·dy Thurs·day *eccl.* [ˈmɔːndɪ ˈθɜːzdɪ] Gründonnerstag *m.*

mauve [məʊv] **1.** Malvenfarbe *f;* **2.** hellviolett.

maw *zo.* [mɔː] (Tier)Magen *m,* bsd. Labmagen *m;* Rachen *m;* Kropf *m.*

mawk·ish □ [ˈmɔːkɪʃ] rührselig, sentimental.

max·i [ˈmæksɪ] **1.** Maximode *f;* Maximantel *m,* -kleid *n,* -rock *m;* **2.** Maxi...

max·i- [ˈmæksɪ] Maxi..., riesig, Riesen...

max·im [ˈmæksɪm] Grundsatz *m.*

max·i·mum [ˈmæksɪməm] **1.** (*pl.* *-ma* [-mə], *-mums*) Maximum *n,* Höchstmaß *n,* -stand *m,* -betrag *m;* **2.** höchste(r, -s), maximal, Höchst...

May[1] [meɪ] Mai *m.*

may[2] *v/aux.* [ˌ] (*pret.* *might*) mögen, können, dürfen.

may·be [ˈmeɪbiː] vielleicht.

may|-bee·tle *zo.* [ˈmeɪbiːtl], **~-bug** *zo.* Maikäfer *m.*

May Day [ˈmeɪdeɪ] der 1. Mai.

mayor [meə] Bürgermeister *m;* △ *nicht* Major.

may·pole [ˈmeɪpəʊl] Maibaum *m.*

maze [meɪz] Irrgarten *m,* Labyrinth *n; fig.* Verwirrung *f; in a* ~ = **~d** [meɪzd] verwirrt.

me [miː; mɪ] mich; mir; F ich.

mead[1] [miːd] Met *m.*

mead[2] *poet.* [ˌ] = *meadow.*

mead·ow [ˈmedəʊ] Wiese *f.*

mea·gre, *Am.* **-ger** □ [ˈmiːgə] mager (*a. fig.*); dürr; dürftig

meal[1] [miːl] Mahl(zeit *f*) *n;* Essen *n;* Mehl *n.*

mean[1] □ [miːn] gemein, niedrig, gering; armselig; knauserig; schäbig; *Am.* boshaft, ekelhaft.

mean[2] [ˌ] **1.** mittel, mittlere(r, -s); Mittel..., Durchschnitts...; **2.** Mitte *f;* ~s *pl.* (Geld)Mittel *pl.*; (*a. sg.*) Mittel *n; by all* ~s auf alle Fälle, unbedingt; *by no* ~s keineswegs; *by* ~s of mittels (*gen.*).

mean[3] [ˌ] (*meant*) meinen; beabsichtigen; bestimmen; bedeuten; ~ *well* (*ill*) es gut (schlecht) meinen.

mean·ing [ˈmiːnɪŋ] **1.** □ bedeutsam; **2.** Sinn *m,* Bedeutung *f;* △ *nicht* Meinung; **~·ful** □ [ˌfl] bedeutungsvoll; sinnvoll; **~·less** □ [ˌlɪs] bedeutungslos; sinnlos.

meant [ment] *pret. u. p.p. von mean*[3].

mean|·time [ˈmiːntaɪm] **1.** mittlerweile, inzwischen; **2.** *in the* ~ inzwischen; **~·while** = meantime 1.

mea·sles 𝔰 [ˈmiːzlz] *sg.* Masern *pl.*

mea·su·ra·ble □ [ˈmeʒərəbl] meßbar.

mea·sure [ˈmeʒə] **1.** Maß *n;* Maß *m,* Meßgerät *n;* ♪ Takt *m;* Maßnahme *f; fig.* Maßstab *m;* ~ *of capacity* Hohlmaß *n; beyond* ~ über alle Maßen; *in a great* ~ großenteils; *made to* ~ nach Maß gemacht; *take* ~s Maßnahmen treffen *od.* ergreifen; *set* in ~ (ab-, aus-, ver)messen; *j-m* Maß nehmen; ~ *up to* den Ansprüchen (*gen.*) genügen; **~d** gemessen; wohlüberlegt; maßvoll; **~·less** □ [ˌlɪs] unermeßlich; **~·ment** [ˌmənt] Messung *f;* Maß *n.*

meat [miːt] Fleisch *n; fig.* Gehalt *m; cold* ~ kalte Platte; **~·y** [ˈmiːtɪ] (*-ier, -iest*) fleischig; *fig.* gehaltvoll.

me·chan|·ic [mɪˈkænɪk] Handwerker *m;* Mechaniker *m;* **~·i·cal** □ [ˌkl] mechanisch; Maschinen...; **~·ics** *phys. mst sg.* Mechanik *f.*

mech·a·nis·m [ˈmekənɪzəm] Mechanismus *m;* **~·nize** [ˌaɪz] mechanisieren; ~*d* ✗ motorisiert, Panzer...

med·al [ˈmedl] Medaille *f;* Orden *m;* **~·(l)ist** [ˌɪst] *Sport:* Medaillengewinner(in).

med·dle [ˈmedl] sich einmischen (*with, in* in acc.); **~·some** [ˌsəm] zu-, aufdringlich.

me·di·a [ˈmiːdjə] *pl.* die Medien *pl.* (*Zeitung, Fernsehen, Rundfunk*).

med·i·ae·val □ [medɪˈiːvl] = medieval.

me·di·al □ [ˈmiːdjəl] Mittel...

me·di·an [ˈmiːdjn] die Mitte bildend *od.* einnehmend, Mittel...

me·di|·ate [ˈmiːdɪeɪt] vermitteln; **~·a·tion** [miːdɪˈeɪʃn] Vermittlung *f;* **~·a·tor** [ˈmiːdɪeɪtə] Vermittler *m.*

med·i·cal □ [ˈmedɪkl] medizinisch, ärztlich; ~ *certificate* ärztliches Attest; ~ *man* F Doktor *m* (*Arzt*).

med·i·cate [ˈmedɪkeɪt] medizinisch behandeln; mit Arzneistoff(en) versetzen; ~*d bath* medizinisches Bad.

me·dic·i·nal □ [meˈdɪsɪnl] medizinisch; heilend, Heil...; *fig.* heilsam.

med·i·cine [ˈmedsɪn] Medizin *f* (*Heilkunde, Arznei*).

med·i·e·val □ [medɪˈiːvl] mittelalterlich.

me·di·o·cre [miːdɪˈəʊkə] mittelmäßig, zweitklassig.

med·i|tate ['medɪteɪt] *v/i.* nachdenken, überlegen; meditieren; *v/t.* im Sinn haben, planen, erwägen; **~ta-tion** [medɪ'teɪʃn] Nachdenken *n*; Meditation *f*; **~·ta·tive** □ ['medɪtətɪv] nachdenklich, meditativ.

Med·i·ter·ra·ne·an [medɪtə'reɪnjən] Mittelmeer...

me·di·um ['miːdjəm] **1.** (*pl. -dia* [-djə], *-diums*) Mitte *f*; Mittel *n*; Vermittlung *f*; Medium *n*; (*Lebens*-) Element *n*; **2.** mittlere(r, -s), Mittel..., Durchschnitts...

med·ley ['medlɪ] Gemisch *n*; ♩ Medley *n*, Potpourri *n*.

meek □ [miːk] sanft-, demütig, bescheiden; **~·ness** ['miːknɪs] Sanft-, Demut *f*.

meer·schaum ['mɪəʃəm] Meerschaum(pfeife *f*) *m*.

meet [miːt] (*met*) *v/t.* treffen (auf *acc.*); begegnen (*dat.*); abholen; stoßen auf (*den Gegner*); *e-m Wunsch*, *e-r Verpflichtung etc.* nachkommen; *j-n* kennenlernen; *Am. j-m* vorgestellt werden; *fig. j-m* entgegenkommen; *v/i.* sich treffen; zusammenstoßen; sich versammeln; sich kennenlernen; *Sport:* sich begegnen; **~ with** stoßen auf (*acc.*); erleiden; **~·ing** ['miːtɪŋ] Begegnung *f*; (Zusammen)Treffen *n*; Versammlung *f*; Tagung *f*.

mel·an·chol·y ['melənkəlɪ] **1.** Melancholie *f*, Schwermut *f*; **2.** melancholisch, traurig.

me·li·o·rate ['miːljəreɪt] (sich) (ver-) bessern.

mel·low ['meləʊ] **1.** □ mürbe; reif; weich; mild; **2.** reifen (lassen); weich machen *od.* werden; (sich) mildern.

me·lo·di·ous □ [mɪ'ləʊdjəs] melodisch.

mel·o|dra·mat·ic [melədrə'mætɪk] melodramatisch; **~·dy** ['melədɪ] Melodie *f*; Lied *n*.

mel·on ♬ ['melən] Melone *f*.

melt [melt] (zer)schmelzen; *fig.* zerfließen; *Gefühl* erweichen.

mem·ber ['membə] (Mit)Glied *n*; Angehörige(r *m*) *f*; ⚥ of Parliament *parl.* Mitglied *n* des Unterhauses; **~·ship** [~ʃɪp] Mitgliedschaft *f*; Mitgliederzahl *f*; **~ card** Mitgliedsausweis *m*.

mem·brane ['membreɪn] Membran(e) *f*, Häutchen *n*.

me·men·to [mɪ'mentəʊ] (*pl. -toes*, *-tos*) Mahnzeichen *n*; Andenken *n*.

mem·o ['meməʊ] (*pl. -os*) = *memorandum*.

mem·oir ['memwɑː] Denkschrift *f*; **~s** *pl.* Memoiren *pl.*

mem·o·ra·ble □ ['memərəbl] denkwürdig.

mem·o·ran·dum [memə'rændəm] (*pl. -da* [-də], *-dums*) Notiz *f*; *pol.* Note *f*; ✎ Schriftsatz *m*.

me·mo·ri·al [mɪ'mɔːrɪəl] Denkmal *n* (*to* für); Gedenkfeier *f*; Denkschrift *f*; Eingabe *f*; *attr.* Gedächtnis..., Gedenk...

mem·o·rize ['meməraɪz] auswendig lernen, memorieren.

mem·o·ry ['memərɪ] Gedächtnis *n*; Erinnerung *f*; Andenken *n*; *Computer:* Speicher *m*; **commit to ~** auswendig lernen; **in ~ of** zum Andenken an (*acc.*).

men [men] *pl. von man* 1; Mannschaft *f*.

men·ace ['menəs] **1.** (be)drohen; **2.** (Be)Drohung *f*; drohende Gefahr.

mend [mend] **1.** *v/t.* (ver)bessern; ausbessern, flicken; besser machen; **~ one's ways** sich bessern; *v/i.* sich bessern; **2.** ausgebesserte Stelle; **on the ~** auf dem Wege der Besserung.

men·da·cious □ [men'deɪʃəs] lügnerisch, verlogen; unwahr.

men·di·cant ['mendɪkənt] **1.** bettelnd, Bettel...; **2.** Bettler(in); Bettelmönch *m*.

me·ni·al ['miːnjəl] **1.** □ knechtisch; niedrig; **2.** *contp.* Diener(in), Knecht *m*.

men·in·gi·tis ✻ [menɪn'dʒaɪtɪs] Meningitis *f*, Hirnhautentzündung *f*.

men·stru·ate *physiol.* ['menstrʊeɪt] menstruieren, die Regel *od.* Periode haben.

men·tal □ ['mentl] geistig, Geistes...; *bsd. Brt.* F geisteskrank, -gestört; **~ arithmetic** Kopfrechnen *n*; **~ handicap** geistige Behinderung; **~ home**, **~ hospital** Nervenklinik *f*; **~·ly handicapped** geistig behindert; **~·i-ty** [men'tælətɪ] Mentalität *f*.

men·tion ['menʃn] **1.** Erwähnung *f*; **2.** erwähnen; *don't ~ it!* bitte (sehr)!

men·u ['menjuː] Speise(n)karte *f*; Speisenfolge *f*; △ *nicht Menü*.

mer·can·tile ['mɜːkəntaɪl] kaufmännisch, Handels...

mer·ce·na·ry ['mɜːsɪnərɪ] **1.** feil,

käuflich; gedungen; gewinnsüchtig; 2. ⚔ Söldner m.

mer·cer ['mɜːsə] Seiden-, Stoffhändler m.

mer·chan·dise ['mɜːtʃəndaɪz] Ware(n pl.) f.

mer·chant ['mɜːtʃənt] 1. Kaufmann m; bsd. Am. Ladenbesitzer m, Krämer m; 2. Handels..., Kaufmanns...; **~man** (pl. -men) Handelsschiff n.

mer·ci|**ful** □ ['mɜːsɪfʊl] barmherzig; **~·less** □ [~lɪs] unbarmherzig.

mer·cu·ry ['mɜːkjʊrɪ] Quecksilber n.

mer·cy ['mɜːsɪ] Barmherzigkeit f; Gnade f; be at the ~ of s.o. j-m auf Gedeih u. Verderb ausgeliefert sein.

mere □ [mɪə] (~r, ~st) rein; bloß; **~·ly** ['mɪəlɪ] bloß, nur, lediglich.

mer·e·tri·cious □ ['merɪ'trɪʃəs] protzig; bombastisch (Stil).

merge [mɜːdʒ] verschmelzen (in mit); econ. fusionieren; **merg·er** ['mɜːdʒə] Verschmelzung f; econ. Fusion f.

me·rid·i·an [mə'rɪdɪən] geogr. Meridian m; fig. Gipfel m.

mer|**it** ['merɪt] 1. Verdienst n; Wert m; Vorzug m; ~s pl. Hauptpunkte pl., Wesen n (e-r Sache); 2. verdienen; **~·i·to·ri·ous** □ ['merɪ'tɔːrɪəs] verdienstvoll.

mer·maid ['mɜːmeɪd] Nixe f.

mer·ri·ment ['merɪmənt] Lustigkeit f; Belustigung f.

mer·ry □ ['merɪ] (-ier, -iest) lustig, fröhlich; make~ lustig sein, feiern; ~**an·drew** Hanswurst m; **~-go-round** Karussell n; **~-mak·ing** [~meɪkɪŋ] Feiern n.

mesh [meʃ] 1. Masche f; fig. oft ~es pl. Netz n; be in ~ ⊕ (ineinander-) greifen; in e-m Netz fangen.

mess¹ [mes] 1. Unordnung f; Schmutz m; F Schweinerei f; F Patsche f; △ nicht eccl. Messe; make a ~ of verpfuschen; 2. v/t. in Unordnung bringen; verpfuschen; v/i. ~ about, ~ around F herumrühren; sich herumtreiben.

mess² [~] Kasino n, Messe f; △ nicht eccl. Messe.

mes·sage ['mesɪdʒ] Botschaft f (to an acc.); Mitteilung f, Bescheid m.

mes·sen·ger ['mesɪndʒə] Bote m.

mess·y □ ['mesɪ] (-ier, -iest) unordentlich; unsauber, schmutzig.

met [met] pret. u. p.p. von meet.

met·al ['metl] 1. Metall n; Brt.

Schotter m; 2. (bsd. Brt. -ll-, Am. -l-) beschottern; **me·tal·lic** [mɪ'tælɪk] (~ally) metallisch, Metall...; **~·lur·gy** ['metəlɜːdʒɪ] Hüttenkunde f.

met·a·mor·phose [metə'mɔːfəʊz] verwandeln, umgestalten.

met·a·phor ['metəfə] Metapher f.

me·te·or ['miːtjə] Meteor m.

me·te·o·rol·o·gy [miːtjə'rɒlədʒɪ] Meteorologie f, Wetterkunde f.

me·ter ⊕ ['miːtə] Messer m, Meßgerät n, Zähler, △ Brt. nicht Meter.

meth·od ['meθəd] Methode f; Art f u. Weise f; Verfahren n; Ordnung f, System n; **me·thod·ic** [mɪ'θɒdɪk] (~ally), **me·thod·i·cal** □ [~kl] methodisch, planmäßig; überlegt.

me·tic·u·lous □ [mɪ'tɪkjʊləs] peinlich genau, übergenau.

me·tre, Am. -ter ['miːtə] Meter m, n; Versmaß n.

met·ric ['metrɪk] (~ally) metrisch; Maß...; Meter...; ~ system metrisches (Maß- u. Gewichts)System.

me·trop·o·lis [mɪ'trɒpəlɪs] Metropole f, Hauptstadt f; **met·ro·pol·i·tan** [metrə'pɒlɪtən] hauptstädtisch.

met·tle ['metl] Eifer m, Mut m, Feuer n; be on one's ~ sein Bestes tun.

mews Brt. [mjuːz] sg. veraltet Stallungen pl.; daraus entstandene Garagen pl. od. Wohnungen pl.

Mex·i·can ['meksɪkən] 1. mexikanisch; 2. Mexikaner(in).

mi·aow [mɪ'aʊ] miauen.

mice [maɪs] pl. von mouse.

Mich·ael·mas ['mɪklməs] Michaelstag m, Michaeli(s) n (29. September).

mi·cro- ['maɪkrəʊ] Mikro..., (sehr) klein.

mi·cro|**phone** ['maɪkrəfəʊn] Mikrophon n; **~·pro·ces·sor** Mikroprozessor m; **~·scope** Mikroskop n.

mid [mɪd] mittlere(r, -s), Mitt(el)...; in ~ air (mitten) in der Luft; **~·day** ['mɪdeɪ] 1. Mittag m; 2. mittägig; Mittag(s)...

mid·dle ['mɪdl] 1. Mitte f; Mitte f (des Leibes), Taille f; △ nicht Mittel; 2. mittlere(r, -s), Mittel...; **~-aged** mittleren Alters; ♀ **Ag·es** pl. Mittelalter n; **~-class** Mittelstands...; **~-class(·es pl.)** Mittelstand m; **~-man** (pl. -men) Mittelsmann m; **~-name** zweiter Vorname m; **~-sized** mittelgroß; ~ **weight** Boxen: Mittelgewicht(ler m) n.

mid·dling ['mɪdlɪŋ] mittelmäßig, Mittel...; leidlich.

midge zo. [mɪdʒ] kleine Mücke; **midg·et** ['mɪdʒɪt] Zwerg m, Knirps m.

mid|land ['mɪdlənd] binnenländisch; ~**most** mittelste(r, -s), innerste(r, -s); ~**night** Mitternacht f; ~**riff** anat. ['mɪdrɪf] Zwerchfell n; ~**ship·man** (pl. -men) Midshipman m: Brt. unterster Marineoffiziersrang; Am. Seeoffiziersanwärter m; ~**st** [mɪdst] Mitte f: in the ~ of mitten in (dat.); ~**sum·mer** ast. Sommersonnenwende f; Hochsommer m; ~**way 1.** adj. in der Mitte befindlich, mittlere(r, -s); **2.** adv. auf halbem Wege; ~**wife** (pl. -wives) Hebamme f; ~**wif·e·ry** [~wɪfərɪ] Geburtshilfe f; ~**win·ter** ast. Wintersonnenwende f; Mitte f des Winters; in ~ mitten im Winter.

mien lit. [mi:n] Miene f.

might [maɪt] **1.** Macht f, Gewalt f; Kraft f; with ~ and main mit aller Kraft od. Gewalt; **2.** pret. von may²; ~**y** □ ['maɪtɪ] (-ier, -iest) mächtig, gewaltig.

mi·grate [maɪ'greɪt] (aus)wandern, (fort)ziehen (a. zo.); **mi·gra·tion** [~ʃn] Wanderung f; **mi·gra·to·ry** ['maɪɡrətərɪ] wandernd; zo. Zug...

mike F [maɪk] Mikro n (Mikrophon).

mil·age ['maɪlɪdʒ] = mileage.

mild □ [maɪld] mild; sanft; gelind; leicht.

mil·dew ♀ ['mɪldju:] Mehltau m.

mild·ness ['maɪldnɪs] Milde f.

mile [maɪl] Meile f (1,609 km).

mile·age ['maɪlɪdʒ] zurückgelegte Meilenzahl od. Fahrtstrecke, Meilenstand m; a. ~ allowance Meilen-, appr. Kilometergeld n.

mile·stone ['maɪlstəʊn] Meilenstein m (a. fig.).

mil·i·tant □ ['mɪlɪtənt] militant; streitend; streitbar, kriegerisch; ~**ta·ry** [~ərɪ] **1.** □ militärisch, Militär...; Heeres..., Kriegs...; ♀ Government Militärregierung f; **2.** das Militär, Soldaten pl., Truppen pl.

mi·li·tia [mɪ'lɪʃə] Miliz f, Bürgerwehr f.

milk [mɪlk] **1.** Milch f; it's no use crying over spilt ~ geschehen ist geschehen; **2.** v/t. melken; v/i. melken; Milch geben; ~**maid** ['mɪlkmeɪd] Melkerin f; Milchmädchen n;

~**man** (pl. -men) Milchmann m; ~ **pow·der** Milchpulver n; ~ **shake** Milchmixgetränk n; ~**sop** Weichling m, Muttersöhnchen n; ~**y** [~kɪ] (-ier, -iest) milchig; Milch...; ♀ Way ast. Milchstraße f.

mill¹ [mɪl] **1.** Mühle f; Fabrik f, Spinnerei f; **2.** Korn etc. mahlen; ⊕ fräsen; Münze rändeln.

mill² Am. [~] ¹/₁₀₀₀ Dollar m.

mil·le·pede zo. ['mɪlɪpi:d] Tausendfüß(l)er m.

mill·er ['mɪlə] Müller m.

mil·let ['mɪlɪt] Hirse f.

mil·li·ner ['mɪlɪnə] Hut-, Putzmacherin f, Modistin f; ~**ne·ry** [~rɪ] Putz-, Modewaren(geschäft n) pl.

mil·lion ['mɪljən] Million f; ~**aire** [mɪljə'neə] Millionär(in); ~**th** ['mɪljənθ] **1.** millionste(r, -s); **2.** Millionstel n.

mil·li·pede zo. ['mɪlɪpi:d] = millepede.

mill|-pond ['mɪlpɒnd] Mühlteich m; ~**stone** Mühlstein m.

milt [mɪlt] Milch f (der Fische).

mim·ic ['mɪmɪk] **1.** mimisch; Schein...; **2.** Imitator m; **3.** (-ck-) nachahmen; nachäffen; ~**ry** [~rɪ] Nachahmung f; zo. Mimikry f.

mince [mɪns] **1.** v/t. zerhacken, -stückeln; he does not ~ matters er nimmt kein Blatt vor den Mund; v/i. sich zieren; **2.** a. ~d meat Hackfleisch n; ~**meat** ['mɪnsmi:t] e-e süße Pastetenfüllung; ~ **pie** mit mincemeat gefüllte Pastete; **minc·er** [~ə] Fleischwolf m.

mind [maɪnd] **1.** Sinn m, Gemüt n, Herz n; Geist m (a. phls.); Verstand m; Meinung f, Ansicht f; Absicht f; Neigung f, Lust f; Gedächtnis n; to my ~ meiner Ansicht nach; out of one's ~, not in one's right ~ von Sinnen; change one's ~ sich anders besinnen; bear od. keep s.th. in ~ (immer) an et. denken; have (half) a ~ to (beinahe) Lust haben zu; have s.th. on one's ~ et. auf dem Herzen haben; make up one's ~ sich entschließen; s. presence; **2.** merken od. achten auf (acc.); sich kümmern um; etwas (einzuwenden) haben gegen; ~! gib acht!; never ~! macht nichts!; ~ the step! Achtung, Stufe!; I don't ~ (it) ich habe nichts dagegen; do you ~ if I smoke? stört es Sie, wenn ich rauche?; would you ~ taking off your hat? würden Sie bitte den Hut abnehmen?; ~ *your own business!* kümmern Sie sich um Ihre Angelegenheiten!; **~ful** □ ['mamdfl] (*of*) eingedenk (*gen.*); achtsam (auf *acc.*); **~less** □ [~lɪs] (*of*) unbekümmert (um), ohne Rücksicht (auf *acc.*).

mine¹ [maɪn] der, die, das meinige *od.* meine.

mine² [~] 1. Bergwerk *n*, Mine *f*, Zeche *f*, Grube *f*; ⚔ Mine *f*; *fig.* Fundgrube *f*; △ *nicht* (*Kugelschreiber- etc.*)*Mine*; 2. *v/i.* graben; minieren; *v/t.* graben in (*dat.*); ⚔ fördern; ⚔ verminen; **min·er** ['maɪnə] Bergmann *m.*

min·e·ral ['mɪnərəl] 1. Mineral *n*; *~s pl. Brt.* Mineralwasser *n*; 2. mineralisch, Mineral...

min·gle ['mɪŋgl] *v/t.* (ver)mischen; *v/i.* sich mischen *od.* mengen (*with* unter).

min·i ['mɪnɪ] 1. Minimode *f*; Minimantel *m*, -kleid *n*, -rock *m*; 2. Mini...

min·i- ['mɪnɪ] Mini..., Klein(st)...

min·i·a·ture ['mɪnjətʃə] 1. Miniatur(gemälde *n*) *f*; 2. in Miniatur; Miniatur..., Klein...; **~ camera** Kleinbildkamera *f.*

min·i|mize ['mɪnɪmaɪz] auf ein Mindestmaß herabsetzen; als geringfügig hinstellen, bagatellisieren; **~mum** [~əm] 1. (*pl.* -ma [-mə], -mums) Minimum *n*, Mindestmaß *n*, -betrag *m*; 2. niedrigste(r, -s), minimal, Mindest...

min·ing ['maɪnɪŋ] Bergbau *m*; *attr.* Berg(bau)..., Bergwerks...; Gruben...

min·i·on *contp.* ['mɪnjən] Lakai *m*, Kriecher *m.*

min·i·skirt ['mɪnɪskɜːt] Minirock *m.*

min·is·ter ['mɪnɪstə] 1. Geistliche(r) *m*; Minister *m*; Gesandte(r) *m*; 2. **~ to** helfen (*dat.*), unterstützen (*acc.*).

min·is·try ['mɪnɪstrɪ] geistliches Amt; Ministerium *n*; Regierung *f.*

mink *zo.* [mɪŋk] Nerz *m.*

mi·nor ['maɪnə] 1. kleinere(r, -s), geringere(r, -s); *fig. a.* unbedeutend, geringfügig; *J* Moll...; *A* ~ *J* a-Moll *n*; **~ key** *J* Moll(tonart *f*) *n*; **~ league** *Am. Baseball*: untere Spielklasse; 2. ⚖ Minderjährige(r *m*) *f*; *Am. univ.* Nebenfach *n*; *J* Moll *n*;

~·i·ty [maɪˈnɒrətɪ] Minderheit *f*; ⚖ Minderjährigkeit *f.*

min·ster ['mɪnstə] Münster *n.*

min·strel ['mɪnstrəl] Minnesänger *m*; *Varietékünstler, der als Neger geschminkt auftritt.*

mint¹ [mɪnt] 1. Münze *f*, Münzamt *n*; *a ~ of money* e-e Menge Geld; 2. münzen, prägen.

mint² ♀ [~] Minze *f.*

min·u·et *J* [mɪnjuˈet] Menuett *n.*

mi·nus ['maɪnəs] 1. *prp.* minus, weniger; *F* ohne; 2. *adj.* negativ.

min·ute¹ ['mɪnɪt] Minute *f*; Augenblick *m*; **in a ~** sofort; *just a ~* Moment mal!; **~s** *pl.* Protokoll *n.*

mi·nute² □ [maɪˈnjuːt] sehr klein, winzig; unbedeutend; sehr genau; **~ness** [~nɪs] Kleinheit *f*; Genauigkeit *f.*

mir·a·cle ['mɪrəkl] Wunder *n* (*übernatürliches Ereignis*); **mi·rac·u·lous** □ [mɪˈrækjʊləs] wunderbar.

mi·rage ['mɪrɑːʒ] Luftspiegelung *f.*

mire ['maɪə] 1. Sumpf *m*; Schlamm *m*; Kot *m*; 2. mit Schlamm *od.* Schmutz bedecken.

mir·ror ['mɪrə] 1. Spiegel *m*; 2. (wider)spiegeln (*a. fig.*).

mirth [mɜːθ] Fröhlichkeit *f*, Heiterkeit *f*; **~ful** □ ['mɜːθfl] fröhlich, heiter; **~less** □ [~lɪs] freudlos.

mir·y ['maɪərɪ] (-*ier*, -*iest*) sumpfig, schlammig.

mis- [mɪs] miß..., falsch, schlecht.

mis·ad·ven·ture ['mɪsədˈventʃə] Mißgeschick *n*; Unglück(sfall *m*) *n.*

mis·an|thrope ['mɪzənθrəʊp], **~thro·pist** [mɪˈzænθrəpɪst] Menschenfeind *m.*

mis·ap·ply ['mɪsəˈplaɪ] falsch anwenden.

mis·ap·pre·hend ['mɪsæprɪˈhend] mißverstehen.

mis·ap·pro·pri·ate ['mɪsəˈprəʊprɪeɪt] unterschlagen, veruntreuen.

mis·be·have ['mɪsbɪˈheɪv] sich schlecht benehmen.

mis·cal·cu·late [mɪsˈkælkjʊleɪt] falsch berechnen; sich verrechnen.

mis·car|riage [mɪsˈkærɪdʒ] Mißlingen *n*; Verlust *m*, Fehlleitung *f* (*von Briefen etc.*); ⚕ Fehlgeburt *f*; **~ of justice** Fehlspruch *m*, -urteil *n*; **~ry** [~ɪ] mißlingen, scheitern; verlorengehen (*Brief*); ⚕ e-e Fehlgeburt haben.

mis·cel·la·ne·ous □ [mɪsɪˈleɪnjəs]

ge-, vermischt; verschiedenartig; **~ny** ['mɪ'selənɪ] Gemisch *n*; Sammelband *m*.

mis·chief ['mɪstʃɪf] Schaden *m*; Unfug *m*; Mutwille *m*, Übermut *m*; **~maker** Unheil-, Unruhestifter(in).

mis·chie·vous □ ['mɪstʃɪvəs] schädlich; boshaft, mutwillig; schelmisch.

mis·con·ceive ['mɪskən'siːv] falsch auffassen, mißverstehen.

mis·con·duct 1. [mɪs'kɒndʌkt] schlechtes Benehmen; Eheverfehlung *f*; schlechte Verwaltung; **2.** ['mɪskən'dʌkt] schlecht verwalten; **~ o.s.** sich schlecht benehmen; e-n Fehltritt begehen.

mis·con·strue ['mɪskən'struː] falsch auslegen, mißdeuten.

mis·deed ['mɪs'diːd] Missetat *f*, Vergehen *n*; Verbrechen *n*.

mis·de·mea·no(u)r r̂z̆ ['mɪsdɪ'miːnə] Vergehen *n*.

mis·di·rect ['mɪsdɪ'rekt] fehl-, irreleiten; *e-n Brief etc.* falsch adressieren.

mis·do·ing ['mɪs'duːɪŋ] *mst* **~s** *pl.* = *misdeed*.

mise en scène *thea.* ['miːzɑ̃ːn'seɪn] Inszenierung *f*.

mi·ser ['maɪzə] Geizhals *m*.

mis·e·ra·ble □ ['mɪzərəbl] elend; unglücklich; erbärmlich.

mi·ser·ly ['maɪzəlɪ] geizig, F knick(e)rig.

mis·e·ry ['mɪzərɪ] Elend *n*, Not *f*.

mis·fire ['mɪs'faɪə] versagen (*Waffe*); *mot.* fehlzünden, aussetzen.

mis·fit ['mɪsfɪt] schlechtsitzendes Kleidungsstück; Außenseiter *m*, Einzelgänger *m*.

mis·for·tune [mɪs'fɔːtʃən] Unglück(sfall *m*) *n*; Mißgeschick *n*.

mis·giv·ing ['mɪs'gɪvɪŋ] böse Ahnung, Befürchtung *f*.

mis·guide ['mɪs'gaɪd] fehl-, irreleiten.

mis·hap ['mɪshæp] Unglück *n*; Unfall *m*; Mißgeschick *n*; Panne *f*.

mis·in·form ['mɪsɪn'fɔːm] falsch unterrichten.

mis·in·ter·pret ['mɪsɪn'tɜːprɪt] mißdeuten, falsch auffassen.

mis·lay [mɪs'leɪ] (*-laid*) *et.* verlegen.

mis·lead [mɪs'liːd] (*-led*) irreführen; verleiten.

mis·man·age ['mɪs'mænɪdʒ] schlecht verwalten *od.* führen *od.* handhaben.

mis·place ['mɪs'pleɪs] an e-e falsche Stelle legen *od.* setzen; *et.* verlegen; falsch anbringen.

mis·print 1. [mɪs'prɪnt] verdrucken; **2.** ['mɪsprɪnt] Druckfehler *m*.

mis·read ['mɪs'riːd] (*-read* [-red]) falsch lesen *od.* deuten.

mis·rep·re·sent ['mɪsreprɪ'zent] falsch darstellen, verdrehen.

miss¹ [mɪs] (*mit nachfolgendem Namen* 2) Fräulein *n*.

miss² [~] **1.** Fehlschlag *m*, -schuß *m*, -stoß *m*, -wurf *m*; Versäumen *n*, Entrinnen *n*; **2.** *v/t.* (ver)missen; verfehlen, -passen, -säumen; auslassen, übergehen; übersehen; überhören; *he* **~ed** ... ihm entging ...; *v/i.* nicht treffen; mißglücken.

mis·shap·en ['mɪs'ʃeɪpən] mißgebildet.

mis·sile ['mɪsaɪl, *Am.* 'mɪsəl] **1.** (Wurf)Geschoß *n*; ✕ Rakete *f*; **2.** ✕ Raketen...

miss·ing ['mɪsɪŋ] fehlend, weg, nicht da; ✕ vermißt; *be* **~** fehlen, weg sein (*Sache*); vermißt sein *od.* werden.

mis·sion ['mɪʃn] *pol.* Auftrag *m*; (innere) Berufung, Sendung *f*, Lebensziel *n*; *pol.* Gesandtschaft *f*; *eccl.*, *pol.* Mission *f*; ✕ Einsatz *m*, (Kampf-) Auftrag *m*; **~a·ry** ['mɪʃənrɪ] **1.** Missionar *m*; **2.** Missions...

mis·sive ['mɪsɪv] Sendschreiben *n*.

mis·spell ['mɪs'spel] (*-spelt od. -spelled*) falsch buchstabieren *od.* schreiben.

mis·spend ['mɪs'spend] (*-spent*) falsch verwenden; vergeuden.

mist [mɪst] **1.** (feiner *od.* leichter) Nebel; △ *nicht* Mist; **2.** (um)nebeln; sich trüben; beschlagen.

mis·take [mɪs'teɪk] **1.** (*-took, -taken*) sich irren, verkennen; mißverstehen; verwechseln (*for* mit); **2.** Mißverständnis *n*; Irrtum *m*; Versehen *n*; Fehler *m*; **~tak·en** □ [~ən] irrig, falsch (verstanden); *be* **~** sich irren.

mis·ter ['mɪstə] (*mit nachfolgendem Namen* 2) Herr *m* (*abbr.* **Mr**).

mis·tle·toe ♀ ['mɪsltəʊ] Mistel *f*.

mis·tress ['mɪstrɪs] Herrin *f*; Frau *f* des Hauses; *bsd.* *Brt.* Lehrerin *f*; Geliebte *f*; Meisterin *f*.

mis·trust ['mɪs'trʌst] **1.** mißtrauen (*dat.*); **2.** Mißtrauen *n*; **~ful** □ [~fl] mißtrauisch.

mist·y □ ['mɪstɪ] (*-ier, -iest*) neb(e)lig; unklar.

mis·un·der·stand [ˈmɪsʌndəˈstænd] (*-stood*) mißverstehen; *j-n* nicht verstehen; **~ing** [~ɪŋ] Mißverständnis *n*.

mis|us·age [mɪsˈjuːzɪdʒ] Mißbrauch *m*; Mißhandlung *f*; **~use 1.** [ˈmɪsˈjuːz] mißbrauchen, -handeln; **2.** [~s] Mißbrauch *m*.

mite [maɪt] *zo.* Milbe *f*; Würmchen *n* (*Kind*); Heller *m*; *fig.* Scherflein *n*.

mit·i·gate [ˈmɪtɪgeɪt] mildern, lindern.

mi·tre, *Am.* **-ter** [ˈmaɪtə] Mitra *f*, Bischofsmütze *f*.

mitt [mɪt] *Baseball*: (Fang)Handschuh *m*; *sl.* Boxhandschuh *m*; = *mitten*.

mit·ten [ˈmɪtn] Fausthandschuh *m*; Halbhandschuh *m* (*ohne Finger*).

mix [mɪks] (sich) (ver)mischen; mixen; verkehren (*with* mit); **~ed** gemischt; *fig.* zweifelhaft; **~ed school** *bsd. Brt.* Koedukationsschule *f*; **~ up** durcheinanderbringen; *be* **~ed up** *with in e-e Sache* verwickelt sein; **~ture** [ˈmɪkstʃə] Mischung *f*.

moan [məʊn] **1.** Stöhnen *n*; **2.** stöhnen.

moat [məʊt] Burg-, Stadtgraben *m*.

mob [mɒb] **1.** Mob *m*, Pöbel *m*; **2.** (*-bb-*) (lärmend) bedrängen; (in e-r Rotte) herfallen über (*acc.*) *od.* angreifen.

mo·bile [ˈməʊbaɪl] beweglich; mobil, motorisiert; lebhaft (*Gesichtszüge*); **~ home** *bsd. Am.* Wohnwagen *m*.

mo·bil·i·za·tion ✗ [ˌməʊbɪlaɪˈzeɪʃn] Mobilmachung *f*; **~ze** ✗ [ˈməʊbɪlaɪz] mobil machen.

moc·ca·sin [ˈmɒkəsɪn] weiches Leder; Mokassin *m* (*Schuh*).

mock [mɒk] **1.** Spott *m*; **2.** Schein...; falsch, nachgemacht; **3.** *v/t.* verspotten; nachmachen; täuschen; spotten (*gen.*); *v/i.* spotten (*at* über *acc.*); **~e·ry** [ˈmɒkərɪ] Spott *m*, Hohn *m*, Spötterei *f*; Gespött *n*; Nachäfferei *f*; **~ing-bird** *zo.* [~ɪŋbɜːd] Spottdrossel *f*.

mode [məʊd] (Art *f* u.) Weise *f*; (Erscheinungs)Form *f*; Mode *f*, Brauch *m*; △ *nicht* (*Damen-* etc.) *Mode*.

mod·el [ˈmɒdl] **1.** Modell *n*; Muster *n*; Vorbild *n*; Mannequin *n*, (Foto-)Modell *n*; *male* **~** Dressman *m*; **2.** Muster...; **3.** *v/t. bsd. Brt.* (*-ll-*, *Am.* *-l-*) modellieren; (ab)formen; *Klei-*

der etc. vorführen; *fig.* formen, bilden; *v/i.* (*e-m Künstler*) Modell stehen; als Mannequin *od.* (Foto)Modell arbeiten.

mod·e·rate 1. □ [ˈmɒdərət] (mittel-)mäßig; gemäßigt; vernünftig, angemessen; **2.** [~reɪt] (sich) mäßigen; **~ra·tion** [mɒdəˈreɪʃn] Mäßigung *f*; Mäßigkeit *f*.

mod·ern [ˈmɒdən] modern, neu; **~ize** [~aɪz] modernisieren.

mod·est □ [ˈmɒdɪst] bescheiden; anständig, sittsam; **~es·ty** [~ɪ] Bescheidenheit *f*.

mod·i·fi·ca·tion [mɒdɪfɪˈkeɪʃn] Abänderung *f*; Einschränkung *f*; **~fy** [ˈmɒdɪfaɪ] (ab)ändern; mildern.

mods *Brt.* [mɒdz] *pl.* betont dandyhaft gekleidete Halbstarke *pl.*

mod·u·late [ˈmɒdjʊleɪt] modulieren.

mod·ule [ˈmɒdjuːl] Verhältniszahl *f*; ⊕ Baueinheit *f*; ⊕ Modul *n* (*austauschbare Funktionseinheit*), *⅋ a.* Baustein *m*; *Raumfahrt*: (*Kommando-* etc.)Kapsel *f*.

moi·e·ty [ˈmɔɪətɪ] Hälfte *f*; Teil *m*.

moist [mɔɪst] feucht; **~en** [ˈmɔɪsn] *v/t.* be-, anfeuchten; *v/i.* feucht werden; **mois·ture** [~stʃə] Feuchtigkeit *f*.

mo·lar [ˈməʊlə] Backenzahn *m*.

mo·las·ses [məˈlæsɪz] *sg.* Melasse *f*; *Am.* Sirup *m*.

mole¹ *zo.* [məʊl] Maulwurf *m*.

mole² [~] Muttermal *n*.

mole³ [~] Mole *f*, Hafendamm *m*.

mol·e·cule [ˈmɒlɪkjuːl] Molekül *n*.

mole·hill [ˈməʊlhɪl] Maulwurfshügel *m*; *make a mountain out of a* **~** aus e-r Mücke e-n Elefanten machen.

mo·lest [məʊˈlest] belästigen.

mol·li·fy [ˈmɒlɪfaɪ] besänftigen, beruhigen.

mol·ly·cod·dle [ˈmɒlɪkɒdl] **1.** Weichling *m*, Muttersöhnchen *n*; **2.** verweichlichen, -zärteln.

mol·ten [ˈməʊltən] geschmolzen.

mom *Am.* F [mɒm] Mami *f*, Mutti *f*.

mo·ment [ˈməʊmənt] Moment *m*, Augenblick *m*; Bedeutung *f*; = *momentum*; **mo·men·ta·ry** □ [~ərɪ] momentan, augenblicklich; vorübergehend; **mo·men·tous** □ [məˈmentəs] bedeutend, folgenschwer; △ *nicht* momentan; **mo·men·tum** *phys.* [~əm] (*pl. -ta* [-tə], *-tums*) Moment *n*; Triebkraft *f*.

561   **morsel**

mon|arch ['mɒnək] Monarch(in);
~·ar·chy [~ɪ] Monarchie f.
mon·as·tery ['mɒnəstrɪ] (Mönchs-)
Kloster n.
Mon·day ['mʌndɪ] Montag m.
mon·e·ta·ry econ. ['mʌnɪtərɪ] Wäh-
rungs...; Geld...
mon·ey ['mʌnɪ] Geld n; ready ~
Bargeld n; ~-box Sparbüchse f; ~
chang·er [~tʃeɪndʒə] (Geld)Wechs-
ler m (Person); Am. Wechselautomat
m; ~ or·der Postanweisung f.
mon·ger ['mʌŋgə] mst in Zusammen-
setzungen: Händler m, Krämer m.
mon·grel ['mʌŋgrəl] Mischling m,
Bastard m; attr. Bastard...
mon·i·tor ['mɒnɪtə] ⊕, TV: Monitor
m; Schule: (Klassen)Ordner m.
monk [mʌŋk] Mönch m.
mon·key ['mʌŋkɪ] 1. zo. Affe m; ⊕
Rammblock m; put s.o.'s ~ up F j-n
auf die Palme bringen; ~ business F
fauler Zauber; 2.~ about, ~ around F
(herum)albern; ~ (about od. around)
with F herummurksen an (dat.); ~-
wrench ⊕ Engländer m (Schraubenschlüssel); throw a ~ into s.th. Am. et.
über den Haufen werfen.
monk·ish ['mʌŋkɪʃ] mönchisch.
mon·o F ['mɒnəʊ] (pl. -os) Radio etc.:
Mono n; Monogerät n; attr. Mono...
mon·o- ['mɒnəʊ] ein(fach), einzeln.
mon·o·cle ['mɒnəkl] Monokel n.
mo·nog·a·my [mɒ'nɒgəmɪ] Einehe
f.
mon·o|logue, Am. a. ~log ['mɒnə-
lɒg] Monolog m.
mo·nop·o|list [mə'nɒpəlɪst] Mono-
polist m; ~·lize [~aɪz] monopolisie-
ren; fig. an sich reißen; ~·ly [~ɪ]
Monopol n (of auf acc.).
mon·ot·o|nous [mə'nɒtənəs] mono-
ton, eintönig; ~·ny [~ɪ] Monotonie
f.
mon·soon [mɒn'su:n] Monsun m.
mon·ster ['mɒnstə] Ungeheuer n (a.
fig.); Monstrum n; attr. Riesen...
mon|stros·i·ty [mɒn'strɒsɪtɪ] Unge-
heuer(lichkeit f) n; ~·strous □
['mɒnstrəs] ungeheuer(lich), gräßlich.
month [mʌnθ] Monat m; this day ~
heute in e-m Monat; ~·ly ['mʌnθlɪ]
1. monatlich; Monats...; 2. Monatsschrift f.
mon·u·ment ['mɒnjʊmənt] Denkmal n; ~·al □ [mɒnjʊ'mentl] monu-
mental; großartig; Gedenk...

moo [mu:] muhen.
mood [mu:d] Stimmung f, Laune f;
~s pl. schlechte Laune; ~·y □ ['mu:-
dɪ] (-ier, -iest) launisch; übellaunig;
niedergeschlagen.
moon [mu:n] 1. Mond m; once in a
blue ~ F alle Jubeljahre (einmal); 2.~
about, ~ around F herumirren; träumen, dösen; ~·light ['mu:nlaɪt]
Mondlicht n, -schein m; ~·lit mond-
hell; ~·struck mondsüchtig; ~ walk
Mondspaziergang m.
Moor ¹ [mʊə] Maure m, Mohr m.
moor² [~] Moor n; Ödland n, Heide-
land n.
moor³ ⚓ [~] vertäuen; ~·ings ⚓
['mʊərɪŋz] pl. Vertäuung f; Liege-
platz m.
moose zo. [mu:s] nordamerikanischer
Elch.
mop [mɒp] 1. Mop m; (Haar)Wust
m; 2. (-pp-) auf-, abwischen.
mope [məʊp] den Kopf hängen lassen.
mo·ped Brt. mot. ['məʊped] Moped
n.
mor·al ['mɒrəl] 1. □ moralisch; Moral..., Sitten...; 2. Moral f; Lehre f;
~s pl. Sitten pl.; mo·rale [mɒ'ra:l]
bsd. ⚓, Moral f, Stimmung f, Haltung f; mo·ral·i·ty [mə'rælətɪ] Mo-
ralität f; Sittlichkeit f, Moral f;
mor·al·ize ['mɒrəlaɪz] moralisieren.
mo·rass [mə'ræs] Morast m, Sumpf
m.
mor·bid □ ['mɔ:bɪd] krankhaft.
more [mɔ:] mehr; noch (mehr); no ~
nicht mehr; no ~ than ebensowenig
wie; once ~ noch einmal, wieder;
(all) the ~ so (nur) um so mehr; so
much the ~ as um so mehr als.
mo·rel ⚘ [mɒ'rel] Morchel f.
more·o·ver [mɔ:'rəʊvə] außerdem,
überdies, weiter, ferner.
morgue [mɔ:g] Am. Leichenschau-
haus n; F (Zeitungs)Archiv n.
morn·ing ['mɔ:nɪŋ] Morgen m; Vormittag m; good ~! guten Morgen!; in
the ~ morgens; morgen früh; tomorrow ~ morgen früh; ~ dress Anzug m
(für offizielle Anlässe).
mo·ron ['mɔ:rɒn] Schwachsinnige(r
m) f; contp. Idiot m.
mo·rose □ [mə'rəʊs] mürrisch.
mor|phi·a ['mɔ:fjə], ~·phine ['mɔ:-
fi:n] Morphium n.
mor·sel ['mɔ:sl] Bissen m; Stückchen
n, das bißchen.

mor·tal ['mɔːrtl] **1.** □ sterblich; tödlich; Tod(es)...; **2.** Sterbliche(r *m*) *f*; **~·i·ty** [mɔː'tælətɪ] Sterblichkeit *f*.

mor·tar ['mɔːtə] Mörser *m*; Mörtel *m*.

mort|gage ['mɔːgɪdʒ] **1.** Hypothek *f*; **2.** verpfänden; **~gag·ee** [mɔːgə'dʒiː] Hypothekengläubiger *m*; **~gag·er** ['mɔːgɪdʒə], **~ga·gor** [mɔːgə'dʒɔː] Hypothekenschuldner *m*.

mor·tice ⊕ ['mɔːtɪs] = mortise.

mor·ti·cian *Am.* [mɔː'tɪʃn] Leichenbestatter *m*.

mor·ti|fi·ca·tion [mɔːtɪfɪ'keɪʃn] Kränkung *f*; Ärger *m*; **~·fy** ['mɔːtɪfaɪ] kränken; ärgern.

mor·tise ⊕ ['mɔːtɪs] Zapfenloch *n*.

mor·tu·a·ry ['mɔːtjʊərɪ] Leichenhalle *f*.

mo·sa·ic [mə'zeɪɪk] Mosaik *n*.

mosque [mɒsk] Moschee *f*.

mos·qui·to *zo.* [mə'skiːtəʊ] (*pl.* -toes) Moskito *m*; Stechmücke *f*.

moss ♣ [mɒs] Moos *n*; **~·y** ♣ ['mɒsɪ] (-ier, -iest) moosig, bemoost.

most [məʊst] **1.** *adj.* □ meiste(r, -s); die meisten; **~** *people pl.* die meisten Leute *pl.*; **2.** *adv.* am meisten; *vor adj.*: höchst, äußerst; *zur Bildung des Superlativs:* the **~** important point der wichtigste Punkt; **3.** das meiste, das Höchste; das meiste; die meisten *pl.*; at (the) **~** höchstens; make the **~** of möglichst ausnutzen; △ *nicht* Most; **~·ly** ['məʊstlɪ] hauptsächlich, meistens.

mo·tel [məʊ'tel] Motel *n*.

moth *zo.* [mɒθ] Motte *f*; **~·eat·en** ['mɒθiːtn] mottenzerfressen.

moth·er ['mʌðə] **1.** Mutter *f*; **2.** bemuttern; **~ coun·try** Vater-, Heimatland *n*; Mutterland *n*; **~·hood** [~hʊd] Mutterschaft *f*; **~-in-law** [~rɪnlɔː] (*pl.* mothers-in-law) Schwiegermutter *f*; **~·ly** [~lɪ] mütterlich; **~-of-pearl** [~rəv'pɜːl] Perlmutter *f*, Perlmutt *n*; **~ tongue** Muttersprache *f*.

mo·tif [məʊ'tiːf] (Leit)Motiv *n*.

mo·tion ['məʊʃn] **1.** Bewegung *f*; Gang *m* (*a.* ⊕); *parl.* Antrag *m*; ♣ Stuhlgang *m*, *oft* **~s** *pl.* Stuhl *m*; **2.** *v/t. j-m* (zu)winken, *j-m* ein Zeichen geben; *v/i.* winken; **~·less** [~lɪs] bewegungslos; **~ pic·ture** Film *m*.

mo·ti|vate ['məʊtɪveɪt] motivieren, begründen; **~·va·tion** [məʊtɪ'veɪʃn] Motivierung *f*, Begründung *f*; Motivation *f*.

mo·tive ['məʊtɪv] **1.** Motiv *n*, Beweggrund *m*; **2.** bewegend, treibend (*a. fig.*); **3.** veranlassen.

mot·ley ['mɒtlɪ] bunt, scheckig.

mo·tor ['məʊtə] **1.** Motor *m*; Kraftwagen *m*, Auto(mobil) *n*; *anat.* Muskel *m*; *fig.* treibende Kraft; **2.** motorisch; bewegend; Motor...; Kraft...; Auto...; **3.** (*in e-m Kraftfahrzeug*) fahren; **~ bi·cy·cle** Motorrad *n*; *Am.* Moped *n*; *Am.* Mofa *n*; **~·bike** F Motorrad *n*; *Am.* Moped *n*; *Am.* Mofa *n*; **~·boat** Motorboot *n*; **~·bus** Autobus *m*; **~·cade** [~keɪd] Autokolonne *f*; **~ car** (Kraft)Wagen *m*, Kraftfahrzeug *n*, Auto(mobil) *n*; **~ coach** Reisebus *m*; **~·cy·cle** Motorrad *n*; **~·cy·clist** Motorradfahrer(in); **~·ing** [~rɪŋ] Autofahren *n*; school of **~** Fahrschule *f*; **~·ist** [~rɪst] Kraft-, Autofahrer(in); **~·ize** [~raɪz] motorisieren; **~ launch** Motorbarkasse *f*; **~·way** *Brt.* Autobahn *f*.

mo(u)ld [məʊld] ✔ Gartenerde *f*; Humus(boden) *m*; Schimmel *m*, Moder *m*; ⊕ (Guß)Form *f* (*a. fig.*); *geol.* Abdruck *m*; Art *f*; **2.** formen, gießen (on, upon nach).

mo(u)l·der ['məʊldə] zerfallen.

mo(u)ld·ing *arch.* ['məʊldɪŋ] Fries *m*.

mo(u)ld·y ['məʊldɪ] (-ier, -iest) schimm(e)lig, dumpfig, mod(e)rig.

mo(u)lt [məʊlt] (sich) mausern; *Haare* verlieren.

mound [maʊnd] Erdhügel *m*, -wall *m*.

mount [maʊnt] **1.** Berg *m*; Reitpferd *n*; **2.** *v/i.* (auf-, hoch)steigen; aufsitzen, aufs Pferd steigen; *v/t.* be-, ersteigen; montieren; aufziehen, -kleben; *Edelstein* fassen; **~ed** police berittene Polizei.

moun·tain ['maʊntɪn] **1.** Berg *m*; **~s** *pl.* Gebirge *n*; **2.** Berg..., Gebirgs...; **~·eer** [maʊntɪ'nɪə] Bergbewohner(in); Bergsteiger(in); **~·eer·ing** [~rɪŋ] Bergsteigen *n*; **~·ous** ['maʊntɪnəs] bergig, gebirgig.

moun·te·bank ['maʊntɪbæŋk] Marktschreier *m*, Scharlatan *m*.

mourn [mɔːn] (be)trauern; trauern um; **~·er** ['mɔːnə] Trauernde(r *m*) *f*; **~·ful** □ [~fl] traurig; Trauer...; **~·ing** [~ɪŋ] Trauer *f*; *attr.* Trauer...

mouse [maʊs] (*pl.* mice [maɪs]) Maus *f*.

mous·tache [məˈstɑːʃ], *Am.* **mustache** [ˈmʌstæʃ] Schnurrbart *m*.

mouth [mauθ] (*pl.* **mouths** [mauðz]) Mund *m*; Maul *n*; Mündung *f*; Öffnung *f*; **~ful** [ˈmauθful] Mundvoll *m*; **~organ** Mundharmonika *f*; **~piece** Mundstück *n*; *fig.* Sprachrohr *n*.

mo·va·ble □ [ˈmuːvəbl] beweglich.

move [muːv] 1. *v/t.* (fort)bewegen; in Bewegung setzen; (weg)rücken; (an)treiben; *Schach:* e-n Zug machen mit; *et.* beantragen; *j-n* er-, aufregen; *fig.* bewegen, rühren, ergreifen; **~ down** *Schüler* zurückstufen; **~ up** *Schüler* versetzen; **~ house** *Brt.* umziehen; **~ heaven and earth** Himmel und Hölle in Bewegung setzen; *v/i.* sich (fort)bewegen; sich rühren; *Schach:* ziehen; (um)ziehen (*to* nach) (*Mieter*); ⚕ sich entleeren (*Darm*); *fig.* voran-, fortschreiten; **~ away** weg-, fortziehen; **~ for** *s.th.* et. beantragen; **~ in** einziehen; anrücken (*Polizei etc.*); vorgehen (*on* gegen *Demonstranten etc.*); **~ on** weitergehen; **~ out** ausziehen; 2. (Fort-) Bewegung *f*, Aufbruch *m*; Umzug *m*; *Schach:* Zug *m*; *fig.* Schritt *m*; *on the* **~** in Bewegung; auf den Beinen; *get a* **~** *on!* Tempo!, mach(t) schon!, los!; *make a* **~** aufbrechen; *fig.* handeln; **~a·ble** [ˈmuːvəbl] = *movable*; **~ment** [~mənt] Bewegung *f*; Bestrebung *f*, Tendenz *f*, Richtung *f*; ♩ Tempo *n*; ♩ Satz *m*; ⊕ (Geh-) Werk *n*; ⚔ Stuhl(gang) *m*.

mov·ie *bsd. Am.* F [ˈmuːvɪ] Film *m*; **~s** *pl.* Kino *n*.

mov·ing □ [ˈmuːvɪŋ] bewegend (*a. fig.*); sich bewegend, beweglich; **~ staircase** Rolltreppe *f*.

mow [məu] (**~ed**, **~n** *od.* **~ed**) mähen; **~er** [ˈməuə] Mäher(in); Mähmaschine *f*, *bsd.* Rasenmäher *m*; **~ing-ma·chine** [~ɪŋməʃiːn] Mähmaschine *f*; **~n** [məun] *p.p. von* mow.

much [mʌtʃ] 1. *adj.* (*more*, *most*) viel; 2. *adv.* sehr; *in Zssgn:* viel...; *vor comp.:* viel; *vor sup.:* bei weitem; fast; **~** *as I would like* so gern ich möchte; *I thought as* **~** das dachte ich mir; 3. Menge *f*, große Sache, Besondere(s) *n*; *make* **~** *of* viel Wesens machen von; *I am not* **~** *of a dancer* ich bin kein großer Tänzer.

muck [mʌk] Mist *m* (F *a. fig.*); **~rake** [ˈmʌkreɪk] 1. Mistgabel *f*; 2. Skanda-

le aufdecken; *contp.* im Schmutz wühlen.

mu·cus [ˈmjuːkəs] (Nasen)Schleim *m*.

mud [mʌd] Schlamm *m*; Kot *m*, Schmutz *m* (*a. fig.*).

mud·dle [ˈmʌdl] 1. *v/t.* verwirren; *a.* **~ up**, **~ together** durcheinanderbringen; F benebeln; *v/i.* pfuschen, stümpern; **~ through** F sich durchwursteln; 2. Durcheinander *n*; Verwirrung *f*.

mud·dy □ [ˈmʌdɪ] (*-ier*, *-iest*) schlammig; trüb; **~guard** Kotflügel *m*; Schutzblech *n*.

muff [mʌf] Muff *m*.

muf·fin [ˈmʌfɪn] Muffin *n* (*rundes heißes Teegebäck, mst mit Butter gegessen*).

muf·fle [ˈmʌfl] *oft* **~ up** ein-, umhüllen, umwickeln; *Stimme etc.* dämpfen; **~r** [~ə] (dicker) Schal; *Am. mot.* Auspufftopf *m*.

mug¹ [mʌg] Krug *m*; Becher *m*.

mug² F [~] (*-gg-*) überfallen u. ausrauben; **~ger** F [ˈmʌgə] Straßenräuber *m*; **~ging** F [~ɪŋ] Raubüberfall *m* (*auf die Straße*).

mug·gy [ˈmʌgɪ] schwül.

mug·wump *Am. iro.* [ˈmʌgwʌmp] hohes Tier (*Person*); *pol.* Unabhängige(r) *m*.

mu·lat·to [mjuːˈlætəu] (*pl. -tos*, *Am. -toes*) Mulatt|e *m*, -in *f*.

mul·ber·ry ⚜ [ˈmʌlbərɪ] Maulbeerbaum *m*; Maulbeere *f*.

mule [mjuːl] *zo.* Maultier *n*, -esel *m*; störrischer Mensch; **mu·le·teer** [mjuːlɪˈtɪə] Maultiertreiber *m*.

mull¹ [mʌl] Mull *m*.

mull² [~]: **~ over** überdenken.

mulled [mʌld]: **~** *claret*, **~** *wine* Glühwein *m*.

mul·li·gan *Am.* F [ˈmʌlɪgən] Eintopfgericht *n*.

mul·li·on *arch.* [ˈmʌljən] Mittelpfosten *m* (*am Fenster*).

mul·ti- [ˈmʌltɪ] viel..., mehr..., ...reich, Mehrfach..., Multi...

mul·ti·far·i·ous □ [mʌltɪˈfeərɪəs] mannigfaltig; **~form** [ˈmʌltɪfɔːm] vielförmig, -gestaltig; **~lat·er·al** [mʌltɪˈlætərəl] vielseitig; *pol.* multilateral, mehrseitig; **~ple** [mʌltɪpl] 1. vielfach; 2. ⅍ Vielfache(s) *n*; **~pli·ca·tion** [mʌltɪplɪˈkeɪʃn] Vervielfachung *f*; Vermehrung *f*; ⅍ Multiplikation *f*; **~ table** Einmaleins n; **~·pli·ci·ty** [~'plɪsətɪ] Vielfalt f; **~·ply** ['mʌltɪplaɪ] (sich) vermehren (a. biol.); vervielfältigen; & multiplizieren, malnehmen (by mit); **~·tude** [~tjuːd] Vielheit f; Menge f; **~·tu·di·nous** [mʌltɪ'tjuːdɪnəs] zahlreich.

mum[1] [mʌm] 1. still; 2. pst!

mum[2] Brt. F [~] Mami f, Mutti f.

mum·ble ['mʌmbl] murmeln, nuscheln; mümmeln (mühsam essen).

mum·mer·y contp. ['mʌmərɪ] Mummenschanz m.

mum·mi·fy ['mʌmɪfaɪ] mumifizieren.

mum·my[1] ['mʌmɪ] Mumie f.

mum·my[2] Brt. F [~] Mami f, Mutti f.

mumps ∉ [mʌmps] sg. Ziegenpeter m, Mumps m.

munch [mʌntʃ] geräuschvoll od. schmatzend kauen, mampfen.

mun·dane □ [mʌn'deɪn] weltlich.

mu·ni·ci·pal □ [mjuː'nɪsɪpl] städtisch, Stadt..., kommunal, Gemeinde...; **~·i·ty** [mjuːnɪsɪ'pælətɪ] Stadt f mit Selbstverwaltung; Stadtverwaltung f.

mu·nif·i·cence [mjuː'nɪfɪsns] Freigebigkeit f; **~·cent** [~t] freigebig.

mu·ni·tions ✕ [mjuː'nɪʃnz] pl. Munition f.

mu·ral ['mjʊərəl] 1. Wandgemälde n; 2. Mauer..., Wand...

mur·der ['mɜːdə] 1. Mord m; 2. (er)morden; fig. F verhunzen; **~·er** [~rə] Mörder m; **~·ess** [~rɪs] Mörderin f; **~·ous** □ [~rəs] mörderisch; Mord...

murk·y □ ['mɜːkɪ] (-ier, -iest) dunkel, finster.

murmur ['mɜːmə] 1. Murmeln n; Gemurmel n; Murren n; 2. murmeln; murren.

mur·rain ['mʌrɪn] Viehseuche f.

mus·cle ['mʌsl] Muskel m; **~-cle-bound:** be ~ bei Gewichthebern etc.: e-e starke, aber erstarrte Muskulatur haben; **~·cu·lar** ['mʌskjʊlə] Muskel...; muskulös.

Muse[1] ['mjuːz] Muse f.

muse[2] [~] (nach)sinnen, (-)grübeln.

mu·se·um [mjuː'zɪəm] Museum n.

mush [mʌʃ] Brei m, Mus n; Am. Maisbrei m.

mush·room ['mʌʃrʊm] 1. ♀ Pilz m, bsd. Champignon m; 2. rasch wachsen; ~ up (wie Pilze) aus dem Boden schießen.

mu·sic ['mjuːzɪk] Musik f; Musikstück n; Noten pl.; set to ~ vertonen; **~·al** [~əl] 1. Musical n; 2. □ musikalisch; Musik...; wohlklingend; ~ box bsd. Brt. Spieldose f; ~ box bsd. Am. Spieldose f; **~·hall** Brt. Varieté (-theater) n; **mu·si·cian** [mjuː'zɪʃn] Musiker(in); **~·stool** Klavierstuhl m.

musk [mʌsk] Moschus m, Bisam m; **~·deer** zo. ['mʌsk'dɪə] Moschustier n.

mus·ket ✕ hist. ['mʌskɪt] Muskete f.

musk·rat ['mʌskræt] zo. Bisamratte f; Bisampelz m.

mus·lin ['mʌzlɪn] Musselin m.

mus·quash ['mʌskwɒʃ] zo. Bisamratte f; Bisampelz m.

muss Am. F [mʌs] Durcheinander n.

mus·sel ['mʌsl] (Mies)Muschel f.

must[1] [mʌst] 1. v/aux. ich, du etc. muß(t) etc., darf(st) etc., pret. mußte(st) etc., durfte(st) etc.; I ~ not (F mustn't) ich darf nicht; 2. Muß n.

must[2] [~] Schimmel m, Moder m.

must[3] [~] Most m.

mus·tache Am. ['mʌstæʃ] = moustache.

mus·ta·chio [mə'stɑːʃɪəʊ] (pl. -os) mst ~s pl. Schnauzbart m.

mus·tard ['mʌstəd] Senf m.

mus·ter ['mʌstə] 1. ✕ Musterung f; pass ~ fig. Zustimmung finden (with bei); △ nicht (Stoff- etc.)Muster; 2. ✕ mustern; a. ~ up Mut etc. aufbieten, zusammennehmen; △ nicht Stoff etc. mustern.

must·y □ ['mʌstɪ] (-ier, -iest) mod(e)rig, muffig.

mu·ta·ble □ ['mjuːtəbl] veränderlich; fig. wankelmütig; **~·tion** [mjuː'teɪʃn] Veränderung f; biol. Mutation f.

mute [mjuːt] 1. □ stumm; 2. Stumme(r m) m f; Statist(in); 3. dämpfen.

mu·ti·late ['mjuːtɪleɪt] verstümmeln.

mu·ti·neer [mjuːtɪ'nɪə] Meuterer m; **~·nous** □ ['mjuːtɪnəs] meuterisch; rebellisch; **~·ny** [~ɪ] 1. Meuterei f; 2. meutern.

mut·ter ['mʌtə] 1. Gemurmel n; Murren n; 2. murmeln; murren.

mut·ton ['mʌtn] Hammel-, Schaffleisch n; leg of ~ Hammelkeule f; **~·chop** Hammelkotelett n.

mu·tu·al □ ['mjuːtʃʊəl] gegenseitig; gemeinsam.

muz·zle [ˈmʌzl] **1.** zo. Maul n, Schnauze f; Mündung f (e-r Feuerwaffe); Maulkorb m; **2.** e-n Maulkorb anlegen (dat.); fig. den Mund stopfen (dat.).

my [maɪ] mein(e).

myrrh ♀ [mɜː] Myrrhe f.

myr·tle ♀ [ˈmɜːtl] Myrte f.

my·self [maɪˈself] (ich) selbst; mir; mich; by ~ allein.

mys·te·ri·ous □ [mɪˈstɪərɪəs] geheimnisvoll, mysteriös; ~**ry** [ˈmɪstərɪ] Mysterium n; Geheimnis n; Rätsel n.

mys|tic [ˈmɪstɪk] **1.** a. ~**ti·cal** □ [~kl] mystisch; geheimnisvoll; **2.** Mystiker(in); ~**ti·fy** [~faɪ] täuschen; verwirren; in Dunkel hüllen.

myth [mɪθ] Mythe f, Mythos m, Sage f.

N

nab F [næb] (-bb-) schnappen, erwischen.

na·cre [ˈneɪkə] Perlmutt(er f) n.

na·dir [ˈneɪdɪə] ast. Nadir m (Fußpunkt); fig. Tiefpunkt m.

nag [næg] **1.** F Gaul m, Klepper m; **2.** (-gg-) v/i. nörgeln; ~ at herumnörgeln an; v/t. bekritteln; △ nicht nagen.

nail [neɪl] **1.** (Finger-, Zehen)Nagel m; ⊕ Nagel m; zo. Kralle f, Klaue f; **2.** (an-, fest)nageln; Augen etc. heften (to auf acc.); ~ **e·nam·el**, ~ **pol·ish** Am. Nagellack m; ~ **scis·sors** pl. Nagelschere f; ~ **var·nish** Brt. Nagellack m.

na·ïve □ [naːˈiːv], **na·ive** □ [neɪv] naiv; ungekünstelt.

na·ked □ [ˈneɪkɪd] nackt, bloß; kahl; fig. ungeschminkt; schutz-, wehrlos; ~**ness** [~nɪs] Nacktheit f, Blöße f; Kahlheit f; Schutz-, Wehrlosigkeit f; fig. Ungeschminktheit f.

name [neɪm] **1.** Name m; Ruf m; by the ~ of ... namens ...; what's your ~? wie heißen Sie?; call s.o. ~s j-n beschimpfen; **2.** (be)nennen; ernennen zu; ~**less** □ [ˈneɪmlɪs] namenlos; unbekannt; ~**ly** [~lɪ] nämlich; ~**plate** Namens-, Tür-, Firmenschild n; ~**sake** [~seɪk] Namensvetter m.

nan·ny [ˈnænɪ] Kindermädchen n; ~ **goat** zo. Ziege f.

nap[1] [næp] (Tuch)Noppe f.

nap[2] [~] **1.** Schläfchen n; have od. take a ~ = **2**; **2.** (-pp-) ein Nickerchen machen.

nape [neɪp] mst ~ of the neck Genick n, Nacken m.

nap|kin [ˈnæpkɪn] Serviette f; Brt. Windel f; ~**py** Brt. F [~ɪ] Windel f.

nar·co·sis ♀ [naːˈkəʊsɪs] (pl. -ses [-siːz]) Narkose f.

nar·cot·ic ♀ [naːˈkɒtɪk] **1.** (~ally) narkotisch, betäubend, einschläfernd; Rauschgift...; ~ addiction Rauschgiftsucht f; ~ drug Rauschgift n; **2.** Betäubungsmittel n; Rauschgift n; ~s squad Rauschgiftdezernat n.

nar|rate [nəˈreɪt] erzählen; ~**ra·tion** [~ʃn] Erzählung f; ~**ra·tive** [ˈnærətɪv] **1.** □ erzählend; **2.** Erzählung f; ~**ra·tor** [nəˈreɪtə] Erzähler(in).

nar·row [ˈnærəʊ] **1.** eng, schmal; beschränkt; knapp (Mehrheit, Entkommen); engherzig; **2.** ~s pl. Engpaß m; Meerenge f; **3.** (sich) verengen; beschränken; einengen; Maschen abnehmen; ~**chest·ed** engbrüstig; ~**mind·ed** engherzig, -stirnig, beschränkt; ~**ness** [~nɪs] Enge f; Beschränktheit f (a. fig.); Engherzigkeit f.

na·sal □ [ˈneɪzl] nasal; Nasen...

nas·ty □ [ˈnaːstɪ] (-ier, -iest) schmutzig; garstig; eklig, widerlich; böse; häßlich; abstoßend, unangenehm.

na·tal [ˈneɪtl] Geburts...

na·tion [ˈneɪʃn] Nation f, Volk n.

na·tion·al [ˈnæʃənl] **1.** □ national, National..., Landes..., Volks..., Staats...; **2.** Staatsangehörige(r m) f; ~**i·ty** [næʃəˈnælətɪ] Nationalität f, Staatsangehörigkeit f; ~**ize**

['næʃnəlaɪz] naturalisieren, einbürgern; verstaatlichen.

na·tion-wide ['neɪʃnwaɪd] die ganze Nation umfassend, landesweit.

na·tive ['neɪtɪv] **1.** ☐ angeboren; heimatlich, Heimat...; eingeboren; einheimisch; ~ *language* Muttersprache *f;* **2.** Eingeborene(r *m*) *f;* ~**born** gebürtig.

Na·tiv·i·ty *eccl.* [nə'tɪvətɪ] Geburt *f* (Christi).

nat·u·ral ☐ ['nætʃrəl] natürlich; angeboren; ungezwungen; unehelich (*Kind*); ~ *sience* Naturwissenschaft *f;* ~**sist** [~ɪst] Naturwissenschaftler(in), *bsd.* Biologe *m;* *phls.* Naturalist(in); ~**ize** [~aɪz] einbürgern; ~**ness** [~nɪs] Natürlichkeit *f.*

na·ture ['neɪtʃə] Natur *f;* ~ *reserve* Naturschutzgebiet *n;* ~ *trail* Naturlehrpfad *m.*

-na·tured ['neɪtʃəd] *in Zssgn:* ...artig, ...mütig.

naught [nɔːt] Null *f;* *set at* ~ *et.* ignorieren, in den Wind schlagen.

naugh·ty ☐ ['nɔːtɪ] (*-ier, -iest*) unartig, frech, ungezogen.

nau·se·a ['nɔːsjə] Übelkeit *f;* Ekel *m;* ~**ate** ['nɔːsɪeɪt] *s.o.* (bei) j-m Übelkeit verursachen; *be* ~*d* sich ekeln; ~**at·ing** [~ɪŋ] ekelerregend; ~**ous** ☐ ['nɔːsjəs] ekelhaft.

nau·ti·cal ['nɔːtɪkl] nautisch, See...

na·val ✠ ['neɪvl] See...; Marine...; ~ *base* Flottenstützpunkt *m.*

nave[1] *arch.* [neɪv] (Kirchen)Schiff *n.*

nave[2] [~] (Rad)Nabe *f.*

na·vel ['neɪvl] *anat.* Nabel *m;* *fig.* Mittelpunkt *m.*

nav·i·ga·ble ☐ ['nævɪgəbl] schiffbar; fahrbar; lenkbar; ~**gate** [~eɪt] *v/i.* fahren, segeln; steuern; *v/t. See etc.* befahren; steuern; ~**ga·tion** [nævɪ'geɪʃən] Schiffahrt *f;* Navigation *f;* ~**ga·tor** ['nævɪgeɪtə] ✠ Seefahrer *m;* ✠ Steuermann *m;* ✈ Navigator *m.*

na·vy ['neɪvɪ] Kriegsmarine *f.*

nay Nein *n;* *parl.* Neinstimme *f;* *the* ~*s have it* der Antrag ist abgelehnt.

near [nɪə] **1.** *adj. u. adv.* nahe; kurz (*Weg*); nahe (verwandt); eng (befreundet *od.* vertraut); knapp; genau, wörtlich; sparsam, geizig; ~ *at hand* dicht dabei; **2.** *prp.* nahe, in der Nähe (von), nahe an (*dat.*) *od.* bei; **3.** sich nähern (*dat.*); ~**by** ['nɪəbaɪ] *in der Nähe* (gelegen); nahe; ~**ly** [~lɪ]

nahe; fast, beinahe; annähernd; genau; ~**ness** [~nɪs] Nähe *f;* ~**side** *mot.* Beifahrerseite *f;* ~ *door* Beifahrertür *f;* ~**sight·ed** kurzsichtig.

neat ☐ [niːt] ordentlich; sauber; gepflegt; hübsch, adrett; geschickt; rein; *bsd. Brt.* pur (*Whisky etc.*); ~**ness** [niːtnɪs] Sauberkeit *f;* Gefälligkeit *f;* Gewandtheit *f;* Reinheit *f.*

neb·u·lous ☐ ['nebjʊləs] neb(e)lig.

ne·ces·sa·ry ☐ ['nesəsərɪ] **1.** notwendig; unvermeidlich; **2.** *mst necessaries pl.* Bedürfnisse *pl.;* ~**si·tate** [nɪ'sesɪteɪt] *et.* erfordern, verlangen; ~**si·ty** [~ətɪ] Notwendigkeit *f;* Bedürfnis *n;* Not *f.*

neck [nek] **1.** (*a. Flaschen*)Hals *m;* Nacken *m,* Genick *n;* Ausschnitt *m* (*Kleid*); ~ *and* Kopf an Kopf; ~ *or nothing* auf Biegen od. Brechen; **2.** F (ab)knutschen, knutschen *od.* schmusen (mit); △ *nicht* necken; ~**band** ['nekbænd] Halsbund *m;* ~**er·chief** ['nekətʃɪf] Halstuch *n;* ~**ing** F [~ɪŋ] Geschmuse *n,* Geknutsche *n;* ~**lace** ['neklɪs], ~**let** [~lɪt] Halskette *f;* ~**line** (*Kleid*)Ausschnitt *m;* ~**tie** *Am.* Krawatte *f,* Schlips *m.*

nec·ro·man·cy ['nekrəʊmænsɪ] Zauberei *f.*

née, *Am. a.* **nee** [neɪ] *vor dem Mädchennamen:* geborene.

need [niːd] **1.** Not *f;* Notwendigkeit *f;* Bedürfnis *n;* Mangel *m,* Bedarf *m;* *be od. stand in* ~ *of* dringend brauchen; **2.** nötig haben, brauchen, bedürfen (*gen.*); müssen, brauchen; ~**ful** ☐ ['niːdfl] notwendig.

nee·dle ['niːdl] **1.** Nadel *f;* Zeiger *m;* **2.** nähen; *fig.* F aufziehen, reizen; *fig.* anstacheln.

need·less ☐ ['niːdlɪs] unnötig.

nee·dle|wom·an ['niːdlwʊmən] (*pl. -women*) Näherin *f;* ~**work** Handarbeit *f.*

need·y ☐ ['niːdɪ] (*-ier, -iest*) bedürftig, arm.

ne·far·i·ous ☐ [nɪ'feərɪəs] schändlich.

ne·gate [nɪ'geɪt] verneinen; **ne·ga·tion** [~ʃn] Verneinung *f;* Nichts *n;* **neg·a·tive** ['negətɪv] **1.** ☐ negativ; verneinend; **2.** Verneinung *f;* *phot.* Negativ *n;* *answer in the* ~ verneinen; **3.** verneinen; ablehnen.

ne·glect [nɪ'glekt] **1.** Vernachlässigung *f;* Nachlässigkeit *f;* **2.** vernachlässigen; ~**ful** ☐ [~fl] nachlässig.

nick

neg·li|gence ['neglidʒəns] Nachlässigkeit f; **~gent** ☐ [~t] nachlässig.
neg·li·gi·ble ['neglidʒəbl] nebensächlich; unbedeutend.
ne·go·ti·ate [nɪ'gəʊʃɪeɪt] verhandeln (über acc.); zustande bringen; bewältigen; Wechsel begeben; **~a·tion** [nɪgəʊʃɪ'eɪʃn] Begebung f (e-s Wechsels etc.); Ver-, Unterhandlung f; Bewältigung f; **~a·tor** [nɪ'gəʊʃɪeɪtə] Unterhändler m.
Ne·gress ['ni:grɪs] Negerin f; **Ne·gro** [~əʊ] (pl. -groes) Neger m.
neigh [neɪ] **1.** Wiehern n; **2.** wiehern.
neigh·bo(u)r ['neɪbə] Nachbar(in); Nächste(r m) f; **~hood** [~hʊd] Nachbarschaft f, Umgebung f, Nähe f; **~ing** [~rɪŋ] benachbart; **~ly** [~lɪ] nachbarlich, freundlich; **~ship** [~ʃɪp] Nachbarschaft f.
nei·ther ['naɪðə, Am. 'ni:ðə] **1.** keine(r, -s) (von beiden); **2.** noch, auch nicht; **~ ... nor ...** weder ... noch ...
ne·on ⚛ ['ni:ɒn] Neon n; **~ lamp** Neonlampe f; **~ sign** Leuchtreklame f.
neph·ew ['nevju:] Neffe m.
nerve [nɜ:v] **1.** Nerv m; Sehne f; (Blatt)Rippe f; Kraft f, Mut m; Dreistigkeit f; lose one's ~ den Mut verlieren; get on s.o.'s ~s j-m auf die Nerven gehen; you've got a ~! F Sie haben Nerven!; **2.** kräftigen; ermutigen; **~ null nerven**; **~less** ☐ ['nɜ:vlɪs] kraftlos.
ner·vous ☐ ['nɜ:vəs] Nerven...; nervös; nervig, kräftig; **~ness** [~nɪs] Nervigkeit f; Nervosität f.
nest [nest] **1.** Nest n (a. fig.); **2.** nisten.
nes·tle ['nesl] (sich) (an)schmiegen od. kuscheln (to, against an acc.); a. ~ down sich behaglich niederlassen.
net¹ [net] **1.** Netz n; **2.** (-tt-) mit e-m Netz fangen od. bedecken.
net² [~] **1.** netto; Rein...; **2.** (-tt-) netto einbringen.
neth·er ['neðə] niedere(r, -s); Unter...
net·tle ['netl] **1.** ♀ Nessel f; **2.** ärgern.
net·work ['netwɜ:k] (Straßen-, Kanal- etc.)Netz n; Rundfunk: Sendernetz n, -gruppe f.
neu·ro·sis ⚛ [njʊə'rəʊsɪs] (pl. -ses [-si:z]) Neurose f.
neu·ter ['nju:tə] **1.** geschlechtslos; gr. sächlich; **2.** kastriertes Tier; gr. Neutrum n.

neu·tral ['nju:trəl] **1.** neutral; unparteiisch; **~ gear** mot. Leerlauf(gang) m; **2.** Neutrale(r m f); Null(punkt m) f; mot. Leerlauf(stellung f) m; **~i·ty** [nju:'trælətɪ] Neutralität f; **~ize** ['nju:trəlaɪz] neutralisieren.
neu·tron phys. ['nju:trɒn] Neutron n; **~ bomb** ⚔ Neutronenbombe f.
nev·er ['nevə] nie(mals); gar nicht; **~more** [~'mɔ:] nie wieder; **~the·less** [nevəðə'les] nichtsdestoweniger, dennoch.
new [nju:] neu; frisch; unerfahren; **~born** ['nju:bɔ:n] neugeboren; **~com·er** [~kʌmə] Neuankömmling m; Neuling m; **~ly** ['nju:lɪ] neulich; neu.
news [nju:z] mst sg. Neuigkeit(en pl.) f, Nachricht(en pl.) f; **~a·gent** ['nju:zeɪdʒənt] Zeitungshändler m; **~boy** Zeitungsjunge m, -austräger m; **~cast** Rundfunk, TV: Nachrichtensendung f; **~cast·er** Rundfunk, TV: Nachrichtensprecher(in); **~deal·er** Am. Zeitungshändler m; **~mon·ger** Klatschmaul n; **~pa·per** [~speɪpə] Zeitung f; attr. Zeitungs...; **~print** [~zprɪnt] Zeitungspapier n; **~reel** Film: Wochenschau f; **~room** Nachrichtenredaktion f; **~stand** Zeitungskiosk m.
new year ['nju:'jɜ:] Neujahr n, das neue Jahr; New Year's Day Neujahrstag m; New Year's Eve Silvester m, n.
next [nekst] **1.** adj. nächste(r, -s); (the) ~ day am nächsten Tag; ~ to gleich neben od. nach; fig. fast; ~ but one übernächste(r, -s); ~ door to fig. beinahe, fast; **2.** adv. als nächste(r, -s), gleich darauf; das nächste Mal; **3.** der, die, das Nächste; **~-door** benachbart, nebenan; **~ of kin** der, die nächste Verwandte, die nächsten Angehörigen pl.
nib·ble ['nɪbl] v/t. knabbern an (dat.); v/i. ~ at nagen od. knabbern an (dat.); fig. (herum)kritteln an (dat.).
nice ☐ [naɪs] (~r, ~st) fein; wählerisch; (peinlich) genau; heikel; nett; sympathisch; schön; hübsch; **~ly** ['naɪslɪ] (sehr) gut; **ni·ce·ty** [~ətɪ] Feinheit f; Genauigkeit f; Spitzfindigkeit f.
niche [nɪtʃ] Nische f.
nick [nɪk] **1.** Kerbe f; in the ~ of time im richtigen Augenblick; im letzten

Moment; 2. (ein)kerben; *Brt. sl. j-n* schnappen.

nick·el ['nɪkl] 1. *min.* Nickel *m* (*Am. a.* Fünfcentstück); 2. vernickeln.

nick·nack ['nɪknæk] = *knick-knack*.

nick·name ['nɪkneɪm] 1. Spitzname *m*; 2. *j-m* den Spitznamen ... geben.

niece [niːs] Nichte *f*.

nif·ty F ['nɪftɪ] (-ier, -iest) hübsch, schick, fesch; stinkend.

nig·gard ['nɪgəd] Geizhals *m*; ~·ly [~lɪ] geizig, knaus(e)rig; karg.

night [naɪt] Nacht *f*; Abend *m*; at ~, by ~, in the ~ nachts; ~·cap ['naɪtkæp] Nachtmütze *f*; Schlaftrunk *m*; ~·club Nachtklub *m*, -lokal *n*; ~·dress (Damen-, Kinder)Nachthemd *n*; ~·fall Einbruch *m* der Nacht; ~·gown *bsd. Am.*, ~·ie F [~ɪ] = *nightdress*; **night·in·gale** zo. [~ɪŋgeɪl] Nachtigall *f*; ~·ly [~lɪ] nächtlich; jede Nacht *od.* jeden Abend (stattfindend); ~·mare Alptraum *m*; ~ school Abendschule *f*; ~·shirt (Herren)Nachthemd *n*; ~·y F [~ɪ] = *nightie*.

nil [nɪl] *bsd. Sport*: Nichts *n*, Null *f*.

nim·ble ☐ ['nɪmbl] (~r, ~st) flink, behend(e).

nine [naɪn] 1. neun; ~ to five normale Dienststunden; a ~-to-five job e-e (An)Stellung mit geregelter Arbeitszeit; 2. Neun *f*; ~·pin ['naɪnpɪn] Kegel *m*; ~s *sg.* Kegeln *n*; ~·teen ['naɪn'tiːn] 1. neunzehn; 2. Neunzehn *f*; ~·teenth [~θ] neunzehnte(r, -s); ~·ti·eth ['naɪntɪɪθ] neunzigste(r, -s); ~·ty ['naɪntɪ] 1. neunzig; 2. Neunzig *f*.

nin·ny ['nɪnɪ] Dummkopf *m*.

ninth [naɪnθ] 1. neunte(r, -s); 2. Neuntel *n*; ~·ly [~lɪ] neuntens.

nip [nɪp] 1. Kneifen *n*; ⊕ Knick *m*; scharfer Frost; Schlückchen *n*; 2. (-pp-) kneifen, klemmen; schneiden (*Kälte*); *sl.* flitzen; nippen (an *dat.*); ~ in the bud im Keim ersticken.

nip·per ['nɪpə] zo. (*Krebs*)Schere *f*; (*a pair of*) ~s *pl.* (e-e) (Kneif)Zange.

nip·ple ['nɪpl] Brustwarze *f*.

ni·tre, *Am.* **-ter** ⊖ ['naɪtə] Salpeter *m*.

ni·tro·gen ⊖ ['naɪtrədʒən] Stickstoff *m*.

no [nəʊ] 1. *adj.* kein(e); at ~ time nie; in ~ time im Nu; ~ one keiner; 2. *adv.* nein; nicht; 3. (*pl. noes*) Nein *n*.

no·bil·i·ty [nəʊ'bɪlətɪ] Adel *m* (*a. fig.*).

no·ble ['nəʊbl] 1. ☐ (~r, ~st) adlig; edel; vornehm; vortrefflich; ⚠ *nicht* nobel; 2. Adlige(r *m*) *f*; ~·man (*pl. -men*) Adlige(r) *m*; ~·mind·ed edelmütig.

no·bod·y ['nəʊbədɪ] niemand, keiner.

noc·tur·nal [nɒk'tɜːnl] Nacht...

nod [nɒd] 1. (-dd-) nicken (mit); (*im Sitzen*) schlafen; sich neigen; ~ off einnicken; ~·ding acquaintance oberflächliche Bekanntschaft; 2. Nicken *n*, Wink *m*.

node [nəʊd] Knoten *m* (*a.* ♀, ♃, *ast.*); ✚ Überbein *n*, (*Gicht*)Knoten *m*.

noise [nɔɪz] 1. Lärm *m*; Geräusch *n*; Geschrei *n*; big ~ *contp.* großes Tier (*Person*); 2. ~ abroad (*about, around*) verbreiten; ~·less ☐ ['nɔɪzlɪs] geräuschlos.

noi·some ['nɔɪsəm] schädlich; unangenehm; widerlich (*Geruch*).

nois·y ☐ ['nɔɪzɪ] (-ier, -iest) geräuschvoll; laut; lärmend; grell, aufdringlich (*Farbe*).

nom·i·nal ☐ ['nɒmɪnl] nominell; (nur) dem Namen nach (vorhanden); namentlich; ~ value econ. Nennwert *m*; ~·nate [~eɪt] ernennen; nominieren, (zur Wahl) vorschlagen; ~·na·tion [nɒmɪ'neɪʃn] Ernennung *f*; Nominierung *f*, Aufstellung *f* (*e-s Kandidaten*); ~·nee [~'niː] Kandidat(in).

nom·i·na·tive gr. ['nɒmɪnətɪv] *a.* ~ case Nominativ *m*, erster Fall.

non- [nɒn] *in Zssgn*: nicht..., Nicht..., un...

no·nage ['nəʊnɪdʒ] Minderjährigkeit *f*.

non-al·co·hol·ic ['nɒnælkə'hɒlɪk] alkoholfrei.

non·a·ligned pol. [nɒnə'laɪnd] blockfrei.

nonce [nɒns]: for the ~ nur für diesen Fall.

non-com·mis·sioned [nɒnkə'mɪʃnd] nicht bevollmächtigt; ~ officer ⚔ Unteroffizier *m*.

non-com·mit·tal [nɒnkə'mɪtl] unverbindlich.

non-con·duc·tor *bsd.* ⚡ ['nɒnkən'dʌktə] Nichtleiter *m*.

non·con·form·ist ['nɒnkən'fɔːmɪst] Nonkonformist(in); ⚭ *Brt. eccl.* Dissident(in).

non-de·script ['nɒndɪskrɪpt] nichtssagend; schwer zu beschreiben(d).

none [nʌn] **1.** keine(r, -s); nichts; **2.** keineswegs, gar nicht; ~ *the less* nichtsdestoweniger.

non·en·ti·ty [nɒˈnentətɪ] Nichtsein n; Unding n, Nichts n; *fig.* Null f.

non-ex·ist·ence [ˈnɒnɪɡˈzɪstəns] Nicht(vorhanden)sein n; Fehlen n.

non-fic·tion [ˈnɒnˈfɪkʃn] Sachbücher pl.

non-par·ty [ˈnɒnˈpɑːtɪ] parteilos.

non-per·form·ance ⚖ [ˈnɒnpəˈfɔːməns] Nichterfüllung f.

non·plus [nɒnˈplʌs] **1.** Verlegenheit f; **2.** (-ss-) j-n (völlig) verwirren.

non-pol·lut·ing [ˈnɒnpəˈluːtɪŋ] umweltfreundlich, ungiftig.

non-res·i·dent [ˈnɒnˈrezɪdənt] nicht im Haus od. am Ort wohnend.

non·sense [ˈnɒnsəns] Unsinn m; **~·sen·si·cal** □ [nɒnˈsensɪkl] unsinnig.

non-skid [ˈnɒnˈskɪd] rutschfest.

non-smok·er [ˈnɒnˈsməʊkə] Nichtraucher(in); 🚃 Nichtraucher(abteil n) m.

non-stop [ˈnɒnˈstɒp] Nonstop..., ohne Halt, durchgehend (*Zug*), ohne Zwischenlandung (*Flugzeug*).

non-u·ni·on [ˈnɒnˈjuːnjən] nicht (gewerkschaftlich) organisiert.

non-vi·o·lence [ˈnɒnˈvaɪələns] (Politik f der) Gewaltlosigkeit f.

noo·dle [ˈnuːdl] Nudel f.

nook [nʊk] Ecke f, Winkel m.

noon [nuːn] Mittag m; *at* (*high*) ~ um 12 Uhr mittags; **~·day** [ˈnuːndeɪ], **~·tide**, **~·time** *Am.* = noon.

noose [nuːs] **1.** Schlinge f; **2.** mit der Schlinge fangen; schlingen.

nope F [nəʊp] ne(e), nein.

nor [nɔː] noch; auch nicht.

norm [nɔːm] Norm f, Regel f; Muster n; Maßstab m; **nor·mal** □ [ˈnɔːml] normal; **nor·mal·ize** [~laɪz] normalisieren; normen.

north [nɔːθ] **1.** Nord(en m); **2.** nördlich, Nord...; **~·east** [nɔːθˈiːst] **1.** Nordost(en m); **2.** a. **~·east·ern** [~ən] nordöstlich; **nor·ther·ly** [ˈnɔːðəlɪ], **nor·thern** [~ðən] nördlich, Nord...; **~·ward(s)** [ˈnɔːθwəd(z)] adv. nördlich, nordwärts; **~·west** [ˈnɔːθˈwest] **1.** Nordwest(en m); **2.** a. **~·west·ern** [~ən] nordwestlich.

Nor·we·gian [nɔːˈwiːdʒən] **1.** norwegisch; **2.** Norweger(in); *ling.* Norwegisch n.

nose [nəʊz] **1.** Nase f; Spitze f; Schnauze f; **2.** v/t. riechen; ~ *one's way* vorsichtig fahren; v/i. schnüffeln; **~·bleed** [ˈnəʊzbliːd] Nasenbluten n; *have a* ~ Nasenbluten haben; **~·cone** Raketenspitze f; **~·dive** ✈ Sturzflug m; **~·gay** [~geɪ] Sträußchen n.

nos·ey [ˈnəʊzɪ] = nosy.

nos·tal·gia [nɒˈstældʒɪə] Nostalgie f, Sehnsucht f.

nos·tril [ˈnɒstrəl] Nasenloch n, bsd. zo. Nüster f.

nos·y F [ˈnəʊzɪ] (-ier, -iest) neugierig.

not [nɒt] nicht; ~ *a* kein(e).

no·ta·ble [ˈnəʊtəbl] **1.** □ bemerkenswert; **2.** angesehene Person.

no·ta·ry [ˈnəʊtərɪ] mst ~ *public* Notar m.

no·ta·tion [nəʊˈteɪʃn] Bezeichnung f.

notch [nɒtʃ] **1.** Kerbe f, Einschnitt m; Scharte f; *Am. geol.* Engpaß m; **2.** (ein)kerben.

note [nəʊt] **1.** Zeichen n; Notiz f; *print.* Anmerkung f; Briefchen n, Zettel m; *bsd. Brt.* Banknote f; (*bsd.* Schuld)Schein m; *Diplomatie*, ♪: Note f; △ *nicht* (Schul)Note; ♪ Ton m (*a. fig.*); *fig.* Ruf m; Beachtung f; *take* ~*s* sich Notizen machen; **2.** bemerken; (besonders) beachten od. achten auf (*acc.*); besonders erwähnen; *a.* ~ *down* niederschreiben, notieren; **~·book** [ˈnəʊtbʊk] Notizbuch n; **not·ed** bekannt, berühmt (*for* wegen); **~·pa·per** Briefpapier n; **~·wor·thy** bemerkenswert.

noth·ing [ˈnʌθɪŋ] **1.** nichts; **2.** Nichts n; Null f; ~ *but* nichts als, nur; *for* ~ umsonst; *good for* ~ zu nichts zu gebrauchen; *come to* ~ zunichte werden; *to say* ~ *of* ganz zu schweigen von; *there is* ~ *like* es geht nichts über (*acc.*).

no·tice [ˈnəʊtɪs] **1.** Nachricht f, Bekanntmachung f; Anzeige f, Ankündigung f; Kündigung f; Be(ob)achtung f; △ *nicht* Notiz; *at short* ~ kurzfristig; *give* ~ *that* bekanntgeben, daß; *give* (*a week's*) ~ (acht Tage vorher) kündigen; *take* ~ *of* Notiz nehmen von; *without* ~ fristlos; **2.** bemerken; (besonders) beachten od. achten auf (*acc.*); △ *nicht* notieren; **~·a·ble** □ [~əbl] wahrnehmbar; bemerkenswert; ~ **board** *Brt.* Schwarzes Brett.

no·ti·fi·ca·tion [nəʊtɪfɪˈkeɪʃn] Anzei-

gef, Meldung f; Bekanntmachung f;
~·fy ['nəʊtɪfaɪ] et. anzeigen, melden;
j-n benachrichtigen.

no·tion ['nəʊʃn] Begriff m, Vorstellung f; Absicht f; ~s pl. Am. Kurzwaren pl.

no·to·ri·ous □ [nəʊ'tɔːrɪəs] notorisch; all-, weltbekannt; berüchtigt.

not·with·stand·ing prp. ['nɒtwɪθ-'stændɪŋ] ungeachtet, trotz (gen.).

nought [nɔːt] Null f; poet. od. veraltet Nichts n.

noun gr. [naʊn] Substantiv n, Hauptwort n.

nour·ish ['nʌrɪʃ] (er)nähren; fig. hegen; ~·ing [~ɪŋ] nahrhaft; ~·ment [~mənt] Ernährung f; Nahrung(smittel n) f.

nov·el ['nɒvl] 1. neu; ungewöhnlich; 2. Roman m; △ nicht Novelle; ~·ist [~ɪst] Romanschriftsteller(in); ~·vel·la [nəʊ'velə] (pl. -las, -le [-liː]) Novelle f; ~·ty ['nɒvltɪ] Neuheit f.

No·vem·ber [nəʊ'vembə] November m.

nov·ice ['nɒvɪs] Neuling m, Anfänger(in) (at auf e-m Gebiet); eccl. Novize m.

now [naʊ] 1. nun, jetzt; eben; just ~ gerade eben; ~ and again od. then dann u. wann; 2. cj. a. ~ that nun da.

now·a·days ['naʊədeɪz] heutzutage.

no·where ['nəʊweə] nirgends.

nox·ious □ ['nɒkʃəs] schädlich.

noz·zle ⊕ ['nɒzl] Düse f; Tülle f.

nu·ance [njuːˈɑ̃ːns] Nuance f, Schattierung f.

nub [nʌb] Knötchen n; kleiner Klumpen; the ~ fig. der springende Punkt (of bei e-r Sache).

nu·cle·ar ['njuːklɪə] nuklear, Nuklear..., atomar, Atom..., Kern...; ~-free atomwaffenfrei; ~-pow·ered atomgetrieben; ~ pow·er sta·tion Kernkraftwerk n; ~·re·ac·tor Kernreaktor m; ~ war·head ✕ Atomsprengkopf m; ~ weap·ons pl. Kernwaffen pl.; ~ waste Atommüll m.

nu·cle·us ['njuːklɪəs] (pl. -clei [-klɪaɪ]) Kern m.

nude [njuːd] 1. nackt; 2. paint. Akt m.

nudge [nʌdʒ] 1. j-n anstoßen, (an-)stupsen; 2. Stups(er) m.

nug·get ['nʌgɪt] (bsd. Gold)Klumpen m.

nui·sance ['njuːsns] Ärgernis n, Un-

fug m, Plage f; lästiger Mensch, Nervensäge f; what a ~! wie ärgerlich!; be a ~ to s.o. j-m lästig fallen; make a ~ of o.s. den Leuten auf die Nerven gehen od. fallen.

nuke Am. sl. [njuːk] Kernwaffe f.

null [nʌl] 1. nichtssagend; ~ and void null u. nichtig; 2. ⊕, ⚡ Null f; **nul·li·fy** ['nʌlɪfaɪ] zunichte machen; aufheben, ungültig machen; **nul·li·ty** [~ətɪ] Nichtigkeit f, Ungültigkeit f.

numb [nʌm] 1. starr (with vor); 2. (empfindungslos); 2. starr od. taub machen; ~ed erstarrt.

num·ber ['nʌmbə] 1. ⚡ Zahl f; (Auto-, Haus- etc.) Nummer f; (An)Zahl f; Heft n, Ausgabe f, Nummer f (e-r Zeitschrift etc.); (Autobus- etc.)Linie f; without ~ zahllos; in ~ an der Zahl; 2. zählen; numerieren; ~·less zahllos; ~·plate bsd. Brt. mot. Nummernschild n.

nu·me·ral ['njuːmərəl] 1. Zahl(en)...; 2. ⚡ Ziffer f; ling. Numerale n, Zahlwort n; ~·rous □ [~əs] zahlreich.

nun [nʌn] Nonne f; ~·ne·ry ['nʌnərɪ] Nonnenkloster n.

nup·tial ['nʌpʃl] 1. Hochzeits..., Ehe...; 2. ~s pl. Hochzeit f.

nurse [nɜːs] 1. Kindermädchen n; a. dry-~ Säuglingsschwester f; a. wet-~ Amme f; (Kranken)Pflegerin f, (Kranken)Schwester f; at ~ in Pflege; put out to ~ in Pflege geben; 2. stillen; nähren; großziehen; pflegen; hätscheln; ~·ing ['nɜːsɪŋ] Säugling m; Pflegling m; ~·maid Kindermädchen n; **nur·se·ry** [~sərɪ] Kinderzimmer n; ✿ Baum-, Pflanzschule f; ~ rhymes pl. Kinderlieder pl., -reime pl.; ~ school Kindergarten m; ~ slope Ski: Idiotenhügel m.

nurs·ing ['nɜːsɪŋ] Stillen n; (Kranken)Pflege f; ~·bot·tle (Säuglings-Saug)Flasche f; ~ home Brt. Privatklinik f.

nurs·ling ['nɜːslɪŋ] = nurseling.

nur·ture ['nɜːtʃə] 1. Pflege f; Erziehung f; 2. aufzie(h)en; (er)nähren.

nut [nʌt] ✿ Nuß f; ⊕ (Schrauben-)Mutter f; sl. verrückter Kerl; be ~s sl. verrückt sein; ~·crack·er ['nʌt-krækə] mst ~s pl. Nußknacker m; ~·meg ✿ ['nʌtmeg] Muskatnuß f.

nu·tri·ment ['njuːtrɪmənt] Nahrung f.

nu·tri|tion [nju:'trɪʃn] Ernährung *f*; Nahrung *f*; **~tious** □ [~ʃəs], **~tive** □ ['nju:trɪtɪv] nahrhaft.

nut|shell ['nʌt∫el] Nußschale *f*; *in a ~* in aller Kürze; **~ty** ['nʌtɪ] (*-ier*, *-iest*) voller Nüsse; nußartig; *sl.* verrückt.

ny·lon ['naɪlɒn] Nylon *n*; **~s** *pl.* Nylonstrümpfe *pl.*

nymph [nɪmf] Nymphe *f.*

O

o [əʊ] **1.** oh!; ach!; **2.** *in Telefonnummern:* Null *f.*

oaf [əʊf] Dummkopf *m*; Tölpel *m.*

oak ♀ [əʊk] Eiche *f.*

oar [ɔ:] **1.** Ruder *n*; **2.** rudern; **~s·man** ['ɔ:zmən] (*pl. -men*) Ruderer *m.*

o·a·sis [əʊ'eɪsɪs] (*pl. -ses* [-si:z]) Oase *f* (*a. fig.*).

oat [əʊt] *mst* **~s** *pl.* ♀ Hafer *m*; *feel one's ~s* F groß in Form sein; *Am.* sich wichtig vorkommen; *sow one's wild ~s* sich die Hörner abstoßen.

oath [əʊθ] (*pl. oaths* [əʊðz]) Eid *m*, Schwur *m*; Fluch *m*; *be on ~* unter Eid stehen; *take* (*make*, *swear*) *an ~* e-n Eid leisten, schwören.

oat·meal ['əʊtmi:l] Hafermehl *n.*

ob·du·rate □ ['ɒbdjʊrət] verstockt.

o·be·di|ence [ə'bi:djəns] Gehorsam *m*; **~ent** □ [~t] gehorsam.

o·bei·sance [əʊ'beɪsəns] Ehrerbietung *f*; Verbeugung *f*; *do* (*make*, *pay*) *~ to s.o.* j-m huldigen.

o·bese [əʊ'bi:s] fett(leibig); **o·bes·i·ty** [~ətɪ] Fettleibigkeit *f.*

o·bey [ə'beɪ] gehorchen (*dat.*); *Befehl etc.* befolgen, Folge leisten (*dat.*).

o·bit·u·a·ry [ə'bɪtjʊərɪ] Todesanzeige *f*; Nachruf *m*; *attr.* Todes..., Toten...

ob·ject 1. ['ɒbdʒɪkt] Gegenstand *m*; Ziel *n*, Zweck *m*, Absicht *f*; Objekt *n* (*a. gr.*); **2.** [əb'dʒekt] *v/t.* einwenden (*to* gegen); *v/i.* et. dagegen haben (*to ger.* daß).

ob·jec·tion [əb'dʒek∫n] Einwand *m*, -spruch *m*; **~tio·na·ble** □ [~əbl] nicht einwandfrei; unangenehm.

ob·jec·tive [əb'dʒektɪv] **1.** □ objektiv, sachlich; **2.** Ziel *n*; *opt. phot.* Objektiv *n.*

ob·li·ga·tion [ɒblɪ'geɪ∫n] Verpflichtung *f*; *econ.* Schuldverschreibung *f*; *be under an ~ to s.o.* j-m (zu Dank)

verpflichtet sein; *be under ~ to inf.* die Verpflichtung haben, zu *inf.*;

ob·lig·a·to·ry □ [ə'blɪgətərɪ] verpflichtend, (rechts)verbindlich.

o·blige [ə'blaɪdʒ] (zu Dank) verpflichten; nötigen, zwingen; *~ s.o.* j-m e-n Gefallen tun; *much ~d* sehr verbunden, danke bestens; **o·blig·ing** □ [~ɪŋ] verbindlich, zuvor-, entgegenkommend, gefällig.

o·blique □ [ə'bli:k] schief, schräg.

o·blit·er·ate [ə'blɪtəreɪt] auslöschen, tilgen (*a. fig.*); *Schrift* ausstreichen; *Briefmarken* entwerten.

o·bliv·i|on [ə'blɪvɪən] Vergessen(heit *f*) *n*; **~ous** □ [~əs]: *be ~ of s.th.* et. vergessen haben; *be ~ to s.th.* blind sein gegen et., et. nicht beachten.

ob·long ['ɒblɒŋ] länglich; rechteckig.

ob·nox·ious □ [əb'nɒk∫əs] anstößig; verabscheuungswürdig, verhaßt.

ob·scene □ [əb'si:n] unanständig.

ob·scure [əb'skjʊə] **1.** □ dunkel; *fig.* dunkel, unklar; unbekannt; **2.** verdunkeln; **ob·scu·ri·ty** [~rətɪ] Dunkelheit *f* (*a. fig.*); Unbekanntheit *f*; Niedrigkeit *f* (*der Herkunft*).

ob·se·quies ['ɒbsɪkwɪz] *pl.* Trauerfeier(lichkeiten *pl.*) *f.*

ob·se·qui·ous □ [əb'si:kwɪəs] unterwürfig (*to* gegen).

ob·ser|va·ble □ [əb'zɜ:vəbl] bemerkbar; bemerkenswert; **~vance** [~ns] Befolgung *f*; Brauch *m*; **~vant** □ [~t] beachtend; aufmerksam; **~va·tion** [ɒbzə'veɪʃn] Beobachtung *f*; Bemerkung *f*; *attr.* Beobachtungs...; Aussichts...; **~va·to·ry** [əb'zɜ:vətrɪ] Observatorium *n*, Stern-, Wetterwarte *f.*

ob·serve [əb'zɜ:v] *v/t.* be(ob)achten; sehen; *Brauch etc.* (ein)halten; *Gesetz etc.* befolgen; bemerken, äußern; *v/i.* sich äußern.

ob·sess [əb'ses] heimsuchen, quälen; ~ed by od. with besessen von; **ob·ses·sion** [~eʃn] Besessenheit f; **ob·ses·sive** □ psych. [~sɪv] zwanghaft, Zwangs...

ob·so·lete ['ɒbsəliːt] veraltet.

ob·sta·cle ['ɒbstəkl] Hindernis n.

ob·sti·na·cy ['ɒbstɪnəsɪ] Hartnäckigkeit f; Eigensinn m; **~·nate** □ [~t] halsstarrig; eigensinnig; hartnäckig.

ob·struct [əb'strʌkt] verstopfen, -sperren; blockieren; (be)hindern; **ob·struc·tion** [~kʃn] Verstopfung f; Blockierung f; Behinderung f; Hindernis n; **ob·struc·tive** □ [~ktɪv] blockierend; hinderlich.

ob·tain [əb'teɪn] erlangen, erhalten, erreichen, bekommen; **ob·tai·na·ble** econ. [~əbl] erhältlich.

ob·trude [əb'truːd] (sich) aufdrängen (on dat.); **ob·tru·sive** □ [~sɪv] aufdringlich.

ob·tuse □ [əb'tjuːs] stumpf; dumpf; begriffsstutzig.

ob·vi·ate ['ɒbvɪeɪt] beseitigen; vorbeugen (dat.).

ob·vi·ous □ ['ɒbvɪəs] offensichtlich; augenfällig, klar, einleuchtend.

oc·ca·sion [ə'keɪʒn] 1. Gelegenheit f; Anlaß m; Veranlassung f; (festliches) Ereignis n; on the ~ of anläßlich (gen.); 2. veranlassen; **~·al** □ [~l] gelegentlich, Gelegenheits...

Oc·ci·dent ['ɒksɪdənt] Westen m; Okzident m, Abendland n; ♀**den·tal** □ [ɒksɪ'dentl] abendländisch, westlich.

oc·cu·pant ['ɒkjʊpənt] bsd. ♏ Besitzergreifer(in); Besitzer(in); Bewohner(in); Insasse m, -in f; **~·pa·tion** [ɒkjʊ'peɪʃn] Besitz(nahme f) m; ✗ Besetzung f, Besatzung f, Okkupation f; Beruf m; Beschäftigung f; **~·py** ['ɒkjʊpaɪ] einnehmen; in Besitz nehmen; ✗ besetzen; besitzen; innehaben; bewohnen; in Anspruch nehmen; beschäftigen.

oc·cur [ə'kɜː] (-rr-) vorkommen; sich ereignen; it ~red to me mir fiel ein; **~·rence** [ə'kʌrəns] Vorkommen n; Vorfall m, Ereignis n.

o·cean ['əʊʃn] Ozean m, Meer n.

o'clock [ə'klɒk] Uhr (bei Zeitangaben); (at) five ~ (um) fünf Uhr.

Oc·to·ber [ɒk'təʊbə] Oktober m.

oc·u·lar □ ['ɒkjʊlə] Augen...; **~·list** [~ɪst] Augenarzt m.

odd □ [ɒd] ungerade (Zahl); einzeln;

nach Zahlen: und einige od. etwas darüber; überzählig; gelegentlich; sonderbar, merkwürdig; **~·i·ty** ['ɒdətɪ] Seltsamkeit f; **~s** [ɒdz] oft sg. (Gewinn)Chancen pl.; Vorteil m; Vorgabe f (im Spiel); Verschiedenheit f; Unterschied m; Uneinigkeit f; be at ~ with s.o. mit j-m im Streit sein, uneins sein mit j-m; the ~ are that es ist sehr wahrscheinlich, daß; ~ and ends Reste pl.; Krimskrams m.

ode [əʊd] Ode f (Gedicht).

o·di·ous □ ['əʊdjəs] verhaßt; ekelhaft.

o·do(u)r ['əʊdə] Geruch m; Duft m.

of prp. [ɒv, əv] von; Ort: bei (the battle ~ Quebec); um (cheat s.o. ~ s.th.); von, an (dat.) (die ~); aus (~ charity); vor (dat.) (afraid ~); auf (acc.) (proud ~); über (acc.) (ashamed ~); nach (smell ~ roses; desirous ~); von, über (acc.) (speak ~ s.th.); an (acc.) (think ~ s.th.); Herkunft: von, aus; Material: aus, von; nimble ~ foot leichtfüßig; the city ~ London die Stadt London; the works ~ Dickens Dickens' Werke; your letter ~ ... Ihr Schreiben vom ...; five minutes ~ twelve Am. fünf Minuten vor zwölf.

off [ɒf] 1. adv. fort, weg; ab, herunter(...), los(...); entfernt; Zeit: bis hin (3 months ~...); aus(-), ab(geschaltet) (Licht etc.), zu (Hahn etc.); ab(-), los(gegangen) (Knopf etc.); frei (von Arbeit); ganz, zu Ende; econ. flau; verdorben (Fleisch etc.); fig. aus, vorbei; be ~ fort od. weg sein; (weg)gehen; ~ and on ab u. an; ab u. zu; well (badly) ~ gut (schlecht) daran; 2. prp. fort von, weg von; von (... ab, weg, herunter); abseits von, entfernt von; frei von (Arbeit); ♣ auf der Höhe von; be ~ duty dienstfrei haben; be ~ smoking nicht mehr rauchen; 3. adj. (weiter) entfernt; Seiten..., Neben...; (arbeits-, dienst-)frei; econ. flau, still, tot; int. fort!, weg!, raus!

of·fal ['ɒfl] Abfall m; ~s pl. bsd. Brt. Fleischerei: Innereien pl.

of·fence, Am. **-fense** [ə'fens] Angriff m; Beleidigung f, Kränkung f, Ärgernis m, Anstoß m; Vergehen n, Verstoß m; ♏ Straftat f.

of·fend [ə'fend] beleidigen, verletzen, kränken; verstoßen (against

once

gegen); **~er** [~ə] Übel-, Missetäter(in); ⚖ Straffällige(r *m*) *f*; *first ~* ⚖ nicht Vorbestrafte(r *m*) *f*, Ersttäter(in).

of·fen·sive [ə'fensıv] **1.** □ beleidigend; anstößig; ekelhaft; Offensiv..., Angriffs...; **2.** Offensive *f*.

of·fer ['ɒfə] **1.** Angebot *n*; Anerbieten *n*; ~ *of marriage* Heiratsantrag *m*; **2.** *v/t.* anbieten (*a.* econ.); *Preis, Möglichkeit etc.* bieten; *Preis, Belohnung* aussetzen; *Gebet, Opfer* darbringen; sich bereit erklären; zu; *Widerstand* leisten; *v/i.* sich bieten; **~ing** [~rıŋ] *eccl.* Opfer(n) *n*; Anerbieten *n*, Angebot *n*.

off·hand ['ɒf'hænd] aus dem Stegreif, auf Anhieb; Stegreif..., unvorbereitet; ungezwungen, frei.

of·fice ['ɒfıs] Büro *n*; Geschäftsstelle *f*; Amt *n*; Pflicht *f*; Dienst *m*, Gefälligkeit *f*; *eccl.* Gottesdienst *m*; ♀ Ministerium *n*; ~ *hours pl.* Dienststunden *pl.*, Geschäftszeit *f*; **of·fi·cer** [~ə] Beamt|e(r *m*) -in *f*; Polizist *m*, Polizeibeamte(r *m*); ✕ Offizier *m*.

of·fi·cial [ə'fıʃl] **1.** □ offiziell, amtlich; Amts...; **2.** Beamt|e(r *m*) -in *f*.

of·fi·ci·ate [ə'fıʃıeıt] amtieren.

of·fi·cious □ [ə'fıʃəs] aufdringlich, übereifrig; offiziös, halbamtlich.

off·-licence *Br.* ['ɒf'laısəns] Schankkonzession *f* über die Straße; **~·print** Sonderdruck *m*; **~·set** ausgleichen; **~·shoot** ♀ Sproß *m*, Ableger *m*; **~·side** ['ɒf'saıd] **1.** *Sport:* Abseits(stellung *f*, -position *f*) *n*; *mot.* Fahrerseite *f*; ~ *door* Fahrertür *f*; **2.** *Sport:* abseits; **~·spring** ['ɒfsprıŋ] Nachkomme(nschaft *f*) *m*; *fig.* Ergebnis *n*.

of·ten ['ɒfn] oft(mals), häufig.

o·gle ['əʊgl]: ~ (*at*) liebäugeln mit, schöne Augen machen (*dat.*).

o·gre ['əʊgə] (menschenfressender) Riese.

oh [əʊ] oh!; ach!

oil [ɔıl] **1.** Öl *n*; **2.** ölen; schmieren (*a. fig.*); **~·cloth** ['ɔılklɒθ] Wachstuch *n*; **~ rig** (Öl)Bohrinsel *f*; **~·skin** Ölleinwand *f*; **~s** *pl.* Ölzeug *n*; **~·y** □ ['ɔılı] (*-ier, -iest*) ölig (*a. fig.*); fettig; schmierig (*a. fig.*).

oint·ment ['ɔıntmənt] Salbe *f*.

O.K., o·kay K ['əʊ'keı] **1.** richtig, gut, in Ordnung; **2.** *int.* einverstanden!; gut!, in Ordnung!; **3.** genehmigen, zustimmen (*dat.*).

old [əʊld] (*~er, ~est, a. elder, eldest*) alt; altbekannt; erfahren; ~ *age* (das) Alter; ~ *people's home* Alters-, Altenheim *n*; **~-age** ['əʊld'eıdʒ] Alters...; **~-fash·ioned** ['əʊld'fæʃnd] altmodisch; ♀ **Glo·ry** Sternenbanner *n* (*Flagge der U.S.A.*); **~·ish** ['əʊldıʃ] ältlich.

ol·fac·to·ry *anat.* [ɒl'fæktərı] Geruchs...

ol·ive ['ɒlıv] ♀ Olive *f*; Olivgrün *n*.

O·lym·pic Games [ə'lımpık'geımz] *pl.* Olympische Spiele *pl.*; *Summer* (*Winter*) ~ *pl.* Olympische Sommer-(Winter)spiele *pl.*

om·i·nous □ ['ɒmınəs] unheilvoll.

o·mis·sion [əʊ'mıʃn] Unterlassung *f*; Auslassung *f*.

o·mit [ə'mıt] (*-tt-*) unterlassen; auslassen.

om·nip·o·tence [ɒm'nıpətəns] Allmacht *f*; **~·tent** □ [~t] allmächtig.

om·nis·ci·ent □ [ɒm'nısıənt] allwissend.

on [ɒn] **1.** *prp. mst* auf (*dat., acc.*); an (*dat.*) ~ *the wall*, ~ *the Thames*); Richtung, Ziel: auf (*acc.*) ... (hin), an (*acc.*), nach (*dat.*) ... (hin) (*march* ~ *London*); *fig.* auf (*acc.*) ... (hin) (~ *his authority*); Zeitpunkt: an (*dat.*) (~ *Sunday*, ~ *the 1st of April*); (gleich) nach, bei (~ *his arrival*); gehörig zu, beschäftigt bei (~ *a committee*, ~ *the "Daily Mail"*); Zustand: in (*dat.*), auf (*dat.*), zu (~ *duty*, ~ *fire*, ~ *leave*); Thema: über (*acc.*) (*talk* ~ *a subject*); nach (*dat.*) (~ *this model*); von (*dat.*) (*live* ~ *s.th.*); ~ *the street Am.* auf der Straße; *get* ~ *a train bsd. Am.* in e-n Zug einsteigen; ~ *hearing it* als ich etc. es hörte; **2.** an(geschaltet) (*Licht etc.*), eingeschaltet, laufend, auf (*Hahn etc.*); (dar)auf(*legen, -schrauben etc.*); *Kleidung:* an(*haben, -ziehen*) (*have a coat* ~); auf(*behalten*) (*keep one's hat* ~); weiter(*gehen, -sprechen etc.*); *and so* ~ und so weiter; ~ *and* ~ immer weiter; ~ *to ...* auf (hinaus *od.* hinaus); *be* ~ im Gange sein, los sein; *thea.* gespielt werden; laufen (*Film*).

once [wʌns] **1.** *adv.* einmal; je(mals); einst; *at* ~ (so)gleich; sofort; zugleich; *all at* ~ plötzlich; *for* ~ diesmal, ausnahmsweise; ~ (*and*) *for all* ein für allemal; ~ *again* od. ~ *more* noch einmal; ~ *in a while* dann und wann; **2.** *cj. a.* ~ *that* sobald.

one [wʌn] ein(e); einzig; eine(r, -s); man; eins; ~'s sein(e); ~ day eines Tages; ~ Smith ein gewisser Smith; ~ another einander; ~ by ~, ~ after another, ~ after the other e-r nach dem andern; be at ~ with s.o. mit j-m einig sein; I for ~ ich für meinen Teil; the little ~s pl. die Kleinen pl.

one·ner·ous □ ['ɒnərəs] schwer(wiegend).

one·self [wʌn'self] sich (selbst); (sich) selbst; ~·sid·ed □ ['wʌn'saidid] einseitig; ~·way ['wʌnwei]: ~ street Einbahnstraße f; ~ ticket Am. einfache Fahrkarte; ⚙ einfaches Ticket.

on·ion ♀ ['ʌnjən] Zwiebel f.

on·look·er ['ɒnlʊkə] Zuschauer(in).

on·ly ['əʊnli] **1.** adj. einzige(r, -s); **2.** adv. nur, bloß; erst; ~ yesterday erst gestern; **3.** cj. ~ (that) nur daß.

on·rush ['ɒnrʌʃ] Ansturm m.

on·set ['ɒnset], **on·slaught** ['ɒnslɔːt] Angriff m; Anfang m; ⚕ Ausbruch m (e-r Krankheit).

on·ward ['ɒnwəd] **1.** adj. fortschreitend; **2.** a. ~s adv. vorwärts, weiter.

ooze [uːz] **1.** Schlamm m; **2.** v/i. sickern; ~ away fig. schwinden; v/t. ausströmen, -schwitzen.

o·paque □ [əʊ'peik] (~r, ~st) undurchsichtig.

o·pen ['əʊpən] **1.** □ offen; geöffnet; auf; frei (Feld etc.); öffentlich; offen, unentschieden, offen, freimütig; freigebig; fig. zugänglich (to dat.), aufgeschlossen (to für); **2.** in the ~ (air) im Freien; come out into the ~ an die Öffentlichkeit treten; **3.** v/t. öffnen; eröffnen (a. fig.); v/i. sich öffnen, aufgehen; fig. öffnen, aufmachen; anfangen; ~ into führen nach (Tür etc.); ~ on to hinausgehen auf (acc.) (Fenster etc.); ~ out sich ausbreiten; ~·air ['əʊpən'eə] im Freien (stattfindend), Freiluft..., Freiluft...; ~·armed ['əʊpən'ɑːmd] herzlich, warm; ~·er ['əʊpənə] (Büchsen- etc.)Öffner m; ~·eyed ['əʊpən-'aid] staunend; wach; mit offenen Augen; ~·hand·ed ['əʊpən'hændid] freigebig, großzügig; ~·heart·ed ['əʊpənhɑːtid] offen(herzig), aufrichtig; ~·ing ['əʊpənɪŋ] (Er)Öffnung f; freie Stelle; Gelegenheit f; attr. Eröffnungs...; ~·mind·ed fig. ['əʊpən'maindid] aufgeschlossen.

op·er·a ['ɒpərə] Oper f; ~·glass(·es pl.) Opernglas n.

op·e·rate ['ɒpəreit] v/t. bewirken, (mit sich) bringen; ⊕ Maschine bedienen, et. betätigen; Unternehmen betreiben; v/i. ⊕ arbeiten, funktionieren, laufen; wirksam werden od. sein; ✕ operieren; ⚕ operieren (on od. upon s.o. j-n); operating room Am., operating-theatre Brt. Operationssaal m; ~·ra·tion [ɒpə'reiʃn] Wirkung f (on auf acc.); ⊕ Betrieb m, Tätigkeit f; ✗, ✕ Operation f; be in ~ in Betrieb sein; come into ~ ⚖️ in Kraft treten; ~·ra·tive ['ɒpərətiv] **1.** □ wirksam, tätig; praktisch; ⚕ operativ; **2.** Arbeiter m; ~·ra·tor [~eitə] ⊕ Bedienungsperson f; Telephonist(in).

o·pin·ion [ə'pinjən] Meinung f; Ansicht f; Stellungnahme f; Gutachten n; in my ~ meines Erachtens.

op·po·nent [ə'pəʊnənt] Gegner m.

op·por·tune □ ['ɒpətjuːn] passend; rechtzeitig; günstig; ~·tu·ni·ty [ɒpə-'tjuːnəti] (günstige) Gelegenheit f.

op·pose [ə'pəʊz] entgegen-, gegenüberstellen; sich widersetzen, bekämpfen; **op·posed** entgegengesetzt; be ~ to gegen ... sein; **op·po·site** ['ɒpəzit] **1.** □ gegenüberliegend; entgegengesetzt; **2.** prp. u. adv. gegenüber; **3.** Gegenteil n, -satz m; **op·po·si·tion** [ɒpə'ziʃn] das Gegenüberstehen; Widerstand m; Gegensatz m; Widerspruch m; Opposition f (a. pol.).

op·press [ə'pres] be-, unterdrücken; **op·pres·sion** [~ʃn] Unterdrückung f; Druck m, Bedrängnis f; Bedrücktheit f; **op·pres·sive** □ [~siv] (be-) drückend; hart, grausam; schwül (Wetter).

op·tic ['ɒptik] Augen..., Seh...; = **op·ti·cal** □ [~l] optisch; **op·ti·cian** [ɒp'tiʃn] Optiker m.

op·ti·mis·m ['ɒptimizəm] Optimismus m.

op·tion ['ɒpʃn] Wahl(freiheit) f; Alternative f; econ. Vorkaufsrecht n, Option f; ~·al □ [~l] freigestellt, wahlfrei.

op·u·lence ['ɒpjʊləns] (großer) Reichtum m, Überfluß m.

o·rac·u·lar □ [ɒ'rækjʊlə] orakelhaft.

o·ral □ ['ɔːrəl] mündlich; Mund...

or·ange ['ɒrindʒ] **1.** Orange n (Farbe); ♀ Orange f, Apfelsine f; **2.**

orange(farben); **~ade** ['ɒrɪndʒ'eɪd] Orangenlimonade f.

o·ra·tion [ɔː'reɪʃn] Rede f; **or·a·tor** ['ɒrətə] Redner m; **or·a·to·ry** [~rɪ] Redekunst f, Rhetorik f; eccl. Kapelle f.

orb [ɔːb] Ball m; Himmelskörper m; poet. Augapfel m, Auge n.

or·bit ['ɔːbɪt] 1. Kreis-, Umlaufbahn f; get od. put into ~ in e-e Umlaufbahn gelangen od. bringen; 2. v/t. die Erde etc. umkreisen; Satelliten etc. auf e-e Umlaufbahn bringen; v/i. die Erde etc. umkreisen, sich auf e-r Umlaufbahn bewegen.

or·chard ['ɔːtʃəd] Obstgarten m.

or·ches·tra ['ɔːkɪstrə] ♪ Orchester n; Am. thea. Parkett n.

or·chid ♀ ['ɔːkɪd] Orchidee f.

or·dain [ɔː'deɪn] anordnen, verfügen; zum Priester weihen.

or·deal fig. [ɔː'diːl] schwere Prüfung; Qual f, Tortur f.

or·der ['ɔːdə] 1. Ordnung f; Anordnung f, Reihenfolge f; Befehl m; econ. Bestellung f, Auftrag m; econ. Zahlungsauftrag m; parl. etc. (Geschäfts)Ordnung f; Klasse f, Orden m (a. eccl.); take (holy) ~s in den geistlichen Stand treten; in ~ to inf. um zu inf.; in ~ that damit; out of ~ nicht in Ordnung; defekt; nicht in Betrieb; make to ~ auf Bestellung anfertigen; 2. (an-, ✠ ver)ordnen; befehlen; econ. bestellen; j-n schicken; **~ly** ['ɔːdəlɪ] 1. ordentlich; fig. ruhig; 2. ✠ (Offiziers)Bursche m; ✠ Sanitätssoldat m; Krankenpfleger m.

or·di·nal ['ɔːdɪnl] 1. Ordnungs...; 2. a. ~ number ⅃ Ordnungszahl f.

or·di·nance ['ɔːdɪnəns] Verordnung f.

or·di·nar·y □ ['ɔːdnrɪ] üblich, gewöhnlich, normal; △ nicht ordinär.

ord·nance ✠ ['ɔːdnəns] Artillerie f; Geschütze pl.; Feldzeugwesen n.

ore [ɔː] Erz n.

or·gan ['ɔːgən] ♪ Orgel f; Organ n; **~grind·er** ['ɔːgəngraɪndə] Leierkastenmann m; **~ic** [ɔː'gænɪk] (~ally) organisch; **~is·m** ['ɔːgənɪzəm] Organismus m; **~i·za·tion** [ɔːgənaɪ'zeɪʃn] Organisation f; **~ize** ['ɔːgənaɪz] organisieren; **~iz·er** [~ə] Organisator(in).

o·ri·ent ['ɔːrɪənt] 1. ♀ Osten m; Orient m, Morgenland n; 2. orientieren;

~en·tal [ɔːrɪ'entl] 1. □ orientalisch, östlich; 2. ♀ Orientale m, -in f; **~en·tate** [ɔː'renteɪt] orientieren.

or·i·fice ['ɒrɪfɪs] Mündung f; Öffnung f.

or·i·gin ['ɒrɪdʒɪn] Ursprung m; Anfang m; Herkunft f.

o·rig·i·nal [ə'rɪdʒənl] 1. □ ursprünglich; originell; Original...; 2. Original n; **~i·ty** [ərɪdʒə'nælətɪ] Orginalität f; **~ly** [ə'rɪdʒnəlɪ] originell; zuerst.

o·rig·i·nate [ə'rɪdʒɪneɪt] v/t. hervorbringen, schaffen; v/i. entstehen; **~na·tor** [~ə] Urheber(in).

or·na·ment 1. ['ɔːnəmənt] Verzierung f; fig. Zierde f; 2. [~ment] verzieren, schmücken; **~men·tal** □ [ɔːnə'mentl] schmückend, Zier...

or·nate □ [ɔː'neɪt] reichverziert, reichgeschmückt; überladen.

or·phan ['ɔːfn] 1. Waise f; 2. a. ~ed verwaist; **~age** [~ɪdʒ] Waisenhaus n.

or·tho·dox □ ['ɔːθədɒks] orthodox; strenggläubig; üblich, anerkannt.

os·cil·late ['ɒsɪleɪt] schwingen; fig. schwanken.

o·si·er ♀ ['əʊʒə] Korbweide f.

os·prey zo. ['ɒsprɪ] Fischadler m.

os·ten·si·ble □ [ɒ'stensəbl] angeblich.

os·ten·ta·tion [ɒstən'teɪʃn] Zurschaustellung f; Protzerei f; **~tious** □ [~ʃəs] großtuerisch, prahlerisch.

os·tra·cize ['ɒstrəsaɪz] verbannen; ächten.

os·trich zo. ['ɒstrɪtʃ] Strauß m.

oth·er ['ʌðə] andere(r, -s); the ~ day neulich; the ~ morning neulich morgens; every ~ day jeden zweiten Tag; **~wise** [~waɪz] anders; sonst.

ot·ter ['ɒtə] zo. Otter m; Otterfell n.

ought v/aux. [ɔːt] (verneint: ~ not, oughtn't) ich, du etc. sollte(st) etc.; you ~ to have done it Sie hätten es tun sollen.

ounce [aʊns] Unze f (= 28,35 g).

our ['aʊə] unser; **~s** ['aʊəz] der, die, das uns(e)re; unser; **~selves** [aʊə-'selvz] uns (selbst); wir selbst.

oust [aʊst] verdrängen, -treiben, hinauswerfen; e-s Amtes entheben.

out [aʊt] 1. aus; hinaus(gehen, -werfen etc.); heraus(kommen etc.); aus(brechen etc.); außen, draußen; nicht zu Hause; Sport: aus, draußen; aus der Mode; vorbei; erloschen; aus(ge)gangen); verbraucht; (bis) zu Ende;

~ *and about* (wieder) auf den Beinen; *way* ~ Ausgang *m*; ~ *of* aus (... heraus); hinaus; außerhalb; außer *Atem etc.*; (hergestellt) aus; aus *Furcht etc.*; von (*in nine cases* ~ *of ten*); *be* ~ *of* s.th. et. nicht mehr haben; **2.** Ausweg *m*; *the* ~*s pl. parl.* die Opposition; **3.** *econ.* übernormal, Über... (*Größe*); **4.** *int.* hinaus!, raus!

out|bal·ance ['aʊtbæləns] überwiegen, -treffen; ~**bid** [aʊt'bɪd] (*-dd-*; *-bid*) überbieten; ~**board** ['aʊtbɔːd] Außenbord...; ~**break** ['aʊtbreɪk] Ausbruch *m*; ~**build·ing** ['aʊtbɪldɪŋ] Nebengebäude *n*; ~**burst** ['aʊtbɜːst] Ausbruch *m* (*a. fig.*); ~**cast** ['aʊtkɑːst] **1.** ausgestoßen; **2.** Ausgestoßene(r *m*) *f*; ~**come** ['aʊtkʌm] Ergebnis *n*; △ *nicht das Auskommen*; ~**cry** ['aʊtkraɪ] Aufschrei *m*, Schrei *m* der Entrüstung; ~**dat·ed** ['aʊt'deɪtɪd] überholt, veraltet; ~**dis·tance** [aʊt'dɪstəns] (weit) überholen; ~**do** [aʊt'duː] (*-did, -done*) übertreffen; ~**door** ['aʊtdɔː] Außen..., außerhalb des Hauses, im Freien, draußen; ~**doors** [aʊt'dɔːz] draußen, im Freien.

out·er ['aʊtə] äußere(r, -s); Außen...; ~**most** [⁓məʊst] äußerst.

out|fit ['aʊtfɪt] Ausrüstung *f*, Ausstattung *f*; F Haufen *m*, Trupp *m*, (Arbeits)Gruppe *f*; *Am.* ✗ Einheit *f*; ~**fit·ter** *Brt.* [⁓ə] Herrenausstatter *m*; ~**go·ing** ['aʊtgəʊɪŋ] **1.** weg-, abgehend; **2.** Ausgehen *n*; ~*s pl.* (Geld)Ausgaben *pl.*; ~**grow** [aʊt'grəʊ] (*-grew, -grown*) herauswachsen aus (*Kleidern*); größer werden als, hinauswachsen über (*acc.*); ~**house** ['aʊthaʊs] Nebengebäude *n*; *Am.* Außenabort *m*.

out·ing ['aʊtɪŋ] Ausflug *m*.

out|last [aʊt'lɑːst] überdauern, -leben; ~**law** ['aʊtlɔː] Geächtete(r *m*) *f*; ~**lay** ['aʊtleɪ] (Geld)Auslage(n *pl.*) *f*, Ausgabe(n *pl.*) *f*; ~**let** ['aʊtlet] Auslaß *m*, Abfluß *m*, Austritt *m*, Abzug *m*; *econ.* Absatzmarkt *m*; *Am.* ≨ Anschluß *m*, Steckdose *f*; *fig.* Ventil *n*; ~**line** ['aʊtlaɪn] **1.** Umriß *m*; Überblick *m*; Skizze *f*; **2.** umreißen; skizzieren; ~**live** [aʊt'lɪv] überleben; ~**look** ['aʊtlʊk] Ausblick *m* (*a. fig.*); Auffassung *f*; ~**ly·ing** ['aʊtlaɪɪŋ] entlegen; ~**match** [aʊt'mætʃ] weit übertreffen; ~**num·ber** [aʊt'nʌmbə] an Zahl übertreffen; ~**pa·tient** ['aʊtpeɪʃnt] ambulanter Patient, ambulante Patientin; ~**post** ['aʊtpəʊst] Vorposten *m*; ~**pour·ing** ['aʊtpɔː-rɪŋ] (*bsd.* Gefühls)Erguß *m*; ~**put** ['aʊtpʊt] Output *m*: *econ.* u. ⊕ Arbeitsertrag *m*, -leistung *f*; *econ.* Produktion *f*, Ausstoß *m*, Ertrag *m*; ≨ Ausgangsleistung *f*; ≨ Ausgang *m* (*an Geräten*); *Computer:* (Daten)Ausgabe *f*; ~**rage** ['aʊtreɪdʒ] **1.** Ausschreitung *f*; Gewalttat *f*; **2.** gröblich verletzen *od.* beleidigen; Gewalt antun (*dat.*); ~**ra·geous** □ [aʊt'reɪdʒəs] abscheulich; empörend, unerhört; ~**reach** [aʊt'riːtʃ] weiter reichen als; ~**right** [*adj.* 'aʊtraɪt, *adv.* aʊt'raɪt] gerade heraus; völlig; direkt; ~**run** [aʊt'rʌn] (*-nn-*; *-ran, -run*) schneller laufen als; *fig.* übertreffen, hinausgehen über (*acc.*); ~**set** ['aʊtset] Anfang *m*; Aufbruch *m*; ~**shine** [aʊt'ʃaɪn] (*-shone*) überstrahlen; *fig. a.* in den Schatten stellen; ~**side** [aʊt'saɪd] **1.** Außenseite *f*; *das* Äußere; *Sport:* Außenstürmer *m*; *at the* (*very*) ~ (*aller-)höchstens; *attr.:* ~ *left* (*right*) *Sport:* Links-(Rechts-)Außen *m*; **2.** *adj.* äußere(r, -s), Außen...; äußerste(r, -s) (*Preis*); **3.** *adv.* draußen, außerhalb; heraus, hinaus; **4.** *prp.* außerhalb; ~**sid·er** [⁓ə] Außenseiter(in), -stehende(r *m*) *f*; ~**size** ['aʊtsaɪz] Übergröße *f*; ~**skirts** ['aʊtskɜːts] *pl.* Außenbezirke *pl.*, (Stadt)Rand *m*; ~**smart** F ['aʊt'smɑːt] überlisten; ~**spo·ken** [aʊt'spəʊkən] offen, freimütig; △ *nicht ausgesprochen*; ~**spread** ['aʊt'spred] ausgestreckt, -breitet; ~**stand·ing** [aʊt'stændɪŋ] hervorragend (*a. fig.*); ausstehend (*Schuld*); ungeklärt (*Frage*); unerledigt (*Arbeit*); ~**stretched** ['aʊtstretʃt] = *outspread*; ~**strip** [aʊt'strɪp] (*-pp-*) überholen (*a. fig.*).

out·ward ['aʊtwəd] **1.** äußere(r, -s); äußerlich; nach (dr)außen gerichtet; **2.** *adv. mst* ~*s* (nach) auswärts, nach (dr)außen; ~**ly** [⁓lɪ] äußerlich; an der Oberfläche.

out|weigh ['aʊt'weɪ] schwerer sein als; *fig.* überwiegen; ~**wit** [aʊt'wɪt] (*-tt-*) überlisten; ~**worn** ['aʊtwɔːn] erschöpft; *fig.* abgegriffen; überholt.

o·val [ˈəʊvl] **1.** □ oval; **2.** Oval n.
ov·en [ˈʌvn] Backofen m.
o·ver [ˈəʊvə] **1.** über; hinüber; darüber; herüber; drüben; über (acc.) ...darüber(...); et. über(geben etc.); über(kochen etc.); um(fallen, -werfen etc.); herum(drehen etc.); von Anfang bis Ende, durch(lesen etc.), ganz, über u. über; (gründlich) über(legen etc.); nochmals, wieder; übermäßig, über...; darüber, mehr; übrig; zu Ende, vorüber, vorbei, aus; (all) ~again noch einmal, (ganz) von vorn; ~ against gegenüber (dat.); all ~ ganz vorbei; ~ and ~ again immer wieder; **2.** prp. über; über (acc.) ...hin(weg); ~ and above neben, zusätzlich zu.

o·ver|act [ˈəʊvərˈækt] e-e Rolle übertreiben; **~all** [ˈəʊvərˈɔːl] **1.** Brt. (Arbeits)Kittel m; ~s pl. Arbeitsanzug m, Overall m; **2.** gesamt, Gesamt...; **~awe** [ˈəʊvərˈɔː] einschüchtern; **~bal·ance** [ˈəʊvəˈbæləns] **1.** Übergewicht n; **2.** das Gleichgewicht verlieren; umkippen; aus dem Gleichgewicht bringen; überwiegen (a. fig.); **~bear·ing** □ [ˈəʊvəˈbeərɪŋ] anmaßend; **~board** ⚓ [ˈəʊvəbɔːd] über Bord; **~cast** [ˈəʊvəkɑːst] bewölkt; **~charge** [ˈəʊvəˈtʃɑːdʒ] **1.** ⚡, ⊕ überladen; e-n Betrag zuviel verlangen (for für); **2.** Überpreis m; Aufschlag m; **~coat** [ˈəʊvəkəʊt] Mantel m; **~come** [ˈəʊvəˈkʌm] (-came, -come) überwinden, -wältigen; **~crowd** [ˈəʊvəˈkraʊd] überfüllen; **~do** [ˈəʊvəˈduː] (-did, -done) zu viel tun; übertreiben; zu sehr kochen od. braten; überanstrengen; **~draw** [ˈəʊvəˈdrɔː] (-drew, -drawn) econ. Konto überziehen; fig. übertreiben; **~dress** [ˈəʊvəˈdres] (sich) übertrieben anziehen; **~due** [ˈəʊvəˈdjuː] (über)fällig; **~eat** [ˈəʊvəˈriːt] (-ate, -eaten): a. ~ o.s. sich übersessen; **~flow 1.** [ˈəʊvəˈfləʊ] v/t. überfluten, -schwemmen; v/i. überfließen, -laufen; **2.** [ˈəʊvəfləʊ] Überschwemmung f; Überfluß m; ⊕ Überlauf m; **~grow** [ˈəʊvəˈgrəʊ] (-grew, -grown) v/t. überwuchern; v/i. zu groß werden; **~grown** [ˌʌn] überwuchert; übergroß; **~hang 1.** [ˈəʊvəˈhæŋ] (-hung) v/t über (dat.) hängen; v/i. überhängen; **2.** [ˈəʊvəhæŋ] Überhang m; **~haul** [ˈəʊvəˈhɔːl] Maschine überholen; **~head 1.**

adv. [ˈəʊvəˈhed] (dr)oben; **2.** adj. [ˈəʊvəhed] Hoch..., Ober...; econ. allgemein (Unkosten); **3.** mst Brt. ~s pl. econ. allgemeine Unkosten pl.; **~hear** [ˈəʊvəˈhɪə] (-heard) (zufällig) belauschen, (mit an)hören; ⚠ nicht überhören; **~joyed** [ˈəʊvəˈdʒɔɪd] überglücklich (at über acc.); **~kill** [ˈəʊvəkɪl] ⚔ Overkill n; fig. Übermaß n, Zuviel n (of an dat.); **~lap** [ˈəʊvəˈlæp] (-pp-) übergreifen auf (acc.); sich überschneiden (mit); ⊕ überlappen; **~lay** [ˈəʊvəˈleɪ] (-laid) belegen, überziehen; **~leaf** [ˈəʊvəˈliːf] umseitig; **~load** [ˈəʊvəˈləʊd] überladen; **~look** [ˈəʊvəˈlʊk] übersehen (a. fig.); ~ing the sea mit Blick auf das Meer; **~much** [ˈəʊvəˈmʌtʃ] zu viel; **~night** [ˈəʊvəˈnaɪt] **1.** über Nacht; stay ~ übernachten; **2.** Nacht..., Übernachtungs...; **~pass** bsd. Am. [ˈəʊvəpɑːs] (Straßen-, Eisenbahn)Überführung f; **~pay** [ˈəʊvəˈpeɪ] (-paid) zu viel bezahlen; **~peo·pled** [ˈəʊvəˈpiːpld] übervölkert; **~plus** [ˈəʊvəplʌs] Überschuß m (of an dat.); **~pow·er** [ˈəʊvəˈpaʊə] überwältigen; **~rate** [ˈəʊvəˈreɪt] überschätzen; **~reach** [ˈəʊvəˈriːtʃ] übervorteilen; ~ o.s. sich übernehmen; **~ride** fig. [ˈəʊvəˈraɪd] (-rode, -ridden) sich hinwegsetzen über (acc.); umstoßen; **~rule** [ˈəʊvəˈruːl] überstimmen; ⚖ Urteil umstoßen; **~run** [ˈəʊvəˈrʌn] (-nn-; -ran, -run) Land überfluten; ⚔ herfallen über (acc.); überwuchern; Signal überfahren; Zeit überziehen; be ~ with wimmeln von; **~sea(s)** [ˈəʊvəˈsiː(z)] **1.** überseeisch, Übersee...; **2.** in od. nach Übersee; **~see** [ˈəʊvəˈsiː] (-saw, -seen) beaufsichtigen; **~seer** [ˈəʊvəsɪə] Aufseher m; Vorarbeiter m; **~shad·ow** [ˈəʊvəˈʃædəʊ] überschatten (a. fig.); fig. in den Schatten stellen; **~sight** [ˈəʊvəsaɪt] Versehen n; **~sleep** [ˈəʊvəˈsliːp] (-slept) verschlafen; **~state** [ˈəʊvəˈsteɪt] übertreiben; **~state·ment** [ˌmənt] Übertreibung f; **~strain 1.** [ˈəʊvəˈstreɪn] überanstrengen; ~ o.s. sich übernehmen; **2.** [ˈəʊvəstreɪn] Überanstrengung f.
o·vert □ [ˈəʊvɜːt] offen(kundig).
o·ver·take [ˈəʊvəˈteɪk] (-took, -taken) einholen; j-n überraschen; überholen; **~tax** [ˈəʊvəˈtæks] zu hoch be-

steuern; *fig.* überschätzen; überfordern; **~·throw** 1. ['ɔʊvəˈθrəʊ] (*-threw*, *-thrown*) (um)stürzen (*a. fig.*); besiegen; 2. ['ɔʊvəˈθrəʊ] (Um-) Sturz *m*; Niederlage *f*; **~·time** *econ.* ['ɔʊvətaɪm] Überstunden *pl.*; *be on* **~**, *do* **~** Überstunden machen.

o·ver·ture ['ɔʊvətjʊə] *♪* Ouvertüre *f*; *♪* Vorspiel *n*; *mst* **~s** *pl.* Vorschlag *m*, Antrag *m*.

o·ver·turn ['ɔʊvəˈtɜːn] (um)stürzen (*a. fig.*); **~·weight** ['ɔʊvəweɪt] Übergewicht *n*; **~·whelm** ['ɔʊvəˈwelm] überschütten (*a. fig.*); überwältigen (*a. fig.*); **~·work** ['ɔʊvəˈwɜːk] 1. Überarbeitung *f*; 2. sich überarbeiten; überanstrengen; **~·wrought** ['ɔʊvəˈrɔːt] überarbeitet; überreizt.

owe [əʊ] Geld, Dank *etc.* schulden, schuldig sein; verdanken.

ow·ing ['əʊɪŋ]: *be* **~** zu zahlen sein; **~** *to* infolge (*gen.*); wegen (*gen.*); dank (*dat.*).

owl *zo.* [aʊl] Eule *f*.

own [əʊn] 1. eigen; selbst; einzig, (innig) geliebt; 2. *my* **~** mein Eigentum; *a house of one's* **~** ein eigenes Haus; *hold one's* **~** standhalten; 3. besitzen; zugeben; anerkennen; sich bekennen (*to* zu).

own·er ['əʊnə] Eigentümer(in); **~·ship** ['əʊnəʃɪp] Eigentum(srecht) *n*.

ox *zo.* [ɒks] (*pl. oxen* ['ɒksn]) Ochse *m*; Rind *n*.

ox·i·da·tion *🜍* [ɒksɪˈdeɪʃn] Oxydation *f*, Oxydierung *f*; **ox·ide** *🜍* ['ɒksaɪd] Oxyd *n*; **ox·i·dize** *🜍* ['ɒksɪdaɪz] oxydieren.

ox·y·gen *🜍* ['ɒksɪdʒən] Sauerstoff *m*.

oy·ster *zo.* ['ɔɪstə] Auster *f*.

o·zone *🜍* ['əʊzəʊn] Ozon *n*.

P

pace [peɪs] 1. Schritt *m*; Gang *m*; Tempo *n*; 2. *v/t.* abschreiten; durchschreiten; *v/i.* (einher)schreiten; **~** *up and down* auf u. ab gehen.

pa·cif·ic [pəˈsɪfɪk] (*~ally*) friedlich.

pac·i·fi·ca·tion [pæsɪfɪˈkeɪʃn] Beruhigung *f*, Besänftigung *f*; **~·fi·er** *Am.* ['pæsɪfaɪə] Schnuller *m*; **~·fy** [~aɪ] beruhigen, besänftigen.

pack [pæk] 1. Pack(en) *m*, Paket *n*, Ballen *m*, Bündel *n*; *Am.* Packung *f* (*Zigaretten*); Meute *f* (*Hunde*); Rudel *n* (*Wölfe*); Pack *n*, Bande *f*; **~**, *Kosmetik*: Packung *f*; *a.* **~** *of cards* Spiel *n* Karten; *a.* **~** *of films phot.* Filmpack *n*; *a* **~** *of lies* ein Haufen Lügen; 2. *v/t.* (voll)packen; bepacken; vollstopfen; zusammenpferchen; *econ.* eindosen; ⊕ (ab-) dichten; *Am.* ℱ *Revolver etc.* (bei sich) tragen; *oft* **~** *up* zusammen-, ver-, ein-, abpacken; *mst* **~** *off* (rasch) fortschicken, -jagen; *v/i.* sich *gut etc.* verpacken *od.* konservieren lassen; *oft* **~** *up* (zusammen)packen; *send s.o.* **~·ing** j-n fortjagen; **~·age** ['pækɪdʒ] Pack *m*, Ballen *m*; Paket *n*; Packung *f*; Frachtstück *n*; **~** *tour* Pauschalreise *f*; **~·er** [~ə] Packer(in); *Am.* Konservenhersteller *m*; **~·et** [~ɪt] Päckchen *n*; Packung *f* (*Zigaretten*); *a.* **~·boat** ♣ Postschiff *n*; **~·ing** [~ɪŋ] Packen *n*; Verpackung *f*; **~·thread** Bindfaden *m*.

pact [pækt] Vertrag *m*, Pakt *m*.

pad [pæd] 1. Polster *n*; *Sport:* Beinschutz *m*; Schreib-, Zeichenblock *m*; Abschußrampe *f* (*für Raketen*); *a.* ink-**~** Stempelkissen *n*; 2. (-*dd*-) (aus)polstern, wattieren; **~·ding** ['pædɪŋ] Polsterung *f*, Wattierung *f*.

pad·dle ['pædl] 1. Paddel *n*; ♣ (Rad-) Schaufel *f*; 2. paddeln; planschen; **~·wheel** ♣ Schaufelrad *n*.

pad·dock ['pædək] (Pferde)Koppel *f*; *Pferderennsport:* Sattelplatz *m*; *Motorsport:* Fahrerlager *n*.

pad·lock ['pædlɒk] Vorhängeschloß *n*.

pa·gan ['peɪɡən] 1. heidnisch; 2. Heid|e *m*, -in *f*.

page¹ [peɪdʒ] 1. Seite *f* (*e-s Buches, e-r Zeitung etc.*); 2. paginieren.

page² [~] 1. (Hotel)Page *m*; 2. j-n ausrufen lassen.

papa

pag·eant ['pædʒənt] historisches Festspiel; Festzug *m*.

paid [peɪd] *pret. u. p.p. von pay* 2.

pail [peɪl] Eimer *m*.

pain [peɪn] 1. Schmerz(en *pl.*) *m*; Kummer *m*; ~s *pl.* Mühe *f*; on od. under ~ of death bei Todesstrafe; be in (great) ~ (große) Schmerzen haben; take ~s sich Mühe geben; 2. *j-n* schmerzen, *j-m* weh tun; **~ful** □ ['peɪnfl] schmerzhaft; schmerzlich; peinlich; mühsam; **~less** □ [~lɪs] schmerzlos; **~s·tak·ing** □ [~zteɪkɪŋ] sorgfältig, gewissenhaft.

paint [peɪnt] 1. Farbe *f*; Schminke *f*; Anstrich *m*; 2. (an-, be)malen; (an-)streichen; (sich) schminken; **~box** ['peɪntbɒks] Malkasten *m*; **~brush** (Maler)Pinsel *m*; **~er** [~ə] Maler(in); **~ing** [~ɪŋ] Malen *n*; Malerei *f*; Gemälde *n*, Bild *n*.

pair [peə] 1. Paar *n*; a ~ of ... ein Paar ..., ein(e) ...; a ~ of scissors e-e Schere; 2. *zo.* sich paaren; zusammenpassen; ~ off Paare bilden; paarweise weggehen.

pa·ja·ma(s) *Am.* [pə'dʒɑːmə(z)] = pyjama(s).

pal [pæl] Kumpel *m*, Kamerad *m*.

pal·ace ['pælɪs] Palast *m*, Schloß *n*.

pal·a·ta·ble □ ['pælətəbl] wohlschmeckend, schmackhaft (*a. fig.*).

pal·ate ['pælɪt] *anat.* Gaumen *m*; *fig.* Geschmack *m*.

pale¹ [peɪl] Pfahl *m*; *fig.* Grenzen *pl.*

pale² [peɪl] 1. □ (~r, ~st) blaß, bleich, fahl; ~ ale helles Bier; 2. blaß od. bleich werden; erbleichen lassen; **~ness** ['peɪlnɪs] Blässe *f*.

pal·ings ['peɪlɪŋz] *pl.* Pfahlzaun *m*.

pal·i·sade [pælɪ'seɪd] Palisade *f*; ~s *pl. Am.* Steilufer *n*.

pall·let ['pælɪt] Strohsack *m*, -lager *n*.

pal·li|ate ['pælɪeɪt] 🖋 lindern; *fig.* bemänteln; **~a·tive** 🖋 [~ɪtɪv] Linderungsmittel *n*.

pall|id □ ['pælɪd] blaß; **~lid·ness** [~nɪs], **~lor** [~ə] Blässe *f*.

palm [pɑːm] 1. Handfläche *f*; ♀ Palme *f*; 2. in der Hand verbergen; ~ s.th. off on od. upon s.o. *j-m* et. andrehen; **~tree** ♀ ['pɑːmtriː] Palme *f*.

pal·pa·ble □ ['pælpəbl] fühlbar; *fig.* handgreiflich, klar, eindeutig.

pal·pi|tate 🖋 ['pælpɪteɪt] klopfen (*Herz*); **~ta·tion** 🖋 [pælpɪ'teɪʃn] Herzklopfen *n*.

pal·sy ['pɔːlzɪ] 1. 🖋 Lähmung *f*; *fig.* Ohnmacht *f*; 2. *fig.* lähmen.

pal·ter ['pɔːltə] sein Spiel treiben (*with s.o.* mit *j-m*).

pal·try □ ['pɔːltrɪ] (-ier, -iest) armselig; wertlos.

pam·per ['pæmpə] verzärteln.

pam·phlet ['pæmflɪt] Broschüre *f*; (kurze, kritische) Abhandlung; △ *nicht* Pamphlet.

pan [pæn] Pfanne *f*; Tiegel *m*.

pan- [~] all..., ganz..., gesamt..., pan..., Pan...

pan·a·ce·a [pænə'sɪə] Allheilmittel *n*.

pan·cake ['pænkeɪk] Pfann-, Eierkuchen *m*.

pan·da *zo.* ['pændə] Panda *m*; ~ car *Brt.* (Funk)Streifenwagen *m*; **~ cross·ing** *Brt.* Fußgängerübergang *m* mit Druckampel.

pan·de·mo·ni·um *fig.* [pændɪ'məʊnjəm] Hölle(nlärm *m*) *f*.

pan·der ['pændə] 1. Vorschub leisten (*to dat.*); *veraltet* sich als Kuppler betätigen; 2. *veraltet* Kuppler *m*.

pane [peɪn] (Fenster)Scheibe *f*.

pan·e·gyr·ic [pænɪ'dʒɪrɪk] Lobrede *f*.

pan·el ['pænl] 1. *arch.* Fach *n*, (*Tür-*) Füllung *f*, (*Wand*)Täfelung *f*; 🔩 ⊕ Instrumentenbrett *n*, Schalttafel *f*; 🔩 Geschworenenliste *f*; 🔩 *die* Geschworenen *pl.*; *die* Diskussionsteilnehmer *pl.*; 2. (*bsd. Brt.* -ll-, *Am.* -l-) täfeln.

pang [pæŋ] plötzlicher Schmerz; *fig.* Angst *f*, Qual *f*.

pan·han·dle ['pænhændl] 1. Pfannenstiel *m*; *Am.* schmaler Fortsatz (*e-s Staatsgebiets*); 2. *Am.* F betteln.

pan·ic ['pænɪk] 1. panisch; 2. Panik *f*; 3. (-ck-) in Panik geraten.

pan·sy ♀ ['pænzɪ] Stiefmütterchen *n*.

pant [pænt] nach Luft schnappen, keuchen, schnaufen.

pan·ther *zo.* ['pænθə] Panther *m*; *Am.* Puma *m*.

pan·ties ['pæntɪz] *pl.* (Damen-) Schlüpfer *m*; Kinderhöschen *n*.

pan·ti·hose *bsd. Am.* ['pæntɪhəʊz] Strumpfhose *f*.

pan·try ['pæntrɪ] Speisekammer *f*.

pants [pænts] *pl. bsd. Am.* Hose *f*; *bsd. Brt.* Unterhose *f*; *bsd. Brt.* Schlüpfer *m*.

pap [pæp] Brei *m*; △ *nicht* Papp, Pappe.

pa·pa [pə'pɑː] Papa *m*.

P

pa·pal □ ['peɪpl] päpstlich.

pa·per ['peɪpə] 1. Papier n; Zeitung f; schriftliche Prüfung; Prüfungsarbeit f; Vortrag m, Aufsatz m; ~s pl. (Ausweis)Papiere pl.; 2. tapezieren; ~back Taschenbuch n, Paperback n; ~bag (Papier)Tüte f; ~clip Büroklammer f; ~hang·er Tapezierer m; ~mill Papierfabrik f; ~weight Briefbeschwerer m.

pap·py ['pæpɪ] (-ier, -iest) breiig.

par [pɑː] econ. Nennwert m, Pari n; at ~ zum Nennwert; be on a ~ with gleich od. ebenbürtig sein (dat.).

par·a·ble ['pærəbl] Gleichnis n.

par·a|chute ['pærəʃuːt] Fallschirm m; ~chut·ist [~ɪst] Fallschirmspringer(in).

pa·rade [pə'reɪd] 1. ⚔ (Truppen-) Parade f; Zurschaustellung f, Vorführung f; (Strand)Promenade f; (Um)Zug m; make a ~ of fig. zur Schau stellen; 2. ⚔ antreten (lassen); ⚔ vorbeimarschieren (lassen); zur Schau stellen; ~ground ⚔ Exerzier-, Paradeplatz m.

par·a·dise ['pærədaɪs] Paradies n.

par·a·gon ['pærəgən] Vorbild n, Muster n.

par·a·graph ['pærəgrɑːf] print. Absatz m, Abschnitt m; kurze Zeitungsnotiz; △ nicht ⚌ Paragraph.

par·al·lel ['pærəlel] 1. parallel; 2. A Parallele f (a. fig.); Gegenstück n; Vergleich m; without (a) ~ ohnegleichen; 3. (-l-, Brt. a. -ll-) vergleichen; entsprechen; gleichen; parallel (ver)laufen zu.

par·a·lyse, Am. **-lyze** ['pærəlaɪz] ⚕ lähmen (a. fig.); fig. zunichte machen; **pa·ral·y·sis** [pə'rælɪsɪs] (pl. -ses [-siːz]) Paralyse f, Lähmung f.

par·a·mount ['pærəmaunt] höher stehend (to als), übergeordnet, oberste(r, -s); höchste(r, -s); fig. größte(r, -s).

par·a·pet ['pærəpɪt] ⚔ Brustwehr f; Brüstung f; Geländer n.

par·a·pher·na·li·a [pærəfə'neɪljə] pl. Ausrüstung f; Zubehör n, m.

par·a·site ['pærəsaɪt] Schmarotzer m.

par·a·sol ['pærəsɒl] Sonnenschirm m.

par·a·troop|er ⚔ ['pærətruːpə] Fallschirmjäger m; ~s ⚔ [~s] pl. Fallschirmtruppen pl.

par·boil ['pɑːbɔɪl] ankochen.

par·cel ['pɑːsl] 1. Paket n, Päckchen n; Bündel n; Parzelle f; 2. (bsd. Brt. -ll-, Am. -l-) ~ out aus-, aufteilen.

parch [pɑːtʃ] rösten, (aus)dörren.

parch·ment ['pɑːtʃmənt] Pergament n.

pard Am. sl. [pɑːd] Partner m.

par·don ['pɑːdn] 1. Verzeihung f; ⚌ Begnadigung f; 2. verzeihen; ⚌ begnadigen; ~? wie bitte?; ~ me! Entschuldigung!; ~a·ble □ [~əbl] verzeihlich.

pare [peə] (be)schneiden (a. fig.); schälen.

par·ent ['peərənt] Elternteil m, Vater m, Mutter f; fig. Ursache f; ~s pl. Eltern pl.; ~teacher meeting Schule: Elternabend m; ~age [~ɪdʒ] Abstammung f; **pa·ren·tal** [pə'rentl] elterlich.

pa·ren·the·sis [pə'renθɪsɪs] (pl. -ses [-siːz]) Einschaltung f; print. (runde) Klammer.

par·ing ['peərɪŋ] Schälen n; (Be-) schneiden n; ~s pl. Schalen pl.; Schnipsel pl.

par·ish ['pærɪʃ] 1. Kirchspiel n, Gemeinde f; 2. Pfarr..., Kirchen...; pol. Gemeinde...; ~ council Gemeinderat m; **pa·rish·io·ner** [pə'rɪʃənə] Gemeindemitglied n.

par·i·ty ['pærətɪ] Gleichheit f.

park [pɑːk] 1. Park m, Anlagen pl.; Naturschutzgebiet n, Park m; Am. (Sport)Platz m; the ~ Brt. F der Fußballplatz; mst car-~ Parkplatz m; 2. mot. parken.

par·ka ['pɑːkə] Parka f, m.

park·ing mot. ['pɑːkɪŋ] Parken n; no ~ Parkverbot, Parken verboten; ~ disc Parkscheibe f; ~ fee Parkgebühr f; ~ lot Am. Parkplatz m; ~ me·ter Parkuhr f; ~or·bit Raumfahrt: Parkbahn f; ~ tick·et Strafzettel m (wegen falschen Parkens).

par·lance ['pɑːləns] Ausdrucksweise f, Sprache f.

par·ley ['pɑːlɪ] 1. bsd. ⚔ Verhandlung f; 2. bsd. ⚔ verhandeln; sich besprechen.

par·lia|ment ['pɑːləmənt] Parlament n; ~men·tar·i·an [pɑːləmen·'teərɪən] Parlamentarier(in); ~men·ta·ry □ [pɑːlə'mentərɪ] parlamentarisch, Parlaments...

par·lo(u)r ['pɑːlə] veraltet Wohnzimmer n; Empfangs-, Sprechzimmer n; beauty ~ Am. Schönheits-

salon *m*; ~ *car Am.* 🚃 Salonwagen *m*;
~**maid** Stuben-, Hausmädchen *n*.

pa·ro·chi·al □ [pə'rəʊkjəl] Pfarr...,
Kirchen..., Gemeinde...; *fig.* engstirnig, beschränkt.

pa·role [pə'rəʊl] **1.** ✗ Parole *f*; ⚖️
bedingte Haftentlassung; ⚖️ Hafturlaub *m*; *he is out on ~* ⚖️ er wurde
bedingt entlassen; er hat Hafturlaub; **2.** ~ *s.o.* ⚖️ j-n bedingt entlassen; j-m Hafturlaub gewähren.

par·quet ['pɑːkeɪ] Parkett(fußboden
m) *n*; *Am. thea.* Parkett *n*.

par·rot ['pærət] **1.** *zo.* Papagei *m* (*a.
fig.*); **2.** nachplappern.

par·ry ['pærɪ] abwehren, parieren.

par·si·mo·ni·ous □ [pɑːsɪ'məʊnjəs]
sparsam, geizig, knaus(e)rig.

pars·ley ♀ ['pɑːslɪ] Petersilie *f*.

par·son ['pɑːsn] Pfarrer *m*; ~**age**
[~ɪdʒ] Pfarrei *f*, Pfarrhaus *n*.

part [pɑːt] **1.** Teil *m*; Anteil *m*; Seite *f*,
Partei *f*; *thea., fig.* Rolle *f*; Stimme *f*;
Gegend *f*; *Am.* (*Haar*)Scheitel *m*; *a
man of (many)* ~s ein fähiger
Mensch; *take ~ in s.th.* an e-r Sache
teilnehmen; *take s.th. in bad (good)*
~ et. (nicht) übelnehmen; *for my* ~
ich für mein(en) Teil; *for the most* ~
meistens; *in* ~ teilweise, zum Teil;
on the ~ von seiten, seitens (*gen.*);
on my ~ meinerseits; **2.** *adj.* Teil...; **3.**
adv. teils; **4.** *v/t.* (ab-, ein-, zer)tei-
len; trennen; *Haar* scheiteln; ~ *company* sich trennen (*with* von); *v/i.*
sich trennen (*with* von).

par·take [pɑː'teɪk] (*-took, -taken*)
teilnehmen, -haben; ~ *of Mahlzeit*
einnehmen.

par|tial □ ['pɑːʃl] Teil..., teilweise,
partiell; parteiisch, eingenommen
(*to* für); ~**ti·al·i·ty** [pɑːʃɪ'ælətɪ] Par-
teilichkeit *f*; Vorliebe *f* (*for* für).

par·tic·i|pant [pɑː'tɪsɪpənt] Teilneh-
mer(in); ~**pate** [~eɪt] teilnehmen,
sich beteiligen (*in an dat.*); ~**pa·tion**
[pɑːtɪsɪ'peɪʃn] Teilnahme *f*, Beteiligung *f*.

par·ti·ci·ple *gr.* ['pɑːtɪsɪpl] Partizip *n*,
Mittelwort *n*.

par·ti·cle ['pɑːtɪkl] Teilchen *n*.

par·tic·u·lar [pə'tɪkjʊlə] **1.** □ beson-
dere(r, -s), einzeln, Sonder...; genau, eigen; wählerisch; **2.** Einzelheit
f; ~s *pl.* nähere Umstände *pl. od.*
Angaben *pl.*; Personalien *pl.*; *in* ~
insbesondere; ~**i·ty** [pətɪkjʊ'lærətɪ]
Besonderheit *f*; Ausführlichkeit *f*;

Eigenheit *f*; ~**ly** [pə'tɪkjʊləlɪ] besonders.

part·ing ['pɑːtɪŋ] **1.** Trennung *f*, Abschied *m*; (*Haar*)Scheitel *m*; ~ *of the
ways bsd. fig.* Scheideweg *m*; **2.** Ab-
schieds...

par·ti·san [pɑːtɪ'zæn] Parteigän-
ger(in); ✗ Partisan *m*; *attr.* Partei...

par·ti·tion [pɑː'tɪʃn] **1.** Teilung *f*;
Scheidewand *f*; Verschlag *m*; Fach
n; **2.** ~ *off* abteilen, abtrennen.

part·ly ['pɑːtlɪ] teilweise, zum Teil.

part·ner ['pɑːtnə] **1.** Partner(in); **2.**
zusammenbringen; sich zusammen-
tun mit (*j-m*); ~**ship** [~ʃɪp] Teilha-
ber-, Partnerschaft *f*; *econ.* Handelsgesellschaft *f*.

part-own·er ['pɑːtəʊnə] Miteigen-
tümer(in).

par·tridge *zo.* ['pɑːtrɪdʒ] Rebhuhn
n.

part-time ['pɑːt'taɪm] **1.** *adj.* Teil-
zeit..., Halbtags...; **2.** *adv.* halbtags.

par·ty ['pɑːtɪ] Partei *f*; ✗ Abteilung
f; (*Arbeits-, Reise*)Gruppe *f*; (*Ret-
tungs- etc.*)Mannschaft *f*; Party *f*,
Gesellschaft *f*; Beteiligte(r *m*) *f*; *co.*
Type *f*, Individuum *n*; ⚖️ *nicht Partie*; ~ *line pol.* Parteilinie *f*; ~
pol·i·tics *sg. od. pl.* Parteipolitik *f*.

pass [pɑːs] **1.** Passier-, Erlaubnis-
schein *m*; △ *nicht (Reise)Pass*; ✗
Urlaubsschein *m*; Bestehen *n* (*e-s
Examens*); *Brt. univ.* einfacher
Grad; kritische Lage; *Sport:* Paß *m*,
(*Ball*)Abgabe *f*, Vorlage *f*, Zuspiel *n*;
(*Gebirgs*)Paß *m*; Durch-, Zugang *m*;
Karten: Passen *n*; (*Zauber*)Trick *m*; 📻 Annäherungs-
versuch *m*; *free* ~ Freikarte *f*; **2.** *v/i.*
(vorbei)gehen, (-)fahren, (-)kom-
men, (-)ziehen *etc.*; *in andere Hände*
übergehen, übertragen werden (*to
auf acc.*); *von e-m Zustand* übergehen; herumgereicht werden, von
Hand zu Hand gehen; *Sport:* (den
Ball) abspielen *od.* abgeben *od.* passen (*to* zu); vergehen, vorübergehen
(*Zeit, Schmerz etc.*); angenommen
werden, gelten; durchkommen; (die
Prüfung) bestehen; *parl.* Rechts-
kraft erlangen; *Karten:* passen; *bsd.
biblisch:* sich zutragen, passieren, geschehen (*it came to* ~ *that* es begab
sich *od.* es geschah, daß); △ *nicht
passen = fit*; ~ *away* sterben; ~ *by*
vorüber- *od.* vorbeigehen an (*dat.*),
passieren; ~ *for od.* as gelten für *od.*

als, gehalten werden für; ~ off vonstatten gehen; ~ out F ohnmächtig werden; v/t. vorbei-, vorübergehen, -fahren, -fließen, -kommen, -ziehen etc. an (dat.); et. passieren; vorbeifahren an (dat.), überholen (a. mot.); durch-, überschreiten, durchqueren, passieren; vorbeilassen; reichen, geben; streichen (mit der Hand); Sport: Ball abspielen, abgeben, passen (to zu); Examen bestehen; Prüfling bestehen od. durchkommen lassen; et. durchgehen lassen; Zeit ver-, zubringen; Geld in Umlauf bringen; Gesetz verabschieden; Vorschlag etc. durchbringen, annehmen; Urteil abgeben; Meinung äußern; Bemerkung machen; fig. (hinaus)gehen über (acc.), übersteigen; ~·a·ble □ ['pɑːsəbl] passierbar; gangbar; gültig (Geld); leidlich.

pas·sage ['pæsɪdʒ] Durchgang m; Durchfahrt f; Durchreise f; Korridor m, Gang m; Reise f, (Über)Fahrt f, Flug m; parl. Annahme f (e-s Gesetzes); ♪ Passage f; (Text)Stelle f; bird of ~ Zugvogel m.

pass·book econ. ['pɑːsbʊk] Bankbuch n; Sparbuch n.

pas·sen·ger ['pæsɪndʒə] Passagier m, Fahr-, Fluggast m, Reisende(r m) f, (Auto- etc.)Insasse m.

pass·er-by ['pɑːsə'baɪ] (pl. passers-by) Vorbei-, Vorübergehende(r m) f, Passant(in).

pas·sion ['pæʃn] Leidenschaft f; (Gefühls)Ausbruch m; Wut f, Zorn m; ♀ eccl. Passion f; ♀ Week eccl. Karwoche f; ~·ate □ [~ət] leidenschaftlich.

pas·sive □ ['pæsɪv] passiv (a. gr.); teilnahmslos (a. gr.).

pass·port ['pɑːspɔːt] (Reise)Paß m.

pass·word ['pɑːswɜːd] Kennwort n.

past [pɑːst] 1. vergangen, pred. vorüber; gr. Vergangenheits...; frühere(r, ~s); for some time ~ seit einiger Zeit; ~ tense gr. Vergangenheit f, Präteritum n; 2. adv. vorbei; 3. prp. Zeit: nach, über (acc.); über ... (acc.) hinaus; an ... (dat.) vorbei; half ~ two halb drei; ~ endurance unerträglich; ~ hope hoffnungslos; 4. Vergangenheit f (a. gr.).

paste [peɪst] 1. Teig m; Kleister m; Paste f; 2. (be)kleben; ~·board ['peɪstbɔːd] Pappe f; attr. Papp...

pas·tel [pæ'stel] Pastell(zeichnung f) n.

pas·teur·ize ['pæstəraɪz] pasteurisieren, keimfrei machen.

pas·time ['pɑːstaɪm] Zeitvertreib m, Freizeitbeschäftigung f.

pas·tor ['pɑːstə] Pastor m, Seelsorger m; ~·al □ [~rəl] Hirten...; idyllisch; eccl. pastoral.

pas·try ['peɪstrɪ] Kuchen m, Torte f; Konditorwaren pl., Feingebäck n; ~·cook Konditor m.

pas·ture ['pɑːstʃə] 1. Weide(land n) f; Grasfutter n; 2. (ab)weiden.

pat [pæt] 1. Klaps m; Portion f (Butter); 2. (-tt-) tätscheln; klopfen; 3. gerade recht; parat, bereit.

patch [pætʃ] 1. Fleck m; Flicken m; Stück n Land; ♂ Pflaster n; in ~es stellenweise; 2. flicken; ~·work ['pætʃwɜːk] Patchwork n; contp. Flickwerk n.

pate F [peɪt]: bald ~ Platte f (Glatze).

pa·tent ['peɪtnt, Am. 'pætnt] 1. offen(kundig); patentiert; Patent...; ~ agent, Am. ~ attorney Patentanwalt m; letters ~ ['pætənt] pl. Patenturkunde f; ~ leather Lackleder n; 2. Patent n; Privileg n, Freibrief m, Patenturkunde f; 3. patentieren (lassen); ~·ee [peɪtən'tiː] Patentinhaber(in).

pa·ter·nal □ [pə'tɜːnl] väterlich(erseits); ~·ni·ty [~tɪ] Vaterschaft f.

path [pɑːθ] (pl. paths [pɑːðz]) Pfad m; Weg m.

pa·thet·ic [pə'θetɪk] (~ally) kläglich, bemitleidenswert, mitleiderregend; △ nicht pathetisch.

pa·thos ['peɪθɒs] Mitleid n; das Mitleiderregende; △ nicht Pathos.

pa·tience ['peɪʃns] Geduld f; Ausdauer f; Brt. Patience f (Kartenspiel); **pa·tient** [~t] 1. ◊ geduldig; 2. Patient(in).

pat·i·o ['pætɪəʊ] (pl. -os) Terrasse f; Innenhof m, Patio m.

pat·ri·mo·ny ['pætrɪmənɪ] väterliches Erbteil.

pat·ri·ot ['pætrɪət] Patriot(in); ~·ic [pætrɪ'ɒtɪk] (~ally) patriotisch.

pa·trol [pə'trəʊl] 1. ✕ Patrouille f; (Polizei)Streife f; on ~ auf Patrouille, auf Streife; 2. (-ll-) (ab)patrouillieren, auf Streife sein (in dat.), s-e Runde machen (in dat.); ~·car (Funk)Streifenwagen m; ~·man [~mæn] (pl. -men) Am. Polizist m (auf Streife); *Brt.* motorisierter Pannenhelfer (*e-s Automobilclubs*).

pa·tron ['peɪtrən] Schirmherr *m*; Gönner *m*; (Stamm)Kunde *m*; Stammgast *m*; ~ **saint** *eccl.* Schutzheilige(r) *m*; △ *nicht* Patrone; **pat·ron·age** ['pætrənɪdʒ] Schirmherrschaft *f*; Gönnerschaft *f*; Kundschaft *f*; Schutz *m*; **pat·ron·ize** [~aɪz] fördern, unterstützen; (Stamm)Kunde *od.* Stammgast sein bei; gönnerhaft *od.* herablassend behandeln.

pat·ter ['pætə] plappern; prasseln (*Regen*); trappeln (*Füße*).

pat·tern ['pætən] **1.** Muster *n* (*a. fig.*); Modell *n*; **2.** (nach)bilden, formen (*after, on* nach).

paunch [pɔːnʃ] (dicker) Bauch.

pau·per ['pɔːpə] Arme(r *m*) *f*.

pause [pɔːz] **1.** Pause *f*; △ *nicht thea.*, *Schule*: Pause; **2.** e-e Pause machen.

pave [peɪv] pflastern; ~ *the way for fig.* den Weg ebnen für; **~ment** ['peɪvmənt] *Brt.* Bürgersteig *m*; Pflaster *n*; *Am.* Fahrbahn *f*.

paw [pɔː] **1.** Pfote *f*, Tatze *f*; **2.** F betatschen; F derb *od.* ungeschickt anfassen; ~ (*the ground*) (mit den Hufen *etc.*) scharren.

pawn [pɔːn] **1.** *Schach*: Bauer *m*; Pfand *n*; *in od. at* ~ verpfändet; **2.** verpfänden; **~bro·ker** ['pɔːnbrəʊkə] Pfandleiher *m*; **~shop** Leihhaus *n*.

pay [peɪ] **1.** (Be)Zahlung *f*; Sold *m*; Lohn *m*; **2.** (*paid*) *v/t.* (be)zahlen; (be)lohnen; sich lohnen für; *Aufmerksamkeit* schenken; *Besuch* abstatten; *Ehre* erweisen; *Kompliment* machen; ~ *attention od. heed to* achtgeben auf (*acc.*); ~ *down*, ~ *cash* bar bezahlen; ~ *in* einzahlen; ~ *into* einzahlen auf (*ein Konto*); ~ *off* et. ab(be)zahlen; *j-n* bezahlen u. entlassen; *j-n* voll auszahlen; *v/i.* zahlen; sich lohnen; ~ *for* (*fig.* für) *et.* bezahlen; **~·a·ble** ['peɪəbl] zahlbar, fällig; **~day** Zahltag *m*; **~·ee** [peɪ'iː] Zahlungsempfänger(in); ~ **en·ve·lope** *Am.* Lohntüte *f*; **~·ing** ['peɪɪŋ] lohnend; **~·mas·ter** Zahlmeister *m*; **~·ment** [~mənt] (Be-, Ein-, Aus-) Zahlung *f*; Lohn *m*, Sold *m*; ~ **pack·et** *Brt.* Lohntüte *f*; ~ **phone** *Brt.* Münzfernsprecher *m*; **~·roll** Lohnliste *f*; ~ **slip** Lohn-, Gehalts-

---

streifen *m*; ~ **sta·tion** *Am.*, ~ **tel·e·phone** Münzfernsprecher *m*.

pea ♀ [piː] Erbse *f*.

peace [piːs] Frieden *m*; Ruhe *f*; *at* ~ *in* Frieden; **~·a·ble** □ ['piːsəbl] friedliebend, friedlich; **~·ful** [~fl] friedlich; **~·mak·er** Friedensstifter(in).

peach ♀ [piːtʃ] Pfirsich(baum) *m*.

pea·cock *zo.* ['piːkɒk] Pfau(hahn) *m*; **~·hen** *zo.* Pfauhenne *f*.

peak [piːk] Spitze *f*; Gipfel *m*; Mützenschild *n*, -schirm *m*; *attr.* Spitzen..., Höchst..., Haupt...; ~ *hours pl.* Hauptverkehrs-, Stoßzeit *f*; **~ed** [~t] spitz.

peal [piːl] **1.** (Glocken)Läuten *n*; Glockenspiel *n*; Dröhnen *n*; ~*s of laughter* schallendes Gelächter; **2.** erschallen (lassen); dröhnen.

pea·nut ♀ ['piːnʌt] Erdnuß *f*.

pear ♀ [peə] Birne *f*; Birnbaum *m*.

pearl [pɜːl] **1.** Perle *f* (*a. fig.*); *attr.* Perl(en)...; **2.** tropfen, perlen; **~·y** ['pɜːlɪ] (*-ier, -iest*) perlenartig, Perl(en)...

peas·ant ['peznt] **1.** Kleinbauer *m*; **2.** kleinbäuerlich, Kleinbauern...; **~·ry** [~rɪ] Kleinbauernstand *m*; *die* Kleinbauern *pl.*

peat [piːt] Torf *m*.

peb·ble ['pebl] Kiesel(stein) *m*.

peck [pek] **1.** Viertelscheffel *m* (= *9,087 Liter*); *fig.* Menge *f*; **2.** picken, hacken (*at* nach); *Körner etc.* aufpicken.

pe·cu·li·ar □ [pɪ'kjuːljə] eigen(tümlich); besondere(r, -s); seltsam; **~·i·ty** [pɪkjuːlɪ'ærɪtɪ] Eigenheit *f*; Eigentümlichkeit *f*.

pe·cu·ni·a·ry [pɪ'kjuːnjərɪ] Geld...

ped·a·gog·ics [pedə'gɒdʒɪks] *mst sg.* Pädagogik *f*; **~·gogue**, *Am. a.* **~·gog** ['pedəgɒg] Pädagoge *m*; F Pedant *m*, Schulmeister *m*.

ped·al ['pedl] **1.** Pedal *n*; *attr.* Fuß...; **3.** (*bsd. Brt. -ll-*, *Am. -l-*) das Pedal treten; radfahren; *Rad* fahren, treten.

pe·dan·tic [pɪ'dæntɪk] (~*ally*) pedantisch.

ped·dle ['pedl] hausieren gehen (mit); ~ *drugs* mit Drogen handeln; **~r** [~lə] *Am.* = *pedlar*; Drogenhändler *m*.

ped·es·tal ['pedɪstl] Sockel *m* (*a. fig.*).

pe·des·tri·an [pɪ'destrɪən] **1.** zu Fuß; *fig.* prosaisch, trocken; **2.** Fußgänger(in); ~ **cross·ing** Fußgängerübergang m; ~ **pre·cinct** Fußgängerzone f.

ped·i·gree ['pedɪgriː] Stammbaum m.

ped·lar ['pedlə] Hausierer m; Drogen-, Rauschgifthändler m.

peek [piːk] 1. spähen, gucken, lugen; 2. flüchtiger od. heimlicher Blick.

peel [piːl] 1. Schale f, Rinde f, Haut f; 2. v/t. schälen; a. ~ off abschälen, Folie etc. abziehen; Kleid abstreifen; v/i. a. ~ off sich (ab)schälen, abblättern.

peep [piːp] 1. neugieriger od. verstohlener Blick; Piep(s)en n; 2. gucken, neugierig od. verstohlen blicken; a. ~ out hervorschauen; fig. sich zeigen; piep(s)en; ~**hole** ['piːphəʊl] Guckloch n.

peer [pɪə] 1. spähen, lugen; ~ at (sich) genau ansehen, anstarren; 2. Gleiche(r m) f; Brt. Peer m; ~**less** □ ['pɪəlɪs] unvergleichlich.

peev·ish □ ['piːvɪʃ] verdrießlich, gereizt.

peg [peg] 1. (Holz)Stift m, Zapfen m, Dübel m, Pflock m; (Kleider)Haken m; Brt. (Wäsche)Klammer f; (Zelt-)Hering m; ♪ Wirbel m; fig. Aufhänger m; take s.o. down a ~ (or two) j-m e-n Dämpfer aufsetzen; 2. (-gg-) festpflocken; mst ~ out Grenze abstecken; ~ away, ~ along F dranbleiben (at an e-r Arbeit); ~**top** ['pegtɒp] Kreisel m.

pel·i·can zo. ['pelɪkən] Pelikan m.

pel·let ['pelɪt] Kügelchen n; Pille f; Schrotkorn n.

pell-mell ['pel'mel] durcheinander.

pelt [pelt] 1. Fell n, (rohe) Haut, (Tier)Pelz m; 2. v/t. bewerfen; v/i. a. ~ down (nieder)prasseln (Regen etc.).

pel·vis anat. ['pelvɪs] (pl. -vises, -ves [-viːz]) Becken n.

pen [pen] 1. (Schreib)Feder f; Federhalter m; Füller m; Kugelschreiber m; Pferch m; (Schaf)Hürde f; 2. (-nn-) schreiben; ~ in, ~ up einpferchen, -sperren.

pe·nal □ ['piːnl] Straf...; strafbar; ~ code Strafgesetzbuch n; ~ servitude Zwangsarbeit f; ~**ize** ['piːnalaɪz] bestrafen; **pen·al·ty** ['penltɪ] Strafe f; Sport: a. Strafpunkt m; Fußball: Elfmeter m; ~ area Fußball: Strafraum m; ~ goal Fußball: Elfmetertor n; ~ kick Fußball: Frei-, Strafstoß m.

pen·ance ['penəns] Buße f.

pence [pens] pl. von penny.

pen·cil ['pensl] 1. (Blei-, Zeichen-, Farb)Stift m; 2. (bsd. Brt. -ll-, Am. -l-) zeichnen; (mit Bleistift) aufschreiben od. anzeichnen od. anstreichen; Augenbrauen nachziehen; ~**sharp·en·er** Bleistiftspitzer m.

pen|dant, ~**dent** ['pendənt] (Schmuck)Anhänger m.

pend·ing ['pendɪŋ] 1. ♣ schwebend; 2. prp. während; bis zu.

pen·du·lum ['pendjʊləm] Pendel n.

pen·e·tra·ble □ ['penɪtrəbl] durchdringbar; ~**trate** [~eɪt] durchdringen; fig. ergründen; eindringen (in acc.); vordringen (to bis zu); ~**trat·ing** □ [~ɪŋ] durchdringend, scharf (Verstand); scharfsinnig; ~**tra·tion** [penɪ'treɪʃn] Durch-, Eindringen n; Scharfsinn m; ~**tra·tive** □ ['penɪtrətɪv] s. penetrating.

pen-friend ['penfrend] Brieffreund (-in).

pen·guin zo. ['peŋgwɪn] Pinguin m.

pen·hold·er ['penhəʊldə] Federhalter m.

pe·nin·su·la [pə'nɪnsjʊlə] Halbinsel f.

pe·nis anat. ['piːnɪs] Penis m.

pen·i|tence ['penɪtəns] Buße f, Reue f; ~**tent** [~t] 1. □ reuig, bußfertig; 2. Büßer(in); ~**ten·tia·ry** Am. [penɪ'tenʃərɪ] (Staats)Gefängnis n.

pen|knife ['pennaɪf] (pl. -knives) Taschenmesser n; ~**name** Schriftstellername m, Pseudonym n.

pen·nant ♣ ['penənt] Wimpel m.

pen·ni·less □ ['penɪlɪs] ohne e-n Pfennig (Geld), mittellos.

pen·ny ['penɪ] (pl. -nies, coll. pence [pens]) a. new ~ Brt. Penny m (= 1 p = £ 0.01); Am. Cent(stück n) m; fig. Pfennig m; ~**weight** englisches Pennygewicht (= 1,5 g).

pen·sion ['penʃn] 1. Rente f, Pension f, Ruhegeld n; △ nicht Pension (Fremdenheim); 2. oft ~ off pensionieren; ~**er** [~ə] Pensionär(in).

pen·sive □ ['pensɪv] nachdenklich.

pen·tath|lete [pen'tæθliːt] Sport: Fünfkämpfer(in); ~**lon** [~ɒn] Sport: Fünfkampf m.

Pen·te·cost ['pentɪkɒst] Pfingsten n.

pent·house ['penthaʊs] Penthouse n, -haus n, Dachterrassenwohnung f; Vor-, Schutzdach n.

permissive

pent-up ['pent'ʌp] an-, aufgestaut (*Ärger etc.*).

pe·nu·ri·ous □ [pɪ'njʊərɪəs] arm; geizig; **pen·u·ry** ['penjʊrɪ] Armut *f*, Not *f*; Mangel *m*.

peo·ple ['piːpl] **1.** Volk *n*, Nation *f*; Leute *pl.*; Angehörige *pl.*; *coll.* die Leute *pl.*; man; **2.** besiedeln, bevölkern.

pep F [pep] **1.** Elan *m*, Schwung *m*, Pep *m*; ~ **pill** Aufputschpille *f*; **2.** (*-pp-*) *mst* ~ up j-n *od. et.* in Schwung bringen.

pep·per ['pepə] **1.** Pfeffer *m*; **2.** pfeffern; ~**mint** ♀ Pfefferminze *f*; Pfefferminzbonbon *m, n*; ~**y** [~rɪ] pfefferig; *fig.* hitzig.

per [pɜː] per, durch; pro, für, je.

per·am·bu·la·tor *bsd. Brt.* ['præmbjʊleɪtə] = *pram*.

per·ceive [pə'siːv] (be)merken, wahrnehmen, empfinden; erkennen.

per cent, *Am.* **per·cent** [pə'sent] Prozent *n*.

per·cen·tage [pə'sentɪdʒ] Prozentsatz *m*; Prozente *pl.*; (An)Teil *m*.

per·cep|ti·ble □ [pə'septəbl] wahrnehmbar, merklich; ~**tion** [~pʃn] Wahrnehmung(svermögen *n*) *f*; Erkenntnis *f*; Auffassung(sgabe) *f*.

perch [pɜːtʃ] **1.** *zo.* Barsch *m*, Rute *f* (= 5,029 *m*); (Sitz)Stange *f* (*für Vögel*); **2.** sich setzen *od.* niederlassen, sitzen (*Vögel*); *auf et.* Hohes setzen.

per·co|late ['pɜːkəleɪt] *Kaffee etc.* filtern, durchsickern lassen; durchsickern (*a. fig.*); gefiltert werden; ~**la·tor** [~ə] Kaffeemaschine *f*, -automat *m*.

per·cus·sion [pə'kʌʃn] Schlag *m*, Erschütterung *f*; ♪ Abklopfen *n*; ♪ *coll.* Schlagzeug *n*; ~ **instrument** ♪ Schlaginstrument *n*.

per·e·gri·na·tion [perɪgrɪ'neɪʃn] Wanderschaft *f*; Wanderung *f*.

pe·remp·to·ry □ [pə'remptərɪ] bestimmt; zwingend; herrisch.

pe·ren·ni·al □ [pə'renjəl] immer wiederkehrend, beständig; immerwährend; ♀ perennierend.

per|fect 1. ['pɜːfɪkt] □ vollkommen; vollendet; virtuos; gänzlich, völlig; **2.** [~] *a.* ~ *tense gr.* Perfekt *n*; **3.** [pə'fekt] vervollkommnen; vollenden; ~**fec·tion** [~kʃn] Vollendung *f*; Vollkommenheit *f*; *fig.* Gipfel *m*.

per|fid·i·ous □ [pə'fɪdɪəs] treulos (*to*

gegen), verräterisch; ~**fi·dy** ['pɜːfɪdɪ] Treulosigkeit *f*, Verrat *m*.

per·fo·rate ['pɜːfəreɪt] durchlöchern.

per|form [pə'fɔːm] verrichten, ausführen, tun; *Pflicht etc.* erfüllen; *thea.*, ♪ aufführen, spielen, vortragen (*a. v/i.*); ~**ance** [~əns] Verrichtung *f*, Ausführung *f*; Leistung *f*; *thea.*, ♪ Aufführung *f*, Vorstellung *f*, Vortrag *m*; ~**er** [~ə] Künstler(in).

per·fume 1. ['pɜːfjuːm] Duft *m*, Wohlgeruch *m*; Parfüm *n*; **2.** [pə'fjuːm] mit Duft erfüllen, parfümieren.

per·func·to·ry □ [pə'fʌŋktərɪ] mechanisch; oberflächlich.

per·haps [pə'hæps, præps] vielleicht.

per|il ['perəl] **1.** Gefahr *f*; **2.** gefährden; ~**ous** □ [~əs] gefährlich.

pe·rim·e·ter [pə'rɪmɪtə] ♣ Umkreis *m*; Umgrenzungslinie *f*, Grenze *f*.

pe·ri·od ['pɪərɪəd] Periode *f*; Zeitraum *m*; *gr. bsd. Am.* Punkt *m*; *gr.* Gliedsatz *m*, Satzgefüge *n*; (Unterrichts)Stunde *f*; *physiol.* Periode *f* (*der Frau*); ~**ic** [pɪərɪ'ɒdɪk] periodisch; ~**i·cal** [~ɪkl] **1.** □ periodisch; **2.** Zeitschrift *f*.

per·ish ['perɪʃ] umkommen, zugrunde gehen; ~**a·ble** □ [~əbl] leicht verderblich; ~**ing** □ [~ɪŋ] *bsd. Brt.* F sehr kalt; F verdammt, -flixt.

perk [pɜːk] ~ *up v/i.* sich wieder erholen, munter werden (*Person*); *v/t.* Kopf heben, Ohren spitzen; schmücken, verschönern; j-n aufmöbeln, munter machen.

perk·y □ ['pɜːkɪ] (*-ier, -iest*) munter; keck, dreist, flott.

perm F [pɜːm] **1.** Dauerwelle *f*; **2.** j-m e-e Dauerwelle machen.

per·ma|nence ['pɜːmənəns] Dauer *f*; ~**nent** □ [~t] dauernd, ständig; dauerhaft; Dauer...; ~ *wave* Dauerwelle *f*.

per·me|a·ble □ ['pɜːmjəbl] durchlässig; ~**ate** [~eɪt] durchdringen; dringen (*into* in *acc.*, *through* durch).

per·mis·si|ble □ [pə'mɪsəbl] zulässig; ~**sion** [~ʃn] Erlaubnis *f*; ~**sive** □ [~sɪv] zulässig; erlaubt; tolerant; (sexuell) freizügig; ~ *society* tabufreie Gesellschaft.

permit

per·mit 1. [pə'mɪt] (*-tt-*) erlauben, gestatten; **2.** ['pɜːmɪt] Erlaubnis *f*, Genehmigung *f*; Passierschein *m*.

per·ni·cious □ [pə'nɪʃəs] verderblich, schädlich; *♣* bösartig.

per·pen·dic·u·lar □ [pɜːpən'dɪkjʊlə] senkrecht; aufrecht; steil.

per·pe·trate ['pɜːpɪtreɪt] verüben.

per·pet·u·al □ [pə'petʃʊəl] fortwährend, ständig, ewig; **~ate** [~eɪt] bewahren; verewigen.

per·plex [pə'pleks] verwirren; **~i·ty** [~ətɪ] Verwirrung *f*.

per·se·cute ['pɜːsɪkjuːt] verfolgen; **~cu·tion** [pɜːsɪ'kjuːʃn] Verfolgung *f*; **~cu·tor** ['pɜːsɪkjuːtə] Verfolger (*-in*).

per·se·ver·ance [pɜːsɪ'vɪərəns] Beharrlichkeit *f*, Ausdauer *f*; **~e** [pɜːsɪ'vɪə] beharren; aushalten.

per|sist [pə'sɪst] beharren, bestehen (*in an dat.*); fortdauern, anhalten; **~sis·tence, ~sis·ten·cy** [~əns, ~ɪ] Beharrlichkeit *f*; Hartnäckigkeit *f*, Ausdauer *f*; **~sis·tent** □ [~ənt] beharrlich, ausdauernd; anhaltend.

per|son ['pɜːsn] Person *f* (*a. gr., ⚥*); **~age** [~ɪdʒ] (hohe *od.* bedeutende) Persönlichkeit *f*; **~al** □ [~l] persönlich (*a. gr.*); *attr.* Personal...; Privat...; **~ data** ♦ Personalien *pl.*; **~al·i·ty** [pɜːsə'nælətɪ] Persönlichkeit *f*; *personalities pl.* anzügliche *od.* persönliche Bemerkungen *pl.*; **~i·fy** [pɜːˈsɒnɪfaɪ] verkörpern; **~nel** [pɜːsə'nel] Personal *n*, Belegschaft *f*; *✗* Mannschaften *pl.*; *♣, ≇* Besatzung *f*; **~ department** Personalabteilung *f*; **~ manager, ~ officer** Personalchef *m*.

per·spec·tive [pə'spektɪv] Perspektive *f*; Ausblick *m*, Fernsicht *f*.

per·spic·u·ous □ [pə'spɪkjʊəs] klar.

per|spi·ra·tion [pɜːspə'reɪʃn] Schwitzen *n*; Schweiß *m*; **~spire** [pə'spaɪə] (aus)schwitzen.

per|suade [pə'sweɪd] überreden; überzeugen; **~sua·sion** [~ʒn] Überredung *f*; Überzeugung *f*, (feste) Meinung; Glaube *m*; **~sua·sive** □ [~sɪv] überredend; überzeugend.

pert □ [pɜːt] keck (*a. fig. Hut*), vorlaut, frech, naseweis.

per·tain [pɜːˈteɪn] (*to*) gehören (*dat. od.* zu); betreffen (*acc.*).

per·ti·na·cious □ [pɜːtɪ'neɪʃəs] hartnäckig, zäh.

per·ti·nent □ ['pɜːtɪnənt] sachdienlich, relevant, zur Sache gehörig.

per·turb [pə'tɜːb] beunruhigen.

pe·rus|al [pə'ruːzl] sorgfältige Durchsicht *f*; **~e** [~z] (sorgfältig) durchlesen; prüfen.

per·vade [pə'veɪd] durchdringen.

per|verse □ [pə'vɜːs] *psych.* pervers; eigensinnig, verstockt; vertrackt (*Sache*); **~ver·sion** [~ʃn] Verdrehung *f*; Abkehr *f*; *psych.* Perversion *f*; **~ver·si·ty** [~ətɪ] *psych.* Perversität *f*; Eigensinn *m*, Verstocktheit *f*.

per·vert 1. [pə'vɜːt] verdrehen; verführen; **2.** *psych.* ['pɜːvɜːt] perverser Mensch.

pes·si·mis·m ['pesɪmɪzəm] Pessimismus *m*.

pest [pest] lästiger Mensch, Nervensäge *f*; lästige Sache, Plage *f*; *zo.* Schädling *m*; *△ nicht Pest (Seuche)*.

pes·ter ['pestə] belästigen.

pes·ti|lent □ ['pestɪlənt], **~len·tial** □ [pestɪ'lenʃl] *bsd. veraltet* schädlich; *mst co.* ekelhaft, abscheulich.

pet¹ [pet] **1.** (zahmes) (Haus)Tier; Liebling *m*; **2.** Lieblings...; Tier...; **~ dog** Schoßhund *m*; **~ name** Kosename *m*; **~ shop** Tierhandlung *f*, Zoogeschäft *n*; **3.** (*-tt-*) (ver)hätscheln; streicheln, liebkosen; F Petting machen.

pet² [~]: *in a ~* verärgert.

pet·al ⚘ ['petl] Blütenblatt *n*.

pe·ti·tion [pɪ'tɪʃn] **1.** Bittschrift *f*, Eingabe *f*, Gesuch *n*; **2.** bitten, ersuchen; ein Gesuch einreichen (*for um*), e-n Antrag stellen (*for auf acc.*).

pet·ri·fy ['petrɪfaɪ] versteinern.

pet·rol ['petrəl] Benzin *n*; *△ nicht Petroleum*; **~ pump** Zapfsäule *f*; **~ station** Tankstelle *f*.

pe·tro·le·um ♠ [pɪ'trəʊljəm] Petroleum *n*, Erd-, Mineralöl *n*; **~ refinery** Erdölraffinerie *f*.

pet·ti·coat ['petɪkəʊt] Unterrock *m*.

pet·ting F ['petɪŋ] Petting *n*.

pet·tish □ ['petɪʃ] launisch, reizbar.

pet·ty □ ['petɪ] (*-ier, -iest*) klein, geringfügig, Bagatell...; **~ cash** Portokasse *f*; **~ larceny** *⚥* einfacher Diebstahl.

pet·u·lant □ ['petjʊlənt] gereizt.

pew [pjuː] Kirchenbank *f*.

pew·ter ['pjuːtə] Zinn *n*; Zinngeschirr *n*; Zinnkrug *m*.

phan·tom ['fæntəm] Phantom *n*, Trugbild *n*; Gespenst *n*.

phar·ma·cy ['fɑ:məsɪ] Pharmazie *f*; Apotheke *f*.

phase [feɪz] Phase *f*.

pheas·ant *zo.* ['feznt] Fasan *m*.

phe·nom·e·non [fɪ'nɒmɪnən] (*pl. -na* [-ə]) Phänomen *n*, Erscheinung *f*.

phi·al ['faɪəl] Phiole *f*, Fläschchen *n*.

phi·lan·thro·pist [fɪ'lænθrəpɪst] Philanthrop *m*, Menschenfreund *m*.

phi·lol·o·gist [fɪ'lɒlədʒɪst] Philologe *m*, -in *f*; **~·gy** [~ɪ] Philologie *f*.

phi·los·o·pher [fɪ'lɒsəfə] Philosoph *m*; **~·phize** [~aɪz] philosophieren; **~·phy** [~ɪ] Philosophie *f*.

phlegm [flem] Schleim *m*; Phlegma *n*.

phone F [fəun] = *telephone*.

pho·net·ics [fə'netɪks] *sg.* Phonetik *f*, Lautlehre *f*.

pho·n(e)y *sl.* ['fəunɪ] 1. Fälschung *f*; Schwindel(in); 2. (*-ier*, *-iest*) falsch, unecht.

phos·pho·rus ↗ ['fɒsfərəs] Phosphor *m*.

pho·to F ['fəutəu] (*pl. -tos*) Foto *n*, Bild *n*.

pho·to- [~] Licht..., Photo..., Foto...; **~·cop·i·er** Fotokopiergerät *n*; **~·cop·y** 1. Fotokopie *f*; 2. fotokopieren.

pho·to·graph ['fəutəgrɑ:f] 1. Fotografie *f* (*Bild*); △ *nicht Fotograf*; 2. fotografieren; **~·tog·ra·pher** [fə'tɒgrəfə] Fotograf(in); **~·tog·ra·phy** [~ɪ] Fotografie *f*; △ *nicht Fotografie* (*Bild*).

phras·al ['freɪzl]: **~** *verb* Verb *n* mit Adverb (und Präposition); **phrase** [freɪz] 1. (Rede)Wendung *f*, Redensart *f*, (idiomatischer) Ausdruck; △ *nicht Phrase (leere Redensart)*; **~·book** Sprachführer *m*; 2. ausdrücken.

phys·i·cal □ ['fɪzɪkl] physisch; körperlich; physikalisch; **~** *education*, **~** *training* Leibeserziehung *f*; **~** *handicap* Körperbehinderung *f*; **~·ly** *handicapped* körperbehindert; **phy·si·cian** [fɪ'zɪʃn] Arzt *m*; △ *nicht Physiker*; **~·i·cist** ['fɪzɪsɪst] Physiker *m*; **~·ics** [~ɪks] *sg.* Physik *f*.

phy·sique [fɪ'zi:k] Körper(bau) *m*, Statur *f*; △ *nicht Physik*.

pi·an·o F ['pjænəu] (*pl. -os*) Klavier *n*.

pi·az·za [pɪ'ætsə] Piazza *f*, (Markt-) Platz *m*; *Am.* (große) Veranda.

pick [pɪk] 1. = *pickaxe*; (Aus)Wahl *f*; *take your ~* suchen Sie sich etwas

aus; 2. (auf)hacken; (auf)picken (*Vogel*); entfernen; pflücken; *Knochen* abnagen; bohren *od.* stochern in (*dat.*); *Schloß* mit e-m Dietrich öffnen, F knacken; *Streit* vom Zaun brechen; (sorgfältig) (aus)wählen; *Am.* ♪ *Saiten* zupfen, *Banjo* spielen; **~** *one's nose* in der Nase bohren; **~** *one's teeth* in den Zähnen (herum-) stochern; **~** *s.o.'s pocket* j-n bestehlen; *have a bone to ~ with s.o.* mit j-m ein Hühnchen zu rupfen haben; **~** *out et.* auswählen; heraussuchen; **~** *up* aufhacken; aufheben, -lesen, -nehmen; aufpicken (*Vogel*); *Spur* aufnehmen; *Täter* aufgreifen; F *et.* aufschnappen; sich e-e *Fremdsprache* aneignen; (*im Auto*) mitnehmen *od.* abholen; F *j-n* zufällig kennenlernen, auflesen; sich erholen; *a. ~ up speed* *mot.* schneller werden; **~·a·back** ['pɪkəbæk] huckepack; **~·axe**, *Am.* **~·ax** Spitzhacke *f*.

pick·et ['pɪkɪt] 1. Pfahl *m*; ✕ Feldwache *f*; Streikposten *m*; **~** *line* Streikpostenkette *f*; 2. mit Steikposten besetzen, Streikposten aufstellen vor (*dat.*); Streikposten stehen.

pick·ings ['pɪkɪŋz] *pl.* Überbleibsel *pl.*, Reste *pl.*; Ausbeute *f*; Profit *m*, (unehrlicher) Gewinn.

pick·le ['pɪkl] 1. (Salz)Lake *f*; *mst ~s* *pl.* Eingepökelte(s) *n*, Pickles *pl.*; F mißliche Lage; 2. einlegen, (-)pökeln; **~d** *herring* Salzhering *m*.

pick·lock ['pɪklɒk] Einbrecher *m*; Dietrich *m*; **~·pock·et** Taschendieb *m*; **~·up** Ansteigen *n*; Tonabnehmer *m*; Kleinlieferwagen *m*; F Straßenbekanntschaft *f*.

pic·nic ['pɪknɪk] 1. Picknick *n*; 2. (*-ck-*) ein Picknick machen, picknicken.

pic·to·ri·al [pɪk'tɔ:rɪəl] □ 1. malerisch; illustriert; 2. Illustrierte *f*.

pic·ture ['pɪktʃə] 1. Bild *n*; Gemälde *n*; bildschöne Sache *od.* Person; Film *m*; *attr.* Bilder...; **~s** *pl. bsd. Brt.* Kino *n*; *put s.o. in the ~* j-n ins Bild setzen; j-n informieren; 2. abbilden; *fig.* schildern, beschreiben; *fig.* sich *et.* vorstellen; **~ post·card** Ansichtskarte *f*; **pic·tur·esque** [pɪktʃə'resk] malerisch.

pie [paɪ] Pastete *f*; gedeckter Obstkuchen.

pie·bald ['paɪbɔ:ld] (bunt)scheckig.

piece [pi:s] 1. Stück *n*; Teil *m*, *n* (*e-r*

Maschine etc., ~e-s Services); Schach: Figur f; Brettspiel: Stein m; by the ~ stückweise; im Akkord; a ~ of advice ein Rat; a ~ of news e-e Neuigkeit; of a ~ einheitlich; give s.o. a ~ of one's mind j-m gründlich die Meinung sagen; take to ~s zerlegen; 2. ~ together zusammensetzen, -stük-keln, -flicken; **~meal** ['pi:smi:l] stückweise; **~work** Akkordarbeit f; do ~ im Akkord arbeiten.

pier [pɪə] Pfeiler m; Pier m, Hafendamm m, Mole f; Landungsbrücke f.

pierce [pɪəs] durchbohren, -stechen, -stoßen; durchdringen; eindringen (in acc.).

pi·e·ty ['paɪətɪ] Frömmigkeit f; Pietät f.

pig [pɪɡ] zo. Schwein n (a. fig. F); bsd. Am. Ferkel n; sl. contp. Bulle m (Polizist).

pi·geon ['pɪdʒɪn] Taube f; **~hole** 1. Fach n; 2. in Fächer einordnen.

pig|head·ed ['pɪɡ'hedɪd] dickköpfig; **~-i·ron** ['pɪɡaɪən] Roheisen n; **~skin** Schweinsleder n; **~sty** Schweinestall m; **~tail** (Haar)Zopf m.

pike [paɪk] ✕ hist. Pike f, Spieß m; zo. Hecht m; Schlagbaum m; Mautstraße f; Maut f.

pile [paɪl] 1. Haufen m; Stapel m, Stoß m; F Haufen m, Masse f; ⚡ Batterie f; Pfahl m; (Stoff, Teppich), ~s pl. ☞ Hämorrhoiden pl.; (atomic) ~ Atommeiler m, (Kern)Reaktor m; 2. oft ~ up, ~ on (an-, auf)häufen, (auf)stapeln, aufschichten.

pil·fer ['pɪlfə] stehlen, F stibitzen.

pil·grim ['pɪlɡrɪm] Pilger(in); **~age** [~ɪdʒ] Pilger-, Wallfahrt f.

pill [pɪl] Pille f (a. fig.); the ~ die (Antibaby)Pille.

pil·lage ['pɪlɪdʒ] 1. Plünderung f; 2. plündern.

pil·lar ['pɪlə] Pfeiler m, Ständer m; Säule f; **~box** Brt. Briefkasten m.

pil·li·on mot. ['pɪljən] Soziussitz m.

pil·lo·ry ['pɪlərɪ] 1. Pranger m; 2. an den Pranger stellen; fig. anprangern.

pil·low ['pɪləʊ] (Kopf)Kissen n; **~case**, **~slip** (Kopf)Kissenbezug m.

pi·lot ['paɪlət] 1. ✈ Pilot m; ♱ Lotse m; fig. Führer m; 2. Versuchs..., Probe..., Pilot...; **~film** TV Pilotfilm m; **~scheme** Versuchsprojekt n; 3. lotsen; steuern.

pimp [pɪmp] 1. Kuppler m; Zuhälter m; 2. sich als Kuppler betätigen; Zuhälter sein.

pim·ple ['pɪmpl] Pickel m, Pustel f.

pin [pɪn] 1. (Steck-, Krawatten-, Hut- etc.)Nadel f; ⊕ Pflock m, Bolzen m, Stift m, Dorn m; ♪ Wirbel m; Kegeln: Kegel m; Bowling: Pin m; (clothes) ~ bsd. Am. Wäscheklammer f; (drawing-) ~ Brt. Reißzwecke f; 2. (-nn-) (an)heften, anstecken (to an acc.), befestigen (to an dat.); pressen, drücken (against, to gegen, an acc.).

pin·a·fore ['pɪnəfɔ:] Schürze f.

pin·cers ['pɪnsəz] pl. (a pair of ~ e-e) (Kneif)Zange.

pinch [pɪntʃ] 1. Kneifen n; Prise f (Salz, Tabak etc.); fig. Druck m, Not f; 2. v/t. kneifen, zwicken, (ein)-klemmen; drücken (Schuh etc.); F klauen; v/i. drücken (Schuh, Not etc.); a. ~ and scrape sich einschränken, knausern.

pin·cush·ion ['pɪnkʊʃn] Nadelkissen n.

pine [paɪn] 1. ♀ Kiefer f, Föhre f; 2. sich abhärmen; sich sehnen (for nach); **~ap·ple** ♀ ['paɪnæpl] Ananas f; **~cone** ♀ Kiefernzapfen m.

pin·ion ['pɪnjən] 1. zo. Flügelspitze f; zo. Schwungfeder f; ⊕ Ritzel n (Antriebsrad); 2. die Flügel stutzen (dat.); fesseln (to an acc.).

pink [pɪŋk] 1. ♀ Nelke f; Rosa n; be in the ~ (of condition od. health) in Top- od. Hochform sein; 2. rosa(farben).

pin-mon·ey ['pɪnmʌnɪ] (selbstverdientes) Taschengeld (der Hausfrau).

pin·na·cle ['pɪnəkl] arch. Spitztürmchen n; (Berg)Spitze f; fig. Gipfel m, Höhepunkt m.

pint [paɪnt] Pint n (= 0,57 od. Am. 0,47 Liter); Brt. F Halbe f (Bier).

pi·o·neer [paɪə'nɪə] 1. Pionier m (a. ✕); 2. den Weg bahnen (für).

pi·ous ['paɪəs] □ fromm, religiös.

pip [pɪp] vet. Pips m; F miese Laune; (Obst)Kern m; Auge n (auf Würfeln etc.); ✕ Brt. F Stern m (Rangabzeichen); kurzer, hoher Ton.

pipe [paɪp] 1. Rohr n, Röhre f; Pfeife f (a. ♪); △ nicht (Triller)Pfeife; ♪ Flöte f; Pfeifen n, Lied n (e-s Vogels); Luftröhre f; Pipe f (Weinfaß = 477, 3 Liter); 2. (durch Rohre) leiten;

pfeifen; flöten; piep(s)en (*Vogel etc.*); **~line** ['paɪplaɪn] Rohrleitung *f*; *Erdöl, Erdgas etc.*: Pipeline *f*; **~r** [~ə] Pfeifer *m*.

pip·ing ['paɪpɪŋ] 1. pfeifend, schrill; ~ *hot* siedend heiß; 2. Rohrleitung *f*, -netz *n*; *Schneiderei*: Paspel *f*, Biese *f*; Pfeifen *n*, Piep(s)en *n*.

pi·quant □ ['pi:kənt] pikant.

pique [pi:k] 1. Groll *m*; 2. kränken, reizen; ~ *o.s. on* sich brüsten mit.

pi·ra·cy ['paɪərəsɪ] Piraterie *f*, Seeräuberei *f*; **pi·rate** [~ət] 1. Pirat *m*, Seeräuber *m*; Piratenschiff *n*; ~ *radio station* Piratensender *m*.

piss V [pɪs] pissen; ~ *off!* verpiß dich!, hau ab!

pis·tol ['pɪstl] Pistole *f*.

pis·ton ⊕ ['pɪstən] Kolben *m*; **~rod** Kolben-, Pleuelstange *f*; **~stroke** Kolbenhub *m*.

pit [pɪt] 1. Grube *f* (*a.* ⚒, *anat.*); ~ Miete *f*; Fallgrube *f*, Falle *f*; *Motorsport*: Box *f*; *Sport*: Sprunggrube *f*; *thea.* Brt. Parterre *n*; *a. orchestra* ~ *thea.* Orchestergraben *m*; *Am.* (Obst)Stein *m*, Kern *m*; Pockennarbe *f*; 2. (*-tt-*) 🖉 einmieten; mit Narben bedecken; *Am.* entsteinen, -kernen.

pitch [pɪtʃ] 1. *min.* Pech *n*; Brt. Stand(platz) *m* (*Straßenhändler etc.*); ♪ Tonhöhe *f*; Grad *m*, Stufe *f*, Höhe *f*; Gefälle *n*, Neigung *f*; Wurf *m* (*a.* Sport); *bsd.* Brt. Sport: Spielfeld *n*, Platz *m*; ⚓ Stampfen *n* (*Schiff*); 2. *v/t.* werfen; schleudern; Zelt, Lager aufschlagen, -stellen; ♪ (an)stimmen; ~ *too high fig.* Erwartungen zu hoch stecken; *v/i.* ⚒ (sich) lagern; hinschlagen; ⚓ stampfen (*Schiff*); ~ *into* F herfallen über (*acc.*); **~black** ['pɪtʃ'blæk], **~dark** pechschwarz; stockdunkel.

pitch·er ['pɪtʃə] Krug *m*; *Baseball*: Werfer *m*.

pitch·fork ['pɪtʃfɔːk] Heu-, Mistgabel *f*.

pit·e·ous □ ['pɪtɪəs] kläglich.

pit·fall ['pɪtfɔːl] Fallgrube *f*; *fig.* Falle *f*.

pith [pɪθ] Mark *n*; *fig.* Kern *m*; *fig.* Kraft *f*; **~y** □ ['pɪθɪ] (*-ier, -iest*) markig, kernig.

pit·i·a·ble □ ['pɪtɪəbl] bemitleidenswert; erbärmlich; **~ful** □ [~fl] bemitleidenswert; erbärmlich; jäm-

merlich (*a. contp.*); **~less** □ [~lɪs] unbarmherzig.

pit·tance ['pɪtəns] Hungerlohn *m*.

pit·y ['pɪtɪ] 1. Mitleid *n* (*on* mit); *it's a* ~ es ist schade; 2. bemitleiden.

piv·ot ['pɪvət] 1. ⊕ (Dreh)Zapfen *m*; *fig.* Dreh-, Angelpunkt *m*; 2. sich drehen (*on, upon* um).

piz·za ['pi:tsə] Pizza *f*.

pla·ca·ble □ ['plækəbl] versöhnlich.

plac·ard ['plækɑːd] 1. Plakat *n*; Transparent *n*; 2. anschlagen; mit e-m Plakat bekleben.

place [pleɪs] 1. Platz *m*; Ort *m*; Stelle *f*; Stätte *f*; (Arbeits)Stelle *f*, (An-) Stellung *f*; Wohnsitz *m*, Haus *n*, Wohnung *f*; Wohnort *m*; *soziale* Stellung *f*; ~ *of delivery econ.* Erfüllungsort *m*; *give* ~ *to j-m* Platz machen; *in* ~ *of* an Stelle (*gen.*); *out of* ~ fehl am Platz; 2. stellen, legen, setzen; *j-n* ein-, anstellen; *Auftrag* erteilen (*with s.o.* j-m); *be* ~*d* Sport: sich placieren; *I can't* ~ *him fig.* ich weiß nicht, wo ich ihn hintun soll (*identifizieren*); **~name** ['pleɪsneɪm] Ortsname *m*.

plac·id □ ['plæsɪd] sanft; ruhig.

pla·gia|rism ['pleɪdʒərɪzəm] Plagiat *n*; **~rize** [~raɪz] plagiieren.

plague [pleɪg] 1. Seuche *f*; Pest *f*; Plage *f*; 2. plagen, quälen.

plaice *zo.* [pleɪs] Scholle *f*.

plaid [plæd] Plaid *n*.

plain [pleɪn] 1. □ klar; deutlich; einfach, schlicht; unscheinbar, wenig anziehend; häßlich (*Frau*); offen (u. ehrlich); einfarbig; rein (*Wahrheit, Unsinn etc.*); 2. *adv.* klar, deutlich; 3. Ebene *f*, Flachland *n*; *the Great* ~*s pl. Am.* die Prärien *pl.* (*im Westen der USA*); **~choc·olate** (zart)bittere Schokolade; **~clothes man** ['pleɪn'kləʊðzmən] (*pl.* -men) Polizist *m od.* Kriminalbeamte(r) *m* in Zivil; ~ *deal·ing* Redlichkeit *f*; **~s·man** (*pl.* -men) *Am.* Präriebewohner *m*.

plain|tiff ['pleɪntɪf] Kläger(in); **~tive** □ [~v] traurig, klagend.

plait [plæt, *Am.* pleɪt] 1. (Haar-*etc.*)Flechte *f*; Zopf *m*; 2. flechten.

plan [plæn] 1. Plan *m*; 2. (*-nn-*) planen; entwerfen; ausarbeiten.

plane [pleɪn] 1. flach, eben; 2. Ebene *f*, (ebene) Fläche *f*; ✈ Tragfläche *f*; Flugzeug *n*; ⊕ Hobel *m*; *fig.* Stufe *f*, Niveau *n*; *by* ~ mit dem Flugzeug, auf dem Luftweg; **3.** (ein)ebnen; ⊕ hobeln; ✈ fliegen.

plan·et *ast.* ['plænɪt] Planet *m*.

plank [plæŋk] **1.** Planke *f*, Bohle *f*, Diele *f*; *pol.* Programmpunkt *m*; **2.** dielen; verschalen; ~ *down* F *et.* hinknallen; *Geld auf den Tisch legen*, blechen.

plant [plɑ:nt] **1.** ♀ Pflanze *f*; ⊕ Anlage *f*; Fabrik *m*; **2.** (an-, ein)pflanzen (*a. fig.*); bepflanzen; besiedeln; anlegen; (auf)stellen; *Schlag* verpassen; **plan·ta·tion** [plæn'teɪʃn] Pflanzung *f*, Plantage *f*; Besied(e)-lung *f*; **~er** [plɑ:ntə] Pflanzer *m*; Plantagenbesitzer *m*; ⊕ Pflanzmaschine *f*; Übertopf *m*.

plaque [plɑ:k] (Schmuck)Platte *f*; Gedenktafel *f*; ✻ Zahnbelag *m*.

plash [plæʃ] platschen.

plas·ter ['plɑ:stə] **1.** ✻ Pflaster *n*; *arch.* (Ver)Putz *m*; *a.* ~ *of Paris* Gips *m* (*a.* ✻); Stuck *m*; **2.** verputzen; bekleben; ✻ ein Pflaster legen auf (*acc.*); ~ **cast** Gipsabdruck *m*, -abguß *m*; ✻ Gipsverband *m*.

plas·tic ['plæstɪk] **1.** (~ally) plastisch; Plastik...; **2.** *oft* ~*s sg.* Plastik(material) *n*, Kunststoff *m*.

plate [pleɪt] **1.** Platte *f*; Teller *m*; (Bild)Tafel *f*; Schild *n*; (Kupfer-, Stahl)Stich *m*; (Tafel)Besteck *n*; *Baseball*: Heimbase *f*; ⊕ Grobblech *n*; **2.** plattieren; panzern.

plat·form ['plætfɔ:m] Plattform *f*; *geol.* Hochebene *f*; ⊕ Bahnsteig *m*; *Brt.* Plattform *f* (*bsd. am Busende*, *Am.* ⊕ *bsd. am Wagenende*); (Red-ner)Tribüne *f*, Podium *n*; ⊕ Rampe *f*, Bühne *f*; *pol.* Parteiprogramm *n*; *bsd. Am. pol.* Aktionsprogramm *n* (*im Wahlkampf*).

plat·i·num *min.* ['plætɪnəm] Platin *n*.

plat·i·tude *fig.* ['plætɪtju:d] Plattheit *f*.

pla·toon ✕ [plə'tu:n] Zug *m*.

plat·ter *Am. od. veraltet* ['plætə] (Servier)Platte *f*.

plau·dit ['plɔ:dɪt] Beifall *m*.

plau·si·ble □ ['plɔ:zəbl] glaubhaft.

play [pleɪ] **1.** Spiel *n*; Schauspiel *n*, (Theater)Stück *n*; ⊕ Spiel *n*; *fig.* Spielraum *m*; **2.** spielen; ⊕ Spiel (-raum) haben; ✻ sich bewegen (*Kolben etc.*); ~ *back Ball* zurück-spielen (*to zu*); *Tonband* abspielen; ~ *off fig.* ausspielen (*against gegen*); ~ *on*, ~ *upon fig. j-s Schwächen* aus-

nutzen; ~*ed out fig.* erledigt, erschöpft; **~back** ['pleɪbæk] Playback *n*, Wiedergabe *f*, Abspielen *n*; **~bill** Theaterplakat *n*; *Am.* Programm (-heft) *n*; **~boy** Playboy *m*; **~er** [~ə] (Schau)Spieler(in); Plattenspieler *m*; **~fel·low** Spielgefährt|e *m*, -in *f*; **~ful** □ [~fl] verspielt; spielerisch, scherzhaft; **~girl** Playgirl *n*; **~go·er** [~gəʊə] (*bsd.* häufige[r]) Theaterbe-sucher(in); **~ground** Spielplatz *m*; Schulhof *m*; **~house** *thea.* Schau-spielhaus *n*; Spielhaus *n* (*für Kinder*); **~mate** = *playfellow*; **~thing** Spielzeug *n*; **~wright** Dramatiker *m*.

plea [pli:] ✻ Einspruch *m*; Ausrede *f*; Gesuch *n*; *on the* ~ *of* od. *that* unter dem Vorwand (*gen.*) od. daß.

plead [pli:d] (~*ed*, *bsd. schott.*, *Am.* *pled*) *v/i.* ✻ plädieren; ~ *for* für *j-n* sprechen; sich einsetzen für; ~ (*not*) *guilty* sich (nicht) schuldig beken-nen; *v/t.* sich berufen auf (*acc.*), *et.* vorschützen; *Sache* vertreten; ✻ (als Beweis) anführen; **~ing** ✻ ['pli:dɪŋ] Plädoyer *n*.

pleas·ant □ ['pleznt] angenehm, er-freulich; freundlich; sympathisch; **~ry** [~rɪ] Scherz *m*, Spaß *m*.

please [pli:z] (*j-m*) gefallen, ange-nehm sein; befriedigen; belieben; ~ bitte; (*yes*,) ~ (ja,) bitte; (*oh ja*,) gerne; ~ *come in!* bitte, treten Sie ein!; ~ *yourself* (ganz) wie Sie wün-schen; **~d** erfreut, zufrieden; *be* ~ *at* erfreut sein über (*acc.*); *be* ~ *to do et.* gerne tun; ~ *to meet you!* ange-nehm!; *be* ~ *with* befriedigt sein von; *Vergnügen haben an (*dat.*).

pleas·ing □ ['pli:zɪŋ] angenehm, ge-fällig.

plea·sure ['pleʒə] Vergnügen *n*, Freude *f*; Belieben *n*; *attr.* Vergnü-gungs...; *at* ~ nach Belieben; **~boat** Vergnügungs-, Ausflugsdampfer *m*; **~ground** (Park)Anlage(n *pl.*) *f*; Vergnügungspark *m*.

pleat [pli:t] **1.** (Plissee)Falte *f*; **2.** fälteln, plissieren.

pled [pled] *pret. u. p.p. von plead*.

pledge [pledʒ] **1.** Pfand *n*; Zutrinken *n*, Toast *m*; Versprechen *n*, Gelöbnis *n*; **2.** verpfänden; *j-m* zutrinken; *he* ~*d himself* er gelobte.

ple·na·ry ['pli:nərɪ] Voll..., Plenar...

plen·i·po·ten·ti·a·ry [plenɪpə'tenʃərɪ] (General)Bevollmächtigte(r *m*) *f*.

plen·ti·ful □ ['plentɪfl] reichlich.
plen·ty ['plentɪ] 1. Fülle f, Überfluß m; ∼ of reichlich; 2. F reichlich.
pli·a·ble □ ['plaɪəbl] biegsam; fig. geschmeidig, nachgiebig.
pli·ers ['plaɪəz] pl. (a pair of ∼ e-e) (Draht-, Kombi)Zange.
plight [plaɪt] (schlechter) Zustand, schwierige Lage, Notlage f.
plim·soll Brt. ['plɪmsəl] Turnschuh m.
plod [plɒd] (-dd-) a. ∼ along, ∼ on sich dahinschleppen; ∼ away sich abplagen (at mit), schuften.
plop [plɒp] (-pp-) plumpsen od. (bsd. ins Wasser) platschen (lassen).
plot [plɒt] 1. Stück n Land, Parzelle f, Grundstück n; (geheimer) Plan, Komplott n, Anschlag m, Intrige f; Handlung f (e-s Dramas etc.); 2. (-tt-) v/t. auf-, einzeichnen; planen, anzetteln; v/i. sich verschwören (against gegen).
plough, Am. **plow** [plaʊ] 1. Pflug m; 2. (um)pflügen; **∼·share** ['plaʊʃeə] Pflugschar f.
pluck [plʌk] 1. Rupfen n, Zupfen n, Zerren n, Reißen n; Zug m, Ruck m; Innereien pl.; fig. Mut m, Schneid m; 2. pflücken; Vogel rupfen (a. fig.); zupfen, ziehen, zerren, reißen (at an dat.); ♪ Saiten zupfen; ∼ up courage Mut fassen; **∼·y** F □ ['plʌkɪ] (-ier, -iest) mutig.
plug [plʌg] 1. Pflock m, Dübel m, Stöpsel m; ⚡ Stecker m; ⚡ F Steckdose f; Hydrant m; mot. (Zünd-) Kerze f; (Zahn)Plombe f; Priem m (Kautabak); Rundfunk, TV: F Empfehlung f, Tip m, Werbung f; 2. v/t. (-gg-) Zahn plombieren; F im Rundfunk etc. (ständig) Reklame machen für; a. ∼ up zu-, verstopfen, zustöpseln; ∼ in ⚡ Gerät einstecken.
plum [plʌm] ♣ Pflaume(nbaum) f; Rosine f (a. fig.).
plum·age ['pluːmɪdʒ] Gefieder n.
plumb [plʌm] 1. lot-, senkrecht; 2. (Blei)Lot n; 3. v/t. lotrecht machen; loten; sondieren (a. fig.); Wasser od. Gasleitungen legen in; v/i. als Rohrleger arbeiten; **∼·er** ['plʌmə] Klempner m, Installateur m; **∼·ing** [∼ɪŋ] Klempnerarbeit f; Rohrleitungen pl.; sanitäre Installation.
plume [pluːm] 1. Feder f; Federbusch m; 2. mit Federn schmücken;

das Gefieder putzen; ∼ o.s. on sich brüsten mit.
plum·met ['plʌmɪt] Senkblei n.
plump [plʌmp] 1. adj. drall, prall, mollig; □ F glatt (Absage etc.); △ nicht plump; 2. a. ∼ down (hin-) plumpsen (lassen); 3. Plumps m; 4. adv. F unverblümt, geradeheraus.
plum pud·ding ['plʌm'pʊdɪŋ] Plumpudding m.
plun·der ['plʌndə] 1. Plünderung f; Raub m, Beute f; △ nicht Plunder; 2. plündern.
plunge [plʌndʒ] 1. (Ein-, Unter-) Tauchen n; (Kopf)Sprung m; Sturz m; take the ∼ fig. den entscheidenden Schritt wagen; 2. (ein-, unter-) tauchen; (sich) stürzen (into in acc.); e-e Waffe ins Herz etc. stoßen; ♣ stampfen (Schiff).
plu·per·fect gr. ['pluː'pɜːfɪkt] a. ∼ tense Plusquamperfekt n, Vorvergangenheit f.
plu·ral gr. ['plʊərəl] Plural m, Mehrzahl f; **∼·i·ty** [plʊəˈrælətɪ] Mehrheit f, Mehrzahl f; Vielzahl f.
plus [plʌs] 1. prp. plus; 2. adj. positiv; Plus...; 3. Plus n; Mehr n.
plush [plʌʃ] Plüsch m.
ply [plaɪ] 1. Lage f, Schicht f (Stoff, Sperrholz etc.); Strähne f (Garn etc.); fig. Neigung f; three-∼ dreifach (Garn etc.); dreifach gewebt (Teppich); 2. v/t. handhaben; umgehen mit; fig. j-m zusetzen; j-n überhäufen (with mit); v/i. regelmäßig fahren (between zwischen); **∼·wood** ['plaɪwʊd] Sperrholz n.
pneu·mat·ic [njuːˈmætɪk] (∼ally) Luft-; pneumatisch; ∼ (tyre) ⊕ Luftreifen m.
pneu·mo·ni·a ♣ [njuːˈməʊnjə] Lungenentzündung f.
poach[1] [pəʊtʃ] wildern.
poach[2] [∼] pochieren; ∼ed eggs pl. verlorene Eier pl.
poach·er ['pəʊtʃə] Wilddieb m, Wilderer m.
pock ♣ [pɒk] Pocke f, Blatter f.
pock·et ['pɒkɪt] 1. (Hosen- etc.)Tasche f; ✈ air pocket; 2. einstecken (a. fig.); Am. pol. Gesetzesvorlage nicht unterschreiben; Gefühl unterdrücken; 3. Taschen...; **∼·book** Notizbuch n; Brieftasche f; Am. Geldbeutel m; Am. Handtasche f; Taschenbuch n; ∼ **cal·cu·la·tor**

Taschenrechner *m*; **~knife** (*pl. -knives*) Taschenmesser *n*.

pod ♀ [pɒd] Hülse *f*, Schale *f*, Schote *f*.

po·em ['pəʊɪm] Gedicht *n*.

po·et ['pəʊɪt] Dichter *m*; **~ess** [~ɪs] Dichterin *f*; **~ic** [pəʊ'etɪk] (*~ally*), **~i·cal** □ [~kl] dichterisch; **~ics** [~ks] *sg.* Poetik *f*; **~ry** ['pəʊɪtrɪ] Dichtkunst *f*; Dichtung *f*; *coll.* Dichtungen *pl.*, Gedichte *pl.*

poi·gnan|cy ['pɔɪnənsɪ] Schärfe *f*; **~t** [~t] scharf; *fig.* bitter; *fig.* ergreifend.

point [pɔɪnt] **1.** Spitze *f*; *geogr.* Landspitze *f*; *gr.*, Å, *phys. etc.* Punkt *m*; Å (Dezimal)Punkt *m*, Komma *n*; *phys.* Grad *m* (*e-r Skala*); ♠ Kompaßstrich *m*; Auge *n* (*auf Spielkarten etc.*); Punkt *m*, Stelle *f*, Ort *m*; springender Punkt; Zweck *m*, Ziel *n*; Pointe *f*; *fig.* hervorstehende Eigenschaft; **~s** *pl.* Brt. ⬛ Weiche *f*; **~ of view** Stand-, Gesichtspunkt *m*; **the ~ is that** ... die Sache ist die, daß ...; **make a ~ of s.th.** auf e-r Sache bestehen; **there is no ~ in doing es** hat keinen Zweck, zu tun; **in ~ of** hinsichtlich (*gen.*); **to the ~** zur Sache (gehörig); **off od. beside the ~** nicht zur Sache (gehörig); **on the ~ of inf.** im Begriff zu *inf.*; **beat s.o. on ~s** j-n nach Punkten schlagen; **win od. lose on ~s** nach Punkten gewinnen *od.* verlieren; **winner on ~s** Punktsieger *m*; **2.** *v/t.* (zu)spitzen; **~ at** Waffe *etc.* richten auf (*acc.*); (*mit dem Finger*) zeigen auf (*acc.*); **~ out** zeigen auf; *fig.* hinweisen auf (*acc.*); *v/i.* **~ at** deuten, weisen auf (*acc.*); **~ to** nach *e-r Richtung* weisen; hinweisen auf (*acc.*); **~ed** □ ['pɔɪntɪd] spitz(ig); Spitz...; *fig.* scharf; **~er** [~ə] Zeiger *m*; Zeigestock *m*; *zo.* Vorstehhund *m*; **~less** [~lɪs] stumpf; witzlos; zwecklos.

poise [pɔɪz] **1.** Gleichgewicht *n*; (Körper-, Kopf)Haltung *f*. **2.** *v/t.* im Gleichgewicht halten; *Kopf etc.* tragen, halten; *v/i.* schweben.

poi·son ['pɔɪzn] **1.** Gift *n*; **2.** vergiften; **~ous** □ [~əs] giftig (*a. fig.*).

poke [pəʊk] **1.** Stoß *m*, Puff *m*; *F* Faustschlag *m*; **2.** *v/t.* stoßen, puffen; *Feuer* schüren; **~ fun at** sich über j-n lustig machen; **~ one's nose into everything** F s-e Nase überall hineinstecken; *v/i.* stoßen; stochern.

pok·er ['pəʊkə] Feuerhaken *m*.

pok·y ['pəʊkɪ] (*-ier, -iest*) eng; schäbig.

po·lar ['pəʊlə] polar; **~ bear** *zo.* Eisbär *m*.

Pole[1] [pəʊl] Pole *m*, Polin *f*.

pole[2] [~] Pol *m*; Stange *f*; Mast *m*; Deichsel *f*; *Sport:* (Sprung)Stab *m*.

pole·cat *zo.* ['pəʊlkæt] Iltis *m*; *Am.* Skunk *m*, Stinktier *n*.

po·lem|ic [pə'lemɪk], *a.* **~i·cal** □ [~kl] polemisch.

pole-star ['pəʊlstɑː] *ast.* Polarstern *m*; *fig.* Leitstern *m*.

pole-vault ['pəʊlvɔːlt] **1.** Stabhochsprung *m*; **2.** stabhochspringen; **~er** [~ə] Stabhochspringer *m*; **~ing** [~ɪŋ] Stabhochspringen *n*, -sprung *m*.

po·lice [pə'liːs] **1.** Polizei *f*; △ *nicht Police*; **2.** überwachen; **~·man** (*pl. -men*) Polizist *m*; **~·of·fi·cer** Polizeibeamte(r) *m*, Polizist *m*; **~ sta·tion** Polizeiwache *f*, -revier *n*; **~·wom·an** (*pl. -women*) Polizistin *f*.

pol·i·cy ['pɒləsɪ] Politik *f*; Taktik *f*; Klugheit *f*; (Versicherungs)Police *f*; *Am.* Zahlenlotto *n*.

po·li·o ⚕ ['pəʊlɪəʊ] Polio *f*, Kinderlähmung *f*.

Pol·ish[1] ['pəʊlɪʃ] **1.** polnisch; **2.** *ling.* Polnisch *n*.

pol·ish[2] ['pɒlɪʃ] **1.** Politur *f*; Schuhcreme *f*; *fig.* Schliff *m*; **2.** polieren; *Schuhe* putzen; *fig.* verfeinern.

po·lite □ [pə'laɪt] (*~r, ~st*) artig, höflich; **~ness** [~nɪs] Höflichkeit *f*.

pol·i|tic □ ['pɒlɪtɪk] diplomatisch; klug; **po·lit·i·cal** □ [pə'lɪtɪkl] politisch; staatlich, Staats...; **~·ti·cian** [pɒlɪ'tɪʃn] Politiker *m*; **~·tics** ['pɒlɪtɪks] *oft sg.* Politik *f*.

pol·ka ['pɒlkə] Polka *f*; **~ dot** Punktmuster *n* (*auf Stoff*).

poll [pəʊl] **1.** Wählerliste *f*; Stimmenzählung *f*; Wahl *f*; Stimmenzahl *f*; (Ergebnis *n e-r*) (Meinungs)Umfrage *f*; **2.** *v/t. Wahlstimmen* erhalten; *v/i.* wählen.

pol·len ♀ ['pɒlən] Blütenstaub *m*.

poll·ing ['pəʊlɪŋ] Wählen *n*, Wahl *f*; **~ booth** Wahlkabine *f*, -zelle *f*; *district* Wahlbezirk *m*; **~ place** *Am.*, **~ station** *bsd. Brt.* Wahllokal *n*.

poll-tax ['pəʊltæks] Kopfsteuer *f*.

pol·lu|tant [pə'luːtənt] Schadstoff *m*; **~tute** [~t] be-, verschmutzen; verunreinigen; *eccl.* entweihen; **~·lu·tion** [~ʃn] Verunreinigung *f*; (Luft-, Wasser-, Umwelt)Verschmutzung *f*.

pose

po·lo ['pəʊləʊ] *Sport*: Polo *n*; **~neck** Rollkragen(pullover) *m*.

pol|yp *zo.* ✶ ['pɒlɪp], **~·y·pus** ✶ [~əs] (*pl.* **-pi** [-paɪ], **-puses**) Polyp *m*.

pom·mel ['pʌml] **1.** (Degen-, Sattel)Knopf *m*; **2.** (*bsd. Brt. -ll-, Am. -l-*) = **pummel**.

pomp [pɒmp] Pomp *m*, Prunk *m*.

pom·pous □ ['pɒmpəs] pompös, prunkvoll; aufgeblasen; schwülstig.

pond [pɒnd] Teich *m*, Weiher *m*.

pon·der ['pɒndə] *v/t.* erwägen; *v/i.* nachdenken; **~·a·ble** [~rəbl] wägbar; **~·ous** □ [~rəs] schwer(fällig).

pon·tiff ['pɒntɪf] Hohepriester *m*; Papst *m*.

pon·toon [pɒn'tu:n] Ponton *m*; **~ bridge** Pontonbrücke *f*.

po·ny *zo.* ['pəʊnɪ] Pony *n*, kleines Pferd; *Am.* Mustang *m*, (halb)wildes Pferd.

poo·dle *zo.* ['pu:dl] Pudel *m*.

pool [pu:l] **1.** Teich *m*; Pfütze *f*, Lache *f*; (Schwimm)Becken *n*; Pool *m*; *Karten*: Gesamteinsatz *m*; *econ.* Ring *m*, Kartell *n*; *mst* **~s** *pl.* (Fußball- *etc.*)Toto *n*, *m*; **~room** *Am.* Billardspielhalle *f*; Wettannahmestelle *f*; **2.** *econ.* ein Kartell bilden; *Geld, Unternehmen etc.* zusammenlegen.

poop ⚓ [pu:p] Heck *n*; *a.* **~ deck** (erhöhtes) Achterdeck.

poor □ [pʊə] arm(selig); dürftig; schlecht; **~·ly** ['pʊəlɪ] **1.** *adj.* kränklich, unpäßlich; **2.** *adv.* arm(selig), dürftig; **~·ness** [~nɪs] Armut *f*.

pop¹ [pɒp] **1.** Knall *m*; F Limo *f* (*Limonade*); **2.** (*-pp-*) *v/t.* knallen lassen; *Am.* Mais rösten; schnell *wohin* tun *od.* stecken; *v/i.* knallen; *mit adv.* huschen; **~ in** hereinplatzen (*Besuch*).

pop² [~] **1.** *a.* **~ music** Schlagermusik *f*; Pop(musik *f*) *m*; **2.** volkstümlich, beliebt; Schlager...; Pop...; **~ concert** Popkonzert *n*; **~ singer** Schlagersänger(in); **~ song** Schlager *m*.

pop³ *Am.* F [~] Paps *m*, Papa *m*; Opa *m* (*alter Herr*).

pop·corn ['pɒpkɔ:n] Popcorn *n*, Puffmais *m*.

pope [pəʊp] *mst* ♀ Papst *m*.

pop-eyed F ['pɒpaɪd] glotzäugig.

pop·lar ♀ ['pɒplə] Pappel *f*.

pop·py ♀ ['pɒpɪ] Mohn *m*; **~cock** F Quatsch *m*, dummes Zeug.

pop·u·lace ['pɒpjʊləs] *die* breite Masse, *das* Volk; *contp.* Pöbel *m*; **~·lar** □ [~ə] Volks...; volkstümlich, populär, beliebt; **~·lar·i·ty** [pɒpjʊ'lærətɪ] Popularität *f*, Beliebtheit *f*.

pop·u|late ['pɒpjʊleɪt] bevölkern, besiedeln; *mst pass.* bewohnen; **~·la·tion** [pɒpjʊ'leɪʃn] Bevölkerung *f*; **~·lous** □ ['pɒpjʊləs] dichtbesiedelt, -bevölkert.

porce·lain ['pɔ:slɪn] Porzellan *n*.

porch [pɔ:tʃ] Vorhalle *f*, Portal *n*, Vorbau *m*; *Am.* Veranda *f*.

por·cu·pine *zo.* ['pɔ:kjʊpaɪn] Stachelschwein *n*.

pore [pɔ:] **1.** Pore *f*; **2.** **~ over** *et.* eifrig studieren.

pork [pɔ:k] Schweinefleisch *n*; **~·y** ['pɔ:kɪ] **1.** (*-ier, -iest*) fett; dick; **2.** *Am.* = **porcupine**.

porn F [pɔ:n] = **porno**.

por|no F ['pɔ:nəʊ] **1.** (*pl. -nos*) Porno(-film) *m*; **2.** Porno...; **~·nog·ra·phy** [pɔ:'nɒgrəfɪ] Pornographie *f*.

po·rous □ ['pɔ:rəs] porös.

por·poise *zo.* ['pɔ:pəs] Tümmler *m*.

por·ridge ['pɒrɪdʒ] Haferbrei *m*.

port¹ [pɔ:t] Hafen(stadt *f*) *m*.

port² [~] ⚓ (Lade)Luke *f*; ⚓, ✗ Bullauge *n*.

port³ ⚓, ✗ [~] Backbord *n*.

port⁴ [~] Portwein *m*.

por·ta·ble ['pɔ:təbl] tragbar.

por·tal ['pɔ:tl] Portal *n*, Tor *n*.

por|tent ['pɔ:tent] (Vor)Zeichen *n*, Omen *n*; Wunder *n*; **~·ten·tous** □ [pɔ:'tentəs] unheilvoll; wunderbar.

por·ter ['pɔ:tə] (Gepäck)Träger *m*; *bsd. Brt.* Pförtner *m*, Portier *m*; *Am.* ✕ Schlafwagenschaffner *m*; Porter (-bier *n*) *m*, *n*.

port·hole ⚓, ✗ ['pɔ:thəʊl] Bullauge *n*.

por·tion ['pɔ:ʃn] **1.** (An)Teil *m*; Portion *f* (*Essen*); Erbteil *n*; Aussteuer *f*; *fig.* Los *n*; **2.** **~ out** aus-, verteilen (*among unter acc.*).

port·ly ['pɔ:tlɪ] (*-ier, -iest*) korpulent.

por·trait ['pɔ:trɪt] Porträt *n*, Bild *n*.

por·tray [pɔ:'treɪ] (ab)malen, porträtieren; schildern; **~·al** [~əl] Porträtieren *n*; Schilderung *f*.

pose [pəʊz] **1.** Pose *f*; Haltung *f*; **2.** aufstellen; *Problem, Frage* stellen, aufwerfen; posieren; Modell sitzen *od.* stehen; **~ as** sich ausgeben als *od.* für.

posh F [pɒʃ] schick, piekfein.

po·si·tion [pəˈzɪʃn] Position f, Lage f, Stellung f (a. fig.); Stand m; fig. Standpunkt m.

pos·i·tive [ˈpɒzətɪv] **1.** □ bestimmt, ausdrücklich; feststehend, sicher; unbedingt; positiv; bejahend; überzeugt; rechthaberisch; **2.** phot. Positiv n.

pos|sess [pəˈzes] besitzen, haben; beherrschen; fig. erfüllen; ~ o.s. of et. in Besitz nehmen; **~·sessed** besessen; **~·session** [~ʃn] Besitz m; fig. Besessenheit f; **~·ses·sive** gr. [~sɪv] **1.** □ possessiv, besitzanzeigend; ~ case Genitiv m; **2.** Possessivpronomen n, besitzanzeigendes Fürwort; Genitiv m; **~·ses·sor** [~sə] Besitzer(in).

pos·si·bil·i·ty [pɒsəˈbɪlətɪ] Möglichkeit f; **~·ble** [ˈpɒsəbl] möglich; **~·bly** [~lɪ] möglicherweise, vielleicht; if I ~ can wenn ich es irgend kann.

post [pəʊst] **1.** Pfosten m; Posten m; Stelle f, Amt n; bsd. Brt. Post f; ~ exchange Am. Einkaufsstelle f; **2.** Plakat etc. anschlagen; aufstellen; postieren; eintragen; bsd. Brt. Brief etc. einstecken, abschicken, aufgeben; ~ up j-n informieren.

post- [pəʊst] nach..., Nach...

post·age [ˈpəʊstɪdʒ] Porto n; ~ stamp Briefmarke f.

post·al □ [ˈpəʊstl] **1.** postalisch, Post...; ~ order Brt. Postanweisung f; **2.** a. ~ card Am. Postkarte f.

post|-bag bsd. Brt. [ˈpəʊstbæg] Postsack m, -beutel m; **~-box** bsd. Brt. Briefkasten m; **~-card** Postkarte f; a. picture ~ Ansichtskarte f; **~-code** Brt. Postleitzahl f.

post·er [ˈpəʊstə] Plakat n; Poster n, m.

pos·te·ri·or [pɒˈstɪərɪə] **1.** □ später (to als); hinter; **2.** oft ~s pl. Hinterteil n.

pos·ter·i·ty [pɒˈsterətɪ] Nachwelt f; Nachkommen(schaft f) pl.

post-free bsd. Brt. [ˈpəʊstˈfriː] portofrei.

post-grad·u·ate [ˈpəʊstˈgrædjʊət] **1.** nach dem ersten akademischen Grad; **2.** j., der nach dem ersten akademischen Grad weiterstudiert.

post-haste [ˈpəʊstˈheɪst] schnellstens.

post·hu·mous □ [ˈpɒstjʊməs] nachgeboren; post(h)um.

post|man bsd. Brt. [ˈpəʊstmən] (pl. -men) Briefträger m; **~·mark 1.** Poststempel m; **2.** (ab)stempeln; **~·mas·ter** Postamtsvorsteher m; **~·of·fice** Post(amt n) f; **~-of·fice box** Post(schließ)fach n; **~-paid** portofrei.

post·pone [pəʊstˈpəʊn] ver-, aufschieben; **~·ment** [~mənt] Verschiebung f, Aufschub m.

post·script [ˈpəʊsskrɪpt] Postskriptum n.

pos·ture [ˈpɒstʃə] **1.** (Körper)Haltung f, Stellung f; **2.** posieren, sich in Positur werfen.

post-war [ˈpəʊstˈwɔː] Nachkriegs...

po·sy [ˈpəʊzɪ] Sträußchen n.

pot [pɒt] **1.** Topf m; Kanne f; Tiegel m; F Sport: Pokal m; sl. Hasch n (Haschisch); sl. Grass n (Marihuana); **2.** (-tt-) in e-n Topf tun; einlegen.

po·ta·to [pəˈteɪtəʊ] (pl. -toes) Kartoffel f; s. chip 1, crisp 3.

pot-bel·ly [ˈpɒtbelɪ] Schmerbauch m.

po·ten|cy [ˈpəʊtənsɪ] Macht f; Stärke f; physiol. Potenz f; **~t** [~t] mächtig; stark; physiol. potent; **~·tial** [pəˈtenʃl] **1.** potentiell; möglich; **2.** Potential n; Leistungsfähigkeit f.

poth·er [ˈpɒðə] Aufregung f.

pot-herb [ˈpɒthɜːb] Küchenkraut n.

po·tion [ˈpəʊʃn] (Arznei-, Gift-, Zauber)Trank m.

pot·ter[1] [ˈpɒtə] ~ about herumwerkeln.

pot·ter[2] [~] Töpfer(in); **~·y** [~rɪ] Töpferei f; Töpferware(n pl.) f.

pouch [paʊtʃ] Tasche f; Beutel m (a. zo.); anat. Tränensack m.

poul·ter·er [ˈpəʊltərə] Geflügelhändler m.

poul·tice ⚕ [ˈpəʊltɪs] Packung f.

poul·try [ˈpəʊltrɪ] Geflügel n.

pounce [paʊns] **1.** Satz m, Sprung m; Herabstoßen n (e-s Raubvogels); **2.** sich stürzen, Raubvogel: herabstoßen (on, upon auf acc.).

pound[1] [paʊnd] Pfund n (Gewicht); ~ (sterling) Pfund n (Sterling) (abbr. £; £ = 100 pence).

pound[2] [~] Tierheim n; Abstellplatz m (für polizeilich abgeschleppte Fahrzeuge).

pound[3] [~] (zer)stoßen; stampfen; hämmern, trommeln, schlagen.

-pound·er [ˈpaʊndə] ...pfünder m.

pour [pɔː] v/t. gießen, schütten; ~ out

Getränk eingießen; *v/i.* strömen, rinnen.

pout [paʊt] 1. Schmollen *n*; 2. *v/t.* Lippen aufwerfen; *v/i.* schmollen.

pov·er·ty ['pɒvətɪ] Armut *f*; Mangel *m*.

pow·der ['paʊdə] 1. Pulver *n*; Puder *m*; 2. pulverisieren; (sich) pudern; bestreuen; **~box** Puderdose *f*; **~room** Damentoilette *f*.

pow·er ['paʊə] 1. Kraft *f*; Macht *f*; Gewalt *f*; ⚖ Vollmacht *f*; ⚛ Potenz *f*; *in* ~ an der Macht, im Amt; 2. ⊕ antreiben; *rocket-~ed* raketengetrieben; **~cur·rent** ⚡ Starkstrom *m*; **~cut** ⚡ Stromsperre *f*; Strom-, Netzausfall *m*; **~ful** □ [~fl] mächtig; kräftig; wirksam; **~less** □ [~lɪs] macht-, kraftlos; **~plant** = *powerstation*; **~pol·i·tics** *oft sg.* Machtpolitik *f*; **~sta·tion** Elektrizitäts-, Kraftwerk *n*.

pow·wow *Am.* F ['paʊwaʊ] Versammlung *f*.

prac·ti|ca·ble □ ['præktɪkəbl] durchführbar; begeh-, befahrbar (*Weg*); **~cal** [~l] praktisch; tatsächlich; sachlich; ~ *joke* Streich *m*; **~cal·ly** [~lɪ] so gut wie.

prac·tice, *Am. a.* **-tise** [~] 1. Praxis *f*; Übung *f*; Gewohnheit *f*; Brauch *m*; Praktik *f*; *it is common* ~ es ist allgemein üblich; *put into* ~ in die Praxis umsetzen; 2. *Am.* = *practise*.

prac·tise, *Am. a.* **-tice** [~] *v/t.* in die Praxis umsetzen; ausüben; betreiben; üben; *v/i.* (sich) üben; praktizieren; ~ *on*, ~ *upon j-s Schwäche* ausnutzen; **~d** geübt (*in in dat.*) (*Person*).

prac·ti·tion·er [præk'tɪʃnə]: *general* ~ praktischer Arzt; *legal* ~ Rechtsanwalt *m*.

prai·rie ['preərɪ] Grasebene *f*; Prärie *f* (*in Nordamerika*); **~schoo·ner** *Am.* Planwagen *m*.

praise [preɪz] 1. Lob *n*; 2. loben, preisen; **~wor·thy** ['preɪzwɜːðɪ] lobenswert.

pram *bsd. Brt.* F [præm] Kinderwagen *m*.

prance [prɑːns] sich bäumen, steigen; tänzeln (*Pferd*); (einher)stolzieren.

prank [præŋk] Streich *m*.

prate [preɪt] 1. Gefasel *n*, Geschwafel *n*; 2. faseln, schwafeln.

prat·tle ['prætl] 1. Geplapper *n*; 2. (*et. daher*)plappern.

prawn *zo.* [prɔːn] Garnele *f*.

pray [preɪ] beten; inständig (er)bitten; bitte!

prayer [preə] Gebet *n*; inständige Bitte; *oft* ~*s pl.* Andacht *f*; *the Lord's* ⚜ das Vaterunser; **~book** ['preəbʊk] Gebetbuch *n*.

pre- [priː, prɪ] *zeitlich*: vor, vorher, früher als; *räumlich*: vor, davor.

preach [priːtʃ] predigen; **~er** ['priːtʃə] Prediger(in).

pre·am·ble [priː'æmbl] Einleitung *f*.

pre·car·i·ous □ [prɪ'keərɪəs] unsicher, bedenklich; gefährlich.

pre·cau·tion [prɪ'kɔːʃn] Vorkehrung *f*, Vorsicht(smaßregel, -smaßnahme) *f*; **~a·ry** [~ʃnərɪ] vorbeugend.

pre·cede [priː'siːd] voraus-, vorangehen (*dat.*); **~ce·dence**, **~ce·den·cy** [~əns, ~sɪ] Vorrang *m*; **~ce·dent** ['presɪdənt] Präzedenzfall *m*.

pre·cept ['priːsept] Grundsatz *m*.

pre·cinct ['priːsɪŋkt] Bezirk *m*; *Am.* Wahlbezirk *m*, -kreis *m*; *Am.* (Polizei)Revier *n*; ~*s pl.* Umgebung *f*; Bereich *m*; Grenzen *pl.*; *pedestrian* ~ Fußgängerzone *f*.

pre·cious ['preʃəs] 1. □ kostbar; edel (*Steine etc.*); F schön, nett, fein; 2. *adv.* F reichlich, herzlich.

prec·i·pice ['presɪpɪs] Abgrund *m*.

pre·cip·i|tate 1. [prɪ'sɪpɪteɪt] *v/t.* (hinab)stürzen; ⚛ (aus)fällen; *fig.* beschleunigen; *v/i.* ⚛, *meteor.* sich niederschlagen; 2. □ [~tət] überstürzt, hastig; 3. ⚛ [~] Niederschlag *m*; **~ta·tion** [prɪsɪpɪ'teɪʃn] Sturz *m*; ⚛ Niederschlagen *n*; *meteor.* Niederschlag *m*; *fig.* Überstürzung *f*, Hast *f*; **~tous** □ [prɪ'sɪpɪtəs] steil (abfallend), jäh.

pré·cis ['preɪsiː] (*pl.* -*cis* [-siːz]) (gedrängte) Übersicht, Zusammenfassung *f*.

pre·cise □ [prɪ'saɪs] genau; **~ci·sion** [~'sɪʒn] Genauigkeit *f*; Präzision *f*.

pre·clude [prɪ'kluːd] ausschließen; *e-r Sache* vorbeugen; *j-n* hindern.

pre·co·cious □ [prɪ'kəʊʃəs] frühreif; altklug.

pre·con|ceived ['priːkən'siːvd] vorgefaßt (*Meinung*); **~cep·tion** [~'sepʃn] vorgefaßte Meinung.

pre·cur·sor [priː'kɜːsə] Vorläufer(in).

pred·a·to·ry ['predətərɪ] Raub...

pre·de·ces·sor ['priːdɪsesə] Vorgänger(in).

pre·des·ti·nate [priːˈdestɪneɪt] vorherbestimmen; **~tined** auserwählt, vorherbestimmt.

pre·de·ter·mine ['priːdɪˈtɜːmɪn] vorher festsetzen; vorherbestimmen.

pre·dic·a·ment [prɪˈdɪkəmənt] mißliche Lage, Zwangslage f.

pred·i·cate 1. ['predɪkeɪt] behaupten; gründen, basieren (on auf dat.); 2. gr. [~kət] Prädikat n, Satzaussage f.

pre·dict [prɪˈdɪkt] vorhersagen; **~·dic·tion** [~kʃn] Prophezeiung f.

pre·di·lec·tion [priːdɪˈlekʃn] Vorliebe f.

pre·dis·pose ['priːdɪˈspəʊz] j-n (im voraus) geneigt od. empfänglich machen (to für); **~·po·si·tion** [~pə-ˈzɪʃn]: ~ to Neigung f zu; bsd. ℱ Anfälligkeit f für.

pre·dom·i·nance [prɪˈdɒmɪnəns] Vorherrschaft f; Vormacht(stellung) f; fig. Übergewicht n; **~·nant** □ [~t] vorherrschend; **~·nate** [~eɪt] die Oberhand haben; vorherrschen.

pre·em·i·nent □ [priːˈemɪnənt] hervorragend.

pre·emp·tion [priːˈempʃn] Vorkauf(srecht n) m; **~·tive** [~tɪv] Vorkaufs...; ✕ Präventiv...

pre·ex·ist ['priːɪgˈzɪst] vorher dasein.

pre·fab F ['priːfæb] Fertighaus n.

pre·fab·ri·cate [ˈpriːˈfæbrɪkeɪt] vorfabrizieren.

pref·ace ['prefɪs] 1. Vorrede f, Vorwort n, Einleitung f; 2. einleiten.

pre·fect ['priːfekt] Präfekt m; Schule: Brt. Aufsichts-, Vertrauensschüler(in).

pre·fer [prɪˈfɜː] (-rr-) vorziehen, bevorzugen, lieber haben od. mögen od. tun; ℱ Klage einreichen; befördern.

pref·er·a·ble □ ['prefərəbl] (to) vorzuziehen(d) (dat.), besser (als); **~·ra·bly** [~lɪ] vorzugsweise, besser; **~·rence** [~əns] Vorliebe f; Vorzug m; **~·ren·tial** [prefəˈrenʃl] bevorzugt; Vorzugs...

pre·fer·ment [prɪˈfɜːmənt] Beförderung f.

pre·fix ['priːfɪks] Präfix n, Vorsilbe f.

preg·nan·cy ['pregnənsɪ] Schwangerschaft f; Trächtigkeit f (Tier); fig. Bedeutung(sgehalt m) f, Tragweite

f; **~t** □ [~t] schwanger; trächtig (Tier); fig. ideenreich; fig. bedeutungsvoll; △ nicht prägnant.

pre·judge ['priːˈdʒʌdʒ] im voraus od. vorschnell be- od. verurteilen.

prej·u·dice ['predʒʊdɪs] 1. Voreingenommenheit f, Vorurteil n; Nachteil m, Schaden m; 2. j-n (günstig od. ungünstig) beeinflussen, einnehmen (in favour of für; against gegen); benachteiligen; e-r Sache Abbruch tun; **~d** [predʒʊˈdɪʃl] nachteilig.

pre·lim·i·na·ry [prɪˈlɪmɪnərɪ] 1. □ vorläufig; einleitend; Vor...; 2. Einleitung f; Vorbereitung f.

prel·ude ['preljuːd] Vorspiel n.

pre·ma·ture □ [preməˈtjʊə] vorzeitig, verfrüht; fig. vorschnell.

pre·med·i·tate [priːˈmedɪteɪt] vorher überlegen; **~d** vorsätzlich; **~·ta·tion** [priːmedɪˈteɪʃn] Vorbedacht m.

prem·i·er ['premjə] 1. erste(r, -s); 2. Premierminister m.

prem·is·es ['premɪsɪz] pl. Grundstück n, Gebäude n od. pl., Anwesen n; Lokal n.

pre·mi·um ['priːmjəm] Prämie f; econ. Agio n; Versicherungsprämie f; at a ~ über pari; fig. sehr gefragt.

pre·mo·ni·tion [priːməˈnɪʃn] (Vor-) Warnung f; (Vor)Ahnung f.

pre·oc·cu·pied [priːˈɒkjʊpaɪd] gedankenverloren; **~·py** [~aɪ] ausschließlich beschäftigen; j-n (völlig) in Anspruch nehmen.

prep F [prep] = preparation, preparatory school.

prep·a·ra·tion [prepəˈreɪʃn] Vorbereitung f; Zubereitung f; **pre·par·a·to·ry** □ [prɪˈpærətərɪ] vorbereitend; ~ (school) Vor(bereitungs)schule f.

pre·pare [prɪˈpeə] v/t. vorbereiten; zurechtmachen; (zu)bereiten; (aus-) rüsten; v/i. sich vorbereiten, sich anschicken; **~d** □ bereit.

pre·pay ['priːˈpeɪ] (-paid) vorausbezahlen; frankieren.

pre·pon·der·ance [prɪˈpɒndərəns] Übergewicht n; **~·rant** [~t] überwiegend; **~·rate** [~reɪt] überwiegen.

prep·o·si·tion gr. [prepəˈzɪʃn] Präposition f, Verhältniswort n.

pre·pos·sess [priːpəˈzes] einnehmen; **~·ing** □ [~ɪŋ] einnehmend, anziehend.

pre·pos·ter·ous [prɪ'pɒstərəs] absurd; lächerlich, grotesk.

pre·req·ui·site ['pri:'rekwɪzɪt] Vorbedingung *f*, (Grund)Voraussetzung *f*.

pre·rog·a·tive [prɪ'rɒgətɪv] Vorrecht *n*.

pres·age ['presɪdʒ] **1.** (böses) Vorzeichen; (Vor)Ahnung *f*; **2.** (vorher) ankündigen; prophezeien.

pre·scribe [prɪ'skraɪb] vorschreiben; ✗ verschreiben.

pre·scrip·tion [prɪ'skrɪpʃn] Vorschrift *f*, Verordnung *f*; ✗ Rezept *n*.

pres·ence ['prezns] Gegenwart *f*, Anwesenheit *f*; ~ of mind Geistesgegenwart *f*.

pres·ent¹ ['preznt] **1.** ☐ gegenwärtig; anwesend, vorhanden; jetzig; laufend (*Jahr etc.*); vorliegend (*Fall etc.*); ~ tense *gr.* Präsens *n*, Gegenwart *f*; **2.** Gegenwart *f*, *gr.* a. Präsens *n*; Geschenk *n*; at ~ jetzt; for the ~ vorläufig.

pre·sent² [prɪ'zent] (dar)bieten; *thea., Film:* bringen, zeigen; *Rundfunk, TV:* bringen, moderieren; vorlegen, (-)zeigen; *j-n* ~ vorstellen; (über)reichen; (be)schenken.

pre·sen·ta·tion [prezən'teɪʃn] Schenkung *f*; Überreichung *f*; Geschenk *n*; Vorstellung *f* (*Person*); Schilderung *f*; *thea., Film:* Darbietung *f*; *Rundfunk, TV:* Moderation *f*; Einreichung (*Gesuch*); Vorlage *f*.

pres·ent-day ['preznt'deɪ] heutig, gegenwärtig, modern.

pre·sen·ti·ment [prɪ'zentɪmənt] Vorgefühl *n*, (*mst* böse Vor)Ahnung *f*.

pres·ent·ly ['prezntlɪ] bald (darauf); *Am.* zur Zeit, jetzt.

pres·er·va·tion [prezə'veɪʃn] Bewahrung *f*, Schutz *m*, Erhaltung *f* (*a. fig.*); Konservierung *f*; Einmachen *n*, -kochen *n*; **pre·ser·va·tive** [prɪ'zɜːvətɪv] **1.** bewahrend; konservierend; **2.** Konservierungsmittel *n*.

pre·serve [prɪ'zɜːv] **1.** bewahren, behüten; erhalten; einmachen; *Wild* hegen; **2.** *hunt.* Revier *n*, (Jagd-, Fisch)Gehege *n*; *fig.* Reich *n*; *mst* ~s *pl.* das Eingemachte.

pre·side [prɪ'zaɪd] den Vorsitz führen (at, over bei).

pres·i·den·cy ['prezɪdənsɪ] Vorsitz *m*; Präsidentschaft *f*; **~dent** [~t] Präsident(in); Vorsitzende(r *m*) *f*; Rektor *m*; *Am. econ.* Direktor *m*.

---

press [pres] **1.** Druck *m* (*a. fig.*); (Wein- *etc.*)Presse *f*; Druckerei *f*; Verlag *m*; Druck(en *n*) *m*; *a.* printing-~ Druckerpresse *f*; *die* Presse (*Zeitungswesen*); *bsd.* (Wäsche-) Schrank *m*; Bügeln *n*; Andrang *m*, (Menschen)Menge *f*; **2.** *v/t.* (aus-) pressen; (zusammen)drücken; drücken auf (*acc.*); *Kleider* plätten, bügeln; (be)drängen; bestehen auf (*dat.*); aufdrängen (*on dat.*); be ~ed for time es eilig haben; *v/i.* pressen, drücken; plätten, bügeln; (sich) drängen; ~ for dringen *od.* drängen auf (*acc.*), fordern; ~ on (zügig) weitermarchen; ~ **a·gen·cy** Nachrichtenbüro *n*, Presseagentur *f*; ~ **a·gent** Presseagent *m*; ~**but·ton** ✗ ['presbʌtn] Druckknopf *m*; ~**ing** ☐ [~ɪŋ] dringend; ~**but·ton** Druckknopf *m*; **pres·sure** [~ʃə] Druck *m* (*a. fig.*); Bedrängnis *f*, Belastung *f*.

pres·tige [pre'stiːʒ] Prestige *n*.

pre·su·ma·ble ☐ [prɪ'zjuːməbl] vermutlich; **~me** [~'zjuːm] *v/t.* annehmen, vermuten, voraussetzen; sich *et.* herausnehmen; *v/i.* sich erdreisten; anmaßend sein; ~ on, ~ upon ausnutzen *od.* mißbrauchen (*acc.*).

pre·sump·tion [prɪ'zʌmpʃn] Vermutung *f*; Wahrscheinlichkeit *f*; Anmaßung *f*; **~tive** ☐ [~tɪv] mutmaßlich; **~tu·ous** ☐ [~tjʊəs] überheblich; vermessen.

pre·sup·pose [priːsə'pəʊz] voraussetzen; **~po·si·tion** ['priːsʌpə'zɪʃn] Voraussetzung *f*.

pre·tence, *Am.* **-tense** [prɪ'tens] Vortäuschung *f*; Vorwand *m*; Schein *m*, Vorspiegelung *f*.

pre·tend [prɪ'tend] vorgeben; vortäuschen; heucheln; Anspruch erheben (to auf *acc.*); **~ed** ☐ angeblich.

pre·ten·sion [prɪ'tenʃn] Anspruch *m* (to auf *acc.*); Anmaßung *f*.

pre·ter·it(e) *gr.* ['pretərɪt] Präteritum *n*, erste Vergangenheit *f*.

pre·text ['priːtekst] Vorwand *m*.

pret·ty ['prɪtɪ] **1.** ☐ (-ier, -iest) hübsch, niedlich; nett; **2.** *adv.* ziemlich.

pre·vail [prɪ'veɪl] die Oberhand haben *od.* gewinnen; (vor)herrschen; maßgebend *od.* ausschlaggebend sein; ~ on *od.* upon s.o. to do s.th. j-n dazu bewegen, et. zu tun; **~ing** ☐ [~ɪŋ] (vor)herrschend.

prev·a·lent □ ['prevələnt] (vor)herrschend, weitverbreitet.

pre·var·i·cate [prɪ'værɪkeɪt] Ausflüchte machen.

pre|vent [prɪ'vent] verhindern, -hüten, e-r *Sache* vorbeugen; j-n hindern; **~·ven·tion** [~ʃn] Verhinderung f, Verhütung f; **~·ven·tive** □ [~tɪv] *bsd.* ✠ vorbeugend.

pre·view ['pri:vju:] Vorschau f; Vorbesichtigung f.

pre·vi·ous □ ['pri:vjəs] vorher-, vorausgehend, Vor...; voreilig; **~ to** bevor, vor (*dat.*); **~ knowledge** Vorkenntnisse *pl.*; **~·ly** [~lɪ] vorher, früher.

pre–war ['pri:'wɔː] Vorkriegs...

prey [preɪ] 1. Raub m, Beute f; *beast of* **~** Raubtier n; *bird of* **~** Raubvogel m; *be od. fall a* **~** *to* die Beute (*gen.*) werden; *fig.* geplagt werden von; 2. **~ on**, **~ upon** zo. Jagd machen auf (*acc.*), fressen (*acc.*); *fig.* berauben (*acc.*), ausplündern (*acc*); *fig.* ausbeuten (*acc.*); *fig.* nagen *od.* zehren an (*dat.*).

price [praɪs] 1. Preis m; Lohn m; 2. *Waren* auszeichnen; den Preis festsetzen für; *fig.* bewerten, schätzen; **~·less** [~lɪs] von unschätzbarem Wert, unbezahlbar.

prick [prɪk] 1. Stich m; V Schwanz m (*Penis*); **~s of conscience** Gewissensbisse *pl.*; 2. *v/t.* (durch)stechen; *fig.* peinigen; *a.* **~ out** *Muster* ausstechen; **~ up one's ears** die Ohren spitzen; *v/i.* stechen; **~·le** ['prɪkl] Stachel m, Dorn m; **~·ly** [~lɪ] (*-ier, -iest*) stach(e)lig.

pride [praɪd] 1. Stolz m; Hochmut m; *take* (*a*) **~** *in* stolz sein auf (*acc.*); 2. **~ o.s. on** *od.* **upon** stolz sein auf (*acc.*).

priest [pri:st] Priester m.

prig [prɪg] Tugendbold m, selbstgefälliger Mensch; Pedant m.

prim □ [prɪm] (*-mm-*) steif, prüde.

pri·ma|cy ['praɪməsɪ] Vorrang m; **~·ri·ly** [~rəlɪ] in erster Linie; **~·ry** □ [~rɪ] 1. ursprünglich; hauptsächlich; primär; elementar; höchst; Erst..., Ur..., Anfangs...; Haupt...; 2. *a.* **~ election** *Am. pol.* Vorwahl f; **~·ry school** *Brt.* Grundschule f.

prime [praɪm] 1. □ erste(r, -s), wichtigste(r, -s), Haupt...; erstklassig, vorzüglich; **~ cost** *econ.* Selbstkosten *pl.*; **~ minister** Premierminister m, Ministerpräsident m; **~ num-**

ber ℀ Primzahl f; **~ time** TV Hauptsendezeit f, beste Sendezeit; 2. *fig.* Blüte(zeit) f; *das* Beste, höchste Vollkommenheit; 3. *v/t.* vorbereiten; *Pumpe* anlassen; instruieren; *paint.* grundieren.

prim·er ['praɪmə] Fibel f, Elementarbuch n.

pri·m(a)e·val [praɪ'mi:vl] uranfänglich, Ur...

prim·i·tive □ ['prɪmɪtɪv] erste(r, -s), ursprünglich, Ur...; primitiv.

prim·rose ♣ ['prɪmrəʊz] Primel f.

prince [prɪns] Fürst m; Prinz m; **prin·cess** [prɪn'ses, *attr.* 'prɪnses] Fürstin f; Prinzessin f.

prin·ci·pal ['prɪnsəpl] 1. □ erste(r, -s), hauptsächlich, Haupt...; △ *nicht prinzipiell*; 2. Hauptperson f; Vorsteher m; (Schul)Direktor m, Rektor m; Chef(in) f; ✠ Haupttäter(in); *econ.* (Grund)Kapital n; **~·i·ty** [prɪnsɪ'pælɪtɪ] Fürstentum n.

prin·ci·ple ['prɪnsəpl] Prinzip n, Grundsatz m; *on* **~** grundsätzlich, aus Prinzip.

print [prɪnt] 1. *print.* Druck m (*a. Schriftart*); Druckbuchstaben *pl.*; (Finger- *etc.*)Abdruck m; bedruckter Kattun, Druckstoff m; (Stahl-, Kupfer)Stich m; *phot.* Abzug m; Drucksache f, *bsd. Am.* Zeitung f; *in* **~** gedruckt; *out of* **~** vergriffen; 2. (ab-, auf-, be)drucken; in Druckbuchstaben schreiben; *fig.* einprägen (*on dat.*); **~ (off od. out)** *phot.* abziehen, kopieren; **~ out** *Computer*: ausdrucken; **~·out** *Computer*: Ausdruck m; **~ed matter** ✉ Drucksache f; **~·er** ['prɪntə] (Buch- *etc.*)Drucker m.

print·ing ['prɪntɪŋ] Druck m; Drucken n; *phot.* Abziehen n, Kopieren n; **~·ink** Druckerschwärze f; **~–of·fice** (Buch)Druckerei f; **~–press** Druckerpresse f.

pri·or ['praɪə] 1. früher, älter (*to* als); 2. *adv.* **~ to** vor (*dat.*); 3. *eccl.* Prior m; **~·i·ty** [praɪ'ɒrɪtɪ] Priorität f; Vorrang m; *mot.* Vorfahrt(srecht n) f.

prise *bsd. Brt.* [praɪz] = *prize²*.

pris·m ['prɪzəm] Prisma n.

pris·on ['prɪzn] Gefängnis n; **~·er** [~ə] Gefangene(r m) f, Häftling m; *take s.o.* **~** j-n gefangennehmen.

pri·va·cy ['prɪvəsɪ] Zurückgezogenheit f; Privatleben n; Intim-, Privatsphäre f; Geheimhaltung f.

pri·vate ['praɪvɪt] **1.** ☐ privat, Privat...; persönlich; vertraulich; geheim; ~ **parts** pl.; **2.** ✕ gemeiner Soldat; in ~ privat, im Privatleben; unter vier Augen.

pri·va·tion [praɪ'veɪʃn] Not f, Entbehrung f.

priv·i·lege ['prɪvɪlɪdʒ] Privileg n; Vorrecht n; **~d** privilegiert.

priv·y ☐ ['prɪvɪ] (-ier, -iest): ~ to eingeweiht in (acc.); **♀ Council** Staatsrat m; **♀ Councillor** Geheimer Rat (Person); **♀ Seal** Geheimsiegel n.

prize¹ [praɪz] **1.** (Sieges)Preis m, Prämie f, Auszeichnung f; (Lotterie-) Gewinn m; **2.** preisgekrönt; Preis...; **~winner** Preisträger(in); **3.** (hoch-)schätzen.

prize², bsd. Brt. **prise** [praɪz] (auf-) stemmen; ~ **open** aufbrechen.

pro¹ [prəʊ] für; △ nicht pro = per.

pro² F [~] Sport: Profi m.

pro- [prəʊ] (eintreten) für, pro..., ...freundlich.

prob·a·bil·i·ty [prɒbə'bɪlətɪ] Wahrscheinlichkeit f; **~ble** ☐ ['prɒbəbl] wahrscheinlich.

pro·ba·tion [prə'beɪʃn] Probe f, Probezeit f; **♣** Bewährung(sfrist) f; ~ **officer** Bewährungshelfer(in).

probe [prəʊb] **1.** ♣, ⊕ Sonde f; fig. Sondierung f; △ nicht Probe; lunar ~ Mondsonde f; **2.** sondieren; untersuchen; △ nicht proben, probieren.

prob·lem ['prɒbləm] Problem n; ♠ Aufgabe f; **~at·ic** [prɒblə'mætɪk] (~ally), **~at·i·cal** ☐ [~kl] problematisch, zweifelhaft.

pro·ce·dure [prə'siːdʒə] Verfahren n; Handlungsweise f.

pro·ceed [prə'siːd] weitergehen (a. fig.); sich begeben (to nach); fortfahren; vor sich gehen; vorgehen; Brt. univ. promovieren; ~ **from** kommen od. ausgehen od. herrühren von; ~ **to** schreiten od. übergehen zu, sich machen an (acc.); **~ing** [~ɪŋ] Vorgehen n; Handlung f; **~s** pl. ♣ Verfahren n, (Gerichts)Verhandlung(en pl.) f; (Tätigkeits)Bericht m; **~s** ['prəʊsiːdz] pl. Erlös m, Ertrag m, Gewinn m.

pro·cess ['prəʊses] **1.** Fortschreiten n, Fortgang m; Vorgang m; Verlauf m (der Zeit); Prozeß m, Verfahren n; △ nicht ♣ Prozeß; in ~ im Gange; in ~ of construction im Bau (befindlich); **2.** ⊕ bearbeiten; ♣ gerichtlich be-

langen; △ nicht prozessieren; **~·ces·sion** [prə'seʃn] Prozession f; **~·ces·sor** ['prəʊsesə] Prozessor m.

pro·claim [prə'kleɪm] proklamieren, erklären, ausrufen.

proc·la·ma·tion [prɒklə'meɪʃn] Proklamation f, Bekanntmachung f; Erklärung f.

pro·cliv·i·ty fig. [prə'klɪvətɪ] Neigung f.

pro·cras·ti·nate [prəʊ'kræstɪneɪt] zaudern.

pro·cre·ate ['prəʊkrɪeɪt] (er)zeugen.

proc·u·ra·tor ♣ ['prɒkjʊəreɪtə] Bevollmächtigte(r) m.

pro·cure [prə'kjʊə] v/t. be-, verschaffen; v/i. Kuppelei betreiben.

prod [prɒd] **1.** Stich m, Stoß m; fig. Ansporn m; **2.** (-dd-) stechen, stoßen; fig. anstacheln, anspornen.

prod·i·gal ['prɒdɪgl] **1.** ☐ verschwenderisch; the ~ son der verlorene Sohn; **2.** Verschwender(in).

pro·di·gious ☐ [prə'dɪdʒəs] erstaunlich, ungeheuer; **prod·i·gy** ['prɒdɪdʒɪ] Wunder n (Sache od. Person); child od. infant ~ Wunderkind n.

pro·duce¹ ['prɒdjuːs] (Natur)Erzeugnis(se pl.) n, (Landes)Produkte pl.; Ertrag m; ⊕ Leistung f, Ausstoß m.

pro·duce² [prə'djuːs] produzieren, erzeugen, herstellen; hervorbringen; Zinsen etc. (ein)bringen; heraus-, hervorziehen; (vor)zeigen; Beweis etc. beibringen; Gründe vorbringen; ♠ Linie verlängern; Film produzieren; fig. hervorrufen, erzielen; **~·duc·er** [~ə] Erzeuger(in), Hersteller(in); Film, TV: Produzent(in); thea., Rundfunk: Brt. Regisseur(in).

prod·uct ['prɒdʌkt] Produkt n, Erzeugnis n.

pro·duc·tion [prə'dʌkʃn] Produktion f; Erzeugung f, Herstellung f; Erzeugnis n; Hervorbringen n; Vorlegung f, Beibringung f; thea. etc. Inszenierung f; **~·tive** ☐ [~ɪv] produktiv; ertragreich, fruchtbar; schöpferisch; **~·tive·ness** [~nɪs], **~·tiv·i·ty** [prɒdʌk'tɪvətɪ] Produktivität f.

prof F [prɒf] Professor m.

pro·fa·na·tion [prɒfə'neɪʃn] Entweihung f; **~·fane** [prə'feɪn] **1.** ☐ profan, weltlich; gottlos, lästerlich; **2.** entweihen; **~·fan·i·ty** [~'fænətɪ] Gottlosigkeit f; Fluchen n.

P

pro·fess [prə'fes] (sich) bekennen (zu); erklären; beteuern; *Reue etc.* bekunden; *Beruf* ausüben; lehren; **~fessed** □ erklärt; angeblich; Berufs...; **~fes·sion** [~ʃn] Bekenntnis *n*; Erklärung *f*; Beruf *m*; **~fes·sion·al** [~nl] **1.** □ Berufs...; Amts...; professionell; beruflich; fachmännisch; freiberuflich; **~** man Akademiker *m*; **2.** Fachmann *m*; *Sport*: Berufsspieler(in), -sportler(in), Profi *m*; Berufskünstler(in); **~fes·sor** [~sə] Professor(in); *Am.* Dozent(in).

prof·fer ['prɒfə] **1.** anbieten; **2.** Anerbieten *n*.

pro·fi·cien·cy [prə'fɪʃənsɪ] Tüchtigkeit *f*; **~t** [~t] □ tüchtig; bewandert.

pro·file ['prəʊfaɪl] Profil *n*.

prof·it ['prɒfɪt] **1.** Gewinn *m*, Profit *m*; Vorteil *m*, Nutzen *m*; **2.** *v/t.* j-m nützen; *v/i.* **~** from od. by Nutzen ziehen aus; **~i·ta·ble** [~əbl] nützlich; vorteilhaft; gewinnbringend, einträglich; **~i·teer** [prɒfɪ'tɪə] **1.** Schiebergeschäfte machen; **2.** Profitmacher *m*, Schieber *m*; **~it·shar·ing** ['prɒfɪt∫eərɪŋ] Gewinnbeteiligung *f*.

prof·li·gate ['prɒflɪgət] lasterhaft; verschwenderisch.

pro·found □ [prə'faʊnd] tief; tiefgründig, gründlich, profund.

pro·fuse □ [prə'fju:s] verschwenderisch; (über)reich; **~fu·sion** *fig.* [~ʒn] Überfluß *m*, (Über)Fülle *f*.

pro·gen·i·tor [prəʊ'dʒenɪtə] Vorfahr *m*, Ahn *m*; **prog·e·ny** ['prɒdʒənɪ] Nachkommen(schaft *f*) *pl.*; *zo.* Brut *f*.

prog·no·sis ⚕ [prɒg'nəʊsɪs] (*pl.* -ses [~si:z]) Prognose *f*.

prog·nos·ti·ca·tion [prəgnɒstɪ'keɪʃn] Vorhersage *f*.

pro·gram ['prəʊgræm] **1.** *Computer*: Programm *n*; *Am.* = *Brt.* programme **1**; **2.** (-mm-) *Computer*: programmieren; *Am.* = *Brt.* programme **2**; **~er** [~ə] = programmer.

pro·gramme, *Am.* **-gram** ['prəʊgræm] **1.** Programm *n*; *Rundfunk, TV*: *a.* Sendung *f*; **2.** (vor)programmieren; planen; **~gram·mer** [~ə] *Computer*: Programmierer(in).

pro·gress 1. ['prəʊgres] Fortschritt(e *pl.*) *m*; Vorrücken *n* (*a.* ✗); Fortgang *m*; *in* **~** im Gang; **2.** [prə'gres] fortschreiten; **~gres·sion** [~ʃn] Fort-

schreiten *n*; Weiterentwicklung *f*; ✗ Reihe *f*; **~gres·sive** [~sɪv] **1.** □ fortschreitend; fortschrittlich; **2.** *pol.* Progressive(r *m*) *f*.

pro·hib·it [prə'hɪbɪt] verbieten; verhindern; **~hi·bi·tion** [prəʊɪ'bɪʃn] Verbot *n*; Prohibition *f*; **~hi·bi·tion·ist** [~ʃənɪst] Prohibitionist *m*; **~hib·i·tive** □ [prə'hɪbɪtɪv] verbietend; Schutz...; unerschwinglich (*Preis*).

proj·ect[1] ['prɒdʒekt] Projekt *n*; Vorhaben *n*, Plan *m*.

pro·ject[2] [prə'dʒekt] *v/t.* planen, entwerfen; werfen, schleudern; projizieren; *v/i.* vorspringen, -ragen; **~jec·tile** [~aɪl] Projektil *n*, Geschoß *n*; **~jec·tion** [~kʃn] Werfen *n*; Entwurf *m*; Vorsprung *m*, vorspringender Teil *m*; *phot.* Projektion *f*; **~jec·tor** [~tə] Projektor *m*.

pro·le·tar·i·an [prəʊlɪ'teərɪən] **1.** proletarisch; **2.** Proletarier *m*.

pro·lif·ic [prə'lɪfɪk] (**~ally**) fruchtbar.

pro·logue, *Am. a.* **-log** ['prəʊlɒg] Prolog *m*.

pro·long [prə'lɒŋ] verlängern.

prom·e·nade [prɒmə'nɑ:d] **1.** (Strand)Promenade *f*; **2.** promenieren.

prom·i·nent □ ['prɒmɪnənt] vorstehend, hervorragend (*a. fig.*); *fig.* prominent.

pro·mis·cu·ous □ [prə'mɪskjʊəs] unordentlich, verworren; sexuell freizügig.

prom·ise ['prɒmɪs] **1.** Versprechen *n*; *fig.* Aussicht *f*; **2.** versprechen; **~is·ing** □ [~ɪŋ] vielversprechend; **~is·so·ry** [~ərɪ] versprechend; **~** note *econ.* Eigenwechsel *m*.

prom·on·to·ry ['prɒməntrɪ] Vorgebirge *n*.

pro·mote [prə'məʊt] *et.* fördern; *j-n* befördern; *Am. Schule*: versetzen; *parl.* unterstützen; *econ.* gründen; *Verkauf durch Werbung* steigern; *econ.* werben für; *Boxkampf etc.* veranstalten; **~mot·er** [~ə] Förderer *m*, Befürworter *m*; *Sport*: Veranstalter *m*; **~mo·tion** [~əʊʃn] Förderung *f*; Beförderung *f*; *econ.* Gründung *f*; *econ.* Verkaufsförderung *f*, Werbung *f*; ⚕ incl. Promotion.

prompt [prɒmpt] **1.** □ umgehend, unverzüglich, sofortig; bereit(willig); pünktlich; **2.** *j-n* veranlassen; *Gedanken* eingeben; *j-m* vorsagen, soufflieren; **~er** ['prɒmptə] Souffleu|r *m*, -se *f*; **~ness** [~nɪs] Schnelligkeit *f*; Bereitschaft *f*.

prom·ul·gate ['prɒməlgeɪt] verkünden; verbreiten.

prone □ [prəʊn] *(~r, ~st)* mit dem Gesicht nach unten (liegend); hingestreckt; *be ~ to fig.* neigen zu.

prong [prɒŋ] Zinke *f*; Spitze *f*.

pro·noun *gr.* ['prəʊnaʊn] Pronomen *n*, Fürwort *n*.

pro·nounce [prə'naʊns] aussprechen; verkünden; erklären für.

pron·to F ['prɒntəʊ] fix, schnell.

pro·nun·ci·a·tion [prənʌnsɪ'eɪʃn] Aussprache *f*.

proof [pru:f] **1.** Beweis *m*; Probe *f*; *print.* Korrekturfahne *f*, -bogen *m*; *print.*, *phot.* Probeabzug *m*; **2.** fest; *in Zssgn:* ...fest, ...widrig, ...dicht, ...sicher; **~read** ['pru:fri:d] *(-read [-red])* Korrektur lesen; **~read·er** Korrektor *m*.

prop [prɒp] **1.** Stütze *f* (*a. fig.*); **2.** *(-pp-) a. ~ up* stützen; *sich, et.* lehnen *(against* gegen).

prop·a·gate ['prɒpəgeɪt] (sich) fortpflanzen; verbreiten; **~ga·tion** [prɒpə'geɪʃn] Fortpflanzung *f*; Verbreitung *f*.

pro·pel [prə'pel] *(-ll-)* (vorwärts-, an)treiben; **~ler** [~ə] Propeller *m*, (Schiffs-, Luft)Schraube *f*; **~ling pen·cil** [~ɪŋ'pensl] Drehbleistift *m*.

pro·pen·si·ty *fig.* [prə'pensətɪ] Neigung *f*.

prop·er □ ['prɒpə] eigen(tümlich); passend; richtig; anständig, korrekt; zuständig; *bsd. Brt.* F ordentlich, tüchtig, gehörig; Eigen...; *~ name* Eigenname *m*; **~ty** [~tɪ] Eigentum *n*, Besitz *m*; Vermögen *n*; Eigenschaft *f*.

proph·e·cy ['prɒfɪsɪ] Prophezeiung *f*; **~sy** [~saɪ] prophezeien, weissagen.

proph·et ['prɒfɪt] Prophet *m*.

pro·pi·ti·ate [prə'pɪʃɪeɪt] günstig stimmen, versöhnen; **~tious** □ [~ʃəs] gnädig; günstig.

pro·por·tion [prə'pɔ:ʃn] **1.** Verhältnis *n*; Gleichmaß *n*; (An)Teil *m*; **~s** *pl.* (Aus)Maße *pl.*; **2.** in das richtige Verhältnis bringen; **~al** □ [~l] proportional; **= ~ate** □ [~nət] im richtigen Verhältnis *(to* zu) angemessen.

pro·pos·al [prə'pəʊzl] Vorschlag *m*, *(a.* Heirats)Antrag *m*; Angebot *n*; **~e**

[~z] *v/t.* vorschlagen; beabsichtigen, vorhaben; e-n Toast ausbringen auf *(acc.)*; *~ s.o.'s health* auf j-s Gesundheit trinken; *v/i.* e-n Heiratsantrag machen *(to dat)*; **prop·o·si·tion** [prɒpə'zɪʃn] Vorschlag *m*, Antrag *m*; *econ.* Angebot *n*; Behauptung *f*.

pro·pound [prə'paʊnd] *Frage etc.* vorlegen; vorschlagen.

pro·pri·e·ta·ry [prə'praɪətərɪ] Eigentümer..., Besitzer...; Eigentums...; *econ.* gesetzlich geschützt *(Arznei, Ware)*; **~tor** [~ə] Eigentümer *m*, Geschäftsinhaber *m*; **~ty** [~ɪ] Richtigkeit *f*; Schicklichkeit *f*, Anstand *m*; *the proprieties pl.* die Anstandsformen *pl.*

pro·pul·sion ⊕ [prə'pʌlʃn] Antrieb *m.*

pro·rate *Am.* [prəʊ'reɪt] anteilmäßig auf- od. verteilen.

pro·sa·ic *fig.* [prəʊ'zeɪk] *(~ally)* prosaisch, nüchtern, trocken.

prose [prəʊz] Prosa *f*.

pros·e·cute ['prɒsɪkju:t] *(a.* strafrechtlich) verfolgen; *Gewerbe etc.* betreiben; ⚖ anklagen *(for* wegen); **~cu·tion** [prɒsɪ'kju:ʃn] Durchführung *f (e-s Plans etc.)*; Betreiben *n (e-s Gewerbes etc.)*; ⚖ Strafverfolgung *f*, Anklage *f*; **~cu·tor** ⚖ ['prɒsɪkju:tə] Ankläger *m*; *public ~* Staatsanwalt *m*.

pros·pect 1. ['prɒspekt] Aussicht *f (a. fig.)*; *econ.* Interessent *m*; △ *nicht* Prospekt; **2.** [prə'spekt]: *~ for* ⚒ schürfen nach; bohren nach *(Öl).*

pro·spec·tive □ [prə'spektɪv] (zu-)künftig, voraussichtlich.

pro·spec·tus [prə'spektəs] *(pl. -tuses)* (Werbe)Prospekt *m.*

pros·per ['prɒspə] *v/i.* Erfolg haben; gedeihen, blühen; *v/t.* begünstigen; segnen; **~i·ty** [prɒ'sperətɪ] Gedeihen *n*, Wohlstand *m*, Glück *n*; *econ.* Wohlstand *m*, Konjunktur *f*, Blüte (-zeit) *f*; **~ous** □ ['prɒspərəs] erfolgreich, blühend; wohlhabend; günstig.

pros·ti·tute ['prɒstɪtju:t] Prostituierte *f*, Dirne *f*; *male ~* Strichjunge *m.*

pros·trate 1. ['prɒstreɪt] hingestreckt; erschöpft; daniederliegend; demütig; gebrochen; **2.** [prɒ'streɪt] niederwerfen; erschöpfen; *fig.* niederschmettern; **~tra·tion** [~ʃn] Niederwerfen *n*, Fußfall *m*; Erschöpfung *f.*

pros·y *fig.* ['prəʊzɪ] (-ier, -iest) prosaisch; langweilig.

pro·tag·o·nist [prəʊ'tægənɪst] *thea.* Hauptfigur *f*; *fig.* Vorkämpfer(in).

pro|tect [prə'tekt] (be)schützen; **~·tec·tion** [ˌkʃn] Schutz *m*; ᵗᵗ (Rechts)Schutz *m*; *econ.* Schutzzoll *m*; △ *nicht* Protektion; **~·tec·tive** [ˌtɪv] (be)schützend; Schutz...; ~ *duty* Schutzzoll *m*; **~·tec·tor** [ˌə] (Be)Schützer *m*; Schutz-, Schirmherr *m*; **~·tec·tor·ate** [ˌərət] Protektorat *n*.

pro·test 1. ['prəʊtest] Protest *m*; Einspruch *m*; **2.** [prə'test] *v/i.* protestieren (*against* gegen); *v/t. Am.* protestieren gegen; beteuern.

Prot·es·tant ['prɒtɪstənt] **1.** protestantisch; **2.** Protestant(in).

prot·es·ta·tion [prɒte'steɪʃn] Beteuerung *f*; Protest *m* (*against* gegen).

pro·to·col ['prəʊtəkɒl] **1.** Protokoll *n*; **2.** (-ll-) protokollieren.

pro·to·type ['prəʊtətaɪp] Prototyp *m*, Urbild *n*.

pro·tract [prə'trækt] in die Länge ziehen, hinziehen.

pro|trude [prə'truːd] heraus-, (her)vorstehen, -ragen, -treten; herausstrecken; **~·tru·sion** [ˌʒn] Herausragen *n*, (Her)Vorstehen *n*, Hervortreten *n*.

pro·tu·ber·ance [prə'tjuːbərəns] Auswuchs *m*, Beule *f*.

proud □ [praʊd] stolz (*of* auf *acc.*).

prove [pruːv] (proved, proved *od.* bsd. Am. proven) *v/t.* be-, er-, nachweisen; prüfen; *v/i.* sich herausstellen *od.* erweisen (als); ausfallen; **prov·en** ['pruːvən] **1.** Am. *p.p. von* prove; **2.** be-, erwiesen; bewährt.

prov·e·nance ['prɒvənəns] Herkunft *f*.

prov·erb ['prɒvɜːb] Sprichwort *n*.

pro·vide [prə'vaɪd] *v/t.* besorgen, beschaffen, liefern; bereitstellen; versorgen, ausstatten; ᵗᵗ vorsehen, festsetzen; *v/i.* (vor)sorgen, **~d** (*that*) vorausgesetzt, daß; sofern.

prov·i·dence ['prɒvɪdəns] Vorsehung *f*; Voraussicht *f*, Vorsorge *f*; **~·dent** □ [ˌt] vorausblickend, vorsorglich; haushälterisch; **~·den·tial** □ [prɒvɪ'denʃl] durch die (göttliche) Vorsehung bewirkt; glücklich, günstig.

pro·vid·er [prə'vaɪdə] Ernährer *m*

(*der Familie*); *econ.* Lieferant *m*.

prov·ince ['prɒvɪns] Provinz *f*; *fig.* Gebiet *n*; *fig.* Fach *n*, Aufgabenbereich *m*; **pro·vin·cial** [prə'vɪnʃl] **1.** □ Provinz..., provinziell; kleinstädtisch; **2.** Provinzbewohner(in).

pro·vi·sion [prə'vɪʒn] Beschaffung *f*; Vorsorge *f*; ᵗᵗ Bestimmung *f*; Vorkehrung *f*, Maßnahme *f*; **~s** *pl.* (Lebensmittel)Vorrat *m*, Proviant *m*, Lebensmittel *pl.*; △ *nicht* Provision; **~·al** □ [ˌl] provisorisch.

pro·vi·so [prə'vaɪzəʊ] (*pl.* -sos, Am. *a.* -soes) Bedingung *f*, Vorbehalt *m*.

prov·o·ca·tion [prɒvə'keɪʃn] Herausforderung *f*; **pro·voc·a·tive** [prə'vɒkətɪv] herausfordernd; aufreizend.

pro·voke [prə'vəʊk] reizen; herausfordern; provozieren.

prov·ost ['prɒvəst] Rektor *m* (*gewisser Colleges*); *schott.* Bürgermeister *m*; ✕ [prə'vəʊ]: ~ *marshal* Kommandeur *m* der Militärpolizei.

prow ♣ [praʊ] Bug *m*.

prow·ess ['praʊɪs] Tapferkeit *f*.

prowl [praʊl] **1.** *v/i. a.* ~ *about*, ~ *around* herumstreichen; *v/t.* durchstreifen; **2.** Herumstreifen *n*; **~ car** Am. ['praʊlkɑː] (Funk)Streifenwagen *m*.

prox·im·i·ty [prɒk'sɪmətɪ] Nähe *f*.

prox·y ['prɒksɪ] (Stell)Vertreter(in); (Stell)Vertretung *f*, Vollmacht *f*; *by* ~ in Vertretung.

prude [pruːd] prüder Mensch; *be a* ~ prüde sein.

pru|dence ['pruːdns] Klugheit *f*, Vernunft *f*; Vorsicht *f*; **~·dent** □ [ˌt] klug, vernünftig; vorsichtig.

prud·er·y ['pruːdərɪ] Prüderie *f*; **~·ish** □ [ˌɪʃ] prüde, spröde.

prune [pruːn] **1.** Backpflaume *f*; **2.** ✄ beschneiden (*a. fig.*); *a.* ~ *away*, ~ *off* wegschneiden.

pru·ri·ent □ ['prʊərɪənt] geil, lüstern.

pry¹ [praɪ] neugierig gucken *od.* sein; ~ *about* herumschnüffeln; ~ *into* s-e Nase stecken in (*acc.*).

pry² [ˌ] = *prize²*.

psalm [sɑːm] Psalm *m*.

pseu·do- ['psjuːdəʊ] Pseudo..., falsch.

pseu·do·nym ['psjuːdənɪm] Pseudonym *n*, Deckname *m*.

psy·chi·a·trist [saɪ'kaɪətrɪst] Psychiater *m*; **~·try** [ˌɪ] Psychiatrie *f*.

psy·chic ['saɪkɪk] (~ally), ~·**chi·cal** □ [~kl] psychisch, seelisch.

psy·cho·log·i·cal □ [saɪkə'lɒdʒɪkl] psychologisch; ~·**chol·o·gist** [saɪ'kɒlədʒɪst] Psychologe m, -in f; ~·**chol·o·gy** □ [~dʒɪ] Psychologie f.

pub Brt. F [pʌb] Pub n, Kneipe f.

pu·ber·ty ['pju:bətɪ] Pubertät f.

pu·bic anat. ['pju:bɪk] Scham...; ~ **bone** Schambein n; ~ **hair** Schamhaare pl.

pub·lic ['pʌblɪk] **1.** □ öffentlich; staatlich, Staats...; allgemein bekannt; ~ **spirit** Gemein-, Bürgersinn m; **2.** Öffentlichkeit f; die Öffentlichkeit, das Publikum, die Leute; △ nicht Publikum = audience.

pub·li·can bsd. Brt. ['pʌblɪkən] Gastwirt m.

pub·li·ca·tion [pʌblɪ'keɪʃn] Bekanntmachung f; Veröffentlichung f; Verlagswerk n; monthly ~ Monatsschrift f.

pub·lic con·ve·ni·ence Brt. ['pʌblɪk kən'vi:njəns] öffentliche Bedürfnisanstalt; ~ **health** öffentliches Gesundheitswesen; ~ **hol·i·day** gesetzlicher Feiertag; ~ **house** Brt. s. pub.

pub·lic·i·ty [pʌb'lɪsətɪ] Öffentlichkeit f; Reklame f, Werbung f.

pub·lic li·bra·ry ['pʌblɪk 'laɪbrərɪ] Leihbücherei f; ~ **re·la·tions** pl. Public Relations pl., Öffentlichkeitsarbeit f; ~ **school** Brt. Public School f (exklusives Internat); Am. staatliche Schule.

pub·lish ['pʌblɪʃ] bekanntmachen, veröffentlichen; Buch etc. herausgeben, verlegen; ~**ing house** Verlag m; ~**er** F Herausgeber m; Verleger m; ~**s** pl. Verlag(sanstalt f) m.

puck·er ['pʌkə] **1.** kleine Falte; **2.** a. ~ **up** Lippen, Mund: (sich) verziehen od. spitzen; Stirn: (sich) runzeln; Falten bilden in (dat.) od. werfen.

pud·ding ['pʊdɪŋ] Pudding m; (feste) Süßspeise, Nachspeise f, -tisch m; (Art) Fleischpastete f; black ~ Blutwurst f; white ~ Preßsack m.

pud·dle ['pʌdl] Pfütze f.

pu·er·ile ['pjʊəraɪl] kindisch.

puff [pʌf] **1.** kurzer Atemzug, Schnaufer m; leichter Windstoß, Hauch m; Zug m (beim Rauchen); (Dampf-, Rauch)Wölkchen n; (Puder)Quaste f; **2.** (auf)blasen, pusten, paffen; schnauben, schnaufen, keuchen; ~ **out**, ~ **up** sich (auf)blähen;

~**ed eyes** geschwollene Augen; ~**ed sleeve** Puffärmel m; ~ **pas·try** ['pʌf 'peɪstrɪ] Blätterteiggebäck n; ~·**y** [~ɪ] (-ier, -iest) böig; kurzatmig; geschwollen; aufgedunsen; bauschig.

pug zo. [pʌg] a. ~**-dog** Mops m.

pug·na·cious □ [pʌg'neɪʃəs] kampflustig; streitsüchtig.

pug-nose ['pʌgnəʊz] Stupsnase f.

puke sl. [pju:k] (aus)kotzen.

pull [pʊl] **1.** Ziehen n, Zerren n; Zug m; Ruck m; print. Fahne f, (Probe-) Abzug m; Ruderpartie f; Griff m; Zug m (at an e-r Zigarette etc.); Schluck m (at aus e-r Flasche); fig. Einfluß m; Beziehungen pl., Vorteil m; **2.** ziehen; zerren; reißen; zupfen; pflücken; rudern; ~ **about** herumzerren; ~ **ahead of** vorbeiziehen an (dat.), überholen (acc.) (Auto etc.); ~ **away** anfahren (Bus etc.); sich losreißen (from von); ~ **down** niederreißen; ~ **in** einfahren (Zug); anhalten (Fahrzeug, Boot); ~ **off** F zustande bringen, schaffen; ~ **out** herausfahren (of aus), abfahren (Zug etc.); ausscheren (Fahrzeug); fig. sich zurückziehen, aussteigen; ~ **over** (s-n Wagen) an die od. zur Seite fahren; ~ **round** Kranken durchbringen; durchkommen (Kranker); ~ **through** j-n durchbringen; ~ **o.s. together** sich zusammennehmen, sich zusammenreißen; ~ **up** Fahrzeug, Pferd anhalten; (an)halten; ~ **up with**, ~ **up to** j-n einholen.

pul·ley ⊕ ['pʊlɪ] Rolle f; Flaschenzug m; Riemenscheibe f.

pull-in Brt. ['pʊlɪn] Raststätte (bsd. a. für Fernfahrer); ~-**o·ver** Pullover m; ~-**up** Brt. = pull-in.

pulp [pʌlp] Brei m; Fruchtfleisch n; ⊕ Papierbrei m; ~ **magazine** Schundblatt n.

pul·pit ['pʊlpɪt] Kanzel f.

pulp·y □ ['pʌlpɪ] (-ier, -iest) breiig; fleischig.

pul·sate [pʌl'seɪt] pulsieren, schlagen; **pulse** [pʌls] Puls(schlag) m.

pul·ver·ize ['pʌlvəraɪz] v/t. pulverisieren; v/i. zu Staub werden.

pum·mel ['pʌml] (bsd. Brt. -ll-, Am. -l-) mit den Fäusten bearbeiten, verprügeln.

pump [pʌmp] **1.** Pumpe f; Pumps m; **2.** pumpen; F j-n aushorchen, -fragen; ~ **up** Reifen etc. aufpumpen; ~ **at·tend·ant** Tankwart m.

P

pump·kin ♀ ['pʌmpkɪn] Kürbis *m*.

pun [pʌn] 1. Wortspiel *n*; 2. (-*nn*-) ein Wortspiel machen.

Punch¹ [pʌntʃ] Kasperle *n*, *m*; ~-*and-Judy show* Kasperletheater *n*.

punch² [~] 1. Locheisen *n*; Locher *m*; Lochzange *f*; (Faust)Schlag *m*; Punsch *m*; 2. (aus)stanzen; lochen; aufnehmen (*auf Lochkarten*); *bsd.* *Am.* Kontrolluhr stechen, Karte stempeln; schlagen (*mit der Faust*), boxen; (ein)hämmern auf (*acc.*); *Am.* Rinder treiben; ~(*ed*) *card* Lochkarte *f*; ~(*ed*) *tape* Lochstreifen *m*.

punc·til·i·ous □ [pʌŋk'tɪlɪəs] peinlich genau; (übertrieben) förmlich.

punc·tu·al □ ['pʌŋktjʊəl] pünktlich; ~**i·ty** [pʌŋktjʊ'ælətɪ] Pünktlichkeit *f*.

punc·tu·ate *gr.* ['pʌŋktjʊeɪt] interpunktieren; ~**a·tion** *gr.* [pʌŋktjʊ'eɪʃn] Interpunktion *f*, Zeichensetzung *f*; ~ *mark* Satzzeichen *n*.

punc·ture ['pʌŋktʃə] 1. (Ein)Stich *m*, Loch *n*; Reifenpanne *f*; 2. durchstechen; ein Loch machen in (*dat. od. acc.*); platzen (*Ballon*); *mot.* e-n Platten haben.

pun·gen·cy ['pʌndʒənsɪ] Schärfe *f*; ~**t** [~t] stechend, beißend, scharf.

pun·ish ['pʌnɪʃ] (be)strafen; ~**a·ble** □ [~əbl] strafbar; ~**ment** [~mənt] Strafe *f*; Bestrafung *f*.

punk [pʌŋk] *sl.* kleiner *od.* junger Ganove; Punk *m* (*a.* ♪), Punker *m*; ~ *rock*(*er*) ♪ Punkrock(er) *m*.

pu·ny □ ['pju:nɪ] (-*ier*, -*iest*) winzig; schwächlich.

pup *zo.* [pʌp] Welpe *m*, junger Hund.

pu·pa *zo.* ['pju:pə] (*pl.* -*pae* [-pi:], -*pas*) Puppe *f*.

pu·pil ['pju:pl] *anat.* Pupille *f*; Schüler(in); Mündel *m*, *n*.

pup·pet ['pʌpɪt] Marionette *f* (*a. fig.*); △ *nicht Puppe = doll*; ~**show** Puppenspiel *n*.

pup·py ['pʌpɪ] *zo.* Welpe *m*, junger Hund; *fig.* Schnösel *m*.

pur·chase ['pɜːtʃəs] 1. (An-, Ein)Kauf *m*; *tₜ* Erwerb(ung *f*) *m*; Anschaffung *f*; ⊕ Hebevorrichtung *f*; Halt *m*; *make* ~*s* Einkäufe machen; 2. (er)kaufen; *tₜ* erwerben; ⊕ hochwinden; ~**chas·er** [~ə] Käufer(in).

pure □ [pjʊə] (~*r*, ~*st*) rein; pur; ~**bred** ['pjʊəbred] reinrassig.

pur·ga·tive *‰* ['pɜːgətɪv] 1. abführend; 2. Abführmittel *n*; ~**to·ry** [~ərɪ] Fegefeuer *n*.

purge [pɜːdʒ] 1. *‰* Abführmittel *n*; *pol.* Säuberung *f*; 2. *mst fig.* reinigen; *pol.* säubern; *‰* abführen.

pu·ri·fy ['pjʊərɪfaɪ] reinigen; läutern.

pu·ri·tan ['pjʊərɪtən] (*hist.* ♀) 1. Puritaner(in); 2. puritanisch.

pu·ri·ty ['pjʊərətɪ] Reinheit *f* (*a. fig.*).

purl [pɜːl] murmeln (*Bach*).

pur·lieus ['pɜːljuːz] *pl.* Umgebung *f*.

pur·loin [pɜːˈlɔɪn] entwenden.

pur·ple ['pɜːpl] 1. purpurn, purpurrot; 2. Purpur *m*; 3. (sich) purpurn färben.

pur·port ['pɜːpət] 1. Sinn *m*, Inhalt *m*; 2. behaupten, vorgeben.

pur·pose ['pɜːpəs] 1. Absicht *f*, Vorhaben *n*; Zweck *m*; Entschlußkraft *f*; *for the* ~ *of* ger. um zu *inf.*; *on* ~ absichtlich; *to the* ~ zweckdienlich; *to no* ~ vergebens; 2. beabsichtigen, vorhaben; ~**ful** □ [~fl] zweckmäßig; absichtlich; zielbewußt; ~**less** □ [~lɪs] zwecklos; ziellos; ~**ly** [~lɪ] absichtlich.

purr [pɜː] schnurren (*Katze*); summen (*Motor*).

purse [pɜːs] 1. Geldbeutel *m*, -börse *f*; *Am.* (Damen)Handtasche *f*; Geldgeschenk *n*; Siegprämie *f*; Boxen: Börse *f*; ~ *snatcher Am.* Handtaschenräuber *m*; 2. ~ (*up*) *one's lips* die Lippen schürzen.

pur·su·ance [pəˈsjuːəns]: *in* (*the*) ~ *of* bei der Ausführung *od.* Ausübung (*gen.*); ~**ant** □ [~t]: ~ *to* gemäß *od.* entsprechend (*dat.*).

pur·sue [pəˈsjuː] verfolgen (*a. fig.*); streben nach; *Beruf* nachgehen; *Studium* betreiben; fortsetzen, -fahren in (*dat.*); ~**su·er** [~ə] Verfolger (-in); ~**suit** [~t] Verfolgung *f*; *mst* ~*s pl.* Beschäftigung *f*.

pur·vey [pəˈveɪ] *Lebensmittel* liefern; ~**or** [~ə] Lieferant *m*.

pus [pʌs] Eiter *m*.

push [pʊʃ] 1. (An-, Vor)Stoß *m*; Schub *m*; Druck *m*; Notfall *m*; Anstrengung *f*, Bemühung *f*; F Schwung *m*, Energie *f*, Tatkraft *f*; 2. stoßen; schieben; drängen; *Knopf* drücken; (an)treiben; *a.* ~ *through* durchführen; *Anspruch etc.* durchsetzen; F vorwärtshelfen; ~ *s.th. on s.o.* j-m et. aufdrängen; ~ *one's way* sich durch- *od.* vordrängen; ~ *along*, ~ *on*, ~ *forward*

weitermachen, -gehen, -fahren *etc.*;
~·but·ton ⊕ [ˈpʊʃbʌtn] Druckknopf
m, -taste *f*; **~-chair** *Brt.* (Falt)Sport-
wagen *m* (*für Kinder*); **~·er** F [~ə]
Pusher *m* (*Rauschgifthändler*); **~·
o·ver** Kinderspiel *n*, Kleinigkeit *f*;
be a ~ for auf *j-n od. et.* hereinfallen.
pu·sil·lan·i·mous ☐ [pjuːsɪˈlæni-
məs] kleinmütig.
puss [pʊs] Mieze *f*, Kätzchen *n*, Katze *f* (*alle a. fig. = Mädchen*); **pus·sy**
[ˈpʊsɪ], *a.* **~-cat** Mieze *f*, Kätzchen *n*;
pus·sy·foot F leisetreten, sich nicht
festlegen.
put [pʊt] (*-tt-*; *put*) *v/t.* setzen, legen,
stellen, stecken, tun; bringen (*ins
Bett*); verwenden; *Frage* stellen,
vorlegen; *Sport: Kugel* stoßen; werfen; ausdrücken, sagen; *~ to school*
zur Schule schicken; *~ s.o. to work*
j-n an die Arbeit setzen; *~ about*
Gerüchte verbreiten; ⚓ den Kurs
(*e-s Schiffes*) ändern; *~ across Idee
etc.* an den Mann bringen, verkaufen; *~ back* zurückstellen (*a. Uhr*),
-tun; *fig.* aufhalten; *~ by Geld* zurücklegen; *~ down v/t.* hin-, niederlegen, -setzen, -stellen; *j-n* absetzen,
aussteigen lassen; (auf-, nieder-)
schreiben; eintragen; zuschreiben
(*to dat.*); *Aufstand* niederschlagen;
Mißstand unterdrücken (*a. Uhr*);
landen, aufsetzen; *~ forth Kräfte*
aufbieten; *Knospen etc.* treiben; *~
forward Uhr* vorstellen; *Meinung
etc.* vorbringen; *~ o.s. forward* sich
bemerkbar machen; *~ in v/t.* herein-,
hineinlegen, -setzen, -stellen, -stek-
ken; hineintun; *Anspruch* erheben;
Gesuch einreichen; *Urkunde* vorlegen; *Antrag* stellen; *j-n* einstellen;
Bemerkung einwerfen; *v/i.* einkehren
(*at in dat.*); ⚓ einlaufen (*at in dat.*); *~
off v/t. Kleider* ablegen (*a. fig.*); auf-,
verschieben; vertrösten; *j-n* abbringen; hindern; *Passagiere* aussteigen
lassen; *v/i.* ⚓ auslaufen; *~ on Kleider*
anziehen, *Hut, Brille* aufsetzen; *Uhr*
vorstellen; *Tempo* beschleunigen;
an-, einschalten; vortäuschen; -spie-

len; *~ on airs* sich aufspielen; *~ on
weight* zunehmen; *~ out v/t.* ausmachen, (-)löschen; verrenken; (her-)
ausstrecken; verwirren; ärgern; *j-m*
Ungelegenheiten bereiten; *Kraft*
aufbieten; *Geld* ausleihen; *v/i.* ⚓
auslaufen; *~ right* in Ordnung bringen; *~ through teleph.* verbinden (*to*
mit); *~ together* zusammensetzen;
zusammenstellen; *~ up v/t.* hinauf-
legen, -stellen, hochheben, -schie-
ben, -ziehen; *Bild etc.* aufhängen;
Haar hochstecken; *Schirm* aufspan-
nen; *Zelt etc.* aufstellen, errichten,
bauen; *Ware* anbieten; *Preis* erhöhen; *Widerstand* leisten; *Kampf* liefern; *Gäste* unterbringen, (bei sich)
aufnehmen; *Bekanntmachung* anschlagen; *v/i.* ~ *up at* einkehren *od.*
absteigen in (*dat.*); *~ up for* kandidieren für; sich bewerben um; *~ up
with* sich gefallen lassen, sich abfinden mit.
pu·tre·fy [ˈpjuːtrɪfaɪ] verwesen.
pu·trid ☐ [ˈpjuːtrɪd] faul, verfault,
-west; *sl.* scheußlich, saumäßig; **~·i·
ty** [pjuːˈtrɪdətɪ] Fäulnis *f*.
put·ty [ˈpʌtɪ] **1.** Kitt *m*; **2.** kitten.
put-you-up *Brt.* F [ˈpʊtjuːʌp]
Schlafcouch *f*, -sessel *m*.
puz·zle [ˈpʌzl] **1.** Rätsel *n*; schwierige
Aufgabe; Verwirrung *f*; Geduld(s)-
spiel *n*; **2.** *v/t.* verwirren; *j-m* Kopf-
zerbrechen machen; *~ out* austüf-
teln; *v/i.* verwirrt sein; sich den
Kopf zerbrechen; **~·head·ed** konfus.
pyg·my [ˈpɪgmɪ] Pygmäe *m*; Zwerg
m; *attr.* zwergenhaft.
py·ja·ma *Brt.* [pəˈdʒɑːmə] Schlaf-
anzugs..., Pyjama...; **~s** *Brt.* [~əz] *pl.*
Schlafanzug *m*, Pyjama *m*.
py·lon [ˈpaɪlən] (Leitungs)Mast *m*.
pyr·a·mid [ˈpɪrəmɪd] Pyramide *f*.
pyre [ˈpaɪə] Scheiterhaufen *m*.
Py·thag·o·re·an [paɪθægəˈrɪən] **1.**
pythagoreisch; **2.** Pythagoreer *m*.
py·thon *zo.* [ˈpaɪθn] Pythonschlange
f.
pyx *eccl.* [pɪks] Hostienbehälter *m*.

P

Q

quack¹ [kwæk] 1. Quaken *n*; 2. quaken.

quack² [~] 1. Scharlatan *m*; *a.* ~ *doctor* Quacksalber *m*, Kurpfuscher *m*; 2. quacksalberisch; 3. quacksalbern (an *dat.*); **~·er·y** ['kwækərɪ] Quacksalberei *f*.

quad·ran·gle ['kwɒdræŋgl] Viereck *n*; viereckiger Innenhof (*e-s College*); **~·gu·lar** [kwɒ'dræŋgjʊlə] viereckig.

quad·ren·nial [kwɒ'drenɪəl] vierjährig; vierjährlich (wiederkehrend).

quad·ru·ped ['kwɒdrʊped] Vierfüß(l)er *m*; **~·ple** [~pl] 1. □ vierfach; Vierer...; 2. (sich) vervierfachen; **~·plets** [~plɪts] *pl.* Vierlinge *pl.*

quag·mire ['kwægmaɪə] Sumpf(land *n*) *m*, Moor *n*; Morast *m*.

quail¹ *zo.* [kweɪl] Wachtel *f*.

quail² [~] verzagen; (vor Angst) zittern (*before vor dat.*; *at* bei).

quaint □ [kweɪnt] anheimelnd, malerisch; wunderlich, drollig.

quake [kweɪk] 1. zittern, beben (*with, for* vor *dat.*); 2. F Erdbeben *n*.

Quak·er ['kweɪkə] Quäker *m*.

qual·i·fi·ca·tion [kwɒlɪfɪ'keɪʃn] Qualifikation *f*, Eignung *f*, Befähigung *f*; Einschränkung *f*; *gr.* nähere Bestimmung; **~·fy** ['kwɒlɪfaɪ] (sich) qualifizieren; befähigen; bezeichnen; *gr.* näher bestimmen; einschränken; abschwächen, mildern; **~·ty** [~ɒtɪ] Eigenschaft *f*; Beschaffenheit *f*; *econ.* Qualität *f*.

qualm [kwɑːm] Übelkeit *f*; *oft* ~*s pl.* Skrupel *m*, Bedenken *n*; △ *nicht* Qualm.

quan·da·ry ['kwɒndərɪ] verzwickte Lage, Verlegenheit *f*.

quan·ti·ty ['kwɒntətɪ] Quantität *f*, Menge *f*; große Menge.

quan·tum ['kwɒntəm] (*pl.* -ta [-tə]) Quantum *n*, Menge *f*; *phys.* Quant *n*.

quar·an·tine ['kwɒrəntiːn] 1. Quarantäne *f*; 2. unter Quarantäne stellen.

quar·rel ['kwɒrəl] 1. Streit *m*; 2. (*bsd.* Brt. *-ll-*, *Am. -l-*) (sich) streiten; **~·some** [~səm] zänkisch, streitsüchtig.

quar·ry ['kwɒrɪ] 1. Steinbruch *m*; *hunt.* (Jagd)Beute *f*; *fig.* Fundgrube *f*; 2. *Steine* brechen.

quart [kwɔːt] Quart *n* (= 1,136 *l*).

quar·ter ['kwɔːtə] 1. Viertel *n*, vierter Teil; Viertel(stunde *f*) *n*; Vierteljahr *n*, Quartal *n*; Viertelpfund *n*; Viertelzentner *m*; *Am.* Vierteldollar *m* (= 25 *Cents*); *Sport*: (Spiel)Viertel *n*; (*bsd.* Hinter)Viertel *n* (*e-s Schlachttiers*); (Stadt)Viertel *n*; (Himmels-, Wind)Richtung *f*; Gegend *f*, Richtung *f*; ✕ Gnade *f*, Pardon *m*; ~*s pl.* Quartier *n* (*a.* ✕), Unterkunft *f*; *a* ~ (*of an hour*) eine Viertelstunde; *a* ~ *to* (*Am. of*) od. *a* ~ *past* (*Am. after*) *Uhrzeit*: (ein) Viertel vor od. nach; *at close* ~*s* in od. aus nächster Nähe; *from official* ~*s* von amtlicher Seite; 2. vierteln, in vier Teile teilen; beherbergen; ✕ einquartieren; **~·back** *American Football*: wichtigster Spieler der Angriffsformation; **~·day** Quartalstag *m*; **~·deck** ♣ Achterdeck *n*; **~·fi·nal** *Sport*: Viertelfinalspiel *n*; ~*s pl.* Viertelfinale *n*; **~·ly** [~lɪ] 1. vierteljährlich; 2. Vierteljahresschrift *f*; **~·mas·ter** ✕ Quartiermeister *m*.

quar·tet(te) ♪ [kwɔːˈtet] Quartett *n*.

quar·to ['kwɔːtəʊ] (*pl.* -tos) Quart (-format) *n*.

quartz *min.* [kwɔːts] Quarz *m*; ~ *clock* Quarzuhr *f*; ~ *watch* Quarzarmbanduhr *f*.

qua·si ['kweɪzaɪ] gleichsam, sozusagen; Quasi..., Schein...

qua·ver ['kweɪvə] 1. Zittern *n*; ♪ Triller *m*; 2. mit zitternder Stimme sprechen *od.* singen; ♪ trillern.

quay [kiː] Kai *m*.

quea·sy □ ['kwiːzɪ] (-*ier*, -*iest*) empfindlich (*Magen, Gewissen*); *I feel* ~ mir ist übel *od.* schlecht.

queen [kwiːn] Königin *f* (*a. zo.*); *Karten, Schach*: Dame *f*; *sl.* Schwule(r) *m*, Homo *m*; ~ *bee* Bienenkönigin *f*; **~·like** ['kwiːnlaɪk], **~·ly** [~lɪ] wie e-e Königin, königlich.

queer [kwɪə] sonderbar, seltsam; wunderlich; komisch; F schwul (*homosexuell*).

quench [kwentʃ] *Flammen, Feuer* (aus)löschen; *Durst etc.* löschen, stillen; *Hoffnung* zunichte machen.

quer·u·lous □ ['kwerʊləs] quengelig, mürrisch, verdrossen.

que·ry ['kwɪərɪ] 1. Frage(zeichen *n*) *f*;

Zweifel *m*; **2.** (be)fragen; (be-, an-) zweifeln.

quest [kwest] **1.** Suche *f*; **2.** suchen (*for* nach).

ques·tion ['kwestʃən] **1.** Frage *f*; Problem *n*, (Streit)Frage *f*, (Streit-) Punkt *m*; Zweifel *m*; Sache *f*, Angelegenheit *f*; *beyond* (*all*) ~ ohne Frage; *in* ~ fraglich; *call in* ~ *et.* anbezweifeln; *that is out of the* ~ das kommt nicht in Frage; **2.** (be)fragen; ⚖ vernehmen, -hören; *et.* an-, bezweifeln; **~·a·ble** [~əbl] fraglich; fragwürdig; **~·er** [~ə] Fragesteller (-in); **~ mark** Fragezeichen *n*; **~·mas·ter** Brt. Quizmaster *m*; **~·naire** [kwestɪə'neə] Fragebogen *m*.

queue [kju:] **1.** Reihe *f* (*von Personen etc.*), Schlange *f*; **2.** *mst* ~ *up* Schlange stehen; anstehen; *et.* anstellen.

quib·ble ['kwɪbl] **1.** Spitzfindigkeit *f*, Haarspalterei *f*; **2.** spitzfindig sein; ~ *with s.o. about od. over s.th.* sich mit j-m über et. herumstreiten.

quick [kwɪk] **1.** schnell, rasch; prompt; aufgeweckt, wach (*Verstand*); scharf (*Auge, Gehör*); lebhaft; hitzig, aufbrausend; *be* ~*!* mach schnell*!*; **2.** lebendes Fleisch; *cut s.o. to the* ~ j-n tief verletzen; **~·en** ['kwɪkən] anregen, beleben; (sich) beschleunigen; **~·freeze** (-*froze, -frozen*) einfrieren, tiefkühlen; **~·ie** F [~ɪ] auf die schnelle gemachte Sache; kurze Sache; **~·ly** [~lɪ] schnell, rasch; **~·ness** [~nɪs] Schnelligkeit *f*; rasche Auffassungsgabe; Schärfe *f* (*des Auges etc.*); Lebhaftigkeit *f*; Hitzigkeit *f*; **~·sand** Treibsand *m*; **~·set hedge** *bsd. Brt.* lebende Hecke; Weißdornhecke *f*; **~·sil·ver** Quecksilber *n*; **~·wit·ted** geistesgegenwärtig; schlagfertig.

quid¹ [kwɪd] Priem *m* (*Kautabak*).

quid² [kwɪd] *Brt. sl.* [~] (*pl.* ~) Pfund *n* (*Sterling*).

qui·es·cence [kwaɪ'esns] Ruhe *f*, Stille *f*; **~·cent** [~t] ruhend; *fig.* ruhig, still.

qui·et ['kwaɪət] **1.** ruhig, still; *be* ~*!* sei still*!*; **2.** Ruhe *f*; *on the* ~ heimlich (, still u. leise); **3.** *bsd. Am.* **~·en** *bsd. Brt.* [~tn] *v/t.* beruhigen; *v/i. mst* ~ *down* sich beruhigen; **~·ness** [~nɪs], **qui·e·tude** ['kwaɪɪtju:d] Ruhe *f*, Stille *f*.

quill [kwɪl] *a.* **~·feather** *zo.* (Schwung-, Schwanz)Feder *f*; *a.*

~·pen Federkiel *m*; *zo.* Stachel *m* (*des Stachelschweins*).

quilt [kwɪlt] **1.** Steppdecke *f*; **2.** steppen; wattieren.

quince ⚘ [kwɪns] Quitte *f*.

quin·ine [kwɪ'ni:n, *Am.* 'kwaɪnaɪn] Chinin *n*.

quin·quen·ni·al [[kwɪŋ'kwenɪəl] fünfjährig; fünfjährlich. .

quin·sy ⚕ ['kwɪnzɪ] Mandelentzündung *f*.

quin·tal ['kwɪntl] Doppelzentner *m*.

quin·tes·sence [kwɪn'tesns] Quintessenz *f*; Inbegriff *m*.

quin·tu·ple ['kwɪntjʊpl] **1.** fünffach; **2.** (sich) verfünffachen; **~·plets** [~lɪts] *pl.* Fünflinge *pl.*

quip [kwɪp] **1.** geistreiche Bemerkung; Stichelei *f*; **2.** (-*pp*-) witzeln, spötteln.

quirk [kwɜ:k] Eigenart *f*, seltsame Angewohnheit; Laune *f* (*des Schicksals etc.*); *arch.* Hohlkehle *f*.

quit [kwɪt] **1.** (-*tt-*; *Brt.* ~*ted od.* ~, *Am. mst* ~) *v/t.* verlassen; *Stellung* aufgeben; aufhören mit; *v/i.* aufhören; weggehen; ausziehen (*Mieter*); *give notice to* ~ j-m kündigen; **2.** *pred. adj.* frei, los.

quite [kwaɪt] ganz, völlig, vollständig; ziemlich, recht; ganz, sehr, durchaus; ~ *nice* ganz *od.* recht nett; ~ (*so*)*!* ganz recht; ~ *the thing* F ganz große Mode; *she's* ~ *a beauty* sie ist e-e wirkliche Schönheit.

quits *pred. adj.* [kwɪts]: *be* ~ *with s.o.* mit j-m quitt sein.

quit·ter F ['kwɪtə] Drückeberger *m*.

quiv·er¹ ['kwɪvə] zittern, beben.

quiv·er² [~] Köcher *m*.

quiz [kwɪz] **1.** (*pl. quizzes*) Prüfung *f*, Test *m*; Quiz *n*; **2.** (-*zz-*) ausfragen; j-n prüfen; **~·mas·ter** *bsd. Am.* ['kwɪzmɑ:stə] Quizmaster *m*; **~·zi·cal** [~ɪkl] spöttisch; komisch.

quoit [kɔɪt] Wurfring *m*; ~*s sg.* Wurfringspiel *n*.

quo·rum ['kwɔ:rəm] beschlußfähige Anzahl *od.* Mitgliederzahl.

quo·ta ['kwəʊtə] Quote *f*, Anteil *m*, Kontingent *n*.

quo·ta·tion [kwəʊ'teɪʃn] Anführung *f*, Zitat *n*; Beleg(stelle *f*) *m*; *econ.*: (Börsen-, Kurs)Notierung *f*; Preis (-angabe *f*) *m*; Kostenvoranschlag *m*; **~ marks** *pl.* Anführungszeichen *pl.*

quote [kwəʊt] anführen, zitieren;

econ. Preis nennen, berechnen; *Börse:* notieren (*at* mit).

quoth *veraltet* [kwəʊθ]: ~ *I* sagte ich.

quo·tid·i·an [kwɒˈtɪdɪən] täglich.

quo·tient ᛒ [ˈkwəʊʃnt] Quotient *m.*

R

rab·bi [ˈræbaɪ] Rabbiner *m.*

rab·bit [ˈræbɪt] Kaninchen *n.*

rab·ble [ˈræbl] Pöbel *m*, Mob *m;* ~**rous·er** [~ə] Aufrührer *m*, Demagoge *m;* ~**rous·ing** □ [~ɪŋ] aufwieglerisch, demagogisch.

rab·id □ [ˈræbɪd] tollwütig (*Tier*); *fig.* wild, wütend.

ra·bies *vet.* [ˈreɪbiːz] Tollwut *f.*

rac·coon *zo.* [rəˈkuːn] Waschbär *m.*

race[1] [reɪs] Rasse *f;* Geschlecht *n*, Stamm *m;* Volk *n*, Nation *f;* (*Menschen*)Schlag *m.*

race[2] [~] 1. Lauf *m* (*a. fig.*); (*Wett*)Rennen *n;* Strömung *f;* ~*s pl.* Pferderennen *n;* 2. rennen; rasen; um die Wette laufen *od.* fahren (mit); ⊕ durchdrehen; ~**course** [ˈreɪskɔːs] Rennbahn *f*, -strecke *f;* ~**horse** Rennpferd *n;* **rac·er** [ˈreɪsə] Läufer (-in); Rennpferd *n;* Rennboot *n;* Rennwagen *m;* Rennrad *n.*

ra·cial □ [ˈreɪʃl] rassisch; Rassen...

rac·ing [ˈreɪsɪŋ] (Wett)Rennen *n;* (Pferde)Rennsport *m; attr.* Renn...

rack [ræk] 1. Gestell *n;* Kleiderständer *m;* Gepäcknetz *n;* Raufe *f*, Futtergestell *n;* Folter(bank) *f; go to ~ and ruin* verfallen (*Gebäude, Person*); dem Ruin entgegentreiben (*Land, Wirtschaft*); 2. strecken; foltern, quälen (*a. fig.*); ~ *one's brains* sich den Kopf zermartern.

rack·et [ˈrækɪt] 1. (*Tennis*)Schläger *m;* Lärm *m;* Trubel *m;* F Schwindel (-geschäft *n*) *m*, Gaunerei *f;* Strapaze *f;* 2. lärmen; sich amüsieren.

rack·e·teer [rækəˈtɪə] Gauner *m*, Erpresser *m;* ~**ing** [~ərɪŋ] Gaunereien *pl*, Beutelschneiderei *f.*

ra·coon *Brt. zo.* [rəˈkuːn] = *raccoon.*

rac·y □ [ˈreɪsɪ] (*-ier, -iest*) kraftvoll, lebendig; stark; würzig; urwüchsig; gewagt.

ra·dar [ˈreɪdə] Radar(gerät) *n.*

ra·di·ance [ˈreɪdɪəns] Strahlen *n,* strahlender Glanz (*a. fig.*); ~**ant** □ [~t] strahlend, leuchtend (*a. fig.* with vor *dat.*).

ra·di·ate [ˈreɪdɪeɪt] (aus)strahlen; strahlenförmig ausgehen; ~**a·tion** [reɪdɪˈeɪʃn] (Aus)Strahlung *f;* ~**a·tor** [ˈreɪdɪeɪtə] Heizkörper *m; mot.* Kühler *m.*

rad·i·cal [ˈrædɪkl] 1. □ ᛒ, ᛒ Wurzel...; Grund...; radikal, drastisch; eingewurzelt; *pol.* radikal; 2. *pol.* Radikale(r *m*) *f;* ᛒ Wurzel *f;* ᛦ Radikal *n.*

ra·di·o [ˈreɪdɪəʊ] (*pl. -os*) 1. Radio (-apparat *m*) *n;* Funk(spruch) *m;* Funk...; ~ *play* Hörspiel *n;* ~ *set* Radiogerät *n; by* ~ über Funk; *on the* ~ im Radio; 2. funken; ~**ac·tive** radioaktiv; ~ *waste* Atommüll *m;* ~**ac·tiv·i·ty** Radioaktivität *f;* ~**ther·a·py** Strahlen-, Röntgentherapie *f.*

rad·ish ᛦ [ˈrædɪʃ] Rettich *m;* (*red*) ~ Radieschen *n.*

ra·di·us [ˈreɪdɪəs] (*pl. -dii* [-dɪaɪ], *-uses*) Radius *m.*

raf·fle [ˈræfl] 1. Tombola *f*, Verlosung *f;* 2. verlosen.

raft [rɑːft] 1. Floß *n;* 2. flößen; ~**er** ⊕ [ˈrɑːftə] (Dach)Sparren *m;* ~**s·man** (*pl. -men*) Flößer *m.*

rag[1] [ræg] Lumpen *m;* Fetzen *m;* Lappen *m; in* ~*s* zerlumpt; ~*-and-bone man bsd. Brt.* Lumpensammler *m.*

rag[2] *sl.* [~] 1. Unfug *m;* Radau *m;* Schabernack *m;* 2. (*-gg-*) *j-n* aufziehen; *j-n* anschnauzen; *j-m* e-n Schabernack spielen; herumtollen, Radau machen.

rag·a·muf·fin [ˈrægəmʌfɪn] zerlumpter Kerl; Gassenjunge *m.*

rage [reɪdʒ] 1. Wut(anfall *m*) *f*, Zorn *m*, Raserei *f;* Wüten *n*, Toben *n* (*der Elemente etc.*); Sucht *f*, Gier *f* (*for* nach); Manie *f;* Ekstase *f; it is (all)* *the* ~ es ist jetzt die große Mode; **2.** wüten, rasen (*a. fig.*).

rag·ged □ ['ræɡɪd] rauh; zottig; zackig; zerlumpt; ausgefranst.

raid [reɪd] **1.** (feindlicher) Überfall, Streifzug *m*; (Luft)Angriff *m*; Razzia *f*; **2.** einbrechen in (*acc.*); überfallen; plündern.

rail¹ [reɪl] schimpfen.

rail² [~] **1.** Geländer *n*; Stange *f*; ♣ Reling *f*; ⛟ Schiene *f*; (Eisen)Bahn *f*; *by* ~ mit der Bahn; *off the* ~s *fig.* aus den Geleise, durcheinander; verrückt; *run off* (*leave, jump*) *the* ~s entgleisen; **2.** *a.* ~ *in* mit e-m Geländer umgeben; *a.* ~ *off* durch ein Geländer (ab)trennen.

rail·ing ['reɪlɪŋ], *a.* ~s *pl.* Geländer *n*.

rail·ler·y ['reɪlərɪ] Neckerei *f*, Stichelei *f*.

rail·road *Am.* ['reɪlrəʊd] Eisenbahn *f*.

rail·way *bsd. Brt.* ['reɪlweɪ] Eisenbahn *f*; ~**man** (*pl.* -**men**) Eisenbahner *m*.

rain [reɪn] **1.** Regen *m*; ~s *pl.* Regenfälle *pl.*; *the* ~s *pl.* die Regenzeit (*in den Tropen*); ~ *or shine* bei jedem Wetter; **2.** regnen; *it never* ~s *but it pours* es kommt immer gleich knüppeldick; ein Unglück kommt selten allein; ~**bow** ['reɪnbəʊ] Regenbogen *m*; ~**coat** Regenmantel *m*; ~**fall** Regenmenge *f*; ~**proof 1.** regen-, wasserundurchlässig; imprägniert (*Stoff*); **2.** Regenmantel *m*; ~**y** □ ['reɪnɪ] (-*ier*, -*iest*) regnerisch; Regen...; *a* ~ *day fig.* Notzeiten *pl.*

raise [reɪz] *oft* ~ *up* (auf-, hoch-) heben; (*oft fig.*) errichten, erhöhen (*a. fig.*); Geld *etc.* aufbringen; *Anleihe* aufnehmen; *Familie* gründen; *Kinder* aufziehen; (auf-) wecken; anstiften; züchten, ziehen; *Belagerung etc.* aufheben.

rai·sin ['reɪzn] Rosine *f*.

rake [reɪk] **1.** Rechen *m*, Harke *f*; Wüstling *m*; Lebemann *m*; **2.** *v/t.* (glatt)harken, (-)rechen; *fig.* durchstöbern; *v/i.* ~ *about* (herum)stöbern; ~**off** F ['reɪkɒf] (Gewinn)Anteil *m*.

rak·ish □ ['reɪkɪʃ] schnittig; liederlich, ausschweifend; verwegen, keck.

ral·ly ['rælɪ] **1.** Sammeln *n*; Treffen *n*; (Massen)Versammlung *f*; Kundgebung *f*; Erholung *f*; *mot.* Rallye *f*; **2.** (sich ver)sammeln; sich erholen~

ram [ræm] **1.** *zo.* Widder *m*, Schafbock *m*; ♀ *ast.* Widder *m*; ⊕, ♣ Ramme *f*; **2.** (-*mm*-) (fest)rammen; ♣ rammen; ~ *s.th. down s.o.'s throat fig.* j-m et. eintrichtern.

ram·ble ['ræmbl] **1.** Streifzug *m*; Wanderung *f*; **2.** umherstreifen; abschweifen; ~**bler** [~] Wanderer *m*; *a.* ~ *rose* ♣ Kletterrose *f*; ~**bling** [~ɪŋ] abschweifend; weitschweifend; weitläufig.

ram·i·fy ['ræmɪfaɪ] (sich) verzweigen.

ramp [ræmp] Rampe *f*.

ram·pant □ ['ræmpənt] wuchernd; *fig.* zügellos.

ram·part ['ræmpɑːt] Wall *m*.

ram·shack·le ['ræmʃækl] baufällig; wack(e)lig; klapp(e)rig.

ran [ræn] *pret. von* **run 1.**

ranch [rɑːntʃ, *Am.* ræntʃ] Ranch *f*, Viehfarm *f*; ~**er** ['rɑːntʃə, *Am.* 'ræntʃə] Rancher *m*, Viehzüchter *m*; Farmer *m*.

ran·cid □ ['rænsɪd] ranzig.

ran·co(u)r ['ræŋkə] Groll *m*, Haß *m*.

ran·dom ['rændəm] **1.** *at* ~ aufs Geratewohl, blindlings; **2.** ziel-, wahllos; zufällig; willkürlich.

rang [ræŋ] *pret. von* **ring¹ 2.**

range [reɪndʒ] **1.** Reihe *f*; (Berg-) Kette *f*; *econ.* Kollektion *f*, Sortiment *n*; Herd *m*; Raum *m*; Umfang *m*, Bereich *m*; Reichweite *f*; Schußweite *f*; Entfernung *f*; (ausgedehnte) Fläche; Schießstand *m*; offenes Weidegebiet; *at close* ~ aus nächster Nähe; *within* ~ *of vision* in Sichtweite; *a wide* ~ *of* ... eine große Auswahl an ...; **2.** *v/t.* (ein)reihen, ordnen; *Gebiet etc.* durchstreifen; *v/i.* in e-r Reihe od. Linie stehen; (umher)streifen; sich erstrecken; reichen; zählen, gehören (*among, with* zu); ~ *from* ... *to* ..., ~ *between* ... *and* ... sich zwischen ... und ... bewegen (*von Preisen etc*); ~**ang·er** ['reɪndʒə] Förster *m*; Aufseher *m* e-s Forsts od. Parks; Angehörige(r) *m* e-r berittenen Schutztruppe.

rank [ræŋk] **1.** Reihe *f*, Linie *f*; ✗ Glied *n*; Klasse *f*; Rang *m*, Stand *m*; ~s *pl.*, *the* ~ *and file* die Mannschaften *pl.*; *fig.* die große Masse; **2.** *v/t.* einreihen, (ein)ordnen; einstufen; *v/i.* sich reihen, sich ordnen; gehören (*among, with* zu); e-n Rang od. e-e Stelle einnehmen (*above* über *dat.*); ~ *as* gelten als; **3.** üppig; ranzig; stinkend; scharf; kraß; △ *nicht rank* (= *slim, slender*).

ran·kle *fig.* ['ræŋkl] nagen, weh tun.

ran·sack ['rænsæk] durchwühlen, -stöbern, -suchen; ausrauben.

ran·som ['rænsəm] **1.** Lösegeld *n*; Auslösung *f*; **2.** loskaufen, auslösen.

rant [rænt] **1.** Schwulst *m*; **2.** Phrasen dreschen; mit Pathos vortragen.

rap¹ [ræp] **1.** Klaps *m*; Klopfen *n*; **2.** (*-pp-*) schlagen; pochen, klopfen.

rap² *fig.* [~] Heller *m*, Deut *m*.

ra·pa·cious [rə'peɪʃəs] habgierig; (raub)gierig; **~·ci·ty** [rə'pæsətɪ] Habgier *f*; (Raub)Gier *f*.

rape¹ [reɪp] **1.** Notzucht *f*, Vergewaltigung *f* (*a. fig.*); **2.** rauben; vergewaltigen.

rape² *fig.* [~] Raps *m*.

rap·id ['ræpɪd] **1.** □ schnell, rasch, rapid(e); steil; **2.** ~*s pl.* Stromschnelle(n *pl.*) *f*; **ra·pid·i·ty** [rə'pɪdətɪ] Schnelligkeit *f*.

rap·proche·ment *pol.* [ræ'prɒʃmɑ̃ːŋ] Wiederannäherung *f*.

rapt [ræpt] entzückt; versunken; **rap·ture** ['ræptʃə] Entzücken *n*; *go into* ~*s* in Entzücken geraten.

rare □ [reə] (*~r, ~st*) selten; *phys.* dünn (*Luft*); halbgar, nicht durchgebraten (*Fleisch*); F ausgezeichnet, köstlich.

rare·bit ['reəbɪt]: *Welsh* ~ überbackener Käsetoast.

rar·e·fy ['reərɪfaɪ] (sich) verdünnen.

rar·i·ty ['reərətɪ] Seltenheit *f*; Rarität *f*.

ras·cal ['rɑːskəl] Schuft *m*; *co.* Gauner *m*; **~·ly** [~ɪ] schuftig; erbärmlich.

rash¹ □ [ræʃ] hastig, vorschnell; übereilt; unbesonnen; waghalsig; △ *nicht rasch.*

rash² ⚕ [~] (Haut)Ausschlag *m*.

rash·er ['ræʃə] Speckscheibe *f*.

rasp [rɑːsp] **1.** Raspel *f*; **2.** raspeln; kratzen; krächzen.

rasp·ber·ry ⚘ ['rɑːzbərɪ] Himbeere *f*.

rat [ræt] *zo.* Ratte *f*; *pol.* Überläufer *m*; *smell a* ~ Lunte *od.* den Braten riechen; ~*s! sl.* Quatsch!

rate [reɪt] **1.** (Verhältnis)Ziffer *f*; Rate *f*; (Verhältnis *n*; (Aus)Maß *n*; Satz *m*; Preis *m*, Gebühr *f*; Taxe *f*; (Gemeinde)Abgabe *f*, (Kommunal-) Steuer *f*; Grad *m*, Rang *m*, Klasse *f*; Geschwindigkeit *f*; *at any* ~ auf

jeden Fall; ~ *of exchange* (Umrechnungs-, Wechsel)Kurs *m*; ~ *of interest* Zinssatz *m*, -fuß *m*; **2.** (ein)schätzen; besteuern; △ *nicht raten*; ~ *among* rechnen, zählen zu (*dat.*).

ra·ther ['rɑːðə] eher, lieber; vielmehr; besser gesagt; ziemlich, fast; ~*!* F und ob!, allerdings!; *I had od. would* ~ (*not*) *go* ich möchte lieber (nicht) gehen.

rat·i·fy *pol.* ['rætɪfaɪ] ratifizieren.

rat·ing ['reɪtɪŋ] Schätzung *f*; Steuersatz *m*; ⚓ Dienstgrad *m*; ⚓ (Segel-) Klasse *f*; Matrose *m*; *TV* Einschaltquote *f*.

ra·ti·o ⚕ ['reɪʃɪəʊ] (*pl. -os*) Verhältnis *n*.

ra·tion ['ræʃn] **1.** Ration *f*, Zuteilung *f*; **2.** rationieren.

ra·tion·al ['ræʃənl] vernunftgemäß; vernünftig; (*a.* ⚕) rational; △ *nicht rationell*; **~·i·ty** [ræʃə'nælətɪ] Vernunft *f*; **~·ize** *econ.* ['ræʃnəlaɪz] rationalisieren.

rat race ['rætreɪs] harter (Konkurrenz)Kampf.

rat·tle ['rætl] **1.** Gerassel *n*; Geklapper *n*; Geplapper *n*; Klapper *f*; Röcheln *n*; **2.** rasseln (mit); klappern; rütteln; rattern; plappern; röcheln; ~ *off* herunterrasseln; **~·brain**, **~·pate** Hohl-, Wirrkopf *m*; Schwätzer(in) *f*; **~·snake** *zo.* Klapperschlange *f*; **~·trap** *fig.* Klapperkasten *m* (*Fahrzeug*).

rat·tling ['rætlɪŋ] **1.** *adj.* rasselnd; F schnell, flott; **2.** F *adv.* sehr, äußerst; ~ *good* prima.

rau·cous □ ['rɔːkəs] heiser, rauh.

rav·age ['rævɪdʒ] **1.** Verwüstung *f*; **2.** verwüsten; plündern.

rave [reɪv] rasen, toben; schwärmen (*about, of* von).

rav·el ['rævl] (*bsd. Brt. -ll-, Am. -l-*) *v/t.* verwickeln; ~ (*out*) auftrennen; *fig.* entwirren; *v/i. a.* ~ *out* ausfasern; aufgehen.

ra·ven *zo.* ['reɪvn] Rabe *m*.

rav·e·nous □ ['rævənəs] gefräßig; heißhungrig; gierig; raubgierig.

ra·vine [rə'viːn] Hohlweg *m*; Schlucht *f*; Klamm *f*.

rav·ings ['reɪvɪŋz] *pl.* irres Gerede; Delirien *pl.*

rav·ish ['rævɪʃ] entzücken; hinreißen; **~·ing** □ [~ɪŋ] hinreißend, entzückend; **~·ment** [~mənt] Entzücken *n*.

raw □ [rɔ:] roh; Roh...; wund; rauh (*Wetter*); ungeübt, unerfahren; **~boned** ['rɔ:bəund] knochig, hager; **~hide** Rohleder *n*.

ray [reɪ] Strahl *m*; *fig.* Schimmer *m*.

ray·on ['reɪən] Kunstseide *f*.

raze [reɪz] *Haus etc.* abreißen; *Festung* schleifen; *fig.* ausmerzen, tilgen; **~** *s.th. to the ground* et. dem Erdboden gleichmachen.

ra·zor ['reɪzə] Rasiermesser *n*; Rasierapparat *m*; **~blade** Rasierklinge *f*; **~edge** *fig.* kritische Lage; *be on a* **~** auf des Messers Schneide stehen.

re- [ri:] wieder, noch einmal, neu; zurück, wider.

reach [ri:tʃ] **1.** Griff *m*; Reichweite *f*; Fassungskraft *f*; *beyond* **~**, *out of* **~** unerreichbar; *within easy* **~** leicht erreichbar; **2.** *v/i.* reichen; langen, greifen; sich erstrecken; △ *nicht* (*aus*)*reichen*; *v/t.* (hin-, her)reichen, (hin-, her)langen; erreichen, erzielen; *a.* **~** *out* ausstrecken.

re·act [rɪ'ækt] reagieren (*to auf acc.*); (ein)wirken (*on, upon auf acc.*).

re·ac·tion [rɪ'ækʃn] Reaktion *f* (*a.* ⚛ *pol.*); Rückwirkung *f*; **~a·ry** [~nərɪ] **1.** reaktionär; **2.** Reaktionär(in).

re·ac·tor *phys.* [rɪ'æktə] (Kern-) Reaktor *m*.

read 1. [ri:d] (*read* [red]) lesen; deuten; (an)zeigen (*Thermometer*); studieren; sich *gut etc.* lesen (lassen); lauten; **~** *to s.o.* j-m vorlesen; **~** *medicine* Medizin studieren; **2.** [red] *pret. u. p.p. von* 1; **rea·da·ble** □ ['ri:dəbl] lesbar; leserlich; lesenswert; **read·er** [~ə] (Vor)Leser(in); *typ.* Korrektor *m*; Lektor *m*; *univ.* Dozent *m*; Lesebuch *n*.

read·i·ly ['redɪlɪ] *adv.* gleich; leicht; bereitwillig, gern; **~ness** [~nɪs] Bereitschaft *f*; Bereitwilligkeit *f*; Schnelligkeit *f*.

read·ing ['ri:dɪŋ] Lesen *n*; Lesung *f* (*a. parl.*); Stand *m* (*des Thermometers*); Belesenheit *f*; Lektüre *f*; Lesart *f*; Auslegung *f*; Auffassung *f*; *attr.* Lese...

re·ad·just ['ri:ə'dʒʌst] wieder in Ordnung bringen; wieder anpassen; ⊕ nachstellen; **~ment** [~mənt] Wiederanpassung *f*; Neuordnung *f*; ⊕ Korrektur.

read·y □ ['redɪ] (*-ier, -iest*) bereit, fertig; bereitwillig; im Begriff (*to do* zu tun); schnell; schlagfertig, ge-

wandt; leicht; *econ.* bar; **~** *for use* gebrauchsfertig; *get* **~** (sich) fertig machen; **~** *cash*, **~** *money* Bargeld *n*; **~made** fertig, Konfektions...

re·a·gent ⚛ [ri:'eɪdʒənt] Reagens *n*.

real □ [rɪəl] wirklich, tatsächlich, real, wahr, eigentlich; echt; △ *nicht reell*; **~ estate** Grundbesitz *m*, Immobilien *pl*.

re·a·lis·m ['rɪəlɪzəm] Realismus *m*; **~t** [~ɪst] Realist *m*; **~tic** [rɪə'lɪstɪk] (*~ally*) realistisch; sachlich; wirklichkeitsnah.

re·al·i·ty [rɪ'ælətɪ] Wirklichkeit *f*.

re·a·li·za·tion [rɪəlaɪ'zeɪʃn] Realisierung *f* (*a. econ.*); Verwirklichung *f*; Erkenntnis *f*; **~ze** ['rɪəlaɪz] sich klarmachen; erkennen, begreifen, einsehen; verwirklichen; realisieren (*a. econ.*); zu Geld machen.

real·ly ['rɪəlɪ] wirklich, tatsächlich; **~!** ich muß schon sagen!

realm [relm] Königreich *n*; Reich *n*; Bereich *m*.

real·tor *Am.* ['rɪəltə] Grundstücksmakler *m*; **~ty** ⚖ [~ɪ] Grundeigentum *n*, -besitz *m*.

reap [ri:p] *Korn* schneiden; *Feld* mähen; *fig.* ernten; **~er** ['ri:pə] Schnitter(in); Mähmaschine *f*.

re·ap·pear ['ri:ə'pɪə] wieder erscheinen.

rear [rɪə] **1.** *v/t.* auf-, großziehen; züchten; (er)heben; *v/i. Pferd:* sich aufbäumen; **2.** Rück-, Hinterseite *f*; Hintergrund *m*; *mot.*, ♣ Heck *n*; ✗ Nachhut *f*; *at* (*Am. in*) *the* **~** *of* hinter (*dat.*); **3.** Hinter..., Rück...; **~** *wheel drive* Hinterradantrieb *m*; **~ad·mi·ral** ♣ ['rɪə'ædmərəl] Konteradmiral *m*; **~guard** ✗ Nachhut *f*; **~lamp**, **~light** *mot.* Rücklicht *n*.

re·arm ✗ ['ri:'ɑ:m] (wieder)aufrüsten; **re·ar·ma·ment** ✗ [~mə-mənt] (Wieder)Aufrüstung *f*.

rear|most ['rɪəməust] hinterste(r, -s); **~view mir·ror** *mot.* Rückspiegel *m*; **~ward** [~wəd] **1.** *adj.* rückwärtig; **2.** *adv. a.* **~s** rückwärts.

rea·son ['ri:zn] **1.** Vernunft *f*; Verstand *m*; Recht *n*, Billigkeit *f*; Ursache *f*, Grund *m*; *by* **~** *of* wegen; *for this* **~** aus diesem Grund; *listen to* **~** Vernunft annehmen; *it stands to* **~** *that* es leuchtet ein, daß; **2.** *v/i.* vernünftig *od.* logisch denken; argumentieren; *v/t.* folgern, schließen (*from* aus); *a.* **~** *out* (logisch) durchdenken; ~ **away** wegdiskutieren; ~ *s.o.* **into** (*out of*) *s.th.* j-m et. ein-(aus)reden; **rea·so·na·ble** □ [~əbl] vernünftig; angemessen; berechtigt.

re·as·sure ['ri:ə'ʃʊə] (nochmals) versichern; beteuern; beruhigen.

re·bate ['ri:beɪt] *econ.* Rabatt *m*, Abzug *m*; Rückzahlung *f*.

reb·el[1] ['rebl] **1.** Rebell *m*; Aufführer *m*; Aufständische(r) *m*; **2.** rebellisch, aufrührerisch.

re·bel[2] [rɪ'bel] rebellieren, sich auflehnen; **~lion** [~ljən] Empörung *f*; **~lious** [~ljəs] = *rebel* 2.

re·birth ['ri:'bɜ:θ] Wiedergeburt *f*.

re·bound [rɪ'baʊnd] **1.** zurückprallen; **2.** [*mst* 'ri:baʊnd] Rückprall *m*; *Sport:* Abpraller *m*.

re·buff [rɪ'bʌf] **1.** schroffe Abweisung, Abfuhr *f*; **2.** abblitzen lassen, abweisen.

re·build ['ri:'bɪld] (*-built*) wieder aufbauen.

re·buke [rɪ'bju:k] **1.** Tadel *m*; **2.** tadeln.

re·but [rɪ'bʌt] (*-tt-*) widerlegen, entkräften.

re·call [rɪ'kɔ:l] **1.** Zurückrufung *f*; Abberufung *f*; Widerruf *m*; *beyond* ~, *past* ~ unwiderruflich; **2.** zurückrufen; ab(be)rufen; sich erinnern an (*acc.*); j-n erinnern (*to* an *acc.*); widerrufen; *econ. Kapital* kündigen.

re·ca·pit·u·late [ri:kə'pɪtjʊleɪt] kurz wiederholen, zusammenfassen.

re·cap·ture ['ri:'kæptʃə] wieder ergreifen; ✕ zurückerobern; *fig.* wiedereinfangen.

re·cast ['ri:'kɑ:st] (*-cast*) ⊕ umgießen; umarbeiten, neu gestalten; *thea. Rolle* umbesetzen.

re·cede [rɪ'si:d] zurücktreten; *receding* fliehend (*Kinn, Stirn*).

re·ceipt [rɪ'si:t] **1.** Empfang *m*; Eingang *m* (*von Waren*); Quittung *f*; △ *nicht* 🍳, *Koch-Rezept*; ~*s pl.* Einnahmen *pl.*; **2.** quittieren.

re·ceiv·a·ble [rɪ'si:vəbl] annehmbar; *econ.* ausstehend; **re·ceive** [~v] empfangen; erhalten; bekommen; aufnehmen; annehmen; anerkennen; **re·ceived** (allgemein) anerkannt; **re·ceiv·er** [~ə] Empfänger *m*; *teleph.* Hörer *m*; Hehler *m*; (*Steuer- etc.*) Einnehmer *m*; *official* ~ 🏛 Konkursverwalter *m*.

re·cent □ ['ri:snt] neu; frisch; mo-

dern; ~ *events pl. die* jüngsten Ereignisse *pl.*; ~**ly** [~lɪ] kürzlich, vor kurzem, neulich.

re·cep·ta·cle [rɪ'septəkl] Behälter *m*.

re·cep·tion [rɪ'sepʃn] Aufnahme *f* (*a. fig.*); Empfang *m* (*a. Rundfunk, TV*); Annahme *f*; ~ **desk** Rezeption *f* (*im Hotel*); ~**ist** [~ɪst] Empfangsdame *f*, -chef *m*; Sprechstundenhilfe *f*; ~ **room** Empfangszimmer *n*.

re·cep·tive □ [rɪ'septɪv] empfänglich, aufnahmefähig (*of*, *to* für).

re·cess [rɪ'ses] Unterbrechung *f*, (*Am. a.* Schul)Pause *f*; *bsd. parl.* Ferien *pl.*; (entlegener) Winkel; Nische *f*; ~*es pl. fig. das* Innere, Tiefe(n *pl.*) *f*; **re·ces·sion** [~ʃn] Zurückziehen *n*, Zurücktreten *n*; *econ.* Rezession *f*, Konjunkturrückgang *m*.

re·ci·pe ['resɪpɪ] (Koch)Rezept *n*.

re·cip·i·ent [rɪ'sɪpɪənt] Empfänger (-in).

re·cip·ro·cal □ [rɪ'sɪprəkl] wechselseitig, gegenseitig; ~**cate** [~eɪt] *v/i.* sich erkenntlich zeigen; ⊕ sich hin- und herbewegen; *v/t. Glückwünsche etc.* erwidern; **~ci·ty** [resɪ'prɒsətɪ] Gegenseitigkeit *f*.

re·cit·al [rɪ'saɪtl] Bericht *m*; Erzählung *f*; ♩ (Solo)Vortrag *m*, Konzert *n*; **re·ci·ta·tion** [resɪ'teɪʃn] Hersagen *n*; Vortrag *m*; **re·cite** [rɪ'saɪt] vortragen; aufsagen; berichten.

reck·less □ ['reklɪs] unbekümmert; rücksichtslos; leichtsinnig.

reck·on ['rekən] *v/t.* (er-, be)rechnen; *a.* ~ *for*, ~ *as* schätzen als, halten für; ~ *up* zusammenzählen; *v/i.* rechnen; denken, vermuten; ~ *on*, ~ *upon* sich verlassen auf (*acc.*); **~ing** ['rekɪŋ] Rechnen *n*; (Ab-, Be-) Rechnung *f*; *be out in one's* ~ sich verrechnet haben.

re·claim [rɪ'kleɪm] zurückfordern; j-n bekehren, bessern; zivilisieren; urbar machen; ⊕ (zurück)gewinnen.

re·cline [rɪ'klaɪn] (sich) (zurück)lehnen; liegen, ruhen; ~*d* liegend.

re·cluse [rɪ'klu:s] Einsiedler(in).

rec·og·ni·tion [rekəg'nɪʃn] (Wieder)Erkennen *n*; ~**ze** ['rekəgnaɪz] anerkennen; (wieder-) erkennen; zugeben, einsehen.

re·coil 1. [rɪ'kɔɪl] zurückprallen; zurückschrecken; **2.** ['ri:kɔɪl] Rückstoß *m*, -lauf *m*.

rec·ol·lect[1] [rekə'lekt] sich erinnern an (*acc.*).

re·col·lect[2] ['ri:kə'lekt] wieder sammeln; ~ *o.s.* sich fassen.

rec·ol·lec·tion [rekə'lekʃn] Erinnerung *f* (*of an acc.*); Gedächtnis *n*.

rec·om·mend [rekə'mend] empfehlen; **~·men·da·tion** [rekəmen'deɪʃn] Empfehlung *f*; Vorschlag *m*.

rec·om·pense ['rekəmpens] **1.** Belohnung *f*, Vergeltung *f*; Entschädigung *f*; Ersatz *m*; **2.** belohnen, vergelten; entschädigen; ersetzen.

rec·on·cile ['rekənsaɪl] aus-, versöhnen; in Einklang bringen; schlichten; **~·cil·i·a·tion** [rekənsɪlɪ'eɪʃn] Ver-, Aussöhnung *f*.

re·con·di·tion ['ri:kən'dɪʃn] wieder herrichten; ⊕ überholen.

re·con·nais·sance [rɪ'kɒnɪsəns] ✕ Aufklärung *f*, Erkundung *f*; *fig.* Übersicht *f*; **~·noi·tre**, *Am.* **~·noi·ter** [rekə'nɔɪtə] erkunden, auskundschaften.

re·con·sid·er ['ri:kən'sɪdə] wieder erwägen; nochmals überlegen.

re·con·sti·tute ['ri:'kɒnstɪtju:t] wiederherstellen.

re·con·struct ['ri:kən'strʌkt] wiederaufbauen; **~·struc·tion** [~kʃn] Wiederaufbau *m*, Wiederherstellung *f*.

re·con·vert ['ri:kən'vɜ:t] umstellen.

re·cord[1] ['rekɔ:d] Aufzeichnung *f*; ⅀ Protokoll *n*; (Gerichts)Akte *f*; Urkunde *f*; Register *n*, Verzeichnis *n*; (schriftlicher) Bericht; Ruf *m*; Leumund *m*; Schallplatte *f*; *Sport:* Rekord *m*; *place on* ~ schriftlich niederlegen; ~ *office* Archiv *n*; *off the* ~ inoffiziell.

re·cord[2] [rɪ'kɔ:d] aufzeichnen, schriftlich niederlegen; *auf Schallplatte etc.* aufnehmen; **~·er** [~ə] Aufnahmegerät *n*, *bsd. Tonband*-Gerät *n*, *Kassetten*-Recorder *m*; ♪ Blockflöte *f*; **~·ing** [~ɪŋ] *Rundfunk, TV:* Aufzeichnung *f*, -nahme *f*; ~ **play·er** ['rekɔ:d-] Plattenspieler *m*.

re·count [rɪ'kaʊnt] erzählen.

re·coup [rɪ'ku:p] *j-n* entschädigen (*for* für); *et.* wiedereinbringen.

re·course [rɪ'kɔ:s] Zuflucht *f*; *have* ~ *to* (s-e) Zuflucht nehmen zu.

re·cov·er [rɪ'kʌvə] *v/t.* wiedererlangen, -bekommen, -finden; *Verluste* wiedereinbringen, wiedergutmachen; *Schulden etc.* eintreiben; *Fahrzeug, Schiff etc.* bergen; *be* ~ed

wiederhergestellt sein; *v/i.* sich erholen; genesen; **~·y** [~rɪ] Wiedererlangung *f*; Bergung *f*; Genesung *f*; Erholung *f*; *past* ~ unheilbar krank.

re·cre·ate ['rekrɪeɪt] *v/t.* erfrischen; *v/i. a.* ~ *o.s.* ausspannen, sich erholen; **~·a·tion** [rekrɪ'eɪʃn] Erholung *f*.

re·crim·i·na·tion [rɪkrɪmɪ'neɪʃn] Gegenbeschuldigung *f*.

re·cruit [rɪ'kru:t] **1.** Rekrut *m*; *fig.* Neuling *m*; **2.** ergänzen; *Truppe* rekrutieren; ✕ *Rekruten* ausheben.

rec·tan·gle ['rektæŋgl] Rechteck *n*.

rec·ti·fy ['rektɪfaɪ] berichtigen; verbessern; ⚡ gleichrichten; **~·tude** [~tju:d] Geradheit *f*, Redlichkeit *f*.

rec·tor ['rektə] Pfarrer *m*; Rektor *m*; **~·to·ry** [~rɪ] Pfarre(i) *f*; Pfarrhaus *n*.

re·cum·bent □ [rɪ'kʌmbənt] liegend.

re·cu·per·ate [rɪ'kju:pəreɪt] sich erholen; *Gesundheit* wiedererlangen.

re·cur [rɪ'kɜ:] (-*rr*-) wiederkehren (*to* zu), sich wiederholen; zurückkommen (*to* auf *acc.*); **~·rence** [rɪ'kʌrəns] Rückkehr *f*, Wiederauftreten *n*; **~·rent** □ [~nt] wiederkehrend.

re·cy·cle [ri:'saɪkl] *Abfälle* wiederverwerten; **~·cling** [~ɪŋ] Wiederverwertung *f*.

red [red] **1.** rot; ~ *heat* Rotglut *f*; ~ *tape* Bürokratismus *m*; **2.** Rot *n*; *bsd. pol.* Rote(r *m*) *f*; *be in the* ~ in den roten Zahlen sein.

red|·breast *zo.* ['redbrest] *a. robin* ~ Rotkehlchen *n*; **~·cap** Militärpolizist *m*; *Am.* Gepäckträger *m*; **~·den** ['redn] (sich) röten; erröten; **~·dish** [~ɪʃ] rötlich.

re·dec·o·rate ['ri:'dekəreɪt] *Zimmer* neu streichen od. tapezieren.

re·deem [rɪ'di:m] zurück-, loskaufen; ablösen; *Versprechen* einlösen; büßen; entschädigen für; erlösen; **2·er** *eccl.* [~ə] Erlöser *m*, Heiland *m*.

re·demp·tion [rɪ'dempʃn] Rückkauf *m*; Auslösung *f*; Erlösung *f*.

re·de·vel·op [ri:dɪ'veləp] *Gebäude, Stadtteil* sanieren.

red|·hand·ed ['red'hændɪd]: *catch s.o.* ~ *j-n auf frischer Tat ertappen*; **~·head** Rotschopf *m*; **~·head·ed** rothaarig; **~·hot** rotglühend; *fig.* hitzig; **2 In·di·an** Indianer(in); **~·let·ter day** Festtag *m*; *fig.* Freuden-, Glückstag *m*; denkwürdiger Tag; **~·ness** [~nɪs] Röte *f*; **~·nosed** rotnasig.

red·o·lent ['redələnt] duftend.

re·dou·ble [riːˈdʌbl] (sich) verdoppeln.

re·dress [rɪˈdres] **1.** Abhilfe *f*; Wiedergutmachung *f*; ♊ Entschädigung *f*; **2.** abhelfen (*dat.*); abschaffen, beseitigen; wiedergutmachen.

red-tap·ism [ˈredˈteɪpɪzəm] Bürokratismus *m*.

re·duce [rɪˈdjuːs] verringern, -mindern; einschränken; *Preise* herabsetzen; zurückführen, bringen (*to* auf, in *acc.*, zu); verwandeln (*to* in *acc.*), machen zu; ⚗, ♔ reduzieren; ⚗ einrenken; ~ *to writing* schriftlich niederlegen; **re·duc·tion** [rɪˈdʌkʃn] Herabsetzung *f*, (Preis)Nachlaß *m*, Rabatt *m*; Verminderung *f*; Verkleinerung *f*; Reduktion *f*; Verwandlung *f*; ♔ Einrenkung *f*.

re·dun·dant □ [rɪˈdʌndənt] überflüssig; übermäßig; weitschweifig.

reed [riːd] ♣ Schilfrohr *n*; Rohrflöte *f*.

re·ed·u·ca·tion [ˈriːedjʊˈkeɪʃn] Umschulung *f*, Umerziehung *f*.

reef [riːf] (Felsen)Riff *n*; ♣ Reff *n*.

ree·fer [ˈriːfə] Seemannsjacke *f*; *sl.* Marihuanazigarette *f*.

reek [riːk] **1.** Gestank *m*, unangenehmer Geruch; **2.** stinken, unangenehm riechen (*of* nach).

reel [riːl] **1.** Haspel *f*; (Garn-, Film-) Rolle *f*, Spule *f*; **2.** *v/t.* ~ (*up*) (auf-) wickeln, (-)spulen; *v/i.* wirbeln, schwanken; taumeln.

re·e·lect [ˈriːɪˈlekt] wiederwählen.

re·en·ter [riːˈentə] wieder eintreten (in *acc.*).

re·es·tab·lish [ˈriːɪˈstæblɪʃ] wiederherstellen.

ref F [ref] = *referee*.

re·fer [rɪˈfɜː]: ~ *to* ver- *od.* überweisen an (*acc.*); sich beziehen auf (*acc.*); erwähnen (*acc.*); zuordnen (*dat.*); befragen (*acc.*), nachschlagen in (*dat.*); zurückführen auf (*acc.*), zuschreiben (*dat.*).

ref·er·ee [refəˈriː] Schiedsrichter *m*; *Boxen:* Ringrichter *m*.

ref·er·ence [ˈrefrəns] Referenz *f*, Empfehlung *f*, Zeugnis *n*; Verweis(ung *f*) *m*, Hinweis *m*; Erwähnung *f*, Anspielung *f*; Bezugnahme *f*; Beziehung *f*; Nachschlagen *n*, Befragen *n*; *in od. with* ~ *to* was ... betrifft, bezüglich (*gen.*); ~ *book* Nachschlagewerk *n*; ~ *library* Handbibliothek *f*; ~ *number* Aktenzei-

chen *n*; *make* ~ *to* et. erwähnen.

ref·er·en·dum [refəˈrendəm] Volksentscheid *m*.

re·fill 1. [ˈriːˈfɪl] Nachfüllung *f*; Ersatzpackung *f*; Ersatzmine *f* (*Kugelschreiber etc.*); **2.** [ˈriːˈfɪl] (sich) wieder füllen, auffüllen.

re·fine [rɪˈfaɪn] ⊕ raffinieren, veredeln; verfeinern, kultivieren; (sich) läutern; ~ *on,* ~ *upon* et. verfeinern, -bessern; *fig.* fein, vornehm; ~**ment** [~mənt] Vered(e)lung *f*; Verfeinerung *f*; Läuterung *f*; Feinheit *f*, Vornehmheit *f*; **re·fin·er·y** [~ərɪ] Raffinerie *f*; *metall.* (Eisen)Hütte *f*.

re·fit ♣ [ˈriːˈfɪt] (*-tt-*) *v/t.* ausbessern; neu ausrüsten; *v/i.* ausgebessert werden; neu ausgerüstet werden.

re·flect [rɪˈflekt] *v/t.* zurückwerfen, reflektieren; widerspiegeln (*a. fig.*); zum Ausdruck bringen; *v/i.* ~ *on,* ~ *upon* nachdenken über (*acc.*); sich abfällig äußern über (*acc.*); ein schlechtes Licht werfen auf (*acc.*); **re·flec·tion** [~kʃn] Reflexion *f*, Zurückstrahlung *f*; Widerspiegelung *f* (*a. fig.*); Reflex *m*; Spiegelbild *n*; Überlegung *f*; Gedanke *m*; abfällige Bemerkung; **re·flec·tive** □ [~tɪv] reflektierend, zurückstrahlend; nachdenklich.

re·flex [ˈriːfleks] **1.** Reflex...; **2.** Widerschein *m*, Reflex *m* (*a. physiol.*).

re·flex·ive □ *gr.* [rɪˈfleksɪv] reflexiv, rückbezüglich.

re·for·est [ˈriːˈfɒrɪst] aufforsten.

re·form¹ [rɪˈfɔːm] **1.** Verbesserung *f*, Reform *f*; **2.** verbessern, reformieren; (sich) bessern.

re·form² [ˈriːˈfɔːm] (sich) neu bilden; ⚔ (sich) neu formieren.

ref·or·ma·tion [refəˈmeɪʃn] Reformierung *f*; Besserung *f*; *eccl.* ⚖ Reformation *f*; **re·for·ma·to·ry** [rɪˈfɔːmətərɪ] **1.** Besserungs..., Reform...; **2.** *Brt. veraltet, Am.* Besserungsanstalt *f*; **re·form·er** [~ə] *eccl.* Reformator *m*; *bsd. pol.* Reformer *m*.

re·fract [rɪˈfrækt] *Strahlen etc.* brechen; **re·frac·tion** [~kʃn] (*Strahlen-*) Brechung *f*; **re·frac·to·ry** □ [~ktərɪ] widerspenstig; ♔ hartnäckig; ⊕ feuerfest.

re·frain [rɪˈfreɪn] **1.** sich enthalten (*from gen.*), unterlassen (*from acc.*); **2.** Kehrreim *m*, Refrain *m*.

re·fresh [rɪˈfreʃ] (*o.s.* sich) erfrischen, stärken; *Gedächtnis etc.* auffrischen; **~ment** [~mənt] Erfrischung f (a. Getränk etc.).

re·fri·ge·rate [rɪ'frɪdʒəreɪt] kühlen; **~ra·tor** [~ə] Kühlschrank m, -raum m; **~ van**, Am. **~ car** ⊞ Kühlwagen m.

re·fu·el ['riː'fjʊəl] (auf)tanken.

ref·uge ['refjuːdʒ] Zuflucht(sstätte) f; Verkehrsinsel f; **~·gee** [refjʊ'dʒiː] Flüchtling m; **~ camp** Flüchtlingslager n.

re·fund 1. [riː'fʌnd] zurückzahlen; ersetzen; **2.** ['riː'fʌnd] Rückzahlung f; Erstattung f.

re·fur·bish ['riː'fɜːbɪʃ] aufpolieren (a. fig.).

re·fus·al [rɪ'fjuːzl] abschlägige Antwort; (Ver)Weigerung f; Vorkaufsrecht n (of auf acc.).

re·fuse¹ [rɪ'fjuːz] v/t. verweigern; abweisen, ablehnen; **~ to do s.th.** sich weigern, etwas zu tun; v/i. sich weigern; verweigern (Pferd).

ref·use² ['refjuːs] Ausschuß m; Abfall m, Müll m.

re·fute [rɪ'fjuːt] widerlegen.

re·gain [rɪ'geɪn] wiedergewinnen.

re·gal □ ['riːgl] königlich, Königs...

re·gale [rɪ'geɪl] fürstlich bewirten; **~ o.s. on** sich gütlich tun an (dat.), schwelgen in (dat.).

re·gard [rɪ'gɑːd] **1.** (Hoch)Achtung f; Rücksicht f; Hinblick m, -sicht f; **with ~ to** hinsichtlich (gen.); **~s** pl. Grüße pl. (bsd. in Briefen); **kind ~s** herzliche Grüße; **2.** ansehen; betrachten; (be)achten; betreffen; **~ s.o. as** j-n halten für; **as ~s** was ... betrifft; **~ing** □ [~ɪŋ] hinsichtlich (gen.); **~less** □ [~lɪs] **~ of** ohne Rücksicht auf (acc.), ungeachtet (gen.).

re·gen·e·rate [rɪ'dʒenəreɪt] (sich) erneuern; (sich) regenerieren; (sich) neu bilden.

re·gent ['riːdʒənt] Regent(in); **Prince ♀** Prinzregent.

re·gi·ment ✗ ['redʒɪmənt] **1.** Regiment n; **2.** [~ment] organisieren; reglementieren; **~als**✗ [redʒɪ'mentlz] pl. Uniform f.

re·gion ['riːdʒən] Gegend f, Gebiet n; fig. Bereich m; **~al** □ [~l] regional; örtlich; Regional..., Orts...

re·gis·ter ['redʒɪstə] **1.** Register n, Verzeichnis n; ⊕ Schieber m, Ventil n; ♩ Register n; Zählwerk n; **cash ~** Registrierkasse f; **2.** registrieren; (sich) eintragen od. -schreiben (las-

sen); (sich) anmelden; (an)zeigen; auf-, verzeichnen; Postsache einschreiben (lassen); Brt. Gepäck aufgeben; sich polizeilich melden; **~ed letter** Einschreibebrief m.

re·gis·trar [redʒɪ'strɑː] Standesbeamte(r) m; **~·tra·tion** [~eɪʃn] Eintragung f; Anmeldung f; mot. Zulassung f; **~ fee** Anmeldegebühr f; **~·try** ['redʒɪstrɪ] Eintragung f; Registratur f; Register n; **~ office** Standesamt n.

re·gress [riː'gres], **re·gres·sion** [rɪ'greʃn] Rückwärtsbewegung f; rückläufige Entwicklung.

re·gret [rɪ'gret] **1.** Bedauern n; Schmerz m; **2.** (-tt-) bedauern; Verlust beklagen; **~·ful** □ [~fl] bedauernd; **~·ta·ble** □ [~əbl] bedauerlich.

reg·u·lar □ ['regjʊlə] regelmäßig; regulär, normal, gewohnt; geregelt; geordnet; genau, pünktlich; richtig, recht, ordentlich; F richtig(gehend); ✗ regulär; **~·i·ty** [regjʊ'lærətɪ] Regelmäßigkeit f; Richtigkeit f, Ordnung f.

reg·u·late ['regjʊleɪt] regeln, ordnen; regulieren; **~·la·tion** [regjʊ'leɪʃn] **1.** Regulierung f; **~s** pl. Vorschrift f, Bestimmung f; **2.** vorschriftsmäßig.

re·hash fig. ['riː'hæʃ] **1.** wiederaufwärmen; **2.** Aufguß m.

re·hears·al [rɪ'hɜːsl] thea., ♩ Probe f; Wiederholung f; **~·e** [rɪ'hɜːs] thea. proben; wiederholen; aufsagen.

reign [reɪn] **1.** Regierung f; a. fig. Herrschaft f; **2.** herrschen, regieren.

re·im·burse ['riːɪm'bɜːs] j-n entschädigen; Kosten erstatten.

rein [reɪn] **1.** Zügel m; **2.** zügeln.

rein·deer zo. ['reɪndɪə] Ren(tier) n.

re·in·force ['riːɪn'fɔːs] verstärken; **~·ment** [~mənt] Verstärkung f.

re·in·state ['riːɪn'steɪt] wiedereinsetzen; wieder instand setzen.

re·in·sure ['riːɪn'ʃʊə] rückversichern.

re·it·e·rate [riː'ɪtəreɪt] (dauernd) wiederholen.

re·ject [rɪ'dʒekt] ab-, zurückweisen; abschlagen; verwerfen; ablehnen; **re·jec·tion** [~kʃn] Verwerfung f; Ablehnung f; Zurückweisung f.

re·joice [rɪ'dʒɔɪs] v/t. sich erfreuen; v/i. sich freuen (at, over über acc.); **re·joic·ing** [~ɪŋ] **1.** □ freudig; **2.** Freude f; **~s** pl. Freudenfest n.

re·join ['riː'dʒɔɪn] sich wieder ver-

Q
R

einigen; wieder zurückkehren zu; [rɪˈdʒɔɪn] erwidern.

re·ju·ve·nate [rɪˈdʒuːvɪneɪt] verjüngen.

re·kin·dle [ˈriːˈkɪndl] (sich) wieder entzünden.

re·lapse [rɪˈlæps] **1.** Rückfall *m*; **2.** zurückfallen, rückfällig werden; e-n Rückfall haben.

re·late [rɪˈleɪt] *v/t.* erzählen; in Beziehung bringen; *v/i.* sich beziehen (*to* auf *acc.*); **re·lat·ed** verwandt (*to* mit).

re·la·tion [rɪˈleɪʃn] Bericht *m*, Erzählung *f*; Verhältnis *n*; Verwandtschaft *f*; Verwandte(r *m*) *f*; ~*s pl.* Beziehungen *pl.*; *in* ~ *to* in bezug auf (*acc.*); **~·ship** [~ʃɪp] Verwandtschaft *f*; Beziehung *f*.

rel·a·tive [ˈrelətɪv] **1.** □ relativ, verhältnismäßig; bezüglich (*to gen.*); *gr.* Relativ..., bezüglich; entsprechend; **2.** *gr.* Relativpronomen *n*, bezügliches Fürwort *n*; Verwandte(r *m*) *f*.

re·lax [rɪˈlæks] (sich) lockern; nachlassen (in *dat.*); (sich) entspannen, ausspannen; **~·a·tion** [riːlækˈseɪʃn] Lockerung *f*; Nachlassen *n*; Entspannung *f*, Erholung *f*.

re·lay¹ [ˈriːleɪ] Ablösung *f*; ⚡ Relais *n*; *Rundfunk:* Übertragung *f*; *Sport:* Staffel *f*; **2.** [riːˈleɪ] *Rundfunk:* übertragen.

re·lay² [ˈriːˈleɪ] *Kabel etc.* neu verlegen.

re·lay race [ˈriːleɪreɪs] *Sport:* Staffellauf *m*.

re·lease [rɪˈliːs] **1.** Freilassung *f*; Befreiung *f*; Freigabe *f*; *Film:* oft first~ Uraufführung *f*; ⊕, *phot.* Auslöser *m*; **2.** freilassen; erlösen; freigeben; *Recht* aufgeben, übertragen; *Film* uraufführen; ⊕ auslösen.

rel·e·gate [ˈrelɪgeɪt] verbannen, verweisen (*to* an *acc.*).

re·lent [rɪˈlent] sich erweichen lassen; **~·less** □ [~lɪs] unbarmherzig.

rel·e·vant □ [ˈrelɪvənt] sachdienlich; zutreffend; relevant, erheblich.

re·li·a·bil·i·ty [rɪlaɪəˈbɪlətɪ] Zuverlässigkeit *f*; **~·ble** □ [rɪˈlaɪəbl] zuverlässig.

re·li·ance [rɪˈlaɪəns] Vertrauen *n*; Verlaß *m*.

rel·ic [ˈrelɪk] (Über)Rest *m*; Reliquie *f*.

re·lief [rɪˈliːf] Erleichterung *f*; (angenehme) Unterbrechung; Unter-

stützung *f*; ⚔ Ablösung *f*; ⚔ Entsatz *m*; Hilfe *f*; *arch. etc.* Relief *n*.

re·lieve [rɪˈliːv] erleichtern; mildern, lindern; *Arme etc.* unterstützen; ⚔ ablösen; ⚔ entsetzen; (ab)helfen (*dat.*); entlasten, befreien; (angenehm) unterbrechen, beleben; *to* ~ *o.s. od. nature* seine Notdurft verrichten.

re·li·gion [rɪˈlɪdʒən] Religion *f*; **~·gious** □ [~dʒəs] Religions...; religiös; gewissenhaft.

re·lin·quish [rɪˈlɪŋkwɪʃ] aufgeben; verzichten auf (*acc.*); loslassen.

rel·ish [ˈrelɪʃ] **1.** (Wohl)Geschmack *m*; Würze *f*; Genuß *m*; *fig.* Reiz *m*; *with great* ~ mit großem Appetit; *fig.* mit großem Vergnügen, *bsd. iro.* mit Wonne; **2.** genießen; gern essen; Geschmack *od.* Gefallen finden an (*dat.*).

re·luc·tance [rɪˈlʌktəns] Widerstreben *n*; *bsd. phys.* Widerstand *m*; **~·tant** □ [~t] widerstrebend, widerwillig.

re·ly [rɪˈlaɪ]: ~ *on*, ~ *upon* sich verlassen auf (*acc.*), bauen auf (*acc.*).

re·main [rɪˈmeɪn] **1.** (ver)bleiben; übrigbleiben; **2.** ~*s pl.* Überbleibsel *pl.*, (Über)Reste *pl.*; *a.* mortal ~*s* die sterblichen Überreste *pl.*; **~·der** [~də] Rest *m*.

re·mand ⚖ [rɪˈmɑːnd] **1.** ~ *s.o.* (*in custody*) j-n in die Untersuchungshaft zurückschicken; **2.** *a.* ~ *in custody* Zurücksendung *f* in die Untersuchungshaft; *prisoner on* ~ Untersuchungsgefangene(r *m*) *f*; ~ *home centre* Brt. Untersuchungsgefängnis *n* für Jugendliche.

re·mark [rɪˈmɑːk] **1.** Bemerkung *f*; Äußerung *f*; **2.** *v/t.* bemerken; äußern; *v/i.* sich äußern (*on, upon* über *acc.*, zu); **re·mar·ka·ble** □ [~əbl] bemerkenswert; außergewöhnlich.

rem·e·dy [ˈremədɪ] **1.** (Heil-, Hilfs-, Gegen-, Rechts)Mittel *n*; (Ab)Hilfe *f*; **2.** heilen; abhelfen (*dat.*).

re·mem·ber [rɪˈmembə] sich erinnern an (*acc.*); denken an (*acc.*); beherzigen; ~ *me to* me her grüße sie von mir; **~·brance** [~rəns] Erinnerung *f*; Gedächtnis *n*; Andenken *n*; ~*s pl.* Empfehlungen *pl.*, Grüße *pl.*

re·mind [rɪˈmaɪnd] erinnern (*of* an *acc.*); **~·er** [~ə] Mahnung *f*.

rem·i·nis·cence [remɪˈnɪsns] Erin-

nerung *f*; **~cent** □ [~t] (sich) er-
innernd.

re·miss □ [rɪˈmɪs] (nach)lässig; **re·mis·sion** [~ʃn] Vergebung *f* (der Sünden); Erlaß *m* (*von Strafe etc.*); Nachlassen *n*.

re·mit [rɪˈmɪt] (*-tt-*) *Sünden* vergeben; *Schuld etc.* erlassen; nachlassen in (*dat.*); überweisen; **~tance** *econ.* [~əns] (Geld)Sendung *f*, Überweisung *f*, Rimesse *f*.

rem·nant [ˈremnənt] (Über)Rest *m*.

re·mod·el [ˈriːˈmɒdl] umbilden.

re·mon·strance [rɪˈmɒnstrəns] Einspruch *m*; Protest *m*; **re·mon·strate** [ˈremənstreɪt] Vorhaltungen machen (*about* wegen; *with s.o.* j-m); protestieren.

re·morse [rɪˈmɔːs] Gewissensbisse *pl.*; Reue *f*; *without* ~ unbarmherzig; **~·less** [~lɪs] unbarmherzig.

re·mote □ [rɪˈməʊt] (*~r, ~st*) entfernt, entlegen; ~ **control** ⊕ Fernlenkung *f*, -steuerung *f*; Fernbedienung *f*; **~·ness** [~nɪs] Entfernung *f*.

re·mov·al [rɪˈmuːvl] Entfernen *n*; Beseitigung *f*; Umzug *m*; Entlassung *f*; ~ **van** Möbelwagen *m*; **~e** [~uːv] 1. *v/t.* entfernen; wegräumen, wegschaffen; beseitigen; entlassen; *v/i.* (aus-, um-, ver)ziehen; 2. Entfernung *f*; *fig.* Schritt *m*, Stufe *f*; (Verwandtschafts)Grad *m*; **~er** [~ə] (Möbel)Spediteur *m*.

re·mu·ne·rate [rɪˈmjuːnəreɪt] entlohnen; belohnen; entschädigen; vergüten; **~·ra·tive** □ [~rətɪv] lohnend.

Re·nais·sance [rəˈneɪsəns] *die* Renaissance.

re·nas·cence [rɪˈnæsns] Wiedergeburt *f*; Erneuerung *f*; Renaissance *f*; **~cent** [~nt] wiederauflebend, -erwachend.

ren·der [ˈrendə] berühmt, schwierig, möglich *etc.* machen; wiedergeben; *Dienst etc.* leisten; *Ehre etc.* erweisen; *Dank* abstatten; übersetzen; ♪ vortragen; *thea.* gestalten, interpretieren; *Grund* angeben; *econ. Rechnung* vorlegen; übergeben; machen zu; *Fett* auslassen; **~ing** [~ərɪŋ] Wiedergabe *f*; Vortrag *m*; Interpretation *f*; Übersetzung *f*; Übertragung *f*; *arch.* Rohbewurf *m*.

ren·di·tion [renˈdɪʃn] Wiedergabe *f*; Interpretation *f*; Vortrag *m*.

ren·e·gade [ˈrenɪɡeɪd] Abtrünnige(r *m*) *f*.

re·new [rɪˈnjuː] erneuern; *Gespräch etc.* wiederaufnehmen; *Kraft etc.* wiedererlangen; *Vertrag, Paß* verlängern; **~al** [~əl] Erneuerung *f*; Verlängerung *f*.

re·nounce [rɪˈnaʊns] entsagen (*dat.*); verzichten auf (*acc.*); verleugnen.

ren·o·vate [ˈrenəʊveɪt] renovieren; erneuern.

re·nown [rɪˈnaʊn] Ruhm *m*, Ansehen *n*; **re·nowned** berühmt, namhaft.

rent¹ [rent] Riß *m*; Spalte *f*.

rent² [~] 1. Miete *f*; Pacht *f*; △ *nicht* Rente; *for* ~ zu vermieten; 2. (ver-)mieten, (-)pachten; *Auto etc.* leihen; **~al** [ˈrentl] Miete *f*; Pacht *f*; Leihgebühr *f*.

re·nun·ci·a·tion [rɪnʌnsɪˈeɪʃn] Entsagung *f*; Verzicht *m* (*of* auf *acc.*).

re·pair [rɪˈpeə] 1. Ausbesserung *f*, Reparatur *f*; **~s** *pl.* Instandsetzungsarbeiten *pl.*; ~ **shop** Reparaturwerkstatt *f*; *in good* ~ in gutem Zustand, gut erhalten; *out of* ~ baufällig; 2. reparieren, ausbessern; wiedergutmachen.

rep·a·ra·tion [repəˈreɪʃn] Wiedergutmachung *f*; Entschädigung *f*; **~s** *pl. pol.* Reparationen *pl.*

rep·ar·tee [repɑːˈtiː] schlagfertige Antwort; Schlagfertigkeit *f*.

re·past *lit.* [rɪˈpɑːst] Mahl(zeit *f*) *n*.

re·pay [riːˈpeɪ] (*-paid*) *et.* zurückzahlen; *Besuch* erwidern; *et.* vergelten; *j-n* entschädigen; **~ment** [~mənt] Rückzahlung *f*.

re·peal [rɪˈpiːl] 1. Aufhebung *f* (*von Gesetzen*); 2. aufheben; widerrufen.

re·peat [rɪˈpiːt] 1. (sich) wiederholen; nachsprechen; aufsagen; nachliefern; aufstoßen (*on dat.*) (*Essen*); 2. Wiederholung *f*; ♪ Wiederholungszeichen *n*; *oft* ~ **order** *econ.* Nachbestellung *f*.

re·pel [rɪˈpel] (*-ll-*) *Feind* zurückschlagen; *fig.* zurückweisen; *j-n* abstoßen; **~lent** [~ənt] abstoßend (*a. fig.*).

re·pent [rɪˈpent] bereuen; **re·pent·ance** [~əns] Reue *f*; **re·pen·tant** [~t] reuig, reumütig.

re·per·cus·sion [riːpəˈkʌʃn] Rückprall *m*; *mst pl* **~s** Auswirkungen *pl.*

rep·er·to·ry [ˈrepətərɪ] *thea.* Repertoire *n*; *fig.* Fundgrube *f*.

rep·e·ti·tion [repɪˈtɪʃn] Wiederholung *f*; Aufsagen *n*; Nachbildung *f*.

re·place [rɪˈpleɪs] wieder hinstellen

od. -legen; ersetzen; an *j-s* Stelle treten; ablösen; **~ment** [~mənt] Ersatz *m*.

re·plant ['riː'plɑːnt] umpflanzen.

re·plen·ish [rɪ'plenɪʃ] (wieder) auffüllen; ergänzen; **~ment** [~mənt] Auffüllung *f*; Ergänzung *f*.

re·plete [rɪ'pliːt] reich ausgestattet, voll (gepfropft) (*with* mit).

rep·li·ca ['replɪkə] *Kunst:* Originalkopie *f*; Nachbildung *f*.

re·ply [rɪ'plaɪ] 1. antworten, erwidern (*to* auf *acc.*); 2. Antwort *f*, Erwiderung *f*; *in* ~ *to your letter* in Beantwortung Ihres Schreibens; **~-paid** *envelope* Freiumschlag *m*.

re·port [rɪ'pɔːt] 1. Bericht *m*; Meldung *f*, Nachricht *f*; Gerücht *n*; Ruf *m*; Knall *m*; (*school*) ~ (Schul)Zeugnis *n*; 2. berichten (über *acc.*); melden; anzeigen; *it is* ~*ed that* es heißt (daß); ~*ed speech gr.* indirekte Rede; **~er** [~ə] Reporter(in), Berichterstatter(in).

re·pose [rɪ'pəʊz] 1. Ruhe *f*; 2. *v/t.* (*o.s.* sich) ausruhen; (aus)ruhen lassen; ~ *trust, etc.* in Vertrauen *etc.* setzen auf *od.* in (*acc.*); *v/i.* (sich) ausruhen; ruhen; beruhen (*on* auf *dat.*).

re·pos·i·to·ry [rɪ'pɒzɪtərɪ] (Waren-) Lager *n*; *fig.* Fundgrube *f*, Quelle *f*.

rep·re·hend [reprɪ'hend] tadeln.

rep·re·sent [reprɪ'zent] darstellen; verkörpern; *thea.* Rolle darstellen, *Stück* aufführen; (fälschlich) hinstellen, darstellen (*as, to be* als); vertreten; **~·sen·ta·tion** [reprɪzən-'teɪʃn] Darstellung *f*; *thea.* Aufführung *f*; Vertretung *f*; **~·sen·ta·tive** □ [reprɪ'zentətɪv] 1. darstellend (*of acc.*); (stell)vertretend; *a. parl.* repräsentativ; typisch; 2. Vertreter (-in); Bevollmächtigte(r *m*) *f*; Repräsentant(in); *parl.* Abgeordnete(r *m*) *f*; *House of* ⊇s *Am. parl.* Repräsentantenhaus *n*.

re·press [rɪ'pres] unterdrücken; *psych.* verdrängen; **re·pres·sion** [~ʃn] Unterdrückung *f*; *psych.* Verdrängung *f*.

re·prieve [rɪ'priːv] 1. Begnadigung *f*; (Straf)Aufschub *m*; *fig.* Gnadenfrist *f*; 2. begnadigen; *j-m* Strafaufschub *od. fig.* e-e Gnadenfrist gewähren.

rep·ri·mand ['reprɪmɑːnd] 1. Verweis *m*; 2. *j-m* e-n Verweis erteilen.

re·print 1. [rɪː'prɪnt] neu auflegen *od.*

drucken, nachdrucken; 2. ['riːprɪnt] Neuauflage *f*, Nachdruck *m*.

re·pri·sal [rɪ'praɪzl] Repressalie *f*, Vergeltungsmaßnahme *f*.

re·proach [rɪ'prəʊtʃ] 1. Vorwurf *m*; Schande *f*; 2. vorwerfen (*s.o. with s.th.* j-m *et.*); Vorwürfe machen; **~ful** □ [~fl] vorwurfsvoll.

rep·ro·bate ['reprəbeɪt] 1. verkommen, verderbt; 2. verkommenes Subjekt; 3. mißbilligen; verdammen.

re·pro·cess [riː'prəʊses] *Kernbrennstoffe* wiederaufbereiten; **~ing plant** Wiederaufbereitungsanlage *f*.

re·pro·duce [riːprə'djuːs] (wieder-) erzeugen; (sich) fortpflanzen; wiedergeben, reproduzieren; **~duc·tion** [~'dʌkʃn] Wiedererzeugung *f*; Fortpflanzung *f*; Reproduktion *f*; **~duc·tive** [~tɪv] Fortpflanzungs...

re·proof [rɪ'pruːf] Tadel *m*, Rüge *f*.

re·prove [rɪ'pruːv] tadeln, rügen.

rep·tile *zo.* ['reptaɪl] Reptil *n*.

re·pub·lic [rɪ'pʌblɪk] Republik *f*; **~li·can** [~ən] 1. republikanisch; 2. Republikaner(in).

re·pu·di·ate [rɪ'pjuːdɪeɪt] nicht anerkennen; ab-, zurückweisen; *j-n* verstoßen.

re·pug·nance [rɪ'pʌɡnəns] Abneigung *f*, Widerwille *m*; **~nant** □ [~t] abstoßend; widerlich.

re·pulse [rɪ'pʌls] 1. ✕ Abwehr *f*; Zurück-, Abweisung *f*; 2. ✕ zurückschlagen, abwehren; zurück-, abweisen; **re·pul·sion** Abscheu *m*, Widerwille *m*; *phys.* Abstoßung *f*; **re·pul·sive** □ [~ɪv] abstoßend (*a. phys.*), widerwärtig.

rep·u·ta·ble □ ['repjʊtəbl] angesehen, achtbar; ehrbar, anständig; **~tion** [repjʊ'teɪʃn] Ruf *m*, Ansehen *n*; **re·pute** [rɪ'pjuːt] 1. Ruf *m*; 2. halten für; *be* ~*d* (*to be*) gelten als; **re·put·ed** vermeintlich; angeblich.

re·quest [rɪ'kwest] 1. Bitte *f*, Gesuch *n*; Ersuchen *n*; *econ.* Nachfrage *f*; *by* ~, *on* ~ auf Wunsch; *in* (*great*) ~ (sehr) gesucht *od.* begehrt; ~ *stop* Bedarfshaltestelle *f*; 2. *um et.* bitten *od.* ersuchen; *j-n* (höflich) bitten *od.* ersuchen.

re·quire [rɪ'kwaɪə] verlangen, fordern; brauchen, erfordern; *if* ~*d* falls notwendig; ~*d* erforderlich; **~ment** [~mənt] (An)Forderung *f*; Erfordernis *n*; ~*s pl.* Bedarf *m*.

req·ui·site ['rekwɪzɪt] **1.** erforderlich; **2.** Erfordernis *n*; (Bedarfs-, Gebrauchs)Artikel *m*; *toilet* ~*s pl.* Toilettenartikel *pl.*; △ *nicht* (*Bühnen*-)*Requisit*; ~**si·tion** [rekwɪ'zɪʃn] **1.** Anforderung *f*; ⚔ Requisition *f*; **2.** anfordern; ⚔ requirieren.

re·quite [rɪ'kwaɪt] *j-m et.* vergelten.

re·sale ['riːseɪl] Wieder-, Weiterverkauf *m*; ~ *price* Wiederverkaufspreis *m*.

re·scind [rɪ'sɪnd] *Urteil* aufheben; *Vertrag* annullieren; **re·scis·sion** [rɪ'sɪʒn] Aufhebung *f*; Annullierung *f*.

res·cue ['reskjuː] **1.** Rettung *f*; Hilfe *f*; Befreiung *f*; **2.** retten; befreien.

re·search [rɪ'sɜːtʃ] **1.** Forschung *f*; Untersuchung *f*; Nachforschung *f*; **2.** forschen, Forschungen anstellen; *et.* untersuchen, erforschen; ~**er** [~ə] Forscher(in).

re·sem·blance [rɪ'zembləns] Ähnlichkeit *f* (*to* mit); ~**ble** [rɪ'zembl] gleichen, ähnlich sein (*dat.*).

re·sent [rɪ'zent] übelnehmen; sich ärgern über (*acc.*); ~**ful** □ [~fl] übelnehmerisch; ärgerlich; ~**ment** [~mənt] Ärger *m*; Groll *m*; △ *nicht Ressentiment*.

res·er·va·tion [rezə'veɪʃn] Reservierung *f*, Vorbestellung *f* (*von Zimmern etc.*); Vorbehalt *m*; Reservat(ion *f*) *n*; *central* ~ *Brt.* Mittelstreifen *m* (*der Autobahn*).

re·serve [rɪ'zɜːv] **1.** Reserve *f* (*a.* ⚔); Vorrat *m*; *econ.* Rücklage *f*; Zurückhaltung *f*; Vorbehalt *m*; *Sport*: Ersatzmann *m*; **2.** aufbewahren, aufsparen; (sich) vorbehalten; (sich) zurückhalten mit; *Platz etc.* reservieren (lassen), belegen, vorbestellen; ~**d** □ *fig.* zurückhaltend, reserviert.

res·er·voir ['rezəvwɑː] Behälter *m* (*für Wasser etc.*); Sammel-, Staubecken *n*; *fig.* Reservoir *n*.

re·side [rɪ'zaɪd] wohnen, ansässig sein, s-n Wohnsitz haben; ~ *in fig.* innewohnen (*dat.*).

res·i·dence ['rezɪdəns] Wohnsitz *m*, -ort *m*; Aufenthalt *m*; (Amts)Sitz *m*; (herrschaftliches) Wohnhaus; Residenz *f*; ~ *permit* Aufenthaltsgenehmigung *f*; ~**dent** [~t] **1.** wohnhaft; ortsansässig; **2.** Ortsansässige(r *m*) *f*, Einwohner(in); Bewohner(in); Hotelgast *m*; *mot.* Anlieger *m*; ~**den-**

tial [rezɪ'denʃl] Wohn...; ~ *area* Wohngegend *f*.

re·sid·u·al [rɪ'zɪdjʊəl] übrig(geblieben); zurückbleibend; restlich; **res·i·due** ['rezɪdjuː] Rest *m*; Rückstand *m*.

re·sign [rɪ'zaɪn] *v/t.* aufgeben; *Amt* niederlegen; überlassen; verzichten auf (*acc.*); ~ *o.s. to* sich ergeben in (*acc.*); sich abfinden mit; *v/i.* zurücktreten; **res·ig·na·tion** [rezɪg-'neɪʃn] Rücktritt(sgesuch *n*) *m*; Resignation *f*; ~**ed** □ ergeben, resigniert.

re·sil·i·ence [rɪ'zɪlɪəns] Elastizität *f*; *fig.* Unverwüstlichkeit *f*; ~**ent** [~t] elastisch; *fig.* unverwüstlich.

res·in ['rezɪn] **1.** Harz *n*; **2.** harzen.

re·sist [rɪ'zɪst] widerstehen (*dat.*); Widerstand leisten (*dat.*); sich widersetzen (*dat.*); ~**ance** [~əns] Widerstand *m* (*a.* ⚡, *phys.*); *med.* Widerstandsfähigkeit *f*; *line of least* ~ Weg *m* des geringsten Widerstands; **re·sis·tant** [~nt] widerstandsfähig.

res·o·lute □ ['rezəluːt] entschlossen, energisch; ~**lu·tion** [rezə'luːʃn] Entschlossenheit *f*; Bestimmtheit *f*; Beschluß *m*; *pol.* Resolution *f*; Lösung *f*.

re·solve [rɪ'zɒlv] **1.** *v/t.* auflösen; *fig.* lösen; *Zweifel etc.* zerstreuen; beschließen, entscheiden; *v/i. a.* ~ *o.s.* sich auflösen; beschließen; ~ *on, ~ upon* sich entschließen zu; **2.** Entschluß *m*; Beschluß *m*; ~**d** □ entschlossen.

res·o·nance ['rezənəns] Resonanz *f*; ~**nant** □ [~t] nach-, widerhallend.

re·sort [rɪ'zɔːt] **1.** Zuflucht *f*; Ausweg *m*; Aufenthalt(sort) *m*; Erholungsort *m*; *health* ~ Kurort *m*; *seaside* ~ Seebad *n*; *summer* ~ Sommerfrische *f*; **2.** ~ *to et.* besuchen; seine Zuflucht nehmen zu.

re·sound [rɪ'zaʊnd] widerhallen (lassen).

re·source [rɪ'sɔːs] Hilfsquelle *f*, -mittel *n*; Zuflucht *f*; Findigkeit *f*; ~*s pl.* (*natürliche*) Reichtümer *pl.*, Mittel *pl.*, Bodenschätze *pl.*; ~**ful** □ [~fl] einfallsreich, findig.

re·spect [rɪ'spekt] **1.** Beziehung *f*, Hinsicht *f*; Achtung *f*, Respekt *m*; Rücksicht *f*; *with* ~ *to* ... was ... (an)betrifft; *in this* ~ in dieser Hinsicht; ~*s pl.* Empfehlungen *pl.*, Grüße *pl.*; *give my* ~*s to* ... grüßen Sie ...

von mir; **2.** v/t. achten, schätzen; respektieren; betreffen; *as ~s* ... was ... (an)betrifft; **re·spec·ta·ble** □ [~əbl] ehrbar; anständig; angesehen, geachtet (*Mensch*); ansehnlich, beachtlich (*Summe*); **~ful** □ [~fl] ehrerbietig; *yours ~ly* hochachtungsvoll; **~ing** [~ɪŋ] hinsichtlich (*gen.*).

re·spec·tive □ [rɪ'spektɪv] jeweilig; *we went to the ~ places* wir gingen jeder an seinen Platz; **~ly** [~lɪ] beziehungsweise.

res·pi·ra·tion [respə'reɪʃn] Atmung f; **~tor** [ˈrespəreɪtə] Atemgerät n.

re·spire [rɪ'spaɪə] atmen.

re·spite [ˈrespaɪt] Frist f; Aufschub m; Stundung f; Ruhepause f (*from* von); *without* (a) ~ ohne Unterbrechung.

re·splen·dent □ [rɪ'splendənt] glänzend, strahlend.

re·spond [rɪ'spɒnd] antworten, erwidern; ~ *to* reagieren *od.* ansprechen auf (*acc.*).

re·sponse [rɪ'spɒns] Antwort f, Erwiderung f; *fig.* Reaktion f; *meet with little* ~ wenig Anklang finden.

re·spon·si·bil·i·ty [rɪspɒnsə'bɪlətɪ] Verantwortung f; *on one's own* ~ auf eigene Verantwortung; *sense of* ~ Verantwortungsgefühl n; *take (accept, assume) the* ~ *for* die Verantwortung übernehmen für; **~ble** □ [rɪ'spɒnsəbl] verantwortlich; verantwortungsvoll.

rest¹ [rest] **1.** Ruhe f; Rast f; Pause f, Unterbrechung f; Erholung f; ⊕ Stütze f; (*Telefon*)Gabel f; *have od. take a* ~ sich ausruhen; *be at* ~ ruhig sein; **2.** v/i. ruhen; rasten; schlafen; (sich) lehnen, sich stützen (*on* auf *acc.*); ~ *on, ~ upon* ruhen auf (*Blick, Last*); *fig.* beruhen auf (*dat.*); ~ *with fig.* liegen bei (*Fehler, Verantwortung*); v/t. (aus)ruhen lassen; stützen (*on* auf); lehnen (*against* gegen).

rest² [~]: *the* ~ der Rest; *and all the* ~ *of it* und so weiter und so fort; *for the* ~ im übrigen.

res·tau·rant [ˈrestərɔ̃:ŋ, ~rɒnt] Restaurant n, Gaststätte f.

rest·ful [ˈrestfl] ruhig, erholsam.

rest·ing-place [ˈrestɪŋpleɪs] Ruheplatz m; (*letzte*) Ruhestätte.

res·ti·tu·tion [restɪˈtjuːʃn] Wiederherstellung f; Rückerstattung f.

res·tive □ [ˈrestɪv] widerspenstig.

rest·less □ [ˈrestlɪs] ruhelos; rastlos;

unruhig; **~ness** [~nɪs] Ruhelosigkeit f; Rastlosigkeit f; Unruhe f.

res·to·ra·tion [restəˈreɪʃn] Wiederherstellung f; Wiedereinsetzung f; Restaurierung f; Rekonstruktion f; Nachbildung f; (Rück)Erstattung f; **~tive** [rɪ'stɒrətɪv] **1.** stärkend; **2.** Stärkungsmittel n.

re·store [rɪ'stɔ:] wiederherstellen; wiedereinsetzen (*to* in *acc.*); restaurieren; (rück)erstatten, zurückgeben; zurücklegen; ~ *s.o.* (*to health*) j-n wiederherstellen.

re·strain [rɪ'streɪn] zurückhalten (*from* von); in Schranken halten; bändigen, zügeln; *Gefühle* unterdrücken; **~t** [~t] Zurückhaltung f; Beschränkung f, Zwang m.

re·strict [rɪ'strɪkt] be-, einschränken; **re·stric·tion** [~kʃn] Be-, Einschränkung f; *without* ~s uneingeschränkt.

rest room *Am.* [ˈrestruːm] Toilette f (*e-s Hotels etc.*).

re·sult [rɪ'zʌlt] **1.** Ergebnis n, Resultat n; Folge f; **2.** folgen, sich ergeben (*from* aus); ~ *in* hinauslaufen auf (*acc.*), zur Folge haben.

re·sume [rɪ'zjuːm] wiederaufnehmen; fortsetzen; *Sitz* wieder einnehmen; **re·sump·tion** [rɪ'zʌmpʃn] Wiederaufnahme f; Fortsetzung f.

re·sur·rec·tion [rezə'rekʃn] Wiederaufleben n; ♀ *eccl.* Auferstehung f.

re·sus·ci·tate [rɪ'sʌsɪteɪt] wiederbeleben; *fig.* wieder aufleben lassen.

re·tail 1. [ˈriːteɪl] Einzelhandel m; *by* ~, *adv.* ~ im Einzelhandel; **2.** [~] Einzelhandels...; **3.** [riː'teɪl] im Einzelhandel verkaufen; **~er** [~ə] Einzelhändler(in).

re·tain [rɪ'teɪn] behalten; zurück(be)halten.

re·tal·i·ate [rɪ'tælɪeɪt] v/t. *Unrecht* vergelten; v/i. sich rächen; **~a·tion** [rɪtælɪ'eɪʃn] Vergeltung f.

re·tard [rɪ'tɑːd] verzögern, aufhalten, hemmen; (*mentally*) ~ed *psych.* (geistig) zurückgeblieben.

retch [retʃ] würgen (*beim Erbrechen*).

re·tell [riː'tel] (*-told*) nacherzählen; wiederholen.

re·ten·tion [rɪ'tenʃn] Zurückhalten n; Beibehaltung f; Bewahrung f.

re·think [riː'θɪŋk] (*-thought*) *et.* nochmals überdenken.

ret·i·cent □ [ˈretɪsənt] verschwiegen; schweigsam; zurückhaltend.

ret·i·nue [ˈretɪnjuː] Gefolge n.

re·tire [rɪ'taɪə] v/t. zurückziehen; pensionieren; v/i. sich zurückziehen; zurück-, abtreten; sich zur Ruhe setzen; in Pension od. Rente gehen, sich pensionieren lassen; **~d** □ zurückgezogen; pensioniert, im Ruhestand (lebend); ~ *pay* Ruhegeld n; **~ment** [\~mənt] Sichzurückziehen n; Ausscheiden n, Aus-, Rücktritt m; Ruhestand m; Zurückgezogenheit f; **re·tir·ing** [\~rɪŋ] zurückhaltend; ~ *pension* Ruhegeld n.

re·tort [rɪ'tɔːt] 1. (scharfe od. treffende) Erwiderung; 2. (scharf od. treffend) erwidern.

re·touch ['riː'tʌtʃ] *et.* überarbeiten; *phot.* retuschieren.

re·trace [rɪ'treɪs] zurückverfolgen; ~ *one's steps* zurückgehen.

re·tract [rɪ'trækt] v/t. *Angebot* zurückziehen; *Behauptung* zurücknehmen; *Krallen,* ✈ *Fahrgestell* einziehen; v/i. eingezogen werden (*Krallen,* ✈ *Fahrgestell*).

re·train ['riː'treɪn] umschulen.

re·tread 1. [riː'tred] *Reifen* runderneuern; 2. ['riː'tred] runderneuerter Reifen.

re·treat [rɪ'triːt] 1. Rückzug m; Zuflucht(sort m) f; Schlupfwinkel m; *sound the ~* ✕ zum Rückzug blasen; 2. sich zurückziehen.

ret·ri·bu·tion [retrɪ'bjuːʃn] Vergeltung f.

re·trieve [rɪ'triːv] wiederfinden, -bekommen; wiedergewinnen, -erlangen; wiedergutmachen; *hunt.* apportieren.

ret·ro- ['retrəʊ] (zu)rück...; **~ac·tive** □ ✍ [retrəʊ'æktɪv] rückwirkend; **~grade** ['retrəʊgreɪd] rückläufig; rückschrittlich; **~spect** [\~spekt] Rückblick m; **~spec·tive** □ [retrəʊ'spektɪv] (zu)rückblickend; ✍ rückwirkend.

re·try ✍ ['riː'traɪ] wiederaufnehmen, neu verhandeln.

re·turn [rɪ'tɜːn] 1. Rück-, Wiederkehr f; Wiederauftreten n; *Brt.* Rückfahrkarte f, ✈ Rückflugticket n; *econ.* Rückzahlung f; Rückgabe f; Entgelt n, Gegenleistung f; (amtlicher) Bericht; (*Steuer*)Erklärung f; *parl.* Wahl f (*e-s Abgeordneten*); *Sport:* Rückspiel n; *Tennis etc.* Rückschlag m, Return m; Erwiderung f; *attr.* Rück...; **~s** *pl. econ.* Umsatz m; Ertrag m, Gewinn m;

many happy ~s of the day herzliche Glückwünsche zum Geburtstag; *in ~ for* (als Gegenleistung) für; *by ~* (*of post*), *by ~ mail Am.* postwendend; ~ *match Sport:* Rückspiel n; ~ *ticket Brt.* Rückfahrkarte f, ✈ Rückflugticket n; 2. v/i. zurückkehren, -kommen; wiederkommen; v/t. zurückgeben; *Geld* zurückzahlen; zurückschicken, -senden; zurückstellen, -bringen, -tun; *Gewinn* abwerfen; (zur Steuerveranlagung) angeben; *parl. Abgeordneten* wählen; *Tennis etc.:* *Ball* zurückschlagen, -geben; erwidern; vergelten; ~ *a verdict of guilty* ✍ *j-n* schuldig sprechen.

re·u·ni·fi·ca·tion *pol.* ['riːjuːnɪfɪ-'keɪʃn] Wiedervereinigung f.

re·u·nion ['riː'juːnjən] Wiedervereinigung f; Treffen n, Zusammenkunft f.

re·val·ue *econ.* [riː'væljuː] *Währung* aufwerten.

re·veal [rɪ'viːl] enthüllen; offenbaren; **~ing** [\~ɪŋ] aufschlußreich.

rev·el ['revl] (*bsd. Brt. -ll-, Am. -l-*) ausgelassen sein; ~ *in* schwelgen in (*dat.*); sich weiden an (*dat.*).

rev·e·la·tion [revə'leɪʃn] Enthüllung f; Offenbarung f.

rev·el·ry ['revlrɪ] lärmende Festlichkeit.

re·venge [rɪ'vendʒ] 1. Rache f; *bsd. Sport, Spiel:* Revanche f; *in ~ for* als Rache für; 2. rächen; **~ful** □ [\~fl] rachsüchtig; **re·veng·er** [\~ə] Rächer(in).

rev·e·nue *econ.* ['revənjuː] Staatseinkünfte *pl.*, -einnahmen *pl.*

re·ver·ber·ate *phys.* [rɪ'vɜːbəreɪt] zurückwerfen; zurückstrahlen; widerhallen.

re·vere [rɪ'vɪə] (ver)ehren.

rev·er·ence ['revərəns] 1. Verehrung f; Ehrfurcht f; 2. (ver)ehren; **~rend** [\~d] 1. ehrwürdig; 2. Geistliche(r) m.

rev·er·ent □ ['revərənt], **~ren·tial** □ [revə'renʃl] ehrerbietig, ehrfurchtsvoll.

rev·er·ie ['revərɪ] (Tag)Träumerei f.

re·vers·al [rɪ'vɜːsl] Umkehrung f, Umschwung m; **~e** [\~s] 1. Gegenteil n; Rück-, Kehrseite f; *mot.* Rückwärtsgang m; Rück(wärts)gang m; □ umgekehrt; Rück(wärts)...; *in ~ order* in umgekehrter Reihenfolge; ~ *gear mot.* Rückwärtsgang m; ~ *side* linke (*Stoff*)Seite f; 3. umkehren; *Ur-*

teil umstoßen; **~·i·ble** □ [~əbl] doppelseitig (tragbar).

re·vert [rɪ'vɜːt] *(to)* zurückkehren (zu *dat.*); zurückkommen (auf *acc.*); wieder zurückfallen (in *acc.*); ⚖ zurückfallen (an *j-n*).

re·view [rɪ'vjuː] **1.** Nachprüfung *f*, (Über)Prüfung *f*, Revision *f*; ⚔ Parade *f*; Rückblick *m*; (Buch)Besprechung *f*, Kritik *f*, Rezension *f*; *pass s.th. in ~* et. Revue passieren lassen; **2.** (über-, nach)prüfen; ⚔ besichtigen; *Buch etc.* besprechen, rezensieren; *fig.* überblicken, -schauen; **~·er** [~ə] Rezensent(in).

re·vise [rɪ'vaɪz] überarbeiten, durchsehen, revidieren; *Brt.* (den Stoff) wiederholen (*Buch etc.* für *e-e Prüfung*); **re·vi·sion** [rɪ'vɪʒn] Revision *f*; Überarbeitung *f*; *Brt.* Wiederholung *f* (des Stoffs) (*für e-e Prüfung*).

re·viv·al [rɪ'vaɪvl] Wiederbelebung *f*; Wiederaufleben *n*, -blühen *n*; Erneuerung *f*; *fig.* Erweckung *f*; **re·vive** [~aɪv] wiederbeleben; wiederaufleben (lassen); wiederherstellen; sich erholen.

re·voke [rɪ'vəʊk] widerrufen, zurücknehmen, rückgängig machen.

re·volt [rɪ'vəʊlt] **1.** Revolte *f*, Aufstand *m*, -ruhr *m*; **2.** *v/i.* sich auflehnen, revoltieren (*against* gegen); *v/t. fig.* abstoßen; **~·ing** □ [~ɪŋ] abstoßend; ekelhaft; scheußlich.

rev·o·lu·tion [revə'luːʃn] ⊕ Umdrehung *f*; *fig.* Revolution *f* (*a. pol.*), Umwälzung *f*, Umschwung *m*; **~·ar·y** [~ərɪ] **1.** revolutionär; Revolutions...; **2.** *pol. u. fig.* Revolutionär(in); **~·ize** *fig.* [~naɪz] revolutionieren.

re·volve [rɪ'vɒlv] *v/i.* sich drehen (*about, round* um); *~ around fig.* sich um *j-n od. et.* drehen; *v/t.* drehen; **re·volv·ing** [~ɪŋ] sich drehend, Dreh...

re·vue *thea.* [rɪ'vjuː] Revue *f*; Kabarett *n*.

re·vul·sion *fig.* [rɪ'vʌlʃn] Abscheu *m*.

re·ward [rɪ'wɔːd] **1.** Belohnung *f*; Entgelt *n*; **2.** belohnen; **~·ing** □ [~ɪŋ] lohnend; dankbar (*Aufgabe*).

re·write ['riː'raɪt] (-wrote, -written) neu (*od.* um)schreiben.

rhap·so·dy ['ræpsədɪ] ♪ Rhapsodie *f*; *fig.* Schwärmerei *f*, Wortschwall *m*.

rhe·to·ric ['retərɪk] Rhetorik *f*; *fig. contp.* leere Phrasen *pl.*

rheu·ma·tism ✲ ['ruːmətɪzəm] Rheumatismus *m*.

rhu·barb ♀ ['ruːbɑːb] Rhabarber *m*.

rhyme [raɪm] **1.** Reim *m*; Vers *m*; *without ~ or reason* ohne Sinn u. Verstand; **2.** (sich) reimen.

rhythm ['rɪðəm] Rhythmus *m*; **~·mic** [~mɪk] (~*ally*), **~·mi·cal** □ [~mɪkl] rhythmisch.

rib [rɪb] **1.** *anat.* Rippe *f*; **2.** (-*bb*-) F hänseln, aufziehen.

rib·ald ['rɪbəld] lästerlich, zotig.

rib·bon ['rɪbən] Band *n*; Ordensband *n*; Farbband *n*; Streifen *m*; **~s** *pl.* Fetzen *pl.*

rib cage *anat.* ['rɪbkeɪdʒ] Brustkorb *m*.

rice ♀ [raɪs] Reis *m*.

rich [rɪtʃ] **1.** □ reich (*in* an *dat.*); prächtig, kostbar; fruchtbar, fett (*Erde*); voll (*Ton*); schwer, nahrhaft (*Speise*); schwer (*Wein, Duft*); satt (*Farbe*); **2.** *the* ~ *pl.* die Reichen *pl.*; **~es** ['rɪtʃɪz] *pl.* Reichtum *m*, Reichtümer *pl.*

rick ✗ [rɪk] (Stroh-, Heu)Schober *m*.

rick·ets ✲ ['rɪkɪts] *sg. od. pl.* Rachitis *f*; **rick·et·y** [~ɪ] ✲ rachitisch; wack(e)lig (*Möbel*).

rid [rɪd] (-*dd*-; *rid*) befreien, frei machen (*of* von); *get ~ of* loswerden.

rid·dance F ['rɪdəns]: *Good ~!* Den (die, das) wären wir (Gott sei Dank) los!

rid·den ['rɪdn] **1.** *p.p. von ride* 2; **2.** *in Zssgn:* geplagt von ...

rid·dle¹ ['rɪdl] Rätsel *n*.

rid·dle² [~] **1.** grobes (Draht)Sieb; **2.** durchsieben; durchlöchern.

ride [raɪd] **1.** Ritt *m*; (Aus)Ritt *m*; Reitweg *m*; **2.** (*rode*, *ridden*) *v/i.* reiten; fahren (*on a bicycle* auf e-m Fahrrad; *in, Am. on a bus* im Bus); *v/t. Pferd etc.* reiten; *Fahr-, Motorrad* fahren, fahren auf (*dat.*); **rid·er** ['raɪdə] Reiter(in).

ridge [rɪdʒ] **1.** (Gebirgs)Kamm *m*, Grat *m*; *arch.* First *m*; ✲ Rain *m*.

rid·i·cule ['rɪdɪkjuːl] **1.** Spott *m*; **2.** lächerlich machen, verspotten; **ri·dic·u·lous** □ [rɪ'dɪkjʊləs] lächerlich.

rid·ing ['raɪdɪŋ] Reiten *n*; *attr.* Reit...

riff-raff ['rɪfræf] Gesindel *n*.

ri·fle¹ ['raɪfl] Gewehr *n*; Büchse *f*.

ri·fle² [~] (aus)plündern; durchwühlen.

rift [rɪft] Riß *m*, Sprung *m*; Spalte *f*.

rig¹ [rɪg] (*-gg-*) manipulieren.

rig² [~] **1.** ⚓ Takelage *f*; ⊕ Bohranlage *f*, -turm *m*, Förderturm *m*; F Aufmachung *f*; **2.** (*-gg-*) *Schiff* auftakeln; ~ *up* F (behelfsmäßig) herrichten, zusammenbauen; **~ging** ⚓ ['rɪgɪŋ] Takelage *f*.

right [raɪt] **1.** □ recht; richtig; rechte(r, -s), Rechts...; *all ~!* in Ordnung!, gut!; *that's all ~!* das macht nichts!, schon gut!, bitte!; *I am perfectly all ~* mir geht es ausgezeichnet; *that's ~!* richtig!, ganz recht!, stimmt!; *be ~* recht haben; *put ~*, *set ~* in Ordnung bringen; berichtigen, korrigieren; **2.** *adv.* rechts; recht, richtig; gerade(wegs), direkt; ganz (und gar); genau, gerade; ~ *away* sofort; ~ *on* geradeaus; *turn ~* (sich) nach rechts wenden, rechts abbiegen; **3.** Recht *n*; Rechte *f* (*a. pol., Boxen*), rechte Seite od. Hand; *by ~* of auf Grund (*gen.*); *on od. to the ~* rechts; **4.** aufrichten; *et.* wiedergutmachen; in Ordnung bringen; **~down** ['raɪtdaʊn] regelrecht; **~eous** □ ['raɪtʃəs] rechtschaffen; selbstgerecht; gerecht(fertigt), berechtigt; **~ful** □ [~l] rechtmäßig; gerecht; **~hand** rechte(r, -s); ~ *drive* Rechtssteuerung *f*; **~handed** rechtshändig; **~ly** [~lɪ] richtig; mit Recht; **~ of way** Durchgangsrecht *n*; *mot.* Vorfahrt(srecht *n*)*f*; **~wing** *pol.* rechte(r, -s), rechtsgerichtet.

rig·id □ ['rɪdʒɪd] starr, steif; *fig.* streng, hart; **~i·ty** [rɪ'dʒɪdətɪ] Starrheit *f*; Strenge *f*, Härte *f*.

rig·ma·role ['rɪgmərəʊl] Geschwätz *n*.

rig·or·ous □ ['rɪgərəs] streng, rigoros; (peinlich) genau.

rig·o(u)r ['rɪgə] Strenge *f*, Härte *f*.

rile F [raɪl] ärgern, reizen.

rim [rɪm] Rand *m*; Krempe *f*; Felge *f*; Radkranz *m*; **~less** ['rɪmlɪs] randlos (*Brille*); **~med** mit (e-m) Rand.

rime *lit.* [raɪm] Rauhreif *m*.

rind [raɪnd] Rinde *f*, Schale *f*; (Speck)Schwarte *f*.

ring¹ [rɪŋ] Klang *m*; Geläut(e) *n*; Klingeln *n*, Läuten *n*; (Telefon)Anruf *m*; *give s.o. a ~* j-n anrufen; **2.** (*rang, rung*) läuten; klingeln; klingen; erschallen; *bsd. Brt. teleph.* anrufen; ~ *the bell* läuten, klingeln; *bsd. Brt. teleph.:* ~ *back* zurückrufen;

~ *off* (den Hörer) auflegen, Schluß machen; ~ *s.o. up* j-n *od.* bei j-m anrufen.

ring² [~] **1.** Ring *m*; Kreis *m*; Manege *f*; (Box)Ring *m*; (Verbrecher-, Spionage- *etc.*)Ring *m*; **2.** umringen; beringen; **~bind·er** ['rɪŋbaɪndə] Ringbuch *n*; **~lead·er** Rädelsführer *m*; **~let** [~lɪt] (Ringel)Locke *f*; **~mas·ter** Zirkusdirektor *m*; ~ *road Brt.* Umgehungsstraße *f*; Ringstraße *f*; **~side**: *at the ~ Boxen:* am Ring; ~ *seat* Ringplatz *m*; Manegenplatz *m*.

rink [rɪŋk] (*bsd. Kunst*)Eisbahn *f*; Rollschuhbahn *f*.

rinse [rɪns] *oft ~ out* (ab-, aus)spülen.

ri·ot ['raɪət] **1.** Aufruhr *m*; Tumult *m*; Krawall *m*; *run ~* randalieren; **2.** Krawall machen, randalieren; e-n Aufstand machen; **~er** [~ə] Aufrührer(in); Randalierer *m*; **~ous** □ [~əs] aufrührerisch; lärmend; ausgelassen, wild.

rip [rɪp] **1.** Riß *m*; **2.** (*-pp-*) (auf-, zer)reißen, (-)schlitzen; F sausen, rasen.

ripe □ [raɪp] reif; **rip·en** ['raɪpən] reifen (lassen), reif werden; **~ness** [~nɪs] Reife *f*.

rip·ple ['rɪpl] **1.** kleine Welle; Kräuselung *f*; Rieseln *n*; **2.** (sich) kräuseln; rieseln.

rise [raɪz] **1.** (An-, Auf)Steigen *n*; (Preis-, Gehalts-, Lohn)Erhöhung *f*; Steigung *f*; Anhöhe *f*; Ursprung *m*; *fig.* Aufstieg *m*; *give ~ to* verursachen, führen zu; **2.** (*rose, risen*) sich erheben, aufstehen; die Sitzung schließen; auf-, hoch-, emporsteigen; (an)steigen; sich erheben, emporragen; aufkommen (*Sturm etc.*); *eccl.* auferstehen; aufgehen (*Sonne, Samen*); entspringen (*Fluß*); (an)wachsen, sich steigern; sich erheben, revoltieren; *beruflich etc.* aufsteigen; ~ *to the occasion* sich der Lage gewachsen zeigen; **ris·en** ['rɪzn] *p.p. von rise 2*; **ris·er** ['raɪzə]: *early ~* Frühaufsteher(in).

ris·ing ['raɪzɪŋ] (An-, Auf)Steigen *n*; *ast.* Aufgehen *n*, -gang *m*; Aufstand *m*.

risk [rɪsk] **1.** Gefahr *f*, Wagnis *n*, Risiko *n* (*a. econ.*); *be at ~* in Gefahr sein; *run the ~ of doing s.th.* Gefahr laufen, et. zu tun; *run od. take a ~* ein Risiko eingehen; **2.** wagen, riskieren; **~y** □ ['rɪskɪ]

(-*ier*, -*iest*) riskant, gefährlich, gewagt.

rite [raɪt] Ritus *m*; Zeremonie *f*;
rit·u·al [ˈrɪtjʊəl] **1.** □ rituell; Ritual...; **2.** Ritual *n*.

ri·val [ˈraɪvl] **1.** Rival|e *m*, -in *f*, Konkurrent(in); **2.** rivalisierend, Konkurrenz...; **3.** (*bsd. Brt.* -*ll*-, *Am.* -*l*-) rivalisieren *od.* konkurrieren mit; **~ry** [~rɪ] Rivalität *f*; Konkurrenz (-kampf *m*) *f*.

riv·er [ˈrɪvə] Fluß *m*, Strom *m* (*a. fig.*); **~side 1.** Flußufer *n*; **2.** am Ufer (gelegen).

riv·et [ˈrɪvɪt] **1.** ⊕ Niet(e *f*) *m*, *n*; **2.** ⊕ (ver)nieten; *fig.* Blick *etc.* heften; *fig.* fesseln.

riv·u·let [ˈrɪvjʊlɪt] Flüßchen *n*.

road [rəʊd] (Auto-, Land)Straße *f*; *fig.* Weg *m*; *on the* ~ unterwegs; *thea.* auf Tournee; **~ ac·ci·dent** Verkehrsunfall *m*; **~block** [ˈrəʊdblɒk] Straßensperre *f*; **~ map** Straßenkarte *f*; **~ safe·ty** Verkehrssicherheit *f*; **~side 1.** Straßen-, Wegrand *m*; **2.** an der Landstraße (gelegen); **~way** Fahrbahn *f*; **~works** *pl.* Straßenbauarbeiten *pl.*; **~wor·thy** *mot.* verkehrssicher.

roam [rəʊm] *v/i.* (umher)streifen, (-)wandern; *v/t.* durchstreifen.

roar [rɔː] **1.** brüllen, brausen, tosen, donnern; **2.** Brüllen *n*, Gebrüll *n*; Brausen *n*; Krachen *n*, Getöse *n*; schallendes Gelächter.

roast [rəʊst] **1.** Braten *m*; **2.** braten; rösten; **3.** gebraten; **~ beef** Rost- *od.* Rinderbraten *m*.

rob [rɒb] (-*bb*-) (be)rauben; **~ber** [ˈrɒbə] Räuber *m*; **~ber·y** [~rɪ] Raub *m*; **~ with violence** ⚖ schwerer Raub.

robe [rəʊb] (Amts)Robe *f*, Talar *m*; Bade-, Hausmantel *m*, Morgenrock *m*.

rob·in *zo.* [ˈrɒbɪn] Rotkehlchen *n*.

ro·bot [ˈrəʊbɒt] Roboter *m*.

ro·bust □ [rəˈbʌst] robust, kräftig.

rock [rɒk] **1.** Fels(en) *m*; Klippe *f*; Gestein *n*; *Brt.* Zuckerstange *f*; ⚠ *nicht Rock; on the* ~s mit Eiswürfeln (*Whisky etc.*); kaputt, in die Brüche gegangen (*Ehe*); **~ crystal** Bergkristall *m*; **2.** schaukeln, wiegen; erschüttern (*a. fig.*).

rock·er [ˈrɒkə] Kufe *f*; *Am.* Schaukelstuhl *m*; *Brt.* Rocker *m*; *off one's* ~ *sl.* übergeschnappt.

rock·et [ˈrɒkɪt] Rakete *f*; *attr.* Raketen...; **~-pro·pelled** mit Raketenantrieb; **~ry** [~rɪ] Raketentechnik *f*.

rock·ing|-chair [ˈrɒkɪŋtʃeə] Schaukelstuhl *m*; **~-horse** Schaukelpferd *n*.

rock·y [ˈrɒkɪ] (-*ier*, -*iest*) felsig, Felsen...

rod [rɒd] Rute *f*; Stab *m*; ⊕ Stange *f*.

rode [rəʊd] *pret. von* ride 2.

ro·dent *zo.* [ˈrəʊdənt] Nagetier *n*.

ro·de·o [rəʊˈdeɪəʊ] (*pl.* -os) Rodeo *m*, *n*.

roe¹ *zo.* [rəʊ] Reh *n*.

roe² *zo.* [~] *a. hard* ~ Rogen *m*; *a. soft* ~ Milch *f*.

rogue [rəʊg] Schurke *m*, Gauner *m*; Schlingel *m*, Spitzbube *m*; **ro·guish** □ [ˈrəʊgɪʃ] spitzbübisch.

role, rôle *thea.* [rəʊl] Rolle *f* (*a. fig.*).

roll [rəʊl] **1.** Rolle *f*; Brötchen *n*, Semmel *f*; (*bsd.* Namens-, Anwesenheits)Liste *f*; Brausen *n*; (*Donner*-) Rollen *n*; (*Trommel*)Wirbel *m*; ♫ Schlingern *n*; **2.** *v/t.* rollen; wälzen; walzen; *Zigarette* drehen; ~ *up Ärmel* hochkrempeln; *mot. Fenster* hochkurbeln; *v/i.* rollen; rattern; sich wälzen; (g)rollen (*Donner*); dröhnen; brausen; wirbeln (*Trommel*); ♫ schlingern; **~-call** [ˈrəʊlkɔːl] Namensaufruf *m*; ✗ Appell *m*.

roll·er [ˈrəʊlə] Rolle *f*, Walze *f*; (*Locken*)Wickler *m*; ♫ Sturzwelle *f*, Brecher *m*; △ *nicht Rollee*; **~-coast·er** Achterbahn *f*; **~-skate** Rollschuh *m*; **~-skate** Rollschuh laufen; **~skat·ing** Rollschuhlaufen *n*; **~tow·el** Rollhandtuch *n*.

roll·ick·ing [ˈrɒlɪkɪŋ] übermütig.

roll·ing [ˈrəʊlɪŋ] rollend *etc.*; Roll..., Walz...; ~ *mill* ⊕ Walzwerk *n*; ~ *pin* Nudelholz *n*.

roll-neck [ˈrəʊlnek] **1.** Rollkragen (-pullover) *m*; **2.** Rollkragen...; **~ed** [~t] Rollkragen...

Ro·man [ˈrəʊmən] **1.** römisch; **2.** Römer(in).

ro·mance¹ [rəʊˈmæns] **1.** (Ritter-, Vers)Roman *m*; Abenteuer-, Liebesroman *m*; Romanze *f* (*a. fig.*); Romantik *f*, Zauber *m*.

Ro·mance² *ling.* [~] *a.* ~ *languages* die romanischen Sprachen *pl.*

Ro·ma·ni·an [ruːˈmeɪnjən] **1.** rumänisch; **2.** Rumän|e *m*, -in *f*; *ling.* Rumänisch *n*.

ro·man|tic [rəˈmæntɪk] **1.** (~ally)

romantisch (veranlagt); **2.** Romantiker(in); Schwärmer(in); **~ti·cis·m** [~sɪzəm] Romantik f.

romp [rɒmp] **1.** Tollen n, Toben n; Range f, Wildfang m; **2.** a. ~ about, ~ around herumtollen, -toben; **~ers** ['rɒmpəz] pl. einteiliger Spielanzug.

roof [ru:f] **1.** Dach n (a. fig.); ~ of the mouth anat. Gaumen m; **2.** mit e-m Dach versehen; ~ in, ~ over überdachen; **~ing** ['ru:fɪŋ] **1.** Material n zum Dachdecken; **2.** Dach...; ~ felt Dachpappe f; **~ rack** bsd. Brt. mot. Dachgepäckträger m.

rook [rʊk] **1.** Schach: Turm m; zo. Saatkrähe f; **2.** betrügen (of um).

room [ru:m] **1.** Raum m; Platz m; Zimmer n; fig. Spielraum m; ~s pl. (Miet)Wohnung f; **2.** Am. wohnen; **~er** ['ru:mə] bsd. Am. Untermieter(in); **~ing-house** [~ɪŋhaʊs] Fremdenheim n, Pension f; **~mate** Zimmergenosse m, -in f; **~y** [~ɪ] (-ier, -iest) geräumig.

roost [ru:st] **1.** Schlafplatz m (von Vögeln); Hühnerstange f; **2.** sich zum Schlaf niederhocken (Vögel); **~er** bsd. Am. zo. ['ru:stə] (Haus-) Hahn m.

root [ru:t] **1.** Wurzel f; **2.** v/i. Wurzeln schlagen; wühlen (for nach); ~ about, ~ around herumwühlen (among in dat.); v/t. tief einpflanzen; ~ out ausrotten; ~ up ausgraben; **~ed** ['ru:tɪd] eingewurzelt; deeply ~ fig. tief verwurzelt; stand ~ to the spot wie angewurzelt stehen(bleiben).

rope [rəʊp] **1.** Tau n; Seil n; Strick m; Schnur f (Perlen etc.); be at the end of one's ~ mit s-m Latein am Ende sein; know the ~s sich auskennen; **2.** verschnüren; festbinden; ~ off (durch ein Seil) absperren od. abgrenzen; **~ lad·der** Strickleiter f; **~ tow** Schlepplift m; **~way** ['rəʊpweɪ] (Seil)Schwebebahn f.

ro·sa·ry eccl. ['rəʊzərɪ] Rosenkranz m.

rose[1] [rəʊz] ♀ Rose f; (Gießkannen-) Brause f; Rosa-, Rosenrot n.

rose[2] [~] pret. von rise[1].

ros·trum ['rɒstrəm] (pl. -tra [-trə], -trums) Rednertribüne f, -pult n.

ros·y □ ['rəʊzɪ] (-ier, -iest) rosig.

rot [rɒt] **1.** Fäulnis f; Brt. F Quatsch m; **2.** (-tt-) v/t. (ver)faulen lassen; v/i. (ver)faulen, (ver)modern, verrotten.

ro·ta·ry ['rəʊtərɪ] rotierend, sich

drehend; Rotations...; **ro·tate** [rəʊ'teɪt] rotieren od. kreisen (lassen), (sich) drehen; ✔ die Frucht wechseln; **ro·ta·tion** [~n] Rotation f, (Um)Drehung f, Umlauf m; Wechsel m, Abwechslung f.

ro·tor bsd. ✈ ['rəʊtə] Rotor m.

rot·ten □ ['rɒtn] verfault, faul(ig); morsch; mies; gemein; feel ~ sl. sich beschissen fühlen.

ro·tund □ [rəʊ'tʌnd] rundlich.

rough [rʌf] **1.** adj. □ rauh; roh; grob; barsch; hart; holp(e)rig, uneben, grob, ungefähr (Schätzung); unfertig, Roh...; ~ copy erster Entwurf, Konzept n; ~ draft Rohfassung f; **2.** adv. roh, rauh, hart; **3.** Rauhe n, Grobe n; holp(e)riger Boden; Golf: Rough n; **4.** an-, aufrauhen; ~ it F primitiv od. anspruchslos leben; **~age** ['rʌfɪdʒ] Ballaststoffe pl.; **~cast 1.** ⊕ Rohputz m; **2.** unfertig; **3.** (-cast) ⊕ roh verputzen; roh entwerfen; **~en** [~n] rauh werden; an-, aufrauhen; **~neck** Am. F Grobian m; Ölbohrarbeiter m; **~ness** [~nɪs] Rauheit f; rauhe Stelle; Roheit f; Grobheit f; **~shod**: ride ~ over j-n rücksichtslos behandeln; rücksichtslos über et. hinweggehen.

round [raʊnd] **1.** adj. □ rund; voll (Stimme etc.); abgerundet (Stil); unverblümt; a ~ dozen ein rundes Dutzend; in ~ figures auf- od. abgerundet (Zahlen); **2.** adv. rund-, rings(her)um; überall, auf od. von od. nach allen Seiten; ask s.o. ~ j-n zu sich einladen; ~ about ungefähr; all the year ~ das ganze Jahr hindurch; the other way ~ umgekehrt; **3.** prp. (rund)um; um (... herum); in od. auf (dat.) ... herum; **4.** Runde f, Kreis m; Runde f (Leiter)Sprosse f; Brt. Scheibe f (Brot etc.); (Dienst-) Runde f, Rundgang m; ♣ Visite f (in e-r Klinik); ♪ Kanon m (Lachetc.)Salve f; 100 ~s ✗ 100 Schuß (Munition); **5.** rund machen od. werden; (herum)gehen od. (-)fahren um, biegen um; ~ off abrunden; fig. krönen, beschließen; ~ up Zahl etc. aufrunden (to auf acc.); Vieh zusammentreiben; Leute etc. zusammentrommeln, auftreiben; **~a·bout** ['raʊndəbaʊt] **1.** ~ way od. route Umweg m; in a ~ way fig. auf Umwegen; **2.** Brt. Karussell n; Brt. Kreisverkehr m; **~ish** [~ɪʃ] rundlich;

~ trip Rundreise *f*; *Am.* Hin- u. Rückfahrt *f*, ✈ Hin- u. Rückflug *m*; ✈ Rückflugticket *n*; **~trip:** ~ ticket *Am.* Rückfahrkarte, ✈ Rückflugticket *n*; **~up** Zusammentreiben *n* (*von Vieh*).

rouse [rauz] *v/t.* wecken; *Wild* aufjagen; *j-n* aufrütteln; *j-n* reizen, erzürnen; *Zorn* erregen; ~ *o.s.* sich aufraffen; *v/i.* aufwachen.

route [ru:t, ✕ *a.* raut] (Reise-, Fahrt)Route *f*, (-)Weg *m*; (Bahn-, Bus-, Flug)Strecke *f*; ✕ Marschroute *f*.

rou·tine [ru:'ti:n] **1.** Routine *f*; **2.** üblich, routinemäßig, Routine...

rove [rəuv] umherstreifen, -wandern; durchstreifen, -wandern.

row¹ [rəu] Reihe *f*.

row² F [rau] **1.** Krach *m*, Lärm *m*; (lauter) Streit, Krach *m*; **2.** (sich) streiten.

row³ [rəu] **1.** Rudern *n*; Ruderpartie *f*; **2.** rudern; **~·boat** *Am.* ['rəubəut] Ruderboot *n*; **~·er** [~ə] Ruder|er, *m*, -in *f*; **~·ing boat** *Brt.* [~ıŋbəut] Ruderboot *n*.

roy·al □ ['rɔɪəl] königlich; **~·ty** [~tı] Königtum *n*; Königswürde *f*; *coll.* das Königshaus, die königliche Familie; Tantieme *f*.

rub [rʌb] **1.** *give s.th. a good* ~ et. (ab)reiben; et. polieren; **2.** (*-bb-*) *v/t.* reiben; polieren; (*wund*) scheuern; ~ *down* abschmirgeln, abschleifen; trockenreiben; (ab)frottieren; ~ *in* einreiben; ~ *it in* fig. F darauf herumreiten; ~ *off* ab-, wegreiben, abwegwischen; ~ *out Brt.* ausradieren; ~ *up* aufpolieren; ~ *s.o. up the wrong way j-n* verstimmen; *v/i.* reiben (*against, on* an *dat.,* gegen).

rub·ber ['rʌbə] **1.** Gummi *n*, *m*; (Radier)Gummi *m*; Wischtuch *n*; ~*s pl. Am.* (Gummi)Überschuhe *pl.*; *Brt.* Turnschuhe *pl.*; ~ **band** Gummiband *n*; ~ **cheque**, *Am.* ~ **check** geplatzter Scheck; **~·neck** *Am.* F **1.** Gaffer(in); **2.** gaffen; **~·y** [~rı] gummiartig; zäh, wie Gummi (*Fleisch*).

rub·bish ['rʌbıʃ] Schutt *m*; Abfall *m*, Müll *m*, Kehricht *m*; *fig.* Schund *m*; Quatsch *m*, Blödsinn *m*; ~ **bin** *Brt.* Mülleimer *m*; ~ **chute** Müllschlucker *m*.

rub·ble ['rʌbl] Schutt *m*.

ru·by ['ru:bı] Rubin(rot *n*) *m*.

ruck·sack ['rʌksæk] Rucksack *m*.

rud·der ['rʌdə] ⏚ (Steuer)Ruder *n*; ✈ Seitenruder *n*.

rud·dy □ ['rʌdı] (*-ier, -iest*) rot, rötlich; frisch, gesund.

rude □ [ru:d] (~*r,* ~*st*) unhöflich, grob; unanständig; heftig, wild; ungebildet; einfach, kunstlos.

ru·di|men·ta·ry [ru:dı'mentərı] elementar, Anfangs...; **~·ments** ['ru:dımənts] *pl.* Anfangsgründe *pl.*

rue·ful □ ['ru:fl] reuig.

ruff [rʌf] Halskrause *f*.

ruf·fi·an ['rʌfjən] Rüpel *m*, Grobian *m*; Raufbold *m*, Schläger *m*.

ruf·fle ['rʌfl] **1.** Krause *f*, Rüsche *f*; Kräuseln *n*; **2.** kräuseln; *Haare, Federn* sträuben; zerknüllen; *fig.* aus der Ruhe bringen; (ver)ärgern.

rug [rʌg] (Reise-, Woll)Decke *f*; Vorleger *m*, Brücke *f*, (kleiner) Teppich.

rug·ged □ ['rʌgıd] rauh (*a. fig.*); wild, zerklüftet, schroff.

ru·in ['ruın] **1.** Ruin *m*, Verderben *n*, Untergang *m*; *mst* ~*s pl.* Ruine(n *pl.*) *f*, Trümmer *pl.*; **2.** ruinieren, zugrunde richten, zerstören, zunichte machen, zerrütten; **~·ous** □ [~əs] verfallen; ruinös.

rule [ru:l] **1.** Regel *f*; Spielregel *f*; Vorschrift *f*; Satzung *f*; Herrschaft *f*, Regierung *f*; Lineal *n*; *as a* ~ in der Regel; *work to* ~ Dienst nach Vorschrift tun; ~*s pl.* (Geschäfts-, Gerichts- *etc.*)Ordnung *f*; ~(*s*) *of the road* Straßenverkehrsordnung *f*; **2.** *v/t.* beherrschen, herrschen über (*acc.*); lenken, leiten; anordnen, verfügen; liniieren; ~ *out* ausschließen; *v/i.* herrschen; **rul·er** ['ru:lə] Herrscher(in); Lineal *n*.

rum [rʌm] Rum *m*; *Am.* Alkohol *m*.

rum·ble ['rʌmbl] rumpeln, poltern, (g)rollen (*Donner*), knurren (*Magen*).

ru·mi|nant *zo.* ['ru:mınənt] **1.** wiederkäuend; **2.** Wiederkäuer *m*; **~·nate** [~eıt] *zo.* wiederkäuen; *fig.* grübeln (*about, over* über *acc.*).

rum·mage ['rʌmıdʒ] **1.** gründliche Durchsuchung; Ramsch *m*; ~ *sale Am.* Ramschverkauf *m*; Wohltätigkeitsbasar *m*; **2.** *a.* ~ *about* herumstöbern, -wühlen (*among, in* in *dat.*).

ru·mo(u)r ['ru:mə] **1.** Gerücht *n*; ⚠ *nicht rumoren*; *it is* ~*ed* man sagt *od.* munkelt, es geht das Gerücht.

rump [rʌmp] Steiß *m*, Hinterteil *n*, -keulen *pl.*

rum·ple [ˈrʌmpl] zerknittern, -knüllen, -wühlen; △ *nicht rumpeln.*

run [rʌn] **1.** (*-nn-; ran, run*) *v/i.* laufen, rennen, eilen; fahren; verkehren, fahren, gehen (*Zug, Bus*); fließen, strömen; verlaufen (*Straße*), führen (*Weg*); ⊕ laufen in Betrieb *od.* Gang sein; (*Uhr etc.*); schmelzen (*Butter etc.*); zer-, auslaufen (*Farbe*), lauten (*Text*); gehen (*Melodie*); laufen (*Theaterstück, Film*), gegeben werden; ⅋ gelten, laufen; *econ.* stehen auf (*dat.*) (*Preis etc.*); *bsd. Am. pol.* kandidieren (*for* für); ~ *across s.o.* j-n zufällig treffen, auf j-n stoßen; ~ *after* hinterher-, nachlaufen; ~ *along!* F ab mit dir!; ~ *away* davonlaufen; ~ *away with* durchbrennen mit; durchgehen mit (*Temperament etc.*); ~ *down* ablaufen (*Uhr etc.*); *fig.* herunterkommen; ~ *dry* austrocknen; ~ *into* (hinein)laufen *od.* -rennen in (*acc.*); fahren gegen; j-n zufällig treffen; geraten in (*Schulden etc.*); sich belaufen auf (*acc.*); ~ *low* knapp werden; ~ *off with* = ~ *away with*; ~ *out* ablaufen (*Zeit*); ausgehen, knapp werden; ~ *out of petrol* kein Benzin mehr haben; ~ *over* überlaufen, -fließen; überfliegen, durchgehen, -lesen; ~ *short* knapp werden; ~ *short of petrol* kein Benzin mehr haben; ~ *through* überfliegen, durchgehen, -lesen; ~ *up to* sich belaufen auf (*acc.*); *v/t.* Strecke durchlaufen, *Weg* einschlagen; fahren; laufen lassen; *Zug, Bus* fahren *od.* verkehren lassen; *Hand etc.* gleiten lassen; *Geschäft* betreiben; *Betrieb* führen, leiten; fließen lassen; *Temperatur, Fieber* haben; ~ *down* an-, überfahren; *fig.* schlechtmachen; herunterwirtschaften; ~ *errands* Besorgungen *od.* Botengänge machen; ~ *s.o. home* F j-n nach Hause bringen *od.* fahren; ~ *in Auto* einfahren; F *Verbrecher* einbuchten; ~ *over* überfahren; ~ *s.o. through* j-n durchbohren; ~ *up Preis etc.* in die Höhe treiben; *Rechnung etc.* auflaufen lassen. **2.** Laufen *n*, Rennen *n*, Lauf *m*; Verlauf *m*; Fahrt *f*; Spazierfahrt *f*; Reihe *f*, Folge *f*, Serie *f*; *econ.* Ansturm *m*, Run *m*; *Am.* stürmische Nachfrage; *Am.* Bach *m*; *Am.* Laufmasche *f*; Gehege *n*; Auslauf *m*, (Hühner)Hof *m*; *Sport:* Bob-, Ro-

delbahn *f*; (Ski)Abfahrt(sstrecke) *f*; freie Benutzung; *thea., Film:* Laufzeit *f*; *have a* ~ *of 20 nights thea.* 20mal nacheinander gegeben werden; *in the long* ~ auf die Dauer; *in the short* ~ fürs nächste; *on the* ~ auf der Flucht.

run·a·bout F *mot.* [ˈrʌnəbaut] kleiner leichter Wagen; ~**a·way** Ausreißer *m.*

rung¹ [rʌn] *p.p. von* ring¹ 2.

rung² [~] (Leiter)Sprosse *f* (*a. fig.*).

run·let [ˈrʌnlit] Rinnsal *n*; ~**nel** [~l] Rinnsal *n*; Rinnstein *m.*

run·ner [ˈrʌnə] Läufer(in); Bote *m* (Schlitten-, Schlittschuh)Kufe *f*; Schieber *m* (*am Schirm*); Läufer *m*; Tischläufer *m*; *Am.* Laufmasche *f*; ⅋ Ausläufer *m*; ~ *bean Brt.* ⅋ Stangenbohne; ~**up** [~rˈʌp] (*pl. runners-up*) *Sport:* Zweite(r *m*) *f.*

run·ning [ˈrʌnin] **1.** laufend, fließend; *two days* ~ zwei Tage hintereinander; **2.** Laufen *n*; Rennen *n*; ~**board** Trittbrett *n.*

run·way ⊁ [ˈrʌnwei] Start-, Lande-, Rollbahn *f.*

rup·ture [ˈrʌptʃə] **1.** Bruch *m*, Riß *m*; (Zer)Platzen *n*; **2.** brechen; bersten, (zer)platzen.

ru·ral □ [ˈruərəl] ländlich, Land...

ruse [ruːz] List *f*, Kniff *m*, Trick *m.*

rush¹ ⅋ [rʌʃ] Binse *f.*

rush² [~] **1.** Jagen *n*, Hetzen *n*, Stürmen *n*; Eile *f*; (An)Sturm *m*; Andrang *m*; *econ.* stürmische Nachfrage; Hetze *f*, Hochbetrieb *m*; **2.** *v/i.* stürzen, jagen, hetzen, stürmen; ~ *at* sich stürzen auf (*acc.*); ~ *in* hereinstürzen, -stürmen; *v/t.* jagen, hetzen, drängen, (an)treiben; losstürmen auf (*acc.*), angreifen; schnell (*wohin*) bringen; ~ **hour** [ˈrʌʃauə] Hauptverkehrszeit *f*, Stoßzeit *f*; ~**hour traf·fic** Stoßverkehr *m.*

Rus·sian [ˈrʌʃn] **1.** russisch; **2.** Russ|e *m*, -in *f*; *ling.* Russisch *n.*

rust [rʌst] **1.** Rost *m*; Rostbraun *n*; **2.** (ver-, ein)rosten (lassen).

rus·tic [ˈrʌstik] **1.** (~*ally*) ländlich, rustikal; bäurisch; **2.** Bauer *m.*

rus·tle [ˈrʌsl] **1.** rascheln (mit *od.* in *dat.*); rauschen; *Am. Vieh* stehlen; **2.** Rascheln *n.*

rust|less [ˈrʌstlis] rostfrei; ~**y** □ [~i] (*-ier, -iest*) rostig; *fig.* eingerostet.

rut¹ [rʌt] Wagenspur *f*; *bsd. fig.* ausgefahrenes Geleise.

Q
R

rut² *zo.* [~] Brunst *f*, Brunft *f*.
ruth·less □ ['ru:θlɪs] umbarmherzig;
rücksichts-, skrupellos.

rut|ted ['rʌtɪd], **~ty** [~ɪ] (*-ier, -iest*)
ausgefahren (*Weg*).
rye ¥ [raɪ] Roggen *m*.

S

sa·ble ['seɪbl] *zo.* Zobel *m*; Zobelpelz
m; △ *nicht* Säbel.
sab·o·tage ['sæbətɑ:ʒ] 1. Sabotage *f*;
2. sabotieren.
sa·bre, *Am. mst* **-ber** ['seɪbə] Säbel *m*.
sack [sæk] 1. Plünderung *f*; Sack *m*;
Am. (Einkaufs)Tüte *f*; Sackkleid *n*;
get the ~ F entlassen werden; F den
Laufpaß bekommen; *give s.o. the* ~
F j-n entlassen; F j-m den Laufpaß
geben; 2. plündern, einsacken; F
rausschmeißen, entlassen; F *j-m den
Laufpaß geben*; **~cloth** ['sækklɒθ],
~ing [~ɪŋ] Sackleinen *n*, -leinwand
f.
sac·ra·ment *eccl.* ['sækrəmənt] Sa-
krament *n*.
sa·cred □ ['seɪkrɪd] heilig; geistlich.
sac·ri·fice ['sækrɪfaɪs] 1. Opfer *n*; *at a
~ econ.* mit Verlust; 2. opfern; *econ.*
mit Verlust verkaufen.
sac·ri·lege ['sækrɪlɪdʒ] Sakrileg *n*;
Entweihung *f*; Frevel *m*; **~·le·gious**
□ [sækrɪ'lɪdʒəs] frevelhaft.
sad □ [sæd] traurig; jämmerlich,
elend; schlimm; dunkel, matt.
sad·den ['sædn] traurig machen *od.*
werden.
sad·dle ['sædl] 1. Sattel *m*; 2. satteln;
fig. belasten; **~r** [~ə] Sattler *m*.
sa·dis·m ['seɪdɪzəm] Sadismus *m*.
sad·ness ['sædnɪs] Traurigkeit *f*.
safe [seɪf] 1. □ (*~r, ~st*) sicher; unversehrt; zuverlässig; 2. Safe *m*, *n*,
Geldschrank *m*; Fliegenschrank *m*;
con·duct freies Geleit; Geleitbrief
m; **~guard** ['seɪfgɑ:d] 1. Schutz *m*
(*against* gegen, vor *dat.*); 2. sichern,
schützen (*against* gegen, vor *dat.*).
safe·ty ['seɪftɪ] Sicherheit *f*; Sicher-
heits...; **~belt** Sicherheitsgurt *m*; **~
is·land** *Am.* Verkehrsinsel *f*; **~lock**
Sicherheitsschloß *n*; **~pin** Sicher-
heitsnadel *f*; **~ ra·zor** Rasierapparat
m.
saf·fron ['sæfrən] Safran(gelb *n*) *m*.

sag [sæg] (*-gg-*) durchsacken; ⊕
durchhängen; abfallen, (herab)hän-
gen; sinken, fallen, absacken.
sa·ga·cious □ [sə'geɪʃəs] scharfsinnig; **~·ci·ty** [sə'gæsətɪ] Scharfsinn *m*.
sage¹ [seɪdʒ] 1. □ (*~r, ~st*) klug, weise;
2. Weise(r) *m*.
sage² ¥ [~] Salbei *m, f*.
said [sed] *pret. u. p.p. von* say 1.
sail [seɪl] 1. Segel *n od. pl.*; (Segel-)
Fahrt *f*; Windmühlenflügel *m*;
(Segel)Schiff(e *pl.*) *n*; *set* ~ auslaufen
(*for* nach); 2. *v/i.* segeln, fahren;
auslaufen (*Schiff*); absegeln; *fig.*
schweben; *v/t.* ⚓ befahren; *Schiff*
steuern; *Segelboot* segeln; **~·boat**
Am. ['seɪlbəʊt] Segelboot *n*; **~·er**
[~ə] Segler *m* (*Schiff*); **~·ing-boat**
Brt. [~ɪŋbəʊt] Segelboot *n*; **~·ing-
ship** [~ɪŋʃɪp], **~·ing-ves·sel** [~ɪŋvesl]
Segelschiff *n*; **~·or** [~ə] Seemann *m*,
Matrose *m*; *be a good* (*bad*) ~ (nicht)
seefest sein; **~·plane** Segelflugzeug
n.
saint [seɪnt] 1. Heilige(r *m*) *f*; [*vor npr.*
snt] Sankt ...; 2. heiligsprechen; **~·ly**
['seɪntlɪ] heilig, fromm.
saith *veraltet od. poet.* [seθ] 3. *sg. pres.
von* say 1.
sake [seɪk]: *for the* ~ *of* um ... (*gen.*)
willen; *for my* ~ meinetwegen; *for
God's* ~ um Gottes willen.
sa·la·ble ['seɪləbl] = *saleable*.
sal·ad ['sæləd] Salat *m*.
sal·a·ried ['sælərɪd] (fest)angestellt,
(-)bezahlt; ~ *employee* Angestellte(r
m) *f*, Gehaltsempfänger(in).
sal·a·ry ['sælərɪ] Gehalt *n*; **~ earn·er**
[~ɜ:nə] Angestellte(r *m*) *f*, Gehalts-
empfänger(in).
sale [seɪl] Verkauf *m*; Ab-, Umsatz *m*;
(Saison)Schlußverkauf *m*; Auktion
f; *for* ~ zu verkaufen; *be on* ~ verkauft werden, erhältlich sein.
sale·a·ble *bsd. Brt.* ['seɪləbl] verkäuf-
lich.

sales|clerk *Am.* [ˈseɪlzklɑːk] (Laden)Verkäufer(in); **~man** [~mən] (*pl. -men*) Verkäufer *m*; (Handels-)Vertreter *m*; **~wom·an** (*pl. -women*) Verkäuferin *f*; (Handels)Vertreterin *f*.

sa·li·ent □ [ˈseɪljənt] vorspringend; *fig.* ins Auge springend, hervorstechend.

sa·line [ˈseɪlaɪn] salzig, Salz...

sa·li·va [səˈlaɪvə] Speichel *m*.

sal·low [ˈsæləʊ] blaß, gelblich, fahl.

sal·ly [ˈsælɪ]: **~ forth**, **~ out** sich aufmachen.

salm·on *zo.* [ˈsæmən] Lachs *m*, Salm *m*.

sa·loon [səˈluːn] Salon *m*; (Gesellschafts)Saal *m*; erste Klasse (*auf Schiffen*); *Am.* Kneipe *f*, Wirtschaft *f*, Saloon *m*; **~** (*car*) *Brt. mot.* Limousine.

salt [sɔːlt] **1.** Salz *n*; *fig.* Würze *f*; **2.** salzig; gesalzen, gepökelt; Salz...; Pökel...; **3.** (ein)salzen; pökeln; **~cel·lar** [ˈsɔːltselə] Salzfäßchen *n*, -streuer *m*; **~·pe·tre**, *Am.* **~·pe·ter** ♈ [~piːtə] Salpeter *m*; **~·wa·ter** Salzwasser...; **~·y** [~ɪ] (*-ier*, *-iest*) salzig.

sa·lu·bri·ous □ [səˈluːbrɪəs], **sal·u·ta·ry** □ [ˈsæljʊtərɪ] heilsam, gesund.

sal·u·ta·tion [sæljuːˈteɪʃn] Gruß *m*, Begrüßung *f*; Anrede *f* (*im Brief*).

sa·lute [səˈluːt] **1.** Gruß *m*; ✕ Salut *m*; **2.** (be)grüßen; ✕ salutieren.

sal·vage [ˈsælvɪdʒ] **1.** Bergung(sgut *n*) *f*; Bergegeld *n*; **2.** bergen; retten.

sal·va·tion [sælˈveɪʃn] Erlösung *f*; (Seelen)Heil *n*; Rettung *f*; ♀ *Army* Heilsarmee *f*.

salve¹ [sælv] retten, bergen.

salve² [~] **1.** Salbe *f*; *fig.* Balsam *m*, Trost *m*; ⚠ *nicht Salve*; **2.** *fig.* beschwichtigen, beruhigen.

same [seɪm]: *the* **~** der-, die-, dasselbe; *all the*~ trotzdem; *it is all the*~ *to me* es ist mir (ganz) gleich.

sam·ple [ˈsɑːmpl] **1.** Probe *f*, Muster *n*; **2.** probieren; kosten.

san·a·to·ri·um [sænəˈtɔːrɪəm] (*pl. -ums, -a [-ə]*) Sanatorium *n*.

sanc·ti|fy [ˈsæŋktɪfaɪ] heiligen; weihen; **~·ti·mo·ni·ous** □ [sæŋktɪˈməʊnjəs] scheinheilig; **~·tion** [ˈsæŋkʃn] **1.** Sanktion *f*; Billigung *f*, Zustimmung *f*; **2.** billigen; **~·ti·ty** [~tətɪ] Heiligkeit *f*; **~·tu·a·ry** [~jʊərɪ] Heiligtum *n*; *das* Allerheiligste; Asyl

n; Schutzgebiet *n* (*für Tiere*); *seek* **~** *with* Zuflucht suchen bei.

sand [sænd] **1.** Sand *m*; **~s** *pl.* Sand (-fläche *f*) *m*; Sandbank *f*; **2.** mit Sand bestreuen; schmirgeln.

san·dal [ˈsændl] Sandale *f*.

sand|-glass [ˈsændglɑːs] Sanduhr *f*, Stundenglas *n*; **~·hill** Sanddüne *f*; **~·pip·er** *zo.* Strandläufer *m*; *common* **~** Flußuferläufer *m*.

sand·wich [ˈsænwɪdʒ] **1.** Sandwich *n*; **2.** einklemmen, -zwängen; *a.* **~** *in fig.* ein-, dazwischenschieben.

sand·y [ˈsændɪ] (*-ier*, *-iest*) sandig; rotblond.

sane [seɪn] (~*r*, ~*st*) geistig gesund; ⚖ zurechnungsfähig; vernünftig.

sang [sæŋ] *pret. von sing.*

san|gui·na·ry □ [ˈsæŋgwɪnərɪ] blutdürstig; blutig; **~·guine** □ [~wɪn] leichtblütig; zuversichtlich; rot, frisch, blühend (*Gesichtsfarbe*).

san·i·tar·i·um *Am.* [sænɪˈteərɪəm] (*pl. -ums, -a [-ə]*) = *sanatorium.*

san·i·ta·ry □ [ˈsænɪtərɪ] Gesundheits..., gesundheitlich, sanitär... (*a.* ⊕); **~** *napkin Am.*, **~** *towel* Damenbinde *f*.

san·i·ta·tion [sænɪˈteɪʃn] Hygiene *f*; sanitäre Einrichtungen *pl.*

san·i·ty [ˈsænətɪ] geistige Gesundheit; ⚖ Zurechnungsfähigkeit *f*; gesunder Verstand.

sank [sæŋk] *pret. von sink 1.*

San·ta Claus [ˈsæntəˈklɔːz] der Weihnachtsmann, der Nikolaus.

sap [sæp] **1.** Saft *m* (*in Pflanzen*); *fig.* Lebenskraft *f*; **2.** (-*pp-*) untergraben (*a. fig.*); **~·less** [ˈsæplɪs] saft-, kraftlos; **~·ling** [~lɪŋ] junger Baum.

sap·phire [ˈsæfaɪə] Saphir *m*.

sap·py [ˈsæpɪ] (*-ier*, *-iest*) saftig; *fig.* kraftvoll.

sar·cas·m [ˈsɑːkæzəm] Sarkasmus *m*.

sar·dine *zo.* [sɑːˈdiːn] Sardine *f*.

sash [sæʃ] Schärpe *f*; (schiebbarer) Fensterrahmen; **~-win·dow** [ˈsæʃwɪndəʊ] Schiebefenster *n*.

sat [sæt] *pret. u. p.p. von sit.*

Sa·tan [ˈseɪtən] Satan *m*.

satch·el [ˈsætʃəl] Schulmappe *f*, -tasche *f*, -ranzen *m*.

sate [seɪt] übersättigen.

sa·teen [sæˈtiːn] (Baum)Wollsatin *m*.

sat·el·lite [ˈsætəlaɪt] Satellit *m*; *a.* **~** *state* Satellit(enstaat) *m*.

sa·ti·ate [ˈseɪʃɪeɪt] übersättigen.

sat·in [ˈsætɪn] (Seiden)Satin *m*.

S

sat|ire [ˈsætaɪə] Satire f; **~ir·ist** [~ərɪst] Satiriker(in); **~ir·ize** [~raɪz] verspotten.

sat·is·fac·tion [sætɪsˈfækʃn] Befriedigung f; Genugtuung f; Zufriedenheit f; eccl. Sühne f; Gewißheit f; **~to·ry** □ [~ˈfæktərɪ] befriedigend, zufriedenstellend.

sat·is·fy [ˈsætɪsfaɪ] befriedigen, zufriedenstellen; überzeugen; be satisfied with zufrieden sein mit.

sat·u·rate ⚗ u. fig. [ˈsæt|ərɪt] sättigen.

Sat·ur·day [ˈsætədɪ] Sonnabend m, Samstag m.

sat·ur·nine □ [ˈsætənaɪn] düster, finster.

sauce [sɔ:s] 1. Soße f; △ nicht Bratensoße; Am. Kompott n; fig. Würze f, Reiz m; F Frechheit f; none of your ~! werd bloß nicht frech!; 2. F frech sein zu j-m; **~boat** [ˈsɔ:sbəʊt] Soßenschüssel f; **~pan** Kochtopf m; Kasserolle f.

sauc·er [ˈsɔ:sə] Untertasse f.

sauc·y □ [ˈsɔ:sɪ] (-ier, -iest) frech; F flott, keß.

saun·ter [ˈsɔ:ntə] 1. Schlendern n, Bummel m; 2. schlendern, bummeln.

saus·age [ˈsɒsɪdʒ] Wurst f; a. small ~ Würstchen n.

sav|age [ˈsævɪdʒ] 1. □ wild; roh, grausam; 2. Wilde(r m) f; Rohling m, Barbar(in); **~ag·e·ry** [~ərɪ] Wildheit f; Roheit f, Grausamkeit f.

sav·ant [ˈsævənt] Gelehrte(r) m.

save [seɪv] v. retten; eccl. erlösen; bewahren; (auf-, er)sparen; schonen; 2. rhet. prp. u. cj. außer (dat.); ~ for bis auf (acc.); ~ that nur daß.

sav·er [ˈseɪvə] Retter(in); Sparer(in); it is a time-~ es spart Zeit.

sav·ing [ˈseɪvɪŋ] 1. □ ...sparend; rettend, befreiend; 2. Rettung f; ~s pl. Ersparnisse pl.

sav·ings | **ac·count** [ˈseɪvɪŋzəˈkaʊnt] Sparkonto n; **~ bank** Sparkasse f; **~ de·pos·it** Spareinlage f.

sa·vio(u)r [ˈseɪvjə] Retter m; the ♀ eccl. der Erlöser, der Heiland.

sa·vo(u)r [ˈseɪvə] 1. (Wohl)Geschmack m; fig. Beigeschmack m; fig. Würze f, Reiz m; 2. fig. genießen; fig. schmecken, riechen (of nach); **~y** □ [~rɪ] schmackhaft; appetitlich, pikant.

saw¹ [sɔ:] pret. von see¹.

saw² [~] Sprichwort n.

saw³ [~] 1. (~ed od. ~n, ~ed) sägen; 2. Säge f; Gewißheit f; **~dust** [ˈsɔ:dʌst] Sägemehl n, -späne pl.; **~mill** Sägewerk n; **~n** [sɔ:n] p.p. von saw³ 1.

Sax·on [ˈsæksn] 1. sächsisch; ling. oft germanisch; 2. Sachse m, Sächsin f.

say [seɪ] 1. (said) sagen; auf-, hersagen; berichten; ~ grace das Tischgebet sprechen; what do you ~ to ...?, oft what ~ you to ...? was hältst du von ...?, wie wäre es mit ...?; it ~s lautet (Schreiben etc.); it ~s here hier heißt es; that is to ~ das heißt; (and) that's ~ing s.th. (und) das will was heißen; you don't ~! was Sie nicht sagen!; I ~ sag(en Sie) mal!; ich muß schon sagen!; he is said to be ...; er soll ... sein; no sooner said than done gesagt, getan; 2. Rede f, Wort n; Mitspracherecht n; let him have his ~ laß(t) ihn (doch auch mal) reden od. s-e Meinung äußern; have a od. some (no) ~ in s.th. et. (nichts) zu sagen haben bei et.; **~ing** [ˈseɪɪŋ] Reden n; Sprichwort n, Redensart f; Ausspruch m; it goes without ~ es versteht sich von selbst; as the ~ goes wie es so schön heißt.

scab [skæb] ꙮ, ♀ Schorf m; vet. Räude f; sl. Streikbrecher m.

scab·bard [ˈskæbəd] (Schwert-) Scheide f.

scaf·fold [ˈskæfəld] (Bau)Gerüst n; Schafott n; **~ing** [~ɪŋ] (Bau)Gerüst n.

scald [skɔ:ld] 1. Verbrühung f; 2. verbrühen; Milch abkochen; ~ing hot kochendheiß; glühendheiß (Tag etc.).

scale¹ [skeɪl] 1. Schuppe f; Kesselstein m; ♀ Zahnstein m; 2. (sich) (ab)schuppen, ablösen; ⊕ Kesselstein abklopfen; ♀ Zähne vom Zahnstein reinigen.

scale² [~] 1. Waagschale f; (a pair of) ~s pl. (e-e) Waage f; 2. wiegen.

scale³ [~] 1. Stufenleiter f; ♪ Tonleiter f; Skala f; Maßstab m; fig. Ausmaß n; 2. ersteigen; ~ up (down) maßstab(s)getreu vergrößern (verkleinern).

scal·lop [ˈskɒləp] 1. zo. Kammmuschel f; Näherei: ⌐Langette f; 2. ausbogen.

scalp [skælp] 1. Kopfhaut f; Skalp m; 2. skalpieren.

scal·y [ˈskeɪlɪ] (-ier, -iest) schuppig.

scamp [skæmp] **1.** Taugenichts *m*; **2.** pfuschen bei.

scam·per ['skæmpə] **1.** *a.* ~ *about*, ~ *around* (herum)tollen, herumhüpfen; hasten; **2.** (Herum)Tollen *n*, Herumhüpfen *n*.

scan [skæn] (*-nn-*) *Verse* skandieren; genau prüfen; forschend ansehen; *Horizont etc.* absuchen; *Computer, Radar, TV*: abtasten; *Überschriften etc.* überfliegen.

scan·dal ['skændl] Skandal *m*; Ärgernis *n*; Klatsch *m*; ~**ize** [~dəlaɪz]: *be* ~*d at s.th.* über et. empört *od.* entrüstet sein; ~**ous** □ [~əs] skandalös, anstößig.

Scan·di·na·vi·an [skændɪ'neɪvjən] **1.** skandinavisch; **2.** Skandinavier(in); *ling.* Skandinavisch *n*.

scant □ [skænt] knapp, gering; ~**y** □ ['skæntɪ] (*-ier, -iest*) knapp, spärlich, kärglich, dürftig.

-scape [skeɪp] *in Zssgn*: ...landschaft, Bild.

scape|goat ['skeɪpgəʊt] Sündenbock *m*; ~**grace** [~greɪs] Taugenichts *m*.

scar [skɑː] **1.** Narbe *f*; *fig.* (Schand-) Fleck *m*, Makel *m*; Klippe *f*; **2.** (*-rr-*) e-e Narbe *od.* Narben hinterlassen (auf *dat.*); ~ *over* vernarben.

scarce [skeəs] (~*r*, ~*st*) knapp; rar, selten; ~**ly** ['skeəslɪ] kaum; **scar·ci·ty** [~ətɪ] Mangel *m*, Knappheit *f* (*of* an *dat.*).

scare [skeə] **1.** erschrecken; ~ *away*, ~ *off* verscheuchen; *be* ~*d* (*of s.th.*) (vor et.) Angst haben; **2.** Schreck(en) *m*, Panik *f*; ~**crow** ['skeəkrəʊ] Vogelscheuche *f* (*a. fig.*).

scarf [skɑːf] (*pl.* scarfs [~fs], scarves [~vz]) Schal *m*, Hals-, Kopf-, Schultertuch *n*.

scar·let ['skɑːlət] **1.** Scharlach(rot *n*) *m*; **2.** scharlachrot; ~ *fever* ⚕ Scharlach *m*; ~ *runner* ⚘ Feuerbohne *f*.

scarred [skɑːd] narbig.

scarves [skɑːvz] *pl. von* scarf.

scath·ing *fig.* ['skeɪðɪŋ] vernichtend.

scat·ter ['skætə] (sich) zerstreuen; aus-, verstreuen; auseinanderstieben (*Vögel etc.*); ~**brain** F Schussel *m*; ~**ed** verstreut; vereinzelt.

sce·na·ri·o [sɪ'nɑːrɪəʊ] (*pl. -os*) Film: Drehbuch *n*.

scene [siːn] Szene *f*; Schauplatz *m*; ~*s pl.* Kulissen *pl.*; **sce·ne·ry** ['siːnərɪ] Szenerie *f*; Bühnenbild *n*, Kulissen *pl.*, Dekoration *f*; Landschaft *f*.

scent [sent] **1.** (*bsd.* Wohl)Geruch *m*, Duft *m*; *bsd. Brt.* Parfüm *n*; *hunt.* Witterung *f*; *gute etc.* Nase; Fährte *f* (*a. fig.*); **2.** wittern; *bsd. Brt.* parfümieren; ~**less** ['sentlɪs] geruchlos.

scep|tic, *Am.* **skep-** ['skeptɪk] Skeptiker(in); ~**ti·cal**, *Am.* **skep-** □ [~l] skeptisch.

scep·tre, *Am.* **-ter** ['septə] Zepter *n*.

sched·ule ['ʃedjuːl, *Am.* 'skedʒuːl] **1.** Verzeichnis *n*, Tabelle *f*; Plan *m*; *bsd. Am.* Fahr-, Flugplan *m*; *be ahead of* ~ dem Zeitplan voraus sein; *be behind* ~ Verspätung haben; im Rückstand sein; *be on* ~ (fahr)planmäßig *od.* pünktlich ankommen; **2.** (in e-e Liste *etc.*) eintragen; festlegen, -setzen, planen; ~*d* planmäßig (*Abfahrt etc.*); ~ *flight* ✈ Linienflug *m*.

scheme [skiːm] **1.** Schema *n*; Plan *m*, Projekt *n*, Programm *n*; Intrige *f*; **2.** *v/t.* planen; *v/i.* Pläne machen; intrigieren, Ränke schmieden.

schol·ar ['skɒlə] Gelehrte(r *m*) *f*; Gebildete(r *m*) *f*; *univ.* Stipendiat(in); *veraltet:* Schüler(in); ~**ly** *adj.* [~lɪ] gelehrt; ~**ship** [~ʃɪp] Gelehrsamkeit *f*; *univ.* Stipendium *n*.

school [skuːl] **1.** *zo.* Schwarm *m*; Schule *f* (*a. fig.*); *univ.* Fakultät *f*; *Am.* Hochschule *f*; *at* ~ auf *od.* in der Schule; **2.** schulen, ausbilden; *Tier* dressieren; ~**boy** ['skuːlbɔɪ] Schüler *m*; ~**chil·dren** *pl.* Schulkinder *pl.*, Schüler *pl.*; ~**fel·low** Mitschüler(in); ~**girl** Schülerin *f*; ~**ing** [~ɪŋ] (Schul)Ausbildung *f*; ~**mas·ter** Lehrer *m*; ~**mate** Mitschüler(in); ~**mis·tress** Lehrerin *f*; ~**teach·er** Lehrer(in).

schoo·ner ['skuːnə] ⚓ Schoner *m*; *Am.* großes Bierglas; *Brt.* großes Sherryglas; *Am.* = prairie schooner.

sci·ence ['saɪəns] Wissenschaft *f*; *a. natural* ~ die Naturwissenschaft(en *pl.*); Kunst(fertigkeit) *f*, Technik *f*; ~ *fic·tion* Science-fiction *f*.

sci·en·tif·ic [saɪən'tɪfɪk] (~*ally*) (natur)wissenschaftlich; exakt, systematisch; kunstgerecht.

sci·en·tist ['saɪəntɪst] (Natur)Wissenschaftler(in).

scin·til·late ['sɪntɪleɪt] funkeln.

sci·on ['saɪən] Sproß *m*, Sprößling *m*.

scis·sors ['sɪzəz] *pl.* (*a pair of* ~ e-e) Schere.

scoff [skɒf] **1.** Spott *m*; **2.** spotten.

scold

scold [skəʊld] **1.** zänkisches Weib; **2.** (aus)schelten; schimpfen.

scol·lop ['skɒləp] = *scallop*.

scone [skɒn] weiches Teegebäck.

scoop [sku:p] **1.** Schaufel *f*, Schippe *f*; Schöpfkelle *f*; F Coup *m*, gutes Geschäft; *Zeitung*: F Exklusivmeldung *f*, Knüller *m*; **2.** schöpfen, schaufeln; ~ *up* (auf)schaufeln; hochheben, -nehmen; zusammenraffen.

scoot·er ['sku:tə] (Kinder)Roller *m*; (Motor)Roller *m*.

scope [skəʊp] Bereich *m*; Gesichtskreis *m*, (geistiger) Horizont; Spielraum *m*.

scorch [skɔ:tʃ] *v/t.* versengen, -brennen; *v/i.* F (dahin)rasen.

score [skɔ:] **1.** Kerbe *f*; Zeche *f*, Rechnung *f*; 20 Stück; *Sport*: (Spiel)Stand *m*, Punkt-, Trefferzahl *f*, (Spiel)Ergebnis *n*; große (An-)Zahl, Menge *f*; ♪ Partitur *f*; ~ of viele; *four* ~ achtzig; *run up a* ~ Schulden machen; *on the* ~ *of* wegen (*gen.*); **2.** einkerben; die Punkte anschreiben; *Sport: Punkte, Treffer* erzielen, *Tore* schießen; ♪ instrumentieren; *Am.* F scharf kritisieren.

scorn [skɔ:n] **1.** Verachtung *f*; Spott *m*; **2.** verachten; verschmähen; ~·ful □ ['skɔ:nfl] verächtlich.

Scot [skɒt] Schott|e *m*, -in *f*.

Scotch [skɒtʃ] **1.** schottisch; **2.** *ling.* Schottisch *n*; schottischer Whisky; *the* ~ die Schotten *pl.*; ~·man ['skɒtʃmən], ~·wom·an = *Scotsman, Scotswoman*.

scot-free ['skɒt'fri:] ungestraft.

Scots [skɒts] = *Scotch*; *the* ~ *pl.* die Schotten *pl.*; ~·man ['skɒtsmən] (*pl.* -men) Schotte *m*; ~·wom·an (*pl.* -women) Schottin *f*.

Scot·tish ['skɒtɪʃ] schottisch.

scoun·drel ['skaʊndrəl] Schurke *m*.

scour¹ ['skaʊə] scheuern; reinigen.

scour² ['skaʊə] ♣ durchsuchen, -stöbern.

scourge [skɜ:dʒ] **1.** Geißel *f* (*a. fig.*); *fig.* Plage *f*; **2.** geißeln.

scout [skaʊt] **1.** *bsd.* ✗ Späher *m*, Kundschafter *m*; *Sport*: Spion *m*, Beobachter *m*; ♣ Aufklärungskreuzer *m*; ✈ Aufklärer *m*; *Brt. mot.* motorisierter Pannenhelfer; (*boy*) ~ Pfadfinder *m*; (*girl*) ~ *Am.* Pfadfinderin *f*; *talent* ~ Talentsucher *m*; **2.** auskundschaften; *bsd.* ✗ auf Erkundung sein; ~ *about*,

scowl [skaʊl] **1.** finsteres Gesicht; **2.** finster blicken.

scrab·ble ['skræbl] (be)kritzeln; scharren; krabbeln.

scrag *fig.* [skræg] Gerippe *n* (*dürrer Mensch etc.*).

scram·ble ['skræmbl] **1.** klettern; sich balgen (*for* um); ~*d eggs pl.* Rührei *n*; **2.** Kletterei *f*; Balgerei *f*; *fig.* Gerangel *n*.

scrap [skræp] **1.** Stückchen *n*, Fetzen *m*; (*Zeitungs*)Ausschnitt *m*, Bild *n* (*zum Einkleben*); Altmaterial *n*; Schrott *m*; ~*s pl.* Abfall *m*, (*bsd.* Speise)Reste *pl.*; **2.** (-*pp-*) ausrangieren; verschrotten; ~·book ['skræpbʊk] Sammelalbum *n*.

scrape [skreɪp] **1.** Kratzen *n*, Scharren *n*; Kratzfuß *m*; Kratzer *m*, Schramme *f*; *fig.* Klemme *f*; **2.** schaben; kratzen; scharren; (*entlang*-) streifen.

scrap|-heap ['skræphi:p] Abfall-, Schrotthaufen *m*; ~·i·ron, ~·met·al Alteisen *n*, Schrott *m*; ~·pa·per Schmierpapier *n*; Altpapier *n*.

scratch [skrætʃ] **1.** Kratzer *m*, Schramme *f*; Kratzen *n*; *Sport*: Startlinie *f*; **2.** zusammengewürfelt; improvisiert; *Sport*: ohne Vorgabe; **3.** (*zer*)kratzen; (*zer*)schrammen; (*sich*) kratzen, *Tier* kraulen; ~ *out*, ~ *through*, ~ *off* aus-, durchstreichen; ~ *pad Am.* Notizblock *m*; ~ *pa·per Am.* Schmierpapier *n*.

scrawl [skrɔ:l] **1.** kritzeln; **2.** Gekritzel *n*.

scraw·ny ['skrɔ:nɪ] (-*ier*, -*iest*) dürr.

scream [skri:m] **1.** Schrei *m*; Gekreisch *n*; *he is a* ~ F er ist zum Schreien komisch; **2.** schreien, kreischen.

screech [skri:tʃ] = *scream*; ~·owl *zo.* ['skri:tʃaʊl] Schleiereule *f*.

screen [skri:n] **1.** Wand-, Ofen-, Schutzschirm *m*; (*Film*)Leinwand *f*; *der* Film, *das* Kino; *Radar, TV, Computer*: Bildschirm *m*; Sandsieb *n*; Fliegengitter *n*; *fig.* Schutz *m*, Tarnung *f*; **2.** abschirmen (*a.* ~ *off*) (*from* gegen); (*be*)schützen (*from* vor *dat.*); ✗ tarnen; *Sand etc.* (*durch*)sieben; *Bild* projizieren; *TV* senden; *Film* vorführen, zeigen; verfilmen; *fig. j-n* decken; *fig. Personen* überprüfen; ~·play ['skri:npleɪ] Drehbuch *n*.

screw [skru:] **1.** Schraube f; (Flugzeug-, Schiffs)Schraube f; Propeller m; **2.** schrauben, vögeln; ~ **up** zuschrauben; ~ **up one's courage** sich ein Herz fassen; ~**ball** Am. sl. ['skru:bɔ:l] komischer Kauz, Spinner m; ~**driv·er** Schraubenzieher m; ~**jack** Wagenheber m.

scrib·ble ['skrɪbl] **1.** Gekritzel n; **2.** kritzeln.

scrimp [skrɪmp], ~**·y** ['skrɪmpɪ] (-ier, -iest) = skimp(y).

script [skrɪpt] Schrift f; Handschrift f; print. Schreibschrift f; Manuskript n; Film, TV: Drehbuch n.

Scrip·ture ['skrɪptʃə]: (Holy) ~, The (Holy) ~s pl. die Heilige Schrift.

scroll [skrəʊl] Schriftrolle f; arch. Volute f; Schnecke f (am Geigenhals); Schnörkel m.

scro·tum anat. ['skrəʊtəm] (pl. -ta [-tə], -tums) Hodensack m.

scrub[1] [skrʌb] Gestrüpp n, Buschwerk n; Knirps m; contp. Null f (Person); Am. Sport: zweite (Spieler)Garnitur.

scrub[2] [~] **1.** Schrubben n, Scheuern n; **2.** (-bb-) schrubben, scheuern.

scru·ple ['skru:pl] **1.** Skrupel m, Zweifel m, Bedenken pl.; **2.** Bedenken haben; ~**pu·lous** □ [~jʊləs] voller Skrupel; gewissenhaft; ängstlich.

scru·ti·nize ['skru:tɪnaɪz] (genau) prüfen; ~**ny** [~ɪ] forschender Blick; genaue (bsd. Wahl)Prüfung.

scud [skʌd] **1.** (Dahin)Jagen n; (dahintreibende) Wolkenfetzen pl.; Bö f; **2.** (-dd-) eilen, jagen.

scuff [skʌf] schlurfen.

scuf·fle ['skʌfl] **1.** Balgerei f, Rauferei f; **2.** sich balgen, raufen.

scull [skʌl] **1.** Skull n (kurzes Ruder); Skullboot n; **2.** rudern, skullen.

scul·le·ry ['skʌlərɪ] Spülküche f.

sculp·tor ['skʌlptə] Bildhauer m; ~**tress** [~trɪs] Bildhauerin f; ~**ture** [~tʃə] **1.** Bildhauerei f; Skulptur f, Plastik f; **2.** (heraus)meißeln, formen.

scum [skʌm] (Ab)Schaum m; the ~ of the earth fig. der Abschaum der Menschheit.

scurf [skɜ:f] (Haut-, bsd. Kopf-) Schuppen pl.

scur·ri·lous □ ['skʌrɪləs] gemein, unflätig; △ nicht skurril.

scur·ry ['skʌrɪ] hasten, huschen.

scur·vy[1] ['skɜ:vɪ] Skorbut m.

scur·vy[2] □ [~] (-ier, -iest) (hunds-) gemein.

scut·tle ['skʌtl] **1.** Kohleneimer m; **2.** = scurry; sich hastig zurückziehen.

scythe 🖊 [saɪð] Sense f.

sea [si:] See f; Meer n (a. fig.); hohe Welle; at ~ auf See; (all) at ~ fig. (völlig) ratlos; by ~ auf dem Seeweg, mit dem Schiff; ~**board** ['si:bɔ:d] Küste(ngebiet n) f; ~**coast** Meeresküste f; ~**far·ing** ['si:feərɪŋ] seefahrend; ~**food** Meeresfrüchte pl.; ~**go·ing** (hoch)seetüchtig; (Hoch)See...; ~**gull** zo. (See)Möwe f.

seal[1] [si:l] **1.** Siegel n; Stempel m; ⊕ Dichtung f; fig. Bestätigung f; **2.** versiegeln; fig. besiegeln; ~ **off** fig. abriegeln; ~ **up** (fest) verschließen od. abdichten.

seal[2] zo. [~] Robbe f, Seehund m.

sea-lev·el ['si:levl] Meeresspiegel m, -höhe f.

seal·ing-wax ['si:lɪŋwæks] Siegellack m.

seam [si:m] **1.** Naht f; ⚓ Fuge f; geol. Flöz n; Narbe f; △ nicht Saum; **2.** ~ **together** zusammennähen; ~**ed with** Gesicht: zerfurcht von.

sea·man ['si:mən] (pl. -men) Seemann m, Matrose m.

seam·stress ['semstrɪs] Näherin f.

sea|plane ['si:pleɪn] Wasserflugzeug n; ~**port** Seehafen m; Hafenstadt f; ~ **pow·er** Seemacht f.

sear [sɪə] versengen, -brennen; 🖊 ausbrennen; verdorren (lassen); fig. verhärten.

search [sɜ:tʃ] **1.** Suche f, Suchen n, Forschen n; ⚖ Fahndung f (for nach); Unter-, Durchsuchung f; in ~ of auf der Suche nach; **2.** v/t. durch-, untersuchen; 🖊 sondieren; Gewissen erforschen, prüfen; ~ me! F keine Ahnung!; v/i. suchen, forschen (for nach); ~ into untersuchen, ergründen; ~**ing** □ ['sɜ:tʃɪŋ] forschend, prüfend; eingehend (Prüfung etc.); ~**light** (Such)Scheinwerfer m; ~**par·ty** Suchmannschaft f; ~**war·rant** ⚖ Haussuchungs-, Durchsuchungsbefehl m.

sea|-shore ['si:ʃɔ:] See-, Meeresküste f; ~**sick** seekrank; ~**side:** at the ~ am Meer; go to the ~ ans Meer fahren; ~ **place**, ~ **resort** Seebad n.

sea·son ['si:zn] **1.** Jahreszeit f; (rechte) Zeit; Saison f; Brt. F = season-

ticket; cherries are now in ~ jetzt ist Kirschenzeit; *out of* ~ nicht (auf dem Markt) zu haben; *fig.* zur Unzeit; *with the compliments of the* ~ mit den besten Wünschen zum Fest; **2.** (aus)reifen (lassen); würzen; *Holz:* ablagern; abhärten (*to* gegen); **sea-so-na-ble** □ [~əbl] zeitgemäß; rechtzeitig; **~al** [~ənl] saisonbedingt, Saison...; **~ing** [~ɪŋ] Würze *f* (*a. fig.*); Gewürz *n*; **~-tick-et** 🚂 Zeitkarte *f*; *thea.* Abonnement *n*.

seat [si:t] **1.** Sitz *m*; Sessel *m*, Stuhl *m*, Bank *f*; (Sitz)Platz *m*; Platz *m*, Sitz *m* (*im Theater etc.*); Landsitz *m*; Gesäß *n*; Hosenboden *m*; *fig.* Sitz *m* (*Mitgliedschaft*), *pol. a.* Mandat *m*; *fig.* Stätte *f*, Ort *m*, Schauplatz *m*; *s. take* **1**; **2.** (hin)setzen; e-n (neuen) Hosenboden einsetzen in (*acc.*); fassen, Sitzplätze haben für; ~**ed** sitzend; *...sitzig; be* ~*ed* sitzen; *be* ~*ed!* nehmen Sie Platz!; *remain* ~*ed* sitzen bleiben; **~-belt** 🚗, *mot.* ['si:tbelt] Sicherheitsgurt *m*.

sea|-ur-chin *zo.* ['si:ə:tʃɪn] Seeigel *m*; **~ward** ['si:wəd] **1.** *adj.* seewärts gerichtet; **2.** *adv. a.* ~**s** seewärts; **~weed** 🌿 (See)Tang *m*; **~wor-thy** seetüchtig.

se-cede [sɪ'si:d] sich trennen, abfallen (*from* von).

se-ces-sion [sɪ'seʃn] Abfall *m*, Abspaltung *f*, Sezession *f*; **~ist** [~ɪst] Abtrünnige(r *m*) *f*.

se-clude [sɪ'klu:d] abschließen, absondern; **se-clud-ed** einsam; zurückgezogen; abgelegen; **se-clu-sion** [~ʒn] Zurückgezogen-, Abgeschiedenheit *f*.

sec-ond ['sekənd] **1.** □ zweite(r, -s); ~ *to none* unübertroffen; *on* ~ *thought* nach reiflicher Überlegung; **2.** als zweite(r, -s), an zweiter Stelle; **3.** *der, die, das* Zweite; Sekundant *m*; Beistand *m*; Sekunde *f*; ~**s** *pl.* Ware(n *pl.*) *f* zweiter Wahl, zweite Wahl; **4.** sekundieren (*dat.*); unterstützen; **~-a-ry** [~ərɪ] sekundär, untergeordnet; Neben...; Hilfs...; Sekundär..; ~ *education* höhere Schulbildung; ~ *modern* (*school*) *Brt.* (*etwa*) Kombination *f* aus Real- u. Hauptschule; ~ *school* höhere Schule; **~-hand** aus zweiter Hand; gebraucht; antiquarisch; **~-ly** [~lɪ] zweitens; **~-rate** zweitklassig.

se-cre|cy ['si:krɪsɪ] Heimlichkeit *f*;

Verschwiegenheit *f*; **~t** [~t] **1.** □ geheim; Geheim...; verschwiegen; verborgen; **2.** Geheimnis *n*; *in* ~ heimlich, insgeheim; *be in the* ~ eingeweiht sein; *keep s.th. a* ~ *from s.o.* j-m et. verheimlichen.

sec-re-ta-ry ['sekrətrɪ] Schriftführer *m*; Sekretär(in) *f*; ♀ *of State Brt.* Staatssekretär *m*; *Brt.* Minister *m*; *Am.* Außenminister *m*.

se-crete [sɪ'kri:t] verbergen; *biol.* absondern; **se-cre-tion** [~ʃn] Verbergen *n*; *biol.*, 🐾 Absonderung *f*; **se-cre-tive** [~tɪv] verschlossen, geheimnistuerisch.

se-cret-ly ['si:krɪtlɪ] heimlich.

sec-tion ['sekʃn] 🔬 Sektion *f*; Schnitt *m*; Teil *m*; Abschnitt *m*; ⚖ Paragraph *m*; *print.* Absatz *m*; Abteilung *f*; Gruppe *f*.

sec-u-lar □ ['sekjələ] weltlich.

se-cure [sɪ'kjʊə] **1.** □ sicher; fest; gesichert; **2.** (sich *et.*) sichern; schützen; garantieren; befestigen; (fest) (ver)schließen; **se-cu-ri-ty** [~rətɪ] Sicherheit *f*; Sicherheitsmaßnahmen *pl.*; Sorglosigkeit *f*; Garantie *f*; Bürge *m*; Kaution *f*; *securities pl.* Wertpapiere *pl.*; ~ *check* Sicherheitskontrolle *f*.

se-dan [sɪ'dæn] *Am. mot.* Limousine *f*; **~(-chair)** Sänfte *f*.

se-date □ [sɪ'deɪt] gesetzt; ruhig.

sed-a-tive *mst* 🐾 ['sedətɪv] **1.** beruhigend; **2.** Beruhigungsmittel *n*.

sed-en-ta-ry □ ['sedntrɪ] sitzend; seßhaft.

sed-i-ment ['sedɪmənt] Sediment *n*; (Boden)Satz *m*; *geol.* Ablagerung *f*.

se-di-tion [sɪ'dɪʃn] Aufruhr *m*; **~-tious** [~əs] aufrührerisch.

se-duce [sɪ'dju:s] verführen; **se-duc-er** [~ə] Verführer *m*; **se-duc-tion** [sɪ'dʌkʃn] Verführung *f*; **se-duc-tive** [~tɪv] verführerisch.

sed-u-lous □ ['sedjʊləs] emsig.

see¹ [si:] (*saw, seen*) *v/i.* sehen; nachsehen; einsehen; sich überlegen; *I* ~! ich verstehe; ach so!; ~ *about* sich kümmern um; *I'll* ~ *about it* ich will es mir überlegen; ~ *into* untersuchen, nachgehen; ~ *through* j-n *od. et.* durchschauen; ~ *to* sich kümmern um; *v/t.* sehen; besuchen; dafür sorgen (~ *daß*); j-n aufsuchen *od.* konsultieren; einsehen; ~ *s.o. home* j-n nach Hause bringen *od.* begleiten; ~ *you!* bis dann!, auf bald!; ~ *off* j-n verabschieden (*at* am *Bahnhof etc.*); ~ *out j-n* hinausbegleiten; *et.* zu Ende *sehen od.* erleben; ~ *through et.* durchhalten; *j-m* durchhelfen; *live to* ~ erleben.

see² [~] (erz)bischöflicher Stuhl.

seed [si:d] **1.** Same(n) *m*, Saat(gut *n*) *f*; (Obst)Kern *m*; *coll.* Samen *pl.*; ~*s pl. fig.* Saat *f*, Keim *m*; *go od.* run *to* ~ schießen (*Salat etc.*); *fig.* herunterkommen; **2.** *v/t.* (be)säen; entkernen; *v/i.* in Samen schießen; ~**less** ['si:dlɪs] kernlos (*Obst*); ~**·ling** [~ɪŋ] Sämling *m*; ~**·y** □ F [~ɪ] (*-ier, -iest*) schäbig; elend.

seek [si:k] (*sought*) suchen; begehren; trachten nach.

seem [si:m] (er)scheinen; ~**ing** □ ['si:mɪŋ] scheinbar; ~**ly** [~lɪ] (*-ier, -iest*) schicklich.

seen [si:n] *p.p. von* see¹.

seep [si:p] (durch)sickern.

seer [siə] Seher(in), Prophet(in).

see-saw ['si:sɔ:] **1.** Wippen *n*; Wippe *f*, Wippschaukel *f*; **2.** wippen; *fig.* schwanken.

seethe [si:ð] sieden; schäumen (*a. fig.*); *fig.* kochen.

seg·ment ['segmənt] Abschnitt *m*; Segment *n*.

seg·re·gate ['segrɪgeɪt] absondern, (*a. nach Rassen, Geschlechtern etc.*) trennen; ~**·ga·tion** [segrɪ'geɪʃn] Absonderung *f*; Rassentrennung *f*.

seize [si:z] ergreifen, packen, fassen; an sich reißen; ⚖ beschlagnahmen; *j-n* ergreifen, festnehmen; (ein)nehmen, erobern; *fig.* erfassen.

sei·zure ['si:ʒə] Ergreifung *f*; ⚖ Beschlagnahme *f*; ✚ Anfall *m*.

sel·dom *adv.* ['seldəm] selten.

se·lect [sɪ'lekt] **1.** auswählen, -lesen, -suchen; **2.** ausgewählt; erlesen; exklusiv; **se·lec·tion** [~kʃn] Auswahl *f*; Auslese *f*; ~**·man** (*pl. -men*) Stadtrat *m* (*in den Neuenglandstaaten*).

self [self] **1.** (*pl. selves* [selvz]) Selbst *n*, Ich *n*; **2.** *pron.* selbst; *econ. od.* F = *myself, etc.*; ~**·as·sured** ['selfə'ʃʊəd] selbstbewußt, -sicher; ~**·cen·t(e)red** egozentrisch; ~**·col·o(u)red** einheitlich in der Farbe; *bsd.* ⚘ einfarbig; ~**·com·mand** Selbstbeherrschung *f*; ~**·con·ceit** Eigendünkel *m*; ~**·con·ceit·ed** eingebildet, überheblich; ~**·con·fi·dence** Selbstvertrauen *n*, -bewußtsein *n*; ~**·con·fi·dent** □ selbstsicher, -bewußt; ~**·**

con·scious □ befangen, gehemmt, unsicher; △ *nicht selbstbewußt*; ~**·con·tained** (in sich) geschlossen, selbständig; *fig.* verschlossen; ~ *flat Brt.* abgeschlossene Wohnung; ~**·con·trol** Selbstbeherrschung *f*; ~**·de·fence**, *Am.* ~**·de·fense** Selbstverteidigung *f*; *in* ~ in Notwehr; ~**·de·ni·al** Selbstverleugnung *f*; ~**·de·ter·mi·na·tion** *pol.* Selbstbestimmung *f*; ~**·em·ployed** selbständig (*Handwerker etc.*); ~**·evi·dent** selbstverständlich; ~**·gov·ern·ment** *pol.* Selbstverwaltung *f*, Autonomie *f*; ~**·help** Selbsthilfe *f*; ~**·in·dul·gent** nachgiebig gegen sich selbst; zügellos; ~**·in·struc·tion** Selbstunterricht *m*; ~**·in·ter·est** Eigennutz *m*, eigenes Interesse; ~**·ish** □ [~ɪʃ] selbstsüchtig; ~**·made** selbstgemacht; ~ *man* Selfmademan *m*; ~**·pit·y** Selbstmitleid *n*; ~**·pos·ses·sion** Selbstbeherrschung *f*; ~**·re·li·ant** [~rɪ'laɪənt] selbstsicher, -bewußt; ~**·re·spect** Selbstachtung *f*; ~**·right·eous** □ selbstgerecht; ~**·serv·ice 1.** mit Selbstbedienung, Selbstbedienungs...; **2.** Selbstbedienung *f*; ~**·willed** eigenwillig, -sinnig.

sell [sel] (*sold*) *v/t.* verkaufen (*a. fig.*); *j-m et.* aufschwatzen; *v/i.* sich verkaufen (lassen), gehen (*Ware*); verkauft werden (*at, for* für); ~ *off*, ~ *out econ.* ausverkaufen; ~**·er** ['selə] Verkäufer(in); *good* ~ *econ.* gutgehender Artikel.

selves [selvz] *pl. von* self 1.

sem·blance ['sembləns] Anschein *m*; Gestalt *f*.

se·men *biol.* ['si:men] Samen *m*, Sperma *n*.

sem·i- ['semɪ] halb..., Halb...; ~**·co·lon** Semikolon *n*, Strichpunkt *m*; ~**·de·tached (house)** Doppelhaushälfte *f*; ~**·fi·nal** *Sport:* Halb-, Semifinalspiel *n*; ~*s pl.* Halb-, Semifinale *n*, Vorschlußrunde *f*.

sem·i·nar·y ['semɪnərɪ] (Priester)Seminar *n*; *fig.* Schule *f*.

semp·stress ['sempstrɪs] Näherin *f*.

sen·ate ['senɪt] Senat *m*.

sen·a·tor ['senətə] Senator *m*.

send [send] (*sent*) senden, schicken; ⚡ senden; (*mit adj. od. p.pr.*) machen; ~ *s.o. mad j-n* wahnsinnig machen; ~ *for* nach *j-m* schicken, *j-n* kommen lassen; *j-n* holen *od.* rufen (lassen); ~ *forth* aussenden, -strahlen; hervorbringen; veröffentlichen; ~ *in* einsenden, -schicken, -reichen; ~ *up fig.* Preise etc. steigen lassen, in die Höhe treiben; ~ *word to s.o.* j-m Nachricht geben; **~er** ['sendə] Absender(in).

se·nile ['si:naɪl] greisenhaft, senil; **se·nil·i·ty** [sɪ'nɪlɪtɪ] Senilität f.

se·nior ['si:njə] 1. *nachgestellt:* senior; älter; rang-, dienstälter; Ober...; ~ *citizens* pl. ältere Mitbürger pl., Senioren pl.; ~ *partner econ.* Seniorpartner m; 2. Ältere(r m) f; Rang-, Dienstältere(r m) f; Senior(in); *he is my ~ by a year* er ist ein Jahr älter als ich; **~i·ty** [si:nɪ'ɒrətɪ] höheres Alter *od.* Dienstalter.

sen·sa·tion [sen'seɪʃn] (Sinnes)Empfindung f; Gefühl n; Eindruck m; Sensation f; **~al** □ [~l] sensationell; aufsehenerregend.

sense [sens] 1. Sinn m (*of* für); Empfindung f, Gefühl n; Verstand m; Bedeutung f; Ansicht f; *in (out of) one's ~s* bei (von) Sinnen; *bring s.o. to his od. her ~s* j-n zur Vernunft bringen; *make ~* Sinn haben; *talk ~* vernünftig reden; 2. spüren, fühlen. **sense·less** □ ['senslɪs] bewußtlos; unvernünftig, dumm; sinnlos; **~ness** [~nɪs] Bewußtlosigkeit f; Unvernunft f; Sinnlosigkeit f.

sen·si·bil·i·ty [sensɪ'bɪlətɪ] Sensibilität f, Empfindungsvermögen n; *phys. etc.* Empfindlichkeit f; *sensibilities* pl. Empfindsamkeit f, Zartgefühl n.

sen·si·ble □ ['sensəbl] vernünftig; spür-, fühlbar; △ *nicht sensibel; be ~ of s.th.* sich e-r Sache bewußt sein; *et.* empfinden.

sen·si·tive □ ['sensɪtɪv] empfindlich (*to* gegen); Empfindungs...; sensibel, empfindsam, feinfühlig; **~tive·ness** [~nɪs], **~tiv·i·ty** [sensɪ'tɪvətɪ] Sensibilität f; Empfindlichkeit f.

sen·sor ⊕ ['sensə] Sensor m.

sen·su·al □ ['sensjʊəl] sinnlich.

sen·su·ous □ ['sensjʊəs] sinnlich; Sinnes...; sinnenfroh.

sent [sent] *pret. u. p.p. von* send.

sen·tence ['sentəns] 1. ⚖ (Straf)Urteil n; *gr.* Satz m; *serve one's ~* e-e Strafe absitzen; 2. verurteilen.

sen·ten·tious □ [sen'tenʃəs] aufgeblasen; salbungsvoll.

sen·tient □ ['senʃnt] empfindungsfähig.

sen·ti·ment ['sentɪmənt] (seelische) Empfindung, Gefühl n; Meinung f; = *sentimentality;* **~men·tal** □ [sentɪ'mentl] empfindsam; sentimental; **~men·tal·i·ty** [sentɪmen-'tælɪtɪ] Sentimentalität f.

sen·ti·nel ⚔ ['sentɪnl], **~try** ⚔ [~rɪ] Wache f, (Wach[t])Posten m.

sep·a·ra·ble □ ['sepərəbl] trennbar; **~rate** 1. □ ['seprət] (ab)getrennt, gesondert, separat; einzeln; 2. ['separeit] (sich) trennen; (sich) absondern; (sich) scheiden; aufteilen (*into* in *acc.*); **~ra·tion** [sepə'reɪʃn] Trennung f; Scheidung f.

sep·sis ⚕ ['sepsɪs] (*pl.* -ses [-si:z]) Sepsis f (*Blutvergiftung*).

Sep·tem·ber [sep'tembə] September m.

sep·tic ⚕ ['septɪk] (*~ally*) septisch.

se·pul·chral □ [sɪ'pʌlkrəl] Grab...; *fig.* düster, Grabes...

sep·ul·chre, *Am.* **-cher** ['sepəlkə] Grab(stätte f, -mal n) n.

se·quel ['si:kwəl] Folge f; Nachspiel n; (Roman- *etc.*)Fortsetzung f; *a four-~ program(me) TV* ein Vierteiler m, e-e vierteilige Serie.

se·quence ['si:kwəns] (Aufeinander-, Reihen)Folge f; *Film:* Szene f; ~ *of tenses gr.* Zeitenfolge f; **se·quent** [~t] (aufeinander)folgend.

se·ques·trate ⚖ [sɪ'kwestreɪt] *Eigentum* einziehen; beschlagnahmen.

ser·e·nade ♪ [serə'neɪd] 1. Serenade f, Ständchen n; 2. *j-m* ein Ständchen bringen.

se·rene □ [sɪ'ri:n] klar; heiter; ruhig; **se·ren·i·ty** [sɪ'renətɪ] Heiterkeit f; Ruhe f.

ser·geant ['sɑ:dʒənt] ⚔ Feldwebel m; (Polizei)Wachtmeister m.

se·ri·al □ ['sɪərɪəl] 1. serienmäßig, Reihen..., Serien...; Fortsetzungs...; 2. Fortsetzungsroman m; (Hörspiel-, Fernseh)Folge f, Serie f.

se·ries ['sɪərɪ:z] (*pl.* -*ries*) Reihe f; Serie f; Folge f.

se·ri·ous □ ['sɪərɪəs] ernst; ernsthaft, ernstlich; △ *nicht seriös; be ~ es* ernst meinen (*about* mit); **~ness** [~nɪs] Ernst(haftigkeit f) m.

ser·mon ['sɜ:mən] *eccl.* Predigt f; *iro.* (Moral-, Straf)Predigt f.

ser·pent *zo.* ['sɜ:pənt] Schlange f; **~pen·tine** [~aɪn] schlangenförmig;

gewunden, kurvenreich, Serpentinen...

se·rum ['sɪərəm] (*pl.* -rums, -ra [-rə]) Serum *n*.

ser·vant ['sɜːvənt] *a.* domestic ~ Diener(in), Hausangestellte(r *m*) *f*, Dienstbote *m*, -mädchen *n*, Bedienstete(r *m*) *f*; civil ~ s. civil; public ~ Staatsbeamt(er, -in; Angestellte(r *m*) *f* im öffentlichen Dienst.

serve [sɜːv] **1.** *v*/*t*. dienen (*dat.*); Dienstzeit (*a.* ✗) ableisten; Lehre machen; ✗ Strafe verbüßen; genügen (*dat.*); j-n, Kunden bedienen; Essen servieren, auftragen, reichen; Getränk servieren, einschenken; versorgen (with mit); j-n schändlich behandeln; nützen, dienlich sein (*dat.*); Zweck erfüllen; Tennis etc.: Ball aufschlagen; Volleyball: Ball aufgeben; (it) ~s him right (das) geschieht ihm ganz recht; ~ out et. aus-, verteilen; *v*/*i*. dienen (*a.* ✗; as, for als); econ. bedienen; nützen; genügen; Tennis etc.: aufschlagen; Volleyball: aufgeben; ~ at table (bei Tisch) servieren, bedienen; **2.** Tennis etc.: Aufschlag *m*.

ser·vice ['sɜːvɪs] **1.** Dienst *m*; econ. etc. Bedienung *f*; Gefälligkeit *f*; Gottesdienst *m*; Versorgung(sdienst *m*, -sbetrieb *m*) *f*; ✗ (Wehr-, Militär-) Dienst *m*; ⊕ Wartung *f*; Inspektion *f*; Service *m*, Kundendienst *m*; (Zug- etc.)Verkehr *m*; Service *n*; Tennis etc.: Aufschlag *m*; Volleyball: Aufgabe *f*; be at s.o.'s ~ j-m zur Verfügung stehen; **2.** ⊕ warten, pflegen; ~·vi·cea·ble □ [~əbl] brauchbar, dienlich (*a. fig.*); praktisch; strapazierfähig; ~ ar·e·a Brt. (Autobahn)Raststätte *f*; ~ charge Bedienungszuschlag *m*; Bearbeitungsgebühr *f*; ~ sta·tion Tankstelle *f*; (Reparatur)Werkstatt *f*.

ser·vile □ ['sɜːvaɪl] sklavisch (*a. fig.*); unterwürfig, kriecherisch; ~·vil·i·ty [sɜː'vɪlətɪ] Unterwürfigkeit *f*, Kriecherei *f*.

serv·ing ['sɜːvɪŋ] Portion *f*.

ser·vi·tude ['sɜːvɪtjuːd] Knechtschaft *f*; Sklaverei *f*.

ses·sion ['seʃn] Sitzung(speriode) *f*; be in ~ ✗✗ parl. tagen.

set [set] **1.** (-tt-; set) *v*/*t*. setzen; stellen; legen; in e-n Zustand (ver-) setzen, bringen; veranlassen zu; ein-, herrichten, ordnen; ⊕ (ein-

stellen; Uhr, Wecker stellen; Edelstein fassen; besetzen (with mit Edelsteinen); Flüssigkeit erstarren lassen; Haar legen; ✗ Bruch, Knochen einrenken, -richten; ♪ vertonen; print. absetzen; Aufgabe stellen; Zeitpunkt, Preis festsetzen; Rekord aufstellen; ~ s.o. laughing j-n zum Lachen bringen; ~ an example ein Beispiel geben; ~ one's hopes on s-e Hoffnung setzen auf (acc.); ~ the table den Tisch decken; ~ one's teeth die Zähne zusammenbeißen; ~ at ease beruhigen; ~ s.o.'s mind at rest j-n beruhigen; ~ great (little) store by großen (geringen) Wert legen auf (acc.); ~ aside beiseite legen, weglegen; ✗ aufheben; verwerfen; ~ forth darlegen; ~ off hervorheben; ~ up errichten; aufstellen; einrichten, gründen; Regierung bilden; j-n etablieren; *v*/*i*. untergehen (Sonne etc.); gerinnen, fest werden; erstarren (*a.* Gesicht, Muskel); ✗ sich einrenken; hunt. vorstehen (Hund); ~ about doing s.th. sich daranmachen, et. zu tun; ~ about s.o. F über j-n herfallen; ~ forth aufbrechen; ~ in einsetzen (beginnen); ~ off aufbrechen; ~ on angreifen; ~ out aufbrechen; ~ to sich daran machen (to do zu tun); ~ up sich niederlassen; ~ up as sich ausgeben für; **2.** fest; starr; festgesetzt, bestimmt; bereit, entschlossen; vorgeschrieben; ~ fair Barometer: beständig; ~ phrase feststehender Ausdruck; ~ speech wohlüberlegte Rede; **3.** Satz *m*, Garnitur *f*; Service *n*; Set *n*, *m* (Platzdeckchen); gesammelte Ausgabe (e-s Autors); (Schriften)Reihe *f*, (Artikel)Serie *f*; Radio, TV: Gerät *n*, Apparat *m*; thea. Bühnenausstattung *f*; Film: Szenenaufbau *m*; Tennis: Satz *m*; hunt. Vorstehen *n* (Hund); ♪ Setzling *m*; (Personen-) Kreis *m*, contp. Clique *f*; Sitz *m*, Schnitt *m* (Kleidung); poet. Untergang *m* (Sonne); fig. Richtung *f*, Tendenz *f*; have a shampoo and ~ sich die Haare waschen und legen lassen; ~-back Rückschlag *m*.

set·tee [se'tiː] kleines Sofa.

set the·o·ry Å ['set 'θɪərɪ] Mengenlehre *f*.

set·ting ['setɪŋ] Setzen *n*; Einrichten *n*; Fassung *f* (Edelstein); Gedeck *n*; ⊕ Einstellung *f*; thea. Bühnenbild *n*;

S

Film: Ausstattung *f;* ♪ Vertonung *f;* *(Sonnen-* etc.)Untergang *m;* Umgebung *f;* Schauplatz *m; fig.* Rahmen *m.*

set·tle ['setl] **1.** Sitzbank *f;* **2.** *v/t.* vereinbaren, abmachen, festsetzen; erledigen, in Ordnung bringen, regeln; *Frage* etc. klären, entscheiden; *Geschäft* abschließen; *Rechnung* begleichen; *econ. Konto* ausgleichen; *Streit* beilegen; *a.* ~ *down* beruhigen; *Kind* versorgen; *j-n beruflich, häuslich* unterbringen; vermachen (*on dat.*); *Rente* aussetzen (*on dat.*); *Land* besiedeln; ~ *o.s.* sich niederlassen; ~ *one's affairs* s-e Angelegenheiten (*vor dem Tode*) in Ordnung bringen; *that* ~*s it* F damit ist der Fall erledigt; *that's* ~*d then* das ist also klar; *v/i.* sich niederlassen *od.* setzen; *a.* ~ *down* sich ansiedeln *od.* niederlassen; sich (häuslich) niederlassen; sich senken (*Grundmauern* etc.); beständig werden (*Wetter*); *a.* ~ *down fig.* sich beruhigen, sich legen; sich setzen (*Trübstoffe*); sich klären (*Flüssigkeit*); sich legen (*Staub*); *a.* ~ *back* sich (gemütlich) zurücklehnen; ~ *down to* sich widmen (*dat.*); ~ *in* sich einrichten; sich einleben *od.* eingewöhnen; ~ *on, ~ upon* sich entschließen zu; ~**d** fest; geregelt (*Leben*); beständig (*Wetter*); ~**ment** [~mənt] (Be)Siedlung *f;* Klärung *f,* Erledigung *f;* Übereinkunft *f,* Abmachung *f;* Bezahlung *f;* Schlichtung *f,* Beilegung *f;* ⅄⅄ (Eigentums)Übertragung *f;* ~**r** [~ə] Siedler *m.*

sev·en ['sevn] **1.** sieben; **2.** Sieben *f;* ~**teen** [~'ti:n] **1.** siebzehn; **2.** Siebzehn *f;* ~**teenth** [~'ti:nθ] **1.** □ sieb(en)te(r, -s); **2.** Sieb(en)tel *n;* ~**th·ly** [~lɪ] sieb(en)tens; ~**ti·eth** [~tɪɪθ] siebzigste(r, -s); ~**ty** [~tɪ] **1.** siebzig; **2.** Siebzig *f.*

sev·er ['sevə] (sich) trennen; zerreißen; *fig.* (auf)lösen.

sev·er·al ['sevrəl] mehrere; verschieden; einige; einzeln; eigen; getrennt; ~**ly** [~lɪ] einzeln, gesondert, getrennt.

sev·er·ance ['sevərəns] (Ab)Trennung *f; fig.* (Auf)Lösung *f,* Abbruch *m.*

se·vere □ [sɪ'vɪə] (~*r,* ~*st*) streng; scharf; hart; rauh (*Wetter*); hart

(*Winter*); ernst, finster (*Ausdruck* etc.); heftig (*Schmerz* etc.); schlimm, schwer (*Krankheit* etc.); **se·ver·i·ty** [sɪ'verətɪ] Strenge *f,* Härte *f;* Heftigkeit *f,* Stärke *f;* Ernst *m.*

sew [səʊ] (*sewed, sewn od. sewed*) nähen; heften.

sew·age ['sju:ɪdʒ] Abwasser *n.*

sew·er[1] ['səʊə] Näherin *f.*

sew·er[2] [sjʊə] Abwasserkanal *m;* ~**age** ['sjʊərɪdʒ] Kanalisation *f.*

sew·ing ['səʊɪŋ] Nähen *n;* Näharbeit *f; attr.* Näh...; ~**n** [səʊn] *p.p. von* sew.

sex [seks] Geschlecht *n;* Sexualität *f;* Sex *m.*

sex·ton ['sekstən] Küster *m* (u. Totengräber *m*).

sex·u·al □ ['seksjʊəl] geschlechtlich, Geschlechts..., sexuell, Sexual...; ~ *intercourse* Geschlechtsverkehr *m;* ~**y** F [~ɪ] (*-ier, -iest*) sexy, aufreizend.

shab·by □ ['ʃæbɪ] (*-ier, -iest*) schäbig; gemein.

shack [ʃæk] Hütte *f,* Bude *f.*

shack·le ['ʃækl] **1.** Fessel *f* (*fig. mst pl.*); **2.** fesseln.

shade [ʃeɪd] **1.** Schatten *m* (*a. fig.*); (*Lampen-* etc.)Schirm *m;* Schattierung *f; Am.* Rouleau *n; fig.* Nuance *f; fig.* F Spur *f;* **2.** beschatten; verdunkeln (*a. fig.*); abschirmen; schützen; schattieren; ~ *off* allmählich übergehen (*lassen*) (*into* in *acc.*).

shad·ow ['ʃædəʊ] **1.** Schatten *m* (*a. fig.*); Phantom *n; fig.* Spur *f;* **2.** e-n Schatten werfen auf (*acc.*); *fig.* j-n beschatten, überwachen; ~**y** [~ɪ] (*-ier, -iest*) schattig, dunkel; unbestimmt, vage.

shad·y □ ['ʃeɪdɪ] (*-ier, -iest*) schattenspendend; schattig, dunkel; F zweifelhaft.

shaft [ʃɑːft] Schaft *m;* Stiel *m; poet.* Pfeil *m* (*a. fig.*); *poet.* Strahl *m;* ⊕ Welle *f;* Deichsel *f;* ⚒ Schacht *m.*

shag·gy ['ʃægɪ] (*-ier, -iest*) zottig.

shake [ʃeɪk] **1.** (*shook, shaken*) *v/t.* schütteln; rütteln an (*dat.*); erschüttern; ~ *down* herunterschütteln; ~ *hands* sich die Hand geben *od.* schütteln; ~ *off* abschütteln (*a. fig.*); ~ *up* Bett aufschütteln; *fig.* aufrütteln; *v/i.* zittern, beben, wackeln, (sch)wanken (*with* vor *dat.*); ♪ trillern; ~ *down* kampieren; **2.** Schütteln *n;* Erschütterung *f;* Beben *n;* ♪

sheaves

Triller *m*; (*Milch- etc.*)Shake *m*; **~·down** ['ʃeɪkdaʊn] **1.** (Behelfs-) Lager *n*; *Am.* F Erpressung *f*; *Am.* F Durchsuchung *f*; **2.** *adj.*: ~ flight ✈ Testflug *m*; ~ voyage ♪ Testfahrt *f*; **shak·en** [~ən] **1.** *p.p. von* shake 1; **2.** *adj.* erschüttert.

shak·y □ ['ʃeɪkɪ] (*-ier, -iest*) wack(e)lig (*a. fig.*); (sch)wankend; zitternd; zitt(e)rig.

shall *v/aux.* [ʃæl] (*pret.* should; *verneint:* ~ not, shan't) ich, du etc. soll(st) *etc.*; ich werde, wir werden.

shal·low ['ʃæləʊ] **1.** □ seicht; flach; *fig.* oberflächlich; **2.** seichte Stelle, Untiefe *f*; **3.** (sich) verflachen.

sham [ʃæm] **1.** falsch; Schein...; **2.** (Vor)Täuschung *f*, Heuchelei *f*; Fälschung *f*; Schwindler(in); △ *nicht* Scham; **3.** (*-mm-*) *v/t.* vortäuschen; *v/i.* sich verstellen; simulieren; ~ ill(ness) sich krank stellen.

sham·ble ['ʃæmbl] watscheln; **~s** *sg.* Schlachtfeld *n*, wüstes Durcheinander, Chaos *n*.

shame [ʃeɪm] **1.** Scham *f*; Schande *f*; *for* ~!, ~ *on you!* pfui!, schäm dich!; *put to* ~ beschämen; **2.** beschämen; *j-m* Schande machen; **~·faced** □ ['ʃeɪmfeɪst] schamhaft, schüchtern; **~·ful** [~fl] schändlich, beschämend; **~·less** [~lɪs] schamlos.

sham·poo [ʃæm'puː] **1.** Shampoo *n*, Schampon *n*, Schampun *n*; Kopf-, Haarwäsche *f*; *s.* set 3; **2.** Kopf, Haare waschen; *j-m* den Kopf *od.* die Haare waschen.

sham·rock ♣ ['ʃæmrɒk] Kleeblatt *n*.

shank [ʃæŋk] (Unter)Schenkel *m*, Schienbein *n*; △ *nicht* (Ober)Schenkel; ♣ Stiel *m*; (⚓ Anker)Schaft *m*.

shan·ty ['ʃæntɪ] Hütte *f*, Bude *f*; Seemannslied *n*.

shape [ʃeɪp] **1.** Gestalt *f*, Form *f* (*a. fig.*); körperliche *od.* geistige Verfassung; **2.** *v/t.* gestalten, formen, bilden; anpassen (*to dat.*); *v/i. a.* ~ up sich entwickeln; **~d** [~t] ...förmig; **~·less** ['ʃeɪplɪs] formlos; **~·ly** [~lɪ] (*-ier, -iest*) wohlgeformt.

share [ʃeə] **1.** (An)Teil *m*; Beitrag *m*; *econ.* Aktie *f*; ⚒ Kux *m*; ♪ Pflugschar *f*; *have a* ~ *in* Anteil haben an (*dat.*); *go* ~s teilen; **2.** *v/t.* teilen; *v/i.* teilhaben (*in an dat.*); **~·crop·per** ['ʃeəkrɒpə] *kleiner* Farmpächter (*in den USA*); **~·hold·er** *econ.* Aktionär(in).

shark [ʃɑːk] *zo.* Hai(fisch) *m*; Gauner *m*, Betrüger *m*; (*Kredit- etc.*)Hai *m*; *Am. sl.* Kanone *f* (*Könner*).

sharp [ʃɑːp] **1.** □ scharf (*a. fig.*); spitz; steil, jäh; schneidend; stechend; heftig; hitzig; beißend; scharf; durchdringend; schrill; schnell; pfiffig, schlau, gerissen; ♪ (*um e-n Halbton*) erhöht; C ~ ♪ Cis *n*; **2.** *adv.* scharf; jäh, plötzlich; ♪ zu hoch; pünktlich, genau; *at eight o'clock* ~ Punkt 8 (Uhr); *look* ~! F paß auf!, gib acht!; F mach fix *od.* schnell!; **3.** ♪ Kreuz *n*; ♪ durch ein Kreuz erhöhte Note; F Gauner *m*; **~·en** ['ʃɑːpən] (ver)schärfen; spitzen; verstärken; **~·en·er** [~nə] (*Messer*)Schärfer *m*; (*Bleistift*)Spitzer *m*; **~·er** [~ə] Gauner *m*, Schwindler *m*; Falschspieler *m*; **~·eyed** [~'aɪd] scharfsichtig; *fig. a.* scharfsinnig; **~·ness** [~nɪs] Schärfe *f* (*a. fig.*); **~·shoot·er** Scharfschütze *m*; **~·sight·ed** [~'saɪtɪd] scharfsichtig; *fig. a.* scharfsinnig; **~·wit·ted** [~'wɪtɪd] scharfsinnig.

shat·ter ['ʃætə] zerschmettern, -schlagen; *Gesundheit, Nerven* zerstören, -rütten.

shave [ʃeɪv] **1.** (shaved, shaved *od. als adj.* shaven) (sich) rasieren; (ab)schaben; (glatt)hobeln; streifen; *a.* knapp vorbeikommen an (*dat.*); **2.** Rasieren *n*, Rasur *f*; *have* (*od.* get) *a* ~ sich rasieren (lassen); *have a close od. narrow* ~ mit knapper Not davonkommen *od.* entkommen; *that was a close* ~ das ist gerade noch einmal gutgegangen!; **shav·en** ['ʃeɪvn] *p.p. von* shave 1; **shav·ing** [~ɪŋ] **1.** Rasieren *n*; **~s** *pl.* (*bsd.* Hobel)Späne *pl.*; **2.** Rasier...

shawl [ʃɔːl] Umhängetuch *n*; Kopftuch *n*.

she [ʃiː] **1.** sie; **2.** Sie *f*; *zo.* Weibchen *n*; **3.** *adj. in Zssgn, bsd. zo.*: weiblich, ...weibchen *n*; **~·dog** Hündin *f*; **~·goat** Geiß *f*.

sheaf [ʃiːf] (*pl.* sheaves) ♪ Garbe *f*; Bündel *n*.

shear [ʃɪə] **1.** (sheared, shorn *od.* sheared) scheren; **2.** (*a pair of*) ~s *pl.* (*e-e*) große Schere.

sheath [ʃiːθ] (*pl.* sheaths [~ðz]) Scheide *f*; Futteral *n*, Hülle *f*; **~·e** [ʃiːð] in die Scheide *od.* in ein Futteral stecken; *bsd.* ⊕ umhüllen.

sheaves [ʃiːvz] *pl. von* sheaf.

S

she·bang bsd. Am. sl. [ʃə'bæŋ]: the whole ~ der ganze Kram.

shed¹ [ʃed] (-dd-; shed) aus-, vergießen; verbreiten; Blätter etc. abwerfen.

shed² [~] Schuppen m; Stall m.

sheen [ʃiːn] Glanz m (bsd. Stoff).

sheep [ʃiːp] (pl. sheep) zo. Schaf n; Schafleder n; **~dog** zo. ['ʃiːpdɔg] Schäferhund m; **~fold** Schafhürde f; **~ish** □ [~iʃ] einfältig; verlegen; **~man** (pl. -men) Am., **~skin** Schaffell n; Schafleder n; Am. F Diplom n.

sheer [ʃiə] rein; bloß; glatt; hauchdünn; steil; senkrecht; direkt.

sheet [ʃiːt] Bett-, Leintuch n, Laken n; (Glas- etc.)Platte f; ⊕ ...blech n; Blatt n, Bogen m (Papier); weite Fläche (Wasser etc.); ⚓ Schot(e) f, Segelleine f; the rain came down in ~s es regnete in Strömen; **~ i·ron** ⊕ Eisenblech n; **~ light·ning** Wetterleuchten n.

shelf [ʃelf] (pl. shelves) (Bücher-, Wand- etc.)Brett n, Regal n, Fach n; Riff n; on the ~ fig. ausrangiert.

shell [ʃel] 1. Schale f; ⚓ Hülse f, Schote f; Muschel f; Schneckenhaus n; zo. Panzer m; Gerüst n, Gerippe n, arch. a. Rohbau m; ⚔ Granate f (Geschoß-, Patronen)Hülse f; Am. Patrone f; 2. schälen; enthülsen; ⚔ (mit Granaten) beschießen; **~fire** ['ʃelfaiə] Granatfeuer n; **~fish** zo. Schal(en)tier n; ~ pl. Meeresfrüchte pl.; ⚠ nicht Schellfisch; **~proof** bombensicher.

shel·ter ['ʃeltə] 1. Schutzhütte f, -raum m, -dach n; Zufluchtsort m; Obdach n; Schutz m, Zuflucht f; take ~ Schutz suchen; bus~ Wartehäuschen n; 2. v/t. (be)schützen; beschirmen; j-m Schutz od. Zuflucht gewähren; v/i. Schutz od. Zuflucht suchen.

shelve [ʃelv] v/t. in ein Regal stellen; fig. et. auf die lange Bank schieben; fig. et. zurückstellen; v/i. sanft abfallen (Land).

shelves [ʃelvz] pl. von shelf.

she·nan·i·gans F [ʃɪ'nænɪgənz] pl. Blödsinn m, Mumpitz m; übler Trick.

shep·herd ['ʃepəd] 1. Schäfer m, Hirt m; 2. hüten; führen; leiten.

sher·iff Am. ['ʃerɪf] Sheriff m.

shield [ʃiːld] 1. (Schutz)Schild m;

Wappenschild m, n; fig. Schutz m; 2. (be)schützen (from vor dat.); j-n decken.

shift [ʃift] 1. Veränderung f, Verschiebung f, Wechsel m; Notbehelf m; List f, Kniff m, Ausflucht f; (Arbeits)Schicht f; work in ~s Schicht arbeiten; make ~ es fertigbringen (to do zu tun); sich behelfen; sich durchschlagen; 2. v/t. (um-, aus)wechseln, verändern; a. fig. verlagern, -schieben, -legen; Schuld etc. (ab)schieben (onto auf acc.); ~ gear(s) bsd. Am. mot. schalten; v/i. wechseln; sich verlagern od. -schieben; bsd. Am. mot. schalten (into, to in acc.); ~ from one foot to the other von e-m Fuß auf den anderen treten; ~ in one's chair auf s-m Stuhl unruhig etc. hin u. her rutschen; ~ for o.s. sich selbst (weiter)helfen; **~less** □ ['ʃɪftlɪs] hilflos; faul; **~y** □ [~ɪ] (-ier, -iest) (augen)gerissen; verschlagen; unzuverlässig.

shil·ling ['ʃɪlɪŋ] altes englisches Währungssystem: Schilling m.

shin [ʃɪn] 1. a. **~bone** Schienbein n; 2. (-nn-) ~ up hinaufklettern.

shine [ʃaɪn] 1. Schein m; Glanz m; 2. v/i. (shone) scheinen; leuchten; fig. glänzen, strahlen; v/t. (shined) polieren, putzen.

shin·gle ['ʃɪŋgl] Schindel f; Am. F (Firmen)Schild n; grober Strandkies; **~s** sg. ✻ Gürtelrose f.

shin·y ['ʃaɪnɪ] (-ier, -iest) blank, glänzend.

ship [ʃɪp] 1. Schiff n; F Flugzeug n; F Raumschiff n; 2. (-pp-) ⚓ an Bord nehmen od. bringen; ⚓ verschiffen; econ. transportieren, versenden; ⚓ (an)heuern; ⚓ sich anheuern lassen; **~board** ⚓ ['ʃɪpbɔːd]: on ~ an Bord; **~ment** [~mənt] Verschiffung f; Versand m; Schiffsladung f; **~own·er** Reeder m; **~ping** [~ɪŋ] Verschiffung f; Versand m; coll. Schiffe pl., Flotte f; attr. Schiffs...; Versand...; **~wreck** Schiffbruch m; **~wrecked** 1. be ~ schiffbrüchig werden od. sein; 2. schiffbrüchig, fig. a. gescheitert; **~yard** (Schiffs-) Werft f.

shire ['ʃaɪə, in Zssgn: ...ʃə] Grafschaft f.

shirk [ʃɜːk] sich drücken (vor dat.); **~er** ['ʃɜːkə] Drückeberger(in).

short-winded

shirt [ʃɜːt] (Herren-, Ober)Hemd n; a. ~ blouse Hemdbluse f; **~-sleeve** [ˈʃɜːtsliːv] **1.** Hemdsärmel m; **2.** hemdsärmelig; leger, ungezwungen; **~-waist** Am. Hemdbluse f.

shit V [ʃɪt] **1.** Scheiße f (a. fig.); Scheißen n; **2.** (-tt-; shit) scheißen.

shiv-er [ˈʃɪvə] **1.** Splitter m; Schauer m, Zittern n, Frösteln f; **2.** zersplittern; zittern, (er)schauern, frösteln; **~-y** [~rɪ] fröstelnd.

shoal [ʃəʊl] **1.** Schwarm m (bsd. von Fischen); Masse f; Untiefe f, seichte Stelle; Sandbank f; **2.** flach(er) werden.

shock [ʃɒk] **1.** Garbenhaufen m; (Haar)Schopf m; (heftiger) Stoß; (a. seelische) Erschütterung; Schock m; Schreck m, (plötzlicher) Schlag (to für); ♯ (Nerven)Schock m; **2.** erschüttern; fig. schockieren, empören; **~ ab-sorb-er** ⊕ Stoßdämpfer m; **~-ing** □ [ˈʃɒkɪŋ] schockierend, empörend, anstößig; haarsträubend; F scheußlich.

shod [ʃɒd] pret. u. p.p. von shoe 2.

shod-dy [ˈʃɒdɪ] **1.** Reißwolle f; fig. Schund m; **2.** (-ier, -iest) falsch; minderwertig, schäbig.

shoe [ʃuː] **1.** Schuh m; Hufeisen n; **2.** (shod) beschuhen; beschlagen; **~-black** [ˈʃuːblæk] Schuhputzer m; **~-horn** Schuhanzieher m; **~-lace** Schnürsenkel m; **~-mak-er** Schuhmacher m; **~-shine** bsd. Am. Schuhputzen m; ~ boy Am. Schuhputzer m; **~-string** Schnürsenkel m.

shone [ʃɒn, Am. ʃəʊn] pret. u. p.p. von shine 2.

shook [ʃʊk] pret. von shake 1.

shoot [ʃuːt] **1.** Jagd f; Jagd(revier n) f; Jagdgesellschaft f; ♀ Schößling m, (Seiten)Trieb m; **2.** (shot) v/t. (ab)schießen; erschießen; werfen, stoßen; fotografieren, aufnehmen, Film drehen; unter e-r Brücke etc. hindurchschießen, über et. hinwegschießen; ♀ treiben; ♯ (ein)spritzen; ~ up sl. Heroin etc. drücken; v/i. schießen; jagen; stechen (Schmerz); (dahin-, vorbei- etc.)schießen, (-)jagen, (-)rasen; ♀ sprießen, keimen; fotografieren; filmen; ~ ahead of überholen (acc.); **~-er** [ˈʃuːtə] Schütze, -in; F Schießeisen n (Schußwaffe).

shoot-ing [ˈʃuːtɪŋ] **1.** Schießen n; Schießerei f; Erschießung f; Jagd f;

Film: Dreharbeiten pl.; **2.** stechend (Schmerz); **~-gal-le-ry** Schießstand m, -bude f; **~-range** Schießplatz m; ~ star Sternschnuppe f.

shop [ʃɒp] **1.** Laden m, Geschäft n; Werkstatt f; Betrieb m; talk ~ fachsimpeln; **2.** (-pp-) mst go ~ping einkaufen gehen; ~ as-sis-tant Brt. [ˈʃɒpəsɪstənt] Verkäufer(in); **~-keep-er** Ladenbesitzer(in); **~-lift-er** [~lɪftə] Ladendieb(in); **~-lift-ing** [~lɪftɪŋ] Ladendiebstahl m; **~-per** [~ə] Käufer(in); **~-ping** [~ɪŋ] **1.** Einkauf m, Einkaufen n; Einkäufe pl. (Ware); do one's ~ (s-e) Einkäufe machen; **2.** Laden..., Einkaufs...; **~ bag** Am. Trag(e)tasche f; ~ centre (Am. center) Einkaufszentrum n; ~ street Geschäfts-, Ladenstraße f; **~ stew-ard** [~stjʊəd] gewerkschaftlicher Vertrauensmann; **~-walk-er** Brt. [~wɔːkə] Aufsicht(sperson) f (im Kaufhaus); **~-win-dow** Schaufenster n.

shore [ʃɔː] **1.** Küste f, Ufer n, Strand m; Strebebalken m, Stütze f; on ~ an Land; **2.** ~ up abstützen.

shorn [ʃɔːn] p.p. von shear 1.

short [ʃɔːt] **1.** adj. kurz; klein; knapp; kurz angebunden, barsch (with gegen); mürbe (Gebäck); stark, unverdünnt (alkoholisches Getränk); in ~ kurz(um); ~ of knapp an (dat.); **2.** adv. plötzlich, jäh, abrupt; ~ of abgesehen von, außer (dat.); come od. fall ~ of et. nicht erreichen; cut ~ plötzlich unterbrechen; stop ~ plötzlich innehalten, stutzen; stop ~ of zurückschrecken vor (dat.); s. run 1; **~-age** [ˈʃɔːtɪdʒ] Fehlbetrag m; Knappheit f, Mangel m (of an dat.); **~-com-ing** [~ˈkʌmɪŋ] Unzulänglichkeit f; Fehler m, Mangel m; **~ cut** Abkürzung(sweg m) f; take a ~ (den Weg) abkürzen; **~-dat-ed** econ. kurzfristig; **~-dis-tance** Nah...; **~-en** [ˈʃɔːtn] v/t. (ab-, ver)kürzen; v/i. kürzer werden; **~-en-ing** [~ɪŋ] Backfett n; **~-hand** [ˈʃɔːthænd] Kurzschrift f; ~ typist Stenotypist(in); **~-ly** [~lɪ] adv. kurz; bald; **~-ness** [~nɪs] Kürze f; Mangel m; Schroffheit f; **~-s** pl. (a pair of ~s) Shorts pl.; bsd. Am. (e-e) (Herren)Unterhose f; **~-sight-ed** □ [ˈʃɔːtsaɪtɪd] kurzsichtig (a. fig.); **~-term** econ. [ˈʃɔːtɜːm] kurzfristig; ~ **wave** ♭ Kurzwelle f; ~ **wind-ed** □ [ˈʃɔːtˈwɪndɪd] kurzatmig.

S

shot [ʃɒt] 1. *pret. u. p.p. von* shoot 2; 2. Schuß *m*; Abschuß *m*; Geschoß *n*, Kugel *f*; *a. small* ~ Schrot(kugeln *pl.*) *m*, *n*; Schußweite *f*; *guter etc.* Schütze; Fußball *etc.*: Schuß *m*, Basketball *etc.*: Wurf *m*, Tennis, Golf: Schlag *m*; *phot.*, *Film*: Aufnahme *f*; 💉 F Spritze *f*, Injektion *f*; F Schuß *m* (*Drogeninjektion*); *fig.* Versuch *m*; *fig.* Vermutung *f*; *have a* ~ *at et.* versuchen; *not by a long* ~ F noch lange nicht; *big* ~ F großes Tier; ~**gun** [ˈʃɒtɡʌn] Schrotflinte *f*; ~ *marriage od. wedding* F Mußheirat *f*; ~**put** *Sport*: Kugelstoßen *n*; Stoß *m* (*mit der Kugel*); ~**put·ter** [~pʊtə] *Sport*: Kugelstoßer(in).

should [ʃʊd, ʃəd] *pret. von* shall.

shoul·der [ˈʃəʊldə] 1. Schulter *f* (*a. v. Tieren*; *fig.* Vorsprung); Achsel *f*; *Am.* Bankett *n* (*Straßenrand*); 2. auf die Schulter *od. fig.* auf sich nehmen; ✖ schultern; drängen; ~**blade** *anat.* Schulterblatt *n*; ~**strap** Träger *m* (*am Kleid etc.*); ✖ Schulter-, Achselstück *n*.

shout [ʃaʊt] 1. (lauter) Schrei *od.* Ruf; Geschrei *n*; 2. (laut) rufen; schreien.

shove [ʃʌv] 1. Schubs *m*, Stoß *m*; 2. schieben, stoßen.

shov·el [ˈʃʌvl] 1. Schaufel *f*; 2. (*bsd. Brt. -ll-*, *Am. -l-*) schaufeln.

show [ʃəʊ] 1. (showed, shown *od.* showed) *v/t.* zeigen; ausstellen; erweisen; beweisen; ~ *in* herein-, hineinführen; ~ *off* zur Geltung bringen; ~ *out* heraus-, hinausführen, -bringen; ~ *round* herumführen; ~ *up* herauf-, hinaufführen; *j-n* bloßstellen; *et.* aufdecken; *v/i. a.* ~ *up* sichtbar werden *od.* sein; sich zeigen; zu sehen sein; ~ *off* angeben, prahlen, sich aufspielen; ~ *up* F auftauchen, sich blicken lassen; 2. (Her)Zeigen *n*; Zurschaustellung *f*; Ausstellung *f*, Vorführung *f*, -stellung *f*, Schau *f*; F (Theater-, Film-) Vorstellung *f*, (Rundfunk-, Fernseh-) Sendung *f*, Show *f*; *leerer* Schein *m*; *on* ~ zu besichtigen; ~**biz** F [ˈʃəʊbɪz], ~ **busi·ness** Showbusineß *n*, Showgeschäft *n*, Vergnügungs-, Unterhaltungsbranche *f*; ~**case** Schaukasten *m*, Vitrine *f*; ~**down** Aufdecken *n* der Karten (*a. fig.*); *fig.* Kraftprobe *f*.

show·er [ˈʃaʊə] 1. (Regen- *etc.*) Schauer *m*; Dusche *f*; *fig.* Fülle *f*; 2. *v/t.* überschütten, -häufen; *v/i.* gießen; (sich) brausen *od.* duschen; ~ *down* niederprasseln; *v·y* [~rɪ] (*-ier*, *-iest*) regnerisch.

show-jump·er [ˈʃəʊdʒʌmpə] *Sport*: Springreiter(in); ~**jump·ing** [~ɪŋ] *Sport*: Springreiten *n*; ~**n** [~n] *p.p. von* show 1; ~**room** Ausstellungsraum *m*; ~**win·dow** Schaufenster *n*; ~**y** □ [~ɪ] (*-ier*, *-iest*) prächtig; protzig.

shrank [ʃræŋk] *pret. von* shrink.

shred [ʃred] 1. Stückchen *n*; Fetzen *m* (*a. fig.*); *fig.* Spur *f*; 2. (*-dd-*) zerfetzen; in Streifen schneiden.

shrew [ʃruː] zänkisches Weib.

shrewd □ [ʃruːd] scharfsinnig; schlau.

shriek [ʃriːk] 1. schriller Schrei; Gekreisch *n*; 2. kreischen, schreien.

shrill [ʃrɪl] 1. □ schrill, gellend; 2. schrillen, gellen; *et.* kreischen.

shrimp [ʃrɪmp] zo. Garnele *f*, Krabbe *f*; *fig. contp.* Knirps *m*.

shrine [ʃraɪn] Schrein *m*.

shrink [ʃrɪŋk] (shrank, shrunk) (ein-, zusammen)schrumpfen (lassen); einlaufen; zurückweichen (*from* vor *dat.*); zurückschrecken (*from*, *at* vor *dat.*); ~**age** [ˈʃrɪŋkɪdʒ] Einlaufen *n*; (Ein-, Zusammen)Schrumpfen *n*; Schrumpfung *f*; *fig.* Verminderung *f*.

shriv·el [ˈʃrɪvl] (*bsd. Brt. -ll-*, *Am. -l-*) (ein-, zusammen)schrumpfen (lassen), (ver)welken (lassen).

shroud [ʃraʊd] 1. Leichentuch *n*; *fig.* Schleier *m*; 2. in ein Leichentuch (ein)hüllen; *fig.* hüllen.

Shrove·tide [ˈʃrəʊvtaɪd] Fastnachts-, Faschingszeit *f*; ~ **Tues·day** Fastnachts-, Faschingsdienstag *m*.

shrub [ʃrʌb] Strauch *m*; Busch *m*; ~**be·ry** [ˈʃrʌbərɪ] Gebüsch *n*.

shrug [ʃrʌɡ] 1. (*-gg-*) (die Achseln) zucken; 2. Achselzucken *n*.

shrunk [ʃrʌŋk] *p.p. von* shrink; ~**en** [ˈʃrʌŋkən] *adj.* (ein-, zusammen)geschrumpft.

shuck *bsd. Am.* [ʃʌk] 1. Hülse *f*, Schote *f*; ~*s!* F Quatsch!; 2. enthülsen.

shud·der [ˈʃʌdə] 1. schaudern; (er-)zittern, (er)beben; 2. Schauder *m*.

shuf·fle [ˈʃʌfl] 1. *Karten*: mischen; schlurfen (mit); Ausflüchte machen; ⚠ *nicht schaufeln*; ~ *off Klei-*

dung abstreifen; *fig. Verantwortung etc.* abwälzen (*on, upon* auf *acc.*); **2.** (Karten)Mischen *n*; Schlurfen *n*; Umstellung *f*, (*Kabinetts*)Umbildung *f*; *fig.* Ausflucht *f*, Schwindel *m*.

shun [ʃʌn] (*-nn-*) (ver)meiden.

shunt [ʃʌnt] **1.** Rangieren *n*; ⚡ Weiche *f*; ⚡ Nebenschluß *m*; **2.** ⚡ rangieren; ⚡ nebenschließen; beiseite schieben; *fig. et.* aufschieben.

shut [ʃʌt] (*-tt-; shut*) (sich) schließen; zumachen; ~ *down Betrieb* schließen; ~ *off Wasser, Gas etc.* abstellen; ~ *up* einschließen; *Haus etc.* verschließen; einsperren; ~ *up!* F halt die Klappe!; ~**ter** [ʃʌtə] Fensterladen *m*; *phot.* Verschluß *m*; ~ **speed** *phot.* Belichtung(szeit) *f*.

shut·tle [ʃʌtl] **1.** ⊕ Schiffchen *n*; Pendelverkehr *m*; ~ **space** ~; **2.** *etc.* pendeln; ~**cock** *Sport:* Federball *m*; ~ **di·plo·ma·cy** *pol.* Pendeldiplomatie *f*; ~ **ser·vice** Pendelverkehr *m*.

shy [ʃaɪ] **1.** □ (~*er od.* shier, ~*est od.* shiest) scheu; schüchtern; **2.** scheuen (*at vor dat.*); ~ *away from fig.* zurückschrecken vor (*dat.*); ~**ness** [ʃaɪnɪs] Schüchternheit *f*; Scheu *f*.

Si·be·ri·an [saɪˈbɪərɪən] **1.** sibirisch; **2.** Sibirier(in).

sick [sɪk] krank (*of an dat.; with* vor *dat.*); überdrüssig (*of gen.*); *fig.* krank (*of von dat.; for* nach); *be* ~ sich übergeben (müssen); *be* ~ *of s.th. et.* satt haben; *fall* ~ krank werden; *I feel* ~ mir ist schlecht *od.* übel; *go* ~, *report* ~ sich krank melden; ~**ben·e·fit** *Brt.* [ˈsɪkbenɪfɪt] Krankengeld *n*; ~**en** [~ən] *v/i.* krank werden; krank machen; ~ *at* sich ekeln vor (*dat.*); *v/t.* krank machen; anekeln.

sick·le [sɪkl] Sichel *f*.

sick|-leave [ˈsɪkliːv] Fehlen *n* wegen Krankheit; *be on* ~ wegen Krankheit fehlen; ~**ly** [~lɪ] (*-ier, -iest*) kränklich; schwächlich; bleich, blaß; ungesund (*Klima*); ekelhaft; matt (*Lächeln*); ~**ness** [~nɪs] Krankheit *f*; Übelkeit *f*.

side [saɪd] **1.** Seite *f*; ~ *by* ~ Seite an Seite; *take* ~*s with* Partei ergreifen für; **2.** Seiten...; **3.** Partei ergreifen (*with* für); ~**board** [ˈsaɪdbɔːd] Anrichte *f*, Sideboard *n*; ~**car** *mot.* Beiwagen *m*; **sid·ed** ...seitig; ~

dish Beilage *f* (*Essen*); ~**long 1.** *adv.* seitwärts; **2.** *adj.* seitlich; Seiten...; ~**road**, ~**street** Nebenstraße *f*; ~**stroke** *Sport:* Seitenschwimmen *n*; ~**track 1.** ⚡ Nebengleis *n*; **2.** ⚡ auf ein Nebengleis schieben; *fig.* ablenken; ~**walk** *Am.* Bürgersteig *m*; ~**ward(s)** [~wəd(z)], ~**ways** seitlich; seitwärts.

sid·ing ⚡ [ˈsaɪdɪŋ] Nebengleis *n*.

si·dle [ˈsaɪdl]: ~ *up to s.o.* sich an j-n heranmachen.

siege [siːdʒ] Belagerung *f*; △ *nicht Sieg; lay* ~ *to* belagern; *fig. j-n* bestürmen.

sieve [sɪv] **1.** Sieb *n*; **2.** (durch)sieben.

sift [sɪft] sieben; *fig.* sichten, prüfen.

sigh [saɪ] **1.** Seufzer *m*; **2.** seufzen; sich sehnen (*for* nach).

sight [saɪt] **1.** Sehvermögen *n*, Sehkraft *f*; Auge(nlicht) *n*; Anblick *m*; Sicht *f* (*a. econ.*); Visier *n*; *fig.* Auge *n*; ~*s pl.* Sehenswürdigkeiten *pl.*; *at* ~, *on* ~ sofort; *at* ~ vom Blatt (*singen etc.*); *at the* ~ *of* beim Anblick (*gen.*); *at first* ~ auf den ersten Blick; *catch* ~ *of* erblicken; *know by* ~ vom Sehen kennen; *lose* ~ *of* aus den Augen verlieren; (*with*)*in* ~ in Sicht(weite); **2.** sichten, erblicken; (an)visieren; ~**ed** [ˈsaɪtɪd] ...sichtig; ~**ly** [~lɪ] (*-ier, -iest*) ansehnlich, stattlich; ~**see** (-saw, -seen): *go* ~*ing se*~ Besichtigungstour machen; ~**see·ing** [~ɪŋ] Besichtigung *f* von Sehenswürdigkeiten; ~ *tour* Besichtigungstour *f*, (Stadt)Rundfahrt *f*; ~**se·er** [~ə] Tourist(in).

sign [saɪn] **1.** Zeichen *n*; Wink *m*; Schild *n*; *in* ~ *of* zum Zeichen (*gen.*); **2.** winken, Zeichen geben; (unter)zeichnen, unterschreiben.

sig·nal [ˈsɪgnl] **1.** Signal *n* (*a. fig.*); Zeichen *n*; **2.** bemerkenswert; außerordentlich; **3.** (*bsd. Brt. -ll-, Am. -l-*) (ein) Zeichen geben; signalisieren; ~**ize** [~nəlaɪz] auszeichnen; hervorheben.

sig·na|to·ry [ˈsɪgnətərɪ] **1.** Unterzeichner(in); **2.** *pol.* ~ *powers pl. pol.* Signatarmächte *pl.*; ~**ture** [~tʃə] Signatur *f*; Unterschrift *f*; ~ *tune Rundfunk, TV:* Kennmelodie *f*.

sign|board [ˈsaɪnbɔːd] (Aushänge-) Schild *n*; ~**er** [~ə] Unterzeichner(in).

sig·net [ˈsɪgnɪt] Siegel *n*.

S

sig·nif·i·cance ['sɪg'nɪfɪkəns] Bedeutung f; ~**cant** □ [~t] bedeutsam; bezeichnend (of für); ~**ca·tion** [sɪgnɪfɪ'keɪʃn] Bedeutung f, Sinn m.

sig·ni·fy ['sɪgnɪfaɪ] andeuten; zu verstehen geben; bedeuten.

sign·post ['saɪnpəʊst] Wegweiser m.

si·lence ['saɪləns] 1. (Still)Schweigen n; Stille f, Ruhe f; ~! Ruhe! put od. reduce to ~ = 2. zum Schweigen bringen; ~**lenc·er** [~ə] ⊕ Schalldämpfer m; mot. Auspufftopf m.

si·lent ['saɪlənt] still; schweigend; schweigsam; stumm; ~ partner Am. econ. stiller Teilhaber.

silk [sɪlk] Seide f; attr. Seiden...; ~**en** ['sɪlkən] seiden, Seiden...; ~**stock·ing** Am. seiden zo. Seidenraupe f; ~**y** □ [~ɪ] (-ier, -iest) seidig, seidenartig.

sill [sɪl] Schwelle f; Fensterbrett n.

sil·ly □ ['sɪlɪ] (-ier, -iest) albern, töricht, dumm, verrückt.

silt [sɪlt] 1. Schlamm m; 2. mst ~ up verschlammen.

sil·ver ['sɪlvə] Silber n; 2. silbern, Silber...; 3. versilbern; silb(e)rig od. silberweiß werden; ~ **plate**, ~**ware** Tafelsilber n; ~**y** [~rɪ] silberglänzend; fig. silberhell.

sim·i·lar □ ['sɪmɪlə] ähnlich, gleich; ~**i·ty** [sɪmɪ'lærətɪ] Ähnlichkeit f.

sim·i·le ['sɪmɪlɪ] Gleichnis n.

si·mil·i·tude [sɪ'mɪlɪtjuːd] Gestalt f, Ebenbild n; Gleichnis n.

sim·mer ['sɪmə] leicht kochen, od. sieden (lassen); fig. kochen (with vor dat.), gären (Gefühl, Aufstand); ~ down sich beruhigen od. abregen.

sim·per ['sɪmpə] 1. einfältiges Lächeln; 2. einfältig lächeln.

sim·ple □ ['sɪmpl] (~r, ~st) einfach; schlicht; einfältig; arglos, naiv; ~**heart·ed**, ~**mind·ed** einfältig, arglos, naiv; ~**ton** [~tən] Einfaltspinsel m.

sim·plic·i·ty [sɪm'plɪsətɪ] Einfachheit f; Unkompliziertheit f; Schlichtheit f; Einfalt f; ~**fi·ca·tion** [sɪmplɪfɪ'keɪʃn] Vereinfachung f; ~**fy** ['sɪmplɪfaɪ] vereinfachen.

sim·ply ['sɪmplɪ] einfach; bloß.

sim·u·late ['sɪmjʊleɪt] vortäuschen; simulieren; ✗, ⊕ a. Bedingungen, Vorgänge (wirklichkeitsgetreu) nachahmen.

sim·ul·ta·ne·ous □ [sɪml'teɪnjəs] gleichzeitig, simultan.

sin [sɪn] 1. Sünde f; 2. (-nn-) sündigen.

since [sɪns] 1. prp. seit; 2. adv. seitdem; 3. cj. seit(dem); da (ja).

sin·cere □ [sɪn'sɪə] aufrichtig, ehrlich, offen; Yours ~ly Briefschluß: Mit freundlichen Grüßen; **sin·cer·i·ty** [~'serətɪ] Aufrichtigkeit f; Offenheit f.

sin·ew anat. ['sɪnjuː] Sehne f; ~**y** [~juː] sehnig; fig. kraftvoll.

sin·ful □ ['sɪnfl] sündig, sündhaft.

sing [sɪŋ] (sang, sung) singen; ~ to s.o. j-m vorsingen.

singe [sɪndʒ] (ver-, ab)sengen.

sing·er ['sɪŋə] Sänger(in).

sing·ing ['sɪŋɪŋ] Gesang m, Singen n; ~ bird Singvogel m.

sin·gle ['sɪŋgl] 1. □ einzig; einzeln; Einzel...; einfach; ledig, unverheiratet; bookkeeping by ~ entry einfache Buchführung; in ~ file im Gänsemarsch; 2. Brt. einfache Fahrkarte, ⚡ einfaches Ticket; Single f (Schallplatte); Single m, Unverheiratete(r m) f; Brt. Einpfund-, Am. Eindollarschein m; ~s sg., pl. Tennis: Einzel n; 3. ~ out auswählen, -suchen; ~**breast·ed** einreihig (Jacke etc.); ~**en·gined** ⚡ einmotorig; ~**hand·ed** eigenhändig, allein; ~**heart·ed** □, ~**mind·ed** □ aufrichtig; zielstrebig.

sin·glet Brt. ['sɪŋglɪt] ärmelloses Unterhemd od. Trikot.

sin·gle-track 🚂 ['sɪŋgltræk] eingleisig; F fig. einseitig.

sin·gu·lar ['sɪŋgjʊlə] 1. □ einzigartig; eigenartig; sonderbar; 2. a. ~ number gr. Singular m, Einzahl f; ~**i·ty** [sɪŋgjʊ'lærətɪ] Einzigartigkeit f; Eigentümlich-, Seltsamkeit f.

sin·is·ter □ ['sɪnɪstə] unheilvoll, böse.

sink [sɪŋk] 1. (sank, sunk) v/i. sinken; ein-, nieder-, unter-, versinken; sich senken; (ein)dringen, (-)sickern; v/t. (ver)senken; Brunnen bohren; Geld fest anlegen; 2. Ausguß m, Spüle f; ~**ing** ['sɪŋkɪŋ] (Ein-, Ver)Sinken n; Versenken n; ♥ Schwäche(gefühl n) f; econ. Tilgung f; ~**fund** (Schulden)Tilgungsfonds m.

sin·less □ ['sɪnlɪs] sünd(en)los, sündenfrei.

sin·ner ['sɪnə] Sünder(in).

sin·u·ous □ ['sɪnjʊəs] gewunden.

sip [sɪp] 1. Schlückchen n; 2. (-pp-)

v/t. nippen an (*dat.*) *od.* von; schlückchenweise trinken; *v/i.* nippen (*at* an *dat. od.* von).

sir [sɜː] Herr *m* (*Anrede*); ♀ [sə] Sir *m* (*Titel*).

sire ['saɪə] *mst poet.* Vater *m*; Vorfahr *m*; *zo.* Vater(tier *n*) *m*.

si·ren ['saɪərən] Sirene *f*.

sir·loin ['sɜːlɔɪn] Lendenstück *n*.

sis·sy F ['sɪsɪ] Weichling *m*.

sis·ter ['sɪstə] (*a.* Ordens-, Ober-, Kranken)Schwester *f*; **~hood** [~hʊd] Schwesternschaft *f*; **~in-law** [~rɪnlɔː] (*pl. sisters-in-law*) Schwägerin *f*; **~ly** [~lɪ] schwesterlich.

sit [sɪt] (*-tt-; sat*) *v/i.* sitzen; e-e Sitzung halten, tagen; *fig.* liegen, stehen; ~ *down* sich setzen; ~ *in* ein Sit-in veranstalten; ~ *in for* für j-n einspringen; ~ *up* aufrecht sitzen; aufbleiben; *v/t.* setzen; sitzen auf (*dat.*).

site [saɪt] Lage *f*; Stelle *f*; Stätte *f*; (Bau)Gelände *n*.

sit-in ['sɪtɪn] Sit-in *n*.

sit·ting ['sɪtɪŋ] Sitzung *f*; **~ room** Wohnzimmer *n*.

sit·u·at·ed ['sɪtjʊeɪtɪd] gelegen; *be* ~ liegen, gelegen sein; **~a·tion** [sɪtjʊ'eɪʃn] Lage *f*; Stellung *f*, Stelle *f*.

six [sɪks] 1. sechs; 2. Sechs *f*; **~teen** ['sɪks'tiːn] 1. sechzehn; 2. Sechzehn *f*; **~teenth** [~θ] sechzehnte(r, -s); **~th** [sɪksθ] 1. sechste(r, -s); 2. Sechstel *n*; **~th·ly** ['sɪksθlɪ] sechstens; **~ti·eth** [~tɪɪθ] sechzigste(r, -s); **~ty** [~tɪ] 1. sechzig; 2. Sechzig *f*.

size [saɪz] 1. Größe *f*; Format *n*; 2. nach Größe(n) ordnen; ~ *up* F abschätzen; **~d** von *od.* in ... Größe.

siz(e)·a·ble ☐ ['saɪzəbl] (ziemlich) groß.

siz·zle ['sɪzl] zischen; knistern; brutzeln; *sizzling (hot)* glühendheiß.

skate [skeɪt] 1. Schlittschuh *m*; Rollschuh *m*; 2. Schlittschuh laufen, eislaufen; Rollschuh laufen; **~board** ['skeɪtbɔːd] 1. Skateboard *n*; 2. Skateboard fahren; **skat·er** [~ə] Schlittschuhläufer(in); Rollschuhläufer(in); **skat·ing** [~ɪŋ] Schlittschuh-, Eislaufen *n*, Eislauf *m*; Rollschuhlauf(en *n*) *m*.

ske·dad·dle F [skɪ'dædl] abhauen.

skein [skeɪn] Strang *m*, Docke *f*.

skel·e·ton ['skelɪtn] Skelett *n*; Gerippe *n*; Gestell *n*; *attr.* Skelett...; ✕

Stamm...; ~ *key* Nachschlüssel *m*.

skep|tic ['skeptɪk], **~ti·cal** [~l] *Am.* = *sceptic(al)*.

sketch [sketʃ] 1. Skizze *f*; Entwurf *m*; *thea.* Sketch *m*; 2. skizzieren; entwerfen.

ski [skiː] 1. (*pl. skis, ski*) Schi *m*, Ski *m*; *attr.* Schi..., Ski...; 2. Schi *od.* Ski laufen *od.* fahren.

skid [skɪd] 1. Bremsklotz *m*; ✈ (Gleit)Kufe *f*; *mot.* Rutschen *n*, Schleudern *n*; ~ *mark mot.* Bremsspur *f*; 2. (*-dd-*) rutschen; schleudern.

skid·doo *Am. sl.* abhauen.

ski·er ['skiːə] Schi-, Skiläufer(in); ⚠ *nicht Skier*; **~ing** [~ɪŋ] Schi-, Skilauf(en *n*) *m*, -fahren *n*, -sport *m*.

skil·ful ☐ ['skɪlfl] geschickt; geübt.

skill [skɪl] Geschicklichkeit *f*, Fertigkeit *f*; **~ed** geschickt; ausgebildet; Fach...; ~ *worker* Facharbeiter *m*.

skill·ful *Am.* ☐ ['skɪlfl] = *skilful*.

skim [skɪm] 1. (*-mm-*) abschöpfen; *Milch* entrahmen; (hin)gleiten über (*acc.*); *Buch* überfliegen; ~ *through* durchblättern; 2. ~ *milk* Magermilch *f*.

skimp [skɪmp] *j-n* knapphalten; sparen an; knausern (*on* mit); **~y** ☐ ['skɪmpɪ] (*-ier, -iest*) knapp; dürftig.

skin [skɪn] 1. Haut *f*; Fell *n*; Schale *f*; 2. (*-nn-*) *v/t.* (ent)häuten; abgalgen; schälen; *v/i. a.* ~ *over* zuheilen; **~deep** ['skɪn'diːp] (nur) oberflächlich; ~ *div·ing* Sporttauchen *n*; **~flint** Knicker *m*; **~ny** [~ɪ] (*-ier, -iest*) mager; **~ny-dip** F nackt baden.

skip [skɪp] 1. Sprung *m*; 2. (*-pp-*) *v/i.* hüpfen, springen; seilhüpfen; *v/t.* überspringen.

skip·per ['skɪpə] ♣ Schiffer *m*; ♣, ✕, *Sport:* Kapitän *m*.

skir·mish ['skɜːmɪʃ] 1. ✕ *u. fig.* Geplänkel *n*; 2. plänkeln.

skirt [skɜːt] 1. (Damen)Rock *m*; (Rock)Schoß *m*; *oft* ~*s pl.* Rand *m*, Saum *m*; 2. (um)säumen; (sich) entlangziehen an (*dat.*); **~ing-board** *Brt.* ['skɜːtɪŋbɔːd] Scheuerleiste *f*.

skit [skɪt] Stichelei *f*; Satire *f*; **~tish** ☐ ['skɪtɪʃ] ausgelassen; scheu (*Pferd*).

skit·tle ['skɪtl] Kegel *m*; *play (at)* ~*s* kegeln; **~al·ley** Kegelbahn *f*.

skulk [skʌlk] (herum)schleichen; lauern; sich drücken.

skull [skʌl] Schädel m.

skul(l)·dug·ge·ry F [skʌl'dʌgərɪ] Gaunerei f.

skunk zo. [skʌŋk] Skunk m, Stinktier n.

sky [skaɪ] oft **skies** pl. Himmel m; **~jack** F ['skaɪdʒæk] Flugzeug entführen; **~jack·er** F [~ə] Flugzeugentführer(in); **~lab** Am. Raumlabor n; **~lark** 1. zo. Feldlerche f; 2. F Blödsinn treiben; **~light** Oberlicht n, Dachfenster n; **~line** Horizont m; Silhouette f; **~rock·et** F in die Höhe schießen (Preise), sprunghaft ansteigen; **~scrap·er** Wolkenkratzer m; **~ward(s)** [~wəd(z)] himmelwärts.

slab [slæb] Platte f, Fliese f; (dicke) Scheibe (Käse etc.).

slack [slæk] 1. □ schlaff; locker; (nach)lässig; flau (a. econ.); 2. ♪ Lose f (schlaffes Taustück); Flaute f (a. econ.); Kohlengrus m; **~en** ['slækən] nachlassen; (sich) verringern; (sich) lockern; (sich) entspannen; (sich) verlangsamen; **~s** pl. Freizeithose f.

slag [slæg] Schlacke f.

slain [sleɪn] p.p. von slay.

slake [sleɪk] Kalk löschen; Durst löschen, stillen.

slam [slæm] 1. Zuschlagen n; Knall m; 2. (-mm-) Tür etc. zuschlagen, zuknallen; et. auf den Tisch etc. knallen.

slan·der ['slɑːndə] 1. Verleumdung f; 2. verleumden; **~ous** □ [~rəs] verleumderisch.

slang [slæŋ] 1. Slang m; Berufssprache f; lässige Umgangssprache f; 2. j-n wüst beschimpfen.

slant [slɑːnt] 1. schräge Fläche; Abhang m; Neigung f; Standpunkt m, Einstellung f; Tendenz f; 2. schräg legen od. liegen; sich neigen; **~ing** adj. □ ['slɑːntɪŋ], **~wise** adv. [~waɪz] schief, schräg.

slap [slæp] 1. Klaps m, Schlag m; 2. (-pp-) e-n Klaps geben (dat.); schlagen; klatschen; **~jack** Am. ['slæpdʒæk] Art Pfannkuchen m; **~stick** (Narren)Pritsche f; a. ~ comedy thea. Slapstickkomödie f.

slash [slæʃ] 1. Hieb m; Schnitt(wunde f) m; Schlitz m; 2. (auf)schlitzen; schlagen, hauen; fig. scharf kritisieren.

slate [sleɪt] 1. Schiefer m; Schiefertafel f; bsd. Am. pol. Kandidatenliste f;

2. mit Schiefer decken; Brt. F heftig kritisieren; Am. F Kandidaten aufstellen; **~pen·cil** ['sleɪt'pensl] Griffel m.

slat·tern ['slætən] Schlampe f.

slaugh·ter ['slɔːtə] 1. Schlachten n; fig. Blutbad n, Gemetzel n; 2. schlachten; fig. niedermetzeln; **~house** Schlachthaus n, -hof m.

Slav [slɑːv] 1. Slaw|e m, -in f; 2. slawisch.

slave [sleɪv] 1. Sklav|e m, -in f (a. fig.); 2. sich (ab)placken, schuften.

slav·er ['slævə] 1. Geifer m, Sabber m; 2. geifern, sabbern.

sla·ve·ry ['sleɪvərɪ] Sklaverei f; Plackerei f; **slav·ish** □ [~ɪʃ] sklavisch.

slay rhet. [sleɪ] (slew, slain) erschlagen; töten; △ nicht schlagen.

sled [sled] 1. = sledge[1] 1; 2. (-dd-) = sledge[1] 2.

sledge[1] [sledʒ] 1. Schlitten m; 2. Schlitten fahren, rodeln.

sledge[2] a. **~hammer** Schmiedehammer m.

sleek [sliːk] 1. □ glatt, glänzend (Haar, Fell); geschmeidig; 2. glätten.

sleep [sliːp] 1. (slept) v/i. schlafen; ~ (up)on od. over et. überschlafen; ~ with s.o. mit j-m schlafen (Geschlechtsverkehr haben); v/t. schlafen; j-n für die Nacht unterbringen; ~ away Zeit verschlafen; 2. Schlaf m; get od. go to ~ einschlafen; put to ~ Tier einschläfern; **~er** ['sliːpə] Schlafende(r m) f; ♣ Schwelle f; ♣ Schlafwagen m; **~ing** [~ɪŋ] schlafend; Schlaf...; ♀**ing Beau·ty** Dornröschen n; ♀**ing-car(·riage)** ♣ Schlafwagen m; **~ing part·ner** Brt. econ. stiller Teilhaber; **~less** □ [~lɪs] schlaflos; **~walk·er** Schlafwandler(in); **~y** □ [~ɪ] (-ier, -iest) schläfrig; müde; verschlafen.

sleet [sliːt] 1. Schneeregen m; Graupelschauer m; 2. it was ~ing es gab Schneeregen; es graupelte.

sleeve [sliːv] Ärmel m; ⊕ Muffe f; Brt. (Schall)Plattenhülle f; **~link** ['sliːvlɪŋk] Manschettenknopf m.

sleigh [sleɪ] 1. (bsd. Pferde)Schlitten m; 2. (im) Schlitten fahren.

sleight [slaɪt]: ~ of hand (Taschenspieler)Trick m; Fingerfertigkeit f.

slen·der □ ['slendə] schlank; schmächtig; fig. schwach; dürftig.

slept [slept] *pret. u. p.p. von* sleep 1.

sleuth [slu:θ] *a.* ~**-hound** Spürhund *m* (*a. fig.* Detektiv).

slew [slu:] *pret. von* slay.

slice [slaɪs] **1.** Schnitte *f*, Scheibe *f*, Stück *n*; (An)Teil *m*; **2.** (in) Scheiben schneiden; aufschneiden.

slick [slɪk] **1.** □ *adj.* glatt, glitschig; F geschickt, raffiniert; **2.** *adv.* direkt; **3.** Ölfleck *m*, -teppich *m*; ~**er** *Am.* F ['slɪkə] Regenmantel *m*; gerissener Kerl.

slid [slɪd] *pret. u. p.p. von* slide 1.

slide [slaɪd] **1.** (*slid*) gleiten (lassen); rutschen; schlittern; ausgleiten; ~ *into fig.* in *et.* hineinschlittern; *let things* ~ *fig.* die Dinge laufen lassen; **2.** Gleiten *n*, Rutschen *n*, Schlittern *n*; Rutschbahn *f*; Rutsche *f*; ⊕ Schieber *m*; *phot.* Dia(positiv) *n*; *Brt.* (Haar)Spange *f*; *a. land*~ Erdrutsch *m*; ~**rule** ['slaɪdru:l] Rechenschieber *m*.

slid·ing □ ['slaɪdɪŋ] gleitend, rutschend; Schiebe...; ~ *time Am. econ.* Gleitzeit *f*.

slight [slaɪt] **1.** □ leicht; schmächtig; schwach; gering, unbedeutend; **2.** Geringschätzung *f*; **3.** geringschätzig behandeln; beleidigen, kränken.

slim (-*mm*-) [slɪm] **1.** □ schlank, dünn; *fig.* gering, dürftig; **2.** e-e Schlankheitskur machen, abnehmen.

slime [slaɪm] Schlamm *m*; Schleim *m*; **slim·y** ['slaɪmɪ] (-*ier*, -*iest*) schlammig; schleimig; *fig.* schmierig; kriecherisch.

sling [slɪŋ] **1.** (Stein)Schleuder *f*; Schlinge *f* (*zum Tragen*); Tragriemen *m*; ☞ Schlinge *f*, Binde *f*; **2.** (*slung*) schleudern; auf-, umhängen; *a.* ~ *up* hochziehen; △ *nicht* schlingen.

slink [slɪŋk] (*slunk*) schleichen.

slip [slɪp] **1.** (-*pp*-) gleiten (lassen); rutschen; ausgleiten, -rutschen; (ver)rutschen; loslassen; ~ *away* wegschleichen, sich fortstehlen; ~ *in* Bemerkung dazwischenwerfen; ~ *into* hineinstecken *od.* hineinschieben in (*acc.*); ~ *off* (*on*) Ring, Kleid etc. abstreifen (überstreifen); ~ *up* (e-n) Fehler machen; *have* ~*ped s.o.'s memory od. mind* j-m entfallen sein; **2.** (Aus)Gleiten *n*, (-)Rutschen *n*; Fehltritt *m* (*a. fig.*); (Flüchtigkeits-)Fehler *m*; Fehler *m*, Panne *f*; Strei-

fen *m*, Zettel *m*; *econ.* (Kontroll)Abschnitt *m*; (Kissen)Bezug *m*; Unterkleid *n*, -rock *m*; △ *nicht* Slip; *a.* ~ *of a boy* (*girl*) ein schmächtiges Bürschchen (ein zartes Ding); ~ *of the tongue* Versprecher *m*; *give s.o. the* ~ j-m entwischen; ~**ped disc** ☞ [slɪpt 'dɪsk] Bandscheibenvorfall *m*; ~**per** ['slɪpə] Pantoffel *m*, Hausschuh *m*; ~**per·y** □ [~rɪ] (-*ier*, -*iest*) glatt, schlüpfrig; ~**road** *Brt.* Autobahnauffahrt *f*, -ausfahrt *f*; ~**shod** [~ʃɒd] schlampig, nachlässig.

slit [slɪt] **1.** Schlitz *m*, Spalt *m*; **2.** (-*tt*-; *slit*) (auf-, zer)schlitzen.

slith·er ['slɪðə] gleiten, rutschen.

sliv·er ['slɪvə] Splitter *m*.

slob·ber ['slɒbə] **1.** Sabber *m*, Geifer *m*; **2.** (be)geifern, (be)sabbern.

slo·gan ['sləʊgən] Slogan *m*; Schlagwort *n*; Werbespruch *m*.

sloop ⚓ [slu:p] Schaluppe *f*.

slop [slɒp] **1.** Krankensüppchen *n*; ~**s** *pl.* Spül-, Schmutzwasser *n*; **2.** (-*pp*-) *v/t.* verschütten; *v/i.* ~ *over* überschwappen.

slope [sləʊp] **1.** (Ab)Hang *m*; Neigung *f*, Gefälle *n*; **2.** ⊕ abschrägen; abfallen; schräg verlaufen; (sich) neigen.

slop·py □ ['slɒpɪ] (-*ier*, -*iest*) naß, schmutzig; schlampig; labb(e)rig (*Essen*); rührselig.

slot [slɒt] Schlitz *m*, (Münz)Einwurf *m*.

sloth [sləʊθ] Faulheit *f*; *zo.* Faultier *n*.

slot-ma·chine ['slɒtməʃi:n] (Waren-, Spiel)Automat *m*.

slouch [slaʊtʃ] **1.** krumm *od.* (nach)lässig dastehen *od.* dasitzen; F (herum)latschen; **2.** schlaffe, schlechte Haltung; ~ *hat* Schlapphut *m*.

slough¹ [slaʊ] Sumpf(loch *n*) *m*.

slough² [slʌf] Haut abwerfen.

slov·en ['slʌvn] unordentlicher Mensch; Schlampe *f*; ~**·ly** [~lɪ] schlampig.

slow [sləʊ] **1.** □ langsam; schwerfällig; träge; *be* ~ nachgehen (*Uhr*); **2.** *adv.* langsam; **3.** ~ *down*, ~ *up v/t.* Geschwindigkeit verlangsamen, -ringern; *v/i.* langsamer werden; ~**coach** ['sləʊkəʊtʃ] Langweiler *m*; ~**down (strike)** *Am. econ.* Bummelstreik *m*; ~ **mo·tion** *phot.* Zeitlupe *f*; ~**poke** *Am.* = slowcoach; ~**worm** *zo.* Blindschleiche *f*.

sludge

sludge [slʌdʒ] Schlamm *m*; Matsch *m*.

slug [slʌg] 1. *zo.* Wegschnecke *f*; Stück *n* Rohmetall; *bsd. Am.* (Pistolen)Kugel *f*; *Am.* (Faust)Schlag *m*; 2. (-*gg-*) *Am.* F *j-m* e-n harten Schlag versetzen.

slug|gard [slʌgəd] Faulpelz *m*; **~gish** □ [~ɪʃ] träge; *econ.* schleppend.

sluice ⊕ [slu:s] Schleuse *f*.

slums [slʌmz] *pl.* Slums *pl.*, Elendsviertel *n od. pl.*

slum·ber [slʌmbə] 1. *mst* ~s *pl.* Schlummer *m*; 2. schlummern.

slump [slʌmp] 1. plumpsen; *econ.* fallen, stürzen (*Preise*); 2. *econ.* (Kurs-, Preis)Sturz *m*; (starker) Konjunkturrückgang.

slung [slʌŋ] *pret. u. p.p. von* sling 2.

slunk [slʌŋk] *pret. u. p.p. von* slink.

slur [slɜ:] 1. (-*rr-*) verunglimpfen, verleumden; undeutlich (aus)sprechen; ♪ *Töne* binden; 2. Verunglimpfung *f*, Verleumdung *f*; undeutliche Aussprache; ♪ Bindebogen *m*.

slush [slʌʃ] Schlamm *m*, Matsch *m*; Schneematsch *m*; Kitsch *m*.

slut [slʌt] Schlampe *f*; Nutte *f*.

sly □ [slaɪ] (~*er*, ~*est*) schlau, listig; hinterlistig; *on the* ~ heimlich.

smack [smæk] 1. (Bei)Geschmack *m*; Schmatz *m* (*Kuß*); Schmatzen *n*; klatschender Schlag, Klatsch *m*, Klaps *m*; (Peitschen)Knall *m*; *fig.* Spur *f*, Andeutung *f*; 2. schmecken (*of* nach); klatschend schlagen; knallen (mit); *j-m* e-n Klaps geben; ~ *one's lips* schmatzen.

small [smɔ:l] 1. klein; gering; wenig; unbedeutend; bescheiden; (sozial) niedrig; kleinlich; △ *nicht schmal*; *feel* ~ sich schämen; sich ganz klein und häßlich vorkommen; *look* ~ beschämt *od.* schlecht dastehen; *the* ~ *hours* die frühen Morgenstunden *pl.*; *in a* ~ *way* bescheiden; 2. ~ *of the back anat.* Kreuz *n*; ~*s pl. Brt.* F Unterwäsche *f*, Taschentücher *pl. etc.*; *wash one's* ~*s* kleine Wäsche waschen; ~ *arms* [smɔ:lɑ:mz] *pl.* Handfeuerwaffen *pl.*; ~ **change** Kleingeld *n*; ~**ish** [~ɪʃ] ziemlich klein; ~**pox** ✼ Pocken *pl.*; ~ **talk** oberflächliche Konversation; ~**time** F unbedeutend.

smart [smɑ:t] 1. □ klug; gewandt, geschickt; gerissen, raffiniert; elegant, schick, fesch; forsch; flink; hart, scharf; heftig; schlagfertig; ~ *aleck* F Klugscheißer *m*; 2. stechender Schmerz; 3. schmerzen; leiden; ~**ness** [smɑ:tnɪs] Klugheit *f*; Gewandtheit *f*; Gerissenheit *f*; Eleganz *f*; Schärfe *f*.

smash [smæʃ] 1. *v/t.* zerschlagen, -trümmern; (zer)schmettern; *fig.* vernichten; *v/i.* zersplittern; krachen; zusammenstoßen; *fig.* zusammenbrechen; 2. heftiger Schlag; Zerschmettern *n*; Krach *m*; Zusammenbruch *m* (*a. econ.*); Schmetterball *m*; *a.* ~ *hit* F toller Erfolg; ~**ing** *bsd. Brt.* F [smæʃɪŋ] toll, sagenhaft; ~**up** Zusammenstoß *m*; Zusammenbruch *m*.

smat·ter·ing [smætərɪŋ] oberflächliche Kenntnis.

smear [smɪə] 1. (be-, ein-, ver)schmieren; *fig.* verleumden; 2. Schmiere *f*; Fleck *m*.

smell [smel] 1. Geruch(ssinn) *m*; Duft *m*; Gestank *m*; 2. (*smelt od. smelled*) *v/t.* riechen (*an dat.*); *v/i.* riechen (*at an dat.*); duften; stinken; ~**y** [smelɪ] (-*ier*, -*iest*) übelriechend, stinkend.

smelt¹ [smelt] *pret. u. p.p. von* smell 2.

smelt² *metall.* [~] Erz (ein)schmelzen, verhütten.

smile [smaɪl] 1. Lächeln *n*; 2. lächeln; ~ *at j-n* anlächeln.

smirch [smɜ:tʃ] besudeln.

smirk [smɜ:k] grinsen.

smith [smɪθ] Schmied *m*.

smith·e·reens [smɪðəˈri:nz] *pl.* Stücke *pl.*, Splitter *pl*, Fetzen *pl.*

smith·y [smɪðɪ] Schmiede *f*.

smit·ten [smɪtn] betroffen, heimgesucht; *fig.* hingerissen (*with von*); *humor.* verliebt, -knallt (*with in acc.*).

smock [smɒk] Kittel *m*.

smog [smɒg] Smog *m*.

smoke [sməʊk] 1. Rauch *m*; *have a* ~ (eine) rauchen; 2. rauchen; qualmen; dampfen; räuchern; ~**dried** [sməʊkdraɪd] geräuchert; **smok·er** [~ə] Raucher(in); 🚃 F Raucher(abteil *n*) *m*; ~**stack** 🚢, ⚓ Schornstein *m*.

smok·ing [sməʊkɪŋ] Rauchen *n*; *attr.* Rauch(er)...; ~**com·part·ment** 🚃 Raucherabteil *n*.

smok·y □ ['sməʊkɪ] (-*ier*, -*iest*) rauchig; verräuchert.

smooth [smu:ð] **1.** □ glatt; eben; ruhig (⊕, *Meer, Reise*); sanft (*Stimme*); flüssig (*Stil etc.*); mild (*Wein*); (aal)glatt, gewandt (*Benehmen*) **2.** glätten; *fig.* besänftigen; ~ *away fig.* wegräumen; ~ *down* sich glätten; glattstreichen; ~ *out Falte* glattstreichen; ~-**ness** □ ['smu:ðnɪs] Glätte *f.*

smoth·er ['smʌðə] ersticken.

smo(u)l·der ['sməʊldə] schwelen.

smudge [smʌdʒ] **1.** (ver-, be)schmieren; schmutzig werden; **2.** Schmutzfleck *m.*

smug [smʌg] (-*gg-*) selbstgefällig.

smug·gle ['smʌgl] schmuggeln; **~r** [~ə] Schmuggler(in).

smut [smʌt] Ruß(fleck) *m*; Schmutzfleck *m*; Zote(n *pl.*) *f*; △ *nicht Schmutz*; **2.** (-*tt-*) beschmutzen; **~·ty** □ ['smʌtɪ] (-*ier*, -*iest*) schmutzig.

snack [snæk] Imbiß *m*; *have a* ~ *e-e Kleinigkeit essen*; **~·bar** ['snækbɑ:] Snackbar *f*, Imbißstube *f.*

snaf·fle ['snæfl] *a.* ~ *bit* Trense *f.*

snag [snæg] (Ast-, Zahn)Stumpf *m*; *bsd. Am.* Baumstumpf *m* (*bsd. unter Wasser*); *fig.* Haken *m.*

snail *zo.* [sneɪl] Schnecke *f.*

snake *zo.* [sneɪk] Schlange *f*; △ *nicht Schnecke.*

snap [snæp] **1.** (Zu)Schnappen *n*, Biß *m*; Knacken *n*, Krachen *n*; Knacks *m*; Knall *m*; Schnappschloß *n*; *F phot.* Schnappschuß *m*; *fig.* Schwung *m*, Schmiß *m*; *cold* ~ Kälteeinbruch *m*; **2.** (-*pp-*) *v/i.* schnappen (*at nach*); zuschnappen (*Schloß*); knacken; knacken; knallen; (zer)brechen; zerkrachen, -springen, -reißen; schnauzen; *a. at s.o.* j-n anschnauzen; ~ *to it!, Am. a.* ~ *it up!* sl. beeil dich!, Tempo!; ~ *out of it!* sl. hör auf (damit)!, komm, komm!; *v/t.* (er)schnappen, beißen; schnell greifen nach; knallen mit; (auf- *od.* zu)schnappen *od.* (-)knallen lassen; *phot.* knipsen; zerbrechen; *j-n* anschnauzen, anfahren; ~ *one's fingers* mit den Fingern schnalzen; ~ *one's fingers at fig. j-n, et.* nicht ernst nehmen; ~ *out Worte* hervorstoßen; ~ *up* wegschnappen; an sich reißen; **~·fas·ten·er** ['snæpfɑːsnə] Druckknopf *m*; **~·pish** □ [~ɪʃ] bissig; schnippisch; **~·py** [~ɪ] (-*ier*, -*iest*) bissig; F flott; F schnell; *make*

it ~*!, Brt. a. look* ~*!* F mach fix!; **~·shot** Schnappschuß *m*, Momentaufnahme *f.*

snare [sneə] **1.** Schlinge *f*, Falle *f* (*a. fig.*); **2.** fangen; *fig.* umgarnen.

snarl [snɑːl] **1.** wütend knurren; **2.** Knurren *n*, Zähnefletschen *n*; Knoten *m*; *fig.* Gewirr *n.*

snatch [snætʃ] **1.** schneller Griff; Ruck *m*; Stückchen *n*; **2.** schnappen; ergreifen; *et.* an sich reißen; nehmen; ~ *at* greifen nach.

sneak [sni:k] *v/i.* schleichen; *Brt. sl.* petzen; *v/t. sl.* stibitzen; **2.** F Leisetreter *m*, Kriecher *m*; *Brt. sl.* Petze *f*; **~·ers** *bsd. Am.* ['sni:kəz] *pl.* Turnschuhe *pl.*

sneer [snɪə] **1.** höhnisches Grinsen; höhnische Bemerkung; **2.** höhnisch grinsen; spotten; *et.* höhnen.

sneeze [sni:z] **1.** niesen; **2.** Niesen *n.*

snick·er ['snɪkə] *bsd. Am.* kichern; *bsd. Brt.* wiehern.

sniff [snɪf] schnüffeln, schnuppern; *fig.* die Nase rümpfen.

snig·ger *bsd. Brt.* ['snɪgə] kichern.

snip [snɪp] **1.** Schnitt *m*; Schnipsel *m*, *n*; **2.** (-*pp-*) schnippeln, schnipseln.

snipe [snaɪp] **1.** *zo.* Schnepfe *f*; **2.** aus dem Hinterhalt schießen; **snip·er** ['snaɪpə] Heckenschütze *m.*

sniv·el ['snɪvl] (*bsd. Brt. -ll-, Am. -l-*) schniefen; schluchzen; plärren.

snob [snɒb] Snob *m*; **~·bish** □ ['snɒbɪʃ] versnobt.

snoop F [snu:p] **1.** ~ *about,* ~ *around* F *fig.* herumschnüffeln; **2.** Schnüffler(in).

snooze F [snu:z] **1.** Nickerchen *n*; **2.** ein Nickerchen machen; dösen.

snore [snɔː] **1.** schnarchen; **2.** Schnarchen *n.*

snort [snɔːt] schnauben; prusten.

snout [snaʊt] Schnauze *f*; Rüssel *m.*

snow [snəʊ] **1.** Schnee *m*; sl. Snow *m* (*Kokain, Heroin*); **2.** schneien; *sl. ed in od. up* eingeschneit; *be ~ed under fig.* erdrückt werden; **~·bound** ['snəʊbaʊnd] eingeschneit; **~·capped**, **~·clad**, **~·cov·ered** schneebedeckt; **~·drift** Schneewehe *f*; **~·drop** ♀ Schneeglöckchen *n*; **~·white** schneeweiß; ♀ **White** Schneewittchen *n*; **~·y** □ [~ɪ] (-*ier*, -*iest*) schneeig; schneebedeckt, verschneit; schneeweiß.

snub [snʌb] **1.** (-*bb-*) *j-n* vor den Kopf stoßen, brüskieren; *j-m* über den Mund fahren; *j-n* schneiden; 2. Brüskierung *f*; **~nosed** ['snʌbnəʊzd] stupsnasig.

snuff [snʌf] 1. Schnuppe *f* (*e-r Kerze*); Schnupftabak *m*; *take* ~ schnupfen; 2. *Kerze* putzen; schnuppen.

snuf·fle ['snʌfl] schnüffeln; näseln.

snug □ [snʌg] (*-gg-*) geborgen; behaglich; enganliegend; **~·gle** ['snʌgl] sich anschmiegen *od.* kuscheln (*up to s.o.* an *j-n*).

so [səʊ] so; also; deshalb; *I hope* ~ ich hoffe es; *I think* ~ ich glaube od. denke schon; *are you tired?* - ~ *I am* bist du müde? Ja; *you are tired,* ~ *am I* du bist müde, ich auch; ~ *far* bisher.

soak [səʊk] *v/t.* einweichen; durchnässen; (durch)tränken; ~ *in* einsaugen; ~ *up* aufsaugen; *v/i.* sich vollsaugen; ein-, durchsickern.

soap [səʊp] 1. Seife *f*; *soft* ~ Schmierseife *f*; *fig.* Schmeichelei *f*; 2. ab-, einseifen; **~·box** ['səʊpbɒks] Seifenkiste *f*; improvisierte Rednerbühne; **~·y** □ [~ɪ] (*-ier, -iest*) seifig; *fig.* F schmeichlerisch.

soar [sɔː] (hoch) aufsteigen, sich erheben; in großer Höhe fliegen *od.* schweben; ✈ segeln, gleiten.

sob [sɒb] 1. Schluchzen *n*; 2. (*-bb-*) schluchzen.

so·ber ['səʊbə] 1. □ nüchtern; 2. ernüchtern; ~ *down,* ~ *up* nüchtern machen *od.* werden; **so·bri·e·ty** [səʊˈbraɪətɪ] Nüchternheit *f*.

so-called ['səʊˈkɔːld] sogenannt.

soc·cer ['sɒkə] Fußball *m* (*Spiel*).

so·cia·ble ['səʊʃəbl] 1. □ gesellig; gemütlich; 2. geselliges Beisammensein.

so·cial ['səʊʃl] 1. □ gesellig; gesellschaftlich; sozial; sozialistisch; Sozial...; 2. geselliges Beisammensein; ~ *in·sur·ance* Sozialversicherung *f*.

so·cial·is·m ['səʊʃəlɪzəm] Sozialismus *m*; **~·ist** [~ɪst] 1. Sozialist(in); 2. = **~·is·tic** [səʊʃəˈlɪstɪk] (*~ally*) sozialistisch; **~·ize** ['səʊʃəlaɪz] sozialisieren; verstaatlichen; gesellschaftlich verkehren (*with* mit).

so·cial| sci·ence Sozialwissenschaft *f*; ~ **se·cu·ri·ty** Sozialhilfe *f*; *be on* ~ Sozialhilfe beziehen; ~ **serv·ic·es** *pl.* staatliche Sozialleistungen *pl.*; ~ **work** Sozialarbeit *f*; ~ **work·er** Sozialarbeiter(in).

so·ci·e·ty [səˈsaɪətɪ] Gesellschaft *f*; Verein *m*, Vereinigung *f*.

so·ci·ol·o·gy [səʊsɪˈɒlədʒɪ] Soziologie *f*.

sock [sɒk] Socke *f*; Einlegesohle *f*.

sock·et ['sɒkɪt] *anat.* (Augen-, Zahn-) Höhle *f*; *anat.* (Gelenk)Pfanne *f*; ⊕ Muffe *f*; ⚡ Fassung *f*; ⚡ Steckdose *f*; ⚡ (Anschluß)Buchse *f*.

sod [sɒd] Grasnarbe *f*; Rasenstück *n*.

so·da ['səʊdə] ⚗ Soda *f, n*; Soda (-wasser) *n*; **~·foun·tain** Siphon *m*; *Am.* Erfrischungshalle *f*, Eisbar *f*.

sod·den ['sɒdn] durchweicht; teigig.

soft [sɒft] 1. □ weich; mild; sanft; sacht, leise; gedämpft (*Licht etc.*); leicht, angenehm (*Arbeit*); weichlich; *a.* ~ *in the head* F einfältig, doof; alkoholfrei (*Getränk*); weich (*Drogen*); 2. *adv.* sanft, leise; **~·en** ['sɒfn] *v/t.* weich machen; *Farbe, Stimme etc.* dämpfen; *Wasser* enthärten; *j-n* erweichen; *fig.* mildern; *v/i.* weich(er) *od.* sanft(er) *od.* mild(er) werden; **~·heart·ed** weichherzig; **~·head·ed** doof; **~·land** *Raumfahrt:* weich landen; ~ **land·ing** *Raumfahrt:* weiche Landung; **~·ware** *Computer:* Software *f* (*Programme etc.*); *Sprachlabor:* Software *f*; **~·y** F [~ɪ] Trottel *m*; weichlicher Typ; Schwächling *m*.

sog·gy ['sɒgɪ] (*-ier, -iest*) durchnäßt; feucht.

soil [sɔɪl] 1. Boden *m*, Erde *f*; Fleck *m*; Schmutz *m*; 2. (be)schmutzen; schmutzig machen *od.* werden.

so·journ ['sɒdʒɜːn] 1. Aufenthalt *m*; 2. sich (vorübergehend) aufhalten.

sol·ace ['sɒləs] 1. Trost *m*; 2. trösten.

so·lar ['səʊlə] Sonnen...

sold [səʊld] *pret. u. p.p. von* **sell**.

sol·der ⊕ ['sɒldə] 1. Lot *n*; 2. löten.

sol·dier ['səʊldʒə] Soldat *m*; **~·like,** **~·ly** [~lɪ] soldatisch; **~·y** [~rɪ] Militär *n*, Soldaten *pl.*

sole[1] □ [~] [səʊl] alleinig, einzig, Allein...; ~ *agent* Alleinvertreter *m*.

sole[2] [~] 1. (Fuß-, Schuh)Sohle *f*; △ *nicht* Sole; 2. besohlen.

sole[3] *zo.* [~] Seezunge *f*.

sol·emn □ ['sɒləm] feierlich; ernst; **so·lem·ni·ty** [səˈlemnətɪ] Feierlichkeit *f*; **~·em·nize** ['sɒləmnaɪz] feiern; *Trauung* feierlich vollziehen.

so·lic·it [səˈlɪsɪt] (dringend) bitten (um); sich anbieten (*Prostituierte*).

so·lic·i·ta·tion [səlɪsɪˈteɪʃn] dringende Bitte; **~tor** [səˈlɪsɪtə] *Brt.* ⚖ (*nicht plädierender*) Anwalt; *Am.* Agent *m*, Werber *m*; **~tous** □ [~əs] besorgt (*about*, for um, wegen); ~ *of* begierig nach; ~ *to do* bestrebt zu tun; **~tude** [~juːd] Sorge *f*, Besorgnis *f*.

sol·id [ˈsɒlɪd] **1.** □ fest; derb, kräftig; stabil; massiv; A körperlich, räumlich, Raum...; gewichtig, triftig; solid(e), gründlich; solid(e), zuverlässig (*Person*); einmütig, solidarisch; *a* ~ *hour* e-e volle Stunde; **2.** fester Stoff; *geom.* Körper *m*; **~s** *pl.* feste Nahrung; **sol·i·dar·i·ty** [sɒlɪˈdærətɪ] Solidarität *f*.

so·lid·i·fy [səˈlɪdɪfaɪ] fest werden (lassen); verdichten; **~ty** [~tɪ] Solidität *f*.

so·lil·o·quy [səˈlɪləkwɪ] Selbstgespräch *n*; *bsd. thea.* Monolog *m*.

sol·i·taire [sɒlɪˈteə] Solitär *m*; *Am.* Karten: Patience *f*.

sol·i·ta·ry □ [ˈsɒlɪtərɪ] einsam; einzeln; einsiedlerisch; **~tude** [~juːd] Einsamkeit *f*; Verlassenheit *f*; Öde *f*.

so·lo [ˈsəʊləʊ] (*pl. -los*) Solo *n*; ♫ Alleinflug *m*; **~ist** ♪ [~ɪst] Solist(in).

sol·u·ble [ˈsɒljʊbl] löslich; *fig.* lösbar; **so·lu·tion** [səˈluːʃn] (Auf)Lösung *f*.

solve [sɒlv] lösen; **sol·vent** [ˈsɒlvənt] **1.** 🧪 (auf)lösend; *econ.* zahlungsfähig; **2.** 🧪 Lösungsmittel *n*.

som·bre, *Am.* **-ber** □ [ˈsɒmbə] düster, trüb(e); *fig.* trübsinnig.

some [sʌm, səm] (irgend)ein; *vor pl.*: einige, ein paar, manche; etwas; etwa; F beachtlich, vielleicht ein (*in Ausrufen*); ~ *20 miles* etwa 20 Meilen; *to* ~ *extent* einigermaßen; **~body** [ˈsʌmbədɪ] (irgend) jemand; irgendeiner; **~day** eines Tages; **~how** irgendwie; ~ *or other* irgendwie; **~one** (irgend) jemand, irgendeiner; **~place** *Am.* = *somewhere*.

som·er·sault [ˈsʌməsɔːlt] **1.** Salto *m*; Purzelbaum *m*; *turn a* ~ = **2.** e-n Salto machen; e-n Purzelbaum schlagen.

some·thing [ˈsʌmθɪŋ] (irgend) etwas; ~ *like* so etwas wie, so ungefähr; **~time** **1.** irgendwann; **2.** ehemalige(r, -s); **~times** manchmal; **~what** etwas, ziemlich; **~where** irgendwo(hin).

son [sʌn] Sohn *m*.

sonde [sɒnd] *Raumfahrt:* Sonde *f*.

song [sɒŋ] Lied *n*; Gesang *m*; Ge-

dicht *n*; *for a* ~ für ein Butterbrot; **~bird** [ˈsɒŋbɜːd] Singvogel *m*; **~ster** [~stə] Singvogel *m*; Sänger *m*; **~stress** [~rɪs] Sängerin *f*.

son·ic [ˈsɒnɪk] Schall...; ~ **boom**, *Brt.* *a.* ~ **bang** Überschallknall *m*.

son-in-law [ˈsʌnɪnlɔː] (*pl. sons-in-law*) Schwiegersohn *m*.

son·net [ˈsɒnɪt] Sonett *n*.

so·nor·ous □ [səˈnɔːrəs] klangvoll.

soon [suːn] bald; früh; gern; *as od. so* ~ *as* sobald als *od.* wie; **~er** [ˈsuːnə] eher; früher; lieber; ~ *or later* früher oder später; *the* ~ *the better* je eher, desto besser; *no* ~ ... *than* kaum ... als; *no* ~ *said than done* gesagt, getan.

soot [sʊt] **1.** Ruß *m*; **2.** verrußen.

soothe [suːð] beruhigen, besänftigen, beschwichtigen; lindern, mildern; **sooth·ing** □ [ˈsuːðɪŋ] besänftigend; lindernd; **sooth·say·er** [ˈsuːθseɪə] Wahrsager(in).

soot·y □ [ˈsʊtɪ] (*-ier, -iest*) rußig.

sop [sɒp] **1.** eingetunkter *od.* -weichter Bissen; **2.** (*-pp-*) eintunken.

so·phis·ti·cat·ed [səˈfɪstɪkeɪtɪd] anspruchsvoll, kultiviert; intellektuell; blasiert; ⊕ hochentwickelt; ⊕ kompliziert; verfälscht; **soph·ist·ry** [ˈsɒfɪstrɪ] Spitzfindigkeit *f*.

soph·o·more [ˈsɒfəmɔː] College-Student(in) *od.* Schüler(in) e-r High-School im zweiten Jahr.

so·po·rif·ic [sɒpəˈrɪfɪk] **1.** (~*ally*) einschläfernd; **2.** Schlafmittel *n*.

sor·cer·er [ˈsɔːsərə] Zauberer *m*, Hexenmeister *m*; **~ess** [~ɪs] Zauberin *f*, Hexe *f*; **~y** [~ɪ] Zauberei *f*, Hexerei *f*.

sor·did □ [ˈsɔːdɪd] schmutzig; schäbig, elend, miserabel.

sore [sɔː] **1.** □ (~*r*, ~*st*) schlimm, entzündet; wund, weh; gereizt; verärgert, böse; *a* ~ *throat* Halsschmerzen *pl.*; **2.** Wunde *f*, Entzündung *f*; **~head** *Am.* F [ˈsɔːhed] mürrischer Mensch.

sor·rel [ˈsɒrəl] **1.** rotbraun; **2.** *zo.* Fuchs *m* (*Pferd*); ♣ Sauerampfer *m*.

sor·row [ˈsɒrəʊ] **1.** Kummer *m*, Leid *n*; Schmerz *m*, Jammer *m*; **2.** trauern; sich grämen; **~ful** □ [~fl] traurig, betrübt.

sor·ry □ [ˈsɒrɪ] (*-ier, -iest*) betrübt, bekümmert; traurig, erbärmlich; *be* ~ *about s.th.* et. bereuen *od.* bedauern; *I am* (*so*) ~*!* es tut mir (sehr) leid, Verzeihung!; ~*!* Verzeihung!,

S

Entschuldigung!; *I am ~ for him* er tut mir leid; *we are ~ to say* wir müssen leider sagen.

sort [sɔːt] 1. Sorte *f*, Art *f*; *what ~ of* was für *m*; *of a ~, of ~s* F so was wie; *~ of* F gewissermaßen; *out of ~s* F nicht auf der Höhe; 2. sortieren; *~ out* (aus-)sortieren; *fig.* in Ordnung bringen.

sot [sɒt] Säufer *m*, Trunkenbold *m*.

sough [saʊ] 1. Rauschen *n*; 2. rauschen.

sought [sɔːt] *pret. u. p.p. von* **seek**.

soul [səʊl] Seele *f* (*a. fig.*); Inbegriff *m*; ♪ Soul *m*.

sound [saʊnd] 1. □ gesund; intakt; *econ.* solid(e), stabil, sicher; vernünftig; ♣ gültig; zuverlässig; kräftig, tüchtig; fest, tief (*Schlaf*); 2. Ton *m*, Schall *m*, Laut *m*, Klang *m*; ♪ Sound *m*; ♣ Sonde *f*; Sund *m*, Meerenge *f*; ♣ Fischblase *f*; 3. (*er*)tönen, (-)klingen; erschallen (lassen); sich *gut etc.* anhören; sondieren; ♣ (aus-)loten; ♣ abhorchen; *Film:* **~ bar·ri·er** Schallgrenze *f*, -mauer *f*; **~film** ['saʊndfɪlm] Tonfilm *m*; **~ing** ♣ [~ɪŋ] Lotung *f*; **~s** *pl.* lotbare Wassertiefe; **~less** □ [~lɪs] lautlos; **~ness** [~nɪs] Gesundheit *f* (*a. fig.*); **pol·lu·tion** Lärmbelästigung *f*; **~proof** schalldicht; **~track** *Film:* Tonspur *f*; Filmmusik *f*; **~wave** Schallwelle *f*.

soup [suːp] 1. Suppe *f*; (*some*) *~ e-e* Suppe; 2. *~ up* F *Motor* frisieren.

sour ['saʊə] 1. □ sauer; *fig.* verbittert; 2. *v/t.* säuern; *fig.* ver-, erbittern; *v/i.* sauer (*fig.* verbittert) werden.

source [sɔːs] Quelle *f*; Ursprung *m*.

sour|ish □ ['saʊərɪʃ] säuerlich; **~ness** [~nɪs] Säure *f*; *fig.* Bitterkeit *f*.

souse [saʊs] eintauchen; (mit Wasser) begießen; *Fisch etc.* einlegen, -pökeln.

south [saʊθ] 1. Süd(en *m*); 2. südlich, Süd...; **~east** ['saʊθ'iːst] 1. Südosten *m*; 2. südöstlich; **~east·ern** Südostwind *m*; **~east·ern** südöstlich.

south·er|ly ['sʌðəlɪ], **~n** [~n] südlich, Süd...; **~n·most** südlichste(r, -s).

south·ward(s) *adv.* ['saʊθwəd(z)] südwärts, nach Süden.

south|-west ['saʊθ'west] 1. Südwesten *m*; 2. südwestlich; **~west·er** [~ə] Südwestwind *m*; ♣ Südwester *m*; **~west·er·ly**, **~west·ern** südwestlich.

sou·ve·nir [suːvə'nɪə] Souvenir *n*, Andenken *n*.

sove·reign ['sɒvrɪn] 1. □ höchste(r, -s); unübertrefflich; unumschränkt, souverän; 2. Herrscher(in), Monarch(in); Sovereign *m* (*alte brit. Goldmünze von 20 Shilling*); **~ty** [~ntɪ] höchste (Staats)Gewalt; Souveränität *f*, Landeshoheit *f*.

So·vi·et ['səʊvɪət] Sowjet *m*; *attr.* sowjetisch, Sowjet...

sow¹ [saʊ] *zo.* Sau *f*, (Mutter-) Schwein *n*; ⊕ Sau *f*; ⊕ Massel *f*.

sow² [səʊ] (*sowed, sown od. sowed*) (aus)säen, ausstreuen; besäen; **~n** [~n] *p.p. von* **sow²**.

spa [spaː] Heilbad *n*; Kurort *m*.

space [speɪs] 1. (Welt)Raum *m*; Raum *m*, Platz *m*; Abstand *m*, Zwischenraum *m*; Zeitraum *m*; 2. *mst ~ out* *print.* sperren; **~ age** Weltraumzeitalter *n*; **~ cap·sule** ['speɪskæpsjuːl] Raumkapsel *f*; **~craft** Raumfahrzeug *n*; **~ flight** (Welt)Raumflug *m*; **~lab** Raumlabor *n*; **~port** (Welt-)Raumfahrtzentrum *n*; **~ probe** (Welt-)Raumsonde *f*; **~ re·search** (Welt-)Raumforschung *f*; **~ship** Raumschiff *n*; **~ shut·tle** Raumfähre *f*; **~ sta·tion** (Welt)Raumstation *f*; **~suit** Raumanzug *m*; **~ walk** Weltraumspaziergang *m*; **~wom·an** (*pl. -women*) (Welt)Raumfahrerin *f*.

spa·cious □ ['speɪʃəs] geräumig; weit; umfassend.

spade [speɪd] Spaten *m*; *Karten:* Pik *n*, Grün *n*; *king of ~s* Pik-König *m*; *call a ~ a ~* das Kind beim (rechten) Namen nennen.

span [spæn] 1. Spanne *f*; *arch.* Spannweite *f*; △ *nicht* Span; 2. (*-nn-*) um-, überspannen; (aus)messen.

span·gle ['spæŋgl] 1. Flitter *m*, Paillette *f*; 2. mit Flitter *od.* Pailletten besetzen; *fig.* übersäen.

Span·iard ['spænjəd] Spanier(in).

Span·ish ['spænɪʃ] 1. spanisch; 2. *ling.* Spanisch *n*; *the ~ pl. coll.* die Spanier *pl.*

spank F [spæŋk] 1. verhauen; 2. Klaps *m*, Schlag *m*; **~ing** ['spæŋkɪŋ] 1. *adj.* □ schnell, flott; tüchtig, gehörig; 2. *adv.*: *~ clean* blitzsauber; *~ new* funkelnagelneu; 3. F Haue *f*, Tracht *f* Prügel.

span·ner ⊕ ['spænə] Schraubenschlüssel *m*.

spar [spaː] 1. ♣ Spiere *f*; ✈ Holm *m*; 2. (*-rr-*) *Boxen:* sparren; *fig.* sich streiten.

spare [speə] **1.** □ sparsam; kärglich, mager; überzählig; überschüssig; Ersatz..., Reserve...; ~ **part** Ersatzteil n, a. m; ~ **room** Gästezimmer n; ~ **time** od. **hours** Freizeit f, Mußestunden pl.; **2.** ⊕ Ersatzteil n, a. m; **3.** (ver)schonen; erübrigen; entbehren; (übrig)haben (für); ersparen, sparen mit; scheuen; △ nicht Geld etc. sparen.

spar·ing [ˈspeərɪŋ] sparsam.

spark [spɑːk] **1.** Funke(n) m; **2.** Funken sprühen; ~**ing-plug** Brt. mot. [ˈspɑːkɪnplʌg] Zündkerze f.

spar|kle [ˈspɑːkl] **1.** Funke(n) m; Funkeln n; **2.** funkeln; blitzen; perlen (Wein); ~**kling** □ [~ɪŋ] funkelnd, sprühend; fig. geistsprühend, spritzig; ~ **wine** Schaumwein m.

spark-plug Am. mot. [ˈspɑːkplʌg] Zündkerze f.

spar·row zo. [ˈspærəʊ] Sperling m, Spatz m; ~**hawk** zo. Sperber m.

sparse □ [spɑːs] spärlich, dünn.

spas·m [ˈspæzm] Krampf m; Anfall m; **spas·mod·ic** [spæzˈmɒdɪk] (~ally) ⚕ krampfhaft, -artig; fig. sprunghaft.

spas·tic ⚕ [ˈspæstɪk] **1.** (~ally) spastisch; **2.** Spastiker(in).

spat [spæt] pret. u. p.p. von spit².

spa·tial □ [ˈspeɪʃl] räumlich.

spat·ter [ˈspætə] (be)spritzen.

spawn [spɔːn] **1.** zo. Laich m; fig. contp. Brut f; **2.** zo. laichen; fig. hervorbringen.

speak [spiːk] (spoke, spoken) v/i. sprechen, reden (to mit; about über acc.); ~ **out**, ~ **up** laut u. deutlich sprechen; offen reden; ~ **to s.o.** in j-m od. mit j-m sprechen; v/t. (aus)sprechen; sagen; äußern; **Sprache** sprechen (können); ~**er** [ˈspiːkə] Sprecher(in), Redner(in); ⚷ parl. Sprecher m, Präsident m; **Mr** ⚷! Herr Vorsitzender!

spear [spɪə] **1.** Speer m; Spieß m, Lanze f; **2.** durchbohren, aufspießen.

spe·cial [ˈspeʃl] **1.** □ besondere(r, -s); speziell; Sonder...; Spezial...; **2.** Hilfspolizist m; Sonderausgabe f; Sonderzug m; Rundfunk, TV: Sondersendung f; Am. Tagesgericht n (im Restaurant); Am. econ. Sonderangebot n; on ~ Am. econ. im Angebot; ~**ist** [~əlɪst] Spezialist(in), Fachmann m; ⚕ Facharzt m, -ärztin

f; **spe·ci·al·i·ty** [speʃɪˈælətɪ] Besonderheit f; Spezialfach n; econ. Spezialität f; ~**ize** [ˈspeʃəlaɪz] besonders anführen; (sich) spezialisieren; ~**ty** bsd. Am. [~tɪ] = speciality.

spe·cies [ˈspiːʃiːz] (pl. -cies) Art f, Spezies f.

spe|cif·ic [spɪˈsɪfɪk] (~ally) spezifisch; besondere(r, -s); bestimmt; ~**ci·fy** [ˈspesɪfaɪ] spezifizieren, einzeln angeben; ~**ci·men** [~mɪn] Probe f, Muster n; Exemplar n.

spe·cious □ [ˈspiːʃəs] blendend, bestechend; trügerisch; Schein...

speck [spek] Fleck(en) m; Stückchen n; △ nicht Speck; ~**le** [ˈspekl] Fleck(en) m, Sprenkel m, Tupfen m; ~**led** gefleckt, gesprenkelt, getüpfelt.

spec·ta·cle [ˈspektəkl] Schauspiel n; Anblick m; △ nicht das Spektakel; (a pair of) ~**s** pl. (e-e) Brille f.

spec·tac·u·lar [spekˈtækjʊlə] **1.** □ spektakulär, sensationell, aufsehenerregend; **2.** große (Fernseh)Schau, Galavorstellung f.

spec·ta·tor [spekˈteɪtə] Zuschauer (-in).

spec|tral □ [ˈspektrəl] gespenstisch; ~**tre**, Am. ~**ter** [~ə] Gespenst n.

spec·u·late [ˈspekjʊleɪt] grübeln, nachsinnen; econ. spekulieren; ~**la·tion** [spekjʊˈleɪʃn] theoretische Betrachtung; Nachdenken n; Grübeln n; econ. Spekulation f; ~**la·tive** □ [ˈspekjʊlətɪv] grüblerisch; theoretisch; econ. spekulativ; ~**la·tor** [~eɪtə] econ. Spekulant m.

sped [sped] pret. u. p.p. von speed 2.

speech [spiːtʃ] Sprache f; Reden n, Sprechen n; Rede f, Ansprache f; **make a** ~ e-e Rede halten; ~**day** Brt. [ˈspiːtʃdeɪ] Schule: (Jahres-) Schlußfeier f; ~**less** □ [~lɪs] sprachlos.

speed [spiːd] **1.** Geschwindigkeit f, Tempo n, Schnelligkeit f, Eile f; ⊕ Drehzahl f; mot. Gang m; phot. Lichtempfindlichkeit f; phot. Belichtungszeit f; sl. Speed n (Aufputschmittel); **2.** (sped) v/i. (dahin)eilen, schnell fahren, rasen; ~ **up** (pret. u. p.p. speeded) die Geschwindigkeit erhöhen; v/t. rasch befördern; ~ **up** (pret. u. p.p. speeded) beschleunigen; ~**boat** [ˈspiːdbəʊt] Rennboot n; ~**ing** mot. [~ɪŋ] zu schnelles Fahren, Geschwindigkeitsüberschreitung f; **~ lim·it** Geschwindigkeitsbegrenzung f, Tempolimit n; **~·o** ⊦ mot. [~ɔʊ] (pl. -os) Tacho m; **~·om·e·ter** mot. [spɪ'dɒmɪtə] Tachometer m, n; **~·up** ['spiːdʌp] Beschleunigung f, Temposteigerung f; econ. Produktionserhöhung f; **~·way** Sport: Speedwayrennen n; Speedwaybahn f; Am. mot. Schnellstraße f; Am. Sport: mot. Rennstrecke f; **~·y** □ [~ɪ] (-ier, -iest) schnell, rasch.

spell [spel] **1.** Weile f, Weilchen n; Anfall m; Zauber(spruch) m; fig. Zauber m; a ~ of fine weather e-e Schönwetterperiode; hot ~ Hitzewelle f; **2.** ~ s.o. at s.th. j-n bei et. ablösen; (spelt od. Am. spelled) buchstabieren; richtig schreiben; bedeuten; geschrieben werden, sich schreiben; **~·bound** ['spelbaʊnd] (wie) gebannt, fasziniert, gefesselt; **~·er** [~ə]: be a good od. bad ~ in Rechtschreibung gut od. schlecht sein; **~·ing** [~ɪŋ] Buchstabieren n; Rechtschreibung f; **~·ing-book** Fibel f.

spelt [spelt] pret. u. p.p. von spell 2.

spend [spend] (spent) verwenden; Geld ausgeben; verbrauchen; verschwenden; Mühe aufwenden; Zeit zu-, verbringen; △ nicht spenden; ~ o.s. sich erschöpfen; **~·thrift** ['spendθrɪft] Verschwender(in).

spent [spent] **1.** pret. u. p.p. von spend; **2.** adj. erschöpft, matt.

sperm [spɜːm] Sperma n, Samen m.

sphere [sfɪə] Kugel f; Erd-, Himmelskugel f; fig. Sphäre f; (Wirkungs)Kreis m, Bereich m, Gebiet n; **spher·i·cal** □ ['sferɪkl] sphärisch; kugelförmig.

spice [spaɪs] **1.** Gewürz(e pl.) n; fig. Würze f; Anflug m; **2.** würzen.

spick and span ['spɪkən'spæn] blitzsauber; wie aus dem Ei gepellt; funkelnagelneu.

spic·y □ ['spaɪsɪ] (-ier, -iest) würzig; gewürzt; fig. pikant.

spi·der zo. ['spaɪdə] Spinne f.

spig·ot ['spɪgət] (Faß)Zapfen m; (Zapf-, Am. Leitungs)Hahn m.

spike [spaɪk] **1.** Stift m; Spitze f; Dorn m; Stachel m; ⚘ Ähre f; Sport: Spike m; ~s pl. Rennschuhe, mot.: Spikes pl.; **2.** festnageln; mit (Eisen)Spitzen etc. versehen; ~ heel Pfennigabsatz m.

spill [spɪl] **1.** (spilt od. spilled) v/t. ver-, ausschütten; Blut vergießen; verstreuen; Reiter abwerfen; sl. ausplaudern; s. milk 1; v/i. überlaufen; sl. auspacken, singen; **2.** Sturz m (vom Pferd etc.).

spilt [spɪlt] pret. u. p.p. von spill 1.

spin [spɪn] **1.** (-nn-; spun) v/t. spinnen; schnell drehen, (herum)wirbeln; Wäsche schleudern; Münze hochwerfen; fig. sich et. ausdenken, erzählen; ~ s.th. out et. in die Länge ziehen, et. ausspinnen; v/i. spinnen; sich drehen; ✈ trudeln; durchdrehen (Räder); ~ along dahinrasen; **2.** schnelle Drehung; Schleudern n (Wäsche); ✈ Trudeln n; go for a ~ e-e Spritztour machen.

spin·ach ⚘ ['spɪnɪdʒ] Spinat m.

spin·al anat. ['spaɪnl] Rückgrat...; ~ column Wirbelsäule f, Rückgrat n; ~ cord, ~ marrow Rückenmark n.

spin·dle ['spɪndl] Spindel f.

spin·dri·er ['spɪndraɪə] (Wäsche-)Schleuder f; **~·dry** Wäsche schleudern; **~·dry·er** = spin-drier.

spine [spaɪn] anat. Wirbelsäule f, Rückgrat n; Stachel m, ⚘ Dorn m; (Gebirgs)Grat m; (Buch)Rücken m.

spin·ning-mill ['spɪnɪŋmɪl] Spinnerei f; **~·top** Kreisel m; **~·wheel** Spinnrad n.

spin·ster ['spɪnstə] ⚥ unverheiratete Frau; alte Jungfer.

spin·y ⚥, zo. ['spaɪnɪ] (-ier, -iest) stach(e)lig.

spi·ral ['spaɪərəl] **1.** □ spiralig; Spiral...; gewunden; ~ staircase Wendeltreppe f; **2.** Spirale f.

spire [spaɪə] (Turm-, Berg- etc.)Spitze f; Kirchturm(spitze f) m.

spir·it ['spɪrɪt] **1.** Geist m; Schwung m; Elan m; Mut m; Gesinnung f; 🜂 Spiritus m; ~s pl. alkoholische od. geistige Getränke pl., Spirituosen pl.; high (low) ~s pl. gehobene (gedrückte) Stimmung; **2.** ~ away od. off wegschaffen, -zaubern; **~·ed** [~ɪd] lebhaft; energisch; feurig (Pferd etc.); geistvoll; **~·less** □ [~lɪs] geistlos; temperamentlos; mutlos.

spir·i·tu·al ['spɪrɪtjʊəl] **1.** □ geistig; geistlich; geistreich; **2.** ♪ (Neger-)Spiritual n; **~·ism** [~ɪzəm] Spiritismus m.

spirt [spɜːt] = spurt².

spit¹ [spɪt] **1.** (Brat)Spieß m; geogr. Landzunge f; **2.** (-tt-) aufspießen.

spit² [~] **1.** Speichel *m*, Spucke *f*; Fauchen *n*; F Ebenbild *n*; **2.** (*-tt-*; *spat od. spit*) spucken; fauchen; sprühen (*fein regnen*); *a.* ~ **out** (aus-)spucken.

spite [spaɪt] **1.** Bosheit *f*; Groll *m*; *in* ~ *of* trotz (*gen.*); **2.** *j-n* ärgern; **~ful** □ ['spaɪtfl] boshaft, gehässig.

spit·fire ['spɪtfaɪə] Hitzkopf *m*.

spit·toon [spɪ'tuːn] Spucknapf *m*.

splash [splæʃ] **1.** Spritzer *m*, (Spritz-)Fleck *m*; Klatschen *n*, Platschen *n*; **2.** (be)spritzen; platschen; planschen; (hin)klecksen; ~ **down** wassern (*Raumkapsel*); **~down** Wasserung *f*.

splay [spleɪ] **1.** Ausschrägung *f*; **2.** *v/t.* spreizen; ausschrägen; ~ sein; **~foot** ['spleɪfʊt] Spreizfuß *m*.

spleen [spliːn] *anat.* Milz *f*; schlechte Laune.

splen|did □ ['splendɪd] glänzend, prächtig, herrlich; F großartig, hervorragend; **~do(u)r** [~ə] Glanz *m*, Pracht *f*, Herrlichkeit *f*.

splice [splaɪs] spleißen; *Film* zusammenkleben.

splint ⚕ [splɪnt] **1.** Schiene *f*; **2.** schienen.

splin·ter ['splɪntə] **1.** Splitter *m*; **2.** (zer)splittern; ~ **off** (*fig.* sich) absplittern.

split [splɪt] **1.** Spalt *m*, Riß *m*, Sprung *m*; *fig.* Spaltung *f*; **2.** gespalten; **3.** (*-tt-*; *split*) *v/t.* (zer)spalten; zerreißen; sich in *et.* teilen; ~ *hairs* Haarspalterei treiben; ~ *one's sides laughing od. with laughter* sich totlachen; *v/i.* sich spalten; zerspringen, (-)platzen, (-)bersten; **~ting** ['splɪtɪŋ] heftig, rasend (*Kopfschmerz*).

splut·ter ['splʌtə] (heraus)stottern; zischen; stottern (*Motor*).

spoil [spɔɪl] **1.** *mst* ~**s** *pl.* Beute *f*; *fig.* Ausbeute *f*, Gewinn *m*; **2.** (*spoilt od. spoiled*) verderben; ruinieren; *Kind* verwöhnen, -ziehen; **~er** *mot.* ['spɔɪlə] Spoiler *m*; **~sport** Spielverderber(in) *f*; **~t** [~t] *pret. u. p.p. von spoil 2.*

spoke¹ [spəʊk] Speiche *f*; (Leiter-) Sprosse *f*.

spoke² [~] *pret. von speak*; **spok·en** ['spəʊkən] **1.** *p.p. von speak*; **2.** gesprochen (*Sprache*); **~s·man** [~smən] (*pl. -men*) Wortführer *m*,

Sprecher *m*; **~s·wom·an** (*pl. -women*) Wortführerin *f*, Sprecherin *f*.

sponge [spʌndʒ] **1.** Schwamm *m*; F *fig.* Schmarotzer(in); *Brt.* = *sponge-cake*; **2.** *v/t.* mit e-m Schwamm (ab)wischen; ~ **off** weg-, abwischen; ~ **up** aufsaugen, -wischen; *v/i.* F *fig.* schmarotzen; ~**cake** ['spʌndʒkeɪk] Biskuitkuchen *m*; **spong·er** F *fig.* [~ə] Schmarotzer(in); **spong·y** [~ɪ] (*-ier, -iest*) schwammig.

spon·sor ['spɒnsə] **1.** Bürg|e *m*, -in *f*; (Tauf-)Pat|e *m*, -in *f*; Förderer *m*, Gönner(in); Schirmherr(in); Geldgeber(in), Sponsor(in); **2.** bürgen für; fördern; die Schirmherrschaft (*gen.*) übernehmen; *Rundfunk-, TV-Sendung, Sportler* sponsern; **~ship** [~ʃɪp] Bürgschaft *f*; Patenschaft *f*; Schirmherrschaft *f*; Unterstützung *f*, Förderung *f*.

spon·ta·ne|i·ty [spɒntə'neɪətɪ] Spontaneität *f*, eigener Antrieb; Ungezwungenheit *f*; **~ous** □ [spɒn-'teɪnjəs] spontan; unvermittelt; ungezwungen, natürlich; von selbst (entstanden); Selbst...

spook [spuːk] Spuk *m*; **~y** ['spuːkɪ] (*-ier, -iest*) gespenstisch, Spuk...

spool [spuːl] Spule *f*; Rolle *f*; *a.* ~ *of thread Am.* Garnrolle *f*.

spoon [spuːn] **1.** Löffel *m*; **2.** löffeln; **~ful** [spuːnfʊl] (*ein*) Löffel(voll) *m*.

spo·rad·ic [spə'rædɪk] (*~ally*) sporadisch, gelegentlich, vereinzelt.

spore ♦ [spɔː] Spore *f*, Keimkorn *n*.

sport [spɔːt] **1.** Sport(art *f*) *m*; Zeitvertreib *m*; Spaß *m*, Scherz *m*; F feiner Kerl; ~**s** *pl.* Sport *m*; *Brt. Schule:* Sportfest *n*; **2.** *v/i.* herumtollen; spielen; *v/t.* F stolz (*zur Schau*) tragen; protzen mit; **spor·tive** □ ['spɔːtɪv] verspielt; **~s** [~s] Sport...; **~s·man** (*pl. -men*) Sportler *m*; **~s·wom·an** (*pl. -women*) Sportlerin *f*.

spot [spɒt] **1.** Fleck *m*; Tupfen *m*; Makel *m*; Stelle *f*, Ort *m*; ⚕ Leberfleck *m*; ⚕ Pickel *m*; *Rundfunk, TV:* (Werbe)Spot *m*; *Brt.* F Tropfen *m*, Schluck *m*; *a.* ~ *of Brt.* F etwas; *on the* ~ auf der Stelle, sofort; **2.** *econ.* sofort liefer- *od.* zahlbar; **3.** (*-tt-*) beflecken; sprenkeln; entdecken, erspähen, erkennen; fleckig werden; **~less** □ ['spɒtlɪs] fleckenlos; **~light** *thea.*

Scheinwerfer(licht *n*) *m*; **~ter** [~ə]
Beobachter *m*; ✕ Aufklärer *m*; **~ty**
[~ɪ] (*-ier, -iest*) fleckig; pickelig.

spouse [spauz] Gatt|e *m*, -in *f*.

spout [spaut] 1. Tülle *f*, Schnabel *m*;
Strahlrohr *n*; (Wasser)Strahl *m*; 2.
(heraus)spritzen; hervorsprudeln.

sprain ✗ [sprein] 1. Verstauchung *f*;
2. sich *et*. verstauchen.

sprang [spræŋ] *pret. von* spring 2.

sprat *zo*. [spræt] Sprotte *f*.

sprawl [sprɔ:l] sich rekeln; ausge-
streckt daliegen; ⚘ wuchern.

spray [sprei] 1. Sprühregen *m*,
Gischt *m*, Schaum *m*; Spray *m*, *n*; **~**
sprayer; 2. zerstäuben; (ver)sprü-
hen; besprühen; *Haar* sprayen; **~er**
['spreiə] Zerstäuber *m*, Sprüh-,
Spraydose *f*.

spread [spred] 1. (*spread*) *v/t. a.* **~**
out ausbreiten; ausstrecken; spreizen; ausdehnen; verbreiten; belegen; *Butter etc.* (auf)streichen; *Brot
etc.* streichen; **~** *the table* den Tisch
decken; *v/i.* sich aus- *od.* verbreiten;
sich ausdehnen; 2. Aus-, Verbreitung *f*; Ausdehnung *f*; Spannweite *f*;
Fläche *f*; (*Bett*)Decke *f*; (*Brot*)Auf-
strich *m*; F Festessen *n*.

spree F [spri:] *go* (*out*) *on a* **~** e-e
Sauftour machen; *go on a buying*
(*shopping, spending*) **~** wie verrückt
einkaufen.

sprig ⚘ [sprig] kleiner Zweig.

spright·ly ['spraitli] (*-ier, -iest*) lebhaft, munter.

spring [spriŋ] 1. Sprung *m*, Satz *m*; ⊕
(Sprung)Feder *f*; Sprungkraft *f*,
Elastizität *f*; Quelle *f*; *fig.* Triebfeder
f; *fig.* Ursprung *m*; Frühling *m* (*a.
fig.*), Frühjahr *n*; 2. (*sprang od. Am.
sprung, sprung*) *v/t.* springen lassen; (zer)sprengen; *Wild* aufjagen; **~**
a leak ⚓ leck werden; **~** *a surprise
on s.o.* j-n überraschen; *v/i.* springen; entspringen (*from dat.*), *fig.*
herkommen, stammen (*from von*); ⚘
sprießen; **~** *up* aufkommen (*Ideen
etc.*); **~board** ['spriŋbɔ:d] Sprungbrett *n*; **~tide** Springflut *f*; *a.* **~tide**
poet., **~time** Frühling(szeit *f*) *m*,
Frühjahr *n*; **~y** [~ɪ] (*-ier, -iest*)
federnd.

sprin|kle ['spriŋkl] (be)streuen;
(be)sprengen; *impers.* sprühen (*fein
regnen*); **~kler** [~ə] Berieselungs-
anlage *f*; Sprinkler *m*; Rasenspren-
ger *m*; **~kling** [~ɪŋ] Sprühregen

m; *a* **~** *of fig.* ein wenig, ein paar.

sprint [sprint] *Sport* 1. sprinten;
spurten; 2. Sprint *m*; Spurt *m*; **~er**
['sprintə] *Sport*: Sprinter(in), Kurz-
streckenläufer(in).

sprite [sprait] Kobold *m*.

sprout [spraut] 1. sprießen; wachsen
(lassen); 2. ⚘ Sproß *m*; (*Brussels*)**~s**
pl. ⚘ Rosenkohl *m*.

spruce[1] □ [spru:s] schmuck, adrett.

spruce[2] ⚘ [~] *a.* **~** *fir* Fichte *f*, Rot-
tanne *f*.

sprung [spraŋ] *pret. u. p.p. von*
spring 2.

spry [sprai] munter, flink.

spun [spʌn] *pret. u. p.p. von* spin 1.

spur [spɜ:] 1. Sporn *m* (*a. zo.*, ⚘);
Vorsprung *m*, Ausläufer *m* (*e-s Ber-
ges*); *fig.* Ansporn *m*; △ *nicht Spur*;
on the **~** *of the moment* der Eingebung des Augenblicks folgend,
spontan; 2. (*-rr-*) *e-m Pferd die Sporen geben*; *oft* **~** *on fig.* anspornen.

spu·ri·ous □ ['spjuəriəs] unecht, gefälscht.

spurn [spɜ:n] verschmähen, veracht-
lich zurückweisen.

spurt[1] [spɜ:t] 1. plötzlich aktiv werden; *Sport*: spurten, sprinten; 2.
plötzliche Aktivität *od.* Anspannung; *Sport*: Spurt *m*, Sprint *m*.

spurt[2] [~] 1. (heraus)spritzen;
(*Wasser- etc.*)Strahl *m*.

sput·ter ['spʌtə] = splutter.

spy [spai] 1. Spion(in); Spitzel *m*; 2.
erspähen, entdecken; (aus)spähen;
~ *on*, **~** *upon* j-m nachspionie-
ren; j-n bespitzeln; *Gespräch etc.*
abhören; **~glass** ['spaiglɑ:s] Fernglas *n*; **~hole** Guckloch *n*, Spion *m*.

squab·ble ['skwɒbl] 1. Zank *m*, Ge-
belei *f*; 2. sich zanken.

squad [skwɒd] Gruppe *f* (*a.* ✕); *Poli-
zei*: (*Überfall- etc.*)Kommando *n*;
Dezernat *n*; **~** *car Am.* (Funk)Strei-
fenwagen *m*; **~ron** ✕ ['skwɒdrən]
Schwadron *f*; (Panzer)Bataillon *n*;
✈ Staffel *f*; ⚓ Geschwader *n*.

squal·id □ ['skwɒlid] schmutzig,
verwahrlost, verkommen, armselig.

squall [skwɔ:l] 1. *meteor.* Bö *f*; Schrei
m; **~s** *pl.* Geschrei *n*; 2. schreien.

squal·or ['skwɒlə] Schmutz *m*.

squan·der ['skwɒndə] verschwenden, -geuden.

square [skweə] 1. □ (vier)eckig; quadratisch, Quadrat...; ... im Quadrat;
rechtwink(e)lig; vierschrötig (*Per-*

son); stimmend, in Ordnung; quitt, gleich; anständig, ehrlich, offen; F altmodisch, spießig; **2.** Quadrat *n*; Viereck *n*; Feld *n* (*e-s Brettspiels*); *öffentlicher* Platz; Winkel(maß *n*) *m*; *sl.* altmodischer Spießer; **3.** quadratisch *od.* rechtwink(e)lig machen; *Zahl* ins Quadrat erheben; *Schultern* straffen; *Sport: Kampf* unentschieden beenden; *econ.* Konten ausgleichen; *econ. Schuld* begleichen; *fig.* in Einklang bringen *od.* stehen (*with* mit); anpassen (*to an acc.*); passen (*with* zu); **~·built** ['skweə'bɪlt] vierschrötig; ~ **dance** *bsd. Am.* Square dance *m*; ~ **mile** Quadratmeile *f*; **~·toed** *fig.* altmodisch, steif.

squash¹ [skwɒʃ] **1.** Gedränge *n*; Brei *m*, Matsch *m*; *Brt.* (*Orangen- etc.*) Saft *m*; *Sport:* Squash *n*; **2.** (*zer-, zusammen*)quetschen; zusammendrücken.

squash² 🍃 [~] Kürbis *m*.

squat [skwɒt] **1.** (*-tt-*) hocken, kauern; sich ohne Rechtstitel ansiedeln (auf *dat.*); *leerstehendes Haus* besetzen; ~ **down** sich hinhocken; **2.** in der Hocke; untersetzt, vierschrötig; **~·ter** ['skwɒtə] Squatter *m*, illegaler Siedler; Schafzüchter *m* (*in Australien*); Hausbesetzer(in); *~ movement* Hausbesetzerszene *f*.

squawk [skwɔːk] **1.** kreischen, schreien; **2.** Gekreisch *n*, Geschrei *n*.

squeak [skwiːk] quiek(s)en, piepen, piepsen; quietschen.

squeal [skwiːl] schreien, kreischen; quietschen, kreischen (*Bremsen etc.*); quiek(s)en, piep(s)en.

squeam·ish □ ['skwiːmɪʃ] empfindlich; mäkelig; heikel; penibel.

squeeze [skwiːz] **1.** (aus-, zusammen)drücken, (-)pressen, (aus)quetschen; sich zwängen *od.* quetschen; **2.** Druck *m*; Gedränge *n*; **squeez·er** ['skwiːzə] (*Frucht*)Presse *f*.

squelch *fig.* [skweltʃ] unterdrücken.

squid *zo.* [skwɪd] Tintenfisch *m*.

squint [skwɪnt] schielen; blinzeln.

squire ['skwaɪə] Großgrundbesitzer *m*, Gutsherr *m*.

squirm F [skwɜːm] sich winden.

squir·rel *zo.* ['skwɪrəl, *Am.* 'skwɜːrəl] Eichhörnchen *n*.

squirt [skwɜːt] **1.** Spritze *f*; Strahl *m*; F Wichtigtuer *m*; **2.** spritzen.

stab [stæb] **1.** Stich *m*, (*Dolch- etc.*)Stoß *m*; ⚠ *nicht* Stab!; **2.** (*-bb-*)

v/t. niederstechen; *et.* aufspießen; *v/i.* stechen (*at* nach).

sta·bil·i·ty [stə'bɪlətɪ] Stabilität *f*; Standfestig-, Beständigkeit *f*; **~·ize** ['steɪbəlaɪz] stabilisieren.

sta·ble¹ □ ['steɪbl] stabil, fest.

sta·ble² [~] **1.** Stall *m*; **2.** in den Stall bringen; im Stall halten; im Stall stehen (*Pferd*).

stack [stæk] **1.** ✔ (Heu-, Stroh-, Getreide)Schober *m*; Stapel *m*; F Haufen *m*; Schornstein(reihe *f*) *m*; ~s *pl.* (Haupt)Magazin *n* (*e-r Bibliothek*); **2.** *a.* ~ **up** (auf)stapeln.

sta·di·um ['steɪdjəm] (*pl.* *-diums*, *-dia* [-djə]) *Sport:* Stadion *n*.

staff [stɑːf] **1.** Stab *m* (*a.* ✗), Stock *m*; Stütze *f*; (*pl. staves* [steɪvz]) ♪ Notensystem *n*; (Mitarbeiter)Stab *m*; Personal *n*, Belegschaft *f*; Beamtenstab *m*; Lehrkörper *m*; **2.** (mit Personal, Beamten *od.* Lehrern) besetzen; ~ **mem·ber** Mitarbeiter(in); ~ **room** Lehrerzimmer *n*.

stag *zo.* [stæg] Hirsch *m*.

stage [steɪdʒ] **1.** *thea.* Bühne *f*; *das* Theater; *fig.* Schauplatz *m*; Stufe *f*, Stadium *n*, Phase *f*; Teilstrecke *f*, Fahrzone *f* (*Bus etc.*); Etappe *f*; ⊕ Bühne *f*, Gerüst *n*; ⊕ Stufe *f* (*e-r Rakete*); **2.** inszenieren; veranstalten; **~·coach** *hist.* ['steɪdʒkəʊtʃ] Postkutsche *f*; **~·craft** dramaturgisches *od.* schauspielerisches Können; ~ **de·sign** Bühnenbild *n*; ~ **de·sign·er** Bühnenbildner *m*; ~ **di·rec·tion** Regieanweisung *f*; ~ **fright** Lampenfieber *n*; ~ **man·ag·er** Inspizient *m*; ~ **prop·er·ties** *pl.* Requisiten *pl.*

stag·ger ['stægə] **1.** *v/i.* (sch)wanken, taumeln, torkeln; *fig.* (sch)wanken(d werden); *v/t.* ins Wanken bringen; *Arbeitszeit etc.* staffeln; *fig.* überwältigen, sprachlos machen; **2.** (Sch)Wanken *n*, Taumeln *n*; ⚙ Staffelung *f*.

stag·nant □ ['stægnənt] stehend (*Gewässer*); stagnierend; stockend; *econ.* still, flau; *fig.* träge; **~·nate** [stæg'neɪt] stagnieren, stillstehen, stocken.

staid □ [steɪd] gesetzt; ruhig.

stain [steɪn] **1.** Fleck *m*; Beize *f*; *fig.* Schandfleck *m*; **2.** *v/t.* beschmutzen, beflecken; färben, *Holz* beizen, *Glas* bemalen; *v/i.* Flecken verursachen; schmutzen; *~ed glass* Buntglas *n*;

~·less □ ['steɪnlɪs] rostfrei, nichtrostend; *bsd. fig.* fleckenlos.

stair [steə] Stufe *f*; **~s** *pl.* Treppe *f*, Stiege *f*; **~·case** ['steəkeɪs], **~·way** Treppe(nhaus *n*) *f*.

stake [steɪk] **1.** Pfahl *m*, Pfosten *m*; Marterpfahl *m*; (Wett-, Spiel)Einsatz *m* (*a. fig.*); **~s** *pl.* Pferderennen: Dotierung *f*; Rennen *n*; *pull up* **~s** *bsd. Am. fig.* F s-e Zelte abbrechen; *be at* **~** *fig.* auf dem Spiel stehen; **2.** wagen, aufs Spiel setzen; **~** *off,* **~** *out* abstecken.

stale □ [steɪl] (**~·r,** **~st**) alt (*nicht frisch*); schal, abgestanden; verbraucht (*Luft*); *fig.* fad.

stalk¹ ⚘ [stɔ:k] Stengel *m*, Stiel *m*, Halm *m*.

stalk² [~] *v/i. hunt.* (sich an)pirschen; *oft* **~** *along* (einher)stolzieren; *v/t.* sich heranpirschen an (*acc.*); verfolgen, hinter *j-m* herschleichen.

stall¹ [stɔ:l] **1.** Box *f* (*im Stall*); △ *nicht* Stall; (Verkaufs)Stand *m* (Markt)Bude *f*; Chorstuhl *m*; **~s** *pl. Brt. thea.* Parkett *n*; **2.** *v/t.* Tier in Boxen unterbringen; *Motor* abwürgen; *v/i.* absterben (*Motor*).

stall² [~] ausweichen; *a.* **~** *for time* Zeit schinden; *Sport:* auf Zeit spielen.

stal·li·on *zo.* ['stæljən] (Zucht-) Hengst *m*.

stal·wart □ ['stɔ:lwət] stramm, kräftig; *bsd. pol.* treu.

stam·i·na ['stæmɪnə] Ausdauer *f*, Zähigkeit *f*; Durchhaltevermögen *n*, Kondition *f*.

stam·mer ['stæmə] **1.** stottern, stammeln; **2.** Stottern *n*.

stamp [stæmp] **1.** (Auf)Stampfen *n*; Stempel *m* (*a. fig.*); △ *nicht* Poststempel; (Brief)Marke *f*; *fig.* Gepräge *n*; *fig.* Art *f*; **2.** (auf)stampfen; aufstampfen mit; (ab)stempeln (*a. fig.*); frankieren; (auf)prägen; **~** *out* (aus)stanzen.

stam·pede [stæm'pi:d] **1.** Panik *f*, wilde, panische Flucht; (Massen-) Ansturm *m*; **2.** *v/i.* durchgehen; *v/t.* in Panik versetzen.

stanch [stɑ:ntʃ] *s.* **staunch**¹·²

stand [stænd] **1.** (*stood*) *v/i.* stehen; sich befinden; bleiben; *fig.* festbleiben; *mst* **~** *still* stillstehen, stehenbleiben; *v/t.* stellen; aushalten; (v)ertragen; sich *et.* gefallen lassen; ertragen; sich *e-r Sache* unterziehen;

Probe bestehen; *e-e Chance* haben; F spendieren; **~** *a round* F e-e Runde schmeißen; **~** *about* herumstehen; **~** *aside* beiseite treten; **~** *back* zurücktreten; **~** *by* dabeistehen, -stehen; bereitstehen; *fig.* zu *j-m* halten *od.* stehen, helfen; **~** *for* kandidieren für; bedeuten; eintreten für; F sich *et.* gefallen lassen; **~** *in* einspringen (*for s.o.* für *j-n*); **~** *in for* Film: *j-n* doubeln; **~** *off* sich entfernt halten; *fig.* Abstand halten; **~** *on* (*fig.* be)stehen auf (*dat.*); **~** *out* hervorstehen, -treten; sich abheben (*against* gegen); aus-, durchhalten; *fig.* herausragen; standhalten (*dat.*); **~** *over* liegenbleiben; (sich) vertagen (*to auf acc.*); **~** *to* stehen zu; ⚔ in Bereitschaft stehen *od.* versetzen; **~** *up* aufstehen, sich erheben; sich aufrichten (*Stacheln etc.*); **~** *up for* eintreten für; **~** *up to* mutig gegenüberstehen (*dat.*); standhalten (*dat.*); **~** *upon* = **~** *on*; **2.** Stand *m*; Stillstand *m*; (Stand)Platz *m*, Standort *m*; Stand(platz) *m* (*für Taxis*); (Verkaufs-, Messe)Stand *m*; *fig.* Standpunkt *m*; Ständer *m*; Tribüne *f*; *bsd. Am.* Zeugenstand *m*; *make a* **~** *against* sich entgegenstellen (*dat.*).

stan·dard ['stændəd] **1.** Standarte *f*, Fahne *f*, Flagge *f*; Standard *m*, Norm *f*; Maßstab *m*; Niveau *n*, Stand *m*, Grad *m*; Münzfuß *m*; (*Gold- etc.*)Währung *f*; Ständer *m*; **2.** maßgebend; normal; Normal...; **~·ize** [~aɪz] norm(ier)en, standardisieren, vereinheitlichen.

stand-by ['stændbaɪ] **1.** (*pl.* -bys) Beistand *m*, Hilfe *f*; Bereitschaft *f*; Ersatz *m*; **2.** Not..., Ersatz..., Reserve...; Bereitschafts...; **~·in** Film: Double *n*; Ersatzmann *m*, Vertreter(in).

stand·ing ['stændɪŋ] **1.** stehend (*a. fig.*); (fest)stehend; *econ.* laufend; ständig; **2.** Stellung *f*, Rang *m*; Ruf *m*, Ansehen *n*; Dauer *f*; *of long* **~** alt; **~** *or·der econ.* Dauerauftrag *m*; **~·room** Stehplatz *m*.

stand-off·ish ['stænd'ɒfɪʃ] reserviert, (sehr) ablehnend, zurückhaltend; **~·point** Standpunkt *m*; **~·still** Stillstand *m*; *be at a* **~** stocken, ruhen, an e-m toten Punkt angelangt sein; **~·up** stehend; im Stehen (eingenommen) (*Essen*); **~** *collar* Stehkragen *m*.

stank [stæŋk] *pret. von* stink 2.

stan·za ['stænzə] Stanze *f*; Strophe *f*.

sta·ple[1] ['steɪpl] Haupterzeugnis *n*; Hauptgegenstand *m*; *attr.* Haupt...

sta·ple[2] [~] **1.** Krampe *f*; Heftklammer *f*; **2.** heften; △ *nicht stapeln*; **~r** [~ə] Heftmaschine *f*.

star [sta:] **1.** Stern *m*; *thea.*, *Film*, *Sport*: Star *m*; △ *nicht zo.* Star; *The* ♀s *and Stripes pl.* das Sternenbanner (*der USA*); **2.** (-*rr*-) mit Sternen schmücken; die *od.* e-e Hauptrolle spielen; in der *od.* e-r Hauptrolle zeigen; *a film ~ring* ... ein Film mit ... in der Hauptrolle.

star·board ♣ ['sta:bəd] Steuerbord *n*.

starch [sta:tʃ] **1.** (Wäsche)Stärke *f*; *fig.* Steifheit *f*; **2.** Wäsche stärken.

stare [steə] **1.** Starren *n*; starrer *od.* erstaunter Blick; **2.** (~ *at*) anstarren; erstaunt blicken.

stark [sta:k] **1.** *adj.* □ starr; rein, bar, völlig (*Unsinn*); △ *nicht stark*; **2.** *adv.* völlig.

star·light ['sta:laɪt] Sternenlicht *n*.

star·ling *zo.* ['sta:lɪŋ] Star *m*.

star·lit ['sta:lɪt] stern(en)klar.

star|ry ['sta:rɪ] (-*ier*, -*iest*) Stern(en)...; **~·ry-eyed** *F* naiv; romantisch; **~-span·gled** [~spæŋgld] sternenbesät; *The* ♀ *Banner* das Sternenbanner (*Flagge u. Nationalhymne der USA*).

start [sta:t] **1.** Auffahren *n*, -schrecken *n*; Schreck *m*; Start *m*; Aufbruch *m*, Abreise *f*, Abfahrt *f*, ✈ Abflug *m*, Start *m*; Beginn *m*, Anfang *m*; *Sport*: Vorgabe *f*; *fig.* Vorsprung *m*; *get the ~ of s.o.* j-m zuvorkommen; **2.** *v/i.* auffahren, hochschrecken; stutzen; sich auf den Weg machen, aufbrechen; abfahren (*Zug*), auslaufen (*Schiff*), ✈ abfliegen, starten; *Sport*: starten; ⊕ anspringen (*Motor*), anlaufen (*Maschine*); anfangen, beginnen; *~ from scratch F* ganz von vorne anfangen; *v/t.* in Gang setzen *od.* bringen; ⊕ *a.* anlassen; anfangen, beginnen; *Sport*: starten (lassen); **~·er** ['sta:tə] *Sport*: Starter *m*; *mot.* Anlasser *m*, Starter *m*; **~s** *pl. F* Vorspeise *f*.

start|le ['sta:tl] erschrecken; aufschrecken; **~·ling** [~lɪŋ] erschreckend; überraschend, aufsehenerregend.

starv|a·tion [sta:'veɪʃn] Hungern *n*; Verhungern *n*, Hungertod *m*; *attr.* Hunger...; **~e** [sta:v] verhungern (lassen); *fig.* verkümmern (lassen).

state [steɪt] **1.** Zustand *m*; Stand *m*; Staat *m*; *mst* ♀ *pol.* Staat *m*; *attr.* Staats...; *in ~* feierlich aufgebahrt liegen; **2.** angeben; erklären, darlegen; feststellen; festsetzen, -legen; ♀ **De·part·ment** *Am. pol.* Außenministerium *n*; **~·ly** ['steɪtlɪ] (-*ier*, -*iest*) stattlich; würdevoll; erhaben; **~·ment** [~mənt] Angabe *f*; (Zeugen*etc.*)Aussage *f*; Darstellung *f*; Erklärung *f*, Verlautbarung *f*, Statement *n*; Aufstellung *f*, *bsd. econ.* (Geschäfts-, Monats- *etc.*)Bericht *m*; *~ of account* Kontoauszug *m*; **~·room** Staatszimmer *n*; ♣ (Einzel)Kabine *f*; **~·side**, ♀**side** *Am.* **1.** *adj.* USA-..., Heimat...; **2.** *adv.* in den Staaten; nach den *od.* in die Staaten (zurück); **~s·man** *pol.* [~smən] (*pl.* -men) Staatsmann *m*.

stat·ic ['stætɪk] (~*ally*) statisch.

sta·tion ['steɪʃn] **1.** Platz *m*, Posten *m*; Station *f*; (Polizei- *etc.*)Wache *f*; (Tank- *etc.*)Stelle *f*; (Fernseh-, Rundfunk)Sender *m*; ☵ Bahnhof *m*; ♣, ✕ Stützpunkt *m*; Stellung *f*, Rang *m*; **2.** aufstellen, postieren; ♣, ✕ stationieren; **~·a·ry** □ [~ərɪ] (still)stehend; fest(stehend); gleichbleibend; **~·er** [~ə] Schreibwarenhändler *m*; **~'s** (*shop*) Schreibwarenhandlung *f*; **~·er·y** [~rɪ] Schreibwaren *pl.*; Briefpapier *n*; **~-mas·ter** ☵ Stationsvorsteher *m*; **~ wag·on** *Am. mot.* Kombiwagen *m*.

sta·tis·tics [stə'tɪstɪks] *pl. u. sg.* Statistik *f*.

stat|u·a·ry ['stætjʊərɪ] Bildhauer (-kunst *f*) *m*; **~·ue** [~u:] Standbild *n*, Plastik *f*, Statue *f*.

stat·ure ['stætʃə] Statur *f*, Wuchs *m*.

sta·tus ['steɪtəs] Zustand *m*; (Familien)Stand *m*; Stellung *f*, Rang *m*; Status *m*.

stat·ute ['stætju:t] Statut *n*, Satzung *f*; Gesetz *n*.

staunch[1] [stɔ:ntʃ] *Blut(ung)* stillen.

staunch[2] □ [~] treu, zuverlässig.

stave [steɪv] **1.** Faßdaube *f*; Strophe *f*; **2.** (*staved od.* stove) *mst ~ in* eindrücken; ein Loch schlagen in (*acc.*); *~ off* abwehren.

stay [steɪ] **1.** ⊕ Strebe *f*, Stütze *f*; ⚖ Aufschub *m*; (vorübergehender) Aufenthalt; *~s pl.* Korsett *n*; **2.** blei-

S

stead

660

ben (*with s.o.* bei j-m); sich (vor-übergehend) aufhalten, wohnen (*at, in* in *dat.*; *with s.o.* bei j-m); △ *nicht stehen*; ~ *away* (*from*) fernbleiben (*dat.*), wegbleiben (von); ~ *up* aufbleiben, wach bleiben.

stead [sted]: *in his* ~ an s-r Stelle; **~fast** □ ['stedfəst] fest, unerschütterlich; standhaft; unverwandt (*Blick*).

stead·y ['stedɪ] **1.** *adj.* □ (-*ier*, -*iest*) fest; gleichmäßig, stetig, (be)ständig; zuverlässig; ruhig, sicher; **2.** *adv.*: *go* ~ *with s.o.* F (fest) mit j-m gehen; **3.** festigen, fest *od.* sicher *od.* ruhig machen *od.* werden; sich beruhigen; **4.** F feste Freundin, fester Freund.

steak [steɪk] Steak *n*.

steal [sti:l] (*stole, stolen*) *v/t.* stehlen (*a. fig.*); *v/i.* stehlen; ~ *away* sich davonstehlen.

stealth [stelθ]: *by* ~ heimlich, verstohlen; **~·y** □ ['stelθɪ] (-*ier*, -*iest*) heimlich, verstohlen.

steam [sti:m] **1.** Dampf *m*; Dunst *m*; *attr.* Dampf...; **2.** *v/i.* dampfen; ~ *up* (sich) beschlagen (*Glas*); *v/t.* Speisen dünsten, dämpfen; **~·er** ⚓ ['sti:mə] Dampfer *m*; **~·y** □ [~ɪ] (-*ier*, -*iest*) dampfig, dampfend; dunstig; beschlagen (*Glas*).

steel [sti:l] **1.** Stahl *m*; **2.** stählern, Stahl...; **3.** *fig.* stählen, wappnen; **~·work·er** ['sti:lwɜ:kə] Stahlarbeiter *m*; **~·works** *sg.* Stahlwerk *n*.

steep [sti:p] **1.** □ steil, jäh; F toll; **2.** einweichen; eintauchen; ziehen lassen; *be* ~*ed in s.th. fig.* von et. durchdrungen sein.

stee·ple ['sti:pl] (spitzer) Kirchturm; **~·chase** *Pferdesport:* Hindernisrennen *n*; *Leichtathletik:* Hindernislauf *m*.

steer¹ *zo.* [stɪə] junger Ochse; △ *nicht Stier*.

steer² [~] steuern, lenken; **~·age** ⚓ ['stɪərɪdʒ] Steuerung *f*; Zwischendeck *n*; **~·ing col·umn** *mot.* [~ɪŋkɒləm] Lenksäule *f*; **~·ing wheel** ⚓ Steuerrad *n*; *mot. a.* Lenkrad *n*.

stem [stem] **1.** (Baum-, Wort)Stamm *m*; Stiel *m*; Stengel *m*; **2.** (-*mm*-) stammen (*from* von); eindämmen; *Blut(ung)* stillen; ankämpfen gegen.

stench [stentʃ] Gestank *m*.

sten·cil ['stensl] Schablone *f*; *print.* Matrize *f*.

ste·nog·ra·pher [ste'nɒɡrəfə] Stenograph(in); **~·phy** [~ɪ] Stenographie *f*.

step [step] **1.** Schritt *m*, Tritt *m*; kurze Strecke; (Treppen)Stufe *f*; Trittbrett *n*; *fig.* Fußstapfe *f*; (*a pair of*) ~*s pl.* (e-e) Trittleiter; *mind the* ~! Vorsicht, Stufe!; *take* ~*s fig.* Schritte unternehmen; **2.** (-*pp*-) *v/i.* schreiten, treten; ~ *on it* F Tempo machen; ~ *out* forsch ausschreiten; *v/t.* ~ *off,* ~ *out* abschreiten; ~ *up* ankurbeln, steigern.

step- [~] *in Zssgn:* Stief...; **~·fa·ther** ['stepfɑ:ðə] Stiefvater *m*; **~·moth·er** Stiefmutter *f*.

steppe [step] Steppe *f*.

step·ping-stone *fig.* ['stepɪŋstəʊn] Sprungbrett *n*.

ster·e·o ['sterɪəʊ] (*pl.* -*os*) *Radio etc.*: Stereo *n*; Stereogerät *n*; *attr.* Stereo...

ster·ile ['steraɪl] unfruchtbar; steril; **ste·ril·i·ty** [ste'rɪlətɪ] Sterilität *f*; **~·il·ize** ['sterəlaɪz] sterilisieren.

ster·ling ['stɜ:lɪŋ] **1.** lauter, echt, gediegen; **2.** *econ.* Sterling *m* (*Währung*).

stern [stɜ:n] **1.** □ ernst; finster, streng, hart; **2.** ⚓ Heck *n*; **~·ness** ['stɜ:nnɪs] Ernst *m*; Strenge *f*.

stew [stju:] **1.** schmoren, dämpfen; **2.** Eintopf *m*, Schmorgericht *n*; *be in a* ~ in heller Aufregung sein.

stew·ard [stjʊəd] Verwalter *m*; ⚓, ✈ Steward *m*; (Fest)Ordner *m*; **~·ess** ⚓, ✈ ['stjʊədɪs] Stewardeß *f*.

stick [stɪk] **1.** Stock *m*; Stecken *m*; trockener Zweig; Stengel *m*, Stiel *m*; (*Lippen- etc.*)Stift *m*; Stab *m*; Stange *f*; (*Besen- etc.*)Stiel *m*; ~*s pl.* Kleinholz *n*; **2.** (*stuck*) *v/i.* stecken(bleiben); (fest)kleben (*to an dat.*); sich heften (*to an acc.*); ~ *at nothing* vor nichts zurückschrecken; ~ *out* ab-, hervor-, heraushalten; ~ *to* bleiben bei; *v/t.* (ab)stechen; stecken, heften (*to an acc.*); kleben; F *Messer* stoßen; F *et.-j-n* (v)ertragen, ausstehen; ~ *out* herausst(r)ecken; ~ *it out* F durchhalten; **~·er** F ['stɪkə] Aufkleber *m*; *antinuke* ~ *sl.* Anti-Kernwaffen-Aufkleber *m*; **~·ing plas·ter** [~ɪŋplɑ:stə] Heftpflaster *n*.

stick·y □ ['stɪkɪ] (-*ier*, -*iest*) klebrig; schwierig, heikel.

stiff [stɪf] **1.** □ steif, starr; hart; fest; mühsam; stark (*alkoholisches Getränk*); *be bored* ~ F zu Tode gelangweilt sein; *keep a ~ upper lip* Haltung bewahren; 2. *sl.* Leiche *f;* **~en** ['stɪfn] (sich) versteifen; steif werden, erstarren; **~necked** [~'nekt] halsstarrig.

sti·fle ['staɪfl] ersticken; *fig.* unterdrücken.

stile [staɪl] Zauntritt *m.*

sti·let·to [stɪ'letəʊ] (*pl.* -tos, -toes) Stilett *n;* **~ heel** Pfennigabsatz *m.*

still [stɪl] 1. *adj.* □ still; ruhig; unbeweglich; 2. *adv.* noch (immer), (immer) noch; 3. *cj.* und doch, dennoch; 4. stillen; beruhigen; 5. Destillierapparat *m;* **~born** ['stɪlbɔːn] totgeboren; *~ life* (*pl.* still lifes *od.* lives) *paint.* Stilleben *n;* **~ness** [~nɪs] Stille *f,* Ruhe *f.*

stilt [stɪlt] Stelze *f;* **~ed** □ ['stɪltɪd] gestelzt (*Stil*).

stim·u·lant ['stɪmjʊlənt] 1. 🗡 stimulierend; 2. 🗡 Reiz-, Aufputschmittel *n;* Genußmittel *n;* Anreiz *m;* **~late** [~leɪt] 🗡 stimulieren (*a. fig.*), anregen, aufputschen; *fig. a.* anspornen; **~la·tion** [stɪmjʊ'leɪʃn] 🗡 Reiz *m,* Reizung *f;* Anreiz *m,* Antrieb *m,* Anregung *f;* **~lus** ['stɪmjʊləs] (*pl.* -li [-liː]) 🗡 Reiz *m;* (An)Reiz *m,* Antrieb *m.*

sting [stɪŋ] 1. Stachel *m;* Stich *m,* Biß *m;* 2. (*stung*) stechen; brennen; schmerzen; *fig.* anstacheln, reizen.

stin·gi·ness ['stɪndʒɪnɪs] Geiz *m;* **~gy** □ [~ɪ] (*-ier, -iest*) geizig, knaus(e)rig; dürftig.

stink [stɪŋk] 1. Gestank *m;* 2. (*stank od. stunk, stunk*) stinken.

stint [stɪnt] 1. Einschränkung *f;* Arbeit *f;* 2. knausern mit; einschränken; *j-n* knapphalten.

stip·u·late ['stɪpjʊleɪt] *a. ~ for* ausbedingen, ausmachen, vereinbaren; **~la·tion** [stɪpjʊ'leɪʃn] Abmachung *f;* Klausel *f,* Bedingung *f.*

stir [stɜː] 1. Rühren *n;* Bewegung *f;* Aufregung *f,* Aufruhr *m;* Aufsehen *n;* 2. (*-rr-*) (sich) rühren; (sich) bewegen; erwachen; (um)rühren; *fig.* erregen; *~ up* aufhetzen; *Streit etc.* entfachen.

stir·rup ['stɪrəp] Steigbügel *m.*

stitch [stɪtʃ] 1. Stich *m;* Masche *f;* Seitenstechen *n;* 2. nähen; heften.

stock [stɒk] 1. (Baum)Strunk *m;* Pfropfunterlage *f;* Griff *m;* (Gewehr)Schaft *m;* △ *nicht Stock;* Stamm *m,* Familie *f,* Herkunft *f,*

Rohstoff *m;* (Fleisch-, Gemüse-) Brühe *f;* Vorrat *m; econ.* Waren(lager *n*) *pl.;* (Wissens)Schatz *m; a. live~* Vieh(bestand *m*) *n; econ.* Stammkapital *n; econ.* Anleihekapital *n;* ~*s pl. econ.* Effekten *pl.;* Aktien *pl.;* Staatspapiere *pl.; in* (*out of*) ~ *econ.* (nicht) vorrätig *od.* auf Lager; *take~ econ.* Inventur machen; *take~ of fig.* sich klarwerden über (*acc.*); 2. vorrätig; Serien..., Standard...; *fig.* stehend, stereotyp; 3. ausstatten, versorgen; *econ. Waren* führen, vorrätig haben.

stock·ade [stɒ'keɪd] Palisade(nzaun *m*) *f.*

stock|breed·er ['stɒkbriːdə] Viehzüchter *m;* **~brok·er** *econ.* Börsenmakler *m;* **~ex·change** *econ.* Börse *f;* **~ farm·er** Viehzüchter *m;* **~hold·er** *bsd. Am. econ.* Aktionär(in).

stock·ing ['stɒkɪŋ] Strumpf *m.*

stock|job·ber *econ.* ['stɒkdʒɒbə] Börsenhändler *m; Am.* Börsenspekulant *m;* **~mar·ket** *econ.* Börse *f;* **~still** stockstill, unbeweglich; **~tak·ing** *econ.* Bestandsaufnahme *f* (*a. fig.*), Inventur *f;* **~y** [~ɪ] (*-ier, -iest*) stämmig, untersetzt.

stok·er ['stəʊkə] Heizer *m.*

stole [stəʊl] *pret. von* steal 1; **sto·len** ['stəʊlən] *p.p. von* steal 1.

stol·id □ ['stɒlɪd] gleichmütig, stur.

stom·ach ['stʌmək] 1. Magen *m;* Leib *m,* Bauch *m;* Lust *f;* 2. *fig.* (v)ertragen; **~ache** Magenschmerzen *pl.,* Bauchweh *n;* **~up·set** Magenverstimmung *f.*

stone [stəʊn] 1. Stein *m;* (Obst)Stein *m;* (-)Kern *m;* (*pl. stone*) *Brt. Gewichtseinheit* (= 14 lb. = 6,35 kg); 2. steinern; Stein...; 3. steinigen; entsteinen, -kernen; **~blind** ['stəʊn'blaɪnd] stockblind; **~dead** mausetot; **~deaf** stocktaub; **~ma·son** Steinmetz *m;* **~ware** [~weə] Steinzeug *n.*

ston·y □ ['stəʊnɪ] (*-ier, -iest*) steinig; *fig.* steinern, kalt.

stood [stʊd] *pret. u. p.p. von* stand 1.

stool [stuːl] Hocker *m,* Schemel *m;* △ *nicht Stuhl;* △ Stuhl(gang) *m;* **~pigeon** ['stuːlpɪdʒɪn] Lockvogel *m;* Spitzel *m.*

stoop [stuːp] 1. *v/i.* sich bücken; gebeugt gehen; *fig.* sich erniedrigen *od.* herablassen; *v/t.* neigen, beugen; 2. gebeugte Haltung.

stop [stɒp] 1. (-pp-) v/t. aufhören (mit); stoppen; anhalten; aufhalten; hindern; *Zahlungen, Tätigkeit etc.* einstellen; *Zahn* plombieren; *Blut* stillen; *a.* ~ **up** ver-, zustopfen; v/i. (an)halten, stehenbleiben, stoppen; aufhören; bleiben; ~ **dead** plötzlich stehenbleiben *od.* aufhören; ~ **off** F kurz haltmachen; ~ **over** kurz haltmachen; *Zwischenstation machen*; ~ **short** plötzlich anhalten; 2. Halt *m*; Stillstand *m*; Ende *n*; Pause *f*; 🚌 *etc.* Aufenthalt *m*; 🚌 Station *f*; (Bus-) Haltestelle *f*; ⚓ Anlegestelle *f*; *phot.* Blende *f*; *mst full* ~ *gr.* Punkt *m*; ~**gap** ['stɒpgæp] Notbehelf *m*; ~**light** *mot.* Brems-, Stopplicht *n*; ~**o·ver** *bsd. Am.* Zwischenstation *f*; ✈ Zwischenlandung *f*; ~**page** [~ɪdʒ] Unterbrechung *f*; Stopp *m*; (Verkehrs)Stockung *f*, Stau *m*; Verstopfung *f*; (Gehalts-, Lohn)Abzug *m*; Sperrung *f* (*e-s Schecks*); (Arbeits-, Zahlungs- *etc.*)Einstellung *f*; ~**per** [~ə] Stöpsel *m*, Pfropfen *m*; ~**ping** ⚕ [~ɪŋ] Plombe *f*; ~**sign** *mot.* Stopp-schild *n*; ~**watch** Stoppuhr *f*.

stor·age ['stɔːrɪdʒ] Lagerung *f*, Speicherung *f*; *Computer*: Speicher *m*; Lagergeld *n*; *attr.* Speicher... (*a. Computer*).

store [stɔː] 1. Vorrat *m*; Lagerhaus *n*; *Brt.* Kauf-, Warenhaus *n*; *bsd. Am.* Laden *m*, Geschäft *n*; *fig.* Fülle *f*, Reichtum *m*; △ *nicht* Store; *in* ~ vorrätig, auf Lager; 2. versorgen; *a.* ~ **up**, ~ **away** (auf)speichern, (ein)lagern; ⚡, *Computer*: speichern; ~**house** ['stɔːhaus] Lagerhaus *n*; *fig.* Fundgrube *f*; ~**keep·er** Lagerverwalter *m*; *bsd. Am.* Ladenbesitzer (-in).

sto·rey, *bsd. Am.* -**ry** ['stɔːrɪ] Stock (-werk *n*) *m*.

-**sto·reyed**, *bsd. Am.* -**sto·ried** ['stɔːrɪd] mit ... Stockwerken, ...stöckig.

stork *zo.* [stɔːk] Storch *m*.

storm [stɔːm] 1. Sturm *m*; Unwetter *n*; Gewitter *n*; 2. stürmen; toben; ~**y** □ ['stɔːmɪ] (-*ier*, -*iest*) stürmisch.

sto·ry¹ ['stɔːrɪ] Geschichte *f*; Erzählung *f*; *thea. etc.* Handlung *f*; F Lüge *f*, Märchen *n*; *short* ~ Kurzgeschichte *f*; Erzählung *f*.

sto·ry² *bsd. Am.* [~] = storey.

stout □ [staut] stark, kräftig; derb; dick; tapfer.

stove¹ [stəuv] Ofen *m*; Herd *m*.

stove² [~] *pret. u. p.p. von* stave 2.

stow [stəu] (ver)stauen, packen; ~ **away** wegräumen; ~**a·way** ⚓, ✈ ['stəuəweɪ] blinder Passagier.

strad·dle ['strædl] die Beine spreizen; rittlings sitzen auf (*dat.*).

strag·gle ['strægl] verstreut liegen *od.* stehen; herumstreifen; (hinterher-) bummeln; ⚘ *etc.* wuchern; ~**gly** [~ɪ] (-*ier*, -*iest*) verstreut (liegend); ⚘ *etc.* wuchernd; unordentlich (*Haar*).

straight [streɪt] 1. *adj.* □ gerade; glatt (*Haar*); pur (*Whisky etc.*); aufrichtig, offen, ehrlich; *put* ~ in Ordnung bringen; 2. *adv.* gerade(aus); gerade(wegs); direkt; klar (*denken*); ehrlich, anständig; *a.* ~ **out** offen, rundheraus; ~ **away** sofort; ~**en** ['streɪtn] v/t. gerademachen, (ge-rade)richten; ~ **out** in Ordnung bringen; v/i. gerade werden; ~ **up** sich aufrichten; ~**for·ward** □ [~'fɔː-wəd] ehrlich, redlich, offen; einfach.

strain [streɪn] 1. *biol.* Rasse *f*, Art *f*; (Erb)Anlage *f*, Hang *m*, Zug *m*; ⊕ Spannung *f*; (Über)Anstrengung *f*; Anspannung *f*; Belastung *f*; Druck *m*; ⚕ Zerrung *f*; *fig.* Ton(art *f*) *m*; *mst* ~**s** *pl.* ♪ Weise *f*, Melodie *f*; 2. v/t. (an)spannen; (über)anstrengen; ⚕ sich *et.* zerren *od.* verstauchen; *fig et.* strapazieren; überfordern; durch-seihen, filtern; v/i. sich spannen; sich anstrengen; sich abmühen (*after* um); zerren (*at* an *dat.*); ~**ed** [~d] gezwungen, unnatürlich; ~**er** ['streɪnə] Sieb *n*, Filter *m*.

strait [streɪt] (*in Eigennamen* ⊇*s pl.*) Meerenge *f*, Straße *f*; ~**s** *pl.* Not (-lage) *f*; ~**ened** ['streɪtnd]: *in* ~ **circumstances** in beschränkten Verhältnissen; ~**jack·et** Zwangsjacke *f*.

strand [strænd] 1. Strang *m*; (Haar-) Strähne *f*; *poet.* Gestade *n*, Ufer *n*; △ *nicht* Strand; 2. auf den Strand setzen; *fig.* stranden (lassen).

strange □ [streɪndʒ] (~*r*, ~*st*) fremd; seltsam, sonderbar; **strang·er** ['streɪndʒə] Fremde(r *m*) *f*.

stran·gle ['stræŋgl] erwürgen.

strap [stræp] 1. Riemen *m*; Gurt *m*; Band *n*; Träger *m* (*Kleid*); 2. (-pp-) festschnallen; mit e-m Riemen schlagen.

strat·a·gem ['strætədʒəm] (Kriegs-) List *f*.

stra·te·gic [strə'tiːdʒɪk] (~*ally*) strategisch; **strat·e·gy** ['strætɪdʒɪ] Strategie *f.*

stra·tum *geol.* ['strɑːtəm] (*pl.* -ta [~tə]) Schicht *f* (*a. fig.*), Lage *f.*

straw [strɔː] 1. Stroh(halm *m*) *n*; 2. Stroh...; **~·ber·ry** ♣ ['strɔːbərɪ] Erdbeere *f.*

stray [streɪ] 1. (herum)streunen; (herum)streifen; sich verirren; 2. verirrt, streunend; vereinzelt; 3. verirrtes *od.* streunendes Tier.

streak [striːk] 1. Strich *m*, Streifen *m*; *fig.* Spur *f*; *fig.* (*Glücks- etc.*)Strähne *f*; **~ of lightning** Blitzstrahl *m*; 2. streifen; rasen, flitzen.

stream [striːm] 1. Bach *m*, Flüßchen *n*; Strom *m*, Strömung *f*; 2. strömen; tränen; triefen; flattern, wehen; **~·er** ['striːmə] Wimpel *m*; (flatterndes) Band.

street [striːt] Straße *f*; *attr.* Straßen...; *in* (*Am. on*) *the* ~ auf der Straße; *up Am.* ['striːtkɑː] Straßenbahn(wagen *m*) *f.*

strength [streŋθ] Stärke *f*, Kraft *f*; *on the* ~ *of* auf ... hin, auf Grund (*gen.*); **~·en** ['streŋθən] *v/t.* (ver)stärken; *fig.* stärken; *v/i.* stark werden.

stren·u·ous □ ['strenjʊəs] rührig, emsig; eifrig; anstrengend.

stress [stres] 1. Ton *m*, Akzent *m*, Betonung *f*; *fig.* Nachdruck *m*; *fig.* Belastung *f*, Anspannung *f*, Druck *m*; Stress *m*; 2. betonen.

stretch [stretʃ] 1. *v/t.* strecken; (aus)dehnen; (an)spannen; recken; *fig.* übertreiben; *fig.* es nicht allzu genau nehmen mit; ~ *out* ausstrecken; *v/i.* sich erstrecken; sich dehnen (lassen); 2. Strecken *n*; Dehnen *n*; Anspannung *f*; Übertreibung *f*; Zeit (-raum *m*, -spanne) *f*; Strecke *f*, Fläche *f*; **~·er** ['stretʃə] (Kranken-) Trage *f.*

strew [struː] (*strewed, strewn od. strewed*) (be-, ver)streuen; **~n** [~n] *p.p. von strew.*

strick·en *adj.* ['strɪkən] heimgesucht, schwer betroffen; ergriffen.

strict [strɪkt] streng; genau; **~·ly speaking** genaugenommen; **~·ness** ['strɪktnɪs] Genauigkeit *f*; Strenge *f.*

strid·den ['strɪdn] *p.p. von stride 1.*

stride [straɪd] 1. (*strode, stridden*) (*a.* ~ *out* aus)schreiten; überschreiten; 2. großer Schritt.

strife [straɪf] Streit *m*, Hader *m.*

strike [straɪk] 1. *econ.* Streik *m*; (Öl-, Erz)Fund *m*; ⚔ (Luft)Angriff *m*; ⚔ Atomschlag *m*; *be on* ~ streiken; *go on* ~ in (den) Streik treten; *a lucky* ~ ein Glückstreffer; 2. (*struck*) *v/t.* schlagen; treffen; stoßen; schlagen *od.* stoßen gegen *od.* auf (*acc.*); stoßen *od.* treffen auf (*acc.*); *Flagge, Segel* streichen; ♪ *Ton* anschlagen; *Streichholz* anzünden; *ein Feuer machen*; *Zelt* abbrechen; einschlagen in (*acc.*) (*Blitz*); *Wurzel* schlagen; *j-n* beeindrucken; *j-m* auf- *od.* einfallen; ~ *off, ~ out* (aus)streichen; ~ *up* ♪ anstimmen; *Freundschaft* schließen; *v/i.* schlagen; ⚓ auflaufen (*on* auf *acc.*); *econ.* streiken; ~ *home fig.* ins Schwarze treffen; **strik·er** *econ.* ['straɪkə] Streikende(r *m*) *f*; **strik·ing** □ [~ɪŋ] Schlag...; auffallend; eindrucksvoll; treffend.

string [strɪŋ] 1. Schnur *f*; Bindfaden *m*; Band *n*; Faden *m*, Draht *m*; (Bogen)Sehne *f*; ♣ Faser *f*; Reihe *f*, Kette *f*; ♪ Saite *f*; ~s *pl.* ♪ Streichinstrumente *pl.*, die Streicher *pl.*; *pull the* ~s *fig.* der Drahtzieher sein; *no* ~s *attached* ohne Bedingungen; 2. (*strung*) spannen; *Perlen etc.* aufreihen; ♪ besaiten, bespannen; (ver-, zu)schnüren; *Bohnen* abziehen; *be strung up* angespannt *od.* erregt sein; **~ band** ♪ ['strɪŋbænd] Streichorchester *n.*

strin·gent □ ['strɪndʒənt] streng, scharf; zwingend; knapp.

string·y ['strɪŋɪ] (*-ier, -iest*) faserig, sehnig; zäh.

strip [strɪp] 1. (*-pp-*) entkleiden (*a. fig.*); *a.* ~ *off* abziehen, abstreifen, (ab)schälen; (sich) ausziehen; *a.* ~ *down* ⊕ zerlegen, auseinandernehmen; *fig.* entblößen; berauben; 2. Streifen *m.*

stripe [straɪp] Streifen *m*; ⚔ Tresse *f.*

strip·ling ['strɪplɪŋ] Bürschchen *n.*

strive [straɪv] (*strove, striven*) streben; sich bemühen; ringen (*for* um).

striv·en ['strɪvn] *p.p. von strive.*

strode [strəʊd] *pret. von stride 1.*

stroke [strəʊk] 1. Schlag *m*; Streich *m*, Stoß *m*; Strich *m*; ⚕ Schlag(anfall) *m*; ~ *of* (*good*) *luck* Glücksfall *m*; 2. streichen über; streicheln.

stroll [strəʊl] 1. schlendern, (herum)bummeln; herumziehen; 2. Bummel *m*, Spaziergang *m*; **~·er** ['strəʊlə] Bummler(in), Spaziergänger(in); *Am.* (Falt)Sportwagen *m.*

S

strong ☐ [strɒŋ] stark; kräftig; energisch; überzeugt; fest; stark, schwer (*Getränk etc.*); **~-box** [ˈstrɒŋbɒks] Geld-, Stahlkassette *f*; **~-hold** Festung *f*; *fig.* Hochburg *f*; **~-mind·ed** willensstark; **~-room** Stahlkammer *f*, Tresor(raum) *m*.

strove [strəʊv] *pret. von* strive.

struck [strʌk] *pret. u. p.p. von* strike 2.

struc·ture [ˈstrʌktʃə] Bau(werk *n*) *m*; Struktur *f*, Gefüge *n*; Gebilde *n*.

strug·gle [ˈstrʌgl] **1.** sich (ab)mühen; kämpfen, ringen; sich winden, zappeln, sich sträuben; **2.** Kampf *m*, Ringen *n*; Anstrengung *f*.

strum [strʌm] (*-mm-*) klimpern (auf).

strung [strʌŋ] *pret. u. p.p. von* string 2.

strut [strʌt] **1.** (*-tt-*) *v/i.* stolzieren; *v/t.* ⊕ abstützen; **2.** Stolzieren *n*; ⊕ Strebe(balken *m*) *f*, Stütze *f*.

stub [stʌb] **1.** (Baum)Stumpf *m*; Stummel *m*; Kontrollabschnitt *m*; **2.** (*-bb-*) (aus)roden; sich *die Zehe* anstoßen; **~ out** *Zigarette etc.* ausdrücken.

stub·ble [ˈstʌbl] Stoppel(n *pl.*) *f*.

stub·born ☐ [ˈstʌbən] eigensinnig; widerspenstig; stur; hartnäckig.

stuck [stʌk] *pret. u. p.p. von* stick 2; **~-up** F [ˈstʌkˈʌp] hochnäsig.

stud¹ [stʌd] **1.** Beschlagnagel *m*; Ziernagel *m*; Knauf *m*, Manschetten-, Kragenknopf *m*; **2.** (*-dd-*) mit Nägeln *etc.* beschlagen; übersäen.

stud² [~] Gestüt *n*; △ *nicht* Stute; *a.* **~-horse** (Zucht)Hengst *m*; **~-book** Gestütbuch *n*; **~-farm** Gestüt *n*; **~-mare** Zuchtstute *f*.

stu·dent [ˈstjuːdnt] Student(in); *Am.* Schüler(in).

stud·ied ☐ [ˈstʌdɪd] einstudiert; gesucht, gewollt; wohlüberlegt.

stu·di·o [ˈstjuːdɪəʊ] (*pl. -os*) Atelier *n*, Studio *n*; (Fernseh-, Rundfunk-) Studio *n*, Aufnahme-, Senderaum *m*.

stu·di·ous ☐ [ˈstjuːdjəs] fleißig; eifrig bemüht; sorgfältig, peinlich.

stud·y [ˈstʌdɪ] **1.** Studium *n*; Studier-, Arbeitszimmer *n*; *paint. etc.* Studie *f*; *studies pl.* Studium *n*, Studien *pl.*; *in a brown ~* in Gedanken versunken, geistesabwesend; **2.** (ein)studieren; lernen; studieren, erforschen; sich bemühen um.

stuff [stʌf] **1.** Stoff *m*; Zeug *n*; **2.** *v/t.* (voll-, aus)stopfen; füllen; △ *nicht* stopfen (*ausbessern*); *v/i.* sich vollstopfen; **~-ing** [ˈstʌfɪŋ] Füllung *f*; **~-y** ☐ [~ɪ] (*-ier, -iest*) dumpf, muffig, stickig; langweilig, fad; F spießig; prüde.

stum·ble [ˈstʌmbl] **1.** Stolpern *n*, Straucheln *n*; Fehltritt *m*; **2.** stolpern, straucheln; **~ across, ~ on, ~ upon** zufällig stoßen auf (*acc.*).

stump [stʌmp] **1.** Stumpf *m*, Stummel *m*; **2.** *v/t.* F verblüffen; *v/i.* stampfen, stapfen; **~-y** ☐ [ˈstʌmpɪ] (*-ier, -iest*) gedrungen; plump.

stun [stʌn] (*-nn-*) betäuben (*a. fig.*).

stung [stʌŋ] *pret. u. p.p. von* sting 2.

stunk [stʌŋk] *pret. u. p.p. von* stink 2.

stun·ning ☐ F [ˈstʌnɪŋ] toll, phantastisch.

stunt¹ [stʌnt] Kunststück *n*; (Reklame)Trick *m*; Sensation *f*; **~ man** *Film:* Stuntman *m*, Double *n*.

stunt² [~] (*im Wachstum etc.*) hemmen; **~-ed** [ˈstʌntɪd] verkümmert.

stu·pe·fy [ˈstjuːpɪfaɪ] betäuben; *fig.* verblüffen.

stu·pen·dous ☐ [stjuːˈpendəs] verblüffend, erstaunlich.

stu·pid ☐ [ˈstjuːpɪd] dumm, einfältig; stumpfsinnig, blöd; **~-i·ty** [stjuːˈpɪdətɪ] Dummheit *f*; Stumpfsinn *m*.

stu·por [ˈstjuːpə] Erstarrung *f*, Betäubung *f*.

stur·dy ☐ [ˈstɜːdɪ] (*-ier, -iest*) robust, kräftig; *fig.* entschlossen.

stut·ter [ˈstʌtə] **1.** stottern; stammeln; **2.** Stottern *n*; Stammeln *n*.

sty¹ [staɪ] Schweinestall *m*.

sty², stye 🖋 [~] Gerstenkorn *n*.

style [staɪl] **1.** Stil *m*; Mode *f*; (Mach)Art *f*; Titel *m*, Anrede *f*; **2.** nennen; entwerfen, gestalten.

styl·ish ☐ [ˈstaɪlɪʃ] stilvoll; elegant; **~-ish·ness** [~nɪs] Eleganz *f*; **~-ist** [~ɪst] Stilist(in).

suave ☐ [swɑːv] verbindlich; mild.

sub- [sʌb] Unter..., unter...; Neben..., untergeordnet; Hilfs...; fast ...

sub·di·vi·sion [ˈsʌbdɪvɪʒn] Unterteilung *f*; Unterabteilung *f*.

sub·due [səbˈdjuː] unterwerfen; bezwingen; bändigen; dämpfen.

sub·ject 1. [ˈsʌbdʒɪkt] unterworfen; untergeben; abhängig; untertan; ausgesetzt (*to dat.*); *be ~ to* neigen zu; ∼ *to* vorbehaltlich (*gen.*); **2.** [∼] Untertan(in); Staatsbürger(in), -angehörige(r *m*) *f*; *gr.* Subjekt *n*, Satzgegenstand *m*; Thema *n*, Gegenstand *m*; (Lehr-, Schul-, Studien-) Fach *n*; **3.** [sʌbˈdʒekt] unterwerfen; *fig.* unterwerfen, -ziehen, aussetzen (*to dat.*); ∼**·jec·tion** [∼kʃn] Unterwerfung *f*; Abhängigkeit *f*.

sub·ju·gate [ˈsʌbdʒʊɡeɪt] unterjochen, -werfen.

sub·junc·tive *gr.* [səbˈdʒʌŋktɪv] *a.* ∼ *mood* Konjunktiv *m*.

sub·lease [ˈsʌbˈliːs], ∼**·let** (*-tt-; -let*) untervermieten.

sub·lime □ [səˈblaɪm] erhaben.

sub·ma·chine gun [ˈsʌbməˈʃiːn ɡʌn] Maschinenpistole *f*.

sub·ma·rine [ˈsʌbməriːn] **1.** unterseeisch, Untersee...; **2.** ⚓, ✕ Unterseeboot *n*.

sub·merge [səbˈmɜːdʒ] (unter)tauchen; überschwemmen.

sub·mis·sion [səbˈmɪʃn] Unterwerfung *f*; Unterbreitung *f*; ∼**·sive** □ [∼sɪv] unterwürfig; ergeben.

sub·mit [səbˈmɪt] (*-tt-*) (sich) unterwerfen *od.* -ziehen; unterbreiten, vorlegen; sich fügen *od.* ergeben (*to dat. od.* in *acc.*).

sub·or·di·nate 1. □ [səˈbɔːdɪnət] untergeordnet; nebensächlich; ∼ *clause gr.* Nebensatz *m*; **2.** [∼] Untergebene(r *m*) *f*; **3.** [∼eɪt] unterordnen.

sub·scribe [səbˈskraɪb] *v/t.* Geld stiften, spenden (*to* für); *Summe* zeichnen; mit *s-m* Namen unterzeichnen, unterschreiben mit; *v/i.* ∼ *to Zeitung etc.* abonnieren (*teleph.* [∼ə] (Unter)Zeichner(in); Spender(in); Abonnent(in); *teleph.* Teilnehmer(in), Anschluß *m*.

sub·scrip·tion [səbˈskrɪpʃn] Vorbestellung *f*, Subskription *f*; (Mitglieds)Beitrag *m*; Spende *f*.

sub·se·quent [ˈsʌbsɪkwənt] (nach-) folgend; später; ∼**·ly** nachher; später.

sub·ser·vi·ent □ [səbˈsɜːvjənt] dienlich; unterwürfig.

sub·side [səbˈsaɪd] sinken; sich senken; sich setzen; sich legen (*Wind etc.*); ∼ *into* verfallen in (*acc.*); ∼**·sid·i·ary 1.** □ [∼ˈsɪdjərɪ] Hilfs...; Neben..., untergeordnet; **2.** *econ.* Tochter(gesellschaft) *f*; ∼**·si·dize** [ˈsʌbsɪdaɪz] subventionieren; ∼**·si·dy** [∼ɪ] Beihilfe *f*; Subvention *f*.

sub·sist [səbˈsɪst] leben, sich ernähren (*on* von); ∼**·sis·tence** [∼əns] Dasein *n*, Existenz *f*; (Lebens)Unterhalt *m*.

sub·stance [ˈsʌbstəns] Substanz *f*; *das* Wesentliche, Kern *m*, Gehalt *m*; Vermögen *n*.

sub·stand·ard [ˈsʌbˈstændəd] unter der Norm; ∼ *film* Schmalfilm *m*.

sub·stan·tial □ [səbˈstænʃl] wesentlich; wirklich (vorhanden); beträchtlich; reichlich; kräftig; stark; solid; vermögend; namhaft (*Summe*).

sub·stan·ti·ate [səbˈstænʃɪeɪt] beweisen, begründen.

sub·stan·tive *gr.* [ˈsʌbstəntɪv] Substantiv *n*, Hauptwort *n*.

sub·sti·tute [ˈsʌbstɪtjuːt] **1.** an die Stelle setzen *od.* treten (*for* von); ∼ *s.th. for s.th.* et. durch et. ersetzen, et. gegen et. austauschen *od.* -wechseln; **2.** Stellvertreter(in), Vertretung *f*; Ersatz *m*; ∼**·tu·tion** [sʌbstɪˈtjuːʃn] Stellvertretung *f*; Ersatz *m*; *Sport:* Auswechslung *f*.

sub·ter·fuge [ˈsʌbtəfjuːdʒ] Vorwand *m*, Ausflucht *f*; List *f*.

sub·ter·ra·ne·an □ [ˈsʌbtəˈreɪnjən] unterirdisch.

sub·ti·tle [ˈsʌbtaɪtl] Untertitel *m*.

sub·tle □ [ˈsʌtl] (∼*r*, ∼*st*) fein(sinnig); subtil; scharf(sinnig).

sub·tract Ⓐ [səbˈtrækt] abziehen, subtrahieren.

sub·trop·i·cal [ˈsʌbˈtrɒpɪkl] subtropisch.

sub·urb [ˈsʌbɜːb] Vorstadt *f*, -ort *m*; ∼**·ur·ban** [səˈbɜːbən] vorstädtisch.

sub·ven·tion [səbˈvenʃn] Subvention *f*.

sub·ver·sion [səbˈvɜːʃn] Umsturz *m*; ∼**·sive** □ [∼sɪv] umstürzlerisch, subversiv; ∼**t** [∼t] stürzen.

sub·way [ˈsʌbweɪ] (Straßen-, Fußgänger)Unterführung *f*; *Am.* Untergrundbahn *f*, U-Bahn *f*.

suc·ceed [səkˈsiːd] *v/i.* Erfolg haben; glücken, gelingen; ∼ *to* folgen (*dat.*) *od.* auf (*acc.*), nachfolgen (*dat.*); *v/t.* (nach)folgen (*dat.*), j-s Nachfolger werden.

suc·cess [səkˈses] Erfolg *m*; ∼**·ful** □ [∼fl] erfolgreich.

suc·ces·sion [səkˈseʃn] (Nach-, Erb-, Reihen)Folge *f*; *in* ∼ nacheinander; ∼**·sive** □ [∼sɪv] aufeinanderfolgend; ∼**·sor** [∼ə] Nachfolger(in).

S

suc·co(u)r [ˈsʌkə] 1. Hilfe f; 2. helfen.

suc·cu·lent □ [ˈsʌkjʊlənt] saftig.

suc·cumb [səˈkʌm] unter-, erliegen.

such [sʌtʃ] solche(r, -s); derartige(r, -s); so; ~ *a man* ein solcher Mann; ~ *as* diejenigen, welche; wie.

suck [sʌk] 1. saugen (an *dat.*); aussaugen; lutschen (an *dat.*); 2. Saugen n; **~er** [ˈsʌkə] Saugorgan n; ♀ Wurzelschößling m; F Trottel m, Simpel m; **~le** [~l] säugen, stillen; **~ling** [~lɪŋ] Säugling m.

suc·tion [ˈsʌkʃn] (An)Saugen n; Sog m; *attr.* (An)Saug...

sud·den □ [ˈsʌdn] plötzlich; (*all*) *of a* ~ (ganz) plötzlich.

suds [sʌdz] *pl.* Seifenlauge f; Seifenschaum m; **~y** [ˈsʌdzɪ] (-ier, -iest) schaumig.

sue [sjuː] *v/t.* verklagen (*for auf acc.*, *wegen*); *a.* ~ *out* erwirken; *v/i.* nachsuchen (*for um*); klagen.

suede, suède [sweɪd] Wildleder n.

su·et [ˈsjʊɪt] Nierenfett n, Talg m.

suf·fer [ˈsʌfə] *v/i.* leiden (*from an*, *unter dat.*); büßen; *v/t.* erleiden, erdulden; (zu)lassen; **~ance** [~rəns] Duldung f; **~er** [~ə] Leidende(r m) f; Dulder(in); **~ing** [~ɪŋ] Leiden n.

suf·fice [səˈfaɪs] genügen; ~ *it to say* es genügt wohl, wenn ich sage.

suf·fi·cien·cy [səˈfɪʃnsɪ] genügende Menge; Auskommen n; **~t** [~t] genügend, genug, ausreichend; *be* ~ genügen, (aus)reichen.

suf·fix [ˈsʌfɪks] Suffix n, Nachsilbe f.

suf·fo·cate [ˈsʌfəkeɪt] ersticken.

suf·frage [ˈsʌfrɪdʒ] (Wahl)Stimme f; Wahl-, Stimmrecht n.

suf·fuse [səˈfjuːz] übergießen; überziehen.

sug·ar [ˈʃʊgə] 1. Zucker m; 2. zuckern; **~ba·sin**, *bsd. Am.* ~ bowl Zuckerdose f; **~cane** ♀ Zuckerrohr n; **~coat** überzuckern; *fig.* versüßen; **~y** [~rɪ] zuckerig; *fig.* zuckersüß.

sug|gest [səˈdʒest, *Am. a.* səgˈdʒest] vorschlagen, anregen; nahelegen; hinweisen auf (*acc.*); *Gedanken* eingeben; andeuten; denken lassen an (*acc.*); **~·ges·tion** [~tʃən] Anregung f, Vorschlag m; *psych.* Suggestion f; Eingebung f; Andeutung f; **~·ges·tive** □ [~tɪv] anregend; vielsagend; zweideutig; *be* ~ *of s.th.* auf et. hindeuten; an et. denken lassen; den Eindruck von et. erwecken.

su·i·cide [ˈsjʊɪsaɪd] 1. Selbstmord m; Selbstmörder(in); *commit* ~ Selbstmord begehen; 2. *Am.* Selbstmord begehen.

suit [sjuːt] 1. (Herren)Anzug m; (Damen)Kostüm n; Anliegen n; Werben n (*um e-e Frau*); *Karten:* Farbe f; ᵗᵗ Prozeß m; *follow* ~ *fig.* dem Beispiel folgen, dasselbe tun; 2. *v/t.* j-m passen, zusagen, bekommen; j-n kleiden, j-m stehen, passen zu; ~ *oneself* tun, was e-m beliebt; ~ *yourself* mach, was du willst; ~ *s.th. to* et. anpassen (*dat.*) *od.* an (*acc.*); *be* ~*ed* geeignet sein (*for, to* für, zu); *v/i.* passen; **sui·ta·ble** □ [ˈsjuːtəbl] passend, geeignet (*for, to* für, zu); **~case** (Hand)Koffer m.

suite [swiːt] Gefolge n; ♪ Suite f; Zimmerflucht f, Suite f; (Möbel-, Sitz)Garnitur f, (Zimmer)Einrichtung f.

sui·tor [ˈsjuːtə] Freier m; ᵗᵗ Kläger(in).

sul·fur, *etc. Am.* [ˈsʌlfə] *s.* sulphur, *etc.*

sulk [sʌlk] schmollen, eingeschnappt sein; **~·i·ness** [ˈsʌlkɪnɪs], **~s** *pl.* Schmollen n; **~·y** [~ɪ] 1. □ (-ier, -iest) verdrießlich; schmollend; 2. *Sport:* Sulky n, Traberwagen m.

sul·len □ [ˈsʌlən] verdrossen, mürrisch; düster, trübe.

sul·ly *mst fig.* [ˈsʌlɪ] beflecken.

sul|phur ॳ [ˈsʌlfə] Schwefel m; **~phu·ric** ॳ [sʌlˈfjʊərɪk] Schwefel...

sul·tri·ness [ˈsʌltrɪnɪs] Schwüle f.

sul·try □ [ˈsʌltrɪ] (-ier, -iest) schwül; *fig.* heftig, hitzig.

sum [sʌm] 1. Summe f; Betrag m; Rechenaufgabe f; *fig.* Inbegriff m; *do* ~*s* rechnen; 2. (*-mm-*) *a.* ~ *up* zusammenzählen, addieren; j-n kurz einschätzen; *Situation* erfassen; zusammenfassen.

sum|ma·rize [ˈsʌmə] zusammenfassen; **~·ma·ry** [~ɪ] 1. □ kurz (zusammengefaßt); ᵗᵗ Schnell...; 2. (kurze) Inhaltsangabe, Zusammenfassung f.

sum·mer [ˈsʌmə] Sommer m; ~ *school* Ferienkurs m; **~·ly** [~lɪ], **~·y** [~rɪ] sommerlich.

sum·mit [ˈsʌmɪt] Gipfel m (*a. fig.*).

sum·mon [ˈsʌmən] auffordern; (einbe)rufen; ᵗᵗ vorladen; ~ *up Mut etc.* zusammennehmen, aufbieten; **~s** Aufforderung *f*; ⁱ⁄₂ Vorladung *f*.

sump·tu·ous □ ['sʌmptjʊəs] kostspielig; üppig, aufwendig.

sun [sʌn] **1.** Sonne *f*; *attr.* Sonnen...; **2.** (*-nn-*) der Sonne aussetzen; **~** (*o.s.*) sich sonnen; **~bath** ['sʌnbɑːθ] Sonnenbad *n*; **~beam** Sonnenstrahl *m*; **~burn** Sonnenbräune *f*; Sonnenbrand *m*.

sun·dae ['sʌndeɪ] Eisbecher *m* mit Früchten.

Sun·day ['sʌndɪ] Sonntag *m*; *on ~* (am) Sonntag; *on ~s* sonntags.

sun·di·al ['sʌndaɪəl] Sonnenuhr *f*; **~down** = *sunset*.

sun·dries ['sʌndrɪz] *pl.* Diverse(s) *n*, Verschiedene(s) *n*; **~dry** [‿ɪ] verschiedene.

sung [sʌŋ] *p.p. von sing*.

sun·glass·es ['sʌŋglɑːsɪz] *pl.* (*a pair of ~ e-e*) Sonnenbrille *f*.

sunk [sʌŋk] *pret. u. p.p. von sink* 1.

sunk·en *adj.* ['sʌŋkən] versunken; tiefliegend; *fig.* eingefallen.

sun·ny □ ['sʌnɪ] (*-ier, -iest*) sonnig; **~rise** Sonnenaufgang *m*; **~set** Sonnenuntergang *m*; **~shade** Sonnenschirm *m*; Markise *f*; **~shine** Sonnenschein *m*; **~stroke** Sonnenstich *m*; **~tan** (Sonnen)Bräune *f*.

su·per ⨍ ['suːpə] super, toll, prima, Spitze, Klasse.

su·per· ['sjuːpə] Über..., über...; Ober..., ober...; Super..., Groß...; **~a·bun·dant** □ [‿rə'bʌndənt] überreichlich; überschwenglich; **~an·nu·ate** [‿r'ænjʊeɪt] pensionieren; **~d** pensioniert; veraltet.

su·perb □ [sjuː'pɜːb] prächtig, herrlich, großartig; ausgezeichnet.

su·per·charg·er *mot.* ['sjuːpətʃɑːdʒə] Kompressor *m*; **~cil·i·ous** □ [‿'sɪliəs] hochmütig; **~fi·cial** □ [‿'fɪʃl] oberflächlich; **~flu·i·ty** [‿'fluːətɪ] Überfluß *m*; **~flu·ous** □ [sjuː'pɜːfluəs] überflüssig; überreichlich; **~heat** ⨍ ['sjuːpə'hiːt] überhitzen; **~hu·man** [‿'hjuːmən] übermenschlich; **~im·pose** [‿rɪm'pəʊz] darauf-, darüberlegen; überlagern; **~in·tend** [‿rɪn'tend] die (Ober)Aufsicht haben über (*acc.*), überwachen; leiten; **~in·tend·ent** [‿ənt] **1.** Leiter *m*, Direktor *m*; (Ober)Aufseher *m*, Inspektor *m*; *Brt.* Kommissar (*-in*); *Am.* Polizeichef *m*; *Am.*

Hausverwalter *m*; **2.** aufsichtführend.

su·pe·ri·or [sjuː'pɪərɪə] **1.** □ höhere(r, -s), höherstehend, vorgesetzt; besser, hochwertiger; überlegen (*to dat.*); hervorragend; **2.** Höherstehende(r *m*) *f*, *bsd.* Vorgesetzte(r *m*) *f*; *mst* Father **2** *eccl.* Superior *m*; *mst* Lady **2**, Mother **2** *eccl.* Oberin *f*; **~i·ty** [sjuːpɪərɪ'ɒrətɪ] Überlegenheit *f*.

su·per·la·tive [sjuː'pɜːlətɪv] **1.** □ höchste(r, -s); überragend; **2.** *a.* **~ degree** *gr.* Superlativ *m*.

su·per|mar·ket ['sjuːpəmɑːkɪt] Supermarkt *m*; **~nat·u·ral** □ [‿'nætʃrəl] übernatürlich; **~nu·me·ra·ry** [‿'njuːmərərɪ] **1.** überzählig; zusätzlich; **2.** Zusatzperson *f*, -sache *f*; *thea.*, *Film*: Statist(in); **~scrip·tion** [‿'skrɪpʃn] Über-, Aufschrift *f*; **~sede** [‿'siːd] ersetzen; verdrängen; absetzen; ablösen; **~son·ic** *phys.* [‿'sɒnɪk] Überschall...; **~sti·tion** [‿'stɪʃn] Aberglaube *m*; **~sti·tious** □ [‿əs] abergläubisch; **~vene** [‿'viːn] (noch) hinzukommen; dazwischenkommen; **~vise** [‿vaɪz] beaufsichtigen, überwachen; **~vi·sion** [‿'vɪʒn] (Ober)Aufsicht *f*; Beaufsichtigung *f*, Überwachung *f*; **~vi·sor** [‿vaɪzə] Aufseher(in); Leiter(in).

sup·per ['sʌpə] Abendessen *n*; *the* (*Lord's*) **2** das heilige Abendmahl.

sup·plant [sə'plɑːnt] verdrängen.

sup·ple ['sʌpl] **1.** □ (*~r, ~st*) geschmeidig; **2.** geschmeidig machen.

sup·ple|ment 1. ['sʌplɪmənt] Ergänzung *f*; Nachtrag *m*; (Zeitungs*etc.*)Beilage *f*; **2.** [‿ment] ergänzen; **~men·tal** □ [sʌplɪ'mentl], **~men·ta·ry** [‿ərɪ] Ergänzungs...; nachträglich; Nachtrags...

sup·pli·ant ['sʌplɪənt] **1.** □ demütig bittend, flehend; **2.** Bittsteller(in).

sup·pli·cate ['sʌplɪkeɪt] demütig bitten; (an)flehen; **~ca·tion** [sʌplɪ'keɪʃn] demütige Bitte.

sup·pli·er [sə'plaɪə] Lieferant(in); *a.* **~s** *pl.* Lieferfirma *f*.

sup·ply [sə'plaɪ] **1.** liefern; *e-m Mangel* abhelfen; *e-e Stelle* ausfüllen; beliefern, ausstatten, versorgen; ergänzen; **2.** Lieferung *f*; Versorgung *f*; Zufuhr *f*; *econ.* Angebot *n*; (Stell)Vertretung *f*; *mst* supplies *pl.* Vorrat *m*; *econ.* Artikel *m*, Bedarf *m*;

S

parl. bewilligter Etat; ~ *and demand econ.* Angebot u. Nachfrage.

sup·port [sə'pɔ:t] **1.** Stütze *f*; Hilfe *f*; ⊕ Träger *m*; Unterstützung *f*; (Lebens)Unterhalt *m*; **2.** tragen, (ab)stützen; unterstützen; unterhalten, sorgen für (*Familie etc.*); ertragen; ~**er** Anhänger(in) (*a. Sport*), Befürworter(in).

sup·pose [sə'pəʊz] annehmen; voraussetzen; vermuten; *he is ~d to do* er soll tun; *we go* gehen wir!; *wie wär's, wenn wir gingen?; what is that ~d to mean?* was soll denn das?; *I ~ so* ich nehme es an, vermutlich.

sup|posed [sə'pəʊzd] vermeintlich; ~**pos·ed·ly** [~ɪdlɪ] angeblich.

sup·po·si·tion [sʌpə'zɪʃn] Voraussetzung *f*; Annahme *f*, Vermutung *f*.

sup|press [sə'pres] unterdrücken; ~**pres·sion** [~ʃn] Unterdrückung *f*.

sup·pu·rate 🗲 ['sʌpjʊəreɪt] eitern.

su·prem|a·cy [sju'preməsɪ] Oberhoheit *f*; Vorherrschaft *f*; Überlegenheit *f*; Vorrang *m*; ~**e** □ [sju:'pri:m] höchste(r, -s); oberste(r, -s); Ober...; größte(r, -s).

sur·charge 1. [sɜ:'tʃɑ:dʒ] e-n Zuschlag *od.* ein Nachporto *etc.* erheben auf (*acc.*); **2.** ['sɜ:tʃɑːdʒ] Zuschlag *m*; Nach-, Strafporto *n*; Über-, Aufdruck *m* (*auf Briefmarken*).

sure [ʃʊə] **1.** *adj.* □ (~*r*, ~*st*): ~ (*of*) sicher, gewiß (*gen.*), überzeugt (von); *make ~ that* sich (davon) überzeugen, daß; **2.** *adv. Am.* F wirklich; *it ~ was cold Am.* F es war vielleicht kalt!; ~! klar!; *make sure!; ~ enough* ganz bestimmt; tatsächlich; ~**ly** [~'ʃʊəlɪ] sicher(lich); **sure·ty** [~tɪ] Kaution *f*; Bürge *m*.

surf [sɜ:f] **1.** Brandung *f*; **2.** *Sport*: surfen.

sur·face ['sɜ:fɪs] **1.** (Ober)Fläche *f*; ✈ Tragfläche *f*; **2.** ⚓ auftauchen (*U-Boot*).

surf|board ['sɜ:fbɔːd] Surfbrett *n*; ~**boat** Brandungsboot *n*.

sur·feit ['sɜ:fɪt] **1.** Übersättigung *f*; Überdruß *m*; **2.** (sich) übersättigen *od.* -füttern.

surf·er ['sɜ:fə] *Sport*: Surfer(in), Wellenreiter(in); ~**ing** [~ɪŋ], ~**rid·ing** [~raɪdɪŋ] *Sport*: Surfen *n*, Wellenreiten *n*.

surge [sɜ:dʒ] **1.** Woge *f*; **2.** wogen; (vorwärts)drängen; *a. ~ up* (auf)wallen (*Gefühle*).

sur|geon ['sɜ:dʒən] Chirurg *m*; ~**ge·ry** [~rɪ] Chirurgie *f*; operativer Eingriff, Operation *f*; *Brt.* Sprechzimmer *n*; ~ *hours pl. Brt.* Sprechstunde(n *pl.*) *f*.

sur·gi·cal □ ['sɜ:dʒɪkl] chirurgisch.

sur·ly □ ['sɜ:lɪ] (*-ier*, *-iest*) mürrisch, grob.

sur·mise 1. ['sɜ:maɪz] Vermutung *f*; **2.** [sɜ:'maɪz] vermuten.

sur·mount [sɜ:'maʊnt] überwinden.

sur·name ['sɜ:neɪm] Familien-, Nach-, Zuname *m*.

sur·pass *fig.* [sə'pɑ:s] übersteigen, -treffen; ~**ing** [~ɪŋ] unvergleichlich.

sur·plus ['sɜ:pləs] **1.** Überschuß *m*, Mehr *n*; **2.** überschüssig; Über(schuß)...

sur·prise [sə'praɪz] **1.** Überraschung *f*; ✕ Überrump(e)lung *f*; **2.** überraschen; ✕ überrumpeln.

sur·ren·der [sə'rendə] **1.** Übergabe *f*; Kapitulation *f*; Aufgabe *f*, Verzicht *m*; Hingabe *f*; **2.** *v/t. et.* übergeben; aufgeben; *v/i.* sich ergeben (*to dat.*), kapitulieren; sich hingeben *od.* überlassen (*to dat.*).

sur·ro·gate ['sʌrəgɪt] Ersatz *m*; ~ *mother* Leihmutter *f*.

sur·round [sə'raʊnd] umgeben; ✕ umzingeln, -stellen; ~**ing** [~ɪŋ] umliegend; ~**ings** *pl.* Umgebung *f*.

sur·tax ['sɜːtæks] Steuerzuschlag *m*.

sur·vey 1. [sə'veɪ] überblicken; sorgfältig prüfen; begutachten; *Land* vermessen; **2.** [sɜː'veɪ] Überblick *m* (*a. fig.*); sorgfältige Prüfung, Inspektion *f*, Besichtigung *f*; Gutachten *n*; (Land)Vermessung *f*; (Lage-)Karte *f*, (-)Plan *m*; ~**or** [sə'veɪə] Landmesser *m*; (amtlicher) Inspektor.

sur|viv·al [sə'vaɪvl] Überleben *n*; Fortleben *n*; Überbleibsel *n*; ~ *kit* Überlebensausrüstung *f*; ~**vive** [~aɪv] überleben, am Leben bleiben; noch leben; fortleben; bestehen bleiben; ~**vi·vor** [~ə] Überlebende(r *m*) *f*.

sus·cep·ti·ble □ [sə'septəbl] empfänglich (*to* für); empfindlich (*to* gegen); *be ~ of et.* zulassen.

sus·pect 1. [sə'spekt] (be)argwöhnen; in Verdacht haben, verdächtigen; vermuten, glauben; **2.** ['sʌspekt] Verdächtige(r *m*) *f*; **3.** [~] = ~**ed** [sə'spektɪd] verdächtig.

sus·pend [sə'spend] (auf)hängen;

aufschieben; in der Schwebe lassen; *Zahlung* einstellen; ⚖ *Verfahren etc.* aussetzen; suspendieren; *Sport: j-n* sperren; **~ed** [~ɪd] schwebend; hängend; ⚖ zur Bewährung ausgesetzt; suspendiert; **~er** [~ə] *Brt.* Strumpf-, Sockenhalter *m; (a. a pair of)* **~s** *pl. Am.* Hosenträger *pl.*

sus∙pense [sə'spens] Ungewißheit *f;* Unentschiedenheit *f;* Spannung *f;* **~∙pen∙sion** [~ʃn] Aufhängung *f;* Aufschub *m;* (einstweilige) Einstellung; Suspendierung *f,* Amtsenthebung *f; Sport:* Sperre *f;* **~ bridge** Hängebrücke *f;* **~ railroad,** *bsd. Brt.* **~ railway** Schwebebahn *f.*

sus∙pi∙cion [sə'spiʃn] Verdacht *m;* Mißtrauen *n; fig.* Spur *f;* **~∙cious** □ [~əs] verdächtig; mißtrauisch.

sus∙tain [sə'steɪn] stützen, tragen; *et.* (aufrecht)erhalten; aushalten *(a. fig.);* erleiden; *Familie* ernähren; *j-m* Kraft geben; ⚖ *e-m Einspruch* stattgeben.

sus∙te∙nance ['sʌstɪnəns] (Lebens-) Unterhalt *m;* Nahrung *f.*

swab [swɒb] **1.** Scheuerlappen *m,* Mop *m;* ⚚ Tupfer *m;* ⚚ Abstrich *m;* **2.** *(-bb-)* **~ up** aufwischen.

swad∙dle ['swɒdl] *Baby* wickeln; **~dling-clothes** [~ɪŋkləʊðz] *pl.* Windeln *pl.*

swag∙ger ['swægə] stolzieren; prahlen, großtun.

swal∙low¹ *zo.* ['swɒləʊ] Schwalbe *f.*

swal∙low² □ **1.** Schlund *m;* Schluck *m;* **2.** (hinunter-, ver)schlucken; *Beleidigung* einstecken, schlucken; F für bare Münze nehmen.

swam [swæm] *pret. von* swim 1.

swamp [swɒmp] **1.** Sumpf *m;* **2.** überschwemmen *(a. fig.); Boot* vollaufen lassen; **~y** ['swɒmpɪ] *(-ier, -iest)* sumpfig.

swan *zo.* [swɒn] Schwan *m.*

swank F [swæŋk] **1.** Angabe *f,* Protzerei *f;* **2.** angeben; protzen; **~y** □ ['swæŋkɪ] *(-ier, -iest)* protzig, angeberisch.

swap F [swɒp] **1.** Tausch *m;* **2.** *(-pp-)* (ein-, aus)tauschen.

swarm [swɔːm] **1.** (Bienen- *etc.*) Schwarm *m;* Haufen *m,* Schar *f;* Horde *f;* **2.** schwärmen *(Bienen);* wimmeln *(with* von).

swar∙thy □ ['swɔːðɪ] *(-ier, -iest)* dunkel(häutig).

swash [swɒʃ] plan(t)schen.

swat [swɒt] *(-tt-) Fliege etc.* totschlagen.

sway [sweɪ] **1.** Schwanken *n;* Einfluß *m;* Herrschaft *f;* **2.** schwanken; (sich) wiegen; schwingen; beeinflussen; beherrschen.

swear [sweə] *(swore, sworn)* schwören; fluchen; **~ s.o. in** *j-n* vereidigen.

sweat [swet] **1.** Schweiß *m;* Schwitzen *n; by the ~ of one's brow* im Schweiße seines Angesichts; *in a ~, fig.* all of a ~ in Schweiß gebadet *(a. fig.);* **2.** *(sweated, Am. mst sweat) v/i.* schwitzen; *v/t.* (aus)schwitzen; in Schweiß bringen; *econ.* schuften lassen, ausbeuten; **~er** ['swetə] Sweater *m,* Pullover *m; econ.* Ausbeuter *m;* **~shirt** Sweatshirt *n;* **~ suit** *Sport: bsd. Am.* Trainingsanzug *m;* **~y** □ [~ɪ] *(-ier, -iest)* schweißig; verschwitzt.

Swede [swiːd] Schwed|e *m,* -in *f.*

Swed∙ish ['swiːdɪʃ] **1.** schwedisch; **2.** *ling.* Schwedisch *n.*

sweep [swiːp] **1.** *(swept)* fegen *(a. fig.),* kehren; gleiten *od.* schweifen über *(acc.) (Blick);* (majestätisch) einherschreiten *od.* (dahin)rauschen; **2.** *(fig. Dahin)*Fegen *n;* Kehren *n;* schwungvolle Bewegung; Schwung *m;* Spielraum *m,* Bereich *m; bsd. Brt.* Schornsteinfeger *m; make a clean ~* gründlich aufräumen *(of* mit); *Sport:* überlegen siegen; **~er** ['swiːpə] (Straßen)Kehrer(in); Kehrmaschine *f;* **~ing** □ [~ɪŋ] schwungvoll; umfassend; **~ings** *pl.* Kehricht *m,* Müll *m.*

sweet [swiːt] **1.** □ süß; lieblich; freundlich; frisch; duftend; *have a ~ tooth* gern Süßes essen; **2.** *Brt.* Süßigkeit *f,* Bonbon *m, n; Brt.* Nachtisch *m;* Süße(r *m) f,* Schatz *m (als Anrede);* **~en** ['swiːtn] (ver)süßen; **~heart** Schatz *m,* Liebste(r *m) f;* **~ish** [~ɪʃ] süßlich; **~meat** Bonbon *m, n;* kandierte Frucht; **~ness** [~nɪs] Süße *f,* Süßigkeit *f;* **~ pea** ⚘ Gartenwicke *f;* **~shop** *Brt.* Süßwarenladen *m.*

swell [swel] **1.** *(swelled, swollen od. swelled) v/i.* (an)schwellen; sich (auf)blähen; sich bauschen; *v/t.* (an)schwellen lassen; aufblähen; **2.** *Am.* F prima; **3.** Anschwellen *n;* Schwellung *f;* ⚓ Dünung *f;* **~ing** ['swelɪŋ] Schwellung *f,* Geschwulst *f.*

swel·ter ['sweltə] vor Hitze umkommen.

swept [swept] *pret. u. p.p. von* sweep 1.

swerve [swɜːv] 1. ausbrechen (*Auto, Pferd*); *mot.* das Steuer *od.* den Wagen herumreißen; schwenken (*Straße*); 2. *mot.* Schlenker *m*; Ausweichbewegung *f*; Schwenk *m* (*e-r Straße*).

swift □ [swɪft] schnell, eilig, flink; **~ness** ['swɪftnɪs] Schnelligkeit *f*.

swill [swɪl] 1. (Ab)Spülen *n*; Spülicht *n*; 2. (ab)spülen; F saufen.

swim [swɪm] 1. (-mm-; swam, swum) durch(schwimmen; schweben; *my head ~s* mir ist schwind(e)lig; 2. Schwimmen *n*; *go for a ~* schwimmen gehen; *have od. take a ~* baden, schwimmen; *be in the ~* auf dem laufenden sein; **~mer** ['swɪmə] Schwimmer(in); **~ming** [~ɪŋ] *n*; 1. Schwimmen *n*; 2. Schwimm...; **~bath(s** *pl.*) Brt. *bsd.* Hallenbad *n*; **~pool** Schwimmbecken *n*, Swimmingpool *m*; **~trunks** *pl.* (e-e) Badehose; **~suit** Badeanzug *m*.

swin·dle ['swɪndl] 1. beschwindeln; betrügen; △ *nicht schwindeln*; 2. Schwindel *m*, Betrug *m*.

swine [swaɪn] Schwein *n*.

swing [swɪŋ] 1. (swung) schwingen; schwenken; schlenkern; baumeln (lassen); (sich) schaukeln; sich (*in den Angeln*) drehen (*Tür*); F baumeln, hängen; 2. Schwingen *n*, Schwung *m*; Schaukel *f*; Spielraum *m*; *in full ~* in vollem Gange; **~door** ['swɪŋdɔː] Drehtür *f*.

swin·ish □ ['swaɪnɪʃ] schweinisch.

swipe [swaɪp] 1. schlagen (*at* nach); F klauen; 2. harter Schlag.

swirl [swɜːl] 1. (herum)wirbeln, strudeln; 2. Wirbel *m*, Strudel *m*.

Swiss [swɪs] 1. schweizerisch, Schweizer...; 2. Schweizer(in); *the ~* *pl.* die Schweizer *pl.*

switch [swɪtʃ] 1. Gerte *f*; *Am.* 🚂 Weiche *f*; ⚡ Schalter *m*; falscher Zopf; 2. peitschen; *bsd. Am.* 🚂 rangieren; ⚡ (um)schalten; *fig.* wechseln, überleiten; **~ off** ⚡ ab-, ausschalten; **~ on** ⚡ an-, einschalten; **~board** ⚡ ['swɪtʃbɔːd] Schaltbrett *n*, -tafel *f*.

swiv·el ['swɪvl] 1. ⊕ Drehring *m*; *attr.* Dreh...; 2. (*bsd. Brt.* -ll-, *Am.* -l-) (sich) drehen; schwenken.

swol·len ['swəʊlən] *p.p. von* swell 1.

swoon [swuːn] *veraltet* 1. Ohnmacht *f*; 2. in Ohnmacht fallen.

swoop [swuːp] 1. **~** *down on od. upon* herabstoßen auf (*acc.*) (*Raubvogel*); *fig.* herfallen über (*acc.*); 2. Herabstoßen *n*; Razzia *f*.

swop F [swɒp] = swap.

sword [sɔːd] Schwert *n*; **~s·man** ['sɔːdzmən] (*pl.* -men) Fechter *m*.

swore [swɔː] *pret. von* swear.

sworn [swɔːn] *p.p. von* swear.

swum [swʌm] *p.p. von* swim 1.

swung [swʌŋ] *pret. u. p.p. von* swing 1.

syc·a·more ⚘ ['sɪkəmɔː] Bergahorn *m*; *Am.* Platane *f*.

syl·la·ble ['sɪləbl] Silbe *f*.

syl·la·bus ['sɪləbəs] (*pl.* -buses, -bi [-baɪ]) (*bsd.* Vorlesungs)Verzeichnis *n*; *bsd.* Lehrplan *m*.

sym·bol ['sɪmbl] Symbol *n*, Sinnbild *n*; **~ic** [sɪm'bɒlɪk], **~i·cal** □ [~kl] sinnbildlich; **~is·m** ['sɪmbəlɪzəm] Symbolik *f*; **~ize** [~aɪz] symbolisieren.

sym|met·ric [sɪ'metrɪk], **~met·ri·cal** □ [~kl] symmetrisch, ebenmäßig; **~me·try** ['sɪmɪtrɪ] Symmetrie *f*; Ebenmaß *n*.

sym·pa·thet·ic [sɪmpə'θetɪk], (**~ally**) mitfühlend; △ *nicht sympathisch*; **~ strike** Sympathiestreik *m*; **~thize** ['sɪmpəθaɪz] sympathisieren, mitfühlen; **~thy** [~ɪ] Anteilnahme *f*, Mitgefühl *n*; △ *nicht Sympathie*.

sym·pho·ny ♪ ['sɪmfənɪ] Symphonie *f*.

symp·tom ['sɪmptəm] Symptom *n*.

syn·chro|nize ['sɪŋkrənaɪz] *v/i.* gleichzeitig sein; synchron gehen (*Uhr*) *od.* laufen (*Maschine*) *v/t.* Uhren, Maschinen, Film, TV synchronisieren; *Geschehen* aufeinander abstimmen; **~nous** □ [~əs] gleichzeitig; synchron.

syn·di·cate ['sɪndɪkət] Syndikat *n*.

syn·o·nym ['sɪnənɪm] Synonym *n*; **sy·non·y·mous** □ [sɪ'nɒnɪməs] synonym; gleichbedeutend.

sy·nop·sis [sɪ'nɒpsɪs] (*pl.* -ses [-siːz]) Übersicht *f*, Zusammenfassung *f*.

syn·tax *gr.* ['sɪntæks] Syntax *f*.

syn|the·sis ['sɪnθəsɪs] (*pl.* -ses [-siːz]) Synthese *f*; **~thet·ic** [sɪn'θetɪk], **~thet·i·cal** □ [~kl] synthetisch.

sy·ringe ['sɪrɪndʒ] 1. Spritze *f*; 2. (be-, ein-, aus)spritzen.
syr·up ['sɪrəp] Sirup *m*.
sys|tem ['sɪstəm] System *n*;

physiol. Organismus *m*, Körper *m*; Plan *m*, Ordnung *f*; **~·te·mat·ic** [sɪstɪ'mætɪk] (*~ally*) systematisch.

T

ta *Brt. int.* F [tɑː] danke.
tab [tæb] Streifen *m*; Etikett *n*, Schildchen *n*, Anhänger *m*; Schlaufe *f*, (Mantel)Aufhänger *m*; F Rechnung *f*.
ta·ble ['teɪbl] 1. Tisch *m*; Tafel *f*; Tisch-, Tafelrunde *f*; Tabelle *f*, Verzeichnis *n*; = *tableland*; *at* ~ bei Tisch; *turn the* ~s den Spieß umdrehen (*on s.o.* j-m gegenüber); 2. auf den Tisch legen; tabellarisch anordnen; **~·cloth** Tischtuch *n*, -decke *f*; **~·land** Tafelland *n*, Plateau *n*, Hochebene *f*; **~·lin·en** Tischwäsche *f*; **~·mat** Set *n*; **~ set** *Rundfunk, TV:* Tischgerät *n*; **~·spoon** Eßlöffel *m*.
tab·let ['tæblɪt] Täfelchen *n*; (Gedenk)Tafel *f*; (Schreib- *etc.*)Block *m*; Stück *n* (*Seife*); Tafel *f* (*Schokolade*); Tablette *f* △ *nicht Tablett*.
table|top ['teɪbltɒp] Tischplatte *f*; **~·ware** Geschirr *n* u. Besteck *n*.
ta·boo [tə'buː] 1. tabu, unantastbar; verboten; verpönt; 2. Tabu *n*; 3. *et.* für tabu erklären.
tab·u|lar □ ['tæbjʊlə] tabellarisch; **~·late** [~eɪt] tabellarisch (an)ordnen.
ta·cit □ ['tæsɪt] stillschweigend.
ta·ci·turn □ [~ɜːn] schweigsam.
tack [tæk] 1. Stift *m*, Reißnagel *m*, Zwecke *f*; Heftstich *m*; ♣ Halse *f*; ♣ Gang *m* (*beim Lavieren*); *fig.* Weg *m*; 2. *v/t.* heften (*to an acc.*); *v/i.* ♣ wenden; *fig.* lavieren.
tack·le ['tækl] 1. Gerät *n*; ♣ Takel-, Tauwerk *n*; ⊕ Flaschenzug *m*; *Fußball:* Angreifen *n*; 2. (an)packen; *Fußball:* angreifen; in Angriff nehmen; *fig.* angreifen.
tack·y ['tækɪ] (*-ier, -iest*) klebrig; *Am.* F schäbig.
tact [tækt] Takt *m*, Feingefühl *n*; **~·ful** □ ['tæktfl] taktvoll.
tac·tics ['tæktɪks] *pl. u. sg.* Taktik *f*.
tact·less □ ['tæktlɪs] taktlos.

tad·pole *zo.* ['tædpəʊl] Kaulquappe *f*.
taf·fe·ta ['tæfɪtə] Taft *m*.
taf·fy *Am.* ['tæfɪ] = *toffee*; F Schmus *m*, Schmeichelei *f*.
tag [tæg] 1. (Schnürsenkel)Stift *m*; Schildchen *n*, Etikett *n*; loses Ende, Fetzen *m*, Lappen *m*; Redensart *f*, Zitat *n*; *a.* *question* ~ *gr.* Frageanhängsel *n*; Fangen *n* (*Kinderspiel*); 2. (*-gg-*) etikettieren, auszeichnen; anhängen (*to, on to an acc.*); ~ *along* F mitkommen; ~ *along behind s.o.* hinter j-m hertrotten *od.* -zockeln.
tail [teɪl] 1. Schwanz *m*; Schweif *m*; hinteres Ende, Schluß *m*; ~*s pl.* Rückseite *f* (*e-r Münze*); F Frack *m*; *turn* ~ davonlaufen; ~*s up* in Hochstimmung, fidel; 2. ~ *after s.o.* j-m hinterherlaufen; ~ *s.o.* F j-n beschatten; ~ *away*, ~ *off* abflauen, sich verlieren; nachlassen; **~·back** *mot.* ['teɪlbæk] Rückstau *m*; **~·coat** [~'kəʊt] Frack *m*; **~·light** *mot. etc.* [~laɪt] Rück-, Schlußlicht *n*.
tai·lor ['teɪlə] 1. Schneider *m*; 2. schneidern; *et.* ~ Maß...; **~·made** Schneider..., Maß...
taint [teɪnt] 1. (Schand)Fleck *m*, Makel *m*; (verborgene) Anlage (*zu e-r Krankheit*); 2. beflecken; verderben; ✽ anstecken; verderben, schlecht werden (*Fleisch etc.*).
take [teɪk] 1. (*took, taken*) *v/t.* nehmen; (an-, ein-, entgegen-, heraus-, hin-, mit-, weg)nehmen; fassen; packen, ergreifen; fangen; × gefangennehmen; sich aneignen, Besitz ergreifen von; (hin-, weg)bringen; △ *nicht herbringen*; *et. gut etc.* aufnehmen; *Beleidigung* hinnehmen; *et.* ertragen, aushalten; halten (*for für*); auffassen; *fig.* fesseln; *phot. et.* aufnehmen, *Aufnahme* machen; *Temperatur* messen; *Notiz* machen, nie-

derschreiben; *Prüfung* machen, ablegen; *Rast, Ferien etc.* machen; *Urlaub, ein Bad* nehmen; *Kleidergröße etc.* haben; sich *e-e Krankheit* holen; *Speisen* zu sich nehmen, *Mahlzeit* einnehmen; *Zeitung* beziehen; *Zug, Bus etc.* nehmen; *Weg* wählen; *j-n wohin* führen; *Preis* gewinnen; *Gelegenheit, Maßnahmen* ergreifen; *Vorsitz etc.* übernehmen; *Eid* ablegen; *Zeit, Geduld* erfordern, brauchen; *Zeit* dauern; *Mut* fassen; *Anstoß* nehmen; *I ~ it* that ich nehme an, daß; *~ it or leave it* F mach, was du willst; *~n all in all* im großen (u.) ganzen; *be ~n* besetzt sein; *be ~n* ill *od.* F *bad* krank werden; *be ~n with* begeistert *od.* entzückt sein von; *~ breath* verschnaufen; *~ comfort* sich trösten; *~ compassion on* Mitleid mit *j-m* haben; sich erbarmen (*gen.*); *~ counsel* beraten; *~ a drive* e-e Fahrt machen; *~ fire* Feuer fangen; *~ in hand* unternehmen; *~ hold* of ergreifen; *~ a look* e-n Blick tun *od.* werfen (*at* auf *acc.*); *Can I ~ a message?* Kann ich et. ausrichten?; *~ to pieces* auseinandernehmen, zerlegen; *~ pity on* Mitleid haben mit; *~ place* stattfinden, spielen (*Handlung*); △ *nicht Platz nehmen*; *~ a risk* ein Risiko eingehen *od.* auf sich nehmen; *~ a seat* Platz nehmen; *~ a walk* e-n Spaziergang machen; *~ my word for it* verlaß dich drauf; *~ along* mitnehmen; *~ apart* auseinandernehmen, zerlegen; *~ around j-n* herumführen; *~ away* wegnehmen; *... to ~ away* Brt. Schild: ... zum Mitnehmen; *~ down* herunternehmen; *Gebäude* abreißen; notieren; *~ from j-m* wegnehmen; ⚔ abziehen von; *~ in* kürzer *od.* enger machen; *Zeitung* halten; aufnehmen (*als Gast etc.*); *Lage* überschauen; *fig.* einschließen; verstehen; erfassen; F *j-n* reinlegen; *be ~n in* reingefallen sein; *~ in lodgers* (Zimmer) vermieten; *~ off* ab-, wegnehmen; *Kleidungsstück* ablegen, ausziehen; *Hut etc.* abnehmen; *e-n Tag etc.* Urlaub machen; *~ on* an-, übernehmen; *Arbeiter etc.* einstellen; *Fahrgäste* zusteigen lassen; *~ out* heraus-, entnehmen; *Fleck* entfernen; *j-n* ausführen; *Versicherung* abschließen; *~ over* Amt, *Aufgabe, Idee etc.* übernehmen; *~ up* aufheben, -nehmen; sich befassen

mit; *Fall, Idee etc.* aufgreifen; *Raum, Zeit* in Anspruch nehmen; *v/i.* ⚓ wirken, anschlagen (*Medikament*); F gefallen, ankommen, ziehen; *~ after j-m* nachschlagen; *~ off* abspringen ✈, *Raumfahrt:* starten; *~ on* Anklang finden; *~ over* die Amtsgewalt *etc.* übernehmen; *~ to* sich hingezogen fühlen zu, Gefallen finden an; *~ to doing s.th.* anfangen et. zu tun; *~ up with* sich anfreunden mit; 2. F *Fischerei:* Fang m; (*Geld*)Einnahme(n *pl.*) f; *hunt.* Beute f; Anteil m (*of* an *dat.*); *Film:* Szene(naufnahme) f; *~*

a·way ['teɪkəweɪ] 1. zum Mitnehmen; 2. Restaurant n mit Straßenverkauf; *~-in* F [~ɪn] Schwindel m, Betrug m; **tak·en** [~ən] *p.p. von* take 1; *~-off* [~ɒf] Absprung m ✈, *Raumfahrt:* Start m, Abflug m; Abheben n; F Nachahmung f.

tak·ing ['teɪkɪŋ] 1. □ F anziehend, fesselnd, einnehmend; ansteckend; 2.(An-, Ab-, Auf-, Ein-, Ent-, Hin-, Weg- *etc.*)Nehmen n; Inbesitznahme f; ⚔ Einnahme f; F Aufregung f; *~s pl. econ.* Einnahme(n *pl.*) f.

tale [teɪl] Erzählung f; Geschichte f; Märchen n, Sage f; *tell ~s* klatschen; *it tells its own ~* es spricht für sich selbst; **~·bear·er** ['teɪlbeərə] Zuträger(in), Klatschmaul n.

tal·ent ['tælənt] Talent n, Begabung f, Anlage f; **~ed** talentiert, begabt.

talk [tɔːk] 1. Gespräch n; Unterhaltung f; Unterredung f; Plauderei f; Vortrag m; Geschwätz n; Sprache f; Art f zu reden; 2. sprechen; reden; plaudern; *~ to s.o.* mit *j-m* sprechen *od.* reden; **~·a·tive** □ ['tɔːkətɪv] gesprächig, geschwätzig; **~·er** [~ə] Schwätzer(in); Sprechende(r m) f; *~ show* TV Talk-Show f; **~·show host** TV Talkmaster m.

tall [tɔːl] groß; lang; hoch; F übertrieben, unglaublich; *that's a ~ order* F das ist ein bißchen viel verlangt.

tal·low ['tæləʊ] Talg m.

tal·ly ['tælɪ] 1. *econ.* (Ab-, Gegen-) Rechnung f; Kontogegenbuch n; Etikett n, Kennzeichen n; *Sport:* Punkt(zahl f) m; 2. in Übereinstimmung bringen; übereinstimmen.

tal·on ['tælən] Kralle f, Klaue f.

tame [teɪm] 1. □ (*~r, ~st*) zahm; folgsam; harmlos; lahm, fad(e); 2. zähmen, bändigen.

tam·per ['tæmpə]: *~ with* sich (unbefugt) zu schaffen machen an (*dat.*); j-n zu bestechen suchen; *Urkunde* fälschen.

tam·pon ⚕ ['tæmpən] Tampon *m*.

tan [tæn] **1.** Lohe *f*; Lohfarbe *f*; (Sonnen)Bräune *f*; **2.** lohfarben; **3.** (*-nn-*) gerben; bräunen; braun werden.

tang [tæŋ] scharfer Geruch *od.* Geschmack; (scharfer) Klang; ♀ Seetang *m*.

tan·gent ['tændʒənt] ☊ Tangente *f*; *fly od.* go off at a ~ plötzlich (vom Thema) abschweifen.

tan·ge·rine ♀ [tændʒə'riːn] Mandarine *f*.

tan·gi·ble ☐ ['tændʒəbl] fühl-, greifbar; klar.

tan·gle ['tæŋgl] **1.** Gewirr *n*; *fig.* Verwirrung *f*, -wicklung *f*; **2.** (sich) verwirren, -wickeln.

tank [tæŋk] **1.** *mot.*, ✕ *etc.* Tank *m*; (Wasser)Becken *n*, Zisterne *f*; **2.** ~ (*up*) auf-, volltanken.

tank·ard ['tæŋkəd] Humpen *m*, *bsd.* (Bier)Seidel *n*.

tank·er ['tæŋkə] ⚓ Tanker *m*; ✈ Tankflugzeug *n*; *mot.* Tankwagen *m*.

tan|ner ['tænə] Gerber *m*; **~·ne·ry** [⌐rɪ] Gerberei *f*.

tan·ta·lize ['tæntəlaɪz] quälen.

tan·ta·mount ['tæntəmaʊnt] gleichbedeutend (*to* mit).

tan·trum ['tæntrəm] Wutanfall *m*.

tap [tæp] **1.** leichtes Klopfen; (Wasser-, Gas-, Zapf)Hahn *m*; Zapfen *m*; Schankstube *f*; *on* ~ vom Faß (*Bier*); *~s pl. Am.* ✕ Zapfenstreich *m*; **2.** (*-pp-*) leicht pochen, klopfen, tippen (*on, at auf, an, gegen acc.*); anzapfen (*a. Telefonleitung*); abzapfen; **~·dance** ['tæpdɑːns] Steptanz *m*.

tape [teɪp] **1.** schmales Band, Streifen *m*; *Sport:* Zielband *n*; *tel.* Papierstreifen *m*; *Computer, Fernschreiber:* Lochstreifen *m*; (Magnet-, Video-, Ton)Band *n*; *s. red tape*; **2.** mit e-m Band befestigen; mit Klebestreifen verkleben; auf (Ton)Band aufnehmen; *TV* aufzeichnen; ~ **cas·sette** Tonbandkassette *f*; ~ **deck** Tapedeck *n*; ~ **li·bra·ry** Bandarchiv *n*; ~ **meas·ure** Bandmaß *n*.

ta·per ['teɪpə] **1.** dünne Wachskerze; **2.** *adj.* spitz (zulaufend); **3.** *v/i. oft* ~ *off* spitz zulaufen; *v/t.* zuspitzen.

tape|-re·cord ['teɪprɪkɔːd] auf (Ton)Band aufnehmen; ~ **re·cord·er**

(Ton)Bandgerät *n*; ~ **re·cord·ing** (Ton)Bandaufnahme *f*; ~ **speed** Bandgeschwindigkeit *f*.

ta·pes·try ['tæpɪstrɪ] Gobelin *m*; △ *nicht Tapete.*

tape·worm *zo.* ['teɪpwɜːm] Bandwurm *m*.

tap·room ['tæprʊm] Schankstube *f*.

tar [tɑː] **1.** Teer *m*; **2.** (*-rr-*) teeren.

tar·dy ☐ ['tɑːdɪ] (*-ier, -iest*) langsam; *Am.* spät.

tare *econ.* [teə] Tara *f*.

tar·get ['tɑːgɪt] (Schieß-, Ziel)Scheibe *f*; ✕, *Radar:* Ziel *n*; *fig.* (*Leistungs- etc.*)Ziel *n*; ☐ Soll *n*; *fig.* Zielscheibe *f* (*des Spottes etc.*); ~ **area** ✕ Zielbereich *m*; ~ **group** *econ.* Werbung: Zielgruppe *f*; ~ **language** *ling.* Zielsprache *f*; ~ **practice** Scheiben-, Übungsschießen *n*.

tar·iff ['tærɪf] (*bsd.* Zoll)Tarif *m*.

tar·nish ['tɑːnɪʃ] **1.** *v/t.* ⊕ matt *od.* blind machen; *fig.* trüben; △ *nicht tarnen*; *v/i.* matt *od.* trüb werden, anlaufen; **2.** Trübung *f*; Belag *m*.

tar·ry ['tɑːrɪ] (*-ier, -iest*) teerig.

tart [tɑːt] **1.** ☐ sauer, herb; *fig.* scharf, beißend; **2.** *bsd. Brt.* Obstkuchen *m*; (Obst)Torte *f*; *sl.* Flittchen *n*.

tar·tan ['tɑːtn] Tartan *m*: Schottentuch *n*; Schottenmuster *n*.

task [tɑːsk] **1.** Aufgabe *f*; Arbeit *f*; *take to* ~ zur Rede stellen; **2.** beschäftigen; in Anspruch nehmen; ~ **force** ⚓, ✕ Sonder-, Spezialeinheit *f*; Sonderdezernat *n* (*der Polizei*).

tas·sel ['tæsl] Troddel *f*, Quaste *f*.

taste [teɪst] **1.** Geschmack *m*; (Kost-) Probe *f*; Neigung *f*, Vorliebe *f* (*for* für, zu); **2.** kosten; (ab)schmecken; *Essen* anrühren; schmecken (*of* nach); versuchen; **~·ful** ☐ ['teɪstfl] schmackhaft; *fig.* geschmackvoll; **~·less** ☐ [⌐lɪs] fad(e); *fig.* geschmacklos.

tast·y ☐ ['teɪstɪ] (*-ier, -iest*) schmackhaft.

ta·ta *int.* F ['tæ'tɑː] auf Wiedersehen !

tat·ter ['tætə] Fetzen *m*.

tat·tle ['tætl] **1.** klatschen, tratschen; **2.** Klatsch *m*, Tratsch *m*.

tat·too [tə'tuː] **1.** (*pl. -toos*) ✕ Zapfenstreich *m*; Tätowierung *f*; **2.** *fig.* trommeln; tätowieren.

taught [tɔːt] *pret. u. p.p. von teach.*

taunt [tɔːnt] **1.** Stichelei *f*, Spott *m*; **2.** verhöhnen, -spotten.

taut

taut □ [tɔːt] straff; angespannt.

tav·ern *veraltet* ['tævn] Wirtshaus *n*, Schenke *f*.

taw·dry □ ['tɔːdrɪ] (*-ier, -iest*) billig, geschmacklos; knallig.

taw·ny ['tɔːnɪ] (*-ier, -iest*) lohfarben.

tax [tæks] **1.** Steuer *f*, Abgabe *f*; *fig.* Inanspruchnahme *f* (*on, upon gen.*); **2.** besteuern; ≈ *Kosten* schätzen; *fig.* stark in Anspruch nehmen; auf e-e harte Probe stellen; *j-n* zur Rede stellen; ~ *s.o. with s.th.* j-n e-r Sache beschuldigen; **~·a·tion** [tæk'seɪʃn] Besteuerung *f*; Steuer(n *pl.*) *f*; *bsd.* ≈ Schätzung *f*.

tax·i F ['tæksɪ] **1.** *a.* ~**-cab** Taxi *n*, Taxe *f*; **2.** (*~ing, taxying*) mit e-m Taxi fahren; ✈ rollen; ~ **driv·er** Taxifahrer(in); ~ **rank**, *bsd. Am.* ~ **stand** Taxistand *m*.

tax|pay·er ['tækspeɪə] Steuerzahler(in); ~ **re·turn** Steuererklärung *f*.

tea [tiː] Tee *m*; *s. high tea;* ~**·bag** ['tiːbæg] Tee-, Aufgußbeutel *m*.

teach [tiːtʃ] (*taught*) lehren, unterrichten, *j-m* et. beibringen; ~**·a·ble** ['tiːtʃəbl] gelehrig; lehrbar; ~**·er** [~ə] Lehrer(in); ~**·in** [~ɪn] Teach-in *n*.

tea|·co·sy ['tiːkəʊzɪ] Teewärmer *m*; ~ **cup** Teetasse *f*; *storm in a* ~ Sturm *m* im Wasserglas; ~**·ket·tle** Tee-, Wasserkessel *m*.

team [tiːm] Team *n*, Arbeitsgruppe *f*; Gespann *n*; *Sport u. fig.:* Mannschaft *f*, Team *n*; ~**·ster** *Am.* ['tiːmstə] LKW-Fahrer *m*; ~**·work** Zusammenarbeit *f*, Teamwork *n*; Zusammenspiel *n*.

tea·pot ['tiːpɒt] Teekanne *f*.

tear¹ [teə] *h.* (*tore, torn*) zerren; (zer-) reißen; rasen, stürmen; **2.** Riß *m*.

tear² [tɪə] Träne *f*; *in* ~*s* weinend, in Tränen (aufgelöst); ~**·ful** □ ['tɪəfl] tränenreich; weinend.

tea·room ['tiːrʊm] Teestube *f*.

tease [tiːz] necken, hänseln; ärgern.

teat [tiːt] *zo.* Zitze *f*; *anat.* Brustwarze *f* (*der Frau*); (Gummi)Sauger *m*.

tech·ni·cal □ ['teknɪkl] technisch; *fig.* rein formal; Fach...; ~**·i·ty** [teknɪ'kælətɪ] technische Besonderheit *od.* Einzelheit; Fachausdruck *m*; reine Formsache.

tech·ni·cian [tek'nɪʃn] Techniker(in); Facharbeiter(in).

tech·nique [tek'niːk] Technik *f*, Verfahren *n*, Methode *f*; △ *nicht Technik* (*Technologie*).

tech·nol·o·gy [tek'nɒlədʒɪ] Technologie *f*.

ted·dy| bear ['tedɪbeə] Teddybär *m*; **≈ boy** Halbstarke(r) *m*.

te·di·ous □ ['tiːdjəs] langweilig, ermüdend; weitschweifig.

teem [tiːm] wimmeln, strotzen (*with von*).

teen|-age(d) ['tiːneɪdʒ(d)] im Teenageralter; für Teenager; ~**·ag·er** [~ə] Teenager *m*.

teens [tiːnz] *pl.* Teenageralter *n*; Teenager *pl.*; *be in one's* ~ ein Teenager sein.

tee·ny F ['tiːnɪ] Teeny *m* (*Teenager*); ~**-bopper** F *junger Teenager* (*bsd. Mädchen), der alles mitmacht, was gerade 'in' ist.*

tee·ny² F [~], *a.* ~**-wee·ny** F [~'wiːnɪ] (*-ier, -iest*) klitzeklein, winzig.

tee shirt ['tiːʃɜːt] = T-shirt.

teeth [tiːθ] *pl. von* tooth; ~**e** [tiːð] zahnen, (die) Zähne bekommen.

tee·to·tal·(l)er [tiː'təʊtlə] Abstinenzler(in).

tel·e·cast ['telɪkɑːst] **1.** Fernsehsendung *f*; **2.** (*-cast*) im Fernsehen übertragen *od.* bringen.

tel·e·course ['telɪkɔːs] Fernsehlehrgang *m*, -kurs *m*.

tel·e·gram ['telɪgræm] Telegramm *n*.

tel·e·graph ['telɪgrɑːf] **1.** Telegraf *m*; **2.** telegrafieren; ~**·ic** [telɪ'græfɪk] (*~ally*) telegrafisch; im Telegrammstil.

te·leg·ra·phy [tɪ'legrəfɪ] Telegrafie *f*.

tel·e·phone ['telɪfəʊn] **1.** Telefon *n*, Fernsprecher *m*; **2.** telefonieren; anrufen; ~ **booth**, ~ **box** *Brt.* Telefon-, Fernsprechzelle *f*; **tel·e·phon·ic** [telɪ'fɒnɪk] (*~ally*) telefonisch; ~ **ki·osk** *Brt.* = *telephone booth*; **te·leph·o·ny** [tɪ'lefənɪ] Fernsprechwesen *n*.

tel·e·pho·to lens *phot.* ['telɪ'fəʊtəʊ 'lenz] Teleobjektiv *n*.

tel·e·print·er ['telɪprɪntə] Fernschreiber *m*.

tel·e·scope ['telɪskəʊp] **1.** Fernrohr *n*; **2.** (sich) ineinanderschieben.

tel·e·type·writ·er *Am.* ['telɪ'taɪpraɪtə] Fernschreiber *m*.

tel·e·vise ['telɪvaɪz] im Fernsehen übertragen *od.* bringen.

tel·e·vi·sion ['telɪvɪʒn] Fernsehen *n*; *on* ~ im Fernsehen; *watch* ~ fernsehen; *a.* ~ **set** Fernsehapparat *m*, -gerät *n*.

tel·ex ['teleks] **1.** Telex *n*, Fernschreiben *n*; **2.** *j-m et.* telexen *od.* per Fernschreiben mitteilen.

tell [tel] (told) *v/t.* sagen, erzählen; erkennen; nennen; unterscheiden; zählen; ~ *s.o. to do s.th.* j-m sagen, er solle et. tun; ~ *off* abzählen; F abkanzeln; *v/i.* erzählen (*of* von; *about* über *acc.*); sich auswirken (*on at acc.*); sitzen (*Hieb etc.*); ~ *on s.o.* j-n verpetzen; *you never can ~* man kann nie wissen; **~er** *bsd. Am.* ['telə] (Bank)Kassierer *m*; **~ing** □ [~ɪŋ] wirkungsvoll; aufschlußreich, vielsagend; **~tale** ['telteɪl] **1.** Klatschbase *f*, Petze *f*; **2.** *fig.* verräterisch.

tel·ly *Brt.* F ['telɪ] Fernseher *m*.

te·mer·i·ty [tɪ'merətɪ] Verwegenheit *f*; Frechheit *f*.

tem·per ['tempə] **1.** mäßigen, mildern; ⊕ tempern; *Stahl* härten; **2.** ⊕ Härte(grad *m*) *f*; Temperament *n*, Charakter *m*; Laune *f*, Stimmung *f*; Wut *f*; *keep one's* ~ sich beherrschen; *lose one's* ~ in Wut geraten.

tem·pe·ra·ment ['tempərəmənt] Temperament *n*; **~·ra·men·tal** □ [tempərə'mentl] von Natur aus; launisch; **~·rance** ['tempərəns] Mäßigkeit *f*; Enthaltsamkeit *f*; **~·rate** □ [~rət] gemäßigt; zurückhaltend; maßvoll; mäßig; **~·ra·ture** [~prətʃə] Temperatur *f*.

tem·pest ['tempɪst] Sturm *m*; Gewitter *n*; **~·pes·tu·ous** □ [tem'pestjəs] stürmisch; ungestüm.

tem·ple ['templ] Tempel *m*; *anat.* Schläfe *f*.

tem·po·ral □ ['tempərəl] zeitlich; weltlich; **~·ra·ry** □ [~ərɪ] zeitweilig; vorläufig; vorübergehend; Not..., (Aus)Hilfs..., Behelfs...; **~·rize** [~aɪz] Zeit zu gewinnen suchen.

tempt [tempt] *j-n* versuchen; verleiten; (ver)locken; **temp·ta·tion** [temp'teɪʃn] Versuchung *f*; Reiz *m*; **~·ing** □ ['temptɪŋ] verführerisch.

ten [ten] **1.** zehn; **2.** Zehn *f*.

ten·a·ble ['tenəbl] haltbar (*Argument etc.*); verliehen (*Amt*).

te·na·cious □ [tɪ'neɪʃəs] zäh; gut (*Gedächtnis*); *be* ~ *of s.th.* zäh an et. festhalten; **~·ci·ty** [tɪ'næsətɪ] Zähigkeit *f*; Festhalten *n*; Verläßlichkeit *f* (*des Gedächtnisses*).

ten·ant ['tenənt] Pächter *m*; Mieter *m*.

tend [tend] *v/i.* sich bewegen, streben

(*to* nach, auf ... zu); *fig.* tendieren, neigen (*to* zu); *v/t.* pflegen; hüten; ⊕ bedienen; **ten·den·cy** ['tendənsɪ] Tendenz *f*; Richtung *f*; Neigung *f*; Zweck *m*.

ten·der ['tendə] **1.** □ zart; weich; empfindlich; heikel (*Thema*); sanft, zart, zärtlich; **2.** Angebot *n*; *econ.* Kostenanschlag *m*; ⓕ, ♨ Tender *m*; *legal* ~ gesetzliches Zahlungsmittel; **3.** anbieten; *Entlassung* einreichen; **~·foot** (*pl.* -foots, -feet) *Am.* F Neuling *m*, Anfänger *m*, Greenhorn *n*; **~·loin** Filet *n*; **~·ness** [~nɪs] Zartheit *f*; Zärtlichkeit *f*.

ten·don *anat.* ['tendən] Sehne *f*.

ten·dril ♣ ['tendrɪl] Ranke *f*.

ten·e·ment ['tenɪmənt] Wohnhaus *n*; Mietwohnung *f*; *a.* ~ *house* Mietshaus *n*.

ten·nis ['tenɪs] Tennis *n*; ~ **court** Tennisplatz *m*.

ten·or ['tenə] Fortgang *m*, Verlauf *m*; Inhalt *m*; ♪ Tenor *m*.

tense [tens] **1.** *gr.* Zeit(form) *f*, Tempus *n*; **2.** □ (~*r*, ~*st*) gespannt (*a. fig.*); straff; (über)nervös, verkrampft; **ten·sion** ['tenʃn] Spannung *f*.

tent [tent] **1.** Zelt *n*; **2.** zelten.

ten·ta·cle *zo.* ['tentəkl] Fühler *m*; Fangarm *m* (*e-s Polypen*).

ten·ta·tive □ ['tentətɪv] versuchend; Versuchs...; vorsichtig, zögernd, zaghaft; **~·ly** versuchsweise.

ten·ter·hooks *fig.* ['tentəhʊks]: *be on* ~ wie auf (glühenden) Kohlen sitzen.

tenth [tenθ] **1.** zehnte(r, -s); **2.** Zehntel *n*; **~·ly** ['tenθlɪ] zehntens.

ten·u·ous □ ['tenjʊəs] dünn; zart, fein; *fig.* dürftig.

ten·ure ['tenjʊə] Besitz(art *f*, -dauer *f*) *m*; ~ *of office* Amtsdauer *f*.

tep·id □ ['tepɪd] lau(warm).

term [tɜːm] **1.** (bestimmte) Zeit, Dauer *f*; Frist *f*; Termin *m*; Zahltag *m*; Amtszeit *f*; ⚖ Sitzungsperiode *f*; Semester *n*, Quartal *n*, Trimester *n*; (Fach)Ausdruck *m*, Wort *n*, Bezeichnung *f*; Begriff *m*; ~*s pl.* (Vertrags)Bedingungen *pl.*; Beziehungen *pl.*; *be on good* (*bad*) ~*s with* gut (schlecht) stehen mit; *they are not on speaking* ~*s* sie sprechen nicht (mehr) miteinander; *come to* ~*s* sich einigen; **2.** (be)nennen; bezeichnen als.

ter·mi·nal ['tɜːmɪnl] **1.** □ End...;

letzte(r, -s); ♂ unheilbar; ~ly zum Schluß. 2. Endstück n; ≠ Pol m; ⚍ etc. Endstation f; Terminal m, n: Flughafenabfertigungsgebäude n; Brt. Endstation der Zubringerlinie zum u. vom Flughafen; Zielbahnhof für Containerzüge; Computer: Terminal n, Datenendstation f, Abfragestation f; ~nate [~neɪt] begrenzen; beend(ig)en; Vertrag lösen, kündigen; ~na·tion [~mɪˈneɪʃn] Beendigung f; Ende n; gr. Endung f.
ter·mi·nus ['tɜːmɪnəs] (pl. -ni [-naɪ], -nuses) Endstation f.

ter·race ['terəs] Terrasse f; Häuserreihe f (an erhöht gelegener Straße); ~d terrassenförmig (angelegt); ~d house Brt. = ~ house Brt. Reihenhaus n.

ter·res·tri·al □ [tɪˈrestrɪəl] irdisch; Erd...; bsd. zo., ♣ Land...

ter·ri·ble □ ['terəbl] schrecklich.

ter·rif·ic F [təˈrɪfɪk] (~ally) toll, phantastisch; irre (Geschwindigkeit, Hitze etc.).

ter·ri·fy ['terɪfaɪ] j-m Angst u. Schrecken einjagen.

ter·ri·to·ri·al □ [terɪˈtɔːrɪəl] territorial, Land...; ~ry ['terɪtərɪ] Territorium n, (Hoheits-, Staats)Gebiet n.

ter·ror ['terə] (tödlicher) Schrecken, Entsetzen n; Terror m; ~is·m [~rɪzm] Terrorismus m; ~ist [~rɪst] Terrorist(in); ~ize [~raɪz] terrorisieren.

terse □ [tɜːs] (~r, ~st) knapp; kurz u. bündig.

test [test] 1. Probe f; Versuch m; Test m; Untersuchung f; (Eignungs)Prüfung f; ⚗ Reagens n; 2. probieren; prüfen; testen; 3. Probe..., Versuchs..., Test...

tes·ta·ment ['testəmənt] Testament n; last will and ~ ⚖ Testament n.

tes·ti·cle anat. ['testɪkl] Hode(n m) m, f.

tes·ti·fy ['testɪfaɪ] bezeugen; (als Zeuge) aussagen.

tes·ti·mo·ni·al [testɪˈməʊnjəl] (Führungs)Zeugnis n; Zeichen n der Anerkennung; ~ny ['testɪmənɪ] ⚖ Zeugenaussage f; Beweis m.

test tube ['testtjuːb] 1. ⚗ Reagenzglas n; 2. ⚗ Retorten...

tes·ty □ ['testɪ] (-ier, -iest) gereizt, reizbar, kribbelig.

teth·er ['teðə] 1. Haltestrick m; fig. Spielraum m; at the end of one's ~

fig. am Ende s-r Kräfte; 2. anbinden.

text [tekst] Text m; Bibelstelle f; ~·book ['tekstbʊk] Lehrbuch n.

tex·tile ['tekstaɪl] 1. Textil..., Gewebe...; 2. ~s pl. Webwaren pl., Textilien pl.

tex·ture ['tekstʃə] Gewebe n; Gefüge n; Struktur f.

than [ðæn, ðən] als; △ nicht dann.

thank [θæŋk] 1. danken (dat.); ~ you danke; no, ~ you nein, danke; (yes), ~ you ja, bitte; 2. ~s pl. Dank m; ~s danke (schön); no, ~s nein, danke; ~s to dank (dat. od. gen.); ~·ful □ ['θæŋkfl] dankbar; ~·less □ [~lɪs] undankbar; ~s·giv·ing [~sɡɪvɪŋ] bsd. Dankgebet n; 2 (Day) Am. (Ernte-)Dankfest n.

that [ðæt, ðət] 1. pron. u. adj. (pl. those [ðəʊz]) jene(r, -s), der, die, das, der-, die-, dasjenige; solche(r, -s); ohne pl.: das; 2. adv. F so, dermaßen; ~ much so viel, so sehr; 3. relative pron. (pl. that) der, die, das, welche(r, -s); 4. cj. daß; damit; weil; da; als.

thatch [θætʃ] 1. Dachstroh n; Strohdach n; 2. mit Stroh decken.

thaw [θɔː] 1. Tauwetter n; (Auf-)Tauen n; 2. (auf)tauen.

the [ðiː; vor Vokalen: ðɪ; vor Konsonanten: ðə] 1. bestimmter art. der, die, das, pl. die; 2. adv. desto, um so; ~ ... ~ je ... desto; je. sooner.

the·a·tre, Am. -ter ['θɪətə] Theater n; fig. (Kriegs)Schauplatz m; the·at·ri·cal □ [θɪˈætrɪkl] Theater...; fig. theatralisch.

thee Bibel od. poet. [ðiː] dich; dir.

theft [θeft] Diebstahl m.

their [ðeə] pol. ihr(e); ~s [~z] der (die, das) ihrige od. ihre.

them [ðem, ðəm] sie (acc. pl.); ihnen.

theme [θiːm] Thema n.

them·selves [ðəmˈselvz] sie (acc. pl.) selbst; sich (selbst).

then [ðen] 1. adv. dann; damals; da; denn; also, folglich; by ~ bis dahin; inzwischen; every now and ~ ab u. zu, gelegentlich; there and ~ sofort; now ~ also (nun); 2. attr. adj. damalig.

thence lit. [ðens] daher; von da.

the·o·lo·gian [θɪəˈləʊdʒən] Theologe m; the·ol·o·gy [θɪˈɒlədʒɪ] Theologie f.

the·o·ret·ic [θɪəˈretɪk] (~ally), ~·ret·i·cal □ [~kl] theoretisch; ~ry ['θɪərɪ] Theorie f.

ther·a·peu·tic [θerə'pju:tɪk] **1.** (~ally) therapeutisch; **2.** ~s mst sg. Therapeutik f; ~·py ['θerəpɪ] Therapie f.

there [ðeə] da, dort; darin; (da-, dort)hin; int. da!, na!; ~ is, pl. ~ are es gibt, es ist, es sind; ~·a·bout(s) ['ðeərəbaʊt(s)] da herum; so ungefähr; ~·af·ter [ðeər'ɑːftə] danach; ~·by ['ðeə'baɪ] dadurch; ~·fore ['ðeəfɔ:] darum, deswegen, deshalb, daher; ~·up·on [ðeərə'pɒn] darauf (-hin); ~·with [ðeə'wɪð] damit.

ther·mal ['θɜ:ml] **1.** Thermal..., phys. thermisch, Wärme..., Hitze...; **2.** Thermik f.

ther·mom·e·ter [θə'mɒmɪtə] Thermometer n.

these [ði:z] pl. von this.

the·sis ['θi:sɪs] (pl. -ses [-si:z]) These f; Dissertation f.

they [ðeɪ] pl. sie; man.

thick [θɪk] **1.** ☐ dick; dicht; trüb; legiert (Suppe); heiser; dumm; F dick befreundet; ~ with über u. über bedeckt von; voll von, voller; that's a bit ~! sl. das ist ein starkes Stück!; **2.** dickster Teil; fig. Brennpunkt m; in the ~ of mitten in (dat.); ~·en ['θɪkən] (sich) verdicken; (sich) verstärken; legieren; (sich) verdichten; dick(er) werden; ~·et [~ɪt] Dickicht n; ~·head·ed dumm; ~·ness [~nɪs] Dicke f, Stärke f; Dichte f; ~·set dicht(gepflanzt); untersetzt; ~·skinned fig. dickfellig.

thief [θi:f] (pl. thieves [θi:vz]) Dieb(in); **thieve** [θi:v] stehlen.

thigh anat. [θaɪ] (Ober)Schenkel m.

thim·ble ['θɪmbl] Fingerhut m.

thin [θɪn] **1.** ☐ (-nn-) dünn; licht; mager; spärlich; dürftig; schwach; fadenscheinig (bsd. fig.); **2.** (-nn-) verdünnen; (sich) lichten; abnehmen.

thine Bibel od. poet. [ðaɪn] dein(e); der (die, das) deinige od. deine.

thing [θɪn] Ding n; Sache f; Gegenstand m; Geschöpf n; ~s pl. Sachen pl.; die Dinge pl. (Umstände); the ~ das Richtige.

think [θɪnk] (thought) v/i. denken (of an acc.); überlegen, nachdenken (about über acc.); meinen; glauben; ~ of sich erinnern an (acc.); sich et. ausdenken; daran denken, beabsichtigen; v/t. et. denken; meinen, glauben; sich vorstellen; halten für; et. halten (of von); beabsichtigen, vor-

haben; ~ s.th. over sich et. überlegen, über et. nachdenken.

third [θɜ:d] **1.** ☐ dritte(r, -s); **2.** Drittel n; ~·ly ['θɜ:dlɪ] drittens; ~·rate [~'reɪt] drittklassig.

thirst [θɜ:st] Durst m; ~·y ['θɜ:stɪ] (-ier, -iest) durstig; dürr (Boden); be ~ Durst haben, durstig sein.

thir·teen ['θɜ:'ti:n] **1.** dreizehn; **2.** Dreizehn f; ~·teenth [~ti:nθ] dreizehnte(r, -s); ~·tieth ['θɜ:tɪɪθ] dreißigste(r, -s); ~·ty ['θɜ:tɪ] **1.** dreißig; **2.** Dreißig f.

this [ðɪs] (pl. these [ði:z]) diese(r, -s); ~ morning heute morgen; ~ is John speaking teleph. hier (spricht) John.

this·tle ♀ ['θɪsl] Distel f.

thong [θɒn] (Leder)Riemen m.

thorn [θɔ:n] Dorn m; ~·y ['θɔ:nɪ] (-ier, -iest) dornig; fig. schwierig; heikel.

thor·ough ☐ ['θʌrə] gründlich, genau; vollkommen; vollständig, völlig; vollendet; ~·bred Vollblut (-pferd) n; attr. Vollblut...; ~·fare Durchgangsstraße f, Hauptverkehrsstraße f; no ~! Durchfahrt verboten!; ~·go·ing gründlich; kompromißlos; durch u. durch.

those [ðəʊz] pl. von that **1.**

thou Bibel od. poet. [ðaʊ] du.

though [ðəʊ] obgleich, obwohl, wenn auch; zwar; jedoch, doch; as ~ als ob.

thought [θɔ:t] **1.** pret. u. p.p. von think; **2.** Gedanke m, Einfall m; (Nach)Denken n; on second ~s nach reiflicher Überlegung; ~·ful ☐ ['θɔ:tfl] gedankenvoll, nachdenklich; rücksichtsvoll (of gegen); ~·less ☐ [~lɪs] gedankenlos, unbesonnen; rücksichtslos (of gegen).

thou·sand ['θaʊzənd] **1.** tausend; **2.** (pl. ~, ~s) Tausend n; ~·th [~ntθ] **1.** tausendste(r, -s); **2.** Tausendstel n.

thrash [θræʃ] verdreschen, -prügeln; Sport: j-m e-e Abfuhr erteilen; ~ about, ~ around sich im Bett etc. hin u. her werfen; um sich schlagen; zappeln (Fisch); ~ out fig. gründlich erörtern; ~·ing ['θræʃɪn] Dresche f, Tracht f Prügel.

thread [θred] **1.** Faden m (a. fig.); Zwirn m, Garn n; ⊕ (Schrauben-) Gewinde n; **2.** einfädeln; aufreihen; fig. sich durchwinden (durch); ~·bare ['θredbeə] fadenscheinig (a. fig.); fig. abgedroschen.

threat [θret] (Be)Drohung *f*; **~en** ['θretn] (be-, an)drohen; **~en·ing** [~nıŋ] drohend; bedrohlich.

three [θri:] 1. drei; 2. Drei *f*; **~fold** ['θri:fəʊld] dreifach; **~pence** ['θrepəns] *altes englisches Währungssystem*: Dreipencestück *n*; **~score** ['θri:'skɔ:] sechzig.

thresh ✔ [θreʃ] dreschen; **~er** ['θreʃə] Drescher *m*; Dreschmaschine *f*; **~ing** [~ıŋ] Dreschen *n*; **~ing-ma·chine** Dreschmaschine *f*.

thresh·old ['θreʃhəʊld] Schwelle *f*.

threw [θru:] *pret. von* throw 1.

thrice *veraltet od. lit.* [θraıs] dreimal.

thrift [θrıft] Sparsamkeit *f*; Wirtschaftlichkeit *f*; **~less** ⬜ ['θrıftlıs] verschwenderisch; **~y** [~ı] (-*ier*, -*iest*) sparsam; *poet.* gedeihend.

thrill [θrıl] 1. *v/t.* erschauern lassen, erregen, packen; *v/i.* (er)beben, erschauern, zittern; 2. Zittern *n*, Erregung *f*; (Nerven)Kitzel *m*, Sensation *f*; Beben *n*; **~er** ['θrılə] Reißer *m*, Thriller *m* (*Kriminalfilm*, *-roman etc.*); **~ing** [~ıŋ] spannend, aufregend.

thrive [θraıv] (*thrived od. throve*, *thrived od. thriven*) gedeihen; *fig.* blühen; Erfolg haben; **~n** ['θrıvn] *p.p. von* thrive.

throat [θrəʊt] Kehle *f*, Gurgel *f*, Schlund *m*; Hals *m*; *clear one's* **~** sich räuspern.

throb [θrɒb] 1. (-*bb*-) (heftig) pochen, klopfen, schlagen; pulsieren; 2. Pochen *n*; Schlagen *n*; Pulsschlag *m*.

throm·bo·sis ⚕ [θrɒm'bəʊsıs] (*pl. -ses* [-si:z]) Thrombose *f*.

throne [θrəʊn] Thron *m*.

throng [θrɒŋ] 1. Gedränge *n*; (Menschen)Menge *f*; 2. sich drängen (in *dat.*).

thros·tle *zo.* ['θrɒsl] Drossel *f*.

throt·tle ['θrɒtl] 1. erdrosseln; **~** *back*, **~** *down mot.* ⊕ drosseln, Gas wegnehmen; 2. *a.* **~valve** *mot.* ⊕ Drosselklappe *f*.

through [θru:] 1. *prp.* durch; hindurch; *Am.* (von ...) bis; *Monday* **~** *Friday Am.* von Montag bis Freitag; 2. *adj.* Durchgangs...; durchgehend; **~** *car Am.*, **~** *carriage*, **~** *coach Brt.* 🚃 Kurswagen *m*; **~** *flight* ✈ Direktflug *m*; **~** *travel(l)er* Transitreisende(r *m*) *f*; **~out** [θru:'aʊt] 1. *prp.* überall in (*dat.*); während; 2. *adv.*

durch und durch, ganz und gar, durchweg; **~put** *econ. Computer*: Durchsatz *m*.

throve [θrəʊv] *pret. von* thrive.

throw [θrəʊ] 1. (*threw, thrown*) (ab)werfen, schleudern; *Am. Wettkampf etc.* absichtlich verlieren; *Würfel* werfen; *Zahl* würfeln; ⊕ ein-, ausschalten; **~** *away* weg-, fortwerfen; **~** *over* *fig.* aufgeben; **~** *up* hochwerfen; erbrechen, sich übergeben; *fig. et.* aufgeben, hinwerfen; 2. Wurf *m*; **~a·way** ['θrəʊəweı] 1. et. zum Wegwerfen, *z. B.* Reklamezettel *m*; 2. Wegwerf...; Einweg...; **~n** [θrəʊn] *p.p. von* throw 1.

thru *Am.* [θru:] = through.

thrum [θrʌm] (-*mm*-) klimpern auf (*od. on* auf) (*dat.*).

thrush *zo.* [θrʌʃ] Drossel *f*.

thrust [θrʌst] 1. Stoß *m*; Vorstoß *m*; ⊕ Druck *m*, Schub *m*; 2. (*thrust*) stoßen; stecken, schieben; **~** *o.s. into* sich drängen in (*acc.*); **~** *upon s.o.* j-m aufdrängen.

thud [θʌd] 1. (-*dd*-) dumpf (auf-) schlagen, F bumsen; 2. dumpfer (Auf)Schlag, F Bums *m*.

thug [θʌg] (Gewalt)Verbrecher *m*, Schläger *m*.

thumb [θʌm] 1. Daumen *m*; 2. **~** *a lift od. ride* per Anhalter fahren; **~** *through a book* ein Buch durchblättern; *well-*~*ed* Buch *etc.*: abgegriffen; **~tack** *Am.* ['θʌmtæk] Reißzwecke *f*, -nagel *m*, Heftzwecke *f*.

thump [θʌmp] 1. dumpfer Schlag *f*; 2. *v/t.* heftig schlagen *od.* hämmern *od.* pochen gegen *od.* auf (*acc.*); *v/i.* (auf)schlagen; (laut) pochen (*Herz*).

thun·der ['θʌndə] 1. Donner *m*; 2. donnern; **~bolt** Blitz *m* (u. Donner *m*); **~clap** Donnerschlag *m*; **~ous** ⬜ [~rəs] donnernd; **~storm** Gewitter *n*; **~struck** *fig.* wie vom Donner gerührt.

Thurs·day ['θɜ:zdı] Donnerstag *m*.

thus [ðʌs] so; also, somit.

thwart [θwɔ:t] 1. durchkreuzen, vereiteln; 2. Ruderbank *f*.

thy *veraltet od. poet.* [ðaı] dein(e).

tick¹ *zo.* [tık] Zecke *f*.

tick² [~] 1. Ticken *n*; (Vermerk)Häkchen *n*, Haken *m*; 2. *v/i.* ticken; *v/t.* anhaken; **~** *off* abhaken.

tick³ [~] Inlett *n*; Matratzenbezug *m*.

tick·er tape ['tıkəteıp] Lochstreifen

m; ~ **parade** bsd. Am. Konfettiparade f.

tick·et ['tıkıt] **1.** Fahrkarte f, -schein m; Flugkarte f, Ticket n; (Eintritts-, Theater- etc.)Karte f; mot. Strafzettel m, gebührenpflichtige Verwarnung; Etikett n, Schildchen n; (Preis- etc.)Zettel m; bsd. Am. pol. (Wahl-, Kandidaten)Liste f; **2.** etikettieren, Ware auszeichnen; ~**can·cel·(l)ing ma·chine** (Fahrschein)Entwerter m; ~ **col·lec·tor** 🚊 (Bahnsteig)Schaffner m; (**au·to·mat·ic**) ~ **ma·chine** Fahrkartenautomat m; ~ **of·fice** 🚊 Fahrkartenschalter m; thea. Kasse f.

tick|le ['tıkl] kitzeln (a. fig.); ~**lish** □ [~ıʃ] kitz(e)lig; fig. heikel.

tid·al ['taıdl]: ~ **wave** Flutwelle f.

tid·bit Am. ['tıdbıt] = titbit.

tide [taıd] **1.** Gezeiten pl.; Ebbe f u. Flut f; fig. Strom m, Strömung f; in Zssgn: high ~ Flut f; low ~ Ebbe f; **2.** ~ **over** fig. hinwegkommen od. j-m hinweghelfen über (acc.).

ti·dy ['taıdı] **1.** □ (-ier, -iest) ordentlich, sauber, reinlich, aufgeräumt; F ganz schön, beträchtlich (Summe); **2.** Behälter m; Abfallkorb m; **3.** a. ~ **up** zurechtmachen; in Ordnung bringen; aufräumen.

tie [taı] **1.** (Schnür)Band n; Schleife f; Krawatte f, Schlips m; fig. Band n, Bindung f; fig. (lästige) Fessel, Last f; Sport: Punkt-, parl. Stimmengleichheit f; Sport: (Ausscheidungs)Spiel n; Am. 🚊 Schwelle f; **2.** v/t. (an-, fest-, fig. ver)binden; v/i. Sport: punktgleich sein; mit Adverbien: ~ **down** fig. binden (to an acc.); ~ **in with** passen zu; verbinden od. koppeln mit; ~ **up** zu-, an-, verzusammenbinden; ~**in** econ. ['taıın] Kopplungsgeschäft n, -verkauf m; a book movie ~ Am. etwa: das Buch zum Film.

tier [tıə] Reihe f; Rang m.

tie-up ['taıʌp] (Ver)Bindung f; econ. Fusion f; Stockung f; bsd. Am. Streik m.

ti·ger zo. ['taıgə] Tiger m.

tight [taıt] **1.** □ dicht; fest; eng; knapp (sitzend); straff, (an)gespannt; econ. knapp; F blau, besoffen; F knick(e)rig, geizig; be in a ~ corner sl. place od. F spot fig. in der Klemme sein; **2.** adv. fest; hold ~ festhalten; ~**en** ['taıtn] fest-, anzie-

hen; Gürtel enger schnallen; a. ~ **up** (sich) zusammenziehen; ~**fist·ed** knick(e)rig, geizig; ~**ness** Festigkeit f; Dichte f; Straffheit f; Knappheit f; Enge f; Geiz m; ~**s** [taıts] pl. (Tänzer-, Artisten)Trikot n; bsd. Brt. Strumpfhose f.

ti·gress zo. ['taıgrıs] Tigerin f.

tile [taıl] **1.** (Dach)Ziegel m; Kachel f; Platte f; Fliese f; **2.** (mit Ziegeln etc.) decken; kacheln; fliesen.

till¹ [tıl] (Laden)Kasse f.

till² [~] **1.** prp. bis (zu); **2.** cj. bis.

till³ [~] bestellen, bebauen; ~**age** ['tılıdʒ] (Land)Bestellung f; Ackerbau m; Ackerland n.

tilt [tılt] **1.** (Wagen)Plane f; Kippen n; Neigung f; Stoß m; **2.** (um)kippen.

tim·ber ['tımbə] **1.** (Bau-, Nutz)Holz n; ⚓ Spant m; Baumbestand m, Bäume pl.; **2.** zimmern.

time [taım] **1.** Zeit f; Uhrzeit f; Frist f; Mal n; ♪ Takt m; Tempo n; ~**s** pl. mal, …mal; ~ is up die Zeit ist um od. abgelaufen; for the ~ being vorläufig; have a good ~ sich gut unterhalten od. amüsieren; what's the ~?, what ~ is it? wieviel Uhr ist es?, wie spät ist es?; ~ and again immer wieder; all the ~ ständig, immer; at a ~ auf einmal, zusammen; at any ~, at all ~s jederzeit; at the same ~ gleichzeitig, zur selben Zeit; in ~ rechtzeitig; in no ~ im Nu, im Handumdrehen; on ~ pünktlich; **2.** messen, (ab)stoppen; zeitlich abstimmen; timen (a. Sport), den richtigen Zeitpunkt wählen od. bestimmen für; ~ **card** Stechkarte f; ~ **clock** Stechuhr f; ~**hon·o(u)red** ['taımɒnəd] altehrwürdig; ~**ly** [~lı] (-ier, -iest) (recht)zeitig; ~**piece** Uhr f; ~ **sheet** Stechkarte f; ~ **sig·nal** Rundfunk, TV: Zeitzeichen n; ~**ta·ble** Terminkalender m; Fahr-, Flug-, Stundenplan m.

tim|id ['tımıd], ~**or·ous** □ [~ərəs] ängstlich; schüchtern.

tin [tın] **1.** Zinn n; Weißblech n; bsd. Brt. (Konserven)Dose f, (-)Büchse f; **2.** (-nn-) verzinnen; bsd. Brt. (in Büchsen) einmachen, eindosen.

tinc·ture ['tıŋktʃə] **1.** Farbe f; Tinktur f; fig. Anstrich m; **2.** färben.

tin·foil ['tın'fɔıl] Stanniol(papier) n.

tinge [tındʒ] **1.** Tönung f; fig. Anflug m, Spur f; 2. tönen, färben; *fig.* e-n Anstrich geben (*dat.*).

tin·gle ['tɪŋgl] klingen; prickeln.

tink·er ['tɪŋkə] herumpfuschen, -basteln (*at an dat.*).

tin·kle ['tɪŋkl] klingeln (mit).

tin| o·pen·er *bsd. Brt.* ['tɪnəʊpnə] Dosenöffner m; **~ plate** Weißblech n.

tin·sel ['tɪnsl] Flitter m; Lametta n.

tint [tɪnt] 1. (zarte) Farbe; (Farb)Ton m, Tönung f, Schattierung f; 2. (leicht) färben; tönen.

ti·ny □ ['taɪnɪ] (*-ier, -iest*) winzig, sehr klein.

tip [tɪp] 1. Spitze f; Filter m (*e-r Zigarette*); Trinkgeld n; Tip m, Wink m; leichter Stoß; *Brt.* Schuttabladeplatz m; 2. (*-pp-*) mit e-r Spitze versehen; (um)kippen; *j-m* ein Trinkgeld geben; *a.* **~ off** *j-m* e-n Tip *od.* Wink geben.

tip·sy □ ['tɪpsɪ] (*-ier, -iest*) angeheitert.

tip·toe ['tɪptəʊ] 1. auf Zehenspitzen gehen; 2. **on ~** auf Zehenspitzen.

tire¹ *Am.* ['taɪə] = tyre.

tire² [~] ermüden, müde machen *od.* werden; **~d** □ müde; **~less** □ ['taɪəlɪs] unermüdlich; **~some** □ [~səm] ermüdend; lästig.

tis·sue ['tɪʃuː] Gewebe n; Papiertaschentuch n; = **~ pa·per** Seidenpapier n.

tit¹ [tɪt] = teat.

tit² *zo.* [~] Meise f.

tit·bit *bsd. Brt.* ['tɪtbɪt] Leckerbissen m.

tit·il·late ['tɪtɪleɪt] kitzeln.

ti·tle ['taɪtl] (Buch-, Ehren- *etc.*)Titel m; Überschrift f; ⚖ Rechtsanspruch m; **~d** ad(e)lig.

tit·mouse *zo.* ['tɪtmaʊs] (*pl. -mice*) Meise f.

tit·ter ['tɪtə] 1. kichern; 2. Kichern n.

tit·tle ['tɪtl]: *not one od.* a **~** of it kein *od.* nicht ein Jota (davon); **~-tat·tle** [~tætl] Schnickschnack m.

to [tuː, tʊ, tə] 1. *prp.* zu; gegen, nach, an, in, auf; bis zu, bis an (*acc.*); um zu; für; *a quarter ~ one* (ein) Viertel vor eins; *from Monday ~ Friday Brt.* von Montag bis Freitag; **~ me** *etc.* mir *etc.*; *I weep ~ think of it* ich weine, wenn ich daran denke; *here's ~ you!* auf Ihr Wohl!, prosit!; 2. *adv.* zu, geschlossen; *pull ~* Tür zuziehen; *come ~* (wieder) zu

sich kommen; **~ and fro** hin u. her, auf u. ab.

toad *zo.* [təʊd] Kröte f; **~stool** ♀ ['təʊdstuːl] (größerer Blätter)Pilz; Giftpilz m; **~·y** [~ɪ] 1. Speichellecker(in); 2. *fig.* vor *j-m* kriechen.

toast [təʊst] 1. Toast m; Toast m, Trinkspruch m; 2. toasten; rösten; *fig.* wärmen; trinken auf (*acc.*).

to·bac·co [tə'bækəʊ] (*pl. -cos*) Tabak m; **~·nist** [~ənɪst] Tabakhändler m.

to·bog·gan [tə'bɒgən] 1. Rodelschlitten m; 2. rodeln.

to·day [tə'deɪ] heute.

tod·dle ['tɒdl] auf wack(e)ligen Beinen gehen (*bsd. Kleinkind*); F (da-hin)zotteln.

tod·dy ['tɒdɪ] Toddy m (*Art Grog*).

to-do F [tə'duː] Lärm m; Getue n, Aufheben n.

toe [təʊ] 1. *anat.* Zehe f; Spitze f (*von Schuhen etc.*); 2. mit den Zehen berühren.

tof·fee, *a.* **~·fy** ['tɒfɪ] Sahnebonbon m, n, Toffee n.

to·geth·er [tə'geðə] zusammen; zugleich; *Tage etc.* nacheinander.

toil [tɔɪl] 1. mühselige Arbeit, Mühe f, Plackerei f; 2. sich plagen.

toi·let ['tɔɪlɪt] Toilette f; **~·pa·per** Toilettenpapier n.

toils *fig.* [tɔɪlz] *pl.* Schlingen *pl.*, Netz n.

to·ken ['təʊkən] Zeichen n; Andenken n, Geschenk n; *as a ~*, *in ~ of* als *od.* zum Zeichen (*gen.*).

told [təʊld] *pret. u. p.p. von* tell.

tol·e|ra·ble □ ['tɒlərəbl] erträglich; **~rance** [~ns] Toleranz f; Nachsicht f; **~rant** □ [~t] tolerant (*of gegen*); **~rate** [~eɪt] dulden; ertragen; **~ra·tion** [tɒlə'reɪʃn] Duldung f.

toll [təʊl] 1. Straßenbenutzungsgebühr f, Maut f; Standgeld n (*auf dem Markt etc.*); *fig.* Tribut m, (Zahl f der) Todesopfer *pl.*; *the ~ of the road* die Verkehrsopfer *pl.*; 2. läuten; **~·bar** ['təʊlbɑː], **~·gate** Schlagbaum m.

to·ma·to ♀ [tə'mɑːtəʊ, *Am.* tə'meɪtəʊ] (*pl. -toes*) Tomate f.

tomb [tuːm] Grab(mal) n.

tom·boy ['tɒmbɔɪ] Wildfang m.

tomb·stone ['tuːmstəʊn] Grabstein m.

tom·cat *zo.* ['tɒmkæt] Kater m.

tom·fool·e·ry [tɒm'fuːlərɪ] Unsinn m.

to·mor·row [təˈmɒrəʊ] morgen.

ton [tʌn] Tonne f (*Gewichtseinheit*); △ *nicht* Ton.

tone [təʊn] 1. Ton m, Klang m, Laut m; (Farb)Ton m; 2. (ab)tönen; ~ *down* (sich) abschwächen *od.* mildern.

tongs [tɒŋz] pl. (a pair of ~ e-e) Zange.

tongue [tʌŋ] *anat.* Zunge f; Sprache f; (Schuh)Lasche f; hold one's ~ den Mund halten; ~**tied** *fig.* [ˈtʌŋtaɪd] stumm, sprachlos.

ton·ic [ˈtɒnɪk] 1. (~ally) tonisch; stärkend, belebend; 2. ♪ Grundton m; Stärkungsmittel n, Tonikum n.

to·night [təˈnaɪt] heute abend *od.* nacht.

ton·nage ♣ [ˈtʌnɪdʒ] Tonnage f.

ton·sil *anat.* [ˈtɒnsl] Mandel f; ~**li·tis** ♣ [tɒnsɪˈlaɪtɪs] Mandelentzündung f.

too [tuː] zu, allzu; auch, ebenfalls.

took [tʊk] *pret. von* take 1.

tool [tuːl] Werkzeug n, Gerät n; ~**bag** [ˈtuːlbæg] Werkzeugtasche f; ~**box** Werkzeugkasten m; ~**kit** Werkzeugtasche f.

toot [tuːt] 1. blasen, tuten; hupen; 2. Tuten n.

tooth [tuːθ] (pl. teeth [tiːθ]) Zahn m; ~**ache** [ˈtuːθeɪk] Zahnschmerzen pl.; ~**brush** Zahnbürste f; ~**less** [~lɪs] zahnlos; ~**paste** Zahnpasta f, -creme f; ~**pick** Zahnstocher m.

top¹ [tɒp] 1. ober(st)es Ende; Oberteil n; Spitze f (a. fig.); Gipfel m (a. fig.); Wipfel m; Kopf(ende n) m; (Topf- etc.)Deckel m; *mot.* Verdeck n; Stulpe f (am Stiefel); at the ~ of one's voice aus vollem Halse; on ~ oben(auf); obendrein; on ~ of (oben) auf (dat.); 2. oberste(r, -s), höchste(r, -s), Höchst..., Spitzen...; 3. (-pp-) oben bedecken; überragen (a. fig.); an der Spitze e-r Liste etc. stehen; ~ up Tank etc. auf-, nachfüllen; ~ s.o. up j-m nachschenken.

top² [~] Kreisel m.

top·boots [ˈtɒpˈbuːts] pl. Stulpenstiefel pl.; ~ **hat** Zylinder(hut) m.

top·ic [ˈtɒpɪk] Gegenstand m, Thema n; ~**al** [~l] lokal; aktuell.

top·less [ˈtɒplɪs] oben-ohne..., Oben-ohne-...; ~**most** höchste(r, -s), oberste(r, -s).

top·ple [ˈtɒpl]: ~*down*, ~ *over* um-) kippen.

top·sy-tur·vy □ [ˈtɒpsɪˈtɜːvɪ] auf den Kopf (gestellt), das Oberste zuunterst; drunter u. drüber.

torch [tɔːtʃ] Fackel f; a. electric ~ bsd. Brt. Taschenlampe f; ~**light** [ˈtɔːtʃlaɪt] Fackelschein m; ~ procession Fackelzug m.

tore [tɔː] *pret. von* tear¹ 1.

tor·ment 1. [ˈtɔːment] Qual f, Marter f; 2. [tɔːˈment] quälen, peinigen, plagen.

torn [tɔːn] p.p. *von* tear¹ 1.

tor·na·do [tɔːˈneɪdəʊ] (pl. -does, -dos) Wirbelsturm m, Tornado m.

tor·pe·do [tɔːˈpiːdəʊ] (pl. -does) 1. Torpedo m; 2. ♣ torpedieren (a. fig.).

tor·pid □ [ˈtɔːpɪd] starr; apathisch; träge; ~**i·ty** [tɔːˈpɪdətɪ], ~**ness** [~nɪs], **tor·por** [~] Apathie f, Stumpfheit f; Erstarrung f, Betäubung f.

tor·rent [ˈtɒrənt] Sturz-, Wildbach m; reißender Strom; fig. Strom m, Schwall m; ~**ren·tial** [təˈrenʃl]: ~ rain(s) sintflutartige Regenfälle.

tor·toise zo. [ˈtɔːtəs] Schildkröte f.

tor·tu·ous □ [ˈtɔːtjʊəs] gewunden.

tor·ture [ˈtɔːtʃə] Folter(ung) f; Tortur f; 2. foltern.

toss [tɒs] 1. (Hoch)Werfen n, Wurf m; Zurückwerfen n (Kopf); 2. werfen, schleudern; a. ~ *about* (sich) hin- u. herwerfen; schütteln; ~ *off* Getränk hinunterstürzen; Arbeit hinhauen; a. ~ up hochwerfen; losen (for um) (durch Münzwurf).

tot F [tɒt] Knirps m (kleines Kind).

to·tal [ˈtəʊtl] 1. □ ganz, gänzlich; total; gesamt; 2. Gesamtbetrag m, -menge f; 3. (bsd. Brt. -ll-, Am. -l-) sich belaufen auf (acc.); ~**i·tar·i·an** [təʊtælɪˈteərɪən] totalitär; ~**i·ty** [təʊˈtælətɪ] Gesamtheit f.

tot·ter [ˈtɒtə] torkeln, (sch)wanken, wackeln.

touch [tʌtʃ] 1. (sich) berühren; anrühren; anfassen; grenzen *od.* stoßen an (acc.); fig. rühren; erreichen; ♪ anschlagen; a bit ~ed fig. ein bißchen verrückt; ~ at ♣ anlegen in (dat.); ~ *down* ✈ aufsetzen; ~ up auffrischen; retuschieren; 2. Berührung f; Tastsinn m; -gefühl n; Verbindung f, Kontakt m; leichter Anfall; Anflug m; besondere Note; ♪ Anschlag m; (Pinsel)Strich m; ~**and-go** [ˈtʌtʃənˈgəʊ] gewagte Sache; *it is* ~ es steht auf des Messers Schneide; **~ing** □ [~ɪŋ] rührend; **~stone** Prüfstein *m*; **~y** □ [~ɪ] (*-ier, -iest*) empfindlich; heikel.

tough □ [tʌf] zäh (*a. fig.*); robust, stark; hart, grob, brutal, übel; **~en** ['tʌfn] zäh machen *od.* werden; **~ness** [~nɪs] Zähigkeit *f*.

tour [tʊə] **1.** (Rund)Reise *f*, Tour *f*; Rundgang *m*, -fahrt *f*; *thea.* Tournee *f* (*a. Sport*); *s. conduct 2*; **2.** (be)reisen; **~ist** ['tʊərɪst] Tourist(in); ~ *agency*, ~ *bureau*, ~ *office* Reisebüro *n*; Verkehrsverein *m*; ~ *season* Reisesaison *f*, -zeit *f*.

tour·na·ment ['tʊənəmənt] Turnier *n*.

tou·sle ['taʊzl] (zer)zausen.

tow [təʊ] **1.** Schleppen *n*; *take in* ~ ins Schlepptau nehmen; **2.** (ab)schleppen; treideln; ziehen.

to·ward(s) [tə'wɔ:d(z)] gegen; nach ... zu, auf (*acc.*) ... zu; (*als Beitrag*) zu.

tow·el ['taʊəl] **1.** Handtuch *n*; **2.** (*bsd. Brt. -ll-, Am. -l-*) (ab)trocknen; (ab)reiben.

tow·er ['taʊə] **1.** Turm *m*; *fig.* Stütze *f*, Bollwerk *n*; *a.* ~ *block* (Büro-, Wohn)Hochhaus *n*; **2.** (hoch)ragen, sich erheben; **~ing** □ ['taʊərɪŋ] (turm)hoch; rasend (*Wut*).

town [taʊn] **1.** Stadt *f*; **2.** Stadt...; städtisch; ~ *cen·tre*, *Am.* ~ *cen·ter* Innenstadt *f*, City *f*; ~ *clerk* Brt. städtischer Verwaltungsbeamter; ~ *coun·cil* Stadtrat *m* (*Versammlung*); ~ *coun·ci(l)·lor* Brt. Stadtrat *m*, -rätin *f*; ~ *hall* Rathaus *n*; **~s·folk** ['taʊnzfəʊk] *pl.* Städter *pl.*; **~·ship** Stadtgemeinde *f*; Stadtgebiet *n*; **~s·man** (*pl. -men*) Städter *m*; (Mit-) Bürger *m*; **~s·peo·ple** *pl.* = *townsfolk*; **~s·wom·an** (*pl. -women*) Städterin *f*; (Mit)Bürgerin *f*.

tox·ic ['tɒksɪk] (*~ally*) giftig; Gift...; **~in** [~ɪn] Giftstoff *m*.

toy [tɔɪ] **1.** Spielzeug *n*; Tand *m*; **~s** *pl.* Spielsachen *pl.*, -waren *pl.*; **2.** Spielzeug...; Miniatur...; Zwerg...; **3.** spielen.

trace [treɪs] **1.** Spur *f* (*a. fig.*); **2.** nachspüren (*dat.*), *j-s* Spur folgen; verfolgen; herausfinden; (auf)zeichnen; (durch)pausen.

trac·ing ['treɪsɪŋ] Pauszeichnung *f*.

track [træk] **1.** Spur *f*, Fährte *f*; 🚂 Gleis *n*; Geleise *n u. pl.*; Pfad *m*;

Computer, *Tonband*: Spur *f*; (Raupen)Kette *f*; *Sport*: (Renn-, Aschen-) Bahn *f*; **~-and-field** *Sport*: Leichtathletik...; ~ *events pl. Sport*: Laufdisziplinen *pl.*; ~ *suit* Trainingsanzug *m*; **2.** nachgehen, -spüren (*dat.*), verfolgen; ~ *down*, ~ *out* aufspüren; **~ing station** *Raumfahrt*: Bodenstation *f*.

tract [trækt] Fläche *f*, Strecke *f*, Gegend *f*; Traktat *n*, Abhandlung *f*.

trac·ta·ble □ ['træktəbl] lenk-, fügsam.

trac|tion ['trækʃn] Ziehen *n*, Zug *m*; ~ *engine* Zugmaschine *f*; **~·tor** ⊕ [~ə] Trecker *m*, Traktor *m*.

trade [treɪd] **1.** Handel *m*; Gewerbe *n*, Beruf *m*; Handwerk *n*; **2.** Handel treiben, handeln; ~ *on* ausnutzen; ~ *mark* Warenzeichen *n*; **~ price** Großhandelspreis *m*; **trad·er** ['treɪdə] Händler *m*; **~s·man** [~zmən] (*pl. -men*) (Einzel)Händler *m*; **~(s) un·i·on** Gewerkschaft *f*; **~(s) un·i·on·ist** Gewerkschaftler(in); ~ *wind* Passat(wind) *m*.

tra·di·tion [trə'dɪʃn] Tradition *f*; Überlieferung *f*; **~·al** □ [~l] traditionell.

traf·fic ['træfɪk] **1.** Verkehr *m*; Handel *m*; **2.** (*-ck-*) (*a. illegal*) handeln (*in* mit).

traf·fi·ca·tor *Brt. mot.* ['træfɪkeɪtə] (Fahrt)Richtungsanzeiger *m*, Blinker *m*.

traf·fic| cir·cle *Am.* ['træfɪk'sɜ:kl] Kreisverkehr *m*; ~ **jam** (Verkehrs-) Stau *m*, Verkehrsstockung *f*; ~ **light(s** *pl.*) Verkehrsampel *f*; ~ **sign** Verkehrszeichen *n*, -schild *n*; ~ **sig·nal** = *traffic light(s)*; ~ **war·den** *Brt.* Politesse *f*.

tra|ge·dy ['trædʒɪdɪ] Tragödie *f*; **~·gic** [~ɪk] (*~ally*), **trag·i·cal** □ [~kl] tragisch.

trail [treɪl] **1.** Schleppe *f*; Spur *f*; Pfad *m*, Weg *m*; *fig.* Schweif *m*; **2.** *v/t.* hinter sich herziehen; verfolgen, *j-n* beschatten; *v/i.* schleifen; sich schleppen; sich ranken; **~·er** ['treɪlə] ♀ Kriechpflanze *f*; *mot.* Anhänger *m*; *Am. mot.* Wohnwagen *m*, Wohnanhänger *m*, Caravan *m*; *Film*, *TV*: (Programm)Vorschau *f*.

train [treɪn] **1.** (Eisenbahn)Zug *m*; *allg.* Zug *m*; Gefolge *n*; Reihe *f*, Folge *f*, Kette *f*; Schleppe *f* (*am Kleid*); **2.** erziehen; (sich) schulen;

abrichten; (sich) ausbilden; *Sport*:
trainieren; sich üben; **~ee** [treɪˈniː]
in der Ausbildung Stehende(r *m*) *f*;
Auszubildende(r *m*) *f*; **~er** [ˈtreɪnə]
Ausbilder *m*; *Sport*: Trainer *m*;
~ing [~ɪŋ] Ausbildung *f*; Üben *n*;
bsd. Sport: Training *n*.

trait [treɪ] (Charakter)Zug *m*.

trai·tor [ˈtreɪtə] Verräter *m*.

tram(-car) *Brt.* [ˈtræm(kɑː)] Stra-
ßenbahn(wagen *m*) *f*.

tramp [træmp] **1.** Getrampel *n*;
Wanderung *f*; Tramp *m*, Landstreicher *m*; **2.** trampeln, treten; (durch-)
wandern; **tram·ple** [ˈtræmpl] (her-
um-, zer)trampeln.

trance [trɑːns] Trance *f*.

tran·quil [ˈtræŋkwɪl] ruhig; gelassen; **~(l)i·ty** [træŋˈkwɪlətɪ] Ruhe *f*;
Gelassenheit *f*; **~(l)ize** [ˈtræŋ-
kwɪlaɪz] beruhigen; **~(l)iz·er** [~aɪzə]
Beruhigungsmittel *n*.

trans- [trænz] jenseits; durch; über.

trans|act [trænˈzækt] abwickeln, ab-
machen; **~·ac·tion** [~kʃn] *Geld*
Erledi-
gung *f*; Geschäft *n*, Transaktion *f*.

trans·al·pine [ˈtrænzˈælpaɪn] trans-
alpin(isch).

trans·at·lan·tic [ˈtrænzətˈlæntɪk]
transatlantisch, Übersee...

tran|scend [trænˈsend] überschrei-
ten, hinausgehen über (*acc.*); übertreffen; **~·scen·dence**, **~·scen·den-
cy** [~əns, ~sɪ] Überlegenheit *f*; *phls.*
Transzendenz *f*.

tran·scribe [trænˈskraɪb] abschreiben; *Kurzschrift* übertragen.

tran|script [ˈtrænskrɪpt], **~·scrip-
tion** [trænˈskrɪpʃn] Abschrift *f*; Umschrift *f*.

trans·fer 1. [trænsˈfɜː] (-rr-) *v/t.*
übertragen; versetzen, -legen; *Geld*
überweisen; *Sport*: Spieler transfe-
rieren (*to* zu), abgeben (*to an acc.*);
v/i. übertreten; *Sport*: wechseln
(*Spieler*); 🚆 *etc.* umsteigen; **2.**
[ˈtrænsfɜː] Übertragung *f*; Verset-
zung *f*, -legung *f*; *econ.* (Geld)Über-
weisung *f*; *Sport*: Transfer *m*, Wechsel *m*; *Am.* 🚆 *etc.* Umsteigefahr-
schein *m*; **~·a·ble** [trænsˈfɜːrəbl]
übertragbar.

trans·fig·ure [trænsˈfɪgə] umgestalten; verklären.

trans·fix [trænsˈfɪks] durchstechen;
~ed *fig.* versteinert, starr (*with* vor
dat).

trans|form [trænsˈfɔːm] umformen;

um-, verwandeln; **~·for·ma·tion**
[trænsfəˈmeɪʃn] Umformung *f*;
Um-, Verwandlung *f*.

trans|fuse 🩸 [trænsˈfjuːz] *Blut* über-
tragen; **~·fu·sion** 🩸 [~ʒn] (Blut-)
Übertragung *f*, (-)Transfusion *f*.

trans|gress [trænsˈgres] *v/t.* über-
schreiten; *Gesetze etc.* übertreten,
verletzen; *v/i.* sich vergehen;
~·gres·sion [~ʃn] Überschreitung *f*;
Übertretung *f*; Vergehen *n*; **~·gres-
sor** [~sə] Übeltäter(in); Rechtsbre-
cher(in).

tran·sient [ˈtrænzɪənt] **1.** □ = *transitory*; **2.** *Am.* Durchreisende(r *m*) *f*.

tran·sis·tor [trænˈsɪstə] Transistor
m.

tran·sit [ˈtrænsɪt] Durchgang *m*;
Transit-, Durchgangsverkehr *m*;
econ. Transport *m* (*von Waren*).

tran·si·tion [trænˈsɪʒn] Übergang *m*.

tran·si·tive □ *gr.* [ˈtrænsɪtɪv] transitiv.

tran·si·to·ry □ [ˈtrænsɪtərɪ] vorübergehend; vergänglich, flüchtig.

trans|late [trænsˈleɪt] übersetzen,
-tragen; *fig.* umsetzen; **~·la·tion**
[~ʃn] Übersetzung *f*, -tragung *f*;
~·la·tor [~ə] Übersetzer(in).

trans·lu·cent [trænsˈluːsnt] licht-
durchlässig.

trans·mi·gra·tion [ˈtrænzmaɪ-
ˈgreɪʃn] Seelenwanderung *f*.

trans·mis·sion [trænzˈmɪʃn] Übermittlung *f*; Übertragung *f*; *biol.* Vererbung *f*; *phys.* Fortpflanzung *f*;
mot. Getriebe *n*; *Rundfunk, TV*:
Sendung *f*.

trans·mit [trænzˈmɪt] (-*tt*-) übermit-
teln, -senden; übertragen; *Rundfunk, TV*: senden; *biol.* vererben;
phys. (weiter)leiten; **~·ter** [~ə] Über-
mittler(in); *tel. etc.* Sender *m*.

trans·mute [trænzˈmjuːt] um-, verwandeln.

trans·par·ent □ [trænsˈpærənt]
durchsichtig (*a. fig.*).

tran·spire [trænˈspaɪə] ausdünsten,
-schwitzen; *fig.* durchsickern.

trans|plant [trænsˈplɑːnt] umpflan-
zen; verpflanzen (*a.* 🩸); **~·plan·ta-
tion** [ˈtrænsplɑːnˈteɪʃn] Verpflan-
zung *f* (*a.* 🩸).

trans|port 1. [trænsˈpɔːt] transpor-
tieren, befördern, fortschaffen; *fig.*
j-n hinreißen; **2.** [ˈtrænspɔːt] Transport *m*, Beförderung *f*; Versand *m*;
Verkehr *m*; Beförderungsmittel *n*;

Transportschiff *n*, -flugzeug *n*; *in a ~ of rage* außer sich vor Wut; *be in ~s of* außer sich sein vor (*Freude etc.*); ~·por·ta·tion ['trænspɔː'teɪʃn] Transport *m*, Beförderung *f*.

trans·pose [træns'pəʊz] versetzen, umstellen; ♪ transponieren.

trans·verse □ ['trænzvɜːs] querlaufend; Quer...

trap [træp] **1.** Falle *f* (*a. fig.*); ⊕ Klappe *f*; *sl.* Schnauze *f* (*Mund*); *keep one's ~ shut sl.* die Schnauze halten; *set a ~ for s.o.* j-m e-e Falle stellen; **2.** (*-pp-*) (in e-r Falle) fangen; *fig.* in e-e Falle locken; **~·door** ['træpdɔː] Falltür *f*; *thea.* Versenkung *f*.

tra·peze [trə'piːz] Trapez *n*.

trap·per ['træpə] Trapper *m*, Fallensteller *m*, Pelztierjäger *m*.

trap·pings *fig.* ['træpɪŋz] *pl.* Schmuck *m*, Putz *m*, Drum u. Dran *n*.

trash [træʃ] *bsd. Am.* Abfall *m*, Abfälle *pl.*, Müll *m*; Unsinn *m*, F Blech *n*; Gesindel *n*; Kitsch *m*; **~·can** *Am.* Abfall-, Mülleimer *m*; *Am.* Abfall-, Mülltonne *f*; **~·y** □ ['træʃɪ] (*-ier, -iest*) wertlos, kitschig.

trav·el ['trævl] **1.** (*bsd. Brt. -ll-, Am. -l-*) *v/i.* reisen; sich bewegen; *bsd. fig.* schweifen, wandern; *v/t.* bereisen; **2.** *das* Reisen; ⊕ (Kolben)Hub *m*; **~s** *pl.* Reisen *pl.*; **~·a·gen·cy**, **~·bu·reau** Reisebüro *n*; **~·(l)er** [-lə] Reisende(r *m*) *f*; **~'s cheque** (*Am. check*) Reisescheck *m*.

tra·verse ['trævəs] durch-, überqueren; durchziehen; führen über (*acc.*).

trav·es·ty ['trævɪstɪ] **1.** Travestie *f*; Karikatur *f*, Zerrbild *n*; **2.** travestieren; ins Lächerliche ziehen.

trawl ♣ [trɔːl] **1.** (Grund)Schleppnetz *n*; **2.** mit dem Schleppnetz fischen; **~·er** ♣ ['trɔːlə] Trawler *m*.

tray [treɪ] (Servier)Brett *n*, Tablett *n*; Ablagekorb *m*.

treach·er·ous □ ['tretʃərəs] verräterisch, treulos; (heim)tückisch; trügerisch; **~·y** [-ɪ] (*to*) Verrat *m* (an *dat.*), Treulosigkeit *f* (gegen).

trea·cle ['triːkl] Sirup *m*.

tread [tred] **1.** (*trod, trodden od. trod*) treten; (be)schreiten; trampeln; **2.** Tritt *m*, Schritt *m*; ⊕ Lauffläche *f*; *mot.* Profil *n*; **trea·dle** ['tredl] Pedal

n; Tritt *m*; **~·mill** Tretmühle *f* (*a. fig.*).

trea|son ['triːzn] Verrat *m*; **~·so·na·ble** □ [-əbl] verräterisch.

treas|ure ['treʒə] **1.** Schatz *m*, Reichtum *m*; ~ *trove* Schatzfund *m*; **2.** sehr schätzen; ~ *up Schätze* sammeln, anhäufen; **~·ur·er** [-rə] Schatzmeister *m*; Kassenwart *m*.

treas·ur·y ['treʒərɪ] Schatzkammer *f*; ♀ Finanzministerium *n*; ♀ **Bench** *Brt. parl.* Regierungsbank *f*; ♀ **De·part·ment** *Am.* Finanzministerium *n*.

treat [triːt] **1.** *v/t.* behandeln, umgehen mit; betrachten; *s.o. to s.th.* j-m et. spendieren; *v/i.*: ~ *of* handeln von; ~ *with* verhandeln mit; **2.** Vergnügen *n*; *school* ~ Schulausflug *m*, -fest *n*; *it is my ~* es geht auf meine Rechnung.

trea·tise ['triːtɪz] Abhandlung *f*.

treat·ment ['triːtmənt] Behandlung *f*.

trea·ty ['triːtɪ] Vertrag *m*.

tre·ble ['trebl] **1.** □ dreifach; **2.** ♪ Diskant *m*, Sopran *m*; *Radio:* Höhen *pl.*; **3.** (sich) verdreifachen.

tree [triː] Baum *m*.

tre·foil ♣ ['triːfɔɪl] Klee *m*.

trel·lis ['trelɪs] **1.** ♣ Spalier *n*; **2.** vergittern; ♣ am Spalier ziehen.

trem·ble ['trembl] zittern.

tre·men·dous □ [trɪ'mendəs] schrecklich, ungeheuer, gewaltig; F enorm.

trem·or ['tremə] Zittern *n*; Beben *n*.

trem·u·lous □ ['tremjʊləs] zitternd, bebend.

trench [trentʃ] **1.** ⚔ (Schützen)Graben *m*; Furche *f*; **2.** *v/t.* mit Gräben durchziehen; *v/i.* ⚔ (Schützen)Gräben ausheben.

tren·chant □ ['trentʃənt] scharf.

trend [trend] **1.** Richtung *f*; *fig.* (Ver)Lauf *m*; *fig.* Trend *m*, Entwicklung *f*, Tendenz *f*; **2.** tendieren, neigen; **~·y** *bsd. Brt.* F ['trendɪ] (*-ier, -iest*) modern.

trep·i·da·tion [trepɪ'deɪʃn] Zittern *n*; Angst *f*, Beklommenheit *f*.

tres·pass ['trespəs] **1.** ⚖ unbefugtes Betreten; Vergehen *n*; **2.** ~ (*up*)*on* ⚖ widerrechtlich betreten; über Gebühr in Anspruch nehmen; *no ~ing* Betreten verboten; **~·er** ⚖ [-ə] Rechtsverletzer *m*; Unbefugte(r *m*) *f*.

tres·tle ['tresl] Gestell n, Bock m.

tri·al ['traɪəl] **1.** Versuch m; Probe f, Prüfung f (a. fig.); ⚖ Prozeß m, Verhandlung f; fig. Plage f; on ~ auf od. zur Probe; give s.th. od. s.o. a ~ e-n Versuch mit et. od. j-m machen; be on ~ ⚖ angeklagt sein; put s.o. on ~ j-n vor Gericht bringen; **2.** Versuchs..., Probe...

tri·an·gle ['traɪæŋgl] Dreieck n; **~gu·lar** [traɪˈæŋgjʊlə] dreieckig.

tribe [traɪb] (Volks)Stamm m; contp. Sippe f; ⚥, zo. Klasse f.

tri·bu·nal ⚖ [traɪˈbjuːnl] Gericht(shof m) n; **trib·une** ['trɪbjuːn] Tribun m; Tribüne f.

trib·u·ta·ry ['trɪbjʊtərɪ] **1.** □ zinspflichtig; fig. abhängig; geogr. Neben...; **2.** Nebenfluß m; **~ute** [~juːt] Tribut m (a. fig.), Zins m; Anerkennung f.

trice [traɪs]: in a ~ im Nu.

trick [trɪk] **1.** Kniff m, List f, Trick m, Kunststück n; Streich m; (schlechte) Angewohnheit; play a ~ on s.o. j-m e-n Streich spielen; **2.** überlisten, F hereinlegen; **~e·ry** ['trɪkərɪ] Betrügerei f.

trick·le ['trɪkl] tröpfeln, rieseln.

trick·ster ['trɪkstə] Gauner(in); **~y** □ [~ɪ] (-ier, -iest) verschlagen, F heikel; verzwickt, verwickelt, schwierig.

tri·cy·cle ['traɪsɪkl] Dreirad n.

tri·dent ['traɪdənt] Dreizack m.

tri·fle ['traɪfl] **1.** Kleinigkeit f; Lappalie f; a ~ ein bißchen, ein wenig, etwas; **2.** v/i. spielen; spaßen; v/t. ~ away verschwenden; **~fling** □ [~ɪŋ] geringfügig; unbedeutend.

trig·ger ['trɪgə] Abzug m (am Gewehr); phot. Auslöser m.

trill [trɪl] **1.** Triller m; gerolltes r; **2.** trillern; bsd. das r rollen.

tril·lion ['trɪljən] Brt. Trillion f; Am. Billion f.

trim [trɪm] **1.** □ (-mm-) ordentlich, schmuck; gepflegt; **2.** (guter) Zustand; Ordnung f; in good ~ in Form; **3.** (-mm-) zurechtmachen, in Ordnung bringen (a. ~ up herausputzen, schmücken; Kleider etc. besetzen; stutzen, trimmen, (be)schneiden; ⚡, ⚓ trimmen; **~ming** ['trɪmɪŋ]: ~s pl. Besatz m, Zutaten pl., Beilagen pl. (e-r Speise).

Trin·i·ty eccl. ['trɪnɪtɪ] Dreieinigkeit f.

trin·ket ['trɪŋkɪt] wertloses Schmuckstück.

trip [trɪp] **1.** (kurze) Reise, Fahrt f; Ausflug m, Spritztour f; Stolpern n, Fallen n; Fehltritt m (a. fig.); fig. Versehen n, Fehler m; F Trip m (Drogenrausch); **2.** (-pp-) v/i. trippeln; stolpern; fig. (e-n) Fehler machen; v/t. a. ~ up j-m ein Bein stellen (a. fig.).

tri·par·tite [traɪˈpɑːtaɪt] dreiteilig.

tripe [traɪp] Kaldaunen pl., Kutteln pl.

trip·le □ ['trɪpl] dreifach; ~ jump Sport: Dreisprung m; **~lets** [~ɪts] pl. Drillinge pl.

trip·li·cate 1. ['trɪplɪkɪt] dreifach; **2.** [~keɪt] verdreifachen.

tri·pod ['traɪpɒd] Dreifuß m; phot. Stativ n.

trip·per bsd. Brt. ['trɪpə] Ausflügler(in).

trite □ [traɪt] abgedroschen, banal.

tri·umph ['traɪəmf] **1.** Triumph m, Sieg m; **2.** triumphieren; **~um·phal** [traɪˈʌmfl] Sieges..., Triumph...; **~um·phant** □ [~ənt] triumphierend.

triv·i·al □ ['trɪvɪəl] bedeutungslos; unbedeutend; trivial; alltäglich.

trod [trɒd] pret. u. p.p. von tread 1; **~den** ['trɒdn] p.p. von tread 1.

trol·l(e)y ['trɒlɪ] Brt. Handwagen m, Gepäckwagen m, Kofferkuli m, Einkaufswagen m, Sackkarre(n m) f, Golf: Caddie m; Brt. ⚡ Draisine f; Brt. Tee-, Servierwagen m; ⚡ Kontaktrolle f (e-s Oberleitungsfahrzeugs); Am. Straßenbahn(wagen m) f; **~bus** O(berleitungs)bus m.

trol·lop ['trɒləp] F Schlampe f; leichtes Mädchen, Hure f.

trom·bone ♪ [trɒmˈbəʊn] Posaune f.

troop [truːp] **1.** Trupp m, Haufe(n) m; ~s pl. ⚔ Truppen pl.; **2.** sich scharen; (herein- etc.)strömen, marschieren; ~ away, ~ off F abziehen; ~ the colours Brt. ⚔ e-e Fahnenparade abhalten; **~er** ⚔ ['truːpə] Kavallerist m.

tro·phy ['trəʊfɪ] Trophäe f.

trop·ic ['trɒpɪk] **1.** Wendekreis m; ~s pl. Tropen pl.; **2.** (~ally), **~i·cal** □ [~kl] tropisch.

trot [trɒt] **1.** Trott m, Trab m; **2.** (-tt-) trotten; traben (lassen).

trou·ble ['trʌbl] **1.** Mühe f, Plage f; Last f, Belästigung f, Störung f;

Unannehmlichkeiten *pl.*, Schwierigkeiten *pl.*, Scherereien *pl.*, Ärger *m*; *ask od.* look for ~ unbedingt Ärger haben wollen; *take (the)* ~ sich (die) Mühe machen; 2. stören, beunruhigen, belästigen; quälen, plagen; *j-m* Mühe machen; (sich) bemühen; bitten (*for* um); *don't* ~ *yourself* bemühen Sie sich nicht; *what's the* ~? was ist los?; **~·mak·er** Unruhestifter(in); **~·some** □ [~səm] beschwerlich; lästig.

trough [trɒf] Trog *m*; Rinne *f*; Wellental *n.*

trounce [traʊns] verprügeln.

troupe *thea.* [truːp] Truppe *f.*

trou·ser ['traʊzə]: *(a pair of)* ~s *pl.* (e-e) (lange) Hose; Hosen *pl.*; *attr.* Hosen...; ~ **suit** Hosenanzug *m.*

trous·seau ['truːsəʊ] Aussteuer *f.*

trout *zo.* [traʊt] Forelle(n *pl.*) *f.*

trow·el ['traʊəl] Maurerkelle *f.*

tru·ant ['truːənt] Schulschwänzer(in); *play* ~ (die Schule) schwänzen.

truce ✗ [truːs] Waffenstillstand *m.*

truck [trʌk] 1. 🚃 offener Güterwagen; *bsd. Am.* Last(kraft)wagen *m*, Lkw *m*; Transportkarren *m*; Tausch(handel) *m*; *Am.* Gemüse *n*; 2. (ver)tauschen; **~·er** *Am.* ['trʌkə] Lastwagen-, Fernfahrer *m*; ~ **farm** *Am.* Gemüsegärtnerei *f.*

truc·u·lent □ ['trʌkjʊlənt] wild, roh, grausam; gehässig.

trudge [trʌdʒ] sich (mühsam dahin-) schleppen, (mühsam) stapfen.

true □ [truː] *(~r, ~st)* wahr; echt, wirklich; treu; genau; richtig; *(it is)* ~ gewiß, freilich, zwar; *come* ~ in Erfüllung gehen; wahr werden; ~ *to nature* naturgetreu.

tru·ly ['truːlɪ] wirklich; wahrhaft; aufrichtig; genau; treu; *Yours* ~ *Briefschluß*: Hochachtungsvoll.

trump [trʌmp] 1. Trumpf(karte *f*) *m*; 2. (über)trumpfen; ~ *up* erfinden.

trum·pet ['trʌmpɪt] 1. ♪ Trompete *f*; 2. trompeten; *fig.* ausposaunen.

trun·cheon ['trʌntʃən] (Gummi-) Knüppel *m*, Schlagstock *m.*

trun·dle ['trʌndl] rollen.

trunk [trʌŋk] (Baum)Stamm *m*; Rumpf *m*; Rüssel *m*; (Schrank)Koffer *m*, Truhe *f*; *Am. mot.* Kofferraum *m*; **~·call** *Brt. teleph.* ['trʌŋkɔːl] Ferngespräch *n*; **~·line** 🚃 Hauptlinie *f*; *teleph.* Fernleitung *f*; **~s**

[trʌŋks] *pl.* Turnhose *f*; Badehose *f*; *Sport:* Shorts *pl.*; *bsd. Brt.* (Herren-) Unterhose *f.*

truss [trʌs] 1. Bündel *n*, Bund *n*; 🌀 Bruchband *n*; *arch.* Träger *m*, Fachwerk *n*; 2. (zs.-)binden; *arch.* stützen.

trust [trʌst] 1. Vertrauen *n*; Glaube *m*; Kredit *m*; Pfand *n*; Verwahrung *f*; ⚖ Treuhand *f*; ⚖ Treuhandvermögen *n*; *econ.* Trust *m*; *econ.* Kartell *n*; ~ **company** ✝ Treuhandgesellschaft *f*; *in* ~ zu treuen Händen; 2. *v/t.* (ver)trauen (*dat.*); anvertrauen, übergeben (*s.o. with s.th., s.th. to s.o.* j-m et.); zuversichtlich hoffen; *v/i.* vertrauen (*in, to* auf *acc.*); **~·ee** ⚖ [trʌs'tiː] Sach-, Verwalter *m*; Treuhänder *m*; **~·ful** □ ['trʌstfl], **~·ing** □ [~ɪŋ] vertrauensvoll; **~·wor·thy** □ [~wɜːðɪ] vertrauenswürdig, zuverlässig.

truth [truːθ] *(pl. ~s* [truːðz, *bsd.* truːθs]) Wahrheit *f*; Wirklichkeit *f*; Genauigkeit *f*; **~·ful** □ ['truːθfl] wahr (-heitsliebend).

try [traɪ] 1. versuchen; probieren; prüfen; verhandeln über *et. od.* gegen *j-n*; vor Gericht stellen; *die Augen etc.* angreifen; sich bemühen *od.* bewerben (*for* um); ~ *on Kleid* anprobieren; ~ *out* ausprobieren; 2. Versuch *m*; **~·ing** □ ['traɪɪŋ] anstrengend; kritisch.

tsar *hist.* [zɑː] Zar *m.*

T-shirt ['tiːʃɜːt] T-Shirt *n.*

tub [tʌb] 1. Faß *n*; Zuber *m*, Kübel *m*; *Brt.* F (Bade)Wanne *f*; *Brt.* F (Wannen)Bad *n.*

tube [tjuːb] Rohr *n*; ⚡ Röhre *f*; Tube *f*; (*inner* ~ Luft)Schlauch *m*; Tunnel *m*; *die* (Londoner) U-Bahn; *the* ~ *Am.* F die Röhre, die Glotze (*Fernseher*); **~·less** ['tjuːblɪs] schlauchlos.

tu·ber ♀ ['tjuːbə] Knolle *f.*

tu·ber·cu·lo·sis 🌀 [tjuːbɜːkjʊ'ləʊsɪs] Tuberkulose *f.*

tu·bu·lar □ ['tjuːbjʊlə] röhrenförmig.

tuck [tʌk] 1. Biese *f*; Abnäher *m*; 2. stecken; ~ *away* weg-, verstecken; ~ *in*, ~ *up* (warm) zudecken; ~ *s.o. up in bed* j-n ins Bett packen; ~ *up Rock* schürzen; *Ärmel* hochkrempeln.

Tues·day ['tjuːzdɪ] Dienstag *m.*

tuft [tʌft] Büschel *n*; (Haar)Schopf *m.*

tug [tʌg] 1. Zerren, heftiger Ruck; *a.*

~boat ♣ Schlepper m; fig. Anstrengung f; 2. (-gg-) ziehen, zerren; ♣ schleppen; sich mühen; ~ **of war** Tauziehen n.

tu·i·tion [tjuːˈɪʃn] Unterricht m; Schulgeld n.

tu·lip ♀ [ˈtjuːlɪp] Tulpe f.

tum·ble [ˈtʌmbl] **1.** fallen; stürzen; purzeln; taumeln; sich wälzen; **2.** Sturz m; Wirrwarr m; ~**down** baufällig; ~**r** [~ə] Becher m; zo. Tümmler m.

tu·mid □ [ˈtjuːmɪd] geschwollen.

tum·my F [ˈtʌmɪ] Bäuchlein n.

tu·mo(u)r ♂ [ˈtjuːmə] Tumor m.

tu·mult [ˈtjuːmʌlt] Tumult m; **tu·mul·tu·ous** □ [tjuːˈmʌltjʊəs] lärmend; stürmisch.

tun [tʌn] Faß n.

tu·na zo. [ˈtuːnə] Thunfisch m.

tune [tjuːn] **1.** Melodie f; ♪ (Ein-)Stimmung f; fig. Harmonie f; in ~ (gut)gestimmt; out of ~ verstimmt; **2.** ♪ stimmen; ~ **in** v/i. (das Radio etc.) einschalten; v/t. das Radio etc. einstellen (to auf acc.); ~ **up** die Instrumente stimmen; Motor tunen; ~**ful** □ [ˈtjuːnfl] melodisch; ~**less** □ [~lɪs] unmelodisch.

tun·er [ˈtjuːnə] Radio, TV: Tuner m.

tun·nel [ˈtʌnl] **1.** Tunnel m; ⚒ Stollen m; **2.** (bsd. Brt. -ll-, Am. -l-) e-n Tunnel bohren (durch).

tun·ny zo. [ˈtʌnɪ] Thunfisch m.

tur·bid □ [ˈtɜːbɪd] trüb; dick(flüssig); fig. verworren, wirr.

tur·bine ⊕ [ˈtɜːbaɪn] Turbine f.

tur·bot zo. [ˈtɜːbət] Steinbutt m.

tur·bu·lent □ [ˈtɜːbjʊlənt] unruhig; ungestüm; stürmisch, turbulent.

tu·reen [təˈriːn] Terrine f.

turf [tɜːf] **1.** (pl. ~s, turves) Rasen m; Torf m; the ~ die (Pferde)Rennbahn; der Pferderennsport m; **2.** mit Rasen bedecken.

tur·gid □ [ˈtɜːdʒɪd] geschwollen.

Turk [tɜːk] Türk|e m, -in f.

tur·key [ˈtɜːkɪ] zo. Truthahn m, -henne f; Pute(r m) f; talk ~ bsd. Am. F offen od. sachlich reden.

Turk·ish [ˈtɜːkɪʃ] **1.** türkisch; **2.** ling. Türkisch n.

tur·moil [ˈtɜːmɔɪl] Aufruhr m, Unruhe f; Durcheinander n.

turn [tɜːn] **1.** v/t. (um-, herum)drehen; (um)wenden; Seite umdrehen, -blättern; lenken, richten; verwandeln; j-n abbringen (from von); ab-

wenden; Text übertragen, -setzen; bilden, formen; ⊕ drechseln; Laub verfärben; ~ **a corner** um eine Ecke biegen; ~ **loose** los-, freilassen; ~ **s.o. sick** j-n krank machen; ~ **sour** Milch sauer werden lassen; s. somersault; ~ **s.o. against** j-n aufhetzen gegen; ~ **aside** abwenden; v/i. away abwenden; ~ **down** umbiegen; Kragen umschlagen; Bett aufdecken; Decke zurückschlagen; Gas etc. klein(er) stellen; Radio etc. leiser stellen; ~ **in** ablehnen; ~ **in** bsd. Am. einreichen, -senden; ~ **off** Gas, Wasser etc. abdrehen; Licht, Radio etc. ausschalten, -machen; ~ **on** Gas, Wasser etc. aufdrehen; Gerät anstellen; Licht, Radio etc. anmachen, einschalten; F antörnen; F anmachen (a. sexuell); ~ **out** econ. Waren produzieren; hinauswerfen; = turn off; ~ **over** econ. Waren umsetzen; umdrehen; Seite umblättern; umwerfen; übergeben (to dat.); überlegen; ~ **up** nach oben drehen od. biegen; Kragen hochschlagen; Ärmel hochkrempeln; Hose etc. auf-, umschlagen; Gas etc. aufdrehen; Radio etc. lauter stellen; v/i. sich drehen (lassen); sich (um-, herum)drehen; mot. wenden; sich (ab-, hin-, zu)wenden; (ab-, ein)biegen; e-e Biegung machen (Straße etc.); sich (ver)wandeln; umschlagen (Wetter etc.); Christ, grau etc. werden (Milch); ~ **about** sich umdrehen; ⚔ kehrtmachen; ~ **aside**, ~ **away** sich abwenden; ~ **back** zurückkehren; ~ **in** F ins Bett gehen; ~ **off** abbiegen; ~ **out** v/t. ausfallen, -gehen; sich herausstellen (als); ~ **over** sich umdrehen; ~ **to** nach rechts etc. abbiegen; sich zuwenden (dat.); sich an j-n wenden; werden zu; ~ **up** fig. auftauchen; **2.** (Um)Drehung f; Biegung f, Kurve f, Kehre f; (einzelne) Windung f (e-s Kabels etc.); Wendung f; Wendepunkt m (a. fig.); Wende f; Wechsel m; Gestalt f, Form f; (kurzer) Spaziergang; (kurze) Fahrt; Reihe(nfolge) f; Dienst m, Gefallen m, Zweck m; Neigung f, Talent n; F Schrecken m; ~ (of mind) Denkart f, -weise f; at every ~ auf Schritt und Tritt; by ~s abwechselnd; in ~ der Reihe nach; it is my ~ ich bin an der Reihe; take ~s (mit-)einander od. sich (gegenseitig) abwechseln (*at* in *dat.*, bei); *does it serve your* ~? ist Ihnen damit gedient?; ~**coat** ['tɜːnkəʊt] Abtrünnige(r) *m*, Überläufer(in); ~**er** [~ə] Drechsler *m*; Dreher *m*.

turn·ing ['tɜːnɪŋ] ⊕ Drehen *n*, Drechseln *n*; Biegung *f*; Straßenecke *f*; (Weg)Abzweigung *f*; Querstraße *f*; ~**point** *fig.* Wendepunkt *m*.

tur·nip ♀ ['tɜːnɪp] (*bsd.* Weiße) Rübe.

turn·out ['tɜːnaʊt] Aufmachung *f*, *bsd.* Kleidung *f*; Teilnahme *f*, Besucher(zahl *f*) *pl.*, Beteiligung *f*; *econ.* Gesamtproduktion *f*; ~**o·ver** ['tɜːnəʊvə] *econ.* Umsatz *m*; Personalwechsel *m*, Fluktuation *f*; ~**pike** *a.* ~ road *Am.* gebührenpflichtige Schnellstraße; ~**stile** Drehkreuz *n*; ~**ta·ble** 🖦 Drehscheibe *f*; Plattenteller *m*; ~**up** *Brt.* Hosenaufschlag *m*.

tur·pen·tine 🜍 ['tɜːpəntaɪn] Terpentin *n*.

tur·pi·tude ['tɜːpɪtjuːd] Verworfenheit *f*.

tur·ret ['tʌrɪt] Türmchen *n*; ⚔, ⚓ Geschützturm *m*.

tur·tle *zo.* ['tɜːtl] (See)Schildkröte *f*; ~**dove** *zo.* Turteltaube *f*; ~**neck** Rollkragen *m*; *a.* ~ sweater Rollkragenpullover *m*.

tusk [tʌsk] Fangzahn *m*; Stoßzahn *m*; Hauer *m*.

tus·sle ['tʌsl] 1. Rauferei *f*, Balgerei *f*; 2. raufen, sich balgen.

tus·sock ['tʌsək] (Gras)Büschel *n*.

tut *int.* [tʌt] ach was!; Unsinn!

tu·te·lage ['tjuːtɪlɪdʒ] ⚖ Vormundschaft *f*; (An)Leitung *f*.

tu·tor ['tjuːtə] 1. Privat-, Hauslehrer *m*; *Brt. univ.* Tutor *m*; *Am. univ.* Assistent *m* (*mit Lehrauftrag*); 2. unterrichten; schulen, erziehen; **tu·to·ri·al** [tjuːˈtɔːrɪəl] 1. *Brt. univ.* Tutorenkurs *m*; 2. Tutor(en)...

tux·e·do *Am.* [tʌkˈsiːdəʊ] (*pl.* -dos, -does) Smoking *m*.

TV F ['tiːviː] 1. TV *n*, Fernsehen *n*; Fernseher *m*, Fernsehapparat *m*; *on* ~ im Fernsehen; Fernseh...

twang [twæŋ] 1. Schwirren *n*; *mst nasal* ~ näselnde Aussprache; 2. schwirren (lassen); näseln; klimpern *od.* kratzen auf (*dat.*), zupfen.

tweak [twiːk] zwicken, kneifen.

tweet [twiːt] zwitschern.

tweez·ers ['twiːzəz] *pl.* (*a pair of* ~ e-e) Pinzette *f*.

twelfth [twelfθ] 1. zwölfte(r, -s); 2. Zwölftel *n*; ⚯**night** ['twelfθnaɪt] Dreikönigsabend *m*.

twelve [twelv] 1. zwölf; 2. Zwölf *f*.

twen·ti·eth ['twentɪɪθ] zwanzigste(r, -s); ~**ty** [~ɪ] 1. zwanzig; 2. Zwanzig *f*.

twice [twaɪs] zweimal.

twid·dle ['twɪdl] herumdrehen (an *dat.*); (herum)spielen mit (*od. with* mit).

twig [twɪg] dünner Zweig, Ästchen *n*.

twi·light ['twaɪlaɪt] Zwielicht *n*; (*bsd.* Abend)Dämmerung *f*; *fig.* Verfall *m*.

twin [twɪn] 1. Zwillings...; doppelt; Zwilling *m*; ~*s pl.* Zwillinge *pl.*; *attr.* Zwillings...; ~**bedded room** Zweibettzimmer *n*; ~ **brother** Zwillingsbruder *m*; ~ **engined** ✈ zweimotorig; ~**jet** ✈ zwei-, doppelstrahlig; ~**lens reflex camera** *phot.* Spiegelreflexkamera *f*; ~ **sister** Zwillingsschwester *f*; ~ **town** Partnerstadt *f*; ~ **track** Doppelspur *f* (*e-s Tonbands*).

twine [twaɪn] 1. Bindfaden *m*, Schnur *f*; Zwirn *m*; 2. zs.-drehen; verflechten; (sich) schlingen *od.* winden; umschlingen, -ranken.

twinge [twɪndʒ] stechender Schmerz, Zwicken *n*, Stich *m*.

twin·kle ['twɪŋkl] 1. funkeln, blitzen; huschen; zwinkern; 2. Funkeln *n*, Blitzen *n*; (Augen)Zwinkern *n*, Blinzeln *n*.

twirl [twɜːl] 1. Wirbel *m*; 2. wirbeln.

twist [twɪst] 1. Drehung *f*; Windung *f*; Biegung *f*; (Gesichts)Verzerrung *f*; Twist *m*, Garn *n*; Kringel *m*, Zopf *m* (*Backwaren*); ♪ Twist *m*; *fig.* Verfall *m*; *fig.* (ausgeprägte) Neigung *od.* Veranlagung *f*; 2. (sich) drehen *od.* winden; zs.-drehen; verdrehen; (sich) verziehen *od.* -zerren; ♪ twisten, Twist tanzen.

twitch [twɪtʃ] 1. zupfen (an *dat.*); zucken (*od. with* vor); 2. Zuckung *f*.

twit·ter ['twɪtə] 1. zwitschern; 2. Gezwitscher *n*; *in a* ~, *all of a* ~ aufgeregt.

two [tuː] 1. zwei; *in* ~s zu zweit, zu zweien; *in* ~ entzwei; *put* ~ *and* ~ *together* sich einen Vers darauf machen; 2. Zwei *f*; ~**bit** *Am.* F ['tuːbɪt] 25-Cent-...; *fig.* unbedeutend, klein; ~**cy·cle** *Am.* ⊕ Zweitakt...;

edged ['tu:'edʒd] zweischneidig;
~fold ['tu:fəʊld] zweifach; **~pence** Brt. ['tʌpəns] zwei Pence pl.; **~pen·ny** Brt. ['tʌpnɪ] zwei Pence wert; **~piece** ['tu:pi:s] 1. zweiteilig; 2. a. ~ dress Jackenkleid; a. ~ swimming-costume Zweiteiler m; **~seat·er** mot., ✈ ['tu:'si:tə] Zweisitzer m; **~stroke** bsd. Brt. ⊕ ['tu:strəʊk] Zweitakt...; **~way** Doppel...; ~ adapter ✦ Doppelstecker m; ~ traffic Gegenverkehr m.

ty·coon Am. F ['taɪ'ku:n] Industriemagnat m; oil ~ Ölmagnat m.

type [taɪp] 1. Typ m; Urbild n; Vorbild n; Muster n; Art f, Sorte f; print. Type f, Buchstabe m; true to ~ artgemäß, typisch; set in ~ print. setzen; 2. v/t. et. mit der Maschine (ab)schreiben, (ab)tippen; v/i. maschineschreiben, tippen; **~writ·er**

['taɪpraɪtə] Schreibmaschine f; ~ ribbon Farbband n.

ty·phoid ✦ ['taɪfɔɪd] 1. typhös; ~ fever = (Unterleibs)Typhus m.

ty·phoon [taɪ'fu:n] Taifun m.

ty·phus ✦ ['taɪfəs] Flecktyphus m, -fieber n; △ nicht Typhus.

typ·i·cal □ ['tɪpɪkl] typisch; bezeichnend, kennzeichnend (of für); **~fy** [~faɪ] typisch sein für; versinnbildlichen.

typ·ist ['taɪpɪst] Maschinenschreiber(in); Schreibkraft f.

ty·ran·nic [tɪ'rænɪk] (~ally), **~ni·cal** □ [~kl] tyrannisch.

tyr·an·nize ['tɪrənaɪz] tyrannisieren; **~ny** [~ɪ] Tyrannei f.

tyr·ant ['taɪərənt] Tyrann(in).

tyre Brt. ['taɪə] (Rad-, Auto)Reifen m.

Tyr·o·lese [tɪrə'li:z] 1. Tiroler(in); 2. tirolisch, Tiroler...

tzar hist. [zɑ:] Zar m.

U

u·biq·ui·tous □ [ju:'bɪkwɪtəs] allgegenwärtig, überall zu finden(d).

ud·der ['ʌdə] Euter n.

ug·ly □ ['ʌglɪ] (-ier, -iest) häßlich; schlimm; gemein; widerwärtig, übel.

ul·cer ✦ ['ʌlsə] Geschwür n; **~ate** ✦ [~reɪt] eitern (lassen); **~ous** ✦ [~rəs] eiternd.

ul·te·ri·or □ [ʌl'tɪərɪə] jenseitig; weiter; tiefer(liegend), versteckt.

ul·ti·mate □ ['ʌltɪmət] äußerste(r, -s), letzte(r, -s); End...; **~ly** [~lɪ] letztlich; schließlich.

ul·ti·ma·tum [ʌltɪ'meɪtəm] (pl. -tums, -ta [-tə]) Ultimatum n.

ul·tra ['ʌltrə] übermäßig; extrem; super...; Ultra..., ultra...; **~fash·ion·a·ble** [~'fæʃənəbl] hypermodern; **~mod·ern** hypermodern.

um·bil·i·cal cord anat. [ʌm'bɪlɪkl kɔ:d] Nabelschnur f.

um·brel·la [ʌm'brelə] Regenschirm m; ✕, ✈ Abschirmung f; fig. Schutz m.

um·pire ['ʌmpaɪə] 1. Schiedsrichter m; 2. als Schiedsrichter fungieren

(bei); schlichten; Sport: a. Spiel leiten.

un- [ʌn] un..., Un...; ent...; nicht...

un·a·bashed [ʌnə'bæʃt] unverfroren; unerschrocken.

un·a·bat·ed [ʌnə'beɪtɪd] unvermindert.

un·a·ble ['ʌn'eɪbl] unfähig, außerstande, nicht in der Lage.

un·ac·com·mo·dat·ing ['ʌnə'kɒmədeɪtɪŋ] unnachgiebig; ungefällig.

un·ac·coun·ta·ble □ [ʌnə'kaʊntəbl] unerklärlich, seltsam.

un·ac·cus·tomed ['ʌnə'kʌstəmd] ungewohnt; ungewöhnlich.

un·ac·quaint·ed ['ʌnə'kweɪntɪd]: be ~ with s.th. et. nicht kennen, mit e-r Sache nicht vertraut sein.

un·ad·vised □ ['ʌnəd'vaɪzd] unbesonnen, unüberlegt; unberaten.

un·af·fect·ed □ ['ʌnə'fektɪd] unberührt; ungerührt; ungekünstelt.

un·aid·ed ['ʌn'eɪdɪd] ohne Unterstützung, (ganz) allein; bloß (Auge).

un·al·ter·a·ble □ [ʌn'ɔ:ltərəbl] unveränderlich; **un·al·tered** ['ʌn'ɔ:ltəd] unverändert.

u·na·nim·i·ty [ju:nə'nɪmətɪ] Einmütigkeit *f*; **u·nan·i·mous** □ [ju:'nænɪməs] einmütig, -stimmig.

un·an·swe·ra·ble □ [ʌn'ɑːnsərəbl] unwiderleglich; **un·an·swered** ['ʌn'ɑːnsəd] unbeantwortet.

un·ap·proa·cha·ble □ ['ʌnə'prəʊtʃəbl] unzugänglich, unnahbar.

un·apt □ [ʌn'æpt] ungeeignet.

un·a·shamed □ ['ʌnə'ʃeɪmd] schamlos.

un·asked ['ʌn'ɑːskt] ungefragt; ungebeten; uneingeladen.

un·as·sist·ed □ ['ʌnə'sɪstɪd] ohne Hilfe *od.* Unterstützung.

un·as·sum·ing □ ['ʌnə'sjuːmɪŋ] anspruchslos, bescheiden.

un·at·tached ['ʌnə'tætʃt] nicht gebunden; ungebunden, ledig, frei.

un·at·trac·tive □ ['ʌnə'træktɪv] wenig anziehend, reizlos, unattraktiv.

un·au·thor·ized ['ʌn'ɔːθəraɪzd] unberechtigt; unbefugt.

un·a·vai·la·ble □ ['ʌnə'veɪləbl] nicht verfügbar; **un·a·vail·ing** [~ɪŋ] vergeblich.

un·a·void·a·ble □ [ʌnə'vɔɪdəbl] unvermeidlich.

un·a·ware ['ʌnə'weə]: *be* ~ *of et.* nicht bemerken; ~s [~z] unversehens, unvermutet; versehentlich.

un·backed ['ʌn'bækt] ohne Unterstützung; ungedeckt (*Scheck*).

un·bal·anced ['ʌn'bælənst] unausgeglichen; *of* a ~ *mind* geistesgestört.

un·bear·a·ble □ [ʌn'beərəbl] unerträglich.

un·beat·en ['ʌn'biːtn] ungeschlagen, unbesiegt; unübertroffen.

un·be·com·ing □ ['ʌnbɪ'kʌmɪŋ] unkleidsam; unpassend, unschicklich.

un·be·known(st) ['ʌnbɪ'nəʊn(st)] (*to*) ohne (*j-s*) Wissen; unbekannt (*to dat.*).

un·be·lief *eccl.* ['ʌnbɪ'liːf] Unglaube *m*.

un·be·lie·va·ble □ ['ʌnbɪ'liːvəbl] unglaublich; **un·be·liev·ing** □ ['ʌnbɪ'liːvɪŋ] ungläubig.

un·bend ['ʌn'bend] (*-bent*) (sich) entspannen; aus sich herausgehen, auftauen; ~**ing** □ [~ɪŋ] unbiegsam; *fig.* unbeugsam.

un·bi·as(s)ed □ ['ʌn'baɪəst] unvoreingenommen; **r̄t̄s** unbefangen.

un·bid·(den) ['ʌn'bɪd(n)] unaufgefordert; ungebeten; ungeladen.

un·bind ['ʌn'baɪnd] (*-bound*) losbinden, befreien; lösen; den Verband abnehmen von.

un·blush·ing □ ['ʌn'blʌʃɪŋ] schamlos.

un·born ['ʌn'bɔːn] (noch) ungeboren; (zu)künftig, kommend.

un·bos·om [ʌn'bʊzəm] offenbaren.

un·bound·ed □ ['ʌn'baʊndɪd] unbegrenzt; *fig.* grenzen-, schrankenlos.

un·bri·dled ['ʌn'braɪdld] ungezügelt; ~ *tongue* lose Zunge.

un·bro·ken □ ['ʌn'brəʊkən] ungebrochen; unversehrt; ununterbrochen; nicht zugeritten (*Pferd*).

un·bur·den ['ʌn'bɜːdn]: ~ *o.s.* (*to s.o.*) (j-m) sein Herz ausschütten.

un·but·ton ['ʌn'bʌtn] aufknöpfen.

un·called-for ['ʌn'kɔːldfɔː] unerwünscht; unverlangt; unpassend.

un·can·ny □ [ʌn'kænɪ] (*-ier*, *-iest*) unheimlich.

un·cared-for ['ʌn'keədfɔː] unbeachtet; vernachlässigt; ungepflegt.

un·ceas·ing □ [ʌn'siːsɪŋ] unaufhörlich.

un·ce·re·mo·ni·ous □ ['ʌnserɪ'məʊnjəs] ungezwungen; grob; unhöflich.

un·cer·tain □ [ʌn'sɜːtn] unsicher; ungewiß; unbestimmt; unzuverlässig; ~**ty** [~tɪ] Unsicherheit *f*.

un·chal·lenged ['ʌn'tʃæləndʒd] unangefochten.

un·change·a·ble □ ['ʌn'tʃeɪndʒəbl] unveränderlich, unwandelbar; **un·changed** ['ʌn'tʃeɪndʒd] unverändert; **un·chang·ing** □ ['ʌn'tʃeɪndʒɪŋ] unveränderlich.

un·char·i·ta·ble □ ['ʌn'tʃærɪtəbl] lieblos; unbarmherzig; unfreundlich.

un·checked ['ʌn'tʃekt] ungehindert; unkontrolliert.

un·civ·il □ ['ʌn'sɪvl] unhöflich; **un·civ·i·lized** [~vəlaɪzd] unzivilisiert.

un·claimed ['ʌn'kleɪmd] nicht beansprucht; unzustellbar (*bsd. Brief*).

un·clasp ['ʌn'klɑːsp] loshaken, loshaken, auf-, losschnallen; aufmachen.

un·cle ['ʌŋkl] Onkel *m*.

un·clean ['ʌn'kliːn] unrein.

un·close ['ʌn'kləʊz] (sich) öffnen.

un·come·ly [ʌn'kʌmlɪ] (*-ier*, *-iest*) unattraktiv, unschön; reizlos; unpassend.

un·com·for·ta·ble □ [ʌn'kʌmfətəbl]

unbehaglich, ungemütlich; unangenehm.

un·com·mon □ [ʌnˈkɒmən] ungewöhnlich.

un·com·mu·ni·ca·tive □ [ˈʌnkəˈmjuːnɪkətɪv] wortkarg, verschlossen.

un·com·plain·ing □ [ˈʌnkəmˈpleɪnɪŋ] klaglos, ohne Murren, geduldig.

un·com·pro·mis·ing □ [ʌnˈkɒmprəmaɪzɪŋ] kompromißlos.

un·con·cern [ˈʌnkənˈsɜːn] Unbekümmertheit f; Gleichgültigkeit f; **~ed** □ unbekümmert; unbeteiligt; gleichgültig; uninteressiert (*with* an *dat.*).

un·con·di·tion·al □ [ˈʌnkənˈdɪʃənl] bedingungs-, vorbehaltlos.

un·con·firmed [ˈʌnkənˈfɜːmd] unbestätigt; *eccl.* nicht konfirmiert.

un·con·nect·ed □ [ˈʌnkəˈnektɪd] unverbunden; unzusammenhängend.

un·con·quer·a·ble □ [ʌnˈkɒŋkərəbl] unüberwindlich, unbesiegbar; **un·con·quered** [ʌnˈkɒŋkəd] unbesiegt.

un·con·scio·na·ble □ [ʌnˈkɒnʃnəbl] gewissen-, skrupellos; F unverschämt, unmäßig, übermäßig.

un·con·scious □ [ʌnˈkɒnʃəs] unbewußt; 💉 bewußtlos; **~·ness** 💉 [~nɪs] Bewußtlosigkeit f.

un·con·sti·tu·tion·al □ [ˈʌnkɒnstɪˈtjuːʃənl] verfassungswidrig.

un·con·trol·la·ble □ [ˈʌnkənˈtrəʊləbl] unkontrollierbar; unbeherrscht; **un·con·trolled** [ˈʌnkənˈtrəʊld] unbeaufsichtigt; unbeherrscht.

un·con·ven·tion·al □ [ˈʌnkənˈvenʃənl] unkonventionell; unüblich; ungezwungen.

un·con·vinced [ˈʌnkənˈvɪnst] nicht überzeugt (*of* von); **un·con·vinc·ing** [~ɪŋ] nicht überzeugend.

un·cork [ˈʌnˈkɔːk] entkorken.

un·count·a·ble [ˈʌnˈkaʊntəbl] unzählbar; **~ed** ungezählt.

un·cou·ple [ˈʌnˈkʌpl] ab-, aus-, loskoppeln.

un·couth □ [ʌnˈkuːθ] ungehobelt.

un·cov·er [ʌnˈkʌvə] aufdecken, freilegen; entblößen.

unc·tion [ˈʌŋkʃn] Salbung f (*a. fig.*); Salbe f; **~·tu·ous** □ [~tjʊəs] fettig, ölig; *fig.* salbungsvoll.

un·cul·ti·vat·ed [ˈʌnˈkʌltɪveɪtɪd], **un·cul·tured** [~tʃəd] unkultiviert.

un·dam·aged [ʌnˈdæmɪdʒd] unbeschädigt, unversehrt, heil.

un·daunt·ed □ [ʌnˈdɔːntɪd] unerschrocken, furchtlos.

un·de·ceive [ˈʌndɪˈsiːv] *j-m* die Augen öffnen; *j-n* aufklären.

un·de·cid·ed □ [ˈʌndɪˈsaɪdɪd] unentschieden, offen; unentschlossen.

un·de·fined □ [ˈʌndɪˈfaɪnd] unbestimmt; unbegrenzt.

un·de·mon·stra·tive □ [ˈʌndɪˈmɒnstrətɪv] zurückhaltend, reserviert.

un·de·ni·a·ble □ [ˈʌndɪˈnaɪəbl] unleugbar; unbestreitbar.

un·der [ˈʌndə] 1. *adv.* unten; darunter; 2. *prp.* unter; 3. *adj.* untere(r, -s); *in Zssgn:* unter..., Unter...; ungenügend, zu gering; **~·bid** [ʌndəˈbɪd] (*-dd-; -bid*) unterbieten; **~·brush** [ˈʌndəbrʌʃ] Unterholz n; **~·car·riage** [ˈʌndəkærɪdʒ] ✈ Fahrwerk n, -gestell n; *mot.* Fahrgestell n; **~·clothes** [ˈʌndəkləʊðz] *pl.*, **~·clothing** [~ðɪŋ] Unterkleidung f, -wäsche f; **~·cut** [ʌndəˈkʌt] (*-tt-; -cut*) Preise unterbieten; **~·dog** [ˈʌndədɒg] Verlierer m, Unterlegene(r m) f; *der* sozial Schwächere *od.* Benachteiligte; **~·done** [ʌndəˈdʌn] nicht gar, nicht durchgebraten; **~·es·ti·mate** [ʌndərˈestɪmeɪt] unterschätzen; **~·fed** [ʌndəˈfed] unterernährt; **~·go** [ʌndəˈgəʊ] (*-went, -gone*) durchmachen; erdulden; sich unterziehen (*dat.*); **~·grad·u·ate** [ʌndəˈgrædjʊət] Student(in); **~·ground** 1. unterirdisch; Untergrund...; 2. *bsd. Brt.* Untergrundbahn f, U-Bahn f; **~·growth** [ˈʌndəgrəʊθ] Unterholz n; **~·hand** [ʌndəˈhænd] unter der Hand; heimlich; **~·lie** [ʌndəˈlaɪ] (*-lay, -lain*) zugrunde liegen (*dat.*); **~·line** [ʌndəˈlaɪn] unterstreichen; **~·ling** *contp.* [ˈʌndəlɪŋ] Untergebene(r m) f; **~·mine** [ʌndəˈmaɪn] unterminieren; *fig.* untergraben; schwächen; **~·most** [ˈʌndəməʊst] unterste(r, -s); **~·neath** [ʌndəˈniːθ] 1. *prp.* unter(halb); 2. *adv.* unten; darunter; **~·pass** [ˈʌndəpɑːs] Unterführung f; **~·pin** [ʌndəˈpɪn] (*-nn-*) untermauern (*a. fig.*); **~·plot** [ˈʌndəplɒt] Nebenhandlung f; **~·priv·i·leged** [ʌndəˈprɪvɪlɪdʒd] benachteiligt; **~·rate** [ʌndəˈreɪt] unterschätzen; **~·sec·re·ta·ry** [ʌndəˈsekrətərɪ] Staatssekretär m; **~·sell** *econ.* [ʌndəˈsel] (*-sold*) *j-n* unterbieten; *Ware* verschleudern; **~shirt** *Am.* ['ʌndəʃɜːt] Unterhemd *n*; **~signed** ['ʌndəsaɪnd]: *the ~* der, die Unterzeichnete; **~size(d)** ['ʌndə-saɪz(d)] zu klein; **~skirt** ['ʌndə-skɜːt] Unterrock *m*; **~staffed** ['ʌndə'stɑːft] (personell) unterbesetzt; **~stand** ['ʌndə'stænd] (-stood) verstehen; sich verstehen auf (*acc.*); (als sicher) annehmen; erfahren, hören; (sinngemäß) ergänzen; *make o.s. understood* sich verständlich machen; *an understood thing* e-e abgemachte Sache; **~stand·a·ble** [~əbl] verständlich; **~stand·ing** [~ɪŋ] Verstand *m*; Einvernehmen *n*; Verständigung *f*, Abmachung *f*, Einigung *f*; Voraussetzung *f*; **~state** ['ʌndə'steɪt] zu gering angeben; abschwächen; **~state·ment** [~mənt] Understatement *n*, Untertreibung *f*; **~take** ['ʌndə'teɪk] (-took, -taken) unternehmen; übernehmen; sich verpflichten; **~tak·er** ['ʌndəteɪkə] Leichenbestatter *m*; Beerdigungs-, Bestattungsinstitut *n*; △ *nicht Unternehmer*; **~tak·ing** [ʌndə'teɪkɪŋ] Unternehmen *n*; Zusicherung *f*; ['ʌndəteɪkɪŋ] Leichenbestattung *f*; **~tone** ['ʌndətəʊn] leiser Ton; *fig.* Unterton *m*; **~val·ue** ['ʌndə'væljuː] unterschätzen; **~wear** ['ʌndəweə] Unterkleidung *f*, -wäsche *f*; **~wood** ['ʌndəwʊd] Unterholz *n*.

un·de·served ['ʌndɪ'zɜːvd] unverdient; **un·de·serv·ing** □ [~ɪŋ] unwürdig.

un·de·signed □ ['ʌndɪ'zaɪnd] unbeabsichtigt, unabsichtlich.

un·de·si·ra·ble ['ʌndɪ'zaɪərəbl] **1.** □ unerwünscht; **2.** unerwünschte Person.

un·de·vel·oped [ʌndɪ'veləpt] unerschlossen (*Gelände*); unentwickelt.

un·de·vi·at·ing □ ['ʌn'diːvɪeɪtɪŋ] unentwegt.

un·dies F ['ʌndɪz] *pl.* (Damen)Unterwäsche *f*.

un·dig·ni·fied □ [ʌn'dɪgnɪfaɪd] unwürdig, würdelos.

un·dis·ci·plined [ʌn'dɪsɪplɪnd] undiszipliniert; ungeschult.

un·dis·guised □ ['ʌndɪs'gaɪzd] nicht verkleidet; *fig.* unverhohlen.

un·dis·put·ed □ ['ʌndɪ'spjuːtɪd] unbestritten.

un·do [ʌn'duː] (-did, -done) aufmachen; (auf)lösen; ungeschehen ma-

chen, aufheben; vernichten; **~ing** [~ɪŋ] Aufmachen *n*; Ungeschehenmachen *n*; Vernichtung *f*; Verderben *n*; **un·done** ['ʌn'dʌn] zugrunde gerichtet, ruiniert, erledigt.

un·doubt·ed □ [ʌn'daʊtɪd] unzweifelhaft, zweifellos.

un·dreamed [ʌn'driːmd], **un·dreamt** [ʌn'dremt]: *~-of* ungeahnt.

un·dress ['ʌn'dres] (sich) entkleiden *od.* ausziehen; **~ed** unbekleidet.

un·due □ ['ʌn'djuː] unpassend; übermäßig; *econ.* noch nicht fällig.

un·du|late ['ʌndjʊleɪt] wogen, wallen; wellenförmig verlaufen; **~la·tion** [ʌndjʊ'leɪʃn] wellenförmige Bewegung.

un·du·ti·ful □ ['ʌn'djuːtɪfl] ungehorsam; pflichtvergessen.

un·earth ['ʌn'ɜːθ] ausgraben; *fig.* aufstöbern; **~ly** [ʌn'ɜːθlɪ] überirdisch; unheimlich; *at an ~ hour* F zu e-r unchristlichen Zeit.

un·easi·ness [ʌn'iːzɪnɪs] Unruhe *f*; Unbehagen *n*; **~y** □ [ʌn'iːzɪ] (-ier, -iest) unbehaglich; unruhig; unsicher.

un·ed·u·cat·ed ['ʌn'edjʊkeɪtɪd] ungebildet.

un·e·mo·tio·nal □ ['ʌnɪ'məʊʃənl] leidenschaftslos; passiv; nüchtern.

un·em·ployed ['ʌnɪm'plɔɪd] **1.** arbeitslos; ungenützt; **2.** *the ~ pl.* die Arbeitslosen *pl.*; **~ploy·ment** [~mənt] Arbeitslosigkeit *f*.

un·end·ing □ [ʌn'endɪŋ] endlos.

un·en·dur·a·ble □ ['ʌnɪn'djʊərəbl] unerträglich.

un·en·gaged ['ʌnɪn'geɪdʒd] frei.

un·e·qual □ ['ʌn'iːkwəl] ungleich; nicht gewachsen (*to dat.*); **~(l)ed** unerreicht, unübertroffen.

un·er·ring □ ['ʌn'ɜːrɪŋ] unfehlbar.

un·es·sen·tial ['ʌnɪ'senʃl] unwesentlich, unwichtig.

un·e·ven □ ['ʌn'iːvn] uneben; ungleich(mäßig); ungerade (*Zahl*).

un·e·vent·ful □ ['ʌnɪ'ventfl] ereignislos; ohne Zwischenfälle.

un·ex·am·pled ['ʌnɪg'zɑːmpld] beispiellos.

un·ex·cep·tio·na·ble □ ['ʌnɪk'sep-ʃnəbl] untadelig; einwandfrei.

un·ex·pec·ted □ ['ʌnɪk'spektɪd] unerwartet.

un·ex·plained ['ʌnɪk'spleɪnd] unerklärt.

un·fad·ing [ʌn'feɪdɪŋ] nicht welkend; unvergänglich; echt (*Farbe*).

un·fail·ing □ [ʌnˈfeɪlɪŋ] unfehlbar, nie versagend; unerschöpflich; *fig.* treu.

un·fair □ [ˈʌnˈfeə] unfair; ungerecht; unehrlich.

un·faith·ful □ [ˈʌnˈfeɪθfl] un(ge)-treu, treulos; nicht wortgetreu.

un·fa·mil·i·ar [ˈʌnfəˈmɪljə] unge-wohnt; unbekannt; nicht vertraut (*with mit*).

un·fas·ten [ˈʌnˈfɑːsn] aufmachen; lö-sen; ∼ed unbefestigt, lose.

un·fath·o·ma·ble □ [ʌnˈfæðəməbl] unergründlich.

un·fa·vo(u)·ra·ble □ [ˈʌnˈfeɪvə-rəbl] ungünstig; unvorteilhaft.

un·feel·ing □ [ʌnˈfiːlɪŋ] gefühllos.

un·fil·i·al □ [ˈʌnˈfɪljəl] respektlos, pflichtvergessen (*Kind*).

un·fin·ished [ˈʌnˈfɪnɪʃt] unvollendet; unfertig; unerledigt.

un·fit [ˈʌnˈfɪt] **1.** □ ungeeignet, un-tauglich; *Sport:* nicht fit, nicht in (guter) Form; **2.** (-*tt*-) ungeeignet *od.* untauglich machen.

un·fix [ˈʌnˈfɪks] losmachen, lösen.

un·fledged [ˈʌnˈfledʒd] ungefiedert, (noch) nicht flügge; *fig.* unreif.

un·flinch·ing □ [ʌnˈflɪntʃɪŋ] ent-schlossen, unnachgiebig; uner-schrocken.

un·fold [ˈʌnˈfəʊld] (sich) entfalten *od.* öffnen; [ʌnˈfəʊld] darlegen, ent-hüllen.

un·forced [ˈʌnˈfɔːst] ungezwungen.

un·fore·seen [ˈʌnfɔːˈsiːn] unvorher-gesehen, unerwartet.

un·for·get·ta·ble □ [ˈʌnfəˈgetəbl] unvergeßlich.

un·for·giv·ing [ˈʌnfəˈgɪvɪŋ] unver-söhnlich, nachtragend.

un·for·got·ten [ˈʌnfəˈgɒtn] unver-gessen.

un·for·tu·nate [ʌnˈfɔːtʃnət] **1.** □ un-glücklich; **2.** Unglückliche(r *m*) *f*; ∼**ly** [∼lɪ] unglücklicherweise, leider.

un·found·ed □ [ˈʌnˈfaʊndɪd] unbe-gründet, grundlos.

un·friend·ly [ʌnˈfrendlɪ] (-*ier*, -*iest*) unfreundlich; ungünstig.

un·furl [ˈʌnˈfɜːl] entfalten, aufrollen.

un·fur·nished [ˈʌnˈfɜːnɪʃt] unmö-bliert.

un·gain·ly [ʌnˈgeɪnlɪ] unbeholfen, plump, linkisch.

un·gen·er·ous □ [ˈʌnˈdʒenərəs] nicht freigebig; kleinlich; unfair.

un·god·ly □ [ˈʌnˈgɒdlɪ] gottlos; F scheußlich; *at an* ∼ *hour* F zu e-r unchristlichen Zeit.

un·gov·er·na·ble □ [ʌnˈgʌvənəbl] unlenksam; zügellos, wild.

un·grace·ful □ [ˈʌnˈgreɪsfl] ungra-ziös, ohne Anmut; unbeholfen.

un·gra·cious □ [ˈʌnˈgreɪʃəs] ungnä-dig; unfreundlich.

un·grate·ful □ [ʌnˈgreɪtfl] undank-bar.

un·guard·ed □ [ˈʌnˈgɑːdɪd] unbe-wacht; ungeschützt; unvorsichtig.

un·guent *pharm.* [ˈʌŋgwənt] Salbe *f*.

un·ham·pered [ˈʌnˈhæmpəd] unge-hindert.

un·hand·some □ [ʌnˈhænsəm] un-schön.

un·han·dy □ [ˈʌnˈhændɪ] (-*ier*, -*iest*) unhandlich; ungeschickt; un-beholfen.

un·hap·py □ [ʌnˈhæpɪ] (-*ier*, -*iest*) unglücklich.

un·harmed [ˈʌnˈhɑːmd] unversehrt.

un·health·y □ [ʌnˈhelθɪ] (-*ier*, -*iest*) ungesund.

un·heard-of [ʌnˈhɜːdɒv] unerhört; beispiellos.

un·heed·ed □ [ˈʌnˈhiːdɪd] unbeach-tet; ∼**ing** [∼ɪŋ] sorglos.

un·hes·i·tat·ing □ [ʌnˈhezɪteɪtɪŋ] ohne Zögern; anstandslos.

un·ho·ly □ [ˈʌnˈhəʊlɪ] (-*ier*, -*iest*) un-heilig; gottlos; F *s. ungodly*.

un·hook [ˈʌnˈhʊk] auf-, loshaken.

un·hoped-for [ʌnˈhəʊptfɔː] unver-hofft, unerwartet.

un·hurt [ˈʌnˈhɜːt] unverletzt.

u·ni- [ˈjuːnɪ] uni..., ein..., einzig.

u·ni·corn [ˈjuːnɪkɔːn] Einhorn *n*.

u·ni·fi·ca·tion [juːnɪfɪˈkeɪʃn] Ver-einigung *f*; Vereinheitlichung *f*.

u·ni·form [ˈjuːnɪfɔːm] **1.** □ gleich-förmig, -mäßig, gleich; einheitlich; **2.** Uniform *f*, Dienstkleidung *f*; **3.** uniformieren; ∼**i·ty** [juːnɪˈfɔːmətɪ] Gleichförmigkeit *f*; Einheitlichkei *f*, Übereinstimmung *f*.

u·ni·fy [ˈjuːnɪfaɪ] verein(ig)en; ver-einheitlichen.

u·ni·lat·e·ral □ [ˈjuːnɪˈlætərəl] ein-seitig.

un·i·ma·gi·na·ble □ [ˈʌnɪˈmædʒɪ-nəbl] unvorstellbar; ∼**tive** □ [ˈʌn-ɪˈmædʒɪnətɪv] phantasie-, einfalls-los.

un·im·por·tant □ [ˈʌnɪmˈpɔːtənt] unwichtig, unbedeutend.

U
V

un·im·proved [ˈʌnɪmˈpruːvd] nicht kultiviert, unbebaut (*Land*); unverbessert.

un·in·formed [ˈʌnɪnˈfɔːmd] nicht unterrichtet *od.* eingeweiht.

un·in·hab·i·ta·ble [ˈʌnɪnˈhæbɪtəbl] unbewohnbar; **~it·ed** [~tɪd] unbewohnt.

un·in·jured [ˈʌnˈɪndʒəd] unbeschädigt, unverletzt.

un·in·tel·li·gi·ble ☐ [ˈʌnɪnˈtelɪdʒəbl] unverständlich.

un·in·ten·tion·al ☐ [ˈʌnɪnˈtenʃənl] unabsichtlich, unbeabsichtigt.

un·in·te·rest·ing ☐ [ˈʌnˈɪntrɪstɪŋ] uninteressant.

un·in·ter·rupt·ed ☐ [ˈʌnɪntəˈrʌptɪd] ununterbrochen.

u·ni·on [ˈjuːnjən] Vereinigung *f*; Verbindung *f*; Union *f*; Verband *m*, Verein *m*, Bund *m*; *pol.* Vereinigung *f*, Zusammenschluß *m*; Gewerkschaft *f*; **~ist** [~ɪst] Gewerkschaftler(in); ♃ **Jack** Union Jack *m* (*britische Nationalflagge*); **~ suit** *Am.* Hemdhose *f* (mit langem Bein).

u·nique ☐ [juːˈniːk] einzigartig, einmalig.

u·ni·son ♪ *u. fig.* [ˈjuːnɪzn] Einklang *m*.

u·nit [ˈjuːnɪt] Einheit *f*; ⊕ (Bau)Einheit *f*; ♣ Einer *m*.

u·nite [juːˈnaɪt] (sich) vereinigen, (sich) verbinden; **u·nit·ed** vereinigt, vereint; **u·ni·ty** [ˈjuːnətɪ] Einheit *f*; Einigkeit *f*, Eintracht *f*.

u·ni·ver·sal ☐ [juːnɪˈvɜːsl] allgemein; allumfassend; Universal...; Welt...; **~i·ty** [ˈjuːnɪvɜːˈsælətɪ] Allgemeinheit *f*; umfassende Bildung; Vielseitigkeit *f*.

u·ni·verse [ˈjuːnɪvɜːs] Weltall *n*, Universum *n*.

u·ni·ver·si·ty [juːnɪˈvɜːsətɪ] Universität *f*; **~ graduate** Akademiker *m*.

un·just ☐ [ˈʌnˈdʒʌst] ungerecht; **un·jus·ti·fi·a·ble** ☐ [ʌnˈdʒʌstɪfaɪəbl] nicht zu rechtfertigen(d), unentschuldbar.

un·kempt [ˈʌnˈkempt] ungekämmt, zerzaust; ungepflegt.

un·kind ☐ [ʌnˈkaɪnd] unfreundlich.

un·know·ing ☐ [ˈʌnˈnəʊɪŋ] unwissend; unbewußt; **un·known** [~n] 1. unbekannt; **~ to me** ohne mein Wissen; 2. der, die, das Unbekannte.

un·lace [ˈʌnˈleɪs] aufschnüren.

un·latch [ˈʌnˈlætʃ] *Tür* aufklinken.

un·law·ful ☐ [ˈʌnˈlɔːfl] ungesetzlich, widerrechtlich, illegal.

un·lead·ed [ˈʌnˈledɪd] bleifrei.

un·learn [ˈʌnˈlɜːn] (-ed *od.* -learnt) verlernen.

un·less [ənˈles] wenn ... nicht, außer wenn ..., es sei denn, daß ...

un·like [ˈʌnˈlaɪk] 1. *adj.* ☐ ungleich; 2. *prp.* unähnlich (*s.o.* j-m); anders als; im Gegensatz zu; **~ly** [ʌnˈlaɪklɪ] unwahrscheinlich.

un·lim·it·ed [ʌnˈlɪmɪtɪd] unbegrenzt.

un·load [ˈʌnˈləʊd] ent-, ab-, ausladen; ♣ *Ladung* löschen.

un·lock [ˈʌnˈlɒk] aufschließen; **~ed** unverschlossen.

un·looked-for [ʌnˈlʊktfɔː] unerwartet, überraschend.

un·loose, un·loos·en [ˈʌnˈluːs, ʌnˈluːsn] lösen; lockern; losmachen.

un·love·ly [ˈʌnˈlʌvlɪ] reizlos, unschön; **un·lov·ing** ☐ [~ɪŋ] lieblos.

un·luck·y ☐ [ʌnˈlʌkɪ] (-ier, -iest) unglücklich; unheilvoll; **be ~** Pech haben.

un·make [ˈʌnˈmeɪk] (-made) aufheben, widerrufen, rückgängig machen; umbilden; *j-n* absetzen.

un·man [ˈʌnˈmæn] (-nn-) entmannen; entmutigen; **~ned** *Raumflug*: unbemannt.

un·man·age·a·ble ☐ [ʌnˈmænɪdʒəbl] unkontrollierbar.

un·mar·ried [ˈʌnˈmærɪd] unverheiratet, ledig.

un·mask [ˈʌnˈmɑːsk] (sich) demaskieren; *fig.* entlarven.

un·matched [ˈʌnˈmætʃt] unerreicht, unübertroffen, unvergleichlich.

un·mean·ing ☐ [ʌnˈmiːnɪŋ] nichtssagend.

un·mea·sured [ʌnˈmeʒəd] ungemessen; unermeßlich.

un·mer·it·ed [ʌnˈmerɪtɪd] unverdient.

un·mind·ful ☐ [ʌnˈmaɪndfl]: **be ~ of** nicht achten auf (*acc.*); nicht denken an (*acc.*).

un·mis·ta·ka·ble ☐ [ˈʌnmɪˈsteɪkəbl] unverkennbar; unmißverständlich.

un·mit·i·gat·ed [ʌnˈmɪtɪgeɪtɪd] ungemildert; *an ~ scoundrel* ein Erzhalunke.

un·mo·lest·ed [ˈʌnməˈlestɪd] unbelästigt.

un·mount·ed [ˈʌnˈmaʊntɪd] unbe-

U V

ritten; ungefaßt (*Schmuckstein*); nicht aufgezogen (*Bild*).

un·moved ['ʌn'muːvd] unbewegt; ungerührt.

un·named ['ʌn'neɪmd] ungenannt.

un·nat·u·ral □ [ʌn'nætʃrəl] unnatürlich.

un·nec·es·sa·ry □ [ʌn'nesəsərɪ] unnötig; überflüssig.

un·neigh·bo(u)r·ly ['ʌn'neɪbəlɪ] nicht gutnachbarlich; unfreundlich.

un·nerve ['ʌn'nɜːv] entnerven.

un·no·ticed ['ʌn'nəʊtɪst] unbemerkt.

un·ob·jec·tio·na·ble □ ['ʌnəb'dʒek-ʃnəbl] einwandfrei.

un·ob·serv·ant □ ['ʌnəb'zɜːvənt] unachtsam; **un·ob·served** □ [~d] unbemerkt.

un·ob·tai·na·ble ['ʌnəb'teɪnəbl] unerreichbar.

un·ob·tru·sive □ ['ʌnəb'truːsɪv] unaufdringlich, bescheiden.

un·oc·cu·pied ['ʌn'ɒkjʊpaɪd] unbesetzt; unbewohnt; unbeschäftigt.

un·of·fend·ing ['ʌnə'fendɪŋ] harmlos.

un·of·fi·cial □ ['ʌnə'fɪʃl] nichtamtlich, inoffiziell.

un·op·posed ['ʌnə'pəʊzd] ungehindert.

un·os·ten·ta·tious □ ['ʌnɒstən-'teɪʃəs] anspruchslos; unauffällig; schlicht.

un·owned ['ʌn'əʊnd] herrenlos.

un·pack ['ʌn'pæk] auspacken.

un·paid ['ʌn'peɪd] unbezahlt.

un·par·al·leled [ʌn'pærəleld] einmalig, beispiellos, ohnegleichen.

un·par·don·a·ble □ [ʌn'pɑːdnəbl] unverzeihlich.

un·per·ceived □ ['ʌnpə'siːvd] unbemerkt.

un·per·turbed ['ʌnpə'tɜːbd] ruhig, gelassen.

un·pick [ʌn'pɪk] *Naht etc.* auftrennen.

un·placed [ʌn'pleɪst]: *be* ~ *Sport*: sich nicht placieren können.

un·pleas·ant □ [ʌn'pleznt] unangenehm, unerfreulich; unfreundlich; ~**ness** [~nɪs] Unannehmlichkeit *f*; Unstimmigkeit *f*.

un·pol·ished ['ʌn'pɒlɪʃt] unpoliert; *fig.* ungehobelt, ungebildet.

un·pol·lut·ed ['ʌnpə'luːtɪd] unverschmutzt, unverseucht, sauber (*Umwelt*).

un·pop·u·lar □ ['ʌn'pɒpjʊlə] unpopulär, unbeliebt; ~**i·ty** ['ʌn-pɒpjʊ'lærətɪ] Unbeliebtheit *f*.

un·prac·ti·cal □ ['ʌn'præktɪkl] unpraktisch; ~**tised**, *Am.* ~**ticed** [ʌn-'præktɪst] ungeübt.

un·pre·ce·dent·ed □ [ʌn'presɪdən-tɪd] beispiellos; noch nie dagewesen.

un·prej·u·diced □ [ʌn'predʒʊdɪst] unbefangen, unvoreingenommen.

un·pre·med·i·tat·ed □ ['ʌnprɪ'medɪteɪtɪd] unüberlegt; nicht vorsätzlich.

un·pre·pared □ ['ʌnprɪ'peəd] unvorbereitet.

un·pre·ten·tious □ ['ʌnprɪ'tenʃəs] bescheiden, schlicht.

un·prin·ci·pled [ʌn'prɪnsəpld] ohne Grundsätze; gewissenlos.

un·prof·i·ta·ble □ [ʌn'prɒfɪtəbl] unrentabel.

un·proved, **un·prov·en** ['ʌn'pruːvd, 'ʌn'pruːvn] unbewiesen.

un·pro·vid·ed ['ʌnprə'vaɪdɪd]: ~ *with* nicht versehen mit, ohne; ~ *for* unversorgt, mittellos.

un·pro·voked □ ['ʌnprə'vəʊkt] ohne Anlaß, grundlos.

un·qual·i·fied [ʌn'kwɒlɪfaɪd] unqualifiziert, ungeeignet; uneingeschränkt.

un·ques·tio·na·ble □ [ʌn'kwestʃə-nəbl] unzweifelhaft, fraglos; ~**tion·ing** □ [~ɪŋ] bedingungslos, blind.

un·quote ['ʌn'kwəʊt]: ~! Ende des Zitats!

un·rav·el [ʌn'rævl] (*bsd. Brt. -ll-*, *Am. -l-*) auftrennen; (sich) entwirren.

un·re·al □ ['ʌn'rɪəl] unwirklich, irreal; **un·re·a·lis·tic** ['ʌnrɪə'lɪstɪk] (~*ally*) wirklichkeitsfremd, unrealistisch.

un·rea·so·na·ble □ [ʌn'riːznəbl] unvernünftig; unsinnig; unmäßig.

un·rec·og·niz·a·ble □ ['ʌn'rekəg-naɪzəbl] nicht wiederzuerkennen(d).

un·re·deemed □ ['ʌnrɪ'diːmd] *eccl.* unerlöst; nicht eingelöst (*Rechnung*, *Pfand*); ungetilgt (*Schuld*).

un·re·fined ['ʌnrɪ'faɪnd] nicht raffiniert, roh, Roh...; *fig.* unkultiviert.

un·re·flect·ing □ ['ʌnrɪ'flektɪŋ] gedankenlos, unüberlegt.

un·re·gard·ed ['ʌnrɪ'gɑːdɪd] unbeachtet; unberücksichtigt.

un·re·lat·ed ['ʌnrɪ'leɪtɪd] ohne Beziehung (*to* zu).

U
V

unrelenting

un·re·lent·ing □ ['ʌnrɪ'lentɪŋ] erbarmungslos; unvermindert.

un·re·li·a·ble □ ['ʌnrɪ'laɪəbl] unzuverlässig.

un·re·lieved □ ['ʌnrɪ'liːvd] ungemildert; ununterbrochen.

un·re·mit·ting □ ['ʌnrɪ'mɪtɪŋ] unablässig, unaufhörlich; unermüdlich.

un·re·quit·ed □ ['ʌnrɪ'kwaɪtɪd]: ~ love unerwiderte Liebe.

un·re·served □ ['ʌnrɪ'zɜːvd] rückhaltlos; frei, offen; nicht reserviert.

un·re·sist·ing □ ['ʌnrɪ'zɪstɪŋ] widerstandslos.

un·re·spon·sive □ ['ʌnrɪ'spɒnsɪv] unempfänglich (to für); teilnahmslos.

un·rest ['ʌn'rest] Unruhe f, pol. a. Unruhen pl.

un·re·strained □ ['ʌnrɪ'streɪnd] ungehemmt; uneingeschränkt.

un·re·strict·ed □ ['ʌnrɪ'strɪktɪd] uneingeschränkt.

un·right·eous □ ['ʌn'raɪtʃəs] ungerecht; unredlich.

un·ripe ['ʌn'raɪp] unreif.

un·ri·val(l)ed □ ['ʌn'raɪvld] unvergleichlich, unerreicht, einzigartig.

un·roll ['ʌn'rəʊl] ent-, aufrollen; sich entfalten.

un·ruf·fled ['ʌn'rʌfld] glatt; fig. gelassen, ruhig.

un·ru·ly ['ʌn'ruːlɪ] (-ier, -iest) ungebärdig, widerspenstig.

un·safe □ ['ʌn'seɪf] unsicher.

un·said ['ʌn'sed] unausgesprochen.

un·sal(e)·a·ble □ ['ʌn'seɪləbl] unverkäuflich.

un·san·i·tar·y □ ['ʌn'sænɪtərɪ] unhygienisch.

un·sat·is·fac·to·ry □ ['ʌnsætɪs'fæktərɪ] unbefriedigend, unzulänglich; **~fied** ['ʌn'sætɪsfaɪd] unbefriedigt; **~fy·ing** □ [~ɪŋ] = unsatisfactory.

un·sa·vo(u)r·y □ ['ʌn'seɪvərɪ] unappetitlich (a. fig.), widerwärtig.

un·say ['ʌn'seɪ] (-said) zurücknehmen, widerrufen.

un·scathed ['ʌn'skeɪðd] unversehrt, unverletzt.

un·schooled ['ʌn'skuːld] ungeschult, nicht ausgebildet; unverbildet.

un·screw ['ʌn'skruː] v/t. ab-, los-, aufschrauben; v/i. sich abschrauben lassen.

un·scru·pu·lous □ [ʌn'skruːpjʊləs] bedenken-, gewissen-, skrupellos.

un·sea·soned ['ʌn'siːznd] nicht abgelagert (Holz); ungewürzt; fig. nicht abgehärtet.

un·seat ['ʌn'siːt] Reiter abwerfen; j-n s-s Postens entheben; j-m s-n Sitz (im Parlament) nehmen.

un·see·ing □ ['ʌn'siːɪŋ] fig. blind; with ~ eyes mit leerem Blick.

un·seem·ly ['ʌn'siːmlɪ] ungehörig.

un·self·ish □ ['ʌn'selfɪʃ] selbstlos, uneigennützig; **~ness** [~nɪs] Selbstlosigkeit f.

un·set·tle ['ʌn'setl] durcheinanderbringen; beunruhigen; aufregen; erschüttern; **~d** unbeständig, veränderlich (Wetter).

un·shak·en ['ʌn'ʃeɪkən] unerschüttert; unerschütterlich.

un·shaved, un·shav·en ['ʌn'ʃeɪvd, ~n] unrasiert.

un·ship ['ʌn'ʃɪp] ausschiffen.

un·shrink·a·ble ['ʌn'ʃrɪŋkəbl] nicht einlaufend (Stoff); **~ing** □ [ʌn'ʃrɪŋkɪŋ] unverzagt, furchtlos.

un·sight·ly [ʌn'saɪtlɪ] häßlich.

un·skil(l)·ful □ ['ʌn'skɪlfl] ungeschickt; **un·skilled** ungelernt.

un·so·cia·ble □ [ʌn'səʊʃəbl] ungesellig; **un·so·cial** [~l] unsozial; asozial; work ~ hours Brt. außerhalb der normalen Arbeitszeit arbeiten.

un·sol·der ['ʌn'sɒldə] los-, ablöten.

un·so·lic·it·ed ['ʌnsə'lɪsɪtɪd] unaufgefordert; ~ goods econ. unbestellte Ware(n).

un·solv·a·ble □ [ʌn'sɒlvəbl] ⚗ unlöslich; fig. unlösbar; **un·solved** [~d] ungelöst.

un·so·phis·ti·cat·ed ['ʌnsə'fɪstɪkeɪtɪd] ungekünstelt, natürlich, naiv.

un·sound □ ['ʌn'saʊnd] ungesund; verdorben; wurmstichig, morsch; nicht stichhaltig (Beweis); verkehrt; of ~ mind ⚖ unzurechnungsfähig.

un·spar·ing □ [ʌn'speərɪŋ] freigebig; schonungslos, unbarmherzig.

un·spea·ka·ble □ [ʌn'spiːkəbl] unsagbar, unbeschreiblich, entsetzlich.

un·spoiled, un·spoilt ['ʌn'spɔɪld, ~t] unverdorben; nicht verzogen (Kind).

un·spo·ken ['ʌn'spəʊkən] ungesagt; ~of unerwähnt.

un·stead·y □ ['ʌn'stedɪ] (-ier, -iest) unsicher; schwankend, unbeständig; unregelmäßig; fig. unsolide.

un·strained ['ʌn'streɪnd] unfiltriert; fig. ungezwungen.

un·strap [ˈʌnˈstræp] (-pp-) ab-, auf-, losschnallen.

un·stressed *ling.* [ˈʌnˈstrest] unbetont.

un·strung [ˈʌnˈstrʌŋ] ♪ saitenlos; ♪ entspannt (*Saite*); *fig.* zerrüttet, entnervt (*Person*).

un·stuck [ˈʌnˈstʌk]: *come* ∼ sich lösen, abgehen; *fig.* scheitern (*Person, Plan*).

un·stud·ied [ˈʌnˈstʌdɪd] ungekünstelt, natürlich.

un·suc·cess·ful □ [ˈʌnsəkˈsesfl] erfolglos, ohne Erfolg.

un·suit·a·ble □ [ˈʌnˈsjuːtəbl] unpassend; unangemessen.

un·sure [ˈʌnˈʃɔː] (∼r, ∼st) unsicher.

un·sur·passed [ˈʌnsəˈpɑːst] unübertroffen.

un·sus·pect|ed □ [ˈʌnsəˈspektɪd] unverdächtig; unvermutet; ∼**ing** [∼ɪŋ] nichts ahnend; arglos.

un·sus·pi·cious □ [ˈʌnsəˈspɪʃəs] nicht argwöhnisch, arglos; unverdächtig.

un·swerv·ing □ [ʌnˈswɜːvɪŋ] unbeirrbar.

un·tan·gle [ʌnˈtæŋgl] entwirren.

un·tapped [ʌnˈtæpt] ungenutzt (*Reserven, Energie*).

un·teach·a·ble [ˈʌnˈtiːtʃəbl] unbelehrbar (*Person*); nicht lehrbar (*Sache*).

un·ten·a·ble [ˈʌnˈtenəbl] unhaltbar (*Theorie etc.*).

un·ten·ant·ed [ˈʌnˈtenəntɪd] unbewohnt.

un·thank·ful □ [ˈʌnˈθæŋkfl] undankbar.

un·think|a·ble [ʌnˈθɪŋkəbl] undenkbar; ∼**ing** □ [ʌnˈθɪŋkɪŋ] gedankenlos.

un·thought [ʌnˈθɔːt] unüberlegt; ∼*of* unvorstellbar; unerwartet.

un·ti·dy □ [ʌnˈtaɪdɪ] (-*ier*, -*iest*) unordentlich.

un·tie [ˈʌnˈtaɪ] aufknoten, *Knoten etc.* lösen; losbinden.

un·til [ənˈtɪl] 1. *prp.* bis; 2. *cj.* bis (daß); *not* ∼ erst als *od.* wenn.

un·time·ly [ʌnˈtaɪmlɪ] vorzeitig; ungelegen.

un·tir·ing □ [ʌnˈtaɪərɪŋ] unermüdlich.

un·to [ˈʌntʊ] = *to*.

un·told [ˈʌnˈtəʊld] unerzählt; ungesagt; unermeßlich; unsäglich.

un·touched [ˈʌnˈtʌtʃt] unberührt (*Essen etc.*); *fig.* ungerührt.

un·trou·bled [ˈʌnˈtrʌbld] ungestört; ruhig.

un·true □ [ˈʌnˈtruː] unwahr, falsch.

un·trust·wor·thy [ˈʌnˈtrʌstwɜːðɪ] unzuverlässig, nicht vertrauenswürdig.

un·truth·ful □ [ˈʌnˈtruːθfl] unwahr; unaufrichtig; falsch.

un·used¹ [ˈʌnˈjuːzd] unbenutzt, ungebraucht.

un·used² [ˈʌnˈjuːst] nicht gewöhnt (*to an acc.*); nicht gewohnt (*to doing* zu tun).

un·u·su·al □ [ʌnˈjuːʒʊəl] ungewöhnlich.

un·ut·ter·a·ble □ [ʌnˈʌtərəbl] unaussprechlich.

un·var·nished *fig.* [ˈʌnˈvɑːnɪʃt] ungeschminkt.

un·var·y·ing □ [ʌnˈveərɪŋ] unveränderlich.

un·veil [ʌnˈveɪl] entschleiern; *Denkmal etc.* enthüllen.

un·versed [ˈʌnˈvɜːst] unbewandert, unerfahren (*in in dat.*).

un·want·ed [ˈʌnˈwɒntɪd] unerwünscht.

un·war·rant·ed [ʌnˈwɒrəntɪd] ungerechtfertigt, unberechtigt.

un·wel·come [ʌnˈwelkəm] unwillkommen.

un·well [ʌnˈwel]: *she is od. feels* ∼ sie fühlt sich unwohl *od.* unpäßlich, sie ist unpäßlich.

un·whole·some [ˈʌnˈhəʊlsəm] ungesund (*a. fig.*).

un·wield·y □ [ʌnˈwiːldɪ] unhandlich, sperrig; unbeholfen.

un·will·ing □ [ˈʌnˈwɪlɪŋ] widerwillig; ungern; *be* ∼ *to do et.* nicht wollen.

un·wind [ˈʌnˈwaɪnd] (-*wound*) auf-, loswickeln; (sich) abwickeln; F sich entspannen, abschalten.

un·wise □ [ˈʌnˈwaɪz] unklug.

un·wit·ting □ [ʌnˈwɪtɪŋ] unwissentlich, unabsichtlich.

un·wor·thy □ [ʌnˈwɜːðɪ] unwürdig; *he is* ∼ *of it* er verdient es nicht, er ist es nicht wert.

un·wrap [ˈʌnˈræp] auswickeln, auspacken, aufwickeln.

un·writ·ten [ˈʌnˈrɪtn]: ∼ *law* ungeschriebenes Gesetz.

un·yield·ing □ [ʌnˈjiːldɪŋ] starr, fest; *fig.* unnachgiebig.

un·zip [ʌnˈzɪp] (-pp-) den Reißverschluß öffnen (*gen.*).

up [ʌp] **1.** *adv.* nach oben, hoch, (her-, hin)auf, in die Höhe, empor, aufwärts; oben; von ... an; flußaufwärts; in der *od.* in die (*bsd.* Haupt-)Stadt; *Brt.* in *od.* nach London; in (*dat.*) (*up North*): aufrecht, gerade; *Baseball*: am Schlag; ~ *to* hinauf nach *od.* zu; bis (zu); **2.** *prp.* hinauf; ... an; **3.** *adj.* aufwärts..., nach oben; oben; hoch; aufgegangen (*Sonne*); gestiegen (*Preise*); abgelaufen, um (*Zeit*); auf (-gestanden); ~ *and about* wieder auf den Beinen; *it is* ~ *to him* es liegt an ihm; es hängt von ihm ab; *what are you* ~ *to?* was machst du (*there* da)?; *what's* ~*?* was ist los?; ~ *train* Zug *m* nach der Stadt; **3.** *prp.* hinauf; ~ (*the*) *country* landeinwärts; **4.** (*-pp-*) *v/i.* aufstehen, sich erheben; *v/t. Preise etc.* erhöhen; **5.** *the* ~*s and downs* die Auf u. Ab, die Höhen u. Tiefen (*of life des Lebens*).

up-and-com·ing [ˈʌpənˈkʌmɪŋ] aufstrebend, vielversprechend.

up·bring·ing [ˈʌpbrɪŋɪŋ] Erziehung *f.*

up·com·ing *Am.* [ˈʌpkʌmɪŋ] bevorstehend.

up·coun·try [ˈʌpˈkʌntrɪ] landeinwärts; im Inneren des Landes (gelegen).

up·date [ʌpˈdeɪt] auf den neuesten Stand bringen.

up·end [ʌpˈend] hochkant stellen; *Gefäß* umstülpen.

up·grade [ʌpˈgreɪd] *j-n* (im Rang) befördern.

up·heav·al *fig.* [ʌpˈhiːvl] Umwälzung *f.*

up·hill [ˈʌpˈhɪl] bergauf; *fig.* mühsam.

up·hold [ʌpˈhəʊld] (*-held*) aufrechterhalten, unterstützen; ⅔ bestätigen.

up·hol·ster [ʌpˈhəʊlstə] *Möbel* polstern; ~·**hol·ster·er** [~rə] Polsterer *m*; ~·**hol·ster·y** [~rɪ] Polsterung *f*; (*Möbel*)Bezugsstoff *m*; Polstern *n*; Polsterei *f.*

up·keep [ˈʌpkiːp] Instandhaltung(skosten *pl.*) *f*; Unterhalt(ungskosten *pl.*) *m.*

up·land [ˈʌplənd] *mst* ~*s pl.* Hochland *n.*

up·lift *fig.* [ʌpˈlɪft] aufrichten, erbauen.

up·on [əˈpɒn] = *on*; *once* ~ *a time there was* es war einmal.

up·per [ˈʌpə] obere(r, -s), höhere(r, -s), Ober...; ~*most* **1.** *adj.* oberste(r, -s), höchste(r, -s); **2.** *adv.* obenan, ganz oben.

up·raise [ʌpˈreɪz] er-, hochheben.

up·right [ˈʌpraɪt] **1.** □ aufrecht; *fig.* rechtschaffen; **2.** (senkrechte) Stütze, Träger *m.*

up·ris·ing [ˈʌpraɪzɪŋ] Erhebung *f*, Aufstand *m.*

up·roar [ˈʌprɔː] Aufruhr *m*; ~·**i·ous** □ [ʌpˈrɔːrɪəs] lärmend, laut, tosend (*Beifall*), schallend (*Gelächter*).

up·root [ʌpˈruːt] entwurzeln; (her-)ausreißen.

up·set [ʌpˈset] (*-set*) umwerfen, (um)stürzen; umkippen, umstoßen; durcheinanderbringen (*a. fig.*); *Magen* verderben; *fig. j-n* aus der Fassung bringen; *be* ~ aufgeregt sein, aus der Fassung sein, durcheinander sein.

up·shot [ˈʌpʃɒt] Ergebnis *n.*

up·side down [ˈʌpsaɪdˈdaʊn] das Oberste zuunterst; verkehrt (herum).

up·stairs [ˈʌpˈsteəz] die Treppe hinauf, (nach) oben.

up·start [ˈʌpstɑːt] Emporkömmling *m.*

up·state *Am.* [ˈʌpsteɪt] im Norden (des Bundesstaates).

up·stream [ˈʌpˈstriːm] fluß-, stromaufwärts.

up·tight F [ˈʌptaɪt] nervös.

up-to-date [ˈʌptəˈdeɪt] modern; auf dem neuesten Stand.

up·town *Am.* [ˈʌpˈtaʊn] im *od.* in das Wohn- *od.* Villenviertel.

up·turn [ˈʌptɜːn] Aufschwung *m.*

up·ward(s) [ˈʌpwəd(z)] aufwärts (gerichtet).

u·ra·ni·um 🜍 [jʊəˈreɪnjəm] Uran *n.*

ur·ban [ˈɜːbən] städtisch, Stadt...; ~**e** □ [ɜːˈbeɪn] höflich; gebildet.

ur·chin [ˈɜːtʃɪn] Bengel *m.*

urge [ɜːdʒ] **1.** *j-n* (be)drängen (*to do* zu tun); dringen auf *et.*; *Recht* geltend machen; *oft* ~ *on j-n* drängen, (an)treiben; **2.** Drang *m*; **ur·gen·cy** [ˈɜːdʒənsɪ] Dringlichkeit *f*; Drängen *n*; **ur·gent** □ [~t] dringend; dringlich; eilig.

u·ri·nal [ˈjʊərɪnl] Harnglas *n*; (Männer)Toilette *f*, Pissoir *n*; ~**nate** [~eɪt] urinieren; **u·rine** [~ɪn] Urin *m*, Harn *m.*

urn [ɜːn] Urne *f*; Tee-, Kaffeemaschine *f*.

us [ʌs, əs] uns; *all of* ~ wir alle; *both of* ~ wir beide.

us·age [ˈjuːzɪdʒ] Brauch *m*, Gepflogenheit *f*; Sprachgebrauch *m*; Behandlung *f*; Verwendung *f*, Gebrauch *m*.

use 1. [juːs] Gebrauch *m*, Benutzung *f*, Verwendung *f*; Gewohnheit *f*, Übung *f*, Brauch *m*; Nutzen *m*; *(of)* no ~ nutz-, zwecklos; *have no* ~ *for* keine Verwendung haben für; *Am.* F nicht mögen; **2.** [juːz] gebrauchen, benutzen, ver-, anwenden; handhaben; ~ *up* ver-, aufbrauchen; *I* ~*d to do* ich pflegte zu tun, früher tat ich; ~**d** [juːzd] ge-, verbraucht; [juːst] gewöhnt *(to an acc.)*, gewohnt *(to zu od. acc.)*; ~**ful** □ [ˈjuːsfl] brauchbar, nützlich; Nutz...; ~**less** □ [ˈjuːslɪs] nutz-, zwecklos, unnütz.

ush·er [ˈʌʃə] **1.** Türhüter *m*, Pförtner *m*; Gerichtsdiener *m*; Platzanweiser *m*; **2.** *mst.* ~ *in* herein-, hineinführen; ~**ette** [ˈʌʃəˈret] Platzanweiserin *f*.

u·su·al □ [ˈjuːʒʊəl] gewöhnlich, üblich, gebräuchlich.

u·sur·er [ˈjuːʒərə] Wucherer *m*.

u·surp [juːˈzɜːp] sich *et.* widerrechtlich aneignen, an sich reißen; ~**er** [~ə] Usurpator *m*.

u·su·ry [ˈjuːʒʊrɪ] Wucher(zinsen *pl.*) *m*.

u·ten·sil [juːˈtensl] Gerät *n*.

u·te·rus *anat.* [ˈjuːtərəs] *(pl. -ri* [-raɪ]) Gebärmutter *f*.

u·til·i·ty [juːˈtɪlətɪ] **1.** Nützlichkeit *f*, Nutzen *m*; *utilities pl.* Leistungen *pl.* der öffentlichen Versorgungsbetriebe; **2.** Gebrauchs...

u·ti·li·za·tion [juːtɪlaɪˈzeɪʃn] (Aus-)Nutzung *f*, Verwertung *f*, -wendung *f*; ~**lize** [ˈjuːtɪlaɪz] (aus)nutzen, verwerten, -wenden.

ut·most [ˈʌtməʊst] äußerste(r, -s).

U·to·pi·an [juːˈtəʊpjən] **1.** utopisch; **2.** Utopist(in).

ut·ter [ˈʌtə] **1.** □ *fig.* äußerste(r, -s), völlig; **2.** äußern; *Seufzer etc.* ausstoßen, von sich geben; *Falschgeld etc.* in Umlauf setzen; ~**ance** [ˈʌtərəns] Äußerung *f*, Ausdruck *m*; Aussprache *f*; ~**most** [ˈʌtəməʊst] äußerste(r, -s).

U·turn [ˈjuːtɜːn] *mot.* Wende *f*; *fig.* Kehrtwendung *f*.

u·vu·la *anat.* [ˈjuːvjʊlə] *(pl. -lae* [-liː], -*ləs)* (Gaumen)Zäpfchen *n*.

V

va|can·cy [ˈveɪkənsɪ] Leere *f*; freies Zimmer *(Hotel)*; offene *od.* freie Stelle; *fig.* geistige Leere; ~**cant** □ [~t] leer *(a. fig.)*; frei *(Zimmer, Sitzplatz)*; leer(stehend), unbewohnt *(Haus)*; offen, frei *(Stelle)*; unbesetzt, vakant *(Amt)*; *fig.* geistesabwesend.

va·cate [vəˈkeɪt, *Am.* ˈveɪkeɪt] räumen, *Stelle* aufgeben, aus *e-m Amt* scheiden, *Amt* niederlegen; **va·ca·tion** [vəˈkeɪʃn, *Am.* veɪˈkeɪʃn] **1.** *bsd. Am.* Ferien *pl.*; univ. Semesterferien *pl.*; ½⅓ Gerichtsferien *pl.*; *bsd. Am.* Urlaub *m*, Ferien *pl.*; *be on* ~ *bsd. Am.* im Urlaub sein, Urlaub machen; *take a* ~ *bsd. Am.* sich Urlaub nehmen, Urlaub machen; **2.** *bsd. Am.* Urlaub machen;

va·ca·tion·ist *bsd. Am.* [~ʃənɪst] Urlauber(in).

vac·ci·nate [ˈvæksɪneɪt] impfen; ~**ci·na·tion** [væksɪˈneɪʃn] (Schutz-)Impfung *f*; ~**cine** 🐄 [ˈvæksiːn] Impfstoff *m*.

vac·il·late *mst fig.* [ˈvæsɪleɪt] schwanken.

vac·u·ous □ *fig.* [ˈvækjʊəs] leer, geistlos.

vac·u·um [ˈvækjʊəm] **1.** *(pl. -uums, -ua* [-jʊə]) *phys.* Vakuum *n*; ~ *bottle* Thermosflasche *f*; ~ *cleaner* Staubsauger *m*; ~ *flask* Thermosflasche *f*; ~*-packed* vakuumverpackt; **2.** *v/t. (mit dem Staubsauger)* saugen; *v/i.* (staub)saugen.

vag·a·bond [ˈvægəbɒnd] Landstreicher(in).

va·ga·ry ['veɪgərɪ] wunderlicher Einfall; Laune *f*, Schrulle *f*.

va·gi·na *anat.* [və'dʒaɪnə] Vagina *f*, Scheide *f*; **~·nal** *anat.* [~nl] vaginal, Vaginal..., Scheiden...

va|grant ['veɪgrənt] **1.** □ wandernd, vagabundierend; *fig.* unstet; **2.** Landstreicher(in).

vague □ [veɪg] (*~r, ~st*) vage, verschwommen; unbestimmt; unklar.

vain [veɪn] eitel, eingebildet; nutzlos, vergeblich; *in ~* vergebens, vergeblich, umsonst.

vale [veɪl] *poet. od. in Namen:* Tal *n*.

val·e·dic·tion [vælɪ'dɪkʃn] Abschied(sworte *pl.*) *m*.

val·en·tine ['væləntaɪn] Valentinsgruß *m* (*am Valentinstag, 14. Februar, gesandt*); am Valentinstag erwählte(r) Liebste(r).

va·le·ri·an ♣ [və'lɪərɪən] Baldrian *m*.

val·et ['vælɪt] (Kammer)Diener *m*; Hoteldiener *m*.

val·e·tu·di·nar·i·an [vælɪtjuːdɪ'neərɪən] **1.** kränklich; hypochondrisch; **2.** kränklicher Mensch; Hypochonder *m*.

val·i·ant □ ['væljənt] tapfer, mutig.

val|id □ ['vælɪd] triftig, stichhaltig, berechtigt; gültig; *~ become ~* Rechtskraft erlangen; **~·i·date** *ztz* [~eɪt] für gültig erklären, bestätigen; **~·id·i·ty** [və'lɪdətɪ] (*ztz* Rechts)Gültigkeit *f*; Stichhaltigkeit *f*; Richtigkeit *f*.

va·lise [və'liːz] Reisetasche *f*.

val·ley ['vælɪ] Tal *n*.

val·o(u)r ['vælə] Mut *m*, Tapferkeit *f*.

val·u·a·ble ['væljʊəbl] **1.** □ wertvoll; **2.** *~s pl.* Wertsachen *pl.*

val·u·a·tion [vælju'eɪʃn] Bewertung *f*, Schätzung *f*; Schätz-, Taxwert *m*.

val·ue ['væljuː] **1.** Wert *m*; *econ.* Währung *f*; *mst ~s pl. fig.* (*kulturelle od. sittliche*) Werte *pl.*; *at ~ econ.* zum Tageskurs; *give* (*get*) *good ~ for money econ.* reell bedienen (bedient werden); **2.** (ab)schätzen, veranschlagen; *fig.* schätzen, bewerten; **~·ad·ded tax** *econ.* (*abbr.* VAT) Mehrwertsteuer *f*; **~d** veranschlagt; geschätzt; **~·less** [~jʊlɪs] wertlos.

valve [vælv] ⊕ Ventil *n*; (*Herz- etc.*) Klappe *f*; Brt. ∮ (Radio-, Fernseh-) Röhre *f*.

vam·pire ['væmpaɪə] Vampir *m*.

van¹ [væn] Lieferwagen *m*; *bsd.* Brt.

₲ Güter-, Gepäckwagen *m*; F Wohnwagen *m*.

van² ✕ [~] = *vanguard*.

van·dal·ize ['vændəlaɪz] wie die Vandalen hausen in (*dat.*), mutwillig zerstören, verwüsten.

vane [veɪn] Wetterfahne *f*; (Propeller)Flügel *m*; ⊕ Schaufel *f*.

van·guard ✕ ['vængɑːd] Vorhut *f*.

va·nil·la [və'nɪlə] Vanille *f*.

van·ish ['vænɪʃ] verschwinden.

van·i·ty ['vænətɪ] Eitelkeit *f*; Nichtigkeit *f*; **~ bag** Kosmetiktäschchen *n*; **~ case** Kosmetikkoffer *m*.

van·quish ['væŋkwɪʃ] besiegen.

van·tage ['vɑːntɪdʒ] *Tennis:* Vorteil *m*; **~·ground** günstige Stellung.

vap·id □ ['væpɪd] schal; fad(e).

va·por·ize ['veɪpəraɪz] verdampfen, verdunsten (lassen).

va·po(u)r ['veɪpə] Dampf *m*, Dunst *m*; **~ trail** ⚡ Kondensstreifen *m*.

var·i·a·ble ['veərɪəbl] **1.** □ veränderlich, wechselnd, unbeständig; ⊕ ver-, einstellbar; **2.** veränderliche Größe; **~·ance** [~ns]: *be at ~* (*with*) uneinig sein (mit *j-m*), anderer Meinung sein (als *j-d*); im Widerspruch stehen (zu); **~·ant** [~nt] **1.** abweichend, verschieden; **2.** Variante *f*; **~·a·tion** [veərɪ'eɪʃn] Schwankung *f*, Abweichung *f*; Variation *f*.

var·i·cose veins ✱ ['værɪkəʊs veɪnz] *pl.* Krampfadern *pl.*

var·ied □ ['veərɪd] verschieden, mannigfaltig; verändert.

va·ri·e·ty [və'raɪətɪ] Mannigfaltigkeit *f*, Vielzahl *f*, Abwechslung *f*; *econ.* Auswahl *f*; Sorte *f*, Art *f*; Spielart *f*, Variante *f*; *for a ~ of reasons* aus den verschiedensten Gründen; **~ show** Varietévorstellung *f*; **~ theatre** Varieté(theater) *n*.

var·i·ous □ ['veərɪəs] verschiedene, mehrere; verschiedenartig.

var·mint F ['vɑːmɪnt] *zo.* Schädling *m*; Halunke *m*.

var·nish ['vɑːnɪʃ] **1.** Firnis *m*; Lack *m*; Politur *f*; *fig.* Tünche *f*; **2.** firnissen; lackieren; *Möbel* (auf)polieren; *fig.* beschönigen.

var·si·ty ['vɑːsətɪ] *Brt.* F Uni *f* (*Universität*); *a.* **~ team** *Am.* Universitäts-, College-, Schulmannschaft *f*.

var·y ['veərɪ] (sich) (ver)ändern; variieren, wechseln (mit *et.*); abweichen *od.* verschieden sein (*from* von); **~·ing** □ [~ɪŋ] unterschiedlich.

vase [vɑːz, *Am.* veɪs, veɪz] Vase *f*.

vast □ [vɑːst] ungeheuer, gewaltig, riesig, umfassend, weit.

vat [væt] Faß *n*, Bottich *m*.

vau·de·ville *Am.* ['vəʊdəvɪl] Varieté *n*.

vault[1] [vɔːlt] 1. (Keller)Gewölbe *n*; Wölbung *f*; Stahlkammer *f*, Tresorraum *m*; Gruft *f*; 2. (über)wölben.

vault[2] [~] 1. *bsd. Sport:* Sprung *m*; 2. *v/i.* springen (*over* über *acc.*); *v/t.* überspringen, springen über (*acc.*); **~ing-horse** ['vɔːltɪŋhɔːs] *Turnen:* Pferd *n*; **~ing-pole** *Stabhochsprung:* Sprungstab *m*.

've *abbr.* [v] = have.

veal [viːl] Kalbfleisch *n*; **~ chop** Kalbskotelett *n*; **~ cutlet** Kalbsschnitzel *n*; *roast* **~** Kalbsbraten *m*.

veer [vɪə] (sich) drehen; *Auto:* a. plötzlich die Richtung ändern, ausscheren.

vege·ta·ble ['vedʒtəbl] 1. Gemüse...; pflanzlich; 2. Pflanze *f*; *mst* **~s** *pl*. Gemüse *n*.

veg·e·tar·i·an [vedʒɪ'teərɪən] 1. Vegetarier(in); 2. vegetarisch; **~·tate** *fig.* ['vedʒɪteɪt] (dahin)vegetieren; **~·ta·tive** □ [~tətɪv] vegetativ; wachstumsfördernd.

ve·he·mence ['viːɪməns] Heftigkeit *f*, Gewalt *f*; **~·ment** □ [~t] heftig; ungestüm.

ve·hi·cle ['viːɪkl] Fahrzeug *n*, Beförderungsmittel *n*; *fig.* Vermittler *m*, Träger *m*; *fig.* Ausdrucksmittel *n*.

veil [veɪl] 1. Schleier *m*; 2. (sich) verschleiern; *fig.* verbergen.

vein [veɪn] *anat.* Vene *f*; Ader *f* (*a. fig.*); *fig.* Veranlagung *f*, Neigung *f*; *fig.* Stimmung *f*.

ve·loc·i·pede *Am.* [vɪ'lɒsɪpiːd] (Kinder)Dreirad *n*.

ve·loc·i·ty ⊕ [vɪ'lɒsətɪ] Geschwindigkeit *f*.

vel·vet ['velvɪt] 1. Samt *m*; 2. aus Samt, Samt...; **~·y** [~ɪ] samtig.

ve·nal □ ['viːnl] käuflich; bestechlich, korrupt.

vend [vend] verkaufen; **~·er** ['vendə] (Straßen)Händler *m*, (-)Verkäufer *m*; **~·ing-ma·chine** ['vendɪŋmə'ʃiːn] (Verkaufs)Automat *m*; **~·or** [~ɔː] *bsd.* ‡‡ Verkäufer(in); (Verkaufs)Automat *m*.

ve·neer [və'nɪə] 1. Furnier *n*; *fig.* äußerer Anstrich, Tünche *f*; 2. furnieren.

ven·e·ra·ble □ ['venərəbl] ehrwürdig; **~·rate** [~eɪt] (ver)ehren; **~·ra·tion** [venə'reɪʃn] Verehrung *f*.

ve·ne·re·al [vɪ'nɪərɪəl] Geschlechts...; **~ disease** ♠ Geschlechtskrankheit *f*.

Ve·ne·tian [vɪ'niːʃn] 1. venezianisch; 2 *blind* (Stab)Jalousie *f*; 2. Venezianer(in).

ven·geance ['vendʒəns] Rache *f*; *with* a **~** F wie verrückt, ganz gehörig.

ve·ni·al □ ['viːnjəl] verzeihlich; *eccl.* läßlich (*Sünde*).

ve·ni·son ['venɪzn] Wildbret *n*.

ven·om ['venəm] (*bsd.* Schlangen-) Gift *n*; *fig.* Gift *n*, Gehässigkeit *f*; **~·ous** □ [~əs] giftig (*a. fig.*).

ve·nous ['viːnəs] Venen...; venös.

vent [vent] 1. (Abzugs)Öffnung *f*, Luft-, Spundloch *n*; Schlitz *m*; *give* **~ to** = 2. *v/t. fig.* **~ s-m** Zorn *etc.* Luft machen, *s-e* Wut *etc.* auslassen, abreagieren (*on* an *dat.*).

ven·ti·late ['ventɪleɪt] ventilieren, (be-, ent-, durch)lüften; *fig.* erörtern; **~·la·tion** [ventɪ'leɪʃn] Ventilation *f*, Lüftung *f*; *fig.* Erörterung *f*; **~·la·tor** ['ventɪleɪtə] Ventilator *m*.

ven·tril·o·quist [ven'trɪləkwɪst] Bauchredner *m*.

ven·ture ['ventʃə] 1. Wagnis *n*, Risiko *n*; Abenteuer *n*; *econ.* Unternehmen *n*; *econ.* Spekulation *f*; *at a* **~** auf gut Glück; 2. (sich) wagen; riskieren.

ve·ra·cious □ [və'reɪʃəs] wahrhaftig; wahrheitsgemäß.

verb *gr.* [vɜːb] Verb *n*, Zeitwort *n*; **~·al** □ ['vɜːbl] wörtlich; mündlich; **ver·bi·age** ['vɜːbɪɪdʒ] Wortschwall *m*; **ver·bose** □ [vɜː'bəʊs] wortreich, langatmig.

ver·dant □ ['vɜːdənt] grün; *fig.* unreif.

ver·dict ['vɜːdɪkt] ‡‡ (Urteils)Spruch *m* (*der Geschworenen*); *fig.* Urteil *n*; *bring in od. return a* **~** *of guilty* auf schuldig erkennen.

ver·di·gris ['vɜːdɪgrɪs] Grünspan *m*.

ver·dure ['vɜːdʒə] (frisches) Grün.

verge [vɜːdʒ] 1. Rand *m*, Grenze *f*; Bankett *n* (*Straße*); *on the* **~** *of am* Rande (*gen.*), dicht vor (*dat.*); *on the* **~** *of despair* (*tears*) der Verzweiflung (den Tränen) nahe; 2. **~** (*up*)*on* grenzen an (*acc.*) (*a. fig.*).

ver·i·fy ['verɪfaɪ] (nach)prüfen; beweisen; bestätigen.

U
V

ver·i·si·mil·i·tude [verɪsɪˈmɪlɪtjuːd] Wahrscheinlichkeit f.

ver·i·ta·ble □ [ˈverɪtəbl] wahr, wirklich.

ver·mi·cel·li [vɜːmɪˈselɪ] Fadennudeln pl.

ver·mic·u·lar [vɜːˈmɪkjʊlə] wurmartig.

ver·mi·form ap·pen·dix anat. [ˈvɜːmɪfɔːm əˈpendɪks] Wurmfortsatz m.

ver·mil·i·on [vəˈmɪljən] 1. Zinnoberrot n; 2. zinnoberrot.

ver·min [ˈvɜːmɪn] Ungeziefer n; Schädling(e pl.) m; fig. Gesindel n, Pack n; **~ous** [~əs] voller Ungeziefer.

ver·nac·u·lar [vəˈnækjʊlə] 1. □ einheimisch; Volks...; □ Landes-, Volkssprache f; Jargon m.

ver·sa·tile □ [ˈvɜːsətaɪl] vielseitig, flexibel.

verse [vɜːs] Vers(e pl.) m; Strophe f; Dichtung f; **~d** [~t] bewandert; be (well) ~ in sich (gut) auskennen in (dat.).

ver·si·fy [ˈvɜːsɪfaɪ] v/t. in Verse bringen; v/i. Verse machen.

ver·sion [ˈvɜːʃn] Übersetzung f; Fassung f, Darstellung f; Lesart f; ⊕ Ausführung f, Modell n (Auto etc.).

ver·sus [ˈvɜːsəs] ♌ Sport: gegen.

ver·te|bra anat. [ˈvɜːtɪbrə] (pl. -brae [~riː]) Wirbel m; **~brate** zo. [~rət] Wirbeltier n.

ver·ti·cal □ [ˈvɜːtɪkl] vertikal, senkrecht.

ver·tig·i·nous □ [vɜːˈtɪdʒɪnəs] schwindlig; schwindelnd (Höhe).

ver·ti·go [ˈvɜːtɪgəʊ] (pl. -gos) Schwindel(anfall) m.

verve [vɜːv] Schwung m, Begeisterung f.

ver·y [ˈverɪ] 1. adv. sehr; vor sup.: aller...; the ~ best das allerbeste; 2. adj. gerade, genau; bloß; rein; der-, die-, dasselbe; the ~ same ebenderselbe; in the ~ act auf frischer Tat; gerade dabei; the ~ thing genau das (richtige); the ~ thought der bloße Gedanke (of an acc.).

ves·i·cle [ˈvesɪkl] Bläschen n.

ves·sel [ˈvesl] Gefäß n (a. anat., ♀, fig.); ♺ Fahrzeug n, Schiff n.

vest [vest] Brt. Unterhemd n; Am. Weste f.

ves·ti·bule [ˈvestɪbjuːl] anat. Vorhof m; (Vor)Halle f; Am. ♺ (Harmonika)Verbindungsgang m; **~ train** Am.

♺ Zug m mit (Harmonika)Verbindungsgängen.

ves·tige fig. [ˈvestɪdʒ] Spur f.

vest·ment [ˈvestmənt] Amtstracht f, Robe f.

ves·try eccl. [ˈvestrɪ] Sakristei f; Gemeindesaal m.

vet F [vet] 1. Tierarzt m; Am. ✗ Veteran m; 2. (-tt-) co. verarzten; gründlich prüfen.

vet·e·ran [ˈvetərən] 1. altgedient; erfahren; 2. Veteran m.

vet·e·ri·nar·i·an Am. [vetərɪˈneərɪən] Tierarzt m.

vet·e·ri·na·ry [ˈvetərɪnərɪ] 1. tierärztlich; 2. a. ~ surgeon Brt. Tierarzt m.

ve·to [ˈviːtəʊ] 1. (pl. -toes) Veto n; 2. sein Veto einlegen gegen.

vex [veks] ärgern; schikanieren; **~a·tion** [vekˈseɪʃn] Verdruß m; Ärger(nis n) m; **~a·tious** [~ʃəs] ärgerlich.

vi·a [ˈvaɪə] über, via.

vi·a·duct [ˈvaɪədʌkt] Viadukt m, n.

vi·al [ˈvaɪəl] Phiole f, Fläschchen n.

vi·brate [vaɪˈbreɪt] vibrieren; zittern; **vi·bra·tion** [~ʃn] Schwingung f; Zittern n, Vibrieren n.

vic·ar eccl. [ˈvɪkə] Vikar m; **~age** [~rɪdʒ] Pfarrhaus n.

vice¹ [vaɪs] Laster n; Untugend f; Fehler m; **~ squad** Sittenpolizei f, -dezernat n.

vice² Brt. ⊕ [~] Schraubstock m.

vi·ce³ prp. [ˈvaɪsɪ] an Stelle von.

vice⁴ F [vaɪs] Vize m; attr. stellvertretend, Vize...; **~roy** [ˈvaɪsrɔɪ] Vizekönig m.

vi·ce ver·sa [ˈvaɪsɪˈvɜːsə] umgekehrt.

vi·cin·i·ty [vɪˈsɪnətɪ] Nachbarschaft f; Nähe f.

vi·cious □ [ˈvɪʃəs] lasterhaft; bösartig; boshaft; fehlerhaft.

vi·cis·si·tude [vɪˈsɪsɪtjuːd] Wandel m, Wechsel m; **~s** pl. Wechselfälle pl., das Auf u. Ab.

vic·tim [ˈvɪktɪm] Opfer n; **~ize** [~aɪz] (auf)opfern; schikanieren; (ungerechterweise) bestrafen.

vic·tor [ˈvɪktə] Sieger(in); **2·to·ri·an** hist. [vɪkˈtɔːrɪən] Viktorianisch; **~to·ri·ous** □ [~ɪəs] siegreich; Sieges...; **~to·ry** [ˈvɪktərɪ] Sieg m.

vict·ual [ˈvɪtl] 1. (bsd. Brt. -ll-, Am. -l-) (sich) verpflegen od. verproviantieren; 2. mst **~s** pl. Lebensmittel pl.,

Proviant *m*; **~·(l)er** [~ə] Lebensmittellieferant *m*.

vid·e·o ['vɪdɪəʊ] **1.** (*pl. -os*) Video(gerät *n*, -recorder *m*) *n*; *Computer*: Bildschirm-, Bildsicht-, Datensichtgerät *n*; *Am.* Fernsehen *n*; **2.** Video...; *Am.* Fernseh...; **~ cas·sette** Videokassette *f*; **~ disc** Bildplatte *f*; **~ game** Videospiel *n*; **~·phone** Bildtelefon *n*; **~·tape 1.** Videoband *n*; **2.** auf Videoband aufnehmen; **~·tape re·cord·er** Videorecorder *m*.

vie [vaɪ] wetteifern (*with* mit; *for* um).

Vi·en·nese [vɪə'niːz] **1.** Wiener(in); **2.** wienerisch, Wiener...

view [vjuː] **1.** Sicht *f*, Blick *m*; Besichtigung *f*; Aussicht *f* (*a.* acc.); Anblick *m*; Ansicht *f* (*a.* fig.); Absicht *f*; *in* ~ sichtbar, zu sehen; *in* ~ *of* im Hinblick auf (*acc.*); angesichts (*gen.*); *on* ~ zu besichtigen; *with a* ~ *to* inf. od. *of* ger. in der Absicht zu *inf.*; *have* (*keep*) *in* ~ im Auge haben (behalten); **2.** *v/t.* ansehen, besichtigen; *fig.* betrachten; *v/i.* fernsehen; **~ da·ta** *pl.* Bildschirmtext *m*; **~·er** ['vjuːə] Fernsehzuschauer(in), Fernseher(in); ⊕ Diabetrachter *m*; **~·find·er** *phot.* [~faɪndə] (Bild)Sucher *m*; **~·less** [~lɪs] ohne eigene Meinung; *poet.* unsichtbar; **~·point** Gesichts-, Standpunkt *m*.

vig|il ['vɪdʒɪl] Nachtwache *f*; **~·i·lance** [~əns] Wachsamkeit *f*; **~·i·lant** [~t] wachsam.

vig|or·ous [ ] ['vɪgərəs] kräftig; energisch; nachdrücklich; **~·o(u)r** ['vɪgə] Kraft *f*; Vitalität *f*; Energie *f*; Nachdruck *m*.

Vi·king ['vaɪkɪŋ] **1.** Wiking(er) *m*; **2.** wikingisch, Wikinger...

vile [ ] [vaɪl] gemein, abscheulich.

vil·lage ['vɪlɪdʒ] Dorf *n*; ~ **green** Dorfanger *m*, -wiese *f*; **~·lag·er** [~ə] Dorfbewohner(in).

vil·lain ['vɪlən] Schurke *m*, Schuft *m*, Bösewicht *m*; **~·ous** [ ] [~əs] schurkisch; *F* scheußlich; **~·y** [~ɪ] Schurkerei *f*.

vim *F* [vɪm] Schwung *m*, Schmiß *m*.

vin·di·cate ['vɪndɪkeɪt] rechtfertigen; rehabilitieren; **~·ca·tion** [vɪndɪ-'keɪʃn] Rechtfertigung *f*.

vin·dic·tive [ ] [vɪn'dɪktɪv] rachsüchtig, nachtragend.

vine ♀ [vaɪn] Wein(stock) *m*, (Wein-) Rebe *f*; △ *nicht* Wein (*Getränk*).

vin·e·gar ['vɪnɪgə] (Wein)Essig *m*.

vine|-grow·ing ['vaɪngrəʊɪŋ] Weinbau *m*; **~·yard** ['vɪnjəd] Weinberg *m*.

vin|tage ['vɪntɪdʒ] **1.** Weinlese *f*; (Wein)Jahrgang *m*; **2.** klassisch; erlesen; altmodisch; ~ *car mot.* Oldtimer *m*; **~·tag·er** [~ə] Weinleser(in).

vi·o·la ♪ [vɪ'əʊlə] Bratsche *f*.

vi·o|late ['vaɪəleɪt] verletzen; *Eid etc.* brechen; vergewaltigen; **~·la·tion** [vaɪə'leɪʃn] Verletzung *f*; (Eid- *etc.*) Bruch *m*; Vergewaltigung *f*.

vi·o·lence ['vaɪələns] Gewalt(tätigkeit) *f*; Heftigkeit *f*; **~·lent** [ ] [~t] gewaltsam, -tätig; heftig.

vi·o·let ♀ ['vaɪələt] Veilchen *n*.

vi·o·lin ♪ [vaɪə'lɪn] Violine *f*, Geige *f*.

VIP *F* ['viː'aɪ'piː] prominente Persönlichkeit.

vi·per *zo.* ['vaɪpə] Viper *f*, Natter *f*.

vi·ra·go [vɪ'rɑːgəʊ] (*pl. -gos, -goes*) Zankteufel *m*, Drachen *m*.

vir·gin ['vɜːdʒɪn] **1.** Jungfrau *f*; **2.** *a.* **~·al** [ ] [~l] jungfräulich; Jungfern...; **~·i·ty** [və'dʒɪnətɪ] Jungfräulichkeit *f*.

vir·ile ['vɪraɪl] männlich; Mannes...; **vi·ril·i·ty** [vɪ'rɪlətɪ] Männlichkeit *f*; *physiol.* Mannes-, Zeugungskraft *f*.

vir·tu·al [ ] ['vɜːtʃʊəl] eigentlich; **~·ly** [~ɪ] praktisch.

vir|tue ['vɜːtʃuː] Tugend *f*; Vorzug *m*; *in od. by* ~ *of* kraft, vermöge (*beide gen.*); *make a* ~ *of necessity* aus der Not e-e Tugend machen; **~·tu·os·i·ty** [vɜːtjʊ'ɒsətɪ] Virtuosität *f*; **~·tu·ous** [ ] ['vɜːtʃʊəs] tugendhaft; rechtschaffen; △ *nicht* virtuos.

vir·u·lent [ ] ['vɪrʊlənt] ✗ (sehr) giftig, bösartig (*a.* fig.).

vi·rus ✗ ['vaɪərəs] Virus *n*, *m*; *fig.* Gift *n*.

vi·sa ['viːzə] Visum *n*, Sichtvermerk *m*; **~ed, ~'d** [~d] mit *od.* e-m Sichtvermerk *od.* Visum (versehen).

vis·cose ['vɪskəʊs] Viskose *f*; ~ *silk* Zellstoffseide *f*.

vis·count ['vaɪkaʊnt] Vicomte *m*; **~·ess** [~ɪs] Vicomtesse *f*.

vis·cous ['vɪskəs] zähflüssig.

vise *Am.* ⊕ [vaɪs] Schraubstock *m*.

vis·i·bil·i·ty [vɪzɪ'bɪlətɪ] Sichtbarkeit *f*; Sichtweite *f*; **~·ble** [ ] ['vɪzəbl] sichtbar; *fig.* (er)sichtlich; *pred.* zu sehen (*Sache*); zu sprechen (*Person*).

vi·sion ['vɪʒn] Sehvermögen *n*, -kraft *f*; *fig.* Seherblick *m*; Vision *f*; **~·a·ry** [~ərɪ] **1.** phantastisch; **2.** Hellseher(in); Phantast(in).

vis|it ['vɪzɪt] **1.** *v/t.* besuchen; aufsuchen; besichtigen; *fig.* heimsuchen; ~ *s.th. on s.o. eccl.* j-n für et. (be)strafen; *v/i.* e-n Besuch *od.* Besuche machen; *Am.* plaudern (*with* mit); **2.** Besuch *m*; △ *nicht* ☞ *Visite* (*im Krankenhaus*); **~i·ta·tion** [vɪzɪ'teɪʃn] Besuch *m*; Besichtigung *f*; *fig.* Heimsuchung *f*; **~i·tor** ['vɪzɪtə] Besucher(in), Gast *m*.

vi·sor ['vaɪzə] Visier *n*; (Mützen-) Schirm *m*; *mot.* Sonnenblende *f*.

vis·ta ['vɪstə] (Aus-, Durch)Blick *m*.

vis·u·al □ ['vɪzjʊəl] Seh..., Gesichts...; visuell; ~ *aids pl. Schule:* Anschauungsmaterial *n*; ~ *display unit Computer:* Bildschirm-, Bildsicht-, Datensichtgerät *n*; ~ *instruction Schule:* Anschauungsunterricht *m*; **~ize** [~aɪz] sich vorstellen, sich ein Bild machen von.

vi·tal □ ['vaɪtl] **1.** Lebens...; lebenswichtig; wesentlich; (hoch)wichtig; vital; ~ *parts pl.* = **2.** ~*s pl.* lebenswichtige Organe *pl.*, edle Teile *pl.*; **~i·ty** [vaɪ'tælətɪ] Lebenskraft *f*, Vitalität *f*; **~ize** ['vaɪtəlaɪz] beleben.

vit·a·min ['vɪtəmɪn] Vitamin *n*; ~ *deficiency* Vitaminmangel *m*.

vi·ti·ate ['vɪʃɪeɪt] verderben; beeinträchtigen.

vit·re·ous □ ['vɪtrɪəs] Glas..., gläsern.

vi·va·cious □ [vɪ'veɪʃəs] lebhaft; **vi·vac·i·ty** [vɪ'væsətɪ] Lebhaftigkeit *f*.

viv·id □ ['vɪvɪd] lebhaft, lebendig.

vix·en ['vɪksn] Füchsin *f*; zänkisches Weib, Drachen *m*.

V-neck ['viːnek] V-Ausschnitt *m*; **V-necked** [~t] mit V-Ausschnitt.

vo·cab·u·la·ry [və'kæbjʊlərɪ] Wörterverzeichnis *n*; Wortschatz *m*.

vo·cal □ ['vəʊkl] stimmlich, Stimm...; laut; ♪ Vokal..., Gesang...; klingend; *ling.* stimmhaft; **~ist** [~əlɪst] Sänger(in), **~ize** [~aɪz] (*ling.* stimmhaft) aussprechen.

vo·ca·tion [vəʊ'keɪʃn] Berufung *f*; Beruf *m*; **~al** □ [~ənl] beruflich, Berufs...; ~ *adviser* Berufsberater *m*; ~ *education* Berufsausbildung *f*; ~ *guidance* Berufsberatung *f*; ~ *school Am.* (*etwa*) Berufsschule *f*; ~ *training* Berufsausbildung *f*.

vo·cif·er|ate [və'sɪfəreɪt] schreien; **~ous** □ [~əs] schreiend; lautstark.

vogue [vəʊg] Mode *f*; *be in* ~ (in) Mode sein.

voice [vɔɪs] **1.** Stimme *f*; *active* (*passive*) ~ *gr.* Aktiv *n* (Passiv *n*); *give* ~ *to* Ausdruck geben *od.* verleihen (*dat.*); **2.** äußern, ausdrücken; *ling.* (stimmhaft) (aus)sprechen.

void [vɔɪd] **1.** leer; ‡‡ (rechts)unwirksam, ungültig; ~ *of* frei von, arm an (*dat.*), ohne; **2.** Leere *f*, *fig.* Lücke *f*.

vol·a·tile ['vɒlətaɪl] ⚗ flüchtig (*a. fig.*); flatterhaft.

vol·ca·no [vɒl'keɪnəʊ] (*pl.* -noes, -nos) Vulkan *m*.

vo·li·tion [və'lɪʃn] Wollen *n*, Wille(nskraft *f*) *m*; *of one's own* ~ aus eigenem Entschluß.

vol·ley ['vɒlɪ] **1.** Salve *f*; (*Geschoß- etc.*)Hagel *m*; *fig.* Schwall *m*; *Tennis*: Flugball *m*; **2.** *mst* ~ *out* e-n Schwall von *Worten etc.* von sich geben; e-e Salve *od.* Salven abgeben; *fig.* hageln; dröhnen; **~ball** *Sport:* Volleyball(spiel *n*) *m*.

volt ⚡ [vəʊlt] Volt *n*; **~age** ⚡ ['vəʊltɪdʒ] Spannung *f*; **~me·ter** ⚡ Volt-, Spannungsmesser *m*.

vol·u·bil·i·ty [vɒljʊ'bɪlətɪ] Redegewandtheit *f*; **~ble** □ ['vɒljʊbl] (rede)gewandt.

vol·ume ['vɒljuːm] Band *m* (*e-s Buches*); Volumen *n*; *fig.* Masse *f*, große Menge; (*bsd.* Stimm)Umfang *m*; ⚡ Lautstärke *f*; **vo·lu·mi·nous** □ [və'ljuːmɪnəs] vielbändig; umfangreich, voluminös.

vol·un|ta·ry □ ['vɒləntərɪ] freiwillig; **~teer** [vɒlən'tɪə] **1.** Freiwillige(r *m*) *f*; **2.** *v/i.* freiwillig dienen; sich freiwillig melden; sich erbieten; *v/t.* *Dienste etc.* freiwillig anbieten; sich *e-e Bemerkung* erlauben.

vo·lup·tu·a·ry [və'lʌptjʊərɪ] Lüstling *m*; **~ous** □ [~əs] wollüstig; üppig; sinnlich.

vom·it ['vɒmɪt] **1.** *v/t.* (er)brechen; *v/i.* (sich er)brechen; **2.** Erbrochene(s) *n*; Erbrechen *n*.

vo·ra·cious □ [və'reɪʃəs] gefräßig, gierig, unersättlich; **vo·rac·i·ty** [vɒ'ræsətɪ] Gefräßigkeit *f*, Gier *f*.

vor·tex ['vɔːteks] (*pl.* -texes, -tices* [-tɪsiːz]) Wirbel *m*, Strudel *m* (*mst fig.*).

vote [vəʊt] **1.** (Wahl)Stimme *f*; Abstimmung *f*; Stimm-, Wahlrecht *n*; Beschluß *m*, Votum *n*; ~ *of no confidence* Mißtrauensvotum *n*; *take a* ~ *on s.th.* über et. abstimmen; **2.** *v/t.* wählen; bewilligen; *v/i.* abstimmen;

wählen; ~ *for* stimmen für; F für *et.* sein; **vot·er** ['vəʊtə] Wähler(in).

vot·ing ['vəʊtɪŋ] Abstimmung *f*, Stimmabgabe *f*; *attr.* Wahl...; ~ **pa·per** Stimmzettel *m*.

vouch [vaʊtʃ]: ~ *for* (sich ver)bürgen für; **~·er** ['vaʊtʃə] Beleg *m*, Unterlage *f*; Gutschein *m*; **~·safe** [vaʊtʃ'seɪf] gewähren; geruhen (*to do* zu tun).

vow [vaʊ] **1.** Gelübde *n*; (Treu-) Schwur *m*; *take a* ~, *make a* ~ ein Gelübde ablegen; **2.** geloben.

vow·el *ling.* ['vaʊəl] Vokal *m*, Selbstlaut *m*.

voy·age ['vɔɪdʒ] **1.** *längere* (See-,

Flug)Reise; **2.** *lit.* reisen; **~·ag·er** ['vɔɪdʒə] (See)Reisende(r *m*) *f*.

vul·gar □ ['vʌlgə] gewöhnlich, unfein, ordinär; vulgär; pöbelhaft; geschmacklos; ~ *tongue* Volkssprache *f*; **~·i·ty** [vʌl'gærətɪ] ungehobeltes Wesen; Ungezogenheit *f*; Geschmacklosigkeit *f*.

vul·ne·ra·ble □ ['vʌlnərəbl] verwundbar (*a. fig.*); ✕, *Sport:* ungeschützt, offen; *fig.* angreifbar.

vul·pine ['vʌlpaɪn] Fuchs..., fuchsartig; schlau, listig.

vul·ture *zo.* ['vʌltʃə] Geier *m*.

vy·ing ['vaɪɪŋ] wetteifernd.

W

wad [wɒd] **1.** (*Watte*)Bausch *m*; Pfropf(en) *m*; Banknotenbündel *n*; **2.** (-*dd*-) wattieren, auspolstern; zu e-m Bausch zusammenpressen; **~·ding** ['wɒdɪŋ] Einlage *f*, Füllmaterial (*zum Verpacken etc.*); Wattierung *f*; Watte *f*.

wad·dle ['wɒdl] **1.** watscheln; **2.** watschelnder Gang, Watscheln *n*.

wade [weɪd] *v/i.* waten; ~ *through fig.* F sich (hin)durcharbeiten; *v/t.* durchwaten.

wa·fer ['weɪfə] Waffel *f*; Oblate *f*; *eccl.* Hostie *f*.

waf·fle¹ ['wɒfl] Waffel *f*.

waf·fle² *Brt.* F [~] schwafeln.

waft [wɑːft] **1.** wehen; **2.** Hauch *m*.

wag [wæg] **1.** (-*gg*-) wackeln *od.* wedeln (mit); **2.** Schütteln *n*; Wedeln *p*; Spaßvogel *m*.

wage¹ [weɪdʒ] *Krieg* führen, *Feldzug* unternehmen (*on*, *against* gegen).

wage² [~] *mst* ~*s pl.* (Arbeits)Lohn *m*; **~·earn·er** *econ.* ['weɪdʒɜːnə] Lohnempfänger(in); **~·freeze** *econ.* Lohnstopp *m*; ~ **pack·et** *econ.* Lohntüte *f*.

wa·ger ['weɪdʒə] **1.** Wette *f*; **2.** wetten.

wag·gish □ ['wægɪʃ] schelmisch.

wag·gle ['wægl] wackeln (mit).

wag·(g)on ['wægən] (Last-, Roll-)Wagen *m*; *Brt.* 🚃 (offener) Güterwagen; **~·er** [~ə] Fuhrmann *m*.

wag·tail *zo.* ['wægteɪl] Bachstelze *f*.

waif *lit.* [weɪf] verlassenes *od.* verwahrlostes Kind.

wail [weɪl] **1.** (Weh)Klagen *n*; **2.** (weh)klagen; schreien, wimmern, heulen (*a. Wind*).

wain·scot ['weɪnskət] (Wand)Täfelung *f*.

waist [weɪst] Taille *f*; schmalste Stelle; ♣ Mitteldeck *n*; **~·coat** ['weɪskəʊt] Weste *f*; **~·line** ['weɪstlaɪn] *Schneiderei:* Taille *f*.

wait [weɪt] **1.** *v/i.* warten (*for* auf *acc.*); *a.* ~ *at* (*Am. on*) *table* bedienen, servieren; ~ *on*, ~ *upon* j-n bedienen; *v/t. abwarten;* **2.** Warten *n*; *lie in* ~ *for s.o.* j-m auflauern; **~·er** ['weɪtə] Kellner *m*; ~, *the bill* (*Am. check*), *please!* (Herr) Ober, bitte zahlen!

wait·ing ['weɪtɪŋ] Warten *n*; Dienst *m*; *in* ~ diensttuend; **~·room** Wartezimmer *n*; 🚃 *etc.* Wartesaal *m*.

wait·ress ['weɪtrɪs] Kellnerin *f*, Bedienung *f*; ~, *the bill* (*Am. check*), *please!* Fräulein, bitte zahlen!

waive [weɪv] verzichten auf (*acc.*).

wake [weɪk] **1.** ♣ Kielwasser *n* (*a. fig.*); *in the* ~ *of* im Kielwasser (*e-s Schiffes*); *fig.* im Gefolge (*gen.*); **2.** (*woke od. waked, woken od. waked*) *v/i. a.* ~ *up* aufwachen; *v/t. a.* ~ *up* (auf)wecken; *fig.* wachrufen; **~·ful** □ ['weɪkfl] wachsam; schlaflos; **wak·en** [~ən] = *wake 2.*

wale [weɪl] Strieme(n *m*) *f*.

walk [wɔːk] **1.** *v/i.* gehen (*a. Sport*), zu Fuß gehen, laufen; spazierengehen; wandern; im Schritt gehen; ∼ *out econ.* streiken; ∼ *out on* F im Stich lassen; *v/t.* (zu Fuß) gehen; führen; *Pferd* im Schritt gehen lassen; begleiten; durchwandern; auf *u.* ab gehen in *od.* auf (*dat.*); **2.** (Spazier-)Gang *m*; Spazierweg *m*; ∼ *of life* (soziale) Schicht; Beruf *m*; **∼er** [ˈwɔːkə] Spaziergänger(in); *Sport*: Geher *m*; *be a good* ∼ gut zu Fuß sein.

walk·ie-talk·ie [ˈwɔːkɪˈtɔːkɪ] Walkie-talkie *n*, tragbares Funksprechgerät.

walk·ing [ˈwɔːkɪŋ] (Zufuß)Gehen *n*; Spazierengehen *n*, Wandern *n*; *attr.* Spazier...; Wander...; ∼ **pa·pers** *pl. Am.* F Laufpaß *m* (*Entlassung*); ∼ **stick** Spazierstock *m*; ∼ **tour** Wanderung *f*.

walk|-out *econ.* [ˈwɔːkaʊt] Ausstand *m*, Streik *m*; ∼ **over** Spaziergang *m*, leichter Sieg; ∼ **up** *Am.* (Miets-)Haus *n* ohne Fahrstuhl; Wohnung *f* in e-m Haus ohne Fahrstuhl.

wall [wɔːl] **1.** Wand *f*; Mauer *f*; **2.** *a.* ∼ *in* mit e-r Mauer umgeben; ∼ *up* zumauern.

wal·let [ˈwɒlɪt] Brieftasche *f*.

wall·flow·er *fig.* [ˈwɔːlflaʊə] Mauerblümchen *n*.

wal·lop F [ˈwɒləp] *j-n* verdreschen.

wal·low [ˈwɒləʊ] sich wälzen.

wall|-pa·per [ˈwɔːlpeɪpə] **1.** Tapete *f*; **2.** tapezieren; ∼ **sock·et** ⚡ (Wand-)Steckdose *f*; ∼ **to**-∼ *carpet* Spannteppich *m*; ∼ *carpeting* Teppichboden *m*.

wal·nut ♀ [ˈwɔːlnʌt] Walnuß(baum *m*) *f*.

wal·rus *zo.* [ˈwɔːlrəs] Walroß *n*.

waltz [wɔːls] **1.** Walzer *m*; **2.** Walzer tanzen.

wan □ [wɒn] (**-nn-**) blaß, bleich, fahl.

wand [wɒnd] Zauberstab *m*.

wan·der [ˈwɒndə] herumwandern, -laufen, umherstreifen; △ *nicht in e-m Gebiet wandern* = *hike*; *fig.* abschweifen; irregehen; phantasieren.

wane [weɪn] **1.** abnehmen (*Mond*); *fig.* schwinden; **2.** Abnehmen *n*.

wan·gle F [ˈwæŋgl] *v/t.* deichseln, hinkriegen; *v/i.* mogeln.

want [wɒnt] **1.** Mangel *m* (*of an dat.*);

Bedürfnis *n*; Not *f*; **2.** *v/i.* ermangeln (*for gen.*); *he* ∼*s for nothing* es fehlt ihm an nichts; *v/t.* wünschen, (haben) wollen; bedürfen (*gen.*), brauchen; nicht (genug) haben; *it* ∼*s s.th.* es fehlt an et. (*dat.*); *he* ∼*s energy* es fehlt ihm an Energie; ∼*ed* gesucht; **∼ad** F [ˈwɒntæd] Stellenangebot *n*, -gesuch *n*; ∼ **ing** [-ɪŋ]: *be* ∼ es fehlen lassen (*in an dat.*); unzulänglich sein.

wan·ton [ˈwɒntən] **1.** □ mutwillig; ausgelassen; **2.** herumtollen.

war [wɔː] **1.** Krieg *m*; *attr.* Kriegs...; *make od. wage* ∼ Krieg führen (*on, against gegen*); **2.** (**-rr-**) streiten, kämpfen.

war·ble [ˈwɔːbl] trillern; trällern.

ward [wɔːd] **1.** (Krankenhaus)Station *f*, Abteilung *f*; Krankenzimmer *n*; (Gefängnis)Trakt *m*; Zelle *f*; (Stadt-, Wahl)Bezirk *m*; ⚖ Mündel *n*; *in* ∼ ⚖ unter Vormundschaft (stehend); **2.** ∼ *off* abwehren; **war·den** [ˈwɔːdn] Aufseher *m*; *univ.* Rektor *m*; *Am.* (Gefängnis)Direktor *m*; **∼er** [ˈwɔːdə] *Brt.* Aufsichtsbeamte(r) *m* (*im Gefängnis*).

war·drobe [ˈwɔːdrəʊb] Garderobe *f*; Kleiderschrank *m*; ∼ *trunk* Schrankkoffer *m*.

ware [weə] *in Zssgn*: Ware(n *pl.*) *f*, Artikel *m od. pl.*; △ *nicht* (*Einkaufs-*) *Ware*.

ware·house 1. [ˈweəhaʊs] (Waren-)Lager *n*; Lagerhaus *n*, Speicher *m*; △ *nicht Warenhaus* = *department store*; **2.** [-z] auf Lager bringen, (ein)lagern.

war|fare [ˈwɔːfeə] Krieg(führung *f*) *m*; ∼ **head** ⚔ Spreng-, Gefechtskopf *m* (*e-r Rakete etc.*).

war·i·ness [ˈweərɪnɪs] Vorsicht *f*.

war·like [ˈwɔːlaɪk] kriegerisch.

warm [wɔːm] **1.** □ warm (*a. fig.*); heiß; *fig.* hitzig; **2.** *et.* Warmes; (Auf-An)Wärmen *n*; **3.** *v/t. a.* ∼ *up* (auf-, an-, er)wärmen; *v/i. a.* ∼ *up* warm werden, sich erwärmen; warmlaufen (*Motor etc.*); **∼th** [-θ] Wärme *f*.

warn [wɔːn] warnen (*of, against von od. dat.*); verwarnen; ermahnen; verständigen; ∼ **ing** [ˈwɔːnɪŋ] (Ver-)Warnung *f*; Mahnung *f*; Kündigung *f*; *attr.* warnend; Warn...

warp [wɔːp] *v/i.* sich verziehen (*Holz*); *v/t. fig.* verdrehen, -zerren; beeinflussen; *j-n* abbringen (*from von*).

war|rant ['wɒrənt] **1.** Vollmacht f; Rechtfertigung f; Berechtigung f; ɪʦ (Vollziehungs-, Haft- etc.)Befehl m; Berechtigungsschein m; ~ of arrest ɪʦ Haftbefehl m; **2.** bevollmächtigen; rechtfertigen; verbürgen, garantieren; **~ran·ty** econ. [~ɪ]: it's still under ~ darauf ist noch Garantie.

war·ri·or ['wɒrɪə] Krieger m.

wart [wɔːt] Warze f; Auswuchs m.

war·y □ ['weərɪ] (-ier, -iest) wachsam, vorsichtig.

was [wɒz, wəz] 1. und 3. sg. pret. von be: war; pret. pass. von be: wurde.

wash [wɒʃ] **1.** v/t. waschen; (ab)spülen; ~ up abwaschen, abspülen; v/i. sich waschen (lassen); vom Wasser gespült od. geschwemmt werden; ~ up Brt. Geschirr spülen; **2.** Waschen n; Wäsche f; Wellenschlag m; Spülwasser n; mouth~ Mundwasser n; **3.** Wasch...; **~·a·ble** ['wɒʃəbl] waschbar; **~and-wear** bügelfrei; pflegeleicht; **~·ba·sin** Waschbecken n; **~cloth** Am. Waschlappen m; **~er** ['wɒʃə] Wäscherin f; Waschmaschine f; = dishwasher; ⊕ Unterlegscheibe f; **~·er·wom·an** (pl. -women) Waschfrau f; **~·ing** ['wɒʃɪŋ] **1.** Waschen n; Wäsche f; ~s pl. Spülwasser n; **2.** Wasch...; **~·ing ma·chine** Waschmaschine f; **~·ing pow·der** Waschpulver n, -mittel n; **~·ing-up** Brt. Abwasch m; **~rag** Am. Waschlappen m; **~·y** ['wɒʃɪ] (-ier, -iest) wässerig, wäßrig.

wasp zo. [wɒsp] Wespe f.

wast·age ['weɪstɪdʒ] Verlust m; Vergeudung f.

waste [weɪst] **1.** wüst, öde; unbebaut; überflüssig; Abfall...; lay ~ verwüsten; **2.** Verschwendung f, -geudung f; Abfall m; Ödland n, Wüste f; **3.** v/t. verwüsten; verschwenden; verzehren; v/i. verschwendet werden; **~·ful** □ ['weɪstfl] verschwenderisch; **~ paper** Abfallpapier n; Altpapier n; **~·pa·per bas·ket** [weɪst'peɪpəbɑːskɪt] Papierkorb m; **~ pipe** ['weɪstpaɪp] Abflußrohr n.

watch [wɒtʃ] **1.** Wache f; (Taschen-, Armband)Uhr f; **2.** v/i. zusehen, zuschauen; wachen; ~ for warten auf (acc.); ~ out (for) aufpassen, achtgeben (auf acc.); sich hüten (vor dat.); ~ out! Achtung!, Vorsicht!; v/t. bewachen; beobachten; achtgeben auf

(acc.); Gelegenheit abwarten; **~·dog** ['wɒtʃdɒg] Wachhund m; fig. Überwacher(in); **~·ful** □ [~fl] wachsam; **~·mak·er** Uhrmacher m; **~·man** [~mən] (pl. -men) (Nacht)Wächter m; **~·word** Kennwort n, Parole f.

wa·ter ['wɔːtə] **1.** Wasser n; Gewässer n; drink the ~s Brunnen trinken; **2.** v/t. bewässern; (be)sprengen; (be-)gießen; mit Wasser versorgen; tränken; verwässern (a. fig.); v/i. wässern (Mund); tränen (Augen); **~·clos·et** (Wasser)Klosett n; **~·col·o(u)r** Wasser-, Aquarellfarbe f; Aquarell(malerei f) n; **~·course** Wasserlauf m; Fluß, Strombett n; Kanal m; **~·cress** ♀ Brunnenkresse f; **~·fall** Wasserfall m; **~·front** an ein Gewässer grenzender Stadtbezirk, Hafengebiet n, -viertel n; **~ ga(u)ge** ⊕ Wasserstands(an)zeiger m; Pegel m; **~·hole** Wasserloch n.

wa·ter·ing ['wɔːtərɪŋ] Bewässern n; (Be)Gießen n; Tränken (von Vieh); **~·can** Gießkanne f; **~·place** Wasserstelle f; Tränke f; Bad(eort m) n; Seebad n; **~·pot** Gießkanne f.

wa·ter| lev·el ['wɔːtəlevl] Wasserspiegel m; Wasserstand(slinie f) m; ⊕ Wasserwaage f; **~·logged** [~lɒgd] ♣ voll Wasser (Boot); vollgesogen (Erdreich); **~ main** ⊕ Hauptwasserrohr n; **~·mark** Wasserzeichen n (Papier); **~·mel·on** ♀ Wassermelone f; **~ pol·lu·tion** Wasserverschmutzung f; **~ po·lo** Sport: Wasserball(spiel n) m; **~·proof 1.** wasserdicht; **2.** Regenmantel m; **3.** imprägnieren; **~·shed** geogr. Wasserscheide f; fig. Wendepunkt m; **~·side** Fluß-, Seeufer n; **~ ski·ing** Sport: Wasserski(laufen) n; **~·tight** wasserdicht; fig. unanfechtbar; stichhaltig (Argument); **~·way** Wasserstraße f; **~·works** oft sg. Wasserwerk n; turn on the ~ fig. F losheulen; **~·y** [~rɪ] wässerig, wäßrig.

watt ⚡ [wɒt] Watt n.

wave [weɪv] **1.** Welle f (a. phys.); Woge f; Winken n; **2.** v/t. wellen; schwingen; schwenken; ~ s.o. aside j-n beiseite winken; v/i. wogen, wehen, flattern; ~ at od. to s.o. j-m (zu)winken, j-m ein Zeichen geben; **~·length** ['weɪvleŋθ] phys. Wellenlänge f (a. fig.).

wa·ver ['weɪvə] (sch)wanken; flakkern.

wav·y □ ['weɪvɪ] (*-ier, -iest*) wellig; wogend.

wax[1] [wæks] **1.** Wachs *n*; Siegellack *m*; Ohrenschmalz *n*; **2.** wachsen; bohnern.

wax[2] [~] zunehmen (*Mond*).

wax|en *fig.* ['wæksən] wächsern; **~works** *sg.* Wachsfigurenkabinett *n*; **~·y** □ [~ɪ] (*-ier, -iest*) wachsartig; weich.

way [weɪ] **1.** Weg *m*; Straße *f*; Art *u.* Weise *f*; (Eigen)Art; Strecke *f*; Richtung *f*; *fig.* Hinsicht *f*; ~ *in* Eingang *m*; ~ *out* Ausgang *m*; *fig.* Ausweg *m*; *right of* ~ ⚡️ Wegerecht *n*; *bsd. mot.* Vorfahrt(srecht *n*) *f*; *this* ~ hierher, hier entlang; *by the* ~ übrigens; *by* ~ *of* durch; *on the* ~, *on one's* ~ unterwegs; *out of the* ~ ungewöhnlich; *under* ~ in Fahrt; *give* ~ zurückweichen; *mot.* die Vorfahrt lassen (*to dat.*); nachgeben; abgelöst werden (*to* von); sich hingeben (*to dat.*); *have one's* ~ s-n Willen haben; *lead the* ~ vorangehen; **2.** *adv.* weit; **~·bill** ['weɪbɪl] Frachtbrief *m*; **~·far·er** *veraltet od. lit.* [~fɛərə] Wanderer *m*; **~·lay** [weɪ'leɪ] (*-laid*) j-m auflauern; *j-n* abfangen, abpassen; **~·out** F äußerst ungewöhnlich; toll, super; **~·side** ['weɪsaɪd] **1.** Wegrand *m*; **2.** am Wege; **~·sta·tion** *Am.* Zwischenstation *f*; **~ train** *Am.* Bummelzug *m*; **~·ward** □ [~wəd] launisch; eigensinnig.

we [wiː, wɪ] wir.

weak □ [wiːk] schwach; schwächlich; dünn (*Getränk*); **~·en** ['wiːkən] *v/t.* schwächen; *v/i.* schwach werden; **~·ling** [~lɪŋ] Schwächling *m*; **~·ly** [~lɪ] (*-ier, -iest*) schwächlich; **~·mind·ed** [wiːk'maɪndɪd] schwachsinnig; **~·ness** Schwäche *f*.

weal [wiːl] Strieme(n *m*) *f*.

wealth [welθ] Reichtum *m*; *econ.* Besitz *m*, Vermögen *n*; *fig.* Fülle *f*; **~·y** □ ['welθɪ] (*-ier, -iest*) reich; wohlhabend.

wean [wiːn] entwöhnen; ~ *s.o. from s.th.* j-m et. abgewöhnen.

weap·on ['wepən] Waffe *f*.

wear [weə] **1.** (*wore, worn*) *v/t.* am Körper tragen; zur Schau tragen; *a.* ~ *away*, ~ *down*, ~ *off*, ~ *out Kleidung etc.* abnutzen, abtragen, verschleißen, *Reifen* abfahren; *a.* ~ *out* ermüden; *j-s Geduld* erschöpfen; *a.* ~

away, ~ *down* zermürben; entkräften; *v/i.* sich *gut etc.* tragen *od.* halten; *a.* ~ *away*, ~ *down*, ~ *off*, ~ *out* sich abnutzen *od.* abtragen, verschleißen; sich abfahren (*Reifen*); ~ *off fig.* sich verlieren; ~ *on* sich dahinschleppen (*Zeit etc.*); ~ *out fig.* sich erschöpfen; **2.** Tragen *n*; (Be-)Kleidung *f*; Abnutzung *f*; *for hard* ~ strapazierfähig; *the worse for* ~ abgetragen; ~ *and tear* Verschleiß *m*; **~·er** ['weərə] Träger(in).

wear·i·ness ['wɪərɪnɪs] Müdigkeit *f*; Überdruß *m*; **~·i·some** □ [~səm] ermüdend; langweilig; **~·y** ['wɪərɪ] **1.** □ (*-ier, -iest*) müde; überdrüssig; ermüdend; anstrengend; **2.** ermüden; überdrüssig werden (*of gen.*).

wea·sel *zo.* ['wiːzl] Wiesel *n*.

weath·er ['weðə] **1.** Wetter *n*, Witterung *f*; **2.** *v/t.* dem Wetter aussetzen; ⚓️ *Sturm* abwettern; *fig.* überstehen; *v/i.* verwittern; **~·beat·en** vom Wetter mitgenommen; *fig.* abgehärtet; **~ bu·reau** Wetteramt *n*; ~ *chart* Wetterkarte *f*; **~·fore·cast** Wetterbericht *m*, *-vorhersage f*; **~·worn** verwittert.

weave [wiːv] (*wove, woven*) weben, flechten; *fig.* ersinnen, erfinden; **weav·er** ['wiːvə] Weber *m*.

web [web] Gewebe *n*, Netz *n*; *zo.* Schwimm-, Flughaut *f*; **~·bing** ['webɪŋ] Gurtband *n*.

wed [wed] (*-dd-; wedded od. selten: wed*) heiraten; *fig.* verbinden (*to* mit); **~·ding** ['wedɪŋ] **1.** Hochzeit *f*; **2.** Hochzeits..., Braut..., Trau...; ~ *ring* Ehe-, Trauring *m*.

wedge [wedʒ] **1.** Keil *m*; **2.** (ver)keilen; (ein)keilen, (-)zwängen (*in in acc.*).

wed·lock ['wedlɒk]: *born in (out of)* ~ ehelich (unehelich) geboren.

Wednes·day ['wenzdɪ] Mittwoch *m*.

wee [wiː] klein, winzig; *a* ~ *bit* ein klein wenig.

weed [wiːd] **1.** Unkraut *n*; **2.** jäten; säubern (*of* von); ~ *out fig.* aussondern, -sieben; **~·kill·er** ['wiːdkɪlə] Unkrautvertilgungsmittel *n*; **~s** [wiːdz] *pl. mst widow's* ~ Witwenkleidung *f*; **~·y** ['wiːdɪ] (*-ier, -iest*) voll Unkraut, verunkrautet; F schmächtig.

week [wiːk] Woche *f*; *this day* ~ heute in *od.* vor e-r Woche; **~·day** ['wiːkdeɪ] Wochentag *m*; **~·end** [wiːk'end] Wochenende *n*; **~·end·er** [~ə] Wo-

chenendausflügler(in); **~ly** ['wiːklɪ]
1. wöchentlich; Wochen...; 2. *a.* ~
paper Wochenblatt *n*, Wochen-
(zeit)schrift *f*.

weep [wiːp] (*wept*) *v/i.* weinen; tropfen;
~ing ['wiːpɪŋ]: ~ *willow* ♀ Trauer-
weide *f*; **~y** *F* [~ɪ] (*-ier, -iest*) weiner-
lich; rührselig, sentimental.

weigh [weɪ] *v/t.* (ab)wiegen; *fig.* ab-,
erwägen; ~ *anchor* ♱ den Anker
lichten; **~ed down** niedergedrückt;
v/i. wiegen (*a. fig.*); ausschlaggebend sein; ~ *on*, ~ *upon* lasten auf
(*dat.*).

weight [weɪt] 1. Gewicht *n* (*a. fig.*);
Last *f*; *fig.* Bedeutung *f*; *fig.* Last *f*,
Bürde *f*; *put on* ~, *gain* ~ zunehmen;
lose ~ abnehmen; 2. beschweren;
belasten; **~less** ['weɪtlɪs] schwere-
los; **~·less·ness** [~nɪs] Schwerelosig-
keit *f* (*a. Raumfahrt*); ~ **lift·ing**
[~lɪftɪŋ] *Sport:* Gewichtheben *n*; **~y**
□ [~ɪ] (*-ier, -iest*) (ge)wichtig;
wuchtig.

weir [wɪə] Wehr *n*; Fischreuse *f*.

weird □ [wɪəd] Schicksals...; unheimlich; *F* sonderbar, seltsam.

wel·come ['welkəm] 1. willkommen;
you are ~ *to inf.* es steht Ihnen frei,
zu *inf.*; (*you are*) ~! nichts zu danken!, bitte sehr!; 2. Willkomm(en) *n*
m; 3. willkommen heißen; *fig.* begrüßen.

weld ⊕ [weld] (ver-, zusammen-)
schweißen.

wel·fare ['welfeə] Wohl(ergehen) *n*;
Sozialhilfe *f*; *Am.* Wohlfahrt *f*; ~ **state**
pol. Wohlfahrtsstaat *m*; ~ **work** So-
zialarbeit *f*; ~ **work·er** Sozialarbei-
ter(in).

well[1] [wel] 1. Brunnen *m*; Quelle *f*; ⊕
Bohrloch *n*; Fahrstuhl-, Licht-,
Luftschacht *m*; 2. quellen.

well[2] [~] 1. (*better, best*) wohl; gut;
ordentlich, gründlich; gesund; *be* ~,
feel ~ sich wohl fühlen; *be* ~ *off in*
*guten Verhältnissen leben, wohlha-
bend sein; 2. *int.* nun!, na!; **~·**
bal·anced ['wel'bælənst] ausgewo-
gen (*Diät*); (*innerlich*) ausgeglichen;
~·being Wohl(befinden) *n*; **~·born**
aus guter Familie; **~·bred** wohlerzo-
gen; **~·de·fined** deutlich; klar um-
rissen; **~·done** gutgemacht; (*gut*)
durchgebraten (*Fleisch*); **~·in·ten·**
tioned [~ɪn'tenʃnd] wohlmeinend;
gutgemeint; **~·known** bekannt; **~·**
man·nered mit guten Manieren;

~·nigh ['welnaɪ] beinahe; **~·off**
[wel'ɒf] wohlhabend; **~·read** bele-
sen; **~·timed** (*zeitlich*) günstig, im
richtigen Augenblick; *Sport:* gutge-
timed (*Paß etc.*); **~·to-do** wohlhabend; **~·worn** abgetragen; *fig.* abgedroschen.

Welsh [welʃ] 1. walisisch; 2. *ling.*
Walisisch *n*; *the* ~ *pl.* die Waliser *pl.*;
~ **rab·bit**, ~ **rare·bit** überbackener
Käsetoast.

welt [welt] Strieme(n *m*) *f*.

wel·ter ['weltə] Wirrwarr *m*, Durcheinander *n*.

wench *veraltet* [wentʃ] (*bsd. Bauern-*)
Mädchen *n*.

went [went] *pret. von* go 1.

wept [wept] *pret. u. p.p. von* weep.

were [wɜː, wə] 1. *pret. von* be: *du*
warst, Sie waren, wir, sie waren, ihr
wart; 2. *pret. pass. von* be: *wurde(n);*
3. *subj. pret. von* be: *wäre(n)*.

west [west] 1. West(en *m*) *n*; *a.* Westen
m, westlicher Landesteil; *the* ♀ *der*
Westen, die Weststaaten *pl.* (*der*
USA); *pol.* der Westen; 2. West...,
westlich; 3. westwärts, nach Westen; **~·er·ly** ['westəlɪ] westlich;
~·ern [~ən] 1. westlich; 2. Western
m, Wildwestfilm *m*; **~·ward(s)**
[~wəd(z)] westwärts.

wet [wet] 1. naß, feucht; 2. Nässe *f*,
Feuchtigkeit *f*; 3. (*-tt-; wet od wet-*
ted) naß machen, anfeuchten.

weth·er *zo.* ['weðə] Hammel *m*.

wet-nurse ['wetnɜːs] Amme *f*.

whack [wæk] (*knallender*) Schlag; *F*
(*An*)Teil *m*; **~ed** [~t] fertig, erledigt
(*erschöpft*); **~ing** ['wækɪŋ] 1. *F*
Mords...; 2. (*Tracht f*) Prügel *pl.*

whale *zo.* [weɪl] Wal *m*; **~·bone**
['weɪlbəʊn] Fischbein *n*; ~ **oil** Tran
m.

whal·er ['weɪlə] Walfänger *m* (*a.*
Schiff); **~ing** [~ɪŋ] Walfang *m*.

wharf [wɔːf] (*pl. wharfs, wharves*
[~vz]) Kai *m*.

what [wɒt] 1. was; wie; was für ein(e),
welche(r, -s), *vor pl.:* was für; (*das,*)
was; *know* ~'*s* ~ Bescheid wissen;
about ...? wie steht's mit ...?; ~ *for?*
wozu?; ~ *of it?, so* ~? na und?; ~
next? was sonst noch?; *iro.* sonst
noch was?, das fehlte noch!; ~ *a*
blessing! was für ein Segen!; ~ *with*
..., ~ *with* ... teils durch ..., teils
durch ...; 2. *int.* was!, wie!;
fragend: was?, wie?; **~·(so·)ev·er**

[wɒt(səʊ)'evə] was (auch immer); alles, was.

wheat ⚶ [wi:t] Weizen m.

whee·dle ['wi:dl] beschwatzen; ~ s.th. out of s.o. j-m et. abschwatzen.

wheel [wi:l] 1. Rad n; Steuer(rad) n; Lenkrad n; bsd. Am. F (Fahr)Rad n; Töpferscheibe f; Drehung f; ⚔ Schwenkung f; 2. rollen, fahren, schieben; sich drehen; ⚔ schwenken; bsd. Am. F radeln; **~·bar·row** ['wi:lbærəʊ] Schubkarre(n m) f; **~chair** Rollstuhl m; **~ed** mit Rädern; fahrbar; in Zssgn: ...räd(e)rig.

-wheel·er ['wi:lə] in Zssgn: Wagen od. Fahrzeug mit ... Rädern.

wheeze [wi:z] schnaufen, keuchen.

whelp [welp] 1. zo. Welpe m; Junge(s) n; F Balg m, n (ungezogenes Kind); 2. (Junge) werfen.

when [wen] 1. wann; 2. wenn; als; während, obwohl, wo ... (doch).

whence [wens] woher, von wo.

when·(so·)ev·er [wen(səʊ)'evə] (immer) wenn, sooft (als); fragend: wann denn.

where [weə] wohin; ~ ... from? woher?; ~ ... to? wohin?; **~·a·bouts** 1. [weərə'baʊts] wo etwa; 2. ['weərəbaʊts] Aufenthalt(sort) m, Verbleib m; **~·as** [weər'æz] wohingegen, während (doch); **~·at** [~r'æt] woran, wobei, worauf; **~·by** [weə'baɪ] wodurch; **~·fore** ['weəfɔ:] weshalb; **~·in** [weər'ɪn] worin; **~·of** [~r'ɒv] wovon; **~·u·pon** [~rə'pɒn] worauf(hin); **wher·ev·er** [~r'evə] wo(hin) (auch) immer; **~·with·al** ['weəwɪðɔ:l] die (nötigen) Mittel pl., das nötige (Klein)Geld.

whet [wet] (-tt-) wetzen, schärfen; fig. anstacheln.

wheth·er ['weðə] ob; ~ or no so oder so.

whet·stone ['wetstəʊn] Schleifstein m.

whey [weɪ] Molke f.

which [wɪtʃ] 1. welche(r, -s); 2. der, die, das; was; **~·ev·er** [~'evə] welche(r, -s) (auch) immer.

whiff [wɪf] 1. Hauch m; Duftwolke f; Geruch m; F Zigarillo m, n; Zug m (beim Rauchen); have a few ~s ein paar Züge machen; F paffen; F duften (unangenehm riechen).

while [waɪl] 1. Weile f, Zeit f; for a ~ e-e Zeitlang; 2. mst ~ away sich die Zeit vertreiben; verbrin-

gen; 3. a. **whilst** [waɪlst] während.

whim [wɪm] Laune f, Grille f.

whim·per ['wɪmpə] 1. wimmern, winseln; 2. Wimmern n, Winseln n; △ nicht Wimper.

whim·si·cal □ ['wɪmzɪkl] wunderlich; launisch (a. Wetter etc.); **~·sy** ['wɪmzɪ] Grille f, Laune f.

whine [waɪn] winseln; wimmern.

whin·ny ['wɪnɪ] wiehern.

whip [wɪp] 1. (-pp-) v/t. peitschen; geißeln (a. fig.); j-n verprügeln; schlagen; a. Eier, Sahne schlagen; **~ped cream** Schlagsahne f, -rahm m; **~ped eggs** pl. Eischnee m; v/i. sausen, flitzen; 2. Peitsche f; (Reit-) Gerte f.

whip·ping ['wɪpɪŋ] (Tracht f) Prügel pl.; **~·top** Kreisel m.

whip·poor·will zo. ['wɪpʊəwɪl] Ziegenmelker m.

whirl [wɜ:l] 1. wirbeln; (sich) drehen; 2. Wirbel m, Strudel m; **~·pool** ['wɜ:lpu:l] Strudel m; **~·wind** [~wɪnd] Wirbelwind m, -sturm m.

whir(r) [wɜ:] (-rr-) schwirren.

whisk [wɪsk] 1. schnelle od. heftige Bewegung; Wisch m; Staubwedel m; Küche: Schneebesen m; 2. v/t. (ab-, weg)wischen, (ab-, weg)fegen; mit dem Schwanz schlagen; Eier schlagen; ~ away schnell verschwinden lassen, wegnehmen; v/i. huschen, flitzen. **whis·ker** ['wɪskə] Barthaar n; ~s pl. Backenbart m.

whis·per ['wɪspə] 1. flüstern; 2. Flüstern n, Geflüster n; in a ~, in ~s flüsternd, im Flüsterton.

whis·tle ['wɪsl] 1. pfeifen; 2. Pfeife f; Pfiff m; F Kehle f; ~ **stop** Am. ⚓ Bedarfshaltestelle f; Kleinstadt f; pol. kurzes Auftreten (e-s Kandidaten im Wahlkampf).

Whit [wɪt] in Zssgn: Pfingst...

white [waɪt] 1. (~r, ~st) weiß; rein; F anständig; Weiß...; 2. Weiß(e) n; Weiße(r m) f (Rasse); **~·col·lar** [waɪt'kɒlə] Büro...; **~ worker** (Büro-) Angestellte(r m) f; ~ **heat** Weißglut f; ~ **lie** Notlüge f, fromme Lüge; **whit·en** ['waɪtn] weiß machen od. werden; bleichen; **~·ness** [~nɪs] Weiße f; Blässe f; **~·wash** 1. Tünche f; 2. weißen, tünchen; fig. reinwaschen.

whit·ish ['waɪtɪʃ] weißlich.

Whit·sun ['wɪtsn] Pfingst...; **~·tide** Pfingsten n od. pl.

whit·tle ['wɪtl] schnitze(l)n; ~ away schwächen, beschneiden, herabsetzen, kürzen.

whiz(z) [wɪz] (-zz-) zischen, sausen.

who [huː; hu] wer; welche(r, -s), der, die, das.

who·dun(n)·it F [huː'dʌnɪt] Krimi *m* (*Kriminalroman, -stück, -film*).

who·ev·er [huː'evə] wer (auch) immer.

whole [həʊl] **1.** □ ganz; voll(ständig); heil, unversehrt; **2.** Ganze(s) *n*; the ~ of London ganz London; on the ~ im großen (u.) ganzen; im allgemeinen; **~-heart·ed** □ [həʊl'hɑːtɪd] aufrichtig; **~-meal** ['həʊlmiːl] Vollkorn...; ~ *bread* Vollkornbrot *n*; **~sale** *econ.* Großhandel *m*; **2.** *econ.* Großhandels...; *fig.* Massen...; ~ *dealer* = **~-sal·er** [~ə] *econ.* Großhändler *m*; **~-some** [~səm] gesund; **~ wheat** *bsd. Am.* = whole-meal.

whol·ly *adv.* ['həʊllɪ] ganz, gänzlich.

whom [huːm, hum] *Objektkasus von* who.

whoop [huːp] **1.** (*bsd.* Freuden)Schrei *m*; ⚕ Keuchen *n* (*bei Keuchhusten*); **2.** schreien, *a.* ~ *with joy* jauchzen; ~ *it up* F auf den Putz hauen (*ausgelassen feiern*); **~·ee** F ['wʊpiː]: *make* ~ auf den Putz hauen (*ausgelassen feiern*); **~·ing-cough** ['huːpɪŋkɒf] Keuchhusten *m*.

whore [hɔː] Hure *f*.

whose [huːz] *gen. sg. u. pl. von* who.

why [waɪ] **1.** warum, weshalb; ~ *so?* wieso?; **2.** *int.* nun (gut); ja doch.

wick [wɪk] Docht *m*.

wick·ed [~] ['wɪkɪd] böse, schlecht, schlimm; **~·ness** [~nɪs] Bosheit *f*.

wick·er [~] ['wɪkə] aus Weiden geflochten, Weiden..., Korb...; ~ *basket* Weidenkorb *m*; ~ *bottle* Korbflasche *f*; ~ *chair* Korbstuhl *m*; **~·work** Korbwaren *pl.*; Flechtwerk *n*.

wick·et ['wɪkɪt] Pförtchen *n*; *Kricket*: Dreistab *m*, Tor *n*.

wide [waɪd] *adj.* □ *u. adv.* weit; ausgedehnt; großzügig; breit; weitab; ~ *awake* völlig (*od.* hell)wach; aufgeweckt, wach; *3 feet* ~ 3 Fuß breit; **wid·en** ['waɪdn] (sich) verbreitern; (sich) erweitern (*Wissen etc.*); **~-o·pen** ['waɪd'əʊpən] weitgeöffnet; *Am.* äußerst großzügig (*in der Gesetzesdurchführung*); **~·spread** weitverbreitet; ausgedehnt.

wid·ow ['wɪdəʊ] Witwe *f*; *attr.* Witwen...; **~·ed** verwitwet; **~·er** [~ə] Witwer *m*.

width [wɪdθ] Breite *f*, Weite *f*.

wield [wiːld] *Einfluß etc.* ausüben.

wife [waɪf] (*pl.* wives [~vz]) (Ehe-) Frau *f*, Gattin *f*.

wig [wɪg] Perücke *f*.

wild [waɪld] **1.** *adj.* □ wild; toll; rasend; wütend; ausgelassen; planlos; ~ *about* (ganz) verrückt nach; **2.** *adv.*: *run* ~ verwildern (*Garten etc.*; *a. fig. Kinder etc.*); *talk* ~ (wild) drauflosreden; dummes Zeug reden; **3.** *a.* ~*s pl.* Wildnis *f*; **~·cat** ['waɪldkæt] **1.** *zo.* Wildkatze *f*; *econ. Am.* Schwindelunternehmen *n*; **2.** wild (*Streik*); *econ. Am.* Schwindel...; **wil·der·ness** ['wɪldənɪs] Wildnis *f*, Wüste *f*; **~·fire** ['waɪldfaɪə]: *like* ~ wie ein Lauffeuer; **~·life** *coll.* wildlebende Tiere (u. wildwachsende Pflanzen).

wile [waɪl] List *f*; ~*s pl. a.* Schliche *pl.*

will [wɪl] **1.** Wille *m*; Wunsch *m*; Testament *n*; *of one's own free* ~ aus freien Stücken; **2.** *v/aux.* (*pret.* would; *verneint:* ~ not, won't) ich, du *etc.* will(st) *etc.*; *ich werde, wir werden; wollen; werden;* **3.** wollen; durch Willenskraft zwingen; entscheiden; ⚖ vermachen.

wil(l)·ful □ ['wɪlfl] eigensinnig; absichtlich, *bsd.* ⚖ vorsätzlich.

will·ing ['wɪlɪŋ] *pred.* gewillt, willens, bereit; (bereit)willig.

will-o'-the-wisp ['wɪləʊ'wɪsp] Irrlicht *n*.

wil·low ♀ ['wɪləʊ] Weide *f*; **~·y** *fig.* [~ɪ] geschmeidig; gertenschlank.

will·pow·er ['wɪlpaʊə] Willenskraft *f*.

wil·ly-nil·ly ['wɪlɪ'nɪlɪ] wohl oder übel.

wilt [wɪlt] (ver)welken.

wi·ly □ ['waɪlɪ] (-ier, -iest) listig, gerissen.

win [wɪn] **1.** (-nn-; won) *v/t.* gewinnen, erringen; erlangen; erreichen; *j-n dazu bringen* (*to do* zu tun); ~ *s.o. over od. round* j-n für sich gewinnen; *v/i.* gewinnen, siegen; **2.** *Sport*: Sieg *m*.

wince [wɪns] (zusammen)zucken.

winch [wɪntʃ] Winde *f*; Kurbel *f*.

wind[1] [wɪnd] **1.** Wind *m*; Atem *m*, Luft *f*; ⚕ Blähung(en *pl.*) *f*; *the* ~ *sg. od. pl.* ♪ die Bläser; **2.** *hunt.* wittern;

W

außer Atem bringen; verschnaufen lassen.

wind² [waɪnd] (*wound*) *v/t.* winden, wickeln, schlingen; kurbeln; (*winded od. wound*) *Horn* blasen; ~ *up Uhr* aufziehen; *Rede etc.* beschließen; *v/i.* sich winden; sich schlängeln; ~ *up* (*bsd. s-e Rede*) schließen (*by saying* mit den Worten); F enden, landen.

wind|bag F ['wɪndbæg] Schwätzer *m*; **~fall** Fallobst *n*; Glücksfall *m*.

wind·ing ['waɪndɪŋ] 1. Windung *f*; 2. sich windend; ~ **stairs** *pl.* Wendeltreppe *f*; ~ **sheet** Leichentuch *n*.

wind-in·stru·ment ♪ ['wɪndɪnstrʊmənt] Blasinstrument *n*.

wind·lass ⊕ ['wɪndləs] Winde *f*.

wind·mill ['wɪnmɪl] Windmühle *f*.

win·dow ['wɪndəʊ] Fenster *n*; Schaufenster *n*; Schalter *m*; ~ **dress·ing** Schaufensterdekoration *f*; *fig.* Aufmachung *f*, Mache *f*; ~ **shade** *Am.* Rouleau *n*; ~ **shop·ping** Schaufensterbummel *m*; *go* ~ e-n Schaufensterbummel machen.

wind|pipe *anat.* ['wɪndpaɪp] Luftröhre *f*; **~screen**, *Am.* **~shield** *mot.* Windschutzscheibe *f*; ~ **wiper** Scheibenwischer *m*; **~surf·ing** *Sport:* Windsurfing *n*, -surfen *n*.

wind·y □ ['wɪndɪ] (*-ier, -iest*) windig (*a. fig. inhaltlos*); geschwätzig.

wine [waɪn] Wein *m*; **~press** ['waɪnpres] (Wein)Kelter *f*.

wing [wɪŋ] 1. Flügel *m* (*a.* ✕ *u. arch.*, *Sport, pol.*); Schwinge *f*; *Brt. mot.* Kotflügel *m*; ✈ Tragfläche *f*; ✕ Geschwader *n*; ~*s pl. thea.* Seitenkulisse *f*; *take* ~ weg-, auffliegen; *on the* ~ im Flug; 2. fliegen; *fig.* beflügeln.

wink [wɪŋk] 1. Blinzeln *n*, Zwinkern *n*; *not get a* ~ *of sleep* kein Auge zutun; *s. forty*; 2. blinzeln od. zwinkern (mit); blinken (*Licht*); △ *nicht winken*; ~ *at* anblinzeln; *fig.* ein Auge zudrücken bei *et.*

win|ner ['wɪnə] Gewinner(in), Sieger(in); **~ning** ['wɪnɪŋ] 1. □ einnehmend, gewinnend; 2. ~*s pl.* Gewinn *m*.

win|ter ['wɪntə] 1. Winter *m*; 2. überwintern; den Winter verbringen; **~ter sports** *pl.* Wintersport *m*; **~try** [~trɪ] winterlich; *fig.* frostig.

wipe [waɪp] 1. (ab-, auf)wischen; reinigen; (ab)trocknen; ~ *out* auswischen; wegwischen, (aus)löschen;

fig. vernichten; ~ *up* aufwischen; *Geschirr* abtrocknen; **wip·er** *mot.* ['waɪpə] Scheibenwischer *m*.

wire ['waɪə] 1. Draht *m*; ⚡ Leitung *f*; F Telegramm *n*; *pull the* ~*s* der Drahtzieher sein; *s-e Beziehungen* spielen lassen; 2. (ver)drahten; telegrafieren; **~drawn** spitzfindig; **~less** [~lɪs] 1. □ drahtlos, Funk...; 2. *Brt.* Radio(apparat *m*) *n*; *on the* ~ im Radio *od.* Rundfunk; 3. funken; **net·ting** ['waɪə'netɪŋ] Maschendraht *m*; **~tap** ['waɪətæp] (*-pp-*) Telefongespräche abhören, die Telefonleitung anzapfen.

wir·y □ ['waɪərɪ] (*-ier, -iest*) drahtig, sehnig.

wis·dom ['wɪzdəm] Weisheit *f*, Klugheit *f*; ~ **tooth** Weisheitszahn *m*.

wise¹ □ [waɪz] (*-r, ~st*) weise, klug; verständig; erfahren; ~ *guy* F Klugscheißer *m*.

wise² *veraltet* [~] Weise *f*, Art *f*.

wise·crack F ['waɪzkræk] 1. witzige Bemerkung; 2. witzeln.

wish [wɪʃ] 1. wünschen; wollen; ~ *for* (sich) *et.* wünschen; ~ *s.o. well* (*ill*) j-m Gutes (Böses) wünschen; 2. Wunsch *m*; **~ful** □ ['wɪʃfl] sehnsüchtig; ~ *thinking* Wunschdenken *n*.

wish·y-wash·y ['wɪʃɪwɒʃɪ] wäßrig, dünn; *fig.* seicht, saft- u. kraftlos.

wisp [wɪsp] Bündel *n*; Strähne *f*.

wist·ful □ ['wɪstfl] wehmütig.

wit¹ [wɪt] Geist *m*, Intelligenz *f*, Witz *m*; *a.* ~*s pl.* Verstand *m*; geistreicher Mensch; △ *nicht Witz = joke*; *be at one's* ~*s od.* ~*s' end* mit s-r Weisheit am Ende sein; *keep one's* ~*s about one* e-n klaren Kopf behalten.

wit² [~]: *to* ~ *bsd.* ⚖ nämlich, das heißt.

witch [wɪtʃ] Hexe *f*, Zauberin *f*; **~craft** ['wɪtʃkrɑːft], **~ery** [~ərɪ] Hexerei *f*; **~hunt** *pol.* Hexenjagd *f* (*for*, *against* auf *acc.*).

with [wɪð] mit; nebst; bei; von; durch; vor (*dat.*); ~ *it* F up to date, modern.

with·draw [wɪð'drɔː] (*-drew, -drawn*) *v/t.* ab-, ent-, zurückziehen; zurücknehmen; *Geld* abheben; *v/i.* sich zurückziehen; zurücktreten; *Sport:* auf den Start verzichten; **~al** [~əl] Zurückziehung *f*, -nahme *f*; Rücktritt *m*; *bsd.* ✕ Ab-, Rückzug *m*; *econ.* Abheben *n* (*von Geld*); *Sport:*

Startverzicht m; ⚕ Entziehung f; ~
cure ⚕ Entziehungskur f; ~ *symp-*
toms pl. ⚕ Entzugserscheinungen
pl.

with·er ['wɪðə] *v/i.* (ver)welken, verdorren, austrocknen; *v/t.* welken lassen.

with·hold [wɪð'həʊld] (*-held*) zurückhalten; ~ *s.th. from s.o.* j-m et.
vorenthalten.

with|in [wɪ'ðɪn] **1.** *adv.* im Innern,
drin(nen); zu Hause; **2.** *prp.* in(ner-
halb); ~ *doors* im Hause; ~ *call* in
Rufweite; ~**out** [wɪ'ðaʊt] **1.** *adv.*
(dr)außen; äußerlich; **2.** *prp.* ohne.

with·stand [wɪð'stænd] (*-stood*) widerstehen (*dat.*).

wit·ness ['wɪtnɪs] **1.** Zeug|e m, -in f;
bear ~ *to* Zeugnis ablegen von, *et.*
bestätigen; **2.** bezeugen; Zeuge sein
von *et.*; beglaubigen; ~ *box, Am.* ~
stand Zeugenstand m.

wit·ti·cis·m ['wɪtɪsɪzəm] witzige Bemerkung; ~**ty** □ [~ɪ] (*-ier, -iest*)
witzig; geistreich.

wives [waɪvz] *pl. von* wife.

wiz·ard ['wɪzəd] Zauberer m; Genie
n, Leuchte f.

wiz·en(ed) ['wɪzn(d)] schrump(e)lig.

wob·ble ['wɒbl] schwanken, wackeln.

woe [wəʊ] Weh n, Leid n; ~ *is me!*
wehe mir!; ~**be·gone** ['wəʊbɪgɒn]
jammervoll; ~**ful** □ ['wəʊfl] jammervoll, traurig, elend.

woke [wəʊk] *pret. u. p.p. von* wake 2;
wok·en ['wəʊkən] *p.p. von* wake 2.

wold [wəʊld] hügeliges Land.

wolf [wʊlf] **1.** (*pl.* wolves [~vz]) *zo.*
Wolf m; **2.** *a.* ~ *down* (gierig) ver- *od.*
hinunterschlingen; ~**ish** □ ['wʊlfɪʃ]
wölfisch; Wolfs-.

wom·an ['wʊmən] **1.** (*pl.* women
['wɪmɪn]) Frau f; F (Ehe)Frau f;
Freundin f; F Geliebte f; **2.** weiblich;
~ *doctor* Ärztin f; ~ *student* Studentin f; ~**hood** [~hʊd] die Frauen pl.;
Weiblichkeit f; ~**ish** □ [~ɪʃ] weibisch; ~**kind** [~'kaɪnd] die Frauen
(-welt f) pl.; ~**like** [~laɪk] fraulich;
~**ly** [~lɪ] weiblich.

womb [wuːm] Gebärmutter f; Mut-
terleib m; *fig.* Schoß m.

wom·en ['wɪmɪn] *pl. von* woman; ♀'s
Liberation (Movement), F ♀'s **Lib**
[lɪb]   Frauenemanzipationsbewe-
gung f; ~**folk, ~kind** die Frauen
pl.; F Weibervolk n.

won [wʌn] *pret. u. p.p. von* win 1.

won·der ['wʌndə] **1.** Wunder n; Verwunderung f, Erstaunen n; *work* ~*s*
Wunder wirken; **2.** sich wundern;
gern wissen mögen, sich fragen; *I* ~ *if*
you could help me vielleicht können
Sie mir helfen; ~**ful** □ [~fl] wunderbar, -voll; ~**ing** □ [~rɪŋ] staunend, verwundert.

wont [wəʊnt] **1.** gewohnt; *be* ~ *to do*
gewohnt sein zu tun, zu tun pflegen;
2. Gewohnheit f; *as was his* ~ wie es
s-e Gewohnheit war.

won't [~] = will not.

wont·ed ['wəʊntɪd] gewohnt.

woo [wuː] werben um; locken.

wood [wʊd] Holz n; *oft* ~*s pl.* Wald m,
Gehölz n; Holzfaß n; = *woodwind;*
touch ~! unberufen!, toi, toi, toi!; *he*
cannot see the ~ *for the trees* er sieht
den Wald vor lauter Bäumen nicht;
~**cut** ['wʊdkʌt] Holzschnitt m;
~**cut·ter** Holzfäller m; *Kunst:* Holz-
schnitzer m; ~**ed** [~ɪd] bewaldet;
~**en** □ [~n] hölzern, aus Holz,
Holz...; *fig.* ausdruckslos; ~**man**
[~mən] (*pl. -men*) Förster m; Holzfäller m; ~**peck·er** *zo.* [~'pekə]
Specht m; ~**s·man** [~zmən] (*pl.*
-men) Waldbewohner m; ~**wind** ♪
[~wɪnd] Holzblasinstrument n; *the* ~
sg. od. pl. die Holzbläser pl.; ~**work**
Holzwerk n; ~**y** [~ɪ] (*-ier, -iest*)
waldig; holzig.

wool [wʊl] Wolle f; ~**gath·er·ing**
['wʊlgæðərɪŋ] Verträumtheit f; ~-
(l)en [~'wɒlən] **1.** wollen, Woll...; **2.**
~*s pl.* Wollsachen pl.; ~**ly** ['wʊlɪ] **1.**
(*-ier, -iest*) wollig, Woll...; **2.** verschwommen (*Ideen*); **2.** woollies *pl.*
F Wollsachen pl.

word [wɜːd] **1.** Wort n; Vokabel f;
Nachricht f; ✗ Losung(swort n) f;
Versprechen n; Befehl m; Spruch m;
~*s pl.* Wörter pl.; Worte pl.; Text m;
Wortwechsel m, Streit m; Text m (*e-s*
Liedes); *have a* ~ *with* mit j-m sprechen; **2.** (*in Worten*) ausdrücken,
(ab)fassen; ~**ing** ['wɜːdɪŋ] Wortlaut
m, Fassung f; ~ **or·der** gr. Wortstel-
lung f (*im Satz*); ~ **pro·cess·ing**
Computer: Textverarbeitung f; ~
pro·ces·sor *Computer:* Textverar-
beitungsanlage f, -system n; ~**split-**
ting Wortklauberei f.

word·y □ ['wɜːdɪ] (*-ier, -iest*) wortreich; Wort...

wore [wɔː] *pret. von* wear 1.

work [wɜːk] **1.** Arbeit f; Werk n; *attr.*

Arbeits...; ~s *pl.* ⊕ (Uhr-, Feder-) Werk *n*; ✗ Befestigungen *pl.*; ~s *sg.* Werk *n*, Fabrik *f*; ~ *of art* Kunstwerk *n*; *at* ~ bei der Arbeit; *be in* ~ Arbeit haben; *be out of* ~ arbeitslos sein; *set to* ~, *set od. go about one's* ~ an die Arbeit gehen; ~s *council* Betriebsrat *m*; 2. *v/i.* arbeiten (*at, on* an *dat.*); ⊕ funktionieren, gehen; wirken; *fig.* gelingen, klappen; ~ *to rule econ.* Dienst nach Vorschrift tun; *v/t.* ver-, bearbeiten; *Maschine etc.* bedienen; betreiben; *fig.* bewirken; ~ *one's way* sich durcharbeiten; ~ *off* ab-, aufarbeiten; *Gefühl* abreagieren; *econ. Ware* abstoßen; ~ *out Plan* ausarbeiten; *Aufgabe* lösen; ausrechnen; ~ *up* verarbeiten (*into* zu); *Interesse* wecken; ~ *o.s. up* sich aufregen.

wor·ka·ble □ ['wɜːkəbl] bearbeitungs-, betriebsfähig; ausführbar.

work|a·day ['wɜːkədeɪ] Alltags...; ~ **bench** ⊕ Werkbank *f*; ~ **book** *Schule:* Arbeitsheft *n*; ~ **day** Werktag *m*; *on* ~s werktags; ~ **er** [~ə] Arbeiter(in).

work·ing ['wɜːkɪŋ] 1. ~s *pl.* Arbeitsweise *f*, Funktionieren *n*; 2. arbeitend; Arbeits...; Betriebs...; ~ **class** Arbeiter...; ~ **day** Werk-, Arbeitstag *m*; ~ **hours** *pl.* Arbeitszeit *f*.

work·man ['wɜːkmən] (*pl. -men*) Arbeiter *m*; Handwerker *m*; ~ **like** [~laɪk] kunstgerecht, fachmännisch; ~ **ship** [~ʃɪp] Kunstfertigkeit *f*.

work|out ['wɜːkaʊt] F *Sport:* (Konditions)Training *n*; Erprobung *f*; ~ **shop** Werkstatt *f*; Werkraum *m*; ~ **shy** arbeitsscheu, faul; ~ **to-rule** *econ.* Dienst *m* nach Vorschrift; ~ **woman** (*pl. -women*) Arbeiterin *f*.

world [wɜːld] Welt *f*; *a* ~ *of* e-e Unmenge (von); *bring* (*come*) *into the* ~ zur Welt bringen (kommen); *think the* ~ *of* große Stücke halten auf (*acc.*); ~ **class** (von) Weltklasse, von internationalem Format (*Sportler, etc.*); ♀ **Cup** Fußballweltmeisterschaft *f*; *Skisport:* Weltcup *m*.

world·ly ['wɜːldlɪ] (*-ier, -iest*) weltlich; Welt...; ~ **wise** weltklug.

world| pow·er *pol.* ['wɜːldpaʊə] Weltmacht *f*; ~ **wide** weltweit, weltumspannend; Welt...

worm [wɜːm] 1. *zo.* Wurm *m* (*a. fig.*); 2. *ein Geheimnis* entlocken (*out of dat.*); ~ *o.s.* sich schlängeln; *fig.* sich

einschleichen (*into* in *acc.*); ~ **eat·en** ['wɜːmiːtn] wurmstichig; *fig.* veraltet, altmodisch.

worn [wɔːn] *p.p. von wear* 1; ~ **out** ['wɔːnaʊt] abgenutzt; abgetragen; verbraucht (*a. fig.*); müde, erschöpft; abgezehrt; verhärmt.

wor·ried □ ['wʌrɪd] besorgt, beunruhigt.

wor·ry ['wʌrɪ] 1. (sich) beunruhigen, (sich) ängstigen, sich sorgen, sich aufregen, ärgern; zerren an (*dat.*); (ab)würgen; plagen, quälen; *don't* ~! keine Angst *od.* Sorge!; 2. Unruhe *f*; Sorge *f*; Ärger *m*.

worse [wɜːs] (*comp. von bad*) schlechter, schlimmer, ärger; ~ *luck!* leider!; *um so* schlimmer!; **wors·en** ['wɜːsn] (sich) verschlechtern.

wor·ship ['wɜːʃɪp] 1. Verehrung *f*; Gottesdienst *m*; Kult *m*; 2. (*bsd. Brt. -pp-, Am. -p-*) *v/t.* verehren; anbeten; *v/i.* den Gottesdienst besuchen; ~ **(p)er** [~ə] Verehrer(in); Kirchgänger(in).

worst [wɜːst] 1. *adj.* (*sup. von bad*) schlechteste(r, -s), schlimmste(r, -s), ärgste(r, -s); 2. *adv.* (*sup. von badly*) am schlechtesten, am schlimmsten, am ärgsten; 3. *der, die, das* Schlechteste *od.* Ärgste; *at (the)* ~ schlimmstenfalls.

wor·sted ['wʊstɪd] Kammgarn *n*.

worth [wɜːθ] 1. wert; ~ *reading* lesenswert; 2. Wert *m*; ~ **less** □ ['wɜːθlɪs] wertlos; unwürdig; ~ **while** [~waɪl] der Mühe wert; ~ **y** □ ['wɜːðɪ] (*-ier, -iest*) würdig; wert.

would [wʊd] *pret. von will* 2; *I* ~ *like* ich hätte gern; ~ **be** ['wʊdbiː] Möchtegern...; angehend, zukünftig.

wound[1] [wuːnd] 1. Wunde *f*, Verletzung *f* (*beide a. fig.*), Verwundung *f*; *fig.* Kränkung *f*; 2. verwunden, verletzen (*beide a. fig.*).

wound[2] [waʊnd] *pret. u. p.p. von wind*[2].

wove [wəʊv] *pret. von weave*; **wov·en** ['wəʊvn] *p.p. von weave*.

wow *int.* F [waʊ] Mensch!, toll!

wran·gle ['ræŋgl] 1. sich streiten *od.* zanken; 2. Streit *m*, Zank *m*.

wrap [ræp] 1. (*-pp-*) *v/t.* oft ~ *up* (ein)wickeln; *fig.* (ein)hüllen; *be* ~ *ped up in* gehüllt sein in (*acc.*); ganz aufgehen in (*dat.*); *v/i.* ~ *up* sich einhüllen *od.* -packen; 2. Hülle *f*;

Decke f; Schal m; Mantel m; ~**per** ['ræpə] Hülle f, Umschlag m; a. postal ~ Streifband n; ~**ping** [~ɪŋ] Verpackung f; ~-**paper** Einwickel-, Pack-, Geschenkpapier n.

wrath lit. [rɔːθ] Zorn m, Wut f.

wreak lit. [riːk] Rache üben, Wut etc. auslassen (on, upon an j-m).

wreath [riːθ] (pl. wreaths [~ðz]) (Blumen)Gewinde n, Kranz m, Girlande f; Ring m, Kreis m; ~**e** [riːð] v/t. (um)winden; v/i. sich ringeln od. kräuseln.

wreck [rek] **1.** Wrack n; Trümmer pl.; Schiffbruch m; fig. Untergang m; **2.** zertrümmern, -stören; zugrunde richten, ruinieren; be ~**ed** ⚓ scheitern, Schiffbruch erleiden; in Trümmer gehen; 🚊 entgleisen; ~**age** ['rekɪdʒ] Trümmer pl.; Wrackteile pl.; ~**ed** [rekt] schiffbrüchig; ruiniert; ~**er** ['rekə] ⚓ Bergungsschiff n, -arbeiter m; bsd. hist. Strandräuber m; Abbrucharbeiter m; Am. mot. Abschleppwagen m; ~**ing** [~ɪŋ] bsd. hist. Strandraub m; ~ company Am. Abbruchfirma f; ~ service Am. mot. Abschleppdienst m.

wren zo. [ren] Zaunkönig m.

wrench [rentʃ] **1.** reißen, zerren, ziehen; entwinden (from s.o. j-m); 🩺 verrenken, -stauchen; ~ open aufreißen; **2.** Ruck m; 🩺 Verrenkung f, -stauchung f; fig. Schmerz m; ⊕ Schraubenschlüssel m.

wrest [rest] reißen; ~ s.th. from s.o. j-m et. entreißen.

wres|tle ['resl] ringen (mit); ~**tler** [~ə] bsd. Sport: Ringer m; ~**tling** [~lɪŋ] bsd. Sport: Ringen n.

wretch [retʃ] Elende(r m) f; Kerl m.

wretch·ed □ ['retʃɪd] elend.

wrig·gle ['rɪgl] sich winden od. schlängeln; ~ out of s.th. sich aus e-r Sache herauswinden.

-**wright** [raɪt] in Zssgn: ...macher m, ...bauer m.

wring [rɪŋ] (wrung) Hände ringen; (aus)wringen; pressen; Hals umdrehen; abringen (from s.o. j-m); ~ s.o.'s heart j-m zu Herzen gehen.

wrin·kle ['rɪŋkl] **1.** Runzel f, Falte f; **2.** (sich) runzeln.

wrist [rɪst] Handgelenk n; ~**watch** Armbanduhr f; ~**band** ['rɪstbænd] Bündchen n, (Hemd)Manschette f; Armband n.

writ [rɪt] Erlaß m; gerichtlicher Befehl; Holy ♀ die Heilige Schrift.

write [raɪt] (wrote, written) schreiben; ~ down auf-, niederschreiben; **writ·er** ['raɪtə] Schreiber(in); Verfasser(in); Schriftsteller(in).

writhe [raɪð] sich krümmen.

writ·ing ['raɪtɪŋ] Schreiben n (Tätigkeit); Aufsatz m; Werk n; (Hand-) Schrift f; Schriftstück n; Urkunde f; Stil m; attr. Schreib-; in ~ schriftlich; ~**case** Schreibmappe f; ~ **desk** Schreibtisch m; ~ **pad** Schreibblock m; ~ **pa·per** Schreibpapier n.

writ·ten ['rɪtn] **1.** p.p. von write; **2.** adj. schriftlich.

wrong [rɒŋ] **1.** □ unrecht; verkehrt, falsch; be ~ unrecht haben; nicht in Ordnung sein; falsch gehen (Uhr); go ~ schiefgehen; be on the ~ side of sixty über 60 (Jahre alt) sein; **2.** Unrecht n; Beleidigung f; Irrtum m, Unrecht n; be in the ~ unrecht haben; **3.** unrecht tun (dat.); ungerecht behandeln; ~**do·er** ['rɒŋdʊə] Übeltäter(in); ~**ful** □ [~fl] ungerecht; unrechtmäßig.

wrote [rəʊt] pret. von write.

wrought|**i·ron** [rɔːt'aɪən] Schmiedeeisen n; ~-**i·ron** ['rɔːt'aɪən] schmiedeeisern.

wrung [rʌŋ] pret. u. p.p. von wring.

wry □ [raɪ] (-ier, -iest) schief, krumm, verzerrt.

X

X·mas F ['krɪsməs] = Christmas.

X-ray [eks'reɪ] **1.** ~s pl. Röntgenstrahlen pl.; **2.** Röntgen...; **3.** durchleuchten, röntgen.

xy·lo·phone ♪ ['zaɪləfəʊn] Xylophon n.

Y

yacht ⚓ [jɒt] **1.** (Segel-, Motor)Jacht *f*; (Renn)Segler *m*; **2.** auf e-r Jacht fahren; segeln; **~club** [ˈjɒtklʌb] Segel-, Jachtklub *m*; **~ing** [~ɪŋ] Segelsport *m*; *attr.* Segel.

Yan·kee F [ˈjæŋkɪ] Yankee *m* (*Spitzname für Nordamerikaner*).

yap [jæp] (-pp-) kläffen; F quasseln; F meckern.

yard [jɑːd] Yard *n* (= 0,914 *m*); ⚓ Rah(e) *f*; Hof *m*; (Bau-, Stapel)Platz *m*; *Am.* Garten *m*; **~ meas·ure** [ˈjɑːdmeʒə], **~·stick** Yardstock *m*, -maß *n*.

yarn [jɑːn] Garn *n*; F Seemannsgarn *n*; abenteuerliche Geschichte.

yawl ⚓ [jɔːl] Jolle *f*.

yawn [jɔːn] **1.** gähnen; **2.** Gähnen *n*.

yea F [jeɪ] ja.

year [jɜː] Jahr *n*; **~·ly** [ˈjɜːlɪ] jährlich.

yearn [jɜːn] sich sehnen (*for* nach); **~·ing** [ˈjɜːnɪŋ] **1.** Sehnen *n*, Sehnsucht *f*; **2.** □ sehnsüchtig.

yeast [jiːst] Hefe *f*; Schaum *m*.

yell [jel] **1.** (gellend) schreien; aufschreien; **2.** (gellender) Schrei; Anfeuerungs-, Schlachtruf *m*.

yel·low [ˈjeləʊ] **1.** gelb; F hasenfüßig (*feig*); Sensations...; **2.** Gelb *n*; **3.** (sich) gelb färben; **~ed** vergilbt; **fe·ver** 🩺 Gelbfieber *n*; **~ish** [~ɪʃ] gelblich; **~ pag·es** *pl.* teleph. *die* gelben Seiten, Branchenverzeichnis *n*.

yelp [jelp] **1.** (auf)jaulen (*Hund etc.*); aufschreien; **2.** (Auf)Jaulen *n*; Aufschrei *m*.

yeo·man [ˈjəʊmən] (*pl. -men*) freier Bauer.

yep F [jep] ja.

yes [jes] **1.** ja; doch; **2.** Ja *n*.

yes·ter·day [ˈjestədɪ] gestern.

yet [jet] **1.** *adv.* noch; schon (*in Fragen*); sogar; *as ~* bis jetzt; *not ~* noch nicht; **2.** *cj.* aber (dennoch), doch.

yew ♧ [juː] Eibe *f*.

yield [jiːld] **1.** *v/t.* (ein-, hervor)bringen; Gewinn abwerfen; *v/i.* 🌱 tragen; sich fügen, nachgeben; **2.** Ertrag *m*; **~·ing** □ [ˈjiːldɪŋ] nachgebend; *fig.* nachgiebig.

yip·pee *int.* F [jɪˈpiː] hurra!

yo·del [ˈjəʊdl] **1.** Jodler *m*; **2.** (*bsd. Brt. -ll-, Am. -l-*) jodeln.

yoke [jəʊk] **1.** Joch *n* (*a. fig.*); Paar *n* (Ochsen); Schultertrage *f*; **2.** an-, zusammenspannen; *fig.* paaren (*to* mit).

yolk [jəʊk] (Ei)Dotter *m, n*, Eigelb *n*.

yon [jɒn], **~·der** *lit.* [ˈjɒndə] da *od.* dort drüben.

yore [jɔː]: *of ~* ehemals, ehedem.

you [juː, jʊ] du, ihr, Sie; man.

young [jʌŋ] **1.** □ jung, klein; **2.** (Tier)Junge *pl.*; *the ~* die jungen Leute, die Jugend; *with ~* trächtig; **~·ster** [ˈjʌŋstə] Junge *m*.

your [jɔː] dein(e), euer(e), Ihr(e); **~s** [jɔːz] deine(r, -s), euer, euere(s), Ihre(r, -s), Bill ~, Bill Briefschluß: Dein Bill; **~·self** [jɔːˈself] (*pl. yourselves* [~vz]) du, ihr, Sie selbst; dir, dich, euch, sich; *by ~* allein.

youth [juːθ] (*pl. ~s* [~ðz]) Jugend *f*; junger Mann, Jüngling *m*; **~ hostel** Jugendherberge *f*; **~·ful** □ [ˈjuːθfʊl] jugendlich.

Yu·go·slav [juːgəʊˈslɑːv] **1.** jugoslawisch; **2.** Jugoslaw|e *m*, -in *f*.

yule·tide *bsd. poet.* [ˈjuːltaɪd] Weihnachten *n*, Weihnachtszeit *f*.

Z

zeal [ziːl] Eifer *m*; **~·ot** [ˈzelət] Eiferer *m*; **~·ous** □ [ˈzeləs] eifrig; eifrig bedacht (*for* auf *acc.*); innig, heiß.

ze·bra *zo.* [ˈziːbrə] Zebra *n*; **~ cross·ing** [ˈzebrə-] Zebrastreifen *m* (*Fußgängerübergang*).

ze·nith [ˈzenɪθ] Zenit *m*; *fig.* Höhepunkt *m*.

ze·ro [ˈzɪərəʊ] **1.** (*pl. -ros, -roes*) Null *f*; Nullpunkt *m*; **2.** Null...; **~ (economic) growth** Nullwachstum *n*; **~ option** *pol.* Nullösung *f*; *have ~*

zoom

interest in s.th. F null Bock auf et. haben.

zest [zest] **1.** Würze *f* (*a. fig.*); Lust *f*, Freude *f*; Genuß *m*; **2.** würzen.

zig·zag ['zɪgzæg] **1.** Zickzack *m*; Zickzacklinie *f*, -kurs *m*, -weg *m*; **2.** im Zickzack laufen *od.* fahren *etc.*

zinc [zɪŋk] **1.** *min.* Zink *n*; **2.** verzinken.

zip [zɪp] **1.** Schwirren *n*; F Schwung *m*; = *zip-fastener*; **2.** (-*pp*-): ~ *s.th. open* den Reißverschluß von et. öffnen; ~ *s.o. up* j-m den Reißverschluß zumachen; ~ **code** *Am.* Postleitzahl *f*; **~-fas·ten·er** *bsd. Brt.*

['zɪpfɑ:snə], **~·per** *Am.* [~ə] Reißverschluß *m*.

zo·di·ac *ast.* ['zəʊdɪæk] Tierkreis *m*.

zone [zəʊn] Zone *f*; *fig.* Gebiet *n*.

zoo [zu:] (*pl.* ~s) Zoo *m*.

zo·o·log·i·cal □ [zəʊə'lɒdʒɪkl] zoologisch; ~ *garden(s)* zoologischer Garten.

zo·ol·o·gy [zəʊ'ɒlədʒɪ] Zoologie *f*.

zoom [zu:m] **1.** surren; ⚡ steil hochziehen; F sausen; *phot. Film:* zoomen; ~ *in on s.th. phot. Film:* et. heranholen; ~ *past* F vorbeisausen; **2.** Surren *n*; ⚡ Steilflug *m*.

Z

APPENDIX

German Proper Names

Aachen ['ɑːxən] *n* Aachen, Aix-la-Chapelle.

Adenauer ['ɑːdənaʊər] *first chancellor of the German Federal Republic.*

Adler ['ɑːdlər] *Austrian psychologist.*

Adria ['ɑːdria] *f* Adriatic Sea.

Afrika ['ɑːfrika] *n* Africa.

Ägypten [ɛ'gyptən] *n* Egypt.

Albanien [al'bɑːnjən] *n* Albania.

Algerien [al'geːrjən] *n* Algeria.

Algier ['alʒiːr] *n* Algiers.

Allgäu ['algɔʏ] *n* Al(l)gäu (*region of Bavaria*).

Alpen ['alpən] *pl.* Alps *pl.*

Amerika [a'meːrika] *n* America.

Anden ['andən] *pl.* the Andes *pl.*

Antillen [an'tilən] *f/pl.* Antilles *pl.*

Antwerpen [ant'verpən] *n* Antwerp.

Apenninen [ape'niːnən] *m/pl.* the Apennines *pl.*

Argentinien [argen'tiːnjən] *n* Argentina, the Argentine.

Ärmelkanal ['ɛrməlkanaːl] *m* English Channel.

Asien ['ɑːzjən] *n* Asia.

Athen [a'teːn] *n* Athens.

Äthiopien [ɛti'oːpjən] Ethiopia.

Atlantik [at'lantik] *m* Atlantic.

Australien [aʊ'strɑːljən] *n* Australia.

Bach [bax] *German composer.*

Baden-Württemberg ['bɑːdən-'vyrtəmberk] *n* Land of the German Federal Republic.

Barlach ['barlax] *German sculptor.*

Basel ['bɑːzəl] *n* Bâle, Basle.

Bayern ['baɪərn] *n* Bavaria (*Land of the German Federal Republic*).

Becher ['bɛçər] *German poet.*

Beckmann ['bɛkman] *German painter.*

Beethoven ['beːthoːfən] *German composer.*

Belgien ['bɛlgjən] *n* Belgium.

Belgrad ['bɛlgrɑːt] *n* Belgrade.

Berg [bɛrk] *Austrian composer.*

Berlin [bɛr'liːn] *n* Berlin.

Bermuda-Inseln [bɛr'muːdaʔinzəln] *f/pl.* Bermudas *pl.*

Bern [bɛrn] *n* Bern(e).

Bismarck ['bismark] *German statesman.*

Bloch [blɔx] *German philosopher.*

Böcklin ['bœkliːn] *German painter.*

Bodensee ['boːdənzeː] *m* Lake of Constance.

Böhm [bøːm] *Austrian conductor.*

Böhmen ['bøːmən] *n* Bohemia.

Böll [bœl] *German author.*

Bonn [bɔn] *n* capital of the German Federal Republic.

Brahms [brɑːms] *German composer.*

Brandt [brant] *German politician.*

Brasilien [bra'ziːljən] *n* Brazil.

Braunschweig ['braʊnʃvaɪk] *n* Brunswick.

Brecht [brɛçt] *German dramatist.*

Bremen ['breːmən] *n* Land of the German Federal Republic.

Bruckner ['bruknər] *Austrian composer.*

Brüssel ['brysəl] *n* Brussels.

Budapest ['buːdapest] *n* Budapest.

Bukarest ['buːkarest] *n* Bucharest.

Bulgarien [bul'gɑːrjən] *n* Bulgaria.

Calais [ka'lɛ] *n:* Straße von ~ Straits of Dover.

Calvin [kal'viːn] *Swiss religious reformer.*

Chile ['tʃiːlə] *n* Chile.

China ['çiːna] *n* China.

Christus ['kristus] *m* Christ.

Daimler ['daɪmlər] *German inventor.*

Dänemark ['dɛːnəmark] *n* Denmark.

Deutschland ['dɔʏtʃlant] *n* Germany.

Diesel ['diːzəl] *German inventor.*

Döblin [dø'bliːn] *German author.*

Dolomiten [dolo'miːtən] *pl.* the Dolomites *pl.*

Donau ['doːnaʊ] *f* Danube.

722

Dortmund ['dɔrtmunt] *n industrial city in West Germany.*
Dresden ['dre:sdən] *n capital of Saxony.*
Dublin ['dʌblin] *n* Dublin.
Dünkirchen ['dy:nkirçən] *n* Dunkirk.
Dürer ['dy:rər] *German painter.*
Dürrenmatt ['dyrənmat] *Swiss dramatist.*
Düsseldorf ['dysəldɔrf] *n capital of North Rhine-Westphalia.*

Ebert ['e:bərt] *first president of the Weimar Republic.*
Egk [ɛk] *German composer.*
Eichendorff ['aiçəndɔrf] *German poet.*
Eiger ['aigər] *Swiss mountain.*
Einstein ['ainʃtain] *German physicist.*
Elbe ['ɛlbə] *f German river.*
Elsaß ['ɛlzas] *n* Alsace.
Engels ['ɛŋəls] *German philosopher.*
England ['ɛŋlant] *n* England.
Essen ['ɛsən] *n industrial city in West Germany.*
Europa [ɔy'ro:pa] *n* Europe.

Feldberg ['fɛltbɛrk] *German mountain.*
Finnland ['finlant] *n* Finland.
Florenz [flo'rɛnts] *n* Florence.
Fontane [fɔn'ta:nə] *German author.*
Franken ['fraŋkən] *n* Franconia.
Frankfurt ['fraŋkfurt] *n* Frankfort.
Frankreich ['fraŋkraiç] *n* France.
Freud [frɔyt] *Austrian psychologist.*
Frisch [friʃ] *Swiss author.*

Garmisch ['garmiʃ] *n health resort in Bavaria.*
Genf [gɛnf] *n* Geneva; *~er See m* Lake of Geneva.
Genua ['ge:nua] *n* Genoa.
Gibraltar [gi'braltər] *n* Gibraltar.
Goethe ['gø:tə] *German poet.*
Grass [gras] *German author.*
Graubünden [grau'byndən] *n the Grisons.*
Griechenland ['gri:çənlant] *n* Greece.
Grillparzer ['grilpartsər] *Austrian dramatist.*
Grönland ['grø:nlant] *n* Greenland.
Gropius ['gro:pjus] *German architect.* [Great Britain.)
Großbritannien [gro:sbri'tanjən] *n*

Großglockner [gro:s'glɔknər] *Austrian mountain.*
Grünewald ['gry:nəvalt] *German painter.*

Haag [ha:k]: *Den ~* The Hague.
Habsburg *hist.* ['ha:psburk] *n* Hapsburg (*German dynasty*).
Hahn [ha:n] *German chemist.*
Hamburg ['hamburk] *n Land of the German Federal Republic.*
Händel ['hɛndəl] Handel (*German composer*).
Hannover [ha'no:fər] *n* Hanover (*capital of Lower Saxony*).
Hartmann ['hartman] *German composer.*
Harz [ha:rts] *m* Harz Mountains *pl.*
Hauptmann ['hauptman] *German dramatist.*
Haydn ['haidən] *Austrian composer.*
Hegel ['he:gəl] *German philosopher.*
Heidegger ['haidegər] *German philosopher.*
Heidelberg ['haidəlbɛrk] *n university town in West Germany.*
Heine ['hainə] *German poet.*
Heinemann ['hainəman] *president of the German Federal Republic.*
Heisenberg ['haizənbɛrk] *German physicist.*
Heißenbüttel ['haisənbytəl] *German poet.*
Helgoland ['hɛlgolant] *n* Heligoland.
Helsinki ['hɛlziŋki] *n* Helsinki.
Henze ['hɛntsə] *German composer.*
Hesse ['hɛsə] *German poet.*
Hessen ['hɛsən] *n* Hesse (*Land of the German Federal Republic*).
Heuß [hɔys] *first president of the German Federal Republic.*
Hindemith ['hindəmit] *German composer.*
Hohenzollern *hist.* [ho:ən'tsɔlərn] *n German dynasty.*
Hölderlin ['hœldərli:n] *German poet.*
Holland ['hɔlant] *n* Holland.

Indien ['indjən] *n* India.
Inn [in] *m affluent of the Danube.*
Innsbruck ['insbruk] *n capital of the Tyrol.*
Irak [i'ra:k] *m* Iraq, *a.* Irak.
Irland ['irlant] *n* Ireland.
Island ['i:slant] *n* Iceland.
Israel ['israel] *n* Israel.
Italien [i'ta:ljən] *n* Italy.

Japan ['jɑːpan] *n* Japan.

Jaspers ['jaspərs] *German philosopher.*

Jesus ['jeːzus] *m* Jesus.

Jordanien [jɔrˈdɑːnjən] *n* Jordan.

Jugoslawien [jugoˈslɑːvjən] *n* Yugoslavia.

Jung [juŋ] *Swiss psychologist.*

Jungfrau ['juŋfrau] *f Swiss mountain.*

Kafka ['kafka] *Czech author.*

Kanada ['kanada] *n* Canada.

Kant [kant] *German philosopher.*

Karajan ['kɑːrajan] *Austrian conductor.*

Karlsruhe [karlsˈruːə] *n city in South-Western Germany.*

Kärnten ['kerntən] *n* Carinthia.

Kassel ['kasəl] *n* Cassel.

Kästner ['kestnər] *German author.*

Kiel [kiːl] *n capital of Schleswig-Holstein.*

Kiesinger ['kiːziŋər] *German politician.*

Klee [kleː] *Swiss-born painter.*

Kleist [klaist] *German poet.*

Klemperer ['klempərər] *German conductor.*

Koblenz ['koːblents] *n* Coblenz, Koblenz.

Kokoschka [koˈkɔʃka] *Austrian painter.*

Köln [kœln] *n* Cologne.

Kolumbien [koˈlumbjən] *n* Columbia.

Kolumbus [koˈlumbus] *m* Columbus.

Königsberg ['køːniçsberk] *n capital of East Prussia.*

Konstanz ['kɔnstants] *n* Constance.

Kopenhagen [kopənˈhɑːgən] *n* Copenhagen.

Kordilleren [kɔrdilˈjeːrən] *f/pl. the* Cordilleras *pl.*

Kreml ['kreːməl] *m the* Kremlin.

Leibniz ['laibnits] *German philosopher.*

Leipzig ['laiptsiç] *n* Leipsic.

Lessing ['lesiŋ] *German poet.*

Libanon ['liːbanɔn] *m* Lebanon.

Liebig ['liːbiç] *German chemist.*

Lissabon ['lisabɔn] *n* Lisbon.

London ['lɔndɔn] *n* London.

Lothringen ['loːtriŋən] *n* Lorraine.

Lübeck ['lyːbɛk] *n city in West Germany.*

Luther ['luːtər] *German religious reformer.*

Luxemburg ['luksəmburk] *n* Luxemb(o)urg.

Luzern [luˈtsern] *n* Lucerne.

Maas [mɑːs] *f* Meuse.

Madrid [maˈdrit] *n* Madrid.

Mahler ['mɑːlər] *Austrian composer.*

Mailand ['mailant] *n* Milan.

Main [main] *m German river.*

Mainz [maints] *n* Mayence (*capital of Rhineland-Palatinate*).

Mann [man] *name of three German authors.*

Marokko [maˈrɔko] *n* Morocco.

Marx [marks] *German philosopher.*

Matterhorn ['matərhɔrn] *Swiss mountain.*

Meißen ['maisən] *n* Meissen.

Meitner ['maitnər] *Austrian-born female physicist.*

Memel ['meːməl] *f frontier river in East Prussia.*

Menzel ['mentsəl] *German painter.*

Mexiko ['meksiko] *n* Mexico.

Mies van der Rohe ['miːsfandərˈroːə] *German architect.*

Mittelamerika ['mitəlʔaˈmeːrika] *n* Central America.

Mitteleuropa ['mitəlʔɔyˈroːpa] *n* Central Europe.

Mittelmeer ['mitəlmeːr] *n* Mediterranean (Sea).

Moldau ['mɔldau] *f Bohemian river.*

Mörike ['møːrike] *German poet.*

Mosel ['moːzəl] *f* Moselle.

Mössbauer ['mœsbauər] *German physicist.*

Moskau ['mɔskau] *n* Moscow.

Mozart ['moːtsart] *Austrian composer.*

München ['mynçən] *n* Munich (*capital of Bavaria*).

Neapel [neˈɑːpəl] *n* Naples.

Neisse ['naisə] *f German river.*

Neufundland [nɔyˈfuntlant] *n* Newfoundland.

Neuseeland [nɔyˈzeːlant] *n* New Zealand.

Niederlande ['niːdərlandə] *n/pl. the* Netherlands *pl.*

Niedersachsen ['niːdərzaksən] *n* Lower Saxony (*Land of the German Federal Republic*).

Nietzsche ['niːtʃə] *German philosopher.*

724

Nil [niːl] *m* Nile.
Nordamerika [ˈnɔrtˀaˈmeːrika] *n* North America.
Nordrhein-Westfalen [ˈnɔrtraɪnvestˈfaːlən] *n* North Rhine-Westphalia (*Land of the German Federal Republic*).
Nordsee [ˈnɔrtzeː] *f* German Ocean, North Sea.
Norwegen [ˈnɔrveːgən] *n* Norway.
Nürnberg [ˈnyrnbɛrk] *n* Nuremberg.

Oder [ˈoːdər] *f* German river.
Orff [ɔrf] *German composer*.
Oslo [ˈɔslo] *n* Oslo.
Ostasien [ˈɔstˈaːzjən] *n* Eastern Asia.
Ostende [ɔstˈɛndə] *n* Ostend.
Österreich [ˈøːstəraɪç] *n* Austria.
Ostsee [ˈɔstzeː] *f* Baltic.

Palästina [paleˈstiːna] *n* Palestine.
Paris [paˈriːs] *n* Paris.
Persien [ˈperzjən] *n* Persia.
Pfalz [pfalts] *f* Palatinate.
Philippinen [filiˈpiːnən] *f/pl.* Philippines *pl.*, Philippine Islands *pl.*
Planck [plaŋk] *German physicist*.
Polen [ˈpoːlən] *n* Poland.
Pommern [ˈpɔmərn] *n* Pomerania.
Porsche [ˈpɔrʃə] *German inventor*.
Portugal [ˈpɔrtugal] *n* Portugal.
Prag [praːg] *n* Prague.
Preußen *hist.* [ˈprɔʏsən] *n* Prussia.
Pyrenäen [pyreˈnɛːən] *pl.* Pyrenees *pl.*

Regensburg [ˈreːgənsburk] *n* Ratisbon.
Reykjavik [ˈraɪkjaviːk] *n* Reykjavik.
Rhein [raɪn] *m* Rhine.
Rheinland-Pfalz [ˈraɪnlantˈpfalts] *n* Rhineland-Palatinate (*Land of the German Federal Republic*).
Rilke [ˈrilkə] *Austrian poet*.
Rom [roːm] *n* Rome.
Röntgen [ˈrœntgən] *German physicist*.
Ruhr [ruːr] *f* German river; **Ruhrgebiet** [ˈruːrgəbiːt] *n* industrial centre of West Germany.
Rumänien [ruˈmɛːnjən] *n* Ro(u)mania.
Rußland [ˈruslant] *n* Russia.

Saale [ˈzaːlə] *f* German river.
Saar [zaːr] *f affluent of the Moselle;* **Saarbrücken** [zaːrˈbrykən] *n*

capital of the Saar; **Saarland** [ˈzaːrlant] *n* Saar (*Land of the German Federal Republic*).
Sachsen [ˈzaksən] *n* Saxony.
Scherchen [ˈʃɛrçən] *German conductor*.
Schiller [ˈʃilər] *German poet*.
Schlesien [ˈʃleːzjən] *n* Silesia.
Schleswig-Holstein [ˈʃleːsviçˈhɔlʃtaɪn] *n Land of the German Federal Republic*.
Schönberg [ˈʃøːnbɛrk] *Austrian composer*.
Schottland [ˈʃɔtlant] *n* Scotland.
Schubert [ˈʃuːbərt] *Austrian composer*. [*poser.*]
Schumann [ˈʃuːman] *German composer*.
Schwaben [ˈʃvaːbən] *n* Swabia.
Schwarzwald [ˈʃvartsvalt] *m* Black Forest.
Schweden [ˈʃveːdən] *n* Sweden.
Schweiz [ʃvaɪts] *f:* die ~ Switzerland.
Sibirien [ziˈbiːrjən] *n* Siberia.
Siemens [ˈziːməns] *German inventor*.
Sizilien [ziˈtsiːljən] *n* Sicily.
Skandinavien [skandiˈnaːvjən] *n* Scandinavia.
Sofia [ˈzɔfja] *n* Sofia.
Sowjetunion [zɔˈvjetˀunjoːn] *f the* Soviet Union.
Spanien [ˈʃpaːnjən] *n* Spain.
Spitzweg [ˈʃpitsveːk] *German painter*. [*losopher.*]
Spranger [ˈʃpraŋər] *German philosopher.*
Steiermark [ˈʃtaɪərmark] *f* Styria.
Stifter [ˈʃtiftər] *Austrian author*.
Stockholm [ˈʃtɔkhɔlm] *n* Stockholm.
Storm [ʃtɔrm] *German poet*.
Strauß [ʃtraʊs] *Austrian composer*.
Strauss [ʃtraʊs] *German composer*.
Stresemann [ˈʃtreːzəman] *German statesman*.
Stuttgart [ˈʃtutgart] *n capital of Baden-Württemberg*.
Südamerika [ˈzyːtˀaˈmeːrika] *n* South America.
Sudan [zuˈdaːn] *m* S(o)udan.
Syrien [ˈzyːrjən] *n* Syria.

Themse [ˈtɛmzə] *f* Thames.
Thoma [ˈtoːma] *German author*.
Thüringen [ˈtyːriŋən] *n* Thuringia.
Tirana [tiˈraːna] *n* Tirana.
Tirol [tiˈroːl] *n* the Tyrol.
Trakl [ˈtraːkəl] *Austrian poet*.

Tschechoslowakei [tʃeçoslovaˈkaɪ] *f*: die ~ Czechoslovakia.
Türkei [tyrˈkaɪ] *f*: die ~ Turkey.

Ungarn [ˈuŋgarn] *n* Hungary.
Ural [uˈrɑːl] *m* Ural (Mountains *pl.*).

Vatikan [vatiˈkɑːn] *m* the Vatican.
Venedig [veˈneːdiç] *n* Venice.
Vereinigte Staaten [vərˈaɪnɪçtə ˈʃtɑːtən] *m/pl.* the United States *pl.*
Vierwaldstätter See [fiːrˈvaltʃtetər ˈzeː] *m* Lake of Lucerne.

Wagner [ˈvɑːgnər] *German composer.*
Wankel [ˈvaŋkəl] *German inventor.*
Warschau [ˈvarʃau] *n* Warsaw.

Weichsel [ˈvaɪksəl] *f* Vistula.
Weiß [vaɪs] *German dramatist.*
Weizsäcker [ˈvaɪtszekər] *German physicist.*
Werfel [ˈverfəl] *Austrian author.*
Weser [ˈveːzər] *f German river.*
Westdeutschland *pol.* [ˈvestdɔʏtʃlant] *n* West Germany.
Wien [viːn] *n* Vienna.
Wiesbaden [ˈviːsbɑːdən] *n capital of Hesse.*

Zeppelin [ˈtsepəliːn] *German inventor.*
Zuckmayer [ˈtsukmaɪər] *German dramatist.*
Zweig [tsvaɪg] *Austrian author.*
Zürich [ˈtsyːriç] *n* Zurich.
Zypern [ˈtsyːpərn] *n* Cyprus.

German Abbreviations

a. a. O. *am angeführten Ort* in the place cited, *abbr.* loc. cit., l. c.

Abb. *Abbildung* illustration.

Abf. *Abfahrt* departure, *abbr.* dep.

Abg. *Abgeordnete* Member of Parliament, *etc.*

Abk. *Abkürzung* abbreviation.

Abs. *Absatz* paragraph; *Absender* sender.

Abschn. *Abschnitt* paragraph, chapter. [dept.]

Abt. *Abteilung* department, *abbr.*]

a. D. *außer Dienst* retired.

Adr. *Adresse* address.

AG *Aktiengesellschaft* joint-stock company, *Am.* (stock) corporation.

allg. *allgemein* general.

a. M. *am Main* on the Main.

Ank. *Ankunft* arrival.

Anm. *Anmerkung* note.

a. O. *an der Oder* on the Oder.

a. Rh. *am Rhein* on the Rhine.

Art. *Artikel* article.

atü *Atmosphärenüberdruck* atmospheric excess pressure.

Aufl. *Auflage* edition.

b. *bei* at; with; *with place names*: near, *abbr.* nr; care of, *abbr.* c/o.

Bd. *Band* volume, *abbr.* vol.; **Bde.** *Bände* volumes, *abbr.* vols.

beil. *beiliegend* enclosed.

Bem. *Bemerkung* note, comment, observation.

bes. *besonders* especially.

betr. *betreffend, betrifft, betreffs* concerning, respecting, regarding.

Betr. *Betreff, betrifft letter*: subject, re. [reference to.]

bez. *bezahlt* paid; *bezüglich* with]

Bez. *Bezirk* district.

Bhf. *Bahnhof* station. [sionally.]

bisw. *bisweilen* sometimes, occa-]

BIZ *Bank für Internationalen Zahlungsausgleich* Bank for International Settlements.

Bln. Berlin Berlin.

BRD *Bundesrepublik Deutschland* Federal Republic of Germany.

BRT *Bruttoregistertonnen* gross register tons.

b. w. *bitte wenden* please turn over, *abbr.* P.T.O.

bzw. *beziehungsweise* respectively.

C *Celsius* Celsius, *abbr.* C.

ca. *circa, ungefähr, etwa* about, approximately, *abbr.* c.

cbm *Kubikmeter* cubic met|re, *Am.* -er.

ccm *Kubikzentimeter* cubic centimet|re, *Am.* -er, *abbr.* c.c.

CDU *Christlich-Demokratische Union* Christian Democratic Union.

cm *Zentimeter* centimet|re, *Am.* -er.

Co. *Kompagnon* partner; *Kompanie* Company.

CSU *Christlich-Soziale Union* Christian Social Union.

d. Ä. *der Ältere* senior, *abbr.* sen.

DB *Deutsche Bundesbahn* German Federal Railway.

DDR *Deutsche Demokratische Republik* German Democratic Republic.

DGB *Deutscher Gewerkschaftsbund* Federation of German Trade Unions.

dgl. *dergleichen, desgleichen* the like.

d. Gr. *der Große* the Great.

d. h. *das heißt* that is, *abbr.* i. e.

d. i. *das ist* that is, *abbr.* i. e.

DIN, Din *Deutsche Industrie-Norm (-en)* German Industrial Standards.

Dipl. *Diplom* diploma.

d. J. *dieses Jahres* of this year; *der Jüngere* junior, *abbr.* jr, jun.

DM *Deutsche Mark* German Mark.

d. M. *dieses Monats* instant, *abbr.* inst.

do. *dito* ditto, *abbr.* do.

d. O. *der (die, das) Obige* the above-mentioned.

dpa, DPA *Deutsche Presse-Agentur* German Press Agency.

Dr. *Doktor* Doctor, *abbr.* Dr; ~ **jur.** *Doktor der Rechte* Doctor of Laws (LL.D.); ~ **med.** *Doktor der Me-*

dizin Doctor of Medicine (M.D.); **~ phil.** *Doktor der Philosophie* Doctor of Philosophy (D. ph[il]., Ph. D.); **~ theol.** *Doktor der Theologie* Doctor of Divinity (D. D.).

DRK *Deutsches Rotes Kreuz* German Red Cross.

dt(sch). *deutsch* German.

Dtz., Dtzd. *Dutzend* dozen.

d. Verf. *der Verfasser* the author.

ebd. *ebenda* in the same place.

ed. *edidit* = *hat* (*es*) *herausgegeben*.

eig., eigtl. *eigentlich* properly.

einschl. *einschließlich* including, inclusive, *abbr.* incl.

entspr. *entsprechend* corresponding.

Erl. *Erläuterung* explanation, (explanatory) note.

ev. *evangelisch* Protestant.

e. V. *eingetragener Verein* registered association, incorporated, *abbr.* inc.

evtl. *eventuell* perhaps, possibly.

EWG *Europäische Wirtschaftsgemeinschaft* European Economic Community, *abbr.* EEC.

exkl. *exklusive* except(ed), not included.

Expl. *Exemplar* copy.

Fa. *Firma* firm; *letter*: Messrs.

FDGB *Freier Deutscher Gewerkschaftsbund* Free Federation of German Trade Unions.

FDP *Freie Demokratische Partei* Liberal Democratic Party.

FD(-Zug) *Fernschnellzug* long-distance express.

ff. *sehr fein* extra fine; *folgende Seiten* following pages.

Forts. *Fortsetzung* continuation.

Fr. *Frau* Mrs.

frdl. *freundlich* kind.

Frl. *Fräulein* Miss.

g *Gramm* gram(me).

geb. *geboren* born; *geborene* ... née; *gebunden* bound.

Gebr. *Gebrüder* Brothers.

gef. *gefällig(st)* kind(ly).

gegr. *gegründet* founded.

geh. *geheftet* stitched.

gek. *gekürzt* abbreviated.

Ges. *Gesellschaft* association, company; society. [registered.]

ges. gesch. *gesetzlich geschützt⟩*

gest. *gestorben* deceased.

gez. *gezeichnet* signed, *abbr.* sgd.

GmbH *Gesellschaft mit beschränkter Haftung* limited liability company, *abbr.* Ltd., *Am.* closed corporation under German law.

ha *Hektar* hectare.

Hbf. *Hauptbahnhof* central *or* main station.

Hbg. *Hamburg* Hamburg.

h. c. *honoris causa* = *ehrenhalber academic title*: honorary.

Hr., Hrn. *Herr(n)* Mr.

hrsg. *herausgegeben* edited, *abbr.* ed.

Hrsg. *Herausgeber* editor, *abbr.* ed.

i. *im*, *in* in.

i. A. *im Auftrage* for, by order, under instruction.

i. allg. *im allgemeinen* in general, generally speaking.

i. Durchschn. *im Durchschnitt* on an average. [sive.)

inkl. *inklusive, einschließlich* inclu-)

i. J. *im Jahre* in the year.

Ing. *Ingenieur* engineer.

Inh. *Inhaber* proprietor.

'Interpol *Internationale Kriminalpolizei-Kommission* International Criminal Police Commission, *abbr.* ICPC. [substitute.)

i. V. *in Vertretung* by proxy, as a⟩

Jb. *Jahrbuch* annual.

jr., jun. *junior, der Jüngere* junior *abbr.* jr, jun.

Kap. *Kapitel* chapter.

kath. *katholisch* Catholic.

Kfm. *Kaufmann* merchant.

kfm. *kaufmännisch* commercial.

Kfz. *Kraftfahrzeug* motor vehicle.

kg *Kilogramm* kilogram(me).

KG *Kommanditgesellschaft* limited partnership.

Kl. *Klasse* class; *school*: form.

km *Kilometer* kilomet|re, *Am.* -er.

'Kripo *Kriminalpolizei* Criminal Investigation Department, *abbr.* CID.

Kto. *Konto* account, *abbr.* a/c.

kW *Kilowatt* kilowatt, *abbr.* kW.

kWh *Kilowattstunde* kilowatt hour.

l *Liter* lit|re, *Am.* -er.

LDP *Liberal-Demokratische Partei* Liberal Democratic Party.

lfd. *laufend* current, running.
lfde. Nr. *laufende Nummer* consecutive number.
Lfg., Lfrg. *Lieferung* delivery; instalment, part.
Lit. *Literatur* literature.
Lkw. *Lastkraftwagen* lorry, truck.
lt. *laut* according to.

m *Meter* met|re, *Am,* -er.
m. A. n. *meiner Ansicht nach* in my opinion.
M. d. B. *Mitglied des Bundestages* Member of the Bundestag.
m. E. *meines Erachtens* in my opinion.
MEZ *mitteleuropäische Zeit* Central European Time.
mg *Milligramm* milligram(me[s]), *abbr.* mg.
Mill. *Million(en)* million(s).
mm *Millimeter* millimet|re, *Am.* -er.
möbl. *möbliert* furnished.
MP *Militärpolizei* Military Police.
mtl. *monatlich* monthly.
m. W. *meines Wissens* as far as I know.

N *Nord(en)* north.
nachm. *nachmittags* in the afternoon, *abbr.* p. m.
n. Chr. *nach Christus* after Christ, *abbr.* A. D.
n. J. *nächsten Jahres* of next year.
n. M. *nächsten Monats* of next month.
No., Nr. *Numero, Nummer* number, *abbr.* N°.
NS *Nachschrift* postscript, *abbr.* P. S.

O *Ost(en)* east.
o. B. *ohne Befund* ❀ without findings.
od. *oder* or.
OEZ *osteuropäische Zeit* time of the East European zone.
OHG *Offene Handelsgesellschaft* ordinary partnership.
o. J. *ohne Jahr* no date.

p. Adr. *per Adresse* care of, *abbr.* c/o.
Pf *Pfennig German coin:* pfennig.
Pfd. *Pfund German weight:* pound.
PKW, Pkw. *Personenkraftwagen* (motor) car.
P. P. *praemissis praemittendis* omitting titles, to whom it may concern.

p.p., p.pa., ppa. *per procura* by proxy, *abbr.* per pro.
Prof. *Professor* professor.
PS *Pferdestärke(n)* horse-power, *abbr.* H.P., h.p.; *postscriptum, Nachschrift* postscript, *abbr.* P. S.

qkm *Quadratkilometer* square kilomet|re, *Am.* -er.   [*Am.* -er.)
qm *Quadratmeter* square met|re,)

Reg. Bez. *Regierungsbezirk* administrative district.
Rel. *Religion* religion.
resp. *respektive* respectively.

S *Süd(en)* south.
S. *Seite* page.
s. *siehe* see, *abbr.* v., vid. (= *vide*).
s. a. *siehe auch* see also.
Sa. *Summa, Summe* sum, total.
s. d. *siehe dies* see this.
SED *Sozialistische Einheitspartei Deutschlands* United Socialist Party of Germany.
sen. *senior, der Ältere* senior.
sm *Seemeile* nautical mile.
s. o. *siehe oben* see above.
sog. *sogenannt* so-called.
SPD *Sozialdemokratische Partei Deutschlands* Social Democratic Party of Germany.
St. *Stück* piece; *Sankt* Saint.
St(d)., Stde. *Stunde* hour, *abbr.* h.
Str. *Straße* street, *abbr.* St.
s. u. *siehe unten* see below.
s. Z. *seinerzeit* at that time.

t *Tonne* ton.
tägl. *täglich* daily, per day.
Tel. *Telephon* telephone; *Telegramm* wire, cable.
TH *Technische Hochschule* technical university *or* college.

u. *und* and.
u. a. *und andere(s)* and others; *unter anderem or anderen* among other things, inter alia.
u. ä. *und ähnliche(s)* and the like.
U.A.w.g. *Um Antwort wird gebeten* an answer is requested, *répondez s'il vous plaît, abbr.* R.S.V.P.
u. dgl. (m.) *und dergleichen (mehr)* and the like.
u. d. M. *unter dem Meeresspiegel* below sea level; **ü. d. M.** *über dem Meeresspiegel* above sea level.

UdSSR *Union der Sozialistischen Sowjetrepubliken* Union of Soviet Socialist Republics.

u. E. *unseres Erachtens* in our opinion.   [following.]

u. f., u. ff. *und folgende* and the]

UKW *Ultrakurzwelle* ultra-short wave, very high frequency, *abbr.* VHF.

U/min. *Umdrehungen in der Minute* revolutions per minute, *abbr.* r.p.m.

urspr. *ursprünglich* original(ly).

US(A) *Vereinigte Staaten (von Amerika)* United States (of America).

usw. *und so weiter* and so on, *abbr.* etc.   [stances permitting.]

u. U. *unter Umständen* circum-]

v. *von, vom* of; from; by.

V *Volt* volt; *Volumen* volume.

V. *Vers* line, verse.

v. Chr. *vor Christus* before Christ, *abbr.* B. C.

VEB *Volkseigener Betrieb* People's Own Undertaking.

Verf., Vf. *Verfasser* author.

Verl. *Verlag* publishing firm; *Verleger* publisher.

vgl. *vergleiche* confer, *abbr.* cf.

v.g.u. *vorgelesen, genehmigt, unterschrieben* read, confirmed, signed.

v. H. *vom Hundert* per cent.

v. J. *vorigen Jahres* of last year.

v. M. *vorigen Monats* of last month.

vorm. *vormittags* in the morning, *abbr.* a. m.; *vormals* formerly.

Vors. *Vorsitzender* chairman.

v. T. *vom Tausend* per thousand.

VW *Volkswagen* Volkswagen, People's Car.

W *West(en)* west; *Watt* watt(s).

WE *Wärmeeinheit* thermal unit.

WEZ *westeuropäische Zeit* Western European time (Greenwich time).

WGB *Weltgewerkschaftsbund* World Federation of Trade Unions, *abbr.* WFTU.

Wwe. *Witwe* widow.

Z. *Zahl* number; *Zeile* line.

z. *zu, zum, zur* at; to.

z. B. *zum Beispiel* for instance, *abbr.* e. g.

z. H(d). *zu Händen* attention of, to be delivered to, care of, *abbr.* c/o.

z. S. *zur See* of the navy.

z. T. *zum Teil* partly.

Ztg. *Zeitung* newspaper.

Ztr. *Zentner* centner.

Ztschr. *Zeitschrift* periodical.

zus. *zusammen* together.

zw. *zwischen* between; among.

z. Z(t). *zur Zeit* at the time, at present, for the time being.

American and British Proper Names

Aberdeen [æbə'di:n] *Stadt in Schottland.*

Adam ['ædəm] *Adam m.*

Adelaide ['ædəleɪd] *Stadt in Australien.*

Aden ['eɪdn] *Hauptstadt des Südjemen.*

Africa ['æfrɪkə] *Afrika n.*

Aix-la-Chapelle ['eɪksla:'ʃæ'pel] *Aachen n.*

Alabama [ælə'bæmə] *Staat der USA.*

Alaska [ə'læskə] *Staat der USA.*

Alberta [æl'bɜːtə] *Provinz in Kanada.*

Alderney ['ɔːldənɪ] *e-e der Kanalinseln.*

Alleghany ['ælɪgeɪnɪ] *Fluß u. Gebirge in USA.*

Alsace [æl'sæs] *Elsaß n.*

America [ə'merɪkə] *Amerika n.*

Andes ['ændi:z] *die Anden.*

Andrew ['ændruː] *Andreas m.*

Ann(e) [æn] *Anna f.*

Anthony ['æntənɪ, 'ænθənɪ] *Anton m.*

Antilles [æn'tɪliːz] *die Antillen.*

Appalachians [æpə'leɪtʃjənz] *die Appalachen (Gebirge in USA).*

Arizona [ærɪ'zəunə] *Staat der USA.*

Arkansas ['ɑːkənsɔː] *Fluß u. Staat der USA.*

Arlington ['ɑːlɪŋtən] *Nationalfriedhof bei Washington.*

Ascot ['æskət] *Stadt in England mit berühmter Rennbahn.*

Asia ['eɪʃə] *Asien n.*

Athens ['æθɪnz] *Athen n.*

Atlantic [ət'læntɪk] *der Atlantik.*

Auckland ['ɔːklənd] *Hafenstadt in Neuseeland.*

Austen ['ɒstɪn] *engl. Autorin.*

Australia [ɒ'streɪljə] *Australien n.*

Austria ['ɒstrɪə] *Österreich n.*

Avon ['eɪvən] *Fluß u. Grafschaft in England.*

Azores [ə'zɔːz] *die Azoren.*

Bahamas [bə'hɑːməz] *die Bahamainseln.*

Balkans ['bɔːlkənz] *der Balkan.*

Balmoral [bæl'mɒrəl] *Königsschloß in Schottland.*

Basle [bɑːl] *Basel n.*

Baltimore ['bɔːltɪmɔː] *Hafenstadt in USA.*

Bath [bɑːθ] *Badeort in England.*

Bavaria [bə'veərɪə] *Bayern n.*

Bedfordshire ['bedfədʃə] *Grafschaft in England.*

Belfast [bel'fɑːst] *Hauptstadt von Nordirland.*

Belgium ['beldʒəm] *Belgien n.*

Ben Nevis [ben'nevɪs] *höchster Berg in Großbritannien.*

Berkshire ['bɑːkʃə] *Grafschaft in England.*

Berlin [bɜː'lɪn] *Berlin n.*

Bermudas [bə'mjuːdəz] *die Bermudainseln.*

Bern(e) [bɜːn] *Bern n.*

Bess(ie) ['bes(ɪ)] *Kurzform von Elizabeth.*

Bill(y) ['bɪl(ɪ)] *Kurzform von William.*

Birmingham ['bɜːmɪŋəm] *Industriestadt in England.*

Bob [bɒb] *Kurzform von Robert.*

Boston ['bɒstən] *Stadt in USA.*

Bournemouth ['bɔːnməθ] *Seebad in England.*

Bridget ['brɪdʒɪt] *Brigitte f.*

Brighton ['braɪtn] *Seebad in England.*

Bristol ['brɪstl] *Hafenstadt in England.*

British Columbia ['brɪtɪʃ kə'lʌmbɪə] *Provinz in Kanada.*

Britten ['brɪtn] *engl. Komponist.*

Brontë ['brɒntɪ] *Name dreier engl. Autorinnen.*

Brooklyn ['brʊklɪn] *Stadtteil von New York.*

Brussels ['brʌslz] *Brüssel n.*

Buckingham Palace ['bʌkɪŋəm 'pæls] *Königsschloß in London.*

Buckinghamshire ['bʌkɪŋəmʃə] *Grafschaft in England.*

Buddha ['budə] *Buddha m.*

Burma ['bɜːmə] *Birma n.*

Burns [bɜːnz] *schott. Dichter.*

Byron ['baɪərən] *engl. Dichter.*

Calcutta [kæl'kʌtə] Kalkutta n.

California [kælɪ'fɔːnjə] Kalifornien n (Staat der USA).

Cambridge ['keɪmbrɪdʒ] **1.** engl. Universitätsstadt; **2.** Stadt in USA, Sitz der Harvard-Universität; **3.** a. ~shire [~ʃə] Grafschaft in England.

Canada ['kænədə] Kanada n.

Canary Islands [kə'neərɪ 'aɪləndz] die Kanarischen Inseln.

Canberra ['kænbərə] Hauptstadt von Australien.

Canterbury ['kæntəbərɪ] Stadt in England, Erzbischofssitz.

Capetown ['keɪptaʊn] Kapstadt n.

Cardiff ['kɑːdɪf] Hauptstadt von Wales.

Carinthia [kə'rɪnθɪə] Kärnten n.

Carlyle [kɑː'laɪl] schott. Autor.

Carnegie [kɑː'neɡɪ] amer. Industrieller.

Caroline ['kærəlaɪn] Karoline f.

Carrie ['kærɪ] Kurzform von Caroline.

Carter ['kɑːtə] Präsident der USA.

Catherine ['kæθərɪn] Katharina f.

Cecil ['sesl, 'sɪsl] männlicher Vorname.

Cecilia [sɪ'sɪljə], **Cecily** ['sɪsɪlɪ, 'sesɪlɪ] Cäcilie f.

Ceylon [sɪ'lɒn] Ceylon n.

Chamberlain ['tʃeɪmbəlɪn] Name mehrerer brit. Staatsmänner.

Charlemagne ['ʃɑːləmeɪn] Karl der Große.

Charles [tʃɑːlz] Karl m.

Chaucer ['tʃɔːsə] engl. Dichter.

Cheshire ['tʃeʃə] Grafschaft in England.

Chesterfield ['tʃestəfiːld] Industriestadt in England.

Cheviot Hills ['tʃevɪət 'hɪlz] Grenzgebirge zwischen England u. Schottland.

Chicago [ʃɪ'kɑːɡəʊ] Industriestadt in USA.

China ['tʃaɪnə] China n.

Churchill ['tʃɜːtʃɪl] brit. Staatsmann.

Cincinatti [sɪnsɪ'nætɪ] Stadt in USA.

Cissie ['sɪsɪ] Cilli f.

Cleveland ['kliːvlənd] **1.** Grafschaft in England; **2.** Industrie- u. Hafenstadt in USA.

Clyde [klaɪd] Fluß in Schottland.

Coleridge ['kəʊlərɪdʒ] engl. Dichter.

Cologne [kə'ləʊn] Köln n.

Colorado [kɒlə'rɑːdəʊ] Name zweier Flüsse u. Staat der USA.

Columbia [kə'lʌmbɪə] Fluß in USA.

Connecticut [kə'netɪkət] Fluß u. Staat der USA.

Constance ['kɒnstəns] **1.** Konstanze f; **2.** Konstanz n; Lake ~ Bodensee m.

Cooper ['kuːpə] amer. Autor.

Copenhagen [kəʊpn'heɪɡən] Kopenhagen n.

Cordilleras [kɔː'dɪ'ljeərəz] die Kordilleren (amer. Gebirge).

Cornwall ['kɔːnwəl] Grafschaft in England.

Coventry ['kɒvəntrɪ] Industriestadt in England.

Cromwell ['krɒmwəl] engl. Staatsmann.

Cumbria ['kʌmbrɪə] Grafschaft in England.

Cyprus ['saɪprəs] Zypern n.

Czechoslovakia ['tʃekəʊsləʊ'vækɪə] die Tschechoslowakei.

Dallas ['dæləs] Stadt in USA.

Daniel ['dænjəl] Daniel m.

Danube ['dænjuːb] Donau f.

Darwin ['dɑːwɪn] engl. Naturforscher.

David ['deɪvɪd] David m.

Defoe [dɪ'fəʊ] engl. Autor.

Delaware ['deləweə] Fluß u. Staat der USA.

Denmark ['denmɑːk] Dänemark n.

Denver ['denvə] Stadt in USA.

Derbyshire ['dɑːbɪʃə] Grafschaft in England.

Detroit [də'trɔɪt] Industriestadt in USA.

Devon(shire) ['devn(ʃə)] Grafschaft in England.

Diana [daɪ'ænə] Diana f.

Dick [dɪk] Kurzform von Richard.

Dickens ['dɪkɪnz] engl. Autor.

Disraeli [dɪs'reɪlɪ] engl. Staatsmann.

District of Columbia ['dɪstrɪkt əv kə'lʌmbɪə] Bezirk um Washington, Bundesdistrikt der USA.

Dorset(shire) ['dɔː'sɪt(ʃə)] Grafschaft in England.

Dover ['dəʊvə] Hafenstadt in England.

Downing Street ['daʊnɪŋ striːt] Straße in London mit der Amtswohnung des Prime Minister.

Doyle [dɔɪl] schott. Autor.

Dublin ['dʌblɪn] Hauptstadt der Republik Irland.

Dunkirk [dʌn'kɜːk] Dünkirchen n.

Durham ['dʌrəm] *Grafschaft in England.*

East Sussex ['iːst 'sʌsɪks] *Grafschaft in England.*

Edinburgh ['edɪnbərə] Edinburg *n.*

Edison ['edɪsn] *amer. Erfinder.*

Egypt ['iːdʒɪpt] Ägypten *n.*

Eire ['eərə] *irischer Name der Republik Irland.*

Eisenhower ['aɪznhaʊə] *Präsident der USA.*

Eliot ['elɪət] 1. *engl. Autorin*; 2. *engl. Dichter, geboren in USA.*

Elizabeth [ɪ'lɪzəbəθ] Elisabeth *f.*

Emerson ['eməsn] *amer. Philosoph.*

England ['ɪŋlənd] England *n.*

Epsom ['epsəm] *Stadt in England mit Pferderennplatz.*

Erie ['ɪərɪ]: *Lake ~ Eriesee m (e-r der fünf Großen Seen Nordamerikas).*

Essex ['esɪks] *Grafschaft in England.*

Ethel ['eθl] *weiblicher Vorname.*

Ethiopia [iːθɪ'əʊpjə] Äthiopien *n.*

Eton ['iːtn] *berühmte Public School.*

Europe ['jʊərəp] Europa *n.*

Eve [iːv] Eva *f.*

Falkland Islands ['fɔːlklənd 'aɪləndz] *die Falklandinseln.*

Faulkner ['fɔːnɪs] *amer. Autor.*

Fawkes [fɔːks] *Haupt der Pulververschwörung (1605).*

Finland ['fɪnlənd] Finnland *n.*

Florida ['flɒrɪdə] *Staat der USA.*

Folkestone ['fəʊkstən] *Hafenstadt in England.*

Ford [fɔːd] 1. *amer. Industrieller*; 2. *Präsident der USA.*

France [frɑːns] Frankreich *n.*

Frances ['frɑːnsɪs] Franziska *f.*

Francis ['frɑːnsɪs] Franz *m.*

Franklin ['fræŋklɪn] *amer. Staatsmann u. Physiker.*

Gainsborough ['geɪnzbərə] *engl. Maler.*

Galveston(e) ['gælvɪstən] *Hafenstadt in USA.*

Geneva [dʒɪ'niːvə] Genf *n*; *Lake ~ Genfer See m.*

Geoffrey ['dʒefrɪ] Gottfried *m.*

George [dʒɔːdʒ] Georg *m.*

Georgia ['dʒɔːdʒjə] *Staat der USA.*

Germany ['dʒɜːmənɪ] Deutschland *n.*

Gershwin ['gɜːʃwɪn] *amer. Komponist.*

Gettysburg ['getɪzbɜːg] *Stadt in USA.*

Gibraltar [dʒɪ'brɔːltə] Gibraltar *n.*

Giles [dʒaɪlz] Julius *m.*

Gill [gɪl] *weiblicher Vorname.*

Gladstone ['glædstən] *brit. Staatsmann.*

Glasgow ['glɑːsgəʊ] *Hafenstadt in Schottland.*

Gloucester ['glɒstə] *Stadt in England*; *a. ~shire [~ʃə] Grafschaft in England.*

Great Britain ['greɪt 'brɪtn] Großbritannien *n.*

Greece [griːs] Griechenland *n.*

Greene [griːn] *engl. Autor.*

Greenland ['griːnlənd] Grönland *n.*

Greenwich ['grɪnɪdʒ] *Vorort von London.*

Guernsey ['gɜːnzɪ] *e-e der Kanalinseln.*

Guy [gaɪ] Guido *m*, Veit *m.*

Hague [heɪg]: *The ~ Den Haag.*

Halifax ['hælɪfæks] *Name zweier Städte in England u. Kanada.*

Hampshire ['hæmpʃə] *Grafschaft in England.*

Hanover ['hænəʊvə] Hannover *n.*

Harlem ['hɑːləm] *Stadtteil von New York.*

Harrow ['hærəʊ] *Nordwestl. Stadtbezirk Groß-Londons mit berühmter Public School.*

Harvard University ['hɑːvəd juːnɪ'vɜːsətɪ] *amer. Universität.*

Harwich ['hærɪdʒ] *Hafenstadt in England.*

Hawaii [hə'waiiː] *Staat der USA.*

Hebrides ['hebrɪdiːz] *die Hebriden.*

Heligoland ['helɪgəʊlænd] Helgoland *n.*

Helsinki ['helsɪŋkɪ] Helsinki *n.*

Hemingway ['hemɪŋweɪ] *amer. Autor.*

Henry ['henrɪ] Heinrich *m.*

Hereford and Worcester ['herɪfədən'wʊstə] *Grafschaft in England.*

Hertfordshire ['hɑːfədʃə] *Grafschaft in England.*

Hogarth ['həʊgɑːθ] *engl. Maler.*

Hollywood ['hɒlɪwʊd] *Filmstadt in Kalifornien, USA.*

Houston ['hjuːstən] *Stadt in USA.*

Hudson ['hʌdsn] *Fluß in USA.*

Hugh [hjuː] Hugo *m.*

Hull [hʌl] *Hafenstadt in England.*

Humberside ['hʌmbəsaɪd] *Graf-schaft in England.*

Hungary ['hʌŋgərɪ] Ungarn *n.*

Huron ['hjuːərən]: *Lake* ~ Huronsee *m* (*e-r der fünf Großen Seen Nord-amerikas*).

Huxley ['hʌkslɪ] *engl. Autor.*

Iceland ['aɪslənd] Island *n.*

Idaho ['aɪdəhəʊ] *Staat der USA.*

Illinois [ɪlɪ'nɔɪ] *Fluß u. Staat der USA.*

India ['ɪndjə] Indien *n.*

Indiana [ɪndɪ'ænə] *Staat der USA.*

Indies ['ɪndɪz]: *East* ~ Ostindien *n*; *West* ~ Westindien *n.*

Iowa ['aɪəʊə] *Staat der USA.*

Iran [ɪ'rɑːn] Iran *m.*

Iraq [ɪ'rɑːk] Irak *m.*

Ireland ['aɪələnd] Irland *n.*

Isle of Man ['aɪləv'mæn] *Insel in der Irischen See.*

Isle of Wight ['aɪləv'waɪt] *Insel u. Grafschaft vor der Südküste Eng-lands.*

Israel ['ɪzreɪəl] Israel *n.*

Italy ['ɪtəlɪ] Italien *n.*

Jack [dʒæk] *Kurzform von James.*

James [dʒeɪmz] Jakob *m.*

Jane [dʒeɪn] Johanna *f.*

Japan [dʒə'pæn] Japan *n.*

Jefferson ['dʒefəsn] *Präsident der USA, Verfasser der Unabhängig-keitserklärung von 1776.*

Jeremy ['dʒerɪmɪ] *männlicher Vor-name.*

Jersey ['dʒɜːzɪ] *e-e der Kanalinseln;* ~ *City Stadt in USA.*

Jesus (Christ) ['dʒiːzəs ('kraɪst] Je-sus (Christus) *m.*

Jim [dʒɪm] *Kurzform von James.*

Joan [dʒəʊn] Johanna *f.*

Job [dʒəʊb] Hiob *m.*

Joe [dʒəʊ] *Kurzform von Joseph.*

John [dʒɒn] Johann(es) *m*, Hans *m.*

Johnson ['dʒɒnsn] 1. *engl. Autor*; 2. *Präsident der USA.*

Joseph ['dʒəʊzɪf] Joseph *m.*

Joule [dʒuːl] *engl. Physiker.*

Joyce [dʒɔɪs] *irischer Autor.*

Kansas ['kænzəs] *Fluß u. Staat der USA.*

Karachi [kə'rɑːtʃɪ] *Hafenstadt in Pakistan.*

Kashmir [kæʃ'mɪə] Kaschmir *n.*

Kate [keɪt] Käthe *f.*

Keats [kiːts] *engl. Dichter.*

Kennedy ['kenɪdɪ] *Präsident der USA;* ~ *Airport Flughafen von New York.*

Kent [kent] *Grafschaft in England.*

Kentucky [ken'tʌkɪ] *Fluß u. Staat der USA.*

King [kɪŋ] *amer. Bürgerrechtskämp-fer.*

Kipling ['kɪplɪŋ] *engl. Dichter.*

Klondike ['klɒndaɪk] *Fluß u. Land-schaft in Kanada u. Alaska.*

Kremlin ['kremlɪn] *der Kreml.*

Labrador ['læbrədɔː] *Halbinsel Nordamerikas.*

Lancashire ['læŋkəʃə] *Grafschaft in England.*

Lancaster ['læŋkəstə] *Name zweier Städte in England u. USA; s. Lancashire.*

Lawrence ['lɒrəns] *engl. Autor.*

Lebanon ['lebənən] *der Libanon.*

Leeds [liːdz] *Industriestadt in Eng-land.*

Leicester ['lestə] *Stadt in England; a.* ~**shire** [~ʃə] *Grafschaft in England.*

Leslie ['lezlɪ] *männlicher u. weiblicher Vorname.*

Lewis ['luːɪs] Ludwig *m.*

Libya ['lɪbɪə] Libyen *n.*

Lincoln ['lɪŋkən] 1. *Präsident der USA*; 2. *Stadt in USA*; 3. *Stadt in England*; 4. *a.* ~**shire** [~ʃə] *Graf-schaft in England.*

Lisbon ['lɪzbən] Lissabon *n.*

Liverpool ['lɪvəpuːl] *Hafen- u. In-dustriestadt in England.*

London ['lʌndən] 1. London *n*; 2. *amer. Autor.*

Los Angeles [lɒs'ændʒɪliːz] *Stadt in USA.*

Louisiana [luːiːzɪ'ænə] *Staat der USA.*

Lucerne [luː'sɜːn] Luzern *n; Lake of* ~ Vierwaldstätter See *m.*

Luxembourg ['lʌksəmbɜːg] Lu-xemburg *n.*

Mabel ['meɪbl] *weiblicher Vorname.*

Mackenzie [mə'kenzɪ] *Strom in Nordamerika.*

Madge [mædʒ] *weiblicher Vorname.*

Madrid [mə'drɪd] Madrid *n.*

Maine [meɪn] *Staat der USA.*

Malta ['mɔːltə] Malta *n.*

Manchester ['mæntʃɪstə] *Industrie-stadt u. Grafschaft in England.*

Manhattan [mænˈhætn] *Stadtteil von New York.*

Manitoba [mænɪˈtəʊbə] *Provinz in Kanada.*

Margaret [ˈmɑːgərɪt] Margarete *f.*

Mark [mɑːk] Markus *m.*

Mary [ˈmeərɪ] Maria *f.*

Maryland [ˈmeərɪlænd] *Staat der USA.*

Massachusetts [mæsəˈtʃuːsɪts] *Staat der USA.*

Mat(h)ilda [məˈtɪldə] Mathilde *f.*

Ma(t)thew [ˈmæθjuː] Matthäus *m.*

Maud [mɔːd] *Kurzform von* Mat(h)ilda.

Maugham [mɔːm] *engl. Autor.*

Maurice [ˈmɒrɪs] Moritz *m.*

May [meɪ] *Kurzform von* Mary.

Melbourne [ˈmelbən] *Stadt in Australien.*

Merseyside [ˈmɜːzɪsaɪd] *Grafschaft in England.*

Miami [maɪˈæmɪ] *Badeort in Florida, USA.*

Michigan [ˈmɪʃɪgən] *Staat der USA*; *Lake* ~ Michigansee *m* (*e-r der fünf Großen Seen Nordamerikas*).

Miller [ˈmɪlə] *amer. Dramatiker.*

Millicent [ˈmɪlɪsnt] *weiblicher Vorname.*

Milton [ˈmɪltən] *engl. Dichter.*

Milwaukee [mɪlˈwɔːkiː] *Stadt in USA.*

Minneapolis [mɪnɪˈæpəlɪs] *Stadt in USA.*

Minnesota [mɪnɪˈsəʊtə] *Staat der USA.*

Mississippi [mɪsɪˈsɪpɪ] *Strom u. Staat der USA.*

Missouri [mɪˈzʊərɪ] *Fluß u. Staat der USA.*

Mohammed [məʊˈhæmed] Mohammed *m.*

Monroe [mənˈrəʊ] **1.** *Präsident der USA*; **2.** *amer. Filmschauspielerin.*

Montana [mɒnˈtænə] *Staat der USA.*

Montgomery [məntˈgʌmərɪ] *brit. Feldmarschall.*

Montreal [mɒntrɪˈɔːl] *Stadt in Kanada.*

Moore [mʊə] *engl. Bildhauer.*

Morocco [məˈrɒkəʊ] Marokko *n.*

Moscow [ˈmɒskəʊ] Moskau *n.*

Moselle [məʊˈzel] Mosel *f.*

Munich [ˈmjuːnɪk] München *n.*

Nancy [ˈnænsɪ] *weiblicher Vorname.*

Nebraska [nɪˈbræskə] *Staat der USA.*

Nelson [ˈnelsn] *engl. Admiral.*

Netherlands [ˈneðələndz] *die Niederlande.*

Nevada [neˈvɑːdə] *Staat der USA.*

New Brunswick [njuːˈbrʌnzwɪk] *Provinz in Kanada.*

Newcastle [ˈnjuːkɑːsl] *Hafenstadt in England.*

New Delhi [njuːˈdelɪ] *Hauptstadt von Indien.*

New England [njuːˈɪŋglənd] Neuengland *n.*

Newfoundland [ˈnjuːfəndlənd] Neufundland *n.*

New Hampshire [njuːˈhæmpʃə] *Staat der USA.*

New Jersey [njuːˈdʒɜːzɪ] *Staat der USA.*

New Mexico [njuːˈmeksɪkəʊ] Neumexiko *n* (*Staat der USA*).

New Orleans [njuːˈɔːlɪəns] *Hafenstadt in USA.*

Newton [ˈnjuːtn] *engl. Physiker.*

New York [njuːˈjɔːk] *Stadt u. Staat der USA.*

New Zealand [njuːˈziːlənd] Neuseeland *n.*

Niagara [naɪˈægərə] Niagara *m* (*Fluß zwischen Erie- u. Ontariosee*).

Nicholas [ˈnɪkələs] Nikolaus *m.*

Nixon [ˈnɪksən] *Präsident der USA.*

Norfolk [ˈnɔːfək] *Grafschaft in England.*

Northampton [nɔːˈθæmptən] *Stadt in England*; *a.* **~shire** [~ʃə] *Grafschaft in England.*

North Carolina [ˈnɔːθ kærəˈlaɪnə] Nordkarolina *n* (*Staat der USA*).

North Dakota [ˈnɔːθ dəˈkəʊtə] Norddakota *n* (*Staat der USA*).

Northumberland [nɔːˈθʌmbələnd] *Grafschaft in England.*

Northwest Territories [nɔːθˈwest ˈterɪtərɪz] Nordwestterritorien *pl.* (*Kanada*).

North Yorkshire [ˈnɔːθ ˈjɔːkʃə] *Grafschaft in England.*

Norway [ˈnɔːweɪ] Norwegen *n.*

Norwich [ˈnɒrɪdʒ] *Stadt in England.*

Nottingham [ˈnɒtɪŋəm] *Stadt in England*; *a.* **~shire** [~ʃə] *Grafschaft in England.*

Nova Scotia [ˈnəʊvəˈskəʊʃə] *Provinz in Kanada.*

Oceania [əʊʃɪˈeɪnjə] Ozeanien *n.*

736

Ohio [əʊˈhaɪəʊ] *Fluß u. Staat der USA.*

Oklahoma [əʊkləˈhəʊmə] *Staat der USA.*

Oliver [ˈɒlɪvə] *männlicher Vorname.*

Omaha [ˈəʊməhɑː] *Stadt in USA.*

O'Neill [əʊˈniːl] *amer. Dramatiker.*

Ontario [ɒnˈteərɪəʊ] *Provinz in Kanada;* Lake ~ *Ontariosee m (e-r der fünf Großen Seen Nordamerikas).*

Oregon [ˈɒrɪgən] *Staat der USA.*

Orkney Islands [ˈɔːknɪ ˈaɪləndz] *der Orkneyinseln.*

Orwell [ˈɔːwəl] *engl. Autor.*

Osborne [ˈɒzbən] *engl. Dramatiker.*

Ostend [ɒˈstend] *Ostende n.*

Ottawa [ˈɒtəwə] *Hauptstadt von Kanada.*

Oxford [ˈɒksfəd] *engl. Universitätsstadt; a.* ~shire [~ʃə] *Grafschaft in England.*

Pacific [pəˈsɪfɪk] *der Pazifik.*

Pakistan [pɑːkɪˈstɑːn] *Pakistan n.*

Paris [ˈpærɪs] *Paris n.*

Patricia [pəˈtrɪʃə] *weiblicher Vorname.*

Patrick [ˈpætrɪk] *männlicher Vorname.*

Paul [pɔːl] *Paul m.*

Pearl Harbor [ˈpɜːl ˈhɑːbə] *Hafenstadt auf Hawaii.*

Peg(gy) [ˈpeg(ɪ)] *Kurzform von Margaret.*

Pennsylvania [pensɪlˈveɪnjə] *Pennsylvanien n (Staat der USA).*

Peter [ˈpiːtə] *Peter m.*

Philadelphia [fɪləˈdelfjə] *Stadt in USA.*

Philippines [ˈfɪlɪpiːnz] *die Philippinen.*

Pittsburgh [ˈpɪtsbɜːg] *Stadt in USA.*

Plymouth [ˈplɪməθ] *Hafenstadt in England.*

Poe [pəʊ] *amer. Autor.*

Poland [ˈpəʊlənd] *Polen n.*

Portsmouth [ˈpɔːtsməθ] *Hafenstadt in England.*

Portugal [ˈpɔːtjʊgl] *Portugal n.*

Potomac [pəˈtəʊmæk] *Fluß in USA.*

Prague [prɑːg] *Prag n.*

Prince Edward Island [prɪnsˈedwəd ˈaɪlənd] *Provinz in Kanada.*

Pulitzer [ˈpʊlɪtsə] *amer. Journalist.*

Purcell [ˈpɜːsl] *engl. Komponist.*

Quebec [kwɪˈbek] *Provinz u. Stadt in Kanada.*

Reagan [ˈreɪgən] *Präsident der USA.*

Reynolds [ˈrenldz] *engl. Maler.*

Rhine [raɪn] *Rhein m.*

Rhode Island [rəʊdˈaɪlənd] *Staat der USA.*

Rhodesia [rəʊˈdiːzjə] *Rhodesien n.*

Richard [ˈrɪtʃəd] *Richard m.*

Robert [ˈrɒbət] *Robert m.*

Rockefeller [ˈrɒkɪfelə] *amer. Industrieller.*

Rocky Mountains [ˈrɒkɪˈmaʊntɪnz] *Gebirge in USA.*

Roger [ˈrɒdʒə] *männlicher Vorname.*

Romania [ruːˈmeɪnjə] *Rumänien n.*

Rome [rəʊm] *Rom n.*

Roosevelt [ˈrəʊzəvelt] *Name zweier Präsidenten der USA.*

Rugby [ˈrʌgbɪ] *berühmte Public School.*

Russell [ˈrʌsl] *engl. Philosoph.*

Russia [ˈrʌʃə] *Rußland n.*

Salinger [ˈsælɪndʒə] *amer. Autor.*

Salop [ˈsæləp] *Grafschaft in England.*

Sam [sæm] *Kurzform von Samuel.*

Samuel [ˈsæmjʊəl] *Samuel m.*

San Francisco [sænfrənˈsɪskəʊ] *Hafenstadt in USA.*

Saskatchewan [səsˈkætʃɪwən] *Provinz in Kanada.*

Scandinavia [skændɪˈneɪvjə] *Skandinavien n.*

Scotland [ˈskɒtlənd] *Schottland n;* ~ Yard *Polizeipräsidium in London.*

Seattle [sɪˈætl] *Hafenstadt in USA.*

Shakespeare [ˈʃeɪkspɪə] *engl. Dichter.*

Shaw [ʃɔː] *engl. Dramatiker.*

Shelley [ˈʃelɪ] *engl. Dichter.*

Shetland Islands [ˈʃetlənd ˈaɪləndz] *die Shetlandinseln.*

Sillitoe [ˈsɪlɪtəʊ] *engl. Autor.*

Singapore [sɪŋgəˈpɔː] *Singapur n.*

Snowdon [ˈsnəʊdn] *Berg in Wales.*

Somerset(shire) [ˈsʌməsɪt(ʃə)] *Grafschaft in England.*

South Carolina [ˈsaʊθ kærəˈlaɪnə] *Südkarolina n (Staat der USA).*

South Dakota [ˈsaʊθ dəˈkəʊtə] *Süddakota n (Staat der USA).*

South Yorkshire [ˈsaʊθ ˈjɔːkʃə] *Grafschaft in England.*

Spain [speɪn] *Spanien n.*

Staffordshire [ˈstæfədʃə] *Grafschaft in England.*

Stevenson [ˈstiːvnsn] *schott. Autor.*

St. Lawrence [snt ˈlɒrəns] *der St.-Lorenz-Strom.*

St. Louis [snt'lɔɪs] *Industriestadt in USA.*

Stratford ['strætfəd]: ~-on-Avon *Geburtsort Shakespeares.*

Styria ['stɪrɪə] *Steiermark f.*

Suffolk ['sʌfək] *Grafschaft in England.*

Superior [su:'pɪərɪə]: *Lake ~ Oberer See m (e-r der fünf Großen Seen Nordamerikas).*

Surrey ['sʌrɪ] *Grafschaft in England.*

Susan ['su:zn] *Susanne f.*

Sweden ['swi:dn] *Schweden n.*

Swift [swɪft] *engl. Autor.*

Switzerland ['swɪtsələnd] *die Schweiz.*

Sydney ['sɪdnɪ] *Hafen- u. Industriestadt in Australien.*

Tennessee [tenə'si:] *Fluß u. Staat der USA.*

Tennyson ['tenɪsn] *engl. Dichter.*

Texas ['teksəs] *Staat der USA.*

Thackeray ['θækərɪ] *engl. Autor.*

Thames [temz] *Themse f.*

Thatcher ['θætʃə] *engl. Politikerin.*

Thomas ['tɔməs] *Thomas m.*

Tokyo ['təʊkɪəʊ] *Tokio n.*

Tom(my) ['tɔm(ɪ)] *Kurzform von Thomas.*

Toronto [tə'rɒntəʊ] *Stadt in Kanada.*

Trafalgar [trə'fælgə] *Vorgebirge bei Gibraltar (Seesieg Nelsons 1805).*

Truman ['tru:mən] *Präsident der USA.*

Turkey ['tɜ:kɪ] *die Türkei.*

Turner ['tɜ:nə] *engl. Maler.*

Twain [tweɪn] *amer. Autor.*

Tyne and Wear ['taɪnən'wɪə] *Grafschaft in England.*

Tyrol ['tɪrəl] *Tirol n.*

Ulster ['ʌlstə] *Ulster n (Nordirland).*

United States of America [ju:'naɪtɪd 'steɪtsəvə'merɪkə] *die Vereinigten Staaten von Amerika.*

Utah ['ju:tɑː] *Staat der USA.*

Vancouver [væn'ku:və] *Stadt in Kanada.*

Vatican ['vætɪkən] *Vatikan m.*

Venice ['venɪs] *Venedig n.*

Vermont [vɜ:'mɒnt] *Staat der USA.*

Vienna [vɪ'enə] *Wien n.*

Virginia [və'dʒɪnjə] *Staat der USA.*

Vivian ['vɪvɪən] *männlicher u. weiblicher Vorname.*

Wales [weɪlz] *Wales n.*

Wallace ['wɒlɪs] *engl. Autor.*

Wall Street ['wɔ:l stri:t] *Straße u. Finanzzentrum in New York.*

Warsaw ['wɔ:sɔ:] *Warschau n.*

Warwickshire ['wɒrɪkʃə] *Grafschaft in England.*

Washington ['wɒʃɪŋtən] **1.** *Präsident der USA;* **2.** *Staat der USA;* **3.** *Bundeshauptstadt der USA.*

Waterloo [wɔ:tə'lu:] *Dorf in Belgien (Niederlage Napoleons 1815).*

Watt [wɒt] *schott. Erfinder.*

Wellington ['welɪŋtən] **1.** *engl. Feldherr u. Staatsmann;* **2.** *Hauptstadt von Neuseeland.*

West Midlands ['west 'mɪdləndz] *Grafschaft in England.*

West Sussex ['west 'sʌsɪks] *Grafschaft in England.*

West Virginia ['west və'dʒɪnjə] *Staat der USA.*

West Yorkshire ['west 'jɔ:kʃə] *Grafschaft in England.*

White House ['waɪt haʊs] *das Weiße Haus (Amtssitz des Präsidenten der USA).*

Whitman ['wɪtmən] *amer. Dichter.*

Wilde [waɪld] *engl. Autor u. Dramatiker.*

Wilder ['waɪldə] *amer. Dramatiker.*

Will [wɪl] *Kurzform von William.*

William ['wɪljəm] *Wilhelm m.*

Wilson ['wɪlsn] **1.** *Präsident der USA;* **2.** *brit. Politiker.*

Wiltshire ['wɪltʃə] *Grafschaft in England.*

Wimbledon ['wɪmbldən] *Vorort von London (Tennisturniere).*

Winnipeg ['wɪnɪpeg] *See u. Stadt in Kanada.*

Wisconsin [wɪs'kɒnsɪn] *Fluß u. Staat der USA.*

Wolfe [wʊlf] *amer. Autor.*

Woolf [wʊlf] *engl. Autorin.*

Worcester ['wʊstə] *Industriestadt in England.*

Wordsworth ['wɜ:dzwəθ] *engl. Dichter.*

Wyoming [waɪ'əʊmɪŋ] *Staat der USA.*

Yale University ['jeɪl ju:nɪ'vɜ:sətɪ] *amer. Universität.*

Yellowstone ['jeləʊstəʊn] *Fluß u. Nationalpark der USA.*

York [jɔ:k] *Stadt in England;* ~shire [~ʃə] *Grafschaft in England.*

738

Yosemite [jəʊˈsemɪtɪ] *Nationalpark der USA.*

Yugoslavia [juːɡəʊˈslɑːvjə] Jugoslawien *n.*

Yukon [ˈjuːkɒn] *Fluß und Territorium in Kanada.*

Zimbabwe [zɪmˈbɑːbwɪ] Simbabwe *n.*

American and British Abbreviations

abbr. *abbreviated* abgekürzt; *abbreviation* Abk., Abkürzung *f.*

ABC *American Broadcasting Company* (*amer. Rundfunkgesellschaft*).

AC *alternating current* Wechselstrom *m.*

A/C *account* (Bank)Konto *n.*

acc(t). *account* Konto *n*, Rechnung *f.*

AEC *Atomic Energy Commission* Atomenergie-Kommission *f.*

AFL–CIO *American Federation of Labor & Congress of Industrial Organizations* (*größter amer. Gewerkschaftsverband*).

AFN *American Forces Network* (*Rundfunkanstalt der amer. Streitkräfte*).

AI *Amnesty International.*

AL *Alabama.*

Alta *Alberta.*

AK *Alaska.*

AM *amplitude modulation* MW, Mittelwelle *f.*

a.m. *ante meridiem* (*lateinisch = before noon*) vormittags.

AP *Associated Press* (*amer. Nachrichtenbüro*).

AR *Arkansas.*

ARC *American Red Cross* Amer. Rotes Kreuz.

arr. *arrival* Ank., Ankunft *f.*

ASA *American Standards Association* Amer. Normungs-Organisation *f.*

AZ *Arizona.*

BA *Bachelor of Arts* Bakkalaureus *m* der Philosophie; *British Airways* (*brit. Fluggesellschaft*).

BBC *British Broadcasting Corporation* (*brit. Rundfunkgesellschaft*).

BC *British Columbia.*

B/E *bill of exchange* Wechsel *m.*

Beds. *Bedfordshire.*

Benelux *Belgium, Netherlands, Luxembourg* (*Zollunion*).

Berks. *Berkshire.*

BFN *British Forces Network* (*Sender der brit. Streitkräfte in Deutschland*).

BL *Bachelor of Law* Bakkalaureus *m* des Rechts.

bldg *building* Gebäude *n.*

BM *Bachelor of Medicine* Bakkalaureus *m* der Medizin.

BO *body odour* Körpergeruch *m.*

BOT *Board of Trade* Handelsministerium *n* (*in Großbritannien*).

BR *British Rail* (*Eisenbahn in Großbritannien*).

Brit. *Britain* Großbritannien *n*; *British* britisch.

Bros. *brothers* Gebrüder *pl.* (*in Firmenbezeichnungen*).

BS *Bachelor of Science* Bakkalaureus *m* der Naturwissenschaften; *British Standard* Brit. Norm *f.*

BSI *British Standards Institution* Brit. Normungs-Organisation *f.*

Bucks. *Buckinghamshire.*

C *Celsius, centigrade* (*Thermometereinteilung*).

c. *cent(s)* Cent *m od. pl.*; *circa* ca., ungefähr, zirka; *cubic* Kubik...

CA *California.*

C/A *current account* Girokonto *n.*

Cambs. *Cambridgeshire.*

Can. *Canada* Kanada *n*; *Canadian* kanadisch.

CBS *Columbia Broadcasting System* (*amer. Rundfunkgesellschaft*).

CD *compact disc* CD-Platte *f*, Kompaktschallplatte *f.*

cf. *confer* vgl., vergleiche.

Ches. *Cheshire.*

CIA *Central Intelligence Agency* (*amer. Geheimdienst*).

CID *Criminal Investigation Department* (*brit. Kriminalpolizei*).

c.i.f. *cost, insurance, freight* Kosten, Versicherung und Fracht einbegriffen.

CO *Colorado.*

Co. *Company* Gesellschaft *f*; *County* Grafschaft *f*, Kreis *m.*

c/o *care of* p.A., per Adresse, bei.

COD *cash* (*Am. collect*) *on delivery* Zahlung bei Empfang, gegen Nachnahme.

C of E Church of England (englische Staatskirche).
Corn. Cornwall.
cp. compare vgl., vergleiche.
CT Connecticut.
Cumb. Cumberland.
cwt. hundredweight (etwa 1) Zentner m.

DC direct current Gleichstrom m.
D.C. District of Columbia (mit der amer. Hauptstadt Washington).
DE Delaware.
dep. departure Abf., Abfahrt f.
Dept. Department Abt., Abteilung f.
Derby. Derbyshire.
Devon. Devonshire.
disc. discount Diskont m, Abzug m.
div. dividend Dividende f.
DJ disc jockey Diskjockey m.
Dors. Dorsetshire.
doz. dozen Dutzend n od. pl.
Dpt. Department Abt., Abteilung f.
Dur(h). Durham.
dz. dozen Dutzend n od. pl.

E east Ost(en m); eastern östlich; English englisch.
ea. each jeder.
ECU European Currency Unit europäische Währungseinheit.
Ed., ed. edition Auflage f; edited hrsg., herausgegeben; editor Hrsg., Herausgeber m.
EDP electronic data processing EDV, elektronische Datenverarbeitung.
EEC European Economic Community EWG, Europäische Wirtschaftsgemeinschaft.
EFTA European Free Trade Association EFTA, Europäische Freihandelsgemeinschaft od. -zone.
e.g. exempli gratia (lateinisch = for instance) z. B., zum Beispiel.
Enc. enclosure(s) Anlage(n pl.) f.
Ess. Essex.

F Fahrenheit (Thermometereinteilung).
f. feminine weiblich; foot, pl. feet Fuß m od. pl.; following folgend.
FAO Food and Agricultural Organization Organisation f für Ernährung und Landwirtschaft (der UN).
FBI Federal Bureau of Investigation (Bundeskriminalamt der USA).

fig. figure(s) Abb., Abbildung(en pl.) f.
FL Florida.
FM frequency modulation UKW, Ultrakurzwelle f.
FO Foreign Office Brt. Auswärtiges Amt.
f.o.b. free on board frei Schiff.
fol. folio Folio n, Seite f.
fr. franc(s) Franc(s pl.) m.
ft foot, pl. feet Fuß m od. pl.

g gramme g, Gramm n.
GA Georgia.
gal. gallon Gallone f.
GATT General Agreement on Tariffs and Trade Allgemeines Zoll- und Handelsabkommen.
GB Great Britain Großbritannien n.
GI government issue von der Regierung ausgegeben; Staatseigentum n; fig. amer. Soldat.
Glos. Gloucestershire.
GMT Greenwich Mean Time WEZ, Westeuropäische Zeit.
GP general practitioner Arzt m (Ärztin f) für Allgemeinmedizin.
GPO General Post Office Hauptpostamt n.
gr. gross brutto.

h. hour(s) Std., Stunde(n pl.) f.
Hants. Hampshire.
HBM His (Her) Britannic Majesty Seine (Ihre) britannische Majestät.
H.C. House of Commons Unterhaus n.
Herts. Hertfordshire.
hf. half halb.
HI Hawaii.
H.L. House of Lords Oberhaus n.
H.M. His (Her) Majesty Seine (Ihre) Majestät.
H.M.S. His (Her) Majesty's Ship (Steamer) Seiner (Ihrer) Majestät Schiff n (Dampfschiff n).
H.O. Home Office Brt. Innenministerium n.
H.P., hp horsepower PS, Pferdestärke f.
H.Q., Hq. Headquarters Stab(squartier n) m, Hauptquartier n.
H.R. House of Representatives Repräsentantenhaus n (der USA).
H.R.H. His (Her) Royal Highness Seine (Ihre) Königliche Hoheit.

IA *Iowa.*
ICBM *intercontinental ballistic missile* interkontinentaler ballistischer Flugkörper.
ID *Idaho.*
I.D. *Intelligence Department* Nachrichtenamt *n.*
i.e. *id est (lateinisch = that is to say)* d. h., das heißt.
IL *Illinois.*
IMF *International Monetary Fund* Internationaler Währungsfonds.
IN *Indiana.*
in. *inch(es)* Zoll *m od. pl.*
Inc. *Incorporated* (amtlich) eingetragen.
inst. *instant* d. M., dieses Monats.
IOC *International Olympic Committee* Internationales Olympisches Komitee.
I of W *Isle of Wight.*
IOU *I owe you* Schuldschein *m.*
Ir. *Ireland* Irland *n; Irish* irisch.
IRC *International Red Cross* Internationales Rotes Kreuz.

JP *Justice of the Peace* Friedensrichter *m.*
Jr *junior* jr., jun., der Jüngere.

k.o. *knock(ed) out* Boxen: k.o. (ge)schlagen; *fig.* erledigt.
KS *Kansas.*

l. *litre(s)* Liter *n, m od. pl.*
£ *pound sterling* Pfund *n* Sterling *(Währung).*
LA *Louisiana.*
Lab *Labrador.*
Lancs. *Lancashire.*
lb. *pound(s)* Pfund *n od. pl. (Gewicht).*
L/C *letter of credit* Kreditbrief *m.*
Leics. *Leicestershire.*
Lincs. *Lincolnshire.*
LP *long playing record* LP, Langspielplatte *f.*
Ltd. *limited* mit beschränkter Haftung.

m. *male* männlich; *metre* m, Meter *n, m; mile* Meile *f; minute* Min., Minute *f.*
MA *Massachusetts.*
M.A. *Master of Arts* Magister *m* der Philosophie.
Man *Manitoba.*
MD *Maryland.*
M.D. *Medicinae Doctor (lateinisch =*

Doctor of Medicine) Dr. med., Doktor *m* der Medizin.
ME *Maine.*
MI *Michigan.*
MN *Minnesota.*
MO *Missouri.*
M.O. *money order* Postanweisung *f.*
Mon. *Monmouthshire.*
MP, M.P. *Member of Parliament* Parlamentsabgeordnete(r *m) f; Military Police* Militärpolizei *f.*
m.p.h. *miles per hour* Stundenmeilen *pl.*
Mr *Mister* Herr *m.*
MRP *manufacturer's recommended price* unverbindliche Preisempfehlung.
Mrs *Mistress* Frau *f.*
MS *Mississippi; manuscript* Manuskript *n.*
Ms *Anrede für Frauen ohne Berücksichtigung des Familienstandes.*
Mt *Mount* Berg *m.*

N *north* Nord(en *m); northern* nördlich.
n. *noon* Mittag *m.*
NASA *National Aeronautics and Space Administration* NASA *f (amer. Luftfahrt- und Raumforschungsbehörde).*
NATO *North Atlantic Treaty Organization* NATO *f,* Nordatlantikpakt-Organisation *f.*
NB *New Brunswick.*
N.B. *nota bene (lateinisch = note well)* NB, notabene.
NBC *National Broadcasting Company (amer. Rundfunkgesellschaft).*
NC *North Carolina.*
ND *North Dakota; Newfoundland.*
NE *north-east* Nordost(en *m); north-eastern* nordöstlich; *Nebraska.*
NH *New Hampshire.*
N.H.S. *National Health Service* Nationaler Gesundheitsdienst *(in Großbritannien).*
NJ *New Jersey.*
NM *New Mexico.*
Norf. *Norfolk.*
Northants. *Northamptonshire.*
Northumb. *Northumberland.*
Notts. *Nottinghamshire.*
NS *Nova Scotia.*
NV *Nevada.*
NW *north-west* Nordwest(en *m); north-western* nordwestlich.

NY *New York.*
N.Y.C. *New York City* Stadt *f* New York.

o/a *on account of* für Rechnung von.
OAS *Organization of American States* Organisation *f* amerikanischer Staaten.
O.E.C.D. *Organization for Economic Cooperation and Development* Organisation *f* für wirtschaftliche Zusammenarbeit und Entwicklung.
OH *Ohio.*
O.H.M.S. *On His (Her) Majesty's Service* im Dienste Seiner (Ihrer) Majestät; Dienstsache *f.*
OK *Oklahoma.*
O.K. o.k., in Ordnung.
Ont *Ontario.*
OPEC *Organization of Petroleum-Exporting Countries* Organisation *f* erdölexportierender Staaten.
OR *Oregon.*
Oxon. *Oxfordshire.*
oz. *ounce* Unze.

p *(new) penny od. pence* Penny *m.*
PA *Pennsylvania.*
p.a. *per annum (lateinisch = yearly)* jährlich.
Pan Am *Pan American World Airways (amer. Fluggesellschaft).*
PC *Personal Computer* PC, Personalcomputer *m.*
P.C. *police constable* Schutzmann *m.*
p.c. *per cent* %, Prozent *n od. pl.*
pd. *paid* bezahlt.
P.E.N., *mst* **PEN Club** *Poets, Playwrights, Editors, Essayists, and Novelists* Pen-Club *m (Internationale Vereinigung von Dichtern, Dramatikern, Redakteuren, Essayisten und Romanschriftstellern).*
Ph.D. *Philosophiae Doctor (lateinisch = Doctor of Philosophy)* Dr. phil., Doktor *m* der Philosophie.
PM *Prime Minister* Premierminister(in).
p.m. *post meridiem (lateinisch = after noon)* nachmittags, abends.
P.O. *Post Office* Postamt *n; postal order* Postanweisung *f.*
POD *pay on delivery* Nachnahme *f.*
P.S. *postscript* PS, Nachschrift *f.*
pt *pint* Pinte *f (etwa ¹/₂ l).*

P.T.O., p.t.o. *please turn over* b.w., bitte wenden.
PX *Post Exchange* Verkaufsläden *pl (der amer. Streitkräfte).*

Que *Quebec.*
qt *quart* Quart *n (etwa 1 l).*

R.A.F. *Royal Air Force* Königlich-Brit. Luftwaffe *f.*
RC *Roman Catholic* rk, r.-k., römisch-katholisch.
Rd. *Road* Str., Straße *f.*
ref. *(in) reference (to)* (mit) Bezug *m* (auf); Empfehlung *f.*
regd. *registered* eingetragen; eingeschrieben.
reg.tn. *register ton* RT, Registertonne *f.*
resp. *respective(ly)* bzw., beziehungsweise.
ret. *retired* i.R., im Ruhestand.
Rev. *Reverend* Pfarrer *m.*
rev *revolution* Umdrehung *f.*
RI *Rhode Island.*
R.N. *Royal Navy* Königlich-Brit. Marine *f.*
R.R. *Railroad Am.* Eisenbahn *f.*
RSVP *répondez s'il vous plaît (französisch = please reply)* u.A.w.g., um Antwort wird gebeten.

S *south* Süd(en *m); southern* südlich.
s. *second(s)* Sek., Sekunde (*n pl.) f.*
$ *dollar* Dollar *m.*
S.A. *South Africa* Südafrika *n; South America* Südamerika *n; Salvation Army* Heilsarmee *f.*
Salop. *Shropshire.*
Sask *Saskatchewan.*
SC *South Carolina; Security Council* Sicherheitsrat *m (der UN).*
SD *South Dakota.*
SE *south-east* Südost(en *m); south-eastern* südöstlich; *Stock Exchange* Börse *f.*
SEATO *South East Asia Treaty Organization* Südostasienpakt-Organisation *f.*
Soc. *society* Gesellschaft *f;* Verein *m.*
Som. *Somersetshire.*
Sq. *Square* Platz *m.*
sq. *square* ... Quadrat...
Sr *senior* sen., der Ältere.
S.S. *steamship* Dampfer *m.*
St(.) *Saint* ... Sankt ...; *Station* Bahnhof *m; Street* Straße *f.*
Staffs. *Staffordshire.*

St.Ex. *Stock Exchange* Börse *f.*
stg. *sterling* Sterling *m (brit. Währungseinheit).*
Suff. *Suffolk.*
SW *south-west* Südwest(en *m); south-western* südwestlich.
Sx *Sussex.*
Sy *Surrey.*

t *ton*(s) Tonne(n *pl.*) *f.*
TM *trademark* Warenzeichen *n.*
TMO *telegraph money order* telegraphische Geldanweisung.
TN *Tennessee.*
TO *Telegraph (Telephone) Office* Telegraphen-(Fernsprech)amt *n.*
TU *Trade(s) Union(s)* Gewerkschaft(en *pl.*) *f.*
TUC *Trade(s) Union Congress* brit. Gewerkschaftsverband *m.*
TV *television* Fernsehen *n.*
TWA *Trans World Airlines (amer. Fluggesellschaft).*
TX *Texas.*

UK *United Kingdom* Vereinigtes Königreich *(England, Schottland, Wales und Nordirland).*
UN(O) *United Nations (Organization)* UN(O) *f,* (Organisation *f* der) Vereinte(n) Nationen *pl.*
UNESCO *United Nations Educational, Scientific, and Cultural Organization* Organisation *f* der Vereinten Nationen für Erziehung, Wissenschaft und Kultur.
UNICEF *United Nations International Children's Emergency Fund* Weltkinderhilfswerk *n* der UNO.
UPI *United Press International (amer. Nachrichtenagentur).*
US(A) *United States (of America)*

US(A) *pl.,* Vereinigte Staaten *pl.* (von Amerika).
UT *Utah.*

v. *verse* Vers *m; versus (lateinisch = against)* gegen; *vide (lateinisch = see)* s., siehe.
VA *Virginia.*
VF *video frequency* Videofrequenz *f.*
viz. *videlicet (lateinisch = namely)* nämlich.
vol(s). *volume*(s) Band *m* (Bände *pl.*).
VT *Vermont.*

W *west* West(en *m); western* westlich.
WA *Washington.*
Warks. *Warwickshire.*
WC *water closet* WC *n,* Wasserklosett *n.*
W.F.T.U. *World Federation of Trade Unions* Weltgewerkschaftsbund *m.*
W.H.O. *World Health Organization* Weltgesundheitsorganisation *f (der UN).*
WI *Wisconsin.*
W.I. *West Indies* Westindien *n.*
Wilts. *Wiltshire.*
Worcs. *Worcestershire.*
wt. *weight* Gewicht *n.*
W.V. *West Virginia.*
WY *Wyoming.*

Xmas *Christmas* Weihnachten *n.*

yd(s). *yard*(s) Elle(n *pl.*) *f.*
Y.M.C.A. *Young Men's Christian Association* CVJM, Christlicher Verein Junger Männer.
Yorks. *Yorkshire.*
Y.W.C.A. *Young Women's Christian Association* Christlicher Verein Junger Mädchen.

Alphabetical List of the German Irregular Verbs

Infinitive – Preterite – Past Participle

backen - backte (buk) - gebacken
bedingen - bedang (bedingte) - bedungen (*conditional*: bedingt)
befehlen - befahl - befohlen
beginnen - begann - begonnen
beißen - biß - gebissen
bergen - barg - geborgen
bersten - barst - geborsten
bewegen - bewog - bewogen
biegen - bog - gebogen
bieten - bot - geboten
binden - band - gebunden
bitten - bat - gebeten
blasen - blies - geblasen
bleiben - blieb - geblieben
bleichen - blich - geblichen
braten - briet - gebraten
brauchen - brauchte - gebraucht (*v/aux.* brauchen)
brechen - brach - gebrochen
brennen - brannte - gebrannt
bringen - brachte - gebracht
denken - dachte - gedacht
dreschen - drosch - gedroschen
dringen - drang - gedrungen
dürfen - durfte - gedurft (*v/aux.* dürfen)
empfehlen - empfahl - empfohlen
erlöschen - erlosch - erloschen
erschrecken - erschrak - erschrokken
essen - aß - gegessen
fahren - fuhr - gefahren
fallen - fiel - gefallen
fangen - fing - gefangen
fechten - focht - gefochten
finden - fand - gefunden
flechten - flocht - geflochten
fliegen - flog - geflogen
fliehen - floh - geflohen
fließen - floß - geflossen
fressen - fraß - gefressen
frieren - fror - gefroren
gären - gor (*esp. fig.* gärte) - gegoren (*esp. fig.* gegärt)
gebären - gebar - geboren

geben - gab - gegeben
gedeihen - gedieh - gediehen
gehen - ging - gegangen
gelingen - gelang - gelungen
gelten - galt - gegolten
genesen - genas - genesen
genießen - genoß - genossen
geschehen - geschah - geschehen
gewinnen - gewann - gewonnen
gießen - goß - gegossen
gleichen - glich - geglichen
gleiten - glitt - geglitten
glimmen - glomm - geglommen
graben - grub - gegraben
greifen - griff - gegriffen
haben - hatte - gehabt
halten - hielt - gehalten
hängen - hing - gehangen
hauen - haute (hieb) - gehauen
heben - hob - gehoben
heißen - hieß - geheißen
helfen - half - geholfen
kennen - kannte - gekannt
klingen - klang - geklungen
kneifen - kniff - gekniffen
kommen - kam - gekommen
können - konnte - gekonnt (*v/aux.* können)
kriechen - kroch - gekrochen
laden - lud - geladen
lassen - ließ - gelassen (*v/aux.* lassen)
laufen - lief - gelaufen
leiden - litt - gelitten
leihen - lieh - geliehen
lesen - las - gelesen
liegen - lag - gelegen
lügen - log - gelogen
mahlen - mahlte - gemahlen
meiden - mied - gemieden
melken - melkte (molk) - gemolken (gemelkt)
messen - maß - gemessen
mißlingen - mißlang - mißlungen
mögen - mochte - gemocht (*v/aux.* mögen)

müssen - mußte - gemußt (v/aux. müssen)
nehmen - nahm - genommen
nennen - nannte - genannt
pfeifen - pfiff - gepfiffen
preisen - pries - gepriesen
quellen - quoll - gequollen
raten - riet - geraten
reiben - rieb - gerieben
reißen - riß - gerissen
reiten - ritt - geritten
rennen - rannte - gerannt
riechen - roch - gerochen
ringen - rang - gerungen
rinnen - rann - geronnen
rufen - rief - gerufen
salzen - salzte - gesalzen (gesalzt)
saufen - soff - gesoffen
saugen - sog - gesogen
schaffen - schuf - geschaffen
schallen - schallte (scholl) - geschallt (*for* **erschallen** *a.* erschollen)
scheiden - schied - geschieden
scheinen - schien - geschienen
schelten - schalt - gescholten
scheren - schor - geschoren
schieben - schob - geschoben
schießen - schoß - geschossen
schinden - schund - geschunden
schlafen - schlief - geschlafen
schlagen - schlug - geschlagen
schleichen - schlich - geschlichen
schleifen - schliff - geschliffen
schließen - schloß - geschlossen
schlingen - schlang - geschlungen
schmeißen - schmiß - geschmissen
schmelzen - schmolz - geschmolzen
schneiden - schnitt - geschnitten
schrecken - schrak - † geschrocken
schreiben - schrieb - geschrieben
schreien - schrie - geschrie(e)n
schreiten - schritt - geschritten
schweigen - schwieg - geschwiegen
schwellen - schwoll - geschwollen
schwimmen - schwamm - geschwommen
schwinden - schwand - geschwunden [gen]
schwingen - schwang - geschwun-}
schwören - schwor - geschworen
sehen - sah - gesehen
sein - war - gewesen
senden - sandte - gesandt
sieden - sott - gesotten
singen - sang - gesungen

sinken - sank - gesunken
sinnen - sann - gesonnen
sitzen - saß - gesessen
sollen - sollte - gesollt (v/aux. sollen)
spalten - spaltete - gespalten (gespaltet)
speien - spie - gespie(e)n
spinnen - spann - gesponnen
sprechen - sprach - gesprochen
sprießen - sproß - gesprossen
springen - sprang - gesprungen
stechen - stach - gestochen
stecken - steckte (stak) - gesteckt
stehen - stand - gestanden
stehlen - stahl - gestohlen
steigen - stieg - gestiegen
sterben - starb - gestorben
stieben - stob - gestoben
stinken - stank - gestunken
stoßen - stieß - gestoßen
streichen - strich - gestrichen
streiten - stritt - gestritten
tragen - trug - getragen
treffen - traf - getroffen
treiben - trieb - getrieben
treten - trat - getreten
triefen - triefte (troff) - getrieft
trinken - trank - getrunken
trügen - trog - getrogen
tun - tat - getan
verderben - verdarb - verdorben
verdrießen - verdroß - verdrossen
vergessen - vergaß - vergessen
verlieren - verlor - verloren
verschleißen - verschliß - verschlissen
verzeihen - verzieh - verziehen
wachsen - wuchs - gewachsen
wägen - wog (⚹ wägte) - gewogen (⚹ gewägt)
waschen - wusch - gewaschen
weben - wob - gewoben
weichen - wich - gewichen
weisen - wies - gewiesen
wenden - wandte - gewandt
werben - warb - geworben [den*)}
werden - wurde - geworden (wor-}
werfen - warf - geworfen
wiegen - wog - gewogen
winden - wand - gewunden
wissen - wußte - gewußt [wollen}
wollen - wollte - gewollt (v/aux.}
wringen - wrang - gewrungen
ziehen - zog - gezogen
zwingen - zwang - gezwungen

* only in connexion with the past participles of other verbs, *e.g.* er ist *gesehen worden* he has been seen.

Alphabetical List of the English Irregular Verbs

Infinitive – Preterite – Past Participle

Irregular forms marked with asterisks (*) can be exchanged for the regular forms.

arise (*sich erheben*) – arose – arisen
awake (*erwachen*) – awoke – awoke*
be (*sein*) – was – been
bear (*tragen; gebären*) – bore – ge- tragen: borne – geboren: born
beat (*schlagen*) – beat – beat(en)
become (*werden*) – became – become
beget (*zeugen*) – begot – begotten
begin (*anfangen*) – began – begun
bend (*beugen*) – bent – bent
bereave (*berauben*) – bereft* – bereft*
beseech (*dringend bitten*) – besought – besought
bet (*wetten*) – bet* – bet*
bid (*[ge]bieten*) – bade, bid – bid(den)
bide (*abwarten*) – bode* – bided
bind (*binden*) – bound – bound
bite (*beißen*) – bit – bitten
bleed (*bluten*) – bled – bled
bless (*segnen; preisen*) – blest* – blest*
blow (*blasen*) – blew – blown
break (*brechen*) – broke – broken
breed (*aufziehen*) – bred – bred
bring (*bringen*) – brought – brought
build (*bauen*) – built – built
burn (*brennen*) – burnt* – burnt*
burst (*bersten*) – burst – burst
buy (*kaufen*) – bought – bought
cast (*werfen*) – cast – cast
catch (*fangen*) – caught – caught
choose (*wählen*) – chose – chosen
cleave (*[sich] spalten*) – cleft, clove* – cleft, cloven*
cling (*sich [an]klammern*) – clung – clung
clothe (*[an-, be]kleiden*) – clad* – clad*
come (*kommen*) – came – come
cost (*kosten*) – cost – cost
creep (*kriechen*) – crept – crept
crow (*krähen*) – crew* – crowed
cut (*schneiden*) – cut – cut
deal (*handeln*) – dealt – dealt
dig (*graben*) – dug – dug
dive (*[unter]tauchen*) – dived, *Am. a.* dove – dived

do (*tun*) – did – done
draw (*ziehen*) – drew – drawn
dream (*träumen*) – dreamt* – dreamt*
drink (*trinken*) – drank – drunk
drive (*treiben; fahren*) – drove – driven
dwell (*wohnen*) – dwelt* – dwelt*
eat (*essen*) – ate – eaten
fall (*fallen*) – fell – fallen
feed (*füttern*) – fed – fed
feel (*fühlen*) – felt – felt
fight (*kämpfen*) – fought – fought
find (*finden*) – found – found
fit (*[an]passen*) – fitted, *Am. a.* fit – fitted, *Am. a.* fit
flee (*fliehen*) – fled – fled
fling (*schleudern*) – flung – flung
fly (*fliegen*) – flew – flown
forbid (*verbieten*) – forbade – forbidden
forget (*vergessen*) – forgot – forgotten
forsake (*aufgeben; verlassen*) – forsook – forsaken
freeze (*[ge]frieren*) – froze – frozen
get (*bekommen*) – got – got, *Am.* gotten
gild (*vergolden*) – gilt* – gilt*
give (*geben*) – gave – given
go (*gehen*) – went – gone
grind (*mahlen*) – ground – ground
grow (*wachsen*) – grew – grown
hang (*hängen*) – hung – hung
have (*haben*) – had – had
hear (*hören*) – heard – heard
heave (*heben*) – hove* – hove*
hew (*hauen, hacken*) – hewed – hewn*
hide (*verbergen*) – hid – hidden
hit (*treffen*) – hit – hit
hold (*halten*) – held – held
hurt (*verletzen*) – hurt – hurt
keep (*halten*) – kept – kept
kneel (*knien*) – knelt* – knelt*
knit (*stricken*) – knit* – knit*

know (*wissen*) - knew - known
lay (*legen*) - laid - laid
lead (*führen*) - led - led
lean ([*sich*] [*an*]*lehnen*) - leant* - leant*
leap ([*über*]*springen*) - leapt* - leapt*
learn (*lernen*) - learnt* - learnt*
leave (*verlassen*) - left - left
lend (*leihen*) - lent -lent
let (*lassen*) - let - let
lie (*liegen*) - lay - lain
light (*anzünden*) - lit* - lit*
lose (*verlieren*) - lost - lost
make (*machen*) - made - made
mean (*meinen*) -meant - meant
meet (*begegnen*) - met - met
mow (*mähen*) - mowed - mown*
pay (*zahlen*) - paid - paid
plead (*plädieren*) - pleaded, *bsd. schott., Am.* pled - pleaded, *bsd. schott., Am.* pled
put (*setzen, stellen*) - put - put
read (*lesen*) - read - read
rid (*befreien*) - rid - rid
ride (*reiten*) - rode - ridden
ring (*läuten*) - rang - rung
rise (*aufstehen*) - rose - risen
run (*laufen*) - ran - run
saw (*sägen*) - sawed - sawn*
say (*sagen*) - said - said
see (*sehen*) - saw - seen
seek (*suchen*) - sought - sought
sell (*verkaufen*) - sold - sold
send (*senden*) - sent - sent
set (*setzen*) - set - set
sew (*nähen*) - sewed - sewn*
shake (*schütteln*) - shook - shaken
shave ([*sich*] *rasieren*) - shaved - shaven*
shear (*scheren*) - sheared - shorn
shed (*ausgießen*) - shed - shed
shine (*scheinen*) - shone - shone
shit (*scheißen*) - shit - shit
shoe (*beschuhen*) - shod - shod
shoot (*schießen*) - shot - shot
show (*zeigen*) - showed - shown*
shrink ([*ein*]*schrumpfen*) - shrank - shrunk
shut (*schließen*) - shut - shut
sing (*singen*) - sang - sung
sink (*sinken*) - sank - sunk
sit (*sitzen*) - sat - sat
slay (*erschlagen*) - slew - slain
sleep (*schlafen*) - slept - slept
slide (*gleiten*) - slid - slid
sling (*schleudern*) - slung - slung
slink (*schleichen*) - slunk - slunk

slit (*schlitzen*) - slit - slit
smell (*riechen*) - smelt* - smelt*
sow ([*aus*]*säen*) - sowed - sown*
speak (*sprechen*) - spoke - spoken
speed (*eilen*) - sped* - sped*
spell (*buchstabieren*) - spelt* - spelt*
spend (*ausgeben*) - spent - spent
spill (*verschütten*) - spilt* - spilt*
spin (*spinnen*) - spun - spun
spit ([*aus*]*spucken*) - spat - spat
split (*spalten*) - split - split
spoil (*verderben*) - spoilt* - spoilt*
spread (*verbreiten*) - spread - spread
spring (*springen*) - sprang, *Am.* sprung - sprung
stand (*stehen*) - stood - stood
stave (*den Boden einschlagen*) - stove* - stove*
steal (*stehlen*) - stole - stolen
stick (*stecken*) - stuck - stuck
sting (*stechen*) - stung - stung
stink (*stinken*) - stank, stunk - stunk
strew ([*be*]*streuen*) - strewed - strewn*
stride (*über-, durchschreiten*) - strode - stridden
strike (*schlagen*) - struck - struck
string (*spannen*) - strung - strung
strive (*streben*) - strove - striven
swear (*schwören*) - swore - sworn
sweat (*schwitzen*) - sweat* - sweat*
sweep (*fegen*) - swept - swept
swell ([*an*]*schwellen*) - swelled - swollen
swim (*schwimmen*) - swam - swum
swing (*schwingen*) - swung - swung
take (*nehmen*) - took - taken
teach (*lehren*) - taught - taught
tear (*ziehen*) - tore - torn
tell (*sagen*) - told - told
think (*denken*) - thought - thought
thrive (*gedeihen*) - throve* - thriven*
throw (*werfen*) - threw - thrown
thrust (*stoßen*) - thrust - thrust
tread (*treten*) - trod - trodden, trod
wake (*wachen*) - woke* - woke(n)*
wear ([*Kleider*] *tragen*) - wore - worn
weave (*weben*) - wove - woven
wed (*heiraten*) - wedded, *selten* wed - wedded, *selten* wed
weep (*weinen*) - wept - wept
wet (*nässen*) - wet* - wet*
win (*gewinnen*) - won - won
wind (*winden*) - wound - wound
wring ([*aus*]*wringen*) - wrung - wrung
write (*schreiben*) - wrote - written

Numerals

Cardinal Numbers

0	null *nought, zero, cipher*	51	einundfünfzig *fifty-one*
1	eins *one*	60	sechzig *sixty*
2	zwei *two*	61	einundsechzig *sixty-one*
3	drei *three*	70	siebzig *seventy*
4	vier *four*	71	einundsiebzig *seventy-one*
5	fünf *five*	80	achtzig *eighty*
6	sechs *six*	81	einundachtzig *eighty-one*
7	sieben *seven*	90	neunzig *ninety*
8	acht *eight*	91	einundneunzig *ninety-one*
9	neun *nine*	100	hundert *a or one hundred*
10	zehn *ten*	101	hundert(und)eins *a hundred and one*
11	elf *eleven*		
12	zwölf *twelve*	200	zweihundert *two hundred*
13	dreizehn *thirteen*	300	dreihundert *three hundred*
14	vierzehn *fourteen*	572	fünfhundert(und)zweiundsiebzig *five hundred and seventy-two*
15	fünfzehn *fifteen*		
16	sechzehn *sixteen*		
17	siebzehn *seventeen*	1000	tausend *a or one thousand*
18	achtzehn *eighteen*	1972	neunzehnhundertzweiundsiebzig *nineteen hundred and seventy-two*
19	neunzehn *nineteen*		
20	zwanzig *twenty*		
21	einundzwanzig *twenty-one*	500 000	fünfhunderttausend *five hundred thousand*
22	zweiundzwanzig *twenty-two*		
23	dreiundzwanzig *twenty-three*	1 000 000	eine Million *a or one million*
30	dreißig *thirty*		
31	einunddreißig *thirty-one*	2 000 000	zwei Millionen *two million*
40	vierzig *forty*		
41	einundvierzig *forty-one*	1 000 000 000	eine Milliarde *a or one milliard (Am. billion)*
50	fünfzig *fifty*		

Ordinal Numbers

1.	erste *first (1st)*	11.	elfte *eleventh*
2.	zweite *second (2nd)*	12.	zwölfte *twelfth*
3.	dritte *third (3rd)*	13.	dreizehnte *thirteenth*
4.	vierte *fourth (4th)*	14.	vierzehnte *fourteenth*
5.	fünfte *fifth (5th), etc.*	15.	fünfzehnte *fifteenth*
6.	sechste *sixth*	16.	sechzehnte *sixteenth*
7.	siebente *seventh*	17.	siebzehnte *seventeenth*
8.	achte *eighth*	18.	achtzehnte *eighteenth*
9.	neunte *ninth*	19.	neunzehnte *nineteenth*
10.	zehnte *tenth*	20.	zwanzigste *twentieth*

21. einundzwanzigste *twenty-first*
22. zweiundzwanzigste *twenty-second*
23. dreiundzwanzigste *twenty-third*
30. dreißigste *thirtieth*
31. einunddreißigste *thirty-first*
40. vierzigste *fortieth*
41. einundvierzigste *forty-first*
50. fünfzigste *fiftieth*
51. einundfünfzigste *fifty-first*
60. sechzigste *sixtieth*
61. einundsechzigste *sixty-first*
70. siebzigste *seventieth*
71. einundsiebzigste *seventy-first*
80. achtzigste *eightieth*
81. einundachtzigste *eighty-first*

90. neunzigste *ninetieth*
100. hundertste *(one) hundredth*
101. hundert(und)erste *(one) hundred and first*
200. zweihundertste *two hundredth*
300. dreihundertste *three hundredth*
572. fünfhundert(und)zweiundsiebzigste *five hundred and seventy-second*
1000. tausendste *(one) thousandth*
1970. neunzehnhundert(und)siebzigste *nineteen hundred and seventieth*
500000. fünfhunderttausendste *five hundred thousandth*
1000000. millionste *(one) millionth*
2000000. zweimillionste *two millionth*

Fractional Numbers and other Numerical Values

$1/2$ halb *one or a half*
$1/2$ eine halbe Meile *half a mile*
$1\,1/2$ anderthalb *or* eineinhalb *one and a half*
$2\,1/2$ zweieinhalb *two and a half*
$1/3$ ein Drittel *one or a third*
$2/3$ zwei Drittel *two thirds*
$1/4$ ein Viertel *one fourth, one or a quarter*
$3/4$ drei Viertel *three fourths, three quarters*
$1\,1/4$ ein und eine viertel Stunde *one hour and a quarter*
$1/5$ ein Fünftel *one or a fifth*
$3\,4/5$ drei vier Fünftel *three and four fifths*
0,4 null Komma vier *point four (.4)*
2,5 zwei Komma fünf *two point five (2.5)*

einfach *single*
 zweifach *double, twofold*
 dreifach *threefold, treble, triple*
 vierfach *fourfold, quadruple*
 fünffach *fivefold, quintuple*

einmal *once*
 zweimal *twice*
 drei-, vier-, fünfmal *three or four or five times*
 zweimal soviel(e) *twice as much or many*

erstens, zweitens, drittens *first(ly), secondly, thirdly; in the first or second or third place*

$2 \times 3 = 6$ zwei mal drei ist sechs, zwei multipliziert mit drei ist sechs *twice three are or make six, two multiplied by three are or make six*

$7 + 8 = 15$ sieben plus acht ist fünfzehn *seven plus eight are fifteen*

$10 - 3 = 7$ zehn minus drei ist sieben *ten minus three are seven*

$20 : 5 = 4$ zwanzig (dividiert) durch fünf ist vier *twenty divided by five make four*

German Weights and Measures

I. Linear Measure

1 mm	*Millimeter* millimet|re, *Am.* -er = 0.039 inch
1 cm	*Zentimeter* centimet|re, *Am.* -er = 10 mm = 0.394 inch
1 m	*Meter* met|re, *Am.* -er = 100 cm = 1.094 yards = 3.281 feet
1 km	*Kilometer* kilomet|re, *Am.* -er = 1000 m = 0.621 mile
1 sm	*Seemeile* nautical mile = 1852 m

II. Square Measure

1 mm²	*Quadratmillimeter* square millimet|re, *Am.* -er = 0.002 square inch
1 cm²	*Quadratzentimeter* square centimet|re, *Am.* -er = 100 mm² = 0.155 square inch
1 m²	*Quadratmeter* square met|re, *Am.* -er = 10000 cm² = 1.196 square yards = 10.764 square feet
1 a	*Ar* are = 100 m² = 119.599 square yards
1 ha	*Hektar* hectare = 100 a = 2.471 acres
1 km²	*Quadratkilometer* square kilomet|re, *Am.* -er = 100 ha = 247.11 acres = 0.386 square mile

III. Cubic Measure

1 cm³	*Kubikzentimeter* cubic centimet|re, *Am.* -er = 1000 mm³ = 0.061 cubic inch
1 m³	*Kubikmeter* cubic met|re, *Am.* -er = 1000000 cm³ = 35.315 cubic feet = 1.308 cubic yards
1 RT	*Registertonne* register ton = 2,832 m³ = 100 cubic feet

IV. Measure of Capacity

1 l	*Liter* lit|re, *Am.* -er = 1.760 pints = *U.S.* 1.057 liquid quarts *or* 0.906 dry quart
1 hl	*Hektoliter* hectolit|re, *Am.* -er = 100 l = 2.75 bushels = *U.S.* 26.418 gallons

V. Weight

1 g	*Gramm* gram(me) = 15.432 grains
1 Pfd.	*Pfund* pound (German) = 500 g = 1.102 pounds avdp.
1 kg	*Kilogramm* kilogram(me) = 1000 g = 2.205 pounds avdp. = 2.679 pounds troy
1 Ztr.	*Zentner* centner = 100 Pfd. = 0.984 hundredweight = 1.102 *U.S.* hundredweights
1 dz	*Doppelzentner* = 100 kg = 1.968 hundredweights = 2.204 *U.S.* hundredweights
1 t	*Tonne* ton = 1000 kg = 0.984 long ton = *U.S.* 1.102 short tons

American and British Weights and Measures

1. Linear Measure

1 inch (in.) = 2,54 cm
1 foot (ft)
  = 12 inches = 30,48 cm
1 yard (yd)
  = 3 feet = 91,439 cm
1 perch (p.)
  = 5$\frac{1}{2}$ yards = 5,029 m
1 mile (m.)
  = 1,760 yards = 1,609 km

2. Nautical Measure

1 fathom (f., fm)
  = 6 feet = 1,829 m
1 nautical mile
  = 6,080 feet = 1853,18 m

3. Square Measure

1 square inch (sq. in.)
  = 6,452 cm²
1 square foot (sq. ft)
  = 144 square inches
  = 929,029 cm²
1 square yard (sq. yd)
  = 9 square feet = 8361,26 cm²
1 square perch (sq. p.)
  = 30$\frac{1}{4}$ square yards = 25,293m²
1 rood
  = 40 square perches = 10,117 a
1 acre (a.) = 4 roods = 40,47 a
1 square mile
  = 640 acres = 258,998 ha

4. Cubic Measure

1 cubic inch (cu. in.)
  = 16,387 cm³
1 cubic foot (cu. ft)
  = 1,728 cubic inches = 0,028 m³
1 cubic yard (cu. yd)
  = 27 cubic feet = 0,765 m³
1 register ton (reg. ton)
  = 100 cubic feet = 2,832 m³

5. Measure of Capacity
Dry and Liquid Measure

1 British or imperial gill (gl, gi.)
  = 0,142 l
1 British or imperial pint (pt)
  = 4 gills = 0,568 l
1 British or imperial quart (qt)
  = 2 pints = 1,136 l
1 British or imp. gallon (imp. gal.)
  = 4 imperial quarts = 4,546 l

Dry Measure

1 British or imperial peck (pk)
  = 2 imperial gallons = 9,092 l
1 Brit. or imp. bushel (bu., bus.)
  = 8 imperial gallons = 36,366 l
1 Brit. or imp. quarter (qr)
  = 8 imperial bushels = 290,935 l

Liquid Measure

1 Brit. or imp. barrel (bbl, bl)
  = 36 imperial gallons = 163,656 l

*

1 U.S. dry pint = 0,551 l
1 U.S. dry quart
  = 2 dry pints = 1,101 l
1 U.S. dry gallon
  = 4 dry quarts = 4,405 l
1 U.S. peck
  = 2 dry gallons = 8,809 l
1 U.S. bushel
  = 8 dry gallons = 35,238 l
1 U.S. gill = 0,118 l
1 U.S. liquid pint
  = 4 gills = 0,473 l
1 U.S. liquid quart
  = 2 liquid pints = 0,946 l
1 U.S. liquid gallon
  = 8 liquid pints = 3,785 l
1 U.S. barrel
  = 31$\frac{1}{2}$ liquid gallons = 119,228 l

1 U.S. barrel petroleum
   = 42 liquid gallons = 158,97 l

= 50,802 kg (*U.S.A.* 100 pounds
= 45,359 kg)

6. Avoirdupois Weight

1 grain (gr.) = 0,065 g
1 dram (dr.)
   = 27.344 grains = 1,772 g
1 ounce (oz.)
   = 16 drams = 28,35 g
1 pound (lb.)
   = 16 ounces = 453,592 g
1 quarter (qr)
   = 28 pounds = 12,701 kg
   (*U.S.A.* 25 pounds
   = 11,339 kg)
1 hundredweight (cwt.)
   = 112 pounds

1 ton (t.)
   (*a.* long ton) = 20 hundred-
   weights = 1016,05 kg (*U.S.A.*,
   a. short ton, = 907,185 kg)
1 stone (st.) = 14 pounds = 6,35 kg

7. Troy Weight

1 grain = 0,065 g
1 pennyweight (dwt.)
   = 24 grains = 1,555 g
1 ounce
   = 20 pennyweights = 31,103 g
1 pound = 12 ounces = 373,242 g